"Value-packed, accurate, and comprehensive..."

—Los Angeles Times

"Unbeatable..."

—The Washington Post

Let's Go
EUROPE

is the best book for anyone traveling on a budget. Here's why:

■ No other guidebook has as many budget listings.

Take İstanbul, for example. We found 6 places to stay for $10 or less. In Barcelona, we found 17 for under $20. In London, we'll show you 20 restaurants where a full meal comes to less than $8. We tell you how to get there the cheapest way, whether by bus, plane, or bike, and where to get an inexpensive and satisfying meal once you've arrived. We give hundreds of money-saving tips that anyone can use, plus invaluable advice on discounts and deals for students, children, families, and senior travelers.

■ Let's Go researchers have to make it on their own.

Our Harvard-Radcliffe researcher-writers travel on budgets as tight as your own—no expense accounts, no free hotel rooms.

■ Let's Go is completely revised each year.

We don't just update the prices, we go back to the place. If a charming café has become an overpriced tourist trap, we'll replace the listing with a new and better one.

■ No other guidebook includes all this:

Honest, engaging coverage of both the cities and the countryside; up-to-the-minute prices, directions, addresses, phone numbers, and opening hours; in-depth essays on local culture, history, and politics; comprehensive listings on transportation between and within regions and cities; straight advice on work and study, budget accommodations, sights, nightlife, and food; detailed city and regional maps; and much more.

■ Let's Go is for anyone who wants to see Europe on a budget.

Books by Let's Go, Inc.

EUROPE

Let's Go: Europe

Let's Go: Austria

Let's Go: Britain & Ireland

Let's Go: France

Let's Go: Germany & Switzerland

Let's Go: Greece & Turkey

Let's Go: Ireland

Let's Go: Italy

Let's Go: London

Let's Go: Paris

Let's Go: Rome

Let's Go: Spain & Portugal

NORTH & CENTRAL AMERICA

Let's Go: USA & Canada

Let's Go: Alaska & The Pacific Northwest

Let's Go: California & Hawaii

Let's Go: New York City

Let's Go: Washington, D.C.

Let's Go: Mexico

MIDDLE EAST & ASIA

Let's Go: Israel & Egypt

Let's Go: Thailand

Let's Go

The Budget Guide to

EUROPE

1994

Elizabeth J. Stein
Editor

Sujatha Baliga
Assistant Editor

Jahan Sagafi-nejad
Assistant Editor

Written by
Let's Go, Inc.
A subsidiary of
Harvard Student Agencies, Inc.

M
Macmillan Reference

HELPING LET'S GO

If you have suggestions or corrections, or just want to share your discoveries, drop us a line. We read every piece of correspondence, whether a 10-page letter, a velveteen Elvis postcard, or, as in one case, a collage. All suggestions are passed along to our researcher-writers. Please note that mail received after May 5, 1994 will probably be too late for the 1995 book, but will be retained for the following edition. Address mail to:

> **Let's Go: Europe**
> **Let's Go, Inc.**
> **I Story Street**
> **Cambridge, MA 02138**
> **USA**

In addition to the invaluable travel advice our readers share with us, many are kind enough to offer their services as researchers or editors. Unfortunately, the charter of Let's Go, Inc. and Harvard Student Agencies, Inc. enables us to employ only currently enrolled Harvard students.

Published in Great Britain 1994 by Pan Macmillan Ltd., Cavaye Place, London SW10 9PG.

10 9 8 7 6 5 4 3 2 1

Maps by David Lindroth, copyright © 1994, 1993, 1992, 1991, 1990, 1989, 1986 by St. Martin's Press, Inc.

Published in the United States of America by St. Martin's Press, Inc.

ISBN: 0 333 61152 7

Let's Go: Europe is written by the Publishing Division of Let's Go, Inc., 1 Story Street, Cambridge, MA 02138.

Let's Go® is a registered trademark of Let's Go, Inc.
Printed in the U.S.A. on recycled paper with biodegradable soy ink.

Editor	Elizabeth J. Stein
Assistant Editors	Sujatha Baliga
	Jahan Sagafi-nejad
Managing Editor	Nina Nowak
Publishing Director	Mark N. Templeton
Production Manager	Edward Owen
Office Coordinator	Susan P. Krause
Assistant General Manager	Anne E. Chisholm

Researcher-Writers

Burgos, León, Santiago de Compostela	Lisa Abend
Iceland, Norway	Peter Belmont Alderman
Belgium, Denmark, Luxembourg, The Netherlands	Clifford B. Anderson
Loire Valley, Bordeaux	John P. Anderson
Portugal	Ingrid Bassett
Rome	Justin Y. Bernold
Central Germany, The Black Forest	Tanya Vivienne Bezreh
Liechtenstein, Switzerland	Karin Braverman
Eastern Germany (except Berlin and Thuringian Forest)	Christopher J. Capozzola
Central and North England, Central and Southern Scotland	Allen C. Chen
Southern Italy (except Ancona)	Massimo Chiocca
Southwest Ireland	Heather Clark
Northeast Austria	Edward J. Collins, Jr.
London	Jenny Davidson
Czech Republic, Hungary	Julio DePietro
Bulgaria, Romania, Ukraine	John J. Didiuk
London, Heart of England, South and Southeast England, East Anglia	Lia Beth Epperson
East Coast, Central and Southeast Ireland	Sean Fitzpatrick
Northern Germany (except Harz Mountains) and Greater Berlin	Declan T. Fox
Northwest Austria	Adam Freudenheim
Central Greece, Peloponnese, Northern Greece, Ionian Islands	Eleni Gage
Andorra, Aquitaine (except Bordeaux), Basque Country, Corsica, Languedoc-Roussillon	Daniel G. C. Glover
Northern Scotland	Elaine Janet Goldenberg
Cyclades, Sporades, Athens, Western Crete, Central Greece	Susan Gray
Western Ireland	Tracy Grikscheit
Rome	Blythe N. Grossberg
Sardinia, Tuscany, Umbria	Rebecca Hellerstein
Bavaria, Baden Württemberg (except the Black Forest)	Moses MacDuff Hohman

Acknowledgments

Thanks from the Europe team to:

Ed, always there when you need him, the man with true stamina and patience. **Nina,** for tea with or without scones, keeping body and soul of the *NNGROUP together. **John,** without whom this book would never have made it off the Zeos, for thousands of pages of proofing, indexing, and organizing. **Lynne, Peter, Pete,** and **J-than** for pitching in when we needed it most, and offering helpful insights, smiles, and late-night discussion. **Sue,** for keeping the ball rolling. **Anne,** for mature insight and encouragement. **Mark,** for staff-meeting agendas, free bagels, and guiding enthusiasm.

Peter Alderman, who survived 275 days of rain a year, all of them in July, to give us a take on Iceland and Norway that was anything but boring as poop.

Cliff Anderson, who braved screaming Scandinavian children and skinhead room-mates to send in stunningly documented description of Benelux and Denmark.

Julio DePietro, who energetically let us know exactly what was or wasn't worth listing in the Czech Republic and Hungary.

John "Duke" Didiuk, for fleshing out Ukraine and for discovering the potential of Bulgaria and Romania; hope you let us know if the water of Kazonlak takes effect.

Minna Järvenpää, for her brilliant descriptions of Russia and the Baltic States; best of luck and don't get sick from all the partying.

Geneviève Roach, for taking on Poland and the Slovak Republic, and safely sending back a bajillion brochures and elegant copy.

Mark Roth, who brought the beauty of Sweden and his native Finland to life on the page, and whose gift for planning will hopefully bring him back to LG next year.

JustinL and Marc, for tainted cooler water and the joys of therapy goo; **Mike and Tracey,** for fun editorial marginalia and the UK intro; **Beth and Deborah,** we'll always have Paris; **Amy and Mimi,** who handcrafted Germany and even Switzer-land, a country more than any other defined by its topography; **Katherine and Alex-andra,** our partners in diacritic hell; **Steve and Eve** for inspired Irish prose; **MarkG and Anna** for inspiring a sharp Italy reorganization; **Natasha and Verity,** the team of kookiness and class; **JustinB,** for crunching Rome between bites of lobster ravioli; and **Rachel and Brian,** the fastest words in the West—of Europe, that is.

Sarthak for lots of typing and proofing before and after the chips were down. **Tanya Bezreh,** for an entire day of spellchecking. To **Mark Fish, Rob Jacoby,** and **Jane Yeh,** for tons of typing. **Mark Moody, Maia Gemmill,** and **Ben Peskoe,** for proofing with style. **Ms. Toby Pyle** of Hostelling International, and **Ms. Wenche Berger** of the Norwegian State Railway. The **Budapest Back Pack hostel,** for the T-shirts. **Sab's,** for the greatest sushi deal in the tri-state area.

Liz thanks

Sujatha and Jahan, loopy as they are (yes. oh, my, yes. Brown doggie), for smiles and songs, beautiful fonts, an education on race and gender realities, and one hell of a good job. Nina, for cooling my head off when it needed it desperately. Natasha, for email heart-to-hearts, and a friendship I hope we'll continue. My summer room-mates, for cheerfully coping with too many people on one shower. Mom and Dad for tired phone calls and welcome Copake hugs. Alex, in the summer he swam the lake, for being a great brother and letting me share in a fun Cousins weekend. Zack, for reminding me how close brothers and sisters can be even when they're on the opposite sides of the earth. John, for Paris, Chamonix, and Knoxville. John, for Kats and pooches and keeping me sane. ❋ In memory of Fletcher.

Sujatha thanks

First and foremost, I must immortalize in print the fact that Europe 1994 had a phenomenal editor. Thanks, Liz, for humoring my 2am inspired format questions. Working with you this summer has given me complete faith that I will someday own an amazing dictionary, perfectly organized, with Hindu Gods and Goddesses capitalized, edited by Elizabeth J. Stein. And Jahan, font god, your sharp wit, even keel, wrist-pad battles, and loooopy self in general made 1 Story St. such a happy place for me. I formally retract all references to lime-green leisure suits. Thanks, Mike Ng, for my *NON-WHITE poster. Lynne, I'll miss our fire-escape talks. Gita, your Europe trip inspired mine, and thus my work on this book. Sarthak, I love you. Let's use our books someday soon and rediscover our amazing traveling relationship. Take good care of Ghanoush, until he's reunited with his twin and Baba. Amma, thank you for giving birth to me, raising me, and for becoming such an amazing friend. ॐ shanti.

Jahan thanks

Before all others, to **Liz** and **Sujatha,** officemates and confidants. Together, my consummate editor—an awesome organizer and kind person with boundless tolerance for the abundant "Hey, Liz"s and late mornings—and my loopy, open, singing, meowing, 3:00-laughing-fit AE-comrade made the Europe room a lively and comfortable home.☺ To **Marc,** the urban cowboy and new friend; G&T **Justin,** my partner in crime; **Dov,** for the first of many real talks; **BenP,** for truly noble hospitality; **DaveG,** for a great evening watching the Yanks down the Red Sox; **Dave,** for stoking my Japanophilic fires; **Mike** and **Sarthak,** for soccer, tennis, and tequila; when-a-little-means-a-lot **Lynne;** all of Andorra: gentle **Deborah,** Chicken Tikka Masala **Brian,** toothsome **Rachel,** and fellow Redskins fan, **Beth;** enthusiastic **Nina; Ěďʼ,** for inspiring mé to tačkłe thôśē dåřń fõņtš. To my pliable yet faithful **therapy goo,** for great comfort. To **Abraham Simpson,** for a new voice. To **lovely Janine** for your much-needed faxes (oh, my morals!), UB40 and the amazing skyline, and chicken tenders in the very beginning☺. To **Kurt** and **Matt,** for few weeks out of your busy schedules to look after the kids and each other. To **Jen,** for your trust. Most of all, as always, to **Mom, Dad, Gramma,** and **Dave.** Little traveling brother, this one's for you, in a summer too unlike the glorious ones past. ☿ ☺

■ About Let's Go

Back in 1960, a few students at Harvard got together to produce a 20-page pamphlet offering a collection of tips on budget travel in Europe. For three years, Harvard Student Agencies, a student-run nonprofit corporation, had been doing a brisk business booking charter flights to Europe; this modest, mimeographed packet was offered to passengers as an extra. The following year, students traveling to Europe researched the first full-fledged edition of *Let's Go: Europe*, a pocket-sized book featuring advice on shoestring travel, irreverent write-ups of sights, and a decidedly youthful slant.

Throughout the 60s, the guides reflected the times: one section of the 1968 *Let's Go: Europe* talked about "Street Singing in Europe on No Dollars a Day." During the 70s, *Let's Go* gradually became a large-scale operation, adding regional European guides and expanding coverage into North Africa and Asia. The 80s saw the arrival of *Let's Go: USA & Canada* and *Let's Go: Mexico*, as well as regional North American guides; in the 90s we introduced five in-depth city guides to Paris, London, Rome, New York, and Washington, DC.

This year we're proud to announce three new guides: *Let's Go: Austria* (including Prague and Budapest), *Let's Go: Ireland*, and *Let's Go: Thailand* (including Honolulu, Tokyo, and Singapore), bringing our total number of titles up to twenty.

We've seen a lot in thirty-four years. *Let's Go: Europe* is now the world's #1 best selling international guide, translated into seven languages. And our guides are still researched, written, and produced entirely by students who know firsthand how to see the world on the cheap.

Every spring, we recruit nearly 100 researchers and an editorial team of 50 to write our books anew. Come summertime, after several months of training, researchers hit the road for seven weeks of exploration, from Bangkok to Budapest, Anchorage to Ankara. With pen and notebook in hand, a few changes of underwear stuffed in our backpacks, and a budget as tight as yours, we visit every *pensione*, *palapa*, pizzeria, café, club, campground, or castle we can find to make sure you'll get the most out of *your* trip.

We've put the best of our discoveries into the book you're now holding. A brand-new edition of each guide hits the shelves every year, only months after it was researched, so you know you're getting the most reliable, up-to-date, and comprehensive information available. And even as you read this, work on next year's editions is well underway.

At *Let's Go*, we think of budget travel not only as a means of cutting down on costs, but as a way of breaking down a few walls as well. Living cheap and simple on the road brings you closer to the real people and places you've been saving up to visit. This book will ease your anxieties and answer your questions about the basics—to help *you* get off the beaten track and explore. We encourage you to put *Let's Go* away now and then and strike out on your own. As any seasoned traveler will tell you, the best discoveries are often those you make yourself. If you find something worth sharing, drop us a line and let us know. We're at Let's Go, Inc., 1 Story Street, Cambridge, MA, 02138, USA.

Happy travels!

Contents

Maps

Paris

London

Rome

How To Use This Book

Back in 1961, *Let's Go: Europe* lasted all of 64 pages, spent 7 lines on Russia, and listed one accommodation in Scotland. We've branched out a little since then, and after sending a growing armada of researcher-writers to the Old World year after year, we hope we can claim to have our collective finger on the pulse of Europe.

This year we've redesigned our format, so the guide could more effectively serve you. *Let's Go: Europe* is divided into five parts. The opening section, **Essentials,** will guide you through the quagmire of preparations, with tips on passport and visa acquisition, packing, getting to Europe, and the budget travel opportunities once you're there. It also addresses specific concerns, such as those of women, bisexuals, gays, lesbians, travelers with disabilities, senior citizens, and travelers with kids.

The rest of the book is in four sections: Western Europe, Northern Europe, Southern Europe, and Eastern Europe. Within each part, individual countries are listed alphabetically (Estonia, Latvia, and Lithuania are listed as the Baltic States) and begin with a historical, cultural, political, and linguistic introduction, followed by country-specific Essentials (analagous to the Essentials section at the front of the book), where you'll find such tidbits as visa requirements and the lowdown on transportation, hostel associations, and regional cuisine.

For each major city, the **Orientation and Practical Information** section gives you a clue about the city's layout, as well as how to get there, how to communicate with folks back home, and where to seek transportation and help in medical emergencies and crisis situations. Then we shower you with information on **Accommodations, Food, Camping, Sights,** and **Entertainment.** Smaller towns are usually divided in half: first we describe the sights and entertainment hotspots, then we dig into the nitty-gritty: accommodations, food, and practical information.

Although our intrepid researcher-writers beat a trail across the continent annually, there are countless undiscovered travel gems in Europe. Please keep an eye out for any amazing places we've missed, follow your own spirit and imagination, and feel free to write us about what you find. For more detailed coverage of various European areas, consider one of our regional guides: *Let's Go: Austria, Let's Go: Britain & Ireland, Let's Go: France, Let's Go: Germany & Switzerland, Let's Go: Greece & Turkey, Let's Go: Ireland, Let's Go: Italy,* and *Let's Go: Spain & Portugal,* or our city guides, *Let's Go: London, Let's Go: Paris,* and *Let's Go: Rome.*

WITH OUR RAIL PASSES YOU'LL HAVE UP TO 70% MORE MONEY TO WASTE.

With savings of up to 70% off the price of point-to-point tickets, you'll be laughing all the way to the souvenir stand. Rail passes are available for travel throughout Europe or the country of your choice—we can also book air travel, rental cars, and hotel reservations. So all you'll have to do is leave some extra room in your suitcase. For more information just call **1-800-4-EURAIL**.

ESSENTIALS

PLANNING YOUR TRIP

Europe's a big place. Fortunately, there are tons of industries out there devoted to helping travelers tackle it. The organizations listed below and various national tourist offices will send you mounds of daunting literature. Dive in and plan a trip tailored to your specific interests, without forgetting that you are going on vacation; attempting to see everything in Scandinavia in 5 days probably won't be enjoyable.

Give careful consideration to those with whom you travel and the time of year in which you travel. Friends can insulate you from local culture, but they're also an invaluable source of energy and comfort, provide extra safety, and share in food and lodging costs. If you choose to travel with others, discuss your trip in detail before you leave to make sure your interests are compatible. Going solo can be the best way to travel and the worst. Freedom of movement is counterbalanced by the danger of loneliness and extra safety precautions, particularly for women (see Women and Travel). A budget travel subculture fills Europe's hostels and ensures that you will only be as lonely as you want to be. Remember that summer is the high season for traveling in Europe, with the masses coming in around July and August; June may be a better time to go.

■■■ USEFUL TRAVEL ORGANIZATIONS

The following student- and youth-oriented travel organizations provide so many services that we will refer to them over and over again. Many of the same services are offered by **Let's Go Travel,** Harvard Student Agencies, Inc., 53a Church St., Harvard University, Cambridge, MA 02138 (tel. (617) 495-9649 or (800) 553-8746) and **Travel Management International,** 39 JFK St., 3rd Floor, Cambridge, MA, 02138 (tel. (617) 661-8187 or (800) 245-3672).

Council on International Educational Exchange (CIEE/Council Travel): Provides low-cost travel arrangements, books, ISIC, ITIC, hostel cards, and gear. CIEE also arranges homestays, and helps students secure work visas and find employment through its work-exchange programs. 43 U.S. offices. **Boston,** 729 Boylston St. #201, MA 02116 (tel. (617) 266-1926). **Chicago,** 1153 N. Dearborn St., IL 60610 (tel. (312) 951-0585). **Dallas,** 6923 Snider Plaza B, TX 75205 (tel. (214) 363-9941). **Los Angeles,** 1093 Broxton Ave. #220, CA 90024 (tel. (310) 208-3551). **New York,** 205 E. 42nd St., NY 10017 (tel. (212) 661-1450). **Portland,** 715 S.W. Morrison #600, OR 97205 (tel. (503) 228-1900). **San Diego,** 953 Garnet Ave., CA 94108 (tel. (619) 270-6401). **San Francisco,** 919 Irving St. #102, CA 94122 (tel. (415) 566-6222). **Seattle,** 1314 N.E. 43rd St. #210, WA 98105 (tel. (206) 632-2448). Also in Providence, RI; Amherst and Cambridge, MA; Berkeley, La Jolla, and Long Beach, CA. CIEE has **affiliates abroad** providing many of the same services. In **Australia,** contact SSA/STA Swap Program, P.O. Box 399 (1st Floor), 220 Faraday St., Carlton South, Melbourne, Victoria 3053 (tel. 033 47 69 11). In the **United Kingdom,** contact London Student Travel, 52 Grosvenor Gardens, London WC1 (tel. (071) 730 34 02). In **Canada** write to Travel CUTS (see below). If you can't locate an office in your country, contact CIEE's New York office or the **International Student Travel Confederation,** Gothersgade 30, 1123 Copenhagen K, Denmark (tel. 33 99 93).

STA Travel, 17 E. 45th St., New York, NY 10017 (tel. (800) 777-0112 or (212) 986-9470). Discount airfares for travelers under 26 and full-time students under 32,

railpasses, accommodations, tours, insurance, and ISICs. **Boston,** 273 Newbury St., MA 02116 (tel. 617) 266-6014). **Los Angeles,** 7202 Melrose Ave., CA 90046 (tel. (213) 934-8722). **New York,** 48 E. 11th St., NY 10003 (tel. (212) 477-7166). **Philadelphia,** University City Travel, 3730 Walnut St., PA 19104 (tel. (215) 382-2928). **San Francisco,** 51 Grant Ave., CA 94108 (tel. (415) 391-8407). In the **U.K.,** offices at 86 Old Brompton Rd., **London** SW7 3LQ, and 117 Euston Rd., London NW1 2SX England (tel. (071) 937 9921 for European travel; (071) 937 1733 for round-the-world travel). In **New Zealand,** 10 High St., **Auckland** (tel. (09) 309 9995).

Travel CUTS (Canadian University Travel Services Limited), 187 College St., Toronto, Ont. M5T 1P7 (tel. (416) 979-2406). Offices across Canada. In the **U.K.,** 295-A Regent St., London W1R 7YA (tel. (071) 637 3161). Discounted transatlantic and domestic flights; ISIC, FIYTO, and HI hostel cards; and discount travel passes. Student Work Abroad Program (SWAP). Offers The Student Traveller (free).

Campus Travel, 52 Grosvenor Gardens, London SW1W 0AG (tel. (071) 730 8832; fax (071) 730 5739). Student and youth fares on travel by train, boat, and bus, as well as flexible airline tickets. Provides ID cards for youths, special travel insurance for students and those under 35, maps, and guides.

International Student Exchange Flights (ISE), 5010 East Shea Blvd. #A104, Scottsdale, AZ 85254 (tel. (602) 951-1177). Budget student flights, BritRail and Eurail passes, traveler's checks, and travel guides, including *Let's Go.* Free catalog.

USIT Ltd., Aston Quay, O'Connell Bridge, Dublin 2 (tel. (01) 679 8833; fax (01) 677 8843).

■ National Tourist Offices

Austrian National Tourist Office

U.S.: 500 Fifth Ave. #2009, New York, NY 10110. Tel. (212) 944-6880. Fax (212) 730-4568.

NATIONAL TOURIST OFFICES

Canada: 2 Bloor St. East #3330, Toronto, Ont. M4W 1A8. Tel. (416) 967-3381.
U.K.: 30 St. George St., London W1R 0AL. Tel. (071) 629 0461.
Australia: 36 Carrington St. 1st Floor, Sydney NSW 2000. Tel. (02) 299 36 21. Fax (02) 299 38 08.

Belgian National Tourist Office

U.S.: 745 Fifth Ave., #714, New York, NY 10151. Tel. (212) 758-8130.
U.K.: Premier House, 2 Gayton Rd., Harrow, Middlesex HA1 2XU. Tel. (081) 861 3300.

British Tourist Authority

U.S.: 551 Fifth Ave., 7th Floor, New York, NY 10176-0799. Tel. (212) 986-2200.
Canada: 111 Avenue Rd., Ste. 450, Toronto M5R 3J8, Ont. Tel. (416) 925-6326.
Australia: The University Centre, 210 Clarence St., Sydney NSW 2000. Tel. (02) 267 4555.

Balkan Holidays (Bulgaria)

U.S.: 41 E. 42nd St. #508, New York, NY 10017. Tel. (212) 573-5530.
U.K.: Sofia House, 19 Conduit St., London W1R 9TD. Tel. (071) 491 4499.

Bulgarian Embassy

U.S.: 1621 22nd St., NW, Washington, DC 20008

Čedok (Private Czech Tourist Agency)

U.S.: 10 E. 40th St., New York, NY 10016. Tel. (212) 689-9720. Fax (212) 481-0597.
U.K.: 17-18 Old Bond St., London W1X 4RB. Tel. (071) 629 6058.

Czech Embassy and Consulate

Australia (Embassy): 38 Culgoa Circuit, O'Malley, Canberra, ACT 2606. Tel. (616) 290 1386. Fax (616) 290 0006.

Canada (Consulate): 1305 Av. des Peins ouest, Montréal, Qué. H3G 1B2. Tel. (514) 849-4495. Fax (514) 849-4117.

Danish Tourist Board

U.S.: 655 Third Ave., 18th Floor, New York, NY 10017. Tel. (212) 949-2333.
Canada: P.O. Box 115, Station N, Toronto, Ont. M8V 3S4. Tel. (416) 823-9620.

Estonian Consulate-General

U.S.: 630 Fifth Ave., Suite 2415, New York, NY 10111. Tel. (212) 247-7634.
Canada: 958 Broadview Ave., Toronto, Ont. M4K 2R6. Tel. (416) 461-0764.
U.K.: 16 Hyde Park, London SW7 5D6. Tel. (071) 589 3428.

Finnish Tourist Board

U.S.: 655 Third Ave., New York, NY 10017. Tel. (212) 949-2333.
U.K.: 66/68 Haymarket, London SW1Y 4RF. Tel. (071) 839 4048.

French Government Tourist Office

U.S.: 610 Fifth Ave., New York, NY 10020. Tel. (900) 990-0040; costs US50¢/min.
Canada: 1981 av. McGill College #490, Montréal, Qué. H3A 2W9. Tel. (514) 288-4264.
U.K.: 178 Piccadilly, London W1V OAL. Tel. (01) 629 1272.
Australia: BNP building, 12th Fl., 12 Castlereagh St., Sydney NSW 2000. Tel. (02) 231 52 44.

German National Tourist Office

U.S.: 122 East 42nd St., 52nd Floor, New York, NY 10168-0072. Tel. (212) 661-7200. Fax (212) 661-7174.
Canada: 175 Bloor St. E., E. North Tower, 6th Floor, Toronto, Ont. M4W 3R8. Tel. (416) 968-1570. Fax (416) 968-1986.
U.K.: Nightingale House, 65 Curzon St., London W1Y 7PE. Tel. (071) 495 3990. Fax (071) 495 61 29.

Australia: Lufthansa House, 9th Floor, 143 Macquarie St., Sydney NSW 2000. Tel. (02) 367 38 90. Fax (02) 367 38 95.

Greek National Tourist Organization

U.S.: Olympic Tower, 645 Fifth Ave., 5th Floor, New York, NY 10022. Tel. (212) 421-5777. Fax (212) 826-6940.
Canada: 1300 Bay St., Toronto, Ont. M5R 3K8. Tel. (416) 968-2220. Fax (416) 968-6533.
U.K.: 4 Conduit St., London WIR DOJ. Tel. (01) 734 59 97.
Australia: 1-57 Pitt St., Sydney, NSW 2000. Tel. (02) 241 16 63.

IBUSZ (Hungarian Tourist Organization)

U.S.: 1 Parker Plaza #1104, Fort Lee, NJ 07024. Tel. (201) 592-8585.
U.K.: Danube Travel, 6 Conduit St., London W1R 9TG. Tel. (071) 493 0263.

Hungarian Consulate

U.S.: 223 E. 52nd St., New York, NY 10022. Tel. (212) 752-0661
Australia: Suite 405, Edgecliffe Centre, 203-233 New South Head Rd., Edgecliff NSW 2027. Tel. (02) 328 7859 or 328 7860. Fax (02) 327 7208.

Icelandic Tourist Board

U.S.: 655 Third Ave., New York, NY 10017. Tel. (212) 949-2333 ext. 130. Fax (212) 983-5260.

Irish Tourist Board

U.S.: 757 Third Ave., 19th Floor, New York, NY 10017. Tel. (800) 223-6470 or (212) 418-0800. Fax (212) 371-9052.
Canada: 160 Bloor St. E., Suite 1150, Toronto, Ont. M4W 1B9. Tel. (416) 929-2777. Fax (416) 929-6783.
U.K.: 150 New Bond St., London W1Y 0AQ. Tel. (071) 493 3201.
Australia: Level 5, 36 Carrington Street, Sydney NSW 2000. Tel. (02) 299 6177. Fax (02) 299 6323.

Italian Government Travel Office

U.S.: 630 Fifth Ave. #1565, Rockefeller Center, New York, NY 10111. Tel. (212) 245-4822. Fax (212) 586-9249.
Canada: 1 Pl. Ville Marie #1914, Montréal, Qué. H3B 3M9. Tel. (514) 866-7667. Fax (514) 392-1429.
U.K.: 1 Princes St., London WIR 8AY. Tel. (01) 408 12 54. Fax (01) 493 66 95.

Latvian Embassy and Honorary Consul

U.S. (Embassy): 4325 17th St., NW, Washington, DC 20011. Tel. (202) 726-8213. Fax (202) 726-6785.
Canada (Embassy): 230 Clemow Ave., Ottawa, Ont. K1S 2B6. Tel. (613) 238-6868.
U.K. (Embassy): 72 Queensborough Terr., London W2 3SP. Tel. (071) 727 1698.
Australia (Honorary Consul): P.O. Box 23, Kew, Victoria, 3101, Melbourne. Tel. (03) 499 69 20.

Lithuanian Embassy, Consulate, and Honorary Consul

U.S. (Embassy): 2622 16th St. NW, Washington, DC 20009. Tel. (202) 234-5860. Fax (202) 328-0466.
U.S. (Consulate): P.O. Box 7406, FDR Station, New York, NY 10150. Tel. (212) 582-1345. Fax (212) 247-3451
Canada (Honorary Consul): 235 Yorkland Blvd., Willowdale, Ont. M2J. Tel. (416) 494-4099. Fax (416) 494-4382.
U.K. (Embassy): 17 Essex Villas, London W8 7BP. Tel. (071) 937 1588 or (071) 938 2481. Fax (071) 938 3329.
Australia (Honorary Consul): 26 Jalanga Crescent, Aranda ACT 2614 Tel. and fax (616) 253-2063.

Luxembourg National Tourist Office

U.S.: 17 Beekman Pl., New York, NY 10022. Tel. (212) 370-9850. Fax (212) 922-1685.
U.K.: 122 Regent St., London W1R 5FE. Tel. (071) 434 2800.

Netherlands Board of Tourism

U.S.: 355 Lexington Ave., 21st floor, New York, NY 10017. Tel. (212) 370-7367.
U.K.: 25-28 Buckingham Gate, London SW1E 6LD. Tel. (071) 828 7900.

Northern Ireland Tourist Board

U.S.: 276 Fifth Ave., Suite 500, New York, NY 10001-4509. Tel. (212) 992-0101.
U.K.: 11 Berkeley St., London W1X 5AD. Tel. (071) 493 0601. Fax (071) 499 3731.

Norwegian Tourist Board

U.S.: 655 Third Ave., New York, NY 10017. Tel. (212) 949-2333.
U.K.: Charles House, 5-11 Lower Regent St., London SW1Y 4LR. Tel. (071) 839 2650.

Polish National Tourist Office

U.S.: 333 N. Michigan Ave., Ste. 224, Chicago, IL, 60601. Tel. (312) 236-9013.

Polish Embassy

U.S.: 223 Madison Ave., New York, NY 10016. Tel. (212) 889-8360.
Canada: 1500 Pine Ave., Montréal, Que. H3G 1B4. Tel. (514) 937-9481.

Portuguese National Tourist Office

U.S.: 590 Fifth Ave., New York, NY 10036. Tel. (212) 354-4403.
Canada: 60 Bloor St. W., Suite 1005, Toronto, Ont. M4W 3B8. Tel. (416) 921-7376.
U.K.: 22/25A Sackville St., London W1X 1DE. Tel. (071) 494 14 41.

Romanian Embassy

U.S.: 1607 23rd St., NW, Washington, DC 20008. Tel. (202) 232-4747.
Canada: 655 Rideau St., Ottawa, Ont. K1N 6A3. Tel. (613) 789-3709 or 789 5345. Fax (613) 789-4365.

Romanian National Tourist Office

U.S.: 342 Madison Ave. Suite 210, New York, NY 10173. Tel. (212) 697-6971.
U.K.: 17 Nottingham St., London W1M 3RD. Tel. (071) 224 3692.

Intourist Travel Information Office (Russia)

U.S.: 630 Fifth Ave., #868, New York, NY 10111. Tel. (212) 757-3884.
Canada: 1801 McGill College Ave. #630, Montréal, Qué. H3A 2N4. Tel. (514) 849-6394.
U.K.: 219 Marsh Wall, London E14 9FJ. Tel. (071) 538 8600.

Scandinavian Tourist Board

U.S.: 655 Third Ave., New York, NY 10017. Tel. (212) 949-2333.
U.K.: 29-31 Oxford St., London W1R 1RE. Tel. (071) 437 5816.

Tourist Office of Spain

U.S.: 665 Fifth Ave., New York, NY 10022. Tel. (212) 759-8822. Fax (212) 658-1061.
Canada: 102 Bloor St. W., 14th Fl., Toronto, Ont. M55 1M8. Tel. (416) 961-3131. Fax (416) 961-1992.
U.K.: 57-58 St. James St., London SW1A ILD. Tel. (071) 499 11 69 or (071) 499 09 01. Fax (71) 609 42 57.
Australia: 203 Castlereagh St., #21A, Sydney South, NSW 2000. Tel. (02) 264-7966. Fax (02) 267 5111.

Swiss National Tourist Office (including Liechtenstein)

U.S.: 608 Fifth Ave., New York, NY 10020. Tel. (212) 757-5944. Fax (212) 262-6116.

Canada: 154 University St., #610, Toronto, Ont. M5H 3Y9. Tel. (416) 971-9734. Fax (416) 971-6425.

U.K.: Swiss Centre, 1 New Coventry St., London W1V 8EE. Tel. (071) 734 1921. Fax (071) 437 4577.

Turkish Cultural and Information Office

U.S.: 821 United Nations Plaza, New York, NY 10017. Tel. (212) 687-2194.

U.K.: 170-173 Piccadilly, London W1V 9DD. Tel. (441) 734 86 81.

Embassy of Ukraine

U.S.: 3350 M St., NW, Washington, DC 20007. Tel. (202) 333-0606.

■■■ DOCUMENTS AND FORMALITIES

Be sure to file all applications several weeks or months in advance of your planned departure date. Remember, you are relying on government agencies to complete these transactions. A backlog in processing can spoil your plans.

When you travel, always carry on your person two or more forms of identification, including at least one photo ID. A passport combined with a driver's license or birth certificate usually serves as adequate proof of your identity and citizenship. Many establishments, especially banks, require several IDs before cashing traveler's checks. Never carry all your forms of ID together, as you risk being left entirely without ID or funds in case of theft or loss. Carry half a dozen extra passport-size photos that you can attach to the sundry IDs or railpasses you will eventually acquire. If you plan an extended stay, register your passport with the nearest embassy or consulate.

U.S. citizens seeking information about documents and formalities and travel abroad should request the booklet Your Trip Abroad from the U.S. Dept. of State, Bureau of Consular Affairs, Public Affairs, Room 5807, Washington, DC 20520-4818.

■ Entrance Requirements

Citizens of the U.S., Canada, the U.K., Ireland, Australia, New Zealand, and South Africa all need valid passports to enter any European country and to re-enter their own country. Some countries will not allow entrance if the holder's passport will expire in less than 6 months, and returning to the U.S. with an expired passport may result in a fine. Some countries in Europe will require a visa.

When you enter a country, dress neatly and carry **proof of your financial independence,** such as a visa to the next country on your itinerary, an air ticket to depart, enough money to cover the cost of your living expenses, etc. Admission as a visitor does not include the right to work, which is authorized only by a work permit (see Alternatives to Tourism below). Entering certain countries to study requires a special visa, and immigration officers may also want to see proof of acceptance from a school, proof that the course of study will take up most of your time in the country, and, as always, proof that you can support yourself.

PASSPORTS

Before you leave, photocopy the page of your passport that contains your photograph and identifying information, especially your passport number. Carry this photocopy in a safe place apart from your passport, and leave another copy at home. These measures will help prove your citizenship and facilitate the issuing of a new passport. Consulates also recommend that you carry an expired passport or an official copy of your birth certificate in a part of your baggage separate from other documents. You can request a duplicate birth certificate from the Bureau of Vital Records and Statistics in your state or province of birth.

If you do lose your passport, it may take weeks to process a replacement, and your new one may be valid only for a limited time. In addition, any visas stamped in your old passport will be irretrievably lost. If it happens, however, immediately notify the local police and the nearest embassy or consulate of your home government. To expedite its replacement, you will need to know all the information that you had previously recorded and photocopied and to show identification and proof of citizenship. Some consulates can issue new passports within 2 days if you give them proof of citizenship. In an emergency, ask for immediate temporary traveling papers that will permit you to return to your home country. If your passport is lost or stolen in the U.S., report it in writing to Passport Services, 1425 K St., NW, Department of State, Washington, DC 20522-1705, or to the nearest passport agency.

Your passport is a public document that belongs to your nation's government. You may have to surrender it to a foreign government official; if you don't get it back in a reasonable time, inform the nearest mission of your home country.

Applying for a Passport

U.S. and Canada U.S. citizens may apply for a passport, valid for 10 years (5 yrs. if under 18) at any federal or state **courthouse** or **post office** authorized to accept passport applications, or at a **U.S. Passport Agency,** located in Boston, Chicago, Honolulu, Houston, Los Angeles, Miami, New Orleans, New York, Philadelphia, San Francisco, Seattle, Stamford, and Washington, DC. Refer to the "U.S. Government, State Department" section of the telephone directory or call your local post office for addresses. Parents must apply in person for children under age 13. You must apply in person if this is your first passport, if you're under age 18, or if your current passport is more than 12 years old or was issued before your 18th birthday. It will cost US$65 (under 18 US$40). You can **renew** your passport by mail (or in person) for US$55. Processing usually takes 3 to 4 weeks. Passport agencies offer **rush service** if you have proof that you're departing within 5 working days (e.g. an airplane ticket). For more info, contact the U.S. Passport Information's **24-hour recorded message** (tel. (202) 647-0518).

Canadian application forms in English and French are available at all passport offices, post offices, and most travel agencies. Citizens may apply in person at any one of 29 regional Passport Offices across Canada. Travel agents can direct the applicant to the nearest location. In the U.S., contact a Canadian diplomatic mission; outside Canada and the U.S., contact the nearest embassy or consulate. You can apply by mail by sending a completed application form with appropriate documentation and the CDN$35 fee to Passport Office, External Affairs, Ottawa, Ont., K1A OG3. Keep in mind that some countries require that a child carry his or her own passport whether traveling with a parent or not. A passport is valid for 5 years and is not renewable. If a passport is lost abroad, Canadians must be able to prove citizenship with another document. For additional info, call the **24-hour number** (tel. (800) 567-6868). In Metro Toronto call 973-3251. Montrealers should dial 283-2152. Refer to the booklet Bon Voyage, But... for further help and a list of Canadian embassies and consulates abroad. It is available free of charge from any passport office or from Info-Export (BPTE), External Affairs, Ottawa, Ont., K1A OG2.

U.K., Ireland, Australia, New Zealand, and South Africa British

citizens can obtain either a full passport or a more restricted Visitor's Passport. For a **full passport** valid for 10 years (5 yrs. if under 16), apply in person or by mail to the London Passport Office or by mail to a passport office located in Liverpool, Newport, Peterborough, Glasgow, or Belfast. Children under 16 may be included on a parent's passport. Processing usually takes 4 to 6 weeks. The London office offers same-day walk-in rush service; arrive early. For a **Visitor's Passport,** valid for 1 year

DOCUMENTS AND FORMALITIES

in Western Europe only, apply in person at major post offices. You must bring identification, 2 identical photos, and the fee (around UK£9).

Irish citizens can apply for a passport by mail to one of two passport offices: Department of Foreign Affairs, Passport Office, Setanta Centre, Molesworth St., Dublin 2 (tel. (01) 671 1633), or Passport Office, 1A South Mall, Cork (tel. (021) 272 525). You can obtain an application form at a local Garda station or request one from a passport office. Passports cost IR£45 and are valid for 10 years. Citizens under 18 or over 65 can request a 3-year passport that costs IR£10.

Australian citizens must apply for a passport in person at a post office, a passport office, or an Australian diplomatic mission overseas. An appointment may be necessary. Passport offices are located in Adelaide, Brisbane, Canberra, Darwin, Hobart, Melbourne, Newcastle, Perth, and Sydney. A parent may file an application for a child who is under 18 and unmarried. Application fees are adjusted every 3 months; call the toll free information service for current details (tel. 13 12 32).

Applicants for **New Zealand passports** must contact their local Link Centre, travel agent, or New Zealand Representative for an application form, which they must complete and mail to the New Zealand Passport Office, Documents of National Identity Division, Department of Internal Affairs, Box 10-526, Wellington (tel. (04) 474 81 00). The application fee is NZ$56.25 for an application lodged in New Zealand and NZ$110 for one lodged overseas (if under age 16, NZ$25.30 and NZ$49.50, respectively). Overseas citizens should send the passport application to the nearest embassy, high commission, or consulate that is authorized to issue passports. Unless you need the passport urgently, it will be processed in New Zealand.

South African citizens can apply for a passport at any Home Affairs Office. Two photos, either a birth certificate or an identity book, and the R30 fee must accompany a completed application. For further information, contact the Home Affairs Office nearest you.

VISAS

A visa is an endorsement that a foreign government stamps into a passport; it allows the bearer to stay in that country for a specified purpose and period of time. Most visas cost US$10-30 and allow you to spend about a month in a country, within 6 months to a year from the date of issue.

Most Western European nations do not require visas of American, Canadian, British, Australian, or New Zealand citizens staying for less than 3 months; France requires a visa from Australians. Eastern European countries' visa requirements have been eroding steadily since 1989 but vary greatly for citizens of different countries. We list specific visa requirements and consulate addresses in the "Getting There" section of each Eastern European country introduction. Check the country's visa requirements and restrictions as close to your departure date as possible.

Some visas are incompatible: Greece won't let you in if you have a passport stamp from Northern Cyprus; Morocco and most Arab countries turn away those with Israeli stamps; and South Africans have been denied entry to Scandinavia. You may ask that these visa or entry stamps be placed on a removable page in your passport. Border officials run the gamut from not nice to downright nasty, so stay informed about visa requirements and restrictions.

If you want to stay for longer, apply for a visa at the country's embassy or consulate in your home country well before your departure (see Useful Travel Organizations: National Tourist Offices, above, for addresses). Unless you are a student, extending your stay once you are abroad is more difficult. You must contact the country's immigration officials or local police well before your time is up, and show sound proof of financial resources (see Entrance Requirements).

For more information, send for the U.S. government pamphlet Foreign Visa Requirements. Mail a check for US50¢ to Consumer Information Center, Dept. 454V, Pueblo, CO 81009 (tel. (719) 948-3334), or contact **Visa Center, Inc.,** 507 Fifth Ave., Ste. 904, New York, NY 10017 (tel. (212) 986-0924).

■ Customs

Unless you plan to import a BMW or a barnyard beast, you will probably pass right over the customs barrier with minimal ado. Most countries prohibit or restrict the importation of firearms, explosives, ammunition, fireworks, controlled drugs, most plants and animals, lottery tickets, and obscene literature and films. To avoid problems when you transport prescription drugs, ensure that the bottles are clearly marked, and carry a copy of the prescription.

Upon returning home, you must declare all articles you acquired abroad and must pay a duty on the value of those articles that exceeds the allowance established by your country's customs service. Holding onto receipts for purchases made abroad will help establish values when you return. It is wise to make a list, including serial numbers, of any valuables (not that you would travel with any!) that you carry with you from home; if you register this list with customs before your departure and have an official stamp it, you will avoid import duty charges and ensure an easy passage upon your return. Be especially careful to document items manufactured abroad.

Goods and gifts purchased at **duty-free** shops abroad are not exempt from duty or sales tax at your point of return; you must declare these items, as well. "Duty-free" merely means that you need not pay a tax in the country of purchase.

■ Hostel Membership

Hostelling International (HI) is the new and universal trademark name adopted by the former International Youth Hostel Federation (IYHF). The 6000 official youth hostels worldwide will normally display the HI logo (a blue triangle) alongside the symbol of one of the 70 national hostel associations.

A 1-year HI membership permits you to stay at youth hostels all over Europe at unbeatable prices. And, despite the name, you need not be a youth; travelers over 25 pay only a slight surcharge for a bed. Save yourself potential trouble by procuring a membership card at home; some hostels don't sell them on the spot. For more details on youth hostels, see Accommodations in each country's Essentials section.

One-year hostel membership cards are available from some travel agencies, including Council Travel, Let's Go Travel, and STA Travel (see Useful Travel Organizations, above), and from the following organizations:

Hostelling International (HI), 9 Guessens Rd., Welwyn Garden City, Hertfordshire AL8 6QW, England (tel. (0707) 33 24 87).

American Youth Hostels (AYH), 733 15th St., NW, Ste. 840, Washington, DC, 20005 (tel. (202) 783-6161; fax (202) 783-6171); also dozens of regional offices across the U.S. (call above number for information). Fee US$25, under 18 US$10, over 54 US$15. AYH is the U.S. member of HI. 200 hostels in U.S. Contact AYH for ISICs, student and charter flights, travel equipment, literature on budget travel, and information on summer positions as a group leader for domestic outings.

Hostelling International—Canada (HI-C), National Office, 1600 James Naismith Dr. #608, Gloucester, Ont. K1B 5N4 (tel. (613) 748-5638). 1-year membership fee CDN$26.75, under 18 CDN$12.84, 2-year CDN$37.45.

Youth Hostel Association of England and Wales (YHA), Trevelyan House, 14 Southampton St., London WC2E 7HY (tel. (0727) 855 215).

An Óige (Irish Youth Hostel Association), 61 Mountjoy Sq., Dublin 7 (tel. (01) 304 555; fax (01) 305 808). Fee £9, under 18 £3.

Australian Youth Hostels Association (AYHA), Level 3, 10 Mallett St., Camperdown, NSW, 2050 (tel. (02) 565 1699).

Youth Hostels Association of New Zealand, P.O. Box 436, corner of Manchester and Gloucester St., Christchurch 1 (tel. 379 99 70). Fee NZ$24.

Budget Accommodation Vol. 1: Europe and the Mediterranean (US$13.95), lists up-to-date information on HI hostels; it's available from any hostel association.

Always travel with a friend.

Get the International
Student Identity Card,
recognized worldwide.

For information call toll-free **1-800-GET-AN-ID**.
or contact any Council Travel office. (See inside front cover.)

Council on International Educational Exchange
205 East 42nd Street, New York, NY 10017

HI has recently instituted an **International Booking Network.** To reserve space in high season, obtain an International Booking Voucher from any national youth hostel association (in your home country or the one you will visit) and send it to a participating hostel 4 to 8 weeks in advance of your stay, along with US$2 in local currency. You can contact some hostels, indicated in the guide, by fax. If your plans are firm enough to allow it, pre-booking is wise.

■ Youth, Student, and Teacher Identification

The **International Student Identity Card (ISIC)** is the most widely accepted form of student identification. Flashing this card can garner you discounts for sights, theaters, museums, accommodations, train, ferry, and airplane travel, and other services throughout Europe. Present the card wherever you go, and ask about discounts even when none are advertised. It also provides accident insurance of up to US$3000 as well as US$100 per day of in-hospital care for up to 60 days. In addition, cardholders have access to a toll-free Traveler's Assistance hotline whose multilingual staff can provide help in medical, legal, and financial emergencies overseas.

Many student travel offices issue ISICs, including Council Travel, Let's Go Travel, and Student Travel Network in the U.S.; Travel CUTS in Canada; and any of the organizations under the auspices of the International Student Travel Confederation (ISTC) around the world (see Useful Travel Organizations). When you apply for the card, request a copy of the International Student Identity Card Handbook, which lists by country some of the available discounts. You can also write to CIEE for a copy (see Useful Travel Organizations). The card is valid from September to December of the following year. The fee is US$15. Applicants must be at least 12 years old and must be a student of a secondary or post-secondary school. Because of the proliferation of phony ISICs, many airlines and some other services now require other proof of student identity: have a signed letter from the registrar attesting to your student status and stamped with the school seal, and carry your school ID card. The new, US$16 **International Teacher Identity Card (ITIC)** offers identical discounts, in theory, but because of its recent introduction many establishments are reluctant to honor it. The application process is the same as for an ISIC.

Federation of International Youth Travel Organisations (FIYTO) issues a discount card to travelers who are not students but are under 26. Also known as the **International Youth Discount Travel Card** or the **GO 25 Card,** this 1-year card offers many of the same benefits as the ISIC, and most organizations that sell the ISIC also sell the Go 25 Card. A brochure that lists discounts is free when you purchase the card. To apply, bring: (1) proof of birthdate (copy of birth certificate, passport, or valid driver's license); and (2) a passport-sized photo (with your name printed on the back). The fee is US$10, CDN$12, or £4. For information, contact FIYTO at Bredgage 25H, DK-1260, Copenhagen K, Denmark (tel. 3333 9600; fax 3393 9676).

■ International Driving Permit

Unless you have a valid driver's license from an EC country, you must have an International Driving Permit (IDP) to drive in Europe, though certain countries allow travelers to drive with a valid American or Canadian license for a limited number of months. Most car rental agencies don't require the permit. A valid driver's license from your home country must always accompany the IDP.

Your IDP must be issued in your own country before you depart. U.S. license holders can obtain an International Driving Permit (US$10), valid for 1 year, at any **American Automobile Association (AAA)** office or by writing to its main office, AAA Florida, Travel Agency Services Department, 1000 AAA Drive, Heathrow, FL 32746-5080 (tel. (800) 222-4357 or (407) 444-7883; fax (407) 444-7380). For further information, contact a local AAA office.

Canadian license holders can obtain an IDP (CDN$10) through any **Canadian Automobile Association (CAA)** branch office in Canada, or by writing to CAA Toronto, 60 Commerce Valley Dr. East, Markham, Ont., L3T 7P9 (tel. (416) 771-3170).

Most credit cards cover standard insurance, but you will need a **green card,** or **International Insurance Certificate,** to prove that you have liability insurance. The application forms are available at any AAA or CAA office, or you can get one through the car rental agency; most of them include coverage in their prices. If you lease a car, you can obtain a green card from the dealer.

■■■ MONEY

> The prices listed here were compiled in the summer of 1993, when our researchers were in the field. Inflation and currency fluctuations have changed both our listed exchange rates as well as prices. Check the financial pages of a large newspaper for up-to-the-minute exchange rates before embarking on your journey, and count on at least some of the organizations and services listed in this guide being 10-15% more costly by the summer of 1994.

If you stay in hostels and prepare your own food, expect to spend anywhere from US$12-50 per day plus transportation, depending on the local cost of living and your needs. Don't sacrifice your health or safety for a cheaper tab; if you end up with pneumonia after pitching a tent on that cliff in northern Iceland, ain't no one to blame but yourself, baby.

■ Currency and Exchange

Banks in Europe often use a three-letter code based on the name of the country and the name of the currency (for example, New Zealand dollars are NZD and Norwegian kroner are NOK). We list this code at the beginning of each country section, with the abbreviation we use for that country's currency and the September, 1993 exchange rate for U.S. dollars (US$), Canadian dollars (CDN$), British pounds (UK£), Irish pounds (IR£), Australian dollars (AUS$), New Zealand dollars (NZ$) and South African Rand (SAR).

It's more expensive to buy foreign currency than to buy domestic; i.e., pounds will be less costly in the U.K. than in the U.S. Converting a small amount of money before you go, however, will allow you to breeze through the airport while others languish in exchange lines, and is a good practice in case you find yourself stuck with no money after banking hours or on a holiday, or if your flight arrives late in the evening. Observe commission rates closely, and check newspapers to get the standard rate of exchange. Bank rates are generally the best. Of course, services vary; in Germany, post offices generally offer the best exchange rates, while in Britain and Ireland, they're the worst. Since you lose money with every transaction, convert in large sums (provided the exchange rate is either staying constant or deteriorating), but not more than you will need.

American Express offices usually charge no commission, but often have slightly poorer rates. Tote bills or checks in small denominations, especially for those moments when you are forced to exchange money at train stations or, worse yet, at luxury hotels or restaurants.

Australian and New Zealand dollars are impossible to exchange in some countries. Keep a few U.S. dollars or German marks handy when heading into Eastern Europe; they can lubricate some squeaky situations. Western currency will often be the preferred payment in Eastern European hotels; find out which hotels and restaurants require hard currency before going there, and don't use Western money when you don't need to. Don't throw dollars around visibly to gain preferential treatment, however; besides being offensive, it'll make you an instant target for theft. Some res-

MONEY

Don't forget to write.

Now that you've said, "Let's go," it's time to say
"Let's get American Express® Travelers Cheques." If they are lost or
stolen, you can get a fast and full refund virtually anywhere you
travel. So before you leave be sure and write.

taurant owners, proprietors, or even taxi drivers may pick up on the fact that you're a foreigner and try to force you to pay in hard currency when it's not necessary. Stick to your guns or go somewhere else.

Purchase no more of one currency than you'll need; you lose money whenever you convert. Save transaction receipts; some countries require them to reconvert local currency. Exchanging some of your old currency before moving on to a new country, is, although a little more costly, good insurance against arriving after hours in a bankless town.

■ Traveler's Checks

Keep check receipts and a record of which checks you've cashed in a separate place from the checks themselves. Leave a photocopy of check serial numbers with someone at home as back-up in case you lose your copy. Never countersign checks until you're prepared to cash them.

American Express: (Call (800) 221-7282 in the U.S. and Canada; (0800) 52 13 13 in the U.K.; (02) 886 0689 in Australia, New Zealand, and the South Pacific with questions or to report lost or stolen Cheques. Elsewhere, call U.S. collect (801) 964-6665). AmEx Traveler's Cheques are the most widely recognized worldwide and easiest to replace if lost or stolen—call the information number or the AmEx Travel office nearest you. AmEx offices cash their Cheques commission-free (except where prohibited by national government) and sell Cheques which can be signed by either of 2 people traveling together ("Cheque for Two"). American Automobile Association members can obtain AmEx Traveler's Cheques commission-free at AAA offices. Request AmEx's booklet Traveler's Companion, listing travel office addresses and stolen Cheque hotlines for each European country.

Barclays Bank: Sells Visa traveler's checks. For lost or stolen checks, call Visa (U.S. tel. (800) 645-6556); for Barclays information, call (800) 221-2426 in the U.S. and Canada, (202) 671 212 in the U.K.; from elsewhere call New York collect at (212) 858-8500. Branches throughout Britain. Commission on check purchase varies (usually 1-3%). Barclays branches cash any Visa brand traveler's checks for free.

Citicorp: Sells Visa traveler's checks. Call (800) 645-6556 in the U.S. and Canada, (071) 982 4040 in London, elsewhere call the U.S. collect at (813) 623-1709. Commission 1-2% on check purchases. Check-holders automatically enrolled in **Travel Assist Hotline** (800) 523-1199 for 45 days: provides travelers with English-speaking doctor, lawyer, and interpreter referrals as well as check refund assistance.

MasterCard International: (tel. (800) 223-9920 in U.S. and Canada; elsewhere call U.S. collect (609) 987-7300.) Commission 1-2% for purchases. Checks issued in U.S. dollars.

Thomas Cook: Distributes traveler's checks with both the MasterCard and Thomas Cook names printed on them. Checks available in U.S. dollars as well as 10 other currencies. In U.S., call (800) 223-7373 for refunds, (800) 223-4030 for orders. Elsewhere call U.S. collect (212) 974-5696. 0-2% commission on purchase. Master-Card/Thomas Cook checks available at any bank displaying a MasterCard sign.

Visa: (tel. (800) 227-6811 in the U.S. and Canada; elsewhere, call New York collect (212) 858-8500 or London (071) 937-8091.)

■ Credit Cards and Cash Cards

Credit cards are not always useful to the budget traveler, but they can prove invaluable in a financial emergency. Visa and MasterCard are the most common, followed by American Express and Diner's Club. The British "Barclaycard" and "Access" are equivalent to Visa and MasterCard, respectively. You can often reduce conversion fees by charging a purchase instead of changing traveler's checks. With credit cards such as American Express, Visa, and MasterCard, associated banks will give you an instant cash advance in the local currency as large as your remaining credit line, but in most cases you will pay mortifying rates of interest for such an advance.

American Express (tel. (800) 528-4800) has a hefty annual fee (US$55) but offers a number of services. AmEx cardholders can cash personal checks at AmEx offices abroad. Global Assist, a 24-hour hotline offering information and legal assistance in emergencies, is also available (tel. (800) 333-2639 in U.S. and Canada; from abroad call U.S. collect (202) 554-2639). Cardholders can also take advantage of the American Express Travel Service; benefits include assistance in changing airline, hotel, and car rental reservations, sending mailgrams and international cables, and holding your mail at one of the more than 1500 AmEx offices around the world. **Master-Card** (tel. (800) 999-0454) and **Visa** (tel. (800) 336-8472) credit cards are sold by individual banks, and each bank offers different services in conjunction with the card. **Working Assets** (tel. (800) 522-7759) offers a Visa card, and donates a portion of money from purchases on their cards to 36 different non-profit, save-the-world organizations, and prints their bills and statements on recycled paper.

Automatic Teller Machines (ATMs; operated by bank cards) in Europe are not quite as prevalent as in North America, but most banks in larger cities are connected to an international money network, usually **PLUS** (U.S. tel. (800) 843-7587) or **CIR-RUS** (U.S. tel. (800) 424-7787). Depending on your home bank's system, you will probably be able to access your own personal bank account whenever you're in need of funds. Do this whenever possible, because ATM machines get the wholesale exchange rate which is generally 5% better than the retail rate most banks use. European ATMs may not have letters on their keypads, so make sure you memorize your PIN by its numbers before you take off.

■ Sending Money Abroad

The easiest way to get money from home is to bring an **American Express card;** AmEx allows green-card holders to draw cash from their checking accounts at any of its major offices and many of its representatives' offices, up to US$1000 every 21 days (no service charge, no interest). You can also wire money through the money transfer services operated by **Western Union** (tel. (800) 225-5227) or **American Express** (tel. (800) 543-4080; in Canada (800) 933-3278). The sender visits one of their offices or calls and charges it to a credit card; the receiver can pick up the cash at any overseas office within minutes (fee about US$25-35 to send US$250, US$70 for US$1000). American Express serves more countries than Western Union, but Western Union may be cheaper, especially in Western Europe. To pick up the money, you'll need either ID or the answer to a test question. The simplest and stodgiest route is to **cable money** from bank to bank. Find a local bank big enough to have an international department; bring the address of the receiving bank and the destination account number. Both sender and receiver must usually have accounts at the respective institutions. Transfer can take up to a few days; the fee is usually a flat US$20-30. Outside an AmEx office, avoid trying to cash checks in foreign currencies; they take weeks and a US$30 fee to clear.

If you're an American and suddenly find yourself in big trouble, you can have money sent to you via the Department of State's **Citizens Emergency Center** (tel. (202) 647-5225), which provides repatriation loans to pay for destitute Americans' direct return to the U.S. For more information, order the pamphlet The Citizens' Emergency Center (Department of State Publication 9746) from the Superintendent of Documents, U.S. Government Printing Office (see Visas for complete address). Citizens of other countries should see if their government provides a similar service.

■■■ HEALTH

■ Before You Go

Common sense is the simplest prescription for good health while you travel: eat well, drink enough, get enough sleep, and don't overexert yourself. If you're going to be doing a lot of walking, take some quick-energy foods to keep your strength up. You'll need plenty of protein (for sustained energy) and fluids (to prevent dehydration and constipation, two of the most common health problems for travelers). Carry a canteen or water bottle and drink frequently. If you are prone to sunburn, be sure to bring a potent sunscreen with you from home (it can be a expensive item while abroad), cover up with long sleeves and a hat, and drink plenty of fluids. Finally, remember to treat your most valuable resource well: lavish your feet with attention. Make sure your shoes are appropriate for extended walking, change your socks often, use talcum powder to keep dry, and have some moleskin on hand to pad hotspots before they become excruciating blisters.

For minor health problems, a compact **first-aid kit** should suffice. Some hardware stores carry ready-made ones, but it's just as easy to assemble your own: include bandages, aspirin, antiseptic soap or antibiotic cream, a thermometer in a sturdy case, a Swiss Army knife with tweezers, moleskin, a decongestant (to clear your ears if you fly with a cold), motion sickness remedy, medicine for diarrhea and stomach problems, sunscreen, insect repellent, burn ointment, and an elastic bandage.

Always go prepared with any **medication** you may need, as well as a copy of the prescription and/or a statement from your doctor, especially if you will be bringing insulin, syringes, or any narcotics into European countries. Travelers with chronic medical conditions should consult with their physicians before leaving.

If you wear **glasses** or **contact lenses,** take an extra prescription with you and arrange for someone at home to send you a replacement pair in an emergency. If you wear contacts, take along a pair of glasses to rest tired eyes. Bring extra solutions, enzyme tablets, and eyedrops; the price for lens solution can be exorbitant.

Any traveler with a medical condition that cannot be easily recognized (i.e. diabetes, epilepsy, heart conditions, allergies to antibiotics) may want to obtain a **Medic Alert Identification Tag.** In an emergency, their internationally recognized tag indicates the bearer's condition and the number of Medic Alert's 24-hour hotline. Lifetime membership begins at US$35. Contact Medic Alert Foundation, P.O. Box 1009, Turlock, CA 95381-1009 (tel. (800) 432-5378). The **American Diabetes Association**, 1660 Duke St., Alexandria, VA 22314 (tel. (000) 232-3472) provides copies of an article Travel and Diabetes and diabetic ID cards—messages in 18 languages on the carriers diabetic status. Contact your local ADA office for information.

All travelers should be concerned about **Acquired Immune Deficiency Syndrome (AIDS),** transmitted through the exchange of body fluids with an infected individual (HIV-positive). Remember that there is no assurance that someone is not infected: HIV tests only show antibodies after a six-month lapse. Do not have sex without using a condom or share intravenous needles. Travelers who are HIV-positive or have AIDS should check on possible immigration restrictions in the country which they wish to visit. The Center for Disease Control's **AIDS Hotline** provides information on AIDS in the U.S. and can refer you to other organizations with information on European countries (tel. (800) 342-2437; TTD (800) 243-7889). Call the **U.S. State Department** for country-specific restrictions for HIV-positive travelers (tel. (202) 647-1488; fax (202) 647-3000) or write to the Bureau of Consular Affairs, Rm. 5807, Dept. of State, Washington D.C. 20520. The **World Health Organization** provides written material on AIDS internationally (tel. (202) 861-3200).

Reliable **contraception** may be difficult to come by while traveling. Women on the pill should bring enough to allow for possible loss or extended stays. Although **condoms** are increasingly available, you might want to stock up on your favorite national brand before you go; availability and quality vary in European countries, and it's best to be prepared in case you need some during the flight over.

Attitudes towards and availability of **abortions** vary from country to country in Europe. The United States **National Abortion Federation's hotline** (tel. (800) 772-9100; Mon.-Fri. 9:30am-5:30pm) can direct you to organizations which provide information on abortion in other countries. Contact your embassy to receive a list of ob/gyn doctors who perform abortions.

For additional information before you go, you may wish to contact the **International Association for Medical Assistance to Travelers (IAMAT).** IAMAT provides several brochures on health for travelers, an ID card, a chart detailing advisable immunizations for 200 countries and territories, and a worldwide directory of English-speaking physicians who have had medical training in Europe or North America. Membership to the organization is free (although donations are welcome) and doctors are on call 24 hours a day for IAMAT members. Contact chapters in the **U.S.,** 417 Center St., Lewiston, NY, 14092 (tel. (716) 754-4883), in **Canada,** 40 Regal Rd. Guelph, Ontario, N1K 1B5 (tel. (519) 836-0102), and 1287 St. Clair Ave. West, Toronto, M6E 1B8 (tel. (416) 652-0137), and in **New Zealand,** P.O. Box 5049, 438 Pananui Rd., Christchurch 5 (tel. (03) 352-9053; fax (03) 352-4630).

Complete health information for travelers is available from a variety of published sources. The **Superintendent of Documents,** U.S. Government Printing Office, Washington D.C. 20402 (tel. (202) 783-3238), publishes Health Information for International Travel, detailing immunization requirements and other health precautions for travelers ($5).

■ Medical Attention While Abroad

While you travel, pay attention to the signals of pain and discomfort that your body may send you. This may be due to a new climate, diet, water quality, or pace when you first arrive or even after a couple of weeks. Once you get going, some of the milder symptoms that you may safely ignore at home may be signs of something more serious on the road; your increased exertion may wear you out and make you more susceptible to illness. Check with the publications and organizations listed above for more information or send for the **American Red Cross'** First-Aid and Safety Handbook (US$14.95), purchasable by writing to your local office or to American Red Cross, 99 Brookline Ave., Boston MA, 02215.

When traveling in summer, protect yourself against **heatstroke,** which can cause death; in the early stages, sweating stops, body temperature rises, and an intense headache develops, followed by confusion. To treat heatstroke, cool the victim off immediately with fruit juice or salted water, wet towels, and shade. Rush the victim to the hospital. Extreme cold is no less dangerous. The signs of **hypothermia** are uncontrollable shivering, poor coordination, and exhaustion, followed by slurred speech, hallucinations, and amnesia. Do not let victims fall asleep—unconsciousness can lead to death. To avoid hypothermia, keep dry, wear wool, dress in layers, and wear a wool hat. **Frostbite** turns skin white, waxy, and cold. NEVER rub frostbite—the skin is easily damaged. See a doctor as soon as possible.

Travelers in **high altitudes** should allow a couple of days to adjust to lower oxygen levels before engaging in strenuous activity, particularly long hikes. Those new to high altitudes may feel drowsy; alcoholic beverages will have stronger effects.

Food poisoning can spoil any trip. Some of the cheapest and most convenient eating options are also most prone: street vendors, tap water, and carrying perishable food for hours in a hot backpack. Generally, the less developed the nation you are visiting, the greater the likelihood of encountering contaminated water and food.

Diarrhea, known variously as turista, Montezuma's revenge, and "what a way to spend my vacation," has unmistakable symptoms but also, thankfully, some means of relief, such as the over-the-counter remedy Immodium. Since dehydration is the most common side effect of diarrhea, those suffering should drink plenty of fruit juice and water. The simplest anti-dehydration formula is still the most effective: 8oz. of water with a ½tsp. of sugar or honey and a pinch of salt. Down several of these a day, rest, and let the heinous disease run its course. If it does not subside within a few days, see a doctor immediately. Traveler's diarrhea may be the symptom of dysentery, giardia, or other parasitic conditions which can haunt your gastrointestinal track for years after your trip is over. Get these diseases treated in the country you're visiting, as your home health care provider may lack the knowledge necessary to detect the new friends who are eating your food.

Women traveling in unsanitary conditions are vulnerable to **urinary tract and bladder infections**, common and severely uncomfortable bacterial diseases which cause a burning sensation and pain during urination. Drink tons of juice (like cranberry) rich in vitamin C, plenty of water, and urinate (even though you really won't want to) frequently. Untreated, they can become very serious and develop into kidney infections or PID (pelvic inflammatory disease), both of which can lead to sterility and death. If symptoms persist, see a doctor.

■■■ SAFETY AND SECURITY

Tourists are particularly vulnerable to crime for two reasons: they often carry large amounts of cash, and they are not as savvy as locals. To avoid such unwanted attention, the best tactic is therefore to blend in as much as possible: the gawking camera-toter is much easier prey than the casual local look-alike. This is often harder than it sounds—chances are you will not be able to fully hide the fact that you're a tourist. Muggings are more often impromptu than planned; walking with nervous, over-the-shoulder glances can be a tip that you have something valuable to protect. Carry all your valuables (including your passport, railpass, traveler's checks, and airline ticket) either in a money belt or neckpouch stashed securely inside your clothing. These will protect you from skilled thieves who use razors to slash open backpacks and fanny packs (particular favorites of skilled bag-snatchers). Making photocopies of important documents will allow you to recover them in case they are lost or filched. Carry one copy separate from the documents and leave another copy at home.

When exploring new **cities,** extra vigilance may be wise, but don't let fear inhibit your ability to experience another culture. When walking at night, turn day-time precautions into mandates. Stay near crowded, well-lit places and do not attempt to cross through parks, parking lots, or any other large, deserted areas. Among the more colorful aspects of many large cities are the **con artists.** Be aware of certain classics: sob stories that require money, rolls of bills "found" on the street, mustard spilled (or saliva spit) onto your shoulder distracting you for enough time to snatch your bag. Always put on a bag so that the strap passes over your head and runs diagonally across your torso. Hustlers often work in groups, and children, unfortunately, are among the most effective. A firm "no" should communicate that you are no dupe. Contact the police if a hustler feels particularly insistent or aggressive.

Trains are other notoriously easy spots for thieving. Professionals wait for tourists to fall asleep and then carry off everything they can. When traveling in pairs, sleep in alternating shifts; when alone use good judgement in selecting a train compartment: never stay in an empty one. When sleeping, wrap the straps of your luggage securely about you. A product intended to prevent exactly this sort of theft is **The Jammer,** a US$3 plastic suction cup designed to be wedged into train compartment doors to prevent thieves from entering.

Sleeping in your **automobile** is one of the most dangerous ways to get your rest. Park in a well-lit area as close to a police station or 24-hour service station as possible. **Sleeping outside** can be even more dangerous—camping is recommendable only in official, supervised, campsites.

There is no sure-fire set of precautions that will protect you from all situations you might encounter when you travel. A good self-defense course will give you more concrete ways to react to different types of aggression, but it might cost you more money than your trip. **Model Mugging** (east coast tel. (617) 232-2900; midwest tel. (312) 338-4545; west coast tel. (415) 592-7300), a U.S. national organization with offices in several major cities, teaches a comprehensive course on self-defense (US$400-500; women's and men's courses offered). Call for details. The **U.S. Department of State's** (tel. (202) 783-3238) pamphlet A Safe Trip Abroad (US$1) summarizes safety information for travelers. It is available by calling the above number or by writing the Superintendent of Documents, U.S. Government Printing

Office, Washington D.C. 20402. For official Dept. of State **travel advisories** on European countries, including crime and security, call their 24-hour hotline at (202) 647-5225. More complete information on safety while traveling may be found in Travel Safety: Security and Safeguards at Home and Abroad, from Hippocrene Books, Inc., 171 Madison Ave., New York, NY 10016 (tel. (212) 685-4371; orders tel. (718) 454-2360; fax (718) 454-1391).

■ Insurance

Beware of unnecessary coverage—your current policies might well extend to many travel-related accidents. **Medical insurance** (especially university policies) often cover costs incurred abroad. Canadians are protected by their home province's health insurance plan: check with the provincial Ministry of Health or Health Plan Headquarters. Your **homeowners' insurance** (or your family's coverage) often covers theft during travel. Homeowners are generally covered against loss of travel documents (passport, plane ticket, railpass, etc.) up to US$500.

An **ISIC,** International Teacher ID or Student Card in the U.S. provides US$3000 worth of accident and illness insurance and US$100 per day up to 60 days of hospitalization. **CIEE** offers the Trip-Safe plan, with options covering medical treatment and hospitalization, accidents, baggage loss, and even charter flights missed due to illness; **STA** offers a more expensive, more comprehensive plan. **American Express** cardholders receive car-rental and flight insurance on purchases made with the card. (For addresses, see Useful Travel Organizations and Money, above.)

Insurance companies usually require a copy of the police report for thefts, or evidence of having paid medical expenses (doctor's statements, receipts) before they will honor a claim, and may have time limits on filing. Have documents written in English to avoid translating fees. Always carry policy numbers and proof of insurance. Note that some of the plans listed below offer cash advances or guaranteed bills. Check with each insurance carrier for specific restrictions.

Globalcare Travel Insurance, 220 Broadway, Lynnfield, MA, 01940 (tel. (800) 821-2488; fax (617) 592-7720). Complete medical, legal, emergency, and travel-related services. On-the-spot payments and special student programs.

Travelers Aid International, 918 16th St., N. W., Washington D. C. 20006 (tel. (202) 659-9468; fax (202) 659-2910). Help for theft, car failure, illness, and other "mobility-related problems." No fee, but you are expected to reimburse them for expenses.

Travel Assistance International, 1133 15th St., N. W., Washington D. C. 20005 (tel. (202) 821-2828; fax (202) 331-1609). Provides on-the-spot medical coverage (US$15,000-US$90,000) and unlimited medical evacuation insurance, 24-hr. emergency multilingual assistance hotline and worldwide local presence. Trip cancellation/interruption, baggage and accidental death and dismemberment insurance are also offered. Short-term and long-term plans available.

Travel Guard Internationale, 1145 Clark St., Stevens Point, WI 54481 (tel. (800) 826-1300 or (715) 345-0505; fax (715) 345-0525). "Travel Guard Gold" packages: Basic ($19), Deluxe ($39), and Comprehensive (8% of total trip cost) for medical expenses, baggage and travel documents, travel delay, baggage delay, emergency assistance, and trip cancellation/interruption. 24-hr. emergency hotline.

The Traveler's Insurance Company, 1 Tower Sq., Hartford, CT 06183-5040 (tel. (800) 243-3174). Insurance against accident, baggage loss, sickness, trip cancellation/interruption, and company default. Covers emergency medical evacuation.

■■■ PACKING

PACK LIGHT. Your backpack or suitcase may be light as a feather when you buy it, but in Europe, it will transform itself into a heavy, frustrating beast. Before you leave, pack your bag and take it for a walk. At the slightest sign of heaviness, unpack something. A good rule is to set out what you think you'll need, then take half of it and more money.

If you plan to cover a lot of ground by foot, a sturdy **backpack** is hard to beat. Internal frames stand up to airline baggage handlers and can often be converted to shoulder bags; external frames distribute weight more evenly. Whichever style you choose, avoid extremely low economy prices (good packs usually cost at least US$100). If checking a backpack on your flight, tape down loose straps, which can catch in the conveyer belt. Take a light **suitcase** or a large **shoulder bag** if you will not be doing much walking. A plastic bag packed inside your luggage will be useful for dirty laundry, while a small **daypack** is indispensable for plane flights, sight-seeing, carrying a camera, and/or keeping some of your valuables with you.

Comfortable **shoes** are essential. In sunny climates, sandals or other light shoes serve well. For heavy-duty hiking, sturdy lace-up walking boots are necessary. Make sure they have good ventilation. A double pair of socks—light absorbent cotton inside and thick wool outside—will cushion feet, keep them dry, and help prevent blisters. Bring a pair of light flip-flops for protection against the fungal floors of some station and hostel showers.

In wet regions, **raingear** is essential. A fold-up umbrella plus a waterproof Gore-Tex jacket plus a backpack rain cover will take care of you and your pack at a moment's notice; a rain poncho is more cumbersome but lightweight.

Also consider taking a pocketknife (with all the gizmos), tweezers, a flashlight, needle and thread, string, waterproof matches, a sturdy plastic water bottle, clothespins and clothesline, electrical tape, a small notebook, a traveler's clock, earplugs, rubber bands, sturdy plastic containers (for soap and detergent, for example), ziplock baggies, a squash ball (to use as a sink plug), and a padlock. Carry extra toiletries—especially aspirin, razor blades, and tampons—in Eastern Europe. The toilet paper in some areas of Europe can be rough on tender Western bottoms—if you're concerned, bring your own.

In most European countries, **electricity** is 220 volts AC, enough to fry any 110V North American appliance. Visit a hardware store for an adapter (which changes the

shape of the plug) and a converter (which changes the voltage). Do not make the mistake of using only an adapter, or you'll melt your radio. Travelers who heat-disinfect their contact lenses should consider switching temporarily to a chemical disinfection system. Contact **Franzus,** Murtha Industrial Park, P.O. Box 142, Railroad Ave., Beacon Falls, CT 06403 (tel. (203) 723-6664) for their free pamphlet, Foreign Electricity is No Deep Dark Secret.

■■■ ALTERNATIVES TO TOURISM

■ Study

Foreign study programs vary tremendously in expense, academic quality, living conditions, degree of contact with local students, and exposure to the local culture and language. Most American undergraduates enroll in programs sponsored by U.S. universities, and many colleges staff offices to give advice and information on study abroad. Take advantage of these counselors and put in some hours in their libraries. Ask for the names of recent participants in the programs, and get in touch.

American Field Service (AFS), 313 E. 43rd St., New York, NY 10017 (tel. (800) 237-4636 or (212) 949-4242). High school, summer, and year-long homestay exchange programs. Financial aid available. Austria, Belgium, Czech Republic, Denmark, Finland, France, Germany, Hungary, Iceland, Italy, Latvia, Netherlands, Norway, Portugal, Russia, Slovak Republic, Spain, Sweden, Switzerland, Turkey, U.K.

American Institute for Foreign Study/American Council for International Studies, 102 Greenwich Ave., Greenwich, CT 06830 (tel. (800) 727-2437; for high school students, call Boston office at (617) 421-9575). Organizes high school and college study in European universities. Programs in Paris, Grenoble, Cannes, London, Berlin, Salzburg, Florence, Grenada, and Salamanca.

ALTERNATIVES TO TOURISM: STUDY

What can you do with a Bachelor's Degree?

Travel to a foreign country and teach someone to speak English. WorldTeach offers you the opportunity to share your skills and knowledge with those in need, while they share their unique culture with you.

WorldTeach is a non-profit organization that matches dedicated volunteers with schools in developing countries. Our volunteers spend a year teaching English in Thailand, Namibia, South Africa, Costa Rica, Ecuador, Russia, or Poland. Programs for undergraduates include spending a semester coaching sports in South Africa or teaching English for a summer in China.

For a program fee ranging from $3300 to $4000, volunteers receive housing and board or a living allowance from their school or community as well as airfare, health insurance, training, placement, and field support. Many volunteers find private sponsors in their own community to help pay the fee, and student loans can be deferred while you teach. WorldTeach also offers a minimal amount of financial aid for outstanding applicants.

You can do something with your Bachelor's degree, something that will make a difference in the lives of others and your own. To apply you need a Bachelor's Degree in any subject area and a desire to share. For an application and more information, call us at (617) 495-5527, or write WorldTeach, Harvard Institute for International Development, One Eliot St., Cambridge, MA. 02138-5705.

WORLDTEACH

Association of Commonwealth Universities, John Foster House, 36 Gordon Square, London, WC1H 0PF, Great Britain (tel. (071) 387 8572). Administers scholarship programs such as the British Marshall Scholarships and publishes information about Commonwealth universities and support travel between them; 416 member institutions; information center with 16,000 volume reference library. Publishes Commonwealth Universities Yearbook, available for US$265 from Stockton Press, 257 Park Avenue South, NY, NY 10010, which provides information on study at institutions throughout the Commonwealth.

Central Bureau for Educational Visits and Exchanges, Seymour Mews House, Seymour Mews, London W1H 9PE, England (tel. (071) 486 5101). Publishes Study Holidays (£7.75 in bookstores, postage extra): basic information on over 600 language study programs in 25 European countries. Distributed in North America by IIE (see below).

Institute of International Education Books (IIE Books), 809 United Nations Plaza, New York NY 10017-3580 (tel. (212) 984-5412; fax (212) 984-5358) puts out several annual reference books on study abroad. Academic Year Abroad (US$42.95 plus US$4 postage) and Vacation Study Abroad (US$36.95 plus US$4 postage) detail over 3,600 programs offered by U.S. colleges and universities overseas. Distributes several books published by the **Central Bureau for Educational Visits and Exchanges** in the U.K., including Study Holidays, Working Holidays, and Home from Home (all **CB** books are US$22.95 plus US$4 postage each.) They also operate the International Education Information Center at the UN Plaza address, open Tues.-Fri. 11am-4pm.

Unipub Co., 4611-F Assembly Dr., Lanham, MD 20706-4391 (tel. (800) 274-4888). Distributes International Agency Publications including UNESCO's Study Abroad (US$24, postage US$2.50). International scholarships and courses for students of various ages. Unwieldy but excellent book.

World Learning, Inc., Summer Abroad, P.O. Box 676, Brattleboro, VT 05302 (tel. (802) 257-7751, ext. 3452, or (800) 345-2929). Founded in 1932 as **The Experiment in International Living,** now titled World Learning, Inc. Same address for semester programs. Positions as tour group leaders are available world-wide. For

the programs themselves, most U.S. colleges will transfer credit for semester work done abroad. Some financial aid is available.

■ Work

There's no better way to submerge yourself in a foreign culture than to become part of its economy. The good news is that it's very easy to find a temporary job abroad; the bad news is that unless you have connections, it will rarely be glamorous and may not even pay for your plane ticket over.

Officially, you can hold a job in European countries only with a work permit, applied for by your prospective employer (or by you, with supporting papers from the employer). Many countries are tight-fisted with work permits due to large numbers of working-age immigrants; often, an employer must demonstrate that a potential employee has skills that locals lack. The real catch-22 is that normally you must physically enter the country in order to have immigration officials validate your work permit papers and note your status in your passport. This means that if you can't set up a job from afar (which requires contacts and time) and have the work permit sent to you, you must enter the country to look for a job, find an employer, and have them start the permit process, then leave the country until the permit is sent to you (up to 6 weeks), and finally reenter the country and start work.

In practice, it's rarely so complicated. Friends in Europe can help expedite work permits or arrange work-for-accommodations swaps. Many permit-less agricultural workers go untroubled by local authorities, who recognize the need for seasonal help. European Community citizens can work in any other EC country without working papers, and if your parents or grandparents were born in an EC country, you may be able to claim dual citizenship or at least the right to a work permit. (Beware, however, of countries where claiming citizenship obligates you to do military service.) Students can check with their universities' foreign language departments, which may have official or unofficial connections to job openings abroad.

(right margin, vertical) ALTERNATIVES TO TOURISM: STUDY

If you are a full-time student at a U.S. or Canadian university, the simplest way to get a job abroad is through work permit programs run by **CIEE** and its member organizations (see Useful Travel Organizations above). For a US$125 application fee, CIEE can procure 3- to 6-month work permits (and a handbook to help you find work and housing) for Britain, France, Germany, Ireland, and Spain. French and German positions require evidence of language skills; the British program is the best for neophytes, since a special CIEE office helps with finding openings and making friends. **Travel CUTS**'s Canadian program is similar, but does not include Germany.

The number of books listing work-abroad opportunities has ballooned in the past few years. Start with CIEE's free booklet Work Abroad, then graduate to the excellent publications put out by **Vacation Work,** 9 Park End St., Oxford OX1 1HJ, England (tel. (0865) 24 19 78). Many of their books are also available in bookstores in the United States, through Travel CUTS, or from **Peterson's Guides,** 202 Carnegie Center, P.O. Box 2123, Princeton, NJ 08543 (tel. (800) 338-3282 or (609) 243-9111). CIEE also publishes many work-abroad pamphlets and guides. **InterExchange Program,** 161 Sixth Avenue, New York, NY 10013 (tel. (212) 924-0446), provides information in pamphlet form on international work programs and au pair positions in France, Germany, Austria, Norway, Finland, Spain, and Italy.

World Trade Academy Press, 50 East 42nd St. Suite 509, New York, NY 10017 (tel. (212) 697-4999), publishes Looking for Employment in Foreign Countries (US$16.50) which gives information on federal, commercial, and volunteer jobs abroad and advice on resumes and interviews. Other guides to check out are Working Holidays (US$22.95 from IIE), an annual guide to short-term paid and voluntary work in Britain and around the world, and Home From Home (£6.99 plus postage), a guide to international homestays, termstays, and exchanges, available from the Central Bureau for Educational Visits and Exchanges (see Study, above).

The best tips on jobs for foreigners come from other travelers, so be alert and inquisitive. Many travelers follow the grape harvest in the fall—mostly in France, but also in Switzerland and Germany's Mosel Valley. More or less menial jobs can be found anywhere in Europe; for instance, Swiss ski resorts leave much of the grunt-work to foreigners. (Be aware of your rights as an employee; should a crafty national try to refuse payment at the end of the season, it'll help to have a written confirmation of your agreement.) Youth hostels frequently provide room and board to travelers willing to stay a while and help run the place. Au pair baby-sitting and household jobs abound in Great Britain, France, and, to some extent, in Germany and Scandinavia. Look for newspaper ads and bulletin board notices.

In non-English-speaking countries, consider **teaching English.** Post a sign in markets or learning centers stating that you are a native speaker, and scan the classifieds of local newspapers, where residents often advertise for language instruction. Teaching English may be your only option in Eastern Europe. Various organizations in the U.S. will place you in a (low-paying) teaching job, but securing a position will require patience and legwork, because teaching English abroad has become enormously popular in the past few years. Professional English-teaching positions are harder to get; most European schools require at least a bachelor's degree and most often training in teaching English as a foreign language. Call or write **WorldTeach,** HIID, 1 Eliot St., Cambridge, MA 02138 (tel. (617) 495-5527) for information.

■ Volunteering

Volunteer jobs are readily available almost everywhere. You may receive room and board in exchange for your labor, and the work can be fascinating. Opportunities include archeological digs and community and workcamp projects. Keep in mind: the organizations that arrange placement sometimes charge high application fees in addition to the workcamps' charges for room and board. You can sometimes avoid this extra fee by contacting the individual workcamps directly; check with the organization. Listings in Vacation Work's International Directory of Voluntary Work (£8.95; see ordering information under Work above) can be helpful.

Archaeological Institute of America, 675 Commonwealth Ave., Boston, MA 02215 (tel. (617) 353-9361). The 1994 edition of Archaeological Fieldwork Opportunities Bulletin, (US$10.50 for nonmembers) is available from Kendall Hunt Publishers at (800) 338-5578. Lists field projects throughout the world.

Council on International Educational Exchange (CIEE), see listing above.

Service Civil International/International Voluntary Service-USA, Rte. 2, Box 506, Crozet, VA 22932 (tel. (804) 823-1826). Arranges placement in workcamps in Europe (ages 18 and over). Registration fees in 1992 US$40-200, depending on the camp location, will most likely go up for 1994.

Volunteers for Peace, 43 Tiffany Rd., Belmont, VT 05730 (tel. (802) 259-2759). Arranges placement in over 800 workcamps in 37 countries, primarily in Europe. Opportunities from reclaiming an abandoned island near Venice to repairing bicycles in Belgium for export to South African refugees, to excavating concentration camps in Germany. Gives perhaps the most complete and up-to-date listings in the annual International Workcamp Directory (US$10 postpaid). Registration fee US$125.

■■■ SPECIFIC CONCERNS

■ Women and Travel

Women exploring any area on their own inevitably face additional safety concerns. In all situations it is best to trust your instincts: if you'd feel better somewhere else, don't hesitate to move on. You may want to consider staying in hostels which offer single rooms which lock from the inside or religious organizations that offer rooms for women only. Stick to centrally-located accommodations and avoid late-night treks or metro rides. Hitching is never safe for lone women, or even for two women traveling together. Choose train compartments occupied by other women or couples. In some parts of the world women (foreign or local) are frequently beset by unwanted and tenacious followers. Exercise reasonable caution without feeling that you must avoid all local men. To escape unwanted attention, follow the example of local women. In general, dress conservatively, especially in more rural areas. If you spend time in cities, you may be harassed no matter how you're dressed. Look as if you know where you're going (even when you don't) and ask women or couples for directions if you're lost or if you feel uncomfortable. Your best answer to verbal harassment is no answer at all (a reaction is what the harasser wants). In crowds, you may be pinched or squeezed by oversexed slimeballs; wearing a wedding band may help prevent such incidents. Don't hesitate to seek out a police officer or a passerby if you are being harassed. Memorize the emergency numbers in the countries you visit, and always carry change for the phone and enough extra money for a bus or taxi. Carry a whistle or an airhorn on your keychain, and don't hesitate to use it in an emergency. A **model mugging** course will not only prepare you for a potential mugging, but will also raise your level of awareness of your surroundings as well as your confidence. (See Safety and Security, above.) Women also face additional health concerns when traveling (see Health, above). All of these warnings and suggestions should not discourage women from traveling alone. Don't take unnecessary risks, but don't lose your spirit of adventure either.

A series of recent travelogues by women outline their sojourns: Nothing to Declare: Memoirs of a Woman Traveling Alone (Penguin Books; US$9) and Wall to Wall: From Beijing to Berlin by Rail (Penguin Books; US$10) by Mary Morris; One Dry Season (Knopf) by Caroline Alexander; Tracks (Pantheon) by Robin Davidson; The Road Through Miyama (Random House/Vintage) by Leila Philips, and anything by Isak Dinesen, especially Out of Africa (Random House). For additional tips and suggestions, consult The Handbook for Women Travelers (£7.99) by Maggie and Gemma Moss, published by Piatkus Books, 5 Windmill St., London W1P 1HF England (tel. 44 (071) 631 0710). Women Going Places, a new women's travel and resource guide, emphasizing women-owned enterprises, is geared towards lesbians, but offers advice appropriate for all women. (US$14. Available from Inland Book Company, P.O. Box 120261, East Haven, CT 06512; tel. (203) 467-4257).

■ Older Travelers and Senior Citizens

Proof of senior citizen status is required for many of the discounts listed below.

AARP (American Association of Retired Persons), 601 E St. NW, Washington, DC 20049 (tel. (202) 434-2277 or (800) 927-0111). U.S. residents over 50 and their spouses receive benefits which include travel programs and discounts on lodging, car, and RV rental, air arrangements, and sight-seeing. US$8 annual fee.

Elderhostel, 75 Federal St., 3rd floor, Boston, MA 02110. You must be 60 or over, and may bring a spouse who is over 50. Programs at colleges and universities in over 40 countries focus on varied subjects and generally last 1 week.

Gateway Books, P.O. Box 10244, San Rafael, CA 94912. Publishes Gene and Adele Malott's Get Up and Go: A Guide for the Mature Traveler (US$10.95, postage US$1.90). Recommendations and general hints for the budget-conscious senior. Call (800) 669-0773 for orders.

National Council of Senior Citizens, 1331 F St. NW, Washington, DC 20004 (tel. (202) 347-8800). For US$12 a year or US$150 for a lifetime an individual or couple can receive hotel and auto rental discounts, a senior citizen newspaper, use of a discount travel agency, and supplemental Medicare insurance (if you're over 65).

Pilot Books, 103 Cooper St., Babylon, NY 11702 (tel. (516) 422-2225). Publishes The International Health Guide for Senior Citizens (US$4.95, postage US$1) and The Senior Citizens' Guide to Budget Travel in Europe (US$5.95 postpaid).

■ Travelers with Children

Tyke-toting travelers will want to check out the following books and publishers:

Wilderness Press, 2440 Bancroft Way, Berkeley, CA 94704 (tel. (800) 443-7227 or (510) 843-8080). Publishes Sharing Nature with Children (US$7.95) and Back-packing with Babies and Small Children (US$8.95).

John Muir Publications, P.O. Box 613, Santa Fe, NM 87504 (tel. (800) 888-7504). The Kidding Around series of illustrated books for children includes one about London that might be educational and distracting on long trips (US$9.95; postage US$2.75 for the 1st book, US50¢ thereafter).

Lonely Planet Publications, Embarcadero West, 112 Linden St., Oakland, CA 94607 (tel. (510) 893-8555 or (800) 275-8555); also P.O. Box 617, Hawthorn, Victoria 3122, Australia. Publishes Maureen Wheeler's Travel with Children (US$10.95, postage US$1.50 in the U.S.).

■ Travelers with Disabilities

Countries vary in their general accessibility to travelers with disabilities. Some national and regional tourist boards provide directories on the accessibility of various accommodations and transportation services. If these services are not available, contact institutions of interest directly. The amount of information for travelers with disabilities is still quite small; if you find additional publications or other information, please let us know for next year's edition.

Rail is probably the most convenient form of travel. Large stations in Britain are equipped with wheelchair facilities, and the French national railroad offers wheelchair compartments on all TGV (high speed) and Conrail trains. Contact your destination's station in advance for specific information, or call **Rail Europe** in the U.S. at (800) 345-1990 (fax (914) 682-2821). Most countries require a 6-month quarantine for all animals, including guide dogs. To obtain an import license, owners must supply current certification of the animal's rabies, distemper and contagious hepatitis inoculations, and a veterinarian's letter attesting to its health.

American Foundation for the Blind, 15 W. 16th St., New York, NY 10011 (tel. (212) 620-2147). ID cards (US$10); write for an application, or call the Product Center at (800) 829-0500. Also call this number to order AFB catalogs in braille, print, or on cassette or disk.

Directions Unlimited, 720 North Bedford Rd., Bedford Hills, NY 10507 (tel. (800) 533-5343 or (914) 241-1700). Specializes in arranging individual and group vacations, tours, and cruises for those with disabilities.

Disability Press, Ltd., Applemarket House, 17 Union St., Kingston-upon-Thames, Surrey KT1 1RP, England (tel. (081) 549 6399). Publishes the Disabled Traveler's International Phrasebook, including French, German, Italian, Spanish, Portuguese, Swedish, and Dutch phrases (UK£1.75). Supplements in Norwegian, Hungarian, and Serbo-Croatian (60p each).

Evergreen Travel Service, 4114 198th St. SW, Suite #13, Lynnwood, WA 98036 (tel. (800) 435-2288 or (206) 776-1184). Arranges wheelchair-accessible tours and individual travel worldwide; also tours for blind persons and deaf persons.

The Guided Tour, Inc. Elkins park house, Suite 114B, 7900 Old York Road, Elkins Park, PA 19117-2348 (tel. (215) 782-1370 or (800) 738-5843). Year-round travel programs for persons with developmental and physical challenges as well as those geared to the needs of persons requiring renal dialysis. Trips and vacations planned both domestically and internationally. Call or write for a free brochure.

Mobility International, USA (MIUSA), P.O. Box 3551, Eugene, OR 97403 (tel. (503) 343-1284 voice and TDD). International headquarters in Britain, 228 Borough High St., London SE1 1JX (tel. (071) 403 5688). Contacts in 30 countries. Information on travel programs, international work camps, accommodations, access guides, and organized tours. Membership costs US$20/year, newsletter US$10. Sells updated and expanded A World of Options: A Guide to International Educational Exchange, Community Service, and Travel for Persons with Disabilities (US$14, nonmembers US$16, postpaid).

Moss Rehabilitation Hospital Travel Information Service, 1200 W. Tabor Rd., Philadelphia, PA 19141 (tel. (215) 456-9603). Information on international travel accessibility: nominal fee charged for packet of information on tourist sights, accommodations, and transportation.

Pauline Hephaistos Survey Projects, 39 Bradley Gardens, West Ealing, London W13 8HE, England. Distributes access guides to London and Paris (£4 each), researched by people with disabilities.

Society for the Advancement of Travel for the Handicapped, 347 Fifth Ave., Suite 610, New York, NY 10016 (tel. (212) 447-7284); fax (212) 725-8253). Publishes quarterly travel newsletter SATH News and information booklets (free for members, US$3 each for nonmembers). Advice on trip planning for people with disabilities. Annual membership is US$45, students and seniors US$25.

Twin Peaks Press, P.O. Box 129, Vancouver, WA 98666 (tel. (206) 694-2462, orders only (800) 637-2256). Travel for the Disabled lists tips and resources for disabled travelers (US$19.95). Also available are the Directory for Travel Agencies of the Disabled (US$19.95) and Wheelchair Vagabond (US$14.95). Postage US$2 for first book, US$1 for each additional.

■ Bisexual, Gay, and Lesbian Travelers

Are You Two Together?, published by Random House; available at bookstores (US$18). Gay and lesbian guide to spots in Europe. Written by a lesbian couple; covers Western European capitals and gay resorts.

Ferrari Publications, P.O. Box 37887, Phoenix, AZ 85069 (tel. (602) 863-2408). Publishes Ferrari's Places of Interest (US$14.95), Ferrari's Places for Men (US$13.95), Ferrari's Places for Women (US$12), and Inn Places: USA and Worldwide Gay Accommodations (US$14.95). Also available from Giovanni's Room (see below).

Gay's the Word, 66 Marchmont St., London WC1N 1AB, England (tel. (071) 278 7654). Tube: Russel Sq. Open Mon.-Fri. 11am-7pm, Sat. 10am-6pm, Sun. and holidays 2-6pm. Information for gay and lesbian travelers. Mail order service available.

Giovanni's Room, 345 S. 12th St., Philadelphia, PA 19107 (tel. (215) 923-2960; fax (215) 923-0813). International feminist, lesbian, and gay bookstore with mail-order service.

Spartacus International Gay Guide, (US$29.95). Order from 100 East Biddle St., Baltimore, MD 21202 (tel. (410) 727-5677) or c/o Bruno Lützowstraße, P.O. Box 301345, D-1000 Berlin 30, Germany (tel. (30) 25 49 82 00); also available from Giovanni's Room (see above) and from Renaissance House, P.O. Box 292 Village Station, New York, NY 10014 (tel. (212) 674-0120). Extensive list of gay bars, restaurants, hotels, bookstores, and hotlines throughout the world. Very specifically for men.

Women Going Places, (US$14). A new women's travel and resource guide emphasizing women-owned enterprises. Geared towards lesbians, but offers advice appropriate for women of all sexual orientations. Available from Inland Book Company, P.O. Box 120261, East Haven, CT 06512 (tel. (203) 467-4257).

■ Kosher and Vegetarian Travelers

National tourist offices often publish lists of kosher and vegetarian restaurants.

Jewish Chronicle Publications, London EC4A 1JT, England. The Jewish Travel Guide is available in the U.S. from Sepher-Hermon Press, 1265 46th St., Brooklyn, NY 11219 (tel. (718) 972-9010) for US$11.95, postage US$1.75. In the U.K., order from Jewish Chronicle Publications, 25 Furnival St., London EC4A England. Lists synagogues, kosher restaurants, and institutions in over 80 countries.

North American Vegetarian Society, P.O. Box 72, Dolgeville, NY 13329 (tel. (518) 568-7970). Ask about their publications which relate to travel.

Vegetarian Society of the U.K., Parkdale, Dunham Rd., Altringham, Cheshire WA14 4QG (tel. (61) 928 0793). The International Vegetarian Travel Guide.

■ Minority Travelers

We have been hard-pressed to find any resources that advise members of visible minorities on specific travel concerns; if our readers have knowledge of any such information, please write to us and let us know.

In certain regions, tourists of color or members of certain religious groups may feel unwelcomed by local residents. Furthermore, either historical or newly-developed discrimination against established minority residents may surface against travelers who are members of those minority groups. In your travels, you may find signs stating things such as "Interdit aux Africains" ("No Africans"). Let's Go asks that our researchers do not include such establishments in our guides. If, in your travels, you encounter discriminatory treatment, you should firmly state your disapproval, but do not push the matter; make it clear to the owners that another hotel or restaurant will be receiving your patronage.

In terms of safety, we don't have any easy answers. Traveling in groups and taking a taxi whenever you are uncomfortable are always good ideas; your personal safety should always be your first priority. For the traveler, the best answer to xenophobic comments and other verbal harassment is no answer at all. Keep abreast of the particular cultural attitudes of the countries you're planning to visit. But above all, keep in mind that your ethnicity or religion will not necessarily be problematic; you very well may find your vacation trouble-free and your hosts open-minded.

■■■ BOOKS, GUIDES, MAPS, ETC.

The College Connection, 19 Newtown Turnpike, Westport CT 06880. Publishes The Passport, a booklet listing hints about every aspect of traveling and studying abroad. Distributed free of charge to universities; call (800) 952-7277.

European Festivals Association, 122, rue de Lausanne, 1202 Geneva, Switzerland (tel. (022) 732 28 03). Their booklet Festivals lists dates and programs of major music galas. Student rates are often available.

Forsyth Travel Library, P.O. Box 2975, Shawnee Mission, KS 66201 (tel. (800) 367-7984). Maps, guidebooks, railpasses, and timetables.

John Muir Publications, P.O. Box 613, Santa Fe, NM 87504 (tel. (505) 982-4078 or (800) 888-7504). Publishes an excellent series of books by veteran traveler Rick Steves, including *Europe Through the Back Door,* offering great advice on the dos and don'ts of budget travel (US$16.95), *2 to 22 Days in Great Britain* (US$10.95), and *Mona Winks: Self-Guided Tours of Europe's Top Museums* (US$16.95). Also available in bookstores. See also Traveling with Children, above, for more John Muir publications.

Hippocrene Books, Inc. 171 Madison Ave., New York, NY 10016 (orders: tel. (718) 454-2366). Strong concentration on Eastern Europe. Offers **Handy Dictionaries** (US$6.95) for travelers and language tapes.

Michelin Maps and Guides, Davy House, Lyon Rd., Harrow, Middlesex HA1 2DQ, England (tel. (081) 861 2121). Their Green Guides for Western Europe can't be matched for historical and cultural background. Visit your bookstore or, in the U.S., call or write P.O. Box 3305, Spartanburg, SC 29304 (tel. (803) 599-0850).

Travelling Books, PO Box 77114, Seattle, WA 98177, publishes a catalogue of travel guides which will make the armchair traveler weep with wanderlust.

Wide World Books and Maps, 1911 N. 45th St., Seattle, WA 98103 (tel. (206) 634-3453). Open Mon.-Fri. 10am-7pm, Sat. 10am-6pm, Sun. noon-5pm. Write them for hard-to-find maps.

GETTING THERE

The first challenge in European budget travel is getting there. The airline industry attempts to squeeze every dollar from customers; finding a cheap airfare in their computerized jungle will be easier if you understand the airlines' systems better than they think you do. Call every toll-free number and don't be afraid to ask about discounts. Have a knowledgeable travel agent guide you; better yet, have several knowledgeable travel agents guide you. Remember that travel agents may not want to do the legwork to find the cheapest fares (for which they receive the lowest commissions). Students and people under 26 should never need to pay full price for a ticket. Seniors can also get great deals; many airlines offer senior traveler clubs or airline passes and discounts for their companions as well. Sunday newspapers have travel sections that list bargain fares from the local airport. Outfox airline reps with the phone-book-sized Official Airline Guide (at large libraries), a monthly guide listing every scheduled flight in the world (with prices). The Airline Passenger's Guerilla Handbook (US$14.95; last published in 1990) is a more renegade resource.

Most airfares peak between mid-June and early September. Midweek (Mon.-Thurs.) flights run about US$30 cheaper each way than on weekends. Leaving the States from a travel hub such as New York, Atlanta, Dallas, Chicago, Los Angeles, San Francisco, Vancouver, or Toronto will win a more competitive fare than from smaller cities; the gains are not as great when departing from travel hubs monopolized by one airline. Flying to London is usually the cheapest way across the Atlantic, though special fares to other cities such as Amsterdam, Luxembourg, or Brussels can be even lower. Return-date flexibility is usually not an option for the budget traveler; except on youth fares purchased through the airlines, traveling with an "open return" ticket can be pricier than fixing a return date and paying to change it. Be wary of one-way tickets, too: the flight to Europe may be economical, but the return fares are outrageous. Whenever flying internationally, pick up your ticket well in advance of the departure date and arrive at the airport several hours before your flight.

■■■ COMMERCIAL AIRLINES

Even if you pay an airline's lowest published fare, you may waste hundreds of dollars. The commercial airlines' lowest regular offer is the **APEX** (Advance Purchase Excursion Fare); specials advertised in newspapers may be cheaper, but have more restrictions and fewer available seats. APEX fares provide you with confirmed reservations and allow "open-jaw" tickets (landing in and returning from different cities). Reservations usually must be made at least 21 days in advance, with 7- to 14-day minimum and 60- to 90-day maximum stay limits, and hefty cancellation and change penalties. For summer travel, book APEX fares early; by May you will have a hard time getting the departure date you want.

Most airlines no longer offer standby fares, once a staple of the budget traveler. Standby in the United States has given way to the **3-day-advance-purchase youth fare**, a cousin of the 1-day variety prevalent in Europe. It's available only to those under 25 (sometimes 24) and only within 3 days of departure, a gamble that can backfire. Return dates are open, but you must come back within a year, and again, can book your return seat no more than 3 days ahead. Youth fares in summer aren't really cheaper than APEX, but off-season prices drop deliciously.

Look into flights to less-popular destinations or on smaller carriers. **Icelandair** (tel. (800) 223-5500) sports last-minute offers and a "get-up-and-go" fare from New York to Luxembourg (June-Sept. US$299 weekdays, US$329 weekends; Oct.-May US$268 weekdays, US$288 weekends). Reservations must be made within 3 days of departure. After arrival, Icelandair offers discounts on trains and buses from Luxembourg to other parts of Europe. **Virgin Atlantic Airways** (tel. (800) 862-8621) offers the Instant Purchase Plan (New York to London round trip US$432), under which reservations can be made no more than 10 days before departure.

■■■ STUDENT TRAVEL AGENCIES

Students and people under 26 with proper ID qualify for enticing reduced airfares. These are rarely available from airlines or travel agents, but instead from student travel agencies like **Let's Go Travel, STA, Travel CUTS, University Travel Network, Travel Management International,** and CIEE's **Council Travel** (see under Useful Travel Organizations at the beginning of the book). These agencies negotiate special reduced-rate bulk purchases with the airlines, then resell them to the youth market; in 1993, peak season round-trip rates from the east coast of North America to even the offbeat corners of Europe rarely topped US$700 (though flights to Russia were higher), and off-season fares were considerably lower. Return-date change fees also tend to be low (around US$50). Most of their flights are on major airlines, though in peak season some seats may be on less reliable chartered aircraft. Student travel agencies can also help non-students and people over 26, but probably won't be able to get the same low fares.

■■■ TICKET CONSOLIDATORS AND CHARTER FLIGHTS

Ticket consolidators resell unsold tickets on commercial and charter airlines. Look for their tiny ads in weekend papers (in the U.S., the Sunday New York Times is best), and start calling them all. There is rarely a maximum age; tickets are also heavily discounted, and may offer extra flexibility or bypass advance purchase requirements, since you aren't tangled in airline bureaucracy. But unlike tickets bought through an airline, you won't be able to use your tickets on another flight if you miss yours, and you will have to go back to the consolidator to get a refund, rather than the airline. Phone around and pay with a credit card so you can stop payment if you never receive your tickets. Don't be tempted solely by the low prices; find out everything you can about the agency you're considering, and get a copy of their refund policy in writing. Ask also about accommodations and car rental discounts; some consolidators have fingers in many pies. Insist on a **receipt** that gives full details about the tickets, refunds, and restrictions, and if they don't want to give you one or just generally seem clueless or shady, use a different company.

It's best to buy from a major organization that has experience in placing individuals on charter flights. One of the most reputable is the CIEE-affiliated **Council Charter,** 205 E. 42nd St., New York, NY 10017 (tel. (800) 800-8222); their flights can also be booked through Council Travel offices. **Unitravel** (tel. (800) 325-2222) offers discounted airfares on major scheduled airlines from the U.S. to over 50 cities in Europe and holds all payments until completion of your trip. Try also **Access International** (tel. 800 825-3633); **Interworld** (tel. (800) 331-4456; in Florida, (305) 443-4929); **Rebel** (tel. (800) 227-3235); and **Travac** (tel. (800) 872-8800). Don't be afraid to call every number and hunt for the best deal.

Consolidators sell some tickets on scheduled airlines, some on **charter flights.** Once a system in its own right, the charter business has effectively merged with the ticket consolidator network. The theory behind a charter is that a tour operator contracts with an airline (usually one specializing in charters) to fly extra loads of passengers to peak-season destinations. Charter flights fly less frequently than major airlines and have more restrictions. They are also almost always fully booked, and schedules and itineraries may change or be canceled at the last moment; you'll be much better off purchasing a ticket on a regularly scheduled airline. As always, pay with a credit card if you can; consider travelers insurance against trip interruption.

Airhitch, 2790 Broadway #100, New York, NY 10025 (tel. (212) 864-2000), advertises a similar service: you choose a date range in which to travel and a list of preferred European destinations, and they try to place you in a vacant spot on a flight. Complete flexibility on both sides of the Atlantic is necessary, but the savings may be worth it: flights cost US$169 each way when departing from the East Coast, US$269 from the West Coast, and US$229 from most places between. Airhitch only guarantees that you'll end up in Europe; check all flight times and departure sites

directly with the airline carrier, read all the fine print, and compare it to what people tell you. The Better Business Bureau of New York City has received complaints about this company; at this time they neither recommend nor condemn it.

Eleventh-hour **discount clubs** and **fare brokers** offer members savings on European travel, including charter flights and tour packages. Research your options carefully. **Last Minute Travel Club,** 1249 Boylston St., Boston, MA 02215 (tel. (800) 527-8646 or (617) 267-9800), is one of the few travel clubs that doesn't charge a membership fee. Others include **Discount Travel International** (tel. (800) 324-9294), **Moment's Notice** (tel. (212) 486-0503; US$25 annual fee), **Traveler's Advantage** (tel. (800) 835-8747; US$49 annual fee), and **Worldwide Discount Travel Club** (tel. (305) 534-2082; US$50 annual fee). For US$25, **Travel Avenue** (tel. (800) 333-3335) will search for the lowest international airfare available and then discount it 5-17%. Study these organizations' contracts closely; you don't want to stop over in Luxembourg for 11 hours.

■■■ COURIER FLIGHTS AND FREIGHTERS

Those who travel light should consider flying to Europe as a courier. The company hiring you will use your checked luggage space for freight; you're only allowed to bring carry-ons. Restrictions to watch for: most flights are round-trip only with fixed-length stays (usually short); you may not be able to travel with a companion (single tickets only); and most flights are from New York (including a scenic visit to the courier office in the 'burbs). Round-trip fares to Western Europe from the U.S. range from US$200-350 (during the off-season) to US$400-550 (during the summer). **NOW Voyager,** 74 Varick St., #307, New York, NY 10013 (tel. (212) 431-1616), acts as an agent for many courier flights worldwide from New York, with some flights available from Houston. They offer special last-minute deals to such cities as London, Paris, Rome, and Frankfurt for as little as US$300 round-trip. **Halbart Express,** 147-05 176th St., Jamaica, NY 11434 (tel. (718) 656-8279), and **Courier Travel Service,** 530 Central Avenue, Cedarhurst, NY 11516 (tel. (516) 374-2299), are other courier agents to try.

You can also go directly through courier companies in New York, or check your bookstore or library for handbooks such as The Insider's Guide to Air Courier Bargains (US$14.95). The Courier Air Travel Handbook (US$10.70) explains the procedure for traveling as an air courier and contains names, phone numbers, and contact points of courier companies. It can be ordered directly from Thunderbird Press, 5930-10 W. Greenway Rd., Suite 112, Glendale, AZ 85306 (tel. (800) 345-0096). **Travel Unlimited**, P.O. Box 1058, Allston, MA 02134-1058 (no phone), publishes a comprehensive, monthly newsletter that details all possible options for courier travel (often 50% off discount commercial fares). A 1-year subscription is US$25 (outside of the U.S. US$35).

If you really have travel time to spare, **Ford's Travel Guides,** 19448 Londelius St., Northridge, CA 91324 (tel. (818) 701-7414) lists **freighter companies** that will take trans-Atlantic passengers. Ask for the Freighter Travel Guide and Waterways of the World (US$14.95, plus $2.50 postage if mailed outside the U.S.).

ONCE THERE

■■■ TRAVELING IN EUROPE

■ By Train

European trains retain the charm and romance their North American counterparts lost long ago. In Western Europe, 2nd-class travel is pleasant, and the 6-person compartments are terrific places to meet folks of all ages and nationalities. In Eastern Europe, first class is worth it, though second class (compartments seat 8) is bearable. Bring some food and a plastic water bottle you can fill at your hostel and take with you on all train trips; the train café can be expensive, and train water undrinkable. Trains are not theft-proof; lock the door of your compartment if you can, and keep your valuables on your person at all times.

Many train stations have different counters for domestic and international tickets, seat reservations, and information; check before lining up. On major lines, reservations are always advisable, and often required, even with a railpass; make them at least a few hours in advance at the train station (usually less than US$3). Faster trains, such as France's famed TGV, require a special supplement (US$4-5), which you can sometimes pay for on board, but it'll cost a bit more.

You may be tempted to save on accommodations by taking an overnight train in a regular coach seat, but there are problems; if you get to sleep you are sure to wake up exhausted and aching, security problems are rampant, and if you spread yourself over several seats in an empty compartment, someone is sure to come in at 2am and claim one of them. A sleeping berth in a bunkbedded couchette car is an affordable luxury (about US$10; reserve at the station at least several days in advance). Very few countries give students or young people discounts on regular domestic rail tickets, but many will sell a student or youth card valid for one-half or one-third off all fares for an entire year. Check the introductory sections of each country chapter for details.

Buying a **railpass** is both a popular and sensible option under many circumstances. Ideally conceived, a railpass allows you to jump on any train in Europe, go wherever you want whenever you want, and change your plans at will. The handbook that comes with your railpass tells you everything you need to know and includes a timetable for major routes, a map, and details on ferry discounts. In practice, of course, it's not so simple. You still must stand in line to pay for seat reservations, for supplements, for couchette reservations, and to have your pass validated when you first use it. More importantly, railpasses don't always pay off. Find a travel agent with a copy of the Eurailtariff manual (or call **Rail Europe** in the U.S. at (800) 438-7245 and ask for the latest edition of the Rail Europe Traveler's Guide), add up the second-class fares for the major routes you plan to cover, deduct 5% (the listed price includes a commission), deduct a rough 35% if you're under 26 and eligible for BIJ (see below), and compare. You may find it tough to make your railpass pay for itself in Belgium, Greece, Ireland, Italy, Luxembourg, Netherlands, Portugal, Spain, and all of Eastern Europe, where train fares are reasonable or distances short. If, however, the total cost of your trips nears the price of the pass, the convenience of avoiding ticket lines may well be worth the difference. Avoid an obsession with making the pass pay for itself; you may come home with only blurred memories of train stations.

Eurailpass is now the best option in European rail passes for Americans and Canadians. Eurailpasses are valid in most of Western Europe. Contact Rail Europe, 230 Westchester Ave., White Plains, NY 10604 (in U.S. tel. (800) 438-RAIL or (800) 848-RAIL, fax (800) 432-1329; in Canada tel. (800) 361-RAIL, fax (416) 602-4198) for information on different railpasses. The first-class Eurailpass is very rarely economical, valid for 15 days (US$498), 21 days (US$648), 1 month (US$798), 2 months

IN LONDON : 2 for 1 THEATRE MUSEUM (COVENT GARDEN) • 25% OFF
SMOLLENSKY'S BALLOON • 2 for 1 L'AMIRAL RESTAURANT•25% OFF
XENON NIGHTCLUB • 2 for 1 VAL TARO RISTORANTE • 25% OFF
WIDOW APPLEBAUMS • 25% OFF SMITH'S RESTAURANT • FREE
MEMBERSHIP 100 CLUB • 25% OFF SMOLLENSKY'S ON THE STRAND
• 25% OFF SOL Y SOMBRA • 25% OFF FERRI'S RESTAURANT • 2 for 1
DINO'S • 25% OFF ROCK GARDEN • 2 for 1 ADMISSION LE PALAIS •
2 for 1 ADMISSION THE HIPPODROME • 2 for 1 CAFE ST PIERRE • 2 for
1 LEONI'S QUO⬚⬚⬚⬚⬚⬚⬚⬚⬚⬚⬚⬚⬚⬚⬚⬚ ODLANDS•
2 for 1 ROYAL⬚⬚⬚⬚⬚⬚⬚⬚⬚⬚⬚⬚⬚⬚⬚⬚⬚⬚⬚ GETARIAN
RESTAURANT⬚⬚⬚⬚⬚⬚⬚⬚⬚⬚⬚⬚⬚⬚⬚⬚⬚⬚ • 2 for 1
ADMISSION S⬚⬚⬚⬚⬚⬚⬚⬚⬚⬚⬚⬚⬚⬚⬚⬚⬚ HTINGALE
MUSEUM • HA⬚⬚⬚⬚⬚⬚⬚⬚⬚⬚⬚⬚⬚⬚⬚⬚ HOUSE • 2
for 1 • 2 for 1⬚⬚⬚⬚⬚⬚⬚⬚⬚⬚⬚⬚⬚⬚⬚ ICKET • 2
for 1 OLD ROY⬚⬚⬚⬚⬚⬚⬚⬚⬚⬚⬚⬚⬚⬚ USE • 2 for
1 THE DESIGN⬚⬚⬚⬚⬚⬚⬚⬚⬚⬚⬚⬚⬚ THE CLINK
• 2 for 1 WINST⬚⬚⬚⬚⬚⬚⬚⬚⬚⬚⬚⬚ EUM SHOP
• 50% OFF THE⬚⬚⬚⬚⬚⬚⬚⬚⬚⬚⬚⬚ TMINSTER
• **IN EDINBU**⬚⬚⬚⬚⬚⬚⬚⬚⬚⬚⬚ TLE • 50%
OFF ROYAL S⬚⬚⬚⬚⬚⬚⬚⬚⬚⬚⬚ USTEAUS
SEAFOOD • 2⬚⬚⬚⬚⬚⬚⬚⬚⬚⬚⬚ UDES: THE
ROYAL OBSER⬚⬚⬚⬚⬚⬚⬚⬚⬚ DSTONE'S
LAND • 2 for⬚⬚⬚⬚⬚⬚⬚⬚ • 2 for 1
CHARLOTTE S⬚⬚⬚⬚⬚⬚⬚⬚ LASGOW:

2 for 1 NATIONAL TRUST FOR SCOTLAND INCLUDES: GREENBANK
GARDEN HUTCHESON'S HALL, AND THE VICEROY • 2 for 1 GANDHI
• 2 for 1 THE TENEMENT HOUSE • **IN DUBLIN**: 2 for 1 THE FLAME ON
THE HILL • 2 for 1 THE IRISH WHISKEY CORNER • 2 for 1 FRY MODEL
RAILWAY • 2 for 1 THE PINK BICYCLE • 2 for 1 CHIMES RESTAURANT
• 50% OFF ADMISSION ROCK GARDEN • **IN PARIS:** 30% OFF FARE
BATEAUX PARISIENS • **IN AMSTERDAM:** 2 for 1 ADMISSION VAN GOGH
MUSEUM • 2 for 1 ALLARD PIERSON MUSEUM • 2 for 1 ADMISSION
AMSTELKRING OUR LORD IN THE ATTIC • 2 for 1 ADMISSION JEWISH
HISTORICAL MUSEUM • 30% OFF ADMISSION THE OLD CHURCH • 2
for 1 THE ROYAL PALACE • 30% OFF DE BRAKKE GROND • 30% OFF
FRASCATI THEATER • 25% OFF ADMISSION JOSEPH LAM • **IN
FI**⬚⬚⬚⬚⬚⬚⬚⬚⬚⬚⬚⬚⬚⬚⬚⬚⬚⬚⬚⬚⬚⬚⬚ d

ALCAZABA • **IN LISBON:** FREE ENTRY ALCANTARA MAR • FREE ENTRY
DISCO PALM BEACH • 50% OFF SOLCLUB • 50% OFF TRANS

(US$1098), or 3 months (US$1398). If you are traveling in a group, you might prefer the **Eurail Saverpass**, which allows unlimited first-class travel for 15 days (US$430), 21 days (US$550), or 1 month (US$678) per person for 2 or more people traveling together (April-Sept. 3 or more). Travelers under age 26 on their first day of travel can buy a **Eurail Youthpass,** good for 15 days (US$398), 1 month (US$578), or 2 months (US$768) of second-class travel. It's tough to get your money's worth from a 1-month pass; the 2-month pass is better. First-class **Eurail Flexipasses** allow limited travel within a 2-month period: 5 days (US$348), 10 days (US$560), or 15 days (US$740). **Youth Flexipasses** are available for US$255, US$398, or US$540, respectively. Overnight trips starting after 7pm count only as the next day on your pass. Rail Europe advises that an appropriate criterion to determine if a pass is a good buy is the distance of your anticipated journeys. If you are planning even one long journey, a pass may be the way to go; in 1993, for example, Paris to Rome (one-way) cost about US$264 first class and US$164 second class. For only US$84 more, you could buy a first-class Eurail Flexipass; for US$91 more, you can get a second-class Eurail Youth Flexipass, and both provide 5 days rail travel within a 2 month period.

You'll almost certainly find it easiest to buy a Eurailpass before you arrive in Europe; contact Council Travel, Travel CUTS, or Let's Go Travel (see Useful Travel Organizations above), or any of many other travel agents. A few major train stations in Europe sell them too (though American agents usually deny this). If you're stuck in Europe and unable to find someone to sell you a Eurailpass, make a transatlantic call to an American railpass agent, who should be able to send a pass to you by express mail. Eurailpasses are not refundable once validated; you will be able to get a replacement if you lose one only if you have purchased insurance on the pass from Eurail, something that cannot be done through a travel agent. 1992 was the first year that this insurance program went into effect; ask a travel agent for specifics.

If you plan to focus your travels in one country, consider a national railpass. Also look into regional passes such as the Nordturist pass in Scandinavia (soon to be eliminated in favor of the ScanRail pass), the BritFrance pass, the Benelux Pass for Belgium, the Netherlands, and Luxembourg, and the EastRail or European East pass, which covers Poland, the Czech Republic, the Slovak Republic, Hungary, and Austria. Some of these passes can be bought only in Europe, some only outside of Europe, and for some it doesn't matter; check with a railpass agent or with national tourist offices. Those national passes that can be bought in Europe are usually cheaper there, but travel agents rarely tell you this.

For those under 26, **BIJ** tickets (Billets Internationals de Jeunesse, sold under the names **Wasteels, Eurotrain,** and **Route 26**) are a great alternative to railpasses. Available for international trips within Europe and for travel within France, they knock 25-45% off regular second-class fares; you buy your ticket for a single destination, and are allowed free and unlimited stopovers along the way. However, you cannot take longer than 2 months to complete your trip, and can stop only at points along the specific direct route of your ticket. In 1993, for instance, Wasteels's London office (tel. (071) 834 7066) offered round-trip tickets to Berlin for £90, and a London-Berlin-Prague-Budapest-Vienna-London ticket for £190—significantly less than the cost of a 2-month youth railpass. You can buy BIJ tickets at Wasteels or Eurotrain offices (usually in or near train stations). BIJ tickets are also available from ticket counters in some countries (including Denmark, Germany, and Switzerland) and from some travel agencies (such as ORBIS in Poland). In the U.S., contact Wasteels at (407) 351-2537.

Look for Lenore Baken's Camp Europe by Train (US$14.95), which covers all aspects of train travel and includes sections on railpasses, packing, and the specifics of rail travel in each country. The Eurail Guide (US$14.95), also available at bookstores, lists train schedules and brief cultural information for almost every country on earth. The ultimate reference is the Thomas Cook European Timetable (US$23.95; US$31.95 includes a map of Europe highlighting all train and ferry routes). The timetable, updated monthly, covers all major and many minor train routes in Europe. In the U.S., order it from **Forsyth Travel Library,** P.O. Box 2975, Shawnee Mission, KS 66201 (tel. (800) 367-7984 or (913) 384-3440). Add US$4.50 for postage.

■ By Bus

Though European trains and railpasses are extremely popular, the long-distance bus networks of Britain, Ireland, Portugal, Morocco, Greece, Turkey, and Yugoslavia are more extensive, efficient, and often more comfortable than train services; in Spain, Hungary, Albania, and northern Scandinavia, the bus and train systems are on a par; and in Iceland, bus service is the only ground transportation available. In the rest of Europe bus travel is more of a crapshoot, where scattered offerings from private companies are often cheap, but unreliable. All over Europe, short-haul buses reach rural areas inaccessible by train.

Bus travel in Europe is significantly more comfortable than in North America, though you can never have a true non-smoking section, and some companies force you to watch videos or listen to the radio. The biggest problem is deregulation; since there is little pan-European organization, it can be difficult to negotiate the route you need. Amsterdam, Athens, İstanbul, London, Munich, and Oslo are centers for lines that offer long-distance rides across Europe and, from time to time, all the way to India; see the Buses listings under the Practical Information sections for those cities.

■ By Car and Van

Yes, there really is no speed limit on the Autobahn. Cars offer great speed, great freedom, access to the countryside, and an escape from the town-to-town mentality of trains. Unfortunately, they also insulate you from the esprit de corps European rail travelers enjoy. Although a single traveler won't save by renting a car, 4 usually will; keep in mind that gas in Europe costs US$3-4 per gallon. If you can't decide

TRAVELING IN EUROPE: BY BUS, CAR, OR VAN

between train and car travel, you may benefit from a combination of the two; Avis and Hertz offer rail and car packages, and Rail Europe and other railpass vendors (see above) offer economical "Euraildrive" passes.

You can **rent** a car from either a U.S.-based firm (Avis, Budget, or Hertz) with its own European offices, from a European-based company with local representatives (National and American International represent Europcar and Ansa, respectively), or from a tour operator (Europe by Car, Auto Europe, Foremost, Kemwel, and Wheels International), which will arrange a rental for you from a European company at its own rates. Not surprisingly, the multinationals offer greater flexibility, but the tour operators often strike good deals and may have lower rates. Rentals vary considerably by company, season, and pick-up point; expect to pay at least US$140 a week, plus tax, for a teensy car. (Picking up your car in Brussels or Luxembourg is usually cheaper than renting from Paris.) Reserve well before leaving for Europe and pay in advance if you can; rates within Europe are harsh. Always check if prices quoted include tax and collision insurance; some credit card companies will cover this automatically. Ask about student and other discounts and be flexible in your itinerary. Ask your airline about special packages; sometimes you can get up to a week of free rental. Minimum age restrictions vary by country; rarely, if ever, is it below 21. Try **Auto Europe** (tel. (800) 223-5555); **Avis Rent a Car** (tel. (800) 331-1084); **Budget Rent a Car** (tel. (800) 472-3325); **Connex** (tel. (800) 333-3949); **Europe by Car**, Rockefeller Plaza, New York, NY 10020 (tel. (800) 223-1516) or (212) 581-3040); **Foremost Euro-Car** (tel. (800) 272-3299; in Canada (800) 253-3876); **France Auto Vacances** (tel. (800) 234-1426); **Hertz Rent a Car** (tel. (800) 654-3001), **The Kemwel Group** (tel. (800) 678-0678); or **Payless Car Rental** (tel. (800) PAYLESS).

For longer than 3 weeks, **leasing** can be cheaper than renting; it is sometimes the only option for those aged 18-20. The cheapest leases are actually agreements where you buy the car and then sell it back to the manufacturer at a pre-agreed price. As far as you're concerned, though, it's a lease and doesn't entail galactic financial transactions. Leases include insurance coverage and are not taxed. The most affordable ones usually originate in Belgium or France and start at around US$500 for 23 days and US$1000 for 60 days. Contact **Foremost**, **Europe by Car**, and **Auto Europe**. You will need to make arrangements in advance.

If you're brave or know what you're doing, **buying** a used car or van in Europe and selling it just before you leave can provide the cheapest wheels on the Continent. Check with consulates for different countries' import-export laws concerning used vehicles, registration, and safety and emission standards. David Shore and Patty Campbell's Europe By Van And Motorhome (US$13.95 postpaid, US$6 for overseas airmail) guides you through the entire process, from buy-back agreements to insurance and dealer listings. To order, write to 1842 Santa Margarita Dr., Fallbrook, CA 92028 (tel. (619) 723-6184). How to Buy and Sell a Used Car in Europe (U.S. $6.00 plus $.75 postage, from Gil Friedman, P.O. Box 1063, Arcata, CA 95521, tel. (707) 822-5001), also contains useful tips.

Driving a camper/van or motorhome gives the advantages of car rental without the hassle of finding lodgings or cramming 6 friends into a Renault. You'll need those friends to split the gasoline bills, however, although many European vehicles use diesel or propane, which are cheaper. The car rental firms listed above have more information, as does Shore and Campbell's book.

Before setting off, be sure you know the laws of the country in which you're driving (for instance, both seat belts and headlights must be on at all times in Scandinavia, and remember to keep left in Ireland and the U.K.). Scandinavians and Western Europeans use unleaded gas almost exclusively, but it's essentially nonexistent in Eastern Europe and North Africa. At most agencies in Europe, all that's required to rent a car is a U.S. license and proof that you've had it for a year. Before you buy an **International Driver's Permit**, check with the car rental agency in Europe; they may not require it. The permit (US$10), valid for one year, must be procured in the country in which your license was issued, and is available from any AAA branch in the U.S. or by mail from the American Automobile Association, 1000 AAA Drive (mail stop 100), Heathrow, FL 32746-5063 (tel. (407) 444-7883); in Canada, contact the Canadian Automobile Association (CAA), 60 Commerce Valley Drive East, Markham, Ont. L3T 7P9 (tel. (416) 771-3170). The **International Insurance Certificate,** sometimes called the "green card," is standard auto insurance and is available at an insurance company or rental agency. Again, check with the rental agency you plan to use before buying additional insurance to see what they offer in the cost of rental and what they require from you. If you have a collision while in Europe, the accident will show up on your domestic records. Theft insurance is not paid by the rental agency in some countries (especially in Spain and Italy, where cars are stolen more often); in any case, you will be required to pay for insurance when the agency does not.

■ By Airplane

Unless you're under 25, flying across Europe on regularly scheduled flights will eat your budget. If you are 24 or under, special fares on most European airlines requiring ticket purchase either the day before or the day of departure are a lovely exception to this rule. These are often cheaper than the corresponding regular train fare, though not always as cheap as student rail tickets or railpasses. Student travel agencies also sell cheap tickets, and budget fares are also frequently available in the spring and summer on high-volume routes between northern Europe and resort areas in Spain, Italy, and Greece. Consult budget travel agents and local newspapers and magazines. The **Air Travel Advisory Bureau,** 41-45 Goswell Road, London EC1V 7DN England (tel. (071) 636 5000), can put you in touch with discount flights to worldwide destinations, for free.

■ By Boat

Travel by boat is a bewitching alternative much favored by Europeans but overlooked by most foreigners. Most European ferries are comfortable and well-equipped; the cheapest fare class sometimes includes use of a reclining chair or couchette where you can sleep the trip away. You should check in at least 2 hours early for a prime spot and allow plenty of time for late trains and getting to the port. It's a good idea to bring your own food and avoid the astronomically priced cafeteria cuisine. Fares jump sharply in July and August. Always ask for discounts; ISIC holders can often get student fares and Eurail passholders get many reductions and free trips (check the brochure that comes with your railpass). You'll occasionally have to pay a small port tax (under US$10). Advance planning and reserved ticket purchases through a travel agency can spare you several tedious days of waiting in dreary ports for the next sailing.

Ferries in Europe divide into 4 major groups. **Mediterranean** ferries may be the most glamorous, but are also the most treacherous. Reservations are recommended, especially in July and August, when ships are insufferably crowded and expensive (bring some toilet paper). Ferries run on erratic schedules, with similar routes and varying prices; shop around and watch out for dinky, unreliable companies which will often not accept reservations. Ferries across the **English Channel** are steely and workaday; see the United Kingdom and Ireland Getting There section for more details. Ferries in the **North Sea** and **Baltic Sea** are prized by Scandinavians for their duty-free candy and alcohol shops; they also offer student and youth discounts, are universally reliable, and go everywhere (in summer, you can go from St. Petersburg to Iceland or Scotland without once using land transport). Those content with deck passage rarely need to book ahead. The best American source for information on Scandinavian ferries and visa-free cruises to Russia is **EuroCruises,** 303 W. 13th St., New York, NY 10014 (tel. (212) 691-2099 or (800) 688-3876). **Riverboats** acquaint you with many towns that trains can only wink at. The Moselle, Rhine, and Danube steamers have been overrun by gaudy tourists; less commercial-looking lines can be more seductive.

■ By Bicycle

Today, biking is one of the key elements of the classic budget Eurovoyage. Everyone else in the youth hostel is doing it, and with the proliferation of mountain bikes, you can do some serious natural sight-seeing. For information about touring routes, consult national tourist offices or any of the numerous books available. Europe By Bike, by Karen and Terry Whitehill (US$14.95), is a great source of specific area tours. Cycling Europe: Budget Bike Touring in the Old World by N. Slavinski (US$12.95) may also be a helpful addition to your library. Michelin road maps are clear and detailed guides. Be aware that touring involves pedaling both yourself and whatever you store in the panniers (bags which strap to your bike). Take some reasonably challenging day-long rides at home to prepare yourself before you leave. Have your bike tuned up by a reputable shop. Wear visible clothing, drink plenty of water (even if you're not thirsty), and ride on the same side as the traffic. Learn the international signals for turns and use them. Learn how to fix a modern derailleur-equipped mount and change a tire, and practice on your own bike before you have to do it overseas. A few simple tools and a good bike manual will be invaluable. If you are nervous about striking out on your own, **College Bicycle Tours** (tel. (800) 736-BIKE in the U.S. and Canada) offers co-ed bicycle tours through 7 countries in Europe that are exclusively for the college-aged and arrange discounted airfares for their participants.

Most airlines will count your bike as your second free piece of luggage (you're usually allowed 2 pieces of checked baggage and a carry-on). As an extra piece, it will cost about US$85 each way. Policies on charters and budget flights vary; check with the airline. The safest way to send your bike is in a box, with the handlebars, pedals, and front wheel detached. Within Europe, most ferries let you take your bike for free. You can always ship your bike on trains, though the cost varies from a small fixed fee to a substantial fraction of the ticket price.

Riding a bike with a frame pack strapped on it or on your back is about as safe as pedaling blindfolded over a sheet of ice; panniers are essential. The first thing to buy, however, is a suitable **bike helmet.** At about US$50-100, they're a much better buy than head injury or death. To lessen the odds of theft, buy a U-shaped **Citadel** or **Kryptonite** lock. These are expensive (about US$20-55), but the companies insure their locks against theft of your bike for 1 or 2 years. Bicycling magazine has the lowest sale prices. **Bike Nashbar,** 4112 Simon Rd., Youngstown, OH 44512 (tel. (800) 627-4227), has excellent prices and cheerfully beats all competitors' offers by US5¢.

Renting a bike beats bringing your own if your touring will be confined to 1 or 2 regions. A sturdy if unexciting 1-speed model will cost US$8-12 per day; be prepared to lay down a sizable deposit. Let's Go lists bike rental shops in most cities and towns. Some youth hostels (especially in France) rent bicycles for low prices. In many countries (including France and Belgium), train stations rent bikes and often allow you to drop them off elsewhere without charge.

■ By Moped and Motorcycle

Motorized bikes have long spiced southern European roads with their flashy colors and perpetual buzz. They offer an enjoyable, relatively inexpensive way to tour coastal areas and countryside, particularly where there are few cars. They don't use much gas, can be put on trains and ferries and are a good compromise between the high cost of car travel and the limited range of bicycles. However, they're uncomfortable for long distances, and are also dangerous in the rain and unpredictable on rough roads or gravel. Always wear a helmet and never ride with a backpack. If you've never been on a moped before, a twisting Alpine road is not the place to start. In general expect to pay US$15-35 per day; try auto repair shops and remember to bargain. Motorcycles normally require a license. Before renting, ask if the quoted price includes tax and insurance or you may be hit for an unexpected additional fee. Avoid handing your passport over as a deposit; if you have an accident or mechanical failure you may not get it back until you cover all repairs. Pay ahead of time instead.

■ By Thumb

> *Let's Go* strongly urges you to seriously consider the risks before you choose to hitch. We do not recommend hitching as a safe means of transportation and none of the information presented here is intended to do so.

No one should hitch without careful consideration of the risks involved. Not everyone can be an airplane pilot, but almost any bozo can drive a car. Hitching means risking theft, assault, sexual harassment, and unsafe driving, entrusting your life to a random person who happens to stop beside you on the road. In spite of this, the gains are many: favorable hitching experiences allow you to meet local people and get where you're going, especially in northern Europe and Ireland, where public transportation is sketchy. In many areas of Eastern Europe, the line between hitching and taking a taxi is quite thin. The choice, however, remains yours. Consider this section as akin to handing out condoms to high school students: we don't endorse using it, but if you're going to do it anyway, we'll tell you how to make it safer and therefore more enjoyable.

Depending on the circumstances and the norms of the country, men and women traveling in groups and men traveling alone might consider hitching (called "autostop" in much of Europe) to locations beyond the scope of bus or train routes. If you're a woman traveling alone, don't hitch. It's just too dangerous. A man and a woman are a safer combination, 2 men will have a harder time finding a ride, and 3 will go nowhere.

If you do decide to hitch, consider where you are. Britain and Ireland are probably the easiest places in Western Europe to get a lift. Hitching in Scandinavia is slow but steady. Long-distance hitching in the developed countries of northwestern Europe demands close attention to expressway junctions and rest stop locations, and often a destination sign. Hitching in southern Europe is generally mediocre; France is the worst. Hitching remains common in Eastern Europe, though Westerners are a definite target for theft. In the former Soviet Union, the Baltics, and some other Eastern European countries, there is no clear difference between hitchhiking and hailing a taxi.

Where you stand is also vital. Experienced hitchers pick a spot outside of built-up areas, where drivers can stop, return to the road without causing an accident, and have time to look over potential passengers as they approach. Hitching (or even standing) on super-highways is generally illegal: you may only thumb at rest stops, or at the entrance ramps to highways—in front of the cute blue and white superhighway pictograph (a bridge over a road). In the Practical Information section of many cities, we list the tram or bus lines that will take travelers to strategic points for hitching out.

Finally, success will depend on what you look like. Successful hitchers travel light and stack their belongings in a compact but visible cluster. Most Europeans signal with an open hand, rather than a thumb; many write their destination on a sign in large, bold letters and draw a smiley-face under it. Drivers prefer hitchers who are neat and wholesome. No one stops for anyone wearing sunglasses.

Safety issues are always imperative, even when you're traveling with another person. Avoid getting in the back of a 2-door car, and never let go of your backpack. Hitchhiking at night can be particularly dangerous; stand in a well-lit place and expect drivers to be leery of nocturnal thumbers. Don't get into a car that you can't get out of again in a hurry. If you ever feel threatened, insist on being let off, regardless of where you are. If the driver refuses to stop, try acting as though you're going to open the car door or vomit on the upholstery.

Europe: A Manual for Hitchhikers gives directions for hitching out of hundreds of cities, rates rest areas and entrance ramps, and deciphers national highway and license plate systems. It's available from Vacation Work Publications (see Work section for complete address).

Most Western European countries offer a ride service, a cross between hitchhiking and the ride boards common at many university campuses, which pairs drivers with riders, with a fee to both agency (about US$25) and driver (per km). **Eurostop International** (called **Verband der Deutschen Mitfahrzentralen** in Germany and **Allostop** in France) is one of the largest in Europe. Not all of these organizations screen drivers and riders; ask in advance.

■ By Foot

Europe's grandest scenery can often be seen only by foot. *Let's Go* describes many daytrips for those who want to hoof it, but native inhabitants (Europeans are fervent, almost obsessive hikers), hostel proprietors, and fellow travelers are the best source of tips. Many European countries have hiking and mountaineering organizations; alpine clubs in Germany, Austria, Switzerland, and Italy, as well as tourist organizations in Scandinavia, provide inexpensive, simple accommodations in splendid settings. One good book is J. Sydney Jones' *Tramping in Europe: A Walking Guide* (US$7.95); check your local bookstore for others.

■■■ ACCOMMODATIONS

If you arrive in a town without a reservation, your first stop should be the local tourist office. These offices distribute extensive accommodations listings free of charge and will also reserve a room for a small fee (though some favor their friends' establishments). As a rule, expect all prices to rise each January.

Often, hostel proprietors or locals with rooms to rent will approach you in ports or train stations. This may seem dangerous, but it is an accepted custom in many areas. However, there is no guarantee of these hawkers' trustworthiness or of the quality of their establishments. Carry your own baggage, ask for their identification, and have them write down the offered price.

■ Hostels

Especially in summer, Europe is overrun by young, budget-conscious travelers. Hostels are the hub of this gigantic subculture, providing innumerable opportunities to meet students from all over the world, find new traveling partners, trade stories, and learn about places to visit. At US$7-20 per night, prices are extraordinarily low; only camping is cheaper. Guests tend to be in their teens and twenties, but most hostels welcome travelers of all ages. In northern Europe, where hotel prices are astronomical, hostels have special family rooms, a higher standard of cleanliness, and correspondingly less of a student atmosphere. In the average hostel, though, you and anywhere from 1 to 50 roommates will sleep in a sex-segregated room full of bunk beds, with common bathrooms and a lounge down the hall. The hostel warden may be a laid-back student, a hippie dropout, or a crotchety disciplinarian. Most hostels have well-equipped kitchens; some serve hot meals.

The basic disadvantage of hostels is their regimentation. Most have an early curfew—fine if you're climbing a mountain the next morning, but a distinct cramp in your style if you plan to rage in town. There is also usually a lockout from morning to mid-afternoon. Conditions are generally spartan and cramped, with little privacy, and you may run into more screaming pre-teen tour groups than you care to remember. Hostel quality also varies dramatically. Some are set in strikingly beautiful castles, others in run-down barracks far from the town center. Rural hostels are

generally more appealing than those in large cities. Hostels usually prohibit sleeping bags for sanitary reasons and provide blankets and sheets instead. Some require **sleepsacks;** make your own by folding a sheet and sewing it shut on two sides. If you're lazy or less domestic, you can order one (about US$14) from Let's Go Travel or a youth hostel federation.

Large hostels are reluctant to take advance telephone reservations because of the high no-show rate; citing an exact train arrival time or promising to call again and confirm can sometimes help. In large city hostels in Western Europe, take advantage of hostel-to-hostel fax booking services where the hostel you're staying at faxes another to see if there's space, then charges you the overnight fee plus a booking fee (less than US$1) and finally issues you a confirmation slip which you present to the other hostel.

Prospective hostel-goers should become members of the official youth hostel association in their country; all national hostel associations are part of **Hostelling International (HI),** formerly the International Youth Hostel Federation (IYHF). If you haven't become a member in advance, show up at an HI hostel and ask for a blank membership card with space for 6 validation stamps. Each night you'll pay a nonmember supplement (equal to one-sixth the membership fee) and earn one Guest Stamp; get 6 stamps and you're a member. This system works well in most of Western Europe, though in some countries you may need to remind the hostel reception to issue you a guest card. In Eastern Europe, many hostels don't care whether you're a member or not. Some hostels, notably in Germany and Austria, will not accept nonmembers under any circumstances. Most student travel agencies sell HI cards on the spot; otherwise, contact one of the national hostel organizations listed below. Ask about the *Budget Accommodation: Volume I: Europe and the Mediterranean* (about US$11).

HI headquarters is located at 9 Guessens Rd., Welwyn Garden City, Herts, AL8 6QW, England (tel. (0707) 33 24 87). National member associations include:

ACCOMMODATIONS: HOTELS, GUESTHOUSES, AND HOMES

American Youth Hostels (AYH), Dept. 481, P.O. Box 37613, Washington, DC 20013-7613, or 733 15th St. NW, Suite 840, Washington, DC 20005 (tel. (202) 783-6161). Cards cost US$25 (renewals US$20, under 18 US$10, over 54 US$15); family cards US$35. Other countries' card prices are often lower.

Hostelling International-Canada, 1600 James Naismith Dr., Suite 608, Gloucester, Ottawa, Ont. K1B 5N4 (tel. (613) 748-5638).

Youth Hostels Association of England and Wales (YHA), Trevelyan House, 8 St. Stephen's Hill, St. Albans, Herts AL1 2DY (tel. 44 (727) 85 52 15); in Ireland, 61 Mountjoy St., Dublin 7, (tel. (01) 304 555).

Scottish Youth Hostel Association (SYHA), 7 Glebe Crescent, Stirling FK8 2JA (tel. (0786) 45 11 81).

Youth Hostel Association of Northern Ireland (YHANI), 56 Bradbury Pl., Belfast BT7 1RU (tel. (0232) 324 733).

Australian Youth Hostels Association (AYHA), Level 3, 10 Mallett St., Camperdown NSW 2050 (tel. (2) 565 16 99).

Youth Hostels Association of New Zealand (YHANZ), P.O. Box 436, 173 Gloucester St., Christchurch 1 (tel. (3) 379 99 70).

Privately owned hostels are found in major tourist centers and throughout some countries (particularly Ireland). No membership is required, and you won't always have to contend with early curfews or daytime lockouts, but their quality varies widely. The YMCA runs 29 **Interpoint** hostels in major northern European cities (July-Aug.); membership cards are available at each location.

■ Hotels, Guesthouses, and Private Homes

Hotels are quite expensive in Britain, Switzerland, Austria, and northern Europe: rock bottom for singles is US$14-17, for doubles US$18-22. In the rest of Europe, couples can usually get by fairly well (rooms with a double bed are generally cheaper than those with 2 twin beds), as can groups of 3 or 4. Inexpensive European ho-

tels may come as a rude shock to pampered North American travelers. You'll share a bathroom down the hall; one of your own is a rarity and costs extra when provided. Hot showers may also cost more. Don't confuse the toilet with the *bidet* (that little sink-like thing next to the toilet). In Britain and Ireland a large breakfast is generally included; elsewhere a continental breakfast of a roll, jam, coffee or tea, and maybe an egg is served. Some hotels offer "full pension" (all meals) and "half pension" (breakfast and lunch). Unmarried couples will generally have no trouble getting a room together, although couples under age 21 may occasionally encounter resistance.

Smaller, family-run **guesthouses** and **pensions** are usually a little cheaper than the cheapest hotels. Even less expensive are rooms in **private homes,** of which the local tourist office usually has a good list. If you're traveling alone, this is an economical way to get your own room and meet real Europeans. The British **bed and breakfast** is a breed of private room that's extra heavy on the bacon and eggs. Private rooms are an excellent option in Eastern Europe, where youth hostels are primitive and hotels in flux; in the absence of good tourist offices, travel agencies book most private rooms in the east, and proprietors flag down tourists at the train station (try not to get stuck in a distant, vapid suburb).

If you reserve in writing, indicate your night of arrival and the number of nights you plan to stay. The hotel will send you a confirmation and may request payment for the 1st night. Not all hotels take reservations, and few accept checks in foreign currency. Enclosing two International Reply Coupons (available at any post office) will ensure a prompt reply, but will cost as much as a short transatlantic phone call.

■ Camping

Camping in Europe can be the best or worst of worlds. **Organized campgrounds** exist in almost every European city, most accessible by foot, car, or public transportation. Showers, bathrooms, and a small restaurant or store are common; some sites

have more elaborate facilities. Prices range from US$1-10 per person with an additional charge for a tent. Money and time expended in getting to the campsite may eat away at your budget and your patience; if you're doing the Eurail thing, hostels are probably more pleasant.

Europa Camping and Caravanning, an annually updated catalog of campsites in Europe, is available through **Recreational Equipment, Inc.,** REI, Sumner, WA 98352-0001 (tel. (800) 426-4840) for US$19.95. The excellent *Camp Europe by Train* (US$17, including postage; available from the **Forsyth Travel Library**—see Books, Guides, Maps, Etc.) offers general camping tips and suggests camping areas along Eurail lines. Finally, the **Automobile Association,** Fanum House, Basingstoke, Hampshire RG21 2EA, England (tel. (0256) 491 510), publishes *Camping and Caravanning in Europe.* An International Camping Carnet (membership card) is required by some European campgrounds but can usually be bought on the spot. The card entitles you to a discount at some campgrounds, and often may be substituted for your passport as a security deposit. In the U.S., it's available for US$30 through the **National Campers and Hikers Association, Inc.,** 4804 Transit Rd., Bldg. #2, Depew, NY 14043 (tel. (716) 668-6242; carnet price includes a membership fee).

Prospective campers will need to invest a lot of money in good camping equipment and a lot of energy carrying it on their shoulders. Use the reputable mail-order firms to gauge prices; order from them if you can't do as well locally. In the fall, last year's merchandise may be reduced by as much as 50%. **Campmor,** 810 Rte. 17N, P.O. Box 997-H, Paramus, NJ 07653 (tel. (800) 526-4784), has a monstrous selection of equipment at low prices. **Cabela's,** 812 13th Ave., Sidney, NE 69160 (tel. (800) 237-4444), also offers great prices. **REI** (listed above) stocks a wide range of the latest gear and holds great seasonal sales. And 24 hours a day, 365 days a year, **L.L. Bean,** Freeport, ME 04033-0001 (tel. (800) 341-4341), supplies its own equipment and national-brand merchandise.

American packs are generally more durable and comfortable, and less expensive, than European ones. **Backpacks** (US$100-300) come with either an external frame or an internal frame; if your load isn't that heavy and you plan to use the pack mainly as a suitcase, choose an internal-frame model. It's more manageable on crowded trains and when hitching, and it's less likely to be mangled by rough handling. Make sure your pack has a strong, padded hip belt, which transfers much of the pack's weight from delicate shoulders to sturdier legs.

Most of the better **sleeping bags**—down (lightweight and warm) or synthetic (cheaper, heavier, more durable, and warmer when wet)—have ratings for specific minimum temperatures. The lower the mercury, the higher the price. Estimate the most severe conditions you may encounter, subtract a few degrees, and then buy a bag. Expect to pay at least US$60 for a synthetic bag and up to US$250 for a down bag suitable for use in sub-freezing temperatures. **Sleeping bag pads** range from US$12-80, while **air mattresses** go for about US$30-60. The best **tents** are freestanding, with their own frames and suspension systems. They set up quickly and require no staking. Remember to use the tent's protective rain fly and seal the seams to protect against water seepage. Backpackers and cyclists will require especially small, lightweight models, costing US$100 and up. **Sierra Design**, 2039 4th St., Berkeley, CA 94710, sells a 2-person tent that weighs less than 1.4 kg (3 lbs.).

Other camping basics include a battery-operated **lantern** (*never* gas) and a simple plastic **groundcloth** to protect the tent floor. When camping in autumn, winter, or spring, bring along a "space blanket," a technological wonder that helps you retain your body heat. Large, collapsible **water sacks** will significantly improve your lot in primitive campgrounds and weigh practically nothing when empty. **Campstoves** come in all sizes, weights, and fuel types, but none are truly cheap (US$30-120) or light. Consider GAZ, a form of bottled propane gas that is easy to use and widely available in Europe and remember waterproof matches. A canteen, Swiss army knife, and insect repellent are small, essential items. For further information about camping equipment and other camping concerns, contact **Wilderness Press**, 2440

Bancroft Way, Berkeley, CA 94704-1676 (tel. (800) 443-7227 or (510) 543-8080), which publishes useful books such as *Backpacking Basics* (US$8.95, including postage) and *Backpacking with Babies and Small Children* (US$9.95).

■ Wilderness Concerns

The first thing to preserve in the wilderness is you—health, safety, and food should be your primary concerns. See the Health section for information about basic medical concerns and first-aid. One comprehensive guide to outdoor survival is *How to Stay Alive in the Woods*, by Bradford Angier (Macmillan, $8). Many rivers, streams, and lakes are contaminated with bacteria such as giardia, which causes gas, cramps, loss of appetite, and violent diarrhea. To protect yourself from the effects of this microscopic trip-wrecker, always boil your water vigorously for at least 5 minutes before drinking it, or use a purifying iodine solution. Filters do not remove all bacteria. *Never go camping or hiking by yourself for any significant time or distance*. If you're going into an area that is not well-traveled or well-marked, let someone know where you're hiking and how long you intend to be out. If you fail to return on schedule, searchers will at least know where to look for you.

The second thing to protect while you are outdoors is the wilderness. The thousands of outdoor enthusiasts that pour into the parks every year threaten to trample the land to death. Because firewood is scarce in popular parks, campers are asked to make small fires using only dead branches or brush; using a campstove is the more cautious way to cook. Some parks prohibit campfires altogether. Pitch your tent on high, dry ground, don't cut vegetation, and don't clear campsites. If there are no toilet facilities, bury human waste at least 4 inches deep and 100 feet or more from any water supplies and campsites. Use only biosafe soap or detergents in streams or lakes. Always pack up your trash in a plastic bag and carry it with you until you reach the next trash can; burning and burying pollute the environment. In more civ-

IF YOU CAN'T AFFORD TO TRAVEL, JOIN THE CLUB.

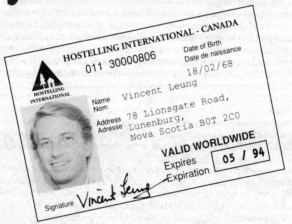

Traveling doesn't have to mean snobby hotels that cost $200 a night. With a Hostelling International card you can stay in Paris for just $16, New York for $19 or Tokyo for $23. Hostels even offer special discounts on everything from museum fees and ski lifts to air, rail and ferry tickets. Plus they have fully equipped do-it-yourself kitchens, which not only save you money but also are great for meeting fellow world travelers. So if you're looking for a less expensive way to travel, join the club. Call (202) 783-6161 in the U.S., or 1-800-663-5777 in Canada.

HOSTELLING INTERNATIONAL

The new seal of approval of the International Youth Hostel Federation.

HOSTELLING
INTERNATIONAL®

ilized camping circumstances, it's important to respect fellow campers. Keep light and noise to a minimum, particularly if you arrive after dark.

■ Alternative Accommodations

In university and college towns, **student dormitories** may be open to travelers when school is not in session. Prices are usually comparable to those of youth hostels, and you usually won't have to share a room with strangers or endure stringent curfew and eviction regulations. Many **monasteries** and **convents** will open their doors to those seeking corporeal or spiritual relief, particularly in Italy. A letter of introduction from a clergy member could facilitate matters.

A number of host networks will help you find accommodations with families throughout Europe. **Servas** is an organization devoted to promoting world peace and understanding among people of different cultures. Traveling members may stay free for 2 nights in other members' homes in over 100 countries. You are asked to contact hosts in advance, and you must be willing to fit into the household routine. Membership is US$55, and for a US$25 deposit you will receive up to 5 host lists, which provide a short self-description of each host member. Write to U.S. Servas, Inc., 11 John St., #407, New York, NY 10038 (tel. (212) 267-0252).

Sleeping in European train stations is a time-honored tradition. While it's free and often tolerated by authorities, it's neither comfortable nor safe. Don't spend the night in an urban park unless you place a similarly low value on your life.

■■■ KEEPING IN TOUCH

■ Mail

Mail can be sent internationally through **Poste Restante** (the international phrase for General Delivery) to any city or town; it's well worth using and much more reliable than you might think. Mark the envelope "HOLD" and address it, for example, "Matt BAUGHMAN, Poste Restante, City, Country." The last name should be capitalized and underlined. The mail will go to a special desk in the central post office, unless you specify a post office by street address or postal code. In Central and Eastern Europe, you should put a "1" after the city name to ensure mail goes to the central post office. As a rule, it is best to use the largest post office in the area; when possible, it is safer, quicker, and more reliable to send mail express or registered.

It helps to use the appropriate translation of Poste Restante (*Lista de Correos* in Spanish and *Postlagernde Briefe* in German). When picking up your mail, bring your passport or other ID. If the clerk insists that there is nothing for you, try checking under your first name as well. In a few countries you will have to pay a minimal fee (perhaps 50¢) per item received. *Let's Go* lists post offices in the Practical Information section for each city and most towns.

Postcards and letters cost the following amounts, when mailed from the US: US19¢ and US29¢ within the US; US40¢ and US50¢ to all other overseas destinations. The post office also sells aerograms, which provide a limited amount of writing space, for US45¢. It helps to mark air mail in the appropriate language if possible (*par avion* in French, *por avion* in Spanish, *mit luftposte* in German, *per via aerea* in Italian, *lotnicza* in Polish), though *par avion* is universally understood. Many U.S. city post offices offer **International Express Mail** service, which sends packages under 8 oz. to major overseas cities in 40 to 72 hours for US$11.50 to US$14.

Sending mail c/o **American Express** offices is quite reliable; they will hold your mail for free if you have AmEx Traveler's Cheques or a card. Even if you use another brand of traveler's checks, you can use this service by buying some AmEx Cheques. Mail will automatically be held 30 days; to have it held longer, write "Hold for x days" on the envelope. Again the sender should capitalize and underline your last name, marking the envelope "Client Letter Service." Check the Practical Informa-

KEEPING IN TOUCH: MAIL

IT'S A VISIT
WITH YOUR MOTHER.

IT'S THE SCORES
OF YOUR HOME TEAM.

IT'S NEWS
OF YOUR PET GOLDFISH.

IT'S ORDERING JEANS
FROM YOUR FAVORITE STORE.

IT'S THE LATEST
CAMPUS GOSSIP.

IT'S A LAUGH
WITH YOUR BEST FRIEND.

BECAUSE NO MATTER
WHERE YOU TRAVEL,

IT CAN ALWAYS GET YOU HOME.

*For more information,
call AT&T at
1 800 435-0812, Ext. 7812.*

THE AT&T CALLING CARD. THE WAY HOME.

ORDER YOUR AT&T CALLING CARD NOW FOR FREE.

With an AT&T Calling Card, you can stay close to home
even when you're thousands of miles away. Use
the Card with AT&T **USADirect**® Service and you'll
get an English-speaking operator who can complete your call
to the U.S. or between any of over 60 countries with
AT&T **World Connect**℠ Service. It's fast. It's easy. And all you
have to do to apply is fill out the coupon below.

☐ Mr.   ☐ Mrs.
☐ Miss ☐ Ms. _____

How would you like your name to appear on the Card? Please print. Spell your last name completely.

_____
Mailing Address   City   State   Zip Code

_____
Telephone Number (Area Code and Number)

Please charge my AT&T calls
to my current* (check one)
☐ American Express® Card
☐ MasterCard®
☐ VISA®

| | | | | | | | | | | | | | | | | | | | | |

My Bank Credit Card (or American Express® Card)
Number

Expiration Date: Year/Month _____

AT&T

Also, provide the name and address of the American Express office or the issuing bank for your
MasterCard or VISA account.

X _____

Signature   Date   Please print full name

Return to: AT&T Global Customer Service Center, P.O. Box 23300, Ft. Lauderdale, FL 33307-3300

For AT&T Use Only: Auth. Code _____ Date _____ Initials _____ EUS781W

Statement of Authorization Please consider my application† for an AT&T Calling Card. If this application is
granted, I authorize AT&T to bill me for charges incurred with the AT&T Calling Card issued to me.

I understand and agree that any charges made with an AT&T Calling Card and billed to my American Express
Card account will be subject to the same terms and conditions governing my American Express Card account. Any
charges billed to my MasterCard or VISA account will be subject to the same MasterCard or VISA finance charges
as may be applicable to other items appearing on my MasterCard or VISA account. I will notify AT&T and American
Express, MasterCard or VISA, if my American Express Card, MasterCard or VISA Card is lost, stolen, expires or is
terminated for any reason, or if I wish to terminate the Authorization to bill my American Express, MasterCard or
VISA account. I will also notify AT&T whenever I change my mailing address.

*Your credit card provider may charge interest in conformity with the terms and conditions of your agreement with
them.

†Approval or selection of this application is made by American Telephone and Telegraph Company in the U.S.A.

©1993 AT&T

tion section of the countries you plan to visit; we list AmEx office locations for most large cities. A complete list is available for free from AmEx (tel. (800) 528-4800) in the booklet *Traveler's Companion*.

Between the U.S. and Europe airmail averages a week to 10 days. Although the Post Office claims mail can get anywhere in that period, allow at least 2 weeks for Australia, New Zealand, Eastern Europe, North Africa, and South Africa. Parts of Eastern Europe can require up to 4 or 6 weeks.

Private mail services provide the fastest, most reliable overseas delivery. **DHL** (tel. (800) 225-5345 in the U.S. and Canada; tel. (81) 890 9393 in London; tel. (353) 1 844 47 44 in Dublin; tel. (2) 317 8300 in Sydney; tel. (9) 636 5000 in Auckland; tel. (11) 921 3600 in Johannesburg) covers every country in this book. Mail to Western Europe costs US$30 and takes 2-3 days, to Eastern Europe, US$70 and 3-4 days. By **Federal Express** (tel. (800) 238-5355 in the U.S. and Canada; tel. (81) 844 2344 in London; tel. (353) 1 847 34 73 in Dublin; tel. (2) 317 66 66 in Sydney; tel. (9) 256 83 00 in Auckland; tel. (11) 921 7500 in Johannesburg), an express letter from North America to Western Europe costs US$32 and takes 2-3 days; service to Eastern Europe costs US$68, takes 3-4 days, and is often limited to cities. **Airborne Express** (tel. (800) 472-4900 in the U.S. and Canada; tel. (81) 899 9876 in London; tel. (353) 1 844 41 83 in Dublin; tel. (2) 263 15 66 in Sydney; tel. (9) 275 80 34 in Auckland; tel. (11) 452 3701 in Johannesburg) charges US$34-39 to mail 8oz. to Western Europe in 2 days, US$69 to mail to Eastern Europe in 4-5 days. Packages can be sent from Europe to the U.S., but costs vary widely between dozens and several hundreds of dollars.

Surface mail is by far the cheapest and slowest way to send mail. It takes 1-3 months to cross the Atlantic, appropriate for sending large quantities of items you won't need to see for a while. It is vital, therefore to distinguish your airmail from surface mail by explicitly labeling air mail in the appropriate language. When ordering books and materials from another country, include an **International Reply Coupon (IRC),** available at the post office, with your request. IRCs provide the recipient of your order with postage to cover delivery.

■ Telephones

In Essentials and country listings, the **country code** is not included with phone numbers; pleases consult the beginning of each country's chapter, where the country code is listed with exchange rates. The same thing applies to cities: the Practical Information section lists the **city code** under Telephones (in parentheses in the Practical Information listings for large cities); numbers within that city are listed without the code. Some **international dialing codes** (listed at the beginning of each country chapter along with the country code) and country codes, respectively, are 011 and 1 (for both the US and Canada), 010 and 44 (Great Britain), 0011 and 61 (Australia), 00 and 64 (New Zealand), 16 and 353 (Ireland), and 09 and 27 (South Africa).

International direct dial is not complicated. First dial the **international dialing prefix/international access code** for the country you are in, then the **country code** for the country you are calling. Next punch in the **area code** or **city code.** Finally, dial the **local number.** In most countries (the U.S., Canada, the former Soviet Union, and Hungary are some exceptions) the first digit of the city code is the **domestic long-distance prefix** (usually 0, 1, or 9); omit it when calling from abroad, but use it when dialing another region in the same country.

Some countries in Eastern Europe do not have an international dialing code; you must go through the operator. In some other countries you must wait for a tone after the international dialing code. Denmark, Luxembourg, and most of Europe's microstates have neither city codes nor domestic long-distance prefixes; just skip that step. For more information, see each country's Practical Information section.

You can usually make direct international calls from a pay phone, but you may need a companion to feed money in as you speak. In some countries, pay phones may be card-operated. Some even accept major credit cards. The best places to call from are phone booths and post offices, since phones in cafés, hotels, and restaurants tend to carry surcharges of 30% or more.

English-speaking operators are often available for both local and international assistance. Operators in most European countries will place **collect calls** for you. It's cheaper to find a pay phone and deposit just enough money to be able to say "Call me" and give your number (though some pay phones in Europe can't receive calls). A better alternative is **AT&T's USA Direct** service, which allows you to dial a number in Europe (either toll-free or charged as a local call), to connect instantly to an operator in the U.S. Rates run about US$1.75-1.85 for the first minute plus about US$1 per additional minute. Calls must be either collect (US$5.75 surcharge) or billed to an AT&T calling card (US$2.50); the people you call need not subscribe to AT&T. USA Direct service (listed in each country's Essentials section) is available from every country in this book (though not always every region within that country) except Bulgaria, Russia, Ukraine, Estonia, Latvia, and Lithuania; for more information, call AT&T at (800) 874-4000. **Canada Direct, Australia Direct,** and **New Zealand Direct** are similar to USA Direct, though not as extensive. For information call (800) 561-8868 (Canada), 0102 (Australia), or 018 (New Zealand). These services can also be used for international calls within Europe. **MCI's Call USA** program allows its customers to call the U.S. from over 65 countries. Calls cost US$3.60-5.35 for the first minute plus US$1-2 per additional minute. MCI also offers **World Reach**, a more expensive program through which you can use a calling card to call from one European country to another. For information on these programs, call MCI at (800) 444-4444 or (800) 444-3333.

Phone rates tend to be highest in the morning, low in the evening, and lowest on Sunday and at night. Also, remember **time differences** when you call. Britain and Ireland, Portugal, and Iceland are on Greenwich Mean Time (GMT), 5 hours ahead of New York. Finland, Estonia, Latvia, Lithuania, western Russia, Romania, Bulgaria, Greece, Turkey, Israel, and Egypt are 2 hours ahead of GMT. Moscow is 3 hours ahead. Everywhere else in this book is 1 hour ahead of GMT. Some countries (like Iceland) ignore daylight savings time, and fall and spring switchover times differ between those countries that do use it.

■ Other Modes of Communication: Telegrams, Faxes, and More

To send a **telegram** overseas from the U.S., Western Union (tel. (800) 625-6000) charges a base fee of US$8, plus US71¢ per word, including name and address (to Mex US45¢/word; Canada US50¢; UK US56¢). There is a US$10 surcharge for telegrams not in English or Spanish. **Mailgrams** require 1 day for delivery and cost US$17.90.

In Eastern Europe domestic and international telegrams can be faster and cheaper than using the phone. Fill out a form at any post or telephone office; cables to North America arrive in 2 days. In Western Europe, telegrams are slower, more expensive, and much less fun. Major cities across Europe also have bureaus where you can pay to send and receive **faxes.**

If you're spending a year abroad and want to keep in touch with friends or colleagues in a college or research institution, **electronic mail** ("e-mail") is an attractive option. It takes a minimum of computer knowledge and a little prearranged planning, and it beams messages anywhere for free.

Between May 2 and Octoberfest, EurAide (P.O. Box 2375, Naperville, IL 60567; tel. (708) 420-2343) offers **Overseas Access**, a service most useful to travelers without a set itinerary. It costs US$15 per week or US$40 per month for an electronic message box. To reach you, people call the "home base" in Munich (Bahnhofplatz

2, 8000 München 2 (tel. (089) 59 38 89) and leave a message; you receive it by calling Munich whenever you wish, which is cheaper than calling overseas. For an additional US$20 per month, EurAide will forward mail sent to Munich to any addresses you specify.

Published media dailies including the London *Times*, *Financial Times*, *Observer*, *International Herald-Tribune*, *Wall Street Journal* (European Edition), and, less frequently, *USA Today* are available at train stations and kiosks in major European cities. Furthermore, the *Economist* and international versions of *Time* and *Newsweek* are easy to come by.

■■■ WEIGHTS AND MEASURES

1 centimeter (cm) = 0.39 inches	1 inch = 2.54cm
1 meter (m) = 3.28 feet	1 foot = 0.31m
1 kilometer (km) = 0.62 miles	1 mile = 1.61km
1 gram (g) = 0.04 ounces	1 ounce = 28g
1 kilogram (kg) = 2.2 pounds	1 pound = 0.45kg
1 liter = 0.26 gallons	1 gallon = 3.76 liter
1 Imperial gallon (U.K.) = 1.2 gallons	1 gallon = .83 Imperial Gallons
°F = (°C x 1.8) + 32	°C = (°F-32) x .56

RETURNING HOME: CUSTOMS

United States citizens returning home may bring US$400 worth of accompanying goods duty-free and must pay a 10% tax on the next US$1000. You must declare all purchases, so have sales slips ready. Goods are considered duty-free if they are for personal or household use (this includes gifts) and cannot include more than 100 cigars, 200 cigarettes (1 carton), and 1 liter of wine or liquor. You must be over 21 to bring liquor into the U.S. To be eligible for the duty-free allowance, you must have remained abroad for at least 48 hours and cannot have used this exemption or any part of it within the preceding 30 days.

You can mail unsolicited gifts duty-free if they are worth less than US$50, though you may not mail liquor, tobacco, or perfume. Officials occasionally spot check parcels, so mark the price and nature of the gift and the words "Unsolicited Gift" on the package. If you send back a non-gift parcel or a gift worth more than US$50, the Postal Service will collect a duty for its value plus a handling charge to deliver it. If you mail home personal goods of U.S. origin, you can avoid duty charges by marking the package "American goods returned." For more information, consult the brochure *Know Before You Go*, available from R. Woods, Consumer Information Center, Pueblo, CO 81009 (item 477Y). You can direct other questions to the U.S. Customs Service, P.O. Box 7407, Washington, DC 20004 (tel. (202) 927-6724). Foreign nationals living in the U.S. are subject to different regulations; refer the leaflet *Customs Hints for Visitors (Nonresidents)*.

Canadian citizens who remain abroad for at least one week may bring back up to CDN$300 worth of goods duty-free once every calendar year; goods that exceed the allowance will be taxed at 20%. You are permitted to ship goods home under this exemption as long as you declare them when you arrive. Citizens over the legal age (which varies by province) may import in-person (not through the mail) up to 200 cigarettes, 50 cigars, 400g loose tobacco, 1.14L wine or alcohol, and 355ml beer; the value of these products is included in the CDN$300 allowance. For more information, contact External Affairs, Communications Branch, Mackenzie Ave., Ottawa, Ontario, K1A 0l5 (tel. (613) 957-0275).

EC nationals who travel between EC countries (Belgium, Denmark, France, Germany, Greece, Ireland, Italy, Luxembourg, the Netherlands, Portugal, Spain, and the

U.K.) no longer need to declare the goods they purchase abroad. Goods for personal use are not taxed or dutied further, provided that duty and tax are paid in the other country. Note that sales of duty-free and tax-free goods to individual travelers are restricted by duty-free shop operators in all EC countries.

British citizens are allowed an exemption of up to UK£36 of goods purchased outside the EC, including not more than 200 cigarettes, 100 cigarillos, 50 cigars, or 250kg of tobacco; and no more than 2L of still table wine plus 1L of alcohol over 22% volume. You must be over 17 to import liquor or tobacco. For more information about U.K. customs, contact Her Majesty's Customs and Excise, Custom House, Heathrow Airport North, Hunslow, Middlesex TW6 2LA (tel. (081) 750 1603; fax 081 750 1549). HM Customs & Excise Notice 1 explains the allowances for people travelling to the U.K. both from within and without the European Community.

Irish citizens may return home with the equivalent of IR£34 (IR£17 under age 17) of goods purchased outside the EC, including: 1) 200 cigarettes, 100 cigarillos, 50 cigars, or 250g tobacco; 2) 1L liquor or 2L wine, or apportioned fractions thereof; 3) 2L still wine; 4) 50g perfume; and 5) 250ml toilet water. Citizens under 17 are not entitled to any allowance for tobacco or alcoholic products. For more information, contact The Revenue Commissioners, Dublin Castle (tel. (01) 679 2777; fax (01) 671 2021).

Australian citizens may import AUS$400 (under 18 AUS$200) of goods duty-free, including 250 cigarettes, 250g tobacco, and 1L alcohol. You must be over 18 to import either. For information, contact the nearest Australian consulate.

New Zealand citizens may bring home up to NZ$700 worth of goods duty-free if they are intended for personal use or are unsolicited gifts. The concession is 200 cigarettes (1 carton) or 250g tobacco or 50 cigars or a combination of all 3 not to exceed 250g. You may also bring in 4.5L of beer or wine and 1.125L of liquor. Only travelers over 17 may bring tobacco or alcoholic beverages into the country. For more information, consult the *New Zealand Customs Guide for Travelers*, available from customs offices, or contact New Zealand Customs, 50 Anzac Avenue, Box 29, Auckland (tel. (09) 377-3520; fax (09) 309-2978).

South African citizens may import duty-free: 400 cigarettes, 50 cigars, 250g tobacco, 2L wine, 1L of spirits, 250mL toilet water, and 50mL perfume. You can import other items up to a value of R500. Golf clubs, watches, firearms, and furs do not fall within the duty-free allowances for travelers who have been absent from the Republic for less than 6 months, and goods acquired abroad and sent to the Republic as unaccompanied baggage do not qualify for any allowances. You may not export or import South African Bank notes in excess of R500. Persons who require specific information or advice concerning customs and excise duties can address their inquiries to: The Commissioner for Customs and Excise, Private Bag X47, Pretoria, 0001. This agency distributes the pamphlet *South African Customs Information*, for visitors and residents who travel abroad. South Africans residing in the U.S. should contact: South African Mission, 3201 New Mexico Ave. NW, Suite 390, Washington, DC 20016 (fax (202) 364-6008).

PARTING WORDS

The best way to sample a new culture is to dissolve discreetly in it; there's no faster way to learn about new people than to let them think you're one of them. As a foreigner, you'll probably be conspicuous—but you will be welcomed if you make a sincere effort to fit in. An afternoon of quiet relaxation at a park in Prague or a café in Colmar will often teach you more about a country and its people than a museum. Make the effort to actually meet people. A photo of Hans and Gisela Kriege who put you up for the night in Munich will contain many more memories than a postcard of the Eiffel Tower. Europeans are earnestly interested in other lands and cultures but have a very strong sense of their own cultural history; if you insult or belittle it, you'll only seem ignorant. Don't expect things to work the way they do at home; half the fun is untangling a new system. Culture shock can really happen, but go for the *pâté* and goulash anyway and leave McDonald's for when you get home.

A word of warning. Many travelers find themselves succumbing to budget obsession on the road: to stay in the cheapest lodgings, no matter how miserable, to eat grim, tasteless food, and to make each day's goal to spend less than yesterday. Perhaps the worst sin of the entire *Let's Go* series is that it perpetuates this mindset among our readers. When you hit the doldrums, use some of your money to cushion the shock. A hearty meal or a quiet evening in a soothing pension might add 10 dollars to your bill, but it will make you feel rich and pampered rather than destitute and ignored. Better to go home raving about 3 lovely weeks of down pillows and *Sachertorte* than bitching about 4 weeks of night-train accommodations and grocery store cuisine. You're on a vacation, not a crusade.

Falling into the mentality that "they all speak English" can offend; every time you address Europeans in English, you're asking a favor that you probably couldn't return were they to visit your home town. Humbly ask "Do you speak English?" before launching into a question. Better yet, try to learn a little about the foreign languages you'll be encountering and don't be afraid of trying them out. Except for Finnish, Estonian, and Hungarian (related to each other), Turkish (related to Central Asian tongues), and Basque (related to nothing in particular), all the languages in Europe are part of the Indo-European language family. Indo-European languages are remarkably similar: for instance, the words for "three" in French, Lithuanian, Norwegian, and Russian are *trois, trys, tre,* and *tri,* respectively. You can learn any pronunciation system, plus the words for yes, no, where is, how much, and the numbers up to 10, in about 15 minutes. Really. Or at least you can make some new friends in the attempt.

WESTERN EUROPE

◾ Andorra

Embracing fewer than 250 sq. km between France and Spain in the hermetic confines of the Pyrénées, fingernail-sized Andorra (pop. 50,000) is Europe's greatest anomaly: French President François Mitterand and Bishop of Urgell Dr. Joan Martí Alanis share the title "Co-Princes" of Andorra, while a popularly elected, 28-member "General Council of the Valleys" conducts day-to-day government. Andorra offers soaring peaks and near-pristine wilderness, but it is the humility of its sales taxes rather than the grandeur of its sights that draws most visitors. Though many maps fail to acknowledge the country's existence, European tourists overrun the capital in search of bargains in the duty-free perfume and electronics shops lining the main avenue of **Andorra la Vella,** the capital city. Andorran establishments are legally bound to accept French and Spanish currencies, but there is a conspicuous preference for pesetas (exchange rate is about 125 pesetas to the U.S. dollar; 23 pesetas to the franc). Spanish is widely spoken and French will get you by, but Catalan is the country's official language. **Phones** require an STA *teletarja* (telecard), which costs a minimum of 920ptas; the cards are available at any post office. Andorra's **city code** is 682. Collect calls are not available, and AT&T does not access Andorra.

To best appreciate Andorra, visit the picturesque Lilliputian villages cradled within a Brobdignagian mountain range. All traffic from France must enter Andorra at the town of **Pas de la Casa; Sant Julià de Lòria** is the gateway on the Spanish side. To approach Andorra by **French train,** stop at the SNCF station l'**Hospitalet** (a stop on the Toulouse-Ax-les-Thermes-Barcelona line, 4/day in each direction) or **La Tour de Carol** (a stop on the same line, as well as a stop on the **petit train jaune** from Perpignan, 5/day, 107F). From l'Hospitalet, **Société Franco-Andorrane de Transports (SFAT),** Carres la Llucuna, 12 Andorra la Vella (tel. 213 72), runs a bus through Pas de la Casa to the capital, Andorra la Vella. (2/day, 1¾hr., 759ptas each way.) From La Tour de Carol, **Autos Pujol Huguet** (tel. 410 19) sends a bus to the capital (2/day; Oct.-June 1/day; 2½hr.; 966ptas). The same bus also goes to Sant Julià de Lòria on the Spanish border (2/day, 20min.). Several private bus companies run to more distant points beyond the French border towns. **Alsina Graells,** 34, rue Prat de la Creu (tel. 273 79), runs to Barcelona, 215km south of Andorra la Vella. (2/day; Mon.-Sat. 100F, Sun. 2645ptas.)

Andorra la Vella The centerpiece of Andorra la Vella's old quarter is the **Casa de la Vall** (House of the Valleys). Built in the 16th century and graced with mini-Barbican towers, the edifice is the tiniest little parliament you ever saw. The main **tourist office** in Andorra la Vella (tel. 202 14), on av. Docteur Villanova at the foot of the **Barri Antic** (Old Quarter), dispenses information on lodgings and on the surrounding countryside. (Open daily 9am-1pm and 3-7pm; Sept.-June Mon.-Sat. 10am-1pm and 3-7pm, Sun. 10am-1pm.) The French-speaking staff of **Departament de Cultura I Joventut,** on the second floor of **Fundació Clara Rabassa,** 30, av. Príncep Benlloch (tel. 608 60), offers info on everything from AIDS to accommodations. **Pensió La Rosa,** Antic Carrer Major, 18 (tel. 218 10), just south of av. Príncep Benlloch, provides immaculate rooms, all with showers and happy flowered wallpaper. (Singles 3082ptas, doubles 3841ptas, triples 8050ptas.) **Camping Valira** (tel. 223 84), located behind the **Estadi Comunal d'Andorra la Vella,** offers shade, video games, hot showers, and an indoor pool. (414ptas/person, tent, or car.)

Austria (Österreich)

US$1 = 11.28AS (schilling, or ATS)	**10AS = US$0.89**
CDN$1 = 8.57AS	**10AS = CDN$1.17**
UK£1 = 17.48AS	**10AS = UK£0.57**
IR£ = 16.35AS	**10AS = IR£0.61**
AUS$1 = 7.34AS	**10AS = AUS$1.36**
NZ$1 = 6.24AS	**10AS = NZ$1.60**
SAR1 = 2.35AS	**10AS = SAR4.26**
Country Code: 43	**International Dialing Prefix: 900**

The Federal Republic of Austria binds Eastern and Western Europe. For centuries, the Austrian lands have sheltered Magyars, Germans, Italians, and myriad other ethnic groups under a common political order. The Danube's majestic flow reflects the commercial conduit between the industrial democracies of Western Europe and the fledgling market economies of the east. This Alpine nation, swathed in edelweiss, nurtured the ineffable genius of Mozart, Schönberg, Beethoven, Brahms, Strauss, Freud, Klimt, and Kokoschka, as well as the xenophobic mania of Adolf Hitler.

The once-sprawling Austro-Hungarian empire is now a tiny fragment of its imperial self, but the Court's cultural footprints remain. Despite the lack of a prior democratic tradition, postwar Austria has seen a successful, stable blend of social welfare and democratic pragmatism. The country has established a marriage of socialism-with-a-brain and conservatism-with-a-heart that will serve it well in the European Community.

> For extensive and entertaining information on the country, pick up a copy of Levitt and Zelanko's truly inimitable *Let's Go: Austria*.

GETTING THERE AND GETTING AROUND

Rail travel in Austria is extraordinarily reliable and efficient, but can be expensive. Eurail is valid. The **Rabbit Card** gives 4 days of unlimited travel over a 10-day period

(2nd-class 1130AS; juniors (under 27) 700AS). The **Bundes-Netzkarte** provides unlimited travel on Austrian trains for one month and scores a 50% discount on railway-operated boats and Danube steamers (2nd-class 3600AS). Seniors (men over 65, women over 60) are entitled to **half-price tickets** *(Umweltticket für Senioren)* on trains, long-distance buses, Danube steamers, and many cable cars; you must show an official **Reduction Card** *(Ermässigungsausweis),* valid for 1 year (240AS). All cards are available at major post offices and train stations.

The Austrian **bus** system consists of orange **Bundes Buses** and yellow **Post buses.** Both are efficient and cover mountain areas inaccessible by train. They usually cost a bit more than trains, and railpasses are not valid. For river **steamers** and **hydrofoils,** see the Danube section.

Austria is a **hitchhiker's** nightmare—Austrians rarely pick them up, and many mountain roads are all but deserted. The thumb signal is recognized, but signs with a destination and the word *bitte* (please) are just as common. More formal arrangements for longer, inter-city routes can be arranged through a **Mitfahrzentrale** office, which charges roughly half the going rail fare to connect travelers with somebody traveling by car in the same direction.

About 160 Austrian rail stations rent **bikes.** They can be returned to any participating station and cost 90AS per day—half-price if you have a train ticket *to* the station from which you are renting and have arrived on the day of rental. Look for signs with a bicycle and the word *Verleih.* Pick up the list *(Fahrrad am Bahnhof)* of participating stations at any station. Tourist offices provide regional bike route maps. 30AS will get your bike aboard a train; look for the *Gepäckbeförderung* symbol on departure schedules to see if bikes are permitted. Most Austrian train stations offer luggage storage (up to several months) for 20AS per piece; many offer lockers as well (10-20AS, depending on size).

AUSTRIA ESSENTIALS

The Austrian government operates a network of chipper and clued-in **tourist offices** *(Verkehrsamt* or *Verkehrsverein);* even the smallest towns have them. Most tourist offices will reserve private rooms, usually for free.

Banks throughout Austria are usually open weekdays 8am to 12:30pm and 2 to 5:30pm. In Vienna, most banks are open Monday to Wednesday and Friday 8am to 3pm, Thursday 8am to 5:30pm; branch offices close from 12:30 to 1:30pm. Many banks offer cash advances to Visa holders (the **Zentralsparkasse und Kommerzialbank** does this at most branches). A town's main post office *(Hauptpostamt)* is usually the best place to exchange money. All banks are legally required to charge a commission for cashing foreign traveler's checks.

Stores in Austria close Saturday afternoons and Sunday, and many museums take Monday off. Stores in many small towns take most of the afternoon off for lunch (usually noon-3pm). Everything closes on Austrian National Day (Oct. 26), Epiphany (Jan. 6), Whit Monday (May 31, 1993), Corpus Christi (June), Assumption (Aug. 15), All Saints' (Nov. 1), Immaculate Conception (Dec. 8), and Christmas and St. Stephen's Day (Dec. 25-26).

Western Austria is one of the world's best **skiing** regions. The areas around Innsbruck and Kitzbühel in the Tyrol are saturated with lifts and runs. There's good skiing year-round on several glaciers, including the Stubaital near Innsbruck and the Dachstein in the Salzkammergut. High season runs from mid-December to mid-January, from February to March, and from July to August. Local tourist offices provide information on regional skiing and can point you to budget travel agencies that offer ski packages. Lift tickets generally run 250-300AS per day.

Unless you're on top of a mountain, Austria doesn't usually get brutally cold, even in the dead of winter. Nevertheless, warm sweaters are the rule from September to May, with a parka, hat, and gloves added in the winter months. Summertime brings frequent rains—almost every other day in Salzburg—so suitable gear is a must.

Communication should not be a tremendous problem; English is the most common second language. Any effort, however incompetent, to use the mother tongue will win you loads of fans; *Grüß Gott* (God bless) is the typical Austrian greeting.

You can make international **phone** calls at telephone centers (usually only in the larger cities), in most post offices, and from pay phones. **Telephone cards** *(Wertkarten)*, available in post offices, train stations, and some stores, come in 50AS, 100AS, and 200AS denominations. For AT&T's **USA Direct,** dial 022 903 011, for **MCI's World Reach,** dial 022 903 012, and for **Canada Direct,** dial 022 903 013. For assistance calling abroad, dial 08. For directory assistance, call 16 11. For the **police** anywhere in Austria, dial 133; for an **ambulance,** dial 144; in case of **fire,** dial 122. With older pay phones, you must push the red button when your party answers. Austria is currently converting its phone system to a digital network; phone numbers may change as a result, especially in Vienna and Innsbruck.

Accommodations and Camping Rooms in Austria are usually spotless; even the most odious of Austria's 120-odd **youth hostels** *(Jugendherberge)* are, by international standards, quite tolerable. Most charge about 100AS per night (130AS in larger cities), breakfast included. Nonmembers are normally charged an extra 40AS and sometimes turned away completely. For information about Austria's hostels or for a membership card (170AS, under 26 100AS), contact the **Österreichischer Jugendherbergsverband** (Austrian Youth Hostel Association), Schottenring 28, Wien (tel. (0222) 533 53 53), and the **Österreichisches Jugendherbergswerk,** Helferstorferstr. 4, A-1010 Wien (tel. (0222) 533 18 33 or 533 18 34).

Hotels are expensive, but smaller pensions and *Gasthäuser* are often within the budget traveler's range. Local tourist offices will help set you up and also give advice on camping. Otherwise, look for *Zimmer Frei* or *Privat Zimmer* signs; they advertise typically inexpensive rooms in private houses (150-200AS/person). **Campgrounds** are the cheapest option, charging about 30-60AS per person, tent, or car.

Hiking The various Alpine associations in Austria currently maintain more than 1100 **huts** *(Schuzhütten)* which provide accommodations, cooking facilities, and, occasionally, hot meals. Prices for an overnight stay are 50-150AS and no reservations are necessary; if they're crowded, you may end up sleeping on a cot, but you won't be turned away. Topographic maps *(Alpenvereinskarten),* available in most bookstores, show hut locations. If you plan carefully, you can undertake week-long hikes that bring you to a hut every night, thus freeing yourself from the burden of carrying a tent and cooking gear. Several guidebooks such as *Walking Austria's Alps Hut to Hut* by Jonathan Hurdle (US$11) plot out such hikes. Those planning extensive walking tours of the Austrian Alps may want to purchase membership in the largest of the Alpine associations, the **Österreichischer Alpenverein** (430AS, under 26 345AS; one-time fee 70AS). This will entitle you to a 50% discount at their refuges, all of which have beds, as well as discounts on some cable car rides and organized hikes. Their main office is at Wilhelm-Greil-Str. 15, Innsbruck 6010 (tel. (0512) 58 41 07).

Even if you're going for only a day hike, check terrain and weather conditions; weather in the Alps changes instantaneously. *Always* carry waterproof clothing and some high-energy food, wear durable footwear, and tell someone where you're going. If you get into serious trouble, use the *Alpinenotsignal* (Alpine Distress Signal)—6 audible (such as blows on a whistle) or visual signals spaced evenly over 1 minute and followed by a break of 1 minute before repetition. Paths marked "Für Geübte" are for experienced climbers only. Finally, remember that those gorgeous Alpine meadows are extremely fragile habitats. Leave trails and campsites exactly as you found them.

Food and Drink One of life's great enigmas is how a country with such unremarkable cuisine can produce such heavenly desserts. In mid-afternoon, Austrians flock to *Café-Konditoreien* to nurse the national sweet tooth with *Kaffe und Kuchen* (coffee and cake). Try *Sachertorte,* a rich chocolate pastry layered with marmalade. Staple foods include *Schweinfleisch* (pork), *Kalbsfleisch* (veal), *Wurst* (sausage), *Eier* (eggs), *Käse* (cheese), *Brot* (bread), and *Kartoffeln* (potatoes). Austria's best-known dish is *Schnitzel,* a meat cutlet (usually veal or pork) fried in butter with bread crumbs. Most butchers sell a hefty *Wurstsemmel* (sliced sausage on a bulkie roll) for under 10AS. The best discount supermarkets in Austria are **Billa, Sparmarkt, Hofer,** and **Konsum.** Most restaurants expect you to seat yourself; a small tip (usually rounding up the bill) is customary. The server won't bring your check without first being asked. Say *zahlen, bitte* (TSAH-len BIT-uh) to settle up.

Imbibing in Austria is trouble-free—beer is sold more commonly than soda, and anyone old enough to see over the counter can buy it (although those under 18 will have trouble purchasing liquor and getting into nightclubs). Eastern Austria is famous for its white wine. Grüner Veltliner's *Klosterneuburger* is both reasonably priced and dry. Austrian beers are outstanding; try *Stiegl Bier,* a Salzburg brew, *Zipfer Bier* from upper Austria, and *Gösser Bier* from Graz. Austria imports lots of Budweiser beer, a.k.a. *Budwar*—the Czech original, not the watery American imitation. For a more potent potable, try *Loköre* (liqueurs) and *Schnäpse* (schnapps); every region has a local specialty.

■■■ VIENNA (WIEN)

A relentlessly self-absorbed metropolis even as it ruled over the vast Habsburg empire, Vienna dwarfs the rest of its country to a degree unmatched even by Paris or London. Most of the old empire lay east of what is now Austria, and the Viennese made no secret of their contempt for the subject peoples. "Asia," declared Metternich, "begins at the Landstraße," the street leading east out of town.

The Habsburg monolith eventually fell—World War I saw to that—but its cultural legacy remains impressive. Imperial palaces and cathedrals are scattered throughout the city, and the flurry of aesthetic achievement that gripped the *fin-de-siècle* city endures in a number of architectural and artistic masterpieces; frequently, the buildings that house Vienna's museums are as impressive as the art inside. Finally, Vienna is the Mecca of European music; almost all composers in the classic Austro-German tradition lived here at one time or another. Don't leave without paying homage to the Opera House, once the stomping ground of Mozart, Schubert, and Mahler.

ORIENTATION AND PRACTICAL INFORMATION

Vienna is in eastern Austria, 40km from the Hungarian, Czech, and Slovakian borders. Vienna is divided into 23 **districts** (*Bezirke*); the oldest area, *die Innere Stadt,* is the first. The **Ringstraße** separates the 1st district from the 2nd through 9th districts. The districts spiral around the center in a clockwise formation; the 10th through 23rd districts begin once one crosses the **Gürtel** (literally "belt," a larger ring and 2-way thoroughfare). Street signs indicate the district number (e.g. "18, Auhofstraße" is in the 18th district) and postal codes depend on the district number (1010 represents the 1st district, 1020 the 2nd, etc.). The epicenter of Viennese life, the intersection of the **Opernring, Kärntner Ring,** and **Kärntner Straße,** is home to the Opera House, tourist office, and the **Karlsplatz** U-Bahn stop.

Tourist Offices: 1010 Kärntner Str. 38 (tel. 51 88 92), behind the Opera House. Pick up the excellent free city map. Books rooms (from 350-400AS); 35AS fee. Open daily 9am-7pm. Other offices at Westbahnhof (open daily 6:15am-11pm), the airport (open daily 9am-11pm; Oct.-May 9am-10pm), and at the "Richtung Zentrum" exit off the A1 *Westautobahn*. **Information stands** also at U-Bahn stations: Karlsplatz, Stephansplatz, Praterstein, Philadelphiabrücke, Landstraße, and

VIENNA

Volkstheater. All open Mon.-Fri. 10am-7pm; Karlsplatz and Stephansplatz also open Sat.-Sun. 8:30am-4pm. **Jugend-Info Wien (Youth Information Service)**, Bellariapassage (tel. 526 46 37), in the underground passage at the Bellaria intersection. Entrance at the Dr.-Karl-Renner-Ring/Bellaria tram stop (lines #1, 2, 46, 49, D, and J). Additional entrance from the Volkstheater U-Bahn station. Info on cultural events. Get the indispensible *Youth Scene* brochure and pick up the hostels and pensions list, as well as cheap tickets to rock and pop music events. Open Mon.-Fri. noon-7pm, Sat. 10am-7pm. Call **Wiener Stadtinformation** (tel. 403 89 89; Mon.-Fri. 8am-4pm) for answers to any questions about Vienna.

Budget Travel: ÖKISTA, 1090 Türkenstr. 6 (tel. 40 14 80). Discount flights; newsy bulletin boards with personal ads. Open Mon.-Fri. 9:30am-5:30pm. Branch at 1040 Karlsgasse 3 (tel. 505 01 280) offers the same hours and services and shorter lines. **ÖS Reisen** (Austrian Student Travel), 1010 Reichsratstr. 13 (tel. 402 15 41), for cheap train, plane, and bus tickets. Open Mon.-Fri. 9:30am-5:30pm. **Österreichisches Verkehrsbüro** (Austrian National Travel Office), 1010 Operngasse 3-4 (tel. 588 62 38), opposite the Opera House. Patient English-speaking staff sells BIJ tickets, the *Thomas Cook Timetable* (240AS), and Eastern European train timetables (100AS). Open Mon.-Fri. 8:30am-6:30pm, Sat. 9am-noon.

Embassies: U.S., 1090 Boltzmangasse 16 (tel. 31 55 11), off Währingerstr.; U.S. **consulate** is at 1010 Gartenbaupromenade 2 (tel. 31 55 11), off Parkring. Open Mon.-Fri. 8:30am-noon and 1:30-3:30pm. **Canada**, 1010 Schubertring 12, 6th floor (tel. 533 36 91), near Schwarzenburgplatz. Open Mon.-Fri. 8:30am-12:30pm and 1:30-3:30pm. **U.K.**, 1030 Jauresgasse 10 (tel. 713 15 75). Open Mon.-Fri. 9:15am-noon, for British citizens also 2-5pm. **Ireland**, 1030, The Hilton Center, 16th floor, Landstr. Haupstr. 2 (tel. 715 42 46 0). **Australia**, 1040 Mattiellistr. 2-4 (tel. 51 28 58 0164), behind Karlskirche. Open Mon.-Fri. 8:45am-1pm and 2-5pm. **New Zealand**, 1010, Lugeck 1 (tel. 52 66 36). Open Mon.-Fri. 8:30am-5pm. **South Africa**, 1190, Sandgasse 33 (tel. 326 49 30). **Czech Republic**, 1140 Penzingerstr. 11-13 (tel. 894 37 41 or 894 62 36). Open Mon.-Fri. 9-11am. **Hungary**, 1010, Bankgasse 4-6 (tel. 533 26 31). Open Mon.-Fri. 8:30am-12:30pm.

Currency Exchange: Banks open Mon.-Wed. and Fri. 8am-3pm, Thurs. 8am-5:30pm. Bank and airport exchanges use same official rates (min. commission 65AS for traveler's checks, 10AS for cash). Longer hours (Mon.-Fri.) and lighter commission at train stations: Opernpassage 9am-7pm, Westbahnhof 4am-10pm, Südbahnhof 6:30am-10pm, the City Air Terminal 8am-12:30pm and 2-6pm, and Schwechat airport 6:30am-11pm. Cash advance with Visa at numerous banks, including the **Zentralersparkasse**, 1010 Kärntner Str. 32. Open Mon.-Wed. 8:30am-12:30pm and 1:30-3pm, Thurs. 8:30-12:30pm and 1:30-5:30pm.

American Express: 1010 Kärntnerstr. 21-23 (tel. 515 40; 24-hr. refund service toll-free 066 02 79), down from Stephansplatz. Holds mail. 40AS min. for Traveler's Cheques, 15AS min. for cash. Open Mon.-Fri. 9am-5:30pm, Sat. 9am-noon.

Post Office: 1010 Fleischmarkt 19. During renovations, it's at the corner of Barbaragasse and Postgasse. Open 24hrs., as are branches at Westbahnhof, Südbahnhof, and Franz-Josefs Bahnhof. All these change currency. Address **Poste Restante** to *Postlagernde Briefe*, 1 Fleischmarkt 19, A-1010 Wien. **Postal Codes:** in the 1st district 1010, in the 2nd 1020, etc.

Telephones: 1010 Börseplatz 1, near the Schottenring. Open daily 6am-midnight. Also at 4 main post offices. Buy telephone cards at post offices and train stations (48AS and 95AS). Push red button on older pay phones to connect. 1AS and up for local calls, 9AS for long-distance. **City Code:** in Austria, 0222; from abroad, 1.

Flights: Wien Schwechat airport (tel. 711 10 22 33), 19km from the city center, linked by bus (60AS) to Westbahnhof, Südbahnhof, and the City Air Terminal (next to the Hilton in 3rd district; take U-3 or U-4 to Landstr. or train to Wien-Mitte). *Schnell-Bahn* metro railway also runs there hourly from "Wien Mitte" or "Wien Nord" stations (30AS, Eurail and Vienna public transport passes valid).

Trains: tel. 17 17, 24hrs. English spoken. There are 4 principal stations in Vienna. **Wien-Mitte**, in the center, handles commuter trains. **Franz-Josefs-Bahnhof** handles local trains and trains to Berlin via Prague; tram D (direction "Südbahnhof") runs to the Ring. **Westbahnhof** sends trains to France, western Germany, Switzerland, the Netherlands, Belgium, the U.K., Bulgaria, Romania, Hungary, and

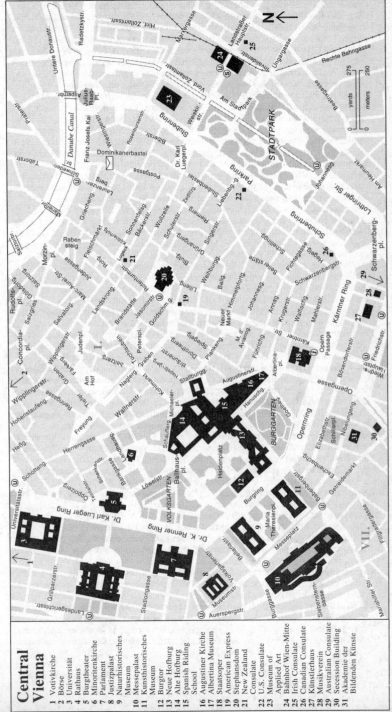

VIENNA

Central Vienna

1 Votivkirche
2 Börse
3 Universität
4 Rathaus
5 Burgtheater
6 Minoritenkirche
7 Parlament
8 Justizpalast
9 Naturhistorisches Museum
10 Messepalast
11 Kunsthistorisches Museum
12 Burgtor
13 Neue Hofburg
14 Alte Hofburg
15 Spanish Riding School
16 Augustiner Kirche
17 Albertina Museum
18 Staatsoper
19 American Express
20 Stephansdom
21 New Zealand Consulate
22 U.S. Consulate
23 Museum of Applied Art
24 Bahnhof Wien-Mitte
25 Irish Consulate
26 Canadian Consulate
27 Künstlerhaus
28 Musikverein
29 Australian Consulate
30 Secession Building
31 Akademie der Bildenden Künste

western Austria; take U-6 then U-4 to Karlsplatz or take tram #52 or 58 to the Ring. **Südbahnhof** has trains to Italy, Greece, Czech Republic, Slovakia, Poland, and (June-Sept.) Bulgaria and Hungary; take tram D (direction "Nußdorf") to the Ring. To: Prague (2/day, 5-6hr., 364-370AS); Berlin (2/day, 15hr., 628-654AS); Warsaw (1/day, 11hr., 494AS); Budapest (4/day, 4-5hr., 372AS plus 80AS inner city supplement); and Kraków (1/day, 8hr., 396AS). Showers and baths available in the Westbahnhof at **Friseursalon Navratil,** on the ground floor. 40AS/30-min. shower; 60AS/30-min. bath. Open Mon.-Sat. 7am-8pm, Sun. 8am-1pm.

Buses: City bus terminal at **Wien-Mitte** rail station. Post and Bundesbahn buses across Austria; private international buses. Currency exchange and lockers available. Domestic ticket desk open daily 6:15am-6pm; international private lines maintain travel agencies in the station. Call 711 01 for info (daily 6am-9pm).

Public Transportation: Excellent **U-Bahn** (subway), bus, and tram systems. Tickets 20AS, 24-hr. pass 45AS, 72-hr. pass 115AS. The 8-day ticket (235AS) must be stamped for each ride; with this card, 4 people can ride for 2 days, 8 for 1, etc. Week pass 125AS (requires passport-sized photo). All passes allow unlimited travel on system during period of validity; to validate, punch your ticket in the machine on board. Purchase tickets from *Tabak* kiosks or machines in major U-Bahn stations. 490AS fine for riding without a valid ticket. System closes shortly before midnight. Special night buses (one-way 25AS, passes not valid) run Fri.-Sat. nights 12:30-4am between city center (at Schwedenplatz) and various outlying districts; stops designated by "N." signs. Tram lines and U-Bahn stops are listed on tourist office's free city map.

Ferries: Cruise with **DDSG Donaureisen** to Budapest for 830AS, round-trip 1200AS (daily April 24-Sept. 18). Buy tickets at tourist offices. Boats dock at the Reichsbrücke on the New Danube. Take U-1 to Reichsbrücke.

Taxis: tel. 17 12, 313 00, 401 00, 601 60, or 910 11. Base charge 22AS. 10AS surcharge for taxis called by radiophone, for trips on Sun. and holidays 11pm-6am, or for luggage over 20kg, 20AS surcharge for luggage over 50kg.

Bike Rental: Best bargain at **Wien Nord** and **Westbahnhof** train stations. 90AS/day, with train ticket 45AS after 3pm on day of arrival. Elsewhere in the city rental averages 30AS/hr. Pick up the *Vienna By Bike* brochure at tourist office.

Hitchhiking: Those who hitch to Salzburg take the tram to the end of the line at "Hütteldorf" station and walk over to the beginning of the Autobahn. Those hitching south try the traffic circle near Laaerberg (tram #67 to the last stop). **Mitfahrzentrale Wien,** 1030 Invalidenstr. 15 (tel. 715 00 66), pairs drivers and riders (Salzburg 190AS, Innsbruck 240AS). Open Mon.-Fri. 9am-1pm and 3-6pm, Sat. 10am-2pm; off-season Mon.-Fri. 9am-1pm and 3-6pm, Sat. 10am-1pm.

Luggage Storage: Lockers at all train stations (24hr. 20AS). Adequate for sizable backpacks. Checked luggage 15AS. Open daily 4am-midnight.

Lost Property: Central Lost Property Office, 1090 Wasagasse 22 (tel. 313 44 91 11). Open Mon.-Fri. 8am-noon. For objects lost on public transport system, call 50 13 00 within 3 days.

Bookstore: British Bookshop, 1010 Weihburggasse 8. Stocks *Let's Go.* Open Mon.-Fri. 9am-6pm, Sat. 9am-noon.

Laundromat: Münzwäscherei Kalksburger & Co., 1030 Schlachthausgasse 19 (tel. 78 81 91). Wash 90AS/6kg, dry 10AS. Soap 10AS. Open Mon.-Fri. 7:30am-6:30pm, Sat. 7:30am-1pm. **Münzwäscherei Margaretenstraße,** 1040 Margaretenstr. 52 (tel. 587 04 73). Wash 85AS/6kg, dry 10AS. Soap included. Open Mon.-Fri. 7am-6pm, Sat. 8am-noon.

Crises: House for Threatened and Battered Women, emergency hotline 545 48 00 or 408 38 80. Open 24hrs. **Rape Crisis Hotline,** tel. 93 22 22. Answered Mon. 10am-1pm, Tues. and Thurs. 6-9pm.

Medical Assistance: Allgemeines Krankenhaus, 1090 Währinger Gürtel 18-20 (tel. 404 00). Your consulate can provide a list of physicians.

Emergencies: Police: tel. 133. *Fremdenpolizei* (foreign police) headquarters at Bäckerstr. 13 (tel. 63 06 71). **Ambulance:** tel. 144. **Fire:** tel. 122.

ACCOMMODATIONS AND CAMPING

The only unpleasant aspect of Vienna is the hunt for cheap rooms. The June crunch abates slightly from July to September, when university dorms metamorphose into hostels. Write ahead or call the day before for reservations, and pick up the lists of hostels and hotels from the tourist office. Beware of offers made at the station and shady talk of *Studentenzimmer* (student rooms), which are often closet-sized. Tourist offices handle private homes (3-day min. stay) in the 180-250AS range, but many of these are in the 'burbs. **ÖKISTA** (see Budget Travel) finds cheaper rooms and charges no commission. The office is at 1090 Türkenstr. 4-6 #314 (tel. 34 75 26 23), adjacent to the budget travel office. (Open Mon.-Wed. and Fri. 9:30am-4pm, Thurs. 9:30am-5:30pm.) In summer, the **Mitwohnzentrale** at Laudongasse 7 (tel. 402 60 61) will find you a room or apartment from 500AS/day (commission included); for stays of a month or longer, rooms start at 2500AS (book 4 weeks in advance). Bring your passport. (Open Mon.-Thurs. 10am-5pm, Fri. 10am-1pm.)

Hostels

Myrthengasse (HI), 1070 Myrthengasse 7 (tel. 523 92 49). From Westbahnhof, take U-6 to Burggasse, then bus #48A to Neubaugasse; walk back about a block, and take the 1st right. About 15min. by bus to city center or Westbahnhof. Sparkling modern rooms with 2-6 beds, washroom, and big lockers. Enthusiastic management, game room. 127 beds. Reception open 7:30am-1am. Lockout 9am-2pm. Curfew 1am. 140AS. Breakfast (7-8:30am) and sheets included. Laundry 50AS/load. Reservations recommended. Wheelchair access.

Neustiftgasse (HI), 1070 Neustiftgasse 85 (tel. 523 74 62). Around the corner from Myrthengasse and managed by the same folks. 118 beds. Reception open 7:30am-1am. Lockout 9am-noon. Curfew 1am. Members only. 140AS. Breakfast included. Laundry 50AS/load. Reservations recommended. Wheelchair access.

Gästehaus Ruthensteiner (HI), 1150 Robert-Hamerlinggasse 24 (tel. 893 42 02 or 893 27 96). From Westbahnhof, walk down Mariahilferstr., take 1st left at Palmgasse, then 1st right (3min.). Small, sunny rooms. Courtyard and kitchen. 76 beds. Reception open 24hrs. Dorm bed (bring sheets or sleeping bag) 129AS. Doubles 418AS. Breakfast 25AS. 50AS key deposit for big lockers. Bicycle rental 78AS/day. Reservations recommended.

Jugendgästehaus Wien Brigittenau (HI), 1200 Friedrich-Engels-Platz 24 (tel. 338 29 40). Take U-Bahn U-1 or U-4 to Schwedenplatz and then tram N to Floridsdorfer Brücke/Friedrich-Engels-Platz. Efficient and helpful management oversees brigades of high-school kids. 334 beds. Reception open 24hrs. Lockout 9am-3pm. Curfew midnight (flexible). Members only. 140AS. Breakfast included.

Believe-It-Or-Not, 1070 Myrthengasse 10, #14 (tel. 526 46 58). Same directions as Myrthengasse hostel across the street. Cramped but homey quarters. Fully equipped kitchen, sheets, down quilts, hot water, and very thoughtful owner. Believe it. Lockout 10:30am-12:30pm. 160AS; Nov.-Easter 110AS. Call ahead.

Schloßherberge am Wilhelminenberg (HI), 1160 Savoyenstr. 2 (tel. 458 50 37 00). From Westbahnhof, take U-6 (direction "Friedensbrücke") to tram #46 to bus #46B or 146B at "Maroltingerstraße." On a hill, abutting a beautiful palace. 164 beds in comfortable quads, all with shower and toilet. Reception open 7am-11:45pm. 205AS. Breakfast included. Open March-Oct. Wheelchair access.

Hostel Zöhrer, 1080 Skodagasse 26 (tel. 43 07 30), just off Alserstr. From Westbahnhof, take U-6 (direction "Heiligenstadt") to "Alserstraße," then take streetcar 43 (direction "Dr. Karl Lueger Ring") 2 stops to Skodagasse. 36 beds. Hospitable owner tends to the garden courtyard and furnished kitchen. 50AS for front door and locker key deposit. Reception open 8am-10pm. Checkout 9am. 160AS. Showers, breakfast, sheets, and kitchen included.

Jugendgästehaus Hütteldorf-Hacking (HI), 1130 Schloßberggasse 8 (tel. 877 02 63). From Karlsplatz, take U-4 to Hütteldorf; cross footbridge and follow signs. From Westbahnhof, take train S-50 (Eurail valid) to "Hütteldorf" (last train 10:15pm; all international trains bound for Westbahnhof stop here). Secluded, with great views of northwest Vienna. 281 dorm beds. Reception open 7am-

VIENNA

11:45pm. Lockout 9am-4pm. Curfew 11:45pm. Members 137AS, 24nonmembers 177AS. Sheets and breakfast included. Laundry 60AS/load.

University Dormitories

The following dorms usually become summer hostels from July to September. Expect mass-produced university cubicles.

Studentenwohnheim der Hochschule für Musik, 1010 Johannesgasse 8 (tel. 514 84). Walk 3 blocks on Kärntnerstr. away from Stephansdom; turn left onto Johannesgasse. Great location. Reception open 24hrs. Singles 380AS. Doubles 660AS. Quads 960AS. Breakfast and showers included.

Porzellaneum der Wiener Universität, 1090 Porzellangasse 30 (tel. 34 72 82). From Südbahnhof, take tram D (direction "Nußdorf") and get off at "Fürstengasse." From Westbahnhof, take tram #5 to Franz-Josefs-Bahnhof, then tram D (direction: "Südbahnhof") to "Fürstengasse." Reception open 24hrs. Renovated singles and doubles 160AS/person. Triples and quads also available. Showers and sheets included. Reservations recommended.

Haus Pfeilheim, 1080 Pfeilgasse 6 (tel. 426 37 40), in the Hotel Avis. From Südbahnhof, take bus #13a to Piaristeng. From Westbahnhof, take U-Bahn U-6 to "Thaliastr.," then walk a block north to Pfeilgasse and take a right (15-20min.). Spartan but adequate rooms. 400 beds. Reception open 24hrs. Singles 240AS. Doubles 400AS. Triples 540AS. Breakfast included.

Katholisches Studentenhaus, 1190 Peter-Jordan-Str. 29 (tel. 34 92 64). From Westbahnhof, take U-6 (direction "Heiligenstadt") to "Nußdorferstr.," then bus #38 to Franz-Jonas-Platz to the "Hardtgasse" stop, then turn left onto Peter-Jordanstr. From Südbahnhof, take tram D to Schottentor, then #38 to Hardtgasse. The reception's on the 2nd floor. Singles 220AS. Doubles 320AS. An affiliated dorm with doubles only is at 1210 Zaunschertgasse 4 (tel. 38 21 97).

Studentenheim Josefstadt, 1080 Buchfeldgasse 16 (tel. 43 52 11), behind the *Rathaus.* Take U-2 to the Rathaus stop and walk 1 block up Schmidtgasse to Buchfeldgasse. Great location, cushy rooms, lots of hot water, and a large breakfast. Reception open 24hrs. Singles 395AS. Doubles 620AS. Triples 900AS.

Hotels and Pensions

Irmgard Lauria, 1070 Kaiserstr. 77, apt. 8 (tel. 5 222 555). From Westbahnhof, take U-6 to "Burggasse-Stadthalle," take a right onto Burggasse, walk 1 block, and turn left (10min.). From Südbahnhof, take bus #13A to Kellermahngasse, then #45A to Kaiserstr. Enchanting rooms. Warm, thoughtful owner and staff. Billowy down quilts, color TVs, refrigerators, hot pots, and front door keys provided. 2-night min. stay on advance bookings. Dorm beds 160AS. Doubles 530AS, with bath 700AS. Triples 700AS, with bath 800AS. Quads 850AS, with bath 940AS.

Pension Kraml, 1060 Brauergasse 5 (tel. 587 85 88), off Gumpendorferstr. From Westbahnhof, take Mariahilferstr. to the 3rd right onto Otto-Bauer-Str., make the 1st left on Königsgasse, then take the 1st right (15min.). From Südbahnhof, take bus #13a. Tidy, comfortable, new, and run by a cordial family. Singles 260AS. Doubles 490-660AS. Triples 720-930AS. Quads 1120AS. Breakfast included.

Hospiz-Hotel CVJM, 1070 Kenyongasse 15 (tel. 93 13 04). From Westbahnhof, walk 1 block down Stallgasse and turn left on Kenyongasse (3min.). Could be the quietest hotel in town. Large, sunny rooms. Interdenominational mass every weekend. Singles 320-360AS. Doubles 540-640AS. Triples 810-900AS. Quads 1040-1120AS. Generous breakfast included. Call ahead.

Pension Falstaff, 1090 Müllnergasse 5 (tel. 34 91 86). From Westbahnhof, take U-6 to "Heiligenstadt," then U-4 to "Rossauer Lande." From Südbahnhof, take tram D to Schlickgasse. High-ceilinged entry and airy dining room overlook a wooded courtyard. Singles 330AS, with shower 440AS. Doubles 540AS, with shower 650AS. Triples 850AS. Extra bed 200AS. Breakfast included. Make reservations.

Camping

Wien-West I and **II**, at Hüttelbergstr. 40 (tel. 94 14 49) and 80 (tel. 94 23 14), respectively, are the most convenient (both in the 14th district about 8km from the city center; both 58AS/person, children 33AS; 53AS/tent or car). I is open July-August; II year-round. II also rents 4-person bungalows (380AS). For either, take U-4 to the end, then switch to bus #52b.

FOOD

Viennese cuisine was born of the city's imperial position, and its specialties betray the influence of Eastern Europe; try *Serbische Bohnensuppe* (Serbian bean soup) and *Ungärische Gulaschsuppe* (Hungarian spicy beef stew). Even the vaunted *Wiener Schnitzel* (fried pork or veal with bread crumbs) originated in Milan. *Wurstelstande* (wurst stands) vend tasty and inexpensive fare. Vienna's desserts are impossibly rich, as you'll want to be when paying for them.

The restaurants in the touristy **Kärntnerstraße** area are generally overpriced. A better bet is the neighborhood just north of the university where **Universitätsstraße** and **Währingerstraße** meet; reasonably priced *Gaststätten, Kneipen* (bars), and restaurants are easy to find. Otherwise, nibble the aromatic delicacies at the open-air **Naschmarkt,** an especially filling option for vegetarians who travel to this carnivorous city (U-4 to Kettenbrückengasse; open Mon.-Fri. 7am-6pm, Sat. 7am-1pm). For discount supermarket fare, try the ubiquitous **Billa.** Except at train stations, all grocery stores close from Saturday afternoon to Monday morning. To conquer the summer heat, try **Gelateria Hoher Markt,** 1010, Hoher Markt just off Rotenturmstr. (Open daily March-Oct. 9am-11pm.)

Restaurants

Schnitzelwirt Schmidt, 1070 Neubaugasse 52. From the Burgring, take bus #49 until it stops at Neubaugasse (5min.). Huge portions at low, low prices to sate your desires. (*Wiener Schnitzel* 55AS). Open Mon.-Fri. 11am-10pm, Sat. 11am-2:30pm and 5-10pm. Closed Dec. 24-Jan. 6 plus 3 weeks in Aug.

Espresso "Teddy"/Rumpelkammerbar, 1090, Liechtensteinstr. 10. Pay attention, baby: take U-2 to "Schottentor," walk up Währingerstr. to Hörlgasse (next to *Votivkirche*), make a right, and go 1 block to Liechtensteinstr. Incredible food, including fish, poultry, salads, and vegetarian fare. *Cordon Bleu* 80AS. Call for a reservation on Fri. and Sat. nights. Open Mon.-Fri. 7am-1am, Sat. 9am-1am.

Tunnel, 1080 Florianigasse 39. From the Rathaus U-Bahn stop, turn left onto Florianigasse (10min.). Young bohemians downing beers and nibbling at Italian, Austrian, and Middle Eastern food. Entrees 35-120AS. Open daily 9am-2pm.

Trzesniewski, 1010 Dorotheergasse 1, 3 blocks from Stephansdom. A famous stand-up sandwich restaurant where Franz Kafka used to stuff his face. Small sandwiches about 7AS/*Brötchen*. Open Mon.-Fri. 9am-7:30pm, Sat. 9am-1pm. Another branch at 1070 Mariahilferstr. 26-30, in the Herzmansky department store. Open Mon.-Fri. 9am-6pm, Sat. 8:30am-1pm.

Fisherbräu, 1190 Billrothstr. 17. Take streetcar #38 from "Schoentor/Universität" to "Hardtgasse," and walk back about 50m. A hangout for youngish locals who revel in home-brewed beer, fantastic Austrian food, and the shaded patio. Jazz brunch on Sundays. Entrees 35-110AS. Open Mon.-Sat. 4pm-1am, Sun. 11am-1am.

Cafés and Konditoreien

The café is a centerpiece of Vienna's unhurried charm. Choose a piece of cake at the counter before sitting down; often you'll pay for it immediately and give your receipt to the server when you order beverages. The server then returns with your pastry. Coffee can be ordered *schwarzer* (black), *brauner* (a little milk), *melange* (light), and *mazagron* (iced with rum).

Demel, 1010 Kohlmarkt 14. Walk 5min. from Stephansdom or Imperial Palace. Deservedly the most famous bakery in Austria. Heavenly cakes (35-45AS) arranged like jewels in glass cases in *fin-de-siècle* elegance. Open daily 10am-6pm.

Sperl, 1060 Gumpendorferstr. 11, 15min. from Westbahnhof. The Vienna art nouveau circle gathered here long before the tourists. Coffee 20-33AS, cake 28AS. Open Mon.-Sat. 7am-11pm, Sun. 3-11pm; Sept.-June closed Sun.

Café Central, 1010, corner of Herrengasse and Strauchgasse, inside Palais Ferstel. Steeped in history, this opulent café was once the favorite hangout of satirist Karl Kraus; both Lenin and Trotsky also used to stop by. Open Mon.-Sat. 9am-8pm.

Hotel Sacher, 1010 Philharmonikerstr. 4, around the corner from the main tourist information office. This historic sight has been serving its world-famous *Sacher Torte* (a delicious chocolate-raspberry cake, 45AS) in red velvet elegance for years. Jeans and shorts are frowned upon, dear. Open daily 6:30am-midnight.

SIGHTS

Vienna from A to Z (30AS from the tourist office, more in bookstores) gives all you need for a self-created tour. The free *Museums Vienna* brochure from the tourist office lists all opening hours and admission prices. Individual museum tickets usually cost 15AS; 150AS will buy you a book of 14.

Ecclesiastic and Imperial Vienna Start your odyssey at the Gothic **Stephansdom** (U-1 or U-3: "Stephansplatz"). The smoothly tapering stone lace spire of this magnificent cathedral has become Vienna's emblem, appearing on every second postcard. (Tours in English Mon.-Sat. 10:30am and 3pm, Sun. and holidays 3pm; June-Sept. also Sat. 7pm; July-Aug. also Fri. 7pm.) View Vienna from the **Nordturm** (North Tower; open daily 9am-5:30pm; elevator ride 30AS). Next to the elevator, descend to the catacombs, the final resting place of the Habsburgs.

The enormous complex rising from the southeast of the *Michaelerplatz* is the humongous home of the Habsburg emperors until 1918, is currently the Austrian president's office. Wander through the *Schweizerhof* (Swiss Courtyard), the *Schatzkammer* (treasuries), the *Burgkapelle* (chapel, where the Vienna Boys' Choir sings mass on Sun. and religious holidays), the *Schauräume* (state rooms), the *Neue Burg* (New Palace), built from 1881-1913, and the *Kaiser Appartment.* (Open Tues.-Fri. and Sun. 9am-1pm. 30AS, students 5AS.) Between Josefsplatz and Michaelerplatz sit the Palace Stables *(Stallburg),* home to the Royal Lipizzaner stallions of the **Spanische Reitschule** (Spanish Riding School). Performances (April-June and Sept. Sun. at 10:45am and Wed. at 7pm; March and Nov. to mid-Dec. Sun. at 10:45am) are always sold out; you must reserve tickets six months in advance. Write to Spanische Reitschule, Hofburg, A-1010 Wien (tel. 533 90 32). Write only for reservations; don't send money. (Tickets 200-600AS, standing-room 150AS.) Watching the horses train is much cheaper. (March-June and Nov. to mid-Dec. Tues.-Sat. 10am-noon; Feb. Mon.-Sat. 10am-noon, except when the horses tour. Tickets sold at door at Josefsplatz, Gate 2, from about 8:30am. 50AS, children 15AS. No reservations.)

Fin-de-Siècle, Cosmopolitan Vienna, Outside the Ring Follow Burgring west through the **Volksgarten's** hundreds of varieties of roses to reach the neoclassical, sculpture-adorned **Parliament** building. Just up Dr.-Karl-Renner-Ring is the **Rathaus,** an intriguing remnant of late 19th-century neo-Gothic with Victorian mansard roofs and red geraniums in the windows. The **Burgtheater** opposite contains frescoes by Klimt. Immediately to the north on Dr.-Karl-Lueger-Ring is the **Universität.** The surrounding sidestreets gush cafés, bookstores, and bars.

Kärntner Straße connects Stephansdom to the **Staatsoper** (State Opera House). During the summer, street music fills the air with everything from Bolivian mountain music to Bob Dylan to Schubert. If you miss the shows (standing-room tickets 15-20AS) at the Opera House, tour the glittering gold, crystal, and red velvet interior (featured in the movie *Amadeus* and once home to Mahler's skilled conducting). (Tours daily 11am-3pm on the hour; Sept.-June on request.) Alfred Hrdlicka's poignant 1988 sculpture **Mahnmal Gegen Krieg und Faschismus** (Memorial Against War and Fascism), behind the opera in the Albertinapl., memorializes the suffering of Austria's people—especially its Jews—during World War II.

Next door to the Künstlerhaus on Karlspl. is the acoustically miraculous **Musikverein**, home of the Vienna Philharmonic Orchestra; the blue-and-gold interior is reminiscent of a beautifully wrapped chocolate box. Music lovers might also trek out to the **Zentralfriedhof** (Central Cemetery), XI, Simmeringer Hauptstr. 234, where Beethoven, Wolf, the Strausses, and Schönberg are buried. Take tram #71. (Open May-July daily 7am-7pm; Sept.-Oct. and March-April 7am-6pm; Nov.-Feb. 8am-5pm.) One of the more unforgettable buildings in Vienna is the **Hundertwasser Haus,** at the corner of Löwenstr. and Kegelgasse in the third district, a municipal housing project named for the artist who designed it in 1983. The structure is a wild fantasia of pastel colors, ceramic mosaics, and tilted tile columns.

Another must-see is the **Schloß Schönbrunn** and its surrounding gardens, which encompass 1.6 sq. km of glorious space. This former summer residence of the Habsburgs holds the **Wagenburg** (coach collection), where the coronation carriage and the imperial hearse are on display. A tour through the palace interior brings you to the **Bergl** rooms, where frescoes of peacocks perched on rose bushes create the impression of a refined royal jungle. (Tours 8:30am-5:30pm; April-June and Oct. 8:30am-5pm; Nov.-March 9am-4pm. 50AS, students 20AS.)

Museums On the other side of Burgring from the *Hofburg* is the world-famous **Kunsthistorisches Museum,** home to one of the world's best art collections, including entire rooms of prime Brueghels, Vermeer's *Allegory of Painting,* and numerous works by Rembrandt, Rubens, Titian, Dürer, and Velázquez. Cellini's famous golden salt cellar is here, along with a superb collection of ancient art and a transplanted Egyptian burial chamber. Gustav Klimt decorated the lobby. (Open Tues.-Fri. 10am-6pm, Sat.-Sun. 9am-6pm; Nov.-March Tues.-Fri. 10am-4pm, Sat.-Sun. 9am-4pm. 95AS, students and seniors 45AS.) Fans of Klimt and his fellow radicals, Egon Schiele and the always colorful Oskar Kokoschka, should visit the **Austrian Gallery,** in the **Belvedere Palace,** entrance at Prinz-Eugen-Str. 27. Also check out the *Biedermeier* paintings and the breathtaking view of the city from the upper floors. (Open Tues.-Sun. 10am-5pm. 60AS, students 30AS.)

If your appetite for art is still only whetted, take tram D to the **Museum Moderner Kunst** (Museum of Modern Art) in Liechtenstein Palace at IX Fürstengasse 1, which displays Klimt's *Portrait of Adele Block-Bauer,* Schiele's *Portrait of Eduard Kosmack,* a Picasso Harlequin, and various Magrittes, Légers, and Ernsts. (Open Wed.-Mon. 10am-6pm. 28AS.) The **Albertina,** I, Augustinerstr. 1, is one of the world's finest collections of graphic art, with 200,000 original etchings and prints and 20,000 drawings and watercolors, including works by Dürer, Michelangelo, Rembrandt, and Rubens—though only facsimiles of the real treasures are displayed. (Open Mon.-Tues. and Thurs. 10am-4pm, Wed. 10am-6pm, Fri. 10am-2pm, Sat.-Sun. 10am-1pm; July-Aug. Mon.-Sat. only. 30AS.) Vienna's Old Masters repose in the **Akademie der Bildenden Künste** (Academy of Fine Arts), I, Schillerplatz 3, which contains Hieronymus Bosch's spooky *Last Judgment* and works by a score of Dutch painters. (Open Tues. and Thurs.-Fri. 10am-2pm, Wed. 10am-1pm and 3-6pm, Sat.-Sun. 9am-1pm. 30AS, students 15AS.)

The greatest monument of *fin-de-siècle* Vienna is the **Secession Building,** I, Friedrichstr. 12, built by Wagner's pupil Josef Maria Olbrich to accommodate the artists, led by Gustav Klimt, who scorned historical style and broke with the uptight Viennese art establishment. Olbrich designed this extraordinary ivory-and-gold edifice as a reaction against the overblown neoclassicism of the Ring museums. Exhibits by contemporary artists adorn the walls, as does Klimt's 30m *Beethoven Frieze.* Note the inscription above the door: *Der Zeit, ihre Kunst, der Kunst, ihre Freiheit* (to the age, its art; to art, its freedom). (Open Tues.-Fri. 10am-6pm, Sat.-Sun. 10am-4pm. 20AS, 10AS for Frieze only.) The **Künstlerhaus,** from which the Secession seceded, is to the east at Karlsplatz 5. This is the conservative museum in Vienna, and you can tell by the statues of Old Masters on either side of the entrance. Every year the primary exhibit changes; in 1993 it was Aztec and Mayan art.

For more of the art nouveau movement, visit the **Österreichisches Museum für Angewandte Kunst** (Museum of Applied Art), I, Stubenring 5, the oldest museum of applied arts in Europe. Otto Wagner furniture and Klimt sketches pose amid crystal, china, furniture, and rugs from the Middle Ages to the present. (Open Wed.-Mon. 11am-6pm. Last entry 5:30pm. 30AS, students 15AS.) Unmissable creations are Otto Wagner's **Pavilion** at Karlsplatz, the major U-Bahn station, his **Kirche am Steinhof**, 1140 Baumgartner Höhe 1 (take bus #48a to the end of the line), and his **Postsparkassenamt** (Post Office Savings Bank), on the Postgasse.

The meager **Sigmund Freud Haus Museum**, XIX Berggasse 19, is where Freud lived from 1891 to 1938. (Open daily 9am-3pm. 60AS, students 40AS.)

ENTERTAINMENT

Music and Theater

You can enjoy Viennese opera in the imperial splendor of the **Staatsoper** (State Opera House) for a mere 15-35AS. Get in line on the west side about 3:30-4pm for standing room (*Stehplätze*, sold only on day of performance). Get tickets for the center; you see nothing standing at the side. Bring a scarf to tie on the rail to save your place during the show. Costlier advance tickets (100-850AS) are on sale at the **Bundestheaterkassen**, I, Goethegasse (tel. 514 44 22 18; open Mon.-Fri. 8am-6pm, Sat. 9am-2pm, Sun. 9am-noon). They also sell tickets for Vienna's other public theaters: the **Volksoper, Burgtheater,** and **Akademietheater.** Discount tickets for these go at the door an hour before performances. (50-400AS, under 27 50AS.) The **Wiener Philharmoniker** (Vienna Philharmonic Orchestra) is world-renowned, performing in the **Musikverein**, I, Dumbastr. 3, on the northeast side of Karlsplatz.

Vienna, the most musical of cities, wanes somewhat in summer; the **Staatsoper** and the **Wiener Sängerknaben** (Vienna Boys' Choir) vacation during July and August. During the rest of the year, the *Sängerknaben* sing 9:15am mass each Sunday at the **Burgkapelle** (Royal Chapel) of the Hofburg. Reserve tickets at least 2 months in advance from **Verwaltung der Hofmusikkapelle,** Hofburg, Schweizerhof, A-1010 Wien. Do not enclose money. Unreserved seats are sold starting at 5pm on the preceding Friday. Standing room is free. Sunday High Masses in the major churches (Augustinerkirche, Michaelerkirche, Stephansdom) are accompanied by choral or organ music that approaches the celestial.

The **Theater an der Wien,** VI, Linke Wienzeile 6, opens with musicals in July (performances 7:30pm; 100-990AS), and the **Wiener Kammeroper** (Chamber Opera) performs during the summer in *Schönbrunner Schloßpark* (tickets 50-350AS). The **Arkadenhof,** the courtyard inside the **Rathaus,** holds orchestral concerts. (July-Aug. Tues.-Thurs. 8pm. 120AS.) During the summer, free tidbits of music by all the famous Viennese composers are performed in front of the Rathaus (Tues. and Fri. at 5pm). Also try *Jugend-Info Wien,* or pick up a brochure on *Wiener Musiksommer* from the tourist office for concert and discount ticket info.

English theater is offered at **Vienna's English Theatre,** VIII, Josefsgasse 12 (tel. 42 12 60 or 42 82 84; box office open Mon.-Sat. 10am-6pm, evening box office opens at 7pm; tickets 150-420AS, students 100AS on night of performance). Something of a tradition in Vienna, this theater still has enough artistic vision to host world premieres; Edward Albee debuted his most recent play, *Three Tall Women,* here. If you yearn to hear still more English, head to the **International Theater,** IX Porzellangasse 8 (tel. 31 62 72; tickets 220AS, students under 26 120AS).

Heurigen and Nightlife

Vienna is almost as famous for its *Heurigen* (outside seating at picnic tables, with mugs of wine hung over the door) as for its art and music. Unique to Vienna, *Heuri-*

gen began when Emperor Joseph II, in a fit of largesse, allowed the local wine-growers to sell and serve their wine in their homes at certain times of the year. The mood is festive and informal; in most places, you can carry out food served inside or bring a picnic. Only wine produced on the property is served. After the feast of Martinas on November 11, the wine remaining from last year's crop becomes "old"—no longer authentic *Heurigen*—so the Viennese mount a huge effort to spare the wine this fate by consuming it. Since the wine can be sickly sweet, learn the word for "dry," *trocken*.

Heurigen freckle the northern, western, and southern suburbs, where grapes are grown. **Grinzing** is the largest *Heurigen* area, but the atmosphere and the wine are more authentic in **Nußdorf** (tram D from the Ring), in **Sievering,** and in **Salmanns-dorf.** At XIX, Pfarrplatz 3, is **Ing. Mayer Franz Mayer am Pfarrplatz Beethoven-haus.** Take tram #37 to the last stop, walk down Wollergasse and through the park, take a right, then your first left on Pfarrplatz. Near the home of Beethoven, this *Heuriger* is one of the most festive in Vienna. Ask the tourist office for its list of *Heurigen*. Most are open daily from 4pm to midnight; wine costs about 30AS per mug.

There are some wonderful *Weinkeller* (wine cellars) downtown as well. **Zwölf Apostelkeller,** I, Sonnenfelsgasse 3, like Hell, has many levels—the lowest is the liveliest. This is one of the best Viennese cellars, with much atmosphere and lots of locals. (Open Aug.-June daily 4:30pm-midnight.) **Esterházykeller,** I, Haarhof, off Naglergasse, is perhaps the least expensive *Weinkeller* in Vienna; try the *Grüner Veltliner* wine. (24AS. Open Mon.-Fri. 10am-1pm and 4-9pm, Sat.-Sun. 4-9pm.)

Vienna's nightlife is elusive but—make no mistake—electric. The city parties 'til dawn, though public transportation goes to sleep at midnight. The 8th district is renowned for student-oriented establishments such as **The Tunnel,** featuring live music in a Euro-chic atmosphere. (Cover 30-90AS, Mon. free. Open daily 9am-2am; music from 8:30pm.) **Fischerbräu,** XIX, Billrothstr. 17, serves up homemade brew in a hardwood interior and leafy garden. (Open Mon.-Sat. 4pm-1am, Sun. 11am-1pm.) Nightlife centers around the **Bermuda Dreieck,** just north of Stephansdom. For techno, a major rager is **P1,** I, Rotgasse 3, 2 blocks north of Stephansdom. (Open Mon.-Thurs. 9pm-4am, Fri.-Sat. 9pm-5am). Try **Jazzland,** I, Franz-Josefs-Kai 29 (cover 50-100AS; open Tues.-Sat. 7pm-2am), for Austrian-style jazz music, or **Opus One,** I, Mahlerstr. 11 (cover 50-100AS; open daily 9:30pm-4am). **Clubhouse Wiener Freizeit,** V, Franzengasse 2, is a hangout for gays and lesbians, with disco on Friday and Saturday nights. (Open Tues.-Thurs. 8pm-4am, Fri.-Sat. 8pm-5am.)

THE DANUBE (DONAU)

The "Blue Danube" is largely the invention of Johann Strauss's imagination, but the mighty, muddy-green river still merits a cruise. The **Erste Donau Dampfschiffahrts-Gesellschaft (DDSG)** runs ships daily from May to late October. They operate offices in Vienna (Handelskai 265, by the *Reichsbrücke;* tel. (0222) 21 75 00), Linz (*Nibelungenbrücke;* tel. (0732) 27 10 90), and Passau (Im Ort 14a, *Dreiflußeck;* tel. (0851) 330 35). Cruises run from Vienna to Grein (passing Melk and Krems en route) and between Linz and Passau, Germany. East of Vienna, hydrofoils run to Bratislava, Slovakia, and Budapest, Hungary. Eurailpasses are valid, while the Rabbit Card merits a 30% discount. Everyone pays full fare for the eastbound hydrofoils.

Between Krems and Melk along the Vienna-Grein route, ruined castles bear crumbling testimony to Austria's glorious past. **Ferries** run from Vienna to Krems (294AS, round-trip 442AS) and from Krems to Melk (20AS, round-trip 330AS). You can also sail from Vienna to Melk (490AS, round-trip 736AS). See the DDSG and tourist offices for prices on other special ship/bus and ship/train ticket combinations.

Cyclists should take advantage of the Lower Danube Cycle Track, a riverside bike trail between Vienna and Naarn linking several Danube villages, including Melk. Ask at an area tourist office for a map and rental information.

Krems an der Donau and Melk

Like a fashion model with a speech impediment, Krems is beautiful and virtually silent. Climb the covered stairway to the 15th-century **Piaristenkirche,** a Gothic structure with baroque altars. The **Jugendherberge (HI)** at Ringstr. 77 (tel. (02732) 834 52) accommodates 52 in 4- to 6-bed rooms. (Reception open 5-10pm. Lockout 9am-5pm. Members only. 170AS.) **Donau Camping,** Wiedengasse 7 (tel. (02732) 844 55) is by the marina. (Reception open July-Aug. 7:30-10:30am and 4-8pm; April-June and Sept. to mid-Oct. 8-10am and 4:30-5:30pm. 35AS/person plus 10.50AS tax, children 25AS; 20-40AS/tent, 35AS/car. Warm showers included.) The **tourist office,** Undstr. 6 (tel. (02732) 82 76), shares oodles of info on accommodations, sports, and entertainment. (Open Mon.-Fri. 8am-6pm, Sat.-Sun. 10am-noon and 1-6pm; mid-Nov. to March Mon.-Fri. 8am-5pm.) **Trains** connect Krems to the outside world; the station sits off Ringstr.

Sprawled along the south bank of the Danube upstream from Krems, **Melk** is dwarfed by the recently restored **Benediktinerstift** (Benedictine monastery). (Open daily 9am-5pm; Nov.-April daily 9am-4pm. 45AS, students 20AS. Tour 10AS extra.) A 5km bus ride or walk out of town is the **Schallaburg,** one of the most magnificent Renaissance castles in central Europe. Take Kirschengraben (off Lindestr., itself off Bahnhofstr.) out of town and turn right under the *Autobahn.* (Open May-Sept. Mon.-Fri. 9am-5pm, Sat.-Sun. 9am-6pm. 50AS, students 15AS. Buses leave from Melk's *Bahnhof* daily at 10:30am and 3:10pm; each departs from castle 15min. later. One way 30AS, students ½-price.) Melk's **Jugendherberge (HI),** Abt-Karl-Str. 42 (tel. (02752) 26 81), under renovations in 1994, is slated to have 104 beds, all in quads with showers and toilets. Walk down Bahnhofstr. and turn right on Abt-Karl-Str. (Reception open 5-10pm. Lockout 10am-5pm. 134AS, 117AS after 2 nights; under 19 114AS, 97AS. 10.50AS tax/night.) **Camping Melk** (tel. (02752) 32 91) overlooks the Danube near the ferry landing. (Reception open 8am-midnight. 35AS/person, children 20AS; 35AS/tent, 25AS/car. 10.50AS tax. Showers 15AS.) The genial **tourist office,** Rathauspl. 11 (tel. (02752) 23 07 32 or 23 07 33), next to the *Rathausplatz* is equipped with plenty of pamphlets. (Open April-June Mon.-Fri. 9am-noon and 3-6pm, Sat.-Sun. 10am-2pm; July-Sept. daily 9am-7pm.) The **train station** (tel. (02752) 23 21) is on Bahnhofstr., a 10-minute walk from the tourist office.

Linz and Mauthausen

Linz proffers museums and galleries, a major music festival, and all the bookstores, cafés, and nightclubs of a university town. Both the main **train station** and **bus station** are on Bahnhofstr. The main **tourist office** (tel. (0732) 23 93 17 77) awaits at Hauptplatz 54. (Open Mon.-Fri. 8am-7pm, Sat.-Sun. and holidays 8-11:30am and 12:30-7pm; Oct.-April Mon.-Fri. 8am-6pm, Sat.-Sun. 8-11:30am and 1:30-6pm.) Linz has 3 **HI youth hostels.** The **Linz Jugendherberge,** Kapuzinerstr. 14 (tel. (0732) 78 27 20), offers the cheapest beds and the best location. (Reception open 8-10am and 5-7pm. No curfew; get a key from reception desk. 110AS, under 10 90AS, nonmembers 30AS surcharge for 1st night.) **Landesjugendherberge Lentia,** Blütenstr. 23 (tel. (0732) 23 70 78), is a skyscraperesque structure across the river from the Hauptplatz. (Reception open 8am-10pm. Curfew 10pm. 110AS, under 19 85AS. Wheelchair access.) The **Jugendgästehaus,** Stanglhofweg 3 (tel. (0732) 66 44 34), presents a soulless exterior but a liveable interior. (Reception open 7:30am-4pm and 6-11pm. Singles 280AS. Doubles 360AS. Quads 520AS. Call ahead.)

Austrians take no pride in the main tourist attraction of **Mauthausen,** about a half-hour down the river from Linz—a forced-labor camp where thousands perished under the Nazis. The museum does its best to underplay Austria's enthusiasm for Hitler in the late 1930s. From Linz, take a train (round-trip 100AS) or a bus (60AS) to Mauthausen. The camp is a 5km walk away. Follow signs to "KZ Mauthausen" and remember Santayana's admonition to those who would forget the past. (Open Feb.-mid-Dec. daily 8am-4pm. Callous admission 15AS, students 5AS.)

■■■ SALZBURG

Protected by forested mountains, Salzburg is a city of castles, horse-drawn carriages and church towers, whose voice is the sublime music of favorite son Wolfgang Amadeus Mozart. Salzburg's adulation of the composer crescendoes during its annual summer music festival, the **Salzburger Festspiele.** For those wishing to pay homage to moviedom's sweetly trilling Von Trapp family singers, Salzburg is the place to be; *The Sound of Music* was largely filmed here, as the tour guides won't let you forget.

ORIENTATION AND PRACTICAL INFORMATION

Salzburg straddles the **Salzach River** a few km from the German border. The expansive *Altstadt* (old town) clusters around **Residenzplatz** on the west bank of the river. The train station is in the (relatively) new town, which centers around **Mirabellplatz** and **Marktplatz,** east of the river. Both towns are a 15- to 20-minute walk down **Rainerstraße** from the train station. You can also get to either by taking bus #5, 6, or 55 from the bus stop across the street from the station.

Tourist Office: Mozartplatz 5 (tel. 84 75 68 or 88 9 87 332; fax 88 9 87 342), in the *Altstadt.* Open daily 8am-10pm; Sept.-Oct. and April-June daily 9am-7pm; Nov.-March Mon.-Sat. 9am-6pm. Hours may vary in spring and autumn. Free hotel map is almost the same as the 5AS city map. Other branches at train station, #10 (open Mon.-Sat. 8:45am-8:30pm) and at the airport (open daily 9am-9pm).
Budget Travel: Ökista, Wolf-Dietrich-Str. 31, A-5020 Salzburg (tel. 88 32 52; fax 88 18 19), near the International Youth Hotel. Open Mon.-Fri. 9:30am-5:30pm. **Young Austria,** Alpenstr. 108a (tel. 25 75 80 0; fax 257 58 21). Open Mon.-Fri. 9am-6pm, Sat. 9am-noon.
Consulates: U.S., Giselakai 51 (tel. 286 01), in the 2nd building past the Nonntaler Brücke, take bus #6 or 49. Open Mon.-Fri. 9-11am and 2-4pm. **U.K.,** Alter Markt 4 (tel. 84 81 33). Open Mon.-Fri. 9am-noon.
Currency Exchange: Banking hours are Mon.-Fri. 8am-noon and 2-4:30pm. Currency exchange at train station open daily 7am-10pm. The post office and AmEx office offer the best rates.
American Express: Mozartplatz 5-7 (tel. 84 25 01; fax 84 25 01 9). All banking services. Open Mon.-Fri. 9am-5:30pm, Sat. 9am-noon.
Post Office: Residenzplatz 9 (tel. 84 41 21 16). Open Mon.-Fri. 7am-7pm, Sat. 8-10am. **Poste Restante** at a branch office in the train station. Address to "Postlagernde Briefe, Bahnhofspostamt, A-5020 Salzburg." Pickup Mon.-Fri. 7am-6:30pm. **Postal code:** A-5010.
Telephones: At the train station post office, open 24hrs. **City Code:** 0662.
Airport: Flughafen Salzburg (tel. 85 29 00; fax 85 29 00 44). Bus #77 (20AS; direction "Bahnhof") runs to the train station every 15min.
Trains: Hauptbahnhof (tel. 888 87), on Südtiroler Platz in the new city. For train info call 17 17. Trains run hourly to Vienna (380AS), hourly to Munich (256AS), 3 times/day to Budapest (648AS).
Buses: Main depot across from the train station on Südtiroler Platz (tel. 87 21 45). Ticket window open Mon.-Fri. 7-9:25am, 9:45am-2:30pm, and 2:50-6:20pm, Sat. 7-9:25am and 9:45am-2:20pm.
Local Public Transportation: Information at Griesgasse 21 (tel. 205 51, ext. 553). Extensive 18-bus network. 20AS/ride if you pay the driver, 13AS if you purchase at a *Tabak/Trafik* stand, 16AS if you buy from an automatic vending machine, 65AS/book of 5 rides. A 24-hr. pass costs 27AS. Ages 6-15 half-price, under 6 free.
Bike Rental: At the train station, platform #3 (tel. 88 87 54 27).
Hitchhiking: Those hitchers headed to Innsbruck, Munich, or Italy (except Venice) first take bus #77 to the German border. Thumbers bound for Vienna or Venice take bus #2 (direction: "Maxglan") to "Mirabellplatz" and then switch to #29

(direction: "Forellenwegsiedlung") until the *Autobahn* entrance at "Schmiedlinger Str." They also take bus #15 (direction: "Bergheim") to the *Autobahn* entrance at "Grüner Wald." The **Mitfahrzentrale** at W. Philharmonikergasse 2 (tel. 84 13 27) in the Studentenhaus Katholische Hochschulgemeinde, matches riders and drivers. Demand for rides outstrips the supply. Open Mon.-Thurs. 9am-noon and 2-5pm, Fri. 9am-noon.

Luggage Storage: At the train station. Large lockers, 20AS/48hr. Small lockers 10AS. Open 24hrs.

Bookstore: Bücher Schneid, Rainerstr. 24 (tel. 87 17 05). Sells *Let's Go* and other English-language books. Open Mon.-Fri. 8:30am-6pm, Sat. 8am-noon.

Laundromat: Wäscherei Constructa, Kaiserschutzenstr. 10 (tel. 87 62 53), opposite the station. 92AS/load for wash and dry. Open Mon.-Fri. 7:30am-6:30pm, Sat. 8am-noon.

Pharmacies: Elisabeth-Apotheke, Elisabethstr. 1 (tel. 714 84), a few blocks left of the train station. Pharmacies open Mon.-Fri. 8am-12:30pm and 2:30-6pm, Sat. 8am-noon. Check the door of any closed pharmacy to find an open one.

Medical Assistance: Hospital, Müllner-Hauptstr. 48 (tel. 315 81).

Emergencies: Ambulance: tel. 144. **Fire:** tel. 122. **Police:** tel. 133. Headquarters at Alpenstr. 90 (tel. 295 11).

ACCOMMODATIONS AND CAMPING

Ask for the tourist office's list of private rooms (*not* the hotel map). During the summer festival (late July-Aug.), hostels fill by mid-afternoon; call ahead. The tourist office charges 30AS to reserve accommodations, plus a 50AS deposit.

Gasthaus Naturfreundehaus, Mönchsberg 19c (tel. 84 17 29). Take bus #1 or 2 (direction: "Maxglan") to "Mönchsbergaufzug," then take elevator built into the cliff (round-trip 21AS). At its summit, turn right and go down paved path through stone arch of the old fortress, and take the small dirt path to the immediate left. Magnificent vista of the *Altstadt* from the terrace café. Accommodates 28 in quads and 6-bed rooms. Reception open daily 7:30am-10pm. 110AS/person. Showers 10AS/3min. Breakfast 45AS. Sheets 5AS. Open May to mid-Oct.

International Youth Hotel, Paracelcustr. 9 (tel. 87 96 49), off Franz-Josef-Str. From town, take bus #15 (direction: "Bergheim") to "Paracelsusstr." Full of drinking Americans. Reception open daily 8am-10pm. No curfew; theoretical quiet time 10pm. Dorms 120AS. Doubles 160AS/person. Quads 140AS/person. Showers 10AS/6min. Breakfast 15-40AS. Dinner entrees 60-75AS. Lockers 10AS. Stylish sheetsacks 20AS.

Institut St. Sebastian, Linzer Gasse 41 (tel. 87 13 86 or 88 26 06). From the station, turn left onto Rainerstr., take a left onto Bergstr., and then a left at the end onto Linzer Gasse. Primarily a residence for female university students, this dormitory opens its doors to travelers of both genders. Reception open Mon.-Fri. 8am-noon and 3-10pm, Sat.-Sun. 8-10am and 6-10pm. No lockout. No curfew. Dorms 120AS. Doubles 180AS/person. Triples 160AS/person. Showers and lockers included. Breakfast 30AS. Sheets 25AS. Reservations recommended.

Jugendgästehaus Salzburg (HI), Josef-Preis-Allee 18 (tel. 842 67 00 or 84 68 57; fax 89 14 87). Take bus #5 (direction: "Birkensiedlung") to "Justizgebäude." Sunny, spacious rooms. Often overrun with school groups. Sporadic reception hours. Lockout 9-11am. Curfew midnight. Dorms 130AS/person. Double with shower 225AS/person. Quads 177AS/person. Shower, breakfast, and sheets included. Lunches, bag lunches, and dinners 63AS. Kitchen, laundry facilities, and lockers available. Bike rental 70AS/day. *Sound of Music* tour 210AS. No reservations accepted; come before 11am to get a place. Wheelchair accessible.

Glockengasse (HI), Glockengasse 8 (tel. 87 62 41, fax 876 24 13). Gabelsbergerstr., turn right on Bayerhamerstr. to the foot of the Kapuzinerberg (mountain). A labyrinth of dormitories with few showers. Reception open 3:30pm-midnight. Curfew midnight. First night 115AS, 105AS thereafter. Showers, breakfast, and sheets included. Lockers 50AS. Open April-Sept.

Haunspergstraße (HI), Haunspergstr. 27 (tel. 87 50 30, fax 88 34 77). From Kaiserschützenstr., which becomes Jahnstr., turn left onto Haunspergstr. Reception open 7am-2pm and 5pm-midnight, but it fills by late afternoon. Curfew 11pm. 135AS/person in doubles, triples, and quads. Sheets and breakfast included. Wash 25AS, dry 25AS. HI advance booking voucher for reservations. Open July-Aug.

Eduard-Heinrich-Haus (HI), Eduard-Heinrich-Str. 2 (tel. 25 9 76; fax 27 9 80). Clean, modern facilities, but a bit out of the way. Take bus #51 (direction: "Alpensiedlung Süd") to "Polizeidirektion." Walk down Billrothstr., turn left on Robert Stolz Promenade. Reception open daily 7-9am and 5-11pm. Dorms 110AS. Showers and lockers included. Breakfast 25AS.

Haus Kernstock, Karolingerstr. 29 (tel. 82 74 69). Take bus #77. Friendly hostess, commodious rooms, and an ample breakfast. 220-250AS/person for doubles, triples, and quads, including breakfast and shower.

Haus Rosemarie Seigmann, Kasern Berg 48 (tel. 500 01). Welcoming, English-speaking hostess. Stone terrace overlooking the Alps. Doubles 320-340AS. Triples 480AS. Breakfast and showers included. If it's full, she'll call around for you.

Haus Moser, Kasern Berg 59 (tel. 45 66 76), above Haus Rosemarie Seigmann. Dark-timbered home with spacious rooms. Singles 160AS. Doubles 330-350AS. Triples 480AS. Fortifying breakfast and shower included.

Germana Kapeller, Kasern Berg 44 (tel. 45 66 71). *Dirndl*-clad hostess oversees enchantingly traditional rooms and screens *The Sound of Music* daily. Doubles 320AS. Triples 450AS. Quads 600AS. Showers and complete breakfast included.

Pension Haus Christl, Kasern-Berg 57 (tel. 51 1 87). Great rooms with gorgeous Alpine views. Doubles 320-440AS. Triples 480-680AS. Quads 640-880AS. Breakfast 30AS. Laundry 85AS.

Haus Elisabeth, Rauchenbichlerstr. 18 (tel. 507 03). Take bus #51 to the end station, walk up Rauchenbichlerstr. over the footbridge, and continue right along the gravel path. Amazing rooms with great views of the city. Singles with shower 300AS. Doubles 260AS/person. Breakfast included.

Camping Stadtblick, Rauchenbichlerstr. 21 (tel. 50 6 52), next to Haus Elisabeth. Sweeping view of the city. Reception open daily 7:30am-10pm. 60AS/person, 15AS/tent, 15AS/car; Sept.-June 50AS/person, 15AS/tent, 15AS/car. Showers included.

FOOD

Blessed with fantastic **beer gardens** and innumerable **Konditoreien** (pastry shops), Salzburg begs its guests to eat outdoors. *Knoblauchsuppe,* a Salzburger specialty—rich cream soup loaded with croutons and pungent garlic—shouldn't daunt the confident (or the asocial). **Hofer,** at Schallmooser Hauptstr. and Franz-Josef-Str., is a discount supermarket. (Open Mon.-Fri. 8am-6pm, Sat. 7:30am-noon.) **KGM,** Karl-Wurmb-Str. 3, across from the train station, is also well-stocked (open Mon.-Fri. 8am-6pm, Sat. 8am-12:30pm). Open-air markets bloom (Mon.-Fri. 6am-7pm, Sat. 6am-1pm) in the *Altstadt's* squares.

Michael Haydn Stube, Mirabellplatz 1, in the Aicher Passage by Mirabell Gardens. A student hangout run by the Mozarteum, Salzburg's College of Music and Fine Arts. Best deal in town. Vegetarian, fish, *Schnitzel,* and *Wurst* dishes 37-73AS. Open Mon.-Fri. 9:30am-8pm. Hot food served 11am-7:30pm.

Restaurant Zur Bürgerwehr-Einkehr, Mönchsberg 19c (tel. 84 17 29), below the Gasthaus Naturfreundehaus. Splendid setting atop the Mönchsberg in the *Altstadt. Wurst* and other sandwiches 30-40AS. Open Thurs.-Tues. 10:30am-10pm, mid-Sept. to May Thurs.-Tues. 10:30am-8pm. Meals served until 8:30pm.

Restaurant Paracelsus Stub'n, Kaigasse 8 (tel. 84 32 77), in the *Altstadt.* Quiet café/bar/restaurant wedged in a less-touristed street of the old city. Hearty *Gulaschsuppe* 38AS, *Wienerschnitzel mit Kartoffeln* 98AS. Open daily 11am-2am.

Priesterhausstube, Priesterhausgasse 12 (tel. 87 83 17). Inexpensive local fare right off Linzergasse. Entrees 70-100AS. Open Tues.-Sun. 5-11:30pm.

SIGHTS

Salzburg sprang up under the protective watch of the hilltop fortress **Hohen-salzburg,** built atop the imposing Mönchsberg between the 11th and 17th centuries by the ruling Archbishops. The first-rate tours wind through medieval torture chambers and the castle's impressive staterooms and pregnate its impregnable watchtower. (Fortress open daily 8am-7pm; Oct.-May 8am-6pm. 45-min. tours daily 9am-5:30pm; April-June and Sept.-Oct. 9:30am-5pm; Nov.-March 10am-4:30pm. 20AS, under 19 10AS; with tour 25AS, ages 16-19 15AS, ages 6-15 10AS, seniors 20AS.) The **Rainer Museum,** inside the fortress, displays more medieval weapons and instruments of torture. (Open May-Oct. Free with tour. Otherwise 10AS, students and children 5AS.) The cable car from Festungsgasse runs every 10 minutes (18AS, round-trip 28AS).

Wolfgang Amadeus Mozart was unleashed upon the world from what is now called **Mozarts Geburtshaus** (birthplace) at Getreidegasse 9. The street itself is worth a look; the guild signs and painted walls remain as they were when the composer was just a tyke. The house exhibits pictures, letters, stage sets for Mozart's operas, and the Hammerklavier on which he composed *The Magic Flute.* (Open daily 9am-7pm; Sept.-March 9am-6pm. 50AS, students and seniors 35AS, ages 15-18 15AS, ages 6-14 10AS.) Mozart's **Wohnhaus** (residence), Marktplatz 8, suffered major damage in WWII air raids, but has since been restored; it now displays period musical instruments and facsimilies of the maestro's manuscripts. (Open daily 10am-6pm; Sept.-March 9am-5pm. 40AS, students 25AS, ages 15-18 20AS, ages 6-14 10AS. To both houses 70AS, students and seniors 45AS, ages 15-18 20AS, ages 6-14 15AS.)

Turning right at the Alter Markt and venturing down to Residenzplatz, you arrive at the Archbishop Wolf Dietrich's palace, the **Residenz,** Residenzpl. 1, which features baroque staterooms and a gallery filled with works by Rembrandt, Rubens, Brueghel, and Titian. (Gallery open daily 10am-5pm. 40AS, students and seniors 30AS, under 15 free.) Mozart was christened in the adjacent baroque **Dom** in 1756 and later worked here as *Konzertmeister* and court organist. The connecting **Dom Museum** holds the **Kunst- und Wunderkammer** (art and miracles chamber), which includes conch shells, mineral formations, and a 2-ft. whale's tooth. (Open May to mid-Oct. Mon.-Sat. 10am-5pm, Sun. 11am-5pm. 30AS, ages 16-18 10AS, ages 6-15 5AS.)

From the cathedral, cross the giant chess grid on Kapitelplatz and walk toward the mountain to the entrance to the elaborate **St. Peter's Abbey.** Tucked between the church and the Mönchsberg lies **Petersfriedhof,** best known as the spot where Liesl's Nazi boyfriend Rolf blew the whistle on the von Trapp family in THAT movie. Behind the church is the entrance to the **Katakomben** (catacombs), St.-Peter-Bezirk 1, where Christians worshiped in secret as early as 250 AD. (Open daily 10am-5pm. Tours in English on the hour; Oct.-April 11am, noon, 1:30pm, 2:30pm, and 3:30pm; min. 5 people. 12AS, students and seniors 8AS.)

If you stroll from the cathedral across Domplatz, you'll find the distinctive dome of the **Kollegienkirche** (Collegiate Church), Fischer von Erlach's masterpiece, standing watch over the Universitätsplatz. The *Staatsbrücke* is the only bridge from the *Altstadt* over the Salzach open to motorized traffic; in the new city, the bridge opens into **Linzer Gasse,** an enchanting, less-touristed medieval street. Ascend the stairs from under the stone arch on the right side of Linzer Gasse 14 to the **Kapuzinerkloster** (Capuchin Monastery), built in the late 16th century. The etymology of the word *cappuccino* lies in the resemblance of coffee topped with steamed milk to the trademark brown robes and white hoods of the resident monks.

From Linzer Gasse you can cut across Dreifältigkeitstr. to the marvelous **Schloß Mirabell** and the delicately manicured **Mirabellarten.** Archbishop Wolf Dietrich built this wonder in 1606 for his mistress Salome Alt. Inspect the excesses of the **Angel Staircase.** (Open daily 8am-noon and 2-5pm.) A tourist office pamphlet lists dates of chamber music concerts in the *Schloß.*

ENTERTAINMENT

The renowned **Salzburger Festspiele** (Summer Music Festivals) run from late July
to the beginning of September. Most of the activities revolve around Hofstallgasse
and the expanse of the **Festspielhaus** (festival hall) built flush against the Mönchsberg wall. Tickets for individual concerts run 100-3600AS. Festival programs are
available in November from "Direktion der Salzburger Festspiele, Festspielhaus, Hofstallgasse 1, A-5010 Salzburg," or from an Austrian National Tourist Office. The few
tickets still available by summer are sold at the Festspielhaus box office (tel. 84 25
41; open April-June Mon.-Fri. 10am-2pm, July Mon.-Sat. 10am-5pm; during the
Festspiele daily 10am-5pm). Many travel agencies in Salzburg add a 20% service
charge to the ticket price. Standing room may be available from 50AS. At **Mario-
netten Theater,** Schwarzstr. 24 (tel. 87 24 06; fax 88 21 41), a lighthearted show is
accompanied by tapes of past festival opera performances (tickets 250-350AS).

The **Stadtkino,** Anton-Neumayr-Pl. 2 (tel. 84 03 49 13), puts on everything from
jazz and rock concerts to postmodern dance. Every summer the **Szene** (tel. 84 34
48) sponsors an international theater and dance festival that coincides with the
Festspiele. (Tickets 120-160AS. Open Mon.-Fri. 10am-5pm, Sat. 10am-noon; in winter closed Sat.)

For an evening of steinhoisting and general *Gemütlichkeit,* go to **Augustiner
Bräustüble,** Augustinergasse 4, home of Salzburg's first brewery. Grab a stein, rinse
it out in the tub, then have it filled by the enormous man who rolls out the wooden
beer barrels and taps them with a brass bung and a massive mallet. (40AS/liter.
Open Mon.-Fri. 3-11pm, Sat.-Sun. 2:30-11pm.) **Frauen Café** on Sittikusstr. 17 (tel.
87 16 39), near the train station, is a relaxed hangout where women drink coffee,
read, and converse. (Open Wed.-Sat. 8pm-midnight.)

Panorama Tours (tel. 87 40 29, 88 32 11 17; fax 87 16 18) presents "The Original
Sound of Music Tour," (300AS) departing daily at 9:30am and 2pm. For those who
interpreted the film as a tragic tale of a dysfunctional family whose domineering
father had an unhealthy fixation on nuns, the expedition is probably a loss.

■ Near Salzburg

The tremendous wealth provided by the **Salzbergwerke** (salt mines) around the
Salzkammergut long buttressed the ruling bishops' political hegemony. The closest
mines, at **Bad Dürrnberg** near Hallein, are quite an experience. On the 90-minute
tour you wear traditional miner's clothes, slide down passages in the dark, take a
miniature train ride, and sometimes a raft ride on the salt lakes. The Salzbergbahn
cable car ride to the entrance provides an outstanding view. (Open May-Sept. daily
8:50am-5:50pm; early Oct. 11am-4:50pm. 185AS, students 170AS, under 15 88AS,
includes round-trip cable car, tour, and museum.) For more info, call (06245) 52 85
15 or 73 00 15. You can reach the mines at Bad Dürrnberg by bus (from Salzburg's
train station, take bus #3083, direction "Hallein"; 32AS each way, 45min., buses
leave every 30-60min.) or rail (frequent trains daily, 20min., one way 32AS, round-
trip 49AS). The cable car will then take you from Hallein to Bad Dürrnberg; it leaves
from the "Salzbergbahn Parkplatz" on Dr.-Viktor-Zatloukal-Str. From the train station, walk straight down Bahnhofstr., turn right at the intersection, and cross the
Salzach via the Staatsbrücke. Then walk straight down to Bayrhamer Platz, bear left
on Raitenaustr., and turn left on Gampertorplatz.

■■■ SALZKAMMERGUT

East of Salzburg, the landscape swells into towering mountains pockmarked by
frigid, unfathomably deep lakes. The Salzkammergut is named for the abandoned
salt mines which, in their glory days, underwrote Salzburg's architectural treasures.

Transportation and Accommodations The Vienna-Salzburg rail line skirts the northern edge of the Salzkammergut. At Attnang-Puchheim, 50km east of Salzburg, a spur line begins its way south through Gmünden, Ebensee, Bad Ischl, Obertraun, and Bad Aussee to Steinbach. If you're traveling by bus or have your own wheels, you can enter directly from Salzburg along Highway 158. Within the region there is a dense network of **post buses;** most run 4-12 times a day. Ask at the Salzburg kiosk for a comprehensive schedule, or call for information: Salzburg tel. (0662) 167, Gmünden tel. (07612) 46 13, Mondsee tel. (06232) 26 69, St. Gilgen tel. (06227) 425, Bad Ischl tel. (06132) 31 13 and Bad Aussee tel. (06152) 20 50. The pamphlet *Wandern mit dem Postauto* (Hiking with the post bus), available at the main bus stations in these towns, details hikes that coincide with the post bus network. There is also a less complete network of **Bahnbuses;** their schedule is available at local rail stations. **Hitchers** from Salzburg reportedly take bus #29 to Gnigl and come into the Salzkammergut at Bad Ischl. The lake district itself is known as one of the rare Austrian regions in which hitchhikers make good time. Most of the train stations in the region rent **bikes.** Reasonably priced **ferries** serve each of the larger lakes. The **Wolfgangsee** line is operated by the Austrian railroad, so railpasses get you free passage; on the **Attersee** and **Traunsee** lines, Eurailpass holders receive a discount.

Hostels abound, though you can often find far superior rooms in private homes and Pensionen at just-above-hostel prices. The local tourist offices can make reservations for you, and it rarely charge a fee. **Campgrounds** dot the region, but many are trailer-oriented; away from large towns, one can camp discreetly almost anywhere without trouble. Hikers can capitalize on dozens of **cable cars** in the area to gain altitude before setting out on their own, and almost every community has a local trail map publicly posted and/or available at the tourist office. At higher elevations there are **alpine huts** leased through the **Alpenverein,** who are more knowledgeable about them than tourist offices; their central office is in Bad Ischl, at Kaltenbach 308 (tel. (06132) 482 62 or 52 50).

St. Gilgen, St. Wolfgang, and Weißenbach The erstwhile hometown of Mozart's mother and sister, **St. Gilgen** in the western Salzkammergut is squeezed between the placid waters of the **Wolfgangsee** and the **Schafberg** summit. The **HI youth hostel** in St. Gilgen, Mondseerstr. 7 (tel. (06227) 365), is positively luxurious, with dreamy, lakeside rooms and balconies. (Reception open 8-9am and 5-7pm. Lockout 9am-noon. Curfew 11pm. Singles 170-230AS. Doubles 140-180AS/person. Triples 120-160AS. Quads 120-140AS. Quints 110-130AS.) The **tourist office** tel. (06227) 348 or 72 67), in the *Rathaus,* details alternative budget accommodations. (Open 9am-noon and 2-6pm, Sat. 9am-noon, Sun. 10am-noon; Sept.-June Mon.-Fri. 9am-noon and 2-6pm.) For a heart-stopping ride, ascend the 1783m Schafberg on the cog-wheeled **Schafbergbahn.** A hike back takes 3 hours. (Open early May-early Oct. Up 110AS, down 90AS, free with railpass.) A steamer runs from St. Gilgen to the base of the railway in nearby St. Wolfgang (disembark at "Wolfgang Schafbergbahnhof"; 40AS, free with railpass); ask for the schedule at the tourist office. The lovely lakeside village of **St. Wolfgang** is itself worthy of exploration. A world-renowned masterpiece fashioned by Michael Pacher in 1481, the delicate and intricate carved wooden altar, , still sits in the dainty **parish church.**

On the other side of the Schafberg from St. Gilgen in the tiny village of **Weißenbach** on the Attersee lake, proletarians and capitalists alike are welcomed at the **Europa-Camp (HI),** owned by the Austrian Young Socialists (tel. (07663) 220). Here, the campground, psychedelic hostel, and modest disco are run with an efficiency worthy of the free market. (Reception open 8am-12:30pm and 2:30-7pm. Dorms 80AS/person. Camping 38AS/person, 30AS small tents, 45AS large tents. Call ahead.) A ferry service links the small villages around the Attersee. The lake is easily accessible from Mondsee, St. Gilgen, Bad Ischl, and Gmunden.

Bad Ischl The cultural and geographic center of the Salzkammergut, **Bad Ischl** is best known for its purportedly curative mineral baths and mud packs. Skeptical visitors can still enjoy the free outdoor concerts (mid-May to Sept. 2-3/day) and the **Ischl Operetta Festival,** which recalls the town's heyday as a rest home for stressed-out composers such as Brahms, Bruckner, and Lehár. (Festival runs July-Aug. Tickets 150-460AS.) Traffic and crowds can create a sort of frenzied feeling in Bad Ischl, but a stroll along the town esplanade allows one to relax amid the sounds of birds and rushing water. The **tourist office** *(Kurdirektion),* Bahnhofstr. 6 (tel. (06132) 35 20), finds rooms in private homes (from 130AS) and *Pensionen* (from 160AS) at no charge. (Open Mon.-Fri. 8am-6pm, Sat. 9am-4pm, Sun. 9-11:30am; Oct.-May Mon.-Fri. 8am-noon and 2-5pm, Sat. 8am-noon.) Bad Ischl's roomy **Jugendgästehaus (HI)** is at Am Rechensteg 5 (tel. (06132) 65 77), in the town center. Show up early if you want a spot. (Reception open 8-9am and 5-7pm. Flexible 10pm curfew. 139AS; in winter 136AS.) Near Bad Ischl, Austria's last emperor, Kaiser Franz-Josef, built the **Kaiservilla,** his summer getaway palace, and stuffed it full of expensive kitsch. (Open May-Sept. daily 9am-noon and 1-5pm. Tours 68AS, with guest card 64AS. Estate grounds and surrounding park 25AS, children 15AS.) The **Katrin Cable Car** runs to the top of 1500m Mt. Katrin, laced with fine hiking trails. (Open daily 9am-4pm. Up 130AS, down 100AS, round-trip 150AS, with guest card 125AS.) **Bike rental** and **luggage check** are at the station (open daily 5am-8:10pm).

Hallstatt South of Bad Ischl poses **Hallstatt,** isolated and breathtaking in its austere, mountainous setting. In the 19th century, Hallstatt was the site of one of the largest Iron Age archeological finds in history. The **Prähistorisches Museum** exhibits some of the relics. (Open daily 10am-6pm; Oct.-April 10am-4pm. 35AS, with guest card 30AS, students 20AS.) If piles of dirt are your thing, take the **Salzbergbahn** (cable car) to the site of the dig. (Open daily 9am-6pm; Oct.-April 9am-4:30pm. 50AS, under 15 30AS. Round-trip 90AS, under 15 45AS.) The **Salzbergwerke,** just up the path from the ancient groves, are the still-operating oldest salt works in the world (2500 years). (Open June to mid-Sept. daily 9:30am-4:30pm; May and mid-Sept. to mid-Oct. 9:30am-3pm. 125AS, with guest card 110AS, children under 14 and students 60AS.) Paths lead back to Hallstatt from the foot of the mountain. The **Skischule Zauner,** Markt 51 (tel. (06134) 246), and the Hallstatt tourist office provide guidance to ski bunnies and hares in all seasons.

The **hostel (Jugendherberge, HI)** at Salzbergstr. 50 (tel. (06134) 212), 10 minutes from the town center, offers basic, inexpensive lodgings in a tidy, flower-bedecked house. (Reception open 6-9pm. Lockout 10am-6pm. Curfew 9pm. 85AS. Open May-early Oct.) **TVN Naturfreunde Herberge,** Kirchenweg 36 (tel. (06134) 318), also called *Gasthaus Zur Mühle,* is a quasi-hostel with very cheap 4- to 8-bed rooms. (Reception open daily 8-10am and 5-10pm. 100AS.) Equally cheap *privat Zimmer* speckle the town. **Camping Klausner-Höll** is at Lahnstr. 6 (tel. (06134) 329), 2 blocks from the bus terminal. (35AS/person, children 18AS, 30AS/tent, 25AS/car.) The Hallstatt **tourist office** (tel. (06134) 208, fax (06134) 352), in the **Kultur und Kongresshaus,** off Seestr., finds cheap rooms (there are plenty). (Open Mon.-Fri. 9am-6pm, Sat.-Sun10am-2pm; Sept.-May Mon.-Fri. 9am-noon and 1-5pm.) If you arrive by **train,** alight at the Hallstatt Bahnhof, across the lake from the village itself. Ferries cross to the village after each train's arrival (18AS). **Post buses** also make the journey from Bad Ischl (42AS).

Dachstein Ice Caves At the other end of the lake in Obertraun, the prodigious **Dachstein Ice Caves,** though marred by cheesy names like "Cave Venus" and "Hall of Oblivion," give eloquent testimony to the geological hyperactivity that forged the region's natural beauty. (Open May-mid-Oct. daily 9am-5pm. To Giant Ice Cave 72AS, to Mammoth Cave 66AS, combined 98AS.) To reach the caves from Hallstatt, take the boat to Obertraun and ride the Dachstein cable car up 1350m to Schönbergalm (round-trip 142AS). For info on the caves, call (06131) 362.

■■■ KITZBÜHEL

A little over an hour by train from Innsbruck, Kitzbühel is the St. Moritz of Austria, where wealthy visitors pump enough Deutschmarks and dollars into the local economy to keep the cobblestone streets in good repair and the sidewalk cafés flourishing. Site of Austria's first cable car, Kitzbühel challenges skiers and hikers with an ever-ascending network of lifts and runs. At night, international playchildren gather in cozy pubs to squander their parents' money.

An extensive network of hiking trails snakes up the surrounding mountains. To reach some of the lower trails and meadow walks, ride the **Hahnenkammbahn** from Hahnenkamm station (140AS, with guest card 120AS; children 70AS). Or climb up yourself; the descent is free on all area cable cars. The **Kitzbüheler Hornbahn** cable cars will take you up to the **Alpenblumengarten,** where over 120 different types of Alpine flowers blossom each season. (Open mid-Oct. to April daily 8:30am-5:30pm; each of 3 sections of the cable car 65AS.) Those with guest cards can take advantage of the tourist office's *wunderbar* free mountain hiking program. Guided hikes begin daily (June to mid-Oct.) at 9am at the office. The Kitzbühel **ski area** is simply one of the world's best. 64 lifts and shuttle buses are yours with a 1-day ski pass (320-340AS; in early morning, under 15 ½-price). Downhill ski rental runs 95-140AS for the 1st day, and lessons cost 340AS/day. Ask at the tourist office about ski packages: 1 week of lodging, ski instruction, and ski passes (available before Christmas and after Easter; rock bottom 2900AS without instruction). For a **snow report** (in German), call (05356) 181 or (0536) 182.

Accommodations, Food, and Practical Information Kitzbühel has more guest beds (10,000) than inhabitants (8070), but you'll pay for the convenience; the only youth hostel is far from town and restricted to groups. Call the **Gasthof Alpenhof,** Aurach 176 (tel. 45 07), 3km outside Kitzbühel, and they'll pick you up at the rail station. The British staff oversees rooms with fantastic balconies. (150-200AS. Reservations recommended.) To get to **Camping Schwarzsee,** take the train to "Schwarzsee" (just before "Hahnenkamm"), and flit toward the lake. (60AS/person, winter 55AS). Grocery shoppers can hit the **SPAR Markt** on the corner of Ehrengasse and Bichlstr. (Open Mon.-Fri. 8am-6:30pm, Sat. 8:30am-1pm.) A **Tyrolean market** takes place in front of the tourist office (Wed. and Sat.). The **post office,** 11 Josef-Pirchl-Str., lists bus schedules and has telephones. (Open Mon.-Fri. 8am-noon and 4-7pm, Sat. 8-11am.)

Tiny Kitzbühel has 2 **train stations,** one at either side of the U-curve that the railroad makes around the town. From Salzburg, you arrive first at **Hauptbahnhof;** from Innsbruck or Wörgl, at **Hahnenkamm.** From there, go left, and, at the end of the street, turn right and walk toward the shops. When you reach the wall, climb the steps on your left and make an immediate left; before you step into the *Fußgängerzone,* turn right to see the **tourist office,** Hinterstadt 18 (tel. (05356) 22 72 or 21 55). The office doesn't make reservations; use the free phone at the electronic accommodations board outside. (Open Mon.-Fri. 8:30am-noon and 3-6:30pm, Sat. 8:30am-noon. Accommodations board open daily 8am-10pm.) Opposite the tourist office, **Reisebüro Eurotours** exchanges money. (Open Mon.-Fri. 8am-12:30pm and 3-6:30pm, Sat. 8am-12:30pm and 4:30-6:30pm, Sun. 10am-noon and 4:30-6:30pm.)

■■■ INNSBRUCK

Thrust into the international limelight by the Winter Olympics of 1964 and 1976, the ancient capital of the Tyrol is lined with Baroque façades, over-laden with rose bushes, and ringed by snow-capped mountains. More than 150 cable cars and chairlifts and an extensive network of mountain paths radiate from Innsbruck, making the Alps surrounding the city accessible to winter skiers and summer hikers alike.

ORIENTATION AND PRACTICAL INFORMATION

Because of Innsbruck's compact size, nearly any two points lie within easy walking distance of each other, and public transportation, though available, is largely unnecessary. To reach the *Altstadt* from the main train station, turn right and walk until you reach Museumstr., then turn left and walk about 10 minutes. Or take streetcars #1 or 3, or city bus K or O from the train station to "Maria-Theresien-Str." You can join **Club Innsbruck** (summer 310AS; winter 280AS) at no charge if you register at any central-Innsbruck accommodation for at least 3 nights, and membership has privileges: you get cable car and museum discounts, free bike tours, and the option of participating in the club's fine hiking program (June-Sept.; ask at the tourist office).

Tourist Office: Fremdenverkehrsverband Innsbruck-Igls, Burggraben 3, 3rd floor (tel. 598 50; fax 598 50 7), on the edge of the *Altstadt,* just off the end of Museumstr. A kindly face, free brochures and city map, ski info, and an ultra-valuable list of private room accommodations in Innsbruck and Igls. Open Sun.-Fri. 8am-6pm, Sat. 8am-noon. The **Jugendwarterraum,** in the *Hauptbahnhof* (tel. 58 63 62), near the lockers. Brochures, maps, free accommodations service, and mutual understanding. (Open Mon.-Fri. 11am-7pm and Sat. 10am-1pm.) **Innsbruck-Information,** Burggraben 3, 1st floor (tel. 53 56; fax 53 56 43). Same building as the tourist office. The place to arrange tours, buy concert tickets, etc. Not really budget-minded accommodations; room reservations 30AS. Open daily 8am-7pm. Branches at the *Hauptbahnhof* (tel. 58 37 66; open daily 9am-10pm). **Tirol Information Office,** Wilhelm-Greil-Str. 17 (tel. 532 01 70, fax 532 01 50). Open Mon.-Fri. 8:30am-6pm, Sat. 9am-noon.

Budget Travel: Tiroler Landesreisebüro, Wilhelm-Greil-Str. at Boznerplatz (tel. 598 85). Discounts on international train, plane, and bus tickets. Open Mon.-Fri. 8:30am-12:30pm and 2-6pm.

Consulates: U.K., Mathias-Schmidt-Str. 12-I (tel. 58 83 20). Open Mon.-Fri. 9am-noon.

Currency Exchange: Best rates at main post office and its main train station branch. Open daily 7:30am-noon, 12:45-6pm, and 6.30-8pm. Innsbruck's banks are open Mon.-Fri. 7:45am-12:30pm and 2:15-4pm.

American Express: Brixnerstr. 3 (tel. 58 24 91), in front of the main train station. Address letters to, for example, David Sagafi-nejad, Client Letter Service, American Express, Brixnerstr. 3, A-6020 Innsbruck, Austria. Open Mon.-Fri. 9am-5:30pm, Sat. 9am-noon.

Post Office: Maximilianstr. 2, down from the Triumph Arch. Open 24hrs. **Poste Restante.** Branch next to the train station. Open Mon.-Sat. 7am-9pm, Sun. 9am-noon. **Postal Code:** A-6020.

Telephones: At post office. **City Code:** 0512.

Trains: Hauptbahnhof, Südtiroler Pl. (tel. 17 17), a 10-min. walk down Museumstr. from the *Altstadt.* Buses J, K, O, 4, and S take you there. Has lockers, luggage storage, bike rental, and showers.

Buses: Post buses leave for all areas of Tyrol from the station on Sterzinger Str., adjacent to the *Hauptbahnhof.* Open Mon.-Fri. 7am-5:30pm, Sat. 7am-1pm. For information, contact the *Postautodienst,* Maximilianstr. 23 (tel. 57 66 00).

Taxis: Innsbruck Funktaxi (tel. 53 11 or 455 00). About 100AS from the airport to the *Altstadt.*

Bike Rental: At the main train station. 90AS/day, 45AS/day with Eurailpass or train ticket to Innsbruck. Return them to any train station in Austria. Open April-early Nov. daily 9am-11pm.

Hitchhiking: Hitchers go to the Shell gas station by the DEZ store off Geyrstr. near Amras; bus K delivers to Geyrstr. Most cars leaving Innsbruck take this exit.

Lockers: 20-30AS/48hr. at the train station. **Baggage check** at the station 20AS. Open 24hrs.; Nov.-April daily 7am-midnight.

Laundromat: Waltraud Hell, Amraserstr. 15, behind the station. Wash and dry 80AS. Open Mon.-Fri. 8am-6pm, Sat. 8am-1pm.

Medical Assistance: University Hospital, Anichstr. 35 (tel. 50 40).

Emergencies: Ambulance: tel. 144, 594 44. **Fire:** tel. 122. **Police:** tel. 133. Headquarters at Kaiserjägerstr. 8 (tel. 590 00). Police precinct adjacent to the main train station.

ACCOMMODATIONS AND CAMPING

Beds are scarce during June, when only three hostels are open. In July, university housing opens up to travelers, making lodgings somewhat easier to find. The **Jugendwarterraum** at the main train station will aid you in your search for accommodations and will telephone hostels to check availability and reserve beds.

Jugendherberge Innsbruck (HI), Reichenauer Str. 147 (tel. 461 79 or 461 80). Take bus O to "Rossbachstr." Often crowded with Americans, but they'll honor phone reservations as long as you show up by 5pm. 4- to 6-bed dorms. Reception 5-10pm. Lockout 10am-5pm. Curfew 11pm. Kitchen facilities. Laundry 45AS including soap but you must notify the desk by 5pm if you intend to do laundry. Members only. 125AS first night, 95AS subsequent nights. Breakfast and sheets included. Open early-Jan. to late Dec.

Jugendheim St. Paulus (HI), Reichenauer Str. 72 (tel. 442 91). Take bus R to "Pauluskirche." Negatives: 20-bed dorm rooms. Positives: kitchen facilities, incredibly helpful staff, the cheapest beds in town. 3-night max stay. Reception 7-9am and 5-10pm. Lockout 10am-5pm. Curfew 10pm; ask for a key. 90AS. Breakfast 25AS. Sheets 20AS. Open mid-June to mid-Aug.

Jugendherberge St. Nicklaus (HI), Innstr. 95 (tel. 28 65 15). Walk across the river from the *Altstadt* along Rennweg to Innstr., or take bus K from the station to "St. Nicklaus." Clean rooms (6-8 beds/room) and a party-hearty, English-speaking crowd. Reception 8-10am and 5-8pm. No curfew or lockout, though deposit is required for a key. Theoretical quiet time 10pm, though the "Igloo" bar downstairs is open later. Checkout 9am. 115AS first night, 100AS for subsequent nights. Non-members surcharge 10AS . Shower tokens 10AS. Breakfast 40-75AS. Meals at adjacent restaurant 55AS. Laundry 100AS/load. Mountain bike rental 150AS/day 9am-6pm. Glacier ski packages 200-300AS/day; winter ski packages 2900AS/week including lodging, equipment, lift tickets, and bus to the slopes.

Hostel Torsten-Arneus Schwedenhaus (HI), Rennweg 17b (tel. 58 58 14), along the river. Guests rave about this spotless, warm hostel with private bathrooms and an excellent location on the river. Take bus C from the station to the "Handelsakademie". Reception 5-7pm. Lockout 8am-5pm. Curfew 10pm. Triples and quads 100AS/person. Breakfast 45AS. Dinner 60AS. Sheets 20AS. Reservations heartily recommended. Open July-Aug.

Jugendherberge MK (HI), Sillgasse 8a (tel. 57 13 11), near the station. A funky place with friendly management and a delirious café next door. Reception open 7-9am and 5-7pm. Lockout 9am-5pm. Curfew 11pm. 1st night 150AS, 140AS thereafter. Breakfast and showers included. Sheets 10AS. Open July to mid-Sept.

Volkshaus Innsbruck (HI), Radetzkystr. 41 (tel. 46 66 82), around the corner from Jugendherberge Innsbruck and Jugendzentrum St. Paulus. Radetzkystr. is off Reichenauerstr., before the Campingplatz. Accommodates 52 in spartan doubles, triples, quads, and quints. 100AS. Breakfast 40AS. Showers and sheets included.

Haus Wolf, Dorfstr. 48 (tel. 58 40 88), in the suburb of Mutters. Take the *Stubaitalbahn* (STB) to "Birchfeld," and walk down Dorfstr. Unload your pack, and bask in the maternal comfort; there's no place like home, but this comes close. Singles, doubles, and triples 180AS/person. Breakfast and shower included.

Camping Seewirt, Amras, Geyrstr. 25 (tel. 461 53). From the *Hauptbahnhof*, take a right on Amrasser Str., left on Amrasser Seestr., and then a right on Geyrstr. Or take bus K to "Amras." Hot showers and restaurant. 50AS/person, 35AS/tent.

FOOD

An indoor **market** is in the Markthalle along the Inn behind the *Altstadt*. (Open Mon.-Fri. 7:30am-8pm, Sat. 7:30am-12:30pm.) The **M-Preis** discount supermarket is near 4 hostels, on the corner of Reichenauer Str. and Andechsstr. (Open Mon.-Fri. 8am-6pm, Sat. 9am-noon.)

University Mensa, Herzog-Siegmund-Ufer 15, on the 2nd floor of the new university between the *Markthalle* and Blasius-Hueber-Str. Tasty lunches (40-60AS) and crisp salads. No student ID necessary. Open Mon.-Fri. 11am-2pm.

China-Restaurant Asia, Angerzellgasse 10, just past the Eurasia Chinese Pizzeria near Treibhaus. Lunch *Mittagsmenu* Mon.-Sat. is probably the best deal in Innsbruck (59AS). Open daily 11:30am-2:30pm, 6pm-midnight.

Hafele, on the corner of Innrain and Rechengasse, in the Innsbruck University complex. Cheap, tried-and-true Austrian meals like a succulent ½-chicken (34AS) and *Kotlett mit Pommes* (fried cutlet with fries; 48AS). Daily menus and salads as well. Open Mon.-Fri. 7am-6pm, Sat. 8am-noon.

Wienerwald, on Museumstr.; branch on Maria-Theresien-Str. Austria's chain version of the family steak (*Schnitzel*) house. Feast on fowl and salads as well (70-120AS). English menus. Open daily 10am-midnight. Major credit cards accepted.

Philippine Vegetarische Küche, Müllerstr. 9, at Templstr. a block from the post office. A veggie rest stop on a highway of meat. Polish off the *Schnitzel* (85AS) with *Erdbeeren "Grossmutterart"* (sauce-dipped strawberries, 38AS). Entrees 82-130AS. English menus. Open Mon.-Sat. 11:30am-2:30pm and 6-10:30pm.

SIGHTS AND ENTERTAINMENT

The **Altstadt** is the center of Innsbruck, and the **Goldenes Dachl** (Golden Roof) is both the center of the *Altstadt* and the city's emblem. It once served as a vantage point for spectators during the medieval tournaments held in the square below. Inside the building is the **Olympiamuseum,** which commemorates the 1964 and 1976 Winter Games with relics and films. (Open daily 9:30am-5:30pm; Nov.-Feb. closed Mon. 22AS, children 15AS, students and seniors 11AS.) Don't miss the adjacent **Stadtturm,** the 14th-century city tower. Combined tickets to the city tower and Olympiamuseum are available. (Open daily 10am-6pm. To tower 18AS, children 9AS. With Olympiamuseum 32AS, students 16AS.) From the Goldenes Dachl, look to your left on the Herzog-Friedrich-Str. to see the 16th-century **Goldener Adler** Inn. Countless dignitaries and artists—among them Goethe, Heine, and Sartre—have stayed or dined here. The area immediately behind the Goldenes Dachl houses the stunning baroque **St. Jakob Dom,** with its superb *trompe l'oeil* ceiling and an altar decorated with Cranach's *Intercession of the Virgin.*

At **Rennweg** and **Hofgasse** stands the grand **Hofburg** (Imperial Palace). Built between the 16th and 18th centuries, the Hofburg is filled with portraits of its one-time royal residents. Empress Maria Theresa glowers over nearly every room; a portrait of Maria's youngest daughter, Marie Antoinette (with head) is in the palace's main hall. (Open daily 9am-4pm; mid-Oct. to mid-May Mon.-Sat. 9am-4pm. 30AS, students 10AS. English guidebook 5AS.) The nearby **Hofkirche** also houses aristocrats, conquerors and monarchs—this time, as mammoth bronze statues. (Open daily 9am-5pm; Oct.-April 9am-noon and 2-5pm. 25AS, students 14AS.) A combined ticket (40AS, students 25AS) will also admit you to the collection of the **Tiroler Volkskunstmuseum** (Tyrolean Handicrafts Museum) next door. Dusty implements, peasant costumes and furnished period rooms give a brief introduction to Tyrolean culture. (Open Mon.-Sat. 9am-5pm; Oct.-April 9am-noon and 2-5pm. Museum also open Sun. 9am-noon. To museum 20AS, students 15AS.) The collection of the **Tiroler Landesmuseum Ferdinandeum,** Museumstr. 15, several blocks from the main train station, includes exquisitely colored, delicately etched stained-glass windows, and several outstanding medieval altars and paintings. (Open Tues.-Wed., Fri.-Sun 10am-5pm, Thurs. 10am-5pm and 7-9pm.; Oct.-April Tues.-Sat. 10am-noon and 2-5pm, Sun. 10am-1pm. 50AS, students 30AS.)

Cross the covered bridge over the Inn River, and follow the signs to the **Alpenzoo,** the highest zoo in Europe, where you can see every vertebrate species indigenous to the Alps in its natural habitat and enjoy a bird's-eye view of the city. Don't miss the zoo's network of scenic trails weaving through the hillside. Catch tram #1, 6, or the STB to the "Hungerburg Funicular Railway" and take the cable car across the Inn River directly to the zoo. (Open 9am-6pm; mid-Nov. to March 9am-5pm. 56AS, students 28AS.) Outside the city, Archduke Ferdinand left behind heaps of armor and paintings at **Schloß Ambras.** (Open April-Oct. Mon. and Weds.-Sun. 10am-5pm.) To reach Ambras, take steetcar #6 (direction "Pradl"). If you ever doubted that ski jumpers have a few screws loose, a trip out to the **Olympische Schischanze** jump will convince you. Take streetcar #1, 6, or the STB to "Bergisel."

During July and August, Innsbruck hosts the **Festival of Early Music,** featuring concerts at the **Schloß Ambras** on period instruments and organ recitals in the **Hofkirche** on the 16th-century Ebert organ. (tel. (512) 535 60 or fax (512) 53 56 43 to book tickets.) Several of the festival's concerts are also held at the **Tiroler Landestheater** (tel. 52 07 44), across from the Hofburg on Rennweg, the finest theater in the region. (Tickets available Mon.-Sat. 8:30am-8:30pm or at the door before performance; 40-250AS.)

Treibhaus (tel. 58 68 74), Angerzellgasse 8, hidden in an alley to the right of China-Restaurant, is Innsbruck's favorite student hangout. Left-wing protest music serenades the young crowd in the evening with jazz on Sunday mornings. (Open Mon.-Sat. 4pm-1am, Sun. 9am-2pm. Evening cover 50-150AS; no cover Sun. Generous beers 26AS.) During the summer, the Treibhaus presents its "Sommergarten" series, which includes concerts every Saturday evening, a June Blues festival, a June Jazz festival, and other hip events.

■ Near Innsbruck

Igls (pronounced "eagles"), one of Innsbruck's suburban skiing spots, lies about 5km out of the city proper. To reach Igls from Innsbruck, take tram #6 to the end of the line (one way 22AS, day pass 33AS). During the summer Igls makes a fine hiking base; pick up free maps at the tourist office (tel. (2) 771 01, fax (3) 789 65). From the tram stop, walk straight through the first intersection and continue through the narrow pathway in the park. At the next street, turn left; the tourist office is on the right. (Open Mon.-Fri. 9am-noon and 2-5pm.) During winter, Igls's **Patscherkofel Pass** (named for the nearby mountain) offers skiers 5 lifts (day pass 265AS, 660AS 3 days, 1200AS 6 days). A round-trip ride on the cable car is 63AS. Bobsledding and luge brought Igls fame in the '64 and '76 Olympics; 300AS buys you a simulated gold: a ride in a 4-person sled with an experienced driver. (Available Nov.-Feb. Call (3) 775 25, (3) 771 60). The **emergency number** for an **avalanche warning** is 15 87. For **ski rescue** it is (3) 771 63 and for a **snow report** it is 15 85 (German only).

■■■ LIENZ

Between the angry peaks of the *Dolomites* and gentle summits of the *Hohe Tauern* mountains, Lienz is quietly captivating. The unofficial capital of **East Tyrol** (*Osttirol*), the city is 3 hours by train from Innsbruck or Salzburg. Above Lienz is the **Schloß Bruck,** home of the **East Tyrolean Regional Museum,** which houses everything from Roman remains and local artifacts to carved Christmas *crèches.* Take the "Matreier Tauernhaus" bus from the train station (16AS), or foot it for 15-20 minutes. (Open mid-June to mid-Sept. daily 10am-6pm; mid-Sept. to Oct. and April to mid-June Tues.-Sun. 10am-5pm. 35AS, students and seniors 23AS, ages 16-18 18AS, under 16 10AS.) For a moderate 4- to 5-hour hike, take the Hochsteinbahnen chairlift, which starts near the castle (90AS, round-trip 130AS; open late June to mid-Sept. 9:15am-12:15pm and 1-5:30pm), then climb **Hochstein** (2057m) and descend to the valley. The **Zettersfeld** chairlift (70AS) provides access to hiking on the Zettersfeld peak (1930m). And from Boznerstr. 2, buses run to another good hiking base, the **Lienzer Dolomitenhütte** in the mountains above town. (Buses leave mid-June to late Sept. daily 8am, 1:10pm, and 4:30pm; 95AS.) Some 14 ski lifts operate between November and April. Full-day **ski passes** cost 290AS (seniors 230AS); ½-day tickets are 230AS (seniors 185AS). Prices drop after the first day. The **Skischule Lienzer**

Dolomiten, at the Zettersfeld lift (tel. (04852) 656 90), gives private lessons for 370AS (groups 170AS/person).

Accommodations, Food, and Practical Information From the station, walk through the Hauptpl., bear left on Rosengasse and right on tree-lined Alleestr. to the cool, fresh doubles and triples of **Egger,** Alleestr. 33 (tel. (04852) 487 72; 150-160AS/person, 10AS surcharge for stays under 3 nights). From the train station, cross Tiroler Str. and bear left into Hauptpl., cross the square, veer right onto Muchargasse, and continue straight (8min.) to **Gasthof Goldener Stern,** Schweizergasse 40 (tel. (04852) 621 92), for spacious rooms in a gorgeous 15th-century mansion. (Curfew 10pm. July-mid.-Sept. Singles 190-290AS. Doubles and triples 180AS/person; mid.-Sept.-June 180-260AS. 10AS surcharge for stays under 3 nights.) If private rooms are more your yen, consult the friendly staff at the tourist office for an exhaustive list of lodgings. Down the street at **Café Wha,** Schweizergasse 3, rocks a bandana-wearing, slightly alternative crowd. (Open daily 6pm-1am.) At **Imbiß Köstl,** Kreuzgasse 4, a mother-daughter duo prepares the cheapest eats in town. (19-49AS. Open Mon.-Fri. 7:30am-7:30pm, Sat. 7:30am-2pm.) The **tourist office** Europapl. (tel. 652 65), distributes the pamphlet *Lienzer Dolomiten Preisliste*, listing accommodations, and the booklet *Informationen für unserre Gäste*, detailing recreational opportunities and cultural activities. From the station, turn left onto Tiroler Str. and turn right onto Europapl. at the SPAR Markt. (Open Mon.-Fri. 8am-7pm, Sat. 9am-noon and 3-5pm, Sun. 10am-noon and 5-7pm; Oct.-June Mon.-Fri. 8am-6pm, Sat. 9am-noon and 3-5pm.)

Großglocknerstraße Outside Lienz begins the scenic **Großglocknerstraße,** one of the highest—and the most beautiful—mountain roads in Europe. At 3797m, **Großglockner** peak is Austria's highest mountain. The brochure *Wandern mit dem Bundesbus: Nationalpark Höhe Tauern* (available at the bus stations in Lienz and Zell am See and at the tourist office in Heiligenblut) contains a schedule of Bundesbus departure times, destinations, maps, hiking paths, and general info about the **Höhe Tauern National Park,** which surrounds the Großglockner. Break up the trip by stopping in **Heiligenblut.** A comfortable, chalet-style **Jugendherberge (HI),** Hof 36 (tel. (04824) 22 59), sleeps 84 in dorms and offers bed, sheets, and breakfast for 140AS/night. (Reception open Dec.-Aug. daily 7-9am and 5-10pm. Members only.) Stop at Franz-Josefs-Höhe, at the foot of Großglockner, and take the **Gletscherbahn** (round-trip 80AS) for a stunning view of the glacier. For information on hiking on the mountain, call the **Regional Großglockner Association** at (04824) 20 01 21.

■■■ GRAZ

Ever since Charlemagne claimed this strategic crossroads for the Germanic empire, Graz has been at battle. The celebrated castles are the few remaining testaments to Graz's long history of political and military upheaval. Today it's war of a different sort: narrow cobblestone streets compete with a hectic network of trams and buses; chic department stores display their inventory in buildings scarred and battered by centuries of weathering. The **Hauptplatz** pedestrian zone is the heart of the city.

The **Landeszeughaus** (provincial arsenal) on Herrengasse is worth exploring. Five floors of spears, muskets, and pistols—enough, in fact, for 28,000 mercenaries—are on display in this former armory of the Styrian estates. (Open April-Oct. Mon.-Fri. 9am-5pm, Sat.-Sun. 9am-1pm. 25AS, seniors 10AS, students free.) Next door is the Renaissance **Landhaus,** longtime seat of the provincial government.

From high atop the **Schloßberg,** a hill overlooking the city that for centuries served as a military vantage point, looms the 16th-century bell tower, the city's hallmark. Take the cable car from Kaiser-Franz-Josef-Kai 38. (Open April 9am-10pm; May-June 8am-11pm; July-Aug. 8am-midnight; Oct.-March 10am-10pm. 15AS, round-trip 20AS, children ½-price.) The exhilarating 15- to 20-minute hike to the top features excellent views of the city all along the well-marked paths. The **Schloß Eggenberg** (Eggenberg Castle) at Eggenberger Allee 90, houses a diverse collection of 17th-century artifacts. To see the castle's elegant **Prunkräume,** you must join one of the free tours. (In German only, on the hour. Admission to entire complex 25AS, students 2AS. *Prunkräume* open April-Oct. daily 10am-1pm and 2-5pm.) Roam with the peacocks through an enchanting **game preserve** adjacent to the castle. (Open May-Aug. daily 8am-7pm; reduced hours off-season.)

Graz's remarkable **Opernhaus** (opera house), at Opernring and Burgasse, sells standing-room tickets (15-25AS) at the door an hour before curtain, as does the **Schauspielhaus** (theater; tel. 80 05) at Freiheitsplatz off Hofgasse. Regular tickets and performance schedules are available at the **Theaterkasse,** Kaiser-Josef-Platz 10 (tel. (0316) 80 00; open Mon.-Fri. 8am-8pm, Sat. 8am-1pm).

Accommodations, Food, and Practical Information Accommodations in Graz are generally affordable and easy to find, except in July and August. The cheapest bed in town is at the **youth hostel (HI)** at Idlhofgasse 74 (tel. (0316) 91 48 76), a 20-minute walk from the train station. Head right on Bahnhofgürtel, take a left at Josef-Huber-Gasse, then the first right at Idlhofgasse. Its congenial staff offsets the noisy, insomniac tour groups. (Reception open 5-10pm. Lockout 9am-5pm. Curfew 10pm. Dorms 130AS, nonmembers 40AS extra.) A more comfortable and expensive option is the **Hotel Strasser,** Eggenberger Gürtel 11 (tel. (0316) 91 39 77, 91 68 56), a 3-minute walk from the train station, with big rooms on a busy street. (Singles 280AS. Doubles 480AS, with showers 580AS. Quads 840AS.)

30,000 students sustain a blitz of cheap eateries (and vice versa). The best deal in town is the **Mensa** of the University of Graz, just east of the Stadtpark at Zinzendorfgasse and Schuberstr. (Set menus 30-55AS. Vegetarian (*Vollwert*) meals available.) Escape this land's cholesterol-laden cuisine at **Margolds Vollwert Restaurant,** Griesgasse 11. Daily lunch specials (39-50AS) include soup, salad, and desserts. (Open Mon.-Fri. 11am-8pm, Sat. 11am-4pm.) The cobblestone sidestreets off Mehlplatz, especially **Färbergasse, Prokopigasse,** and **Engegasse,** are sprinkled with lively pubs where you can quaff *Gösser,* a tasty Styrian brew. For a bargain night on the town, stroll down **Herrengasse** and let the street musicians serenade you.

The **Hauptbahnhof** lies a short ride from the Hauptplatz by streetcars #1, 3, or 6. An easy 2- to 3-minute jaunt away is the **tourist office,** at Herrengasse 16 (tel. (0316) 83 52 41, ext. 11 or 12), where the cordial staff sells city maps (10AS) and books rooms. (30AS fee. Open Mon.-Fri. 9am-7pm, Sat. 9am-6pm, Sun. and holidays 10am-3pm.) You can change money at any of the banks along Herrengasse, but the **American Express** office, Hamerlingasse 6 (tel. 81 70 10), gives the best rates. (Open Mon.-Fri. 9am-5:30pm, Sat. 9am-noon.)

Belgium
(België, Belgique)

US$1 = 34.40BF (francs, or BEF)	**10BF** =	**US$0.29**
CDN$1= 26.09BF	**10BF** =	**CDN$0.38**
UK£1 = 53.13BF	**10BF** =	**UK£0.19**
IR£ = 49.84BF	**10BF** =	**IR£ 0.20**
AUS$1= 22.25BF	**10BF** =	**AUS$0.45**
NZ$1 = 18.90BF	**10BF** =	**NZ$0.53**
SAR1 = 7.09BF	**10BF** =	**SAR 1.41**
Country Code: 32	**International Dialing Prefix: 00**	

Despite its status as one of Europe's "little countries," Belgium's appeal is wide and varied. In the south, the wooded Ardennes decorate gentle hills; near the North Sea, Bruges and Ghent bask in guildhoused medieval splendor; and centrally located Brussels revels in decorous frenzy. Belgium has served as a perennial battleground for larger continental powers, whose partitions gave rise to the nation's present cultural tensions between the Flemish in the north, who speak a Dutch dialect, and the

French-speaking Walloons in the south. As the voices of Flemish nationalists in Antwerp call for the partitioning of the Belgian state and the country mourns for its departed monarch, a steady bureaucratic hum rings through Brussels, where government officials are quietly drawing up plans for the federation of all Europe.

GETTING THERE AND GETTING AROUND

Belgium's **train** network is one of the most reliable in Europe. Prices are low, if only because the country is small (at most 4 rail-hours across). **Eurail** is valid on intercity buses as well as trains. The **Benelux Tourrail Pass** is a good option, covering 5 days of travel in Belgium, the Netherlands, and Luxembourg during a 17-day period (3780BF, under 26 2860BF). The best deal could be the **Go Pass** (990BF for 8 trips within Belgium). A **Half-Fare Card** (550BF for 1 month) is also available, and tourist offices sell a **24-hr. pass** covering all municipal transport in the country (180BF).

Biking is very popular, and many roads are equipped with bike lanes (which you must use even if they're studded with potholes). When you see 2 side paths next to the street, the inner one is for bicycles and mopeds, the outer for pedestrians. Of Belgium's 150 train stations, 65 rent bikes (150BF/day, 280BF/day without rail ticket); you can return them to any of 115 designated stations (100BF to return a bike to a station that doesn't lend them). Pick up the brochure *Train et Vélo/Trein en Fiets* at any station. **Hitching** in Belgium is generally auspicious. Bilingual signs ("please" is *s.v.p.* in French, *a.u.b.* in Flemish) are reportedly more successful. **Taxi Stop** (tel. (02) 646 86 10) has offices in major cities and matches travelers with Belgian drivers to destinations all over Europe (1.3BF/km, 150-500BF/trip). **Ferries** from Zeebrugge and Oostende, near Bruges, cross to Dover and other British ports.

BELGIUM ESSENTIALS

Belgium's network of efficient tourist offices is supplemented by **Infor-Jeunes/Info-Jeugd,** a nationwide information service which helps young people with short- or long-term accommodations in Belgium. The English-language weekly *Bulletin* (75BF at newsstands) lists everything from movies in English to job opportunities.

National holidays in Belgium are Ascension Day (6th Thurs. after Easter), Whit Monday (7th Mon. after Easter), July 21 (Belgian National Day), and August 15. Most public **phones** require a phone card (200BF or 1000BF) which can be purchased at **PTT** (post, telephone, and telegraph) offices or at magazine stands; the few remaining coin-operated phones take an initial deposit of 10BF. Belgium's **MCI World Reach** number is 078 11 00 10, and the **Canada Direct** number is 11 00 11. In an **emergency** anywhere in Belgium, dial 100 for medical service and the fire brigade, and 101 for the police. To reach the domestic operator, dial 1307; the European operator, 1304; the international operator, 1322. Note that the digit "3" in the preceding numbers becomes a "2" in Flemish areas.

Accommodations, Camping, Food, and Drink
Most visitors to Belgium make the mistake of staying in Brussels and day-tripping to neighboring cities. Try using Namur, Bruges or Ghent as a base instead. **Hotels** in Belgium are expensive, with trench-bottom prices for singles 800BF and doubles 1000-1100BF. Avoid bankruptcy by staying in one of the 31 **HI hostels,** which charge about 335BF per night. Pick up *Budget Holidays* at any tourist office for complete hostel listings. **Campgrounds** charge about 100BF per night. The pamphlet *Camping*, with complete listings and prices, is available free at tourist offices. Belgian cuisine can be wonderful, but a native dish may cost as much as a night in a decent hotel. Steamed mussels are usually tasty and mildly affordable (a whole pot for around 295BF). Belgian beer provides both national pride and a national pastime; more varieties (over 500) are produced here than in any other country. Regular or quirky blonde goes for as little as 30BF, and dark beers cost about 60BF. Leave room in the wallet and the belly for Belgian *gaufres* (waffles) and those famous Godiva chocolates.

■■■ BRUSSELS (BRUXELLES, BRUSSEL)

A city with a lineage of leadership, Brussels has become "the capital of Europe," but not without paying a heavy architectural price; the headquarters of NATO and glass towers of the European Community rise uncomfortably beside the belfries of ancient cathedrals and the magical art nouveau creations of Victor Horta. The soul of the city is found in its secluded cafés and intimate neighborhoods, not the grand boulevards through which countless Eurocrats speed to work each morning.

ORIENTATION AND PRACTICAL INFORMATION

Tourist Brussels is roughly bounded by **Gare du Nord** in the north, **Parc de Bruxelles** in the east, the **Palais de Justice** in the south, and the **Bourse** (stock exchange) in the west. **Gare Centrale** and the **Grand-Place** share the center. Brussels and its suburbs are officially bilingual, but since most Bruxellians speak French, and since French is more familiar to most travelers than Flemish, *Let's Go* uses French.

Tourist Offices: National, 61, rue du Marché aux Herbes (tel. 504 03 90). From the Grand-Place, walk away from Town Hall 1 block. Books rooms throughout Belgium. Exhaustive *What's On* brochure (free). Open Mon.-Fri. 9am-7pm; Oct.-June 9am-1pm and 2-7pm. **TIB (Tourist Information Brussels),** in the Town Hall on the Grand-Place. Helpful but crowded (tel. 513 89 40). Free room reservations, *Brussels Guide and Map* (70BF). Theater, opera, and ballet tickets sold Mon.-Sat. 11am-5pm. Open daily 9am-6pm; Oct.-March Mon.-Sat. 9am-6pm.

Tours: Le Bus Bavard/De Babbelbus (tel. 673 18 35). Walking tour of the old city, then a bus to attractions on the outskirts. Tours (3hr.) leave daily May 20-Sept. 26 at 10am (in July also at 2pm) from the entrance to the St-Hubert Galleries at 90, rue Marché aux Herbes. (300BF; discount if staying in a youth hostel.)

Budget Travel: Acotra World, 51, rue de la Madeleine (tel. 512 70 78). Free room-finding; budget flights for those under 26. Open Mon.-Sat. 10am-5:30pm. **Infor-Jeunes,** 27, rue du Marché aux Herbes (tel. 512 32 19). Budget bonanza. Open Mon.-Fri. noon-5:45pm. Also at Gare du Midi (tel. 522 58 56) March-Oct.

Embassies: U.S., 27, bd. du Régent (tel. 513 38 30). **Canada,** 2, av. Tervurin (tel. 735 60 40). **U.K.,** 28, rue Joseph II (tel. 287 62 11). **Australia,** 6, rue Guimard (tel. 231 05 00). **New Zealand,** 47-48, bd. du Régent (tel. 512 10 40).

Currency Exchange: At Gare du Nord (open daily 7am-9:45pm, 20BF commission), Gare Centrale (open daily 8am-8pm; no commission, mediocre rates) and Gare du Midi (open daily 7am-11pm, 20BF commission). Almost every bank and *change* booth charges 100-150BF to cash checks, but banks have better rates.

American Express: 2, pl. Louise (tel. 512 17 40). Mo. Louise. Decent exchange rates. Open Mon.-Fri. 9am-5pm, Sat. 9:30am-noon. Holds mail for 30 days. Charges 50BF to retrieve mail if you don't have an AmEx card or Cheques.

Post Office: Mo. de Brouckere. **Main office** on the 2nd floor of the Centre Monnaie, the tall building on pl. de la Monnaie. Open Mon.-Fri. 9am-6pm, Sat. 9am-noon. **Poste Restante Code:** 1000 Bruxelles 1.

Telephones: 17, bd. de l'Impératrice, near Gare Centrale. Open daily 8am-10pm. Far superior rates to privately owned competitors. **Public Phone** (a private company) at 30a, rue de Lombard, open daily 10am-8pm. High rates in a more pleasant atmosphere. For operator assistance in Brussels, dial 1280. **City Code:** 02.

Flights: Tel. 722 31 11. Flight info tel. 723 60 10. Trains to **Brussels International Airport** (80BF) depart Gare Centrale 5:39am-11:14pm; all stop at Gare du Nord.

Trains: Tel. 219 28 80. Most trains stop at **Gare Centrale,** and many stop at either **Gare du Nord** (in a neighborhood that could have served as the movie set for "Blade Runner") or **Gare du Midi** as well. Traffic to **Gare du Quartier Leopold** generally passes through one of the main stations.

Buses: STIB (Société des Transports Intercommunaux Bruxellois). Offices in Gare du Midi (open Mon.-Fri. 7:30am-6pm, Sat. 8:30-4:30pm), and at 20, Galeries de la Toison d'Or, 6th floor (tel. 515 30 64). **L'Épervier,** 50, pl. de Brouckere (tel.

217 00 25). Mo. Brouckere. Belgian representative of Europabus; low fares to major cities. Open Mon.-Fri. 9am-6pm, Sat. 9am-12:30pm and 1:30-4:30pm.

Luggage Storage: Lockers and offices at the 3 major train stations; 60BF/day.

Public Transportation: 50BF buys 2hrs. of travel on buses, the **Métro** (Mo.), and trams. Tickets at any Métro or train station, or on the bus. Forego the many passes; the city is quite walkable. Public transportation runs 6am-midnight.

Hitchhiking: Hitchhiking is on the decline in Belgium; it is illegal to hitch on motorways and sliproads. Those hitching to Antwerp and Amsterdam take tram #52 from Gare du Midi or Gare du Nord to Heysel, the terminus. About 300m from the terminus, they fork right for Antwerp. Those going to Liège and Cologne take tram #90 from the Gare du Nord to Mo. Diamant to reach the E40. Those headed to Ghent, Bruges and Oostende take bus #85 from the Bourse to one stop before the terminus and follow the E40 signs. Those going to Paris take tram #52 (direction "Gare du Midi") to rue de Stalle and walk toward the E19.

Bookstore: W.H. Smith, 71-75, bd. Adolphe Max (tel. 219 27 08). Mo. de Brouckere. Vast and pricey. Open Wed.-Mon. 9am-6:30pm, Tues. 10am-6:30pm.

Laundromat: Salon Lavoir, 5, rue Haute, around the corner from Breugel's youth hostel. Mo. Gare Centrale. Wash and dry 210BF. Open Mon.-Fri. 8am-6pm.

Crisis Hotline: SOS-Jeunes, 27, rue Mercellis (tel. 512 90 20). 24 hrs.

Pharmacies: Pharma-Congrès, 56, rue du Congrès, at rue du Nord, near the Jacques Brel hostel. Mo. Gare Centrale. Open Mon.-Fri. 8:30am-1pm and 1:30-5:30pm. **Neos-Bourse Pharmacie,** bd. Anspach at rue du Marché aux Polets. Mo. Bourse. Open Mon.-Fri. 8:30am-6:30pm, Sat. 9am-6:30pm.

Medical Assistance: Free Clinic, 154a, chaussée de Wavre (tel. 512 13 14). Don't be misled by the name; you do have to pay for medical attention. Open Mon.-Fri. 9am-6pm. **24-hr. medical services** (tel. 479 18 18 or 648 80 00).

Emergencies: Ambulance or **First Aid:** tel. 112. **Police:** tel. 101.

ACCOMMODATIONS AND CAMPING

Should you decide to stay the night, Brussels offers a small herd of hostels. The tourist office in the Grand-Place and Acotra will help you find other places.

Gîtes d'Étape: Auberge de Jeunesse "Jacques Brel" (HI), 30, rue de la Sablonnière (tel. 218 01 87), on the pl. des Barricades; 10min. from Gare du Nord, 15min. from Gare Centrale. Mo. Madou. Institutional rooms, each with shower. Bar and terrace. Reception open 7am-1am. Curfew 1am. Dorms 380BF. Singles 620BF. Doubles 510BF. Triples and quads 425BF. Breakfast included. Sheets 120BF. Wheelchair accessible. Call ahead because hostel fills up quickly.

CHAB, 8, rue Traversière (tel. 217 01 58). Mo. Botanique. From Gare du Nord, take bus #61 or walk 10min. From Gare Centrale, take bus #65 or 66 to rue du Méridien. Vincent van Gogh wrote that "my modest room costs 50 francs a month. Bread is included, and a cup of coffee every morning..." Prices may have changed, but breakfast is still free. Kitchen. Lockout 10am-4pm. Curfew 2am. Large dorms 290BF. Smaller dorms 370BF. Singles 600BF. Doubles 500BF. Triples and quads 430BF/person. Large lockers 100BF deposit. Sheets 100BF. Laundry 150BF.

Sleep Well, 27, rue de la Blanchisserie (tel. 218 50 50). Mo. Rogier. From Gare du Nord, walk to pl. Rogier and continue to rue Neuve, then take 1st left. Tintin and his little dog are the official mascots. Fading murals and cramped hallways, but friendly and relaxed staff. Lockout 10am-5pm; lounge and small lockers (20BF) open 24 hrs. Curfew 1am. "Sleep-ins" (huge dorms) 220BF (July-Aug.). Dorms 295BF. Singles 495BF. Doubles 425BF. Triples and quads 375BF. 10% off with ISIC, 25% off if your passport number has "27" anywhere in it, 50% off if it contains the letters "SLEEP WELL," and free if it's your birthday! Showers and breakfast included. Sheets 80BF. Restaurant and bar open Mon.-Sat. 6-11pm. In summer of 1994 it'll move next door (22, rue de Damier) to become **Brusswell,** with wheelchair access and laundry facilities. Similar quirky discounts: you'll have the lucky passport if it contains the letters "BRUSSWELL" or the number 22.

Bruegel (HI), 2, rue du St. Esprit (tel. 511 04 36), behind Notre-Dame-de-la-Chapelle. Mo. Gare Centrale. Excellent location. Lockout 10am-2pm. Curfew midnight. Dorms 380BF. Singles 620BF. Doubles 510BF. Quads 425BF. Showers and breakfast included. Dinner 250BF. Packed lunch 140BF. Free lockers with 100BF deposit. Sheets 120BF. Wheelchair accessible. Make reservations in summer.

Hôtel Pacific, 57, rue Antoine Dansaert (tel. 511 84 59). Mo. Bourse. Fine location, and friendly English-speaking management. Flexible midnight curfew. Singles 900BF. Doubles 1250-1450BF. Showers 100BF. Breakfast included.

Pension Bosquet, 70, rue Bosquet (tel. 538 52 30). Mo. Hotel des Monnaies. Plaster falling off the walls, but fairly inexpensive rooms, some with small terraces. Reception open 8am-11pm. Singles 900BF, with shower 1200-1300BF. Doubles 1200BF, with shower 1650BF. Quads with shower 2600BF. Hall showers 100BF. Breakfast included. Reserve in summer.

Camping: All sites are outside Brussels. First choice is **Paul Rosmant,** 52 Warandeberg (tel. 782 10 09), in Wezembeck-Oppem. Reception open 9am-12:30pm and 2-10pm. 120BF/person. Open April-Sept. Just north of Brussels in Grimbergen is **Veldkant,** 64 Veldkantstr. (tel. 269 25 97). Take bus G or H from Gare du Nord; alight at Grimbergen. 100BF/person, 100BF/tent. Open April-Oct.

FOOD

Brussels restaurants range from expensive to outrageous. Inexplicably renowned in this landlocked city are the seafood establishments along the touristy rue des Bouchers. Also try the city's plentiful *frites* stands and snack bars, supplemented with an ever-so-scrumptious Belgian waffle. Find daily **markets** at pl. Ste-Catherine (daily 7am-5pm), pl. Emile Bockstael (Sat. 7am-2pm), and Chauss. D'Anvers (Wed. 7am-1pm). **GB** supermarkets are at 248, rue Vierge Noire (Mo. Bourse; open Sat.-Thurs. 9am-7:50pm, Fri. 9am-8:50pm) and in the "City 2" shopping center, 50m from the Sleep Well. (Mo. Rogier. Open Sat.-Thurs. 10am-7pm, Fri. 10am-8pm.)

Chez Léon, 18-20, rue des Bouchers, just off the Grand-Place. Mo. Gare Centrale. Deep in the tourist maelstrom, but fun. Hamburgers and Brussels' famed mussels (large portions 315-595BF). *Plat du jour* 315BF. Open daily noon-1am.

Le Grand Café, 78, bd. Anspach, on the other side of the *Bourse*. Mo. Bourse. Generous menus include appetizer, main course and dessert (465-695BF). Open Sun.-Mon. 7am-midnight, Fri.-Sat. 7am-1am.

L'École Buissonnière, 13, rue de Traversière (tel. 217 01 65), opposite CHAB youth hostel. Mo. Botanique. Great lunch menus (300BF). Ask to dine on the patio. Open Mon.-Fri. noon-2:30pm and 6:30-10:00pm.

SIGHTS AND ENTERTAINMENT

Victor Hugo dubbed the magnificent collection of guildhalls and public buildings that is the **Grand-Place** "the most beautiful square in the world." The 15th-century **Town Hall** on the *place* is open to the curious. (Open Tues.-Fri. 9:30am-12:15pm and 1:45-5pm, Sun. 10am-noon and 2-4pm, Oct.-March 9:30am-12:12pm and 1:45-4pm.) Three blocks behind the Town Hall on rue de l'Etuve at rue du Chêne is Brussels's most giggled-at sight, the **Mannekin-Pis,** a fountain of a small boy urinating. One story goes that a 17th-century mayor of Brussels promised to build a statue in the position that his lost son was found; another says it commemorates a boy who ingeniously extinguished a fuse which had been lit to blow up the Town Hall.

The **Musée d'Art Ancien,** 3, rue de la Régence (Mo. Gare Centrale or Parc), displays a huge collection of early Flemish masters, including Pieter Brueghel the Elder's *Fall of Icarus* and *Census in Bethlehem*. (Open Tues.-Sun. 10am-noon and 1-5pm. Free.) Next door is the spruced-up **Musée d'Art Moderne,** 1, pl. Royale, a huge, 8-level underground museum housing the best of 19th and 20th-century Belgian Modernists. (Open Tues.-Sun. 10am-1pm and 2-5pm. Free.) The **Musées Royaux d'Art et d'Histoire,** 10, parc du Cinquantenaire (Mo. Merode), cover a wide variety of periods and genres—Roman torsos missing their heads, Syrian heads missing their torsos, and Egyptian caskets with protruding wooden feet. (Open Tues.-Fri. 9:30am-12:30pm and 1:30-4:45pm, Sat.-Sun. and holidays 10am-4:45pm. Free.) The **Botanical Gardens,** on rue Royal, provide a picturesque, quiet spot to relax in the heart of downtown Brussels. (Mo. Botanique. Open daily 10am-10pm. Free.) The recently renovated but still dull **Atomium** (Mo. Heysel), a gigantic model of an iron atom, is the putative symbol of Brussels. (Open daily 10am-8pm. 160BF.)

Brussels, the "Comic Strip Capital of the World," is home to the **Belgian Comic Strip Centre,** in the art-nouveau Waucquez Warehouse, 20, rue des Sables, near the rue de St-Laurent. It contains originals of the most famous Belgian comic strips and many Tintin comics. (Open Tues.-Sun. 10am-6pm. 150BF.) For more of the city's art nouveau architecture, visit the classy café and dance hall **De Ultieme Hallucinatie,** 316, rue Royale (tel. 217 06 14). Take tram #92 or 94. (Bar open Mon.-Fri. from 11am, Sat.-Sun. from 4pm.) Baron Victor Horta is the style's greatest representative; his house, the **Musée Horta,** is at 25, rue Américaine; take tram #81 or 92. (Open Tues.-Sun. 2-5:30pm. 100BF, weekends 200BF.) The newly refurbished **St. Michael's Cathedral,** Brussels' most impressive Gothic edifice, will give you a glimpse of how the city's older buildings looked before smog came to town.

The **Cinema Museum,** 9, rue Baron Horta (tel. 513 41 55), Mo. Gare Centrale, shows 2 silent movies per night with piano accompaniment and 3 talkies, sometimes in English with French subtitles. (Open 5:30-10:30pm. 80BF/2-hrs.) To get more frenzy for your franc, string along the nightclubs, discos, and bars around av. Louise and rue de Livourne. **La Mort Subite,** 7, rue Montagne-aux-Herbes-Potagères, is one of Brussels' oldest and best-known cafés, located across the street from the entrance to Galeries St. Hubert opposite the Grand-Place. (Open daily 10:30am-midnight. Beer 50BF. Coffee 55BF.) **L'Ecume des Nuits,** 122a, Galerie Louise, at pl. Stéphanie, spins funk. (Open Fri.-Sat. 10pm-dawn.) For live jazz hang out in the mellow 17th century tavern, **Au bon vieux Temps,** tucked away in a dark alley at 12 Rue aux Herbes, just off the Grand-Place. (Open Sun.-Thurs. 11am-11pm, Fri.- Sat 11am-2am. Beers from 70BF.) From June through September, concerts frequently pop up on the **Grand-Place,** on pl. de la Monnaie, and in the **Parc de Bruxelles.** The **Théâtre Royal des Galleries** offers popular theater but presents it only in French (tel. 513 23 28; tickets 150-800BF). For more events information, snag a calendar at the tourist office or call **BBB Agenda** (tel. 512 82 77).

■ Near Brussels

Louvain Twenty minutes outside of Brussels, just over the language border, stands the ancient university town of **Louvain (Leuven).** The colorful Flemish Renaissance façades provide a flamboyant cover for scores of tiny cafés and bars, frequented by an often raucous student population. The **Stadhuis** (Town Hall) is perhaps the most sculpture-burdened Gothic edifice in Europe. (Visit by guided tour only. Open Mon.-Fri. 11am and 3pm, Sun. 3pm; March-Oct. 3pm.) Across from the Stadhuis is **St. Pieterskerk,** a 15th-century church with a collection of paintings by Dirk Bouts, including his *Last Supper.* (Open Mon.-Sat. 10am-noon and 2-5pm, Sun 2-5pm; Oct.15-March 15 Tues.-Sat. 10am-noon and 2-5pm.) The 50BF admission includes the **Museum Vander Kalen-Mertens** at Savoyestraat 6. Down Naamsestr. is the **Groot Begijnhof,** a lovely "city within a city." Built with brick and sandstone during the 17th and 18th centuries, the buildings once housed *Beguines,* women scorned because they insisted on keeping their own property and supporting themselves *(mon dieu,* what brazenness!); university students now frolic in the area. Louvain is home both to Belgium's largest (Interbrew) and smallest (Domus) **breweries.** The latter, at Tiensestraat 8, has taps running directly from its brewery to its tavern (beer 45BF). Thursday is party night, since most students return home for the weekend. Each Friday in July hosts a different festival; the first is a **classical music festival,** with violinists playing on rooftops and balconies. On August 13-15 Louvain busts loose for the **Markt Rock festival** (most concerts free; finale 100BF).

Students in Louvain live in *Kots,* houses overseen by often stern women known as *Kotmadams;* during the summer, some of them open their doors to travelers. Try the *Kot* at De Beriotstraat 13. (tel. (016) 40 02 88. Singles 800BF, doubles 1400BF, triples 200BF.) Trains leave hourly from Brussels (130 BF). From the station, walk down Bondgenotenlaan to pick up a map (10BF) at the **tourist office,** Naamsestr. 1a (tel. (016) 21 15 39; open Mon.-Fri. 8am-5pm, Sat.-Sun. 10am-5pm).

Waterloo   Napoleon was caught with both hands in his shirt at **Waterloo,** south of Brussels. Climb the **Lion Mound** for a superb view of the plains where he was defeated. (Open 9:30am-6:30pm; Nov.-March 10:30am-4pm. Last entry ½hr. before closing. 40BF.) The **Musée Wellington** explains European politics before and after the little guy, and has hour-by-hour descriptions of the battles. (Open daily 9:30am-6:30pm; mid-Nov. to March 10:30am-5pm. 70BF, students 50BF, children 40BF.) To reach Waterloo, take bus W (every 1½-2hr.; 40BF each way) from pl. Rouppe in Brussels (accessible via tram #90), or take the train from Brussels (130BF) and walk 1km to the city center. From there, bus #34 will deliver you to the Lion Mound.

■■■ BRUGES (BRUGGE)

Bruges, the capital of Flanders, is Europe's sleeping beauty. This wealthy Renaissance town went into hibernation 500 ago, as accumulating silt from the River Zwin cut it off from the sea and its livelihood. But in 1907, a 2nd seaport—Zeebrugge—was attached to the town, and Bruges awoke. The result: northern Renaissance architecture is better preserved here than anywhere else in Europe. Remarkable façades reflect in the canals, and horse-drawn carriages clop over cobblestones. The romance and beauty draws travelers from all over the world: Bruges is becoming a popular place for Japanese marriages and honeymoons.

ORIENTATION AND PRACTICAL INFORMATION

Many make Bruges a daytrip from Antwerp or Brussels, but it's wiser to make Brussels a daytrip from Bruges. A highway and canal encircle the town; other canals flow through it. All converge at the **Markt,** a handsome square presided over by the **belfort** (belfry). The train station lies just outside the ring, due south of the Markt.

Tourist Office: Burg 11 (tel. 44 86 86), just east of the Markt, in the town's other main square, the Burg. Turn left out of the station and enter 't Zand Sq., then turn right on Zuid-Zuidzandstr. Books rooms (400BF deposit) and sells a good map for 20BF. Open Mon.-Fri. 9:30am-6:30pm, Sat.-Sun. 10am-noon and 2-6:30pm; Oct.-March Mon.-Fri. 9:30am-5pm, Sat. 9:30am-12:45pm and 2-5pm. Smaller office at the train station also sells maps and books hotels (open Mon.-Sat. 2:45-9pm; Nov.-Feb. Mon.-Sat. 1:45-8pm). **Youth Information Center: JAC,** Kleine Hertsbergestr. 1 (tel. 33 83 06), near the Burg, just off Hoogstraat. Lists cheap rooms and restaurants. Also a youth crisis center. Open Mon. and Wed. 9am-noon and 1:30-8pm, Tues. 1:30-8pm, Fri. 9am-noon and 1:30-6pm, Sat. 10am-12:30pm.
Post Office: Markt 5. Poste Restante. Open Mon.-Fri. 9am-6pm. **Postal Code:** 8000.
Telephones: City Code: 050.
Trains: Train station on Stationsplein (tel. 38 23 82), a 15min. walk south of the city center. Open daily 6:30am-10:30pm. Frequent connections to Antwerp (360BF), Brussels (345BF), and Ghent (155BF).
Bike Rental: At the train station, it's 150BF/day with train ticket, 280BF without. **Koffieboontje,** Hallestr. 4 (tel. 33 80 27), off the Markt next to the belfry, charges 250BF 1st day, 150BF thereafter; students 110BF, 850BF/week.
Hitchhiking: The train system is so efficient and so (relatively) cheap that hitching is not that attractive an option. Those hitching to Brussels take bus #7 to St. Michiels or pick up the highway behind the station.
Luggage Storage: At the train station 60BF. Lockers (15BF) at the tourist office.
Laundromat: Belfort, Ezelstr. 51, next to Snuffel's Traveller's Inn. Wash 'n' dry 120-240BF. Open daily 7am-10pm.
Emergencies: Ambulance, tel. 100, **Police** tel. 101.

ACCOMMODATIONS, CAMPING, AND FOOD

While the official hostel is spotless, the private hostels are more central and heaps more fun. Arrive before noon in June, July, and August.

Bauhaus International Youth Hotel, Langestr. 135-137 (tel. 34 10 93), 10min. from the Markt. Bus #6 from the station (30BF). The party never stops. Restaurant open 6pm-midnight (entrees 185BF-400BF). Co-ed dorms 295BF. Singles 550BF. Doubles 950BF. Triples and quads 320BF/person. Showers and breakfast included. Lockers available (30BF). Reception open 8am-2am.

The Passage, Dweersstr. 26 (tel. 34 02 32), 1 block from 't Zand. Sparkling clean, above a cozy bar. Restaurant serves Belgian specialities and vegetarian meals 6pm-midnight (195BF-370BF); free Belgian beer with meal if you're staying here. No lockout or curfew. Dorms 310-375BF. Showers and breakfast included. Reception open 9am-midnight; bar open 5pm-3am. Live concerts every 2 weeks (free if staying in the hostel). 5% discount off more expensive rooms with a *Let's Go*.

Snuffel's Traveller's Inn, Ezelstr. 49 (tel. 33 31 33), 10min. from the Markt; follow Sint-Jakobstr., which turns into Ezelstr. Bus #3, 8, 9, or 13 from the station. A funhouse. Hip bar and café downstairs. No lockout or curfew. Co-ed dorms 325BF. Doubles 450BF. Showers and breakfast included. Reception open 10am-midnight. Ask about doing chores in exchange for a free night's stay.

Europa Jeugdherberg (HI), Baron Ruzettelaan 143 (tel. 35 26 79), 25min. south from the Markt; take bus #2 to "Steenbrugge" (2nd stop). Clean and slick, but comparatively dull and far away. Attracts grammar-school groups. Reception open 7:30-10am and 1-11pm. Lockout 10am-1pm. No curfew. Dorms 335BF. 4-bed rooms with shower 1700BF. Nonmembers add 100BF. Showers and breakfast included. Dinner 230BF. Wheelchair access. Free lockers. Sheets 120BF. Bar open 6pm-midnight. Cheapest beer in city (30BF). Reserve ahead.

Hotel Lybeer, Korte Vulderstraat 31 (tel. 33 43 55), just off 't Zand Sq. Fresh and pretty rooms and an elegant reception area. Singles 900BF. Doubles 1500BF. Triples 2100BF. Breakfast and showers included. Reception open 8am-midnight.

Camping: Memling, Veltemweg 109 (tel. 35 58 45), 2km from town center. Bus #11 or 58A from the station. Friendly, cozy camping spot off the beaten path. 150BF/person, 100BF/tent. Restaurant open 6-10:30pm (130BF-450BF).

Bruges offers 2 unusually cheap but tasty restaurants. **Ganzespel,** Ganzestr. 37, cooks up delicious Flemish specialties; don't be put off by the coarse and vocal service. Soup 80BF. *Dagschotel* 210BF. (Open Wed.-Sun noon-2pm and 6-10pm.) **The Lotus,** near the Markt at Wapenmakerstr. 5, dishes out vegetarian plates (210-230BF) in a mellow atmosphere. (Open mid-Aug. to July 10am-2pm.) Forage through the **Nopri Supermarket** at Noordzanstr. 4, near the Markt. (Open Mon.-Thurs. and Sat. 9am-6:30pm, Fri. 9am-7pm.) **Markets** take over **'t Zand Sq.** every Saturday morning and the **Burg** every Wednesday morning until 1pm.

SIGHTS AND ENTERTAINMENT

Bruges is best seen on foot; the tourist office suggests excellent walking tours. You can't miss the Markt's grand architectural flagship, the **belfort,** subtly luminous by night. Climb its 366 steps for a stupefying panorama but go early to enjoy it alone. (Open daily 9:30am-5:30pm (tickets sold only until 4:15pm); Nov.-March 9:30am-12:30pm and 1:30-5pm. 100BF, students 80BF.) The 14th-century **Stadhuis** (Town Hall) on nearby Burg Sq. is flamboyantly Gothic. (Open daily 9:30am-5pm; Oct.-March 9:30am-noon and 2-5pm. 60BF.) Masterpieces of Jan van Eyck and Gerard David are displayed in the splendid **Groeninge Museum** on Dijverstr. (Open daily 9:30am-5pm; Oct.-March Wed.-Sun. 9:30am-noon and 2-5pm. 130BF, students 70BF.) Next door is the **Gruuthuse Museum,** in the 15th-century residence of wealthy beer magnates. The museum today hosts a collection of historic weapons, musical instruments, pottery, lace, and coins. (Open daily 9:30am-5pm; Oct.-March Wed.-Mon. 9:30am-noon and 2-5pm. 130BF, students 70BF.) The **Church of Our Lady** contains the only Michelangelo to leave Italy during the master's lifetime, a touching *Madonna and Child.* (Open Mon.-Sat. 10-11:30am and 2:30-5pm, Sun. 2:30-5pm; Oct.-March closes ½hr. earlier in the evenings. 30BF.)

If **cycling** is more your speed, try **Bruges with Bart** bike tours, which depart from the Markt at 10am (350BF includes bike rental; tickets at Boekhandel De Reyghere, Markt 12). **The Back Road Bike Co.** explores remote windmills and castles by mountain bike. Tours leave the tourist office on op de Burg. (July-Aug. daily at 10am, 400BF; at 2pm, 450BF; March-June and Sept.-Oct. daily at 1pm, 400BF. Groups limited to 15 and fill quickly. Call 34 30 45 for more information.) **Boat tours** along Bruges's picturesque and winding canals leave every ½-hour (10am-6pm) from 5 points on the main canal (150BF); call the tourist office for more information.

The best nightlife in Bruges is free—wandering through gloomy, romantic streets and over cobblestone bridges after sunset. Serious beer-drinkers will go nuts in **Brugs Beertje,** Kemelstr. 5, where proprietor Jan De Bruyne bubbles with enthusiasm about the proper way to serve and drink the 300-plus brands he stocks. (Open Mon.-Tues. and Thurs. 4pm-1am, Sat.-Sun. 4pm-2am. Beers 50BF and up.) Sample lemon or apple *jenever*, a potent Dutch liquor, next door at **Dreiple Huis.** The crowd at **L'ObCèDè,** right off 't Zand, dances the night away (8pm-3am, no cover).

During the **Festival van Vlaanderen** (July 23-Aug. 11), the entire town pulses with the **International Fortnight of Music.** On Ascension Day, while the rest of Belgium snoozes, Bruges oozes with medieval fare during the **Festival of the Holy Blood** (May 12 in 1994). Snatch the monthly program *Agenda Brugge* (free) at the tourist office for a schedule of local events.

■ Near Bruges

Informative **Quasimodo** tours (tel. (050) 37 04 70) are one way to explore Flanders while keeping Bruges as a base. One tour somberly patrols the battlefields of the World Wars (Mon. and Sat. 1300BF); another giddily hops through Flemish breweries (Tues. and Thurs. 1300BF—samples included); a 3rd checks out the North Sea coast (Wed. and Fri. 1300BF). Conducted in English, these tours leave various hostels and hotels around 9am, return around 5pm, and include a picnic lunch.

The towns of the North Sea coast of Belgium win fans largely for their beaches. Ferries, ships, and jetfoils chug daily to the U.K. from **Zeebrugge** and **Oostende,** easily accessible by train from Bruges. Get tickets from travel agents, at ports, or in the Oostende train station. **P&O European Ferries** (Brussels tel. (02) 231 19 37; Oostende tel. (059) 70 76 01; Zeebrugge tel. (050) 54 22 22) sails between Oostende and Dover (7/day), Zeebrugge and Dover (6/day), and Zeebrugge and Felixstowe (2/day). (One way 1370BF, 60-hr. round-trip 1370BF, 5-day round-trip 2000BF.) In Oostende, the **De Ploate youth hostel (HI),** Langestr. 82 (tel. (059) 80 52 97), is 5 minutes from the station (reception open 8am-6pm). Campgrounds freckle the coast; 2 options are **De Vuurtoren,** Heistlaan 168, in Knokke (tel. (050) 51 17 82; 90BF/person, 190BF/tent; open mid-March to mid-Oct.) and **Jamboree,** Polderlaan 55, in Blankenberge (tel. (050) 41 45 45; 120BF/person, 150BF/tent).

■■■ GHENT (GENT)

Three great medieval towers rise above the central squares in Ghent, attesting to the city's wealthy heritage. In the 14th-century, a raging textile industry lifted Ghent into the ranks of Europe's great cities, and on the continent, only Paris exceeded it in size and splendor. The modern city has lost some of its Renaissance glory, but a twilight stroll along the gloriously illuminated canals shows that it still challenges the beauty of Bruges and the *savoir faire* of Antwerp.

PRACTICAL INFORMATION

Tourist Office: Municipal Tourist Office, in the crypt of the town hall on Botermarkt (tel. 224 15 55). Take tram #1 or 12 from the train station to the main post office, then head down Klein Turkije. Maps and informative walking-tour booklets. Open daily 9:30am-6:30pm; Nov.-March 9:30am- 4:30pm.

Budget Travel: JOKER/Acotra, Overpoorstr. 58 (tel. 221 97 94). BIJ tickets and helpful advice. Open Mon.-Fri. 10am-1:15pm and 2-6pm, Sat. 10am-1pm; Sept.-April Mon.-Fri. 10am-1:15pm and 2-6pm. **Taxi-Stop,** Onderbergen 51 (tel. 223 23 10). Matches drivers with riders (1.3BF/km), books cheap last-minute flights (tel. 224 00 23) and sells **Eurolines** bus tickets. Open Mon.-Fri. 9am-6pm.

Post Office: Korenmarkt 16 (tel. 225 20 34). Poste Restante. One of the lovelier buildings in town. Open Mon.-Fri. 8am-6pm Sat. 9am-noon. **Postal Code:** 9000.

Telephones: Keizer Karelstr. 1. Buy telephone cards here or at any newsstand. Open Mon.-Thurs. 8am-4pm, Fri. 8am-6pm. **City Code:** 09.

Trains: Trams #1, 10, 11 and 12 run between **Sint-Pieters Station** (tel. 222 44 44) on the southern edge of the city, and Korenmarkt, the center of the old city. Frequent trains to Bruges (155BF), Brussels (250BF), and Antwerp (230BF).

Hitchhiking: Ghent lies at the intersection of the E40, connecting Brussels and Germany with Oostende, and the E17, linking Paris and Amsterdam. Hitchers turn right out of the station onto Clementinalaan, which becomes Burggravenlaan, and continue until they reach the E17.

Laundromat: St. Jacobsnieuwstr. 85. Open daily 8am-10pm. Wash and dry 140BF; bring plenty o' 20BF coins.

Emergencies: Ambulance: tel. 100, **Police:** tel. 101; headquarters: tel. 266 61 11.

ACCOMMODATIONS, CAMPING, AND FOOD

Ghent is a fairly expensive place to stay. Travelers can often find an open bed in the dorms of Ghent's **university** (June 15-Sept. 15; single with sink 500BF, breakfast and shower included). Call the office at Stalhof 6 (tel. 222 09 11) for information and reservations. In a pinch, **De IJzer,** Vlaanderenstr. 117 (tel. 225 98 73), near Woodrow Wilsonplein, has small, dimly-lit rooms. Take tram #12 from the station to "Kouter." (Singles and doubles 1150BF. Showers and breakfast included.) **Camping Blaarmeersen,** Zuiderlaan 12 (tel. 221 53 99), is 15 blocks or a bus ride (#38) northwest of Sint-Pietersstation (100BF/person, 110BF/tent; open March to mid-Oct.).

When bread and cheese just won't do it anymore, treat yourself to a meal at **De Appelier,** Citadellaan 47 (tel. 221 67 33), near the Museum of Fine Arts. Their vegetarian plates (240-290BF) are scrumptious; ask to sit in the rose garden in back. (Open Sun.-Fri. 11:30am-2pm and 5:30-8pm, Sat. 11:30am-2:30pm.) At the student cafeteria **Overpoort,** in the Restaurant Rijksuniversiteit Gent building on Overpoortstr., near Citadellaan, you'll find typical student subsistence: macaroni, spaghetti and hamburgers (100-200BF; open 10:30am-2:30pm). Lovers of sweets will die and go to heaven when they enter the **Bloch Alsacienne Patisserie,** Veldstr. 60-62, a bakery shop stuffed with sinful, dripping platters of honey, nuts, and dough. (Open Mon.-Fri. 8am-7:30pm.) Atone with fruits and vegetables at the **Groentenmarkt** (open Mon.-Fri. 7am-1pm, Sat. 7am-7pm). Cheap *menus du jour (dagschotel)* can be found at several restaurants across from the post office (270BF-300BF).

SIGHTS AND ENTERTAINMENT

Ghent has more than its share of medieval edifices. The forbidding fortress **Gravensteen** stands on the Canal Sint-Veerleplein. (Open daily 9am-6pm; Oct.-March 9am-5pm. 80BF, students 40BF.) The august **Belfort** (belfry), in the city center, offers a 15th-century cloth hall, torture equipment, and a bronze dragon. (Open daily 10am-12:30pm and 2-5:30pm. 100BF with guide, 80BF without. Students 60BF.) The **Stadhuis** (Town Hall) on the corner is an arresting juxtaposition of Gothic and Renaissance architecture. Another block down on Limburgstr. lies **Sint-Baafskathedraal,** built between the 14th and 16th centuries; its real pearl is Jan van Eyck's *Adoration of the Mystic Lamb,* an imposing polyptych on wood panels. (Open Mon.-Sat. 9:30am-noon and 2-6pm, Sun. 1-6pm; Oct.-March Mon.-Sat. 10:30am-noon and 2:30-4pm, Sun. 2-5pm. Cathedral free. *Adoration* 50BF, students 40BF.) Also worth a visit is the **Museum voor Schone Kunsten** (Museum of Fine Arts), in the Citadel

Park, which lodges a strong Flemish collection and an outstanding exhibit of contemporary art. (Open Tues.-Sun. 9:30am-5pm. 80BF, students 40BF.)

Ghent houses a large university, and the city's nightlife lives and dies by its student population. From October to July 15, students cavort in the cafés and discos near the university restaurant on Overpoortstr. **Vooruit,** on Sint Petersniewstr., is a huge art-deco bar popular with collegiates. Its concert hall (tel. (09) 223 82 01 for reservations) features everything from rock to jazz to avant-garde. The café is always crowded. (Open Aug. 13-July 16 daily 10pm-3am.)

■■■ ANTWERP (ANTWERPEN)

The early commercial capital of Europe, Antwerp rode to the center of the Northern Renaissance behind the painting of the Flemish Old Masters—most notably, favorite son Rubens. Today commerce still rules; Antwerp's port is an international hub for the garment and diamond trade. Be sure to explore the mind-boggling art-deco mansions lining Cogels Osylei and the Orthodox Jewish quarter.

ORIENTATION AND PRACTICAL INFORMATION

Antwerp rests 40km north of Brussels on the Amsterdam-Brussels-Paris rail line. **Centraal Station** is true to its name. The **Meir,** an avenue lined with shops and eateries, connects it to the **Grote Markt** and **Groenplaats,** Antwerp's 2 major squares.

Tourist Office: Municipal Tourist Office, Grote Markt 15 (tel. 232 01 03). From the train station, turn left onto DeKeyserlei, which becomes Meir, and follow it to Groenplaats; turn right past the cathedral. Free hotel reservations. City map 10BF; whopping package of info plus map 20BF. Open Mon.-Sat. 9am-7:45pm, Sun. 9am-4:45pm.

Budget Travel: VTB, St. Jacobsmarkt 45-47 (tel. 234 34 34). Travel info and youth tickets. Open Mon.-Fri. 9am-5:30pm, Sat. 9am-12:30pm. **Jeugd-Info-Antwerpen,** Apostelstr. 20-22 (tel. 232 27 28). Open Mon.-Fri. 10am-7:30pm, Sat. 2-5pm.

Consulates: U.S., Nationalestr. 5 (tel. 225 00 71) **U.K.,** Korte Klarenstr. 7 (tel. 232 69 40). Open Mon. 8:30am-12:30pm, Tues.-Wed. 8:30am-12:30pm and 2-6pm, Thurs.-Fri. 8:30am-12:30pm.

Currency Exchange: Bureaus at Centraal Station have poor rates (10-50BF commission for cash, 50BF for traveler's checks), but one is open daily 8am-11pm. If the banks aren't open, you'll find the best rates at **American Express** and the **Thomas Cook** bureau on Koningen Astridplein, in front of the train station.

American Express: Frankrijklei 21 (tel. 232 59 20). Exchange and mail desk close at 5pm Mon.-Fri. 50BF to retrieve mail without AmEx card or Traveler's Cheque.

Post Office: Main office and Poste Restante on Groenplaats. Open Mon.-Fri. 7am-7pm, Sat. 7am-noon. Open Mon.-Fri. 9am-6pm. **Postal Code: 2000.**

Telephones: Jezusstr. 1. Open daily 8am-8pm. Also at Centraal Station. Open Mon.-Fri. 9am-noon and 12:30-5:15pm. **City Code: 03.**

Trains: Centraal Station, 15min. from the Grote Markt and most of the sights. 20 trains/day to Rotterdam (530BF) and Amsterdam (870BF), 4/hr. to Brussels (175BF). Lockers (15BF) are cheaper than checking your bags (60BF). Open Mon.-Fri. 3:30am-1:30am and Sat.-Sun. 4:30am-1:30am.

Public Transportation: Trams and buses 40BF; buy an 8-ride ticket for 185BF at Centraal Station and in tram and subway stops. Trains run 6am-midnight. Tourist offices offer a 24-hr. pass for all municipal transportation in Belgium (180BF).

Hitchhiking: Those heading to Germany, the Netherlands, and Ghent take bus #20 from the train station to the big interchange (Plantin en Moretuslei) outside town. Those going to Brussels and points south take tram #2 to the intersection of Jan Devoslei and Jan van Rijswijklaan.

Laundromat: Was-A-Tom, 34 Lange Koepoort, near the Grote Markt. Wash 80-110BF, dry 10-20BF. Open daily 7am-11pm.

Pharmacy: Apoteek devollesmacht, Nationalestr. 119. Open Mon.-Fri. 9am-12:30pm and 2-6:30pm. Pharmacies post the current *pharmacie de garde.*

Medical Assistance: Stuivenberg Hospital, Lange Beeldekenstr. 267 (tel. 217 71 11).

Emergencies: Ambulance: tel. 100. **Police:** tel. 101; headquarters, Oudlaan 5 (tel. 231 68 80).

ACCOMMODATIONS, CAMPING, AND FOOD

Budget accommodation possibilities are less than spectacular. Some cafés around the train station advertising "rooms for tourists" rent lodgings by the hour.

Jeugdherberg Op-Sinjoorke (HI), Eric Sasselaan 2 (tel. 238 02 73). Take tram #2 (direction "Hoboken") to "Bouwcentrum" or bus #27 to "Camille Huysmanslaan" and follow the signs. A hike, but handsome, modern, and moated. Kitchen, laundry, game room. Lockers for groups. Work 3hrs. and stay free, work 2 more and get 3 meals. Lockout 10am-5pm. Flexible midnight curfew. 335BF, nonmembers 435BF. Breakfast included. Lunch 120BF. Dinner 230BF. Bar open 5-11:30pm.

Boomerang Youth Hostel, Volkstr. 49 (tel. 238 47 82). From Centraal Station, take bus #23 to "Museum," or walk 25min. Vagabonds keep coming for the mellow, post-Amsterdam aura. Reception open 9am-10pm. Free lockers take padlocks. Movie every night at 8pm, terrace with barbecue. Dorms 350BF. Doubles 1000BF. Breakfast included. Dinner 200BF. Sheets 100BF.

New International Youth Home, Provinciestr. 256 (tel. 230 05 22). Take tram #11 from Centraal Station or walk left down Pelikaanstr., and another left onto Provinciestr.; 5th underpass under the railroad tracks (10min.). Squeaky clean and not far from the station. Changes money and sells maps. Reception open 8am-11pm. No lockout. Curfew 11pm, but night key available. Dorms 410BF. Singles 870BF. Doubles 1250-1350BF. Triples 1950BF. Quads 2200BF. Dinner at 7:30pm, 330BF. Sheets 120BF. Phone reservations encouraged.

Camping: Jan van Rijswijklaan, on Vogelzanglaan (tel. 238 57 17). Reception open 7am-10pm. 35BF/person, 35BF/tent. Shower 30BF. **De Molen,** on St. Annastrand (tel. 219 60 90). Reception open 7am-7pm. 35BF/person, 35BF/tent. Shower 20BF. Both open April-Sept.

Many Italian restaurants and pizzerias around the Groenplaats and the Grote Markt spoon out surprisingly tasty and cheap pasta. Try **Pizzeria Toni** (tel. 226 03 00), across from the Stadhuis (pasta and pizza from 230BF). Snag a seat on the 2nd floor for a spendid view. Or search out a "brown pub" such as **De Ware Jacob,** Vlasmarkt 19; the moniker is derived from their oak interiors (menu 350BF; open Mon.-Sat. 5pm-2am). Sink into the vegetarian **Atlantis,** Korte Nieuwstr. 6, where omelettes and cheese toast cost 125-220BF. (Open Mon. and Wed.-Fri. noon-2pm and 5-9:30pm, Sat.-Sun. 5-9:30pm.) Restaurant prices drop away from the main square. Look for signs advertising cheap (195-295BF) *dagschotel*, or wander south down Pelikaanstr. to the **Jewish District** for fine kosher shops and restaurants. A huge supermarket, **GB,** weighs down Schoenmarkt just off the Groenplaats. (Open Mon.-Thurs. 9am-8pm, Fri. 9am-9pm, Sat. 9am-8pm.)

SIGHTS AND ENTERTAINMENT

The **Stadhuis** (Town Hall), in Grote Markt in the **oude stad** (old city), is a noble example of Renaissance architecture. (Open Mon. 9am-noon, Tues.-Fri. 9am-3pm, Sat. noon-4pm. Closed during (frequent) official functions. 30BF.) The nearby **Kathedraal van Onze-Lieve-Vrouw,** Groenplaats 21, has a showy Gothic tower. Its interior is decorated with stained glass and Flemish masterpieces, notably Rubens's *Descent from the Cross* and *Exaltation of the Cross.* (Open Mon.-Fri. 9am-6pm, Sat. 9am-3pm, Sun. 1-4pm. 60BF.) Few tourists get to **Cogels Osylei,** an avenue in southeastern Antwerp with a procession of eclectic art nouveau mansions. The little-known **Mayer van den Bergh Museum** at Lange Gasthuisstr. 19 harbors Brueghel's *Mad Meg* and other works. (Open Tues.-Sun. 10am-5pm. 75BF, students 30BF.)

Antwerp has a mild obsession with Peter Paul Rubens, who built **Rubens Huis,** Wapper 9 (off Meir), and filled it with a trove of art. (Open daily 10am-5pm. 75BF, students 30BF.) The **Royal Art Gallery,** Leopold De Waelplaats 1-9, showcases one of the best collections of Old Flemish Masters (from the 14th-17th centuries) in the world, as well as some monumental Rubens canvases. Natural lighting and the originality of its exhibit designs have made this gallery a model for many others. (Open Tues.-Sun. 10am-5pm. Main galleries free; special exhibits be pricey.)

Antwerp's best night is Monday, when from mid-June to mid-September the bells ring from 9 to 10pm, signaling everyone to file into the bars surrounding the Grote Markt. The **Pelgrom,** Pelgrimsstr. 15, is a converted 16th-century wine cellar specializing in Belgian ale (from 55BF). (Open daily 11:30am-late.) **Bierland,** Korte Nieuwstr. 28, offers over 400 varieties of Belgian beer (from 40BF; open Sun.-Thurs. 11am-late, Fri.-Sat. noon-late). For movie listings or a guide to events, pick up the monthly *Antwerpen* at the tourist office.

■■■ NAMUR AND THE ARDENNES

Heart of Wallony and gateway to the Ardennes Forest, **Namur** is an ideal base for venturing into the Belgian provinces of Namur, Liège, and Luxembourg (not the independent country); castles, caves, and kayaks greet those who forge beyond the city. Trains link the larger towns, and buses, though infrequent, cover the rest.

Not quite an hour's train ride from Brussels, Namur itself deserves exploration. The scars of 20 sieges have faded, but the city's immense **citadel** still glowers from its rocky perch. Start the steep climb or ride the *téléférique* (cable car) from Grognon, a hill on the southern edge of the city. (Open daily 10am-7pm; July-Aug. 10am-11pm; in winter Sat.-Sun. only, 10am-7pm. 160 BF, round-trip 190 BF.) The 2-hour visit includes a historical film, a museum, a guided tour through underground passages, and a train ride around the fort (195BF). To get down from the citadel in a hurry, rent a **mountain bike** at the high station of the *télésiège* (150BF). A host of small museums populates Namur. For those inspired by spirits of all sorts, the **Abbaye de Floreffe** gives tours of both its 18th-century monastery and its brewery. Take bus #10, direction "Chatelineau" to Floreffe. (Open March-Oct. Mon.-Fri. 11am-6pm, Sat.-Sun. 11am-8pm. 80BF, students 60BF. Beer 60BF.)

Accommodations, Food, and Practical Information For a complete list of all 13 museums visit the **city tourist office** in the train station (tel. (081) 23 07 70; open April-Sept. daily 8am-5pm; city map 10BF). First stop for those itching to get out of the city and into the cool valleys of the Ardennes should be the **provincial tourist office,** 3, rue de Notre Dame (tel. (081) 22 29 98; open Mon.-Fri. 8am-5pm). For youth travel information, consult **Infor-Jeunes,** Beffroi 4 (tel. (081) 22 38 12), in Namur's medieval belfry. (Open daily 11:30am-6pm.)

The **Auberge Félicien Rops (HI),** 8, av. Félicien Rops (tel. (081) 22 36 88), in a residential neighborhood on the banks of the Meuse river, ranks among the classiest youth hostels ever to hit the budget traveler scene, with laundry service (240BF), kitchen facilities, bountiful meals, and bargain brew. It also rents bikes (100BF a day), and books 10% dicount kayaking trips. Ask about working for free lodging and food (3 week- 1 month periods). (Take bus #3 or #4 across the street from the station to La Plante. 335BF, nonmembers 435BF. Breakfast included. Packed lunch 120BF. Dinner 230BF. Sheets 120BF. Flexible midnight curfew.) **Les Trieux,** 99, rue des Tris (tel. (081) 44 55 83), in Malonne, is your best "wilderness" option. Take bus #6 for 6km to Malonne. (75BF/person, 50BF/tent. 30BF/hot shower. Cold showers free. Brrrr. Open April-Oct.) **Le Parisien,** 16, rue Emile Cuvelier, has a lunchtime *menu* for 290BF. (Open daily noon-2pm.)

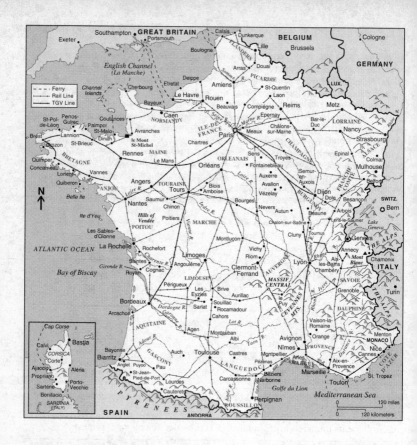

France

US$1 = 5.61F (francs)
CDN$1 = 4.27F
UK£1 = 8.69F
IR£1 = 8.15F
AUS$1 = 3.64F
NZ$1 = 3.09F
SAR1 = 1.16F
Country Code: 33

1F = US$0.18
1F = CDN$0.23
1F = UK£0.12
1F = IR£0.12
1F = AUS$0.28
1F = NZ$0.32
1F = SAR0.86
International Dialing Prefix: 19

Temple of culture, cuisine, fashion, snobbery, and cheese, France is an extraordinary mosaic of tiny villages, walled medieval cities, seamy ports, and, of course, Paris. Charles de Gaulle, WWII Resistance hero and French President for much of the postwar era, summed up the French spirit with the words, "France cannot be France without greatness." In the center of all this, the crowded brilliance of Paris presents only one of France's many facets. In the north, the industry of Lille resides close by the bubbly of the Champagne region. The cliffs and fertile countryside of Normandy posed for the Impressionists and embraced an Anglo-American liberation, while Brittany and Corsica clung to distinct cultural identities. The Loire Valley blossoms with the architecture of the French Renaissance, while the Alps illustrate the architecture of raw geological force. The Dordogne River Valley, dubbed "The Capital of Prehistory," shelters 20,000-year-old cave paintings, while the Côte d'Azur is just too glorious for its own good.

France was originally inhabited by the Gauls, a Celtic people who fell prey first to Caesar's legions and then to decentralized turmoil after the collapse of the Roman Empire. Charlemagne brought renewed unity to France in the 8th century, and over the next several centuries, the feudal lords of Paris consolidated power over the rest of the region, forging for the first time a true French "nation." During the Renaissance, the nation grew grand, as François I planted the Loire Valley with luxuriant châteaux. The opulence crescendoed during the reign of Louis XIV, the Sun King, whose ostentatious palace at Versailles was imitated in castles across the continent. By 1789, the French citizens could no longer support such extravagance; the ensuing years of furious barricade-building, rabble-rousing, and unrequited violence served as the inspiration for later revolutions in France and across Europe.

In the afterglow of the Revolution, Napoleon's armies mastered Europe, and the marching song of Marseille's tattered regiment became the country's national anthem—*La Marseillaise*. (The song's bloody lyrics have recently spurred something of a national debate.) The unstable 19th century saw France swap republic for monarchy, for republic, for empire, and for republic once again. Later in the 19th century, Bonaparte's bravado faded into a grim and gray process of industrialization. Journalists and literary titans such as Hugo, Zola, and Balzac portrayed the dirty drudgery of France's miners and the indulgences of its wealthy bourgeoisie.

French and German armies ripped through the countryside in the Franco-Prussian War (1870-71) and both World Wars. French Impressionists such as Monet and Renoir redefined painting, and after WWI, Paris became the shrine of Hemingway, Gertrude Stein, and the rest of the Lost Generation.

President Charles de Gaulle pursued his claims to French Greatness as the foremost public figure of the post-WWII era, and his words still ring in French ears. Today, though France's political scene is as rocky as ever, the country holds its position as a world leader in the avant garde of aesthetic, cultural, and intellectual movements, and its tourist industry, as always, is poised and waiting to receive.

> For more detailed, fact- and flavor-filled coverage, pick up a copy of *Let's Go: France* or *Let's Go: Paris.*

GETTING THERE AND GETTING AROUND

France does not require visas of U.S., Canadian, New Zealand, or EC citizens, but it does of Australians. Contact the French consulate in Australia at 31 Market St., 20th floor, Sydney NSW 2000 (tel. (02) 261 5779).

With over 15,000 departures daily, the **Société Nationale de Chemins de Fer (SNCF)** manages one of Europe's most extensive rail networks. Timetables are complicated but well-organized, consisting of 3 color-designated periods. "Blue periods" have minimum train traffic, usually Monday afternoon through Friday morning and Saturday afternoon to Sunday afternoon; "white periods" coincide with heavier train use (most other times), while important holidays are "red periods." Point-to-point ticket prices vary according to the period. Train tickets are not valid for use until inserted in the orange machine at the entrance to the platforms. Seat **reservations,** recommended for international trips and during red periods, are mandatory on France's legendary TGV *(train à grande vitesse).* Reservation fees run about US$8 and are waived for Eurailpass holders. The SNCF's premier pass offering, the **France Railpass,** allows 4 days of 2nd-class travel within a 15-day period (US$125), with up to 5 additional days available (US$27 each), and must be purchased outside France; contact a travel agent for details. Other special tickets apply during specified periods. The **Carissimo** (190F for 4 trips, 350F for 8 trips) allows you and up to 3 friends (all under 26) discounts of 20% during white periods and 50% during blue periods. A **Carte Vermeille** (230F for 1 year of unlimited trips, 130F for 4 trips) entitles travelers over 60 to essentially the same discounts. Passes are available from most large train stations. Bring a photo when you make your purchase.

French **buses,** usually slow and cheap, are useful for filling the gaps in the rail network. The bus station, usually located near the train station, is called the *gare routière.* France is known as one of the worst countries in Europe for **hitching.** The larger the city, the more difficult it will be to get a ride. **Allostop-Provoya** is a nationwide service that pairs drivers and riders. It charges 220F for 8 trips within a 2-year period, or 27-67F for individual trips depending on the distance traveled. Gas and tolls are extra. Their main office at 84, passage Brady, 75010 Paris (tel. 42 46 00 66), can give you the addresses of offices throughout the country.

With a wealth of well-paved minor routes, French roads are terrific for **cycling.** Prime regions include the Loire Valley, Normandy, Provence, the Dordogne River Valley, Alsace-Lorraine, and Burgundy. SNCF's pamphlet *Guide du train et du vélo* offers details on combining cycling and railroading in France. Bikes cost 42F to transport on trains, and they often take 3 days to arrive. Many train stations rent bikes (around 50F/day); you may sometimes return it to another station.

FRANCE ESSENTIALS

The extensive French tourism support network revolves around **syndicats d'initiative** and **offices de tourisme,** both of which *Let's Go* labels as "tourist office." Either will help you find accommodations (for about 15F), distribute maps, and suggest excursions to the countryside. The basic unit of currency in France is the franc, subdivided into 100 centimes and issued in both coins and paper notes. The smallest unit of French currency is the 5-centime piece.

Just about everything snoozes in France from noon to 2pm and closes on Sundays, and many provincial areas also shut down on Mondays. Most museums close for at least one day per week, usually Tuesday. The major national holidays in France, on which banks, museums, and other public buildings close, are: January 1, Easter Monday, May 1 (Labor Day), May 8 (Victory in Europe Day), Ascension Day (40th day after Easter—a Thurs.), Whit Monday (7th Mon. after Easter), July 14 (Bastille Day), August 15 (Assumption Day), November 1 (All Saints' Day), November 11 (Armistice Day), and December 25 (Christmas).

Summer brings daytime highs of around 23°C to most of France, although it is cooler in the North and in the Alps, and southern France hosts a plethora of 32°C scorchers every summer. Winters are generally mild, with temperatures rarely dipping below freezing, although frequent rains will dampen more than just spirits.

Communication Everything you've heard about the rudeness of the French may prove true if you address people in English without a prefatory *Parlez-vous anglais, Madame/Monsieur?* (PAR-lay VOO an-GLAY, mah-DAHM/muh-SYUR; "Do you speak English, ma'am/sir?"). Contrary to popular opinion, even flailing efforts to speak French will be appreciated, especially in urban areas. Be lavish with your *Monsieurs, Madames,* and *Mademoiselles;* greet people with a friendly *bonjour* (*bonsoir* after 6pm). Other helpful phrases include *combien* (kohm-BYEHN, "how much"), *je voudrais* (ZHUH voo-DRAY, "I would like"), *Où est/sont* (OO AY/SOHN, "where is/are"), and *je ne comprends pas* (ZHUH NUH kohm-PRAHN pah, "I don't understand").

France's **telephone** system splits into 2 halves: Paris (city code 1) and everything else (no city code). To dial the provinces from Paris, preface the 8-digit number with 16; in reverse, dial 1 and then the 8-digit Paris number. To operate payphones, buy a *télécarte* (telephone credit card). Available at train stations, post offices and *tabacs,* they cost 40F (*petite*) or 96F (*grande*). To call collect, tell the operator *"en PCV"* (on-PAY-say-VAY). For AT&T's **USA Direct,** dial 19, wait for the tone, then dial 0011. For MCI's **World Reach,** dial 19 00 19. For **Canada Direct,** dial 19 00 16. Anywhere in France, dial **10** for an operator, **12** for directory assistance, **15** for medical emergencies, **17** for police assistance and **18** for the fire department. Dial 19 33 11 for the international operator, and be prepared to wait for up to an hour.

Accommodations and Camping Youth hostels (*auberges de jeunesse*) cover France, ranging from well-kept, centrally located castles to run-down barracks. Most are affiliated with HI and charge nonmembers slightly more. Hostels run 40-80F per person, with breakfast about 15F (usually not obligatory). The quality of **hotels** in France generally matches their standardized rating on the government scale of zero to 4 stars. Rock-bottom hotels start at about 80-100F for singles, 90-110F for doubles, both without private bath or breakfast. Rates are often the same for single- and double-occupancy. Showers are usually not included in the price, and can run 10-25F. Inquire whether the breakfast or meals at the hotel are *obligatoire*. Breakfast (15-25F) usually means bread, jam, and coffee or hot chocolate. Make reservations (confirm with 1 night's deposit) for the larger cities in summer.

Campgrounds, plentiful in France, are also rated on a 4-star system. *Michelin's Camping and Caravanning in France* details the best sites. The **Club Alpin Français** maintains a network of mountain huts in upland regions. For further information, contact the office at 24, av. de Laumière, 75019 Paris (tel. 42 02 68 64).

Tourist offices list local *gîtes d'étape* (shelters forbidden to motorists) and *chambres d'hôte* (rustic farmhouse accommodations). Most tourist offices in rural areas have a list of *campings à la ferme*—campsites located on private farms.

Food and Drink French chefs cook for one of the most finicky clienteles in the world: the French. Traditionally, the complete French dinner includes an *apéritif* (pre-dinner drink), an *entrée* (appetizer), a *plat* (main course), salad, cheese, dessert, fruits, coffee, and a *digestif* (after-dinner drink); it takes several hours. A meal to tell your grandchildren about will run about 160F. The French *always* take wine with their meals. You might hear the story of how Woody Allen was kicked out of a French restaurant for ordering a Coke with his meal. Of him it was said, *"Il manque du savoir vivre."* (He doesn't know how to live.)

In restaurants, fixed-price 3-course meals (called *menus*) begin at a reasonable 50F. Service is always included; tips are only necessary for (rare) sensational treatment. Be careful when ordering *à la carte; l'addition* (the check) may exceed your weekly budget. You can buy sandwiches at most French bakeries and cafés; for 12-25F you get a foot-long *baguette* with cheese or meat inside. Cafés are a forum for continuous conversation, but you pay for the right to sit and watch the world go by: drinks and food are often 10-30% more if served in the dining room (*salle*) or outside (*sur la terrasse*) rather than at the bar (*comptoir* or *zinc*).

Boulangeries, pâtisseries, and *confiseries* tempt with bread, pastries, and candy, respectively. *Fromageries* and *crémeries* present an astonishing array of cheeses. *Charcuteries* sell salads and meats. For supermarket shopping, look for **Uniprix, Prisunic,** or **Monoprix.** The many local markets (*marchés*) are picturesque, animated, and often offer better quality than supermarkets. Smaller towns hold them once or twice per week; they are a fixed feature in larger cities, coloring the streets every morning except Sunday and Monday.

■■■ PARIS

Paris is a place that exists in most peoples' imaginations before they ever see the city—Paris as the City of Lights, the romantic Paris of the movies, the mysterious city described in books and letters. The actual city, though different from the imaginary one, is not a disappointment. The city constantly evolves. It is the center of the changing French political landscape and ground for artistic innovation as well as tradition. Baudelaire called Paris a "teeming city, city full of dreams, where the specter in full daylight, accosts the passerby." These phantoms are part of the city's mystery. And while Paris may not be the mythic city full of dreams (it is quite possible to go

Paris

1 Accueil Central de France:
   127 Champs Elysée
2 Transalpino: 16, rue La Fayette
3 American Express: 11, rue Scribe
4 Post Office: 52, rue du Louvre

5 Musée Marmottan
6 l'Arc de Triomphe
7 Sacré-Coeur
8 Musée d'Art Moderne
   de la Ville de Paris
9 Grand Palais
10 Petit Palais
11 Opéra Garnier
12 Place Vendôme
13 Comedie Française
14 Palais Royal
15 Orangerie
16 St-Eustache
17 Centre National d'Art et
   Culture George Pompidou
18 Hôtel de Ville
19 Musée Picasso
20 Musée Carnavalet

21 Place des Vosges
22 Opéra Bastille
23 Sainte Chapelle and Palais de Justice
24 Notre Dame
25 St-Germain-des-Prés
26 Musée de Cluny
27 Sorbonne
28 Panthéon
29 Palais du Luxembourg
30 Musée d'Orsay
31 Musée Rodin
32 Les Invalides

33 Tour Eiffel
34 Cité Internationale
   de l'Université de Paris
35 Louvre

to Paris and not fall in love; you may not even finish your novel), its complexities are part of its charm, and the web of myth is part of its everyday realities. It is, in Hemingway's words, "a moveable feast," a city with a flavor so irresistible that once you taste it, you will carry memories of the experience around with you forever after.

> For comprehensive, detailed, entertaining coverage of the wonders of Paris and its environs, pick up a copy of *Let's Go: Paris*.

ORIENTATION AND PRACTICAL INFORMATION

Paris is in northern France, 200km and 2-3 rail hours from the English Channel (*La Manche*), a similar distance from Brussels, and no more than 12 hours from any major city in France. The city is divided into 20 *arrondissements,* or districts, whose numbers rise clockwise in a rough spiral from the 1st or *premier* district around the Louvre to outer *arrondissements* near the periphery. *Let's Go* gives the *arrondissement* with every address: 5ème means *cinquième* or 5th. Most of the popular sights are within the first 8 *arrondissements*. The River Seine, which flows from east to west, splits the city; **Rive Gauche** (Left Bank) lies to the south, and **Rive Droite** (Right Bank) to the north. Paris's efficient *Métropolitain* (abbreviated here as "Mo.") will whisk you from one quarter to the next, and each metro station has a detailed map of the surrounding streets (see Public Transportation below).

Tourist Offices: Bureau d'Accueil Central, 127, av. des Champs-Elysées, 8ème (tel. 49 52 53 54). Mo. Charles de Gaulle-Etoile. Helpful, English-speaking, and packed. Open daily 9am-8pm. Branches at Gare de Lyon (tel. 43 43 33 24), major train stations, and the Eiffel Tower. **Tourist Information:** tel. 49 52 53 56, French 49 52 53 55. A taped message in English gives the week's major events.

Budget Travel: Accueil des Jeunes en France (AJF), 119, rue St-Martin, 4ème (tel. 42 77 87 80), in front of the Pompidou Center. Mo. Rambuteau. Reduced-price student train and bus tickets. Open Mon.-Sat. 9:30am-6:30pm. Another office at Gare du Nord. **Centre Franco-Américain Odéon,** pl. de l'Odéon, 6ème (tel. 46 34 16 10; fax 43 26 97 45). Mo. Odéon. CIEE's work and study center for American students in Paris. Open Mon.-Fri. 9am-6pm. **Council Travel,** 51, rue Dauphine, 6ème (tel. 43 26 79 65). Mo. Odéon. Sells cheap charter flights, BIJ tickets and ISICs (45F). All open Mon.-Fri. 10am-6pm, Sat. 10am-5pm. **Office de Tourisme Universitaire,** 39, av. G. Bernanos, 5ème (tel. 43 36 80 27). Mo. Port-Royal. A CIEE-esque French student travel agency. Open Mon. 11am-6:45pm, Tues.-Fri. 10am-6:45pm. **CROUS** next door (tel. 40 51 36 00) has pamphlets on student housing, employment, university restaurants, and health care.

Embassies and Consulates: U.S.: 2, av. Gabriel, 8ème (tel. 42 96 12 02). Mo. Concorde. **Consulate,** 2, rue St-Florentin (tel. 42 96 12 02), 3 blocks away. Open Mon.-Fri. 9am-3pm. **Canada:** 35, av. Montaigne, 8ème (tel. 44 43 29 00). Mo. Franklin Roosevelt. Open Mon.-Fri. 9-10:30am and 2-3pm. **U.K.:** 35, rue du Faubourg-St-Honoré, 8ème (tel. 42 66 91 42). Mo. Concorde. **Consulate,** 16, rue d'Anjou. Visa bureau open Mon.-Fri. 9am-noon. **Australia:** 4, rue Jean Rey, 15ème (tel. 40 59 33 00). Mo. Bir-Hakeim. Open Mon.-Fri. 9am-noon and 2-5pm. **New Zealand:** 7ter, rue Léonard-de-Vinci, 16ème (tel. 45 00 24 11). Mo. Victor-Hugo. Open Mon.-Fri. 9am-1pm and 2-5:30pm. **Ireland:** 12, av. Foch, 16ème (tel 45 00 20 87). Mo. Dauphine. Not a consulate, but in an emergency call this number for instructions. **South Africa:** 59, quai d'Orsay, 7ème (tel. 45 55 92 37).

Currency Exchange: Banks usually give the best rates; try the 9th *arrondissement*. **Change Automatique,** 66, av. des Champs-Elysées, 8ème. ATM machine accepts US$5, 10, and 20 bills. Poor rates. Open 24 hrs. All **train stations** (except Gare Montparnasse) have currency exchanges with mediocre rates. (Open daily 7am-9pm.) Most cash machines will give you francs off MasterCard or Visa.

American Express: 11, rue Scribe, 9ème (tel. 47 77 77 07), across from the Opéra. Mo. Opéra or Auber. All regular services. Mediocre exchange rates. Always packed. Open daily 9am-5:30pm.

Post Office: 52, rue du Louvre, 1er (tel. 40 28 20 00), by the Bourse du Commerce. Mo. Châtelet-Les-Halles. Poste Restante. Only urgent telegrams, and no mailings over 2kg, outside normal business hours. Open 24 hrs. The **postal code** can be formed by adding the *arrondissement* to the number 750 (e.g., 1er becomes 75001, 16ème becomes 75016, etc.).

Telephones: At the main post office. Open 24 hrs. No collect calls to the U.S. on Sun. Buy a *télécarte* (40 or 98F) at any rail station ticket window, post office, or *tabac;* coin-operated phones are scarce. For calls outside Paris, dial 16. To Paris from the provinces, dial 161. From abroad, use the **city code:** 1.

Flights: Most international flights land at **Aéroport Roissy-Charles de Gaulle** (tel. 48 62 22 80) 23km northeast of Paris. Terminal 2 serves Air France (tel. 43 20 14 55). The cheapest, fastest way to get into town is by Roissy Rail, a bus-train combination to central Paris. Take the free shuttle bus from Aérogare 1, arrival gate 28; Aérogare 2A, gate 5; Aérogare 2B, gate 6 or Aérogare 2D, gate 6 to the Roissy train station, where you can ride the RER B3 to the city (45min., 37F, includes transfer to metro). **Aéroport Orly** (tel. 49 75 15 15), 12km south of Paris, handles charters and many European flights. From Orly Sud, Gate H or Orly Ouest, Gate F, you can take the free shuttle bus to Orly train station and the RER C2 to central Paris (35min., 27F).

Trains: SNCF (tel. 45 82 50 50 for info; 45 65 60 60 for reservations). Guard your valuables; don't buy train or metro tickets from anyone except the uniformed personnel in the booths. **Gare du Nord** for northern France, Belgium, Netherlands, Scandinavia, and northern Germany. To: Brussels (10/day, 3hr., 221F); Amsterdam (6/day, 5-6hr., 356F); Cologne (6/day, 5-6hr., 322F); Copenhagen (4/day, 16hr., 1036F). **Gare de l'Est** for eastern France, Luxembourg, northern Switzerland, southern Germany, and Austria. To: Zürich (7/day, 6hr., 375F). **Gare de Lyon** for southeastern France, southern Switzerland, Italy, and Greece. To: Geneva (5/day, 4hr. by TGV, 397F plus 10-80F reservation); Rome (3/day, 14-16hr., 678F). **Gare d'Austerlitz** for southwestern France, Spain, and Portugal. To: Barcelona (3/day, 11-14hr., 575F); Madrid (5/day, 12-16hr., 561F). **Gare St-Lazare** for Normandy. **Gare de Montparnasse** for Brittany. All train stations are also metro stops for at least 2 lines.

Buses: Many international buses arrive at **Gare Routière Internationale**, av. du Général de Gaulle, Bagnolet 93170 (tel. 49 72 51 51; Mo. Gallieni; formerly at Porte de la Villette). Check with your company for the precise location. For international bus info, call **International Express Eurolines Coach Station** (tel. 40 38 93 93).

Public Transportation: The Paris subway, **Métropolitain** or **Métro** (Mo.), is quick and efficient. It is said that no point in the city is more than 5min. from the nearest stop. Lines are referred to by final destination *(direction)*, not by number. Connections are called *correspondances*. Tickets anywhere within the city cost 6F; a *carnet* of 10 is 37F. Several passes allow unlimited travel on the metro and buses. *Formule 1* is valid for one day (25F). *Carte Jaune* is valid Mon.-Sun., regardless of what day you buy it, and requires a photo. Hold onto your ticket until you pass the point marked *"Limite de Validité des Billets";* you could be asked for it by a uniformed *contrôleur*. Any *correspondances* to the **RER** (Réseau Express Régional—commuter train to the suburbs, express subway within central Paris) require inserting your validated (and uncrumpled) ticket into a turnstile. Metro service runs approximately 5:30am-12:15am (check the *Principes de Tarification* poster on every platform for specifics on each line). **Buses** require their own 6F tickets (purchased from driver); on trips crossing 2 zones (refer to route map on buses) you'll need 2 tickets, both of which must be validated in the machine by the driver's seat. Buses run until 8:30pm, *autobus du soir* until 12:30am and a few *noctambus* (3-4 tickets) run all night. Schedules are available at the RATP office, 53ter, quai des Grands-Augustins, 6ème (tel. 43 46 14 14). Mo. St-Michel. Open daily 6am-9pm.

Taxis: Cab stands near train stations and major bus stops. 3-person max. Taxis are expensive, especially if you don't speak French. When you call (tel. 47 39 47 39, 42 41 50 50, or 42 70 41 41), the meter starts running immediately (i.e., before you are picked up). A 12-15% tip is customary.

Hitchhiking: Thumbing out of Paris is difficult and unsafe. Toward the east (Strasbourg, Munich), hitchers take the metro to Porte de Charenton and walk along bd. Massena to catch the A4. Toward the north (Brussels, Cologne, Berlin), hitchers take the metro to Porte de la Chapelle, right next to the A1. Toward the west (Rouen, Mont St-Michel, St-Malo), they take the metro to Porte de St-Cloud, and up bd. Murat toward pl. de la Porte d'Auteuil, where the A13 begins. Toward the south, they take the metro to Porte d'Orléans, down av. de la Porte d'Orléans, and left to a number of *autoroutes:* A16 goes to Lyon, the French Riviera, Switzerland, Italy, and Barcelona; A10 to Bordeaux and Madrid; A11 branches off A10 toward Brittany.

Luggage Lockers: At all train stations. 15F.

Lost Property: Bureau des Objets Trouvés, 36, rue des Morillons, 15*ème* (tel. 45 31 14 80). Mo. Convention. Yeah, right. No information given by phone. Open Mon.-Fri. 8:30am-5pm; Sept.-June Mon., Wed., and Fri. 8:30am-5pm, Tues. and Thurs. 8:30am-8pm.

Bookstores: Shakespeare and Co., 37, rue de la Bucherie, 5*ème,* across the Seine from Notre-Dame. Mo. St. Michel. This cozy, upscale shop seeks to reproduce the atmosphere of the shop from which Sylvia Beach published Ulysses. More a landmark than a place to buy cheap books. Open daily noon-midnight. **Brentano's,** 37, av. de l'Opéra, 2*ème* (tel. 42 61 52 50). Mo. Opéra. American literature and guidebooks. Open Mon.-Sat. 10am-7pm.

Libraries: Bibliothèque Publique d'Information, at the Centre Pompidou (tel. 42 77 12 33). Mo. Rambuteau. Many books in English. Open Mon.-Fri. noon-10pm, Sat.-Sun. 10am-10pm.

Public Baths: Beat the high cost of hotel showers at 8, rue des Deux Ponts, 4*ème* (tel. 43 54 47 40). Mo. Pont-Marie. Showers 5F, with soap and towel 11F. Check under *Bains Douches Municipaux* in the phone book for other addresses. All open Thurs. noon-7pm, Fri. 8am-7pm, Sat. 7am-7pm, Sun. 8am-noon.

Crises: SOS Friendship (tel. 47 23 80 80). Crisis help line staffed daily 3-11pm. Assistance in English for the depressed and lonely. **Rape: SOS Viol** (tel. 05 05 95 95). Call free from anywhere in France. Open Mon.-Fri. 10am-6pm.

Pharmacy: Les Champs Elysées, 84, av. des Champs-Elysées, 8*ème* (tel. 45 62 02 41). Mo. George V. Open 24hrs.

Medical Assistance: Hôpital Franco-Britannique de Paris, 3, rue Barbès, in the suburb of Levallois-Perret (tel. 47 58 13 12). Mo. Anatole France. Consultations with English-speaking doctors. **Hôpital Americain,** 63, bd. Victor Hugo, Neuilly (tel. 46 41 25 25), also in the 'burbs. Mo. Porte Maillot, then bus #82 until the end of the line. More expensive. Blue Cross-Blue Shield accepted if you fill out the forms first. Dental service.

Emergency: Ambulance: SOS Médecins: tel. 15. **Fire:** tel. 18. **Police:** tel. 17. Police station in every *arrondissement;* call the operator (tel. 12) for the nearest.

ACCOMMODATIONS

If at all possible, make a reservation *before* coming to Paris; it will make your first day in the luminous city far more pleasant, and you just might be able to stay in the city center without paying a fortune for it. Otherwise, don't panic. Instead of calling around or showing up at hotels, try the booking services listed below:

La Centrale de Réservations (FUAJ-HI), 4, bd. Jules Ferry, 11*ème* (tel. 43 57 02 60; fax 40 21 79 92). Mo. République. The best way to get a bed in a hostel and one of the best to find any budget accommodation in Paris. Near the Jules Ferry hostel, the *Centrale* can provide you with same-day reservations in one of the youth hostels or budget hotels with which it's affiliated: a total of 10,000 beds in and around the city. Reservations require a 10F on-the-spot deposit, which is deducted from the bill. Also books beds throughout France and Europe, and arranges excursions. Open daily 8am-10pm.

Accueil des Jeunes en France (AJF), 119, rue St-Martin, 4*ème* (tel. 42 77 87 80). Mo. Rambuteau; open Mon.-Sat. 9:30am-6pm. Other offices are at 139, bd. St-Michel, 5*ème* (tel. 43 54 95 86; Mo. Port-Royal; open Tues.-Sat. 10am-12:30pm and 1:30-6:15pm) and Gare du Nord, 10ème (tel. 42 85 86 19; Mo. Gare du Nord; open June 1-Sept. 4 daily 7:30am-10pm). Guarantees "decent and low-cost lodging with immediate reservation" for the same day only. You pay the full price when you make your reservation, even before seeing the room. Often they can't find you a room for the full duration of your stay; you may have to use AJF more than once. 10F fee/reservation.

The **Office du Tourisme** listed in the Practical Information section can also book rooms, although the lines may be long and the selections not the cheapest in Paris.

Hostels and Foyers

Paris's big-city hostels don't bother with many of the restrictions—sleep sheets, curfews and the like—that characterize most hostels in the world, but they do have maximum stays (though even these are flexible). Only 2 hostels in Paris require HI membership. The rest of the dorm-like accommodations in Paris are either non-HI hostels or *foyers,* many of which are full-time dorms during the academic year, and have different characters, rules, and prices.

Centre International de Paris (BVJ). A relatively luxurious chain of youth hostels. **Paris Louvre,** 20, rue Jean-Jacques Rousseau, 1er (tel. 42 36 88 18; fax 42 33 40 53). Mo. Louvre. 200 beds in spacious, dorm-style rooms. 2-8 beds/room. Lunch or dinner 50F. Groups must pay for 1 meal a day. **Paris Opéra,** 11, rue Thérèse, 1er (tel. 42 60 77 23; fax 42 33 40 53). Mo. Pyramides. Bigger rooms, fewer beds, and a more subdued atmosphere than Paris Louvre. **Paris Les Halles,** 5, rue du Pélican, 1er (tel. 40 26 92 45; fax 42 33 40 53). Mo. Palais Royal. 55 beds. Cramped rooms, less common space, and toilets and showers on alternate floors. **Paris Quartier Latin,** 44, rue des Bernardins, 5ème (tel. 43 29 34 80; fax 42 33 40 53). Mo. Maubert-Mutualité. 138 beds. Modern white tile and chrome décor. Large, spotless, but densely packed rooms. Lockers 10F. All hostels open 6am-2am. No families. Singles available (except in Paris Louvre) 120F. Doubles, triples, and quads 110F/person, available at 2:30pm, breakfast and showers included. Individual reservations not accepted—call or show up at 8am.

Auberge de Jeunesse "Jules Ferry" (HI), 8, bd. Jules Ferry, 11ème (tel. 43 57 55 60). Mo. République. About 100 beds in this well-located hostel. Clean, large rooms. Noisy party atmosphere, and jovial, multilingual management. Most spaces filled by 10am. Adequate kitchen facilities. 4-day max. stay. Open 24hrs. Lockout 10am-1:30pm, but reception staff will answer questions or accept reservations anytime. No curfew. Single-sex lodging, but accommodations made for male-female couples. 2-6 bed rooms 100F/person. Singles 110F. Sheets 14F or use your own sleeping bag. Showers and breakfast (self-serve 7-9:30am) included. Lockers 5F. Laundry, including dryer and soap, 33F. Bike storage in basement.

Auberge de Jeunesse "Le d'Artagnan" (HI), 80, rue Vitruve, 20ème (tel. 43 61 08 75; fax 43 61 75 40). Mo. Porte de Bagnolet or Porte de Montreuil. A cross between a hostel and a mall. 7-floor complex with 411 beds, a restaurant, a bar, even a small movie theater. Vending machines and microwaves. Most rooms are triples, some have 8 beds; a few are doubles. Rooms designed for maximum space utilization without creating a cramped atmosphere. Friendly English-speaking staff. Wheelchair access. Flexible 3-day max. stay. Reception open 24hr. Lockout 10am-2pm. Doubles 115-125F/person. Triples and dorms 100F/person, including breakfast and sheets. Lockers 15F. Laundry 15F/wash, 5F/dry; soap 3F. Make reservations—the hostel is packed Feb.-Oct. Individual reservations can be made through other HI member hostels around the world.

Hôtel des Jeunes (MIJE): "Le Fauconnier," 11, rue du Fauconnier (tel. 42 74 23 45). Mo. St-Paul or Pont-Marie. **"Le Fourcy,"** 6, rue de Fourcy (tel. 42 74 23 45). Mo. St-Paul or Pont-Marie. **"Maubisson,"** 12, rue des Barres (tel. 42 74 23 45). Mo. Hôtel de Ville or Pont-Marie. All in the 4ème. These star *foyers* are all located in former aristocratic residences *(hôtels particuliers)* of the Marais district, close to the sights and to one another. Le Fauconnier is luxury in modern hostelry. Spacious rooms with 2-, 4-, and 8-bed rooms. Lively Maubisson, the smallest of the 3, has newer but smaller rooms. All give priority to groups of 10 or more (but no discounts). Guests must be ages 18-30. 7-day max. stay. Lockout noon-4pm. Curfew 1-6am. 110F/person. Showers and breakfast included (showers in the room, toilets down the hall). Lockers 2F. Reservations (in person only) require advance payment. Within walking distance of all hostels is the **Restaurant la Table d'Hôtes**, 16, rue du Pt. St-Louis-Phillipe. 3 courses for 50F if you're staying at one of the hostels and show up at 12:30, 6:30, or 7:30pm.

Maisons des Jeunes Rufz de l'Avison, 18, rue J.-J. Rousseau, 1er (tel. 45 08 02 10). Mo. Louvre or Palais-Royal. From Louvre *métro* stop, take rue du Louvre away from the river, turn left on rue St-Honoré, and turn right on rue J.-J. Rousseau. During the academic year it's a private residence hall for male students, but in summer it fills with tourists of both sexes. Some rooms may be open during school year as well. Stunning open-air courtyard. Doubles, triples, and crowded quads. 3-day min. stay. Reception open 7am-7pm. No curfew. 95F. Shower and breakfast included. Reserve by mail with 1 night's payment, or arrive early.

Young and Happy (Y&H) Hostel, 80, rue Mouffetard, 5ème (tel. 45 35 09 53; fax 47 07 22 24). Mo. Censier-Daubenton. A lively youth hostel with clean, cramped rooms. Ideally located in the heart of the raucous student quarter on the rue Mouffetard. Claustrophobes beware the serpentine staircase and incredibly tight hallways. Rooms with 2-6 beds. Lockout 11am-5pm. Curfew 1am. 95F. Breakfast and shower included. Reservations accepted with 1 night's deposit.

UCJF (Union Chrétienne de Jeunes Filles) or **YWCA,** 22, rue Naples, 8ème (tel. 45 22 23 49). Mo. Europe or Villiers. Extremely organized, well-kept, and homey environment. This *foyer* accepts women for a 3-day min. stay June-Sept. in spacious, airy rooms with wood floors and large beds. Friendly staff, large and elegant oak-panelled common room with fireplace, TV and VCR, theater performance space, and family-style dining room with a varied daily *menu*. In summer: singles 148F/day (444F/3 days) and 125F/person in a double (375F/3 days). Sept.-May, the *foyer* caters to longer stays by women ages 18-24, with breakfast and dinner included. 1 week: singles 650F, doubles 567F. 1 month: doubles 2070F. All guests must pay 30F membership fee and 100F processing fee, which guarantees world-wide YWCA membership. 200F key deposit. Reception open Mon.-Fri. 9am-6:30pm, Sat.-Sun. 9:30am-4:30pm. Curfew 12:30am, but negotiable. Reserve if you can (500F deposit required). Other locations at 65, rue Orfila, 20ème (tel. 46 36 82 80; Mo. Gambetta), and 168, rue Blanet, 15ème (tel. 45 33 48 21; Mo. Convention). Men should contact the YMCA *foyer* **Union Chrétienne de Jeunes Gens,** 14, rue Trévis, 9ème (tel. 47 70 90 94).

Foyer International des Etudiantes, 93, bd. St-Michel, 6ème (tel. 43 54 49 63), across from the Jardin du Luxembourg. Mo. Luxembourg. Wood floors, large windows, beautiful desks, and excellent facilities: this is one of the best. TV lounge, piano, kitchenettes on each floor (bring your own equipment), irons, hair dryers, and laundry facilities. International students galore, and a friendly director. Open Sun.-Fri. 6am-1:30am, Sat. all night. Curfew 1:30am. July-Sept.: singles 153F, doubles 102F, shower included. Oct.-June: singles 133F, doubles 82F, breakfast and shower included. Reserve in writing 2 months in advance, 200F if confirmed. Call or arrive at 9:30am to check for no-shows. July-Sept. coed. Oct.-June women only.

Résidence Bastille (AJF), 151, av. Ledru-Rollin, 11ème (tel. 43 79 53 86). Mo. Voltaire. Recently renovated airy rooms with wooden bunks. 167 beds; rooms for 2-4 people. Some triples and quads have bathrooms in the room. Doubles use older hall bathrooms. Hair dryers in hall. Less crowded and more subdued. Friendly multilingual staff. Ages 18-35 only. Reception open 7am-12:30pm and 2pm-1am. Curfew 1am. 105F. Showers, breakfast, and sheets included. No reservations, so arrive early in the morning.

Maison Internationale des Jeunes, 4, rue Titon, 11ème (tel. 43 71 99 21; fax 43 71 78 58). Mo. Faidherbe-Chaligny. Well-located, exceptionally clean, airy, and tranquil, with a garden in the back. Mostly bright rooms with 2-8 beds for ages 18-30, with beautiful new duplexes. Single-sex by room, but exceptions made for traveling buddies, couples, and consenting groups. Coed bathrooms. Some family housing. 3-day max. stay. They'll find you another place if they're full. Reception open 8am-2am. Lockout 10am-5pm. Curfew 2am. Quiet hours 10pm-8am. 110F. Sheets 15F. Showers and breakfast (served 8-9:30am) included.

Hôtel Ste-Marguerite, 10, rue Trousseau, 11ème (tel. 47 00 62 00). Mo. Ledru-Rollin. Affiliated with Jules Ferry hostel. 240 beds. Small, airy rooms with real mattresses; atmosphere of happy chaos and youthful enthusiasm. Most rooms 2-6 beds. Small showers. Hall or room bathrooms. Safe available for valuables. Common room. Vending machine sells beer for 5F—need we say more? No lockout. 90F. Breakfast included. Same-day reservations available through Jules Ferry. Otherwise, show up at 8am to get a room.

Aloha Hostel, 1, rue Borromée, 15ème (tel. 42 73 03 03), on a tiny side street across from 243, rue de Vaugirard. Mo. Volontaires. Despite the cheesy name, this newly-renovated hostel is one of the best. Young management is full of advice. Bright rooms with new beds, new mattresses, and freshly painted interiors have space for 2, 3, or 4 guests. Kitchen facilities, communal refrigerator, and café-style common room. Lockout 11am-5pm. 85F. Breakfast 5F. Arrive at 9am or send 1 night's deposit to reserve.

Three Ducks Hostel, 6, pl. Etienne Pernet, 15ème (tel. 48 42 04 05). Mo. Commerce. To the right of the church. One of the most rowdy and fun hangouts in the city for young backpackers. Three Ducks offers all the amenities (clean dorm-style rooms with bunk beds for 2-8 people). The ivy-covered central courtyard becomes a loud and fun café at night when a young, mostly Anglo backpacking crowd drinks cheap beer from the hostel's watering hole, **Richie's Bar.** 1-week max. stay. Small kitchen. Lockout 11am-5pm. Curfew 1am. Weekly rate 530F. Reservations accepted with 1 night's deposit. Fabulous **Mountain Bike Trip** (tel. 48 42 57 87) bike tours of Paris begin here.

FIAP Jean-Monet, 30, rue Cabanis, 14ème (tel. 45 89 89 15; fax 45 81 63 91). Mo. Glacière. From *métro*, walk down bd. St-Jacques, turn left on rue Ferrus, turn right onto rue Cabanis. International student center with 507 beds, most of which are full in summer with tour groups. Comfortable, well-furnished rooms, all with toilet and shower, are impeccably maintained. Offers disco and jazz concerts at night (free), French language classes, and stacks of tourist info, as well as 12 conference rooms, a game room, a laundry room, and a cheap cafeteria (54F for full meal). Some rooms wheelchair accessible. 3-day max. stay. Singles 240F. Doubles 160F/person. Quads 140F/person. 8-bed rooms 120F/person. Reservations essential. Open April-Sept.

Centre International du Séjour de Paris: CISP "Ravel," 6, av. Maurice Ravel, 12ème (tel. 43 43 19 01; fax 43 44 45 30). Mo. Porte de Vincennes. On the edge of the city. Large and professional with extensive facilities, this hostel caters primarily to groups. Large rooms (most with 4 or fewer beds; 216 beds total), a bar, restaurant, and access to municipal pool next door (15F). Some rooms available for guests with disabilities. Flexible 3-day max. stay. Reception open daily 6:30am-1:30am. Singles 143F, rooms with 2-5 beds 122F, with 8-12 beds 97F. Reduction for ISIC holders: 132F, 114F, 91F respectively. Breakfast included. Self-service restaurant open 7:30-9:30am, noon-1:30pm, and 7-8:30pm. Room reservations accepted no more than 36 hrs. in advance.

Association des Foyers de Jeunes: Foyer des Jeunes Filles, 234, rue Tolbiac, 13ème (tel. 45 89 06 42; fax 45 65 46 20). Mo. Glacière. From the *métro*, take a right on rue de Glacière and then a left on rue Tolbiac. Large, modern *foyer* for women ages 18-25. Excellent facilities include kitchens on all floors, cable TV, washers and dryers, piano, exercise room, library, cafeteria, and garden. Exceptionally friendly and helpful staff. Sunny singles with attractive brick walls equipped with a sink and closet space. Reception open 24hrs.; excellent security. Sept.-June 2910F/month, plus 30F registration fee; breakfast and dinner included. July-Aug. 100F/night. Showers and breakfast included. Dinner 45F. Reservations accepted by mail, but there are usually vacancies during summer.

Maison des Clubs UNESCO, 43, rue de Glacière, 13ème (tel. 43 36 00 63; fax 45 35 05 96). Mo. Glacière. From the *métro*, take a left on rue de la Glacière. Enter through the garden on the right. Small simple rooms—some newly renovated—run by a friendly, multilingual management. Wheelchair access. Flexible 3-day max. stay. Reception open 8am-1am; someone on duty 24hrs. Singles 150F. Doubles 130F/person. Triples 110F/person. Showers and breakfast included. Individual reservations not accepted; call to check for vacancies.

Hotels

Of the 3 classes of Parisian budget accommodations, hotels may be the most practical for the majority of travelers. There are no curfews, no school groups, total privacy, and often concerned managers—features hostels and *foyers* usually can't offer. Budget hotels in Paris are not significantly more expensive than their hostel or *foyer* counterparts. Groups of 3 and 4 may actually find it more economical to stay in a hotel. Note that Parisian law forbids hanging laundry from windows or over balconies to dry; proprietors will remind you that food in the rooms attracts mice.

Expect to pay at least 110-160F for a single, but only 40-60F more for a single-bedded double; 2-bed doubles are rare and cost considerably more. In less expensive hotels, few rooms come with private bath, though most have *bidets* (a toilet-like apparatus used for cleansing those more private body parts) and sinks with hot and cold water. No matter how desperate you are, *do not* use your *bidet* as a toilet. If you book a room without a shower, you will usually have to pay 15-25F for the key to the hall shower.

Rooms disappear quickly after morning checkout (generally 10am-noon), so try to arrive early or reserve ahead; all hotels accept reservations unless otherwise noted. Instead of parading yourself and your bags around town all morning, call first.

Left Bank (Rive Gauche)

A high concentration of inexpensive restaurants and fashionable cafés and bars puts the Left Bank closer to the nightlife. And although conveniently close to the major sights, it escapes the daily flood of tourists to the Louvre and the Pompidou Center across the river.

Hôtel d'Esmeralda, 4, rue St-Julien Le Pauvre, 5ème (tel. 43 54 19 20; fax 40 51 00 68). Mo. St-Michel. Next door to Shakespeare and Co. Romantic hotel with great view of Notre-Dame. Cozy wooden interior, traditional furniture, and floral wallpaper complement homey atmosphere. Reserve at least a month ahead in summer. Singles 150F, with shower 310F. Doubles with shower 410-470F. Triples with shower and toilet 520F. Quads with shower and toilet 580F. Breakfast 40F.

Hôtel des Médicis, 214, rue St-Jacques, 5ème (tel. 43 54 14 66). Mo. Luxembourg. Don't despair when you see the entrance; the rooms are in much better repair than the lobby. Young and energetic clientele; convenient location near cafés and groceries. Singles 75-85F. Doubles 140-160F. Showers 10F.

Hôtel des Grandes Ecoles, 75, rue Cardinal Lemoine, 5ème (tel. 43 26 79 23; fax 43 25 28 15). Mo. Cardinal Lemoine. If you want to go all-out on a hotel, this is the place. Ivy-covered hotel built around flowery garden where guests breakfast in warm weather. Impeccably clean and tastefully decorated rooms. Faithful guests return year after year. Singles 450F, with shower 480. Doubles 530F, with shower 550F. Breakfast 40F. Reserve well in advance, deposit required.

Hôtel des Allies, 20, rue Berthollet, 5ème (tel. 43 31 47 52; fax 45 35 13 92), off bd. Port Royal. Mo. Censier Daubenton. Not quite as scenic or centrally located as other hotels in the 5ème, but clean and comfy rooms for next to nothing. Singles 130F, with shower 165F. Doubles 200F, with shower and toilet 280F. Showers 15F. Breakfast 27F. Reservations accepted with 1 night's deposit.

Hôtel Gay Lussac, 29, rue Gay Lussac, 5ème (tel. 43 54 23 96), at rue St-Jacques. Mo. Luxembourg. Affable owner loves *Let's Go* readers. Carefully cleaned, sunlit rooms in an old, well-preserved hotel on noisy street. Renovation in progress. Tour groups may limit space. Doubles 280F, with shower 350-400F. Triples 300F, with shower and toilet 500F. Breakfast included, served in bar attached to hotel.

Grand Hôtel du Progrès, 50, rue Guy Lussac, 5ème (tel. 43 54 53 18). Mo. Luxembourg. Multilingual proprietors. Clean, bright rooms with great windows and simple decor. Charming, top-floor, garret-like rooms over the Panthéon. Singles

168-220F, with shower and toilet 310F. Doubles 240-285F, with shower and toilet 330F. Triples 360F. Showers 15F. Breakfast included.

Hôtel Nesle, 7, rue de Nesle, *6ème,* (tel. 43 54 62 41), off rue Dauphine. Mo. Odéon. Impeccably clean rooms feature wooden rafters decorated with caricatures depicting Paris history. Outrageously low price in the heart of the *6ème.* Turkish bath and laundry facilities. Singles with breakfast and shower 130F. Doubles 160F, with breakfast and shower 250-300F. Showers 25F. Turkish bath 25F. Breakfast 25F. No reservations accepted; arrive around 11am.

Hôtel St-Michel, 17, rue Git le Coeur, *6ème* (tel. 43 26 98 70), near pl. St-Michel, steps away from Seine. Mo. St-Michel. Conveniently located, but on a quiet street. Large, comfortable rooms with bright floral prints. Friendly management. Curfew 1am. Singles 195F, with shower 290F, with shower and toilet 325F. Doubles 220F, with shower 315F-350F, with shower and toilet 350F-390F. Showers 12F. Breakfast included. Reservations accepted with 1 night's payment.

Hôtel Stella, 41, rue Monsieur le Prince, *6ème* (tel 43 26 43 49; fax 43 54 97 28). Mo. Odéon or Luxembourg. Rooms are pleasant and breezy. Singles with shower and toilet 188F. Doubles with shower and toilet 258F. Reservations with 1 night's payment, or call in morning to reserve.

Hôtel de la Paix, 19, rue du Gros Caillou, *7ème* (tel. 45 51 86 17). Mo. Ecole Militaire, up av. Bosquet and left on rue de Grenelle. The only true budget accommodations in the *7ème* and it shows. Worn carpets, soft mattresses, and peeling paint, but clean and quiet. Reception open 9am-9pm. Singles 135F, with shower 198F. Doubles with shower 250F, with shower and toilet 330F. 2-bed doubles with shower and toilet 290F. Triples with shower and toilet 420F. Showers 15F. Breakfast 30F, served 7-10:30am. Reservations with deposit recommended.

Hôtel du Palais Bourbon, 49, rue de Bourgogne, *7ème* (tel. 45 51 63 32 or 47 05 29 26; fax 45 55 20 21). Mo. Varenne or Invalides. Recent renovations have produced ultra-modern bathrooms. Prices as high as the ceilings, but doubles remain an affordable option. Reception open 24hr. Singles with toilet 220F, with toilet and shower 259F. Doubles with toilet 251F, with toilet, TV, and shower 368F. Showers 12F. Breakfast included, served in elegant salon or rooms. Reservations recommended confirm by letter or fax with credit card number.

Hôtel de Blois, 5, rue des Plantes, *14ème* (tel. 45 40 99 48, fax 45 40 45 62) Mo. Mouton-Duvernet. Rooms decked-out with full bathrooms, TVs, telephones, and Laura Ashley décor. Gracious proprietor offers tourist advice, directions. Doubles 210F, with bath or shower 240F, with shower or bath and toilet 260F-350F. Triples 360F. Showers 15F. Breakfast 25F.

Hôtel Plaisance, 53, rue de Gergovie, *14ème* (tel. 45 42 11 39). Mo. Pernety. From the *métro,* turn right on rue Raymond Losserand, left on rue de Gergovie. On a quiet street in a dull neighborhood. Institutional but clean and comfortable. Singles 126F, with shower 180F, with shower and toilet 210F. Doubles 160F, with shower 200F, with shower and toilet 250F. Showers 20F. Breakfast 20F.

Hôtel du Parc, 6, rue Jolivet, *14ème* (tel. 43 20 95 54; fax 42 79 82 62). Mo. Montparnasse-Bienvenue. Large, modern hotel with a marble interior. Clean, spacious, bright—you won't feel like a deprived budget traveler. Singles 230F. Doubles with shower and toilet 350F. Showers 20F. Breakfast 20F.

Right Bank (Rive Droite)

Since most bargain hunters head first for the Left Bank, this side of the Seine is more likely to yield vacancies. In general, hotel prices here rise with proximity to the Louvre and the Opéra. Exceptions do exist, but supermarkets and inexpensive restaurants are fewer and farther between than in the Left Bank.

Hôtel de Lille, 8, rue du Pelican, 1*er* (tel. 42 33 33 42). Mo. Palais Royal. Clean and pleasant. Great location in a quiet street, insanely close to the Louvre. No private bathrooms. Singles 170F. Doubles 200-250F. Showers 30F.

Hôtel Saint-Honoré, 85, rue St-Honoré, 1*er* (tel. 42 36 20 38 or 42 21 46 96; fax 42 21 44 08). Mo. Louvre, Châtelet, or Les Halles. From Mo. Louvre, take rue du Louvre (away from the river) and turn right on rue St-Honoré. In the throes of all-out renovation; sparkling rooms glimmer in the distance. Ask about renovations before reserving. Friendly, English-speaking staff and young clientele. Singles or doubles 180-200F, with shower and toilet 280F. Triples or quads with shower and toilet 380-420F. Showers 15F. Breakfast 24F. In summer, confirm reservations by phone the night before, or by telephone upon arriving in Paris.

Hôtel Lion d'Or, 5, rue de la Sourdière, 1er (tel. 42 60 79 04; fax 42 60 09 14). Mo. Tuileries or Pyramides. Newly refurbished rooms are clean and carpeted though spare. Singles 180F, with shower 220F. Doubles 220F, with shower 280F, with bath and toilet 360F. Extra bed 60F. Showers 20F. Breakfast 25F. 5% discount on stays of over 3 days.

Hôtel de Rouen, 42, rue Croix des Petits Champs, 1er (tel. or fax 42 61 38 21). Mo. Louvre or Palais-Royal. Climb the steep and narrow staircase to small rooms with phones and grape-sized bathrooms. Proprietors aim to please. Singles or doubles 180F, with shower 240F, with shower, toilet, and TV 290F. Triples with shower and toilet 290F. Quads with shower and toilet 350F. Breakfast 20F.

Hôtel La Marmotte, 6, rue Léopold Bellan, 2ème (tel. 40 26 26 51). Mo. Sentier. Pristine rooms and firm beds. Inexpensive restaurant on 1st floor. TV and phone in every room. Singles 180F, with toilet 200F, with shower and toilet 260F. Doubles 200F, with toilet 220F, with shower and toilet 280F. Extra bed 80F. Showers 15F. Breakfast 20F. Reservations recommended.

Hôtel Zora, 4, rue Léopold Bellan, 2ème (tel. 45 08 18 75). Mo. Sentier. Not particularly well-lit and somewhat worn, but clean, adequate rooms make this a decent option. This family-run hotel is located on beautiful, safe, and quiet pedestrian street and does not require a deposit for reservations. Singles 120F, with shower and toilet 150F. Doubles 160F, with shower and toilet 220F. Showers 20F.

Hôtel Tiquetonne, 6, rue Tiquetonne, 2ème (tel. 42 36 94 58). Mo. Etienne-Marcel. Near the intersection of rue St-Denis and rue de Turbigo. Rooms are clean and the price is right. Singles 120F, with shower and toilet 190F. Doubles with shower and toilet 220F. Showers 22F. Breakfast 22F. Open Sept.-July.

Grand Hôtel des Arts et Métiers, 4, rue Borda, 3ème (tel. 48 87 73 89; fax 48 87 66 58). Mo. Arts et Métiers. Trades appealing decor for great prices and central location. 20-30F discount with Let's Go. Singles with toilct 160F. Doubles with toilet 200F. Singles or doubles with shower 220F, with toilet and shower 280F. Showers 20F. Breakfast 25F.

Hôtel Picard, 26, rue de Picardie, 3ème (tel. 48 87 53 82). Mo. République or Filles du Calvaire. 2-star hotel run by proprietor who likes American students. Charming, clean little rooms. 10% Let's Go discount. Singles 200F, with shower 250F, with bath and toilet 320F. Doubles 240-260F, with shower 320F, with bath and toilet 390F. Triples 360F. Extra bed 120F. Showers 20F. Breakfast 30F.

Hôtel Bretagne, 87, rue des Archives, 3ème (tel. 48 87 83 14). Mo. République, Temple, or Filles du Calvaire. Wide range in prices reflects the wide range in room quality. Reception open 24hrs. Singles 150F, with bath, toilet, and TV 300F. Doubles 190F, with bath, toilet, and TV 350F. Triples 300F, with 3 beds and bath, toilet, and TV 600F. Breakfast 30F.

Hôtel Paris France, 72, rue de Turbigo 4ème, (tel. 42 78 00 04, for reservations 42 78 64 92; fax 42 71 99 43). Mo. République or Temple. From the République métro, walk down the noisy rue de Turbigo. Fairly clean and well-lit, with a convenient elevator. Phone in rooms. No hall showers. Singles or doubles 220F, with shower 280F, with bath, toilet, and TV 350F. Extra bed 100F. Breakfast 20F.

Hôtel Practic, 9, rue d'Ormesson, 4ème (tel. 48 87 80 47). Mo. St-Paul or Bastille. Spare but sunny rooms, some with views of pl. du Marché-Ste-Catherine. Clean as a whistle. If orange and green bedspreads don't grab you, the location and price will. Singles with toilet 150F. Doubles with toilet 220F, with shower 260F, with shower, bath, and toilet 320F. Showers 35F. Breakfast 25F.

Hôtel de la Herse d'Or, 20, rue St-Antoine, 4ème (tel. 48 87 84 09). Mo. Bastille or St-Paul. Freshly painted, refurbished rooms around an enclosed courtyard. Telephones in rooms with toilet and shower. Some parking spaces. Singles 150F. Doubles 190F, with shower 250F, with shower and toilet 375F.

Grand Hôtel du Loiret, 8, rue des Mauvais-Garçons, 4ème (tel. 48 87 77 00; fax 48 04 96 56). Mo. Hôtel de Ville. Located a few blocks from the Hôtel de Ville, the

Loiret's décor may be a bit frayed around the edges, but you get what you pay for. One of the last real bargains in the Marais. Singles and doubles with toilet 160F, with shower 210F. Showers 15F. Breakfast 15F.

Hôtel Andréa, 3, rue St-Bon, 4ème (tel. 42 78 43 93). Mo. Châtelet or Hôtel de Ville. Clean, comfortable rooms, all with phone, some with TV. Rooms face Pizza Hut or gray wall, but good location and moderate prices. Singles 120-180F. Doubles with shower and toilet 310-330F. Showers 15F. Breakfast 25F.

Hôtel des Trois Poussins, 15, rue Clauzel, 9ème (tel. 48 74 38 20). Mo. St-Georges. Lovely courtyard, clean rooms, and editions of *Let's Go* from 1982. Singles 140-150F. Doubles with shower 220-230F, with shower and toilet 250F. Showers 15F. Breakfast 25F. Reserve at least a week in advance.

Palace Hôtel, 3, rue Bouchardon, 10ème (tel. 42 06 59 32). Mo. Strasbourg/St-Denis. Small, cheerful rooms face a plant-filled courtyard. Recently renovated. Quiet, back-street location. TV and drink machines. Singles 100F. Doubles 140F, with bath and toilet 250F. Triples 180F, with shower and toilet 280F. Quad 230F, with shower and toilet 350F. Breakfast 20F. No reservations.

Cambrai Hôtel, 129*bis*, bd. de Magenta, 10ème (tel. 48 78 32 13; fax 48 78 43 55). Mo. Gare du Nord. Clean and airy rooms with high ceilings. Wide, firm beds. Large clean showers. Phones in every room. A step away from the Gare. Singles 129F, with shower 196F. Doubles 170F, with shower 216F, with shower and toilet 220-240F. Triples 315F, with shower 330F. Showers 20F. Breakfast included.

Hôtel Mêtropole Lafayette, 204, rue Lafayette, 10ème (tel. 46 07 72 69). Mo. Louis Blanc. Wildly clashing fabrics and dark rooms, but if you close your eyes, firm mattresses take you away from this world of paisley and plaid. Very clean, with friendly reception. Singles 110F, with shower 150F. Doubles 130F, with shower 180F-200F. Triples with shower 230F-250F. Showers 25F. Breakfast 15F.

Hôtel des Familles, 216, rue du Faubourg St-Denis, 10ème (tel. 46 07 76 56). Mo. Gare du Nord. A little dark, a little modest looking, but big beds and clean, hot showers. Singles 130-150F, with shower 200F. Doubles 180F, with shower 220F. Triples 250F, with shower 300F. Quads 300F-350F. Showers 17F. Breakfast 20F.

Hôtel Baudin, 113, av. Ledru-Rollin, 11ème (tel. 47 00 18 91; fax 48 07 04 66). Mo. Ledru-Rollin. A real find: 20 big, recently renovated rooms near the Bastille. Very clean, with a tranquil décor. Singles 120F. Doubles 170-200F, with shower 230F, with bath and toilet 270F. Extra bed 100F. Showers 20F. Breakfast 25F.

Hôtel de Vienne, 43, rue de Malte, 11ème (tel. 48 05 44 42). Mo. Oberkampf or République. From Oberkampf *métro* stop, exit at Crussol. Peaceful, floral rooms. Firm mattresses and clean bathrooms. Family atmosphere. Singles 105F. Doubles 155F, with shower 215F. Breakfast 30F. No hall showers. Open Sept.-July.

FOOD

"Paris is just like any other city, only people eat better..." Thus intones the gravelly voice of Maurice Chevalier in the film *Love in the Afternoon*. Parisians do not simply eat—they eat well, often, and at length. Fortunately, they don't necessarily eat expensively. In a city with some of the world's most fabulous restaurants, you can spend as much as you care to, but Parisians seldom spend more than 100F on a meal. You can eat satisfactorily for 50F, enjoyably for 65F, superbly for 90F, and unforgettably for 130F. The restaurants of Paris are a diverse lot; don't hesitate to try one of the many wonderful and inexpensive Vietnamese, North African, or Middle Eastern restaurants that dot the city. Otherwise, crunch a *croque monsieur* or a plate of quiche at a sidewalk café. Or absorb the best of both at a *bistro,* an amusingly pretentious café-restaurant hybrid. For a light meal accompanied by excellent wine, hit one of Paris's many wine bars, cozy places that seem to sidestep the tourist onslaught. Every *arrondissement* has at least one outdoor market (most last Mon.-Sat. 7am-noon). Ask at your hotel for the nearest one. Finally, university restaurants (some closed on weekends and in summer) serve institutional meals for as little as 12F; you will ordinarily be asked to show a student ID. For more information, including summer and weekend schedules, stop at **CROUS,** 39, av. Georges Bernanos, 5ème (tel. 40 51 36 00; Mo. Port-Royal). Above all, be bold, be adventurous,

FOOD

and splurge at least once: you may never get another chance to slurp snails by the Seine.

The Left Bank (Rive Gauche)

Hungarian restaurants, American bars, Tunisian *pâtisseries,* Breton *crêperies* and eateries of every other variety pack the ancient streets of the 5th arrondissement. Look past the ubiquitous tourist traps on the bd. St-Michel to find some terrific bargains on rue de la Harpe and rue Mouffetard. In the neighboring 6th arrondissement, a myriad of restaurants jostle for space between place de l'Odéon and place St-Sulpice. The daily market on rue de Seine (Mon.-Sat. mornings) is an inexpensive stop for fresh fruit, fish, and cheese. If in doubt, do what the French might do—stock up on picnic supplies and head for the Jardin de Luxembourg. Beware the tourist restaurants, betrayed by their multilingual menus.

L'Apostrophe, 34, rue de la Montagne Ste-Geneviève, 5ème (tel. 43 54 10 93). Mo. Maubert-Mutualité. Tiny, unpretentious French restaurant on a lovely street that winds down from the Panthéon. A great bargain. 49F *menu* served until 8pm, 59F until 9pm, 75F all night. Open Tues.-Sat. noon-2pm and 7-10pm.

Chez Lena et Mimille, 32, rue Tournefort, 5ème (tel. 47 07 72 47). Mo. Censier Daubenton. Everything you imagine a classic French restaurant to be, and more. Traditional cuisine in an elegant, intimate setting. In summer, dine on the flowered terrace. Lunch menu at 98F. Dinner with cocktail, *entrée, plat,* dessert, wine, coffee, and true love 185F. Open Wed.-Mon. noon-2pm and 7:30-11pm.

Restaurant Perraudin, 157, rue St-Jacques, 5ème (tel. 46 33 15 75). Mo. Luxembourg. Rub elbows with locals at this family-style bistro. Gamble on the chef's special or try old favorites like *sautée d'agneau aux flageolets* (lamb with white beans, 55F). Come early to avoid crowds. Lunch *menu* 60F. Main dishes 50-60F. Open Tues.-Fri. noon-2:15pm and 7:30-10:15pm, Mon. and Sat. 7:30-10:15pm.

Orestias, 4, rue Gregoire de Tours, 15ème (tel. 43 54 62 01), off bd. St-Germain. Mo. Odéon. Generous 3-course *menu* 44F for lunch *and* dinner. Middle-of-the-road French, with lots of grilled meats (the lamb skewers are the best offering) accompanied by fries and green beans. You can't eat more for the price anywhere in the area. Open Mon.-Sat. noon-2:30pm and 6-11:30pm.

Così, 54, rue de Seine, 15ème (tel. 46 33 35 36), off rue de Buci. Mo. Odéon. Strains of *Così Fan Tutte* emanate from this hip little sandwich shop. A myriad of tantalizing ingredients like curried turkey, goat cheese, and tomato and basil salad, all stuffed into freshly baked *focaccia* bread (33-48F). Respectable wines (14F/glass) complement the gargantuan creations. Open daily noon-midnight.

Le Petit Vatel, 5, rue Lobineau, 15ème (tel. 43 54 28 49). Mo. Odéon or Mabillon. Little ambience but delicious, inexpensive meals. Choose from 2-course 59F *menu* scribbled on a chalkboard. Specialties include *poivrons farcis, gratin d'épinards au jambon, moussaka,* vegetarian stews. Take-out available. Open Mon.-Fri. noon-3pm and 7pm-midnight, Sat. noon-1am, Sun. 7pm-midnight.

Sampieru Corsu, 12, rue de l'Amiral Roussin, 15ème. Mo. Cambronne. Worth a hike to 15ème. Run by a Marxist Corsican separatist. Share tables with other members of *lumpenproletariat.* Pay according to your means; 40F is suggested for a copious, 3-course *menu* (beer or wine included). On some nights there is entertainment; give a little extra for the artist. Open Mon.-Fri. noon-2pm and 7-9:30pm.

Le Jerobam, 72, rue Dido, 14ème (tel. 45 39 39 13), off rue d'Alésia. Mo. Plaisance. Superb traditional offerings. 65F lunch *menu* includes delectable *Tarine de Poisson aux olives et citron confit* (fish stew with lemon preserves and olives). Dinner *menu* 95F. Open Tues.-Sat. noon-2pm and 7-10pm, Mon. noon-2pm.

Crêperie St-Malo, 53, rue de Montparnasse, 14éme (tel. 43 20 87 19). Mo. Edgar Quinet. An appealing *crêperie.* 49F *menu* includes meat *crêpe,* dessert *crêpe,* hard cider, coffee. Open Mon.-Fri. noon-3pm and 6pm-1am, Sat.-Sun. noon-midnight.

La Coupole, 102, bd. du Montparnasse, 14ème and **Le Séléct,** 99, bd. du Montparnasse, 6ème. Both Mo. Vavin. 2 of the most famous cafés in Paris, these animated and oh-so-chic establishments have served geo-pols (Lenin and Trotsky); musicians (Stravinsky and Satie); writers (Hemingway and Cocteau) and artists (Picasso and Eisenstein). So...who are you? Coffee 12F. Both open daily noon-2am.

The Right Bank (Rive Droite)

Most Right Bank restaurants are more elegant than cheap. Rue des Rosiers in the Marais (4th *arrondissement)* is the nucleus of Paris's Jewish neighborhood. Come here for kosher delis and *pâtisseries,* many of which are open on Sunday, when much else in Paris is closed. Many of Paris's finest and most famous restaurants have assembled in the 8'*eme.* Farther east, the 9'*eme* and 10'*eme* sequester phenomenal Middle Eastern and North African bargains in colorful, multiethnic neighborhoods.

Lescure, 7, rue de Mondovi, 1er (tel. 42 60 18 91). Mo. Concorde. Lively ambience has accompanied hearty French cuisine for over 70 years in this popular restaurant. 98F *menu* (includes 3 courses and wine) offers a wide selection and huge servings. Open Sept.-July Mon.-Fri. noon-2:15pm and 7-10pm, Sat. noon-2:15pm.

Au Petit Ramoneur, 74, rue St-Denis, 1er (tel. 42 36 39 24). Mo. Les Halles. The food is hearty, the price is right, and the word is out. Exceptional value. 64F *menu* includes appetizer, main course, and ½-liter of wine. Open Mon.-Sat. 11:30am-2:30pm and 6:30-9:30pm, Sun. 11:30am-2:30pm.

Chez Jo Goldenberg, 7, rue des Rosiers, 4ème. Mo. St-Paul. In the heart of the Jewish quarter, Goldenberg's is a landmark. A slice of the old world—almost. *Plat du jour* 70F, soups 50F. Take-out borscht, sauerkraut, pickles, pastries, other traditional foods. Deli open daily 8:30am-11pm; dining room daily noon-midnight.

La Dame Tartine, 2, rue Bisemiche, 4'*eme* (tel. 42 77 32 22). Mo. Rambuteau. From the terrace, watch the sculptures in the Stravinsky fountain. Atmosphere as lively as the fountain. Young crowd. Main courses 20-36F. Open daily noon-11:30pm.

Chez Marianne, 2, rue des Hôspitalières St-Gervais 4ème (tel. 42 72 18 86). Mo. St-Paul. Popular restaurant with Israeli and Eastern European dishes. Known for falafel (30F), blini, and *vatrouchka,* a *gâteau de fromage.* Sit in a cozy dining room and order 4, 5, or 6 specialties (50F, 60F, or 70F) from options such as chopped liver, tabouli, and hummus. Take-out available. Open Sat.-Thurs. 11am-midnight.

Paris-Dakar, 95, rue du Faubourg St-Martin, 9ème (tel. 42 08 16 64). Mo. Gare de l'Est. Run by Senegalese family, heralded as "the most African of all African restaurants." Brochettes and curries abound; try *Tiep Bou Dieone.* 59F lunch *menu.* Open daily noon-4pm and 7pm-midnight.

Au Trou Normand, 9, rue Jean-Pierre Timbaud, 11ème (tel. 48 05 80 23). Mo. Oberkampf. A neighborhood institution with orange tablecloths and low-priced no-fuss French food. Youthful crowd. *Onglet rocquefort* with *frites* (30F) is a favorite. Appetizers 9-13F, *plats du jour* 29-39F, tasty desserts 9-13F. Open Mon.-Fri. noon-2:30pm and 7:30-11pm, Sat. 7:30-11pm. Open Sept.-July.

Au Grain de Folie, 24, rue la Vienville, 18ème. Mo. Abbesses. A vegetarian restaurant for one and all, with a vast array of dishes from *couscous* to salads to every kind of cheese. On a quiet street. Dinner à la carte about 100F; also 65F and 100F *menus.* Open Tues.-Sun. noon-3pm and 7:30-11:30pm, Mon. 7:30-11:30pm.

Chez les Fondues, 17, rue des Trois Frères, 18ème (tel. 42 55 22 65). Mo. Abbesses. Choose between *fondue bourguignonne* (meat fondue) and *fondue savoyarde* (cheese fondue). What did you expect? Fun and crowded at night. 80F *menu* includes appetizer, fondue, dessert (such as *ananas au kirsch*), and half *pichet* (jug) of wine. Open daily 5pm-2am.

Berthillon, 31, rue St-Louis-en-l'Ile, 4ème, on the Ile-St-Louis. Mo. Cité or Pont Marie. The best ice cream and sorbet in Paris. Their ice cream, which is lighter and less creamy than the American version, is also available at various cafés and restaurants around town. Open Tues.-Sun. 10am-8pm. Open Sept.-July.

SIGHTS

You're not the first person to be fascinated by Paris. Over the centuries people have sung her praises, penned her history, acted out her trails and tribulations, painted her portrait, and immortalized her façades in film and photographs. What is it about this city that creates such mystique and evokes such attraction? For one, a historic monument on every corner and in every *place.* For another, an aesthetic quality enhanced by the eclectic melange of architectural styles and the graceful curves of the Seine. With map in hand, comfortable shoes on feet, and adventurous spirit, you are ready to discover what makes Paris tick.

Ile de la Cité and Ile St-Louis   If any one location could be called the sentimental and physical heart of Paris, it is the **Ile de la Cité.** Since the 3rd century BC, when it was inhabited by a primitive Gallic tribe of hunters, sailors, and fisherfolk called the Parisii, it has been the administrative center of Paris and the home of kings. When Baron von Haussmann rolled through, he destroyed the island's traditional appearance, reducing its medieval monuments to anachronistic relics. Now the island sinks under the weight of countless tour buses whose passengers spill into souvenir shops to buy the only berets you're likely to see in Paris. **The Cathédrale de Notre-Dame de Paris** (Mo. Cité) was begun in 1163 but not completed until 1361. After the Revolution, the building fell into disrepair and was even used to shelter livestock, but Victor Hugo's 1831 novel, *Notre-Dame de Paris (The Hunchback of Notre Dame)* inspired thousands of citizens to push for restoration. The modifications by the architect Eugène Viollet-le-Duc (including the addition of the spire, the gargoyles, and a statue of himself admiring his own work) remain highly controversial. Thousands of visitors float in sweeping torrents past the doors of the cathedral, overlooking one the most glorious aspects of the entire structure: the **façade.** Break away from the line of marching souls to admire the delicate, intricate curves that adorn the 3 central wooden portals. Once you pass inside, you'll be overawed by the soaring light and seeming weightlessness of the walls—effects produced by brilliant engineering and optical illusions. The cathedral's biggest draw is the enormous stained-glass **rose windows** that dominate the north and south ends of the transept. Free **guided tours** are an excellent way to acquire a deeper understanding of the cathedral's history and architecture; inquire at the information booth to the right as you enter. (Tours in English Wed. at noon. In French Mon.-Fri. noon, Sat.-Sun. 2pm. Free.) A perilous and claustrophobic staircase inside the **towers** emerges onto a spectacular perch, where weather-worn gargoyles survey a stunning view of the city's heart. (Open Sept. and April-July daily 9:30-11:30am and 2-5:30pm; Oct.-March daily 10am-4:30pm; Aug. daily 10am-6:30pm. 31F, students and seniors 17F, under 17 6F.)

Far below the cathedral towers, in a cool and dark excavation beneath the pavement of the *Parvis* (the square in front of the cathedral), the **Archeological Museum,** pl. du Parvis du Notre-Dame, shelters an archeological dig of the remarkably preserved Roman village that once covered the island. (Open daily 10am-6pm. 25F, students and seniors 14F.)

The Palais de Justice harbors numerous tribunals where you can see the law in action, as Paris's district courts have clustered here since the 13th century. At the heart of the Palais, **Ste-Chapelle** remains one of the foremost examples of 13th-century French architecture, though its imprisonment in the middle of the 19th-century Palais de Justice obscures its medieval flavor. The church was begun in 1241 to house the most precious of King Louis IX s possessions, the crown of thorns from Christ's Passion. In the upstairs chapel, reserved for royalty and their court, an overwhelming array of stained-glass windows lights the church with a burgundy hue, hence the saying, "wine the color of Ste-Chapelle's windows." (Open daily 9:30am-6:30pm. 25F, students and seniors 17F, under 17 6F.) **The Conciergerie,** one of Paris's most infamous prisons, lurks ominously around the corner of the Palais from the entrance to the Chapelle, jealously brooding over the souls and memories of the prisoners who died here during the Revolution. Among those imprisoned here were Marie Antoinette and Robespierre. (Open daily 9:30am-6pm; Oct.-March

10am-5pm. 25F includes guided tour in French, students and seniors 14F, under 17 6F. Combo ticket to Conciergerie and Ste-Chapelle 40F.)

A short walk across the Pont St-Louis will take you to **Ile St-Louis,** among the city's most charming and elegant neighborhoods. Some of the most privileged of Paris's exceedingly privileged elite, including the Rothschilds and Pompidou's widow, now call this scrap of land home. At night, Ile St-Louis comes alive with the glow of cast-iron lamps, outlined against the shadows of the Seine. Sweeping arcs of light from *bateaux-mouches* highlight the 17th-century *hôtels* on the *quais* and the 19th-century buildings on either side of the island.

The Left Bank Only one part of the Left Bank deserves a bohemian reputation: *Le Quartier Latin.* The Romans built some of the area's ancient streets, but the *Latin* in the *Quartier's* name refers to the language of scholarship heard here until 1798. Traditionally home base to many Parisian schools and scholars, the *Quartier* has changed greatly in the last 20 years, imperiling its youthful and scholarly ambience. After the student uprisings of May 1968, the University of Paris was decentralized, and in one blow, the *Quartier* lost many of its inhabitants. Then a tidal wave of tourist gold swept over the area and crushed many of its small bookstores and cafés. Much of the area now resembles any other Parisian commercial center.

If an average walk in the park bores you, stroll through the **Jardin des Plantes,** 57, rue Cuvier (Mo. Jussieu). Opened in 1640 for the sole purpose of growing medicinal plants to promote His Majesty's health, it now supports a conglomeration of museums, including a natural history museum, a mineral museum, an insect gallery, a hedge maze, an arboretum, a tropical-flower greenhouse, and, best of all, a full-fledged **zoo.** A walk through the park is, of course, free, but the many museums charge admission. (Zoo open Mon. and Wed.-Sat. 10am-5pm, Sat.-Sun. 11am-6pm. 25F, students ands ages 6-16 13F.) The **boulevard St-Michel,** with its fashionable cafés, restaurants, bookstores and movie theaters, courses with student life. **Place St-Michel,** at the northern tip of this grand avenue, offers a microcosm of the entire quarter—the beautiful fountain, the students, and the street people.

The Panthéon, its proud dome visible from any point in the Latin Quarter, towers over the highest point of the Left Bank (Mo. Cardinal Lemoine, RER Luxembourg). In the **crypt** you ll find the remains of Voltaire, Rousseau, Victor Hugo, Emile Zola, Jean Jaurès, and Louis Braille decaying peacefully in their stone tombs, which can be viewed from behind locked iron gates at each of their niches. The dome lavishes you with an up-close view of a horrifyingly garish set of neoclassical frescoes proclaiming the glory and justice of France, and a disappointing view of the surrounding neighborhood to boot. One ticket provides entry to both. (Crypt and dome open daily 10am-5:45pm. 25F, students 17F, children 13F.)

West of the Panthéon, the **Jardin du Luxembourg** is one of the most beautiful parks in Europe. A block north of the garden's northern edge is the awesome **Eglise St-Sulpice** (Mo. St-Sulpice), containing Delacroix frescoes and one of the world's largest organs. (Open daily 7:30am-7:30pm.) The **Eglise St-Germain-des-Prés,** pl. St-Germain-des-Prés (Mo. St-Germain-des-Prés), showing the wear of its many centuries, is officially the oldest standing church in modern-day Paris, dating from 1163.

7th Arrondissement and Right Bank The **Hôtel des Invalides,** 2, av. de Tourville (Mo. Invalides, Latour-Maubourg, or St-François Xavier) includes the **Musée de l'Armée** (see museums, below); the same ticket admits you to **Napoleon's Tomb,** lovingly placed under Jules Hardouin-Mansart's royal dome. (Open daily 10am-7pm; Oct.-March 10am-5pm; April-Dec. 10am-6pm.)

The railroad bridge cut in half and planted on end that is the **Eiffel Tower** (Mo. Bir-Hakeim) pierces the Paris skyline, symbolizing the City of Light. Built in 1889 to celebrate the centennial of the storming of the Bastille, the world's largest Gallic symbol is breathtaking. Try it at night—even the most blasé will be impressed. (Tower open daily July-Aug. 9:30am-midnight; Sept.-June 9:30am-11pm. Elevator to:

1st floor 18F, 2nd floor 25F, 3rd floor 52F. Under 12 and over 60 1st floor 8F, 2nd floor 17F, 3rd floor 24F. Under 4 free. Wheelchair accessible.)

Charles V built the Right-Bank prison called the Bastille to confine his enemies and to guard the eastern entrance to his capital. On July 14, 1989, François Mitterand inaugurated the glittering **Opéra Bastille**, 120, rue de Lyon, 12ème (Mo. Bastille) to celebrate the destruction of Charles's hated fortress 200 years earlier. West of the Bastille are the 3rd and 4th *arrondissements*, known together as *Le Marais*. With Henry IV's construction of the **place des Vosges** (Mo. St-Paul) at the beginning of the 17th century, the area became the center of fashionable living. Several of the many mansions left in the area now house museums.

Le Jardin des Tuileries, 1er (Mo. Palais-Royal/Musée du Louvre), was built in 1649 and has since become one of the most popular open spaces in Paris. The **place Vendôme**, 3 blocks north along the rue de Castiglione, hides 20th-century office buildings behind 17th-century façades. In the center of the *place* is a column cast from 1,250 Austrian and Russian bronze cannon captured in battle by Napoleon. Its spiral frieze is based on Trajan's column in Rome.

The **place de la Concorde** (Mo. Concorde), Paris's largest and most infamous public square, forms the western boundary of the Tuileries. Constructed between 1757 and 1777 to provide a home for a monument to Louis XV, the vast area soon became the place de la Revolution, the site of the guillotine that severed 1,343 necks. The gargantuan, rose-granite **Obélisque de Louqsor** dates back to the 13th century BC and recalls the deeds of Ramses II.

Stretching west from the *place,* the **avenue des Champs-Elysées**, 8ème, is lined with salons and boutiques of *haute couture* and sprinkled with embassies. At its western terminus, the **Arc de Triomphe,** pl. Charles de Gaulle, moves every heart not made of stone (Mo. Charles de Gaulle-Etoile). The world's largest triumphal arch, and an internationally recognized symbol of France, this behemoth was commissioned in 1806 by Napoleon in honor of his Grande Armée. The *terrasse* at the top of the Arc provides a terrific view of the gorgeous av. Foch and the sprawling city. (Observation deck open daily 9am-6pm. 31F, students 18-25 and over 59 17F, ages 7-17 6F, under 7 free. Expect lines even on weekdays and buy your ticket before going up to the ground level.)

Avenue Foch, one of Haussmann's finest creations, runs from l'Arc de Triomphe to the **Bois de Boulogne**, 16ème (Mo. Porte Maillot, Sablons, Pont de Neuilly, Porte Dauphine, or Porte d'Auteuil), a popular place for walks, jogs, and picnics. Although the police have recently cleaned out many of the drug dealers and prostitutes who once did business here, it's still a poor choice for a romantic, moonlight stroll.

The **Basilique du Sacré-Coeur (Basilica of the Sacred Heart),** 35, rue du Cheval de la Barre, 18ème (Mo. Anvers, Abbesses, or Château-Rouge), crowns the **butte Montmartre** like an enormous, puffy white meringue. Its onion dome is visible from almost any corner of Montmartre and from much of the city down below. Climb the 112m bell tower for the highest point in Paris (yes, you *can* go higher than the Eiffel Tower) and a view that can stretch as far as 50km. (Open daily 7am-11pm. Free. Dome and crypt open daily 9am-7pm; in winter 9am-6pm. To dome 15F, students and seniors 8F. To crypt 10F, students and seniors 5F.)

The **Cimetière Père-Lachaise,** on bd. de Ménilmontant, 20ème (Mo. Père-Lachaise), encloses the remains of Balzac, Colette, Corot, Danton, David, Delacroix, La Fontaine, Haussmann, Molière, and Proust within its peaceful, winding paths and elaborate sarcophagi. Foreigners inhumed here include Chopin, Jim Morrison, Sarah Bernhardt, Gertrude Stein, Modigliani, and Oscar Wilde. French Leftists pay homage to the **Mur des Fédérés** (Wall of the Federals), where 147 *communards* were executed and buried after the suppression of the Commune. (Open Mon.-Fri. 7:30am-6pm, Sat. 8:30am-6pm, Sun. and holidays 9am-6pm; in winter Mon.-Fri. 8am-5:30pm, Sat.-Sun. and holidays 9am-5:30pm.)

Museums

Paris is not a museum, but you could certainly spend all your time going from one to the next. Every institution, artistic movement, ethnic group, and custom seems to have a museum devoted to its history, art, and memorabilia. For listings of temporary exhibits, consult the bimonthly *Le Bulletin des Musées et Monuments Historiques,* available at the tourist office. *Musées et Monuments, Paris,* published by the tourist office, describes the museums and indexes them by theme and *arrondissement. Pariscope, 7 à Paris* and *L'Officiel des spectacles* also list museums with hours and temporary exhibits. Frequent museum-goers, especially those ineligible for discounts, may want to invest in a **Carte Musée,** which grants entry to 65 Parisian museums as well as in the suburbs and environs. The card is available at major museums and metro stations (1 day 60F, 3 days 120F, 5 days 170F).

Les Catacombs, 1, pl. Denfert-Rochereau, 15ème (Mo. Denfert-Rochereau), contain the bones of 5 to 6 million Parisians in former limestone mines. Bring a sweater, a flashlight, and a friend for support. Open Tues.-Fri. 2-4pm, Sat.-Sun. 9-11am and 2-4pm. 15F, students 10F.

Centre National d'Art et de Culture Georges-Pompidou (Palais Beaubourg), 4ème. (Mo. Rambuteau, Hôtel de Ville, or Châtelet-Les Halles). The dazzlingly shameless building-turned-inside-out bares its circulatory system to all passers-by, and has inspired architectural controversy ever since its inauguration in 1977. The **Musée National d'Art Moderne,** the center's main attraction, houses a rich selection of 20th-century art, from fauves and cubists to pop and conceptual art. Open Mon. and Wed.-Fri. noon-10pm, Sat.-Sun. 10am-10pm. Wheelchair access through back entrance on rue Beaubourg. 30F, under 26 20F, under 18 free, Sun. 10am-2pm free. Admission to temporary exhibits varies with the show. Buy your tickets downstairs; they are not available at the museum entrance.

Hôtel de Cluny, 6, pl. Paul-Painlevé, 5ème, not only houses one of the world's finest collections of medieval art, jewelry and tapestries, but is itself a perfectly preserved medieval manor, built on top of restored Roman ruins. Open Wed.-Mon. 9:30am-5:15pm, 26F; under 25, over 60, and Sun. 17F; under 18 free.

Musée de l'Armée, 2, av. de Tourville (Mo. Invalides, Latour-Maubourg, or St-François Xavier), in the Hôtel des Invalides, celebrates centuries of French military history, examining heroes ranging from Napoleon to de Gaulle. Open daily 10am-6pm; Oct.-March 10am-5pm.

Musée Carnavalet, 23, rue de Sévigné, 3ème (Mo. Rivoli or Carnavalet), in a 16th-century *hôtel.* Paris's main display of its own history. Open Tues.-Sun. 10am-5:30pm. 20F, Sun. free. Temporary exhibits extra. Wheelchair access.

Musée des Egouts de Paris (Sewers Museum), actually inside the sewers at the corner of the quai d'Orsay and the place de la Résistance, 7ème (Mo. Pont de l'Alma). Take a self-guided tour with a French, English, German, and Spanish pamphlet, or one of the impromptu tours with a real live *égoutier* (sewer worker). Open Sat.-Wed. 11am-6pm; winter 11am-5pm. Last ticket sold 1hr. before closing. 22F, students 17F. Closed for 3 weeks in Jan.

Musée du Louvre, 1er (Mo. Palais-Royal/Musée du Louvre). Don't try to cover the entire museum in 2hrs.; the most satisfaction you're likely to derive is seeing the *Mona Lisa* through a forest of golf hats. Spending a full day in the museum is more likely to dull your powers of perception than to sharpen your appreciation of the art. Try to take in a few galleries over the course of several days. The extra admission charges are a small price to pay for the satisfaction. Better yet, come on Mon. or Wed. evening, when there are more paintings than people. Open Mon. and Thurs.-Sun. 9:30am-5:30pm, Wed. 9am-9:30pm. Last entry 45min. before closing. 35F, under 26 and over 60 30F, under 18 free. If buying full-priced tickets, save up to 30min. by using one of the automatic ticket machines. Tours in English, Wed.-Sat. every ½hr. 10-11:30am and 2-3:30pm, 30F. Meet at the "Acceuil Groupes" area. Recorded tours of 25 masterpieces—available in English—25F.

Musée d'Orsay, 1, rue de Bellechasse, 7ème (Mo. Solférino; RER Musée d'Orsay), Often reckoned as Paris's Impressionist museum, but in fact devoted to French art in all forms from 1848-1914. Its most engaging displays highlight the lesser-known artists who anticipated Impressionism's revolutionary approach. Contrasting architecture, sculpture, painting, and furniture all showcased beneath the breathtaking ceiling of a former train station. Open Tues.-Wed. and Fri.-Sun. 9am-6pm, Thurs. 9am-9:30pm; Sept. 21-June 19 Tues.-Wed. and Fri.-Sat. 10am-6pm, Thurs. 10am-9:45pm, Sun. 9am-6pm. Last tickets sold 5:15pm, Thurs. 9pm. 31F; ages 18-25, over 60, and Sun. 16F; under 18 free. Guided 90-min. tours Tues.-Sat. 11:30am, Thurs. also at 7pm; in summer also 2pm. 30F.

Musée Picasso, 5, rue de Thorigny, 3ème (Mo. Chemin Vert). Many works of minor significance, but the collection as a whole is fascinating, thanks largely to the tasteful and informative layout. Open Wed.-Mon. 9:30am-6pm; Oct. 1-March 31 9:30am-5:20pm. 33F, reduced 24F. Wheelchair access.

Musée Rodin, 77, rue de Varenne, 7ème (Mo. Varenne), in elegant 18th-century Hôtel Biron. Containing all the major works of France's most famous sculptor, Auguste Rodin, it ranks among the top attractions in Paris. Open Tues.-Sun. 10am-5:45pm; Oct.-March Tues.-Sun. 10am-5pm. Last entry 30min. before closing. To museum and park 26F; under 18, students, and seniors 17F. To park alone 4F.

ENTERTAINMENT

Paris after dark—you've heard a lot about it. The city has much to offer, but don't expect the whole shebang of glamorous options to fall into your lap. The hottest spots in town change at the flight and fancy of elite Parisian party-goers. "In" spots are usually tough to find and frequented by a moderately exclusive crowd that will not go out of its way to accommodate newcomers. Meeting a local may be your only chance to enter a highly private culture that loves to disappear behind intolerably smoky air to stomp, shimmy, sing, or mellow out until dawn. Although nightclubs, jazz *caves,* theater, and even opera don't have to cost an arm and a leg, they grow more expensive in geometric proportion to their exclusivity.

The first thing to do is buy an entertainment weekly, of which the best are the glossy magazine *Pariscope* (issued Wed., 3F) and the Entertainment section in the Thursday *Figaro* (Paris's major newspaper, 6F). These publications, used by hip Parisians, give listings of everything going on, from theater and films to concerts, discothèques and late-night bistros. Look here for your Godard festival, your tango party, or your free Mozart requiem. Even if you don't understand French, you should be able to decipher the listings of times and locations. You can also contact **Info-Loisirs,** a multilingual recording that keeps tabs on events in Paris (in English tel. 47 20 88 98; in French tel. 47 20 94 94).

Fortunately, the most traditional Parisian entertainment—*la flânerie,* strolling, observing other passers-by—is free. The area around the Pompidou Center fills with an aging, rotund fire-eater, sword-swallowers, Chilean guitar bands, and other performers. Around place St-Germain, you'll find throngs of people parading by in the latest fashions and a few bars where unlimited jazz comes with the price of one drink. At Ile St-Louis you'll find more refined tourists strolling the banks of the Seine. To see a movie or to linger in the more fashionable cafés, wander around Montparnasse, the touristy Champs-Elysées, and the streets radiating from bd. St-Michel, bd. St-Germain, and bd. Sébastopol. Keep in mind that several sections of Paris have developed entertainment businesses of a different sort. The areas around Pigalle, Gare St-Lazare, and Beaubourg fill nightly with prostitutes and drug dealers. Everyone should avoid the Bois de Boulogne after dark.

Theater tickets can run as high as 200F, but students can often pay lower prices, and some theaters sell standby tickets a half-hour before the performance. Most theaters close for August. *Pariscope* and *l'Officiel des Spectacles* print complete listings of current shows. Far and away the best place for reduced-rate theater tickets is the **Kiosque-Théâtre,** 15, pl. de la Madeleine, 8ème (Mo. Madeleine), which sells tickets at half-price the day of the show. (Open Tues.-Sat. 12:30-8pm, Sun 12:30-4pm.) For more advanced planning, the student organization **COPAR** (Service des Activités Culturelles), whose ticket agency is at 39, av. Georges Bernanos, 5ème (tel. 40 51 37 13, Mo. Port-Royal), sells discounted tickets and publishes a monthly list of plays. The agency also sells reduced-priced concert tickets, even in summer. They accept any student ID. (Open Sept.-July Mon.-Fri. 9am-4:30pm; July-Aug. 9:30am-noon and 2-4:30pm.) Another useful service for theater, concert, and festival tickets is **Alpha FNAC: Spectacles** at 136, rue de Rennes, 6ème (tel. 49 45 30 00; Mo. Montparnasse-Bienvenue); Forum des Halles, 1-7, rue Pierre Lescot, 1er (Mo. Châtelet-Les Halles); 26-30, av. des Ternes (tel. 44 09 18 00; Mo. Ternes); and 71, bd. St-Germain, 5ème (tel. 44 41 31 50). They sell tickets for theater, concerts, and festivals. Their Carte FNAC (150F for 3 years, students 100F) entitles you to discounts of up to 40% on classical music and theater tickets. (Open Mon.-Sat. 10am-7pm.) Another place to get tickets to concerts and shows is at the **Virgin Megastore,** 52, av. des Champs Elysées, 8ème (tel. 40 74 06 48; Mo. George V). Finally, contact the theater itself—many offer last minute rush tickets.

Jazz

Some critics mourn that Paris is no longer the jazz center it once was. Although big names find it more profitable to play huge summer festivals in southern France and in Switzerland, Paris still nourishes dozens of interesting clubs. Not only do many excellent, lesser-known American musicians play here, the variety of music—including African, Antillean, and Brazilian—is astounding. For complete listings, check out the monthly *Jazz Magazine* or one of the entertainment weeklies.

New Morning, 7-9, rue des Petites-Ecuries, 10ème (tel. 45 23 51 41). Mo. Château d'Eau. 500 seats. All the greats have played here; expect long lines. Open Sept.-July from 9:30pm (times vary—check *Pariscope).* 110F.

Le Petit Opportun, 15, rue des Lavandières-St-Opportune, 1er (tel. 42 36 01 36). Mo. Châtelet. Relaxed and unpolished, featuring the best modern jazz around. Come early to get a place in the tiny 60-seat club. Open Sept.-July Tues.-Sat. from 11pm; bar open until 3am. 1st drink 100F, 50F thereafter.

Au Duc des Lombards, 42, rue des Lombards, 1er (tel. 42 33 22 88). Mo. Châtelet. French jazz groups, occasional American singers or soloists. Great ambiance—dark and smoky and enthusiastic clientele. Come on nights without cover to hear free music. Call for prices—1st drink about 60F. Open daily from 10:30pm.

Discos and Rock Clubs

Paris is not Barcelona, Montréal, or Buenos Aires; you won't find streets filled with young people waiting to get into discos. Instead, the clubs are small, private, and nearly impossible to sniff out unless you're a native. Many Parisian clubs are officially private, which means they have the right to pick and choose their clientele. The management can evaluate prospective customers through peepholes in the handle-less front doors. Parisians tend to dress up more than Americans for a night on the town; haggard backpackers might be wise to try a bar instead.

Les Bains, 7, rue de Bourg l'Abbée, 3ème (tel. 48 87 01 80). Mo. Réaumur-Sébastopol. Ultra-selective and ultra-expensive, but worth it—if you can get in past the fearless bouncers. Prince established its reputation with a surprise concert a few years ago and still drops in occasionally. Models and super-attractive people dressed to those proverbial nines. 140F (includes 1 drink), second drink 100F. Can you stand a third? Open Tues.-Sun. midnight-6am.

Le Palace, 8, rue du Faubourg Montmartre, 9ème (tel. 42 46 10 87). Mo. Montmartre. Huge (up to 2000 people/night), funky disco with multi-level dance floors, each with separate bars and music. American cocktails and occasional rock concerts. Its reputation as the hottest club in Paris no longer holds. Top-40 hits and happy high-school students hoping to hook up. Some older people as well. Cover and 1 drink Tues.-Thurs. 100F; Fri.-Sat. 130F; Sun. 130F for men, free for women. Subsequent drinks 85F. Open Tues.-Sun. 11pm-6am, Fri.-Sat. 11pm-10am. British owners also run **Le Central,** 102, av. des Champs-Elysées, 8ème. Mo. George V. Same prices, older clientele, and a higher percentage of foreigners.

Scala de Paris, 188bis, rue de Rivoli, 1er (tel. 42 61 64 00). Mo. Tuileries. Not as well known or trendy as some, but becoming more popular. Youngish (18-24) crowd dances to house and techno. Lots of foreigners. Sun.-Thurs. 80F, free for women; Fri. 80F for all; Sat. 90F for all. Open daily 11pm-6am.

Le Balajo, 9, rue de Lappe, 11ème (tel. 47 00 07 87). Mo. Bastille. Formerly the favorite stage of Edith Piaf. Founded in 1936. Jammed with a youthful crowd. Cover and first drink 100F. Open Mon. and Wed.-Sat. 11pm-5am.

Le Cirque, 49, rue de Ponthieu, 8ème (tel. 42 25 12 13). Mo. Franklin D. Roosevelt. Currently one of the hottest clubs in Paris. Mixed gay and straight crowd. Mon.-Thurs. night no cover, Fri.-Sun. 90F. Open daily 10:30pm-noon.

Bars

Almost as common as cafés, the bars feature heavier drinking and heavier socializing. Expect to meet new people and engage in absurd conversation. Law dictates a price increase after 10pm, but no one really goes out to drink before then.

Le Bar sans Nom, 49, rue de Lappe, 11ème. Mo. Bastille. There's nothing cooler than this bar—cavernous, deep crimson, and packed with the hippest of the hip. Beer 20F. Cocktails 44F. Open daily 10:30pm-2am.

Pub St-Germain-des-Prés, 17, rue de l'Ancienne Comédie, 6ème. Mo. Odéon. Perhaps the largest and least interesting pub in Europe, this mammoth bar is a long-time favorite of American students. 100 types of whisky. 450 types of bottled beer, 24 on tap. Beers and cocktails start at a whopping 75F. Open 24hr.

Bisexual, Gay, and Lesbian Entertainment

While it's not London or Berlin, Paris has a lively and venerable bi, gay, and lesbian scene. The indisputable center of the scene is still the Marais, but also consider the quieter restaurants and cafés that line the rue Vieille-du-Temple. For the most comprehensive listing of bi, gay, and lesbian restaurants, clubs, hotels, organizations, and services, consult Gai Pied's *Guide Gai 1994* (45F at any kiosk). *Lesbia's* ads are a good gauge of what's hot, or at least what's open (22F at kiosks).

La Champmeslé, 4, rue Chabanais, 2ème (tel. 42 96 85 20). Mo. Opéra. Intimate, relaxed women's bar. Young, yuppie clientele. Cabaret shows Thurs. No cover. Drinks 25-40F. Open Mon.-Sat. 6pm-2am, Sun. 5pm-2am.

Le Bar Central, 33, rue Vieille-du-Temple, 4ème (tel. 42 72 16 94). Mo. Hôtel de Ville. Small and crowded, this friendly bar is popular among locals and tourists alike. Mostly men. Drinks 20-60F. Open daily 4pm-2am.

Le Swing, 42, rue Vieille-du-Temple, 4ème (tel. 42 72 16 94). Mo. Hôtel de Ville. Bar with 50s decor and Elvis music. Drinks 11-40F. Open Mon.-Sat. noon-2am, Sun. 2pm-2am.

Le Piano Zinc, 49, rue des Blancs Manteaux, 4ème (tel. 42 74 32 42). Mo. Rambuteau. Piano bar (after 10:30pm) where campy performers pay homage to Judy, Liza, Eartha, Madonna, Better, Grace Jones, and, of course, Edith Piaf. We're talking campy. Drinks 36-42F. Open Tues.-Sat. 6pm-2am.

Le Piano Show, 20, rue de la Ververie, 4ème (tel. 42 72 23 81). Mo. Hôtel de Ville. Restaurant-cabaret performs a drag cabaret that'll knock your pantyhose off! Dinner and show Sun.-Thurs. 9-11:30pm. 260F. Reservations required.

Offbeat Entertainment

Paris lives up to its reputation as the City of Lights every night from sundown to midnight. Walk around and see the Panthéon, Eiffel Tower, Notre-Dame, Arc de Triomphe, and Obélisque transformed. As a variation on this theme, the French have invented a new art form: take an impressive building, add a light show, superimpose a recorded message about the glorious history of the building, the region, or the country, *et voilà:* **son et lumière.** It's as tacky as it sounds, but that's half the fun. Check the entertainment weeklies for listings or the pamphlet *Paris Illuminé,* available at the tourist office.

A ride on the **bateaux-mouches** (tel. 42 25 96 10) river boats may seem goofy until you try it. The high embankments on both sides of the Seine obscure everything but the tops of the highest buildings, but it's a worthwhile trip at night. Be prepared to laugh at 1½ hours of continuous sight-commentary in 5 languages and dozens of tourists straining their necks to peer over the next guy. (Departures every ½hr. from 10am-10:30pm from the Right Bank pier near pont d'Alma. Mo. Alma-Marceau. 30F, under 14 15F.) The **Batobus** (tel. 47 05 50 00) makes frequent stops along both sides of the river from April to September. A spin on this ridiculous form of transportation costs 10F. (Daypass 50F.) Buy tickets on board.

■ Near Paris

La Défense Paris has laws governing the size and shape of buildings within the city limits; these were instituted to prevent repeating the architectural mistakes of the 1960s (ugly tower blocks that are not only aesthetic disasters, but also contribute to traffic congestion). La Défense, just outside city limits and reachable by metro, forms a sharp contrast to this regimentation. The headquarters of 14 of France's top 20 corporations vie to outdo each other with sleek, modern design. The boldest plan is that of the **Grande Arche,** a 35-story office block in the shape of a hollowed cube. Go through the roof for a great view. (Open Sun.-Thurs. 9am-8pm, Fri.-Sat. 9am-9pm; roof closes 1 hr. after ticket office. 32F, under 18 25F. Wheelchair accessible.) Shops, galleries, trees and a liberal sprinkling of sculpture make the large pedestrian esplanade a pleasant place for a stroll. Major roads run underneath the esplanade, but you'll feel less oppressed by pollution and cars here than you ever will in central Paris.

Versailles, Chartres, and Giverny The magnificent palace of Louis XIV, **Versailles** perfectly embodies the Sun King's absolute power and his famous statement, *"L'État, c'est moi"* (I am the State). Louis gathered the aristocracy of France to this glorified hunting lodge, forcing them to vie for his attention while paying crippling taxes. The incredibly lavish building embodies the old-regime's extravagance that led to the Revolution. Le Nôtre's geometric gardens are studded with unforgettable fountains, which spurt every Sunday (May-Sept). (Château open daily 9am-6:30pm; Oct.-April 9am-5:30pm. Last entry 1hr. before closing. To State Apartments and Hall of Mirrors 40F; ages 18-25, over 60, and Sun. 26F; under 18 free. For info, call 30 84 76 76, -74 00.) Take RER Line C5 to the Versailles Rive Gauche station from downtown Paris (roughly every 20min., 35min., round-trip 20F).

The stunning **Cathédrale de Chartres,** spared by bureaucratic inefficiency after being condemned during the Revolution, survives today as one of the most sublime creations of the Middle Ages. Arguably the finest example of Gothic architecture in the world, the cathedral gained fame for its stained-glass windows and the magnificent sculptures adorning each of the main portals. (Open daily 7:30am-7:30pm; in winter 7:30am-7pm. No casual visits allowed Sat. 5:45-7pm or Sun. 9-10:15am and 10:45am-noon because of religious services.) The town of Chartres provides a refreshing change from the grand boulevards and cosmopolitan atmosphere of Paris. Chartres is accessible by frequent trains from Gare Montparnasse (1hr., round-trip 122F). In Paris call 45 82 50 50 for info; in Chartres call 37 28 50 50. Many trains run only on certain days or occasions—make sure you aren't caught waiting in vain.

While most of Monet's own works have been scattered to the world's greatest museums, the subject of many of his paintings was his garden in the village of **Giverny,** including the famous Japanese-style bridge and the water lilies below. The **Musée Claude Monet** (tel. 32 51 28 21) includes the garden and renovated house. Arrive early, as the line often stretches into a 2-hour wait. (House and garden open April-Oct. Tues.-Sun.) Trains arrive from Paris St.-Lazare to **Vernon,** across the river and 6km from the museum (every 2hr., 45min., 60F). To get to Giverny, rent a **bike** from the station (55F/day, 1000F deposit), or take a **bus** from the front of the station (3/day each way; 10min.; 10F, round-trip 16F).

ROUEN

Euro Disney® It's a small world after all; it's a small, small world. Although Euro Disney® Resort (tel. 64 74 28 82) may eventually develop its 600 hectares, the current theme park isn't even the size of an *arrondissement*. From the gate it takes only 10 minutes to walk to the farthest point inside the park, nothing like the vast reaches of Florida's Disneyworld. On the other hand, this is the most technologically advanced Disney park yet, and the special effects on some of the rides are enough to knock your Reeboks off. The easiest way to get to Euro Disney® is to take the RER A4 from Gare de Lyon or Châtelet-Les Halles. Before hopping on the train, check the illuminated electric boards hanging above the platform to make sure there is a light next to the Marne-La-Vallée/Chessy stop, otherwise the train won't end up there (every 30min., 50min., round-trip 66F). Buy tickets to the park at the park or at the Paris tourist office on the Champs-Elysées, which is definitely the fastest method if you plan to visit on a weekend. (Park open daily 9am-midnight. 225F. Hours subject to change during the winter.)

NORMANDY (NORMANDIE)

Inspiration to Impressionists and generals, fertile Normandy is a land of gently undulating farmland, tiny fishing villages, and soaring cathedrals. Vikings seized the region in the 9th century, and invasions have twice secured Normandy's place in military history: in 1066, when William of Normandy conquered England, and on D-Day, June 6, 1944, when Allied armies began the liberation of France here.

Normandy supplies a fat percentage of the country's butter. Try the creamy, pungent *Camembert* cheese, but be sure it's ripe (soft in the middle). Eating *tripes à la Normandaise* (made from cow guts) requires intestinal fortitude (yours, that is). The province's traditional drink *(cidre)* is fermented apple juice that comes both dry *(brut)* and sweet *(doux)*. A harder cousin is *Calvados,* aged apple brandy, whose fumes alone are lethal.

■■■ ROUEN

Best known as the city where Joan of Arc was burned and Emma Bovary was bored, Rouen is no provincial town. From the 10th through the 12th centuries, Rouen witnessed a flowering of Gothic architecture while enjoying great power and prestige as the capital of the Norman empire. More recently, American and German troops bombed the city's history to pieces. Victor Hugo dubbed Rouen "the city of 100 spires," the most famous of which are the needles, gargoyles and gables of the **Cathédrale de Notre Dame,** with the tallest tower (151m) in France. The now-grimy Gothic façade so fascinated Monet that he painted it over and over again in varying lights and seasons. Behind the cathedral lies **Eglise St-Maclou,** a fine example of the later, flamboyant Gothic style. Its charnel house, **Aitre St-Maclou** (turn left into 186, rue de Martinville), with its cloister of macabre wood carvings, has also been preserved. (Open daily 8am-9pm. Free.) Joan of Arc burned at the stake on **place du Vieux Marché,** east of the center of town; a cross near the modern, boat-shaped **Eglise Jeanne d'Arc** marks the spot. Pedestrian precincts full of cafés and restaurants radiate from the charmingly inaccurate **Gros Horloge,** a 14th-century clock tower and Renaissance gatehouse. (Open April-Oct. Thurs.-Mon. 10am-noon and 2-6pm, Wed. 2-6pm. 10F, students free.) The **Musée Flaubert et d'Histoire de la Médecine,** 51, rue de Lecat, houses a gruesome array of pre-anesthesia medical instruments, including gallstone crushers and a battlefield amputation kit. (Open Tues.-Sat. 10am-noon and 2-6pm. Free.)

Accommodations, Food, and Practical Information Rouen's clean, modern, discordant **auberge de jeunesse (HI)** is at 118, bd. de l'Europe (tel. 35 72

06 45), across the river. Take bus #12 from the station or walk straight across the river on rue Jeanne d'Arc and its extensions, av. Jacques Cartier and av. de Bretagne, to bd. de l'Europe (½hr.). (Reception open 5-10pm. Lockout 10am-5pm. Curfew 11pm. 55F. 100F deposit for linen and a locker key.) **Hôtel Normandya,** 32, rue du Cordier (tel. 35 71 46 15), offers attractive, bright rooms only 10 minutes from the train station. (Singles and doubles 80-100F, with shower 130F.) **The Hôtel St-Ouen,** 43, rue des Faulx (tel. 35 71 46 44), across from the Eglise St-Ouen, has spacious rooms kept by a friendly owner. (Singles 75-130F. Doubles 105-140F.) For information on university **CROUS** lodgings, which are cheap but usually available only on summer weekends, ask the tourist office or call 35 74 18 68.

A **market** enlivens pl. du Vieux Marché (Tues.-Wed. and Fri.-Sun. 7am-12:30pm). Buy fish, cheese and fresh produce there or at **Monoprix supermarket,** 67, rue du Gros Horloge. (Open Mon.-Sat. 9am-7pm.) For the ferocious *calvados* of yore, buy directly from the farmers in the Norman countryside. **La Petite Flambée,** 24, rue Chauchoise, just off pl. Vieux-Marché, flips super *crêpes.* (10-28F. Open Tues.-Fri. noon-2:30pm and 7-11:30pm, Sat.-Sun. 7-11:30pm.) Near the cathedral, **Natural Vital,** 3, rue du Petit Salut, serves great vegetarian *plats du jour,* including drink, dessert, and coffee for 68F. (Open Tues.-Sat. noon-3pm. Health food store open Tues.-Sat. 8:30am-7pm.)

From Rouen's train station (lockers 15-30F), walk straight down rue Jeanne d'Arc and turn left onto rue Gros Horloge for pl. de la Cathédrale and the **tourist office** (tel. 35 71 41 77). Rouen is easily accessible by **train** from Paris's Gare St-Lazare (1/hr., 70min., 95F), from Lille (3/day, 3hr., 154F), Le Havre (1/hr., 1hr., 64F), and Caen (every 2hr., 2hr., 112F).

■■■ NORMANDY COAST

With its seaside cliff relief and thriving pedestrian district, **Dieppe** is now one of the largest passenger ports in France. Many visitors come to roast on the long pebbly beach, bordered by protective cliffs to the west and the port to the east. The **auberge de jeunesse (HI),** 48, rue Louis Fromager (tel. 35 84 85 73), has recently been renovated. From the station, take bus #1 (direction "Les Bruyères") from the station and ask the driver to drop you at the *auberge;* or call ahead for directions. (Members only. Lockout 11pm. 42F.)

Fécamp is famous for the massive **Abbatiale de la Trinité,** whose 127m nave is as long as that of Paris's Notre-Dame. (Open daily 9am-7pm. Free.) The relic of the **Précieux Sang,** a fig trunk that allegedly carried a few drops of Christ's blood and washed ashore in the 6th century, rests within the nave. An **auberge de jeunesse (HI)** (tel. 35 29 75 79) overlooks town from rue du Commandant Roquigny. (Members only. 42F. Camping 22F. Open May-Oct. 15.) The **tourist office,** 113, rue Alexandre Le Grand (tel. 35 28 51 01), dispenses free maps and books rooms. (Open daily 9am-12:15pm and 1:45-6pm; Nov.-April also Sat.-Sun. 10am-1pm and 2-6pm.)

Le Havre, the country's largest transatlantic port, connects France with Rosslare and Cork in Ireland and Portsmouth in England. **P&O European Ferries,** quai de Southampton (tel. 35 21 36 50), serves Portsmouth year-round. (Ticket and info office open Mon.-Sat. 7am-noon and 2-11:30pm). Take bus #3 from the train station or the Hôtel de Ville. **Irish Ferries,** quai du Môle Central (tel. 35 53 28 83), alternates service to Rosslare and Cork (Eurail valid). Take bus #4 from the train station or the Hôtel de Ville to the "Marceau" stop. Avoid walking alone at night in Le Havre, especially near the station and the port. Try the homey **Hôtel Jeanne d'Arc,** 91, rue Emile-Zola (tel. 35 41 26 83), off rue de Paris with singles from 120F and doubles from 135F, or the pleasant **Hôtel Séjour Fleuri,** 71, rue Emile-Zola (tel. 35 41 33 81), where singles and doubles are 100-130F, with shower 145F. The **tourist office** (tel. 35 21 22 88) is across the bridge in the Hôtel de Ville. (Open Mon.-Sat. 8:45am-12:15pm and 1:30-7pm; Oct.-March 8:45am-12:15pm and 1:30-6:30pm.)

C A E N

Trains connect Le Havre to Rouen, Paris, and Fécamp. The **bus station,** bd. de Strasbourg (tel. 35 26 67 23), runs various buses along the coast west of Le Havre all the way to Cabourg and then on to Caen.

■■■ CAEN

Despite a punishing Allied bombardment during WWII, the Romanesque churches of **Caen** recall the prosperous 11th century, when the town was William the Conqueror's ducal seat. In the town center, the imposing ruins of William's **château** (open daily 6am-9:30pm; Oct.-April 6am-7:30pm) enclose two notable museums: the **Musée des Beaux Arts,** with paintings by Monet, Rubens, and Perugino; and the **Musée de Normandie,** which traces Norman peasant life. (Beaux Arts will reopen from renovations in early 1994. Normandie open Wed.-Fri. 10am-12:30pm and 2-6pm; April-Sept. Sat.-Mon. 9:30am-12:30pm and 2-6pm. 10F, students 5F. Wed. free.) In the shadow of the château stands the **Eglise St-Pierre,** whose bell tower and detailed exterior illustrate the evolution of the Gothic style from the 13th through the 16th centuries. (Open daily 9am-noon and 2-6pm.) Perched above the city center, the **Abbaye-aux-Dames** and its twin, the **Abbaye-aux-Hommes,** were built by William and his cousin Mathilda to expiate the sin of their incestuous marriage. North of the center, the excellent **Mémorial: Un Musée Pour la Paix** makes a cogent plea for world peace with high-tech audio-visual aids and actual WWII footage. Take bus #17 from *centre ville* (direction "Mémorial"). (Open daily 9am-10pm; Sept.-May daily 9am-7pm. 41F.) The super-organized, English-speaking **tourist office,** pl. St-Pierre (tel. 31 86 27 65), finds rooms. (15F in town. Open Mon.-Sat. 9am-7pm, Sun. and holidays 10am-12:30pm and 3-6pm; mid-Sept. to May Mon. 10am-noon and 2-7pm, Tues.-Sat. 9am-noon and 2-7pm.)

Accommodations, Food, and Practical Information To reach Caen's **Auberge de Jeunesse (HI),** foyer Robert Reme, 68bis, rue Eustache-Restout (tel. 31 52 19 96) from the station, walk right, take a left up the hill at the end of the street, and catch bus #5 or 17 (direction "Fleury" or "Grâce de Dieu") to "Lycée Fresnel." (Reception open June-Sept. daily 5-10pm. Lockout during day. Members only. 65F.) The more conveniently located **Hôtel de la Paix,** 14, rue Neuve-St-Jean (tel. 31 86 18 99), near the château, has a helpful proprietor. (Comfortable singles 105F, with shower 165F. Doubles 115F, with shower 185F. Showers 20F.) The clean rooms of the **Hôtel St-Jean,** 20, rue des Martyrs (tel. 31 86 23 35), next to Eglise St-Jean, are in a quiet setting. (Singles and doubles with shower 140-180F.)

Several inexpensive *crêperies* and *brasseries,* as well as a smattering of ethnic restaurants, line the **quartier Vaugeux,** near the château. **La Petite Auberge,** 17, rue des Equipes-d'Urgence, next to Eglise St-Jean, offers excellent Norman-style *menus.* (Open Tues.-Sat. noon-2pm and 7-9pm, Sun. 7-9pm.) Caen's staid old streets pulsate by moonlight, especially by the university. At the **Pub Concorde,** 7, rue Montoir Poissonnerie (tel. 31 93 61 29), the "century-and-a-half-club" samples 150 beers from around the world. (Open Mon.-Sat. 6pm-4am.) Locals frequent the **Retro Piano-Bar,** 9, rue Fresnel (tel. 31 44 09 19), for mellow atmosphere and nightly jazz concerts. (Open Tues.-Sat. 9pm-4am.) The brochure *Le Mois à Caen* lists plays, concerts, and exhibitions for the month. Free copies are available at the youth hostel and at the student center, **CROUS,** 23, av. de Bruxelles (tel. 31 94 73 37).

From pl. de la Gare (tel. 31 83 50 50) **trains** depart to: Paris (17/day, 2hr., 153F) and Rouen (4/day, 1½hr., 111F), and **Bus Verts** (tel. 31 44 77 44) to: Bayeux (2/day, 1hr., 34F) and Le Havre (2/day, 2½hr., 111F).

■■■ BAYEUX, D-DAY BEACHES, AND CHERBOURG

Bayeux Beautiful, ancient Bayeux is an ideal launching pad for the D-Day beaches, and is itself renowned for the **Bayeux Tapestry,** which recounts the Norman conquest of Britain at the 1066 Battle of Hastings. The linen embroidery, probably commissioned for Bayeux's cathedral, now hangs in the **Centre Guillaume le Conquérant** on rue de Nesmond (tel. 31 92 05 48). (Exhibitions and audio cassette in French and English. Open May 16-Sept. 15 daily 9am-7pm; Sept. 16-Oct. 15 and March 16-May 15 9am-12:30pm and 2-6:30pm; Oct. 16-March 15 9:30am-12:30pm and 2-6pm. 28F, students 13F.)

The helpful, English-speaking staff of the **tourist office,** 1, rue des Cuisiniers (tel. 31 92 16 26), makes hotel reservations for the price of a phone call, hunts down rooms in private homes, and changes money when banks are closed. (Open Mon.-Sat. 9:30am-12:30pm and 2-6:30pm, Sun. 10am-12:30pm and 3-6:30pm; mid-Sept. to May 9:30am-12:30pm and 2-6:30pm.) The coziest place to stay is the converted 16th-century residence, **Family Home (HI),** 39, rue Général-de-Dais (tel. 31 92 15 22), off rue de la Juridiction. (Follow signs from the train station. Reception open daily 7:30am-11pm. 75F, nonmembers 85F. Make reservations.) The **Centre d'Accueil Municipal,** 21, rue des Marettes (tel. 31 92 08 19), has sterile singles for 78F (Reception open daily 7am-10pm.) Check out the beautiful, modern rooms at **Hôtel des Sports,** 19, rue Saint-Martin (tel. 31 92 28 53), a block down from the tourist office. (Singles and doubles with shower 160F and 180F; quads 310F.) For fantastic Norman cuisine, try **Le Petit Normand,** 35, rue Larcher (tel. 31 22 88 66), overlooking the cathedral; *menus* start at 49F. (Open Mon.-Sat. noon-2pm and 7-9:30pm, Sun. noon-2pm. Reservations recommended.)

D-Day Beaches and Cherbourg Ten km north of Bayeux on the D514 is **Arromanches,** easternmost of the **D-Day beaches.** Look for special events in 1994, as it's the 50th anniversary of the invasion. Arromanches's fascinating **Musée du Débarquement** displays photographs of the British and Canadian landings. (Open daily 9am-6:30pm; Sept.-June 9-11:30am and 2-5:30pm. 25F, students 12F.) The high cliffs of **Omaha Beach,** scaled by invading American troops, lie to the west. The American Cemetery is in **Colleville-St-Laurent;** the Canadian Cemetery is at **Bény-sur-Mer-Reviers,** near Courseulles; there are British cemeteries at **Hermanville-sur-Mer** and **Ranville.** English-speaking tours based in Bayeux are more convenient than buses. In Bayeux, **Normandy Tours** (tel. 31 92 10 70) runs small, flexible tours for 1-8 people (2/day, 100F, students 90F), and **Bus Fly,** 24, rue Montfiquet (tel. 31 22 00 08) leaves from the Family Home (daily 9am and 2pm, 120F, students 100F).

Northwest of Bayeux at the northern tip of the Cotentin peninsula lies **Cherbourg,** WWII's "Port de la Libération," which shuttles passengers to and from Portsmouth, Poole, and Southampton, England. **Irish Ferries** (tel. 33 44 28 96) run to Rosslare, Ireland 3 times a week in high season, less in off-season. The train station is a 15-minute walk from the ferry terminal; trains run to Paris (7/day, 3½hr., 240F), Rouen (3/day, 3hr., 174F), Caen (6/day, 1½hr., 90F), Bayeux (9/day, 1hr., 72F), and points south in Normandy and Brittany. If you stay overnight in this city of concrete blockhouses, try the **auberge de jeunesse (HI)** av. Louis Lumière (tel. 33 44 26 31), a converted elementary-school 15 minutes by foot from the train station. Take bus #5 from behind the station (direction "Tourlaville," every 30min., last bus 7:20pm, 5F20) to the "Fleming" stop, or walk right on the highway toward Tourlaville and hang a right at the first light after the round-about, onto av. Maréchal de Lattre de Tassigny; the hostel is one block away on the left corner. (Reception open daily 8am-noon and 7-11pm. Lockout noon-7pm. Members only. 56F.)

■■■ MONT SAINT-MICHEL

No matter how many times you've seen it in pictures, your heart will flutter when you first glimpse Mont-St-Michel. A venerable abbey and exquisite cloister balance precariously on the jutting rock, surrounded by military fortifications and a *ville basse* built to serve medieval pilgrims. Pack a lunch and make the Mont a daytrip; ignore its tourist swarms. You can pay to visit just limited parts of the abbey on your own or take a one-hour guided tour to see more. (Open daily 9:30am-6pm; Sept. 16-Nov. 10 and Feb. 16-May 14 9:30-11:45am and 1:45-5pm; Nov. 12-Feb. 15 9:30-11:45am and 1:45-4:15pm. Tours in English daily at 10am, 11am, noon, 1:30pm, 2:30pm, 3:30pm, 4:30pm, and 5:30pm. Tours in French every 20min. 32F, ages 18-25 and over 60 21F, under 18 6F, Sun. ½-price.) The 2-hour *visites conférences* (French only) are a special treat; they allow you to walk atop a flying buttress and creep inside the pre-Roman crypts. (Tours daily at 10am, 11am, 2:30pm, and 3:30pm. 52F, ages 18-25 and over 60 41F, under 18 26F.) The tide rushes in to envelop the Mont at 2m per second; an extraordinary sight. Try to time your visit with the highest tides: 36 to 48 hours after the new and full moons respectively. You must be on the Mont 2 hours ahead of time, as the causeway becomes impassable. Mont St-Michel is illuminated during all church festivals and feasts, on high-tide nights, and nightly from July to September (dusk-11pm).

Prices rise higher than the bay's famous tides, but the **Centre Duguesclin (HI)** (tel. 33 60 18 65), rue Gén. Patton, a 10-minute walk from the Pontorson station, has good facilities. (Reception open daily 9-11am and 6-10pm. Lockout 9am-6pm. Members only. 41F.) In **Pontorson**, stay in the comfortable rooms of the **Hôtel de l'Arrivée**, pl. de la Gare (tel. 33 60 01 57), across from the station. (Singles and doubles 80-100F. 3-4 people 150-180F.) Count on walking the 5km from Pontorson to **Pleine-Fougères (HI)**, rue de la Gare (tel. 99 48 75 59; 45F.)

To get to Mont St-Michel, take a train to **Pontorson;** from Paris, change at Rennes (2/day, 4hr., 235F), Folligny (2/day, 197F), or Caen (2/day, 219F), or take the TGV from Paris to Rennes and change there (3-4/day, 3hr., 235F plus 36-90F required reservation). The last train from Pontorson to Rennes leaves around 7pm. Conquer the remaining 9km to the Mont by boarding the **STN bus** outside the Pontorson station (the last leaves the Mont at 5:45pm) or by renting a **bike** at the station (55F/day with a 100F deposit or major credit card). Lock your baggage at the station (3F) or with the gracious toilet attendant at the Porte Bavole (10F/day).

BRITTANY (BRETAGNE)

This rugged peninsula, with cliffs gnawed by the sea into long crags and inlets, tugs away from mainland France, intent on its own direction. Unlike most of their compatriots, Bretons are a Celtic people whose ancestors crossed over from Britain to escape Anglo-Saxon invaders in the 5th and 6th centuries. Today's locals aver that they are Bretons first and French second, and lilting *Breizh* (Breton) is spoken energetically at the pubs and ports in the western part of the province. Recently the French government has granted more autonomy to the local Breton leadership and has begun to support the preservation of Breton culture.

The French have great affection for the spectacular beaches and misty, almost apocalyptic headlands that line this province. June is a perfect month to see Brittany, as the weather is mild, the restaurants and hotels open, and the towns not yet swarmed. Off-season, many of the coastal resorts essentially shut down, but the churches, beaches, and cliffs will seduce with their eerie and romantic solitude. *Menhirs, cromlechs,* and *dolmens*—all megalithic rock monuments left by Brittany's first neolithic inhabitants—dot the Breton islands and mainland.

The region's 1800-odd *crêperies* set their tables with the regional specialty, accompanied by *cidre brut* (the local cider) or by the sweeter *cidre doux*. Such delectable seafood dishes as *coquilles St-Jacques* (scallops), *saumon fumé* (smoked salmon), and *moules marinières* (steamed mussels in a white wine-based broth) are served with *muscadet*, a dry white from the vineyards around Nantes. Brittany's *pâtisseries* display *kouign amann* (flaky sheets dripping with butter and sugar).

While getting to Brittany is hardly a problem (high-speed trains from Paris's Gare Montparnasse arrive in Rennes and Brest 2 and 4 hr. later, respectively), getting around Brittany is a different matter. The main train lines run between Rennes and Brest (passing through none of the scenic towns), between Rennes and Quimper and between Nantes and Quimper. Smaller, less frequent trains and SNCF buses connect such towns as St-Malo, Dinan, Paimpol, Camaret, and Quiberon to the main lines, but not necessarily to each other. Cycling is the best way to travel. Hikers can choose from a number of routes, including the long-distance footpaths *(Grandes Randonnées)* GR341, GR37, GR38, GR380 and the spectacular GR34 along the northern coast. Tourist offices can help you coordinate your hiking or biking tour.

■■■ RENNES

In 1720, a drunken carpenter knocked over his lamp and set most of Rennes ablaze. This misbegotten bonfire consumed all but the heart of the wood-heavy *vieille ville*, but Rennes has survived and become the administrative center of Brittany. The **Musée de Bretagne** and the **Musée des Beaux Arts** are housed in the same building at 20, quai Emile Zola, by the canal. The Musée de Bretagne provides an informative introduction to the region's history and traditions; the Musée des Beaux Arts displays local landscapes as well as an interesting (if obscure) collection of art from the 14th century to the present. (Both open Wed.-Mon. 10am-noon and 2-6pm. To each 15F, under 14 8F.) The pamphlet *Spectacles, Informations* at the tourist office lists everything going on around town. In early July, Rennes hosts **Les Tombées de la Nuit,** 9 days of non-stop music, dance, theater, song, and mime by international performers who prowl the streets from noon to midnight. For information, write to the Office de Tourisme, Festival de TN, 8, pl. du Maréchal Juin, 35000 Rennes (tel. 99 79 01 98, 99 30 38 01). For hiking and biking information, head to the **Association Bretonne des Relais et Itinéraires (ABRI),** also known as **maison de la Randonée,** 9, rue des Portes Mordelaises (tel. 99 31 59 44). It offers piles of invaluable information on Brittany's extensive network of Grande Randonée routes as well as lists of *gîtes d'étape*. (Open Mon.-Sat. 9:30am-12:30pm and 2-7pm.)

Accommodations, Food, and Practical Information The **tourist office,** pont de Nemours (tel. 99 79 01 98), has accommodations info as well as good city maps. (Open Mon.-Sat. 9am-7pm, Sun. 10am-1pm and 3-5pm; mid-Sept. to mid-June 10am-12:30pm and 2-6:30pm.) To reach the newly renovated **auberge de jeunesse (HI),** 10-12 Canal St-Martin (tel. 99 33 22 33), walk (30min. from station) or take bus #20 or 22, or #2 on weekends (direction "Centre Commercial Nord") to "Pont de Legraverend." (Reception open Mon.-Fri. 7:45am-11pm, Sat.-Sun. 8-10am and 6-11pm. Curfew midnight; 30F key deposit to get in later. Members only. Singles 103F. Doubles 146F. Triples 189F. Quads 252F. Sheets 16F.) The well-located **Hôtel de Léon,** 15, rue de Léon (tel. 99 30 55 28), near the Vilaine River off quai de Richemont, has 110F singles and 127F doubles. (Floor showers 16F. Breakfast 23F. Closed 2 weeks in July or Aug.) Formerly a prison, the **Crêperie du Boulingrain,** 25, rue St-Melaine, serves *galettes* worth doing some jail time for. *(Crêpe* 35F. Open Mon.-Fri. 11:30am-2pm and 6:30-11pm, Sat.-Sun. 6:30-11pm.) Otherwise, take some bread and cheese to a bench in the beautiful **Jardin du Thabor.**

Rennes is 2 hours from Paris's Gare Montparnasse by TGV (3½hr. by regular train) and accessible from Normandy via Caen. **Trains** leave from the station on pl. de la Gare (tel. 99 65 50 50; reservations 99 65 18 65), running to St-Malo (11/day, 1hr.,

61F), Nantes (8/day, 2hr., 104F), Caen (3/day, 3hr., 166F), and Paris (3/day, 3½hr., 210F; 9 TGVs/day, 2hr., 210F plus 36-90F TGV reservation). **Buses,** bd. Magenta (tel. 99 30 87 80), off pl. de la Gare, serve St-Malo (2/day in summer, 6/day in winter; 90min.; 48F) and Vannes (2/day, 2¾hr., 88F) The **post office,** 27, bd. du Colombier (tel. 99 31 42 72) **exchanges currency.** (Open Mon.-Fri. 8am-7pm, Sat. 8am-noon.) **Postal Code:** 35000.

■■■ ST-MALO AND DINAN

St-Malo To writer Châteaubriand, St-Malo's ever-changing shore provided Romantic inspiration. Today, the town is the ultimate vacation spot; walk on the high walls, explore the tiny streets, duck into the many small restaurants and shops, and luxuriate on its miles of beach. Porte St-Thomas looks out onto the **Fort National,** accessible only at low tide. Climb down to the beach and continue along the stone walkway to **Le Grand Bé,** the small island that holds Châteaubriand's lonely grave. Within the walls of the *vieille ville,* the **Musée de la Ville** (tel. 99 40 71 11), at the Hôtel de Ville near Porte St-Vincent, leads you through caches of maps, models, maritime documents, and other pirate paraphernalia. The turret has a phenomenal panorama of St-Malo. (Open daily 10am-noon and 2-6pm; Nov.-March Wed.-Mon. 10am-noon and 2-6pm. 18F, students 9F.)

During July and August, accommodations are wicked hard to come by. To get to the **auberge de jeunesse (HI),** 37, av. du Père Umbricht (tel. 99 40 29 80), walk (25min. from station) or catch bus #5 (direction "Paramet;" last bus at 7:30pm) and get off after the hostel flags on the left. (Open 24hr. No lockout. Members only. 64F. Modern doubles 72F/person.) Next door, the **Foyer des Jeunes Travailleurs** has laundry facilities (20F). Basic, comfortable rooms await you at **Les Chiens du Guet,** 4, pl. du Guet (tel. 99 40 46 77; singles 150-170F, with shower 180-240F; prices may increase during high tourist season). Info on campgrounds is available at the tourist office. **Camping de la Cité d'Aleth,** near promenade de la Corniche in **St-Servan** (tel. 99 81 60 91), is the closest and most scenic site, equipped with running water and hot shower. (18F/adult, 9F/child, 7F/car, 9F/tent.)

The **tourist office,** Esplanade St-Vincent (tel. 99 56 64 48), near the entrance to the old city, distributes a city map and a list of campsites. (Open Mon.-Sat. 9am-8pm, Sun. 10am-6pm; Sept.-June Mon.-Sat. 9am-noon and 2-7pm, Sun. 10am-noon and 2-5pm.) **Trains** chug daily to Paris-Montparnasse (3/day, 5hr., 356F) and the TGV books to Paris via Rennes (7-9/day, 3½hr., 356F plus 36-90F reservation fee). The pavilion opposite the tourist office doles out information on buses and ferries. **Mont St-Michel** makes a convenient daytrip from St-Malo. Reserve a day in advance at any of the bus tour offices by the tourist office. Most cost 87F.

Dinan Thirty-five km southwest of St-Malo, tranquil Dinan was once the focus of a medieval tug-of-war between England and France, and today boasts proudly of its reputation as the best preserved medieval town in Brittany. The **Promenade des Petits-Fossés** begins near the post office and follows the looming ramparts to the 13th-century **Porte du Guichet,** the entrance to the formidable **Château de la Duchesse Anne.** Inside its oval tower, the **Musée de Dinan** displays 18th-century multicolored statuettes and bas-reliefs and a selection of medieval and Roman weapons and artifacts. (Château and museums open June-Oct. 14 daily 10am-6:30pm; Oct. 15-Nov. 15 and March 16-May Wed.-Mon. 10am-noon and 2-6pm; Nov. 16-Dec. 31 and Feb. 7-March 15 Wed.-Mon. 1:30-5:30pm. 20F, students 10F.) In the *vieille ville,* rue Général de Gaulle leads to the **Promenade de la Duchesse Anne,** at the end of which stands the beautiful **Jardin Anglais.** From the port, reenter the walled city by **rue de Petit Fort,** which becomes **rue du Jerzval,** one of Dinan's prettiest roads. On rue de l'Horloge, the 15th-century **Tour de l'Horloge** commands a brilliant view of Dinan's jumbled medieval streets. (Open June-Aug. daily 10am-7pm. 10F. Call tourist office to ascend off-season.)

There's no bus to the **auberge de jeunesse (HI),** Moulin du Méen in Vallée de la Fontaine-des-Eaux (tel. 96 39 10 83), but if you're arriving at night and call ahead, the hostel will arrange to pick you up at the station. If you're walking (30min.), turn left from the train station's main exit, then turn left across the tracks and follow the signs. (Reception open daily 8-11am and 3-11pm. Curfew 11pm; make arrangements if you'll be out later. Members only. 43F. If the hostel is full, cots in tent outside are only 23F. Sheets 15F.) **The Hôtel du Théâtre,** 2, rue Ste-Claire (tel. 96 39 06 91), around the corner from the tourist office, has comfortable rooms in a crackerjack location. (Singles and doubles 80-120F. Doubles with showers 145F.) **Camp** at the youth hostel in a beautiful location (23F/night). Featured in the *New York Times,* **the Crêperie des Artisans,** 6, rue du Petit Fort, serves a feast of *galettes* and *crêpes. (Menus* 45-60F. Open daily noon-10:30pm; Sept.-June open Tues.-Sun.) Dinan is accessible by train (change at Dol) from Rennes (6/day, 2hr., 64F) and St-Malo (7/day, 1¼min., 42F). From July to September, 3 daily buses run to St-Malo (1hr., 32F). The **tourist office,** 6, rue de l'Horloge (tel. 96 39 75 40), in the *vieille ville,* offers walking tours of the town (25F, children 15F) and excellent guides (10F) and maps. (Open Mon.-Sat. 9am-6:45pm, Sun. 10am-1pm and 3-5:45pm; Sept.-May. Mon.-Sat. 8:30am-12:30pm and 2-6pm.)

■■■ NORTHERN COAST (CÔTES D'ARMOR)

Brittany's northern coast features some of the most spectacular scenery in France. Conveniently located near the most worthwhile sites, youth hostels and *gîtes d'étape* range from the rugged tent-camp near Cap Fréhel to the well-equipped hostel in Brest. (Motorists cannot stay in most *gîtes d'étape.*) Transportation poses problems, but don't let it deter you. **Tourisme Verney** (tel. 99 82 26 26) or **Companie Armoricaine de Transports** (CAT; tel. 96 33 36 60 in St-Brieuc) run buses along the coast. Many tourist offices give out the *Guide Régional des Transports,* which lists bus, train, even boat connections, and is issued twice a year.

■ Côte d'Emeraude and Côte de Granite Rose

St-Brieuc is a great place to launch a tour of the Côte d'Emeraude and even the eastern part of the Côte de Granite Rose, but not for much else. It has a train station (most towns around here don't) and is a hub for the buses which service the area. Frequent **trains** arrive from (and depart for) Paris as well as Rennes (12/day, 1hr., 75F), to Morlaix (10/day, 1hr., 67F), and Dinan (2-3/day, 49F).

Northeast of St-Brieuc, **Cap Fréhel** marks the northern point of the Côte d'Emeraude, a windswept peninsula whose tip drops 70m into the ocean below. The Cap itself is served by **CAT buses** once a day (38F from St-Brieuc), although the nearby Le Vieux Bourg sees more frequent service (4/day from St-Brieuc, also 38F). If your spirit is as rugged as the Cap's cliffs, you'll love the **auberge de jeunesse Plévenon (HI),** Kerivet, la Ville Hadrieux (tel. 96 41 48 98). Take a bus to the Cap and walk 20 minutes toward Plévenon on the D16. (36F. Camping 20F. Sheets 15F. Open May-Aug.) The hostel also rent **bikes.** Ask at the hostel about the 15F **fishing excursions** that locals organize for travelers. The boats leave from Port St-Géran.

The sweet town of **Paimpol** anchors the eastern end of the Côte de Granite Rose. **Trains** connect to St-Brieuc (4/day, 45min., 53F) via Guincamp (20min., 34F). Six **CAT buses** run daily direct from St-Brieuc to Paimpol (1½hr., 37F). Paimpol's **auberge de jeunesse/gîte d'etape (HI),** an old manor house at Château de Keraoul (tel. 96 20 83 60), is 25 minutes from the station. (Members only. 42F. Camping 23F. Sheets 16F.) Five minutes by boat from Arcouest (6km north of Paimpol), footpaths crisscross the idyllic **Ile de Bréhat. Les Vedettes de Bréhat** ferries 15 times daily (Oct.-May 5/day, round-trip 33F, 30F for bikes).

■ Nord Finistère

Morlaix and Brest Like the venerable, wind-burned Bretons who keep its many lighthouses, the Nord Finistère, the northern peninsula of Brittany's western-most *département*, is hardy, aloof, and perhaps a bit rough around the edges. **Morlaix,** whose motto is "If they bite you, bite them back," clings picturesquely to the high green hills that flank the edge of 2 merging rivers. The **auberge de jeunesse (HI),** 3, rte. de Paris (tel. 98 88 13 63), is a 20-minute walk from the station. (Reception open 8-11am and 6-9pm. Lockout 10am-6pm. Curfew 11pm. Members only. 40F. Sheets 15F.) Although not quintessential, **Camping Municipal Lannorgant** (tel. 98 61 35 06) is worth the money. (35F, 70F/2 people, 10F/person thereafter; hot water included.) Those without camping equipment can stay in one of the 4 area **gîtes d'étape.** All cost 26-36F per night. Ask the tourist office in Morlaix for more info. **Trains** run to St-Brieuc (7-9/day, 1hr., 67F), Brest (9/day, 45min., 49F), and Quimper (89F). **CAT buses** run between Morlaix and Lannion (1/day, 38F). The helpful and multilingual **tourist office,** pl. des Otages (tel. 98 62 14 94), can give you a city map or a self-guided walking tour brochure (5F each). (Open Mon.-Sat. 9am-7:30pm, Sun. 10am-12:30pm; Sept.-June Mon.-Sat. 9am-12:30pm and 1:30-7:30pm, Sun. 10am-12:30pm.)

   Situated on the southern side of Finistère's northern peninsula, **Brest** has a natural harbor so ideal that in 1631 Cardinal de Richelieu designated it as France's major naval base. The **auberge de jeunesse (HI)** (tel. 98 41 90 41) is about 4km from the train station and right near Océanopolis. From the Port de Plaisance bus stop, take the first left and turn left again at the first street. (Reception open 8-9am and 5-8pm. Lockout 10am-6pm. Curfew 11pm. Members only. 63F.) A pleasant 2 ½-hour boat ride from Brest is windswept **Ile d'Ouessant,** its green pastures dotted with gray sheep and white stone crosses. Boats dock at **Port du Stiff** on the northeastern shore, and the main town of **Lampaul** is just a 45-minute southwestern stroll (or an 8F bus ride) across the island. You can rent a **bike** at the dock from one of the island's two rental agencies, **Savina** (tel. 98 48 80 44) and **Malgorn** (tel. 98 48 83 44). In Lampaul, you'll find the **tourist office** (tel. 98 48 85 83), replete with maps. (Open Mon.-Sat. 10:30am-12:30pm and 2-5pm; Sun. 10:30am-12:30pm.)

Camaret, Morgat, and Crozon At the western end of the Crozon penin-sula, little **Camaret** is a jewel of a town; once you see the beach below the hostel, you'll want to stay forever. Just beyond the edge of town on the D8 is a modest cir-cle of stone *menhirs.* The **Pointe de Penhir,** 3½km away on the D8, is one of the finest capes in Brittany. Climb out onto the rocks for a blood-boiling view of the iso-lated rock masses of the **Tas de Pois.** Farther north, the road passes another stone circle, the **Alignements de Lagatjar,** some 100 *menhirs* arranged in intersecting lines and ending in a Stonehenge-like circle. Camaret's **tourist office,** quai Toudouze (tel. 98 27 93 60), is on the corner of rue de la Gare. (Open Mon.-Sat. 9am-7:30pm, Sun. 9am-12:30pm; June and Sept. closed Sun.; Oct.-May Mon.-Sat. 9am-noon and 2-6:30pm.) To reach the **auberge de jeunesse de l'Iroise (HI),** rte. de Toulinguet (tel. 98 27 98 24), walk down the quay (along the port), turn left in front of Hôtel Styvel, then bear right and walk up the hill about 200m. (35F. Open mid-June to Sept.) **Camping Municipal de Lannic** (tel. 98 27 91 31), off rue du Gronnach, is fairly close to town center. (9F/person, 8F/site, 6F/car. Showers 8F. Open May-Sept.)

   Morgat and **Crozon** are practically indistinguishable, although for the record, Crozon is more commercial, while everything in Morgat pales before its big, touristy beach. The 9F bus ride from Camaret will drop you atop the hill in Crozon. From there it's a 2.6km (25min.) hike to Morgat. The Crozon **tourist office** (tel. 98 26 17 18) has a slew of info on both towns and the surrounding area. (Open Mon.-Sat. 9am-8pm, Sun. 9:30am-12:30pm; Sept.-June Tues.-Sun. 9am-noon and 2-7pm.) Mor-gat's **tourist office,** across from the beach on bd. de la France Libre (tel. 98 27 07 92), waylays visitors as they enter from Crozon. (Open July-Aug. Mon.-Sat. 9:30am-7:30pm, Sun. 4-7pm; Sept. 1-15 Mon.-Sat. 9:30am-noon and 2-6pm, Sun. 9am-noon.)

If you plan to spend the night, try Morgat's pleasant **Hôtel Julia,** 43, rue de Tréflez (tel. 98 27 05 89; singles and doubles 120-150F, with shower 190F; open Feb. 15-Oct.). Cheaper and right across from the beach is **Hôtel de la Baie,** 46, bd. de la Plage (tel. 98 27 07 51; singles 100F, doubles 150-260F, triples 250-310F; quads 260F). There are several *gîtes d'étapes* in this region. **Landévennec**—one of the stops for buses to and from Quimper and Brest—has a beautiful facility on a hill just above the port. Call the *mairie* (tel. 98 27 72 65) to reserve a place (36F/night). The whole Crozon peninsula is strewn with **campgrounds.** Ask at the Crozon tourist office for a complete listing. **Pen-Ar-Ménez,** on bd. de Pralogan toward Camaret (tel. 98 27 12 36), is closest to this town-and-beach. (15F/person, 18F/tent and car.)

■■■ SOUTHERN BRITTANY

Quimper Although staunch, half-timbered houses with crooked façades share cobblestone streets in the *vieille ville* (old town) with legions of tourists and hordes of fashion-conscious teens, Quimper (KEM-pear), capital of La Cornouaille, has managed to retain its Breton flavor. Each year during the last week of July, Quimper recalls its heritage with the *Festival de Cornouaille,* a cavalcade of mirth and music in Breton costume. The **tourist office,** 7, rue Déese (tel. 98 53 04 05), has free maps and brochures, sells bus excursion tickets to nearby sights such as Pointe du Raz and may help find accommodations in local homes. (Open Mon.-Sat. 8:30am-8pm, Sun. 9:30am-12:30pm, all day during the festival; Sept.-June Mon.-Sat. 9am-noon and 2-6pm.) **Trains,** running out of the station on av. de la Gare (tel. 98 90 26 21, 98 90 50 50), leave for Paris (2-3/day normal, 5/day TGV; 298F, plus 36-90F reservation for TGV), Nantes (6/day, 3hr., 167F), and Brest (6/day, 1½hr., 76F). All **buses** leave from the parking lot to the right of the train station or across the street in front of the **Café Nantais.** Ask at the tourist office for schedules or peruse the ones posted around the parking lot next to the train station.

To reach the **auberge de jeunesse (HI),** 6, av. des Oiseaux (tel. 98 55 41 67), about 2km out of town, take bus #1 to Chaptal from the rue du Parc stop across from the tourist office. (Reception open 8-10am and 6-8pm. Kitchen and bathroom areas open during day, but rooms locked 10am-6pm. 42F. HI card required. Open April-Oct.) Near the train station, the **Hôtel de l'Ouest,** 63, rue le Déan (tel. 98 90 28 35), proffers clean rooms in a quiet neighborhood. (Singles 100F, with toilet 150F, with shower 180F. Doubles 150F, with shower 190F. Extra bed 30F. Showers 15F.) Next to the hostel, **Camping Municipal,** av. des Oiseaux in the Bois du Séminaire, allows you to pitch your tent in the woods. (Office closed June 15-July 1. Call the mayor's office (tel. 98 98 89 89) for more info. Open Mon.-Sat. 9-11am and 1-7pm. 6F/person, 2F/tent. Showers 20F.)

Concarneau and Quiberon The crenulated walls, round towers, and cobblestone streets of **Concarneau's** touristy *ville close* conceal the city's identity as France's largest tuna fishing port. You'll smell it, however, along the quai Carnot, lined by warehouses packing the daily catch. Escape the cute crafts shops fishing for their own catch of tourists, and head away to the town's beaches. The **Plage des Sables Blancs** is the town's most popular beach. Take bus #1 from av. Pierre Guéguin across from the quai d'Aiguillon to "Les Sables Blancs." The superb **auberge de jeunesse (HI),** 5-10 minutes from the center of town on quai de la Croix (tel. 98 97 03 47), looks out over the ocean. (Reception open daily 9am-noon and 6-8pm. Curfew midnight. HI card required. 42F.) **Camping du Dorlett** (tel. 98 97 16 44) lies about 2km out of town near the Plage des Sables Blancs. Take bus #1 from the bus station to Le Dorlett. (13/day, last bus 6:20pm. 5F. Reception open 8:30am-noon and 2-7pm. 12F/person, 21F/site, 6F/car. Open late June to mid-Sept.)

All roads in **Quiberon** lead to the sandy and wonderfully clean **Grande Plage** in the heart of town. To escape the congested port area, head for smaller, rockier **Plage du Goviro** near the campgrounds. From the port, follow bd. Chanard east along the water as it becomes bd. de la Mer and then bd. du Goviro. To reach the small, centrally located **auberge de jeunesse (HI),** 45, rue du Roch-Priol (tel. 97 50 15 54), turn left at the station, then take rue de la Gare through pl. du Repos, take rue de Lille, turn left on rue Roch-Priol, and continue bearing left about 2 blocks. (43F. 2-bed tents 60F. Kitchen. Sheets 16F. Open May-Sept. 30.) The **Hôtel de L'Océan,** 7, quai de l'Océan (tel. 97 50 07 58) lets clean, color-coordinated rooms on the boardwalk facing the harbor. (Singles and doubles 145-170F, with shower 200F, with shower and toilet 290F.) The campsite nearest the city is **Camping du Goviro** (tel. 97 50 13 54), adjacent to the lovely beach of the same name. (Reception open 8:30am-noon and 2-5:30pm. 9F/adult, 6F/tent, 5F/car.)

Train service to Quiberon operates only in July and August; in the off-season, buses are frequent and dependable. **TTO buses** (tel. 97 47 29 64) run to Auray (6-8/day, 4 on Sun.; 1hr.; 34F) via Carnac (30min., 20F50). To find the **tourist office** (tel. 97 50 07 84) from the train station, turn left and walk down rue de la Gare. Veer to the right of the church, down rue de Verdun; the tourist office is on the right. The professional staff can help you find a B&B for 100-200F.

Belle-Ile At least 10 boats depart daily from Quiberon's Port-Maria for Belle-Ile, an island that merges high cliffs, narrow creeks, and crashing seas. The crossing takes 25-45 minutes (80F/person, 35F/bike round-trip). Biking is the best way to tour the island. **Didier Banet,** quai de l'Acadie (tel. 97 31 84 74), rents them from the harbor. (40F/½-day, 50F/day; mountain bikes 80F/½-day, 100F/day. 800F deposit. Open April-Sept. 9am-7pm.) An impressive 15th-century walled citadel protects **Le Palais,** once a strategic port and currently the island's largest town. The **tourist office** (tel. 97 31 81 93) at the end of the quai in Le Palais distributes a comprehensive brochure on the island. (Open July-Sept. 15 8:30am-12:30pm and 2-7:30pm; Oct.-June 9am-noon and 2-6pm.) Bike 6km to **Sauzon,** a tiny fishing port with picture-book façades. From Sauzon, continue another 4km to the **Pointe des Poulains,** at the northernmost tip of the island. Four km southwest on the Côte Sauvage lies the impressive **Grotte de L'Apothicairerie.** Heed the signs and stay out of the caves; people have perished in this grotto. From the grotto, follow D25 south to the rough **Aiguilles de Port-Coton,** which Monet captured in an 1886 painting.

Inexpensive accommodations on the island include 2 campgrounds, 3 *gîtes d'étapes,* and an **HI youth hostel.** The hostel (tel. 97 31 81 33) is located near the citadel, a 20-minute hike from Le Palais port. Turn right from the port and follow the *quay* to the footbridge leading to the citadel; cross the bridge, walk diagonally left through the parking lot, and enter **Camping Les Glacis.** (Reception open July-Aug. 9am-2:30pm and 3:30-10pm; Sept. to mid-Oct. and April-June 9-11:30am and 4:30-6:30pm. 11F/person, 20F/tent, 6F/car, 2F/bike. Showers 8F.) To reach the hostel, continue on and turn right at the road by the showers, climb another hill, follow the road through a small residential neighborhood and look for the sign to the *auberge* on the right. (Reception open 8:30-10am and 6-8pm. Members only. 45F. Camping 35F. Breakfast 17F. Sheets 16F.) Besides selling fresh vegetables, the *gîte d'étape* in **Port Guen** (tel. 97 31 55 88), about 3km south of Le Palais, rents beds (31F) in dorm-style rooms in a colorful barn. Reservations are recommended.

■■■ NANTES

Nantes bears a resemblance to Paris, with public parks and gardens, and wide boulevards marking the boundaries between administrative *arrondissements.* And, like the capital, Nantes molts in summer when the students leave and the tourists arrive. Stuffed to the gills with historic sights, diverse museums, and nightclubs, Nantes deserves more than a lazy afternoon of sight-seeing.

Thanks to their lightweight Vendée stone, the Gothic vaults of **Cathédrale St-Pierre** soar 37m into the heavens, higher than the arches of Notre-Dame in Paris. (Open daily 8:45am-noon and 2-7pm.) Built by François II, Nantes's heavily fortified

15th-century **château** once held Gilles de Rais (Bluebeard), who was convicted of sorcery in 1440. Henri IV signed the Edict of Nantes here in 1598, granting religious freedom to Protestants. The better of two museums inside the château, the **Musée des Arts Populaires Régionaux,** displays traditional Breton costumes and furniture. The **Musée des Salorges** presents Nantes's commercial history since the 18th century. (Château and museums open Wed.-Mon. 10am-noon and 2-6pm. To both museums 30F, students 15F, Sun. free. Courtyard and ramparts open Wed.-Mon. 10am-7pm. 6F, students 3F.)

Two blocks from the cathedral at 10, rue Georges Clemenceau, is Nantes's **Musée des Beaux Arts,** with a large collection of fine canvases by Rubens, Courbet, de la Tour, and many contemporary artists. (Open Wed.-Mon. 10am-noon and 1-5:45pm, Sun. 11am-5pm. 20F, students 10F, Sun. free.) The **Musée d'Histoire Naturelle,** 12, rue Voltaire, showcases a mind-boggling array of stuffed mammals, birds, reptiles, and insects. (Open Tues.-Sat. 10am-noon and 2-6pm, Sun. 2-6pm. 15F, students 8F.) Let your imagination run wild at the innovative **Musée Jules Verne,** 3, rue de l'Hermitage, near the river in pl. M. Schwob, which re-creates the world of Captain Nemo and other Verne characters through a collection of the author's novels, letters, and photographs. Take bus #21 to "Garennes." (Open Mon. and Wed.-Sat. 10am-noon and 2-5pm, Sun. 2-5pm. 8F, students 4F, Sun. free.) Nearby is Nantes's **planetarium,** 8, rue des Acadiens. (Showings and *séances* Tues.-Sat. 10:30am, 2:15pm, and 3:45pm; Sun. 2:15pm and 3:45pm. 22F, students 11F.) A **global pass** to the château museums, the Musée des Beaux Arts, the Musée d'Histoire Naturelle and the Musée Jules Verne costs 30F (students 15F).

West of the château is a *quartier* of elegant 18th-century buildings. Prosperous sea merchants relied on the slave trade profits to build lavish houses on the **Ile Feydeau,** between allée Turenne and allée Tuouin. Locals have so perfected the art of loafing down **rue Crébillon** to the **place Graslin** that the verb "crébilloner" has entered their vocabulary. Take bus #31 from the Commerce stop on cours Franklin Roosevelt to Le Corbusier's **Cité Radieuse,** a place of pilgrimage for John Ruark and other architecture and Corbu buffs.

Although university buildings are scattered throughout the city, the area north of rue Crébillon is most popular in the evening, and rue Scribe has an array of late-night bars and cafés. Nightly at 10pm, a live jazz ensemble tunes up at **The Tie Break Club,** 1, rue des Petites Ecuries. (Open Mon.-Sat. 10pm-3:30am.) During the first 2 weeks of July, Nantes hosts the annual **Les Fêtes de l'Eté,** a harmonic convergence of more than 1000 dance, music, and theater groups. (Tickets around 100F, festival pass 250F.) For information and reservations, contact the tourist office.

Accommodations, Food, and Practical Information To get to the center of town and the tourist office, turn left out of the station onto bd. de Stalingrad, which becomes cours John Kennedy. Place du Commerce and the tourist office are 1km ahead. The spacious **auberge de jeunesse (HI),** 2, pl. de la Manufacture (tel. 40 29 18 57), is open only in July and August. From the station, turn right onto bd. de Stalingrad, left onto rue Manille and then left onto pl. de la Manufacture (10min.). Alternatively, take the tram from the train station (7F) to "Manufacture." (Reception open 7-noon and 2-11pm. 50F. Sheets 16F.) Clean, dimly lit 2-, 3-, or 4-bed rooms await you at the **Centre Jean Macé,** 90, rue du Préfet Bonnefoy (tel. 40 74 55 74). To get there, turn left onto cours John Kennedy, then right at pl. de la Duchesse Anne onto rue Henri IV, which becomes rue Sully. The *centre* is on rue Sully at rue du Préfet Bonnefoy. Otherwise, take bus #12 from the SNCF station to pl. Maréchal Foch and continue up rue Sully. (Reception open 9am-11:30pm and 2:30-6pm. 52F.) To reach the superb **Camping du Val de Cens,** 21, bd. du Petit Port (tel. 40 74 47 94), 3km from town, take bus #51 or #53 from pl. du Commerce to "Marhonnière." (Reception open 7-11pm. 15F/person, 20F/site. No phone reservations; arrive early in summer.)

Try Nantes's delicious seafood, prepared *au beurre blanc* (with butter sauce), and *Canard Nantais* made with grapes, as well as the white wines *Muscadet* and *Gros Plant*. **Markets** erupt daily except Monday from 9am to 1pm in pl. du Bouffay and at the **Marché de Talensac,** along rue de Bel Air near pl. St-Similien. A **Decré supermarket** is in the basement of Nouvelles Galeries, rue du Moulin, in the *centre ville.* (Open Mon.-Sat. 9am-7pm.) **Chez Rémy-La Brasserie des Sportifs,** rue de la Bâclerie, has an outdoor *terrasse* as well as delicious *couscous.* (60-100F. Open Tues.-Sat. noon-2pm and 7-11pm.)

The **tourist office** (tel. 40 47 04 51), on pl. du Commerce, a stone's throw from McDonald's, has a very professional and courteous staff that doles out free maps. (Open Mon.-Fri. 9am-7pm, Sat. 10am-6pm.) **Trains** leave from the station at 27, bd. Stalingrad (tel. 40 08 50 50), running to Paris (4-5/day, 3-4hr., 218F; 12-14 TGVs/day, 2hr., 218F plus 36-90F TGV reservation), Bordeaux (5-8/day, 4hr., 216F), and Rennes (7/day, 2 on Sun., 2hr., 104F). A **Tan Air** shuttle (tel. 40 29 39 39) runs from the pl. du Commerce and the SNCF station, *Gare Sud* (Mon.-Fri. 14/day, 6 on Sat., 3 on Sun.; 25min.; 28F), to the **airport** 10km from Nantes. **Air Inter** (tel. 51 88 31 08) sends 6-8 flights/day to Paris, and **Air France** (tel. 40 47 12 33) sends 1 flight/day to London. The **post office,** pl. de Bretagne, exchanges currency. (Open Mon.-Fri. 8:30am-7pm, Sat. 8:30am-noon.) **Postal Code:** 44000.

LOIRE VALLEY (PAYS DE LA LOIRE)

For years, people have come to the region between Paris and Brittany to see the Loire River and the châteaux: the surprisingly sordid history of many of these dignified mansions presents a mixed bag of mischief, genius, promiscuity, and dirty-dealing; rich fodder for the imagination. Some of the finest châteaux, notably Blois and Chambord, were built in the era of scandalous intrigue and multiple mistresses. While the dukes and the counts chased stags with armies of hounds, their wives hosted bacchanalian orgies and decorated the castles with the finest Italian masters, fostering an opulence never before imagined.

Take your time and don't try to see more than two châteaux a day, or you'll go numb. The excellent hostels in Blois, Saumur, and Orléans are comfortable bases, but they pose daunting logistical challenges to those without their own wheels; public transportation routes fan out of the larger cities, but infrequent service can leave you stranded. Four of the most spectacular châteaux—Ussé, Villandry, Cheverny, and Chambord—can be reached only by bike, tour bus, or thumb. Unquestionably the best way to see the valley is by bike, and nearly all towns have bike rentals. Distances are relatively short, and the terrain is flat and lush. Those spending more than a day in the saddle should purchase *Michelin's* road map of the region, which will steer you away from the truck-laden highways and onto delightful country roads. Equally helpful is SNCF's *Châteaux pour Train et Vélo,* with train schedules, distances, and information on bike and car rental. We've heard that hitching to the isolated châteaux, such as Chambord and Chenonceau, is difficult; fortunately, many châteaux lie near well-traveled roads.

■■■ ORLÉANS

In 1429, Joan of Arc wrested Orléans, then the most important city in France after Paris, from the English. Today, the city proudly sports her name on restaurants, cafés, and hotels. Stop in Orléans en route to chateau country, if only to witness Orléans' modern battle between cobblestone and plastic. The stained-glass windows telling Joan's story in the **Cathédrale Ste-Croix** will knock your smelly socks off. (Open daily 9am-noon and 2-6pm.) The **Maison de Jeanne d'Arc,** 3, pl. de Gaulle, features period costumes and an audio-visual recreation of the siege of

Orléans. (Open Tues.-Sun. 10am-noon and 2-6pm; Nov.-April Tues.-Sun. 2-6pm. 10F, students 5F, under 16 free.) When you tire of churches and museums, take bus S from pl. Albert 1*er* to the **Parc Floral,** a peaceful garden of purple irises and tulips. (Open daily 9am-6pm; Nov.-March 2-5pm. 19F, students 10F; Nov.-March 10F.) Lunch with locals at **Le K. T. Self,** 13, rue des Pastoureaux, off rue Jeanne d'Arc before the cathedral. (*Plats du jour* 21–37F. Open Mon.-Sat. 11:30am-2:15pm.)

The **tourist office,** pl. Albert 1*er* (tel. 38 53 05 95), next to the train station, sponsors walking tours (35F, students 18F) and books rooms for a 6F fee. (Open Mon.-Sat. 9am-7pm, Sun. 9:30am-12:30pm and 3-6:30pm; Sept.-June Mon.-Sat. 9am-7pm.) One of the brightest spots in Orléans is the homey, well-appointed **auberge de jeunesse (HI)** at 14, rue Faubourg Madeleine (tel. 38 62 45 75), on the west side of town; take bus B (direction "Paul-Bert") from in front of the train station (8F). (Reception open daily 7-9:30am and 5:30-10pm; Feb-March Sun.-Fri. only. Lockout 9:30am-5:30pm. Members only. 34F. Wheelchair access.) The owner of the **Hôtel de Paris** (tel. 38 53 39 58), 29, rue Faubourg Bonnier, speaks English and keeps clean rooms with firm, new mattresses. (Singles and doubles 100-180F.)

■■■ BLOIS

Though Blois's château lies right in the middle of town, diehard Eurail users should still head to Tours, from which more châteaux are accessible by rail. The **Château de Blois** glistens as a result of a massive restoration project. The spiral staircase crawls with King François I's stone salamanders. (Open daily 9am-6:30pm; Nov.-March 9am-noon and 2-5pm. 27F, students 15F.) A mid-sized city bursting at its seams, Blois corrals a herd of attractive churches and gardens. A tinted hodgepodge of Renaissance and Gothic, the **Abbaye St-Lomer** impresses inside and out. Don't miss the old quarter around the **Cathédrale St-Louis.**

The **tourist office,** 3, av. Jean Laigret (tel. 54 74 06 49 or 54 78 23 21), will change money for an 18F commission. (Open Mon.-Sat. 9am-7pm, Sun. 10am-1pm and 4-7pm; Oct.-March Mon.-Sat. 9am-noon and 2-6pm.) Ask here about bus passes to create your own itinerary of chateaux. Accommodations in Blois fill up fast. The homey and rustic **auberge de jeunesse (HI),** 18, rue de l'Hôtel Pasquier (tel. 54 78 27 21), is 4½km outside Blois in Les Grouets. Take bus #4 (direction "Les Grouets," last bus at 7:30pm; 5F40) from pl. Valin by the river. (Lockout 10am-6pm. 39F. Open March-Nov. 15.) Get a warm welcome and bright, tidy rooms at the **Hôtel St-Jacques,** 7, rue Ducoux (tel. 54 78 04 15; singles and doubles 95-110F, with toilet 155F). Near the Eglise St-Nicolas and the château, **Hôtel St-Nicolas,** 33, rue des Trois Marchands (tel. 54 78 41 09), purveys quiet singles (90F) and doubles (125F; open Jan. 15-Dec. 15; reserve 2 weeks in advance). To find the quiet **Hôtel du Bellay,** 12, rue des Minimes (tel. 54 78 23 62), turn left onto Minimes at the top of porte Chartraine. (Singles 100F. Doubles 120F.)

Eating is most blissful on lively, restaurant- and bar-lined rue Foulerie. Elsewhere, **Côté Sel Côté Cour,** 5, rue du Grenier à Sel (tel. 54 56 17 08), is left off rue de la Foulerie walking away from the rond pont de la Résistance. Every wackily carved glass-holder in the eatery is for sale. (80F *menu.* Open Tues.-Sat. 1-4pm and 6:30pm-midnight.) For 58F, enjoy the all-you-can-eat buffet with dessert at **La Forge,** 18, rue Bourg Neuf. The specialty is meat cooked over a wooden fire. (Open Mon. noon-2pm, Tues.-Sat. noon-2pm and 7:30-11pm.)

■■■ BLOIS TO TOURS

Chambord, Cheverny, and Chaumont-sur-Loire Built by François I for his frequent hunting trips and orgiastic fêtes, **Chambord** is the largest and most extravagant of the Loire châteaux. Access to the grounds and surrounding wildlife preserve is free and unlimited. 700 of François I's trademark stone salamanders, symbols of bravery, lurk on Chambord's walls, ceilings, and ingenious double-helix staircase. 365 fireplaces scattered through the 400 rooms create a miniature rooftop city of decorated chimneys. (Open daily 9:30am-6:15pm; Sept.-June 9:30-12:15am and 2-5:15pm. 31F, students 20F.) Chambord is accessible by bus or bike from Blois; take the D956 south for 2-3km and turn left onto the D33 for 11km.

Cheverny, also served by bus from Blois, soothes with stately classical lines and the most elegant interior of all the châteaux. A compound on the ground houses 70 bloodhounds; watch them ravenously devour their dinner. (Dinner served Mon-Sat. at 5pm; Sept.-March Mon. and Wed.-Fri. at 3pm. Château open daily 9:15am-6:45pm; mid-Sept.-May 9:30am-noon and 2:15-5pm. 29F, students 20F.) Those hitching to Cheverny from Blois follow the D956 south.

Turreted, moated, and drawbridged **Chaumont-sur-Loire** reminds us that castles were first built to defend kingdoms, not to appear in *Brideshead Revisited.* The château is also known for its luxurious *écuries* (stables). (Open daily 9:30am-6:30pm; Oct.-March 10am-5pm. 26F, students 17F.) Trains run from Blois (12/day, 10min., 17F) or Tours (12/day, 35min., 14F) to Onzain, 2km north of Chaumont.

Amboise and Chenonceaux The château at **Amboise** marks the beginning of the decorative Renaissance style that later inspired Blois and Chambord. It also saw two Kings expire: the 4-ft. Charles VIII fatally bumped his head on a *really* low door here, and Charles V tripped onto a torchbearer and burned himself alive. Well, Chuck, I guess it sucks to be you. Leonardo da Vinci spent the last 3 years of his life in the nearby Clos Lucé, and his bones are said to rest in the flamboyant **Chapelle St-Hubert,** the gem of the château's remaining structures. (Open daily 9am-6:30pm; Sept.-March 9am-noon and 2-5pm; April-June 9am-noon and 2-6:30pm. 28F, students 18F.) You can also visit the **Clos-Lucé,** where Leonardo painted, pondered, and invented; his sketches include inventions that presaged the paddle steam boat, the airplane, and the stick-shift car. (Open daily 9am-7pm; Nov.-Dec. and Feb. 9am-6pm. 30F, students 22F.) Amboise's comfortable **auberge de jeunesse** (tel. 47 57 06 36) lies on the delightful Ile d'Or. (Reception open Tues.-Sun. 3-8pm. 46F. Nov.-Feb. 32F. Call ahead and arrive 6-8pm to be let in on Mon.) About half the trains on the Blois-Tours route stop midway at Amboise.

The graceful château of **Chenonceaux** (tel. 47 23 90 07) arches effortlessly over the languid River Cher. Three women overlooked and influenced the construction of this romantic palace: Catherine Briçonnet, Diane de Poitiers (Henri II's mistress), and Cathérine de Médicis (Henri's wife). The long gallery served as a military hospital during WWI, and a passageway from annexed France to Vichy France during WWII. Chenonceau's stunning exterior, viewed from the spacious garden or from a 10F rowboat, will move even the most jaded castle-goer. (Open daily March 16-Sept. 15 9am-7pm; call for closing times at other times. 35F, students and ages 7-15 25F.) Your best bet is to make Chenonceaux a daytrip from Tours (3 trains/day, 1 on Sun.; 45min.; 29F).

■■■ **TOURS**

Tours is too large to be cute, and too impersonal to be endearing. But with a large, cosmopolitan student population, it's the hotspot of the Loire, and an excellent urban base from which to explore the Valley. East of pl. Plumereau, **Cathédrale St-Gatien,** rue Jules Simon, may be the most dazzling compilation of stained glass in the Loire. (Open daily 7:15am-7pm; Oct.-Easter 7:15am-noon and 2-6:45pm.) If it isn't, the amazing **Musée du Gemmail,** 7, rue du Murier, flaunts several *gemmaux* (a step beyond stained glass) signed by Picasso. (Open April-Oct. 15 Tues.-Sun. 10am-noon and 2-6:30. 25F, students 15F.) Tours's **tourist office,** rue Bernard Palissy (tel. 47 05 58 08), arranges bus tours to the chateaux. (Open Mon.-Sat. 8:30am-7pm, Sun. 10am-12:30pm and 3-6pm; Sept.-May Mon.-Sat. 8:30am-6:30pm.)

Tours's **auberge de jeunesse (HI)** (tel. 47 25 14 45), 4km from the station in a park by the freeway, is accessible via buses #1 and 6 from the stop on the right side of av. de Grammont, 30m down from pl. Jean Jaurès. (Reception open 5-11pm; off-season 5-10pm. Lockout 10am-4pm. Curfew 11pm. 60F; 2-person rooms 11F extra/person.) **Le Foyer,** 16, rue Bernard Palissy (tel. 47 05 38 81), is well-located and lets large rooms to those aged 16-25. (Office open Mon. afternoon-Sat. morning. Singles 70F. Doubles 130F.) **Hôtel Vendôme,** 24, rue Roger-Salengro (tel. 47 64 33 54), 1 block off av. Grammont, has a family atmosphere. (Singles 95F. Doubles 100F. Triples 200-220F. Showers 15F.) Or try **Mon Hôtel,** 40, rue de la Préfecture (tel. 47 05 67 53. Singles 100F. Doubles 200F). Inexpensive hotels cluster near the train station. Tasty treats abound on rue Colbert and around pl. Plumereau. **Aux Trois Canards,** 16, rue de la Rotisserie, serves an elegant 47F 3-course *menu* and a more delicate 69F *menu.* (Open Mon.-Fri. noon-2pm and 7:30-10pm, Sat. 7:30-10pm.) Join the locals at **Le Foyer cafeteria,** 16, rue Bernard Palissy, where a 3F membership card entitles you to a 5-course *menu* for 39F. (Open Mon.-Sat. 11:30am-1:45pm.)

■■■ TOURS TO ANGERS

Azay-le-Rideau château gazes vainly at its reflection from an island in the Indre river. Colorful 16th-century French tapestries ornament the interior, and 2 miniature waterfalls cascade down from the moat. (Open daily 10am-noon and 2-6pm; Oct.-Dec. and Feb.-March 10am-noon and 2-5pm. 31F, students 20F.)

Engulfed by the thick woods of the Forêt de Chinon **Ussé's** pointed towers, white turrets, and chimneys inspired *Sleeping Beauty.* The château is decorated with wax figures which give a sense of theme to the place, but if 52F for the whole ball of wax seems a little steep, just relish the view with a picnic outside. (Open March 15-Nov. 11 daily 9am-noon and 2-6:45pm. 52F, students 19F.)

Just west of Tours and connected to Ussé by a pastoral cyclist's dream-road (the D16) is the feudal and forbidding **Langeais.** Notice the stone slabs along the upper fortifications which contain slots for pouring boiling oil on attackers. (Open daily 9am-6:30pm; Nov. 3-March 14 9am-noon and 2-5pm. 35F, students 17F. Call 47 96 72 60 for more info.) Trains run from Saumur and Tours. Rent a 10-speed bike at **Station Glorex,** 24, rue de Tours (tel. 47 96 81 17; 40F/day, plus 1000F deposit; open Mon.-Fri. 8am-8pm).

Villandry maintains fantastic formal gardens with vine-covered walkways and 3 terraces of sculpted shrubs and flowers, but the château pales before its regal cousins. (Gardens open daily 9am-8pm; Sept.-May 9am-dusk. Château open daily March 15-Nov. 11 from 9am-8pm. To gardens 25F, to château an extra 15F.)

Once famous for St-Louis's extravagant feasts and parties, **Saumur** is now Europe's largest producer of carnival masks. Many of the town's sights and museums have a horsey bent, with the resident *Cadre Noir* equestrian corps still staging competitions and public presentations. Saumur's proud name adorns a fine white, a subtle rosé, and an earthy red wine. Thinly sliced *champignons* (mushrooms) marinated in wine are another locally-grown specialty. Ask at the **tourist office,** pl. Bilange (tel. 41 51 03 06), for information about horse exhibitions, wine *dégustations,* and fungus tours. The modern **auberge de jeunesse (HI)** (tel. 41 67 45 00), on Ile d'Offard between the station and tourist office, has a free swimming pool and a superb view of Saumur's château. (Reception open 8-10am and 5-10pm. Lax lockout 10am-5pm. Curfew 10pm. Loud 6-berth rooms 43F, nonmembers 45F.) There are several daily trains to Tours (51F) and Angers (38F).

■■■ ANGERS

Guarding the western gateway to the château region, Angers's massive stone walls once daunted Norman hordes, then narrowly escaped destruction during the Wars of Religion; today they remain imposing despite a stifling urban onslaught. The 17 formidable towers of the château and the deep moat's waters have been replaced with formal gardens and a deer park. Inside, the priceless **Tapestries of the Apoca-**

lypse depict the Book of Revelations. Spun in gold thread, this tour de force of medieval art is large enough to carpet a small street. (Château open daily 9am-7pm; Sept. 16-April 9:30am-12:30pm and 2-6pm. 31F, students 17F.)

Angers's **tourist office** (tel. 41 23 51 11), across from the château, organizes castle trips and changes money when banks are closed. (Open Mon.-Sat. 9am-7pm, Sun. 10:30am-6:30pm; Oct.-May Mon.-Sat. 9am-12:30pm and 2-6:30pm.) The largest hostel in France (and soon in Europe, too), the **Foyer des Jeunes Travailleurs (HI),** is on rue Darwin (tel. 41 72 00 20), 4km from the station. Take bus #8 (direction "Beaucouzé") to "CFA" (46F, nonmembers 65F). The **Centre d'Accueil du Lac de Maine,** av. du Maine (tel. 41 22 32 10) awaits at lakeside; take bus #6 from the station. (Singles 101F. Doubles 144F. Quads 232F.) At **Hotel des Lices,** 25, rue des Lices (tel. 41 87 44 10), near the cathedral and château, welcoming owners present immaculate, small singles and doubles for 100F, with shower and toilet 155F. (Reserve ahead in summer.) Appetizing eateries garnish the pedestrian district around pl. Romaine. **Le Spirit Factory,** 14-16, rue Bressigny, serves mussels (43-65F) any which way but loose in a fun factory interior; the owner proudly displays the Rube Goldberg-esque machinery in which he brews the house beer.

AQUITAINE

This region's forested hills, soporific river valleys, and dramatic cliffs first drew Paleolithic people here some 150,000 years ago. Soon thereafter, Paleolithic people drew the region; paintings and engravings embellish the caves of the area, while the ancient skeletons and other artifacts have revealed more about prehistory than have relics in any other region on earth. Today, the Dordogne, Vézère, Isle, and Lot Rivers snake past 12th-century Byzantine-Romanesque churches, chapels clinging to the rocks in the pilgrimage town of Rocamadour, *bastides* (fortified mountaintop towns) built during the Hundred Years War, and pastoral villages near Sarlat and Périgueux. The sudden rise in tourism has brought prosperity and even a demand for the culinary specialties that were once the region's livelihood: delectable-but-unaffordable *foie gras* (goose liver), *crêpes,* and *truffes* (mushrooms sniffed out by pigs), as well as the more budget-happy *confit de canard* (potted duck leg cooked in its own fat), accompanied by *pommes sarladaise,* potatoes fried in garlic.

■■■ PERIGORD

Périgueux and Les-Eyzies-de-Tayac The capital of the Périgord region within Guienne, **Périgueux** makes a good base for the caves. In town, modern façades mask the labyrinthine *vieille ville* and the multiply domed **Cathédrale St-Front.** The **Foyer des Jeunes Travailleurs Résidence Lakanal,** off bd. Lakanal (tel. 53 53 52 05), at the end of rue des Thèmes, features comfortable beds, intimate insects, and peeling paint. From the tourist office, turn left down cours Fénelon and take a right onto bd. Lakanal; 15m before the dead-end at the train tracks, turn right and walk around the club Périgueux and through the gate out back. (Reception open Mon.-Fri. 5-7pm, Sat.-Sun. noon-1pm and 7-8pm. 60-80F/person.) The **Hôtel des Voyageurs** (tel. 53 53 17 44), opposite the train station at #26, offers simple, clean rooms at prices the whole family will love. (Singles and doubles 74-100F.) There's always camping 1½km away in Boulazac at **Barnabé-Plage,** 80, rue des Bains (tel. 53 53 41 45). Hop the city bus D (direction "Cité Belaire") from cours Montaigne. (14F/person, 13F/tent.) **Le Fromage à Malices,** 3, rue Port de Graule, the first right turn when walking up av. Daumesnil from the river, is a neat little mousehole of a restaurant with *plates* (65-75F) highlighting types of cheese. Ask the **tourist office,** 26, pl. Francheville (tel. 53 53 10 63), for their invaluable free brochures, *La Fête en Périgord* and *Guide des Commerces.* (Open Mon.-Fri. 9am-7pm,

Sat. 9am-noon and 2-7pm, Sun. 10am-5pm; Sept.-May Mon.-Sat. 9am-noon and 2-6pm.) The town receives several **trains** a day from Bordeaux (2½hr., 91F); Paris (7hr., 251F), and Toulouse (168F, change at Agen).

Five trains per day from Périgueux (40min., 39F) make **Les Eyzies-de-Tayac** a perfect daytrip. **Prehistoric caves**—nearly bursting with tourists from July to mid-September—house fascinating paintings and carvings, as well as spectacular stalagmites and stalactites. Call at least 2 weeks in advance to get tickets during summer; the days of waiting in line to get them are long gone. The best paintings near town are at the **Grotte de Font-de-Gaume**, just outside of town, where 15,000-year-old horses, bison, reindeer and woolly mammoth cavort along the cave walls. (Open Wed.-Mon. 9am-noon and 2-6pm; Oct.-March Wed.-Mon. 10am-noon and 2-4pm. 31F; ages 18-25 and over 60 17F; ages 7-18 6F; under 7, artists, and art students free.) In town, the **Musée National de La Préhistoire** has an excellent collection of paintings, carvings, skeletons, and other fascinating artifacts. (Open Wed.-Mon. 9:30am-6pm; April-June and Sept.-Nov. 9:30am-noon and 2-6pm; Dec.-March 9:30am-noon and 2-5pm. 7F; ages 18-25, over 60, and Sun. 11F; under 18 free.) Hotels are scarce in summer. Try the idyllic *gîte d'étape* at **Ferme des Eymaries,** rte. de St-Cirq (tel. 53 06 94 73). Cross the tracks at the station, go over the bridge, and turn left at the Elf station. Walk along the road 2km and turn right 3m before crossing the train tracks. Follow the gravel-then-dirt road for 1km (40min). (Reception open 6pm-10am. 38F. Breakfast 18F. Call ahead.)

Sarlat, Montignac, and Rocamadour Despite the dense mobs swarming **Sarlat** each summer, its remarkable *vieille ville,* a medieval sculpture of golden sandstone, merits a mosey. The Saturday **market** is renowned throughout France. Sarlat's run-down **auberge de jeunesse (HI),** 15bis, av. de Selves (tel. 53 59 47 59), 30 minutes from the train station but only 10 minutes from the *vieille ville,* has an easy-going atmosphere and outdoor showers and toilets. (Reception open 6-8pm. 39F. Camping 23F. Sheets 16F. Open July-Oct. 15.) **Hôtel des Récollets,** 4, rue Jean-Jacques Rousseau (tel. 53 59 00 49), has pristine rooms close to all the action. (Singles and doubles 165-230F. Breakfast 32F.) Camp at **Le Montant** (tel. 53 59 18 50), 2.5km from town on the D57. (18F/person, 20F/tent. Open Easter-Sept.) **Restaurant du Commerce,** 4, rue Albéric Cahuet, has a 55F *menu* on one of the liveliest terraces in town. Stop by Sarlat's **tourist office,** pl. de la Liberté (tel. 53 59 27 67), for the crucial (and free) *Guide Pratique,* which includes transportation schedules and useful practical info. (Open Mon.-Sat. 9am-7pm, Sun. 10am-noon and 3-7pm; Oct.-May Mon.-Sat. 9am-noon and 2-7pm.)**Trains** run to Bordeaux (3-4/day, 2½hr., 113F) and Périgueux (3/day, 1½hr., 63F) via Les Eyzies (1hr., 39F). SCETA **buses** truck to Souillac (4/day, 50min., 25F), and from there trains chug to Toulouse.

One or two buses per day (30min., 19F) run north to **Montignac,** where the man-made **Lascaux II** cave convincingly impersonates **Lascaux,** the largest cave paintings on earth—themselves closed to the public since 1963 due to devastating deterioration. (Open July-Aug. daily 9:30am-7pm; Feb.-June and Sept.-Dec. Tues.-Sun. 10am-noon and 2-5:30pm. 45F.)

Built into the face of a sheer cliff, the sanctity and staggering beauty of historic **Rocamadour** bring 1½ million pilgrims and tourists a year to this town of 800. **Le Grand Escalier** climbs from the town's lone street; some devotees still journey here to kneel at each of its 216 steps. At the top hovers the 12th-century **Cité Religieuse,** a complex of chapels including the **Chapelle de Notre-Dame,** home to the venerated Black Virgin. (Cité open daily 9am-6pm and 6:30-10pm; June-Sept. 9am-6pm.) Perched precariously at the top of the cliff—and more zigzagging steps—is the 14th-century **château.** Its ramparts command exceptional views of the valley. (Ramparts open July-Aug. daily 9am-7pm; April-June and Sept.-Oct. 9am-noon and 1:30-8pm. 10F.) **Elevators** ascend to both Cité and château every 3 minutes (24F). Expect to pay at least 200F for a single or double; if trying to reserve less than 2 weeks in advance in July or August, you'll be laughed at. The **Hôtel Panorama** (tel. 65 33 62

13), up in L'Hospitalet, has 5 nice rooms with showers and TV for 170F. (Breakfast 28F. Open April-Nov. 15.) Rocamadour is most easily reached via Brive-la-Gaillarde, to the north, by **train** (5/day, 45min., 39F). Coming from Sarlat, take a **bus** to St-Denis-Près-Martel, then a train.

■■■ BORDEAUX

Like many of the fine vintage reds for which it is renowned, Bordeaux has grown noticeably darker with age, an apparent victim of its own success. The layer of grime that coats the city's once-resplendent high Gothic cathedrals speaks of a rapid, post-haste industrialization, but Bordeaux's twinkle is far from defunct; the *bordelais* are scrubbing down their monuments, and city planners are in the midst of expanding this globally acclaimed wine haven.

ORIENTATION AND PRACTICAL INFORMATION

Bordeaux is 40km from France's Atlantic coast, about 200km north of the Spanish border. **Rue Ste-Catherine** connects **place de la Victoire** and **place de la Comédie,** the city's main squares. Buses #7 and 8 connect the train station with the *centre ville* (8F). Bordeaux is a big city: guard your wallet and yourself, especially at night.

Tourist Office: 12, cours du 30 Juillet (tel. 56 44 28 41). Take bus #7 or 8 from the train station, get off at the Grand Théâtre and walk one block toward the Monument des Girondins. 1-day bus ticket 19F. Arranges bus tours of local wineries. Open Mon.-Sat. 9am-8pm, Sun. 9am-7pm; Oct.-May Mon.-Fri. 9am-7pm. **Information booth** at train station. Open Mon.-Sat. 9am-7pm; Oct.-May Mon.-Sat. 9am-12:30pm and 1:30-6pm, Sun. 9:30am-12:30pm. 24-hr. English **information hotline** (tel. 56 48 04 61).

Consulates: U.S., 22, cours Maréchal Foch (tel. 56 52 65 95). Open Mon.-Fri. 9am-5pm. Visa division open Mon.-Fri. 10am-noon. **U.K.,** 15, cours de Verdun (tel. 56 42 34 13). Open Mon.-Fri. 9am-12:30pm and 2:30-5pm. In the case of serious emergency after hours, call 57 22 01 43.

Currency Exchange: Thomas Cook, at the train station (tel. 56 91 58 80). Open daily 8am-8pm.

American Express: 14, cours de l'Intendance (tel. 56 81 70 02). Open Mon.-Fri. 8:45am-noon and 1:30-6pm. Client mail. 24-hr. refund (tel. 05 90 86 00).

Post Office: 52, rue Georges Bonnac (tel. 56 48 87 48). Open Mon.-Fri. 8am-7pm, Sat. 8am-noon. Currency exchange. **Postal Code:** 33000.

Trains: Gare St-Jean, rue Charles Domercq (tel. 56 92 50 50). To: Paris (10-14/day, 5-8hr., 285F; TGV 3¼hr., 375F), Nantes (5-8/day, 4hr., 216F), Toulouse (10/day, 2½hr., 168F), Nice (4/day, 9½hr., 395F), St-Emilion (2/day, 45min., 39F). Lockers 15-30F. Showers in station 15F. Info office open daily 9am-7pm.

Buses: Citram, 14, rue Fondaudège (tel. 56 43 04 04). St-Emilion via Libourne (3-4/day, 1hr., 36F), and most nearby towns. Info office open Mon.-Sat. 9am-noon and 2-6pm.

Public Transportation: CGTE urban and suburban buses. Tickets 8F. Maps available at the train station and at the CGTE information office, 4, rue Georges Bonnac, off pl. Gambetta (tel. 57 57 88 88). Open Mon.-Sat. 8am-7:30pm.

Laundromat: cours de Marne, 5min. from station. Wash 16F, dry 2F/5min. Open daily 7am-9pm.

Medical Assistance: Hôpital St-André, 1, rue Jean Burguet (tel. 56 79 56 79). 24-hr. emergency room. **SAMU** ambulance service (tel. 56 96 70 70).

Police: Headquarters at 87, rue de l'Abbé de l'Epée, also known as rue Castéja. (tel. 56 90 92 75). Also at the train station (tel. 56 92 18 90). **Emergency:** tel. 17.

ACCOMMODATIONS, CAMPING, AND FOOD

The *accueil* bureau (*quai* #1 in the train station) provides maps and accommodations listings. Call ahead in July and August.

Auberge de Jeunesse Foyer Barbey (HI), 22, cours Barbey (tel. 56 91 59 51). Take Cours de la Marne from the right end of the *gare* for about 5 blocks and turn left onto cours Barbey (5min.). Reasonably clean. Loads of backpackers. Single-sex rooms. Kitchen. Reception open 8-9:30am and 6-11pm. Strict lockout 9:30am-6pm. Curfew 11pm. 39F, nonmembers with passports 43F. Sheets 16F.

Maison des Etudiants, 50, rue Ligier (tel. 56 96 48 30). Take bus #7 or 8 from the train station to "Bourse du Travail" and continue in the same direction on cours de la Libération to rue Ligier. From the *gare*, follow cours de la Marne through pl. de la Victoire to cours Aristide Briand and turn right onto rue Ligier (30min.). Quiet, clean, and closer to the town center than the hostel. From Oct.-June, pri-marily monthly residents, but may have a few beds available for women travelers. No lockout or curfew. 67F, with ISIC 47F. TV. Showers and sheets included.

Hôtel la Boétie, 4, rue de la Boétie (tel. 56 81 76 68), on a quiet street between pl. Gambetta and the Musée des Beaux Arts. Attentive management lends personal touch to spacious, comfortable rooms with shower, toilet, TV, telephone, and mini-bar. Reception open 24 hr. VCR (10F) and movie rentals (10F). Singles 120-135F. Doubles 135F, with two beds 160F. Triples 180F. Breakfast 18F.

Hôtel d'Amboise, 22, rue de la Vieille Tour (tel. 56 81 62 67), in *centre ville*. Attractive rooms overlooking a busy side street. Singles 65-70F, with shower 100F. Doubles 90F, with shower 110F. Breakfast 15F. Call to reserve during the summer.

Hôtel-Bar-Club Les 2 Mondes, 10, rue St-Vincent-de-Paul (tel. 56 91 63 09), a block from train station. Spacious rooms above a bar. Singles 85F, with shower 105F. Doubles 100F, with shower 126-136F. Triples 189F. Breakfast 20F.

Camping: Camping les Gravières, Pont-de-la-Maye (tel. 56 87 00 36), in Ville-neuve D'Ornon. In a riverside forest. Reception open 8am-11pm; off-season, 8am-10pm. 17F/person, 16F/tent, 7F/car.

Bordeaux, known as *La Région de Bien Manger et de Bien Vivre* (The region of Fine Eating and Living), has some of the most affordable restaurants in the country, especially in pl. St-Michel, between *centre ville* and the station. **Baud et Millet,** 19, rue Huguerie, off pl. Tournu, boasts 650 wines and over 200 cheeses. Cheese plus dessert costs 95F. (Open daily 9am-2am.) Call **CROUS** (tel. 56 33 86 86) for info on university cafeterias, where you can eat for 25F, 12F with ISIC or *Carte Jeune*.

SIGHTS

Nearly 900 years after its consecration by Pope Urban II, **Cathédrale St-André** remains the *grande dame* of Bordeaux's high Gothic masterpieces. (Free organ concerts every other Tues. evening, mid-May to mid-Sept. Cathedral open daily 9am-noon and 2-6pm.) The warehouse-like **Basilica St-Michel** is accompanied by an immense, free-standing 15th-century bell tower. The **Musée d'Aquitaine,** 20, cours Pasteur, houses a comprehensive collection of *bordelais* agricultural, maritime, and commercial treasures. (Open Tues.-Sun. 10am-6pm. 15F, students 8F, Wed. free.) The **Galerie des Beaux Arts,** pl. du Colonel-Raynal, features 3-4 expositions per year of satirical cartoons, landscapes in crayon, and rough pencil sketches. (Open Wed.-Mon. 10am-12:30pm and 1:30-7pm.) The **Maison du Vin/CIVB,** 1, cours du 30 Juillet, pours free samples of regional labels, answers any wine questions, and dis-tributes a list of the smaller wine-producing châteaux in the area. Ask about screen-ing times for their 15-minute film on *bordelais* wines. (Open Mon.-Fri. 8:30am-6pm, Sat. 9am-12:30pm and 1:30-5pm.)

■ Near Bordeaux

Many châteaux around **St-Emilion** welcome visitors and have guided tours, such as **Château La Brande** (tel. 57 74 36 38) in nearby Fronsac. Ask at the **tourist office** (tel. 57 24 72 03; open daily 9:30am-12:30pm and 1:45-7pm; Nov.-March until 6pm) about guided tours of the various châteaux. The village's spectacular **Eglise Mono-**

lithe is an underground behemoth painstakingly carved from a single massive rock. **Trains** run from Bordeaux to St-Emilion (2/day, 30min., 42F).

Trains leave Bordeaux daily for **Arcachon** (1hr., 48F), the first leg of a daytrip to the **Dune du Pilat.** A mountain of sand that brings out the acrobat in everyone, the Dune may be the most sublime beach in the world. Its 60 million sandy tons, 104-114m high, pose an encroaching threat to the homes lying at its base. Buses leave from the Arcachon station for **Pyla-sur-Mer** (about 20/day, last return around 8pm; 30min.; 16F round-trip), which is a 10- to 15-minute walk from the Dune.

BASQUE COUNTRY (PAYS BASQUE)

Bayonne A grand port with small-town appeal, Bayonne enjoys a prominent position on the Gulf of Gascony close to the Spanish border. Its spiny twin steeples biting into Bayonne's skies, the northern-Gothic **Cathédrale Sainte-Marie** intimidates from afar and impresses from within. (Open Mon.-Sat. 8am-7:15pm, Sun. 8:30am-7pm.) Highlights of the unbeatable **Musée Bonnat,** 5, rue Jacques Laffitte, in Petit-Bayonne, include a ghoulish El Greco portrait and Goya's grim *La Dernière Communion de San José de Calasanz*. (Open Wed.-Mon. 10am-noon and 3-7pm, Fri. open until 9pm; Sept. 11-June 14 reduced hours. 15F, students 5F.)

The **tourist office,** (tel. 59 46 01 46), pl. des Basques, provides a shoddy map and can help find rooms. (Open Mon.-Sat. 9am-7pm, Sun. 10am-1pm; Oct.-May Mon.-Fri. 9am-12:30pm and 1:30-6:30pm, Sat. 9am-12:30pm.) Inexpensive hotels abound in Bayonne. Try the **Hôtel des Arceaux,** 26, rue Pont Neuf (tel. 59 59 15 53), 15 minutes from the station in Grand-Bayonne's pedestrian shopping district. Bright, clean doubles go for 125, triples 200F. (Reception open 7:30am-10:30pm. Call ahead.) The **Hôtel Paris-Madrid,** pl. de la Gare (tel. 59 55 13 98), features fine rooms and 24-hour reception. (Singles 85F. Doubles 125F, with shower 165F. Triples 195F.) Bayonne is linked by bus and train to Bordeaux (9/day, 2hr., 130F and reservation).

Anglet The only hostel within 100km is in **Anglet;** the well-equipped, carefree **Auberge de Jeunesse (HI),** 19, rte. de Vignes (tel. 59 63 86 49), lies directly uphill from the beach. From the Hôtel de Ville in Biarritz, take line #4 (every 50min.; direction "Bayonne Sainsontain"). From pl. de la République or pl. de Reudit in Bayonne, take line #4 to "La Barre," then change to bus #4N (direction "Mairie Biarritz"). (Tickets 7F, good for 1hr. after validation on bus.) The 95-bed hostel is the hub of southwestern France's surfing subculture. (Reception open 8:30-10am and 6-10pm. No lockout. 65F/person. Cot in the circus-style tent 61F. Camping 43F.) Try to arrive at least an hour before opening and reserve in person at the reception.

Biarritz Originally a whaling village at the base of the Pyrenees and now home to the "queen of French beaches," Biarritz embodies all that is quintessentially regal. While this town is not a budget traveler's dream, a little ingenuity renders it accessible. At the **Grande Plage,** you'll find a wealth of surfers and bathers. Just north are **plage Miramar,** cozied against the base of the cliffs, and **Pointe St-Martin,** where bathers peacefully repose *au naturel*. Jutting out from the plateau, the craggy peninsula of the **Rocher de la Vierge** gazes over magical views at sunset. At low tide, the **plage des Basques** boasts the cleanest water and the most open sand in Biarritz.

Biarritz hotels have more stars than the Milky Way. Write a month or two ahead for a space in July or August or enlist the help of the tourist office. Centrally located **Hôtel Berhouet,** 29, rue Gambetta (tel. 59 24 63 36), offers singles and doubles for 100-180F. A few hundred feet from a cliff overlooking the water, the **Hôtel du Rocher de la Vierge,** 13, rue Port Vieux (tel. 59 24 11 74), has clean singles (100F) and doubles with shower (170F). You might try commuting from Anglet's hostel or from Bayonne. The **tourist office,** Javalquinto, 1, square d'Ixelles (tel. 59 24 20 24), dispenses reams of maps and bouquets of brochures and will track down a room or a campsite for you. Be warned: Affordable accommodations go fast. (Open daily 8am-8pm; Oct. 4-May 9am-6:45pm.) Trains cruise through **Biarritz-la-Négresse,** 3km out of town. To get to the *centre ville,* take blue bus #2 (direction "Bayonne via Biarritz"; 6:30am-7:38pm every 20-40min.) or bus #9 (direction "Biarritz HDV," same schedule). Both buses leave directly across from the station. Since many Paris-Hendaye trains don't stop in Biarritz, another option is to get off the train in Bayonne and hop a bus to downtown Biarritz (30min.). All buses cost 7F.

St-Jean-de-Luz and St-Jean-Pied-de-Port A formerly fishy cousin of glitzier Biarritz, nearby **St-Jean-de-Luz** also sees some of southwestern France's finest stretches of sand. **Trains** run from Biarritz (10/day, 15min., 14F) and Bayonne (10/day, 25min., 23F), but rooms fill quickly. Eight km from the Spanish border and accessible by rail from Bayonne (4-6/day, 1hr., 42F), **St-Jean-Pied-de-Port** epitomizes the natural splendor of Basque country. The tourist office, 14, av. Charles de Gaulle (tel. 59 37 03 57), foots hiking information on the Forêt d'Iraty. (Open Mon.-Sat. 9am-12:30pm and 2-7pm, Sun. 10:30am-12:30pm and 3-6pm; Sept.-June Mon.-Fri. 9am-noon and 2-7pm, Sat. 9am-noon and 2-6pm.)

LANGUEDOC-ROUSSILLON

■■■ TOULOUSE

Toulouse came of age in the 16th and 17th centuries when merchants who had amassed fortunes through the pastel (a plant used to dye fabrics blue) trade gained appointments as consuls or *capitouls* and built extravagant townhouses to symbolize their new power and status. Former capital of southern Aquitaine, the youthful city, thriving with spicy influences of Spanish and North African immigrants, now enjoys a role as the capital of historic Languedoc as well as France's aeronautics research center; it's hometown to Ariane rockets and the Airbus jumbo jet.

Perennially a bastion of Catholicism in a Protestant region, Toulouse boasts an assemblage of distinctive churches. The **Basilique St-Sernin,** on rue du Taur, is the world's largest Romanesque structure, within which is a subterranean crypt. (Church open Mon.-Sat. 8-11:45am and 2-5:45pm, Sun. 2-5:45pm. Crypt open Mon.-Sat. 10-11:30am and 2:30-5pm, Sun. 2:30-5pm. 8F.) In the austere interior of **Les Jacobins,** rue Lakanal, stained glass and the calm cloister, site of weekly summer piano concerts, complement the elegant proportions of the church. St. Thomas Aquinas is buried in the modest crypt. (Church open Mon.-Sat. 10am-noon and 2:30-6pm, Sun. 2:30-6pm. To cloister 10F. Concert tickets from 70F available at tourist office.) The **Musée des Augustins,** 21, rue de Metz, off rue Alsace-Lorraine, exhibits exquisite Romanesque and Gothic sculpture. (Open daily 10am-6pm; Oct.-May Wed.-Mon. 10am-5pm. 10F.) Next to St-Sernin, the **Musée St-Raymond** houses an impressive collection of regional archeological finds; check out the sculpture gallery of Roman emperors on the entry level. (Open daily 10am-6pm; Oct.-May Wed.-Mon. 10am-5pm. 8F, students free.) Many *hôtels particuliers* (mansions) near the Garonne River shelter 17th-century courtyards open to the public; try the opulent **Hôtel d'Assezat,** pl. D'Assezat, on rue de Metz. The least expensive and most eccentric places lie along **rue des Blanchers. Place St-Georges** is the heart of *toulousain* student life. The free *Regard* magazine, available in newsstands and tabacs, lists concerts and theater events in the area. Pick up a copy of *50 festivals de musique en Midi-Pyrénées* from the tourist office.

Accommodations, Food, and Practical Information The auberge de jeunesse **Villa des Rosiers (HI),** 125, rue Jean Rieux (tel. 61 80 49 93), is friendly

TOULOUSE

but remote, and its bathrooms are no place for bare feet. From the station, take bus #14 (direction "Purpan") to pl. Dupuy and change to bus #22 (direction "Gonin-La Terrasse"). Get off at Leygues. (39F.) **Hôtel des Arts,** 1bis, rue Cantegrol (tel. 61 23 36 21), at rue des Arts, off pl. St-Georges, offers lively, central rooms with artsy posters and is run by a delightful, young English-speaking couple. (Singles 80-105F, with shower and toilet 135F. Doubles 125F, with shower 145F.) St-Exupéry (best known for his book *Le Petit Prince*) stayed in room 32 of the **Hôtel du Grand Balcon,** 8, rue Romiguières (tel. 61 21 48 08), at a corner of the pl. du Capitôle. (Singles 105F, with shower 146F. Doubles 125F, with shower 146-195F. Triples and quads 146F, with shower 195F. Closed much of Aug.; call first.)

Markets line bd. Victor Hugo, pl. des Carmes, and bd. Strasbourg (Tues.-Sun. 9am-1pm), and food stands spill over the ground floor of the Parking Victor Hugo, Les Halles. **Restaurants** thrive on the tiny streets on either side of rue St-Rome, but the most economical eateries lie along the **rue du Taur** on the way to the university. **Auberge Louis XIII,** 1bis, rue Tripière, with its shaded terrace and country cuisine, draws an interesting student crowd. (60F and 70F *menus*. Open Sept.-July Mon.-Fri. noon-2pm and 7-9:45pm.) **La Tantina de Burgos,** 27, av. de la Garonnette, is worth the lengthy walk from the center. Hearty Spanish specialties include sizzling *paella* (60F) and a *bar à tapas* in an relaxed atmosphere. (48F lunch *menu*. Open Tues.-Sat. noon-1:30pm and 7:30pm-midnight.) Let the regional specialties of **Salade Gasconne,** 75, rue du Taur, tantalize your taste buds. Students love it. (Salads 29-49F. 49F *menu* includes a ¼-carafe of wine. Open Mon.-Fri. noon-2pm and 7:30-10pm, Sat. noon-2pm and 7:30pm-midnight.)

The **tourist office,** rue Lafayette (tel. 61 11 02 22), in the park behind the Capitôle, changes money when banks are closed and books rooms. (Open Mon.-Sat. 9am-7pm, Sun. 9am-1pm and 2-5:30pm; Oct.-April Mon.-Fri. 9am-6pm, Sat. 9am-12:30pm and 2-6pm.)

■ Near Toulouse

Albi An hour northeast of Toulouse by train, Albi, which derived its name from the bloody 13th-century Albigensian crusade initiated by the Pope against its population, today presides over culture instead of carnage. The extraordinary **Musée Toulouse-Lautrec,** in the Palais de la Berbie, presents a stunning collection of the controversial artist's work, including the lithographs that earned him his international reputation. (Open daily 9am-noon and 2-6pm; Oct.-March Wed.-Mon. 10am-noon and 2-5pm. April-May 10am-noon and 2-6pm. 20F, students 10F.) Across from the museum, the enormous **Basilique Ste-Cécile** hides bright 16th-century frescoes and Burgundian and Gothic statuary. The nearby **Eglise St-Salvy** provides a fragrant garden and an intimate contrast to the imposing basilica.

The **tourist office,** 19, pl. Ste-Cécile (tel. 63 54 22 30), has rooming info. (Open Mon.-Sat. 9am-7:30pm, Sun. 10:30am-1pm and 3:30-5:30pm; Sept.-June Mon.-Sat. 9am-noon and 2-6pm.) The **Maison des Jeunes et de la Culture,** 13, rue de la République (tel. 63 54 53 65), offers dorm bunks for 24F. (Reception open daily 6-7pm. 20F key deposit. Dorm bunks 26F.) **Hôtel Régence,** 27, av. Maréchal-Joffre (tel. 63 54 01 42), near the station, offers antique furniture and tasteful rooms from 100-110F. Camp at **Parc de Caussels** (tel. 63 60 37 06), 2km east of Albi on rte. de Millau (40F/2 people). **Le Petit Bouchon,** 77, rue Croix Verte, serves a 57F *menu* featuring 4 courses and wine. (Open Mon.-Fri. 8am-10pm, Sat. 8am-3pm.)

Cordes-sur-Ciel Set on a hillside overlooking the patchwork farmland of the Cerou River Valley, Cordes-sur-Ciel served as a sentinel on the Cathar frontier during the Albigensian crusades, and still beckons to approaching visitors today. A flux of lesser artists and artisans have followed Sartre and Camus here; the double-walled, 13th-century bastide features Gothic houses flanking steep, cobblestone walkways in a flawlessly preserved medieval setting. The unique **Musée de l'Art du Sucre,** to the left of the tourist office on pl. de la Bride, will leave you drooling over the display of sculptures crafted entirely of sugar, and, in a few instances, chocolate: the private efforts of Yves Thuriès—a two-time French champion *pâtissier*—and his assistants. (Open daily 10am-noon and 2-6pm; Oct.-April Tues.-Sun. 3-5pm. 5F.) Hotels here are exorbitant; daytrip from Albi, but plan ahead. From pl. Jean Jaurès in Albi, SNCF mini-vans depart for Cordes (1/day except Sun., 35F). Alternatively, take the train (33F) to Vindrac-Cordes and walk the remaining 4km to town, or **Minicar** can pick you up at the station (tel. 63 56 14 80; 18F, 26F at night).

■■■ CARCASSONNE

The **Cité de Carcassonne** is a life-sized toy castle, a 13th-century Disneyland, a double-walled, fortified city with towers and turrets rising from a precipitous plateau in the Garonne valley, and, last but not least, the backdrop for the 1991 movie *Robin Hood: Prince of Thieves.* First attacked in the 1st century by Roman invaders (who subsequently gave way to Visigoths, Invisigoths, and Arabs), Europe's largest fortress fell into an egregious state of disrepair following the 13th-century Wars of Religion. Rising interest in medieval France spurred the rebuilding of the Cité, directed by architect Viollet-le-Duc in 1844.

On the black line, bus #4 serves the **medieval Cité** from both the train station and pl. Gambetta (every ½hr. until 7pm, 5F); you can also hike 30 minutes up the hill. Originally constructed as a palace, the **Château Comtal** fortress overlooks the south side of the Cité. Admission is by guided tour. (Open daily July-Aug. 9:30am-7:30pm; Sept. 1-15 and May-June 9:30am-12:30pm and 2-6:30pm; Sept. 16-April 9:30am-12:30pm and 2-5pm. French tours begin at 9am. 26F, ages 18-25 and over 60 17F, under 18 6F, under 7 free.) The **Basilique St-Nazaire,** with its radiant stained-glass windows and delicate Gothic ribbed vaulting, is considered the finest in southern France. The entire Cité medievalizes during the **Médiévales** festival in August (tickets 30F).

Accommodations, Food, and Practical Information The immaculate **auberge de jeunesse (HI)** (tel. 68 25 23 16) is on rue Vicomte Trencavel in the Cité. (Reception open July-Aug. daily 8-11am and 6pm-midnight; June and Sept. until 11pm; April until 10:30pm; Feb.-March and Nov. until 10pm. 65F. Call a few days in advance. Max. stay 3 days.) At the intersection of rue Montpellier and rue Tourtel, the **Hôtel Astoria** (tel. 68 25 31 38) doles out pristine singles for 80F and doubles for 105F, with shower 130F. (Reception open 6am-midnight.)

Cassoulet, the local specialty, is a hearty stew with white beans, herbs, and usually lamb or pork. Near the entrance to the castle is **La Taverne Medievale,** rue Cros-Mayrevieille, serving the cheapest *cassoulet* around (30F). **L'Ostal des Troubadours,** 5, rue Viollet-le-Duc, posts one of the cheapest *menus* around (49F, plus service) and remains animated all year with live performers nightly. (Open noon to midnight. *Menus* served noon-2pm and 7-11pm.) **L'Hippocampe,** 38, rue du 4 Septembre, is a relaxed counter-top restaurant with miraculously low prices—hold on to your brain! (Pizza 26F. Open Mon.-Sat. 11:30am-2pm and 6:45-10pm.) For provisions, visit the **market** in pl. Carnot (Tues., Thurs., and Sat. mornings). To reach the **tourist office,** 15, bd. Camille Pelletan (tel. 68 25 07 04), from the train station, walk over the canal on rue G. Clemenceau; turn left onto rue de la Liberté and then right onto bd. Jean Jaurès; the office is on the right. (Open Mon.-Sat. 9am-7pm; Sept.-June 9am-12:15pm and 1:45-7pm; Oct.-March 9am-noon and 2-6:30pm.)

PROVENCE

The region the Romans named Provincia (literally, "the province") is carpeted with olive groves and vineyards on hills dusted with lavender and mimosa. Situated midway between Spain and Italy, its enchanting sweetness and too-blue light has inspired medieval troubadours to verses of courtly love, and such artists as Cézanne, Picasso, and Van Gogh to masterpieces. Summer boils with festivals, often staged in old arenas and palaces. Do as the Romans did and spend a few centuries here.

■■■ AVIGNON

The walled city of Avignon sparkles with artistic brilliance among the lush vineyards of the Rhône Valley. Film festivals, street musicians, and the famed **Festival d'Avignon** keep this university town shining. The **Palais des Papes,** built in the 14th century when the popes moved from Rome, stands in white-granite majesty at the highest point in Avignon. (Open daily 9am-7pm; April-June and Oct. 9am-12:15pm and 2-6pm; Nov.-March 9am-noon and 2-5pm. 38F, students and over 65 29F. English guided tours daily 10am and 3pm; 46F, students 37F.) Next to the *Palais,* the popes' expansive garden, **Le Rocher des Doms,** overlooks the 12th-century **Pont St-Bénezet,** the "Pont d'Avignon" of nursery-rhyme fame. The bridge, which now ends abruptly mid-stream, affords a great view of sunset but is not worth the 10F admission fee. Watch the sun set from more modern Pont Daladier, which yields an equally spectacular view and costs nary a centime.

From early July through early August, the **Festival d'Avignon** (tel. 90 82 67 08) puts on everything from avant-garde plays to all-night readings of the *Odyssey.* (Tickets 90-165F/event, some are free. Events start 9:30-11pm.) The festival has at least 65 official locations, but you can have fun for free in most of the surrounding streets.

Accommodations, Food, and Practical Information Avignon lacks an official youth hostel, but **Foyer Bagatelle** (tel. 90 86 30 39), Ile de Barthelasse, just over Pont Daladier, has inexpensive accommodations. (53F in 6- to 8-bed rooms. Sheets 16F.) The **Hôtel Mignon,** 12, rue Joseph Vernet (tel. 90 82 17 30), has newly renovated rooms and cable TV. (Singles with shower 130F. Doubles with shower 165F. Triples with shower and toilet 250F.) The managers at the **Squash Club,** 32, bd. Limbert (tel. 90 85 27 78), will give you a discount on lodgings if you can beat them at squash. (Reception open 8-11am and 5-11pm. Lockout 11am-5pm. Curfew 11pm. 46F. Breakfast on squash courts mandatory 15F. Sheets 14F. Call ahead during festival and off-season.) The **Hôtel le Parc,** 18, rue Perdigurer (tel. 90 82 71 55), off cours Jean Jaurès near the tourist office, has impeccably bright rooms. (Singles and doubles 110F, with shower 140F. Triples with shower 180-200F. Quads with shower 200F.) And the **Hôtel Splendid,** 17, rue Perdiguier (tel. 90 86 14 46), off cours Jean Jaurès near the tourist office, offers a central location, spacious rooms and an enthusiastic owner. (Singles with shower 140F. Triples with shower 200F. Quads with shower 250F. 10-20F less during off-season.) The best site for camping is **Camping Bagatelle** (tel. 90 86 30 39), a big ol' site next to the Piscine Municipale, with a cafeteria, laundromat, and supermarket (15F/person, 7F/tent).

Buy provisions in **Les Halles,** the huge indoor market in pl. Pie. (Open Tues.-Sun. 8am-1pm.) **Restaurant Oanh,** 31bis, rue Bonneterie, is a family-run Vietnamese restaurant with great food at great prices, such as curry chicken for 31F. (Open daily 11am-2pm and 6-11pm.) For the musically inclined, try **Tache d'Encre,** 22, rue des Teinturiers, a pleasant *café-théâtre* with live jazz and blues on most weeknights. The excellent French cuisine includes 49F (3-course, lunchtime), 74F, and 89F *menus.* (Open Tues.-Sat. noon-2pm and 7:30pm-midnight, Sun.-Mon. 7:30pm-midnight.)

The **tourist office,** 41, cours Jean Jaurès (tel. 90 82 65 11), 3 blocks from the train station, has a list of all accommodations, restaurants, and museums. (Open Mon.-Sat. 9am-1pm and 2-6pm; during festival, Mon.-Fri. 9am-6pm, Sat. 9am-1pm and 2-5pm.)

■ Near Avignon

Fifteen minutes north by train (27F), **Orange** has a pair of famous monuments from the Roman city of Aurasio: an imposing **triumphal arch** and the best preserved **Roman theater** in France. Concerts, theater, and opera spring up regularly here through July and August. The **tourist office** on the cours Aristide Briand (tel. 90 34 70 88) has free maps. Large, carpeted rooms await you at recently renovated **Arcotel**, 8, pl. aux Herbes (tel. 90 34 09 23), between the Roman theater and rue St-Martin. (Singles and doubles 100-140F, with shower and toilet 150-190F. Triples 150F, with shower 210F. Quads with shower and toilet 220F. Discount with *Let's Go*.) For a memorable French meal, try **La Roselière**, 4, rue du Renoyer, off pl. Clemenceau. (65F *menu* of local specialties. Open daily noon-2pm and 7-11pm.)

Vaison-la-Romaine, a village in the heart of the Rhône wine valley, features partially excavated Roman villas, a medieval city, and a hillside castle. The **tourist office** is on pl. du Chanoine Santel (tel. 90 36 02 11) and has guided French or English tours (30F, students 15F, under 19 10F) of the region. (Open daily 9am-noon and 2-7pm; Sept.-June Mon.-Sat. 9:30am-noon and 2-6pm.) The **auberge de jeunesse (HI)** in nearby **Séguret** (tel. 90 46 93 31), in a rambling farmhouse surrounded by vineyards, enjoys unrivaled scenery. (Last bus leaves Vaison at 4pm. 63F. Breakfast included. Dinner with local wine 66F, members 58F. Pool out back.) Back in Vaison, the **Centre Culturel à Coeur Joie,** on av. César Geoffrey near the campground (tel. 90 36 00 78), rents spartan but spotless singles (111F, with shower 135F) and doubles (155F, with shower 175F), breakfast included. (Office open March-Dec. 8am-9pm.) **Les Voconces,** pl. Montfort (tel. 90 36 00 94), is a small hotel with big rooms. (Singles and doubles 110-120F, with shower 150-160F. Breakfast 25F.) Vaison is an 80-minute bus ride from Avignon (37F).

■■■ ARLES

Roman grandeur haunts the sun-baked remnants of Arles's **Roman baths,** lingers in the beautiful **Arènes** (now used for bullfights), and endures in the city's **Théâtre Antique** (now used for frequent summer concerts). Proudly Provençal, Arles inscribes plaques in the regional tongue and celebrates the **Fête de la Tradition** (the last weekend in June) in local costume, with bonfires blazing in the streets. Arles's beautiful monuments and vistas lured both Picasso and Van Gogh (who spent his final years—and his ear—here). The **Musée Réattu,** rue du Grand Prieuré, exhibits contemporary art including 57 Picasso drawings donated by the master himself. (Open daily 8:30am-7pm; Nov.-Feb. 9am-noon and 2-4:30pm; March and Oct. 9am-12:30pm and 2-6pm; April-May 9am-12:30pm and 2-7pm. 15F, students 9F.) The mid-July **Rencontres Internationales de la Photographie** (10-20F/exhibit, global ticket 140F, students 110F) courts photographers and agents alike.

The sleek **auberge de jeunesse (HI)** is on av. Maréchal Foch (tel. 90 96 18 25), 10 minutes behind the tourist office. (Reception open 7-10am and 5pm-midnight. Curfew 2am. 75F 1st night, 65F thereafter. Arrive early.) **La Gallia Hôtel,** 22, rue de l'Hôtel de Ville (tel. 90 96 00 63), is a real gem in an excellent location. (Singles or doubles with shower 115F. Doubles with shower and toilet 135F.)

Regional produce fills the **open markets** on bd. Emile Courbes (Wed. 7am-1pm) and on bd. des Lices (Sat. 7am-1pm). A **Monoprix supermarket** faces pl. Lamartine. The popular **Lou Gardian,** 70, rue 4 du Septembre, at the end of rue d'Hôtel de Ville, is run by a proud *provençale* family. Wonderful food in heaping portions will stuff even the most accomplished eaters. (4-course *menu* 63F. Open Mon.-Sat. noon-2pm and 7-9:30pm.) For more cheap eats, check out pl. Voltaire; for people-watching head to the cafés on pl. du Forum.

The **tourist office,** in esplanade Charles de Gaulle at bd. des Lices (tel. 90 96 29 35), has festival information, currency exchange, and a 4F accommodations service. (Open Mon.-Sat. 9am-8pm, Sun. 9am-1pm; March-June 9am-7pm; Oct.-March 9am-

6pm.) There is also a **branch office** at the train station. Inexpensive **hotels** cluster around rue de l'Hôtel de Ville and pl. Voltaire, filling fast during the photography festival. Frequent **buses** run from the *gare routière* (next to the train station) to the **Camargue,** an enormous natural reserve where flamingoes and wild horses run free (8/day, 1hr., 32F) and the **beaches** at nearby Stes-Marie-de-la-Mer (same bus). Trains roll from the **train station,** av. P. Talabot, to Avignon (hourly, 20min., 33F), Marseille (16/day, 1hr., 68F), Nîmes (15/day, 25min., 38F), and Aix-en-Provence (10/day, 1¾hr., 82F).

■■■ AIX-EN-PROVENCE

Blessed with plentiful restaurants, elegant cafés, spellbinding museums, and exuberant festivals, Aix (pronounced "Ex") truly marks the spot as the gastronomic and cultural core of Provence. Pass the afternoon sitting in a café on the **cours Mirabeau,** or walk the **chemin de Cézanne** and check out the artist's original studios.

Aix hosts an internationally renowned **Music Festival** from mid-July to early August (call 42 17 34 00 for info) and supports several museums of note. The **Musée Granet,** pl. St-Jean-Marie-de-Malte, displays bushels of Dutch and French works and 8 small paintings by Cézanne. (Open Wed.-Mon. 10am-noon and 2:30-6pm. 20F, students and children 15F.) The **Musée des Tapisseries,** pl. des Martyrs de la Résistance, houses a lovely collection of 17th- and 18th-century tapestries. (Open Wed.-Mon. 10am-noon and 2-6pm. 11F, students 5F.) The **Fondation Vasarely,** 1, av. Marcel Pagnol, next to the youth hostel, is worth a trip for its modern art experiments. (Open daily 9am-12:30pm and 2-5pm. Off-season Wed.-Sun. 30F, ages 7-18 15F.)

Accommodations, Food, and Practical Information The crowded **auberge de jeunesse (HI),** 3, av. Marcel Pagnol (tel. 42 20 15 99), is next to the Fondation Vasarely. Follow av. des Belges from la Rotonde and turn right on av. de l'Europe. At the first rotary after the highway overpass, bear left and climb the hill. The hostel is on your left; or take bus #12 (every 30min. until 5:30pm, 7F) from "La Rotonde." (Reception open 7:30-10am and 5:30-10pm. Lockout 10am-5:30pm. Curfew 11pm. 76F 1st night, 65F thereafter. Sheets 16F.) Friendly **Hôtel du Casino,** 38, rue Victor Leydet (tel. 42 26 06 88), has comfy rooms. (Singles 160F. Doubles 200-220F.) Near la Rotonde, **Hôtel des Arts,** 69, bd. Carnot (tel. 42 38 11 77), has extremely modern, bright, clean rooms. (Doubles with shower 175F.)

The streets north of cours Mirabeaus are packed with restaurants for all palates and wallets. **Hacienda,** 7, rue Mérindol, in the pl. des Fontêtes, is a good value; the delicious 57F *menu* includes wine. (Open Sept.-Aug. Mon.-Sat. noon-2pm and 7-10:30pm.) The well-liked **Bistrot Aixois,** 37 cours Sextius, cooks up regional specialties for 40-60F. (Open daily noon-2pm and 7-10pm.) Buy a picnic lunch at the **market** at pl. de Verdun (Tues., Thurs., and Sat. 7am-1pm), or stock up at **Monoprix** supermarket, 25, cours Mirabeau. (Open Mon.-Sat. 8:45am-7:30pm.) Be sure to sample Aix's famed almonds, used in cakes and cookies, at one of the numerous *pâtisseries* or *salons de thé* along rue d'Italie or rue Espariàt.

The **tourist office,** 2, pl. du Général de Gaulle (tel. 42 26 02 93), makes hotel reservations (5F) and has the comprehensive guide *Aix la Vivante,* packed with walking tours, museums, and local recipes. From the train station, bear left up av. Victor Hugo for the tourist office and the central city bus terminus. (Open Mon.-Sat. 8am-10pm, Sun. 6-10pm; Sept. 16-June Mon.-Sat. 8am-7pm, Sun. 8:30am-12:30pm.) To get anywhere by **train** from Aix, one must first go to Marseille by train (23/day, last train 9:40pm; 40min; 34F) or on cheaper **buses** (every 15min.; 45min.; 20F, students 23F round-trip). Six buses per day run to Avignon (1½hr., 65F).

FRENCH RIVIERA (CÔTE D'AZUR)

Paradises are made to be lost. Sparkling between Marseille and the Italian border, the sun-drenched beaches and waters of the Mediterranean form the backdrop for this fabled playground of the rich and famous. But its seductive loveliness has almost been its undoing, as shrewd developers have turned the coast's beauty to profit and its pleasures into big business. Today, the area is as crammed with low-budget tourists as with high-handed millionaires, and many French condemn it as a shameless Fort Lauderdale, a mere shadow of its former self.

In the 18th and 19th centuries, English and Russian aristocrats came to the Riviera's unspoiled fishing villages to cure winter ailments. The Côte became a favorite destination of French sunseekers only after WWII, when new highways and railroads and a government-mandated increase in vacation time made the area accessible to the masses. Besides attracting tourists and aristocracy, the Côte has also drawn some of the past century's greatest artists to its shores. Nearly every town along the eastern stretch of the Côte has a chapel, room, or wall decorated by Matisse or Chagall, and there are superb museums everywhere. Jazz festivals mount throughout the summer; Nice's *Carnaval* is held in February, the Cannes Film Festival and Monte-Carlo Grand Prix in May, and Monaco's Fireworks Festival in August.

The coast is well-served by frequent, inexpensive trains and buses. Trains for the Côte leave Paris's Gare de Lyon every hour in summer; the trip takes 5 hours on the TGV to Marseille and 7-8 hours to Nice. Trains and roads are packed in summer; you might want to base yourself in the less expensive coastal towns and take daytrips to the purse-emptying cities. Like western Provence, the Riviera is best visited during early June and in September when crowds are low and hotel vacancies high.

In high season, youth hostels and hotels are often booked months in advance. Although sleeping on the beach is illegal, many travelers end up where they lay their towels during the day. Several beaches provide showers, toilets, and even towels for a small fee (10-15F). Be careful, as you may find yourself next to groups of "respectable" looking youths who enjoy relieving tourists of their mopeds, jewelry, and spare cash. Daytrippers can make use of the lockers (15F-20F) available at most train stations—always hide the key—or can check luggage at the desk.

■■■ MARSEILLE

France's third city, Marseille is sort of like the *bouillabaisse* for which it is famous: steaming hot and full of spice. Unlike *bouillabaisse,* the town is hardly delectable. The rather grimy city enjoys a universal reputation for roguishness and danger. Although racial tensions pervade Marseilles, it remains charged throughout with color and commotion. Its daily fish market, nearby beaches, wild nightclubs, and big-city adventure merit a (brief) stop-over on the way to Nice or Avignon.

The city's heart is the humming **Vieux Port** (old port) and the adjacent streets of the *vieille ville*. Extending straight out of the port is Marseille's main artery, **La Canebière,** affectionately known to English sailors as "Can o' beer." The **North African quarter** twists through the narrow, dusty streets between the train station and La Canebière. At night these areas can be dangerous for travelers of either sex.

Accommodations, Food, and Practical Information A former château now houses a well-kept but isolated **Auberge de Jeunesse de Bois-Luzy (HI),** 76, av. de Bois-Luzy (tel. 91 49 06 18); take bus #6 from pl. de la Libération, #8 from La Canebière by day, or bus K after 8:20pm (until 10pm) from La Canebière (8F). Exit at "Bois-Luzy." (Reception open 7:30-10am and 5-10:30pm. Curfew 10:30pm. 42F.) Inexpensive hotels abound in Marseille, especially on rue Breteuil and rue Aubagne. A herd of 1- and 2-star hotels grazes on allé Gambetta. Turn right off rue Paradis to arrive at the great location of **Hôtel Montgrand,** 50, rue Montgrand (tel.

91 33 33 81). The immaculate rooms are squeaky clean. (Singles 110-150F. Doubles with bath and toilet 160-180F. Triples with bathroom 160-220F.) Chow down on *bouillabaisse* or a 5-course seafood *menu* (each 75F) at **Racasse-Dauphin,** 6, quai de Rive-neuve, in the *vieux port.*

Marseille is a **transportation** hub with connections to Paris (4 TGV/day, 4¾hr., 392F plus 16F required reservation) and Lyon (about every 2hr., 3½hr., 200F). A cheaper but slower option are the buses that leave from pl. Victor Hugo, behind the train station. For information on ferries to Corsica, Sardinia, and North Africa, try the **SNCM office** at 61, bd. des Dames (tel. 91 56 30 10, for reservations -80 20). To reach the local **hospital,** Hôpital Timone, bd. Jean Moulin (tel. 91 38 60 00), take metro line #1 to "Castéllane," then bus #91. The phone for SAMU **ambulances** is 91 49 91 91. The **police** are at 2, rue du Commissaire Becker (tel. 91 39 80 00).

The **tourist office,** 4, La Canebière (tel. 91 54 91 11), near the *vieux port*, has a free accommodations service. Turn left from the station steps, walk along bd. d'Athènes, and take a right onto La Canebière at McDonald's. (Open daily 8am-8pm; Oct.-June Mon.-Sat. 9am-7:30pm, Sun. 10am-5:30pm.) The **annex** at the train station (tel. 91 50 59 18) performs the same services. (Open Mon.-Sat. 9am-7pm; Sept.-June Mon.-Fri. 10am-1pm and 1:30-6pm.) The **U.S.** (12, bd. Paul Peytral; tel. 91 54 92 00) and the **U.K.** (24, av. du Prado; tel. 91 53 02 08) maintain **consulates.**

■■■ ST-TROPEZ

Hollywood and *Lifestyles of the Rich and Famous* have popularized an image of St-Tropez as a veritable modern-day *El Dorado*. One expects a city in which Hermès goes to bathe with Yves St-Laurent and Lamborghinis prowl streets paved with gold. While swanky Cannes to the east might fit this image, the St-Tropez of reality bears mercifully little resemblance to that of myth. To reach the beaches, take a **Sodetrav bus** from the *gare routière* on av. du Général de Gaulle ("St-Tropez-Ramatuelle" line; runs Mon.-Sat.). Or, rent a pair of wheels from **Louis Mas,** 3 and 5, rue Quarenta (tel. 94 97 00 60; **bicycles** 40F/day, deposit 500F; mountain bikes 70F, deposit 1500F, and mopeds 80-135F, deposit 2000-4000F, gas 25F, helmets 6F; open Easter-Oct. 15 Mon.-Sat. 9am-7:30pm, Sun. 9am-12:45pm and 5:30-7:30pm).

The **tourist office** (tel. 94 97 41 21; fax 94 97 79 08), between avs. du Général de Gaulle and Général Leclerc, has an invaluable free room-finding service. (Open daily 9am-7:30pm; Oct.-March. Mon.-Sat. 9am-noon and 2-6pm; April-June 15 daily 9am-7pm.) There *are* some semi-affordable hotels in St-Tropez, but by mid-June, they're booked nearly solid. Call ahead to **Hôtel le Méditerranée,** 21 bd. Louis Blanc (tel. 94 97 39 59) across from the Hôtel de Paris. (Singles and doubles 250F, with shower 280F, with toilet 380-410F. Quads with shower and toilet 530F.) **Camping** is by far the cheapest option, but again, make reservations. The tourist office can tell you which sites have space (few will in July and Aug.). Try 4-star **La Croix du Sud,** route de Pampelonne (tel. 94 79 80 84; 25F/person, 36F/tent; open Easter-Sept.), or **Kon Tiki** (tel. 94 79 80 17; 67F/tent). Both lie just behind the Pampelonne beach.

The **Vieux Port** and the narrow cobblestone streets of the hillside *vieille ville* behind the waterfront form the hub of St-Tropez's culinary activity. For dinner, hang out at **Mario,** 9, rue Aire du Chemin, which offers a 68F French-Italian *menu* on a pink and lavender terrace. (Open daily 7-11pm.) To create your own ambience, head to **Prisunic Supermarché,** 7, av. du Général Leclerc (open Mon.-Sat. 8am-8pm), or to the outdoor *grand marché* in pl. des Lices (Tues. and Sat. 6:30am-1pm). Great picnic spots lounge along the water 10 minutes from the Vieux Port.

To reach "St. Trop d'Aise" (St. Too much Luxury, as locals affectionately call it) take the bus (but don't admit it) from St-Raphaël (8/day, 1½-3hr., 41F) or Toulon (8/day, 2½-4hr., 80F). Call **Sodetrav buses** (tel. 94 97 62 77), or ask the tourist office for details. The faster, more scenic boat ride from St-Raphaël is much more suave, and not much more expensive (mid-June to mid-Sept. 3-4/day, April-June and Sept.-Oct. 4/day; 50min.; one-way 50F, round-trip 100F, only 68F if you stay at the Fréjus hostel). Call **Gare Maritime de St-Raphaël** at 94 95 17 46 for details. (Open daily 9am-noon and 2-6pm.) Hitching is poor; you'd soil the upholstery, darling.

■■■ ST-RAPHAËL AND FRÉJUS

Sandwiched between St-Tropez and Cannes, the twin cities of St-Raphaël and Fréjus boast all the wide, sandy beaches, seafood restaurants, and coastal charm of their swanky Côte d'Azur cousins at half the cost. Bake in the sun along the long and sandy **Plage Fréjus**, just 10 minutes along the waterfront from the St-Raphaël train station. You can visit the huge **Parc Zoologique Safari de Fréjus** (tel. 94 40 70 65) by car or—if you're brave—by foot. Take the "Fayence-St-Raphaël" bus line from St-Raphaël to the "Le Camps le Coq" stop. Go right at the fort and continue for about 10 minutes. (Open daily 10am-5:30pm. 50F, ages 3-10 28F.) The **Grand Canyon de Verdon** reigns as the deepest canyon in Europe. Here, massive cliffs streaked with yellow and pink wildflowers plunge to swift rivers and forested valleys. The tourist offices in St.-Raphaël and Fréjus have hiking maps and sundry information on the canyon. **Voyages Cagnard,** av. Karr (tel. 94 95 24 78), at the *gare routiere,* runs tours every Thursday.

Kind managers and a great crowd of backpackers hang out at the **Auberge de Jeunesse de St-Raphaël-Fréjus (HI),** chemin du Counillier (tel. 94 52 18 75), 4km from the St-Raphaël train station. A direct shuttle bus runs from quai #6 of the *gare routière* to the hostel daily at 6pm (6.5F); a return shuttle leaves at 9:15am. (Lockout 10am-6pm. Curfew 11pm. 59F.) Or head to the simple but well-located **La Bonne Auberge,** 54, rue de la Garonne (tel. 94 95 69 72) in St-Raphaël. (Doubles 150F, with shower 200F. Open March-Oct.) Affordable restaurants center around the Vieux Port and bd. de la Libération. **Restaurant La Grillade,** 32, rue Boëtman, serves delicious *brochette d'agneau* (lamb skewers, 62F) and a 78F seafood *menu.* Pizzas run 36-55F. (Open Mon.-Fri. and Sun. noon-2:30pm and 7-10:30pm, Sat. 7-10:30pm.)

The **tourist office** in St-Raphaël (tel. 94 82 15 68, -69; fax 94 82 15 70), across the street from the train station, has the scoop on transportation and room availability. (Open Mon.-Sat. 8:15am-12:30pm and 1:30-7:30pm, Sun. 8:15am-noon; Oct.-June Mon.-Sat. 8:15am-noon and 1:30-6pm.) St-Raphaël has frequent **trains** to Toulon (20/day, 50min., 71F), Cannes (25/day, 25min., 32F), and Nice (25/day, 1hr., 51F). **Sodetrav buses** connect St-Raphaël to St-Tropez (8/day, 2hr., 43F), and **Forum Cars** (tel. 94 95 16 71) makes the scenic trip from Cannes to St-Raphaël (with a fantastic view of the *calanques;* 8/day, 70min., 29F). Buses leave from quai #7 for the St-Raphaël to Fréjus voyage every half hour (Mon.-Sat. 7am-7pm, Sun. 7am-6pm; 5F).

■■■ CANNES

All preconceived notions of the French Riviera materialize in Cannes. Sister city to Beverly Hills, Cannes is a favorite stop of the international jet-set. Less reclusive than St-Tropez, Cannes allows even the unshaven budget traveler to tan on the beach with Gerard Depardieu or browse in boutiques with Madonna. In May, Cannes's **Festival International du Film** skims the cream of Hollywood across the ocean. Executives will sign deals for 50-million-dollar flops on cocktail napkins and Spike Lee wanna-be's will leave in a huff, proclaiming they've been robbed. None of the festival's 350 screenings is open to the public (that means you). Most of Cannes's daytime activity (and spending) pulses between rue Félix-Faure and the waterfront. Of Cannes's 3 casinos, the most accessible is **Le Casino Croisette,** 1, jetée Albert Eduoard (tel. 93 38 12 11), next to the Palais des Festivals, with slots, blackjack, and roulette. (Gambling daily 5pm-3am; open for slots at 11am. No shorts. Must be 18. Free.) If your luck sours, take to the clubs, but prepare to feel underdressed. From 11pm to dawn, dance at **Jane's,** 38, rue des Serbes (tel. 92 99 79 59), in the Hôtel Gray d'Albion. (Cover and 1st drink 120F.) Cannes has about as many gay nightspots as straight ones. **Les 3 Cloches** (tel. 93 68 32 92) rings with jazz, rock, and blues every night. (Cover 50F. Open 11pm-dawn.)

Accommodations and Food   There is no youth hostel in Cannes, but the **Auberge de Jeunesse Fréjus-St-Raphaël (HI)** (tel. 94 52 18 75; 31F) is just 20 minutes by train. The city's hotels have enough stars to fill a galaxy, but a few bargains lurk just off rue d'Antibes and close to the beach. Try to book ahead—an absolute must in July and August. **Hôtel Chanteclair,** 12, rue Forville (tel. 93 39 68 88), off the Forville market to the right of the station, has firm beds and an enclosed courtyard. (Singles 170-200F. Doubles 180-230F. Quad 230-360F.) Across from the train station at the **Hôtel du Nord,** 6, rue Jean-Jaurès (tel. 93 38 48 79), the owner loves the U.S., speaks English, and readily gives advice on how to do Cannes right. (Singles 140-180F. Doubles 200-230F, with showers 250F. Quads with shower 368F. Open Dec.-Oct.) The best **camping** is the 3-star site at **Le Grand Saule,** 24, bd. Jean Moulin (tel. 93 90 55 10), in nearby Ranguin. Take bus #9 (65F) from pl. de l'Hôtel de Ville toward Grasse. (50F/person, 81-121F/two, tent included. Open April-Oct.)

The elegant sidewalk cafés on bd. de la Croisette, Cannes's center of conspicuous consumption, attract violinists and accordion players but cost an arm, a leg, and your soul as deposit. The smaller cafés and restaurants on rue Meynardier are just as lovely and much less expensive. The delightful **Chez Mamichette,** 1, rue St-Antoine, has *fondue savoyarde* (50F), a 65F *menu,* and a 40F *plat du jour.* (Open Mon.-Sat. noon-3pm and 7-11pm.) **Restaurant le Pacific,** 14, rue Venizélos, across from the train station on the right, serves excellent pizzas (32-50F), a 57F 4-course *menu,* and an 95F 6-course *menu.* (Open Sun.-Thurs. 11am-2:30pm and 6:30-9:30pm, Fri. 11am-2pm.) For a picnic, buy supplies at **Monoprix Supermarket,** 9, rue Maréchal Foch, across from the train station (open daily 9am-7:30pm), and head to the breezy, palm-tree-filled **Jardin de la Croisette.** The Cannes **outdoor markets** find happy homes in pl. Gambetta and rue Forville (Tues.-Sun. 7am-1pm).

Practical Information   The helpful **tourist office** at 1, bd. de la Croisette (tel. 93 39 01 01 or 93 39 24 53; fax 93 99 37 06), in the Palais des Festivals next to the *vieux port,* has loads of information on Cannes and the surrounding area, as well as a free accommodations service. (Open daily 9am-7:30pm; Sept.-June Mon.-Sat. 9am-6:30pm.) The train station has a **branch office.** (Open Mon.-Sat. 9am-12:30pm and 2-6pm.) On the major coastal **train** line, Cannes has frequent connections to Nice (35min., 28F), Monaco (50min., 39F), and Marseille (2hr., 112F). The station, 1, rue Jean-Jaurès (tel. 93 99 50 50), has baggage service for those who want to make Cannes a daytrip. Buses leave from the **gare routière** (Buz Azur; tel. 93 64 50 17), near Palais de Festivals, every 20 minutes to Antibes (30min., 13F), Nice (1½hr., 28F), and to St-Raphaël (70min., 23F). The nearest **hospital** is at 13, av. des Broussailles (tel. 93 69 91 33).

■ Near Cannes

Antibes boasts beautiful beaches, new theater and music festivals, and a seaside youth hostel. Once home to celebrated English writer Graham Greene, the town has become one of the Riviera's newest budget backpacker hotspots. The **Musée Picasso,** in the Château Grimaldi on pl. Mariejol (tel. 93 34 91 91), displays works by the master and his contemporaries. (Open June 15-Aug. Wed.-Mon. 10am-noon and 3-7pm; Sept.-Oct. and Dec.-June 14 10am-noon and 2-6pm. 20F, students 10F.)

Coed bathrooms, cheap rooms, and a fun backpacking crowd make the **Relais International de la Jeunesse,** at the intersection of bd. de la Garoupe and av. l'Antiquité (tel. 93 61 34 40), a good option. Just don't expect the Ritz. Take bus #2a from the *gare routière* to the L'Antiquité stop on bd. de la Garoupe (5F). (Lockout 10am-6pm. Curfew midnight. 60F. Dinner 45F. Sheets 20F. Open June-Sept.) Place Nationale, in the heart of the *vieille ville,* holds a great selection of cheap restaurants. Try the *crêpes salés* (65-80F) at **Adieu Berthe,** 26, rue Vauban. Or resign yourself to the

Codec Supermarket, 8, av. Niqué, near pl. de Gaulle. (Open Mon.-Sat. 8am-7:30pm.) The **tourist office**, 11, pl. de Gaulle (tel. 93 33 95 64), has information on accommodations, camping, and restaurants. (Open Mon.-Sat. 8:30am-8pm, Sun. 10am-1pm; Oct.-June Mon.-Sat. 9am-noon and 2-6pm.)

■■■ NICE

Blessed with a beautiful beach and all the nightlife, arts, and entertainment of a big city, Nice is the unofficial capital of the French Riviera. Don't let Nice's popularity and crowds scare you away; it's a big place and there's room for everyone, with reasonably priced hotels, excellent local and regional transport, a population accustomed to visitors, and all the other conveniences of an authentic metropolis. Every spring on Fat Tuesday, Nice erupts into song and dance during the annual *Carnaval,* the grandmother of New Orleans's *Mardi Gras.* Even if you can't make it then, you'll find plenty of revelry in Vieux Nice, a labyrinth of tiny streets. Just be careful of purse-snatchers there and around the train station and rue Masséna.

ORIENTATION AND PRACTICAL INFORMATION

With excellent rail connections, Nice is a fab place from which to make daytrips to surrounding coastal towns. The SNCF train station (Gare "Nice-Ville") is in the center of town, next to the tourist office on **avenue Thiers.** To the left, **avenue Jean-Médecin** runs toward the water to **place Masséna.** Vieux Nice lies just south of pl. Masséna. Heading right from the train station, you'll run into **boulevard Gambetta,** the other main street running directly to the water. Sweeping along the coast, the majestic and festive **promenade des Anglais** is rock-covered, crowded, and noisy. Unfortunately, Nice's big-city appeal is coupled increasingly with big-city crime. Women should avoid walking alone after sundown, and both sexes should exercise caution at night near the train station and Vieux Nice.

Tourist office: av. Thiers (tel. 93 87 07 07), beside the station. Books a limited number of rooms after 10am (12F). Stake out a place in line early. Free map of Vieux Nice. Open daily Mon.-Sat. 8:45am-6:45pm, Sun. 8:45am-12:15pm and 2-5:45pm; Oct.-May Mon.-Sat. 8:45am-12:15pm and 2-5:45pm. **Branch office** at 5, av. Gustave V (tel. 93 87 60 60), near the intersection of av. de Verdun and promenade des Anglais. Open same hours, but closed noon-2pm July-Sept.

Consulate: U. S., 31, rue Maréchal Joffre (tel. 93 88 89 55). Open Mon.-Sat. 9-11:30am and 1:30-4:30pm.

Currency Exchange: Cambio, 17, av. Thiers (tel. 93 88 56 80), across from the train station. No commission; good rates. Open daily 7am-midnight.

American Express: 11, promenade des Anglais (tel. 93 87 29 82), at the corner of rue des Congrès. Open Mon.-Fri. 9am-noon and 2-6pm, Sat. 9am-1pm.

Post Office: 23, av. Thiers (tel. 93 16 53 53), near the train station. Open Mon.-Fri. 8am-7pm, Sat. 8am-noon. **Poste Restante** and **telephones. Postal code:** 06000.

Trains: Gare SNCF Nice-Ville, av. Thiers (tel. 93 87 50 50). Trains about every 20min. (5:40am-midnight) to Cannes (35min., 28F) and Antibes (18min., 14F); about every 15min. (6:30am-11:30pm) to Monaco (25min., 13F) and Menton (35min., 18F). Also to other coastal towns, northern France, Italy, and Spain. **Showers** 12F. **Toilets** 2F. Open daily 7am-7pm. **Lockers** 20F for 72 hr. **Luggage storage** 15F/day/piece (open daily 5:30pm-midnight).

Buses: gare routière, promenade du Paillon (tel. 93 85 61 81), between av. Félix-Faure and bd. Jean Jaurès. Buses every 20min. (6:30am-7:30pm). To Monaco (45min., 18F); Antibes (1hr., 22F); and Cannes (1¼hr., 26F).

Public Transportation: Station Centrale, the TN (Transports Urbains de Nice) bus system has its base at 10, av. Félix Faure (tel. 93 16 52 10). Bus #12 from the train station goes to pl. Masséna and the beach (Mon.-Sat. 6am-midnight, Sun. 7:45am-midnight). Tickets for all buses (8F), *carnet* of 5 (28F), or a day pass (23F) available at the av. Thiers tourist office, kiosks, and *tabacs.*

NICE

Ferries: SNCM, quai du Commerce (tel. 93 13 66 66), at the port. Take bus #1 or #2 from pl. Masséna. Passage to and from Corsican cities: Bastia (4-5hr.; one-way 255F, students 190F, ages 4-12 145F) and Ajaccio (6-7hr., same prices as for Bastia). Open Mon.-Fri. 8am-noon and 1:30-6:30pm, Sat. 8am-noon.

Bike Rental: Nicea Location Rent, 9, av. Thiers (tel. 93 82 42 71), near the train station. Bikes 120F/day; 2000F deposit. Open Mon.-Sat. 9am-7:30pm. **Cycles Arnaud,** 4, pl. Grimaldi (tel. 93 87 88 55), near the pedestrian zone and the beach. Bikes 80F; credit card deposit. Open Mon.-Fri. 8am-noon and 2-7pm.

Laundromats: Suisse Laundrette, rue de Suisse, between rue Paganini and rue d'Angleterre (tel. 93 51 13 04). Close to hotels around the station. Wash 18F. Dry 2F/5min. Open 7am-9pm. **Point Laveria,** bd. Raimbaldi off rue Jean Médecin away from the station. Wash 16F, dry 2F for 6min. Open Mon.-Sat. 9am-8pm and Sun. 9am-7pm.

Hospital: St-Roch, 5, rue Pierre Devoluy (tel. 93 13 33 00). From av. Jean Médecin, turn left on rue Pastorelli, which turns into rue P. Devoluy.

Medical Services: SOS Medical Service (tel. 93 53 03 03). Available 24 hr.

Emergency: tel. 17. **Police:** tel. 93 92 62 22, at the opposite end of bd. Maréchal Foch from bd. Jean Médecin. English interpreter on call.

ACCOMMODATIONS

Rooms in summer are like Marlboros in Moscow: gone as soon as they're on sale. Arrive at the av. Thiers tourist office early for help in finding a room, or call individual hotels in advance. Although police do sporadically enforce a law that prohibits sleeping on the beach, groups of young people often check their baggage at the concierge and head for the rocky waterfront. The largest concentrations of decent, affordable hotels cluster around Notre Dame, on rue d'Angleterre, rue de la Suisse, and rue de Russie. Nice's two youth hostels and two *résidences* (temporary youth hostels set up in university dorms) are great, but often full.

Auberge de Jeunesse (HI), rte. Forestière du Mont-Alban (tel. 93 89 23 64), 4km away from it all—but worth the commute. Take bus #5 from the train station or walk to pl. Masséna, then take bus #14 from bd. Jean-Jaurès (every 25-40min. until 7:30pm). Reception opens at 5pm. Lockout 10am-5pm. Curfew 11:30pm. 60F. Showers and breakfast included. Kitchen. Laundry 35F.

Relais International de la Jeunesse "Clairvallon," 26, av. Scudéri (tel. 93 81 27 63), in Cimiez, 10km out of town. Take bus #15 from pl. Masséna (every 10min., 20min.). A large, luxurious hostel in an old villa with a free swimming pool. Reception at 6pm. Curfew 12:30am. 70F. Breakfast included.

Résidence Les Collinettes, 3, av. Robert Schumann (tel. 93 97 10 33), near the train station, off pl. St-Philippe. Summer hostel in a great location. Curfew midnight. Open for reservations all day; lockout 10am-6pm. 90F. Open July 7-Aug. 31.

Espace Magnan, 31, rue de Coppet (tel. 93 86 28 75), near the promenade des Anglais and the beach. From the train station, take bus #3, 9, 10, 12, 22, or 24 (8F). Clean and efficient, if somewhat impersonal. Open for reservations 8:30am-12:30pm and 2pm-midnight. Lockout 10am-6pm. 50F. Baggage rooms 10F. Open June 12-Sept. 22.

Hôtel Belle Meunière, 21, av. Durante (tel. 93 88 66 15), near the station. This quasi-villa was a gift from one of Napoleon's generals to his mistress. 75F/person in 3- to 5-bed rooms. Singles 90F. Doubles 140-250F. Showers 10F. Breakfast included. Baggage room 5F. Open Feb.-Dec.

Hôtel Les Orangers, 10bis, av. Durante (tel. 93 87 51 41) across from Hôtel Belle Meuniere. Newly renovated, with balconies in most rooms, and all with kitchenette and fridge. Dorm rooms 85F/person. Singles 80-100F. Doubles 160F, with showers 180-190F. Triples with showers 270F. Breakfast 18F. Open Dec.-Oct.

Hôtel Central, 10, rue de Suisse (tel. 93 88 85 08), off rue d'Angleterre. Clean and airy rooms, most recently renovated. Singles with shower 90F. Doubles with shower 150F. Breakfast 20F (17F for students). Call ahead.

Hôtel Idéal Bristol, 22, rue Paganini (tel. 93 88 60 72), off of rue Alsace-Lorraine. Ideal hotel in an ideal spot. TV room. Dorm-style rooms (4-5 in room) with kitchenette and refrigerator 87F. Singles 117F. Doubles 184F.

FOOD

Nice offers a smorgasbord of seafood, North African and Italian gastronomic delights. *Niçois* specialties include *bouillabaisse, pissaladière* (onion, olive, and anchovy pizza), and, of course, the *salade niçoise*. Avoid the cheap, touristy places near the train station in favor of the fine restaurants that cluster around the Vieux Port. Or munch at one of Nice's many university cafeterias; filling meals are about 36F. The convenient **Restaurant Université,** 3, av. Robert Schumann (tel. 93 97 10 20), is open from September through June. The cafeteria at **Montebello,** 96, av. Valrose (tel. 93 52 56 59), near the Musée Matisse, is open until mid-August. All student cafeterias are open daily 11:30am-1:30pm and 6-8pm. Stock up at the supermarket **Prisunic,** 42, av. Jean Médecin. (Open Mon.-Thurs. and Sat. 8:30am-8pm, Fri. 8:30am-8pm.)

Le Säetone, 8, rue d'Alsace Lorraine, off rue d'Angleterre near the train station. Serves regional dishes; fills up quickly. Try the *soupe au pistou* (34F) and the *mousse au café.* 60-85F *menus.* Open Tues.-Sat. 11:30am-2pm and 6-10pm.

Restaurant de Paris, 28, rue d'Angleterre (tel. 93 88 99 88), near the train station. Specialties at affordable prices, including beef *fondue* (with fries or salad 60F). *Menus* 40F, 50F, 60F. Open Dec.-Oct. daily 11:30am-2:30pm and 7pm-midnight.

Le Faubourg Montmartre, 32, rue Pertinax, off av. Jean Médecin. Fantastic beef, chicken, and pork *couscous* (55-70F). Excellent *bouillabaisse* (70F, 110F for 2). *Menu* 68F. Manager loves students. Open daily 1-3pm and 5pm-midnight.

Via Veneto, 37 bis, rue d'Angleterre (tel. 93 82 02 10), near the station. Delicious and delectable 4-course meals for 59F. Open Mon.-Sat. 7-11pm.

Cafétéria Flunch, av. Thiers, next door to the train station. A budget traveler's best friend. Good food, large portions, and the cheapest prices in town. Roast chicken or sausages with 2 vegetables and Coke 29F. Open daily 11am-midnight.

SIGHTS

Even museum-haters will have a hard time resisting Nice's varied collections. Since most are hidden among attractive houses in quiet suburbs, visiting them gives you a respite from the beach and a glimpse of the luxurious residential areas. Furthermore, they're virtually all free. The pride of Nice's museum collection, the **Musée Matisse,** 164, av. des Arènes de Cimiez, is unfortunately closed for renovations indefinitely. The elegant **Musée National Marc Chagall,** av. du Docteur Ménard, is a 15-minute walk north of the station. Or take bus #15 (every 20min., 8F) to the "Docteur Moriez" stop. The collection contains the works into which Chagall said he injected all his sadness and happiness. (Open Wed.-Mon. 10am-7pm; Oct.-June 10am-12:30pm and 2-5:30pm. 17F; students, seniors, and Sun. 8F. Under 18 free.) The **Musée des Beaux-Arts,** 33, av. Baumettes (tel. 93 44 50 72), is a must-see for fans of the surreal and of Degas, Monet, Sisley, and Renoir. Take bus #38 from the train station to "Chéret," or #12 to "François Gross." (Open Tues.-Sun. 10am-noon and 3-6pm; Oct.-April 10am-noon and 2-7pm. Free.) The **Musée d'Art Moderne et d'Art Contemporain,** promenade des Arts, at the intersection of av. St-Jean Baptiste and Traverse Garibaldi (take bus #5 from the station) features over 400 French and American avant-garde pieces from 1960 to the present. (Open Sat.-Mon. and Wed.-Thurs. 11am-6pm, Fri. 11am-10pm. Free.)

Fiddle with your rosaries at the **Cathédrale Orthodoxe Russe St-Nicolas,** 17, bd. du Tsarévitch, off bd. Gambetta, a 5-minute walk east of the train station. This gorgeous church was built in 1912 under the patronage of Tsar Nicholas II. (Open 9am-noon and 2:30-6pm; Sept.-May 9:30am-noon and 2:30-5pm. 12F. No shorts or sleeveless shirts allowed.) The **Monastère Cimiez,** pl. du Monastère, housed Nice's Franciscan brethren from the 13th to the 18th centuries. You can see the monastery's cloister, the Eglise Gothique, and 350 works of religious art. Take bus #15 or 17 from the station. (Open Mon.-Sat. 10am-noon and 3-6pm. Free.)

Nice maintains many beautiful parks and public gardens, the most central of which is the sprawling **Jardin Albert 1er.** Located at promenade des Anglais and quai des Etats-Unis, this quiet refuge has benches, fountains, plenty of shade, and the ornate 18th-century Triton fountain. The fragrant, equally sprawling **Esplanade du Paillon,** near pl. Masséna, surrounds a spectacular central fountain and is an ideal setting for a picnic. Like many centers on the Côte, Nice has a colorful, convoluted old section, known to residents as **Vieux Nice.** Just east of Vieux Nice lies **Le Château,** a hillside public park where you can enjoy a spectacular view of the city, its beaches, the port, and the Baie des Anges (Bay of Angels).

ENTERTAINMENT

Nice guys do finish last. Nice's party crowd swings long after the folks in St-Tropez and Antibes have called it a night. The bars and nightclubs around rue Massena and Vieux Nice are constantly rollicking with jazz, snazz, and rock 'n' roll. The area around the clubs in Vieux Nice can be dangerous at night and should not be visited alone. Nice's nightclubs are relentlessly expensive. The **Hot Spot,** 10, Cité du Parc (tel. 93 80 49 84) deserves its name. The party lasts from 9pm 'til dawn but only for those in proper attire—no shorts or sandals. (50F, free most Sundays.) **The Blue Boy,** a gay disco on rue Spinetta in West Nice, is always blowing its horn. For pubs, crawl into the lively **Hole in the Wall,** 3, rue de l'Abbaye (tel. 93 80 40 16), about a block from rue de la Préfecture in Vieux Nice. (Open Tues.-Sun. 8pm-midnight.) **Scarlet O'Hara's,** 22, rue Droite (tel. 93 80 43 22), off rue Rossetti in Vieux Nice, attracts a French crowd. (Open Mon.-Sat. 7pm-12:30am.)

The **Théâtre du Cours,** 2, rue Poissonnerie in Vieux Nice, stages traditional dramatic performances. (Thurs.-Sat. 9pm, Sun. 7pm. 75F.) The more experimental **Central Dramatique National,** promenade des Arts (tel. 93 80 52 60 or 93 13 90 90), at the corner of av. St-Jean Baptiste and Traverse Garibaldi, offers a show almost every weekend (50-160F). The **Nice Opéra,** 4, rue St-François de Paule (tel. 93 85 67 31) showcases visiting orchestras and soloists (75-250F).

Nice's **La Grande Parade du Jazz** in mid-July at the Parc et Arènes de Cimiez (tel. 93 37 17 17), near the Musée Matisse, attracts world-famous European and American jazz musicians to its 3 stages. Past performers have included B. B. King, Miles Davis, and Wynton Marsalis. The **Festival de Folklore International** and the **Batailles des Fleurs,** pageants of music and flowers along promenade des Anglais, bloom every year on the last weekend of July (reserved seats 80F). *Semaine des Spectacles,* published every Wednesday, carries entertainment listings for the entire Côte and is available at newsstands (8F). The **Comité des Fêtes,** 5, promenade des Anglais (tel. 93 87 16 28), has festival information. (Open Mon.-Fri. 10am-noon and 2-5pm.) The **FNAC** in the Nice Etoile shopping center on 24, av. Jean Médecin, sells tickets for virtually every performance in town. Call the tourist office for more info.

■ Near Nice

The finest beach east of Antibes is at **Cap d'Ail,** 20 minutes by train from Nice. Several km inland from Nice, **St-Paul-de-Vence** is among the best-preserved hill towns in France. Walk along the ramparts, virtually unchanged since the 16th century. The pride of car-less St-Paul-de-Vence is the **Fondation Maeght** (tel. 93 32 81 63), a 1km walk from the center of town. If you can go to only one museum in the whole Riviera, make this the one. Get off at the second St-Paul bus stop, just outside the center of town on the way to Vence, and follow the signs up a steep, winding hill, chemin des Gardettes. The Fondation is actually part museum and part park, with fountains, wading pools, and split-level terraces. (Open daily 10am-7pm; Oct.-June 10am-noon and 3-6pm. 45F, students 30F, but worth every centime.) Matisse considered the interior of the **Chapelle du Rosaire,** 1.5km from the last bus stop on av. Henri Matisse, his masterpiece. (Open Dec. 15-Oct. Tues. and Thurs. 10-11:30am and 2-5:30pm. Free. No photographs.) The St-Paul-de-Vence **tourist office** (tel. 93 32 86 95) is near the entrance of the village at the beginning of rue Grande. (Open Mon.-Tues. and Thurs.-Sat. 10am-6pm, Sun. 2-6pm; Oct.-June Mon.-Tues. and Thurs.-Sat.

10am-noon and 2-6pm, Sun. 2-6pm.) **Buses** roll regularly to St-Paul-de-Vence from Nice's *gare routière* (20/day, 55min., 26F).

■■■ MONACO/MONTE-CARLO

The world's wealthiest come to play nightly at Monaco's casino, and these days, all of Monaco—the *monégasques* number only 4500, and the entire principality occupies only 2 sq. km—is under constant construction in an effort to impress them. Be sure to make Monaco one stop on your itinerary, but don't plan to stay long; the city costs too much for the average budget tourist.

All the wealth, mystery, and intrigue of Monte-Carlo revolves around the famed **Casino,** where Mata Hari once shot a Russian spy. The slot machines open at noon, and the *salle américaine* (where blackjack, craps, and roulette require a 30F min. bet) at 4pm; hard core veterans don't arrive until after 10pm. Admission to the main room—or "kitchen"—is free (you must be over 21 and cannot wear shorts, sneakers, sandals, or jeans), but it costs 50F to enter the chic *salons privés*. After losing your shirt, admire the royal robes at the **Palais Princier,** the some-time home of Prince Rainier and the one-time home of his bride, Princess Grace. Guards change outside the palace daily at 11:55am. Next door is the stately **Cathédrale de Monaco,** 4, rue Colonel Bellando de Castro. Each of the former Princes of Monaco is buried within this Romanesque-Byzantine church; Grace Kelly's simple grave is behind the altar. (Open Mon.-Sat. 10am-6pm, Sun. 2-6pm.) Once directed by Jacques Cousteau, the tremendous **Musée de l'Océanographie,** av. St-Martin, houses thousands of species of fish and marine animals from every sea on earth. (Open daily 9am-8pm; Sept.-June 9am-7pm. 60F, ages 6-18 and students 30F.)

Accommodations, Food, and Practical Information Monaco is a nice place to visit, but it's expensive as the Dickens to sleep here. Try the **Centre de Jeunesse Princesse Stéphanie,** 24, av. Prince Pierre (tel. 93 50 83 20), 100m up the hill from the train station. In summer, arrive before 9am if you want a bed; reservations are accepted off-season only. Admits only foreign students ages 16-31 (ID required). (Reception open 7am-12:45am; off-season 7am-11:45pm. Curfew 12:45am. 60F.) Sitting by the ocean in the shade with a breeze blowing, you'll look like you stepped straight out of an Orangina commercial at **Le Calypso,** off bd. Louis II. Savor especially the *escalope de veau* (veal cutlet, 65F) or the lasagna (47F). The **Codec Supermarket,** 30, bd. Princesse Charlotte (open Mon.-Fri. 8:30am-noon and 3-7pm, Sat. 8:30am-7pm), is by the **tourist office,** 2a, bd. des Moulins (tel. 92 16 61 66), which provides a helpful map of the city and makes room reservations. **Annexes** are set up in the train station and in the port in summer. (Open Mon.-Sat. 9am-7pm, Sun. 10am-noon.) The **train station** at av. Prince Pierre (tel. 93 87 50 50), connects Monaco to Nice (every 30min., 25min., 15F), Antibes (every 30min., 45min., 30F), and Cannes (every 30min., 70min., 45F) from 5:30am to 11pm. (Information desk open daily 9am-7pm.) For emergencies, go to **Centre Hospitalier Princesse Grace,** av. Pasteur (tel. 93 25 99 00) or call the **police,** 3, rue Louis Notari (tel. 93 30 42 46 or in an emergency tel. 17). For **lost and found,** call 93 15 30 15.

CORSICA (CORSE)

Appropriately called Kallysté, "the most beautiful," by the Greeks, the island combines the mountainous splendor of the Alps with the beaches and crystal-blue Mediterranean water of the Riviera. Try to visit in the off-season; although ferries and other tourist services multiply between June 15 and the end of September, prices soar by 50%. Half the island's one million annual tourists (mostly French, Italian, and German) visit then, and the beaches and hotels in the coastal resorts are packed.

Getting There and Getting Around The **Société National Maritime Corse Méditerranée (SNCM)** sends car ferries from Marseille, Toulon, and Nice on the continent to Bastia, Calvi, Ile Rousse, Ajaccio, and Propriano on Corsica. About 2 boats per day travel between Corsica and the mainland in the off-season, a few more per day during summer. The trip from Marseille or Toulon costs 285F (255F off-season); from Nice, 255F (230F off-season). Travelers under 25 jaunting to and from Nice get a 30% reduction. From October to April, SNCM boasts a "blue period," when people under 25 receive a 25% discount and those over 60 a 50% discount. SNCM has offices in Ajaccio, quai l'Herminier (tel. 95 29 66 99, -88); Bastia, Nouveau Port (tel. 95 54 66 99, -88); Calvi, quai Landry (tel. 95 65 01 38). On the mainland, SNCM offices are in Nice, quai du Commerce (tel. 93 13 66 99); Marseille, 61, bd. des Dames (tel. 91 56 80 20); Toulon, 21, av. de l'Infanterie de Marine (tel. 94 41 25 76); and Paris, 12, rue Godot-de-Mauroy, 9ème (tel. 49 24 24 24). **Corsica Ferries** crosses from the Italian ports of Livorno, Genoa, and La Spezia to Bastia (145-175F).

Air France and **Air Inter** fly to Bastia, Ajaccio, and Calvi from Paris (810F, with discounts 630F), Nice (390F, with discounts 282F), and Marseille (424F, with discounts 300F). Discounted fares apply to everyone under 25 or over 60, and to students under 27, for off-peak "blue flights" (several/week, boxed in blue on the schedule). Air France maintains offices at 3, bd. du Roi-Jérome in Ajaccio (tel. 95 29 45 45) and at 6, av. Emile Sari, in Bastia (tel. 95 54 54 95). Air Inter's offices are at the airports in Ajaccio (tel. 95 29 45 45), Bastia (tel. 95 54 54 95), and Calvi (tel. 95 65 20 09). Reservations are advisable; call daily between 8am and 6pm.

Train service in Corsica is slow and limited; it doesn't serve all the major towns (no rail to Bonifacio or Porto-Vecchio) and accepts no passes. **Buses** mire in a seemingly endless maze of carriers, connections, and times (many before 8am). Bus services connect major towns but are neither cheaper nor more frequent than trains. **Hitchhiking** is reportedly near impossible. Renting a **car** is convenient but costs 120-250F per day for the least expensive models, plus 1F37-3F30 per km. Weekly rentals (from 1700F) usually include unlimited free mileage. **Hiking** is the best way to explore the island's mountainous interior. The longest marked route, the **Grande Randonnée-20,** is a difficult, 160km, 15- to 21-day trail which takes hikers across the island from Calenzana (southeast of Calvi) to Conca (northeast of Porto-Vecchio). The **Comité Régional du Tourisme Corse,** at 17, bd. Roi Jérôme (tel. 95 21 56 56), in Ajaccio, publishes thorough guides (free in most tourist offices) to all of Corsica's hotels, hostels, and campsites. There are about 25 hostels on Corsica; most are inland and far from the major towns. Hostel cards are rarely necessary, and most set no age restrictions. Campgrounds lie close to most major cities, and many rent tents. The government ban on unofficial camping is strictly enforced.

Ajaccio, Calvi, and Bastia Ajaccio is both a picturesque beachside resort and a humming industrial center, whose claim to fame is its notorious son, Napoleon Bonaparte. The **tourist office** (tel. 95 21 40 87, 95 21 53 39), Hôtel de Ville, pl. Maréchal Foch, makes no hotel reservations, but knows where there's room. (Open daily 8am-8pm; Sept. 16-June 14 Mon.-Sat. 9am-6:30pm.) Try the **Hôtel Colomba,** 8, av. de Paris (tel. 95 21 12 66), in the center of town, near pl. de Gaulle. (Singles 130F, with shower 150F. Doubles and triples with shower 160F.) *Boulangeries, pâtisseries, charcuteries,* and Corsican specialty shops congregate along rue Cardinal Fesch, flanked by pizzerias.

With its well-preserved Genoan citadel and stretches of white-sand beaches, **Calvi** is an ideal place to bask in the island's sun and beauty—ideal, that is, until July and August, when tourists flood in. The **tourist office,** at Port de Plaisance (tel. 95 65 16 67, fax -14 09), describes excursions and hotel availability and distributes the indispensible *Guide Calvi,* which includes a map and a list of hostels. (Open daily 10am-6pm; Sept.-June Mon.-Fri. 9am-noon and 2-6pm, Sat. 9am-noon.) **Hôtel Christophe Colomb,** pl. Bel Ombra (tel. 95 65 06 04), at the foot of the citadel, offers large, clean rooms. (Doubles 200F. Triples 240F. Quads 300F. Prices vary by season.) **SuperCalvi,** 42, rue Clemenceau, sells a wide array of Corsican cuisine. (Open May-Sept. daily 8:30am-midnight.)

The sections of **Bastia** that aren't under construction look like they should be, but the crowded, student-filled streets bestow color and life upon the city. The **tourist office** (tel. 95 31 00 89) at pl. St-Nicolas (open daily 7am-11pm; March-June 8am-noon and 2-7pm; Oct.-Feb. Mon.-Sat. 8:30am-noon and 2-6pm) distributes a free leaflet (in English) suggesting an excellent 2-hour walking tour. The **Hôtel San Carlu,** 10, bd. Auguste Gaudin (tel. 95 31 70 65), has about 100 times as much character as the other hostels. (Singles 150F, doubles 160F, triples 180F, all with showers. Oct.-May about 30F less.) Intimate **Le Dépot,** 22, rue César Campinchi, has a winding wood staircase and fire-cooked pizza. (28-48F. Open Tues.-Sat. noon-1pm, 2-4pm, and 6pm-midnight.)

THE ALPS (SAVOIE-DAUPHINÉ)

After museum corridors in urban centers have exhausted you, the Alps come as a refreshing relief. Snow-capped crests, tumbling waterfalls, and rich pastures exhilarate the weary soul, and crystal-clear air makes Paris smog seem a distant memory.

Skiing in the Alps has always been expensive. Make arrangements 6-8 weeks in advance or, better yet, in late summer. The least crowded and cheapest months to go are January, March, and April. Most resorts close in October and November, between the hiking and skiing seasons. **FUAJ,** the French Youth Hostel Federation, offers affordable week-long winter skiing and summer sports packages. For more info, contact local FUAJ offices, youth hostels, or the central office at 27, rue Pajol, 75018 Paris (tel. 46 07 00 01).

Food here takes a Swiss twist. Sample a warm pot of cheesily rich *fondue savoyarde* (made from local cheese, white wine, and garlic); locals cure excellent ham and net superb rainbow trout, which ends up on the table as the buttery *truite meunière*. Desserts won't disappoint you, what with the liqueur-laced *roseaux d'Annecy,* the light and spongy *gâteau de Savoie,* and the head-spinning *eaux de vie,* strong liqueurs distilled from fruits.

The beauty of the Alps does little good to the traveler who wants to go anywhere quickly or directly. While TGV **train** service will whisk you from Paris to Aix-les-Bains or Annecy at the gateway to the serious mountains, from there it's either slow trains, special mountain trains, or more often, torturously slow **buses. Hiking** ranges from simple strolls through mountain meadows to some of the most difficult climbing in the world, including Europe's highest mountain, Mont Blanc. Many towns maintain chalet dorms, as well as hostels and campgrounds; in less accessible spots, the **Club Alpin Français** runs refuges. Get a list from one of their offices: 136, av. Michel-Croz, Chamonix (tel. 50 53 16 03); 38, av. du Parmelan, Annecy (tel. 50 45 52 76); 32, av. Félix Vialet, Grenoble (tel. 76 87 03 73).

■■■ ANNECY

With winding cobblestone streets, overstuffed flower boxes, and the purest mountain lake in France, Annecy resembles those homecoming queens you resented for their perfection but fell in love with anyway. Hordes of vacationers enjoy the lakeside beaches and stroll along the flower-dotted canals around the **Palais d'Ile,** a 12th-century prison rising out of a tiny island. Climb up to the **Château d'Annecy,** which doubles as a museum, for a splendid view of the town's aquatic labyrinth. (Open daily 10am-noon and 2-6pm; Sept.-June Wed.-Mon. 10am-noon and 2-6pm. To museum and observatory 30F, students 15F. Museum or observatory alone 20F, students 10F. Free Wed. Sept.-May.) Sun-seekers can use the free beach, the **plage des**

Marquisats, while restless sailors might want to pay a hefty 100F to rent a boat or windboard on the transparent **Lac d'Annecy.** The **Fête du Lac** enlivens the first Saturday in August with fireworks and water shows (45-190F).

Accommodations, Food, and Practical Information Reservations are vital throughout the summer, particularly during July and August. The **tourist office,** 1, rue Jean Jaurès (tel. 50 45 00 33), at pl. de la Libération on the ground floor of the *Bonlieu,* dispenses a list of hotels and a bevy of brochures on both Annecy and the quieter towns on the upper part of the lake. (Open daily 9am-6:30pm; Sept.-June Mon.-Sat. 9am-noon and 1:45-6:30pm, Sun. 3-6pm.) **Hôtel Rive du Lac,** 6, rue des Marquisats (tel. 50 51 32 85), offers spectacular mountain views, and its simple rooms are the best bargain in town. (Singles and doubles from 130F. Triples 175F. Quads 190F. Showers 15F. Breakfast 23F. Reservations recommended.) The **Auberge de Jeunesse "La Grande Jeanne" (HI),** 16, rte. de Semnoz (tel. 50 45 33 19), is in a quiet, wooded area but requires a 45-minute uphill haul (from the tourist office, walk down quai Chappuisto to the Hôtel de Ville) or a ride on the infrequent bus marked "Semnoz" across the street from the Hôtel de Ville (7F). (Reception open 5-10pm. 60F, non-members 79F. Curfew 11pm. Sheets 16F.) **Hôtel Savoyard,** 41, av. de Cran (tel. 50 57 08 08), in a residential area behind the train station, is hospitable and comfortable. (Singles 100F, with luxurious bathroom 170F. Doubles 140F. Triples 140F. Showers 10F. Breakfast 20F.) On the road to the HI youth hostel is the oft-mobbed **Camping area,** rte. de Semnoz (tel. 50 45 48 30; open Dec. 15-Oct. 15). Dozens of small campgrounds border the lake in the town of **Albigny,** reachable by Voyages Crolard buses or by following av. d'Albigny from the tourist office.

You'll hate the prices this prom queen commands when it comes to food. Lakeside picnics are the only real budget options; a **Prisunic supermarket** fills the better part of the pl. de Notre Dame (open Mon.-Sat. 8:30am-12:15pm and 2:15-7pm), and **open-air markets** are held on pl. Ste-Claire (Tues., Fri. and Sun. mornings) and on bd. de Taine (Sat. mornings). Try *fondue savoyarde* (52-92F) and *raclette* (57F) at **Taverne du Freti,** 12, rue Ste-Claire. (Open Tues.-Sat. 7-11:30pm, Sun. 7-10:30pm.)

Take a train to Lovagny (3/day, 10min., 10F) and then walk 800m to the **Gorges du Fier,** a canyon carved by prehistoric glaciers. (Open March 15-Oct. 15 daily 9am-noon and 2-6pm. 22F for the 40-min. walk. Call 50 46 23 07 for info.)

■■■ CHAMONIX

Just as Nice *is* the Riviera, Chamonix *is* the French Alps, snug between the bookend peaks of Le Brévent to the west and L'Aiguille du Midi to the east. Both shrink before the majesty of nearby Mont Blanc, which at 4807m is Europe's highest peak. Even if hiking and skiing aren't your thing, don't forsake this town; numerous *téléphériques* (cable cars) will take you on breathtaking tours over the cloud-covered peaks of France and even Italy.

For *télépherique* travel, get under way as early as you can—crowds and clouds usually gather by late morning. The simplest trip takes you to **Plan de l'Aiguille** (54F, round-trip 70F), but you really gotta continue to the dazzling **Aiguille du Midi** (130F, round-trip 170F). From the Midi, you can continue to a 3rd stage, Gare Helbronner in Italy (170F, round-trip 240F; take your passport). Bring warm clothes and lunch, don't forget your camera, and remember that mountain weather can change rapidly. Special trains run from a small station next to the main train station to the huge **Mer de Glace** glacier (May-Sept. 8am-6pm; 42F, round-trip 56F), but you might prefer the 2-hour hike. A more rewarding hike is to **Lac Blanc,** a turquoise pool encircled by jagged peaks and Alpine flowers. To get there, walk 25 minutes along rue Vallot/rte. de Praz to the town of Les Praz, then board the *téléphérique* for La Flégère (round-trip 46F). From there it's 1½ hours to the lake.

Accommodations, Food, and Practical Information Mountain chalets with dormitory accommodations combine affordability with splendid settings, but many of them close off-season (Oct.-Nov. and May). All hotels and many dormitories require reservations (preferably 6 weeks in advance) for the hectic school vacations (Dec. and Feb.). For breathtaking views and hordes of schoolchildren, try the **auberge de jeunesse (HI)** in Les Pélerins (tel. 50 53 14 52). Take the bus from pl. de l'Eglise in Chamonix toward Les Houches; get off at "Pélerins Ecole," and follow signs uphill. If coming by train, get off at Les Pélerins and follow the signs. You can also walk there along rte. des Pélerins (25min). (Reception open daily 8-noon and 2-10pm. 68F, nonmembers 87F. Wheelchair access and vegetarian meals. Sheets 17F.) Close to town, **Les Grands Charmoz,** 468, chemin de Cristalliers (tel. 50 53 45 57), has excellent rooms and reasonable prices. From the station, turn right and go under the bridge, take a right across the tracks, then a left onto ch. des Cristalliers (10min.). (4-bed dorm 62F/person. Doubles 164F. Reserve ahead and confirm the day before arrival.) The **Chalet Ski Station,** 6, rte. des Moussoux (tel. 50 53 20 25), is near the télécabine de Planpraz, up the hill from the tourist office. (Reception open Dec. 20-May 10 and mid-June to mid-Sept. 8:30am-11pm. 50F. 5- to 9-bunk dorms. Showers 5F. Sheets 30F.) The clientele of **Chalet le Chamoniard Volant,** 45, rte. de la Frasse (tel. 50 53 14 09), is a veritable global melting pot. (Reception open daily 10am-10pm. 60F. Dorms 4-8/room. Sheets 20F.) To get to **L'Ile des Barrats,** rte. des Pélerins (tel. 50 53 51 44), from the *téléphérique*, turn left and look right. (24F/person, 16F/tent. Reception open May-Sept. 8am-9pm.) It's illegal to pitch tents in the Bois du Bouchet.

   Poco Loco, 45, rue du Dr. Paccard, serves sandwiches for 12-34F. (Open daily noon-4am.) **Le Sabot,** 254, rue Paccard, serves a sexy cheese fondue in a wooden chalet-type place. (*Crêpes* 15-40F; *menu* 68F. Open daily noon-2pm and 7-10pm.) Frugal folks like John and Liz retreat to **Supermarché Payot Pertin,** 117, rue Joseph Vallot. (Open Mon.-Sat. 8:15am-7:30pm, Sun. 8:30am-12:15pm.)

   The **tourist office,** pl. du Triangle de l'Amitié (tel. 50 53 00 24), lists hotels and dormitories and a map of campgrounds; they sell good 20F hiking maps. (Open July-Aug. and winter vacation weeks daily 8:30am-7:30pm; otherwise 8:30am-12:30pm and 2-7pm.) Across the street, the **Maison de la Montagne** houses the **Compagnie des Guides** (tel. 50 53 00 88) and a ski school. Upstairs in the **Office de Haute Montagne** (tel. 50 53 22 08), there's vital information on trails and mountain refuges.

■■■ GRENOBLE AND VOIRON

The historic capital of Dauphiné, Grenoble combines cultural excellence and an active nightlife with plenty of opportunities to enjoy the mountains. Take the bubble-shaped cable car (the *téléphérique de la Bastille)* up to the **Bastille** for a jarring view of Grenoble and the landscape that inspired Shelley to ethereal free verse. Several mountain **hikes** begin here. (Open Mon. 10am-midnight, Tues.-Sun. 9am-midnight; Sept. 13-Oct. and April-June 13 Sun. 9am-7:30pm, Mon. 10am-7:30pm., Tues.-Sat. 9am-midnight; Nov.-Dec. and Feb.-March Mon. 11am-6pm, Tues.-Sun. 10am-6pm. 19F, round-trip 30F; students 11F, round-trip 16F. Wheelchair access.) In town are several interesting museums, including the **Musée de Peinture et de Sculpture,** pl. de Lavalette (open Wed.-Mon. 10am-noon and 2-6pm; 15F, students 10F, Wed. free), and the **Musée de la Résistance et de la Déportation,** 14, rue J-J Rousseau. (Open Mon. and Wed.-Sat. 2-5:30pm; Sept.-June Wed.-Sat. 2-5:30pm. Free.)

   To reach the **auberge de jeunesse (HI),** 18, av. du Grésivaudan (tel. 76 09 33 52), 4km out of town, take bus #8 (direction "Pont Rouge") to "La Quinzaine." (Reception open Mon.-Sat. 7:30am-11pm, Sun. 7:30-10:30am and 5:30-11pm. 4- to 6-bed dorms 63F, nonmembers 82F. Sheets 16F.) In the center of town, **Hôtel de la Poste,** 25, rue de la Poste (tel. 76 46 67 25), has friendly management, a barking dog, and spacious rooms. (Singles 112F. Doubles 134F. Triples 166F.) **Hôtel Victoria,** 17, rue Thiers (tel. 76 46 06 36), is 5 minutes from the train station. (Singles and doubles

120F, with shower 155-170F. Breakfast 26F.) Wander around **rue Chenoise** for cheap North African eats, or try the regional delights at **Bleu Nuit,** 9, pl. de Metz. (Open Mon. 11:30am-2pm, Tues.-Sat. 11:30am-2pm and 7:30-10:30pm; closed 1st half of Aug.) The **Prisunic supermarket** is across from the tourist office. (Open Mon.-Sat. 8:30am-7:15pm.) The **tourist office,** 14, rue de la République (tel. 76 42 41 41), has excellent maps, accommodations information, and *Grenoble Magazine*, a guide to events in town. (Open Mon.-Sat. 9am-6:30pm, Sun. 10am-12:30pm.)

Voiron In 1605 in **Voiron,** the monks of the **Monastère de la Grande Chartreuse** tried to manufacture the elixir of long life and created the celebrated Chartreuse liqueur. Today, only 3 monks know the 130-ingredient secret recipe, but you can try to figure it out at the **Caves de la Grande Chartreuse,** 10, bd. Edgar Kofler; the free tour ends with a free tasting. Although the monastery is not open to visitors, the **museum** in **Correrie,** 1km. from the main road, faithfully depicts the monks' daily routine. (Open Easter-Nov. 1 daily 9:30am-noon and 2-6:30pm. 12F.) Five buses per day run to Voiron from Grenoble's *gare routière* (45min., 18F).

CENTRAL FRANCE

■■■ LYON

One would expect France's second-largest city to quiver in the gargantuan shadow cast by Paris, but Lyon has established itself as a cultural and economic alternative to, rather than subordinate of, the capital. Lyon also has a more tangible attraction: the city's world-renowned cuisine. Some of the greatest chefs in the world—Paul Bocuse, Georges Blanc, Jean-Paul Lacombe—call Lyon home, and even the cheapest restaurants seem always to delight the palate. The city is also known for its wealth and its mascot (a marionette named Guignol who has been disparaging kings, ministers, and presidents since 1808). Off-beat neighborhoods, 26 museums, energetic nightlife, and reasonably priced accommodations all make for a fine destination.

ORIENTATION AND PRACTICAL INFORMATION

The Saône and the Rhône cleave Lyon into 3 parts. **Vieux Lyon** (the old city) unfolds on the west bank of the Saône. East of the Rhône spreads a quieter residential neighborhood, an extensive shopping district, and the mammoth Part-Dieu commercial center and train station. Between the rivers, the pedestrian zone runs from the Perrache train station north to pl. Carnot, up rue Victor Hugo to pl. Bellecour, and along rue de la République to pl. des Terreaux. For a walking tour of the old town, pick up the pamphlet at the tourist office. Lyon is a reasonably safe city and solitary travelers can walk almost anywhere during the day, but exercise caution at night, especially inside Perrache and at pl. des Terreaux.

Tourist Office: pl. Bellecour, 2ème (tel. 78 42 25 75). Incredibly efficient office with a smorgasbord of information. Distributes *Lyon Vous Aimerez...* and the *Guide de Lyon*, which lists hotels, restaurants, bars. Superb map. Open Mon.-Fri. 9am-7pm, Sat. 9am-6pm, Sun. 10am-6pm; mid-Sept. to mid-June closes 1hr. earlier. **Branch office** in the Centre d'Echange, attached to the Perrache train station. Open Mon.-Fri. 9am-12:30pm and 2-6pm, Sat. 9am-5pm.
Budget Travel: La Bigerie Wasteels, in the Perrache's **Galerie Marchand.** BIJ and Transalpino tickets. Long lines. Open Mon.-Fri. 9am-7pm, Sat. 9am-6pm.
Consulates: Canada, 74 rue de Bonnel, 3ème (tel. 72 61 15 25), one block towards the river from Part-Dieu. Open Mon.-Fri. 10am-noon. **U.K.,** 24, rue Childebert, 2ème (tel. 78 37 59 67), off rue de la République. Open Mon.-Fri. 10am-noon, 2:30-5pm. **Ireland,** 4 rue Jean Desparmet (tel. 78 76 44 85). Call first.

Currency Exchange: AOC, in the tourist offices on pl. Bellecour and Perrache.
Thomas Cook (tel. 78 33 48 55), in the Part-Dieu train station. Open Mon.-Sat.
8am-8pm, Sun. 10am-7pm.
American Express: 6, rue Childebert (tel. 78 37 40 69), up rue de la République
from pl. Bellecour. Open Mon. Fri. 9am noon and 2-6:15pm, Sat. 9am-noon, Oct.-
April Mon.-Fri. 9am-noon and 2-6:15pm. Currency exchange closes at 5:30pm.
Post Office: pl. Antonin Poncet (tel. 78 42 60 50), next to pl. Bellecour. Regular
service and **Poste Restante** open Mon.-Fri. 8am-7pm, Sat. 8am-noon. **Tele-
phone** and telegraph services open Mon.-Sat. 8am-midnight, Sun. 8am-2pm.
Postal Code: 69002. Last digit indicates the *arrondissement*.
Flights: Aéroport Lyon-Satolas (tel. 72 22 72 21), 25km east of Lyon. **Buses**
leave from Perrache via Part-Dieu (daily every 20min. 6am-11pm, 50F). **Air
France,** 69, rue de la République, 2*ème* (tel. 78 42 79 00). Open Mon.-Fri.
8:30am-12:30pm and 1:30-6pm, Sat. 8:30am-12:30pm.
Trains: Lyon has 2 train stations; TGV trains to Paris pass through both. Check the
schedule posters at either station to find out about other destinations. **Perrache**
(tel. 78 92 50 50), between the Saône and Rhône rivers, is more central of the 2.
Sprawling mall with shops, bars, and **currency exchange.** SNCF information and
reservation desk open Mon.-Sat. 8am-7:30pm. **Part-Dieu** (tel. 78 92 50 50), in the
business district on the east bank of the Rhône. SNCF information desk open
Mon.-Sat. 8am-7:30pm, Sun. 9am-noon and 2-6:30pm. To: Paris (36/day, most are
TGV, 4½hr. (non-TGV), 261F plus reservation), Dijon (frequent, 2¼hr., 132F),
Grenoble (13/day, 1½hr., 91F), Strasbourg (8/day, 5hr., 251F), Geneva (11/day,
2hr., 121F), Marseille (13/day, 3½hr., 200F), and Nice (15/day, 7hr., 283F).
Buses: (tel. 78 71 70 00), on the bottom floor of the Perrache train station. Open
Mon.-Sat. 7:30am-6:30pm; Sept.-June Mon.-Sat. 6:30am-5pm. Daily service to
Annecy and Grenoble.
Public Transportation: TCL (tel. 78 62 67 69), information offices at both train
stations and major *métro* stops. Open Mon.-Fri. 7:30am-6:30pm, Sat. 9am-5pm.
Métro operates 5am-midnight. Tickets good for 1hr. in 1 direction, bus and trol-
ley connections included. 7F/ticket, 38F for a *carnet* of 6, students 31F. **Trolleys**
(funiculaires) operate until 8pm and go from pl. St-Jean to the Théâtre Romain
and the Musée Gallo-Romain.
Taxis: Allô Taxi (tel. 78 28 23 23). **Taxi Radio de Lyon** (tel. 78 30 86 86). 24 hr.
A trip to the airport will run about 150F.
Hitchhiking: Those hitching to Paris are aware that the *autoroute* approaches are
difficult places to catch rides; taking bus #2, 5, 19, 21, 22, or 31, and standing past
pont Monton at the intersection with the N6 is reportedly easier. Those heading
to Grenoble usually take bus #39 as far as the rotary at bd. Pinel.
Bookstore: Eton, 1, rue du Plat (tel. 78 92 92 36), 1 street west of pl. Bellecour
toward the Saône. The only all-English bookshop in Lyon.
Laundry: Salon Lavoir GTI, 38, rue Jean Jaurès. Wash 15F/5kg, dry 2F/7min.
Open daily 7am-9pm. **LavPlus,** 28, rue Condé, near Perrache. Turn right from pl.
Carnot. Wash 20F, dry 2F/5min. Soap 2F. Open daily 7am-9pm.
Crises: CISL (tel.78 01 23 45), an international center for visitors to Lyon. For the
lonely traveler, **SOS Amitié** (tel. 78 29 88 88). **SOS Depression** (tel. 78 65 98
92). **SOS Racisme** (tel. 78 39 24 44). **Maison de l'Homosexualité,** 16 rue St-
Polycarpe, 1*er* (tel. 78 47 10 10). Open Mon.-Fri. 6:30-8:30pm. **Assistance for
People with Disabilities: L'Association des Paralysés France,** 73, rue Francis
de Préssené (tel. 72 43 01 01).
Pharmacy: Pharmacie Blanchet, 5, pl. des Cordeliers (tel. 78 42 12 42), in the
centre ville between pont Lafayette and rue de la République. If you need something from midnight-7am, call ahead.
Medical Assistance: Hôpital Edouard Herriot, 5, pl. Arsonval (tel. 78 53 81 11).
Best-equipped to handle serious emergencies, but far from center of town. For
non-emergencies, go to **Hôpital Hôtel-Dieu,** 1, pl. de l'Hôpital, 2*ème* (tel. 78 41
30 00), near quai du Rhône.
Emergencies: tel. 17. **Police:** pl. Antonin Poncet (tel. 78 28 92 93), next to pl. Bellecour and the post office.

ACCOMMODATIONS AND CAMPING

France's second financial center, Lyon fills with businesspeople during the week. The centrally located hotels are often packed Monday to Thursday nights but then empty over the weekend. Even if the hotels near Perrache are full, cheap rooms should be available near pl. des Terreaux. Plan ahead; a few days should suffice.

Auberge de Jeunesse (HI), 51, rue Roger Salengro, Vénissieux (tel. 78 76 39 23), just outside the city limits. Take bus #35 from pl. Bellecour to "George Lévy" (30min.); after 9pm, take bus #53 (direction "St. Priest") from Perrache to "Etats-Unis-Viviani," and walk 500m along the abandoned train tracks. From Part-Dieu, take bus #36 to "Vivani Joliot-Curie" (last bus at 11:15pm, but call ahead if you'll be late). Friendly modern hostel makes up for the hike with comfortable 4- to 6-bunk dorms, kitchen, bar, TV, laundry facilities, and international crowd. Lockout 11:30am-5pm, but you can leave bags all day. 45F, non-members 64F. Sheets 16F. Wash and dry 30F. Breakfast 18F. Phone reservations accepted.

Résidence Benjamin Delessert, 145, av. Jean Jaurès, 7ème (tel. 78 61 41 41). From Perrache, take any bus that goes to "J. Macé," walk under the train tracks (5-10min.), and look to your left. From Part-Dieu, take the *métro* to "Macé." Large, plain dorm rooms, all with telephones and comfortable beds. TV room. 90F, July-mid-Sept. 55F. Showers and sheets included. Reserve a week ahead in the summer; 6 months ahead for the school year.

Hôtel Croix-Pâquet, 11, pl. Croix-Pâquet, 1er (tel. 78 28 51 49), in Terreaux. Mo. Croix-Pâquet, or walk up rue Romarin from pl. des Terreaux to pl. Croix-Pâquet. Superb rooms in a beautiful neighborhood. Singles 110F. Doubles 120F, with shower 160-180F. Showers 15F. Breakfast 20F.

Centre International de Séjour, 46, rue du Commandant Pegoud, 8ème (tel. 78 01 23 45), near the youth hostel. From Perrache, take bus #53 to "Etats-Unis-Beau-visage" (last bus at 11:30pm). From Part-Dieu, take bus #36 towards "Minquettes" (last bus 11:15pm). A hopping polyglot place with 24-hr. reception. Modern rooms with showers. Singles 110F. Doubles 83F/person. Triples 74F/person. Quads 69F/person. Self-service meals from 30F. Reserve well ahead.

Hôtel Alexandra, 49, rue Victor Hugo, 2ème (tel. 78 37 75 79). A large, old hotel in an ideal location. Smallish but elegant rooms with TV and phone. Often close-to-full during the week. Singles 146F, with shower 195F. Doubles 150F, with shower 214F. Breakfast 22F.

Hôtel Vaubecour, 28, rue Vaubecour, 2ème (tel. 78 37 44 91). Mo. Ampère/Victor Hugo. Some of the cheapest rooms in town. Cozy, but not cramped. Singles 89F. Doubles 113-127F, with shower 168-257F. Breakfast 22F. Showers 13F.

Camping: Dardilly (tel. 78 35 64 55). From the Hôtel de Ville, take bus #19 (direction "Ecully-Dardilly") to "Parc d'Affaires." One of the most beautiful camp-grounds in the Rhône Valley. Hot showers, swimming pool, grocery store, bar, and restaurant. 49F/tent and car.

FOOD

Lyon's galaxy of *Michelin* stars proclaims this city the gastronomic capital of western civilization, but there are plenty of affordable options for budget travelers. Head for a *bouchon,* descendant of the inns where travelers would stop to dine and to have their tired horses *bouchonné* (rubbed down) with straw. Today, the 20 or so remaining *bouchons* serve *cochonailles* (hot pork dishes), *tripes à la lyonnaise* (heavy on the onions and vinegar), and *andouillette* (sausage made of chitterlings, Mark Moody's favorite). Original *bouchons* concentrate around pl. des Terreaux (the oldest is **Le Soleil,** 2, rue St-Georges). The most pleasant (and tourist-laden) places in Vieux Lyon will seat you outdoors on narrow, cobblestone streets. The culturally diverse restaurants on rue St-Jean provides another affordable alternative.

The **university restaurants** in Villeurbanne serve cheap but unappetizing food. Ask at the CRIJ for names and locations. The market at **Les Halles,** 102, cours Lafayette, 3ème, sells celery, *escargots,* and truffles. (Open Tues.-Sat. 7am-noon and 3-7pm. Sun. 7am-noon.) Open **markets** are held at quai St-Antoine and on bd. de la

Croix Rousse (both Tues.-Sun. 7:30am-12:30pm). The **Carrefour Supermarché,** one of the largest in France, looms across the highway from the hostel.

Chocolate lovers swoon at Lyon's grandest and most famous *pâtisserie,* **Berna-chon,** 42, cours Franklin Roosevelt, 6ème. To get there, cross Pont Morand to the east bank of the Rhône and continue straight through the park to cours Franklin Roosevelt. The showcase sparkles with heavenly pastries and the ambrosial *Palets d'Or,* probably the best chocolate in France. (Open Tues.-Sat. 8am-7pm, Sun. 8am-1pm; Sept. 16-June 14 Tues.-Sat. 8am-7pm, Sun. 8am-5pm.)

Café de Jura, 25, rue Tupin, 2ème. Mo. Cordeliers. Near pl. des Cordeliers. An authentic *bouchon* where the selection changes daily at the whim of chef Henri. Dishes 36-72F. Open Mon.-Fri. at 7:30am; lunch noon-2pm; dinner 7:30-10:30pm.

Chez Mounier, 3, rue des Marroniers, 2ème (tel. 78 42 88 92), on the street across from the post office. Another *bouchon;* the *Gnafron* (sausage in fresh cream sauce) alone justifies the visit. 57F, 80F, and 90F *menus* change daily. Open Tues. and Thurs.-Sun. noon-2pm and 7-10pm, Wed. noon-2pm.

Garioud, 14, rue du Palais-Grillet, 2ème (tel. 78 37 04 71). Mo. Cordeliers. Great *cuisine lyonnaise* by Paul Griard, a Bocuse acolyte. 135F *menu* includes wine. Dress appropriately (no shorts). Open Mon.-Fri. noon-2pm and 7:30-10pm, Sat. 7:30-10pm. Reservations recommended.

Chez Carlo, 22, rue du Palais Grillet, 2ème, near Restaurant Garioud. Recommended by locals for the greatest pasta and pizza (42-44F) in Lyon. *Hyper-populaire.* Open Tues.-Sat. noon-1:30pm and 7-11pm, Sun. noon-1:30pm.

L'Etoile de l'Orient, 31, rue des Ramparts d'Ainay, 2ème. Mo. Ampère/Victor Hugo. Cozy restaurant full of regulars; the best North African cuisine in town. Fresh *couscous* 50-100F. 105F *menu.* Open Thurs.-Tues. noon-2pm and 7-11pm.

Le Pâtisson, 17, rue Port du Temple, 2ème. Mo. Bellecour. A rarity in France: a vegetarian and non-smoking restaurant. 57F and 64F *menus; plat du jour* 47F. Open Mon.-Fri. 11:30am-2pm and 7-9pm, Sat. 7-9:30pm.

SIGHTS

To enjoy Lyon, cultivate a taste for *la flânerie* (strolling). Start at **place Bellecour,** fringed by shops and flower stalls and encircling an equestrian statue of Louis XIV. At pl. des Terreaux, the ornate Renaissance **Hôtel de Ville** stands guard opposite the **Musée des Beaux Arts,** in the Palais St-Pierre, whose strengths include a small but distinguished collection of French painting, works by Spanish and Dutch masters, and a wing devoted to the Italian Renaissance. (Open Wed.-Sun. 10:30am-6pm. 20F, students 15F, under 18 free. Day pass for most museums in town 30F, students 15F.) The **Musée d'Art Contemporain,** located in the same building but with an entrance at 16, rue Edouard-Herriot, displays excellent temporary exhibitions of works from 1960 on. (Open Wed.-Mon. noon-6pm. 20F, students 15F, under 18 free.) A few blocks north of the museums on rue Burdeau, 1er, are the ruins of the Roman **Amphithéâtre des Trois Gaulles,** built in 19 AD and the site of the martyrdom of a band of Christians in 177. (Open dawn-dusk. Free.)

Lyon revels in its long-standing dominance of the European **silk** industry. At the turn of the 18th century, 28,000 looms operated in Lyon, and although silk manufacturing is based elsewhere today, an extraordinary collection of silk and embroidery ranging from the Coptic to the Oriental remains at the **Musée Historique des Tissus,** 34, rue de la Charité, 1er. (Open Tues.-Sun. 10am-5:30pm. 20F, students 10F. Wed. free.) Weave through the **Musée Lyonnais des Arts Decoratifs,** down the street at 30, rue de la Charité, which displays furniture, porcelain, silver, and tapestries from the 17th and 18th centuries. (Open Tues.-Sun. 10am-noon and 2-5:30pm. Free with ticket from Musée des Tissus.) **La Maison des Canuts,** 10-12, rue d'Ivry, demonstrates the actual weaving techniques of the *canuts lyonnais.* (Open Mon.-Fri. 8:30am-noon and 2-6:30pm, Sat. 9am-noon and 2-6pm. 6F.)

Leave urban fatigue and city noise behind for the roses of the **Parc de la Tête d'Or,** Lyon's botanical garden, so called because it is believed that a golden bust of

LYON

Christ is buried somewhere within. Bounce about on a pony or tour around the park in a go-cart or a mini-train. (Open daily 6am-11pm; off-season daily 6am-9pm.)

Vieux Lyon A brief walk across the Saône leads to the most intriguing part of town, Vieux Lyon. A particularly interesting church in the St-Jean quarter is the *bourguignon*-style **Cathédrale St-Jean.** Its northern transept holds a 14th-century astronomical clock that shows the feast days from 600 years ago all the way through 2000. (Open Mon.-Fri. 7:30am-noon and 2-7:30pm, Sat.-Sun. 2-5pm. Free.)

You can gaze upon Lyon's urban sprawl from the **Fourvière Esplanade,** high above the old city. The most scenic route follows rue de la Bombarde to rue du Boeuf. Take the montée des Chazeaux staircase and turn left on montée St-Barthélémy. On the right lie the **Jardins du Rosaire,** from which a beautiful uphill path climbs to the extravagant 19th-century **Basilique de Fourvière.** (Open daily 8am-noon and 2-6pm.) This hillside was the site where Julius Caesar founded Lugdunum—the commercial and military center of Gaul—in 43 BC. The **Musée Gallo-Romain,** 17, rue Cléberg, 5ème, on the Fourvière hill, displays a collection of mosaics, swords, rings, statues, and money from Lyon's Roman past. (Open Wed.-Sun. 9:30am-noon and 2-6pm. 20F, students 10F, under 18 free.)

Back in the lower section of Vieux Lyon, the **Musée de la Marionette,** pl. du Petit Collège in the Hôtel Gadagne, 5ème, exhibits the famous *lyonnais* puppets, including their proud mascot Guignol himself. (Open Tues.-Sun. 10:45am-6pm, Fri. 10:45am-8:30pm. 20F, students 10F.)

The **Musée de la Résistance,** 14, av. Bertholet, 7ème, has assembled documents and photos of the *Résistance,* which was centered in Lyon. (Open Wed.-Sun. 10:30am-noon and 1-6pm. Free.) The **Musée Africain,** 150, cours Gambetta, examines the culture of West Africa and its integral part in France's colonial history and modern economy. (Open Wed.-Sun. 2-6pm. 10F, students 5F.) Film and photography buffs will want to see the **Institut Lumière,** 25, rue du Premier-Film, 8ème, a museum which examines the lives of the brothers who invented the first film projector. (Open Tues.-Sun. 2-7pm. 25F.)

ENTERTAINMENT

To find out what's up in Lyon each week, pick up a copy of *Lyon Poche* (9F) at a newsstand. Lyon supports a variety of resident theaters as well as an opera company, but the highlight of its cultural activities arrives in June, with one of two annually alternating music and dance festivals. (Schedules available from tourist office.) In May, **Festival des Musiques Européennes** draws musicians from all across Europe (contact the Centre Charlie Chaplin-Vaux-en-Velin; tel. 72 04 37 03), and the **Festival de Théâtre Amateur** gives aspiring thespians a chance to show their stuff. (Call 78 25 00 58 for info.) July 1 starts off the **Festival du Jazz à Vienne,** a celebration that lasts nearly 2 weeks and welcomes international jazz celebrities to **Vienne,** a town just outside Lyon, accessible by bus or train. For info, call 74 85 00 05 or the Vienne **tourist office** (tel. 74 85 12 62) on 11, quai Reonded.

Lyon is a terrific place to see silver screen classics. The **Cinéma Opéra,** 6, rue J. Serlin (tel. 78 28 80 08), and **Le Cinéma,** 18, impasse St-Polycarpe (tel. 78 39 09 72), specialize in black-and-whites, all in the original language (30-40F). Avant-garde flicks and more classics roll at the **CNP Terreaux Cinéma,** 40, rue Président Edouard Herriot (37F).

Lyon may well have more pubs per capita than any other French city. For the twentysomething crowd, **Eddie and Domino,** 6, quai Gailleton, 2ème, off Pont de l'Université, is a Scottish-style pub with a huge selection of whiskeys. (Open Mon.-Sat. 6pm until dawn.) Local students kill the night at **Albion,** 12, rue Ste-Cathérine, 1er. (Open Mon.-Sat. 5pm-2am, Sun. 5pm-1am.)

BURGUNDY (BOURGOGNE)

Burgundy's best ambassadors to the world are its annual 40 million bottles of wine, which graciously represent a grand, sparse landscape splashed with vineyards and peppered by monasteries, cathedrals, and châteaux. Burgundy was an ecclesiastical center in medieval times, and the religious orders that constructed the monumental abbeys at Tournus, Cluny, and Vézelay also planted the green vineyards that now carpet the hills. Their wines were originally reserved for liturgical celebrations but are now an integral part of the region's gastronomy, imparting flavor to *boeuf bourguignon, coq au vin,* and Dijon's famous mustard. Other regional specialties include *gougère* (a soft pastry with cheese), *escargots,* and *jambon persillé* (a gelatin mold of ham and parsley). Go to Dijon and the smaller cities for culture and excitement, but leave time to explore the charming villages of the surrounding countryside.

■■■ DIJON

While Dijon is universally synonymous with the spicy, wine-based mustards it produces, the town does not survive on Grey Poupon alone; it is an important industrial center and home to a respected university. Burgundy's animated capital stands at the tip of one of the world's finest wine producing regions: the Côte d'Or. It also encompasses a colorful and tastefully restored *vieille ville,* myriad churches, museums, festivals, and sidewalk cafés filled with a lively student population that keeps this ancient city fresh.

Dijon's greatest attraction is the **Musée des Beaux Arts,** occupying a wing of the splendid **Palais des Ducs de Bourgogne.** Its most famous gallery is the **Salle des Gardes,** dominated by the huge sarcophagi of Philippe le Hardi and Jean sans Peur. (Open Mon. and Wed.-Sat. 10am-6pm, Sun. 10am-12:30pm and 2-6pm. 12F, students and Sun. free. A 15F card, available at the Musée des Beaux Arts, admits you to all of Dijon's museums.) Its façade a morass of gargoyles, the 13th-century **Eglise de Notre Dame** exemplifies the Burgundian Gothic style, while the **Eglise St-Michel** is a mélange of Gothic and Renaissance artistry. The elegant 93m apse and spire of the **Cathédrale St-Bénigne,** rue Docteur Maret, memorialize a 2nd-century missionary priest whose martyred remains were unearthed near Dijon in the 6th century. Next door to the Cathédrale St-Bénigne, the **Musée Archéologique,** 5, rue Docteur Maret, depicts the history of the Côte d'Or. (Open Wed.-Mon. 9:30am-6pm; Sept.-May Wed.-Sun. 9am-noon and 2-6pm. 9F, students free.) And no trip to Dijon is complete without a stop at the **Grey Poupon** store, 32, rue de la Liberté, where they've been making *moutarde au vin* since 1777.

In June, Dijon's **Eté Musical** stages many of the world's best symphony orchestras and chamber groups. From mid-June to mid-August, **Estivade** (call 80 30 31 00 for info) brings dance, music, and theater to the streets. Dijon devotes a week in the first half of September to the **Fête de la Vigne** (call 80 30 37 95 for info) a well-attended celebration of the grape with various folklore ensembles. The best source (aside from *Divio 94*) of entertainment information is *Dijon Nuit et Jour,* available free from the tourist office.

Accommodations, Food, and Practical Information The **tourist office,** pl. Darcy (tel. 80 43 42 12), is a 5-minute walk down av. Maréchal Foch from the train station. (Open daily 9am-9pm; April 10-May 31 and Sept. 16-Nov. 15 9am-8pm; Nov. 16-April 9 9am-noon and 2-7pm.) It also offers a 15F accommodations service. The cheapest beds in Dijon are at the **auberge de jeunesse (HI),** 1, bd. Champollion (tel. 80 71 32 12), a concrete mega-hostel with electronic surveillance, bar, and screaming school groups. (Dorms 61F). To reach it, take bus #5 from the Bar Bleu in pl. Grangier (direction "Epirey"). The **Foyer International d'Etudiants,**

6, rue Maréchal Leclerc (tel. 80 71 51 01), is a sleek, noisy place with 300 beds. Take bus #4 (direction "St. Apollinaire") to the "Vélodrome" stop. (55F.) Hotels in the center fill quickly in summer. Try **Hôtel du Sauvage,** 64, rue Monge (tel. 80 41 31 21), near Eglise St-Jean below rue Bosset off rue de la Liberté. (Singles 180F, doubles 200F, both with shower. Extra bed 50F. Showers 20F.) **Hôtel Confort,** 12, rue Jules Mercier (tel. 80 30 37 47), on an alley off rue de la Liberté, has plain but delightful chambers. (Singles 115F. Doubles 120F, with shower 155F.) Take bus #12 to "Chartreux" to arrive at **Camping du Lac** (tel. 80 43 54 72), at bd. Kir and av. Albert 1er, on a picturesque lake. (9F/person, 4F/car or tent. Open April-Nov. 15).

The most elegant way to sample Burgundy's fabulous wines is with a gourmet meal. **Au Bec Fin,** 47, rue Jeannin, has an outstanding 65F *menu* at lunch and 74F and 94F *menus* at dinner. (Open Mon.-Fri. noon-1:30pm and 7:30-10:30pm, Sat. 7:30-10:30pm.) Otherwise, pick up vital vittles in the basement of the **Nouvelles Galeries** at 41, rue de la Liberté.

■ Near Dijon

Beaune and Côte d'Or The wealthy and touristed town of **Beaune,** half an hour south of Dijon on the Lyon rail line (12/day, 33F), has disgorged wine for centuries. Surrounded by the famous **Côte de Beaune** vineyards, the town itself is packed with wineries offering free *dégustations.* Visit the **Marché aux Vins,** near the Hôtel-Dieu. For 40F (imitation silver tasting spoons 10F), you can sample 37 of Burgundy's finest wines (the best of which come last, so don't get too rocked on the early labels). (Open daily 9:30-11:30am and 2:30-6:30pm; Nov.-March 9:30am-noon and 2:30-4:30pm.) The **Hôtel-Dieu,** built in the 15th century as a hospital for the poor, is a landmark of Burgundian architecture with colorful roof tiles. (Open daily 9am-6:30pm. 27F, students 21F, ages 10-14 11F, under 10 free.) The **tourist office,** rue de l'Hôtel-Dieu (tel. 80 22 24 51), lists *caves* in the region offering tours. (Open daily 9am-midnight; March-May and Oct-Nov. 9am-10pm; Dec.-Feb. 9am-7:15pm.) The 60km **Côte d'Or,** dubbed the "golden hillside," has produced some of the world's greatest wines. The fascinating **Château du Clos de Vougeot** is home to the Confrèrie des Chevaliers du Tastevin, a ritualized fraternity founded in 1934 to defend the honor of Burgundian wines. (Open daily 9am-6:30pm; Oct-March Mon.-Sat. 9-11:30am and 2-5:30pm. 20F.) Also check out the *caves* at the **Château de Gevre-Chambertin,** just south of Dijon. Both the Dijon and Beaune tourist offices can provide you with information on bus services, fares, and schedules.

Cluny and Auxerre Once the center of Western Christendom, **Cluny** is the site of a critically acclaimed cathedral so impressive that architects all over Europe used it as a model for their own graceful Romanesque edifices. Due to the ravages of revolution, war, and other avarice, only a fraction of the once-stunning abbey survives. The grandeur of these remnants is still evident in the informative tour that leaves from the Musée Ochier. **Cluny Séjour** (tel. 85 59 08 83), behind the bus stop, is the least expensive place to say in Cluny. (Reception open 7-11am and 5:30-10pm. Singles 115F. Doubles, triples, or quads 66F/person.) SNCF buses run to Cluny from Mâcon and Chalon-sur-Saône, both on the main rail line (4-6/day, 1½hr., 44F). The **tourist office,** 6, rue Mercière (tel. 85 59 05 34), distributes maps of the town and region. (Open daily 10am-7pm; April-June and Oct. 10am-noon and 2-6pm; Jan.-March 2-4:30pm.)

Once soaked with grape vines, industrial **Auxerre** provides those traveling by boat, car, bike, or foot with a superb base from which to venture into northern Burgundy. The **Abbaye St-Germain's** frescoes of St. Stephen getting stoned (no, with rocks) are the oldest in France. (Open Wed.-Mon. 9-11:30am and 2-5:30pm, mandatory tour of crypt every ½hr.; Sept.-June open 9-11am and 2-5pm, tours every hr. 18F, students, under 16, and Wed. free.) The **Foyer des Jeunes Travailleuses (HI),** 16, bd. Vaulabelle (tel. 86 52 45 38), accepts men and women (singles 75F). To reach it, follow signs to *centre ville,* cross the bridge and turn left; the first right is rue Vaulabelle. The **tourist office,** 1-2, quai de la République (tel. 86 52 06 19), below the cathedral on the bank of the Yonne, provides maps and a free accommodations service. (Open Mon.-Sat. 9am-7pm, Sun. 9:30am-12:30pm and 2-7pm; Sept. 16-June 14 daily 9am-12:30pm and 2 6:30pm.) **Trains** run to Paris (13/day, 2hr., 112F) and Lyon (9/day, 4½hr., 206F).

ALSACE AND LORRAINE

Acrimoniously disputed during the 19th and early 20th centuries, Alsace and Lorraine figured prominently in 3 modern wars between France and Germany; the cultural battle has never stopped. The Route du Vin, a ribbon of wine-producing villages, threads through the lakes, valleys, and wooded slopes of the Vosges region. Dividing the provinces, the Vosges make for ideal hiking, camping, and cross-country skiing, with hundreds of miles of marked trails and overnight shelters.

■■■ STRASBOURG

Sophisticated and elegant, Strasbourg impressed both Goethe and Rousseau. Home of the Council of Europe and one of 3 bases of the European Parliament, the city today is a symbol of international cooperation, but retains a distinctive local flavor with its half-timbered houses, covered bridges, and flower-lined canals. Start a tour at the **cathedral,** whose airy spire soars 142m above the historic center. While you wait for the tuneful tinkle of the **horloge astronomique** (astrological clock) at 12:30pm, take a gander at the **Pilier des Anges** (Angels' Pillar), a masterpiece of Gothic sculpture; both are in the south transept (4F to see the tiny apostles parade around and the rooster crow). The palatial **Château des Rohan,** 2, pl. du Château, houses a trio of small, noteworthy museums; the **Maison de l'Oeuvre Notre-Dame** has a huge collection of medieval and Renaissance art. The **Musée d'Art Moderne,** also across from the cathedral, holds a collection of paintings and sculpture by Chagall, Arp, Klee, and the usual gang of Impressionists. Many of the more famous works are in storage, awaiting the opening of a new museum in 1994. (Museums open Mon., Wed.-Sat. 10am-noon and 1:30-6pm, Sun. 10am-5pm. Call 88 52 50 00 for info on these and other local museums. To each museum 15F, students 8F. Visits to 2 museums 22F, students 10F.)

Accommodations, Food, and Practical Information Everyone stays the night here, so make reservations, call ahead, or arrive early. The **Auberge de Jeunesse René Cassin (HI),** 9, rue de l'Auberge de Jeunesse (tel. 88 30 26 46), 2km from the station, has a friendly and fun young staff, and a game room. Take bus #3, 13, or 23 from rue du Vieux-Marché-aux-Vins. (Reception open 7am-11:30pm and 2pm-midnight. Curfew 1am. No lockout. Members only. 6-bed dorms 64F. Doubles, triples, and quads 92F/person. Singles 141F. Sheets 16F. Camping 40F/person.) The sparkling **CIARUS (Centre International d'Accueil de Strasbourg),** 7, rue Finkmatt (tel. 88 32 12 12), flags terrific rooms just 15 minutes from the train station. Take rue du Maire-Kuss to the canal, turn left, then make a left onto rue Finkmatt. (Curfew 1am. 6- to 8-bunk room 80F. 12-bunk room 71F. Triples and quads 95F/person. Doubles 106F/person. Singles 170F. Wheelchair accessible.) **Hôtel Patricia,** 1a, rue du Puits (tel. 88 32 14 60), in the *vieille ville* between rue de l'Ail and rue de Serruriers, behind Eglise St-Thomas, gloats over a perfect location with loads of charm. (Singles from 110F. Doubles from 140F, with shower from 180F.)

Strasbourgeois restaurants are known for delicious *choucroute garnie,* spiced sauerkraut served with meat. You can't miss the triple-decker **Au Pont St-Martin,** at 13-15, rue des Moulins. Sit overlooking the canal locks and savor huge servings of seafood, salads, and *choucroute.* (Mon.-Fri. 3-course 54F lunch *menu.* Open daily noon-2pm and 7-11pm; no Sat. lunch.) **Pizzaria Aldo,** 8, rue du Faisan, is a wildly popular joint where you design your own pizza (35-45F), salad (34-37F), or pasta. (29-48F). (Open daily noon-2pm and 6:30pm-1:30am.)

A **tourist office** on pl. de la Gare (tel. 88 32 51 49), opposite the train station, dispenses guides to entertainment and 3F city maps, and will find you a room for 6F. (Open Mon.-Sat. 9am-12:30pm and 1:45-6pm, Sun. 9am-12:30pm and 1:45-5pm; Oct.-May closed Sun.) The **U.S. consulate** is on 15, av. d'Alsace (tel. 88 35 31 04), next to pont John F. Kennedy. (Open Mon.-Fri. 9:30am-noon and 2-5pm.) There is also a **Canadian consulate** on rue du Ried (tel. 88 96 65 02; open Mon.-Fri. 11am-noon). For BIJ/Eurotrain tickets, BritRail passes, French railpasses, and ISICs, head to the **CROUS youth center** at 1, quai du Maire-Dietrich (tel. 88 36 16 91; open Mon.-Fri. 9-11am and 2-4pm). If you have a student ID, they can set you up in a dorm for 55F per night (July-Aug. only). Strasbourg is a major European rail junction; **trains** go to Paris (14/day, 6hr., 259F), Luxembourg (4/day, 2½hr., 140F), Frankfurt (2 direct/day, 3hr., 203F), and Zürich (1 direct/day, 3hr., 214F).

■■■ COLMAR AND METZ

Ringed by vineyards and overshadowed by the craggy Vosges Mountains, **Colmar** slices Alsatian life authentically, but the word is out, and the streets are flooded with tourists. The restored tanners' lodgings and **La Petite Venise** area preserve the feeling of a medieval town. Don't miss the extraordinary **Musée Unterlinden,** on pl. Unterlinden, a Dominican convent housing medieval religious art, including Matthias Grünewald's gruesome and beautiful *Isenheim Altarpiece.* (Open daily 9am-6pm; Nov.-March Wed.-Mon. 9am-noon and 2-5pm. 25F, students 15F.) The annual **Alsatian Wine Festival,** held in early August, spouts wine, beer, and agricultural equipment for all. Early September brings the **Jours Choucroute** (Sauerkraut Days), 2 weeks of feasting and dancing. A 5-minute walk from the station, the **Maison des Jeunes (Centre Internationale de Séjour),** 17, rue Camille Schlumberger (tel. 89 41 26 87), is the best deal in town. (Registration Mon.-Sat. 8am-noon and 2-11pm. Curfew 11pm. 40F. Sheets 16F.) Colmar is 30 minutes south of Strasbourg by frequent **train** (51F).

In the neighboring region of Lorraine, the public buildings of **Metz** are constructed of a regional stone, *pierre de jaumont,* which lends the city its warm mustard overtone. The 6500 square meters of sensational stained-glass windows, including several by Chagall, have earned the **Cathédrale St-Etienne** the moniker "Lantern to God." (Open daily 7am-6:30pm.) Nearby, the fascinating **Musée de l'Art et de l'Histoire,** built over ruins of Roman baths, reconstructs medieval and Renaissance home interiors. (Open Wed.-Mon. 10am-noon and 2-6pm, Tues. 10am-6pm. 25F, students 18F, Wed. and Sun. mornings free.) The fantastic **auberge de jeunesse (HI),** 1, allée de Metz Plage (tel. 87 30 44 02), is on the river across town from the station. Hop bus #3 or 11 (last bus 8:50pm) from the station to "Pontiffroy." (Reception open 7-10am and 5-10pm. Lockout 10am-5pm. 6-bed dorms 59F/person. Singles and doubles 65F.) **Trains** run to Paris (8/day, 3hr., 219F), Strasbourg (10/day, 1½hr., 107F), and Lyon (4/day, 5½hr., 250F).

CHAMPAGNE

Champagne, the region between Lorraine and Paris, is under French law the only source of real champagne, which must be vinted according to the rigorous *méthode champenoise.* The best way to see and taste the results is to visit the underground **caves** of Reims and Epernay, both a little over an hour from Paris's Gare de l'Est, where prestigious champagne houses carefully guard their precious troves.

■■■ REIMS AND EPERNAY

Pounded to rubble during WWI, Reims has been tenaciously reconstructed; the modern city gracefully combines contemporary structures (such as funky egg-shaped fountains) with a restored fleet of Gothic and Roman buildings. The **Cathédrale de Notre Dame,** ornamented with dreamlike Chagall windows, was built with blocks of golden limestone quarried beginning in 1211. From Clovis to Charles X, 25 kings of France were crowned beneath its vaulted roof. (Open daily 7:30am-7:30pm.) The **Palais du Tau** next door, once the archbishop's palace, houses medieval sculptures and cathedral treasures. (Open daily 9:30am-6:30pm; March 16-June and Sept. 1-Nov. 14 9:30am-12:30pm and 2-6pm; Nov. 15-March 15 Mon.-Fri. 10am-noon and 2-5pm, Sat.-Sun. 10am-noon and 2-6pm. 26F, under 17 and students 17F.) To the east lies the **Basilique St-Remi,** reputed resting place of France's earliest kings. The graceful **Musée des Beaux-Arts,** 8, rue Chazny, built in the 18th century as an abbey, has a fine Corot collection and some Impressionist works. (Open Mon. and Wed.-Fri. 10:30am-noon and 2-6pm, Sat.-Sun. opens at 10am. 10F, students free.) For a look at the simple schoolroom where the Germans surrendered to the Allies on May 8, 1945, head over to the **Salle de Reddition.** It shows maps, period newspapers, photos, and an excellent film. (Open Wed.-Mon. 10am-noon and 2-6pm. 10F, students free.) Snag a brochure with maps and hours of Reims's underground city of **champagne caves** from the tourist office. Most offer free tours in French and English. The most engaging *caves* (and perhaps the best wines) belong to **Pommery,** 5, pl. du Général Gouraud (tel. 26 61 62 55).

Accommodations, Food, and Practical Information The **Centre International de Séjour (HI),** 1, chaussée Bocquaine (tel. 26 40 52 60), next to La Comédie-Espace André Malraux, is a 15-minute walk from the station. Continue straight through the park (1 block) then turn right onto bd. Général Leclerc. Follow it to the canal and cross the first bridge you come to (pont de Vesle). Chaussée Bocquaine is your first left. The place is as close to heaven as a hostel gets, and just as hard to get into. (Reception open daily 7am-11pm. 11pm curfew. Singles 75F. Doubles 72F.) **Hôtel d'Asace,** 6, rue Général Sarrail (tel. 26 47 44 08), is steps away from the station. (Singles 120F, with shower 155F. Doubles 130F, with shower 165-220F. Showers 12F.) **Au Bon Accueil,** 31, rue Thillois (tel. 26 88 55 74), right off pl. d'Erlon, has large, bright rooms with comfy beds—if you make it up the amusingly perilous staircase. (Singles from 60F. Doubles from 100F, with shower 140F.) Place Drouet-Erlon is crammed with fast food joints, cafés, and bars. **Les Brisants,** 13, rue de Chativesle, is right off pl. d'Erlon; sit in the pastel dining room or bask in the courtyard. (73F and 120F *menus.* Open Mon.-Fri. noon-2pm and 7-10:30pm, Sat. 7-11pm. Reservations recommended on weekends.) The **tourist office,** 2, rue Guillaume de Machault (tel. 26 47 25 69), is in the ruins of the old charterhouse. (Open Mon.-Sat. 9am-8pm, Sun. 9:30am-7pm; Easter-June 30 and Sept. closes ½hr early; Oct.-Easter closes 1hr earlier.) They have info on Reims's numerous *foyers,* which start at about 60F and may accept travelers for 1 or 2 nights.

Epernay There are no cathedrals in Epernay, but the golden *caves* under av. de Champagne inspire worship of a different sort. The best known is **Moët et Chandon,** 20, av. de Champagne, home of James Bond's preferred vintage, *Dom Perignon.* For information on Epernay's bubbly makers and about lodging (25F), consult the **tourist office,** 7, av. de Champagne (tel. 26 55 33 00; open Mon.-Sat. 9:30am-12:30pm and 1:30-7pm, Sun. and holidays 11am-4pm; mid-Oct. to mid-April Mon.-Sat. 9:30am-12:30pm and 1:30-5:30pm). Epernay is not the place for the budget traveler to stay; instead, rest your bones in Reims, only 20 minutes and 30F away.

THE NORTH

The world's battlefronts have swept across northern France four times in this century alone, and nearly every town bears scars from the wanton bombing of WWII. In spite of the numerous memorials to the soldiers who gave their lives here, as well as some of the most magnificent Gothic cathedrals in the world, the North remains the final frontier of tourist-free France, probably because of the region's unfavorable reputation as an early 20th-century industrial center. The best course for a tourist here is to head inland to the grand cathedral towns and dodge the coast entirely.

■■■ THE CHANNEL PORTS

Calais and Boulogne Ever since Richard the Lion-Hearted and his crusaders passed through en route to Jerusalem, **Calais** has been the Continent's primary portal to Britain. The tourist mobs will only get denser after the long-awaited **Channel Tunnel** linking Calais with Dover, England is completed. For now, Calais is the most frequently used transfer point for **ferries** to Dover, England: **Sealink** (tel. 21 34 55 00; 290F, 5-day return 460F) and **P&O** (tel. 21 97 21 21; 1½hr., 220F). **Hoverspeed,** in the Hoverport (tel. 21 96 67 10), fires its space-age craft to Dover every hour (35min.; 230F, 5-day round-trip 350F). A free shuttle bus connects port to train station; from there it's a 3- to 4-hour trip to Paris Nord. Ferry tickets can be purchased in advance from travel agencies in London and Paris. There are 24-hour **currency exchanges** at both the ferry terminals and the Hoverport, but rates are obscene. The town's **tourist office**, 12, bd. Clemenceau, provides a free accommodations list. (Open Mon.-Sat. 9am-1pm and 2-7pm.) Should you have to stay the night, try the brand-new **Centre Européen de Séjour/Auberge de Jeunesse (HI),** av. Maréchal de Lattre de Tassingy (tel. 21 34 70 20; 65F), or drop your bags at **Hôtel le Littoral,** 71, rue Aristide Briand (tel. 21 34 47 28), with its huge, comfy rooms. (Singles 100F. Doubles 120-140F.) The large, friendly **Taverne Kronenbourg,** 46, rue Royale, has a 75F 3-course menu. (Open daily noon-3pm and 7-11pm.)

In 636, an unpiloted boat carrying a statue of the Virgin Mary washed up on the beach at **Boulogne,** and the town immediately became a magnet for pilgrims. Towering over the *vieille ville* is the 19th-century **Basilique de Notre Dame.** Beneath it are labyrinthine crypts containing the remains of a Roman temple. (Crypt open Tues.-Sat. 2-5pm, Sun. 2:30-5pm. 10F, children 5F.) **Hoverspeed** crafts (tel. 21 30 27 26) shuttle to Folkestone (every 3hr., one way 160F, round-trip 250F; bikes sail free.). The **tourist office,** pl. Frédéric Sauvage (tel. 21 31 68 38), has a free accommodations service and ferry brochures. (Open Mon.-Sat. 9am-8pm, Sun. 10am-7pm; Oct.-May Mon.-Sat. 9am-7pm, Sun. 9am-1pm.) Boulougne's **auberge de jeunesse (HI),** 36, rue de la Port Gayole (tel. 21 31 48 22), just outside the *vieille ville,* offers cramped but clean dorms. (Reception open 8-10am and 5-11pm. Curfew 11pm, but manager will give you code to open door. 60F, nonmembers must buy a 19F stamp. In July-Aug. reserve a week in advance.) Large, airy rooms and efficient, personable management await at the **Hôtel le Mirador,** 2-4, rue de la Lampe (tel. 21 31 38 08), off bd. Daunou, which boasts TVs and private bathrooms for each room. (Singles 125F. Doubles 120-220F. Extra bed 45F.) **Restaurants,** bistros and their quintalingual menus line rue de Lille in the *vieille ville.*

Dunkerque A fishing town since the 10th century and now the 3rd-largest port in France, Dunkerque endured Flemish, Spanish, and English rule before becoming French in 1662, and remains unaffected by the waves of foreigners washing over its tiled sidewalks and clean beaches. The **Musée d'Art Contemporain,** rue des Bains, across the bridge from the hostel (tel. 28 59 21 65), has eccentrically manicured paths enclosing a modern sculpture garden. (Museum open Wed.-Mon. 10am-8:50pm; Oct.-March 10am-5:50pm. 6F, students 3F.) Also worth a peek is the **Musée**

des Beaux Arts, pl. du Général de Gaulle, which houses 16th- and 18th-century French and Flemish paintings. (Open Wed.-Mon. 10am-noon and 2-6pm. 6F, students 3F; Sun. free.) The **tourist office,** rue Amiral Ronarch (tel. 28 66 79 21), offers an excellent 2F city map, locates accommodations, and changes cash after banks close. (Open Mon.-Sat. 9am-6:30pm; Sept.-June 9am-noon and 2-6:30pm.) The **auberge de jeunesse (HI),** pl. Paul Asseman (tel. 28 63 36 34), by the beach, is crowded but clean. (Lockout 9am-5:30pm. Curfew 11pm. Members only. 42F.) In a prime location, the 2-star **Hôtel du Tigre,** 8, rue Clemenceau (tel. 28 66 75 17), offers singles from 90F, doubles from 120F. Take bus #3 (every 20min., 6am-9pm) to the campsite **Dunkerque-Malo-les-Bains** for grounds with shower, TV, and swimming pool. (11F/person, 7F/tent or car. Open March-Nov.) Huge, crowded, and overlooking the ocean, **L'Iguane,** 15, digue des Alliés, serves scrumptious mussels (45F) and other seafood. (Open daily 10am-10pm.)

■■■ LILLE

Founded in the 11th century as a transit station for boats on the Deûle River, Lille remains a center for trade. The largest city in the north, Lille puts aesthetics before practicality, but possesses the best features of a city: an ultra-modern *métro,* a huge shopping district, sidewalk cafés, street festivals, and enough students to foster a fun nightlife. Acknowledged as one of the finest French museums, Lille's **Musée des Beaux Arts,** on pl. de la République, shelters works by Rubens, Goya, El Greco, David, Delacroix, and Renoir in a majestic 19th-century building on pl. de la République. Restorations currently underway are to be completed in late 1994. **Charles de Gaulle's birthplace** at 9, rue Princesse, now marred by graffiti, has a vast collection of photographs and newspaper clippings on the leader of the Resistance and two-time French president. (Open Tues., Thurs., Sat., and Sun. 10am-noon and 2-5pm. 7F, children 2F.) The **tourist office,** pl. Rihour (tel. 20 30 81 00), haunts a 15th-century castle. (Open Mon.-Sat. 9am-7pm, Sun. 10am-noon and 2-5pm.) Five minutes away, the **post office** is at 7, pl. de la République. (Open Mon.-Fri. 8am-6:30pm, Sat. 8am-noon.) If you are staying in town a while, ask about summer university housing at **CROUS,** 70, rue de Cambrai (tel. 20 52 84 00), or **Fédération des Etudiants,** 125, rue Meurein (tel. 20 30 60 26). Clean, dark, and padded with brown shag, the **Hôtel Faidherbe,** 42, pl. de la Gare (tel. 20 06 27 93), offers 100F singles and 130F doubles. The 40-60F mussels at **Aux Moules,** 34, rue de Béthune, are unavailable until 1994 due to renovations. (Open daily 11:30am-11:30pm.)

■■■ FROM LILLE TO PARIS

The route from Lille to Paris hides some of northern France's best-kept secrets, largely uncompromised by tourists. **Arras** is built over tunnels *(les Boves)* that have-housed both medieval chalk miners and British soldiers (the latter during WWII). The friendly folks of the **tourist office** (tel. 21 51 26 95) in the 15th-century **Hôtel de Ville** provide an accommodations service. (Open summer Mon.-Sat. 9am-6pm, Sun. 10am-6:30pm; reduced winter hours.) Ask the concierge of the **Hôtel de Ville** to show you the marriage chamber, where all marriages officially take place (a church wedding is not sufficient, and most French have both ceremonies). The town has a central **auberge de jeunesse (HI),** 59, Grand Place (tel. 21 25 54 53), with dorm-style rooms in a newly renovated Flemish townhouse. (Reception open May-Sept. daily 7:30-10am and 6-11pm; Oct. and March-April 7:30-10am and 5-10pm. Curfew 11pm. Members only. 42F.) Inexpensive cafés skirt pl. des Héros; more elegant restaurants are found on the Grand Place. Eight km north of Arras lie the monument of **Vimy,** a memorial to the 60,000 Canadians killed in WWI. (Open daily 10am-6pm. Tours April-Nov. 15. Free.) Frequent buses and trains serve Vimy (15min each), but you still have to hike about 2km from the station to the memorial.

When the leaders of **Amiens** rebuilt their **Cathédrale de Notre Dame** in 1220, they sought to outdo the cathedrals of Paris and Laon, and the result is a monument not only to God but also to Gothic architecture. Its nave is the highest in France at 42m, and the astounding west façade boasts 4000 figures in Biblical scenes. (Open Mon.-Sat. 8:30am-7pm, Sun. 8:30am-12:30pm and 2:30-7pm; Oct. 1-March 31 Mon.-Sat. 8:30am-noon and 2-5pm.) The home of **Jules Verne** is at 2, rue Charles Dubois (open Tues.-Sat. 9:30am-noon and 2-6pm; 25F); the early science fiction writer rests 0.000046 leagues under the ground in an impressive tomb in the **Cimetière de la Madeleine.** The elegant **Hôtel Victor Hugo,** 2, rue l'Oratoire (tel. 22 91 57 91), offers singles (95F) and doubles (245F; showers 10F).

Perched dramatically on an upstart butte in the middle of a flat prairie, **Laon** huddles under the tremendous **Cathédrale de Notre Dame,** the first of the great Gothic cathedrals. Its 5 towers display the heads of oxen, in memory of the ox who mysteriously appeared to help cart building materials to the top of the hill. (Open daily 8am-7pm.) Ask at the **tourist office** (tel. 23 20 28 62), beside the cathedral in what was France's first hospital, for a free map of town with walking tours. (Open Mon.-Sat. 9am-12:30pm and 2-6:30pm, Sun. 10am-12:30pm and 2:30-6:30pm.) The pumpkin-colored interior of the **Maison des Jeunes,** 20, rue du Cloître (tel. 23 20 27 64), squats near the cathedral. (65F. Call ahead.)

Germany (Deutschland)

US$1   = DM1.60 (Deutschmarks)   DM1 =   US$0.63
CDN$1 = DM1.22   DM1 = CDN$0.82
UK£1   = DM2.48   DM1 = UK£0.40
IR£1   = DM2.32   DM1 = IR£ 0.43
AUS$1 = DM1.04   DM1 = AUS$0.97
NZ$1   = DM0.88   DM1 = NZ$1.14
SAR1   = DM0.33   DM1 = SAR3.03
Country Code: 49   **International Dialing Prefix: 00**

It seems somehow appropriate that as the world reinvents itself, Germany once again stands at the center of it all. Despite its long history of reactionary governments, Germany has always been a wellspring of revolutionaries—for better and for worse. One of the greatest heroes of German history, Karl der Große (Charlemagne), was the first to unify post-Roman Europe under enlightened rule. An obscure German monk, Martin Luther, stands as one of the most influential figures in Western history for the revolutionary forces unleashed when he triggered the Protestant reformation. Lessing, Bach, and Beethoven turned the worlds of drama and music upside-down. Socialist pioneers Karl Marx and Friedrich Engels equipped the revolutionary ground swell of 19th-century Europe with an ideology and a goal whose power has only been blunted and redirected, never defused. Adolf Hitler, the most loathsome figure in Western history, organized in this country the capacity to perform deeds—the seizure of power, the conquest of Europe, the Holocaust—that simply defy explanation. This last image, of course, indelibly colors all subsequent German history. Germans must grapple with the wrenching fact that the cradle of Goethe and Beethoven also nurtured Dachau and Buchenwald. As the only country to acknowledge collectively the moral bankruptcy of its nationalism, Germany brings a unique perspective—and a unique motivation—to the revolutionary transformation of Europe into a democratic super-state. Although eternally burdened with the crimes of the Third Reich, Germany is also blessed with a cultural tradition without compare. No major European artistic movement of the last 500 years is entirely without debt to Germans, and quite a few would be unthinkable without German influence.

While the historical truths underlying popular stereotypes do provide some insight into what it means to be German, the nation that has finally emerged from the horrors of World War II and the surreal bipolarism of the Cold War is decidedly non-stereotypical. There are, to be sure, certain "German" characteristics—industriousness, efficiency, and a mystifying refusal to cross the street against the light, even in the absence of traffic—but the broad social and political range that comprises the nation defies easy categorization.

Not that you'll hear this from any Germans themselves, who these days are busy typecasting each other as either snooty, materialistic *Wessis* (Westerns) or lazy, gap-toothed *Ossis* (Easterners) as they go about the painful process of reconciling their recently divergent pasts. The Wall had barely come down when West Berlin dilettantes started cracking jokes about putting it back up, and some 40-odd years of socialism won't be erased in the next decade, or probably even the next generation. Yet at precisely the same moment that the Germans are turning inward to resolve their own internal problems, their position is becoming increasingly relevant in a global sense. In the wake of Europe's most recent wave of revolution, the newly reunited Germany's position at the border of east and west is even more important than during the Cold War, and in the European Community, German initiative is a primary engine of European integration.

It's worth remembering all of this as you pass through the country—that the legacy represented by the wealth of artistic, historical, and cultural treasures that Germany has managed to accumulate throughout centuries of war and division defines a healthy chunk of Western civilzation's collective past, but may conceal more than just of a glimpse into the future.

> For a scintillating, witty, and breathtakingly well-written look at Germany, pick up a copy of *Let's Go: Germany & Switzerland.*

GETTING THERE AND GETTING AROUND
German Train Systems and Railpasses
In the midst of integrating the western **Deutsche Bundesbahn (DB)** and old eastern **Reichsbahn (DR),** Germany is also on the verge of privatizing the entire federal rail system. The plan is to replace both companies with one, the **Deutsche Bahn.** Signs of this process may already be

visible, but "*Ein Land, zwei Bahnen*," (one country, two railroads) is still the motto to travel by. Moving from west to east there are significant differences in quality and service. Averaging over 120km per hour including stops, the DB network is one of Europe's best (and most expensive). The Reichsbahn is getting better, but it's still not up to par. One problem is complex connections; on an indirect route, allow about twice as much time as you would in the west. Commuter trains, marked "City-Bahn" (CB), "S-Bahn," or, "Nahverkehrszug" (N), are very slow; "D" and "E" (Eilzug) trains are slightly faster and "FD" trains are faster still. "Interregio" (IR) trains, between neighboring cities, are speedy and comfortable. From metropolis to metropolis, "IC" (inter-city) trains approach the luxury and speed of an airplane. Unless you have a full-fare railpass, you must purchase a supplementary "IC Zuschlag" to ride an IC or EC train (DM6 when bought in the station, DM8 on the train). Even the IC yields to the brand-new super-sleek InterCity Express (ICE), which zips from Hamburg to Munich in 6 hours flat.

If you intend a long stay in Germany, or if you decide to purchase a **railpass** once in Germany, there are a few passes that can only be purchased once you've arrived. For anyone under age 23, and for students under age 27, the best deal going is the **tramper-Monats** ticket, good for one month of unlimited 2nd-class travel on all DB trains (except the ICE), the railroad-run buses (*Bahnbusse*), and the local S-Bahn (DM300; combined DB/DR ticket DM350; with ICE DM465). Bring proof of age and a student ID. International train stations (Frankfurt's, for example) may not sell the Tramper-Monats ticket to foreigners over 23 who are not students at a German university; go to a nearby, smaller station and try again. The **Bahncard,** available to travelers ages 18-22 and students under 27 (DM110), is valid for 1 year and gets you a 50% discount on all rail tickets, DB and DR alike. It offers the same deal for everyone between 12 and 17 (DM50), and anyone over age 60 (DM110). Passes are only available at major train stations, and all require a small photo.

Eurail, Buses, Flights, Bikes, and Cars Eurail holders get free passage on the S-Bahn (commuter rail) and on DB bus lines (marked *Bahn*). Passholders also get free rides and discounts on Romantic Road buses and some Rhine steamers, and railpasses are valid for the ferries from Puttgarden, Warnemünde and Saßnitz to Denmark and Sweden, although most trains just drive right onto the ferry. Regional **bus** systems are, at least in the west, a blessing. Long-distance bus travel is more of a crap-shoot, with scattered offerings from private companies. Within Germany, **air travel** is expensive; the few student discounts around tend to be restricted to native Germans. Frankfurt International Airport, Europe's second-largest, is the German hub, though the international terminals at Hamburg and Munich are also busy.

Bikes are sight-seeing power tools; Germany makes it easy with its wealth of trails and bike tours. Cities and towns usually have designated bike lanes, sometimes in the street, and sometimes laid out in the sidewalk itself. Bike rentals are available at approximately 250 stations throughout the country, where German Rail's *Fahrrad am Bahnhof* (Bikes at the Station) program has rentals at DM6-10 per day. Bikes usually can be rented from one station and returned at another with a deposit; ask for details at the station. For information about bike routes, regulations and maps, contact **Allgemeiner Deutscher Fahrrad-Club,** Postfach 10 77 44, 2800 Bremen. A bike tour guidebook, including extensive maps, is available from **Deutsches Jugendherbergswerk (DJH)** (see address in Accommodations).

Germans drive *fast;* before venturing out, be *very* familiar with traffic rules and especially signs and symbols. It is permitted and quite common to **hitch** on the German *Autobahnen* (expressways), but hitchers may stand only at **Raststätten** (rest stops), **Tankstellen** (gas stations), and in front of the *Autobahn* signs on-ramps. *Autobahn* hitchers will need a good map to navigate the tangled interchanges in the Rhine Valley. Thumbers pay attention to license plates: B—Berlin, M—Munich, F—Frankfurt, HH—Hamburg. Hitching is also common on the heavily traveled *Bundesstraßen,* scenic secondary roads marked by signs with a yellow diamond.

Mitfahrzentralen offices in many cities pair drivers and riders. For a fee of DM10-25, the MFZ will give you the telephone number of the driver, whom you can then call to make arrangements and set a price (usually determined by splitting gas costs). Check in the white and yellow pages *(Gelbe Seiten)* under "Mitfahrzentrale."

Urban **public transit** is excellent in the west and fair to middling in the east. You'll see 4 types: the **Straßenbahn** (streetcar), the **S-Bahn** (commuter rail), the **U-Bahn** (subway), and regular **buses.** Consider purchasing a day card *(Tagesnetzkarte)* or multiple-ride ticket *(Mehrfahrkarte)*, which will usually pay for itself by the 3rd ride. Often you must get your ticket beforehand at an *Automat* and then validate *(entwerten)* it in one of the little boxes either in the station or on board.

GERMANY ESSENTIALS

In certain regions, tourists of color or members of certain religious groups may feel threatened by local residents. Neo-Nazi skinheads in the large cities of former East Germany, as well as in Western Germany, have been known to attack foreigners, especially travelers of color. Furthermore, either historical or newly-developed discrimination against established minority residents may be directed towards travelers who are members of those minority groups. In any situation, however, common sense will serve you better than paranoia.

Every city in western Germany has a **tourist office,** usually located near the main train station *(Hauptbahnhof)* or in the central market square *(Marktplatz)* of each town's old city *(Altstadt)* and marked with signs reading *"Verkehrsamt"* or *"Verkehrsverein."* They provide city maps and book rooms (usually for a small fee).

The German mark is divided into 100 pfennigs (pf); find **currency exchange** *(Wechsel)* in all large train stations and in virtually all banks. (Open Mon.-Fri. 9am-noon and 2-4pm.) The best rates are often at post offices (in major cities usually open Sat.-Sun.), which will cash American Express checks for DM3 per check. **Credit card** acceptance is markedly less common in Germany than in the U.S. or U.K.; locals tend to carry large wads of hard cash in their wallets. All this means is that you shouldn't rely on plastic; carry traveler's checks. A new barrage of bills has been unleashed upon the people of Germany; don't be disconcerted if you find yourself in possession of two very different-looking bills worth the same amount (the new ones have a silver stripe). Old issue bills are still very much in use, but automats will only accept the new breed.

Shops are generally open weekdays from 8:30am to 6pm, and Saturday from 8:30am to 1pm. In some smaller towns, stores close from noon to 3pm for *Mittagspause*. In larger cities, stores stay open until 6pm on the first Saturday of each month *(langer Samstag)*.

Communication English **language** ability is common in the west, but far less so in the east. In all cases, introduce yourself with a polite, universally applicable *bitte* ("please," "excuse me," "thanks," "help"), the even politer *bitte schön* or the definitive *Entschuldigung* ("excuse me," "sorry I bumped into you," "help me *now"* or "get the #!ş%& out of my way"). The letter *ß* is equivalent to a double *s*.The climate in Germany is generally comparable to New England in the U.S. Summers are rarely hot—32°C is about tops. The Alps in the south are perpetually cool, while everything north of Hamburg is extremely rainy.

In the west, most **post offices** are open Monday through Friday from 8am to 6pm, Saturday from 8am to noon; all accept **Poste Restante,** known as *Postlagernde Briefe.* In western **phone** booths, a local call costs 30pf. Deposit coins first, even for toll-free calls. Change will not be returned, but if you hang up, then quickly pick up the receiver again, you can make another call. The *Kartentelefon* accepts cards sold at the post office in DM12 and DM50 denominations; it saves loose change and time in line, and is displacing coin-ops in many cities. Oddly enough, only phones marked "international" can be used for international calls. The old national information number, 11 88, has been replaced by 011 88. For information within the EC, call 00 11 88. For international collect calls, go to the post office; for AT&T's **USA Direct,** dial 01 30 00 10. AT&T recently issued new cards for European service. Your old card may no longer work; call AT&T before you go to make sure. The **MCI World Reach** number is 0130-0012. Keep these phone numbers in mind: **police** (tel. 110) and **fire or medical emergency** (tel. 112).

Accommodations and Camping Local tourist offices can usually find you a bed for a DM1-6 fee. Hotels are generally expensive. *Pensionen* and *Gasthäuser,* less elegant but equally comfortable, are more reasonably priced. Rooms in a private home *(Zimmer Frei)* are usually a few marks less but are often unavailable (or more expensive) for one-night stays; the same holds true for many rural pensions. **Mitwohnzentralen** offices in large cities can help find lodging for both short and long stays. Living in the cheaper suburbs of a town may be false economy, as public transportation is often costly.

A German schoolteacher founded the world's first youth hostel in 1909, and there are now more than 750 *(Jugendherberge)* in Germany—Europe's most extensive system. Signs for hostels read "DJH." In June 1990, the **Deutsches Jugendherbergswerk (DJH)** festively engulfed its eastern counterpart, but western hostels are still more convenient. Beds in the west normally cost DM13-19 for "juniors" (under 27) and 2 or 3 marks more for "seniors" (27 and up). Bavarian hostels accept *only* juniors; elsewhere, they are given priority (until 7pm). Curfews at western hostels are normally early, between 9:45pm and 11pm. A small breakfast is almost always included (not always in the east). Sheetless guests must rent bed linen (DM3.50-5); sleeping bags are often unacceptable. All hostels are required to hold extra beds for unannounced individual travelers, although these can fill quickly. In some western cities, the new-generation **Jugendgästehaus** is displacing the hostel, with higher prices (from DM21.50, sheets included) and a later curfew, catering more to young adults than schoolchildren. DJH publishes a guidebook (DM6), which details all federated German hostels, available at all German bookstores and many news stands, or write DJH-Hauptverband, Bismarckstr. 8, Postfach 1455, 32756 Detmold, Germany.

Campgrounds are everywhere and usually cost only DM4-7 per person, DM3-4 per tent; ask at the local tourist office for the most convenient sites. Freelance camping is now illegal, to protect the environment.

Food and Drink Though German cuisine is generally fatty and ponderous, a visit here need not torture your taste buds. Some of the more savory German dishes include *Schnitzel* (a thin cutlet of veal lightly fried in butter), *Spätzle* (noodles from the South), and almost anything that swims (from the North Sea). Pork and potatoes in all forms are staples of the German diet. Vegetarians will have a tough time with sit-down meals, although most eateries offer a salad plate *(Salatteller),* and Germany's palette of breads and cheeses puts the baguette to shame. The fresh rolls *(Brötchen* or *Semmeln)* sold at any bakery are unforgettable. **Supermarkets** are open Monday to Friday from 8am to 1pm and 3 to 6:30pm, and on Saturday from 9am to 1pm. **Aldi, Plus,** and **Penny Markt** are popular, very cheap discount chains.

German breakfasts *(Frühstück)* are simple, consisting of coffee and buttered rolls with cheese or salami and the occasional hard-boiled egg. The main meal, *Mittagessen,* is served at noon. At about 4pm, you may notice Germans with sweet tooths and coffee addictions heading to the *Konditorei* for *Kaffee und Kuchen* (coffee and cake). The evening meal, *Abendbrot* or *Abendessen,* is traditionally a repeat performance of breakfast—bread, cheese, and cold cuts.

In a restaurant or *Gaststätte* (a simpler, less expensive restaurant), order from the *Tageskarte* (daily menu). All restaurant prices include tax and service *(Mehrwertsteuer und Bedienung).* If you wish to tip, simply round up the bill to the nearest mark or two. For inexpensive food, go to a department-store cafeteria or *Mensa* (dining halls located at most universities). Most *Mensas* are supposed to admit only their own students, but you'd never guess it. Stop at an *Imbiß* for anything fast; they dot the pedestrian zones. Most German towns have relatively inexpensive Greek, Yugoslavian and Turkish restaurants. Italian restaurants, almost as common as BMWs, generally offer a decent, low-priced plate of pasta.

In good weather, stein-hoisters flock to the ubiquitous open-air *Biergarten. Ein Helles* is a standard light-colored beer; *Dunkles* is darker and sweeter. *Weißbier* or *Weizenbier* is a delicious, smooth, rich wheat beer. *Pilsner* or *Pils* gets its clear complexion and bitter taste from the addition of extra hops. *Radler* is a tasty, thirstquenching mix of beer and lemon soda. Also try German wine, especially the sweet *(lieblich* or *süß)* whites of the Rhine and Mosel Valleys and the comparatively unknown dry *(trocken)* whites of southwestern Baden.

EASTERN GERMANY

Those visiting Eastern Germany for the first time will be surprised to find that the lion's share of Germany's cultural and historic monuments lie in the east. That's the good news; the bad news is that the corpse of Communism still rots across most of the former GDR. Careless industrialization has decimated much of the environment, casting whole regions a depressing, sooty gray. The disparity in living standards between Eastern and Western Germany is still astounding: the majority of Eastern homes lack telephones and central heating. Trains, buses, and service personnel move at about half the speed of their Western German counterparts, but the slower pace and lifestyle breed a sense of hospitality long forgotten: ask an Easterner for directions and you may find yourself being escorted to your destination.

Those who have been here before will marvel at how quickly things are changing, how much cleaner the air is, and how much difference a little paint can make. Everywhere businesses are opening, remodeling, or closing. In a country where just about everything was named after a socialist hero, socialism's demise means that streets, schools, hospitals, and universities are all being rechristened. The former German Democratic Republic is undergoing a major transformation.

For travelers, the confusion takes its toll. There is probably nothing more irritating than searching for a hotel or street that no longer exists. Don't expect to enter the *neue Bundesländer* and actually find exactly what you thought you'd find the way you thought you'd find it. Take heart; no one is more frustrated than the people who live here. For 40 years this planned society changed so slowly that astute observers could usually predict the headlines in the party papers. Today no one can guess what titillating sex scandal the trashy (and wildly popular) *Bild Zeitung* will think up next, let alone predict what the future holds in terms of employment and financial security; and this in a country where the government once planned, directed, and financed the lives of its citizens from cradle to grave. At first such spontaneity was exciting, but unification has not yet brought the prosperity that it seemed to promise. As unemployment persists at staggering levels, the unpredictability of life in the new East Germany has translated into anger directed at the Western Germans for their condescension, and fear that everything the party said about the horrors of capitalism may yet prove true. Radical right gangs loiter in many eastern cities, distinguishable by their black boots with white laces. With a beleaguered and divided left, these gangs are quietly gaining tacit acceptance by Germans.

If you have come expecting to dance on the Wall, you're late. Caught somewhere between division and unity, many Germans are having second thoughts. Few doubt the long-term prospects of unification; East Germany is being rebuilt with the best and most modern infrastructure available, but the payoff is at least a decade away.

■■■ BERLIN

Berlin is one of the most fascinating cities on earth. For half a century, the divided city responded to the undeclared Cold War with a storm of urban activity and the sort of nightlife you might expect from a population with its back against the Wall. When governments fell across Eastern Europe, Berlin became a gateway—*the* gateway, in fact—between distinct but no longer separate worlds. The result has been a period of dizzying change, and the city is both better and worse off as a result. Suddenly, Berlin is once again the capital of Germany (though the bureaucrats stay in Bonn), reunification has brought artists and authors from east and west into one burgeoning cultural scene, and the entire city has access to Eastern Berlin's outstanding museums. But alongside the bohemian squatter's scene which has emerged along its sidestreets, Eastern Berlin suffers from unemployment and alienation, as evidenced by the growing number of neo-Nazis who frequent its streets.

Berlin is not honestly picturesque, and the sudden change in its borders has left the city without a single center. The Wall's legacy still crops up occasionally in wide, empty spaces of cracked concrete. There's something about Berlin that doesn't make sense; it sneaks up on you and hides things. But Berlin's dark side pales in comparison to the exhilaration of being on the cutting edge. As Weimar decadent Karl Zuckmayer wrote, "Berlin tasted of future, and for that one happily accepted the dirt and coldness as part of the bargain."

ORIENTATION AND PRACTICAL INFORMATION

Berlin surveys the Prussian plain in the northeastern corner of reunited Germany, about 4 rail hours southeast of Hamburg and double that time north of Munich, with excellent rail and air connections to Eastern and Western European capitals.

Berlin is *immense*, and its eastern and western halves are 2 worn puzzle pieces that no longer fit together smoothly, connected by the grand tree-lined boulevard, **Straße des 17 Juni,** which runs through the massive **Tiergarten** park. The blue and yellow **Falk Plan** (DM8.80; available at most kiosks) is indispensable.

The commercial district of Western Berlin centers around **Bahnhof Zoo** (Zoo Station) and **Breitscheidplatz,** site of the bombed-out Kaiser-Wilhelm-Gedächtniskirche, the boxy tower of Europa Center, and the main tourist office. A star of streets radiates from Breitscheidpl. Toward the west run **Hardenbergstraße, Kantstraße** and the **Kurfürstendamm,** or **Ku'damm.** Down Hardenbergstr. 800m is Steinpl. and the enormous Berlin Technical University. Down Kantstr. 800m is **Savignyplatz,** home to cafés, restaurants, and pensions. The newly asphalted **Ebert Straße** runs uncomfortably along the path of the deconstructed Berlin Wall from the Reichstag to **Potsdamer Platz.** The landmark **Brandenburg Gate** and surrounding Pariser Platz, reconstructed with the aid of EC funds, open onto **Unter den Linden,** which leads to the historic heart of Berlin around **Lustgarten,** and the neighboring commercial district of **Alexanderplatz.** The region near the Brandenburg Gate still shows the scars of what Berliners called "wall sickness." The alternative **Kreuzberg** and **Mitte,** for 40 years fringe back-against-the-wall neighborhoods of the West and East respectively, are once again at the crossroads.

In newly united Berlin, many municipal services are still divided between East and West. When services are duplicated in both parts of the city, *Let's Go* lists those in Western Berlin first, then their Eastern counterparts.

Safety Warning! Although neo-Nazis represent a tiny minority of Berliners, any conspicuously non-German individuals should be on guard in the less-touristed areas of Eastern Berlin. Extreme-right groups have also been known to target gay and lesbian couples.

> **Tourist Offices: Berlin-Touristen-Information, Europa Center,** in the Europa Center at Budapesterstr. 45 (tel. 262 60 31). From Bahnhof Zoo, walk along Budapesterstr. past the Kaiser-Wilhelm-Gedächtniskirche about 5 min. Open Mon.-Sat. 8am-10:30pm, Sun. 9am-9pm. **Branch offices** at Bahnhof Zoo (tel. 313

90 63 or 313 90 64) and Tegel Airport (tel. 41 01 31 45) open daily 8am-11pm. Branch at **Hauptbahnhof** in the east (tel. 279 52 09) open daily 8am-8pm. All offices provide a simple city map, *Berlin Tut Gut* (a pamphlet about the city), and a very useful and up-to-date pamphlet, *Unterkünfte für Junge Besucher*, which lists Berlin's budget accommodations with directions and prices. All offices will also book rooms for a DM5 fee. A handy book, *Berlin for Young People*, with suggested walks and information about the city, is also available at no cost.

Budget Travel: ARTU Reisebüro, Hardenbergstr. 9 (tel. 31 04 66), down the street from Bahnhof Zoo. **Branch offices** at Takustr. 47 (tel. 831 50 94; U-Bahn: Dahlem-Dorf), Nollendorfpl. 7 (tel. 216 30 91; U-Bahn: Nollendorfpl.), and in Kreuzberg, at Mariannenstr. 7 (tel. 614 68 22; U-Bahn: Kottbusser Tor). Sells Transalpino passes and books flights; last minute specials. **Hardenbergstr. branch** open Mon.-Tues. and Thurs.-Fri. 10am-6pm, Wed. 11am-6pm, Sat. 10am-1pm. Other branches open same hours, but closed an hour for lunch. **SRS**, Marienstr. 25 (tel. 281 67 61; fax 281 51 33); U-Bahn 6: Friedrichstr. Books student flights; useful binder of last minute specials. Open Mon.-Fri. 9am-6pm, Sat. 9am-2pm.

Embassies and Consulates: U.S., Clayalle 170 (tel. 832 40 87). Open Mon.-Fri. 2:30-4pm. **Canadian Consulate,** Friedrichstr. 95 (tel. 261 11 61). Open Mon.-Fri. 8:30am-noon and 2-4pm. **U.K. embassy,** Unter den Linden 32-4 (tel. 220 24 31). Open Mon. Fri. 8:30am-noon and 2-4pm. **Austrian Consulate,** Uhlandstr. 181-3 (tel. 880 08 80). Open Mon.-Fri. 9am-noon and 2-4pm. **South African Consulate,** Douglasstr. 9 (tel. 82 50 11). Open Mon.-Fri. 8am-4:15pm. **Bulgaria,** Leipzigerstr. 20 (tel. 200 09 22). Open Mon.-Fri. 10am-12:30pm and 1:30-5pm. **Hungary,** Unter den Linden 76 (tel. 220 25 61). Visa section open Mon., Wed., and Fri. 9am-1pm, Tues. and Thurs. 2-5pm. **Russian Federation,** Under den Linden 63-65 (tel. 229 11 10). Visa section open Mon.-Fri. 9am-noon. **Czech Republic,** Toleranzstr. 21 (tel. 220 04 81). Visa section open 8:30-11am. **Poland,** Under den Linden 72-74 (tel. 220 25 51). Visa section open Mon.and Wed.-Fri. 9am-1pm.

Currency Exchange: Deutsche Verkehrs-Kredit Bank at Bahnhof Zoo, on Hardenbergstr. Open Mon.-Sat. 7:30am-10pm, Sun. 8am-7pm. Decent rates for exchange; 1% commission on traveler's checks (DM7.50 min.). **Berliner Bank** in Tegel Airport is open daily 8am-10pm. Branches of commercial banks are sprouting in East Berlin. You can also change money at most post offices.

American Express: Uhlandstr. 173 (tel. 882 75 75). The usual. Open Mon.-Fri. 9am-5:30pm, Sat. 9am-noon.

Post Office: In Bahnhof Zoo (tel. 313 97 99). Open 24hrs. **Poste Restante** (at window #9) should be addressed: Poste Restante/Hauptpostlagernd, Postamt Bahnhof Zoo, 10612 Berlin. Branch office at Tegel Airport (tel. 430 85 23) open daily 6:30am-9pm. In Eastern Berlin, at the **Hauptbahnhof**, Postamt Berlin 17, Str. der Pariser Kommune 8-10, 10243 Berlin. Open Mon.-Fri. 7am-9pm, Sat. 8am-8pm.

Telephones: At Bahnhof Zoo. Open 24hrs. **City Code**: 030. When calling Eastern Berlin from overseas, if dialing (30) doesn't work, you'll probably need operator assistance. You may occasionally see a (9) in front of an Eastern Berlin number; this old prefix has almost entirely been phased out; the number itself may be out of date. Give it a try both ways, or call directory assistance to check the number. *Let's Go* lists Eastern numbers without the (9) before them.

Flights: Flughafen Tegel (tel. 410 11) is Western Berlin's main airport, connected to Bahnhof Zoo by bus #109. **Flughafen Tempelhof** (tel. 690 91) is making a post-reunification comeback, especially for flights within Europe. **Flughafen Schönefeld** (tel. 67 20), in East Berlin, is connected by S-Bahn to the city.

Trains: Bahnhof Zoo is Berlin's principal station for locations in the west, **Hauptbahnhof** is the focus of eastern and southern-bound trains. Stations are connected by S-Bahn. Trains from the east also arrive at **Bahnhof Lichtenberg. Connections:** Dresden (2hr.), Leipzig (2½hr.), Hamburg (3-4hr.), Hanover (4hr.), Frankfurt am Main (9hr.), Prague (9hr.), Warsaw (8hr.), Vienna (11hr.). **Information: Bundesbahn** and **Reichsbahn Information** (tel. 194 19). Be prepared for a long wait. Similarly long lines at info offices in **Bahnhof Zoo** and **Hauptbahnhof.**

Buses: ZOB, the central bus station (tel. 301 80 28), is by the Funkturm near Kaiserdamm. U-Bahn: Kaiserdamm. Check *Zitty* and *Tip* for deals on long-distance buses (often only slightly cheaper than the train or plane).

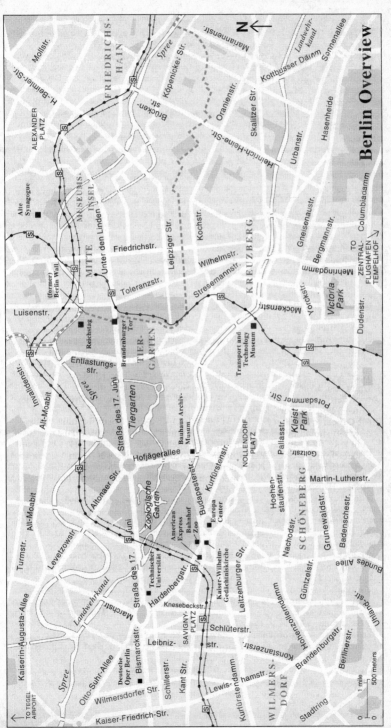

Berlin Overview

Luggage Storage: In the Bahnhof Zoo. Lockers DM2, larger ones DM3. 72-hr. max. At **Hauptbahnhof;** lockers DM2, larger DM4, 72hr. max. At Bahnhof **Lichtenberg** and S-Bahnhof **Alexanderplatz,** lockers DM2, 24-hr. max.

Public Transportation: The transit system is as indispensable and efficient as it is expensive. The extensive **bus, U-Bahn** (subway), and **S-Bahn** (surface rail) systems of Eastern and Western Berlin now operate as one network, the **BVG.** A single ticket for the network *(Einzelfahrschein Normaltarif)* costs DM3.20 and is good for 2hr. after validation. An *Einzelfahrschein Kurzstreckentarif* (short-trip fare, DM2.10) allows travel up to 6 bus stops (no transfers; not valid on airport bus lines) or 3 U- or S-Bahn stations (with one transfer). 4-ride *Sammelkarte* (multiple ticket), DM11; short-trip 4-ride *Sammelkarte* DM6.40. You can buy tickets from machines, bus drivers, or ticket windows in the U-Bahn and S-Bahn stations. The fine for cheating is steep (DM60) and inspections are frequent. Children under 6 accompanied by an adult travel free. All tickets must be cancelled in the red validation box before boarding to be valid. The **Berlin Ticket** (DM12, ages 6-14 DM6) is a 24-hr. pass on the bus, U-, and S-Bahn. A **6-Day Berlin Ticket** (Mon.-Sat.) costs DM30. An extensive **Liniennetz** map costs DM3 and can be bought from subway ticket offices. The **Falk Plan** also has all routes indicated. U- and S-Bahn do not run 1-4am, except for the **U-1** and **U-9**, which run all night Fri.-Sat. There is an extensive system of **night buses** which stops every ½hr.

Lost Property: BVG Fundbüro, Lorenzweg 5 (tel. 17 51 80 21). For items lost on the bus or U-Bahn. Open Mon.-Tues. and Thurs. 9am-3pm, Wed. 9am-6pm, Fri. 9am-2pm. **Fundbüro Deutsche Reichsbahn,** in the Hackescher Markt S-Bahn station (tel. 29 72 16 71). For items lost on trains or S-Bahn. Open Mon. and Wed.-Thurs. 10am-4pm, Tues. 10am-6pm, Fri. 8am-noon.

Bike Rental: Fahrradbüro Berlin, Hauptstr. 146 (tel. 784 55 62). U-Bahn: Kleistpark. DM15/day, DM60/week. Tandems DM25/day. Deposit DM50; bring ID. Open Mon.-Wed. and Fri. 10am-6pm, Thurs. 10am-7pm, Sat. 10am-2pm.

Hitchhiking: Those hitching west or south (Hanover, Munich, Weimar, Leipzig) take the S-Bahn to Wannsee, then bus #211 to the Autobahn entrance ramp. Those hitching north (Hamburg, Rostock) take the U-Bahn to Tegel, then bus #224; they ask the driver to stop at the *Trampenplatz.* **Mitfahrzentrale** has its **City Netz** office at Kurfürstendamm 227 (tel. 882 76 04; open daily 8am-9pm) and branches at Südstern 2 (tel. 693 60 95), open 9am-8pm, and Bahnhof Zoo (tel. 31 03 31), open daily 8am-9pm. Berlin has Mitfahrzentralen not belonging to the national chain; see *Zitty* or *Tip* magazines for addresses and phone numbers. There is a Mitfahrzentralen exclusively for gays and lesbians (tel. 216 40 20). The Mitfahrzentrale in U-Bahnhof Alexanderpl. specializes in the East (tel. 242 36 42).

Pharmacies: Europa-apotheke, Tauentzienstr. 9-12 (tel. 261 41 42), by Europa Center (close to Bahnhof Zoo). Open 9am-9pm. Closed *Apotheken* post signs direct you to the nearest open one. **In East Berlin: Apotheke am Alexanderplatz,** Hans-Beimler-Str. 70-72 (tel. 212 57 66).

Bookstore: Kiepert's, on Hardenbergstr. 4, across from the Technical University, includes works in English. Open Mon.-Fri. 9am-6pm, Sat. 9am-1pm.

Laundromat: Wasch Centers at Leibnizstr. 72, Wexstr. 34, Rheinstr. 62, Markstr. 4, Behmstr. 12, and (in Eastern Berlin's Prenzlauer Berg) Jablonskistr. 21. All open daily 6am-midnight. Wash DM8/6kg, dry DM2/30 min. Soap included.

Crisis Lines: Sexual Assault Hotline (tel. 251 28 28). Open Tues. and Thurs. noon-9pm, Sun. noon-2pm. **Schwüles Überfall** (gay-bashing) hotline and legal help (tel. 216 33 36). Open Sun.-Fri. 6-9pm, Sat. 6pm-4am.

Medical Assistance: The tourist office has a list of English-speaking doctors. **Emergency Doctor,** tel. 31 00 31 (Western), 12 59 (Eastern). **Emergency Dentist,** tel. 11 41. In Eastern Berlin try the emergency room of **Rettungsamt Berlin,** Marienburgerstr. 41-46 (tel. 282 05 61).

Emergencies: Ambulance and Fire: tel. 112. **Police:** tel. 110. Headquarters at Pl. der Luftbrücke 6 (tel. 69 90; lost and found 69 93 64 44). **In East Berlin: Ambulance:** tel. 115. **Fire:** tel. 112. **Police:** tel. 110.

ACCOMMODATIONS AND CAMPING

The immediate euphoria and tourist influx after the fall of the Wall has leveled out and the prices and quality of Berlin accommodations have stabilized. Nonetheless, Berlin is a major tourist center and it is advisable to book ahead.

For a DM5 fee, **tourist offices** will find you a hotel room or private accommodations. Plan to spend at least DM60 for a single, DM100 for a double, though they also have private accommodations from DM40 per person with breakfast (2-night min. stay). The office prefers to fill up the *pensions* first, so you may have to ask for private rooms. Reserve a room by writing directly to a *pension* or to the **Verkehrsamt Berlin,** Martin-Luther-Str. 105, 10825 Berlin. The Verkehrsamt requires that you state precisely how much you want to spend (min. DM60 for a single, DM95 for a double). Write at least 4 weeks in advance.

For visits of more than 4 days, the various *Mitwohnzentralen* can arrange for you to sublet an apartment. Prices start at DM35 per night and go down the longer you stay. The **Mitwohnzentrale,** Kurfürstendamm 227/228, 2nd floor (tel. 88 30 51), in Ku'damm Eck, is the biggest. (Open Mon.-Fri. 10am-6:30pm, Sat.-Sun. 11am-2pm.)

Hostels and Dormitories

Hostels quickly fill with German school groups (especially in summer and on weekends); call ahead. All admit members only, but some will give nonmembers a guest stamp for DM4. To buy an HI card, head to Tempelhofer Ufer 32 (tel. 262 30 24; open Mon., Wed., and Fri. 10am-3pm, Tues. and Thurs. 2-5:30pm).

Jugendgästehaus am Zoo, Hardenbergstr. 9a (tel. 312 94 10). Bus #145 or a short walk from the Zoo. The central location almost makes up for the crowded rooms. No curfew. Singles DM47. Doubles DM85. Small dorms DM35.

Jugendgästehaus (HI), Kluckstr. 3, 10785 Berlin (tel. 261 10 97). Bus #129 from Kurfürstendamm (direction "Hermannpl."). Look for the 8m conceptual "DJH" archway. Central location, many school groups. Reception open 1-1:45pm, 2:35-9:45pm, and 10:15pm to midnight. Lockout 9am-noon. Curfew midnight. DM27, over 26 DM33. Sheets and breakfast included. Lockers, laundry facilities. Key deposit DM10. Reservations strongly recommended.

Jugendgästehaus Wannsee (HI), Kronprinzessinnenweg 27 (tel. 803 20 34; fax 803 59 08). S-Bahn 1, 3: Nikolassee, walk 10 min. toward the Strand Bad Wannsee beach. Far from the center, a bit institutional, likely to have space. Curfew 1am. DM27, over 26 DM33. Sheets and breakfast included. Key deposit DM20.

Jugendherberge Ernst Reuter (HI), Hermsdorfer Damm 48 (tel. 404 16 10). U-Bahn #6 to "Tegel", then bus #125 (direction "Frohnau") to "Jugendherberge." Similarly remote, so also likely to have space. Curfew midnight. DM22, over 26 DM27. Sheets and breakfast included. Key deposit DM10.

Studentenhotel Berlin, Meiningerstr. 10, 10823 Berlin (tel. 784 67 20). U-Bahn: Rathaus Schöneberg. From Bahnhof Zoo, hop on bus #146, get off at "Rathaus Schöneberg," and walk across Martin-Luther-Str. Decent dorm lodgings in a green, quiet neighborhood. Reception open 24 hr. Doubles DM38/person. Quads DM34/person. Breakfast included. Reservations recommended.

Jugendgästehaus Tegel, Ziekowstr. 161, 13509 Berlin (tel. 433 30 46). U-Bahn: Tegel, then bus #222. Old brick outside, new and bright inside, on the north end of town by the Tegel parks. Under 27 only. Often has space. No curfew. DM31.50. Breakfast included. Written reservations only.

Jugendgästehaus Nordufer, Nordufer 28 (tel. 451 70 30). U-Bahn 9: Westhafen, then left over the bridge and left again onto Nordufer. Away from the center but on a pretty, swimmable lake. Some singles, but more 4-bed rooms. Reception open 7am-midnight. No curfew. DM35. Buffet breakfast and sheets included.

Jugendgästehaus Central, Nikolsburgerstr. 2-4 (tel. 870 188). U-Bahn: Güntzelstr. Looks like a high school, with drab green walls, but worth it if you can get a double. Curfew 1am. 2- to 6-bed rooms (many with showers and toilet) DM32/person. Breakfast included. Full pension DM4 extra. Sheets DM7.

Jugendgästehaus Feurigstraße, Feurigstr. 63 (tel. 781 52 11). U-Bahn: Kleistpark. Near the Schöneberg bars and clubs. Reception open 24hrs. Dorms DM34. Singles DM54. Doubles DM88. Sheets and breakfast included. Make reservations.

CVJM-Haus, Einemstr. 10 (tel. 264 91 00). German YMCA. Institutional setting, but it'll make you feel young again. Reception open 8-11am and 4-9pm. Singles DM40. Doubles DM80. Breakfast included.

Hotels and Pensions

Prices have finally stabilized as owners of small pensions and hotels once more cater to small budgets. Most *Pensionen* and small hotels listed in *Let's Go* are amenable to *Mehrbettzimmer:* extra beds moved into a large double or triple. Look for cheap hotel rooms around Savignyplatz and down along Wilmerdorfstr. and its side-streets.

Hotelpension Bialas, Carmerstr. 16 (tel. 312 50 25). Bus #149 to "Steinpl." Unusually convenient for Berlin; the rooms have sculptured ceilings. Reception open 24hr. Singles DM65, with shower DM95. Doubles DM65-95, with shower DM150.

Pension Kreuzberg, Grossbeerenstr. 64 (tel. 251 13 62). U-Bahn: Mehringdamm or bus #119. Near the bars and clubs of Kreuzberg. Reception open 9am-8pm. Singles DM60. Doubles DM90. *Mehrbettzimmer* DM40/person. Breakfast included.

Hotelpension Gloria, Wielandstr. 27 (tel. 881 80 60). Bus #119 to "Bleibtreustr." Just off the Ku'damm. Reception open 7am-8pm. Singles DM60, with shower DM80. Doubles with shower DM130. Breakfast included.

Centrum Pension Berlin, Kantstr. 31 (tel. 316 153). Bus #149 Savignypl. Convenient location in a big pink building. Singles DM50. Doubles DM75. Triples DM90. Quads DM120. Breakfast DM7.50.

Hotelpension Cortina, Kantstr. 140 (tel. 313 90 59). S-Bahn 3, 5, 6, 9, or Bus #149 Savignypl. Bright, convenient, and hospitable. Singles DM65. Doubles DM95, with shower DM120. *Mehrbettzimmer* upon agreement. Breakfast included.

Pension Knesebeck, Knesebeckstr. 86 (tel. 31 72 55). North of Savignypl. Big rooms with sinks. Reception open 24hr. Singles DM75. Doubles DM120, with shower DM140. *Mehrbettzimmer* DM140, with shower DM150. Breakfast included.

Hotel Transit, Hagelbergerstr. 53-54 (tel. 785 50 51). U-Bahn: Mehringdamm, bus #119, or night bus N19 (every 10-15min.). In a renovated factory in Kreuzberg, with bar and 24-hr. (M)TV lounge. Laundry. Reception open 24hr. Singles DM70. Doubles DM95. Triples DM120. Dorms DM30. Breakfast included.

Hamburger Hof, Kinkelstr. 6 (tel. 333 46 02), in the old quarter of Spandau. Easily accessible, next to U-Bahn #7: Altstadt Spandau. A tiny, comfortable hotel with only 15 beds, but so far from the action that they usually have room. Singles DM45. Doubles DM90. Showers and breakfast included.

Charlottenburger Hof, Stuttgarterpl. 14 (tel. 324 48 19). Across from S-Bahn: Charlottenburg. Sparkling rooms with cable TV and phones. Singles DM65. Doubles DM80-100, with shower DM120-140. Triples DM160. Quads DM180.

Hotelpension Pariser Eck, Pariserstr. 19 (tel. 881 21 45), near Ludwigpl. Bright rooms on a café-lined corner. Singles DM50. Doubles DM85. Showers DM1.50.

Hotel-Pension Hansablick, Flotowstr. 6 (tel. 391 40 48; fax 392 69 37). Near Tiergarten. A bit pricey, but it's an architectural pearl, from the decorative ceilings to the marble entranceway. Call, write, or fax ahead for reservations. Reception open 7am-9pm. Singles DM85. Doubles DM115, with shower DM125, with shower, bath, and color TV DM165.

Pension Münchener, Güntzelstr. 62 (tel. 854 22 26). U-Bahn: Güntzelstr. Small, art-filled *pension*. Clean rooms. Singles DM50. Doubles DM78. Breakfast DM9.

Camping

All 3 of the major campgrounds in Berlin are adjacent to the former Berlin Wall. **Kladow,** Krampnitzer Weg 111-117 (tel. 365 27 97), is in Spandau; take U-Bahn to "Rathaus Spandau," then take bus #135 to the end and follow Krampnitzer Weg another 500m. Closer to the center of Spandau is **Haselhorst,** Pulvermühlenweg (tel. 334 59 55); take U-Bahn to "Haselhorst," then head north on Daumster to Pulvermühlenweg. Perhaps the most unusual is **Dreilinden** (tel. 805 12 01), which is surrounded on 3 sides by the vestiges of the Berlin Wall. Take the U-Bahn to "Oskar-Helene Heim," then bus #118, then follow Kremnitzufer to Albrechts-Teergfen (about 20min.). All charge DM6.90 per person, DM5.50 per tent. All are open year round. Make reservations with **Deutscher Camping Club,** Mandlstr. 28, 80802 München, or call in advance. Also, try the **Internationales Jugendcamp,** Ziekowstr. 161 (tel. 433 86 40), U-Bahn 6: Tegel, then bus #222 or night bus N22: Titusweg. Next to Jugendgästehaus Tegel (see Hostels, above), it's far away, but gets you a mat under a giant tent with shower facilities. (Under 27 only. Lockout 9am-5pm. DM9. No written reservations accepted. Open June 21-Aug. 31.)

FOOD

Berlin's restaurant scene is as international as its population; German cuisine should not be a priority here. *Berliner Weißbier,* a must-try concoction of beer and fruit syrup, is one exception. Typical Berlin food is Turkish; almost every street in the city has its own Turkish *Imbiß* or restaurant. The *Döner Kepab,* a sandwich of lamb and salad, has cornered the fast food market, with *falafel* running a close second. For DM4-5, either makes a small meal. A second wave of immigration has brought quality Indian restaurants to Berlin, and Italian is always a safe choice.

Although budget eateries are scarce in Eastern Berlin, new cafés in Mitte and Prenzlauer Berg are rapidly providing stiff competition for their western counterparts. Street vendors with all shapes, sizes, and flavors of cheap food fill **Alexanderplatz** every day. Like all big cities, Berlin has numerous supermarkets. **Aldi, Bolle,** and **Penny Markt** are the cheapest. (Markets open Mon.-Fri. 9am-6pm, Sat. 9am-1pm.) The best **open-air market** is Saturday mornings in Winterfeldpl.

Western Berlin

Mensa der Freie Universität, in the huge complex at Habelschwerdter Allee 45. U-Bahn: Thielpl. Meals from DM2 with ISIC. Open Mon.-Fri. 11:15am-2:30pm.

Mensa TU, Hardenbergstr. 34. Bus #145 to Steinpl. Hard to miss; says "MENSA" in big letters on the building. More conveniently located, but slightly worse food than the above. Meals from DM2. Open Mon.-Fri. 11:15am-2:30pm.

Tiergartenquelle, Stadtbahnhogen 482, under the S-Bahn bridge at S-Bahn: Tiergarten. Huge portions of food in friendly, student-filled atmosphere. Most entrees under DM12. Open daily 6pm-midnight.

Rogacki, Wilmersdorferstr. 145. A huge delicatessen, with every sort of hot and cold food imaginable. Something good in every price range (lobster only DM50). Also take out. Open Mon.-Fri. 9am-6pm, Sat. 9am-1pm.

Schwarzes Café, Kantstr. 148, near Savignypl. Loads of young people. Breakfast at all hours (omelettes DM7). Open 24hrs., except for Tues. 3am-Wed.11am.

Restaurant Marché, down the street from Zoo with an elegant Ku'damm view. Vegetarians as well as ice cream fans will be pleased. Open daily 8am-midnight.

Baharat Falafel, Winterfeldtstr., 37 U-Bahn 1 or 4: Nollendorfplatz. Falafel from heaven (DM5). Open Mon.-Sat. noon-2am, Sun. 1pm-2am.

Dicke Wirtin, Carmerstr. 9, around the corner from Savigny Platz. Huge bowls of thick soup and stew for DM4-6. Open daily noon-4am.

Café Voltaire, Stuttgarterpl. 14. Café-bistro-gallery with a colorful and talkative crowd. Great breakfasts (5am-3pm, DM6-8); warm meals noon-5am. Open 24hrs., except for a brief hiatus Mon. 1-7am.

Eastern Berlin

Valentino, Auguststr. 84. Active art deco café, with food until late and changing exhibits by young Berliner artists. Brunch Sundays at the *Frühstücksbüffett* (DM10). Open Mon.-Fri. 4pm-3am, Sat. 2pm-3am, Sun. 10am-3am.

Zur Rippe, Poststr. 17. Near the Mühlendamm bridge. Satisfying meals DM10-14, and the *Berlin Weiße mit Rippenshosse* (DM3.80), a bizarre red cocktail, tickles your tongue. Open daily 11am-midnight.

Café Rastauration 1900, Husemannstr. at Kollwitzpl. in Prenzlauer Berg. Alternative interior. Decent food at reasonable prices. Open daily noon-2am.

Die Krähe, Kollwitzstr. 84, off Kollwitzpl. Ochre walls, old wooden tables, and a bright crowd. Superb breakfasts; *Großes Frühstück* (DM9.50) comes with 3 cheeses, 3 meats, smoked salmon, and fruit. Basement bar opens at 9pm. Open Tues.-Sun. 9am-2am, Mon. 5pm-2am.

SIGHTS

Between Eastern and Western Berlin

For decades a gateway to nowhere, the **Brandenburger Tor** (Brandenburg Gate) is the structure that most commonly symbolizes the future of Berlin and a united Germany. It is now the center point of the city, opening east onto Unter den Linden (S-Bahn: Unter den Linden). Built during the reign of Friedrich Wilhelm II as a symbol of peace, the gate became a symbol of East-West division as a locked door embedded in the Berlin Wall. The gate was not actually opened until December 22, 1989, more than a month after the wall came down. The **Berlin Wall** itself is a dead dinosaur, with only fossil remains still visible. Fenced in overnight on August 13, 1961, the 160-km-long wall separated families and friends, sometimes running through people's homes. Portions of it are preserved near the *Hauptbahnhof* and the Reichstag. The longest remaining bit is the brightly painted **East Side Gallery** (S-Bahn: Hauptbahnhof), the world's largest open-air gallery.

The **Haus am Checkpoint Charlie,** Friedrichstr. 44 (U-bahn: Kochstr. or bus #129), narrates the history of the Wall through film and photo. Upstairs there are exhibits on human rights, as well as artistic renderings of the Wall. (Open daily 9am-10pm. DM7.50, students DM4.50.)

Western Berlin

The Reichstag, Tiergarten, and the Ku'damm Just to the north of the Brandenburger Tor sits the **Reichstag** building, the once and future seat of unified Germany's parliament. In August 1914, Karl Liebknecht's famous "Nein!" was one of a few votes in its halls against the impending First World War. In 1918, after Kaiser Wilhelm II had abdicated, The Social Democrat Philip Scheidemann proclaimed the German Republic from one of its windows. His move turned out to be wise, since 2 hours later Karl Liebknecht announced a German Socialist Republic down the street in **Palast der Republik.** Civil war conditions in Berlin and much of the rest of Germany resulted. In February 1933, just one month after Hitler became chancellor, the Reichstag mysteriously burnt down. Hitler used the Reichstag fire to woo support for the infamous Enabling Act, managing to convince the "moderate" parties in parliament to help him become legal dictator of Germany. At the moment, the Reichstag is not a government building, although the major political parties have opened offices here.The lush **Tiergarten,** a vast landscaped park formerly used by the Prussian monarchs for hunting, spreads itself over the northeast corner of western Berlin. In the heart of the Tiergarten, the **Siegessäule** (victory column) celebrates Prussia's campaign against France in 1870. In 1938, the Nazis moved the monument from its spot in front of the Reichstag to increase its height and make it more impressive. Climb the 285 steps to the top for a panorama of the city. (Open April-Nov. Mon. 1-5:30pm, Tues.-Sun. 9am-5:30pm. DM1.50, students DM1.) The **Soviet Army Memorial** (yes, you're still in Western Berlin) stands at the end of Str. des 17. Juni, flanked by a pair of giant toy tanks.

A sobering reminder of the devastation caused by World War II, the shattered **Kaiser-Wilhelm-Gedächtniskirche** now houses an exhibit dedicated to peace which has lost some of its didactic force amidst the giddy neon of the Ku'damm and the Europa Center. (Exhibit open Tues.-Sat. 10am-4pm.) The renowned **Zoo,** entrance at Budapesterstr. 34 (the Elephant Gate), across from the tourist office in the Europa Center, houses an exotic collection of fauna as well as the spectacular **Aquarium,** Budapesterstr. 32. (Zoo open daily 9am-6pm; Oct.16-Feb. daily 9am-5pm; March-daily April 9am-5:30pm. Aquarium open daily 9am-6pm. To zoo DM9, students DM7.50, ages 3-15 DM4.50. To aquarium DM8, students and children DM4. Comprehensive admission DM13.50, students DM11.50, ages 3-15 DM6.50.)

Schöneberg and Charlottenburg South of Nollendorfpl. is the **Rathaus Schöneberg,** where West Berlin's city government convened. On June 26, 1963, 1½ million Berliners swarmed the streets to hear John F. Kennedy reassure them of the Allies' continued commitment to the city 15 years after the 11-month Berlin Airlift. Kennedy's speech ended with the now-famous words, "All free men, wherever they may live, are citizens of Berlin. And therefore, as a free man, I take pride in the words *Ich bin ein Berliner.*" Not too far away is **Fehrbelliner Platz** (U-Bahn: Fehrbelliner Pl.), an example of Nazi architecture. The huge, prison-like blocks were meant to be model apartment houses; try to imagine a city full of them.

Schloß Charlottenburg, the vast baroque palace built by Friedrich I for his second wife, stands on the western edge of town amid Baroque landscaping. The ornate **Knobelsdorff Wing** is the most lavish of the palace suites. Take U-Bahn #2 to "Sophie-Charlotte-Pl." or bus #145 from Bahnhof Zoo. (Open Tues.-Sun. 9am-5pm. To palace complex DM6, students DM3. Knobelsdorff Wing alone DM2.50, students DM1.50, under 14 free.) Seek out the **Palace Gardens,** with their carefully planted rows of trees, small lake, footbridge, and fountains (open Tues.-Sun. 6am-9pm) which surround the **Royal Mausoleum** (open Tues.-Sun. 9am-5pm); **Belvedere,** an 18th-century residence housing a porcelain exhibit; and the **Schinkel Pavilion,** with furniture designed by Schinkel. (Open Tues.-Sun. 9am-5pm.)

Kreuzberg and Plötzensee Indispensable for a sense of Berlin's counterculture is a visit to **Kreuzberg,** an area loaded with cafés and bars. For its more respectable face, get off at U-Bahn #6 or 7: Mehringdamm and wander around; Bergmannstr. features an especially large number of old buildings and second-hand shops. At night many bohemian and punk clubs overflow onto Yorckstr., which heads west from its intersection with Mehringdamm. Other good streets are the more radical Oranienstr. (U-Bahn: Kottbusser Tor) and the east end of Kreuzberg, (U-Bahn: Schlesisches Tor), which houses Balkan and Turkish neighborhoods.

A chilling monument to the victims of Nazism, the **Gedenkstätte Plötzensee Memorial** exhibits documents recording death sentences of "enemies of the people" (including the officers who attempted to assassinate Hitler in 1944) in the former execution chambers of the Third Reich. The stone urn in front of the memorial contains soil from Nazi concentration camps. Take bus #123 from S-Bahn: Tiergarten to "Goerdelerdamm" and follow Hüttingpfad 200m away from the Kanal, along a tall brick wall. (Open daily 8am-6pm; Oct. and Feb. 8:30am-5:30pm; Nov. and Jan. 8:30am-4:30pm; Dec. 8:30am-4pm. Free.)

Eastern Berlin

An excellent and easy way to get a quick overview of most of the sights in Eastern Berlin is by **bus #100,** which takes the scenic route from Zoo to Alexanderpl., going down Unter den Linden. (Standard Berlin rapid transit ticket valid.)

Unter den Linden and Gendarmenmarkt The Brandenburg Gate opens eastward onto **Unter den Linden,** once one of Europe's best-known boulevards and the spine of old Berlin. All but the most famous buildings have been destroyed, but farther down many 18th-century structures have been restored to their original Prussian splendor. Past Friedrichstr., the first massive building on your left is the **Deutsche Staatsbibliothek** (Library), with a pleasant café inside. Beyond the library is the **Humboldt Universität,** once one of the finest in the world. Next door, the old **Neue Wache** (New Guard House), designed by the renowned Prussian architect Friedrich Schinkel, is today the somber **Monument to the Victims of Fascism and Militarism.** Buried inside are urns filled with earth from the Nazi concentration camps of Buchenwald and Mauthausen and from the battlefields of Stalingrad, El Alamein, and Normandy. The honor guard in front changes on the hour, with the full ceremony on Wednesdays at 2:30pm. Across the way is **Bebelplatz,** the site of Nazi book burnings, now named for the old Social Democratic Party leader August Bebel. The building with the curved façade is the **Alte Bibulosity.** The most striking of the monumental buildings is the **Zeughaus,** now the **Museum of German History.** From the museum you can enter the courtyard and see the tormented faces of Andreas Schlüter's *Dying Warriors.*

Berlin's most impressive ensemble of 18th-century buildings is a few blocks south of Unter den Linden at **Gendarmenmarkt,** graced by the twin cathedrals of the **Deutscher Dom** and the **Französischer Dom.** Enclosing the far end of the square, the classical **Schauspielhaus,** designed by Schinkel, is Berlin's most elegant concert space and hosts many international orchestras and classical performers. Destroyed by an air attack in 1945, it was painstakingly reconstructed and reopened in 1984.

Lustgarten, the Museumsinsel, and Alexanderplatz

As it crosses the bridge, Unter den Linden opens out onto the **Museumsinsel** (Museum Island). To the left is the **Altes Museum,** with a big polished granite bowl in front, and the multiple domed **Berliner Dom** (Berlin Cathedral). Severely damaged by an air raid in 1944, the cathedral has just emerged from 20 years of reconstruction. (Open daily 9am-7:30pm. Free.) Behind the Altes Museum lie 3 other enormous museums and the ruins (now being restored) of a fourth. At the center of this jungle of pediments, porticoes, and colonnades is the **Lustgarten** park, formerly Marx-Engels Platz.

Across the Liebknecht Brücke, in the middle of a park stands a park and "conceptual memorial" consisting of steel tablets engraved with images of worker struggle and protest surrounding a twin statue of Marx and Engels. The park and the street behind it used to be collectively known as the **Marx-Engels Forum;** the park has yet to be renamed, while the street is now called **Rathausstr.**

On the other side of the Museumsinsel, Unter den Linden leads into the teeming, concrete **Alexanderplatz.** This atrociously ugly square was meant to be a showpiece for socialism; construction has begun to remove the edge from the buildings, but it's unclear whether the revamped version will be any more satisfying. Friends from both Germanies often meet at the plaza's **Weltzeituhr,** the international clock, but the undisputed landmark of the district is the Death-Star-esque **Fernsehturm** (television tower), the tallest structure in Berlin. (Open daily 9am-midnight; open the 2nd and 4th Tues. of each month 1pm-midnight only. Last entry 11:30pm. Expect a 1-hr. wait. To tower DM5, students, seniors, and children DM3.)

Nikolaiviertel and Scheuenviertel-Oranienburger Str.

The **Marienkirche,** a graceful 15th-century church, stands on the wide open plaza behind the *Fernsehturm.* Nearby is the gabled **Rotes Rathaus,** Old Berlin's famous red-brick town hall. Behind the *Rathaus,* the twin spires of the **Nikolaikirche** mark Berlin's oldest building. Inside the 13th-century structure, a small museum documents the early history of the city. (Open Tues.-Fri. 9am-5pm, Sat. 9am-6pm, Sun. 10am-5pm.) The church gives the surrounding **Nikolaiviertel,** a carefully reconstructed *Altstadt,* its name; among the two dozen historic buildings are the **Knoblauchhaus** and the Rococo **Ephraim-Palais.**

Northwest of Alexanderpl. is the **Scheuenviertel,** the former ghetto of Berlin. It was later home to the Jews who fled the Eastern European pogroms only to end up in Hitler's concentration camps, and it contains many reminders of Berlin's former Jewish community, once the most emancipated and cultured in the world. It later became a showpiece for the East German government; many buildings have been restored, and some new constructions have a flair unusual for Berlin. The area has also become a center of the squatter scene, with a corresponding amount of cultural and café life. Down Oranienburgerstr. at no. 30 is the burnt-out shell of Berlin's major **synagogue,** once the center of West European Judaism. Torched by Nazis during *Reichkristallnacht* (November 9, 1938), the building is still being restored. The façade is nonetheless gorgeous. A sign on the side reads "Never forget this."

Prenzlauer Berg, Elsewhere in Mitte, and Treptow Take Oranienburgerstr. all the way to Friedrichstr. and bear left to reach the **Brecht-Haus Berlin,** Chausseestr. 125, where Bertolt Brecht lived and worked from 1953 to 1956. If you understand German you should take the guided tour, given in a flamboyant Brechtian style. (Tours every ½hr. Open Tues.-Wed. and Fri. 10-11:30am, Thurs. 10-11:30am and 5-6:30pm, Sat. 9:30am-1:30pm.) Just before Brecht's house, the **Dorotheenstädtischer Friedhof** contains the graves of a host of German luminaries, including Brecht, Fichte, and Hegel. (Open daily 9am-6pm.)

East of Oranienburgerstr. is **Prenzlauer Berg,** a former working-class district largely neglected by East Germany's reconstruction efforts. Many of its old buildings are falling apart; others still have shell holes and embedded bullets from WWII. The result is the charm of age and graceful decay, slightly less charming for phoneless local residents with bad plumbing. Home to cafés, restaurants, and several museums, restored **Husemannstraße** is especially worthy of a stroll. The area's population belies the aging architecture; there are heaps of students, artists, cafés, clubs, and communes, but the city government's anti-commune policy is in danger of destroying this counter-cultural renaissance.

The powerful **Sowjetische Ehrenmal** (Soviet War Memorial) is a mammoth promenade built with marble taken from Hitler's Chancellery (S-Bahn: Treptower Park). The Soviets dedicated the site in 1948, honoring the soldiers of the Red Army who fell in the "Great Patriotic War." The memorial sits in the middle of **Treptower Park,** a spacious wood ideal for morbid picnics. The neighborhood adjoining the park is known for its pleasant waterside cafés and handsome suburban mansions.

Museums

With 85 museums, Berlin is one of the world's great museum cities. Four major complexes—Charlottenburg, Dahlem, Museumsinsel, and Tiergarten—form the hub of the city's museum culture; smaller museums deal with every subject imaginable. The Charlottenburg complex is closed Friday, Museumsinsel Monday and Tuesday, and the Dahlem and Tiergarten on Monday. While permanent collections are generally free, special exhibits can be expensive (DM6-10); bring a student ID.

Pergamonmuseum, Kupfergraben, Museumsinsel. One of the world's great ancient history museums. The scale of the exhibits is mind-boggling: the Babylonian Ishtar Gate (575 BC), the Roman Market Gate of Miletus, and one of the ancient wonders of the world, the majestic Pergamon Altar of Zeus (180 BC). The museum also has extensive collections of Greek, Islamic, and Far Eastern art. Open Wed.-Sun. 10am-6pm; architecture halls (including altar) only open Mon.-Tues. Last entry 30min. before closing. DM4, students and seniors DM2. Tours of Pergamon Altar at 11am and 3pm.

Alte Nationalgalerie, Bodestr., Museumsinsel. Good collection of expressionism, including Feininger, Kokoschka, and the Brücke school. Open Wed.-Sun. 10am-6pm. DM4, students DM2.

Bodemuseum, Monbijoubrücke, Museumsinsel. World-class Egyptian art exhibit, as well as late Gothic wood sculptures, early Christian art, and an ancient history exhibit. Open Wed.-Sun. 10am-6pm. DM4, seniors and students DM2.

Dahlem Museum, Arnimallee 23-27 and Lansstr. 8. U-Bahn: Dahlem-Dorf. Huge complex of 7 museums, each worth a ½-day. Particularly superb are the **Gemäldegalerie** (painting Gallery), a collection of Italian, German, Dutch, and Flemish Old Masters (including 26 Rembrandts), and the **Museum für Indische und Islamische Kunst.** Open Tues.-Fri. 9am-5pm, Sat.-Sun. 10am-5pm. Free.

Schloß Charlottenburg, Spandauer Damm (U-Bahn #2: Sophie-Charlotte-Pl. or bus #145) contains several museums. The **Ägyptisches Museum,** across Spandauer Damm from the castle's main entrance, houses a fascinating collection of ancient Egyptian art, including the 3300-year-old bust of Queen Nefertiti. Also check out the **Antikensammlung** and the **Galerie der Romantik.** All open Sat.-Thurs. 9am-5pm. Free.

Reichstag Museum, Pl. der Republik, near Brandenburg Gate. Bus #100 from Bahnhof Zoo. The huge Wilhelmine building is half the spectacle; its oversized plaza, where angry crowds of Weimar Germans threatened the Republic, was perfect for Reunification Day celebrations. Contains an absorbing exhibit on German history from 1800 to 1949. Open Tues.-Sun. 10am-5pm. Free.

Martin-Gropius Bau, Stresemannstr. 110. S-Bahn: Anhalter Bahnhof. Numerous museums and exhibits including the world-famous **Metropolis** exhibition of modern art; the **Topographie des Terrors,** which describes the development of fascism in Germany (open Tues.-Sun. 10am-6pm, free) and **Juden in Berlin,** with documents, pictures, and paintings about and by Berlin's Jewish community. Most exhibits open Tues.-Sun. 10am-8pm. DM10, students DM5.

Bauhaus Archiv-Museum für Gestaltung, Klingenhöferstr. 13-14. Take bus #129 to Lützowpl. Designed by Walter Gropius, this shimmering modern building displays exemplary works by Bauhaus members (among them Kandinsky and Klee). Open Wed.-Mon. 10am-5pm. DM3, students DM1.

Brücke Museum, Bussardsteig 9. From the Zoo, take bus #115 to Pücklerstr. at Clayallee. The Expressionist museum in Berlin, with works by the German expressionist Brücke school, which flourished in Dresden and Berlin from 1909 to 1913. Open Wed.-Mon. 11am-5pm. DM4, students DM2.

Deutsches Historisches Museum, Unter den Linden 2, Zeughaus. Across from the Museumsinsel. Once a paean to the advent of socialism, now the site of provocative multi-media exhibitions on recent German history. Open Thurs.-Tues. 10am-6pm. DM4, students DM2.

Lesben-Archiv Spinnboden, Burdgorfstr. Lesbian history archive and information center. Open Mon.-Thurs. 2-6pm, Fri. 5-9pm. DM5.

ENTERTAINMENT

Berlin is *wild,* all night, every night. The best guides to theater, cinema, nightlife, and the extremely active musical scene are the biweekly magazines *Tip* and *Zitty.* The monthly *Berlin Program* lists more "cultural" events and includes good theater information. *Berlin von hinten* (Berlin from the rear) is a guide to gay life.

Nightlife

In Western Berlin, the best places to look are the **Savignypl., Schöneberg, Wilmersdorf, Kreuzberg,** and **Scheunenviertel** districts. Mainstream activity centers around 2 areas to the north and south of the Ku'damm. The north is a bit more inviting; the middle point is **Savignyplatz** and it includes Grolmanstr., Knesebeckstr., Bleibtreustr., and Schlütterstr., as well as Steinpl. South of the Ku'damm, the area between Uhlandstr. and Olivaer Platz is littered with crowded late-night cafés. Traditionally, the social nexus of bisexual, gay, and lesbian life has centered around the **Nollendorfplatz**—Christopher Isherwood lived at Nollendorfstr. 17 while writing his collection of stories *Goodbye to Berlin,* later adapted as the Broadway musical *Cabaret.* A marble pink triangel plaque outside the Nollendorfpl. U-Bahn station reads "Beaten to death; abandoned to death," and remembers the thousands of bisexuals, gays, lesbians deported to concentration camps from the station. The **Kreuzberg** *Szene* is near Viktoria Park, along Yorckstr. and Gneisenaustr. This scene is pretty intense, with radically alternative bars along Oranienstr, between U-Bahn 1: Kottbusser Tor and U-Bahn 1: Görlitzer Bahnhof; it is not well lit at night and can be unsafe for women and solo travelers.

The clubs which have been sprouting in Eastern Berlin are giving their counterparts a run for their money. Some of the more interesting bars abound in the Scheunenviertel. The Prenzlauer Berg area also boasts some fun, interesting places. The café and bars of the east tend to have a grittier, more vital feel to them and attract an exciting mixture of people. Most of the listings in *Let's Go* lean toward the alternative; if you want a beer hall, go to Munich.

Metropol, Nollendorfpl. 5 (tel. 216 41 22). U-Bahn: Nollendorfpl., or night buses N19, N29, or N85. Still the place to go. Nude statues fraternize on the façade. Live or disco music. Cover about DM10. Music until 4am. Open Fri.-Sat. from 10pm.

M, Goltzstr. 33 (tel. 216 70 92). U-Bahn 7: Eisenacherstr, One of the more interesting Schöneberg bars, slightly wild late at night. Black is eternally "in." Open Sun.-Thurs. 8:30am-midnight, Fri.-Sat. 8:30am-3am.

Quasimodo, Kantstr. 12a (tel. 312 80 86). A basement pub with live jazz and rock (frequent big names) and a lively crowd. Open daily from 8pm; concerts usually begin at 10pm. Cover free to DM30. Concert tickets available daily from 5pm or at Kant Kasse ticket service (tel. 313 45 54).

Ex, Mehringhof, Gneisenaustr. 2a. A Kneipe in a courtyard run by a famed collective; hangout for the people from the independent scene. Piped-in music and punk rock. Open Mon.-Thurs. 11am-1am, Fri.-Sun. 8pm-1am.

Alibi, Oranienstr. 166. U-Bahn 1 or 8: Kottbusser Tor. Crowded bar with offbeat regulars, up to something at all hours. Open Sun.-Thurs. 10pm-2am, later Fri.-Sat.

Café Wirtschaftswunder, Yorckstr. 81 (tel. 786 99 99). U-Bahn 7 or S-Bahn 1 or 2: Yorckstr, Colorful Kreuzberg café with tiny tables virtually overlapping. Name ironically refers to Germany's Economic Miracle. Serves drinks daily 4pm-4am.

Tacheles, Oranienburgerstr. 53-56 (tel. (9) 282 61 85). U-Bahn: Oranienburger Tor. Huge alternative art commune with a busy bar. The squatters here have kept the party going through some crazy incidents over the past 4 years. Live music and a dance club playing lots of house Sat. Open daily around 4pm-late.

Franz-Klub, Schönhauser Allee 36-39 (tel. 448 55 67). U-Bahn 2: Eberswalder Str. Another favorite among Prenzlauer Bergers and Wessies in the know. Live music or performances; cover varies.

Lipstick, Richard-Wagner-Platz 5. U-Bahn 7: Richard-Wagner-Platz. A teeming lesbian dance hall, the hottest in the city. Men (mostly gay) can creep in Tues., Thurs., or Sun. nights and the first Fri. of the month. Open daily from 10pm.

Anderes Ufer, Hauptstr. 157 (tel. 784 15 78). U-Bahn 7:Kleistpark. Stylish bi/gay/lesbian mixed café with rotating art exhibits. Open daily 11am-2am.

Concerts, Opera, and Dance

Berlin reaches its musical zenith during the fabulous **Berliner Festwochen,** lasting almost the entire month of September and drawing the world's best orchestras and soloists, and the **Berliner Jazztage** in November. For more information on all these events (and tickets, which sell out far in advance), write to Berliner Festspiele, Budapesterstr. 48-50, 10787 Berlin 30 (tel. 25 48 92 50; open daily noon-6pm). In mid-July, **Bachtage** (Bach Days) offer an intense week of classical music; every Saturday night in August **Sommer Festspiele** turns the Ku'damm into a multifaceted concert hall with punk, steel drum, and folk groups competing for attention.

In the monthly pamphlet *Kultur in Berlin* and *Berliner Programm,* as well as the biweekly magazines *Tip* and *Zitty,* you'll find notice of concerts in the courtyard of the old Arsenal, on the **Schloßinsel Köpenick** (Castle Island), or in the parks. Tickets for the *Philharmonie* and the *Oper* are often impossible to acquire through conventional channels. Instead, try standing out in front before performances with a small sign saying, *"Suche Karte"* (I seek a ticket).

Philharmonie, Matthäikirchstr. 1 (tel. 25 48 80). Take bus #129 from Ku'damm to "Potsdamerstr." and walk 3 blocks north. The big yellow building is as acoustically perfect within as it is unconventional without, and the Berliner Philharmoniker—led for decades by the late Herbert von Karajan—may be the world's finest orchestra. It's nigh impossible to get a seat; check an hour before concerts or write far in advance. Sadly, the Philharmonie is often closed during the summer months. Ticket office open Mon.-Fri. 3:30-6pm, Sat.-Sun. and holidays 11am-2pm.

Deutsche Staatsoper, Unter den Linden 7 (tel. (9) 200 47 62). East Berlin's leading opera company. Ballet and classical music, too. Box office open Mon.-Sat. noon-6pm, Sun. 2-6pm. Tickets DM18-35.

Deutsche Oper Berlin, Bismarckstr. 35 (tel. 341 02 49). U-Bahn #1: Deutsche Oper. Berlin's best opera. Box office open Mon.-Sat.11:30am-5:30pm, Sun. 10am-

2pm and 1hr. before performances. 10min. before performances, you can get student discounts of up to 50% off. Tickets DM10-125.

Tanzfabrik, Möckernstr. 68 (tel. 786 58 61). U-Bahn #1 or 7: Möckernbrücke. Modern dance performances and a center for dance workshops. Ticket office open Mon.-Thurs. 10am-1pm and 5-8pm. Down the alley and to your left, up 3 flights of stairs. Tickets DM15. Occasional weekend performances at either 8 or 8:30pm.

Theater and Film

Berlin has a lively English-language theater scene; look for listings in *Tip* or *Zitty* that say *"in englischer Sprache"* next to them. On any night in Berlin, you can choose from 100 different films, many in the original language. ("O. F." next to a movie listing means "original version"; "O.m.U." means original with German subtitles. Everything else is dubbed.) Check *Tip, Zitty,* or the subway posters. There is an international **Film Festival** (late Feb.-March) and a **Theater Festival** (May).

Das Schiller Theater, Bismarckstr. 110 (tel. 312 65 05). U-Bahn: Ernst-Reuter-Pl. The most respected theater in the country; with occasional inspired works. Box office open daily 9am-noon. Tickets DM10-45.

Deutsches Theater, Schumannstr. 13a (tel. 28 44 10). U- or S-Bahn: Friedrichstr. The best theater in the country. Innovative productions of both classics and newer works. The **Kammerspiel des Deutschen Theaters** (tel. 284 42 26) has smaller productions. Tickets DM15-40; 50% student discount often available.

Maxim Gorki Theater, Am Festungsgraben 2 (tel. 208 27 83), just off Unter den Linden. Excellent contemporary theater. Box office open Mon.-Sat. 1-6:30pm, Sun. 3-6:30pm. Tickets DM5-25.

Die Distel, Friedrichstr. 101 (tel. 200 47 04). A cabaret of political satire. Box office open Mon.-Fri. noon-6pm, Sat.-Sun. 2hr. before performance.

Filmtheater Babylon, Rosa-Luxemburg-Str. 30. Classics and art films often in original language. DM8, students DM7.

Kino-Arsenal, Welserstr. 25. Berlin's best repertory film house. DM9.

■ Near Berlin: Potsdam

Potsdam, city of Frederick the Great and get-away spot for the Kaisers, is an essential foray from Berlin. S-Bahn #3 runs directly from Berlin-Zoo to both Potsdam-Stadt, in the town center, and Potsdam-West, by the palaces. Berlin rapid transit tickets are valid on the S-Bahn and for public transportation within Potsdam.

The 600-acre **Sanssouci Park** houses 4 baroque palaces and countless exotic pavilions. The largest of the quartet, the **Neues Palais,** was built by Frederick the Great while pouting over several unsuccessful wars. Inside is the 19th-century Grottensaal, a reception room whose ribbed walls glitter with seashells and semi-precious stones. At the opposite end of the park stands **Schloß Sanssouci,** where Fred used to escape his wife and other troubles. Next door, the fabulous **Bildergalerie** houses works by Caravaggio, van Dyck, and Rubens beneath its gilded ceiling. Romantic **Schloß Charlottenhof** melts into its landscaped gardens and grape arbors. Overlooking the park from the north, the pseudo-Italian **Orangerie-Schloß** is famous for its 67 dubious Raphael imitations and for the **Neue Kammern** (royal guest chambers). The most bizarre of the park's pavilions are its "oriental" houses; the **Chinesisches Teehaus** is a gold-plated opium dream, complete with rooftop Buddha. (Park open 9am-sundown; free. Palaces open 9am-5pm; Oct. and Feb.-March 9am-4pm; Nov.-Jan. 9am-3pm. Neue Kammern closed Fri. All palaces closed 1st and 3rd Mon. of each month. To each palace DM6, students DM3. Compulsory German tours of Sanssouci, Neue Kammern, Schloß Charlottenhof—in others you can wander on your own.)

The **Brandenburger Tor,** a less famous cousin of Berlin's Brandenburg Gate, sits awkwardly in the middle of Luisenplatz. **Schloß Cecilienhof** exhibits the **Potsdam Treaty,** signed at the Palace in 1945. (Open daily 9am-5:15pm; Nov.-April daily 9am-4:15pm; closed 4th Mon. of each month. DM3, students and seniors DM2, under 6 free.) From here, **Brandenburger Str.** leads down to the 19th-century **Peter-Pauls-Kirche.** One block before the church, Friedrich-Ebertstr. heads left to the red-brick **Dutch Quarter.** The sumptuous if somewhat decrepit mansions along **Hegelallee** hint at Potsdam's bygone grandeur. Fritz Lang made *Metropolis* and Marlene Dietrich got her first break in what today is known as **Filmstadt Babelsberg,** August-Bebelstr. 26-52 (tel. (0331) 72 27 55). There are plans to renew production, but now the old ghost towns and costume closets are the main attractions. (Open daily 9am-6pm. Last entry 4:30pm. DM11, students DM8.)

The **tourist office,** Friedrich-Ebertstr. 5 (tel. (0331) 211 00), is near the "Pl. der Einheit" or the "Alter Markt" tram station. The office provides info on local events, a modest map, and private rooms. (Accommodations tel. (0331) 233 85. Rooms DM15-25/person. Bungalows DM35-50/person. Open Mon.-Fri. 9am-8pm, Sat.-Sun. 9am-6pm.)

■■■ DRESDEN

No matter where you go in Dresden, you won't be able to forget the fact that the "Florence on the Elbe," a city of minimal military importance but incredible cultural value, was incinerated by Allied bombers during WWII, claiming over 50,000 lives. For 40 years, Dresden lived in the shadow of its former glory and great destruction. Unlike Munich or Hamburg, where reconstruction quickly obscured the wounds of war, Dresden remains scarred. Yet contemporary Dresden is staging a comeback; reunification brought with it the money and will to rebuild the city in all its former glory. Sadly, it also seems to be teeming with neo-Nazis, who have designated the city as the capital of their movement. Consequently, any conspicuous non-Germans should exercise appropriate caution.

ORIENTATION AND PRACTICAL INFORMATION

The capital of Saxon, Dresden stands magnificently on the Elbe River about 80km northwest of the Czech Republic and 180km south of Berlin on the train line to Prague. As usual in Eastern Germany, huge numbers of streets and public places have had their names changed recently; be wary of any map published before 1991.

Tourist Office: Fremdenverkehrsbüro, Pragerstr. 10/11 (tel. 495 50 25). Turn left out of the front door of the Hauptbahnhof, cross Wienerpl. and walk straight down Pragerstr. 5min.; the office is on the right. Rooms, maps, theater tickets, and tours. Open Mon.-Sat. 9am-8pm, Sun. 9am-noon; Nov.-Feb. Mon.-Sat. 9am-6pm, Sun. 9am-noon.

Currency Exchange: Deutsche Verkehrs Bank, in the Hauptbahnhof. Open Mon.-Fri. 7:30am-7:30pm, Sat. 8am-4pm. More banks on Pragerstr.

American Express: Köpckestr. 15, (tel. 566 28 65), in the Bellevue Hotel across the Elbe from the Opera. Open Mon.-Fri. 10am-noon and 1-5:30pm, Sat. 9am-noon.

Post Office: Hauptpostamt currently fills several trailers on Hertha-Lindner-Str.; while renovation continues, the actual office is in Dresden-Neustadt at Königbrückerstr. 21/29, 01099 Dresden (tel. 584 40). Open Mon.-Fri. 8am-6pm, Sat. 8am-noon. **Postal code:** O-8010.

Telephones: At the post offices. **City code:** 0351.

Trains: From **Dresden Hauptbahnhof** (the main station), travelers shoot off to Warsaw, Paris, Kraków, Berlin, Budapest, Copenhagen, Munich, and Frankfurt. Trams #3, 11, and 26 connect it to **Dresden Neustadt** station on the other side of the Elbe. Some trains to destinations within Eastern Germany stop only at Neustadt. Watch out; the two stations look exactly the same. Both have lockers.

Public Transportation: Extensive but noisy. As you board, punch your ticket (DM1, day pass DM5, week pass DM12).

Hitchhiking: Mitfahrzentrale Dresden, Nürnbergerstr. 57 (tel. 463 60 60), matches rides and drivers. Open Mon.-Fri. 10am-7pm, Sat. noon-2pm.

Crisis Lines: Frauen in Not (tel. 33 22 33) is for women in emergency situations. **Ausländer in Bedrängis** (tel. 484 55 08) is for victims of racially motivated hate crimes.
Emergencies: Ambulance: tel. 115. **Fire:** tel. 112. **Police:** tel. 110.

ACCOMMODATIONS, CAMPING, AND FOOD

Arrive early and expect a struggle. Contact the tourist office for private rooms. (Singles DM20-30. Doubles DM40-100. DM5 fee.) To reach the **Jugendherberge Dresden (HI)**, Hübnerstr. 11 (tel. 471 06 67; fax 472 89 59), take tram #5 (direction "Südvorstadt") or #11 (direction "Plauen"): Nürnberger Platz, continue down Nürnbergerstr. and turn right onto Hübnerstr.; the hostel is at the first corner on your right. From the Hauptbahnhof, walk down 2 blocks on Fritz-Löffler-Str. turn right on Reichenbach, which becomes Altenzellerstr., go about 4 blocks, and turn left onto Hübnerstr. The 73-bed hostel was built by the sewing machine magnate Isaac Singer. (DM19.50, over 26 DM23.) **Jugendherberge Oberloschwitz (HI)**, Sierksstr. 33 (tel. and fax 366 72), has a beautiful location worth the hour-long trip. Take tram#10 (direction "Laubegast") or 26 (direction "Johannstadt"): Fetscherpl.; switch to tram #1 (direction "Tolkewitz"): Schillerpl.; then walk across the Elbe to Körnerpl. and ride the *Schwebebahn* (DM2.50; the hill train—not the *Standseilbahn*) up to Sierkstr. (Reception open 4-8pm. DM16, over 26 DM19. Phone first.) **Campingplatz Mockritz** Borderitzer Str. 30 (tel. 471 82 26), is also an hour away from the *Hauptbahnhof:* take the bus (direction "Moritzburg" or "Moritzburg/Radeburg") to "Sonnenland." (Reception open until 10pm. Camping DM10/person, DM6/tent. Bungalows with kitchens DM20.)

Restaurants open and close daily in Dresden, as the new market mentality shuffles the status quo.The cheapest seats are at supermarkets or *Imbiß* stands on Pragerstr. There's a **Karstadt** supermarket on Pragerstr. (Open Mon.-Wed. 9am-6:30pm, Thurs. 9am-8:30pm, Fri. 9am-6:30pm, Sat. 9am-2pm, 1st Sat. in month 9am-4pm.)

SIGHTS AND ENTERTAINMENT

The extravagant collection of Augustus the Strong, and the magnificent private gallery he built to house it, the **Zwinger,** once rivaled the Louvre in Paris. Today the **Alte Meister** collection, centered around Raphael's Sistine *Madonna*, remains one of Germany's best. The **Porzellansammlung** traces the history of Dresden's famous porcelain. (Open Fri.-Wed. 10am-6pm. DM3, students and seniors DM1.50.) The northern wing of the palace was designed by Gottfried Semper, revolutionary activist and master architect.

Semper's famed Opera House, the **Semper-Oper,** echoes the robust style of the palace wing. Its painstaking restoration has made it Dresden's major attraction. Near the Zwinger lie the ruins of the **Palace of Saxony's Electors and Kings,** leveled by firebombing on February 13, 1945. The lighter stonework is all spanking new, evidence of the speed with which restoration has been proceeding since reunification. A private walkway connects the palace to the **Katholische Hofkirche** (Catholic Cathedral), originally the royal family's private chapel. Adorning the alley leading to the main entrance of the Catholic cathedral is the **Fürstenzug** (Procession of Kings), a porcelain pictorial tracing the history of Saxony.

From the Catholic cathedral, the 16th-century **Brühlsche Terrasse** offers a prime photo opportunity of the River Elbe (best at sunset). Turn right at the end of the terrace to reach the **Albertinum,** another of Dresden's fabulous museum complexes. The **Gemäldegalerie der Neuen Meister's** small collection of Gaugins and Monets pales beside the power and intensity of pre-war paintings by local Jewish and antifascist artists. (Open Fri.-Wed. 10am-6pm. DM7, students and seniors DM3.50.) The **Grünes Gewölbe** dazzles with priceless coins and gem-studded treasures. At the end of WWII, the Soviet Union snatched the collection for "cataloguing" and only returned it in 1955 after West German protests. In all fairness, considerable restoration was done, and the Germans did their share of art looting during the war in Russia as well. So there. (Open Fri.-Tues. 9am-5pm, Wed. 9am-6pm. Long lines, so come early. DM5, students and seniors DM2.50.) From the Albertinum, walk down Neumarkt to the **Frauenkirche,** once Germany's most splendid Protestant church, now overscored by trees and vegetation. The ruins were intended to remain as a memorial to the destroyed city; there's now talk of building a hotel on the spot. The first Protestant communion took place in the **Protestant Kreuzkirche** on the Altmarkt. You might even catch the **Kreuzchor,** one of the world's most famous boys' choirs. Jog south to the start of Ernst-Thälmann-Str., where the 18th-century neoclassical **Landhaus** houses the **Museum für Geschichte der Stadt Dresden.** The exhibit contains some numbing photos from 1945. (Open Sat.-Thurs. 10am-6pm. DM2, students and seniors DM1.)

Paradoxically, Dresden's **Neustadt** is now the oldest part of the city, since it escaped the worst of the bombing. In front of the Catholic church, the picturesque Georgij-Dimitroff Brücke spans the Elbe to the **Goldener Reitter,** a gold-plated statue of Friedrich August II (after fathering over 365 children, he was renamed Augustus the Strong). The pedestrian **Hauptstraße,** a tree-lined avenue of shops and restaurants, promenades from the river bank to **Albertplatz** (formerly Platz der Einheit) still surrounded by handsome 19th-century mansions. Vonnegut aficionados can take tram #9 (direction "Friedrichstadt") from the Hauptbahnhof to the last stop to reach the **Schlachthofringe** (slaughterhouses), little-changed since they were used as a camp for prisoners of war.

For centuries, Dresden has been a focal point for theater, opera, and music. The incredible **Semper Oper** has premiered many of Strauss and Wagner's greatest, and for German-speakers, Dresden offers all kinds of drama. With the availability of American movies and the disappearance of state-sponsored 25pf tickets, many locals have sworn off the arts for a while, making tickets a bit easier to come by. **Schauspielhaus,** Ostra-Allee 3 (tel. 484 25 67; box office 484 24 29), produces classics from Goethe's *Faust* to Brecht's *Three Penny Opera.* Satirical cabaret sneers at the **Dresdener BREttL,** Maternistr. 17 (tel. 495 41 23). For those who don't speak, the **Podium,** Hauptstr. 11 (tel. 532 66), offers good mime. (Phone for dates and times. Do they mime on the phone?) **Die Tonne,** Tzschirnerpl. 3 (tel. 495 13 54) grooves to great jazz. (Performances most nights at 9pm. Cover DM5-12.) The local magazine **SAX,** DM2.50 at any newsstand, lists local events.

■ Near Dresden

Take the train (or a Weiße Flotte boat) from Dresden toward Bad Schandau and Prague and alight at the town of **Königstein.** The spectacular medieval fortress on the cliff was used by the Nazis as a stash for stolen art. It now houses museums of everything from weaponry to porcelain. (Open daily 8am-8pm; Oct.-April 9am-5pm. DM5, students and seniors DM3.50; Oct.-April DM3.50, students and seniors DM2.) The Königstein **tourist office,** Dresdner Str. 1 (tel. (03521) 261), may convince you to spend weeks exploring. (Open Mon.-Tues. and Thurs.-Fri. 9am-5:30pm, Sat. 9am-noon; Nov.-March officially open Tues. 9am-6pm, Fri. 9am-noon, but may be open at other times.) The nearest **Jugendherberge (HI)** is across the river by ferry (from under the train station), and upstream 5 to 10 minutes by foot at Halbestadt 13 (DM14, over 26 DM17). Take the ferry across to the **Lilienstein** for a spectacular view of the Saxon countryside. The gem of this area is Germany's newest national park, the **Bastei,** a breathtaking stretch of gigantic sandstone boulders and sharp ravines. The quickest way there is via **Rathen.**

The town of **Meißen** was the center of the porcelain craft from the 18th-century on; many have been obsessed with the eerie beauty of Meißen dolls. The **Albrechtsburg** is a castle/cathedral/fortress overlooking the city. (Open Feb.-Dec. daily 10am-6pm. DM4, students and seniors DM2.) Augustus the Strong built Europe's first top-secret porcelain factory here; today anyone can tour the **Staatliche Porzellanmanufaktur** at Talstr. 9. (Open April-Oct. Tues.-Sun. 8:30am-12:30pm and 1-4:30pm. DM4, students and seniors DM3.) In the village, the porcelain bells of the **Frauen-**

kirche will lead you to the **tourist office,** An der Frauenkirche 3 (tel. (03521) 44 70), which arranges rooms and guides wayward tourists to the **Jugendherberge (HI)** at Wilsdrufferstr. 28 (tel. (03521) 45 30 65; reception open 7-10am and 5-8pm; DM12.50, over 26 DM15).

■■■ WITTENBERG

The Protestant Reformation, which threw Europe into centuries of convulsive upheaval, began quietly in **Lutherstadt Wittenberg** on October 13, 1517, when Martin Luther, a local professor, nailed his 95 theses to the wooden door of the castle church (Schloßkirche). This small town on the Leipzig-Berlin train route makes for a relaxing daytrip from either city. As you exit the train station, head straight and swing right under the tracks onto **Collegienstraße.** On your right, note the sickly elm tree; under it Luther proudly burned a papal order of excommunication. At no. 54 stands Luther's former home, the **Lutherhalle,** where he lived from 1508. Grab an English guide from the ticket desk to follow the exhibition through the course of the Reformation and of Luther's groundbreaking Bible translation. The family living room has been preserved intact, as has obnoxious tourist Peter the Great's signature, scribbled on the door when he stopped by in 1702. (Open Tues.-Sun. 9am-6pm. Last entry 5:30pm. DM4, students and seniors DM2.) Farther down the street is **St. Marienkirche** (St. Mary's Church); its distinctive altar, painted by pharmacist-*cum*-artistic genius **Cranach the Elder,** incorporates Luther in the biblical scene. (Open Mon.-Sat. 9am-noon and 2-5pm; Nov.-April Mon.-Sat. 10am-noon and 2-4pm.) Nearby rises the town's **Rathaus,** with an imposing Renaissance façade and statues to Luther and the philosopher-humanist Melancthon. Also in the square is the **Jungfernröhrwasser** (fountain of youth), a 16th-century well whose refreshing and drinkable waters still flow through the original wooden pipes, proof that East German infrastructure was once quite reliable. Farther down the street, a sumptuous baroque cupola crowns the tower of the **Schloß.** It was here that Luther nailed his theses to the door; his original draft is inside.

Wittenberg Information (tel. (03491) 511 44), at Collegienstr. 29 just off the market, will help find rooms. (Open Mon.-Fri. 9am-6pm, Sat. 10am-2pm, Sun. 11am-3pm.) The **Jugendherberge (HI)** in the castle has a unique atmosphere and reasonable prices (tel. (03491) 32 55; DM15, over 26 DM18).

■■■ LEIPZIG

Badly bruised in WWII, Eastern Germany's second-largest city compensates for its lack of beauty with one of Europe's more brilliant cultural pedigrees. Originally, Leipzig gained its fame through music and letters: the university, founded in 1409, upholds an illustrious tradition that embraces the names of Leibniz, Lessing, and Nietzsche. More recently, Leipzig has become Germany's *Heldenstadt* (city of heroes) for its role as the crucible of *die Wende,* the sudden toppling of the GDR, in 1989. Dozens of bookstores recall Leipzig's pre-war position as capital of European publishing, and several major international book fairs take place here annually.

In **Sachsenplatz,** the sooty façades of the early 18th century **Bürgerhäuser** (Burgers' House) can be seen clearly if you look past the tired cement. The heart of the city centers on the **Marktplatz,** a colorful, cobblestone square guarded by the somewhat crooked, 16th-century **Altes Rathaus.** The **Museum der Bildenden Künste** at Georg-Dimitroff-Pl. 1 has a ponderously impressive collection of over 2500 paintings and sculptures, including works by van Eyck, Dürer, Rubens, Rembrandt, and Rodin. (Open Tues. and Thurs.-Sun. 9am-5pm, Wed. 1-9:30pm. DM5, students DM2.50; free on Sun.) Close to the Marktplatz is the **Thomaskirche** where J.S. Bach served as cantor; his remains were interred here in front of the altar. (Open daily 8am-6pm; in winter 9am-5pm. Services Sun. 9:30am and 6pm.) Not far north of the Thomaskirche is Leipzig's newest and most moving museum, the **Museum der**

"Runden Ecke," Dittrichring 24, the former headquarters of the East German Ministry for State Security, or **STASI,** now home to a permanent exhibition "STASI-Macht und Banalität" (Power and Banality) on excesses of paranoia and power. The museum also chronicles the process by which Leipzig's citizens overthrew the STASI terror. Outside of the city, the **Völkerschlachtdenkmal** on the *süd-Friedhof* remembers the 400,000 soldiers engaged in the 1813 Battle of Nations. Climb the 500 steps to the platform for a view all the way to the Harz Mountains. Take tram #15 or 20 (direction "Meusdorf" or "Probstheida") from the Hauptbahnhof (20min.). (Open daily 9am-5pm. DM2, students and seniors DM1.)

Leipzig's streets echo with the very best in classical music. In 1723, Johann Sebastian Bach settled here, entrancing local churchgoers with his early works. A century later, Felix Mendelssohn founded the *Leipzig Gewandhaus Orchester,* still a superb ensemble. When the orchestra performs at home in the **Gewandhaus,** Augustus Pl. (tel. (0341) 77 96 or 913 20), tickets go fast. (Tickets from DM7; 30% student discount. Ticket office open Mon. 1-6pm, Tues.-Fri. 10am-6pm, Sat. 10am-2pm; no concerts in August.) Leipzig's **Opera** (tel. 29 10 36) is also the entry point to Leipzig's diverse theater scene. In 1994, Leipzig will celebrate a musical and political triumph as the 69th **Bach Festival** runs from March 30 to April 5. For tickets, write the **Bach-Archiv,** Thomaskirchhof 16, 04109 Leipzig, or call (0341) 78 66, or fax (0341) 27 53 08. For entirely different festivities, head to **Moritzbastei,** just off Augustusplatz. Sometimes you'll think that the entire student population is here to take in live jazz, rock, and folk concerts, or to dance away the late-night hours. In this diverse alternative crowd, gay and lesbian couples barely get a second look. (Café/bar open daily 2pm-midnight. Disco or concerts from 9 or 10pm. DM4-10.)

Accommodations, Food, and Practical Information

Leipzig's **tourist office,** Sachsenpl. 1 (tel. (0341) 795 90), books private rooms (DM40-50). From the train station, walk through Pl. der Republik and bear right past the Park Hotel. (Open Mon.-Fri. 9am-7pm, Sat. 9:30am-2pm.) Budget travelers are still a novelty here, though they are not, unfortunately, as rare as budget rooms. The **Jugendherberge (HI)** is at Käthe-Kollwitz-Str. 64 (tel. (0341) 47 05 30). Take tram #1 or 2 west 4 stops. (Reception open 7-9am and 2:30-10pm. Curfew 1am. DM17.50, over 26, DM21.) The **Jugendherberge Leipzig am Auensee (HI),** Gustav-Esche-Str. 4, Leipzig 04159 (tel. 517 89), in the nearby suburb of Wahren (tram #10 or 28 to Rathaus Wahren, turn left at the city hall and follow the signs) is a restful abode. (Reception open 7am-8pm. No curfew. DM14, over 26 DM17.) **Campingplatz am Auensee,** Gustav-Esche-Str. 5 (tel. 212 30 31), lies down the road past the youth hostel. (Tents DM5.) The **Innenstadt** offers a whole range of *Imbisse* (snack joints), bistros, and restaurants. Greek and Turkish merchants offer their fresh produce Tuesdays and Fridays in **Sachsenplatz,** in front of the tourist office. **Universität Leipzig Mensa** (tram #17 direction "Böhlitz-Ehrenberg" to the 4th stop) is a student cafeteria with plain fare for pretty prices. (Meals DM3-8. Open mid-Oct. to Feb. and April to mid-July.) Leipzig lies on the Berlin-Munich **rail** line with regular InterCity service to Frankfurt am Main (tel. 702 11). The information counter is near track 15. **Trams** cover the city. (DM0.50, 9am-midnight day-card DM3.)

To the north, about 30 minutes by train from Leipzig on the way to Berlin, lies Germany's dirtiest city, **Bitterfeld,** whose highly appropriate name means "bitter fields." Thousands have made a pilgrimage here to see for themselves what humans can do to the environment. Particularly disturbing is nearby **Wolfen,** where the lakes have a chlorine content 600 times that of the Rhine and high concentrations of cyanide, arsenic, and chrome.

■■■ HALLE

Halle an der Saale, the fortunate town saved by Katrin's drumming in the climactic scene of Brecht's *Mother Courage and Her Children,* was also lucky enough to emerge from WWII more or less unscathed. The city's luck ran out 3 months later, when the occupying Americans traded the city to the Soviets for a piece of Berlin. From that point on, pollution and neglect devastated what the war had spared, but Halle's cobblestone streets, gabled apartment blocks, and screeching streetcars still provide a glimpse of how this historic German city might have been.

Halle has two favorite sons: composer Georg Friedrich Händel and political *Wunder* Hans-Dietrich Genscher, Germany's well-respected ex-foreign minister. The city revolves around the **Marktplatz,** which buzzes with streetcar traffic and international vendors around the haunting red **Roter Turm,** a bell tower built 400 years ago. Across from the tower lies the **Marktkirche unsere lieben Frauen,** with the organ where little Händel began his studies. (Open Mon.-Wed. and Fri. 10am-noon and 3-6pm, Thurs. 4-5pm, Sat. 9am-noon and 3-5pm, Sun. service at 10am. Free 30-min. organ concerts Tues. at 5:30pm and Fri. at 11:30pm.) The **Händelhaus,** the composer's family home at Große Nikolaistr. 5-6, offers high-quality stereo soundtracks in 19 languages to guide pilgrims through Händel's career in Germany, Italy, and England. (Museum open Mon.-Wed. and Fri.-Sun. 9:30am-5:30pm, Thurs. 9:30am-7pm. DM2, students DM0.50, seniors DM1; Thurs. free.)

From Händel's home to the **Dom** (cathedral) is a 5-minute walk down Nikolaistr. Just a few steps from the *Dom* lies the **Moritzburg fortress,** one of whose towers hosts the city's **Studentenclub.** Foreign students with ID are heartily welcomed; join Germans for a cheap drink and a dance. (Open Mon.-Sat. 7pm-midnight; closed during university vacations.) Most of the 15th-century giant is reserved for the **Staatliche Galerie Moritzburg-Halle,** a mid-sized art museum focusing mostly on 19th- and 20th-century German painters. Much of the museum's extensive expressionist collection was deemed "degenerate" and burned or sold by the Nazis.

The **tourist office** (tel. (0345) 233 40), in the *Roter Turm* on the marketplace, sells maps and books rooms. From the main train station cross beneath the underpass to the left as you exit the building, follow the pedestrian tunnel, and follow Leipzierstr. past the *Leipziger Turm* to the Marktplatz (15min). Or take tram #4 (direction "Heide/Hubertuspl.") or #7 (direction "Kröllwitz") to Markt (4 stops). The **Jugendherberge (HI),** August-Bebel-Str. 48a (tel. (0345) 247 16), is in a newly restored mansion north of the market. Take tram #7 (direction "Kröllwitz"), 6 stops from the train station or 2 from the market. Follow Große Ulrichstr. one block, turn right onto Puschkinstr., and turn right onto August-Bebel-Str. (Reception open 7-10am and 5-11pm. Lockout 10am-5pm. Curfew 11pm. DM14, over 26 DM17.)

■■■ WEIMAR

The name Weimar still evokes many contradictory pictures: the 1920's Weimar Culture, which resolved itself in economic crisis and the defeat of democracy; the birthplace of the Bauhaus art school; site of the Buchenwald concentration camp; the city where Germany's first republic was founded; and the city where Goethe, Schiller, Herder, Liszt, and Nietzsche all unleashed their genius.

Goethe, Germany's very own Renaissance man, still presides over these streets 150 years after his death. Especially impressive are his flawless manuscripts and private chambers in the **Goethe Haus,** Frauenplan 1. A stalwart English booklet, *Goethe's House on the Frauenplan at Weimar,* will guide you through the rooms where Goethe entertained, wrote, studied, and eventually died. (Open Tues.-Sun. 9am-5pm; Nov.-Feb. 9am-4pm. DM5, students DM3.) Between the Frauenplan and the **marktplatz** is the beginning of Weimar's central artery, **Schillerstraße,** a pedestrian zone crammed with antique shops and bookstores. At the end of the street, **Schillerhaus,** Schillerstr. 12, the former residence of the playwright, displays original drafts, early editions of plays, and a biographical chronicle of the life of Goethe's friend and rival. (Open Wed.-Mon. 9am-5pm; Nov.-Feb. 9am-4pm. DM5, students DM3.) Around the corner, the pair are reconciled in stone before the **Deutsches**

Nationaltheater, which first breathed life into their works, and from whose balcony the doomed Weimar Republic was proclaimed in 1919.

The **Bauhaus school,** now at the **Hochschule für Architektur und Bauwesen** (college for Architecture and Construction), offers no exhibits related to the iconoclastic design movement. Bauhaus work is better represented by the **Denkmal der Märzgefallenen,** designed by Gropius to honor those killed in the 1919 revolution, past the Goethe and Schiller graves in the historic cemetery, **Historischer Friedhof.** (Open Mon.-Sun. 9am-1pm and 2-5pm.) The two poets lie side by side in the local ducal sarcophagus. The neighboring **Park an der Ilm,** landscaped by Goethe, sprouts numerous 18th-century pavilions and shelters grazing sheep and goats. Of particular note are Goethe's fake ruins and the statue of William Shakespeare, still bearing the scars of a coat of black paint applied by the Nazis in 1939. On the park's slopes rests Goethe's **Gartenhaus,** Corona-Schröter-Str., the poet's first home in Weimar, and later his retreat from the city. (Open Tues.-Sun. 9am-noon and 1-5pm. DM3, students DM1.) At the edge of the park is the **Franz Liszt Haus,** Marienstr. 17, where the composer spent his last years. The instruments and furnishings are supposedly original, but given Liszt's torrid love life, the small single bed seems unlikely. (Open Tues.-Sun. 9am-1pm and 2-5pm; Nov.-Feb. 9am-1pm and 2-4pm. DM2, students and seniors DM1.)

Accommodations, Food, and Practical Information Weimar's 3 youth hostels make finding a place to stay here easier than in other Eastern cities. Try the friendly, convenient **Jugendherberge Germania (HI),** Carl-August-Allee 13 (tel. (03643) 20 76), 2 minutes from the station. (Lockout 10am-1pm. Curfew 11pm. Reception open 3-11pm. DM16.50, over 26 DM20.50.) The **Jugendgästehaus Weimar (HI),** Zum Wilden Graben 12 (tel. and fax (03643) 34 71) is pleasantly located amid old villas. (Reception open 4-8pm. DM18.50, over 26 DM22.50.) Weimar serves up very rich cooking for tourists; console yourself at the daily **produce market** in the Marktplatz, or at the **Ladenmarkt** grocery store at the corner of Markstr. and Windischenstr.; facing the tourist office, turn left and walk a block. (Open Mon.-Fri. 8am-6pm, Sat. 8am-noon.)

Bus #4 links Weimar's train station with Goethepl. in the center of town. From there, the **tourist office,** Marktstr. 4 (tel. (03643) 21 73), is just off the Markt down a side street near the Rathaus. (Open Mon.-Fri. 9am-7pm, Sat. 9am-4pm; Nov.-Feb. Mon.-Fri. 9am-6pm, Sat. 9am-1pm.)

■ Near Weimar

From 1937 to 1945, the concentration camp of **Buchenwald** held over 250,000 Jews, political prisoners, gypsies, and gays; most did not survive the Holocaust. What remains is the **Nationale Mahn-und Gedenkstätte Buchenwald** (National Buchenwald Memorial). Signs point to the **KZ Lager** and the **Gedenkstätte:** the former refers to the remains of the camp; the latter is a solemn monument overlooking the valley. Since reunification, the focus of the camp exhibits has shifted from the internment of German communists under the Third Reich to the Soviet use of the camp from 1945-50, when 32,000 Germans were interned here by the Soviet Army. Almost no mention is made of the other victims of the camp: Jews, gypsies, gays, and other groups towards which neither regime holds a spotless record. A **memorial stone** on the site of a former Jewish children's barracks will be laid on November 9, 1993, the 55th anniversary of *Kristallnacht*. (Museum and film buildings open Tues.-Sun. 9:30am-5:30pm; Oct.-March 8:45am-4:45pm.) Reach Buchenwald by bus from the Weimar train station (several departures/day).

■■■ ERFURT

Erfurt offers a stunning cathedral, a handful of museums, and a cultural life fueled by its three colleges. Because of its political importance and its 1250th birthday celebration last year, most of the inner city has been beautifully restored, giving Erfurt a look of style all too rare in the cities of the East. Towering above the city skyline on the Domhügel hill is one of Eastern Germany's most impressive cathedrals. Luther was invested as a priest here, and interrupted his first mass by throwing the Bible across the altar. He claimed that his target was the devil himself. The simple sandstone interior of the **Church of St. Severi** is dominated by the Saint's sarcophagus. (Cathedral and church open Mon.-Fri. 9-11:30am and 12:30-5pm, Sat. 9-11:30am and 12:30-4:30pm, Sun. 2-4pm). From the sprawling Domplatz, a broad **Marktstr.** leads down to the Fischmarkt, bordered by former guild houses with rather wild façades, and the 1869 Rathaus. Marktstr. runs to the Gera River, spanned by the **Krämerbrücke,** a covered medieval bridge teeming with small shops dating from the 12th century. From the far side of the bridge, follow Gotthardrstr., and cut left through Kirchengasse to reach the **Augustinerkloster,** where Martin Luther spent 10 years. He got his way; the cloister now functions as a Protestant college. (Tours Tues.-Sat. hourly 10am-noon and 2-4pm; Nov.-March Tues.-Sat. at 10am, noon, and 2pm, as well as after the 9:30am Sun. services.)

The **tourist office (Erfurt Fremdenverkehrsamt),** Bahnhofstr. 37 (tel. (0361) 262 67; fax 233 55), is 5 minutes straight from the train station. They sell maps and book rooms in private homes. (Singles DM30-50. Doubles DM40-60. DM5 fee. Open Mon.-Fri. 10am-6pm, Sat. 10am-1pm.) Housing options are limited. Try the **Jugendherberge (HI),** Hochheimerstr. 12 (tel. (0361) 267 05), whose newly renovated interior is much more accommodating than the overgrown exterior. Take tram #5 from the train station and get off at "Steigerstr.," backtrack a little, and turn right down Steigerstr.; the hostel is on the left corner at the first intersection. (DM14, over 26 DM17.) In a pinch, Weimar's hostels are only a 15-minute train ride away.

■■■ THURINGIAN FOREST

"The area is magnificent, quite magnificent...I am basking in God's world," wrote Goethe from the Thuringian Forest more than 200 years ago. Stretching south of Eisenach, Weimar, and Erfurt to the border with Bavaria, the time-worn mountains and the peaceful pine woods fostered and inspired many of Germany's composers, philosophers, and poets. The **Rennsteig,** a 168km-long scenic hiking trail, snakes from Hörschel near Eisenach right into Bavaria; history books date the trail at 1330, but locals claim that it was first worn down by prehistoric hunter-gatherers. **Erfurt** is without question the door to the Thuringian Forest; the **tourist office** there (see Erfurt) will equip you with guides and maps.

Arnstadt Thirty km beyond Erfurt lies Arnstadt, the oldest town in Thuringia. Johann Sebastian Bach began his career as an organist in what is now the **Bachkirche.** (Open March-Sept. 10:30am-12:30pm and 2-4pm.) The **Neues Schloß** (new palace), Schloßplatz 1, houses the **doll museum "mon Plaisier."** More than 400 dolls are displayed in 24 dollhouses, in a total of 84 furnished rooms. (Open Tues.-Sun. 8:30am-noon and 1-4:30pm; Nov.-April 9:30am-4pm. DM2.50, students DM2.) The **tourist office, Arnstadt Information,** Markt 3 (tel. (03628) 20 49), finds rooms from DM25 (fee DM3); turn left from the station and then right on Bahnhofstr., and walk up Ledermarkt. (Open Mon.-Fri. 9:30-noon and 12:30-6pm, Sat. 9am-noon.) They also organize bus tours (DM5-10) to the **Drei Gleichen** (3 matching castles), and have info on hiking trails. Near Arnstadt, the ruined monastery of **Paulinzella,** on the train line to Saalfeld and Rudostadt, remains one of Thuringia's most striking monuments of the Romanesque period.

Ilmenau and the Goethe Trail Goethe first worked in Ilmenau, 45 minutes south of Arnstadt, reorganizing the Thuringian mining industry, and came back to the area as a poet looking for a place of his own. South of the city center, parallel to Waldstr., stretches the 18km **Goethe Trail (Goethewanderung)**, marked by Goethe's over-flourished **"G"** monogram. About 4km into the uphill trail is his hut on the **Kickelhahn,** where you can read the poetry he scratched on the walls as a young man. A year before his death at age 83, Goethe himself returned to the hut on a tour of his past. The hike ends in **Stützerbach,** where the local glass-works magnate hosted the poet. His house is now a **Goethe Memorial,** with demonstrations of traditional **glass-blowing** on the 1st floor. (Open Tues.-Sun. 9am-noon and 1-5pm. DM3, students DM2.) Ilmenau also makes a good starting point for a hike along the **Rennsteig.** (Take the train to Schmiedefeld.)

Ilmenau's **youth hostel,** Waldstr. 22 (tel. 24 13), lies at the beginning of the trail, straight ahead from **Bahnhof Ilmenau-Bad.** (Reception open 7am-8pm. Curfew 10pm. DM14.50, over 26 DM18.50.) Behind the Raiffeisenbank on the right side of Bahnhofstr., the **market** offers fresh fruits and vegetables. (Open Mon.-Fri. 8am-5pm, Sat. 8am-11am.) The **tourist office** is at Lindenstr. 12 (tel. (03677) 23 58); walk down Bahnhofstr. across Wetzlarer Platz and follow the pedestrian zone (15min.). They provide Goethe Trail maps and hiking brochures (DM5) and book private rooms (from DM15) for DM2 per person. (Open Mon.-Fri 9am-6pm, Sat. 9am-noon.)

Rudolstadt and Bad Blankenburg Underneath Weimar, the Saale River Valley winds down to **Rudolstadt,** where Richard Wagner got his first break. **Schillerstraße 25** marks the spot where Goethe and Schiller met for the first time, thus beginning one of literature's greatest symbiotic relationships. During the 18th century, social life centered on the Baroque-towered **Heidecksburg palace,** accessible through Vorwerkgasse, a path behind the *Rathaus.* (Open Tues.-Sun. 10am-6pm; Nov.-April 9am-4pm. DM5, children DM2.50.) Rudolstadt is also a route to **Schloß Kochberg,** once the summer home of **Charlotte von Stein,** the inspiration for many of Goethe's powerful love poems; take bus #21 (10/day, 40min.), or hike 8km north to the beautiful moated palace. (Castle open Tues.-Sun. 9am-noon and 1-5pm; Sept.-April Wed.-Sun. 9am-noon and 1-5pm. DM3, students DM2. Last bus from Groß Kochberg to Rudolstadt around 6pm.)

The nearest **hostel** is in **Bad Blankenburg,** Am Kesselberg 1 (tel. (03674) 25 28), a 20-minute bus ride away. From Anton-Sommer-Str. (across from the Rudolstadt station) take bus A, B, or C (every 20min.) to the Bad Blankenburg *Bahnhof.* Walk straight on Bahnhofstr., then right on Zeigerheimer Weg, up the stairs, and keep slightly to the right. (Reception open 2-7pm. Curfew 10pm. 5-day max. stay. DM15.50, over 26 DM18.50.) You can buy fresh vegetables and fruits at the **farmer's market** on the *Marktplatz.* (Wed. 6am-6pm and Sat 6am-noon.) To reach the **tourist office,** Marktstr. 57 (tel. and fax (03672) 245 43), walk down Bahnhofstr. to Marktstr. and turn left. (Open Mon.-Fri 9am-5pm, Sat. 9am-1pm.) Trains and buses from Weimar (bus #14) and Erfurt (bus #13) take about an hour.

Saalfeld Twenty-five minutes by train from Rudolstadt lies Saalfeld, famous for its underground **Feengrotten** (fairy grottoes), Feengrottenweg 2. The phosphorescent caverns are intensely colorful; the main orange and amber **Märchendom** (fairy cathedral) chamber branches off into the **Balugrüne Grotte** (blue-green grotto) which glows with teal light. From the marketplace go straight on Brudergasse and then on to Pfortenstr., take a left on Melanchthonstr. and follow the signs. (Open Feb. to mid-Nov. daily 9am-5pm. Guided tours every 45min. DM5, students DM4, children DM3, not open to children under 4. Not wheelchair accessible.)

Saalfeld's **tourist office,** Blankenburger Str.4 (tel. and fax (03671) 339 50), scouts out rooms (from DM25) for a DM1 fee. From the station walk left on Bahnhofstr. and across the bridge; at the Saaltor gate, take Saalstr., and turn right at Markt. (Open Mon.-Fri 9am-6pm, Sat 9am-1pm.) Saalfeld's **youth hostel,** Schieferhof 4 (tel. 28 02 or 51 03 94), is a 25-min. hike from the station. At the Saaltor gate go right on Am Bleichanger and follow it until Schieferhof. (Reception open 3-7pm. Curfew 10pm. DM14, over 26 DM17.) **Roter Hirsch,** Markt 6 (tel. 22 85), offers Thuringian wild game. (Venison "stag plate" DM10. Open Mon.-Sun. 9am-10pm.)

■■■ EISENACH

Birthplace of Johann Sebastian Bach and home-in-exile of Martin Luther, Eisenach boasts impressive humanist credentials. Yet inside the walls of the town's Wartburg castle, student fraternities convened in 1817 to promote their bizarre admixture of democracy and xenophobia; the writings of Karl Marx and Friedrich Engels were so well received that the duo called the local faction "our party." Adolf Hitler called Wartburg "the most German of German castles," and fought a pitched battle with the local church to replace its cross with a swastika. It is oddly fitting that Eisen-ach—this humanist, romantic, conservative, radical, democratic, despotic bundle of contradictions—should be one of Germany's most treasured national symbols.

Eisenach's medieval half-timbered houses ornament the northwestern slope of the Thuringian forest. The Romanesque **Wartburg Schloß** sheltered Martin Luther after his excommunication. The reformer translated the Bible into German here, and after working a bit too late one night, was visited by...SATAN! By Luther's account, it only took a toss of an ink pot to dispel the beast; later visitors mistook a smudge of stove grease for the damned ink spot, gutting the wall in their scramble for a fleck. Otherwise, the simple study has been preserved. The castle's **Festsaal** commemorates the 1817 meeting of university fraternities. Wagner's opera *Tannenhäuser,* inspired by a 12th-century musical contest here, is illustrated with Romantic murals. The view from the top of the Wartburg's courtyard tower is amazing; the 1st floor is a former dungeon. Wartburg sits on the south side of Eisenach, down Wartburger Allee from the train station. Take the **Wartburg Express** (DM3) up the hill, or hike through the woods (30min.). The interior can be visited only with a tour. (Open daily 8:30am-5pm; Nov.-March 9am-3:30pm. Entire complex DM10, students DM6, seniors DM7. Museum and study, DM5, DM4, DM3.)

The **Bachhaus,** Frauenplan 21 (tel. (03691) 37 14), where Johann Sebastian stormed into the world in 1685, recreates the family quarters with period instruments. Turn off Wartburger Allee at Grimmelgasse. (Open Mon. noon-5:45pm, Tues.-Sun. 9am-5:45pm. DM5, students and seniors DM4.) Town life centers on the **Markt,** bounded by the **Lutherhaus,** Lutherplatz 8, home to young man Martin from 1458 to 1501. (Open daily 9am-1pm and 2-5pm. DM3, students DM1.50.)

Accommodations, Food, and Practical Information Jugendherberge **Artur Becker (HI),** Marientalstr. 24 (tel. (03691) 3613), fills an old villa beyond the castle. From the station, take Bahnhofstr. to Wartburger Allee, to Marientalstr.; the hostel is a long walk down and to the right (35min.). Or, take the infrequent bus #3 from the station, get off at Lillenstr., and the path to the hostel will be a few meters in front of you. (Reception open 9am-8pm. Curfew 10pm. DM16, over 26 DM19.50. Breakfast included.) **Camp** at **Am Altenberger See** (tel. (03691) 741 37), in the hamlet of Eckardshausen. From the Eisenach station, take the Bad Liebenstein bus (4/day 7:35am-5:35pm); tell the driver your destination. (Reception open until 8pm. DM10/person.) Lunch specials at **Zum Schwan** go for under DM8 (open Mon.-Fri 8am-6pm). The **tourist office,** Bahnhofstr. 3-5 (tel. 761 62, fax 761 61), books private rooms for no fee. (Open Mon. 10am-6pm, Tues.-Fri. 9am-6pm, Sat. 10am-2pm).

BAVARIA (BAYERN)

From the hidden villages of the Bavarian Forest and the glittering baroque cities along the Danube to the medieval churches punctuating the Romantic Road and the turreted castles in the Alps, Bavaria is the Germany of fairy tale, Teutonic myth, and Wagnerian opera. In fact, when many foreigners conjure up images of Germany, they are thinking of Bavaria-land of beer halls, oom-pah bands, and *Lederhosen*. Nevertheless, the fiercely independent locals have always been Bavarians first and Germans second; it took wars with France and Austria to pull the Kingdom of Bavaria into Bismarck's orbit. Though largely rural, predominantly Catholic, and (save Munich) staunchly conservative, this largest of Germany's federal states harbors strong commerce and industry, including Kugel-Fischer, Siemens, and BMW. Remember that HI-affiliated hostels in Bavaria do not admit guests over age 26.

■■■ MUNICH (MÜNCHEN)

A glamorous, cosmopolitan sprawl amid the bucolic Bavarian heartland and the solidly conservative southern German population, Munich breathes with the vitality of Germany's postwar economic boom. Its world-class museums, stately parks, and architecture, theater, and art scene thrive, and an ebullient, arrogant mixture of sophistication and earthy Bavarian *Gemütlichkeit* keeps the city awake all hours. Münchners party particularly zealously during *Fasching* (Germany's equivalent of Mardi Gras or Carnival) and the legendary *Oktoberfest*.

ORIENTATION AND PRACTICAL INFORMATION

Touring by foot is easy in Munich's compact center. **Schützenstraße,** straight ahead from the main train station, leads toward **Neuhauser Straße,** the pedestrian shopping street. Neuhauser Str. connects **Karlsplatz am Stachus** and the famed **Marienplatz.** Keeping straight ahead, first Im Tal and then Zweibrückenstr. lead to the Isar River. North of Marienplatz, the pedestrian zone ranges past magnificent **Odeonplatz,** next to the *Residenz,* to glittering Ludwigstr. Farther north lie the university and **Schwabing,** Munich's student district. To the east, the enormous **Englischer Garten** sprawls along the Isar. West of Schwabing lies genteel **Nymphenburg,** surrounding **Nymphenburg Palace.** Southwest of Marienplatz, **Sendlingerstraße** heads toward Sendlingertor, from which Lindwurmstr. leads to Goetheplatz. Mozartstr. proceeds onward to **Theresienwiese,** site of the annual *Oktoberfest.*

Radius Touristik (tel. 59 61 13), opposite track #35 in the main train station, offers a 2-hour walking tour of the old city (DM12) daily at 10:30am; a 3-hour, 16-km bicycle tour (DM25, with own bike DM18) Sat. at 10:30am; and a "Munich in a Day" tour covering most major sights.

Tourist Office: Fremdenverkehrsamt (tel. 239 12 56 or 239 12 57), opposite track #11 in the main train station. A near must, but you'll wait 15min. or more in summer. Books rooms (DM5 plus DM3 deposit) and sells accommodations lists (DM0.50). Excellent free map and the invaluable *Munich for Young People* (DM1). Open daily 8am-10pm. Branch office at the new **Flughafen München** airport (tel. 97 59 28 15) in the *Zentralgebäude.* Open Mon.-Sat. 8:30am-10pm, Sun. 1-9pm. **Fremdenverkehrsband München-Oberbayern,** Sonnenstr. 10 (tel. 59 73 47), has brochures, maps, and information for the upper Bavaria region. **EurAide in English** (tel. 59 38 89), in the station at track 11. Provides free train info and reserves rooms (DM6). Their *Inside Track* (free) is available at their office and at the *Reisezentrum.* Thomas Cook timetables sold (DM37) and Eurailpasses validated. Open daily 7:30-11:30am and 1-6pm.
Budget Travel: Studiosus Reisen an der Uni, Amalienstr. 73 (tel. 50 06 05 40, ext. 544), near the university. Open Mon.-Fri. 9am-6pm. Sells FIYTO cards and

ISICs Mon.-Fri. 10am-2pm. **Travel Overland,** Leopoldstr. 13 (tel. 34 67 21), behind the pink library in the university cafeteria. Open Mon.-Fri. 10am-2pm.

Consulates: U.S., Königinstr. 5 (tel. 288 80). **Canada,** Tal 29 (tel. 22 26 61). **U.K.,** Bürkleinstr. 10 (tel. 21 10 90). **Ireland,** Mauerkircherstr. 1a (tel. 98 57 23 25).

Currency Exchange: Go to the **post office** across from the station to exchange large denomination traveler's checks (DM3/check). **Deutsche Verkehrs-Bank (DVB),** at the main station, also changes currency and checks and advances cash with Visa and MasterCard. Open daily 6am-11:30pm. Pick up the free publication *Inside Track* at the EurAide office for a 50% commission reduction for U.S. traveler's checks totaling over US$50 at the Deutsche Verkehrs-Bank.

American Express: Promenadepl. 6 (tel. 219 90). From the train station, walk straight through Karlsplatz to Neuhauserstr. and turn left on Ettstr. Cashes AmEx Cheques for no fee. Open Mon.-Fri. 9am-5:30pm, Sat. 9am-noon.

Post Office: Post/Telegrafamt, Bahnhofplatz 1, 80335 München (tel. 53 88 27 32), opposite the train station. **Poste Restante** open daily 7am-11pm. All other services 24hrs.

Telephones: Make credit card and collect calls from the **post office** on the 2nd level of the train station or across the street. **City code:** 089.

Flights: The spiffy new **Flughafen München** is accessible from the train station by S-Bahn #8 every 20min. from 3:13am-11:13pm. DM12 or 8 stripes on a 12-stripe ticket *(Streifenkarte);* railpasses valid.

Trains: The **Hauptbahnhof** is the transport hub of southern Germany. For schedules, call 194 19; fare info 55 41 41; reservations (in German only), 128 59 94. Station open daily 5am-12:30am. To: Frankfurt (40/day, 3½hr.); Berlin (25/day, 9½hr.); Prague (10/day, 7hr.); Vienna (19/day, 5½hr.); and Zürich (5/day, 4½hr.).

Public Transportation: Runs from about 5am-12:30am on weekdays, until 1:30am on weekends. Eurail is valid on any S-Bahn (commuter rail) train, but *not* on the U-Bahn (subway), *Straßenbahn* (trams), or buses. Single rides within the *Innenraum* (inner city) cost DM3. The *Tageskarte Innenraum* (inner-city day pass; DM10) is valid for up to 2 people on all public transport in Munich proper until 4am. Cancel your ticket in the boxes marked with an "E" *before* you go to the platform. Transit maps can be found at the tourist office, EurAide, and the MVV counters near the subway entrance in the train station.

Bike Rental: Bikes can be rented from the Deutsche Bahn at 15 S-Bahn locations and returned to train stations throughout upper Bavaria. Most convenient to town center is English-speaking **Radius Touristik** (tel. 59 61 13), near platform #35 at the station. Bikes DM5/hr., DM20/day. DM50 deposit. Students and Eurailpass holders get 10% discount. Friendly owners loan rain gear to bikers in inclement weather. Open daily 9am-6:30pm. They also run a bike rental at the southern entrance to the *Englischer Garten* (same prices and phone).

Hitchhiking: Mitfahrzentrale, Lämmerstr. 4 (tel. 59 45 61), near train station, and **Känguruh,** Amalienstr. 87 (tel. 194 44), in the Amalienpassage. Open Mon.-Fri. 8:30am-7pm, Sat. 9am-3pm, Sun. 10am-3pm. **Frauenmitfahrzentrale,** Klenzestr. 57b (tel. 201 46 90), 2 blocks from the Frauenhoferstr. U-Bahn stop, matches women passengers with women drivers. Open Mon.-Fri. 8am-8pm. Ride-seekers also scan bulletin boards in the *Mensa* at Leopoldstr. 13. Those who hitch head for *Autobahn* on-ramps. To head to Salzburg, Vienna, or Italy, they reach Autobahn E11 by taking U-Bahn #1 or 2 to Karl-Preis-Platz. For E11 in the opposite direction (Stuttgart/France), hitchers take U-1 to Rotkreuzplatz and tram #12 to Amalienburgstr. *or* S-2 to Obermenzing. Either way, hitchers then take bus #73 or 75 to Blutenburg. For points north, they take Autobahn E6, ride the U-6 to Sudetenstadt, and walk 500m to the Frankfurter Ring. For Autobahn to Lake Constance and Switzerland, they take U-4 or U-5 to Heimeranplatz, then bus #33 to Siegenburgerstr. For Garmisch-Partenkirchen, hitchers take Autobahn E6 to the south, ride the U-3 or U-6 to Westpark, and then take bus #33 to Luise-Kesselbach-Platz.

Laundromat: Wasch-Center, Klenzestr. 18. S-Bahn (from the main station) to "Isartor" (2 stops). Walk 1 block down Rumforstr., turn left. Wash DM6, dry DM0.50/15min. Soap included. Open daily 6am-10:30pm.

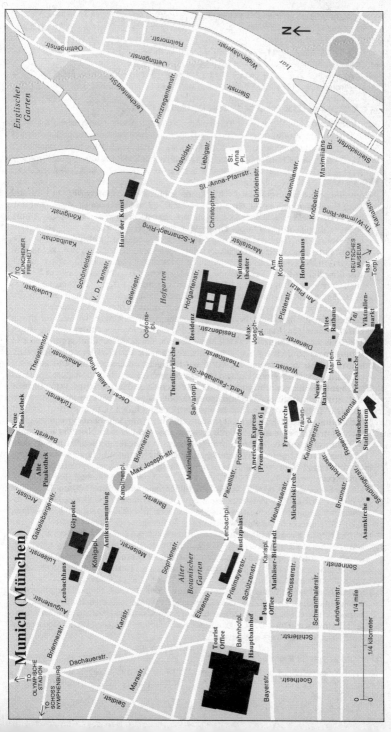

MUNICH (MÜNCHEN)

Munich (München)

TO OLYMPISCHE STADION
TO SCHLOSS NYMPHENBURG

Englischer Garten

TO MUNCHENER FREIHEIT

TO DEUTSCHES MUSEUM

Oettingenstr.
Leichtenfelsstr.
Veitingenstr.
Prinzregentenstr.
Sternstr.
Wider-Mayerstr.
Isar
Heimstr.

Unsoldstr.
Liebigstr.
St. Anna Pl.
St.-Anna-Pfarrstr.
Christophstr.
Bürkleinstr.
Maximilianstr.
Knöbelstr.
Maximilians Br.
Steinsdorfstr.
Kellerstr.
Th.-Wimmer-Ring

Königinstr.
Kaulbachstr.
Schönfeldstr.
V. D. Tannstr.
Galeriestr.
Ludwigstr.
Haus der Kunst
K.-Scharnagl-Ring
Hofgartenstr.
Hofgarten
National-theater
Marstallstr.
Am Kosttor
Hofbräuhaus
Am Platzl
Isar Torpl.

Theresienstr.
Amalienstr.
Türkenstr.
Oscar v. Miller Ring
Odeons-pl.
Residenz
Residenzstr.
Max-Joseph-pl.
Pfisterstr.
Dienerstr.
Altes Rathaus
Marien-pl.
Viktualien-markt
Tal
Peterskirche

Neue Pinakothek
Barerstr.
Alte Pinakothek
Arcisstr.
Theatinerstr.
Theatinerkirche
Salvatorpl.
Kard.-Faulhaber-Str.
Weinstr.
Neues Rathaus
Frauenkirche
Frauen-pl.
Rosenstr.
Rosental
Münchener Stadtmuseum

Gabelsbergerstr.
Glypotek
Königspl.
Antikensammlung
Meiserstr.
Karolinenpl.
Brennerstr.
Max-Joseph-str.
Maximiliansspl.
Promenadepl.
Pacellistr.
American Express [Promenadeplatz 6]
Kaufingerstr.
Augustenstr.
Lenbachhaus
Luisenstr.
Karlstr.

Sophienstr.
Barerstr.
Lenbachpl.
Justizpalast
Alter Botanischer Garten
Elisenstr.
Prielmayerstr.
Schützenstr.
Karlspl.
Mathäser-Bierstadt
Neuhauserstr.
Michaelskirche
Brunnstr.
Hotterstr.
Sendlingerstr.
Asamkirche
Sonnenstr.
Schlosserstr.
Schwanthalerstr.
Landwehrstr.

Brennerstr.
Briennerstr.
Seidlstr.
Dachauerstr.
Marsstr.
Marsstr.
Bayerstr.
Goethestr.
Schillerstr.
Bahnhofpl.
Hauptbahnhof
Tourist Office
Post Office

1/4 kilometer
1/4 mile

Pharmacy: Bahnhof Apotheke (tel. 59 41 19), on the corner outside the station. Open Mon.-Fri. 8am-6:30pm, Sat. 8am-2pm. 24-hr. service rotates; call 59 44 75 for information or get a free schedule from the tourist office or EurAide.

Medical Assistance: University clinic, across the river on Ismaningerstr. U.S. and British consulates have lists of English-speaking doctors.

Emergencies: Ambulance: tel. 192 22. **Emergency medical service:** tel. 55 86 61. **Police:** tel. 110.

ACCOMMODATIONS AND CAMPING

Accommodations in Munich fall into 1 of 3 categories: slimy, expensive, or booked solid. Everything should be reserved in advance in summer and during *Oktoberfest*. Sleeping in the Englischer Garten is unsafe and illegal. With a railpass, Augsburg's hostel (30-45min. by train) is a viable option, but check the curfew.

Hostels

Jugendlage Kapuzinerhölzl ("the Tent"), Frank-Schrank-Str. (tel. 141 43 00). Take U-1 to Rotkreuzplatz, then tram #12 (direction "Amalienburgstr."), and hop off at Botanischer Garten (ticket inspectors are especially rigorous on this route). Sleep with 400 others in a big circus tent. DM7 gets you a foam pad, blankets, a dry spot on the floor, bathrooms, a shower, hot tea, and enthusiastic management. 3-night max. stay. Reception open 5pm-9am. No reservations. No lockers; use the ones at the station. No reservations. Under 24 only (flexible). Open late June-early Sept.

Jugendherberge Burg Schwaneck (HI), Burgweg 4-6 (tel. 793 06 43), in a castle far from the city. Take S-Bahn #7 (direction "Wolfratshausen," last train 10:40pm) to "Pullach" and follow the signs that begin on Margaretenstr. (15min.). Unmajestic but entirely adequate. Swarms of schoolchildren. Reception open 5-11pm. Curfew 11:30pm. 6- to 8-bed dorms. Under 27 only. DM14.50. Shower token DM2. Breakfast included.

Jugendgästehaus München (HI), Miesingstr. 4 (tel. 723 65 50). Take U-1 or 2 to Sendlinger Tor, then U-3 to "Thalkirchen (Tierpark)," walk south on Pognerstr., and turn left onto Frauenbergstr.; cross Plinganserstr., walk 2 blocks and turn right onto Miesingstr. (30min.). Crowded and distant, but rooms are spacious and immaculate. Reception open 7am-1am; rooms available after 3pm. Curfew 1am. Under 27 only. 8- to 15-bed dorms DM23. Singles DM31. Doubles DM54. Triples DM75. Quads DM100. Sheets and breakfast included.

Jugendherberge (HI), Wendl-Dietrichstr. 20 (tel. 13 11 56). Take U-1 to Rotkreuzplatz; enter on Winthirplatz. Central, with noise and crowds. *Use the new safes in the reception area,* or leave your valuables in a locker at the station. Check-in starts at 10am; lines form at 9am. Reception open 10am-1am. Lockout 9am-noon. Curfew 1am. Under 27 only. DM19.80-21. Breakfast and sheets included.

Haus International Youth Hotel, Elisabethstr. 87, 80797 München (tel. 12 00 60; fax 12 00 62 51). Take U-2 to Hohenzollernplatz (direction "Dülferstr."), then tram #12 or bus #33 to Barbarastr. Clean; bare concrete interior. Disco, swimming pool, cafeteria. Singles DM51. Doubles DM96. Triples DM129. Quads DM156. Quints DM190. Reservations by mail or fax.

CVJM (YMCA) Jugendgästehaus, Landwehrstr. 13 (tel. 552 14 10), 2 blocks south of the station. Convenient, with clean, no-frills rooms in a shabby neighborhood. Reception open 8am-12:30am. Curfew 12:30am. Singles DM45. Doubles DM78. Triples DM108. Over 27 add 14% surcharge. Breakfast included. Reservations by mail or phone.

Jugendhotel Marienberge, Goethestr. 9 (tel. 55 58 91), less than a block south of the train station. Catholic hostel open only to women ages 18-25. Rough neighborhood but secure building; the rooms are spotless. Reception open 5-9pm. Curfew midnight. Singles DM31. Doubles 54DM. Triples DM81. Giant 6-bed dorms DM25/person. Showers included.

Hotels and Pensions

When the city is full, finding singles under DM60 or doubles under DM100 is nearly impossible. The tourist office charges DM5 to find rooms. When they say nothing available under DM60, believe it. At the train station, EurAide also finds rooms (DM6 fee).

Hotel-Pension Am Markt, Heiliggeiststr. 6 (tel. 22 50 14), between Viktualien-markt and Im Tal, next to Heiliggeist Kirche. Aging photographs recall the celeb-rities who have graced the hotel's sparsely furnished, immaculate rooms. Singles DM62, with shower DM89. Doubles DM110, with shower DM124-150. Reserve these highly sought-after rooms 3-4 weeks in advance by phone only.

Pension am Kaiserplatz, Kaiserplatz 12 (tel. 34 91 90). U-Bahn 1 or 2 (from the main station): "Odeonsplatz;" then U-Bahn 3 or 6: "Münchner Freiheit," take the escalator to Herzogstr., follow it, and take a left onto Viktoriastr.; then walk to Kaiserplatz (10min.). Carefully decorated, elegant, high-ceilinged rooms. Recep-tion open daily 7am-8pm. Singles DM45-49. Doubles DM69-79. Triples DM98-105. Quads DM120. Quints DM140. 6-person room DM160. Showers and breakfast included. Phone reservations only.

Pension Geiger, Steinheilstr. 1 (tel. 52 15 56), across the street from the Tech-nische Universität. Walk up Luisenstr. from the train station 5 blocks and it's on the left. Homey, with fluffy pillows. Singles DM45-59. Doubles DM74-90.

Pension Frank, Schellingstr. 24, 80799 München (tel. 28 14 51). Take U-3 or 6 to Universität. A curious mélange of scruffy backpackers and dolled-up models. Sin-gles DM55. Doubles DM75-85. Share a room wherever a bed is available for DM40. Showers and breakfast included. Book ahead during summer.

Hotel Helvetia, Schillerstr. 6 (tel. 55 47 45), near the train station. Bare walls and smiling hostess. Singles DM65. Doubles DM95. Triples DM120. Quads DM160. Quints DM200. Showers and breakfast included. Phone reservations only.

FOOD

Munich's gastronomic center is the vibrant **Viktualienmarkt,** 2 minutes south of Marienplatz, with a rainbow of bread, fruit, meat, pastry, cheese, wine, vegetable, and sandwich shops. (Open Mon.-Fri. 6am-6:30pm, Sat. 6am-noon.) Try Munich's *Leberkäs* (a mixture of beef and bacon) and *Weißwurst* (veal sausage).

University Mensas are located at: Arcisstr. 17, near the Pinakothekstr., Leopoldstr. 13, Dachauer-Str. 98b, and Helene-Mayer-Ring in the former Olympic village. Big slops of institutional food only DM2.70-4. Open Mon.-Fri. 11am-1:45pm. At Leopoldstr. 15, there's a **student café** with sandwiches (DM2-3). Open Mon.-Fri. 9am-5pm. *Mensas* and cafeterias open Nov.-July; student ID technically required.

Münchener Suppenküche, at the Viktualienmarkt and at Schellingstr. 24, near the university. Soups are authentic and eat like a meal. Really, they do. *Krustis* DM3.50-4.80. Open Mon.-Fri. 8am-6:30pm, Sat. 10am-5pm.

Türkenhof, Türkenstr. 78, west of the university. Favorite student hangout; packed evenings. Creative entrees DM6.50-16.80. Open daily 11am-1am.

Gaststätte Engelsburg, Türkenstr. at Schellingstr. A mix of students and Bavarian locals. 3-course lunches DM9.90-15.90. Salads DM11-14. Open daily 10am-11pm.

Beim Sendlmayr, Westenriederstr. 6, just off the Viktualienmarkt. So very... Bavar-ian. Terrific local specialties DM8.50-21.50.

Mango, Rosental 3-4, between Marienplatz and the Viktualienmarkt. Self-serve veg-etarian, DM6-12. Open Mon.-Fri. 11am-7pm, Thurs. until 9pm, Sat. until 4pm.

Café Oase, Amelienstr. 89. Quirky mix of the intellectual and whimsical. Sand-wiches DM6.80-7.80. Salads DM5.10. Entrees DM9-15. Open Mon.-Fri. 8:30am-1am, Sat.-Sun. 9:30am-1am.

SIGHTS

The 15th-century **Frauenkirche,** one of the city's most beloved landmarks, domi-nates Munich's skyline (closed for renovations until 1994). At the **Neues Rathaus,** the famous **Glockenspiel** steals the show with an elaborate mechanized display of jousting knights and dancing coopers. (Daily 11am, noon, 5pm, and 9pm; Nov.-April 11am and 9pm only.) At 9pm, a mechanical watchman marches out and the Guard-ian Angel escorts the Münchner Kindl, the little monk who is the symbol of Munich, to bed. The interior of the 11th-century **Peterskirche,** whose tower has been affectionately christened *Alter Peter* (Old Peter) by locals, was Baroquified in the 18th century. (Tower DM2.)

The richly decorated rooms built from the 14th to 19th centuries in the magnificent **Residenz,** Max-Joseph-Platz 3 (U-3, 4, 5, or 6: Odeonsplatz), form the earthly remains of the Wittelsbach dynasty. The grounds now house several museums, including the state collection of coins and the state treasury. (Open Tues.-Sun. 10am-4:30pm. DM4.) Even posher is **Schloß Nymphenburg,** the royal summer residence. A baroque wonder set in a winsome park, the palace hides unexpected treasures, including a 2-story granite marble hall seasoned with stucco and frescoes, and a Chinese lacquer cabinet. Check out King Ludwig's "Gallery of Beauties;" whenever a woman caught his fancy, he would have her portrait commissioned (a particularly scandalous habit as most were mere commoners). Take U-1 to Rotkreuzplatz, then tram #12 (direction "Amalienburgstr."). (Main palace open Tues.-Sun. 9am-12:30pm and 1:30-5pm; Oct.-March 10am-12:30pm and 1:30-4pm. Pagodas and palaces have similar hours. To main palace DM2.50, students DM1.50, to entire complex DM6. Wander the grounds for free.)

Abutting the city center is the vast **Englischer Garten,** one of Europe's oldest landscaped public parks. Nude sunbathing areas are designated FKK *(Freikörperkultur)* on signs and park maps.

Museums Munich is a superb museum city. Take tram #18 to "Isartor," where the **Deutsches Museum,** one of the world's most extensive museums of science and technology, fills an island in the Isar River with displays on just about anything ever invented. The planetarium (DM2) and the daily electrical show will warm the heart of any young Galileo or Franklin. (Open daily 9am-5pm. DM8, students DM3.) The **Alte Pinakothek,** Bärenstr. 27, and the **Neue Pinakothek,** just next door, rank with the world's finest art museums. Take U-2 or steetcar #18 to Königsplatz. The older museum holds an extensive collection of masterpieces from the 13th to 17th centuries, including a number of works by Dürer and Rubens, and Albrecht Altdorfer's mind-bogglingly detailed *Battle of Alexander.* The sleek quarters of the newer museum house an array of 18th- and 19th-century works. (Both open Wed. and Fri.-Sun. 9:15am-4:30pm, Tues. and Thurs. 9:15am-4:30pm and 7-9pm. To either DM5, students DM3.50; joint admission with the Neue Pinakothek DM10, students DM5. Sun. free.) The **Lenbachhaus,** Luisenstr. 33, just off Königspl., houses an extensive collection including works by Kandinsky, Klee, and the *Blaue Reiter* school. (Open Tues.-Sun. 10am-6pm. DM5, students DM2.50, Sun. free.) Facing one another on Königsplatz, the **Glyptothek,** Königspl. 3, and the **Antikensammlung,** Königspl. 1, hold Germany's best collections of Greek, Etruscan, and Roman sculpture. (Both museums open Tues.-Wed. and Fri.-Sun. 10am-4:30pm, Thurs. noon-8:30pm. To either DM5, students DM3; joint admission DM8, students DM4. Sun. free.)

ENTERTAINMENT

Munich's streets erupt with bawdy beer halls, rowdy discos, and cliquey cafés every night of the week. Pick up the *Young People's Guide to Munich* or buy a copy of the biweekly *Münchener Stadtmagazin* at any newsstand to find out what's up.

Beer To most visitors, Munich means beer. The 6 great city labels are *Augustiner, Hacker-Pschorr, Hofbräu, Löwenbräu, Paulaner-Thomasbräu,* and *Spaten-Franzinskaner.* Each brand supplies its own beer halls. (Most open daily until 11pm or midnight. Beer is served by the *Maß,* about a liter, DM8-11.) *Helles Weißbier* is a smooth, light beer; *dunkles Weißbier,* a rich, brown beer, is the dark variety. *Hefeweizenbier* is a mix of the two. *Bockbier* has a high alcohol content (5.5%). A *Radler* is a mixture of *Helles* beer and *Limonade* (a bright soft drink), a favorite among German lightweights—don't knock it 'til you've tried it. The biggest keg party in the world, Munich's **Oktoberfest** runs from the second-to-last Saturday in September to the first Sunday in October (Sept. 17-Oct. 2, 1994).

Munich's world-famous **Hofbräuhaus,** Am Platzl 9, 2 blocks from Marienpl., has been tapping barrels since 1859, but is now hopelessly touristy. (*Maß* DM9. Oom-pah band after 7pm. Open daily 10am-midnight.) To sample great suds with Ger-mans, head to one of Munich's other brewery-sponsored beerhalls: **Hacker-Pschorr,** Theresienhöhe 4 and 7; **Augustiner,** Neuhauserstr. 16; **Löwenbräukeller,** Nymphenburgerstr. 2 (U-1 to Stiglmaierpl.) or **Hofbräukeller,** Innere Wiener Str. 19. **Forschungsbrauerei,** Unterhachingerstr. 76, means "research brewery," so in their pleasant atmosphere you can imbibe mystery potions hitherto undiscovered by humankind. (*Maß* DM8-8.80. Open Tues.-Sat. 11am-11pm, Sun. 10am-10pm.) For outdoor Stein-hoisting, the best-known locale is the **Chinesischer Turm** beer gar-den, hidden away in the *Englischer Garten*. Take the U-3 or 6 to Giselastr., follow Giselastr. into the park and then take any one of the paths to the right and look for the pagoda; or take bus #54 from Südbahnhof to "Chinesischer Turm." (*Maß* DM9.40. Open daily in balmy weather 10am-11pm.)

Nightlife and Performances   Beer is a mere fanfare to nightlife in Munich. The **Schwabing** district, especially **Leopoldstraße,** is littered with bars, cafés, caba-rets, discos, and galleries. The area in Schwabing around **Münchener Freiheit** is the most touristy, but you'll also find the most serious partying and loudest discos here. More low-key is the southwestern section of Schwabing, directly behind the univer-sity on Amalienstr. and Türkenstr.; this area swims with student cafés, cheap restau-rants, and mellow bars. The blocks between **Viktualienmarkt** and **Gärtnerpl.** are the center of the city's gay nightlife.

The **Allotria Jazz Saloon,** Türkenstr. 33 (tel. 28 58 58), features excellent jazz. (Cover varies. Beer DM5.50. Open Tues.-Sun. from 10:30pm.) At night, raucous rev-elers of many sexual orientations gather at the **Villanis Café-Bistro,** Kreuzstr. 3b, in the passage (*Asamhof*) between Sendlinger Str. and Kreuzstr. (Beers DM4. Open Mon.-Sat. 10am-1am, Sun. and holidays 11am-1am. Sun. is unofficially gay night.) **Oly,** Helene-Mayer-Ring, is a slick and loud student dance spot with cheap beer (DM4) and a bohemian crowd.

The tourist office's monthly program (*Monatsprogramm,* in German) provides thorough schedule and ticket information for concerts and theater performances. Standing-room (DM9) and reduced-rate student tickets to the operas and ballets of the **Bavarian State Opera** are sold at Maximillianstr. 11 (tel. 22 13 16) behind the Opera House, or one hour before the performance at the side entrance to the opera itself. (Box office open Mon.-Fri. 10am-1pm and 3:30-5:30pm, Sat. 10am-12:30pm.) The **Gasteig** cultural center features the Munich Philharmonic's performance space as well as that for numerous other events. The **Staatstheater,** Gärtnerpl. 3 (tel. 201 67 67), stages comic opera and musicals; standing-room tickets start at DM6. Take U-1 or 2 to "Frauenhoferstr.," or tram #18 or 20. Munich's **Opera Festival** runs through July, as does a concert series in the Nymphenburg and Schleißheim pal-aces. The **Cinema Programmkino,** Nymphenburgerstr. 31 (tel. 55 52 55), screens English-language films.

■ Near Munich

"Once they burn books, they'll end up burning people," wrote the 19th-century German poet Heinrich Heine. This eerily prophetic statement is posted at **Konzen-trationslager-Gedenkstätte,** the concentration camp (Germany's first) at Dachau, next to a photograph of one of Hitler's book burnings. Though most of the buildings were destroyed in 1962, the walls, gates, guard towers, and crematoria remain. The terrifying legacy of Dachau lives in photographs and on film in the museum, the two reconstructed barracks and the several memorials and chapels on the grounds. Take S-2 toward Petershausen, get off at Dachau and catch bus #722 (DM2) in front of the station to the *KZ Gedenkstätte* (Memorial), a 20-minute ride. (Grounds open Tues.-

Sun. 9am-5pm.) EurAide offers a guided tour in English that leaves at 9:30am from the Munich Hauptbahnhof. (June-Aug. 21 on Tues. and Thurs.; Aug. 22-Sept. on Wed. DM25, with railpass DM17.)

The monastery at **Andechs** combines Bavaria's two most acclaimed attributes—Catholicism and beer gardens—on a gorgeous mountaintop. The monks brew a tasty light beer and a strong *Bockbier* that isn't served on Sundays *(Maß* DM6.20). The adjacent **Klosterkirche Heiliger Berg** houses over 250 centuries-old votive candles—giant, ornate candles commemorating departed brothers. (Beer hall open Mon.-Sat. 10am-7pm. Church open daily 10am-7pm.) Take S-5 from Munich to Herrsching, then switch to the private bus line Omnibus-Verkehr Rauner (outbound: Mon.-Sat. 7-10/day 7am-6:30pm; inbound 9-12/day, last return Mon.-Tues. and Thurs.-Fri. 5:50pm, Wed. 6:45pm, Sat. 5:30pm; Sun. 11/day 7:56am-6:33pm, returning 9:30am-6:45pm), or work up a thirst on the 3km hiking trail up the mountain. Follow signs marked "Fußweg nach Andechs" and stick to the trail; a sign reminds hikers of 11 people who met their death short-cutting down the precipitous slope.

Farther south, on the cusp of the Alps, lies the breathtakingly beautiful **Chiemsee,** Bavaria's largest lake and a favorite German holiday spot. Ludwig II of Bavaria built the third and last of his extravagant castles, **Königsschloß Herrenchiemsee,** on the **Herreninsel,** the largest of the lake's islands. The dozen completed rooms are replicas of rooms at Versailles. (Obligatory tours in German every 10min.; tours in English 10:30am, 11:30am, 2pm, and 3pm. DM6; students, seniors, and disabled DM3.50.) To reach Chiemsee and Herrenchiemsee, take the train from Munich to **Prien,** the main town on the lake.

■■■ NUREMBERG (NÜRNBERG)

In 1332, Nuremberg was declared a "free city" by the Holy Roman Emperor—meaning that its citizens answered only to the authority of the Emperor—and the Reichstag (parliament) was held here until 1543. It was this long connection with the empire that first attracted Hitler to Nuremberg, where he established the Reichsparteitag of the Nazi Party in 1927. The racial purity laws, which came to be known as the "Nuremberg Laws," were passed here in 1935. These events and the 1945-1949 Nuremberg war criminal trials have left the city indelibly tainted by the memory of Nazism, although the city's official tourist pamphlets cites *Bratwurst,* Albrecht Dürer, and the local soccer team as its most memorable attractions.

From the station, walk down Königstr. to the **Lorenzkirche,** which houses an exquisite 20m tabernacle and the **Engelsgruß,** a large free-hanging wooden carving by Veit Stoss, over the main altar. (Open Mon.-Sat. 9am-5pm, Sun., 2-4pm.) Across the Pegnitz River on Hauptmarktpl. is the **Frauenkirche,** a Gothic church with beautiful stained-glass windows. (Open Mon.-Sat. 9am-5pm, Sun., and holidays 12:30-6pm.) Every day at noon you can watch the antics of Emperor Karl IV and his 7 elector-princes on the church clock. On the other side of the square is the pastel and gold **Schöner Brunnen** (beautiful well). The **Kaiserburg** (Emperor's castle), housed all the Holy Roman Emperors after Konrad III. (40min. tour in German covers all parts of the Kaiserberg. DM3, students DM2. Open daily 9am-noon and 12:45-5pm; Oct.-March 9am-noon and 12:45-4pm.) Below the castle is the **Albrecht Dürer House,** a perfectly preserved monument to the 15th-century painter. (Open Tues. and Thurs.-Sun. 10am-5pm, Wed. 10am-7pm. DM3, students DM1.)

Germany's uglier contributions to modern civilization are on display at the **Dutzendteich Park.** Site of the Nuremberg rallies in the 1930s, the park still envelops the **New Congress Hall** and broad **Great Road.** (S-Bahn #5 direction "Neumarkt": "Dutzendteich Bahnhof" or tram #9 direction "Luitpoldhain": last stop, and continue walking to your left.) On the other side of town on Fürtherstr., many of the Nazi leaders faced a less enthusiastic audience of Allied military judges in Room 600 of the **Justizgebände.** The building still serves as a busy courthouse. (U-Bahn #1: "Bärenschanze" and continue walking away from the old town on Fürtherstr.)

Accommodations, Food, and Practical Information The comfortable and well-run **Jugendgästehaus (HI),** Burg 2 (tel. (0911) 22 10 24), is in the imperial castle. From the train station, continue north through the *Altstadt* to Burgstr.; the hostel is on top of the hill. (Reception open 7am-1am. Curfew 1am. Checkout 9am. Under 27 only. DM22.) The **Jugend-Hotel Nuremburg,** Rathsbergstr. 300 (tel. (0911) 521 60 92), is 25 minutes north of town. (Tram #3: "Ziegelstein", or bus #41: "Felsenkeller". Dorm-style rooms DM21-24/person.) Close behind the train station, **Pension Vater Jahn,** Jahnstr. 13 (tel. (0911) 44 45 07), offers comfortable, tidy rooms. (Singles DM40. Doubles DM70.) **Campingplatz am Stadion,** Hans-Kalb-Str. 56 (tel. (0911) 81 11 22), waits behind the soccer stadium; take the U-Bahn south to "Messenzentrum". (DM7/person, DM6/tent, DM5.50/car. Call ahead.)

Rostbratwurst, a mild sausage, is the thing to eat in Nuremberg, and the place to do so is beneath the smoking chimney of the tiny **Bratwurst-Häusle,** next to St. Sebald's Church. (6 *Rostbratwürst* DM8-15 served with sauerkraut or spiced potato salad. Open Mon.-Sat. 9:30am-10pm.) The **University Mensa,** Andrej-Sacharov Platz 1, is new, modern, efficient, and spanking white. (Lunch DM4-5. Open mid-Sept. to mid-July daily 11:30am-2pm.)

Nuremberg's **tourist offices** (tel. (0911) 23 36 32) are in the main train station (open Mon.-Sat. 9am-7pm) and downtown on Hauptmarktpl. (Open Mon.-Sat. 9am-1pm and 2-6pm; March-Sept. Sun. 10am-1pm and 2-4pm.) The **Mitfahrzentrale** office is a 10-minute walk from behind the station at Allerbergerstr. 31a (tel. (0911) 194 40; open Mon.-Fri. 9am-6pm, Sat. 8:30am-1pm, Sun. 11am-2pm). **American Express** (tel. (0911) 23 23 97) has an office at Adlerstr. 2. (Open Mon.-Fri. 9am-5:30pm; cashier closed noon-2pm, Sat. 9am-12:30pm.)

■■■ ROMANTIC ROAD
(ROMANTISCHE STRAßE)

Between Würzburg and Füssen, at the foothills of the Alps, lies a beautiful countryside of walled cities, castles, and elaborate churches. Sensing opportunity, the German tourist industry christened these bucolic backwaters the Romantic Road in 1950. The world has responded—this is the most visited region in Germany, so be prepared.

Deutschebahn's **Europabus** runs daily from Frankfurt to Munich (11hr.) and from Würzburg to Füssen (11hr.) from mid-March to late October (March-May only 1/day). The trip can also be done in segments, or you can stop anywhere along the line and catch the bus the next day (must be specified in your reservations). Eurail and all Deutschebahn passes cover the charge. The DB's regular *Lintenbuses* go to all the towns on the Europabus route and then some (3-10/day) and are far less crowded. Schedules are posted in train stations and tourist offices. For general information, contact the **Romantische Straße Arbeitgemeinschaft,** Marktplatz, 91550 Dinkelsbühl (tel. (09851) 902 71).

Würzburg Straddling the Main River and surrounded by vineyards, Würzburg sports an expansive baroque palace, a muscular fortress, and numerous alcohol-oriented festivals. In front of the train station, a **tourist office** (tel. (0931) 374 36) helps find rooms for a DM3 fee. (Open Mon.-Sat. 8am-8pm.) In March, the **Kulturamt,** also in the pink Falkenhaus at the Marktpl. will begin selling tickets for June's **Mozartfest.** Würzburg's answer to *Oktoberfest*—the **Kiliani Festival**—is held in July, and an annual **Wine Festival** takes place in late September. The striking 13th-century **Marienburg Fortress** stands vigil from high upon a hillside over the Main. Masochists can climb (40min.); otherwise take bus #9 (DM1.80), which runs every half-hour (May to mid-Oct. 9:43am-5:43pm) from the Spitäle bus stop at the western end of the Alte Mainbrücke bridge. (Open Tues.-Sun. 9am-12:30pm and 1-5pm; Oct.-March 10am-12:30pm and 1-4pm. DM3, students DM2, under 15 accompanied by adult free.) The **Residenz** (ecclesiastical palace), containing the largest ceiling fresco in the world, lies in **Residenzplatz.** (Open Tues.-Sun. 9am-5pm; Oct.-March 10am-4pm. Free.) In front of the Residenz stands the 900-year-old **Dom** of St. Killian, rebuilt in the mid-1960s after obliteration in 1945. (Tours April-Oct. Mon.-Sat. at noon, Sun. at 12:30pm. Open Mon.-Fri. 10am-5pm, Sun. 1-6pm; Nov.-Easter Mon.-Fri. 10am-noon and 2-5pm, Sun. 12:30-1:30pm and 2:30-6pm. DM2, children DM1.)

Würzburg's **Jugendgästehaus (HI),** Burkarderstr. 44 (tel. (0931) 425 90), is in the lee of St. Burkard's Basilica, across the river from downtown. Take tram #3 or 5 from the station (direction "Heidingsfeld") to "Löwenbrücke." (Reception open 2-10pm. Lockout 9am-2pm. Curfew 1am. Under 27 only. Top floor beds DM20, others DM24. Wheelchair access.) **Europabuses** head down the Romantic Road daily at 9am and 10:15am, departing from beside the station.

Rothenburg to Augsburg Though **Rothenburg ob der Tauber** is undoubtedly the most touristed spot in Germany, it may be your only chance to ever see a completely intact walled medieval city. Not as pre-packaged as Rothenburg, **Dinkelsbühl,** 40km south, maintains a full complement of half-timbered houses. The walled city of **Nördlingen,** 35km south of Dinkelsbühl, sits near the center of a circular meteor crater, the **Ries,** nearly 12km in diameter, which you can eye from **Der Daniel,** the tower of the 15th-century **St. Georgskirche** (DM2).

Founded by Caesar Augustus in 15 BC, **Augsburg** became the financial center of the Holy Roman Empire through the industry of the Fugger banking dynasty, later the personal financiers to the Habsburgs. The **Fuggerei** was founded by Jakob Fugger the Rich as a haven for the elderly destitute, who earn their keep by praying for the departed souls of the Fuggers. (Open March-Dec. daily 9am-6pm. DM1, students, senior and groups DM0.50.) The **Brecht Haus** on Auf dem Raim, birthplace of influential 20th-century playwright Bertolt Brecht, now chronicles his life through photos and letters. (Open Tues.-Sun. 10am-5pm; Nov.-April 10am-4pm. DM2.50, students and children DM1.50.)

Augsburg's resourceful **tourist office,** Bahnhofstr. 7 (tel. (0821) 50 20 70), is about 300m in front of the station, and will book rooms for a DM3 fee. (Open Mon.-Fri. 9am-6pm; Sat.-Sun. at the Rathaus, on Sat. 10am-6pm, Sun. 10am-1pm; at Rathaus tel. (0821) 502 07 24.) To find the clean, cramped, and central **Jugendherberge (HI),** Beim Pfaffenkeller 3 (tel. (0821) 339 03), take streetcar #2 (DM1.60) from the Bahnhof (direction "Kriegshaber") to the Stadtwerke stop, and continue on foot in the same direction; turn right onto Inneres Pfaffengäßchen. (Reception open 7:30am-11pm. Curfew 11pm. Under 27 only. DM15.50. Call ahead. Open Jan 2.-Dec.11.) The **Europabus** stops in Augsburg on its way south to Füssen. The **Mitfahrzentrale** is at Barthof 3 (tel. (0821) 15 70 19; open Mon.-Sat. noon-9pm).

■■■ BAVARIAN ALPS (BAYERISCHE ALPEN)

South of Munich, the land buckles into dramatic peaks and valleys which keep on tossing through Austria into Italy. Rail lines are scarce in this terrain; buses fill the gaps. For regional info, contact the **Fremdenverkehrsverband** (gotta love those German nouns) **Oberbayern,** Sonnenstr. 10, 8000 München (tel. (089) 59 73 47).

Füssen At the southern terminus of the Romantic Road, **Füssen** draws an inordinate number of visitors to the nearby **Königschlösser** (royal castles), two extravagant architectural concoctions of the fading Bavarian monarchy. Turn left from the train station to reach the town center, dominated by the **Hohes Schloß** (High Castle), former summer residence of Augsburg's bishops. Inside is the **Gemäldegalerie,** a collection of regional late-Gothic and Renaissance art. (Open Tues.-Sun. 11am-4pm; Nov.-March 2-4pm. DM3, students and seniors DM2.) The Romanesque **St. Mangkirche,** below the castle, had baroque alterations in the early 18th century.

The adjacent **Chapel of St. Anne** harbors the skeleton-bedecked *Totentanz* (Death Dance), a mural depicting the misfortunes that death bestows upon the living.

The Füssen **tourist office,** Augsburger-Tor-Pl. (tel. (08362) 70 77), 3 minutes from the station toward the town center, gives advice on hiking and finds rooms. Singles in *Gasthäuser* run DM30-35; in *Pensionen,* DM40 and up. Private rooms are cheaper but generally go only for 3 or more nights. (Office open Mon.-Fri. 8am-noon and 2-6:15pm, Sat. 10am-noon and 2-6:15pm, Sun. 9am-12:30pm; Oct.-May Mon.-Fri. 8am-noon and 2-6pm, Sat. 10am-noon.) Though decaying, Füssen's **Jugendherberge (HI),** Mariahilfstr. 5 (tel. (08362) 77 54), is generally packed. Turn right from the station and follow the railroad tracks. (Reception open 5-7pm. Lockout 9-11am. Curfew 10pm; in summer 11pm. Under 27 only. DM17.80. Sheets DM5. Wash DM2.50, dry DM2.50; soap DM2. Open mid-Dec. to Oct. Reservations recommended.) To reach Füssen from Munich or Augsburg, change trains in Buchloe.

From Füssen, take the bus marked "Königschlösser," which departs from the train station more or less hourly (DM2.10, Eurail valid). It was in neo-Gothic **Hohenschwangau,** built by Maximilian II, that Ludwig II, Bavaria's "crazy king," spent his childhood. Though lacking that lived-in look, **Neuschwanstein,** inspiration for the Disney World "Fantasyland" castle and pinnacle of Ludwig's desperate building spree across Upper Bavaria, is far more impressive in its excesses. The lines tend to be endless for the obligatory tours. Consider taking the tour first thing in the morning and spending the rest of the day hiking around the spectacular castle environs, particularly the **Pöllat Gorge** behind Neuschwanstein. (Castles open daily 9am-5:30pm; Nov.-March 10am-4pm. To either castle DM8; students, seniors, and disabled persons DM5.) Other **buses** to the castles depart from the Garmisch train station and stop in Hohenschwangau village (8am, 12:10pm, and 4:50pm; 2hr.; DM14.70, round-trip DM23.40, free with Eurail). From Munich, take a **train** to Buchloe or Kaufbeuren and transfer to the regional train to Füssen (2hr., DM30).

Oberammergau and Garmisch-Partenkirchen

Since 1634, the tiny Alpine town of **Oberammergau** has been the site of the world-famous **Passion Play** every 10 years. The next performances will be in the summer of 2000. Book a good 2 years ahead. The **tourist office,** Eugen-Papst-Str. 9a (tel. (08822) 10 21), has free maps and finds rooms for DM1. To reach the **Jugendherberge (HI),** Malensteinweg 10 (tel. (08822) 41 14), follow the right bank of the Ammer upstream (7min. from the station). The atmosphere is a bit loud and unpredictable. (Reception open 5-9:30pm. Curfew 10pm. Under 27 only. DM15.50. Open Dec. 27 to mid-March and April to mid-Nov.) Between Oberammergau and Garmisch-Partenkirchen stands **Schloß Linderhof,** Ludwig II's small hunting palace, surrounded by an elegant, manicured park with a 25m fountain. (Palace and grounds open daily 9am-5:30pm; Oct.-March 10am-12:15pm and 12:45-4pm. To all buildings in summer DM7, students DM4; in winter DM5 and DM2.50, respectively.) **Buses** (round-trip DM7.20) run to and from Oberammergau (7/day, 10am-7:02pm; last bus leaves Linderhof at 5:35pm). Get to Oberammergau by bus from Garmisch-Partenkirchen (round-trip DM10.40), Schongau (round-trip DM12.60) or Füssen (round-trip DM18). Railpasses are valid on all of these routes. **Trains** from Munich run to Oberammergau, switching at Murnau (11/day, 100min., DM21).

The two small resort villages of **Garmisch** and **Partenkirchen** united in 1935 in anticipation of the following year's Winter Olympics, and today Garmisch-Partenkirchen, in the shadow of the **Zugspitze,** Germany's highest mountain, is a thriving ski paradise. There are two ways up the peak: the first is to take a cog railway from the Zugspitzbahnhof (50m behind the Garmisch main station) to the Hotel Schneefernerhaus stop, then cable car "Gipfelseilbahn" to the top; the trip lasts 80 minutes, 65 minutes to the ski area (round-trip DM60). Another cable car, "Eibseeseilbahn," runs from Eibsee to the summit (10min.). Tickets are interchangeable and include the cog railway between the two base stations. **Hiking trails** of every grade radiate from town. Get a free map of local hiking trails at the **tourist office**

(Verkehrsamt), Richard-Strauss-Pl. (tel. (08821) 18 06); walk left from the train station, then turn left on Von-Brug-Str. (Open Mon.-Sat. 8am-6pm, Sun. and holidays 10am-noon.) When the office is closed, check out the *automat* in front of the building or call (08821) 194 12 for hotel information; the cheaper hotels are at the end of the recording. The **Jugendherberge (HI),** Jochstr. 10 (tel. (08821) 29 80), is 4km from town in Burgrain; take bus #6 or 7, direction "Farchant" to Burgain (DM2). (Reception open 7-10am and 5-10pm. Curfew 11:30. Under 27 only. Dorms DM15.50. Open late Dec.-Oct.) **Camping Zugspitze** (tel. (08821) 31 80) is on highway B24 at the base of the Zugspitze; take the blue-and-white bus from the station toward Eibsee/Grainau and get off at "Schmölzabzweigung." (DM6.50/person, DM9.50/site; in summer DM5.70 and DM8.50; in winter call ahead.) The cheapest **ski equipment rental** is at **Sepp Hohenleitner's,** at the Zugspitzbahnhof (tel. (08821) 506 10; DM 23/day, DM90/5days.) Procure **mountain bikes** at **Sportfreizeit Werdenfels,** Münchnerstr. 11 (tel. (08821) 81 62; DM25/day).

■■■ THE DANUBE

Northeast of Munich, the Danube Valley, with baroque Passau and Gothic Regensburg, is every bit as inviting as the Romantic Road. Rolling hills and lovely riverscapes attract visitors year-round—Germans themselves summer in cottages here.

Regensburg and the Bavarian Forest Regensburg was once the capital of Bavaria; it later became the administrative seat of the Holy Roman Empire. The halls where the Imperial Parliament met live on in the **Reichstags Museum,** housed in the Gothic **Altes Rathaus.** (Tours every 30min. Mon.-Sat. 9:30am-4pm, English tour 3:15pm; Nov.-March Mon.-Sat. 9:30am, 10:30am, 11:30am, 2pm, 3pm, and 4pm, Sun. 10am, 11am, and noon. Admission DM3, students DM1.50.) The splendid high-Gothic **Cathedral of St. Peter** towers over the city. (Open daily 6:30am-6pm; Nov.-March 6:30am-4pm.) The **Jugendherberge (HI),** Wöhrdstr. 60 (tel. (0941) 574 02), has been renovated into pleasant, roomy modernity. (Reception open most of the time 7am-11:30pm. Lockout 9am-1pm. Curfew 11:30pm. DM16.50. Reservations encouraged. Partial wheelchair access.) Campers should head for the **Campingplatz** (tel. (0941) 268 39) on Weinweg 40 outside of town. Take the Hochweg or bus #6 out of town and turn right on Hans-Sachs-Str., go about 2½km and the campsite will be on your right. (DM5/person, DM3.50/tent, DM3/car. Open March-Oct.) The **tourist office** *(Fremdenverkehrsamt),* Altes Rathaus (tel. (0941) 507 44 10) finds rooms (DM1.50), provides a free map and sells tickets to city events. From the station, walk down Maximilianstr. and take a left on Grasgasse. Take a right onto Obere Bachgasse and follow it to Rathauspl. **Trains** depart to Munich via Landshut (2-3hr., DM31). Trains to Passau (1hr., DM29) run every 30-60 minutes.

Northeast of Regensburg and Passau along the Austrian and Czech borders, the **Bavarian Forest** (Bayerischer Wald) is Central Europe's largest range of wooded mountains. The **Bavarian Forest National Park** is strictly protected from any activities that may alter the forest ecosystem. You can hoof it alone or sign up for guided walking tours, botanical tours, natural history tours, and tours of virgin woodlands. For information and schedules, contact the **Nationalparkverwaltung Bayerischer Wald,** Freyunger Str. 2, 8352 Grafenau (tel. (08552) 427 43). For news of the rest of the forest, contact the **Fremdenverkehrsverband Ostbayern,** Landshuterstr. 13 (tel. (0941) 571 86), off Maximilianstr., a 10-minute walk from the station in Regensburg. (Open Mon.-Sat. 9am-noon and 2-6pm, Sun. 10am-noon.) The park's thick, cool woods conceal glass factories and 17 **HI youth hostels;** Regensburg's tourist office has an omniscient brochure. **Jugendherberge Mauth (HI),** Jugendherbergstr. 11 (tel. (08557) 289), is accessible from Passau. (Under 27 only. DM16.50.)

Passau Elegant, baroque Passau spans two peninsulas formed by the confluence of the Danube, Inn, and Ilz Rivers. A center of trade and of both sacred and profane power for centuries, Passau teems with beautiful churches, palaces and cloisters. Its architecture reaches its apex in the sublime **St. Stephen's Cathedral.** Hundreds of chubby cherubs line the ceiling, and the world's largest church organ, gilded and filigreed, rests weightily above the choir. (Cathedral open Mon.-Sat. 8-11am and 12.30-6pm. Free. Organ concerts May-Oct. Mon.-Fri. noon, Thurs. 8pm; no concerts on holidays. Noon concerts DM3, students and seniors DM1; evening concerts DM6, students and seniors DM3.) Nearby are the **Residenz,** former home of the bishops of Passau, and the 14th-century Gothic **Rathaus.** The **Domschatz** (cathedral treasury), in the Residenz, testifies to the erstwhile wealth and power of the German church. (Open May-Oct., Christmas to early Jan., and the week after Easter Mon.-Sat. 10am-4pm. DM2, children DM1. Great Hall of *Rathaus* open Easter-Oct. Mon.-Fri. 10am-noon and 1:30-4pm, Sat.-Sun. 10am-4pm. DM1.)

The ominous 13th-century military complex of **Veste Oberhaus,** formerly the palace of the bishopric, now houses a regional **Cultural History Museum** (open March-Jan. Tues.-Sun. 9am-5pm; DM3, students DM1.50, free on Sun.), as well as the **Jugendherberge (HI)** (tel. (0851) 413 51), an aging hostel redeemed by the fantastic view of Austria through the windows. Take the infrequent shuttle from Rathauspl. to the front door or cross the bridge by the docks and brace yourself for the arduous hike. (After Easter to mid-Oct. every 30min. 11:30am-5pm. Reception open 9am-2pm and 4-11:30pm. Curfew 11:30pm. DM16.50.) **Gasthof zum Hirschen,** Im Ort 6 (tel. (0851) 362 38), has clean rooms in a central location on a cobblestone street; follow the Fritz-Schäffer-Promenade as far as possible toward the tip of the Passau peninsula, then turn right. (Singles DM30. Doubles DM55.) The **tourist office,** Rathauspl. 3 (tel. (0851) 334 21), has free maps, schedules, and hiking and camping info, and can find you a room for a DM2.50 fee. (Open Mon.-Fri. 8:30am-6pm, Sat.-Sun. and holidays 10am-2pm.) **Trains** run to Munich (DM46) and Vienna (8/day, fewer on weekends; DM64). **Steamers** cruise to Linz, Austria, (5½hr., round-trip DM47), with connections to Vienna (full round-trip DM221.40).

■■■ BAYREUTH AND BAMBERG

Bayreuth   When composer Richard Wagner first moved to Bayreuth in 1872, he saw in the small provincial town the perfect setting for his music and the perfect wealthy patroness (the Margravine Wilhelmine) to support him. Every year in late summer (late July-late Aug.), thousands of visitors pour in for the **Bayreuther Festspiele,** a vast and bombastic celebration of Wagner's works in the **Festspielhaus,** the theater Wagner built for his "music of the future." Tickets (DM35-255, obstructed view DM17-25) go on sale a year in advance and sell out almost immediately. For the 1995 festival, order tickets in writing by November 15, 1994. Write to Bayreuth Festspiele 95402 Bayreuth. Reserve a room as soon as you get tickets. Ticketless visitors can console themselves with a tour of Wagner's house, **Villa Wahnfried,** Richard-Wagner-Str. 48. Snippets from Wagner's compositions are performed daily in the drawing room at 10am, noon, and 2pm. (Open daily 9am-5pm. DM4, students DM1.50; Sept.-June DM3, students DM1.50.)

Except during the Festspiele, accommodations in Bayreuth are abundant and reasonable. To reach the roomy and modern **Jugendherberge HI,** Universitätsstr. 28 (tel. (0921) 252 62), take bus #4 (DM1.60) from the Marktpl. to "Mensa," walk past the buildings straight ahead, take the first left after the Mensa, then take a right after the bridge underpass. (Reception open 9-11:30am and 6-10pm. Curfew 10pm. Under 27 only. DM11. Open March to mid-Dec.) **Gasthof Vogel,** Friedrichstr. 13 (tel. (0921) 682 68), is centrally located and offers clean, pleasant rooms. (Singles DM30. Doubles DM60.) The **Schützenhaus,** Am Schießhaus 2, offers authentic Franconian delights and a large beer garden. (Open Tues.-Sat. 9:30am-midnight. Kitchen open Tues.-Sun. 9:30am-2pm and 5-10pm.) The **tourist office,** Luitpoldpl. 9 (tel. (0921) 885 88), to the left and about 4 blocks from the train station, provides a free map, a list of hotels, and information about surrounding areas. (Open Mon.-Fri. 9am-

6pm, Sat. 9am-noon.) Bayreuth can be done as a daytrip; but frequent **trains** connect it to Nuremberg (DM21.40).

Bamberg Few travelers think to explore the treasures of the Franconian cathedral city of Bamberg. The **Altes Rathaus,** half *Fachwerk* (timber and plaster) and half Baroque fresco, guards the middle of the Regnitz River like an anchored ship. Across the river and up the hill is the **Dom** (cathedral). Dating from 1004, the *Dom* began Romanesque and ended up Gothic. Inside is the mysterious horse-and-rider statue called the *Bamberger Reiter*. (Open daily 9am-6pm except during services. ½hr. organ concerts Sat. noon. Free.) Across the square, the **Neue Residenz,** Bamberg's former episcopal residence, poses baroquely; from its **rose garden,** the town is a sea of roofs. (Open daily 9am-noon and 1:30-5pm; Oct.-March daily 9am-noon and 1:30-4pm. DM3, students DM2.)

Though far from the center of town, both of Bamberg's hostels are clean and pleasant. To reach **Wolfsschlucht (HI),** Oberer Leintritt 70 (tel. (0951) 560 02), take bus #18 from the Zentralomnibusbahnhof (ZOB) to "Am Regnitzufer." (Reception open 3-5pm and 6-10pm. Curfew 10pm. Under 26 only. DM15.50. Sheets DM5. Breakfast included. Open Feb. to mid-Dec.) **Stadion (HI),** Pödeldorferstr. 178 (tel. (0951) 123 77), is loads of fun. Take bus #2 from ZOB to "Stadion". (Reception open 5-7pm. Lockout 9am-4pm. Curfew 10pm. Under 26 only. DM15. Sheets DM4.50. Breakfast included. Open April-Sept. Call ahead.) The **Maiselbräustübl,** Obere Königstr. 38 (tel. (0951) 255 03), has large rooms overlooking a serene courtyard. (Reception 11am-midnight. Singles DM35. Doubles DM65, with shower DM75. Breakfast included; delectable dinners from DM11.) The university **Mensa,** centrally located at Ausstr. 37, off Grüner Markt, serves the cheapest edible meals in town at DM3.50. Any student ID will do. (Open Nov.-July 11:30am-2pm.) **Polarbär,** Judenstr. 7, has vegetarian dishes for under DM12, a beer garden, and a hip student clientele. (Open daily noon-11pm.)

The **tourist office** at Geyerwörthstr. 3 (tel. (0951) 87 11 61) dispenses city maps. (DM0.30. Open Mon.-Fri. 9am-7pm, Sat. 9am-5pm.) Frequent **trains** connect Bamberg to Würzburg (DM24) and Nuremberg (DM15).

BADEN-WÜRTTEMBERG

Two of the most prominent German stereotypes—the brooding romantic of the Brothers Grimm and the economic empowerment exemplified by Mercedes Benz—shake hands in Baden-Württemberg. Pretzels, cuckoo clocks, and cars were all invented here, and the region is as diverse as its products. Rural custom and tradition are still widely evident in the scenic, foreboding hinterlands of the Black Forest and the Swabian Jura, while the modern capital city of Stuttgart is rooted in the latter-day ascendancy of the German industrial machine. The province also hosts the snooty millionaires' resort of Baden-Baden, the vacation getaways of Lake Constance, and the ancient university towns of Freiburg, Tübingen, and Heidelberg.

■■■ STUTTGART

Stuttgart epitomizes the "New Germany"—the prosperous, stable democracy that emerged from the horrors of the Third Reich to become the economic juggernaut of post-war Europe. The birthplace of Porsche, Mercedes, and a host of high-tech coffee makers, Stuttgart basks in a standard of living that's impressive even by contemporary German standards. While it lacks the architectural verve of other major German cities, the remarkable range of Stuttgart's cultural offerings and its less aggressively German atmosphere will refresh any visitor.

The **Schloßgarten,** Stuttgart's main municipal park, runs from the train station south to the *Neues Schloß* and northeast to the Neckar. Across from the *Schloßgarten* at Adenauer-Str. 30 is the superb **Staatsgalerie,** the modern wing of which contains works by Picasso, Kandinsky, Beckmann, and Dalí. At the other end of the *Schloßgarten* is the **Schloßplatz,** upon which reposes the elegant, Baroque **Neues Schloß,** now infested with bureaucrats. This and the 16th-century **Altes Schloß** across the street on Schillerplatz comprise the whole of Stuttgart's architecturally notable sights, but Stuttgart's dearth of venerable buildings is more than compensated for by numerous excellent museums, most of them free. **Hegel's birthplace,** Eberhardtstr. 53, is a few blocks down Adenauer-Str. near a busy porn shop. The museum provides a thorough, if somewhat inscrutable, exegesis of the philosopher's life. (Open Tues. and Fri. 11am-5pm, Thurs. 11am-8pm, Sat. 11am-4pm.)

The **Gottlieb Daimler Museum** is housed in the workshop where Herr Daimler, the inventor of the automobile, built the first generation of Mercedes-Benz. Take bus #56 to "Stadion" or S-Bahn #1 to "Neckarstadion." (Open Tues.-Sun. 9am-5pm. Free.) Not to be outdone, Dr. Porsche's **Porsche-Museum** tells the same story with different cars. Take S-Bahn #6 (direction "Wielderstadt") to "Neuwirkshaus." (Open Mon.-Fri. 9am-noon and 1:30-5pm. Free.)

The **Staatstheater,** across the plaza from the *Neues Schloß,* is Stuttgart's most famous. (Tickets available Mon.-Fri. 9am-1pm and 2-5pm. DM10-90.) The 25 other local theaters are usually much cheaper. (DM10-25, students DM5-15.) The tourist office provides schedules and sells tickets. The walls sweat and the music blasts at **OZ,** a hard-rock dance outlet on Büchsenstr. 10 (entrance on Kronprinzstr.; open Fri. 8pm-5am, Sat. 8pm-8am and Sun. 6pm-midnight). Two discos, **Kings Club,** Calverstr. 21 (tel. 22 45 58), and **Lauras Club,** Lautenschlagerstr. 20 (tel. 29 01 60), cater to gay men and lesbians, respectively. (Open daily 10pm-5am.)

Accommodations, Food, and Practical Information

The **tourist office, I-Punkt,** Königstr. 1 (tel. (0711) 222 80), directly in front of the escalator down into the Klett-Passage, books rooms for free and sells the **Monatsspiegel** (in German, DM1), which lists museum hours, cultural events, and musical performances and includes a guide to restaurants and nightlife. (Open Mon.-Sat. 9am-8pm, Sun. 11am-5pm; Nov.-Dec. Mon.-Sat. 8:30am-8pm, Sun. 1-5pm; Jan.-April Mon.-Sat. 9am-8pm.) The main **post office** is at Lautenschlagerstr. 17, 70173 Stuttgart. (Open Mon.-Fri. 8am-6pm, Sat. 8:30am-12:30pm, Sun. 11am-noon.) The **American Express** office, Lautenschlagerstr. 3 (tel. (0711) 187 50), is 1 block south of the station. (Open Mon.-Fri. 9am-5:30pm, Sat. 9am-noon.) Tickets for Stuttgart's **public transportation** are DM3; a 24-hour *Tageskarte* is DM14.

Most of Stuttgart's budget beds are located on the two ridges surrounding the downtown area and are easily accessible by tram. The **Jugendherberge (HI),** Haußmannstr. 27 (tel. (0711) 24 15 83; fax (0711) 60 83 51), is left from the station on Schillerstr. and up the hill; otherwise, take U-Bahn 15 or 16 (direction "Heumaden") to Eugensplatz and walk right down Kernerstr. (Reception open 7-9am and noon-11pm. Strict lockout 9am-noon. Curfew 11:30pm. DM18.50, over 26 DM23.50. Sheets DM5.50. Sleepsack DM3.50. Reserve by mail or fax.) If the Stuttgart hostel's full, try **Jugendherberge Ludwigsburg (HI),** Gemsenbergstr. 21 (tel. (07141) 515 64), in nearby Ludwigsburg. Take S-Bahn 4 or 5 (direction "Marbach" or "Biegetheim") to "Ludwigsburg" (about 15min.) and walk 10 minutes from the station. (Reception open 5pm to shortly before the 10pm curfew. DM17.70, over 26 DM22.70. Breakfast included. Sheets DM5.50.)

At the **University Mensa,** Holzgartenstr. 9-11, quantity compensates for quality (meals DM3-4). Get a Mensa credit card at the entrance and leave a DM20 deposit. (Open daily 11:15am-2pm; Aug.-Sept. until 1:30pm. Student ID required.) **Iden,** Eberhardstr. 1, serves inexpensive vegetarian fare cafeteria-style. (Entrees DM6.40-7.90. Open Mon.-Wed. and Fri. 11am-8pm, Thurs. until 9pm, Sat. 10am-4pm.)

Southwestern Germany's transport hub, Stuttgart has direct rail links to most major German cities. **Trains** roll out to Munich 30 times a day.

■■■ HEIDELBERG

In 1386, the sages of Heidelberg turned from illuminating manuscripts to illuminating young German minds. This, the oldest of Germany's university towns, is perhaps also the most quintessentially German. Set against a backdrop of wooded hills along an ancient river, the crumbling edifices of the once-majestic *Schloß* and the cobblestone streets of the *Altstadt* exert a magnetism that draws thousands of shutter-clicking, beer-swilling tourists every year.

ORIENTATION AND PRACTICAL INFORMATION

To get in, out and around the city, buy a 24-hour *Multi-ticket* pass good for 2 people on all trams and buses (DM7) at the **HSB kiosk,** opposite the side entrance to the train station. Single ride tickets are a serious DM2.70. To get to the *Altstadt* from the train station, take almost any bus or streetcar going into the city. (From Bismarckplatz, bus #33, direction "Köpfel" to "Bergbahn," or bus #11 to "Universitätsplatz.")

Tourist Office: Directly in front of the station (tel. 277 35). Rooms reserved for a DM4 fee plus a 5% down payment. Try calling hotels yourself, as the tourist office may steer guests toward more expensive lodging. Open Mon.-Sat. 9am-7pm, Sun. 10am-6pm; Nov.-Dec. same but Sun. until 3pm; Jan.-Feb. same but closed Sun.

Budget Travel: HS Reisebüros, am Bismarckplatz, next to Woolworth's (tel. 271 51). Special student deals; any student ID will do. Open Mon.-Fri. 9am-12:30pm and 2-6pm, Sat. 9am-noon.

American Express: Friedrich-Ebert-Anlage 16 (tel. 290 01). Open Mon.-Fri. 9am-5:30pm, Sat. 9am-noon. Banking services closed noon-2pm.

Post Office: Hauptpostamt, Belforstr., 69115 Heidelberg, diagonally to the right across from front of station. Open Mon.-Fri. 7am-6pm, Sat. 7am-noon.

Telephones: At post office and main train station. **City Code:** 06221.

Bike Rental: At the *Expreßgut* counter at the back of the train station. DM12, with railpass DM8. Open April-Sept. Mon.-Fri.7am-7pm, Sat. 7am-11:30pm.

Hitchhiking: Hitchers walk to the western end of Bergheimerstr. for all directions. The **Mitfahrzentrale** is at Kurfürsten Anlage 57 (tel. 246 46 or 194 44), 200m in front of the station. Open Mon.-Fri. 9am-6:30pm, Sat. 10am-2pm, Sun. 11am-2pm.

Women's Resources: Information for women tel. 213 17; **Frauencafé** (Women's Café), Blumenstr. 43 (tel. 213 17); **Women's Bookstore,** Theaterstr. 16.

Laundromat: Wasch Salon SB, Post Str. 49, next to Kurfürst Hotel. Wash DM7, dry DM1 (20min.). Open Mon.-Sat. 7am-11pm.

Emergencies: tel. 110 for all emergencies, including medical.

Police: Rohrbacherstr. 11 (tel. 52 00).

ACCOMMODATIONS, CAMPING, AND FOOD

Finding accommodations can be a nightmare in Heidelberg. In the summer, try to arrive early in the day. If Heidelberg fills up, the tourist office's listings in nearby Kirchheim (20min. on bus #40) may be worth investigating. Heidelberg's tourist office does not always have correct information about whether or not a place is full; check again by phone.

Jugendherberge (HI), Tiergartenstr. 5 (tel. 41 20 66). Bus #33 from Bismarckplatz or train station (direction "Zoo-Sportzentrum") to "Jugendherberge" (1st stop after Zoo). After 8pm, streetcar #1 to "Chirurgisches Klinik" and then bus #33 as above. Fairly far from the action. Reception open 7-9am, 1-3:30pm, and 4:30-11pm. Lockout 9am-1pm. Curfew 11:30pm. Members only. DM18.20, over 26 DM22.20. Sheets DM5.50. Partial wheelchair access. Reserve ahead if possible.

Jeske Hotel, Mittelbadgasse 2 (tel. 237 33). Bus #33 from train station (direction "Köpfel") or #11 (direction "Karlstor") to "Bergbahn." Perfect location, helpful management, and barnburner price. 2- to 5-bed rooms DM22/person. Floor with sleeping bag and cushion DM11. Showers DM2. Open Feb. to mid-Nov.; other times call ahead: the owners may be on vacation.

Hotel-Pension Schmitt, Blumenstr. 54 (tel. 272 96). 10-min. walk from station and 10min. to the *Altstadt.* Large rooms located just off Kurfürsten-Anlage. Singles DM60. Doubles with shower DM110; with shower and TV DM120. Triples DM150. Breakfast included.

Hotel-Pension Elite, Bunsenstr. 15 (tel. 257 33). From Bismarckplatz, follow Rohrbacher Str. away from the river, turn right onto Bunsenstr. Singles DM75. Doubles DM95; DM15/extra person in a double. Shower and breakfast included. Reservations by mail or phone.

Pensione Brandstätter, Friedrich-Ebert Anlage 60 (tel. 239 44). Bus #33 to "Peterskirche." Doubles DM79. Call way way way in advance. Way.

Camping: Haide (tel. (06223) 21 11) between Ziegelhausen and Kleingemünd. Bus #35 to "Orthopedisches Klinik," and cross the river. DM7/person, DM6/tent. Cabins DM14-16 depending on number of people. The more expensive **Camping Heidelberg-Schlierbach** (tel. 80 25 06) is on the other side of the river, near the Orthopedic Clinic.

FOOD

Eating out is costly in Heidelberg. Avoid the pedestrian zone; just outside its confines are historic student pubs and restaurants that offer better value. Buy groceries at **Handelshof,** Kurfürsten-Anlage 60, 200m in front of the train station on the right. (Open Mon.-Wed. and Fri. 8am-6:30pm, Thurs. 8am-8:30pm, Sat. 8am-2pm.)

Mensa, on Marstallstr. perpendicular to the river. State-subsidized cafeteria turns into an afternoon café. Cheap food, beer, cheesecake. Best to have a student ID.

Higher Taste, Kornmarkt 9. Vegetarian dishes DM5-8. Open 10:45am-6:30pm.

Zur Alten Brücke, Oberneckarstr. near the Karl-Theodor Brücke. Salads, sandwiches, fish, and vegetarian cuisine DM6-20. Kitchen open until 11pm.

Goldener Hecht, Steingasse 2, by the Alte Brücke. A 270-year-old Wagnerian pub. Filling meals DM20; appetizers DM7. Credit cards accepted.

Wirtshaus Zum Spreisel, Neckarstaaden 66, in Hotel Holländischer Hof, next to Goldener Hecht. Individual meals are not cheap (DM15-40), but the portions are huge. Open Sun.-Thurs. 5pm-midnight, Fri.-Sat. 2pm-midnight.

SIGHTS

The **Heidelberger Schloß** is the jewel in the crown of an already beautiful city. Destroyed both by war (1622 and 1693) and nature (lightning struck the tower arsenal in 1764), the castle is best viewed from the Philosophenweg high above the northern bank of the Neckar. The *Schloß* is easily accessible by foot or by *Bergbahn* (cable car), which runs from "Bergbahn/Rathaus" (bus #11 or 33) to the castle (round-trip DM4.50) and farther up to Königstuhl (DM7). (Departures every 10min. from Kornmarkt 9am-6:20pm.) The obligatory tour of the *Schloß* includes a visit to the **Faß,** reputedly the world's largest wine barrel. (Tours in English and German 9am-4pm. Castle open daily 9am-5pm; Nov.-March 9am-4pm. DM5, students and children DM2.50, including *Faß.*) The **Apothekenmuseum,** also in the castle, features a 17th-century pharmacy and alchemist's laboratory. (Open daily 10am-5pm; Nov.-March Sat.-Sun. 11am-5pm. DM3, students DM1.50.)

In town, several sights are clustered near the **Marktplatz,** a cobblestone square that holds an open air market every Wednesday and Saturday. In the center of the square stands **Hercules's Fountain,** where accused witches and heretics were burned in the 15th century. Here stand the two oldest structures in Heidelberg: the 15th-century **Heiliggeistkirche** and the 16th-century **Hotel zum Ritter.** The stately **Rathaus** presides over the far end of the square. From the Marktplatz, take Hauptstr. west for more Heidelbergian beauty; 5 blocks down, the **Universitätsplatz,** centered about a stone-lion fountain, is the former headquarters of the **Alte Universität.** Between 1778 and 1914, naughty students were jailed in the **Studentkranzer** (enter via Augustinergasse behind the old university building). (Open Tues.-Sat. 10am-noon and 2-5pm; Nov.-March Sat. 10am-1pm. DM1.50, students and children DM1.) At Hauptstr. 97, the **Kurpfälzisches Museum** features the jawbone of *homo Heidelbergensis,* or "Heidelberg Man" (one of the oldest humans yet unearthed), works of art by Van der Weyden and Dürer, and a spectacular 15th-century Gothic altarpiece. (Open Tues. and Wed.-Sun. 10am-5pm, Thurs. 10am-9pm. DM4; students DM2; children and Sun. free)

A stroll across the elegant **Karl-Theodor-Brücke** reveals a statue of the Prince-Elector himself, which he commissioned as a symbol of his modesty. From the far end of the bridge, clamber up the **Schlangenweg,** a winding stone stairway, to the **Philosophenweg,** a famous pedestrian walkway where Hegel indulged in afternoon promenades. Atop the **Heiligenberg,** the mountain traversed by the Philosophenweg, lie the ruins of the 9th-century **St. Michael Basilika,** the 13th-century **St. Stephen Kloster,** and an **amphitheater** built under Hitler in 1934 on the site of an ancient Celtic gathering place.

Heidelberg's **Faschings Parade** struts through the city on Shrove Tuesday, the day before Ash Wednesday. The 2-week **Spring Festival** begins at the end of May. A **wine festival** is held in mid-September, and the **Christmas market** runs from late November to December 22.

■ Near Heidelberg

The cathedral sites of **Speyer** and **Worms** to the west and the ancient castles of the Neckar Valley to the east are both simple day trips from Heidelberg. The Rhein-Neckar-Fahrgastschiffahrt (tel. (06221) 201 81) runs passenger cruises daily from June through early September between Heidelberg (departing from in front of the *Stadthalle*) and Neckarsteinach (daily, round-trip DM15.50). You can also view the valley from the Heidelberg-Heilbronn rail line, which follows the river with frequent stops in the medieval towns of **Neckarsteinach** and **Hirschhorn.** Along a slightly different Heidelberg-Heilbronn line lies the picture-perfect hamlet of **Bad Wimpfen,** a living fairy-tale where cobbled streets and rough-worked, half-timbered houses are the rule rather than the exception.

Bus #7007 continues on to **Speyer** (1½hr.), which can also be reached by train via Mannheim. The 12th-century **Kaiserdom (Imperial Cathedral)** is the largest structure of the Romanesque period. The crypt under its east end keeps the remains of 8 Holy Roman Emperors. (Open daily 9am-7pm except during Sunday services; Nov.-March 9am-5pm.) Just south of the *Dom* is the **Historisches Museum der Pfalz,** whose adjacent **Dommuseum** harbors what is touted as the **oldest bottle of wine in the world,** from a wild Roman bash around 300 AD. (Museums open Tues.-Thurs.-Sun. 10am-6pm, Wed. 10am-8pm. Under renovations until May 1994. DM2, students DM1.) Speyer's **tourist office** (tel. (06232) 143 92 or 143 95) is on Maximilianstr. 11, near the main entrance to the cathedral; take the city shuttle from the train station. (Open Mon.-Fri. 9am-5pm, Sat. 10am-noon.)

The site of Martin Luther's brave stand before the Imperial Diet in 1521, little **Worms** (VUHRMS) is now home to 7 pre-1900 churches, all located within a stone's throw in the *Altstadt.* Towering above all the rest is the **Dom St. Peter,** a Romanesque cathedral whose vaulted interior is both eerie and awe-inspiring. Across from the *Dom* to the east on Neumarkt 14, the **tourist office** provides maps of the town highlighting Worms's other 6 churches. (Open Mon.-Fri. 9am-noon and 2-5pm, Sat. 9am-noon.) The 1000-year legacy of Worms's Jewish community survives today in the **Heiliger Sand** cemetery on Andreasring west of the *Dom* and in the former Jewish quarter around **Judengasse** at the north end of the *Altstadt.* Just off the Judengasse are the **synagogue,** which houses the yeshiva of the famous Talmudic commentator Rabbi Shlomo Ben-Yitzhak (Rashi), and the **Rashi-Haus Museum,** which traces the history of the community. (Open Tues.-Sun. 10am-noon and 2-5pm. DM1, students DM0.50, free 1st Sun. of each month.)

■■■ TÜBINGEN

Radical graffiti smeared across 15th-century public buildings leaves no doubt that Tübingen is one of Germany's venerable academic towns, The students are gone in August and September, but at other times the buzz of young people and the relative lack of tourists enhance Tübingen's charm.

The focal point of the old city, the 15th-century **Stiftskirche,** is surrounded by winding alleys and gabled houses. The church's chancel contains the tombs of 14 members of the former House of Württemberg; climb the rickety stairs of the church tower for a commanding view. (Church open daily 9am-5pm. Chancel and tower open April-July and Oct. Fri.-Sun. 10:30am-5pm; Aug.-Sept. daily 10:30am-5pm. To chancel and tower DM1 each, students DM0.50.) The ornate, painted façade of the **Rathaus** faces the old market square in the middle of the *Altstadt.* On top of the hill that rudely separates the university from most of the city stands the **Schloß Hohentübingen,** a castle with a rough stone cowboy overlooking the old town. (Obligatory tour Sat. 5pm, Sun. 11am and 3pm. Open April-Oct. DM3.) Without a tour, you can still go out on the balcony for a view of the *Altstadt.* From the *Rathaus,* follow the signs marked "*Schloß*" leading up to the right in order to reach the castle. Along the river, the tree-lined path of the **Platanenallee**—which runs the length of an artificial island in the Neckar—makes for a pleasant walk with a scenic view of the *Altstadt.* On the northern riverbank is the **Hölderlinturm,** a tower where the great 18th-century poet Friedrich Hölderlin lived out the final 36 years of his life in a state of clinical insanity. The tower now houses a memorial museum. (Open Tues.-Fri. 10am-noon and 3-5pm, Sat.-Sun. 2-5pm. Tours Sat.-Sun. 5pm. DM2, students DM1.)

Accommodations, Food, and Practical Information Tübingen's **tourist office** (tel. (07071) 350 11) sits on the south side of the Eberhardt Bridge. From the front of the train station, turn right and walk to Karlstr., turn left, and walk to the river. The office will book hotel rooms for a DM4.50 fee and lodging in private homes (DM25-40) for DM3. (Open Mon.-Fri. 9am-6:30pm, Sat. 9am-5pm, Sun. 2-5pm; Oct.-April closed Sun.) The **Mitfahrzentrale,** Münzgasse 6 (tel. (07071) 267 89 or 50 81), can find you a ride to Munich for DM9, plus DM15-20 for gas. (Open Mon.-Fri. 9am-6:30pm, Sat. 9am-2pm, Sun. 10am-1pm. Call 1-2 days in advance.)

The large, worn **Jugendherberge (HI),** Gartenstr. 22-2 (tel. (07071) 230 02), overlooks the Neckar just downstream from the bridge at the tourist office. Take bus #11 from the station (DM2.50) to the "Jugendherberge" stop. (Reception open 7:30-9am, noon-1pm, 5-8pm, and 10-10:15pm. Curfew midnight. Members only. DM17.70, over 26 DM21. Wheelchair access.) Camp at **Rappernberghalde** (tel. (07071) 431 45) on the river. Go upstream from the old town or left from the station, cross the river on the Alleenbrücke, and turn left again. Follow the blue camping signs (20-25min.). (Reception open April to mid-Oct. daily 8am-12:30pm and 2:30-10pm. DM7/person, DM5-6/tent.)

Tübingen's students keep a number of superb yet inexpensive restaurants busy. The student-run **Marquardtei,** Herrenbergstr. 34, serves whole-wheat pizza and a vast selection of vegetarian and meat dishes to a mostly Red and Green clientele. Bus #8 or 9 to Rappstraße stops just outside the door. (Entrees DM6-15. Open Sun.-Fri. 11:30am-1am, Sat. 6pm-1am.) For the miserly, the **Mensa,** at Wilhelmstr. and Keplerstr., offers generic fare at low prices. (Open late Aug.-late July Mon.-Fri. 11:30am-1:30pm and 6-8:15pm. Tübingen University ID theoretically required.) In the *Altstadt,* **Restaurant beim Hölderlinturm,** Bursagasse 4, cooks up Swabian specialties for DM10.50-25. (Beer DM3-4. Open daily 11am-2pm and 5:30-10pm.)

Nearly every block in Tübingen claims one or two student pubs. The **Zentrum-Zoo** disco, Schliefmühleweg 86, a 10-minute walk from the old city, is popular with college students but occasionally gets overrun by a younger crowd. (Beer DM3.50-

4. Cover varies, usually DM5.) Inside the *Altstadt*, **Alter Simpel,** Haaggasse 24, proffers the standard assortment of beer and beverages (DM3-4) from 6pm to 2am.

■■■ BLACK FOREST (SCHWARZWALD)

Stretching west of the Rhine from Karlsruhe to Basel, the Black Forest looms large in the German cultural consciousness. Fairy tales, storybooks, and romantic lyrical poetry all owe their inspiration to the tangled expanse of evergreens where Hänsel and Gretel were left to their own devices. Still a bastion of local tradition, the forest is home to venerable farm houses sporting trademark straw roofs and venerable farmers sporting rural garb. Hiking is a favorite pastime here; trails are frequent and well-marked, and many are used in winter for cross-country skiing.

The main entry points to the Black Forest are Freiburg, at its center, Baden-Baden to the northwest, Stuttgart to the east, and Basel, Switzerland to the southwest. Public transportation is sparse in this mountain region; rail lines run along the perimeter from Baden-Baden to Freiburg and east from Freiburg to Donaueschingen and Stuttgart, but many of the innermost regions are accessible only by infrequent bus service. Check return connections in advance before setting off on daytrips. Many bus lines are privately owned, rendering railpasses invalid.

Freiburg In May 1940, a squadron of *Luftwaffe* pilots accidentally bombed Freiburg when they mistook the city for a French border town. Historically and culturally, at least, this is an easy mistake to make; a political football that has spent most of its 800-odd years under Austrian or French control, the undisputed metropolis of the Black Forest maintains a relaxed and cosmopolitan air. The pride of Freiburg is the **Münster,** a tremendous stone cathedral built at intervals between the 13th and 16th centuries. Its 116m tower can be climbed for DM1.50, offering dizzying views of the city and the forest beyond. A stroll through the surrounding *Altstadt* will uncover several of the **Bächle,** narrow streams of swiftly flowing water that run through the city. In medieval times, these open gutters were used to water cattle and protect against fires; today, they exist only to soak the shoes of unwary tourists. Two medieval gates—the **Schwabentor** and the **Martinstor**—still stand within a few blocks of one another in the southeast corner of the *Altstadt*. The latter is indelibly profaned by a McDonald's sign. From the Schwabentor, take the pedestrian overpass across the heavily trafficked Schloßbergring and climb the **Schloßberg** for an excellent view of the city. Freiburg's museums cater to a variety of interests. The **Augustiner Museum** on Augustinerplatz has a large collection of mostly medieval artifacts. (Open Tues.-Fri. 9:30am-5pm, Sat.-Sun. 10:30am-5pm. DM4, students DM2.) Farther south at Marienstr. 10a is the **Museum für Neue Kunst** (Museum of Modern Art), with a modest collection of 20th-century German works. (Museums open Tues.-Fri. 9:30am-5pm, Sat.-Sun. 10:30am-5pm. Free.)

Accommodations in Freiburg tend toward the pricey; the tourist office books cheaper rooms (single DM22-40, doubles DM40-80) in private homes, but a stay of at least 3 nights is usually required. The modern **Jugendherberge (HI),** Kartäuserstr. 151 (tel. (0761) 676 56), is one of the largest in Germany. Take S-Bahn #1 (direction: "Littenweiler") to "Römerhof," walk down Fritz-Geiges-Str., cross the stream, and turn right. (Reception open 7am-11:30pm. Curfew 11:30pm. Members only. DM17, over 26 DM22.50.) **Hotel Schemmer,** Eschholzstr. 63 (tel. (0761) 27 24 24), is friendly and centrally located. From the train station, take the overpass that crosses over the tracks, then go past the church and turn left. (Singles DM45. Doubles DM75.) Take S-Bahn #1 (direction "Littenweiler") "Lassbergstr.", then hop on bus #17 to "Kleintalstr." and follow Peterhof up to the large wooden farmhouse and **Haus Lydia Kalchtaler,** Peterhof 11 (tel. (0761) 671 19; DM18). For a truly unique culinary experience, try **Toast Reich,** at Münsterplatz 14 next to the cathedral. Europe's first—and probably last—toasteria, it features a variety of open-faced combinations for under DM10. (Open daily 9am-11pm.) The **tourist office** at Rotteck-ring 14 (tel. (0761) 368 90 90 or 368 90 97), 2 blocks down Eisenbahnstraße from the train station, finds rooms and distributes the comprehensive *Freiburg Official Guide*. (DM5, German or English. Open Mon.-Sat. 9am-8pm, Sun. 10am-noon; Nov.-April Mon.-Fri. 9am-6pm, Sat. 9am-3pm, Sun. 10am-noon.)

Titisee and Schluchsee Thirty km east of Freiburg lies the resort town of **Titisee** along the lake of the same name, attractively set against a backdrop of dark pine-forested ridges, but somewhat marred by the kitsch trappings of consumer tourism. Twice-hourly trains connect Freiburg to Titisee; the train ride, running through the **Höllental** (Hell's Valley), is one of the most scenic in Germany. The **tourist office** is in the *Kurhaus*, Strandbadstr. 4 (tel. (07651) 81 01); to reach the building, turn right in front of the train station, walk to the first intersection and turn right at the entrances to the pedestrian zone. Look for the flags dotting the lawn. The office books rooms for DM4; detailed maps (DM7.80-DM9.80) of the 130km of hiking trails surrounding the lake are also available. (Open Mon.-Fri. 8am-noon and 1:30-5:30pm, Sat.-Sun. 10am-noon.) **Paddleboats** can be rented from several vendors along Seestr. for DM11-15 per hour, and **guided boat tours** of the lake (DM5, 25min.) depart from the same area. **Jugendherberge Veltishof (HI)**, Bruderhalde 27 (tel. (07652) 238), is comfortable but out in the boondocks at the far end of the lake. From the train station, take the Südbaden bus, direction "Todtnau" (every 2hr., DM2) to Feuerwehrheim. By foot, it's a 30-minute walk along the main road from the *Kurhaus*. At DM8, the hostel serves the cheapest meal in the area. (Reception open 5-6pm and 7:30-8pm. Curfew 10pm. DM17.50, over 26 DM22.50.) Several campgrounds lie along the same road; **Campingplatz Weiherhof** (tel. (07652) 14 68) is on the water near the hostel and has laundry facilities. (April-Oct. DM6.50/person, DM8.50/tent.)

South of Titisee is the larger, less-touristed **Schluchsee**, whose **Jugendherberge Schluchsee-Wolfsgrund (HI)** (tel. (07656) 329) is ideally situated on the shore; from the station, with your back to the water, turn left and follow the tracks across the bridge to Wolfsgrund 28. (Curfew 11pm. DM17.70, over 26 DM22.70. Dinner DM8. Laundry DM6.)

St. Peter, St. Märgen, and Triberg North of Titisee and about 20km due east of Freiburg, the twin villages of **St. Peter** and **St. Märgen** lie within the High Black Forest. Eight buses per day depart from Freiburg's Omnibushof, adjacent to the train station, to reach these scenic locales (bus #7216; DM5.50 to St. Peter, DM6.50 to St. Märgen). **St. Peter's**, designed by architect Peter Thumb, perches up where a halo of green farmland breaks through the dark crust of pine forests. Its Klosterkirche may not be much on the outside, but inside it's rocking with Baroque angels. (Tours in summer Tues. 2:30pm. Bus: "St. Peter Post.") The bus puts you right in front of the **tourist office** (tel. (07660) 274; open Mon.-Thurs. 8am-noon, 2-5pm; June-Oct. also Sat. 11am-1pm). Well-marked **trails** cover the surrounding area; one of the trails from the abbey leads directly to St. Märgen, 8km away.

At the center of the High Black Forest is **Triberg**, a hiker's paradise accessible by a half-hour train ride from Donaueschingen to the southeast. From the train station, the city center is a 15-minute uphill walk; turn right in front of the station, head down the stairs at the overpass and follow the road past the large post office building. At the top of the street is Triberg's prime attraction, the **largest waterfall in Germany.** Mobs of visitors shell out DM2 (students DM1) to see the water plunge 162m in 7 separate drops. (Open daily 9am-7pm.) One-and-a-half blocks to the left of the waterfall's entrance is the **tourist office,** Luisenstr. 10 (tel. (07722) 812 30), in the *Kurhaus*. It books rooms and sells city maps (in English, DM1) and detailed hiking maps. (DM5.50. Open Mon.-Fri. 8am-noon, 2-5pm; May-Oct. also Sat. 10am-noon.) Triberg's **Jugendherberge (HI)**, Rohrbacherstr. 37 (tel. (07722) 41 10), is scenically located, but the journey there—a grueling 20-minute walk uphill from the

BADEN-BADEN

waterfall or 40 minutes from the station—may dismay you. (Reception open 5-7pm and at 9:45pm. Curfew 10pm. Members only. DM17.20, over 26 DM22.20.)

The dark, meandering valleys of the Northern Black Forest, spanned by an extensive network of trails, make for terrific trekking. The transportation hub of the region is **Freudenstadt.** Three major (9- and 12-day) trails traversing the entire Black Forest from north to south originate in the city of **Pforzheim;** for more information and the detailed brochure *Tips für Schwarzwaldwanderer,* write to: Stadtinformation, Marktplatz, W-7530 Pforzheim.

■■■ BADEN-BADEN

If you're fabulously wealthy, Baden-Baden can be a lot of fun. Even if you're not, it can still be a great place to visit, as long as you get at least some pleasure out of watching rich people on vacation; minor royalty and the like convene here to bathe in the curative mineral spas and drop fat sums of money in the casino.

Baden-Baden's history as a resort goes back nearly two millennia, when the Romans built the first **thermal baths** here. The **Friedrichsbad,** Römerplatz 1 (tel. 27 59 20), is a palatial 19th-century bathing palace where you can enjoy a 2-hour "Roman" "Irish Bath," guaranteed to cure any malady, almost. Not a stitch of clothing is permitted. (Open Mon.-Sat. 9am-10pm. Last entry 7:30pm. Baths are coed Tues. and Fri. 4-10pm and all day Wed. and Sat. DM28, with soap and brush massage DM38.) More modest and budget-minded cure-seekers should try next door at the also astoundingly beautiful **Caracalla-Thermen,** Römerplatz 11 (tel. 27 59 40), which offers placid soaking in the same water (and in bathing suits) at half the price. (DM18, with youth hostel coupon DM14.40. Open daily 8am-10pm.)

When they're not busy getting all pruney at the baths, Baden-Baden's affluent guests head to the **Casino,** whose opulent decor—modeled on the palace at Versailles—can be viewed via daily guided tours. (Open daily 10am-noon; Oct.-March 9:30am-noon. Last tour leaves at 11:30am. DM3). Attendance during gaming hours (Sun.-Thurs. 2pm-2am, Fri.-Sat. 2pm-3am) costs DM5, but you must be 21, present ID proving you're not a Baden-Baden resident, and wear appropriate dress (coat and tie for men). Technically, students are not allowed in. Bus #1 stops just outside the door. Next to the casino is the **Trinkhalle** (Pump Room), which contains a gold-plated fountain that dispenses the town's trademark spring water. (Open daily 10am-5:30pm. Tours and a drink DM4, students DM2.)

For a sumptuous view of the Black Forest, mount the 668m **Merkur** peak east of town. Take bus #5 to the Merkurwald stop, then take the railway to the top. (Combined round-trip DM6.) On the hill, the **Neues Schloß** houses a museum of the town's history. (Tours Mon.-Fri. 3pm; open Tues.-Sun. 10am-12:30pm, 2-5pm. Admission DM2, students DM1.) From the neighboring garden, you can get an excellent view of the entire town; there's an even better one, extending all the way to France, from the 12th-century ruins of the **Altes Schloß** in the upper hills a few km from the Neues Schloß. (Take bus #15 from Augustaplatz to "Altes Schloß.")

Accommodations, Food, and Practical Information The cheapest bed in town is at the modern **Jugendherberge (HI),** Hardbergstr. 34 (tel. (07221) 522 23), halfway between the station and the town center; take line #1 to "Große-Dollen-Straße" and follow the signs uphill. (Reception open 5-6pm and briefly at 8 and 10pm. Curfew 11:30pm. Members only. DM18.20, over 26 DM23.20. Wheelchair-accessible.) Rooms in the center of town are ritzy and overpriced, with the exception of the **Hotel Löhr,** Adlerstr. 2 (tel. (07221) 313 70). Reception is 1½ blocks away at **Café Löhr,** Lichtentaler Str. 19, across the street from the Augustaplatz bus stop. (One single at DM35, other singles DM50, with shower DM55. Doubles DM85, with shower DM90.)

You're probably not wealthy enough to eat out in Baden-Baden, but if you're in search of young, rich, marriageable Europeans, scope out **Club Taverne,** located in the basement of the Kurhaus, under the casino. (Cover DM10. Open 9pm-3am.)

Baden-Baden's **train station** is several km northwest of town. To avoid the blistering 90-minute walk, take bus #1. (Direction "Lichtental/Oberbeuren." DM2.50, 24-hr. pass DM6.50.) The appropriately opulent **tourist office** is at Augustapl. 8 (tel. (07221) 27 52 00), inside the massive Haus des Kurgastes. (Open Mon.-Sat. 9am-10pm, Sun. 10am-10pm.) The **post office** on Leopoldpl. has phones (daily 8am-7pm) and changes money, as does the casino.

■■■ LAKE CONSTANCE (BODENSEE)

The third-largest lake in Europe, the Bodensee forms a graceful three-cornered border at the conjunction of Austria, Switzerland, and Germany. Ancient castles, manicured islands, and endless opportunities to tan to an oily crisp draw residents of all three countries to the lake all summer long.

Spanning the Rhine's exit from the lake, the elegant university city of **Konstanz** is among the few German cities never struck by a bomb, and the local architecture shows it. Particularly inspiring is the **Münster** (cathedral); don't miss the view from the top of its Gothic spire. (Open April 15-Oct. 15 Mon.-Sat. 10am-5pm, Sun. 1-5pm. Free. Tower DM2, students DM1.) Konstanz's 3 free public beaches are packed in good weather. **Strandbad Horn** is the largest and most popular. (Take bus #5.) The twentysomething set frolics on the beach at the university. (Take bus #4 to "Egg" and walk past the playing fields.)

The **tourist office** (tel. (07531) 28 43 76), in the arcade to the right of the train station, provides an excellent walking map. (Open Mon.-Fri. 9am-8pm, Sat. 10am-1pm and 4-7pm, Sun. 10am-1pm; reduced hours off-season.) Konstanz has two **HI youth hostels. Jugendherberge Kreuzlingen,** (tel. (072) 75 26 63), rests in an old manor south of the border in Kreuzlingen. Take bus #8 to the Kreuzlingen train station and follow Bahnhofstr. until you see the signs. (Reception open 8am-10am and 5-11pm. DM19.) The hostel in Konstanz proper, **Jugendherberge "Otto-Moericke-Turm"** at Allmannshohe 18 (tel. (07531) 322 60), is neither as close nor as clean. Take bus #4 (DM1.80) from the "Marktstätte" stop (around the corner from the post office in front of the station) to the "Jugendherberge" stop. (Curfew 10pm. DM16, over 26 DM18.50). Fill up on Konstanz's cheapest food at the **University Mensa,** where lunch costs DM3-4 (DM1 discount with student ID). Take bus #9 from the station. (Open Mon.-Fri. 8am-7pm, Sat. 8am-1pm.) Health food stores, leftist graffiti, and student cafés pepper the area around **Rheingasse. Ships** depart about every hour from behind the train station to all the ports on the Bodensee. Consider the cruise that stops at Meersburg, Mainau, Unteruhldigen, and Überlingen. (Daily June-late Sept. Round-trip DM19.20, half-price with railpass.) For info and schedules, contact the **Weiße Bodenseeflotte** counter (tel. (07531) 28 13 89) at the harbor behind the train station.

CENTRAL GERMANY

■■■ FRANKFURT AM MAIN

A city of skyscrapers and investment bankers, Frankfurt belongs properly to the Germany of the future; it has the reputation of being the most Americanized city in Europe, a dubious distinction given Frankfurt's designation as the crime capital of Germany. Not much of historic Frankfurt escaped the bombings of World War II, but the treasures of the surviving *Altstadt,* coupled with an extraordinary variety of museums and one of the best zoos in the world, amply reward a few days' stay.

Sights and Entertainment The train station lies at the end of Frankfurt's moderately sleazy red-light district; the rest of the city is considerably more amenable. What's left of old Frankfurt is in the **Römerberg** area, a 20-minute walk down Münchener Str. from the station. The **Römer,** a distinctively gabled red sandstone structure at the west end of Römerberg, has been Frankfurt's city hall since 1405. The upper floors contain the **Kaisersaal,** a banquet hall whose walls are adorned with portraits of 52 German emperors. (Open Tues.-Sun. 11am-3pm; obligatory tour on the hour DM3.) The east end of Römerberg is overshadowed by the **Dom,** a huge red Gothic cathedral that was the site of coronation ceremonies for German emperors between 1562 and 1792. The view from the cathedral's tower is worth the climb to the top. (Under renovation until mid-1994. Tours 3pm. Open daily 9am-1pm and 2:30-6pm. Tower DM2, students and children DM1.) Near the Römer at Saalgasse 19, the **Historisches Museum** presents a first-rate series of exhibitions on the history of the city and the German nation. (Open Tues. and Thurs.-Sun. 10am-5pm, Wed. 10am-8pm. DM3, students DM1.) A few blocks from the Römer at Großer Hirschgraben 23-25 stands the **Goethe Haus,** birthplace of the poet and now a carefully preserved museum. The sumptuous interior is evidence that you don't have to suffer to produce great art. (Tours Mon.-Sat. 10:30am and 2pm, Sun. 2pm. Open Mon.-Sat. 9am-6pm and Sun. 10am-1pm. DM3, students DM2.)

From Römerberg, it's an easy 10-minute walk across the Eiserner Steg footbridge to the the **Museumsufer,** a string of 7 museums along Schaumainkai on the southern bank of the Main. There's something for everyone here, including collections devoted to ethnography, architecture, and filmmaking; the highlight is the **Städel,** one of Europe's leading art museums. (All 7 museums open Tues. and Thurs.-Sun. 10am-5pm, Wed. 10am-8pm. All are free except the architecture museum, which costs DM4, students DM2; and the Städel, which costs DM6, students DM3, Sun. free.) For less cerebral entertainment, head to Frankfurt's 4-star **Zoo** on the eastern side of town (U-6 or U-7). The feeding of the apes (daily at 4:30pm) and the big cats (daily at 5pm) excite a certain visceral pleasure. (Open daily 8am-7pm; Oct. to mid-March 8am-5pm. DM9.50, students DM4.50.)

The **Alt Sachsenhausen** district between Dreieichstr. and Brückenstr. is crawling with pubs and outdoor restaurants. Frankfurt's renowned jazz scene centers around Kleine Bockenheimer Str.—also known as Jazzgasse—in the city center. The most famous of the venues is **Der Jazzkeller,** Kleine Bockenheimer Str. 18a (tel. (069) 28 85 37; open Tues.-Sun. 9pm-3am; cover varies). Gay nightlife flourishes in the area between Zeil and Bleichstr.

Accommodations and Food The **HI youth hostel,** Deutschherrnufer 12 (tel. (069) 61 90 58), is conveniently located near the Sachsenhausen pubs. From the station, take bus #46 (DM2.10, during rush hours DM2.80) to Frankensteiner-platz. The hostel is 50m west in the large yellow building. After 7:30pm, take tram #16 to the Lokalbahnhof, walk north on Dreieichstr. and take a left on Deutschherrnufer. (Reception open 11am-10pm. Lockout 9am-1pm. Curfew midnight. DM19.50, over 20 DM23.50. Sheets DM10. Key deposit for smaller rooms DM10.) **Pension Backer,** Mendelssohnstr. 92 (tel. (069) 74 79 92), has clean rooms and a pleasant location near the university. Take the U-Bahn to "Westend." (Singles DM30-40. Doubles DM60.) **Pension Bruns,** Mendelssohnstr. 42 (tel. (069) 74 88 96), has tastefully decorated, comfortable rooms. Take bus #33 to "Bettinaplatz"; or, facing the train station, turn right down Düsseldorfer Str., which will become Friedrich-Ebert-Anlage, turn right on Mendelssohnstr., and it's on the right. (Singles DM54. Doubles DM76.) **Hotel Goldener Stern,** Karlsruher Str. 8 (tel. (069) 23 33 09), is one block behind the station to the right. (Reception open until 11pm. Singles DM39-50. Doubles DM60-75.)

Frankfurter sausages (the locals know them as *Wieners*) are not a Frankfurt specialty and should probably be avoided; try instead *gegrillte Rippchen* (grilled ribs) or *Handkäse mit Musik* ("handcheese with music"; really curd cheese with raw onions). Many of the taverns and pubs in the Alt Sachsenhausen district also serve food, and you can always find fairly cheap cuisine around Lipzigerstr. in the Bockenheim district (U-Bahn 6 or 7). **Ulli's Backstube,** Jordanstr. 1, near the university, is a small outdoor café serving sandwiches, salads, and quiche as well as breakfasts, all for under DM8. (Open Mon.-Fri. 6am-7:30pm.)

Practical Information Frankfurt's airport and train station are among the busiest in Europe. From the **airport,** S-Bahn lines #14 and 15 travel every 10 minutes to the main train station (DM4 from a blue automat, Eurail valid). Frequent **trains** leave the station for all the other major cities in Germany and the rest of central Europe. The **Mitfahrzentrale,** Baselerstr. 7 (tel. (069) 23 64 45 or 23 64 55), is 200m from the side exit (track 1) of the main train station. (Open Mon.-Fri. 8am-6:30pm, Sat. 8am-2pm. Call ahead.) The **tourist office,** in the main train station across from track 23 (tel. (069) 21 23 88 49 or 21 23 88 51), will book rooms for DM5, plus a DM8 deposit. (Open Mon.-Sat. 8am-9pm.) **American Express** is at Kaiserstr. 8 (tel. (069) 210 50; open Mon.-Fri. 9:30am-5:30pm, Sat. 9am-noon). There's a 24-hour **post office** on the 2nd floor of the train station; fetch **Poste Restante** at counter 6 or 7 of the main branch at Zeil 110, 60313 Frankfurt (U-Bahn: "Hauptwache;" open Mon.-Fri. 8am-6pm, Sat. 8am-noon).

■■■ MARBURG

The brothers Grimm spun their fairy tales in these rolling hills; from a distance Marburg an der Lahn seems more of their world than ours. The world's first Protestant university was founded here in 1527 and is still the heart of the town. Its alumni include Martin Heidegger, Boris Pasternak, T.S. Eliot, and Richard Bunsen (of burner fame). Climb more than 250 steps or take bus #16 to the exalted **Landgrafenschloß,** former haunt of the Teutonic knights. **Elisabethkirche,** the oldest Gothic church in Germany (c.1285), commemorates the town's patron, a countess-and-widowed-child-bride-turned-altruist-and-saint. (Tours Mon.-Fri. at 3pm, and Sun. at 11am and 3pm. Open Mon.-Sat. 9am-6pm, Sun. 11:15-6pm. DM2, students DM1.) Call (06421) 194 14 for **24-hour information** on hotel vacancies. The riverside **Jugendherberge (HI),** Jahnstr. 1 (tel. (06421) 234 61), catches the nighttime music of the *Altstadt* from across the Lahn. From the train station, take a city bus (#1-6, 16, or S) to Rudolfspl., cross the river and turn immediately right onto Trojedamm, then follow the riverside road until you turn left onto Jahnstr. (10min.). To find Rudolfspl. on foot, head up Bahnhofstr., turn left on Elisabethstr., which becomes Pilgrimstein, and walk 10 minutes. (Reception officially open 3:30-11:30pm. DM19.50, over 26 DM23.) **Camping Lahnaue** (tel. (06421) 213 31) is on the Lahn River; take bus #1 toward Sommerbad. (DM5/person, DM4/tent.) **Café Barfuß,** Barfüßerstr. 33, fills up at night, with Jever on tap (DM3), Guinness in bottles, and "American coffee" (i.e., free refills) at breakfast. (Meals DM12 and up. Open daily 10am-1am.) The **tourist office** (tel. (06421) 20 12 49 and 20 12 62), to the right of the train station, finds rooms from DM35 free of charge. (Open Mon.-Fri. 8am-12:30pm and 2-5pm, Sat. 9:30am-noon; Nov.-March closed Sat.) Marburg is served by frequent **trains** from Frankfurt (1hr.) and Kassel (1hr.).

■■■ THE RHINE: MAINZ TO KOBLENZ

The Rhine may run all the way from Switzerland to the North Sea, but in the popular imagination it exists only in the 80km of the Rhine Gorge that stretches from Bonn to just north of Mainz. This is the Rhine of legend, a sailor's nightmare and a poet's dream, where robber-baron castles overlook treacherous whirlpools and craggy riverbanks. From the Lorelei Cliff above St. Goarshausen, fair sirens once lured passing sailors to their deaths on the sharp rocks below, and the Rhine wines from the hillside vineyards have been the source of many lesser tragedies.

The Mainz-Koblenz train affords excellent views, but the best way to see the Rhine is by boat. The **Köln-Düsseldorfer (KD) Line** makes the complete Mainz-Koblenz run thrice daily in summer and along shorter stretches more frequently. (Fewer trips off-season. Mainz-Koblenz one-way DM72.60, round-trips discounted, free with Eurail.) English copies of the schedule are available at local tourist offices or at the docks; for more information call (0221) 208 83 18 or 208 83 19.

Mainz and Bacharach An easy 30 minutes by S-Bahn (line 14) from Frankfurt, **Mainz** makes a convenient starting point for Rhine tours; **Köln-Düsseldorfer ferries** depart from the docks across from the postmodern façade of the **Rathaus.** As the capital of the Rhineland-Palatinate region, Mainz has better things to do than cater to tourists. Mainz's most famous son, Johannes Gutenberg, is immortalized along with his most important creations in the **Gutenberg Museum** on Liebfrauenpl. (Open Tues.-Sat. 10am-6pm, Sun. 10am-1pm; movie shown at 11:15am; free.) Across the square stands the colossal 11th-century red sandstone **Martinsdom,** one of the most impressive cathedrals in Germany and the final resting place of several Archbishops of Mainz, whose extravagant tombs line the walls. (Open Mon.-Fri. 9am-6:30pm, Sat. 9am-4pm, Sun. 1-2:45pm and 4-6:30pm; Oct.-March Mon.-Fri. 9am-5pm, Sat. 9am-4pm, Sun. 1-5pm.) The adjacent **Dom Museum** houses sculptural artifacts dating from the early years of the Holy Roman Empire. (Open Mon.-Wed. and Fri. 10am-4pm, Thurs. 10am-8pm, Sat. 10am-2pm. Free.)

To make the maze of Mainz more maneuverable, streets running parallel to the Rhine have blue nameplates and streets running toward the river have red nameplates. The **tourist office,** Bahnhofstr. 15 (tel. (06131) 28 62 10), down the street opposite the train station, reserves rooms for DM5; unfortunately, the town offers few inexpensive ones. (Open Mon.-Fri. 9am-6pm, Sat. 9am-1pm.) Mainz's well-run **Jugendgästehaus (HI)** (tel. (06131) 853 32) is in the Volkspark in Weisenau (bus #1: "Jugendgästehaus" or #22: "Viktorstift"). (Reception open 5-10pm. Curfew 11:30pm. DM17, over 26 DM20.50.) **Campingplatz Maaraue** (tel. 43 83), lies close to the Theodor-Heuss bridge; cross it and turn right. (Reception open 7am-1pm and 3-10pm. DM5.50/person, DM4.50/tent, DM4/car. Open April-Sept.) For good, reasonably cheap food, head to the *Altstadt* in the streets behind the *Dom.*

On the west bank of the Rhine between Mainz and Koblenz is the cozy village of **Bacharach,** whose many **Weinkeller** (wine cellars) and **Weinstuben** (wine pubs) do their best to live up to the town's name ("altar to Bacchus"). The **tourist office,** a 3-minute walk up to the right from the train station at Overstr. 1 (tel. (06743) 12 97), has maps of area hiking trails. (Open Mon.-Fri. 8:30am-12:30pm and 1:30-5pm.) A grueling 15-minute walk uphill from the *Wernerkapelle* ends at **Jugendherberge Stahleck (HI)** (tel. (06743) 12 66), a gorgeously old castle with a fabulous view of the Rhine Gorge. The manager will bowl you over with friendliness. (Curfew 10pm. DM16.50, over 26 DM20.50.)

Koblenz At the north end of the Rhine Gorge stands **Koblenz,** whose location at the confluence of the Rhine and the Mosel has ensured prosperity since Roman days. Koblenz turns 2002 in 1994; the annual **Rhein in Flammen** (Rhine in Flames) festival on the second weekend in August features a burst of pyrotechnics.

Koblenz is a popular jumping-off point for Rhine and Mosel **cruises.** Bus line #1 connects the train station to the main docks at the Rheinfähre stop (one-way DM1.60); on foot, it's a 25-minute walk from the station down Markenbildchen Weg and then left along the river. Cruises lasting anywhere from one hour to all day depart frequently from the docks. The **tourist office** (tel. (0261) 313 04), across the street from the station, gladly gives away boat schedules and city maps complete with hotel, restaurant, and pub listings. (Open Mon.-Sat. 8:30am-8:15pm, Sun. 2-7pm; Nov.-April Mon.-Fri. 8:30am-1pm and 2-5pm.)

The focal point of the city is the **Deutsches Eck** (German Corner), the peninsula that supposedly saw the birth of the German nation when the Teutonic Order of Knights settled there in 1216. The monumental **Mahnmal Der Deutschen Einheit** (Monument to German Unity) now dominates this little corner of history; first erected in 1897 in honor of Kaiser Wilhelm I, the 14m equestrian statue that once crowned it was destroyed in 1945. Most of the nearby *Altstadt* was flattened during WWII, but several important buildings have been carefully restored. The **Mittel Rhein Museum,** Florinsmarkt 15-17, contains a reputable collection of German art and antiquities. (Open Tues. and Thurs.-Sun. 10am-4:30pm, Wed. 10am-9pm. Free.) From the docks on the Rhine, a frequent ferry (DM1.20) runs across the river to **Festung Ehrenbreitstein,** a fortress that in Prussian days was the largest in Europe. The 20-minute climb to the battlements is worth it for the view; a chairlift *(Sesselbahn)* also makes the trip. (May-Oct. 9am to about 5pm. DM4, round-trip DM7.)

Inside the fortress is the recently renovated **Jugendherberge (HI),** which may have the most scenic location of any hostel in Germany (tel. (0261) 737 37). From the train station, take bus #7, 8, 9, or 10 to "Charlottenstr.," then continue up the river and turn right onto the "main road" towards the castle (follow the signs). (Curfew 11:30pm. DM18.20, over 26 DM22.20.) **Campingplatz Rhein-Mosel** (tel. (0261) 80 24 89) is across the Mosel from the *Deutsches Eck;* a ferry journeys across the river during the day. (DM5/person, DM4/tent. Open April to mid-Oct.)

■■■ THE MOSEL VALLEY (MOSELTAL)

An arresting landscape, a smattering of ancient castles, and many fewer tourists make the Mosel Valley as intriguing as the Rhine to the east. The river meanders northeast across more than 200km of German territory from Trier on the Luxembourg border to Koblenz, where it flows into the Rhine. The valley's slopes aren't quite as steep as the Rhine's narrow gorge, and the countless vineyards that crowd the gentle hillsides have been producing quality vintages since Roman times. See the valley's splendid scenery by boat, bus, or bicycle, since the train line between Koblenz and Trier strays frequently from the river into remarkably dull countryside. Some train stations will rent you a sturdy, heavy one-speed for DM12 per day, DM6 per day with a train ticket, Bundesbahn bus ticket, or railpass. You can drop off the bike at another train station at no extra charge and have your baggage sent ahead. Although passenger boats no longer make the complete Koblenz-Trier run, several companies run daily summer trips along shorter stretches; local tourist offices will provide details.

Cochem and Beilstein   Cozied in a bend in the river 35 minutes from Koblenz is the town of **Cochem,** which exists solely to produce wine and coddle tourists. High on a vineyard-blanketed hill above the town, the majestic turrets of the **Reichsburg** castle reign over the setting. Originally built in the 11th century, the castle—like much of the Palatinate—was destroyed in 1689 by French troops under King Louis XIV. In 1868, it was rebuilt in neo-Gothic style by a wealthy Berlin merchant. The interior can be seen today only on a guided tour. (Frequent tours last 40min; written English translations available. Open mid-March to Oct. daily 9am-5pm. DM4, students DM3.50.) Even if you bag the tour, the view from the castle grounds alone is worth the 20-minute uphill climb along Schloßstr. from the Marktpl. Cochem itself is a maze of twisting streets and tourist establishments. The flower-lined **promenade** along the river offers some respite from the endless succession of beer steins and postcard trees.

The **tourist office** (tel. (02671) 39 71) is on Enderpl. right next to the bridge; from the train station, head to the river and turn right. The office will book rooms free of charge. (Open Mon.-Fri. 9am-1pm and 2-5pm, Sat. 10am-3pm; Nov.-May closed Sat.) Cochem's friendly but minimalist **Jugendherberge (HI)** is 30 minutes from the station on the opposite shore at Klottener Str. 9 (tel. (02671) 86 33). Cross the Mosel bridge and turn left on Burgstr., which turns into Klottener Str. (Reception open 8-9am and 6-6:30pm. Latecomers should ring bell. Curfew 10pm. DM17, over 26 DM21.) **Campingplatz am Freizeitzentrum** (tel. (02671) 44 09) is on Stadionstr. just below the youth hostel. (Reception open 8am-10pm. DM4.50/person, DM3.50-7.50/site. Open April-Oct.)

Ten km upstream from Cochem lies **Beilstein,** an attractive hamlet with little-touristed half-timbered houses and crooked cobblestone streets. A private bus line (railpasses not valid) makes several trips a day between Cochem (stopping at the train station and on Endertpl.) and Beilstein (15min., one-way DM3.60); the passenger boats of **Personenschiffahrt Kolb** (tel. (02673) 15 15) make 4 round-trips per day. (1hr. each way, round-trip DM15. Railpasses not valid.) **Wine cellars** abound in Beilstein; make it a point to try one of the full-bodied local whites. Not to be missed here are the ruins of **Burg Metternich,** another casualty of the pyromaniacal French tourists of 1689; the view from its broken-down edifices sweeps the valley. (Open April-Oct. daily 8:30am-7pm. DM2, students DM1.)

Trier At the western end of the Mosel Valley lies **Trier,** the oldest city in Germany. Now just over 2000 years old, Trier had its heyday in the 4th century as the capital of the Western Empire and residence of Emperor Constantine. It's been a long but graceful 1600-year decline; today, some of the most extensive Roman ruins outside Italy and an *Altstadt* that's as attractive and well-preserved as they come make Trier more than worth your time. A short 5- to 10-minute walk down Theodor-Heuss-Allee from the train station brings you to the 2nd-century **Porta Nigra** (Black Gate), named for the centuries of grime that have turned its sandstone face varying shades of gloomy. (Open daily 9am-5:30pm; Oct.-Nov. and Jan.-March 9am-4:30pm. DM2, students DM1.) In the shadow of the Porta Nigra is Trier's **tourist office** (tel. (0651) 97 80 80; open Mon.-Sat. 9am-6pm, Sun. 9am-3:30pm; Nov.-March Mon.-Sat. 9am-6pm, Sun. 9am-1pm). From there, stroll down Simeonstr. to the **Hauptmarkt,** which is the northern leg of Trier's remarkably large pedestrian shopping district. A left onto Sternstr. brings you to the impressive interiors of the 11th-century **Dom.** (Open daily 6am-6pm; Nov.-March 6am-noon and 2-5:30pm. Free.) From the *Dom,* Liebfrauenstr. leads to the **Konstantin Basilika,** Constantine's 4th-century throne room, now about as exciting as an airplane hangar. From here, it's a 5-minute walk uphill along Olewiger Str. to the remains of the 2nd-century **amphitheater,** a 20,000-seat venue which would have been a required stop on any Roman world tour. The masses may want to make a pilgrimage to the **Karl-Marx Haus,** Brückenstr. 10, the birthplace of the bearded philosopher; it now houses a slightly dry account of his life. (Open Mon. 1-6pm, Tues.-Sat. 10am-6pm. DM3, students DM2.)

Trier's **Jugendgästehaus (HI),** An der Jugendherberge 4 (tel. (0651) 292 92), has all the comforts of home. From the station, it's a 30-minute walk; take Theodor-Heuss-Allee to the Porta Nigra, turn right on Paulinstr., take the first left onto the narrow, poorly marked Maarstr. and follow it until it ends. Or take bus #2 or 8 (direction "Trierweilerweg" or "Pfalzel/Quint") to "Moselbrücke" and walk 10 minutes downstream on the path along the top of the river embankment. (Lockout 9:30am-1pm. Curfew midnight. DM24-31.50, over 26 DM28-35.50. Wheelchair accessible.) The **Jugendhotel Kolpinghaus,** with dorm rooms, and the adjacent **Hotel Kolpinghaus** with singles and doubles, are clean, friendly, and one block off the Hauptmarkt at Dietrichstr. 42 (tel. (0651) 751 31; reception open 8am-11pm; dorm bed DM22; singles DM30, doubles DM60; call ahead). Camp at **Schloß Monaise,** at Monaiser Str. (tel. (0651) 862 10) on the grounds of an 18th-century castle. From the station, take bus #40 toward "Zewen" to "Flugplatz." (DM5/person, DM6/car.) **Astarix,**

Karl-Marx-Str. 11, serves ridiculously inexpensive meals in a casual student-dominated environment. (Open Mon.-Sat. 11am-1am, Sun. 6pm-1am.)

Several **trains** a day make the 1½-hour trip from Trier to Koblenz in the east and the one-hour jaunt from nearby Luxembourg to the west. From May to October, one **boat** per day departs for Bernkastel Kues in the Mosel Valley (9:15am, DM41).

■■■ COLOGNE (KÖLN)

Cologne, whose eight bridges straddle the Rhine just north of Bonn, began as a Roman colony, gaining fame and fortune as a medieval crossroads rich in academic life. The city pulled itself up by its bootstraps after WWII, which left 90% of its inner parts in ruins; the magnificent façade of the reconstituted cathedral was once a national symbol of the postwar reconstruction effort.

PRACTICAL INFORMATION

Tourist Office: Verkehrsamt, Unter Fettenhennen 19 (tel. 221 33 45), across from the main entrance to the cathedral. City maps (free) and rooms booked (fee DM3-5). Open Mon.-Sat. 8am-10:30pm, Sun. 9am-10:30pm; mid-Oct. to April Mon.-Sat. 8am-9pm, Sun. 9:30am-7pm.

Currency Exchange: At the train station daily 7am-9pm, but service charges are lower at the post office.

American Express: Burgmauerstr. 14, near the Dom. ATM. Client letter service only for cardholders. Open Mon.-Fri. 9am-5:30pm, Sat. 9am-noon. Cash window closed noon-2pm.

Post Office: Main office, An den Dominikanern. **Poste Restante** at windows 3 and 4. **Postal Code:** 50668.

Telephones: City Code: 0221.

Flights: Take bus #170 from the Hauptbahnhof to the Köln-Bonn Flughafen. Call (02203) 40 40 01 for flight information.

Trains: Hauptbahnhof, next to the cathedral. To: Düsseldorf (25min.); Hamburg (4hr.); Frankfurt (2hr.); Brussels (2½-3hr.), and Amsterdam (3hr.). The auxiliary **Köln-Deutz Bahnhof** is across the river.

Public Transportation: VRS (Verkehrsverbund Rhein-Seig) offices have a plan of the S- and U-Bahn lines and the city bus and tram lines. Tickets are priced by distance: short-ride single cards (DM1.70), 4-ride cards (DM6), and day-cards (DM8)

Hitchhiking: Citynetz Mitfahrzentrale, Saarstr. 22, tel. 194 44. Open Mon.-Sat. 9am-7pm.

Laundry: Öko-Express, Neue Weyerstr. 1. Wash DM6, dry 15min./DM1. Soap included. Open Mon.-Sat. 6am-11pm. The Köln-Deutz hostel also has machines.

Pharmacy: Dom-Apotheke, Komodienstr. 5, near the station, offers advice in English. A list of late-night pharmacies is posted outside.

ACCOMMODATIONS AND FOOD

Cologne's 2 hostels are both filled to the beams from June to September.

Jugendherberge Köln-Deutz (HI), Siegesstr. 5a (tel. 81 47 11), just over Hohenzollern Bridge. Cramped rooms in a prime location and a great juke box. From the Deutz station, go one stop on S-Bahn #6, 11 or 12; cross Ottoplatz and you're there (2min.). 374 beds. Fills quickly. Check in 6-9am. Riskier reception noon-10pm. Curfew 12:30am. DM23, over 26 DM27. Breakfast included. AmEx, MC, V.

Jugendgästehaus Köln-Riehl (HI), An der Schanz 14 (tel. 76 70 81), on the Rhine north of the zoo. From the station, take tram #5 (Mon.-Fri. until 7pm) or U-Bahn #16 or 18 (direction "Eberplatz/Mülheim") to "Boltonsternstr.," or walk (40min.) along the Rhine on Konrad-Adenauer-Uferstr. More luxurious but less convenient. 1st-floor **Köln-Treff Café** open 8pm-12:30am daily. Reception open 24hrs. No curfew. DM28.50. Breakfast included.

Hotel Rossner, Jakordenstr. 19 (tel. 12 27 03). From the back of the *Hauptbahnhof* (2min.); the 4th left off Johannisstr. A good value and convenient. Classic noble German rooms. Singles DM55, with shower DM75. Doubles DM80, with shower DM110.

Campingplatz Poll (tel. 83 19 66), southeast of the *Altstadt*, on the Rhine. Take U-Bahn #16 to "Marienburg" and cross the Roddenkirchener Bridge. DM5.50/person, DM3-7.50/tent.

You shouldn't desert Cologne without sampling the city's extraordinarily smooth beer, Kölsch. Inexpensive food—and just about anything else—is available along **Schildergasse** and **Hohe Straße**, the main pedestrian shopping thoroughfares by the cathedral. Stands between the station and the cathedral offer *Rievekochen* (potato pancakes) with *Apfelmuß* late into the night. The basement of the **Karstadt** department store on Hohe str. sells groceries. Off **Aulpicherplatz**, supermarket **Plus** gives the deepest price cuts. The most interesting area for inexpensive food is on **Weidengasse**, in the Turkish district. Restaurants, Imbiß, and specialty stores compose the street, though at night they edge on the red-light district.

SIGHTS AND ENTERTAINMENT

Overwhelming in intricacy and scale, the colossal **Dom** (cathedral) took 6 centuries to build. Inside is the **Shrine of the Magi**, a reliquary of the town's holy patrons in blinding gold, under the 19th-century bell known affectionately as **Der Große Peter** (at 24 tons, the world's heaviest swinging bell). All it takes are 509 steps to reach the top of the **Südturm** (south tower) and peer down at the city below. Time and pollution have erased much of the cathedral's original detail; each piece is being reproduced and replaced in new and treated stone. (Cathedral open daily 7am-7pm. Tower open 9am-5:30pm; March-April and Oct. 9am-4:30pm; Nov.-Feb. 9am-3:30pm. DM2, students DM1.)

The exterior of the 12th-century **Groß St. Martin**, once on an island surrounded by the then-Rhine-flooded pedestrian zone, is striking despite extensive wartime damage. In the shadow of the cathedral, the **Hohenzollern Brücke** crosses the Rhine. The majestic bridge empties out onto a promenade, guarded by equestrian statues of the imperial family.

If you stay at a Köln hostel, be sure to pick up the **Köln Bonbon,** a packet of 12 vouchers only available through the hostel system. A 3-day pass is good for free entry into the city's 9 museums. (DM15, bonbon with discount voucher for 2hr. city bus tour DM26.) On the other side of the *Dom* from Heinrich-Böll-Platz, the **Römisch-Germanisches Museum**, Roncallipl. 4, displays artifacts from the city's Roman days. Imperial mementos include the risqué **Dionysos-Mosaik,** a nearly complete tile floor. (Open Tues.-Sun. 10am-5pm. Tour Sun. 11:30am. DM5, students DM2.50.) Near the station, the unusual building (Bischofsgartenstr. 1) housing both the **Wallraf-Richartz** and **Ludwig-Museum** provides a maximum of indirect, natural light. The museum's early medieval and very modern collections are integrated, so it's only a few steps from the sublime to the ridiculous. (Open Tues.-Thurs. 10am-8pm, Fri.-Sun. 10am-6pm. Comprehensive admission DM8, students DM4. Special exhibits extra.) Smaller museums hide in every *Kölsch* corner; one of the best is the **Beatles Museum,** Heinsbergstr. 13 off Zülpicherstr., absolutely crammed with Fab Four memorabilia. They say they want a renovation, well well, you know, they don't want to change the price. (Open Sept.-July Wed.-Sat. 10am-7pm. DM3.)

Cologne becomes a living spectacle during the **Carneval,** celebrated in the opulent spirit of the city's Roman past. For the dancing-in-the-street **Rosenmontag** procession on the last Monday before Lent (February 21, 1994), everyone in costume gets a couple of dozen *Bützchen*—Kölsch for a kiss on a stranger's cheek. Arrive early; this is Cologne's specialty, and half of Germany wants in.

Students congregate in the **Quartier Lateng,** a.k.a. Bermuda Dreieck (triangle), the area bounded by Zülpicherstr., Zülpicher Platz, Roonstr. and Luxemburgstr. The center of **gay nightlife** runs up Matthiasstr. to Möhlenbach, Hohe Pforte, Marienplatz, and up to Heumarkt in the area by the Deutzer Brücke. The tradition of getting plastered is most respected by the various *Brauhäuser*, where the original

Kölsch is brewed and served in house. Here the Köbes will bring one beer after the other until you fall under the table, or lay your coaster across your glass.

■■■ BONN

Poor Bonn. A historical nonentity for most of its 2000 years, the so-called *Hauptdorf* (capital village) made it big by chance: since Konrad Adenauer, the revered postwar chancellor, had a house in its suburbs, the ever-considerate occupying powers promoted humble Bonn to capital status. Easy come, easy go; newly resurgent Berlin is poised to become what it always really was, Germany's capital. Snide Berliners like to say that Bonn is "half the size of a Chicago cemetery and twice as dead," but with more than its share of museums and a respectable university, this "small town in Germany" is a worthwhile destination even without the political clout.

Before the Bundestag, Bonn had Beethoven. Ludwig wailed his first notes in what's now called **Beethovens Geburtshaus** (Birthplace), Bonngasse 20, now a museum dedicated to his life and work. (Open Mon.-Sat. 10am-5pm, Sun. 10am-1pm; Oct.-March Mon.-Sat. 10am-4pm, Sun. 10am-1pm. Last entry ½hr. before closing. DM5, students DM1.50.) The symphonic ghost grips Bonn every 2 or 3 years for the summer-long **Beethoven Festival.** At the first scandal-ridden fête in 1845, the composer himself snubbed Queen Victoria, and Lola Montez—the King of Bavaria's mistress—danced on the tables. The 18th-century pastel **Rathaus** presides over the Marktplatz; in the similarly colorful 1960s, de Gaulle, Kennedy, and Elizabeth II all made the building their photo-op backdrop. Nearby stands the **Kurfürstliches Schloß,** an 18th-century palace later converted into the central building of Bonn's university. The **Kunstmuseum Bonn,** Friedrich-Ebert Allee, showcases a superb assembly of Expressionist and contemporary German art. (Open Tues.-Sun. 10am-7pm. DM5, students DM3.) From the bank of the Rhine, you can see the **Bundeshaus,** Germany's Parliament, on Görrestr., the "Least Prepossessing Parliament Building" in the whole world. (Open Mon.-Fri. 9am-4pm, Sat.-Sun. 10am-4pm; Jan. to mid-March Mon.-Fri. 9am-4pm. Obligatory tours on the hour at Hermann-Ehlers-Str. 29, opposite the Hochhaus; bring your passport.)

Accommodations, Food, and Practical Information The recently renovated **Jugendgästehaus Bonn-Venusberg (HI)** is at Haager Weg 42 (tel. (0228) 28 12 00). Take bus #621 (direction "Ippendorf Altenheim"). (Curfew 1am. DM28.50.) The more central **Jugendgästehaus Bonn-Bad Godesberg (HI),** Horionstr. 60 (tel. (0228) 31 75 16), is just as spiffy. Take U-Bahn #63 or 16 from the main station to "Rheinallee" or bus #615 (direction "Stadtwald/Evangelische Krankenhaus") from the Bad Godesberg station to "Venner Str." and look for the sign. (Curfew 1am. Same prices and perks.)

Young Bonners stomach inexpensive but barely palatable meals (DM2.20-3.40, DM1 extra without student ID) at the **University Mensa,** Nassestr. 11, a 15-minute walk from the train station along Kaiserstr., with a ridiculously cheap (DM5/kg) salad bar upstairs. (Open Mon.-Fri. 8am-4pm, lunch served 11:30am-2pm; late Sept. to mid-July open Mon.-Thurs. 8am-8pm, lunch served Mon.-Thurs. 11:30am-2:15pm and 5:30-8pm, Fri. 11:30am-2pm, Sat. noon-1:45pm.) **Cassius Garten,** Maximilianstr. 28d, at the edge of the *Altstadt* facing the station, will fulfill your wildest vegetarian fantasies. (DM2.12/100g. Open Mon.-Wed. and Fri. 11am-8pm, Thurs. 11am-9pm, Sat. 11am-3pm.)

Bonn's **tourist office,** which books hotels for a DM3-5 fee, is in a passageway at Münsterstr. 20 (tel. (0228) 77 34 66). Take the "Stadtmitte" exit from the station, walk 60m up Poststr., turn left at Münsterstr. and left again. (Open Mon.-Sat. 8am-9pm, Sun. 9:30am-12:30pm; Oct.-Feb. Mon.-Sat. 8am-7pm, Sun. 9:30am-12:30pm.) Bonn's got consulates: **U.S.,** Deichman Ave. 29 (tel. (0228) 339 20 53; open Mon.-Fri. 8:30-11:30am); **Australia,** Godesberger Allee 105 (tel. (0228) 810 30; open Mon.-Fri. 9am-noon); **Canada,** Godesberger Allee 119 (tel. (0228) 81 00 60; open

Mon.-Fri. 8am-noon); **New Zealand,** Bundeskanzlerplatz 2-10 (tel. (0228) 22 80 70;
open 9am-1pm.)

■■■ AACHEN

Tramping across 8th-century Europe, Charlemagne fell in love with Aachen and
made it the capital of the nascent Frankish empire. Its octagonal neo-Byzantine
Dom, in the center of the city circle, is one of the world's immortal cathedrals.
Stained-glass panels ring the 15th-century Gothic choir; beneath the chancel lie the
bones of the big guy himself. (Open daily 7am-7pm.) Old Charlie cuts more of a figure in the **Schatzkammer** (treasury) around the corner to the right from the Dom
exit, where the solid gold *Karlsbüste,* the best known likeness of the emperor,
shines. (Open Mon. 10am-2pm, Tues.-Sat. 10am-6pm, Sun. 10:30am-5pm; late-Oct.
to early-April Mon. 10am-2pm, Tues.-Sat. 10am-5pm, Sun. 10:30am-5pm. Last entry
½hr. before closing. DM3, students DM2.) Cathedral tours, the only way to get close
to the imperial throne, begin at the treasury (DM2). On the northern façade of the
14th-century **Rathaus,** over the Marktpl. beside the cathedral, stand 50 statues of
former German sovereigns. (Open Mon.-Fri. 8am-1pm and 2-5pm, Sat.-Sun. 10am-
1pm and 2-5pm.) The **Ludwig Forum für Internationales Kunst,** Jülicherstr. 97-
109, in a converted Bauhaus umbrella factory, opened just in time to invest in a stunning Eastern European collection. Warhol looks stodgy by comparison. (Open
Tues.-Wed. and Fri.-Sun. 11am-7pm, Thurs. 11am-10pm. DM6, students DM3. Free
tours Thurs. 8pm and Sun. 11:30am.)

Accommodations, Food, and Practical Information Aachen's central **tourist office** (tel. (0241) 180 29 60) is in the Atrium Eliserbrunnen on
Friedrich-Wilhelm-Pl. Another office is at Bahnhofpl. 4 (tel. (0241) 180 29 65), opposite the train station. Both book rooms for a DM3 fee. (Open Mon.-Fri. 9am-6:30pm,
Sat. 9am-1pm.) Aachen's whitewashed brick **Jugendherberge (HI),** Maria-Theresa-
Allee 260 (tel. (0241) 711 01), sits on the fringe of a forest south of the city. From
the station, walk left on Lagerhausstr. to the Finanzamt stop at the corner of Mozartstr.; from there, take bus #2 (direction "Preusswald") to "Ronheide" or bus #12
(direction "Diepenbendem") to "Colynshof" stop and walk uphill. (Reception open
until 10pm. Curfew 11:30pm. DM17.30, over 26 DM20.80.) **Pontstraße** is lined
with restaurants and student pubs. **Katakomben Studentenzentrum,** Pontstr. 74-
76, a student co-op, serves wholesome, inexpensive food (meals DM5.50-8.50) and
has occasional live music. (Open Mon.-Fri. 4pm-1am, Sat.6pm-1am.) Pocket some
Aachen Printen, trademark nut-studded ginger cookies, at local bakeries.

At the crossroads between Germany, Belgium, and the Netherlands, Aachen is
also a departure point for **trains** to France, and Cologne is less than an hour away.
Find a ride at the **Mitfahrzentrale,** Röermonderstr. 4 (tel. (0241) 15 20 11). Up to 5
people can ride the city bus network all day with a DM6 *Tagesnetzkarte.*

■■■ DÜSSELDORF

Germany's fashionable advertising center and multinational corporate base, Düsseldorf runneth over with German patricians and poser aristocrats. Residents have a
maxim that Düsseldorf isn't on the Rhine, but on the **Königsallee** (a.k.a. "the Kö"),
a km-long fashion runway that leads down either side of the old town moat. At the
upper end of this see-and-be-seen *Belle Epoque* promenade, the **Hofgarten** park
adds an oasis of green and culture to all the urbanity. Resident Robert Schumann
tried to end it all in the Rhine by jumping off a town bridge, but nationally beloved
Heinrich Heine is a much more favored son: every third restaurant and fast-food
stand on the Bölkerstr. block where he was born bears the Heine name. The
author's dignity is maintained a bit better at the **Heinrich Heine Institut,** Bilkerstr.
12-14, with its collection of manuscripts and a discomfiting death mask cast from

Heinrich's still-warm features. (Open Tues.-Sun. 11am-5pm. Library open Tues.-Fri. 10am-4pm. DM3, students DM1.50.) West of the Hofgarten is the reflecting-glass thing, the **Kunstsammlung Nordrhein-Westfalen,** Grabbepl. 5, an exceptional modern art museum with *the* definitive Paul Klee collection. Take U-Bahn #70, 76, 78, or 79 to Heinrich-Heine-Allee and walk north 2 blocks. (Open Tues.-Sun. 10am-6pm. DM10, students DM5.) A spectacular collection spanning 2 stories and 11 centuries awaits in the **Kunstmuseum Düsseldorf,** Ehrenhof 5. (Open Tues.-Sun. 11am-6pm. DM5, students DM2.50.) Even farther north on the Rhine, but still in Düsseldorf, are the well-preserved ruins of Emperor Friedrich's palace in the tiny town of **Kaiserswerth.** Take U-Bahn #79 to "Klemenspl.," then follow Kaiserwerther Markt to the Rhine and walk left another 150m. (Open Mon.-Fri. 3-7pm, Sat.-Sun. 10am-7pm. Free.)

Accommodations Düsseldorf is a convention city; if you're considering a budget hotel stay, call the tourist office for trade fair *(Messe)* dates and show up during a lull. Most rooms go for at least DM40 per person even in the off-season. The conjoined **Jugendherberge und Jugendgästehaus Düsseldorf (HI),** Düsseldorfer Str. 1 (tel. (0211) 57 40 41), is a better deal, just over the Rheinkniebrücke from the *Altstadt.* From the station, take bus #835 to "Jugendherberge" or U-Bahn #70, 705, or 717 to "Lugepl." and walk 500m down Kaiser-Wilhelm-Ring. Choose between the cheaper but above-average **Jugendherberge** (DM20, over 26 DM24; breakfast included) or the possibility of a single in the adjacent **Jugendgästehaus.** (Singles DM34.50. Double DM63. Quads DM28.50/person. At both, reception open 7-9:30am, 12:30-5:30pm and 6-10:30pm. Curfew 1am, but open briefly at 2, 3, 4 and 5am. Both open early-Jan. to mid-Dec.) Bible literature is the only frill at the standard **CVJM-Hotel,** Graf-Adolf-Str. 102 (tel. (0211) 36 07 64), down the street to the left of the train station. (Singles DM55. Doubles DM90.) **Hotel Manhattan,** Graf-Adolf-Str. 39 (tel. (0211) 37 02 44), is straight up from the station. The mirror-plated lobby glows with 1970s dance fever, but the clean, desk-equipped rooms are surprisingly charming. (Singles DM60-135. Doubles DM95-180. Call in advance, if possible.) Stake out **Camping Unterbacher See,** Kleiner Torfbruch 31 (tel. (0211) 899 20 38). Take the S-Bahn to "Dü Geresheim" and change to bus #737 (direction "Stamesberg") to "Seestr." Or take the S-Bahn to "Dü Eller" and change to bus #735 for "Unterbach." (DM27.50/tent for up to 3 people, DM7/extra person, DM24/ family.)

Food Düsseldorf's specialty is "eating while shopping," but you can't afford most of the spots on the Kö. One exception is **Marché,** in the Kö-galerie mall at Königsallee 60. Herbivores can pick from the *Gemüsebuffet* and fancy-dancy juice bar. (Regular meals for DM8.90-12.50. Open Mon.-Thurs. and Sun. 8am-11pm, Fri.-Sat. 8am-11:30pm.) The **Markt** on Karlsplatz offers all sorts of produce and foods, including a *Sauerbraten* (pickled beef) with greens on the side. (Open Mon.-Sat. 8am-2pm.) **Breweries** sell cheap meals in addition to their house concoctions; **Hausbrauerei "zum Schlüssel"** and **Schumacher Bräu "Im Goldenen Kessel,"** Bolkerstr. 44 and 45 respectively, are two fine examples.

Folklore holds that Düsseldorf's 500 pubs make up *die längste Theke der Welt* (the longest bar in the world). *Prinz* magazine (DM4) is Düsseldorf's fashion cop and scene detective; it's often available free at the youth hostel. **Zum Goldenen Einhorn** and **Brauerei zum Uel,** Rattingerstr. 16-18, in the *Altstadt,* is papered with listings for musical happenings. (Requisite *Schlösser Alt*—0.2 liter for DM2. Open Mon.-Sat. 11am-1am.) The **Burghof** is a big *Biergarten* packed with Düsseldorfers eating sausages in good weather, in Kaiserwerth next to Friedrich's ruins on the Rhine. Take U-Bahn #79 to the Klemenspl. stop.

Practical Information Düsseldorf is 25 minutes by frequent train from Cologne. The prime **tourist office** is on Konrad-Adenauer-Pl. (tel. (0211) 35 05 05), down Immermannhof 50m to the right of the train station. Their free monthly *Düs-*

seldorf Monatsprogramm is packed with information. (Open for ticket sales (fee 10%) and general services Mon.-Fri. 8:30am-6pm, Sat. 9am-12:30pm; for hotel reservations (DM5) Mon.-Sat. 8am-10pm, Sun. 4-10pm.) A second office at Heinrich-Heine-Allee 24 (tel. (0211) 899 23 46) specializes in cultural listings. (Open Mon.-Fri. 9am-5pm; Oct.-March Mon.-Thurs. 9am-5pm, Fri. 9am-1pm.) Brits in need can head to the **U.K. Consulate**, Yorckstr. 19 (tel. (0211) 944 80); the **Canadian Consulate** is at Immermannstr. 40 (tel. (0211) 02 28 96 80). The more worldly **American Express** office is at Heinrich-Heine-Allee 14 (tel. (0211) 802 22; open Mon.-Fri. 9am-5:30pm, Sat. 9am-noon). The central **post office** is on Konrad-Adenauer-Pl. (Open Mon.-Fri. 8am-6pm, Sat. 10am-2pm, Sun. noon-1pm, but open for reduced after-hour service Mon.-Fri. 6-8pm, Sat.-Sun. noon-8pm.) **Postal code:** 40210.

Frequent S-Bahns travel to Düsseldorf's **airport.** Call (0211) 421 22 23 from 6am-midnight for flight information. **Change money** at the airport (daily 6am-10pm) or at **Deutsche Verkehrs Credit Bank** in the Hauptbahnhof. (Open daily 7:30am-8pm.) Better rates with no service charge are available at **AmEx.** The **Mitfahrzen-trale** is at Konrad-Adenauer-Pl. 13 (tel. (0211) 37 60 81). The regional transportation network, the *Rheinbahn,* includes subways, trams, buses, and the S-Bahn. Single rides cost DM1.60-10, depending on distance. The *Tagesticket* (DM7.70, higher prices for longer distances) is the best value around: groups of up to 5 people can travel all day on any line.

■ Near Düsseldorf

Düsseldorf owes a good deal of its modern prosperity to the wealth of the **Ruhr Valley** *(Das Ruhrgebiet),* a sprawling conglomeration of cities joined by the densest concentration of rail lines in the world. Between the 1850s and the 1970s, riverside coal deposits were mined to feed Germany's breakneck industrialization. Infamous 19th-century railroad and armaments mogul Alfred Krupp perfected steel-casting in industrial **Essen.** The **Villa Hügel,** for decades the Krupp family home, was given to the city in the 1950s in an attempt to brighten a company image sooted by unsavory wartime activities. (S-Bahn #6: "Essen-Hügel." Grounds open daily 8am-8pm. Villa open Tues.-Sun. 10am-6pm. DM1.50, special exhibits DM10.) Essen's massive **Alte Synagoge,** Steelerstr. 29, was gutted by Nazis in 1938, but remained standing as the largest synagogue this side of the Alps. Nearby **Dortmund** produces 600 million liters of beer annually, making it the second- largest beer-producing city in the world after Milwaukee.

NORTHERN GERMANY

This region has a history of prosperity and fierce independence that dates back to the medieval Hanseatic League. Hamburg is an immense port and frenzied metropolis; Bremen and Lübeck preserve the heritage that infected all of Scandinavia with German culture and medieval mercantilism.

■■■ HAMBURG

Birthplace of Brahms and the largest German city after Berlin, Hamburg has the oldest democratic structure in the country and a liberal atmosphere, from the licentious sex industry in St. Pauli to a vociferous ecological movement. Though partially devastated in World War II, the copper-roofed brick architecture so characteristic of northern Germany survives, due in large part to the old money that makes Hamburg Germany's richest city. Germany's largest port has been welcoming and bidding farewell to goods and passengers from all over the world for centuries; the result is a vibrant and cosmopolitan metropolis.

ORIENTATION AND PRACTICAL INFORMATION

The center of Hamburg lies on the north bank of the River Elbe. Most major sights lie between the St. Pauli Landungsbrücken ferry terminal in the west, and the tourist office and main train station in the east,

Tourist Offices: The **Hauptbahnhof office**, Kirchenallee exit (tel. 30 05 12 45), open daily 7am-11pm, and the Fühlsbüttel **airport office**, Terminal 3 arrivals (tel. 30 05 12 40), open daily 8am-11pm, will book rooms for a DM6 fee. Information also available at the **St. Pauli Landungsbrücken**, between piers 4 and 5 (tel. 30 05 12 00), open daily 9am-6pm, Nov.-Feb. daily 10am-5pm; and in the **Hansa-Viertel mall,** Poststr. entrance (tel. 30 05 12 20), open Mon.-Fri. 10am-6:30pm, Sat. 10am-3pm, Sun. 11am-3pm.

Budget Travel: SSR Reiseladen, Rothenbaumchaussee 61 (tel. 410 20 81), near the university. BIJ and student discounts. Open Mon.-Fri. 9am-6pm, Sat. 9am-noon.

Currency Exchange: Long hours but high prices at the train station. Open daily 7:30am-10pm. Better rates at banks (open Mon.-Fri. 9am-4pm).

American Express: Rathausmarkt 5 (tel. 33 11 41). Open Mon.-Fri. 9am-5:30pm, Sat. 9am-noon.

Post Office: At the Kirchenallee exit of the train station. **Poste Restante** at window #1. Open Mon.-Sat. 7am-9pm, Sun. 8am-8pm.

Telephones: At train station post office. Open Mon.-Sat. 6:15am-10pm. **City Code:** 040.

Flights: tel. 50 75 25 57. Buses zoom off to **Fühlsbüttel Airport** from outside the Kirchenallee exit of the train station (5:40am-9:20pm every 20min., 30min., DM8), or take the U-Bahn to "Ohlsdorf," then a bus (every 10min., DM3.40).

Trains: The **Hauptbahnhof** handles most traffic. **Dammtor** station is across the Kennedy/Lombardsbrücke. Most trains to and from Kiel, Schleswig, Flensburg, and Westerland stop only at **Altona** station, in the west of Hamburg. Frequent trains and S-Bahn connect the three.

Buses: Near Hauptbahnhof on Adenauerallee. Long-distance buses to Berlin (3½hr., DM50) and points farther afield.

Ferries: Landungsbrücken, pier 9 (tel. 38 90 71), 2km west along the shore from St. Pauli Landungsbrücken. Overnight connections with **Scandinavian Seaways,** Rathausstr. 12 (tel. 389 03 71), to Harwich, England (mid-June to Aug. Tickets Sun.-Wed. DM216, Thurs.-Sat. from DM240; reduced rate Sept.-June; ages 4-15 50% off; students under 26 and seniors 25% off).

Public Transportation: Efficient buses, the U-Bahn and the S-Bahn cost DM2.30-5.20. 24hrs. U-Bahn and S-Bahn tickets DM6.50 from orange automat machines or at tourist office. A 3-day ticket is DM19. Only a few buses run past midnight.

Hitchhiking: Hitchers to Berlin, Copenhagen, and Lübeck take S-1 to "Wandsbeker Chaussee" and walk along Hammerstr. until the Hamburg Horn, a large, treacherous traffic rotary at the base of the *Autobahn.* For points south, hitchers take S-3 (direction "Harburg") to Veddel and walk 5min. to the *Autobahn.* **Mitfahrzentrale,** Lobuschstr. 22 (tel. 39 17 21), at the Altona train station. Open Mon.-Wed. 8am-7pm, Thurs.-Fri. 8am-8pm, Sat. 9am-7pm, Sun. 10am-6pm.

Laundry: Wasch-Center, Nobistor 34, near the Reeperbahn. Wash DM6, dry DM2/15min. Open 6am-10pm.

Bookstore: Internationaler Bücherladen, Eppendorferweg 1, vends scads of English-language books at second-hand prices. Open Mon.-Fri. 10:30am-6pm, Sat. 10am-2pm.

Lesbian and Gay Center: Magnus Hirschfeld Centrum, Borgweg 8 (tel. 279 00 60). U-Bahn 3 or bus #108 to "Borgweg." Daily films and counseling sessions. Evening café open Mon.-Sat. 3pm-midnight, Sun. and holidays 4pm-midnight.

Emergency: Police: tel. 110. Headquarters at Kirchenallee 46, opposite the train station. **Ambulance:** tel. 112.

ACCOMMODATIONS, CAMPING, AND FOOD

Hamburg is not a cheap place to stay; single rooms start at about DM55, with doubles from DM75. A stew of small, inexpensive pensions line **Steindamm, Bremer Weg** and **Bremer Reihe** north of the train station. Check out your hotel before you accept a room—half the establishments along this strip are dubious. For help, pick up a *Hotelführer* (DM0.50) from the tourist office.

> **Jugendherberge auf dem Stintfang (HI),** Alfred-Wegener-Weg 5 (tel. 31 34 88; fax 31 54 07). Take S-Bahn #1, 2, or 3 or U-Bahn #3 from the main station to the Landungsbrücke. Hike up steps to hill above. Large, busy hostel attracts travelers from all over the globe. Reception open 7-9am and 5:30pm-1am. 3-day max. stay. Curfew 1am. DM18, over 26 DM22, nonmembers DM5 extra. Breakfast included.
>
> **Horner-Rennbahn (HI),** Rennbahnstr. 100 (tel. 651 16 71; fax 65 56 516). Clean and peaceful, but a bit far. Take U-Bahn #3 to "Horner-Rennbahn," then walk 10min. or take the bus toward Wandsbek (DM2.80). Strict. Reception open 7:30-9am, 1-6pm and 12:30pm-1am. Curfew 1am. DM25, over 26 DM29.50. Open March-Dec.
>
> **Hotel Terminus Garni,** Steindamm 5 (tel. 280 31 44), near Hauptbahnhof. Better than it looks. Sprightly service and fetching rooms; avoid the raisin-sized singles. Call ahead. Singles DM65. Doubles DM100. Triples DM150. Showers DM1.
>
> **Pension Sarah Peterson,** Lange Reihe 50 (tel.24 30 24). Small, artsy pension in an old building with bohemian flair. Doubles DM89. Triples DM140.
>
> **Campingplatz Buchholz,** Kielerstr. 374 (tel. 540 45 32). Take S-Bahn #3 (direction "Pinneberg") or S-Bahn #21 (direction "Elbgaustr.") to "Stellingren." Reception open 7am-11pm; Oct.-May 8-10am and 4-8pm. DM5/person, DM12.50-16.50/tent. Showers DM2.50. Call ahead.

Walk along **St. Pauli's Quai, Landungsbrücke,** for small fish restaurants. In the middle of the square of the same name, the **Rathausmarkt** offers all things edible at honest prices. Numerous cheap dives line **Kirchenallee,** serving everything from *Schnitzel* to gyros. Find better deals in the numerous inexpensive cafés and restaurants in the university area around **Renteelstr., Grindlehof,** and **Grindallee.** In **Altona** a plethora of inexpensive cafés and restaurants can be found on **Schanzenstraße.** Nearby is a **mensa** at Schlüterstr. 7, which serves lunch Monday through Friday. (DM1, ID officially required.) **Piceno,** Hein-Hoyer-Str. 8, is a simple Italian restaurant which serves the classics. (DM8-15. Open daily 5pm-midnight.) Incidentally, the hamburger did *not* originate in Hamburg.

SIGHTS AND ENTERTAINMENT

The sight of Hamburg's seven copper towers tells visitors they've arrived. At night the **Hamburg Hafen,** the largest port in Germany, is lit up by ships from all over the world. After sailing the East Indies, the 19th century **Windjammer Rickmer Rickmers** was docked at pier 1 and restored as a museum ship. Come for the old navigation equipment, all brass and polished, alongside the newer technology. (Open daily 10am-6pm. DM4, students DM3, children DM2.)

The richly ornamented **Rathaus,** a 19th-century monstrosity, dominates the city center. Tours pass through gorgeous rooms, still used for receptions and meetings. (Hourly in English Mon.-Thurs. 10:15am-3:15pm, Fri.-Sun. 10:15am-1:15pm. *Rathaus* open Mon.-Thurs. 10am-3pm, Fri.-Sun. 10am-1pm. DM1.) Just south of the *Rathaus* on Ost-West-Str. stand the somber ruins of the **St. Nikolaikirche.** One of the earliest examples of neo-Gothic architecture, it was flattened by Allied bombing raids in 1943. A tad farther west is the imposing 18th-century **Große Michaeliskirche,** whose baroque tower is Hamburg's city emblem. (Tower open Mon.-Sat. 9am-5:30pm, Sun. 11:30am-5:30pm; Nov.-April Thurs.-Tues. 10am-4pm. Church free, tower elevator DM4.) At the end of the restored baroque **Peterstraße,** the **Museum of Hamburgische History,** Holstenwall 24, is the parent of the **Historic Emigration Office,** Bei den St. Pauli Landungsbrücken 3, an archive that recorded the names and home towns of the 5 million Germans and East Europeans who emigrated through Hamburg between 1850 and 1914. Take the U-Bahn to the St. Pauli stop. (Open Tues.-Sat. 10am-2pm. DM2, students DM0.70.) One block north of the train station, the **Hamburger Kunsthalle,** Glockengiesserwall 1, holds a huge selection of paintings and drawings ranging from medieval to modern. (Open Tues. Wed. and Fri.- Sun. 10am-6pm, Thurs. 10am-9pm. DM3, students DM0.70.) Consider buying a week-long pass to all of Hamburg's 36 museums for just DM15.

Entertainment The cultural capital of the North, Hamburg invests a lot of effort in the arts. The **Staatsoper,** Dammtorstr. 28, houses one of the best opera companies in Germany, and the attached **ballet** company is the nation's acknowledged dance powerhouse. **Orchestras** abound: the **Philharmonie,** the **Symphony,** and the **Nord-Deutcher-Rundfunk** are the big 3. Lighter music, popular musicals, and transvestite cabarets play the **Operettenhaus Hamburg,** the **Neue Flora Theater,** and smaller venues. Call the tourist office for info on dates and tickets.

Hamburg has an extensive live music scene which spans all tastes. Traditional jazz is at its best at the **Cotton Club** (see below), and on Sunday mornings at the Fish Auction Hall at the **Fischmarkt.** International rock groups frequently play at **Große Freiheit** 36, (tel. 319 36 49), and at **Docks,** Spielbudenplatz 19 (tel. 319 43 78). The renowned **Fabrik,** Barnerstr. 36 (tel. 39 19 70) in Altona, features everything from funk to punk. The best sources of information about what's happening are *Szene, Oxmox,* or *Prinz* (available at newsstands and hostels).

The nexus of Hamburg's nightlife is at the heart of St. Pauli on the **Reeperbahn.** Known world-wide as the home of the St. Pauli girls, the area features the best clubs and bars in Hamburg, as well as seamy sex-clubs and peepshows. **Große Freiheit,** a street lined with explicit revues and cabarets, might be one of the most concentrated sinks of sleaze in the world. **Herbertstraße,** just south of the Reeperbahn of Davidstr., is a legalized prostitution strip. Only men over 18 are permitted down the street.

The red-light district does not by any means represent the social whole of Hamburg: the city also has an active community of bisexual, lesbian, and straight women. If you can read German, pick up the Hamburger Frauenzeitung (DM5), available at the **Frauenbuchladen und Café,** Bismarckstr. 98 (tel 420 47 48; open Mon.-Fri. 10am-6:30pm, Sat. 10am-2pm). **Frauenkneipe,** Stresemanstr. 60, is a bar and meeting place for women of all orientations. Lesbians and gays alike are informed by the *Dorn Rosa* journal, as well as by a publication called *Gay Life.* Much of the Hamburg gay scene is located in the St. Georg area of the city.

Clusters of popular student bars can be found along Grindelallee and Schanzenstr. Swarms of street-side cafés line the three squares **Gänsemarkt** (U-Bahn 2), **Rodningsmarkt** (U-Bahn #3), and **Großneumarkt** (S-Bahn #1 or 2; Stadthausbrücke). In general, clubs open late and close late, with some techno and trance clubs staying open until noon the following day. Check *Szene, Oxmox,* and *Prinz* for more info.

■■■ SCHLESWIG-HOLSTEIN

Lübeck Flat and agrarian Schleswig-Holstein is Germany's northernmost province and the site of countless 19th-century turf wars with Denmark. Schleswig-Holstein's most exciting city (largely by default), **Lübeck** flourished in the Middle Ages as a vital link in the prosperous Baltic overseas trade, and its merchants funneled their profits into architecture and interior decoration. Since 1942, when it was flattened by Allied bombers, Lübeck has been rebuilding its historic *Altstadt;* the efforts were rewarded in 1987 when UNESCO declared it a World Heritage Site. The core of the *Altstadt* is the **Rathaus,** a striking 13th-century structure of glazed black bricks that sets off the vibrant fruit and flower market. (DM3, students DM1. Tours Mon.-Fri. at 11am, noon, and 3pm.) Across the Marktplatz towers the Gothic **Marienkirche;** inside, under the southern tower, the broken pieces of the multi-ton church bells still rest where they fell during an air raid in 1942. (Open daily 10am-6pm; off-season 10am-4pm. Free.) Opposite the Marienkirche on Mangstr. is the **Buddenbrooks House,** now a museum dedicated to the life and works of Thomas and Heinrich Mann; reading knowledge of German is helpful although English guides are available. The organ inside the **Jacobikirche,** farther north on Breitestr., is one of the oldest in Germany. (Open daily 10am-6pm. 30-min. organ recitals every Sat. at 5pm. DM3, students DM2.) Between the inner city and the train station is **Holstentor,** one of the 4 gates built in the 15th century to guard the entrance to Lübeck. Inside the gate, the **Museum Holstentor** has exhibits on ship construction and quaint local implements of torture. (Open Tues.-Sun. 10am-5pm; Oct.-March 10am-4pm. DM3, students DM1.50, under 18 free.)

The **HI youth hostel,** Am Gertrudenkirchhof 4 (tel. (0451) 334 33), is northeast of the historic center, past the Burgtor. Take bus #1 or 3 from the front of the station. (Reception open 8-9am and 1:30-11:30pm. Lockout 9-11:30am. Curfew 11:30pm. Members only. DM17.50, over 26 DM21.50. Open Jan. 11-Dec. 9.) Peter and Kalli welcome you to their clean and friendly **Rucksack Hotel,** Kanalstr. 70 (tel. 70 68 92), in the *Altstadt* by the canal. From the train station walk past the Holstentor, turn left on An der Untertrave, and right on Beckergrube. (Reception open daily 9am-10pm. Singles DM30. Doubles DM120. Dorms DM19-22.)

The miniscule **tourist office** (tel. 86 46 75) in the train station is quite clueless. (Open Mon.-Sat. 9am-7pm.) Unless you want to book a room for DM3, grab a free map and make for the larger and more powerful **branch** at Am Markt 1 (tel. (0451) 122 81 06), across from the *Rathaus*. (Open Mon.-Fri. 9:30am-6pm, Sat.-Sun. 10am-2pm.) The **Mitfahrzentrale** (tel. 710 74) is at Fischergrube 45. (Open Mon.-Fri. 2-6pm, Sat.-Sun. noon-2pm.) Frequent **trains** connect Lübeck and Hamburg's Hauptbahnhof (40min.).

Travemünde This small beach town lies about 15km northeast of Lübeck, and is useful primarily for its beach and ferry connections to Scandinavia. Take the train to "Lübeck-Travemünde-Skandinavienkai" to catch the **Finnjet,** which zooms to Helsinki (23-27hr.; DM210-680, students DM195-620), and **TT-Line** ferries to Trelleborg, Sweden (2/day; 7-8hr.; DM110, students DM82 on day sailings, Eurail 50% off). For more information on both town and ferries, inquire at the jovial **Nordische Touristik Information** (tel. (04502) 66 88; open daily Mon.-Fri 9am-5:30pm). Take the Priwall ferry (DM6) to the **Jugendherberge (HI),** Mecklenburgerlandstr. 69 (tel. (04502) 25 76), which sidles up to Strandcamping and shares its atmosphere. (Reception open 2-10pm. Curfew 10pm. DM19.50, over 26 DM21.50. Open April to mid-Oct.) **Strandcamping-Priwall,** Dünenweg 3 (tel. (04502) 28 35), is 1 minute from the beach, and attracts city kids as well as the eco-conscious. Take the train to the Lübeck-Travemünde-Strand stop (20min.) and cross the River Trave on the Norder ferry to the Priwall side. (DM6/person, DM5-10/tent. Open April-Sept.)

Kiel Capital of Schleswig-Holstein, industrial Kiel boasts the Kiel locks, the largest in the world. If shipping and other maritime activities (including sunbathing) aren't for you, every 2 hours a bus leaves from the station for the Hamburg airport (1½hr., DM20). Leaving from the wharf on the west bank of the city, **Stena Line** (tel. (0431) 90 90) sails to Gothenburg, Sweden daily at 7pm (14hr., DM98-194), and **Color Line** (tel. (0431) 97 40 90) journeys to Oslo, Norway (daily, every other day in Jan.; 18hr.; DM140-188, students 50% off selected sailings). Reach the **Jugendherberge** (tel. (0431) 73 57 23) on bus #4 or 34. Get off at the Karlstraße stop, walk a block north, and go left on Johannesstr. (DM17.50, over 26 DM21.50.)

■■■ BREMEN

Bremen lies along the Weser River, and owes its living to the North Sea, preserving its medieval heritage while capitalizing on such modern assets as Beck's Beer brewery. The early 15th-century **Rathaus** survived World War II because the English pilot ordered to bomb the downtown deliberately dodged his target. (Tours given Mon.-Fri. at 10am, 11am, and noon, Sat.-Sun. at 11am and noon; DM4; children DM2.) Also a war survivor, the impressive **St. Petri Dom,** Sandstr. 10-12, dates from 1042; Charlemagne had the first foundation stone laid in 798. The cathedral hosts a mosaic interior of orange, gold, and gray stone arches. (Cathedral open Mon.-Fri. 10am-5pm, Sat. 10am-noon, Sun. 2-5pm.) Cross the Domsheide to the **Schnoorviertel,** a gingerbread quarter of craft shops and red-roofed houses. Bremen's **Kunsthalle,** Am Wall 207, contains a bouquet of art from the Renaissance to the present, including a strong collection of moody early 20th-century German expressionists. (Open Tues. 10am-9pm, Wed.-Sun. 10am-5pm. DM6, students DM3.) Since 1095 Bremen has celebrated its trading past with the **Freimarkt** (2nd week of Oct.).

Accommodations, Food, and Practical Information The sleek **Jugendgästehaus (HI)**, Kalkstr. 6 (tel. (0421) 17 13 69; fax 171 102), can be reached by bus #26 or tram #6 to the Am Brille stop; then take Bürgermeister-Smidt-Str. to the river, turn right, and walk 2 blocks. (Reception open 24hrs. DM24, over 26 DM28.) Under the bridge between the station and the post office, down Hermann-Böse and right on Hohenlohe, **Hotel Weltevreden,** Am Dobben 62 (tel. 780 15; fax 70 40 91), just off Ostertorsteinweg, has immediate access to late-night Bremen. (Reception open until 10pm. Singles DM 58. Doubles DM95, with shower DM100. Call ahead.) **Hotel Enzensperger,** Brautstr. 9 (tel. (0421) 503 224), has tidy rooms with some street-side terraces. From the Markt, cross the Wilhelm-Kaisern Bridge, turn right on Osterstr. and right again on Brautstr. (Singles DM42, with shower DM47. Doubles DM68, with shower DM78.) Otherwise, rooms in Bremen are ruinously expensive. **Camping** is distant, at Am Stadtwaldsee 1 (tel. 21 20 02); take bus #22 or 23 to the last stop (15min.), then walk along Kuhgangweg to Anwieseck and turn left. (DM6.50/person, DM4-8/tent. Open Easter-Oct.)

In the *Rathaus* visit Bremen's renowned **Ratskeller** (1408), one of the oldest wineries in Germany, and sip one of each of the 600 German labels (DM3-10/0.2 liter glass). Meals here cost at least DM20, but merit every mark. Student pubs await farther east on and around the unsavory **Ostertorsteinweg,** just beyond Goethepl.

The **tourist office** (tel. (0421) 30 80 00; fax 30 80 03), across from the train station carries guides to museum exhibits and the like. (Open Mon.-Wed. and Fri. 9:30am-6:30pm, Thurs. 9:30am-8:30pm, Sat. 9:30am-2pm.) The **post office** and **telephones** are at Domsheide 15, near the Markt. **American Express** (tel.141 71) has a travel agency and full cardmember service at Am Wall 138. (Open Mon.-Fri. 9am-5:30pm, Sat. 9am-noon.)

Up the Weser and to the north, **Bremerhaven** and **Cuxhaven** work deep-sea ports with ferry connections to the vacation isle of **Helgoland.** About an hour to the east, **Oldenburg** opens up the "Southern-North-Sea-Land," an embarkment point for trips to the low-lying **East Frisian Islands.**

■■■ HANNOVER

Hannover, a hyper-modern industrial and commercial center, rose phoenix-like from the ashes of World War II. Among the few architectural gems remaining is the spectacular **Rathaus,** which spent 1943 to 1945 as a parking lot. This painstakingly recreated palace has an amazing tower view. (Tower open April-Oct. daily 10am-12:30pm and 1:30-4:30pm. DM3, students DM2.) The city's crown jewel is the **Großer Garten Herrenhauser,** a baroque garden with manicured rose gardens, geyser-inspired fountains, and the **Herrenhausen Palace.** The frequent concerts, ballets, and plays held in the palace often spill outside in the summer. Take U-Bahn #4 or 5 (direction "Stocken") to the Herrenhausengarten. (Open daily 8am-8pm; in winter 8am-4:30pm.) Inquire at the **tourist office,** Ernst-August-Pl. 8 (tel. 30 14 22; fax 30 14 14), across from the train station and to the left, about tickets to performances at the Herrenhauser and the Opera. The amiable staff also finds rooms (DM5 fee) and gives regional transport information (Hannover is an international transport hub, on the Amsterdam-Berlin and Hamburg-Basel rail lines). The **American Express office**, Georgstr. 54, 30159 Hannover (tel. 36 34 28) has a travel agency and full cardmember services. (Open Mon.-Fri. 8:30am-6pm, Sat. 8:30am-2pm.)

Most of Hannover's cheap eats lie in or near the pedestrian zone between the *Altstadt* and Kröpcke. **Restaurant Marché**, in the Galerie Luise, Luisenstraße 5, offers fresh produce and hearty meals. (Open daily 11am-midnight.) To wash down your feast, head to **Kalauer Bierpub Bistro,** Ballholstr 12, overlooking a pretty cobbled square. (Open daily from 10am.) For 10 days in late June and early July, Hannover crawls with locals for the 452-year-old **Schützenfest** (shooting festival). Shooting quickly gives way to drinking as celebrants get Schützen-faced on the traditional festival drink: the *Lutje Lager*. Without spilling, you drink from two glasses at the same time—held side by side. One glass contains dark beer, the other Schnapps. Hold onto your hat! The **Jugendherberge (HI)** at Ferdinand-Wilhelm-Weg 1 (tel. (0511) 131 76 74; fax 185 55) is the cheapest and most central place to crash. Take bus #24 to Stadionbrücke or U-Bahn #3 or 7 (direction "Mühlenberg") to "Fischerhof/Fachhochschule," cross the tracks and follow the signs along the bike path. (DM18.30, over 26 DM22.30. Camping DM11.50-13.50. Reservations recommended.)

■■■ HARZ MOUNTAINS

Heinrich Heine wrote that even Mephistopheles trembled when he approached the mist-draped Harz Mountains. Unification lifted a less tangible but more palpable veil from the range, which stretches from the western **Oberharz** to the eastern **Ostharz** and to sun-sheltered health resorts in the south. Spring thaws turn ski slopes into webs of hidden hiking trails. The **Harzerquerbahn,** a stylishly antique narrow-gauge railway, steams up, up, and up the Ostharz from Nordhausen.

Goslar In 922 AD, Holy Roman Emperor Heinrich stumbled upon **Goslar,** and the dusty town, 40 minutes by train from Hannover, still fancies itself the unofficial capital of the Harz. The **Kaiserpfalz**, at Kaiserbleek 6, is a massive Romanesque palace that served as the ruling seat for 11th- and 12th-century emperors. (Open daily 10am-5pm; Nov.-March 10am-4pm. DM3.50, students DM2.) Each day, the small mechanical figures of court nobles and the miners whose work made the region prosperous dance to the chime of the **Glocken- und Gigurenspiel** at 9am, noon, 3pm, and 6pm, opposite the Rathaus. The **Mönchehaus**, Mönchestr. 3, at Jakobistr., is an outstanding but tiny modern art museum. (Open Tues.-Sat. 10am-1pm and 3-5pm, Sun. 10am-1pm. DM 3.50, students and children DM2.)

The **Harzer Verkehrsverband regional tourist office,** Marktstr. 45 (tel. (05321) 200 31), is inside the Industrie und Handels Kammer building. (Open Mon.-Thurs. 8am-4pm, Fri. 8am-1pm.) Their indispensable *Grüner Faden für den Harz-Gast* pamphlet lists attractions, and *Jugend und Freizeitheime im Harz und im Harzvorland* is a compilation of area youth hostels and student centers. The **local tourist office,** Markt 7 (tel. (05321) 28 47), across from the *Rathaus,* finds rooms (from DM30) for a DM3 fee. From the station, walk to the end of Rosentorstr. (Open Mon.-Fri. 9am-6pm, Sat. 9am-2pm; Nov.-April Mon.-Fri. 9am-5pm, Sat. 9am-1pm.) The **Jugendherberge (HI),** Rammelsbergerstr. 25 (tel. (05321) 222 40), wins the prize for most confusing address of the year. From the bus C stop at "Theresienhof," walk up Rammelbergerstr. past numbers 27-49. After no. 49, make a sharp left at the "Jugendherberge" sign and walk uphill to no. 25. (Reception open 8:30-11am, 4-7pm and 9:30-10pm. Curfew 10pm. Members only. DM17.80, over 26 DM21.80.) **Campingplatz Sennhütte,** Clausthalerstr. 28 (tel. (05321) 224 98), 3km from town along the B241 highway, has a restaurant and sauna. (DM4/person, DM3.50/tent, showers DM1.)

Bad Harburg, Torfhaus, and Braunlage The train from Hannover to the mountains ends at **Bad Harzburg**, about 10 minutes past Goslar. Next to the station, the **tourist office** is always happy to find you a room (DM5 fee). **Torfhaus**, a humble crossroads 3km from the former inter-German border, offers naught but an airy mountain hostel, near-perfect hiking trails, and the Harz's highest mountain (the 1142m, supposedly witch-haunted **Brocken**). The Bad Harzburg-Braunlage bus pauses here every 1½ hours (Mon.-Fri. 7:45am-9pm, DM3.90). Turn right at the "Altenau-8km" sign for the exceptional **Jugendherberge (HI)**, Torfhaus 3 (tel. (05320) 242; reception open 12:15-1pm and 6:15-7pm; curfew 10pm; DM18.20, over 26 DM22.20). A left turn from the "Altenau 8km" sign leads to **Goethe Weg** and the 16km trail to Brocken's peak. Along the way it skirts the stream that used to divide the two Germanies; look for the abandoned Soviet radar station.

Twelve km south of Torfhaus, the larger town of **Braunlage** also makes an ideal launchpad for hikes and winter sports. The **tourist office** *(Kurverwaltung)*, Elbinger-oderstr. 17 (tel. (05520) 10 54), attends to accommodations. (Open Mon.-Fri. 7:30am-12:30pm and 2-5pm, Sat. 9:30am-noon.) After hours, check the mega-board outside the office. The **Jugendherberge (HI)**, von-Langenstr. 63 (tel. (05520) 22 38), is an uphill climb from town. Take the bus to the Marienhof stop and walk up Am Marienhof to the dirt path; or walk von-Langenstr. past the dirt soccer fields and turn left on the first paved path. (Reception open 9am-1pm and 5-7pm. DM17.30, over 26 DM21.30.)

Wernigerode One of Goethe's secret spots in the hills and the best east-west connection within them, this is a worthy terminus for the narrow-gauge **Harzquerbahn.** The Kaiser came to the **Schloß** above town for the hunting; his room is a wildly brocaded suite of red, green, and gold. Rule the mountains with the view from the terrace. (Open daily 10am-6pm; Oct.-April Tues.-Sun. 9am-4pm. DM5, students DM4, under 14 DM3; tour DM1 extra.) Wernigerode's busy **tourist office,** on Breitstr. (tel. (03943) 330 35) around the corner from the *Rathaus,* books rooms for 10% of the first night's price. (Open Mon.-Fri. 9am-6pm, Sat.-Sun. 10am-3pm.) To reach the **Jugendgästehaus,** Friedrichstr. 53 (tel. (03943) 320 61), take bus line A or D to Kirchstr., or walk from the Westerntor station right on Unter den Zindeln, then turn right on Friedrichstr. (25min.). Guests sleep in motel-style rooms. (Reception open 5-7pm. DM14.50, over 26 DM18.50.) The main train station is next to the **Bus-Bahnhof,** whose tentacles extend to other Ostharz towns. Wernigerode is also the beginning of the line for the **Brockenbahn,** a steam train that spirals up and around to the peak of the witches' mountain.

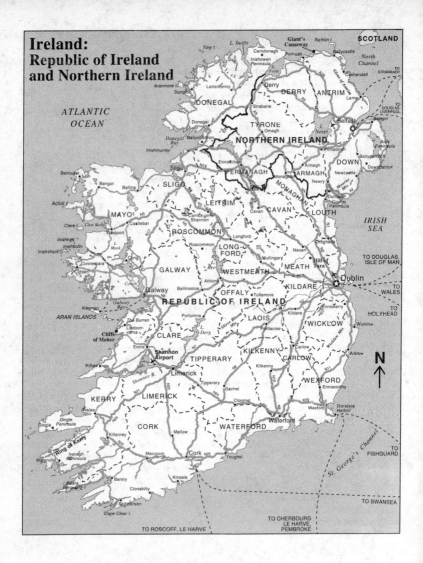

Ireland (Éire)

US$1 = IR£1.45 (pounds, or IEP)
CDN$1 = IR£1.10
UK£1 = IR£2.25
AUS$1 = IR£0.95
NZ$1 = IR£0.80
SAR1 = IR£0.30
Country Code: 353

IR£1 = US$0.69
IR£1 = CDN$0.91
IR£1 = UK£0.44
IR£1 = AUS$1.06
IR£1 = NZ$1.25
IR£1 = SAR3.31
International Dialing Prefix: 16

It can be hard to see Ireland through the mist of stereotypes that surrounds the island even on the clearest days. Yes, it rains a lot. Yes, it's green (for that reason). Yes, Irish people are friendlier than most, and yes, they drink more stout. But other stereotypes can mislead: though much of the country is still rural and religious, there's also a developing urban culture with links to the European continent as well as to Great Britain. Traditional musicians roam Western pubs, while rockers try hard in Dublin and Cork. The Irish language lives both in coastal villages and in national magazines, while literature in English—especially poetry—is in some ways healthier in this highly educated island than it is anywhere else. Long hiking trails, roads, and cliff walks make a chain of windy, watery, spectacular scenery around the western coast; go out of your way for the coastal vistas, by all means, but don't forget that people live here too.

In 1171, Henry II claimed the Emerald Isle for the English throne in a less-than-decisive victory, and both English feudal and Gaelic Irish influences split Ireland during the Middle Ages. The trail to independence and emancipation was blazed by Daniel O'Connell in the 1830s; by the turn of the century, nationalist Fenians agitated passionately for home rule. Following the abortive proclamation of the Irish Republic in Easter 1916, a 5-year-long Anglo-Irish War ended in the partition of the island into the Irish Free State and Northern Ireland, which remains in bloody contention to this day. In 1949 Ireland officially proclaimed itself the Republic of Ireland (*Éire* in Gaelic), an independent land.

Though *Let's Go*'s coverage doesn't mirror this organization, it helps to know that Ireland is traditionally thought of in 4 provinces: Leinster, the east and southeast; Munster, the southwest; Connacht, the province west of the Shannon (except County Clare); and Ulster, 6 of whose 9 provinces make up Northern Ireland, part of the U.K. You shouldn't have to go out of your way in any of the 4 to encounter either Ireland's past—its Round Towers, medieval streets, monasteries, legends, and *curraghs*—or its equally exciting, and more talkative, present.

For more detailed coverage of the country, snag a copy of *Let's Go: Ireland* or *Let's Go: Britain & Ireland*.

GETTING THERE

USIT (Irish Student Travel Agency; Dublin tel. (01) 677 8843), is thrillingly helpful and provides cheap fares, special deals, and ISICs. Almost all ferries in June, July, and August are "controlled sailings": you must book ahead (a day in advance is fine).

Brittany Ferries, Tourist House, 42 Grand Parade, Cork (tel. (021) 27 78 01), sail from Roscoff, France (at least 1/week, 21hr., IR£49-70). **Irish Ferries,** 2-4 Merrion Row, Dublin 2 (tel. (01) 661 05 11), 9 Bridge St., Cork (tel. (021) 50 43 33), and in Rosslare Harbor (tel. (053) 331 58), sail from Le Havre, France (July-Dec. 1/week; 20hr.; IR£63-112, students with ISIC IR£49-97, lower prices for all after Aug.). **Stena-Sealink** (tel. (0233) 64 70 47) and **P&O European Ferries** (London tel. (081) 575 8555) arrive in Dover and Portsmouth, England from ports in France (Calais, Cherbourg, Le Havre), Belgium (Oostende), and Spain (Bilbao). Sealink paddles fervently between Dover and Calais (22/day, 1¾hr., about UK£24 one way). By April, 1994, the undersea road and rail tunnel between Folkestone, England and Coquelles, France (near Calais) should be down and running.

To get to Ireland from Britain, **B&I** (Ireland toll-free after-hours tel. (1 850) 60 66 66; London tel. (071) 734 4681; Holyhead tel. (0407) 76 02 22 or 76 02 23; Pembroke tel. (0646) 68 41 61; Dublin tel. (01) 679 79 77; Rosslare Harbor tel. (053) 333 11; Cork tel. (021) 27 30 24) sails from Holyhead to Dublin (about IR£12-24). **Stena-Sealink** (Dublin tel. (01) 28 08 44; Rosslare Harbor tel. (053) 331 15) goes from Holyhead to Dún Laoghaire (dun-LEER-ee; a Dublin suburb) for about IR£24-30, or IR£19-27 for students. **Cork-Swansea,** 55 Grand Parade, Cork (tel. (021) 27 11 66) sails between Wales and Cork daily in summer, less often other times (IR£18-26, students with ISIC IR£13). **Hoverspeed Seacat** zips between Stranraer (tel. (0776) 22

55) and Belfast (0232) 31 20 02; July-Sept. 4-5/day; 1¼hr.; UK£18-19, students, seniors, and children less), a swell deal for pedestrians. **Slatterly's** travel agency (1 Russell St., Tralee; tel. (066) 216 11) runs a bus-ferry combination between Cork and London. **Supabus** (run by Bus Éireann; book tickets through USIT, above) dashes between Dublin and London for UK£35-63 (more mid-July to Aug.).

Many **flights** of British Airways, Aer Lingus, British Midlands, and Ryan Air hop between Gatwick, Heathrow, Luton, Manchester, Birmingham, Liverpool, and Glasgow airports (in Britain) and Dublin, Shannon, Cork, Knock, and Waterford (in Ireland). Students who book with USIT can fly to Dublin from London for UK£42.

TRAVELING IN IRELAND

Trains run by **Iarnród Éireann (Irish Rail)** (tel. (01) 363 222) fan out like cat's whiskers from Dublin to larger cities, but there is no service between these periphery cities. For schedule information, pick up a free *Inter-City Timetable*, available at most train stations. By far the most useful student travel pass in Ireland is the **Travelsave stamp,** available at any USIT with an ISIC and IR£7. Affixed to your ISIC, this stamp decreases single fares by about 50% on national rail and bus services in Ireland (except on bus fares less than IR£2) and takes 30% off return fares. The **Eurailpass** *is* accepted in Ireland.

Buses in the Republic of Ireland, operated by **Bus Éireann** (tel. (01) 747 733), reach more destinations than trains but run infrequently (even more so on Sun. and in winter). The company operates both long-distance **Expressway** buses, which link larger cities, and **Provincial** buses, which serve the countryside and smaller towns. The bus timetable book (50p) is available at Busáras in Dublin. Ireland has its share of **Rambler** tickets, but you have to move fast to make them pay off.

You can rent 3-, 5-, and 10-speed bikes from **Raleigh Rent-a-Bike** shops almost anywhere in the country (IR£/day, IR£30/week; IR£10-40 deposit). A list of Raleigh dealers is available at most tourist offices and bike shops. Ireland offers rugged hills and small mountains to its **hikers,** and hostels often lie within 20 scenic miles of each other. The best hiking maps are the Ordnance Survey ½-in.-to-1-mi. series (IR£3.70), available at tourist offices.

IRELAND ESSENTIALS

Bord Fáilte (the Irish Tourist Board) operates a nationwide network of offices, selling maps (including IR£3 survey maps for hikers) and detailed local guidebooks. They also distribute the free *Calendar of Events* in Ireland. Their accommodations booking service (locally IR£1, nationwide IR£2; deposit 10%) can be helpful, but do your homework: many fine hostels and B&Bs are not "approved" (which involves paying a regular cut to Bord Fáilte), so the tourist office can't tell you about them.

Weather in Ireland is both temperate (summer temperatures 10-27°C or 50-80°F) and temperamental. Keep a rain poncho or umbrella handy, and carry a warm sweater, as warm sunshine often suddenly yields to chilly dampness.

Ireland has 9 annual bank holidays: New Year's Day, St. Patrick's Day (March 17), Good Friday (April 1), Easter Monday (April 4), first Monday in June (June 6), first Monday in August (Aug. 1), last Monday in October (Oct. 31), Christmas Day (Dec. 25), and St. Stephen's Day (Dec. 26). Also check for local half-day holidays, when banks and stores close. **Banks** are open from Monday to Friday 10am to 12:30pm and 1:30 to 3pm; in Dublin, banks stay open until 5pm on Thursday. The Bank of Ireland has offices throughout the country but no standardized exchange rates, so check around in larger towns. The green-fronted **post offices** are labeled in Irish: *Ofig an Phoist*. Most phones have a miniature rampway on top; line up your coins, and they'll automatically feed into the phone as needed. Press the "FC" button on newer phones (follow-on-call) before hanging up if you want to make another call; otherwise you'll lose whatever change you currently had in the machine. Dial 10 for the operator and 1190 for directory inquiries. To make **international direct calls** from the Republic of Ireland, dial the **international access code:** 00; then the country code, area code, and local number. You can access an international operator at 114. AT&T's **USA Direct** can be reached at 1 800 550 000; MCI's **World Reach** at 1 800 551 001; and **Sprint** at 1 800 552 001. Dial 999 anywhere in the country in an **emergency.**

Accommodations, Camping, and Food Hosteling is the way to go in Ireland. **An Óige,** the Irish Hostelling International association, runs 50 hostels throughout the country which are generally more clean, friendly, and relaxed than the standard HI hostel. Most of them charge IR£4.50-6/night (under 18 IR£3.50-5); nonmembers pay extra. All HI hostels will reserve a bed for you at another HI hostel (no booking charge). Two non-HI hostel organizations, **Independent Hostel Owners (IHO)** (tel. (073) 301 30) and **Irish Budget Hostels** (tel. (065) 740 06), also operate in Ireland. **IHO** hostels generally have no lockout or curfew, accept all ages, and don't charge membership fees. The Irish Budget hostels require no membership but are all approved by the Irish Tourist Board and also offer special transportation deals (such as a round-trip ticket from certain departure points to any destination in Ireland, with one overnight at a budget hostel included). **B&Bs** are a wonderful, luxurious break from hosteling and are occasionally the only accommodations option. Expect to pay IR£12-17 for a bed and cereal, toast, bacon, sausage, and tea or coffee.

Camping in Irish State Forests and National Parks is not allowed; camping on public land is allowed only if there is no official campsite in the area. Caravan and camping parks provide all the trappings of bourgeois civilization (about IR£4-5).

Pubs in Ireland are the forum for banter, singing, and *craic* (KRAK), meaning simply "a good time." In the evening, many pubs play impromptu or organized traditional music; there's quite a bit of variety to these watering holes. Aside from the Holy Trinity, **Guinness,** a rich, dark stout, is the most revered thing in Ireland. **Irish coffee** is sweetened with brown sugar and whipped cream and laced with Irish whiskey, which is sweeter and more stinging than its Scotch counterpart. Pubs are generally open Monday to Saturday 10:30am to 11:30pm (11pm in winter), Sunday 12:30 to 2pm and 4 to 11pm.

Food in Ireland is expensive, especially in restaurants. The basics—and that is what you'll get—are simple and filling. Soda bread is delicious and will keep for about a week, and Irish dairy products are addictive. Colcannon, "Ploughman's lunch," and Irish stew, usually IR£4, are probably the essential Irish dishes.

■■■ DUBLIN

Dublin is where the Irish nation meets international urban trends, traditions, and economies, and where (counting the suburbs) over a third of the Republic's population resides. Its buildings belong to 18th-century England, but its culture belongs to the Dubliners: the life of packed pubs, long walks, and walk-ups recorded in James Joyce's *Dubliners* and *Ulysses*. Subcultures flourish here in a way they couldn't in the rest of the country, making Dublin's social life both more hidden and more various than the rest of Ireland's, while the economics of trade, transport, and education draw the young here from other counties, just as they did 100 years ago

During the fall of 1993, Telecom Éireann began to replace all remaining 6-digit phone numbers in Greater Dublin (the 01 telephone-code area) with new 7-digit numbers. Any 6-digit Dublin phone number that begins with 3, 5, 90, 93, 94, 96, or 97 has probably been changed by the time you read this. *Let's Go* prefixes these phone numbers with a **double-dagger symbol [‡]. Directory Assistance for Ireland** (including Northern Ireland): tel. 1190. **Telecom Éireann information number:** tel. 1 800 330 330.

ORIENTATION AND PRACTICAL INFORMATION

The **River Liffey** cuts central Dublin in half. Most of the best food and famous sights stick to the **South Side,** though plenty of hostels (and the bus station) sprout up in the **North Side.** When streets split into "Upper" and "Lower" Such-and-Such Street, "Lower" is always closer to the mouth of the Liffey. Be safety-conscious on the far North Side, in parks at night, and on the far west of the South Side around the Guinness Brewery; compared to most of Ireland, Dublin has plenty of crime, though with respect to American cities it's relatively safe. Major streets on the South Side are Westmoreland (which becomes Grafton, which becomes Aungier), Dawson, and Patrick St.; and Nassau St. and Dame St. among east-west streets. O'Connell, Gardiner, and Capel St. are the major north-south arteries of the North Side.

Tourist Office: Main Office: 14 Upper O'Connell St. (tel. 284 4768). From Connolly Station, follow Talbot St. Accommodations service (IR£1 fee and 10% booking deposit). *Map of Greater Dublin* (IR£4). Open Mon.-Sat. 8:30am-6pm; July-Aug. Mon.-Sat. 8:30am-8pm, Sun. 1-5pm.; Sept.-May Mon.-Sat. 9am-5pm. **Bord Fáilte Éireann (Irish Tourist Board),** Baggot St. Bridge 2 (tel. 616 6500). Maps 'n' stuff on the rest of the Republic. Open Mon.-Sat. 9am-5pm.

Budget Travel: USIT (Irish Student Travel Agency), 19-21 Aston Quay (tel. 677 8117), near the O'Connell Bridge. ISICs, HI cards. Travelsave stamps IR£7. Plethora of discounts, especially for under 26. Open Mon.-Fri. 9am-6pm, Sat. 11am-4pm.

An Óige (Irish Youth Hostel Association): 39 Mountjoy Sq. (tel. ‡363 111). Membership IR£7.50, under 18 IR£4. Book HI hostels here and pay at time of booking.

Embassies: U.S., 43 Elgin Rd., Ballsbridge (tel. 668 8777). Open Mon.-Fri. 8:30am-5pm. **Canada,** 65 St. Stephen's Green South, (tel. 478 1988; emergencies, call 285 1246). Open Mon.-Fri. 10am-noon and 2-4pm. **U.K.,** 31 Merrion Rd., Dublin 4 (tel. 269 5211). Open Mon.-Fri. 10am-noon and 2-4pm. **Australia,** Fitzwilton House, Wilton Terrace (tel. 676 1517). Open Mon.-Fri. 10am-noon and 2-4pm. **New Zealanders** should contact the British Embassy.

Currency Exchange: Best rates at banks, otherwise try the *bureau de change* in the **General Post Office.**

American Express: 116 Grafton St. (tel. 676 2874), up the street from Trinity Gates. Client mail held. Open Mon.-Sat. 9am-5pm, Sun. 11am-4pm; Sept.-June closed Sun.

Post Office: General Post Office, O'Connell St. (tel. 872 8888), near the tourist office. Dublin is the only city in Ireland with postal codes. Open Mon.-Sat. 8am-8pm. **Postal Code** for **Poste Restante:** Dublin 1.

Telephones: In the General Post Office. International pay phones open Mon.-Sat. 8am-8pm, Sun. and holidays 10:30am-6:30pm. **City Code:** 01.

Flights: Dublin Airport, 7 mi. north of the city center (tel. ‡379 900). Catch Dublin bus #41, 41A, or 41C (every 20min., IR£1.10) to Eden Quay in the city center.

Trains: Most trains arrive at **Heuston Station,** just south of Victoria Quay. The other main terminus is **Connolly Station,** centrally located on Amiens St. **Pearse Station,** on Pearse St. and Westland Row, is served by fewer trains. **Irish Rail Information,** 35 Lower Abbey St. (tel. 836 3333). Open Mon.-Fri. 9am-5:30pm, Sat. 11am-4pm; phones open Mon.-Sat. 9am-6pm, Sun. 10am-6pm.

Buses: Busáras, Store St. (tel. ‡366 111), directly behind the Customs House. Central station for intercity buses. Day **luggage lock-up** IR£1.10, rucksack IR£1.60, each additional day 65p. **Dublin Bus (main office),** 59 Upper O'Connell St. (tel. 873 4222, 872 0000), opposite the tourist office. Quality free maps of the suburbs. Open Mon.-Fri. 9am-5:30pm, Sat. 9am-1pm.

Public Transportation: Fares 55p-IR£1.10; some buses require exact change. **Dublin Area Rapid Transportation (DART)** serves the suburbs; costs a tad over IR£1.

Ferries: Stena-Sealink ferries arrive in Dún Laoghaire, where the DART shuttles weary passengers to Connolly Stn., Pearse Stn., and Tara St. in the city center for about IR£1.20. **B&I** ferries dock at the mouth of the River Liffey; from there,

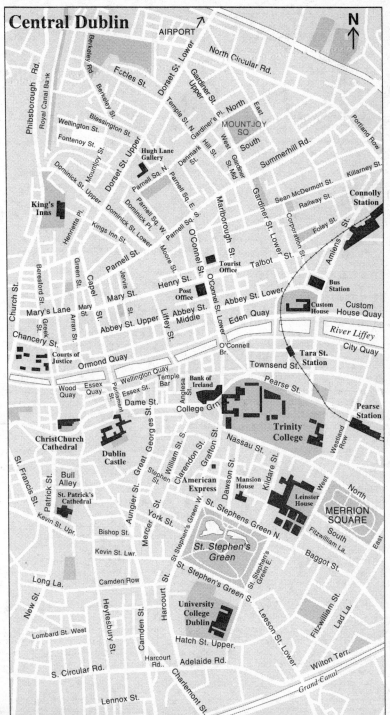

Central Dublin

AIRPORT

N

buses #53 and 53A run by Alexandra Rd. and arrive near the Custom House (80p). **B&I,** 16 Westmoreland St. **Sealink,** 15 Westmoreland St.

Taxis: National Radio Cabs, 40 James St. (tel. 667 2222). 24hrs. IR£1.80 plus 80p/mi. IR£1.20 call-in charge. IR£12-14 to airport from city center.

Bike Rental: Rent-A-Bike, 58 Lower Gardiner St. (tel. 872 5931 or 872 5399). Cross-country and mountain bikes IR£6/first day, IR£5/day thereafter, IR£30/ week, deposit IR£30. Panniers, helmets, and childseats IR£5/week. For IR£5 extra, return the bike to depots in Rosslare, Cork, Limerick, Killarney, Sligo, Galway, or Westport. Open Mon.-Sat. 9am-6pm.

Laundromat: The Laundry Shop, 191 Parnell St. (tel. 872 3541). Wash IR£1.70, dry IR£1. Open Mon.-Wed. and Fri.-Sat. 8:30am-6pm, Thurs. 8:30am-8pm.

Crises: Samaritans, 112 Marlborough St. (tel. 872 7700). **Rape Crisis Centre,** 70 Lower Leeson St. (tel. 661 4911). **Women's Aid** (tel. 872 3122). Open Mon.-Fri. 10am-10pm, Sat. 10am-6pm. **Racial Discrimination: Harmony,** 41 Morehampton Rd., Dublin 4 (tel. ‡964 402 or ‡906 196). **Bisexual, Gay and Lesbian Information: Gay Switchboard Dublin,** Carmichael House, North Brunswick St., Dublin 7 (tel. 872 1055).

Late-Night Pharmacy: O'Connell's, 55 Lower O'Connell St. (tel. 873 0427). Open Mon.-Sat. 8:30am-10pm, Sun. 10am-10pm.

Hospital: Meath Hospital, Heytesbury St. (tel. ‡536 555, ‡536 000, or ‡536 694). Open 24hrs.

Emergency: Dial 999; no coins required.

ACCOMMODATIONS

Hostels

Most hostels are north of the River Liffey and east of O'Connell St., in a working-class neighborhood. Most are independent. In busy summer months, call ahead.

Isaac's (The Dublin Tourist Hostel), 2-4 Frenchman's Lane (tel. 749 321), 1st right on Lower Gardiner St. up from the Custom House. Hip young internationals rub elbows in this wood-raftered grotto. Self-catering kitchen, café, tightly monitored baggage room. Reception open 24hrs. Bed lockout 11am-5pm. No curfew. Dorm room with 12-14 beds IR£5.50; 6-8 beds IR£6.25; 4-6 beds IR£7.25. Singles IR£15.25. Doubles IR£23. Triple IR£33.75. Breakfast included, except in dorms. Lockers 50p. Reserve 1 week in advance for Fri. or Sat. night.

Marlborough Hostel (IHO), 81-81 Marlborough St. (tel. 874 7629 or 874 7812), next to the pro-Cathedral, and directly behind the O'Connell St. tourist office. Brand-spanking-new hostel with super-comfy beds. Kitchen with microwave. Checkout 10:30am. 4- to 10-bed dorms IR£7.50. Singles IR£14. Doubles IR£22. 50p discount when you flash your *Let's Go.* Continental breakfast included. Luggage storage free. Sheets 50p. Laundry 50p. Reserve by phone 1-2 weeks in advance during February's scrum-heavy rugby season.

Avalon House (IHO), 55 Aungier St. (tel. 475 0001). From Dame St. take South Great George St. to Aungier St., 2 blocks west of St. Stephen's Green. Great location. Coed showers, toilets, and dorms. Kitchen w/ microwave. 24-bed room IR£7.50 (Oct.-June IR£7). 4-bed dorm IR£11. 2-bed double IR£12.50. Wheelchair-accessible double (2 beds) IR£13.50. 10% off with European Youth Card.

M.E.C., 43 North Great George St. (tel. 872 6301), off Parnell St. All rooms have extra-long beds, big windows, and sinks. M.E.C. stands for Montessori Education Centre. No curfew. 8-16 bed dorm IR£6. Singles IR£11. Doubles IR£16. Free luggage storage; safe available. Sheet and pillow for hire: IR£1

Dublin International Youth Hostel (HI), Mountjoy St. (tel. ‡301 766), continue straight up O'Connell St./Frederick St. past Dorset St., take next left onto Mountjoy St. A convent (stained-glass windows and confessional boxes) converted to a comfortable, institutional hostel. 3-night max. stay. Kitchen, secure parking. No lockout. No curfew. IR£9, non-members IR£9.50; Oct.-May IR£7, IR£7.50. Continental breakfast included. Luggage storage 50p. Sheets 50p.

Bed and Breakfasts

A pride of august B&Bs covers Dublin and the surrounding suburbs, charging from IR£12 up to IR£25 and clustered along Upper and Lower Gardiner St. Those with a green shamrock sign are registered and approved by Bord Fáilte, the Irish Tourist Board. B&Bs without the shamrock haven't been inspected but are often better-located and cheaper. Bord Fáilte's *Ireland Accommodation Guide* (IR£4) lists all approved B&Bs and their rates.

FOOD

Dublin's open air **Moore St. Market** provides fresh and cheap fixings for those on a tight budget. (Open Mon.-Sat. 9am-5pm.) The **Thomas St. Market** (continue on Dame St./Lord Edward St. past Christ Church) is a calmer alternative for fruit and vegetable shopping. (Open Fri.-Sat. 9am-5pm.) On-the-go food is quick, greasy, and very popular; you can't escape the "Take Away: Fish and Chips" signs. Pub grub is always a good choice for a quick and inexpensive meal. Your cheapest option is **Dunne's Stores,** a supermarket chain with a branch on North Earl St. off O'Connell St. (Open Mon.-Wed. and Fri.-Sat. 9am-6pm, Thurs. 9am-8pm.)

Bewley's Cafes, 3 locations. A delightful crowd of Dublin characters, dark wood paneling, marble table tops, and mirrored walls. (1) The 78 Grafton St. branch, the largest, becomes an informal gay hangout on Sat. and Sun. afternoons. Open Mon.-Wed. 7:30am-1am, Thurs.-Sat. 7:30am-2am, Sun. 9:30am-10pm. (2) James Joyce frequented 12 Westmoreland St. Open Mon.-Wed. 7:30am-9pm, Thurs.-Sat. 7:30am-1am, Sun. 10am-8pm. (3) Also 13 South Great George's St. Open Mon., Tues. 7am-6pm, Wed.-Sat. 7am-2am.

Leo Burdock's, 2 Werburgh St. (tel. ‡540 306). Lucky the steps of the Christ Church Cathedral are near—it's takeout only, and eating these fish and chips is a religious experience. Every Dubliner's pick for best fish and chips in the universe. Haddock and cod IR£2. Large chips 80p. Open Mon.-Fri. 12:30-11pm, Sat. 2-11pm.

Marks Bros., 7 S. Great Georges St., off Dame St. Thick sandwiches (IR£1.30-1.70) and salads for starving artists and punks among artsy posters. Fun game: count the total number of pierced body parts on the waitstaff. Open Mon.-Sat. 10am-5pm.

The Well Fed Café, 6 Crow St., just off Dame St. Inventive vegetarian dishes served by a worker's cooperative. Peace posters on the walls, idealists at the tables. Wheelchair accessible. Open Mon.-Sat. 12:30-8:30pm.

SIGHTS

Dublin is a walkable city; most of the sights lie within a 1-mile radius of O'Connell Bridge. The tourist office sells *Visitor Attractions in Dublin* (IR£1) and Trinity gives 2 good walking tours. The **Historical Walking Tour** (tel. 845 0241 or ‡535 730; IR£4, students IR£3) meets at Trinity's front gate. The witty and irreverent **Trinity College Walking Tour** leaves every 15 minutes from the Information Booth inside the front gate (30min., IR£3.50). **Trinity College,** alma mater of Swift, Beckett, and Wilde, houses Wendy's favorite, the *Book of Kells,* in the **Old Library,** built in 1712. (Open Mon.-Sat. 9:30am-5:30pm, Sun. noon-4:30pm. IR£2.50, students IR£2.) South of the city, on the block between Kildare St. and Upper Merrion St., Irish history and culture reign. The Tara brooch and a live leprechaun share quarters at the **National Museum.** (Open Tues.-Sat. 10am-5pm, Sun. 2-5pm. Free.) Down the street on Merrion Sq., the **National Gallery's** 4-floor winding staircase is lined with portraits of Lady Gregory, Eliza O'Neill, Joyce, Shaw, and Yeats. (Open Mon.-Wed. and Fri.-Sat. 10am-6pm, Thurs. 10am-9pm, Sun. 2-5pm. Free.) Just south of Trinity on Dawson St. sits **Mansion House,** the residence of every Lord Mayor of Dublin since 1715. At the west end of Dame St., at its confluence with Parliament and Castle St., is **Dublin Castle,** built in 1204 by King John, and seat of English rule for more than 700 years. (State Apartments open Mon.-Fri. 10am-12:15pm and 2-5pm. Sat.-Sun. and holidays 2-5pm. Hours vary during official functions. IR£1.50, students and children 75p.)

Ironically, Dublin's only official cathedrals, **Christ Church Cathedral** (on Dame St.; open Mon.-Sat. 9am-5pm, Sun. 10am-4pm; last entry 1hr. before close; IR£4, students and children IR£3) and **St. Patrick's Cathedral,** are both Protestant.

As the **Irish Museum of Modern Art** (formerly the Royal Hospital Kilmainham) builds its collection, Irish art cohabitates with that of other nations. (Open Tues.-Sat. 10am-5:30pm, Sun. noon-5:30pm. Free.) Next door, **Kilmainham Gaol** stands as a silent tribute to those who died for Irish independence. (Open May-Sept. daily 11am-6pm; April Mon.-Fri. 1-4pm, Sun. 1-6pm. IR£1.50, seniors IR£1, students and children 60p.) Take buses #23, 51, 51A, 78, or 79 to the museum and the Gaol. If you crave alcoholic nectar, the huge **Guinness Brewery,** St. James Gate, pumps 2½ million pints a day to sate your thirst. (Open Mon.-Fri. 10am-4:30pm, last tour 3:30pm. IR£2, children 50p.) To get there, take bus #21A, 78, or 78A west along the quays, where murky river water seems to resemble the beverage.

ENTERTAINMENT

Be it Seamus Heaney or the Pogues, Dublin will show you a good time. The *Dublin Event Guide* (free from the tourist office) and *In Dublin* (IR£1.50) offer a smorgasbord of choices: music listings, theater reviews, exhibitions, and comedy shows. "Good puzzle would be cross Dublin without passing a pub," wrote James Joyce. The oldest one in Dublin, the **Brazen Head,** Lower Bridge St., off Merchant's Quay, established in 1198, still welcomes travelers. As a rule, dance spots open at 10:30 or 11pm, but the action gets moving only after 11:30pm, when partyers swarm from closing pubs to the dance floors; most clubs close down at 3 or 4am. Cover runs from IR£4-8, pints IR£2.

The national theater of Ireland, the **Abbey Theatre,** 26 Lower Abbey St. (tel. 787 222), was founded in 1904 by Yeats and Lady Gregory to promote Irish culture and modernist theater. (Box office open Mon.-Sat. 10:30am-7pm. Tickets IR£8-13; student standby discounts available 1hr. before Mon. and Thurs. shows.) The **Gate Theatre,** 1 Cavendish Row (tel. 744 045), produces everything from Restoration comedies to Irish classics. (Box office open Mon.-Sat. 10am-7pm. Tickets IR£10-12; student standby IR£6 Mon.-Thurs. at curtain time.)

In Dublin should be your bible to Dublin's music world. Scheduled concerts usually start at 9pm, impromptu ones even later. Traditional music is not a tourist gimmick, but a vibrant and important element of the Dublin music scene and the Irish culture; try **The Rock Garden,** 3a Crown Alley (tel. 679 9114), the current core of Dublin's rock world. Bigger bands entertain at the **Baggot Inn,** 143 Baggot St. (tel. 676 1430), where U2 played in the early 80s. For classical, the **National Concert Hall,** Earl's Fort Terrace (tel. 971 1533), hosts touring orchestras. (Nightly shows in July and Aug. 8pm. Tickets IR£7-10, students ½-price.)

The celebrations of **Bloomsday** occur every June 16, the day when Joyce loosed his *Ulysses* on Dublin. Besides staged readings, there is a garden party at Merrion St., lunch at Davy Byrne's, a walk based on the narrative of Chapter 8, and men wandering around in Joycean garb. Home games of the Irish **rugby** team are played in Lansdowne Road Stadium from October to March. Ruck over! (Tickets available at the turnstiles. All-Ireland Finals tickets sell out quickly.)

SOUTHEAST IRELAND

Southeast Ireland is its sunniest segment; it's also the part of the Republic which shows the most English influence. Irish people take holidays on the beaches along the south coast, Waterford is a real city, and Cashel has a superbly preserved cathedral complex; stop in Kilkenny to admire the medieval streets.

Rosslare Harbour and the Wicklow Mountains Rosslare Harbour is the region's transportation hub, where daily ferries chug to Britain and France. **Buses** and **trains** connect to: Dublin (bus: 4/day, Sun. 3/day, 3hr., IR£8; train: 3/day, Sun. 2/day, 2hr.); Cork (bus: 3/day, Sun. 4/day); Limerick (bus. 3/day; train: Mon.-Fri. 2/day; 3½hr.); Waterford (bus: 3/day; train: Mon.-Sat. 3/day; 1¼hr.); and Wexford (bus: 7/day, 20min., IR£2.40, return IR£3.40; train: 3/day, Sun. 2/day, 20min., IR£3, return IR£4). Hitching is said to be tough. The **Rosslare Harbour youth hostel (HI),** Goulding St. (tel. (053) 333 99), offers modern facilities and a concentration of continental youth. (Check-in 5:30pm. Lockout 10am-5:30pm. Curfew 11:30pm, lights out at midnight. Kitchen facilities. IR£6.50; Sept.-May IR£5.) **Mrs. J. Foley,** 3, Coastguard Station (tel. (053) 335 22), signposted off *the* main street, offers minimal B&B. (Checkout noon. IR£7. Camping IR£2.) The town has **tourist offices** in the ferry port (tel. (053) 336 22) and a mile from Rosslare Harbour on the road to Wexford (tel. (053) 332 32; open May-Sept.). Both run on ferry-time: 2-5pm and 6-8:30pm, plus Monday and Wednesday 11am-2pm and July through August 6:30-8:30am.

Just inland from the east coast jut the gorse- and heather-covered summits of the **Wicklow Mountains,** pleated by rivers rushing through wooded glens. The 70-mi. **Wicklow Way** hiking trail starts near Dublin and jogs south all the way to Clonegal in County Carlow. Though the path is well-posted with yellow arrows, pick up the Wicklow tourist board's free fact sheet #26B and the Ordnance Survey's *Wicklow Way Map* at the main Dublin tourist office or any mountaineering store. **Glendalough** (GLEN-da-lock), a spectacularly uninhabited valley in the midst of the mountains, cradles two lakes, a pine forest, and the best preserved of Ireland's ruined monastic settlements. Stay at the **Glendalough hostel (HI)** (tel. (0404) 451 43; IR£5.50, Oct.-April IR£3.80) or the **Old Mill Hostel (IHO),** Rathdrum Rd., Glendalough (tel. (0404) 451 56; IR£5.30, camping IR£2.90). **St. Kevin's Bus Service** (tel. (01) 281 8119) runs there from Dublin (return IR£8) or from Bray town hall (return IR£6).

Kilkenny and Cashel Touted as the best preserved medieval town in Ireland, **Kilkenny's** ancient architecture, rocking nightlife, and daytrip-rich locale give it the edge as a southeast base camp. Beware the ghost of 13th-century **Kilkenny Castle.** (Open daily 10am-7pm; Oct.-March Tues.-Sat. 10:30am-12:45pm and 2-5pm, Sun. 11am-12:45pm and 2-5pm; April-May daily 10:30am-5pm. IR£1, seniors 70p, students and children 40p.) The stone steps of **St. Canice's Cathedral** are lined with fragments of sculpture from the cathedral itself. (Open daily 9am-1pm and 2-5:30pm, except during services. 50p, students 30p.) Stay at the **Kilkenny Tourist Hostel (IHO),** 35 Parliament St. (tel. (056) 635 41; IR£5.50; sheets 50p). Demand the free *Kilkenny City and County Guide* at the **tourist office,** Rose Inn St. (tel. (056) 515 00; open Mon.-Sat. 9am-6pm, Sun. 11am-1pm and 2-5pm; Nov.-March Tues.-Sat. 9am-12:45pm and 2-5:15pm.) Kilkenny is on the Dublin-Waterford rail line.

Northwest of Kilkenny, the **Rock of Cashel** rises like a fairy castle out of Cashel town, truly magical when lit at night. Cashel's castle (say that 10 times fast) contains the 13th-century **St. Patrick's Cross.** B&Bs are a dime a dozen. Visit with Mrs. E. Ryan at **Abbey House,** Moor Lane (tel. (062) 611 04; singles IR£18, doubles IR£26). Three mountain ranges rear their moor-covered rumps out of the flatlands near the town of Cahir: the **Galtees,** the **Knockmealdowns,** and the **Comeraughs.** The Galtees boast **Galtymore,** Ireland's third highest mountain at 3654 ft.; the Knockmealdowns have **Knockmealdown Gap,** swarming with sheep and goats; and the Comeraughs flaunt many lakes, each accessible from the **Powers The Pot Hostel (IHO)** (tel. (052) 230 85), 5 miles from Clonmel on the road to Carrick-on-Suir. This may just be the end of the rainbow. (IR£5. Camping IR£2.50. Open May-Oct.)

SOUTHWEST IRELAND

Traveling west or southwest from Cork city means moving from an English-influenced, 20th-century landscape into one that often looks untouched: the scenery is lush rather than grim, the fishermen enthusiastic, and the roads sometimes lousy.

■■■ CORK CITY

Originally no more than an island surrounded by marsh, Cork remains a compact city, in both geography and disposition. Cork stands stoic and steadfast; it can hold its own against the best of them, and challenges are met with a fierce determination. In the early 17th century, the citizens of Cork refused to recognize the English monarchy, and through the first decades of the 20th century, Cork remained a center for Republican activities. Any Corkian will attest that their city is by all means superior to Dublin, a conviction especially evident in their fanatic pride in their soccer team.

The River Lee is a physical and economic divide between the north side (Shandon) and the more affluent commercial south side. Good pubs are generally to be found in the latter area, while the shopping district is in and around Patrick St.

St. Finbarr's Cathedral, at the South Gate entrance to medieval Cork, incorporates a zoo's worth of animals, griffins, and angels into its limestone gingerbread-house façade. (Open Mon.-Sat. 10am-1pm and 2-5:30pm; Oct.-April Mon.-Fri. 10am-1pm and 2-5pm.) North of the River Lee, the red sandstone and white limestone **Shandon Tower** of **St. Anne's Church** rises high above the hodgepodge of factories and warehouses, sporting an 11-ft. salmon weathervane. Climb it for a view of the city and harbor. (Open Mon.-Fri. 9:30am-5pm, Sun. open just for services. IR£1.50; to church only IR£1.) Just opposite the church, artisans practice weaving, porcelain-making, crystal-cutting, and pottery in the **Shandon Craft Centre.** In the city center, the **Crawford Municipal Art Gallery** (tel. (021) 270 433) is one of Ireland's finest public art museums. (Open Mon.-Sat. 10am-5pm. Free.)

Accommodations, Food, and Practical Information Cork is blessed with wonderful hostels; B&Bs run IR£11-13. Both are concentrated on **Western Rd., Glanmire Rd.** (a short walk from the train and bus station), west of the Grand Parade (take bus #8), and the less attractive **Lower Glanmire Rd. Campus House (IHO),** 3 Woodland View, Western Rd. (tel. (021) 343 531), is the tops for friendly hostel owners. (IR£5.50.) Or stay at **Isaac's,** 48 MacCurtain St. (tel. (021) 500 011), where resplendent rays illuminate the old wood floors and brick arches of the industrial-sized hostel. (Reception open 24hrs. Dorms IR£5.50. 4- to 6-person dorms with bath IR£4.50. Singles IR£18.50. Doubles IR£27. Wheelchair access.) Campers head for **Cork City Caravan and Camping Park** (tel. (021) 961 866), southwest of the city center on Togher Rd., ½ mi. beyond Lough Rd. Bus #14 runs every 20 minutes. (IR£5.50/tent, IR£1/person, IR£7.50/caravan, children under 7 25p. Open Easter-Oct.)

Try the **arcade** (entrances off Grand Parade, Patrick St., and Princes St.) for fresh fruit and grilled chickens, and the armada of bakeries along Oliver Plunkett St. and Washington St. for pastries and sandwich breads. **Quay Co-op,** 24 Sullivan's Quay, serves up vegetarian and vegan entrees. (Open daily 9:30am-10:30pm.) **The Other Place,** 7/8 Augustine St. (tel. 317 660), has an alternative library—a haven for budding radicals—as home of Cork's **Lesbian and Gay Center. Kelly's,** 64 Oliver Plunkett St., is a true-blue Cork establishment, serving up *real* Irish food. (Open daily noon-9pm.) Pop a cork at any of the many pubs in town serving local brews **Murphy's Stout** and **Beamish. Nancy Spain's,** 48 Barracks St., is one of the most popular clubs in the city, where live concerts (Fri.-Sun.) go for a IR£5 cover charge (includes a meal).

Cork's **tourist office** (tel. (021) 273 251) is on Grand Parade at South Mall St. (Open June-Sept. daily 9am-7pm; winter Sun.-Fri. 9:15am-5:30pm, Sat. 9am-1pm.) The **Bank of Ireland** changes money at 70 Patrick St., as does **American Express** at **Heffernan's Travel,** Pembroke St. (tel. (021) 271 081) **A.A. Bike Shop,** 68 Shandon St. (tel. (021) 304 154), rents cycles for IR£5 per day. (Open Mon.-Sat. 9:30am-6pm.) The **post office** licks envelopes on Oliver Plunkett St. (Open Mon.-Sat. 9am-1pm and 2–5:30pm.) **Trains** chug into **Kent Station,** Lower Glanmire Rd. (tel. (021) 504 777; across the river in the northeast part of town; open 7am-8pm) from Dublin (7/day, Sun. 3/day, 3hr., return IR£32.50), Limerick (7/day, Sun. 3/day, 2hr., return IR£14.50), and Rosslare Harbour (1/day Mon.-Sat., 6hr., return IR£24.50). **Buses** roll into the Parnell Pl. station (tel. (021) 508 188; 2 blocks from Patrick's Bridge) from Dublin (5/day, Sun. 3/day, IR£12), Blarney (nearly every hr., return IR£2.50), and Kinsale (6/day, Sun. 4/day, IR£3.70, round-trip IR£4.90). **Ferries** from Cork to France and Britain dock at **Ringaskiddy Terminal,** 9 miles south of the city. Call **Brittany Ferries** (tel. (021) 277 801) and **Irish Ferries** (tel. (021) 504 333) for information.

Blarney   Five mi. northwest of Cork is **Blarney,** home of **Blarney Castle** and the terrifically overrated **Blarney Stone.** Buses leave for Blarney from the Cork bus station (15/day, Mon.-Fri., 16/Sat., 10/Sun., 20min., return IR£2).

■■■ SOUTHWEST COAST

Kinsale   An hour's drive southwest of Cork lies Kinsale, a ritzy seaside resort town where you don't need money to have fun because the highlights—its spectacular vistas and peaceful walking trails—are free. A hike up **Compass Hill** south from Main St. or to **Charles Fort,** 2 miles east of town, will brighten any rainy day. (Fort open mid-June to Sept. daily 9am-6:00pm; mid-April to mid-June Tues.-Sat. 9am-4:30pm, Sun. 11-5:30pm. IR£1, students 50p.) Take the **Scilly walk** on your way back; the view of the harbor and ocean is reportedly one of the best in Europe. Stay at **Dempsey's Hostel (IHO),** just outside town on Cork Rd. (tel. (021) 772 124), beside Dempsey's Garage (8 beds/room, IR£4), or at the **An Óige Hostel,** Summer Cove (tel. (021) 772 309), 2 miles from Kinsale on the east side of the harbor up the hill just before Charles Fort. (Chores. Lockout from bedrooms 10:30am-5pm. Curfew 11:30pm. IR£5.50, Sept.-May IR£3.80.) Down Pearse St. and to the left waits **Mother Hubbard's,** Market St. (tel. 021 772 212), a 1-room place whose massive hearth gives it an Irish-cottagey feel. (Breakfast IR£3.50. Open daily 9am-4pm.)

Beara Peninsula   Southwest of Kinsale, off the coast of the tiny fishing village of **Baltimore,** lie Sherkin Island and Cape Clear Island (where Gaelic is still spoken). North of the islands, the Beara Peninsula juts into the sea with similar majesty to the more northerly Iveragh Peninsula and fewer tourists. Don't even bother trying to hitchhike; rent a bike instead.

Bantry makes a fine base for exploring Beara's scenic surroundings. Buses come from Cork daily. (3/day, except 1/day Sun. Return IR£11.50, students IR£7.) The **Bantry Independent Hostel (IHO),** Bishop Lucy Pl. (tel. (027) 510 50), is a small, friendly establishment eying the surrounding hills. (IR£5. Open mid-March to Oct.)

A fishing village and the largest town on the peninsula, **Castletownbere** reverberates with the sounds of ferry engines, cars, loud children, and wind. The **Beara Hostel (IHO)** (tel. (027) 701 84) offers comfortable beds for IR£5 and less comfy ground to camp on for IR£3.50. In the Caha Mountains, the **Adrigole House** (tel. (027) 601 32) is the eponymous hamlet's only hostel, a few minutes from the Castletownbere/Healy Pass junction. The breathtaking pass is a narrow, winding, 6km road which takes you through the green and rocky Caha Mountains.

SOUTHWEST COAST

Kenmare, a colorful town at the elbow of the Beara and Iveragh peninsulas, offers access to both. Sink into the cushy **Fáilte Hostel (IHO),** Henry St. (tel. (064) 410 83; no lockout; no curfew; kitchen; IR£6).

Iveragh Peninsula The **Ring of Kerry** has gone the way of U2; both once embodied the tough, romantic spirit of Ireland, but both have more or less sold out to attract the masses. Stock up but tarry not in Killarney; head for the hills instead. Try the shiplike rooms at **The Súgán,** Lewis Rd. (tel. (064) 331 04), or the **Bunrower House Hostel (IHO)** (tel. (064) 339 14), right next to the Killarney National Park. (Both IR£5. Sheets 50p.) Down a meal deal at **An Taelann,** Bridewell Lane, off New St. **Bus Éireann** does a summer circuit through all the major towns on the Ring (Mon.-Sat 3/day, Sun. 1/day).

What tiny **Caherdaniel** lacks in greeting-card charm she makes up for in inspiring stretches of beach. Across the street form Skellig Aquatics is the **Village Hostel** (tel. 752 77), where flowery comforters console pale peach rooms. (No lockout. Midnight curfew. Kitchen. IR£5. Showers 50p.) The best reason to halt around **Ballinskelligs Bay** is the proprietor of the groovy **Peter's Place** hostel on Main St. in Waterville. (No phone, he hates 'em. No lockout. No curfew. Kitchen. Door open 24hrs. Free laundry. Free coffee, tea, and toast. Free tunes. IR£5; camping IR£3. Incredible vegetarian meals IR£1-2.) Or you can stay at the quiet **Ballinskelligs Youth Hostel (An Óige/HI)** (tel. (066) 792 29), near the beach overlooking the Bay. (Midnight curfew; July-Aug. IR£5.50, April-June and Sept. IR£4.30.) The Ring of Kerry traditionally commences in **Killorglin;** it should be your last stop if driving behind gigantic tour buses isn't your cup of tea. **Laune Valley Farm Hostel** (tel. (066) 614 88), is a farm ½-mile from Killorglin on the Tralee road. Cleanliness abounds (IR£5); "wholefood" meals are an extra IR£3.50.

Dingle Peninsula Dingle Peninsula, County Kerry's northernmost, has one of Ireland's few surviving Gaelic-speaking communities. Skip over Tralee, at the peninsula's base, and head straight for **Dingle,** chock full o' traditional music, craft shops, and small restaurants, before the growing tourist flood drowns all the charm. The ex-hippie owner of **Rainbow Hostel** (tel. 510 44), ½-mile west of town on Strand Rd., his son, and a team of students maintain this small, friendly setup. (IR£5, private rooms IR£15). Good, inexpensive food can be had at **Eirí na Gréine,** Green St., opposite the church, behind Dick Mack's pub. Though fewer than 1500 people live in Dingle, the town has 52 pubs—drink up.

No matter how tight you think your schedule is, you will inevitably be waylaid by glorious **Slea Head** and its inviting, though clandestine, strand. **Dunquin youth hostel (HI)** (tel. (066) 561 21) looks out onto the sea. (Lockout 10:15am-5pm. Curfew 11:30pm. Kitchen. IR£6, Oct.-May IR£4.50. Sheets 60p.) Northeast of Dunquin lies **Ballydavid** and **Brandon Creek,** the exact spot from which St. Brendan, patron saint of Kerry, is said to have set sail for the "Heavenly Isles" (almost certainly America). In Ballydavid proper, follow the signs to the **Tigh TB Hostel** (tel. 553 00; no lockout or curfew; kitchen; IR£5). From Dingle town to the northern side of the peninsula, the 1000-ft.-high **Conor Pass,** a winding cliffside road too narrow for buses to traverse, crosses the mountains and affords ripping views of the bays and valleys.

WESTERN IRELAND

The undesirability of Western land limited foreign influence, preserving spoken Irish in the Connemara, though it's the rugged scenery there that most travelers are understandably seeking. The West was hardest-hit by the potato famine: entire villages emigrated or died, and the population is still less than half of what it was in

1841. Hikers, cyclists, and hitchhikers observe rural depopulation in boggy, rocky, or brilliantly mountainous landscapes.

■■■ LIMERICK AND ENNIS

Linking much of Western Ireland by rail and bus, the city of **Limerick** offers more than a station bench to the traveler waiting for a connection. At **King John's Castle** (on St. Nicholas St. and the N18 to Galway), the pre-Norman excavations and scale models of battle machinery are worth exploring. (IR£3.20, students IR£1.60.) Antiseptic doubles and private rooms are available across town on George's Quay at the **Limerick Holiday Hostel** (tel. (061) 415-222), Barrington House. (IR£5 shared, IR£6.50 private room.) Midway between George's Quay and the station, **Ennis Rd.** graciously lures you to its row of B&Bs. The **train and bus stations** (train info tel. (061) 315-555; bus info tel. (061) 313-333; office open Mon.-Sat. 9am-6pm), just off Parnell St., serve destinations throughout western Ireland. **Buses** foray all over the region; 5-10 per day go to each main destination. **Trains** all change at Limerick Junction to: Dublin (9/day, Sun. 4/day, 2½hr.); Cork (7/day, Sun. 4/day, 2½hr.); to Killarney and Tralee (5/day, Sun. 3/day, 3hr. to Killarney, 3½hr. to Tralee) and to Waterford and Rosslare (Mon.-Sat. 2/day, 2hr. to Waterford, 3½hr. to Rosslare).

Fifteen miles west of Limerick is **Shannon Airport** (for Aer Lingus (061) 614 44, for 24-hr. flight info (061) 616 66), a domestic and transatlantic hub. The airport provides direct ground transport to Ennis, Galway, Westport, Tralee, and Killarney.

The narrow, high-walled streets and buzzing crowds of **Ennis** reside 20 miles northwest of Limerick; the town is also the gateway to the Clare coastal region. Ask for a map at the rambling **Abbey Tourist Hostel (IHO).** (Reception open 9:30am-10:30pm. No curfew or lockout. Kitchen. Laundry. IR£5. Sheets IR£1.) **O'Connell Street** is the place for cheap eats. Ask questions at the tourist office in the **Upstairs Downstairs shop,** O'Connell Sq. (Open daily 9am-9pm; Oct.-May 9am-6pm.) **Buses** run frequently from Station Rd. to Limerick (IR£3.50) and Galway.

■■■ CLARE COAST

Meadows freckled with hollyhocks, dandelions, and B&Bs roll down to the sea along the coast from Kilkee in the south to Miltown Malbay; the 15-mile stretch north of Miltown to Doolin is far more dramatic. To get to the coast, take the Ennis post bus or the bi-daily buses from Limerick and Ennis to the many coastal towns.

Halfway up the coast, past Lahinch, cold blue waves crash against the majestic **Cliffs of Moher,** limestone masses that tower 700ft. over the sea. Vaguely-marked paths meander the cliffs; tourists drop away after the first curve. A nearby **tourist office** (tel. (065) 811 71; open July-Aug. daily 9am-7pm; June and Sept. 10am-6pm) herds the aforementioned tourists past the cliffs. A mile from the cliffs, the **Old Hostel (IHO)** (tel. (065) 813 82), a gabled schoolhouse, keeps a collection of musical instruments around the peat stove. (Kitchen. Dorm beds IR£4. Doubles IR£10.) **Lisdoonvarna** hosts one of Ireland's last remaining **Matchmaking Festivals.** At these traditional fêtes, farmboys and farmgirls, their crops already harvested (but with wild oats left to sow), throw their rakes and buckets aside to collide in uninhibited climax. Irish women tend to stay home and mock the randy bachelors who attend. The **Burren Holiday Tourist Hostel,** Doolin Rd. (tel. (065) 743 00), ranks among the finest in Ireland, with its oak handrails, high ceilings, and antique decor. (No curfew or lockout. Kitchen. IR£5.50. Delicious meals IR£3-6. Laundry IR£3. Bikes IR£5.)

Doolin (called **Fisherstreet** on some maps) is why you came to Ireland. World-class folk music fills the pubs, and the single mile-long street is one hand-painted storefront after another. **O'Connor's,** in the lower village, and **McGann's,** in the upper, have both won awards for the best traditional music in Ireland. Always book ahead for accommodations. The modern **Doolin Hostel** (tel. (065) 740 06), in the lower village, comes complete with a shop, currency exchange, and a volcanic tourist information desk (just waiting to erupt with info). All 3 offices are open daily 8am-9pm. (No curfew. Kitchen. IR£6. Laundry IR£2.50. Sheets 50p. Bikes IR£5/day.) The **Rainbow Hostel (IHO)** (tel. (065) 744 15), in the upper village, has a cheery common room with wooden benches. (Kitchen. IR£4.50. Wash IR£1.50; no dryer.)

■■■ GALWAY CITY

Galway meanders between rivers and sea, full of old merchant houses, traditional music pubs, active independent theaters, and gaggles of hip young people. In summer you must parry and thrust with your furled umbrella to clear space on the tourist-filled streets. The historic sites line the banks of the **River Corrib** in the western part of the city. Galway's **cathedral** dominates the city's skyline and postcards. Two blocks south, the restored **Nora Barnacle House,** Bowling Green (tel. (091) 647 43), exposes the private (ha!) letters and photos of James Joyce and his wife. (Open May-Sept. Mon-Sat. 10am-5pm. IR£1.)

Hostels are conveniently located downtown. **The Galway City Hostel,** 25-27 Dominick St. (tel. (091) 663 67), has spotless new dorms, sizzling showers, and a welcoming cup of tea. (Curfew 1am. IR£6.60, mid-Oct. to May IR£5.50.) At Galway's newest hostel, the **Salmon Weir,** Woodquay (tel. 611 33), owners John and Fiona provide peaceful living in their home. (Curfew 3am. IR£6.90, Sept.-May IR£5.90.) B&Bs hide in **Renmare,** 1 mile east, and Salthill, 1½ mi. southwest of the center. Be sure to book lodgings ahead, especially in July and August. Galway's self-proclaimed Left Bank/Latin Quarter sandwiches vegetarian eateries, theaters, street music, and pubs into a few blocks between Shop St., High St., and Quay St. A few minutes west across the Corrib River, **Dominick St.** is the heart of another similar district.

The main **tourist office,** Victoria Pl. (tel. (091) 630 81), lies just 1 block west of the bus and train station (tel. (091) 621 41; open daily 9am-7pm, Sept.-June 9am-6pm). Another office hides in **Salthill** (same phone; open June to mid-Sept. daily 9am-8:30pm). **Bikes** can be rented in the alley below the train station. (IR£5/day, IR£25/week; IR£40 or ID deposit. Open July-Aug. Mon.-Sat. 9am-6pm, Sun. 9am-noon.) **Trains** run from Eyre Square Station to Athlone (Mon.-Sat. 10/day, Sun. 6/day, 1hr.) and continue to Dublin (3hr., IR£9, students IR£6.50); transfer at Athlone for all other lines. **Buses** depart from the steps outside to Dublin (8/day, Sun. 2/day, IR£9, students IR£6.50), Ennis (every 2-3hr., Sun. 5/day, IR£7.30, students IR£3.90), and Shannon Airport (5/day., Sun. 2/day).

■■■ ARAN ISLANDS (OILEÁIN ÁRANN)

Fifteen miles off the coast of Galway, Irish-speaking Inishmore, Inishmaan, and Inisheer rise defiantly out of the Atlantic. Unless you're a jolly good swimmer, boats and planes are your only transport options. Frequent **ferries** run from Galway, Rossaveal, and Doolin (in County Clare). Direct your ferry queries to the Galway **tourist office** (tel. (091) 689 03, after business hours (091) 924 47; ferry desk open daily 9am-7pm, Sept.-June 9am-6pm; call (091) 554 80 for plane info). Shuttling **inter-island boats** connect with most ferry arrivals. Dozens of ruins, forts, and churches, as well as "minor sites" like holy wells, lighthouses, and kelp kilns, rise from the stony terrain of **Inishmore.** The 18-ft. thick walls of **Dún Aengus Fort** (Dún Aonghasa), 5 miles west of the pier at Kilronan, guard Inishmore's northwest quarter and the strangely brilliant turquoise waves that hollow the base of the surrounding cliffs. Stay at the wonderful **Mainistir House (IHO)** (tel. (099) 611 69), which perches half a mile from Kilronan; go up the hill and take a right after the supermarket. (IR£7.

Doubles IR£20.) **An Sean Chéibh,** with outdoor seating and fresh Aran fish, is a short walk left from the harbor. Ferries land at the pier in **Kilronan** (Cill Rónáin), the island's main harbor; the **tourist office** (tel. (099) 612 63) is at the pier. (Open June to mid-Sept. daily noon-6:15pm.)

Tourists are a rarer breed on the smaller islands, **Inishmaan** and **Inisheer,** than on Inishmore. Here one finds stunning scenery and locals who construct *curraghs* (small boats made from curved wicker rods tied with string and covered with cowskin and black tar). On Inishmaan, stay with **Mrs. Faherty,** Creigmore (tel. (099) 730 12), who runs a jolly good B&B. (IR£9. Open April-Oct.)

■■■ CONNEMARA

The chocolate-brown earth of the Connemara and the cold, still sea stand in unlikely juxtaposition; inhabitants insist that nary a more beautiful place exists in Ireland. Like much of the western coast, the most rewarding way to absorb Connemara is on bike. Otherwise, take the 3-hour public bus from Galway to Clifden via Cong, which passes through the most miraculous areas of the region. On the southern coast of Connemara, Ireland's largest Gaelic-speaking population inhabits an area stretching westward from Galway City to Carna that is perfect for camping. Throngs arrive in the summer for the *curragh* races, the largest of which is held in **Spiddal** (An Spidéal), 12 miles west of Galway City on the main Connemara coast road. The landscape becomes progressively starker west of Spiddal. Consider interrupting your western trek with a stay at the 20-bed **Connemara Tourist Hostel (IHO),** Aille, Inverin (tel. (091) 931 04), 2 miles west of Spiddal. (July-Aug. IR£5.90, Oct.-May IR£4.50.) The coastal bus from Galway stops outside.

Clifden Connemara's western outpost is the only spot in the region that could be properly classified as a town. It manages to accommodate tourists without appearing infested, and the expanded market buoys the local weavers, artists, and Irish music sellers. **Connemara Heritage Tours,** Market St. (tel. (095) 213 79), foray into the history, folklore, and archeology of the region (tours leave Mon.-Sat. from the Island House, Market St., 9am, return 4:45pm; IR£11, students IR£10). The reputation of the "loo with a view" at sunny, whitewashed **Leo's Hostel (IHO)** has spread far and wide. (IR£5, private room IR£5.50. Bikes IR£5/day.) The new **Brookside Hostel** (tel. (095) 218 12) provides a family atmosphere. (IR£5, private rooms negotiable.) Sit on honey-colored wooden picnic benches at **My Teashop,** Main St. (Open daily 9am-9pm.) For a little drink and wink, try **The Central,** Main St.

The amiable **tourist office** (tel. (095) 211 63) is at the bottom of Market St. (Open June-Sept. 15 Mon.-Sat. 9am-7pm, Sun. 10am-6pm.) Rent bikes at **Mannion's,** Bridge St. (tel. (095) 211 60; IR£6/day, IR£30/week, IR£10 deposit; open Mon.-Sat. 9:30am-7pm, Sun. 10:30-11:30am). Buses run to Clifden from Galway through Oughterard; an express service operates during July and August (Mon.-Sat.).

Cleggan and the Twelve Bens Ten miles northwest, **Cleggan,** the center of Connemara's fishing industry, offers the charms of Clifden without the tourists. Explore the pleasant sandhills and small ruins of **Omey Island,** just offshore to the southwest and accessible by foot at low tide. People remain for days at the airy **Master House Hostel (IHO)** (tel. (095) 447 46), full of plants, bright wood, and exposed stone. (IR£5. Private room IR£6. Fishing rods IR£2.50.)

The **Twelve Bens** (Na Benna Beola, also known as the Twelve Pins) are a range of rugged hills 1700-2400 ft. high in the heart of the Connemara. Hikers can base themselves at the **Ben Lettery youth hostel (HI)** (tel. (095) 346 36) in Ballinafad, eight miles east of Clifden, just off the N59 west of the Roundstone turn-off. (IR£5.50, Oct.-May IR£3.80.) Farther east along the N59, **Killary Harbour,** Ireland's only fjord, breaks through the mountains to the town of **Leenane,** wrapping itself in the skirts of the **Devilsmother Mountain.** The remote **Killary Harbour youth hostel (HI)** (tel.

(095) 434 17) is at the very mouth of the harbor, 7 miles west of Leenane. (IR£5.50,Oct.-May IR£3.80.) The Galway-Leenane-Clifden bus stops 3 miles from the hostel, at Kylemore Abbey and in Letterfrack.

Westport This welcoming town is a great base for the West Coast, proximate to the Connemara region, County Mayo, and some of the hoppingest pubs out west. **Street Festival** (the first week in July) draws visitors into musical revelry. The **Old Mill Holiday Hostel,** James St. (tel. (098) 270 45), offers firm pine-framed beds and shockingly hot showers in a renovated mill and brewery. (Bedroom lockout 11am-1pm. IR£6, Sept.-June IR£5.) **The Granary Hostel (IHO)** is a mile from town on the Louisburgh Rd. in a 150-year-old granary with a simple kitchen and outdoor toilets and showers (IR£4.50). Westport's **B&Bs** (IR£12-13) are easily spotted on the Castlebar and Altamount Roads. Locals pile into **McCormack's** on Bridge St. for pastries, tea, and simple meals on flowered tablecloths. (Open daily 10:15am-6pm.) Rock on over to **the West** for live bands (Thurs., Sat., and Sun.).

The **tourist office** (tel. (098) 257 11) occupies the North Mall, down by the river. (Open daily 9am-6pm.) **Bike World,** the Octagon (tel. (098) 596 179), rents 2-wheelers (IR£5/day, IR£25/week; open Mon.-Sat. 10am-6:30pm, Sun. noon-6pm). Transportation connections are poor for such a major town. **Trains** (tel. (098) 252 53) arriving from Dublin terminate in the Octagon (3/day, Sun. 1/day; mid-June to mid-Sept. Mon.-Sat. 1/day). **Buses** leave from the Octagon for Clifden (mid-June to mid-Aug. 1/day, 1½hr.); Galway (1-2/day, 2hr.); and Sligo (June-Sept. 1/day, 2½hr.).

NORTHWEST IRELAND

The upper Shannon's strips of farmland interrupted by monasteries and islands are a gradual windup to the punch of Sligo, a fun bay town close to the heart of the poet William Butler Yeats. Donegal's windy mountains and winding coasts may be your wildest dream come true, and don't leave the country without having seen the Inishowen Peninsula. From there, it's easy to cross into Derry, a history-soaked Northern city filled with nervous energy.

Sligo town, Donegal town, and Killybegs South of County Donegal, **Sligo town,** childhood haunt of W.B. Yeats, is a convenient stopover for northern wanderers and a happening pub town to boot. Yeats fanatics hike up rocky **Knocknarea** but, simply admire more severe **Ben Bulben,** which broods over Yeats's grave in **Drumcliff churchyard,** 4 miles north of town. Back in Sligo, the **bus/train station** (tel. (071) 698 88) is centrally located on Lord Edward St. and the **tourist office** (tel. (071) 612 01) is past the cathedral on Temple St. The hippest hostel in town, the **White House (IHO),** Markievicz Rd. (tel. (071) 451 60), has 3 wardens: 2 who pluck banjos and one who jams a *bodhrán.* (IR£6. Key deposit IR£2.) Wonderful lunches vary daily at ever-authentic **Hardogan's** on O'Connell St.

Gateway to the stunning cliffs and inlets to the west, **Donegal town** is a good springboard for northwest Ireland. The **tourist office** (tel. (073) 211 48) sits just south of the Diamond (the central town square and home of the **bus depot**) on Quay St. (Open Mon.-Fri. 10am-1pm and 2-8pm; Sept.-June Mon.-Fri. 10am-1pm and 2-6pm, Sat.-Sun. 10am-1pm.) With its wide patio, the **Donegal Town Hostel (IHO)** (tel. 228 05), 1 mile down Killybegs Rd., seems as if it should overlook the sea, not the main road. (IR£5. Camping IR£3.) The best dinner deal (IR£3.50) is at **Errigal Restaurant,** Main St. (Open daily 9am-10:30pm.) For basics, head to **Foodland Supermarket,** in the Diamond. **Schooner's** on Main St. has live music and good conversation.

The road heading west along Donegal's southern coast, from Donegal town to Rossan Point at the peninsula's tip, is scenic and varied. Buses run from Donegal town to **Killybegs** (5/day, late Aug.-early July Mon.-Sat. 3/day). Several miles farther on the coast road between Kilcar and Carrick, **Dún Ulun House** provides a luxurious alternative to hostel life. Large flowery beds accompany a continental (IR£11) or full (IR£13) breakfast. Down the road, the **Derrylahan Hostel** (tel. (073) 380 79), is run by the kind Shaun McClosky. With a well-stocked shop, hot showers, and 2 cozy houses, this hostel makes a great stopover. (IR£5, private room IR£7, camping IR£3; hot showers 50p; laundry.) The road south from Carrick leads to **Slieve League,** a 2000-ft. mountain that drops precipitously along the coastline. On one side of One Man's Pass, the cliffs drop 1800ft. straight to the sea; on the other side they fall 1000ft. to a rocky floor. The N15 provides a considerably safer, if less dramatic, route to **Glencolumbcille** at the westernmost point of the peninsula.

Derryveagh Mountains and Letterkenny

The bulky **Derryveagh Mountains** isolate the northwest corner of Donegal, the country's largest Gaelic-speaking area. **Crohy Head youth hostel (HI)** (tel. (075) 213 30; June-Sept. IR£5.80, under 18 IR£3.50; April-May and Oct. IR£3.80 and IR£3), 5 miles west of **Dungloe** (turn off Main St. towards the water on Quay St. and follow it out), overlooks ocean 100 ft. below. Farther north, 1½ miles west from Dunfanaghy and 5½ miles from Falcarragh, is wondrously comfortable **Corcreggan Mill Collage hostel (IHO)** (tel. (074) 364 09, IR£5). On the road to Gweedore via Church Hill, 14 miles northwest of Letterkenny, stretches the **Glenveagh National Park** (tel. (074) 370 88)—10,000 hectares of glens, mountains, and nature walks, plus a castle. (Open June-Aug. Mon.-Sat. 10am-6:30pm, Sun. 10am-7:30pm; early April to May and Sept. daily 10am-6:30pm; Oct. Sat.-Thurs. 10am-6:30pm. IR£1, children and students 40p; same for castle.)

Letterkenny, Donegal's largest town and its ecclesiastical capital, is a fast-expanding place that eases its growing pains with nightly pub crawls. The **Letterkenny Tourist Hostel (IHO),** High Rd. (tel. (074) 252 38), sags in the center of town. From the bus station, go up Port Rd., then take a hard right at the fork. (IR£4; open Feb.-Dec. 23.) The **Chamber of Commerce Visitors Information Centre,** 40 Port Rd. (tel. (074) 266 78), looks like a china shop, but bull on in for the pamphlets and friendly advice. (Open Mon.-Sat. 9am-7pm; Oct.-June Mon.-Fri. 9am-5pm.)

Donegal Peninsulas

Donegal's phenomenal four northern peninsulas are divided into stubby tendrils (Horn Head, Rosguill, Fanad, and Inishowen Peninsulas) by bays and loughs. Derry, Northern Ireland is the largest transport hub in the area; Letterkenny is the acknowledged touring base. By far the best way to see the peninsulas is by bike; rent in Letterkenny or Milford.

Between Lough Swilly and Mulroy Bay lies the **Fanad Peninsula.** North of Rathmullan, the land rises over the Knockala Hills and Glenvar, beyond which the coast is at its most arresting as it arcs between mountain and shore. Follow the signs to **Bunnaton Hostel,** Glenvar (tel. (074) 501 22; kitchen; IR£5; hot showers included). It would be a crime to leave Ireland without experiencing the **Inishowen Peninsula.** A mosaic of rugged mountains, lush forests, sumptuous beaches, and sheep, the peninsula is a microcosm of Ireland. Any tour of the area must begin with a visit to the hilltop fort of **Grianan of Aileach,** the "stone palace of the sun" originally built in 1700 BC. **Buncrana,** on the west side of the peninsula along the shores of Lough Swilly, is an energetic resort where sweeping beaches repose in the long shadow of **Slieve Snacht,** a 2019-ft. peak. Five miles north of Buncrana, the **Gap of Mamore** lies 800 ft. above sea level, offering torrid views of the entire peninsula. Vivid **Malin,** winner of Ireland's cut-throat Tidiest Town Competition, is Inishowen's northernmost outpost before the peninsula reaches out to tag **Malin Head,** from which you can see all the way across to the Paps of Jura on a clear day. Make a pitstop at **Farren's Pub,** Malin Head, Ireland's northernmost pub. One mile from the head is **Hell's Hole,** a 250-ft. chasm that roars with the incoming tide.

Situated on a lovely estuary, the village of **Culdaff** exudes a friendly warmth from its beaches and the great **McGrory's Pub.** The McGrory family also runs a splendid **Guest House** (tel. (077) 791 94; IR£13). Nearby **Kinnagoe Bay,** site of the 1588 wreckage of the Spanish Armada, will take your breath away. On the southeast coast of the Inishowen Peninsula, 5 miles over the border from Derry, Northern Ireland, lies **Muff Hostel** (tel. (077) 841 788), run by the gentle Martin Cooke and his sidekick, a golden retriever named Andrex. (IR£3.50. Hot showers. Open March-Oct.)

Liechtenstein

Liechtenstein uses Swiss currency and the Swiss phone system; its city code is 075.

Famous chiefly for its postage stamps, wines, and royal family, Liechtenstein's minute size renders the principality its own chief tourist attraction. Exhibits rotate about 4 times a year at **Staatliche Kunstsammlung,** in the capital city of **Vaduz,** Städtle 37, next to the tourist office. (Open daily 10am-noon and 1:30-5pm; April-Oct. until 5:30pm. 3SFr, students 1.50SFr.) The **Walser Heimatmuseum** in nearby **Triesenberg** chronicles the simple lifestyle of the Walsers, a group of 13th-century Swiss immigrants. (Open Tues.-Fri. 1:30-5:30pm, Sat. 1:30-5pm, Sun. 2-5pm; Sept.-May closed Sun. 2SFr, students 1SFr.) The Triesenberg **tourist office** (tel. 219 26) is in the same building as the museum and has the same hours. Winter sports breathe life into the mountain communities of **Malbun** and **Steg;** ski passes are 29SFr per day and 120SFr per week. Lift and lodging packages are available at many hotels (473-1011SFr/week); contact the Malbun **tourist office** (tel. 265 77) for specifics. (Open June-Oct. and mid-Dec. to mid-April Mon.-Wed. and Fri.-Sat. 9am-noon and 1:30-5pm.)

Accommodations and Food The lone **youth hostel (HI)** is in **Schaan.** Take the "Schaan" bus from Vaduz and request the "Hotel Mühle" stop; from there, turn on Marianumstr. and follow the signs. This pink and blue wonderland offers all the amenities of home. (Reception open Mon.-Sat. 7-9:30am and 5-10pm, Sun. 6-10pm. Members only. 20.30SFr. Lockers and laundry facilities 6SFr. Open Jan.-Nov. 15.) If the hostel is full, walk about 10 minutes back up the main road toward Vaduz or take the bus (direction "Falknis") for **Hotel Falknis** (tel. 263 77) right near the stop. (Singles and doubles 40SFr/person.) Of the 2 **campgrounds** in Liechtenstein, the more convenient is in **Bendern** (tel. 312 11), accessible by bus. (3SFr/person, 2-4SFr/tent, 3SFr/car. Cooking facilities.) Eating in Liechtenstein is an absolute nightmare; shop at **Denner Superdiscount,** Aulestr. 20, in Vaduz, and find a shady tree. (Open Mon.-Fri. 8:30am-1pm and 1:30-6:30pm, Sat. 8am-4pm.)

Practical Information Though its people have enjoyed the status of a sovereign country since 1806, a customs agreement with Switzerland makes border passage hassle-free. **Postal buses** speed visitors to Vaduz from Buchs or Sargans in Switzerland, or from Feldkirch in Austria. Liechtenstein's national **tourist office** (tel. 214 43), a few paces from the Vaduz bus stop, finds rooms at no charge, and distributes a list of hiking routes and a map of bike routes; bikes can be rented around the corner at **Hans Melliger,** Kirchstr. 10 (tel. 216 06), for 20SFr per day. Although biking is a dream in this flat, green principality, one can also opt for the efficient and cheap **postal bus system** that links all 11 villages (most trips 2SFr).

See *Let's Go: Germany & Switzerland* for in-depth coverage of this itsy little country.

Luxembourg

US$1	**= 34.50LF (francs, or LUF)**	**10LF =**	**US$0.29**
CDN$1	**= 26.20LF**	**10LF =**	**CDN$0.38**
UK£1	**= 53.40LF**	**10LF =**	**UK£0.19**
IR£1	**= 50.00LF**	**10LF =**	**IR£0.20**
AUS$1	**= 22.40LF**	**10LF =**	**AUS$0.45**
NZ$1	**= 19.10LF**	**10LF =**	**NZ$0.52**
SAR1	**= 7.17F**	**10LF =**	**SAR1.39**
Country Code: 352		**International Dialing Code: 00**	

Founded in 963, the Grand Duchy of Luxembourg was first named Luclinburhuc, or "little castle." By the time successive waves of Burgundians, Spaniards, French, Austrians, and Germans had receded, the little castle had become a bristling armored mountain, and the countryside was saturated with fortresses. Only after the last French soldier returned home in 1867 and the Treaty of London restored its neutrality did Luxembourg begin to cultivate its current image of peacefulness and independence. Today Luxembourg is an independent constitutional monarchy, a member of the European Community, and a tax-haven for investors from around the globe, with the Grand Duke and his Cabinet of 12 ministers still wielding supreme executive power over the country's 400,000 residents. From the wooded and hilly

Ardennes in the north to the fertile vineyards of the Moselle Valley in the south, the country's unspoiled rural landscapes markedly contrast with the high-powered banking industry of its capital city.

LUXEMBOURG ESSENTIALS

Luxembourg is only 2600km square, but the tiny territory is split into even smaller travel zones; the price of a trip is calculated according to the number of zones crossed. A *billet courte distance* (short distance ticket) costs 35LF and allows you to traverse up to 6 zones. Most inter-city trips will require at least 2 or 3 tickets. Train and bus stations sell network tickets (**Billets Reseaux,** 140LF) which allow for a day's unlimited 2nd-class travel on any train or national bus. A **Benelux Pass,** good for unlimited travel any 5 days in a 17-day period in Belgium, the Netherlands, and Luxembourg, costs only 2860LF, over 26 3780LF. **Bicycles** are permitted on any train for 35LF. **Hitching** is fair; distances are short, but traffic is light.

The **tourist office** network is exhaustive and highly skilled at ferreting out bargain rooms. Youth hostels frequently offer discounts on tours. The hostel association maintains trails marked with white triangles between each of their houses.

Luxembourg's official **languages** are French and German, but the most common language is Letzebuergesch, a German dialect with a slew of French loanwords. French is often preferred over German, especially by those who remember WWII. Most banks are open Mon.-Fri. from 8:30am to 4:30pm; most shops Tues.-Sat. from 9:30am to 6pm and Mon. from 2 to 6pm. Many shops close at noon for 2 hours, especially in the countryside, where only taverns may be open after 6pm. Luxembourg francs are worth the same as Belgian francs; you can use Belgian money in Luxembourg, and Luxembourg bills are valid in Belgium. The AT&T **USA Direct** number for Luxembourg is 08 00 01 11. The MCI **World Reach** number is 08 00 60 63. **Business holidays** are November 1 and 2, December 25 and 26, January 1, Carnival (in Feb.), Easter, Easter Monday, May 1, Ascension Day, Pentecost, Pentecost Monday, June 23, and August 15.

Accommodations, Camping, and Food The 13 **HI youth hostels** in Luxembourg charge between 300 and 380LF, ages over 26 350 to 440LF, nonmembers 90LF extra. Breakfasts are included, packed lunches cost 110LF, and dinners are 230LF; eating a meal in the hostel wins a 15LF discount. Sheets are 100LF. Lockers require 500LF or your passport deposit. All hostels (except the one in Grevenmacher) have kitchens. Many hostels are clogged with traveling tots in early summer, and many of them also close during December and January; phone ahead. Luxembourg hotels run from 600 to 1500LF per night. **Campgrounds** abound; almost all have hot showers. Two people with a tent will pay 250 to 300LF. Restaurant prices will devour your budget. Luxembourg cuisine is closely linked to that of the neighboring Lorraine region of France, with sliced Ardennes ham a national specialty.

■■■ LUXEMBOURG CITY (VILLE DE LUXEMBOURG)

Rising triumphantly on both sides of the steep gorge that divides it, the city of Luxembourg is one of the most physically dramatic capitals of Europe, cradling a mix of houses, castle ruins, vegetable gardens, and miniature golf sites. Home to international banking firms and the European Court of Justice, Luxembourg adds a dollop of cosmopolitanism to the otherwise overwhelmingly rural Grand Duchy.

PRACTICAL INFORMATION

Tourist Offices: Grand Duchy National Tourist Office, pl. de la Gare (tel. 48 11 99), in the Luxair office. Turn right as you leave the train station. Indispensable map, hotel listings, and reservations service—all free. Open Mon.-Fri. 9am-7:15pm, Sat., Sun., and holidays 9am-noon and 2-6pm; Sept.-May Mon.-Sat. 9am-

6pm. The **Municipal Tourist Office,** pl. d'Armes (tel. 22 28 09), in the center of town, offers info on and services for the city only. Open Mon.-Sat. 9am-7pm, Sun. 10am-noon and 2-6pm; mid-Sept. to Mid-June Mon.-Sat. 9am-1pm and 2-6pm.

Budget Travel: SOTOUR, 15, pl. du Théâtre (tel. 46 15 14). BIJ and other discount tickets. Open Mon.-Fri. 9am-6pm, Sat. 9am-noon.

Embassies: U.S., 22, bd. E. Servais (tel. 46 01 23). **U.K.,** 14, bd. Roosevelt (tel. 22 98 64). Open Mon.-Fri. 9am-12:30pm and 2-5pm. Answering machine gives a 24-hr. emergency number. Travelers from **Canada, Australia,** and **New Zealand** should contact their embassies in France or Belgium.

Currency Exchange: Mediocre rates at the train station. Open Mon.-Sat. 8:30am-9pm, Sun. 9am-9pm. Banks all have nearly the same rates. Many have offices in front of the train station. Standard charge of around 50LF/check. An **automatic currency exchange machine** is across from the station at Banque UCL.

American Express: 34, av. de la Porte-Neuve (tel. 22 85 55). Mail held. Traveler's Cheques cashed, sold, and replaced; wired money accepted. Exchange rates similar to banks. Open Mon.-Fri. 9am-1pm and 2-5pm, Sat. 9:30am-noon.

Post Office: Main office, 38, pl. de la Gare, across the street and to the left of the train station. Poste Restante open Mon.-Sat. 6am-8pm. **Branch office,** 25, rue Aldringern, 2 blocks from pl. d'Armes. Poste Restante open Mon.-Sat. 8am-7pm. **Poste Restante Code:** L-1009 Luxembourg.

Telephones: At both post offices. Main office open Mon.-Fri. 6am-7:15pm, Sat. noon-8pm. The branch on rue Aldringern has the same hours as the post office.

Flights: Bus #9 to the airport (35LF plus a rarely enforced 35LF charge for baggage) is cheaper than the Luxair bus (120LF) and runs the same airport-hostel-train station route more frequently (every 20min.).

Trains: Gare CFL av. de la Gare (tel. 49 24 24), near the foot of av. de la Liberté. In the southern part of the city, a somewhat seedy area, 10min. from the city center. Bus #9 runs between the railway station, the hostel, and the airport. Pick it up on your right as you leave the station, in front of the Luxair office. Luxembourg lies on major train routes from Brussels to Basel, and from Amsterdam to Milan.

Buses: Buy tickets from the driver (35LF; valid 1hr.), or get a package of 10 (270LF) at banks or at the bakery around the corner from the national tourist office.

Luggage Storage: At the station. Check your bags (60LF; open daily 6am-10pm) or use the lockers (80LF, oversized lockers 100LF).

Laundromat: Quick Wash, 31, rue de Strasbourg, near the station. Wash 230LF, dry 20LF for 7min. Open Mon.-Sat. 8am-7pm (closed holidays).

Pharmacy: Pharmacie du Globe, 12, rue Jean Origier (tel. 48 70 09), off av. de la Gare. Open Mon.-Fri. 7:40am-noon and 1:30-6pm. Dial 112 on weekends to find an open pharmacy or look in any pharmacy window for the name and address of the current *pharmacie de garde.*

Medical Assistance: Tel. 112. 24 hrs. (English spoken).

Emergencies: Ambulance: Tel. 112. **Police:** 58-60, rue Glesner (tel. 40 94 01).

ACCOMMODATIONS, CAMPING, AND FOOD

Inexpensive hotels jam the streets near the train station; several offer pleasant rooms, but others are as shabby as their neighborhood. Hotels become increasingly pricey and posh as you move north of the ravine. Both the main and branch tourist offices find rooms for free, but the main (Luxair) office is less crowded.

Auberge de Jeunesse (HI), 2, rue du Fort Olisy (tel. 22 68 89). Take bus #9 from airport or train station to Vallée d'Alzette below rue Sigefroi. Can be noisy, but has exceptionally friendly staff. Clean dorms and rooms for families and groups. 3-day max. stay if it's full. Reception open 7:30-9:30am and 3pm-midnight. Lockout 9:30am-2pm. No curfew. 350LF, over 26 420LF. Breakfast included. Packed lunch 110LF. Dinner 230LF. Lockers 500LF or passport deposit. Bike rental 400LF.

Hotel Carlton, 9, rue de Strasbourg (tel. 48 48 02). From the station, up av. de la Liberté and left on rue de Strasbourg. Cheapest rooms in the city. Lobby with stained-glass windows; clean rooms. 24hr. reception. Singles 650-850LF, with shower 1100-1250LF. Doubles 1500LF. Breakfast included. Make reservations.

Hotel Papillon, 9, rue Jean Origier (tel. 49 44 90). From the station, north on av. de la Gare and left on rue Jean Origier. Decently large rooms, each with shower and furniture resembling a Barbie doll play set. Singles 1050LF. Doubles 1600LF. Breakfast included. Credit cards accepted.

Auberge Le Parisien, 46, rue Ste. Zithe (tel. 49 23 97), 5min. from the station, off pl. de Paris. Small rooms, all with TV. Singles 1000LF, with shower 1150LF. Doubles 1600LF, with shower 1750LF. Breakfast included. Open Jan. 9-Dec. 22.

Camping: Kockelscheuer (tel. 47 18 15). Bus #2 from the station. 90LF, children 50LF, 100LF/tent. Hot showers included. Wheelchair access. Open Easter-Oct.

Restaurant prices are discouraging. **EMS**, 30, pl. de la Gare, packs in locals with moderately priced specialties such as smoked Ardennes ham. **Bella Napoli**, 4, rue de Strasbourg, offers pizza from at 180LF. Located directly across from the Ducal palace, **Restaurant Bacchus,** 32, Marché aux Herbes, serves excellent food in an upscale atmosphere with surprisingly low prices. (Entrees from 200LF.) Or shop at **Nobilis,** the huge, modern supermarket at 47, av. de la Gare, and sit peacefully in the parks by the ravine. (Supermarket open Mon.-Fri. 9am-7:30pm, Sat. 9am-7pm.)

SIGHTS AND ENTERTAINMENT

Luxembourg's ancient façades and battlements are being furiously scrubbed of all graffiti as the city prepares for its year as the cultural capital of Europe in 1995. Unfortunately for visitors in 1994, this means that some of its best attractions are literally under wraps—a giant drape is hanging over the Grand-Ducal Palace until 1995—but most sights are still open and can be seen in one day. The tourist office offers a well-organized **walking route** which begins and ends in front of the train station. A must-see is the **Bock-Casemates,** which looms imposingly over the Alzette valley and sheltered 35,000 people during WWII. (Entrance at rue Sigefroi near chemin de la Corniche. Open daily March-Oct. 10am-5pm. 50LF.) The **Musées de l'Etat** are a salad of ancient and contemporary art, natural history, and local history. (Open Tues.-Fri. 10am-noon and 1-5pm, Sat. 2-6pm, Sun. 10am-noon and 2-6pm. Free.) When you tire of the crowded old city, head for the **parks** along the shaded River Pétrusse. *La Semaine à Luxembourg,* available at the city tourist office, lists the week's events. To find what local bars are "in," stroll along **rue Besseroueg** and **rue St. Unic.** Luxembourg doesn't have the hottest nightlife in Europe by a long shot, but **Scott's Pub and Restaurant,** 4, Bisserweg (tel. 22 64 74), is one place that really rocks. Take the elevator at pl. du St. Esprit down into the valley and cross the bridge. (English pub grub 300-350LF. Open daily noon-1am.)

■■■ THE COUNTRYSIDE

In 1944 the bloody Battle of the Bulge raged through the Ardennes, flattening the forests into slime and mud. Today the revived forests, hilltop castles, and shallow rivers of Luxembourg's countryside entice travelers away from the city. Trains grind regularly between Luxembourg and Ettelbrück (1/hr., 30min., 105LF), or you can take the brown CFL buses to smaller towns. (Luxembourg-Echternach 1/hr., 1hr., 105LF; Ettelbrück-Echternach 2/hr., 30min., 105LF; Echternach-Vianden 2/day, 50min., 105LF; Vianden-Ettelbrück 9/day, 30min., 70LF.) Railpasses are valid. Many towns harbor only an afternoon's worth of sights, so buy the one-day 140LF pass and see several in one jaunt.

■ Ettelbrück and the Moselle Valley

Ettelbrück itself offers little, but its train and bus stations serve as a central hub for the rest of the country. Find the **tourist office** at 1, pl. de la Gare (tel. 820 68; open Mon.-Fri. 8:30am-noon and 1:30-5pm, Sat. 9am-noon and 1-4pm, Sun. 10am-noon and 2-4pm; Sept.-June closed weekends). The **HI youth hostel,** rue Grande-Duchesse Josephine-Charlotte (tel. 822 69), is a 1½km hike from the station. (Reception open 5-6:15pm and 8:15-9:30pm. 300LF, over 26 350LF. Open mid-March to mid-

Oct. and early Dec. to mid-Feb.) **Camp** in Ettelbrück at **Kalkesdelt** (tel. 821 85) 100LF per person, 100LF per site. (Free showers. Open April-Sept.) **Hostels** lurk in the woods at **Beaufort,** 6, rue de l'Auberge (tel. 860 75); **Bourglinster,** 2, rue de Gonderange (tel. 781 46); **La Rochete,** 45, Osterbour (tel. 870 81); **Hollenfels,** 2, rue du Château (tel. 30 70 37); **Lultzhausen,** (tel. 894 24); and **Wilz,** 6, rue de la Montagne (tel. 95 80 39). Most tourist offices have a brochure with all hostels, their addresses, and a brief description of their facilities.

For those interested in exploring the famous vineyards of the **Moselle valley** (home to *Riesling* and *Pinot Gris*), the intimate, family-run **hostel** at **Grevenmacher** makes an excellent base. (300LF, over 26 350LF.) Although few buses or trains serve this secluded area, **river boats** cruise the gentle Moselle river (Grevenmacher-Remich 240LF). Pick up a schedule at the hostel. Kayaking on the river **Sûre** is readily available. **The Outdoor Center,** 34, av. de la Gare, is just off the bus in **Diekirch** (tel. 80 97 92). (One-seaters 650LF. Two-seaters 1000LF. Life jacket 50LF. 50F *Let's Go* discount.) The shop will pick up kayaks at their final destination, but not passengers; stay in Echternach to avoid the bus trip back to Diekirch.

■ Vianden

Victor Hugo found Vianden "consoling and magnificent;" so will you. The village spills down a steep hill beneath a renovated 9th-century **château** containing an exhibit on its own history. Dutch tourists crowd the riverside and Dutch dishes are served in the restaurants, all because Vianden is the ancestral home of the Orange-Nassau dynasty, rulers of Holland and (in the person of William III) England as well. (Château open daily 10am-6pm; Oct. 10am-5pm; Nov.-Dec. 10am-4pm; Jan.-Feb. open only on weekends and holidays; March daily 11am-5pm. 110LF, students 80LF.) The **tourist office** (tel. 842 57) is in the **Victor Hugo House,** on rue de la Gare, beside the bridge over the River Our. (Open April-Oct. Fri.-Wed. 9:30am-noon and 2-6pm; July-Aug. open daily same hours; Nov.-March Wed. and Fri. 2-6pm, Sat. 9:30am-noon.) Ride Vianden's *télésiège* (chairlift) from rue de Sanatorium, 500m upstream from the tourist office (round-trip 150LF, one-way with easy hike down 90LF, students 90LF and 60LF; open daily Easter to mid-Oct. 10am-6pm; July-Aug. 10am-7pm). The ascent affords a phenomenal photo opportunity of the château and, with a small hike, Europe's largest hydroelectric plant, the **Barrage.** Yum. The **HI youth hostel,** 3, Montée du Château (tel. 841 77), sits atop a large hill beneath the castle; cross the bridge from the tourist office and follow the Grande Rue until it curves to the left and ends. In early summer the hostel accepts many groups and often has no space left for individual trekkers; call ahead. (Reception open 5-9pm or later if you call ahead. 300LF, over 26 350LF. Sheets 100LF. Open Feb.-Nov.) Numerous cheap hotels litter the Grande Rue; the tourist office lists rooms in private homes (from 800LF singles, 1000LF doubles), but you can find cheaper rooms yourself. **Camp op dem Deich** (tel. 843 75), a 5min. hike downstream from the tourist office, offers campsites in the shadows of the château on both banks of the river. (120LF/person and /tent. Open Easter-Sept.)

■ Echternach

Echternach is where elderly Europeans vacation with their dogs. The only source of excitement is the month-long **Festival International,** which begins in late May and showcases opera, orchestra, and organ performances. Buy student tickets from the tourist office (200LF); regular tickets run 300-1000LF. Concerts are held in the **Basilica** and the **Eglise Sts-Pierre-et-Paul.** The **tourist office** (tel. 722 30) in the Basilica coolly coordinates it all. From the bus station head left through the pedestrian zone and follow the signs. (Open Mon.-Fri. 9am-noon and 2-6pm; Sept.-June Mon.-Fri. 9am-noon and 1-5pm. Call 72 99 40 for ticket info and reservations.) The **HI youth hostel,** 9, rue Andre Duchscher (tel. 721 58), packs rustic charm only 350m from the bus stop. (Reception open daily 5-11pm; check in by 9pm. No wheelchair access.)

The Netherlands
(Nederland)

US$1 = fl.80 (guilders, or NLG) fl = US$0.56
CDN$1 = fl.37 fl = CDN$0.73
UK£1 = f2.78 fl = UK£0.36
IR£1 = f2.61 fl = IR£0.38
AUS$1 = f0.91 fl = AUS$0.85
NZ$1 = f0.99 fl = NZ$1.01
SAR1 = f0.37 fl = SAR2.67
Country Code: 31 International Dialing Prefix: 09

Limitless horizons, cows grazing at a windmill's base, dike-rimmed fields: this is the Holland of storybooks, and outside the few major cities, it's still the reality in the country more formally known as the Netherlands. In the 1580s, the Dutch East and West India Companies traded as far afield as Java, Africa, and the Caribbean. The 17th century was the Dutch Golden Age, an era of enormous wealth and tolerance; thousands of Europe's Jews and religious and political dissidents fled here to escape persecution, while the country's open intellectual life attracted great minds such as Descartes and Spinoza and produced such painters as Rembrandt and Vermeer.

The forward-thinking Dutch people embraced modernism with a vengeance: the influence of the stark planes of Mondrian's De Stijl school and the architecture of Mies van der Rohe are relentlessly visible. With the notable exception of Rotterdam's cube homes and pencil-shaped towers, however, Dutch cities are still populated by gabled houses peering over quietly flowing canals.

Visitors to the Netherlands come either for high culture or "high" culture, and are usually surprised by how much of the other category confronts them. Holland proper (the country's western half) collects the majority of international tourists due to its fast-paced urban centers and dense rail system; the eastern half remains largely rural and untouristed. This diminutive, industrious country is still home to 17th-century façades, windmills, tulips, and wooden shoes, but the authentic, traditional Dutch lifestyle is overshadowed by the urbanity of Amsterdam and the burgeoning tourist industry. The most glorious spot for springtime tulip-gazing is the region between Oegstgeest, Noordwijkerhout, De Zilk, and Hillegom.

GETTING THERE AND GETTING AROUND

Trains, Buses, and Trams NS, the efficient rail authority, runs up to 4 trains per hour between major cities. Intercity trains generally cruise non-stop, *sneltreins* traverse the quickest route between 2 points, and *stoptreins* pause in most or all of the villages along the way. **Eurail** is valid. A round-trip ticket is valid only on the day of issue. **Day Trip** programs, available at train stations in spring and summer, allow you to pay an all-inclusive, reduced price for a round-trip train ticket, entrance fees for attractions, and often connecting transport and a snack.

Buying the **Holland Rail Pass** (f79 for 3 days of travel in a 10-day period, f109 for 2 people during June-Aug.), or the **Netkaart** tickets (unlimited 2nd-class train travel within the country), will probably prove a rip-off unless you scramble frantically. However, the one-day, (f88 for 2 people, f105 for 3, f150 for 6), can pay off, and under 18s can snare a **Tienertoer,** valid for 4 days out of 10 (f56). If you are planning a lot of tram travel, ask for the "plus" railpass, which, for a 20% surcharge, licenses free use of all non-rail transportation in the Netherlands except ferries.

A nationalized fare system covers city buses, trams, and long-distance buses. The country is divided into zones; you need a certain number of *strippenkaart* (strip tickets) depending on the number of zones through which you travel. The base charge is 2 strips, and travel to smaller towns can exceed 20 strips. Bus and tram drivers sell 2-strip tickets (f3), 3-strip tickets (f4.25), and 8-strip tickets (f10.75). Tickets are *much* cheaper (15-strip ticket f10.75, 45-strip ticket f31) from public transportation counters, post offices, and some tobacco shops and newsstands (look for a *strippenkaart* sign). You can have the bus driver validate two 10-strip tickets as a day-ticket, good for unlimited travel anywhere in the country, or, during the summer, buy a *Zommer Zwerfkaart* from the driver with the same effect (f14.75). Riding without a ticket can result in a f60 fine plus the original cost of the ticket.

Cycling and Hitchhiking Cycling is the way to go in the Netherlands. Distances between cities are short, the countryside is flat, and most streets have separate bike lanes. One-speed bikes abound (f8/day or f40/week, deposit f50-200); utter flatness (except near the coast) renders 3-speeds unnecessary. Eighty train stations rent bicycles (f5/day, f7.50 without a rail ticket, plus f50-100 deposit) upon presentation of your train ticket or railpass. Call the station a day ahead to reserve; phone numbers are in the free booklet *Fiets en Trein.* Purchasing a used bike (about f140) and then reselling it may prove more thrifty than renting one. **Hitchhiking,** where allowed, appears to be generally swift, except out of Amsterdam, where competition is cutthroat.

NETHERLANDS ESSENTIALS

The **VVV** tourist information offices inhabit buildings marked by blue triangular signs. The VVV, as well as museums themselves, sell the one-year **Museumkaart,** good for free admission to over 400 Dutch museums (except special exhibitions) and discounts on various cultural events (f40, under 18 f15, over 64 f25). The **Cultureel Jongeren Paspoort (CJP)** entitles those under 26 to reduced rates at museums and cultural events (f15, valid Sept. to Sept.), at the VVV or the **Amsterdam Uit Buro (AUB),** Leidseplein 26. Bring a passport-size photo for either card.

A profusion of women's centers, coffeehouses, and crisis telephone lines exist, particularly in Amsterdam and the university towns. Check *Man to Man* (f15), available in bookstores or directly from the publisher at Spuistr. 21, Amsterdam, for listings of services for gay men. Travelers with disabilities should obtain the VVV's free and thorough pamphlet, *Holiday in Holland for the Handicapped.*

Drugs are illegal in this country, despite what you may see, hear, and smell. Although police largely ignore the soft drug scene, possession of less than 30g of hashish will make you subject to fines, and possession of more than this amount is a serious offense. Dutch police consider hard drugs a different category altogether and punish offenders accordingly.

Although most Dutch speak English extremely well, do try out their native tongue, which resembles German. "Yes" = *ja;* "no" = *nee;* "please" = *alstublieft;* "thank you" = *dank u;* "hello" = *hallo;* "bathroom" = *toiletten;* "bread" = *broodje;* and "cheese" = *kaas.* Dutch coins have names, just like in the U.S. and Canada: the *stuiver* (5¢), *dubbeltje* (10¢), *kwartje* (25¢), and *rijksdaalder* (f2.50). You can make international calls from pay **phones,** which take US25¢ and f1 coins. For directory assistance, dial 06 80 08 (within the Netherlands) or 06 04 18 (international); for collect calls, dial 06 04 10. To reach AT&T's **USA Direct,** dial 06, wait for a tone then dial 022 91 11. For MCI's **World Reach,** dial 06 022 91 22. For **Canada Direct,** dial 06, wait for the second tone, and dial 022 91 16.

Banks are open weekdays from 10am to 4pm and usually on Thurs. from 6 to 8pm or 7 to 9pm. Post offices, generally open weekdays from 9am to 5pm, exchange money at reasonable rates for a commission. Most shops and supermarkets are open Mon. afternoons, Tues.-Fri. from 9am to 6pm, and Saturday 9am to 5pm. Most museums are open Tues.-Sun. from 9am to 5pm. Shops close for standard European holidays, as well as the Queen's Birthday (April 30), Ascension Day, Whitsunday, and Whitmonday. All of Holland flocks to Amsterdam to celebrate the Queen's birthday, New Year's Day, and Liberation Day (May 5).

Accommodations and Camping The VVV supply accommodations lists, can nearly always find you a room, and will make reservations in other cities (f4 fee). A room in a private home costs about two thirds as much as a hotel, but may not be available everywhere; check with the VVV. During July and August many cities levy a f2.50 "tourist tax," added to the price of all rooms. The country's best values are the 42 **youth hostels** run by the **NJHC (Dutch Youth Hostel Federation),** set into 3 price categories based on quality and charm (f20-23 for bed and breakfast, plus high-season and prime-location supplements). The VVV has a hostel list and the useful *Jeugdherbergen* brochure describes each one (both free). Contact the NJHC at Prof. Tulpplein 4, Amsterdam (tel. (020) 551 31 55; open Mon.-Fri. 9am-5pm). Youth hostel cards are available at hostels (f27.50; bring a passport photo). **Camping** is possible all over the country (the VVV lists campgrounds), but many sites are crowded and trailer-ridden in summer.

Food and Drink Dutch food is hearty and simple: plenty of meat, potatoes, vegetables, bread, cheese, and milk. Pancakes, salted herring, and pea soup are national specialties. Dutch cheeses transcend *gouda* and *edam;* nibble *leiden* and the creamy *kernhem* too. Slices of cold meat and fresh cheese on bread with a soft-boiled egg make for a typical breakfast. For a hearty brunch, order an *uitsmijter,* a dish which piles salad, ham, cheese, and eggs on one plate. At dinner, reap the benefits of Dutch imperialism: *rijsttafel* is an Indonesian specialty comprising up to 25 different dishes, such as curried chicken or lamb with pineapple, served on a mountain of rice. Or try *pannekoeken,* the traditional Dutch supper of buttery, sugary, golden brown pancakes. Wash it all down with a foamy mug of hometown beers Heineken and Amstel, or *jenever,* a strong gin made from juniper berries and traditionally accompanied by eel. In any of the many university towns in Holland, you can eat cheaply and plentifully at student *mensas* when school is in session.

■■■ AMSTERDAM

Anything goes in Amsterdam. On warm evenings, the Leidseplein fills with foreign crowds and the strains of jazz and blues until the early morning. In summer the bars around Rembrandtsplein overflow with orange-clad revelers trying to drink their soccer players on to victory. The pleasures of the city's numerous museums complement outdoor concerts at Vondelpark and boat trips on the canals, many of which date from the imperialist years of the 17th century. The city's colorful Flower Market, seedy red light district, *cannabis*-scented coffeehouses, and love for favorite son Rembrandt reflect a rich imagination and liberal mindset. However, the city that pioneered the dispensing of controlled amounts of methadone and heroin to addicts has now begun to reconsider its long tradition of tolerance in light of steadily worsening crime and drug problems centered in Nieuwmarkt.

ORIENTATION AND PRACTICAL INFORMATION

Amsterdam is a major world transportation center, with budget flights all over the world (especially southeast Asia) and trains all over Europe. Emerging from the train station, you will land on **Damrak,** a key thoroughfare that leads to the **Dam,** its main square. Concentric canals ripple out around the Dam and the **Centraal Station,** so that the city resembles a horseshoe with the train station at the open northern end. Radiating outwards from the station, the canals lined by streets of the same name are **Singel, Herengracht, Keizergracht,** and **Prinsengracht.**

The areas around the train station and up Damrak are the easiest places to lose money, cameras, and credit cards. Don't head immediately left of the train station (into the red light district) until you've locked up your bags either at the train station or where you'll be staying. Pickpockets run rampant between the VVV and the station, and unattended baggage may disappear. Take an extra minute to organize yourself—the hash isn't going anywhere. Women traveling alone should avoid the train station at night. Seek out larger coed dorms; there's often safety in numbers. Amsterdam has some of the best nightlife in Europe, but use your brains as well as your beer-drinking skills. The police are extremely helpful, so report all thefts.

Amsterdam is best conquered by foot or bike. The names of streets change capriciously; buy a *Falk Plan* (f7.50) at the VVV or more cheaply at magazine stands (f4.95). *Use It* (free at the VVV) includes a map, information on inexpensive accommodations, an index of youth agencies, and news about the city. While illegal, marijuana and hashish are tolerated and readily available at cafés and coffeehouses (listed in the *Mellow Pages,* available at bookstores). Ignore the street dealers who will undoubtedly approach you; street hash is usually of poor quality or laced with something else. For information on the legal ins and outs of the Amsterdam drug scene, call 570 23 55. Anyone with drug-related health problems should call 555 55 55.

Tourist Office: VVV, Stationsplein 10 (06 340 340 66; Mon.-Sat. 9am-5pm), in front of Centraal Station, to the left. Try to book your own rooms; they can be reticent about budget alternatives (hefty f4.50 fee). Sells maps (f3.50) and tickets, changes money (poor rates), and plans excursions. Get *What's On,* a fabulous listing of all events in Amsterdam (f3.50). Go early to skirt long lines. Open daily 9am-11pm; Easter-June and Sept. Mon.-Sat. 8am-8:30pm; Sept.-May daily 9am-5pm. **Branch office,** Leidestr. 106, at Korte Leidsedwarsstr open daily 9am-9pm.

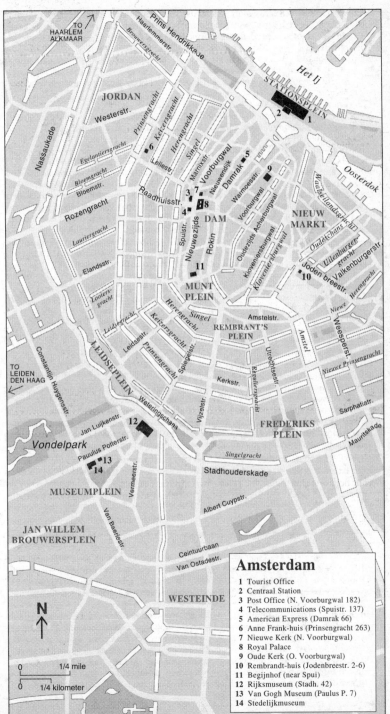

Amsterdam

1 Tourist Office
2 Centraal Station
3 Post Office (N. Voorburgwal 182)
4 Telecommunications (Spuistr. 137)
5 American Express (Damrak 66)
6 Anne Frank-huis (Prinsengracht 263)
7 Nieuwe Kerk (N. Voorburgwal)
8 Royal Palace
9 Oude Kerk (O. Voorburgwal)
10 Rembrandt-huis (Jodenbreestr. 2-6)
11 Begijnhof (near Spui)
12 Rijksmuseum (Stadh. 42)
13 Van Gogh Museum (Paulus P. 7)
14 Stedelijkmuseum

Budget Travel: NBBS, Rokin 38 (tel. 620 50 17). Budget student flights. Open Mon.-Fri. 9:30am-5:30pm, Sat. 10am-4pm; mid-Aug. to mid-May closes Sat. at 3pm. Credit cards not accepted. **Budget Bus,** Rokin 10 (tel. 627 51 51). Good deals on Euroline buses. Open Mon.-Fri. 9:30am-5:30pm, Sat. 10am-4pm.

Consulates: U.S., Museumplein 19 (tel. 664 56 61). Open Mon.-Fri. 8:30am-noon and 1:30-3:30pm. **U.K.,** Koningslaan 44 (tel. 676 43 43). Open Mon.-Fri. 9am-noon and 2-3:30pm. **Australian, Canadian,** and **New Zealand** embassies are in The Hague.

Currency Exchange: Your best bet is the American Express office (see below). For after-hours banking try **Change Express,** Damrak 86 (tel. 624 66 82), for fine rates with a 3% commission. Open daily 8am-midnight. **Branch offices** at Kalverstr. 150, Kalverstr. 150 (both open daily 8am-8pm), and Leidestr. 106 (open daily 8am-midnight). The **GWK** office at Centraal Station has worse rates but is open 24 hrs. Avoid the **Chequepoint** booths' outrageous commissions (up to 10%).

American Express: Damrak 66 (tel. 520 77 77). Excellent rates, no commission on any brand of traveler's checks. Open Mon.-Fri. 9am-5pm, Sat. 9am-noon. Cash machine for cardholders. **Branch Office,** Van Baerlestraat 28, is near the museums and much less crowded. Open Mon.-Fri. 9am-5pm, Sat. 10am-4pm.

Post Office: Singel 250 (tel. 555 89 11), at Raadhuisstr. behind the Dam, holds Poste Restante. Open Mon.-Fri. 9am-9pm, Sat. 9am-noon.

Telephones: Call first and pay afterward at **Telehouse,** Raadhuisstr. 48-50, near the Dam (open 24 hrs.), or **TeleTalk Center,** Leidsestr. 101, near the Leideseplein (open daily 10am-midnight). Both handle faxes. **City Code:** 020.

Flights: Schiphol Airport (tel. 06 350 33 08 for charters; 601 09 66 for other flights). Trains connect to Centraal Station (every 15min., 16min., f2.50).

Trains: Centraal Station, Stationsplein 1, at the end of the Damrak and opposite the tourist office. Lockers f3.50, large f5.50. For international information and reservations, get a number at the booth, then wait inside the office until you're called. In summer, expect waits as long as 1hr. Open for international information Mon.-Fri. 8am-10pm, Sat.-Sun. 9am-8pm; reservations Mon.-Fri. 8am-8pm, Sat.-Sun. 9am-5pm. For info, call 601 05 41 (international) or (06) 92 92 (domestic).

Buses: Trains are usually quicker and more convenient. The **GVB** (see Public Transportation) will tell you if your destination lies on a rail line. If it doesn't, they'll direct you to a bus departure point. **Muiderpoort** (2 blocks east of Oosterpark) serves destinations to the east; **Marnixstation** (at the corner of Marnixstr. and Kinkerstr.), the west; and **Stationsplein depot** the north and south.

Public Transportation: Trams, buses, *nachtbussen* (night buses), and 2 subway lines. Most tram and bus lines radiate from Centraal Station and retire at midnight; get a separate schedule for the *nachtbussen*. Don't buy your *strippenkaart* and *dagkaart* (Amsterdam day-passes, f11.50) on the bus. The **GVB,** Amsterdam's public transportation company, has an office on Stationsplein (tel. (06) 92 92 for transport info) which sells tickets and distributes the handy flyer *Public Transport*. Best deal for light travel over several days is the 15-strip card (f10.75). Open daily 8am-10:30pm, Sat.-Sun. 8am-10:30pm.

Taxis: tel. 677 77 77. Fares start at f4.80 plus f2.62/km or min.; more at night.

Bike Rental: All **train stations** rent plain ol' bikes (f7.50/day, f30-40/week). **Koender's,** Stationsplein 33 (tel. 624 83 91); f7.50/day, f30/week. Open daily 8am-10pm. **Rent-a-Bike,** Pieter Jacobstr. 11, just off Damstr. (tel. 625 50 29), near the Dam; f12.50/day, f50/week; sells used bikes for f140-200. **Yellow Bike Tours,** N.Z. Voorburgwal 66 (tel. 620 69 40), offers 3hr. city tours at 9:30am and 1pm (f29) and 6½-hr. countryside tours at 9am and noon (f42.50) daily April-Oct. (reservations necessary). **ENA's Bike Tours** leave from Amstel station (tel. 69 23 584) for 7-hr. trips June-Oct. at 10am (f40).

Hitchhiking: Those hitching to Utrecht, central and southern Germany, and Belgium take tram #25 to the end and start at the bridge. Those heading to Groningen and northern Germany take bus #56 to Prins Bernhardplein or the metro to Amstel and start along Gooiseweg. Those going to the airport, Leiden, and The Hague take tram #16 or 24 to Stadionplein and start on the other side of the canal on Amstelveenseweg. Those going to Haarlem, Alkmaar, and Noord Holland take bus #22 to Haarlemmerweg and start from Westerpark. The **International Lift**

Center, Nieuwezijds Voorburgwal 256, 1st floor (tel. 622 43 42), matches riders and drivers for destinations all over Europe. Riders pay a f5-25 fee, plus US6¢/km for gas. Open Mon.-Fri. 10am-6pm, Sat. 10am-4pm, Sun. noon-3pm; Oct.-Easter Mon.-Fri. 10am-5pm, Sat. noon-4pm.

Bookstores: Paperbacks at the **American Discount Book Center,** 187 Kalverstr. Open Mon.-Wed. and Fri.-Sat. 10am-8pm, Thurs. 10am-10pm, Sun. 11am-6pm.

Laundry: Look for a *Wasserette* sign, or Oude Doelenstr. 12. Open Mon.-Fri. 8:30am-7pm, Sat. 10am-4pm; last load 1hr. before closing.

Women's Centers: De Kat, Wagenaarstr. 165 (tel. 694 72 14), near the Tropen-museum. Open Tues., Thurs.-Fri. and Sun. 9pm-midnight. **Rechtshulp voor Vrouwen** (legal aid for women) at Willemstr. 246 (tel. 624 03 23). The **Opvang Sexueel Geweld** counsels women threatened by violence (tel. 612 75 76; daily 10:30am-11:30pm).

Gay and Lesbian Services: COC, Rozenstr. 14 (tel. 623 40 79). The main source of info. Open Wed.-Thurs. 1-5pm, Fri. 9pm-4am, Sat.1-5pm. Coffeehouse on Wed. 8pm-midnight. The *Man to Man* guide (f15) has a "gay map" listing bars, shops, saunas, and more. The *Best Gay Guide* lists the top clubs and activities in the Benelux countries (f15). Help for victims of violence or discrimination available Wed. and Sun. 8pm-midnight (tel. 624 27 49). **Intermale,** Spuistr. 251 (tel. 625 00 09), is a gay bookstore. Open Mon. noon-6pm, Tues.-Sat. 10am-6pm. **Gay and Lesbian Switchboard** (tel. 623 65 65) is answered daily 10am-10pm.

Crises: Drug counseling, Binnenkant 46 (tel. 624 47 75), 10min. from Centraal Station, near the Oosterdok. Open Mon.-Fri. 10am-5pm.

Medical Assistance: Tourist Medical Service (tel. 612 37 66), 24hr. For hospital care, call **Academisch Medisch Centrum,** Meibergdreef 9 (tel. 566 33 33), near the Holendrecht metro stop. For free emergency medical care, visit the **Kruis-post,** Oudezijds Voorburgwal 129 (tel. 624 90 21). Open daily 10am-12:30pm and 6:45pm-11pm. **Sexually Transmitted Disease Clinic** at Groenburgwal 44 (tel. 555 58 22; open Mon.-Fri. 8-10:30am). Free and confidential. **AIDS Hotline,** (tel. 060 22 22 20; open Mon.-Fri. 2pm-10pm).

Pharmacies: Everywhere. Open Mon.-Fri. 8:30am-5pm. When closed, each *apotheek* (pharmacy) posts a sign directing you to the nearest open one.

Emergencies: tel. 06 11. **Police headquarters:** Elandsgracht 117 (tel. 559 91 11).

ACCOMMODATIONS AND CAMPING

Amsterdam is packed from late June to mid-September, but you can almost always find a bed at the Sleep-In if the bazillions of hostels and student hotels are full. For most, the best shot is to show up early in the morning or to book a room from another HI hostel and pay for it in advance. Both the HI and Christian hostels have huge, clean rooms, and curfews; the Christian hostels' single-sex dorms are safer, less wild, and easily the best bargain in town. Private hostels generally charge more for later (or nonexistent) curfews, and more laid-back (read: ganja-scented) atmo-spheres. Almost all places lower their rates about f2.50 in the off-season; *Let's Go* lists summer prices. If you arrive at night, just stay in a neighboring city.

In both institutional and private hostels, keep tabs on your valuables at all times. Use the lockers wherever provided; some will require your own padlock, available at **HEMA** (a department store behind the Damrak American Express) for f7-25. At the station and tourist office you'll be accosted by people offering all kinds of lodg-ings; many are from reputable hostels, but be cautious; the legitimate ones usually carry printed cards bearing their hostel's address and prices. Always ask to see the card before you follow, carry your own luggage, and never pay before you look.

Institutional Hostels

Christian Youth Hostel Eben Haëzer, Bloemstr. 179 (tel. 624 47 17), 1 street from Rozengracht. Take tram #13 or 17 to Marnixstr. A pristine bargain with a clean-cut and cheery staff. No large groups accepted in summer (hurray!). The maps cost f1, but the Gospels are free. Rooms close 10am-2pm, but the lobby and snack bar stay open. Curfew midnight, Fri.-Sat. 1am. Ages 16-35 f15. Showers and breakfast included. Dinner f8.50. Lockers f10 deposit. Reservations encouraged.

Jeugdherberg Stadsdoelen (HI), Kloveniersburgwal 97 (tel. 624 68 32), between Nieuwmarkt and Rembrandtsplein. Take tram #4, 9, 16, 24, or 25 to Muntplein. The more desirable of the HI hostels; spacious, clean, and central. Rebuffs tour groups. Bar with pool table and daily happy hour (8-9pm; beers f1.50). Reception open 7am-1am. Curfew 2am. f21.50, nonmembers f26.50 (July-Aug. f2.50 surcharge). Breakfast included. Sheets f6. Free lockers with passport or f25 deposit. Open mid-March to Jan. Reservations accepted but you must arrive by 4pm.

Jeugdherberg Vondelpark (HI), Zandpad 5 (tel. 683 17 44), on a sleepy street bordering Vondelpark. Take tram #1, 2, or 5 to Leidseplein, then cross the Stadhouderskade and walk 2 streets to the left. Facilities include kitchen and small library. Avoid the park when dark. Bar open 7pm-12:30am, happy hour 8-9pm. Reception open 7am-12:30am. Lockout 10:45am-3:30pm. Curfew 2am. f23, nonmembers f28. Breakfast included. Sheets f6. Lockers 25¢/day; deposit f10.

Christian Youth Hostel "The Shelter," Barndesteeg 21-25 (tel. 625 32 30), off the Nieuwmarkt, amid the red lights. Larger and looser than Eben Haëzer, with snack bar (open 8am-2pm and 2:30-11:30pm) and cozy courtyard. Huge dorms with happy religious slogans. Strictly enforced midnight curfew. Ages 16-35 f15. Showers, sheets, and breakfast included. Lockers f1; deposit f10.

Private Hostels

't Ancker, De Ruijterkade 100 (tel. 622 95 60). From the back exit of Centraal Station, walk to your right 80m. Super-fun Irish woman and her Dutch husband keep these rooms in ship-shape condition. Reception and bar open 24 hrs. Dorms f35. Doubles f80. Sheets, lockers (deposit f10), and all-you-can-eat breakfast included. Free maps. Restaurant open 1pm-10pm (meals f4-20); bar food available all night.

Hotel Kabul, Warmoesstr. 38-42 (tel. 623 71 58), 5min. from Centraal Station, in the Red Light District. Huge, clean, and right in the thick of things. Two swinging bars (meals f12.50); live bands Fri. and Sat. (10pm-1 or 2am). 24-hr. reception. No curfew. Dorms f23-32. Singles f67. Doubles f79-94. Triples f116. Breakfast f6.50 or f12.50. Key deposit f15. Safe for valuables (f1) and free lockers in the rooms.

International Budget Hotel, Leidsegracht 76 (tel. 624 27 84). Take tram #1, 2, or 5 to Prinsengracht and walk 1 block to the right facing Leidseplein. Beautiful canal location. Reception open 9am-11pm. No curfew. f30/person in 4-person dorm. Singles f55. Doubles f100. Showers and TV included. Huge breakfast f5.

Euphemia Budget Hotel, Fokke Simonszstr. 1-9 (tel. 622 90 45), 10min. from Leidseplein. Take tram #16, 24, or 25 to Prinsengracht (Weteringcircuit), cross back over Lijnbaansgracht, and turn right. Safe and comfortable, near the museums. Dorms f35. Doubles f95. Triples f135. Sheets included. Breakfast 9am-noon (f6.50). Reception open 8am-11pm. Bikes stored safely in the garden.

Bob's Youth Hostel, Nieuwezijds Voorburgwal 92 (tel. 623 00 63), near the Dam and Centraal Station. Take tram #1, 2, 5, 13, or 17. No smoking in rooms; you'll inhale enough going up the stairs. Curfew 3am. Dorms f20. Mattress on floor f18. Breakfast included. Dinner f5 (July-Aug. only). Free lockers (f10 deposit).

Frisco Inn, Beurstr. 5 (tel. 620 16 10), brushing the Red Light District, close to the station. Cramped rooms and noisy bar but central location. Dorms f30-35. Doubles f70-75. Triples f105. Quads f140. Some rooms have private showers. Breakfast f12.50. Reception and bar open Mon.-Fri. 9am-1am, Sat.-Sun. 9am-2am.

Sleep-In, 's-Gravesandestr. 51-53 (tel. 694 74 44). Major renovations have turned this place into a palace, complete with marble columns and art deco staircases, a recording studio, concert hall, and art gallery. Take trams #3, 6, 9, 10, or 14 to Mauritskade and walk back down Sarphatistr., or hop night bus #77. Over 500 beds. Hip bands play Wed.-Sun. (f2.50 off cover if you're staying here); dances on Fri. Reception closed noon-1:30pm. f17.50/person (60-bed dorms), f22.50/person (8-20 bed dorms), f40/person (doubles and triples). Breakfast f7. Lunch f9.50. Dinner f14. Sheets f5; f20 deposit. Information office open 9am-1pm and 4-9pm. Bike rental (f10/day) open 10am-noon and 7-8pm. Free lockers.

Hotels

Hotel van Onna, Bloemgracht 102 (tel. 626 58 01), in the Jordaan. Take tram #13 or 17 from Centraal Station. Well-kept. Singles, doubles, triples, and quads f55/person. Big breakfast in a canal-view dining room included. Reception open 8am-midnight. Reservations recommended.

Hotel Museumzicht, Jan Luykenstr. 22 (tel. 671 29 54). In a quiet neighborhood near the museums and chock-full of similar budget hotels. Doubles f100, with shower f115. Triples f120-145. Breakfast included. Reserve in advance.

Hotel Bema, Concertgebouwplein 19 (tel. 679 13 96, fax (020) 662 36 88), across from the Concertgebouw. Take tram #16 to Museumplein stop. Spacious, spotless rooms near the museums. Bouncy American owner. Singles f55-65. Doubles f75-105. Triples f125-135. Quads f165. Breakfast in bed included. Reserve in advance. Also handles tours of the red-light district.

Hotel Groenendael, Nieuwendijk 15 (tel. 624 48 22), near the station. Friendly, comfortable, and surrounded by the best Amsterdam vices. Singles f60. Doubles f85. Triples f120. Breakfast included. Reserve ahead—year-round.

City Hotel, Utrechtsestr. 2 (tel. 627 23 23). Great location near Rembrandtsplein will move you away from tourist invasion. Singles f65. Doubles f95. Triples, quads, and quints f45/person. No breakfast, but free coffee. Coin-operated TVs in every room. Reception open 8am-10pm.

Hotel Ronnie, Raadhuisstr. 41b (tel. 624 28 21). Singles f55. Doubles f110. Triples f165. Breakfast f7. 24-hr. reception. Book in advance.

Hotel the Crown, Oude Zijds Voorburgwal 21 (tel. 626 96 64). Hard core drinkers and smokers corral in this red-light district establishment. Bar open 8am-6am (beer f6 pint). Dorms f25-30. Singles f60. Doubles f90-100. Quads with shower f140. Free lockers (f10 deposit). Reception open 24 hr. Breakfast f4-10.

Pensions and Private Accommodations

If you're tired of absorbing smoke from the coffeeshop downstairs, pensions and private homes are a cheap escape usually worth the effort involved in getting there.

Gerda Rikker-Kouwenhoren, Iepenlaan 16 (tel. 02993 639 33). In Volendam, about 20min. from Amsterdam by bus. Hearty Dutch breakfast, clean rooms, knowledgable and friendly owner. f27.50/person. Central to Edam, Hoorn, and Zaanse Schans for windmill-lovers.

Pension Kil, Volendammerpad 19 (tel. 02993 718 27). Take the NZH bus to Edam (7 strips). Complete with small aviary of birds who softly serenade you to sleep. f40/person, Oct.-June f35-40/person. Breakfast and showers included. Reception open 9am-midnight. No reservations.

Camping

Camping Zeeburg, Zuider-Ijdijk 44 (tel. 694 44 30), next to the Amsterdam Rijncanal. Direct ferry to Centraal Station, or take buses #22 or 37, or night bus #170. Youth-oriented, with periodic live music. f5/person, f2.25/tent. Showers f1.50. Reception open 8am-11pm, April-June and Sept.-Aug. 9am-1pm and 5pm-9pm.

Gaasper Camping, Loosdrechtdreef 7 (tel. 696 73 26), in the idyllic Gaasper Park, 20min. from Centraal Station by metro ("Gaasperplas") to the end, or night bus #75. Vast and fully rigged. f5/person, f4.25/tent. Showers f1.25. Washers and dryers f11. Reception open 9am-12:30pm and 1:30-9pm. Open mid-March to Dec.

FOOD

Dutch cuisine is about as subtle as a wounded moose, but Amsterdam's restaurant scene has been colonized by various international cuisines. Taste Surinamian, Indonesian, Chinese, and Indian food in the red-light district around the Nieuwmarkt and off the Dam, on streets such as Hartenstr. Indonesian *rijsttafel* here is ambrosia. *Automatiek* (self-service fast food stands) are reasonably priced; *frikandel* (fried sausage) usually costs as little as f1.50. *Eetcafés* strewn through Amsterdam purvey good meat-and-potatoes fare for about f12-20, especially in the Jordaan. Bakeries vending inexpensive cheese croissants and magnificent breads cluster along Utrechtsestr. south of Prinsengracht.

Fruit, cheese, flowers, and sometimes even live chickens take over the **markets** on Albert Cuypstraat, near the Heineken brewery (open Mon.-Sat. 9:30am-5pm); the VVV publishes a list of markets in its Amsterdam brochure (f6.50). Shop for grocery essentials at the **Mignon Supermarket** at Leidsestr. 74-6 near Prinsengracht (open Mon. 11am-5pm, Tues.-Wed. and Sat. 9am-6pm, Thurs. 9am-9pm, and Fri. 9am-6:30pm); the **Big Banana Nightshop** across the street is more expensive, but open daily until 1am. Health food nuts will shop 'til they drop at **Met de Natuuraan Tafel,** Weteringschans 135. (Open Mon. 11am-5pm, Tues.-Wed. and Fri. 9am-6pm, Thurs. 9am-9pm, and Sat. 9am-5pm.) Some restaurants close during school vacations.

Atrium, Oude Zijds Achterburgwal 237, at Binnengasthuisstr. A huge, spotless university trough on the fringe of the red-light district. Dinner f7.75. Meals served noon-2pm and 5-7pm; snack bar open 9am-7pm. Open Aug.-June.

Bojo, Lange Leidsedwarstr. 51, near the Leidseplein. Crowded at dinner-time with those seeking the terrific *rijsttafel* (f13.50-15.50) and other Indonesian fare (f10-16.50). Open Sun.-Thurs. 5pm-2am, Fri.-Sat. 5pm-5:30am.

Vegetarish Eethuis "Sisters," Nes 102, 300m from Dam Sq. Two women and one cat run this cavernous, bohemian eatery. Daily vegetarian special (f12.50) usually disappears by 7pm. Open Mon.-Fri. noon-4pm and 5-9:30pm, Sat.-Sun. 2-9:30pm. Dinner f16-17. Dinner salads f8.50-11.

Egg Cream, Sint Jacobstr. 19, an alley off N.Z. Voorburgwal. Custom-built sandwiches f3-6.50; complete vegetarian dinner with salad f17. The apple crumble (f3.50) is the sweetest of Amsterdam's many sins. Open daily 11am-8pm.

The Pancake Bakery, Prinsengracht 191 (tel. 625 13 33), a canal-side block down from the Anne Frank Huis. Crowded with locals and out-of-towners. More than 50 varieties of the classic Dutch supper f6.50-18; omelettes f10-14. *Kersen* (cherry) or *mokkakaramel* pancakes make a killer dessert. Open daily noon-9:30pm.

Vishandel de Kreeft, Vijzelstr. 3, near Muntplein. A stand-up seafood counter that'll satisfy your salty, wet desires cheaply. Open Tues.-Sat. 10am-5:30pm.

Bolhoed, 60-62 Prinsengracht, across the canal from the Anne Frank house, specializes in organic vegetarian food (f10-20). Open daily noon-10pm.

SIGHTS

Amsterdam's former town hall, **Koninklijk Paleis,** on the Dam, symbolizes the city's 17th-century commercial activity. (Open June-Aug. daily 12:30-4pm. f5.) The **Rijksmuseum,** on Museumplein at Stadhouderskade 42, has a magnificent Dutch collection including Rembrandt's famous militia portrait *The Nightwatch.* Introductory slide shows every 25 minutes make this bevy o' art manageable. The south wing is closed for renovations until 1995. (Open Tues.-Sat. 10am-5pm, Sun. 1-5pm. f10, under 18, over 64, and CJP holders f5.) **Rembrandthuis,** Jodenbreestr. 4-6 (at the corner of the Oude Schans Canal), is where the master lived, worked, and taught until the house was confiscated by the city for taxes. It holds 250 of Rembrandt's etchings and drypoints, as well as many of his tools and plates. (Open Mon.-Sat. 10am-5pm, Sun. 1-5pm. f5, under 17 f3.50.) The renowned **Van Gogh Museum,** at Paulus Potterstr. 7, traces the artist's frenzied life through 200 of his paintings. (Open Mon.-Sat. 10am-5pm, Sun. 1-5pm. f10, under 18, over 64 and CJP holders f5; free with Museumkaart.) For an informative and moving museum experience, visit the **Tropenmuseum** (Museum of the Tropics), Linnaeusstr. 2 near the Oosterpark, a center devoted to the people and problems of developing countries. (Open Mon.-Fri. 10am-5pm, Sat.-Sun. noon-5pm. f7.50, under 18, over 65, and CJP holders f4.)

A visit to the **Anne Frank Huis,** Prinsengracht 263, is profoundly stirring. In the attic of the annex to the house, the young Jewish girl and her family hid from the Nazis until their capture in 1944. The house now headquarters the city's anti-fascist and anti-racist movements. (Open Mon.-Sat. 9am-6:45pm, Sun. 10am-6:45pm. ½-hr. lines. f7, under 17 f3.50, CJP holders f3.50.) Of related interest is the **Verzetsmu-**

seum **Amsterdam,** Lekstr. 63, which relates the poignant story of the Nazi resistance in the Netherlands. Take trams #4 and 25. (Open Tues.-Fri. 10am-5pm, Sat.-Sun. and holidays 1-5pm. f3.50, free with Museumkaart.) More obscure is the **Joods-Portugese Synagogue** at Jonas Daniël Meijerplein, near Waterlooplein. A handsome 17th-century building, the synagogue was founded by Portuguese Jews expelled from their country. (Open Sun.-Fri. 10am-4pm. Free.) Next door at Jonas Daniël Meijerplein 2-4 is the **Joods Historisch Museum,** with exhibits on Jewish history and culture. (Open daily 11am-12:30pm and 1pm-4pm. f7, with ISIC f3.50.) The **Museum Amstelkring "Ons' Lieve Heer op Solder"** ("Our Lord in the Attic"), O.Z. Voorburgwal 40, in the red-light district, dates from the days of the Reformation, when it was forbidden for Catholics to practice their faith in public. The former Catholic priest's *grachtenhuis* (house on a canal) houses a hidden church in its attic. (Open Mon.-Sat. 10am-5pm, Sun. 1-5pm. f4.50, students and over 65 f3.)

The retired **Heineken Brewery** at Stadhouderskade 78 is now a museum, giving 90-minute tours which culminate in 3 or 4 free rounds (daily at 9, 9:45, and 10:30am, 1, 1:45 and 2:30pm). Tickets go fast (on sale from 9am). The f2 admission fee goes to UNICEF. Of course, a journey to this modern-day Sodom and Gomorrah wouldn't be complete without the **Amsterdam Sex Museum,** on Damrak directly across from the tour boat docks—where else in the world can you have your photo taken on the "lap" of a prodigious 7-ft. penis? (Open daily 10am-11:30pm. f3.95.) Tickle a slightly different fancy at the **Medieval Torture Museum** near Leidseplein. (Open daily 11am-7pm. Adult f7.50, children(?!) f4.)

For a pleasing night of tourist-free strolling or café-hopping, visit the **Jordaan,** bounded roughly by Prinsengracht, Brouwersgracht, Marnixstr., and Lauriersgracht. Built as an artisan district in the Golden Age, it is the most intimate part of the city and still bears the street names of its agricultural origin. Take refuge from Amsterdam's mobbed sights and seamy streets in **Begijnhof,** a beautifully maintained, grassy courtyard surrounded by 18th-century buildings; walk down Kalverstr. and turn onto Begijnensteeg, a small side street between Kalverstr. 130 and 132.

The **red-light district,** bounded by Warmoestr., Gelderskade, and Oude Doelenstr., is the vice sink of Europe; it'll either repulse you or fulfill your wettest dreams. Pushers, porn shops, and live sex theaters do a brisk business. Red neon marks houses of legal, if ill, repute. Unlike the illegal streetwalkers, these prostitutes have regular gynecological exams—but forget not that HIV/AIDS takes 6 months to detect. Cops patrol the district until midnight, and there's a police station on Warmoestr. Women may feel uncomfortable walking through this area. Walk quickly and avoid eye contact with the numerous sleazy characters.

ENTERTAINMENT

Cafés and Bars

Amsterdam's finest cafés are the old, dark, wood-paneled *bruine kroegen* (brown cafés) of the Jordaan, where denizens gather under the nicotine-stained ceilings and dim brass lamps to trade tales and crack jokes. Bars at Leidseplein are predominantly tourist traps, but the jazz is good. Rembrandtsplein has become *the* place to watch soccer and sing with drunk revelers; just pretend you know the words. Most cafés open at 10 or 11am and close at 1am on Fridays and 2am Saturdays.

Café Twee Prinsen, Prisenstr. 27, on the edge of the Jordaan. Crowded at night with upscale Dutch partygoers. Beer from f2.75. Open Sun.-Thurs. 11am-1am, Fri.-Sat. 11am-2am.

Café de Tuin, Tweede Tuindwarsstr. 13 (open Sun.-Thurs. 10am-1am, Fri.-Sat. 10am-2am), and **de Reiger,** Nieuwe Leliestr. 34 (Sun.-Mon. 6pm-1am, Fri.-Sat. 11am-2am; beer from f2.75), both in the Jordaan, attract a young, artsy set.

Saarien, Elandstr. 119, is a hip bar in the Jordaan. Bi, lesbian and straight women only. Open Mon. 8pm-1am, Tues.-Thurs. and Sun. 3pm-1am, Fri.-Sat. 3pm-2am.

Grand Café Dulac, Haarlemserstr. 118, near the station. A decorative fantasy from "1001 Nights." Erotic statues jump out of every metallic corner. Open daily 4pm-1am or 2am.

Coffeehouses

Let's be honest. A lot of people come to Amsterdam to smoke, and most coffee-houses still specialize in Thai stick and Jamaican sensemilla. While police have out-lawed the hemp-leaf stickers that once adorned the windows, any green, leafy foliage in the window or the green, yellow, and red that symbolize Rastafarianism are signs that marijuana, hashish, and sometimes spacecakes may be available within. The **Coffeeshop 36,** Warmoesstr. 36, next to the Hotel Kabul in the red-light district, is an Amsterdam institution. All types hang out here amid the blaring music. (Open Sun.-Thurs. 10am-1am, Fri.-Sat. 10am-2am.) **The Grasshopper,** Nieuwzijds Voorburgwal 57, gently simmers across the street from Bob's Youth Hostel and is much frequented by its guests. (Open Sun.-Thurs. 9am-midnight, Fri.-Sat. 9am-1am.) Bumblebees vanish against the yellow-and-black decor of the **Mellow Yellow,** Vijzel-str. 33. A short walk up Vijzelstr. (away from the center) takes you to a calm canal-side park to chill. (Open Sun.-Thurs. 8:30am-1am, Fri.-Sat. 8:30am-2am.) The farther you travel from the popular and over-touristed spots, the better, the mellower, and less expensive it becomes.

Live Music

Though Amsterdam may lack a thriving, world-class music scene, it does offer you a great deal of variety and occasionally headlines some mainstream pop and jazz groups. The **Jazzlijn** gives information (tel. 626 77 64) about concerts in the Amster-dam area. Many clubs avoid a cover charge by inflating beer prices.

Melkweg, Lijnbaasgracht 234a (tel. 624 17 77), in an old factory off Leidseplein, across from the police station. Amsterdam's legendary nightspot retains a cutting-edge aura despite the crowds. Live bands, theater, films, an art gallery, and a snack bar fashion the joint's multi-media attack on the senses. Open Wed.-Thurs. and Sun. 7pm-2am, Fri.-Sat. 7pm-4am. Cover charge f7-15 plus membership fee (f4, good for 1 month), f13-21 plus membership on the weekends. Box office open Mon.-Fri. noon-5pm, Sat.-Sun. 4-7pm and while the club is open.

Paradiso, Weteringschans 6-8 (tel. 626 45 21). Some of the foremost international punk, new-wave, and reggae bands play here. f10-27, depending on the band. Shows start at 10pm; check outside or call to learn the evening's guests.

De Kroeg, Lijnbaansgracht 163 (tel. 420 02327). Vibrant crowds writhe to live reg-gae, salsa, rock, and blues. Open Sun.-Thurs. 8pm-2am, Fri.-Sat. 8pm-3am. DJ on Fri. Periodic jam sessions (usually Mon. and Wed.). Music starts at 10pm. f5 cover on nights with live music, f2.50 on DJ night, jam sessions free.

The Bimhuis, Oude Schans 73-77 (tel. 623 13 61). The hub of Dutch jazz. More than 200 concerts held yearly. Sun.-Tues. jazz workshops. Wed.-Sat. concerts after 9pm. f10, students f7.50.

Odeon Jazz Kelder, Singel 456, near Leidsestr. Men in sharp suits and women in heels women come here to bebop. Open Sun.-Thurs. 10pm-4am, Fri.-Sat. 10pm-3am. Cover f7.50, weekends f12.50.

Dancing

Many nightclubs in Amsterdam charge a membership fee in addition to the normal cover, so the tab can be hefty. There are expensive discos aplenty on Prinsengracht, near Leidsestr., and on Lange Leidsedwarsstr. Gay discos line Amstelstr.

Roxy, Singel 465. The hippest crowd in town busts a move to acid house. Obvious tourist attire rebuffed. Open Wed.-Thurs. around 9am-4am, Fri.-Sun. 9am-5am. Cover Wed. and Sun. f7.50, Thurs. f10, Fri.-Sat. f12.50.

Mazzo, Rozengracht 114 (tel. 26 75 00), in the Jordaan. Artsy house music disco that changes its display and slideshow every 3 weeks. Open Sun.-Thurs. 11pm-4am, Fri.-Sat. 11pm-5am. Live music Tues. Cover f7.50, weekends f10.

Dansen bij Jansen, Handboogstr. 11, near Spui. Location near the university makes it popular among students (officially, a student ID is required). Happy hour Sun.-Wed. 11pm-midnight. Open Sun.-Thurs. 11pm-4am, Fri.-Sat. 11pm-5am. Cover f4, weekends f5.

iT, Amstelstr. 24, near Waterlooplein. Clients tout this as one of the best and most decadent gay discos in Europe. Open Thurs. and Sun. 11pm-4am, Fri.-Sat. 11pm-5am. Free to members, otherwise f15. Gay only on Sat.

Theater, Dance, and Music

VVV puts out *What's On* (f3.50), with comprehensive cultural listings. In summer, there are free performances Wednesday through Sunday at the **Vondelpark Openluchttheater** (tel. 673 14 99); jazz and folk concerts dominate, but children's theater, political music, and mime also grab the limelight. Check posters at park entrances. The June **Holland Festival** of dance, drama, and music is closely followed by the **Summer Festival** of small theater companies in July. (Contact the Balie Theatre on Leidseplein, tel. 623 36 73. Tickets f10-15.) The sparkling new **Muziektheater,** perched on the junction of the Amstel and the Oude Schans (tel. 625 54 55), hosts the **Netherlands Opera** and the **National Ballet.** The **Royal Concertgebouw Orchestra,** one of the world's finest, is conducted by Ricardo Chailly at the Concertgebouw on Van Baerlestr. (Concerts start at 8:15pm. Tickets f25.) There is English-speaking theater year-round in **De Stalhouderij,** eerste Bloemdwarsstr. 4 (tel. 626 22 82). Frequent English-language performances and cabarets are given at the theater/café **Suikerhof,** Prinsengracht 381 (tel. 22 75 71; open daily from 5pm, Sun. from 2pm). **Boom Chicago,** at Iboya, 20 Korte Liedsedwarsstr., an American comedy ensemble, cracks jokes and improvs with the audience (Wed.-Sun. 8-10pm). Make reservations for any cultural event, in person only, at the **Amsterdams Uit Buro** (AUB) Ticketshop (tel. 621 12 11). The VVV Tourist Office theater desk, Stationsplein 10 (open Mon.-Sat. 10am-4pm) and the larger tourist bureaus in Holland (VVV I) also operate ticket-reservation services.

Organ concerts resound Wednesday evenings at 8:15pm during the summer at **Westerkerk,** where Rembrandt is buried, at Prinsengracht 281 (tel. 624 77 66), and **Nieuwe Kerk,** where Dutch monarchs are sworn in (they're not crowned), on the Dam (tel. 626 81 68). Prices are f5-12.50. The free monthly publication *UITKRANT* list all concerts, films, theater, and club events.

■ Near Amsterdam

When you tire of free and easy Amsterdam, explore the surrounding countryside. Trains are expensive, so buy a cheap day return or get a one-day bus pass (f18.10). **Alkmaar,** 45 minutes away by train (4/hr.), holds a large open-air **cheese market** every Friday from 10am to noon (mid-April to mid-Sept.). When the market is over, there is still plenty to buy along the narrow canal-lined streets. Die-hard windmill fans should flock to **Zaanse Schaanz,** a traditional (and touristy) town sitting alongside a river. Five windmills stand accompanied by a cheese-making facility and traditional crafts (from Amsterdam 15min., round-trip f6).

Discover picturesque cottages and soaring stone towers in **Edam,** Holland's sleeping beauty just outside Amsterdam, accessible by NZH bus from Centraal Station (7 strips). The 15th century **Grote Kerk,** or St. Nicholaaskerk, is the largest 3-ridged church in Europe and has 30 superb stained-glass windows. Farmers still bring their famed edam cheese to market by horse and by boat on Wednesdays in July and August (10am-12:30pm). Rent a bike at **Ronald Schot,** Kleine Kerkstraat 9-11 (f10/day), and head to the source yourself. **Alida Hoeve,** Zeddewed 1, is a **traditional cheese factory** across the street from the bike path as you head toward Volendam (pass by the first cheese factory you see, it's a tourist trap), where Edam cheese is still made by hand and the generous samples are free. (Open daily 9am-6pm. Free.) Further down the same bike path stands a towering **windmill**. For f1, you can climb the steep ladder to the top (while it's turning) and catch a great view of the surrounding pastures. (Open April-Aug. daily 9am-4pm.)

■■■ HOORN

If you need more wholesome pictures of the Netherlands to send to the folks back home, move toward the post-card land of North Holland, where windmills are scattered among affordable bed-and-breakfasts along sleepy canals. (Yes, you can skate on the water in winter.) Hoorn, one of Holland's key whaling towns in the 17th century, still harbors a Golden Age port atmosphere. On Wednesdays in July and August a full market, "Hartie Hoorn," fills the town with old-time Dutch costumes, dancing, and food. The **Westfries Museum** (open Mon.-Fri. 11am-5pm, Sat.-Sun. 2-5pm; f3.50, f2.50 seniors and under 16) is probably the most diverse in the country. Once home to governors and the court of justice, the 17th-century building now maintains a floor-to-ceiling, basement-to-attic collection of native paintings, model shops, furniture, and skeletons. **Jeugdherberg De Toorts (HI),** Schellinkhonterdijk 1a (tel. (02290) 142 56), solves your lodging quandaries with bunk beds near a sandy beachfront. (f20, nonmembers f25. Breakfast included. Open July-Aug. only.) **Hetter Witte Paard,** Lange Kerkstr. 27, located across from the Grote Kerk, specializes in vegetarian dishes. (f11.50-15. Open Mon. 11am-8pm, Tues.-Wed. 10am-8pm, Thurs.-Fri.10am-9pm, Sat. 11am-9pm, Sun. 2pm-9pm.) The **VVV**, Niuewstr. 23, offers maps (f2-4) and 2 walking tours (f2.50), both of which start in its 380-year-old home. (Open Mon. 1-6pm, Tues.-Sat. 9:30am-6pm; Sept.-June Mon. 1-5pm, Tue.-Wed. and Fri. 9:30am-5pm, Thurs. 9:30am-5pm and 7-9pm, Sat. 9:30am-4pm.)

■■■ HAARLEM

Haarlem, 20km from Amsterdam, quietly entices visitors with the same glorious façades and romantic canals that inspired revolutionary Dutch artists during the Golden Age. Seek out the 17th- and 18th-century *hofjes* (almshouses for elderly women), red-brick structures with grassy and blooming courtyards. Try secluded **Hofje van Bakenes,** Wijde Appelaarsteeg 11, near the Teylers Museum, or the **Hofje van Oirschot,** at the end of Kruisstr., where it becomes Barteljorisstr. These are private property and still inhabited—be tactful. From the station, Kruisweg leads to the **Grote Markt** and the glorious medieval **Stadhuis** (Town Hall), originally the 13th-century hunting lodge of the Count of Holland. When the Hall of Counts is not in use, you can sneak a free peek at the lavishly furnished interior; ask at the reception desk. The **Grote Kerk** graces the opposite end of the Grote Markt and still houses the Müller organ, which Mozart played at age 11 (the organ was 28). (Church open Mon.-Sat. 10am-4pm. f2, children and students f1. Free organ recitals May-Oct. Tues. 8:15pm and also July-Aug. Thurs. 3pm.)

From the church, walk down Damstr. to the Netherlands' oldest museum, the **Teylers Museum** at Spaarne 16. Looking like something out of an H.G. Wells novel, the museum lets you see what people in 1788 thought a museum should be: a blend of scientific instruments of the era, fossils, coins, paintings, and superb drawings, including works by Raphael and Michelangelo. (Open Tues.-Sat. 10am-5pm, Sun. 1-5pm. f6.50, seniors and CJP holders f4.50.) The legacy of Haarlem's brash portraitist Frans Hals lives on in the **Frans Hals Museum,** Groot Heiligland 62. Housed in a charming 17th-century almshouse, the collection includes Hals's lively group portraits and a permanent collection of modern art. (Open Mon.-Sat. 10am-5pm, Sun. 1-5pm. f6, seniors and CJP holders f2.) The **Corrie Ten Boomhuis,** better known as The Hiding Place, Barteljorisstr. 19, is where Corrie Ten Boom and her family hid Jewish refugees during WWII. The refugees were never discovered, but the entire Ten Boom family was removed to concentration camps; Corrie was the only survivor. (Tours on the hr. Tues.-Sat. 10am-4pm; Nov.-April Tues.-Sat. 11am-4pm. Free admission but donation appreciated.) On Saturdays, a technicolor **flower and fruit market** fills the Grote Markt (9am-4pm).

Accommodations, Food, and Practical Information

A super-cheery staff keeps the clean but worn **Jeugdherberg Jan Gijzen (HI)**, Jan Gijzenpad 3 (tel. (023) 37 37 93). Bus #2 (direction "Haarlem-Nord") will drive you the 3km from the station to the hostel; tell the driver your destination. In July and August, no groups are accepted. (Reception open 7:30am-midnight. f21.50, nonmembers f26.50. Flexible midnight curfew. Open March-Oct.) Bus round-trip f6.50 makes it almost as much as a **private room**, which the VVV can book for around f26 (f7 fee). Haarlem apparently has not heard of budget hotels, but try the ideally located **Hotel Carillon**, Grote Markt 27 (tel. (023) 31 05 91). (Singles f50-85. Doubles f105. Breakfast included. Reception and bar open 7:30am-1am.) The **Stads Café**, Zijlstr. 56-58 (tel. (023) 32 52 02), offers Dutch cuisine (daily *dagschotel* f9.75) and commodious sleeping quarters. (Singles f50. Doubles f75-100. Breakfast f8.50. Café open Mon.-Thurs. 11am-10:30pm, Fri.-Sat. 11am-11:30pm, Sun. 2-11pm.) When these hotels fill, seek out the cheap pensions in nearby Zandvoort (see Near Haarlem). A **campground** is located at **De Liede,** Liewegje 17 (tel. (023) 33 23 60). Take bus #92 or 93 (direction "Waarderpolder") and walk 10 minutes (f4/person, f4/tent).

Pannekoekhuis De Smikkel, Kruisweg 57, serves plump buttery pancakes (f6.75-16.75) dripping with anything from bananas to seafood. (Open Mon.-Sat. 11:30am-8pm, Sun. 2-8pm.) For healthier fare, try out **Eko Eetcafé,** Zijlstr. 39. They serve a verdant vegetarian plate for f16 and pizzas for f12-16.50. (Open daily 5:30-9:30pm.)

The **VVV,** Stationsplein 1 (tel. (023) 31 90 59), sells an excellent map of Haarlem for f2.50. (Open Mon.-Sat. 9am-5:30pm; Oct.-March Mon.-Fri. 9am-5:30pm, Sat. 10am-4pm.) Haarlem is easily accessible from Amsterdam by **train** (4/hr., f5.25) or by **bus** #80 from Marnixstr., near Leidseplein (2/hr., 6 strips). Five night buses (#86) cruise from Amsterdam's Leidseplein to Haarlem (12:42am-3:20am), but none go from Haarlem to Amsterdam.

■ Near Haarlem

Haarlem is only 10 minutes by train from **Zandvoort** beach (2-6/hr., round-trip f3.50). South of here, between *paal* (wooden posts) #68 and 71, is a popular nude beach. Zandvoort hosts scads of cheap pensions and hotels. The **VVV,** at Schoolplein 1, in the village center, a downhill walk from the beach and the station, sells a indispensable guide to lodgings (f3.50). (Open Mon.-Fri. 9am-7pm, Sat. 9am-5pm; April-June and Sept. Mon.-Sat. 9am-5pm; Oct.-March Mon.-Fri. 10am-12:30pm and 1:30-5pm, Sat. 10am-12:30pm and 1:30-3:30pm.) **Hotel-Pension Noordzee,** Hogeweg 15 (tel. (02507) 13127), is located only 100m from the beach and the casino. (Singles f40. Doubles f65-70.) Hotel van der Aar, Brederodestr. 44, (tel. (02507) 14 802) is a good second choice. (Singles f32.50. Doubles f65. Reception open 8am-midnight.) **Bloemendaal** is a more repressed beach, accessible by bus #81 (1/hr.) from the Haarlem train station. An international flower auction is held year-round in the nearby town of **Aalsmeer.** From Haarlem, take bus #140. (Open Mon.-Fri. 7:30-11am; the most germinal budding flowers from 8-9am.) The **Frans Roozen Gardens** bloom with 500 different types of flowers and plants; summer flower shows are free. Bus #90 (direction "Den Haag") stops in front of the gardens. (Open July-Oct. Mon.-Fri. 9am-5pm. Tulip show April-May daily 8am-6pm.) Bus #50 or 51 runs past some of Holland's famous flower fields. Daffodils blossom in early to late April, hyacinths in mid- to late April, and tulips from late April to mid-May.

■■■ LISSE AND GOUDA

In late March, April, and May, the small town of **Lisse** lights up with color. Over 5 million bulbs flourish at the splendiferous **Keukenhof** garden (f13). Take bus #50 or

51 toward Lisse from the Haarlem train station; a combination bus and admission ticket bought at Centraal Station (f19) saves money. The rest of the year you can examine what goes on under the soil at the **Museum Voor de Bloembollenstreek,** which is devoted entirely to the history and science of tulip raising. (Open Tues.-Sun. 1-5pm. f2.50.) On April 23, 1994, Lisse will stick its petals to the metal in the annual flower parade.

Gouda's late Gothic splendor revolves around the monstrous **St. John's Church,** the longest in the Netherlands. Ravaged by everything from lightning to Reformation iconoclasts, it has managed to maintain a stunning collection of 70 16th-century stained-glass windows. (Open Mon.-Sat. 9am-5pm; Nov.-March Mon.-Sat. 10am-4pm. f2.50, students f1.50.) The **Goudse Pottenbakkerij,** 76 Peperstraat, has been producing traditional Dutch clay pipes since the 17th century. Behind the factory that makes these long, almost lascivious pipes, the **Het Trefpunt Hostel,** at Westhaven 46 (tel. (01820) 128 79), sits primly along a canal (f19. Sheets f5.50. Reception open Mon.-Sat. 8am-11:30pm, Sun. 8am-7pm. No wheelchair access). Wonderful Dutch pancakes are served to hungry souls at **Het Goudse Winkeltje,** just across from the church at 9a Achter de Kerk (f3.00-11.00; open Tues.-Wed. 9am-6pm, Thurs. 9am-9pm, Fri.-Sat. 9am-6pm). Gouda is also one of the few places in Holland where you can climb inside a working windmill, **De Roode Leeuw,** while it's turning. (Open Tues.-Sat. 9am-2pm. f2.50, children f1.00.)

■■■ LEIDEN

As William of Orange's 1574 reward to the people of Leiden for withstanding a Spanish siege, the University of Leiden is Holland's oldest institute of higher learning. The resourceful residents threw open local dikes, flooding the surrounding plain and thwarting the Spanish armies. Leiden is an archetypal college town, brimming with bookstores, cafés, bicycles, and 11 diverse museums. The **VVV,** Stationsplein 210 (tel. (071) 14 68 46), across the street and to the right of the train station, doles out maps (f1) and can locate rooms in private homes (f3.50 fee). Their *Rembrandt Tour* (f3.50) and *Pilgrim Tour* (f1) brochures offer creative ways to see the town on foot. (Open Mon.-Fri. 9am-5:30pm, Sat. 9am-4pm.) The **Rijksmuseum voor Volkenkunde** (National Museum of Ethnology), Steenstr. 1, one of the oldest anthropological museums in the world, boasts a collection of fantastic artifacts from the Dutch East Indies. (Open Tues.-Fri. 10am-5pm, Sat.-Sun. noon-5pm. f5, students f3.50.) The **Rijksmuseum van Oudheden** (National Antiquities Museum), Rapenburg 28, harbors the complete, lovingly restored Egyptian Temple of Taffeh, which the Dutch removed from the reservoir basin of the Aswan Dam and opened to the public in 1979. (Open Tues.-Sat. 10am-5pm, Sun. noon-5pm. f3.50; over 65, under 18, and CJP holders f2.) The university's garden, the **Hortus Botanicus** at Rapenburg 73, is one of Europe's oldest. It includes greenhouses and a Japanese garden. (Garden open Mon.-Sat. 9am-5pm, Sun. 10am-5pm; Oct.-March Mon.-Sat. 9am-5pm. Some greenhouses close at 4:30pm. f3.50; seniors and CJP holders f1.50.) Propel yourself to the top of a functioning Dutch windmill and inspect its mechanical innards at the **Molenmuseum "De Valk,"** 2de Binnenvestgracht 1, built in 1743. (Open Tues.-Sat. 10am-5pm, Sun. 1-5pm. f3; over 65, under 18, and CJP holders f1.50; free with Museumkaart.)

Accommodations, Food, and Practical Information A student housing crunch has made finding inexpensive rooms difficult but not impossible in Leiden. The surest bargain is the **Lits Jumeaux Jeugdhotel,** Lange Scheistr. 9 (tel. (071) 12 84 57), off Oude Singel and just outside the pedestrian district. (Reception open 8:30am-12:30am. 4- to 10-bed dorms f22.50. Singles f35. Doubles f70. Triples f105. Sheets f5. Doors lock at 12:30pm but keys to outside door available upon request.) If you need a break from hostels, set yourself up in either **Pension Witte,** Witte Singel 80 (tel. (071) 12 45 92; singles f38, doubles f78), or the nearby **Pension**

Bik, Witte Singel 92 (tel. (071) 12 26 02; singles f47, doubles f80; breakfast included; reception open 7:30am-10pm). Both offer immaculate rooms overlooking gardens and canals. If it hasn't already filled, try **Pension In de Goede Hoek,** Diefsteeg 19a (tel. (071) 12 10 31), with tidy rooms and a great location near the Stadhuis. You'll have to make your own breakfast, but plenty of good food is available in the kitchen. (Reception open 7am-1pm and 3-10pm. Singles f35. Doubles f60.) Idyllic **Jeugdherberg De Duinark (HI),** Langevelderlaan 45 (tel. (02523) 729 20), is 18km from Leiden in Noordwijk. Take bus #60 to Kappellebosiaan or bus #61 to Sancta Maria and walk 15 minutes. Reserve ahead. (Reception open 8am-1am. f24, non-members f29. July-Aug. f2.50 tourist tax. Sheets f6.00.)

For Leiden's cheapest bite, try the university *mensas:* **Augustinus,** Rapenburg 24 (open Sept.-June Mon.-Fri. 5:30-7:15pm), and **De Bak,** Kaiserstr. 23-25, offer dishes starting at f5. (Open mid-Aug. to late July Mon.-Fri. noon-2pm and 5:30-6:30pm.) **Café de Illegale,** Hooigracht 72, draws an intellectual crowd with scrumptious vegetarian and Dutch cuisine (f15-22). Someone will usually be crooning and playing guitar on Tuesday and Wednesday nights. (Open daily 5pm-midnight; kitchen closes at 10pm.) Or eat a bag lunch culled from the **Dagmarkt** supermarket, on the corner of Stationsweg and Stationsplein, just across from the station. (Open Mon. 1-6pm, Tues.-Fri. 9am-6pm, Sat. 9am-5pm.) The renovated area near Pieterskerk harbors sedate coffee shops. The **Duke,** Oude Singel 2 (tel. (071) 12 19 72), on the canal down the street from the Jeugdhotel, rounds up live jazz nightly at 9:30pm and open jam sessions on Sundays. (Open Sun.-Thurs. 7pm-1am, Fri.-Sat. 7pm-3am. Beer from f2.25.)

Leiden makes an appealing **rail** daytrip from Amsterdam (4/hr. from Centraal Station, 30min., f11.50) or the Hague (2/hr., 20min., f4.50).

■■■ THE HAGUE (DEN HAAG)

Although Amsterdam is the economic center of the Netherlands, the seat of government is The Hague. Here the streets are broader, the buildings grander, and the roses redder. This cool city of diplomats also harbors the royal residence and the International Court of Justice, which meets at the Peace Palace. In **Scheveningen,** a popular beach and nightspot northwest of the city, the fishing folk still don centuries-old traditional costume.

PRACTICAL INFORMATION

Tourist Offices: VVV, Kon. Julianaplein 30 (information hotline tel. (06) 340 350 51), in front of Centraal Station, on the right side under the Hotel Sofitel. Distributes tourist brochures (f1.50), peddles maps (f2.75), books rooms (f3.50 fee) and publishes events listings. Open Mon.-Sat. 9am-9pm, Sun. 10am-5pm; mid-Sept. to March Mon.-Sat. 9am-6pm, Sun. 10am-5pm.

Budget Travel: NBBS, Schoolstr. 24 (tel. 346 58 19). Long lines pay off in cheap tix. Open Mon.-Fri. 9:30am-5:30pm, Sat. 10am-4pm; Sept.-Dec. Mon.-Fri. 9:30am-5:30pm, Sat. 10am-3pm.

Embassies: U.S., Lange Voorhout 102 (tel. 362 49 11). Open Mon.-Fri. 8:30am-5:15pm. **Canada,** Sophialaan 7 (tel. 361 41 11). Open Mon.-Fri. 9am-5:30pm. **U.K.,** Lange Voorhout 10 (tel. 364 58 00). Open Mon.-Fri. 9am-1pm and 2:15-5:30pm. **Australia,** Carnegielaan 12 (tel. 310 82 00). Open Mon.-Fri. 9am-12:30pm and 2-5:30pm. **New Zealand,** Mauritskade 25 (tel. 346 93 24). Open Mon.-Fri. 9am-12:30pm and 1:30-5:30pm.

American Express: Venestr. 20 (tel. 370 11 00), near the Binnenhof. Open Mon.-Fri. 9am-5pm, Sat. 9:30am-12:30pm. Published rates and no charge on Cheques. Mail held (f2.50 charge without AmEx card or Cheques).

Post Office: Nobelstr. and Prinsenstr. (tel. 384 58 45), near the Grote Kerk. Poste Restante code: 25 13 AZ. Open Mon.-Wed. and Fri. 8:30am-6:30pm, Thurs. 8:30am-8:30pm, Sat. 9am-noon. Branch office at Koningin Julianaplein 6, to the left of the station. Open Mon.-Fri. 8am-6pm.

Telephones: City Code: 070. Public phones (and fax!) at the Post Office or across the street from the Kurhaus in Scheveningen.

Trains: Call 06 92 92 for information. Trains serving Amsterdam and Rotterdam use **Holland Spoor;** most others use **Centraal Station.** Reach Centraal Station and the VVV from Holland Spoor by *stoptrein* or tram #9 or 12. Both have **lockers** (small size f3.50, large size f5.50).

Ferries: Regular ferries run between nearby ports and England. **North Sea Ferries,** Luxembourgweg 2 (tel. (01819) 555 55), steams from Rozenburg-Europoort to Hull (1/day, 6pm, students f105 Mon.-Thurs., otherwise f178). **Stena Line** (tel. (017) 47 41 40) sails from Hoek van Holland to Harwich at noon and 10:30pm (f145).

Bike Rental: At both Holland Spoor (tel. 389 08 30) and Centraal Station (tel. 385 32 35). f7.50/day, deposit f100 or passport. Grab cycling maps (f5.40-10) at VVV.

Pharmacies: Hofstad Apotheek, 7a Korte Poten (tel. 46 47 48), just off the Plein. Open Mon.-Fri. 8:30am-10pm, Sat. 10am-6pm, Sun. noon-5pm.

Emergencies: tel. 0611. English spoken.

ACCOMMODATIONS AND FOOD

The Hague's lack of budget accommodations makes it a prime daytrip from Delft or Rotterdam (at least 4 trains/hr. to both). If you stay, **private homes** are a good option (from f30; ask at tourist office). **Jeugdherberg Ockenburgh (HI),** Monsterseweg 4 (tel. (070) 397 00 11), 8km from town in Kijkduin, is accessible by bus #122, 123 or 124 from Centraal Station; alert the driver, then follow the signs (10min.). Enormous, antiseptic, and overflowing with groups, it lies 15 minutes from the beach. (Reception open 7am-11pm. Curfew midnight, but door opens briefly at 1, 2, and 3am. Dorms f25.55. Singles f35. Doubles f65. Triples f92.50. Nonmembers add f5.) The Hague's cheap hotel rooms cluster in the seedy and somewhat dangerous neighborhood around the Holland Spoor train station; ship out to more pleasant quarters in nearby **Scheveningen.** Five minutes from a beautiful beach and huge casino, **Hôtel Lubèl,** Haagsestr. 53 (tel. (070) 354 58 03), will set you up in a tidy single (f45) or double (f90). Take bus #22 from the station (direction "Scheveningen," 3 strips) and tell the driver your destination. Pitch a tent near the beach at **Ockenburgh,** Wijndaelerweg 25 (tel. 325 23 64). Take tram #3 from Centraal Station. (f5/adult, f12/site. Under 18 *(Jeugdplaats)* f12.75. Open April to mid-Oct.)

Eating in this city of diplomats may require an expense account. Join ordinary citizens in the covered market at **Markthof,** Spuistr., a few blocks from Binnenhof, along Grote Marktstr. (Open Mon. 11am-6pm, Tues.-Wed. and Fri. 9am-6pm, Thurs. 9am-9pm, Sat. 9am-5pm.) Enjoy a stroll along **Denneweg,** a street lined with tiny exotic restaurants. For more traditional fare, **Le Perroquet,** Plein 12a (tel. 363 97 86), has entrees from f22.50. On the beach at Scheveningen, expect to pay f12-16 for a *halve kip* (half chicken) or, if you are the brave sort, swallow a herring for f3-4.

SIGHTS

A visit to the **Binnenhof,** the courtyard whose buildings house the Netherlands's Parliament, is enough to make you want a career in Dutch politics. Guided tours (leaving from Binnenhof 8a) begin with an audiovisual presentation and move on to the **Ridderzaal** (Hall of Knights) and usually one or both of the chambers of the States General. (Open Mon.-Sat. 10am-4pm. f5.) Just outside the north entrance of the Binnenhof, the 17th-century **Mauritshuis** features a heavyweight collection of Dutch paintings, including Rembrandt's *The Anatomy Lesson* and Vermeer's *Lady with a Turban.* (Open Tues.-Sat. 10am-5pm, Sun. 11am-5pm. f7.50; seniors, under 18, and CJP holders f4.50.) Mavens of abstraction will adore the **Haags Gemeentemuseum,** Stadhouderslaan 41, which boasts the largest assemblage of Mondrians in the world. (Open Tues.-Sun. 11am-5pm. f7, seniors and children f6, CJP holders f5.)

The extravagant **Peace Palace,** home to the International Court of Justice, glistens at Carnegieplein, 10 minutes from the Binnenhof. The palace often closes when the

Court is in session; call ahead to check if it's open to the public (tel. 346 96 80). Guided tours (required) leave Mon.-Fri. at 10, 11am, 2, 3, and 4pm. (Oct.-May last tour leaves at 3pm. f5, under 13 f3.)

The **Haags Filmhuis,** Spui 191, features oldies and the best of current movies; all films are shown in their original language with Dutch subtitles. (f11-15, students and seniors f8.50-12.50. Screenings nightly at 7:30pm and 9:45pm.) **Muziekcafé La Valletta,** Nieuwe Schoolstr. 13a, is a jazz café with live shows Thursday nights at 10pm. (Open daily 5pm-1am; no cover.) **Fireworks** explode from the pier (f1 entrance fee) in Scheveningen every Friday night in July and August, and in mid-June the beach hosts the **International Fokker Kite Flying Festival** and the **International Sandcastle Festival. Parkpop** in late June is the largest free mainstream rock concert in Europe. From July 9-11 in 1994, the 18th annual **North Sea Jazz Festival** brings 4 straight days of jazz, gospel concerts, and dance contests to the Hague. For a complete list of cultural events, pick up the brochure *Info* from the VVV.

■■■ ROTTERDAM

A barrage of German bombs obliterated Rotterdam's center on May 14, 1940, cowing the Netherlands into a hasty surrender. Dutch efficiency and the influence of the De Stijl school rebuilt the city into a futuristic Fisher-Price-toy construction. Rotterdam's center of gravity is its port, the largest in the world. Ossip Zadkine's incredible **Monument for the Destroyed City,** a statue of a person screaming, arms raised in self-defense and guts wrenched out, illustrates the 1940 bombing raid. (Take the subway or tram #1, 3 or 6 to Churchillplein behind the Maritime Museum). Check out the freaky sci-fi **cube houses,** family living units composed of a square box perched on a thin stalk. Tour the model home for an idea of what daily life in 2050 may be like. Take the subway to Blaak and follow the *Cubuswoning* sign to **Kijk-Kubus.** (Open Mon.-Fri. 10am-5pm, Sat.-Sun. 11am-5pm; Oct.-Dec. and April-May Tues.-Fri. 10am-5pm, Sat.-Sun. 11am-5pm; Jan.-March Sat.-Sun. 11am-5pm. f2.50.) All the modern architecture strikes a strange contrast with nearby **Oude Haven** (Old Harbor), where swanky youths recline at cafés and watch the ships go by.

Accommodations, Food, and Practical Information The **NJHC City-Hostel Rotterdam (HI),** Rochussenstr. 107-109 (tel. (010) 436 57 63), is well-run, with a bar, TV lounge, kitchen, and state-of-the-art lockers (f3.50). The hostel doesn't accept groups during July and August. Take the subway to Dijkzigt or tram #6. (Reception open 7am-2am. Lockout 10am-3pm. Curfew 2am. f23, nonmembers f28. Showers and breakfast included. Sheets f6.) The **Sleep-In,** Mauritsweg 29 (tel. (010) 412 14 20 or 414 32 56) offers bargain dorm beds at f15 a night. (Reception 4pm-1am. Curfew 1am. Lockout 10am-4pm. Breakfast and showers included. Open mid-June to mid-August. No reservations accepted).

Affordable Dutch delights (f9-f16) issue from **De Eend,** Mauritsweg 28. The menu changes daily. (Open Mon.-Fri. 4:30-7:30pm.) Otherwise, plenty of bread and cheese stack the shelves at the **Jac Hemans** supermarket, near the HI youth hostel, at 30a Nieuwe Binnenweg. (Open Mon. 11am-6pm, Tues.-Thurs. 9am-6pm, Fri. 9am-6:30pm, Sat. 9am-5pm.) **Dizzy Jazz-Café,** 's-Gravendijkwal 127, features live jazz on Tuesdays. (Open Mon. 8pm-2am, Tues. 9pm-midnight, Wed.-Sat. 8pm-2am, Sun. 10pm-2am. Beers from f2.50. Dinners f13.50-f22.)

The **VVV** booth at the train station (tel. (010) 413 60 06) sells an informative guide and street map (f1.50) and books rooms (f2.50). (Open Mon.-Sat. 9am-10pm, Sun. 10am-10pm.) The main office at Coolsingel 67 (tel. (063) 403 40 65), near Stadhuisplein, publishes the cultural calendar *This Month* (free) and does theater bookings (f2.50). (Open Mon.-Thurs. 9am-5:30pm, Fri. 9am-9pm, Sat. 9am-5pm, Sun. 10am-4pm; Oct.-March closed on Sun.) For travel information, head to budget hub **NBBS,** Meent 126, near the statehouse (tel. 414 94 85; open Mon.-Fri. 9:30am-5:30pm, Sat. 10am-4pm). The **American Express** office is located down the street at

Meent 92. (Open Mon.-Fri. 9am-5pm, Sat. 10am-1pm.) The office will hold mail (**postal code:** 3011 JP Rotterdam) but charges f2.50 for those without an AmEx card or Traveler's Cheques. **Local buses** (tel. 411 71 00) depart from the train station. Next door at Delftsplein 31 is the **post office.** (Open Mon.-Fri. 8:30am-6pm. Poste Restante, currency exchange, telephones, and fax are all available.)

Rotterdam is a central **rail** hub and offers frequent connections to The Hague (9-10/hr., f6.25), Amsterdam (5-6/hr., f20), and Utrecht (3-4/hr., f13).

■■■ DELFT

Delft's canals and well-preserved edifices live on in unsullied serenity, much as they did when Vermeer froze the city on canvas. To compete with imported Chinese porcelain, Delft potters conjured up their jaw-dropping blue-on-white china in the 16th century. You can gawk at the pricey plates in the main boutique at **Koniklijke Porceleyne Fles,** Rotterdamseweg 196 in South Delft, where there are also hourly painting demonstrations. Take bus #60 from the station. (Open Mon.-Sat. 9am-5pm, Sun. 10am-4pm. Free.) For more in-depth study, tour the factory at **De Delftse Pauw,** Delftweg 133, in the northern reaches of the city, where artisans still painstakingly hand-paint the porcelain. Take tram #1 from the station. (Open daily 9am-4pm; mid-Oct. to March Mon.-Fri. 9am-4pm, Sat.-Sun. 11am-1pm. Free.) Both places unload seconds at 25% off.

Built in 1381, the **Nieuwe Kerk** looms over Delft's central **Markt.** It contains the mausoleum of William of Orange, who liberated the Dutch from the Spanish yoke, along with a statue of his loyal dog, who starved to death out of despair after his master died. (Church open Mon.-Sat. 9am-5pm; Nov.-March. Mon.-Sat. 11am-4pm. f2.50, seniors f2.) Ascend the church tower to see the 48-bell carillon and a ripping view of old Delft. (Tower open June 12-Sept. 4 Mon.-Sat. 10am-4:30pm; April 30-June 12 Tues.-Thurs. 10am-4:30pm. f3.25.) Built in the 15th century as a nun's cloister, **Het Prinsenhof,** at Sint Agathaplein, was William's abode until a crazed Spanish sympathizer assassinated him in 1584. Today it exhibits paintings, tapestries, Delft pottery, and a touch of adventurous contemporary art. In mid-October, the museum sponsors an **antique fair** famous throughout Holland. (Open Tues.-Sat. 10am-5pm, Sun. 1-5pm. f3.50; seniors, under 14, and CJP holders f1.75.)

Accommodations, Food, and Practical Information Delft may be renowned for its china, but it sure isn't known for its budget accommodations. The sage choice is cozy **Van Leeuwen,** Achterom 143 (tel. (015) 12 37 16), overlooking a canal near the train station and the Markt. Don't worry if you don't see a hotel sign, just ring the bell. (Singles f35. Doubles f65-70. Breakfast included.) Surprisingly, several hotels dotting the Markt offer spiffy rooms at decent prices. **La Dalmacija,** Markt 39 (tel. (015) 12 37 14), posts singles at f40-60 and doubles at f70-100. (Reception open 9am-11pm.) Delft also has a private **campground** on Korftlaan (tel. (015) 13 00 40), in the Delftse Hout recreation area. (Reception open 9am-10pm, mid-Sept.-May 9am-6pm. f3.50/person, f17.50/tent. Laundry facilities available.) The camp restaurant serves *Dagschotel* for f13.50. (Open noon-10pm.) Take bus #60 or 64 from the station to the Korftlaan stop.

A large **market** erupts every Thursday (9am-5pm) in the town center; on Saturdays, a **fruit and vegetable market** fills the Brabantse Turfmarkt. The student *mensa* **Eettafel Tyche,** Oude Delft 123 (tel. (015) 12 21 23), practically gives away meat-and-potatoes fare (if you give them f5.25 first). (Open Sept.-May Mon.-Sat. 5:15-7:15pm.) For f5.95, you can savor the small yet tasty sandwich voted the best *broodje* in the Netherlands at **Kleyweg's Stads-Koffyhuis,** down the street at no. 133-135. (Open Mon.-Fri. 9am-7pm, Sat. 9am-6pm.) After dark, the dim yet inviting **Bebop Jazzcafé,** Kromstr. 33, near the Markt, draws local hepcats. (Open Mon.-Thurs. 7pm-1am, Fri.-Sun. 3pm-2am. Live jazz Sept.-June Sun. and the 1st and 3rd Wed. of the month.) Delft has a central square full of activity, especially in the summer. The **Straattheater festival** in June summons street performers from every corner of the city. The third week in August brings the **Oude Stijl Jazz Festival** and the cultural **Delftdag.**

Snag a complete pamphlet on Delft (f3), as well as hiking and cycling maps of the area, from the **VVV,** Markt 85 (tel. (015) 12 61 00; open Mon.-Fri. 9am-6pm, Sat. 9am-5pm, Sun. 11am-3pm; Oct.-March closed Sun.) Delft is one hour southwest of Amsterdam by **train,** with connections at The Hague (f3.50) and Leiden (f6.25). For train or bus info in Delft, call 06 92 92.

■■■ UTRECHT

At the geographical center of the Netherlands, Utrecht presents comely canals, a grandiose cathedral, and a university that is a leftist bastion in a liberal country. Its students support a dynamic cultural scene and nightlife. If you arrive by train, linger not in nightmarish **Hoog Catharijne,** the huge modern shopping complex around Centraal Station—bail out to Utrecht's older quarters. At the center of Utrecht rises the **Domkerk,** begun in 1254 and finished 250 years later. (Open daily 10am-5pm; Oct.-April Mon.-Sat. 11am-4pm. Free.) The **Domtoren,** originally attached to the cathedral but free-standing since a nasty medieval storm blew away the church nave, is the highest tower in the Netherlands. Climb all 465 steps to see Amsterdam on a clear day. (Tower open Mon.-Fri. 10am-5pm, Sat.-Sun. noon-4pm; Nov.-March open Sat.-Sun noon-4pm. Obligatory guided tours on the hour. f4, children under 12 f2.) The **Pandhof,** the church's 15th-century cloister garden, has been converted into a rustic herb garden. (Open Mon.-Fri. 10am-5pm, Sat. 11am-5pm, Sun. noon-5pm; Nov.-March Sat.-Sun. noon-5pm. Free.) At the **Centraal Museum,** Agnietenstr. 1, you can marvel at a 9th-century Viking ship and paintings of the Utrecht school. (Open Tues.-Sat. 10am-5pm, Sun. noon-5pm. f5; seniors, children, and CJP holders f2.50.) **Het Catharijneconvent,** Nieuwe Gracht 63, documents the progress of Christianity in the Netherlands with a comprehensive collection of Dutch religious artwork. (Open Tues.-Fri. 10am-5pm, Sat.-Sun. 11am-5pm. f5; students, seniors, and those under 18 f3.50.)

Accommodations, Food, and Practical Information Utrecht has a lamentable dearth of cheap hotels; the **VVV** charges f3.50 (plus f1 for the phone calls) to locate lodgings, but they can secure special discount rates. Visit the main office, Vredenburg 90 (tel. (06) 34 03 40 85), at the end of the shopping mall—if you arrive by train, ask at the information booth in the station for a free walking map (subsequent maps f1.50) to help you find it. (Open Mon.-Fri. 9am-6pm, Sat. 9am-4pm. A machine outside spews a map and information for f2 at other times.) The delightful **Jeugdherberg Rhijnauwen (HI),** Rhijnauwenselaan 14 (tel. (03405) 612 77), is set in a majestic medieval manor house surrounded by countless country canals. Take bus #40, 41 or 43 from Utrecht's Centraal Station (several/hr., 3 strips; tell driver your destination) and walk 5 minutes. (Reception open 8am-12:30am. Curfew officially 12:30am, but it's flexible. f21.50, nonmembers f26.50. Sheets f6. Lockers f1, with f5 deposit. Showers and breakfast included. Pizza and cheeseburgers f2-7 at the bar.) **Camping De Berekuil,** Ariënslaan 5-7 (tel. (030) 71 38 70), is not far from the center of town; take bus #57 from the station to the Veemarkt stop. (f4/person and f4/tent. Reception open 9am-10pm. Open April-Oct.)

Café De Baas, Lijnmarkt 8, just across the canal from the Domtoren, features yummy vegetarian dishes from f9.50 with occasional live music. (Open Wed. 5pm-10pm, Thurs. 5pm-1am, Fri. 5pm-10pm, Sat. noon-10pm.) The 2 main student *mensas,* open to all, are **Veritas,** Kromme Nieuwe Gracht 54, and **Unitas,** Lucasbolwerk 8. (Meals f5-9. Both open mid-Aug. to late June Mon.-Fri. 5-7:30pm.) **De Goey-Koot,** Nobelstr. 22, vends exotic fruits at basement prices. (Open Mon. noon-6pm, Tues.-Sat. 9am-6pm.) The restaurants lining the Oude Gracht are more atmospheric, but their ambience will cost you. Try the hip and happening **Toque Toque,** Oude

Gracht 138, at Vinkenburgstr. A mongo plate of pasta, with salad and bread, runs f12.50. (Open Mon.-Fri. 10am-midnight, Sat. 9am-midnight, Sun. noon-midnight.)

Utrecht presents ample opportunity to get wild and loose. Things get hopping around 11pm at 2 popular bars: intellectual **De Kneus,** Nobelstr. 303 (open daily 4pm-4am), and the earthier **'t Pandje,** Nobelst. 193. (Open daily 10pm-4am. Beers from f2.50. Bar food f2.50-4.50.) If you're yearning for Americana, escape to the jungle at **Mad Mick and Big Mamou,** Oudekerkhof 29, a rocking Cajun bar and restaurant with drinks like the "Slippery Nipple" and live music every Monday at 9:30pm. (Dishes f7.50-15. Open Sun.-Thurs. 2pm-2am, Fri.-Sat. 11am-3am.)

■■■ ARNHEM AND THE HOGE VELUWE NATIONAL PARK

Rebuilt after punishing WWII bombings, Arnhem, 100km southeast of Amsterdam (2 trains/hr., 70min.) is now one huge outdoor shopping center with little to offer. Nevertheless, the contiguous Hoge Veluwe National Park, a 13,000 acre preserve of woods, heath, dunes, red deer, and wild boars, may well prove one of the highlights of your trip to Europe. Tucked deep within the park and a 35-minute walk from the nearest entrance lies the **Rijksmuseum Kröller-Müller,** one of the finest modern art museums in Europe, with 276 van Goghs and superb paintings by Seurat, Mondrian, and many others, as well as a sculpture garden including pieces by Maillol, Moore, and Lipchitz. Visitors can pedal the park's white bikes for free—pick one up at the visitor center and drop it off at any bike stand. The newly-opened **Museonder,** at the visitor center, is the world's first underground museum, dedicated to the study of the subterranean eco-system. (Exhibits open daily 9am-5pm, Nov.-April 10am-5pm.) From June through August, and at selected times throughout the rest of the year, bus #12 ("Hoge Veluwe") leaves from the Arnhem train station; board and alight as often as you wish (1/hr., 9:40am-4:10pm, 7 strips). The bus will zoom you directly to the museum's doorstep, or you can ride another 1200m to **Koperen Kop,** the visitor center and bike rental station. At other times, take bus #107 to Otterlo and walk 45 minutes from there. (Park open 8am-sunset. Museum and sculpture park open Tues.-Sat. 10am-5pm, Sun. 11am-5pm; Nov.-March Tues.-Sat. 10am-5pm, Sun. 1-5pm. Park f7.50, children f3.75; museum and sculpture park free.)

The **VVV,** to the left of the station on Stationsplein (tel. (085) 42 03 30), finds accommodations and distributes information about the park. (Open Mon.-Fri. 9am-5:30pm, Sat. 9am-4pm.) The placid **Jeugdherberg Alteveer (HI),** Diepenbroeklaan 27 (tel. (085) 42 01 14), is in a crunchy rural setting but gives special attention to groups and families. Every room has a shower. Take bus #3 toward Alteveer and ask the driver to let you off at the hostel, then follow the signs. (Reception open 8am-12:30am. Curfew 12:30am. f23, nonmembers f28. Sheets f6. Breakfast included.) **Hotel-Pension Parkzicht,** Apeldoornsestr. 16 (tel. (085) 42 06 98), is about 15 minutes from the station. (Singles f45. Doubles f80-90. Breakfast included.) Camp at **Kampeercentrum Arnhem,** Kemperbergerweg 771 (tel. (085) 43 16 00), accessible by bus #2. (Direction "Schaarsbergen." f10/person, no site charge. Open March-Sept.) The **Old Inn,** Stationsplein 39a (tel. (085) 42 06 49), is a café and restaurant with a f11.70 *dag*menu. (Open daily 11am-1am; kitchen closes at 11pm.)

■■■ WADDEN ISLANDS (WADDENEILANDEN)

Wadden may mean "mudflat" in Dutch, but it is a surfeit of sand on these 5 islands that draws so many Dutch and German vacationers. Check a weather forecast; there's zippo to do if it's raining.

Texel You can visit **Texel,** the southernmost and largest island, on a daytrip from Amsterdam if you get your act together. Take the train to Den Helder (f20, 2/hr., 70 min.), then bus #3 from the station to the ferry. Boats leave at 35 minutes past the hour, every hour from 6am to 9pm (last boat back 9:05pm, round-trip f11.55). After the ferry drops you at **'t Horntje,** on the southern tip of the island, rent a bike (f7) to pedal between Texel's 3 major villages. **Den Berg,** the largest town, squats in the center of island; **De Koog** lolls on the beaches on the western edge; and **De Cocks-dorp** isolates itself at the northern end of the isle. Texel is a voyeur's paradise: there are 2 popular nude beaches (one south of Den Hoorn and one off De Cocksdorp at paal 28) plus fine bird watching. You can visit the **nature reserves** only on a 2-hour guided tour organized by the State Forest Department (f7.50). Book in advance from **Ecomare,** Ruyslaan 92 (tel. (02220) 177 41), in De Koog, and specify English-speaking tours not requiring rubber boots.

Both of Texel's **HI youth hostels** are immaculate and within walking distance of Den Burg; snag bus #27 or 28 from the ferry landing to reach either one (tell the driver your destination). **Panorama,** Schansweg 7 (tel. (02220) 154 41), snuggles in a nature reserve complete with Texel's own breed of sheep. (Curfew midnight, but night key available with f50 deposit. f24.20, f29.20 non-members.) **De Eyercoogh,** Pontweg 106 (tel. (02220) 154 41), is conveniently near the town center. (Curfew midnight, but night key available. f21.50, nonmembers f26.50. Reception open 9am-midnight. Open March-Oct.) If both the hostels are full, your best bet is **Hotel de Merel,** Warmoestr. 22 (tel. (02220) 131 32), around the corner from the main square in Den Burg. (f40/person; f10 surcharge/person for 1 night stay; f2 tourist tax in summer.) The **VVV** in Den Burg, 66 Emmalaan (tel. (02220) 147 41), sells excellent maps (f5.95) of biking and walking routes and updates you on the island's 20 **campgrounds** and several farms that allow camping. (Open Tues.-Fri. 9am-6pm, Sat. 9am-5pm, Sun. 4-6pm; Sept.-June closed Sun.) Sample the local seafood at **Theodo-rahoeve,** Kogerstr. 26 in Den Burg (fish soup f7.50), which also dishes out great Dutch pancakes (f8.50-15.50). (Open 11am-9pm.) **De 12 Balcken Tavern,** at 20 Weverstr. in Den Burg, is a snug and dimly lighted pub that specializes in *'t Jutterje,* the island's wildly popular alcohol, blended from herbs and wheat. (Open Mon.-Sat. 10am-2am, Sun. noon-2am. Beer f2.75.) On June 11, Texel holds **Ronde Van Texel,** the largest catamaran race in Europe and the culmination of a week-long **jazz festival.** Another jazzfest is held October 16-17.

The Friese Islands The 4 other islands (the Friese Islands) all have extensive dunes and wildlife sanctuaries. **Schiermonnikoog** and **Vlieland** are the most deserted, while **Terschelling** and **Ameland** offer more nightlife. On boat excursions to Vlieland from Texel, you must return the same day. Schiermonnikoog's **VVV,** Reeweg (tel. (05195) 312 33), finds rooms in private homes for about f30 per person. Reserve ahead, even in off-season. (Open Mon.-Fri. 9am-1pm and 2:30-6:30pm.) There are **HI youth hostels** on 3 of the islands: **the Terschelling Hostel (HI),** van Heusdenweg 39 (tel. (05620) 23 38; open year-round), the Ameland **De Kleine Grie (HI),** Oranjeweg 59 (tel. (05191) 41 33; open mid-June to late Aug. plus a week at Easter), and Schiermonnikoog's **Rijsbergen,** Knuppeldam 2 (tel. (05195) 312 57; closed in Jan.) For Terschelling or Vlieland, take the main train line from Amsterdam to **Leeuwarden** (2½hr.), then continue to Harlingen (f7), where you can catch the ferry to either island (2hr., round-trip f30.60, bikes f11). To reach Ameland, take bus #66 from Leeuwarden (6 strips, 50min.) to Holwerd and then the ferry (8-11/day; Sept.-May 4-6/day; 45min., f14.30 round-trip). Reach Schiermonnikoog from Lauwersoog (40min., f14.80 round-trip), itself reached by bus #51 from Leeuwarden (75 min., 11 strips). In July and August, ferries also run between the islands, making it possible to see several in 2 or 3 days.

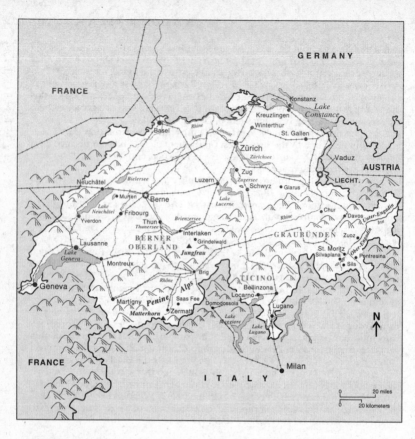

Switzerland (Suisse, Die Schweiz, Svizzera, Confederatio Helvetica)

US$1 = 1.40SFr (francs)	1SFr = US$0.72
CDN$1 = 1.06SFr	1SFr = CDN$0.94
UK£1 = 2.16SFr	1SFr = UK£0.46
IR£1 = 2.03SFr	1SFr = IR£0.49
AUS$1 = 0.91SFr	1SFr = AUS$1.11
NZ$1 = 0.77SFr	1SFr = NZ$1.30
SAR1 = 0.29SFr	1SFr = SAR3.47
Country Code: 41	**International Dialing Prefix: 00**

Divided by impassable Alpine giants and united by neither language nor religion, it's curious that Switzerland is a nation at all. What is now a confederation of 23 largely autonomous cantons was first conceived in 1291 and jelled into its present form at a slothful pace all the way through the 19th century. Swiss politics have an old-fashioned feel; approximately 3000 local communes retain a great deal of power, and major policy disputes are routinely settled by national referenda.

Official neutrality since 1815 has kept the ravages of war away from this postcard-perfect haven. Placidity has also nurtured the growth of Big Money in the staid banking centers of Geneva and Zürich. You may find that personalities in Switzerland exemplify staidness as well; many big-city locals' idea of a good time is sitting in a bank watching gold prices change (dial 166 from any place in Switzerland to reach the stock market bulletins hotline). Spurred by its love of prosperity, Switzerland now seems on the verge of major change. Though the nation remains neutral in relationship to its European neighbors, Swiss citizens have recently shown interest in the country's affairs; voters are turning out in droves to cast their ballots for or against integration into the European Economic Community.

One aspect of Switzerland will likely always overshadow whatever internal divisions exist: the majestic Alps. John Keats glorifies them in his Romantic poetry; others have fallen silent in a landscape that defies words. Snow-capped peaks lord over half the country's area, enticing skiers, bikers, hikers, and paragliders from around the globe to one of the most finely-tuned tourist industries in the world. Victorian scholar John Ruskin called the Swiss Alps "the great cathedrals of the earth"; you're welcome to worship here if you can spare the cash.

> For more information on this, the country in Europe which is, more than any other, defined by its topography, pick up a copy of *Let's Go: Germany & Switzerland*.

GETTING THERE AND GETTING AROUND

Getting around Switzerland is gleefully easy. **Federal and private railways,** and yellow **post buses** (railpasses not valid), which serve many of the remote villages, pick up the slack where trains fail to go. **Eurailpasses** clear the way for passage on most lake cruises and portage on state-run trains, but private companies exert a deathgrip on Alpine rail routes, making travel fatally expensive.

An array of special passes help beat the ruinous transport costs. An absolute must for Eurail-less wayfarers is the **Half-Fare Travel Card,** which entitles you to 50% off all trips on federal and private railroads, postal buses, and steamers. At only 75SFr per month, the card pays for itself in 1 or 2 journeys. Less casual and more expensive is the **Swisspass,** available through Rail Europe or any major travel agency in your home country. The Flexipass option buys you 3 days of travel in 15 for US$148; continuous passes cost US$186 for 8 days, US$214 for 15 days, and US$296 for a month; they give unlimited travel on all government-operated railways, lake steamers, and most private railways and postal buses, but only a 25-50% discount on the most expensive mountain railways and cable cars. Finally, you can opt for one of 8 cantonal **Regional Passes** (50-175SFr), most valid for 15 days; 5 days (consecutive or not) can be used for free travel, the remaining 10 for half-fare travel. Swisspass or Half-Fare Travel Card holders get a 20% discount. The **Berner Oberland Pass** (125SFr), covering Berne, Lucerne, Interlaken, and Zermatt, is the most practical.

Intercity **buses** are virtually nonexistent in this rail-oriented nation, but the postal buses (a barrage of banana-colored-3-brake-system-coaches delivered to you expressly by the Swiss government) take care of transport in rural areas (the only mode of transport near St. Moritz). **Steamers** ply many of the larger lakes. Fares are no bargain, but a Eurailpass often gets you free passage, and a Swisspass almost always wins a free ride. **Cycling,** though strenuous, is a splendid way to see the country; rental at almost any station is standard at 14-16SFr per day (return to any station). **Hitching** is known to be difficult. With sufficient stamina, overland **walking and hiking** are the most enjoyable ways to see Switzerland. Thirty thousand miles of hiking trails lace the entire country; yellow signs give directions and traveling times.

SWITZERLAND ESSENTIALS

Switzerland is quadrilingual: French is spoken in the west, Italian in the south, Romansch (a relative of Latin and Etruscan) in the cantons of Engadin and Graubünden, and Swiss German *(Schwyzerdütsch,* a dialect nearly incomprehensible to other German speakers) everywhere else. Most people know at least 3 languages, including English. **Tourist offices** in every Swiss city *(Verkehrsbüro* or *Kurverein)* locate rooms, distribute maps, and suggest hiking or biking routes. All official tourist offices are marked by a fat blue **"i"**.

Currency exchange at its easiest (and latest) takes place in train stations; rates are usually the same as banks. **Local phone calls** cost 40 centimes. **Post offices** and **PTT centers,** often in the same building, offer international calling on a phone-first, pay-later or collect basis. Dial 191 or 114 for English-friendly assistance. For AT&T's **USA Direct,** dial 155 00 11; for **MCI,** dial 155 02 22; for **Canada Direct,** dial 046 05 83 30. Ring the **police** at 117, an **ambulance** at 144. Most stores are open Monday through Friday from 8am to 6:30pm with a break from noon to 2pm, and Saturday mornings. In cities, shops also close Monday mornings. Museums close on Mondays.

Switzerland is justifiably proud of its winter-wonderland reputation. Far-sighted planning, and avoiding the hoity-toity resorts, allows for inexpensive **skiing.** Lift tickets average 30-50SFr per day, rentals 30SFr. Passes usually cover transportation to the lifts as well as uphill carriage. A week of lift tickets, equipment rental, lessons, lodging, and demi-pension (breakfast plus dinner) averages 475SFr. Like its terrain, Switzerland's weather varies crazily from area to area. Wear layers. Be prepared.

Accommodations, Camping, Food, and Drink All things Swiss are meticulous, orderly, efficient, and expensive. No hosteling horror stories apply to Switzerland; the uniformly cheery **HI Jugendherbergen** are bright, clean, and open to all ages (14-22SFr/night, nonmembers 5-7SFr extra; breakfast and sheets included). **Hotels** are expensive; the gems in *Let's Go* are uniformly one-star but offer bathless rooms. In smaller towns, *Zimmerfrei* (private rooms) abound; the tourist office can supply a list and make reservations. As befits a country so blessed by Mother Nature, Switzerland blossoms with over 1200 **campgrounds.** Some are so beautiful they take on spiritual value; others are glorified backyards (3-6SFr/person and 4-9SFr/tent). This land of order and propriety forbids freelance camping along roads and in public areas. **Swiss Alpine Club (SAC) huts** are modest and extremely practical for those interested in trekking in higher, more remote areas. Bunk rooms sleep 10 to 20 weary hikers, with blankets (but no running water or electricity) provided. SAC huts are open to all, but SAC members get discounted rates. The average rate for one night's stay without food is 30SFr for nonmembers, 20-25SFr for members. Those serious about conquering the summits should contact SAC, Sektion Zermatt, Haus Granit, 3920 Zermatt, Switzerland.

The Swiss are hardly culinary daredevils. In French Switzerland, try the cheese specialties; *fondue* is always excellent, as is *raclette* (melted cheese with pickled onions and boiled new potatoes). Swiss-German food is heartier. Try *Züricher Geschnetzeltes* (veal strips in a delicious cream sauce) and *Rösti* (hashbrowned potato with onion). **Migros** supermarket cafeterias and **Manora** restaurants are the budgeteer's choice for self-service dining. Tips are included in meal prices.

CENTRAL SWITZERLAND AND SWISS JURA

■■■ ZÜRICH

Rich and aloof, Zürich is the quintessential banker's town. The city was the seat of the Reformation in German Switzerland; since then, Protestant asceticism has gradually been overwhelmed by the secular tide of money that floods the city. But there

ZÜRICH

is more to Zürich than money; the city retains something of the avant-garde spirit of 1916, a year in which artistic and philosophical radicalism shook the calm of Zürich. Living at Universitätstrasse 38, James Joyce toiled away on what was to become *Ulysses*, the ultimate modernist novel. Not far away at Spiegelgasse 14, Russian exile V.I. Lenin bided his time, read a lot of Marx, and dreamed of revolution. At the same time, raucous young artists calling themselves Dadaists—some, legend has it, living next door to Lenin and irritating him immensely—were founding the seminal proto-performance-art collective known as the *Cabaret Voltaire*.

ORIENTATION AND PRACTICAL INFORMATION

Zürich sits on the northern tip of the Zürichsee (Lake Zürich); the River Limmat divides it in half. Swissly efficient trams crisscross the city, operating from 5:30am-midnight. Rides cost 1.70-2.80SFr. The 24-hour *Tageskarte* is your best bet (6.40SFr). Buy tickets from machines at tram stops.

Tourist Offices: Main office in the **train station** at Bahnhofplatz 15 (tel. 211 40 00). Exit the station to Bahnhofplatz, and walk to the left. Finds rooms for 5SFr; dispenses maps and the weekly *Zürich News*. Open Mon.-Fri. 8:30am-9:30pm, Sat.-Sun. 8:30am-8:30pm; Nov.-March Mon.-Fri. 8:30am-7:30pm, Sat.-Sun. 8:30am-6:30pm. Also at **airport terminal B** (tel. 816 40 81; open daily 10am-7pm).
Consulates: U.S., Zollikerstr. 141 (tel. 422 25 66). Open Mon.-Fri. 9-11:30am, 1:30-4pm. **U.K.,** Dufourstr. 56 (tel. 261 15 20). Open Mon.-Fri. 9am-noon, 2-4pm.
Currency Exchange: Honest deal at the train station. Open daily 6:15am-10:45pm.
American Express: Bahnhofstr. 20, near Paradeplatz (tel. 211 83 70). All AmEx services. Open Mon.-Fri. 8:30am-5:30pm, Sat. 9am-noon.
Post Office: Main office at Kasernenstr. 95-97. Open Mon.-Fri. 6:30am-10:30pm, Sat. 6:30am-8pm, Sun. 11am-10:30pm. 1SFr Poste Restante charge after 6:30pm.
Poste Restante: Sihlpost, Kasernenstr., Psetlagernde Briefe, CH-8021 Zürich.
Telephones: PTT phones at the train station. **City Code:** 01.
Flights: Trains from Hauptbahnhof to airport, 10min., 4.50SFr, railpasses valid.
Trains: tel. 211 50 10. To Berne (42SFr), Geneva (73SFr), Lugano (58Sfr).
Bike Rental: At the baggage counter *(Gepäckexpedition Fly-Gepäck)* in the station. Open daily 6am-7:40pm. 19SFr/day.
Hitchhiking: Those who hitchhike take tram #4 from the station to the end (Werdhölzli) for Basel, Geneva, Paris, or Bonn. To Lucerne, Italy, and Austria, they take tram #5 or 14 to Bahnhof Wiedikon and walk 1 block down Schimmelstr. to Silhölzli. For Munich, they take tram #14 to Milchbuck, walk to Schaffhauserstr., toward St. Gallen and St. Margarethen. **Mitfahrzentrale** (tel. 261 68 93) pairs drivers and riders.
Bookstore: Daeniker's Bookshop, In Gassen 11. English books, including *Let's Go.* Open Mon.-Fri. 8:15am-6:30pm, Sat. 9am-4pm.
Laundromat: Speed-Wash, at Müllerstr. 55, Matteng. 29, Friesstr. 4. Open Mon.-Sat. 7:30am-noon and 1-6:30pm.
Emergencies: Ambulance: tel. 144. **Medical Emergency:** tel. 47 47 00. **Police:** tel. 117.

ACCOMMODATIONS AND CAMPING

Jugendherberge Zürich (HI), Mutschellenstr. 114 (tel. 482 35 44). Take tram #7 (direction "Wollishofen"): Morgental, and follow the signs (5min.). Impeccably clean and busy. Reception open 2pm-1am. Checkout 6-9am. 22SFr, nonmembers 30SFr. Showers, sheets, and huge breakfast included. Laundry 8SFr. Reserve a few days in advance.
Marthahaus, Zähringerstr. 36 (tel. 251 45 50). Go left out of the station, cross the river and take the 2nd right after the quay. Convenient but busy. Reception open 24hr. Dorms 30SFr. Singles 60SFr. Doubles 90SFr.
Foyer Hottingen, Hottingerstr. 31 (tel. 261 93 15). Take tram #3 from Bahnhofplatz (direction "Albisrieden"): Hottingerplatz. Sparkling, with plants and possessed children. Women, families, and married couples only. Curfew midnight. Dorms 20SFr. Singles 50SFr. Doubles 80SFr. Showers 1SFr. Breakfast included.

ZÜRICH

Glockenhof, Sihlstr. 33 (tel. 221 36 73), next to the expensive Hotel Glockenhof (10min. from station). Men only. Summer only. Reception open Mon.-Fri. 8:15am-7:45pm, Sat. 9:45am-3:45pm, Sun. 8:30am-1pm. Curfew 11pm. Singles 40SFr.

Hotel Regina, Hohlstr. 18 (tel. 242 65 50). Take tram #3 (direction "Albirsrieden") or 14 (direction "Triemli"): Kaserne, walk straight to Zeughausstr., turn right, follow to Hohlstr. Friendly owner. Reception open 24 hr. Renovated singles 85SFr, doubles 110SFr.

Camping: Camping Seebucht, Seestr. 559 (tel. 482 16 12). Distant but by the lake. Take the train to Wollishofen and walk the remaining 15min. Or take bus #161 or 165 from Bürkliplatz, on the lake at the end of Bahnhofstr., to **Grenzsteig.** 5SFr/person, 8SFr/tent. Open early May-late Sept.

FOOD

The cheapest eats in Zürich are at the *Wurstli* stands (sausage and bread for 3-4SFr) and fresh veggie and fruit stalls peppering the streets. Pick up the free brochure *Preiswert Essen in Zürich* at the tourist office.

Mensa der Universität Zürich, Rämistr. 71. Take tram #6 from Bahnhofplatz to ETH Zentrum, or walk. To return to town, take the tram on Tannenstr. Stunningly edible grub—even students who feed here daily approve. Hot dishes 5.50-6.50SFr with ISIC, salads 6.90SFr. Open Mon.-Fri. 11am-1:30pm and 5-7:30pm. **Mensa Polyterrasse,** down the street at #101, has same food and prices. Open Mon.-Fri. 11:15am-1:30pm and 5:30-7:30pm, Sat. and mid-July to mid-Sept. lunch only.

Vier Linden, Gemeindestr. 48, near the Foyer Hottingen Hotel, just above Hottingerplatz. Tasty vegetarian food. Meal-sized salads 8-13.50SFr. *Menus* 17-19SFr. Open Mon.-Fri. 6am-9pm. **Bakery** and **health food store** across the street open Mon.-Fri. 7am-12:30pm and 2-6:30pm, Sat. 7am-4pm.

Cafeteria Freischütz, Freischützgasse 1, at Militärstr., near the main post office. Massive Swiss dishes for 10-14SFr. Open daily 9am-7pm.

SIGHTS AND ENTERTAINMENT

The stately and colorful **Bahnhofstrasse** runs from the station to the Zürichsee. East of the Bahnhofstrasse rises the **Fraumünster,** a Chagall-decorated wonder (open Mon.-Sat. 9am-noon and 2-6pm; March-April and Oct. daily 10am-noon and 2-5pm; Nov.-Feb. daily 10am-noon and 2-4pm), matched only by the Giacometti stained glass of the **Grossmünster** across the river in the *Altstadt.* (Open Mon.-Fri. 9am-6pm, Sat. 9am-5pm, Sun. after services-6pm; Oct.-March Mon.-Sat. 10am-4pm, Sun. after services-6pm.) The **Schweizerische Landesmuseum** (Swiss National Museum) is behind the train station. (Open Tues.-Sun. 10am-5pm; free.) The **Kunsthaus,** Heimplatz 1, is famed for large Impressionist and Expressionist collections. (Open Tues.-Thurs. 10am-9pm, Fri.-Sun. 10am-5pm. 4SFr, students 3SFr.) Boat trips on the **Zürichsee** range from short jaunts to isolated villages (1½hr., 8.40SFr), to a "grand tour" (4hr., 25.20SFr, Eurail valid; leaves from Bürkliplatz).

Zürich's nightlife revolves around Niederdorfstr., Münstergasse, and Limmatquai. Enjoy myriad street performers or follow the mobs to countless cabarets and clubs. Everyone likes **Casa Bar,** Münstergasse 30, a teeny, pricey pub with live jazz. (Open daily 7pm-2am.) **Bar Pigalle,** just uphill from Hirschenplatz, attracts a young, environmentally aware crowd. (Open Mon.-Sat. until 2am.) An arty, mostly gay coterie hangs out at the **Bar Odeon,** Limmatquai 2, near the Quaibrücke. Thornton Wilder and Lenin used to get sloshed here.

■ Near Zürich

Once-placid **Zug,** just south of Zürich, is losing its battle with big business, but the *Altstadt* on the **Zugersee,** a veritable cornucopia of cathedrals and cobblestone, retains its old-world charm. Hop bus #11 from the station to "Stadion" for the cozy **Jugendherberge (HI),** Allmendstr. (tel. (042) 21 53 54; reception open 7-8:30am and 5-10pm; 25SFr, nonmembers 32SFr; wheelchair accessible), or camp on the lake at **Innere Lorzenallmend** (tel. (041) 31 50 35; 5SFr/person, 5SFr/ tent).

■■■ LUCERNE (LUZERN)

While tourism is peripheral to Zürich, Bern, and Geneva, for Lucerne it stands front and center. A steady stream of modern visitors continues to gaze in appreciation at the medieval turrets, 16th-century wall paintings, and myriad museums resting under the watchful gaze of the Lion of Lucerne.

The crowded corridors of old Lucerne blaze with technicolor paintings and gleeful carvings; the **Hirschenplatz** basks in the glow of its polychrome façades. Equally explosive are the decorative wooden bridges straddling the Reuss River: on August 17, 1993, a barge hit the **Kapellbrücke,** setting off a spectacular fire; Kaspar Meglinger's *Totentanz* (Dance of Death) paintings on the **Spreuerbrücke** lend it an eerie cast. The **Towers of Lucerne** on Museggstr. invite the reenactment of a medieval siege. (Open daily 8am-7pm.)

Lucerne's **Verkehrshaus der Schweiz** (Transport Museum), Lidostr. 5, features a neck-wrenching 360° "Swissorama" panorama. (Open daily 9am-6pm. 15SFr, students 11SFr.) The **Richard Wagner Museum,** Wagnerweg 27, allows a peek at original scores, instruments, and letters. (Take bus #6 or 8 to "Wartegg," or walk along the lake from the train station. Open Tues.-Sun. 10am-noon and 2-5pm; Oct.-April. Tues., Thurs., and Sat.-Sun. 10am-noon and 2-5pm. 4SFr, students 2SFr.) The **Picasso Museum,** Am Rhyn Haus, Furrengasse 21, shelters a collection of Picasso's later works, most of them lithographs. (Open daily 10am-6pm; Nov.-March Fri.-Sun. 11am-noon and 2-5pm. 5SFr, students 3SFr.)

Boat trips from the train station cruise the Vierwaldstättersee; get a list of good destinations from the tourist office (13-34SFr, Eurail and Swisspass free). **Mt. Titlis** (69SFr, with Swisspass 49SFr, with Eurail 52.80SFr) and the **Trübsee** glacier (29SFr, with Swisspass 22SFr, with Eurail 24.60SFr), are both easy cable car rides from the nearby village of Engelberg.

Accommodations, Food, and Practical Information

Hop on bus #18 to "Goplismoos" for the friendly **Jugendherberge Am Rotsee (HI),** Sedelstr. 12 (tel. (041) 36 88 00). After 7:30pm, take bus #1 to "Schlossberg" and walk 15 minutes down Friedentalstr. (Reception open 4-10pm. Lockout 9:30am-4pm. Curfew 11:30pm. 21SFr, nonmembers 28SFr. Showers and breakfast included. Laundry 9SFr. Reserve in advance in summer.) The centrally located **Touristen Hotel Luzern,** St. Karliquai 12 (tel. (041) 51 24 74), is by the river. From the station, walk left on Bahnhofstr., continue left on Reuss-steg and cross the Spreuerbrücke; turn left on St. Karliquai. (8-bed room 33SFr/person, 10% discount with ISIC.) **Hotel Schlussel,** Franziskanerplatz 12 (tel. (041) 23 10 61), is comfy and newly renovated. From Pilatusplatz, turn right on Hirschengraben to Rütling, then left to the hotel. (Reception open 8am-6pm. Doubles 86-100SFr, with shower 130-140SFr. Breakfast included.) **Camping Lido,** Lidostr. 8 (tel. (041) 31 21 46), is a ½-hour hike from the station, on the Lido beach. Cross the Seebrücke and turn right along the quay, or take bus #2 (direction "Verkehrshaus"). Swimming, tennis, and mini-golf are nearby. (Reception open 8am-6pm. 6SFr/person, 3SFr/tent. Dorms 12SFr. Open April-Oct.)

Lucerne's **Rathausquai** blooms daily with outdoor markets. There's a **Migros** supermarket at Hertensteinstr. 44. (Open Mon.-Wed. and Fri.-Sat. 8am-6:30pm, Thurs. 8am-9pm.) Next door is a **Migros restaurant,** the cheapest in town. (Open Mon.-Sat. 6:30am-6:30pm.) Enjoy Swiss specialties in Swiss atmosphere at **Restaurant Walliser Spycher Le Mazot,** Eisegasse 15, in the heart of the *Altstadt*. (Entrees 10-23SFr. Open Mon.-Fri. 4pm-12:30am, Sat. 11:15am-12:30am.) Lucerne's nightlife centers around the *Altstadt*. The popular riverfront **Mr. Pickwick Pub** dishes out fish 'n' chips. (Open Mon.-Sat. 11am-12:30am, Sun. 4pm-12:30am.)

The **tourist office,** Frankenstr. 1 (tel. (041) 51 71 71), 1 block from the river on the Zentralstr., overflows with maps and guides. (Open Mon.-Fri. 8:30am-6pm, Sat. 9am-1pm; Nov.-March Mon.-Fri. 8:30am-noon and 2-6pm, Sat. 9am-noon and 2-5pm.) The **post office** is across from the station at Bahnhofstr., 6000 Luzern 1. (Open Mon.-Fri. 7:30am-6:30pm, Sat. 9:30-11am.) The station itself (schedule info tel. (041) 21 33 11) houses **phones** (downstairs; open Mon.-Fri. 7:30am-8pm, Sat. 8am-4pm); **currency exchange** (open Mon.-Fri. 7am-8:45pm, Sat.-Sun. 7:30am-7:30pm; Nov.-April Mon.-Sat. 7:30am-7:30pm, Sun. 8am-6pm); **lockers** (2-5SFr); and **bicycle rental** (19SFr).

■■■ BASEL (BÂLE)

The city of Basel lies on the Rhine River, at the border of both France and Germany. Its churches, fountains, gateways, and its ageless Gothic quarter are testimony to its fecund past, while the chemical-pharmaceutical giants Roche, Sandoz, and Ciba-Geigy, as well as textile, metal, and machine factories rule the industrial sector and jolt the visitor into the present. Above its visible disparities, Basel is a city of culture; where Erasmus once lived, Switzerland's first university still stands. The Humanists have been printing books here since the 15th century, and Basel's 27 museums hold some of the best art, antique, historical, and botanical collections in the world.

The gargantuan **Kunstmuseum,** St. Albino-Graben 16, flaunts masterpieces including van Gogh's *Daubigney's Garden* and Holbein's *Erasmus*. Entire rooms full of works by Picasso, Dalí, and Braque complement masterpieces by Klee, Kandinsky, and Mondrian, many of them bought by a far-sighted museum director when Hitler's Germany deemed them "decadent." (Open Tues.-Sun. 10am-5pm. 6SFr, students 4SFr, Sun. free.) Equally explosive, the **Museum of Contemporary Art,** St. Alban-Rheinweg 60 (a painting's throw from the youth hostel), touches on all the major movements of the last 2 decades; rotating exhibits featuring up-and-coming artists are skillfully chosen. (5SFr, students 3SFr.) The **Cartoon and Caricature Collection,** St. Alban-Vorstadt 9, could make any sourpuss chuckle. (Open Wed. 4-6pm, Sat. 3-5:30pm, Sun. 10am-4pm. 5SFr, students 2.50SFr.)

The symbol of the city, Basel's **Münster,** hulks 500m south of the tourist office. Enclosed within its 11th-century walls are countless sculptures and carvings, as well as Erasmus's bones. (Open Mon.-Fri. 10am-6pm, Sat. 10am-noon and 2-5pm, Sun. 1-5pm; mid-Oct. to Easter Mon.-Sat. 10am-noon and 2-4pm, Sun. 2-4pm.) Impressively crimson, the **Rathaus** glares on Marktplatz; **Totengässlein** leads from Marktplatz past rich patrician homes and guildhouses to the 13th-century **Peterskirche.**

Accommodations, Food, and Practical Information The **tourist office** *(Verkehrsbüro),* Blumenrain 2 (tel. (061) 261 50 50), hands out info on accommodations and events. They have an excellent deal: if you're under 26, you can stay in a hotel for the price of your age times the rating of the hotel (i.e., a 19-yr.-old can stay in a 3-star hotel for 3x19=57SFr/night), including shower but not breakfast. (Office open Mon.-Fri. 8am-noon and 1-5pm.) From the train station, take tram #1 to the Schifflände stop; the office is on the river near the bridge. Basel's genial **Jugendherberge (HI),** St. Alban-Kirchrain 10 (tel. (061) 272 05 72), is a 10- to 15-minute walk from the station down Aeschengraben, then St. Alban Anlage; or take tram #1 to Aeschenplatz, then tram #3 2 stops. (Reception open 3pm-1am; Oct.-May 4pm-midnight. Checkout 7-10am; Oct.-May 7:30-10am. Lockout 10am-4pm. Curfew 1am. 23SFr. Lockers available. Laundry 4SFr.) The nearest **camping** is **Waldhort** (tel. (061) 711 64 29); take tram #1 to Aeschenpl., then tram #11 to Landhof. (Reception open daily 8am-noon and 2:30-10pm. 5SFr/person, 4SFr/tent. Open March-Oct.) Basel's 2 **Migros** markets at Clarapl. and Sternengasse 17 as always, are the cheapest eats in town. (Open Mon.-Fri. 8am-6:30pm, Sat. 7:30am-5pm.) A morning **market** vends produce daily in Marktplatz.

BERNE AND THE BERNER OBERLAND

Pristine, savage, and comfortably remote, the great hulking peaks and isolated lodges in this area are the very picture of Swiss leisure.

■■■ BERNE (BERN)

The home of Toblerone and Swiss cheese, Berne has been Switzerland's capital since 1848. Founded by the Duke of Zähringen in 1191, Berne's mascot and name-sake is the cuddly, lovable bear; spend a few days here and the tourist industry will burn that fact indelibly into your brain. Bears aside, it's an attractive city; burned to the ground in 1405, Berne was rebuilt of sandstone and mahogany, and its cobble-stone streets wrap around splashily painted fountains and long shopping arcades.

PRACTICAL INFORMATION

Tourist Office: Verkehrsbüro, on the ground floor of the train station complex (tel. 22 76 76). Pick up a map and *This Week in Berne*. Room reservations (3SFr); when closed, check the info board. Open daily 9am-8:30pm; Oct.-May Mon.-Sat. 9am-6:30pm, Sun. 10am-5pm.

Budget Travel: SSR, at Rathausgasse 64 (tel. 21 07 22). Bus #12: "Rathaus". BIJ tickets and other student discounts. Open Mon.-Wed. and Fri. 10am-6pm, Thurs. 10am-8pm.

Embassies: U.S., Jubiläumsstr. 93 (tel. 43 70 11). Open Mon.-Fri. 9:30am-noon and 2:30-4pm. **Canada,** consulate at Belpstr. 11 (tel. 25 22 61). Open Mon., Wed., and Fri. 8am-12:30pm and 1-4pm, Tues. and Thurs. 1-4pm. **U.K.,** Thunstr. 50 (tel. 44 50 21). Open Mon.-Fri. 9am-12:30pm and 2-5pm. **Ireland,** Eigstr. 71 (tel. 46 23 53). **Australia,** Alpenstr. 29 (tel. 43 01 43). Open Mon.-Fri. 8am-12:30pm and 1:30-5pm. Citizens of **New Zealand** should consult the consulate in Geneva.

Currency Exchange: Downstairs in the train station. Rates comparable to major banks. Open daily 6:10am-10pm; Jan.-March 6:10am-9pm.

American Express: Bubenbergpl.11 (tel. 22 94 01), by the bus area across Bahnhofpl. from the station. Mail held. All banking services. Open Mon.-Fri. 8:30am-5:30pm, Sat. 9am-noon. 24-hr. toll-free refund service (tel. (046) 05 01 00).

Post Office: Schanzenpost 1, behind the train station. **Poste Restante.** Open Mon.-Fri. 6am-11pm, Sat. 6am-9pm, Sun. 10am-noon and 4-11pm.

Telephones: At the train station. Open Mon.-Sat. 6:30am-10:30pm, Sun. 7am-10:30pm. **City Code:** 031.

Trains: Berne Centrale station (tel. 21 11 11). To: Geneva (47SFr), Lucerne (31SFr).

Public Transportation: For all **SVB** buses and trams (tel. 22 14 44), buy a **Touristen-Karte** (4SFr/day, 6SFr/2 days) from the station (downstairs) or at Bubenbergplatz 5. **Nightbuses** leave station at 12:35am and 1:40am.

Bike Rental: At the train station, 19SFr/day with ID deposit. Open daily 6:10am-9:50pm.

Hitchhiking: Those going to Geneva and Lausanne take bus #11 to "Brückfeld". Those heading for Interlaken and Lucerne were last seen taking tram #5 to "Ostring". Those using the *Autobahn* north take bus #20 to "Wyler".

Pharmacy: In the train station; open 6:30am-8pm.

Emergencies: Police: tel. 117. **Ambulance:** tel. 144. **Doctor's night service:** tel. 22 92 11.

ACCOMMODATIONS AND CAMPING

The outlook is bleak. Unless you stay at the youth hostel, you'll pay at least 40SFr for a single. Guesthouses a few km outside the city offer rooms for less (30-40SFr), and the tourist office helps find accommodations.

Jugendhaus (HI), Weihergasse 4 (tel. 22 63 16). From Bahnhofplatz, walk straight to Christoffergasse until it ends, then continue around the side of the Parliament. Go through the gate marked "1875" and turn left onto the Bundesstr. Take the *Drahtseilbahn* (funicular) down for 1SFr, or walk down the path to the left and turn left onto Weihergasse. Don't make this trip at night; a shady culture thrives near the *Drahtseilbahn*. Spanking new, the hostel is among the best in Switzerland. Reception open 7-9:30am, 5-6pm, 6:30-10:45pm, and 11:15pm-midnight. 16SFr, nonmembers 23SFr. Breakfast 6SFr. Lunch or dinner 10SFr. Laundry 5SFr.

Hotel Goldener Schlüssel, Rathausgasse 72 (tel. 311 02 16; fax 311 56 88). Streetcar #9 or 12: "Zytglogge". Newly renovated hotel, popular restaurant-café downstairs, in the center of town. Reception open until 11pm. Single 60SFr, with shower 82SFr. Doubles 96SFr, with shower 120SFr. Breakfast included.

Camping: Camping Eichholz, Strandweg 49 (tel. 961 26 02). Take tram #9 to terminus Wabern. 5SFr/person, 4SFr/tent. Also rooms with 2 beds, 14SFr plus 5SFr/person. Reserve ahead. Open May-Sept.

FOOD

Shop at markets to beat the pricey restaurants. A daily **fruit market** blossoms at Bärenplatz (open 7am-6pm), Tuesday and Saturday markets are at Bundesplatz and Thursdays at Waisenhausplatz. **Migros** and **Ryfflihof** supermarkets and cafeterias are near the train station, and the **Migros Restaurant** at Zeughausgasse 31, off Bärenplatz, offers well-prepared meals at reasonable prices. (Open Mon.-Wed. and Fri. 8:30am-7:30pm, Thurs. 8:30am-9:30pm, Sat. 8am-4pm.) The **Mensa der Universität,** Gesellschaftstr. 2, past Hochschulstr., northwest of the station and off Sidlerstr. (bus #1: "Universität"), serves better than average institutional fare, and the students are friendly. *(Menus* 7-10SFr. Kitchen open Mon.-Thurs. 11:30am-1:45pm and 5:45-7:30pm, Fri. 11:30am-1:45pm. Cafeteria open Mon.-Thurs. 7:30am-8:30pm, Fri. 7:30am-5pm. Open mid-Sept. to mid-July.) **Restaurant Ratskeller,** Gerechtigkeitsgasse 81, has a great selection of wines, and offers a modern version of traditional Bernese fare. The outside seating area provides a view of *Altstadt* street life. (Open daily 10am-11:30pm.)

SIGHTS AND ENTERTAINMENT

Everything is centered around the *Altstadt;* Bern's compactness is one its best characteristics. Beginning in front of the station at the **Church of the Holy Ghost,** built in 1726 and filled with pastels (open Mon.-Sat. 11am-3pm), the cobblestone route leads past the **Zytglogge** (clock tower), built in the 13th century, now famous for its astronomical clock and its moving figures. Join the crowd of craned necks 4 minutes before each hour. (Guided interior tours May-Oct. at 4:30pm. Tickets 3SFr at tourist office.) Next is **Albert Einstein's house,** Kramgasse 49, where from 1903 to 1905 he developed the special theory of relativity. (Open Feb.-Nov. Tues.-Fri. 10am-5pm, Sat. 10am-4pm. 3SFr.) An alley a few blocks down Münstergasslein leads to the imposing Gothic **Münster,** whose portal depicts the Last Judgment with imagination-defying horrors of Hell. Climb the tower for a fantastic view of Berne's mahogany roofs. (Church open Mon.-Sat. 10am-noon and 2-5pm, Sun. 11am-noon and 2-5pm; Nov.-Easter Tues.-Fri. 10am-noon and 2-4pm, Sat. 10am-noon and 2-5pm, Sun. 11am-noon and 2-5pm. Tower closes 30min. before church; 3SFr.) Cross the Kirchenfeldbrücke to the 500-year-old **Bärengraben** (bear pits), where the mascots of Bern pad back and forth to munch on the carrots you can throw them. (Open daily 7am-6pm; Oct.-March 8:30am-4pm.) Conclude your tour at the **Parliamentsgebäude** with an introduction to Switzerland's political system. (Free 45-min. tours every hr. 9am-noon and 2-4pm. When in session, only galleries open.)

Several of Berne's many outstanding museums cluster together at **Helvetiaplatz** across the Kirchenfeldbrücke (take tram #3 or 5). The **Kunsthalle,** Helvetiapl. 1, features the contemporary work of one or two starving young artists at a time. (Open Tues. 10am-9pm, Wed.-Sun. 10am-5pm. 4SFr, students 2SFr.) On the other side of town, near the Lorrainebrücke, the **Kunstmuseum,** Hodlerstr. 8-12, masses over

2500 of Paul Klee's works, plus tons of Hodler and other Swiss artists. (Open Tues. 10am-9pm, Wed.-Sun. 10am-5pm. 4SFr, students 3SFr.) The **Swiss Alpine Museum,** Helvetiapl. 4, is famed for its topological models. Yodel-ay-hee-hoo. (Open Feb.-Nov. Tues.-Fri. 10am-5pm, Sat. 10am-4pm. 3SFr.)

To explore Berne's underground music scene, head to the graffiti-covered warehouse informally known as **Reithalle.** (Alternative bands, alternative dress.) From the corner of Bollweik and Holderstr. (near the Lorrainebrücke), walk through the parking lot, under the train tracks, and into the building in front on the left. Shows are on Fridays and Saturdays, often on Thursdays, and occasionally on other nights. Have all the fun with none of the angst at **Bar Big Ben,** Zeughausgasse 12, "where nice people meet." Jazz lovers should plan their journeys for early May, when Berne's **International Jazz Fest** blows into town (contact the tourist office for info).

■ Near Berne: Fribourg

Fribourg, Berne's sister city to the southwest, teeters on the border between French and German Switzerland. For centuries the home and refuge of Swiss-German Catholicism, Fribourg today cherishes the richest collection of medieval religious art in the country. Upon arrival, head to the **tourist office,** 1, Square des Places (tel. (037) 81 31 75 or 81 31 76), 5 minutes from the train station. Walk left down av. de la Gare and continue down rue de Romont, then turn right at Georges Python. (Open Mon.-Fri. 8am-noon and 2-6pm, Sat. 9am-noon.) If you turn left at Georges Python, you'll find the new **Auberge de Jeunesse,** 2, rue de l'Hôpital (tel. (037) 23 19 16). (Reception open Mon.-Fri. 7:30-9:30am and 5-10pm, Sat.-Sun. 7:30-9:30am and 6-10pm. Curfew 11pm. 22SFr, nonmembers 29SFr. Laundry, lockers, and kitchen facilities. Open Dec. to mid-Jan. and Feb.-Oct. Reserve in advance.)

■■■ INTERLAKEN

Less than an hour by train from Bern, Interlaken is a starting point for treks into the surrounding mountains and a hub for trains throughout Switzerland. The town lies between the Brienzersee and the Thunersee and offers convenient access to both lakes; it functions better as a way station than as a destination.

Practical Information and Accommodations Any train you want probably starts and stops at the **Ostbahnhof** (tel. (036) 22 30 24). The **Westbahnhof** (tel. (036) 22 35 25) stands in the center of town bordering the Thunersee. Each station features a minute **tourist office** that changes currency at good rates. (Open Mon.-Sat. 7:30am-7pm, Sun. 7:30am-noon and 1:30-6:30pm; Oct.-May Mon.-Sat. 7:30am-noon and 1:30-6pm, Sun. 8am-noon and 2-6pm.) Computers on the platform at either station babble tourist info in English, German, and French. The main **tourist office,** Höheweg 37 (tel. (036) 22 21 21), in the Hotel Metropol near Westbahnhof, finds rooms and provides maps and schedules for free. Ask for their list of rooms in private homes if you'll be staying at least 3 days. (20-30SFr/person. Open Mon.-Fri. 8am-noon and 2-6:30pm, Sat. 8am-noon and 2-5pm, Sun. 5-7pm; Sept.-June Mon.-Fri. 8am-noon and 2-6pm, Sat. 8am-noon.) The **post office,** Marktgasse 1, 3800 Interlaken, is 5 minutes from Westbahnhof (open Mon.-Sat. 7am-9:30pm, Sun. 9am-9:30pm; Oct.-April Mon.-Sat. 7am-9:30pm, Sun. 9am-1pm and 5-8:45pm) and also has **telephones. Bicycles** can be rented at the train stations (19SFr/½-day).

Although Interlaken gushes hotels, very few approach affordability. Take bus #5, "Hotel Sonne," or walk 15 minutes from either station to **Balmer's Herberge,** Haupstr. 23 (tel. (036) 22 19 61). From Westbahnhof go left, veer right onto Bahnhofstr., turn right on Centralstr. and follow the signs. Sign in and return at 5pm, when beds are assigned (no reservations). Balmer's draws a primarily American crowd with its summer-camp atmosphere. "Uncle Erich" provides currency exchange, bike rental (single and tandem), discount excursions, nightly movies, CNN, MTV, book exchange, kitchen facilities (1SFr/20min.), laundry (8SFr/load), mini department store (open until 10pm), and a super-friendly staff. Everyone is welcome—if beds are filled, you can crash on a mattress. (Dorms 16SFr. Doubles 52SFr. Triples 63SFr. Quads 84SFr. Breakfast included.) **Jugendherberge Bönigen (HI),** Aarcweg 21 (tel. (036) 22 43 53), is farther from town; take bus #1 to Lütschinbribrück from either station (every 50min.) or walk from Ostbahnhof (left from station for 20min., then follow signs from fork). On the swimmable Brienzersee, the Jugendherberge counters friendly Balmer's fracas with tranquility and humongous bathrooms. (Reception open Feb.-Oct. daily 6-9am and 5-9pm. 17.60SFr. Dinner 9SFr. Laundry 8SFr.) Seven campgrounds grace Interlaken's gates. **Jungfraublick** (tel. (036) 22 44 14) is 5 minutes past Balmer's on Gsteigstr. (7.50SFr/person, off-season 6.30SFr; 4-10SFr/tent. Open April-Oct.) Just across the river from Ostbahnhof is the small, waterside **Sackgut** (tel. (036) 24 44 34; 5.80SFr/person, 5-11SFr/tent; open May-Oct.). The 5 other sites cluster together near the Lombach River in Unterseen. Follow the signs from Seestr. near Westbahnhof.

Food and Entertainment Avoid the expensive restaurants on Höheweg. Instead, try **Tea Room Spatz,** Spielmatte 46, on an island in the Aare River, for delicious, reasonable (11-13SFr) meals. (Open Mon.-Fri. 8:30am-noon and 1:30-6:30pm, Sat. 8:30am-4pm.) Stock up for hikes at the **Migros** supermarket across from Westbahnhof. (Open Mon.-Fri. 8:30am-noon and 1:30-6:30pm, Sat. 8:30am-4pm.)

Höheweg nightlife heats up in tourist season. The party starts at **Buddy's,** Höheweg 33, an Interlaken tradition with the cheapest beer in town. (2.70SFr. Open Sun.-Thurs. 10am-1am, Fri.-Sat. 10am-1:30am; off-season Sun.-Thurs. 10am-12:30am, Fri.-Sat. 10am-1am.) Herds then migrate to Interlaken's oldest disco, **Johnny's Dancing Club,** Höheweg 92, downstairs in the Hotel Carlton. (Sat. cover 3SFr. Drinks from 5.50SFr. Open Dec.-Oct. Tues.-Sun. 9:30pm-2:30am.)

Interlaken's *other* tradition is the summer production of Schiller's *Wilhelm Tell.* Held in a huge amphitheater around the corner from Balmer's, the cast of hundreds includes residents, children, and local horses and cows, which are paraded through the streets before the performance begins. (Shows late June to early July Thurs. 8pm; mid-July to early Sept. Thurs. and Sat. 8pm. Tickets (12-30SFr) from the *Tell-büro,* Bahnhofstr. 5 (tel. (036) 22 37 23); English synopsis 1SFr.)

■■■ BRIENZERSEE AND THUNERSEE

Appreciate the riotous topography of the Berner Oberland with a cruise on one of Interlaken's lakes, the **Brienzersee** (to the east) or the **Thunersee** (to the west). Relaxing and beautiful, the trips are also one of the few inexpensive excursions around (day passes 37SFr, Sept.-June 29SFr; Eurail and Swisspass valid). Steamers cross the lakes approximately every hour between 8am and 6pm; the best cruising strategy is to disembark at whim and reboard a later boat or catch a train or postal bus back to Interlaken. Hiking and biking are also options.

Thunersee The Thunersee cruise takes a half hour to reach the **Beatushöhlen,** prehistoric caves with stalactites, waterfalls, and the ancient cell of the pallid Augustinian monk St. Beatus. (Open April-Oct. daily 9:30am-5pm. 9SFr, students 8SFr.) Across the lake **Spiez Castle** features authentic period rooms, a mesmerizing tower view, a chapel, and a rose garden. (Open April-Oct. Mon. 2-5pm, Tues.-Sun. 10am-5pm. 3SFr, students 2SFr.) Two castles are accessible from the Thun station: **Schloss Thun** and **Schloss Schadau,** which houses the **Swiss Gastronomy Museum.** (Open June-Aug. Tues.-Sun. 10am-5pm; April-May and Sept. to mid-Oct. 1-5pm. 3SFr.) **Schloss Hünegg** at the Hilterfingen landing resounds with luxury, and **Schloss Oberhofen,** purchased in 1925 by an enterprising American lawyer, is 20 minutes from Thun.

Accommodations on the lake are expensive; ask at the tourist offices for *Zimmer Frei* options. **Spiez** and **Thun,** the Thunersee's metropolises, have offices located adjacent to the train stations. (Spiez tel. (033) 54 21 38; open Mon.-Fri. 8am-noon and 1:30 6:30pm, Sat. 8am-noon; June and Sept. Mon.-Fri. 8am-noon and 2-6pm, Sat. 8am-noon; Oct.-May Mon.-Fri. 8am-noon and 2-5pm. Thun tel. (033) 22 23 40; open Mon.-Fri. 9am-noon and 2-5pm, Sat. 9am-noon.) The lone **Jugendherberge (HI)** on the lake is in **Faulensee,** Quellenhofweg 66 (tel. (033) 54 19 88). Most steamers stop at the hostel; check the itinerary at the landing just to be sure. (Reception open March-Dec. 7-9am and 5-10pm. Lockout 9am-5pm. Members only. 10.90SFr. Breakfast 4SFr. Lunch 7SFr. Dinner 8SFr. Kitchen facilities. Reservations encouraged.) **Campgrounds** are countless; try **Panorama Rossen** (tel. (033) 54 43 77) in Aeschi (take the bus to Mustermattli from Spiez; 5.70SFr/person, 5-7SFr/tent; open May-Oct.) or **Bettlereiche** (tel. (033) 36 40 67) in Gwatt near Thun (15min. along the lake to the right of the station; 8SFr/person, 6-10SFr/tent).

Brienzersee The Brienzersee is the more rugged and less developed of the lakes. **Brienz,** its lone populous village, makes for a serene daytrip from Interlaken (1¼hr. by boat, 20min. by train). The **Ballenberg Swiss Open-Air Museum,** a 50-hectare park, displays examples of traditional rural dwellings from every region of Switzerland, with Swiss artisans busily at work. The park is about an hour's walk from the train station, but an hourly bus (round-trip 5.60SFr) connects the two. (Open April 15-Oct. 25 daily 10am-5pm. 12SFr.) The **tourist office** (tel. (036) 51 32 42) across from the train station gives tips for hikers of all levels. (Open Mon.-Fri. 8am-7pm, Sat. 8am-6pm; Sept.-June Mon.-Fri. 8am-noon and 2-6pm, Sat. 8am-noon.) The train station rents **bicycles.** From the tourist office, cross the tracks, turn left and hug the lake for 15 minutes to the rustic **Brienz Jugendherberge (HI),** Strandweg 10 (tel. (036) 51 11 52), which rents hiking boots (5SFr) and bikes (10SFr/day, 15SFr/2 days) to its guests. (Reception open March-Nov.15 8-9am, 5-6pm, and 7-9pm. 20SFr, nonmembers 25SFr. Breakfast 6SFr. Dinner 9SFr. Kitchen facilities.) Along the same stretch sprawl 2 campgrounds: **Camping Seegärtli** (tel. (036) 51 13 51; 6SFr/person, 3-5SFr/tent; open June-Sept.) and **Camping Aaregg** (tel. (036) 51 18 43; 4.80SFr/person, 6SFr/tent; open April-Oct.).

Giessbach Falls, 10 minutes by steamer from Brienz, typifies the wonder of Nature with 14 frothy cascades. Though a funicular takes you up (3SFr), the hike is an easy 15 minutes—continue on to **Axalp** or **Iseltwald,** a tiny fishing town. Pitch your tent for the night at **Camping du Lac** (tel. (036) 45 11 48; 5.90SFr/person, 6-8SFr/tent; open May-Sept.).

■■■ JUNGFRAU REGION

Spectacular mountain views, wildflower meadows, roaring waterfalls, and unspoiled forests await in the Lauterbrünnen and Grindelwald valleys above Interlaken. Both become busier and considerably more expensive during ski season; on the bright side, they teem with jobs for dishwashers, bartenders, and chalet staff. Rail costs are scandalously steep, and Eurail gets no discount on private lines to Grindelwald, Lauterbrünnen, and beyond. A Swisspass will get you either 25% or 100% off the price. The 15-day **Berner Oberland Regional Pass** (125SFr, 100SFr with Swisspass or Half-Fare Card) can be a bargain with 5 free days and 10 ½-priced days.

Grindelwald The Grindelwald valley is the more touristy of the two; the town of Grindelwald is a skier and climber's nirvana. The **tourist office** (*Verkehrsbüro*; tel. (036) 53 12 12), up the main street to the right in the Sportzentrum, has hiking and skiing maps and can find you rooms in private homes. (Open Mon.-Fri. 8am-noon and 2-6pm, Sat. until 5pm; Oct.-June same except Sat. until noon.) Ride Europe's longest chairlift to the **First** mountain for toe-curling scenery. (25SFr, round-trip 39SFr, guests of Balmer's Herberge 20SFr. Regional Pass valid.) Trips to the **Männlichen** mountain snake up from the **Grund** station (23SFr, round-trip 39SFr); the summit affords a glorious glance at the **Eiger,** the **Mönch,** and **Jungfrau.**

Budget travelers strike it rich in Grindelwald. The **Jugendherberge Die Weid (HI)** (tel. (036) 53 10 09) is a 20-minute climb up Terrassenweg (take the right fork from the train station and turn left at the top), in an old timbered house with a transporting view. Come early and write your name on the list, then check in 5-6pm or 7:30-8:30pm. Some of the small rooms have balconies; the sitting room offers a fireplace and a communal guitar. (Curfew 11pm. Members only. 15SFr. Sheets and showers included. Breakfast 6SFr. Dinner 10SFr.) The rustic **Naturfreundehaus** (tel. (036) 53 13 33) is also on Terrassenweg. (Reception open 8-9am, 5-6pm, and 7-8pm. Curfew 10pm. Students and HI members 21SFr. Showers included. Breakfast 8SFr. Dinner 15SFr. Kitchen facilities. Laundry 7SFr. Sheets 2SFr.) One block to the right and 50m around the corner, **Lehmann's Herberge** (tel. (036) 53 31 41) offers bright wooden rooms to fatigued hikers (25-35SFr; breakfast included). Several hotels in town have dorms; ask the tourist office for a list. Next to the main train station is an info board littered with notices for private rooms. Of Grindelwald's 4 **campgrounds,** the closest is **Gletscherdorf** (tel. (036) 53 14 29), a small site endowed with clean facilities and phenomenal photo opportunities of the mountains. From the station, turn right; take the 1st right after the tourist office, then the 3rd left. (5SFr/person, 4-8SFr/tent.) Another option is **Camping Eigernordwand** (tel. (036) 53 12 42), across the river and to the left of the **Grund** station (5-6SFr/person, 4SFr/tent). The budget-minded avoid restaurants and buy provisions at the **Coop** across from the tourist office.

Lauterbrünnen The glacier-cut valleys of the Lauterbrünnen are stark but beautiful, untamed yet serene. Lauterbrünnen town feels small, dwarfed by sheer rock cliffs. The **tourist office** (tel. (036) 55 19 55) is 200m left of the station on the main street. (Open Mon.-Sat. 8am-noon and 2-6pm, Sun. 2-5pm; Oct.-June Mon.-Fri. 8am-noon and 2-6pm, Sat. 9am-noon and 3-6pm.) A delightful farmhouse-turned-hostel, the **Matratzenlager Stocki** (tel. (036) 55 17 54), offers a full kitchen redolent with spices and a mellow atmosphere. Leave the train station from the back, descend the steps, cross the river, turn right, and walk 200m. The sign on the house reads "Massenlager." (10SFr. Open Jan.-Oct.) **Camping Schützenbach** (tel. (036) 55 12 68), on the Panorama walkway to the falls, has showers and laundry and kitchen facilities. (6.50SFr/person, 5-8SFr/tent, dorms 13-15SFr.) Follow the signs toward Trümmelbach from the station (15min.). **Camping Jungfrau** (tel. (036) 55 20 10), up the main street from the station toward the large waterfall, provides cheap beds, kitchens, showers, lounges, and a snack bar. (6SFr/person, 2-7SFr/tent, dorms 13-15SFr.) Lauterbrünnen's **Coop** roosts between the train station and tourist office.

The fabulous **Trümmelbach Falls,** 10 consecutive glacier-bed chutes, generate mighty winds and a roaring din inside their mountain home. Explore via tunnels, footbridges, and underground funiculars. (Open April-Nov. 8:30am-5:30pm. 8SFr.) Though you can nab a postal bus (2SFr), the ½-hour hike is well-marked and simple. Cable cars leave from **Stechelberg** (45min. from the falls) to Gimmelwald (6.20SFr), to Mürren (11.80SFr), to Birg (21SFr) and to the top of the **Schilthorn** (30.50SFr), the mountain made famous in the Bond flick *In Her Majesty's Secret Service*. **Mürren,** a car-free skiing and sport resort hub, coordinates this area; ask at the **tourist office** (tel. (036) 55 16 16) in the Sports Center (5min. left of the Lauterbrünnen terminus, 10min. right of the Gimmelwald one) for hiking trails and skiing prices. (Open Mon.-Wed. and Fri. 9am-noon and 2-6pm, Thurs. 9am-noon and 2-8pm, Sat.-Sun. 2-6pm.) The single hostel in the valley rewards those who trek to **Gimmelwald** on the steep Stechelberg trail; the **Mountain Hostel** (tel. (036) 55 17 04) is rustic, inexpensive, and friendly. *Don't arrive without food*—there are cooking facilities, but no restaurants, in this microscopic burg (7SFr, showers 1SFr).

The Jungfraujoch The most arresting ascent in this area—or in all of Switzerland—is up the **Jungfraujoch** (3454m). The **Jungfrau** itself is almost always inaccessible. Trains start at Interlaken's Ostbahnhof and travel to either Grindelwald or Lauterbrünnen, continuing to **Kleine Scheidegg** and finally to the peak itself, "the top of Europe." The entire trip costs a dizzying 140SFr. If you take the 6:34am train from Interlaken Ost, the 7:05 from Lauterbrünnen or the 7:18am from Grindelwald, the fare is reduced to 97SFr. The early bargain can only be bought round-trip. (Eurail not valid; Swisspass 25% off.) The rail is chiseled out of solid mountain and penetrates the Eiger and Mönch. Included in the price are visits to the **Ice Palace** (a maze cut into the ice) and the **Sphinx** scientific station. Avoid going on a cloudy day—call (036) 55 10 22 for a weather forecast. Even in mid-summer, the summit is frigid and the elevator line to the Sphinx is often an hour long; bring winter clothing, sunglasses, and food. The hike down takes about 4½ hours. At Kleine Scheidegg, you can sleep in a dorm at the **Restaurant Grindelwaldblick** (tel. (036) 53 30 43; dorms 30SFr; in winter 33SFr; breakfast included).

■ Skiing and Hiking

Overland hiking is the way the Alps were meant to be done. Free maps of the region are available from even the smallest tourist offices; hiking trails are also clearly marked by bright yellow signs indicating the trail time—which may or may not be accurate—to reach nearby destinations. Hikers should pack sunglasses, water, and a sweater; the Alps aren't kind to the unprepared. For more information, write to the **Interlaken Tourist Office,** Höheweg 37, CH-3800 Interlaken.

There are 4 types of **ski passes** for the Oberland; the **Jungfrau Region pass** is the most extensive and expensive (3-day pass 130SFr, 1 week 240SFr, 2 weeks 384SFr). Prices include transportation to lifts. The **Kleine Scheidegg/Männlichen pass** (1-day pass 62SFr, 2 days 114SFr) covers more trails than you'd tire of in a (365SFr) week. **Ski rental** is available throughout the valleys; skis, boots, and poles cost about 44SFr the first day, less each day thereafter. The **ski schools** in Grindelwald (tel. (036) 53 20 21) and Wengen (tel. (036) 55 20 22) supply information on classes. Call (036) 53 26 92 for info on ski conditions at Grindelwald/First, (036) 55 44 33 for Kleine Scheidegg/Männlichen, and (036) 55 26 55 for Mürren/Schilthorn.

Balmer's youth hostel guests have greater options; discount ski packages include transportation to Grindelwald (13SFr), ski rental (30SFr alpine, 15SFr nordic), and expert trail advice as well as ski passes at slashed prices.

LAKE GENEVA AND VALAIS

■■■ GENEVA (GENÈVE)

If peace has a home on this planet, it is Geneva. The city has exemplified Switzerland's policy of neutrality since it joined the Swiss Confederation in 1815. Center of nascent Protestantism and birthplace of both the Red Cross and the League of Nations, Geneva now hosts the European headquarters of the United Nations, a slew of international organizations (one-third of its 375,000 residents are foreigners) and perpetual negotiations between various and sundry belligerents.

ORIENTATION AND PRACTICAL INFORMATION

Genevois sun themselves on the western shore of **Lake Geneva** (Lac Léman), at the southwestern corner of Switzerland. The Rhône River divides the city. Trains arrive at the **Gare Cornavin,** on the *rive droite* (north of the Rhône). To the south, the *rive gauche* hosts the buzzing shopping district and the *vieille ville* around the Cathédrale de St-Pierre.

Tourist Office: In the train station (tel. 738 52 00). Qualified staff books hotel rooms (5SFr fee) and provides information on excursion and local events. Free map and monthly List of Events in French, or get *What's on in Geneva,* published monthly in English. Open daily 8am-8pm; Sept. to mid-June Mon-Sat. 9am-6pm.

CAR (Centre d'Accueil et de Renseignements): Gare Cornavin and rue du Mont Blanc (tel. 731 46 47; off-season tel. 346 79 39), in a car (really!) in front of the train station. Open mid-June to mid-Sept. daily 8am-11pm.

Budget Travel: SSR, 3, rue Vignier (tel. 329 97 33). Open Mon.-Fri. 9am-6pm.

Consulates: U.S., 1-3, av. de la Paix (tel. 738 50 95). **Canada,** 1, chemin du Pré-de-la-Bichette (tel. 733 90 00). **U.K.,** 37-39, rue de Vermont (tel. 733 23 85). **Australia,** 56-58, rue de Moillebeau (tel. 734 62 00). **New Zealand,** 28a, chemin du Petit-Saconnex (tel. 734 95 30).

Currency Exchange: In Gare Cornavin. Good rates, no commission on traveler's checks. Open daily 6am-9:45pm.

American Express: 7, rue du Mont-Blanc, P.O. Box 859, Geneva 1, CH-1208 (tel. 731 76 00). Mail held. All banking services. Open Mon.-Fri. 8:30am-5:30pm, Sat. 9am-noon.

Post Office: Poste Centrale, rue de Mont-Blanc, 1 block from the Gare Cornavin in the huge Hôtel des Postes. Open Mon.-Fri. 7:30am-6pm, Sat. 7:30-11am. Address **Poste Restante** to: Poste Centrale, 1200 Genève 1. Also **Poste de Montbrillant,** 16, rue des Gares, behind the Gare Cornavin. Open Mon.-Fri. 6am-10:45pm, Sat. 6am-9pm, Sun. 9am-noon and 3-10pm.

Telephones: In Gare Cornavin (24 hr.), and in post offices. **City Code:** 022.

Flights: Swissair (tel. 799 31 11). Trains leave Gare Cornavin for **Cointrin Airport** (5:21am-11:18pm every 10min., 4.70SFr, railpasses valid).

Trains: Gare Cornavin (tel. 731 64 50) is the primary station. Zürich (73SFr), Paris (67SFr), Rome (178SFr), Madrid (135SFr), Munich (135SFr), and Vienna (140SFr). Reservations and info office open Mon.-Fri. 8am-7:15pm, Sat. 8am-6:15pm, Sun. 10am-6:15pm. **Gare Genève Eaux-Vives,** on the eastern edge of the city, serves Annecy and Chamonix.

Public Transportation: Get 2 maps—*Le centre* and *Le réseau*—free at **Transport Publics Genevois,** next to the tourist office on the right. Rides of 3 or fewer stops along bus routes marked in dark red cost 1.20SFr, 6-ride pass 11SFr, 1-day pass 8.50SFr, 2-day pass 15SFr, 3-day pass 19SFr. Buses free with Swisspass, but not with Eurail. Buy multifare and day tickets at train station; buy other tickets at automatic vendors located at every stop. Buses run roughly 5:30am-midnight.

Ferries: CGN, quai du Mont-Blanc, at the foot of rue du Mont-Blanc (tel. 722 39 16). To Lausanne (3½hr., 42SFr) and Montreux (5hr., 50SFr). Ferries leave daily at 9:15am and 4:15pm. Eurail valid.

Bike Rental: At the baggage check in Gare Cornavin. From 19SFr/12hr., 16SFr/12hr. ID deposit required. Open daily 7am-7:30pm.

Hitchhiking: Those headed to Germany or northern Switzerland take bus 4/44 to "Jardin Botanique". Those headed to France take bus 4/44 to "Palettes" and switch to line D to "St. Julien." Or call **Telstop** (tel. 731 46 47) or check their list of available rides in front of the CAR information office (0.05Sfr/km).

Bookstore: ELM Video and Books, 5, rue Versonnex, has a fantastic selection of English books at comfortable prices.

Laundromat: Lave Blanc, 29, rue de Monthoux, near corner of rue de Charles Cusin. Open daily 7am-10pm. Wash and dry 8SFr.

Medical Assistance: Hôpital Cantonal, 24, rue Micheli-du-Crest (tel. 346 92 11). Door #3 for outpatient care. Walk-in clinics dot the city; call 320 25 11.

Emergency: Ambulance: tel. 144. **Police:** tel. 117. At 5, rue Pecollat, next to post office.

ACCOMMODATIONS AND CAMPING

Thanks to the large number of hostel and quasi-hostel accommodations, finding a room in Geneva shouldn't be a problem. If the ones below are full, ask the tourist office for the brochure *Youth Accommodation* (**CAR** map lists the same info).

Auberge de Jeunesse (HI), 28-30, rue Rothschild (tel. 732 62 60). Walk 5min. left from the station down rue de Lausanne and then turn right on rue Rothschild. State-of-the-art; huge and well-tended. Flexible 3-night max. stay. Reception open daily 6:30-10am and 5-11pm, but you can dump your baggage anytime. Lockout 10am-5pm. Curfew midnight. 21SFr, nonmembers 28SFr. Showers, breakfast, and sheets included. Dinner 10.50SFr (with seconds). Laundry 7SFr. Kitchen.

Cité Universitaire, 46, av. Miremont (tel. 46 23 55), on the other side of the old town from the station. Take bus #3 from the pl. de 22 Cantons opposite the train station (direction: "Crte de Champel") to the last stop. Respectable rooms in a modern high-rise. Reception open Mon.-Fri. 8am-noon and 2-10pm, Sat. 8am-noon and 6-10pm, Sun. 9-11am and 6-10pm. Curfew 11:30pm. Dorms 14SFr. Singles 33-39SFr. Doubles 48-54SFr. Showers included. Open mid-July to mid-Oct. Cafeteria downstairs: salad bar and *menu* from 8SFr (open daily 7am-10pm). Open mid-July to mid-Oct.

Hôme St-Pierre, 4, cour St-Pierre (tel. 310 37 07), a converted medieval monastery in an unforgettable location in front of the cathedral in the old city. Take bus #5 for 5 stops to pl. Neuve, or walk 15min., crossing the Rhône at the Pont du Mont-Blanc. Women only. Far and away the best place to stay in Geneva. No lockout or curfew. Dorms 16SFr. Rarely-available singles 30-37.50SFr. Doubles 44-59SFr. Showers and lockers included. Breakfast 6SFr. Popular and small, so reserve ahead by phone or mail.

Hôtel St. Gervais, 20 rue des Corps-Saints (tel. 732 45 72). From the train station, cross the street and walk right 3min. down rue Corvain. Slick and luxurious rooms with sink and desk. Reception open 6:30am-midnight. Singles 50-58SFr. Doubles 68-98SFr, shower and breakfast included.

Hôtel de la Cloche, 6, rue de la Cloche (tel. 732 94 81), just off the quai du Mont-Blanc across from Noga Hilton. Attractively wallpapered rooms, many with a balcony and a view of Lake Geneva. Singles 45SFr. Doubles 70SFr. Triples 90SFr. Quads 120SFr. Breakfast 70SFr.

Camping: Pointe-à-la-Bise (tel. 752 12 96). Take bus #9 to Rive stop, then bus E about 7km north to Bise. 6SFr/person, 7SFr/tent. Open April-Sept. Stay on bus E to the last stop, "Hermance" (7km more), for **Camping d'Hermance,** chemin des Glerrets (tel. 751 14 83). 3.50SFr/person, 2SFr/tent. Open April-Sept. Both sites are near the lake.

FOOD

You can eat everything here from sushi to *paella,* but you may need a banker's salary to cover it. Shop at the **Co-op** and **Migros** supermarkets for a picnic in one of the parks; the Migros on rue de Lausanne sits conveniently around the corner from the youth hostel. (Open Mon. 1-6:45pm, Tues.-Fri. 8am-6:45pm, Sat. 8am-5:45pm.) For fresh fruits and cheeses, check out the **market** on rue de Coutance, leading down to the river just above the *ponts de l'Ile* (daily 8am-6pm).

Le Zofage, 6, rue des Voisins, off pl. des Philosophes and rue Leschot. This university restaurant is one of the cheapest spots in town. *Plat du jour* with salad and bread 8SFr. Open Sun.-Fri. 7am-10:30pm.

L'age d'Or, at the foot of rue de Cornavin, near the train station. Small but tasty individual pizzas 7.30-8.80SFr. Salads 3.50-8SFr. Open Mon.-Sat. 7pm-1am.

Restaurant Manora, 4, rue de Cornavin, attached to La Placette department store near the station. A cavernous and popular self-service restaurant featuring a fruit bar (3.50-6SFr), salad bar (3.90-8.90SFr), and hot dishes (5.50-14SFr). Magnificent desserts. Open Mon.-Sat. 7am-9pm, Sun. 9am-9pm.

Les Armures, 1, rue du Puits-St.-Pierre. A small step up in price but a huge leap up in atmosphere. An extension of the expensive Les Armures hotel, around the corner from the Cathédrale de St. Pierre. Eat outside across from the Hôtel de Ville and Maison Tavel. Good-sized fondue 18SFr and an assortment of weekly specials for 16SFr or less. Open Mon.-Fri. 8am-midnight, Sat.-Sun. 11am-midnight.

GENEVA (GENÈVE)

Au Pied de Cochon, 4, pl. du Bourg-de-Four. Across from the Palais de Justice, this authentic *brassiere génévoise* serves *plats du jour* (14.50SFr) and entrees (16-25SFr), with a wine selection. Open daily 10am-midnight.

SIGHTS

Climb the north tower of John Calvin's church, the **Cathédrale de St-Pierre,** for a view of the winding streets and flower-bedecked homes of Geneva's old town. (Cathedral open daily 9am-7pm; Oct. and March-May 9am-noon and 2-6pm; Nov.-Feb. 9am-noon and 2-5pm. Tower open daily 11:30am-noon and 2-5:30pm except during services. 2.50SFr, children 1SFr.) Most of the city's museums are in the old town. The **Musée d'Art et d'Histoire,** 2, rue Charles-Galland, prides itself on its eclecticism; exhibits range from ancient Greek vases to the postwar avant-garde. (Open Tues.-Sun. 10am-5pm. Free.) **Maison Tavel,** 6, rue du Puits-St-Pierre (tel. 28 29 00), next to the *Hôtel de Ville* (town hall), relates the history of Geneva from the 14th through 19th century. (Open Tues.-Sun. 10am-5pm. Free.) The **Petit-Palais,** 2, terrasse St-Victor, displays a wonderful collection of surrealist art in a 19th-century palace. Classical music echoes through its 5 floors, and in the 2nd *sous-sol* (basement) you can see Geneva's ancient ramparts. (Open Tues.-Sun. 10am-noon and 2-6pm, Mon. 2-6pm. 10SFr, students and seniors 3.50SFr.)

Geneva's contemporary monuments stand on the *rive droite,* 10 minutes from the train station. The guided tour of the **United Nations** at the end of rue Montbrillant is, like Orson Welles' conception of peace, quite dull, despite art treasures donated by all the nations of the world. The constant traffic of international diplomats, brightly clothed in their native garb, provides more excitement than anything the tour guides say. (Open daily 9am-noon and 2-6pm; Sept.-Oct. and April-June daily 10am-noon and 2-4pm; Nov.-March Mon.-Fri. 10am-noon and 2-4pm. 7SFr, seniors and students 5SFr, children 3SFr.) More interesting is the nearby **International Red Cross and Red Crescent Museum,** 17, ave. de la Paix, open since 1988. A beautifully designed series of films, slide shows and photographs traces the bloody history of the humanitarian organization and its Muslim counterpart. (Open Wed.-Mon. 10am-5pm. 8SFr, students 4SFr, under 11 free.)

Geneva's lakefront begs to be strolled. Saunter down **quai Gustave-Ador** to the world's tallest fountain, the **Jet d'Eau** ("Calvin's Bidet" to irreverent foreigners). **Le Jardin Anglais,** with its famous **Horloge Fleurie,** a large clock of flowers designed in homage to Geneva's clock industry, sits at the foot of the pont du Mont-Blanc on the *rive gauche.* The old city nurtures scads of antique shops and galleries along the cobblestone (and generally car-free) streets. Two fine beaches front the lake: **Paquis Plage,** at quai du Mont-Blanc (2SFr), is laid-back and popular with the Génévois; upscale **Genève Plage** (5SFr) offers a giant waterslide, volleyball, and basketball tournaments and an Olympic-size pool. Next to biking, the best way to see Lake Geneva is through one of the **ferry tours** leaving from quai du Mont Blanc. From June to September, **CGN,** near the pont du Mont Blanc (tel. 722 39 16), operates day tours with the opportunity to disembark at Montreux or the stupendous Château de Chillon (see Montreux Sights). (Depart at 9:15am and return at 8:40pm; 43SFr, Eurail and Swisspass valid.) **Swiss Boat** cruises by numerous *châteaux* on shorter tours. (2-hr. tours depart at 10:15am and 3pm, 20SFr. 1-hr. tours depart at 3:15pm and 5:15pm, 14SFr. Reduced fares with railpasses.)

ENTERTAINMENT

At the tourist office, pick up the free *List of Events* (French) or *What's on in Geneva* (English), invaluable guides to nighttime activities. Summer nightlife centers around the cafés and the lakeside quays. **Place Molard** can be a lively hangout; so can **place du Bourg-du-Four,** below Cathédrale St-Pierre in the old town (**La Clémence,** at #20, is one of its most popular spots). Anglophones gather at the **Brittania Pub,** on the pl. de Cornavin, across from the Notre Dame. (Open Sun.-Thurs. to 1am; Fri.-Sat. to 2am.) Enjoy a Euro night out at the **Midnight Rambler,** 21, Grande-

Rue, in the *vieille ville,* a disco with frequent live acts or DJs supplying rock, new wave and rap hits. (Doors open at 11pm.) When the weather complies, spontaneous concerts often appear at the **Jardin Anglais.**

Geneva celebrates the first week in August with the **Fêtes de Genève.** Three days of international musical and artistic celebration culminate in boat shows and a fabulous fireworks display. The **Fête du Bois de la Batie,** a folk-music festival traditionally held in September, draws Swiss music lovers down from the hills for 2 weeks of cabaret, theater, and concerts. Many events are free; students pay half-price for the others (regular prices 10-32SFr).

■■■ LAUSANNE

Wedged between Lake Geneva to the south and the Alps to the north, Lausanne's attractions put it on a par with Geneva. Sports are Lausanne's business: the Ouchy waterfront is a summer haven for sailors, swimmers, and waterskiers, and for over a century, Lausanne has proudly hosted the headquarters of the International Olympic Committee. At the other end of the city's 5-stop mini-metro, the *vieille ville* (old town) retains an ecclesiastic, medieval air. The train station sits halfway up, a 15-minute hike from either end.

Lausanne's Gothic **Cathédrale** was consecrated by Pope Gregory X in 1275. Ogle the famous rose window, then check out the stunning view from the tower. (Open Mon.-Fri. 7am-7pm, Sat. 8am-7pm, Sun. 11:30am-7pm; Oct.-Feb. daily 8am-5:30pm. Free. Tower open Mon.-Sat. 9-11:30am and 1:30-5:30pm, Sun. 2-5:30pm. 2SFr, children 12 and under 1SFr.) Nearby, the fountain on **place de la Palud** helps the city perpetuate itself, acting as a locus for young people on the make. The **Collection de l'Art Brut,** 11, av. Bergières, is perhaps Europe's most unusual gallery. Its founder, postwar painter Jean Dubuffet, despised the pretension of the avant-garde art scene, so he filled the gallery with the works of "non-artists"—the criminally insane, the institutionalized, and others who considered themselves only dabblers. (Open Tues.-Fri. 10am-noon and 2-6pm, Sat.-Sun. 2-6pm. 5SFr, students 3SFr, under 16 free.) The **Musée Olympique,** 1, quai d'Ouchy, presents the philosophy and history of the Olympic Games from their re-establishment in Athens in 1896 to the 1992 competitions in Albertville and Barcelona. (Open Tues.-Wed. and Fri.-Sat. 9am-noon and 2-6pm, Thurs. 9am-noon, 2-6pm and 8-10pm, Sun.-Mon. 2-6pm. Free.) Take an evening stroll down the **quai de Belgique** in Ouchy, a lakeside promenade flanked by flowers, immaculate gardens, small fountains, and benches.

Accommodations, Food, and Practical Information Lausanne's comfortable **Auberge de Jeunesse (HI),** 1, chemin de Muguet, corner of rue du Stade (tel. (021) 26 57 82), near Ouchy, looks out to the lake and mountains, across the street from a giant municipal sporting complex that's open to the public. Take bus #1 (direction "La Maladière") to La Batelière, then follow the signs downhill about 200m. (Reception open 7-9am and 5-10pm. Curfew 11:30pm. 22.50SFr, second night 20SFr. Nonmembers over 20, 30.50SFr, second night 29SFr. Lockers. Get there by 5pm to beat the crunch.) **Camping de Vidy** is at 3, chemin du Camping (tel. (021) 24 20 31; 6SFr/person, students 5.50SFr; 6-10SFr/tent). Take av. de Rhodanie west out of the city, loop around the autoroute onto rte. de Vidy and turn left onto chemin des Ruines Romaines.

Many restaurants are just spectator sports for the budget traveler. Visit produce **markets** Wednesday and Saturday at pl. de la Riponne (7:30am-12:30). Nearby, a local favorite, the **Berguglia Boulangerie,** 10, rue Madeleine, serves up scrumptious and cheap delights. (Open Mon. 2:15-6:30pm, Tues.-Fri. 7:30am-12:30pm and 2:15-6:30pm, Sat. 7am-5pm.) Pack your picnic at the **Co-op** supermarket on rue du Petit Chêne, on the way from the station to the city center. **Manora Sainf,** 17, pl. de St-François, is a popular self-service restaurant with fantastic salad, fruit, and dessert bars. (*Menus du jour* 7.15SFr. Open Mon.-Fri. 7am-10:30pm, Sun. 9am-10:30pm.)

MONTREUX

Pinte Besson, 4, rue de l'Ale (tel. 312 72 27), has turned out fondue (16SFr) since its opening in 1780. (Open Mon.-Sat. 7:30am-midnight.) A stroll around Ouchy or Place Daint-François and most side streets by night will reveal an authentic Lausannois bar. Dance the night away at **Frisbee,** 12bis, pl. St-François. (Open daily 10pm-4am.)

The **tourist office,** 2, av. de Rhodanie (tel. (021) 617 14 27), is located across from the lake, in Ouchy. Either take the metro (direction "Ouchy"), or take bus #2 to the last stop at Ouchy. The staff will book hotel rooms free if the request is written or faxed ahead. (Open Mon.-Sat. 8am-7pm, Sun. 9am-noon and 1-6pm; mid-Oct. to Easter Mon.-Fri. 8am-6pm, Sat. 8:30am-noon and 1-5pm.) Pick up the invaluable *Lausanne Official Guide* (free). **SSR,** 20, bd. de Grancy (tel. (021) 617 56 27), supplies budget travel information. (Open Mon.-Fri. 9:30am-5:30pm.) Lausanne is a short ride by land or lake from Geneva and Montreux.

■■■ MONTREUX

Popular resort and retirement pad for the wealthy, Montreux also draws footloose young folks to its music festivals. The most famous is the annual **Montreux Jazz Festival** (2½ weeks in mid-July; tickets 58-150SFr, festival pass 1500SFr) featuring jazz, gospel, blues, big band, salsa, and rap. Write well in advance for info and tickets to **Festival du Jazz,** service de location cp 1451, CH-1820 Montreux 1, or call (021) 963 74 74. In the U.S., try **Ciao Travel,** 2707 Congress St., Suite 1F, San Diego, CA 92110 (tel. (619) 297-8112). Full payment is required when you reserve. With luck, the tourist office may have some tickets available when the festival starts, but most are snapped up over a month before the concerts begin. From late August to early October, the **Classical Montreux-Vevey Music Festival** takes over. Write to **Festival de Musique,** 5, rue de Théâtre, Case Postale 162, CH-1820 Montreux 2, for information (tickets 30-110SFr). In the U.S., contact **Dailey-Thorp Inc.,** 315 W. 57th St., New York, NY 10019 (tel. (212) 307-1555) for info. **Free concerts** from yodeling to rock are held in the pavilion of the Rouvenaz. Check the tourist office for details.

Festival-free Montreux exudes peaceful karma. Exotic plants line the lakeside promenade, which surveys swans and boats below and the Alps beyond. Sunsets dazzle along the 10km stretch. A 10-minute walk past the hostel stands **Château de Chillon,** a remarkably well-preserved 13th-century fortress with all the comforts of home: prison, torture chamber, weapons room, and terrific views. The château inspired narratives by Rousseau, Hugo, and Dumas as well as Lord Byron's *The Prisoner of Chillon.* (Open April-June and Sept. daily 9am-5:45pm; Oct. 10am-4:45pm; Nov.-Feb. 10am-noon and 1:30-4pm; March 10am-noon and 1:30-4:45pm. 5SFr, students 4SFr.)

Accommodations, Food, and Practical Information The newly renovated, wheelchair-accessible **Auberge de Jeunesse Haut Lac (HI),** 8, passage de l'Auberge (tel. 963 49 34), is a 30-minute walk along the lake to the left; or take bus #1 (direction "Villeneuve"), get off at the Territet-Gare stop, and follow the signs downhill. Due to its view of the lake, fantastic showers, and airy comforters, it's wise to make reservations at least a few days in advance. (Reception open 7-9am and 5-10pm. Curfew 11pm. 24.40SFr, nonmembers 31.40. Doubles 34.40SFr/person. Wheelchair access rooms with shower (2 available) 41SFr.) Nearby **Villeneuve** has luxurious lakeside camping at **Les Horizons Bleues** (tel. (021) 960 15 47; reception open 7am-noon and 3-8pm; 5.50SFr/person, 4-6SFr/tent; open April-Sept.). Take bus #1 to Villeneuve. Montreux's lakeside cafés stun visitors both with their elegance and their exorbitant prices. Instead, assemble a lakeside picnic at **Migros** supermarket on av. du Casino. **Restaurant Le Palais,** 14, quai du Casino, serves expensive Iranian specialties and affordable desserts (banana split 9.50SFr) to the beautiful people of Montreux. (Open daily 11am-midnight.) **Restaurant-Glacier Apollo,** 2 Place du Marché (tel. 963 10 26), serves Swiss specialties as well as fresh fish dishes. (Entrees 16-20SFr. Open daily from 9am-11:30pm.)

Montreux's **tourist office,** pl. du Débarcadère (tel. (021) 963 12 12), sits on the lake. Exit the train station onto av. des Alpes, cross the street, descend the steps to the right and walk about 200m to the left. (Open daily 9am-7pm; Sept.-May Mon.-Fri. 9am noon and 2 6pm, Sat. 9am noon.)

■ Near Montreux: Leysin

Southeast of Montreux lies **Leysin,** a major funspot in the Alpes Vaudoises. Once a haven for patients who needed "sun therapy" as treatment for tuberculosis, hikers now set forth from here in summer, and skiers do likewise in winter. Take a train to Aigle, then board a spectacular cog railway that climbs the 2200m to Leysin. (Round-trip 16.40SFr, free with Swiss Holiday Card, Eurail not valid.)

The **tourist office,** pl. du Marché (tel. (025) 34 22 44), is in Leysin-Feydey near the New Sporting building; take the bus to Leysin-Feydey and follow the signs downhill. (Open Mon.-Fri. 8am-6pm, Sat. 9am-noon.) The resourceful staff gives overnight visitors a **Carte de Séjour** that entitles them to use myriad recreational facilities. They also hand out lists of authorized mountain guides and maps of area hiking trails.

The single best place to sleep, eat and drink the night away is **Club Vagabond,** 1854 Leysin (tel. (025) 34 13 21), at the Leysin-Feydey stop past the village. Ascend the stairs on your left as you exit the station, turn left, and bear left at the fork in the road by the Eglise Catholique. The headquarters of the International School of Mountaineering, the Vagabond has regal food and an English-speaking staff that arranges special events like fondue nights, ski races, and costume parties throughout the winter season. (Reception open 8am-noon and 4:30-10:30pm. Singles 36SFr; in winter 42SFr. Doubles 28SFr; in winter 37SFr. 3-4 bed dorm-rooms 25SFr in summer; 31SFr in winter.) Wintertime litters Leysin with skiers. Lift tickets start at 36SFr per day; a 7-day pass runs 161SFr. Rentals start at 39SFr per day.

During mid-July the town hosts the **Leysin Rock Festival.** In past years stars as luminous as Billy Idol, INXS, Simple Minds, and Sinéad O'Connor have headlined here. Tickets, available from the tourist office, cost 50SFr per day, 125SFr for the 3-day series if purchased in advance.

■■■ ZERMATT AND THE MATTERHORN

The Matterhorn is an ornery giant, its peak often shrouded in thick clouds; the best time to catch a glimpse is at dawn or dusk. To climb this beast, you need a mountain of money and a courageous heart; it claims dozens of lives each year. Fortunately, you can hike 388km worth of sign-posted paths around Zermatt without grave danger to life or pocketbook. Information is available at the **Burgführerbüro** (Mountaineering Office; tel. (028) 67 34 56), across from the train station. (Open July to mid-Oct. 8:30am-noon and 4:30-7pm.) Sturdy boots, warm clothing and raingear are essential. Ride the cable car (round-trip 26SFr) or hike (4-5hr.) to the bathtub-sized **Schwarzsee;** from there the path to **Hörnli Hütte** (1½-2hr.) affords stunning glimpses of the region's reigning mount and the sumptuous valley below. Zermatt has more **summer ski trails** than any other Alpine resort; lifts operate daily from 7am-2pm depending on the weather. Ski passes cost 50SFr for a day, 176SFr for one week. Flexible passes allow 2 in 4 days of slopes for 80SFr, 3 in 6 days for 124SFr, and 7 days in 2 weeks for 252SFr. Ski rental runs 40SFr (30SFr if you stay at the youth hostel). For more time on the slopes, rent equipment a day ahead; ski shops are open Monday through Saturday 8am-6:30pm. For **alpine rescue,** call (028) 67 34 87.

The newly renovated **Jugendherberge (HI)** (tel. (028) 67 23 20) oozes fitness freaks and offers sumptuous views of the surrounding mountain ranges. From the train station, walk to the right, down the main street, turn left at the church, cross the river and follow the signs uphill for 5 minutes. (Reception open 6:30-9am and 4-10pm. Curfew 11:30pm. 35SFr, 33.50SFr for additional nights. Nonmembers 42SFr,

40.50SFr for additional nights.) Closer to the station but farther from the mountains is the pleasant **Hotel Bahnhof** (tel. (028) 67 24 06); get off your train and go 100m to the right. (Dorms 25SFr. Singles 39SFr. Doubles from 70SFr.) The lone campground in town is **Camping Matterhorn Zermatt** (tel. (028) 67 39 21), 5 minutes to the left of the station (7SFr/person; showers and toilets included. Open June-Sept.) The **Coop Center** grocery store is next door to the tourist office. (Open Mon.-Fri. 8am-noon and 2-6:30pm, Sat. 8am-noon and 2-6pm.) Cafés are expensive, even for Switzerland. Zermatt's oldest restaurant, the **Café du Pont,** serves hearty Alpine fare. (5-17SFr. Open daily 9am-midnight; food served 9am-10pm.)

The **tourist office** (tel. (028) 66 11 81) is next to the train station. (Open Mon.-Fri. 8:30am-noon and 1:30-6:30pm, Sat. 8:30am-6:30pm.) For rail service to the Italian-speaking Swiss canton of Ticino, go down to Brig (36SFr). Swisspass is valid.

GRAUBÜNDEN

Graubünden is the largest but least populous of the Swiss *cantons* and a microcosm of Swiss cultural heterogeneity; from valley to valley the language changes from German to Romansch to Italian, with a wide range of dialects in between. A few developed resorts draw hutches of ski-bunnies impervious to the lofty prices. High season runs December through March (reservations are *necessary*) and peaks again in July and August. In May and early June, virtually everything shuts down.

■■■ ST. MORITZ

In St. Moritz-Dorf, jet-setters saunter about the nearby Gucci and Cartier boutiques. Laugh at them in all their wretchedness. Across town in St. Moritz-Bad, scruffy (yet sexy) travelers trudge out of the youth hostel and into the Coop. Nijinsky danced his final dance here in 1918 before going insane. Prevent similar mishaps by consulting the **tourist office** *(Kruverein),* via Maistra 12 (tel. (082) 331 47); cross the street from the station and climb Truoch Serlas, then Via Serlas to the left. The *Kruverein* is up the stairs across the street. (Open Mon.-Fri. 9am-noon and 2-6pm, Sat. 9am-noon.) Hotel information, currency exchange, bicycle rental (14SFr), and lockers (2SFr) are also available at the train station. Yellow **postal buses** destined for various valley villages leave just left of the station.

The design of the **Jugendherberge Stille (HI),** via Surpunt 60 (tel. (082) 339 69); merited an architectural award. Walk 45 minutes around the lake or catch the Sils postal bus (2SFr) to the "Hotel Sonne" stop. (Reception open 6:30-9am, 4-5:30pm, 6-8pm, and 9-10pm. 30.40SFr, nonmembers 46.40SFr. Doubles 89.60SFr. Showers, breakfast, dinner, and sleepsacks included. Open June 15-Oct. and Dec. 15-April.) Campers can catch the post-bus to St. Moritz-Bad Post (2SFr) to find **Camping Olympianschanze** (tel. (082) 340 90; 5SFr/person, 6-9SFr/tent). St. Moritz restaurants are a financially disastrous proposition. Forage at the **Coop** grocery 1 block left of the tourist office or on via Greves en route to the hostel. (Open Mon.-Thurs. 8am-noon and 1:30-6:30pm, Fri. 8am-noon and 1:30-8pm, Sat. 8am-noon.)

■ Near St. Moritz: Engadin Valley

Most of the towns along the train routes from St. Moritz make super daytrips. **Pontresina** lolls 5 minutes by train from St. Moritz (3SFr) and is second to it only in style, comfort, and prices. Across from the station is the strict and spotless **Jugendherberge (HI)** (tel. (082) 672 23), a whole 5 centimes cheaper than the hostel in St. Moritz, and the dinner (included) is better. (Reception open 6:45-9am and 5-9pm. Lockout 9:30am-4pm. Curfew 11pm. Dorms 39SFr. Doubles 61SFr. Open June to mid-Oct. and Dec. to mid-April.) The **tourist office,** via Maistra and Cruscheda (tel.

(082) 664 88), finds rooms for free and generally knows all. (Open Mon.-Fri. 8:30am-noon and 2-6pm, Sat. 8:30am-noon and 2-5pm.) **Zuoz,** 30 minutes north of St. Moritz, is an enchanting mixture of Romansch houses, fountains, and carved troughs. Though rooms are expensive, the **tourist office** (tel. (082) 715 10), up the hill and to the right on the main square, won't let you leave reservation-less. (Open Mon.-Fri. 9am-noon and 2-6pm, Sat. 9-11am; Oct.-Nov. Mon.-Fri. 9-noon and 2-6pm.)

Fields of flowers and sparkling streams pull enough tourists to **Sils** to put St. Moritz to shame, but it still *feels* unspoiled, which is why it's such a successful resort town in the first place. While strolling Sils's picturesque lanes, check out the **Nietzsche House,** near Hotel Edelweiss, where the philosopher lived from 1881-88, slowly decaying into syphilitic madness. (Open summer, Tues.-Sun. 3-6pm. 4SFr, students 2SFr.) A 18.40SFr ride from St. Moritz, **Maloja's** charm lies in its convenience; only a few steps from the bus stop are the **tourist office** (tel. (082) 431 88; open Mon.-Fri. 8:30am-noon and 2-6pm, Sat. 8:30am-noon; Oct. to mid-Dec. and May-June Mon.-Fri. 8:30am-noon and 2-6pm) and the **Jugendherberge (HI)** (tel. (082) 432 58), a friendly farmhouse turned hostel. (Reception open 8-9am, 4:30-5:30pm and 8-9pm. Lockout 9:30am-4:30pm. Curfew 10pm. 28SFr. Open July-Nov. 15 and Dec. 22-May.) The **campground** around the lake (tel. (082) 431 81), across the street from the PTT bus stop, to the left, and left on the small street heading towards the lake (after Hotel Scheizerhaus), doubles as a windsurfing landing and beach. (7SFr/person, 4-6SFr/tent. Open summer only.)

Ski rental in this region goes for 35-45SFr per day, 25SFr for cross-country. Novices should head for Zuoz or Corviglia, experts for Diavolezza or Corvatsch, and anyone hoping to catch a glimpse of Hollywood, to St. Moritz. Passes cover transport and T-bars for the entire area (50SFr/day, 240SFr/week, 422SFr for 15 days).

ITALIAN SWITZERLAND

The Italian-speaking canton of **Ticino** (Tessin in German) is renowned for its refreshing juxtaposition of Swiss efficiency and Italian *dolce vita*. The ring of Italian voices is not all that sets the region apart from Switzerland—the southern climate turns it into a Mediterranean garden. The emerald lakes, lush mountains, and vineyards that surround defiant stone houses render Ticino's countryside as romantic as Lugano and Locarno, its famed resorts. Although Italian is the official language, many residents also speak German, English, or French.

■■■ LUGANO

Switzerland's 3rd-largest banking center, Lugano serves up business and pleasure with Italian flavor. Start at the 16th-century **Cathedral of San Lorenzo,** across the street and down the hill from the station; its hidden alcoves contain beautifully carved statues and frescoes. The **Chiesa San Rocco** on via Canova houses a Madonna altarpiece and Passion frescoes under a intricately decorated ceiling. The **Museo Cantonale d'Art,** via Canova 10, features 19th- and 20th-century Swiss and international works. (Open Tues. 2-5pm, Wed.-Sun. 10am-5pm. 6SFr, students 3SFr.) Those inclined towards watersports can visit the **Lido beach** to swim (3SFr) or paddleboat (10-14SFr/hr.) on the sun-kissed waters of **Lago di Lugano.** For a loftier view of the lake, take a car or ride the funicular to **Monte Brè,** with continuous service year round to the 3059-ft.-high summit. Hike up to the 933m summit for a magnificent view of the city below and the Alps beyond.

Accommodations, Food, and Practical Information
Albergo la **Gioventú (HI)** (tel. (091) 56 27 28) is a short ride on bus #5 (catch it left of the train station and across the street) to Crocifisso, the 6th stop (backtrack a few steps and

turn left on via Cantovale), or trudge uphill from the station (25min.). The hostel sprawls over a large plot of land featuring picnic tables, table tennis and a swimming pool. (Reception open 6am-1pm and 3-10pm. Curfew 10pm. 14SFr, nonmembers 21SFr. Sheets 2SFr. Open mid-March to Oct.) **Zurigo,** corse Pestalozzi 13 (tel. (091) 23 43 43), in the center of town across from the piazza Maghetti park, has cheap but comfortable rooms. (Singles 50SFr, with shower 80SFr. Doubles 80SFr, with shower 90SFr. Open Feb.-Nov.) **Campers** must catch the Ferrovia Lugano-Ponte-Tresa (from the train station, head right, cross the street, and go down the stairs by the restaurant) to Agno (every 20min., 3SFr), where 5 campgrounds such as **La Palma** (tel. (091) 59 25 61) and **Golfo del Sole** (tel. (091) 59 48 02) settle near the lake. (All cost 4-7SFr/person, 3-7SFr/tent, and are open April-Oct.)

Shop or dine at the **Migros,** via Pretoria 15, in the center of town. (Market open Mon.-Fri. 8am-6:30pm, Sat. 7:30am-5pm. Restaurant open daily 9am-10pm.) For a more genuine repast, **Pestalozzi,** piazza Indipendenza, serves cheap Italian and vegetarian dishes from 6am-10pm. (Meals 10-15SFr. Salad bar 3.50-10.50SFr.)

The busy **tourist office,** riva Giocondo Albertolli 5 (tel. (091) 21 46 64), finds rooms and provides general info. (Open Mon.-Sat. 9am-6:30pm; Oct.-June Mon.-Fri. 9am-6pm, Sat. 9am-5pm.) To reach the office from the station, walk left on piazzale della Stazione, turn right on via San Gottardo, right on via Paolo Regazzoni, and a left on via Cattedrale to reach the piazza Cioccaro (or take the funicular). From the piazza, follow via Cattedrale, turn right on Pessina, left on via del Pesci, then left on riva via Vela, which turns into riva Giocondo Albertolli. The office is to the left, next to Bar Elite. Frequent **trains** head from Lugano to Milan (round-trip 30SFr), Zürich (58SFr), Berne (65SFr), and Locarno (round-trip 76SFr; change in Bellinzona).

■■■ LOCARNO

On the shores of Lago Maggiore, Locarno basks in Mediterranean breezes and Italian sun. For much of the interwar era, hopes for peace were symbolized by "the Spirit of Locarno"—the visionary German leader Gustav Stresemann signed a conciliatory pact here with France, Great Britain, and Italy in 1925. Above the city towers the brilliantly orange **Madonna del Sasso** (Madonna of the Rock), the town's landmark and symbol. Madonna herself is tucked away in the museum next to the cathedral. (Grounds open 7am-10pm; Nov.-Feb. 7am-9pm. Museum open Sun.-Fri. 10am-noon and 2-5pm. 3SFr, students 1.50SFr.) A cable car ascends to the sanctuary (every 15min., round-trip 6SFr), but the walk is pleasant nonetheless.

To reach Locarno's **tourist office,** Largo Zorzi on piazza Grande (tel. (093) 31 03 33), walk diagonally to the right from the train station for a block, then another block through a pedestrian walkway and then cross the street on the left. (Open Mon.-Fri. 8am-7pm, Sat.-Sun. 9am-noon and 1-5pm; Nov.-March Mon.-Fri. 8am-noon and 2-6pm.) Locarno's youth hostel, the friendly **Pensione Città Vecchia,** via Torreta 13 (tel. (093) 31 45 54), on the corner of via Borghese uphill from the piazza Grande, is always full; make reservations weeks in advance. (Reception open 8am-10pm. Singles 20SFr. Doubles 38-44SFr.) Nearby is the cramped but convenient **Albergo la Zingara,** via delle Monache 1 (tel. (093) 31 12 19), a block up from the Largo Zorzi. (Singles 30-35SFr. Doubles 60-90SFr.) Downstairs is Locarno's hippest nightclub; staying upstairs saves you the cover charge. (Beers 8SFr.) Camp 20 minutes to the left of the station at **Delta Camping** (tel. (093) 31 60 81), on the southern lakeshore. (9SFr/person, 8-10SFr/tent. Open mid-March to late Oct.) Purchase picnic paraphernalia in the piazza Grande at the **Coop** or **Migros** supermarkets (both open Mon.-Fri. 8am-6:30pm, Sat. 7:30am-5pm). The Migros has yet another familiar **restaurant.** (Open Mon.-Sat. 7am-10pm.) The largest number of eateries are to be found near the waterfront, underneath the arcades bordering the piazza Grande.

■ Near Locarno: Verscio and Valle Maggia

In nearby **Verscio** is a world-famous clown school run by a master jester: **Teatro Dimitri** offers plays, mimes, and variety acts in German and Italian during July and August. Performances begin at 8:30pm; reserve tickets 1 or 2 days in advance (ask the tourist office for a schedule). Twelve km northeast of Locarno, Verscio can be reached on the Domodossola-Centovalli railway. (Round-trip 9SFr. Railpasses valid. For information call (tel. (093) 81 15 44).

Perhaps the most striking section of Italian Switzerland is the **Valle Maggia,** a sparsely populated valley of forests and pastures that stretches north of Locarno. Get a one-day "tourist ticket" (17SFr) in the train station for unlimited travel in the Valle. Waterfalls surround German-speaking **Bosco Gurin,** the highest village (1506m) in the Ticino canton, with old wooden houses and great skiing in the winter. Hop on postal bus #10 to Cervio, then switch to #2; Bosco Gurin is the last stop (round-trip 25SFr). The sparkling waves of the **Lago Maggiore** are almost impossible to resist; a boat trip to **Brissago Island** (19SFr) transports nature lovers to a vast botanical garden of fragrant subtropical plants, palms, and stone promenades. (Open April-Oct. daily 9am-6pm. 5SFr.)

UNITED KINGDOM

US$1	= £0.65 (British pounds)		£1 =	US$1.55
CDN$1=	£0.49		£1 =	CDN$2.04
IR£1	= £0.94		£1 =	IR£1.07
AUS$1 =	£0.42		£1 =	AUS$2.39
NZ$1	= £0.36		£1 =	NZ$2.81
SAR1	= £0.13		£1 =	SAR7.49
Country code: 44				

International Dialing Prefix: 011

There have been a couple significant changes in the United Kingdom since Julius Caesar happened upon the Kentish shore nearly 2000 years ago—you probably won't be met by a phalanx of sword-slinging Britons at the airport. Yet for centuries these islands have held captive the world's imagination by deftly mingling ancient tradition with the cutting edge of modern life. These paradoxes remain in force today amid familiar traditions—Beefeaters who stand guard outside Her Majesty's palaces brandish assault rifles nowadays, the skirling of bagpipes rings across modern Scottish towns as well as across mist-swirled glens, and superhighways ring once-silent Roman ruins. Life on these islands means a constant adjustment to what Spenser called the "ever whirling wheels of Change," making these lands among the most culturally fertile spots on the planet.

The United Kingdom comprises four very distinct regions, each with its own notions of identity and of its relation to the others. "England" originally referred to a group of Anglo-Saxon principalities united in the 9th century, but came to mean that region of the British Isles that dominated the other parts. By 1603, the English had established control over Ireland, Scotland and Wales; the "United Kingdom of Great Britain and Ireland" was proclaimed in 1801. Yet by the early 20th century, this union was starting to disintegrate, foreshadowing the collapse of the overseas Empire. Most of Ireland won its independence in 1921; Scotland and Wales were promised regional autonomy in 1975. Though modern times have spread the BBC and Burger King across every glen and dale from Aberdeen to Belfast to Cardiff, the four regions retain surprisingly distinctive characters, resulting in an often problematic co-existence. As ongoing Troubles in Northern Ireland indicate, questions of union and nationalism will likely be contested for years to come.

Deciding just what to call this volatile mosaic calls up a host of regional tempers and political debates. Generally, "Britain" refers to the island that contains England, Scotland and Wales (and don't refer to a Scot or a Welsh person as "English"—it's neither accurate nor polite), while the political term "United Kingdom" encompasses these regions and Northern Ireland as well. For practical purposes, *Let's Go* will use the term "Britain" to refer to England, Scotland, Wales and Northern Ireland, while "Ireland" will refer to the Republic of Ireland. Our use of this terminology is not meant to reflect a political opinion.

> For more detailed, ripping coverage of the United Kingdom, pore over *Let's Go: Britain & Ireland* or *Let's Go: London*.

GETTING THERE

From Continental Europe The cheapest way to reach Britain from continental Europe is to swim the English Channel; this requires extraordinary stamina and has been tackled by only a handful of budget travelers. Plus it's hard to take your luggage. Fortunately, many ferries connect the two lands, and rail tickets between London and the Continent normally include cross-Channel passage. Ask ahead about the train-boat linkage, which can be confusing.

Sealink Stena Line (tel. (0233) 647 047 or (081) 575 8555) and **P&O European Ferries** (tel. (081) 575 8555) offer extensive ferry service across the channel between France (Calais, Cherbourg, and Le Havre) and England (Dover or Portsmouth). Sealink ferries are the most frequent and take about 1½ hours (22 trips/day; one-way roughly US$36). Other routes between the Continent and England include Bergen, Norway, to Newcastle; Cherbourg to Weymouth or Southampton; Dieppe to Newhaven; Esbjerg, Denmark, to Harwich or Newcastle; Gothenburg, Sweden, to Harwich or Newcastle; Hamburg to Harwich; Le Havre to Southampton; Oostende, Belgium, to Dover; Rotterdam to Hull; and Zeebrugge, Belgium to Dover or Hull or Felixstowe. **Brittany Ferries** (tel. (0752) 221 321) has service between Plymouth and Roscoff or Portsmouth and St-Malo.

Traveling by **hovercraft** is quicker (50min.), but seats must be booked in advance. **Hoverspeed** services depart from Boulogne for Dover, with extra craft operating to Ramsgate from Dunkerque during the summer. Contact **Travelloyd,** 8 Berkeley Sq., London SW1, or the **British Rail Travel Centre,** 4-12 Regent St., London SW1Y 4PQ, for information.

As a rule, **air travel** is prohibitively expensive across much of Europe. In high season, however, budget fares make flights between England and the Continent quite affordable. Look for student discounts and holiday charters available through budget travel agents and local newspapers and magazines.

From Ireland **Ferries** are also the best way to get from Ireland to Britain. Boats run from Fishguard and Pembroke in South Wales to Rosslare in southeastern Ireland; from Holyhead in North Wales to Dún Laoghaire (dun LEAR-y) near Dublin; from Liverpool in North England to Dublin and Belfast, Northern Ireland, and from Stranraer, Scotland, to Larne, Northern Ireland. Fares on the Holyhead-Dublin and Fishguard/Pembroke-Rosslare routes, operated by Sealink and B&I Line, both run about £17-23 (bikes free). HI members receive a 25% discount on fares from both Sealink and B&I. ISIC holders receive a 25% discount from B&I, and ISIC holders with Travelsave stamps (see Ireland) save 50%. Almost all sailings in June, July and August are "controlled sailings," which means that you must book the crossing ahead of time (a day in advance does the trick). Sailing time is 3 hours. Contact **B&I** in London at 150 New Bond St., London W1Y 0AQ (tel. (071) 491 8682); in Dublin at 16 Westmoreland St., Dublin 2 (tel. (01) 679 7977). Their after-hours information line in England is (061) 236 3936, in Ireland (01) 606 666. **Sealink** can be reached at 15 Westmoreland St., Dublin 2 (tel. (01) 280 844); and in Rosslare Harbour (tel. (053) 331 15).

TRAVELING IN THE U.K.

In general, fares on all modes of public transportation in Britain and Ireland are either "single" (one way) or "return" (round-trip). "Period returns" require you to return within a specified number of days; "day return" is equivalent to same-day round-trip.

When in Britain, travel by **coach,** a long-distance mode of transport distinct from slow, short-run "buses," which run within cities and between rural villages. Eurail isn't valid in the United Kingdom, and express coaches are cheaper than trains and often almost as fast. Each county or region has its own companies for rural service; **National Express** is the principal operator of long-distance coach services. For info contact Eurolines, Grosvenor Gardens, London SW1 (tel. (071) 730 0202). Those aged 60 or over or between 16 and 23 are eligible for Seniors' and Young Persons' **Discount Coach Cards** (£7 for one year), valid on National Express, which reduce standard coach fares by about 30%.

Britain's nationalized **British Rail** service is extensive but somewhat expensive. British Rail offers a myriad of "Rail Rover" and "Flexi Rover" options for unlimited travel in specific regions of England, Scotland, and Wales—*Let's Go* provides some information on these passes in the relevant regional sections. The **Young Person's Railcard** (£16, valid for one year) offers 33% off most fares, as well as discounts on Sealink Stena Line to the Continental and Irish ports. You can buy this pass at major British Rail Travel Centres in the U.K. You must prove you're either between 16 and 23 (with a birth certificate or passport) or a full-time student over 23 at a British school and submit 2 passport-sized photos. Families, seniors, and travelers in wheelchairs have their own Railcards. If you plan to travel a great deal within Britain, the **BritRail Pass** is a good buy. *You must buy BritRail Passes before arriving in Britain.* They allow unlimited travel in England, Wales, and Scotland; British Rail does not operate in Northern Ireland or the Republic of Ireland. In 1993, BritRail passes cost US$209 for 8 days (ages 16-25 US$169), US$319 for 15 days (ages 16-25 US$255).

Freewheelers is a "lift agency" which can match you up to a driver going your way. Membership is required, and costs £5. Each match-up costs you £1, and the price for the trip itself is agreed between the passenger and driver, based on fuel costs—the agency's 1993 sample rates estimated a £9.40 fare for a London to Manchester trip. The agency requires that members abide by a safety procedure to confirm each other's identity, and keeps records of all members and matches made. Single-sex matching can be arranged. Freewheelers does not take responsibility for members' safety—you are still getting in a car with a stranger. For more details, call (07) 738 6861, or write to Freewheelers, Ltd., Ventura House, 176 Acre La., London SW2 5UL.

Those who've chosen to sample British **hitching** often call it Europe's best, especially in rural areas and on islands. Hitching is reportedly more difficult on Sundays; small highland roads can be terrible. British secondary roads are never very wide and are often bordered by high hedges or stone banks; successful hitchers don't stand in the narrows. Britons drive on the left.

To really see Britain, you must get off the rail or coach routes and **bike** or **hike.** Most cities and villages have bike rental shops and maps of local cycle routes; ask at the tourist office. Britain is the most-mapped, most-written-about island in the world; take along a large-scale Ordnance Survey map of the area you plan to cover, and ask tourist offices and National Park Information Centres about routes.

U.K. ESSENTIALS

There are local **tourist offices** everywhere in the United Kingdom; any of them will book you a room in a local bed and breakfast (up to a £1-2 fee), and most will book a space in a B&B anywhere in the country (£2.50-4 fee). Many offices post an accommodations list after closing.

The pound sterling (£) is the main unit of **currency** in the United Kingdom. The separate currencies issued in the Channel Islands, the Isle of Man, Scotland, and Northern Ireland can be used interchangeably with standard English currency only in the region of issue; elsewhere, few people will accept it. Most banks are closed on Saturday, Sunday, and all public holidays. Usual weekday bank hours are Monday through Friday 9:30am to 3:30pm, although more and more banks are opening Saturdays as well. The United Kingdom charges **value-added tax (VAT),** a national sales tax on most goods and some services; the rate is 17.5% on many services (such as hairdressers, hotels, restaurants, and car rental agencies) and on all goods (except books, medicine, and food). Should you, as a visitor to the U.K., wish to receive a VAT refund, you must ask the shopkeeper from whom you buy your goods for the appropriate form, which British officials will sign and stamp when you take your purchases through customs. Once home, send the form and a self-addressed, British-stamped envelope to the shopkeeper, who will then mail your refund. (Whew!)

The weather in the United Kingdom is subject to frequent changes but few extremes, with an average temperature in the low to mid-60°F in the summer and in the low 40°F in the winter. Throughout the islands, you should expect unstable weather patterns; a bright and cloudless morning sky is often followed by intermittent drizzle throughout the afternoon. Bring something that can instantly cover both you *and* your pack.

Communication The newly remodeled **British pay phone** charges 10p for local calls. A series of harsh beeps will warn you to insert more money when your time is up. For the rest of the call, the digital display ticks off your credit in 1p increments so you can watch your pence in suspense. Only unused coins are returned. You may use all remaining credit on a second call by pressing the "follow on call" button (often marked "FC"). Phones don't accept 1p, 2p, or 5p coins. If you'll be making more than a few calls during your stay in Britain, pick up a handy **Phonecard,** available in denominations of £2, £4, £10, and £20. Get them at post offices, newsagents, or John Menzies stationery shops. Phone booths that take cards are

U.K. ESSENTIALS

labeled in green and are common except in rural areas; coin booths are labeled in yellow.

To make **international direct calls** from the United Kingdom, dial the **international access code (010),** the country code for where you're calling, the area/city code and then the local number. Another option is to access an operator in the country you're dialing—rates are often cheaper than those for direct calls, and service a bit speedier, but they tack on a hefty automatic service charge. The following services will allow you to place **collect calls** (expensive) or charge them to a **calling card** (less so): AT&T **USA Direct** (tel. 0800-8900-11; collect or AT&T calling card), MCI **World Reach** (tel. 0800-8902-22; collect or MCI calling card), **Canada Direct** (tel. 0800-8900-16; collect or calling card), **New Zealand Direct** (tel. 0800-8900-64; collect or NZ Telecom calling card) and **Australia Direct** (tel. 0800-8900-61; collect or AUT calling card). In the event of sudden illness or an accident, dial **999,** the general **emergency** number for Britain and Ireland; it's a free call from any pay phone.

Accommodations and Camping

The United Kingdom has hundreds of **youth hostels,** both HI and independent. The respective hostel associations of England and Wales (YHA), Scotland (SYHA), and Northern Ireland (YHANI), publish inexpensive, essential guides with full maps and descriptions for all their hostels. Rates, which depend on the traveler's age and the grade of the hostel, hover between £4.50-8.50, higher in London. Hostels are generally closed from 10am-5pm and impose an evening curfew (usually about 11pm). All require sleep sacks, which they sell or rent for a nominal fee. If these regulations cramp your style, stick to looser independent establishments. Always book ahead in high season.

Native to Britain, the term "Bed and Breakfast" generally means a small place that offers basic accommodations and breakfast at a reasonable price, often in private homes whose owners have room to spare, or guest houses. B&Bs (£10-15, in London £16-60) are so rampant that it is absurd to single out the establishments we list; when they're full, ask for a referral. Practically all tourist offices book rooms for a fee (usually £1 or 10% deposit); *Let's Go* notes those that don't charge. Most offices also publish *Where to Stay* brochures listing B&Bs and campsites they have approved. B&Bs have less space for single travelers, though proprietors soften toward evening when their doubles don't fill. Vegetarians should declare themselves at once; some proprietors will alter the bacon-and-eggs routine when asked.

Camping brings you closest to the land, the water, the insects, and continued financial solvency. Britain has over 2500 campsites, most of which are open from April through October, though some stay open year-round. You can legally set up camp only in specifically marked areas, unless you get permission from the owner on whose land you plan to squat. It is legal to cross private land by **public rights of way** (marked paths); any other use of private land without permission is considered trespassing. For more info about camping in Britain, send for the British Tourist Authority's free brochure *Caravan and Camping Parks.* In the U.S. contact 40 W. 57th St., 3rd floor, New York, NY 10019 (tel. (212) 581-4700).

Food and Drink

Although enormous traditional breakfasts get all the fame and glory, the rest of English cuisine is not simply a cauldron of boiled blandness. After recovering from your morning tea or coffee, orange juice, cereal, eggs, bacon, sausage, toast, butter, marmalade, grilled tomatoes, mushrooms, kippers (smoked herring), and, in winter, porridge, you will discover that England is a nation of meat-eaters; the best native dishes are roasts—beef, lamb, and Wiltshire hams. Vegetables are the weakest and mushiest part of the meal; go with salads.

Pub grub (meals served in bars) is the classic, fast, and filling lunch. The *ploughman's lunch* (actually the product of a 1960s advertising campaign) is inexpensive: cheese, bread, pickled onions, chutney, and a tomato or two. Fish and chips are traditionally drowned in vinegar and salt. The best supermarket chains are **Asda, Safeway, Sainsbury,** and **Co-op.** To escape English food, try Asian, Greek, Middle

Eastern, or Indian cuisines. The last is especially worth a try; English restaurants (especially those in London and the larger cities) serve some of the best curries outside India. Ubiquitous "wholefoods" shops cater to vegetarians.

Traditional Welsh cooking relies heavily on potatoes and onions, dairy products, mutton and pork, and fish and seaweed. Welsh *rarebit* is buttered toast topped with a thick cheesy mustard beer sauce. Griddle cakes *(crempog)* are made with sour cream and topped with butter. *Cawl* is a thick broth with everything in it, served with a slab of bread. A few Scottish dishes invoke the good old days of the tartan clans and cavorting livestock—most notably black pudding, made with sheep's blood, and the infamous *haggis* (sheep's or calf's heart and liver minced with oats and boiled in the animal's stomach). They sound more exotic than they taste. The Northern Irish just stick to their potatoes.

Britain may be surrounded by water, but tea keeps it afloat. Tea is the preferred remedy for exhaustion, ennui, a rainy morning, or a hot afternoon. It is served strong and milky; if you want it any other way, say so in advance. "Tea" is also a meal. Afternoon high tea as it is still served in rural Britain includes cooked meats, salad, sandwiches, and dessert. Cream tea, a specialty of Cornwall and Devon, includes toast, shortbread, crumpets, scones and jam, along with the essential thick, "clotted" cream.

If tea remains the focus of family life, the pub is where individual and community come together, a place to catch the latest news or gossip, air an opinion, or relax with your mates. Although exact times vary from pub to pub, the most common hours are from 11am to 11pm. Beer—not wine or cocktails—is the standard pub drink. Bear in mind that British beer may have a higher alcohol content than that to which you are accustomed. It is also usually served warm. Traditional cider, a fizzy fermented apple juice, called "scrumpy" in pub argot and served either sweet or dry, is an equally alcoholic and tasty alternative to beer. The Scotch and the Irish compete with their home-brewed whisk(e)ys (spelled with the e in Ireland, without in Scotland). Scotch whisky is either "malt" (from a single distillery) or "blended" (a mixture of several different brands). For information on pubs throughout Britain, stop by the **Pub Information Centre,** 93 Buckingham Palace Rd., London SW1 (tel. (071) 222 3232).

England

Most of the world knows England as a stunning crash of past and present—the royal family at the mercy of flashy tabloids and fickle bookies, modern-day druids dancing around Celtic Stonehenge, and twentysomethings raving til dawn under the shadow of Industrial Revolution cotton mills. England doesn't put its past in museums or rope it off into National Landmarks; history is merely assumed into daily life. The stones under your feet? They might be ancient Roman roads, the shoulder of a superhighway, or exquisite 12th-century tile—you might step on them all in the space of an hour.

England is exceptionally diverse, belying its diminutive size and isolated position. The Empire's legacy has brought large communities of former colonials to British shores, infusing the island with a wide range of cultures and attitudes, from Indian to Caribbean. And within the island, its various regions maintain distinct identities, from the dramatic coastline and moors of the Southwest to the megalopolis of Central England, from the downs and resorts of the Southeast to the national parks of the North, from London's sprawling splendor to the Cotswolds' village charm.

ORIENTATION AND PRACTICAL INFORMATION

■■■ LONDON

At first, London is kind to the expectations of visitors packing their mental baggage with bobbies and Beefeaters, nursery rhymes and "Masterpiece Theatre," Agatha Christies and history books. The Thamescape is still bounded by the over-familiar Big Ben and the archetypal Tower Bridge, the haphazard streets are indeed crammed with old-fashioned black cabs, and the double-decker red buses do transport bowler-hatted City directors.

But Central London is just a speck on the Greater London map. Ever-expanding London fascinates, bewilders, and thrills to the cutting-edge. The Victorian doorway inscribed with an Anglican piety may belong to a Sikh or Muslim in a city internalizing its imperialist past. Peers and punks swirl around Piccadilly, where "culture" means far more than the Royal Opera. The elusive sense of what makes London more than "quite interesting" can be found partly in this tension between the sometimes fictional past of the heritage industry and a riotously modern present. The less elusive pleasure is in picking and choosing, in creating your very own London.

> For a dapper little book absolutely packed with first-rate information on this city, grab a copy of *Let's Go: London.*

ORIENTATION AND PRACTICAL INFORMATION

London is divided into boroughs and postal code areas, and into informal districts. Both the borough name and postal code prefix appear at the bottom of most street signs. The city has grown by absorbing nearby towns, which is reflected in borough names such as "City of Westminster" and "City of London" (or simply "The City").

Central London, on the north side of the Thames and bounded roughly by the Underground's Circle Line, contains most of the major sights. Within central London the vaguely defined **West End** incorporates the understated elegance of Mayfair, the shopping streets around Oxford Circus, the theaters and tourist traps of Piccadilly Circus and Leicester Square, the exotic labyrinth of Soho, chic Covent Garden, and London's unofficial center, Trafalgar Square. East of the West End lies **Holborn,** center of legal activity, and **Fleet Street,** the traditional journalists' haunt.

Around the southeastern corner of the Circle Line is **The City:** London's financial district, with the Tower of London at its eastern edge and St. Paul's Cathedral nearby. Farther east is the **East End,** ethnically diverse and working-class, and the epic construction site of **Docklands.** Moving back west, along the river and the southern part of the Circle Line is the district of **Westminster,** the royal, political, and ecclesiastical center of England, where you'll find Buckingham Palace, the Houses of Parliament, and Westminster Abbey. In the southwest corner of the Circle Line, below the expanse of **Hyde Park,** are gracious **Chelsea,** embassy-laden **Belgravia,** and **Kensington,** adorned with London's posher shops and restaurants.

Around the northwest corner of the Circle Line, tidy terraces border **Regent's Park;** nearby are the faded squares of **Paddington** and **Notting Hill Gate,** home to large Indian and West Indian communities. Moving east towards the Circle Line's northeast corner leads to **Bloomsbury,** which harbors the British Museum, London University colleges, art galleries, and specialty bookshops. Trendy residential districts stretch to the north, including **Hampstead** and **Highgate,** with the enormous Hampstead Heath and fabulous views of the city.

Trying to reach a specific destination in London can be frustrating. Numbers often go up one side of a street and then down the other. One road may change names 4 times in fewer miles and a single name may designate a street, lane, square, and row. A good map is key. For a day's walk, London Transport's free map will do, but those staying a week or longer ought to buy a London street index. *London A to Z* (that's "ay to *zed,*" by the way), *Nicholson's Streetfinder,* and the *ABC London Street Atlas* (all £2 and up) are excellent.

Walking tours, such as **Original London Walks** (tel. 624 3978), fill in the nooks and crannies that bus tours (see Sights) roll over; most walks cost £4, £3 for students and YHA members. The **London Bicycle Tour Company** (tel. 928 6838) peddles a 3-hr city tour (Sat. and Sun. only; £9.95, including bike hire). The *London Silver Jubilee Walkway* guide is available free from tourist offices; the route passes the larger sights and lesser-known treasures.

Tourist Offices: London Tourist Board Information Centre, Victoria Station Forecourt, SW1 (tel. 123 432, recorded message only, 48p/min.). Tube: Victoria. Info and expensive room bookings (£5 fee, £13 deposit). Open daily 8am-7pm; Dec.-March Mon.-Sat. 8am-7pm, Sun. 8am-5pm. Tourist offices also at **Heathrow Airport** (open daily 9am-6pm; Dec.-March 9am-5pm), **Harrods,** and **Selfridges. British Travel Centre,** 12 Regent St., SW1. Tube: Piccadilly Circus. Best for travel outside of London. Fuses the services of the British Tourist Authority, British Rail, American Express, and an accommodations service (£5 booking fee plus deposit). Open Mon.-Fri. 9am-6:30pm, Sat. 9am-5pm, Sun. 10am-4pm; Nov.-March Mon.-Fri. 9:30am-5pm, Sat. 9:30am-12:30pm.

Budget Travel: London is *the* place to shop for cheap bus, plane, and train tickets to North America, Africa, Asia, Australia, and the moon. Browse the ads in *Time Out* or the *Evening Standard.* **STA Travel,** 86 Old Brompton Rd., SW7 (tel. 937 9221 for Euro travel, 937 9971 for North American travel, and 937 9962 for the rest of the world). Tube: South Kensington. Also at 117 Euston Rd., NW1. Tube: Euston. Open Mon.-Fri. 8am-8pm, Sat. 10am-4pm, Sun. 10am-2pm. **YHA Travel,** 14 Southampton St., WC2 (tel. 836 8541). Tube: Covent Garden. For the free-wheeling young and old. Travel guides (*Let's Go* and mere mortals), maps and equipment. Also a branch at 174 Kensington High St., W8 (tel. 938 2948). Open Mon.-Wed. 10am-6pm, Thurs.-Fri. 10am-7pm, Sat. 9am-6:30pm. **Council Travel,** 28a Poland St., W1 (tel. 287 3337). Tube: Oxford Circus. Affiliated with international CIEE; great plane deals. Open Mon.-Wed. and Fri. 9am-7pm, Sat. 9am-6:30pm. **Travel CUTS,** 295a Regent St., W1 (tel. 255 1944). Tube: Oxford Circus. Canadian equivalent of Council Travel. **Trailfinders,** 42-50 Earl's Court Rd., W8 (tel. 937 5400). Tube: High St. Kensington. Clearinghouse for cheap air tickets. Open Mon.-Wed. and Fri.-Sat. 9am-6pm; tel. only Sun. 10am-2pm. **National Express,** 52 Grosvenor Gdns., SW1 (tel. 730 8235). Tube: Victoria. International office also handles coach travel in England. Branch office at 13 Regent St., SW1. Tube: Piccadilly Circus. Open Mon.-Fri. 9am-6pm, Sat. 9am-4pm. **London Student Travel,** 52 Grosvenor Gdns., WC1 (tel. 730 3402). Tube: Victoria. Competitive rail, coach, and air fares on the Continent and beyond.

Embassies and High Commissions: U.S., 24 Grosvenor Sq., W1 (tel. 499 9000). Tube: Bond St. **Canadian High Commission,** MacDonald House, 1 Grosvenor Sq., W1 (tel. 658 6600). Tube: Bond St. **Australian High Commission,** Australia House, The Strand, WC2 (tel. 379 4334). Tube: Aldwych or Temple. **New Zealand High Commission,** New Zealand House, 80 Haymarket, SW1 (tel. 930 8422). Tube: Charing Cross. For visas for **France,** contact the French Consulate, 21/23 Cromwell Pl., SW7 (tel. 581 5292). Tube: South Kensington. **Ireland,** 17 Grosvenor Pl., SW1 (tel. 235 2171). Tube: Hyde Park Corner. **South Africa,** South Africa House, Trafalgar Sq. WC2 (tel. 930 4488).

Currency Exchange: Go to banks, *never to bureaux de change* (such as Chequepoint), which have high fees and/or ridiculously bad rates. If you're stuck outside banking hours, stick to American Express, **Thomas Cook,** 15 Shaftesbury Ave., Piccadilly Circus (24hrs.), or **Exchange International,** Victoria Station (24hrs.).

American Express: 6 Haymarket, SW1 (tel. 930 4411). Tube: Piccadilly Circus. Currency exchange open Mon.-Fri. 9am-5pm, Sat. 9am-5:45pm, Sun. 10am-5:45pm. Message and mail pick-up Mon.-Fri. 9am-5pm, Sat. 9am-noon (60p, free for AmEx users). Other offices at 147 Victoria St., SW1 (Tube: Victoria), opposite Harrods (Tube: Knightsbridge), 54 Cannon St., EC4 (Tube: Cannon St.), and in the British Travel Centre (above). Report lost or stolen Traveler's Cheques 24hrs. at tel. 0 800 52 1313.

London

Regent's Park

Inner Circle

Eversholt St.

Euston Station

Abbey Rd.

Abercorn Pl.

Grove

Wellington Rd.

Circus Rd.

Prince Albert Rd.

Hall Rd.

End Rd.

St. John's Wood Rd.

Lisson Grove

Outer Circle

Chester Rd.

Outer Circle

Park Rd.

Albany St.

Hampstead Rd.

Euston Rd.

Gower St.

Maida Vale

Clifton Rd.

Bloomfield Rd.

Edgware Rd.

Marylebone Rd.

Devonshire St.

Gt. Portland St.

Portland Pl.

Harley St.

Cleveland St.

Tottenham Court Rd.

Univers

Lon

Harrow Rd.

Marylebone Flyover

Crawford St.

Upper Montague St.

Gloucester Pl.

Seymour Pl.

Baker St.

Marylebone High St.

Wigmore St.

Benters St.

Bishop's Bridge Rd.

Praed St.

Paddington Station

Sussex Gdns.

Edgware Rd.

Manchester Square

Duke St.

Oxford Circus

Oxford St.

Regent St.

Dean St.

Queensway

Craven Hill

Marble Arch

Bayswater Rd.

N. Carriage Dr.

Speaker's Corner

Oxford St.

Grosvenor Square

Brook St.

Grosvenor St.

Bond St.

Brewer St.

Shafte

Bayswater Rd.

U.S. Embassy

Berkeley Square

Sth. Audley St.

Piccadilly Circus

Regent

Kensington Gardens

Hyde Park

The Serpentine

Park Lane

Curzon St.

Jermyn St.

Piccadilly

Green Park

St. James's Palace

Pall Mall

The Mall

Kensington Palace

W. Carriage Dr.

S. Carriage Rd.

Knightsbridge

Hyde Park Corner

Constitution Hill

St. James's Park

Birdcage W

Kensington Rd.

Kensington Gore

Kensington Rd.

Sloane St.

Belgrave Square

Grosvenor Pl.

Wes

Royal Albert Hall

Prince Consort Rd.

Victoria & Albert Museum

Brompton Rd.

Basil St.

Pavilion Rd.

Cadogan Pl.

Eaton Square

Victoria

Palace Gate

Gloucester Rd.

Queen's Gate

Exhibition Rd.

Natural History Museum

Walton St.

Pont St.

Buckingham Palace Rd.

Victoria Station

Horsefe Rd.

Cromwell Rd.

Draycott Ave.

Coach Station

Ixworth Pl.

Sloane Ave.

Sloane Sq.

Pimlico Rd.

Warwick Way

Sutherland St.

Vauxhall B

Old Brompton Rd.

Cale St.

Sydney St.

Old Church St.

King's Rd.

Flood St.

Royal Hospital Rd.

Chelsea Br. Rd.

Ebury Br. Rd.

Belgrave Rd.

Lupus St.

Redcliffe Gdns.

Fulham Rd.

Royal Hospital

Chelsea Embankment

Grosvenor Rd.

Finborough Rd.

Beaufort St.

Carlyle's House

Cheyne Walk

Oakley St.

Chelsea Br.

Nine El

Albert Br.

River Thames

Battersea Park

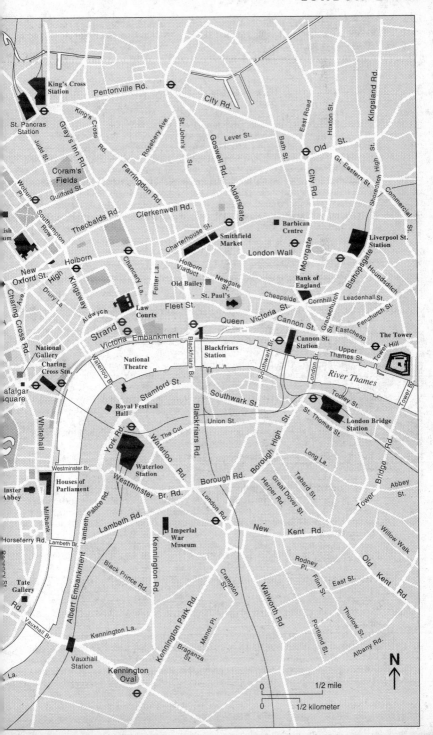

King's Cross Station

St. Pancras Station

Pentonville Rd.

City Rd.

King's Cross Rd.

Roseberry Ave

St. John's St.

Lever St.

Goswell Rd.

East Road

Hoxton St.

Old St.

Bath St.

City Rd.

Gt. Eastern St.

Shoreditch High St.

Kingsland Rd.

Commercial St.

Gray's Inn Rd.

Judd St.

Coram's Fields

Guilford St.

Woburn Pl.

Southampton Row

Farringdon Rd.

Theobalds Rd.

Clerkenwell Rd.

Charterhouse St.

Aldersgate

Barbican Centre

Moorgate

Liverpool St. Station

Bishopsgate

Houndsditch

...ish ...um

Holborn

New Oxford St.

High

Kingsway

Drury La.

Chancery La.

Fetter La.

Holborn Viaduct

Smithfield Market

London Wall

London Wall

Bank of England

Cornhill

Leadenhall St.

Fenchurch St.

Newgate St.

Old Bailey

St. Paul's

Cheapside

Gracechurch St.

Eastcheap

Charing Cross Rd.

Aldwych

Law Courts

Fleet St.

Queen Victoria St.

Cannon St.

Strand

Victoria Embankment

Blackfriars Br.

Blackfriars Station

Cannon St. Station

Upper Thames St.

The Tower

Tower Hill

National Gallery

Charing Cross Stn.

...afalgar ...quare

National Theatre

Royal Festival Hall

Blackfriars Rd.

Stamford St.

Southwark St.

Union St.

Southwark Br.

Cannon St. Br.

London Br.

River Thames

Todley St.

St. Thomas St.

London Bridge Station

Tower Br.

Whitehall

York Rd.

The Cut

Waterloo Rd.

Borough High St.

Long La.

Tower Bridge Rd.

Abbey St.

Westminster Br.

...inster Abbey

Houses of Parliament

Waterloo Station

Westminster Br. Rd.

Borough Rd.

London Rd.

New

Kent Rd.

Tabard St.

Great Dover St.

Harper Rd.

Old Kent Rd.

Willow Walk

Millbank

Lambeth Br.

Lambeth Palace Rd.

Lambeth Rd.

Imperial War Museum

Rodney Pl.

Flint St.

East St.

Thurlow St.

Horseferry Rd.

Lambeth Br.

Black Prince Rd.

Kennington Rd.

Crampton St.

Walworth Rd.

Portland St.

Albany Rd.

Tate Gallery

Albert Embankment

Kennington Park Rd.

Kennington La.

Braganza St.

Manor Pl.

Regency St.

Vauxhall Br.

Vauxhall Station

Kennington Oval

N

0   1/2 mile

0   1/2 kilometer

Post Office: Unless specified otherwise, Poste Restante goes to the Chief Office, King Edward St., EC1 (tel. 239 5047). Tube: St. Paul's. Open Mon.-Tues. and Thurs.-Fri. 8:30am-6:30pm, Wed. 9am-6:30pm. Save hassle and have mail sent to Trafalgar Sq. Post Office, 24-28 William IV St., WC2N 4DL (tel. 930 9580). Tube: Charing Cross. Open Mon.-Sat. 8am-8pm.

Telephones: You can make international calls from any pay phone; use a Phone-card for convenience. The blue Mercurycard phones are cheaper than BT phones, but harder to find. For London directory information call 142; operator 100; international operator 155. London has 2 **city codes:** 071 (central London) and 081 (outer London). Use the code only if you are calling from one area to the other. All London numbers listed in *Let's Go* are (071) unless otherwise indicated.

Flights: Heathrow Airport (tel. (081) 759 4321), is the world's busiest airport. From Heathrow, take the **Underground** to central London (40min.). London Transport's **Airbus** (tel. 222 1234) zips from Heathrow to central points, including hotels (1hr., £5), and a **National Express** (tel. 730 0202) bus runs hourly between Gatwick and Victoria from 6am-8pm (£6). Buses give you more baggage room than the underground, a better view, and run after midnight. Most charter flights land at **Gatwick Airport** (tel. (0293) 535 353). From there, take the BR Gatwick Express train to Victoria Station (every 15min., £8.60). Taxis take twice as long and cost 5 times as much. British Rail's Stansted Express runs to **Stansted Airport** (tel. (0279) 502 380) from Liverpool St. station.

Trains: British Rail runs Travel Centres at its mainline stations and at 12-16 Regent St. (Tube: Piccadilly Circus); The Strand (Tube: Charing Cross); Victoria St.; and Kind William St. (All open Mon.-Fri. 9am-5pm.) To East Anglia, Essex, Southern England, Northeast, East, and South London: tel. 928 5100. To South Midlands, West of England, South Wales, West London, and Ireland via Fishguard: tel. 262 6767. To East and West Midlands, North Wales, Northwest England, Scotland via West Coast, Northwest London, Northern Ireland, and Ireland via Holyhead: tel 387 7070. To East and Northeast England, Scotland via East Coast, and North London: tel. 278 2477. To Europe: tel. (0891) 888 731.

Buses: Green Line (tel. 668 7261) buses serve outer London areas; most routes originate on Buckingham Palace Rd. or Eccleston Bridge, near Victoria Station. Buy a one-day **Rover** ticket (£6, valid on almost all Green Line coach and London Country buses Mon.-Fri. after 9am, Sat.-Sun. all day; 3-day Rover £16.50). **National Express** (tel. 730 0202) serves most of Britain. The main depot is **Victoria Coach Station** on Buckingham Palace Rd. at Elizabeth St. (tel. 730 0202). Tube: Victoria. Private coach companies are frequently the best deal for long-distance trips (to the north, to Scotland, and to Ireland).

Luggage Storage: Very restricted, due to recent bomb threats.

Public Transportation: The **Underground** (or **Tube**) is fast, efficient and crowded. It opens about 6am; the last train runs around midnight. Buy your ticket before you board and pass it through automatic gates at both ends of your journey; fare dodgers can be fined up to £200. Within the central zone 1 (bounded roughly by the Circle line), the fare is a standard 80p; journeys outside this zone cost up to £2.30. Transfers are free. London's languorous **buses** are a great way to see the city. Fares are generally 10-20p lower than the Tube. Pick up a free *London Bus Map* from a Travel Information Centre (Euston, King's Cross, Victoria, Oxford Circus, Heathrow, Piccadilly Circus, Liverpool St., and St. James's Park). Also get a **night bus** schedule; these can save you after midnight. All run through Trafalgar Sq. London Transport's 24-hr. phone information line (tel. 222 1234) can advise you on all routes.

Taxis: Hail your own or call a radio-dispatched taxi (tel. 272 0272 or 253 5000). London fares are steep, and 10% tip is standard. In addition to licensed black cabs, there are tons of unregulated "minicabs" in the Yellow Pages. **Ladycabs** (tel. 272 3019) has only women drivers.

Bike Rental: Mountain Bike and Ski, 18 Gillingham St., SW1. (tel. 834 8933). Tube: Victoria. Mountain bikes £7/day, £13/long weekend. £50 deposit, plus £1/day insurance. Open Mon.-Thurs. 8:30am-5pm, Fri. 8:30am-7:30pm, Sat. 8:30am-4pm.

Hitchhiking: Women, even in groups, should never hitchike—men who value safety should also take a train or bus out of London. Hitchers often check the U of

London Union's **ride board,** on the ground floor of 1 Malet St., WC1 (tube: Russell Sq.), or ask at youth hostels. It's easier to hitch to London than out of it. **Freewheelers** (tel. 738 6861) matches hitchers and drivers, at a £5 yearly membership fee plus 2½p/mile for gas. Single-sex matching available. Write to Freewhellers, Ltd., Ventura House, 176 Acre La., SW2 5UL.

Disabled Travelers: Call the **Disability Information Service** (tel. 630 5994) or **GLAD** (Greater London Association for the Disabled; tel. 274 0107).

Bisexual, Gay, and Lesbian Services: London Lesbian and Gay Switchboard (tel. 837 7324). 24-hr. advice and support service. **Bisexual Helpline:** tel. (081) 569 7500. **London Lesbian and Gay Centre,** 67-69 Cowcross St., EC1 (tel. 608 1471). Tube: Farringdon. Largest in Europe. Open Mon.-Tues. noon-11pm, Wed.-Thurs. and Sun. noon-midnight, Fri.-Sat. noon-3am. *Time Out* magazine provides exhaustive listing of clubs, events, and information.

Crises: Samaritans, 46 Marshall St., W1 (tel. 734 2800). Tube: Oxford Circus. 24-hr. hotline for all sorts of problems. **London Rape Crisis Centre,** (tel. 837 1600), offers advice, counseling and accompaniment to a doctor or court. 24hrs.

Pharmacy: Bliss Chemists, 5 Marble Arch, W1 (tel. 723 6116). Open daily 9am-midnight. Most branches of **Boots** are open Mon.-Sat. 9am-7pm.

Medical Assistance: Call **999** for **ambulance** assistance. You can receive free treatment in the casualty ward (emergency room) of any hospital. Try the **London Hospital** at Whitechapel (Whitechapel Rd., E1; tel. 377 7000) or **Westminster Hospital** at Pimlico (Dean Ryle St., Horseferry Rd., SW1; tel. 746 8000).

Emergencies: Police, fire, or ambulance (tel. **999**). No coins required.

ACCOMMODATIONS

Write well in advance to reserve rooms for summer. Among London's spectrum of accommodations, private hostels and university halls of residence are the best buys; check for reduced weekly rates in hotels. Sleeping outdoors is unsafe and illegal; in a pinch, contact the **Piccadilly Advice Centre,** 100 Shaftesbury Ave., W1 (tel 434 3773; Tube: Piccadilly Circus), which helps the "young, homeless, or new to London." (Open daily 2-6pm and 7-9pm.)

YHA Hostels

Cheap, cheery, and chock full o' youths, London's YHA hostels can be a welcome relief from dreary B&Bs; despite daytime lockouts and curfews, they're buzzing meeting places. Groups gobble space early, but some beds are kept free for individuals. Reserve ahead for July and August; if not, it's still worth calling (central tel. 248 6547). All hostels have personal lockers requiring a padlock, and require international membership cards: £9 at the hostels or YHA London Headquarters, 14 Southampton St., WC2 (tel. 240 5236; Tube: Covent Garden; open Mon.-Wed. and Fri. 10am-6pm, Thurs. 10am-7pm, Sat. 9am-6pm).

City of London, 36 Carter Lane, EC4V 5AD (tel. 236 4965). Tube: St. Paul's. Central, refurbished, and antiseptic, with new facilities. Rooms of 2-15, averaging 5. 24-hr. security, canteen. Reception open 7am-11pm. £19.30, under 18 £16.

Hampstead Heath, 4 Wellgarth Rd., Hampstead, NW11 (tel. (081) 458 9054). Tube: Golder's Green. Sumptuous. Currency exchange. Reception open 7am-midnight. No curfew. £13.90, under 18 £11.80. Wheelchair access.

Holland House (King George VI Memorial Youth Hostel), Holland Walk, Kensington, W8 (tel. 937 0748), next to Holland Park Open Air Theatre. Tube: Holland Park or Notting Hill Gate. Daily pick-up soccer games. Bright and active. Currency exchange. Reception open 7am-11:30pm. No curfew. £19, under 18 £16.

Oxford Street, 14-18 Noel St., W1 (tel. 734 1618). Tube: Oxford Circus. Heart of London and Soho. Small, plush rooms for 2-4. 24-hr. security. Currency exchange. Baggage room. Reception open 7am-11pm. No curfew. £16.70, under 18 £13.50.

Earl's Court, 38 Bolton Gns., SW5 0AQ (tel. 373 7083). Tube: Earl's Court. Townhouse in leafy neighborhood. Kitchen. 24-hr. security. Currency exchange. Reception open 7am-11pm. 4-16/room. No curfew. £16.10, under 18 £14.50.

■ **UNITED KINGDOM**

Highgate, 84 Highgate West Hill, N6 (tel. (081) 340 1831). Tube: Archway. Out-of-the-way Georgian house in beautiful neighborhood—worth the trek. 9- to 16-bed rooms. Reception open 8:45-10am, 1-7pm, and 8-11:30pm. Lockout 10am-1pm. Strict curfew midnight. £11.40, under 18 £7.60.

Rotherhithe, Island Yard., Salter Rd., SE16 (tel. 232 2114). Tube: Rotherhithe. 15-min. walk down Brunel Rd. to Salter. Brand-new Orwellian chrome and glass. Light, immaculate rooms. Bar and video games. Reception open 7am-11:30pm. No curfew. 24-hr. security. £17.10. Wheelchair access.

Private Hostels

These places aren't as crammed with schoolkids, do not require membership cards, and tend to have fewer rules. Open all year, their facilities compare to HI hostels'.

Curzon House Hotel, 58 Courtfield Gdns., SW5 0NF (tel. 581 2116). Tube: Gloucester Rd. Exceptionally friendly staff attracts diverse clientele. Kitchen, TV lounge. Single-sex dorms £13. Singles £26. Doubles £34. Triples £45. Quads £64. Continental breakfast included. Nov.-May dorm £65/week.

Elizabeth House (YWCA Hostel), 118 Warwick Way, SW1 (tel. 630 0741). Tube: Victoria. Any human over 5 welcome. Friendly. Dorms £15. Singles £22. Doubles £36-38. Continental breakfast included. Reserve early by £10 deposit.

Albert Hotel, 191 Queens Gate, SW7 5EU (tel. 584 3019). Tube: South Kensington or Gloucester Rd. Near Royal Albert Hall. Victorian rooms with private facilities. Reception open 24hrs. No lockout. Check-out 10am. Dorms £9-12. Singles £25. Twins £30. Continental breakfast included. Reserve ahead with 1 night's deposit.

Anne Elizabeth House Hostel, 30 Collingham Pl., SW5 (tel. 370 4821). Tube: Earl's Court. Bare, clean, single-sex dorm-style rooms. No curfew. Singles £16.50-21. Doubles £27.50-36. Triples £34.50-48. Reserve way ahead with £10 deposit.

International Student House, 229 Great Portland St., W1 (tel. 631 3223). Tube: Great Portland St. Ugly '60s exterior conceals thriving international network of events and facilities. Well-maintained rooms. 4-bed dorm £12. Singles £22.70. Doubles £38.30. Triples £48.30. English breakfast included. Reserve well ahead.

Central University of Iowa Hostel, 7 Bedford Pl., WC1 (tel. 580 1121). Tube: Holborn or Russell Sq. Bright, spartan, clean rooms. 2-week max. stay. Reception open 8am-1pm and 3-8pm. Dorms £16. Laundry. Open April to mid-Aug.

Centre Français, 61 Chepstow Pl., W2 (tel. 221 8134). Tube: Notting Hill Gate or Bayswater. Delightful ambience, immaculate hostel, chic area. No curfew. Dorms £12. Singles £23.75. Doubles £38. Triples £49.50. Quads £66. Breakfast included. Weekly rates. Book 2 months ahead by mail or phone. Volume discounts.

Palace Hotel, 31 Palace Ct., W2 (tel. 221 5628). Tube: Notting Hill Gate or Queensway. Shiny, happy young'uns in bright 8-bed rooms. Pool table. No curfew. £10.

Talbot Hotel, Talbot Sq., W2 (tel. 402 7202). Tube: Paddington. Basic. Thin mattresses, but that price! 24-hr. security. Kitchen, TV lounge. 3- to 4-bed dorms £8.

Tonbridge School Clubs, Ltd., corner of Judd and Cromer St., WC1 (tel. 837 4406). Tube: King's Cross. Right price for desperadoes. Seedy neighborhood. Blanket and foam pads on gymnasium floor. Non-British students with passports only. Reception open 10-11:30pm. Check-out 10am. Hot showers, storage. £3.

University Halls of Residence

Slightly more expensive than the cheapest hotels, university dorms feature more amenities. Available in summer (mid-July to Sept.), they have singles. Write the bursar in advance. **King's College** of the U. of London handles summer bookings for the first 3 halls listed below. Locations are excellent and include breakfast and linens. To book, write to King's Campus Vacation Bureau, 552 King's Rd., London SW10 0UA (tel. 351 6011). This summer they may have openings as early as June.

Ingram Court, 552 King's Rd., SW10 0UA (tel. 351 6513). Tube: Fulham Broadway; 10-min. walk. Popular hall on main campus, with mostly singles. Tennis courts. Stately, verdant lawn and fish pond. Singles £18.80. Twins £29.40.

Wellington Hall, 71 Vincent Sq., Westminster, SW1P 2PA (tel. 834 4740). Tube: Victoria. Edwardian hall on quiet square. Library, bar, oak-paneled, stained-glass-windowed dining room. On a quiet square. Singles £21. Doubles £31.50.

Lightfoot Hall, Manresa Rd. at King's Rd., SW3 (tel. 351 2488). Tube: Sloane Sq. or South Kensington. Primo location. Modern institutional rooms. Satellite TV room. Singles £19.50. Doubles £31. Continental breakfast included.

Queen Alexandra's House, Kensington Gore, SW7 (tel. 589 3635 or 589 4053), by Royal Albert Hall. Tube: South Kensington. Women only. Ornate Victorian building. Cozy rooms, mostly singles, sunny dining hall. Beaucoup de pianos. Kitchen and laundry. £22. English breakfast included. Open mid-July to mid-Aug. and near Easter. Write weeks in advance.

Tufnell Park Hall, Hudelleston Rd., N7 (tel. 272 4649). Tube: Tufnell Park. Modern tower juts behind row houses. Bar. Singles with wash desk and sink £17. English breakfast included. Make reservations through the Polytechnic Bookings Office (tel. 753 5091). Open Easter and July-Sept.

James Leicester Hall, Market Rd., N7 9PN (tel. 607 3250, -5417). Tube: Caledonian Rd. Drab modern building and bright, new one around corner from Tube. Bar. Same price, reservations, and dates as Tufnell. English breakfast included.

John Adams Hall, 15-23 Endsleigh St., WC1 (tel. 387 4086), off Tavistock Sq. Tube: Euston Sq. Elegant London U. building; some rooms have balconies. Mostly singles. Reception open July-Aug. and around Easter Mon.-Fri. 7:30am-10pm. Laundry, TV, ping-pong. Singles £21. Doubles £37. English breakfast included. Book well in advance, then confirm.

Passfield Hall, 1 Endsleigh Pl., WC1 (tel. 387 3584 or 387 7743). Tube: Euston. London School of Economics hall with many long-term residents; high-ceilinged rooms vary in size. Reception open 8:30am-midnight. Singles £16. Doubles £25. Triples £33. Breakfast included. Laundry. Open July-Sept. and near Easter.

Hughes Parry Hall, Cartwright Gdns., WC1H 9EF (tel. 387 1477). Tube: Russell Sq. Mammoth modern London U. hall with small singles. Slick! Squash, tennis, laundry, bar, TV, libraries, 24-hr. porter. Students £14, including English breakfast and dinner. Non-students £18.50 with breakfast, £22 with dinner. Open July-Aug.

Bed and Breakfast Hotels

The number of London B&Bs boggles the mind, but most are about as distinct as blades of grass, providing functional facilities, a TV lounge, and less attentive service in slightly tawdry neighborhoods. Often location makes the most difference.

Near Victoria Station

Here's the bargain basement of budget B&Bs. Near Victoria Station, scope Belgrave Rd., St. George's Dr., and Warwick Way for £20-25 action. Ebury St.'s calm has a price. Also try Earl's Court, Penywern Rd., and Earl's Court Sq.

Luna and Simone Hotel, 47-49 Belgrave Rd., SW1 (tel. 834 5897, 828 2474), past Warwick Sq. Tube: Victoria. Immaculate, cheap rooms with color TV. English breakfast. Singles £20-22. Doubles £30-44. Triples £39-51. Winter discounts.

Marne Hotel, 34 Belgrave Rd., SW1 (tel. 834 5195). Tube: Victoria. Arranges home stays for students, with Homestay U.K. Laundry. Singles from £25. Doubles £35, with bath £42. Triples £45. Discounts over 5 nights. English breakfast.

Georgian House Hotel, 35 St. George's Dr., SW1 (tel. 834 1438). Tube: Pimlico. Best-decorated. Friendly. Wacky student discounts. TV, phone, tea/coffee maker too. Reception open 8am-11pm. Singles £25-29. Doubles £35-44. Triples £48-53. Quads £59-67. Students: singles £15, doubles £28, triples £39. English breakfast.

Oxford House, 92-94 Cambridge St., SW1 (tel. 834 6467), near the church. Tube: Victoria Sta. Quiet residential area; it's home-like, with pets. TV lounge. Good cooking, commodious rooms, and firm beds. Singles £28-30. Doubles £38-40. Triples £48-51. Quad £64-68. English breakfast. Reserve 3-4 weeks ahead.

Ebury House Hotel, 102 Ebury St., SW1 (tel. 730 1350, 730 1059). Classy, posh, gorgeous. Color TV, comforters on all beds. Patio. Experienced management knows sights. Singles £40. Doubles £50. Triples £66. Quad £76. Reserve a month early.

Earl's Court

The area feeds on the tourist trade; beware the hustlers. Travel agencies, take-away eateries, Australians, and souvenir shops dominate. Earl's Court is home to a significant gay population.

White House Hotel, 12 Earl's Ct. Sq., SW5 (tel. 373 5903). Glassed-in porch. Bedrooms are pleasant and much cheaper than most of their equals. Laundry. Singles £15. Doubles £25-30. Triples £30. Continental breakfast included.

York House Hotel, 27-29 Philbeach Gdns., SW5 9EA (tel. 373 7519). Helpful, experienced manager. French, Spanish, and Arabic spoken. TV lounge, garden. Reception open 7am-11pm. Singles £24.70. Doubles £38.80-55. Triples £49-65. Quads £56. English breakfast included. Reserve in advance with 1 night's deposit.

Kensington and Chelsea

The snazzy Royal Borough of Kensington and Chelsea is hardly a gold mine of budget B&Bs. The few exceptions to this rule are particularly impressive.

Vicarage Hotel, 10 Vicarage Gate, W8 4AG (tel. 229 4030). Tube: Notting Hill Gate. Posh! Red velvet and gold frame a sweeping staircase. Small, comfy, immaculate bedrooms. Luxurious TV lounge. Singles £30. Doubles £52. Triples £65. Quads £70. Full English breakfast included. Reserve in advance.

Hotel Europe, 131-137 Cromwell Rd., SW7 4DU (tel. 370 2336, 370 2337, 370 2338). Tube: Gloucester Rd. Classy dining room and lounge. Fax service. Singles £30-35. Doubles £40-45. Triples £45-55. Continental breakfast included. Reserve in advance.

Bloomsbury

Heaps of comfortable hotels (£16-30/person) line well-situated, busy Gower St. Bedford Pl. is a step up in price and comfort, and Cartwright Gardens outshines all streets in the area. As you go toward King's Cross, the digs lose their luster.

Regency House Hotel, 71 Gower St., WC1 (tel. 637 1804). Tube: Goodge St. Tops in Bloomsbury. Clean. TV. Small garden. Singles £27-35. Doubles £36-52. Triples £52-65. Quads £60. Quint £68. Hefty winter discounts. Book well ahead.

Ridgemount Hotel, 65-67 Gower St., WC1 (tel. 636 1141 or 580 7060). Tube: Goodge St. Another bright choice in Bloomsbury. Cheery pink bedspreads, firm beds, most rooms with TV. Laundry. Garden. Dare to eat a peach. Singles £25-35. Doubles £38-47. Triples £51-61. Quads £60-70. English breakfast.

Repton House Hotel, 31 Bedford Pl., WC1 (tel. 436 4922). Tube: Russell Sq. Cheaper and only slightly less ornate than its neighbors. TV, phone, tea/coffee makers. Laundry. Rose garden. Reception open 8am-11pm. 6-bed dorm £12. Singles £30-43. Doubles £44-56. Triples £56-66. Continental breakfast.

Thanet, 8 Bedford Pl., WC1 (tel. 636 2869, 580 3377). Like above, but patio for garden. Singles £35-45. Doubles £48-58. Triples with bath £69. Quads £80.

Mentone Hotel, 54-55 Cartwright Gdns., WC1 (tel. 387 3927). Tube: Russell Sq. Pleasantly decorated. Color TV. Singles £34-48. Doubles £45-54. Triples with bath £63. Quads with bath £68-72. Reductions Nov.-March. Same street: the similar **Crescent** at #49-50 (tel. 387 1515) and **Jenkins** at #45 (tel. 387 2067).

Hotel Apollo, 43 Argyle St., WC1 (tel. 837 5489). Tube: King's Cross. Actually a guest house for low-income families. Color TV. One of the neater and cleaner on the block. Singles £24. Doubles £32. Discount £2/night for stays over 3-4 nights.

Paddington and Bayswater

Squashed between Paddington Station and Hyde Park, this area seethes with sullen B&Bs. Though almost every building in Norfolk Sq. and Sussex Gardens calls itself a hotel, the ones on smaller Talbot Sq. and Princes Sq. are more peaceful and residential. As you travel west, establishments become less seedy.

Garden Court Hotel, 30-31 Kensington Gdns. Sq., W2 (tel. 229 2553). Tube: Bayswater. Speckless rooms with phones, radios. TV lounge and lounge serving complimentary beverages. Singles £26-28. Doubles £38-51. Triples £49-57. Quads £57.

Ruddimans Hotel, 160 Sussex Gdns., W2 (tel. 723 1026). Tube: Paddington. White-glove clean. All with sink, TV. Singles £25-28. Doubles £35-40. Triples £51.

Hyde Park Rooms Hotel, 137 Sussex Gdns., W2 (tel. 723 0225, 723 0965). Tube: Paddington. Cheery proprietor. Tidy but drab. All with TV, sink. Enticing bathtubs. Singles £20. Doubles £30. Family £45. 5% extra to pay by credit card.

FOOD

London presents a tantalizing range of foreign and English specialties. With Indian, Lebanese, Greek, Chinese, Thai, Italian, West Indian, and African food inexpensive and readily available, the city has few rivals when it comes to diversity. If you eat but one meal in London, let it be Indian—British Indian food is rivaled only by India's and Sarala's. Meals are cheaper on Westbourne Grove (Tube: Bayswater), or near Euston Station (Tube: Euston) than in the West End.

Supermarkets are cheaper than corner shops and stock inexpensive pre-fab dishes. **Safeway** stores punctuate King's Rd., Edgware Rd. (not far from Paddington), and the Brunswick Shopping Centre opposite the Russell Sq. Tube stop. **Sainsbury** has a branch on Victoria Rd. not far from Victoria Station, and another on Cromwell Rd. (Tube: Gloucester Rd.). Ubiquitous **Europa Food** stores are expensive but stay awake until 11pm.

The West End and City of London

Food for Thought, 31 Neal St., WC2. Tube: Covent Garden. Generous vegetarian servings straight from the pot in an intimate plant-filled restaurant. Daily specials from £3.25. Open Mon.-Sat. 9am-7pm.

Calabash Restaurant, 38 King St., WC2. Tube: Covent Garden. Hand-lickin' pancontinental African dishes, £4.10-7.50. Meals usually about £13. Open Mon.-Fri. 12:30-3pm and 6-11:30pm, Sat. 6-11:30pm.

Neal's Yard Dining Room, 14-15 Neal's Yard, WC2. Wide international selection in an airy room, overlooking a vegetarian paradise: nearby are Neal's Yard's takeaway **Soup and Salad Bar** and **Bakery.** Tortilla heaped with cheese £3.10. Open Tues.-Fri. noon-8pm, Mon. and Sat. noon-5pm.

Scott's, corner of Bedfordbury St. and New Row, WC2. Tube: Covent Garden. Crowds line up at lunchtime to get into this sophisticated *pâtisserie.* Sandwiches £1.50-3.50. Open daily 8am-11:30pm.

Alpha One Fish Bar, 43 Old Compton St., W1. Tube: Leicester Sq. or Piccadilly Circus. Good, greasy fun. Fresh fish and chips, "not a deep freeze on the premises." Large Cod £2.40. Open Sun.-Thurs. 11:30am-1am, Fri.-Sat. 11:30am-2am.

Pollo, 20 Old Compton St., W1. Tube: Leicester Sq. or Piccadilly Circus. Packed Italian restaurant/madhouse. Pizzas £3.30. Open Mon.-Sat. 11:30am-11:30pm.

Chuen Cheng Ku, 17 Wardour St., W1. Tube: Leicester Sq. Considered by some to be one of the planet's best. *Dim sum* dishes £1.65. Open daily 11am-midnight.

Pizza Express, 10 Dean St., W1. Tube: Tottenham Ct. Rd. Great pizza £3.15-5.30. Live jazz Mon.-Thurs. from 9pm and Fri.-Sat from 8pm. Open daily noon-midnight.

Blooms, 90 Whitechapel High St., E1. Tube: Aldgate East. London's finest kosher restaurant, with good salt (corned) beef under £3.20. Popular on Sun. Open Sun.-Thurs. noon-9:30pm, Fri. noon-3:30pm. Open Sat. night until early Sun. morn.

The Place Below, St. Mary-le-Bow Church crypt, Cheapside, EC2. Tube: St. Paul's. Hip, unique vegetarian café. Menu changes daily. Quiche and salad £4.95. Open Mon.-Wed. 7:30am-3pm, Thurs.-Fri. 7:30-3pm and 6-10:30pm.

Kensington, Knightsbridge, Chelsea, and Victoria

Chelsea Kitchen, 98 King's Rd., SW3. Tube: Sloane Sq. Locals rave about this place and its cheap, eclectic menu. Chicken mushroom *fricassee* or Spanish omelette each £2.20. Open Mon.-Sat. 8am-11:30pm, Sun. noon-11:30pm.

Stick and Bowl, 131 Kensington High St., W8. Tube: High St. Kensington. Cheap, *quick,* and good Chinese food. £2 minimum. Open daily 11:30am-11:30pm.

Palms Pasta on the Hill, 17 Campden Hill Rd., W8. Tube: High St. Kensington. Italian café popular with trendies. Pasta under £5. 12.5% service. Open daily noon-midnight.

Arco Bars, 46 Hans Crescent, SW1. Cheap and fairly plentiful Italian. Pasta, wine, and coffee is but £4.25. Open Mon.-Fri. 7am-6pm, Sat. 8am-6pm.

Up-All-Night, 325 Fulham Rd., SW10. Bus #14 or #45. Ferns, fans, and sauna booths. Huge Greek salad £3.30. 10% service. 15% discount on entrees noon-8pm. Open daily noon-6am.

Bloomsbury and North London

Diwana Bhel Poori House, 121 Drummond St., NW1. Tube: Warren St. Clean, airy, and tasty. Try *samosas* or *thali* (silver tray with portions of vegetables, rice, sauce, bread, and dessert). Meals £6-7. BYOB. Open daily noon-11:30pm. Also at 50 Westbourne Grove (Tube: Bayswater).

Chutney's, 124 Drummond St., NW1. Tube: Warren St. A light, cheerful Indian vegetarian café with an all-you-can-eat lunch buffet (£4.50). Open daily noon-2:45pm and 6-11:30pm.

Greenhouse, 16 Chenies St. basement, WC1. Tube: Goodge St. Fresh vegetarian dishes. Thick pizza £2.10. Open Mon. 10am-noon, Tues.-Fri. 10am-9pm, Sat. noon-8pm.

Spaghetti House Ristorante, 15-17 Goodge St., W1. Tube: Goodge St. The original of a popular chain of authentic pasta houses. Assorted trendy pastas start at £4.50. Open Mon.-Sat. noon-11pm, Sun. 5:30-10:30pm.

Wot the Dickens, 3 Woburn Walk, WC1. Tube: Euston. Trendier than its neighbors, this slick joint draws lively crows at lunchtime. Strong espresso and big sandwiches. Shaded sidewalk seating. Smoked salmon plate £2.40. Open Mon.-Fri. 7am-6:30pm, Sat. 8am-4pm.

North Sea Fish House, 7-8 Leigh St., WC1, off Cartwright Gdns. Tube: Russell Sq. 16 kinds of fish fried in pure nut oil, egg, matzo meal, or grilled, plus chips or new potatoes. Low prices. Open daily noon-2:30pm and 5:30-11pm.

Indian Veg Bhelpoori House, 92-93 Chapel Market, N1. Tube: Angel. An unmistakable bargain: all-you-can-eat lunch buffet of Indian vegetarian food for a startling £3.25; dinner buffet £3.50. Open daily noon-3pm and 6-11pm.

Nontas, 16 Camden High St., NW1. Tube: Mornington Crescent or Camden Town. Intimate, superior Greek restaurant. Endless *meze* is worth the £8.75; other dishes £4-6. Open Mon.-Sat. noon-3pm and 3:30pm-midnight.

Paddington and Bayswater

Khan's, 13-15 Westbourne Grove, W2. Tube: Bayswater. Deservedly renowned. Most Indian restaurants are cemetery quiet, but not Khan's. Enormous entrees £1.75-4. Chicken *masala* £3.25. Open daily noon-3pm and 6pm-midnight.

Geale's, 2 Farmer St., W8. Tube: Notting Hill Gate. Efficient service and consummately crisp fish and chips around £3.50. Open Tues.-Sat. noon-3pm and 6-11pm.

Penang, 41 Hereford Rd., W2. Tube: Bayswater. The standard interior belies magnificent Malaysian and Thai cuisine. Mixed vegetables in coconut milk £2.95. Open daily 6-11pm.

PUBS

London's 7000 pubs are as colorful as their country counterparts, but in London the clientele varies widely from one neighborhood to the next. Avoid pubs near train stations; they prey on naïve tourists. For the best prices, head to the East End or south of the Thames. Posh prevails in Chelsea and Hampstead. For people-watching, hit the West End. Besides as many as a dozen potent ales and two ciders, many pubs offer cheap, standard British "pub grub," juices, and soft drinks. Most pubs are open Mon.-Sat. 11am-11pm, Sun. 11am-3pm and 7-10:30pm. The heartbreaking "Time, people, PLEASE!" leaves you 10 minutes to down your brew.

Lamb and Flag, 33 Rose St., WC2, off Garrick St. Tube: Covent Garden or Leicester. Bygone fights earned it the name "Bucket of Blood"; poet John Dryden was thrashed here by a mob of angry readers.

Ye Olde Cheshire Cheese, Wine Office Ct., 145 Fleet St., EC4. Tube: Blackfriars or St. Paul's. Authentic 17th-century pub; sawdust on the floors and Yorkshire suds on tap. Dickens and Johnson were regulars.

Drill Hall Women-Only Bar, 16 Chenies St., WC1 (tel. 631 1353). Tube: Goodge St. Crowded and friendly, with cheap drinks. Open Mon. 6-11pm.

Dirty Dick's, 202-204 Bishopgate, EC2. Tube: Liverpool St. Bedecked with cobwebs and 2 stuffed cats.

King's Head and Eight Bells, 50 Cheyne Walk, SW3. Tube: Sloane Sq., then bus #11, 45, 49, or 219. A favorite of Thomas Carlyle, who lived just up the street. Thomas More would have a jar with his dangerous friend Henry VIII.

The Edge, 11 Soho Sq., W1 (tel. 439 1223). Tube: Tottenham Ct. Rd. Possibly the prime café/bar in which to pose and socialize in Soho; sleek BGL and straight customers pack in from Mon.-Sat. 8am-midnight, Sun. 7:30-10:30pm.

The Scarsdale, 23 Pembroke Sq., W8. Tube: Earl's Ct. Not so much a pub as a private garden party in a sea of flowers and ivy. No blaring jukebox.

Spaniards Inn, Spaniard's End, NW3. Tube: Hampstead, then bus #210 along Spaniard's Rd. Dickens enjoyed a pint in this 1585 traditional pub. Intriguing aviary.

The Flask Tavern, 77 Highgate West Hill, N6. Tube: Archway. Near the youth hostel. Popular in summer—terrace overflows into the heart of Highgate.

Slug and Lettuce, 1 Islington Green, N1. Tube: Angel. Observe Islington trendies through the vast windows. Try upstairs for a comfy, cozy setting.

Prospect of Whitby, 57 Wapping Wall, London Docks. Tube: Wapping. 600-year-old tavern where diarist Samuel Pepys used to imbibe. Excellent Thamescape.

SIGHTS

London is best explored on foot. When your soles begin to ache, try an **Original London Transport Sightseeing Tour** (tel. 222 1234), covering central London's landmarks. (Daily 10am-4pm every ½hr. from Baker St., Haymarket and Victoria St., near the station. £8, children £4. Pay conductor.) For a more comprehensive view of London, invest in a copy of *Let's Go: London* or *Let's Go: Britain & Ireland.*

From Mayfair to Parliament An auspicious beginning to a day's wander is **Piccadilly Circus** and its towering neon bluffs (Tube: Piccadilly Circus). North are the tony shops of Regent St. and the renovated seediness of **Soho. Piccadilly,** running off the Circus, is lined with exclusive stores, including **Fortnum and Mason,** with its Earl Greys. Paths across **Green Park** lead to **Buckingham Palace** (Tube: Victoria or Green Park), now open to tourists. (Tours Aug.-Sept.; £8, seniors £5.50, children £4.) The Changing of the Guard occurs daily (April-July) or every other day (Aug.-March) at 11:30am unless it's raining; arrive early or you won't see a thing. The extravagant "Trooping the Colour" is on a Sat. in June, the Queen's official birthday.

The Mall, a wide processional, leads from the palace to **Admiralty Arch** and Trafalgar Square. **St. James's Park,** south of the Mall, shelters a duck preserve and a flock of lawn chairs. Pigeons crowd **Trafalgar Square** (Tube: Charing Cross), where 4 great stone lions disdain the tourists. A 40-ft. statue of Admiral Nelson tops off the 132-ft. column at the center of the square. **Charing Cross Road,** leading north from Trafalgar to the theater district of **Leicester Square,** is renowned for its bookstores.

Political Britain branches off **Whitehall,** just south of Trafalgar. The **Banqueting House** was the backdrop for Charles I's beheading; it now hosts less lethal state dinners. (Open Mon.-Sat. 10am-5pm; £2.75, students £1.75.) The Prime Minister resides off Whitehall at **10 Downing Street,** now closed to tourists and other terrorists. In the middle of Whitehall is the **Cenotaph,** a monument to Britain's war dead. White-hall ends by the sprawling **Houses of Parliament** (Tube: Westminster). To watch the floor debates, stand in the long lines by St. Stephen's Gate. Committee meetings can be seen without the wait. (Commons open Mon.-Thurs. 4-10pm, Fri. 10am-3pm; Lords open Mon.-Wed. 2:30pm-late, Thurs. 3pm-late, Fri. 11am-late.) Pedantically speaking, **Big Ben** is neither the tower nor the clock, but the 13½-ton bell, cast when a similarly proportioned Sir Benjamin Hall served as Commissioner of Works. Church and state tie the knot in **Westminster Abbey,** coronation chamber to English monarchs for the past 684 years, as well as the site of **Poet's Corner,** the **Grave of the Unknown Warrior,** and the elegantly perpendicular **Chapel of Henry VII.** Britain bestows no greater honor than burial within these walls. The abbey plumber is buried here among such greats as Elizabeth I, Darwin, Dickens, and Ben Jonson (whose last name is misspelled with an *h* on his tomb). Ask about the story surrounding the Stone of Scone. (Abbey open Thurs.-Tues. 8am-6pm, Wed. 8am-7:45pm. Free. Chapels and transepts open Mon.-Tues. and Thurs.-Fri. 9am-4:45pm, Wed. 9am-4:45pm and 6-7:45pm, Sat. 9am-2:45pm and 3:45-5:45pm. £3, students £1.50, free Wed. 6-7:45pm. Photography permitted Wed. 6-7:45pm only.) Abbey Guided Super Tours (£6) are, well, super.

From Hyde Park and Kensington to Chelsea Hyde Park shows its best face on Sundays from 11am to dusk, when soapbox orators take freedom of speech to the limit at **Speaker's Corner** (Tube: Marble Arch, *not* Hyde Park Corner). To the west, **Kensington Gardens,** an elegant relic of Edwardian England, celebrates the glories of model yacht racing in the squarish Round Pound. From the gardens you can catch a glimpse of Kensington Palace, home of those models of royal family values, Charles and Diana. The **Royal Albert Hall,** on the south edge of Hyde Park, hosts the Proms, a gloriously British festival of music (see Entertainment). Up Brompton Rd. near Knightsbridge, **Harrods** (Tube: Knightsbridge) vends under their humble motto, *Omnia Omnibus Ubique* ("All things for all people, everywhere"). (Open Mon.-Tues. and Thurs.-Sat. 9am-6pm, Wed. 9am-8pm, may soon open Sun.) Still-fashionable **King's Road** (Tube: Sloane Sq.), to the south in **Chelsea,** attempts to do justice to its bohemian past.

From Regent's Park to Fleet Street Take a picnic from Harrods to the expanse of **Regent's Park,** northeast from Hyde Park across Marylebone (Tube: Regent's Park). The **London Zoo,** in the north end, has mambos, Asian lions, and piranhas. (Open daily 10am-5:30pm; £6, students and seniors £4.70.) **Camden Town** (Tube: Camden Town), bordering the park to the northeast, sports some of the hemisphere's rollickingest street markets.

   Bloomsbury—eccentric, erudite and disorganized—is known for its literary and scholarly connections, including the **British Museum** (see Museums, below). **Covent Garden**—hub of the jostling 18th century—still sports its grand Royal Opera House, but the tattered old market is now a touristy shopping district. **Fleet Street** is the traditional den of the British press, though nearly all the papers have moved to cheaper real estate. Close by are the **Inns of Court,** which have controlled access to the English Bar since the 13th century.

City of London Once upon a time, "London" meant the square-mile enclave of the **City of London;** the rest of today's metropolis were far-flung towns and villages. The **Tower of London** was the grandest fortress in medieval Europe and the palace and prison of English monarchs for over 500 years. Its best-known edifice, the **White Tower,** is also the oldest, begun by William the Conqueror. In 1483, the "Princes in the Tower" (Edward V and his brother) were murdered in the **Bloody Tower** in one of the great unsolved mysteries of history; 2 of the wives of jolly King Henry VIII were beheaded in the courtyard, and in 1941 Hitler's ridiculous deputy Rudolf Hess was sent to the Tower after his parachute dumped him in Scotland. The

Crown Jewels include the Stars of Africa, cut from the enormous Cullinan Diamond, which was mailed 3rd-class from the Transvaal in an unmarked brown paper package; Scotland Yard believed that was the safest way of getting it to England. (Tube: Tower Hill. Open Mon.-Sat. 9:30am-5pm, Sun. 2-5pm; Nov.-Feb. Mon.-Sat. 9:30am-4pm. £6.70, students and seniors £5.10.) Next to the Tower is **Tower Bridge,** one of London's best-known landmarks. The walkways provide one of London's best views. (Tube: Tower Hill. Open daily 10am-5:45pm; Nov.-March daily 10am-4pm. £2.50.) Other shrapnel of history are scattered throughout the City, among them 24 Christopher Wren churches interspersed with the soaring steel of modern skyscrapers. Peruse smaller churches, such as The Strand's **St. Clement Danes** of "Oranges and Lemons" fame, or the superb **St. Stephen Walbrook** near the Bank of England (Tube: Bank). True-blue cockney Londoners are born within earshot of the famous bells of **St. Mary-le-Bow,** Cheapside. The **Old Bailey** (Tube: St. Paul's) is London's most famous criminal court. Observing a trial can be either thrilling or depressing, depending on how you feel about men in wigs. (In session Oct.-May Mon.-Fri. 10am-1pm and 2-4pm. Cameras not allowed inside.) Nearby is the centerpiece of the City, Wren's mammoth masterpiece, **St. Paul's Cathedral.** In the German Blitz in 1940, the cathedral stood firm in a sea of fire. Climb above the graves of Wren, Nelson, and Wellington in the crypt to the dizzying top of the dome; the view is unparalleled. (Tube: St. Paul's. Open Mon.-Sat. 9am-4:15pm; ambulatory and crypt open Mon.-Sat. 9:30am-4:15pm; galleries open Mon.-Sat. 9:45am-4:15pm. Cathedral, ambulatory and crypt £2.50, students £2.) The immense residential and arts complex, the **Barbican Center,** has been both praised and derided for its concretescape.

The South and the Outskirts Lesser-known but equally rewarding treasures lie south of the river. **Southwark Cathedral,** a smallish, quiet church, boasts London's second-best Gothic structure and a chapel dedicated to John Harvard (Tube: London Bridge). West along the riverbank, a reconstruction of Shakespeare's Globe Theatre is underway. South London's entertainment history lives on in the externally brutal but internally festive **South Bank Arts Centre** (Tube: Waterloo).

The transport system that encouraged London's urban sprawl blurs the distinction between the city and its surroundings. If Hyde Park seemed but a small bit of green, **Highgate** and **Hampstead Heath** will prove that there is an English countryside. To the east, Karl Marx and George Eliot repose in the gothic tangle of **Highgate Cemetery.** (Tube: Archway. Eastern Cemetery open Mon.-Fri 10am-4:45pm, Sat.-Sun. 11am-4:45. £1.50. Western Cemetery by tour only; £2.)

Head by train or boat to red-brick **Hampton Court** for a quirky change of pace; its grounds contain the famous hedgerow maze (British Rail: Hampton Court). **Windsor Castle** is the Queen's country retreat. **Greenwich,** home of the Prime Meridian, is on the Thames, east of central London. You can visit Wren's **Old Royal Observatory,** Inigo Jones' grand **Queen's House,** as well as the suprisingly elaborate **National Maritime Museum** (British Rail: Greenwich). Just west of central London on the Thames lie the serene and exotic **Kew Gardens.** Lose yourself in the controlled wilderness of the grounds, or explore the Victorian and modern glasshouses containing thousands of plant species (Tube or British Rail: Kew Gardens).

Museums

British Museum, Tube: Tottenham Ct. Rd. or Holborn. The closest thing this planet has to a complete record of the rise and ruin of world cultures. Among the plunder on display are the Rosetta Stone (whose inscriptions allowed French scholar Champollion to decipher hieroglyphics) and the Elgin Marbles. Also hoards an early manuscript of *Beowulf* and 2 of the 4 surviving copies of the *Magna Carta.* Open Mon.-Sat. 10am-5pm, Sun. 2:30-6pm. Free.

Imperial War Museum, Tube: Lambeth North. Despite its jingoistic name, a moving reminder of the human cost of conflict. Open daily 10am-6pm. £3.70, students £2.65 and children £1.85, free after 4:30.

London Transport Museum Tube: Covent Garden. Transforms the tube from frustrating to fascinating. Open daily 10am-6pm, last entry 5:15pm. £3.95, concessions £2.50. Excellent shop open daily 10am-5:45pm.

Museum of London, Tube: St. Paul's. The City has been ravaged by plague, destroyed by fire, reshaped by the conceits of Christopher Wren, and demolished by the Luftwaffe; the Museum fills you in on the entire story. Open Tues.-Sat. 10am-6pm, Sun. 2-6pm. £3, students £1.50. Free after 4:30.

Museum of Mankind, Tube: Piccadilly Circus. Engrossing assemblage of artifacts from non-Western societies. Open Mon.-Sat. 10am-5pm, Sun. 2:30-6pm. Free.

National Gallery, Trafalgar Sq., Tube: Charing Cross. One of the world's finest collections of European painting; heavyweight works by da Vinci, Turner and Velázquez. The new Micro Gallery, a computerized, illustrated catalogue, will print out a free personal tour. Open Mon.-Sat. 10am-6pm, Sun. 2-6pm. Free.

National Portrait Gallery, Trafalgar Sq. Tube: Charing Cross. Doubles as *Who's Who in Britain.* Open Mon.-Fri. 10am-5pm, Sat. 10am-6pm, Sun. 2-6pm. Free.

Science Museum, Exhibition Rd. Tube: South Kensington. A hands-on extravaganza irresistible to kids of all ages, including *Let's Go* researchers. Open Mon.-Sat. 10am-6pm, Sun. 11am-6pm. £4, concessions £2.10, people with disabilities and children under 5, 4:30-6pm free.

Sir John Soane's Museum, 13 Lincoln's Inn Fields. Tube: Holborn. Brings Holbeins, an ancient Egyptian sarcophagus, and arcane achtitectonics together in an endearing clutter. Open Tues.-Sat. 10am-5pm. Lecture tour Sat. at 2:30pm. Free.

Tate Gallery, Millbank, up the Thames from Parliament Sq. Tube: Pimlico. The best of British artists such as Gainsborough, Reynolds, and Constable, along with works by Monet, Dalí, and Matisse. The vast J.M.W. Turner collection rests in the Clore Gallery, an extension of the main building. Both open Mon.-Sat. 10am-5:50pm, Sun. 2-5:50pm. Free.

Victoria and Albert Museum, Exhibition Rd. Tube: South Kensington. A mind-boggling array of fine and applied arts from all periods and places. Open Mon.-Sat. 10am-5:50pm, Sun. 2:30-5:50pm. "Donation" £3.50, concessions £1.

ENTERTAINMENT

For guidance through London's amazing cultural network, consult *Let's Go: London, Let's Go: Britain & Ireland,* the weekly *Time Out* (£1.40), or *What's On* (£1).

Theater and Music London **theater** is unrivalled. The ubiquitous *London Theatre Guide* leaflet gives comprehensive information. Seats cost £8-22 and up, and student/senior standby (with an "S" or "concessions" in listings) puts even the best seats within reach—around £7 shortly before curtain (come 2hr. early to get a seat). **Day seats** are sold cheaply (9-10am, the day of) to all; queue up earlier to snag one. **Capital Radio** (95.8FM, 1548AM) has current info at 6pm. The **Leicester Square Ticket Booth** sells ½-price tickets on the day of major plays. (Open Mon.-Sat. noon-2pm and 2:30-6:30pm; long wait. £1.50 fee. Cash only.) Standby tickets for the **National Theatre,** on the South Bank (tel. 928 2252; Tube: Waterloo) sell 2 hours beforehand (£7-9, students and seniors £5.50 45min. before). The **Barbican Theatre** (tel. 628 2295; Tube: Moorgate), the London home of the Royal Shakespeare Co., has 1½-hr. student and senior standbys for £5.50-8. **Open Air Theater** (tel. 486 2431; Tube: Baker St. or Regent's Park) stages Shakespeare in summer. (Tickets £7-15.50; student standby tickets £5 1hr. beforehand.) Eschew ticket agencies.

Most major **classical music** is staged at the acoustically superb **Royal Festival Hall** (tel. 928 3002 or 928 8800; Tube: Waterloo) and the **Barbican Hall** (see Sights). Hampstead Heath's **Kenwood House** and the **Marble Hill House** have low-priced outdoor concerts on summer weekends (tel. 973 3427; booking 379 4444). Opera and ballet embellish the **Royal Opera House** (tel. 240 1911 or 240 1066; Tube: Covent Garden) and the **London Coliseum** (tel. 836 3161; Tube: Charing Cross Leicester Sq.). Londoners have been lining up for standing room in the **Royal Albert Hall's "Proms"** (BBC Henry Wood Promenade Concerts), the most popular and endearing feature of the London music scene, for nearly a century. So, how many holes *does* it take to fill the Albert Hall? (Tel. 823 9998; Tube: South Kensington; nightly July-Sept.)

Every **pop music** phenom that didn't take off in London gets there at some point. Ticket offices and record shops list concerts. **The Marquee,** 105 Charing Cross Rd., WC2 (tel. 437 6601; Tube: Leicester Sq. or Tottenham Ct. Rd.), is a loud, up-to-date machine (cover £5-7). **Brixton Academy,** 211 Stockwell Rd., SW9 (tel. 326 1022; Tube: Brixton) is a larger, rowdy venue for a variety of music including rock and reggae (advance tickets £9-15). **Ronnie Scott's,** 47 Frith St., W1 (tel. 439 0747; Tube: Leicester Sq. or Piccadilly Circus), has London's greatest jazz (cover from £14). Find fine folk at **Bunjie's,** 27 Litchfield St., WC2 (tel. 240 1796; Tube: Covent Garden), where the crowd transcends all bounds (cover £3, students £2.50).

Dance Clubs For dance club happenings, consult *Time Out* or *City Limits:* the best events are one-night stands (like "Get up and Use Me"). Many offbeat clubs are not listed; some gay and lesbian ones are. Call ahead for dress code. A relaxed, multi-ethnic crowd clubs **Subterania,** 12 Acklam Rd., W10 (tel. (081) 960 4590; Tube: Ladbroke Grove; cover £5-8; open daily 10pm-3am). **The Fridge,** Town Hall Parade, Brixton Hill, SW2 (tel. 326 5100; Tube: Brixton), is a cool dance dive. Prepare to funk in a steamy atmosphere. Dress: *some* clothes. (Cover £5-10. Garage and house Fri. Mixed gay/straight night Sat. Open Mon.-Thurs. 10pm-3am, Fri.-Sat. 10pm-4am.) **Heaven,** Villiers St., WC2 (tel. 839 3852, Tube: Embankment), underneath The Arches, is a BGL/straight club with capacity of 4000, cavernous dance floors, and high-tech lighting. (Women only Mon. Cover £4-7.50. Open Tues.-Wed. and Fri. 10:30pm-3:30am, Sat 10pm-4am.) The **Camden Palace,** 1a Camden High St., NW1 (tel. 387 0428; Tube: Camden Town), is hugely popular with Brits and tourists alike. Wednesday's "Twist and Shout" sees 60s classics instead of the usual house and funk. (Cover £4-7. Open Tues.-Sat. 9pm-3am.) **Gossips,** 69 Dean St., W1 (tel. 434 4480; Tube: Piccadilly Circus), ranges from "Euros and trendy weirdos" on Wed. to heavy metal to psychedelia. (Cover £3-8; open Mon.-Sat. 10pm-3:30am.)

Sports In late June and early July, London aces **Wimbledon** (tel. (081) 946 2244; Tube: Southfields). Admission to grounds £5-7, less after 5pm; important matches cost up to £30. Final matches sell out centuries in advance. **Football** (soccer) matches are electric, and the "terraces" are simply fierce: beware! International matches are played at **Wembley** (tel. (081) 902 8833); half-a-dozen other fields are scattered around the city: check out **Arsenal** (tel. 359 0131; Tube: Arsenal) or **Tottenham Hotspur** (tel. (081) 808 8080; British Rail: White Hart Lane). **Lord's** (tel. 289 1615; Tube: St. John's Wood) hosts stuffy cricket matches; in contrast, see **rugby,** a revelrous melee of mud, blood, and drink, at Wembley (above).

SOUTH AND SOUTHEAST ENGLAND

■■■ KENT

Canterbury In the Middle Ages, the route from London to Canterbury was England's busiest road, lined with pilgrims striding to Thomas à Becket's shrine in **Canterbury Cathedral.** (Open Mon.-Sat. 8:45am-7pm; Nov.-Easter 8:45am-5pm. Donation £1.50. Check nave pulpit for times of guided tours: tickets £2.40, students £1.20. 25-min. headphone tour £1.70. Services Sun. 11am and 6:30pm.) The rest of the city brims with more religious monuments: the gardens of **Greyfriars,** on Stour St.; **St. Augustine's Abbey,** near the medieval wall; and, round the corner, **St. Martin's,** the oldest parish church in England. Canterbury's **tourist office,** 34 St. Margaret's St. (tel. (0227) 766 567), books accommodations and carries maps and guides for the rest of Kent. (Open daily 9:30am-5:30pm; Nov.-March 9:30am-5pm.) B&Bs bunch near both train stations and on London and Whitstable Rd., with costlier ones near the **HI youth hostel** at 54 New Dover Rd. (tel. (0227) 462 911). (Reception open 8-10am and 1-11pm. £8.40, ages 16-20 £5.90. Open daily March-Oct. Book a week in advance in July and Aug. Call for off-season openings.) The **London Guest House,** 14 London Rd. (tel. 765 860), is a spacious Victorian house in immaculate condition (£15-16.50). **The Tudor House,** 6 Best Ln. (tel. (0227) 765 650), sports bright rooms with TV (£16). **St. Martin's Touring Caravan and Camping Site,** Bekesbourne Lane (tel. (0227) 463 216), off A257 (Sandwich Rd.), lies 1½ mile east of the city center. (£3 pitch fee, £3.30/person. Open April Oct.) The streets around the cathedral seethe with bakeries and sweet shops. **Fungus Mungus,** 34 St. Peter's St., is Canterbury's only vegetarian restaurant. The tasty selections are fresh—despite the name. (Main dishes £4.95, starters £2.10. Open daily 10am-11pm.) **The Sweet Heart Pâtisserie,** in the Weaver's House, St. Peter's St., has light lunches, ice cream, and *wunderbar* German pastries. Across the street, the **Sugarloaf** offers a bevy of midday munchies.

Trains run from London's Victoria Station to Canterbury East Station and from Charing Cross and Waterloo to Canterbury West Station (1½hr.; £11.70, day-return £11.90). Reach both Canterbury stations at (0732) 770 111. **Buses** to Canterbury (station tel. (0227) 472 082) leave London's Victoria Coach Station (1¾hr., £10.50).

Dover The "melancholy roar" of the English Channel at Dover has been drowned out by the puttering of ferries and the squabbling of French families *en vacances.* The view from Castle Hill Rd. reveals why **Dover Castle** is famed both for its setting and for its impregnability. Dover's **tourist office,** Townwall St. (tel. (0304) 205 108), spews info on available accommodations, ferry tickets, hoverport tickets, and rental cars. (Open daily 8am-8:30pm; Oct.-March 9am-6pm.) The **Charlton House Youth Hostel (HI)** is at 306 London Rd. (tel. (0304) 201 314), is a ½-mile walk from the train station. (Strict lockout 10am-1pm. Curfew 11pm. £10.60, under 18 £7.80. May refuse phone bookings in summer.) **Gordon Guest House,** 23 Castle St. (tel. 201 894), is a top notch B&B, where all rooms have both color TV and kettles. (Doubles £34, with shower £36.) If you arrive late, try a B&B on Folkestone Rd. next to the station, or camp at **Harthorn Farm** (tel. (0304) 852 658), at Martin Mill Station off the A258 between Dover and Deal (without car £6.50/person, children under 14 £2; electricity hook-up £1.50). Cheap **food** fries from dawn to dusk in the fish-and-chip shops on London Rd. and Biggin St., and a decent pub lunch can be had almost anywhere in the city center.

Trains for Dover's Priory Station (tel. (0732) 770 111) leave from London's Victoria, Waterloo, Cannon St., London Bridge, and Charing Cross stations approximately every 45 minutes (2hr., £15, return £15.40). From Victoria, express lines continue to the Western Docks Station. **Buses** run regularly from London's Victoria Coach Station; they continue to the Eastern Docks after stopping at the bus station on Pencester Rd. (tel. (0227) 240 024, 2¾hr., £10). Buses also make trips to Canterbury (hourly, £3). Most **ferries** sail from Eastern Docks; Sealink (tel. 240 280) and P&O (tel. 203 388) both serve Calais (72-hr. return £48, students £40). These prices also apply to P&O's Oostende and Boulogne services. **Hovercrafts** hover from the Hoverport (tel. 208 013; reservations 240 241), for Calais or Boulogne (35min.). Book a few days in advance. (Single £26, 3-day return £26, 5-day return £38.)

■■■ SUSSEX

Brighton Garish Brighton is Queen Victoria and Liberace rolled into one—the undisputed home of the "dirty weekend." Recently restored, George IV's **Royal Pavilion** shimmers on Pavilion Parade, next to Old Steine. (Open daily 10am-6pm; Oct.-May 10am-5pm. £4, children £2.) At the **tourist office,** 10 Bartholomew Sq (tel. 264 50), book-a-bed ahead. (£2.50. Open Mon.-Sat. 9am-6pm, Sun. 10am-6pm; winter Mon.-Sat 9am-5pm, Sun. 10am-4pm.) Cheaper and shabbier B&Bs snuggle in the **Kemp Town** area, on the streets opposite Palace Pier. The nearest **HI youth hostel** is on Patcham Pl. (tel. (0273) 556 196), 4 miles north on the A23; take bus #773 or 5a from Old Steine. (£7.50, ages 16-20 £6.30. Breakfast £2.30. Sleep sack 75p. Often full—call ahead in July-Aug.) The **Brighton Backpackers Hostel,** 75-76 Middle St. (tel. (0273) 777 717), is an independent hostel opened by two young English chaps at a great location. (No curfew. £9. 4-8/room.) Prowl "The Lanes" between North and Prince Albert St. in search of sustenance. **Food for Friends,** 17a Prince Albert St., has cheap, well-seasoned vegetarian meals (£2.50-4. Open Mon.-Sat. 9am-10pm, Sun. 9:30am-10pm). Trendy types dance at **The Escape Club** (tel. (0273) 606 906), near the pier on Marine Rd. **The Marlborough** (tel. (0273) 570 028), opposite the Royal Pavilion, blends folk and rock (Wed. and Sat.).

Trains escape regularly from London to Brighton (1¼hr.; £11, day return £17.10). They escape Brighton station (tel. (0273) 206 755) to other southern locales including Arundel via Ford (2/hr.; ½hr.; £4.70, day return £4.80) and Portsmouth (1/hr., 1½hr., £9.30). National Express **buses** go from London to Brighton (2hr., £8.75).

Arundel and Chichester Squat **Arundel** is an affable nugget of a town. **Arundel Castle** is the third oldest in Britain and seat of the Duke of Norfolk, Earl Marshal of England. (Open April-Oct. Sun.-Fri 11am-5pm. Last entry 4pm. £4, students and seniors £3.50, children £3.) Find useful brochures at the **tourist office,** 61 High St. (tel. (0903) 882 268; open Mon.-Fri 9am-6pm, Sat.-Sun. 10am-6pm; off-season Mon.-Fri. 9am-3:30pm). Stay at the **Warningcamp Youth Hostel (HI)** (tel. (0903) 882 204), 1½ miles from town. (Lockout 10am-5pm. Curfew 11pm. £6.30, under 18 £4.20. Kitchen. Open daily April-Aug; Sept.-Oct. and March Tues.-Sat.) Otherwise, prepare to pay at least £14 for B&B. Locals frequent **Belinda's,** 13 Tarrant St., off High St. A barn on the 1560 town map, its only herds today are those that consume steak and kidney pie (£4.25). **Trains** leave London's Victoria Station for Arundel (every hour, 1¼hr., day return £11.80). Most other train and bus routes require connections at Littlehampton to the south or Barnham to the east.

Ringed by the remains of Roman walls and distinguished by its Norman cathedral, **Chichester** is a small city stuck between harbor and downs. The **Cathedral,** begun in 1091, has a Chagall stained-glass window. (Open Mon.-Sat. 9:30am-6pm, Sun. 12:45-5:30. £1, seniors, students, and children 40p.) The **Roman Palace** in nearby Fishbourne is the largest Roman residence yet excavated in Britain. Fishbourne is an easy walk from Chichester; go west along Westgate, which becomes Fishbourne Rd. (the A259) for 1½ miles, or take bus #700 or 701 from Chichester center. (Palace open May-Sept. daily 10am-6pm; March-April and Oct. daily 10am-5pm; Nov.-Dec. daily 10am-4pm; Jan. Sun. 10am-4pm. £3.20, students £2.60.) The **tourist office,** South St. (tel. (0243) 775 888; open Mon.-Sat. 9:15am-5:15pm; April-Sept. also Sun. 10am-4pm), has a 24.-hr. computer information guide listing available accommodations. Rooms for under £15 are virtually nonexistent here. **Hedgehogs,** 45 Whyke Lane (tel. (0243) 780 022), is run by an enthusiastic hound named Sooty (£16-17). Camping is available at **Southern Leisure Centre,** Vinnetrow Rd. (tel. (0243) 787 715), a 5-minute walk southeast of town. (£8.25/large tent, 90p/person. Open April-Oct.) **Noble Rot,** 3 Little London off East St., crouches in 200-year-old wine cellars, serving great food at low prices. (Open Mon.-Sat. noon-2:30pm, Mon.-Thurs. 5:30-11pm, Fri.-Sat. 5:30-12pm.)

Trains run to and from London's Victoria Station (1½hr., day return £13.40); Brighton (1hr., day return £6.10), and Portsmouth (40min., day return £3.80). National Express **buses** run less frequently to London (period return £12.25); Coastline buses serve Brighton (#700, 2hr., £2.90) and Portsmouth (#700, 1hr., £2.50). The bus station (tel. (0243) 783 251) lies diagonally across from the train station (tel. (0243) 206 755) on Southgate St.

■■■ HAMPSHIRE

Portsmouth Portsmouth is the overlord of British maritime history. Henry VIII's **Mary Rose** set sail from Portsmouth in 1545 only to keel over before the monarch's eyes. (Open daily 10am-5:30pm, Nov.-Feb. 10am-5pm. Wheelchair accessible.) Admiral Nelson's flagship **HMS Victory** won the Battle of Trafalgar against the French and Spanish in 1805. (Open daily 10am-4:50pm; Nov.-Feb. 10:30am-4:20pm. £2.50, students and children £1.75.) Moderate **B&Bs** clutter Southsea, a contiguous town 1½ miles east along the coast. Cheaper lodgings lie 2 or 3 blocks inland. Cosham, a bus or train ride away, harbors the **HI youth hostel,** Wymering Manor, Old Wymering Lane, Medina Rd. (tel. (0705) 375 661). (Lockout 10am-5pm. 58 beds. No showers. £7.50, under 18 £5. Open July-Aug. and Jan.1-4 daily; March-June Mon.-Sat.; Sept.-Nov. Tues.-Sat.; mid-Jan.-Feb. Fri.-Sat.) Mrs. Parkes presides at **Testudo House,** 19 Whitwell Rd., Southsea (tel. (0705) 824 324; £15; doubles £28). Decent **restaurants** bunch along Osborne, Palmerston, and Clarendon Rd. in the Southsea shopping district. Portsmouth's **tourist office** is on The Hard (tel. (0705) 826 722), right next to the entrance to historic ships. (Open daily 9:30am-5:45pm.) **Trains** from London's Waterloo station stop at both Portsmouth and Southsea station (the "town station") and at Portsmouth harbor station (tel. (0705) 825 771, 1½hr., day return £14.90). National Express **buses** run from London (2½hr.; £12.25, return £13-15.50).

Winchester Once the capital of England, Winchester retains its majesty. **Winchester Cathedral,** at 556 ft., is the longest medieval building in Europe, and **Winchester College** was founded in 1382 as England's first "public" school. (College open daily 10am-1pm, 2-4pm. £2, seniors, students, and children £1.50.) **B&Bs** cluster southwest of the office on Christchurch and St. Cross Rd. near Ranelagh Rd. The **HI youth hostel** is well-located at 1 Water Ln. (tel. (0962) 853 723). (Lockout 10am-5pm, with stringent curfew 11pm. Expect a chore or two. £6.90, under 18 £4.60. Kitchen. Open July-Aug. daily; March-June and Sept. Tues.-Sat. Call ahead.) **Mrs. P. Patton,** 12 Christchurch Rd. (tel. (0962) 854 272), has graceful, classy doubles. (£12.50, £10 for multiple nights.) Camp at **River Park Leisure Centre,** Gordon Rd. (tel. (0962) 869 525; 3-night max. stay; £6/1-2 person tent; open June-Sept.) **Restaurants** line Jewry St., and most of Winchester's many pubs serve good fare. The **Royal Oak** is another of countless English bars that claim fame as the oldest. Descend into the 900-year-old subterranean foundations. The **tourist office,** The Guildhall, Broadway (tel. (0962) 840 500 or 848 180), gives guided tours. (£2, children 50p. Open Mon.-Sat. 9:30am-6pm, Sun. 10am-1pm; Oct.-April Mon.-Sat. 10am-5pm.) **Trains** run to Winchester from London (2/hr.; 1hr.; single £13.30-15.90, day return £13.40-28.80), and depart for Chichester (hourly after 10am; 1hr., change at Fareham; £7.60-8, day return £7.70-8.20); Portsmouth (45min., £5.50-5.90), and Bath (hourly; 2hr, change at Southampton or Redding; day return £ 12.50£17.50). National Express **buses** run to London via Heathrow (8/day, 2hr., £11.75). Hampshire buses head to Salisbury (#32, 1½hr., £3.15) and Portsmouth (#69, 11/day, 1½hr., round-trip £3.15). Call the train station in Southampton (tel. (0703) 229 393) or the bus station (tel. (0962) 853 129) for all the sordid details.

■■■ SALISBURY AND STONEHENGE

Salisbury Cathedral rises monolithically from its grassy close to the neck-breaking height of 404 ft. The free 45-minute tours feature the oldest working clock in Britain: One of 4 surviving copies of the *Magna Carta* rests in the **Chapter House,** to King John's eternal chagrin. (Open Mon.-Sat. 9:30am-4:45pm, Sun. 1-4:45pm; Nov.-Feb. Mon.-Sat. 11am-3pm, Sun. 1-3:15pm. 30p, students and seniors 20p.) The folks at the **tourist office,** Fish Row (tel. (0722) 334 956), in the Guildhall in Market Sq., are especially helpful. (Open Mon. 9:30am-5pm, Tues.-Sat. 9:30am-6pm, Sun 11am-4pm; Oct.-April Mon.-Sat. 9am-5pm.) There's a **HI youth hostel** at Milford Hill House, Milford Hill (tel. (0722) 327 572; lockout 10am-1pm; curfew 11:30pm; £7.10, ages 16-20 £5.00; July-Aug. £7.50, £6.30; camping £3.30; breakfast £2.30). **Ron and Jenny Coats**, 51 Salt Lane (tel. 327 443), just up for the bus station, keep welcoming and clean 400-year-old house. (2-, 3- and 6-bed rooms. No curfew. £7, with breakfast £9. Sheets 80p.) **Reeve the Baker** (next to tourist office) stocks all the strolling sightseer could crave, from Cornish pasties to caterpillar meringues.

Trains depart Salisbury station (tel. (0703) 229 393) to Winchester (2/hr., change at Southampton, 1½hr., £10); Southampton (2/hr., 40min., £5.50); Portsmouth (1/hr., 1½hr., same-day round-trip £9.80) and London (hourly, £16.90-18.40). National Express **buses** run from Victoria (2/day, 2½hr., £12.25; call the Salisbury bus station at (0722) 336 855). **Wilt's and Dorset** service #X4 runs from Bath, 40 miles north-west of Salisbury (6/day, 2hr., £3.90); buses also drive to Stonehenge (Mon.-Fri. 8/day, Sat.-Sun. 3-5/day, ½hr., return £3.75).

The much-touted **Stonehenge,** only 22 ft. high, may initially be disappointing. Consider, however, that these geometrically-arranged gray slabs were lifted by an infinitely tedious process over many lifetimes (2800-1500 BC), representing an enduring religious and aesthetic dedication that defies modern explanation. Capture the finest view of the site from Amesbury Hill, 1½ miles up the A303. On clear Tuesdays and Fridays in winter the ropes around the stones are taken down to allow a closer view. (Open daily 10am-6pm; Oct.-Easter 10am-4pm. £2.70, students £1.30.) **Wilts & Dorset** (tel. (0722) 336 855) runs buses daily from Salisbury center and Salisbury train station (£3.75). The last leaves Stonehenge at 4:20pm (Sun. 3:50pm, ½hr.). Some hitch on the A345 from Salisbury to Amesbury.

SOUTHWEST ENGLAND

Mists of legend shroud the counties of Dorset, Somerset, Devon, and Cornwall in England's **West Country.** While it is easy to lose the spirit of legend among "King Arthur" parking lots and "Mayflour" bake shops, the terrain itself is unfailingly beautiful. The sunny coast of Cornwall is particularly popular with older travelers.

British Rail **trains** from London pass through Exeter (2½hr., £34), Plymouth (3½hr., £39), and end at Penzance (6hr., £50). From Edinburgh, trains roll through Bristol, Taunton, and Exeter before continuing through Plymouth to Penzance. National Express **buses** run to major points along the north coast via Bristol and to points along the south coast (including Penzance) via Exeter and Plymouth. Within the region, local bus service is less expensive and more extensive than local trains.

The longest coastal path in England, the **South West Peninsula Coast Path,** originates in Dorset and passes through South Devon, Cornwall, and North Devon, ending in Somerset; the final section, **Somerset and North Devon Coastal Path,** offers views from the highest seaside cliffs in Southwest England.

■ ■ ■ EXMOOR NATIONAL PARK

Dramatic sea-plunging cliffs, tranquil woodlands, and purple-heathered moorland cover **Exmoor,** the 265 sq. mile national park on the north coast of England's southwestern peninsula. Access is made easy by frequent buses and trains from Exeter, Plymouth, Bristol, and London to Barnstaple and Minehead, Exmoor's western and eastern gateways. Once you reach the outskirts of the park, exploring its innards by public transport is a nightmare; the meager offerings of the area's sundry bus companies have been collected in a booklet available at the tourist and park offices. The park is best toured on foot (on the **Somerset and North Devon Coast Path**) and by bike (on the **coastal path** that follows the ghost of the Barnstaple railroad).

Stop at one of the many **National Park Information Centres** to pick up detailed Ordnance Survey maps (£4) and the free *Exmoor Visitor,* an annual park publication that includes a map and a detailed accommodations list (including B&Bs, starting at £10-11). The head center is at the **Dulverton Heritage Centre,** Guild Hall, Dulverton (tel. (0398) 238 41), and handles all postal inquiries. Other centers are at **Combe Martin** (tel. (0271) 883 319), **Countisbury** (tel. (05987) 321), **Dunster** (tel. (0643) 821 835), and **Lynmouth** (tel. (0598) 525 09). Additionally, there are **tourist offices** in **Barnstable** (tel. (0271) 471 77), **Ilfracombe** (tel. (0271) 863 001), **Lynmouth and Lynton** (tel. (0598) 522 25), and **Minehead** (tel. (0643) 702 624).

Little villages (some hundreds of years old) interrupt the coastal path about every 15 miles; B&Bs line the streets. **HI youth hostels,** practically all with a lockout (10am-5pm), a curfew (11pm-midnight), and kitchen and laundry facilities, string out along the path in **Crowcombe Heathfield** (tel. (09847) 249; £5.90, ages 16-20 £4.70; open Feb.-Oct. Fri.-Tues.), **Exford** (tel. (064383) 288; £6.80, ages 16-20 £5.50; open July-Aug. daily; April-June and Sept.-Oct. Mon.-Sat.; March-Feb. and Nov. Tues.-Sat.), **Hartland** (tel. (02374) 413 67; £4.70, ages 16-20 £3.80; open July-Aug. daily; mid-April to June and Sept. Fri.-Tues.), and **Ilfracombe** (tel. (0271) 653 37; £6.30, ages 16-20 £5.10; open July-Aug. daily; April-June and Sept. Mon.-Sat.). Campsites are easy to find along the coastal road, but be sure to ask the owner's permission.

■ ■ ■ EXETER

With one of the few universities in the area and an array of theaters and clubs, **Exeter** is distinctly cosmopolitan—for a town in the moors. Large sections of Exeter's hefty Roman wall survived the swift bombing during WWII, as did its fabulous 16th-century **cathedral** (tel. (0392) 555 73). The cathedral library displays the *Exeter Book,* the richest surviving treasury of Anglo-Saxon poetry. Stay at the spacious and cheery **HI youth hostel,** 47 Countess Wear Rd. (tel. (0392) 873 329), 2 miles southeast of the city center. (£7.50. Hearty English breakfast £2.40. Evening meal £3.70. Self-catering kitchen. Towels 90p. £8.40; June-Sept. £7.50.) Head to the restaurant-infested cathedral area to eat in or to **St. George's Market,** 91 High St., to eat out. **Herbie's,** 14 North St. (tel. 584 73), caters to the herbivorous. (Open Mon.-Fri. 11am-2:30pm, Sat. 10:30am-4pm; dinner Tues.-Sat. 6-9:30pm.) A skeleton guards the Roman-era well in the basement of the **Well House Tavern** (annexed to the ancient **Royal Clarence Hotel**) while hearty ale flows upstairs. The **Northcott Theatre** at the **University of Exeter** showcases its own and visiting drama troupes (tel. (0392) 561 82). Grab one of the Ordnance Survey maps of the surrounding moors at the **tourist office,** Civic Centre, Paris St. (tel. (0392) 265 700 or 265 297; open Mon.-Fri. 9am-5pm, Sat. 9am-1pm and 2-5pm). **Trains** (tel. (0392) 433 551) and **buses** (tel. (0392) 562 31) run from London (trains: 9/day, 3hr., £34; buses: 8/day, 4hr., £20).

■ ■ ■ DARTMOOR NATIONAL PARK

The lush, green forests and windy moors of the Dartmoor National Park (south of Exmoor, 10 miles west of Exeter and 7 miles east of Plymouth) will make you forget how hard it was to get there. Call the **Exeter bus station** at (0392) 562 31, the **Plymouth bus station** at (0752) 664 011, or the Devon County Council's **Public Transportation Helpline** (tel. (0392) 382 800; open Mon.-Fri. 8:30am-5pm) for advice. Also be sure to grab a copy of the free *Dartmoor Visitor* at one of the following National Park Information Centres: **Dartmoor (Tavistock)** (tel. (0822) 612 938), **Okehampton** (tel. (0837) 530 20), **Newbridge** (tel. (03643) 303), **Parke Barn** (tel. (0626) 832 093), **Postbridge** (tel. (0822) 882 72), **Princetown** (tel. (082289) 414), and **Steps Bridge** (tel. (0647) 520 18).

Prehistoric remains are scattered about the moor around **Princetown,** the setting for the famous Sherlock Holmes tale *The Hound of the Baskervilles.* The eastern part of the park is a rugged area centered around **Hay Tor.** Dartmoor's celebrated medieval ruins at **Hound Tor,** where excavations unearthed the remains of 13th-century huts and longhouses, lie 2 miles north of Hay Tor village. **Dartmoor Letterboxes,** each complete with an inkpad, rubber stamp, and visitors book, hide themselves all about the moors, though finding them is hardly elementary, my dear Watson. (Collect as many different stamps as possible; cluebooks available.)

B&B signs frequently hang in pubs and farmhouses along the roads; the less adventurous can check the *Dartmoor Visitor.* Both Dunsford village and Yellerton have hostels, **Steps Bridge** (tel. (0647) 524 35; July-Aug. £6.30; Apr.-June and Sept. £5.70; open July-Aug. daily; April-June and Sept. Thurs.-Tues.) and **Bellever** (tel. (0822) 882 27; £7.5; open July-Aug. daily; April-June and Sept.-Oct. Mon.-Sat.), respectively. If you want to camp on the open moor, ask permission before crossing or camping on private land.

■■■ PLYMOUTH

One of England's major naval ports and the largest city in Southwest England, Plymouth knows how to exploit the sentimental potential of its history. Both Sir Francis Drake and the *Mayflower* began their famous voyages from Plymouth's harbor, now lined with restored Elizabethan buildings, a *Mayflower* passenger list, and the "journey through time" of the **Plymouth Dome.**

A fountain of luxurious, low-priced B&Bs irrigates Citadel Rd. and Athenaeum St., between the north end of Royal Parade and the Hoe; prices run from £11.50 to £16. The spacious rooms at the **HI youth hostel** (tel. (0752) 562 189), 2 miles from the city center, lie at the Molesworth St. stop of bus #15 or 15A (70p, day return £1). (Lockout 10am-4pm; Sept.-June 10am-1pm. Curfew 11pm. £7.50. Breakfast £2.40. Evening meals £1.70-2.55.) Gorge on a block of Nelson Square (a fruity bread pudding, 32p) at the **Gorge Café** on Royal Parade. (Open Mon.-Sat. 7:30am-6pm, Sun. 9:30am-5:30pm.)

The **tourist office,** Royal Parade (tel. (0752) 264 849), can be found in the main entrance hall of the Civic Centre. (Open May-Sept. Mon.-Fri. 9am-5pm, Sat. 9am-4pm; Oct. Mon.-Fri. 9am-5pm, Sat. 9am-12:30pm; Nov.-March Mon.-Fri. 9am-5pm.) **Trains** run hourly to London's Paddington station (3½hr., return £39), Exeter (1½hr., £6.75), Bristol (2hr., £21), and Penzance (return £8.70). National Express **buses** serve London (6hr., £31), Exeter (1½hr., £6.75), and Bristol (2½hr., £21). **Brittany Ferries** run from **Millbay Docks** (tel. (0752) 221 321) to **Roscoff, France** (1-3/day, 6hr., £37) and **Santander, Spain** (2/week, 24hr., £75).

■■■ THE CORNISH COAST

Penzance and St. Ives The largest town on Cornwall's Penwith peninsula, **Penzance** manages to combine Cornish Market Town and Mediterranean Resort. Near the top of Chapel St. is the bizarre **Egyptian House,** a rare example of the 1830s craze for Egyptian ornamentation. A few hundred yards off the coast at Marazion is the **St. Michael's Mount** monastery, accessible by ferry. (Visitors' entrance open April-Oct. Mon.-Fri. 10:30am-5:45pm. £3. Ferry return £1.20, children 60p.) The **HI youth hostel,** Castle Horneck (tel. (0736) 626 66), reportedly has a smuggler's tunnel. (Curfew 11pm. £8.40, ages 16-20 £5.90.) The smorgasbord lunch (£2.30) at **The Millhouse,** Victoria Pl., includes *mousaka, kasha, gado gado, suki yaki,* and *ratatouille,* among other vegan delights. (Open Mon.-Sat. 9:30am-8:30pm.) On Chapel St., you can cuss like Long John Silver in the nautical chambers of the 400-year-old **Admiral Benbow.** Penzance's **rail station** (tel. (0872) 762 44), **bus station** (tel. (0736) 660 55), and **tourist office** (tel. (0736) 622 07) stand conveniently together in the same square, adjacent to both the harbor and the town.

Ten miles north of Penzance, the peaked roofs and breathtaking views of **St. Ives** grant a partial reprieve from the commercialization of neighboring towns. Stop by the **Barbara Hepworth Museum,** in the late artist's studio. (Open July-Aug. Mon.-

Sat. 10am-6pm, Sun. 2-6pm; Oct.-March until 4:30pm; April-June until 5:30pm. 50p.) When the surf's up, head to **Porthmeor Beach.** St. Ives has scads of B&Bs; try **Belmont Place, Barnoon Hill,** or **Park Avenue.** Miniscule **Ferrell's Bakery,** at 15 Fore St. (tel. (0736) 797 703), bakes a delicious version of the Cornish pasty (PAH-stee). (Open Mon.-Sat. 9am-6pm). The **tourist office** is in the Guildhall at Street-an-Pol (tel. (0736) 797 600 or 796 297; open mid-May to mid-Sept. Mon.-Sat. 9am-5:30pm; mid-Sept. to mid-May Mon.-Thurs. 9am-5:30pm, Fri. 9am-5pm.) **Trains** run daily to St. Erth, connecting to Penzance (£2.50). Three **buses** per hour run from Penzance (daily; off-season Mon.-Sat.).

Newquay "Surf City" is an outpost of surfer subculture in a region of blue-haired bus tours. The town overlooks 6 beaches, each with its own crowd and reputation. Sack out at the **HI youth hostel,** Alexandra Court, Narrowcliff (tel. (0637) 876 381; £8.40, ages 16-20 £6.30; open July-Aug. daily; March-April and Sept.-Nov. Tues.-Sat.), or at the more cramped and centrally located **Towan Beach Backpackers,** 15 Beachfield Ave. (tel. (0637) 874 668; £6.50). **Ellery's Bakery and Winebar,** 58 East St. (tel. (0637) 872 832), squishes pasties into tourists for under £5. (Open daily 10am-4pm and 7pm-1am. Live jazz Fri.) Newquay's after-hours activities are notorious. **Tall Trees** on Tolcarne Rd. (tel. (0637) 873 894) is the acknowledged giant of the town's club scene (Tues. and Thurs.-Sat.). The town's **tourist office** sits atop Marcus Hill (tel. (0637) 871 345; open July-Sept. Mon.-Sat. 9am-6pm, Sun. 10am-5pm; Oct.-May Mon.-Fri. 9:15am-5pm, Sat. 9:15am-1pm). All **trains** to Newquay run through Par off the main London-Penzance line. National Express **buses** run from Plymouth via Bodmin (2/day, 2hr., £5.75), St. Austell (daily, off-season Mon.-Sat. only, 2/hr., 45min., £2.10), and St. Ives (June-Sept. 3/day, 2hr., £4).

HEART OF ENGLAND

■■■ OXFORD

Shrouded in 800 years of tradition, Oxford's 40 colleges and halls form a sheltered world. Unfortunately, a measure of mayhem, squealing bus brakes, and rattling bicycle chains have forced directors of BBC dramas to shoot Oxford's "dreaming spires" from very select camera angles.

ORIENTATION AND PRACTICAL INFORMATION

Queen, High, St. Aldates, and Cornmarket Streets intersect at right angles in **Carfax,** the town center, surrounded by the colleges; bus and train stations lie to the west.

Tourist Office: St. Aldates St. (tel. 726 871), just south of Carfax. *Vade Mecum* (£1), published by Oxford undergrads, has the low-down on the best pubs and the most elite colleges. Open Mon.-Sat. 9am-5pm, Sun. 10am-3:30pm. Good daily walking tours (10:30-11:30am and 1:30-2:30pm, £3.20). Or take a tour from a student group that offers them (9am-5pm; about 1/hr.; £2.50, students free).
Financial Services: Try the banks near Carfax.
American Express: Keith Bailey Travel Agency, 98 St. Aldates St. (tel. 790 099), a few doors from the tourist office. Client mail held; postal code OX1 1BT. Open Mon. and Wed.-Fri. 9am-5:30pm, Tues. 9:30-5:30, Sat. 9:30am-5pm.
Post Office: 102/104 St. Aldates St. (tel. 814 783). Open Mon.-Wed. and Fri.-Sat. 9am-5:30pm, Thurs. 9:30am-7:30pm. **Postal Code:** OX1 1ZZ.
Telephones: Rows of Phonecard and intercontinental phones at Carfax and on Cornmarket St. **City Code:** 0865.
Trains: Botley Rd. (tel. 722 333 for British Rail timetable), west of Carfax. From London, trains run from Paddington (1hr.; day return £10.20, period return £18).

Buses: Gloucester Green. **Oxford Tube** (tel. 772 250), **Oxford CityLink** (tel. 711 312), and **National Express** (tel. 791 579). **Carfax Travel** (tel. 726 172), books for National Express. **Oxford Tube** and **Oxford CityLink** (both 3/hr.; 1½hr.; day return £5.50, period return £6.50) provide bus services between Oxford's bus station and London's Victoria bus station.

Crises: Samaritans, 123 Iffley Rd. (tel. 722 122). Phone 24hrs.; drop in 8am-10pm. **Drug and Alcohol Hotline** (tel. 244 447 or 248 591). 24-hr. answer phone. **The Women's Line** (tel. 726 295). Open Mon.-Thurs. 7-9pm, Fri. 2-4pm; answering machine other times; in emergency call **London Rape Crisis Center** at (071) 837 1600.

Gay Switchboard, tel. 739 999. Phone answered daily 7-9pm. Oxford Lesbian Line, tel. 242 333. Wed. 7-10pm.

Pharmacy: Boots, 8 Cornmarket St. (tel. 247 461). Open Mon. and Fri.-Sat. 8:45am-6pm, Tues.-Wed. 9am-5:30pm, Thurs. 8:45am-8pm.

Hospital: John Radcliffe Hospital, Woodstock Rd. (tel. 741 66 or 647 11). Take bus #10.

Emergencies: Dial 999; no coins required. **Police:** St. Aldates and Speedwell St. (tel. 266 000).

ACCOMMODATIONS AND CAMPING

B&Bs line the main roads out of town, all of them a 15- to 20-minute walk from Carfax. You'll find cheaper B&Bs on Iffley Rd. and Cowley Rd., both served by buses from Carfax. Expect to pay at least £15-18 per person, and book ahead.

HI youth hostel, Jack Straw's Lane, Headington (tel. 629 97). Catch any minibus departing from the job center south of Carfax (every 15min., last bus 10:30pm). Remote but well-equipped, with showers, kitchen, and food shop. Lockout 10am-1pm. Curfew 11pm. £6.80, ages 16-20 £5.30. Sheets 80p.

Tara, 10 Holywell St. (tel. 244 786 or 248 270). The best B&B in town, with desks, basins, TVs, and refrigerators in every room, and a kitchenette on the 2nd floor. Open July-Sept.; the rest of the year it fills up with students, but check anyway. Reserve at least 2 weeks in advance. Singles £25. Doubles £36.

Whitehouse View, 9 Whitehouse Rd. (tel. 721 626), off Abingdon Rd. Good-sized rooms only 10min. from Carfax. Solicitous proprietors and excellent breakfasts. Rooms with TV. £17-18.

Old Mitre Rooms, 48 Turl St. (tel. 279 821). Lincoln College dorm rooms with authentic ripped-down poster decor. Chic to say you're doing research, even if you're not. Singles £17.25. Doubles £33.50, with bath £36.25. Open late June-Sept.

Camping: Oxford Camping International, 426 Abingdon Rd. (tel. 246 551), behind the Texaco Station. 129 nondescript sites on a manicured lawn. Laundry and warm showers. £6.60/2-person tent.

FOOD

During the summer, walk a few blocks away from the 4 major streets to escape tourists and generic food. For fresh produce and deli goods, visit the **Covered Market** between Market St. and Carfax. (Open Mon.-Sat. 8am-5:30pm.)

The Nosebag, 6-8 Michael's St. Vegetarian meals served in wood-paneled surroundings for under £5. Unfortunate name. Open Mon. 9:30am-5:30pm, Tues.-Thurs. 9:30am-9pm, Fri.-Sat. 9:30am-10:30pm, Sun. 9:30am-9pm.

Munchy Munchy, 6 Park End St., on the way into town from the rail station. Different dishes daily, all Indonesian or Malaysian, with at least 1 vegetarian (£5-8). BYOB but 50p charge/person. Open Tues.-Sat. noon-2pm and 5:30-10pm.

Heros, Ship St. (tel. 723 459) Packs in student clientele and serves up yummy sandwiches with a super selection of stuffings, £1.40-2.50. Open Mon.-Fri 8am-7pm, Sat. 8:30am-5pm, Sun. 10am-5pm. Breakfast 8am-11am.

SIGHTS

A tour of Oxford University, founded in 1167, begins at the college with the grandest quad and the most distinguished and obnoxious students, **Christ Church** (open Mon.-Sat. 9:30am-6pm, Sun. 12:45-5:30pm; £1, students and seniors 40p), whose **Picture Gallery** collects Italian primitives and Dutch paintings. (Open Mon.-Sat. 10:30am-1pm and 2-5:30pm, Sun. 2-5:30pm; Oct.-March, closes at 4:30pm. 80p, students 40p.) **University College** on High St., obviously up Logic Lane from Merton St., dates from 1249 and vies with Merton for the title of oldest college, claiming Alfred the Great as its founder. **Magdalen College** is traditionally considered Oxford's handsomest. Its spiritual patron is probably alumnus Oscar Wilde; the place has always walked on the flamboyant side. (Open daily 2-6:15pm.) Just up High St., **Queen's College** approaches Magdalen's beauty. (Open daily 2-4:30pm.) **New College** has become one of Oxford's most prestigious. Built between 1960 and 1964 by the Danish architect Arne Jacobsen, **St. Catherine's** dining hall was funded by that curmudgeonly eccentric, Esso Petroleum.

Turn up Catte St. to the **Bodleian Library,** which does not lend out its over 6 million books. Across Broad St. you can browse more freely at **Blackwell's,** the famous bookstore. The **Sheldonian Theatre,** set beside the Bodleian, is the Roman-style home of the graduation ceremonies. (Open Mon.-Sat. 10am-12:45pm and 2-4:45pm; Nov.-Feb. until 3:45pm. 50p, children 25p.) The **Ashmolean Museum,** Beaumont St., brandishes an outstanding collection of European art. (Open Tues.-Sat. 10am-4pm, Sun. 2-4pm. Free.) A few blocks up St. Giles stands **Somerville College,** educator of Dorothy Sayers, Indira Gandhi, and Margaret Thatcher.

In **Cowley Road** near the Magdalen Bridge roundabout clutter alternative lifestyles, Marxist bookstores, jumble shops, and scruffy ethnic restaurants.

Music at Oxford is a particularly cherished art; try to attend a concert or a service at one of the colleges, or a performance at the **Holywell Music Rooms.** The **Jericho Tavern,** at the corner of Walton and Jericho St., features local rock and jazz bands. (Open Mon.-Sat. until 2:30am, Sun. noon-2pm and 7-10:30pm.) A favorite pastime in Oxford is **punting** on the River Thames (known in Oxford as the Isis) or on the River Cherwell. The university celebrates **May Day** at the beginning of May, and **Eights Week** at the end of May.

■ Near Oxford

While attending a party at **Blenheim Palace,** Churchill's mother gave birth to the future cigar smoker. (Palace open mid-March to Oct. daily 10:30am-5:30pm. Last entrance 4:45pm. Grounds open daily 9am-5pm. £6.30, children £3.10; includes a boat trip on the lake.) Blenheim Palace sprawls in **Woodstock,** 8 miles north of Oxford on the A34; **South Midlands** (tel. (0993) 776 679) runs an express bus from Oxford's Gloucester Green (3/day, 20min., £2.25, children £1.10). Churchill is buried in nearby **Bladon's** village churchyard.

■■■ COTSWOLDS

Stretching across the west of England from the River Humber to the Dorset coast, the rolling hills of the Cotswolds, origin of the famed Cotswold stone, are flecked with tiny villages dating from the Saxon times. The Cotswolds lie mostly in Gloucestershire, bounded by Banbury in the northeast, Bradford-upon-Avon in the southwest, Cheltenham in the north, and Malmesbury in the south. Local roads are perfect for biking; the frequent villages make ideal watering holes. The 97-mile **Cotswold Way** should appeal to those interested in hiking the hills and staying in unspoiled villages. The **Cotswold Way Handbook** (£1) lists B&Bs along the Way. Camping abounds around Cheltenham but is rather sparse elsewhere. Get *The Cotswolds and Gloucestershire Caravan and Camping Guide* free from local tourist offices.

While they ought not to be omitted from any itinerary, the Cotswolds are not easily accessible by public transportation. Major cities within the area (Cheltenham, Bath, Gloucester, and Cirencester) can be reached by train or bus; the smaller villages are linked by a bus service that is infrequent and slow. Snag the inclusive and far-reaching *Connection* timetable free from all area bus stations and tourist offices.

Stow-on-the Wold, Winchcombe, Cirencester, and Cheltenham Stow-on-the-Wold ("where the winds blow cold") is quintessential Cotswolds: it flourished with the sheep trade and its buildings are of honey-colored stone. An **HI youth hostel** (tel. (0451) 304 97) occupies the center of town. (£5.90, ages 16-20 £4.90. Open March-Oct. daily; Nov.-Dec. and Feb. Fri.-Sun.) West of Stow-on-the-Wold and 6 miles north of Cheltenham on the A46, **Sudeley Castle** dominates **Winchcombe.** Regular falconry shows are held here. (Open April-Oct. daily noon-5pm. £4.75.) Archaeologists have found prehistoric tracks and some 70 habitation sites across the Cotswolds. **Belas Knap,** a laterally chambered long barrow built 4000 years ago, stands about 1½ mile southwest of Sudeley Castle.

The Cotswolds contain some of the best examples of Roman settlements in Britain—most notably in **Cirencester,** the site of "Corinium," founded in 49 AD. The **Corinium Museum,** Park St., houses a formidable collection of Roman artifacts. (Open Mon.-Sat. 10am-5:30pm, Sun. 2-5:30pm; Oct.-March Tues.-Sat. 10am-5pm, Sun. 2-5pm. £1, students and seniors 50p.) On Fridays, the town turns into a rollicking market. **Duntisbourne Abbots hostel (HI)** (tel. (0285) 821 682) is 5 miles outside town. (£6.30, under 18 £4.20. Open March-early Nov. Mon.-Sat. and Dec. 24-28). **The tourist office** is in Corn Hall, Market Pl. (tel. (0285) 654 180).

Cheltenham, the Cotswold's largest town, epitomizes elegance, and proudly possesses the only **naturally alkaline water** in Great Britain. Enjoy the diuretic and laxative effects of the waters at the **Town Hall.** (Open Mon.-Fri. 9am-1pm and 2:15pm-5pm. Free.) The **Gustav MacCallum Holst Birthplace Museum,** 4 Clarence Rd., presents an interesting picture of middle-class family life in the Regency and Victorian periods. (Open Tues.-Sat. 10am-4:20pm. Free.) Four miles northeast of town, the **Cleeve Hill hostel (HI)** (tel. (0242) 672 065), provides bunks. (£6.30; under 18 £4.20. Open March-Oct. Tues.-Sun.) Both men and women can stay at the **YMCA,** Victoria Walk (tel. (0242) 524 024), for £12.25. Supermarkets and the aptly named **Fruity Fruit Store** are strung along High St. and Clarence St. The **tourist office,** 77 Promenade (tel. (0242) 522 878), lies one block east of the bus station. (Open summer Mon.-Fri. 9:30am-6pm, Sat. 9:30am-5pm, Sun. 10am-4pm; Oct.-May Mon.-Sat. 9:30am-5pm.) **Trains** (tel. (0452) 295 01) run regularly to London (1/hr., 2½hr., £22.50), Bristol (1/hr., 1¾hr., £5.70), Bath (1/hr., 1½hr., £9.50), and Exeter (every 2hr., 2hr., £21). Frequent **buses** (tel. (0242) 584 111) run to London (1/hr., 3hr., £16), Bath (2/day, 2½hr., £7.50), and Exeter (every 2hr., 3½hr., £17).

■■■ STRATFORD-UPON-AVON

There's no business like Bard business. Die-hard fans should purchase the joint ticket to the 5 **Shakespeare properties** (£7.50). The least-crowded way to pay homage is to visit his grave in **Holy Trinity Church,** Trinity St. (50p, students 30p.) Start your walking tour at **Shakespeare's Birthplace** on Henley St., half period recreation and half Shakespeare life-and-work exhibition. (Open Mon.-Sat. 9am-5:30pm, Sun. 10am-5:30pm; Nov.-March Mon.-Sat. 10am-4pm, Sun. 1:30-4:30pm. £1.70.) **New Place,** Chapel St., was Stratford's hippest home when Shakespeare bought it back in 1597. (Open Mon.-Sat. 9:30am-5:30pm, Sun. 10:30am-5:30pm; Nov.-March Mon.-Sat. 10am-4:30pm, Sun. 1:30-4:30pm. £1.60.) Shakespeare's eldest daughter once lived in **Hall's Croft,** Old Town Rd. (Hours and admission same as New Place.)

All the world's a stage (and you a player) at the **Royal Shakespeare Company Collection** museum. (Open Mon.-Sat. 9:15am-8pm, Sun. noon-5pm. £1.50, students and seniors £1.) Backstage tours allow you to fiddle with the props and costumes.

(Call (0789) 296 655 for advanced booking. 45-min. tours Mon.-Sat. 1:30 and 5:30pm, except matinee days, Sun. 12:30, 2:15, 3:15, 4:15pm; Nov.-March same except Sun. 11:30am, 12:30, 2:15, 3:15pm. £3.50, students £2.50.) The well-respected **Shakespeare Centre,** Henley St., has a library, a bookshop (across the street), and archives open to students and scholars. The center also holds madrigal concerts and hosts a fine poetry festival in July and August. (For festival information, call (0789) 204 016. Concerts £1-£1.50. Poetry readings Sun. at 8pm; tickets £3.50-5.50.) **Anne Hathaway's Cottage,** the birthplace of Shakespeare's wife, lies about a mile from Stratford in Shottery. (Open Mon.-Sat. 9am-5:30pm, Sun. 10am-5:30pm; Nov.-Feb. Mon.-Sat. 9:30am-4pm, Sun. 6:30am-4pm. £2.10, children £1.) **Mary Arden's House,** the farmhouse restored in a style that a 19th-century entrepreneur determined to be that of Shakespeare's mother, stands 4 miles from Stratford in Wilmcote. (Open Mon.-Sat. 9:30am-5pm, Sun. 10:30am-5pm; Nov.-Feb. Mon.-Sat. 10am-4pm, Sun. 1:30-4pm. £3.) After enduring the cultural-commodity fetishism, seek solace in a performance by the sublime **Royal Shakespeare Company** (seats £4.50-37; tel. (0789) 295 623; 24-hr. recorded information tel. (0789) 269 191). The **Swan Theatre** (tel. (0789) 292 965) is designed for RSC productions of plays by Shakespeare's contemporaries. (Tickets £8-25, standing room £4.50.) **The Other Place** (tel. (0789) 292 965) is the RSC's newest branch, producing modern dramas (£8-14).

Accommodations, Food, and Practical Information

Guest houses (£14-18) line Grove Rd., Evesham Pl., Evesham Rd., and Shipston and Banbury Rd. across the river. The tourist office will put you in touch with local farms that take paying guests (£12.50-16). The **HI youth hostel,** Hemmingford House, Wellesbourne Rd., Alveston (tel. (0789) 297 093), is 2 miles from Stratford. (Reception 7am-11:30pm. Curfew 11pm, post-theater 11:30pm. £11.50, under 18 £8.40). **The Glenavon,** 6 Chestnut Walk (tel. (0789) 292 588), has a prime location. (Singles £14-15. Doubles £30.) Find refreshing lodgings at **Field View Guest House,** 35 Banbury Rd. (tel. (0789) 292 694), an immaculate country home. (Singles £14. Doubles £28.) Camp at **Avon Caravan Park,** Warwick Rd. (tel. (0789) 293 438), 1 mile east of town on the A439. (£4.50, £1.50/additional person. Showers. Open March-Oct.) **Café Natural,** 10 Greenhill St., prepares elaborate vegetarian foods. (Tues. discount (10%) for students and seniors. Entrees £2.50-3.15. Open Mon.-Sat. 9am-4:30pm.) **Vintner Bistro and Café Bar,** 5 Sheep St., serves satisfying ham, beef, and turkey salads. (£4.75-4.95. Open Mon.-Sat. 10:30am-11pm, Sun. 10:30am-10:30pm.)

The **tourist office** is at Bridgefoot (tel. (0789) 293 127; open Mon.-Sat. 9am-6pm, Sun. 9am-5pm; Oct.-March Mon.-Sat. 9am-5pm). Stratford performs 2¼ hours from London Euston by rail or by the bus/rail **"Shakespeare Connection."** (2hr.; £22.50, round-trip £21.) Only the Shakespeare Connection (tel. (0789) 294 466) operates at night after plays. National Express **buses** run to London's Victoria Station (3/day; 3hr.; day return £13.75, period return £17) from the corner of Waterside Rd. and Bridge St. You can buy tickets for National Express buses at the tourist office.

■■■ BATH

Bath was at one time the second social capital of England, but this elegant Georgian city is now more of a museum than a resort. The Romans built an elaborate complex of baths here early in their occupation. Since Queen Anne paid a visit in 1701, a parade of distinguished visitors and residents (Pitt, Burke, Johnson, and Defoe) has come to escape the metropolis while avoiding the boredom of the country.

ORIENTATION AND PRACTICAL INFORMATION

The train and bus stations are near the south end of Manvers St. From either terminal, walk up Manvers St. to the Orange Grove rotary and turn left to the tourist office in the Abbey Churchyard.

Tourist Office: The Colonnades (tel. 462 831 for info and rooms). Efficient staff, crowded office in summer. Map and mini-guide 25p. Open Mon.-Sat. 9:30am-6pm, Sun. 10am-4pm.

Currency Exchange: Barclays, Stall St. (tel. 462 521), behind the Abbey Churchyard. Open Mon.-Tues. and Thurs.-Fri. 9:30am-4:30pm, Wed. 10am-4:30pm, Sat. 9:30am-noon. **Lloyds Bank,** Milsom St. Open Mon.-Fri. 9:30am-4:30pm, Sat 9:30-5pm.

American Express: 5 Bridge St. (tel. 444 767), just before Pulteney Bridge. Open Mon.- Fri. 9am-5pm, Sat. 9am-5pm.

Post Office: New Bond St. (tel. 825 211), at Broad St. Open Mon.-Fri. 9am-5:30pm, Sat. 9am-1pm. **Postal Code:** BA1 1AA.

Telephones: City Code: 0225.

Trains: Railway Pl., at the south end of Manvers St. (tel. 463 075). Booking office open daily 6am-9:30pm. Trains from London's Paddington Station (hourly, 1½hrs., return £32), Exeter (22/day, 1¾hr., £17.50), and Bristol (15min., £3.50).

Buses: Manvers St. (tel. 464 446). National Express **buses** from London's Victoria coach station (9/day, 3hr., return £12.75), Oxford (6/day, 2hr., £11.50), and Salisbury (4/day, 90min., £4.15).

Emergency: Dial 999; no coins required.

ACCOMMODATIONS, CAMPING, AND FOOD

B&Bs (£12-17) cluster on **Pulteney Rd.** and **Pulteney Gdns**. For a more relaxed setting, continue past Pulteney Gdns. to **Widcombe Hill**.

HI youth hostel, Bathwick Hill (tel. 465 674). From N. Parade Rd., turn left on Pulteney Rd., then right on Bathwick. A footpath takes the hardy up the hill (20min.). Badgerline bus #18 (5/hr., until 11pm, return 75p) runs from the bus station or the Orange Grove rotary. Gracious mansion overlooking town. 119 beds, shower, TV, laundry. No lockout. £8.40; Sept.-May £7.50.

Mr. Gay, 14 Raby Pl.(tel. 465 120). From N. Parade, turn left onto Pulteney Rd., then right up Bathwick Hill. Luxuriate in this elegant Georgian house with modern art and superior views of the city. Generous English breakfast. No smoking indoors. Singles £15. Doubles £30.

YMCA International House, Broad St. Place (tel. 460 471). Walk under the arch and up the steps from Walcot St. across from Beaufort Hotel. Men and women allowed. Free hot baths or pulsating showers and midnight curfew. Heavily booked in summer. Singles £12. Doubles £22. Dorm rooms with continental breakfast £9.20/person. Key deposit £5. Laundry facilities.

The Shearns, Prior House, 3 Marlborough Lane (tel. 313 587). Great location on west side of town beside Royal Victoria Park. Take bus #14 or 15 from bus station (every 15min.). Warm, wonderful proprietors. No singles. Doubles with full English breakfast £24.

Camping: Newton Mill Touring Centre, Newton St. Loe (tel. 333 909), 3 mi. west of the city center off the A36/A39. Take bus #5 from bus station (return 75p) to Newton Rd. 105 sites. £6.70/site, £3/person. Free warm showers. Laundry.

For fruits and vegetables, visit the **Guildhall Market,** between High St. and Grand Parade. Splash out for cream tea (£4.25) in the palatial Victorian **Pump Room,** Abbey Churchyard. (Open Mon.-Sat. 10am-noon and 2:45-5pm.) Scoff not at **Scoff's** lunches, served in a woody dining room on Monmouth and Westgate St. (Open Mon.-Sat. 9am-5pm.) Among Bath's pubs, **The Grapes,** Westgate St., attracts an energetic throng. Bath nights wake up at **The Bell**, 103 Walcot St. to live jazz blues.

SIGHTS

Sewer-diggers uncovered the **Roman Baths** in 1880, and recent excavation has yielded a splendid model of Roman engineering. (Open daily 9am-7pm; Aug. daily 9am-6pm and 8-10pm; Sept.-Oct. and March-June daily 9am-6pm; Nov.-Feb. Mon.-Sat. 9am-5pm, Sun. 10am-5pm. £4, children £2.) The 15th-century **Abbey Church** seems an anomaly among Bath's first-century Roman and 18th-century Georgian sights. (Open Mon.-Sat. 9am-4:30pm, Sun. 1-2:30pm and 4:30-5:30pm. Donation £1.) Walk up Gay St. to **The Circus,** which has attracted illustrious residents for 2 centuries; blue plaques mark the houses of Thomas Gainsborough, William Pitt, and David Livingstone. Proceed from there up Brock St. to **Royal Crescent** and its up-ended saucer of a lawn. The interior of **No. 1 Royal Crescent** has been painstakingly restored to a near-perfect replica of a 1770 townhouse. (Open Tues.-Sun. 10:30am-5pm. £3, children, students, and seniors £2.50.) The **Assembly Rooms,** Bennett St., just east of The Circus, staged fashionable social events in the late 18th century. (Open Mon.-Sat. 9:30am-6pm, Sun. 10:30am-5pm; Nov.-Feb. Mon.-Sat. 10am-5pm, Sun. 11am-5pm. £2.50, children £1.40). The 15th-century **Bath Abbey** seems an anomaly among Bath's first-century Roman and 18th-century Georgian sights. (Open daily 9am-6pm. "Donation" £1.)

EAST ANGLIA

The plush green farmlands and dismal watery fens of East Anglia stretch northeast from London, cloaking the counties of Cambridgeshire, Norfolk, and Suffolk. While high-tech industry is modernizing the economies of Cambridge and Peterborough, the college town and cathedral city are still linked by flat fields, hedges, and stone walls. East Anglia's flat terrain and relatively low annual rainfall are a boon to bikers and hikers. The area's two longest and most popular walking trails are **Peddar's Way** and **Weaver's Way**. If you plan to see a lot of the region by public transport, buy an **Anglia Rover** ticket (approximately £35, discount with railcard), available only at rail stations within East Anglia, good for one week's unlimited rail travel.

■■■ CAMBRIDGE

Cambridge the university has lorded it over Cambridge the town for over 700 years. Competing in most everything with Oxford, Cambridge loses in age and boat races but wins on charm and spectacle; the countrified Backs on the west bank of the River Cam lend a pastoral air to the city.

ORIENTATION AND PRACTICAL INFORMATION

Cambridge, about 60 miles north of London, has 2 main avenues. The main shopping street starts at **Magdalene Bridge** (MAWD-lin) and becomes Bridge Street, Sidney Street, St. Andrew's Street, Regent Street, and finally Hills Road. The other—alternately St. John's Street, Trinity Street, King's Parade, Trumpington Street, and Trumpington Road—is the academic thoroughfare.

Tourist Office: Wheeler St. (tel. 322 640), 1 block south of the marketplace. Open Mon.-Tues. and Thurs.-Fri. 9am-6pm, Wed. 9:30am-6pm, Sat. 9am-5pm; Nov.-Feb. closes at 5:30pm. Also open Easter-Sept. Sun. 10:30am-3:30pm. Information on Cambridge events also available at **Corn Exchange** box office (tel. 357 851), Corn Exchange St., opposite the tourist office.

Tours: Unbeatable 2-hr. walking tours of the city and some colleges leave the main tourist office daily April-Sept. (April-June 11am and 2pm; July-Aug. every hr. 11am-3pm; Sept. every hr. 11am-3pm.) Tours less frequent during the rest of the year. £3.30.

American Express: Abbot Travel, 25 Sidney St. (tel. 351 636). Client mail held. Open Mon., Tues., Thurs., Fri. 9am-5:30pm, Wed. 9:30-5:30pm, Sat. 9am-5pm.

Post Office: 9-11 St. Andrew's St. (tel. 323 325). Open Mon.-Tues. and Thurs.-Fri. 9am-5:30pm, Wed. 9:30am-5:30pm, Sat. 9am-12:30pm. **Postal Code:** CB2 3AA.

Telephones: City Code: 0223.

Train Station: Station Rd. (tel. 311 999). Purchase tickets 5am-11pm daily. Travel Centre open Mon.-Sat. 4:30am-11pm, Sun. 6am-11pm. To get to Market Sq. from the train station, take a Cityrail Link bus or walk down Hills Road (25min., 60p).

Bus and Coach Station: Drummer St. Station. **National Express** tel. 460 711. **Cambus** (tel. 423 554) handles city and area service (40p-£1). Some local routes serviced by **Miller's** or **Premier** coaches. **Whippet Coaches** run daytrips from Cambridge. Travel Centre open Mon.-Sat. 8:15am-5:30pm.

Bike Rental: C. Frost, 188 New Market Rd. (tel. 356 464). £5/day, £12/week; £20 deposit. Open Mon.-Fri. 9am-1pm and 2-6pm, Sat. 9:30am-1pm and 2-5:30pm.

Crisis Lines: AIDS: tel. 697 65. Open Tues.-Wed. 7:30-10pm. **Crime Victims:** tel. 630 24. **Rape Crisis:** 24-hr. answering service, tel. 358 314. **Samaritans:** tel. 644 55.

Emergency: tel. 999; no coins required. **Police:** Parkside, (tel. 358 966). **Addenbrookes Hospital,** Hills Rd. (tel. 245 151).

ACCOMMODATIONS, CAMPING, AND FOOD

Cambridge has no shortage of rooms (albeit expensive ones) for visitors, but it's advisable to book ahead during high season. Many of the cheap B&Bs hover around **Portugal St.** and **Tenison Rd.**

HI youth hostel, 97 Tenison Rd. (tel. 354 601; fax 312 780), entrance on Devonshire Rd. Close to train station; walk straight ahead, then right on Tenison Rd. Relaxed, welcoming atmosphere; well-equipped kitchen, laundry room, and TV lounge. £11.50, ages 18 £8.40, breakfast and sleepsack included; crowded in March-Oct.; lockers should be installed by 1994. Call a few days in advance and arrive by 6pm.

Home from Home B&B, Mrs. Flora Miles, 39 Milton Rd. (tel. 323 555). Mrs. Miles graciously welcomes guests into her sunny, immaculate, well-decorated home. Singles £20. Doubles £32. Call a few days ahead.

Highfield Farm Camping Park, Long Rd., Comberton (tel. 262 308). Head west on A603 for 3 mi., then left on B1046. Or take Cambus #118 from the Drummer St. bus station (every 45min.). Flush toilets, showers, and a washing machine. £6-7/tent. Call ahead. Open April-Oct.

Warkworth Guest House, Warkworth Terrace (tel. 636 82). A charming and gracious hostess has 16 sunny rooms near the bus station. Singles £17. Doubles £30. Family £45. Breakfast included. Kitchen, laundry, telephone.

Tenison Towers, Mr. J. DaSivla, 148 Tenison Rd. (tel. 639 24). Clean and comfy rooms located near the train station. Singles £14-18. Doubles £24-28. Triples £32-36. Quads £44-48. Prices depend on season.

Market Square has bright pyramids of fruit and vegetables for the hungry budgetarian. (Open Mon.-Sat. approximately 8am-5:30pm.) Students buy their gin and cornflakes at **Sainsbury's,** 44 Sydney St., the only grocery store in the middle of town. (Open Mon.-Wed. 8:30am-7pm, Thurs.-Fri. 8:30am-8pm.) **Rajbelash,** 36-38 Hills Rd., serves up a spectacular array of curries, *tandooris,* and *biryanis.* (£2.60-6.40. Open daily noon-2:30pm and 6pm-midnight.) The generous portions and low prices make up for the corner-diner atmosphere at the **Corner House Restaurant,** 9 King St. (Open Mon.-Fri. 11:30am-2:30pm and 5-9:30pm, Sat.-Sun. 11:30am-9:30pm.) Practice your Esperanto over cappuccino at **Clown's,** 54 King St., a meeting place for foreigners, bozos, and beautiful people. (Open daily 9am-11pm.)

SIGHTS AND ENTERTAINMENT

Cambridge is an architect's dream, packing some of the most breathtaking examples of English architecture into less than 1 sq. mile. If you are pressed for time, visit at least one chapel (preferably King's), one garden (try Christ's), one library (Trinity's is the most interesting), and one dining hall (difficult without befriending a Cambridge undergrad, although no one will prevent you from sneaking a peek). Cambridge is most busy (read: most interesting) during the university's 3 terms:

Michaelmas (Oct. 6-Dec. 4), Lent (Jan. 12-March 12), and Easter (April 20-June 11). Most of the colleges are open daily from 9am to 5:30pm, though virtually all are closed during exam period (mid-May to mid-June).

Cambridge's colleges stretch along the River Cam. **King's College,** on King's Parade, possesses a spectacular Gothic chapel. (Open term-time Mon.-Sat. 10am-3:45pm, Sun. 2-3pm and 4:30-5:45pm. Free.) **Trinity College,** on Trinity St., includes the notable treasure of A.A. Milne's handwritten manuscript of Winnie-the-Pooh and less momentous works such as John Milton's "Lycidas." **Queens' College** was founded not once, but twice, and possesses the only unaltered Tudor courtyard in Cambridge. **Christ's College,** founded as "God's house" in 1448, has won fame for its gardens. (Open Mon.-Fri. 2-4pm; in summer 9:30am-noon as well.)

You can easily get caught up in the splendor of the colleges, but try to explore a few museums. The **Fitzwilliam Museum,** Trumpington Rd., houses paintings by Leonardo da Vinci, Michelangelo, Dürer, and Seurat. (Open Tues.-Fri. ground floor 10am-2pm, upper floor 2-5pm, Sat. both floors 10am-5pm, Sun. both floors 2:15-5pm. Free.) The **Scott Polar Research Institute,** Lensfield Rd., commemorates icy expeditions with photographic and artistic accounts and equipment. (Open Mon.-Sat. 2:30-4pm. Free.)

Students drink local bitters IPA (India Pale Ale) and Abbott at the **Anchor,** Silver St., on rainy days, and **The Mill,** Mill Lane, off Silver St. Bridge, on sunny ones. **The Geldart,** 1 Ainsworth St., features Irish folk, rock, and R&B, and **Burleigh Arms,** 9-11 Newmarket Rd., serves up beer and lager to a primarily gay, lesbian, and bisexual clientele. The best source of information on student activities is the *Varsity.* Try the **Arts Cinema,** Market Passage (tel. 352 001), which screens comedy classics and undubbed foreign films. (Tickets £2.50-3.50. Box office open daily 1-9:15pm, Sat. 11am-9:15pm, Sun. 1:30-9:15pm.) You can get an earful of concerts at the **Cambridge Corn Exchange** (tel. 357 851), at the corner of Wheeler St. and Corn Exchange, a venue for jazz, and classical concerts (tel. 357 851; tickets £7.50-16, 50% off for student standby day of performance; box office open Mon.-Sat. 10am-6pm). On a sunny afternoon, the river is almost always stocked with narrow, flat-bottomed **punts,** England's retort to the gondola. You can rent one from **Scudamore's Boatyards,** at Magdalene Bridge or Silver St. (tel. 359 750); hourly rates are £7 for punts, rowboats, and canoes, plus a £40 cash deposit. (Open daily 9am-6pm.)

■ Near Cambridge

Fifteen miles north of Cambridge, **Ely** earned national tourist notoriety as the first town in England to charge admission to its **cathedral,** but the massive building and its separate stained glass museum are well worth the pence. (Cathedral open in summer daily 7am-7pm. Other times open Mon.-Fri. 7:30am-6pm, Sun. 7:30am-5pm. Tours Easter-Oct. 11:15am and 2:15pm; July-Aug. also 3:15pm. £2.50, students £2. Stained glass museum open March-Oct. Mon.-Fri. 10:30am-4pm, Sat. 10:30am-4:30pm, Sun. noon-3pm. £1.50, students 70p.) Trains run between Cambridge and Ely (1/hr., 20min., day return £3.10). Twenty-five miles southeast of Cambridge, the less-touristed streets of **Bury St. Edmunds** arrange themselves according to the original 12th-century street plan and house an exquisite **abbey flower garden.** (Abbey and gardens open daily 7:30am-sunset. Free.)

CENTRAL ENGLAND

The 19th century swept into central England, revolutionizing quiet village life with its industrial sandstorms; the "dark satanic mills" that William Blake foresaw indeed overran the Midlands. The region remains the industrial heart of England despite growing unemployment and a dwindling population, but the description "industrial" should not disqualify this region from your route. Manchester and Liverpool are now home to innovative music and arts scenes as well as some of the U.K.'s most vibrant nightlife, cities like Lincoln and Chester tell some of their stories in Latin, and Sheffield...well, Sheffield is near the Peak District.

■■■ NOTTINGHAM

Remnants of a booming lace industry and a working canal prove that life went on in Sherwood Forest after Friar Tuck and Maid Marian. Prince John's famous home (Nottingham Castle) was demolished in the 17th century (and rebuilt) and burned in the 19th century (and repaired). Today's **Castle Museum** exhibits the history of Nottingham. (Museum open daily 10am-5:45pm; Oct.-March 10am-4:45pm. Grounds open Mon.-Fri. 8am-dark, Sat.-Sun. 9am-dark. Museum and grounds free; Sat.-Sun and bank holidays £1, children 50p . .) Across Castle Rd. at 51 Castle Gate is the **Museum of Costume and Textiles,** complete with hundreds of pieces of lace. (Open daily 10am-5pm. Free.) Nearby, at the base of the castle's hill, the **Brewhouse Yard Museum** stocks items of everyday life from the past 300 years—see how toothpaste was packaged during the reign of Queen Victoria. (Open daily 10am-5:45; Mon.-Fri. free; Sat.-Sun. £1, children 50p).

Stay at the **YMCA,** 4 Shakespeare St. (tel. (0602) 473 068; £13; key deposit £4; call 2 weeks ahead), or at **Langley Guest House,** 82-84 Goldsmith St. (tel. (0602) 474 992; singles £11; doubles £20). **Whitwell Delicatessen,** 7-9 Ilkeston Rd., serves delicious mozzarella, basil, and tomato sandwiches. (Open Mon.-Thurs. 8am-5pm, Fri. 8am-6pm, Sat. 8:30am-6pm; sandwiches 10am-3pm only.) Prowl through 13th-century caves before enjoying a pint of local bitter at the 550-year-old **Salutation Inn,** Spaniel Row. (Open Mon.-Sat. 10:30am-11pm, Sun. noon-3pm and 7-10:30pm.)

The **tourist office,** 1-4 Smithy Row (tel. (0602) 470 661), is an info-tainment bonanza that sequesters great free maps and brochures behind the counter. (Open Mon.-Fri. 8:30am-5pm, Sat. 9am-5pm, Sun. 10am-4pm. Nov.-March. Closed Sun.) **Trains** (tel. (0332) 320 51) run to Lincoln (24/day, Sun. 11/day; £3.50, day return £5.30); Sheffield (about every hr., £9.50, return £11-12.50), and London's St. Pancras (every hr.; 2hrs.; £28.50, return from £26.60). **Buses** (tel. (0602) 585 317) run to London (7/day; 2:20am-6:05pm; £16.50, return £17.50-21), Sheffield, Manchester, and other destinations.

■■■ LINCOLN

France has Chartres, Spain has Santiago de Compostela, and England has Lincoln, the home of its great Gothic cathedral. Begun in the 12th century on the ruins of a Norman structure, **Lincoln Minster** was for many centuries the tallest building in Europe, and its position at the top of Castle Hill makes it visible from as far away as Boston (on *really* clear days). (Open Mon.-Sat 7:15am-8pm, Sun. 7:15am-6pm; in winter Mon.-Sat. 7:15am-6pm, Sun. 7:15am-5pm. Suggested donation £2.50, students and seniors £1.) **Lincoln Castle** has been heavily restored, though the Norman walls remain, enclosing a vast area and the best preserved of the 4 copies of the *Magna Carta*. (Open Mon.-Sat. 9:30am-5:30pm, Sun. 11am-5:30pm; Nov.-March Mon.-Sat. 9:30am-4pm. Last entry 30min. before closing. £2, students, seniors, and children £1.50.)

Carline Rd. and Yarborough Rd., west of the castle and cathedral, are lined with B&Bs. The **HI youth hostel,** 77 S. Park (tel. (0522) 522 076), opposite South Common at the end of Canwick Rd., is a top-notch, relaxing hostel across the street from a park. (Reception closed 10am-5pm. Curfew 11pm. £7.50, under 18 £5. Cafeteria meals 5-8pm (£3.50). MC, V. Open July-Aug. daily; April-June Mon.-Sat.; Sept.-Oct. and mid- Feb. to March Tues.-Sat.; Nov. to mid-Dec. Fri.-Sat.) Sit by the window in a house built on a medieval bridge at **Stokes High Bridge Café,** 207 High St. (£3-4 lunchtime specials 11:30am-2pm. Open Mon.-Wed. 9am-5pm, Thurs.-Sat. 9am-5:30pm.) Or down a pint and some grub at the **Lion and Snake,** 79 Bailgate, up by the cathedral. (Food served Mon.-Fri. noon-2pm and 6-8pm.) **Vienna,** Newland Ave., and **Ritzy,** Silver St., supply music and a flat surface.

The **main tourist office,** 9 Castle Hill (tel. (0522) 529 828), perches at the top of the hill near the cathedral. (Open Mon.-Thurs. 9am-5:30pm, Fri. 9am-5pm, Sat.-Sun. 10am-5pm; Oct.-March same weekday hrs., Sat.-Sun. 11-3pm.) **Trains** (tel. (0522) 539 502) run to London via Newark (3/day, Sat. 1/day; £30, return £31-38) and to York (Mon.-Sat. roughly hourly, Sun. 10/day; 1½-3½hr.; £14.30, return £16.50-21.50). National Express sends **buses** (tel. (0522) 534 444) to London (2/day; 5hr.; £22, return £23-27.50).

■■■ SHEFFIELD

While Manchester was clothing the world, Sheffield was setting the table, first with hand-crafted flatware, then with mass-produced goods and eventually stainless steel. Not the most attractive destination in and of itself, Sheffield is the perfect jumping off point to the Peak District. The **Kelham Island Industrial Museum,** Alma St., displays some of the iron, steel, silverware, and unusual metal products manufactured in Sheffield over the past 300 years. (Open March-Nov. Mon.-Thurs. 10am-4pm, Sun. 11am-4pm. £2.20, seniors and children £1.10.)

The tourist office accommodations list, posted in its window, is fairly comprehensive; B&Bs run at least £15. The **YMCA,** 20 Victoria Rd. (tel. (0742) 684 807), offers worn but clean and comfortable rooms to men and women. (Singles £13. Doubles £22.) **Mamas and Leonies,** 111-115 Norfolk St., near Town Hall, serves pasta, burgers, and pizza. (Open Mon.-Thurs. 10am-11pm, Fri.-Sat. 10am-11:30pm.) The **tourist office,** Town Hall Extension, Union St. (tel. (0742) 734 671), answers queries. (Open Mon.-Fri. 9:30am-5:15pm, Sat. 9:30am-4:15pm.) **Trains** (tel. (0742) 726 411) run to Manchester (every ½hr., Sun. every hr.; 1-1½hr.; £7.50, return £9.50), Birmingham (12-14/day; 2hr.; £15.50, return £17-23.50), and London's St. Pancras Station (10-17/day; 2-3hr.; £36.50, saver return £32-40). National Express **buses** (tel. (0742) 754 905) run to London (roughly every 2hr.; 3½hr.; £20.50, economy return £23.50-28), and Nottingham (every 1-2hr.; 1hr.; £6.25, return £6.75-8).

■■■ PEAK NATIONAL PARK

Peak National Park lies at the southern end of the Pennines, covering 555 sq. miles, with Manchester, Sheffield, Nottingham, and Stoke-on-Trent at its corners. Here the landscape is pastoral rather than wild, with chest-high stone walls meandering through fields of grass well-nibbled by sheep and Frisian cattle.

Practical Information To accommodate the pumped-up volume of human traffic in Britain's most touristed national park, public transport and commercial bus tours move the mobs on sunny summer weekends; for a more tranquil visit, try to catch the infrequent buses to the bleaker northern moors, out of the reach of the commuter-rail lines. If you plan to use buses or trains to get around, Derbyshire County Council's *District Timetable* (50p) is an invaluable investment, available at most Peak tourist offices. Although protected from development by national park status, the land is still privately owned, so be respectful to property and environment and stick to designated rights-of-way. For an information pack on the park, write to the Tourism Officer, Town Hall, Matlock, Derbyshire DE4 3NN.

Information centers in the park distribute free park-wide and regional accommodations guides; a camping guide costs 35p. The following **National Park Information Centres** should be helpful: **Castleton** (tel. (0433) 620 679), **Edale** (tel. (0433) 670 207), and **Fairholmes** (tel. (0433) 509 53). You can also ask questions at area **tourist offices: Ashbourne** (tel. (0335) 436 66), **Bakewell** (tel. (0629) 813 227), **Buxton** (tel. (0298) 251 06), and **Matlock Bath** (tel. (0629) 550 82).

There are over 20 **HI youth hostels** in the park, including **Bakewell** (tel. (0629) 812 313) and **Buxton** (tel. (0298) 222 87). The area also has plenty of B&Bs (from £10) and camping barns; ask for comprehensive lists at tourist offices.

The park authority operates 7 **Cycle Hire Centres,** where you can rent a bike. (£3.50-3.70/3hr., £5.70/day; under 16 £3-3.20/3hr., £4/day, £5 deposit. 10% discount for HI members and Wayfarer ticket holders. Open in summer daily 9:30am-6pm, varying hours off-season). Call **Ashbourne** (tel. (0335) 431 56) for information.

Southern and Northern Peaks The **Southern Peak** is better served by buses and trains and is consequently more trampled than the Northern Peak. The former spa town of **Buxton** still fills its swimming pool with spring water; just outside of town, **Poole's Cavern** (tel. (0298) 269 78) is one of many stalagmite-studded showcaves scattered throughout the Peaks. (Open June-Sept. daily 10am-5pm; Oct. and April-May Thurs.-Tues. 10am-5pm. £3, seniors and students £2.40, children £1.50.) In town, try comfortable **Guildford B&B,** 12 Compton Rd. (tel. (0298) 239 85), on a quiet residential avenue (from £13). The **tourist office** (see information centers above) on the Crescent gives guided walks of the town. (1½hr., £1.75. Open daily 9:30am-5pm; Nov.-March Mon.-Sat. 10am-4pm, Sun. noon-4pm). To the east lies **Bakewell,** the best base from which to explore the southern portion of the park and to eat Bakewell pudding (created when a flustered cook, trying to make a tart, poured an egg mixture over strawberry jam instead of mixing it into the dough). Try gracious Mrs. Holden's **Erica Cottage,** Butts Rd. (tel. (0629) 813 241), for £13. Four miles northeast of Bakewell, off the B6012, the Duke and Duchess of Devonshire's palatial **Chatsworth House** attracts gaggles of gawkers at its 100 acres of creative landscaping. (Open mid-March to Oct. daily 11am-5:30pm. £5, seniors £4.25, children £2.50. No wheelchair access.)

The **northern district** area contains some of the wildest and most rugged hill country in England. The village of **Edale** is the terminus of the Pennine Way footpath to the Scottish border. Your tent could be your best friend in this town, where the only accommodations are the 140-bed **HI youth hostel.** (Lockout 10am-5pm. Curfew 11pm. £5.70-£8.40.) Picturesque **Castleton,** in the shadow of the ruined Peveril Castle, has 4 caverns that are the source of the town's characteristic Blue John stone. At **Speedwell Cavern,** you can take a boat tour of the "Bottomless Pit," which once had 40,000 tons of rubble dumped in it without its water level rising. (Open daily 9:30am-5:30pm. £4; seniors, students and HI members £3.25, children £2.50.) Only Brontë diehards should spend an hour or two in sleepy **Hathersage,** the village that probably corresponds to the "Morton" to which Jane Eyre fled from Thornfield Hall.

■■■ MANCHESTER

Manchester recently declared itself a "nuclear-free city," and countless placards and posters reveal that the labor movement and environmentalism are the norm here. An intense cultural core and vibrant arts community pulses beneath the buffed façade, sending its rhythms across the nation in the form of bands with funny names.

Behind the Town Hall Extension is Manchester's jewel, the **Central Library,** one of the largest municipal libraries in Europe. (Open Mon.-Wed. and Fri. 10am-8pm, Sat. 10am-noon and 1-5pm.) In the **Museum of Science and Industry,** on Liverpool Rd., working steam engines and looms provide a dramatic sense of the awesome speed, power, danger, and noise of Britain's industrialization. (Open daily 10am-5pm. £3.50, students, seniors, and visitors with disabilities £1.50; includes entrance to all galleries for one day, which may not be enough.) The brown land of the Ardwick and Rusholme neighborhoods south of the city center is gilded by **Manchester University** and its two fine museums. **Manchester Museum,** on Oxford Rd., houses the university's natural history collections. (Open Mon.-Sat. 10am-5pm. Free.) The

Whitworth Art Gallery, Oxford Rd., features British watercolors, a few stray Warhols and a large collection of international textiles. (Open Mon.-Wed. and Fri.-Sat. 10am-5pm, Thurs. 10am-9pm. Free. Wheelchair access.)

Mancunians have furnished themselves with a lively nightlife. Pick up a free copy of the biweekly *Uptown* at the Central Library's information center or *City Life* (£1.20) at the tourist office for a comprehensive schedule of arts events (from Mozart to dance clubs) before entering the whirlpool. Manchester's club scene remains a national trend-setter, and it centers on the notorious **Hacienda,** 11-13 W. Whitworth St., close to G-Mex. (For concert info call (061) 236 5051. Open daily 9pm-2am.) Buses run to outlying areas regularly until 11pm; less frequent night service runs until 2:30am.

Accommodations, Food, and Practical Information Manchester sends its budget travelers packing to the outskirts of town. The highest concentration of budget accommodations is found 2 or 3 miles south of the city center in the suburbs of **Fallowfield, Withington,** and **Didsbury.** Try **Mrs. Matheson,** 41 Atwood Rd., Didsbury (tel. (061) 434 2268; £10). In the Rusholme area, before the university on the #40 bus, numerous Middle Eastern and Indian restaurants and take-away counters line Wilmslow Rd. At **Camel One,** 107 Wilmslow Rd. in Rusholme, £3 gets you a kebab or curry and a fluffy *naan,* to take away or eat at the counter. (Open daily 11am-5am.) The **Lass-O-Gowrie,** Charles St., serves 2 versions of their own brew to a rambunctious crowd.

The **tourist office,** Town Hall Extension, Albert Sq. on Lloyd St. (tel. (061) 234 3157), will provide a free list of B&Bs on request. (Open Tues.-Fri. 9am-5pm, Mon. and Sat. 10am-5pm.) The office also offers dozens of guided walks (£2, students and seniors £1) on such topics as "Murders and Mysteries of Manchester" and "Feminine Influence." **Trains** (tel. (061) 832 8353) run to London (every hr., 2½hr., return £32-42), Liverpool (every 30min.; 45min.; £5.50, same-day return £6.30), Chester (every hr.; 1hr.; £6.10, same-day return £6.30) and York (every 30min.; 1hr.; £11, same-day return £11.50). **Buses** (tel. (061) 228 7811) roll to Sheffield (9/day every 2hr.; 90min.; one-way £7.25, same-day return £7.50), Glasgow (6/day; 4-5hr.; one-way £20, same-day return £21-25), and London (7 Rapide/day 7:30am-11:50pm; 5hr.; one-way £20.50, same-day return £21.50-26).

■■■ CHESTER

With fashionable shops tucked away in medieval houses, guides in full Roman armor leading tours around the city's walls, and a Barclays Bank occupying a wing of the cathedral, **Chester** sometimes resembles an American theme-park pastiche of Ye Olde English Village. Chester's famous **city walls** completely encircle the town, and you can encircle them for free. The original **Northgate,** with a fine-grained view of the Welsh hills, was rebuilt in 1808 to house the city's jail, 30 ft. below ground level. Just outside Newgate lie the half-unearthed foundations of the largest **Roman amphitheater** in Britain. (Open daily 10am-6pm; Oct.-March Tues.-Sun. 10am-1pm and 2-4pm. Free.) Chester's brooding and massive gothic **cathedral** began its life in the 11th century as the burial place for St. Werburgh, a Mercian abbess, and one of the early founders of the northern monasteries. (Cathedral open daily 7:30am-6:30pm.) For a look at some Cheshire cats, primates, and reptiles, head to the **Chester Zoo** in nearby Upton-by-Chester. (Zoo open daily 10am-dusk. Last entry 5:30pm; in winter 3:30pm. £5.50, ages 3-15 and seniors £3.) The finest pleasure in Chester is also the simplest: strolling beside the River Dee. Rent a boat or simply take tea and watch vessels float by at the **Rex Café** beside the Queen's Park Footbridge, the street that runs along the water. (Open daily 9:30am-dusk.)

Accommodations, Food, and Practical Information The highest concentration of decent B&Bs (average price £12) is along **Hoole Road,** 5 minutes from the train station. The **HI youth hostel,** Hough Green House, 40 Hough Green (tel. (0244) 680 056), is in a beautiful, recently renovated Victorian house on a quiet street. (Lockout 10am-3pm. £10.60, under 18 £7.80. Open Jan.-Nov.) **Dutton's Health Foods,** 8 Godstall Lane, near the cathedral entrance, has packed lunches—a roll with cheese or paté, apple, and Brazil nuts—for a pittance. (Open Mon.-Sat. 8:30am-5pm.) **Hattie's Tea Shop,** 5 Rufus Ct., off Northgate, has scrumptious cakes and inexpensive lunchtime snacks. Try the "giant topless" ham salad sandwich. (£2.25. Open Mon.-Sat. 9am-5pm. Wheelchair access.) For current listings of musical and special events, pick up the free monthly *What's On* from the tourist office. **Rendezvous,** Northgate St. (open Thurs.-Sat. 9:30pm-2am), and **Blimper's,** City Rd. (open Wed.-Sat. 9:30pm-2am), both blast a good variety of music.

The **tourist office,** Town Hall, Northgate St. (tel. (0244) 313 126), offers brochures and info. (Open Mon.-Sat. 9am-5:30pm.) British Rail **trains** (tel. (0244) 340 170) run to London's Euston (every hr.; 3hr.; £38.50, supersaver return £32-42); Holyhead (every 2hr.; £13; supersaver return £13-17.50), and Manchester (every 90min.; 2hr.; £6.10, same-day return £6.30). National Express **buses** (tel. (0244) 381 515) run to London (5 Rapide/day; 4½hr.; £22, return £23-27), Manchester (4/day; 1¼hr.; £6, return £6.25-7.50), and Bristol (11:30am; 3hr.; £20, return £21-25).

■■■ LIVERPOOL

The city that clings tightly to its status as the birthplace of the Beatles maintains a thriving cultural life that has diminished little since the 1960s, when Allen Ginsberg described it as "the center of human consciousness." Liverpool's efforts to bring its waterfront out of the rusty age of freight have yielded **Albert Dock,** an 1846 series of warehouses transformed into a complex of shops, restaurants, and museums. A cornerstone of this development is the **Tate Gallery,** Albert Dock, a branch of the London institution. (Open Tues.-Sun. 10am-6pm. Free; some special exhibitions cost £1, seniors, students, and children 50p. Wheelchair access.) Among the other attractions at Albert Dock is **The Beatles Story,** which presents a chronological look at the four guys that shook the world. (Open daily 10am-6pm. £3.50, students, seniors, and children £2, families £8.) Pick up the **Beatles Map** (£1) at the tourist office, which gives directions to Strawberry Fields and Penny Lane. Along the way, try to determine if the Fab Four were indeed bigger than Jesus.

It's fun to stay at the **YMCA,** 56-60 Mt. Pleasant (tel. (051) 709 9516; singles £12.50; doubles £21.50; full breakfast included), or, if you're a woman, at the **YWCA,** 1 Rodney St. (tel. (051) 709 7791; singles £9). Try **St. John's Market** (above the shopping mall) for fresh produce and local color. Liverpool has many a budget restaurant, especially along Hardman St. Grab a pint at the **Black Horse & Rainbow,** 21-23 Berry St., near Chinatown, which is named after its two home-brewed bitters.

Liverpool's oft-grim demeanor is brightened by a thriving arts scene and an energetic nightlife. The *Liverpool Echo,* a local evening newspaper sold on streetcorners, has the most up-to-date arts information as well as local news and banal royal family gossip (25p). Fight your way inside **Flanagan's Apple,** Matthew St., which offers the best Irish music in town nightly.

The **tourist office** (tel. (051) 709 3631) hides itself in the Clayton Sq. Shopping Centre. (Open Mon.-Sat. 9am-5:30pm.) A smaller branch is located at **Atlantic Pavilion,** Albert Dock (tel. (051) 708 8854; open daily 10am-5:30pm). **Trains** (tel. (051) 709 9696) run to Manchester (every hr.; 1½hr.; £5.50, return £6.30), Birmingham (every hr.; 1¾hr.; £16, return £12.50-20), and London (every hr.; 3hr.; £44, return £32-42). **Buses** (tel. (051) 709 6481) head to London (5 Rapide/day; 4½hr.; £20.50, return £21.50-26), Manchester (every hr.; 1hr.; £4.50, return £4.75-5.75), and Birmingham (5/day; 2½hr.; £11, return £11.50-13.75).

NORTH ENGLAND

Between Central England's industrial belt and Scotland's rugged wilderness is a quiet area of natural beauty. Vertically sliced by the Pennine Mountains, North England's main attractions lie enshrined in 4 national parks and several calm coastal areas. Walkers and ramblers flock here, and no trail tests their stamina more than the Pennine Way, the country's first official long-distance path and still its longest. Isolated villages along the trails continue a pastoral tradition that contrasts with the polluted enormity and din of many English cities to the south.

Two north-south rail lines traverse the far north, one via York to Newcastle (east of the Pennines) and another via Crewe to Carlisle (west of the Pennines). From Carlisle, an east-west line connects to Newcastle. Buses run between some of the scattered hamlets of agricultural England, but without the frequency of their urban counterparts; plan detailed itineraries and check them with transport officials to avoid being stranded for a week in Hebden Bridge.

■■■ PENNINE WAY

The Pennine (PEN-eyen) Peaks form, as the common anthropomorphism goes, England's spine. They arch, like any quality backbone would, south to north up the center of Britain from the Peak National Park to the Scottish border. The **Pennine Way,** the Countryside Commission's 250-mile path, crowns the central ridge of the watershed. Hikers (with a capital "H") have completed the hike in 10 days, but most walkers spend 3 weeks on the long, green trail. The classic Wainwright's *Pennine Way Companion* (£6.50), a pocket-sized volume available from Peak Information Centres, is a worthwhile supplement to Ordnance Survey maps, which run about £5 or £10 with lamination. Sudden mist and rain on the Peaks can reduce visibility to under 20 ft. After a storm, the low-level paths can become boggy, and some paths will leave you knee-deep (or worse) in hungry peat.

HI youth hostels are spaced within a day's hike (7-29 mi.) of one another. Any National Park Information Centre can supply details on trails and alternative accommodations. The *Pennine Way Accommodations and Catering Guide* (90p) could prove as valuable as moleskin. Camping in the open is also permitted.

South Pennines In the midst of the barren **South Pennines,** the tiny villages of **Haworth** and **Hebden Bridge** provide hospitable civilization breaks for an overnight or daytrip from Leeds or Manchester. From Hebden Bridge, you can make dayhikes to the nearby villages of Blackshaw Head, Cragg Vale, or **Hepstonstall,** where you'll find the ruins of a 13th-century church and a 1764 octagonal church, the oldest Methodist house o' worship in the world. The **Birchcliffe Centre,** in a former Baptist chapel on Birchcliffe Rd. (tel. (0422) 843 626), allows travelers who call ahead to fill beds not needed by groups (£12-15). Hebden Bridge's **tourist office,** 1 Bridge Gate (tel. (0422) 843 831), is equipped with maps and guides. (Open Mon.-Sat. 9am-5pm, Sun. 10am-5pm; Oct. to mid-March daily 10am-4pm.) Brontë fans must stop in Haworth to see the **parsonage** near the tourist office, where Emily, Charlotte, and Anne lived with their father and their brother Branwell. (Open daily 10am-5pm; Oct.-March 11am-4:30pm. £3.50, students and seniors £2.50.) Haworth's **HI hostel,** Longlands Dr. (tel. (0535) 642 234), tops a hill a mile from the tourist office. (£7.50, under 18 £5. Open March-Oct. daily; Nov. and mid- to late Feb. Sun.-Thurs.) B&Bs for about £16-17 are at #4, 6, and 8 Main St., and up the hill to the tourist office. Haworth's **tourist office,** 2 West Lane (tel. (0535) 642 239; open daily 9:30am-5:30pm), at the summit of Main St., stocks plenty of maps and guides.

Northern (High) Pennines This stretches area from below Barnard Castle in the south to Hadrian's Wall in the north, about 20 miles west of Durham City. It's best suited to hiking and cars can successfully navigate the roads, but buses tackle the region with distressing hesitancy. Twenty miles southwest of Durham along the River Tees, the busy market town of **Barnard Castle** makes an excellent base for exploring the castles of Teesdale and the North Pennine peaks and waterfalls. In town, stay with **Mrs. Fry,** 66 Newgate (tel. (0833) 372 40; £13). The **tourist office,** 43 Galgate (tel. (0833) 690 909), will tell you about nearby scenic walks. A pleasant 12 miles northwest along the **Pennine Way** lies the mining town **Middleton-in-Teesdale. High Force Waterfall,** one of England's most spectacular, lies nearby.

Near the top of the way, **Alston,** the highest market town in England, is the best hiking base. The **tourist office** (tel. (0434) 381 696) is in the railway station. (Open daily 10am-5pm; Nov.-March 10am-noon and 1-4pm.) Three quarters of a mile from Alston along the Pennine Way stands a superior-grade **HI youth hostel,** The Firs, Alston (tel. (0434) 381 509; open mid-March to Sept. Mon.-Sat.; Oct. Tues.-Sat.; Jan. to mid-Feb. Fri.-Sat.; £6.90, under 18 £4.60).

■■■ YORK

A well-preserved circuit of medieval city walls may have defended York from invaders in the past, but today stands ineffectual before the vicissitudes of marauding tourists. With medieval cottages, Georgian townhouses, and Britain's largest Gothic cathedral, York is a justifiably popular tourist destination that hides its visitors from view in narrow alleyways and winding streets.

ORIENTATION AND PRACTICAL INFORMATION

Tourist Offices: Main Office in De Grey Rooms, Exhibition Sq. (tel. 621 756). Ask for the useful brochure entitled Historic Attractions of York. Open June-July Mon.-Sat. 9am-5pm, Sun. 10am-1pm; Aug. Mon.-Sat. 9am-7pm, Sun. 10am-1pm; Oct.-May Mon.-Sat. 9am-5pm. The one on **Rougier St.** (tel. 620 557) is open Mon.-Sat. 9am-6pm, Sun. 10am-5pm.

Financial Services: Barclays, 2 St. Helen's Sq. (tel. 631 333). Open Mon.-Tues. and Thurs.-Fri. 9:30am-4:30pm, Wed. 10am-4:30pm, Sat. 9:30am-noon. **Thomas Cook,** 4 Nessgate (tel. 639 928). Open Mon.-Thurs. 9am-5:30pm, Fri. 10am-5:30pm, Sat. 9am-5pm.

American Express: 6 Stonegate (tel. 611 727). Open Mon.-Fri. 9am-5:30pm, Sat. 9am-5pm; Nov.-March same weekday hrs., Sat. 9am-1pm.

Post Office: 22 Lendal (tel. 617 285). Open Mon.-Fri. 9am-5:30pm, Sat. 9am-12:30pm. **Postal Code:** YO1 2DA.

Telephones: City Code: 0904.

Trains: Station Rd. (tel. 642 155). Information office open Mon.-Sat. 8am-7:45pm, Sun. 9am-7:45pm. **Luggage lockers** 50p-£2. Luggage office storage: small articles £1.50, packs £2.50. Open Mon.-Sat. 7:15am-9:15pm, Sun. 11:15am-6:45pm. To: King's Cross, London (every 30min.; 2½hr.; £46, return £45); Manchester's Piccadilly (about every hr.; 1¾hr.; £11.50, return £15); Edinburgh (every hr.; 2-3hr.; £38.50, return £38-53).

Buses: Offices and stops at Rougier St. tourist office. **National Express** (tel. (0532) 460 011). **Rider York** local buses (tel. 624 161). Open Mon.-Fri. 8am-5pm, Sat. 9am-4:30pm. To: London (4/day; 5hr.; £31.50, return £33-39.50); Manchester (6/day; 2½hr.; £7.75, return £8.25-10); Edinburgh (1/day; 7hr.; £31.50, return £33-39.50).

Crises: Samaritans, 89 Nunnery Lane (tel. 655 888). **Gay and Lesbian Switchboard,** tel. 411 399. **Rape Crisis,** tel. 610 917.

Emergencies: York District Hospital, Wiggonton Rd. (tel. 631 313). Take bus #1, 2, or 3. **Police:** Fulford Rd. (tel. 631 321). **Emergency:** Dial 999; no coins required.

ACCOMMODATIONS AND FOOD

Competition for inexpensive B&Bs (from £12) can be fierce from June through August. Try **The Mount** area (out past the train station and down Blossom St.);

Haxby Road (take bus #2a, or walk from the tourist office out to the end of Gillygate and take the right fork); or any of the sidestreets along Bootham/Clifton.

The Old Dairy, 10 Compton St. (tel. 623 816). ½ mi. up Bootham from Exhibition Sq. Or bus #19 to Clifton Green. Charming chambers, iron bedframes. £12.

Bishophill House Youth Hotel, 11-13 Bishophill Senior (tel. 625 904 or 630 613). The 20-bed Room #12 is great for meeting fellow travelers; the rest of the building is often booked by youth groups. Dorm beds £8-11 (sheets £1). Singles £13-16.50. Doubles £24-30. Full breakfast £2.50. Wash £2, dry £1.

HI youth hostel, Haverford, Water End, Clifton (tel. 653 147), 1 mi. from the town center. Superior-grade hostel, but at B&B-level prices, is it worth the lack of privacy and the long hike? 158 beds with 4-8 beds/room; often fills with groups. No curfew. Reception open 7am-11:30pm. Lockout 10am-5pm. £12.40, under 18 £9, includes breakfast. Open daily early Jan.-early Dec.

Expensive tea rooms, medium-priced bistros, and cheap eateries bump elbows in even the remote alleyways of York. The **Gillygate Vegetarian Restaurant,** at Millers Yard off Gillygate, has tasty, inventive meatless hot dishes. (£2.50-3. Open Mon.-Sat. 10am-4:30pm. 10% student discount.) Grab a massive plate to load with salads, meats, and desserts (£5-6) at **Oscar's Wine Bar and Bistro,** Little Stonegate, off Stonegate. (Open daily 11am-10pm.) There are more **pubs** in the center of York than gargoyles on the wall of the Minster. The **King's Arms** gathers lively folk in a royal embrace, and the **Roman Bath,** St. Sampson's Sq., serves pints among the ruins.

SIGHTS AND ENTERTAINMENT

The **York Visitor Card** (£1), available at the tourist office, offers discounts on many of the museums and buildings in York; it will pay for itself if 2 adults use it at just 1 or 2 places. Of the bewildering array of organized tours, a few merit attention: the free 2-hour **walking tour** emphasizes York's architectural legacy (meet in Exhibition Sq.; April-Oct. daily at 10:15am and 2:15pm; June-Aug. also at 7pm); and a fascinating **haunted walk** covers some of York's ghostlier spots. (Meet at King's Arms Pub, King's Staith at 8pm. £2.50, children £2. Call 646 463 for more info.) For information on the narrated open-top **Guide Friday bus tour,** call 640 896.

Everyone and everything in York converges on **York Minster,** the largest Gothic cathedral in Britain. An estimated half of all the medieval stained glass in England glitters and holds the walls together. It's a mere 275 steps to the top of the **Central Tower,** from which you can stare down at the red roofs of York. (Open daily 10am-6:30pm. £2, children £1.)

Housed in a former debtor's prison, the huge York **Castle Museum** (tel. 653 611), by the river and Skeldergate Bridge, contains everything from excavations to, quite literally, the kitchen sink. Visit Kirkgate, an intricately reconstructed Victorian shopping street, and the Half Moon Court, its Edwardian counterpart. (Museum open Mon.-Sat. 9:30am-5:30pm, Sun. 10am-5:30pm; Nov.-March Mon.-Sat. 9:30am-4pm, Sun. 10am-4pm. £3.80, students and seniors £2.70.) The titanic steam locomotives at the new **National Railway Museum,** Leeman Rd., are nothing short of sculpture. (Open Mon.-Sat. 10am-6pm, Sun. 11am-6pm. £3.95, students, seniors, and travelers with disabilities £2.60, children £2.)

For the most current information, pick up the weekly *What's On* guide and the seasonal *Evening Entertainment* brochure from the tourist office. The free bimonthly *Artscene* is a good resource for arts information throughout Yorkshire.

■■■ LAKE DISTRICT NATIONAL PARK

Hackneyed hills cover much of England's rural landscape, but only in the northwest corner do sparkling water holes fill the spaces in between. Here, in a cherished national park (intelligently named the Lake District), spreads a mottled arrangement of hills, farms, and mortarless cottages built from the region's blue-green slate. Windermere, Ambleside, Grasmere, and Keswick all make sensible bases for exploring the region. To enjoy the best of the area, however, ascend into the hills and wander through the smaller towns, especially those in the more remote northern and western regions; the farther west you go from the busy bus route serving the towns along the A591, the more countryside you'll have to yourself. Note that many information centers, B&Bs, and nearly all campgrounds close for the winter.

Getting There and Getting Around The most sensible option for reaching the Lake District is either to head straight to Windermere and Keswick or to cross the perimeter of the park at Oxenholme and Penrith and connect from there. **National Express** and **British Rail** run to and through the park (info. tel. (05394) 464 99). The **Mountain Goat Bus** (tel. (05394) 451 61) serves the north Lake District. Once in the park, a vast array of bus, rail, and lake steamer transport is at your disposal. **CMS** buses serve Hawkshead, Coniston, and Newby Bridge, and connect Keswick with Penrith, Carlisle, Seatoller, Whitehaven, and Cockermouth. The free *Explore Lakeland by Bus* presents a list of timetables, available at tourist offices. The **Lakeside and Haverthwaite Railway** (tel. (05395) 315 94) can take you through the scenic River Leven Valley by steam locomotive (late April-Oct. 6-7/day; day return £2.90, children £1.45). The **Ravenglass and Eskdale Railway** (tel. (0229) 717 171) is England's oldest and narrowest (11 in.) narrow-gauge railway (6-14/day, Nov. to early April Mon.-Fri. 1-2/day; 40min.; return £5.40, children £2.70).

Hilly terrain comes with the territory in the Lake District; expect sore muscles if you decide to **bike.** Two-wheelers can be rented in almost all the area towns. Hikers will find an abundance of trails and often an overabundance of fellow walkers. If you plan to take a long or difficult hike, check with the Park Service, call for weather information (tel. (05394) 451 51; 24hrs.), and leave a plan of your route with your B&B proprietor or hostel warden before you set out. Paul Buttle's *Favourite Walks in the Lake District,* which details 14 of the best rambles (£1.95), is available from National Park Information Centres, tourist offices, and bookshops.

Practical Information and Accommodations For an introduction to the area, including exhibits, talks, films, and special events, visit the beautiful landscaped grounds and house of the **National Park Information Centre** (tel. (05394) 466 01) in **Brockhole,** halfway between Windermere and Ambleside. (Open July-Aug. 10am-8pm; Sept.-Oct. and Easter-June 10am-5pm. Free. Parking £2.) The free newspaper *Lake District Guardian* includes a comprehensive calendar of guided walks and events in the park. The following **National Park Information Centres** provide expert information on the Lakes, sell a camping guide (95p), and book accommodations: **Pooley Bridge** (tel. (07684) 865 30), **Ullswater** (tel. (07684) 824 14), **Seatoller Barn** (tel. (07687) 772 94), **Grasmere** (tel. (05394) 352 45), **Ambleside (Waterhead)** (tel. (05394) 327 29), **Hawkshead** (tel. (05394) 365 25), **Coniston** (tel. (05394) 415 33), and **Bowness Bay** (tel. (05394) 428 95).

Although plentiful, accommodations in the Lake District do fill in July and August. Book as far ahead as possible. **B&Bs** line every street in every town (£13-15) and the Lakes have the highest concentration of **HI youth hostels** in the world (27 at last count). You should call to reserve—most places will hold a bed until 6pm. Some hostels have short lockout hours, re-opening at 1pm. Campers should pick up the National Park Authority's comprehensive guide (95p), which includes listings of **camping barns** (£3-5) where you can stay high and dry in the big outdoors.

Windermere and Bowness A first stop for most travelers, Windermere and Bowness together are vacation towns-*cum*-tourist centers. **Bowness Bay Boating** (tel. (05394) 433 60) and the **Windermere Iron Steamboat** (tel. (05395) 311 88) run cruises from the pier; from Easter to October, boats sail north to Waterhead pier in Ambleside (about every ½hr. 10am-6pm; return £4.85, children 5-15 ½-price) and south to Lakeside (at least 1/hr. 10:25am-6:30pm; return £4.85, children 5-15 ½-price). The nearest **HI youth hostel** is in Troutbeck (tel. (05394) 435 43), 2 miles north of Windermere. (£6.30, ages 16-20 £5.10. Open April-Aug. daily; Sept.-Oct. and Jan.-March Wed.-Mon.) Both Windermere and Bowness are chock-full of **B&Bs,** all convenient to train and town. The nearest campground, **Limefitt Park** (tel. (05394) 323 00), lies 4½ miles south of Bowness on the A592 and has all the necessary amenities except access by public transportation (£7-8.60/2-person tent). In Windermere, eat at the cheery **The Coffee Pot,** 15 Main Rd. (Open Mon.-Sat. 9:30am-6:30pm.) In Bowness, try the **Hedgerow Teashop,** on Lake Rd. (Open daily 10:30am-5pm; Nov.-Easter Wed.-Mon. 10:30am-5pm.) The **Windermere tourist office** near the rail station is game for questions (tel. (053945) 464 99; open daily 9am-6pm; Nov.-Easter daily 9am-5pm; wheelchair accessible).

Ambleside and Grasmere The lake-bound villages of Ambleside and Grasmere both do their thing at a slower, more roomy pace. The easy hike between the two is not to be missed. Ambleside's only worthwhile sight is the tiny **House on the Bridge,** off Rydal Rd.; actually, house and bridge are one and the same. Lodging seems to be Ambleside's principal industry; there are almost as many B&Bs and guesthouses here as private residences. Nonetheless, call ahead in summer. The nearest **HI hostel** (tel. (05394) 323 04), 1 mile south on Windermere Rd. (the A591), has a distinctive country-club feel; you can even swim off the pier. (£8.40, ages 16-20 £5.60. Open mid-Feb.; Sept. to mid-Dec. Thurs.-Tues.) **The Old Smithy,** The Slack, off Market Pl. at the Queen's Hotel, serves cheap and excellent fish and chips and boasts lengthy queues to prove it. (Open daily about 11:30am-2pm and 5-10:30pm.) The **tourist office** awaits on Church St. (tel. (05394) 325 82; open daily 9am-6pm; Nov.-March Fri.-Sat. 9am-5pm).

Every establishment in Grasmere tries to cash in on William Wordsworth's legacy, occasionally falling back on the more easily digested Beatrix Potter. Visit 2 of Wordsworth's homes: **Dove Cottage** (open daily 9:30am-5pm; closed mid-Jan. to mid-Feb.; £3.70, children £1.85; tickets sold at the shop nearby) and **Rydal Mount** (estate open daily 9:30am-5pm; Nov.-Feb. Wed.-Mon. 10am-4pm; £2, children 80p). There are 2 **HI youth hostels** within a half-mile of Grasmere. **Butharlip How** (tel. (05394) 353 16) is a Victorian house with flowering gardens north of Grasmere village. (Open April-Aug. daily; Jan.-March and Sept.-Oct. Tues.-Sun. £7.50, under 18 £5.) **Thorney How** (tel. (05394) 355 91) is a converted farmhouse; follow the road to Easedale, turn right at the fork, then turn left. (Open April-Aug. daily; Sept.-early Nov. Wed.-Mon.; mid-Feb. to March and mid-Nov. to mid-Dec. Fri.-Sat. £7.50, under 18 £5.) Sarah Nelson's famous Grasmere Gingerbread is a bargain at 20p per slice in **Church Cottage,** just by St. Oswald's.

Keswick Set between high fell and crag by the side of northerly Lake Derwentwater, once-quiet Keswick (KEZ-ick) rivals Windermere as the Lake District's tourist capital. **Keswick Launch** (tel. (07687) 722 63) stages frequent day and evening narrated cruises around the lake. (£4.25, seniors and children £2. HI discount 15%.) Two **HI hostels** grace this small town: **Honister House** (tel. (07687) 772 67) is at the summit of **Honister Pass,** 9 miles north (£6.30, under 18 £4.20; open July-Aug. Fri.-Wed.; late March-June and Sept.-early Nov. Fri.-Tues.). **Keswick,** Station Rd. (tel. (07687) 724 84), has balconies over the river. (Curfew 11pm. £8.40, under 18 £5.60. Open April-Aug. daily; Sept. to mid-Dec. and mid-Feb. to March Thurs.-Tues. MC, V.) B&Bs are sandwiched between the A591, Station St., St. John St., and Ambleside Rd. **Pillars,** 21 Main St., serves freshly prepared sandwiches (£1.55) and scrumptious pancakes with jam and cream. (£1.40. Open Mon.-Sat. 9:45am-5:30pm; Oct.-Easter daily 9:45am-5:30pm.) The **tourist office,** Moot Hall, Market Sq. (tel. (07687) 726 45), provides an accommodations booklet (80p) and a 20p map. (Open daily 9:30am-7pm; April-June and Sept.-Oct. 9:30am-5:30pm.)

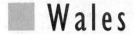# Wales

Wales clings steadfastly to its Celtic heritage, continuing a struggle for independence that has been surging for over a millennium. Especially in the North, the Welsh language endures in conversation, through a revived literature and on bilingual road signs. As churning coal and steel mines fall victim to the vicissitudes of Britain's economy, Wales has turned its economic base from heavy industry to tourism. Avoid calling the Welsh "English" at all costs.

TRAVELING IN WALES

Transportation throughout Wales is easiest by bus, as train stations are few and far between. Two main rail lines in the south and 2 in the north connect the coast with many towns in England, and buses fill the gaps. Beware: the same Welsh bus network that will render you speechless in the north will make you coin new curses in the south. **Cardiff Bus** (tel. (0222) 396 52) serves the area around Cardiff; **Red and White** (tel. (0291) 622 947) buses run the routes from Gloucester and Hereford in England west through the Wye Valley, past Abergavenny and Brecon in the north. **South Wales Transport** (tel. (0492) 475 511) operates between Swansea and Haverfordwest in South Pembrokeshire in the West. **TransCambria** (tel. (0222) 371 331) is a north-south bus line. Call the British Rail offices in Cardiff (tel. (0222) 228 000) or Swansea (tel. (0492) 467 777) for train information. Many travelers **hitchhike** in summer. Cars are said to stop readily for hitchers who stand in lay-by (pull-off) areas along narrow roads.

Wales has hundreds of well-marked **footpaths.** The **Offa's Dyke Path** and the **Pembrokeshire Coast Path** are popular long-distance walks through glorious and often remote countryside. For more info, write to the **Countryside Commission Dispatch Dept.,** Prinworks Lane, Levenshulme, Manchester M19 3JP, England. **Bikers** should obtain a copy of the indispensable *Cyclists' Guide to North Wales.*

SOUTH WALES

The transition from England to Wales is smoothest in the south, where calm hills ease into gritty harbors and seething market towns. The farther north you go, the more characteristically Welsh the terrain and the communities become, but the Southerners' pride in their country is as firm as any Welshman's, and North Wales does not hold a monopoly on Welsh national beauty.

■■■ CARDIFF (CAERDYDD)

The only truly urban center in a land of small villages, Cardiff expresses its intense Welsh pride through a lively arts scene and beautifully restored architecture. The preposterously opulent interior of **Cardiff Castle** is no less flamboyant than the peacocks that mewl inside the gates and pester tourists for food. (Castle open May-Sept. 10am-6pm, tours every 20min.; Oct.-Nov. and Feb.-April less frequently. July-Sept. £3, seniors £1.50.) The **National Museum of Wales** attempts to cover all that's indigenous. (Open Tues.-Sat. 10am-5pm, Sun. 2:30-5pm. £2, seniors and children £1.) The **Lovespoon Gallery,** 25 Castle St., devotes itself exclusively to this stirring Welsh folk tradition. (Open Mon.-Sat. 10am-5:30pm.)

The smaller neighborhoods around Cathedral Rd. are the best bet for less expensive B&Bs (bus #32, 62, or a 15-min. walk from the castle). Meet "Hog" the pig-dog at the comfortable **Cardiff youth hostel (HI),** Wedal Rd., Roath Park (tel. (0222) 462 303), 2 miles from the city center; take bus #78, 80, or 82 from Central Station. (Check-in after 3pm. Curfew 11pm. £8.40. Open March-Oct. daily; Jan.-Feb. and Nov. Tues.-Sat.) **The Homade,** 26 Dumfries Pl., at the end of Queen St., and **Bistro One,** Quay St., off St. Mary St. toward the castle, both serve large rolls enlivened by a variety of fillings. (Open Mon.-Sat. 7:30am-6pm.) Head to the **Four Bars Inn** on Castel St. for a Brains booze-fest—the upstairs houses one of Britain's only all-jazz clubs outside of London. (Cover £2-3, student discounts 50p.)

The **tourist office** (tel. (0222) 227 281) doles out information at Cardiff Central Railway Station and 8-14 Bridge St. (Main office open Mon.-Sat. 10am-8pm, Sun. 10am-6pm.) **Buses** roll into the station at Wood St. National Express Rapide buses (tel. 334 751) run between Cardiff and London (5/day; 3hr.; £18), Penzance (2/day; 8hr.; £36), and Bristol (9/day; 1hr.; £7). Store your luggage or jump on a train at **Central Station,** Wood St. (tel. (0222) 228 000), behind the bus station. British Rail **trains** leave from London's Paddington Station (1/hr., 2hr., £33.50).

■■■ WYE VALLEY

The River Wye (Afon Gwy) joins the broad River Severn at Beachley near **Chepstow,** running through both England and Wales. The **Wye Valley Walk** runs between the picturesque towns of Chepstow and Monmouth along cliffs, wooded hills, and farmland, while across the river **Offa's Dyke Path** runs the entire length of the English-Welsh border, offering over 150 miles of hiking trails.

Chepstow Castle guards the ancient entrance to the valley by stretching its massive bulk right along the river. (Open daily 9:30am-6:30pm; mid-Oct. to mid-March Mon.-Sat. 9:30am-4pm, Sun. 2-4pm. £2.90, seniors and students £1.50.) The **tourist office** (tel. (0291) 623 772), confronts the castle from its car park. (Open in season 9am-5pm daily.) Area walks can lead you to such landmarks as **Wintour's Leap,** a 300-ft. cliff from which the doomed Sir Geoffrey De Wintour supposedly jumped. In Chepstow, stay at the **Lower Hardwick House,** Mt. Pleasant (tel. (0291) 622 162), a wonderful old mansion run by the delightful Eileen Grassby (singles £16, doubles £26), or camp in her exquisite garden (£5/tent). Alternatively, stay at the **HI youth hostel** at **St. Briavel's Castle,** 4 miles from Tintern, complete with dog-turning spit. Take bus #69 from Chepstow and get off at Bigsweir Bridge; walk 2 miles from there. (£7.50. Open mid-Feb. to Oct.)

Five miles north of Chepstow along the A466, find the delicate walls of **Tintern Abbey,** the majestic 12th-century monastery that inspired Wordsworth. (Open daily 9:30am-6:30pm; mid-Oct. to mid.-March Mon.-Sat. 9:30am-4:pm, Sun. 2-4pm. £2, seniors and under 16 £1.25.) Often crowded with tourists, the abbey retains its mystical appearance if viewed from the surrounding hills—hike to the **Devil's Pulpit** (1hr.), an enormous stone from which Satan is said to have tempted the monks. Stay at **Home Farm** (tel. (0291) 689 559), 2 miles away from town. (Single £12.50. Double £27.)

The market town of **Monmouth** lies 17 miles north of Tintern Abbey, birthplace of Henry V and Geoffrey of Monmouth (who gave what little historical credibility there is to King Arthur and Merlin in his *History of the Kings of Britain).* Fascinated by its own history, the Monmouth is always excavating some piece of turf. Monmouth's **HI youth hostel,** Priory St. School (tel. (0600) 715 116), occupies a 15th-century building in the center of town. (£6.30. Open March-Oct.)

Home to the largest colony of second-hand bookstores in the world, **Hay-on-Wye** is a restless hotbed of esotericism. Stay 8 miles outside of town at **Capel-y-Ffin** (tel.

(0873) 890 650), along Offa's Dyke Path (£6.30; open June-early Sept. Thurs.-Tues.; Nov. and Feb. weekends only), or in town at the **Belmont House** (tel. (0497) 820 718), an antique-filled home. (Singles £16, doubles £25.) Stop by **The Granary,** Broad St., for Welsh specialties like *Bara Brith* (a delicious buttered fruitcake), baked fresh every day.

Between the Wye Valley and Brecon Beacons National Park, **Abergavenny** makes a good touring base for either. The **tourist office** and **National Park Information Centre,** Swan Meadow, Monmouth Rd. (tel. (0873) 857 588; national park information tel. (0873) 857 3254), provides oodles of information about the surrounding hills. (Open Easter-Oct. daily 9:30am-5:30pm.)

■■■ BRECON BEACONS NATIONAL PARK (BANNAU BRYCHEINIOG)

The Brecon Beacons National Park has roughly 519 sq. miles of varied terrain and is crisscrossed by 4 mountain ranges. Five **HI youth hostels** dot the park: **Llwyn-y-Celyn youth hostel,** Brecon Beacons (tel. (0874) 624 261), 8 miles south of Brecon (£6.30; open mid-April to mid-July Tues.-Sun.; mid-July to Sept. daily); **Ystradfellte youth hostel** (tel. (0639) 720 301), south in the waterfall district (£5.70; open Aug. daily; March-July and Sept. Fri.-Wed.); **Llanddeusant hostel** (tel. (05504) 634), in the Black Mountains by Llangadog village and accessible from the Trecastle-Llangadog mountain road (£5.10; open March-Oct.); **Capel-y-Ffin youth hostel** (tel. (0873) 890 650), near the River Honddu, at the eastern edge of the Black Mountains (£6.30; open April-Sept. Thurs.-Tues.); and **Ty'n-y-Caeau youth hostel (HI)** (tel. (0874) 628 6270), 3 miles from Brecon, on a lane leading from the A470 through the hamlet of Groesffordd to the A38. (£6.30, ages 16-20 £5.10. Open daily April-Sept.; March and Oct. Mon.-Sat.)

At the center of the park, the **Brecon Beacons** mountain range beckons hikers with its beauty. Climb 2907-ft. **Pen-y-Fan,** the highest mountain in South Wales; or take the trail that skirts **Llyn** (Lake) **Cwm Llwch** (koom-hlooch), a small pool at an altitude of 2000 ft. The **Black Mountains** make great ridge-walking. At **Porth-yr-Ogof** (Welsh for "mouth of the river"), less than a mile from the HI hostel, the River Afon Mellte flows into a cave at the base of a cliff and reappears in a small, natural, ice-cold swimming pool. Near **Abercrave,** midway between Swansea and Brecon off the A4067, the **Dan-yr-Ogof Showcaves** are huge and stunning, with enormous stalagmites. Although not actually in the mountains, **Brecon** is the best base for hiking through the surrounding craggy peaks. The **National Park Information Centre** (tel. (0874) 623 156) is in Cattle Market Car Park. (Open April-Oct. Mon.-Sat. 9:30am-5:30pm.)

■■■ PEMBROKESHIRE COAST NATIONAL PARK AND ABERYSTWYTH

Pembrokeshire Coast National Park's 178-mile coastal path makes the Welsh proud they're not English; magnificent cliffs, natural sea arches, and islands spotted by wild birds and seals create a truly stunning landscape. Enter the region at centrally located **Haverfordwest,** on the main rail line from London (£38) and Cardiff (£13.80). Send inquiries and requests for publications to the **National Park Information Services,** Country Offices, Haverfordwest, Dyfed SA61 1QZ, Wales (tel. (0437) 764 591, ext. 5133). **HI youth hostels** are spaced along the coastal path, all within a day's hike of each other.

Positioned along the sweeping Cardigan Bay coastline, **Aberystwyth's** elaborate pier and promenade hark back to its heyday as a Victorian seaside resort; today, not-

SNOWDONIA FOREST

so-Victorian students make their own mark on the town. At the promenade's south end stands the **Old College,** a neo-Gothic patchwork structure opened in 1877 as Wales's first university. Nearby, the **National Library of Wales,** off Penglais Rd., houses nearly all books and manuscripts written in or pertaining to Wales. (Open Mon.-Fri. 9:30am-6pm, Sat. 9:30am-5pm. Free.) At the other end of the promenade, the **Electric Cliff Railway,** "a conveyance for gentlefolk since 1896," will whisk you to the top of **Constitution Hill** to see the Camera Obscura gazebo, an enormous wide-lens telescope that offers dizzying views of the town. (Open daily 10am-6pm; July-Aug. 10am-9pm; train every 10min. Last entry to Camera Obscura 5:30pm. Rail fare return £1.80, students and seniors £1.50. To Camera Obscura free.)

The nearest **HI hostel** (tel. (0970) 871 498) lies 9 miles north in Borth. (£7.50. Open April-Sept. daily; March and Oct. Mon.-Sat.) In town, stay with **Mrs. E. V. Williams,** 28 Bridge St. (tel. (0970) 612 550) for £11. When hungry, head to **Y Graig Wholefood Café,** 34 Pier St. (tel. (0970) 611 606; open Mon.-Sat. 9am-midnight, Sun. 2pm-midnight). Forty-two **pubs** make Aberystwyth more than just a dayspot.

Aberystwyth's **tourist office,** Terrace Rd. (tel. (0970) 612 125), has photos of area B&Bs. (Open daily 10am-6pm; Nov.-Easter Mon.-Thurs. 10am-5pm, Fri. 10am-4:30pm.) **The post office,** 8 Great Darkgate St. (tel. (0970) 612 536), accepts mail at **postal code:** SY23 1AA.

NORTH WALES

North Wales is even more fiercely nationalistic and linguistically independent of England than is South Wales. From atop the hills of Snowdonia, the vast English flatlands appear soft and placid, in sharp contrast to the jagged and uneven Welsh hills to the west. Avoid the crowded castles and resort towns of the northern coast by heading inland to the mountain footpaths and hamlets of Snowdonia National Park, which covers most of North Wales. Southwest of Snowdonia, the largely unspoiled Lleyn Peninsula attracts visitors to its sandy beaches; to the northwest the Isle of Anglesey sends ferries to Ireland; to the east languishes the lush Vale of Conwy.

■■■ SNOWDONIA FOREST AND NATIONAL PARK

Stretching from Machynlleth in the south to Bangor and Conwy in the north, Snowdonia is the reason you came to Wales. A total of 840 square sheep-dotted miles, the park encompasses coastal areas as well as the rugged hills of the interior. The mountain of **Snowdon** itself, at 3560 ft., is the highest, barest peak in England and Wales. Half a million climbers reach the summit of Mt. Snowdon every year; the result has been the erosion of the mountain and disruption of its ecosystem. Stick to the well-marked trails to avoid damaging the area further. Since other climbs will be less crowded and probably more scenic, it might be wise to skip Snowdon altogether and try a hike up **Tryfan** or nearby **Devil's Kitchen.** Contact the **Snowdonia National Park Information Centre** (tel. (0766) 770 274), Penrhyndeudraeth (pen-ren-DOY-dryth), Gwynedd LL48 6L5, Wales for detailed information. Other National Park Information Centres are at Betws-y-Coed, Harlech, Blaenau Ffestiniog, Dolgellau, Aberdyfi and Bala. Scenic **Beddgelert** offers access to Moel Hebog (2566 ft.), less prone to the traffic jams that plague Snowdon.

The 8 **HI youth hostels** in the mountain area are some of the best in Wales, although they are also often the most crowded. **Pen-y-Pass** (tel. (0286) 870 428) sits 1170 ft. above sea level at the head of Llanberis Pass between the Snowdon and Glyders peaks. (£8.40, Open April-Oct. daily; Feb.-March and Nov. Tues.-Sat.) The **Llanberis hostel** (tel. (0286) 870 280; £7.50; open April-Sept. daily; Oct. and Feb.-March Fri.-Tues.; Nov.-Dec. Fri.-Mon.) and **Snowdon Ranger** (tel. (0286) 85391; £7.50, ages

16-20 £5.50; open April-Sept. daily; Oct. and Feb.-March Thurs.-Mon.) are near main walking trails up Snowdon. Save yourself the hike by taking the **Snowdon Mountain Railway** (tel. (0286) 870 223), which runs from Llanberis. (Round-trip 3hr., £12. Weary hikers can try for a £5 standby back down.)

The **Snowdon Sherpa,** a service of Crosville bus lines on which all Crosville passes are valid, offers relatively easy access to the various Snowdon trailheads, where parking is almost impossible to find. Inform the driver if you intend to switch buses; connections often fail due to late or impatient buses.

Distinguished mainly by the Mountain Railway, **Llanberis** is the largest town in the park and the best place to stock up on food and gear. To reach **Ceunant Mawr,** one of Wales's most impressive waterfalls, take the public footpath on Victoria Terrace by Victoria Hotel, then the first right and then the first left (about 1 mi.). Stoke your engine with a dose of gut-nuking chili (£4.10) at **Pete's Eats.** (Open daily 9am-8pm; off-season 9am-6:30pm.) The **tourist office,** Museum of the North building (tel. (0286) 870 765), in the bypass at the end of High St., doles out tips on hikes and sights. (Open Easter-Sept. daily 10am-6pm.)

LLEYN PENINSULA AND NORTHERN COAST

The towns on the Llyen Peninsula masquerade as beach resorts, but rain and wind often expose the charade. Indigenously Welsh in language and community, the peninsula is partially spared the waves of tourists that crash the northern coast. **Porthmadog,** a resort town and travel hub at the southeastern end of the peninsula, is linked to Blaenau Ffestiniog by the steam **Ffestiniog Railway** (tel. (0766) 512 340), which runs northwest through the Ffestiniog Valley into the hills of Snowdonia. (March—Oct. daily, 1hr., round trip £11.40.) Lacking a hostel, Porthmadog offers fine B&Bs: **Hirgraig,** Morfa Bychan Rd. (tel. (0766) 512 836), promises lovely views of the sea (£13). Porthmadog's **tourist office** is at the end of High St. (tel. (0766) 512 981; open daily 10am-6pm). **Criccieth** calls itself the "pearl of the peninsula," and its castle merits the moniker. **Pwllheli** (pooth-ELLY), 8 miles further west, buzzes as the main transportation hub. The **tourist office,** Station Sq. (tel. (0758) 613 000), books B&Bs. (£10-11. Open March-Sept. daily 10am-6pm.)

Caernarfon and Bangor Perched on the edge of the bay of the same name, **Caernarfon** (can-AR-von) lures visitors with Wales's grandest medieval **castle,** dating from 1283. Built by Edward I of England, the castle features the typically Middle Eastern double gatehouses he discovered while crusading. Prince Charles was appointed Prince of Wales at the castle in 1969. (Open daily 9:30am-6:30pm; mid-Oct. to mid-March Mon.-Sat. 9:30am-5pm. £3.50, seniors and students £2.50.) Stay with **Mrs. Hughes,** Pros Kairon, Victoria Rd. (tel. (0286) 762 29), and you'll be treated like one of the family (£11). **Camping** is available about ½ mile from town at **Cadnant Valley,** Llanberis Rd. (tel. (0286) 673 196; tents £3.60/person). **Real Food and Treasures** on Palace St. serves nothing but. The more expensive craft shops and the **tourist office,** Castle Pitch, Oriel Pendeitsh (tel. (0286) 672 232), lie opposite the castle entrance. (Open daily 10am-6pm.) **Buses** #5 and X5 shuttle between Caernarfon and Bangor every 20 minutes (£1.05). The **Snowdon Sherpa bus** runs southwest to Beddgelert and Llanberis, while buses #1 and 2 heads south to Porthmadog (every 2hr., £2.90).

The pleasant university town of **Bangor** is the transportation hub for North Wales, and boasts a fine castle, a Victorian pier, a thriving Welsh arts scene, and a busy pedestrian shopping district. Just outside Bangor, where the A55 splits off the A5 (walk about 2 mi. or catch any bus heading north), **Penrhyn Castle** is the best buy for your castle-going pound. (Open July-Aug. Wed.-Mon. 11am-5pm; Sept.-Oct. and April-June noon-5pm. Grounds open 11am-6pm. £4.20, children £2.10.) Stay at the **Tany y Bryn youth hostel (HI)** (tel. (0248) 353 516), ½ mile from the town center, with its aristocratic view of Penrhyn Castle. Take the Maesgeirchen bus from the train station. (£7.50. Open daily March-Feb. Tues.-Sat.), or try the B&Bs along Garth Rd. **High St.** has good eats. The **tourist office** at Theatr Gwynedd, off Deiniol Rd. (tel. (0248) 352 786), provides loads of bus schedules, maps, and other good things. (Open April-Sept. daily 10am-6pm.) Call (0248) 353 201 for **train info** and (0248) 370 295 for **bus info** in Bangor. Buses fan out everywhere; trains run along the North Wales Coast rail line that connects Holyhead with Chester.

Holyhead, Conwy, and Llangollen **Holyhead,** on the Isle of Anglesey (Ynys Môn), is a one-horse town with **ferries to Ireland. B&I** (tel. (0407) 760 222) runs to Dublin (2/day, 3½hr., £18-23, round-trip £36-46). **Sealink** (tel. (0407) 766 765) sails to **Dún Laoghaire** (3/day, 3½hr., £17-23, round-trip £34-46), with bus connections to Dublin. In July and August, book several weeks ahead. If you miss the boat, check the list of B&Bs (from £11) posted at Holyhead's **tourist office,** Marine Sq., Salt Island Approach (tel. (0407) 762 622), in a caravan down the main road from the terminal. (Open daily 10am-6pm.) Holyhead can be reached by Crosville Bus #4 from Bangor via Llangefni (every hr., Sun. 3/day, 80min.). The town is also the end of the North Wales Coast rail line with hourly trains to Bangor (½hr., £4.50), Chester (1½hr., £9.80), and London (5hr., £39).

Conwy has an agelessness that even the visitor buses that scrape through its 13th-century arches cannot touch. Fourteenth-century **Aberconwy House** on Castle St. is the oldest dwelling in town; the Elizabethan **Plas Mawr,** around the corner on High St., is an ornately haunted townhouse laced with sordid stories. Mind your head as you step into **Ty Bach,** Britain's smallest house, with a mere 72 in. of frontage on the quay. (Open July-Aug. 10am-9pm. 50p, students and children 30p.) Conwy's **tourist office** (tel. (0492) 592 248) is at the entrance to the castle. (Open Easter-Oct. daily 9:30am-6:30pm.) **B&Bs** cluster in the Cadnant Park area. (Turn left at the town walls by the post office, then walk 10min.) Try one of the two **HI hostels** in the area; buses serve both **Penmaenmawr** (tel. (0492) 623 476), 5 miles west of town (£6.30; open July-Aug. Mon.-Sat; April-June and Sept.-Oct. Fri.-Sat.) and **Colwyn Bay youth hostel,** Foxhill, Nant-y-Glyn (tel. (0492) 530 627), 8 miles east of town. (£6.30. Open May-Aug. daily; mid-Feb. to March and Sept-Oct. Tues.-Sat. April Mon.-Sat.) **Crosville buses** #5 and X5 serve a northern coastal route, passing from Bangor (to the southwest) to Llandudno (across the broad mouth of the River Conwy) via Conwy (every 20min., round-trip £2.30).

Halfway to Shrewsbury, England, is the emphatically Welsh town of **Llangollen** (thlang-OTH-len), which overflows with tourists during the **Llangollen International Musical Eisteddfod** (July 6-11 in 1994). Book tickets and accommodations far in advance through the International Musical Eisteddfod Office, Llangollen, Clywyd, Wales LL20 8NG (tel. (0978) 860 236; office open Mon.-Fri. 9:30am-12:30pm and 1:30-4:30pm). The friendly wardens at the **HI hostel,** Tyndwr Hall (tel. (0978) 860 330), 1 mile out of town, frequently plan days of climbing, archery, or water sports. (£7.50. Open mid-Feb. to Oct.)

■ Scotland

Scotland at its best is a world apart, yet its modern cities often threaten to upstage the natural drama that surrounds them. Exuberant Glasgow is the most Scottish in character, Aberdeen is a postcard set-piece of grand architecture and delightful gardens, and Edinburgh is transformed annually into an epicenter of culture during its famed International Festival in August. A little over half the size of England but with

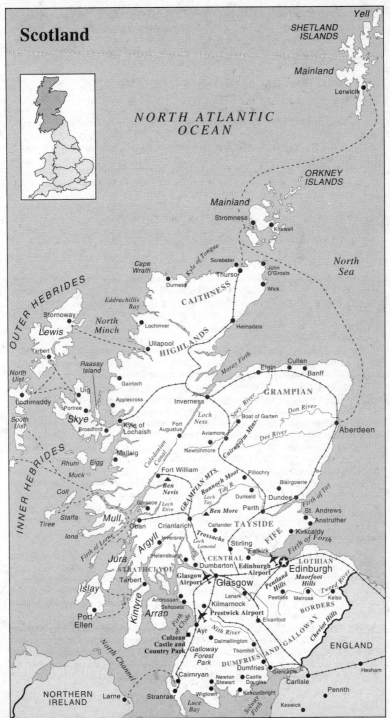

Scotland

NORTH ATLANTIC OCEAN

SHETLAND ISLANDS

Yell

Mainland

Lerwick

ORKNEY ISLANDS

Mainland

Stromness

Kirkwall

North Sea

Cape Wrath

Kyle of Tongue

Scrabster

Thurso

John O'Groats

Durness

Wick

CAITHNESS

Helmsdale

OUTER HEBRIDES

Eddrachillis Bay

Stornoway

North Minch

Lochinver

Lewis

HIGHLANDS

Ullapool

Tarbert

Cullen

North Uist

Raasay Island

Gairloch

Elgin

Banff

GRAMPIAN

Lochmaddy

Uig

Applecross

Spey River

Don River

South Uist

Portree

Inverness

Boat of Garten

Skye

Kyle of Lochalsh

Fort Augustus

Loch Ness

Aviemore

Cairngorm Mtns.

Dee River

Aberdeen

Broadford

Caledonian Canal

Newtonmore

INNER HEBRIDES

Mallaig

Rhum

Eigg

Fort William

GRAMPIAN MTS.

Pitlochry

Muck

Ben Nevis

Rannoch Moor

Blairgowrie

Coll

Glencoe

Loch Etive

Loch Tay

Tay R.

Dunkeld

Dundee

Firth of Tay

Staffa

Ben More

Perth

Tiree

Iona

Mull

Oban

Crianlarich

Callander

TAYSIDE

St. Andrews

Anstruther

Trossachs

Kirkcaldy

Inveraray

Loch Lomond

Stirling

FIFE

Firth of Forth

Jura

Argyll

Helensburgh

CENTRAL

Falkirk

LOTHIAN

Firth of Lorne

STRATHCLYDE

Dumbarton

Edinburgh Airport

Edinburgh

Glasgow Airport

Glasgow

Pentland Hills

Moorfoot Hills

Tweed River

Islay

Tarbert

Lanark

Melrose

Kelso

Kintyre

Androssan

Saltcoats

Kilmarnock

Peebles

BORDERS

Arran

Prestwick Airport

Elvanfoot

Cheviot Hills

Port Ellen

Firth of Clyde

Ayr

Nith River

Culzean Castle and Country Park

Dalmellington

DUMFRIES AND GALLOWAY

ENGLAND

North Channel

Thornhill

Galloway Forest Park

Castle Douglas

Dumfries

Hexham

Cairnryan

Newton Stewart

Glencaple

Carlisle

Penrith

NORTHERN IRELAND

Larne

Stranraer

Wigtown

Kirkcudbright

Luce Bay

Solway Firth

Keswick

one tenth its population, Scotland revels in stark and open space that varies with the geography of the land. The kaleidoscope of mountains and lochs along the west coast and under the luminescent mists of the western isles is divine, while the bucolic borders to the south, the level river valleys along the east coast, and the islands of Orkney in the north all display an intimate beauty.

GETTING THERE AND GETTING AROUND

The cheapest way to Scotland from outside Britain is usually through London. Although the **bus** trip from London's Victoria Station takes more than 7 hours, fares are one half that of trains. **Scottish Citylink** (tel. (071) 636 9373) and **Caledonian Express** (tel. (071) 730 0202) both serve Scotland (Citylink £28, return £35; Caledonian £32, return £34-36). The cheapest option is Citylink's **Londonliner** which departs King's Cross at 11pm and costs £15, return £22. Reserve in advance. From London, **trains** to Scotland take only 5-6 hours, but fares are steep: trains to Edinburgh (14-19/day, most from King's Cross Station) and to Glasgow Central (9-16/day, most from Euston Station) both cost £57 (return £57-67).

While **air travel** is even more expensive (APEX round-trip £75-77), **British Airways** (tel. (081) 897 4000), **British Midland** (tel. (0345) 589 5599), and **Air UK** (tel. (0345) 666 777) all fly north. Scotland is also linked by **ferry** to Northern Ireland (see Northern Ireland or Stranraer) and to Norway and the Faroe Islands (see Thurso and the Shetland Islands).

Bus travel in Scotland is a steal. **Scottish Citylink** and **Caledonian Express** are the main long-distance operators; Citylink generally travels more frequently to more places than its rival, but neither company has printed a comprehensive timetable. Bus stations are often closed or non-existent, but tickets can always be bought on board. In rural areas, wave to signal the driver to stop. **Scottish Rail** trains are clean and punctual, if not especially cheap. Their comprehensive timetable costs 40p (available at all stations); alternatively, pick up free timetables to services in particular regions. The excellent **Go Blue Banana** minibus service (tel. (031) 228 2281) drives a circular route from Edinburgh through Skye and back, stopping at hostels on its way. A complete circuit, completed in under a month, costs an unbeatable £39. Many **hitchhike** in Scotland, except in places like the Northwest and Inverness, where cars crammed full of tourists make up a large percentage of the traffic.

Scotland offers scenic, challenging terrain for **biking.** The area of Fife and regions south of Edinburgh and Glasgow offer gentle pastoral pedaling, while the Highlands are tremendously challenging. You can usually rent bikes even in very small towns and transport them by ferry for little or no charge. Beginning in April, the **Bike Bus** (tel. (031) 229 6274) will take you and your bike from Edinburgh to different points north and south on weekends (£4-6).

For information on Scotland's 2 long-distance footpaths, the **West Highland Way** and the **Southern Upland Way,** write to the **Scottish Tourist Board,** 23 Ravelston Terr., Edinburgh EH4 3EU. Or you can join in the hiking sport of "Munro bagging" by collecting any of the 280 Scottish peaks logged in 1891 by Hugh T. Munro.

SCOTLAND ESSENTIALS

SYHA hostels, part of the Hostelling International stable, are the most economical lodgings in Scotland; hostel standards are perhaps the best in the world. The price range is low (£3.45-7.25), and there are hostels in or near almost every city and region described in this section. Hostels are carefully graded: grade 1 hostels have laundry facilities, free hot showers, shorter lockouts, and a microwave in the kitchen. Most grade 2 hostels charge for hot showers, may have more primitive clothes-washing facilities, and have lockouts until 5pm. Grade 3 hostels, usually more remote, lack hot showers and clothes washers, but compensate with coziness and lenience. A sleepsack (rentable for 60p) and an HI membership card (purchasable as you go) are required at all grades. From June to August, advance booking is *essential.* Hostels generally accept telephone reservations between 7 and 10pm (never on the same day as arrival) and hold them until 6pm (sometimes later if you can specify a train or bus arrival time). Some travelers prefer the growing Scottish network of **independent hostels.** Though their atmosphere and rules are usually more relaxed than those at SYHA hostels, facilities vary considerably

B&Bs are a comfortable but more expensive alternative. It's best to book B&Bs using tourist office literature. All tourist offices participate in the **Book-a-Bed-Ahead** scheme which allows you to reserve a room in any other region in Scotland for a £2.50 fee. You can **camp** free on all public land, but make sure you know which areas are restricted (i.e., preserves or other protected land). Always ask the landowner's permission if you suspect you're on privately owned land.

Weekend clan gatherings, bagpipe competitions, and Highland games occur frequently during the summer here. Check at the tourist office and in the local newspaper for dates of local events. Above all events towers the **Edinburgh International Festival,** the largest international festival in the world and its much less costly sibling, the **Festival Fringe.** (See Edinburgh Entertainment below.)

■■■ EDINBURGH

Scotland's magnificent capital is less a city than an event, a drama of natural rock and molded stone. From the castle-crowned volcano that rises abruptly from the city's center, across the elegant green parks that lace through the trough of a drained loch and over to the summit of King Arthur's seat, Edinburgh makes use of all three dimensions. The city's visual splendor is matched by its cultural wealth: Edinburgh boasts superb museums, bookstores, and pubs, and is transformed into a veritable magnet for thrills (and visitors) during August's Festival season.

ORIENTATION AND PRACTICAL INFORMATION

Small distances and quiet streets make Edinburgh an ideal walking city. Princes St. is the main thoroughfare in the New Town, the northern section of Edinburgh; **"The Royal Mile"** (Lawnmarket, High St., and Canongate) connects **Edinburgh Castle** and **Holyrood Palace** and is the Old Town's major road of the city's southern half.

Tourist Office: Edinburgh and Scotland Information Center, Waverley Market, 3 Princes St. (tel. 557 1700), next to the Waverley train station. Busy but efficient accommodations service (£2.50-3). Pick up *The Essential Guide to Edinburgh* (£1.50), the calendar *Day by Day* (free), and a Edinburgh accommodations booklet (free). Open Mon.-Sat. 9am-8pm, Sun. 11am-8pm; May-June and Sept. Mon.-Sat. 9am-7pm, Sun. 11am-7pm; April and Oct. Mon.-Sat. 9am-6pm, Sun. 11am-6pm; Nov.-March Mon.-Sat. 9am-6pm.

Budget Travel: Edinburgh Travel Centre, Potterow Union, Bristol Sq. (tel. 668 2221). Open Mon.-Fri. 9am-5:30pm. Branches at 196 Rose St. and 92 S. Clark St. also open Sat. 10am-1pm. **SYHA District Office,** 161 Warrender Park Rd. (tel. 229 8660), near Bruntsfield Hostel. Open Mon.-Fri. 9am-5pm, Sat. 9am-12:30pm.

Consulates: U.S., 3 Regent Ter. (tel. 556 8315). Open Mon., Wed and Fri. 10am-noon and 1-4pm, Tues. and Thurs. 10am-noon. **Australia,** 80 Hanover St. (tel. 226 6271). Open Mon.-Fri. 10am-4pm.

Currency Exchange: When banks are closed, go to the tourist office.

American Express: 139 Princes St. (tel. 225 7881). Holds mail. Open Mon.-Fri. 9am-5pm, Sat. 9am-noon.

Post Office: 2-4 Waterloo Place (tel. 550 8229), at North Bridge and Princes St. Open Mon.-Fri. 9am-5:30pm, Sat. 9am-12:30pm. **Postal Code:** EH1 1AL.

Telephones: City Code: 031.

Flights: LRT's **Airlink 100** (tel. 220 4111; £2.80) and the **Edinburgh Airbus Express** (tel. 556 2244; £3) both depart from Waverly Bridge for Edinburgh Airport. Journey time is about 25min.

Trains: Waverley Station, in the center of town. For 24-hr. information, call 56 2451. Ticket office and information office open daily 8am-11pm. To: Glasgow (at least 2/hr., £5.50); Stirling (at least 1/hr., £3.70); Aberdeen (1/hr., £26, return £30); Inverness (5/day direct, 4/day connect at Glasgow, £23, return £31); Thurso (3/day, £30.50, return £40); London (£58, with 2-week advance reservation £29; return £69, reserve 1 week in advance for £44 rate).

Buses: St. Andrew Square Bus Station, St. Andrew Sq. For Scottish Citylink info call 557 5717; for SMT info call 558 1616; for National Express info call 452 8777. After hours, or to avoid crushing lines, buy your ticket on the bus. Open Mon.-Tues. and Thurs.-Fri. 8:40am-6pm, Wed. 9am-6pm, Sat. 8:40am-5pm, Sun. 10am-4pm; Oct.-May Mon.-Tues. and Thurs.-Sat. 8:40am-5pm, Wed. 9am-5pm. **Scottish Citylink** to: Glasgow (#500/501, at least 1/hr., £3.90, return £5.50), Aberdeen (#564/565/568/569, 1/hr., £11.40, return £15); Inverness (#555/557, 1/hr., £10.90, return £14.50); Thurso (change at Inverness, from Inverness #558/559, £9, return £12) **Caledonian Express** (a.k.a. **National Express**) to London (£29.50, return £36; reserve 7 days in advance for £25 return). Overnight buses to London (£15, return £22, departs approx. 9pm).

Taxi: Taxi stands at both stations and almost every corner on Princes St., or call **Capital Cabs** (tel. 220 0404) or **City Cabs** (tel. 228 1211).

Bike Rental: Central Cycle Hire, 13 Lochrin Place (tel. 228 6333), off Home St. in Tollcross near Cameo Cinema. 12-speed town bikes £8/day, 21-speed touring bikes £10/day, mountain bikes £15/day. £35-60/week. Open Mon.-Sat. 10am-5:30pm; Sept.-May Mon. and Wed.-Sat. 10am-5:30pm.

Laundry: Bruntsfield Laundrette, 108 Bruntsfield Pl. tel. 229 2669, near Bruntsfield hostel. Wash £2, dry 20p. Open Mon.-Fri 9am-5pm, Sat. 9am-4pm, Sun. 10am-4pm.

Bisexual, Gay, and Lesbian Services: Gay Switchboard tel. 556 4049. Open daily 7:30-10pm. **Lesbian Line** tel. 557 1751. Open Mon. and Thurs. 7:30-10pm. Pick up a copy of *Gay Scotland* or drop by the **Blue Moon Café** (tel. 556 1471) on Broughton St. for more information.

Services for Disabled: Lothian Coalition of Disabled People, 13 Johnston Terr. (tel. 220 6855). Information available on disabled access to restaurants and sights.

Crises: Nightline tel. 557 4444. Open 10pm-8am. **Rape Crisis Center:** tel. 556 9437. Mon.-7-9pm, Tues. 1-4pm, Thurs. 6-8pm; also answering machine.

Pharmacy: Boots, 48 Shandwick Pl. (tel. 225 6757), past west end of Princes St. Emergency medication Mon.-Fri. 8:30am-9pm, Sat. 8:45am-9pm, Sun. 9am-5pm.

Emergencies: Dial 999; no coins required. **Hospital: Royal Infirmary of Edinburgh,** 1 Lauriston Pl. (tel. 229 2477). From the Mound take buses #23 or 27. **Police:** Fettes Ave. (tel. 311 3131).

ACCOMMODATIONS

Edinburgh's **B&Bs** cluster in 3 well-stocked colonies. The **Bruntsfield** district lies south of the west end of Princes St.; take bus #11, 15, 16, or 17 and try around Gilmore Pl., Viewforth Ter., or Huntington Gdns. **Newington** is south of the east end of Princes St. Hunt along Dalkeith Rd. and Minto St.; take bus #3, 8, 18, 31, 36, 62, 69, 80, 81, or 89. **Leith** lies northeast of the east end of Princes St. Try Pilrig St.; take Leith Walk from the east end of Princes St. or bus #11 or 14. Most of the hundreds of B&Bs in the city are open between May and September and cost £11-16. Edinburgh's **hostels** are cheap and convenient but fill up fast.

High Street Hostel, 8 Blackfriars St. EH1 1NE (tel. 557 3984). From Waverley Station, turn right up North Bridge to the Royal Mile (High St.), then turn left down the hill and take the 2nd right. Centrally located and well-managed, it fills up fast. Atmosphere is lively and relaxed. 130 beds. Reception open 24hrs. No curfew. 4- to 16-bed rooms. £8.50, 7th night free. Continental breakfast £1.20. Kitchen. Laundry service (£2.50). Vigorous (and private) showers. No phone reservations, so arrive before 10am in summer (9am during the Festival). Mailed reservations must be accompanied by payment for 1st night.

Hostel Eglinton (HI), 18 Eglinton Crescent EH12 5DD (tel. 337 1120), about 1 mi. west of the center of town, near Haymarket train station. Take bus #3, 4, 12, 13, 22, 26, 28, 31, 33, or 44 from Princes St. to Palmerston Pl., then take the 2nd left

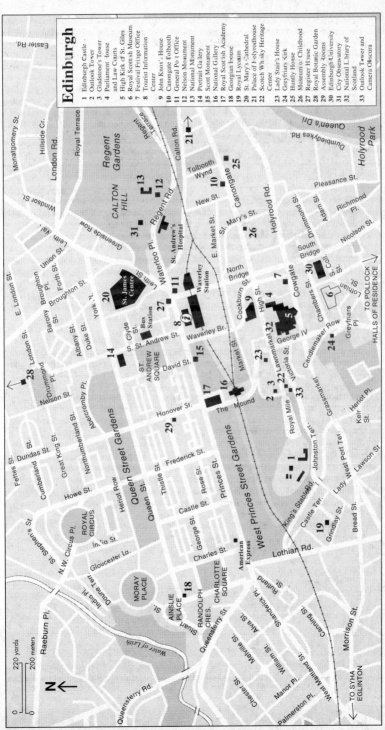

Edinburgh

1 Edinburgh Castle
2 Outlook Tower
3 Gladstone's Tower
4 Parliament House
  and Law Courts
5 High Kirk of St. Giles
6 Royal Scottish Museum
7 Festival Fringe Office
8 Tourist Information
  Center
9 John Knox's House
10 Canongate Tolbooth
11 General Post Office
12 Nelson Monument
13 National Monument
14 Portrait Gallery
15 Scott Monument
16 National Gallery
17 Royal Scottish Academy
18 Georgian House
19 Royal Lyceum
20 St. Mary's Cathedral
21 Palace of Holyroodhouse
22 Scotch Whisky Heritage
   Center
23 Lady Stair's House
24 Huntly House
25 Greyfriars Kirk
26 Museum of Childhood
27 Register House
28 Royal Botanic Garden
29 Assembly Rooms
30 Edinburgh University
31 City Observatory
32 National Library of
   Scotland
33 Outlook Tower and
   Camera Obscura

for Eglinton Crescent. Clean and well-lit, with sumptuous Victorian decor. 186 beds in 4- to 22-bed dorms. Curfew 2am. £9.25; under 18 £8. Paid advance reservations urged Easter-Sept. Open Jan.-Nov. MC,V.

Belford Youth Hostel, 6-8 Douglas Gardens EM4 3DA (tel. 225 6509), near Eglinton Hostel, just continue down Palmerston Pl. The friendly Hunter family has converted this elegant 100-yr.-old church into a modern hostel. Reception open 24hrs. Checkout 10am. No curfew. 90 beds in 4-6 person "hives," some private rooms. Snooker, ping-pong, and videos nightly. £7.95. Kitchen. Laundry. Accepts phone and mail reservations. Bus picks up groups from bus or train stations.

Hostel Bruntsfield (HI), 7 Bruntsfield Crescent EH10 4EZ (tel. 447 2994), about 1 mi. south of the West End of Princes St., in a lovely area by the Meadows. Take bus #11, 15, 16, C1, or C11, or walk down Lothian Rd., which becomes Bruntsfield Pl.; follow Bruntsfield Terrace to Bruntsfield Crescent. 168 beds in 8- to 26-bed rooms. Large store, ample kitchen, and laundry facilities. Reception open 7am-11:30pm. Curfew 2am. £6.85. Open Feb.-Dec. MC, V.

14 Argyle Pl. (Iolaire), EH9 1JL (tel. 667 9991), south of the Meadows and the Royal Mile. Heather and Jed Dignan have lovingly renovated 2 old houses and furnished them with solid wooden furniture and oriental rugs. TV lounge and unlimited kitchen access. 2-4 person rooms. No curfew. A bargain at £8.50-9. MC, V.

Hostel Merchiston (HI), North Merchiston Boys' Club, Watson Crescent. Take bus #9 or 10 to Polwarth and then #30 or 43 to Dundee St. This seasonal hostel is a long hike from the city center but provides 100 desperately needed beds at the peak of summer. Grade 2. £4.80. Hot showers. Full kitchen. No reservations accepted. Open late June-early Sept. Exercise caution when returning late.

Camping: Silverknowes Caravan Park, Marine Drive, by the Forth (tel. 312 6874). Take bus #14. Toilets, showers, and a shop in the campground. Space for 150 tents. Tents from £4.70. Open April-Oct.

FOOD AND PUBS

Most traditional Scottish fare in Edinburgh is served in restaurants that will have you in the alms house for a week, but you can get haggis—if you want to, that is—at many inexpensive cafés. **Littlewoods Department Store,** 92 Princes St., has a basement supermarket where you can pack a container full of salad for a fixed price. (£1.09-2.49. Open Mon.-Wed. 9:30am-5:30pm, Thurs. 9am-7pm, Fri.-Sat. 9am-6pm.)

Corner Stone Coffee House, Lothian Rd., at Princes St., beneath St. John's Church. Cheap "organically grown" meals in a cavernous, non-smoking café. Hot vegetarian meals served after noon for £2.95. Open Mon.-Sat. 10am-4:30pm.

Teviot Restaurant, Teviot Row Union. The best of the university unions. Filling main dishes about £2. Open Oct.-June Mon.-Fri. 8:30am-6:45pm, Sun. 12:30-6:30pm. During the Festival, it becomes the **Fringe Club.**

Kalpna, 2 St. Patrick's Sq. Superb Indian vegetarian fare in a subdued, smoke-free setting. Buffet lunch £3.50. Dinner reservations are wise. Open Mon.-Fri. noon-2pm and 5:30-11pm.

Larry's Diner, 26 Nicolson St. Good chips. Steak pie and those chips (£2.50), or fish and yes, chips (£2.75). Open Mon.-Sat. 8am-5:30pm, Sun. 9am-2pm.

Henderson's Salad Table and Wine Bar, 94 Hanover St., between George and Queen St. Cozy round wooden tables and low ceilings. Heaping hot dishes and unconventional salads (salads 80p). Open Mon.-Sat. 8am-10:45pm, also Sun. 9am-9pm during the Festival.

Parrots, 3-5 Viewforth. A faithful clientele flocks to the parrot-theme dining room for tasty, inexpensive dishes. Aubergine (eggplant, in American) and mushroom mousaka £3.25. Open Sun.-Thurs. 6-10:30pm, Fri.-Sat. 5-10:30pm; under 18 admitted only on Fri.-Sat from 5-7pm. Non-smoking. Reservations are very wise.

It's tough to find yourself without a pub in view anywhere in Edinburgh; some of the best cluster around the university. **Grassmarket,** at the base of Candlemaker Row, blows minds and tuitions with frequent live music and an array of ales. Royal Mile pubs tend to attract an older crowd. **Deacon Brodie's Tavern,** 435 Lawnmarket, pays homage to the schizophrenic Scot who inspired Stevenson to write *Dr. Jekyll and Mr. Hyde.* For bisexual, gay, and lesbian travelers, **The Laughing Duck,** 24 Howe St. offers a hectic buzz on Thursday nights.

SIGHTS

Princes St. Gardens split Edinburgh into gray-stone **Old Town,** where centuries of piecemeal construction overlap haphazardly, and the classically Georgian **New Town,** a marvel of rational city planning. Great locations for people-watching. The **Royal Mile** spills downhill through the middle of the Old Town, from Edinburgh Castle to the Palace of Holyrood.

At one end of the Royal Mile, **Edinburgh Castle** scowls atop an extinct volcano at the city it once protected. Inside it is **St. Margaret's Chapel,** a Norman church believed to be the oldest structure in Edinburgh. (Open Mon.-Sun. 9:30am-5:15pm; in winter Mon.-Sun. 9:30am-4:15pm, Sun. 12:30-4:20pm. £4, children £1.) Everything in the 1620 tenement **Gladstone's Land,** behind the pig at 483 Lawnmarket, remains as it was almost 400 years ago. (Open April-Oct. Mon.-Sat. 10am-5pm, Sun. 2-5pm. £2.40, students £1.20.) Through the passage at 477 Lawnmarket, the 17th-century **Lady Stair's House** harbors relics of Robert Burns, Sir Walter Scott, and Robert Louis Stevenson. (Open Mon.-Sat. 10am-6pm, during Festival also Sun. 2-5pm; Oct.-May Mon.-Sat. 10am-5pm. Free.)

Where Lawnmarket becomes High St., the Mile is dominated by the principal church of Scotland, **St. Giles Cathedral.** From its pulpit John Knox delivered the fiery Presbyterian sermons that drove Mary Queen of Scots into exile. (Open daily 9am-7pm; Sept.-Easter 9am-5pm. Free. Donation requested in Thistle Chapel.) Behind St. Giles in Parliament Sq. is the old **Parliament House,** the current Supreme Court. (Open Tues.-Fri. 9:30am-4:30pm. Free.) The unusual **Museum of Childhood,** 42 High St., displays dolls, games, toys, rods and canes. (Open Mon.-Sat. 10am-6pm, during Festival also Sun. 2-5pm; Oct.-May Mon.-Sat. 10am-5pm. Free.)

The **New Town Conservation Centre,** at 13A Dundas St., will answer your questions and direct you on your merry way. (Open Mon.-Fri. 9am-1pm and 2-5pm. Free.) For a self-guided tour, start at **St. Andrew Square,** walk west up George St. to the **Georgian House,** 7 Charlotte Sq., a well-restored townhouse where audio-visual shows and guides (all named George) explain the evolution of Georgian architecture and the New Town. (Open April-Oct. Mon.-Sat. 10am-5pm, Sun. 2-5pm. £2.50, students and children £1.40.) Beyond Register House is **Calton Hill,** home of the 143-step **Nelson Monument** (open Mon. 1-6pm, Tues.-Sat. 10am-6pm; Oct.-March Mon.-Sat. 10am-3pm; £1), which provides a view well worth the climb.

The *Edinburgh Gallery Guide* at the tourist office will guide you through the marble halls of Edinburgh's vast and varied collections. On **The Mound** between the 2 halves of Princes St. Gardens, the **National Gallery of Scotland** stashes a small but superb collection of works by Renaissance, Romantic, and Impressionist masters. (Open Mon.-Sat. 10am-5pm, Sun. 2-5pm; during Festival Mon.-Sat. 10am-6pm, Sun. 11am-6pm. Free.) The **Scottish National Portrait Gallery,** 1 Queen St., just north of St. Andrew Sq., displays likenesses of famous Scots, including Robert Burns, Sean Connery, and Mary Queen of Scots. (Open Mon.-Sat. 10am-5pm, Sun. 2-5pm. Free.)

Just off the eastern end of the Royal Mile, you can get a wee whiff of the Highlands with a stroll through **Holyrood Park** or a manageable 45-minute climb up **Arthur's Seat** (823 ft.); the exposed volcanic summit offers a stunning view. Edinburgh's requisite romantic oasis is the **Royal Botanic Gardens** on Inverleith Row. Take bus #23 or 27 from Hanover St. and stroll around the splendid rock garden and plant houses. (Open daily 10am-8pm; Sept.-Oct. and March-April 10am-6pm; Nov.-Feb. 10am-4pm.)

ENTERTAINMENT

The summer season overflows with music in the gardens, theater and film events, and *ceilidhs* (KAY-lees, bouts of country dancing, singing, and drinking)—and that's all *before* the Edinburgh International Festival comes to town. In winter, light thickens; shorter days and the crush of students promote a flourishing nightlife. For details, pick up a copy of *The List* (£1.50), a bi-weekly comprehensive guide to events in Glasgow and Edinburgh, at any local bookstore, newsstand or record shop. *Day by Day*, free from the tourist office, is also useful.

The **Royal Lyceum Theatre,** Grindlay St. (tel. 226 9697), presents well-known comedies. The **Traverse Theatre,** West Bow (tel. 226 2633), performs innovative and sometimes controversial drama, and the **Playhouse Theatre,** Greenside Place (tel. 557 2590), often hosts musical shows. Tickets for these theaters run £5-25.

Thanks to an overabundance of hip university students who never let books get in the way of a good night out, Edinburgh's music scene is alive and well. For jazz and blues, head to **Preservation Hall,** 9A Victoria St. (Open 1pm-1am.) The **Blue Moon Café** (60 Broughton St.) and **Madisons** (Greenside Place) are good bi, gay, and lesbian meeting places. **Negociant's,** 45-47 Lothian St. (open daily 9am-3am), is a pub with a wide range of Continental beers upstairs and frequent live shows downstairs, not to mention the best cappuccino in Edinburgh. **Ripping Records,** 91 South Bridge (tel. 226 7010), and the **Virgin Megastore,** 113 Princes St. (tel. 225 4583), have calendars of most rock, reggae, and pop concerts in Edinburgh and sell tickets as well. You'll find Scottish bands and country dancing most evenings at the **Ross Open-Air Theatre** (info. tel. 529 7905), under the tent in the west end of Princes St. Gardens (usually begins about 7pm) and at a number of smaller local pubs.

Festivals The extraordinary **Edinburgh International Festival** (Aug. 14-Sept. 3 in 1994) incites a massive bonfire of music, art, drama, and dance. Tickets (£2-35) are available by mail starting in May, as are full schedules of events. Contact the **Festival Box Office,** 21 Market St. EH1 1BW (inquiries tel. 226 4001, bookings tel. 225 5756; fax 226 7669). Tickets are sold over the counter and by phone starting the third week in April, and by mail from the second week in April. You can book by credit card, except on the day of a performance. From 1-5pm on the day of performance, half-price tickets are available at the bottom of The Mound.

Around the established festival has grown a more spontaneous **Festival Fringe.** The Fringe is generally more weird and whimsical than the official offerings; you may also find it more interesting. The *Fringe Programme* lists performance information; it and tickets are available from the **Fringe Festival Office,** 180 High St., Edinburgh, Scotland EH1 1QS. (Outside Britain, include £1 (from EC countries) or £2 postage; cash, stamps, and foreign currency accepted; from within Great Britain, 60p, available usually in mid-June.) Bookings can be made by mail starting June 27, by credit card beginning July 4 (tel. 226 5257) and in person from August 1. (Box office open Mon.-Fri. 10am-6pm; in Aug. and during the Festival 10am-7pm daily.)

The **Edinburgh International Jazz Festival** (Aug. 6-13, 1994) opens with a day of free jazz at the Princes St. Gardens. Tickets (£8-15) are available at the Ticket Centre on Waverly Bridge from 5 days before the festival, by phone (tel. 557 1642; credit card required), and by mail from the Festival Office, 116 Canongate EH8 8DD.

■ Near Edinburgh: St. Andrews

Scotland's oldest university, the cathedral and castle ruins, restored medieval streets, and active nightlife make St. Andrews equally compelling to the golf fanatic and the sports unenthusiast. The most imposing sights are concentrated by the North Sea at the east end of town. **St. Andrews Cathedral,** once Scotland's religious nexus, now lies in ruin. (Open Mon.-Sat. 9:30am-6pm, Sun. 2-6pm; Oct.-March Mon.-Sat. 9:30am-4pm, Sun. 2-4pm. £1.50, students and seniors 80p.) The nearby ruin of **St. Andrews Castle,** once the local bishop's residence, still contains a network of explorable secret tunnels, bottle-shaped dungeons and high stone walls to keep out (or in) rebellious heretics. (Same hours as cathedral. £2, students, seniors, and children £1.) **St. Andrews University,** founded in the 15th century, stretches just west of the castle between North St. and The Scores. For a 1-hour **Official Tour of St. Andrews**

University, show up to meet the guide at St. Salvator's Chapel Tower on North St. (Mid-June to Aug. Mon.-Sat. 10:30am and 2:30pm. £2.) The tour is your key to the interiors of most university buildings.

Golf pilgrims' holy shrine is the St. Andrews **Old Course,** the oldest golf course in the world, at the northwest edge of town. According to disputed historical evidence, Mary Queen of Scots played here only days after her husband was murdered. Nonmembers must present a handicap certificate or a letter of introduction from a golf club to play the Old Course. The impressively modern **British Golf Museum** lies next door to the private clubhouse. (Open daily 10am-5:30pm; Nov. Thurs.-Tues. 10-4pm; Dec.-Feb. Thurs.-Mon. 11am-3pm; March-April Thurs.-Tues. 10am-5pm. £3, students and seniors £2, under 15 £1. Wheelchair accessible.)

Try **Mrs. Pauline Lusk,** 2 Nelson St. (tel. (0334) 725 75), for some TLC, but don't despair if the B&Bs are all full or beyond your ailing budget. The trek to **Mr. Pennington's Bunkhouse** (tel. (0333) 310 768), 8 miles south of town, is well worth the time and effort. The owner, a diving expert-*cum*-historian, and his family warm the coldest hearts. (£5.50. Bicycles available.) For great take-out food, try **PM,** 1 Union St., at Market St. (Open daily 10am-11:30pm; Sept.-June Sun. from 4pm.) The marvelous **tourist office** is on 78 South St. (tel. (0334) 720 21; 24-hr. answering service), at Church St. (Open Mon.-Sat. 9:30am-7pm, Sun. 11am-5pm; Sept. and June Mon.-Sat. 9:30am-6pm, Sun. 11am-5pm; May Mon.-Sat. 9:30am-1pm and 2-5pm, Sun. 2-5pm; Oct.-April Mon.-Fri. 9:30am-1pm, Sat. 2-5pm.)

Fife Scottish buses (tel. (031) 556 8464) take the cheapest and most scenic route from Edinburgh to St. Andrews (#X59; 5-6/day, later service Fri.-Sun., nearly 2hr., £4, day return £6, student single £2.60). **British Rail** condescends to touch St. Andrews with a 10-ft. pole but remains wary, stopping 8 miles away at **Leuchars** on its London-Edinburgh-Dundee-Aberdeen line. (Hourly from Edinburgh, 1hr., £6.10, return £10.50. 3-4/day from London, including 1 overnight sleeper.)

■■■ GLASGOW

Scotland's largest city matches Edinburgh's capital class with volumes of energy and a Continental elegance. Glasgow University, half a millennium old, overlooks Kelvingrove Park; its student population of 13,000 overlaps with an innovative arts community to breed a lively atmosphere. Named Cultural Capital of Europe 1990 (an honor previously bestowed upon Athens, Amsterdam, Paris, and Dublin), the city has maintained its heady status and continues to support arts of all types, from the only opera in Scotland to kilt-clad streetcorner bagpipers.

ORIENTATION AND PRACTICAL INFORMATION

Glasgow's transportation system includes suburban rail, a confusing variety of private local bus services and the **Underground (U),** a circular subway line. (U trains run Mon.-Sat. 6am-10:45pm, Sun. 11am-6pm. Fare 50p.) Wave your hand to ensure that buses stop for you, and carry exact change (45-50p). Strathclyde Transport authority runs an immensely useful **Travel Centre** (tel. 226 4826) in St. Enoch's Square (U: St. Enoch), 2 blocks from Central Station; (open Mon.-Sat. 9:30am-5:30pm; phone inquiries Mon.-Sat. 7am-9pm, Sun. 9am-7:30pm).

Tourist Office: 35 St. Vincent Place, off George Sq. (tel. 204 4400) and south of Buchanan and Queen St. Stations, northeast of Central Station. U: Buchanan St. Pick up *What's On,* a free schedule of local events; the *Official Quick Guide to Glasgow* (80p) and *Where To Stay,* a guide to accommodations (80p). Open June and Sept. Mon.-Sat. 9am-7pm, Sun. 10am-6pm; July-Aug. Mon.-Sat. 9am-8pm, Sun. 10am-6pm; Oct.-May Mon.-Sat. 9am-6pm, Sun. (only in May) 10am-6pm.

Currency Exchange: Thomas Cook, 15-17 Gordon St. (tel. 221 5522). Open Mon.-Fri. 9am-5:30pm, Sat. 9am-5pm.

American Express: 115 Hope St. (tel. 226 3077). Mail held up to 8 weeks; no charge for nonmembers. Open Mon.-Fri. 9am-5pm, Sat. 9am-noon.

GLASGOW

Post Office: 2-5 George Sq. (tel. 242 4260). Open Mon.-Fri. 9am-5:30pm, Sat. 9am-12:30pm. **Postal Code:** G2 1AA.

Telephones: City Code: 041.

Trains: Central Station, Gordon St. (U: St. Enoch). To: Stranraer (Mon.-Sat. 6/day, Sun. 3/day, 2¼hr., £16.50, return £19-24; most connect with ferry to Larne, Northern Ireland) and Dumfries (£13.50, return £18-23). **Queen St. Station,** beside Coppthorne Hotel, George Sq. (U: Buchanan St.). To: Edinburgh (Mon.-Sat. 34-38/day, Sun. 20/day; 50min., £5.50, day return £6.80); Aberdeen (Mon.-Sat. 15/day, Sun. 7/day, £30, return £33-39); Inverness (Mon.-Sat. 8-9/day, Sun. 3/day, £23, return £28-31); Thurso (9hr., £30.50, return £40.50-43.50). For connections between the two stations, take bus #98 (every 15min., 50p); take a taxi (£1.50) or walk (8-10min.). For 24-hr. passenger inquiries, call 204 2844; for sleeper reservations call 221 2305. **Luggage storage** £1-2.

Buses: Buchanan Station (tel. 332 9191), 2 blocks north of Queen St. Station on N. Hanover St. **Caledonian Express/Stagecoach** (tel. 332 4100) has an office to your left as you come in the front door. To: Perth (£6, return £8-10) and Aberdeen (£11.80, return £5.50-19.50). **Scottish Citylink:** (tel. 332 7133 or 332 9191). To: Edinburgh (41/day, Sun. 27/day, 1¼ hr., £3.90, return £5.50); Oban (3/day, Sun. 2/day, 2¾hr., £8.80, day return £11.50) and Inverness (£11.90, return £16-20). **Anderston Station** (tel. 248 7432), a few blocks beyond Central Station on Argyle St. handles intra-city and suburban journeys.

Flights: Glasgow Airport (tel. 887 1111), 10 mi. west in Abbotsinch. Frequent buses (service #500/501) run to Glasgow's Buchanan (25min., £2) and Anderston stations, as well as to Edinburgh (1¾hr., £5).

Taxi: TOA Taxis tel. 332 7070. Free taxi phone at tourist office.

Laundry: Park Laundrette, 14 Park Rd. Wash £1.20, dry 30p/10min. Express service £3. Open Mon.-Fri. 8:30am-8pm, Sat.-Sun. 9am-7pm.

Gay and Lesbian Switchboard: tel. 221 8372, daily 7-10pm.

Women's Center: 48 Miller St. (tel. 221 1177), near George Sq.

Pharmacy: Boots, 200 Sauchiehall St. (tel. 332 1925). Open Mon.-Wed. 9am-5:30pm, Thurs. 8:30am-7pm, Fri.-Sat. 8:45am-6pm.

Medical Assistance: Glasgow Royal Infirmary, 82 Castle St. (tel. 552 3535).

Emergencies: Dial 999; no coins required. **Police:** Stewart St. (tel. 332 1113).

ACCOMMODATIONS

On the debit side of Glasgow's growing popularity is a perennial bed shortage, most acute in August. Reserve in advance; if you'd rather go a-wandering, most B&Bs lie scattered on the streets to either side of the Great Western in the University area.

HI youth hostel, 7-8 Park Terrace (tel. 332 3004; grade 1), 100m from the old hostel at 11 Woodlands Terrace and in a beautiful residential district overlooking Kelvingrove Park. (U: St. George's Cross.) From Central Station, take bus #44, 59, or 74 and ask for the *first stop* on Woodlands Rd. (at Lynedoch St.). From elsewhere in the city center, take bus #10, 11, 11A, or 12. Luxurious 4- to 6-person rooms with bathroom facilities. TV room, game room, bicycle shed, and in-house disco. No lockout. Curfew 2am. £9.25, includes breakfast; ages 5-17 £8. Sheets 60p.

Glasgow Backpackers Hostel, Kelvin Lodge, 8 Park Circus (tel. 332 5412, U: St. George's Cross). Spacious rooms; no bunkbeds. No lockout. No curfew. £7. Kitchen.

University of Glasgow, administrative offices at 52 Hillhead St. (tel. 330 5385; open Mon.-Fri. 9am-5pm). Summer housing at 6 college dorms. **Queen Margaret Hall,** 55 Bellshaugh Rd. (tel. 334 2192), near Byres Rd., is the most modern but also the farthest from the city center. Tea, coffee, soap, towels, and sheets included. B&B: students £14.10, nonstudents £20.50. Free laundry.

YMCA Aparthotel, David Naismith Court, 33 Petershill Dr. (tel. 558 6166). Take bus #10 or 11 from Buchanan Station or #12 or 16 from Queen St. Station. Clean, institutional rooms. TV lounge, game room. No curfew. Singles £15-17. Doubles £25-28.

FOOD AND PUBS

As in with many university towns, Glasgow has plenty of cheap hole-in-the-wall restaurants with great food. Professors hold *téte-à-tétes* at the cafés behind Byres Rd. on Ashton Lane, a cobblestone alley lined with 19th century brick façades.

The Bay Tree Vegetarian Café, 403 Great Western Rd. Vegetarians rejoice! Just down from the hostel, with superb hot meals (£3.50) and a selection of salads (large plate £3) and sinful desserts. Try the hot breakfast with vegetarian sausage, beans, and potatoes (£2.75) all day Sun. Open Tues.-Sun. 10am-9pm.

Grosvenor Café, 35 Ashton Lane, in a walkway off the middle of Byres Rd. (Behind U: Hillhead.) Students flock to this café's unbelievable subterranean bargains: Open Mon.-Sat. 9am-10:30pm, Sun. 9am-5:30pm.

Magnus Dining Room, in the Glasgow University Refectory ("The Hub"), on Hillhead St. just above University Ave. (U: Hillhead.) The central student cafeteria with salad, snacks, and meals. Open Mon.-Thurs. 8:30am-6:10pm, Fri. 8:30am-3:30pm.

The Basement Restaurant, 14 Otago St., off Great Western Rd. (U: Kelvinbridge.) In a basement cluttered with paintings and gallery posters. Delicious, homemade vegetarian dishes. Quiche 95p, salads 70-90p. Open Mon.-Sat. 9:30am-5:30pm.

The Byres Road pub crawl ("The path is long an' the ale is strong") usually starts with a trip to **Tennant's Bar** and then proceeds in the direction of the River Clyde. Alternatively, try the jazzy **Halt Bar,** 106 Woodlands Rd.; the groovy **O'Brien's Pub,** steps from the HI hostel, or the artsy **Cul de Sac Bar,** 46 Ashton Lane.

SIGHTS

The Gothic **Glasgow Cathedral,** near the center of town on Castle St., is the only cathedral left intact after the fury of the 16th-century Scottish Reformation. Next door is the giant **necropolis,** where most of the city's 19th-century industrialists are buried. (Cathedral open Mon.-Sat. 9:30am-6pm, Sun. 2-5pm; Oct.-March Mon.-Sat. 9:30am-4pm, Sun. 2-4pm. Free.) Rounded crescents and elegant parks in the West End's residential **Park Circus** area, near the youth hostel, present intact examples of early Victorian terracing. Check out **Tenement House,** a late 18th-century apartment on 145 Buccleuch St. (U: Cowcaddens. Open daily 2-5pm; Nov.-Easter Sat.-Sun. 2-4pm. £2, children and seniors £1.) Starting 1 block west of Park Circus is **Kelvingrove Park,** a wooded expanse on the banks of the River Kelvin. In the park's southwest corner, off the intersection of Argyle and Sauchiehall, is the spired **Glasgow Art Gallery and Museum.** The collection ranges from Rembrandt to Dalí. (U: Kelvin Hall. Open Mon.-Sat. 10am-5pm, Sun. 11am-5pm. Free.)

Kelvin Hall, on Dumbarton Rd. near the River Kelvin (U: Kelvin Hall), combines a complete public sports complex and a dazzling museum. The **Museum of Transport,** in the rear half of Kelvin Hall, houses a fascinating collection of full-scale original trains, trams, and automobiles inside an immense warehouse. (Open Mon.-Sat. 10am-5pm, Sun.11am-6pm. Free.) North of the Kelvingrove Park area at the end of Byres Rd. are the **Botanic Gardens,** Great Western Rd. Inside the **Kibble Palace,** one of two large hothouses, white marble statues overlook serene ornamental ponds. (Open daily 10am-4:45pm; late Oct.-March 10am-4:15pm. Free.)

Hidden in the large Pollok Country Park, 3½ miles south of town but worth the trek, is the fabulous **Burrell Collection,** including 19th-century French paintings, Chinese ceramics, and Persian tapestries. (Open Mon.-Sat. 10am-5pm, Sun. 11am-5pm. Free.) Take bus #45, 48, or 57 from Union St. (£1).

ENTERTAINMENT

Glasgow plays more than Edinburgh; take advantage of it, and pick up a copy of the monthly *What's on* at the tourist office. The **Ticket Centre,** City Hall, Candleriggs (tel. 227 5511), will tell you what's up at the city's dozen-odd theaters. (Open Mon.-

Sat. 10:30am-6:30pm.) *The List,* available from city newsstands, is a comprehensive fortnightly guide to the arts and other events in Glasgow and Edinburgh (80p).

Nightly gyrations to the latest club music shake the hip **Tunnel,** 84 Mitchell St. (student discounts on Thurs.). **Club Xchange,** 23 Royal Exchange Square attracts a mixed crowd. Club hours are generally 11pm to 3:30am; cover runs £3-7.

Mayfest, an arts festival during the first 3 weeks in May, offers a good program of Scottish and international theater and music. For information, contact Mayfest, 46 Royal Exchange Sq., Glasgow, Scotland G1 3AR (tel. 221 0232). The annual **Glasgow International Jazz Festival,** in late June or early July, brings the sounds of such greats as B.B. King and Herbie Hancock to town (same address as Mayfest; tel. 226 3813). Folk and traditional music thrive throughout Glasgow, especially during the **Glasgow International Folk Festival** at the beginning of July. (Contact the Festival Office, 8 Westercraigs, Dennistoun; tel. 556 1526.)

SOUTHERN SCOTLAND

Rolling hills, heathered moors, fertile farmland, and forested river valleys stretch south from Edinburgh and Glasgow to the English border. Poet Robert Burns is the Nessie of Ayrshire—sighted everywhere at once, yet strangely elusive. Dumfriesshire is rich in tales of Robert the Bruce, born in nearby Lochmaben, who successfully led the cause of Scottish independence to victory at Bannockburn in 1314.

■■■ STRANRAER

Located on the westernmost peninsula of Dumfries and Gallaway, Stranraer (stren-RAHR) is *the* place to get a **ferry to Northern Ireland,** but don't count on much beyond that. **Sealink ferries** (tel. (0776) 22 62) leave for Larne, Northern Ireland (8-9/day, Sun. 6-8/day, 2½hr., £18-20, students, children, seniors £9-10, off-season £17; bikes free). Show up 45 minutes before scheduled departures; ferries will occasionally leave early depending on weather conditions. Trains connect Glasgow to Stranraer (4/day, Sun. 7/day, £16.50). The **Seacat Hoverspeed** (tel. (041) 204 2266) travels year-round to Belfast, Northern Ireland. (4-9/day, 1½hr., £18-20, seniors and students £14-15, children £9-10. Bikes free.)

Stranraer is well-stocked with **B&Bs;** check the supplies on the A75 toward Newton Stewart (London Rd.). The **tourist office** (tel. (0776) 25 95), in the brown trailer across from the ferry waiting room and booking office, books accommodations and posts a list of B&Bs. (Open daily July-Aug. 10am-6:30pm; April-June and Sept. 10am-5pm.) Frequent **buses** from Stranraer north to Ayr and Glasgow and east to Dumfries all stop behind the tourist office, and some even meet the ferry directly at the pier (ask the ferry crew or the tourist office).

■■■ THE BORDERS

The southernmost Scottish outpost before entering the wilds of England, this aptly named 1800-sq.-mile tract of land south of Edinburgh served for centuries as Scotland's first line of defense against invasion. While border disputes are a thing of the past, practically all villages still hold annual **common ridings,** where "principals" lead their followers on horseback around the town limits to ensure that no encroaching clans have shifted a border-forming fence or stone. **Galashiels,** the homely focal point of the Borders, sends buses west to Peebles (16/day, 45min., £2.30, return £4.60); east to Kelso via Melrose (13-14/day, 45min., £2.30, return £4.60) and north to Edinburgh (£3.10, return 6.20). The seasonal **tourist office** (tel. (0896) 555 51) will help with transport connections. (Open July-Aug. Mon.-Sat. 10am-6:30pm, Sun. 1-5:30pm; Sept. Mon.-Sat. 10am-5:30pm; Oct. Mon.-Sat. 10am-

4:30pm; April-May Mon.-Sat. 10am-5pm; June Mon.-Sat. 10am-5:30pm, Sun. 1-3pm). Fifteen miles west of Galashiels on the A72 and the River Tweed lies **Peebles,** a well-kept town and a good base for exploring the forests of **Tweed Valley, Glentree,** and **Cardrona,** as well as **Lindinny Wood.** Stay with **Mrs. O'Hara,** Rowanbrae, Northgate (tel. (0721) 7216 30; £14). Relax at the cozy **Sunflower Coffee Shop,** 4 Bridgegate. (Open Mon.-Sat. 9am-5:30pm.) The **tourist office** in the Chambers Institute on High St. (tel. (0721) 201 38), sells a slew of local maps and walking guides. (Open July-Aug. Mon.-Sat. 9am-7pm, Sun. 1-6pm; Sept. and June 10am-5:30pm, Sun. 1-6pm; Oct. 10am-4:30pm, Sun. 1:30-4:30pm; April-May 10am-5pm, Sun. 2-4pm.)

One of the loveliest of the region's wee towns, **Melrose** makes a solid touring base. Centerpiece of the town, **Melrose Abbey** was decimated in 1543. Search amid the extensive foundations for a plaque marking the spot where Robert the Bruce's heart is buried. (Open Mon.-Sat. 9:30am-6:30pm, Sun. 2-6:30pm; Oct.-March Mon.-Sat. 9:30am-4:30pm, Sun. 2-4:30pm. £2, children and seniors 90p.) The well-equipped **HI youth hostel** (tel. (089682) 25 21; grade 1), off High Rd., looks out of a magnificent stone mansion at Melrose Abbey. (Lockout 11am-2pm. Curfew 11pm. £6.15, ages 5-17 £5.20. Open March-Oct.) The small **tourist office** (tel. (089682) 25 55) hides in the Priorwood Gardens near the abbey. (Open July-Aug. Mon.-Sat. 9:30am-6:30pm, Sun. 1:30-6:30pm; Sept.-Oct. and Easter-June Mon.-Sat. 10am-5:30pm, Sun. 1:30-5:30pm.)

Buses run from Edinburgh to Galashiels (13-14/day, Sun. 8/day, 1½hr., £3.10), connecting there with Melrose (15min., 95p, return £1.90). Get to Galashiels from the south via Newcastle (National Express #375; Newcastle to Melrose is £4.65). Otherwise, go up to Edinburgh and then south to Galashiels on National Express #591 (London to Edinburgh to Galashiels, £32 single, £36 return).

NORTHEAST SCOTLAND

Scotland's northeastern shoulder hunches up from the forested Perthshire region along the River Tay to the high Grampian and Cairngorm summits and descends to the chilly North Sea. The best scenery in the northeast lies back from the flat coast along the fertile river valleys and among the gentle slopes of mountains. Unfortunately for seekers of scenic views, transportation through the interior of this region is very spotty. Rail and bus routes tend to follow either the coast or the busy A9 trunk road from Perth to Inverness.

■■■ ABERDEEN

Snug between the Rivers Dee and Don, Aberdeen succeeds in cushioning its industrial character as the center of Britain's North Sea oil industry with attractive parks and a vibrant university. The tourist office offers **guided tours of Olde Aberdeene.** (Early June-early Sept. Wed. 7pm and Sun. 2:30pm. £2, children 50p.) Pick up a copy of the tourist office's monthly *What's On in Aberdeen,* or call the 24-hour information line (tel. (0224) 636 363); the *Gallery* has a free calendar of art exhibitions and events.

The Aberdeen Art Gallery, Schoolhill, houses a wide range of English, French, and Scottish paintings; its 20th-century British collection is particularly good. (Open Mon.-Sat. 10am-5pm, Thurs. 10am-8pm, Sun. 2-5pm. Free.) **Provost Skene's House,** on Guestrow near the tourist office, is a beautifully restored 17th-century townhouse "among buildings of lesser vintage." (Open Mon.-Sat. 10am-5pm. Free.) Aberdeen has a fine **sandy beach** that stretches about 2 miles north from the old fishing community of Footdee (fi-TEE) to the Don estuary. For another serene stroll, follow the **Old Deeside Line Walkway,** an abandoned railroad, through southwest Aberdeen; the trail begins at Duthie Park and leads toward the village of Cults.

INVERNESS

Accommodations, Food, and Practical Information King George VI Memorial Hostel (HI), 8 Queen's Rd. (tel. (0224) 646 988; grade 1) is humongous. (Strictly enforced 11:30pm lights-out and 8am wake-up call. Lockout 11am-2pm. Curfew 2am. £6.50. Open mid-Feb. to early Jan.) **Great Western Road,** 25 minutes from the train and bus stations on foot and also accessible by bus #17, 18, or 19, is loaded with B&Bs (£13-18). For wholefoods, try **Fresh Fields,** 49 Netherkirkgate beside Marks & Spencer. (Open Mon.-Wed. and Fri.-Sat. 9am-5pm, Thurs. 9am-6:30pm.) **The Grill,** 213 Union St., is authentically Aberdonian. (Open Mon.-Thurs. 10am-11pm, Fri.-Sat. 11am-midnight, Sun. 7:30-11pm.)

The **tourist office,** St. Nicholas House, Broad St. (tel. (0224) 632 727), has a mountain of leaflets; ask for *It's Free in Aberdeen.* (Open July-Aug. Mon.-Fri. 9am-8pm, Sat. 9am-6pm, Sun. 10am-6pm; Sept. and June Mon.-Sat. 9am-6pm, Sun. 10am-4pm; Oct.-May Mon.-Fri. 9am-5pm, Sat. 10am-2pm.) **The Aberdeen Ferry Terminal,** Jamieson's Quay (tel. (0224) 572 615), is the only place on mainland Britain where you can catch a ferry to the Shetland Islands. There are also ferries to Lerwick (year-round Mon.-Fri. at 6pm; June-Aug. also Tues. at noon; 14hr.; June-Sept. £48, with berth £51.50-99; Oct.-May £42.50, with berth £46-90.50) and Stromness (most Sat. year-round at noon or 6pm; June-Aug. Sat. also Tues. at noon; 8hr.; £34.50, with berth £38-71; off-season £31.50, with berth £34-65). Going down Market St., turn left at the traffic light past the **P&O Scottish Ferries** warehouse. (Office open Mon.-Fri. 8:45am-6pm, Sat. 9am-noon; Oct.-May Sat. 9am-6pm.)

National Express travels to Edinburgh (more than 1/hr., £11.40, return £19.50) and Glasgow (more than 1/hr., £11.80, return £19.50). **Bluebird Northern** serves Inverness (6/day, £8.50, round-trip £10). **ScotRail** (tel. (0224) 594 222) provides service to Edinburgh (Mon.-Sat. 20/day, Sun. 13/day, £26, return £30); Glasgow (Mon.-Sat. 17/day, Sun. 10/day; £30, return £33); Inverness (Mon.-Sat. 12/day, Sun. 5/day, £15.50, round-trip £22) and London (3/day direct, £69, return £68).

■■■ INVERNESS

The charms of Inverness, like Nessie herself, are somewhat elusive—Banquo's ghost has no ruin to haunt, and Nessie lives 15 miles to the south—but this transportation and tourist center for the Highlands offers a bucolic riverside setting in addition to its legendary associations with the Bard and the Monster. The unjustifiably famous **Loch Ness** creeps in its petty pace 5 miles south of town. For a full dose of Nessie-hunting lore and a hearty welcome to the Highlands, take a tour on **Gordon's Minibus.** The entertaining narrative of marine biologist and historian Dr. Gordon Williamson is a refreshing break from the usual area tourist traps. His minibus leaves from the Inverness tourist office at 10:30am and returns at 4:30pm. (£9.90; students, seniors and hostelers £6.90.) **Cawdor Castle** has been the residence of the Thane's descendents since the 15th century; don't miss the "wild" garden and the stunning nature walks. (Open May-early Oct. daily 10am-5:30pm. £3.50, grounds only £1.80.)

While in town, stay at the friendly **Inverness Student Hotel,** 8 Culduthel Rd. (tel. (0463) 236 556. Reception open 6:30am-2:30am. Check-out 10:30am. £6.90. Phone reservations only accepted from High St. Hostel in Edinburgh and Backpacker's Guest House in Kyleakin, Skye.) Near the youth hostel, **The Castle Restaurant** serves filling British meals. (Steak pie £3.05. Open Mon.-Sat. 8am-8:30pm.)

The Inverness **tourist office** in Castle Wynd (tel. (0463) 234 353; fax 710 609) gives out—you guessed it—information. (Open April to late May Mon.-Sat. 9am-5pm, Sun. 10am-4pm; late May-late June. Mon.-Sat. 9am-6pm, Sun. 10am-5pm; late June to mid-Sept. Mon.-Sat. 9am-8:30pm, Sun. 9:30am-6pm; mid-Sept.-end of Sept. Mon.-Sat. 9am-6pm, Sun. 10am-5pm; Oct. Mon.-Sat. 9am-5pm, Sun. 10am-4pm; Nov.-late April Mon.-Fri. 9am-5pm, Sat. 10am-4pm. Whew.) **Scottish Citylink** provides service to Edinburgh (4hr., £10.90, return £18), Glasgow (4¼hr., £11.90, return £20); Thurso and Wick (3½hr., £9, return £15). **Gaelicbus** runs to Fort William and **Morrison's Coaches** serves Thurso and Wick for the same price as Scottish Citylink. For more travel information call **Highland Bus and Coach** (tel.(0463) 233 371) or the **train** station (tel. (0463) 238 924).

HIGHLANDS AND ISLANDS

The Highlands Boundary Fault stretches northeast from Arran Island to Aberdeen, marking the southern boundary of the Highlands and Islands. Scotland's frayed northwestern coast, cut by sea lochs and girded by innumerable islands, remains the most beautiful region in Scotland and one of the last stretches of true wilderness in Europe. Even in tourist season, you can easily hike for a full day without seeing another human being. The Mainland towns of Oban, Fort William, Glencoe, Ullapool, and Thurso act as points of access to the islands. Travel in the Highlands requires a great deal more planning than in the rest of Britain. Although bus routes criss-cross the region and boat services connect more than 40 islands to the mainland, you can't count on making more than one or two journeys per day on any form of transportation, even in high season. Be prepared; if you miss your connection, you may be waiting till tomorrow, and tomorrow, and tomorrow...

Most ferries on the west coast are run by **Caledonian MacBrayne** (head office tel. (0475) 337 55), which publishes an excellent, widely available free timetable and fare sheet; their open-dated **Island Hopscotch** service provides discounts on a succession of ferry trips. Bikes can cross without reservation for a fee of £1-2, but advance booking for cars is strongly recommended.

■■■ OBAN AND FORT WILLIAM

Oban, Mull, Iona, and Glencoe Oban (OH–ben; 3hrs. by bus or train from Glasgow), the busiest ferry port on the west coast, endears itself with sporadic outbursts of small-town warmth. If you tire of the busy pier, gaze at the bay from **McCaig's Tower** (built in the 19th century to employ local masons), or walk 15 minutes north of town to the crumbling tower of **Dunollie Castle.** The **HI youth hostel,** on Corran Esplanade (tel. (0631) 620 25), presides over the bay. (Laundry facilities, store, and kitchen. Curfew 2am. £6.15. Open March-Oct.; frantically busy July-Aug.) **Jeremy Inglis,** 21 Airds Cresc. (tel. (0631) 650 65), is a *Let's Go* institution. (£6—yes, £6. Bath, breakfast, and kitchen included. Key deposit £1.) The **tourist office,** Argyll Sq. (tel. (0631) 631 22), is unflaggingly friendly despite the milling throngs. (Open Mon.-Sat. 9am-8:45pm, Sun. 10am-5pm; May and Sept. Mon.-Sat. 9am-5:30pm, Sun. 10am-5pm; Oct. and April Mon.-Fri. 9am-5:30pm; Nov.-March Mon.-Fri. 9am-1pm and 2-5:30pm.)

Most visitors leave from the Oban pier for **Mull,** the largest of the southern isles. Ferries leave several times per day in summer for **Craignure** (£2.55, next-day round-trip £4.10). There's little to do in Craignure but climb aboard Mull's 10¼-in.-gauge steam train to **Torosay Castle,** a graceful Victorian mansion nearby (open Easter-Oct. daily 10:30am-5:30pm), or else bus it to **Tobermory** (Mull's main town) or **Fionnphort** (where ferries to Iona leave). The **HI youth hostel** (tel. (0688) 24 81) on Main St., has a magnificent panorama of the bay. (£3.65. Open mid-March to Sept.) The isle of **Iona** was the first Christian settlement in Scotland (St. Columba founded its abbey in 563). For B&B, try the **Bishop's House** (tel. (06817) 306; £24.50, students 15% off) or **Finlay, Ross Ltd.** (tel. (06817) 357; £16-18).

A spectacular valley between Oban and Fort William, **Glencoe** is known as the "weeping glen" after a 1692 massacre in which government troops turned on their Highland hosts to make an example of King William III's power over the clans. Today the glen attracts rock climbers to its sheer and often slippery faces where numerous waterfalls cascade into the valley. Stage-Ways Fort William-Glasgow **buses** stop twice daily in Glencoe Village; the Gaelic Bus from Oban will deposit you in Ballachulish, ¾ mi. away. The **Glencoe HI youth hostel** (tel. (08552) 219; £6.15), 2 miles south of the village on the east side of the river, is much more pleasant than the adjacent Leacantium Bunkhouse. In town, the comfortable **Glencoe Outdoor Centre** (tel. (08552) 350) does a £13 B&B and rents sports equipment.

Fort William and Mallaig   Fort William no longer has a fort, but it could use one to fend off summer tourists. Mountaineers come for the challenge of **Ben Nevis** (4418 ft.), the highest peak in Britain. The main tourist path starts just up Glen Nevis past the town park. The **Glen Nevis HI youth hostel** (tel. (0397) 702 336) stands 3 miles east of town on the Glen Nevis Rd.; book 2 days ahead in July and August (£6.15; Dec.-Oct.). On the opposite side of the River Nevis, the **Ben Nevis Bunkhouse** (tel. (0397) 702 240) lies 2 miles from town along Achintee Rd. (£6). When both of these are packed, head 4 miles out of town on the A830 to the immaculate **Smiddy Alpine Lodge** (tel. (0397) 772 467) in Corpach (£6). Buses run to Corpach from High St. The **Glen Nevis Caravan & Camping Park** (tel. (0397) 702 191) stretches canvas on the same road, ½ mile before the HI hostel. (Tents £4.50-5.80 plus £1.10/person. Open mid-March to mid-Oct.) The **tourist office** (tel. (0397) 703 781) functions as the central depot for information of the West Highlands. (Open late May-Sept. Mon.-Sat. 9am-8pm, Sun. 10am-6pm; Oct. Mon.-Thurs. 9am-5:30pm, Fri.-Sat 9am-5pm; Nov.-Dec. Mon.-Thurs. 9am-5:30pm, Fri. 9am-5pm; Jan.-March Mon.-Sat. 9am-5:30pm; April to mid-May daily 9am-5:30pm.)

   Trains wind coastwards from Fort William to **Mallaig** along the famous "Road to the Isles," through mountains and past lochs and the Silver Sands of Morar (white beaches more at home in the Caribbean). Disembark from the train either at Arisaig or the next stop, Morar, to reach the comfortable **Garramore youth hostel (HI)** (tel. (06875) 268; grade 1; £6.15; open March-Oct.), a 3-mile walk along the A830 from either station; it's next to a campsite and close to secluded sandy beaches with misty views of the Inner Hebrides. From Mallaig, ferries shuttle to Skye and the **Small Isles** of Muck, Eigg, and Canna.

■■■ SKYE

Skye radiates unparalleled natural splendor. The **Cuillin Hills,** volcanic peaks surging boldly into a halo of clouds, are perhaps the most dramatic mountain vistas in Britain. Lush peninsulas and bays mark the extremes of the island near Staffin and Armadale. Bridge completion is scheduled for 1995; in the meantime, Skye is easily reached by **ferry** from Mallaig to Armadale (£2.30) or Kyle of Lochalsh to Kyleakin (free). Transportation on the island is not easy; bus service is infrequent and expensive. Biking or hiking may be better options; many hitch.

   Most of Skye's sights are on small country roads and accessible only under your own power. Ask about bus tours, which usually include **Dunvegan Castle** at Skye's northwestern tip, ancient home of the Clan MacLeod. Many accessible walks lead out of **Sligachan,** which has a large campsite and a hotel. The main path here traverses a stately bridge and continues through the river valley between peaks. For a spellbinding view of the Cuillins across the sea, make the strenuous bike trip or catch a bus from Broadford to **Elgol.**

   Skye's 5 **HI hostels** are sweetly situated but distressingly oversubscribed in the summer. Try to call at least one night in advance. **Glenbrittle** (tel. (0478) 640 278; grade 2) is in the heart of the Cuillins, accessible only to hikers and those with their own transportation. (£4.80. Open late March-Sept.) **Uig** (tel. (047042) 211; grade 2), overlooking the bay on the northern peninsula, is the least crowded and is accessible by bus or ferry from the Outer Hebrides. (£4.80. Open late March-Oct.) **Broadford** (tel. (04712) 442; grade 2) is the most central, close to both mountains and beaches. (£4.80. Open early March-Oct.) **Armadale** (tel. (04714) 260), on the southern tip of Skye, is a ½-mile away from the Mallaig ferry and serves well as a base for touring the verdant **Sleat Peninsula.** (£4.55. Open late March-Sept.) **Kyleakin** (tel. (0599) 45 85), Skye's only grade 1 hostel fills very quickly in the summer, so book weeks ahead. (£6.15. Breakfast £2.65, dinner £3.55.) Several independent hostels have recently sprung up in Skye to help cope with excess demand. The **Backpacker's Guesthouse** (tel. (0599) 45 10) in Kyleakin offers low-key comfort for £7.50. Near Broadford, the tiny **Fossil Bothy** (tel. (0471) 822 644 or 822 297) sleeps 8 cozily (£5), and just west of the Cuillins in Portnalong, the **Croft Bunkhouse** (tel. (047842) 254) sleeps 16 in a refurbished cow shed (£4.50).

■■■ OUTER HEBRIDES

The landscape of the Outer Hebrides is uniformly ancient. Much of the exposed rock here has been around for about 3 billion years, more than half as long as the planet itself. The culture and customs of the Hebridean people have also resisted change; most old and some young islanders still speak Gaelic among themselves. The vehemently Calvinist islands of Lewis, Harris, and North Uist observe the Sabbath strictly: all shops, pubs, and restaurants close, and public transportation stops on Sundays. According to legend, Bafinn, a Norwegian princess, rests in a 3000-year slumber under a knoll on North Uist. When she wakes, the weather on the Outer Isles will improve. Until then, expect a regular riot of high winds and rain.

Caledonian MacBrayne ferries travelers out, while spasmodically scheduled buses and ferries connect the islands lengthwise; hitching and cycling are excellent but often rain-soaked. Since ferries arrive at odd hours, try to arrange a bed ahead. The Outer Hebrides are home to the very special **Gatliff Hebridean Trust Hostels** (Urras Osdailean Nan Innse Gall Gatliff, listed in the SYHA handbook), 5 19th-century thatched croft houses converted into simple hostels, open year-round, whose authenticity and atmosphere more than compensate for crude facilities. A green brochure at tourist offices gives more complete details. Camping is allowed on any public land, but freezing winds and sodden ground often make it miserable. For more light on the islands, snag a copy of *The Outer Hebrides Handbook and Guide* (£4.25 at all tourist offices).

Lewis, Harris, and the Uists Lewis island is famous for its atmosphere: pure light and drifting mists off the Atlantic Ocean shroud the untouched miles of moorland and small lochs in quiet luminescence. The unearthly setting is great for exploring the **Callanish Stones,** an extraordinary Bronze Age circle as isolated as Stonehenge is overrun. **Caledonian MacBrayne** ferries from Ullapool on the mainland serve **Stornoway,** the biggest town in the Outer Hebrides (Mon.-Sat. 2-3/day, £9.20). The **tourist office** (tel. (0851) 703 088) is at 26 Cromwell St.—turn right from the ferry terminal, then left on Cromwell St. (Open Mon.-Sat. 9am-6pm and 9-10pm; Nov.-March Mon.-Fri. 9am-5pm; April Mon.-Thurs. 9am-5:30pm and 9-10pm, Fri.-Sat. 9am-5pm and 9-10pm.)

Although **Harris** is part of the same island as Lewis, it preserves its separate identity behind the curiously treeless Forest of Harris (actually a mountain range). Open hills, softened by a carpet of *machair* and wildflowers, make for wonderful off-trail rambling. **Ferries** (tel. (0859) 24 44) serve the town of **Tarbert** from Uig on Skye (Mon.-Sat. 1-2/day, £6.55) and Lochmaddy on North Uist (direct service Tues. and Fri. only, £6.55). A **tourist office** sits on Pier Rd. (tel. (0859) 20 11; open April to mid-Oct. roughly 9am-5pm and for late ferry arrivals). The nearest **HI youth hostel** is 7 miles away in **Stockinish** (tel. (085983) 373; grade 3; £3.65; open April-Sept.).

Under a heavy mist, the flat **Uists** (YOO-ists) are almost invisible. A rare spot of sunlight reveals a strange world of white beaches, crumbling black houses, wild jonquils, and quiet streams. The main villages of **Lochmaddy** on **North Uist** and **Lochboisdale** on **South Uist** are but glorified ferry points. **Ferries** run from Uig on Skye to Lochmaddy (1-2/day, 1¾-4hr., £6.55), connecting with Tarbert on Harris. Additional ferries run from Oban to Lochboisdale (Mon.-Sat. 1/day, £14.30). Some stop at

Castlebay on Barra on the way. **Tourist offices** are on the piers at either end of the string of islands, at Lochmaddy (tel. (08763) 321) and Lochboisdale (tel. (08784) 286). Either will find you a bed. (Both open late April to mid-Oct. roughly 9am-5pm and for all ferries except Sun.) The **Lochmaddy HI youth hostel** (tel. (08763) 368; grade 2), a ½-mile from the pier along the main road, overlooks a garden and a small bay. (Curfew 11pm. £4.80. Open mid-May to Sept. 7-10:30am and 5-11pm.)

■■■ ORKNEY ISLANDS

Less well known than the more northerly Shetland, Orkney rarely fails to enchant its visitors with its impressive mix of nature, history, and hospitality.

Getting There and Getting Around There are more bus companies populating the roads of Mainland than there are islands in the surrounding sea. Ask at the tourist office for details. **Ferries** to the smaller islands run from Kirkwall and Tingwall for the north, Houton and Stromness for the south. The **Orkney Islands Shipping Company (OISC)** (tel. (0856) 872 921) operates most ferries. (Round-trip fares range from £2-8.)

Two ferries connect mainland Scotland to Orkney. **P&O's** St. Ola car ferry (tel. (0224) 572 615 in Aberdeen, (0856) 850 655 in Stromness) runs past the great cliffs of Hoy on its journey from Scrabster to Stromness. (Mon.-Sat. 2-3/day, Sun. 1/day; Nov.-March Mon.-Sat. 1/day; 1¾hr.; £12.50, Oct.-May £11.50, seniors 10% off.) A **bus** leaves from Thurso railway station for Scrabster before each crossing (70p). **Thomas & Bews** (tel (095581) 353) runs from John O'Groats to Burwick on South Ronaldsay (June-Aug. 4/day, May and Sept. 2/day, weather permitting; 45min.; £12, return £18). A reduced £15 return includes free bus service from Burwick to Kirkwall, but you must leave John O'Groats on an afternoon sailing and leave Orkney in the morning.

Kirkwall and Stromness Home to one-third of Orkney's 21,000 souls, **Kirkwall** is Orkney's most busy and modern town. The handsome red sandstone **St. Magnus Cathedral,** built in 1137, stands tall in the town center. (Open Mon.-Sat. 9am-5pm. Free.) Located in a former WWII communications center on Old Scopa Rd. on the edge of town, Kirkwall's recently renovated **HI youth hostel** (tel. (0856) 872 243; grade 1) sports 90 beds in 3- to 4-bed rooms. (Reception open 7-11am and 2-11:30pm. £6.15. Open late March-Oct.) The **Atholl Coffee Shop,** Albert St., is the cheapest sit-down in town. (Sandwiches £1.10, mince pie £1.80, baked potato £1.10-1.35. Open Mon.-Fri. 9:30am-7pm, Sat. 9am-6pm, Sun. 10am-6pm.) The twisting alleyways will send you scurrying straight to the **Orkney Tourist Board,** 6 Broad St. (tel. (0856) 872 856; fax. 875 056) to pick up your free map. (Open daily 8:30am-8pm; Oct.-March Mon.-Sat. 9am-1pm and 2-5pm.)

Stromness, Orkney's second-largest metropolis, is a small port with narrow streets and aging storefronts. **Stromness Museum,** 52 Alfred St., toward the south end of town, mounts exhibits on Orcadian and natural history. (Open Mon.-Sat. 10:30am-5pm; Sept.-April Mon.-Sat. 10:30am-12:30pm and 1:30-5pm. 80p, children 30p.) The **HI youth hostel,** Hellihole Rd. (tel. (0856) 850 589; grade 2), has 8-bunk rooms and a view of the harbor. (Lockout 10:30am-5pm. Curfew 11pm. £4.80.) **The Café** at 22 Victoria St. serves cheap sit-down meals (breakfast £2.50, burger £3.50) at one of the more happening places in Stromness. (Open daily 9am-10pm.) The Stromness **tourist office** (tel. (0856) 850 716), by the pier, finds B&Bs and goes out of its way to help you plan your stay. (Open April-Oct. Mon.-Sat. 8am-6pm, Sun. 9am-4pm. Opens for ferry arrivals year-round.)

■■■ SHETLAND ISLANDS

Getting There and Getting Around Nearly the cheapest and certainly the fastest transit to Shetland is the **British Airways/BABA special** from Orkney. You're eligible for the £31 flight to Shetland *only if you book ahead* at any Shetland B&B or guest house *from Orkney*. The same offer holds for the return to Kirkwall if you book ahead in Shetland. The tourist offices in Stromness, Kirkwall, or Lerwick will handle the bookings. **British Airways** flies from Aberdeen, Inverness, Edinburgh, and Glasgow. All flights are met by buses which run to Lerwick (1hr., £2.90). Inter-Shetland flights use **Tingwall Airstrip** just outside Lerwick (tel. (059548) 246 for reservations).

Ferries arrive at Holmsgarth Terminal in Lerwick, a 20-minute walk northwest of the city center and smaller Victoria Pier. **P&O Scottish Ferries** leave weekdays at 6pm (June-Aug. also Tues. at noon) from Aberdeen for Lerwick (14hr.; £48, Oct.-May £42.50, berth from £3.50 extra). A P&O ferry also runs from Stromness on Orkney to Lerwick (Tues. at 10pm and Sun. at noon, Sept.-May Sun. at noon; 8hr.; £31.50). From June through August, the **Smyril Line** car ferry sails from Lerwick to Bergen, Norway (11pm Mon., £53), the Faroe Islands (2am Tues., £56), and Hanstholm, Denmark (1pm Sun., £73). Connect to Iceland from Faroe. Students get 25% off the fares, which are lower in early June and late August. Bookings and info for P&O and Smyril Line are available from P&O Scottish Ferries, P.O. Box 5, Jamieson's Quay, Aberdeen AB9 8DL (tel. (0224) 572 615).

Shetland's main **bus** companies are **John Leask & Son** (tel. (0595) 31 62) and **Shalder Coaches** (tel. (059588) 217). The tourist office has the indispensable *Inter-Shetland Transport Timetable* (60p), listing bus, ferry, and plane schedules.

Lerwick, Bressay, and Tingwall Nowhere on Shetland's desolate, tireless terrain can you be farther than 3 miles from the sea. **Lerwick** lies on the eastern coast of the main island ("Mainland") and is served by the A970 which runs the length of the island. The best views of Lerwick and its harbor are from the giant pentagonal **Fort Charlotte** in the center of town, a relic of the Cromwellian era. Only 1 mile west of the city center on Clickimin Rd., the ruins of **Clickimin Broch,** a stronghold from the 4th century BC, rest on a strand cutting into a loch. Hourly **ferries** (65p) sail from Lerwick to the isle of **Bressay,** a gentle spot ideal for a slow amble. Hike up conical **Ward of Bressay** (743 ft.) for a sweeping view of the sea. **Tingwall,** 5 miles north of Lerwick, houses the cluttered **Tingwall Agricultural Museum.** (Open June-Sept. daily 2-5pm. £1, seniors 50p.) The view from the top of nearby Wamadale Hill will shatter your camera lens—in clear weather, you can see 40 miles.

Accommodations, Food, and Practical Information The relaxed Lerwick **HI youth hostel,** Islesborough House at King Harald and Union St., is closed for renovations until 1994. Camping **böds** (barns) are a unique Shetland accommodations alternative. Try the **The Böd of Nesbister** on Whiteness Voe, **The Sail Loft** next to the pier in Voe, and **"Johnnie Notions"** at Hamnavoe, Eshaness in far northwest Mainland. All *böds* cost £2.50 per night (£12-50 for exclusive use), are open April through October and must be booked in advance. Reserve through the tourist office and bring everything you need but the roof.

Inexpensive eats cluster in the heart of Lerwick. **Central Bakery** offers fresh filled rolls in a non-smoking environment. (Open Mon.-Tues. and Thurs.-Fri. 9am-4:15pm, Wed. 9am-1:30pm, Sat. 9am-4pm.) The **Fort Café,** 2 Commercial Rd., fries up the local catch. (Open Mon.-Fri. 11am-10:30pm, Sat. 11am-7pm, Sun. 5-10:30pm.)

Shetland Islands Tourism (tel. (0595) 34 34), at Market Cross across from Victoria Pier near the Holmsgarth Ferry Terminal in Lerwick, will book you a bed anywhere in the islands for a £1 fee. (Open Mon.-Fri. 8am-6pm, Sat. 8am-5pm; Oct.-

March Mon.-Fri. 9am-5pm.) A small branch in the ferry terminal greets all seaborne arrivals, even at 1:30am.

■ Northern Ireland

The strife that makes the North famous hides the land's raw shocking beauty from international travelers. What they miss out on includes the pockets of womblike green collectively called the Glens of Antrim; and one of the world's strangest geological sights, the Giant's Causeway, which interrupts the islands and beaches along the north Antrim coasts. Urban neighborhoods, can show you everyday life in a divided (and, most of the time and most everywhere, peaceful) society.

> As part of the United Kingdom, Northern Ireland uses British pounds ("sterling"); its banks print their own sterling notes, which are not accepted in England or Scotland, though English pounds are accepted in Northern Ireland.

GETTING THERE AND GETTING AROUND

Stena-Sealink ferries (Larne tel. (0574) 273 61; Stranraer tel. (0776) 22 62) run from Stranraer, Scotland, to Larne, Northern Ireland (7-9/day; 2½hr.; £18, students £13, seniors and children £8). **P&O Ferries** (Larne tel. (0574) 274 321; Carnyran tel. (05812) 276) run between Carnryan, Scotland and Larne. (Mon.-Fri. 6/day, Sat.-Sun. 4/day; £18, seniors and children £9.) The **Hoverspeed Seacat** leaves Stranraer (tel. (0776) 22 55) and arrives in Belfast (tel. (0232) 312 002; 9/day, 4/day in winter; 1½hr.; £18-19, seniors and students £14-15, ages 4-15 £9-10, bikes and tykes (under 4) free). **British Airways** (tel. (0345) 222 111) and **British Midland Airways** (tel. (0232) 325 151) both run regular flights from London's Heathrow to Belfast International Airport (7/day/airline, 1¼hr.). **Aer Lingus** does not fly to Belfast.

Northern Ireland Railways (tel. (0232) 235 282) service isn't extensive, but covers the Northeastern coastal region well. A valid **Travelsave** stamp (£5.50), bought at the Student Travel Office, 136 Fountain St., Belfast, and affixed to the back of an ISIC, will get you 50% off all trains, but does not give discounts on buses. **Ulsterbus,** Oxford St., Belfast (tel. (0232) 320 011), runs service throughout the province; coverage expands in summer, when open-top buses cover a northeastern coastal route. Full- and half-day tours leave for key tourist spots from Belfast. **Hitching** has become much more dangerous within the past couple of years. Weak in public transportation yet loaded with luscious hiking terrain, Northern Ireland is a rambler's dream. The **Ulster Way** encircles Northern Ireland with 491 miles of marked trail.

If you're planning to cross the border on a bike or in a car, be sure you do so at one of the approved border-crossing checkpoints; crossing at an unapproved point can actually get you followed by the Army. Do *not* hitchhike in or around Newry, South Armagh, or metropolitan Belfast, or, in the Republic, around Dundalk. Do not ever take photographs of soldiers or of military installations or vehicles; if you do, your film will be confiscated, and you may be detained for questioning.

NORTHERN IRELAND ESSENTIALS

Youth Hostel Association of Northern Ireland (YHANI) has 6 permanent HI hostels in Northern Ireland and one temporary one in Derry which opens from June to September. All are well-kept, serve breakfast, and offer family quarters; most provide ample kitchen facilities, and all have free showers and sleepsacks. For complete hostel listings contact YHANI, 56 Bradbury Place, Belfast BT7 1RU (tel. (0232) 324 733). More recently, the **Independent Hostel Organization (IHO)** has popped up throughout Ireland, with 2 hostels located in Northern Ireland: one in Portstewart and one in Dungiven. These generally have no curfew, lockout, or membership fee. For cushier lodgings and a taste of an Ulster Fry breakfast, try one of the region's many **B&Bs**. Northern Ireland treats its **campers** royally; there are well-equipped sites throughout and spectacular parks often house equally mouth-watering sites.

■■■ BELFAST

Home to about one-third of Northern Ireland's population, Belfast has been an active industrial city since its prime at the turn of the century. In recent years, an artistic renaissance has successfully established a new cosmopolitan image for the 90s. However, Belfast cannot ignore the reality of political turmoil; armed soldiers still patrol the town, and burned-out bars await refurbishment.

ORIENTATION AND PRACTICAL INFORMATION

Belfast is loosely centered on **City Hall** in **Donegall Square,** 6 blocks from the River Lagan and the harbor. To the north of the center lies the city's snazzy shopping district and 2 blocks west on Great Victoria St. is the **Golden Mile.**

Tourist Office: St. Anne's Court, 59 North St. (tel. 231 221). Info, brochures, and a terrific free map of the city with bus schedules. Open Mon.-Fri. 9am-5:15pm. The **Northern Ireland Tourist Board** is in the same building. **Irish Tourist Board** (Bord Fáilte), 53 Castle St. (tel. 327 888). Info on the Republic of Ireland. Open Mon.-Fri. 9am-5pm; March-Sept. also Sat. 9am-12:30pm.

Budget Travel Office: USIT, 136 Fountain Centre, College St. (tel. 324 073), near Royal Ave. Open Mon.-Fri. 9:30am-5:30pm, Sat. 10am-1pm.

U.S. Consulate General: Queens House, Queen St. (tel. 228 239).

Currency Exchange: Thomas Cook, 11 Donegall Pl. (tel. 326 934). Open Mon.-Fri. 9am-5:30pm.

American Express: Hamilton Travel, 10 College St. (tel. 322 455). Client mail held. Cashier open Mon.-Fri. 9:30am-4:30pm; travel open 9am-5pm.

Buses: Central Station (tel. 320 011). To Dublin (Mon.-Sat. 4/day, Sun. 3/day; £9.50, return £12). From Derry (Mon.-Sat. 6/day, Sun 4/day; £5.30, return £9.30). All others arrive at **Europa/Glengall St. Station.**

Trains: Belfast Station (tel. 230 310). From Dublin's O'Connolly Station (Mon.-Sat. 7/day, Sun. 3/day; 2hr. 35min.; £13, return £19.50). From Derry (Mon.-Fri. 7/day, Sat. 6/day, Sun. 3/day; 2¼hr.; £7, return £9.70).

Ferries: The Seacat and ferries cross from Scotland to Belfast and Larne, north of the city. (See Getting There and Getting Around above.) A **Flexibus shuttle** runs from Donegall Quay, where the Seacat docks, to Europa Buscentre (50p). From the ferry terminals at Larne, take either a bus or a train into the city center. Buses: Mon.-Fri. 17/day, Sat. 15/day, Sun. 3/day; 1hr.; £2.30, return £4.80. Trains: Mon.-Fri. 20/day, Sat. 16/day, Sun. 6/day; 45min.; £2.80, return £4.70.

Flights: Belfast International Airport (Aldergrove). A shuttle bus runs to Central Station (every ½hr., Sun. every hr.; £3.50).

Post Office: 25 Castle Pl. (tel. 323 740). Open Mon.-Fri. 9am-5:30pm, Sat. 9am-1pm. **Postal Code:** BT1 1BB.

Telephones: City Code: 0232.

Crises: Samaritans: tel. 664 422, 24hrs. **Women's Aid:** (tel. 662 385), 24hrs. **Rape Crisis Center:** 41 Waring St. (tel. 249 696).

Bisexual, Gay, and Lesbian services: Carafriend Counselling (tel. 238 668), Thurs. 7:30-10pm.

Emergencies: Dial 999; no coins required. **Police:** 65 Knock Rd. (tel. 650 222).

ACCOMMODATIONS AND FOOD

Look for safe and convenient lodgings near the university, south of the center.

Belfast youth hostel (HI), 11 Saintfield Rd., Ardmore (tel. 647 865). A 45-min. walk from the center of town or a shorter ride on red bus #38 or 84 from City

FERMANAGH LAKE DISTRICT

Hall, Donegall Sq. E. (tell the bus driver where you want to go). Upper floor dorm windows look out on a tidy walled garden. Showers located outside. Lockout 10:30am-1pm; Sept.-May 10:30am-1:30pm. Curfew 11:30pm. £7.20, under 18 £6, nonmembers add £1.50. MC, V. Closed Christmas week.

Mrs. Davidson's East-Sheen Guest House, 81 Eglantine Ave. (tel. 667 149). The best deal in Belfast, if you can get a room. Mrs. D. will nurse you with scones; every room has a teapot, sugar cubes, and biscuits. £13, with shower £13.50.

Queen's University Accommodations, 78 Malone Rd. (tel. 381 608). Take bus #70 or 71 from Donegall Sq., or walk down Great Victoria Rd. which runs into Malone Rd. Spartan rooms on long corridors. Singles and doubles in residence halls. Kitchen with microwave, TV lounge. UK students £7, international students £8.23, nonstudents £11-16. Open mid-June to mid-Sept.

Dublin Rd. and the **Golden Mile,** stretching from the Grand Opera House down Great Victoria St. to University Rd., have the highest concentration of places to eat; **Bookfinders,** 47 University Rd. (tel. 328 629), serves potato-and-leek soup and homemade bread (£1.40) behind stacks of well-worn books. (Open Mon.-Sat. 10am-5:30pm.) You'll want to be a regular at **The Lamplighter,** 115A Ormeau Rd., which serves heaping portions at rock-bottom prices. (Open Mon.-Sat. 10am-9pm.)

SIGHTS AND ENTERTAINMENT

Belfast's main attraction, the **Ulster Folk and Transport Museum,** lies 7 miles east of the city center in Cultra. This fascinating open-air museum contains traditional buildings from all over Northern Ireland that were dismantled at their original locations and carefully reconstructed on the museum's 180 acres of parkland. (Open Mon.-Sat. 10:30am-6pm, Sun. noon-6pm; April-June and Sept. Mon.-Fri. 9:30am-5pm, Sat. 10:30am-6pm, Sun. noon-6pm; Oct.-March Mon.-Fri. 9:30am-4pm, Sat.-Sun. 12:30-4pm. Closed Christmas week. £2.60, children £1.30, families £6, HI discount 50%.)

Belfast's ornate **City Hall** stands like a wedding cake, set apart by a grassy square. (Free tours Wed. 10:30am, by advance booking only. Call 320 202, ext. 227.) The northwest corner of Donegall Square holds the **Linen Hall Library,** 17 Donegall Sq., famous for its comprehensive collection of political materials relating to the Troubles. (Open Mon.-Wed. and Fri. 9:30am-5:30pm, Thurs. 9:30am-8:30pm, Sat 9:30am-4pm.) Just across College Square, **Old Museum** puts up rotating art exhibits, and holds frequent concerts and performances. (Open Mon.-Fri. 9am-5:30pm, Sat. 10am-5pm. Free.) Follow Great Victoria St. south from City Hall to **Queen's University,** whose attractive Tudor buildings overlook the **Botanic Gardens.** (Open daily 8am-dusk. Free.) The **Ulster Museum and Art Gallery** has an astounding collection of silver and gold looted from the *Girona,* a Spanish Armada ship wrecked off the Giant's Causeway in 1588. (Open Mon.-Fri. 10am-5pm, Sat. 1-5pm, Sun. 2-5pm. Free.)

Belfast's nightlife changes with the wind; the best sources of information are the Arts Council's *Artslink,* Thursday's *Irish News* and the daily *Belfast Telegraph.* You'll find pubs all over the city, but they'll practically bump into you around Great Victoria St. and the city center, or in the vicinity of the university. Try the **Crown Liquor Saloon,** 46 Great Victoria St., or **Kelly's Cellars,** 30 Bank St. Students hop back and forth between **The Botanic Inn** ("The Bot"), 23 Malone Rd., and **Eglantine Inn** ("The Egg"), 32 Malone Rd. They dance at **Lavery's,** 12 Bradbury Pl.

The truly **Grand Opera House** was bombed in the spring of 1993 and will remain closed at least until late Dec. 1993. In November, Queen's University hosts the **Belfast Festival at Queen's,** a 3-week extravaganza of drama, music, and art. (Contact the Festival House, 25 College Gdns., Belfast BT9 6BS by Aug.; tel. 667 687.)

■■■ FERMANAGH LAKE DISTRICT

Located in the southwestern corner of Northern Ireland, the Fermanagh Lake District is the perfect place for an amphibious jaunt. The best way to explore the islands is by boat; ask at the tourist office in **Enniskillen,** the region's main town, for an exhaustive list of renters. **Erne Tours Ltd.** (tel. (0365) 322 822) sets out from Round O Jetty, Beleek Rd., and stops on **Devenish Island,** with its 12th-century castle. (May-June Sun. 2:30pm; July-Aug. 2/day plus Tues., Thurs., and Sun. 7.15pm, Sept. Tues., Sat., and Sun. 2:30pm. £3, under 14 £1.50.) Stay at the modern **HI youth hostel** (tel. (03656) 281 18) in a restored 19th-century house 1 mile off the road from Enniskillen to Kesh. (Lockout 11am-5pm. £6, under 18 £5. Open March.-Dec. 21.) Visit Enniskillen's well-equipped **Lakeland Visitors Center** (tel. (0365) 323 110) on Shore Rd. (Open Mon.-Fri. 9am-6:30pm, Sat. 10am-6pm, Sun. 11am-5pm; Oct.-May Mon.-Sat. 9am-5pm.) **Ulsterbus** (tel. (0365) 322 633) leaves from its swanky new station across from the tourist office to Belfast (3/day; 2¼hr.; £5, return £8.80) and Dublin (Mon.-Sat. 5/day, Sun. 1/day; 3hr.; £5, return £8.20).

■■■ DERRY

Nicknamed "Stroke City" because it's sometimes written "L'derry" so as not to offend rival factions of Unionists and Nationalists, Derry is a city divided—the River Foyle keeps the predominantly Protestant east side and the predominantly Catholic west side from running into each other. At the highest point in the city, **St. Columb's Cathedral** of 1633 was the first built in Britain and Ireland after the Reformation. (Tours Mon.-Sat. 9am-1pm and 2-5pm. Call (0504) 262 746 to reserve space.) The many political murals painted around the streets are sights themselves—look for "The Auld's Days," which is painted at the junction of William and Rossville St. The very institutional but oh-so central **Oakgrove Manor (HI/YHANI),** Magazine St. (tel. 372 273), is brand-new and spacious. (Small dorm £4.50, large dorm £6. Family room with breakfast £40, single with breakfast and shower £15, double with same £28.) Just 5 miles outside of Derry is the relaxed, homey **Muff Hostel** (£3.50, campers £2). **The Sandwich Co.,** the Diamond, at the corner of Ferryquay St. and Bishop St., offers *real* sandwiches with loads of fresh fillings. (£1-2. Open daily 9am-5:30pm, later when there's music.) The **tourist office,** 8 Bishop St. (tel. (0504) 267 284), distributes *Derry Tourist Guide 1994*. (Open Mon.-Sat. 9am-8pm, Sun. 10am-6pm; Oct.-June Mon.-Fri. 9am-5pm.) The **Irish Rail,** The Waterside (tel. 422 28), chugs to Belfast (Mon.-Sat. 8/day, Sun. 6/day; 2½hr.; £7, return £9.70). **Ulsterbus** (tel. 262 261) also services all points in Northern Ireland.

■■■ CAUSEWAY COAST

As the Northern Irish coast rounds Torr Head, between Ballycastle in the east and Portstewart in the west, 600-ft. cliffs plummet into the restless surf. **Ulsterbus** runs tours through the area, and during July and August the open-topped **Bushmills Bus** (tel. (0265) 433 34) follows the coast between Coleraine (5 mi. south of Portrush) and the Giant's Causeway (4/day, Sun. 2/day). Ulsterbus #172 runs along the coast from Ballycastle to Portrush (Mon.-Sat.).

At the eastern edge of the Causeway Coast, **Ballycastle** is a tired but friendly resort stopover point. The new **Castle Hostel,** 62 Quay Rd. (tel. (02657) 623 37), has a central location and overcrowded bunk rooms. (No curfew or lockout. £5.) The **tourist office** is in Sheskburn House at 7 Mary St. (tel. (02657) 620 24; open July-Aug. Mon.-Fri. 9:30am-7pm, Sat. 10am-7pm, Sun. 2-6pm; Sept.-June daily 9:30-am-5pm). Ballycastle's best asset is actually the **ferry** that runs to Rathlin Island, the ultimate in escapism for 20,000 puffins, the odd golden eagle, and about 100 human beings —all of whom lived without electricity until September 1992.

Five miles west of Ballycastle is the village of **Ballintoy,** with a picturesque church and a tiny harbor. **Boat trips** (£1) run every ½-hour on summer weekends past Sheep Island to **Carrick-a-rede Island** ("rock in the road"). If you get seasick (or even if you don't), take the signposted path that branches off the main road over the plank-and-rope **Carrick-a-rede Bridge,** a rattly structure that swings 80 ft. above the swirling waters and connects the island to the mainland; it will thrill you right down to your booties. (Bridge open May to mid-Sept. Free.)

Six miles west of Ballintoy is the world-famous **Giant's Causeway,** deservedly Northern Ireland's most famous sight. Forty thousand hexagonal columns of basalt form a honeycomb path from the foot of the cliffs into the sea. Many paths loop to the causeway from the nearby **Whitepark Bay HI youth hostel** (tel. (02567) 317 45; lockout 11am-2pm; curfew 11:30pm; £5.95, under 18 £4.95, nonmembers £1.50 extra; open Feb.-Nov.). Visit the **Causeway Visitors Centre** (tel. (02657) 318 55) to pick up the excellent trail leaflet (40p) that will guide you on the 8 miles back. (Center open July-Aug. daily 10am-7pm; Sept.-Oct. 10:30am-6pm; mid-March to May 11am-5pm. Causeway always open.)

Two miles west of the National Trust Visitor's Centre is **Bushmills,** home of the oldest functioning whiskey distillery in the world. (Tours with complimentary sample Mon.-Thurs. 9am-noon and 1:30-4:45pm, Fri. 9am-3:45pm, Sat. 10am-3:45pm. Call ahead at (02657) 315 21. £2, seniors £1.50, children free.)

■■■ GLENS OF ANTRIM

Between the Causeway Coast and Belfast, the rolling green hills and high moors of County Antrim drop through 9 deep valleys lush with greenery—the Glens of Antrim—down to the rocky coast. Two **bus** lines serve the area: the #162 service from Belfast (Mon.-Fri. 10/day, Sat. 8/day, Sun. 2/day) and the Antrim Coaster from Belfast to Coleraine (June-Sept. Mon.-Sat. 2/day). Most rides within the Glens average £2-4. Many hitch a ride along these lovely roads; cycling is, as always, fabulous.

Ballygally and Waterfoot Ballygally is an excellent gateway to the Glens. Both the Larne-Cushendall and Antrim Coaster buses stop right outside the friendly **Ballygally Hostel** (tel. (0574) 583 377; £5.95, under 18 £4.95, nonmembers add £1.50; open March-Dec. 21). Outside Ballygally, nearer to Larne, is the **Carnfunnock Country Park.** Pathways lead from the sundials of the time garden to a carefully constructed maze.

Five miles farther down the coast, the village of **Waterfoot** (Glenariff) guards Antrim's broadest glen and the town's namesake, Glenariff. Another 4 miles down the road in **Glenariff Forest Park,** waterfalls feed the River Glenariff (taxonomic originality was not an Irish strength). If you don't want to camp at **Glenariff Forest Park Camping,** 98 Glenariff Rd. (tel. (026673) 232), find one of the many farmers in the area who welcome campers (ask in town), or stay in Waterfoot itself. The Ballymena-Cushendun **bus** (Mon.-Fri. every 2hr., Sat. 4/day) passes the park entrance.

Cushendall, Cushendun, and Fair Head Cushendall, 2 miles north of Waterfoot, offers plenty of rooms and practical convenience for the glen explorer. For a womb of greenery, the **Cushendall HI youth hostel** (tel. (02667) 713 44) is a mile from town on Layde Rd. (£5.95, under 18 £4.95, nonmembers add £1.50. Open March-Dec. 21.) It would be hard to imagine a warmer welcome than the one you will receive from **Mrs. O'Neill** at Glendale, 46 Coast Rd. (tel. (02667) 714 95). Bikes and the like can be rented from **O'Kane's,** a mile outside of town on Ballycastle Rd. (tel. (02667) 718 00; £4/half-day, £6/day).

Farther north via an inland road that climbs up through the moors, the National Trust preserves the tiny village of **Cushendun.** The vast sandy beach and a set of pudding stone sea caves makes the village a terrific afternoon stopover. The **National Trust** (tel. (026674) 506) maintains an office at 1 Main St. (Open July-Aug. daily noon-6pm; Sept.-June Sat.-Sun. noon-6pm.) Catherine Scally at **The Villa,** 185 Torr Rd. (tel. (026674) 252), has a great B&B a mile from town on a particularly scenic portion of the Ulster Way (£13).Seven miles north of Cushendun, just south of Ballycastle, **Fair Head** draws international hikers to its majestic basalt cliffs. On a clear day, you can see Rathlin Island, Donegal, and Scotland.

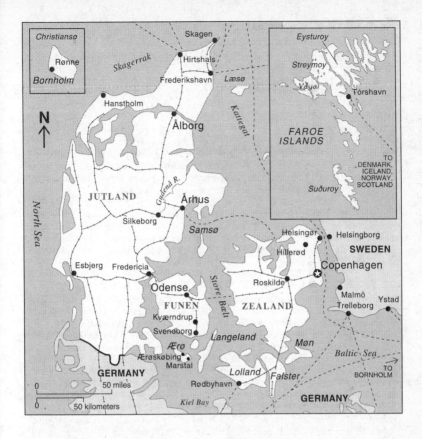

NORTHERN EUROPE

▨ Denmark (Danmark)

US$1 = 6.62kr (kroner, or DKK)		**10kr = US$1.51**
CDN$1 = 5.03kr		**10kr = CDN$1.99**
UK£1 = 10.30kr		**10kr = UK£0.97**
IR£1 = 9.60kr		**10kr = IR£1.04**
AUS$1 = 4.31kr		**10kr = AUS$2.32**
NZ$1 = 3.66kr		**10kr = NZ$2.73**
SAR1 = 1.38kr		**10kr = SAR7.26**
Country Code: 45		**International Dialing Prefix: 009**

The word "Dane" once struck fear into hearts all over Europe, but today the Vikings live only in tourist shops and brochures. On a short visit, Denmark seems such an overwhelmingly *good* country: the Danes (who rarely jaywalk) saved their Jews from the Nazis, invented Legos, spend tons of money on education, and make wonderful ice cream. The only threat Denmark poses is its cuteness. To immunize yourself against the onslaught of Hans Christian Andersen knickknacks, peruse *The Present Age,* by the wry Danish philosopher Søren Kierkegaard, and note that the conservative Danish government has curtailed the vast spending of the social-paradise days of the 1960s and 1970s. Denmark's foreign debt has stopped growing for the first time, but unemployment is rising (and the Social Democrats again say they're the only ones who know how to deal with it).

Well into the 16th century, the Danish crown ruled an empire that united Norway, Sweden, Iceland, and parts of Germany. Strategically positioned at the northern tip of continental Europe, Denmark was the bridge across which first Christianity, then the Protestant Reformation, and then the socialist movements of the late 19th century crossed into Scandinavia. Today, Danes are proud of their self-proclaimed label as *roligans* (*roli* means "peaceful" in Danish).

Danes joke that if you stand on a carton of beer you can see from one end of the country to the other, but Denmark is neither quite that flat nor quite that small—especially when you consider that Greenland, the world's largest island, is Danish territory. Though Copenhagen may be Denmark at its most festive, save time for the sea breezes and snug farmhouses of the countryside, where Danes often enjoy their annual five-week vacations.

GETTING THERE AND GETTING AROUND

Eurailpasses are valid on all state-run **DSB** routes. The **Nordturist pass,** available at rail stations and DSB travel agencies, allows 21 days of unlimited rail travel through Denmark, Sweden, Norway, and Finland (2nd class 1930kr, ages 12-25 1450kr). It's much cheaper than the similar ScanRail pass sold in the USA. If you're under 26 and make your journey during the first 2 weeks of the Danish university's summer vacation (usually late June-early July), you can take advantage of the **UNG pass** (450kr), good for train travel throughout Denmark (Bornholm and Faroe Islands excluded). Check ahead of time with a tourist office, or call **Dan Rail** at 33 14 17 01. Seat reservations are compulsory on some trains, including the plush IC (Intercity—30kr) and some international trains (20kr). They sometimes require long waits, so you may want to stick to the seat-yourself IR and Re trains. Towns not on rail lines are often served by regional buses that stop at the nearest train station.

To reach Copenhagen by train from the rest of Denmark or from any other country you'll need to use at least one **ferry;** however, you may hardly notice, since these ships are specially equipped with rails, and the trains just drive on and off. Trains from Odense cross from Nyborg to Korsør, trains from Hamburg cross from Puttgarden to Rødby Færge, trains from Berlin from Warnemünde to Gedser, and trains from Stockholm and from Helsingborg to Helsingør. Railpasses are also valid on the ferries from Hirtshals to Kristiansand in Norway, and Frederikshavn to Gothenburg in Sweden. The *Danmark Ferry Guide,* available at tourist offices, can help you sort out the dozens of smaller ferries that serve Denmark's outlying islands. Also, remember that while Denmark proper is small, it can take up to 11 hours to travel from the northernmost point of Jutland to Copenhagen.

Flat terrain, bike paths in the countryside, and bike lanes in the towns and cities make Denmark a cyclist's dream. **Bicycles** can be rented for 35-50kr per day from some tourist offices (not Copenhagen's), ubiquitous bicycle rental shops, and a few railway stations in North Zealand (Copenhagen, Helsingør, Hillerød, Klampenborg, and Lyngby). A 200kr deposit is ordinarily required. For quality maps (25-75kr) and tour information, contact the **Dansk Cyklist Forbund** (Danish Cycle Federation), Rømersgade 7, 1362 Copenhagen K (tel. 33 32 31 21; open Mon.-Wed. 10am-5pm, Thurs. 10am-7pm, Sat. 10am-2pm). It's often possible to tote bicycles on the train; check the pamphlet "Bikes and Trains in Denmark" for rules and prices.

DENMARK ESSENTIALS

Stacks of free tourist information in English, published by tourist boards, are an extra bonus when visiting Denmark. Good street maps and comprehensive city guides are waiting at almost every tourist office. Cirrus cash cards work in the red Eurocard machines in Denmark. Danish **phone** numbers are all 8 digits long, and you must dial the whole thing regardless of where you're calling from (no city codes). From pay phones, local calls require a minimum of 1kr, often 2kr. For directory information, dial 118 (free from pay phones). For international information, dial 113. For AT&T's **USA Direct,** dial 80 01 00 10; for MCI's **World Reach,** dial 80 01 00 22; for **Canada Direct,** dial 80 01 00 11. Denmark's **emergency** number is **112;** no coins are required.

Most every Dane speaks English, and a simple "Pardon?" will generally prompt a switch. The Danish alphabet adds *æ* (like the "e" in "egg,"*)*, *ø* (like the "i" in "first,"*)*, and *å* (still sometimes written as *aa;* like the "o" in "lord"*)* at the end; thus Århus would follow Viborg in an alphabetical listing of cities. One particularly useful word to know is *ikke* ("not"), which will help you to figure out such signs as "No smoking" and "Don't walk on the grass." If you're feeling more confident, try *tak* ("thank you"), *undskyld* (UND-scoold, "I'm sorry" or "Excuse me"), and *vær venlig* (VER VEN-li, "please"). Also remember that a *kastel* is a fort and a *slot* is a castle.

Accommodations and Camping The 104 **HI youth hostels** *(vandrerhjem)* throughout Denmark are well-equipped and well-run, have no age limit, and generally include rooms for families. All charge 55-84kr per bed; nonmembers pay 22kr extra for a guest stamp. You can generally feast on an unlimited breakfast for 38kr. Reception desks normally close between noon and 4pm and close for the day at 9 or 11pm. Reservations are required from September to mid-May, recommended in summer, and essential in hostels near beaches. They can be made by phone without a deposit, but you will be asked to show up by 5pm on the first night of the reservation or call that day to confirm. Cards (112kr) and an official hostel guide (free and available in English) are available at **Danmarks Vandrerhjem,** Vesterbrogade 39, 1620 København V (tel. 31 31 36 12; fax 3131 3626). (Open Mon - Thurs. 9am-4pm, Fri. 9am-3pm.) Other options are **hotels,** the cheapest of which run about 250kr for a single without shower, and cheaper rooms in **private homes,** which can often be arranged through tourist offices (100-150kr, 25kr fee).

Before you pitch a tent in Denmark, you must get the landowner's OK. You can also stay at one of the many official **campgrounds** (about 35kr/person/night). Campgrounds rank from one star (basic facilities) to three (the works). You'll need a camping pass; the Danish version is available at all campgrounds (24kr; family pass 48kr) and expires in January; one-time guest passes are 6kr (families 12kr), and international passes are accepted, too. In a pinch, an HI hostel card can sometimes do the trick. The **Dansk Camping Union,** Gammel Kongevej 74d, Copenhagen (tel. 31 21 06 04), will sell you passes and a campground handbook (65kr; also available in bookstores; open Mon.-Fri. 10am-5pm; May 15-July 15 Mon. and Wed.-Fri. 10am-5pm, Tues. 10am-6:30pm). Sleeping in train stations, parks, and streets is illegal.

For a fee of US$25, **Friends Overseas** will connect you with families along your itinerary in Denmark, Sweden, Norway, and Finland who are eager to introduce you to their communities; send a self-addressed, stamped envelope to 68-04 Dartmouth Street, Forest Hills, NY 11375, USA, for more information.

Food and Drink Beyond the "Danish," called *wienerbrød,* there are oodles of other baked goodies: flaky *kringle,* syrupy *brunsvigerkage,* and more. Danish ice cream, especially nut flavors like pistachio, is generally quite good, but better still are the cones it comes in, fresh-baked and filled with whipped cream, plus more cream and jam on top. Remember: ice cream doesn't have any calories if you eat it in a foreign country. For more substantial fare, Danes favor *smørrebrød* (pronounced "smorebro" as one syllable)—small, open-faced sandwiches with such toppings as cheese, smoked salmon, pickled herring, or raw beef. Wash these down with the national brews, Carlsberg and Tuborg. The many varieties of *akvavit*, a distilled liquor, are so expensive that they are served one shot (0.2 liter) at a time.

Menus and restaurant checks include both tax and service; what you see is what you pay. All-you-can-eat buffets are very popular in Denmark. Youth hostels offer unlimited breakfasts of cereal, rolls, cheese, and meat for around 36kr; restaurants may have buffets of pizza, herring, or Mongolian barbeque.

■■■ COPENHAGEN (KØBENHAVN)

A plethora of parks, waterways, and teeming pedestrian streets, the Danish capital is sensuous and exuberant—especially in summer. Copenhagen's countless street performers, outdoor cafés, ice cream vendors, and all-night discos epitomize Nordic *joie de vivre*. In winter, the outdoor seating is packed away and the harsh realities of life above the 55th parallel set in.

ORIENTATION AND PRACTICAL INFORMATION

Copenhagen lies on the east coast of the Danish island of **Zealand** (Sjælland). Malmö, in Sweden, is just across the sound (Øresund). Copenhagen's **Hovedbanegården** (Central Station) lies close to the city's heart. One block north of the station, **Vesterbrogade** passes **Tivoli** and **Rådhuspladsen** (the city's central square, where most bus lines originate) and then leads into **Strøget** (STROY-yet), the longest pedestrian thoroughfare in the world. The districts of Vesterbro, Nørrebro, Østerbro, and Christianshavn fan out from this central area.

Tourist Office: Danmarks Turistråd, Bernstorffsgade 1, 1577 København V (tel. 33 11 13 25), in the corner of Tivoli nearest the train station on the left. Everything you need to know about Copenhagen and the rest of Denmark (much of it hidden behind the counter), plus a free map and the indispensible *Copenhagen This Week*, which lists sights, prices, and hours. Open daily 9am-8pm; mid-April to mid-May daily 9am-6pm; mid-Sept. to mid-April Mon.-Fri. 9am-5pm, Sat. 9am-2pm. **Use It,** Rådhusstræde 13 (tel. 33 15 65 18), on the 2nd floor of the Huset complex 2 blocks east of Rådhuspladsen. A youth-oriented info office with heaps of free assistance, from bed-finding to passport retrieval. Mail held, ride and message boards, flash reports on rooming availability (list posted after-hours), and free baggage storage (1 day; 10kr each day thereafter; 50kr deposit). Publishes 3 helpful guides: *Copenhagen By Bike, Copenhagen By Foot,* and *Copenhagen By Bus.* Get their map (superior to the Turistråd's) and a copy of their guide *Playtime.* Open daily 9am-7pm; mid-Sept. to mid-June Mon.-Fri. 10am-4pm.
Budget Travel: Waastel, at Skoubogade 6 (tel. 33 14 46 33), sells student and youth discount tickets for trains and flights. Open Mon.-Fri. 10am-5pm. Similarly reduced ferry and plane fares also at **Kilroy Travel,** Skindergade 28 (tel. 33 11 00 44). Open Mon. 10am-7pm, Tues.-Fri. 10am-5pm, Sat. 10am-1pm. **Spies,** Nyropsgade 41 (tel. 33 32 15 00), arranges cheap charters to southern Europe. Open daily 6am-midnight.
Embassies: U.S., Dag Hammarskjölds Allé 24 (tel. 31 42 31 44; bus #1 or 6). Open Mon.-Fri. 8:30am-5pm. **Canada,** Kristen Bernikowsgade 1 (tel. 33 12 22 99; bus #27, 28, or 29). **U.K.,** Kastelsvej 36-40 (tel. 35 26 46 00; bus #1, 14, or 40). **Australia,** Kristianiagade 21 (tel. 35 26 22 44; bus #1, 6, or 9). Travelers from **New Zealand** should contact the British embassy. **Estonia** (tel. 33 93 34 62), **Latvia** (tel. 33 93 18 67), and **Lithuania** (tel. 33 93 48 17) all at H.C. Andersens Blvd. 38. **Poland,** Richelieusallé 10 (tel. 31 62 77 02).
Currency Exchange: At Central Station (open daily 6:45am-10pm; Oct. to mid-April 7am-9pm; 22-28kr commission on cash, 20kr/check with a 40kr minimum), the Tivoli office (open in summer daily noon-11pm), or the airport (open daily 6:30am-10pm; traveler's checks and cash only). Avoid the countless change counters on the Støget, which charge up to 9.5% commision. Most banks are clustered on Vesterbrogade, between the train station and Rådhuspladsen, and in the

pedestrian district. Regular bank hours Mon.-Wed. and Fri. 9:30am-4:30pm, Thurs. 9:30am-6pm. Commissions on traveler's checks are high (30-35kr min.), except at American Express.

American Express: Neither a borrower nor a lender be at their office on Amagertorv 18, on the Strøget (tel. 33 12 23 01). No commission on Traveler's Cheques (15kr commission on cash). Holds mail for AmEx card and Chequeholders only. Open Mon.-Fri. 9am-5pm, Sat. 9am-2pm, Sun. 10am-2pm; Sept.-May Mon.-Fri. 9am-5pm, Sat. 9am-noon.

Post Office: Tietgensgade 37-39, behind Central Station. Poste Restante. Open Mon.-Fri. 10am-6pm, Sat. 9am-1pm. **Postal Code:** 1500 København V. Branch office at Central Station. Open Mon.-Fri. 8am-10pm, Sat. 9am-4pm, Sun. and holidays 10am-5pm.

Telephones: Telecom Denmark, at Central Station. Call first and pay later (even by credit card). (Open Mon.-Fri. 8am-10pm, Sat.-Sun. 9am-9pm.) **Faxes** and **telegrams** can also be sent from here.

Flights: tel. 31 54 17 01. Bus #32 (32min.; 14kr or 1 stamp on yellow stripcard) from Rådhuspladsen and the SAS bus (20min.; 28kr) from Central Station both run to and from **Kastrup Airport.** SAS buses run to the airport 5:40am-9:45pm every 10-15min. and from the airport 6:30am-11:10pm every 10-15min.

Trains: All trains stop at **Hovedbanegården.** For information, call 33 14 17 01. To: Stockholm (429kr, under 26 325kr); Oslo (534kr, under 26 354kr); Berlin (323kr, under 26 250kr). The **InterRail Center** in the station, for all holders of BIJ, Nordturist, or Eurailpasses, is one of Copenhagen's most useful and friendly assets. Relax in a special lounge, wait for late-night connections, make phone calls, get information, and take showers (10kr/10min.). Free stove use (no oven) but no utensils. Message board great for finding lost travelers and making new friends. Open mid-June to mid-Sept. daily 6:30am-midnight.

Public Transportation: Bus information: tel. 36 45 45 45. **Train** information: tel. 33 14 17 01. Buses and S-trains (a cross between subways and suburban trains) operate on a shared zone system. Three zones cover central Copenhagen; 11 zones get you all the way to Helsingør. Buy tickets (2 zones 9.50kr, each additional zone 4.75kr) or, better, a yellow *rabatkort* (rebate card), which gets you 10 "clips" for 85kr (each clip good for 1 ride within 3 zones; more zones require more clips). Purchase the cards at kiosks or from bus drivers; they must be clipped in the machines provided each time you begin a journey. Ticket or clipped clip gives 1hr. of unlimited transfers on buses and trains. The 24-hr. bus and train pass permits free use of public transportation in nearly half of Zealand; buy it at the Tivoli tourist office or any railway station (65kr). All railpasses allow free travel on S-trains but not on buses. The **Copenhagen Card** allows unlimited free travel throughout North Zealand, discounts on ferries to Sweden, and free admission to most sights, including Tivoli (1 day 120kr, 2 days 200kr, or 3 days 250kr; available at hotels, travel agencies, tourist offices, and large train stations). Free maps issued by tourist office and Use It both show bus routes and include S-train network maps. Buses and trains run approx. Mon.-Sat. 5am-12:30am, Sun. 6am-12:30am; **night buses** cost an extra 9.50kr and run through the night, but less frequently and on fewer routes.

Ferries: The variety and number of ferry services from Copenhagen boggle the mind; consult the tourist office for more complete details. There are 4 basic groups. To **Norway: DFDS/Scandinavian Seaways** (tel. 33 11 22 55) sails daily departing at 5pm from Copenhagen to Oslo (16hr.; 630kr with berth, 405kr without, 20% Eurail discount, bigger student discounts through Kilroy Travel; see Budget Travel above). To **Sweden:** trains from Copenhagen to the rest of Scandinavia cross over the Helsingør-Helsingborg **Scanlines** ferry at no extra charge. **Hydrofoils** (tel. 33 12 80 88) cross hourly between Havnegade at the end of Nyhavn in Copenhagen and Malmö, Sweden (45min.; 85kr, 64kr with railpasses). To **Poland:** **Polferries** (tel. 33 11 46 45) sails Mon., Wed., and Thurs. at 10pm, Sun. at 11:30am from Nordre Toldbod off Esplanaden in Copenhagen to Świnoujście in the northwest corner of Poland, where there are rail connections to the rest of the country (9½-10½hr.; 280kr, 230kr with ISIC). To **Bornholm:** See the Bornholm section.

Taxis: tel. 31 35 35 35. Expensive. Central Station to Kastrup Airport, 130kr.

Bike Rental: Dan Wheel, Colbjørnsensgade 3 (tel. 31 21 22 27). From 35kr/day, 165kr/week; 200kr deposit. Open Mon.-Fri. 9am-5:30pm, Sat.-Sun. 9am-2pm. **DSB Cykelcenter,** Reventlowsgade 11 (tel. 33 14 07 17), in the train station building. From 40kr/day, 185kr/week; 200kr deposit. Repairs too. Open Mon.-Fri. 7am-6pm.

Hitchhiking: You have a better chance of ice skating across Egypt in July. Try **Use It's** ride boards (see Tourist Offices above) instead. **Interstop,** 54A Vesterbrogade (tel. 31 23 24 40) hooks hitchers up with drivers for a fee of .30kr/km.

Luggage Storage: Use It is good but has limited hours (see Budget Travel above). In **Central Station,** luggage lockers accessible Mon.-Sat. 5:30am-1am and Sun. 6am-1am (20kr per 24 hrs.), and the **DSB Garderobe** is open daily 6:30am-12:15am (suitcases 10kr, backpacks 15kr/24hrs.).

Bookstores: The Book Trader, Skindergade 23 (tel. 33 12 06 69), sells second-hand English books (20-30kr) and offers a 50% discount on exchanges. Open Mon.-Thurs. 11am-5:30pm, Fri. 11am-7pm, Sat. 10am-1pm. Pick up the latest English tabloids at **The British Bookshop,** 8 Badstrustræde (tel. 33 93 11 15). Open Mon.-Thurs. 10am-5:30pm, Fri. 10am-6pm, Sat. 10am-2pm.

Laundromats: Just about everywhere; look for the sign *"møntvask."* At Borgergade 2, Nansensgade 39, and Istedgade 45. Most open daily 8am-10pm (25-30kr). Facilities at the 2 main HI hostels (25kr).

Travelers With Disabilites: Contact the **Danish Tourist Board** (tel. 33 11 13 25) for a copy of *Access in Denmark: A Travel Guide for the Disabled* (60kr).

Women's Centers: Kvindehuset, Gothersgade 37 (tel. 33 14 28 04), runs a bookstore-café. (Open Mon.-Fri. noon-7:30pm.) **Kvindecentret Dannerhuset,** Nansensgade 1 (tel. 33 14 16 76). Overnight shelter for women who have been attacked.

Gay and Lesbian Services: National Organization for Gay Women and Men, Knabrostræde 3 (tel. 33 13 19 48), provides information and advice. Distributes *Copenhagen Gay and Lesbian Guide,* a listing of gay/lesbian nightspots and services in Copenhagen (free). Also operates a small bookstore and library (open Mon.-Fri. 5pm-7pm).

Crisis hotline: tel. 33 66 33 33. **Den Sociale Døgnvagt** offers counseling for travelers experiencing difficult times.

Pharmacy: Steno Apotek, Vesterbrogade 6c (tel. 33 14 82 66). Open 24 hrs. From 8pm-8am Mon.-Fri., 2pm-8am Sat., and all day Sun., ring for entrance; 10.25kr fee on purchases except for prescriptions written that day.

Medical Assistance: Doctors on Call (tel. 33 93 63 00) provides appointments with medical practitioners. (Mon.-Fri. 9am-4pm; at other times, call tel. 31 12 00 41. Doctor's visits cost 120-350kr.

Hospital: Rigshospitalet, Blegdamsvej 9 (tel. 35 45 35 45; bus #3, 10, 43, 84). Denmark offers free medical care to visitors.

Emergencies: Police, Ambulance, and **Fire:** tel. 112. No coins needed from public phones. **Police station** is at Nyropsgade 20 (tel. 33 91 14 48).

ACCOMMODATIONS

Like all of Scandanavia, Copenhagen is rich in hostels and campgrounds but poor in budget hotels. In summer the 3 HI hostels fill early, despite their remote locations. (Allow for at least 19kr to cover bus fare there and back.) Reservations are especially advisable during Karneval (mid-May), the Roskilde Festival (late June), and the Copenhagen Jazz Festival (early July). Failing that, consult **Use It** or **Værelseanvisning,** a hotel reservation service located in the Copenhagen Tourist Information office near Tivoli. (Open daily 9am-midnight; mid-Sept. to mid-April Mon.-Fri 9am-5pm, Sat. 9am-2pm. 13kr fee/person.) Both give a listing of hostels and budget hotels. Slumbering in a park or the station is not a good idea, nor is it legal.

Hostels

YMCA Inter Point, KFUK, Store Kannikestræde 19 (tel. 33 11 30 31). Super-central location. 60 beds in a ballroom divided into 5-bed cubicles. You'll need an

Inter Point pass, which costs 25kr and is good for one calendar year. Reception open daily 8am-noon, 2:30pm-6pm, and 7pm-1:30. Lockout 10am-2pm. Curfew 12:30am. 50kr. Breakfast 20kr. Sheets 20kr. Bike rentals 50kr. Open July to mid-Aug. Also at **Vesterbros KFUM,** Valdemarsgade 15 (tel. 31 31 15 74). Approx. 40 beds. Open July 15-Aug. 15.

Københavns Vandrerhjem (HI), Herbergvejen 8 (tel. 31 28 97 15), in Bellahøj. In a park with a small lake, 15-min. bus or bike ride from Rådhuspladsen. Take bus #2 (direction "Bronshøj" or "Bellahøj") to Fuglsang Allé, or night bus #902. The Godthåbsvej S-train stop is about a 15-min. walk south down Godthåbsvej, but you'll have to transfer at Ryparken to get downtown. 250 beds (in 4- to 6-bed dorms) fill quickly. Reception and lobby open 24 hrs. Lockout 10am-1pm. No curfew. 65kr, nonmembers 87kr. Breakfast 35kr. Backpack-size lockers, optional lock rental 5kr, deposit 20kr. No kitchen. Laundry 25kr/load. Open mid-Feb.-Dec. Wheelchair accessible.

Sleep-In, Per Henrik Lings Allé 6 (tel. 31 26 50 59). From central station, S-train to Østerport and walk up Hammarskjülds to Rådhuspladsen, take bus #1 to "Parken", or #6 or night bus #906 to Sankt Jakobs Plads. 385 beds in a converted ice rink (it's not cold) partitioned into 2- to 4-bed cubicles. Clean, fun and not too far out of town (about 15 min.). The best last-minute place; they'll virtually always find you a spot to crash. Lockout noon-4pm. Dorms 85kr. Singles 120kr. Doubles 240kr. Breakfast included. Thursday night BBQ's (25kr) and a great juice bar. Free lockers, deposit 20kr. Open July-Aug. At the highest point of the high season (July 25-Aug.15), another 320 beds open up down the street.

Copenhagen Youth Hostel (HI), Sjællandsbroen 55 (tel. 32 52 29 08). Take bus #46 (Mon.-Fri. 6am-5pm) from Central Station or #37 (destination Valby Station) from Holmens Bro (across the street from the front of Christiansborg Castle) to Sjællandsbroen, or take the S-train to Valby station and bus #37 from there. Good place to meet screaming Scandinavian children and their overly-permissive parents. 528 beds—the largest hostel in Europe. Slow reception and long lines mean 20-40min. wait to check in. Hotel-like, lockable 2- and 5-bed rooms. Reception open 1pm-10am, bathrooms closed 9am-1pm. No curfew. 65kr, nonmembers 87kr. Breakfast 35kr. Dinner 55kr. Sheets 25kr. Laundry 25kr/load. Kitchen. Free use of safe. Wheelchair access. Open Jan. 2-Dec. 20.

City Public Hostel, Absalonsgade 8 (tel. 31 31 20 70), in the Vesterbro Ungdomsgård. From the station, walk away from the Rådhuspladsen on Vesterbrogade (10 min.). Central location makes it worth the price. In a quiet park, near the red light district. 206 beds. Room size varies; the largest has 68 beds. Reception open 24 hrs. Lockout 10am-noon. 95kr, with all-you-can-eat breakfast 110kr. Kitchen, BBQ facilities. Small unlocked lockers free, locks sold for 30kr. Sleeping bags allowed. Open early May-Aug.

Private Homes and Hotels

Værelseanvisning will find you a room in a hotel or private home (often a haul from the center of town) for a booking fee of 13kr per bed. Private home prices start at 150kr per person. Use It can often beat these prices and does not charge a fee.

Mike's Guest House, Kirkevænget 13 (tel. 36 45 65 40), near Frederiksberg Castle and the Zoological Gardens. Take bus #6 from Rådhuspladsen. Lush gardens and some private balconies are paradise for the weary traveler. 5th-floor "The Sky Light" restaurant serves daily 40-50kr dinner. Reception open 24hr. Singles 200kr. Doubles 260kr. Triples 350kr. Guest kitchen (30kr), laundry facilities (25kr), and free showers. Several cheap supermarkets in the vicinity.

Søfolkenes Mindehotel, Peder Skramsgade 19 (tel. 33 13 48 82), conveniently located near Nyhavn. A seafarer's hotel with clean, simply furnished rooms and an earnest, affable staff. Reception open 24 hrs. Singles 245kr. Doubles 430kr. Triples 600kr. Breakfast included.

Hotel Jørgensen, Rømersgade 11 (tel. 33 13 81 86), in a quiet area about 20 min. from Central Station. Cramped but clean. Reception open 8am-midnight. Coed basement dorm 89kr. Singles 360kr. Doubles 460-575kr. Lockers free (20kr deposit). Huge breakfast included. Rents bikes (50kr with 300kr deposit).

Camping

Bellahøj Camping, Hvidkildevej (tel. 31 10 11 50), 5km from the center. Take bus #2 (direction "Bellahøj") or night bus #902 from Rådhuspladsen. Reception open 24 hrs. 40kr. Kitchen facilities and free showers. Danish breakfast 25kr. Café and market open 7am-midnight. Rents bikes (35kr). Open June-Aug.

Absalon Camping, Korsdalsvej 132 (tel. 31 41 06 00), 9km away. Take S-train line B or L to Brøndbyøster, then walk 10 min. north through the housing projects (ask for directions at the station). 48kr. Reception open 7am-10pm. Also has cabins (195kr plus 42kr/person), store, and laundry.

FOOD

In Copenhagen, food is a party. Stroll down the **Strøget** with peach juice dripping down your chin, munch pickled herring by the waterfront and sample the goodies staring out of every bakery window. All this comes cheaply if you avoid the touristy sit-down restaurants, especially in the pedestrian district and Tivoli. Picnic in a park or by the harbor on take-out *smørrebrød* (from 20kr each, but you'll need more than one), or shop for your own in the discount supermarket, **Fakta,** Landemærket 3, near the round tower (open Mon.-Fri. 8am-7pm, Sat. 8am-2pm). Supermarkets—except the one in Central Station (open daily 8am-midnight)—are closed Sundays. An open **market** occurs daily except Sunday in Israels Plads near Nørreport Station for much of the year (Mon.-Fri. 7am-6pm, Sat. 7am-2pm), and scads of fruit stalls line Strøget. For cheap hot meals, your best bet will be pizza or pasta at one of the many Italian joints that line the city's open spaces, some with outdoor seating.

Centrum Smørrebrød, Vesterbrogade 6c, near Scala and Tivoli. Scrumptious take-out sandwiches for 20-30kr. Open 24 hrs. The affiliated **City Smørrebrød** at Gothersgade 10 is open Mon.-Fri. 8am-7pm.

Nyhavns Færgekro, Nyhavn 5 (tel. 33 15 15 88). Sit indoors or along the canal. Lunch on all-you-can-eat herring (65kr), over a dozen varieties. You can't get much more Danish than that. Dinners around 130kr. Open daily 11:30am-4pm and 5-11:30pm.

Riz Raz, Kompagnistræde 20. Savory all-you-can-eat vegetarian Mediterranean buffet often includes pizza and falafel. 39kr before 5pm, 59kr thereafter. Dinner kebabs 69-145kr (includes buffet). Open daily 11:30am-midnight.

Pasta Basta, Valkendorfsgade 22. Classy establishment with a cold pasta buffet for 69kr, entrees 45-200kr. Open Sun.-Wed. 11:30am-3pm, Thurs.-Sat. 11:30am-5am.

ReeF N' BeeF, Landemarket 27, near Kultorvet. A little piece of Australia in the middle of Denmark. Serves up the best alligator (188kr) and kangaroo (155kr) in Copenhagen. Dinner entrees 85kr-166kr. Open daily 5-10pm.

Alexander's Original Pizza House, Lille Kannikestræde 5. All-you-can-eat pizza and salad 49kr. Open daily noon-11:30pm.

Den Grønne Kælder, 10 Klarehoderne. Fights the good vegetarian fight. Specializes in hummus (small plate 18kr, large 35kr) and veggie burgers (28kr, served with 2 salads). Daliy vegetarian dishes 28-45kr. Open Mon.-Sat. 11am-9pm.

SIGHTS

A fairly compact city, Copenhagen is best seen on foot or by bike. Pick up *Copenhagen This Week* and begin with the celebrated **Tivoli** amusement park. Founded in 1843, it doesn't have the most thrilling rides in the world, but parts are awfully pretty. The wild swans—each painted differently—give a terrific, spinning panorama of the city's skyline. In the evening, the park becomes a spectacle of colorful, illuminated ponds, outdoor concerts, and fireworks (Wed. and Fri.-Sun.). (Open late April to mid-Sept. daily 10am-midnight. Children's rides begin at 11:30am, more serious rides from 1:30pm. 35kr; 10kr discount before 1pm. Single-ride tickets 8kr, 10 for 70kr; most rides cost 2 tickets. Ride-pass 125kr.)

Next to Tivoli, the **Ny Carlsberg Glyptotek,** funded by the Carlsberg beer empire, displays ancient, classical, and impressionist art, including a fine collection of Roman portrait busts. The museum centers on a glass-domed tropical plant conservatory. (Open Tues.-Sun. 10am-4pm; Sept.-April Tues.-Sat. noon-3pm, Sun. 10am-4pm. 15kr, free with ISIC, Sun. and Wed. free.) Nearby, the **National Museum,** at Ny Vestergade 10, contains Danish and European archaeological discoveries. This year their giant Viking exhibit returns from its sojourn in Paris. (Open Tues.-Sun. 10am-5pm. 30kr. Closed on national holidays.) Across the canals on Slotsholmen Island is **Christiansborg Palace,** the meeting place of the *Folketing* (Parliament). (Hourly tours Sun.-Fri. 10am-4pm; Oct.-May Sun. 10am-4pm. Free.)

Continuing north, you'll reach **Kongens Nytorv,** the departure point for harbor and canal boat tours. (July-Aug. every ½hr. 10am-7:30pm; May-June and Sept. hourly 10am-6pm, 50min., 15-36kr.) Boats also leave from **Gammel Strand** (tel. 33 13 31 05 for info) across the canal from Thorvaldsens Museum. Kongens Nytorv marks the ritzy endpoint of **Strøget,** the pedestrian street; the **Royal Theater** here is home to the world-famous Royal Danish Ballet. Half-price tickets are available the day of the performance at **Nørreport Kiosk** on the corner of Fiolstræde and Nørrevold opposite the Nørreport Rail Station. (Open Mon.-Fri. noon-7pm, Sat. noon-3pm; 40-100kr. Call 36 66 22 22 for information.) East of the square is **Nyhavn,** a picturesque canal crammed with yachts and lined with restaurants, where Hans Christian Andersen wrote his first fairy tale. Farther north is **Amalienborg Palace,** a group of four 18th century Rococo mansions that serves as the official royal residence. The changing of the guard takes place at noon on the brick plaza. The western approach to the plaza frames a view of the impressive dome of the 19th-century Romanesque Baroque **Marmorkirken** (marble church). The inside of the dome is almost as elaborate. (Open Mon.-Sat. 11am-2pm. Sunday mass 10:30am. Free.) A few blocks north of Amalienborg is the intriguing **Frihedsmuseet** (Resistance Museum), Churchillparken, which chronicles the Nazi occupation of 1940-1945. While proudly documenting Denmark's heroic rescue of almost all its Jews, the museum also examines the initial period of resigned acceptance of German "protection," when the Danish government arrested anti-Nazi saboteurs. (Open Tues.-Sat. 10am-4pm, Sun. 10am-5pm; mid-Sept. to April Tues.-Sat. 11am-3pm, Sun. 11am-4pm. Free.) On the other side of **Kastellet,** a 17th-century fortress-turned-park (open daily 6am-dusk) is Edvard Eriksen's statue of **Den Lille Havfrue** (The Little Mermaid), the model for all those souvenir paperweights you've been seeing. Watch the sun set over posing tour groups.

The area around Østervoldgade and Sølvgade houses Copenhagen's finest parks and gardens. The **Botanisk Have** (Botanical Gardens), at the corner of Østervolgade and Gothersgade, flower daily from 8:30am-6pm (Sept.-late March 8:30am-4pm; free). Across the street is **Rosenborg Palace and Gardens** (Rosenborg Slot); the palace (entrance on Østervoldgade) houses a collection of royal treasures, including the crown jewels and 3 life-size silver lions. (Open daily 10am-4pm; Sept.-late Oct. and May daily 11am-3pm; late Oct.-April Tues., Fri., and Sun. 11am-2pm. To both 35kr, children 5kr.) Nearby, at Rømersgade 22, the gripping **Arbejdermuseet** (Workers' Museum) graphically portrays the lives of those who could not afford royal treasures. (Open Tues.-Fri. 10am-3pm, Sat.-Sun. 11am-4pm. 25kr, children 15kr.) Three blocks north, at Østervoldgade and Sølvgade—in yet another garden— is the **Statens Museum for Kunst** (State Museum of Fine Arts), worth a visit for its Matisses and Dutch Masters. (Open Tues.-Sun. 10am-4:30pm. 20kr, students and seniors 10kr.)

Back in the pedestrian district, climb the unique spiral ramp of the **Rundetårn** (round tower) for a good view of the city's spires. (Open daily 10am-8pm; Sept.-March Mon.-Sat. 10am-5pm. 12kr, 5kr children.) Southeast of downtown, in the Christianshavn district, lies **Christiania** (entrances on Prinsessegade). This utopian "free city" was founded in 1971 by youthful squatters in abandoned military barracks. A source of continuing controversy, Christiania accepts visitors, and you can wander among its houses, workshops, and meadows. With lots of hash and pot and mess, it's not everyone's cup of tea. Always ask before taking pictures. Beer enthusiasts can tour the city's breweries: **Carlsberg,** Ny Carlsbergvej 140 (take bus #6 west from Rådhuspladsen; tours Mon.-Fri. at 11am and 2pm; meet at the Elephant Gate), and **Tuborg,** Strandvejen 54 (take bus #6 north from Rådhuspladsen; ½hr.-tours Mon.-Fri. at 10am, 12:30pm, and 2:30pm). Both tours are free and both offer free beer (about 2 bottles/person) and soda at the end of the tour.

ENTERTAINMENT

Copenhagen's weekends often begin on Wednesday, and nights rock until 5am. The central pedestrian district reverberates with populous bars and discos, while Kongens Nytorv contains fancier joints and Nyhavn exudes the salty charisma of moored ships. For current events listings, consult *Copenhagen This Week* or contact Use It, which also distributes a lesbian and gay guide to the city. Avid drinkers might consider the "death route," including Vestergade and Skt. Petersstræde just off the Strøget. University students liven up the cheaper bars in the Nørrebro area.

Huset, Rådhusstræde 13. A relaxed, unpretentious cultural center. Use It is on the 2nd floor. The cinema often features film series for around 45kr. On the ground floor, **Kafé pår Zalü** overflows into a student-filled courtyard. Coffee 10kr, beer 17kr. Open daily noon-2am. **Bar Bue,** a techno disco/club jolts to a start later in the evening. Open mid-Aug. to mid-June Mon.-Fri. 10pm-2am, Sat.-Sun. 6pm-2am. Cover 80kr. Upstairs, **Græshoppen** screens American and Danish films (with English subtitles) for 30kr. Open 5:30pm-midnight.

Mojo, Løngangstræde 21. A jamming spot for blues. Open Sun.-Thurs. 8pm-4am, Fri.-Sat. 8pm-5am. Cover Fri.-Sat. 40kr.

Pan Café, Knabrostræde 3. A popular lesbian and gay center. Open Sun.-Tues. 2pm-3am, Wed.-Thurs. 2pm-4am, Fri.-Sat. 2pm-6am. Cover on weekends 55kr. Dancing nightly after 10pm . Café and disco only for women on Thurs.

hos Simon, Løngangstræde 37. Dance like you have never danced. Open Tues.-Thurs. 8pm-1am, Fri.-Sat. 8pm-5am. Live music Fri.-Sat. 11pm-4am. 20kr cover.

Montmartre, Nørregade 41. Regular live music and exhausting all-night dancing. Café open Mon.-Sat. 3pm-midnight. Club night (Thurs.-Sat. midnight-5am) followed by breakfast for the sore and sleepy (served Sat.-Sun. 5-8am). Cover Fri.-Sat. 20kr. Live music on irregular weekdays (9am-1am; cover 50-250kr; call the ticket office (3-7pm) at 33 12 78 36 for more info).

Café Sommersko, Kronprinsensgade 6 (tel. 33 14 81 89), is one of the most popular student hangouts in the city. Open Mon.-Wed. 9am-1am, Thurs.-Sat. 9am-2am, Sun. 10am-1am; beer 18kr. **Bananrepblukken,** Nørrebrogade 13 (tel. 31 39 79 21), is another good place to explore student nightlife.

The **Copenhagen Jazz Festival** draws top musicians from around the globe (July 1-10 in 1994); make accommodations reservations early. **Karneval,** a Brazilian dance extravaganza, is slated for Whitsund. The **Mermaid Theater,** 27, Sct. Pederstræde (tel. 33 11 43 03), presents everything from Twain to Kierkegaard (in English), after which the audience is invited to discuss their reactions to the play with the performers over coffee. (Performances Mon.-Sat. 8:30pm; tickets 65-125kr).

■ Near Copenhagen

Royal castles, scenic beaches, and a stunning museum are all within easy reach of Copenhagen by train. Two rail lines go north from Copenhagen: a more or less coastal line up to Helsingør (paralleled by the very coastal and more scenic bus #388), and an S-train line to Hillerød. **Klampenborg** and **Bellevae,** close in on the coastal line (alternatively, at the end of S-train line C), both offer topless beaches, while **Bakken,** the world's oldest amusement park, delivers more thrills (magnified by untranslated warning signs and unknown safety codes) but is far less ornate than

Tivoli. (Open March-Aug. daily 2pm-midnight. Just north from the train station, turn left, cross the bridge over the road, and head through the park. Free.)

Rungsted and Humlebæk Rungsted, up the coast from Klampenborg, has recently opened the **Karen Blixen Museum,** Rungsted Strandvej 111, which occupies the home of the late author, who wrote as Isak Dinesen; Meryl Streep portrayed her in the film *Out of Africa*. Many of Blixen's Gothic tales paint a sweeping picture of 19th-century Denmark. (Open daily 10am-5pm; Oct.-April Wed.-Sun. 1-4pm. 30kr, children free.) **Humlebæk,** yet a stretch further up the coast, would be completely undistinguished were it not home to the spectacular **Louisiana Museum of Modern Art**. Named after the 3 wives of the estate's original owner, all called Louisa, the museum contains works by Picasso, Warhol, Giacometti, Lichtenstein, and other 20th-century deities. Overlooking the sea and the Swedish coast, the remarkable building and its sculpture-studded grounds are themselves well worth the trip. Follow the signs 1.5km north from the Humlebæk station or snag bus #388. Evening classical concerts on summer Wednesdays cost 85kr, including museum admission. Call 42 19 07 19 for information. (Open Mon.-Tues. and Thurs.-Fri. 10am-5pm, Wed. 10am-10pm, Sat.-Sun. 10am-6pm; mid-Sept. to late Jan. Mon.-Tues. and Thurs. 10am-5pm, Wed. and Fri. 10am-10pm, Sat.-Sun. 10am-6pm. 45kr, students with ISIC and seniors 35kr.)

Helsingør and Hillerød Farther north, castles give evidence of the Danish monarchy's fondness for lavish architecture. Take arms against your sea of troubles at **Helsingør** (Elsinor in Shakespeare's *Hamlet*), the major ferry departure point for Sweden; its many liquor stores cater to Swedes seeking to avoid their country's outrageous fortune of an alcohol tax (from Central Station 3/hr., 50min., 11 zones). **Kronborg Slot** was built in the 15th century to collect tolls from passing merchant ships. Viking chief and Danish national hero Holger Danske sleeps in the castle's dungeon; legend has it that he arises to face menaces to Denmark. The royal apartments boast some impressive furnishings, including a pair of fascinating Renaissance globes. The castle also houses the Danish maritime museum. (Open daily 10:30am-5pm; April and Oct. Tues.-Sun. 11am-4pm; Nov.-March Tues.-Sun. 11am-3pm. To castle 20kr, to casemates and dungeons 10kr; to maritime museum 34kr.) An **HI youth hostel** (tel. 49 21 16 40) stands by the beach at Ndr. Strandvej 24. Take bus #340 from the station. (64kr, non-members 86kr. Reception open 8am-noon and 4-9pm. Sheets 40kr. Free showers and kitchen. Open Feb.-Nov.) The **tourist office** (tel. 49 21 13 33) in Helsingør is to the left of the train station as you exit. They book rooms (25kr fee) and provide ferry info. (Open Mon.-Fri. 9:30am-7pm, Sat. 10am-6pm; mid-Aug. to mid-June Mon.-Fri. 9:30am-5pm, Sat. 10am-1pm).

Moated **Frederiksborg Slot** in **Hillerød** is the most impressive of the castles north of Copenhagen, featuring exquisite gardens, brick ramparts, and the **National Historical Museum,** exhibiting portraits of several centuries' worth of prominent Danes. Concerts are given on the famous **Esaias Compenius organ** in the chapel Sundays at 5pm. Call 42 26 04 39 for information. (Castle open daily 10am-5pm; Oct. 10am-4pm; Nov.-March 11am-3pm; April 10am-4pm. 30kr, students with ID 10kr, children 5kr.) Along the train line halfway between Hillerød and Helsingør is **Fredensborg Castle,** built in 1722 and still in use as the spring and autumn royal residence. When Queen Margrethe is in, there is a colorful changing of the guard. The park is free and open year-round. (Castle open July daily 1-5pm. 10kr, children 5kr.) You can peek into the palace gardens from the famous **Fredensborg youth hostel (HI),** Østrupvej 3 (tel. 42 28 03 15), 1km from the train station. (84kr, non-members 106kr. Reception 8am-11pm). Hillerød is at the end of **S-train** lines A and E from Copenhagen (40min. via Lyngby, 32.25kr or 3 clips on the yellow *rabatkort)* and also accessible direct from Helsingør by train (30min.).

Roskilde and Møns Roskilde, 25-30 minutes west of Copenhagen (33.25kr or 3 clips on the yellow *rabatkort*), is home to much Danish history; King Harald Bluetooth built the first Christian church in Denmark here in 980, and 38 Danish monarchs repose in the **Roskilde Domkirke** cathedral. The **Viking Ship Museum,** down on the shore of Roskilde Fjord, houses the dinosaur-like remains of 5 vessels. The ships were sunk about 1060 AD and are somewhat the worse for wear, but the reconstructions moored in the harbor outside aid the imagination. (Open daily 9am-5pm; Nov.-March 10am-4pm. 28kr includes 15-min. film.) A vegetable, fruit, flea, and flower **market** transforms Roskilde on Wed. and Sat. (8am-2pm). In late June, Roskilde hosts one of northern Europe's largest **music festivals,** with rock, jazz, and folk bands from all over the planet. U2 and Talking Heads played here before they were big. (June 30-July 3 in 1994; 4 days 600kr, Sun. only 300kr. Free camping fills quickly.) Roskilde's **HI youth hostel,** amid rolling fields on Hørhusene 61 (tel. 42 35 21 84; bus #601 or 604, then a 1.5km walk), is geared toward young families (75kr, non-members 97kr; breakfast 38kr). You can **camp** by the beach at **Vigen Strandpark,** Baunehøjvej 7-9 (tel. 46 75 79 96), 4km north of town on bus #602. If you don't have the required 24kr camping card, they'll accept an HI hostel card. (40kr/person. Open early April to mid-Sept. Reception 7am-10pm.) The **tourist office** (tel. 42 35 27 00) near the cathedral can suggest walking tours around the enchanting old quarter and makes bookings in local hotels. (25kr fee. Open Mon.-Fri. 9am-8pm, Sat. 9am-5pm, Sun. 10am-1pm.)

To see what H.C. Andersen called one of the most beautiful spots in Denmark, travel south from Copenhagen 2 hours to the white cliffs of the isle of **Møns.** Take the train to Vordingborg, bus #62 to Stege, then bus #852 to Møns Klint. Be warned: only 3 buses go out and back per day, and the last usually leaves before 4pm.

■■■ BORNHOLM

East of Denmark and southwest of Sweden, the gorgeous island of Bornholm lures vacationers to its expansive sand beaches, cozy fishing villages, and winding bicycle paths. The red-roofed cliffside villas may remind you of southern Europe, but the flowers and tidy half-timbered houses are irretrievably Danish.

From Copenhagen, the fastest way here is the **Bornholmerpilen** service (tel. 56 95 95 95, daily 9am-11pm) that leaves Kastrup Havn near Copenhagen's airport, with bus connections to Central Station (June-Aug. 3/day, 4-5hr., 149kr, seniors and children 9kr). Hydrofoils whisk passengers to Malmö, Sweden, with connections to Ystad and Rønne. The **Bornholmstraffiken** car ferries (tel. 33 13 18 66) are slower and cheaper, and sail overnight from Kvæsthusbroen 2 in Copenhagen (daily, 11:30pm, in summer also Thurs.-Mon. 8:30am; 7hr.; 174kr) and from Ystad in Sweden (3/day, 2½hr., 102kr). The #866 **Bornholmerbussen** service runs from Central Station in Copenhagen to the Ystad ferry, cutting travel time to 5½ hours (1/day, in summer 3/day. Copenhagen-Bornholm 140kr, children 90kr. For reservations call 44 68 44 00.) All ferries run to the harbor in Rønne, where you can rent a **bike** for 50kr at **Cykel-Centret,** Søndergade 7 (open Mon.-Fri. 7:30am-5:30pm, Sat.-Sun. 7:30am-noon and 2-4pm; Sept.-May Mon.-Fri. 8am-5:30pm, Sat. 9am-noon) or for 40-50kr at **Bornholms Cykeludlejning,** Havnegade 11, near the tourist office (open May-Sept. daily 7am-4pm). Bornholm has an efficient local BAT bus service (30kr to Gudhjem or Sandvig-Allinge, 37.50kr to Svanehe), and there are numerous cycling paths. Hostel rooms on Bornholm must be reserved in advance.

Rønne, Gudhjem, and Sandvig-Allinge Part workaday port and part festive resort town, Rønne, on Bornholm's western coast, is brimming with outdoor cafés and red and yellow houses on winding cobblestone streets. **Den Grimme Alling** restaurant, St. Torvegade 22, offers an all-you-can-eat Ugly Duckling Buffet for 69.50kr or lunch dishes for 39kr. (Open daily noon-2:30pm and 5:30-10:30pm.) The **youth hostel (HI),** Arsenalvej 12 (tel. 56 95 13 40; fax 56 95 01 32), is in a quiet, woodsy area. (65-75k. Reception open May-Oct. 8am-10pm.) **Campgrounds** at Strandvejen 4 (tel. 56 95 23 20; open May-Sept.) and Antoinettevej 2 (tel. 56 95 22 81; open May-Sept.) charge 38kr per person. The Rønne **tourist office** (tel. 56 95 95 00), a mirrored-glass building behind the gas station by the Bornholmstraffiken terminal, can help plan your stay on the island and will book you a room in a private home. (135-175kr. Open daily 7am-11:30pm; Oct.-May Mon.-Fri. 9am-4pm.)

The robust towns of **Gudhjem** and **Sandvig-Allinge** anchor Bornholm's spectacular north coast. Both have a hostel, a tourist office, bus connections, and campgrounds. Just outside of **Sandvig** is the **Vandrerhjem Sjøljan (HI),** Hammershusvej 94 (tel. 56 48 03 62; reception open 8am-10pm; 75kr; open June-Oct.). Another km down the same road sulks **Hammershus,** a thrilling heap of stone perched above the sea. Free and always open, it is northern Europe's largest castle ruin. In the middle of the north coast, **Gudhjem**'s harbor appeared in the Academy-Award-winning film *Pelle the Conqueror*. Its popular **Vandrerhjem Sct. Jørgens Gaard (HI)** (tel. 56 48 50 35), right by the harbor and across from the bus stop, has a kitchen of greatness (75kr). A small beach is 1km away, to the right of the harbor.

FUNEN (FYN)

Funen is Denmark's garden. Colorful flowerbeds grace nearly every house, and diverse wildflowers carpet the coast. A bridge connects to Jutland on the east, and regular ferry service shuttles to and from Zealand. The IC trains from Copenhagen cross from Korsør on Zealand to Nyborg on Funen, and require seat reservations.

■■■ ODENSE

Hans Christian Andersen's birthplace, the old manufacturing metropolis of **Odense** (OH-then-sa), has grown to become Denmark's 3rd largest city. Seek out its cobblestone alleyways, pedestrian zones, town gardens, and waterways, all haunted by statues of fairy tale heroes. Odense's sights begin at the train station. The **Railway Museum,** Dannebrogsgade 24, just across the tracks, has locomotives and coaches from various periods, plus a model railway elaborate enough to make any enthusiast drool. (Open daily 10am-4pm; Oct.-April Mon.-Fri. 10am-1pm, Sun. 10am-4pm. 20kr, children 7.50kr, free with railpass.) At **H.C. Andersens Hus,** Hans Jensens Stræde 39-43, you can learn about the author's eccentricities and listen to recordings of his stories in English. (Open daily 9am-6pm; April-May and Sept. 10am-5pm; Oct.-March 10am-3pm. 20kr, children 10kr.) At the other end of the pedestrian district, **Brandts Klædefabrik,** Brandts Passage 37, Odense's cloth-factory-*cum*-art-and-culture center, hosts street performers, plus a model railway, a graphic museum, an art gallery, and a photography museum. (Open daily 10am-5pm; Sept.-June Tues.-Sun. 10am-5pm. 25kr, children 20kr.) In the south part of Odense is **Den Fynske Landsby (Funen Village)**, Sejerskovvej 20, a pleasant collection of 18th and 19th century rural buildings brought here by pillaging curators from towns all around the island. Take bus #25 or 26. (Open daily 10am-7:30pm; Sept.-Oct. and April-May daily 10am-4pm; Nov.-March Sat. and Sun. 10am-4pm. 20kr, children 10kr; off-season prices slightly lower.) The easiest way to see Odense is to buy an **Odense Eventyrpas,** good for travel on all muncipal buses and trains and admission to most museums, river boats, and water parks in the area. (2 days 100kr; definitely worth it in the winter when the price drops to 50kr.) In late June, Odense hosts **Midtfyn,** one of the largest rock festivals in Denmark. The Black Crowes, INXS, Jesus Jones, Joan Baez, and Robert Plant all played here last year. (250kr/day, or 500kr for Fri.-Sun; camping free.)

Accommodations, Food, and Practical Information The **tourist office** (tel. 66 12 75 20), in the City Hall, a few blocks south of the train station, spews free maps, exchanges currency when banks are closed, and books rooms in private homes (100kr/person; 25kr fee). They also have a **Meet the Danes** program: with one or two days' notice, they arrange an evening of tea and conversation with a Danish family who shares your interests. (Lucky folks might get dinner and a guided tour as well.) Follow Jernbanegade, to the right of the station, all the way to Vestergade, and turn left. (Open Mon.-Sat. 9am-7pm, Sun. 11am-7pm; Sept. to mid-June Mon.-Fri. 9am-5pm, Sat. 10am-1pm.) **Vandrerhjem Kragsbjerggården (HI),** Kragsbjergvej 121 (tel. 66 13 04 25), inhabits a pastoral yellow building about 2km from the town center. The hostel manager looks like Woody from Cheers. Take bus #61 or 62 from Klingenberg or the train station. (Reception open 8am-noon and 4-8pm. 64kr, nonmembers 86kr. Laundry 30kr/load. Open mid-Feb. to Nov. Reserve if possible; definitely arrive before 5pm or call.) You can camp next to the enticing Fruens Boge park at **DCU Camping,** Odensevej 102 (tel. 66 11 47 02). Take bus #13. (38kr/person. Reception open 7am-10pm. Open late March-Sept.)

Den Grimme Ælling, across Thomas Thriges Gade from the H.C. Andersen, serves a huge buffest (lunch 69.50kr, dinner 99.50kr; open daily noon-10pm), while **Madhuset,** Albanigade 53, serves light 3-course dinners for 95kr. (Open Tues.-Sun. 5-10pm.) Seek refuge from chilly Odense nights at **Café Cuckoo's Nest,** 73 Vestergade, with a big cup of hot cocoa (14kr). (Open daily 11am-2am).

Bus routes radiate from Klingenberg, south of the city hall; board at the rear of the bus and pay your fare when you disembark (10kr). Regional buses to elsewhere on Funen stop behind the train station.

■■■ EGESKOV SLOT AND SVENDBORG

About 45 minutes south of Odense on the Svendborg rail line is **Egeskov Slot,** a stunning 16th-century castle that appears to float on the lake that surrounds it—it's actually supported by 12,000 oak piles. The interior of the castle is nothing special, but the grounds are a wonderland with formal gardens, a large bamboo labyrinth and a transportation museum. On summer Sundays at 5pm, classical concerts resound in the castle's great hall. (Grounds open June-Aug. daily 9am-6pm; May and Sept. daily 10am-5pm. Castle open May-Sept. daily 10am-5pm. To grounds 45kr; castle 45kr extra.) To get to Egeskov, exit the Svendborg-bound train at **Kværndrup;** leave the station and turn right, until you reach the Bøjdenvej, the main road. You can then wait for the hourly bus #920, or turn right and walk the 2km to the castle.

On Funen's south coast, an hour from Odense by rail, **Svendborg** makes the best base for stays on Funen and for bicycle trips to the islands just south of it. The resort-like town is built on hilly ground dipping into one of the most scenic ports in the country. The 17th-century estate of **Valdemars Slot,** across the bridge on the island of Tåsinge, was built by Christian IV for his son Valdemar. Take bus #200 or buy a boat ticket at the Svendborg tourist office (45kr round trip). (Open May-Sept. daily 10am-5pm; Easter-end of April and Oct. Sat.-Sun. and holidays 10am-5pm. 40kr.) Svendborg's centrally located **youth hostel (HI)** at Vestergade 45 (tel. 62 21 66 99) has 2-4 beds per room (75kr; reception open 8am-10pm; reservations strongly encouraged). **Carlsberg Camping,** Sundbrovej 19 (tel. 62 22 53 84), is across the sound on Tåsinge. (41kr. Reception open 8am-10pm. Open mid-April to mid-Sept.) Rent a bike and explore the surrounding countryside from **Hotel Swendborg,** Centrum Pladsen (tel. 62 21 17 00; 50kr/day, 100kr deposit. Open daily 8am-8pm.) The **tourist office** (tel. 62 21 09 80) is on the café-rimmed *torvet* (town square); it provides a map of beaches (20kr) and finds rooms in private homes (25kr fee). (Open Mon.-Fri. 9am-7pm, Sat. 9am-5pm; Sept. to mid-June Mon.-Fri. 9am-5pm, Sat. 10am-4pm.) On the other side of the train station is the dock for **ferries** to Ærø.

ÆRØ

The serene hamlets and cobblestone streets of Ærø quietly preserve an earlier era in Danish history. If you're seeking an escape from the beaten tourist path, you'll find it on this island, where the only beaten paths are those trampled by the cattle. Ærø is easily accessible to rail travelers, since certain trains from Odense to Svendborg are timed to meet the ferry from Svendborg to Ærø's principal town, Ærøskøbing. (Ferry 40kr, buy ticket on board. Departs Mon.-Fri. 6am, 9am, 1pm, 4pm, 7pm; Sat.-Sun. 7am, 10am, 1pm, 4pm, 7pm. Call 62 52 10 18 for more information.) Once on the island, bus #990 rides between the 3 main towns of Ærøskøbing, Marstal, and Søby (14kr from one town to the next; 44kr day pass).

In **Ærøskøbing,** cobblestone lanes, hollyhocks, and tiny half-timbered houses attract yachtspeople from as far away as Sweden and Germany. The **tourist office** (tel. 62 52 13 00), near the church on the *torv* (main square), arranges rooms in private homes. (Doubles 175kr. 25kr fee rarely exacted. Open Mon.-Sat. 9am-5pm; Sept. to mid-June Mon.-Fri. 9am-4pm, Sat. 10am-4pm.) The gracious **HI youth hostel,** Smedevejen 13 (tel. 62 52 10 44), lies 1km from town. Its magnificent views of the sea make it the most desirable hostel on the island. (65-72kr, non-members 87-94kr. Reception open 7:30am-noon and 4-8pm). **Ærøskøbing Camping,** Sygehusvejen 40b (tel. 62 52 18 54), is 10 minutes to the right as you leave the ferry. (36kr/person. Reception open 7am-10pm. Open May to mid-Sept.) You can rent a **bike** at the hostel (35kr/day), the campground (36kr/day), or the gas station at Pilebækken 7. Ærøskøbing harbors one of Denmark's best kept jazz secrets, **Andelen,** at 28A Søndergade. Musicians from the Copenhagen and other jazz festivals come here for their vacations and to play for the far more intimate and appreciative crowds. The café's rhubarb pie is almost as delicious as the jazz and arguably more popular (20kr). (Concerts 9pm-midnight, 80-125kr depending on the band. Café open daily 11am-midnight or slightly later.) Restaurants line up along Vestergade, the primary street leading into town from the ferry port. The most impressive establishment on the row is **Vaffelbageriet,** Vestergade 21, an ice cream stand whose "Ærø Special" is excellent even by Danish standards (14-28kr; open daily 11am-10pm).

Marstal, 13km away on Ærø's east coast, is less picturesque but has generally cheaper restaurants and accommodations. The **tourist office,** Kirkestræde 29 (tel. 62 53 19 60), on the *torv,* rents bikes and finds rooms in private homes. (Open Mon.-Fri. 10am-5pm, Sat. 10am-3pm; July also Sun. 10am-noon; Sept.-May Mon.-Fri. 9am-4pm.) The **HI youth hostel,** Færgestræde 29 (tel. 62 53 10 64), is by the harbor, a 10-minute walk to the left of the ferry. (72kr, nonmembers 94kr. Reception open 7am-noon and 4-9pm.) Down Havnegaden, past the hotel, you can **camp** (tel. 62 53 19 60) steps away from the town's best beach. (30kr. Open mid-May to Aug.).

JUTLAND (JYLLAND)

Homeland of the Jutes (who made history by hooking up with the Anglos and Saxons to conquer England), the Jutland peninsula is Denmark's largest land lump and its only link to continental Europe. Low rolling hills and sparse forests make for a slightly more variegated topography; numerous beaches and countless campgrounds mark the peninsula as prime summer vacation territory. Jutland may not be suitable for a whirlwind tour, but the plentiful supply of hostels will allow you to take a weekend beach fling without denting your budget.

Scandinavian Seaways runs ferries from **Esbjerg,** on Jutland's west coast, to Harwich, England, 6-8 times a week (mid-June to mid-Aug.; round-trip 995kr, over 26 1390kr; lower fares off-season). From mid-June to mid-August there's also service to Newcastle, England (2/week), and Tórshavn in the Faroe Islands (1/week). (Some reductions for railpass holders; call for information in Esbjerg, tel. 75 12 48 00, or Copenhagen, tel. 33 11 22 55.) There are rail connections from Jutland to Esbjerg and an **HI youth hostel** 3km from town at Gammel Vardevej 80 (tel. 75 12 42 58; 75kr, nonmembers 97kr; open Feb. to mid-Dec.). In northern Jutland, ferries also travel to the Faroes from **Hanstholm** (2780kr round-trip); there are bus connections to Århus and Copenhagen, and to Olso, Norway from **Hirtshals** (310kr; tel. 98 94 19 66; accessible by train, changing at Hjørring).

■■■ FREDERICIA AND BILLUND

The only reason to come to dull **Fredericia** is the **"Pro Pace" hostel (HI),** Skovlobervnget 9 (tel. 75 92 12 87), 2km from the train station; bus #2 runs from the station to within a few blocks of the hostel. The owners have filled their rooms with old books and pottery (much of it for sale). (Reception open 8am-noon and 4pm-10pm. 55-75kr, nonmembers 77- 97kr. Open Jan.15-Dec.15.)

Billund is renowned as the home of **Legoland**—an amusement park built out of 33 million Legos. Don't skip the impressive indoor exhibitions. Unfortunately, private buses and a new price system make Legoland a bit expensive. To get there, take the train from Fredericia to Vejle (1/hr., 17min.), then bus #912, marked "Legoland." The combined ticket for the bus and park admission (including rides) costs a cool 150kr. (To park alone 95kr adults, 75kr children. Open daily 10am-8pm; May-June and mid-Aug. to mid-Sept. open 10am-7pm. Indoor exhibits open Easter to mid-Dec. 10am-5pm. Call 75 33 13 33 for more information.)

■■■ ÅRHUS

Århus, Denmark's second city, is the cultural and student center of Jutland, but thanks to the city's rivalry with Copenhagen, its residents are the traditional butt of Danish jokes. Two milennia ago, people living near Århus sacrificed some of their own and threw them into nearby bogs, whose antiseptic acidity preserved the hideous, squished bodies. Take bus #6 from the train station to the **Moesgård Museum of Prehistory** at the end of the line to see one of the creatures. Eeeuw. (Open daily 10am-5pm, June-Aug. 9am-6pm. 30-40kr, children 10-12kr.) From behind the museum, the open-air **Prehistoric Trail** leads through mock settings all the way down to a splendiferous sand beach (3km). Bus #19 returns you from the beach to the Århus station (summer only). Check out the **Women's Museum** and its café behind the cathedral at Domkirkeplads 5. (Open 10am-5pm; mid-Sept. to June Tues.-Sun. 10am-4pm. 10kr, children 5kr.) The annual **Århus Festuge,** a rollicking week of theater and music, begins on the first Saturday in September.

The **tourist office** (tel. 86 12 16 00) is in the town hall, a block down Park Allé from the train station; pick up a free map and city guide. Contact them a day or two in advance to reconnoiter with a Danish family through the **Meet the Danes** program. The office also books lodgings (around 110kr/bed) for 25kr. (Open daily 9am-8pm; early Aug. to mid-Sept. daily 9am-7pm; mid-Sept. to mid-June Mon.-Fri. 9am-4:30pm, Sat. 9am-1pm.) Århus's **HI youth hostel, "Pavillonen,"** rests peacefully 3km from the city center and 5 minutes from the beach at Marienlundsvej 10 (tel. 86 16 72 98), in the Risskov forest. Take bus #1, 6, 9, or 16 to "Marienlund" (12.50kr) and follow the signs. (70kr, non-members 92kr.) Camp at the beauteous **Blommehaven,** located near a beach in the Marselisborg forest at Ørneredevej 35 (tel. 86 27 02 07). Take bus #19 (summer only) from the rail station directly to the grounds, or bus #6 to Hørhavevej. (Reception open 7am-11pm. Open April 8-Sept. 12) Forage for food along the cafés and stands of the pedestrianized Søndergade. **Kulturgyngen,** Mejlgade 53 (tel. 86 19 22 55) features live music and avant-garde theater as well as the cheapest food in town (breakfast 25-40kr, lunch 15-40kr, dinner 40-50kr). The **Musikcafæeen,** its adjacent underground dance club, hammers out discordant industrial beats every night (9pm-2am, no cover).

■■■ SILKEBORG

Less than an hour west of Århus by train, Silkeborg squats in Jutland's lake and canal country. The town makes a fine launchpad for canoeing and hiking; pick up a map at the **tourist office,** Godthåbsvej 4 (tel. 86 82 19 11). From the train station, turn right, take the first left onto Hostrupsgade, then turn right at the first 4-way traffic light and follow Vestergade through the pedestrian zone to Torvet Square. From there head downhill toward the river on Godthåbsvej. (Open Mon.-Fri. 9am-5pm, Sat. 9am-3pm; Sept.-June Mon.-Fri. 9am-4pm, Sat. 9am-noon.) The Tollund Man, another bog person (see Århus above), resides in the **Silkeborg Museum** in Hovedgården. (Open daily 10am-5pm; Nov.-Easter Wed. and Sat.-Sun. noon-4pm. 20kr, children 5kr.) The **Silkeborg Museum of Art,** Gudenåvej 7-9, contains a striking array of paintings and ceramics by Asger Jorn. (Open Tues.-Sun. 10am-5pm; Nov.-March Tues.-Fri. noon-4pm, Sat.-Sun. 10am-4pm. 20kr, students 10kr.) For marine forays, rent a boat at **Silkeborg Kanocenter,** 7 Åhave Allæ (tel. 86 80 30 03). (40kr first hour, 30kr each additional hour; 200kr/day. Open April-Oct. daily 9am-10pm.) **Cyclecompagniet,** Vestergade 18, rents **bikes** for 35kr/day. (100kr deposit. Open Mon.-Thurs. 90am-5pm, Fri. 9am-7pm, Sat. 9am-1pm.)

Beside a duck-filled canal stretches the grassy lawn of **Vandrerhjemmet Åbo (HI),** Åhavevej 55 (tel. 86 82 36 42). Walk to the right from the train station to the end of the street, turn left, then take the first right. Some wheelchair-accessible rooms. (65-84kr, non-members 87-106kr. Reception open 8am-noon and 4-8pm.) To snooze under the stars, try **Indelukket Camping,** Indelukket (tel. 86 82 22 01). (40kr/person. Reception open noon-10pm. Open April-Sept.) Silkeborg hosts a more traditional **jazz festival** than Copenhagen's (June 17-19 in 1994).

■■■ FREDERIKSHAVN AND SKAGEN

The self-proclaimed busiest ferry terminal in the world, **Frederikshavn** is truly drab. **Stena Line** ferries (tel. 98 42 43 66) leave here for Gothenburg, Sweden (6-8/day; 3¼hr.; 90kr, round-trip 180kr; a mere 2kr for all railpass holders), as well as for Oslo and other points in Norway (1-2/day, 190-260kr, round-trip 330-570kr). The **Sea-Catamaran** offers slightly speedier and less expensive service to Gotheburg, Sweden (5/day; 75 min.; 75kr, 140kr round-trip). Ferries are rarer and cheaper off-season. Frederikshavn's **tourist office** (tel. 98 42 32 66) is near the Stena Line terminal, 400m south of the rail station at Brotorvet 1. (Open Mon.-Sat. 8:30am-8:30pm, Sun. 11am-8:30pm; Sept.-May Mon.-Fri. 9am-4pm, Sat. 11am-2pm; Oct.-March closed Sat.) The **HI youth hostel,** Buhlsvej 6 (tel. 98 42 14 75), group-oriented and packed in summer, is a 15-minute walk from the station and harbor. (Reception open 7am-noon and 4-11:30pm. Sept.-Mar. 4-8pm. Dorms 53kr-68kr. Open Feb. to mid-Dec.)

More majestic is **Skagen,** which lies among the dunes at Denmark's northernmost tip. You can swim along 60km of sand beaches, then stand at the very tip with your feet in two different seas, but be careful! The underwater currents are extremely powerful and every year at least one hapless soul is carried out to sea. To get there, take bus #99 from the Skagen station to Gammel (10kr) or walk the 2.5km down Fyrvey. The Danes who don't go to see where their country ends go for the beachcomber aura of the 19th-century artists' colony. Works by Skagen painters are on display in the **Skagen Museum,** in **Anchers Hus,** and in **Drachmanns Hus.**

Get information on these sights and on the area's many fine beaches at the **tourist office** (tel. 98 44 13 77), inside the train station. (Open Mon.-Fri. 9am-5:30pm, Sun. 11am-2pm; Sept.-May Mon.-Fri. 9am-4pm.) **Nordjyllands Trafikselskab** runs both buses and private trains from Frederikshavn to Skagen as route #79 (30kr each way, railpasses not valid). **The Skagen Vandrerhjem,** Højensvej 32 (tel. 98 44 13 56), in Gammel Skagen, 4km west of Skagen, is somewhat inconvenient. The #79 bus stops right in front of it, or it's a 20-minute walk from the Højen train stop (the last stop before Skagen). (85kr, 75kr off-season. Reception open 9am-11am and 4pm-7pm. Reserve ahead.) Most campgrounds around Skagen are open late April to mid-September (38kr); try **Grenen** (tel. 98 44 25 46) or **Østerklit** (tel. 98 44 31 23). From June 23-26 in 1994 Skagen hosts a large music festival. The rest of the year, live music can be found at the **Plesner,** Holstvej 8 (tel. 98 44 68 44). (Open Easter-Sept. daily noon-2am. Live music Thurs.-Sat. No cover. Beer 20kr).

■■■ AALBORG

If too much exposure to fairy-tale castles has made you wish an oil slick on the Little Mermaid, head back to the Viking settlements of Northern Jutland. The infrequent trains and ferries (sometimes intentionally slow to increase duty-free buying time on the water) make anything past Funen a difficult commute from Copenhagen, but just sever your attachment to the big cities and take in the north country.

The site of the first Viking settlement 1300 years ago, **Aalborg,** Denmark's 4th-largest city, recently celebrated its 650th birthday, and its spotless pedestrian streets and white church garnered it the title of Europe's Tidiest City (1990). **Lindholm Høje,** Vendilavej 11, was filled with reveling Vikings in 693AD. Today, it's covered with 700 of their gravestones, making it one of the most important relics of Denmark's less peaceful days. Take bus #6 (10kr) from near the tourist office. Tell the driver your destination. (Site open dawn-dusk. Museum open daily 10am-7pm; Sept.-Oct. 24 daily 10am-5pm; Oct. 25-Easter Tues.-Sun. 10am-4pm; Easter-May daily 10am-5pm. 20kr.) The **tourist office,** Østera 8 (tel. 98 12 60 22), compulsively dusts their free maps and information about most of Northern Jutland and books rooms in private homes. From the station turn left on Boulevarden Østeragade and continue straight for about 5 minutes. (Open Mon.-Fri. 9am-5pm, Sat. 9am-4pm; Sept.-May Mon.-Fri. 9am-4pm, Sat. 9am-noon.) **Jomfru Ane Gade** boasts the largest continuous stretch of bars and restaurants in Denmark. The **Aalborg Vandrerhjem (HI),** Skydebanevej 50 (tel. 98 11 60 44), isn't exactly central, but it does sit on a beautiful fjord. Take bus #8, direction "Fjordparken," to the end. (Reception open 7:30am-noon and 4-9pm. 84kr, non-members 106kr. More expensive cottages available. Open Jan. 16-Dec. 15. Reservations *highly* recommended.)

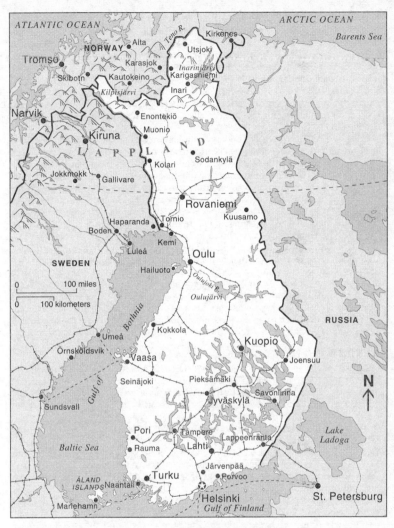

Finland (Suomi)

US$1 = 5.68mk (markka, also known as FIM)
CDN$1 = 4.31mk
UK£1 = 8.80mk
IR£1 = 8.23mk
AUS$1 = 3.70mk
NZ$1 = 3.14mk
SAR1 = 1.18mk
Country Code: 358

10mk = US$1.76
10mk = CDN$2.32
10mk = UK£1.14
10mk = IR£1.21
10mk = AUS$2.71
10mk = NZ$3.19
10mk = SAR8.47
International Dialing Prefix: 990

Between the Scandinavian peninsula and the Russian wilderness lies a long-suffering land of coniferous trees and five million taciturn souls. After enduring seven centuries between the warring Swedish and Russian empires, Finland experienced a romantic nationalism in the 19th century, nurtured by the *Kalevala* folk epic, Jean Sibelius's rousing symphonies, and Akseli Gallen-Kallela's mythic paintings. Once free of Russian domination in 1917, the Finns turned on themselves in a bitter civil war that saw the Right slaughter the Social Democrats. On the principle that the enemy of my enemy is my friend, Finland joined the Nazis in their war against the USSR, later turning against these same "allies" who were reluctant to leave this captivating land.

Finland today incarnates a confident Scandinavian egalitarianism. The country is a legal pioneer, tying speeding penalties to the offender's annual income: a wealthy businessman was recently fined US$11,400. In this first European nation to enfranchise women (1906), women and men stand on equal ground. Paternity leave is becoming nearly as common as maternity leave, and trains often have children's cars complete with baby bottle warmers. Internationally, Finland leads the world in participation in the U.N. Peacekeeping Forces. The nation's acclaimed mediation efforts are memorialized in Namibia, where hundreds of children are named Ahtisaari after the Finnish diplomat who supervised the independence process.

Finland has maintained a delicate Nordic neutrality, with both Western and Eastern influences in its culture. The language, a member of the Finno-Ugric family, is a relative of Hungarian, and contains almost as many grammatical cases as letters in the alphabet. Outside the Helsinki metropolitan area, undisturbed nature reigns. The west coast is dotted with old wooden shacks, and the Swedish-speaking Åland Islands are a biker's green paradise. For the avid sailor, the Lake District in southeastern Finland is the place to be. Lapland, in the north, sports rugged terrain and rolling fells, boundless wilderness and Finland's several thousand indigenous Sami people.

GETTING THERE

Citizens of the U.S., Canada, U.K., Ireland, Australia, and New Zealand can visit Finland visa-free for up to 90 days. The titanic vessels of **Silja Line** are floating shopping malls often jammed with hundreds of partying Scandinavians. Silja (tel. (90) 180 41 in Helsinki, (08) 22 21 40 in Stockholm, (961) 323 36 30 in Vaasa, (060) 12 93 10 in Sundsvall, (090) 409 80 in Umeå, (0910) 141 60 in Skellefteå) sails from Stockholm to Turku (2/day; 9-11hr.; 90mk, students and YIEE holders 65mk, Eurail and Nordturist holders ride free on deck), and to Helsinki (1/day; 15hr.; 285mk, students and YIEE holders 250mk, Eurail 75mk, Nordturist 145mk;breakfast included); from Travemünde, Germany to Helsinki (3/week; 520-660mk, depending on the day, students 460-600mk, Inter-rail 260-330mk); from Sundsvall and Umeå, Sweden across the Gulf of Bothnia to Vaasa on Finland's west coast (135mk from Umeå, 150mk from Sundsvall, students and railpass holders deduct 35mk); from Skellefteå and Umeå, Sweden to Kokkola and Pietarsaari (several/week; 135mk, students and railpass holders 10mk). All fares balloon on Friday and shrivel mid-August to late June.

Viking Line (tel. (90) 123 51 in Helsinki, (08) 644 07 65 in Stockholm), like Silja, steams from Stockholm to Helsinki (180mk, students and railpass holders 120mk, Eurail free) and to Turku via Mariehamn (150mk, students and railpass holders 100mk, Eurail free), and from Kapellskär to Naantali via Mariehamn (75mk, students 50mk, Eurail free). Snatch lower fares mid-August to late June. **Polferries** (tel. (90) 44 54 48 in Helsinki) jaunts from Gdańsk, Poland to Helsinki (2/week; 380mk, with ISIC 260mk) and to Tallinn, Estonia (9/day; 1½-3½ hr.; 100-290mk); in Helsinki call **Estonian New Line** at (90) 680 24 99 or **Tallink** at (90) 60 28 22. **Finnair** (tel. (90) 818 81) flies in and out of Finland for low fares—if you're under 25 and book one day in advance. (Copenhagen 885mk, London or Paris 1060mk.) Buses and trains connect Helsinki to St. Petersburg via Lahti. (See Helsinki Practical Information.)

TRAVELING IN FINLAND

Efficient **trains** zip as far north as Kolari at the usual painful Nordic prices (Turku to Helsinki 80mk); railpasses are valid. The **Nordturist pass** *(Pohjola Junalla)* allows 21 days of boundless travel in Sweden, Denmark, Norway, and Finland for 1660mk (under 26 945mk). After January 1, 1994, Nordturist will no longer be available; only the **ScanRail Pass,** allowing one consecutive month of travel (US$399), 9 days of travel within 21 days (US$275), or 4 days of travel within 15 days (US$159) will be offered, though those under 26 will win a 25% discount. A **Finnrail Pass** offers free rail travel throughout Finland (8 days for 470mk; 15 days, 730mk; 22 days, 920mk). Seat reservations (15-30mk) are necessary on certain express trains. Couchettes (in triples) cost 60mk from Monday to Thursday, 90mk from Friday to Sunday.

Buses cost about the same as trains, though expresses carry a 10mk surcharge. The **Bussilomalippu** pass offers 1000km of travel over 2 weeks for 300mk. For bus information anywhere in Finland, call (9700) 40 00. Students *(opiskelija,* OH-pees-KAY-lee-yah) often receive a 50% discount for distances over 75km; a 30mk card, issued at the station, is required. Railpasses are valid on some buses that follow disused train routes. **Finnair** takes 40% off domestic fares for those under 25. A **Finnair Holiday Ticket** gives 15 days of boundless air travel for US$300, ages 12-24 US$250. Steamers link up many cities in the lake district. **Hitchhikers** find more rides in Finland than elsewhere in Scandinavia, while **cyclists** hanker for Denmark's shorter distances. Campgrounds often rent bikes, as do some youth hostels and tourist offices. (Rates average 40-50mk/day, 180mk/week; plus deposit of 150mk or passport.)

FINLAND ESSENTIALS

Most **shops** close at 5pm on weekdays (Sat. around 1pm), but urban supermarkets may stay awake until 8pm (Sat. 4-6pm). **Kiosks,** especially those marked *elintarvikekioski,* sell basic food, snacks, and toiletries until 9 or 10pm. **Banks** are open weekdays 9:15am-4:15pm. Finns celebrate May Eve and Day (April 30-May 1), Ascension Day (May 12), Midsummer Eve and Day (June 25-26), and Independence Day (Dec. 6). Many stores and museums, as well as all banks and post offices, are also closed on Easter (April 1-4), Christmas (Dec. 24-6), and New Year's Day. During Midsummer, when Finns party all night to the light of *kokko* (bonfires) and the midnight sun, the country shuts down completely.

Local calls usually cost 2mk, and most pay **phones** take 1mk and 5mk coins. Phone cards (local calls 1mk) are available in 30, 70, and 100mk denominations. "Tele" or "Nonstop" cards work nationwide; other cards will only work in the city in which you purchase them. "Nonstop" phones can always be found at post offices. Call 020 for domestic information, 920 20 for international information, 920 22 to place a collect call, 112 in **emergencies,** and 100 22 for the **police.** For AT&T's **USA Direct,** call 980 01 00 10; for MCI's **World Reach,** call 98 00 15 92 81; for **Canada Direct,** dial 980 01 00 11. The mail service is fast and efficient.

The Finnish language is virtually impenetrable to foreigners. Watch out for town names that modify their form on train schedules due to the lack of prepositions in the Finnish language. Swedish, often seen on signs, is the official second language; many Finns speak English, but fluency decreases as you go north. Useful words and phrases include *Missä on* (pronounced MEESS-ah OWN, "Where is?"), *Haluaisin* (HAH-loo-ay-seen, "I would like"), *Kiitos* (KEE-toss, "thank you"), *rautatieasema* (RAO-tah-tee-AH-sehma, "train station"), and *keskus* (KESS-kooss, "center"). Don't be surprised if a strange Finn asks you to throw away all inhibitions and partake in Finland's chief export, the *sauna.* "M" and "N" on bathroom and sauna doors designate men and women, respectively.

Travelers with disabilities can contact the Finnish Tourist Board and the Helsinki tourist office as well as **Rullaten Ry** (see Helsinki), an organization that assists with travel planning.

Accommodations, Camping, and Food Finland has 165 *retkeilymaja* (RET-kay-loo-MAH-yah; **youth hostels**), 60 of which shelter travelers year-round. Prices are based on a four-star system and range from 30-90mk; most charge 40-65mk. Some include saunas, and most prohibit sleeping bags. **Hotels** are generally exorbitant (over 200mk), although *kesähotelli* (summer hotels) usually offer doubles for around 200mk. **Private room** booking is not as common as in Sweden, but local tourist offices will help you find the cheapest accommodations. The **Finnish Youth Hostel Association** (Suomen Retkeilymajajärjestö) is located at Yrjönkatu 38 B, Helsinki (tel. (90) 694 03 77). As in much of the rest of Scandinavia, you may camp anywhere as long as you respect fauna and flora and stay a polite distance away from homes. Well-equipped official **campgrounds** dapple the country, some offering saunas (tents 25-75mk/night, *mökit* (small cottages) 150mk and up).

A *baari* is a café that serves food, coffee, and occasionally beer. *Kahvilat* also serve food and are often a bit classier, while *grillit* are fast-food stands. A *ravintola* is a restaurant; some evolve into dance-spots or bars toward the end of the evening (cover charge 10mk and up; doorkeeper is often tipped a few markka). The standard minimum age is 18, but it can be as high as 25, and alcohol is no bargain. You need not tip servers (the bill is often rounded up). Beer *(olut)* is divided into several groups. Olut IV is the strongest and most expensive (at least 20-25mk/*iso tuoppi*; ½-liter), while olut III (your best value for your money) is slightly weaker and cheaper. Outside bars and restaurants, all alcohol stronger than olut III must be purchased at the state-run **Alko** liquor stores.

Among the less expensive supermarkets are **Alepa** and **Valintatalo.** Many large hotels offer bargain breakfasts open to outsiders. Short of that, lunch is the best deal, often an all-you-can-eat buffet (30-50mk). Fish ranges from *silli* (Baltic herring) to *lohi* (salmon). Finnish dietary staples include robust rye bread, potatoes, malodorous cheeses, and squirming yogurt-like *viili*. In July and August, the land blossoms with blueberries, cranberries, and—in the far north—Arctic cloudberries.

■■■ HELSINKI

Less festive than Copenhagen but friendlier than Stockholm, peaceful Helsinki has long been a meeting point of West and East. Lutheran and Russian Orthodox cathedrals stand almost face to face, and cobblestone streets and well-tended parks make it a city ideal for afternoon strolls; the southeast corner is a nest of diplomats and elegant mansions, though it also features plentiful drunks and aggressive traffic. Helsinki has become synonymous with human rights and international cooperation, and planned streets and neoclassical buildings lend it a radiant aura.

ORIENTATION AND PRACTICAL INFORMATION

Helsinki, "daughter of the Baltic," dangles on the southern edge of Finland. The central city's layout resembles a "V" with a large, bulbous point and several smaller peninsulettes. The train station lies just north of the vertex from which the Mannerheimintie and Unioninkatu thoroughfares radiate. The harbor and most sights are south of the train station. All street signs have both Finnish and Swedish names. For candid and practical information, the free youthful paper *City* is unbeatable, while *Helsinki This Week* provides a comprehensive list of information and current happenings (as does an English recorded message line, tel. 058).

Tourist Offices: City Tourist Office, Pohjoisesplanadi 19 (tel. 169 37 57), near the market square. From the train station, walk 2 blocks south on Keskuskatu and turn left on Pohjoisesplanadi. Open Mon.-Fri. 8:30am-6pm, Sat. 8:30am-1pm; mid-Sept. to mid-May Mon. 8:30am-4:30pm, Tues.-Fri. 8:30am-4pm. **Hotellikeskus** (Hotel Booking Center; tel. 17 11 33), in the train station. Primarily room-finding (10mk fee; hostel beds 5mk), but also has city maps, youth hostel lists and useful brochures. Open Mon.-Fri. 9am-7pm, Sat.-Sun. 10am-6pm; Sept.-May Mon.-Fri.

9am-5pm. Both offices sell the **Helsinki Card,** offering unlimited local transportation, museum discounts, and other treats (1-day 80mk, 2-day 125mk, under 17 half-price). **Finnish Tourist Board,** Eteläesplanadi 4 (tel. 40 30 13 00), covers the whole country, including campgrounds. Open Mon.-Fri. 9am-5pm, Sat. 9am-1pm, Sept.-May Mon.-Fri. 0:30am-4pm. **Finnish Youth Hostel Association,** Yrjönkatu 38 B (tel. 694 03 77), on the south side of the bus station, lists hostels nationwide and arranges Lapland lodgings for hikers. Open Mon.-Fri. 9am-4pm.

Travelers' Center: Lighthouse, will move in 1994 (possibly to Kullio Youth Hostel). Call 402 95 00 or contact the tourist office. Can't keep a good woman down.

Budget Travel: Kilroy Travels, Mannerheimintie 5 (tel. 680 78 11). Sells Transalpino tickets, ISICs, and YIEE cards. Open Mon.-Fri. 9am-6pm, Sat. 10am-1pm; Sept.-May closed Sat.

Embassies: U.S., Itäinen Puistotie 14 A (tel. 17 19 31). Open Mon.-Fri. 9am-noon. **Canada,** Pohjoisesplanadi 25 B (tel. 17 11 41), at Fabianinkatu. Open Mon.-Thurs. 8:30am-4:30pm, Fri. 8:30am-1:30pm. **U.K.,** Itäinen Puistotie 17 (tel. 66 12 93). In emergencies, **Australians** and **New Zealanders** should contact the British Embassy. **Estonia,** Fabianinkatu 13 A (tel. 17 95 28). **Latvia,** Bulevardi 5 A 18 (tel. 60 56 40). **Commonwealth of Independent States,** Tehtaankatu 1 B (tel. 66 18 76). **Poland,** Armas Lindgrenintie 21 (tel. 684 80 77).

Currency Exchange: Rates are generally identical, with a minimum 10mk commission on traveler's checks. Try **Forex,** in the train station. Open daily 8am-9pm; charges 10mk fee for cash, 10mk/traveler's check, no fee to exchange FIM into foreign currency. Same rates at the handy **Poste Restante** office 50m west of the train station. Open Mon.-Fri. 8am-9pm, Sat. 9am-6pm, Sun. 11am-9pm. The airport terminal has money exchange (cash only). Open 6:30am-11pm daily. **KOP** banks at the ferry terminals are open Mon.-Fri. 9am-6pm, Sat. 9am-11:30pm and 3:45-7:30pm, Sun. 9-11:30am and 3:45-6pm. Visa credit card advances are available 24 hrs. from most bank machines.

American Express: Full service at **Area Travel,** Pohjoisesplanadi 2 (tel. 185 51), at Mannerheimintie. Open Mon.-Fri. 9am-1pm and 2:15-4:30pm.

Post Office: Mannerheimintie 11 (tel. 195 51 17). Open Mon.-Fri. 9am-5pm. Poste Restante office sells stamps and exchanges money; open Mon.-Fri. 8am-9pm, Sat. 9am-6pm, Sun. 11am-9pm. **Postal Code:** 00100.

Telephones: In the same building as the post office. Open Mon.-Fri. 9am-10pm, Sat.-Sun. 10am-4pm. Get best rates by using a Tele or Nonstop phone card, which works in all green Nonstop card phones. For international calls dial 990 then country code. City Code: 90.

Flights: Tel. 818 81. Bus #615 runs frequently 5:20am-10:20pm between the **Helsinki-Vantaa** airport and train station platform #12 (15mk). The Finnair bus shuttles between the airport and the Finnair building at Asema-aukio 3, next to the train station (daily every 20 min., 5am-midnight; 35min.; 20mk).

Trains: For information, call 101 01 15. Trains chug to Turku (2½hr., 80mk), Tampere (2hr., 80mk), and Rovaniemi (10hr., 260mk). For trains to St. Petersburg (7½hr., 265mk) and Moscow (16hr., 506mk, sleeper included) call 62 52 16. The station has **lockers** and **luggage service** (10mk each, service open 6:30am-10:25pm). Station open Mon.-Fri. 5:15am-1:30am, Sat.-Sun. 5:15am-midnight.

Buses: Tel. 97 00 40 00. The long-distance station, with routes throughout Finland and to St. Petersburg via Lahti (3/day, 8hr., 190-250mk), sits just west of the post office, between Salomonkatu and Simonkatu. Buy tickets there or on board.

Ferries: For voyage details, see "Getting to Finland," above. **Silja Line,** Mannerheimintie 2 (tel. 180 41) is open Mon.-Fri. 8:30am-6pm, Sat. 9am-2pm). **Viking Line,** Mannerheimintie 14 (tel. 123 51) is open Mon.-Fri. 8:30-5pm, Sat. 9am-3pm. **Viking Line** and **Finnjet** (contact Silja Line) ferries leave from Katajanokka island east of Kauppatori (take tram #2 or 4). **Silja Line, Polferries** (tel. 44 54 48), **Estonian New Line** (tel. 680 24 99), and **Tallink** (tel. 60 28 22) ferries leave from south of Kauppatori (take tram #3T).

Public Transportation: The metro and most trams and buses run approximately 6am-11pm (certain bus and tram lines, including the indispensable tram #3T, continue to 1:30am). On the weekend, trains run until 2:30am. Within Helsinki, 9mk/trip, 10-trip ticket for 75mk. For travel between Helsinki, Espoo, and Vantaa,

15mk, 10-trip ticket 125mk. All tickets are valid for one hour (transfers free) and are available at R-Kiosks and City Transport offices (Simonkatu 1, Rautatientori metro station, Hakaniemi train station). Punch your ticket on board. The **Tourist Ticket** provides boundless transit in Helsinki, Espoo, and Vantaa (1-day 48mk, 3-day 96mk; inside Helsinki 1-day 25mk, 3-day 50mk); available at City Transport and tourist offices. For transit information, call 101 01 11.

Bike Rental: Cheapest at the **Olympic Stadum Youth Hostel** (tel. 49 60 71), 40-50mk/day, 100mk deposit. The **Töölönahti Kioski** (tel. 949) 40 40 12), by the Finlandia House, rents bikes for 50mk/day.

Bookstore: The Academic Bookstore, Pohjoisesplanadi 39 (tel. 121 41). Dazzling selection of books in English. Open Mon.-Fri. 9am-8pm, Sat. 9am-5pm.

Laundromat: Look for the words *Itsepulvelu Pesula.* Try Suonionkatu 1. Wash and dry 46mk. Open Mon.-Fri. 8am-5pm, Sat. 8am-2pm. Or try Punavuorenkatu 3. Wash 25mk, dry 25mk. Open Mon.-Fri. 8am-8pm, Sat. 9am-2pm, Sun. noon-4pm.

Women's Center: The Union of Feminist Women runs **Naisten huone,** Bulevardi 11 A (tel. 64 24 61), a cultivated social center and café. Open mid-Aug. to June Mon.-Fri. 5-9pm, Sat. noon-6pm.

Gay and Lesbian Services: Contact the **Organization for Sexual Equality,** Oikokatu 3 (tel. 135 83 05). Open Wed.-Fri. and Sun. 6-9pm. They host a dance every Mon. 9pm-3am at Museokatu 10. Cover 25mk.

Travelers With Disabilities: For information on facilities and transport, contact **Rullaten Ry,** Malminkatu 38 (tel. 694 11 55).

Sauna and Pool: Uimastadion, Hammarskjöldintie (tel. 402 93 84), behind the Olympic Stadium. Built for the 1952 Olympics. 10mk includes sauna, water-slide 20mk. Open June-late Aug. Mon.-Sat. 7am-8pm, Sun. 9am-8pm; May and early Sept. reduced hrs. If you can't stand the heat, get out of the **Sauna Society** (tel. 67 86 77) in Lauttasaari.

Pharmacy: Yliopiston Apteekki, Mannerheimintie 5 (tel. 17 90 92). Open daily 7am-midnight. The branch at Mannerheimintie 96 (tel. 41 57 78) is open 24 hrs.

Medical Assistance: The **Kallion terveysasema,** Eläintarhantie 3E (tel. 709 92 02) receives and refers foreigners. Take the metro or trams #1, 2, 3, 6, or 7 to Hakanieni and walk one block northwest on Eläintarhantie.

Emergencies: (tel. 112). **Police** (tel. 100 22). Stations at Olavinkatu 1A, Kasarmikatu 25B, 2 Pikku Roobertinkatu 1-3, and the train station near platform #11. Call 18 91 for switchboard.

ACCOMMODATIONS

Kallio Youth Hostel, Porthaninkatu 2 (tel. 70 99 25 90). From the train station, walk 15 min. north on Unioninkatu, or take the metro to Hakaniemi. Cozy 30-bed hostel, amicable and homey staff. TV room and kitchen. Reception open 8-10:30am and 3pm-2am. Lockout 10:30am-3pm. Curfew 2am. 50mk, sheets included. Free small lockers. Laundry 10mk. Open June-Aug.

Stadionin Youth Hostel (HI), Pohj. Stadiontie 3B (tel. 49 60 71), in the Olympic Stadium complex. Take tram #3T or 7A, or walk 25min. from the train station. Enormous (200 beds); high-ceilinged rooms with huge windows. Kitchen TV, bikes (see Bike Rental above). Reception open 7am-11pm, mid-Sept. to May 7-10am and 4-11pm. Lockout 10am-4pm. Curfew 2am. Dorms 45mk, nonmembers 15mk extra. Doubles 65mk. Breakfast 25mk. Backpack-sized lockers (3mk/day). Sheets 20mk. Laundry 15mk.

Hotel Satakuntatalo (HI), Lapinrinne 1 (tel. 69 58 51). 1km southwest of the train station. Another dorm-*cum*-summer hotel; clean and well-run. Phones in all rooms, sauna (20mk), laundry. Dorms 45mk. Singles 165 mk. Doubles 225mk. Nonmembers add 15mk. Students 20% off. Breakfast 25mk. Free baggage storage. Kitchens. Reception open 24hrs. No lockout or curfew. Open June-Aug.

Eurohostel (HI), Linnankatu 9 (tel. 66 44 52, fax 655 04), 2km west of the train station. Take tram #4 (direction: Katajanokka) past the port. Huge (250 beds) with clean rooms. Kitchen on every floor. Reception open 24hr. Singles 145mk. Doubles and triples 95mk/person. Sheets and morning sauna included. Nonmembers add 15mk. Breakfast 25mk. Laundry.

Oranssi Youth Hostel: Funky; run by a squatter's organization. New location in 1994. Call 79 92 81 or contact tourist office for more information.
Camping: Rastila Camping (tel. 31 65 51), 14km east of the center. Take the metro to Itäkeskus and then catch bus #90, 90A, or 96. Vast, cheap, municipal campground with washing, cooking and abluting facilities. One person 30mk, 2-5 people 50mk; cabins 150-200mk. Open mid-May to mid-Sept.

FOOD

Corporate monopolies make even groceries expensive; seek refuge in the **Alepa** chain (the one in the tunnel under the train station is open Mon.-Sat. 10am-10pm, Sun. noon-10pm). Energetic epicureans can dive into **Kauppatori** (Market Square), by the port (open Mon.-Sat. 7am-2pm and 4-8pm; Sept.-May Mon.-Fri. 7am-2pm), and the nearby **Kauppahalli** (Market Hall; open Mon.-Sat. 8am-5pm, Sat. 8am-2pm).

University cafeterias: Humanists relate in the convivial main building, Fabianinkatu 33, while technocrats exchange impulses in outdoor-terraced Porthania, Hallituskatu 6 at Fabianinkatu (both open Mon.-Fri. 8am-3:30pm; Sept.-May Mon.-Fri. 8am-6pm, Sat. 10:30am-2:30pm). Entrees 17-21mk. Students only.
Green Way, Kaisamemenkatu 1. Vegetarian meals with a diverse clientele. 89mk/kg (students 69mk/kg Mon.-Fri. 2-4pm). Open Mon.-Fri. 11am-6pm, Sat. 11am-4pm; July same but Sat. until 2pm.
Palace Café, Eteläranta 10, 2nd floor, next to the Palace Hotel. A homely cafeteria with harborscape and complete lunches (10:30am-1:30pm) for 35mk. Open Mon.-Fri. 7am-3pm.
Café Engel, Aleksanterinkatu 26. Sip boundless coffee for hours (8.50mk) or try the 36mk lasagne at this trendy café.
Kappeli, Eteläesplanadi 1. Has exuded a Parisian air since 1867. Warm pies 32-36mk, pasta dishes 41-45mk. Open daily 9am-4am.

SIGHTS

Tram #3T is the city's cheapest tour (pick up its free itinerary on board). Or just walk—most sights are packed within 2km of the train station. The tourist office will give you the booklet *See Helsinki on Foot;* their only serious omission is the **Temppeliaukio Church**—a modern masterpiece built into a hill of rock, and an acoustical wonder. From the train station, head west on Arkadiankatu and then right on Fredrikinkatu to the square where the church is buried. (Open Sun.-Fri. 10am-8pm, Sat. 10am-6pm.) The striking **Jean Sibelius Monument,** 750m north of the church in Sibelius Park on Mechelininkatu, was dedicated to one of the 20th century's greatest composers by sculptor Eila Hiltunen. It looks like a cloud of organ pipes blasted into outer space. (Take bus #18 from the train station.) The **Kansallismuseo** (National Museum), 500m northwest of the train station at Mannerheimintie 34, sets out intriguing displays of Finnish culture, from Gypsy and Sami costumes to *ryijyt* (rugs), along with a splendid exegesis of the country's tortuous history. (Open Wed.-Mon. 11am-4pm, Tues. 11am-4pm and 6-9pm; Oct.-April Wed.-Sat. and Mon. 11am-3pm, Sun. 11am-4pm, Tues. 11am-3pm and 6-9pm. 10mk, students 5mk, Tues. free.) Across from the train station sprawls Finland's largest art museum, the **Art Museum of the Ateneum,** Kaivokatu 2-4. (Open Tues. and Fri. 9am-5pm, Wed.-Thurs. 9am-9pm, Sat.-Sun. 11am-5pm. 10mk, students and seniors 5mk, under 18 free, special exhibits 25mk.) Finnish finesse in graphic and industrial design is well-documented at the **Museum of Applied Arts,** Korkeavuorenkatu 23. (Open Tues.-Fri. 11am-5pm, Sat.-Sun. 11am-4pm. English tours Sat. 2pm. 20mk, students 10mk.) Head over to **Hietalahden Kirpputori**, Finland's best flea market, at the end of Bulevardi, where you might find a suit for 30mk or grab a couple of 70s LPs for 5mk. (Open late March to mid-Oct. Mon.-Sat. 7am-2pm, Sun. 10am-4pm; mid-May to mid-Sept. also Mon.-Fri. 3:30-9pm.) The crowning glory of neoclassical **Senate Square,** on the corner of Unioninkato and Aleksanterinkatu, is the **Lutheran Cathedral.** (Open Mon.-Fri. 9am-7pm, Sat.-Sun. 9am-6pm; Oct.-April daily 9am-5pm.) A few blocks to the west, on Katajanokka island, the contrasting Byzantine-Slavonic **Uspensky Orthodox Cathedral** guards the island with its red spikes. Elsewhere in the city, the boldly simple creations of the city's great 20th-century architects—notably Aalto and Saarinen—blend with slick neoclassical lines. Aalto said of Finland, "architecture is our form of expression because our language is so impossible."

Helsinki's relaxed surrounding islands counterbalance the hectic center of town. Ferries from the market leave hourly (round-trip 18-20mk) for the now-demilitarized fortress island of **Suomenlinna.** Explore the dark passageways of the old fortress or visit one of the 6 museums on the island. (Open mid-May to Aug. daily 10am-5pm; Sept. daily 11am-3pm. 5mk, students 2.50mk.) When museumed-out, relax on the rocky **beach. Seurasaari,** connected to the mainland by a causeway, is a peaceful place to picnic, swim, or saunter. Its open-air museum contains churches and farmsteads transplanted from the Finnish countryside. Come during Midsummer to witness the *kokko* (bonfire) and Finnish tradition in its full splendor. (Open June-Aug. daily 11am-5pm, Wed. until 7pm; May and Sept. Mon.-Fri. 9am-3pm, Sat.-Sun. 11am-5pm. 10mk, students 5mk, Wed. free.) Take bus #24 from Erottaja, outside the Swedish Theater, to the last stop. There's also boat service from Market Sq. in summer. A 15-minute train ride (take R, H, K, or P to Tikkurila, 15mk) takes you to the **Heureka Science Center,** housing hands-on exhibits, a planetarium, and a fascinating exhibit on the Finno-Ugric languages. (55mk, 75mk includes film in planetarium, students 35mk, seniors 45mk. Open Fri.-Wed. 10am-6pm, Thurs. 10am-8pm; Oct.-April Tues.-Wed. and Fri.-Sun. 10am-6pm, Thurs. 10am-8pm.)

ENTERTAINMENT

Much of Helsinki nods off early. Sway to afternoon street music in the leafy **Esplanadi** or party on warm nights at **Hietaniemi beach. Kaivopuisto park** hosts open-air rock concerts on Sundays in July, while **Hakaniementori** offers waterside beer gardens. Consult *Helsinki This Week* for current happenings and the *City* or the weekly *Clubland* for more bars and nightclubs. In late August, the 2-week **Helsinki Festival** cobbles together a mélange of arts events. Finland is one of the few European countries where the drinking age—18 for beer and wine, 20 for hard alcohol—is usually enforced. Both bouncers and cover charges usually relax on weeknights; speaking English or German may help you get in. Tickets to some discos sell out before the evening begins; the super-cautious can buy in advance at **Tiketti** in the Forum mall at the corner of Mannerheimintie and Simonkatu (3rd floor) or **Lippupalvelu,** Mannerheimintie 5. The cheapest place to get hammered is the state-run liquor store **Alko.** (Branches at Eteläesplanadi 22, Mannerheimintie 1, and Salomonkatu 1. Open Mon.-Thurs. 10am-5pm, Fri. 10am-6pm, Sat. 9am-2pm.)

Cantina West, Kasarminkatu 23 (tel. 63 98 60), south of the train station on Keskuskatu, then east on Eteläesplanadi. Expensive Tex-Mex restaurant and bar with cacti on the tables. *The* happening place in Helsinki. 3 floors, live music nightly. Min. age 22. Cover 15mk on weekends. Open Mon.-Thurs. 11am-3am, Fri. 11am-4am, Sat. noon-4am, Sun. noon-3am.

Old Students' House, Mannerheimintie 3 (tel. 66 73 76). Neoclassical building with pubs, dance floors, restaurant, beer patio, and sociable students. Beer 15-20mk. 20-50mk cover for live bands. Open daily 11am-1am.

Storyville, Museokatu 8 (tel. 40 80 07), near the National Museum. Helsinki's choice jazz club, with diverse clientele. Live music nightly. Open daily 8pm-4am.

Arkadia, Fredrikinkatu 48 (tel. 694 01 51). A lively international disco complete with casino and karaoke bar. Open daily 8pm-4am, cover weekdays 15mk after 10pm, Fri. 25mk after 9pm, Sat. 35mk after 9pm.

■■■ ÅLAND ISLANDS
(AHVENANMAA)

The Åland (OH-land) Islands have long been a cultural and geographic bridge between Sweden and Finland. Swedish for many centuries, they became part of Finland in 1807. Since 1921, Åland has been an autonomous territory within Finland, with its own flag and parliament. The Ålanders are entirely Swedish-speaking and they vigilantly minimize Finnish influence. Political controversy seems out of place here; the gentle landscape more befits leisurely hikes, bike rides, and sun-soaking. Most establishments accept both Finnish marks and Swedish kronor.

Viking Line (tel. (928) 260 11 in Mariehamn) sails daily between the capital city of Mariehamn and Stockholm (6½hr.; 75mk, students and railpass holders 50mk), Turku (5½hr.; 110mk, students and railpass holders 75mk), Naantali (5½-8hr.; 75mk, students 50mk), and Kapellskär (2½ hr.; 37mk, students 22mk). They have lower fares mid-Aug to June, and Eurail Pass gets you free passage on all routes. **Silja Line** (tel. (928) 167 11 in Mariehamn) sails daily between Mariehamn and Turku (5½hr.) and Stockholm (6hr., 80mk, students and seniors 60mk, Eurail and Nordturist free, lower fares mid-Aug. to late June). **Birka Lines'** *Princess* sails daily between Stockholm and Mariehamn (30mk; tel. (928) 270 27 in Marienhamn, (08) 714 55 20 in Stockholm), and **Eckerö Line** (tel. (928) 280 00 in Mariehamn, (0175) 309 20 in Grisslehamn) travels from Eckerö, on the west coast of Åland, to Grisslehamn, Sweden (37.50mk, students and railpass holders 19mk) with bus connections to both Mariehamn (½hr., 20.50mk) and Stockholm (2hr., 15mk).

Inter-island ferries are generally free (though there is a 42mk entry fee for the Turku archipelago). You can pick up the *Skärgårdstrafiken* ferry schedule or the *Ålandstrafiken* **bus** schedule at the Mariehamn tourist office. The main island is best explored by bike. **RoNo Rent,** across from the ferry terminal in Mariehamn, is the most convenient. (Bikes 25mk/day, 125mk/week. Mopeds, windsurfers, and boats, too. Open June-Aug. daily 9am-noon and 1-6pm; May and Sept. reduced hrs.)

Mariehamn On the south coast of the main island, this is the hub of activity on Åland. Local artwork and history springs to life at the **Åland Museum** at Stadshusparken off Storagatan. (Open Wed.-Mon. 10am-4pm, Tues. 10am-8pm; Sept.-April Wed.-Sun. 11am-4pm, Tues. 11am-8pm.) Just 500m north of the ferry terminal, the **Sjöfartsmuseum** displays navigational instruments in a cleverly constructed landbound ship. (Open daily 9am-5pm; Sept.-April daily 10am-4pm. 13mk.)

Botel Alida (tel. (928) 137 55), on Österleden 2km from the ferry terminal, offers sardine-sized doubles on a ship for 70mk. (Reception open May-Sept. 24hrs.) Otherwise, **Ålandsresor,** Storagatan 9 (tel. (928) 280 40), books accommodations for all the islands. (Reception open Mon.-Fri. 9am-5pm. Singles in private homes 130mk. Doubles 170mk. 30mk booking fee.) **Campground Gröna Udden** (tel. (928) 190 41) relaxes by the water, 10 minutes down Skillnadagatan from the town center. (15mk/tent. Open mid-May to Aug.) Mariehamn's restaurant prices make **supermarket** food suddenly alluring; try **Fokus** at Torggatan 14. (Open Mon.-Thurs. 9am-6pm, Fri. 9am-8pm, Sat. 9am-3pm, Sun. 9am-4pm.) At **Älänningen,** Torggatan 1, lunches run 35-37mk, salads 32mk. (Open Mon.-Fri. 9am-8pm, Sat. 10am-8pm, Sun. noon-8pm.) Bite into *Ålands pannkakor,* covered with marmalade and whipped cream, for 22mk at **Amanda Kaffestuga,** Norragatan 15 (open Mon.-Sat. 10am-6pm, Sun. 11am-6pm), or **Café Julius,** Torggatan 10, where a similar portion is 10mk. (Open daily 8am-10pm.) For maps of Åland and an *Åland Islands Guide,* head to the **tourist office** at Storagatan 11 (tel. (928) 273 00), 5 minutes from the Viking Line terminal. (Open daily 9am-6pm; Sept.-May Mon.-Sat. 10am-4pm.)

Sund and Djurvik Deep bays and cliffs predominate in the hilly northern districts; **Sund** is home to 4 attractions located only meters from each other. Once you've gotten on bus #4 (7/day, 15.50mk), get off at the Kastelholm stop and follow the sign to the 13th-century **Kastelholm Castle** (May-Sept. 6 tours/day; 20mk, students and seniors 14mk). Nearby lurks the **Vita Björn** museum, which features prison cells from various centuries (open May-Sept. daily 10am-5pm; 10mk, students and seniors 7mk), as well as an open-air museum, **Jan Karlsgården.** (Open May-Sept. daily 9:30am-5pm. Free.) At nearby **Bomarsund** (also on the bus #4 route) are the ruins of an ancient Russian fortress blown up in the Crimean War. Two **bicycle ferries** (Skarpnåtö-Hällö (20mk) in the north, Långnäs-Bomarsund (40mk) in the southeast) run thrice per day, creating excellent loops for day- to week-long trips, with inexpensive campgrounds and guesthouses situated conveniently along most routes.

In **Djurvik,** on the way to Eckerö in the west, there is an easy-to-afford but hard-to-reach guesthouse called **Djurviks Gästgård** (tel. (928) 324 33) on a secluded inlet full of fish and bluish swimmers. Take bus #1 to Gottby (9km), then walk the 4-5km to the guesthouse; the light traffic hinders hitching. (1- to 2-person room 130-180mk. Call ahead or contact Ålandsresor.) Farther west, in Eckerö, **Käringsunds Camping** (tel. (928) 383 09) charges only 8mk per tent; take bus #1 to Storby and walk 1km. A free wilderness hut with a wood stove, 4 bunks and a portrait of Åland's first prime minister stands proudly atop **Orrdals klint,** Åland's highest peak (a Himalayan 129m). Many take the bus to Saltvik-Kvarnbo, and then hitch toward Långbergsöda and follow the signs for an hour from the Orrdals junction by the logging road and trail. Most people here camp or stay in cottages. Freelance camping is forbidden without the landowner's permission, but the 10 campgrounds are quite cheap. Campgrounds often rent cottages. (2 persons 170mk, 3 persons 195mk.)

■■■ TURKU (ÅBO)

From meek beginnings as a trading outpost, the old city of Turku became Finland's first capital and premier town. It lost that status in 1812, when Tsar Alexander I snatched Finland from Sweden and reined the capital Russiaward to Helsinki. Shortly thereafter, Scandinavia's worst fire devoured 2500 of Turku's wooden buildings. Despite these losses, Turku today remains a flourishing cultural and academic center. Reflecting the city's rich Swedish inheritance, one of its two universities, **Åbo Akademi,** operates in Swedish. Near the campus, the massive **cathedral,** completed in 1300, speaks of the time when Turku was a center for the spiritual and commercial colonization of the Finnish hinterland. (Open Mon.-Fri. 10am-6pm, Sat. 10am-3pm, Sun. 11:30am-4:30pm; mid-Sept. to mid-April Mon.-Sat. 10am-3pm, Sun. after service-4:30pm. Concerts in summer Tues. at 8pm. Free.)

Sheltered from the ferry ports by a screen of trees, the 700-year-old **Turku Castle,** along the Aura River about 3km from the city center, tastefully combines sleek lines, medieval artifacts and an intriguing **historical museum.** (Open daily 10am-6pm; mid-Sept. to mid-April 10am-3pm. Museum 15mk.) **Luostarinmäki,** the only part of Turku to survive the 1827 fire, is now alive as an open-air **handicrafts museum** recalling workaday life. (Open daily 10am-6pm; mid-Sept. to mid-April Tues.-Sun. 10am-3pm. 15mk.) Across the river on Puolalanmäki hill, under the granite spires of the imperial **Turku Art Museum,** hang some of Akseli Gallen-Kallela's vibrant *Kalevala* paintings. (Open Tues., Wed., Sat. 10am-4pm, Thurs. 10am-8pm, Sun. 10am-6pm. 15mk, special exhibits 25mk.) In summer, open-air rock concerts rattle the parks just outside town (schedules at the tourist office), including **Ruisrock** in the 2nd weekend of July (call (921) 51 11 62 for info). The **Down by the Laituri** music festival transplants chunks of 1950s Americana to the river's banks the weekend before midsummer, and street dancing swings at 6pm on most summer Tuesdays by the Auransilta Bridge.

Accommodations, Food, and Practical Information One of Finland's best-appointed youth hostels, **Turun Kaupungin Retkeilymaja (HI),** Linnankatu 39 (tel. (921) 31 65 78), is midway between the ferry terminals (take bus

#1) and the train station (bus #3). From the train station walk west 3-4 blocks on Ratapihankatu, left on Puistokatu to the river and right on Linnankatu, or walk 20 minutes up Linnankatu from the ferry. (Reception open 6-10am and 3pm-midnight. Curfew 2am. Dorms 35mk. Doubles 55mk/person. Nonmembers 15mk extra.) For immaculate singles (170mk) and doubles (260mk), try the **St. Birgittas Convent Guesthouse,** Ursininkatu 15A (tel. (921) 50 19 10). The nearby **Matkakoti Turisti-Aula,** Käsityöläiskatu 11 (tel. (921) 233 44 84), offers 160mk singles and 220mk doubles. (Reception open 24hrs.) The **InterRail Center,** Läntinen Rantakatu 47 (tel. (921) 30 45 51), offers cheap homecooked meals, free luggage storage, and bike rentals. (20mk/day, 40mk deposit. Open Midsummer to mid-Aug. daily 8am-10pm.) **Ruissalo Camping** (tel. (921) 58 92 49) comes complete with sauna, water slide, and nude beach. Take bus #8 from Market Sq. (10km, 2/hr., 7mk. Camping 30mk, families 60mk. Open June-Aug.) Ruissalo Island also makes a refreshing daytrip, with lush forests, sunbathing, and boat rentals at Saaronniemi Beach.

For groceries, hop directly over the river from the Kaupungin hostel. **Kauppatori** (Market Square) peddles produce (open Mon.-Sat. 8am-2pm), while just southwest on Eerikinkatu the red-brick **Kauppahalli** (Market Hall) vends pricey pastries. (Open Mon.-Fri. 8am-5pm, also mid-May to Sept. Mon.-Fri. 3-10pm.) **Tolmuset**, Hämeen-katu 8, practically gives away hearty meals. (22mk daily special. Open Mon.-Fri. 7:30am-6pm.) **Verso,** upstairs at Linnankatu 3, is a riverside veggie bistro extraordinaire. Lunches (served until 2pm) run 34mk; any student ID shaves off 10%. (Open Mon.-Fri. 11am-5pm; Sept.-May also Sat. noon-5pm.) Festive Turku swims in cafés and riverside beer gardens. Stone-walled **Pinella,** by Tuomiokirkko bridge, exchanges a beer for 25mk. (Open Mon.-Sat. 11am-midnight, Sun. noon-10pm.) Nightspots are generally open until 1am, 2-3am on weekends. Live bands (cover 10mk) often play at **Bar 1957,** Eerikinkatu 12. (Open Sun.-Tues. noon-2am, Wed.-Thurs. noon-3am, Fri.-Sat. noon-8am.) The youthful, student-run **Kåren** disco (called **Ibiza** in summer) throbulates at Hämeenkatu 22. (Open Fri.-Sat. 10pm-4am.)

There's no shortage of **tourist offices:** a branch at Aurakatu 4 (open Mon.-Fri. 8:30am-7:30pm, Sat.-Sun. 10am-5pm; mid-Sept. to May Mon.-Fri. 8:30am-6pm, Sat.-Sun. 10am-5pm) supplements the main office, Käsityöläiskatu 3 (tel. (9700) 55 15), in the town center. (Open Mon.-Fri. 8am-4pm; Sept.-May 8:30am-4pm.) Turku is accessible by **train** from Helsinki (8/day, 2hr., 80mk), and from points northward via Toijala. From the terminal 3km from the train station, daily **ferries** ply to Marie-hamn in the Åland Islands and beyond to Stockholm. (See Getting to Finland, above.)

■ Near Turku

Naantali, 15km west of Turku, bills itself as the "sunshine town," a peaceful enclave of old wooden houses with a charming harbor and 700 years of history. The buildings of the **old town,** some dating back to the late 18th century, are situated to the south of the **Convent Church,** built in 1462. (Open daily noon-6pm; mid- to late Aug. daily noon-3pm; Sept.-Apr. Sun. noon-3pm.) Catch up on Naantali's rich history at the **Museum of Naantali,** Katinhäntä 1. (Open daily noon-6pm. 3mk.) From the shore, **Kultaranta,** the president's fortress-like summer residence, is visible (40mk). Even if you've never read *Finn Family Moomintroll,* you can still grow young again at **Moomin World,** a fantasy land spread throughout the town and islands of Naan-tali. (Open midsummer to mid-Aug. daily 10am-8pm. 65mk, children 4-14 35mk.) **Merisali,** situated in a seaside villa, offers a 40mk lunch buffet which includes *kotikalja,* a homemade non-alcoholic Finnish brew. (Open Easter to mid-Sept. daily 9am-midnight.) The **tourist office,** Kaivotori 2 (tel. (921) 85 08 50), can book accommodations and arrange tours. From the bus station walk southwest on Tul-likatu to Kaivokatu, right 300m; the tourist office is on your left. (Open daily 10am-8pm; mid-Aug. to May Mon.-Fri. 8am-4pm.) There are no youth hostels in Naantali, but **Naantali camping,** only 800m south of town, maintains small huts (doubles 180mk, quads 210mk) and tent sites. (34mk/person. Open June to mid-Aug.) **Buses**

run to Naantali from the Puutori square in Turku every 5-15 minutes. (25min., 11.50mk.)

LAKE DISTRICT

The vast Lake District of southeastern Finland is a sylvan fest of canoeing, hiking, and cross-country skiing amidst boundless stretches of water and forest. To truly experience it, avoid tourist centers and stay at one of the area's isolated youth hostels. Tourist offices can arrange rooms in farmhouses and point out wilderness huts.

■■■ TAMPERE

Though officially founded in 1779, Tampere is best described as a child of the industrial revolution. When in 1820 Scotsman James Finlayson harnessed the power of the nearby Tammerkoski rapids for a textile mill, he transformed a provincial town into the country's most industrialized city. Today industry is no longer the centerpiece of "the Manchester of Finland." Some of the red-brick factory buildings on the banks of Tammerkoski now house restaurants, and the old working-class neighborhood of Pispala, perched on a ridge between two lakes, is today the trendy abode of wealthy artists. Preserved workers' housing can be found in the museum of **Amuri**, Makasiininkatu 12, a fascinating showcase of 25 representative living quarters spanning the century before 1973. (Open early May to mid-Sept. Tues.-Sat. 9am-5pm, Sun. 11am-5pm. 10mk, students 3mk.) The proletarian spirit burns most brightly at the **Lenin Museum,** established and still managed by the Finnish-Soviet Friendship Society at Hämeenpuisto 28, site of the first conference of Lenin's revolutionary party. The only museum of its kind outside Eastern Europe, it may soon become the only one left in the world. (Open Mon.-Fri. 9am-5pm, Sat.-Sun. 11am-4pm. 10mk, students 3mk. Lenin pins 3mk.) Climb up the world's highest *esker* (a glacier-formed ridge) at **Pyynikki** park, and catch a view of both Näsijärvi lake and Pyhäjärvi lake from the observation tower (2mk), which also serves a delicious *munkki*, a Finnish pastry. Tampere's **Short Film Festival** (March 9-13 in 1994), featuring contestants from 30 different countries (5-day pass 300mk, seat tickets extra; for info call (931) 23 56 81), is rivaled in cosmopolitan content only by the **International Theater Festival.** (Aug. 9-14 in 1994. Tickets 0-150mk. For info call (931) 19 69 58.)

Accommodations and Food When your Marxist yearnings have faded, treat yourself to the 4-star **Domus hostel (HI),** Pellervonkatu 9 (tel. (931) 55 00 00), 2km east of the train station, where every room comes equipped with kitchenette and bathroom, and where the sauna, indoor pool (both open 7-10am), laundry room and bike rental are free. From the train station, follow Itsenäisyydenkatu and Sammonkatu and turn left onto Joukahaisenkatu, or take bus #25. (Reception open 24hrs. Dorms 50mk, nonmembers 65mk. Breakfast 20mk. Open June-Aug.) The alternative is the **Tampeeren NNKY (YWCA),** Tuomiokirkonkatu 12 (tel. (931) 22 54 46), 400m north on Tuomiokirkonkatu perpendicular to Hämeenkatu a block from the train station. (Max. stay 5 nights. Reception open 8-10am and 4pm-midnight. Triples and quads 45mk/person. Dorms 40mk. Nonmembers add 15mk. Breakfast 25mk. Kitchen. Open June to late Aug.) 5 km southwest on bus #1, **Camping Härmälä** (tel. (931) 65 12 50) overlooks Lake Pyhäjärvi. (Tents 60-62mk, cottages 100-275mk. Open early May to late Aug.)

Sample *mustamakkara,* a Tampere sausage containing flour and cow's blood at **Kauppahalli** (market hall), Hämeenkatu 19. (Open Mon.-Thurs. 8am-5pm, Fri. 8am-6pm, Sat. 8am-2pm.) Inexpensive groceries can be found at **Hanski,** Tuomiokirkonkatu 19. (Open Mon.-Fri. 9am-8pm, Sat. 91m-4pm.) At **Kaks Mattia,** Ilmarinkatu 16, you can heap a plate to your heart's content for 33mk (open Mon.-

LET'S GO® Travel

1994 CATALOG

We give you the world
at a discount!

ORDER
1-800-5-LETS-GO
TOLL FREE!

• Discount Flights • Eurails • Travel Gear

LET'S PACK IT UP

Let's Go Supreme

Innovative hideaway suspension with parallel stay internal frame turns backpack into carry-on suitcase. Includes lumbar support pad, torso and waist adjustment, leather trim, and detachable daypack. Waterproof Cordura nylon, lifetime guarantee, 4400 cu. in. Navy, Green or Black.

A • • • • • • • • • • • • • $175

Let's Go Backcountry

Full size, slim profile expedition pack designed for the serious trekker. New Airflex suspension. X-frame pack with advanced composite tube suspension. Velcro height adjustment, side compression straps. Detachable hood converts into a fanny pack. Waterproof Cordura nylon, lifetime guarantee. Main compartment 6530 cu. in. extends to 7130 cu. in.

C • • • • • • • • • $210

Let's Go Backpack/Suitcase

Hideaway suspension with internal frame turns backpack into carry-on suitcase. Detachable daypack makes it 3 bags in 1. Waterproof Cordura nylon, lifetime guarantee, 3750 cu. in. Navy, Green or Black.

B • • • • • • • • • • • • • • $130

Undercover NeckPouch

Ripstop nylon with soft Cambrelle back. 3 pockets. 6 x 7". Lifetime guarantee. Black or Tan.

D • • • • • • • • • • • • • $9.95

Undercover WaistPouch

Ripstop nylon with soft Cambrelle back. 2 pockets. 12 x 5" with adjustable waistband. Lifetime guarantee. Black or Tan.

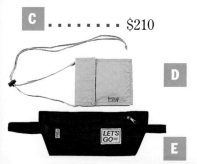

E • • • • • • • • • • • • • • $9.95

WE GIVE YOU THE WORLD...

AT A DISCOUNT!

LET'S GO TRAVEL
53a Church St.
Cambridge, MA 02138
(617) 495-9649 or 1-800-5-LETS-GO
FAX (617) 496-8015

LET'S GO HOSTELING
1994-95 Youth Hostel Card
Required by most international hostels.
Must be a U.S. resident.

F1 Adult (ages 18-55) $25

F2 Youth (under 18) $10

Sleepsack
Required at all hostels. Washable durable
poly/cotton. 18" pillow pocket. Folds into
pouch size.

G $13.95

1993-94 Youth Hostel Guide (IYHG)
Essential information about 4000 hostels in
Europe and the Mediterranean.

H $10.95

LET'S GET STARTED
Please print or type. Incomplete applications will be returned

Last Name	First Name	Date of Birth

Street   *We do not ship to P.O. Boxes. U.S. addresses only.*

City	State	Zip Code

Phone   Date Trip Begins

Item Code	Description, Size & Color	Quantity	Unit Price	Total Price

Shipping & Handling	
If order totals: · · · · · Add	Total Merchandise Price
Up to $30.00 · · · · · · · $4.00	Shipping & Handling (See box at left)
30.01-100.00 · · · · · · · $6.00	For Rush Handling Add $10 for continental U.S., $12 for AK & HI
Over 100.00 · · · · · · · $7.00	MA Residents (Add 5% sales tax on gear & books)
	Total

Mastercard/Visa Order

Cardholder name_____

Card number_____

Expiration date_____

Allow 2-3 weeks for delivery. Rush
orders delivered within one week of
our receipt.

Enclose check or money order
payable to:
Harvard Student Agencies, Inc.
53a Church St. Cambridge, MA 021

Prices subject to change without notice

Fri. 7am-5pm), and at **Myllärit,** Åkerlundinkatu 4, 4 salads and an all-you-can-eat buffet lunch costs 35mk. (Open Mon. 11am-3:30pm, Tues.-Sat. 11am-midnight.) At **Tullikamari,** live music resonates 3-4 nights a week (cover 15-100mk; beer 15mk; min. age 18) in a warehouse where you can lunch during the academic year for 35mk. (Open Mon. and Fri. 11am-4pm, Tues.-Thurs. 11am-2am, Sat. 9pm-4am.)

Practical Information Learn about guided walking tours of the area (1½-2hr., 25mk) at the **tourist office,** Verkatehtaankatu 2 (tel. (931) 12 66 52 or 12 67 75), a block off Hämeenkatu on the east bank of the river. (Open Mon.-Fri. 8:30am-8pm, Sat. 8:30am-6pm, Sun. 11:30am-6pm; Sept.-May Mon.-Fri. 8:30am-5pm.) Tampere connects south by **train** to Helsinki (9/day, 2hr., 80mk) and to Turku (7/day, 2hr., 72mk) and north by train to Oulu (6/day, 5hr., 182mk), or by the steamers that sail thrice a week to Ruovesi (4½hr., 152mk) and beyond to Virrat (7½hr., 204mk).

■ Near Tampere

Rauma, 146 km west of Tampere, is one of Finland's best-preserved medieval communities, lauded for seafaring, lace-making, and an incomprehensible dialect. Trains run from Tampere to Kokemähi, with a bus connection (railpasses valid) to Rauma (2hr., 60mk), though many hitchhike. Amble through the extensive **old town,** protected under the UNESCO World Heritage Convention. The **Rauma Lace Festival,** held the last week of July, celebrates all things lace with exhibits, music, and plays.

The **tourist office,** Valtakatu 2 (tel (938) 34 45 51), is 1 block from the bus station. (Open Mon.-Fri. 9am-5pm.) There is also tourist information (tel. (938) 22 45 66) on the market Square during the summer. (Open June-Aug. Mon.-Fri. 10am-6pm, Sat. 10am-2pm, Sun. noon-3pm.) The **Kesähotelli Rauma (HI),** Satamahatu 20 (tel. (938) 824 01 30), is situated 600m west of the bus station. (Dorms 60mk, nonmembers 75mk. Open June-Aug.)

■■■ JYVÄSKYLÄ

Right in the middle of Finland's lake district, Jyväskylä is famous as the home of architect Alvar Aalto. The compact and modern city is sprinkled with Aalto's buildings which, if you can't pick them out yourself, are presented in a guide (5mk) offered by the **tourist office,** Vapaudenkatu 38 (tel. (941) 62 49 04), one block up Asemakatu (the street perpendicular to the train station) and left one block. (Open Mon.-Fri. 8am-6pm, Sat.-Sun. 10am-6pm; Sept.-May Mon.-Fri. 8am-5pm.) The **Alvar Aalto Museum,** at Alvar Aallon Katu 7, left on Vapaudenkatu to the end, will help you follow the development of his style. (Open Tues.-Sun. 11am-6pm. 10mk, Fri. free.) Nearby, the **University of Jyväskylä,** largely designed by Aalto, occupies an isolated campus in piney woods near the museum. The unique **Finnish National Costume Center,** Gummeruksenkatu 3E, displays a changing selection of national costumes. (Open Tues.-Sun. 11am-6pm. 10mk, Fri. free.) Jyväskylä is a student-oriented town; show your student ID, and admission to any of its 9 museums is free. During the 2nd week of June, Jyväskylä hosts an **Arts Festival,** with concerts, film screenings, and exhibitions. (Call (941) 61 56 24 1 for info. Ticket prices 25-103mk, students win 25-50% discounts.)

Sporty **Laajari (HI),** Laajavuorentie 15 (tel. (941) 25 33 55), has a ski slope and skateboard ramp in its backyard and a free sauna in the basement. Take bus #25 (7.5 mk) from the park across from the tourist office. (Dorms 30mk, nonmembers 45mk. Kitchen.) Lakeside **Tuomiojärvi Camping** (tel (941) 62 48 96) lies 2km north of town by bus #8. (35mk/person. Cabins 170mk for 4 persons. Open June-Aug.) Treat yourself to a lunch special at **Rosso Ristorante,** Kauppakatu 19. (Pizza 34mk, lunch 35-45mk. Open Mon.-Thurs. 11am-11pm, Fri.-Sat. 11am-midnight, Sun. noon-11pm.) **Trains** from Tampere (8/day, 2hr., 68mk) and Helsinki (8/day, 3½hr.,

136mk) plus **bus** connections to towns throughout the Lake District make Jyväskylä a regional transport hub.

■■■ SAVONLINNA

The tsarist aristocracy turned Savonlinna into a fashionable resort 150 years ago; with an attractive harbor, pleasurable islands and ancient fortress, it remains the most alluring of the Lake District towns. While the others merely border lakes, Savonlinna is surrounded by the region's crystal water. During the renowned **Opera Festival** (July 7-30 in 1994), divas come from all over the world to perform in the courtyard of Olavinlinna Castle. Tickets to performances cost 200-500mk and should be ordered as early as the preceding October. Write to Savonlinna Opera Festival, Olavinkatu 35, SF-57130 Savonlinna (tel. (957) 51 47 00; fax (957) 218 66) or contact the tourist office (see below). Unclaimed tickets are sold at the ticket booth on Tallisaari (before castle) at 5pm the day of the show, but individual scalpers often charge less, and prices plunge nearer to showtime. The **Retretti Arts Center** takes culture to new depths; a summer concert series resounds in the wonderful acoustics of a deep cave. (Tickets 20-90mk, students 20-70mk. Inquire at the Opera Festival Ticket Office.) The 1.5km of caverns feature paintings and sculpture amid shimmering reflecting pools. (Open late May to June and Aug. daily 10am-6pm; late June-July daily 10am-7pm. 60mk, students and seniors 55mk.) All trains to Savonlinna will stop at Retretti upon request. During July, special *lättähattu* trains shuttle between Savonlinna and Retretti (15mk, ½hr.). Head east from the bus and train stations on Olavinkatu and cross the bridge, then hug Linnankatu along the south shore until you reach **Olavinlinna Castle,** a weatherworn but intact medieval fortress. A guided tour sallies through steep defense passages, winding stairways, and three 16th-century towers. (Open daily 10am-5pm; mid-Aug. to May 10am-3pm. 14mk.) For some peace and sun, hop north via the two footbridges to the pine-covered isle of **Sulosaari.**

Accommodations, Food, and Practical Information Despite its location behind the casino, **Vuorilinna Hostel (HI),** Kylpylaitoksentie (tel. (957) 575 00), snoozes peacefully on the island 200m across the footbridge from the market. (Reception open June-Aug. 6:30am-10:30pm. 75mk, nonmembers 90mk. Breakfast 25mk.) **Retkeilymaja Malakias (HI),** Pihlajavedenkuja 6 (tel. (957) 232 83), is 1.5km from town. Going up Tulliportinkatu, veer right on Savonkatu, or take bus #1, 2, 3, or 4. (Reception open July to mid-Aug. 7am-11pm. 75mk, nonmembers 90mk. Breakfast 22mk.) **Vuohimäki Camping** (tel. (957) 53 73 53) is 7km out, but bus #3 (2/hr) runs. (Camping 35mk/person, June and Aug. 33mk. Open early June to late Aug.)

Eating and imbibing here centers around Olavinkatu. For a great breakfast deal, visit **Pietari Kylliäinen** at Olavinkatu 15, on the castle side of town. (All-you-can-eat 17mk. Open Mon. and Sat. 7-9:30am, Tues.-Fri. 6:30-9:30am, Sun. 7-10am.) For lunch, try **Steakhouse San Martin,** Olavinkatu 46. (Salads 28mk, lunch special 40mk. Open Mon.-Fri. 10:30am-9pm, Sat. 11am-9pm, Sun. noon-8pm.) Across Olavinkatu from the market, throw back a few beers at **Happy Time Pub,** Kauppatori 1. (Open Sun.-Thurs. noon-1am, Fri.-Sat. noon-2am; live bands Wed. No cover.)

The friendly but busy **tourist office** occupies the yellow building across the bridge from the market at Puistokatu 1 off Olavinkatu (tel. (957) 27 34 92). They will hold your baggage, help you find accommodations and change money when banks are closed. (Open daily 8am-6pm; July 8am-10pm; Aug. 8am-4pm; Sept.-May 9am-4pm.) Savonlinna is yours by **train** from Helsinki (5/day, 160mk) or **bus** (railpasses not valid) from Pieksämäki (2/day, 57mk) or Kuopio (4/day, 75mk). The train stops first at Savonlinna-Kauppatori in the center of town and near the tourist office, then continues to the Savonlinna stop by the main train station. **Water travel** costs a pretty *penni* but provides the best access to the pristine regions of the lakes; vessels cruise between Savonlinna and Kuopio. (Tues.-Sun. 10am; 11½hr; 250mk.)

■ Near Savonlinna

The stretch of land and water between Savonlinna and Kuopio includes many worthwhile stops. One of the best is the isolated farmhouse **Pohjataival (HI)** (tel. (972) 664 19), 12km from Heinävesi, with its own steamboat pier. Unwind with the cows, ducks, and dogs, bloat yourself with glorious homecooked meals (25-30mk), and debauch in the sauna. (Dorms 45mk, nonmembers 60mk. Rowboats available.) The Savonlinna-Kuopio motorboat will drop you literally at the doorstep; otherwise take the bus to Pieksämäki, the train to Heinävesi and then call the farmhouse for a 30mk lift. At the handsome **Valamo Monastery** (tel. (972) 619 59), 35km from Heinävesi along the Savonlinna-Kuopio boat route, guests often outnumber monks 20 to 1. Stay in the guest house for 100mk per night (breakfast included), and chow at the restaurant for 40-65mk. (No shorts or photographs.) Visit the largest wood church in the world in **Kerimäki**, 24km east of Savonlinna. (Bus 15mk. Guided tours 5mk. Free entry.) A more worldly retreat is **Rauhalinna,** a wooden palace built in the 19th century by a Russian commander for his wife. Cruises to this elegant island leave the market square in Savonlinna several times daily. (1¼hr., 30mk round-trip)

■■■ KUOPIO

Strategically situated at the Lake District's northern edge, Kuopio was originally established in 1782 to boost the maritime trade industry. Two hundred years later, Kuopio is playing up its ideal location as Finland's lakeside cruise hub. Steamers sail daily to Heinävesi (5hr., 125mk) and Savonlinna (11hr., 250mk); find out more about cruises at the **tourist office,** Haapaniemenkatu 17 (tel. (971) 18 25 84, -85), next to the market square and the town hall. (Open Mon.-Fri. 8am-5pm, Sat. 9am-1pm; mid-Aug. to May Mon.-Fri. 8am-5pm.) **Retkeilymaja Tekma** is the closest hostel to the train station (2½km), easily accessible by buses #3 and 5 (7.5mk) from the city center. (Reception open 8am-10:30pm. Doubles 80mk/person. Dorms 50mk. Nonmembers add 15mk. Kitchens.) **Rauhalahti Camping** (tel. (971) 31 22 44), 7km from town, has Kuopio's best beach; take bus #20 (2/hr., 7mk). They also rent bikes, mopeds, canoes, and boats. (30mk. 2-person cabins 150mk. Open mid-May to Aug.) Kuopio's lively and colorful **marketplace** (open daily 7am-2pm; June to mid-Aug. until 3pm) has crafts, flowers, and delicious traditional foods. This is the place to sample *kalakukko,* a Finnish fish bread. Finicky cats agree—it's yummy. Lining the market square, several grocery stores keep late hours on weekdays. (Open Mon.-Fri. until 8pm.)

   Trains link Kuopio to Helsinki (5/day, 5hr., 170mk), Jyväskylä (4/day, 2hr., 72mk), and Kajaani (5/day, 2hr., 72mk) and Oulu (3 /day, 4½hr., 140mk) up north.

■■■ OULU

A lively university city, Oulu's flower-bordered streets and well-tended bike paths lend it a Mediterranean grace that belies the city's history as one of Finland's busiest ports and the world's leading tar exporter during the 19th century. See and sniff exotic flora from around the world at the University of Oulu's **Botanical Gardens,** 7km north of the center along bus route #4, 6, 7, or 16. Twin glass pyramids, named Romeo and Julia, house citrus, olive and cocoa trees. (Pyramids open Tues.-Fri. 8am-5pm, Sat.-Sun. 10am-5pm; Sept.-May Tues.-Fri. 8am-3pm, Sat.-Sun. noon-3pm. Open-air gardens open daily 8am-9pm. Free.) A bizarre cultural phenomenon awaits at the shopping center between the rail station and the youth hostel: hundreds of Finnish teens drive cars back and forth for hours on end, with friends jumping in and out of back seats, in an unusual form of "cruising." **Nallikari,** Finland's Côte d'Azur, rims an island 5km northwest of town. The largely untouristed and splendiferous beach is the best place in Northern Finland to enjoy the Bothnian waters, despite its tacky amusement park. You can stay at nearby **Nallikari Camping**. (Tents 30mk/person. 4-person cabins 290mk, May and Sept.-Oct. cabins 240mk.) Take bus #5 (hourly) from Kajaanintie outside the hostel heading toward the center of the city.

Retkeilymaja Välkkylä (HI), Kajaanintie 36 (tel. (981) 37 77 07, in winter 311 52 47), offers the only inexpensive lodgings in town; roomy quads (not heinous bunk beds) ensure a comfy stay. Walk down Rautatienkatu parallel to the railway, take a right onto Kajaanintie, and continue until the cemetery ends and a hostel sign appears. (Reception open 5:30am-midnight. 50mk, nonmembers 65mk. Breakfast 25mk. Kitchen. Free laundry. Sauna (7-10am) 15 mk. Open June-Aug.) Toss one back with the locals at **Madison** (beer 10-20mk, lunch 43mk), on the corner of Isokatu and Pakkahuoneenkatu, and play pool for free. (Open Mon.-Thurs. 10am-1am, Fri.-Sat. 10am-2am, Sun. 11am-1am). Dungeonesque **Rock Club 45 Special,** Saaristonkatu 12, complete with iron bars and shackles, serves "Jailhouse Rock" hamburgers (38mk) and hosts Finnish bands. No Billy Dee Williams, though. (Open nightly 8pm-4am. Cover Fri.-Sat. 20mk, students 15mk.)

The **municipal tourist office,** Torikatu 10 (tel. (981) 314 12 94), greets with good-natured help. Take Hallituskatu, the broad avenue perpendicular to the train station, for 6 blocks, then go left on Torikatu. (Open Mon.-Fri. 9am-4pm. Early June to mid-Aug. tourist info at ice cream stand in Otto Kashin *puisto* (park) Sat.-Sun. 10am-3pm). All **trains** between north and south Finland pass through Oulu's clutches; 4-5 per day leave south to Helsinki (224mk) and north to Rovaniemi (92mk).

■■■ KUUSAMO AND THE KARHUNKIERROS

For foaming rapids and bottomless gorges, lace up your hiking boots and head for the **Karhunkierros** (The Bear's Ring), a 75km hiking trail through untainted landscape near the Russian-Finnish border. To get started, head by bus to Kuusamo from either Oulu (6/day, 3½hr., about 100mk), Kajaani (4/day, 4½hr., 116mk) or Rovaniemi (2/day, 2½hr., 90mk). In **Kuusamo,** stay at **Kuusamon Kansanopisto (HI)** (tel. (989) 221 32), a yellow house across from the bus station. (Reception open June-Aug. 5-9pm. 45-60mk, nonmembers 60-75mk.) Stock up on food at **Kitkan Viisas** in the same building as the bus station. (Open Mon.-Fri. 9am-8pm, Sat. 9am-6pm.) The Kuusamo **tourist office,** Torangintaival 2 (tel. (989) 850 29 10), 2km from town at the corner of highways 20 (Ouluntie) and 5, peddles maps (47mk) and proffers information about the trail, which takes 4-6 days, depending on your condition. If you want to hike just part of the trail, they'll show you which buses to catch. (Open daily 9am-8pm; Sept.-May Mon.-Fri. 9am-5pm.) There are free 10- to 20-person cabins every 10km or so along the way, but bring a tent during the summer in case they're full. You may want rubber boots for the boggy stretches. Bring food and mosquito repellent—there are only 2 supply stations on the trail and billions of pesky pests ready to eat you alive. To fish, you need both a local (50mk/day, 200mk/week) and a national license (30mk/year); get both at the tourist office in Kuusamo.

LAPLAND (LAPPI)

For a different sense of space and time, for untouched fells rising against a clean northern sky, for swarms of reindeer and herds of mosquitoes... visit Lapland, Europe's most desolate wilderness. In the south you'll find crashing river rapids and whitefish. To the north lies 80km-long *Inarijärvi* (Lake Inari) and its countless islands; even farther north, the steep tundra slopes of the Teno River Valley.

The sun never sets on Lapland during the pleasant 2- to 3-month summer. In winter the sun rises for only a few hours a day, but the dry air abates the effects of the low temperatures. Clear sky, moonlight, and white snow produce an eerie blue glow, and the green, red, and yellow streaks of the Northern Lights illuminate a surreal snowscape. Skiing is ideal from February to mid-May, with facilities and rental outlets at almost every tourist center (Pallas, Pyhä, Ruka, Saariselkä, Ylläs, and Ounasvaara, near Rovaniemi). In summer, guides lead hiking expeditions from the same places. Only experienced groups should undertake independent excursions. Hikers should plan their routes around the mountain huts run by the Finnish Youth Hostel Association. The best source for maps, hiking routes, locations of huts and cabins, and information regarding fishing licenses is **Etiäinen** (tel. (960) 36 25 26), located 8km north of Rovaniemi in Santa Claus's Village (see below).

Most of the Sami (Finnish Lapps) and Kolttas (originally Russian Lapps) live in the 4 northernmost parishes of Sodankylä, Enontekiö, Inari, and Utsjoki; at least 800 families still make a living from reindeer herding. Local delicacies include *poroliha* (Rudolph meat), *lohi* (salmon), and liqueurs made from Arctic *lakka* (cloudberries).

■■■ ROVANIEMI

Tucked 8km south of the Arctic Circle, Rovaniemi is the capital of Finnish Lapland. Take bus #8 or 10 from the train station (7.50mk) to **Santa Claus's Village,** from which destinations around the world are served by reindeer shuttle. (Departures yearly in late Dec.; youths free if you've been good.) You can meet the elves and pet the reindeer too; in fact, Mr. and Mrs. Claus's home is one of the nicest in this spread-out metropolis—makes you wonder about the ties between Christianity and capitalism! (Open daily 8am-8pm; Sept.-May 9am-5pm. Free.) A visit to the brand-new **Arktikum** center, Pohgoisranta 4, is a must; it houses the **Arctic Science Center,** with exhibits on life and culture in the north, as well as the **Provincial Museum of Lapland.** (Open daily 10am-8pm; Sept. to mid-June Tues.-Sun. 10am-6pm. 30mk, students 15mk; films 15mk.)

Rovaniemi's **HI youth hostel**, Hallituskatu 16 (tel. (960) 34 46 44), lacks a kitchen. Turn right from the station, go up the hill, and turn right on Hallituskatu just after the bus station. (Reception open 6:30-10am and 5-10pm. 45mk, nonmembers 60mk. Breakfast 24mk.) Across the river from the town center, **Ounaskoski Camping** (tel. (960) 34 53 04) has a prime location and river swimming. (37mk. Open June-Aug.) In the Sampokeskus shopping center, **Ristorante Il Bel Giovanni** serves up pasta dishes and Finnish lunch specials. (43mk. Open daily 11am-10pm.) **Rinnemarket** is the closest market to the station, with a huge selection including several types of *lapinleipä* (Lappish bread). (Open Mon.-Fri. 8am-8pm, Sat. 8am-6pm.)

The **tourist office** at Aallonkatu 1 (tel. (960) 34 62 70 or 322 22 79) finds rooms in private homes (about 120mk) and dishes up a weekly events listing amusingly titled *Let's Go,* as well as information on boat (95-250mk) and snowmobile (220-530mk) safaris. (Open Mon.-Fri. 8am-6pm, Sat.-Sun. 11:30am-4pm; Sept.-May Mon.-Fri. 8am-4pm.) From the train station, head right on Ratakatu and turn right on Hallituskatu; follow Hallituskatu to the end, where you go left on Valtakatu; it becomes Aallonkatu after 3 blocks. **Buses** head east to Kuusamo (2½hr., 90mk), and north to Inari (5½hr., 150mk), Karigasniemi (7hr., 190mk), Kilpisjärvi (6½hr., 180mk), and Muonio (3½hr., 110mk) with connections to Norway. Travel to Sweden by train to Kemi, then by bus (railpasses valid) 25km west to the border town of Tornio. Some buses continue across the border into Haparanda. Stay at the Tornio **HI hostel** (tel. (9698) 416 82), at Kirkkokatu, 1.6km north of the Finnish customs post. Rovaniemi is easily accessible by **trains** coming northward through Oulu (Helsinki-Rovaniemi, 4/day, 260 mk) and by southbound buses from Inari, Muonio, Enontekiö, and Karasjok, Norway. Finnair also flies here from Helsinki (youth fare 470mk).

■■■ NORTHERN LAPLAND

When you set out for northern Lapland, plan ahead; connections will be difficult. From Rovaniemi, there are 2 routes to the north, traversed by buses and hitchers: Highway 79 leads towards Muonio and Enontekiö in the northwest, Highway 4 to Inari and Utsjokidue north. At the info office in the Rovaniemi train station, borrow timetables for Lapland's 2 bus companies: the **Postilinjat** (postal buses), and **J.M. Eskelisen Lapin Linjat Oy.** Prices are fairly similar; the postal line is slower.

Next to Lake Inari, the minute town of **Inari** is both a tourist spot and an old Lapp center. Seaplanes roar off the lake, and befuddled reindeer wander the streets. A well-kept and friendly (but small) **retkeilymaja (HI)** (tel. (9697) 512 44) welcomes travelers. It's a few hundred meters north from the center of town; turn left at the gas station. (Reception open 8am-noon and 4-11pm. Dorms 25mk. Nonmembers 40mk. Open March-Sept.) Six official **campgrounds** punctuate the wilderness. The tiny **tourist office** (tel. (9697) 511 93; open mid-June to mid-Sept. Mon.-Sat. 9am-8pm) sits next to a gallery of regional art in the town center. Ask them about **Lemmenjoki River** hiking, about 40km from Inari (daily bus connection), and about boat trips (50mk). The **Ravadasköngäs Falls** resound for kilometers; make day-hikes and return to Inari, or crash out in the wilderness huts along the trails. A few professional gold-panners still work claims along the river.

North of Inari, the River Teno winds along the Norwegian border below dwarf birches and tundra-covered fells. **Karigasniemi,** an isolated outpost, has an **HI retkeilymaja** (tel. (9697) 611 88) right in the center of "town." (35mk, nonmembers 50mk.) Use your railpass to its max at **Kolari,** the northernmost rail point in Finland. (In summer and ski season 2 train/week.) The train station is 4km north of town, although all buses stop at the TB gas station 400m west of the train station. Stay at **Vaattovaaran retkeilymaja (HI)** (tel. (9695) 610 86) in town. Buses run from Kolari and Rovaniemi to **Muonio,** then continue either north to Kautokeino in Norwegian Lapland (7½hr. from Rovaniemi), or northwest through **Kilpisjärvi** in Finland's most mountainous region (7hr.) before emerging an hour later at Skibotn on the Norwegian coast and connecting with the bus to Tromsø. Hiking in this pure, untainted part of the world is stunning, but the freedom exploring uninhabited wilderness carries with it the responsibility not to fall off the edge of it all: carry a map and compass. Muonio has 2 hostels; while in Kilpisjärvi you can stay at the **Retkeilykeskus (HI)** (tel. (9696) 26 59; 45-55mk, nonmembers add 15mk). Hike from Kilpisjärvi across the gently rounded peaks of the **Malla Nature Reserve** and to the **Three Countries Frontier,** where Finland, Norway, and Sweden meet on the shores of a lonely lake.

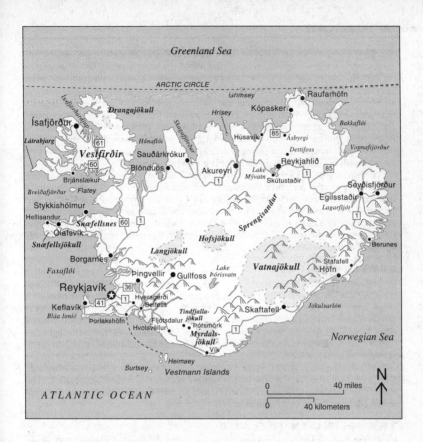

Iceland (Ísland)

US$1	= 69.28kr (krónur, or ISK)	**10kr =** **US$0.15**
CDN$1	= 52.66kr	**10kr =** **CDN$0.19**
UK£1	= 107.38kr	**10kr =** **UK£0.09**
IR£1	= 100.48kr	**10kr =** **IR£0.10**
AUS$1	= 45.08kr	**10kr =** **AUS$0.22**
NZ$1	= 38.31kr	**10kr =** **NZ$0.26**
SAR1	= 14.41kr	**10kr =** **SAR0.66**
Country Code: 354		**International Dialing Prefix: 90**

Land at Iceland's Keflavík Airport and you'll think you're on another planet. As the airport bus twists towards Reykjavík past inland mountains and plumes of geothermal steam, you'll notice that the country is more than the fields of crumbled lava that surround the terminal. Further afield rages a topographical riot of birch shrubs and glacier-tipped valleys, torrential rivers, harsh winds and sheltered coves, spitting volcanos and green hillsides. Iceland is hardly accurate, since the Gulf Stream keeps winters warmer than New York's.

In fact, Iceland pushes social frontiers even more than geological and geographic ones. Icelanders are liberal about ignoring European convention: 55% of children

447

are born out of wedlock, people don't frown on using friendships to get better prices and service, and everyone loves the president, who, incidentally, is a woman. At the same time, Icelanders are fervent homogenizers and traditionalists. Women keep their maiden names, a language committee systematically banishes foreign words, most roads are still unpaved, and milk and meat imports are banned. Despite near-Japanese prices and rampant consumerism (cellular phones are everywhere, and the per capita consumption of Coke is surpassed only by Mexico's), Icelanders know how to live with nature. Eighty-five percent of all households are geothermally heated, hydroelectric power makes fossil fuels redundant, the sea supplies Iceland with 60% of its exports, and trash is nowhere in sight.

The fierce Norwegian noblemen who settled here with their Irish slaves in the 9th century started Iceland's tradition of internal democracy when the country's first parliament met at Þingvellir in 930 AD. Today, it's worth a case of chronic sticker shock to join Iceland's 265,000 residents, who still consider themselves privileged to live half-apart from the rest of Europe—even though they must work the longest week in the world (54-56 hours) to maintain this paradoxical modern life on an island in the middle of the North Atlantic.

GETTING THERE

From North America, flying is the only option. **Icelandair** (tel. (800) 223-5500) flies from New York all year (Thurs.-Tues. in summer), from Orlando (in summer 1/week, early Sept.-late May 1-2/week), and from Baltimore (April-late Oct. 3-4/week). These planes connect each morning with flights to Icelandair's European destinations; Luxembourg is the most popular. The only scheduled non-Icelandair flights to Iceland are on **SAS** from Copenhagen (3/week) and on **Lufthansa** from Frankfurt (1/week, summer only).

The only opportunity to feel the sea wind off Iceland's rugged shores is on the ferry *Norröna*, which circles the North Atlantic via Seyðisfjörður (East Iceland), Tórshavn (Faroe Islands), Bergen (Norway), and Hanstholm (Denmark); see the East Iceland section for more information.

TRAVELING IN ICELAND

Icelanders make it very easy to travel in their country. One tour company, **BSÍ,** coordinates all bus schedules and prices into a single system. There are no trains. Free schedules are available in hostels and tourist offices. The *Iceland 1994* brochure lists selected bus schedules as well as tours and ferry routes.

Buses Though flying is more comfortable, **bus travel** can be cheaper and allows you to appreciate the rugged terrain up close. Land travel focuses on the 1411km **Highway #1,** completed in 1974, which circles the island. (Only partially paved, it often has just one lane.) Plan on at least a week in Iceland if you want to circle the country on the ring road; buses do it in four 5- to 9-hour stages (Reykjavík to Akureyri to Egilsstaðir to Höfn and back to Reykjavík, and vice versa), with daily service on each leg from mid-June through August. Frequency drops dramatically off-season. You can buy tickets in the stations *(umferðarmiðstöð)* in Reykjavík and Akureyri, or from the driver. **BSÍ,** based in the Reykjavík bus station, sells 2 passes that simplify bus travel greatly. The **Full Circle Passport** (11,500kr) allows you to circle the island at your own pace. (Available mid-May to Sept.) The **Omnibus Passport** (available all year) entitles you to a period of unlimited travel on all scheduled bus routes. (1 week 14,000kr, 2 weeks 18,000kr, 3 weeks 23,500kr, 4 weeks 26,000k.r) Both passes entitle you to 10% discounts on many ferries, camping grounds, farms, and *hótel edda* sleeping-bag accommodations. In the off-season, one-week Omnibus Passports are cheaper, since fewer routes are available.

Flights The only quick way to travel in Iceland is by air; flights are on propeller planes with occasionally stellar views over glaciers, mountains, and lava fields, though more often of puffy nimbocumulus clouds. **Flugleiðir** (Icelandair's domestic service) flies primarily between Reykjavík and major towns, **Flugfélag Norðurlands** out of Akureyri, and **Flugfélag Austurlands** between towns in the east. The two available air packages may be cheaper than the bus. The first, the **Air Rover,** is only available for purchase abroad at Icelandair offices, and offers 4 stops from Reykjavík for US$280. The second option, the **Four Sector Icelandair Pass,** allows 3 destinations from Reykjavík and may be purchased in Iceland (US$176). Both are valid on the regional scheduled airlines as well as Icelandair. Another option is the **Air/Bus Rover** (fly one-way, bus the other), offered by Icelandair and BSÍ Travel. Valid from June 1 to Sept. 30, a ticket from Reykjavík to Akureyri costs 7800kr. Icelandair offers 20% student discounts on all flights, and a 50% companion discount. Flugfélag Norðurlands offers 25% discounts for students on all flights. Iceland's dicey weather can ground flights on short notice, so *do not* plan to fly back to Reykjavík the day before your plane leaves Iceland.

Cars Seeing the country by **car** (preferably 4-wheel-drive) allows you the most freedom. Car rental *(bílaleiga)* starts at about 4000kr per day and 30kr per km (ask about special package deals). Patient **hitchers** try the busiest roads in summer, but rides can be hard to come by, especially in the East. The traffic is sparse and the weather unpredictable. A tent, a map and awareness of recent road closings help. **Cycling** is becoming increasingly popular, but ferocious winds, non-existent road shoulders, and thousands of aimless sheep conspire to make the going difficult. The cheapest and most rewarding way to see Iceland is on foot. Well-marked trails are rare, but many areas of the country are suitable for walking. (See The Interior for more information.)

ICELAND ESSENTIALS

The tourist season in Iceland lasts from June through August. Many accommodations, transport and tourist information offices hibernate until June 1. The summer is *the* best time to travel here. Though the sun technically dips beneath the horizon for a few hours each night, it never gets really dark, there's no snow, and it's warm enough to camp and hike. The Gulf Stream keeps temperatures moderate: the mercury rarely gets above 60°F (16°C) in summer, or below 20°F (-6°C) in winter. Bring watertight, lightweight clothing that can be layered. A rain jacket, woolen sweaters, and sturdy shoes are a must any time of the year. Iceland's hot water wells spawn an extensive outdoor bathing culture, so pack a swimsuit. Every town has comfortable pools with special hot pools on the side.

Seek out the tourist information offices in large and important towns for mounds of schedules and brochures, and request information at hotel reception desks in smaller towns for local information. Must-haves are the free brochures **Around Iceland,** with accommodations, restaurant, and museum listings for every town, and **Iceland A-Z,** which presents relevant practical information concisely. The Icelandic language has changed little from Old Norse, but fortunately most Icelanders speak English. Icelandic's two extra letters need not confuse:Þ (lower-case þ) is pronounced as in *th*orn, Ð (lower-case ð) as in *th*e.

On June 17, Independence Day festivals are held all over Iceland, the best of them in Reykjavík. Other legal holidays in 1994, when most everything closes, include Ascension Day (May 12), Whit Sunday (May 22), Whit Monday (May 23), and Bank Holiday Monday (Aug. 1). Regular business hours are weekdays from 9am to 5pm, 6pm in summer. **Banks** open weekdays from 9:15am to 4pm. Currency exchange commissions vary only slightly between banks (except at the airport), and the exchange rates are set by the government. **Post offices** *(póstur)* are generally open on weekdays from 8:30am to 4:30pm, as are **telephone** *(sími)* offices (often in the same building). Post offices and hostels normally hold mail. Pay phones take 5, 10 and 50kr pieces; local calls cost 10kr. AT&T's **USA Direct** is 990-001 (5kr) and MCI **World Reach** is 992-002 (5kr). For assisted international calls, dial 09. **Emergency**

numbers vary across the country; they are listed on the inside front cover of the *símaskrá* (phone book), or you can call the operator 24 hours a day by dialing 03. Since Icelandic surnames are simply the father's name plus "son" or "dóttir," the phone book lists people by first name. Iceland does not observe daylight savings time, so it is even with London in winter but stays an hour behind in summer.

Accommodations and Camping Iceland has 25 **HI youth hostels** (get the free *Hostelling in Iceland* brochure at the tourist office for a complete listing) which charge 1000kr (non-members 1100 or 1250kr) and are invariably clean, with kitchens and common rooms. **Sleeping-bag accommodations** *(svefnpokapláss)*, widely available on farms, at summer hotels, and in guest houses *(gistiheimili)*, are a viable and competitively priced alternative (most often you get at least a mattress); consult the free *Around Iceland* and *Icelandic Farm Holidays* brochures (the latter lists about 100 farms nationwide). Starting in early June, many schoolhouses become *Hótel Eddas,* which offer sleeping-bag accommodations for only 750kr (no kitchens, 10% discount for bus-pass holders). Most of these places also offer breakfast and made-up beds (both of which are *quite* expensive). Be warned: while staying in a tiny farm or hostel may be the highlight of your Icelandic trip, the nearest bus may be 20km away and run once a week. Check the bus schedules *very* carefully and try not to hurry through your trip. Many remote lodgings offer to pick up car-less tourists at the nearest town, sometimes charging a small fee.

In cities and nature reserves **camping** is permitted only at designated campsites. Outside of official sites, camping is free but discouraged; watch out for *Tjaldstæði bönnuð* (No Camping) signs and *always* ask in the nearest farm before you camp anywhere else. Use gas burners; Iceland has no firewood and it is illegal to burn the sparse vegetation. Always bring your waste with you to the nearest disposal. **Official campsites** (summer only) range from rocky fields with cold water taps to the sumptuous facilities in Reykjavík. Upper-crust sites run 400kr per person, more basic ones about 250kr. Rent camping gear suited to Iceland's climate from **ALP Rentals,** located beside BSÍ bus station in Reykjavík (tel. (91) 175-70; open daily 8am-6pm; sleeping bag 1400/week, 2-person tent 3500kr/week). For all camping items, go to **Skátabúðin** in Reykjavík at Snorrabraut 60 (tel. (91) 61 20 45), between Egilsgata and Bergþórugata. (Open Mon.-Fri. 9am-6pm, Sat. 10am-2pm.)

Food and Drink Grocery stores are the basic hunting grounds for travelers in Iceland; most every town has a **Kaupfélag** (cooperative store) and usually a fast-food kiosk. Gas stations (usually open from 9am until 10 or 11pm) sell snacks too. Groceries in many small towns close for an hour at lunch (noon-1pm). Larger towns commonly have supermarkets: the best deal is the comprehensive **Hagkaup**. Most larger towns also have restaurants which serve fish and meat courses. Remember that food is extremely expensive in Iceland; a *cheap* restaurant meal will cost you no less than 800kr. There's no tipping in Iceland.

Icelandic cuisine celebrates animals you might normally have considered wonderful and exotic pets. Check supermarkets or ask around for traditional foods such as *lundar* (puffin), *rjúpa* (ptarmigan) and *selshreifar* (seal flippers). Conservative eaters can stick to fish and lamb, or bust out and try *svið* (singed and boiled sheep's head). Icelanders drink mostly on weekends and pay through the nose for the privilege; a beer at almost any pub costs more than 450kr. Alcoholic beverages are sold only in state-run monopoly outlets (located in few places and open very few hours) and in pubs and restaurants. The drinking age is 20, and driving under the influence is severely punished.

■■■ REYKJAVÍK

Home to only a hundred thousand people, Reykjavík's cosmopolitan frenzy belies its small size. Heavy traffic races along the main streets, and expensive foreign goods shine in shop windows. Nevertheless, the snow-striped inland peaks, visible when not shrouded in persistent rain clouds, serve as a silent reminder that the world's northernmost capital still belongs to the wilderness.

ORIENTATION AND PRACTICAL INFORMATION

Lækjartorg, the main square of old Reykjavík, sits on the northern side of a stubby peninsula on Iceland's southwest coast. To the north and across the harbor looms Mount Esja. Roughly south of Lækjartorg are the lake, the long-distance bus station, and Reykjavík Airport on the peninsula's south shore. Radiating east and west from Lækjartorg is the pedestrian thoroughfare which forms the axis of the city; the street name varies, called **Austerstræti** to the west and **Bankastræti** to the immediate east, then transforming into **Laugavegur.**

All international flights arrive at **Keflavík Airport,** 55km from Reykjavík. Forty-five minutes after each arrival, a "Flybus" (tel. (91) 62 10 11; US$9.50 or 500kr) shuttles passengers to the domestic **Reykjavík Airport** and the adjacent Hótel Loftleiðir, from which bus #17 (100kr) leaves every 20 minutes for Lækjartorg, and bus #5 goes to the Sundlaugarvegur Youth Hostel. Outgoing Flybuses leave the Holiday Inn 2½ hours and Hótel Loftleiðir 2 hours before each departure from Keflavík as well as from the youth hostel at 4:45am June 1 to September 10. Many flights depart before city buses run, so allow time for walking to the Flybus stops or book a cab in advance. From Hótel Loftleiðir's Reykjavík Excursions desk (open 24 hrs.), which runs the Flybus and many tours, you can pick up a free city map and a free copy of *What's On in Reykjavík.* After-hours currency exchange is cheapest at the hotel's **Landsbanki Íslands** branch. (Open Mon.-Fri. 8:15am-4pm and 5-7:15pm, Sat. 8:15am-7:15pm, Sun. 2-6pm. Commissions double on weekends and holidays.)

Tourist Office: Upplýsingamiðstöð Ferðamála á Íslandi, Bankastræti 2 (tel. 62 30 45), at the end of the small courtyard immediately to your right as you walk uphill from Lækjartorg. Free maps, tons of brochures, perfect English, and extensive information on tours, accommodations, cultural events, and weather conditions. Open Mon.-Fri. 8:30am-6pm, Sat. 8:30am-2pm, Sun. 10am-2pm; Sept.-May Mon.-Fri. 10am-4pm, Sat. 10am-2pm. Sunday hours on holidays.

Budget Travel: Ferðaskrifstofa Stúdenta, Hringbraut (tel. 61 56 56), next to the National Museum. Same building as the university bookshop. Discounts on international travel only; sells ISIC and InterRail. Open Mon.-Fri. 9am-5pm.

Embassies: U.S., Laufásvegur 21 (tel. 291 00). Open Mon.-Fri. 8am-12:30pm and 1:30-5pm. **Canadian consulate,** Suðurlandsbraut 10, 3rd floor (tel. 68 08 20). Open Mon.-Fri. 8am-4pm. **U.K.,** Laufásvegur 49 (tel. 158 83). Open Mon.-Fri. 9am-noon; phones answered until 5pm.

Currency Exchange: Banks open Mon.-Fri. 9:15am-4pm; there are many on Austurstræti and Laugavegur. After-hours exchange at the Hótel Loftleiðir bank (see above). Also at the tourist office (June-Sept. Mon.-Fri. 4:30-6pm, Sat. 9am-1pm) and at the Salvation Army (May-Oct.).

American Express: Úrval-Útsýn Travel, Pósthússtræti 13, P.O. Box 9180 (tel. 269 00). Mail held, Travelers Cheques not cashed; no wired money accepted. Additional offices on Lágmúli 4.

Post Office: Póstur, Pósthússtræti 5 (tel. 63 60 00), in the town center. Open Mon.-Fri. 8:30am-4:30pm, Sat. 10am-2pm; Sept.-May Mon.-Fri. 8:30am-4:30pm. Poste Restante. Branch at BSÍ bus station open Mon.-Fri. noon-6pm, Sat. 9am-1pm. **Postal code:** Reykjavík 101.

Telephones: Póstur og Sími Afgreiðsla, across from Kirkjustræti 8, in the center. Open Mon.-Fri. 8:15am-7pm, Sat. 10am-6pm, Sun. noon-6pm. **City Code:** 91.

Flights: Keflavík Airport, for international flights (see above). The Icelandair ticket office is at Lækjargata 2 (information tel. 69 03 00; open Mon.-Fri. 9am-5pm). Domestic **Reykjavík Airport,** just south of town, has 2 distinct halves. On the *western* side of the runways, **Flugleiðir** (tel. 69 02 00) services Iceland, Greenland, and the Faroe Islands. Take bus #5 from Lækjartorg or Sundlaugarvegur, or walk (15 min. along the dirt road near the bus station, at the junction of

Hringbraut and Vatnsmýrarvegur). From the *eastern* side of the airport, next to Hótel Loftleiðir, **Arnarflug** (tel. 61 60 60) flies to several small towns in Iceland, including Vestmannaeyjar. Take bus #17 or walk (15 min. from the bus station).

Buses: Umferðarmiðstöð, Vatnsmýrarvegur 10 (tel. 223 00), off Hringbrau near Reykjavík Airport. Terminal open daily 7am-midnight, tickets sold from 7:30am. Upstairs, **BSÍ Travel** has bus passes and schedules, as well as bike rentals (open June-Aug. Mon-Fri. 7:30am-7pm, Sat. 7am-2pm, Sun. 7am-1pm and 5-7pm).

Public Transportation: Strætisvagnar Reykjavíkur (SVR) runs yellow city buses (tel. 127 00). Fare 100kr. Ask the driver for a free transfer ticket *(skiptimiði)*, good for 45 min. Kiosks at 4 terminals sell sheaves of schedules and bunches of tickets; the 2 main ones are at Lækjartorg (in the building on the north side of the square) and at "Hlemmur" (in the building between Hverfisgata and Laugavegur at Rauðarárstígur). Buses run at 20-30min. intervals Mon.-Sat. 7am-midnight, Sun. and holidays 10am-midnight.

Taxis: BSR, Skolatröð 18 (tel. 117 20). 24-hr. service. About 500kr from Lækjartorg to Hótel Loftleiðir.

Bike Rental: Reiðhjólaverkstæðið Borgarhjól, Hverfisgata 50 (tel. 156 53). 3-speeds 390kr/½-day, 800kr/24hrs.; mountain bikes 580/½-day, 1180kr/24hrs, and 6800kr/week. All bikes come with free repair kit. Open Mon-Fri. 8am-6pm, Sat. 10am-2pm, or try BSÍ Travel (see Buses).

Hitchhiking: Those hitching take buses #15a, 15b, 10 or 100 to the east edge of town, then stand on Vesturlandsvegur for the north, Suðurlandsvegur to go southeast. Exposure is risked if not picked up quickly.

Luggage Storage: At the Sundlaugarvegur hostel. 50kr/day, even for non-guests. Also at the BSÍ terminal (open Mon.-Fri. 7:30am-11:30pm, Sat. 7:30am-2:30pm; 100kr/day, 310kr/week).

Laundromat: Ask your hostel about special arrangements with nearby cleaners. Otherwise, visit **Þvoið Sjálf,** Barónsstígur 3, below Hverfisgata (tel. 314 41). Wash 350kr, dry 250kr. Open Mon.-Fri. 8am-7pm, Sat. 10am-6pm; Sept.-May Mon.-Fri. 8am-7pm, Sat. 10am-6pm.

Weather: Daily radio broadcasts in English on FM 92.4 and FM 93.5, June-Aug. 8:30am. Also try the tourist office or call an English recording (tel. 69 36 90).

Women's crisis hotline: (tel. 99 62 05).

Pharmacies: Vesturbaëgur Apótek, Laugávegur 16. Open Mon.-Fri. 9am-5pm. Or just look for *apótek* signs. For the location of a 24-hr. pharmacy, call 18-888.

Disabled Visitors: Contact **Icelandic Association of the Disabled,** Hátún 10, IS-105, Reykjavík (tel. 267 00).

Medical Assistance: The Medical Center (Laeknavaktin) at Heilsuverndarstöðin, Barónsstígur 47 (tel. 212 30). Open Mon.-Fri. 8am-5pm, Sat.-Sun. and holidays 24hrs. Also, **Borgarspítalinn** (City Hospital), on Sléttuvegur. Take bus #6, 7, 8 or 9. Or call 69 66 00. Telephone number and emergency ward are open around the clock.

Emergencies: Ambulance and **Fire** (tel. 111 00). **Police** (tel. 111 66).

ACCOMMODATIONS AND CAMPING

The tourist office has complete listings of guesthouses that offer sleeping-bag accommodations.

Reykjavík Youth Hostel (HI), Sundlaugarvegur 34 (tel. 381 10). Stay on the Flybus to the Holiday Inn, or take bus #5 from Lækjargata to Sundlaugarvegur. 108 beds in 2- to 8-bed rooms; special rooms have wheelchair access. Large kitchen. Shopping and swimming nearby. Reception open Mon.-Fri. 8am-11am; Sat.-Sun. 8 -11am and 4pm-midnight. Curfew midnight. Sells bus and air tickets and stores baggage (50kr/day). 1000kr, nonmembers 1250kr. No sleeping bags; sheets 250kr. Reservations recommended; held until 7pm or later with advance notice. Breakfast 550kr.

Hjálpræðisherinn Gesta- og Sjómannaheimili (Salvation Army Guest and Seamen's Home), Kirkjustræti 2 (tel. 61 32 03), a pale yellow house on the same street as the Parliament. Cheap, friendly place. 2- to 5-bed rooms. Reception open daily 7am-1am, but try the doorbell if you arrive later. Sleeping-bag accommodations 1000kr. Sheets 200kr. Reservations needed July-Aug.

Camping: Tel. 68 69 44. Right behind the Sundlaugarvegur hostel; take bus #5. The only site in town. Showers, laundry, and cooking facilities. 200kr/tent, 200kr/ person. Reservations recommended. Open June-Aug.

FOOD

Food in Iceland ranges from the culturally unique (ram's testicles) to the attempted imitation (bad pizza). Coffee shops, hot-dog stands and kiosks abound (open 9 or 10am to 10 or 11pm). Many inexpensive restaurants cluster on Tryggvagata by the harbor. The most common supermarket is **Hagkaup.** (Branch at Laugavegur 59; open Mon.-Thurs. 9am-6pm, Fri. 9am-7pm, Sat. 10am-4pm.)

Café Sólon Íslandus, Bankastræti 7. Trendy café with avant-garde art on the walls and artists in the seats. Mostly fish and surprisingly inexpensive. From 480kr. Open Mon.-Fri. 10am-1am, Sat.-Sun. 11am-3am.

Múlakaffi Cafeteria, on Hallarmúli near Ármuli. Ask a waiter to translate the traditional Icelandic menu; it's worth it. From 680kr. Open daily 7am-11pm.

Thailandi, just by Laugavegur 11 on Smiðustígur. Step off the monochromatic streets of Reykjavík into a crowded, bright orange, green, and blue Bangkok alley complete with parking meter. Eight Thai dishes; large servings 490-880kr. Open daily 11:30am-10pm.

Á Næstu Grösum, Laugavegur 20b, entrance on Klapparstígur (1st door on your right coming from Laugavegur). Simple 2nd-floor macrobiotic restaurant—the aroma of boiled lentils and wild rice meets your nostrils as you enter. Iceland's only vegetarian restaurant. Limited selection. Large portions 800kr; small portion without refills 400kr. Open Mon.-Fri. noon-2pm and 6-8pm.

Sveinn Bakari. Many locations of this bakery chain, including one on Laugavegur and one on Lækjargata. Hours generally 9am-7pm. *Kleina* (doughnuts) 47kr, orange juice 70kr.

SIGHTS AND ENTERTAINMENT

For a better idea of the layout of the city, hike up Skólavörðustígur to the **Hallgrímskirkja** (Hallgrímur's Church), modeled after the ubiquitous basalt columns, and visible from almost anywhere in town. The observation deck in the steeple shows how minuscule Reykjavík is compared to Mount Esja. (Open Tues.-Sun. 10am-6pm; 200kr to ascend). For over two hours of seismographic delight, see the **Volcano Show** at Hellusund 6a (almost a continuation of Skothúsvegur as you walk from the lake; tel. 299 75 for info, 132 30 for bookings). Ósvaldur Knudsen and his son Vilhjálmur sniff out all volcanic activity on the island; they've filmed the Mývatn eruptions for 17 years. (Shows in English daily at 10am, 3pm, and 8pm; Sept.-May Tues., Thurs. and Sat. at 8pm. 750kr.)

The **Þjóðminjasafn Íslands** (National Museum of Iceland), at Hringbraut and Suðurgata beside the university, packs a millennium of history into a few well-arranged rooms, written and described only in Icelandic—from disintegrating iron swords of the 10th-century Norse settlers to models of 19th-century fishing boats. (Open Tues.-Sun. 11am-5pm; mid-Sept. to mid-May Tues., Thurs., and Sat.-Sun. noon-5pm. 200kr.) The bright, modern **Listasafn Íslands** (National Gallery of Iceland) by the lake at Fríkirkjuvegur 7 (entrance on Skálholtsstígur) shows Icelandic paintings and frequent international shows. (Open Jan. to mid-Dec. Tues.-Sun. noon-6pm. Free; special exhibits 300kr.) **Árbæjarsafn,** a collection of old buildings from all over the country, traces the history of daily life in Iceland. Take bus #10 or 100 to Rofabær and walk back to the end of the street and through the underpass. (Open June-Aug. Tues.-Sun. 10am-6pm. 250kr, seniors and under 16 free.) **Light Nights,** Tjarnargata 10e, by the lake and across from the concrete town hall monstrosity, is a multi-media show based on Icelandic history and sagas. (Performances mid-June to Aug. Thurs.-Sun. at 9pm. 1500kr, with student I.D. 900kr.) You haven't experienced

Iceland without a plunge into one of Reykjavík's geothermally heated pools. The outdoor **Laugardalslaug**, on Sundlaugarvegur next to the campground, is the largest. (Open Mon.-Fri. 7am-9pm, Sat. 7:30am-5:30pm, Sun. 8am-5:30pm. Closed holidays. 150kr, children 75kr.)

Weekends bring expensive gaiety and drunken 15-year-olds to downtown Reykjavík, and mixed older crowds to pubs and nightclubs. Most pubs are on Laugavegur, Austurstræti, and vicinity; consult *What's On in Reykjavík* for entertainment info. Pubs with cover charges (around 500kr) usually have live music. **Glaumbær**, Tryggvagata 20, serves 450kr beers to a mixed, cosmopolitan crowd. (Open Sun.-Thurs. 6pm-1am, Fri.-Sat. 6pm-3am.) **22**, Laugavegur 22, is an artsy, black-white-and-mirrors hangout where life begins around midnight. (Open Thurs. to 1am, Fri. to 3am.) The morning after, **Reykjavík Flea Market** brings a collection of greying fishermen and farmers together to sell their last herring. (In the garage at the junction of Lækjargata and Tryggvata. Open Sat. 10am-4pm, and Sun. 11am-5pm.)

■ Near Reykjavík

Most travel agents, tourist offices, and hostel wardens arrange one-day tours for the convenience of the wealthy traveler (seldom less than 2000kr). Check the BSÍ bus schedule for cheaper "tours" (really scheduled buses) to the same places. **Þingvellir National Park**, 50km east of Reykjavík, is both the junction of the European and American tectonic plates and the site of the world's first parliament. Crossing the ravine and then emptying into Þingvallavatn (Iceland's largest lake), the river Öxará separates the Lögberg (law rock) from the church on the site where the Icelanders traded paganism for Christianity in 1000 AD. (Buses from Reykjavík to Þingvellir daily at 2pm, returning at 5pm from þingvellir. July-Aug 15 also at 10:30am Tues.-Wed. and Fri.-Sun. 410kr one-way). Call the Ranger's office at (98) 226 77 for information and touring suggestions.

One of the more popular daytrips from Reykjavík takes you to the twin attractions of **Gullfoss** (Golden Falls) and **Geysir**, the etymological parent of geysers worldwide. (Scheduled buses from Reykjavík daily in summer at 9am; 2040kr round-trip.) Geysir, which can shoot as high as 80m, has been inactive for years, but is sometimes made to spout through the addition of large quantities of soap, which breaks the water's surface tension. These eruptions are announced in the papers and at tourist offices. A few steps away, the smaller **Strokkur** makes up for its size with the energetic frequency of its eruptions (every 5-10 min.). Across the road, **Hotel Geysir** (tel. (98) 689 35) offers a free swimming pool, sleeping-bag accommodations (with breakfast 1000kr), and camping (300kr/person; no charge/tent; camping open mid-May to mid-Sept.; call ahead). The canteen sells basic staples. Nine km uproad lies torrential **Gullfoss**, golden-hued from the mud it carries downriver and surrounded by a steady mist; bring raingear if you're planning to go close (bus departs Gullfoss at 12:45pm).

On the road to Gullfoss and Geysir lies **Hveragerði**, called "the flower town" for its hothouse cultivation and known for its rheumatism rehab center and hiking. (Scheduled buses in summer 9am, 11:30am, 1:00pm, 3pm, 5pm, 8pm, and 11pm, and returns at 9:50am, 1:20pm, 4:20pm, 6:50pm, and 9:50pm. 350kr one-way.) **Tourist information** is at Breiðamörk 10 (tel. (98) 342 80). Sleeping bag accommodations are at **Ból youth hostel**, Hveramörk 14 (tel. (98) 345 88).

Southwest Iceland's most popular attraction is **Bláa Lónið (Blue Lagoon)**, steaming white water surrounded by lava, tourists, and a geothermal plant. It costs 300kr to enter and is open daily 10am-10pm. Take the Grindavík bus from Reykjavík. (10:30am and 6:30 pm; returns 1pm and 8:30pm. 780kr round-trip.)

SNÆFELLSNES AND THE WEST FJORDS

Clawing into the Greenland Sea like the gnarled hand of a fisher, the Snæfellsnes peninsula and the West Fjords (Vestfirðir) together form Iceland's most isolated coastal region and the heart of its vital fishing industry. At the western tip of Snæfellsnes, the extinct glacier-capped volcano **Snæfellsjökull** opens the way to the inner world (or so claims Jules Verne in *Journey to the Center of the Earth*). To the north, separated from Snæfellsnes by the island-strewn **Breiðafjörður,** lie the magnificent **West Fjords,** whose deep and narrow inlets mirror towering snow-veined mountain slopes.

Only 150km north of Reykjavík, Snæfellsnes is best reached by road. Daily bus departures from Reykjavík (Mon.-Fri. 9am, Sat. 1pm, Fri. and Sun. 7pm) serve the entire peninsula. To see Snæfellsjökull, connect to Ólafsvík (4hr., 8120kr one-way, 3300kr round-trip) or Hellisandur (4½hr., 1820kr); ask the Reykjavík tourist office about sleeping-bag accommodations and glacier tours. Otherwise, stay on the bus to Stykkishólmur (4hr., 1660kr one-way, 3000kr round-trip). Daily buses return to Reykjavík from Ólafsvík (Sun.-Fri. 5:30pm, Mon. and Sat. 8am; Hellisandur ½hr. earlier) and from Stykkishólmur (Sun., Tues., and Thurs. 6pm, Mon., Wed., and Fri. 4pm and 6pm, Sat. 8:30am).

■ Stykkishólmur

Stykkishólmur is the principal port and major town of the peninsula. As you arrive you'll pass the **campsite** on your right, just before the gas station. **Hótel Egilshús** (tel. (93) 814 50), in the red and white building at the end of Aðalgata (the main street and continuation of the intercity road), offers sleeping-bag accommodations. (11 rooms, 1900-2700kr.) To get to the **HI hostel** at Höfðagata 1, follow Aðalgata around to the left and then take another left up the hill (tel. (93) 810 95; 50 beds; 1000kr, nonmembers 1250kr; sheets 250kr). Ask the Reykjavík tourist office or the boat office (tel. (93) 814 50) beside Egilshús about tours of Breiðafjörður on the speedboat *Eyjafirðir*.

The ferry *Baldur* (tel. (93) 811 20) from Stykkishólmur is the most convenient, scenic, and economical way to the West Fjords; it runs twice daily to **Brjánslækur** in the southern West Fjords. (Mid-May to Aug. leaves Stykkishólmur daily at 10am and 4:30pm, returns from Brjánslækur at 1pm and 7:30pm; 1300kr one-way, 10% discount with bus pass or student card.) On Mondays, Wednesdays, and Fridays (mid-June to Aug.), buses run from Ísafjörður to Brjánslækur and back (3hr. each way), meeting the *Baldur's* 1pm arrival and departure; Tuesdays, Thursdays, and Saturdays see similar service to the cliffs of **Látrabjarg** (3½ hr), Europe's westernmost point, where daring cragsmen gather thousands of bird eggs each June. The *Baldur* also stops mid-journey at the gorgeous island of **Flatey** where you can gambol over coastal dales among shocked sheep and thousands of sibilant seabirds. **Café Vogur** (tel. (93) 814 13) on Flatey stocks some food and has space for sleeping-baggers.

■ Ísafjörður

Walled in by the cliffs of Eyrarfjall and Ernir, **Ísafjörður** is the center of all things in the West Fjords and may be the most beautiful town in Iceland. From mid-June through August, buses connect it to Reykjavík via ferry **Baldur**. (12hr.; schedules available at BSÍ.) Flugleiðir has daily flights from Reykjavík to Ísafjörður, while Árnarflug (tel. (94) 41 50), Flugfélagið Ernir (tel. (94) 42 00), and Flugfélagið Norðurlands (tel. (94) 30 00) provide regular service between Ísafjörður and other Icelandic cities. Still, the *Baldur* is the cheapest transportation option to the area. The only way to get from Ísafjörður to Akureyri is by plane (1/day); by bus, you must backtrack to Reykjavík or Borgarnes.

The main part of Ísafjörður rests on a spit of land that curves out into Skutuls-fjörður, forming a natural harbor. As you approach Ísafjörður from the bottom of the fjord, its **summer hostel** is on your left as you enter the main part of town, in the Menntaskólinn á Ísafirði, a 2-story white building with red trim and roof (tel. (94) 38 76; sleeping-bag accommodations 700kr, beds 1300kr; open mid-June to Aug.). Beside it is a **campsite.** (350kr/1-person tent, 150kr/additional person. Open mid-June to Aug.) There are two **guest houses** in town: **Austurstræti 7** (tel. (94) 38 68; sleeping-bag accommodations 800kr, singles 1500kr) and **Föndurloftið,** above a tourist shop at Mjallargötu 5 (tel. (94) 36 59; sleeping bag accommodations 100kr, bed 1500kr). The **tourist office** is at Aðalstræti 11 (tel. (94) 35 57), on your right past the hotel in the center of town and the post and telephone offices. Follow the waterfront past the trawlers (look for a big sign on a red wall pointing the way) to the 2nd-floor **Sjómannastofan,** a fishers' cafeteria offering huge meals. (Fish 660kr. Meat 960kr.) If Ísafjörður's harmonious beauty tires you, there are two ways to tour the Ísafjarðardjúp (the West Fjords' main inlet) and the fjords branching off it: the regular ferry *Fagranes* (tel. (94) 31 55; full-day tour 1000kr, reservations necessary) and the speedboat *Eyjalín* (2500kr; inquire at the tourist office).

NORTH ICELAND (NORÐURLAND)

■ Akureyri

Basking in the glow of the midnight sun and sheltered from the polar winds by snow-capped mountains lining the Eyjafjörður, **Akureyri** is the hub of the north. Iceland's second city and the capital's alter-ego, temperate summers make Akureyri a welcome respite from Reykjavík's incessant clouds. It is also a launch pad for exploring the lunar landscape near **Lake Mývatn,** 100km to the east, and the village-strewn fjords along the north coast.

Daily **buses** connect Reykjavík and Akureyri all year, leaving Reykjavík at 8am and Akureyri at 9:30am (6½hr., 3400kr one-way, 6200kr round-trip); summer brings extra evening buses in both directions (daily 5pm). Buses depart Akureyri at 8:15am for Lake Mývatn (May-Sept. daily, 2hr., 1000kr one-way) and Egilsstaðir. (Mid-May to mid-June and Sept. 3-4/week; mid-June to Aug. daily: 6hr., 2700kr one-way.) **Flu-gleiðir** flies 5 times daily to and from Reykjavík (50min., 6230-12130kr round-trip), while **Flugfélag Norðurlands** flies direct from Keflavík to Akureyri (5/week) and from Akureyri to smaller Icelandic towns.

The helpful **tourist office** (tel. (96) 277 33) and the **bus station** (tel. (96) 244 42) share a building at Hafnarstræti 82 in the south end of town. (Tourist office open June-Aug. Mon.-Fri. 7:30am-9pm, Sat.-Sun. 7:30-11:30am and 3-6:30pm; Sept.-May Mon.-Fri. 8:30am-5pm.) Their SVA city bus schedules are helpful but slightly confusing (75kr/ride). The **post office** is also on Hafnarstræti, farther north. (Open Mon.-Fri. 9am-4:30pm.) **Phones** are in the same building. (Open Mon.-Fri. 9am-6pm, Sat. 10am-3pm.)

Akureyri has two **HI hostels.** The one on the 2nd floor of Stórholt 1 (tel. (96) 236 57) is a 20-minute walk from the bus station; go left (facing the water) on Drottnin-garbraut, the busy street along the shore; it changes its name to Glerárgata after the town center, and Stórholt is on the right. (Reception open 7:30-11am and 4-11:30pm. 1000kr, nonmembers 1100kr.) A second hostel is 3km north of town in Lónsá; if you call (tel. (96) 250 37), the owners will pick you up. (Same prices.) Clean guesthouses right in the center of town offer **sleeping-bag accommodations** for 1100kr (min. 2 people; only available if the room is unoccupied at the higher bed-and-breakfast rate); the tourist office has an exhaustive list. Try friendly **Salka,** Skipagata 1, 3rd floor (tel. (96) 226 97) or **Ás,** Hafnarstræti 77 (tel. (96) 122 49). The **campsite** (400kr/person) is near downtown on Þórunnarstræti, beside the outdoor swimming pool. For plain but filling meals, head to **Bautinn,** at the corner of Kaupvangsstræti and Hafnarstræti across from the pedestrian district, which serves meals with soup and salad, a rarity on this vegephobic island (from 1050kr; open daily 9am-11pm) or to **Súlnaberg cafeteria,** across the street, which does mediocre (but very full) traditional meals (fish from 850kr, meat from 1050kr, sandwiches from 350kr). **Hagkaup** supermarket at Norðurgata and Grenivellir has the cheapest food (and stocks the complete Paul Newman line). (Open Mon.-Fri. 9am-9pm, Sat. 10am-6pm, Sun. noon-7pm.) Red, orange, and purple line buses go straight to the door.

Wander through Akureyri's **Lystigarður** (Botanical Garden), on Eyrarlandsvegur; you'll have to hunker down to the ground to read the labels on the garden's fascinating collection of Arctic plants. (Open daily June-Sept. Free.) Nearby, the **Minjasafn Akureyrar** (Akureyri Museum), at Aðalstræti 58, recounts the town's history. (Open June-Aug. daily 11am-5pm. 200kr.)

■ Mývatn

Iceland's geological tumult explodes into view in the region surrounding **Mývatn,** a shallow lake shaped by 2000 years of volcanic eruptions. Trails lead through strange lava formations known as "black castles" which fill a jagged area called **Dimmuborgir;** pyramids of ash rise nearby, and in the **Devil's Kitchen** the ground steams madly while sulfurous pits burp and spit fetid blue sludge. Massive volcanic craters, simmering plains of cooling lava, and jets of steam bring a primal spirit to the nearby **Krafla** volcano complex. When exploring these areas, observe the many warning signs and stick to the brown soil, or you may drop through the thin crust to the boiling sulfur pit below.

You'll need several days to appreciate the sites, since many involve lengthy hikes. One time-saving option is renting a **bike** from the gas station by Hotel Reynihíð. (500kr/½-day, 900kr/full day. 1000kr deposit or passport required.) For those short on time, regular one-day **bus tours** of the area leave the Akureyri bus station daily. (Mid-May to Sept. 8:15am, 4000kr, 10% off with either bus pass.) Regular bus service departs Akureyri at 8:15am and 8pm, returning from Mývatn at 8am, 4:15pm, and 7:30pm. (2hrs., 1000kr one-way.)

Buses stop at the small communities of **Skútustaðir** (on Mývatn's south shore) and **Reykjahlíð** (on the northeast side), which from June to August host **camping** (Reykjahlíð tel. (96) 443 05, Skútustaðir tel. (96) 442 79, both 400kr/person) and **sleeping-bag accommodations** (Reykjahlíð 1200kr, tel. (96) 442 20; Skútustaðir 900kr, tel. (96) 442 79 or 442 12). Information on accommodations and tours is provided at Hotel Reynahlíð, and at **Eldá** (tel. (96) 442-20), 300m south of the bus dropoff, on the lake-side of the road. Akureyri makes a fine base for exploring northern Iceland's other attractions; ask about getting to the islands of **Hrísey,** in the fjord north of Akureyri, and **Grímsey,** Iceland's only territory north of the Arctic Circle, or to Europe's most powerful waterfall at **Dettifoss** and the cliffs of **Ásbyrgi** and **Hljóðaklettar**.

EAST ICELAND (AUSTURLAND)

Iceland's eastern fjords are unjustly overlooked; quiet fishing villages and bristling fjordside peaks make the east well worth an unhurried stay.

■ Egilsstaðir

The main town in the east is land-locked **Egilsstaðir,** at the northern tip of the narrow lake **Lagarfljót.** The Kaupfélag Héraðsbúa supermarket and its parking lot make a good reference point; just uphill are the post office and bank, while the **tourist office** (tel. (97) 123 20; open June-Sept. Mon.-Sun. 9am-5pm and 7-11pm) and campsite (400kr/person) are at the far end of the parking lot. Looking lakewards from the Kaupfélag, you can easily spot red-roofed **Egilsstaðir Farm,** a 5- to 10-minute walk away, which has sleeping-bag accommodations for 1200kr (tel. (97) 111 14). Egilsstaðir is the opposite node of the bus ring from Reykjavík, with service to Akureyri (2700kr, see North Iceland) and Höfn. (2360-3060 kr, 5-6hr. Leaves Höfn 9am, Egilsstaðir 4pm. Mid-May to mid-June and Sept. 3-4/week; mid-June to Aug. daily.) Planes arrive from Reykjavík (3-4/day) and Akureyri (1/day).

■ Seyðisfjörður

Twenty-six km from Egilsstaðir, **Seyðisfjörður's** curving, sheltered fjord harbors Iceland's only international car and passenger ferry, the *Norröna* (tel. (97) 211 11; in Reykjavík (91) 62 63 62; bookings in U.S. through Eurocruises, tel. (800) 688-3876). Service is to Tórshavn in the Faroe Islands (16hr., about US$190, with 25% student discounts), and continues to Bergen (Norway, 19,080kr one-way), and Hanstholm (Denmark, 22,680kr one-way). (Arrives Seyðisfjörður June-Aug. Thurs. at 8am, departing at noon.) Seyðisfjörður's excellent **HI hostel** (tel. (97) 214 10) is in the pink house on the north shore of the fjord and has all the "Twin Peaks" episodes on video. (1000kr, nonmembers 1250kr. Sheets 350kr. Make reservations on nights before and after the ferry.) Buses connect Egilsstaðir and Seyðisfjörður over a fogbound pass that sometimes stays snowy all summer. (740kr one-way, Mon.-Fri. leaving Seyðisfjörður between 8:30 and 9:30am, check hostel or ferry office for exact times. Egilsstaðir between 9:30 and 10:30am, check tourist office for times, late June- late Aug. also Sat.-Sun. at 2:45pm and 4:15pm; extra service Wed.-Thurs.)

■ The Coast

The coast between Egilsstaðir and Höfn will make you glad you came east. Buses that stop at Reyðarfjörður take Highway #96, which meanders through small fjord villages before rejoining Highway #1 at Breiðalsvík. The route clings to steep, dark seaside cliffs with dramatic mountain landscapes at every turn. There are two isolated **HI hostels** along the way, at Berunes (off Highway #1; tel. (97) 889 88; 20 beds) and Stafafell (tel. (97) 817 17; 45 beds).

THE SOUTHERN COAST (SUÐURLAND)

Gentler than the east or north, Iceland's southern coast is still a star attraction. Sandy glacial outwash gives way to sheep-filled pastures and green cliffs, beyond which waterfalls, lava fields, glaciers, and volcanoes provide exhilarating hiking.

■ Höfn

This run-of-the-mill town links the southern coast to the eastern fjords; it's the terminus for buses from both Egilsstaðir (see above) and Reykjavík (leaves Reykjavík daily 8:30am, Höfn 9am; mid-Sept. to May Sun., Tues., and Fri. leaves Reykjavík 8:30am, Höfn 10am; 9-10hr., 3600kr), as well as the launching point for tours to **Vatnajökull** (Europe's largest glacier), which dwarfs the town and shimmers a robust gold at sunset. The **campsite** (on your left as you come into town) doubles as a **tourist information center** (tel. (97) 817 01; open June-Sept.) and intercity bus stop. Look on your right for cheap **sleeping-bag accommodations** in the local theater on the main road at Hafnarbraut 17 (tel. (97) 811 61; open June to mid-Sept. Sun.-Thurs.). Further along the street is the **HI youth hostel,** Hafnarbraut 8 (tel. (97) 817 36; reception open 7:30-11:30am and 5-11:30pm; 1000kr, nonmembers 1250kr; open mid-May to mid-Sept.; 30 beds).

■ Skaftafell National Park

The best way to appreciate the vast, rolling mass of Vatnajökull is to hike amid the dense shrubbery and icy alpine vistas of **Skaftafell National Park,** on Highway #1. (3hr. west of Höfn. Bus from Reykjavík 2520kr, from Höfn 980kr.) An excellent **campsite** serves as a good base (tel. (97) 816 27; 400kr, shower 100kr); an information center with maps and a grocery complete this wheelchair-accessible facility. Up the hill, the farmhouse **Bolti** (tel. (97) 816 26) offers year-round sleeping-bag accommodations (from 1300kr) and a kitchen. Buses to Höfn stop briefly at **Jökulsárlón,** a glacial lake with floating blue icebergs that makes a visit to Greenland redundant.

■ The Coast

The coastline to Reykjavík is mostly owned by farmers whose sheep graze freely on the slopes. The Reykjavík-Höfn bus stops at every little town. There are **HI youth hostels** in **Reynisbrekka** (tel. (98) 711 06), **Fljótsdalvr** (tel. (98) 784 98), **Leirubakki** (tel. (98) 765 91), and **Selfoss** (tel. (98) 688 31). Ask about sleeping-bag accommodations in **Vík** or in the farm country near **Selfoss,** center of Iceland's dairy industry.

THE INTERIOR

Iceland's Interior is Europe's most forbidding wilderness, a vast expanse of lava fields, volcanos, glaciers, and swift-flowing unbridged rivers. Traveling here is safest and easiest by bus. In summer, special buses with huge tires run over the black-sanded **Sprengisandur** in the heart of the island; to the luscious valleys of **Þórsmörk** (where much of *Njáls Saga* took place), west of Mýrdalsjökull; to summer skiing at Kerlingarfjöll; and to the warm rivers of **Landmannalaugar** north of Mýrdalsjökull. Some trips continue across the island to Akureyri, an interesting alternative to the coastal bus. Consult **BSÍ Travel** at the Reykjavík bus station (tel. (91) 223 00) for reservations. (To Þórsmörk in summer Mon.-Fri. 8:30am and 5pm. Return to Reykjavík Mon.-Fri. 8am and daily 3:30pm. 3600kr.)

Several companies offer guided hiking trips in the interior. Try **Útivist,** Hallveigarstig 1, P.O. Box 236, 121 Reykjavík (tel. (91) 614 330), or **Austurland Travel,** Dragháls 6, 110 Reykjavík (tel. (91) 67 85 45). Without professional guidance, prepare well. The **Ferðafélag Íslands** (Icelandic Touring Club), at Mörkinni 6, 108 Reykjavík (tel. (91) 682 533), can help. Never venture out without a 4-season sleeping bag, a sturdy, wind-resistant, waterproof tent, a compass, a detailed map, and more provisions than you think you'll need. **Landmælingar Íslands** (the Iceland Geodetic Survey) runs a complete and up-to-date map shop at Laugavegur 178 in Reykjavík (tel. (91) 68 09 99; open Mon.-Fri. 9am-6pm). Leave an itinerary with the **Landssamband Hjálparsveita Skáta** (Association of Icelandic Rescue Teams) at Snorrabraut 60 above the Skátabúðin camping store in Reykjavík (tel. (91) 250 22; 24-hr. hotline (91) 68 60 68; open Mon.-Fri. 9am-5pm). Be sure to get a copy of the brochure *Mountain Roads* at any of the above locations. There are many huts in the interior (marked on good maps) and popular places like Þórsmörk and Landmannalaugar have campsites.

VESTMANN ISLANDS (VESTMANNAEYJAR)

Rising steeply from the ocean floor, the 15 Ve stmann Islands are only barely inhabited by humans. The one town, also called **Vestmannaeyjar,** spreads over the island of **Heimaey**. In 1973, Heimaey threw open its vaults and sent molten lava from the volcano **Eldfell** flowing through the town streets. Luckily, everyone was rescued;

today Vestmannaeyjar stands modernized and rebuilt, surrounded by cooling lava and jagged green mountains which enclose the town and separate the harbor from the sea. The airport sits below Eldfell's twin peak **Helgafell,** a short uphill walk from town. Five Flugleiðir flights per day arrive from Reykjavík (20min., 7670kr round-trip), but prepare for cancellations in bad weather. Sailing is slower but cheaper; connecting buses (1½hr., 460kr) link Reykjavík to **Þorlákshöfn,** meeting the ferry. For information in Reykjavík, call (91) 686 464; in Vestmannaeyjar (98) 128 00. Vestmannaeyjar's **tourist office** is the reception desk at Hótel Gestgjafinn (on Heiðarvegur; 24hr.). Signposts point from both the harbor and airport to the **HI hostel,** Faxastígur 38 (tel. (98) 129 15), which can house 40 people in four rooms and a dorm. (1000kr. Nonmembers 1250kr. Sheets 280kr. Open June to mid-Sept.) The hostel runs clearly signposted **camping,** along Dalvegur (200kr/person, 200kr/tent; open June-Aug.) The **Eyjakaup** supermarket (open Mon.-Fri. 9am-9pm, Sat. 10am-4pm) is near the hostel at Faxastíg 36. Get face-to-face with Iceland's strange sea creatures at the country's only **aquarium,** on Heiðarvegur. (Open daily in summer 11am-5pm; 200kr.) Follow the dirt tracks which lead safely through the still-warm gray-brown lava desert around Eldfell, and save on cooking expenses by letting nature boil an egg or potato for you. (Dig into a steamy patch and bury your food; eggs take 1-1½hr. to boil.)

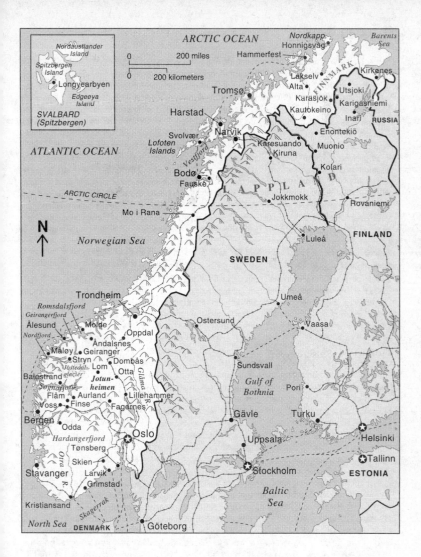

Norway (Norge)

US$1	= 6.99kr (kroner, or NOK)	10kr =	US$1.43
CDN$1	= 5.31kr	10kr =	CDN$1.88
UK£1	= 10.80kr	10kr =	UK£0.92
IR£1	= 10.20kr	10kr =	IR£0.99
AUS$1	= 4.53kr	10kr =	AUS$2.21
NZ$1	= 3.85kr	10kr =	NZ$2.60
SAR1	= 1.45kr	10kr =	SAR6.92
Country Code: 47		International Dialing Prefix: 095	

Stretched over the northwest rim of Europe, Norway is the continent's ineffable encounter with nature. Piney valleys and farming homesteads soften severe fjords and mountains. From Norway's rugged coast, fierce Norsemen spread across the Atlantic and "settled" communities in England, Ireland, and France. The pagan pillaging party subsided in the 10th century, when King Harald Hårfagre (Harold the Fairhaired) unified the realm and Olav Haraldsson imported Christianity (duty free). Runestones, stave churches, and preserved Viking ships still survive from this age, while Icelandic sagas chronicle it and its myths in rich poetry and epics.

The closing years of the 19th century spawned great luminaries of art, drama and music, from Munch to Ibsen, Hamsun to Grieg. After oppressive German occupation in WWII, Norway developed into a modern welfare state. Today its 4 million people pay outrageous taxes but know no poverty. Northern Norway's simple, striplike geography contrasts with the country's wider southern parts, where long valleys run between Oslo and Trondheim, connected by passes over Scandinavia's highest mountains to the fjords in the west.

GETTING THERE AND GETTING AROUND

Every coastal town of any significance from Oslo to Bergen has **ferry** service to Denmark, England, or Germany (more frequent and expensive in summer and on weekends). Most foreigners, cowed by the ferry system, take the **train** to Oslo from Copenhagen (3-4/day, 10hr., 580kr) or Stockholm (1-3/day, 6hr., 484kr). Eurail is valid on all trains in Norway. The Scandinavian **Nordturist pass,** which offers 21 days of unlimited travel for 1980kr (under 26 1470kr), will be available until January 1, 1994, at which time it will pass the torch to the **ScanRail pass,** offering 1 consecutive month of travel (US$399), 9 days of travel within 21 (US$275), or 4 days of travel within 15 (US$159), with about 25% off for those under 26 and 50% reduction on several bus and ferry trips. Eurailpasses get few fringe benefits in Norway, and Nordturist gets some for free. No free brochure gives you a complete, comprehensive picture of the complex domestic transportation scene; you'll have to collect sheaves of free regional schedules, or ask travel agents or train stations for a look at their all-fathoming *Rutebok for Norge.* Norwegian trains run only up to Bodø; the only trains farther north move along the Swedish rail line through Kiruna, which dead-ends at Narvik on the Norwegian coast, and along a line from Murmansk in Russia. You need a seat to ride trains, so book ahead (20kr, sleeping berths 100-200kr).

For those under 25, special youth fares make **flying** a viable option, often cheaper than the train. **SAS** and **Braathens SAFE** are the main airlines, and both offer stand-by tickets for any trip either north or south of Trondheim for 400kr one-way, or 800kr if the trip involves both the northern and southern zones. **Buses** are usually quite expensive (about 1kr/km), but are the only firm surface option north of Bodø and in the fjords. Always ask for student discounts, and try flashing your railpass.

Car ferries *(ferjer)* are usually much cheaper (and slower) than the many **hydrofoils** *(hurtigbåte)* that cruise the coasts; both occasionally allow student discounts. Throughout the chapter you'll see references to the **Hurtigruten** (the famed Coastal Steamer), which takes 6 days for its fantastic voyage from Bergen to Kirkenes; each of the 25 stops en route have one northbound and one southbound departure per day. The *Hurtigruten* often have a free sleeping-bag room; empty cabins run from 70 to 110kr per night. Many Norwegians **hitch** beyond the rail lines in northern Norway and the fjord areas of the west. Those hitching use a sign or flag and try to find a ride before or during a ferry trip to avoid getting stuck at the landing.

In all of Nordland province (including Bodø, Fauske, the Lofotens, and Narvik), Nordturist takes 50% off bus fares. In the Lofotens, students only get the 50% discount, Eurail gets nothing, and car ferries give a 50% student discount, while hydrofoils give no discounts to non-Norweigians.

NORWAY ESSENTIALS

Most towns in Norway have *Turistinformasjon* offices; look for the blue signs with black lower-case "i"s. Try to go the night before planning an excursion, as buses often leave early in the morning or late in the afternoon. **Banks** are open Monday through Friday from 8:15am to 3pm in summer and 3:30pm in winter, Thursday until 5pm. Large **post offices** exchange money and usually charge less commission. (Generally open Mon.-Fri. 7am-5:30pm, Sat. 8:15am-5pm.) Legal **holidays,** when everything closes, include New Year's Day, Maundy Thursday, Good Friday and Easter Monday, Labor Day (May 1), Constitution Day (May 17), and Christmas.

For a few weeks around the summer solstice (June 21), Norway north of Bodø basks in the midnight sun. Skiing is best just before Easter, when the winter has slackened somewhat, and the sun returns after months of darkness. Oslo averages 63°F (17°C) in July, 24°F (-4°C) in January; up north, temperatures dip significantly. Hikers should bring heavy clothing and 4-season sleeping bags.

Telephone calls within and outside Norway butcher the budget. For operator assistance dial 093 (English- and German-speaking), 092 (French), or 091 (Nordic). To make collect calls internationally, dial 0115. Pay phones take 1, 5, and 10kr coins and local calls require at least 2kr. For AT&T's **USA Direct,** dial 050 12 011. **MCI World Reach** is 050 12 912, and **Canada Direct** is 050 12 111. Norway is officially a bilingual country. Reacting to the Danish-influenced *bokmål* Norwegian used in Oslo, 19th-century linguists constructed an alternative standard language *(nynorsk)* based on the more archaic dialects of rural western Norway; the two are taught on an equal footing in schools. Fortunately, the great majority of Norwegians speak fluent English.

Accommodations and Camping When in Norway, camp. Norwegian law allows you to camp for free anywhere you want for 2 nights, provided you keep 150m from all buildings and fences and leave no traces of your frolicking. Take advantage of **Den Norske Turistforening** (DNT, the Norwegian Mountain Touring Association); their Oslo and Bergen offices are particularly helpful. They sell excellent maps and maintain a series of mountain huts *(hytter)* throughout the country. (40-65kr/night. Open to nonmembers for a 45kr surcharge. Membership 270kr, under 25 150kr.) Staffed huts serve full meals and are akin to hostels but have a consistently more attractive ambience and more Norwegian guests than international tourists. Get the entrance key for unattended huts (deposit required) from a DNT or tourist office before heading out. DNT huts are open during Easter and from the end of June to the beginning of September. The indispensable *Vandrerhjem i Norge* brochure lists prices, phone numbers, and so much more for Norway's 94 **HI youth hostels** *(vandrerhjem)*. Beds run 60-110kr; breakfast (often mandatory) costs 40-50kr. Usually only rural hostels have curfews, but only a few are open year-round. Most tourist offices in Norway can book you a room in a private home; they're roughly 160kr for singles, 240kr for doubles. **Campgrounds** usually have cabins at 200-400kr for groups of 2 or 4.

Food and Drink Norwegian food is murder on the wallet; markets and bakeries may become your dearest friends. Seek out the nationwide discount **REMA 1000** supermarkets. (Usually open Mon.-Fri. 9am-8pm, Sat. 9am-6pm.) Though hostel breakfasts are usually dull, they almost always provide the cheapest grub around. Restaurants often have inexpensive *dagens ret* (dish of the day) specials (60-70kr for a full meal); otherwise you're lucky to get out for less than 100kr. Tips are included. Self-service *kafeterias* are a less expensive option. Fish in Norway is unusually fresh, good and cheap. National specialties include cheese *(ost;* try *Jarlsberg* and the brown *geitost),* pork and veal meatballs *(kjøtkaker)* with boiled potatoes, and (for lusty carnivores) controversial *kval* (whale meat). In most Norwegian restaurants, alcohol is served only after 3pm and never on Sundays. Beer is heavily taxed and quite expensive. *Gløgg,* a Scandinavian mulled wine, is popular in winter.

■■■ OSLO

Norway's capital stands tight and modern around its harbor; a few blocks away, people and traffic swirl among the trees and statues of the town center. Much smaller than Copenhagen or Stockholm, Oslo stays laid-back, its green spaces spreading until the suburbs blend into the Norwegian woodlands.

ORIENTATION AND PRACTICAL INFORMATION

Karl Johans Gate, running from Sentralstasjon to the *Slottet* (Royal Palace), is Oslo's principal boulevard and a useful reference point.

Tourist Office: The **Main Tourist Office,** Vestbaneplassen 1 (tel. 22 83 00 50), in a yellow former train station toward the piers, sports gigantic "NORWAY" signs. Free maps and guides. Open Mon.-Fri. 9am-8pm, Sat.-Sun. 9am-4pm; March-May and Sept.-Nov. Mon.-Fri. 9am-4:30pm; Jan.-Feb. and Dec. Mon.-Fri. 9am-4pm. The branch at **Sentralstasjon** is open daily 8am-11pm. For hikers, **Den Norske Turistforening**, Stortingsgata 28, with entrance around the corner on Olav V gate (tel. 22 83 25 50), rents mountain huts and sells trail maps. Open Mon.-Wed. and Fri. 8:30am-4pm, Thurs. 8:30am-6pm. **USE IT,** Møllergata 3, (4 blocks up Carl Johans gate from the station, then right; tel. 22 41 51 32), offers brochures, listings of cheap lodgings and restaurants, and travel tips. Open Mon.-Fri. 7:30am-6pm, Sat. 9am-2pm; Sept.-May Mon.-Fri. 11am-5pm.

Budget Travel: Reisebyrået Terra Nova, Dronningensgate 26 (tel. 22 42 14 10). Discounted rail and plane tickets on international routes. Open Mon.-Fri. 9:30am-4pm, Sat. 10am-2pm.

Embassies: U.S., Drammensveien 18 (tel. 22 44 85 50). Take tram #1, 2 or 9, or bus #27, 29 or 30. Open Mon.-Fri. 9am-3pm. **Canada,** Oscarsgate 20 (tel. 22 46 69 55), near Bislett Stadium. Take tram #2 or 11. Open Mon.-Fri. 8am-3:30pm. **U.K.,** Thomas Heftyesgate 8 (tel. 22 55 24 00). Open Mon.-Fri. 9am-4pm. Travelers from **Australia** or **New Zealand** should contact the British Embassy.

Currency Exchange: Lowest commissions on traveler's checks other than AmEx (see below) at post offices (10kr/check, 15kr for cash). Rail station office open Mon.-Fri. 7am-5:30pm, Sat. 9am-2pm and central post office open late (see Post Office). After-hours exchange in **Bankveksling** next to the post office in the station—but 15-20kr/traveler's check. Open daily 7am-11pm.

American Express: Winge Reisebyrå, Karl Johans Gate 33 (tel. 22 41 95 00; emergency number: 050 11 000). All services. Address mail to American Express, P.O. Box 54, Majorstuen, 0304 Oslo. Open Mon.-Fri. 9am-6pm, Sat. 10am-3pm.

Post Office: Dronningens gate 15 (tel. 22 40 78 23); enter at Prinsens Gate. Open Mon.-Fri. 8am-8pm, Sat. 9am-3pm, Sun. noon-6pm. **Postal Code:** 0101 Oslo 1.

Telephones: Kongens Gate 21, enter at Prinsens gate. Open daily 8am-9pm.

Flights: White SAS buses (30kr) run between **Fornebu Airport** and the Air Bus Terminal (tel. 59 62 20) at Galleri Oslo opposite the station. Frequent service daily 6am-9:30pm. Municipal bus #31 runs to Fornebu (15kr). **SAS** (tel. 22 59 60 50), in the Oslo City shopping mall across from the train station, and **Braathens SAFE** (tel. 22 59 70 70), at Haakon VII's gate 2. To New York: summer 4,700kr round-trip; winter 3,800kr. Under 25 to London 2,200kr round-trip.

Trains: Oslo Sentralstasjon (Central Station, tel. 22 17 14 00). Trains to Bergen (7-8hr., 460kr), Trondheim (7-8hr., 516kr). Open daily 6am-11pm. The **InterRail Center** at Sentralstasjon has **showers** (20kr), a kitchen, and **luggage storage** (free). Open mid-June to late Sept. daily 7am-11pm.

Buses: Norway Bussekspress, Schweigårdsgate 10 (tel. 22 17 52 90) in the Oslo Galleri Mail, behind the train station and to the right, sends buses scurrying throughout Norway (Bergen 486kr) and across Europe. Terminal open Mon.-Fri. and Sun. 8am-10pm, Sat. 8am-5:30pm.

Ferries: Passenger ferries arrive at the port, a 15-min. walk from the center. **Color Line** (tel. 22 83 60 10) has daily ferries to Kiel, Germany (from US$75 summer) and Hirtshals, Denmark (from US$42 summer). No student discount July to mid-Aug. **DFDS Scandinavian Seaways** (tel. 22 41 90 90) sails to Copenhagen daily (from 405kr in summer; 50% student discount Sun.-Thurs.). **Stena Line** (tel. 22 33 50 00) has 1 daily run to Frederikshavn, Denmark (350kr in summer).

Public Transportation: Info at **Trafikanten** (tel. 22 17 70 30), in front of the station. Open Mon.-Fri. 7am-8pm, Sat.-Sun. 8am-6pm. All forms (bus, tram, subway, and ferry) 15kr/trip. A 24-hr. **Dagskort** allows unlimited travel (35kr). For longer stays, the **7-day card** (130kr) makes sense. The **Oslo-Card** (transport plus sights for 24hr. 95kr; 48hr. 140kr) is economical only for *a lot* of sight-seeing.

Bike Rental: Den Rustne Eike, Enga 2 (tel. 22 83 72 31), behind the tourist office. 95kr/day, 465kr/week. 500kr deposit. Open daily 10am-6:30pm, Oct.-May Mon.-Fri. 10am-3:30pm. 15% discount with Oslo card.

Hitchhiking: Leaving Oslo by thumb is often a losing proposition; some try the USE IT ride board. Those heading south try outside West Station. Those going north take bus #30 or 31 to Sinsenkrysset, main intersection of north-bound highways.

Luggage Storage: Station lockers 20-30kr. Open 7am-11pm. Free at InterRail.

Laundromat: Look for the word *Myntvaskeri*. **Selvbetjent Vask,** Ullevålsveien 15, a few blocks from the city center. Wash 30kr, dry 10kr. Soap included.

Bookstore: Tanum Libris, Karl Johans gate 43 (in Paléet). Wide selection of English paperbacks and *Let's Go*s. Open Mon.-Fri. 10am-8pm, Sat. 10am-5pm.

Pharmacy: Look for the word *Apotek*. **Jernbanetorvets Apotek** (tel. 22 41 24 82), in front of the station. Open 24 hr.

Medical Assistance: Oslo Kommunale Legevakt, Storgata 40 (tel. 22 11 70 70). 24-hr. emergency care. **Legevakt** (tel. 22 20 10 90) is also a **rape crisis** line.

Emergencies: Ambulance: tel. 003. **Fire** and **Accidents:** tel. 001. **Police:** tel. 002. Headquarters at Grølandsleiret 44 (tel. 66 90 50). **Women's Crisis Center:** tel. 22 37 47 00. **Men's Crisis Center:** tel. 22 20 91 12.

Gay and Lesbian Services: tel. 22 11 33 60, after 8pm, weekdays.

ACCOMMODATIONS AND CAMPING

Ask at the **Innkvartering** accommodations office in the station, and at the **USE IT** office, which has a list of cheap sleeps. Innkvartering books rooms in private homes for multi-night stays. (Singles 300kr. Doubles 400kr. 17kr fee.) *Pensjonater* (pensions) are usually less expensive than hotels; call for reservations. Many hotels slash prices from late June to mid-August. Wilderness huts outside Oslo are a deal (from 60kr), but 45 minutes from public transport. Inquire at USE IT.

KFUM (YMCA), Møllergata 7 (tel. 22 42 10 66); enter on parallel Grubbegata. The cheapest spot in town. Sleeping-bag accommodations; 60 mats in 2 dorms. Reception open 8-11am and 5pm-midnight. Lock-out 11am-5pm. Kitchen facilities and baggage storage. 75kr plus 20kr membership fee. Open July to mid-Aug.

Haraldsheim (HI), Haraldsheimveien 4 (tel. 22 15 50 43). Take tram #1 or 7 direction "Sinsen" to the end of the line. Friendly, cozy, and crowded. Reception closed 11am-2pm. Lock-out 11am-4pm. 141kr, nonmembers 166kr. Breakfast included. Wash and dry 40kr (soap included). Reservations essential in summer.

Ellingsens Pensjonat, Holtegata 25 (tel. 22 60 03 59). Take tram #1 direction "Majorstuen". Clean, tight ship. Singles 180kr. Doubles 270kr. Call ahead.

Coch's Pensjonat, Parkveien 25 (tel. 22 60 48 36), corner of Hegdehaugsveien by the royal park. Triples 450kr. Quads 520kr. Triple 570kr and quad 640kr with kitchenette and bathroom. Reservations recommended.

Camping: Ekeberg Camping, Ekebergveien 65 (tel. 22 19 85 68), about 3km from town, with marvelous view. Take bus #24 from Central Station. Tent sites 90kr. Open June-Aug. **Free camping** in the forest north of town as long as you avoid public areas. Try the end of the Sognsvann subway line.

FOOD

A full meal in a restaurant will impoverish you. The cheapest shopping area is the **Tøyen/Grønland** immigrant district northeast of Central Station; try along Tøyengata and Urtegata. Another option is the lunch specials (from 44kr) in the **Paléet Shopping Center** (Carl Johans gate 37-41, next to the American Express office). Three discount chains bring an inexpensive selection: **Rimi,** Rosenkrantzgate 20 (open Mon.-Fri. 9am-5pm); **Rema 1000,** Holmesgata 7 (open Mon.-Wed. and Fri. 9am-6pm, Thurs. 9am-8pm); **Tempus,** Youngsgata 11 (open Mon.-Fri. 8am-7pm, Sat. 10am-6pm). The **Seven-Eleven** stores and **Narvesen** kiosks are open late.

Vegeta Vertshus Frisksportrestaurant, Munkedamsveien 3b, off Stortings gate. Unpretentious vegetarian delight with an awesome array of salads, soups, pizzas, and hot dishes. All-you-can-jam-on-a-plate 65-73kr, all-you-can-jam-in-your-face buffet 98kr. Open daily 10am-11pm.
Kafé Celsius, Rådhusgata 19. Pale-yellow buildings shelter a cozy courtyard. Omelette 64kr, pasta from 76kr. Open Tues.-Wed. 11:30am-12:30am, Thurs.-Sat. 11:30am-2am, Sun. 1pm-12:30am.
Darbar Mat & Vinhus, Smedgata 45. Take subway to Tøyen station, walk down path to Sørligata, and continue to Smedgata. Authentic Indian restaurant full of aroma and decor. Vegetarian dishes 55-85kr, meat dishes 90-140kr. Open Mon.-Sat. 4-11pm, Sun. 2-11pm.

SIGHTS AND ENTERTAINMENT

Akershus Castle and Fortress was built in 1300 and transformed into a Renaissance palace by Christian IV. You can explore the castle's underground passages, banquet halls, dungeons, and courtyards. There are concerts on summer Sundays. (Open May to mid-Sept. Mon.-Sat. 10am-4pm, Sun. 12:30-4pm; mid-Sept. to Oct. and April 15-30 Sun. 12:30-4pm. 10kr, students and children 5kr; tours in summer daily at 11am, 1pm, 3pm, spring and fall at 1 and 3pm.) The poignant **Resistance Museum** in the fortress documents Norway's efforts to subvert Nazi occupation. (Open Mon.-Sat. 10am-5pm, Sun. 11am-5pm; Oct. to mid-April Mon.-Sat. 10am-3pm, Sun. 11am-4pm. 15kr; students, seniors, and kids 5kr.)

From the castle, head toward the island of **Bygdøy**; take ferry #91 from pier #3, or bus #30 from Nationaltheatret. The island's draws include the **Folkemuseum's** collection of traditional houses. (Open daily 10am-6pm, mid-Sept. to mid-May daily 10am-4pm. 35kr, students 25kr. English tours daily at 11am, 12 and 2pm.) For information on daily events here and elsewhere in Oslo, consult *What's on in Oslo,* free at the tourist offices. The 3 vessels of the **Viking Ship Museum** include the 9th-century ring-prowed, dragon-keeled Oseberg ship used to bury a queen. (Open daily 10am-6pm; Sept. 11am-5pm; April and Oct. 11am-4pm; Nov.-March 11am-3pm. 20kr, students 10kr.) **Thor Heyerdahl**'s crafts *Kon-Tiki, Ra I,* and *Ra II* have their own museum. (Open daily 10am-6pm; Sept. to mid-May closes 1-3hr. earlier. 20kr, students and children 10kr.) Weather permitting, plunge in the bracing water off **Huk Beach,** Oslo's most popular, located about 1km from the Viking Ship Museum. Or bare it all at nude **Strandskogen,** across the inlet from Huk.

The blunt, powerful sculptures at **Vigeland Park (Frognerpark)** depict each stage of the human life cycle; the park is a playground of grassy knolls, duck ponds, and tennis courts. Gustav Vigeland's obelisk resides here: an eerie, erotic tower of contorted human shapes. (Open 24 hr. Free.) Take tram #2 or bus #20 from Nationaltheatret, or walk up Hegdehaugsveien, with its markets, cafés, and shops.

The **Munch Museum,** Tøyengata 53 (open Mon.-Sat. 10am-6pm, Sun. noon-6pm; Oct.-May Tues.-Sat. 10am-4pm, Sun. noon-6pm; 20kr, students 10kr; take the subway to Tøyen) may be a scream, with an outstanding collection of Edvard Munch's unsettling paintings, woodcuts, and lithographs, but his work of that title is actually at the **National Gallery,** Universitetsgaten 13. (Open Mon., Wed., and Fri.-Sat. 10am-4pm, Thurs. 10am-8pm, Sun. 11am-3pm. Free.)

For a panorama of Oslofjord and the city, take the #15 subway from Stortinget to the stop on the Frognerseteren line and walk to the ski jump **Holmenkollen.** Grease your body and slide on down. As you sail through the air, note that forest and lakes cover over half of the "city" of Oslo. (Open May and Sept. daily 10am-5pm; June 9am-8pm; July 9am-10pm; Aug. 9am-8pm; Oct-April Mon-Fri. 10am-3pm, Sat.-Sun. 11am-5pm. 15kr, students 10kr.) To bask in Norway's natural grandeur, take the Sognsvann subway from Nationaltheatret to the end of the line. USE IT provides free trail maps; in winter, ask the tourist office about cross-country ski rental.

Enjoy a delightful and inexpensive daytrip on one of the islands in the inner Oslofjord. In summer, you can visit the ruins of an old monastery on **Hovedøya**; **Langøyene** offers Oslo's best beach. Boats leave from the piers in front of City Hall and from **Vippetangen**, reached by bus #18. (Round-trip 32kr, free with city transport pass.) The evening cruise is especially enchanting.

Summer sends the opera, philharmonic, and numerous theatre companies scurrying for shade, and the Oslo hordes head for the pubs, bars, and cafés which line **Aker Brygge** quay and the area along Karl Johans gate. **The Beach Club,** Bryggetorget 14, is a quiet outdoor bar at the end of the courtyard in Aker Brygge. (Beer 39kr/½ liter, snacks from 40kr. Open Mon.-Sat. noon-1am, Sun. 1pm-1am.) **Sebastian's Rock Cafe,** on Carl Johans gate next to the American Express office, features live music and outdoor tables for people-watching on Oslo's busiest street. (Open Mon.-Tues. 11am-1am, Wed.-Thurs. 11am-2am, Fri.-Sat. 11am-4am, Sun. 3pm-1am; Beer from 40kr.) One bar with wheelchair access is **Summit 21,** Holbergst.

■■■ SOUTHERN NORWAY

Norway's southern coast substitutes serenity for drama. *Skjærgård,* archipelagos of water-worn rock hugging the shore, stretch from Oslo south to Kristiansand. From Kristiansand to Stavanger, the shoreline smooths to an endless white beach. This coast is Norway's premier summer holiday resort, but foreign tourists are less common here. Inland, dense woods swathe the high cliffs; fishing, hiking, rafting, and canoeing are summer options, as is cross-country skiing in the winter, especially in Telemark, where the sport was born. Two train lines run south from Oslo. The main one extends through Kristiansand around to Stavanger; the other loops through Tønsberg to Skien before reconnecting with the main line at Nordgatu. Most towns along the south coast without rail service are connected by buses (check the NSB schedules). Larger towns have ferry service to Denmark and sometimes Britain.

Tønsberg and Larvik   Reputedly the oldest town in Scandinavia, **Tønsberg** brings the beach to within a daytrip from Oslo. Buses run from the station to **Nøtterøy** (12-15kr) and **Tjøme** islands (25kr), where *skjærgård* and bathing unite. The Slottsfjellet tower offers a voluptuous vista (10kr). The terminally helpful **tourist office** (tel. 333 102 20) is on Nedre Langgate 36B; follow Tolbod from the station, and turn left on Nedre Langgate a block before the harbor. (Open June and Aug. Mon.-Sat. 10am-5pm; July daily 10am-8pm; Sept.-May Mon.-Fri. 9am-4pm.) The homey **HI youth hostel,** Dronning Blancasgate 2 (tel. 333 128 48), is near the station. Take a right on Farmannsveien, then left on Peder Lagmannsgate. (Reception open 6am-11pm. 130kr, nonmembers 150kr. Closed Christmas week.)

Larvik, the small and industrial birthplace of explorer and author Thor Heyerdahl *(Kon-Tiki),* lies 2½ hours south of Oslo. The **tourist office,** Storgata 48 (tel. (331) 301 00), 50m east of the station, helps you find accommodations in *hytte* (pensions). (Open Mon.-Sat. 7am-6pm, Sun. 3-6pm; early Aug.-late June Mon.-Fri. 8:30am-4pm.) **Jahrengård og Færiehytter** (tel. 331 990 30) offers doubles for 250kr, a 15kr bus ride from town. The closest **camping** is at **Gon** (tel. 331 265 11), 4km out of town. Consult the gratis *Larvik Distrikt* booklet for happenings.

Skien, Grimstad, and Kristiansand   **Skien,** the hub of the Telemark province, lies before **Nordgatu** at the junction of the two train lines. Birthplace of iconoclast playwright Henrik Ibsen, its **tourist office** is at Henrik Ibsen gata 2 (tel. 35 52 82 27). From the train station, walk down Rektor Ørns Gate and follow the signs. **Dag Bondeheim,** a hotel at Prinsessegt 7 near the tourist office, offers the cheapest bed at 230kr a room; to get to the 2 **camping sites,** take the Ulefoss bus (**Gåsodden camping**) or the Klyve bus (**Skien camping**).

Grimstad, accessible by Kristiansand buses (1/hr., 52kr, with ISIC 26kr), is a village of neat white cottages and wooden boats bobbing on the busy pier. Ibsen wrote his first play here in 1850. The **house** at Henrik Ibsens gata 14 contains the desk where he secretly penned poetry during his years as a bashful romantic. (Open June-Aug. Mon.-Sat. 11am-5pm, Sun. 1-5pm. 20kr includes entrance to the town/maritime museum in same building.) The **tourist office** at Torskeholmen (tel. 370 440 01) can help find accommodations. (Open June-Aug. Mon.-Fri. 10am-6pm, Sat.-Sun. 11am-5pm.

Kristiansand, "Norway's #1 Vacation Town," lies at the southern tip of Norway. Here the sun shines more often—on tourists and touristy shops. Day hikes wind along the cliffs above the town, and the beach is jumping on a warm day. The helpful **tourist office** on Dronningensgate 2 (tel. 380 260 65), is a 5-block walk from the train station along Vestre Strandgate. (Open Mon.-Fri. 8am-7pm, Sat. 10am-7pm, Sun. noon-7pm; late Aug. to mid-May Mon.-Fri. 8am-4pm.) The **Kristiansand Youth Hostel (HI),** Kongsgårds Allé 33c (tel. 380 953 69), is a long trek across the Otra River from the city center. Take bus #15 or 16 from Henrik Wergelandsgate (direction "Lund"). (Reception open 4-10pm. 120kr, nonmembers 140kr. Open May-Sept.) **Ferries** run to Hirshals, Denmark. (Bookings tel. 380 788 88. 3-4/day; 4hr.; from 84kr in the winter and 294kr July and Aug., 10% round-trip discount, 50% Eurail discount, included in Nordturist, students ½-price except July to mid-Aug.).

Stavanger   At the end of the southern rail line, **Stavanger** radiates oil-boom-town wealth. North Sea cash provided the tax revenue to restore the be-cobbled **old quarter,** Northern Europe's best preserved wooden-house settlement. Built by King Sigurd the Crusader in 1125, the Gothic **Cathedral** retains medieval solemnity amidst Stavanger's light-hearted center. (Open Mon.-Sat. 9am-6pm, Sun. 1-6pm; late Sept.-early May Mon.-Sat. 9am-2pm; services Sun. 11am-1pm.) At the spectacular **Pulpit Rock,** a cliff plunges over 600m into the Lysefjord. From Stavanger, take the frequent ferry to Tau (tel. 51 56 71 71; 23kr, 40min.), a bus (30kr, departs every 40min.) to the base of the mountain, and hike the 2 hours to the top. The **tourist office** (tel. 51 53 51 00), 2 blocks from the train station (turn left as you leave the station), can provide maps, a city guide, and essential ferry information. (Open Mon.-Fri. 9am-5pm; Sept.-May also Sat. 9am-2pm; booth by the fisher's market open June-Aug. daily 10am-8pm.) The **Mosvangen Youth Hostel (HI)** (tel. 51 87 09 77) is one of Norway's poshest (110kr, nonmembers 135kr). The most central campsite is **Mosvangen camping** (tel. 51 53 29 71) by the youth hostel. Take bus #130 to both. (Tents 60kr. Open June-Aug.) Nothing is cheap in the center of town, but for budget food, try **Rema 1000, Mauritz,** and **Obs** markets. Stavanger's streets teem with young people; clown-car-like hordes emerge on weekends, frequenting the **pubs** along Nedre Strandgate and the **waterfront.**

Catamarans run from Stavanger to **Bergen** (2-3/day; 4hr.; 450kr, 50% off for students, 25% off with Nordturist). Slower **ferries** connect the 2 cities, shipping out from Randaberg in Stavanger (1-2/day; 6hr.; 175kr, students 25% discount); **buses** meet Rondaberg-Bergen ferry sailings; inquire in the tourist office for information. **Color Line** (tel. 51 52 45 45) runs ships from Stavanger to **Newcastle,** England (2-3 per week, 18hr., from US$57 in winter and US$114 July-Aug.).

■■■ BERGEN

Bergen's scenery exalts it above most cities in the world, and its Germanic heritage sets it apart from most of Norway. Until the railway to Oslo was completed, it was easier to travel from Bergen to London, and the city acquired an international flair. Originally the capital of Norway, Bergen became a center of commerce in the 14th century and more recently a focal point of resistance to the Nazis. Trees soften the commercial frenzy; from the hills, Bergen looks more like a wooded settlement than a thriving commercial and university city.

ORIENTATION AND PRACTICAL INFORMATION

Bergen's train station lies several blocks above the gleaming harbor, at the top of the city center. Looking towards the water, **Bryggen** (the extension of Kong Oscar's gate) and the town's most imposing mountain are to your right; most of the main buildings are to the left. **The Torget**—an outdoor market—is at the harbor's tip.

Tourist Office: Bryggen 7, on the harbor's right side, just past the Torget (tel. 55 32 14 80). Pick up the all-knowing *Bergen Guide 1994*. Open Mon.-Sat. 8:30am-9pm, Sun. 10am-7pm; Oct.-April Mon.-Fri. 10am-3pm. **DNT** (see Oslo section, tel. 55 32 22 30), Tverrgaten 4-6, off Marken, a pedestrian thoroughfare beginning at the railroad station and leading to the harbor, is a must for travelers headed for the highlands. Open Mon.-Wed. and Fri. 10am-4pm, Thurs. 10am-6pm.

Budget Travel: Kilroy Travel, in the Studentsentret, Parkveien 1 (tel. 55 32 64 00). Discounts on international travel, sells ISICs and Interrail tickets. Open Mon.-Fri. 8:30am-4pm.

Currency Exchange: At the tourist office when banks and post offices are closed; 4% commission.

American Express: Winge Travel Bureau, Christian Michelsens gate 1-3 (tel. 55 90 12 90). Mail held (address to: P.O. Box 1226, 5001 Bergen), but no other services. Open Mon.-Fri. 8:30am-4pm, Sat. 9:30am-2pm.

Post Office: In the green building with the clock on Småstrand gate, 1 block from the Torget. **Poste Restante:** 5000 Bergen, open Mon.-Wed. and Fri. 8am-5pm, Thurs. 8am-6pm, Sat. 9am-2pm.

Telephones: Starvhuse gate 4, across Rådhus gate from the post office. Open Mon.-Fri. 8am-8pm, Sat. 9am-2pm. **City Code:** 55.

Trains: tel. 55 96 60 60 or 55 96 60 50. To Voss (4-6/day, 1hr., 100kr), Myrdal (1¾-2½hr., 145kr), and Oslo (7-8hr., 460kr, seat reservations compulsory). **Luggage storage** 10kr. Open daily 6:45am-10:45pm.

Buses: Bystasjonen, Strømgaten 8 (tel. 55 32 67 80). Service to neighboring areas and the Hardangerfjord district, as well as to Oslo, 460kr.

Ferries: To Stavanger and the nearby fjord regions: from the train station, boats leave from the left side of the harbor. **To other countries:** ships leave from Skoltegrunnskaien, a 20-min. walk past Bryggen along the right side of the harbor. **Smyril Line,** with offices in Engelgården at Bryggen (tel. 55 32 09 70), departs June-Aug. Tues. at 3pm for the Faroe Islands (20hr., 900kr) and Iceland (42hr., 1610kr). Student discount 25%, another 25% off early to mid-June and Aug. **Color Line,** Skuteviksboder 1-2 (tel. 55 54 86 60), sails to Newcastle via Stavanger May-Sept. US$57-114, 50% off with student ID in winter. **P & O Scottish Ferries,** reservations made through Color Line, sails June 4-Aug. 28 to the Shetland Islands (12hr., 660kr, 25% student discount). The **Hurtigruten** leaves daily at 10pm from a separate harbor at Frieleneskaien, behind the Natural History Museum.

Public Transportation: Yellow buses chauffeur you around the city (13kr/ride).

Gay and Lesbian Services: Gay Movement, 2a Nygårdsgaten, (tel. 55 31 21 39). Open Mon.-Thurs. 7-10pm.

Pharmacy: In the bus station. Open daily 8:30am-midnight.

Medical Assistance: Accident Clinic, Lars Hilles gate 30 (tel. 55 32 11 20). Open 24 hr.

Emergencies: Ambulance: tel. 003. **Police:** tel. 002.

ACCOMMODATIONS AND CAMPING

The tourist office books rooms for a 15kr fee (20kr for 2 people) in private homes. (Singles 145-180kr. Doubles 235-260kr.)

Intermission, Kalfarveien 8 (tel. 55 31 32 75). A 15-min. walk from the center up Kong Oscars gate, which turns into Kalfarveien past the train station at the Old Gate House; or take bus #2,4, 7 or 11. Coed dorm, friendly staff, kitchen, showers, and ghost. Lockout 11am-5pm. Flexible curfew. 95kr. Breakfast 20kr. Free laundry. Open mid-June to mid-Aug.; leave name on sign-up sheet or call ahead.

YMCA Interrail Center, Nedre Krskirkealmenningen 4 (tel. 55 31 73 32). Spacious and central. 80kr for mattress on floor; 2- to 50-person rooms. Reception 7:30-midnight. Lockout 11am-4:30pm. Open June 15-Sept. 1. Reserve.

Vågenes, J.L. Mowinckelsvei 95 (tel. 55 16 11 01), 10min. on bus #19 (13kr). In a private home; call for reservations and directions. Doubles with kitchens and made-up beds 100kr. Sleeping bag accommodations 80kr.

Montana Youth Hostel (HI), Johan Blyttsveien 30 (tel. 55 29 29 00), halfway up Mt. Ulriken, 4km from center. Take bus #4 to Lægdene (13kr). 141kr, nonmembers 162kr Open early May-early Oct. Reservations recommended.

Camping: Bergenshallen Camping, Vilhelm Bjerknesveien 29 (tel. 55 27 01 80), in the city. Take bus #3 from Strandgate. 60kr/tent. Open June 24-Aug. 10.

FOOD

Mekka, a discount supermarket, at Marken 3, 5min. from the station on the street parallel to Kaigaten, saves the hungry traveler. (Open Mon.-Fri. 9am-8pm, Sat. 9am-6pm.) Hunt around for *dagens ret* restaurant specials (60-100kr), or try one of the seafood restaurants. **Kaffistova,** on the 2nd floor across from the Torget, offers large hot entrees. *(Dagens ret* 70kr. Open Mon.-Fri. 10am-6pm, Sat. 11:30am-3:30pm, Sun. noon-6pm.) For vegetarian food in a whole-wheat atmosphere, try **Spisestedet Kornelia,** Fosswinckelsgate 8. (Salads from 39kr, pasta from 54kr, student specials Tues. and Fri. Open Mon.-Fri. 11:30am-7:30pm, Sat. 12:30-5:00pm, Sun. 2-6pm; in summer closed weekends.) **Ola's Inn,** Vaskerelvsmuget 1, at the end of Torgalmenningen, in the alley behind "Dickens," is a quiet, inexpensive cafeteria. (Fish and chips 56kr. Open Mon.-Fri. 10am-10pm, Sat. 10:30am-5pm.)

SIGHTS AND ENTERTAINMENT

Looking toward the right side of the harbor from the Torget, you'll see the pointed gables of **Bryggen,** a row of medieval buildings that's survived half a dozen disastrous fires and the explosion of a Nazi munitions ship on Hitler's birthday in 1944. It now features restaurants, offices, and artsy-craftsy workshops. The former city fortress **Bergenhus** teeters at the end of the quay, and the **Rosenkrantz Tower** stands in late medieval splendor. **Håkonshallen,** built by Håkon Håkonsson in the 13th century, is what is left of the original castle. (Open daily 10am-4pm; mid-Sept. to mid-May Sun. noon-3pm. 10kr.) The **Theta Room,** Enhjørningsgården Bryggen, chronicles the Resistance operations during the Nazi occupation. (Open mid-May to mid-Sept. Tues. and Sat.-Sun. 2-4pm. 10kr.)

Lose your head over the **Leprosy Museum,** Kong Oscars gate 59. Since 1970, the university has tastefully documented the history of the disease in a 19th-century hospital. (Open mid-May to Aug. daily 11am-3pm. 15kr, students 6kr.) On the western shore of **Lille Lungegårdsvatnet,** a shimmering pond in the middle of town, the **Rasmus Meyer's Collection** provides a quality overview of Norwegian Naturalists, Impressionists and Expressionists. (Open Mon.-Sat. 11am-4pm, Sun. noon-3pm; mid-Sept. to mid-May Tues.-Sun. noon-3pm. 15kr.) A quick bus trip from downtown is **Gamle Bergen** (Old Bergen), a collection of wooden buildings from the last century. Of the 40 old houses, 17 are open to the public via guided tours. Take city bus #1 or 9 direction "Lønborg" from outside Den Norske Bank to the 1st stop past the 2nd tunnel. (Houses open May 16-Aug. 29 11am-6pm. 25kr, students 15kr.)

With mountains on 3 sides and vast archipelagos to the west, you can take your scenic pick of nearby nature. The ever-popular **Fløibanen** takes you from the city's heart up into a maze of mountaintop paths and views. (Open daily 7:30am-11:30pm; 14kr one-way.) Consult **Bergen Touring Association,** Bergen Turlag, at the DNT office, for detailed maps and inspiration.

Nightclubs and discos pack the town center. (All open Thurs.-Sat. until 3am.) Consult your *Bergen Guide* for other distractions. All the stops are pulled out for the annual **Bergen International Festival,** a 12-day program of music, ballet, folklore, and drama from May 25-June 5 in 1994. Try calling the ticket office (tel. 55 31 09 54 or 55 31 31 04); uncollected tickets are sold at half-price on the day of performance.

■■■ THE FJORDS AND WEST COUNTRY

All along the western coast, sapphire sea and severe mountain ranges will tax your supply of camera film. Bergen is an ideal starting point; the tourist office there will help you plan a trip. Ferries wind through labyrinths of islands and peninsulas, catamarans go to Sognefjord and Nordfjord to the north, and buses connect to Hardangerfjord and the uninhabited Hardangervidda plateau to the southeast.

■ Sognefjord and Trips from Bergen

The longest of the fjords (200km), **Sognefjord's** deep, slender fingers penetrate all the way to the foot of the Jotunheimen mountains. A short ride north of the stunning Oslo-Bergen rail line, Sognefjord is ideal for those seeing Norway by train.

Flåm, Finse, and Aurland A natural starting point tucked deep within Sognefjord, **Flåm** is the only fjord town accessible by rail (connecting to the Oslo-Bergen line through **Myrdal;** 8/day, 50min., 50kr). Catamarans also run between Flåm and Bergen (1-2/day, 5hr., 430kr, 50% off with railpass or ISIC), traveling through **Balestrand** and on to Aurland. A jumble of ferries also tie Flåm to its fjord-bound friends: Godvangen, Aurland, and Balestrand. Flåm has a small, friendly **tourist office** (tel. (576) 321 06), in the hut beside the train station (open June to mid-Aug. daily 8:15am-8:30pm), and a newborn **HI youth hostel** (tel. (576) 321 21), 5 minutes into the valley along the tracks. (75kr, nonmembers 100kr. Open May to mid-Oct.)

The boots 'n' shorts set can alight from the Oslo-Bergen train at **Finse,** just east of Myrdal, and hike for 3 or 4 stunning days down the Aurlandsdalen Valley to **Aurland,** 7km from Flåm—sleeping warmly all the way in evenly spaced DNT *hytter.* For maps and prices, inquire at DNT in Oslo or Bergen; they range from 40kr for a mattress on the floor (nonmembers 90kr) to 350kr for a bed with breakfast and a pack lunch with thermos and dinner. You may also ask the Finse **tourist chalet** (tel. (05) 52 67 32), just by the station. (75kr, nonmembers 120kr. Open late June to mid-Sept.) Buses also connect Aurland and Flåm (13kr). The Aurland **tourist office** (tel. (576) 333 13) serves Flåm in the winter. (Open Mon.-Fri. 8am-7pm, Sat.-Sun. 11am-7pm; Sept.-April Mon.-Fri. 8am-3pm.)

Gudvangen, Voss, and Ørnaberg Ferries run from Flåm and Aurland west through narrow fjords to **Gudvangen** (2/day, 2½hr., 95kr from Flåm, 85kr from Aurland). From Gudvangen, buses (5-8/day, 70min., 49kr) run up to **Voss,** birthplace of the canonized American football figure Knute Rockne, east of Bergen on the Oslo rail line. From the train station, turn left when you face the lake and bear right at the fork by the church to find the **tourist office** in Tinghuse (tel. (56) 51 00 51; open Mon.-Sat. 9am-7pm, Sun. 2-6pm; Sept.-May Mon.-Fri. 9am-4pm). Turning right from the station and walking along the lakeside road brings you to Voss's large, modern **youth hostel (HI)** (tel. (56) 51 22 05) where you can rent canoes and rowboats. (30kr/hr., 85kr/day. Hostel 141kr, nonmembers 171kr. Open Jan.-Oct. Reserve ahead.) The central **Voss Camping** (tel. (56) 51 15 97) is right by the lake and tourist office. (50kr/tent, 4-person hut 250kr.) Local **trains** between Voss and Myrdal stop on demand at **Ørnaberg,** where a steep 300m path leads you down to the slightly decrepit but incredibly well-located **Mjølfjell Youth Hostel (HI)** (tel. (56) 51 81 11). The owner will give you hiking suggestions and maps. (121kr, nonmembers 146kr. Open June-Sept.; call ahead the rest of the year.)

Balestrand On the North side of Sognefjord, **Balestrand** is a spectacular midway point between Flåm and Bergen or Nordfjord. A ferry leaves Balestrand at 12:25pm to cruise up the **Fjærland fjord** to Mundal. Crafty buses meet the boat and transport you to the base of the **Jostedal glacier,** whose blue ice hangs ominously overhead; the ferry returns to Balestrand around 6pm. (Ticket includes stop at interactive glacier museum, 188kr at the tourist office.) The **Balestrand Youth Hostel (HI)** (tel. (576) 913 03) overlooks the fjord, a 5-minute walk up the hill and to the left. (85kr, nonmembers 110kr. Open mid-June to late Aug.) **Sjøtun camping** (tel. (056) 912 23), 500m down the coastal road, provides tent sites and huts. (15kr/person, 30kr/tent. 2-person hut 90kr.) The **tourist office** (tel. (576) 914 57), near the bus station on the quay, can help plan area tours by boat, bike or foot around Kaiser Wilhelm's garden spot. (Open June-Aug. Mon.-Sat. 8am-6pm, Sun. 11am-3pm.) The Bergen **hydrofoils** serve Balestrand twice a day (4½hr., 355kr, railpasses and ISIC 50% off). **Ferries** to Fjærland (9am) connect with buses north over snowy mountains to Stryn in Nordfjord (114kr, 50% ISIC discount).

■ Nordfjord

Twisting over 100km inland to the foot of the **Jostedal glacier,** Nordfjord is less fjantastic than its neighbors to the North and South. Wedged between the mountains near the inner end of the fjord, **Stryn** is a summer ski hub. Buses stop at the edge of town; walk past the Esso station to get to the main street, Tonningsgata. Well-versed downhillers should ask at the tourist office about **summer skiing** at Strynefjellet. Take a bus to Briksdalsbreen (departs 10am, 42kr) to probe the crevasses of the Jostedal glacier. The tasteful **HI youth hostel** (tel. (578) 711 06) is a hefty romp up the hill behind town. (Lockout 10:30am-4pm. Curfew 11pm. 80kr, nonmembers 105kr. Washer and drying room. Open May-Oct.) **Stryn Camping** (tel. (578) 711 36) is the most central of countless sites. (60kr/tent, 10kr/person.) The **tourist office** (tel. (578) 723 33) lies off the main street on the paved square with the *Télé* offices. (Open June-Aug. Mon.-Sun. 9am-6pm.) Stryn is a meeting point for **buses** from Otta on the Oslo-Trondheim rail line via Lom and Jotunheimen (Otta-Stryn 190kr, students 143kr; Lom-Stryn 120kr, students 90kr), from Hellesylt in Geirangerfjord (59kr) and from Fjærland and Balestrand in Sognefjord (114kr, 50% ISIC discount).

Sunbathers can bask on the coast around **Måløy,** at Nordfjord's mouth. Reach Måløy by hydrofoil from Bergen (1-2/day, 420kr, 210kr with ISIC), by daily *Hurtigruten* northbound from Bergen (arrives at 7:30am, 9hr., 457kr) or southbound from Ålesund (arrives at 4:45am, 4½hr., 218kr), or by bus from Stryn (3/day, 106kr). The local **tourist office** (tel. (057) 508 50), in the town hall, will help you with accommodations. (Open mid-June to mid-Aug. daily 10am-6pm.)

■ Geirangerfjord

Resist the temptation to stay snuggled in bed and take the bus to Geirangerfjord, perhaps the most stunning of the Norwegian fjords, and certainly the most visited. The most southerly, inland arm of the fjord system that begins at Ålesund, its 16km of green-blue water reflects stunning cliffs and waterfalls. Watch for the drama of the **Seven Sisters,** the powerful surge of the **Suitor,** and the mist of the **Bride's Veil.** From June through August, several daily ferries (60min, 27kr) connect the tiny towns of Hellesylt and Geiranger, at opposite ends of the fjord. Otherwise, both towns are accessible only by road. From the south or southeast, go through Stryn; from the north, launch yourself from Åndalsnes or Ålesund.

Geiranger and Hellesylt Geiranger is Norway's Yellowstone; in the summer over 5000 tourists visit each day, and an armada of oceanliners maintains a steady presence off-shore. You can join the flotilla by going on the sight-seeing trip of the fjord (1¾hr., 60kr) or enlarge it by renting a boat near the pier (tel. (702) 631 23; motorboats 100kr/hr., 400kr/day; open late June and early Aug. daily 10am-6pm; July 10am-8pm). The Geiranger **tourist office** (tel. (702) 630 99), just up from the landing, provides camping and hiking information. Ask about the walk to **Storseter,** which passes under a waterfall. (Open June-Aug. daily 9am-7pm; 45min.) Geiranger has 10 campgrounds; the closest (and only one with wheelchair access) is **Geiranger Camping** (tel. (702) 631 20; 10kr/person, 40kr/tent).

At the eastern end of the fjord, tiny, unspoiled **Hellesylt** is a base for mountain hiking in some of the wildest scenery in Norway. In the 1800s, cruise ship passengers were led on ponies from Hellesylt to Øye through the extremely narrow **Norangsdalen.** At the turn of the century, a huge avalanche dammed up the valley; farm buildings remain under the murky water. The daily Leknes bus (30kr to Øye) runs through the valley, but the return is the next day. The **Hellesylt Youth Hostel (HI)** (tel. (702) 651 28), up the hill along the road to Stranda, has a ripping view. (Lockout 10am-5pm. 85kr, nonmembers 110kr. Open June-Aug.) The **tourist office** (tel. (702) 650 52), right on the ferry landing, rents fishing equipment (15kr/hr.) and provides hiking maps. (Open mid-June to mid-Aug. daily 8:30am-5:30pm.)

■ Hardangerfjord

Hardangerfjord, east of Bergen and south of Voss, is the subject of endless sight-seeing tours. Either of these towns can serve as a base of operations, although **Odda** is more central. Odda's **tourist office** (tel. (536) 412 97) will provide assistance for trips to the fjord, but a stay at the **Odda Youth Hostel** (tel. 53 64 14 11) will cost you a whopping 130kr (nonmembers 155kr). Beautiful **Eidfjord,** on the main road RV7, 45km southeast of Voss, *"is* a Norwegian fjord," according to its brochure. Glad to hear it. Its **tourist office** (tel. (536) 651 77) will help with sight-seeing and rooms; there are several guest houses that run 120-320kr for singles, and a **campsite: Saebø Camping** (tel. (536) 659 27; 60-200kr/cabin, 20kr/tent, 10kr/person). Take an hour-long hike down to **Vøringstossen,** one of Norway's most famous waterfalls, and check out the stunning scenery from RV7, including the **Hardangerjøkulen glacier.**

■■■ GUDBRANDSDALEN, RONDANE, AND DOVREFJELL

Two train lines shoot north from Oslo to Trondheim; the slower goes eastward through the Østerdalen valley and Røros, the faster one through the **Gudbrandsdalen** valley that runs from Lillehammer northwestward through Otta and Dombås. Traditionally one of Norway's great thoroughfares, Gudbrandsdalen is also famous as the origin of the brown Gudbrandsdalsost cheese, and for its skiing, hiking, canoeing, and old churches and wooden houses. Lillehammer is the largest town and forms the southern edge; farther up the valley, the old, soft slopes of the mountain ranges of **Dovrefjell** and **Rondane** provide easy access to untrampled scenery. Both areas have national parks—the one in Dovrefjell is famous for its musk oxen.

Otta and Dombås Rondane is most accessible from **Otta,** 1½ hours north of Lillehammer. The **tourist office** (tel. (612) 303 65), in the station, has maps and tips on accommodations, white water rafting on the Sjoa River, and hints on the Rondane hiking trails at **Mysuseter** and **Høvringen.** (Open Mon.-Fri. 8:30am-7:30pm, Sat. 10am-6pm, Sun. noon-6pm; mid-Aug. to mid-June Mon.-Fri. 8:30am-4pm.) The **Guesthouse Sagatun** (tel. (612) 308 14) offers singles (160kr), doubles (220kr), and triples (325kr). Spectacular **bus** routes snake from Otta across the Jotunheimen mountains to Sogndal in Sognefjord and Stryn in Nordfjord.

The slightly more challenging **Dovrefjell** is best reached from the rail hub of **Dombås.** The **Dombås tourist office** (tel. (612) 414 44), in the shopping mall at the end of the hill, can help you plan tours along the trails. (Open daily 10am-8pm; late Aug.-early June Mon.-Fri. 9am-4pm.) The **Dombås Youth Hostel (HI)** (tel. (612) 410 45) is uphill from the train station; turn right, away from the city, on the main street. (Reception open 8-10am and 4-11pm. 85kr, nonmembers 110kr. Lockout 10am-4pm, reservations necessary in summer. Open late June to mid-Aug.)

Lillehammer For 2 weeks this winter, this little town will be at the center of the world, as it hosts the opening and closing ceremonies of Norway's second winter Olympic Games (Feb. 12-Feb. 27). The 114 events have been spread across the valley in the neighboring towns of Kvitfjell, Faberg, Hunder, Hamar, and Gjøvik. Despite the construction of several billion kroner's worth of infrastructure, Lillehammer maintains a natural atmosphere; all the sports facilities were designed to be environmentally friendly, and the Olympic housing will be recycled for use by the army. Any aspiring Eddie the Eagle can reach the top of the **ski jump** (15kr; Sat.-Sun. only). A **bobsled simulator** in the Olympic park takes you on a terrifying run. (Open daily 10am-7pm, 35kr.) The adventurous or perhaps just stupid can ride the **real bobsled run** in summer on wheels and in winter on ice. (Take the bus from the station to Hunder, 20kr. Open daily 1-6pm, 100kr).

Gjeste Bu, Gamleveien 110 (tel. 61 25 43 21), is central, snug, and cozy (sleeping bag accommodations 60kr); open all year, it's your best rooming bet, but call ahead. **Speidersenter,** Zystgårdsveien 23 (tel. 61 25 97 24), provides a view of the Olympic facilities, but closes August 15 to July 2 (sleeping bag accommodations 50kr). The **Lillehammer Youth Hostel (HI),** in the **Smestad Sommerhotell,** Smestadreien 14 (tel. 61 25 09 87), is both distant and institutional. (98kr, 120kr non-members.)

Restaurants line the pedestrian thoroughfare, and the best deal may be found in the Olympic Information Center, where the food varies weekly to reflect different areas of Norway. (Mon-Sat. 11am-6pm; Sun. noon-7pm. Lunch specialties from 55kr). Decent fast food hangs near the tourist information office at **M-Burger** (Lysgadsveien 89), with hot dogs from 10kr and hamburgers from 29kr.

The **tourist office** lies at the North end of Storgata (tel. 61 25 92 99; open Mon.-Fri. 9am-9pm, Sat. 9am-7pm, Sun. 11am-7pm; Olympic hours will vary). The **Olympic Information Center** (tel. 61 27 19 50; Mon.-Sat. 10am-8pm, Sun. noon-8pm) is nearby. **Winge Reisebureau,** Jerbanegt. 2 (tel. 61 25 49 05), will function as a full service **American Express** office during the games. **Trains** run up to a dozen times daily for Oslo (2½hr.), and service also runs to Trondheim (4 /day) and Åndalsnes (2/day).

■■■ VALDRES AND JOTUNHEIMEN

The **Valdres** valley, running parallel and to the west of Gudbrandsdalen, has 6 of Norway's 25 medieval wooden stave churches. It terminates in the highest mountain range in Europe north of the Alps, the jagged, reindeer-freckled **Jotunheimen** massif. Covered by endless boulder fields, the region looks like the home of the troll giants for whom it is named. While only 2 of the several hundred peaks require technical gear to climb, only experienced hikers should attempt anything longer than a daytrip. It snows even in July, so always bring warm, wool clothes and raingear, even on short jaunts. Also visit the DNT offices in either Oslo or Bergen for maps and info on trails, huts, and safety precautions. On the east side of Jotunheimen, Route 51 winds north from Fagernes to meet Route 15 at Vågåmo; **Gjendesheim,** an hour north of Fagernes by bus, is the best hiking base. The DNT hut here provides a sleeping bag and lodging (120kr). Buses also run to Gjendesheim from the Oslo-Trondheim train line at Otta, 30km downvalley from Vågåmo. From the **hut** at Gjendesheim, you can hike across the **Besseggen,** a spectacular ridge featuring a deep blue lake at 1200m and an emerald green one at 984m.

Fagernes is the center of things in the valley. The **tourist office** (tel. (613) 604 00), by the bus station, will gladly hand over the comprehensive *Valdres Summer* (or *Winter) Guide.* (Open Mon.-Fri. 8am-9pm, Sat. 10am-6pm, Sun. 11am-6pm; late Aug.-late June Mon.-Fri. 8am-4pm.) Ask at the tourist office about the **stave churches** (30kr each). The more mobile should request a map and further info about the *Vardevandring* (watchtower hike), through most of the valley. The **Fagernes Youth Hostel (HI),** Valdres Folkhøjskole (tel. (613) 620 25), is 4km south of town in

Leira. (80kr, nonmembers 105kr. Open June-Sept.) Reach Fagernes by **bus** from Gol on the Oslo-Bergen rail line (70min., 39kr, students 33% off), from Lillehammer (2hr., 90kr, students 33% off), or by *Valdresekspressen* bus from Oslo (3hr., 170kr).

Lom, Galdesand, and Turtagrø The northwest approach means a spectacular bus ride along Routes 15 and 55 over the main massif of Jotunheimen between Otta on the rail line and Sogndal on Sognefjord (2/day). Sixty-two km out of Otta, the bus stops in **Lom** (48kr), just to the north of Jotunheimen, the branching point for buses to Stryn in Nordfjord. Lom's **tourist office** (tel. (612) 112 86), 300m from the bus stop, does the info thing. (Open Mon.-Sat. 9am-9pm, Sun. noon-7pm; Sept.-May Mon.-Fri. 8:30am-3pm.) In **Galdesand**, 15 km from Lom, stay at the **youth hostel (HI)** (tel. (612) 120 64; 60kr, nonmembers 80kr) and make daytrips to **Galdhøpiggen** (2469m) and its sibling summit **Glittertinden** (2464m), the highest points in Norway. Eighteen km off Route 55, the **tourist chalet** (tel. (612) 114 80) at Spiterstulen is closer to Glittertinden, with cheap beds and story-filled hikers. (60kr, camping 40kr/person.) **Buses** run daily (July 10-Aug. 15; 50kr) from Lom at 4:05pm, and from Galdesand (across from youth hostel) at 5pm (30kr). They return to Lom from Spiterstulen at 11am (70kr). Southwest of Bøverdalen, the plateau between **Krossbu** and **Sognefjellhytta** is strewn with rock cairns tracing the way between snow-covered lakes; cross-country skiing is often possible even in July. Near **Turtagrø**, just above the tip of the Sognefjord system, is one of Norway's premier rock-climbing areas. From the road there's a steep but well-maintained 4-hour path to **Fannaråkhytta** (2069m), highest hut in the DNT system, on Smørstabreen Glacier.

■■■ ÅNDALSNES AND ÅLESUND

The mountains around Åndalsnes are a mecca for mountaineers, rock climbers, and casual hikers. The wagons that split off the Oslo-Trondheim train at Dombås end at Åndalsnes (3/day, from Oslo 6½hr., 440kr), passing by an ultimate mountaineering challenge, Trollveggen, and the most notable peak in the area, Romsdalshorn. The train spends 2 hours running through the visually exhausting **Romsdal Valley,** a narrow canyon bounded by 1000m walls. Dombås-Åndalsnes buses parallel the train. An equally awesome approach is the dizzying road down **Trollstigen,** traversed by the bus to Geiranger, and featuring no fewer than 11 hairpin turns.

Åndalsnes The town itself is splendiferous and comfortable, at the mouth of the Rauma River and the bottom of a wide fjord. It centers on the road leading uphill from the train station and boasts the **Norsk Tindemuseum,** housing legendary mountaineer Arne Randers Heen's collection of expedition paraphernalia. (Open mid-June to mid-Aug. Mon.-Fri. 3-6pm, Sat.-Sun. 2-6pm; other times on request.) To get to the **Setnes Youth Hostel (HI)** (tel. (712) 213 82), walk up Jernberegata and take a left where the road ends onto Storgata. Follow Storgata down to the traffic circle, stay right, pass the gas stations, and cross the river. The hostel is on the left; you can see it from the road. It's a good 30-minute walk, but the breakfast makes you forget the miles. (90kr, nonmembers 115kr. Breakfast 50kr. Open mid-May to mid-Sept.) The knowledgable hostess sometimes arranges trips to Geirangerfjord. To hit the mountains, contact **Aak** (tel. (072) 264 44), 4km east of town on the E69 back toward Dombås; they have beds (50-140kr) with showers and a fireplace and rent both canoes (first hr. 100kr, thereafter 30kr/hr.) and cross-country telemark skis (100kr/day). Follow the signs from the hostel to **Åndalsnes Camping** (tel. (712) 216 29), which lets you set up tents for 12kr per person, 40kr per tent; they rent out huts (125-500kr), bikes (30kr/hr., 70kr/day), and canoes (40kr/hr., 150kr/day). The local **tourist office** (tel. (712) 216 22) is a good source for hiking maps and recreational information. (Open Mon.-Sat. 9:30am-9:30pm, Sun. 3:30-9:30pm; late Aug.-May Mon.-Fri. 9am-3pm.)

Ålesund This largest city between Bergen and Trondheim enjoys a beautiful cliff-side location and is renowned for its art nouveau architecture. For a view of old Åle-sund, the harbor, and the mountains beyond, chug up the 418 steps to **Aksla.** The **Summøre Museum** (10min by bus # 13, 14, 18, or 24; 12kr) displays local fishing boats from days of yore, and a reconstructed vikingship. (Open Mon.-Fri. 10am-5pm, Sat.-Sun. noon-5pm. 25kr, students 15kr.) Newly-opened **Hansen Garden,** Kongensgate 14 (tel. (701) 35 890), provides spotless, cozy rooms. (110kr. Open June 20-Aug. 20.) Call ahead for reservations. **Camp Prinsen** (tel. (701) 552 04), at Gåseid, is 5km outside town (bus 12kr) next to a popular beach. (30kr/tent. Huts or rooms 150-600kr/person. Wheelchair access.) The **tourist office** (tel. (701) 212 02) is across from the bus station in the city hall. (Open Mon.-Fri. 9am-6pm, Sat. 9am-3pm, Sun. noon-5pm; Sept.-May Mon.-Fri. 8:30am-4pm.) Ålesund is reachable by **road** (3 buses/day along the 122km from Åndalsnes, 122kr), by **Hurtigruten,** 623kr, which docks here daily, or by **hydrofoil** from Bergen (Mon.-Fri. 1/day).

There's an old Viking site on **Giske,** a short bus ride from Ålesund (34kr). Ornithu-siasts will thrill to the island of **Runde,** a sanctuary for more than 500,000 birds. A hydrofoil runs from Ålesund to Hareid; a *Soreid* bus leaves from there (one-way 102kr). From Ålesund, it's 2 hours by bus and ferry (90kr) to **Molde,** a seaside town known for its **International Jazz Festival** (July 17-23, 1994). Ask at Ålesund or Åndalsnes for information.

■■■ TRONDHEIM

Medieval capital of Norway, Trondheim is the natural stopping point between Oslo and destinations above the Arctic Circle. Olav Tryggvason founded Trondheim in 997; his image now presides over an outdoor market from a column in the main town square, **Torvet.** Local boy King Olav Haraldsson became Norway's patron saint after he fought to introduce Christianity. A steady stream of pilgrims prompted the construction of **Nidaros Cathedral,** Scandinavia's largest medieval structure, built over a holy well that sprang up beside St. Olav's grave. (Open mid-June to Aug. Mon.-Fri. 9:30am-5:30pm, Sat. 9:30am-2pm, Sun. 1-4pm; reduced hours off-season. 10kr, students 5kr.) The view from the top of the 172-step spiral staircase in the tower is worth the 5kr. The **Gamle Bybro** (old town bridge) and the 18th-century wharves are perhaps the prettiest part of town. On the hill across the river is the white **Kristiansten Fortress** (1681); its restoration should finished by summer 1994. Exhibits of some of Norway's greatest art are displayed at the **Trondhjems Kunst-Forening,** next to the cathedral. Edvard Munch has a hallway to himself, highlighted by the woodcuts *Lust* and *Jealousy.* (Open daily 11am-4pm; Sept.-May Tues.-Sun. noon-4pm. 20kr, students 10kr.) Bus #4, direction "Iade", will take you to the intriguing **Ringve Museum of Musical History.** Displays range from a one-stringed Ethiopian violin to the ornate Mozart Room; guides demonstrate the instruments. (Tours in English daily at 11am, 12:30, 2:30, and 4:30pm in July. 40kr, students 25kr.) Ferry over to **Munkholmen,** an island monastery that became a prison for-tress and then flipped again into a quiet beach and picnic spot. (Round-trip 25kr; fortress 15kr, students 10kr.) From late August until May, the city is alive with stu-dents; visit the red 'n' round **Studentersenter** across the river from the cathedral to dip your toes in their hectic activity.

Accommodations, Food, and Practical Information The **InterRail Center,** Elgeseter gate 1 (tel. (73) 89 95 38), which bears no relation to its hom-onym at the railway station, offers cheap dorms. From the station, cross the bridge, and turn right on Olav Tryggvason's gate, then left on Prinsens gate; it's across the next bridge on the left. (80kr. Angst-ridden student café open July-late Aug.) Stu-dent-run **Singsaker Sommerhotell,** Rogertsgate 1 (tel. (73) 52 00 92), has a grill, pool table, piano, and TV room. (Sleeping-bag accommodations 120kr. Singles 290kr. Doubles 450kr. Open mid-June to mid-Aug.) **Pensjonat Jarken Youth Hos-**

tel, Kongensgate 40 (tel. (73) 51 32 18), is smack-dab in the center, its convenience justifying its price. (150kr, 175kr non-members.) The closest of multiple campsites is large and crowded **Sandmoen Camping** (tel. (73) 88 61 35), 10km south of town. Take bus #44 or 45 from the bus station to Sandbakken. (20kr/tent, 20kr/person.) Camping outside of sites is not permitted in the Trondheim area. Cheap **Rema 1000** stores abound in the town center. Wander along Munkegata, from the **fruit market** at Torvet to the **Ravnkola fish market** by the water, to replenish the vitamins lost to weeks of bread and cheese.

The **train** station faces the center of town, which is circled by the Nid River. From the train station, walk across the bridge, then 6 blocks on Søndregate, turn right on Munkegata, and continue to the main square and the **tourist office** (tel. (73) 92 94 05), which books rooms in private homes. (180kr. Open Mon.-Fri. 8:30am-8pm, Sat. 8:30am-6pm, Sun. 10am-6pm; late Aug.-May Mon.-Fri. 9am-4pm, Sat. 9am-1pm.) The **InterRail Center,** in the train station, has hot plates, showers, and "at-your-own-risk" baggage storage. (Open early July-late Aug. daily 7am-10pm.) A **DNT office,** Munkegata 64, above Paul's Indian Restaurant (tel. (73) 52 38 08), describes huts and trails to the north and south of Trondheim. (Open Mon.-Wed. and Fri. 8am-4pm, Thurs. 8am-6pm.) All **city buses** leave from the Munkegata-Dronningensgate intersection and require exact change (13kr). **Trains** run to Trondheim from Oslo (6-7/day, 7-8hr., 502kr), Stockholm via Storlien (2/day, 13hr.) and Bodø. **Long-distance buses** leave from the *rutebilstasjonen* on Hans Hagrups gate.

■■■ BODØ AND FAUSKE

Bodø Its provincial charm destroyed in WWII, Bodø (BUD-dha) is the northern terminus of the Norwegian rail line and the starting point for buses and boats farther into the Arctic. **Kjerringøy,** an old coastal trading center 30km north of Bodø, recently opened as a highly reputed outdoor museum; several buses (46kr) and ferries (14kr) make the trip each day. (Guided tours daily at 11:15am, 1pm and 3:30pm. 25kr, students 10kr.) The largest maelstrom in the world, **Saltstraumen,** is only 33km from Bodø, but isn't really that exciting; it looks like a patch of mild rapids. Ask at the tourist office for tidal timetables. (Mon.-Fri. 5 buses/day, Sat. 3 buses/day, Sun. 1 bus; 38kr, 19kr with Nordturist.)

The **tourist office,** Sjøgata 21 (tel. (081) 260 00), is about 5 blocks toward the center from the train station. They'll give you the all-knowing, all-seeing *Bodø Guide,* and also have maps and hiking info. (Open Mon.-Fri. 9am-5pm and 7-9pm, Sat. 10am-3pm, Sun. 6-9pm; in winter Mon.-Fri. 9am-4pm.) To get to the **Flatvold Youth Hostel (HI)** (tel. (750) 256 66), turn right on Sjøgata from the bus stop, or left from the ferry landing and train stations; turn left at the traffic circle and walk 10 minutes to the traffic light. It's Nordically clean and modern, with kitchen and laundry facilities. (95kr, nonmembers 120kr. Reception closed noon-5pm. Open June 20 to mid-Aug.) **Bodøsjøen Camping** is 3km from town, by the airport (tel. (081) 229 02 or 229 62; 50kr/tent; 2-person hut 270kr). Follow the directions for the youth hostel, but turn right at the traffic circle. Daily **flights** from Oslo cost only 780kr; from anywhere north of Trondheim, 410kr. By **train,** Bodø is 11 hours north of Trondheim. (1 day and 1 night train/day.) Two **buses** per day run from Bodø north to Narvik (7hr., 305kr).

Fauske To make the Trondheim-Narvik run in 1 bite, get off the train one stop before Bodø at **Fauske** (63km before Bodø), where a bus meets the train and goes directly to Narvik; if you stay on the train to Bodø, the bus will have left. Fauske's **HI youth hostel** (tel. (75) 64 67 06) lies 1km south toward Bodø from the station. (87kr, nonmembers 112kr. Open June to mid-Aug.) **Lundhøgda Camping** (tel. (081) 439 66) is 3km from town (50kr/tent). Call the Statens skoger office (tel. (081) 459 66) for information about hiking in **Rago National Park,** where trails lead all the way to Jokkmokk and Kvikkjokk in Sweden. **Mo i Rana** is 2½ hours further towards

Trondheim. It's home to a hostel (tel. (75) 15 09 63; 90kr, nonmembers 115kr; open May to mid-Sept.) and is the base for excursions to the **Svarteisen glacier;** buses (120kr) leave at 10:30am from the local **tourist office** (tel. (75) 15 04 21).

■■■ NARVIK

In a land where snowcapped peaks reflect in glimmering fjords, **Narvik** is a necessary monstrosity, a tangle of tracks and conveyor belts that bring iron ore from trains to ships. If you doubt its importance, wander through the cemeteries just east of the train station, a testament to the cost of the Allies' first victory over the Nazis (May 28, 1940). The **War Museum,** on the main square, tells the story behind the gravestones. (Open early June-late Aug. Mon.-Sat. 10am-10pm, Sun. 11am-5pm; late Aug. to mid-Sept. and early March-early June Mon.-Fri. 11am-5pm. 20kr, students 10kr.) If you doubt Narvik's sheer ugliness, a dock tour may convince you. (Mid-June to mid-Aug. daily 2pm from LKAB guardhouse on Havnegata. 20kr.) In winter, the city basks in the midnight sun—on the rare days when the clouds part—and Narvik becomes a **skiing** center; slopes run from above tree level to sea level. You can ascend the looming peak by foot or take the new **Gondolbanen** (cable car) to open June 1994. Undoubtedly the most glorious aspect of Narvik is getting there; Nordic nature in its untamed glory is yours on the bus north to Tromsø (251kr, 5hr.) or south to Bodø (305kr, 7hr.), the hydrofoil to Svolvær (255kr; see Lofoten), or the last hour of the train trip through Kiruna in Sweden (3/day, 154kr, 2 22-hr. through-trains/day from Stockholm).

Accommodations, Food, and Practical Information Northbound *Nord-Norge Buss-Ekspressen* buses stop at the **Nordkalotten Youth Hostel (HI),** Havnegata 3 (tel. (769) 425 98); otherwise, turn left from the tourist office and walk 10 minutes down Kongensgate. (135kr, nonmembers 150kr. 4-min. showers 10kr. Open March-Nov. Reservations recommended.) Back up the hill 100m toward town, on Kongensgate, the Swedish Church runs an International Seamen's Center with cheap food, sauna, ping-pong, and showers. **Narvik Camping** (tel. (769) 458 10) is 2km north of town along the main road (70kr/tent. 4-person hut 390kr). The **Rema 1000** discount store is on Snorresgate, 6 blocks uphill and parallel to Kongensgate. (Open Mon.-Fri. 10am-8pm, Sat. 10am-6pm.)

Parallel to the ore-loading tracks is Narvik's main street, Kongensgate, on which you'll find the amicable **tourist office,** Kongensgate 66 (tel. (769) 433 09). From the train station exit, turn right, walk 100m up the hill, then turn left past Gunnars market. The office changes money (bank rates are much better), gives transportation advice, and books private rooms. (Singles 150kr. Doubles 250kr. 20-25kr fee. Open Mon.-Sat. 9am-9pm, Sun. 11am-8pm; mid-Aug. to mid-June Mon.-Fri. 9am-4pm). The **bus station** is in the parking lot just above the tourist office.

■■■ LOFOTEN ISLANDS

Yes, there are enchanted islands, and when they're sunny, they are the Lofotens. Made luscious by the Gulf Stream, their jagged, green-gray mountains shelter fishing villages, farms, and happy sheep. Sun-spangled puffins pontificate from the cliffs at Værøy, while stockfish dry on quayside wooden racks. As late as the 1950s, fisherfolk lived in the small *rorbuer,* yellow and red wooden shacks which cluster along the coast. Today, tourists book the *rorbuer* solid (75-125kr/person/night in a group of 4 or more). The indispensable brochure *Nordland 1994*—available at any tourist office from Bodø north—lists them, among other accommodations, while the *Lofoten Info-Guide 1994,* available at tourist offices in the Lofotens (5kr), also furnishes information on ferries, buses, and sights. The **midnight sun** glows May 27-July 15 over the Lofotens. Any high place or beach is a good vantage point; try **Eggum,** across Vestvågøy from Stamsund, **Laukvik,** across Austvågøy from Svolvær, or ask around. Arctic swimming is possible at shallow, white sandy beaches after the sun has shone for a few days; good places are toward **Utakleiv** on Vestvågøy, where you can also spot the midnight sun, and the beach by **Ramberg** on Flakstadøy.

Transportation Highway E10 binds the 4 largest of the Lofotens—Vågen, Vestvågøy, Flakstad, and Moskenes—which point toward the tiny outlying isles of Værøy and Røst. Narvik and Bodø are the best mainland springboards to the Lofotens; bus service runs daily from Narvik to Svolvær (7hr., 291kr, railpass and student discount 50%) and Bodø, through Fauske, to Svolvær (10½hr., 406kr, railpass and student discount 50%). By **boat,** your best and cheapest bet is the car ferries from Bodø to Moskenes (2-3/day, 4½hrs., 89kr), stopping 2 or 3 times per week at Røst and Værøy. Hydrofoils from Bodø serve Værøy (twice daily, 220kr) and Svolvær (once daily, 219kr). From Narvik, hydrofoils skim the channel to Svolvær daily (255kr; return only Tues.-Sun.). A final approach is the *Hurtigruten* daily connecting Bodø with Stamsund (4½hr., 226kr) and Svolvær (6hr., 243kr).

Try to get where you want in one ferry swoop from the mainland; the **buses** on the 4 northern islands are infrequent, expensive, and have confounding schedules. Wave at them to make sure they stop. **Hitching** is easier on the east coast than on the sparsely populated west coast, but no one's holding their breath. The best way to experience Lofoten's spectacular scenery is to hike inland away from Highway E10. Almost every tourist office or hostel owner can give suggestions and maps.

Røst, Værøy, and Moskenes Røst is the southernmost and smallest of the Lofotens, reachable only by ferry from Bodø (Tues. and Fri., 5hr., 79kr), and Moskenes (Wed. and Sun.). The **HI youth hostel** (tel. (76) 06 61 09) is 500m from the boat landing. (85kr, nonmembers 95kr. Open May-Aug.) Though famed for its puffins, uncharacteristically flat Røst can't compare to craggy **Værøy**, which rises volcano-style between Røst and Moskenes, wallpapered with thousands of seabirds. You can stay at the **Værøy Youth Hostel (HI),** 4km from the ferry stop (tel. (76) 09 53 75 or (76) 09 53 52; 75kr, nonmembers 100kr; open mid-May to mid-Sept.), and hike out to the cliffs. You can take the car ferry from Bodø (Mon.-Wed., Fri.-Sat., 4-7hr., 84kr) or from Moskenes (Mon., Wed., Thurs., Sat., Sun. 1¾hr.) to Værøy.

Ferries to **Moskenes,** the southernmost of the larger Lofotens, dock at the town of **Moskenes.** The **tourist office** (tel. (760) 915 99) by the ferry landing gives advice on rooms and sights. (Open early June daily 10am-4pm; June-late Aug. 9am-8pm.) About 10km to the south is **Å,** a tiny wooden settlement with a **youth hostel (HI)** (tel. (760) 911 21; 95kr, nonmembers 115kr, reservations essential). The hostel also rents *rorbuer*, which are both more rustic and cheaper for groups of 4 or more. Half of Å's buildings make up the **Norsk Fiskeværsmuseum,** an open-air museum documenting life in the old fishing days. (Open June-late Aug. Mon.-Fri. 10am-6pm, Sat.-Sun. 11am-3pm. 25kr.) You can camp on the cliffs behind the town above a snow-fed lake (free), or take a fishing cruise to the **Moskenesstraumen** (260kr), a maelstrom described in the fiction of both Jules Verne and Edgar Allen Poe. A cheap, lovely **fjord cruise** sails daily from Reine (north of Moskenes) to Rostad, Kirkefjord, Engelsnes, Vindstad, and back to Reine (35kr).

Flakstad, Vestvågøy, and Austvågøy Moving north, the next large island is **Flakstad,** centered on the hamlet of **Ramberg.** Flakstad has perhaps the best hiking trails on the islands; get detailed maps at the **tourist office** (tel. (760) 934 50), which opens when the bus stops. The island's red-painted church, built of Russian driftwood in 1780, holds concerts during the summer (early July-early Aug.).

The mountain-backed hamlet of **Stamsund** on **Vestvågøy,** the next island north, is home to a *rorbu* **youth hostel (HI)** (tel. (760) 893 34 or 891 66), where travelers from all over the world come for a night and remain for weeks, cooking their freshly caught fish on wood-burning stoves. (70kr, nonmembers 95kr. Open mid-Dec. to Oct.). The benevolent ruler of this island utopia, Roar Justad, keeps bureaucracy to a minimum and will lend you his rowboats and fishing gear for a 100kr deposit. He also rents mopeds (80kr/day plus 0.50kr/km) and mountain bikes (75kr/day) for quests into the Lofoten wilderness. Two buses run daily to Stamsund from Å (86kr, 50% off with railpass) and Svolvær (72kr, 50% off with railpass) via Vestvågøy's underwhelming main town of **Leknes.**

Svolvær, on the northernmost island of **Austvågøy,** is the bland hub of beautiful Lofoten. The **tourist office** (tel. (760) 730 00) is right near the ferry dock and will energetically provide info on hiking and sight-seeing possibilities. (Open Mon.-Fri. 9am-4pm). **Svolvær Sjøhuscamping** offers clean harborside rooms not far from the center, take the 4th right from Torget on Vestfjordgata going north (tel. (76) 07 03 36; reception open 9am-2pm and 4-11pm; 100kr). More distant, and far more charming, is the friendly **Marinepollen Sjøhus** (sea house; tel. (760) 718 33), north along the E10 for 15 minutes until *Jektveien* on the right—the quay-side WWII hospital ship is visible from the road. (Single cabin 100kr. Double 200kr.) **Camping** is free on a beach 2km north of town, with running water and an ancient toilet.

Above Svolvær is the 2-pronged rock stack called **The Goat;** lunatic rock climbers occasionally attempt the leap from one horn to the other. You can hike up past it to **The Frog,** another weird formation bucking the spine of the mountain. A natural rock bridge at the cliff top overlooks the island's mountains.

■■■ TROMSØ

Tromsø, city of midnight fun and Norway's gateway to the Arctic Ocean, is about 240km up the coast from Narvik on a small island connected to the mainland by bridge. Europe's northernmost university and brewery have both settled here (no coincidence). The locals call the city (celebrating its 200th anniversary on June 25, 1994), with its cafés, discos, and 60 nightclubs, "the Paris of the North;" they are perhaps suffering from cranial frostbite. Nevertheless, Tromsø is a good place to toast the woods and mountains before heading north to Finnmark or the snowfields of **Svalbard.** The striking, modern **Arctic Cathedral** has clean white lines designed to blend with ice and snow. (Open Mon.-Sat. 10am-5pm, Sun. 1-5pm. 5kr.) The **Tromsø Museum** features exhibits on the region's natural history, as well as ethnographic displays on Sami culture. (Open daily 9am-6pm; Sept.-May Mon.-Fri. 8:30am-3:30pm, Sat. noon-3pm, Sun. 11am-4pm. 10kr, students 5kr.) Take bus #21 or 27 to the south end of the island. The 2nd-floor **Polar Museum** chronicles Roald Amundsen's hardy polar exploits, all in Norwegian. (Open daily 11am-6pm; mid-Sept. to mid-May daily 11am-3pm. 20kr.) For a sweeping view of the city in the midnight sun (roughly May 21-July 23), take the **cable car** to the top of Tromsdalstind; reach the cable car station aboard bus #28. (Daily 10am-5pm; midnight sun season 9pm-1:30am in good weather. 45kr.)

To sample the nightlife, wander down **Storgata** and its sidestreets. **Vertshuset Skarven,** on Strandskillet, looking onto the harbor, is a spot for all generations. Look for a whitewashed building. (Beer 35kr. Dinner from 50kr. Open Mon.-Thurs. noon-12:30am, Fri.-Sat. noon-1:30am, Sun. 3pm-12:30am.) **Blå Rock Café,** Strandgata 14, is a sleek 3-story eatery in the Hard Rock Café tradition. (0.5L beer 29kr in summer, large pizza 85kr, small 60kr. Open Mon.-Thurs. 6pm-1:30am, Fri. 2pm-3:30am, Sat. noon-4am, Sun. 6pm-1:30am.) **Middags Kjelleren,** in a basement grotto between Skarven and Blå Rock, has bands most nights. (Cover after 8pm. Open Mon.-Thurs. 3pm-2am, Fri. 3pm-4am, Sat. noon-4am, Sun. 6pm-1:30am.)

Accommodations, Food, and Practical Information The Elverhøy Youth Hostel (HI) (tel. (776) 853 19) is a bland, impersonal student dorm. Take bus #24. (Lockout 11am-5pm. 95kr, nonmembers 120kr, 100kr deposit mandatory for keys. Open June 20-Aug. 19.) Closer but more expensive is **Park Pensjonat,** Skolegate 24 (tel. (776) 822 08), with spacious, comfortable rooms. (Singles 260kr. Doubles 320kr. Triples 360kr.) **Tromsdalen Camping** (tel. (083) 380 37) has its share of

bare ground but still undercuts the competition. Walk across the river to Troms-dalen, 20 minutes from the town center, or take bus #30 or 36. (2- to 4-person huts 250kr. Tents 100kr.) Next to the open-air market is **Domus**, a large market with a cheap salad bar (open Mon.-Fri. 10am-8pm, Sat. 10am-6pm). Fishermen sell fresh goods near the harbor by a statue memorializing their perils at sea.

The **tourist office**, Storgata 61/63 (tel. (776) 100 00), books rooms in private homes for 25kr, and is generally well clued-in. (Open Mon.-Fri. 8:30am-7pm, Sat.-Sun. 10am-5pm; Aug.16-May 31 Mon.-Fri. 8:30am-4pm. Singles 150kr. Doubles 200kr.) Tromsø's location means frequent connections to the rest of the country. The *Nord-Norge Ekspressen* **bus** is 251kr to Narvik and 323kr to Alta (Nordturist gets 50% off). The northbound *Hurtigruten* leaves daily at 6pm; the southbound arrives at 11:45pm. (To Honningsvåg 691kr, to Bodø 701kr.)

■■■ FINNMARK

On most maps, Finnmark appears about as inviting as a walk-in freezer. The sun hides its face here from late November until late January and only the exquisite col-ors of the *aurora borealis* (Northern Lights) illuminate the frigid countryside. But in summer the snow-capped peaks, vast stretches of coastal tundra, and inland forest bask under the midnight sun, and, the landscape becomes an arctic wonderland. The wilderness of **Finnsmarksvidda** that spreads east from Tromsø is Europe's larg-est, a highly popular hiking area spotted with tourist huts. Consult the DNT offices in Oslo or Bergen for maps, prices and other information.

Buses run once or twice per day along the E6, the main highway around the top of Norway; spur lines branch south to Sweden and Finland. Both buses and the *Hur-tigruten* are *very* expensive. Nordturist and ScanRail get 50% off on *Nord-Norge Ekspressen* buses from Bodø to Kirkenes, and students may get some reduction on buses run by **FFR**. Some travelers find **hitchhiking** surprisingly successful, though traffic is light and distances are long. Those who thumb it bring a tent and a warm sleeping bag. If you're under 25, **flying** is the cheapest way to get to Finnmark. SAS offers 800kr standby (*Superbaik*) to Alta, and *Widerøe Airlines* will fly between any 2 cities north of and including Tromsø for 410kr (make reservations); youth standby fares in Sweden (250 Swedish kr from Stockholm to Kiruna or Gällivare in Swedish Lapland) are sometimes an even better option.

Alta and Hammerfest Slate-gray mountains, towering cliffs, and icy green sea make the road from Tromsø north to **Alta**, Finnmark's largest town, the most spectacular bus route in Norway. The **Alta River**, famous for its salmon, runs nearby at the bottom of Europe's longest canyon (tours 100kr). For fishing permits, consult the **tourist office** (tel. (784) 377 70). The **Alta Museum**, winner of "European Museum of the Year Award 1993," includes Scandinavia's only prehistoric UNESCO World Heritage site: spectacular rock carvings from more than 6000 years ago. Take the city bus to its west end along the E6. (Open summer daily 8am-11pm; early June and late August 8am-8pm; off-season reduced hours. 30kr, 25kr in winter). You can stay at the **Frikirkens Elevheim (HI)** (tel. (784) 344 09; 100kr, nonmembers 125kr; mattress on floor 45kr; lockout 11am-5pm; open late June-late Aug.). The **camp-ground** on the river (tel. (084) 343 53) is toward Hammerfest from the bus terminal (50kr/tent, 20kr/person, 4-person huts 330kr). One to 2 **buses** per day run to Tromsø (7-8hr., 323kr); Hammerfest (3hr., 143kr); Honnigsvåg (5hr., 213kr); Kau-tokeino (3hr., 132kr); and Karasjok (4hr., 244kr).

At **Hammerfest**, the world's northernmost town, you can become a member of the Royal and Ancient Polar Bear Society (est. 1963)—if you have 95kr to blow. The *Hurtigruten* stops here for 1½ hours. Daily buses head west to Alta and east to Kirkenes. Contemplate the midnight sun from **Salen**, a short, steep hike up the hill from the **tourist office** (tel. (784) 121 85), up the street from the pier and on the left. (Open Mon.-Fri. 8am-6pm, Sat.-Sun. 10am-3pm; Sept.-May Mon.-Fri. 8am-3pm.) The cheapest beds in town are with **Sara Myrvoll** (tel. (084) 133 44), a 20-minute walk around the bay or by bus #1 or 4 to Fuglenes. Look for the big red "SARA" letters. (Sleeping bag accommodations 100kr. Breakfast included. Open June 20-Aug. 20.)

Nordkapp and Honningsvåg

Looming into the Arctic Ocean from the island of Magerøy, the famed **Nordkapp** is much ado about less than you might have hoped. Not even continental Europe's northernmost point (a title held by Knivskjellodden, a peninsula to the west), Nordkapp is an expensive tourist mecca (ticket, including bus, 190kr). Nordkapp's first budget traveler was a 17th-century Italian monk named Francesci Negri, who made the journey by rowboat and foot. Battered by gale and wave and carrying only a letter from his mom for comfort, Negri managed to caulk leaks in his boat with his habit and, once on land, to spark fires on the desolate rock using his own hair. Exhausted, naked, and bald, he arrived in Nordkapp and was (can you believe it?) ostracized. Perched on and inside the rock is the **Nordkapp Complex,** with a bank, post office, telephones, cafeteria, and a gold-enameled Thai Museum commemorating King Chulalongkorn's visit in 1907. No joke. Around the complex is rough landscape, open ocean bashing beneath the midnight sun (mid-May to July), and a cliff-side champagne bar. Be warned: the complex closes at 2am, and the only rooms are in Honnigsvåg (last bus leaves at 1:15am).

To reach Nordkapp, first travel to **Honningsvåg,** 25km south, whose **tourist office** (tel. (784) 728 94) provides transport info for all of Finnmark. (Open daily 8:30am-7pm; Sept.-May Mon.-Fri. 8:30am-4pm.) The 33km trip to Nordkapp can be made by bus (4/day, round-trip 95kr); some thumb it, but get the weather forecast first—Nordkapp is dullsville in the mist. The cold and primitive **Nordkapp Youth Hostel and Camping (HI)** (tel. (784) 751 13) is 8km up the same road (bus 12kr). There's a kitchen but few utensils, and the toilets are a windy 200m walk away. (100kr, non-members 120kr. 20kr/person, 40kr/tent. Open June-Sept. Reservations recommended.) To visit Nordkapp in winter, call the **Nordkapp Turistheim,** N-9763 Skarsvåg (tel. (784) 752 19), to arrange transportation by motor sleigh. The **bus** to Honningsvåg from Alta (1-2/day, 6hr., 213kr with ferry) or Hammerfest (1-2/day, 4½hr., 156kr) is cheaper than the *Hurtigruten* (from Kirkenes 626kr, Tromsø 649kr, Hammerfest 251kr). Hitchers beware the Kåfjord-Honningsvåg ferry—you can get stuck at the landing for hours.

Karasjok, Kautokeino, and Kirkenes

Fishing, rafting, and hiking are the norm in **Karasjok,** and those who missed last century's gold rushes can ask about panning in local rivers. During Easter, the city hosts concerts, theater, exhibits, games, and a reindeer race on a frozen river. The **tourist office** (tel. (784) 67 360), in the Samelandssentret, dispenses info. (Open Mon.-Sat. 8am-9pm, Sun. 10am-9pm; Sept.-May daily 9am-4pm.) **Karasjok Camping** (tel. 784) 66 135) is down the street toward Alta. (15kr/person, 45kr/tent. 4-bed huts 280-300kr. Open early June-Aug.) There is plenty of freelance camping, but beware of mosquitoes. The **youth hostel** in Karigasniemi, Finland is only 18km away. Karasjok is 4½ hours and 246kr away from Alta, and is a major transit point for buses through Karigasniemi to Inari (1/day, 2½hr., 60 Finnish mk) and Rovaniemi (1-2/day, 7hr., 191 Finnish mk) in Finland. When reading bus schedules, remember that Finland is one time zone ahead.

Probably the emptiest portion of empty Finnmark is between Karasjok and **Kautokeino,** 128km to the west; inquire at local tourist offices or at the Oslo DNT about the area's **mountain huts.** Buses to Kautokeino run from Karasjok (3-4/week), daily from Alta, and daily from Muonio, Finland. From Muonio you can connect farther south to Rovaniemi, or west to Karesuando and Kiruna in Swedish Lapland. For further information on nearby regions, turn to the Finland and Sweden chapters.

A bus ride in the opposite direction from Karasjok brings you to Norway's eastern outpost at **Kirkenes,** 7km from the Russian border, 5102km from Rome, and 93 million very long miles from the sun. Longtime Cold War tensions have softened into hectic Russo-Norwegian cultural exchange; the city is now the starting point for visa-free excursions to Murmansk. Contact **Folkhøgskolen** (tel. (785) 950 92) well in advance about cheaper tours for students and seniors or **FFR** (the bus company) which runs hydrofoil trips (tel. (78) 41 43 44 or (78) 41 10 00); make reservations 4 days in advance. The **tourist office** (tel. (785) 925 44), in the small wooden hut just as you enter town, can help you with info on these trips, as well as shorter excursions along the Russian border. (Open mid-June to late Aug. Tues.-Sun. 9am-9pm, Mon. 8am-9pm. Off-season contact A/S Grenseland at tel. (085) 925 01.) The **Statens skoger** office at Joh. Knudtzens gate 27 (tel. (785) 932 63 or (785) 924 70 or (785) 987 86) has maps and hut locations for hiking in area parks. The cheapest beds are in private homes; **Julie Fermann Jensen,** Fridtjof Nansensgate 6 (tel. (785) 911 44), offers the best place in town. (200-300kr. Reserve ahead.) The closest **camping** (tel. (785) 980 28) is 8km out of town. Take the bus to Hesseng (10kr) and walk 1km toward Kirkenes. (10kr/person, 30kr/tent. Open June-Sept.) Kirkenes is the eastern terminus of both the daily *Nord-Norge Ekspressen* bus from Karasjok (5½hr., 316kr) and Alta (10½hr., 556kr), and of the *Hurtigruten* from Bodø (1599kr), Honningsvåg (626kr), and points south.

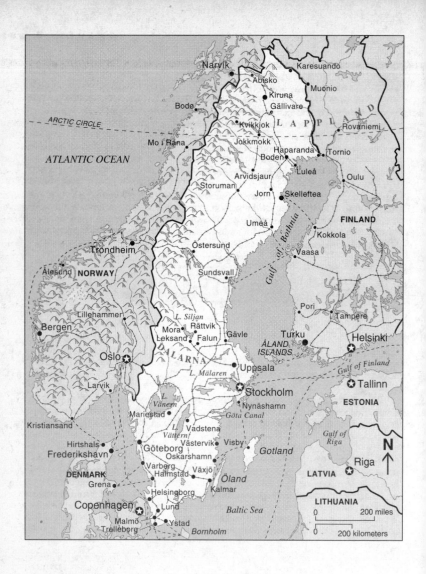

Sweden

US$1 = 7.85kr (kronor)
CDN$1 = 5.97kr
UK£1 = 12.20kr
IR£1 = 11.40kr
AUS$1 = 5.09kr
NZ$1 = 4.32kr
SAR1 = 1.62kr
Country Code: 46

10kr =   US$1.27
10kr = CDN$1.68
10kr =   UK£0.82
10kr =   IR£0.88
10kr = AUS$1.96
10kr =   NZ$2.31
10kr =   SAR6.16
International Dialing Prefix: 009

Some call Sweden the world's success story, a modern miracle. Fervent social democratic idealism and principled neutrality have made Sweden (Sverige) a land whose affluence is widely shared. Thanks to free health care, education, and other services, Sweden some years ago became the first place on earth where physicians could not tell the social class of children by examining their bodies and growth rates.

Sweden's internationalism is unforgettable: Raoul Wallenberg clambered over the roofs of Nazi trains handing out Swedish passports that saved thousands of Jews from concentration camps, Dag Hammarskjöld nurtured the U.N., and Prime Minister Olof Palme marched against the Vietnam War and sheltered draft resisters. Today in impoverished East Africa, so much of the incoming aid bears the Swedish colors that many villagers assume Sweden is a global superpower.

The country's 8.3 million citizen—among them tens of thousands of political refugees—inhabit a land the size and shape of California. A whopping 25 hours by train in length, Sweden defies the whirlwind tour, but unless you're an avid mountaineer, you needn't make the pilgrimage north to Lapland's sleepless sun and the alpine huts of the Kungsleden. If logging and coastal scenery inspire you, head to the northeast coastal cities of Luleå, Umeå, and Sundsvall. Life pulses peacefully in the southern half of the country, where 85% of Swedes reside, many taking their 5-week paid vacations in waterside cottages or on Viking-trodden Gotland or Åland, islands off the southeast coast. At the center of it all lies celestial Stockholm, a city of bland apartment blocks and utopian hopes.

GETTING THERE AND GETTING AROUND

Sweden is easily accessible by boat or train from Denmark and Germany, by ferry from Poland and Finland, and by train and bus from Norway and Finland. A consistent and reliable series of trains greets travelers in the southern half of the country; in the north, long-distance buses (railpasses not valid), are often a better option. As of January 1, 1994, the 21-day **Nordturist pass,** which allows unlimited travel on state-run trains and ferries in Denmark, Sweden, Norway, and Finland (2nd class 1980kr, ages 12-25 1450kr), will give way to the **ScanRail pass,** offering 1 consecutive month of travel (US$399), 9 days of travel within 21 (US$275), or 4 days of travel within 15 (US$159), with about 25% off for those under 26. (seniors and under 16 ½-price; seniors can upgrade a 2nd-class ticket to 1st class for 50kr.) For holders of the **Reslustkortet** card (150kr, seniors 50kr; valid 1 year), fares are reduced 50% on trains marked with a red circle in the timetable, and on all trains from July to mid-August. (25% discount on all trips begun on a Tues., Wed., Thurs., or Sat.) **Eurail** is valid, but reservations (20kr) are still required (though rarely enforced) on nearly all long-distance journeys.

For those under 25, **SAS** offers a standby fare of 220-260kr on all their flights between Stockholm and other Swedish cities (call (08) 24 00 00 for details Mon.-Fri. 7am-9pm, Sat. 8am-6pm, Sun. 8am-8pm). **Hitching** in Sweden can be slow near the major cities, but picks up in the north. In this safety-minded country, all must wear seatbelts, and headlights must be on at all times. Sweden is a biker's heaven; numerous paths cover most of the country, particularly the south; you can complete a trip of Sweden on the hostel-spotted Sverigeleden **bike route**. Contact the Svenska Turistföreningen (STF) (see below) for more information.

SWEDEN ESSENTIALS

Sweden is a nation of bank **holidays** (Jan. 1, Jan. 6, April 1-4, April 30-May 1, May 12, May 23, June 25, Nov.5, and Dec. 24-26 in 1994) and festivals. May 1 brings a rousing solidarity parade in Stockholm, while Midsummer incites Bacchanalian dancing, and the "Crayfish Premiere" and Stockholm Water Festival (beginning on the 2nd Wed. of Aug.) coax out the wildest spirits in every Swede. Plan ahead for these days, as many transportation lines grind to a halt and some hostels close.

Most Swedish **banks** are open weekdays until 5pm (sometimes later in Stockholm). Exchange rates remain constant, but commissions vary. Try to exchange checks in large denominations, as there is usually a 35kr commission per check. Many **post offices** double as banks and are open weekdays from 9am to 5pm or later, Saturdays from 9am to 1pm. Pay **phones** require at least 2kr, although nearly half of all phones in the country only accept phone cards *(Telefonkort)* (widely available at newsstands and post offices). Call 079 75 for directory information in Sweden and 0018 to make a collect call. For AT&T's **USA Direct**, dial (020) 79 56 11. For MCI's **Global Reach**, dial (020) 79 59 82. For **Canada Direct**, dial (020) 79 90 15. For **emergency help** dial 900 00 (free). Almost all Swedes speak some English, and those under 50 are generally fluent. Sweden leads the world in facilities for people with disabilities. Begin by requesting the Swedish Tourist Board's free 260-page *Holiday Guide for the Disabled* from the Swedish Institute.

Accommodations, Camping, and Food Sweden's top-flight **youth hostels** *(vandrarhem)*, at 83kr for HI members and 30kr more for nonmembers, are the only budget option in Sweden; hotels cost at least 275-350kr. If you arrive in the off-season and the local hostel is closed (a problem in the north and in smaller towns), staying in private homes is a bearable alternative (100-200kr/night). Book through the local *turistbyrå* (tourist office). Be warned that in Swedish hostels, sheets are paper disposables.

The **Svenska Turistföreningen (STF)** runs Sweden's hostels, which often fill in a flash during summer, so reserve in advance. Most hostels have kitchen facilities, and receptions are usually open from 8-10am and 5 to 9 or 10pm (shorter hours in winter; around 130 of the 280 hostels are open all year). Outside the cities, *vandrarhem* are often used by Swedish families who can't afford expensive hotels. STF's main office is in downtown Stockholm at Drottninggatan 31, P.O. Box 25, 101 20 Stockholm (tel. (08) 790 31 00; fax (08) 20 13 32), with branches in Göteborg and Malmö; they'll sell you membership (215kr, under 20 60kr) and the indispensable *STF Vandrarhem* book (59kr), listing all hostels with maps, pictures, phone numbers, opening hours, and dates. (Open Mon.-Fri. 10am-6pm, Aug.-April Mon.-Fri. 10am-5:30pm.) The STF also manages mountain huts in the northern wilds. Many **campgrounds** (50-80kr/site) also offer *stugor* (simple cottages, often with kitchen facilities) for around 75-175kr per person. If you don't have an International Camping Card, you'll need a Swedish one (45kr; valid 1 year), available with the booklet *Camping in Sweden* from **Sveriges Campingvärdars Riksförbund** (tel. (0522) 393 45), Box 255, S-451 17 Uddevalla. You may walk or camp for 1 or 2 nights anywhere on *privately* owned land—except for gardens—so long as you respect the privacy of the owners as well as the flora and fauna. Pick up the brochure *The Common Right of Access (Allemansrätten)*, at the STF. Don't let the fact that the natives persist in T-shirts and shorts trick you into thinking that the weather is always warm; summer days are pleasant (around 20°C in the south, 16°C in the north) but nights can get surprisingly chilly (around 10°C in the south, 5°C in the north). Meet youthful Swedes and foreigners by joining a workcamp; contact **Internationella Arbetslag**, Barnångsgatan 23, (tel. (08) 643 08 89) in Stockholm.

Food is very expensive in Sweden, both in restaurants and grocery stores. Rely on supermarkets; most are open until 7pm. Grab a box of strawberries or blueberries, or try *pannkakor* with lingonberry jam. Expect to find numerous potatoes in Swedish cuisine (a meal's worth for about 1kr); spuds are celebrated in Alingsås's annual "Tater Fest" in mid-June. Tasty milk products include *messmör* (spreadable whey cheese) and *fil*, a fluid yogurt good for dousing your cereal. When you tire of cold muesli, seek out restaurants that offer a **dagens rätt**, a daily special usually available only at lunch. This may be the only time you can afford a sit-down meal: the price (40-50kr) includes a main dish, salad, bread, and beverage. Alcohol is not a wise option for the budget traveler; a real beer *(starköl)* usually costs at least 25kr, often 50-60kr, in city bars. The cheaper, weaker, and lousier low-alcohol alternative is *lättöl* (8-12kr).

■■■ STOCKHOLM

Stockholm displays august monuments but no imperial arrogance, genteel cultural life free from injurious class distinctions, opulent consumerism without hardness of heart. Hot-air balloons dot the summer sky while sailboats slip between the city's islands. How, you may ask, could such a serene city nurture the melancholy pensiveness of an Ingmar Bergman or the stoic radicalism of an Olof Palme? Visit in the winter and find out.

ORIENTATION AND PRACTICAL INFORMATION

Gamla Stan (Old City) is the centerpiece of Stockholm's 24,000-island archipelago. To the east lie the museums and hostels of Skeppsholmen island and the cultured greenery of Djurgården; to the south, the artsy island of Södermalm. The train station stands on the southern edge of the mainland, just east of the workaday Kungsholmen island. The *tunnelbana* (subway) links it all up, but given the short distances and disproportionate subway fares, a stroll is often preferable.

Tourist Offices: Stockholm Information Service, in the northeast corner of Kungsträdgården at Hamngatan (tel. 789 24 90). From Centralstation, walk up Klarabergsgatan to Sergels Torg (T-bana: T-Centralen), then bear right on Hamngatan. Books hostels and hotels (30kr fee). Tourist information open Mon.-Fri. 9am-7pm, Sat.-Sun. 9am-5pm; Sept.-May Mon.-Fri. 9am-6pm, Sat.-Sun. 9am-3pm. **Hotellcentralen,** at the train station (tel. 24 08 80). 30kr finding fee for hotels, but just 12kr/person for hostels. No charge if reserved by phone. Also sells a comprehensive color city map (10kr). Open daily 8am-9pm.

Budget Travel: Kilroy Travels Sweden, Kungsgatan 4 (tel. 23 45 15). Cheap and largely refundable student flight tickets. Branch on university campus at Frescati (tel. 16 05 15). Open Mon.-Fri. 9:30am-5pm. **Transalpino,** Birger Jarlsgatan 13 (tel. 679 98 70). Open Mon.-Fri. 10am-5:30pm. T-bana for both: Östermalmstorg.

Embassies: U.S., Strandvägen 101 (tel. 783 53 00). **Canada,** Tegelbacken 4 (tel. 613 99 00). **U.K.,** Skarpögatan 6-8 (tel. 667 01 40). **Australia,** Sergelstorg 12 (tel. 613 29 00). In emergencies, contact the British Embassy. **Estonia,** Storgatan 38 (tel. 665 65 50). **Latvia,** Storgatan 38 (tel. 667 34 00). **Lithuania,** Strandvägen 53 (tel. 667 11 72). **Poland,** Karlavägen 35 (tel. 11 41 32). **Russia,** Gjörwellsgatan 31 (tel. 13 04 40; for visa info call 20 86 52).

Currency Exchange: Forex in Centralstation (open daily 8am-9pm) and in Cityterminalen (open Mon.-Sat. 10am-3pm) take 15kr/traveler's check and a 20kr commission to exchange cash. **Valutaspecialisten,** Kungsgatan 30 (tel. 10 30 00), near Hötorget, charges no commission and has good rates. Open Mon.-Fri. 8am-7pm, Sat. 9am-4pm. See also **Post Offices,** below.

American Express: Birger Jarlsgatan 1 (tel. 679 78 80; for 24-hr. refund assistance (020) 79 51 55). T-bana: Östermalmstorg. Open Mon.-Fri. 9am-6pm, Sat. 10am-1pm; Sept.-May Mon.-Fri. 9am-5pm, Sat. 10am-1pm.

Post Office: Mäster Samuelsgatan 70, near Centralstation. Poste Restante held in indoor courtyard. Open Mon.-Fri. 8am-6:30pm, Sat. 10am-2pm. **Postal code:** 10110 Stockholm 1. Buy cheap postcards (1kr) along Drottninggatan.

Telephones: Telecenter, at Centralstation. Also sells phone cards for 24, 45, 80kr. Open daily 8am-9pm. **Telebutiken,** Kungsgatan 36 (T-bana: Hötorget). Open Mon.-Fri. 9:30am-6pm, Sat. 9:30am-3pm. **City Code:** 08.

Flights: Arlanda Airport, 45km north of the city. **Flygbussar** buses (40 min., 50kr; public transportation passes not valid) run between it and Cityterminalen (see Buses, below), departing Cityterminalen every 10min. from 4:30am-10pm.

Trains: Centralstation (T-bana: T-Centralen) is Stockholm's main gateway. Luggage office (40kr/day) near the Vasagatan entrance; **lockers** 15-25kr/24hr. Open 5am-midnight. Train information: tel. (020) 75 75 75. To Copenhagen (6/day, 8½hr., 524kr) and Oslo (3/day; 6½hr. day, 9hr. overnight; 490kr). Waiting rooms for women *(Damväntsal)* and families *(Familjeväntsal).*

Buses: The **Cityterminalen,** across the street from Centralstation, sends buses to the airport, to the Gotland and Poland ferries, and on routes within Sweden (to

Göteborg, 7-8hr., 220kr; to Malmö, 10-11hr., 240-260kr). Reservations required daily on **Swebus** buses, Fri. and Sun. for all other buses (tel. (020) 64 06 40).

Public Transportation: SL: Office in Sergelstorg (tel. 600 10 00) provides info and sells the *Stockholmskartan* (35kr), a peerless street map complete with bus and subway lines. Open Mon.-Thurs. 8:30am-6:30pm, Fri. 8:30am-5:30pm. Most in-town destinations cost 2 coupons (13kr). **Rabatt-kuponger,** sold at *Pressby-rån* news agents cost 85kr, valid for up to 7 trips; the **SL Tourist Card** costs 60kr (24hr. in all zones), or 115kr (3-day in all zones). Most subway lines run 5am-2am, after which they are replaced by night buses. The **Stockholmskortet** (Stockholm Card) offers unlimited travel by bus, subway, and local trains (not airport buses), boat sight-seeing, a bus tour around the city, admission to over 50 attractions, and a guide to the city (150kr/24hr. up to 3 days).

Ferries: Silja Line, Kungsgatan 2 (tel. 22 21 40), and **Viking Line,** Centralstation (tel. 714 56 00). Daily to Mariehamn, Turku (Åbo), and Helsinki in Finland. Viking Line ferries also sail daily from Kapellskär to Mariehamn and Naantali, Finland (buses to Kapellskär leave from Cityterminalen; 1½hr, 20kr). Silja ferries to Turku and Helsinki free with Eurailpass, though to Helsinki a cabin (100kr) must be reserved; with Nordturist, free to Turku and 50% off to Helsinki. (T-bana: Ropsten, then take a Silja bus to the terminal). Viking Line ferries are free with Eurail (T-bana: Slussen; then bus #45 to the terminal, free). Ferries to **Gotland** leave from Nynäshamn, south of Stockholm by bus or SL commuter rail (see under Gotland); **Polferries** (tel. (0155) 781 00) ships to Gdańsk, Poland leave from Oxelösund, further south (1-3/week; 300kr, students and seniors 230kr).

Bike Rental: Try **Skepp och Hoj** on Djurgårdsbron (tel. 660 57 57). 110kr/day, 360kr/week. Open daily April-Sept. 9am-9pm.

Hitchhiking: Laborious. Gas stations are the hitcher's best bet; it's illegal to wait on a highway. Those headed south take the T-bana to the gas station Kungens Kurva in Skärholmen. Those going north take bus #52 to Sveaplan and stand on Sveavägen at Nortull, or go farther up the E4 to the junction of Uppsalavägen and Enköpingsvägen.

Bookstore: Akademibokhandeln, Almquist, & Wiksell, Mäster Samuelsgatan 32 (tel. 23 79 90). Truckloads of English books. Open Mon.-Fri. 9:30am-6pm, Sat. 10am-3pm; Sept.-May Mon.-Fri. 10am-4pm, Sat. 10am-3pm.

Laundromat: Rare and expensive. Try **Tvättomaten,** Västmannagatan 61. T-bana: Odenplan. Open Mon.-Fri. 9am-6pm, Sat. 10am-2pm. 55kr/load.

Women's Center: Alla Kvinnors Hus, Svartengatan 3 (tel. 644 09 25). Closes in summer. **Kvinnobokhandeln Medusa,** Wollmar Ykullsgatan 33 (tel. 84 50 07), houses a women's bookstore.

Gay and Lesbian Services: The Swedish Federation for Sexual Equality (RFSL) runs a center at Sveavägen 57 (tel. 736 02 12). T-bana: Rådmansgatan. Bookstore open Mon.-Thurs. noon-3pm and 6-9pm, Fri. noon-6pm, Sat.-Sun. noon-3pm. Café open daily 11am-8pm. Restaurant and disco nightly 6pm-3am.

Travelers With Disabilities: Subways and most public places offer facilities.

Pharmacy: Apotek C. W. Scheele, Klarabergsgatan 64 (tel. 21 82 80), under the green-and-white "Apotek" signs at the overpass over Vasagatan. T-bana: T-Centralen. Open 24 hrs.

Medical Assistance: Call 644 92 00 for a referral to the nearest hospital.

Emergencies: Ambulance, Fire, and **Police,** tel. 900 00 (red button on older pay phones). Police station: Bryggargatan 19, north of Centralstation (tel. 769 51 00).

ACCOMMODATIONS AND CAMPING

Hostels (Vandrarhem)

Summer demands reservations, and most hostels limit stays to 5 nights.

Skeppsholmen

af Chapman (HI), (tel. 679 50 15; fax 611 71 55), a full-rigger 1888 sailing ship majestically moored off Skeppsholmen, to the right as you cross the bridge. Take bus #65 from T-Centralen. 136 places in 2- to 10-bed cabins. Reception open 7am-noon and 3pm-2am. Lockout noon-3pm. Curfew 2am. 90kr, nonmembers 125kr.

Breakfast 40kr. Sheets 30kr. In summer reserve 2-3 months in advance or show up 7-8:30am. Open April to mid-Dec.

Skeppsholmens Vandrarhem (HI) (tel. 679 50 17; fax 611 71 55), in the Hantverkshuset, on the shore behind the af Chapman . Less mythic, but bigger rooms. 152 beds, 2-6/room. Reception open 7am-2pm and 3pm-2am. Lockout noon-3pm. Curfew 2am. 90kr, nonmembers 125kr. Breakfast 40kr. Laundry nearby. Lockers 10kr. Sheets 30kr. Open mid-Jan. to mid-Dec. 4 wheelchair-accessible rooms.

Södermalm

Långholmen Vandrarhem (HI), Kronohäktet (tel. 668 05 00; fax 84 10 96), on Långholmen Island. Plush cells in a transmogrified prison, most with TV, phone and private shower. From T-bana: Hornstull, march north on Långholmsgatan, turn left (before the bridge) onto Högalidsgatan, then right on Bergsundsgatan over the bridge onto Långholmen, then follow the "Kronokäktet" signs. No curfew, no lockout, no lockup. Reception open 24 hrs. 90kr, nonmembers 125kr. Sheets 35kr. Breakfast 50kr. Dinner 30kr. Laundry 24kr. Kitchen. Some free lockers. Fewer beds available on winter weekdays. 10 rooms have wheelchair access.

Columbus Hotell-Vandrarhem, Tjärhovsgatan 11 (tel. 644 17 17; fax 702 07 64). Three blocks east of T-bana: Medborgarplatsen. Built in 1780, a former brewery, prison, and plague hospital (none within this century), with the cheapest hotel rooms in town (singles 390kr, doubles 490kr) and a mega-friendly staff. The hostel has 90 beds, 2-6 per room. Kitchen and TV. 1 floor women-only. Reception open 24 hrs. No curfew. 110kr. Breakfast 40kr. Café and bar. Credit cards accepted. Lockers 5kr. Sheets 30kr. Open Jan.-late Dec.

Gustaf af Klint, Stadsgårdskajen 153 (tel. 640 40 77; fax 640 64 16). A snug former Navy ship moored 200m east of T-bana: Slussen. Reception open 24 hrs. No curfew. 130 beds. 2-6 bed cabins, 120kr per person. Breakfast 40kr. Free backpacksized lockers. Sheets 35kr. TV. Laundry 25kr. Open mid-Jan. to mid-Dec.

Zinken Hostel (HI), Zinkens Väg 20 (tel. 668 57 86; fax 658 36 64). From T-bana: Zinkensdamm, head south on Ringvägen 3 blocks; turn right on Zinkens Väg, 200m on right. A peaceful, if institutional and out-of-the-way 340-bed hostel, frequented more by families than by youths; 2-10 bodies per room. No curfew, no lockout if you finagle a key. 90kr, nonmembers 125kr. Breakfast 37kr. Sheets 35kr. Laundry 20kr. Luggage room and safe. Lockers in rooms. Kitchen and TV.

Norrmalm

Located on the mainland portion of Stockholm, Norrmalm consists of quiet residential, embassy, and academic blocks near the shopping district.

Brygghuset, Norrtullsgatan 12N (tel. 31 24 24). Two blocks north of T-bana: Odenplan. Spacious, sterile 2- to 8-bed rooms. Limited kitchen. Ping-pong. 53 beds. Reception open 8am-noon and 3-10pm. Lockout noon-3pm. Curfew 2am. 110kr. Breakfast 30kr. Free lockers. Sheets 30kr. Laundry 30kr. TV. Open June-Aug.

Sleep Inn (formerly Dans Akademien), Döbelnsgatan 56 (tel. 612 31 18 or 612 38 36), opposite the post office. T-bana: Odenplan, or bus #52 from outside the Centralstation balcony to stop opposite "Hard Rock Café." Walk east on Surbrunnsgatan to first cross-street, then turn left. A debonair erstwhile ballet school filled with floor mattresses. Three large rooms: 1 for women, 1 for men, the other mixed. Not well suited for families with children. A/C. 90 beds. Reception open 8am-noon and 4pm-1am. Lockout 1-4pm. Curfew 1am. 90kr. Free lockers. Sheets 25kr. Laundry 25kr. Refrigerator. No breakfast; supermarket next door. Open July to mid-Aug.

Mälarhöjdne

Klubbensborg (tel. 646 12 55; fax 646 45 45), a majestic mansion on its own peninsulette on Lake Mälar awaits those who brave the hearty 10 minute walk from T-bana: Mälarhöjden (follow sign to Klubbensborg). 60 beds, 2-8/room. Reception open 8am-9pm, Sept. to mid-June 8am-5pm. No lockout. No curfew. 95kr. Sheets 35kr. Laundry. Breakfast 20-40kr. Camping 40kr.

Camping

Bredäng Camping (tel. 97 70 71), 10km southwest of the city center near Lake Mälar. T-bana: Bredäng. Follow the signs down the stairs, past the hulking housing project, and parallel to the train tracks along Stora Sällskapets väg to the campsite (7-10min.). Often crowded. Sauna, running water. 65kr/person. Store, laundry. Open daily 7am-11pm; Oct.-April 7am-9pm.

FOOD

Stockholm's best deals are at lunch, when most restaurants offer a *dagens rätt* for 40-55kr. If that leaves you kronorless, head for the supermarket in the basement of **Åhléns** department store at Klarabergsgatan and Drottninggatan (T-bana: T-Centralen; open Mon.-Fri. 9:30am-9pm, Sat. 9:30am-8pm, Sun. noon-8pm). **Hötorget** and **Östermalmstorg** both host outdoor produce markets and indoor deli malls (the underground **Hötorgshallen** is cheaper; open Mon.-Fri. 9:30am-6pm, Sat. 9:30am-3pm). Copy the locals and picnic in idyllic **Djurgården.**

Herman's Lilla Gröna, Katarina Bangata 17 (tel. 640 30 10). T-bana: Medborgarplatsen, 3 blocks south on Götgatan, then left on Katarina Bangata. Generous servings from your choice of Green Cuisine for 49kr on weekdays, 55kr on weekends, refill 10kr; includes biodynamic bread and salad. Herman, the 25-year-old workaholic owner, offers *Let's Go* users 10% off here or at any of the other branches: Fjällgatan 23a (tel. 643 94 80), which shares the building with a New Age center; Stora Nygatan 11; and Regeringsgatan 91. All open Mon.-Fri. 11am-8pm, Sat. noon-8pm (9pm summer), Sun. 1-8pm.

Kafé 44, Tjärhovsgatan 44 (tel. 644 53 12). From T-bana: Medborgarplatsen, walk 3 blocks east. A dirt-cheap candle-lit mecca for poets and free thinkers. Vegetarian *dagens rätt* 30kr, sandwiches 10-18kr. Open Mon.-Fri. 9am-7pm, open to 10pm 2-3 nights/week when bands play (30-50kr; no minimum age).

Café Gråmunken, Västerlånggatan 18 in Gamla Stan. A favorite meeting place for young Stockholmers. Sandwiches 22-39kr. Open Mon.-Thurs. 10am-11pm, Fri.-Sat. 10am-midnight, Sun. 11am-11pm.

La Bamba, Kungsgatan 15 (tel. 20 00 23). T-bana: Hötorget. Down your *dagens rätt* (48kr) with young businessfolk in the heart of the city. Open Mon.-Thurs. 11am-midnight, Fri.-Sat. 11am-1am, Sun. noon-midnight.

Pinocchio, St. Eriksgatan 56. T-bana: St. Eriksplan. Pub/restaurant frequented by men in their 50s in the front, all-you-can-eat salads, fruit, and desserts for 870kr in the back. Open daily noon-midnight; mid-Aug. to mid-June Sat.-Sun. only.

Kungshallen, Kungsgatan 44, on the north edge of Hötorget. 15 restaurants; from tacos to traditional Swedish. Open Mon.-Sat. 9:30am-4am, Sun. 11am-4am.

SIGHTS

For the ultimate city view, walk uphill on Katarinavägen (on the north edge of Södermalm) to the sculpted hand memorializing Spanish Civil War martyrs. Or take Stockholm Sightseeing's 2-hr. **"Under the Bridges"** cruise (tel. 24 04 70), which sails from Strömkajen, across from the Grand Hotel (110kr, ages 10-14 50kr; 10/day in summer). The **Stadshus** (City Hall), on Stadshusbron near Centralstation, holds 19 million gilded tiles in its Golden Hall; you'll feast here when you win your Nobel Prize. (Tours daily at 10am, 11am, noon, and 2pm; Sept.-May 10am and noon. Tower open May-Sept. 10am-4pm. Tour and tower 25kr.)

The **Gamla Stan** quarter is Stockholm's ancient heart, and it still beats healthily, albeit infused with tourist blood. Two-hour **walking tours** of the narrow, winding streets start daily at 6:30pm from the obelisk between the palace and the cathedral (summer only, 40kr). At the northwest corner the 18th-century **Kungliga Slottet** (Royal Palace), hoards within its walls the gold and glitter of menacing weaponry and extravagant living quarters. (About 20kr/exhibit.) Head over to petite Skeppsholmen Island for such cultured monstrosities as a sculpture of a blue lemon paying homage to a pair of bull's horns, at the **Moderna Museet.** (Open Tues.-Thurs. 11am-8pm, Fri.-Sun. 11am-5pm. 40kr, under 17 free.) For more traditional artistic fare, such as Rembrandt's stunning portrayal of the Batavian conspiracy, try the **Nationalmuseum** at the north end of the Skeppsholmen bridge. (Open Tues. 11am-9pm, Wed.-Sun. 11am-5pm. 40kr, students and seniors 20kr, Fri. free.)

Sample Swedish internationalism at the **National Museum of World Ethnography** *(Etnografiska Museet)* (open Tues.-Fri. 11am-4pm, Sat.-Sun. noon-5pm; 30kr, children 10kr), or learn about Swedish inventors at the adjacent **National Museum of Science and Technology** *(Tekniska Museet).* (Open Mon.-Fri. 10am-4pm, Sat.-Sun. noon-4pm. 25kr, students 10kr.) Both museums are located at Djurgårdsbrunnsvägen 34; take bus #69 from Norrmalmstorg. View the less benign internationalism of Sweden's Viking past at **Historiska Museet** on Narvavägen, the street that leads to Djurgårdsbron bridge. (Open Tues.-Wed. and Fri. noon-5pm, Sat.-Sun. 10am-5pm, Thurs. until 8pm. 50kr, students, children and seniors 30kr.)

Djurgården, east of Skeppsholmen, is Stockholm's pleasure island, reached by bus #44 or 47 from the center, by foot from Strandvägen, by the Djurgårdslinjen tram from Nybroplan (13kr/day, tourist cards valid but not transportation passes), or by ferry from Nybroplan or Slussen (10kr). Especially wander-worthy is its south coast, where you'll pass house boats, museums, and a former tar factory **(Beckholmen).** Djurgården's most intriguing sight is the **Vasa,** an intact 17th-century warship dredged up in 1961 from the bottom of Stockholm's harbor. The new **Vasamuseet,** built specially for the ship, will knock your socks off. (Open daily 10am-7pm; Sept.-May 10am-5pm, Wed. 10am-5pm. 40kr, students 25kr, under 15 10kr.) Further inland sprawls **Skansen,** a vivifying open-air cultural museum, zoo, festival forum, and folk dancing center. (Open daily 9am-10pm; in winter daily 9am-5pm. 40kr summer, 30kr winter, under 14 free. Located on the mainland portion of Stockholm, **Millesgården,** the mythic sculpture garden of Carl Milles, perches like an eagle's nest on the cliffs of Lidingö. To set your soul soaring, take bus #201, 202, 204 or 206 or the *Lidingöbaran* train from T-bana: Ropsten to Torviks torg. (Open daily 10am-5pm; Oct.-April Tues.-Sun. 11am-4pm. 30kr, students 25kr.)

ENTERTAINMENT

Let the street musicians of **Gamla Stan** enchant you, or sally through **Kungsträdgården.** City parks host free concerts nightly. Sniff out events in the free booklet *Stockholm This Week* or the Saturday *På Stan* supplement of the *Dagens Nyheter* newspaper. Concerts and dancing animate summer evenings in Skansen, while Skeppsholmen shines with stellar performers during the **Stockholm Jazz and Blues Festival** (late June to early July; for details, call 25 01 80). The city bubbles with excitement during the **Stockholm Water Festival** (2nd week of Aug.), with 10 days of crayfish orgies and a world championship fireworks competition.

Engelen/Kolingen, Kornhamnstorg 59 (tel. 10 07 22), in Gamla Stan. A thumping disco for older "young" people in a crypt-like basement; easygoing pub and roulette upstairs. Frequent live bands. Cover Fri.-Sat. 70kr, Sun.-Thurs. 50kr. Pub open 4pm-3am, disco 10pm-3am. Minimum age 23.

Fasching, Kungsgatan 63 (tel. 21 62 67). T-bana: T-Centralen. Live rhythm and blues and jazz for a 20's crowd. Cover 50-90kr. Open daily 8pm-1am.

Kaos, Stora Nygatan 21 (tel. 20 58 76), in Gamla Stan. Food, but more drink, and samples of Stockholm's garage rock scene. Open Mon.-Fri. 5pm-1am, Sat. 2pm-1am, Sun. 6pm-1am. 30kr at the door, early evenings free.

Tre Backar, Tegnérgatan 12-14 in Norrmalm (tel. 673 44 00). Bands every evening. Plat du jour 47kr, 20% less with International Youth Card. Open Mon.-Thurs. 11am-midnight, Fri. 11am-1am, Sat. 6pm-1am. 20-60kr.

■ Near Stockholm

The peninsulas and islands of Stockholm's surrounding *Skärgård* (archipelago) offer relaxing vacation spots. To the west of Stockholm floats **Björkö,** a booming Viking Age trade center, and its recent excavations. (Ferries from Stadshusbron near the Stadshuset leave daily 10am, returning at 4:45pm, Sat.-Sun. at 5:45pm; round-trip 165kr). Hugging the Baltic coast, the islands of the **Outer Skärgård** are an ideal escape from urban life. Boats depart from Strömkajen (2-4hr., one-way 70kr; contact Waxholmsbolaget (tel. 679 59 60) for info). **Vaxholm,** with its mighty fortress and museum, is closer to central Stockholm; contact Waxholmsbolaget or Strömma Kanalbolaget (tel. 23 33 75) about trips out (1hr. 25min., round-trip 70kr) or take bus #676, 671, 672, or 673 from T-bana: Tekniska Högskolan. For excursions that cover the entire Skärgård, contact Waxholmsbolaget, Strömma Kanalbolaget, or Stockholm Sightseeing (tel. 24 04 70).

The Swedish royal family hangs out at the extravagant **Drottningholm** palace amidst baroque gardens and rococo interiors. Catch the ½-hourly English tour of the palace's **theater** and watch the original stage machinery produce thunderstorm effects. Ballet or opera are yours for 50-400kr (tel. 660 82 25 for ticket information). **Kina Slott,** Drottningholm's Asian pavilion, was an 18th-century royal summer cottage. (Palace and Kina Slott open May-Sept. daily 11am-4:30pm; Oct. Mon.-Fri. 1-3:30pm, Sat.-Sun. noon-3:30pm. 25kr, students and children 10kr. Theater open May-Aug. daily noon-3pm; Sept. daily 1-4pm. 30kr, children 10kr.) Get to Drottningholm via frequent ferries from Stadshusbron (May-Aug., round-trip 70kr), or on buses #301 through 323 from T-bana: Brommaplan.

■■■ SOUTHERN SWEDEN

Islands and skerries line both the east and west coasts of Sweden; the eastern **Småland** coastline, between Västervik and Kalmar, is particularly beautiful, while the western **Halland** coast between Gothenburg and Helsingborg, though pleasant, is less breathtaking. Inland, clear lakes and limitless woods abound. The island of **Öland,** accessible from Kalmar via Europe's longest bridge, supports a nature reserve; it also has its share of archaeological sites. Famous crystal makers like **Orrefors** and **Kosta** roost in towns by the same name (near Växjö in Småland). **Skåne** (the stub of Sweden across from Copenhagen) and **Blekinge** (around Karlskrona), are Sweden's southernmost provinces; Blekinge is traditionally known as Sweden's garden, and Skåne as its breadbasket. *Pågatågen* (local trains; railpasses not valid) run to destinations in most of Skåne (for info, call (040) 720 55).

From **Helsingborg** in northern Skåne, trains bound for Copenhagen cross on ferries to Helsingør in Denmark; reach Helsingborg by SJ train or by *pågatåg* (from Malmö or Lund 50kr). **Trelleborg,** in southern Skåne, sees several ferries per day off to Saßnitz (railpasses valid) and Travemünde in Germany; take an SJ train or bus from Malmö (33kr). From **Ystad,** also in southern Skåne, daily ferries serve Bornholm (see Denmark), and others shuttle to Świnoujście, Poland (2/day, 260kr, with ISIC 210kr). Reach Ystad by *pågatåg* (from Malmö or Lund 55kr).

■ Malmö

Sweden's 3rd-largest city rises on the west coast of Skåne; transformed by trade and modernization, little remains of the old cobblestone streets. The **Form and Design Center,** in an old yellow building at Lilla torg 9, exhibits Sweden's contributions to convenience culture: bike helmets, wheelchairs, and other useful stuff. (Open Tues., Wed., and Fri. 11am-5pm, Thurs. 11am-6pm, Sat. 10am-4pm, Sun. noon-4pm. Free.) From here wander to the **Rooseum,** Gasverksgatan 22, a collection of contemporary art. (Open Tues.-Sun. 11am-5pm. 20kr, under 15 free.) Or meander in the other direction to **Malmöhus,** the city's old fortress, now a group of museums housing everything from historical artifacts to the local aquarium. (Open Mon.-Sat. noon-4pm, Sun. noon-4:30pm; Sept.-May closed Mon. 30kr.) To find out what's happening in Malmö, consult the tourist office, the InterRail center, or the all-knowing *Malmö This Month* guide (free).

Accommodations, Food, and Practical Information The Kirsebergs **Youth Hostel** (tel. (040) 34 26 35) is at Dalhemsgatan 5; take bus #14C or 14D to Kirsebergsskolan. (Reception open 5pm-9am. 75kr. Open late June to mid-Aug.) The alternative is the slightly sterile **HI hostel,** Södergården, Backavägen 18 (tel. (040) 822 20). Take bus #21A to Vandrarhemmet, walk across Trelleborgvägen to Backavägen and turn right. (90kr, nonmembers 125kr. Open mid-Jan. to mid-Dec.) **City Room,** Adelgatan 19 (tel. 795 94), will book rooms in private homes. (150-200kr. Open Mon.-Fri. 9am-5pm, Sat. 9am-1am.) **Sibbarp Camping,** Strandgatan 101 (tel. (040) 15 51 65), is at the end of bus route #11A (tents 120kr).

Browse around **Möllevångstorget** at mealtime; it offers a wide variety of cuisine at the lowest prices, as well as a **vegetable and fruit market.** (Open Mon.-Fri. 10am-2pm.) The least expensive supermarket close to the city center is **AG Favör** on Värnhemtorget. (Open Mon.-Fri. 9am-7pm, Sat. 9am-3pm.) Or feast at **Börshusets Restaruang,** Skeppsbron 2, same building as the tourist office. *(Dagens rätt* 41-49kr. Open Mon.-Fri. 11:30am-2am, Sat. 6pm-2am.)

The train station and ferry harbor lie just north of the old town. Try **Copenhagen Line** for the cheapest trips to Denmark (5/day; 1½hr.; 15kr). **Trains** arrive from Göteborg (320kr) and Stockholm (500kr). The knowledgeable **tourist office,** Skeppsbron 2 (tel. (040) 30 01 50), is right by the ferry quay, across the street from the train station, in the main post office. (Open Mon.-Fri. 9am-7pm, Sat. 9am-5pm, Sun. 11am-4pm; Sept.-May Mon.-Fri. 9am-5pm, Sat. 9am-1pm.) Free **showers** and **baggage storage** lurk in the **InterRail Center,** Stortorget 24 (tel. (040) 11 85 85). (Open daily 10am-6pm; Aug.-May Sun.-Thurs. 3-10pm, Fri.-Sat. 7pm-2am.) Rent **bikes** from **Fridhem Cykelaffär,** Tessinsväg 13 (tel. (040) 26 03 35; 35kr/day; open Mon.-Fri. 9am-noon and 1-6pm, Sat. 10am-1pm).

■ Lund

Malmö just can't compete with the beauty of **Lund,** its smaller sibling city 30km away. Lund houses Sweden's second-largest **university,** which pumps the town with young people in winter. Their sophisticated fraternities—called *nations*—are sleepier during vacations than those of rival Uppsala, but you can try calling the Småland (tel. (046) 12 06 80), Lund (tel. (046) 14 51 20), or Malmö (tel. (046) 12 78 02) *nations* to see what's up. The campus is north of the town's ancient **cathedral,** a 900 year-old remnant of the time when Lund was the religious epicenter of Scandinavia. (Open Mon.-Tues. and Fri. 8am-6pm, Wed.-Thurs. 8am-7pm, Sat. 9:30am-5pm, Sun. 9:30am-6pm.) **Kulturen,** Tegnérplatsen, a collection of old Swedish houses, boasts modern art, archaeological findings, and much more. (Open daily 11am-5pm; Oct.-April daily noon-4pm. 30kr, students 20kr.)

Accommodations, Food, and Practical Information Rest your tired limbs at the unusual **HI Hostel Tåget** (The Train), Bjerredsparken (tel. (046) 14 28 20), with authentic sleeping cars from the 1940's. Turn right as you come from the trains in the central station, and follow the signs. (Reception open 8-10am and 4-8pm. 90kr, nonmembers 125kr. Open Jan. to mid-Dec.). The tourist office books rooms in **private homes** (150kr, 40kr fee). **Camping** is closest at Källbybadet (tel. (046) 35 51 88); take bus #91 toward Klostergården. (40kr. Open mid-June to Aug.) **Mårtenstorget** has a fresh fruit and vegetable market (open Mon.-Sat. 7am-2:30pm), and **supermarkets** abound (the **ICA** store across from the station is open daily 9am-9pm). **Chrougen,** the local student hangout, at Sandgatan 2 in the *Akademiska Föreningen* (student union), moonlights as a restaurant and disco. (Restaurant open daily 7-10pm, music 10pm-2am; cover 60kr.)

Most intercity **SJ trains** from Malmö stop at Lund; the cities are also connected umbilically by *pågatågen* (25kr). Lund's **tourist office,** Kyrkogatan 11 (tel. (046) 35 50 40), is in the city hall, across the street from the cathedral. (Open Mon.-Fri. 10am-6pm, Sat.-Sun. 10am-2pm; Sept.-May Mon.-Fri. 9am-5pm; May also Sat. 10am-2pm.)

■ Gothenburg (Göteborg)

Sweden's second-largest city is an unusual architectural jumble of industry and residential areas. For the best view of the town, climb up to the towering **Masthuggskyrha** (take tram #3 or 4 to Stigbergstorget). Walk back to the city center via Haga Nygata, a cobblestone street with beautifully restored wooden houses. The **Maritime Museum** houses the destroyer Småland and submarine Nordkaparen. (Open May-Aug. daily 11am-5pm; March-April and Sept.-Nov. Sat.-Sun. 11am-5pm. 35kr.) The mighty **Poseidon statue** stands in front of the **Konstmuseum** (art museum) at the upper end of Kungsportsavenyn. (Open Mon.-Fri. 11am-4pm, Sat.-Sun. 10am-5pm; Sept.-April closed Mon. 30kr, under 17 free. Wheelchair access.) The surrounding *skärgård* (archipelago) is Gothenburg's least expensive pleasure, but parts of it are military zones off-limits to foreigners (check at the tourist office or call (031) 69 20 00). **Vrångö** offers secluded beach serenity (take tram #4 from Saltholmen). **Nya Elfsborg** is a fortress where the Göta Älv meets the sea; many a time, this island stronghold saved Gothenburg form the Danish navy. (Tours leave Stenpiren early May to early Sept., 7/day; 55kr).

Try **Magasinet,** Magasinsgatan 3 (tel. (031) 11 10 53), for a taste of some excellent local bands. (Open daily 9pm-2am. Free entry every Tues., Wed., and Fri.-Sat.) **Dojan,** Vallgatan 3 (tel. (031) 11 24 10), serves the cheapest beer in town (24kr) with live bands every night. (Open Sun.-Thurs. 5pm-1am, Fri.-Sat. 5pm-2am. No cover. Min. age 23.) Fantastic jazz swings at **Nefertiti,** Hvitfeldtsplatsen 6 (tel. (031) 11 15 33; open July-May). Consult *Göteborg This Week* for concert and event listings; get tickets at the main tourist office at Kungsportsplatsen 2 (tel. (031) 13 65 00; booth open Mon.-Fri. 9am-5pm, Sat. 10am-2pm).

Accommodations and Food The **HI hostel** closest to the center of town is the enormous, modern **Ostkupan,** Mejerigatan 2 (tel. (031) 40 10 50). Take bus #64 from Brunnsparken to "Gräddgatan," or tram #1, 3, or 6 to "Redbergsplatsen," and bus #62 to "Gräddgatan." (250 beds in dorms. Reception open 7:30-11pm. 90kr, nonmembers 125kr. Wheelchair access. Open June-Aug.) Sleep cheap in the cramped **Nordengården,** Stockholmsgatan 16 (tel. (031) 19 66 31). Take tram #1 or 3 to Stockholmsgatan and walk downhill; it's in the yellow wooden building on your left. (Reception open daily 7-10am and 4-9pm. Lockout 10am-4pm. 75kr. Sleeping bags allowed.) Docked among the ships of the Maritime Museum, **Seaside** tel. (031) 10 10 35),centrally located at Packhuskajen harbor, has newly renovated cabins in a former Norwegian motorship well worth the 100kr— if you don't get seasick. (Reception open 7:30am-10pm. No phone reservations.) The closest **campsite** is **Kärralund Camping,** Olbersgatan (tel. (031) 25 27 61; take tram #5 to "Welandergatan," east 200m on Olbersgatan). There are 48 beds in its hostel (Reception open daily 7am-11pm, Sept.-Apr. 8am-noon and 4-8pm. 90kr, nonmembers 125kr. Wheelchair access.)

Munch on a 38-45kr *dagens rätt* at **Plankan,** Vasaplatsen 3 (tel. (031) 11 63 02; open Mon.-Thurs. 10:30am-1am, Fri. 10:30am-2am, Sat. 1pm-2am, Sun. 1pm-1am). Or fuel up with a 25kr vegetarian lunch with the university students at **Norrlands Café,** Västra Hamngatan 20. (Open Mon.-Thurs. 9am-11pm, Fri. 9am-2am, Sat. 11am-2am, Sun. noon-9am). The readily available *City Nytt* paper provides a comprehensive list of restaurants.

Practical Information The **tourist office,** Kungsportsplatsen 2 (tel. (031) 10 07 40), is in the old town. Pick up your free copy of the *City Nytt* and *Göteborg This Week* here. (Open daily 9am-8pm, early to mid-June and late Aug. daily 9am-6pm, Sept.-April Mon.-Fri. 9am-5pm, Sat. 10am-2pm; May Mon.-Fri. 9am-6pm, Sat.-Sun. 10am-2pm.) **Budget Travel: Kilroy Travels Sweden** peeks out from Berzeliigatan 5 (tel. (031) 20 08 60; open Mon.-Fri. 9:30am-5pm). **Exchange currency** at the **Forex** shops (open daily 8am-9pm in Centralstation and Kungsportsavenyn 22; 15kr/traveler's check, 20kr commission on cash), or at **American Express,** at

Tichet, Östra Hamngatan 35. (Open Mon.-Fri. 10am-1:30pm and 2:30-6pm.) The **post office** is at Drottningtorget, next to Centralstation. (Postal code: 40110 Göteborg 1. Open Mon.-Fri. 10am-6pm, Sat. 10am-noon).

Public transportation is a must if you move out of the city center. Trams, buses, and even boats in the *skärgård* are accessible with the *magnetkort*, fare cards that come with varying numbers of *kuponger* (valid 1hr.; single ticket (2 *kuponger*) 14kr, 9 *kuponger* 50kr, 22 *kuponger* 100kr). The **24-hour-card** (35kr) allows unlimited travel within city limits. All cards are available at the **Tidpunkten** kiosk at Nils Ericsonsplatsen, next to the train station (open Mon.-Thurs. 7am-10pm, Fri. 7am-2:30am, Sat. 9am-2:30am, Sun. 9am-6pm), and in the many **Pressbyrån** kiosks at transit hubs. The **Göteborg Card** gives you free public transportation plus free entry (or discounts) for many attractions and tours (available at tourist offices and hotels; 120kr/24hr., 200kr/48hr., 250kr/72hr.).

Trains arrive at **Centralstation** (to Oslo, 6/day, 5hr., 373kr; to Stockholm, 13/day, 3½-5hr., 425kr.), which offers **lockers** (20kr/24hr.) and **showers** (15kr; open Sun.-Thurs. 7am-9pm, Fri.-Sat. 7am-10pm), as well as a **waiting room** for women traveling alone. Centralstation lies northeast of elegant Brunnsparken, while Kungsportsavenyn, the city's main boulevard, runs south. **Stena Line ferries** (tel. (031) 775 00 00) sail to Fredrikshavn, Denmark (6-8/day, 3hr., free with Eurail or Nordturist) and to Keil, Germany (1/day, 14hr., 570kr). **Sea Cat hydrofoils** (tel. (031) 775 08 00) whisk to Fredrikshavn (5/day, 1¾hr., 75kr). **Scandinavian Seaways** (tel. (031) 80 55 10) sails to Harwich (3/week, 23hr., 895kr), and Newcastle, England (1/week, 20hr., 895kr) and Amsterdam, Netherlands (2-3/week, 23hr., 890kr).

■■■ UPPSALA

Once a hotbed of pagan spirituality and the cradle of Swedish civilization, Uppsala is now a Nordic Oxbridge, sheltering the 20,000 students of Sweden's oldest university. Scandinavia's largest cathedral, the **Domkyrka,** where Swedish monarchs were crowned, looms just over the river. (Open daily 8am-8pm, Sept.-May 8am-6pm. Free.) The **Gustavianum,** across from the Domkyrka, lodges the macabre **Anatomical Theater**—the site of public human dissections—as well as museums of Nordic, classical, and Egyptian antiquities. (Open daily 11am-3pm; Sept.-May Anatomical Theater only daily noon-3pm. 10kr/museum, 20kr for all 4.) The university's millhouse from the 1760s has been converted into **Upplandsmuseet,** a showcase of the province's settlements, as well as its 2-billion-year geological history. (Open daily noon-5pm. Free.) For university events, scope the bulletin board at the massive **Carolina Rediviva Library,** Övre Slottsgatan at Drottninggatan. (Open Mon.-Thurs. 8:30am-8pm, Fri. 8:30am-6pm, Sat. 9am-1pm; late Aug. to mid-June Mon.-Fri. 8:30am-9pm, Sat. 9am-6pm.) A glorious pagan temple stood a millennium ago at **Gamla Uppsala** (Old Uppsala), 4km north of the city center. Little remains save huge burial mounds of monarchs and **Uppsala Kyrka** (Church), one of Sweden's oldest. (Open daily 8:30am-7:30pm; Sept.-March 8:30am-dusk. Take bus #14, 20, or 24 north from Dragarbrunnsgatan. Return within 90min. to re-use ticket.)

After exhausting Uppsala, baroque aficionados should hop the boat to **Skokloster,** a dazzling many-windowed palace. (Round-trip 85kr. Departs 11:45am and returns 5:30pm from Islandsbron on Östra Ågatan and Munkgatan. Summer only.)

Accommodations and Food   **Sunnersta Herrgård (HI),** Sunnerstavägen 24 (tel. (018) 32 42 20), 6km south of town, offers pleasing doubles, a few triples, and swimming in nearby Lake Mälar. Take bus #20 or 50 from Dragarbrunnsgatan to Herrgårdsvägen (12-15min., 15kr), then walk 2 blocks behind the kiosk, turn left and walk 50m. (Reception open 8-10am and 5-9pm. 90kr, nonmembers 125kr. Laundry. Sheets 25kr. Kitchen. Open May-Aug.) From late June to mid-August the YMCA runs an easygoing **InterPoint** at Torbjörnsgatan 2 (tel. (018) 27 66 35), 3km north of the center; walk north on Svartbäcksgatan, or take bus #10 or 12 from Stora

Torget to Torbjörnsgatan. (Reception open 8-11am and 4:30-9pm. 70kr plus 25kr membership. Kitchen.) By the river next to a swimming pool rests **Fyrishov Camping** (tel. (018) 23 23 33), off Svartbäcksgatan 2km from the city center. (Reception open Mon. and Thurs. 8am-11pm, Tues.-Wed. 7am-11pm, Fri. 10am-8pm, Sat. 9am-6pm, Sun 9:30am-11pm. Tents 75kr, huts 350kr; Sept.-May heated huts 275kr.)

All Uppsala university students belong to refined fraternities called *nations,* which practically give away food and drink (meals average 35kr, beer 25kr) and throw flamboyant fests. If you are a university student and arrive on a summer Thursday, bring your ID (not an ISIC) and your passport to the student union office, Övre Slottsgatan 7 (tel. (018) 10 59 54; open Thurs. 5-7pm), at Åsgränd, for a one-week student card (30kr, 10kr extra for each additional week). Or try the direct approach and show up at a *nation*'s door with a smile and a college ID or ISIC in hand. Your best bets are **Uplands Nation,** St. Larsgatan 11 (tel. (018) 13 24 16), with a disco on Fridays during the school year (open daily 7pm-1am; beer 20kr), or the laid-back **Södermanland-Nerikes Nation,** St. Olofsgatan 16 (tel. (018) 12 34 91; summer Tues., Fri., and Sun.; school year Tues. and Sun. only; open nightly 6pm-1am; winter 7pm-1am), which serves an all-you-can-munch lunch open to everybody during the academic year (30kr; Mon.-Fri. 11am-2pm). The cornucopian but pricey **Saluhallen market** lies at St. Eriks Torg. (Open Mon.-Fri. 9:30am-6pm, Sat. 9:30am-2pm; winter closes Sat. 3pm.) For evening food, devour one of the 17 different choices (from vegetarian to pasta to traditional Swedish) of *dagens rätt* for only 39kr at **Kamel Club,** Vaksalagatan 10. (Open daily 11am-2am). Works by Scandinavian and other artists hang on the 15th-century stone walls of **Galleri Dombron,** which serves sandwiches (15-25kr) and coffee (10kr) near the water by Dombron bridge off Fyris Tory. (Open daily 11am-10pm; in winter noon-5pm.)

Practical Information As you exit the Uppsala train station, the center of town is ahead and to the right. The **tourist office,** Fyris Tory 8 (tel. (018) 11 75 00 or (018) 27 48 00), is near the west bank of the River Fyris. From the train station, walk right on Kungsgatan 2-3 blocks, turn left on St. Persgatan, and cross the bridge to pick up a map (25kr) of the city. (Open Mon.-Fri. 10am-6pm; mid-Aug. to mid-June Mon.-Fri. 10am-6pm, Sat. 10am-2pm.) If you insist on wheels in this walkable town, rent them at **Cykel and Skidstället,** Svartbäcksgatan 20 (tel. (018) 12 67 40), for 65kr per day, 200kr per week. (Open Mon.-Fri. 9:30am-6pm, Sat. 10am-2pm.)

Trains from Stockholm's Centralstation run about every hour (45min., 50kr).

■■■ GOTLAND

Vacationing Swedes have long cherished Gotland for its narrow cobblestone streets, seductive sands, and wildlife sanctuaries. Once the Baltic's trading center, Gotland lies off the east coast of Sweden, 320km south of Stockholm. You can tour the countryside by bike, explore the ruins of medieval churches, and party with the international jet setters who surface here at night.

Visby's ancient wall encloses narrow, winding streets, ruined churches, and a wealth of petite squares and gardens. At the **Gotlands Fornsal** history museum, you'll discover that in 1361 this wall sheltered the town's privileged merchants while the peasantry were massacred outside the gates. (Open daily 11am-6pm; mid-Sept. to mid-May Tues.-Sun. noon-4pm. 20kr, students and seniors 10kr, under 17 free.) Outside the walls, a world of nature awaits. Examine the mystical monoliths on **Fårö,** off the northern tip of Gotland, the blazing beaches of **Tofta,** about 15km south of Visby, and the calcified cliffs of **Hoburgen** at the island's southernmost tip. Cycling is a pleasant way to explore Gotland's flat terrain; try **HyrCykel Här,** across the street from the ferry terminal. (40kr/day, 200-225kr/week for 3- to 5-speeds. Open daily 5:30am-6pm.) Contact the Turistcenter (see below) for more information on bike trips. Part of northern Gotland is a military area closed to the public.

Accommodations, Food, and Practical Information Private rooms are cheaper outside the wall; reserve one at **Gotlands Turistcenter,** Korsgatan 2 (tel. (0498) 27 90 95; open Mon.-Fri. 9am-6pm; singles 180kr, doubles 320kr). Or stay at the **STF Vandrarhem Visby,** Gamla A7 området (tel. (0498) 26 32 58). From the Visby bus station (Kung Magnusväg 1, outside the east wall of the *innerstad*), head east along the southern edge of the walled sports complex to Artillerigatan. The hostel is on the right. (Reception open 8-10am and 5-9pm. 83kr. Open mid-June to mid-Aug.) For a more rural setting try **Västerhejde Vandrarhem,** 6km south of the center of Visby (tel. (0498) 26 49 95; fax (0498) 29 62 60). Take bus #31 from the bus station, and ask the bus driver to drop you off. **Campgrounds** abound on Gotland. **Kneippbyns Campingplats** (tel. (0498) 26 43 65), 4km south of Visby, the home of Pippi Longstocking's Villa Villekulla, mini-golf, and a water park, dips its toes in the sea and is accessible by bus. (72kr/tent. Open May-Aug.)

The **Brinken** café, Söder Torg 19, offers a 47kr *dagens rätt.* (Open Mon.-Fri. 10am-7pm, Sat.-Sun. 11am-6pm.). At **Rosa's,** St. Hansgatan 22, daily specials begin at 45kr. (Open mid-May to Sept. Mon.-Fri. 9am-5pm, Sat. 9am-4pm, Sun.11am-6pm.) Admire a crumbling church ruin over coffee and crumbling pastry at **St. Hans Konditori,** St. Hansplan 2; it serves large meals from 55kr and metamorphoses into a mellow nightspot, sometimes with live folk music. (Open May to early-Sept. Mon.-Sat. 8:30am-8:30pm, Sun. 9:30am-8:30pm.)

The simplest way to Gotland is via the **Gotlandslinjen ferries** to Visby from Nynåshamn (2/day Mon.-Thurs., 3/day Fri.-Sun.; late Aug.-early June 1/day; 5-6hr.) or Oskarshamn (2/day; late Aug.-early June 1/day; 4-6hr.). Fares are highest on weekends (175kr) and cheapest during the week (135kr, 85kr students). Nynåshamn is linked to Stockholm by **bus** from Cityterminalen (1hr., 50kr) and by *pendeltåg* from Centralstation (1 hr., 50kr). For details contact Gotlandslinjen (tel. (0498) 29 30 00) or the Gotland office in Stockholm, Kungsgatan 48 (tel. (08) 23 61 70 or (08) 23 31 80; open Mon.-Fri. 9:30am-6pm, Sat. 10am-2pm). Once you're there, find the helpful **tourist office** in Burmeisterska huset, Strandgatan 9 (tel. (0498) 21 09 82), a 10-minute walk to the left of the ferry terminal. (Open June-Aug. Mon.-Fri. 8am-8pm, Sat.-Sun. 10am-4pm.) They **change money** outside banking hours and offer detailed maps of Gotland and Visby (30kr). In the winter, head to **Gotlands Turistförening,** Hamngatan 4 (tel. 24 70 65; open Sept.-May Mon.-Fri. 9am-5pm). Pick up a **bus** timetable at the ferry terminal or at the Visby bus station, Kung Magnusväg 1 (tel. (0498) 141 12; open Mon.-Fri. 8am-5pm).

■■■ DALARNA

An old Ingmar Bergman movie goes by the English title *Wild Strawberries*. The Swedish title, *Smultronstället,* holds two meanings: a place of wild strawberries, or a secret spot where one goes to commune with nature, one's self, and one's significant other. Dalarna, however hokey, is Sweden's *smultronstället.* Scores of Swedes summer here in tidy red and white farmhouses in the woods. The **Silijansleden,** a 310km cycling or 340km hiking trail, winds its way through forests and over mountains around shimmering Lake Siljan. The region lies about 3½ hours northwest of Stockholm; several trains a day run from Stockholm via Uppsala to Borlänge, and from there either northeast to Falun or northwest to Leksand, Rättvik, and Mora.

Leksand Over 20,000 people flock to this small town on bluffs above the lake to take part in the ancient **Midsummer** (summer solstice) festivities: the raising of the maypole, a procession of richly decorated longboats that once ferried people to church, exuberant folk music, and the **Siljansrodden,** a 2-week series of longboat-rowing competitions on Lake Siljan. The annual **Musik vid Siljan** festival in Leksand and Rättvik (1st week of July) arranges a mélange of music from all over the earth (call (0248) 102 90 for more info). Also contact the **tourist office,** on Norsgatan (tel. (0247) 803 00), for details. To get to the office from the train station, walk up Villagatan to Leksandsvägen; turn left, then hang a right on Norsgatan. (Open Mon.-Sat. 9am-9pm, Sun. noon-9pm; mid-Aug. to mid-June Mon.-Fri. 9am-5pm, Sat. 9am-1pm.)

Accommodations are often crowded (packed for Midsummer), but the tourist office can hook you up with a private room for a 25kr fee (doubles from 265kr). Try the **Ungdomsgården** (tel. (0247) 100 90), on Rättviksvägen near Tällbergsvägen, a few minutes from the station; a combination campground, lodge, and country kitchen, the main building is a red farmhouse. (Reception open 8am-9pm. 2- to 4-bed cabin; 60kr/bed. Tents 80kr. Breakfast 30kr. Laundry. Open mid-June to mid-Aug.) With new facilities and lots of common space, Leksand's **HI** hostel (tel. (0247) 152 50) is 2.5km from the train station. Cross the bridge near the tourist office and head left on Insjövägen. (Reception open 8-10am and 5-8pm; May and Sept. open 5-7pm. Oct.-April call before you arrive. 90kr, nonmembers 125kr. Laundry 30kr. Bikes 60kr/day.) A 20-minute walk on the road toward Tällberg brings you to swimming and **camping** (tel. (0247) 803 13) at Orsandbaden (70kr/tent). Hit **Leksands Kebab & Pizza,** Norsgatan 23, for substantial low-cost pizza. (From 30kr. Open Mon.-Thurs. 11am-10pm, Fri.-Sat. 11am-midnight, Sun. noon-10pm.)

From Leksand's quay there are breezy **boat connections** a few times a week to Rättvik (50kr) and Mora (100kr). For info, call (010) 252 32 92 or (010) 204 77 24.

Rättvik Twenty minutes north by train, **Rättvik** blossoms with life during the Musik vid Siljan Festival (see above), and plays no second fiddle to Leksand in celebrating Midsummer. If fiddling is in fact your thing, check out the **Bingsjö Spelmansstämma** (Player's Convention) on the 1st or 2nd Wednesday in July (check the tourist office), when some 30,000 people from all over the world invade a private farm in Bingsjö, 40km from Rättvik, for everything from Swedish folk songs to bluegrass. Nearby attractions include **Rättviks Gammelgård,** a Dalarna farm reincarnated, with local handicrafts and a café. Walk 10 minutes northwest out of the town center towards Sjurberg. (Open mid to late June daily noon-4pm; late June to mid-Aug. Mon.-Sat. 11am-6pm, Sun. noon-6pm. Free. Guided tours at 1 and 2:30pm.) Or rent a canoe, pedal boat, or windsurfer at **Siljansbadet Sommarland** (tel. (0248) 134 00), just south of the train station (20-50kr/hr.).

Rättvik's **tourist office** (tel. (0248) 109 10), across from the train station, sells detailed hiking and biking maps of the Lake Siljan area (35kr) and pins down rooms in private homes. (Singles 200kr. 25kr fee. Open Mon.-Sat. 9am-8pm, Sun. 11am-8pm, open 1hr. later in July; Aug. Mon.-Sat. 9am-6pm, Sun. 11am-6pm; Sept. to mid-June Mon.-Fri. 9am-5pm, Sat. noon-4pm.) Built in the old Dalarna blockhouse style, the **HI youth hostel** (tel. (0248) 105 66) sprawls beneath the pines off Centralgatan, 1km behind the tourist office. (Reception open 8-10am in summer and 5-8pm year-round. 90kr, nonmembers 125kr. Laundry 15kr. Breakfast 40kr.) **Rättviksparkens Camping** (tel. (0248) 116 06 , in winter (0248) 102 51) is down the side road that turns off Centralgatan at the youth hostel. (Reception open 8am-10pm; Sept.-May Sat.-Sun. noon-1pm. 100kr/tent, cabins available.) Gaze at Agneta Svensdotter's *Paradise* while eating a late-night pizza at **Rättviks Kebab and Pizzeria** (Mehdis's All-In-One-Life's-Pizza-and-Kebab), across from the tourist office. (40kr/meal. Cable TV. Open Mon.-Thurs. 11am-10pm, Fri.-Sat. 11am-2am, Sun. 10pm.)

Mora Head north to **Mora** for a voluptuous sea of blueberries, lingonberries, and *svamp* (mushrooms). The **tourist office** (tel. (0250) 265 50), on the lakefront, books beds in private homes (160kr) for a 25kr fee. (Open Mon.-Sat. 9am-8pm, Sun. 11am-8pm; mid-Aug. to mid-June Mon.-Fri. 9am-5pm, Sat. 9am-1pm.) Comprised of buildings up to 200 years old, the hostel at **Åmåsängsgården** (tel. (0250) 133 42) is 4km south from the town center (Reception open 10am-noon and 4-8pm. 90kr. Open mid-June to mid-Aug.) Mora was home to artist Anders Zorn (1860-1920), famous for his paintings of large, naked women. Visit his collection at the **Zornmuseet,** Vasagatan 36. (Open Mon.-Sat. 10am-5pm, Sun. 1-5pm. 20kr, students 15kr.)

Santa Claus's humble abode (or one of them; every snowy village claims the title) is in nearby **Gesunda**, accessible by bus #107 from Mora. It's called **Tomteland** (tel. (0250) 290 00; open daily mid-June to mid-Aug. 10am-6pm, and throughout Dec., of course; 95kr). **Nusnäs**, 10km east of Mora (take bus #108), is famous for its wooden *dalahäst* horses, the Swedish equivalent of American baseball and apple pie. You can tour the factory at **Nils Olsson Hemslöjd** (tel. (0250) 372 50) for free. (Open Mon.-Fri. 9am-4pm, Sat.-Sun. 10am-4pm; mid-Aug. to May Mon.-Fri. 8am-4pm, Sat. 10am-1pm.) Mora is a gateway to northern Sweden; the **Inlandsbanan** train route (see Lapland) begins here (1 train/day).

■■■ ÖSTERSUND

Located at the intersection of the longitudinal Inlandsbanan and the latitudinal railway from Sweden's east coast to Trondheim, Norway, Östersund is a natural stopover (from Trondheim, 4½hr., 273kr; from Stockholm, 6hr., 480kr). Though near the country's geographical heart, this lakeside town is a tad outlandish. No low-key patriots, the inhabitants of Jämtland county boisterously boost their region during **Storsjöyran**. Held the last weekend in July, this "freedom fest" has the locals performing some decidedly un-Swedish dancing in the streets. Their pride becomes more understandable when one glimpses the majestic landscape that surrounds them. **Lake Storsjön** is home to a cousin of the Loch Ness monster that King Oscar II and a crew of Norwegian whalers unsuccessfully tried to capture in 1894. Their harpooning equipment is on display at the **Jämtlands Läns (County) Museum,** 700m north of the city center on Kykgatan. (Open Mon., Wed.-Fri. 9am-4pm, Tues. 9am-9pm, Sat-Sun. noon-4pm. Free.) Rent a mountain bike at **Cykelogen,** Kyrkgatan 45, for 80kr a day and let gravity draw you over the footbridge to **Fröson Island,** formerly the turf of the (Viking) Aesir gods. Wild strawberries grow on the thatched roof of **Frösötornets Härbärge hostel,** which sits at the top of a 176m high ski area overlooking the city (tel. (063) 11 57 67). Take bus #5 from the city center. (Reception open 9am-9pm. 115kr. Showers 1kr/2min. Kitchen. Open May-Sept.) The **tourist office,** Rådhusgatan 44 (tel. (063) 14 40 01), books private rooms (125-150kr) for a 40kr fee. (Open Mon.-Sat. 9am-9pm, Sun. 10am-7pm; Sept.-May Mon.-Fri. 9am-5pm.) To get to **Alléhemmet Youth Hostel (HI),** Tingsgatan 12 (tel. (063) 10 23 43), go right from the train station on Ringvägen 600m to Allégatan, turn left, then right on Tingsgatan. (Reception open 8-9:30am and 5-9:30pm. 84kr, nonmembers 119kr. Open mid-June to early Aug.) Take bus #2 or 6 to **Östersunds Camping** (tel. (063) 14 46 15) at "Fritidsbyn". (Tents 90kr.) A stuffed Rudolph guards the entrance to **Saluhallen,** a gourmet food market on the main square; snack on reindeer chips (18kr/bag) or spread some cloudberry jam (½kg 38kr) on your pancakes. (Open Mon.-Fri. 9am-6pm, Sat. 10am-2pm.) Find both Mexican and Creole cuisine in the old-fashioned Swedish interior of **Brunkullans Café/Restaurang,** Postgränd 5. (Lunch buffet—choice of 10 salads, local bread, and coffee—55kr. Open Mon.-Sat. 11am-11pm.)

■■■ UMEÅ

Return to the sunnier coast in Umeå, a pulsating university town at the mouth of the Ume Älv river. **Silja Line** ferries sail to Vaasa and Pietarsaari (Jakobstad) in Finland (2-4/day, 175kr, 17 and under and railpass holders 130kr). On weekends many of the younger passengers don't disembark at all; they just go for the party. The **HI hostel** (tel. (090) 11 16 50), Järnvägsallén 22, sits 200m east of the train station. (Reception open 8am-noon and 4-10pm. 73kr, nonmembers 108kr. Kitchen. Open early-June to mid-Aug.) If it's full, stroll down Rådhusesplanaden and turn right on Skolgatan to get to the **tourist office,** Renmarkstorget (tel. (090) 16 16 16), which has a list of contacts for private rooms (150kr; open Mon.-Fri. 8am-8pm, Sat. 10am-6pm, Sun. noon-6pm). Camping at **Nydala lake** (tel. (090) 16 16 60) costs 65kr, people-watching included. **Cykeluthyrning** rents bikes (25kr/day) to adventurous souls who head up the river around the 30km **Umeleden** bike trail. (Open June to mid-Aug. Mon.-Fri. 9am-4pm.) Along the Umeleden sit old hydropower stations, gardens, restaurants, and **Baggböle Herrgård,** a delightful café in a 19th-century mansion. (Open Tues.-Sun. noon-8pm). To brave the rapids of Vindelälven in a rubber raft "navigated" by the staff of **Sotarns Forsränning** (tel. (090) 19 39 90; open July daily noon-5pm, reservations required May-June and Aug.-Sept.; 130kr), take bus#15 to Vännäs. Check out the world's oldest ski at the **Swedish Ski Museum,** one of 7 museums built door-to-door in **Gammlia.** (Indoor museums open daily 10am-5pm, mid-Aug. to early June daily 9am-4pm, open-air museum open Midsummer to mid-Aug. 11am-5pm. Free.)

Dine on a hearty Swedish *dagens rätt* (45kr) at **Karl Gustav,** Magasingatan 17. (Open daily 10am-10pm.) The artsy crowd might suit you better at **Teater Café,** Vasaplan, where daily lunch specials run 35-42kr. (Open daily 10am-9pm.) The **Blå Dragon** night club, on Västra Norrlandsgatan by the E4 highway, caters to a young clientele on Wednesday (cover 20kr) and Friday. (70kr, before 10pm 35kr. Open 8pm-1am.) A lively pub atmosphere dominates at **Viskninjar and Rop,** in the Hotel Plaza on Storgatan near Renmarkstorget. (No cover. Open Sun.-Thurs. 10am-1am, Fri.-Sat. 10am-2am.) **Trains** run to Umeå from Boden (4½hr., 320kr).

■■■ LAPLAND

Many "Southerners"—anyone living south of the Arctic Circle—imagine that Lapland consists of herds of reindeer roaming through dense forest, thick snow, unrelenting darkness, and bitter cold for half the year, and perpetual light for the other half. This is all true. Although mining has begun to encroach upon previously virgin land, the lure here is still nature, from swampy birch and pine forests in the vast lowlands to the spectacular fells: old, rounded mountains that rise to meet the Norwegian border. In the lowlands, long clothing and a supple wrist will protect you against the summer's swamp-bred mosquitoes. Many bug repellents were banned for environmental reasons; buy your repellent in Lapland to be on the safe side.

Getting There Swedish Lapland is home to 17,000 reindeer-tending **Sami,** to whom the name "Lapps" is derogatory. Jokkmokk, Gällivare, and Kiruna are the 3 main settlements north of the Arctic Circle, and all make good stopovers on the way to mountains stations such as Kvikkjokk and Abisko. The cheapest way north, and a considerable time-saver, is to fly on **SAS's** youth standby fare (under 26 only; 250kr from Stockholm to Kiruna or Gällivare.) There are 2 **rail routes** to Lapland: the **coastal route** extends from Stockholm through Boden, Gällivare, and Kiruna to Narvik, Norway, along the **Malmbanan** (Stockholm-Kiruna 2/day in either direction, 18hr., 641kr, reservations necessary). Traveling the entire length of touristy the **Inlandsbanan** (inland railway) requires overnight stopovers in Östersund and Storuman or Arvidsjaur. (1/day; Mora-Gällivare 300-500kr. 50% discount with Eurail; Nordturist not valid. Runs early-June to Mid-Aug.) Connections between the parallel train routes can be made at Uppsala-Mora, Sundsvall-Östersund, and Luleå-Boden-Gällivare. **Buses,** many of which accept no railpasses, are the only way to the smaller towns; pick up a copy of the *Länstrafiken i Norrbotten* company schedule. If you plan to use both buses and trains in the north, consider buying the **Norrlandskortet,** valid for 14 days of travel on all trains and buses in Sweden north of Sundsvall (890kr, under 18 445kr, 50% off train/bus travel from Trondheim to Narvik, Norway). The brochure *Summer Routes in Norrland* (available at tourist offices) supplies an exhaustive menu of routes and trails, complete with listings of attractions and events. If you're heading for the mountains, Svenska Turistföreningen's *Turisttrafik i fjällen* brochure is an indispensable transport overview.

Getting Out Transportation out of Lapland can be challenging. Those heading farther north can take the most scenic train ride in Sweden up to Narvik on the Norwegian coast (stop at Abisko Turiststation or lonelier Låktatjåkka for dramatic mountain trails). Three buses a day (130kr) link Kiruna to **Karesuando** on the Finnish border, site of Sweden's northernmost **Youth Hostel** (tel. (0981) 202 85; open June-Aug.; call ahead). From there you can continue to Skibotn, Norway or Kilpisjärvi and Muonio, Finland, or travel Finlandward by backtracking south through **Boden**. Railpasses are valid on all **buses** from Boden to **Haparanda,** on the Finnish border. Be sure to plan ahead: the hostel in **Luleå** (20min. from Boden) is 6km from the city (tel. (0920) 523 25, take bus #6 from Luleå). If you make it to Haparanda, stay at the **HI hostel,** Strandgatan 26 (tel. (0922) 111 71). Remember that Finland is one time zone ahead when consulting schedules. For further information, leaf through the Norway and Finland chapters.

Jokkmokk and Gällivare Ájtte, an outstanding museum of Sami culture, makes a stop in **Jokkmokk** more than worthwhile. (Open Mon.-Fri. 9am-6pm, Wed. until 8pm, Sat.-Sun. 11am-6pm; Sept. to mid-June Mon.-Fri. 9am-4pm, Sat.-Sun. noon-4pm. Closed Mon. Oct.-April. 20kr.) Ask the **tourist office,** Stortorget 4 (tel. (0971) 121 40) on the main square, about the reconstructed Stone Age village of **Vuollerim,** 45km east of Jokkmokk. The office keeps a list of private rooms (85-150kr/person), sells mountain maps, and rents bikes. (50kr/day. Open daily 9am-7pm; Sept.-May Mon.-Thurs. 8am-4pm, Fri. 8am-3pm.) If you didn't intend to head for the mountains, the wilderness photos in **Edvin Nilsson's gallery,** on Klockarvägen, just off Storgatan, may change your mind. (Open July daily 11am-6pm. Free.) To get to the **HI Hostel,** walk up Stationsgatan from the train station, and turn left on Storgatan. (Reception open 8-10am and 5-9pm. 83kr, non-members 108kr. Laundry 25kr. Open mid-June to mid-Aug.) Footsore travelers can stay at the **yellow house** across the street from the station (85kr). The campsite is 3km outside of town at **Jokkmokks Turistcenter** (tel. (0971) 123 70; tents 60kr, 4-bed cabins 540kr). Hike east on Storgatan. **Buses** to Jokkmokk run from Gällivare (1-4/day, 1½hr., 70kr.) and Boden (1-2/day, 2hr., 90kr.).

Spend some time underground in the mining town of **Gällivare.** The **tourist office** (tel. (0970) 166 60) is at Storgatan 16; from the train station, bear right. (Open daily 9am-8pm; mid-Aug. to May Mon.-Fri. 9am-4:30pm.) Their weekday tours will bury you in the **copper and iron mines** (mid-June to early-Aug. daily at 10am to iron mine, 160kr; 1:30pm to copper mine, 135kr). For a real taste of the crags, take a day hike up 820m-high **Dundret mountain** (round-trip 14km, allow 3-6 hr.). If hiking doesn't suit you, take the midnight sun trip up Dundret (mid-June to mid-July 11pm; 135kr; includes coffee and waffle). The **HI youth hostel** (tel. (0970) 143 80) is a 5-minute walk from the station; cross the bridge over the tracks, then the one over the river. (Reception open 8-10am and 5-10:30pm. 84kr, nonmembers 119kr. Laundry 20kr. Kitchen. Sauna 50kr/hr. Call ahead.) **Gällivare Camping** (tel. (0970) 186 79) is home to friendly people and overfriendly mosquitoes; it's by the river 1.5km from the station. (75kr/tent. Open early June-early Sept.)

Kiruna and the Kungsleden Kiruna bills itself as the "City of the Future," but it's a rather dystopian vision of mining, missile launching, and satellite operations. You can see the world's largest underground iron ore mine here. (Sign up at **Kiruna Guidetour,** across from the tourist office, early June to mid-Sept. daily 10am, noon, 2pm, and 4pm. 85kr.) The Sami knew about the stuff long before it was "discovered" but didn't tell anyone because they feared (rightly) that they'd be forced to transport the ore with their reindeer and sleighs. The midnight sun lasts from May 28 to July 15, with the all-night **Festival of Light** on the first weekend in July. The **tourist office** is at Lars Janssonsgatan 17 (tel. (0980) 188 80; open Mon.-Fri. 9am-8pm, Sat.-Sun. 9am-6pm; mid-Sept. to March Mon.-Fri. 10am-4pm; April-early June Mon.-Fri. 9am-5pm, Sat. 10am-1pm). The **HI youth hostel** (tel. (0980)

171 95) is at Skyttegatan 16a. Walk up the hill from the train station, then up the stairs marked "Sommarled," then east on Lars Janssonsgatan which turns into Mangigatan, right on Adolf Hedinsvägen, then left on Skyttegatan. (Reception open 8-9:30am and 4-9:30pm. 83kr, nonmembers 113kr. Open mid-June to mid-Aug.) **Camp** at **Radhusbyn Ripan** (tel. (0980) 131 00), 20 minutes from the train station. (85kr/tent, 4-person cabins 560-660kr.) **Buses** leave across from the city hall on Hjalmar Lundbonsvägen.

A short bus trip from Kiruna or Jokkmokk, the 500km **Kungsleden,** a moderate, well-marked hiking trail, stretches from Abisko in the north (on the Narvik train line) to Hemavan in the south. Many sections, in particular from Abisko to Kvikkjokk, have HI-staffed cabins 8-21km apart (95kr, 125 non-members). To climb **Sweden's highest peak,** Kebnekaise (2112m), take a bus from Kiruna to Nikkaluokta (52kr) and hike 19km to the Kebnekaise mountain cabin. From there, you can reach the summit in a day (travelers must have a guide during the summer). This is rugged country, and there may be snow as late as July. Even if you're just hiking between huts by day, bring food, maps, full raingear, and warm clothing, and leave a copy of your route with someone in town. Be sure to contact STF—the **Svenska Turistföreningen**—before heading north (see Accommodations, Camping, and Food at the beginning of the chapter); they run most of the mountain stations and huts, and publish essential brochures and guides for hikers. Local tourist offices are wellsprings of information.

SOUTHERN EUROPE

Greece (Ελλασ)

US$1	= 231dr (drachmas, or GRD)	100dr =	**US$0.43**
CDN$1	= 176dr	100dr =	**CDN$0.57**
UK£1	= 358dr	100dr =	**UK£0.28**
IR£1	= 335dr	100dr =	**IR£0.30**
AUS$1	= 150dr	100dr =	**AUS$0.66**
NZ$1	= 128dr	100dr =	**NZ$1.78**
SAR1	= 48dr	100dr =	**SAR2.08**
Country Code: 30		**International Dialing Prefix: 00**	

Even before Odysseus made his epic voyage across the Mediterranean, Greece was a place for wanderers. Wanderers today should know they will not be alone, although finding a heavenly piece of solitary Greece remains a possibility. Some areas of Greece are plowed over by the heaviest tourist industry in Europe, while others nearby retain authenticity. The West's oldest, most sacred monuments cringe over conspicuously tacky tourist strips, while untrodden mountainsides arch above beaches resembling human rugs.

In some ways, Greece is an aggressively western country whose capital rivals London, Paris, and Rome. As proud guardians of the classical inheritance, Greeks consider western civilization a home-spun export. But to step into Greece is to walk east—into a stir of Byzantine icons, Orthodox priests trailing long dark robes, and air spiced with the strains of *bouzouki*. Greece owes its Eastern flavor to four centuries of Ottoman rule. Thanks mostly to the integrity of the Orthodox Church, the Greek national identity survived Turkish captivity. Memories of the 1821 War of Independence still excite Greek nationalism; 400 years are not easily forgotten.

Only in the last 15 years has Greece rebounded from a battering century that brought Nazi occupation, mass starvation, civil war, and military rule. Villages began seeing automobiles and electric lights only in the 1960s. Greece still faces severe problems, however; despite its recent entry into the Common Market, per capita income and productivity are half the EC average, and inflation continues to rage. Consequently, volatility and ferocity characterize Greek politics. Today Prime Minister Constantine Mitsotakis attempts to rejuvenate Greece's economy, in part by furiously deregulating industry—including tourism. No longer given upper and lower limits by the government, accommodations and restaurants are free to charge as much or as little as they can get away with. How this will affect the budget traveler is not yet clear.

Macedonia is the latest issue to inflame Greek politics. After the former Yugoslav province declared itself the independent Republic of Macedonia, Greeks felt an important part of their history and culture usurped. Ancient Macedonia, home to Alexander the Great, was very probably a Hellenic civilization and certainly not a Slavic one.

> For more comprehensive coverage of Greece than we can offer here, revel in *Let's Go: Greece & Turkey*.

GETTING THERE

One of the least expensive ways to reach Greece is by **train,** even without a railpass. From Venice or Vienna, expect a 36-hour trip and enormous crowds in summer; insist on a seat reservation. Buses are even cheaper, but a real marathon. **London Student Travel,** 52 Grosvenor Gardens, London SW1W OAG (tel. 44 (071) 730 34 02), runs a bus from London to Athens for about £75. **Magic Bus,** 20 Filellinon St., Athens (tel. 44 (01) 323 74 71), sells discounted bus tickets from Athens to London.

Certainly the most popular way of getting to Greece is by **ferry** from Italy. Boats travel primarily from Bari and Bríndisi to Corfu (9hr.), Igoumenitsa (11hr.), and Patras (19hr.). From Patras, buses leave for Athens frequently and also for points throughout the Peloponnese. If you plan to travel from Bríndisi in the summer, make reservations and arrive at the port well before your departure time. Sample deck class fares to Patras for travelers under 26 and students under 31 with ID are 15,500dr (July 23-Aug. 15) and 8970dr (Aug. 16-July 22); Eurail holders pay only tax and supplement. From March through October, cheaper boats (though not free with railpasses) also travel from Bari, a much more attractive city than Bríndisi. See Bari and Bríndisi, Italy for more details. More expensive boats run from Ancona and Venice in Italy. Two boats steam weekly from Haifa, Israel, to Greece, and a number of small lines connect Turkey's Aegean coast with islands in the northeast Aegean and Dodecanese (usually US$30-40; most run only in summer).

Flying from northern European cities is also a popular way of getting to Greece. Watch for special package fares offered by travel agents or advertised in newspapers, especially from London, Amsterdam, and major cities in Germany and Scandinavia. These are often the cheapest deals available, even if you must take a hotel

So, you're getting away from it all.

Just make sure you can get back.

AT&T Access Numbers
Dial the number of the country you're in to reach AT&T.

*ANDORRA	19◇-0011	GERMANY**	0130-0010	*NETHERLANDS	06◇-022-9111
*AUSTRIA	022-903-011	*GREECE	00-800-1311	*NORWAY	050-12011
*BELGIUM	078-11-0010	*HUNGARY	00◇-800-01111	POLAND¹◆²	0◇010-480-0111
BULGARIA	00-1800-0010	*ICELAND	999-001	PORTUGAL¹	05017-1-288
CROATIA¹◆	99-38-0011	IRELAND	1-800-550-000	ROMANIA	01-800-4288
*CYPRUS	080-90010	ISRAEL	177-100-2727	*RUSSIA¹ (MOSCOW)	155-5042
CZECH REPUBLIC	00-420-00101	*ITALY	172-1011	SLOVAKIA	00-420-00101
*DENMARK	8001-0010	KENYA¹	0800-10	SPAIN	900-99-00-11
*EGYPT¹ (CAIRO)	510-0200	*LIECHTENSTEIN	155-00-11	*SWEDEN	020-795-611
*FINLAND	9800-100-10	LITHUANIA◆	8◇196	*SWITZERLAND	155-00-11
FRANCE	19◇-0011	LUXEMBOURG	0-800-0111	*TURKEY	9◇9-8001-2277
*GAMBIA	00111	*MALTA	0800-890-110	UK	0800-89-0011

Countries in bold face permit country-to-country calling in addition to calls to the U.S. *Public phones require deposit of coin or phone card. **Western portion. Includes Berlin and Leipzig. ◇Await second dial tone. ¹May not be available from every phone. ◆ Not available from public phones. ²Dial ¨02¨ first, outside Cairo. ²Dial 010-480-0111 from major Warsaw hotels. ©1993 AT&T.

Here's a travel tip that will make it easy to call back to the States. Dial the access number for the country you're visiting and connect right to AT&T **USADirect**® Service. It's the quick way to get English-speaking operators and can minimize hotel surcharges.

If all the countries you're visiting aren't listed above, call **1 800 241-5555** before you leave for a free wallet card with all AT&T access numbers. International calling made easy—it's all part of **The i Plan.**℠

THE *i* PLAN™

AT&T

Let's Go wishes you safe and happy travels

These people are only a third of the 150 students who bring you the *Let's Go* guides. Most of us were still out on the road when this photo was taken, roaming the world in search of the best travel bargains.

Of course, *Let's Go* wouldn't be the same without the help of our readers. We count on you for advice we need to make *Let's Go* better every year. That's why we read each and every piece of mail we get from readers around the globe — and that's why we look forward to your response. Drop us a line, send us a postcard, tell us your stories. We're at 1 Story Street, Cambridge, Massachusetts 02138, USA. Enjoy your trip!

package. In addition, you may be able to fly aboard charters to island destinations otherwise inaccessible by direct flight.

TRAVELING IN GREECE

Train service in Greece is slow and infrequent compared with that in the rest of Europe, and no lines go to the western coast. Though Eurail is valid, even Eurail holders should take buses. **OSE** (tel. 524 06 46, or 47, or 48), the national train network, offers discounts of up to 40% to those under 26.

Faster, more extensive, and only slightly more expensive, **buses** are a good alternative to train travel; most are run through **KTEL.** While large towns all have their own bus stations, smaller ones usually use cafés as bus stops. Along the road, little blue signs marked with white buses or the word "ΣΤΑΣΙ" indicate bus stops, but drivers usually stop anywhere if you signal. Let the driver know ahead of time if you want to get off; if your stop is passed, yell "Stasi!"

Greeks are not eager to pick up foreigners. Sparsely-populated areas simply have little or no traffic. Those who do choose to **hitchhike** write their destination on a sign in both Greek and English, and hitch from turn-offs rather than along long stretches of straight road. *Women should never hitch alone.* The mountainous terrain and unpaved roads make **cycling** in Greece difficult. A better means of transport is the humble **moped,** which is perfect for exploring.

There is frequent **ferry** service to the Greek islands, but schedules can be exasperating, misinformation is common, and direct connections exist only between major islands. Don't plan to follow a strict schedule. Wild competition exists between ferry lines and travel agencies. No Greek ferry agent has ever breathed a word about the competition's schedule (or even their existence), so you'll have to visit several—or all—agencies in town to plan your trip. To avoid hassles, go to *limenarxeio* (port police)—every port has one, and they all carry complete ferry information. **Hydrofoils** are speedier, but costlier. In Piraeus, the situation is considerably better, since GNTO publishes a schedule; the schedule loses meaning as the summer progresses. And finally, keep an ear to the ground for boat strikes.

The national airline, **Olympic Airways** (tel. (01) 929 21 11), operates efficient and reasonably priced flights between many islands. Note that these flights are often booked weeks in advance in summer, however. Coverage to remote areas is spotty.

GREECE ESSENTIALS

The **Greek National Tourist Organization (GNTO),** which the Greeks call **EOT,** is far from standardized. Some cities have full-fledged offices that distribute brochures, maps and bus schedules, and help with accommodations. Other towns have no office at all. In the islands, "Tourist Information Centers, Inc." often masquerade as official offices. They can supply useful information, but more often they try to sell you their package tours of the island. Many towns have branches of the **tourist police,** who can give information and assist travelers in trouble. Regular police will step in if there isn't a tourist police officer around; most, however, speak no English. **Tourist information** is available in English by calling 171 (24 hrs.). The **emergency** number for **police** is 100 throughout most of Greece; for **medical assistance,** it's 166.

Though many Greek men are notorious *kamakis* (playboys), women traveling in Greece are relatively safe. If you find yourself in an emergency, call out "vo-EE-thee-a" ("help"). Modest dress (no shorts, short skirts, or revealing tops) is required of both sexes at monasteries and churches. Normal **business hours** in Greece include a break from about 2pm until 5 or 6pm, with **evening hours** usually on Tuesday, Thursday, and Friday. Banks are normally open Monday through Thursday from 8am to 1:30pm, Friday from 7:45am to 2pm. The major **national holidays** in Greece—during which all banks and shops are closed—are New Year's Day, Epiphany (Jan. 6), National Holidays (March 25 and Oct. 28), Labor Day (May 1), The Assumption of the Virgin Mary (Aug. 15) and Christmas (Dec. 25).

Communication Although many Greeks in Athens and other resort towns speak English—particularly young people—those living off the beaten path are unlikely to. Be forewarned that "né" means "yes" in Greek. The following transliteration table should help you decipher things, although prepare for some exceptions to it (for instance, Φ and φ are often spelled *ph*).

Greek	Roman	Greek	Roman	Greek	Roman
Α, α	A, a	Ι, ι	I, i	Ρ, ρ	R, r
Β, β	V, v	Κ, κ	K, k	Σ, σ, ς	S, s
Γ, γ	G, g	Λ, λ	L, l	Τ, τ	T, t
Δ, δ	D, d	Μ, μ	M, m	Υ, υ	Y, y
Ε, ε	E, e	Ν, ν	N, n	Φ, φ	F, f
Ζ, ζ	Z, z	Ξ, ξ	X, x	Χ, χ	Ch, ch
Η, η	I, i	Ο, ο	O, o	Ψ, ψ	Ps, ps
Θ, θ	Th, th	Π, π	P, p	Ω, ω	O, o

Learn a few helpful phrases, given here phonetically: "I don't speak Greek" (dhen mee-LAHO el-leen-ee-KAH), "how much?" (PO-so KAH-nee), "I would like" (thah EE-the-lah), "can I see a room?" (bo-RO nah-DHO E-nah dho-MAH-tee-o), "what time is it?" (tee O-rah EE-ne) and "do you have?" (E-che-te).

Even more important to know is Greek body language, which can lead to endless misunderstandings. To say no, Greeks silently close their eyes or click their tongues while lifting their heads and/or eyebrows. To indicate a yes, they tilt and bow the head in one motion. A hand waving up and down that seems to say "stay there" actually means "come." Be careful when waving good-bye; if you do so with your palm forward, the gesture may be interpreted as an insult.

Greece's **telephone** company is **OTE.** Their offices are usually open from 7:30am to 3pm in small towns and from 7:30am to 10pm in larger towns. In cities, OTE offices are open 24 hours, but you must bang on the door after midnight. For AT&T's **USA Direct,** dial 00 800 1311. For MCI **World Reach,** dial 00 800 1211. **Post offices** are generally open Monday through Friday from 7:30am to 2pm; some larger offices keep longer hours. A letter or postcard to the U.S. costs 120dr and takes about 9 to 11 days, sometimes longer from small villages. **Poste Restante** may be filed under your last name, first name, or randomly.

Accommodations and Camping Lodging in Greece is a bargain; the country's two dozen or so **youth hostels** cost about 700dr per night. Curfew is usually midnight or 1am, and HI membership requirements are not enforced. Since bartering is common, **hotels** are also reasonable; expect to pay 5000dr for a double without bath in a D or E class hotel, plus 100-150dr for a shower, possibly hot. GNTO offices invariably have a list of inexpensive accommodations with prices. In many areas, *dhomatia* (rooms to let) are an attractive and perfectly dependable option. Although you may lack locks or towels, the possibility of sharing coffee or some intriguing conversation with your proprietor is worth it. Often you'll be approached by locals as you enter town or disembark from your boat; see their rooms before you decide. Greece hosts plenty of official **campgrounds,** and discreet freelance camping—though illegal in Greece—is widely tolerated. Under these warm, dry skies, camping may become your favorite way to spend the night, but only if you remember to bring mosquito spray. **Tourist Guide of Greece,** 137 Patission St., Athens 11251 (tel. (01) 864 16 88), puts out a list of official campsites in Greece.

Food and Drink If there's an art to Greek cuisine, it's ingenuity, for the people have managed to do well with the sparse yield of a dry and stony land. A meal without olive oil is unthinkable; pine resin has been put to use in the wine *retsina*. The quality and price in *tavernas* varies notably little. Coffee is syrupy sweet and so strong it comes in miniature doses with a glass of water; you may prefer to order it *metrio* (with a medium amount of sugar) or *sketo* (without sugar). Instant coffee goes by the catch-all name of Nescafé. Specify *zesto* (hot), *me gala* (with milk) or *me zahaki* (with sugar). A *frappé* is an iced coffee, shaken until it's frothy. *Baklava* is a honey-rich flaky pastry filled with chopped nuts; *galaktobouriko* is similar but comes with a creamy filling, and *kataifi* consists of nuts and cinnamon rolled up in shredded wheat.

Budget travelers may find themselves eating a lot of *souvlaki,* a large skewer of meat, available everywhere. *Choriatiki* is a "peasant's salad" of cucumbers, tomatoes, onions, and olives with a wedge of tangy feta cheese. Dinner is a leisurely and late affair; some restaurants open only after 9pm. If your menu isn't multilingual, head for the kitchen and browse—it's accepted (even encouraged) in most places. Start your meal with a salad or *lathera*—any vegetable, usually beans, eggplant, or zucchini—marinated in oil, tomato sauce, and oregano. Meat, whether lamb *(arni),* beef *(moschári),* or pork *(hirini),* is expensive. Cheaper entrees are chicken *(kotópoulo),* spiced meatballs *(keftédes),* or stuffed tomatoes, peppers, or eggplant *(domato, pipéri,* or *melitzána gemistá). Mousaka* (meat and eggplant mixed with a cheese and tomato paste) and *pastitsio* (lasagna-like pasta with a rich cream sauce) are fairly cheap and readily available. Fresh fish and shellfish on the islands are extremely expensive; one affordable option is fried squid *(kalamarakia).*

■■■ ATHENS (ΑΘΗΝΑ)

Under the watchful eye of the ancient Acropolis, this three-million-plus metropolis slowly drags itself towards the hi-tech Age of Efficiency. Visitors harboring mental images of togas and philosophers may be disappointed; this is a *city*, racked with heavy pollution, traffic, and run-down neighborhoods. But though Athens is indeed congested, short of breath and graying in the temples, its firstborn, Western Civ, is no spring chicken either, and a glimpse of the Parthenon from the grimy streets may be enough to remind you of the capital's more ethereal incarnation.

ORIENTATION AND PRACTICAL INFORMATION

Athens is impossible to negotiate without a map. **Syntagma (Constitution) Square** is the focal point for tourists, with the transportation terminals and construction for a subway station. **Filellinon Street** and **Nikis Street,** parallel streets which head out from Syntagma toward the Plaka, contain the city's budget travel offices, cheap hotels, and dance clubs. Next to the Parliament is the **National Garden,** which contains the **Zappeion** and **Exhibition Hall.** The **Plaka,** between Syntagma and the **Acropolis,** is a the oldest section of the city, where you'll now find a number of budget accommodations. Ermou St. leads from Syntagma to **Monastiraki,** home of the Athens **flea market.** Adjacent to the flea market is the **Agora** (marketplace). Northeast of Syntagma—down parallel Stadiou or Panepistimiou Street—is **Platia Omonia,** the central subway station of the metropolis, heaped with inexpensive shops and office buildings. The influx of homeless refugees from Eastern Europe has made this Times Square-esque area increasingly unsafe. South of the Acropolis, divided by Leoforos Singrou, are the **Koukaki** and **Kinossargous** regions. **Piraeus,** a seedy port, is a 15-minute subway ride to the southwest.

Ask for a free map from the tourist office (GNTO). Taxis should be cheap, especially if you're with a group (40dr per km plus 30dr fee, 240dr min. fare). If you are coming from the airport or train station drivers can charge an extra 40dr, but watch the meter. *This Week in Athens,* also available at the GNTO, is a trove of addresses and phone numbers. The daily *Athens News* (90dr) and the monthly *Athenian* magazine (325dr) both provide helpful information on sights and events.

Tourist Offices: Greek National Tourist Organization (GNTO), 2 Karageorgi Servias St. (tel. 322 25 45), inside the National Bank on Syntagma Sq. All-encompassing info sheets on transportation, embassies, and museums. Ask for the Athens city map. Open Mon.-Fri. 8am-2pm and 3:30-8pm, Sat. 9am-2pm; off-season

Mon.-Fri. 8am-2pm and 3:30-6pm, Sat. 9am-2pm. The **Hellenic Chamber of Hotels,** at the same location, will give advice on rooming. Open Mon.-Fri. 8:30am-2pm. A less harried GNTO office is 1 block away at 1 Ermou St. (tel. 325 26 67/68), inside the General Bank of Greece. Open Mon.-Fri. 8am-8pm, Sat. 8am-2pm. Open Mon.-Fri. 8am-2pm, Sat. 9am-1pm. The GNTO office in the East Terminal of the airport (tel. 969 95 00) is open in summer Mon.-Fri. 8am-10pm, Sat. 10am-5pm; off-season Mon.-Fri. 9am-6pm, Sat. 10am-5pm.

Budget Travel: Most offices are on Nikis and Filellinon St., off Syntagma Sq. **Magic Bus,** 20 Filellinon St. (tel. 323 71/74), has an extremely competent, English-speaking staff. Open Mon.-Fri. 9am-5pm, Sat. 9am-1pm. **Sotiriou/Transalpino,** 28 Nikis St. (tel. 322 05 03), sells ½-price train tickets to those under 26 and cut-rate airfare. Open Mon.-Fri. 9am-6pm, Sat. 9am-1pm.

Embassies: U.S., 91 Vassilissis Sofias (tel. 721 29 51 or 721 84 00). Open Mon.-Fri. 8:30am-5pm. Visas 8am-noon. Bring a photo. **Canada,** 4 Ioannou Genadiou St. (tel. 723 95 11). Open Mon.-Fri. 9am-1pm. **U.K.,** 1 Ploutarchou St. (tel. 723 61 11), at Ypsilantou St. Visas Mon.-Fri. 8am-1:30pm. **Australia,** 37 D. Soutson St. (tel. 644 73 03). Open Mon.-Fri. 9am-1pm. **New Zealand,** 15-17 An. Tsoha St. (tel. 641 03 11). Open Mon.-Fri. 9am-1pm. **Ireland,** 7 Vas. Konstantinov Ave., (tel. 723 27 71). **Egypt,** 3 Vassilissis Sofias (tel. 361 86 12); visa window around the corner on Zalokosta St. Bring a photo. 1-day wait. Open Mon.-Fri. 9:30am-noon. **Turkey,** 8 Vassileos Gheorgiou B. St. (tel. 724 59 15); **Jordan,** 30 P. Zervou St. Paleo Psihiko (tel. 647 41 61). Comprehensive embassy list at the GNTO.

Currency Exchange: National Bank of Greece (tel. 322 27 30), Syntagma Sq., on the corner of Karageorgi Servias and Stadios St. Open Mon.-Thurs. 8am-2pm and 3:30-6:30pm, Fri. 8am-6:30pm, Sat. 9am-3pm, Sun. 9am-1pm. East Terminal of the airport is open 24hrs.

American Express: 2 Ermou St., Syntagma Sq. (tel. 324 49 75 or -9). Open Mon.-Fri. 8:30am-2:30pm, Sat. 8:30am-12:30pm. Cash changed for cardholders only. Open Mon.-Fri. 8:30am-5:30pm, Sat. 8:30am-4pm; Nov.-March open Mon.-Fri. 8:30am-4pm, Sat. 8:30am-1:30pm. Branch office (tel. 725 15 01) at the Athens Hilton Hotel on Vassilissis Sophias Ave.

Central Post Office: 100 Eolou St., Omonia Sq.(tel. 321 60 23). Poste Restante on right as you enter. **Postal code:** 10200. Branch office on Syntagma Sq. Open Mon.-Fri. 7:30am-8pm, Sat. 7:30am-2pm, Sun. 9am-1:30pm.

Telephones: OTE, 15 Stadiou St. on the first floor. Open 24hr. Also at 85 Patission St. and 28 October St. Open daily 7am-11pm. International collect calls take up to 1hr., 3hr. on weekends. **City Code:** 01.

Flights: East Air Terminal serves foreign and charter flights. Take the blue, white and yellow Express line #91 bus for Leoforos Amalias at Syntagma (every ½hr., 160dr from 6:20am-midnight, then every hr., 200dr). To return to the airport, take the A and B express buses from Syntagma or Omonia Sq. (6am-midnight every 20min. 160dr, then every hr. 200dr). **West Terminal** serves Olympic Airways. Bus #133 leaves for Syntagma from outside the gates (every 20min., 50dr).

Trains: Larissis Station, take yellow trolley #1 from Deligiani St. to Syntagma. Serves Northern Greece. To Thessaloniki (3440dr). **Peloponnese Railroad Station,** tel. 513 61 01. Behind Larissis at 3 Peloponnesou St. To Patras (1580dr). For more information, call **Hellenic Railways** (OSE) (tel. 522 43 02).

Buses: Kifissou Station, 100 Kifissou St. (tel. 514 88 56), serves all of Greece except for the central regions. To reach Syntagma, take bus #51 to the corner of Ziononos and Menandrou near Omonia Sq. **Liossion St. Station** (terminal B), 260 Lission St. (tel. 831 70 59), serves Delphi, Evia, Lamia and Larissa. Take bus #24 from the entrance to the National Garden.

Ferries: Most dock at **Piraeus.** To reach Syntagma, walk left (facing inland) along the waterfront to Rousvelt St., take the subway to Monastiraki (75dr), turn right up Ermou St. and walk for 5min. Alternately, take green bus #40 from Vassileos Konstandinou across from the Public Theater (every 10min., 75dr). Boats also leave from **Rafina** (a port suburb in the East) to Andros, Tinos, Mykonos and Karystos. Schedules and prices available at the GNTO or in the *Athens News.*

Public Transportation: Bus, subway and trolley rides all cost 75dr. From Syntagma trolleys #1, 2, 4, 5 and 11 run to Omonia Sq.

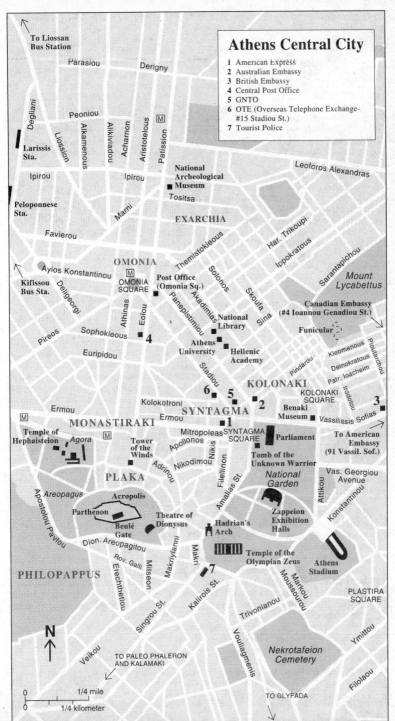

Athens Central City

1 American Express
2 Australian Embassy
3 British Embassy
4 Central Post Office
5 GNTO
6 OTE (Overseas Telephone Exchange–#15 Stadiou St.)
7 Tourist Police

To Liossan Bus Station

Parasiou   Derigny

Degliani
Liossion
Peoniou
Alkamenous
Allkiviadou
Acharnon
Aristotelous
Patission   M

Larissis Sta.

Ipirou   Ipirou

National Archeological Museum

Peloponnese Sta.

Marni   Tositsa

Favierou

EXARCHIA

Leoforos Alexandras

Har. Trikoupi

Ayios Konstantinou

OMONIA   M   Themistokleous   Ippokratous   Sarantapichou

Kifissou Bus Sta.   OMONIA SQUARE   Post Office (Omonia Sq.)   Solonos   Skoufa   Mount Lycabettus

Deligeorgi   Athinas   Panepistimiou   Akadimias   Sina   Canadian Embassy (#4 Ioannou Genadiou St.)

Pireos   Eolou   Sophokleous   National Library   Funicular

Euripidou   Athens University   Hellenic Academy   Kleomenous   Ploutarchou

Stadiou   Pindarou   Deinokratous   Iridotou

KOLONAKI   Patr. Ioacheim

6   5   KOLONAKI SQUARE

Ermou   Kolokotroni   SYNTAGMA   2   Benaki Museum   Vassilisis Sofias   3

M   Ermou   1   Vassilisis Sofias

MONASTIRAKI   Mitropoleas   SYNTAGMA SQUARE   Parliament   To American Embassy (91 Vassil. Sof.)

Temple of Hephaisteion   M   Tower of the Winds   Apollonos   Nikis   Tomb of the Unknown Warrior   Vas. Georgiou Avenue

Agora   Adrinou   Nikodimou   Filelinon   National Garden   Attikou   Konstantinou

PLAKA   Amalias St.

Areopagus   Acropolis   Zappeion Exhibition Halls

Apostolou Pavlou   Parthenon   Theatre of Dionysus

Beulé Gate   Hadrian's Arch   Athens Stadium

Dion. Areopagitou   Temple of the Olympian Zeus   PLASTIRA SQUARE

Rov. Galli   Erechthethiou   Mitseon   Makriyianni   Makri   7   Markou   Moussourou   Trivonianou

PHILOPAPPUS   Singrou St.   Kalirois St.   Ymittou

N   ↑

Veikou   Vouliagmenis   Nekrotafeion Cemetery   Filolaou

TO PALEO PHALERON AND KALAMAKI

0   1/4 mile
0   1/4 kilometer   TO GLYFADA

Luggage Storage: At the airport for 130dr/piece/day. Several offices on Nikis and Fillellinon St. Usually 200dr/piece/day.

Hitchhiking: Hitchhiking out of Athens is nigh impossible and dangerous for women traveling alone. Hitchers have the most luck at the truck parks at the cargo wharves in Piraeus. Those going to northern Greece take the subway to the last stop (Kifissia), walk up to the town's central square, take the bus to Nea Kifissia, walk to the National Road (Ethniki Odos) and start praying. Those heading to the Peloponnese take bus #873 from Eleftheras Sq. to the National Road.

English Bookstores: Eleftheroudakis, 4 Nikis St. (tel. 322 93 88). Open Mon.-Fri. 9am-8:30pm, Sat. 9am-3pm. **Pantelides** on 11 Amerikis St. Open Mon., Wed. and Sat. 8am-3pm, Tues. and Thurs.-Fri. 8am-2:30pm and 5:30-8:30pm.

Pharmacies: Look for the Byzantine-style red cross. (tel. 107) Mon. and Wed. 8:30am-2:30pm; Tues., Thurs., Fri. 8:30am-2:30pm and 5:30-8:30pm, alternate Sat. and Sun.

Medical Assistance: Free emergency medical care for tourists at **Evangelismos Hospital,** 45-47 Ipsilandou St. (tel. 722 00 01 or -01 01 or -15 01), opposite the Hilton. The **National AIDS Center** can be reached at 644 49 06.

Emergencies: Tourist Police: tel. 171. English spoken. Greek-speakers can phone the **Athens Police:** tel. 100 or **Medical Emergency:** tel. 166. **Red Cross First Aid Center:**#21, 3 Septemvriou St. (tel.150 or 522 55 55). Three blocks north of Omonia Sq., on the left. Open 24hr. English spoken.

ACCOMMODATIONS AND CAMPING

In July and August, swarms of tourists buzz into this already noisy city. When hotels fill up, the management often allows guests to sleep on the roof for 100dr per night, a cheaper and cooler option than indoor rooms. (Women should probably avoid this less secure arrangement.) Many hotel hawkers meet trains at the station; some of them may lure tourists into fleabags miles from anywhere and then charge exorbitant prices. Have the hawker point out the place on a large map of the city and set a firm price, in writing if possible, before leaving the station. If you are planning to stay less than 3 nights, a hotel owner can legally add a 10% surcharge to your bill.- Most of the city's cheap hotels cluster in the **Plaka-Syntagma Area;** stay here if sights and nightlife are a priority. Do not sleep in the parks; it's illegal and extremely unsafe.

Festos, 18 Filellinon St. (tel. 323 24 55 or 322 66 52), 3 blocks down from Syntagma Sq. Festive and popular, especially during happy hour at the bar. Free luggage storage and *hot* showers. Check out 9am. Dorm bed 1600dr. Doubles 4400dr. Triples 5550dr. Quads 7400dr.

Thisseos Inn, 10 Thisseos St. (tel. 324 59 60). Walk down Perikleous from Syntagma; 3rd right is Thisseos. On a small street with less noise than most. Kitchen. Dorm bed (4/room) 1500dr/person. Doubles 3500dr. Triples 4500dr.

Youth Hostel #5 Pangrati, 75 Damareos St. (tel. 751 95 30), in Pangrati. Take trolley #2, 11 or 12 from Syntagma. Or walk through the National Garden, down Eratosthenous St. to Plintira Sq., take Efthidou St. to Frinis St., and make a right on Damareos. Residential area. Yiannis, the owner, speaks 6 languages. Dorms (5-6/room) 1200dr/person. Laundry load 500dr. Breakfast 300-500dr. Hot showers.

Joseph's House, 13 Markou Moussourou, Ardistos (tel. 923 12 04 or- 922 11 60). Cheap and semi-quiet. Kitchen. Roof 500dr. Dorms 1000dr. Singles 1500dr with bath. Doubles 1500. Triples 3000dr. Solar-heated showers. Free luggage storage.

HI/IYHF Athens Youth Hostel, 57 Kipselis St. at Agion Meletiou, Kipseli (tel. 822 58 60). From Syntagma, take trolleys #2, 4 or 9 and get off at Zakinthou. Distant, but the price is right. Beds 1200dr.

Hotel Annabel, 28 Koumoundourou St. at Veranzerou (tel. 524 58 34). Family run, plus a cheery bar. Roof 600dr. Dorms 1500dr. Doubles 1800dr, with bath 2000dr. Triples 5100dr. Free luggage storage. 10% discount for *Let's Go* users. No curfew.

Athens House Hotel, 4 Aristotelous St. (tel. 524 05 39), 5th floor, near corner of Halkidrandi. Tidy, snug rooms with balconies. Friendly, helpful proprietor.

Money exchange. Common baths only. Single 2500dr. Doubles 4000dr. Triples 500dr. Quad 6000dr.

FOOD

Eating in Athens is a mélange of stands, open-air cafes, and intriguing dim restaurants frequented by grizzled Greek men. Athens' culinary claim to fame is Greece's answer to fast food: cheap and plentiful *souvlaki* (200dr), either on a *kalamaki* (skewer), or wrapped in *pita*, bought on the street.

The best place to eat is the Plaka. Don't be intimidated by "restaurant pimps" who solicit from the street. If these people have offended, think but this, and all is mended: there's a tiny **supermarket** at 52 Nikis St. and the huge **Makrigiani's of Acropolis,** on Athinas St. between Euripidou St. and Sofokleous St.

Theophilos' Tavern, 1 Vakhou St. (tel. 322 39 01). Walk down Kidathineon toward the Parthenon, turn left at Adrianou St., pass the circular monument of Lysikrates as you enter Vironos St. and turn right onto Vakhou. You might get serenaded by the grandmother who has run the place for 50 years. Just be sure you agree firmly on the menu price before partaking. Open Tues.-Sat. 8am-1pm.

To Gerani (tel. 324 76 05), on the corner of Tripodon St. and Epiharmou St. in the Plaka. From Filellinon, turn right on Kidathineon and follow it to Tripodon. Turn right and walk 2 blocks. Try the delicious hors d'oeuvres (300-500dr) or flaming sausages (500dr). Open 8am-2am.

Tsekouras, 3 Tripodon St., 30m down from To Gerani. Tranquil garden canopied by a fig tree. *Souvlaki* 900dr, *dolmades* 600dr. Open Thurs.-Tues. 7pm-midnight.

Eden Vegetarian Restaurant, 12 Lissou (tel. 324 88 58). On the corner of Mnissicleous. Popular with omnivores too. Meatless *mousaka* and lasagna (800dr each). Open daily noon-midnight.

Restaurant Gardenia (Γαρδενια), 31 Zini St., in Koukaki south of Filopapou Hill. Sign in Greek. Very cheap fare in a residential neighborhood. Sauteed eggplants only 350dr. Open Mon.-Fri. noon-10pm, Sat.-Sun. noon-6pm.

SIGHTS

The heady heights of the famed **Acropolis** ("High City") overlook the Aegean Sea and the Attic plain. This summit, which has served as both fortress and temple, was crowned by the **Parthenon,** the **Temple of Athena Nike,** the **Propylaea** ("Monumental Gates") and the **Erechtheum** during Athens's Golden Age (the 2nd half of the 5th century BC). Despite the ravages of time, earthquakes, explosions and pollution, the Parthenon's monumental size and grace abide. The design relies on subtle curves rather than lines: the columns slant inward, their sides swell about one third of the way up and the floor bows slightly upward. The tiny Temple of Athena Nike, near the entrance, once housed a winged statue of the goddess, wings clipped to keep her from fleeing the city. Other famous females atop the rock are the **Caryatids,** found facing the Parthenon on the Erechtheum. They remain surprisingly complacent despite supporting tons of marble. Ravaged by air pollution, the originals now reside in the **Acropolis Museum,** which also houses other fragments of the Parthenon; most, however, were stolen in the early 19th century and are on display in the British Museum. Visit early in the morning to avoid the massive crowds and midday sun. (Acropolis open Mon.-Fri. 8am-6:45pm, Sat.-Sun. 8:30am-2:45pm; winter 8:30am-4:30pm. Museum open Mon. 12:30-7pm, Tues.-Fri. 8am-7pm, Sat.-Sun. 8:30am3:30pm. Acropolis and museum 1500dr, students 800dr with ISIC.)

At the foot of the Acropolis are the **Athena Agora,** the **Temple of Hephaestos** and the adjacent **Agora Museum,** housed in the reconstructed **Stoa of Attalos.** The Agora contains the ruins of the administrative complex and marketplace of ancient Athens. (Open Tues.-Sun. 8:30am-3pm. Admission to both 800dr, students 400dr.) One of the world's finest selections of classical sculpture, ceramics and bronzework is found in Athens's **National Archeological Museum,** 44 Patission St. Pieces that would shine elsewhere impact only dimly amid the general magnificence. The "Mask of Agamemnon," from Heinrich Schliemann's Mycenae digs, is a must-see. (Museum open Mon. 12:30-7pm, Tues.-Sun. and holidays 8am-7pm. 1500dr, students 750dr, free on Sun. and holidays.) A precious collection of simple marble figurines can be viewed at the air-conditioned **Goulandris Museum of Cycladic and Ancient Greek Art,** 4 Neophytou Douka St., near Kolonaki. (Open Mon.-Fri. 10am-4pm, Sat. 10am-3pm. 200dr, students 100dr.) The Byzantine period is also represented in Athens by the numerous churches that perch in unlikely corners of the Plaka. **Kapnikaria Church,** on Ermou St. at Eolou St., is exemplary. The **Funicular** on Lycabettus Hill offers a stunning view of Athens and the Acropolis and a refreshing respite from the bust and dust below. (Open Wed. and Sat.-Sun. 8:45am-12:15am, Mon.-Tues. and Fri. 9:30am-12:15am. 130dr, 220dr round-trip.)

ENTERTAINMENT

For live, free entertainment, watch the pomp-laden guards strut their stuff every hour on the hour in the **Changing of the Guard** by the **Tomb of the Unknown Soldier** on Syntagma Sq. The **National Garden** is the easiest escape from the noise, fumes, and frantic pace of the city; singers, comedians and acrobats appear nightly at its **Zappeion Exhibition Hall.**

The best summertime alternative to café relaxation is the **Athens Festival.** Concerts and classical theater productions animate the **Odeon of Herodes Atticus.** The festival office is at 4 Stadiou St. Student tickets run 500-1500dr.

■ Near Athens

The sublime view of the Aegean from the **Temple of Poseidon** makes a visit here a spiritual experience, even for lapsed Poseidon worshippers. The 16 remaining Doric columns of this sanctuary, built by Pericles in 440 BC, sit on a promontory high above the coast at **Cape Sounion,** 70km from Athens. (Open Mon.-Sat. 9am-dusk, Sun. 10am-dusk. 300dr, students 150dr. Last Athens bus departs at 9:30pm.) Two **buses** travel to Cape Sounion. One goes along the coast every hour on the half-hour from Mavromateon St. opposite Areos Park. The other bus, following an inland route, leaves from Areos Park (750dr). Don't forget water and a lunch.

The masterful mosaics in the monastery at **Daphni** deserve a visit. The monastery has served as both an army camp and a lunatic asylum, which may explain the pronounced scowl on Jesus' face as he stares down from the dome. (Open daily 8am-3pm. 500dr, students 250dr.) Daphni also hosts an indulgent all-you-can-drink **wine festival** (late June-early Sept. nightly 7:45pm-12:30am; 300dr, students 150dr; tel. 32 27 94). **Camping Daphni** (tel. 581 15 63) is on the road to the monastery (800dr/person, 550dr/small tent, 800dr/large tent). To reach Daphni from Athens, take **bus** #873 for Deligiori St. (every ½hr., 25min., 75dr.)

The oracle at **Delphi** (Δελφοι), where an old woman called a *Pythia* ruled the rulers of the ancient world, maintains its stature as a pilgrimage site. Billions of tourists seek the sanctuary, so visit early in the morning. There are **buses** from 260 Liossion St. in Athens (5/day, 3hr., 1950dr). Take city bus #24 from Omonia Sq. or from Amalias Ave. at the National Garden entrance to get to the Liossion St. station. If you have a railpass, take the **train** to Levadia and catch the Delphi bus there (550dr).

NORTHERN GREECE

The northern provinces of **Macedonia, Thessaly, Thrace** and **Epirus** adamantly cling to the charm that the Greek Islands long ago relinquished. Here, unlike on the islands, no one caters to visitors or puts on a show: nobody whitewashes the buildings, translates the menus, or accepts American Express cards with a smile.

Thessaloniki and Pella A clean, green, and delightfully moped-free city of shops and cafés, **Thessaloniki** is simultaneously low-key and energetic. The capital of Macedonia and second-largest city in Greece, Thessaloniki is riddled with Byzantine churches and Roman ruins, and contains one of the best **archeological museums** in Greece, full of opulent artifacts from the significant Macedonian finds at Vergina. (Open Mon. 10:30am-5pm, Tues.-Fri. 8am-5pm, Sat.-Sun. 8:30am-3pm; winter Mon. noon-5pm, Tues.-Fri. 8am-5pm, Sun. 8:30am-3pm. 1000dr.)

The **GNTO** (tel. (031) 26 31 12), off Aristoelous Sq. at #8, 1 block from the water, has city maps, hotel listings and transport information. (Open Mon.-Fri. 8am-8pm, Sat. 8:30am-2pm.) The **tourist police,** 10 Egnatia St. (tel. (031) 54 41 62), are less helpful than the GNTO. Several bargain hotels cluster on Egnatia St., near the railway station. The **HI youth hostel** (tel. (031) 22 59 46) is at 44 Alex. Svolou St. (Reception open 9-11am and 6-11pm. Curfew 11pm. 1500dr/person. Showers 6-10pm only.) The **Hotel Iliasa**, 24 Egnatia St. (tel. 52 84 92), is probably the best bargain in Thessaloniki. (Singles 4000dr. Doubles 6000dr.) The **YWCA** ("Xen" in Greek) is at 11 Agias Sophia St. (tel. (031) 27 61 44; women only; dorm beds average 1700dr). Stock up at the lively **agora** (marketplace), bordered by Aristotelous, Irakliou, Egnatia, and Venizelou St. **Trains** leave from Monastirou St., in the western part of the city (tel. (031) 51 75 17). Destinations include Athens (8hr., 3440dr); Sofia, Bulgaria (9hr., 10,000dr); and İstanbul (23hr., 11,800dr). The **KTEL bus** company—not available in any stores—operates out of stations across the city. One, across from the train station, sees buses off to Athens (7½hr., 6300dr.)

Pella (Πελλα) was the capital of ancient Macedonia and the birthplace of Alexander the Great. The ruins, including remarkably creative mosaic floors, make a great daytrip. Take a bus from Thessaloniki (45min., 400dr).

Mt. Olympus, Meteora, and Kalambaka Greece's loftiest peak, **Mt. Olympus** (Ορος Ολυμπος), rises from the coastal plain 90km from Thessaloniki. The mountain's eerily beautiful summits require 2 days of challenging hiking but no special equipment. Get there from Thessaloniki via Katerini (2hr.). In **Litohoro,** the gateway village to Olympus, the **tourist office,** Ag. Nickalou 15, in the town hall (tel. (0352) 812 50) can give you a rundown on trails and can reserve a spot for you in one of the mountain refuges. (Open daily Mon.-Sat. 9am-2pm and 5-9pm; Sun. 9am-2pm.)

Southwest of Olympus is **Meteora** (Μετεωρα), where Orthodox monasteries grip the tops of 500m rock formations. Meteora, the setting for the 1981 James Bond flick *For Your Eyes Only*) is one of the top tourist attractions in northern Greece, and it's easy to see why. From the 11th century, monks created Byzantine cloisters to escape the secular world and its marauding infidels. Today the few monks and nuns who remain spend much of their time shepherding crowds of visitors. The most popular base for exploring Meteora is the town of **Kalambaka** (Καλαμβακα), where the **Hotel Astoria** (tel. 222 13 or 235 57), across from the train station, has comfortable singles for 2500dr and doubles for 3000dr. Closer to Meteora, the village of **Kastraki** has the **Hotel Kastraki** (tel. 222 86; doubles 4500dr) and two swell campgrounds. The swimming pool at **Camping Vrachos** (tel. 222 93) provides welcome relief from the parching sun (650dr/person, 350dr/ tent). The 5 monasteries accessible by bus from Kalambaka (5/day, 1/day in winter, 160dr) are open 9am-1pm and 3:30-6pm. Closing days are staggered; all 5 are open Sunday, Wednesday and Thursday. The regulations against picture-taking and revealing dress are enforced with severity.

THE PELOPONNESE
(ΠΕΛΟΠΟΝΝΗΣΟΣ)

The Peloponnese, a divine union of *vouna* (mountains) and *thalassa* (sea), is the Greece of legend. History slumbers in the ruins at Mycenae, Epidavros and Corinth, the Byzantine remains at Mystra and Monemvassia and the Turko-Venetian castle-fortresses at Methoni, Koroni and Pylos. Stay in the serene mountain villages in Arcadia, the lively port towns of Gythion and Nafplion, or the bland but central modern cities of Sparta, Tripolis, Patras and Kalamata. The rugged should explore barren but fascinating Mani, with its dramatic tower houses. Most enter the Peloponnese by sea from Italy to Patras, or by land from Athens to Corinth. The easiest way to explore is by car, but tour buses make trips to the monuments daily. You'll know when you're in the Peloponnese because the air pollution will have dissipated and the oil refineries outside your window will be replaced by fragrant olive leaves.

■■■ ARGOLIS AND CORINTHIA
(ΑΡΓΟΛΛΑ ΚΑΙΚΟΡΙΝΥΑ)

This mountainous region is doused with some of the ancient world's grandest ruins. Corinth, Mycenae and Epidavros recall more than the heyday of the Greek city states; at their fringes whisper the legends of Oedipus Rex and the House of Atreus.

Corinth The first stop for most visitors to the Peloponnese from Athens is Corinth (Κοπιν–θοσ), a town thrice crumpled by earthquakes and rebuilt as a squat, secure, but uninspiring city. The **ruins** of Ancient Corinth are 7km from town; follow either the road to Patras or the one to Argos and look for signs. Alternately, take the buses that leave on the hour for Ancient Corinth from Corinth's main station on Koliatsou St at Ermou St. (169dr, every hr., 20min.). Begin your visit at the **museum,** which houses mosaics from the site and in the Asclepion Room, a collection of cured body parts, votive offerings to the god of medicine. As you exit the museum, to your left the 6th-century BC **Temple of Apollo** keeps a quiet vigil over the city's Roman ruins. (Site and museum open daily 8:45am-7pm high season; 8:45-3pm off season. Admission to both 1000dr, students 500dr; free on Sun. and holidays.) The Turko-Venetian fortress of **Acrocorinth** towers 575m over the classical site; you can take a taxi directly from Corinth or tough the one-hour hike up. Built on the lower of the Acrocorinth's twin peaks, the fortress has foundations dating back to ancient times. The upper summit originally held a **Temple to Aphrodite,** which was served by 1000 "sacred courtesans." From here you could, until about 20 years ago, see all the way to the Acropolis in Athens, but pollution took care of that.

If you stay in New Corinth, try the **Hotel Belle-vue** (tel. (0741) 220 88) on the waterfront. (Doubles 3500dr. Triples 5000dr.) For a local favorite with delicious seafood, try **Taverna O Thodorakis,** on G. Seferis St. at the extreme right side of the waterfront (whole fried *kalamari* 500dr; open daily 12:30-5pm and 8:30pm-2am). **Buses** leave Athens for Corinth from 100 Kifissou St. (6am-9:30pm every 30min., 1½hr., 1000dr). Returns are from Ermou St. at Koliatsou St.

Nafplion Plentiful bus connections make this the ideal base for exploring the ruins of the Argolid Peninsula. From the bus terminal, walk right (facing the bus station) down Singrou to the harbor. The area behind Bouboulinas and Singrou is the old part of town, where reasonably priced hotels dapple the streets. The **HI youth hostel,** Neon Vyzantion St. (tel. (0752) 277 54), is a hike (15-20 min.) from the bus stop. (Curfew 11pm. Usually members only. 1000dr.) **Hotel Epidavros** (tel. (0752) 275 41) offers clean rooms on Ipsilandou St., 1 block below Amalias St. (Doubles 5500dr, with private bath 6600dr.) Or, if you are in the new part of town, try the clean and airy rooms of the **Hotel IRA** (HPA in Greek), 9 Vas. Georgiou B St. (Doubles 4000dr, triples 5000dr, off-season doubles 2300dr.)

Evenings in Nafplion are made for sitting in a waterfront café and watching the *volta* (promenade). At the corner of Bouboulinas and Singrou streets, **Kanaris** serves delicious fish dishes. Try Saromas fish for 800dr-100dr. Soften your arteries on the nearly 999 steps to the **Palamidi Fortress,** with intricate walls and a stunning view. (Open Mon.-Sat. 8:45am-7:30pm, Sun. 8:30am-2:45pm; low season Mon-Fri. 8:45am-2:30pm, Sun. 8:45am-2pm. 400dr, students 200dr.)

Mycenae and Epidavros Mycenae (MYKHNAI), Greece's supreme city from 1600 to 1100 BC, was once ruled by Agamemnon, commander of the Greek forces during the Trojan War. His wife Clytemnestra and her fatal attraction Aegisthus axed him in a bathtub. Most of the treasures from the excavation are in the Athens Museum, but the **Lion's Gate** and the **Beehive Tombs** number among the most celebrated archeological finds in modern history. (Site open Mon.-Fri. 8am-7pm, Sat.-Sun. 8:30am-2:45pm high season. 1000dr, students 500dr; free on Sun.) Arrive ahead of the midday heat and tourist swarms, and hold on to your ticket so you won't have to pay twice. Mycenae has a sunny **HI youth hostel** (tel. (0751) 662 85). The **bus** rambles daily to Mycenae from Nafplion (380dr).

In **Epidavros** (ΕΠΙΔΑΥΡΟΣ), visit the ruins of the **Sanctuary of Asclepius** as well as the best preserved of all Greek theaters. Built in the 4th century BC and still acoustically impeccable, the theater has total capacity of 14,000. Henry Miller wrote that he heard "the great heart of the world beat" here; while you may not have the same experience, you can stand on the top row of seats and hear a *drachma* dropped on stage. Classical drama (in Greek) is still performed at the theater on Friday and Saturday evenings from July to mid-August. Tickets start at 1000-2000dr (600-1000dr for students) and may be purchased at the theater 4 hours before the performance (usually at 9pm) or at travel agencies including **Olympic Airways** (2 Bouboulinas St., Nafplion) and **Bourtzi Tours** (near the bus station in Nafplion).

■■■ PATRAS (ΠΑΤΡΑΣ)

The homogenous high-rises of Patras languish under a shroud of smog, but you can find a decent amount of diversion, especially during the **carnival season** (mid-Jan.-Ash Wednesday). Patra's bash is reputed to be the best carnival in Greece. The **Achaia Clauss Winery,** 9km southeast of town, has a free tour and tasting. Take bus #7 (95dr) from the intersection of Kolokotroni and Kanakari St. (Tours 9am-7:30pm, off-season 9am-5pm. Free.)

The crowded but adequate **HI youth hostel** lies on 68 Iron Polytechniou St. (tel. (061) 42 72 78; 1300dr). Cheap accommodations thread through the tangle of buildings on Agiou Andreou St., a block from the waterfront along the main square. Try the huge rooms of the old **Hotel Parthenon**, 25 Erma St. (tel. (061) 27 34 21). (Singles 1200dr, doubles 1800dr, triples 2200dr.) For general tourist services, a restaurant and toilets, go to the rosy **Europa Centre** at the corner of Othonos Amalias St. and Karolou (tel. (061) 43 48 01; open daily 6:30am-3am). There are also many decent **fast-food** places near Platia Trion Simahon.

Everything you need is on the waterfront. The staff at the **GNTO** (tel. (061) 65 33 68 or -69, or 65 33 60 or -61), right outside customs, knows the ferry schedules cold. The **tourist police** (tel. (061) 22 09 02), on Patreos Korinthon St., are helpful but remote. There is an **OTE** at customs (open daily 7:30am-6:30pmand 7:30-10:30pm) as well as a **post office** (open Mon.-Fri. 7:30am-8pm, Sat. 7:30am-2pm, Sun. 9am-1:30pm). Leaving the customs house, make a right for the bus station and continue (with the water on your right) to the train station.**Trains** roll with glacial speed to Athens (5-6/day, 5hr., 1580dr), stopping in Corinth (780dr). Then head south to Kalamata (summer only, 3/day, 6hr., 1200dr) and Olympia via Pirgos (6/day, 2hr., 820dr). For Delphi take the train to Ceradia. You can leave **baggage** at the train station (200dr per day). **Buses** run to Athens (every hr. until 9:30pm, 4hr., 2400dr) and Kalamata (2/day, 4hr., 3100dr). For **ferry tickets** to Bríndisi (Deck fare with Eurail-pass 3500dr) go to **Mertikas Travel,** 36 Iron Polytechniou (tel. 42 87 50 or 42 36 97). You'll have to shell out a 1500dr port tax. Departures from Bríndisi are at 5 and 10pm, in off-season at 10pm only (18hr.). **Simaras travel** (tel. (061) 27 77 83), 14 Orthonos Amalias St., sells tickets for ferries to Sami on Cephalonia (4hr., 1750dr) and Vathi on Ithaki (5hr., 3800dr).

■■■ WESTERN PELOPONNESE

From the unexciting but inevitable **Pirgos,** take a bus (16/day until 9pm, 45min., 300dr) to **Olympia** (Ολυμπια), the religious sanctuary that hosted the ancient Olympics. In 776 BC young men from cities all over Greece gathered here for the quadrennial festival of Olympian Zeus and the athletic competition that accompa-nied it. The games began with a simple footrace and a few wrestling matches but gradually expanded into a 5-day extravaganza that included 6 different kinds of races, boxing, no-holds-barred wrestling (*pankration*), and the pentathlon. Today the site is scattered and poorly labeled but still lovely; the gleaming **New Museum** is excellent. Inside is Praxiteles' statue of Baby Dionysus, in addition to the famous Little Man with the Big Erection. (Site open Mon.-Fri. 8am-7pm, Sat.-Sun. 8:30am-3pm. 1000dr, students 500dr. Museum hours same as site, except Mon. 12:30-7pm. 1000dr, students 500dr.) In the center of town is a 50-bed **youth hostel (HI)** (tel. (0624) 225 80; 800dr). **Camping Diana** (tel. (0624) 223 14), just 200m above town, costs 1000dr per person, 1200dr per tent, with a 10% reduction for students. Other-wise choose from the dozens of inexpensive hotels. In the center of town near the taxi stand, **Ambrosia** offers tasty, reasonably priced meals and a 10% discount to *Let's Go* users.

The tumbledown **Andritsena** (90min. east of Pirgos) is near Vassae, site of the Temple of Epircurus Apollo. Also near Andritsena is the charming medieval village of **Karitena,** as pictured on the 5000 drachma bill. Buses run to Andritsena twice daily (350dr). Stay at **Stamata Kondopoulo's** (tel. 312 62), across from the post office. (tel. 312 62. Singles 1800dr. Doubles 3500dr.)

■■■ LACONIA (ΛΑΚΩΝΙΑ)

Sparta and Mystra Outside of war, **Sparta** (Σπαρτη) contributed little to Greek history; no philosophy, poetry, or art ever flourished here. Great ruins are lacking; the Spartans considered monumental architecture a luxury that made strong citizens weak. They would have been scandalized by the Byzantine opulence 6km west in **Mystra** (Μυστρα), where 3 tiers of tiled churches and ghostly palaces grope up a steep hillside. (Site open Mon.-Fri. 8am-7pm, Sat.-Sun. 8:30am-3pm. Spring and fall 8am-5pm; winter 9am-3:30pm. 1000dr, students 500dr; free on Sun.) You can camp at **Camping Mystra** (tel. (0731) 227 24) between Sparta and Mystra. (650dr/person, 350dr/tent.) The modern **Camping Castle View** (tel. (0731) 933 03) is also near Mystra (650dr/person, 350dr/tent). Sparta is a convenient, if bland, place to stay. **Hotel Cyprus,** 66 Leonidou St. (tel. 265 90), just off Lykourgou, offers semi-cramped rooms, some with balconies. (Singles 3000dr, doubles 4400dr, triples 5850dr. Open March 15-Nov. 15.) On Paleologou, just past Lykourgou, **Hotel Pan-ellinion** (tel. (0731) 280 31) has clean rooms with balconies. (Singles 3000dr. Dou-bles 4500dr.) To reach either hotel, turn left out of the main bus station onto Paleologou St. and then right onto Lykourgou. **Dhiethnes** is in a corner of the main square across from the **GNTO** office in the town hall; it has good spaghetti (780dr) and standard *taverna* fare. **Buses** run to Athens (5hr., 2850dr), stopping in Corinth (4hr., 1850dr); Monemvassia (2½hr., 1350dr; change in Molai); and Gythion (1hr., 600dr).

Mani and Monemvassia The bold can plunge south into the sparsely settled territory of **Mani** (Μανη), the middle peninsula of the southern Peloponnese, known for a bloody past of family feuds and savage piracy. The entire region is stark; bald mountains drop to a jagged coast, and forbidding, hooded towers guard the abandoned towns. Rooms can be rented in **Kardamili.** From **Areopolis,** you can make daytrips to the spectacular **Glyfatha Lake Caves** of **Pirgos Dirou,** known as *Spilia Dirov.* The ticket includes a 30-minute boat ride and walk through the dense forest of stalactites and stalagmites. The caves are 4km away from the town, accessible by bus, and make for an easy trip from Gythion by moped. Many hitchhike, especially in summer when hordes of tourists converge; you may not get in after 4pm. (Open June-Sept. 8am-6pm; off-season 8am-3pm. 1400dr.) For a bed in **Areopolis,** take Kapetan Matapa St. off the main square and look for a sign dangling off a balcony that advertises rooms to rent. Beneath the sign, **George Versakos** has an impressive antique gun collection and a wonderful sense of humor. (Doubles 5000dr. Quints 10,000dr.) If you don't mind a much bleaker room, George will rent you lodgings across the street. (Singles 3000dr for 2-3 people).

The capital of the Mani is the picturesque port of **Gythion** (Γυθειο). Swim off the wooded islet nearby or in many of the desolate rocky coves to the southeast. In town, try the comfortable, super-clean rooms of **Xenia Karlaftis** (tel. (0733) 227 19) near the port police. (Doubles 3500-4500dr. Bed on the *veranda* 1500dr.) **Aktaion** (tel. (0733) 224 94) is right on the waterfront. (Doubles 8899dr, off season 6675dr.) There are 4 splendid campgrounds: **Mani Beach** (tel. (0733) 234 50), **Gytheio Beach** (tel. (0733) 255 22), **Meltemi** (tel. (0733) 228 33), and **Kronos** (tel. (0733) 930 93). The first is cheapest. There is a **laiki agora** (fruit and produce market) every Tuesday and Friday starting at 4:30am (time to make the donuts!). **Boats** connect with Piraeus (13hr., 3913dr) and Monemvassia (5hr., 2073dr). Contact **Rozakis Travel Agency** (tel. (0733) 222 29) on the waterfront for schedules.

Off the easternmost peninsula of the Peloponnese is **Monemvassia** (Μονεμ βασια), a ruined city atop a huge rock rearing straight from the sea. Still inhabited, this charming medieval village revolves around the church that clings to its rocky summit. Stay in the new town on the mainland at **Hotel Akrogiali** (tel. (0732) 613 60) which wears a sign bearing the owner's name, S. Sofos. (Singles 3426dr; doubles 5161dr.) **Buses** connect Monemvassia with Sparta (2½hr., 1350dr), and Athens (6½-7hr., 4200dr) via Molai (½hr., 360dr).

IONIAN ISLANDS (ΝΗΣΙΑ ΤΟΝΙΟΝΙΟΥ)

This archipelago melds Byzantine tradition with Renaissance culture, hoary South European beaches with crass North European tourism. It's possible to hop from Cephalonia to Ithaka to Corfu, but Zakinthos is reached only by ferry from Killini on the Peloponnese. You can stop in Corfu en route between Brindisi, Italy, and Patras or Igoumenitsa, Greece.

■■■ CORFU (KERKYRA; ΚΕΡΚΥΡΑ)

A verdant island bordered by sparkling beaches, lush **Corfu** is traditionally a favorite haunt of European royalty and aristocrats, and is the most eclectically international of the Ionians. Only here do British palaces sit on an esplanade modeled after the Rue de Rivoli in Paris and next to the shuttered alleyways of an ersatz Venice. Visitors to Corfu in 1994 will be especially catered to and especially overcrowded, as the EEC is holding a convention in July and August.

Corfu Town Decent, reasonably priced rooms are available in Corfu, but hotel managers sometimes fill their rooms with camp beds, which they then offer as dorms but charge the price for singles. Prices drop about 100dr per person in off-season. The cheapest place to stay on Corfu (1000dr/person) is the **HI youth hostel** (tel. (0661) 912 02), located 4.5km north on the main road from the port; take bus #7 (every hr. until 11:30pm, 20min., 85dr) from Platia San Rocco to Kontokali. (Reception open 8am-noon and 5-8pm.) The centrally located and immaculate **Hotel Cyprus,** 13 Agion Pateron (tel. (0661) 406 75), shines nears the ruins of a church around the corner from the National Bank on Voulgareos St. (Doubles 5000dr. Triples 2000dr.) **Hotel Constantinoupolis**, 11 Zavitsanou St. (tel. (0661) 315 95), by the old port, is clean but noisy. (Doubles with shared bath 5600dr.) **Pizza Pete,** 19 Arseniou St., has great grub (entrees 800-1400dr) and a "Pete special" pizza (1150dr). (Open April-Oct. daily 10am-midnight.) Or try **Restaurant Aegli,** on the Spianada. Its outdoor tables are an ideal spot to dine on a warm summer's night (large Greek salad 900dr). **Ferries** from Patras and Italy dock in **Corfu Town's** new port. Follow the water to your left to get to the old town, where you'll find an informative **GNTO** in the agricultural Bank Building (tel. (0661) 302 65; open Mon.-Sat. 7am-2:30pm).

Elsewhere on Corfu KTEL buses leave frequently from New Fortress Sq. in Corfu Town for most of the island's major spots (some are reached by city buses from Platia San Rocco); it's easier but more dangerous to travel by moped. A trip west takes you to **Paleokastritsa** and its whitewashed mountaintop monastery, **Panayia Theotokos** with a **bella vista,** a natural balcony with a great view. (Monastery open April-Oct. daily 7am-8pm.) Nearby are the knee-weakening beaches of **Glyfada** and **Pelekas** and the nearby nude beach **Myrtiotissa.** (Topless sunbathing is the rule on just about all of Corfu.) Pelekas swings at night and has several inexpensive pensions. **Lina's Travel Service** (tel. 945 80; open daily 8:30am-11pm) rents mopeds (2500dr/day) and will help you find a room. The western exposure and elevation of Pelekas offer an ideal vantage for rejoicing with the sunsets. Near town are the stunning cliffs of **Agios Gordios,** arguably Corfu's most spectacular beach, and the site of the **Pink Palace,** a summer camp/frat/hotel, amazingly popular with North Americans. You'll either love it or hate it. (3700dr/person. Terrace cot 3200dr. Showers, breakfast, dinner and disco cover included. Laundry 1800dr.)

A trip north will take you to the quiet sand beaches at **Roda, Chanin,** and **Sidari.** Try **Roda Beach Camping** (tel. 931 20) or just buy supplies at the market here, and wing it. From Sidari, walk the 3.5km west to catch the sunset in Peroulades.

■■■ CEPHALONIA (ΚΕΠΑΛΛΩΝΙΑ)

If Corfu whets your appetite for islands, visit rugged Cephalonia, larger and far less touristed. All boats leave you on the east coast of the island in **Sami,** a tranquil port town surrounded by lush green hills. Though smaller than the capital, Sami has a beach and is closer to the beauty of the island's northern region. Stay at the **Hotel Kyma** (tel. (0674) 220 64) in the town square, with a spectacular view. (Singles 3560dr. Doubles with shared bath 5670dr.) Otherwise, head for the main town of **Argostoli,** the island's transportation center. A **GNTO** at the port gives candid advice on accommodations. (Open Mon.-Sat. 8am-10pm.) The surprisingly interesting and eclectic **Historical and Folk Museum** shows pictures of the town before it was wiped out by a 1953 earthquake. (Open Mon.-Sat. 8:30am-2:30pm.400dr.) Hotels here are expensive. The **Hotel Parthenon** (tel. (0671) 222 46) offers sunny balconies and doubles for 4400dr. Both Sami and Argostoli have superb **campgrounds.** Sami's (700dr/person, 550dr/tent) is right by the town's uncomfortable pebble beach; Argostoli's (1100dr/person, 750dr/tent) is a 1½km trek.

Take the trip north to the fishing town of **Fiskardo,** the only village left intact after the 1953 earthquake. The café toward the bus stop rents rooms (doubles

3000dr); inquire here about excursions to Ithaka. Right along the harbor, the **Restaurant Fiskardo** serves the tasty local specialty *kreatopita* (meat pie). (Open noon-midnight.) On the way are the sensational beaches at **Agia Kyriaki** and **Myrtos,** as well as the little town of **Assos,** joined by a narrow isthmus to an island with a Venetian fortress. Savor the town's sweet-smelling gardens; if you want to spend the night, the **Snack Bar Assos** vends doubles for 2000dr.

In summer, **ferries** link Cephalonia with Patras and Zakinthos. Boats from Corfu and Bríndisi stop here daily in July and August on their way to Patras.

■■■ ITHAKA (ITHAKI; ΙΘΑΚΗ)

The placid beauty of the island's northern villages explain Odysseus' compulsive homesickness for this small, steep, rocky place. The main town of **Vathi** is an amiable cluster of shops and houses in the center of a horseshoe harbor. The **post office** is on the main square (open Mon.-Fri. 7:30am-2pm), while the **OTE** (open Mon.-Sat. 7:30am-3:10pm) sits on the water next to the chunky Hotel Mentor. All hotels here are expensive; the helpful staff at **Polyctor Tours** (tel. (0674) 331 20) can help you find a room. (Doubles 6000-7000dr.) Some travelers **camp** on the nearby beach.

Those of poetic imagination and adequate footwear will want to climb 45 minutes up to the **Cave of the Nymphs,** where Odysseus hid the treasure the Phaeacians bestowed upon him; bring a flashlight or you'll see only the entrance. (200dr.) The site of Odysseus's palace is farther north in **Stavros.** Swim in the tingling waters of the gentle pebble coves of the east coast between charming **Frikes** and **Kioni.** Kioni's only bar is the island's best. An exhilarating **bus** route serves these villages from Vathi. The biggest celebrations of the year on Ithaka take place on August 14th in the village of Anogi and August 15th in Platrighia. There's also a **Wine Festival** in Perahori on the last Sunday in July.

Ferries run from Nidri on Lefkas (3/day, 2½hr., 720dr). There is also a ferry from Patras on the mainland to Vathi via Sami on Cephalonia (1/day, 6hr., 2300dr). Another ferry departs from Astakos on the mainland for Vathi (1/day, 2hr., 900dr) and continues to Agia Efemia on Cephalonia. You can also catch that ferry on its way back to Vathi from Agia Efemia. Check boat schedules with travel agencies at your port of embarking.

CYCLADES (ΚΥΚΛΑΔΕΣ)

For many people, the Cyclades are *the* Greek Islands. Do you dream of boxy white houses tumbling down hills over secluded sandy beaches meeting impossibly blue waters? Well, you're not the only one: the Cyclades hemorrhage tourists each summer. If you want a taste of authentic Greek culture, you should travel in the off-season, but nothing in all Europe can match the Cyclades nightlife in summer. Each island has a unique reputation: Mykonos is a gorgeous, decadent, and increasingly gay resort; Ios is a frathouse party; Santorini is a marvel of geological beauty; and Paros has a little of everything, but nothing special. Space constraints do not allow every island to be mentioned here. But they're all worth checking out. Word of mouth will help you decide which is the best for you.

■■■ MYKONOS AND DELOS (ΜΥΚΟΝΟΣ ΚΑΙ ΔΛΟΣ)

Chic and sleek, Mykonos' sole purpose is partying and sunning, but its sophistication and sense of history (pirates, churches) make it bearable—pleasant, even. The social life, gay and straight, is pricey on this favorite among the Cyclades islands—

you'd need a wallet thicker than your *Let's Go* to enjoy all the flash. But you needn't pay to savor the beaches and the labyrinthine streets of Mykonos Town, dotted with the odd confused mule and pompous pink pelican.

For most visitors, "beach" is synonymous with the renowned, largely gay naked-ness of **Paradise Beach** and **Super Paradise Beach.** Take a bus to **Plati Yialos,** not a bad beach in its own right, and a boat from there (200dr to Paradise, 250dr to Super Paradise). The beaches at **Megali Ammos, St. Stephanos,** and **Psarou** are closer to town and have less of a meat-market atmosphere. At night, the sprawling **Scandinavian Bar** is always packed. (Beers 400dr, cocktails 900dr.) The popular, slick **Windmill Disco** next door growls when thought of as cute. (Beers 500dr, cocktails 1000dr. 1-drink min.) **Montparnasse,** in "Little Venice," has a stately bay window and classical music. (Wine 500dr.) At **Pierro's** on Matogianni St., the mainly gay crowd spills out into the square. (Brews 700dr, mixed drinks 1200dr.) For the party after the party (3-8am), head to **The Yacht Club** on the south side of the waterfront. (Beers 400dr.)

Accommodations, Food, and Practical Information Pushing past the hawkers and their shuttle vans as you step of the ferry, bear right 10m along the water; you can't miss the offices for hotels (tel. 295 40), rooms-to-let (tel. 246 80), camping, and the port police. The following are typical rooms-to-let prices, but don't hesitate to bargain once you meet the owner: singles 5000dr, doubles 7000dr, and triples 10,000dr. Freelance camping is illegal in Mykonos. The official **camp-ground** on Paradise Beach (tel. 221 29 or 228 52) is a spacious and clean self-suffi-cient community. (24-hr. check-in. Open April-Oct.) **Hotel Phillippi** (tel. (0289) 222 94), 32 Kalogera St., is worth the extra dough. (Doubles 10,300dr. Triples 14,250dr.) Right next door, **Rooms Chez Maria** (tel. (0289) 224 80) is cheap but often full. (Doubles 8000dr.) **Hotel Karboni Matoglanni,** (tel. 222 17), on Matoy-anni St. offers truly picturesque rooms. (Doubles 8500dr. Triples 10,000dr.)

On Mykonos, self-consciously trendy food is the rule, but several cheap and/or good places persist nonetheless. **Ta Kiouria** has some interesting specials (veal *sou-vlaki* 1250dr; open 5pm-midnight); **La Scala** serves big plates of Italian food (3990dr for 2-person entree) and **Niko's Taverna** has traditional Greek cuisine (baked *kalamari* with cheese 1000dr; open daily noon-1am).

The **National Bank of Greece** is in the center of the waterfront. (Open Mon.-Thurs. 8am-2pm, Fri. 8am-1:30pm; exchange window open Mon.-Thurs. 8am-2pm, 6:30-9pm, Fri. 8am-1pm and 6:30-9pm, Sat.-Sun. 10am-1pm and 5:30-8:30pm.) The **American Express** office (tel. 224 22), to the left of the bank and inside Delia Travel Ltd., provides a full range of services. (Open daily 9am-9pm.) To find the **police** (tel. (0289) 224 82 for tourist info, 222 35 for general info; open 24 hrs.), fol-low the "Bus to Plati Yialos" signs and turn left on Plateia Dim. Koutsi. The **post office** at the edge of the town beach, next to **Olympic Airways,** changes money (open Mon.-Fri. 7:30am-2pm), and the **OTE** is uphill from the far left of the water-front (facing inland). **Buses** are the best way to cover the island. The **North Station** next to the beach serves the northern and eastern beaches; **South Station,** oddly enough, serves the south. Schedules are posted. Mykonos is 5 hours on the **ferry** from Rafina (2700dr). You can also get there from Piraeus (3000dr) with daily con-nections in summer to all the other major Cyclades.

Delos The nearby island of **Delos,** legendary birthplace of Apollo and his twin sis-ter Artemis, was one of the great spiritual centers of the ancient world. Extensive ruins cover the island, but they can only be visited on a daytrip from Mykonos or Naxos, as overnight stays are forbidden.

■■■ PAROS AND NAXOS
(ΠΑΡΟΣ ΚΑΙ ΝΑΞΟΣ)

Paros The geographical center of the islands, Paros is the place for those who want a taste of everything. To enjoy such variety, however you'll have to skimp on quality. Paros' vast interior is less idyllic, its villages less picturesque, its beaches not as luscious, and its nightlife neither as raucous nor as chic. **Parikia,** the main port of the island, has two redeeming features: a healthy nightlife and the wonderful Byzantine **Panagia Ekatontapiliani** (Church of Our Lady of 100 Gates). (Open daily 6am-noon and 5-9pm.) Ten km south of town is the cool, spring-fed **Valley of the Butterflies,** home to an enormous spawning swarm of the brown-and-white critters. Take the bus from Parikia to Aliki (every 2hr., 10min., 240dr), ask to be let off at the butterflies *(petaloudes)*, and follow the signs. Beautiful **Chryssi Akti** (Golden Beach) is a short bus or windsurf jaunt from town. The next beach south, lovely **Dryos,** is quieter and more isolated. Also worth a visit is the adjacent island of **Antiparos** and its ancient stalactite caves, with graffiti from as far back as 1776.

The Dina (tel. (0284) 213 25) is quiet, immaculate, and right off Market St. (Doubles 7000dr. Triples 8000dr. Reserve ahead.) **Rooms Mimikos** (tel. (0284) 214 37), past the National Bank, has airy rooms in a quiet waterfront neighborhood. (Doubles 6000dr. Triples 7500dr.) **Pensions** east of town generally charge 4000dr for doubles and 6500dr for triples. Since accommodations are an endangered species from late July to mid-August, sleeping on the island's beaches is quite common and, though illegal, is generally tolerated by police everywhere but in Parikia. There are also official **campgrounds: Koula** (tel. (0284) 220 81) is near town; **Parasporas** (tel. (0284) 219 44) lies 2km south of Koula; and **Krios Camping** (tel. (0284) 217 05) on Krios Beach across the harbor. (All charge 600dr/person, 250dr/tent.) Cheap and cheesy restaurants infest the street behind the town beach, where Greek plate specials go for about 900dr. A **laundromat** gurgles off the waterfront just before the bus stop. (Wash, dry, and soap for 1500dr. Open Mon.-Sat. 9am-2:30pm and 5-9pm.) The **Tourist Information Center** (tel. (0284) 220 79) occupies the converted windmill on the dock. (Open daily 9am-11pm.) Paros is 6 ferry hours from Piraeus (5-6/day, 2820dr) and in summer is linked to all the neighboring islands by frequent service. Olympic Airways has flights between Paros and Athens (10/day, 15,000dr).

Naxos Town After Ariadne, daughter of King Minos of Crete, saved Theseus from her father's labyrinth, he expressed his gratitude by abandoning her on **Naxos**. Don't worry about self-centered demi-gods on this largest and least spoiled of the major Cyclades. The twining streets of **Naxos Town** dazzle with flashes of blue ocean behind ice-white walls. Be sure to stroll around the old **Venetian Kastro,** a series of mansions still inhabited by the descendants of the original Frankish and Venetian nobility, and check out the **museum** where Nikos Kazantzakis, author of *The Last Temptation of Christ* and *Zorba the Greek,* studied. Follow the yellow signs through the labyrinth of streets. (Open Tues.-Sun. 8:30am-3pm. 400dr, students 200dr; free on Sun. and holidays.) The **Palatia,** an impressive 6th-century marble archway on the hilltop peninsula near the port, is a perfect photo and picnic spot.

Dock hawks charge about 3000dr for singles and 5000dr for doubles. In the old market section, near the Venetian *kastro* (look for painted red hands pointing the way), is the **Hotel Dionyssos** (tel. (0285) 223 31), cheap, friendly, and boho, but a little run-down. (Dorm beds 1000dr. Roof 1000dr. Doubles 2500dr. Triples 3500dr. Cold showers only.) **Naxos Camping** (tel. (0285) 235 00), off Agios Giorgios Beach, charges 250dr per person, 200dr per tent. Walk down the waterfront with the water on your right for the **National Bank of Greece.** (Open Mon.-Thurs. 8am-2pm, Fri. 8am-1:30pm.) Opposite the bank is the **OTE.** (Open Mon.-Sat. 7:30am-midnight, Sun. 9am-midnight; Oct.-May. daily 7:30am-10pm.) Turn left after Hotel Hermes, then take your first right to the **post office** (open Mon.-Fri. 7:30am-2pm), with **Vesta Laundry** (200dr/piece; open Mon.-Sat. 9am-10pm) nearby. To find the **police** (tel. (0285) 221 00 or 232 80), turn right off Neofitou St., and then first left. (Police station on the building's 2nd floor. Open 24 hrs.). You can rent **mopeds** from **Theoharis** (tel. (0285) 239 00), a patient man with fluent English and endless knowledge about Naxos; turn left after the tourist office. (Open daily 8am-2pm and 5-9pm. Mopeds 1600dr. Helmets and 3rd-party insurance provided.) On the waterfront across from the boat dock is a **Tourist Information Center** (tel. (0285) 252 00 or 252 01; open daily 8am-12:30am, Sept.-June daily 8am-9:30pm) where you can store luggage (180dr), change money, make phone calls, and trade used books.

Naxos Interior Naxos's bewitching interior is easily traversed by bus or, with some difficulty, by moped. **Buses** (in front of the Naxos Town ferry dock) are cheap and frequent. The main road across the island passes through the resplendent **Tragea**, a vast arcadian olive grove. Stop in **Chalki's** parish church, **Panayia Protothonis**, where restoration has uncovered wall paintings from the 11th through the 13th centuries. If the church is closed, ask a local to find the priest who can admit you. In Apiranthos, visit the **Folk Art museum** (open daily 10am-1pm; free) and **Michael Bardani** (Cycladic Art) **museum** (open daily 8am-2pm, but hours are flexible; free), which lie in the shadows of the two castles commanding the town. The road ends at the enticing beach town of **Apollon** on the west coast. Don't miss the 10.5m-high *kouros* (sculpture of an idealized male figure) outside of town.

Amorgos Solitude-seekers should head east of Naxos to rugged **Amorgos,** home of the cliff-hanging **Chozoviotissa Monastery** of the Presentation of the Virgin. At the end of a 750m path, the 900-year-old monastery is pressed into a tiny alcove on the sheer rock face. Be sure to observe the dress code: long pants for men, dresses or skirts for women, no bare shoulders. If you arrive before 2pm, the monks will greet you with coffee or Naxion liqueur and sweets. Early morning (usually 5-6am) **ferries** leave Katapola, the island's main port, daily for Naxos (5-7hr., 1713dr).

■■■ IOS (ΙΟΣ)

Everything that you've heard about Ios is true. If your idea of paradise is to beach-wallow all day and cavort drunkenly all night, Ios is your island: this place, in the words of Nigel Tufnell, goes to eleven. Most places offer happy hours from 10pm to midnight or 1am. Just after midnight, the crowds pack into the bars in the main square of the village and the real drinking begins. Try **Disco 69, The Slammer Bar, Dubliner,** or get some **Satisfaction**. After that, everyone migrates with their sloshed peers to the row of discos on the main road that heads to Milopatos Beach—**Scorpion Disco,** at the end of the line on the way to the beach is *the* outdoor dance emporium. Make sure to try Ios's native drink, the "Slammer" (a mixture of tequila, Tia Maria, and *limonade).*

Ios gushes lodgings (doubles 3000-3500dr), which fill quickly in July and August. First try your luck at the row of pension clones behind the bus stop; if there are no vacancies, seek out the rooms to rent beneath the windmills in the village. **Francesco's** (tel. (0286) 912 23), uphill from the bank with a conversation-starting view of the water, has doubles for 3500dr (call ahead). **The Wind** (tel. (0286) 911 39), behind the bus stop on the right, breezes friendly doubles for 5000dr. **Marko's Pension** (tel. (0286) 910 59), just left of the Wind, is lively and clean with doubles for 5000dr. Backpackers frequently freelance camp on the quieter beaches (such as **Manganari** or **Koumbara).** If you arrive late, go to **Camping Ios** (tel. (0286) 913 29), next to the port (1000dr/person including tent and shower). For great Greek fare, try **Pithari,** near the bank *(kalamari* with tomatoes over yellow rice, 1000dr) or **Saïni's,** on the village's main road.

You can take care of business in Ios within a 3-block radius of the bus stop. Behind it is the **tourist information office** (tel. (0286) 910 28; open daily 9am-3pm and 4:30-10pm) and the **police station** (tel. (0286) 912 22). The **bank** is behind the big church. (Open Mon.-Thurs. 8am-2pm, Fri. 8am-11:30pm.) **Buses** shuttle between the port, the village, and the beach every 15 minutes (140dr).

■■■ SANTORINI (THIRA; ΘΗΡΑ)

Santorini is the diamond at the end of this string of pearls. Dark cliffs salted with sparkling white buildings, burning black-sand beaches, and deeply scarred hills make Santorini's landscape as wildly beautiful and dramatic as the cataclysm that carved it: a massive volcanic eruption that gave rise to the Atlantis legend and is believed by many to have destroyed the Minoan civilization on Crete. Modern Santorini is really only the eastern crescent of what was a circular island. You can climb New Kameni, which remains an active volcano. Be aware that there is a severe water shortage on Santorini.

Larger ferries land at **Athinios** harbor, where you can strike a deal for a room with the homeowners who meet each boat. Try for one of the small towns near **Thira,** the island's dramatically situated capital. You can stay at the large **HI youth hostel,** 400m north of town. (900dr. Roof 700dr. Reception open 8am-1pm and 5-11pm.) The **Villa Maria** (tel. 221 68 or 220 92), weds cheery rooms with gauzy curtains. (Doubles 5000dr.) Follow the blue "camping" signs to **Santorini Camping** (tel. 229 44; 700dr/person; 500dr/tent). The **Commercial Bank** and the **National Bank** in the square exchange money. (Open Mon.-Thurs. 8am-2pm, Fri. 7:45am-1:30pm.) **American Express** (tel. (0286) 226 24) is located in the square at the X-Ray Kilo Travel and Shipping Agency. (Open daily 8am-10:30pm; off-season Mon.-Sat. 9am-1pm and 5-7:30pm.) The **tourist police** station is at 25 Martiou St. (tel. (0286) 226 49), north of the square.

In Thira, the **Archeological Museum** holds an impressive collection of vases, most from the site of ancient Thira. (Open Tues.-Sun. 8:30am-3pm. 400dr, students 200dr.) More fascinating are the excavations at **Akrotiri,** a late Minoan city preserved virtually intact under layers of volcanic rock. (Open Tues.-Sun. 8am-3pm. 1000dr, students 500dr.) Unfortunately, their famed frescoes are in the Archeological Museum in Athens. The **Profitias Ilias Monastery,** about an hour's hike up the mountain from Pyrgos, lugubriously shares its site with a radar station. From Profitias Ilias, it's about an hour's hike to the ancient city of **Thira.** The ancient theater, church, and forum of the island's old capital are still visible, though less spectacular than the Akrotiri excavations. (Open Tues.-Sun. 9am-3pm. Free.) **Oia,** a small village clinging to the rocky promontory at the island's northern tip, 300m above the sea, is a prime spot for appreciating the sunset (and your companion). The sparkling new **Youth Hostel Oia** (tel. 714 65) has wheelchair-accessible mixed dorms for 1700dr and roof beds for 1500dr.

SPORADES (ΣΠΟΡΑΔΕΣ)

Lush islands of fragrant pines, luxurious beaches, and abundant fruit orchards, the Sporades ("the scattered ones") offer travelers a smorgasbord of earthly delights. Although word has gotten out about the Sporades, this small archipelago remains relatively quiet and inexpensive.

Stop at **Alkyon Travel,** 98 Akadimias St., Athens (tel. (01) 362 20 93), to pin down the best way to reach the islands. For Skiathos, Skopelos and Alonissos it's easiest to travel by **bus** from Athens to Agios Konstantinos (2½hr., 2000dr) and from there by **ferry** (to Skiathos 3½hr., 2500dr; to Skopelos 4½hr., 2900dr; to Alonissos 5hr., 3232dr). Skyros is linked to the charming town of **Kimi,** on Evia (5 buses/day from Liossion Station, 3½hr., 1950dr). Most buses to Kimi should continue on to the port area, Paralia Kimi. From there a ferry makes sporadic trips, but at least 2 boats per week serve the group; Skiathos (4½hr., 3398dr); Skopelos (4hr., 3050dr); and Alonissos (3hr., 2870dr). Skyros can be reached by daily ferry from Kimi (3hr., 1510dr), or by hydrofoil from any of the other 3 Sporades (weekends only).

Skiathos and Skopelos Cosmopolitan and expensive, **Skiathos** (Σκιαθοσ) is the place to ogle and be ogled in the Sporades. A bus runs every half-hour along Skiathos's only paved road to the 60 **beaches** on the southern coast. The same bus route also passes the island's 2 campgrounds; **Aselinos Camping** (tel. (0424) 493 12), a 20-minute walk from the road, is the nicer. (200dr/person, 400dr/tent.) At the end of this line, **Koukounaries** beach and nearby nudist **Banana** beach feature pine trees, golden sand, and big crowds. For relative peace 'n' quiet, take one of the treacherous paths continuing away from the Koukonories to the less populated **Eleni beach.** Single rooms are scarce in late July and August; homes advertising "rooms to let" (dhomatia) have the cheapest rates. You'll find restful rooms at **Hadula Tsourou,** 17 Mitrop. Ananiou St., at the end of Pandra St. (Doubles 5000dr. Triples 6000dr.) **Hotel Kastro** (tel. 226 23), down the alley on the right of Evangelistrias St. as you pass the Taverna Stavros, also offers rooms with private baths. (Singles 6000dr. Doubles 7000dr.) For dinner, gobble up the lamb dishes served with well-seasoned vegetables (1200dr) at **Taverna Stavros** on Evangelistrias St. If you want munchies for the beach, try the numerous fruit peddlers and grocery stores; 50m up Papadiamandi St. at the **Souper Market** sign, you should find all you need for a do-it-yourself meal. (Open daily 7-11:30am and 5-9:30pm.) Skiathos bursts with drink and dance. The **Bourtzi Bar,** on the small peninsula at the corner of the harbor, lets you "Swim by day, stargaze by night." (Open 24 hrs.) Across from the Taverna Stavros, the **Adagio Bar** features classical music until midnight, when it *accelerandos* to jazz and light pop. (Open nightly 8:30pm-2:30am.)

The looming cliffs rising from the coastline of **Skopelos** (Σκοπελοσ) gave the island its name: "steep rock from the sea." Tourism here has been kept within sane limits: only the harbor area of Skopelos Town has been transformed to suit foreign expectations. For a superb hike, take the bus to Glossa and walk the dirt track across the island to the **Monastery of Agios Ioannis** clinging to a massive boulder above the ocean. The best beach is the sometimes-nude **Velanio,** reached by bus from either Glossa or Skopelos to Agnondas, and then by a small boat.

Tourist offices on the island are primarily interested in selling their own excursions and rooms; shop around. For the lowest prices, bargain with the *dhomatia* owners who will meet you at the ferry. On a waterfront corner, the **Sotos Pension** (tel. 225 09) offers rooms with private baths, plus an orange-tree-shaded courtyard. (Doubles 7000dr.) Because there are no campgrounds on the island, authorities have been known to tolerate freelance **camping** on any beach except the littered one in Skopelos Town. **Mila Beach,** with its shaded pine-needle beds, is one of the more appealing options. The restaurants in town are fairly expensive, but **Ta Kymata,** at the end of the jetty, has a busy family atmosphere and serves tasty fresh fish and *tzatziki* (400dr). For hefty pasta portions and tangy pizza, try **Aktaion** in the center of the waterfront (spaghetti dishes 600-1000dr).

Alonissos and Skyros Though it lacks polished beauty, **Alonissos** is one of the friendliest and least touristed islands in Greece. The beaches are magnificent, and the mountains and cliffs maintain a pristine, almost icy, emptiness. Set high on the hill to ward off pirate attacks, the rebuilt old town of **Old Alonissos** is a jewel among the craggy rock, a 45-minute uphill hike from **Patitiri,** where the ferry drops you off; you can also take a bus from outside Ikos Travel. While there, stop at the **Paraport Taverna** at the end of the central street for a drink and equally intoxicating views. Among the myriad beaches kissing the Aegean, **Chrismilia** is the best.

In Patitiri, **Ikos Travel** (tel. (0424) 653 20) is run by an amiable English-speaking couple who will help find rooms, give info, and exchange money. Ask at **Boutique Mary,** on Pelagson Ave., about rooms at **Dimakis Pension** (tel. (0424) 652 94; doubles 3500dr, with bath 4700dr). At the waterfront *tavernas,* you have the choice of dining under canvas or a canopy of leaves. Your sweet tooth will appreciate the decadent desserts at **Pub Dennis,** also on the waterfront. **Bars** start to warm up around 9 or 10pm and stay hot until 2 or 3am.

Skyros (Σκυροσ) is the most beautiful of the Sporades, and its hardy island culture outlasts burgeoning tourism. The warrior Achilles spent much of his youth here; to prevent his enlistment in the Trojan War, his mom dressed him up as a girl. **Skyros Travel** runs boat and bus excursions around the island. (Open daily 8:30am-2:30pm and 6:30-11pm.) In **Skyros Town,** visit the **Monastery of St. George** and the **Venetian/Byzantine fortress** that surrounds it. Both sites afford spectacular views of the island's eastern coast. The **Archeological Museum** shows a cult ceramic ring with two snakes devouring a series of ducks. (Open Tues.-Sat. 8:30am-3pm, Sun. 9:30am-2:30pm. 400dr; free on holidays.) Not to be outdone, the **Faltaits Museum** exhibits a superior folk art collection. (Open daily 10am-1pm and 5:30-8pm. Donation.) The museums are located near the **Rupert Brooke Statue,** commemorating the English poet who perished here of fever en route to Gallipoli.

Try to get a room in a traditional home (singles 4000dr; doubles 6000dr); they're smothered with heirlooms and knickknacks from around the world. **Campers** sack out in a field near the beach (tel. (0222) 919 55; 700dr/person, 100dr/tent) or do the freelance thing. Rent a **motor bike** (2500-3500dr/day with gas) at any of the many dealers in town. Maps are available at Skyros Travel. At the beach in Molos, 1km from Skyros Town, **Taverna Marietas** has fresh lobster. Several night-spots revel in town; **On The Rocks,** near the beach, plays Top 40 until 2 or 3am, when Greek music attracts the local youths.

CRETE (KRITI; ΚΡΗΤΗ)

The people of Crete are Cretans first, then Greeks, perhaps because they became Greek only in 1913. The island's strategic location laid it open to centuries of invaders, including armies of tourists, most of whom stick to the eastern half of the easily accessible north coast. Don't make the mistake of following them. Explore the mountains specked with olive groves, tiny ports, and ruins of bygone civilizations.

Iraklion, the port of entry for most visitors, is connected by ferry with Piraeus (2/day at 7 and 7:30pm, 3800dr) and Santorini (mid-July to mid-Sept. 1/day, off-season 3-5/week, 5hr., 3100dr). Boats also run regularly from Piraeus to Chania (11hr., 3580dr); from Rhodes to Agios Nikolaos (2/week, 12hr., 4010dr); and from Piraeus to Agios Nikolaos (2/week, 13hr., 4310dr), via Milos, Folegandros, Santorini, and Anafi. The **hydrofoil** *Nearchos* connects Iraklion with Santorini (3/week, 2½hr.), Ios (3½hr.), Paros (4½hr.), and Mykonos (5hr.). The *Vergina* sails weekly via Iraklion from Athens to Israel. (19,400dr. 20% student/youth discount. 2500dr port tax.)

■■■ CENTRAL CRETE

Iraklion Many visitors' first impression of Crete is the overdeveloped mess of **Iraklion** (Ηρακλειο). All that is impressive in this town is its past: the superb museum and spectacular ruins will explain why Crete is considered the cradle of Western civilization. The **Archaeological Museum** off Elethenias Sq. houses colorful Minoan frescoes. (Open Mon. 12:30-7pm, Tues.-Sun. 8am-7pm. 1000dr, students 500dr; free on Sun.)

Most of Iraklion's cheap accommodations cluster around **Handakos Street,** which runs from the waterfront to Venizelou Sq. Turn right after disembarking at the port and right again at the old city walls, then walk along the waterfront about 700m until you pass the Xenia Hotel; Handakos is to your left. **Hotel Rea,** Kalimeraki St. (tel. (081) 22 36 38), off Handakos St., has spotless pastel-colored doubles for

4000dr. The **Youth Hostel,** 5 Vironos St. (tel. 28 62 81), is just off 25th Augustou Ave. It's family-run, cleanish, cool, and quiet. (11:30pm curfew. 700dr/person.) The best food show in town is the open-air **market** on 1866 St., just off Venizelou Sq. There you can either amass a picnic or sample one of 10 colorful *tavernas* on **Theodosaki Street,** the first left as you enter the market. On 25th Augustou Ave., **Thraka** is the most fun thanks to Plateia Kallergon, the loud and exciting owner. Try the *souvlaki* (200dr). Across from the Archaeological Museum, the **GNTO** office (tel. (081) 22 82 03) has maps of the city, hotel lists and schedules. (Open Mon.-Fri. 8:30am-2:30pm.) The **tourist police,** 10 Dikeosinis St. (tel. 28 31 90), will provide general tourist information as well. (Open daily 7am-11pm.) The main **post office** is in Daskalogiani Platia. You can make international calls at the **OTE,** near El Greco Park. (Open daily 7am-11pm.)

Knossos, Gortinen, Phaestos, and Matala Bus #2 travels from Venizelou Sq. to **Knossos,** 6km south. Here the mytho-historical palace of King Minos and the ancient capital of the Minoan civilization have been imaginatively reconstructed. (Open daily 8am-7pm. 1000dr, students 350dr; free on Sun.) Buses travel from Chania Gate in Iraklion to the Greco-Roman ruins of **Gortyn** at **Gortinen,** where a stone wall is inscribed with one of the earliest records of Greek law. (Site open daily 8:30am-3pm. 400dr, students 200dr.) The same bus continues to the Minoan ruins at **Phaestos,** which may be a disappointment to those not well-versed in Minoan archaeology because it's hard to visualize what the palace must have looked like in its prime. (Open Mon.-Fri. 8am-7pm, Sat.-Sun. 8am-6pm. 800dr, free on Sun.) At the end of this route are the sandy beach and spacious caves of **Matala** (2hr., 1000dr). The grottoes surrounding the town were cut by the Romans, used by the Nazis as hideouts, and became summer homes for 1960s flower children. At the moment, most of the caves are sealed with thin netting. Most travelers stay legally at **Matala Camping** (400dr/person, 400dr/tent), or at one of Matala's few pensions. Flash your *Let's Go* at **Rent Rooms Dimitris** and he'll give you a discount on his posh, clean rooms (doubles 3300dr; inquire at Matala Travel in the center of town).

■■■ WESTERN CRETE

Rethymnon and Chania 81km west of Iraklion, **Rethymnon** (Ρεθυμνο) is an enchanting slice of Crete's past spiced with vestiges of Turkish and Venetian influence. Be sure to visit the colossal **Venetian Fortezza,** dating from around 1580, and if you are traveling in July and August, don't miss the **Renaissance Festival,** held in the fortress. The **HI youth hostel,** 41 Tombasi St. (tel. (0831) 228 48), is cheerful, relaxed, and crammed in summer. (No curfew. HI card not required. 900dr.) **Vrisinas,** 10 Chereti St. (tel. (0831) 260 92), is centrally located and has top-notch rooms. (Doubles 2500dr.) **Olga's Pension,** 57 Souliou St. (tel. (0831) 298 51), is an eternal party, with homemade wine (150dr) at the **Terrarium Café.** (Roof 500dr. Singles 3500dr. Doubles 4000dr. Triples 5000dr. Quads 6000dr. Private bath included.) **Elizabeth Camping** (tel. (0831) 286 94), 3km east of town, charges 1200dr per person, 1000dr per tent; buses run frequently from the bus station. The **GNTO** (tel. (0831) 291 48), on the waterfront, supplies maps and bus and ferry schedules.

In the lively harbor town of **Chania** (Χανια), Ottoman and Venetian architecture converge. Check out the **Venetian Inner Harbor** for a thriving social scene, as well as a **Venetian lighthouse** restored by the Egyptians during their occupation of Crete in the 1830's. The **HI youth hostel,** 33 Drakonianou St. (tel. (0821) 535 65), is on the southern outskirts of town; take the Agios Ioannis bus from Apokoronou St. and ask to be let off at the youth hostel. (800dr. Open March-Nov.) In the old town, most of the inexpensive pensions overlook the harbor. Try **Pension Teris,** 47 Zambeliou St. (tel. (0821) 531 20). The walls are psychedelic pink, the showers are hot, and the price is right (singles 300dr, doubles 4000dr). When you first get off the bus, head to **Yordanni's** (ΙΟΡΔΑΗΝΕΣ) at 18 N. Plastira (tel. 44 710), the insider's place for *bougatsa,* a pie filled with the creamy, slightly salty white cheese unique to Crete (about 280dr for a ½-kilo; sold by weight). **Discos** and live music enliven at the eastern end of the harbor beyond the tourist office. The **GNTO** (tel. (0821) 264 26) is on the 4th floor of the Megaro Pantheon, Platia 1866, above the Greek Agricultural Bank. (Open Mon.-Fri. 8am-2:30pm.)

Samaria Gorge, Agia Roumeli, and Environs One of the "musts" in Crete is a hike through the **Samaria Gorge,** a spectacular ravine that cuts through heavy forests and sheer granite cliffs. (Open May-Oct. Winter flash floods have claimed many lives.) **Buses** run from Chania via Omalos to **Xyloskalo** at the mouth of the gorge daily at 6:30am, 7:30am, 4:30 and 8:30pm (1½hr., 650dr). A hot, dusty hike beyond the official exit from the gorge will bring you to **Agia Roumeli,** a seedy oasis for tired and thirsty hikers. Energetic hikers should explore Crete's unspoiled southwest coast. Peaceful **Loutro,** accessible only by ferry from Agia Roumeli or Chora Sfakion. **Sougia** and **Paleochora,** to the west of Agia Roumeli, are likewise beautiful, though more crowded. In Paleochora, stay at the cozy **Lissos Hotel** (tel. (0821) 412 66) on Venizelou St. (doubles 3500dr).

■■■ EASTERN CRETE

Visit the tawdry resort town of **Malia** (Μαλια) for the ruins of the **Minoan Palace,** one of the 3 great cities of Minoan Crete, or for the brain-melting boogie-orgies of hip discos. The **HI youth hostel** is about 200m past the OTE on the road to Iraklion. (Beds 800dr. Fun owners.) Campers should try **Camping Hersonissos,** Anisara (tel. 229 02). Take bus or walk 3km toward Iraklion. (750dr/person, 350dr/tent.) **Taverna Kavouri** (tel. 211 61) is an enjoyable escape from the commercialized waterfront. Walking toward Iraklion, turn right onto Peace and Friendship St. near the Hard Rock Café. (Opens at 6pm.)

 Agios Nikolaos (Αγιοσ Νικολαοσ) exudes the out-of-control mood of a newly-chic resort town. The **Tourist Information Office** (tel. (0841) 223 57), at the bridge between the "bottomless lake" and the port, changes money and makes room reservations. (Open daily 8:30am-9:30pm.) **The Green House**, 15 Modatsou St. (tel. (0841) 220 25), has a tangled garden, and the multilingual proprietors often proffer homemade Italian ice. (Doubles 3500dr.) For nightlife, stroll around the harbor; check out **Charlie Chan's** nightclub. (Beer 400dr, mixed drinks 700dr.)

 Sitia (Σητεια), at the island's east end, is an etherized port town with a good **HI youth hostel,** 4 Therissou St. (tel. (0843) 226 93; 1000dr/person; reception open 9am-1:30pm and 4:30-9pm). For **ferry** tickets to the Dodecanese, Amorgos, Paros, and Piraeus (Wed.); and Kassos, Karpathos, Halki, and Rhodes (Sat.); try **Porto Belis Travel,** 3 Karamanli St. (tel. 223 70), near the bus station. (Open daily 8:30am-9pm.) From Sitia, it's an easy trip to the fortified monastery of **Toplou.** Notice the holes above the gate where gentle monks poured boiling oil on the heads of invaders. Also nearby are the ravishing and touristy beaches of **Zakros** and **Vai.**

NORTHEAST AEGEAN AND DODECANESE ISLANDS

The intricate, rocky coastlines of the Northeast Aegean Islands enclose thickly wooded mountains and isolated valleys. Proximity to Turkey explains the presence of guns, camouflage, and large numbers of young solders.

Lesvos, Samos, and Nearby Islands Once home of the sensual poet Sappho, **Lesvos** (ΛΕΣΒΟΣ) is Greece's 3rd-largest island. Legend holds that Sappho was a lesbian, and thus the sexual orientation is named after her island. The towns of **Plomari,** in the south, and **Molyvos,** in the north (dominated by a Genoese fortress) are two good destinations. Coming from the main port of Mitilini, the bus stops at Molyvos's **tourist office** (tel. (0253) 713 47), which finds private rooms for about 4000dr per person. In the summer, you will be besieged by locals offering rooms to let. Lesbian travelers make their pilgrimage to the western villages of **Eressos** and **Skala Eressos** and camp along the fine sands of the Aegean. **Boats** run daily to Lesvos via Chios from Piraeus (13/week, 12-14hr., 4250dr), as do several **flights** from Athens (3-4/day, 14,400dr) and Thessaloniki (6/week, 18,400dr).

Samos is perhaps the most beautiful and certainly the most touristed island in the area, although it's quiet compared to most of the Dodecanese and the Cyclades. On the northeastern end of the island, **Samos Town** is among the northeast Aegean's more attractive ports. Ferries run from Samos Town to Piraeus (1-3/day, 12hr.), Chios (2-4/week), Patmos (4/week, 4hr., 6000dr round-trip), and Paros; less frequently to Lesvos, Mykonos, and Syros. Ferries leave from quieter **Pythagorion,** the former capital of Samos, for Patmos and points south. **Samos Tours** (tel. (0273) 277 15), right at the end of the ferry dock, has all the information you'll need. (Open daily 6am-3pm and 5:30-11pm and usually whenever a boat arrives.) The **tourist office** (tel. (0273) 285 30) is signposted from the waterfront (open July-Aug. Mon.-Sat. 9am-1pm and 6-8:30pm). There are barely enough rooms to go around on Samos. The best place to stay is the clean, cheap **Pension Ionia** (tel. (0273) 287 82; singles 2200dr; doubles 4000dr). Another appealing option is the delightful **Pension Avli** (tel. (0273) 229 39), in a renovated 150-year-old convent. **Buses** run every hour from Samos Town to Pythagorion, where you can see the magnificent remains of Polykrates's 6th-century BC engineering projects: the **Tunnel of Eupalinos,** a rock pier built in 40m of water, and the **Temple of Hera,** one of the 7 wonders of the ancient world. The beautiful beaches that rim the northern coast are, excepting picturesque **Kokkari,** uncrowded. **Psili Ammos** on the southern coast becomes nicer after 4pm, when the excursion buses return to Samos Town.

Samos is the main transit point to **Ephesus** on the Turkish coast, the site of perhaps the most extensive classical ruins in the Mediterranean (see Turkey). Ferries leave twice daily in summer (8am and 5pm) to Kuşadası (about 5500dr). The Turkish port tax (not included) is about US$9 but can fluctuate wildly; if you stay overnight you have to pay the tax again. Just a 2-hour ferry hop west from Samos (940dr), **Ikaria** is famous for its therapeutic waters and wax-winged namesake. The verdant, untouristed **Chios** lies midway between Samos and Lesvos. Green **Thassos** and small, mysterious **Samothraki** are easily accessible from northern Greece.

Rhodes Bunched off the coast of Asia Minor, the **Dodecanese** have historical significance, gorgeous beaches and throngs of tourists. An aura of legends permeates **Rhodes** (Ρο–δος), despite the absence of the Colossus (toppled by a devastating earthquake in 226 BC) and the annual inundation of tourists in both the capital city and Lindos. The island is famous for its unparalleled medieval architecture, impressive ancient ruins and splendid coves. The best beaches (**Faliraki, Tsambika,** and **Haraki**) stretch along the east coast toward Lindos. Five km north of Faliraki is **Kalithea,** once an exclusive spa for European aristocrats and one of the few places in the island's north where you can **camp** in peace. On the northern coast are the ruins of an ancient town at **Kamiros,** and farther west, the majestic hilltop castle at **Monolithos.** The interior and southern half of the island are quieter, subsisting on agriculture rather than tourism.

One look at the **Old City** and it's clear that the Knights of St. John were building for keeps. Replacing Hellenistic structures with their own incredible array of medieval castles and fortresses, the knights left the most enduring mark on the city. The best place to begin exploring this quarter is at **Symi Square,** inside Liberty and Arsenal Gates, the main passages between the Old and New Towns and the waterfront. The beautiful halls and courtyards of the former **Hospital of the Knights** now house the **Archeological Museum** in **Museum Square.** (Open Tues.-Sun. 8:30am-3pm. 600dr, students 300dr; free on Sun.) At the top of the street is a second pride of the city, the **Palace of the Knights of St. John.** Also called the Palace of the Grand Masters, the complex has 300 rooms, moats, drawbridges, huge watch towers, and colossal battlements. The modern **new town** has only hotels and expensive shops, but the old town welcomes budget travelers with small pensions and inexpensive restaurants. The **Rhodes tourist office** (tel. (0241) 359 45) is on Rimini Sq. The **GNTO** (tel. (0241) 232 55) is several blocks up the street. Stay at the friendly and international **Steve Kefalas's Pension,** 60 Omirou St. (tel. (0241) 243 57; beds 1500dr). Or drop by **Billy's Pension,** 32 Pericleous St. (tel. (0241) 732 81; doubles 3000dr), or **Iliana Hotel,** 1 Gavala St. (tel. (0241) 302 51; doubles 5000dr, triples 7000dr).

There are **ferries** from Rhodes to all of the Dodecanese islands and Athens (Piraeus) and to Marmaris in Turkey (6000dr). For tickets and schedules, go to **Triton Tours,** 9 Plastira St. (tel. (0241) 306 57; open daily 8am-8pm). Regular **flights** in summer leave from Rhodes to Athens, Crete, Kos, Santorini, Mykonos, Karpathos, and Kassos. The airport (tel. (0241) 929 81) is on the west coast, 17km from town near the city of Paradisi; public buses run hourly (280dr). Book flights 2 weeks in advance and arrive at the airport at least one hour before your scheduled departure.

Kos, Patmos, and Karpathos Keeping the island of **Kos** (Κως) a secret from travel agents is like hiding truffles from a pig. In summer visitors throng to the classical and Hellenic ruins, carpet the wide, sandy beaches, and frisk about bars. The most popular beach is at shady **Tingaki,** 10km west of **Kos Town,** which is notable only for a boisterous nightlife. **Paradise Beach,** about 50km south of Kos Town, has Kos's most unsullied sand. Try **Pension Alexis,** 9 Irodotou at Omirou St. (tel. (0242) 287 98), the first right off Megalou Alexandrou St. (Doubles 4000-4500dr; triples 5500-6000dr.) The main archaeological sites are in town and at **Asclepion,** Hippocrates's school of medicine, 4km away. The mountain villages of **Asfendiou** and the surrounding hills beg to be hiked. For a quieter beach town than Kos itself, try **Mastihari** on the northern coast or petite **Kamari,** near the southern tip of the island. Two **boats** per day travel from Kos to Bodrum, Turkey (8000-10,000dr or US$30 round-trip).

Patmos, the northernmost of the Dodecanese islands, is where St. John is said to have written the Book of Revelation. The sprawling **monastery** dedicated to him, just above the charming and labyrinthine hilltop village of **Chora,** presides over the austere beauty of the island. Stay in the pleasant port of **Skala;** though accommodations can be scarce, you can rent a room from the welcome wagon at the dock or camp for 800dr per person at the well-appointed site at **Meloi,** a nudist beach (tel. 318 21), 2km from Skala. (Open April 15-Oct. 15.)

Karpathos (Καρπαθος), south of Rhodes, is more isolated and features **Olymbos,** a town with two working windmills, women in traditional garb, and the pretty, stony beach at **Vananda.** Both are accessible from the small port of **Diafani** in the northern part of the island; the main administrative port is **Karpathos** in the south. In Karpathos Town, stay at the family-run, English-speaking **Harry's Rooms to Rent** (tel. (0245) 221 88), just up the hill and to the left of the Arva Hotel. (Singles 2400dr. Doubles 3500dr.) The beautiful, nearly deserted beaches of **Ahata** and **Amopi** are perfect for camping and nude bathing. The island is served by boats sailing from Rhodes to Crete; departures are infrequent in winter and always at the mercy of the weather in this, the roughest stretch of the Aegean.

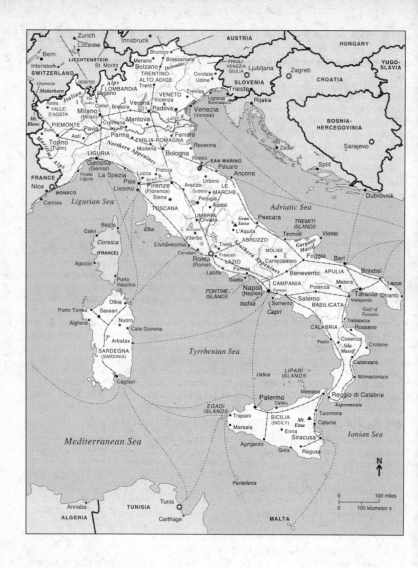

Italy (Italia)

US$1 = L1539 (lire)
CDN$1 = L1171
UK£1 = L2384
IR£1 = L2236
AUS$1 = L998
NZ$1 = L848
SAR1 = L318
Country Code: 39

L1000 = US$0.65
L1000 = CDN$0.85
L1000 = UK£0.42
L1000 = IR£0.45
L1000 = AUS$1.00
L1000 = NZ$1.18
L1000 = SAR3.14
International Dialing Prefix: 00

You may have the universe if I may have Italy.

—Giuseppe Verdi

Stolid, rough-hewn medieval walls still encircle many of Italy's cities. In past centuries they insulated communities from the mayhem of the world beyond, facilitating the development of local dialects and customs, and original artistic and architectural styles. Though the 20th century has left an indelible mark on Italian culture, the outward appearance of many cities has remained virtually unchanged, and a proud individualism still exists within each region. If it's not politics, it's soccer, and if not soccer, then it's wine that provokes heated discussion. Since the fall of Mussolini and the fascists, Italy has seen no fewer than 48 governments, the result of an electoral system that gives power to even the smallest of parties and necessitates unwieldy, tenuous coalitions. Added to this state of near- anarchy is the persistence of politically-motivated acts of violence intended to disrupt the slow process of reforming the government. Despite this, Italy perseveres, with all of its pleasures and laid-back elegance intact.

A trip through the history of Italy begins beneath the grassy hills of Tarquínia, in the brightly painted tombs of the Etruscans; this highly developed civilization ruled central Italy centuries before the birth of Christ. Meanwhile, in Sicily, the Greeks honored their gods with soaring temples in white marble. Traces of the vast Roman Empire define the landscape, from the monumental amphitheaters of Rome and Verona to the volcanically embalmed towns of Pompeii and Herculaneum. Sparkling with Byzantine frescoes, simple early Christian churches distinguish Ravenna as a treasure house of early medieval culture, while San Gimignano bristles with the forbidding towers of the later Middle Ages. In Florence the remnants of the Italian Renaissance can be experienced at its most intoxicating.

> For more detailed and satisfying coverage than can be offered here, turn to *Let's Go: Italy* and *Let's Go: Rome*.

GETTING THERE AND GETTING AROUND

The **Ferrovie dello Stato (FS),** the Italian State Railway, runs on time, more or less, and its network is comprehensive. A *locale* stops at nearly every station; the *diretto* is more direct, while the *espresso* stops only at major stations. The *rapido* zips along but costs a bit more (Eurailpass and BTLC holders exempt). The *Biglietto Chilometrico* (Kilometric Ticket) is good for 20 trips or 3000km, whichever comes first, and can be used for 2 months by as many as 5 people. (1st-class US$238, 2nd-class US$140, plus US$10/person.) If you have no railpass and are under 26, the **cartaverde** (L40,000, good for 3 years) should be your first purchase. Showing this card entitles you to a 20% discount on rail tickets. Trains, however, are not the safest means of travel. When traveling in groups, sleep in shifts, and always padlock your locked backpacks to luggage racks.

Intercity **buses** are often more convenient for shorter hauls off the main rail lines, and they serve countryside points inaccessible by train. The most beautiful rides are, unfortunately, the most nauseating—no fun for motion-sick types. For **city buses,** buy tickets in *tabacchi* stores or most newsstands, and validate them on board. The relatively uncrowded *autostrade* (super-highways) are gorgeous celebrations of engineering, but gas and tolls are prohibitive, and Italian drivers tend to be crazed speed demons. **Mopeds** (rates L25,000-50,000/day) can be a great way to see the islands and the more rural areas of Italy, but are potentially disastrous in major cities, where you should stick to public transportation. **Bicycling** is a popular national sport but not always pleasant. Bike trails are rare, drivers often reckless, and, except in the Po Valley, the terrain challenges even the fittest. **Women traveling alone should never hitchhike.** Hitchers should *never* fall asleep—some drivers consider it tantamount to a wholesale sexual invitation.

ITALY ESSENTIALS

Italian tourist offices come in two varieties: the bureaucratic **Ente Provinciale per il Turismo (EPT)**, in the largest cities, and the fuzzier **Azienda Autonoma di Sogiorno e Turismo (AST)** nearly everywhere else. Most offices can usually help you find a room, often free of charge. Recently, a new brand of tourist office, the **Azienda di Promozione Turismo (APT)** has popped up. Watch out for these—they're allowed to present you with a list of only those hotels that have paid to be listed, and some of the hotels we recommend may not be on the list.

Festivals such as **il Palio** in Siena (July 2 and Aug. 16) and the **Carnevale** in Venice (early March) have age-old histories and rituals. August, especially the weeks around the 15th, is vacation month for most Italians; the cities close down and empty out. Summers are humid and hot in the north, drier and hotter with every step south. In general, early afternoon is good for nothing but a *siesta* (snooze). Winters are ferocious in the Alps and cold and damp in Venice, Florence, and Rome, but Sicilian waters are swimmable year-round.

Nearly everything closes from 1 to 3 or 4pm. Most museums open from 9am-1pm and some again from 4-7pm; Monday is their *giorno di chiusura* (day of closure). Banks are usually open from 8:30am-12:30pm and 2:30-4pm.

Italy's cathedrals are religious institutions and not museums. Don't visit during mass, and cover your legs and shoulders; the more conservative your appearance, the better your treatment.

Italian men, generally speaking, have earned their tarnished reputation. For tips on how to handle unwanted attention and sexual harassment, see Women and Travel in the Essentials section at the front of this book.

Communication Any knowledge of Spanish, French, Portuguese, or Latin will help you understand Italian. Most tourist office staff speak at least some English. If your conversation partner speaks Italian too quickly, ask her or him to *rallenta* (rah-LEN-ta; "slow down"). Useful phrases include: *Quanta costa* (KWAN-tah CO-stah; "How much does it cost?"); *Dov'è* (doh-VEH; "Where is...?"); *Che ore sono* (Kay orah SO-no; "What time is it?"); *Non capisco* (non cah-PEE-sko; "I don't understand"); *Grazie* (GRAHT-zee; "Thank you") and *Il conto, per favore* (ill KON-to pehr fah-VO-ray; "The bill, please").

Everyone is at the mercy of the Italian **phone** system, which this year is undergoing yet another series of major overhauls. In Rome, phone numbers change as quickly as traffic lights. For directory assistance, dial 12. There are 3 types of phones in Italy. Dark ages phones take only tokens *(gettoni),* available for L200 from machines in bus and train stations. (One *gettone*/5min.) *Scatti* calls are made from a phone run by an operator. A meter records the cost of the call, and you pay when you finish. Check first for a service fee. The most common type of phone accepts either coins or **phone cards** (L5000 or L10,000 from machines). For **AT&T's USA Direct,** use your phone card or deposit L200 (which will be returned), then dial 172 10 11; for **MCI** dial 172 10 12; and for **Canada Direct** dial 172 10 01. **Fermo posta** is Italian for Poste Restante.

Accommodations and Camping Associazione Italiana Alberghi per la Gioventù **(AIG),** the Italian **hostel** federation, operates dozens of youth hostels *(ostelli Italiani)* across the country, especially in the north. A complete list is available from most EPT and CTS offices and from many hostels. Prices average about L15,000 per night, including breakfast. Hostels that require HI cards charge L5000 extra for nonmembers or sell the cards for L30,000. Hostels are the best option for solo travelers (single rooms are relatively scarce in hotels), but curfews, lockouts, and out-of-the-way locations detract from their appeal. Two or more people can often stay almost as cheaply in a hotel.

The **hotel** industry is rigorously controlled in Italy; prices are set not by private owners but by the state. Under Italian law all guests must be registered by passport on a special form, so check the room *first,* and then don't be afraid to hand it over for a while (usually overnight). One-star *pensioni* are the best budget option. Prices fluctuate by region, but singles usually start around L23,000, doubles L36,000. By law, the price must be posted on the door of each room; if it isn't, get it in writing from the management. It's illegal to charge more than what's posted. Always check to see if tax (IVA), breakfast, and shower privileges are included and/or mandatory. For doubles, specify *doppia* (2 beds) or a *letto matrimoniale* (double bed). A triple should cost no more than 135% the price of a double. A private bath *(con bagno)* usually costs at least L5000 extra. *Affitta camere* (rooms to let in private residences) can be significantly less.

An even better value in most large cities are the **Protezione della Giovane,** dorms run by religious orders for women travelers only. Quality is high, and beds average only L14,000, but the curfew is generally early. Try to reach your destination and begin looking for accommodations before noon, especially in summer. If you must arrive late, call and reserve a day ahead. **Convents** are an alternative to hostels (and sometimes admit men as well as women). Singles are quiet and clean and cost about L17,000, doubles L22,000. Their curfews are even earlier than the hostels, usually around 10pm. No naked Twister, either.

Camping sites tend to be loud and modern and average L7000 per person plus L7000 per car, much higher in big cities. An annual guide to the country's campsites, *Campeggi in Italia,* is available in bookstores across Italy.

Food and Drink *"Mangia, mangia!"* The production, preparation, and loving consumption of food are all close to the core of Italian culture. For simple, hearty, and inexpensive eating, try *alimentari* stores; they often prepare *panini* (sandwiches) with fresh local salami and slices of excellent Italian cheese: *groviera, Bel Paese, provolone,* or the divinely rich *parmigiano* (parmesan). *Rosticcerie* sell hot food take-out and are often the cheapest option for a filling dinner. Local markets *(mercati)* also offer these delicacies, along with the freshest produce, but supermarkets are often cheaper. A *tavola calda* is a cheap, sit-down option, as is the student *mensa* in every university town. *Osterie, trattorie,* and *ristoranti* are, in ascending order, fancier and more expensive. They are usually open from 12:30-2pm and 7-11pm (later in the south). Menus in smaller restaurants are often incomplete or nonexistent; ask for the *piatti del giorno* (daily specials). A *menù turistico,* when offered, might run only L14,000-18,000 for a full meal, but variety is limited. Sit-down establishments charge *pane e coperto* (a bread and cover charge), with luck not much more than L1500-2500. Check whether service is included *(servizio compreso).*

A full meal consists of an *antipasto* (appetizer), a *primo piatto* (pasta or soup), a *secondo piatto,* meat or fish with a vegetable *(contorno),* and usually salad, fruit, and/or cheese. As one travels south, tomatoes and spices play an increasingly significant role. By the time you reach Naples, the standard pasta dish beads the brow with sweat. Pastries also get progressively sweeter, reaching an all-time glucose high in the sinfully sugary *marzipan* of Sicily.

Coffee is another focus of Italian life. *Espresso* is meant to be quaffed quickly. *Cappuccino,* a mixture of *espresso* and hot, frothy milk, is the normal breakfast beverage. *Caffè macchiato* ("spotted") is *espresso* with a touch of milk, while *latte macchiato* is milk with a splash of coffee. Perhaps the best finish to a meal is a *caffè corretto* ("corrected"), *espresso* spiked with your favorite liqueur.

Starting with the delicate white *Asti Spumante* from Piedmont and *Soave* from Verona, Italian local wines get rougher and earthier as you proceed south, although there are several exceptions. Italian beer leaves something to be desired. Drink *Peroni* or *Wührer* only if there are no imports in sight.

Bars are a good place to sample wines, eat breakfast, or stop for snacks. They also serve a wide collection of Italian liqueurs. Try *grappa,* the gut-wrenching liqueur of the Veneto flavored with various fruits, and Roman *sambuca,* a sweet anise concoction served flaming, with coffee beans floating on top. Sitting down at a table doubles the price of anything you order.

In almost every Italian town you can find numerous shops selling Italy's greatest contribution to civilization: *gelato* (ice cream). Look for the *produzione propria* (homemade) sign. Also delicious on hot summer days are *granite* ("Italian ices") and *frullati* (cool fruit shakes), both guaranteed to please.

■■■ ROME (ROMA)

Any attempt to capture Rome in its entirety fails. There is always one more forgotten church, obscured cornice, or grinning gargoyle that eludes. Rome is the study of failed human efforts to control a city, a civilization that grew from humble (lupine) origins into something divine. The foolish still attempt capture—Mussolini tried it only 65 years ago and was thwarted by the ancient ruins that kept sprouting up from beneath his efforts to create broad modern thoroughfares. And the millions of pilgrims who search Rome every year find themselves wearied by its twisting hot alleyways and multi-layered design. But no matter what you see or how long you stay, you will touch the city's spiritual core. Rome is and always will be *bellissima*.

> For more detailed, decorated, and highly descriptive information on this city, pick up a copy of *Let's Go: Rome*.

ORIENTATION AND PRACTICAL INFORMATION

From **Termini**, the central locus and arrival point for most visitors to Rome, **Città Universitaria** and the student area of **San Lorenzo** are to the east, while most of the major sights slope between hills to the west toward the Tiber. **Via Nazionale** is the central artery connecting Termini with the city center. At its base, via Nazionale joins immense **piazza Venezia,** crowned by the conspicuous white marble pile of the **Victor Emanuele Monument.** From piazza Venezia, **via dei Fori Imperiale** leads southeast to the **Forum** and **Colosseum; corso Vittorio Emanuele** heads west into the historic districts that fill the bend in the Tiber; the **via del Corso,** the backbone of the city, stretches straight north to the **piazza del Popolo** and the **Spanish Steps.**

The 14 *rioni* (districts) of Rome, distinct in appearance and character, emerge from the snarl of traffic that fills these boulevards. To the north, the enormous **Villa Borghese** and **Pincio** parks border the piazza del Popolo, the high-class shopping streets centering round the Spanish Steps, and the (now very faded) glamour of the **via Veneto.** South of here, between via Tritone and via Nazionale, **piazza Barberini** points the way to the stunningly restored **Trevi Fountain.** The **Forum** and **Colosseum** lead out of the city towards the ruins of the **Circus Maximus,** the **Appian Way,** and the **Catacombs.** From piazza Venezia to the west, the **Largo Argentina** marks the start of the corso Vittorio Emanuele, which leads into the **Pantheon** and **piazza Navona** (north of the street) and **Campo dei Fiori** and **piazza Farnese** (between via Giulia and the river), before crossing the Tiber to the overwhelming prospect of **Castel Sant'Angelo** and the **Vatican City.** South of the Vatican is the medieval **Trastevere** quarter, home to countless *trattorie* and the best streets for wandering in the city. Back across the river, the historic **Tiber Island** and **Jewish Ghetto** lie in ruinous calm behind the Victor Emanuele Monument. Bounding the historic city at the south is the peaceful **Aventine Hill,** crowned with gardens and monasteries, and the delicious **Testaccio** district.

Rome is congested day and night with lost, bewildered, and distracted tourists, each loaded with cash and valuables in every pocket. The bright side is that Roman thieves, provided with so many thousands of easy targets, rarely resort to violence. Never, ever count money in public, and watch to see that you are not followed after changing money. Watch out for packs of children begging for change as they thrust flat pieces of cardboard or newspaper at your waist—underneath the flutter of paper they can probe pockets and unzip fanny pouches. The thieving hordes are especially thick around the Forum and the Colosseum, where people are blindly admiring the architecture, and on crowded buses like the #64 and the #492.

For a big city, Rome is relatively safe at night. Women and men will generally feel safe walking through the center of town during all but the darkest hours. Outside the *Centro Storico* (historical center), however, use caution. The area around Termini and to its south (especially near piazza Vittorio Emanuele and the colle Oppio, notorious drug areas) and Testaccio deserve special care; walk in groups at night. Bipedal mugging is particularly bad in the suburbs of Cinecittà and Centocelle. Store your gear in Termini along track #1, or use a bus or train locker—although these are occasionally broken into.

Tourist Offices: EPT, in the Termini Station (tel. 487 12 70 or 482 40 78), between tracks #2 and 3. Lines can be horrendous. Open daily 8:15am-7:15pm. **Central Office,** via Parigi, 5 (tel. 48 89 91 or 48 89 92 00). Walk from the station diagonally to the left across p. del Cinquecento and cross p. della Repubblica to via Parigi. English spoken. **Fiumicino Office,** outside Customs (tel. 65 01 02 55). All 3 offices open Mon.-Sat. 8:15am-7:15pm. At any office, pick up a map and copies of *Romamor* and *Carnet di Roma e della Sua Provincia*. Ask for *Alberghi di Roma e Provincia,* which lists all hotels and *pensioni* registered with the EPT. All offices will help you find a room. **Enjoy Rome,** via Varese 39 (tel. and fax 445 18 43), one block east of Termini station, perpendicular to via Milazzo. Hotel reservations for Rome and all of Italy (free). Open Mon.-Fri. 8:30am-1pm and 3:30-6pm, Sat. 8:30am-1pm. They'll answer the phone Mon.-Sat. until 10pm.

Budget travel: Centro Turistico Studentesco (CTS), via Genova, 16 (tel. 467 91), off via Nazionale, halfway between p. della Repubblica and p. Venezia. Offices at Termini (at track #22, tel. 467 92 54), via Appia Nuova, 434 (tel. 780 84 49), corso Vittorio Emanuele II, 297 (tel. 687 26 72), and Air Terminal Ostiense (tel. 574 79 50), open same hours as main office. ISIC and YIEE cards L15,000 each. Carta Verde L40,000. Discount transport reservations and tickets, free map, and currency exchange. Accommodations service (free). Bulletin boards with notices for rides, special services, etc. Lines can be slow. English spoken. Main office open Mon.-Fri. 9am-1pm and 4-7pm, Sat. 9am-1pm. **Compagnia Italiana di Turismo (CIT),** p. della Repubblica, 64 (tel. 479 43 49, fax 479 41). Books discount train tickets and tours. In Termini (tel. 488 16 78; combined with *Sestante* travel agency), via Veneto, 14c (tel. 481 43 82), Air Terminal Ostiense (tel. 574 57 42, general info tel. 479 41). Offices open Mon.-Fri. 9am-1pm and 2-5:30pm. **Italian Youth Hostels Association (Associazione Italiana Alberghi per la Gioventu) (HI),** via Cavour 44 (tel. 487 11 52). List of hostels throughout Italy. IYHA cards L30,000. Open Mon.-Thurs. 7:30am-5pm, Fri. 7:30am-3pm.

Embassies: U.S., via Veneto, 121 (tel. 467 41). Open Mon.-Fri. 8:30am-noon and 2-4pm. **Canada: Consulate,** via Zara, 30 (tel. 44 59 81 or 44 84 21; non-business hrs., 033 772 71 95; fax 44 59 89 05). Open 10am-noon and 2-4pm. **Embassy,** via G.B. De Rossi, 27 (tel. 44 59 81). **U.K.,** via XX Settembre 80A (tel. 482 55 51; fax 487 33 24). Open Mon.-Fri. 9:30am-12:30pm and 2-4pm; mid-July and Aug. 8am-1pm. **Australia,** via Alessandria, 215 (tel. 85 27 21; fax 85 27 23 00). Consular and passport services at corso Trieste 25. Open Mon.-Thurs. 9am-noon and 1:30-4pm, Fri. 9am-noon. **New Zealand,** via Zara, 28 (tel. 440 29 28/29/30; fax 440 29 84). Open Mon.-Fri. 8:30am-12:45pm and 1:45-5pm.

Currency Exchange: Large banks like **Banco d'Italia** or **Banco Nazionale del Lavoro** have offices all around the city. **Termini** has *cambi* with low rates and/or high commissions. The one by the train information booth is open daily 8am-8pm. **Automatic tellers** will change American dollars into *lire* at usurious rates; machines in Termini; at via Marsala, 4; via del Corso, 230 and 283; via degli Uffici del Vicario, 78; p. San Silvestro; via di Conciliazione; via Veneto 7, 74, and 115. Some **ATMs** accept Visa and MasterCard and give excellent rates around via Veneto, the Vatican, p. Barberini, and via Giovanni Giolitti near Termini.

American Express, p. di Spagna, 38 (tel. 676 41; lost or stolen cards toll-free 24hr. 167 86 40 46; lost or stolen Traveler's Cheques toll-free 24hr. 167 87 20 00). Cha-

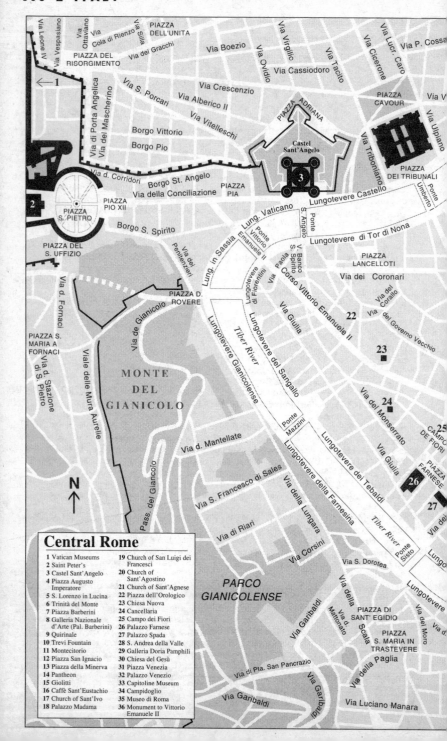

Central Rome

1 Vatican Museums
2 Saint Peter's
3 Castel Sant'Angelo
4 Piazza Augusto Imperatore
5 S. Lorenzo in Lucina
6 Trinità del Monte
7 Piazza Barberini
8 Galleria Nazionale d'Arte (Pal. Barberini)
9 Quirinale
10 Trevi Fountain
11 Montecitorio
12 Piazza San Ignacio
13 Piazza della Minerva
14 Pantheon
15 Giolitti
16 Caffè Sant'Eustachio
17 Church of Sant'Ivo
18 Palazzo Madama

19 Church of San Luigi dei Francesci
20 Church of Sant'Agostino
21 Church of Sant'Agnese
22 Piazza dell'Orologico
23 Chiesa Nuova
24 Cancellaria
25 Campo dei Fiori
26 Palazzo Farnese
27 Palazzo Spada
28 S. Andrea della Valle
29 Galleria Doria Pamphili
30 Chiesa del Gesù
31 Piazza Venezia
32 Palazzo Venezio
33 Capitoline Museum
34 Campidoglio
35 Museo di Roma
36 Monument to Vittorio Emanuele II

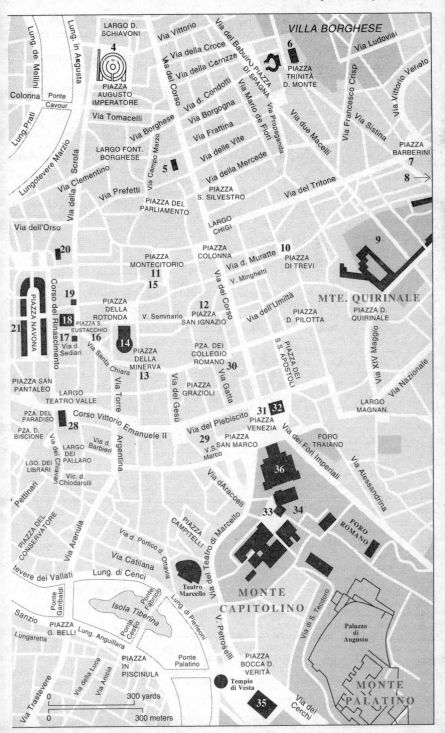

otic at times, but perfect English spoken. Mail held. Postal code 00187. Same rates as any of the small *cambi* all over Rome. Good free maps. Open Mon.-Fri. 9am-5:30pm, Sat. 9am-12:30pm.

Post office: p. San Silvestro, 19 (tel. 67 71), between p. di Spagna and the corso. Stamps at booths #31-33, Fermo Posta booth #65. Currency exchange (no checks) booths #25-28. Stamp machines and computer information in English in lobby. Open Mon.-Fri. 8:25am-7:10pm, Sat. 8:20-11:50am. *Cambio* open Mon.-Fri. 8:20am-5:30pm, Sat. 8:20-11:50am. Fermo Posta postal code: 00186.

Phones: SIP, in the Villa Borghese parking lot. Open 8am-9:30pm. Phone booths throughout the city. Booth in Termini across from aisle 6 (open Mon.-Sat. 8am-11pm, Sun. 9am-noon and 5-10pm) sells magnetic phone cards in L5000 or L10,000 units; are also available at *tabacchi* and newsstands around the city.

Lost Property: Oggetti Rinvenuti, via Nicolo Bettoni, 1 (tel. 581 60 40), north of p. di Ponte Testaccio. Open Mon.-Sat. 10am-noon. **Termini,** at track #22 (tel. 473 06 02). Open 7am-11pm. Also check at your **embassy** and with the police.

Flights: International flights at **Leonardo da Vinci Airport** (tel. 659 51), a.k.a. **Fiumicino.** Currency exchange, baggage check (24hr.; L4650/day). After you exit Customs, you'll find a **tourist office** (tel. 65 01 12 55) immediately to your left; provides maps of the city and room-finding service. Open Mon.-Sat. 8:15am-7:15pm. The **train** into Rome leaves from the 2nd floor of the international arrivals wing for the new **Air Terminal Ostiense** inside the city. Buy your ticket (L6000) from one of the machines on the 1st floor. Trains depart every 20-30min. (6:15am-12:45am; 25min.). 2 new "bullet" trains run to Florence and Naples. One-way L30,000 with Alitalia plane ticket, otherwise L122,500. Most charter and domestic flights arrive at **Ciampino** (tel. 79 49 41). From here take the blue ACO-TRAL bus to the Anagnina stop on Linea A of the *Metropolitana* (6am-9:30pm, every 30min.; L1000).

Trains: Termini is the focal point of most train and both subway lines. Multilingual information booths, currency exchanges, baggage services, restaurants, bars, barbers, telephone offices, gift shops, and even an aquarium. Crowded railway information and Eurail offices at the front. Make reservations in person. Various stations on the fringe of town (**Tiburtina, Trastevere, Ostiense, San Lorenzo, Roma Nord, Prenestina, Stazione S. Pietro**) connected by bus and/or subway to Termini. Watch out for pickpockets in and around the station. **Luggage storage** along tracks 1 and 22. (Open daily 5am-1am, L1500/piece/day.) *Diretto* (direct) trains to: Florence (2hr.; L22,000, *rapido* supplement L9300); Venice (5hr.; L40,200, *rapido* supplement L14,800); Naples (3hr.; L15,400, *rapido* supplement L7300); Brindisi (7-8hr.; L43,500, *rapido* supplement L15,800).

Buses: ACOTRAL, between Rome and the province of **Lazio** (tel. 591 55 51); take the subway to an outlying area and catch the bus from there.

Public Transportation: ATAC *(Aziende Tramvie Autobus Communali),* intra-city **bus** company (tel. 469 51), piazza del Cinquecento. English spoken. Detailed map of bus routes L1000. Buses run until midnight, followed by *servizio notturno* (signal nighttime buses by waving arm). Tickets L800. Stamp ticket in orange machine at back of bus as you board (only from front or back doors); ticket good for transfers over the next 90min. If you exceed 90min. during your last ride, stamp other end of ticket to prove it was still valid when you boarded. Buy tickets at newsstands, *tabacchi,* or kiosks. **B.I.G.** daily ticket valid for 24hr. on Metro and buses (L2800). **Weekly bus pass** *(biglietto settimanale),* valid for 8 nights and days (L10,000), sold at piazza del Cinquecento. **Trams** use same tickets as buses. L50,000 fine for riding without ticket. After midnight, ticket salesmen will sell you a ticket on-board buses. **Metro** entrances marked on the street by white "M" on red square. **Linea A** daily 5:30am-11:30pm; **Linea B** Sun.-Fri. 5:30am-9pm, Sat. and holidays 5:30am-11:30pm. Tickets L700; buy them at newsstands, *tabacchi,* or at coin-operated machines in stations.

Taxis: Expensive. Ride only in yellow or white taxis, and make sure there's a meter. L6400 for first 3km or 9min. waiting period, then L1200/km. Night surcharge L3000; Sunday surcharge L1000; each suitcase L500. **Radio taxis** (tel. 35 70, 66 45, 49 94, 881 77). Taxis to and from the airport cost around L70,000.

Bicycle and Moped Rental: Scooters for Rent, via della Purificazione, 84 (tel. 488 54 85), off p. Barberini. Bicycles L15,000/day, L80,000/week. Mopeds L50,000/day. Vespas L60,000/day. Open 9am-7pm. Visa, MC, and AmEx.

Bookstores: Economy Book and Video Center, via Torino, 136 (tel. 474 68 77), off via Nazionale. Open Mon.-Fri. 9:30am-7:30pm, Sat. 9:30am-1:30pm; Oct.-May Mon. 3-7:30pm, Tues.-Sat. 9:30am-7:30pm. **Open Door Bookshop,** via della Lungaretta, 25 (tel. 271 69 00), off viale Trastevere. Fax (L4000 1st page, L2000/additional page, plus phone bill). Open Mon. 4-8pm, Tues.-Sat. 10am-1pm and 4-8pm.

Laundromat: OndaBlu, via Principe Amedeo, 70/b, off via Cavour 2 blocks south of Termini. Wash L6,000/6.5kg. Dry L6,000/20min.

Crisis Line: Samaritans, via San Giovanni in Laterano, 250 (tel. 70 45 44 44). Native English speakers. Open for calls and visits 4-10pm.

Pharmacies: The closed pharmacies usually post a list. **Farmacia Grieco,** piazza della Repubblica, 67 (tel. 488 04 10 or 48 38 61), steps from Termini. **Farmacia Risorgimento,** p. Risorgimento, 44 (tel. 372 46 22).

Medical Assistance: Rome-American Hospital, via Emilio Longoni, 69 (tel. 22 55 71). Private emergency and lab services. English-speaking physician on call 24hrs. **Red Cross:** via Antonio Pacinotti, 18 (tel. 55 10), in piazza della Radio.

Emergency: First Aid (*Pronto Soccorso*). **Fire** (*fuoco*) tel. 115. **Police** tel. 113. **Carabinieri** tel. 112. **Foreigner's Office** (*Ufficio Stranieri*), via Genova, 2 (tel. 46 86 28 76). English spoken. Report thefts in person. Open 24hrs. **Police Headquarters,** via San Vitale, 15 (tel. 468 61). **Green Line** tel. 1678 632 77 to report anti-gay violence; toll-free.

ACCOMMODATIONS AND CAMPING

A huge quantity of rooms meets the tourist demand, but quality varies significantly and hotel prices in Rome are often astronomical. Although reservations help, they don't always guarantee that a room awaits you for the full length of your intended stay, or at the decided price, as large groups frequently take precedence over a reserved double in the minds of some proprietors. Make sure the hotel charges you no more than the price posted on the back of your room's door; it's the law.

The **tourist offices** in Rome will scrounge (reluctantly in peak season) to find you a room, as will the **Centro Turistico Studentesco e Giovanile (CTS)** and the **Enjoy Rome** agency (see Practical Information). **Protezione delle Giovane,** via Urbana, 158 (tel. 488 14 19), will assist women in finding convent accommodations and moderately priced rooms. Termini is full of "officials" swarming around to find you a place. Many of them are the real thing, and have photo IDs issued by the tourist office. Stay on the safe side: ask for maps and directions (real officials will always have maps), and **always insist on seeing a room first.**

It is illegal and, well, stupid to "camp out" in the public places of Rome. It is also a good idea to be careful even at designated campgrounds. See *Let's Go: Rome* for more information on accommodations and long-term stays.

Hostels and Student Dormitories

If you're looking for a raucous time in Rome, institutions are not the place to go. Most of them are inconveniently located, difficult to arrange, and curfews at the HI hostel and various religious organizations keep you locked away from *la dolce vita*.

Ostello del Foro Italico (HI), viale delle Olimpiadi, 61 (tel. 32 36 279 or 32 36 267; fax 32 42 613). Take Metro Linea A to "Ottaviano" (last stop) and then exit onto via Barletta and take bus #32 to "Cadorna." Inconvenient location. 350 beds. Lockers. 3-day max. stay when full. Reception open noon-11pm. Lockout 9am-2pm. Lunch (1-2pm) or dinner (7-9pm) L12,000. Bar open 7:30am-11pm. Curfew midnight. L18,000/person; nonmembers L25,000 (buy membership at the desk for L30,000). Breakfast and showers included. Wheelchair access.

Esercito della Salvezza (Salvation Army), via degli Apuli, 41 (tel. 446 52 36), off via dei Marsi, northeast of Termini. Take bus #492 or 415 from Termini to "Tiber-tina." 175 tiny but tidy rooms in a pretty quiet area. No lockout or curfew. Singles L28,000-40,000. Doubles L46,000-60,000. Reserve 1 week in advance.

YWCA, via Cesare Balbo, 4 (tel. 48 88 3917 or 48 80 460), off via Torino, south of Termini. Somewhat pricey; no men allowed unless they're married to their roommates. Curfew midnight. Singles L38,000. Doubles L64,000. Triples L78,000. Quads L104,000. Showers and breakfast included. No breakfast offered Sunday.

Hotels and Pensions

North of Termini

There are clusters of clean, reasonably priced *pensioni* and hotels waiting within 15 minutes of Termini in a somewhat run-down but not particularly dangerous area.

Pensione Papa Germano, via Calatafimi, 14A (tel. 48 69 19), off via Volturno between via Gaeta and via Montebello. German discipline and Italian warmth. Reservations a must in summer. Papa may try to match lone travelers with groups to fill a room. Singles L35,000. Doubles L50,000, with bath L60,000. Triples L75,000. Quads L22,000/person. 10% off Nov.-March. Visa, MC.

Pensione Tizi, via Collina, 48 (tel. and fax 474 32 66 or 482 01 28). 15min. from the station. Take via Goito from p. dell'Indipendenza, cross via XX Settembre onto via Piave, then take the 1st left onto via Flavia, which leads to via Collina. Family *pensione,* safer than many places around Termini. Singles L40,000. Doubles L55,000, with shower L65,000. Triples L75,000.

Hotel Castelfidardo, via Castelfidardo, 31 (tel. 474 28 94 or 494 13 78; fax 446 95 96). New rooms, clean showers, grey graph-paper walls. Singles L40,000, with bath L50,000. Doubles L55,000, with bath L70,000. Visa, MC, AmEx.

Pensione Alessandro, via Vicenza, 42 (tel. 446 19 58). Near the corner with via Palestro. Buzz #6. Occasionally co-ed, average dorms, but the price and owner are great. Check in 8am-midnight. No curfew; ask for a key. L20,000/person.

Pensione Piave, via Piave, 14 (tel. 474 34 47; fax 487 33 60). Off via XX Settembre. Worth the extra *lire:* all rooms have private bath and phone. English spoken. Check-out at 10am but luggage can be left all day. Singles L35,000-50,000. Doubles L50,000-70,000. Triples L75,000-90,000. Quads L85,000-115,000.

Pensione Lachea, via San Martino della Battaglia, 11 (tel. 495 72 56), off p. dell'Indipendenza. Warm-hearted owner is *Let's Go*'s biggest fan. Newly renovated. Doubles L48,000-52,000. Triples L65,000-70,000. Try to bargain.

Pensione Reatina, downstairs from Pensione Lachea. (tel. 445 42 79; fax 44 41 27). Interior decorating ain't its forte, but the cellar price includes breakfast. Singles L35,000-39,000. Doubles L50,000-60,000. Triples L75,000. MC, Visa.

Pensione Monaco, via Flavia, 84 (tel. 474 43 35 or 481 56 49), near Tizi. Strict manager, but spanking clean. Curfew midnight. One shower/day included, extras L2500. Singles L35,000. Doubles L50,000. Triples and quads L23,000/person.

Pensione Restivo, via Palestro, 55 (tel. 446 21 72). *La donna simpatica* who runs the place takes great pride in the blinding whiteness of her sheets. Laundry service. Singles L40,000. Doubles L60,000. Triples L75,000. MC.

Hotel Cervia, via Palestro, 55 (tel. 49 10 57 fax 49 10 56). 21 rooms and 41 beds. A bit musty, but the helpful management speaks English. Curfew 1:30am. Singles L35,000-40,000. Doubles L50,000, with bath L75,000.

South of Termini

The closer you get to p. Vittorio Emanuele, the seedier the area becomes at night. Use extra caution if you're a woman traveling alone. In general, the farther one gets from the station, the better the neighborhood becomes.

Pensione di Rienzo, via Principe Amadeo, 79A (tel. 446 71 31). Tranquil; fabulous price. Lovely rooms, most with balcony overlooking courtyard. English spoken. Singles L25,000-40,000. Doubles L50,000-80,000. Triples with bath L104,000.

Hotel San Paolo, via Panisperna, 95 (tel. 474 52 13), at via Caprareccia. Dirtcheap; swell proprietor is cross between Grizzly Adams and Mickey Rourke in *Barfly.* Singles L30,000. Doubles L45,000, with bath L50,000.

Pensione Sandy, via Cavour, 136 (tel. 488 45 85). No sign; look for the Hotel Valle next door and climb to the 4th floor. 25 hostel-style beds at L20,000/person. Winter L15,000 (no heat but lots of blankets). Showers included. Small lockers.

Hotel Orlanda, via Principe Amadeo, 76 (tel. 488 06 37), at via Gioberti. Sparse but clean. Official curfew midnight, but arrangements can be made. Singles L35,000. Doubles L50,000, with bath L65,000. Triples L67,000. Quads L85,000.

Hotel Ferraro, via Cavour, 266 (tel. 474 37 55), just past via degli Annabaldi. Charming place, a stone's throw from the Colosseum. Singles L40,000-51,000. Doubles L51,000-65,500. Triples with bath L88,400. Quads with bath L111,000.

Hotel Scott House and **Hotel Eliana,** via Gioberti, 30 (tel. 446 53 92 or 446 53 79; fax 446 49 86). Inexpensive and undergoing renovation: breakfast room and roof patio coming in. Special *Let's Go* prices. Singles with bath L30,000. Doubles with bath L50,000. Triples with bath L75,000. TV and phone in each room.

Pensione Pezzotti and **Hotel Cantilia,** via Principe Amadeo, 79D (tel. 446 69 42 or 446 68 75; fax 446 69 04). New, pleasing, and pastel. **Pezzotti:** Rooms with bath: singles L40,000, doubles L55,000, triples L71,000. **Cantilia:** Singles L45,000, with bath L60,000. Doubles L60,000, with bath L80,000. Prices drop in the off-season. Phones, balconies, and TVs. Major credit cards accepted.

Around piazza Navona and Campo Dei Fiori

Il Centro Storico (The Historic Center) is an ideal, if expensive, base. Most major sights are within walking distance; expect to pay about 10-15% more to finance the charm, and make reservations, especially in the summer.

Albergo Della Lunetta, p. del Paradiso, 68 (tel. 686 10 80; fax 689 20 28), near the Church of Sant'Andrea della Valle. Take via Chiavari off corso Vittorio, then the first right. Tidy rooms with phones and desks; garden and TV lounge. Singles L35,000-65,000. Doubles L75,000-100,000. Triples L100,000-135,000.

Pensione Mimosa, via Santa Chiara, 61 (tel. 68 80 17 53), off p. di Minerva behind the Pantheon. Fantastic location, plus *kitsch*. Curfew 1am. Singles L45,000. Doubles L70,000. Triples L105,000. Quads L130,000. Breakfast L5000/person.

Albergo Pomezia, via dei Chiavari, 12 (tel. 686 13 71). Renovated rooms on the 1st floor. Phones; winter heat; anally clean bathrooms on 2nd and 3rd floors. Curfew Sun.-Fri. 1:30am. Singles L50,000-85,000. Doubles L70,000-110,000. Triples L90,000-148,000. Prices drop in winter, except around Christmas.

Hotel Piccolo, via dei Chiavari, 32 (tel. 689 23 30 or 68 80 25 60), off corso Vittorio Emanuele II, behind Sant'Andrea della Valle. Clean, quiet, and comfortable. Curfew 1:30am. Singles L58,000-70,000. Doubles L85,000-120,000. Triples L95,000-120,000. Reservations recommended in summer. Visa, MC.

Pensione Navona, via dei Sediari, 8 (tel. 686 42 03). Take via de'Canestrari off p. Navona, cross over corso del Rinascimento, and continue straight. Helpful Italo-Australian family runs a tight ship in this 16th-century Borromini building, a *pensione* for over 150 years. Call *way* in advance; US$100 deposit. Checkout 11am. Singles with bath and breakfast L65,000. Doubles L90,000, with bath and breakfast L95,000. Each extra person L43,000.

Pensione Primavera, p. San Pantaleo, 3 (tel. 68 80 31 09), off corso V. Emanuele. Renovated rooms with a view of Palazzo Braschi. Doubles L80,000-90,000. Triples L120,000. Breakfast included. Prices drop 15% in winter.

Albergo Del Sole, via del Biscione, 76 (tel. 654 08 73). Off p. Campo dei Fiori. Supposedly the oldest *pensione* in Rome. Check-out noon. Singles L70,000-85,000. Doubles L90,000-120,000. Triples with bath L160,000.

Albergo Abruzzi, p. della Rotonda, 69 (tel. 68 80 17 53). Smack dab in front of the Pantheon. Singles L48,000-62,000. Doubles L60,000-82,000. Reservations recommended in summer.

Near The Spanish Steps

This is the Italian equivalent of Paris's *Rive Gauche;* inexpensive rooms are scarce.

ACCOMMODATIONS AND CAMPING

Residenza Brotsky, via del Corso, 509 (tel. 361 23 39 or 323 66 41). Antique furniture, roof terrace, and TV lounge. Singles L55,000-60,000. Doubles L75,000-90,000. Triples with bath L90,000-105,000. Reservations recommended.

Pensione Parlamento, via delle Convertite, 5 (tel. 679 20 82, for reservations 684 16 97 or 69 94 16 97), behind *La Rinascente* off via del Corso. Gorgeous terrace and wonderful views. English spoken. Singles L61,000-85,000. Doubles L80,000-105,000. Each extra person L25,000. Reservations recommended.

Pensione Fiorella, via del Babuino, 196 (tel. 361 05 97), off p. di Spagna near p. del Popolo. Spruce set-up and a charming management. Curfew 1am. English spoken. Singles L40,000. Doubles L70,000. Breakfast included. No reservations.

Across The River: Ottaviano

The *pensioni* on the other side of the Tiber aren't the cheapest in Rome, but they tend to be quiet, clean, and friendly. Those in Ottaviano, near the Vatican, are attractive for their proximity to popular sights and a safer, residential area.

Hotel Pensione Alimandi, via Tunisi, 8 (tel. 39 72 39 48, 39 72 63 00, or 39 72 39 41; fax 39 72 39 43). Take the steps off viale Vaticano down to via Sebastiano Veniero. Literally meters from the Vatican Museum. Gorgeous. Singles L54,000-70,000. Doubles L75,000-120,000. Triples with bath L120,000. L10,000/extra bed. Under 12 free. Credit cards accepted.

Hotel Pensione Joli, via Cola di Rienzo, 243, 6th floor (tel. 324 18 54, fax 324 18 93). At via Tibullo. Sleek and snazzy; the joint sparkles. Singles L55,000-70,000. Doubles with bath L70,000. Triples with bath L128,000.

Hotel Florida, via Cola di Rienzo, 243 (tel. 324 18 72; fax 324 18 57). On the 4th floor, below Joli. Trim, sparse, modern rooms with phones. Singles L57,000-73,000. Doubles L77,000-99,000. Triples with bath L135,000.

Pensione Ottaviano, via Ottaviano, 6 (tel. 370 05 33, 39 73 72 53 or 39 73 81 38), off p. del Risorgimento north of p. San Pietro. Inches from St. Peter's; fine but spare home to international backpackers. English spoken. Dorm beds L20,000.

Across the River: Trastevere

Hedonists and bohemians might prefer to stay in **Trastevere,** scene of much nighttime revelry and home to many young expatriates.

Pensione Manara, via Luciano Manara, 25 (tel. 581 47 13). Take a right off viale di Trastevere onto via delle Fratte di Trastevere to via Luciano Manaro. Homey establishment overlooking colorful p. San Cosimato. Truly a perfect location. English spoken. Doubles L58,000. Triples L75,000. Quads L95,000. Showers L3000 each.

Pensione Esty, viale Trastevere, 108 (tel. 588 12 01), about 1km down viale di Trastevere from the Ponte Garibaldi. Spotless rooms in an Orwellian building removed from the rowdy heart of Trastevere. English spoken. Singles L40,000. Doubles 58,000. Triples L78,000. Quad L100,000. Reserve in advance.

Camping

You probably won't catch the malaria that killed Daisy Miller, but there are still plenty of mosquitoes in campgrounds near the city. In August, arrive early—well before 11am—or you may find yourself without a spot.

Seven Hills, via Cassia, 1216 (tel. 371 08 26), 8km north of Rome. Take bus #910 from Termini to piazza Mancini and transfer to #201; get off on via Cassia and walk 1½km down via Italo Piccagli. A 60s camping commune in the hills. Volleyball, pool, disco (9:30pm-1am). Reasonably priced bar, market, and pizzeria. Daily shuttle bus to the city center at 9:30am, returning at 1:30 and 5:30pm (L4000). L9200/person, L4900/tent. Open March 15-Oct. 30.

Flaminio, via Flaminia Nuova, 821 (tel. 333 26 04), about 7km outside Rome. Take bus #910 from Termini to piazza Mancini, then transfer to bus #200. Get off on via Flaminia Nuova when you see the "Philips" building on your right. Shady grass strewn with closely knit enclaves of tents, campers, and bungalows. 24-hr. pool, market, restaurant, bar, and disco. Laundry. L9000/person, L4500/tent, bungalows L37,000 (less/person with more people). Open March-Oct.

FOOD

Meals in Rome are prolonged affairs (breakfast—a quick gulp of caffeine—is the exception). Stay away from the area near the train station—most ostensibly "bargain" restaurants (offering dirt-cheap fixed-price menus) are actually second-rate tourist snares serving nothing resembling Italian cuisine. Explore the winding streets around **piazza Navona,** particularly around **via del Governo Vecchio,** and **Campo dei Fiori.** Some of the best *pizzerie* known to man call **Trastevere** home. The university district of **San Lorenzo** and the traditional neighborhood of **Testaccio,** on the eastern banks of the Tiber, are the last untouristed restaurant districts in Rome. Romans generally eat dinner around 9pm. For daytime snacks, try any of the numerous places that sell *pizza rustica* (the cruder square pizza, sold by weight) or *panini* (bulging sandwiches). Try p. Vittorio, near the station, or Campo dei Fiori. *Gelato* rarely disappoints at any place that has a *produzione propria* (homemade) sign, but two Roman legends prevail: **Giolitti,** via degli Uffici del Vicario, 40, northeast of the Pantheon (open Tues.-Sun. 7am-2am), and **Fassi Palazzo del Freddo,** via Principe Eugenio, 65/67, off p. Vittorio Emmanuele. (Open Tues.-Fri. 3pm-midnight, Sat.-Sun. 10am-2pm.) Also don't miss out on the numerous *caffè* supplying Rome with its foremost fuel—coffee. **Tazza D'Oro,** off piazza della Rotunda, makes some of the best take-out brew around. (Open Mon.-Sat. 6:45am-8:15pm.) The environs of Trastevere and piazza Navona are ripe with mellow, sit-down cafés. Campo dei Fiori hosts the liveliest food **market;** there's an indoor market off via Cola di Rienzo (at p. dell'Unità), near the Vatican, and outdoor ones on via Montebello, near Termini, and at p. di S. Cosimato, in Trastevere. (Markets open Mon.-Sat. 6am-2pm, closed Thurs. afternoons.) Supermarket **STANDA** offers a huge selection of foodstuffs; there's one on viale Trastevere, and one on via Cola di Rienzo, several blocks down from the Ottaviano Metro stop and several blocks up from piazza del Popolo.

Palladini, via del Governo Vecchio, 29. A *salumiere* (deli) with no sign or place to sit for the lunch crowd eating seconds-old *panini.* Fillings of choice include *prosciutto e fiche* (smoked ham and figs) and *bresaola e rughetta* (smoked meat with arugula). Sandwiches L3500. Open Sept.-July Mon.-Sat. 8am-2pm and 5-8pm.

Il Giardinetto, via del Governo Vecchio, 125 (tel. 686 86 93). Tunisian-run oasis with leaf-lined ceiling. Try the *gnochetti* (L7000) and house wine (L8000/liter). Portions generous enough to skip the *secondi* (L12,000-16,000). Open Tues.-Sun. 12:30-3pm and 7:30pm-midnight. Reservations and credit cards accepted.

Pizzeria Baffetto, via del Governo Vecchio, 114 (tel. 686 16 17), on the corner of via Sora. A Roman household name. Once a meeting place for 60s radicals; now, stand in line with Romans of all political persuasions for *pizza gigante.* Pizzas L5000-9000. *Vino* L6000. Cover L1000. Open Mon.-Sat. 6:30pm-1am.

L'Insalata Ricca, Largo di Chiavari, 85 (tel. 654 36 56), off corso Vittorio Emanuele near p. Sant'Andrea della Valle. Funky modern art, innovative dishes, and traditional *trattoria* food. Title dish *insalata ricca* L6500, smaller portion L5500. Cover L2000. Open Thurs.-Tues. 12:30-3pm and 7-11pm.

Filetti di Baccalà, Largo dei Librari, 88 (tel. 686 40 18). Take via dei Giubbonari off p. Campo dei Fiori. Self-service favorite; unforgettable *filetto di baccalà* (deep fried cod, L4000). Cover L1500. Open Sept.-July Mon.-Sat. 5:30-10:30pm.

Pizzeria Vergillo, Campo dei Fiori, 10 (tel. 68 80 27 46). Delicious pizzas (L7000-12,000) and rich pasta dishes (*fettucine al salmone,* L12,000). Cover L2500. Open Thurs.-Tues. noon-3pm and 7pm-midnight. Major credit cards accepted.

Er Buco, via del Lavatore, 91 (tel. 678 11 54), steps from p. di Trevi. Possibly the oldest pizza oven in the city. The amicable owner, a young soccer-playing Stanford graduate, is the 6th generation to take over the farm. Pizzas L6000-10,000. Cover L2000. Open Mon.-Sat. noon-4pm and 6:30-11:30pm.

La Cappricciosa, Largo dei Lombardi, 8 (tel. 687 84 80), off via del Corso. Abstract New Age paintings, *primi* (L6000-8000), pizza (from L7000) and *dolci* (L5000). Cover L2000. Open Wed.-Mon. 12:30-3pm and 7pm-1am.

Al Piccolo Arancio, Vicolo Scanderberg, 112 (tel. 678 61 39), near the Trevi Fountain in an alley off via del Lavatore, which runs off p. di Trevi. Sign says "Osteria." Unusual and delicious pastas and appetizers. Tues. and Thurs. homemade *gnocchi al salmone* (L7000) or *raviole di pesce* (L8000). Cover L2500. Arrive early. Open Sept.-July Tues.-Sun. 12:30-3pm and 7-11:30pm. Credit cards accepted.

Taverna dei Quaranta, via Claudia, 24 (tel. 700 05 50), 2 blocks up from the piazza del Colosseo. The best food you can afford in the shade of the amphitheater. *Pennette con melanzana* (eggplant) L7500. Wine L3000/500mL. Cover L2500. Open daily noon-3pm and 8pm-1am. AmEx.

Pizzeria Imperiale, Largo C. Ricci, 37, at the start of via Cavour opposite the Forum entrance. Recover from ruins under shady umbrellas. *Peccato del frate* pizza (red peppers, zucchini, sausage, olives, and artichokes) L9500. Pasta L8000-12,000. Cover L1500. Open Mon.-Sat. noon-4pm and 7:30pm-midnight.

Taverno del Moro, via del Moro, 43 (tel. 580 91 65), off via Lungaretta in Trastevere. Beautiful *antipasto* spread L7000. *Pizza con verdura* L12,000. Cheesecake L4000. Cover L2000. Open Tues.-Sun. 7-11pm. Credit cards accepted.

Mario's, via del Moro, 53 (tel. 580 38 09). Take via della Lungaretta off viale Trastevere, and turn right after the church. Consistently phenomenal pasta a mere L4500-6500. *Menù turistico* L16,000. Wine L4400. Cover L1000. Open Sept. to mid-Aug. Mon.-Sat. noon-3pm and 7-11pm. Major credit cards accepted.

Pizzeria Ivo, via di San Francesca a Ripa, 158 (tel. 581 70 82). Take via delle Fratte di Trastevere off viale Trastevere. Mouth-watering pizza is worth the long wait and chaotic atmosphere. Pizza L9500-13,000. Delicious wine, with the restaurant's own label, L9000. Cover L1500. Open Sept.-July Wed.-Mon. 6pm-1am.

Il Tulipano Nero, via Roma Libera, 15 (tel. 581 83 09), in p. San Cosimato. A friendly, rowdy pizzeria—dine outdoors in summer. *Pizza tonno, mais, e rughetta* (with tuna, corn, and arugula, L7000 tastes far better than it sounds. Wine L9000/liter. Cover L1500. Open Thurs.-Tues. 6:30pm-1am.

Armando, via degli Ombrellari, 41 (tel. 686 16 02). North of via di Conciliazione. Delicious lasagne is the house specialty at L8000; the *vino bianco* is a delight at L6000/liter. Cover L2500. Open Thurs.-Tues. 12:30-3pm and 7:30-11pm.

Hostaria dei Bastioni, via Leone IV, 29 (tel. 39 72 30 34), off p. del Risorgimento near the Vatican Museums. Miraculous subterranean restaurant rightly boasts of seafood specialties. Fresh fish L12,000-15,000. Wine L6000/liter. Noisy outdoor lunch. Cover L2000. Service 10%. Open Mon.-Sat. noon-3pm and 7pm-1:30am.

Trattoria da Bucantino, via Luca della Robbia, 84/86. Take via Vanvitelli off via Marmorata, then the 1st left. A Testaccio tavern with fabulous *antipasti.* Indigenous pasta delights like *bucatini all'amatriciana* (L8000). Wine L5000/liter. Cover L2800. Open Aug. 27-July 21 Tues.-Sun. noon-3pm and 7:30-11pm.

Trattoria Turiddo, via Galvani, 64 (tel. 575 04 47), in the Mattatoio district of Testaccio (take bus #27 from Termini or the Colosseum). Locals come here to taste the food they grew up on, like *rigatoni con pagliata* (with tomato and lamb intestine, L8000). Vegetarians strongly cautioned. Cover L2000. Open mid-Sept. to mid-Aug. Mon.-Tues. and Thurs.-Sat. 1-2:30pm and 7-10:30pm, Sun. 1-2:30pm.

Il Pulcino Ballerino, via degli Equi, 66/68 (tel. 49 03 01), off via Tiburtina. Artsy atmosphere with cuisine to match. *Tagliolini del pulcino* (pasta in a lemon cream sauce, L9000). Cover L1500. Open Tues.-Sun. 8pm-midnight. Closed 1st ½ of Aug.

Pizzeria L'Economica, via Tiburtina, 46 (tel. 445 66 69). The name says it all. Some of the most vicious pizza around (L4500-6000). *Antipasto* an incredible L5000. Wine L4000. Open Sept.-July Mon.-Sat. 6:30-11pm.

Il Ristorante Tudini, via Filippo Turati, 5 (tel. 45 75 86), one block from Termini on corner with via Gioberti. Modish marble tables and greenery. *Veal scalloppine* L10,000. Cover L2000. Service 15%. Open Mon.-Sat. 12:30-11:30pm.

La Cantinola da Livio, via Calabria, 26 (tel. 482 05 19 or 474 39 62). Take via Piave off via XX Settembre, then 4th left onto via Calabria. Cozy establishment specializing in *frutti di mare*—live lobsters wait tensely in tanks by the door. *Spaghetti alla Cantinola* L9000. Open Mon.-Sat. 12:30-3pm and 7:30-11:30pm.

SIGHTS

Rome wasn't built in a day, and it's not likely that you'll see much of it in 24 hours either. The city practically implodes with monuments. No other city can lay claim to so many masterpieces of architecture from so many different eras of history—not to mention the treasures of painting and sculpture inside. A hot and dusty place in summer (and crowded and chaotic year-round), Rome is likely to sap the energy of even the most hardened sightseer. Pace yourself, make time for a stop in a bar or *caffè*, and carry a bottle of water (refillable at any of Rome's corner water-spouts; you'll see Romans bending to drink from the streams). With the exception of the Vatican, all museums are closed Mondays. When visiting churches, dress modestly—those in shorts, short skirts, sleeveless dresses, or sleeveless shirts will not be welcome and in some cases (like St. Peter's) will not be admitted.

Vatican City Occupying 108½ acres entirely within Italy's capital, the **Vatican City** is the last territorial toehold of a Catholic church that was once a wheeling and dealing power throughout Europe. Under the Lateran Treaty of 1929, the pope remains supreme monarch of this tiny theocracy, exercising all legislative, judicial, and executive powers over the 300 souls who hold Vatican citizenship; by the same agreement, the church stays out of national and municipal politics. The state maintains an army of Swiss Guards—all descended from 16th-century mercenaries hired by Pope Julius II. Michelangelo designed their resplendent costumes. (Take Metro A to "Ottaviano"—walk south on via Ottaviano toward the colonnade—or buses #64 and 492 from Termini, #62 from p. Barberini, or #19 from San Lorenzo.)

A 10-minute walk around the Vatican City walls, or the bus from the piazza, brings you to the **Vatican Museums.** Of the 4 color-coded tours, Tour A hits only the barest essentials, while tour D hits absolutely everything. The most famous works of classical sculpture cluster in the **Pio-Clementine Museum;** to conciliate the Council of Trent in 1550, naughty bits left by the less inhibited ancients were removed and covered with fig leaves. In the **Belvedere Court** stand the *Apollo Belvedere* and the evocative *Laocoön*, which was carved from a single piece of marble; these two statuaries provided the chief inspiration for much of the Renaissance sculpture throughout Rome and Italy. The remarkable **Etruscan Museum,** a floor above, displays the contents of the splendid **Regolini-Galassi Tomb,** found intact and full of such treasure as an extraordinary bronze chariot and bed.

All routes in the museum lead through the breathtakingly frescoed **Raphael Stanze** (Raphael rooms). The **Stanza della Segnatura** contains the *School of Athens*, in which Raphael painted the features of his contemporaries onto those of great philosophers. The climax of the tour is the **Sistine Chapel.** In the *Creation of Adam*, 8 Old Testament scenes climax in the electric touch of God's and Adam's fingers. Art historians worldwide debate the wisdom of the recent gradual cleaning of the paintings in the Chapel; opponents of restoration argue that scraping off layers of grime as well as paint from previous patch-up jobs has also scraped off an important second layer that Michelangelo would have added to the original fresco for shadowy details. Refrain from taking flash photos, even if you see others doing it; it's detrimental to the fresco and you can buy much better shots (cheaper than using your own film) on professional postcards. Get there early to avoid the mobs.

Once out of the Sistine Chapel, linger at the **Pinacoteca;** Raphael's *Transfiguration* alone is worth the stop. (Museums and Sistine Chapel open Mon.-Sat. 8:45am-1:45pm; Easter and July-Sept. Mon.-Fri. 8:45am-4pm, Sat. 8:45am-1:45pm. Last entry 45min. before closing. Closed on major religious holidays. Last Sun. of every month open 8:45am-1pm, free. Otherwise L12,000, L8000 with ISIC.)

Basilica di San Pietro and Castel Sant'Angelo Approach the **Basilica di San Pietro** (St. Peter's Basilica), the largest Roman Catholic cathedral in the world, through Bernini's peerless Baroque colonnades. Begun by Bramante on the site of St. Peter's tomb, the basilica's design changed hands from da Sangallo to

Michelangelo, Raphael, and finally Maderno, who added the present façade. Michelangelo's sorrowful *Pietà* now sits in grace on the ground level behind bullet-proof glass (a maniac attacked the sculpture with an ax in 1978). Downstairs, the **Vatican Grottoes** harbor the tombs of innumerable popes and saints. The cavernous **dome** of St. Peter's, for centuries the world's largest, was Michelangelo's final opus. To enjoy a matchless view of Rome, make the climb to the top. You *must* wear long pants and clothing that covers your shoulders when visiting St. Peter's. (Open daily 8am-7pm. Dome closes 1hr. earlier. To dome on foot L5000, by elevator L6000.) **Mass** is conducted several times per day, with a particularly beautiful vespers service Sunday at 5pm.

When in town, the Pope grants **public audiences** in p. San Pietro on Wednesdays (11am; Sept.-May 10am). Get free tickets (Mon.-Tues. 9am-1pm) at St. Peter's Gate (bronze doors to right of Basilica), or apply in writing to the **Prefetture della Casa Pontificia,** 00120 Città del Vaticano.

A short walk down via d. Conciliazone from St. Peter's stands the massive **Castel Sant'Angelo.** Built by the Emperor Hadrian (117-138 AD) as a mausoleum for himself and his family, the edifice has served the popes of Rome as a convenient and forbidding fortress, prison, and palace. It now contains a museum of arms and artillery, but the papal apartments and the incomparable views of Rome seen from them are the real reasons to visit. (Open Tues.-Sun. 9am-2pm; Sun. 9am-1pm, last entry at noon; Mon. 2-7pm; last entry one hour before closing; L8000.) The marble **Ponte Sant'Angelo,** lined with Bernini's angels, leads back across the river, and is the starting point for the traditional pilgrimage route from St. Peter's to the Basilica of San Giovanni in Laterano on the other side of Rome.

Piazza del Popolo to Piazza Quirinale

The northern entrance to the city, **piazza del Popolo** (the people's square) is a favorite arena for communal antics; after a victory by one of the city's soccer teams the *piazza* resounds with music and merriment. Tucked away on the north side of the *piazza* near the Porta del Popolo, the small **Church of Santa Maria del Popolo** contains 2 canvases by Caravaggio: the *Conversion of St. Paul* and the *Crucifixion of St. Peter.* (Open Mon.-Sat. 7am-noon and 4-7pm, Sun. 8am-1:30pm and 4:30-7:30pm.)

Designed by an Italian, paid for by the French, occupied by the British, and now haunted by Americans, the **Spanish Steps** (Metro: "Spagna") have a truly international atmosphere. Ideal for people-watching, the Spanish Steps and **piazza di Spagna** take their names from the Spanish Embassy, located since 1647 in the hourglass-shaped *piazza.* Today you're more likely to see con artists than true artists, but in its day the *piazza* attracted Stendhal, Balzac, Wagner, and Liszt; Henry James and the Brownings lived on via Bocca di Leone, a small sidestreet in the area. Above via Frattina, 50, a plaque announces James Joyce's former residence. Another small plaque on the side of p. di Spagna, 26, marks the place where Keats died in 1821. The 2nd floor of the house now houses the charming **Keats-Shelley Memorial Museum,** full of curious relics from the poets' lives. (Open Mon.-Fri. 9am-1pm and 3-6pm; L5000.) Despite its simple design (by Carlo Maderno), the rosy façade of the **Church of Santa Trinità dei Monti** provides a worthy climax to the stairs' grand curves, not to mention a sweeping view over the city. East along via Sabina rises the newly restored **Fontana di Trevi,** at its aesthetic best at night. Tradition says travelers who throw a coin into it will return to Rome; save your *lire,* since coins rust the fountain.

Northwest of the fountain, **piazza Barberini** showcases the Bernini **Fontane delle Api** (Bee Fountain, for the "use of the public and their animals"). The **Palazzo Barberini's Galleria Nazionale d'Arte Antica** in via Quattro Fontane, near the Barberini Fountain, houses a superb collection of paintings from the 13th to 18th centuries. (Open Tues.-Sun. 9am-7pm. After 2pm, visitors only on 1st floor. L6000.)

Piazza del Quirinale, at the end of via del Quirinale, running from via XX Settembre, occupies the summit of the tallest of Rome's 7 hills. In the middle of the piazza, the heroic **statues of Castor and Pollux** (mythical warrior twins embraced by ancient Romans as their protectors) flank yet another of Rome's many obelisks. The **Palazzo del Quirinale** is the official residence of president of the Italian Republic. via del Quirinale leaves the piazza to the north, passing the modest façade of Bernini's **Sant'Andrea al Quirinale,** whose oval interior departs from traditional church plans (the nave is wider than it is long). (Open Wed.-Mon. 8am-noon and 4-7pm.) Further down the street is the undulating façade of Borromini's **Church of San Carlo alle Quattro Fontane** (a.k.a. **San Carlino**). (Open Mon.-Fri. 9am-12:30pm and 4-6pm, Sat. 9am-12:30pm. If interior is closed, ring at the convent next door.)

Closer to Termini at p. della Repubblica, the **Church of Santa Maria degli Angeli** presides over the ruins of the ancient Baths of Diocletian.

Via del Corso to Piazza Navona and Beyond

The glorified traffic circle of **piazza Venezia** is presided over by the bombastic white **Vittorio Emanuele Monument** that King Victor Emanuele II erected to himself. In piazza dei Collegio Romano, the stalwart **Palazzo Doria Pamphili** hides the Rococo frivolity of the **Galleria Doria Pamphili.** (Open Tues. and Fri.-Sun. 10am-1pm. L6000, L3000 more for a tour of the private apartments.)

The majestic **Pantheon,** between via del Corso and piazza Navona, has presided over its busy *piazza* for nearly 2000 years, its marble columns and pediment, bronze doors, and soaring domed interior (save superficial decorative changes) all unchanged from the day it was erected by Hadrian. (Open Mon.-Sat. 9am-4pm, Sun. 9am-1pm; Oct.-June Mon.-Sat. 9am-2pm, Sun. 9am-1pm. Free.) Around the left side of the Pantheon another obelisk marks the center of tiny **piazza Minerva,** supported by Bernini's winsome elephant statue. Behind, the unassuming façade of the **Church of Santa Maria Sopra Minerva** hides some of Renaissance Rome's artistic masterpieces, including the **Carafa Chapel,** with a brilliant fresco cycle by Filippino Lippi (closed for restoration in 1993). Michelangelo's great *Christ Bearing the Cross* stands upright. (Open daily 7am-noon and 4-7pm. Under restoration.)

A few blocks west, across corso Rinascimento, **piazza Navona** is the finest Baroque space in Rome. Modern times have maintained the true-to-Rome uproar of the ancient chariot track and 15th-century festival and marketplace, home to 3 Bernini fountains, most notably the **Fountain of the Four Rivers.** This centerpiece represents the Nile, Ganges, Danube, and Río de la Plata (all identifiable by representative flora and fauna). One story holds that Bernini designed the Nile and Plata statues to shield their eyes, so as to express derision for the **Church of Sant'Agnese** opposite, which was designed by Bernini's great rival Borromini. The legend says that Borromini then added the statue of St. Agnes looking haughtily out past the *piazza,* not deigning to drop her gaze to Bernini's work. Off the northeastern corner of the *piazza* sits the 15th-century **Church of Sant'Agostino,** which shelters a Raphael fresco and Caravaggio's *Madonna of Loreto.* (Open daily 4:30-8pm.)

Corso Vittorio Emanuele II, Campo Dei Fiori, and Via Giulia

The baroque **Gesù,** on corso Vittorio Emanuele, is the parent church of the Jesuit order. (Open daily 6am-12:30pm and 4-7:15pm.) Continuing up the corso, find the recently restored **Church of Sant'Andrea della Valle,** which was begun in 1591 by Grimaldi and completed in 1665 by Baroque bigwig Carlo Maderno. (Open Mon.-Sat. 7:30am-noon and 4:30-9:30pm, Sun. 7:30am-12:45pm and 4:30-7:45pm.)

Across corso Vittorio Emanuele II from piazza Navona (down via della Cancelleria), **campo dei Fiori** is a flower-filled clearing in the middle of a dense medieval quarter. During papal rule, the area was the site of countless executions; now the only carcasses that litter the *piazza* are those of the fish in the colorful **market** that springs up every day but Sunday from 7am to 2pm. Behind the elaborate Baroque façade of the **Palazzo Spada,** in piazza della Quercia, you'll find the jewel-like picture collection of the **Galleria Spada.** (Open Tues.-Sat. 9am-7pm, Sun. 9am-1pm; in winter Tues.-Sat. 9am-2pm, Sun. 9am-1pm; L4000.) Head toward the river to find the harmonious **piazza Farnese** and wander down the elegant Renaissance **via Giulia,** the first direct route to the Vatican.

The Ancient City Across the River Tiber from the Vatican lie the few tangible remnants of ancient Rome. The physical center, the original capitol, and the most sacred part of the ancient city, the **Campidoglio** (Capitoline Hill) still serves as the seat of the city's government and is crowned by a spectacular piazza of Michelangelo's design. From the back of piazza del Campidoglio, behind Rome's **City Hall** (the central building), there's a great daytime view of the Forum. The **Musei Capitolini,** in the twin *palazzi* on either side of the piazza, display one of the largest collections of ancient sculpture in the world, including the famous *Capitoline Wolf,* an Etruscan statue which has symbolized Rome since antiquity (Antonio Pollaiulo added the cherubic figures of Romulus and Remus in 1509). You may find the *pinacoteca*'s lackluster assortment of 16th-century Italian paintings a bit disappointing. (Museums open Tues.-Sun. 9am-1:30pm; in winter, also Tues. and Sat. 5-8pm; in summer, also Tues. 5-8pm and Sat. 8-11pm. Last entry ½hr. before closing. L10,000; L5000 with student ID; free last Sun. of the month.)

Enter the Roman **Forum** (Metro: "Colosseo" or bus #27), once the center of the Empire, from via dei Fori Imperiali, behind the white neoclassical horror of the **Victor Emanuel Monument** (popularly known as the wedding cake or the typewriter). Once a marshy valley prone to flooding, the area which is now the Forum evolved first into an Etruscan market and later into Rome's chief square, and was at its busiest in the 2nd century, after the conquest of ancient Greece. Dwindling at one point to a cow pasture, the Forum endured its first excavations in 1803, and they continue today; unfortunately, archaeologists have rendered the site extremely confusing. To really understand the chaotic collage of stone and brick, invest in a map (L4000). Brace yourself for the traditional headaches of visiting the Forum: slow tour groups, confusing sites, heat, and dust. Go early and take a bottle of water. (Forum, Palatine, and Antiquarium open Mon. and Wed.-Sat. 9am-6pm, Sun. and Tues. 9am-1pm; in winter Mon. and Wed.-Sat. 9am-3pm, Sun. and Tues. 9am-1pm. L10,000.)

The Forum houses dozens of significant monuments. The Senate met at the **Curia;** male citizens voted at the **Comitum Well,** or assembly place, in front of the Curia, until Julius Caesar moved the gathering point to the *campus martius,* today's Campo dei Fiori. Visit the **Tomb of Romulus,** one of Rome's legendary founders, the **Imperial Rostra,** from which politicians orated, and the **Arch of Titus,** which features the famous frieze of Roman legionnaires making off with the great Menorah from the Temple of Jerusalem. Bordering the south side of the Forum is Julius Caesar's **Basilica Giulia** (54 BC), from whose halls justice was administered. Look for inscribed grids and circles in the steps where Romans, anxiously awaiting verdicts, distracted themselves with an ancient form of tic-tac-toe. The **Column of Phocas** in front of the basilica honors the man who seized the throne of Byzantium and awarded the Pantheon to Pope Boniface IV. At the east end of the Basilica Giulia, the **Temple of Castor and Pollux** celebrates the Roman rebellion against their Etruscan king in 510. According to legend, the twin gods descended and routed the Etruscan army at the Battle of Lake Regilles in 499 BC. At the far end of the Forum, the **Palatine Hill** houses a complex of imperial palaces surrounded by parks and gardens. The most impressive structure here is the **Palace of Domitian,** divided into the Domus Flavia (official palace), the Domus Augustana (private residence), and the Stadium. At the southern base of the Palatine is the **Circus Maximus;** you can still see the start and finish lines for the chariot races once held here.

Fori Imperiali and the Colosseum The **Fori Imperiali** sprawl across the street from the old Forum Romanum, a vast conglomeration of temples, basilicas, and public squares constructed by the emperors of the first and 2nd centuries AD. In the 1930s, Mussolini, with imperial aspirations of his own, cleared the area of medieval constructions and built the via dei Fori Imperiali to pass over the newly excavated remains; the broad, barren thoroughfare cuts across the old foundations at an awkward angle. The largest and most impressive of the lot is the **Forum of Trajan** (107-113 AD), including the **Trajan Column;** it is the greatest specimen of Roman relief sculpture ever carved, narrating the Emperor's victorious campaigns against the Dacians, denizens of present-day Romania. **Trajan's Market,** a semi-circular ancient shopping mall that housed 150 *tabernae* (single-room stores), holds frequent art exhibits. (Open Tues.-Sat. 9am-1:30pm and 4-7pm, Sun. 9am-1pm, winter Tues.-Sat. 9am-1:30pm, Sun. 9am-1pm. L3750. EC citizens under 18 and over 60 free. Entrance at via IV Novembre, 94.) The **Forums of Caesar** and **Nerva** are best appreciated from street level, as is the **Forum of Augustus,** dedicated by the Emperor in 2 BC in honor of Mars Ultor (Mars the Avenger). (All *fora* except Trajan's Markets closed for renovation in 1993.)

Dominating the heart of ancient Rome, the **Colosseum** (Metro: "Colosseo"), erected in 80 AD by Emperor Flavius, is the city's grandest symbol. In its heyday, the Colosseum accommodated more than 50,000 spectators, and could be filled with water for mock naval battles. The floor (now gone) lay over a labyrinth of brick cells, corridors, ramps, and elevators used for transporting wild animals from their cages up to the level of the arena. The interior is a bit of a disappointment, since Renaissance popes used most of the marble stands for their own grandiose constructions. Today, due to the incessant onslaught of traffic and pollution, the Colosseum faces serious deterioration. (Ground level open Mon.-Tues. and Thurs.-Sat. 9am-7pm, Wed. 9am-1pm, Sun. 9am-6pm (until 1pm Sept.-May). Free. Upper floors open Sun.-Tues. and Thurs. 9am-6pm, Wed. 9am-1pm, Fri.-Sat. 9am-7pm; winter Sun.-Tues. and Thur. 9am-4pm. L6000, free for Europeans under 18.)

The **Arch of Constantine,** to the side of the Colosseum, was built by Constantine in the 4th century. The well-proportioned triple arch is constructed almost entirely from sculptural fragments pillaged from older Roman monuments. Unfortunately, recent excavations of an earlier garden park have obstructed most access to it.

From the piazza di Porta Capena, via delle Terme di Caracalla passes the hulking remains of the **Baths of Caracalla,** the largest and best-preserved imperial baths in the city. (Open Tues.-Sat. 9am-3pm, Sun.-Mon. 9am-1pm; in summer Tues.-Sat. 9am-6pm. L6000, discount for EC citizens under 18 or over 60.)

Outside the city proper lie the **catacombs,** mysterious multi-story condos for the dead. The most notable are those of **San Sebastiano, San Callisto,** and **Santa Domitilla,** next door to one another on via Appia Antica south of the city. Take bus #118 from via Claudia near the Colosseum (20min.; infrequent service), or more frequent bus #218, also on via Appia Antica; get off before it takes a sharp right turn up via Ardeatina. (Open 8:30am-noon and 2:30-5pm. San Sebastiano closed Thurs., Santa Domitilla closed Tues., San Callisto closed Wed. Obligatory tour L6000.)

The grandiose **Church of San Giovanni in Laterano,** the cathedral of the diocese of Rome, lies east of the Colosseum at the end of via San Giovanni in Laterano, in the *piazza* of the same name. The traditional pilgrimage route from St. Peter's ends here at the city's oldest Christian basilica. The church, accorded the same rights of extraterritoriality as the Vatican, was used by the Pope for mass on certain feast days; in 1993 it was closed to repair severe damage inflicted by a recent bombing.

Across the River: Trastevere

A functioning hospital has occupied **Isola Tiberina** (Tiber Island) since 291 BC, when the Romans turned the island into a replica of the ship of Asclepius, who (according to legend) sailed up the Tiber to Rome.

Across the river, with its meandering streets, hidden churches, lively cafés, and crumbling medieval homes, Trastevere (bus #170 from Termini) proclaims its independence and unrivaled vitality. Today, Trastevere attracts hordes of expatriates, bohemians, and artists, but thanks to rent control and centuries of fiery patriotism, the area retains its local *gusto*. Right off the Ponte Garibaldi, on busy viale di Trastevere, stands the **Torre degli Anguillara,** the only medieval town tower left of those that once forested the area. Via di Giulio Cesare Santini leads east into via dei Genovesi (left of the McDonald's). The **Church of Santa Cecilia in Trastevere** lies 2 blocks ahead, on via di S. Cecilia. Don't miss the *Statua di Santa Cecilia* by Stefano Maderno (1576-1636). Rococo restorers wreaked untold damage on the medieval frescoes by Pietro Cavallini which once covered the church, but his magnificent *Last Judgement* (1293) has no contemporary parallel in Europe. (Open daily 10am-noon and 4-6pm.) At the end of via della Lungaretta, the **Church of Santa Maria in Trastevere** dominates the *piazza* of the same name. It claims to be the first of Rome's churches dedicated to the Virgin, and is the site of the oldest Christian structure in Rome, tracing back to 222 AD. The 13th-century mosaics on the 12th-century façade are only a prelude to those within. (Open daily 7am-7pm.)

The easiest way to ascend **Gianicolo Hill** is by the medieval via Garibaldi on its tortuous route up from the via della Scala in Trastevere (10min.). Atop the hill sits the **Church of San Pietro in Montorio,** on the spot once believed to be the site of St. Peter's upside-down crucifixion. It's home of one of Italy's smallest and most exquisite buildings, the **Tempietto** (1499-1502), a brilliant marriage of Renaissance theory and ancient architecture. At via della Lungara, 10 (on the left as you descend via Garibaldi), is the **Palazzo Corsini,** home to one half of the **Galleria Nazionale d'Arte Antica** (the rest of the collection is in the Palazzo Barberini). Spanning the 13th through 18th centuries, the museum contains no fewer than 41 portrayals of the Virgin Mary, by Fra Angelico, Breughel, van Dyck, Titian, and Poussin. (Open Tues.-Sat. 9am-2pm, Sun. 9am-1pm. L6000.) Across the street, the magnificent **Villa Farnesina** houses several rooms frescoed by Raphael, Peruzzi, il Sodoma, and Giulio Romano. (Open daily 9am-1pm. Free.)

Parks Rome's largest park, the **Villa Borghese** (Metro: "piazza di Spagna"), contains 3 major museums: **Museo Borghese** (take bus #910 from Stazione Termini and get off on via Pinciana), **Galleria Nazionale d'Arte Moderna,** and the **Museo di Villa Giulia** (within easy walking distance of the main gate, or take tram #19 from via Flaminia to viale delle Belle Arti). The **Museo Borghese,** under ongoing restoration, houses Bernini's greatest early sculpture (including *Apollo and Daphne* and *David)*. (Open Tues.-Sat. 9am-7pm, Sun. and holidays 9am-1pm. L4000.) The **Galleria Nazionale d'Arte Moderna** is filled with the best Italian art of the 19th and 20th centuries. (Open Tues.-Sat. 9am-2pm, Sun. and holidays 9am-1pm. L8000, EC students under 19 free.) The **Museo di Villa Giulia,** hides a vast trove of Etruscan art discovered in burial grounds north of Rome. (Open Tues.-Sun. 9am-7pm; Sept.-May 9am-2pm. L8000.)

ENTERTAINMENT

Roman entertainment is a public affair—concerts under the stars, street fairs with acrobats and fire-eaters, and Fellini-esque crowds of Romeos, modern-day minstrels, and enchanted foreigners. Clubs are not necessarily an integral part of nightlife—the real social scene spills out-of-doors. Those clubs that do exist keep erratic hours and often close in summer. Call ahead, or check Thursday's *TrovaRoma,* a comprehensive list of concerts, plays, clubs, movies, and special events in *La Repubblica.*

During weekdays, most Romans rush into a *caffè,* down an *espresso,* and leave, but at night, the *caffès* come alive. The streets around Campo dei Fiori and Trastevere hide some of the best places. **Bar S. Calisto,** p. S. Calisto, 4, in Trastevere, is where Trasteverean youth, expatriates, and Roman elders socialize over inexpensive *cappuccino.* (L1200. Open Mon.-Sat. 6:30am-3am.)

In summer the **Terme di Caracalla** hosts lavish opera productions, beginning with Verdi's *Aida,* worth seeing for the incredible scenery alone. (Performances 9pm-1am.) Special buses (L1200) ferry spectators home. Buy tickets (from L30,000) at the theater before the show or at the opera's headquarters in p. Beniamino Gigli, 9, near via Viminale. Perhaps the best time to appreciate the vigor of Christianity in Rome is during **Holy Week,** when every church hosts concerts and High Mass; the pope traditionally conducts the Way of the Cross in the Colosseum on Good Friday.

Rome's music clubs attract a much hipper Italian crowd than the pubs; some even have dancing and are usually much cheaper than discos. Try **Yes Brasil,** via San Francesco a Ripa, 103, in Trastevere, for live Brazilian music (drinks L8000-10,000; music 10pm-midnight; open Mon -Sat 3pm-2am), or **Caffè Latino,** via di Monte Testaccio, 96, a large, fashionable place with a room for bands (mostly jazz) and one for videos and dancing. (Drinks L5000-12,000. Open Oct.-June 9:30pm-2:30am. Membership fee L2000.) **Caffè Caruso,** next door, has a similar set-up. If your feet have got to meet the beat no matter what price, point your toes toward **La Makumba,** via degli Olimpionici, 19, across the Tiber from the Stadio Olimpico, for hot Brazilian and African music. (Open 11pm-3am.) Rome has only a handful of gay and lesbian bars, and most keep late hours. Pick up a *Pianta Gay di Roma* at any bar or disco for complete entertainment listings. Gay clubs include **Angelo Azzurro,** via Cardinal Merry del Val, 13, in Trastevere, where Friday is women only and Sunday is "Open City," a new theme night with services, shopping, and drinks for a gay clientele. (Mandatory first drink L12,000. Open Tues.-Sun. 10pm-3:30am.)

■ Near Rome

Do as the (ancient) Romans did to escape urban commotion; retreat to **Tivoli,** summer resort for such archaic big-wigs as Horace and Hadrian. The 16th-century **Villa d'Este** is a dazzling, splashy park overflowing with fountains and waterfalls. (Open 9am to 1hr. before sunset. L10,000 if water is at full power, L5000 otherwise.) Just outside of Tivoli is the **Villa Adriana,** where the Emperor Hadrian reconstructed the architectural wonders of his far-flung empire. (Open daily 9am-dusk. L8000.) **ACO-TRAL buses** depart from via Lepanto for Tivoli (5am-midnight, ½hr., L4600).

The romantic remains of **Ostia Antica** offer a cooler, closer, and cheaper alternative to the more famous ruins at Pompeii and Herculaneum. The ruins are so sparsely visited you'll have no trouble finding a spot for a picnic. Take Metro Linea B to the Magliana stop (L700), change to the Lido train, and get off at "Ostia Antica" (20min., same ticket). Cross the overpass and continue to the "T" intersection. Make a left and follow the signs. (Open daily 9am-6pm; in winter 9am-4pm. L8000.)

Overlooking Rome from the volcanic Alban hills, the Castelli Romani are famous for their white wines, Renaissance villas, and annual festivals. **Frascati,** famed for its fruity white wines, is the closest to Rome (20min. by bus). Beneath the Villa Aldo-brandini, the road leading left out of town climbs 5km over winding country roads to the ruins of **Tusculum,** an ancient resort town that hosted such Roman luminaries as Cato and Cicero. Down the other side rests the hamlet of **Grottaferrata,** 3km from Frascati, whose handsome Romanesque 11th-century **abbey** is inhabited by Greek Orthodox monks who run an ancient winery and a museum of Byzantine mosaics. Catch the bus here back to Rome (last one at 9pm). Buses leave Rome for Frascati, Grottaferrata, or Marino (5am-10:30pm, about every ½hr., L1500).

A few km across the hills from Frascati and Grottaferrata, the rest of the Castelli Romani cling to the sides of an extinct volcanic crater, now filled with the shimmering blue (and swimmable) waters of **Lago Albano. Buses** leave for Marino (for a clockwise tour of the lake) or Castel Gandolfo (to go counterclockwise) and other *castelli* locations every half hour from the Anagnina stop at the end of Metro Linea A (L1500 each way).

VENETO

The Veneto encompasses a multitude of culturally independent towns and cities with profound Germanic and Milanese influences, lumped together by Venetian rule. A good indicator of unity can be found in the transcendent medium of cuisine. Rice and *polenta* (a cornmeal concoction used with most local seafood dishes) provide the starch base; wine is strictly regional, featuring the dry white *soave,* the dry, sparkling *prosecco,* the light red *bardolino,* and the full-bodied *valpolicella.*

■■■ VENICE (VENEZIA)

As unreal as it appears, Venice convinces even the most skeptical visitor that its fantastic history has not been lost to modern tourism. Land in the lagoon was at a premium, so only narrow pedestrian passages, most of which are old canals now filled with earth, connect the *campi* (squares). Buildings appear to rise out of the water and as the tide comes in and water laps at the threshold of their doors, you may wonder if they have risen high enough. During the day, boats ferry everything from food supplies to building debris to camera-happy tourists. An evening stroll through the illuminated streets returns the city to its past: Venice has more historic buildings and inspiring vistas per square inch than any other city in Italy. Enjoy the architecture in the cool of the night, with colored lights reflected in the sloshing waters and gondolas lazily passing by. Despite its crowds and inflated prices, Venice beckons anyone interested in the roots of Italian culture to make at least one visit to its sublime combination of water, stone and light.

ORIENTATION AND PRACTICAL INFORMATION

Situated at the northern tip of the Adriatic, Venice is linked by ferry to Greece and the Middle East, and by rail to major European cities. The **Santa Lucia train station** lies on the northwestern edge of the city, while the garages, car rentals, and bus terminals are across the Grand Canal in nearby **piazzale Roma.** To get to **piazza San Marco** (and the central tourist office) directly, take *vaporetto* (canal boat) #2 from the station or piazzale Roma. For a splendid introduction to the *palazzi* along the stately **Canale Grande,** take #1 or 34, or follow the signs on foot to San Marco. The city is a confusing maze; the *edizioni Storto* map-guide of Venice (L5000) shows all the major streets, is color coded, and has an invaluable street index.

The main part of Venice is divided into 6 *sestieri* (districts): **San Marco, Castello, San Polo, Santa Croce, Cannaregio,** and **Dorsoduro.** Within each section, there are no individual street numbers, but one long sequence of numbers (roughly 6000 per *sestiere*) that winds its way haphazardly through the district. Every building is located on a "street"—*fondamenta, salizzada, calle, campi, canale, rio, ponte, and rio terrà*—*Let's Go* also lists these wherever possible. Always be sure you're looking in the proper *sestiere;* some street names are duplicated and no *sestiere* boundaries are marked. Yellow signs posted all over town will direct you to and from **piazza San Marco** (at the border of San Marco and Castello), the **Rialto Bridge** (linking San Marco to San Polo), the **train station** *(ferrovia;* in Cannaregio), **piazzale Roma** (in Santa Croce), and the **Accademia** (in Dorsoduro). Boats plow across the lagoon regularly to Venice's 2 principal islands, **Giudecca** and the **Lido.**

The **Grand Canal,** the central artery of Venice, can be crossed on foot only at the **ponti** (bridges) **Scalzi, Rialto,** and **Accademia.** *Traghetti* (gondola-like ferry boats) are used fairly frequently for canal crossings where there is no bridge. High tides (usually Nov.-April) cause *aque alte,* the periodic floodings that swamp parts of the city, notably San Marco, under as much as 3 feet of water.

Tourist Offices: APT (tel. 71 90 78), at the train station. Usually mobbed. The longer of the 2 lines is just for accommodations. They provide *Un Ospite di Venezia* (A Guest in Venice), a bilingual biweekly (monthly for winter) booklet packed with info and entertainment listings. Open Mon.-Fri. 9am-noon and 3-6pm, Sat. 8am-2pm. **Main Office: San Marco,** Ascensione, 71/F (tel. 552 63 56), opposite the basilica. Shorter lines. English spoken. Open Mon.-Sat. 8:30am-2pm. **Youth Discount Card: Rolling Venice,** at the train station (tel. 72 01 61 or 72 05 19). Open June 15-Sept. 30 daily 8am-8pm. **Main office** at San Marco (tel. 270 76 50 or 270 76 45), near the tourist office. For ages 14-29. Discount card for admission to museums, shops, restaurants, and events throughout Venice, also an invaluable guide. Worth it whether you're in Venice for 1 day or 1 month. Bring L5000 and a passport photo (L3000 at the booth in the station).

Budget Travel: Centro Turistico Studentesco (CTS), Dorsoduro, 3252 (tel. 520 56 60) on fondamenta Tagliapietra. Off the Dorsoduro-to-San Marco route near campo S. Margherita. Take calle Piove to calle Larga Foscari and turn right after crossing the bridge, on the bank of rio Foscari. Open Mon.-Fri. 9am-12:30pm and 3:30-7pm. **Transalpino** (tel. 71 66 00) is to the right as you exit the train station. Open daily 8am-8pm.

Consulates: U.K., Dorsoduro, 1051 (tel. 522 72 07). Open Mon.-Fri. 9am-noon and 2-4pm. The closest **U.S., Canadian,** and **Australian** consulates are in Milan; **New Zealanders** and **South Africans** should contact their embassy in Rome.

Currency Exchange: for the best rates, change money in Padua. Otherwise, try **Banca Ambrosiano Veneto** on calle Larga XXII Marzo, San Marco 2378, between San Marco and the Accademia. Open Mon.-Fri. 8:20am-1:20pm and 2:35-4:05pm. L4500 commission. Many banks cluster around the same *calle*. You can shop here for the best rates, but watch out for sky-high commissions. If you insist upon changing money at the station, spare yourself the lines and get slightly better rates by walking 400m to **Banco San Marco,** next to the bridge spanning the canal. Open Mon.-Fri. 8:30am-1:30pm and 2:45-4:15pm.

American Express: San Marco, Sal. S. Moise, 1471 (tel. 520 08 44), off p. San Marco. Take calle Seconda dell'Ascensione from the end of the *piazza* opposite the basilica and follow it for a couple of blocks (look for the AmEx directional mosaic underfoot). L1500 inquiry charge on mail without card or Traveler's Cheques. Mediocre **exchange** rates but no commission. Open Mon.-Fri. 9am-5:30pm, Sat. 9am-12:30pm. Exchange service open summer Mon.-Sat. 8am-8pm.

Post Office: San Marco, 5554 (tel. 528 93 17), on salizzada Fontego dei Tedeschi near the eastern end of the Rialto bridge. Fermo Posta at desk #4; stamps at #11 and 12. Open Mon.-Sat. 8:15am-6:45pm. **Branch office** through the arcades at the end of p. San Marco. Open Mon.-Sat. 8:15am-12:10pm. Stamps are sold in the *tabacchi* at the station. Also close to the train station in an alley off Lista di Spagna, calle del Spizier. **Postal Code:** 30124.

Telephones: ASST, train station. Open Mon.-Fri. 8am-7:45pm, Sat. 8am-1:45pm. Also at **Iritel,** at San Marco, 5551, next to the main post office. Open daily 8am-7:45pm. **SIP,** in p. Roma and along viale Santa Maria Elisabetta on the Lido. Open daily 8am-9:30pm. **City Code:** 041.

Trains: Stazione di Santa Lucia (tel. 71 55 55; tel. 71 61 22 for lost and found). Information office in station across from tourist office. To: Padua (every 15min., ½hr., L5400); Bologna (14/day, 1½hr., L12,800); Milan (18/day, 2½-3hr., L17,000); Florence (6/day, 2½-3hr., L18,700); Rome (4/day, 5¼hr., L40,200). **Luggage Storage:** L1500. Open 24 hrs.

Buses: ACTV, the local line for buses and boats (tel. 528 78 86) in p. Roma. Open Mon.-Sat. 8am-6:30pm. Roughly every ½hr. to: the villas on the Riviera del Brenta (L1000-L3100), Padua (L3800), Mestre (L1000), and Treviso (L2600). Ticket office open daily 7:30am-11pm. Information office open Mon.-Sat. 8am-6:30pm. The fine for riding without a ticket is L30,000.

Public Transportation: The alternative to walking is taking the *vaporetti* (motorboat buses). Most principal boats run 24hr. but frequency is reduced after 11pm. A *biglietto turistico*, available at any ticket office, allows you unlimited travel on all boats except #2 (L12,000/day; 3-day ticket L17,000). Neither is really worthwhile unless you're on a kamikaze tour. The ACTV office offers a special 3-day ticket for holders of the **Rolling Venice Pass** for L16,000. Tickets purchasable both at booths in front of *vaporetti* stops and at self-service dispensers (at the ACTV office at p.Roma and at the Rialto stop). Tickets may also be bought from the conductor after boarding (L500 surcharge). The fine for riding the *vaporetti* without a ticket is L15,000, but enforcement can be lax.

Bookstore: Il Libraio a San Baranabà, Dorsoduro, 2835/A (tel. 522 87 37), fondamenta Gherardini, off campo San Baranabà. Classics, all American fiction set in Venice, and—joy of joys—the *Let's Go* budget travel series. Claims to be open Mon.-Tues. and Thurs.-Sat. 10:30am-1pm and 4-8pm.

Laundromat: Lavaget, Cannaregio, 1269 (tel. 71 59 76), on fondamenta Pescaria off rio Terà San Leonardo, beside the Ponte Guglie. Self-service wash L12,000. Soap included. Open Mon.-Fri. 8:15am-12:30pm and 3-7pm.

Public Baths: Albergo Diurno (Day Hotel), San Marco, 1266, in the *ramo secondo* (2°), off the west end of p. San Marco. Showers L4000. Toilets L500. Luggage storage L2000-3000. Showers open daily 8am-4pm. Also in the station, next to *binario* 1. Showers L4000. Soap and towel each L500. Open daily 7am-8pm.

Pharmacy: check the *Ospite di Venezia* or call 192.

Hotel Crises: Questura, on fondamenta San Lorenzo in the Castello (tel. 270 36 11). Contact them if you suspect your hotel keeper is pulling a fast one on you.

Emergencies: tel. 113. **Police: Carabinieri,** p. Roma (tel. 523 53 33 or 112 in an emergency). **Medical Assistance:** tel. 520 32 22. **Ospedali Civili Hospital,** campo SS. Giovanni e Paolo (tel. 529 45 17). **Boat ambulances,** tel. 523 00 00.

ACCOMMODATIONS AND CAMPING

Venice is a squirming mass of tourists in summer and expensive to boot; reservations, preferably made as much as a month in advance, will preserve your sanity. To avoid the crowds and expense, visit the city while based in one of the towns nearby (Padua and Treviso, each 30min. away, are good choices). The APT at the train station will book rooms, but if you go directly to the establishment they are more willing to bargain. If the situation becomes desperate, you can always resort to one of the campgrounds at Mestre (ask at the tourist office) or Padua's youth hostel (closes at 11pm, last train at 9:15pm). The police frown on impromptu crashing in parks or on beaches. Dorm-type lodgings are always available in Venice without reservations, even during August and September. In *pensioni,* look out for L10,000 breakfasts and other forms of bill-padding, and always agree on what you'll pay before you hit the sack or surrender your passport.

Hostels and Dormitories

Ostello Venezia (HI), fondamenta di Zitelle, 86 (tel. 523 82 11, fax 523 56 89), on Giudecca. Take *vaporetto* #5 *(sinistra* or *destra)* from the station (25min., L2500), or #8 from San Zaccaria near San Marco (5min., L2500). Get off at Zitelle and walk right. A recently-renovated warehouse on the canal. English spoken. In summer arrive in the morning to secure a place—the tourist office at the train station will let you know if they're already full. Open daily 7:30-9am and 2-11:30pm. Curfew 11:30pm. Members only. L20,000. HI cards L30,000 over 6 nights. Breakfast included. Full meals L12,000. No phone reservations.

Foresteria Valdese, Castello, 5170 (tel. 528 67 97). Take the *vaporetto* to San Zaccharia, then walk to campo Santa Maria Formosa (5min.) and take calle lunga S. M. Formosa; it's over the 1st bridge. The 18th-century guesthouse of Venice's biggest Protestant church. Check-in 9am-1pm and 6-8pm. Lockout 9:45-1pm. Bunk beds in dorms for L25,000, L21,000 each additional night. Breakfast included. Reserve 1 month ahead for their 2 beautiful doubles (L56,000). 2 apartments with bath and kitchen L80,000 for 2; L15,000 for each additional bed up to max. of 5.

Domus Civica (ACISJF), San Polo, 3082 (tel. 72 11 03), across the street from a bar in both directions, on the corner of calle Chiovere, calle Campazzo, and S. Rocco, between the Frari Church and piazzale Roma. Along the road, follow the yellow arrows between piazzale Roma and the Rialto. Cheery nuns, ping-pong table, and a TV room. Check-out 7:30-10am. Curfew 11:30pm. Singles L28,000. Doubles L50,000. Rolling Venice: 20% discount. Open mid-June to mid-Oct.

Suore Cannosiano, fondamenta del Ponte Piccolo, 428 (tel. 522 21 57), also on Giudecca. Take boat #5 to Sant'Eufemia, and walk to your left and over the Ponte Piccolo bridge as you descend. Women only. Run by solicitous nuns. You can arrive at any time of day to leave your bags. Check-out 6-8:30am. Lockout 8:30am-4pm. Curfew 10:30pm. Dorm-style rooms L16,000/person.

Hotels

Locanda Antica Casa Carettoni, Cannaregio, 130 (tel. 7162 31), along rio Terà Lista di Spagna, to the left of the station. "Truly Venetian" antique rooms, but you might have to settle for a cold shower. Curfew midnight. Singles L28,000, doubles L48,000, triples L69,000. Open March-July and Sept.-Jan.

Hotel Minerva and Nettuno, Cannaregio, 230 (tel. 71 59 68), on your left on Lista di Spagna from the station. Spacious, remodeled rooms and convenient locale make this a prime choice. Singles L47,000, with bath L61,000. Doubles L68,000, with bath L89,000. Breakfast included. MasterCard, Visa.

Locanda San Salvador, San Marco, 5264 (tel. 528 91 47), on Calle del Galliazzo, off campo San Bartolomeo. Good views and a spacious terrace. Right in the middle of the action. Singles L40,000, with bath L50,000. Doubles L65,000-70,000, with bath L85,000-95,000.

Penison Casa Verardo, Castello, 4765 (tel. 528 61 27). Take Rimpetto la Sacrestia out of campo San Filippo e Giacomo (just east of San Marco) across the bridge. *The* find in this part of town, run by a hospitable, outgoing family. Singles L43,000-44,000. Doubles 60,000, with bath L85,000. Triples L120,000-130,000. Quad L130,000-140,000. Breakfast L7000. Reserve with 1 night's deposit. They have another establishment, **Hotel da Bepi,** Santa Croce, 160 (tel. 522 67 35), on fondamenta Minotto, near p. Roma. Singles L45,000. Doubles L70,000, with bath L90,000. Breakfast included. MasterCard, Visa.

Albergo Adua, Cannaregio, 233/A (tel. 71 61 84), on Lista di Spagna. Courtly rooms with flowery wallpaper, most with wall-to-wall carpeting. Small, family-run, and quiet for the neighborhood. Singles L42,000. Doubles L58,000, with bath L90,000. 35% more/extra bed. Breakfast L7500. MasterCard, Visa.

Hotel Calderon, Cannaregio, 283 (tel. 71 55 62), in p. San Geremia at the end of lista di Spagna. Friendly, family-run. No English spoken. No private baths, no curfew. Singles L35,000, doubles L50,000, triples L75,000.

Cà Foscari, Dorsoduro, 3887/B (tel./fax 522 58 17), on calle della Frescata, at the foot of calle Crosera where it hits calle Marconi. Take *vaporetto* #1 or 34 to San Tomà. Camouflaged sign. Family-run and tastefully decorated. Singles L40,000. Doubles L70,000. Breakfast included. Call in advance—rooms held until noon. Open Feb.-Nov.

Locanda Montin, Dorsoduro, 1147 (tel. 522 71 51). From campo San Barnabà, go south through the passageway Casin dei Nobili, across the bridge, right on fondamenta Lombardo, and around the corner onto fondamenta di Borgo. Modern paintings and restored antiques abound. Singles L40,000. Doubles L65,000. Showers and breakfast included. Reserve with 1 night's deposit. Closed 20 days in Jan. and 10 days in Aug. AmEx, MasterCard, Visa.

Locanda Casa Petrarca, San Marco, 4386 (tel. 520 04 30). From campo San Luca, go south on calle dei Fuseri, take the 2nd left and then turn right onto calle Schiavone. English spoken. Singles L40,000. Doubles L70,000-75,000, with bath L90,000-99,000. 35% more/extra bed. Breakfast L6000.

Locanda Silva, Castello, 4423 (tel. 522 76 43). Take Cale dell'Anzolo (it starts next to San Marco), then make the 2nd right, continue across the bridge, and go left when you hit Fondamenta del Rimedio. On a canal. Large and fastidiously kept. Singles L45,000. Doubles L65,000, with shower L80,000, with bath L145,000. Includes breakfast. Open Feb.-Nov.

Locanda Sant'Anna, Castello, 269 (tel. 528 64 66). Take via Garibaldi, which becomes fondamenta Santa Anna, turn left on ponte Santa Anna, then right at corte del Bianco (*vaporetto* #1 or 4 to "Giardini"). Worth the hike. Friendly family proprietors and a refreshing absence of tourists. Starched sheets and sparkling rooms. TV downstairs. Curfew midnight. Singles L47,000. Doubles L68,000, with bath L96,000. Triples L99,000, with bath L125,000. Quads L122,000, with bath L150,000. Breakfast included. Reserve ahead with 1 night's deposit.

Camping

Cà Pasquall, via Poerio, 33 (tel. 96 61 10), charges a mere L4500/person and L12,000/tent space. (Open May 10-Sept. 17.) **Campeggio Fusina,** via Moranzani, in the locality of Malcontenta (tel. 547 00 55), costs L8000/person, L6000/tent. (English spoken. Call ahead.) From p. Roma, take bus #4 (L1100) to Mestre and change to bus #13 (across the street from Supermarket PAM). Ride to the last stop (1hr., last bus at 9pm). The boat trip is more picturesque, convenient and expensive. Take *vaporetto* #5 (L2500) left to Zattere, then take #16 (L3500) for 20min. to Fusina.

FOOD

It's getting hard to actually sit down to a good meal in Venice at terrestrial prices. To avoid paying a fortune, visit a *bar* or *osteria* and make a meal from meat- and cheese-filled pastries and *tramezzini,* triangular slices of soft white bread with every imaginable filling. Good deals on tourist *menùs* converge along the broad **via Garibaldi,** a lovely 15-minute walk along the waterfront from p. San Marco. If you're going to spend big bucks on dinner, try the local seafood. A plate of *pesce fritta mista* (mixed fried seafood, at least L9000) usually includes *calamari* (squid), *polpo* (small octopus), shrimp, and the catch of the day. The Veneto and Friuli regions produce an abundance of excellent and inexpensive wines. A good local white wine is the sparkling, dry *prosecco della Marco,* or *collio,* another dry white.

Fruit stands line the Ruga degli Orefici, and on the right are the *Erberia* (vegetables) and *Pescheria* (fish) markets. In Cannaregio, **STANDA,** on Strada Nova, 3660, near Campo S. Felice, has groceries in the back. (Open daily 8:30am-7:20pm.)

Cafe da Poggi, Campo della Maddalena, 2103 (tel. 71 59 71). On the main route from the station to San Marco. A popular student hangout with coffee, drinks, sandwiches, and loud music. Open daily, early to late.

Mensa Universitaria di Cà Foscari, San Polo, 2480 (tel. 71 80 69), on calle del Magazen. Full meals including drink and dessert L6000 with student ID. Open Mon.-Sat. 11:45am-2:30pm and 6:30-8:30pm, Sun. noon-2pm.

Osteria do Spade, San Polo, 860 (tel. 521 05 74), in sottoportego delle Do Spade near the Rialto. Really a winery, but serves sumptuous little sandwiches (L1200-1800). Try the house wine (L800/glass) or any of the hundreds of Friuli and Veneto whites and reds. Open Sept.-July Mon.-Sat. 9am-1pm and 5-8:30pm. Closed Thurs. afternoon.

El Chef, Dorsoduro, 2765 (tel. 522 28 15), on calle Lombardo, under the archway from campo S. Barnabà. If a dish of fish is not your wish, go elsewhere. Local wines L8500/liter. Open mid-March to Dec. Tues.-Sun. noon-3pm and 6:30-10pm.

Vino, Vino, San Marco, 2007/A (tel. 523 70 27), on calle del Sartor da Veste, off calle Larga XXII Marzo, which runs from the Ponte Moisè due west of p. San Marco. Praised in the *New York Times,* and, like the paper, it's black and white, and red all over. A river of wines (L2500-8000/glass) and a sea of tourists. Cover L1000. Rolling Venice discount. Open for drinks Wed.-Mon. 10am-11:30pm; for food, noon-4pm and 7-11pm.

Antiche Botteselle, via Garibaldi, 1621 (tel. 523 72 92), on a street that penetrates Castello near the Arsenale stop, about a 15-min. walk from S. Marco. Economical *menù* L13,000 if you name-drop *Let's Go.* 36 types of pizza (L4800-8000). *Primi* L5000-14,000. *Secondi* L6000-19,000. Wine L8000/liter. Open Thurs.-Tues. 8:30am-3am and 6-10pm (bar til midnight).

Gelati Nico, fondamenta Zattere, 922 (tel. 522 52 93), in Dorsoduro near the *vaporetto* stop of the same name, is the pride of Venice. *Gianduiotto,* a slice of dense chocolate hazelnut ice cream dunked in whipped cream, is their specialty (L3200). Open Fri.-Wed. 7am-11pm; off-season 7am-9pm.

Causin, p. Santa Margherita, 2996, is a *caffè-gelateria* that has pleased customers since 1928. The best and cheapest place in Venice. 2-scoop cone L1500. 5-scoop bowl L3000. Open daily 8am-8pm.

SIGHTS

> In Venetian churches a strict dress code applies. No shorts, sleeveless shirts or miniskirts allowed.

San Marco and Environs Piazza San Marco is the city's nucleus. Construction of the **Basilica of San Marco** began in the 9th century, when 2 Venetian merchants stole St. Mark's remains from Alexandria. The basilica's main treasure is the **Pala d'Oro**, a Veneto-Byzantine gold bas-relief encrusted with precious gems. The ticket to this area will also get you into the small **treasury**, a hoard of gold and relics from the Fourth Crusade. (Open Mon.-Sat. 9:45am-6:30pm, Sun. 1:30-5:30pm. L2000.) The **Galleria della Basilica** displays the recently restored Horses of St. Mark. (Open daily 10am-6:30pm. L2000.) The **Torre dell' Orologio** (clock tower), left of San Marco, is an florid arrangement of sculpture and sundials. Two oxidizing bronze Moors still strike the hour. You can ascend the brick **Campanile** in front of San Marco for a Kodak moment of the whole city. Built in 902 AD, the bell tower crumbled into a pile of rubble just before its 1000th birthday. Nobles on horseback could ascend the stairs in the original tower, but modern Venetians have installed an elevator. (Open daily 9:30am-9:30pm, winter until 7:30pm. L4000.)

The **Palazzo Ducale** (Doge's Palace), next to San Marco, faces Sansovino's exquisite **Libreria**. Admire the exhaustive display of Titians, Veroneses, and Tintorettos (especially his *Paradiso*), as well as the armor museum and the ominous **Ponte dei Sospiri** (Bridge of Sighs), leading out to the prison. (Open daily 9am-7pm. L8000.)

Art Galleries, Churches, and the Lagoon The **Accademia** in Dorsoduro displays the best of Venetian painting. The world-class collection includes a superb Bellini *Madonna,* Giorgione's enigmatic *Tempest,* and Titian's last work, a brooding Pietà. Go early to get your money's worth. (Open Mon.-Sat. 9am-7pm; off-season Mon.-Sat. 9am-1pm. L8000.) For very different art, visit the **Collezione Peggy Guggenheim,** Dorsoduro, 701, housed in the late Ms. Guggenheim's Palazzo Venier dei Leoni, near the tip of Dorsoduro. All the major names in modern art are here, shown in glorious surroundings. (Open Wed.-Mon. 11am-6pm. L7000, seniors, students with ISIC, or Rolling Venice card L4000.) Another art-filled area surrounds the Gothic **Basilica dei Frari** in San Polo (*vaporetto* to San Tomà). The basilica houses a moving wooden sculpture of St. John by Donatello, Bellini's *Madonna and Saints* and Titian's dramatic *Assumption.* (Open Mon.-Sat. 8:30am-noon and 3-6pm, Sun. 3-5:30pm. L1000, Sun. and holidays free.) The *scuole* of Venice, a cross between guilds and fraternities, erected ornate "clubhouses" throughout the city. The richest *scuola* was the **Scuola Grande di San Rocco** (across the campo at the end of the Frari), which gloats over 56 Tintorettos. To see the paintings in chronological order, start on the 2nd floor in the Sala dell'Albergo and follow the cycle downstairs. (Open daily 9am-5:30pm; off-season Mon.-Fri. 10am-1pm, Sat.-Sun. 10am-4pm. L6000, Rolling Venice L5000.)

Across the Giudecca canal on the island of Giudecca stand 2 churches designed by the great late-Renaissance architect Palladio: **San Giorgio Maggiore,** on the Isola di San Giorgio, and the **Chiesa del Redentore,** on Giudecca itself and built after one of the many Venetian plagues. Both can be viewed from the **Church of Santa Maria della Salute,** a baroque extravaganza commemorating yet another plague savior, at the tip of Dorsoduro. Take *vaporetto* #5 or 8 from p. San Marco.

North of Venice stretches the **lagoon.** With a *vaporetto* ticket (L1800-L2500), you can visit the **glass museum** at the island of **Murano** (#5), the fishing village of **Burano** (#12), and **Torcello,** an island with an enchanting Byzantine cathedral and some of the finest mosaics in Italy. The **Lido** separates the Venice lagoon from the Adriatic. Its long sandy beach, setting for Thomas Mann's truly dreadful *Death in Venice,* is as popular as its water is polluted.

■■■ PADUA (PÁDOVA)

By the middle of the 12th century, Padua had overcome its penchant for tyrannical rule and become one of the intellectual hubs of Europe. The university, once host to Dante, Petrarch, and Galileo, still enlivens this small city whose beautiful youth hostel, within close reach of Venice, makes Padua an ideal base camp.

The train station is at the northern edge of town, a 10-minute walk down the corso del Popolo—which becomes corso Garibaldi; the latter leads to the modern, commercially minded heart of town. On the way you'll pass the **Cappella degli Scrovegni,** the masterpiece of medieval innovator Giotto. The 36 panels illustrating the Redemption story constitute the painter's only fresco cycle to have escaped even partial deterioration. (Open daily 9am-7pm, Oct.-March Tues.-Sun. 9am-6pm. L10,000, students L7000. Admission to chapel on Mon. L4000. Tickets are sold (and valid also) at the **Museo Civico.**) Take via Antenore, then turn down via del Santo to get to the **Basilica di Sant'Antonio,** a quirky potpourri of medieval architectural styles and popular pilgrimage destination. The tongue and voice box of St. Anthony are preserved in an appropriately head-shaped reliquary in the apse of the church. (Open daily 6:30am-7:45pm.) On the piazza del Santo, don't miss Donatello's imposing **equestrian statue of Gattemelata,** a mercenary general. Featuring the same pose as the famous *Marcus Aurelius,* this was the first great equestrian bronze cast since antiquity. Across the *piazza,* the **Oratorio di San Giorgio** houses some fine examples of Giotto-school frescoes, and the **Scuola del Santo** on the corner contains 3 by a very young Titian. (Both open daily 9am-12:30pm and 2:30-7pm, Oct.-Jan. daily 9am-12:30pm, Feb.-March daily 9am-12:30pm and 2:30-4:30pm. L2000 for both, group rate L1000/person.)

Accommodations, Food, and Practical Information In summer, start looking for rooms early and call ahead. If you arrive late, try calling (049) 65 42 99 to check on availability of summer housing at the university. The friendly, crowded **Ostello Città di Padova,** via Aleardi, 30 (tel. (049) 875 22 19), has tidy, capacious rooms. From the station, take bus #3, 8, or 12. (Curfew 11pm. L16,000. Showers and breakfast included.) The friendly family at **Albergo Pavia,** via del Papafava, 11 (tel. (049) 875 57 44), offers rooms with wooden floors, and clothesline space on the roof. (Doubles L34,000, with bath L43,000.) **Pensione Bellevue,** via L. Belludi, 11 (tel. (049) 875 55 47), off Prato della Valle, has gorgeous rooms on an ivy-covered courtyard. (Singles L35,000-40,000. Doubles L40,000-64,000.)

Tame your hunger at **Mensa Universitaria,** via San Francesco, 122. (Full meal L9000. Open 11:45am-2:30pm, 6:45-9pm.) Check here for info on the other *mensas'* schedules. The self-service **Brek,** in the *piazza* off via VII Febbraoi, rivals the university *mensa's* prices. (Full meal including wine L11,000. Open Sat.-Thurs. 11:30am-3pm and 6:30-10:30pm.) **Al Pero,** via Santa Lucia, 72, is a neighborhood eatery with fantastic food. (*Salamini arrosti con polenta* (small roasted sausages), L4500. Cover L1500. Open Mon.-Sat. noon-2:30pm and 7-9:30pm.)

The **tourist office** (tel. (049) 875 20 77) in the train station provides free maps and accommodations and entertainment listings. (Open Mon.-Sat. 8am-6pm, Sun. 8am-noon.) The **bus station** at via Trieste, 42, is 5 minutes from the train station; buses run to Venice every half hour (45min., L4200). **Trains** chug to Venice (every 15min., ½hr., L3200, round-trip L4800) and to Milan (every hr., 2½hr., L17,100).

■■■ VERONA

Shakespeare immortalized Verona when he chronicled the story of locals Romeo and Giulietta, but a cursory glance at the city's opulent *palazzi* shows that names greater than Montague or Capulet have made their residences here. The wealth of Roman ruins reveals the classical origins of the modern metropolis.

In July and August, the Colosseum-like **Arena** (100 AD) hosts an annual opera and ballet extravaganza. Parting with L25,000 for tickets is such sweet sorrow. (Tickets available under arches #8 and 9. Call (045) 59 01 09 for information, (045) 59 09 66 for reservations.) The **Teatro Romano** across the river welcomes Shakespearean drama—in Italian—to its recently excavated stage. (Tickets from L19,000. Call (045) 807 71 11 for information, (045) 59 00 89 for reservations.) The train station is a 20-minute walk on corso Porta Nuova or a L1200 ride on bus #2 from Verona's center, **piazza Brà.** From here via Mazzini takes you into **piazza delle Erbe,** where vendors hawk fruit and hokey trinkets amid the Renaissance *palazzi* constructed by several gentlemen of Verona. Through an arch on the right are **piazza dei Signori** and the **Tombs of the Scaligeri,** the peculiar Gothic remnants of the Scala family, top dogs in medieval Verona. The equestrian statue of the Cangrande della Scala, a glorification of raw power, preens in the museum of the **Castelvecchio.** (Open Tues.-Sun. 8am-6:30pm. L5000.) Upstream from the Castelvecchio looms **Chiesa di San Zeno Maggiore,** a Romanesque church noted for its Mantegna altarpiece; pay L500 to illuminate the altarpiece and savor the brilliant coloring. Don't shell out a small fortune for a moment of disillusionment at **Casa Giulietta (Juliet's House),** via Cappello, 23; you'll stand on a diminutive balcony and thrill to a view of camera-happy tourists. (Open Tues.-Sun. 8am-6:30pm. L5000, students L1000.) **Casa Romeo (Romeo's House),** via Arche Scaligori, 2, is now a coffee bar.

Accommodations, Food, and Practical Information To reach the unbeatable **Ostello Verona (HI),** salita Fontana del Ferro, 15 (tel. (045) 59 03 60), hop bus #72 (from the "f" platform of the train station). Get off in p. Isolo, turn right at cia Ponte Pignolo, walk 3 blocks, turn left, then right, then left again. The best hostel in Italy has both 15th-century frescoes and spotless bathrooms. (Curfew 11pm, later if you're at the opera. L14,000. Amazing dinners L11,000. Camping in the garden L7000. 5-night max. stay.) Women might try **Casa della Giovane,** via Pigna, 7 (tel. (045) 59 68 80; curfew 10:30pm, extended for opera-goers; L15,000-L20,000). **Locanda Catullo,** vicolo Catullo, 1 (tel. (045) 800 27 86), has gorgeous singles for L32,000; doubles for L45,000, with bath L65,000. Camp at **Castel S. Pietro,** via Castel S. Pietro, 2 (tel. (045) 59 20 37; open mid-June to mid-Sept.; L5500/person, L4000-7000/tent).

Across the river, the fine *menù* at **Trattoria al Cacciatore,** via Seminario, 4, beckons. (Cover L1500. Open Mon.-Fri. 8:30am-2:30pm and 6:30-10pm, Sat. noon-2:30pm.) **Nuova Grottina** feeds Verona's student body at via Interrato dell'Acqua Morta, 38. (Hearty *menù* L14,000. Cover L1000. Open Fri.-Wed. 9:30am-2:30pm and 6pm-1am.) **Il Grillo Parlante,** vicolo Seghe San Tomaso, 10, is a vegetarian hotspot. (Cover L2500. Open Fri.-Sun. and Tues.-Wed. noon-2pm and 7:30-10pm, Thurs. noon-2pm.) **Supermarket PAM** is at via dei Mutilati, 3, off corso Porta Nuova. (Open Mon.-Tues. and Thurs.-Sat. 8:30am-7:30pm, Wed. 8:30am-noon.)

The **tourist office,** via Dietro Anfiteatro, 6 (tel. (045) 59 28 28), behind the arena (open Mon.-Sat. 8am-8pm, Sun. 8:30am-1:30pm), has an obliging, multilingual staff.

FRIULI-VENEZIA GIULIA: TRIESTE

Evidence of Trieste's multinational history lingers in the numerous buildings and monuments of Habsburg origin and the Slavic nuances in the local cuisine. The city's Italian identity is aggressively asserted by the persistence of fascist and anti-Slav parties, and more passively in **piazza dell'Unità d'Italia.** The product of these conflicting forces is a cosmopolitan transportation hub—a logical departure point for travelers to Eastern Europe. Trieste is a direct train ride from Venice or Udine, and several trains and buses cross over daily to neighboring Slovenia and Croatia. Less frequent ferry service runs the length of the Istrian Peninsula. The **train station,** in the p. della Libertà (tel. (040) 41 82 07), serves Venice (2hr., L12,100), Milan (7½hr., L30,300), and Ljubljana (3½hr., L14,500). **Agemar Viaggi, p.** Duca degli Abruzzi, 1/A (tel. (040) 36 37 37), will arrange ferry bookings with **Adriatica Navigazione** to Pula (4½hr., L32,500) in Yugoslavia. The **Ostello Tegeste (HI),** viale Miramare, 331 (tel. (040) 22 41 02), stacks only members in its bunks. From the station, take bus #36 (L1000). (Registration open noon-11:30pm. Curfew 11:30pm. Checkout 9:30am. L17,000, shower and breakfast included.)

THE LAKES AND THE DOLOMITES

When Italy's monuments and museums all start to blur together, take a breather and explore the country's natural beauty—its lakes and mountains. The Dolomites dominate the landscape in the province of Trentino-Alto Adige, rising from Austrian-influenced valley communities to lofty peaks equipped for skiing, hiking and awe-struck admiration. The lake country, by contrast, has long attracted a less athletic breed of tourist (windsurfers being a prominent exception). Contemplate the meaning of life in the shade of a lake or the isolation of a mountain hut before descending upon Italy's human wonders with renewed enthusiasm.

The Lakes An oddly forked amalgam of 3 lesser lakes, **Lake Como** (Lago di Como) is a ½-hour north of Milan by train (L2700) en route to the nearby Swiss border. The city of **Como** is the lake's largest urban outpost; its stately **duomo** harmoniously combines Gothic and Renaissance elements, and is accompanied by a multitude of luxurious *ville* which overlook the dreamy waters amid the secular splendor of shoreside parks and gardens. Contact the tourist office for information and visiting hours. For excellent hiking and eye-exploding views, take a *funicolare* up to **Brunate.** The cars leave from the far end of lungo Lareio Tieste every ½-hour (L3500). In Como, stay in the **Ostello VIlla Olmo (HI)** behind imposing Villa Olmo, via Bellinzona, 6 (tel. (031) 57 38 00, fax 57 38 00; L13,000); or choose from 2 excellent privately-run HI hostels in **Menaggio** (tel. (0344) 323 56) and **Domaso** (tel. (0344) 960 94). Both charge L12,000. Como's **tourist office** distributes information near the waterfront at p. Cavour, 16 (tel. (031) 27 40 64; open Mon.-Sat. 9am-12:30pm and 2:30-6pm). The **ferry landing** (tel. (031) 27 33 24) is across lungo Larro Trieste from p. Cavour; daily service runs to all the other lake villages (tickets L1300-11,200).

   Lake Garda (Lago di Garda) is the grandest and most popular of the lakes. In the north, **Riva del Garda** has thus far escaped complete commercialization, but **Sirmione,** the southern peninsula, has become a zoo of summer tourists. Get accommodations information at the **tourist office** in Riva (tel. (0464) 55 44 44) or Sirmione (tel. (030) 91 61 14), or choose the indoor economy option at Riva's **Ostello Benacus (HI),** p. Cavour, 9 (tel. (0464) 55 49 11; L13,000). The lake's impressive castles include the **Rocca** at Riva and an equivalent at Sirmione. **Desenzano** lies 2 hours from Venice, 25 minutes from Verona, and 1 hour from Milan. Once there, it's easy to get to the lake towns by bus, hydrofoil, and ferry.

The Dolomites Trent (Trento, Trient) is an hour north of Verona on the Bologna-Brenner train line. Italian prevails culturally and linguistically, but you'll see Austrian influence in the local cuisine and interest in all things mountainous. The Azienda Autonoma **(tourist office)** is across the park from the train station at via Alfieri, 4 (tel. (0461) 98 38 80). Stay at the luxurious, hotel-like **Ostello Giovane Europa (HI),** via Manzoni (tel. (0461) 23 45 67), for L15,000. **Monte Bondone** rises majestically over Trent and begs for pleasant daytrips and overnight excursions. Check with the tourist office (tel. and fax 94 71 88) in **Vanzene,** halfway up the mountain, about accommodations, ski lifts, and maps.

Only an hour and a half north of Trent, also en route to the Brenner Pass, **Bolzano** (Bozen) attempts to ease linguistic feuds with mandatory instruction in both Italian and German for its youth, but the disproportionately large number of fair, rosy-cheeked bilinguals reveals the city's true Austrian bent. The historic center is a combination of spacious *Plätze/piazze* and arcaded alleys, and is an ideal place to acclimate to Südtiroliën valley culture and stock up on essentials for a mountain escape. The **tourist office** at p. Walther, 8 (tel. (0471) 97 56 56), has local information, including some easy hiking recommendations in the neighboring hillsides. To prep for serious mountaineering, go to the **Provincial Tourist Office for South Tyrol,** p. Parracchia, 11 (tel. (0471) 99 38 08), just down from p. Walther, across from the *duomo*. Also pick up their volume of regional accommodations services. For housing in Bolzano itself, head for the hills (you'll find great views and lower prices). **Pensione Reiseggerhof,** Sta. Maddalena di Sotto, 24 (tel. (0471) 97 86 94), offers doubles and breakfast for L25,000 per person. The **Alpe di Suisi** offer a return to nature just 1½ hours away by bus.

LOMBARDY (LOMBARDIA)

Although cosmopolitan Milan, with its international reputation for high style and finance, may loom largest in foreigners' perceptions of the region, Lombardy is in fact far more than a metropolis and its countryside; Mantua, with its hints of Venetian influence, is culturally foreign to its western neighbor. The beginnings of the Alps are not far from the southern plain, combining an Italian climate with strains of Swiss and Austrian culture.

■■■ MILAN (MILANO)

It's said that for every church in Rome, there's a bank in Milan. But there's more to Milan than money; there's the preoccupation with *haute couture* and rampant industrial expansion. The steel and glass face of the city's center reflects its fixation with modernity; the city's adolescents exude the epidemic vanity.

ORIENTATION AND PRACTICAL INFORMATION

Milan is linked by train to all major cities in Western Europe. The layout of the city resembles a giant target, encircled by concentric ancient city walls. The **duomo** and **Galleria Vittorio Emanuele II** comprise the bull's-eye, roughly at the center of the downtown circle. The huge Stazione Centrale sprawls on a radial street to the northeast, and the **Metropolitana Milano (MM)** makes it easy to get around.

Tourist Office: APT, via Marconi, 1 (tel. 80 96 62), in the Palazzo di Turismo in p. del Duomo, to the right as you face the *duomo*. Comprehensive local and regional information, useful map and museum guide. Open Mon.-Sat. 8am-8pm, Sun. 9am-12:30pm and 1:30-5pm. Branch offices at **Stazione Centrale** (tel. 669 05 32 or 669 04 32; open Mon.-Sat. 8am-6pm) and **Linate Airport** (tel. 74 40 65; open Mon.-Fri. 9am-4:30pm). For hotel information and reservations, call **Hotel Reservation Milano** (tel. 76 00 60 95), which may request a deposit during busy periods. The **Associazione Turistrea Giovanile,** via del Amicis, 4 (tel. 89 40 50 75), near the Porta Ticinese, has some discounts and helpful information for young travelers. Open Mon.-Fri. 9:30am-1pm and 2-6:30pm, Sat. 9:30am-1pm.

Budget Travel: CIT, Galleria Vittorio Emanuele (tel. 86 66 61). The most central travel agency. Also **changes money.** Open Mon.-Fri. 9am-5:50pm. Another office at the **Stazione Centrale** (same hours). **CTS,** via S. Antonio, 2 (tel. 583 041 21). Open Mon.-Fri. 9:30am-6pm, Sat. 9:30am-noon; Sept.-May Mon.-Fri. 9:30am-1pm and 2:30-6pm, Sat. 9:30am-noon.

Consulates: U.S., via p. Amedeo, 2/10 (tel. 29 00 18 41). Open Mon.-Fri. 9am-1pm. **Canada,** via Vittor Pisani, 19 (tel. 669 74 51). Open Mon.-Fri. 9am-12:30pm and 1:30-5:15pm. **U.K.,** via S. Paolo, 7 (tel. 869 34 42). Open Mon.-Fri. 9:15am-12:15pm and 2:30-4:30pm. **Australia,** via Borgogna, 2 (tel. 76 01 33 30). Open daily 9:15am-noon and 2-4:30pm. **New Zealand** citizens should contact their embassy in Rome.

Currency Exchange: All **Banca d'America e d'Italia** and **Banca Nazionale del Lavoro** branches give cash advances on Visa cards. The former are usually open Mon.-Fri. 8:30am-1:30pm and 2:45-4:15pm; the latter Mon.-Fri. 8:20am-1:20pm and 2:30-4pm. The **Banca Nazionale delle Comunicazioni** at Stazione Centrale has standard rates. Open Mon.-Sat. 8am-6:30pm, Sun. 9am-1pm. L3000 fee.

American Express: via Brera, 3 (tel. 855 71), on the corner of via dell'Orso. Holds mail free for AmEx members, otherwise L800 per inquiry. Accepts wired money for a fee of US$30 per US$1000. Open Mon.-Fri. 9am-5pm.

Post Office: via Cordusio, 4 (tel. 869 20 69), near p. del Duomo toward the castle. Stamps at #1 and 2. *Fermo Posta* c/o CAI-POST office to the left upon entering. Open Mon.-Fri. 8:30am-5:30pm, Sat. 8:30am-1pm. **Postal Code:** 20100.

Telephones: SIP, in Galleria Vittorio Emanuele. Open 7am-midnight. **ASST,** in Stazione Centrale, past the tourist office. Open 7am-midnight. **City Code:** 02.

Flights: Malpensa Airport, 45km from town. Intercontinental flights. Buses leave every ½hr. in the morning, hourly in the afternoon from p. Luigi di Savoia, on the east side of Stazione Centrale (L12,000). **Linate Airport,** 7km from town. Domestic and European flights and intercontinental flights with European transfers. Much easier logistically: the bus to Linate leaves Stazione Centrale every 20min. from 5:50am-9pm (L4000). It's cheaper (L1200) to take bus #73 from p. San Babila (MM1). **General flight information** for both airports, tel. 74 85 22 00.

Trains: Stazione Centrale, p. Duca d'Aosta (tel. 675 00), on MM2. The primary station. To: Genoa (every hr.; L12,000); Venice (20/day, L18,700); Florence (every hr.; L33,500 with supplement); Rome (every hr.; L59,300 with supplement.) **Luggage storage** L1500. Open 4am-2am. **Lost and Found:** (tel. 67 71 26 77) next to *binario* 21. Open daily 7:20am-8:45pm.

Buses: Intercity buses are less convenient and more expensive than trains; **Autostradale** and many others depart from p. Castello and environs.

Public Transportation: The 3 **Metropolitana Milano** lines serve much of the city. Buses and trains fill the gaps. Municipal buses require pre-purchased ticket (L1100). Day passes for non-residents L3500.

Women's Center Hotline: Centro Azione Milano Donne, viale Tibaldi, 41 (tel. 58 10 40 67). Advises women on legal rights.

Disabled Services: Settore Servici Sociale, Largo Treces, 1 (tel. 62 08 69 10).

Laundromat: Lavanderia Automatica, corso Porta Vittoria, 51 (tel. 55 19 23 15), beyond largo Augusto behind the *duomo,* is the most central.

Late-Night Pharmacy: Though nocturnal duty rotates (call 192 for info), the one in Stazione Centrale stays open 24hrs. (tel. 669 07 35 or 669 09 35).

Hospital: Ospedale Maggiore Policlinico, via Francesco Sforza, 35 (tel. 550 31), 5min. from the *duomo* on the inner ring road.

Emergencies: tel. 113. **Police:** tel. 772 71. **"SOS for Tourists":** tel. 545 65 51 for legal complaints. **Medical Emergency:** tel. 38 83. **Ambulance:** tel. 77 33.

ACCOMMODATIONS

Every season is high season in Milan (except Aug.), and a single in an upright establishment for under L35,000 is a real find. For the best deals, head for the city's center or its southern periphery. In all cases, make reservations well ahead of time.

Ostello Pietro Rotta (HI), viale Salmoiraghi, 2 (tel. 39 26 70 95). Take MM2 to "Cadorna" and change to MM1 (direction "Molino Dorino"). Get off at "QT8." Modern with helpful staff, but very regimented. Open 7-9am and 5-11:30pm (arrive in the evening). Inflexible daytime lockout. Curfew 11:30am. L20,000. Breakfast and lockers included. Wash or dry L6000 each. Open Jan. 13-Dec. 20.

MILAN (MILANO)

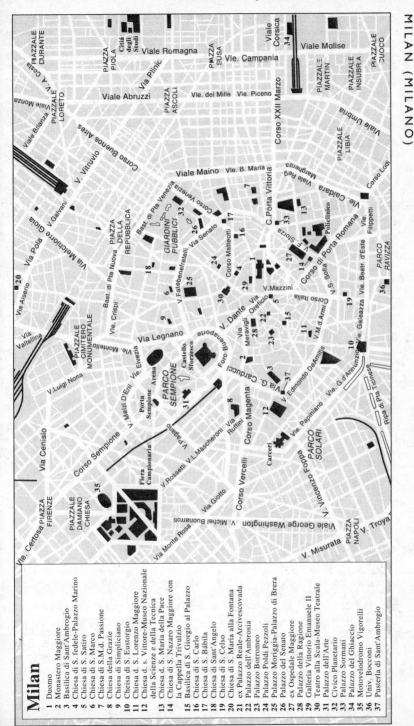

Milan

1 Duomo
2 Monastero Maggiore
3 Basilica di Sant'Ambrogio
4 Chiesa di S. fedele-Palazzo Marino
5 Chiesa di S. Satiro
6 Chiesa di S. Marco
7 Chiesa di S.M.d. Passione
8 Chiesa della Grazie
9 Chiesa di Simpliciano
10 Chiesa di S. Eustorgio
11 Chiesa d. S. Lorenzo Maggiore
12 Chiesa d. s. Vittore-Museo Nazionale
   della Scienze e della Tecnica
13 Chiesa di S. Maria della Pace
14 Chiesa di S. Nazaro Maggiore con
   la Cappella Trivulzio
15 Basilica di S. Giorgio al Palazzo
16 Chiesa di S. Carlo
17 Chiesa di S. Bábila
18 Chiesa di Sant'Angelo
19 Chiesa di S. Celso
20 Chiesa di S. Maria alla Fontana
21 ex Palazzo Reale-Arcivescovada
22 Palazzo dell'Ambrosia
23 Palazzo Borromeo
24 Palazzo Poldi Pezzoli
25 Palazzo Moriggia-Palazzo di Brera
26 Palazzo del Senato
27 ex Ospedale Maggiore
28 Palazzo della Ragione
29 Galleria Vittorio Emanuele II
30 Teatro alla Scala-Museo Teatrale
31 Palazzo dell'Arte
32 Civico Planetario
33 Palazzo Sormani
34 Palazzo del Ghiaccio
35 Motovelodromo Vigorelli
36 Univ. Bocconi
37 Pusterla di Sant'Ambrogio

Hotel Ca' Grande, via Porpora, 87 (tel. 26 14 52 95 or 26 14 40 01). Take MM1-2 to "Loreto." About 7 blocks in from p. Loreto in a free-standing building protected by a spiked fence. Clean rooms, but the street side can be noisy. Good English spoken. Singles L40,000, with bath L60,000. Doubles L60,000, with bath L80,000.

Hotel S. Tomaso, viale Tunisia, 6 (tel. 29 51 47 47), on the 3rd floor. Orderly rooms with hardwood floors, some overlooking a courtyard. Singles L40,000, with bath L45,000. Doubles L70,000. Prices may be a bit higher Sept.-Oct., a bit lower Dec.-Jan. On the 6th floor, **Hotel Kennedy** (tel. 29 40 09 34) has tidy rooms and dreamscape decor. Singles L45,000. Doubles L60,000, with bath L85,000. Reservations recommended.

FOOD

Like its fine *couture,* Milanese cuisine is classic, understated and overpriced. Specialties include *risotto giallo* (rice with saffron) and *cazzouela* (a mixture of pork and cabbage). Strike deals at the **markets** along via Santa Croce on Thursdays; on Saturdays, the **Fiera di Sinigallia,** a 400-year-old tradition, takes over via Calatafimi. For the freshest and fanciest, take your taste buds to the jolly **Viel Frutti Esotici Gelati** on the left as you face the *castello* from largo Cairoli (MM1: Cairoli).

Tarantella, v.le Abruzzi, 35, just north of via Plinio. Lively neighborhood joint with sidewalk dining. Great *antipasti.* Immense specialty salads L10,000. Pizza L8000-20,000 (try the *gorgonzola).* Open Sept.-July Sun.-Fri. noon-3pm and 7-11:30pm.

Flash, via Bergamini, 1. Take MM1 to "Duomo." At p. San Stefano. Delectable Neapolitan pizza (L7000-11,000) and many delicious *panini* (including vegetarian) at the bar (L3500-4000). Open Tues.-Sun. noon-3pm and 7pm-1am.

La Crêperie, via C. Correnti, 24, the continuation of via Torino. Fruit crepes L3000 and the "real food" variety L6000. Lunch special combo L9000. Open Mon. and Wed-Fri. noon-midnight, Sat. noon-1:30am, Sun. 4pm-midnight.

Portnoy, via de Amicis, 1, at corso di Porta Ticinese. Ultra hip. Young, socially conscious management. Writers give readings of their work followed by discussion. *Panini* L2000-4500. Open Mon.-Sat. 7am-2am.

SIGHTS

The *duomo,* with its 135 spires and 96 gargoyles, is a terrifying, radically vertical Gothic creation whose grand stained-glass windows are said to be the largest in the world. Climb to the top of the cathedral to find yourself surrounded by florid outbursts of turrets and spires. (Open daily 7am-7pm; Oct.-May 9am-4:30pm. L4000, elevator L6000. Proper dress required.) Beside the *duomo* is the monumental entrance to the **Galleria Vittorio Emanuele II,** a colossal iron-and-glass arcade housing cafés and shops. Meander through the gallery from the *duomo* to the **Teatro alla Scala (La Scala),** the world's premier opera house. Innumerable opera titans, from Caruso to Pavarotti, made their international debuts here. Enter the lavish hall through the **Museo Teatrale alla Scala.** (Open Mon.-Sat. 9am-noon and 2-6pm, Sun. 9:30am-12:30pm and 2:30-6pm; Oct.-April closed Sun. L5000.)

Via Verdi leads to via Brera and the **Pinacoteca di Brera,** one of Italy's finest museums, a 17th-century *palazzo* with works by Caravaggio, Bellini and Raphael. (Open Tues.-Sat. 9am-2pm, Sun. 9am-1pm. L8000.) The **Museo Poldi-Pezzoli,** at via Manzoni, 12, houses a superb private collection whose masterpieces reside in the Golden Room. (Open Tues. and Fri. 9am-12:30pm and 2:30-6pm, Sat. 9:30am-12:30pm and 2:30-5:30pm, Sun. 9:30am-12:30pm. L5000.)

The **Castello Sforzesco** (MM1: "Cairoli") is the huge 15th-century castle of Milan's Renaissance dukes. Its excellent sculpture collection includes Michelangelo's *Pietà Rondanini.* (Open Tues.-Sun. 9:30am-5:30pm. Free.) Leonardo da Vinci created his *Last Supper* for the refectory wall of the **Basilica di Santa Maria delle Grazie** (MM1:Cairoli). You can glimpse Leonardo's characters and use of perspective through the scaffolding, likely to remain up into the next millenium. (Open Tues.-Sun. 8:15am-1:45pm. L6000. Wheelchair accessible.)

ENTERTAINMENT AND SHOPPING

Milan's pace doesn't let up at night. Pick up the tourist office's *What's on in Milan.* Every Thursday Milan's 2 leading papers—*Corriere della Sera* and *La Repubblica*—also sum up the city's cultural offerings in slick magazine type inserts that include information about performances at **La Scala** (tel. 72 00 37 44; regular season Dec. 7-June; fewer shows in summer and Sept.). Gallery seats (notorious for inducing altitude sickness) go for as little as L30,000. (Box office tel. 72 00 37 44, open Tues.-Sun. 10am-1pm and 3:30-5:30pm; unsold gallery seats and standing room go on sale 1hr. before curtain.)

   Cinema Anteo, via Milazzo, 9, and **Angelicum,** p. Sant'Angelo, 2, show films in their original language (both charge L10,000). **Rolling Stone,** corso XXII Marzo, 32. is a noted rock club. (Open Thurs.-Sun. until 3am. Cover L20,000). Milan's leading jazz venue remains **Le Scimmie,** via Ascanio Sforza, 49. (Open daily 8pm- 2am.) Of Milan's gay discos, **Nuova Idea,** via de Castillia, 30, is the largest and best-known. (Open Tues. and Thurs.-Sun. 9:30pm-1 or 2am; cover L8000-10,000.)

   Fashion is Milan's lifeblood. Reasonably priced, well-designed clothing is sold in the shops along **corso Buenos Aires.** The Saturday **Fiera di Sinigallia** market on via Calatafini (MM2: Sant'Agostino) offers super bargains, as does the **STANDA** department store at via Torino, 37. (Open Tues.-Sun. 9am-7:30pm and Mon. 2-7:30pm.)

■■■ MANTUA (MANTOVA)

Mantua had its heyday as court of the extravagant Gonzaga dynasty. During their 400-year reign, the Gonzaga loaded the center of town with palaces, churches and towers, and lured some of the most important Renaissance artists to their court. Mantua is two hours southeast of Milan by train; the station lies a 10-minute walk up via Solferino e S. Martino and via Fratelli Bandiera from the center of town.

   The **Church of Sant'Andrea** is acclaimed as the most brilliant creation of Florentine architect Leon Battista Alberti. The façade combines the classical triumphal arch motif—barrel-vaulted portal and flanking pilasters—with an antique pedimented temple front. The plan—a vaulted church with a single aisle, flanking side chapels, and a domed crossing—served as a prototype for ecclesiastical architecture for the next 200 years. Cobblestone **Piazza Sordello** forms the center of a vast complex built by the Gonzaga. The **Palazzo Ducale** is one of the largest and most sumptuously decorated palaces in Europe. Its more than 500 rooms include a series of miniature chambers designed for court dwarves. Near the entrance is the Hall of Dukes hang Antonio Pisanelli's frescoes (1439-44), discovered in 1969 under thick layers of plaster. (Open Mon.-Sat. 9am-1pm and 2:30-4pm, Sun. 9am-1pm. L10,000 lets you into everything in the Palazzo.)

   A trek through p. Veneto and down Largo Patri leads to the opulent **Palazzo del Tè,** built in the early 16th century as the Gonzaga family's suburban villa. Idyllic murals of Psyche, remarkable for their vividness and eroticism, fresco Francesco's banquet hall. Another wing of the palace features regular exhibits by modern Italian artists alongside a collection of Egyptian art. (Open Tues.-Sun. 10am-6pm. L10,000, under 18 L4000.)

   The **tourist office** is at p. Mantegna, 6, adjacent to the church of Sant'Andrea (tel. (0376) 35 06 81); open Mon.-Sat. 9am-noon and 3-6pm). Mantua's superb youth hostel, **Ostello Sparafucile (HI)** (tel. (0376) 37 24 65), inhabits a 16th-century castle in the nearby hamlet of Lunetta di San Giorgio. Take bus #2 or 9 from p. Cavallotti. (Lockout 9am-4pm. Curfew 11pm. HI card required. L14,000. Open April-Oct. 15.) Breezy, clean rooms are at **Locanda La Rinascita,** via Concezione, 4 (tel. (0376) 32 06 07; singles L25,000, doubles L40,000). For cheap sit-down meals go to the **Self-Service Virgiliana,** p. Virgiliana, 57; this *mensa* has a *menù* for L11,000. (Open Mon.-Fri. noon-2pm.) For spicier, pricier fare featuring regional specialties, try **Ai**

Ranari, via Trieste, 11, near Porto Catena. (Cover L1500. Open Thurs.-Tues. noon-3:30pm and 7-11pm.)

ITALIAN RIVIERA (LIGURIA)

Genoa divides Liguria, the Italian Riviera, neatly in half—**Riviera di Ponente** to the west and the more splendid **Riviera di Levante** to the east, with its colorful fishing villages and clear turquoise water. This crescent-shaped coastal stretch differs greatly from its French counterpart; here you'll find elegance, not arrogance, and much less hype. Especially lovely are the **Portofino peninsula** (about ½hr. by train from Genoa) and the **Cinque Terre** area (immediately west of La Spézia). In July and August, only reservations or amazingly good fortune will get you a place for the night. Don't miss the *pasta alla genovese,* commonly known as "al pesto," and *focaccia,* a delicious oily bread topped with onions or tomato sauce.

■■■ GENOA (GENOVA)

The descendant of a proud and piratical maritime republic, Genoa's commercial center does not merit a visit; stick to the entanglement of narrow footpaths that wind their way among houses and overhanging gardens; these trails offer a peaceful respite from the chaos of the modern city. The *centro storico* (historical center) preserves many of Genoa's most important monuments; unfortunately, it is also the city's most dangerous quarter. The sights are well worth seeing, but do it with a map, during the day. North of p. de Ferrari is p. Fontane Marose, off which runs **via Garibaldi,** along which the splendid *palazzi* **Bianco, Rosso, Municipale,** and **Parodi** house many of the Flemish and Dutch masterpieces amassed by the Genovese merchants. Two other musts are the **Palazzo Ducale** in p. Matteotti and the **Villetta di Negro,** with its **Museo d'Arte Orientale,** off p. Corvetto. (Museum open Tues.-Sat. 9am-7pm, Sun. 9am-12:30pm.) Admission to all of Genoa's museums is L4000, free to those under 18. Street numbers are marked in red (commercial establishments) or black (residences or offices). Via Balbi extends from Stazione Principe to **piazza de Ferrari,** the center of town, while **via XX Settembre** runs east towards Stazione Brignole.

Accommodations, Food, and Practical Information Genoa's youth hostel, **Ostello per la Gioventù (HI),** via Costanzi, 120 (tel. (010) 24 22 457 or 58 64 07), offers panoramic views and incredible facilities. Take bus #35 5 stops, then transfer to #40 and ride to the end. (Lockout 9am-3pm. Curfew 11:30pm. HI card required. L18,000. Wheelchair access.) Women can also take advantage of the **Casa della Giovane,** p. Santa Sabina, 4 (tel. (010) 20 66 32 or 28 18 02), near p. Annunziate. (Strict 10:45pm curfew. Secure, clean singles L18,000, doubles L36,000.) Avoid the hotels in the *centro storico,* many of which rent rooms by the hour.

Genoa's culinary claim to fame is *pesto,* this editor's favorite pasta sauce, made from basil, cheese, pine nuts, garlic and olive oil. Try *pansotti,* ravioli filled with cheese and herbs served with a walnut sauce. **Osteria du Colombo e Bruno,** at #44r, offers delicious full meals for L11,000. (Open Mon.-Sat. 12:30-2:30pm and 7:30-10pm.) In the *centro storico,* **Sa Pesta,** via Giustiniani, 16r, knows its pesto, and it's cheap. (*Primi* L5000-7000, *secondi* L6000-8000. Open Mon.-Sat. noon-2:30pm.) At **Trattoria da Maria,** vico Testadoro, 14r (tel. 5810 80), off via XXV Aprile, everything's extremely fresh. (*Prezzo fisso* L12,000. Open daily noon-2pm and 4:30-7pm. Closed Fri. and Sat. night.) In summer the action moves to nearby **Nervi,** where they bar-hop or stroll along the *lungomare* lapping *gelato.*

Genoa is easily accessible by rail from Rome (15/day, 5-6hr., L33,600) and Turin (2hr., L12,100). The French border lies 2 hours westward. There are 2 train stations:

Stazione Principe, p. Acquaverde (tel. (010) 26 24 55), to the west near the port, and Stazione Brignole, p. Verdi (tel. (010) 58 63 50), farther east. Bus #40 from Brignole and #41 from Principe run, to p. de Ferrari. There are helpful tourist offices in both Principe (tel. (010) 26 26 33) and Brignole (tel. (010) 56 20 56) stations. (Both open daily 8am-8pm.) Genoa has a U.S. consulate, p. Portobello, 6 (tel. (010) 28 27 41), and one for the U.K., via XII Ottobre, 2 (tel. (010) 56 48 33).

■■■ RIVIERA DI PONENTE AND RIVIERA DI LEVANTE

Finale Ligure Eschewing the glamor and arrogance of other Riveria towns, **Finale Ligure** welcomes weary backpackers with soft sand and luxurious flora. The **Castello Uvillermin (HI),** via Generale Caviglia (tel. (019) 69 05 15), is in a turreted castle overlooking the sea. From the station, take a left onto v. Torino. At tiny p. Milano, turn left and go up the stairs, then turn right onto via Caviglia. (Reception open 7-9:30am and 5-10:30pm. Curfew 11pm, July-Aug. 11:30. Check-in 5pm, but you can leave bags 7-9:30am. Doors locked until 7am. L14,000/person for cardholders (otherwise L19,000; cards cost L30,000). Open March15-Oct.15.) The best culinary options are on via Rossi and via Roma, inland from the waterfront. **Spaghetteria Il Posto,** via Porro, 21, is an elegant locale for pasta-festing. Try *penne zar* (with salmon and caviar) for L8500. (Cover 1500. Open Tues.-Sun. 7:30-10:30pm.) Savor *panini* and MTV at **Paninoteca Pilade,** via Garibaldi, 67 (tel. 69 22 20; open daily 10am-1am; off-season 10am-2:30pm and 4-8pm).

Constant **trains** head to Genoa (L6000), Ventimiglia (L7000), and Santa Margherita Ligure (L8200). To the left of the train station, **SAR buses** run to neighboring beachside towns. Orange city buses will take you to **Finalborgo** for L1000. The **IAT tourist office,** via S. Pietro, 14 (tel. (019) 69 25 81, -82), on the street parallel to the waterfront, provides a free map and loving advice. (Open Mon.-Sat. 8am-1pm and 4-7pm; off-season Mon.-Sat. 8am-1pm and 3-6pm, Sun. 8:30am-12:30pm.) Rent **bikes** at **Oddone,** via Colombo, 20 (tel. (019) 69 42 15), behind the tourist office.

Camogli With a fabulous pebble beach and festive atmosphere, Camogli takes its name from the wives who ran the town while their husbands sailed its once-huge fishing fleet. (Camogli is a contraction of *casa mogli*—wives' house.) Stay at **Albergo La Camogliese,** via Garibaldi, 55 (tel. (0185) 77 14 02), down the loooong stairway near the train station. The wonderful owner offers "Let's Go *amici*" discounts on luxurious rooms. (Singles with bath L45,000; doubles 55,000, with bath L60,000-80,000). Don't miss the joy of eating *camogliese al rhum*, a chocolate-covered rum cream puff, at **Revello,** via Garibaldi, 183 (tel. 77 07 77). (Open daily 7:30am-1pm and 3:30-7:30pm.) Reach Camogli by train (L1500) or bus (L1700) from Santa Margherita. The **tourist office,** via XX Settembre, 33 (tel. 77 10 66), looms to your right as you exit the station. (Open Mon.-Sat. 9am-12:30pm and 4-7pm, Sun. 9am-12:30pm; Sept.-June Mon.-Sat. 9am-12:30pm and 3:30-6:30pm.)

Santa Margherita Ligure When you tire of overpriced, crowded beach towns, come here for an affordable taste of what a real Italian Riviera holiday is supposed to be. Evocative of the elegance of an era now past, you can still experience the fantasy of glamour which has not been ruined by tourist development. Frequent trains from Genoa (L2400) make this an excellent base for exploration of the Portofino peninsula. The English-speaking **tourist office,** via XXV Aprile, 2b (tel. (0185) 28 74 85), provides accommodations service and a town map. Turn right from the train station onto via Roma, then right again on via XXV Aprile. (Open daily 8:45am-12:30pm and 3:30-7pm.) **Corallo,** via XXV Aprile, 14 (tel. (0185) 28 67 74), about a block from the tourist office, offers tidy, recently repainted rooms. (Curfew 2:30am. Singles L28,000. Doubles L48,000.) The large, clean rooms at **Albergo Annabella,** via Costasecca, 10 (tel. (0185) 28 65 31), are another option. (Singles

L35,000. Doubles L53,000. Showers L2000. High season ½–pension required: L65,000/person.) Buy bread, cheese, meat, and produce along corso Matteotti; on Fridays from 8am to 1pm, the shops spill out onto the *corso*. For a hearty meal, try the Giavanuzzi family's **Trattoria Baicin,** via Algeria, 9, off p. Martiri della Libertà. Mamma's *Trofie alla Genovese* (L6500) is stupendous. (Open Tues.-Sun. noon-3pm and 6:45pm-midnight.) **Rosticceria Revelant,** via Gramsci, 15, east of p. Martiri della Libertà, offers unbeatable take-out meals. (Open Thurs.-Tues. 8am-1pm and 4:30-8:30pm, Sun. 7:30am-1pm.)

Portofino and San Fruttuoso Gorgeous yacht- and boutique-filled **Portofino** merits a daytrip from Santa Margherita. Though you won't be able to afford to stay or eat, the harbor view is enthralling. The town is accessible by foot (1½hr) from Portofino and by boat from Camogli (round-trip L10,000); **buses** also leave every ½-hour to and from Santa Margherita (L1400)—get off at Portofino Mare, not Portofino Vetta. Trek up to the **Chiesa di San Giorgio** or the **castle** for enchanting vistas of the bay, or follow the "Al faro" signs to reach the **lighthouse** for a breathtaking view of the coastline. Isolated **San Fruttuoso** is a wonderfully verdant village at the peninsula's western corner. Boats run here (about every hr.) from Camogli (round-trip L10,000), or you can venture on foot (1½.; from Portofino.)

Cinque Terre and La Spézia Tripping down the coast, don't miss the **Cinque Terre**, a group of 5 isolated villages clinging to the cliffs above the sea. The towns, in order of increasing distance from Genoa, are: **Monterosso, Vernazza, Corniglia, Manarola,** and **Riomaggiore,** among which Monterosso is the biggest, easiest to reach, and least charming. The **tourist office** (tel. (0187) 81 75 06) in Monterosso next to the train station, provides accommodations service and currency exchange. (Open April-Oct. Mon.-Sat. 9am-noon and 5:30-8pm, Sun. 9am-noon.) Sack out at **Hostel Mamma Rosa,** p. Unità 2, Riomaggiore (tel. (0187) 92 00 50), an ultra-mellow establishment across from the bar at the train station (L18,000), or check out the *affitta camere* (private rooms) in Corniglia and Vernazza. Munch happily on any of the seafood dishes that abound in the Cinque Terre, and wash them down with *sciacchetrà,* the sweet local white wine.

La Spézia is more commercial and less pleasant than the smaller towns of the surrounding coast, but it serves as a departure point to Corsica. **Corsica Ferries** (tel. (0187) 212 82) and **Navarma Lines** (tel. (0187) 218 44), both at molo Italia, offer comparable service to Bastia, Corsica (L31,000-38,000). If you must stay here, **Albergo Terminus,** via Paleocapa, 21 (tel. (0187) 372 04), has lofty singles (L35,000) and doubles (L47,000). **Osteria con Cucina "del Prione,"** via Prione, 270, will satisfy your every culinary whim. (Pasta from L6000, pizza from L4500. Cover L1500. Open Mon.-Sat. 6-10:30pm.) The new **Tourist Information Booth** in the station provides a detailed map of the city, brochures, and a list of official *affita camere* for all 5 villages of Cinque Terre. (English spoken. Open Mon.-Sat. 8:30am-1pm and 2-6pm, Sun. 8:30am-6pm.)

EMILIA-ROMAGNA

Italy's wealthiest wheat and dairy producing region covers the fertile plains of the Po river valley and fosters the finest culinary traditions on the Italian Peninsula. Plan to go over budget, as you gorge on Parmesan cheese and prosciutto and Bolognese fresh pasta and *mortadella,* washing it down with reds like the sparkling *lambrusco.* The region looks different than the rest of Italy; the uninterrupted plains seem to stretch forever, and the illusion of distance is magnified by the cold gray fog of winter—replaced in summer by a silver haze and stifling heat that make distant towns shimmer.

LET'S GO® By Train

Eurail passes
The least expensive and easiest way to see Europe

Call toll free **1-800-5LETS-GO**

Eurail Pass

	1st class
15 days	$498
21 days	$648
1 month	$798
2 months	$1098
3 months	$1398

Eurail Flexipass

Any 5 days in 2 months	$348
Any 10 days in 2 months	$560
Any 15 days in 2 months	$740

Also Available:

Country Passes

Rain n' Drive

Flexotel

Eurail Youthpass

Under 26	2nd class
15 days	$430
21 days	$550
1 month	$678

Eurail Youth Flexipass

Any 5 days in 2 months	$255
Any 10 days in 2 months	$398
Any 15 days in 2 months	$540

*Prices subject to change at any time.

See reverse for order card
Free UPS mailing

YES! I WANT TO JOIN THE CLUB.

With my Hostelling International card I can stay at 6,000 hostels in 70 countries and enjoy great discounts around the world. Please sign me on as a: ❏ youth (under 18) $10, ❏ adult $25, ❏ family $35, ❏ senior (over 54) $15, or ❏ Life $250, member and send me my 12-month membership and **FREE** directory of all the hostels in North America.

Name _____

Address _____

City _____ State _____ Zip _____

Phone _____ Birth Date (m/d/y)_____

Departure Date_____ Destination _____

Or call 202-783-6161 for the office nearest you.

HOSTELLING INTERNATIONAL

The new seal of approval of the International Youth Hostel Federation.

HOSTELLING INTERNATIONAL®

The right Eurail for me is:

Description	Name (Should appear as on passport)	Price

Free Shipping and Handling with this card! | Total | |

Bill my:

❑ Mastercard ❑ Visa ❑ AmEx ❑ Check or Money Order

Card # _____ Name on Card _____

Ship my Eurail to:

Exp. Date: _____

Name _____ Birthdate _____ Date trip begin _____

Street address _____ City _____ ST _____ ZIP _____ Phone Number _____

We also offer:

Travel Gear
Discounted Airfares
AYH cards

Mail Order to
Let's Go Travel

53A Church Street
Cambridge, MA 02138

Or Call Toll Free
1-800-5LETS-GO

See our Catalog in
this Guide

PLACE
STAMP
HERE

HOSTELLING INTERNATIONAL

American Youth Hostels
Membership Services Department
P.O. Box 37613
Washington, D.C. 20013-7613

ılıılıllıııllıııılllılllııılllıııılllıllılıııll

■■■ BOLOGNA

With one forkful of Bologna's *tortellini,* it becomes clear that this city appreciates the better things in life. The city founded the first university in Europe 900 years ago; the **Università di Bologna** has since graduated the likes of Dante, Petrarch, Copernicus, and Tasso. A general opulence belies wealthy Bologna's contradictory position as the outpost of the Italian Communist Party.

Bologna's most remarkable sight is the endless series of porticoes lining buildings throughout the city, a 14th-century solution to an urban housing crisis. The tranquil expanse of **piazza Maggiore** is the city's heart and center. It adjoins the **piazza del Nettuno,** whose **Palazzo del Podestà** was remodeled by Fioravanti's son Aristotle, who later designed Moscow's Kremlin. Follow the afternoon shade to the steps of the **Basilica of San Petronio,** a huge Gothic structure that some claim would have been bigger than St. Peter's had the Pope not meddled. The bronze *Neptune and Attendants* by Giambologna splash happily in the fountain outside. (Open 7:30am-7pm.) You can climb the less tipsy of the two towers on **piazza di Porta Ravegnana.** (Open daily 9am-6pm; winter 9am-7pm. L3000.)

Down via Santo Stefano, the triangular **piazza Santo Stefano** opens into a complex of Romanesque churches of austere beauty. The grandest is the round **Chiesa del San Sepolcro;** San Petronio, patron of Bologna, rests under a carved pulpit. In the courtyard behind is the **Basin of Pilate,** in which Pontius supposedly cleansed his hands. A few blocks away in the **Church of San Domenico,** the saintly founder of the Dominican order is buried under a marble monument with statuettes by Michelangelo and Nicolò dell'Arca. (Most churches open early morning-noon and 4-6pm.) The **Pinacoteca Nazionale,** via delle Belle Arti, 56, one of Italy's major galleries, contains a beguiling bevy of Bolognese paintings and a spread of Renaissance masterpieces. (Open Tues.-Sat. 9am-2pm, Sun. 9am-1pm. L6000.)

The university ensures classical concerts and a hopping nightlife during the academic year. Get *Bologna Spettacolo News* from the tourist office for listings and times, and bar-hop the university quarter around p. Verdi.

Accommodations, Food, and Practical Information

Prices are high and rooms scarce due to the glut of students and business travelers. Bologna's clean, congenial **Ostello Di San Sisto (HI),** via Viadagota, 5 and 14 (tel. and fax 50 18 10), overlooks fertile farmland 6km away. Ask at the tourist office for the map with specific directions. (Reception open 7-9am and 5-11:30pm. Lockout 9am-5pm. L17,000, nonmembers L22,000. Breakfast included.) In the heart of town, try the cleanliness-obsessed **Albergo Panorama,** via Livraghi 1 (tel. (051) 22 18 02; singles L40,000, doubles L65,000). Nearer the station, **Albergo Minerva,** via de'Monari, 3 (tel. (051) 23 96 52), offers optimal location and decent rooms (singles L45,000, doubles L65,000).

Don't miss Bologna's namesake dish, *spaghetti alla Bolognese,* pasta with a hefty meat and tomato sauce; or, perhaps, "bologna," known locally as *mortadella.* The areas around via Augusto Righi and via Piella, as well as the neighborhood of via Saragozza, are especially good for cheap, traditional *trattorie.* **Antica Trattoria Roberto Spiga,** v. Broccaindosso 21/A, a modest, miraculous Bolognese relic, serves complete meals with wine or water (L18,500) and sublime *gnocchi* (L5000). (Open Sept.-July Mon.-Sat. noon-2pm and 7-10pm.) **Ristorante Clorofilla,** strada Maggiore, 64, serves up innovative vegetarian specialties and imaginative salads (L5500-8000). (Open Mon.-Sat. 11am-3pm and 7pm-midnight.) Pizzeria **La Mamma "Self-Service"** at via Zamboni, 16, offers a 10% discount to students with ID (pizza L5500-10,000; open daily noon-2:30pm and 7-10pm). Or mingle with the student crowd at the **University Mensa,** piazza Puntoni, 1, where you can load up on a full meal for only L1000-7800. (Show any student ID to buy a ticket. Open Sept.-July Mon.-Sat. 11:45am-2:30pm and 6:45-9pm.)

Bologna's **tourist office,** in the train station (tel. (051) 24 65 41), books rooms for free. Pick up a copy of *Bologna Dove* for the latest information and a respectable free map. (Open Mon.-Sat. 9am-7pm.) The main office in Palazzo Comunale at p. Maggiore, 6 (tel. (051) 23 96 60), is more exhaustive. Poste Restante goes to the **post office** at p. Minghetti, southeast of p. Maggiore. (**Postal code:** 40100. Open Mon.-Fri. 8:15am-6:40pm, Sat. 8:15am-12:20pm.) One of Italy's biggest rail hubs, the **train station** (tel. (051) 24 64 90) is in p. delle Medaglio d'Oro at the northern end of town, a 20-minute walk from the center (or hop bus #25 or 30; L1300).

■■■ PARMA

Parma exudes a mannered elegance. Conveniently located on the Bologna-Milan rail line, Parma rivals Bologna as Italy's food capital and is home to the most refined *prosciutto* ham and fragrant *parmigiano* cheese on the peninsula, as well as *lambrusco,* a deliciously intoxicating red wine. Try to arrive famished.

Parma's **duomo** contains two medieval masterpieces: the moving *Descent from the Cross,* precursor of several Renaissance versions, and the *Episcopal Throne* by Benedetto Antelami, Parma's medieval master sculptor. (Open daily 7:30am-noon and 3-7pm.) Correggio painted the interior of the dome of the **Church of San Giovanni Evangelista,** while Antelami festooned the exterior of the **battistero** (baptistry) with bas-reliefs of fantastic animals and biblical allegories. (Open 6:30am-noon and 3:30-8pm.) Nearby, the **Palazzo della Pilotta** houses the **Galleria Nazionale di Parma,** with works by da Vinci, the Holbeins and van Dyck. (Open Tues.-Sat. 9am-2pm. L4000.)

Via Garibaldi, Parma's main street, runs from the station to the center of town. The **Azienda Promozione Turistica,** p. Duomo, 5 (tel. (0521) 23 47 35), has price lists of Parmesan accomodations. (Open Mon.-Fri. 9am-12:30pm and 3:30-6:30pm, Sat. 9am-12:30pm, Oct.-April Mon.-Fri. 9am-12:30pm and 3-6pm, Sat. 9am-12:30pm.) The **Ostello Cittadella (HI),** via Passo Buole (tel. (0521) 58 15 46), lodges in a 17th-century fortress; take bus #9 in front of the station. (Reception open all day. Lockout 9:30am-5pm. Curfew 11pm. Members only, but sometimes accepts student ID. L12,000.) The **Albergo Leon D'Oro,** viale A. Fratti, 4 (tel. (0521) 77 31 81), off via Trento, 2 blocks left from the station, has functional if uninspiring rooms. (Singles L25,000. Doubles L40,000.) **Casa Della Giovane,** via del Conservatorio, 11 (tel. (0521) 28 32 29), offers clean rooms to women under 25 (L17,000).

Eat lustily while in Parma. The wonderful **Sorelle Pachini,** strada Farini, 27, near p. Garibaldi, hide the best *trattoria* in town under the cover of a salami shop. The menu changes daily to suit the sisters' fancies (*primi* L8000, *secondi* L10,000-12,000; open Mon.-Sat. noon-2:30pm). For dinner, hit the **Trattoria Corrieri,** via Conservatorio, 1. Exceptional *tortelli di zucca* (ravioli made with sweet squash in a parmigiano sauce) are L6000; wash them down with L6000 carafes of *lambrusco* . An **open-air market** can be found at p. Ghiaia, off viale Mariotti, past Palazzo Pilotta (8am-1pm and 3-8pm).

TUSCANY (TOSCANA)

The archetypal Italy springs from Tuscany. Its landscapes, familiar from Renaissance paintings, mix sere ochres with groves of holly and olive trees, lines of cypresses and parasol pines. Grapevines and sunflowers follow the contours of the hills that roll from the rocky, forested Apuan Alps to the sea and the hills of the south. Its towns, often walled, preen upon the heights, quintessential hill towns. Its Renaissance culture—an unprecedented explosion of art, architecture, and humanist scholarship—became the culture of Italy, while Tuscan, the language of Dante, Petrarch, and Machiavelli, is today's textbook Italian.

The region has only one drawback: it's too popular. Though Tuscans are generally very gracious, your English may induce sighs from natives, especially in Florence. Efforts to speak Italian, however mangled, will be much appreciated.

An extensive and convenient transportation system makes it easy to tour Tuscany's countryside. The state railroad serves all major towns and many smaller ones, though the many hill towns are better reached by bus. Hitching is not uncommon in the area. Given the ease of transportation and the overcrowding of sightseers, plan your itinerary wisely. Youth hostels abound in Tuscany, but hotels are on the expensive side. Reservations are advisable all summer, especially in Florence, Siena, and Pisa. Camping is possible at the many lakes, mountains, and coastal resorts.

■■■ FLORENCE (FIRENZE)

Epicenter of the Renaissance, Florence retains its beauty and vitality. Michelangelo, Machiavelli, and Cellini—all Florentines—presided over Italy's cultural rebirth, and the Medici court became Italy's political and economic standard-bearer. The fruits of the period are still evident in the city's seemingly endless array of museums, churches and *palazzi*. Florence preserves its wool town beginnings in small churches and family *trattorie* even as it upholds the Renaissance ideal of progress with a flair for fashion, finance and food.

ORIENTATION AND PRACTICAL INFORMATION

Major arteries radiate from the *duomo* and its two *piazze:* piazza San Giovanni encircling the baptistry and piazza del Duomo around the cathedral. The city's main street, via dei Calzaiuoli, runs from between the baptistry and the *duomo* to piazza Signoria towards the river Arno. Parallel to via dei Calzaiuoli on the west, via Roma leads from piazza S. Giovanni through piazza della Repubblica to the Ponte Vecchio, which spans the Arno to the district called the Oltrarno. For guidance through Florence's tangled center, pick up a free map (ask for the one with the street index) either inside the station from the booth marked *Informazioni Turistiche Alberghiere* or just outside at the red and white tourist booth. A more detailed map is the *Litografia Artistica Cartografica* (L3000 at newsstands).

Florence has two entirely independent sequences of street numbers: red indicates a commercial building (noted here with an "r"), and blue or black a residential one (including most *pensioni*).

Tourist Offices: Azienda Promozionale di Turismo: Offices at Chiasso Barconcelli, 19r (tel. 230 21 24), via Cavour, 1r (tel. 276 03 82), and via Manzoni, 16 (tel. 247 81 41). Open Mon.-Sat. 8am-7pm. Other offices at Piazzetta Guelfa, 3 (tel. 28 40 15) and via Martelli, 6 (tel. 21 38 93). Open Mon.-Sat. 9am-3pm. **Consorzio I.T.A.** (tel. 28 28 93), in the train station by track 16 next to the pharmacy. Come in person and they'll find you a room. L3000-5000 fee. Open daily 8:30am-9pm.

Budget Travel: STS (Student Travel Service), via Zanetti 18r (tel. 28 41 83). Student discounts on rail, bus, and plane tickets. Open Mon.-Fri. 9:30am-12:30pm and 3:30-6:30pm, Sat. 9:30am-12:30pm.

Consulates: U.S., lungarno Vespucci, 38 (tel. 239 82 76). Open Mon.-Fri. 8:30am-noon and 2-4pm. **U.K.,** lungarno Corsini, 2 (tel. 28 41 33). Open Mon.-Fri. 9:30am-12:30pm and 2:30-4:30pm. Citizens of **Canada, Australia,** and **New Zealand** should contact their consulates in Rome.

Currency Exchange: Banks have the best rates. Open Mon.-Fri. 8:20am-1:20pm and 2:45-3:45pm. Banks open on Sat. mornings close by 11:20am. **Cassa di Risparmio di Firenze** now has ATMs to change money at via de' Bardi, 73r; via de' Tornabuoni, 23r; via degli Speziali, 16r; and via dei Servi, 40r. Open 24hrs.

American Express: v. Dante Alighieri, 20-22r (tel. 509 81). From the *duomo,* walk down v. Calzaiuoli; turn left onto v. dei Tavolini. AmEx is on the little *piazza* at its end. Open Mon.-Fri. 9am-5:30pm, Sat. 9am-12:30pm. A **branch office** is at via Guicciardini, 49r (tel. 27 87 51), across the Ponte Vecchio from the old city down

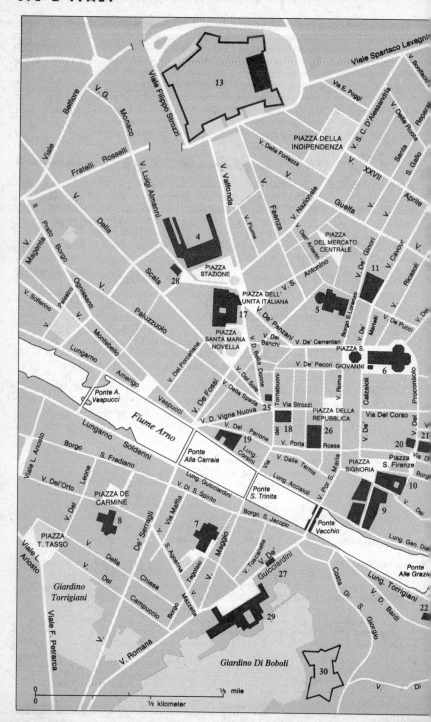

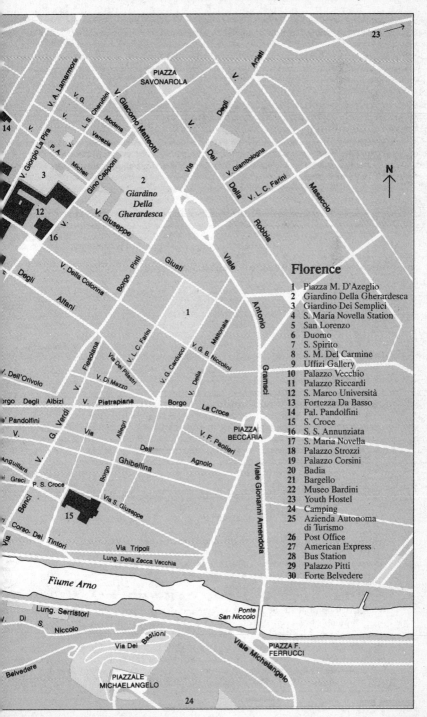

Florence

1   Piazza M. D'Azeglio
2   Giardino Della Gherardesca
3   Giardino Dei Semplici
4   S. Maria Novella Station
5   San Lorenzo
6   Duomo
7   S. Spirito
8   S. M. Del Carmine
9   Uffizi Gallery
10 Palazzo Vecchio
11 Palazzo Riccardi
12 S. Marco Università
13 Fortezza Da Basso
14 Pal. Pandolfini
15 S. Croce
16 S. S. Annunziata
17 S. Maria Novella
18 Palazzo Strozzi
19 Palazzo Corsini
20 Badia
21 Bargello
22 Museo Bardini
23 Youth Hostel
24 Camping
25 Azienda Autonoma
    di Turismo
26 Post Office
27 American Express
28 Bus Station
29 Palazzo Pitti
30 Forte Belvedere

via de Guicciardini on the left. If you pass the Palazzo Pitti, you've also passed the office. Financial services and rail reservations only. Open Mon.-Fri. 9am-5:30pm.

Post Office: via Pellicceria, off p. della Repubblica. **Fermo Posta** at windows #23 and 24. Open Mon.-Fri. 8:15am-7pm, Sat. 8:15am-noon. **Postal Code:** 50100.

Telephones: ASST, at the post office. Open 24hrs. Also at via Cavour, 21r. Open 9am-9pm; in winter 9am-8pm. Shorter lines at **SIP** in the train station. One booth available for international calls. Open daily 7:30am-9:30pm. **City Code:** 055.

Trains: Santa Maria Novella Station, near the center of town. Information office (tel. 27 87 85) open daily 9am-5pm. Try the (English-speaking) computers outside the office to plan your trip. Every hr. to Bologna (1hr., L7200, *rapido* supplement L2700); Venice (3½hr., L18,700, *rapido* supplement L6400); Milan (3½hr., L22,000, *rapido* supplement L9300) and Rome (2½hr., L22,000). All trains arrive here except a few to and from Rome, which use the **Campo di Marte** station on the east side of town. Bus #19 connects the 2 stations about every 20min. around the clock (25min.).

Buses: SITA, via Santa Caterina da Siena, 15r (tel. 48 36 51, Sat.-Sun. tel. 21 14 87). Frequent buses to Siena (2hr., L8300); San Gimignano (13/day, L7100). **LAZZI,** p. Stazione, 4-6r (tel. 21 51 54), to Pisa (L8700). **LAZZI Eurolines** to Rome and Naples.

Public Transportation: ATAF, p. del Duomo, 57r. Tickets (L1000 for 70min.; L5000 for 24hr.) must be bought *before boarding* and are available at the train station or at *tabacchi.* L34,100 fine for ticketless passengers.

Bike and Moped Rental: Promotourist, via B. Bandinelli, 43 (tel. 70 18 63). Bikes start at L7000/3hr., L15,000/day. Mopeds start at L5000/hr., L30,000/day, L180,000/week. No license required, but have ID showing you're at least 16.

Hitchhiking: Expect all the usual hazards. Those going on the A-1 to Bologna and Milan or the A-11 to the Riviera and Genoa take bus #29, 30, or 35 from the train station to the feeder near Peretola. Those desiring the A-1 to Rome and the Siena extension take bus #31 or 32 from the station to exit 23. The **International Lift Center,** corso Tintori, 39 (tel. 28 06 21), matches passengers with drivers for a fee. Open Mon.-Sat. 9am-7:30pm, Sun. noon-3pm.

Bookstores: BM Bookstore, borgo Ognissanti, 4r (tel. 29 45 75). Hugest selection of English language books in Florence. Open Mon.-Sat. 9am-1pm and 3:30-7:30pm, Sun. 9am-1pm; Nov.-Feb. closed Sun.

Lost Property: If on a train: **Ufficio Oggetti Rivenuti** in train station (tel. 235 21 90). Otherwise, **Ufficio Oggetti Smarrito,** via Circondaria, 19 (tel. 36 79 43).

Laundromat: Elensec, via dei Neri, 46r (tel. 28 37 47), near p. San Remigio. L3000/kg. Open Mon.-Fri. 8:30am-1pm and 3:30-7:30pm. **Lavaria Express,** p. S. Pier Maggiore. L3000/kg. Open Mon.-Fri. 8:30am-1pm.

Public Baths: Bagno S. Agostino, via S. Agostino, 8, off p. Santo Spirito. Bath L3000. Soap and towel L1500. Open Tues. and Thurs. 3:30-6:45pm, Sat. 8:30am-noon and 3:30-6:45pm.

Pharmacy: Farmacia Comunale, by track #16 in the station (tel. 28 94 35). Open 24hrs. **Molteni,** via Calzaiuoli, 7r (tel. 28 94 90).

Medical Assistance: Misericordia, p. del Duomo, 20 (tel. 21 22 22). **Tourist Medical Services,** via Lorenzo il Magnifico, 59 (tel. 47 54 11). 24-hr. house calls.

Emergency: tel. 113. **Police: Questura** (headquarters), via Zara, 2 (tel. 497 71). On weekends or after hours go around the corner to via Duca D'Aosta. English-speaking personnel usually available. **Ufficio Stranieri** (for visa, work-permit or passport problems) is at the same address and phone number.

ACCOMMODATIONS AND CAMPING

Florence abounds with one-star *pensioni* and private homes with *affitta camere*. Many reputable hotel proprietors, including those listed in this book, may approach you when you disembark at the train station. If you arrive late in the afternoon, check with the accommodations service at the train station. The best places go early, so reservations *(prenotazioni)* are wise, especially if you plan to visit at Easter or in summer. The vast majority of *pensioni* prefer to take reservations in the form of a letter with at least 1 night's deposit by postal money order, either in dollars or lire. From June to August, and around Easter, there's almost no chance you will find any space in the best lodgings without prior reservations (and a deposit). Calling a day or so in advance may make things easier, but remember that without a deposit most hotels will only hold reservations until noon. It's polite to leave L1000 per day on the pillow for the person who cleans your room. If you have any complaints talk first to the proprietor, and then to the **Ufficio Controllo Alberghi**, via Cavour, 37 (tel. 27 601).

Sleeping in Florence's train stations, streets, or parks is a poor idea, and police discourage it. The city's best budget lodgings can be found at **Pensionale Pio X** and **Istituto Gould** in the Oltrarno.

Hostels

Istituto Gould, via dei Serragli, 49 (tel. 21 25 76), across the river in the Oltrarno. Leave the station by track #16, turn right, and walk to p. della Stazione. Go straight down via degli Avelli, with Santa Maria Novella church on your right. Cross p. Sta. Maria Novella and continue straight down via dei Fossi, over the Ponte alla Carraia, and down via dei Serragli (15min.). One of the best lodgings in Florence: staff is happy to answer questions, and the sunny rooms are spotless. All profits support a local orphanage. Only 2 drawbacks: no checking in or out on Sun., and the rooms over the street are often noisy. Open Mon.-Fri. 9am-1pm and 3-7pm, Sat. 9am-1pm. Singles L35,000, with bath L38,000. Doubles L50,000, with bath L54,000. Triples with bath L69,000. Quads with bath L84,000. Bed in a quad L18,000. Sheets and towels included. Rooms scarce during the academic year. Reserve 3-4 months in advance with deposit in spring. Arrive by 8am for a room.

Pensionato Pio X, via dei Serragli, 106 (tel. 22 50 44). Follow the directions to Istituto Gould (above) then walk a few more blocks down the street. Quiet, no daytime lockout, gregarious management, clean, 4 or 5 beds/room. 2-day min. stay, 5-day max. stay. Check-out 10am. Curfew midnight. L18,000/person. Showers included; L3000 more for bath. No reservations. Usually full in summer, but turnover is high. On weekends arrive before 9am.

Ostello della Gioventù Europa Villa Camerata (HI), viale Augusto Righi, 2-4 (tel. 60 14 51), northeast of town. Leave the station by track #5, then take bus #17b (20-30min.). You can also take this bus from p. del Duomo. In gorgeous villa with *loggia* and gardens. Tidy and popular, though far away. Reception open Mon.-Fri. 9am-1pm and 3-7pm. Check-out 9am. Curfew midnight. L18,000. L14,000 to stay outside in tent, breakfastless. L5000/night extra for nonmembers. Breakfast and sheets included. Dinner L12,000. Open daily 2-11:30pm; off-season 3-10:30pm. Reserve by letter only.

Ostello Santa Monaca, via S. Monaca, 6 (tel. 26 83 38), off via dei Serragli near Istituto Gould. Crowds many beds into the high-ceilinged rooms, but has the best price for this central location. Curfew 1am. No breakfast. Shower included. Sign-up sheet posted 9:30am-1pm. No reservations. Open 8-9:30am and 4-11:30pm.

Hotels: Near the Railroad Station

Beyond the Basilica of Santa Maria Novella and in the immediate vicinity you'll find excellent budget accommodations galore, close to the *duomo* and *centro,* a short walk from the station. Here, along **via Nazionale, via Faenza, via Fiume, via Guelfa,** and nearby, cheap establishments abound—often several to a building.

Pensione La Mia Casa, p. Santa Maria Novella, 23 (tel. 21 30 61). A 14th-century *palazzo* with clean rooms and quiet views. Every night, the proprietor screens—in English and for free—a documentary on Florence (8pm) and a relatively recent American film (9pm). Curfew midnight. Singles L28,000. Doubles L43,000, with bath L54,000. Triples L58,000, with bath L73,000. Quads L73,000, with bath L92,000. Breakfast L6000.

Locanda La Romagnola and **Soggiorno Gigliola,** via della Scala, 40 (tel. 21 15 97 and 28 79 81). Leave the station by track #5, walk across the street and turn right onto via della Scala after a block. Friendly, simple, and likely to have room. Curfew midnight. Singles L33,000, with bath L45,000. Doubles L51,000, with bath L68,000. Triples L65,000, with bath L81,000. Showers L3000.

Albergo Montreal, via della Scala, 43 (tel. 238 23 31). Clean, friendly, professional. Curfew 1:30am. Singles L38,000. Doubles with bath L63,000. Triples with bath L80,000. Quads with bath L100,000.

Hotel Visconti, p. Ottaviani, 1 (tel. 21 38 77). Friendly proprietor. Fussily decorated singles L35,000. Doubles L52,000, with bath L67,000. Triples L98,000, with bath L113,000. Quads L126,000, with bath L145,000. Breakfast included.

Hotel Elite, via della Scala, 12 (tel. 21 53 95). Kind, enthusiastic proprietor is rightly proud of his well-maintained 8-room hotel. Singles with shower L45,000; with bath L55,000. Doubles with bath L75,000. Triples L100,000. Breakfast L10,000. To reserve, send 1 night's deposit or call ahead and show up by noon.

Via Faenza, 56, houses no fewer than 6 separate *pensioni*. From the station follow the directions to via Nazionale, on which via Faenza is the 2nd intersection. **Pensione Azzi** (tel. 21 38 06) styles itself the *locanda degli artisti*—the artists' inn. Friendly management, large, immaculate rooms, and elegant dining room and terrace. Small but growing library ranges from Stephen King to art history (and not much in between). Curfew 1am. Singles L40,000-50,000. Doubles L55,000-80,000. Triples L90,000. Breakfast L3000. 7- to 8-bed dorms L25,000/person. **Albergo Anna** (tel. 239 83 22). Lovely rooms—some ceilings with frescoes, others with fans. Singles L45,000. Doubles L70,000. Triples L95,000. Breakfast L8000. When it's slow, the proprietress may knock L5000 off the price of a room. **Albergo Merlini** (tel. 21 28 48). Light and airy; hip and breezy. Breakfast on the terrace, overlooking a garden to the *duomo* beyond. Curfew 1am. Singles L38,000. Doubles L60,000, with bath L75,000. Triples L69,000. **Albergo Armonia** (tel. 21 11 46). Clean and adequate. Doubles L75,000. Triples L105,000. Quads L132,000. Quints L150,000. Showers and breakfast included; prices significantly lower Nov.-March. **Albergo Marini** (tel. 28 48 24). Simple white rooms with comfy beds. Curfew 1am. Doubles with bath L70,000. Triples with bath L81,000. Quads with bath L100,000. Breakfast L10,000. **Locanda Paola** (tel. 21 36 82). Relaxed; furniture doesn't match. Doubles with private shower (but no toilet) L70,000. Triples L75,000, with shower L90,000. Discounts for longer stays.

Hotel Nazionale, via Nazionale, 22 (tel. 238 22 03), near p. Indipendenza. Sunny rooms and friendly French management. Breakfast (served in your room) included. Curfew midnight. Singles L46,000, with bath L56,000. Doubles L72,000, with bath L80,000. Triples L94,500, with bath L108,000. MC,Visa.

Locanda Nella e Pina, via Faenza, 69 (tel. 21 22 31 and 28 42 56). Kind proprietor will take care of you. One double has view of a spectacular garden. Curfew midnight. Singles L35,400. Doubles L52,000. Triples L70,000. Quads L90,000. **Locanda Giovanna,** (tel. 238 13 53), same address. 7 small, well-kept rooms, some with garden view. Singles L35,000. Doubles L40,000-63,000. Triples L80,000. **Hotel Soggiorno d'Erico,** same address, 4th floor (tel. and fax 21 55 31). Small rooms have views of the hills and free kitchen use. Laundry L1000/kg. Singles L36,000. Doubles L44,000. Triples L74,000. AmEx, Visa.

Pensione Daniel, via Nazionale, 22 (tel. 21 12 93), near p. Indipendenza. Small and a bit dark, but the walls are painted in pinks, yellows, and blues reminiscent of a Fra Angelico fresco. Go figure. Strict curfew midnight. Dorms L24,000/person. Doubles with bath L50,000. Breakfast L5000. No reservations.

Ausonia e Rimini, via Nazionale, 24 (tel. 49 65 47). Leaving the station from track #16, take a right, then a left onto via Nazionale. Welcoming, avuncular owners. The spotless rooms are pleasantly decorated and well-lit. Curfew 1am. Singles L42,000, with bath L55,000. Doubles L68,000, with bath L86,000. Triples L90,000, with bath L111,000. Quads L120,000, with bath L132,000. Breakfast included. Nov. 10-Jan. prices should be about 10% lower. AmEx, Visa.

Hotels: In the University Quarter

This area is considerably calmer and less tourist-ridden than its proximity to the center would suggest.

La Colomba, via Cavour, 21 (tel. 28 91 39). Sunny white modernity. Windows peer out across a charming Florentine roofscape. Italo-Australian proprietor Rosanna is helpful and friendly. Curfew 1:30am. Singles L55,000. Doubles L90,000, with bath L100,000. A real continental breakfast is included. **Hotel Sofia,** just upstairs, offers pleasant, plain rooms at good prices. Curfew 1am. Singles L36,000. Doubles L55,000. Triples L69,000. Quads L92,000.

Hotel Tina, via San Gallo, 31 (tel. 48 35 19, -93). Small *pensione* with high ceilings and artsy posters. Fantastic owners offer excellent advice on everything from local discos to hidden architectural gems in Florence. Breakfast included. Singles, L40,000. Doubles L60,000, with bath L70,000. Triples with bath L90,000.

Albergo Sampaoli, via San Gallo, 14 (tel. 28 48 34). A peaceful hotel with antique furniture and spic 'n' span bathrooms. Refrigerators on each floor. Doubles L56,000, with bath L70,000. Triples with bath L90,000. Quads L88,000. No written reservations; call the night before you arrive.

Hotels: Near the Duomo

The tourist deluge misses many of these establishments; the atmosphere benefits.

Locanda Orchidea, borgo degli Albizi, 11 (tel. 248 03 46). Dante's wife was born in this 12th-century *palazzo*, which features an intact tower. English-speaking proprietor presides over 7 exquisite rooms (some overlook a charming garden). Singles L32,000. Doubles L48,000, with shower L55,000. Triples L66,000, with shower L72,000. Quads L88,000, with shower L92,000. Quints L100,000. Reservations strongly recommended in summer.

Soggiorno Brunori, via del Proconsolo, 5 (tel. 28 96 48), off p. del Duomo. Beautiful and conveniently located building. Friendly manager speaks English. Curfew 12:30am. Doubles L54,000, with bath L68,000. Triples with bath L90,000. Quads L96,000, with bath L120,000. Breakfast L8000 served in your room.

Albergo Firenze, p. Donati, 4 (tel. 21 42 03, 26 83 01), off via del Corso. Tidy, friendly, centrally located. Singles L43,000, with bath L52,000. Doubles L66,000, with bath L77,000. Triples L95,000, with bath L105,000. Breakfast included.

Hotel Maxim, via dei Medici, 4 (tel. 21 74 74; fax 28 37 29). Another entrance at via dei Calzaiuoli, 11. Cheerful proprietor lets clean and sunny rooms near the *duomo*. Doubles L64,000, with bath L84,000. Triples L97,000, with bath L120,000. Breakfast included. Laundry L16,000/5kg. AmEx, MC, Visa.

Camping

Italiani e Stranieri, via le Michelangelo, 80 (tel. 681 19 77), near p. Michelangelo. Take bus #13 from the station. An invigorating view, one you'll share with *many* others. May tell you they're full on the phone, but if you show up with your pack, they'll probably cough up a space. 500 campsites for tents. L6000/person, L7000/tent, L4000/car, L2500/motorcycle. Open mid-March to Nov. 6am-midnight. Also try the slightly cheaper **Camping Villa Camerata,** viale A. Righi, 2-4 (tel. 61 03 00), near the youth hostel. L6000/person, L7500/small tent. Open April-Oct. 7:30am-1pm and 3-9pm.

FOOD

Like all other things Florentine, food here comes with style. White beans and olive oil form the two main staples, and most regional dishes will come loaded with one or the other, if not both. Specialties include such *antipasti* as *bruschette* (grilled Tuscan bread doused with olive oil and garlic, and sometimes topped with tomatoes and basil). For *primi,* Florentines have perfected the Tuscan classics *minestra di fagioli* (a delicious white bean and garlic soup), *trippa alla fiorentina* (tripe cooked in a tomato and cheese sauce), *pecorino* (a cheese made from sheep's milk), and the premium wine, *chianti classico.* For lunch, visit one of the many *rosticcerie gastonomie,* or browse at pushcarts throughout the city. Buy your own fresh produce, tripe, and meats at the **Mercato Centrale,** between via Nazionale and the back of San Lorenzo. (Open Mon.-Sat. 8am-1pm; Oct.-May Mon.-Sat. 6:30am-1pm and 4-8:30pm.) For staples, head to **Supermercato STANDA,** via Pietrapiana, 1r (open Tues.-Sat. 8:30am-8pm, Mon. 3-8pm), or to any of the small markets through-out the city.

No dinner in this gelato capital of Italy would be complete without a luscious lick from one of the many *gelaterie.* You know you've found a true Florentine *gelateria* when the banana is slightly off-grey, indicating only real live bananas are inside. Test **Vivoli,** via della Stinche, 7, behind the Bargello (open Sept.-July Tues.-Sun. 8am-mid-night); **Gelateria dei Neri,** via dei Neri, 20-22r (open daily 10:30am-midnight).

Trattoria da Giorgio, via Palazzuolo, 100r. Filling, down-home-style meals includ-ing *primo, secondo,* salad and wine for L14,000. Menu changes daily. There's usu-ally a wait to get in. Open Mon.-Sat. noon-3pm and 6:30-10pm.

Trattoria Mario, via Rosina, 2r. Share huge wooden tables with the crowds of locals that flock here for lunch. Menu changes daily. *Primi* L3000-5000, *secondi* L4500-9000. Open for lunch noon-3:30pm.

La Maremmana, via dei Macci, 77r (tel. 24 12 26). A rare combination: simple, generous, and affordable. *Menù* starting at L18,000. Tablecloths, cut flowers, pasta, *secondi,* side dishes, a fruit dessert and wine included. Justifiably busy. Open Sept.-July Mon.-Sat. 12:30-3pm and 7:30-10:30pm. MC, Visa.

Oltrrarno Trattoria Casalinga, via Michelozzi, 9r, near p. Santo Spirito. Hearty Tuscan meals in a relaxed, if crowded, establishment. Go for the *ravioli* made with spinach and ricotta (L6000). Menu changes daily. Cover L1500. Open Mon.-Sat. noon-3pm and 7-9:30pm.

Trattoria l'che c'è c'è, via de Mangalotti, 11r (tel. 21 65 89). The owner/chef cares about his food, as you'll taste. *Topini (gnocchi) al gorgonzola,* L7500. Try a Tuscan *secondo* like *salsicce e faglioli* (sausage and beans), L10,000. Cover L2000. Open Tues.-Sun. 11:30am-2pm and 7:30-10:30pm. Reserve in advance.

Amon, via Palazzuolo, 26-28r. Some of the best Middle Eastern food to be found on any continent. Falafel L3000, shish kebab L4000. Stand-up or take-out only. Open Mon.-Sat. noon-3pm and 7-11pm.

CarLie's Bakery, via Brache, 12r. Not just Americans lonely for home will love the fudge brownies and gooey chocolate chip cookies. Owners dole out sympathy and advice. Open Sept. 1-July 15 Tues.-Sun. 10am-1:30pm and 3:30-8pm.

SIGHTS

In past years, visitors have had to battle the crowds to see the most popular muse-ums—the Uffizi, the Accademia, the Bargello. This is no longer true, but the expla-nation for this phenomenon is unfortunate: all Florentine museums recently doubled their admission price to L4000-10,000 at most major venues. Before writing off the Uffizi or the Bargello (L10,000), remember that they house the best collec-tions of Renaissance painting and sculpture in the world. Fill in the gaps left by bud-get strictures by exploring Florence's churches, most of which are also in themselves treasuries of great art.

Piazza Signoria, Piazza San Firenze, and the Accademia In May of 1993, a bomb was detonated in the **Uffizi,** killing 5 people in nearby buildings and destroying priceless works of art. Half the rooms in the Uffizi remain closed to the public and will not open for several years as reconstruction of the bombed out rooms carefully progresses. But don't skip the Uffizi because of the closed rooms: it continues to display an unparalleled collection of Renaissance works, such as Mich-elangelo's *Doni Tondo,* Caravaggio's *Bacchus,* and Titian's *Flora.* (Open Tues.-Sat. 9am-7pm, Sun. 9am-1pm. L10,000.)

The fortress-like **Palazzo Vecchio** in p. della Signoria forms the civic center of Flo-rence. (Open Mon.-Fri. 9am-7pm, Sun. 8am-1pm. L8000.) Sculptures adorn the area, including an awkward Neptune statue to whose sculptor Michelangelo quipped: "Oh Ammannato, Ammannato, what lovely marble you have ruined!" Michelange-lo's **David** used to stand here in self-assured perfection, but it now graces the **Acca-demia,** via Ricasoli, 60. (Open Tues.-Sat. 9am-2pm, Sun. 9am-1pm; L10,000.) The heart of medieval Florence lies between the *duomo* and the Signoria around the 13th-century **Bargello**, in piazza San Firenze, once the chief magistrate's residence. It now houses the **Museo Nazionale**, with Donatello's delicate *David* and Ghiberti and Brunelleschi's *Sacrifices of Abraham*. (Open Tues.-Sat. 9am-2pm, Sun. 9am-1pm. L6000.)

Duomo Florentines often refer to their cathedral as "Santa Maria del Fiore"; asking a local about "*il duomo*" may leave both of you confused. Filippo Brunelleschi directed the construction of the largest dome in Europe since the Roman Pantheon. His revolutionary idea involved building a double-shelled dome with interlocking bricks that would support itself during construction. Michelangelo paid tribute to its harmonious proportions in a ditty he composed upon receiving the commission for the dome of St. Peter's: "*Io farò la sorella,/Già più gran ma non più bella*" ("I'm going to make its sister/Even bigger but not more beautiful"). The church has the world's third longest nave, behind St. Peter's in Rome and St. Paul's in London. The fresco in the left aisle, by a student of Fra Angelico, illustrates the *Divine Comedy* in tribute to Dante. The **orologio**, on the cathedral's back wall, a 24-hour clock designed by Paolo Uccello, runs backwards. Climb up the 463 steps around the inside of the dome to the **lantern**, and on the way survey the city from the external gallery. (*Duomo* open daily 10am-5pm. Mass held 7-10am and 5-7pm. L5000.) The much older **Battistero** (Baptistry), just in front of the *duomo*, is famous for its bronze doors (the southern set by Andrea Pisano, the others by Ghiberti). Entering the cool, cavernous interior, note the mosaics in the cupola—the devils beneath Christ's feet and the intricate tortures of Hell are worthy of Dante, who was baptized here. (Interior open Mon.-Sat. 1:30-6pm, Sun. 9am-1pm.)

Next to the *duomo* rises the bright 82m **Campanile**, the "lily of Florence blossoming in stone." (Its 414 steps open daily 8:30am-6:50pm; Nov.-March 9am-5:30pm. L5000.) Most of the *duomo's* sculpture is housed in the nearby **Museo dell'Opera del Duomo**. The collection includes an unfinished *Pietà* by Michelangelo, nearly destroyed by the frustrated sculptor. The museum now houses 4 frames from the baptistry's *Gates of Paradise* and soon will house the entire collection. (Open Mon.-Sat. 9am-7:30pm; winter until 6pm. L5000.)

Churches and Palazzi The churches of Florence are as much like museums as they are places of worship. Lorenzo il Magnifico, the great Medici political boss and patron of the arts, is buried in Brunelleschi's **Basilica di San Lorenzo**. (Open daily 7am-12:15pm and 3:30-5:30pm.) The neighboring **Biblioteca Mediceo-Laurenziana**, its rooms designed by Michelangelo, was a wellspring of Mannerist architecture. (Open Mon.-Sat. 9am-1pm. Free.) Michelangelo's simple, unfinished **New Sacristy**, the final resting place of Lorenzo and Giuliano de' Medici, stands in sharp contrast to the gaudy, ornate chapel that shelters it. The dubious look of the female figures *Dawn* and *Night* may derive from Michelangelo's refusal to employ female models. (Open Tues.-Sat. 9am-2pm, Sun. 9am-1pm. A steep L9000.)

Near the Accademia, at the **Museum of the Church of San Marco**, mount the stairs to see Fra Angelico's famous *Annunciation*. In the dormitory each cell contains its own Fra Angelico fresco, painted in flatter colors and sparse forms so as to facilitate the monks' meditation on the scene. (Open Tues.-Sat. 9am-2pm, Sun. 9am-1pm. L6000. Exterior under renovation.) Masaccio's *Trinity* may be seen in the Dominican **Basilica di Santa Maria Novella**. (Open Mon.-Sat. 7-11:30am and 3:30-6pm, Sun. 3:30-6pm.) To see Giotto's epoch-making frescoes, visit the **Church of Santa Croce**, the most lavish in the city. Among the famous Florentines buried here are Michelangelo, Machiavelli, Rossini, and Galileo. Dante was supposed to have been buried here, and his empty sarcophagus stands waiting, but the people of Ravenna, the city which took him in after his banishment from Florence, have clung to his remains. (Open Mon.-Sat. 8am-12:30pm and 3-6pm, Sun. 3-5:30pm.)

Florence's grandest frescoes are those by Masaccio, Masolino, and Filippo Lippi in the **Brancacci Chapel** of the **Church of Santa Maria del Carmine.** The finest panels, entirely by Masaccio, depict *The Tribute Money* and *The Expulsion from Paradise.* (Open Mon. and Wed.-Sat. 10am-5pm, Sun. 1-5pm. L5000.)

Strewn about the city in gargantuan glory are various *palazzi,* grand palaces reflecting the architectural magnificence of the Renaissance. The **Palazzo Strozzi,** on via Tornabuoni at via Strozzi, begun in 1489, may be the most august of its kind. With its regal proportions and carefully rusticated façade, it is the best example of the Florentine *palazzo* type. (Open Mon., Wed., and Fri. 4-7pm. Free.) Alberti's architectural triumph of half a millennium ago, the **Palazzo Rucellai,** via della Vigna Nuova, 16, is renowned for its delicate classical façade. Across the Ponte Vecchio, paved with expensive jewelers and souvenir stands, is the **Palazzo Pitti,** another Medici stronghold. It contains 5 museums; the most notable is the **Galleria Palatina.** (Open Tues.-Sat. 9am-2pm, Sun. 9am-1pm. L8000.)

ENTERTAINMENT

For reliable information on what's hot and what's not, consult *Firenze Spettacolo* (L2500). The **passeggiata** promenades along via dei Calzaiuoli; afterwards Florentines frequent the ritzy *caffè* in p. della Repubblica. Street performers draw crowds to the steps of the *duomo,* the arcades of the Mercato Nuovo, and p. Michelangelo. Many discos cater almost exclusively to tourists, with a sprinkling of Italians who have designs on foreigners. Near Santa Maria Novella, **Space Electronic,** via Palazzuolo, 37, reflects a young international crowd with its multitudes of mirrors. (Open Sun.-Fri. 10pm-2am, Sat. 10pm-3am. Sept.-Feb. closed Mon. Cover with 1 drink L20,000, with a copy of *Let's Go* L15,000.) The trendy spot for Italian students is **Rockafè,** Borgo degli Albizi, 66, American infiltration not yet complete. (Cover L15,000. Open Sept.-June Tues.-Sun. 10pm-4am.) In a tiny alleyway across p. della Signoria from the Palazzo Vecchio is **Tabasco Gay Club,** p. S. Cecilia, 3r, Florence's most popular gay disco. (Minimum age 18. No cover, but min. 1 drink. Open Tues.-Sun. 10pm-3am.) For live jazz and a slick scene, try the **Jazz Club,** via Nuova de' Caccini, 3; disregard the "members only" sign. (Open Sept. 21-July 14.)

The most important of Florence's traditional festivals, that of **St. John the Baptist** (June 24), centers around a tremendous fireworks display which rips over the city from p. Michelangelo. The last week of June also brings the traditional games of **Calcio Storico in Costume,** an archaic, hilarious form of soccer played in historical dress. Contact the tourist office for ticket info. The summer swings with music festivals, starting in May with the **Maggio Musicale,** which draws many of the world's eminent classical musicians. The **Estate Fiesolana** fills the old Roman theater in **Fiesole** with concerts, opera, theater, ballet, and movies (June-Aug.). For information on tickets, contact the Biglietteria Centrale in the Teatro Communale, corso Italia, 16 (tel. 21 62 53, 277 92 36), or Universalturismo, via degli Speziali, 7r (tel. 21 72 41), off p. della Repubblica.

■■■ SIENA

Today, Siena suffers in Florence's shadow, but during the 13th century its flourishing wool trade, crafty bankers, and quasi-republican civil administration made it easily its rival's equal. The city remains a living masterpiece; even in Italy, few places are as aesthetically harmonious. Its visual consonance incorporates even the red clay hills in the distance, source of the burnt Siena hue that tints the buildings of the historic center. Siena hits its peak in July and August, when the entire populace wildly celebrates its medieval heritage with the *Palio* horse races.

The salmon-colored, shell-shaped **piazza del Campo** is the focus of Sienese life. At the bottom of the shell is the **Palazzo Pubblico,** a graceful Gothic palace over which soars the **Torre del Mangia,** nicknamed for the gluttonous bellringer. Inside, the **Museo Civico** contains some of Siena's finest Gothic painting; don't miss the *Allego-*

ries of Good and Bad Government by Pietro and Ambrogio Lorenzetti. (*Palazzo* and museum open Mon.-Sat. 9:30am-6:45pm, Sun. 9:30am-1:45pm; Nov.-March daily 9am-1:45pm. L6000, students L3000. Torre del Mangia open daily 10am-7pm; mid-April to mid-June and mid-Sept. to mid-Oct. 10am-6pm; mid-March to mid-April and mid-Oct. to mid-Nov. 10am-5pm; mid-Nov. to mid-March 10am-1:30pm. L4000.)

The construction of Siena's zebra-striped **duomo** took so long that it spanned two architectural epochs, incorporating Romanesque arches and Gothic pinnacles. The **pulpit** is one of Andrea Pisano's best, with allegorical and biblical reliefs wrapping around the barrel. Pay L2000 to enter the **Libreria Piccolomini,** off the left aisle, which holds frescoes by Pinturicchio and some lavish 15th-century illuminated musical scores. (*Duomo* open daily 7:30am-7:30pm; Oct. to early Nov. 7:30am-6:30pm; early Nov. to mid-March 7:30am-1:30pm and 2:30-5pm. No tank-tops or shorts above the knee. Library open daily 9am-7:30pm; Oct. to early Nov. 9am-6:30pm; Nov. to mid-March 10am-1pm and 2:30pm; L2000.) One of the *duomo*'s greatest treasures, the **font,** lies in the baptistry at the back of the church. Its brass relief panels by Ghiberti, della Quercia, and Donatello mark the transition from International Gothic to Renaissance sculpture. The **Museo dell'Opera della Metropolitana,** next to the cathedral, displays some incredible Gothic sculpture by Giovanni Pisano, as well as Duccio di Buoninsegna's splendid *Maestà*. (Open daily 9am-7:30pm; Jan. to mid-March 9am-1pm; Oct. to early Nov. 9am-6:30pm; early Nov. to Dec. 9am-1:30pm. L5000.) For more of this school, take in the exceptional collection of the **Pinacoteca Nazionale,** via San Pietro, 29. (Open Mon. 8:30am-2pm, Tues.-Sat. 8:30am-7pm, Sun. 8:30am-1pm; in winter Mon.-Sat. 8:30am-2pm. L8000.)

All day on **il Palio,** July 2 and August 16, Sienans parade around in 15th-century costume; the central event is a traditional horse race around the packed p. del Campo. Get there 3 days early to watch the rambunctious horse selection in the *campo* and to pick a *contrada* to root for. You can stand in the "infield" of the piazza for free, but access closes early, so stake out a spot early in the day. The winning district holds a torch-lit procession through the city the night after the race. For tickets and a list of hotels and *pensioni*, write to the tourist office by March; arrive without a reservation and you'll be sleepin' on the streets.

Accommodations, Food, and Practical Information

The **tourist office,** p. del Campo, 56 (tel. (0577) 28 05 51), has a list of *affitta camere* (about L125,000/person). (Theoretically open Mon.-Sat. 8:30am-7:30pm.) Its travel agency **changes money** for outrageous rates and sells bus, train, and boat tickets. (Open Mon.-Fri. 9am-1pm and 3:30-7pm, Sat. 9am-1pm.) Finding a room in Siena is usually simple, but call a few days ahead during July and August and book months ahead for either *Palio*. The somewhat inconveniently located **Ostello della Gioventù "Guidoriccio" (HI),** via Fiorentina, 89 (tel. (0577) 522 12), in *località* lo Stellino, is about a 20-minute bus ride from the center. (Curfew 11pm. L18,000. Breakfast included.) Take bus #4 or 15 from the station or p. Matteotti; if coming from Florence by bus, get off at the stop just after the large black and white sign announcing that you've entered Siena. The **Casa del Pellegrino,** via Camporegio, 3 (tel. (0577) 441 77), behind p. San Domenico, is a spotless establishment run by nuns; the rooms have fantastic views of the *duomo*. (Opens at 7:30am. Curfew 11pm. Singles L32,000-40,000. Doubles with bath L55,000. Triples with bath L75,000. Quads with bath L95,000. Reservations preferred.) **Albergo Tre Donzelle,** via Donzelle, 5 (tel. (0577) 28 03 58) offers airy singles (L30,000) and doubles (L50,000).

Siena specializes in rich pastries, the most notable *Panforte,* a concoction of honey, almonds, and candied fruit. Sample it at **Bar/Pasticceria Nannini,** via Banchi di Sopra, 22-24. Shoestringers can pick up supplies at the **Consortio Agrario supermarket,** via Pianigiani, 5, off p. Salimberi. (Open Mon.-Fri. 7:45am-1pm and 5-8pm, Sat. 7:45am-1pm.) Locals frequent **Rosticceria Monti,** via Calzoleria, 12, for prepared food. Pick up great Tuscan bean specialties, including bean soup (L3000) and bean salad (L2500). (Open Sat.-Thurs. noon-3pm and 6:30-11pm.) **Osteria Le**

Logge, via Porrione, 33, is popular and cozy. (Cover L2000. Service 10%, but they give 110%. Open Mon.-Sat. 12:30-3pm and 7:30-10:30pm. MC, Visa.) Just down the street, at #65-67, a young staff serves excellent Tuscan specialties at unbeatable prices at **Grotta del Gallo Nero.** (Open Mon. noon-3pm, Tues.-Sun. noon-3pm and 7pm-1:30am.) A deal you'll strut like a rooster for.

Siena lies off the main Florence-Rome-Rome **rail** line. From Florence, change at Empoli (L7200); from Rome, at Chiusi (L18,700). Take any bus passing across the street from the station to the center of town (L1000), or prepare for a 45-minute uphill trek. Express **TRA-IN/SITA** buses, often faster than the train, link Siena with Florence (L8300) and other Tuscan destinations.

■ Near Siena

The medieval towers of **San Gimignano** bristle skyward only an hour from Siena by bus (L6300). The towers and the perfectly preserved walled *centro* testify to a 13th-century building competition between San Gimignano's two wealthiest families. Of the original 72 edifices, 14 remain. Scale the **Torre Grossa,** the tallest of the remaining towers, attached to **Palazzo del Popolo,** for a 360° panorama of Tuscany. San Gimignano hosts one of the cleanest and friendliest hostels in central Italy, **Ostello della Gioventù,** via della Fonti, 1 (tel. (0577) 94 19 91). (Curfew 11:30pm. L20,000. Showers, breakfast and sheets included. Open mid-Feb. to mid-Dec.) **Rosticerria/Pizzeria Chiribiri,** off via San Giovanni, offers plentiful pasta from L4500, and pizza by the slice. (Open Thurs.-Tues. 11am-10pm.)

If you've had it with city hopping, soak in a few days of sun and swimming on the island of **Elba,** just off the coast of Tuscany. Take the train to Piombino Marittima, where you can hop a Toremar ferry (1hr., L8000). Avoid Elba in July and August, when half of Italy and two-thirds of Germany cram onto its limited shores.

■■■ PISA

Shameless exploitation obscures the splendor of Pisa's republican history and cultural legacy. Though it once rivaled Genoa and Venice for maritime supremacy and Padua and Bologna for scholarly brilliance, today Pisa subsists largely on the daily tide of tourists from Florence (1hr. by train) and other neighboring cities who come to ogle a tilting tower that is closed to the public indefinitely.

Pisa's most revered monuments lie in the **campo dei Miracoli** (Field of Miracles), a grassy expanse on the northern side of the Arno. A L12,000 ticket lets you into all of the Campo's sights. The dazzling **duomo** is a treasury of fine art, including Giovanni Pisano's elaborate **pulpit** and its burlesque Gothic reliefs. (Open daily 7:45am-12:45pm and 3-6:45pm; in winter until 4:45pm. Closed for mass 10-10:45am.) Next door in the **baptistry;** ask the custodian for a demonstration of the acoustics—a sung note resounds for minutes. (Same hours as *duomo.* L5000. Donation expected for the demonstration.) The adjoining **camposanto,** a long white-walled cemetery, has many classical sarcophagi and a series of haunting frescoes by an unidentified 14th-century artist known only as "Master of the Triumph of Death." (Open daily 8am-7:40pm; off-season 9am-4:40pm.) The **Museo delle Sinopie,** across the street, displays *sinopie* (sketches preliminary to the fresco process) discovered during restoration after World War II (Open daily 9am-12:40pm and 3-6:40pm; off-season 9am-12:40pm and 3-4:40pm. L5000.) The **Museo dell' Opera del Duomo,** behind the Tower, displays works by Giovanni Pisano and Guardi, alongside archeological finds. (Open daily 8am-7:30pm; off-season 9am-12:30pm and 3-4:30pm.) Though the famous **Leaning Tower** continues to slip 1-2mm every year, it's losing little ground as a tourist hotspot. One hidden treasure in town is the church of **Santa Maria della Spina,** which faces Lungarno Gambacorti against the river. (Open daily 8am-noon and 3:30-7pm.)

Accommodations, Food, and Practical Information New in April 1992, the **Centro Turistico Madonna dell'Acqua** hostel, via Pietrasantina, 15 (tel. (050) 89 06 22), awaits beneath an old sanctuary. Take bus #3 from the station and ask to be let off at the *ostello*. (Reception open 6-11pm. L17,000.) The **Albergo Gronchi,** p. Archivescovado, 1 (tel. (050) 56 18 23), is just off p. del Duomo. (Curfew midnight. Singles L28,000. Doubles L44,000.) The **Casa della Giovane,** via Corridoni, 31 (tel. (050) 227 32), a 10-minute walk from the station (turn right immediately), offers beds to women. (Curfew 10pm. L22,000 in clean doubles, triples and quads.) **Campeggio Torre Pendente** (tel. (050) 56 06 65) is just outside the gates at viale delle Cascine, 86 (L7800/person, L5000/tent). Pisa's cheapest (and most well-rounded) meals cost L5000 at the **Mensa Universitaria** on via Martiri off p. dei Cavalieri. Buy tickets noon-2:30pm (no student ID necessary) or ask students outside for extras. (Open mid-Sept. to mid-July Mon.-Fri. noon-2:30pm and 7-9pm, Sat.-Sun. noon-2:30pm.) The best alternative is **Trattoria da Matteo,** via l'Aroncio, 46, off via S. Maria. (Open Sun.-Fri. noon-3pm and 7-10:30pm.)

The **tourist office,** p. della Stazione, 11 (tel. (050 422 91) doles out maps with directions to the tower (open Mon.-Sat. 9:30am-1pm and 3:30-7pm). The **branch office** off the Campo dei Miracoli, in p. del Duomo (tel. (050) 56 04 64), has more detailed information. (Open Mon. and Fri. 9am-3pm and 3:30-6:30pm, Tues.-Thurs. 9:30am-3pm, Sat. 9am-noon and 3-6pm.)

UMBRIA

Christened the "Green Heart of Italy," Umbria has enjoyed renown since ancient times for its wooded hills, valleys, and rivers. Often shrouded in an ethereal silvery haze, the landscape also nurtured a mystic tradition that stretches from prehistory through to St. Benedict, who preached the doctrine of the marriage of work and worship, and to Umbria's most famous visionary, the nature-adoring ascetic St. Francis. Generations of visual artists also clambered about these hills, among them Giotto, Signorelli, Perugino and Pinturicchio.

While trains link most major towns, buses provide the most convenient access, especially as they drop you off in the center of town rather than at the bottom of a steep hill. Thermal springs, clear streams, Etruscan ruins, and velvety ravines make the verdant countryside nearly as appealing as the numerous hilltowns.

■■■ PERUGIA

The exceedingly polite population of Perugia may be trying to make up for several millennia of excessive nastiness, during which they regularly stoned each other for fun and even threw tree-hugging St. Francis of Assisi into a dungeon. Perugia has since mellowed into a university town, host of a popular world-class jazz festival from late June to early July, and core of the Italian chocolate-making industry. City buses (L1000) regularly connect the station, in the valley, with p. Italia and p. Matteotti, in the center of town. Perugia is 3 hours by train from both Rome (changing at Teróntola) and Florence. It's also near Assisi (25min.), the acutely picturesque **Gubbio,** the Umbrian hilltop delights of **Orvieto** (which has arguably the finest cathedral façade in Italy), and **Spoleto** (home of Italy's biggest arts festival, the *Festival dei Due Mondi,* in June and July).

The city's most important sights frame **piazza IV Novembre.** The grand fountain in the center is adorned with sculptures and bas-reliefs by Nicola and Giovanni Pisano. The 13th-century **Palazzo dei Priori** presides over the *piazza*, sheltering the **Galleria Nazionale dell'Umbria,** with works by Perugino, Duccio, Piero della Francesca and Fra Angelico. (Open Mon.-Sat. 9am-1:45pm and 3-7pm, Sun. 9am-1pm. L8000.) Perugia's austere Gothic **duomo** looms at the end of the *piazza;* its façade was never completed because the *Perugini* were forced to return the marble they had stolen to build it. Near via Cavour, the **Museo Archeologico Nazionale dell'Umbria,** next to the **Church of San Domenico** (Umbria's largest), emphasizes Perugia's Etruscan heritage. (Open Tues.-Sat. 9am-1:30pm and 2:30-6pm, Sun. 9am-1pm. L4000.) **Rocca Paolina,** by via Marzia, is a 16th-century fortress whose interior juxtaposes Italian antiquity with dubious modern art. Above, the well-maintained **Giardini Carducci** is the place to clutch your *amore.* (That's not a body part, for you who speak no Italian.) A walk down via Ulisse Rocchi leads to the perfectly preserved Roman **Arch of Augustus.**

Accommodations, Food, and Practical Information The **Tourist Office,** on p. IV Novembre (tel. (075) 572 33 27) in the Palazzo dei Priori, provides travel and accommodations information, a misleading city map, and a detailed walking guide. (Open Mon.-Sat. 8:30am-1:30pm and 4-7pm, Sun. 9am-1pm; in winter Mon.-Sat. 3:30-6:30pm.) The **currency exchange** in the train station charges no commission for amounts under L80,000. For a cheap, clean bed, try the independent youth hostel, **Centro Internazionale di Accoglienza per la Gioventù,** via Bontempi, 13 (tel. (075) 572 33 27). (Lockout 9:30am-4pm. Curfew midnight. L14,000. Showers and use of kitchen included. Sheets L1000. Open mid-Jan. to late Dec.) Rooms in **Albergo Anna,** via del Priori, 48, 4th floor (tel. (075) 573 63 04), are clean, cool and 17th-century. (Singles L32,000. Doubles L44,000.) **Paradis d'Ete** (tel. (075) 517 21 17), 5km away in Colle della Trinità, provides a place to camp. Take bus #36 from the station. (L7000/person, L6000/tent.)

Dining in Perugia is tasty and cheap. Sample simple Italian cooking at the **Trattoria Calzoni,** via Cesare Caporali, 12, off p. Repubblica. The saintly *signora* creates complete meals nightly for about L16,000. (Open Mon.-Sat. 12:30-2:30pm and 7:30-9:30pm.) The **Tavola Calda,** p. Danti, 16, offers cheap fare: sandwiches from L3000 and a decent *rosticceria.* (Open Sun.-Fri. 9:30am-3:30pm and 7-11pm.) Top off your meal with any number of goodies from a bakery or sweet shop. **Ceccarani,** p. Matteotti, 16, and the **Co.Fa.Pa.** bakery, at #12, are both outstanding.

■■■ ASSISI

Assisi's serenity originates with the legacy of St. Francis, the nature-adoring monk who preached poverty, obedience, and love 8 centuries ago. After his death in 1226, eminent Florentine and Sienese painters decorated the **Basilica di San Francesco** with a spectacular ensemble of frescoes illustrating his life. The basilica is actually a double decker; the Upper Church is elaborate and sumptuously decorated, while the Lower Church, built around the crypt housing the saint's tomb, is more subdued and pious. (Open daily 6:30am-7pm, no tourists on Holy Days. English-language Mass Sun. 8:30am. English tours Mon.-Sat. 10am and 3pm. Modest dress; no photography.) The modern **Museo Tesoro della Basilica** is worth a visit. (Open April-Oct. Tues.-Sun. 9:30am-noon and 2-6pm; closed on Holy Days. L3000.) Towering above town, the recently restored fortress **Rocca Maggiore** overwhelms with huge proportions and tremendous views. (Open daily 9am-8pm; winter 10am-4pm. Closed in very windy or rainy weather. L3000, university students L1500.)

Check with the **tourist office,** p. del Comune, 12 (tel. (075) 81 25 34), for rooming help, musical events info, and bus and train schedules. (Open Mon.-Fri. 8am-2pm and 3-7pm, Sat. 9am-1pm and 4-7pm, Sun. 9am-1pm.) The new **Ostello della Pace (HI)** charges L16,000 for bed and breakfast. (Lockout 10am-5pm. Curfew 11pm.) A superb **hostel and campground** (tel. (075) 81 36 36) lies a few km from Assisi in the hamlet of Fontemaggio (Hostel L15,000. Camping L6000/person, L4500/tent.) Several houses off p. Matteotti offer *camere* (rooms) for about L25,000/person. Try **Alunni Camere Maria Bocchini,** via dell'Acquario, 3 (tel. (075) 81 31 82), with clean, cool singles for L30,000 and doubles for L40,000. Nearby,

Camere Maria Fortini, via Villamena, 19 (tel. (075) 81 27 15), has singles for
L30,000 and doubles for L42,000.

See Vincenzo at his **pizzeria,** via San Rufino, just off p. del Comune, where the
endearing artist will show you his sociopolitical paintings while feeding you the
best pizza in Assisi. (Open daily 8am-2pm and 4-7:30pm.) Assisi is on the Foligno-
Teróntola **rail** line, ½hour from Perugia (L2400). From Florence (L14,100), change
at Teróntola; from Rome (L13,700) or Ancona (L11,300), change at Foligno. Buses
run to Perugia (L4200) and other Umbrian towns.

THE MARCHES (LE MARCHE): URBINO

If you visit only one town in Italy, make this the one. A perfectly harmonious ensemble created under the aegis of philosopher/warrior Federico da Montefeltro (1444-
1482), Urbino exemplifies the finest in Renaissance style and tradition. It's no wonder that Baldassare Castiglione described Federico as the "light of Italy" and set the
elegant dialogues of his book *The Courtier* in Urbino's Ducal Palace. The town's
fairy-tale skyline has changed little in the last 500 years, and while tourists shape the
character of many cities, Urbino owes its flair to its university students, still imbued
with the creative spirit of native sons Raphael and Bramante.

ORIENTATION AND PRACTICAL INFORMATION

The **SAPUM bus** from Pésaro's p. Matteotti or the train station is cheap, frequent
and direct (10/day, 1hr., L3500). After winding up steep hills, the bus will deposit
you at borgo Mercatale, above which lies the beautiful city center. A short uphill
walk or a ride in the elevator (open summer daily 9am-9pm; L300) takes you to
piazza della Repubblica, the city's hub.

Tourist Office: p. Duca Federico, 35 (tel. 24 41). Distributes a list of hotels and a
small map. Open Mon.-Sat. 9am-1pm and 3-7:30pm; off-season 8:30am-2pm.
Buses: For info, call 97 05 02. Departures from borgo Mercatale. Timetable posted
at the beginning of corso Garibaldi, under the portico at the corner bar on p. della
Repubblica.
Post Office: via Bramante, 22 (tel. 25 75), right off via Raffaello. Open Mon.-Fri.
8:30am-7:40pm, Sat. 8:30am-1pm. **Postal Code:** 61029.
Telephones: SIP, p. Rinascimento, 4, off p. Duca Federico. Open daily 8am-10pm.
City Code: 0722.
Medical Assistance: Hospital, via B. da Montefeltro (tel. 32 93 51, 32 81 21 or 32
81 22), to the north of the city out of p. Roma.
Emergencies: tel. 113. **Police:** p. della Repubblica, 3 (tel. 26 45 or 32 04 91). **Hos-
pital:** via B. da Montefeltro (tel. 32 93 51, 32 81 21, or 32 81 22), north of the city
out of p. Roma.

ACCOMMODATIONS AND CAMPING

Cheap lodging is rare in Urbino. If you can't get into one of the following places, try
one of the many *affitta camere,* inexpensive rentals that target Urbino's students.
Ask for a list at the tourist office, or check at **Trattoria Leone,** in p. della Repubblica. Signposts around **via Budassi** may also prove helpful. For longer stays, write to
the **Università degli Studi,** calle dei Cappuccini.

Albergo Italia, corso Garibaldi, 52 (tel. 27 01), off p. della Repubblica, near the
Palazzo Ducale. Affable management. Patio, great view, and elevator. 48 elegant
rooms. Singles L35,000, with bath L45,000. Doubles L48,000, with bath L64,000.
Pensione Fosca, via Raffaello, 67, on the top floor (tel. 32 96 22). Small, charming
rooms without baths. Singles L30,000-35,000. Doubles L42,000-49,000.

Hotel San Giovanni, via Barocci, 13 (tel. 28 27). A relatively modern hotel with a helpful manager. Restaurant downstairs. Singles L35,000, with bath L48,000. Doubles L50,000, with bath L65,000. Triples with bath L75,000.

Camping Pineta, via San Donato (tel. 47 10), in Cesana, 2km from the city walls. L7000/adult, L3500/child, L14,000/tent. Open June 1-Sept. 15.

FOOD

Many *paninoteche, gelaterie* and burger joints lurk around p. della Repubblica. Execute comprehensive shopping at **Supermarket Margherita,** via Raffaello, 37. (Open Mon.-Sat. 7:45am-12:45pm and 5-7:45pm. Closed Thurs. afternoon.)

Ristorante Rustica, via Nuova, 5 (tel. 25 28), across from Club 83. Delicious pizza from L4000. *Secondi* from L9000. Traditional atmosphere. Open Thurs.-Tues. noon-3pm and 7pm-1am. Closed July 5-25.

Pizza Evoé, p. S. Franceso, 3. Outdoor seating on a secluded piazza. Pizzas from L5000. Cover L500; wine L3000/½-liter.

Pizzeria Le Tre Piante, via Foro Posterula, 1 (tel. 48 63), off via Budassi. Spectacular view from the outside tables and delicious food to boot. Pizza dinners L4000-6000, others from L15,000. Open Tues.-Sun. noon-3pm and 7pm-2am.

Ristorante Ragno d'Oro, on p. Roma at the top of via Raffaello. Quality home cooking on an outdoor patio. Fantastic pasta (L4500). Don't miss the *cresce sfogliate,* an Urbino specialty: flaky, flat bread filled with meat, vegetables, or cheeses, (L3000-5000). Open July-Aug. daily noon-3pm and 7pm-midnight.

SIGHTS

Urbino's most remarkable monument is the Renaissance **Palazzo Ducale** (Ducal Palace). The façade, which overlooks the edge of town, boasts a unique design attributed to Ambrogio Barocchi: 2 tall, slender towers enclosing 3 stacked balconies. Most of the rest of the palace, celebrated in Italy as "the most beautiful in the world," was designed by Luciano Laurana. Enter the palace from p. Duca Federico; the interior **courtyard** is the quintessence of Renaissance harmony and proportion. To the left, a monumental staircase takes you to the private apartments of the Duke, which now house the **National Gallery of the Marches,** a delightful museum whose exhibits, many displaying Duke Federico's penchant for oddity, are incorporated through the meandering hallways of his palace. Eyeball Berruguete's portrait of Duke Federico (who sports the world's most famous broken-nosed profile), Raphael's *Portrait of a Lady,* Paolo Uccello's tiny, strange *Profanation of the Host* and Piero della Francesca's completely unsettling *Flagellation.* The most intriguing room of the palace is the Duke's study on the 2nd floor, where stunning inlaid wooden panels give the illusion of real books and shelves covered with astronomical and musical instruments. Nearby, descend a circular stairway to the **Cappella del Perdono** and the **Tempietto delle Muse,** where the Christian and pagan components of the Renaissance ideal coexist: the chapel once served as a repository for holy relics accumulated by the Duke, and wooden panels representing Apollo, Minerva and the 9 muses at one time covered the walls of the temple, but all have been removed (8 are currently in Florence's Galleria Corsini). The **Archeological Museum,** on the far side of the palace's courtyard, is free with admission to the National Gallery, but you can only enter during the sporadic hours when the guide is on duty. (*Palazzo* open Mon.-Sat. 9am-2pm, Sun. 9am-1pm. L8000.)

At the end of via Barocci lies the 14th-century **Oratorio di San Giovanni Battista,** decorated with brightly colored Gothic fresco-work of Lorenzo and Giacomo Salimbeni, representing events from the life of St. John. If you speak Italian, the *custode* can give you a wonderful explanation of how fresco painters used lamb's blood as ink for their sketches. (Open daily 10am-noon and 3-5pm. L2000, but you will be obliged to see S. Giuseppe next door for another L2000.) **Raphael's house,** via Raffaello, 57, is now a vast and delightful museum with period furnishings. His earliest work, a fresco entitled *Madonna e Bambino,* can be found in the *sala.* (Open

Mon.-Sat. 9am-1pm and 3-7pm, Sun. 9am-1pm. L4000.) Hike up to the **Fortezza Albornoz,** turn left at the end of via Raffaello, where the awe-inspiring view of the Ducal Palace and the rest of the city demands a picnic. (Open daily 8am-6pm. Free.) For information on English-speaking tours, try contacting Marguerite Laciura (tel. 32 89 40).

ENTERTAINMENT

Urbino's p. della Repubblica serves as a modeling runway for local youth in their bohemian threads. Take a walk down this fashion ramp and then stroll (or climb) the serpentine streets at dusk. If you seek more active entertainment, dance the night away at **Club 83** on via Nuova. Throughout July you can attend the **Antique Music Festival** in Church of S. Domenico. A cheaper alternative, more popular with students, is the **University ACLI,** on via Santa Chiona, a bar with music and small crowds. All this begins in August, when the Italian university summer session convenes. August also brings the ceremony of the **Revocation of the Duke's Court,** replete with Renaissance costumes. Check at the tourist office for the 1994 date.

SOUTHERN ITALY

South of Rome, the sun gets brighter, the meals longer and the passions more intense. Though Southern Italy has long been subject to the negative stereotypes and prejudices of the more industrialized North, the so-called "Mezzogiorno" (midday) region remains justly proud of its open-hearted and generous populace, strong traditions, classical ruins, and enchanting beaches. Pampered with the Amalfi coast and a troupe of paradisiacal islands, Campania (the area around Naples) gets the most press. Genuine *Italia* is farther south and east in Calabria, Apulia and Basilicata.

■■■ NAPLES (NAPOLI)

Naples greets the world with haggling market crowds, honking cars and packs of screaming youngsters. But below the surface (and away from the train station) flourishes one of Europe's most convivial cities, where grand *palazzi* and rich museums mesh with humble artisans' shops and fantastic hole-in-the-wall *trattorie.* The infamous Camorra mafia poses less of a threat to tourists than petty theft does; always keep your valuables out of sight and wear your daypack on both shoulders.

ORIENTATION AND PRACTICAL INFORMATION

Naples is on the west coast of Italy, 2 hours south of Rome. It sends regular ferries to Sicily and Sardinia, and trains to and from Rome, Calabria, Sicily and the Adriatic.

Tourist Office: EPT, at the central train station (tel. 26 87 79). Helps with hotels and ferries. Pick up the invaluable *Qui Napoli* (Here's Naples) and a city map. Open Mon.-Sat. 9am-8pm, Sun. 9am-1pm. **AAst Information office,** p. Gesù Nuovo (tel. 552 33 28). Take bus #185 up via Roma toward p. Dante, get off at via Caitelli, and follow it to the *piazza.* The most helpful and professional office in the city. Open Mon.-Sat. 9am-7pm, Sun. 9am-2pm.
Consulates: U.S., p. della Repubblica (p. Principedi Napoli on some maps; tel. 761 43 03, 24hrs.). Open Mon.-Fri. 8am-noon and 2-4pm. **U.K.,** via Francesco Crispi, 122 (tel. 65 35 11; in an emergency call Rome (06) 475 54 41). Open Mon.-Fri. 8am-1:30pm; mid-Sept. to June Mon.-Fri. 9am-12:30pm and 3-5:30pm.
Currency Exchange: Neapolitan banks charge high commissions. Closest to the train station is Banca Nazionale del Lavoro, p. Garibaldi (tel. 799 71 13). Open for exchange Mon.-Fri. 8:30am-1:30pm and 2:45-4pm.

Post Office: p. Matteotti (tel. 551 14 56), off via Diaz. *Fermo Posta* (L250/letter). Open Mon.-Fri. 8:15am-1:30pm, Sat. 8:15am-12:10pm. **Postal code:** 80100.

Telephones: At the train station. Less crowded office at via Depretis, 40, off p. Bovio at the end of corso Umberto. Both open 24 hrs. **City code:** 081.

Trains: Lines and booths open daily 7am-9pm. **Digiplan** machines in the station or call 553 41 88. To: Rome (1-2/hr., 2½hr., L15,400); Syracuse (10hr., L43,500); and Brindisi for ferries to Greece (6½hr., L27,100).

Ferries: Caremar, Molo Beverello. Hydrofoils and ferries to: Cápri (5/day, 70min., L14,000); **Tirrenia,** Molo Angioino. To Palermo (daily at 8pm, 11hr., L61,900; Oct.-May L47,900) and Cagliari (Thurs. and Sat. at 5:30pm, 16hr., L48,400; Oct.-May L37,800).

Emergency: tel. 113. **Ambulance:** tel. 752 06 96. **Police:** tel. 794 11 11. English-speaking *ufficio stranieri* (foreigners' office) at the *Questura* (police station), via Medina, 75, at via Diaz.

ACCOMMODATIONS AND FOOD

In Naples, consider paying a little more for added comfort, security and respectability. Always agree on the price before you unpack, never give up your passport before seeing your room, and be alert for shower charges, obligatory breakfasts, and the like. Call the EPT (tel. 40 62 89) if you have complaints. Naples's lone youth hostel is the **Ostello Mergellina (HI),** salita della Grotta, 23 (tel. and fax 761 23 46), a quick rights onto via Piedigrotta from the Mergellina metro stop. (Lockout 9:30am-4:30pm. Curfew 11:30pm. Check-out 9am. L18,000. Nonmembers L5000 extra/night.) There are better alternatives in the area around the university, between p. Dante and the *duomo.* Take bus #185, CS, or CD from p. Garibaldi. **Albergo Imperia,** p. Miraglia, 386 (tel. 45 93 47), on the 4th floor, has clean, recently renovated rooms. (Singles L21,000. Doubles L34,000.) Near noisy but safe piazza Bovio is the **Albergo Orchidea,** c. Unmerto, 7 (tel. 552 40 07), scala B, on the 5th floor, whose dazzling, high-ceilinged rooms (all with private showers) have small balconies and great views. (Doubles L80,000. Triples L100,000. Quads L120,000.) The area around the train station should be your last choice, but the **Casanova Hotel,** via Venezia, 2 (tel. 26 82 87) is a good option (doubles L40,000). **Hotel Ginevra,** via Genova, 116 (tel. 28 32 10), has bright, pleasant rooms. (Singles L25,000. Doubles L45,000. Show them your *Let's Go.*)

Pizza-making is an art born in Naples. At **Antica Pizzeria da Michele,** via Cesare Sersale, 1/3, off corso Umberto not far from the train station, they've perfected the craft. Try their L3000 *Marinara.* (Open Sept. to mid-Aug. Mon.-Sat. 8am-10pm.) Spaghetti, too, was first cooked up by Neapolitan chefs. Seek it out *alle vongole* (with clams) or *alle cozze* (with mussels). A traditional Neapolitan snack is *sfogliatella* (a ricotta-filled pastry). Some of the best *trattorie* and *pizzerie* are near p. Dante. **Pizzeria Trianon da Ciro,** via Parco Margherita, 27, off p. Amedio, is a stylish and modern place catering to a snobby crowd. Pizza Trianon is their hallmark, with 4 different sections (L12,000). (Cover L2000. Open daily noon-4pm and 6pm-1am.) Huddling under the Dante clock tower, **Pizzeria Port'Alba,** via Port'Alba, 18, is Italy's oldest *pizzeria.* The L8000 *vecchia Port'Alba* is a tasty treat. (Open Thurs.-Tues. 9am-2am.) At **Avellinese da Peppino,** via Silvio Spavneta, 31/35 (from the train station, take the 3rd left on p. Garibaldi), locals and tourists dine in harmony at the outdoor tables. Unparalleled *spaghetti alle vongole* (L6500). (Cover L1000. Service 10%. Open daily 11am-midnight.) For a *trattoria* true to the Neapolitan style, try **Trattoria Da Maria,** via Genova, 115, the 2nd right off corso Novara (no sign). All pasta is L4000. (Open Mon.-Sat. noon-3:30pm and 6:30-10pm.)

SIGHTS

Begin with the world-famous **Museo Nazionale Archeologico,** near the Cavour metro stop, and its collection of frescoes and jewelry excavated from Pompeii and Herculaneum. (Open Tues.-Sat. 9am-2pm, Sun. and holidays 9am-1pm. L8000; under 18 and over 60 free.) Occupying a restored 18th-century royal palace in the hills to the north is the **Museo e Gallerie di Capodimonte;** take bus #110 or 127. Highlights include works by Michelangelo, Botticelli and Raphael. (Open Tues.-Sat. 9am-2pm, Sun. 9am-1pm. L8000, under 18 and over 60 free.) The **Museo Nazionale di San Martino** (tel. 578 17 69), in a Carthusian monastery on the hill of Sant'Elmo, documents the art and history of Naples since the 16th century. (Open Tues.-Sat. 9am-2pm, Sun. 9am-1pm. L6000, under 18 and over 65 free.) The **Palazzo Reale,** on p. del Plebiscito, conceals an 18th-century theater and an impressive museum. (Open Tues.-Sun. 9am-2pm. L6000.) For a nature break, head to the **Villa Floridiana,** on a knoll overlooking the bay, where you'll find a lovely park and the pottery-filled **Museo Duca di Martina.** (Open Tues.-Sat. 9am-2pm, Sun. 9am-1pm. L4000, under 18 and over 65 free.)

Via Roma, a.k.a. **via Toledo,** runs through the heart of **Spaccanapoli (Historic Naples).** Don't miss a visit to Naples's best-kept secret, the **Cappella di San Severo,** via de Sanctis, which houses Sammartino's incredible *Veiled Christ* sculpture, as well as 2 leering and grisly corpses. (Open Mon. and Wed.-Sat. 10am-1pm and 5-7pm, Tues. 10am-1pm, Sun. 9am-1:30pm. L3000.) Off p. Gesù Nuovo, step into the **Chiesa del Gesù Nuovo** and more serene **Chiesa di Santa Chiara** for a few moments of tranquility.

■ Near Naples

Mount Vesuvius and Pompeii Immense **Mount Vesuvius** looms indomitably over the area east of Naples. The eruption of the great volcano in 79 AD buried the nearby Roman city of Herculaneum (Ercolano) in mud, and its neighbor Pompeii (Pompei), in ashes. Excavation continues to uncover the lives of the ancients with astonishing precision. Most travelers take the *circumvesuviana's* Naples-Sorrento line, which lets you off at the Pompeii-Villa dei Misteri stop just outside the west entry. In **Pompeii,** wind your way around the main thoroughfare, via dell'Abbondanza, stopping at the **amphitheater** (near the east entrance) and the **forum** (at the western end of the *via*). To reach the site, walk straight from the station, take a right across the first piazza (piazza Immacolata) and head about 300m down via Roma until you see the east entrance. (Entrances open 9am-1hr. before sunset (off season around 3pm). L10,000.) The corpus of remains at **Herculaneum** (round-trip L1600) is smaller but better preserved. (Open daily 9am-1hr. before sunset. Visitors may remain until 30min. before sunset. L8000.)

Amalfi Coast South of Naples on the far side of the Amalfi Peninsula, clinging cliffside roads and tiled towns make the **Amalfi Coast** the most beautiful stretch of shoreline in Italy. Both **Sorrento,** at the western end of the peninsula (1½hr. by *circumvesuviana* train), and **Salerno** at its eastern base (1hr. by regular rail) are easy jaunts from Naples; buses between them (every 2hr.) pass through all the coastal towns. The towns to see are Positano, Amalfi and Ravello. Beware though—affordable beds are available only in Praiano and Atrani. To fully imbibe the coast's beauty, rent a moped in Sorrento from **Sorrento Rent-A-Car,** corso Italia, 210/A (tel. (081) 878 13 86). In **Praiano,** between Sorrento and Amalfi, marvel at the coastal views from **La Tranquilità,** via Roma, 10 (tel. (089) 87 40 84), a campground/hotel. (Bungalows L25,000-30,000 per person. Campsites L12,000 per person; off-season L10,000.) Above La Tranquilità is the open-air **Ristorante Continental,** whose package deal of mountain air, endless views, and exquisite meals will leave you in Amalfi Coast bliss. (Cover L2000. *Let's Go* bearers receive 15% discount. Open March-Nov. daily noon-3pm and 8pm-midnight.) In **Atrani,** a 10-min. walk from the town of **Amalfi,** stay in **A Scalinatella,** p. Umberto 12 (tel. (089) 87 19 30), in the town's only *piazza.* The congenial family that manages this quasi-hostel caters to students and budget travelers. Special *Let's Go* price of L10,000 (L15,000 in Aug.).

Cápri Since imperial times, the divine landscapes and azure waters of the island of **Cápri** have beckoned wayfarers from the Italian mainland. The **Grotta Azzura**

(Blue Grotto) is the island's symbol, but avoid the rip-off motorboat tours; instead take a bus (L1500 from Ánacapri) to the fluorescent cave, and don't swim. Ferries depart for Cápri several times daily from Naples. On the island, most ships dock at Marina Grande; take the bus up to **Ánacapri** (L1500), where rooms are most agreeable. **Villa Eva,** via della Fabbrica, 8 (tel. (081) 837 20 40), is splendidly isolated. Mamma Eva and Papà Vincenzo will pick you up from Ánacapri center (*Let's Go* prices: L18,000-25,000). Equally wonderful rooms can be found at **Hotel il Girasole,** via Linciano, 43 (tel. (081) 837 23 51). A bed in a double runs L25,000; in a triple L23,000. Dine in style in Ánacapri at **Trattoria il Solitario,** via G. Orlandi, 54, an outdoor flower-filled hideaway serving hand-prepared pasta for L7000-8000. (Cover L1500. Open daily in summer 12:15-3pm and 7pm-midnight; off-season Tues.-Sun.)

■■■ ADRIATIC PORTS

The cities of Ancona, Bari and Bríndisi—all on the Bologna-Lecce train line—are Italy's principal departure points for Greece, Cyprus and Albania. Ancona is a cheerless maritime city, but compared to Bríndisi, it's paradise. The latter is redeemed only by its cheap fares to Greece for Eurailpass holders. Bari is the South's most vibrant city, and has the cheapest passage to Greece for those without railpasses.

Bríndisi and Ancona Bríndisi (1½hr. by train from Bari) has a lone redeeming feature: its ferries to Greece are semi-free for Eurailpass holders and discounted 50% for *cartaverde* bearers. **Adriatica,** via Regina Margherita, 13 (tel. (0831) 52 38 25); **Marlines** c/o Pattimare, corso Garibaldi, 97 (tel. (0831) 52 65 48); **Hellenic Mediterranean Lines,** corso Garibaldi, 8 (tel. (0831) 52 85 31); and **Fragline,** corso Garibaldi, 88 (tel. (0831) 56 82 32) all run to Corfu, Igoumenitsa and Patras in Greece. Eurailers sail free on Adriatica and Hellenic Mediterranean, except for the L10,000 port tax (L18,000 high-season supplement includes tax). Don't spend money on anything more posh than deck class; in summer you'll actually be more comfortable there than in an upright seat in a large, smoke-filled cabin. Bicycles travel free. Railpass holders should go directly to the main offices listed above for tickets; travel agents will try to charge commission. Those without railpasses should consider departing from Bari. Check in at the embarkation office at least 2 hours before departure or risk losing your reservation. Allow plenty of time for late trains and the 1km station-to-port walk.

The **EPT tourist office,** lungomare Regina Margherita, 5 (tel. (0831) 52 19 44), is charming. Two restaurants offer special discounts for *Let's Go* carriers: **Trattoria da Emilia Spaghetti House,** vico dei Raimondo, 11, off via San Lorenzo, serves fresh pasta, salad, bread, and a beverage for L7000. (Open daily 9am-10pm.) **Spaghetti House Osteria Cucina Casalinga,** via Mazzini, 57, serves excellent spaghetti meals for about L7000. (Cover L500. Open Mon.-Sat. 11am-2:30pm and 4-8:30pm. Whoosh, whoosh!) The **Supermarket Eurospar** at the end of corso Garibaldi is convenient for boat-ride provisions. (Open Fri.-Wed. 8:30am-1pm and 4:30-8pm, Thurs. 8:30am-1pm.) Avoid staying in Bríndisi; if you're absolutely stuck and suicide is not a viable option, try **Hotel Altair,** via Tunisia, 4 (tel. (0831) 52 49 11), off corso Garibaldi. (Singles L25,000. Doubles L40,000.) Trains leave Rome for Bríndisi 3 times daily (L46,000).

From **Ancona,** the **Karageorgis** (tel. (071) 27 45 54 or 27 72 04), **Strintzis** (tel. (071) 286 43 31), and **Marlines** (tel. (071) 20 25 66) companies sail to Greece, and **Minoan Lines** (tel. (071) 567 89; fax 411 77 80) goes to Greece and Turkey. To get to the ferries from the train station, take bus #1 (L1000) to the **Stazione Marittima.** Arrive at least 2 hours before departure. There is a **tourist office** at the train station (tel. 417 03), as well as a seasonal branch office at the port (tel. 20 11 83). Don't leave without seeing the **Museo Archeologico's** 2 life-size bronzes of Roman emperors, or the fine painting gallery, **Galleria Comunale.** (Museum open Mon.-Sat. 9am-1:30pm, Sun. 2:30-7:30pm. Gallery open Tues.-Sat. 10am-7pm, Sun. 9am-1pm.) Stay at **Hotel Cavour,** viale della Vittoria, 7 (tel. (071) 20 03 74), 1 block from p. Cavour. (Doubles with bath L50,000.) The **Post Office** is at viale della Vittoria.

Bari Yes, dear, there is a Santa Claus, but he's dead. The burial place of St. Nicholas, **Bari** offers a terrific program designed to serve under-30 backpackers. From mid-June to mid-September, the **"Stop-Over in Bari Program"** (24-hr. English-speaking summer hotline (080) 44 11 86) will cater to your every need. Stop-Over **information offices** in the train and ferry stations have info on free events and discounts (open daily 8:30am-8:30pm); pick up their daily English newsletter or tune into 102FM. They also offer free camping (if you've got a sleeping bag) and free but insufficient bus service throughout the city. If you're sackless, Stop-Over's English-speaking student types will put you up in a private home (L30,000 for 2 nights). In the **old town,** stop in at the **Chiesa di San Nicola** to view the remains of dear old Santa. **Morfimare** (tel. (080) 521 00 22) and **Ventouris Ferries** (tel. (080) 524 43 64) run ferries to Greece. **Trains** come from Rome 3 times daily (1hr., L7800).

SICILY (SICILIA)

Every great Mediterranean civilization of the past 2500 years has left its mark on Sicily: the ancient Greeks scattered temples and theaters; the Romans, bridges and aqueducts; the Saracens, mosques and towers; the Normans, churches and castles. Unlike citizens of other parts of Italy, Sicilians don't revel in their island's traditions: today they speed unabated toward the future, installing condom-vending machines in front of medieval cathedrals and demonstrating against their most well-known institution, the Mafia. A series of seismic and volcanic catastrophes have periodically wiped clean the gains of Sicily's inhabitants, but the island has remained intact through centuries of occupation, creation, and destruction.

The cheapest way to reach Sicily is a train-ferry combination to Messina (from Rome via Règgio di Calabria, L46,000). **Tirrenia** sails from Naples to Palermo (1/day at 8pm; 10½hr.; *Poltrona* L61,900, Oct.-May L47,900) and from Messina to Règgio di Calabria (L1400) and Villa San Giovanni (L1000). Two bus companies, the private, air-conditioned **SAIS** and the public, often steamy **AST** serve many of the destinations inaccessible by train. Expect delays and confusion. **Hitchhiking** is difficult on long hauls; hitchers are reputed to have better luck near turn-offs, on short trips.

■■■ PALERMO

The people and palaces of Palermo proclaim it as a crossroads of Mediterranean cultures. In modern times, Palermo has earned notoriety as the cradle of *Cosa Nostra* (the Mafia). Sicily's capital and cultural center features brightly-lit avenues masking a labyrinth of dark, older streets; despite the dilapidation, the *palazzi* strewn about the town contain some of the most wondrous courtyards in Italy. To reach the exuberant *cattedrale* from the stadium, head straight on via Roma, bearing left on corso Vittorio Emanuele. (Open daily 7am-noon and 5-7pm.) Close by, the **Palazzo dei Normanni** exhibits an impressive fusion of artistic styles and a mucho-mosaicked *cappella palatina*. Go for baroque at the **Church of San Giuseppe dei Teatini,** with its phantasmagorical interior decoration. (Open daily 7:30am-noon and 6:30-8:15pm.) If you like mosaics, don't pass up nearby **Monreale,** where the cathedral mixes Norman architecture with Sicilian and Arabian motifs. From Palermo take bus #9 (L1000) from via Lincoln, across from the train station and to the left. (Open daily 8am-12:30pm and 3:30-6:30pm.) The **Benedictine Cloister** next door frames a garden with fanciful medieval columns. (Open daily 9am-7pm; Nov.-March Mon.-Sat. 9am-1:30pm, Sun. 9am-12:30pm. L2000.)

For maps and information, visit the **APT** office in the train station, or the main branch 2km north (tel. (091) 58 38 47); take bus #7 or 46 going toward Teatro Politeamo; it's the building with the huge *Sicilcassa* sign. (Mon.-Fri. 8am-8pm, Sat. 8am-2pm.) **Hotel Cortese**, via Scarpelli, 16, (tel. (091) 33 17 22), a 10-minute walk from the train station down via Maqueda to via dell'Universitá, has impeccable rooms. (Singles L22,000, with shower L28,000. Doubles L36,000, with shower L45,000. Credit cards accepted.) **Albergo Orientale,** via Maqueda, 26 (tel. (091) 616 57 27), just a few blocks from the station, is a gloriously run-down 17th-century *palazzo.* (Singles L30,000. Doubles L45,000, with bath L50,000. Triple with bath L60,000.) **Albergo Letizia,** via Bottai, 30, (tel. (091) 58 91 10), is a little out-of-the-way, but the rooms are as fresh as the bottles of rainwater the owner collects in his spare time. (Singles L27,000. Doubles L40,000, with bath L50,000. Extra bed L17,500. Prices rise about L10,000 in the summer.)

Despite its name, **Trattoria Shanghai,** vicolo de Mezzani, 34, overlooking piazza Caracciolo, is pure Palermo, with great *gambieri* (shrimp; L8000). (Cover L1000, service 10%; open daily noon-3:30pm and 6:30-midnight.) After dinner, hike up town to Frankie's **Bar Fiore,** via Principe di Belmonte, 84 (tel. 33 25 39) where Palermo's biggest extrovert will give you a *frullato* (frothy Italian milkshake) for only L4000. (Open daily 6am-midnight.) Most of Palermo's nightlife is outside the city proper in nearby **Mondello;** take bus #6, 14 or 15 from via della Libertà or the station, and get off at Mondello Paese.

■■■ AGRIGENTO

Among Sicily's classical remains, the **Valley of Temples** at Agrigento shares top honors with those at Syracuse. **Temple of Concord,** one of the world's best-preserved Greek temples, owes its survival to consecration by St. Gregory. On the road to the archaeological park from the city center lies the **Museo Archeologico Nazionale,** containing a notable collection of artifacts, especially vases from all over central Sicily. (Open Mon.-Fri. 9am-1pm, Sat. 9am-5pm. Free.) The **tourist office** (tel. (0922) 20 454) is on the main street at via Atenea, 123. (Open Mon.-Sat. 8am-2pm and 4:30-6:30pm.) Take bus #8, 9, 10, or 11 from the train station (last bus back at 9:45pm; L600) and ask to be dropped off at the *Quartiere Ellenistico-Romano.*

Trains run from the station to Palermo (11/day, 1½hr., L10,700). **Bella Napoli,** p. Lena, 6 (tel. (0922) 20 435), at the north end of via Atenea, has clean rooms and a terrace overlooking the valley. (Singles L25,000. Doubles L40,000.) Closer to the train station is spotless **Concordia,** via San Francesco, 11 (tel. (0922) 59 62 66; singles L25,000, with bath L30,000; doubles L40,000, with bath L60,000). Hear the chef sing Verdi at **Trattoria Black Horse,** via Celaro, 8, off via Atenea. *Tronchetto dello chef* (L6500) is the specialty: a thick lasagna packed with peas, ham, and meat sauce. (Cover L2000. Open Mon.-Sat. noon-3pm and 7-11pm. AmEx, MC, Visa.)

■■■ SYRACUSE (SIRACUSA)

Founded in 734 BC by Corinthians who fancied its splendid harbor, the Hellenic city of Syracuse produced Pindar, Archimedes, and the world's first cookbook. Cross the bridge on corso Umberto to the island of **Ortigia** to pay homage to the Temples of **Apollo** and **Athena.** The latter, now part of the city's cathedral, has a richly embellished baroque façade, added in the 18th century. From the p. del Duomo, a trip down via Picherale will bring you to the ancient **Fonte Aretusa,** a "miraculous" freshwater spring by the sea. Syracuse's larger monuments are in or near the Archaeological Park on the north side of town; follow corso Gelone until it is intersected by via le Teocrito; the entrance to the park is down via Augusto to the left. The park contains the world's largest **Greek Theater** (5th century BC). (Park open daily 9am-6pm; winter 9am-3pm. L2000.) Check out the **Orecchio di Dionisio** (Ear of Dionysius), a giant artificial grotto with an earlobe-shaped entrance. The cave's acoustics reputedly allowed one to overhear prisoners talking in the lower room. Nearby, the **Altar of Hieron II** (241-215 BC) was used for public sacrifices. At 198m by 23m, it is the largest altar known. The **Roman amphitheater,** constructed in the 2nd century AD, is occasionally used for dance and dramatic performances.

Near the **Catacombs of San Giovanni** (open Thurs.-Tues. 10am-noon and 4-6pm; mid-Nov. to mid-March 10am-noon; L2000, under 18 or over 60 free), the **APT,** via San Sebastiano, 45, distributes maps and brochures. (Open 8am-2pm and 4-7pm.) Rooms vary at the **Hotel Milano,** corso Umberto, 10 (tel. 66 981), but it has a low price and convenient location near the bridge to Ortigia. (Singles L25,000, with bath L35,000. Doubles L40,000, with bath L55,000.) **Pensione Bel Sit,** via Oglio, 5 (tel. (0931) 60 245), on the 5th floor, has caring proprietors and is near the station. (Singles L30,000, with bath L35,000. Doubles L40,000, with bath L50,000.) The city's grandest supermarket is **Supermercato Linguanti,** corso Umberto, 186, to the left of the train station. (Open Mon.-Tues. and Thurs.-Sat. 7am-1pm and 3-8pm, Wed. 7am-1pm.) **Tuttopizza,** lungomare Alfeo, 12, combats Syracuse's high-priced tourist *menùs* (pizzas L4000-10,000; *servizio* 30%; open Thurs.-Tues. 7pm-late). Bus the 18km to **Fontane Bianche** (bus #21 or 22, L600), an endless, silken beach. More popular with the locals is **Arenella,** 8km from the city (bus #23, L600).

■■■ TAORMINA

Perched precariously on a cliff high above the Mediterranean, with the massive profile of Mt. Etna looming nearby, Taormina has drawn visitors since the 8th century BC when it was founded by Greek sailors after a shipwreck on the rocky shore below; it later became a destination for European aristocrats who transformed the town into a resort community. These days it's a precious combination of mansions, pine trees and purple flowers, with a hazy-blue coastline stretching out beyond. The 3rd-century **Greek Theater,** at the very edge of the cliff, is arguably the most dramatically situated theater on earth (Open daily 9am-1hr. before sunset. L2000, under 18 or over 60 free.) Nearby is the **Roman Odeon,** a small theater now partly covered by the Church of Santa Caterina next door. A small set of steep steps snake up the mountainside to the **castello,** hands down Taormina's finest view.

Accommodations can be hard to come by in summer, so arrive early and have the tourist office book a room for you. The **Pensione Svizzera,** via Pirandello 26 (tel. (0942) 237 90; fax 62 59 06), is a bit expensive but its spotless rooms with baths and magnificent views of the coastline are worth every *lira.* (Singles L32,000. Doubles L52,000. Triples L60,000. Breakfast L7000. Open March-Nov.) Another option is the **Villa Pompei,** via Bagnoli Croci, 88 (tel. 238 12), across from the public gardens. You can smell the flowers from the tidy rooms. (Singles L30,000. Doubles L48,000, with bath L54,000. Extra bed L15,000. Showers L2000. Reservations for June-Sept. required a month in advance with deposit.) Dining can be expensive, since restaurants cater almost exclusively to tourists; consider stocking up at the **Standa** supermarket on via Apollo Arcageta, at the end of corso Umberto, one block up from the post office. (Open Mon.-Sat., 8:30am-1pm and 5-9pm.) For a sit-down meal try **U Lantirnaru,** via Apollo Arcageta, 14 (tel. 245 65), also at the end of corso Umberto, and watch the chickens spinning in their huge wood-burning oven. (*Menù turistico* L13,000. Open Mon. and Wed.-Sat. noon-2pm and 5-11pm, Sun. 10:30am-2pm.)

Reach Taormina is by **bus** from Messina (13/day, L5100) or Catania (16/day, L5100). **Trains** are more frequent—from Messina (30/day, L3100) and Catania (29/day, L3900)—but the train station is far below town with access controlled by buses which make the climb every 15 to 75 minutes until 10:25pm (L1500). A helpful and well-organized **tourist office** waits on p. Santa Caterina (tel. 232 43), in Palazzo Corvaia off corso Umberto. (Open Mon.-Sat. 8am-2pm and 4-7pm.)

■■■ AEOLIAN ISLANDS (ISOLE EOLIE)

Home of the smithy god Hephaistos, the wind god Aeolus, and the Sirens, the Aeolian Islands are an enchanting volcanic archipelago off northern Sicily. On **Lípari,** the largest and most beautiful of the islands, the picturesque town of the same name is crowned by the walls of a medieval *castello,* the site of an ancient Greek acropolis. Inside the walls is the **Ostello Lípari (HI)** (tel. (090) 981 15 40, winter 98 12 527; L10,000; breakfast L3000; full meals L10,000-14,000; midnight curfew; kitchen, sheets, and cold showers included; open March-Oct.). Reach Lípari by ferry (Lípari 2hr., L9800 Siremar/L8900 NGI) from the city of **Milazzo,** on the Messina-Palermo train line (from Messina L3500; from Palermo L13,800). **Siremar** (tel. (090) 928 32 42 in Milazzo) and **Navigazione Generale Insulare** (tel. 928 34 15) run reliable ferries out of Milazzo. Take the quicker, more expensive hydrofoils (*aliscafi*) to the nearby islands (Vulcano, Salina and Panarea), but use the slow ferries for visits to Strómboli, Filicudi and Alicudi. Grab a bite to eat at the **Self-Service "Dal Napoletano,"** via Garibaldi, 12 (tel. 988 03 57), down the block from Locanda Salina. *(Gnocchi alla Napoletana* L7000. *Menu* 18,000. Beer on tap. June-Sept. open 24hrs. Oct.-May daily 9am-3pm and 6pm-midnight. Closed Mon.)

The island of **Vulcano,** easily accessed from Lípari (by hydrofoil L3400, by ferry L1800), is the perfect daytrip, with thermal springs and bubbling mud baths. From the dock at Porto di Levante, head to the left up the snaking path to the crater and past the sulfur fumaroles for a breathtaking view of the other isles. **Strómboli** (take the less-expensive *nave* rather than the ferry from Lípari) is the most dramatic and enticing of the islands, with an active volcano, streams o' lava, voluptuous vegetation, and alluring beaches. A night spent at the summit watching red-hot lava against pitch-black sky is unforgettable. Nights are crisp and windy at the crater; bring a plastic groundsheet and sleeping bag, a heavy sweater, 2 liters of water per person, and a flashlight with an extra set of batteries, as the path isn't lit. Always stay within the rocky enclosures. The hike takes 3 hours up, 2 hours down. An authorized guide (L25,000) is legally required, but few hikers hire one. Don't stash your bags in town—try asking at the Villa Petrusa further down the road. Arrive at dusk, as there's nothing to see but smoke during the day. The aforementioned conditions make winter travel on Strómboli particularly impractical. Get away from it all on **Filicudi** or **Alicudi;** neither supports more than 400 people, and electricity only came recently. The beautiful, expensive beaches and crystal-clear waters of **Panarea** and **Salina** are also good daytrips from Lípari.

SARDINIA (SARDEGNA)

Phoenicians, Byzantines, Pisans, Genoans, and Aragones alike have all tried to mainstream the island, but to no avail; Sardinia unabashedly retains its honor and proclaims its autonomy. Sardinia's beaches rival Europe's finest, and the island is still a refuge for marine seals and pink flamingos. Tourism has vanquished the northeastern **Costa Smeralda;** stick to the stunning beaches and ancient ruins farther south.

Tirrenia runs the most extensive ferry network, with service from **Civitavécchia** to Olbia (2/day, 7hr., L31,000) and Cagliari (daily, 13hr., L50,700); Genoa to Olbia (daily, 13hr., L57,400); Genoa to Cagliari (3/week, 20½hr., L80,200); and Naples to Cagliari (1/week, 16hr., L51,400). Prices listed above are for reserved seats; *posto ponte* (deck class) is cheaper. **Flights** arrive in Olbia and Cagliari (Rome-Olbia about L131,500 one way, cheaper night flights). On the island, **ARST** buses link villages while **PANI** buses connect only major cities. **Trains** are picturesque and inexpensive, but can be slow and unreliable. Most ignore railpasses. **Car rental** is not a bad idea. Ask any tourist office for the *Annuarii degli Albergi and Campeggi,* which lists all Sardinian hotels, *pensione* and campsites.

Cagliari, at the southern tip of the island, lies near beautiful beaches, ancient ruins, and flamingoed lagoons. Stay at **Albergo Firenze,** corso Vittorio Emanuele, 50 (tel. (070) 65 36 78; singles L25,000; doubles L30,000), or **Allogio Londra,** via Regina Margherita, 16 (tel. (070) 66 90 83; singles L28,000; doubles L40,000). Try **La Cantina,** via dei Mille, 3, for filling, inexpensive eats. **Sássari** is the second largest Sardinian city and a great base for daytrips. Try **Pensione Famiglia,** viale Umberto, 65 (tel. (070) 23 95 43; doubles L28,000). **Núoro** is an authentic Sardinian town in the heart of the island, largely unblemished by tourism. From Núoro, a 1-hour bus trip will connect you with **Cala Gonone,** a beautiful beach and take-off point for boats to **Grotta del Bue Marino,** a stunning cave where seals still romp at night.

District boundaries are
shown in light gray.
Districts names are the
same as the capital cities.
Regional areas are
named in bold-face:
ALGARVE
Regions have no
administrive boundaries

(Map of Portugal with labels including:)

ATLANTIC OCEAN

SPAIN

Viana do Castelo · MINHO · Serra do Gerês · Bragança · TRÁS-OS-MONTES · Rio Minho · Rio Cávado · Braga · Guimarães · Serra do Marão · Vila Real · Porto · DOURO LITORAL · DOURO ALTO · Rio Douro · BEIRA ALTA · Aveiro · Viseu · Salamanca · BEIRA LITORAL · Rio Mondego · Serra da Estrela · Guarda · Figueira da Foz · COSTA DA PRATA · Coímbra · Serra da Gardunha · Leiria · Batalha · BEIRA BAIXA · Nazaré · Fátima · Castelo Branco · São Martinho do Porto · Alcobaça · Tomar · Ilhas Berlengas · Caldas da Rainha · Cabo Carvoeiro · Óbidos · Rio Tejo · Peniche · Serra do Aire · Serra de São Mamede · ESTREMADURA · RIBATEJO · Cáceres · Vila Franca · Portalegre · Mafra · Sintra · Cascais · Lisboa · Estremoz · Elvas · Estoril · Queluz · Mérida · Cabo Espichel · Setúbal · ALTO ALENTEJO · Évora · Serra de Ossa · COSTA AZUL · Beja · Sines · BAIXO ALENTEJO · Rio Guadiana · COSTA DOURADA · Rio Mira · Mertola · Serra de Monchique · Portimão · Silves · ALGARVE · Cabo São Vicente · Lagos · Tavira · Sagres · Faro · Olhão · Vila Real de Santo Antonio · Golfo de Cádiz

Portugal

US$1 = 164$ (escudos, or PTE)   100$ =   US$0.61
CDN$1 = 125$ 100$ = CDN$0.80
UK£1 = 254$ 100$ =   UK£0.39
IR£1 = 238$ 100$ =   IR£0.42
AUS$1 = 107$ 100$ = AUS$0.94
NZ$1 = 91$ 100$ =   NZ$1.10
SAR1 = 34$ 100$ =   SAR2.93
Country Code: 351 International Dialing Prefix: 097

Centuries ago, Portuguese explorers noticed that the Atlantic Ocean didn't swallow the sun every evening. Their revolutionary navigational and shipbuilding techniques allowed Vasco de Gama to sail around the Cape of Good Hope and Magellan to sail around the world, and their discoveries fed the country's prosperity, transforming art and architecture into the ornate and sometimes eccentric Manueline style. Following the Age of Discovery a period of decline set in, imbuing the culture with a nostalgia still reflected in the folk ballads of *fado*—fate. By 1580, Portugal had exhausted both its resources and its royal line, and after minimal resistance, the Spanish Habsburg Philip II claimed the Portuguese throne. Independence wasn't regained until 1640, when the royal house of Bragança stabilized itself by hooking up with England. An earthquake in 1755 reduced much of Lisbon to rubble, shaking the country's faith and economy so much that when Napoleon invaded in 1807, King Pedro III moved the court of his crumbling empire to Brazil.

A parliamentary republic sprouted in 1910, only to be overthrown by a 1926 military coup. Strongman António Salazar, an economist-turned-dictator, and his successor, Marcelo Caetano, ruled the country for the next 50 years, running down the economy through the exploitation of a domestic peasantry and African laborers under colonial rule. In 1974, a bloodless coup toppled the regime, prompting mass rejoicing—every Portuguese town now has its Rua 25 de Abril to honor the putsch. The new government granted independence to Portugal's African holdings; the ensuing civil wars in Mozambique and Angola set off a rush of immigration into an already unstable Portugal. In 1986, Prime Minister Cavaco Silva supervised Portugal's entry into the European Economic Community, and he initiated a sometimes painful modernization drive for the country. Portugal remains quite poor by European standards; some estimates hold that up to two-fifths of the population now lives abroad in search of better jobs and living standards.

Each year, sun-worshipers migrate to the sands, cliffs, and sparkling waters of the Algarve; fewer visit the rougher northern coast. Notable architecture abounds in the north: Coimbra and Porto have Romanesque churches, while the area north of the Rio Douro is dotted with Roman and Visigothic ruins. In the center and south are massive fortresses lingering from the Moorish occupation.

> For more detailed, energetic, and sunny information on Portugal, grab a copy of *Let's Go: Spain & Portugal.*

GETTING THERE AND GETTING AROUND

International **airports** in Lisbon, Porto, and Faro serve major European and North American cities. **TAP,** the national airline, frequently offers half-price youth fares. Lisbon and Porto are also accessible by daily **trains** from Madrid and Paris.

Eurailpasses are valid on the Portuguese national **train** system, but passholders pay extra on express trains. **Caminhos de Ferro Portugueses,** Portugal's national railway, operates throughout the country, but aside from the Braga-Porto-Coimbra-Lisbon line, it's wisest to take the bus: trains are less comfortable, less frequent, often slower and reach fewer destinations. On the other hand, a 2nd-class train ticket is generally less expensive than the bus fare. **Rodoviária,** the national bus company, links just about every town, while an abundance of private regional companies cover the more obscure routes. Express coach service *(expressos)* between major cities is especially good. **Hitchhiking** in Portugal is not reliable enough to be anyone's main means of transportation.

PORTUGAL ESSENTIALS

The national **tourist board** is the Direção General do Turismo (DGT). Their offices are in virtually every city; look for the "Turismo" sign. They'll give you free maps that usually include brief descriptions of sights, and useful phone numbers. Many *turismos* keep lists of approved accommodations and can point you to a *quarto* (private room).

A strongly Catholic country, Portugal's liveliest festivals are the *festas juninas,* which take place around the feast days of St. John and St. Peter, June 24 and 29. June is bedlam in Lisbon; the feast day of its patron saint Santo Antônio is celebrated June 13 with costume processions and bacchanalian excesses. Two important festivals commemorate the appearances of the Virgin in Fátima (May 12-13 and Oct. 12-13). Holy Week in April brings processions and crowds to Braga; Easter Sunday marks the beginning of the Portuguese bullfighting season. (The bull is wounded, not killed.) Every town has its patron saint; their feast days are local holidays, accompanied by pilgrimages, village fairs, and often makeshift amusement parks, and closed shops. Everything in Portugal closes on New Year's Day, Carnival Tuesday, Good Friday, Easter Sunday, April 25, Labor Day (May 1), June 10, June 24, Corpus Christi, Assumption, Oct. 5, All Saints Day (Nov. 1), Restoration of Independence (Dec. 1), Immaculate Conception (Dec. 8), Christmas Eve, and Christmas Day.

Portuguese **currency** is divided into escudos and centavos; the $ sign is used in *Let's Go* as a currency symbol. Shops are usually open weekdays from 9am to 1pm and from 3 to 6pm, and on Saturday mornings. Normal banking hours are weekdays from 8:30am to 6:30pm and Saturday from 9am to noon. In smaller towns banks close for lunch and weekends.

Communication
Portuguese is a Romance language similar to Spanish, but also accessible to those with a background in French or Italian. In the southern and central provinces, many locals speak English, French, or German.

Mail usually takes 6-8 business days to reach the U.S. or Canada; postage costs 130$. *Posta restante* (Poste Restante) pick-up (at central post offices) costs 20$ per item. A **telegram,** the most reliable means of communication, may be sent from most any post office; offices with telegram service have signs that read "CTT." A message of 10-15 words costs a flat fee of about 1614$ plus a 84$ per word charge. Post offices also house telephone offices, which in larger cities remain open until 11:30pm or midnight. **Phone booths** (marked by signs saying Credifone) are located at phone offices, on the street, and in some post offices. Direct-dialing from a phone booth is the least expensive way to make an international call. Dial 098 for Europe, 097 for everywhere else. Few pay phones accept coins; the Credifone system uses magnetic cards that are sold at locations posted on the phone booth. Local calls cost 17.50$ by Credifone, 20$ by coin. Phone calls from bars and cafés cost whatever the proprietor decides to charge, typically 30-35$; there's usually a posted sign that indicates the charge. Some helpful numbers throughout Portugal are: **directory assistance: 118; local operator: 142; international operator: 099** for inside Europe; 098 for elsewhere. In an **emergency (police, fire, medical): 115.** For MCI's **World Reach,** dial 05 017 1234. Women traveling alone will likely receive inordinate amounts of male attention—annoying, but rarely dangerous. See *Women and Travel,* in the front of this book.

Accommodations and Camping
The **Associação Portuguesa de Pousadas de Juventude (APPJ),** the Portuguese Hostelling International affiliate, runs the country's HI hostels. A bargain bed in a *pousada de juventude* costs 850-1350$ per night, 750-1000$ in off-season (breakfast included). Lunch or dinner costs 750$. Rates are slightly higher for guests 26 or older. Hostels are typically some distance away from the town center. Reception hours are from 9am to 12:30pm and 6 to 9pm. Most hostels enforce a lockout 10:30am to 6pm; the early curfews (11pm or midnight) may cramp your style if you club-hop. To stay in a hostel, an HI card (3000$), sold at many hostels and budget-travel agencies, is mandatory.

Hotels in Portugal are usually more expensive than they're worth. *Pensões,* also called *residencias,* will likely be your mainstay. They're far cheaper and offer fewer amenities than hotels; the primary reason to spend the extra escudos is to get a private room. All are rated by the government on a 3-star scale, and are required to prominently post their category and legal price limits. During high season, many *pensõe* owners won't reserve rooms by phone.

The Portuguese love to camp; their 168 official **campgrounds** *(parques de campismo)* come chock-full of amenities and comforts. With such facilities, it's wise to arrive early; urban and coastal parks may require reservations. Recently, police have been cracking down on illegal camping, so don't try it close by one of the official campgrounds. Larger tourist office branches stock the *Roteiro Campista*, an indispensable multilingual guide to all official campgrounds; or write to the **Federação Portuguesa de Campismo,** Apartado 3168-1304, Lisboa Codex (tel. (1) 886 23 50 or 315 57 15; fax (1) 54 93 72). **Orbitur-Intercâmbio de Turismo, S.A.,** a private company, administers 15 of Portugal's poshest, best-run, and most expensive campgrounds (bungalows available). For reservations write to Orbitur at Av. Almirante Reis, 246 r/c, Dío. Lisboa 1000 (tel. (1) 89 05 75 or 84 29 38; fax (1) 848 18 81). *Quartos* are rooms in private residences, sometimes the only choice in small or less touristed towns, particularly in southern Portugal. The tourist office can usually help find them, and restaurant proprietors and bartenders often supply names and directions. A *pousada* (literally, resting place) is a castle, palace, or monastery converted into an expensive and luxurious government-run guest house (Portugal's version of the Spanish *parador nacional).*

Food and Drink   Olive oil, garlic, herbs, and sea salt routinely season local specialties. As a whole, the aromatic Portuguese cuisine is heavy on herbs and light on spices. *Sopas* (soups) are hearty and filling. Main dishes run a delectable gamut. Seafood lovers get their fix from grilled *peixe espada grelhado* (Madeiran scabbardfish), *lagosta suada* (steamed lobster), *pescada frita* (fried hake, a particularly delish Atlantic fish), *linguado grelhado* (grilled sole), *polvo* (boiled or grilled octopus), and *mexilhões* (mussels). Pork fiends indulge in *bife de porco à alentejana,* made with clams in a coriander sauce. Those who prefer chicken fork into *frango assado* (roasted on a spit) and *frango no churrasco* (barbecued). The entire country feeds on *cozida à portuguesa* (boiled beef, pork, sausage, and vegetables) in winter. Portugal's favorite dessert is *pudim,* a rich caramel custard. Portuguese *vinho* (wine) costs a pittance by North American standards. Sparkling *vinho verde* (literally "green wine"—the name refers to its youth, not its color) comes in red and white versions. Excellent local table wines are *Colares, Dão, Borba, Bairrada, Bucelas,* and *Periquita.* Port, pressed (by feet) from the red grapes of the Douro Valley and fermented with a touch of brandy, is a dessert in itself. A unique heating process gives Madeira wines their odd "cooked" flavor.

The Portuguese eat earlier than the Spanish. The midday meal (dinner, "lunch" to Americans) is served between noon and 2pm, supper between 7:30 and 10pm. A good meal costs 900-1100$ just about anywhere. Oddly, prices don't vary much between ritzy and economy restaurants in Portugal. Half portions *(meia dose)* cost more than half-price but are often more than adequate. The ubiquitous *prato do dia* (special of the day) and *menú* (appetizer, bread, entree, and dessert) satisfy hungry folks. Although restaurant prices certainly won't drive you to it, concocting a meal from the outdoor food stalls is the most inexpensive option. Attention vegetarians— every town you visit is likely to have a **mercado municipal** (open-air produce market); for groceries, shop at the **mercado** (supermarket).

Most restaurants will add a service charge to your bill. It's customary to round off the sum to the next highest unit of currency and leave the change as a tip.

■■■ LISBON (LISBOA)

Though Portugal's colonial empire is only a memory, there's still something imperial about Lisbon. Traffic, smog, and urban decay plague the city, and most of the historic buildings were destroyed in the great earthquake of 1755, but Lisbon's relaxed urbanity still appeals to visitors. Streetcars run down the broad avenues and narrow lanes, and the city still maintains its black-and-white mosaic sidewalks.

ORIENTATION AND PRACTICAL INFORMATION

The **Baixa**, or Lower Town, is Lisbon's downtown and the old business district. Its grid of small streets begins at the **Rossio** (the main square, comprised of the connecting **Praça Dom Pedro IV** and **Praça da Figueira**) and ends at Praça do Comércio, near the **Tagus River** (Rio Tejo). **Praça dos Restauradores,** an active square, is just north of the Rossio. Lisbon's swank shopping district, the **Chiado,** is linked to the Baixa by the Ascensor de Santa Justa. West of Rua da Misericórdia spreads the **Bairro Alto,** or Upper District, a populous working-class area of narrow streets, tropical parks and baroque churches. To the east, the **Alfama,** Lisbon's famous medieval quarter, stacks tiny whitewashed houses along a labyrinth of narrow alleys and stairways beneath the city's *castelo.* The old and new business districts are connected by **Avenida da Liberdade,** a broad, tree-lined boulevard that begins its uphill climb at Pr. Restauradores. **Belém** (Bethlehem), formerly an autonomous town (about 6km west of Praça do Comércio), is home to several museums and palaces.

Tourist Office: Palácio da Foz, Pr. Restauradores (tel. 346 33 14 or 342 52 31). Metro: Restauradores. English and French spoken. Open daily 9am-8pm. Airport branch office open 24hrs. **National Tourist Office Headquarters,** Av. António Augusto de Aguiar, 86 (tel. 57 50 86). Open Mon.-Fri. 9am-12:30pm, 1:30-5:30pm.

Budget Travel: Tagus (Youth Branch), Pr. Londres, 9B (tel. 849 15 31). Metro: Alameda. Books flights on TAP and British Airways. English spoken. **Tagus (Main Office),** R. Camilo Castelo Branco, 20 (tel. 352 55 09). Both offices open Mon.-Fri. 9:30am-1pm and 2:30-6pm.

Embassies: U.S.: Av. Forças Armadas (tel. 726 66 00). **Canada:** Av. da Liberdade, 144, 3rd floor (tel. 347 48 92). **U.K.:** R. São Domingos à Lapa, 37 (tel. 396 11 91). Also handles **New Zealand** affairs. **Australia:** Av. Liberdade, 244, 4th floor (tel. 52 33 50).

Currency Exchange: Estação Santa Apolónia, on the platform. Enormous lines here and at the airport branch. Both open 24hrs.

American Express: Top Tours, Av. Duque de Loulé, 108 (tel. 315 58 85). Metro: Rotunda. Exit toward R. Rod. Samparo and walk up Av. da Liberdade toward the Marques de Pombal Statue, then hang a right. This sole Top Tours office handles all AmEx services. Traveler's Cheques sold and cashed; mail held. English spoken. Open Mon.-Fri. 9:30am-1pm and 2:30-6:30pm.

Post Office: Correio, Pr. Comércio (tel. 346 32 31). Open for **Posta Restante** Mon.-Fri. 9am-7pm. Branch office at Pr. Restauradores open for **telegrams,** international express service, stamps and telephones 8am-10pm. **Postal Code:** 1100 for central Lisbon.

Telephones: Central exchange at Pr. Dom Pedro IV, 68. Metro: Rossio. For **telegrams,** dial 183. Open 8am-11pm. Credifone cards come in 50 units (750$) or 120 units (1725$). Local calls consume at least 1 unit. **City Code:** 01.

Flights: Aeroporto de Lisboa (tel. 80 20 60), on the northern outskirts of the city. Local buses #44 or 45 (20min. from downtown). The express bus *(linha verde,* 300$) is faster. All 3 lines head for the Baixa. Taxis are cheaper for more than 2 people (about 800$ to the Baixa). **TAP Air Portugal** (airport tel. 848 91 81; info 848 91 82). **Iberia** (tel. 356 20 16; reservations 847 50 34).

Trains: (tel. 888 40 25). **Santa Apolónia,** on banks of the Tagus near Alfama, for all international, northern, and eastern lines. **Cais do Sodré** for Estoril and Cascais (every 15min., 40min., 155$). **Barreiro** for the Algarve and southern lines. To reach Barreiro, take a ferry across the Tagus (every 5-10min, 110$, free if coming into Lisbon from the south) from Pr. Comércio. **Rossio** (between Pr. Restauradores and Pr. Dom Pedro IV) for Sintra (every 10min., 45min., 155$) and western lines. Detailed schedules and some assistance at Rossio. Open 8am-11pm. To: Évora (4/day, 3hr., 770$); Porto (4/day, 5hr., 1615$); Lagos (5/day, 6½hr., 1550$); Badajoz, Spain (4/day, 5hr., 2448$); Paris (1/day, 27hr., 19,000$).

Buses: Rodoviária, Av. Casal Ribeiro, 18 (tel. 54 58 63). To find it, from Pr. Marquês de Pombal take Av. Fontes Pereira de Melo to Pr. Duque de Saldanha and bear right around the roundabout. Metro: Picoas. To: Évora (7/day, 2½hr., 1050$); Coimbra (8/day, 3hr., 1150$); Lagos (5/day, 5hr., 1900$); Porto (5/day, 5hr., 1600$). The private company **Caima,** R. Bacalhoeiros, 16 (tel. 87 50 61) runs express buses to the Algarve and Porto. To Lagos (6/day, 2100$).

Public Transportation: Buses, CARRIS (tel. 57 77 15). 130$ within the city. **Subway:** 65$ at window, 55$ from vending machines. Book of 10 475$ at window, 500$ from machines. *Bilhete de assinatura turístico* (tourist pass), good for unlimited travel on CARRIS buses, trolleys, funiculars, and the subway (1200$ for 4 days, 1700$ for 7 days). The passes are sold in CARRIS booths (open 8am-8pm), located in most network train stations and the busier metro stations. **Trolleys (*eléctricos*):** Ubiquitous cars (many pre-WWI) offer beautiful views of the harbor and older neighborhoods. #28 good for sightseeing (stops in Pr. Comércio, 140$).

Taxis: Rádio Táxis de Lisboa (tel. 815 50 61), **Autocoope** (tel. 793 27 56), and **Teletáxi** (tel. 815 20 16). 24-hr. service.

Luggage Storage: At **Estaçãos Rossio and Santa Apolónia.** Lockers 350$, 450$, and 750$ for up to 48 hr. At the **bus station,** 130$/bag/day.

English Bookstore: Livraria Bertrand, R. Garrett, 75 (tel. 346 86 46), Good collection of best-sellers. International maps, and travel guides. Open Mon.-Fri. 9am-7pm, Sat. 9am-1pm.

Laundromat: Lavatax, R. Francisco Sanches, 65A (tel. 82 33 92). Metro: Arroios. Wash, dry, and fold 800$/5kg load. Open 9am-1pm and 3-7pm, Sat. 9am-noon.

Medical Assistance: British Hospital, R. Saraiva de Carvalho, 49 (tel. 60 20 20; at night 60 37 85).

Emergency: tel. 115 anywhere in Portugal. **Police:** R. Capelo, 3 (tel. 346 61 41).

ACCOMMODATIONS AND CAMPING

Expect to pay 2500$ for a single and 4000$ for a double. The vast majority of hotels are in the center of town on **Av. Liberdade** and adjacent sidestreets. Lodgings near the *castelo* or in the Bairro Alto are quieter, nearer to the sights, and more expensive. Be cautious in the Bairro Alto, the Alfama, and the Baixa after dark. If the central accommodations are full, head east to the *pensões* along **Av. Almirante Reis.**

Pousada da Juventude de Lisboa (HI), R. Andrade Corvo, 46 (tel. 353 26 96). Newly renovated and reopened in 1993. A few Metro stops from town center. No curfew, no lockout. Spic 'n' span rooms. Handicap access. No age restriction. Max. stay 3 days in high season. Check-in 8am-noon. Check-out by 10:30am. Multiples 1700$. Doubles with bath 4250$. Low season: 1500$; 2750$. Breakfast included. Lunch or dinner 750$. Reservations highly recommended, in writing. HI card required.

Pousada da Juventude de Catalazete (HI), Estrada Marginal (tel. 443 06 38), in the coastal town of **Oeiras.** Take a train from Estação Cais do Sodré to Oeiras (20min., 95$), exit through the underpass and turn right under the sign "Praia" (beach). Head left and follow the signs. Rooms a bit cramped. Moonlight ocean views rival those from the Captain Steubing's Aloha deck. Reception open 9:30-11am and 6-10:30pm. Curfew midnight. June-Sept., Holy Week, and Christmas 1400$; Oct.-May 1100$. Breakfast included. Lunch or dinner 750$. Make reservations through Lisbon's HI office, R. Andrade Corvo, 46 (tel. 57 10 54).

Pensão Prata, R. Prata, 71, 3rd fl. (tel. 346 89 08), 2 blocks from Pr. Comércio. Sun-kissed rooms in a peaceful apartment setting. Some kitchen use permitted. Singles 3000$, with bath 3500$. Doubles 4000$, with bath 4500$. Triples with bath 4500$. Winter 25% off.

Pensão Campos, R. Jardim do Regedor, 24, 3rd fl. (tel. 346 28 64), on the pedestrian street between Pr. Restauradores and R. Portas de Santa Antão. Cozy, well-furnished rooms and clean bath. Singles 3000$. Doubles 3500$, with bath 4500$.

Pensão Estrela de Chiado, R. Garrett, 29, 4th fl. (tel. 342 61 10). The 95-stair climb is hell but worth it. Clean rooms with hot water. Singles 2500$. Doubles 3000$, with bath 3500$.

Pensão Londres, R. Dom Pedro V, 53 (tel. 346 55 23, fax 346 56 82). Take the funicular by Palácio da Foz in Pr. Restauradores. Facing away from the funicular, walk right (west) up to R. Dom Pedro V. Ideal for nature lovers and bargain hunters; near the parks and the best inexpensive restaurants. Singles 3000$, with bath 4000$. Doubles 4000$, with bath 5000$. Breakfast included.

Pensão Residencial Brasil Africano, Trav. Pedras Negras, 8, 2nd floor (tel. 886 92 66), off R. Madalena. Conveniently located near the cathedral and the Baixa. Don't judge the hotel by the outside; it's been renovated. Spacious rooms with balconies. Singles 1500$. Doubles 2700$, with bath 3800$. Triples 3600$.

Camping: Parque da Câmara Municipal de Lisboa-Monsanto (tel. 70 20 61 or 70 74 74), on the road to Benfica. Swimming pool and a reasonably priced supermarket. Take bus #43 from the Rossio to the Parque Florestal Monsanto. 350$/person, 350$/tent, 230$/car. **Clube de Campismo de Lisboa Costa da Caparica** (tel. 290 01 00), 5km out of Lisbon. Take the metro to Palhavã or the bus from Pr. Espanha. Beaches. Shade. Pool. Fun. 700$/person, /tent, and /car.

FOOD

Lisbon has some of the least expensive restaurants of any European capital. A full dinner costs about 1500$ per person. Restaurants in the **Baixa** are more elegant and more expensive, catering largely to tourists. The **Bairro Alto** feeds many locals. Restaurants there, as in the **Alfama,** are correspondingly small, dark, and cheap.

Bus #40 runs to **Mercado Ribeira,** a market complex on Av. 24 de Julho outside the Cais do Sodré. (Open Mon.-Sat. until 2pm.) There's a larger market in Cascais on Wednesday morning (5min. from the train station). A jumbo supermarket, **Pão de Açucar,** is in the Amoreiras Shopping Center de Lisboa, Av. Duarte Pacheco.

Adega Popular 33, R. Conceiçao, 33 (tel. 84 94 72), 2 blocks from Pr. Comércio. Small and popular, the least expensive on the block. Delicious *lulas grelhadas* (grilled squid) 720$. Entrees 500-850$; ½-portions available. Open Mon.-Fri. 8am-9:30pm.

Restaurante Bonjardim, Trav. de Santo Antão, 12 (tel. 342 74 24), off Pr. Restauradores. Toothsome roast chicken (970$). Nibbly good appetizer *chouriço asado na brasa* (roast sausage, 290$). Open daily noon-3pm and 6:30-10:30pm.

Celeiro, Rua 1 de Dezembro, 65 (tel. 342 24 63), just off the Rossio. The strict herbivore can happily graze at this macrobiotic restaurant (beneath a health food supermarket). Salads, soufflées, and sandwiches all self serve.

Lua de Mel, R. Prata, 242-248 (tel. 87 91 51), on the corner with R. Santa Justa. Possibly the freshest, most scrumptious pastries in the city (85$). Sandwiches 200-400$. Fruit salads and ice cream sundaes 450$. Open Tues.-Sat. 7:30am-8:30pm.

Cervejaria da Trindade, R. Nova Trindade, 20c-d (tel. 32 35 06), a street perpendicular to R. Garrett. Regal imagery on shiny azulejos give rise to the elegant but noisy atmosphere. Grilled specialties and fish entrees. The *Espetada de Tamboril con Gambas* (fish and prawn kebab, 1280$) is particularly yummy. Entrees 600-1450$. Open Mon.-Sat. 9am-11:30pm.

Lua Nova, Trav. Queimada, 4 (tel. 346 57 92), off R. Misericórdia, a couple blocks down from Calçada da Gloria. Great for a cheap dinner before hitting the nearby *fado* houses. Entrees 800-1000$. Open July 16-June 30 Mon.-Sat. 10am-10pm.

Mestre André, Calçadinha de Sto. Estevão, 6, off R. Remédios. Eclectic yet tasteful adornment of old movie posters and stills. Their *murcela frita*, an ugly but savory little blood sausage (400$) is a favorite among regulars. Outdoor seating and grill on a stone terrace above the street. Open Mon.-Sat. noon-3pm and 7-10:30pm.

SIGHTS

Lisbon's 18th-century heart shows the city's modern and sophisticated side. The center of activity is the **Rossio;** the **Teatro Nacional** marks the former site of the Palace of the Inquisition. After the earthquake, Pombal commissioned the **Baixa,** the grid of streets south of the Rossio, to facilitate communication between the town center and the river. **Rua Augusta,** a pedestrian zone, is lined with shops selling furs, shoes, and perfume, and leads past a triumphal arch to **Praça do Comércio.**

North of the Rossio, **Praça dos Restauradores** commemorates the 1640 "restoration" of Portugal's independence from Spain with an obelisk and a bronze sculpture of the Spirit of Independence. Here begins **Avenida da Liberdade,** the city's most imposing boulevard. Boxed in a fanciful Gothic tower by Eiffel, the **Acensor de Santa Justa** connects the Baixa to the Chiado (35$; under construction in 1993). On R. da Misericórdia is the **Igreja de São Roque,** noted for its **Capela de São João Baptista** (4th from the left), a chapel ablaze with precious gems and metals that caused a stir upon its installation in 1747. Three different ships delivered the chapel to Lisbon after it was built in Rome from agate, lapis lazuli, alabaster, and *verde antica*.

Originally a Visgoth settlement and later home to the Moorish aristocracy, the **Alfama** became the noisy, popular section of town it is today when the Christians recaptured the city. Look into **Igreja de São Miguel** (1812), arguably Lisbon's finest church, and the busy **Rua de São Pedro.** Between the Alfama and the Baixa is the quarter known as the **Mouraria** (Moorish ghetto), established after Dom Afonso Henriques and the Crusaders expelled the Moors in 1147. The restored, luxurious **Castelo de São Jorge** looks down at Lisbon from its hill a few blocks up from the cathedral. Built in the 5th century by the Visigoths, this castle was the principal palace of the royal family from the 14th to the 16th centuries. High up on its windswept esplanade shaded by olive trees, the castle gardens are home to odd-looking albino peafowl. (Open daily 9am-9pm; Oct.-March 9am-7pm. Free.)

A ½hr. walk down Av. Infante Santo and a 10-minute jaunt to the left of Calçada da Pampulha is the **Museu Nacional de Arte Antiga,** home to a representative collection of European paintings ranging from Gothic primitives to 18th-century French masterpieces. (Open Tues.-Sat. 10am-1pm and 2-5pm. 250$, students free.) Buses #40 and 60 stop to the right as you leave the museum and head back to the Baixa.

Rising from the banks of the Tagus behind a royally sculpted garden, **Mosteiro dos Jerónimos** stands as Portugal's most refined celebration of the Age of Discovery. (Open Tues.-Sun. 10am-5pm; Oct.-May 10am-1pm and 2:30-5pm. 400$, Oct.-May 250$, students and seniors free.)

The **Torre de Belém,** built to protect the seaward entrance of the Portuguese capital, rises from the Tagus's north bank. It's a half-hour walk along the railroad tracks from the monastery. The 6-cornered turrets, copied from originals in India, and the Venetian balconies and windows demonstrate the crafty eclecticism of Manueline architects. (Open Tues.-Sun. 10am-1pm and 2:30-5pm. 400$; Oct.-May 250$; students and seniors free.)

ENTERTAINMENT

The paper *Sete,* available from kiosks in the Rossio (215$), publishes listings of concerts, movies, plays, exhibits, and bullfights. The more comprehensive, less hip, multilingual *Cultura Agenda* is available free from kiosks in the Rossio and the Turismo. *Fado* is a melancholy wailing expressive of *saudade,* an enigmatic Portuguese emotion of nostalgic yearning. The sensational tales of lost loves and faded glory performed by *fadistas* are Portugal's blues. The Bairro Alto has many *fado* joints off **R. Misericordia,** particularly on sidestreets radiating from the Museu de São Roque. For a particularly melodramatic show try **Sr. Vinho,** R. Meio a Lapa, 18 (tel. 397 26 81), in nearby Madregoa. (Min. food and drink charge 2500$. Open 8:30pm-2am.)

Those in search of rowdier fun shouldn't be deceived by the after-dinner lull; nothing starts up until after midnight. Nightlife clusters around **Rua Diario das Notícias** in the Bairro Alto. Drinkers gather in **Boris,** Travessa Água da Flor, 20, a small but trendy place where the drunken singing carries into the street. (Open 9pm-2am.) Diagonally across the street, **Mascote do Bairro** is calmer and roomier. Figure out the postmodern decor, technopop music, and requisite smoky air of **Cena de Lopos,** R. da Barroca, 105, which gets jammed after midnight. (Open 10pm-2am.)

If dancing's your thing, **La Folie Discoteca,** R. Diario das Noticias, 122-4, runneth over with a bar, air conditioning, and the latest international music. The 900$ cover includes 2 beers or a mixed drink. (Open Tues.-Sun. 10pm-4am.) **Memorial,** R. Gustavo dc Matos Sequeira, 42A (tel. 396 88 91), a block south of R. Escola Politécnica in the Bairro Alto is a hip gay and lesbian disco-bar that doesn't get moving until after midnight. (Cover and 2 beers or 1 drink 1000$. Open 10:30pm-4am.)

June is the month of *feiras populares,* outdoor night fairs with plenty of eating, drinking, and dancing to live music. There's a lively one called "Oreal" at **Campo das Cebolas,** near the waterfront in the Alfama. (Open June Mon.-Fri. 10pm-1am, Sat.-Sun. 10pm-3am.)

■ Near Lisbon

After Lord Byron sang its praises in the epic poem *Childe Harold,* **Sintra** became a must for 19th-century English aristocrats on the Grand Tour. While the town's popularity has made it a bit self-conscious, Sintra retains the air of a fairy-tale city and makes a delightful daytrip from Lisbon. Between the train station and the town center stands a storybook village hall; the conical chimneys of the **Paço Real** (Palácio Real) loom behind. Once the summer residence of Moorish sultans and harems, the palace and its complex gardens were torn down during the Reconquista and replaced with a vaguely Moorish, mostly Gothic and Manueline building. Inside is the Sala dos Cisnes, a banquet hall with 27 swans in different positions decorating the ceiling. (Open Thurs.-Tues. 10am-12:30pm and 2-4:30pm. Tickets sold 10am-4:30pm. 400$, Oct.-May 200$, Sun. free.) Hike or taxi (round-trip 2000$) up the 3km of winding access road to the **Palácio de Pena,** a massive palace built over an old Hieronymite monastery. The palace was built in the 1840s by Prince Ferdinand, the queen's German consort. Nostalgic for his country, the prince commissioned on obscure German architect to design this folly. The utterly fantastic result would do loony King Ludwig proud: a Bavarian castle embellished with Arab minarets, Gothic turrets, and a Renaissance dome. (Open Tues.-Sun. 10am-5pm, none admitted after 4:30pm. 400$, Oct.-May 200$; students with ID and seniors free.) Sintra's **tourist office** (tel. 923 11 57; fax 923 51 76) is at Pr. República, in the same building as the regional museum. Sintra, 30km northwest of Lisbon, is accessible by train from the Rossio station (every 8min., 45min., 155$).

The reputation of **Estoril** and **Cascais,** a half-hour west of Lisbon, as playgrounds for the rich and famous, shouldn't deter you from spending a day at the beach. Although they bristle with their share of luxury hotels and restaurants, at least they're relaxed and informal. In Estoril, you can find a reasonably priced room at **Pensão Costa,** R. Olivença, 2 (tel. 468 16 99), on the corner of Estrada Marginal uphill from the train station. (Singles and doubles 4000$, with shower 5000$; Oct.-June 25% off.) For rooms in Cascais, try **Pensão Residêncial Casa Lena,** Av. Ultramar, #389 (tel. 486 87 43), on the outskirts of town. (Doubles 5000$, with bath 6500$. Triples 7500$.) For a taste of the Mediterranean, dine at **Joshuas Shoarma Grill,** R. Visconde da Luz, 19 (tel. 484 30 64), just past the R. Alex. Herculano and Av. Combatentes da Grande Guerra intersection. (Open Mon.-Fri. noon-4pm and 6pm-2am, Sat.-Sun. 1pm-2am.) Trains to Estoril leave from the Cais do Sodré station in Lisbon (every 15min., 40min., 145$).

CENTRAL PORTUGAL

The meadowed **Ribatejo** is a fertile region that fills most of the basin of the Tagus and its main tributary, the Zêzere. Although farmed intensely—yielding vegetables, olives, and citrus fruits—the area is best known in Portugal as a pastureland for Arabian horses and great black bulls. Stretching south and east of the Tagus, the less fortunate **Alentejo** region covers almost one-third of the Portuguese land mass; with a population of slightly over half a million it remains the least populous region. The requisite olive trees and whitewashed hamlets dot the rolling hills.

Tomar Two cities of particular note lie in or near the Ribatejo. For centuries the mysterious Knights Templar schemed and plotted from **Tomar,** a small town straddling the Rio Nabão. Most of Tomar's monuments reflect its former status as the den of that secretive religious order. The **Convento de Cristo** is a stately fortress, established in 1320 as a refuge for the disbanded Knights. Modeled after the Holy Sepulchre in Jerusalem, the **Templo dos Templares** contains an ornate octagonal canopy that protects the high altar. The Knights supposedly attended Mass on horseback, each under one of the arches. **Claustro dos Felipes** is considered one of Europe's masterpieces of Renaissance architecture; its graceful spiral staircases, Tuscan columns and Ionic pillars frame a large fountain. Tomar's **Museu Luso-Hebraico,** in the 15th-century Sinagoga do Arco at R. Dr. Joaquim Jaquinto (a.k.a. R. da Judiaria), 73, is Portugal's only significant reminder of what was once a great European Jewish community. After the expulsion of the Jews, the building served as a prison, a hayloft, and a grocery warehouse until its classification as a national monument in 1921. (Open Sun.-Fri. 2-5pm. Free.)

The **Rio Nabão** divides Tomar. The train and bus stations and most accommodations and sights lie on the west bank. **Rua Serpa Pinto** connects the Ponte Velha (old bridge) to the main square, **Praça da República.** From Tomar's train or bus station, walk straight down the street out front, turn left at the first light and walk until you reach Av. do Cândido Madureira. Tomar's **tourist office** (tel. (049) 32 34 27), is 2 blocks to your left, facing Parque Mata Nacional. It offers the most comprehensive map on the Portuguese mainland. (Open Mon.-Fri. 9:30am-12:30pm and 2-6pm, Sat.-Sun. 10am-1pm and 3-6pm; Oct.-May Mon.-Fri. 9:30am-12:30pm and 2-6pm, Sat. 10am-1pm.)

The most inexpensive rooms in town are in the **Pensão Tomarense,** R. Torres Pinheiro, 15 (tel. (049) 31 29 48), a block from Nuno Alvares. (Singles 1700$, with bath 2200$. Doubles with bath 2700$.) Another bargain is the **Pensão Nuno Alvares,** Av. Nuno Alvares, 3 (tel. (049) 31 28 73), a block to the right of the bus and train stations. (Singles 1800$. Doubles 2400$, with bath 3200$.) Dine on a riverside patio with a handsome view of the castle in the **Restaurante A Bela Vista,** Fonte Choupo, 6, across Ponte Velha on your left. (Entrees 800-1700$. Open Wed.-Mon. noon-3pm and 7-9:30pm.)

The **train station** is on Av. Combatentes da Grande Guerra (tel. (049) 31 28 15), on the southern edge of town. Tomar is the northern terminus of a minor line, so most destinations require a transfer at Entroncamento; you can buy the ticket for both legs here. To: Lisbon (12/day, 2hr., 770$), Coimbra (9/day, 2hr., 735$), Porto (5/day, 4½hr., 1235$), Faro (via Lisbon, 9hr., 1925$). **Buses** leave from Av. Combatentes da Grande Guerra (tel. (049) 31 27 38), next to the train station, to: Lisbon (6/day, 2hr., 1050$), Coimbra (2/day, 2hr., 1000$), Porto (1/day, 4hr., 1300$), and Lagos (1/day, 8hr., 2020$).

Santarém Capital of the Ribatejo province and its major town, **Santarém** sits on a rocky mound overlooking the Río Tejo. This flourishing medieval center boasted 15 convents, making it the capital of Portugal's Gothic style, and is now the primary market for produce in this fertile region. The core of the town is formed by the densely packed streets between **Praça Sá da Bandeira** and the park **Portas do Sol,** below which flows the Río Tejo. **Rua Capelo Ivêns,** which begins at the *praça,* contains the **tourist office,** R. Capelo Ivêns, 63 (tel. (043) 231 40; open Tues.-Fri. 10am-7pm, Sat.-Mon. 9:30am-12:30pm and 2-6pm) and many *pensões.*

The austere façade of the **Igreja do Seminário dos Jesuitas** is a stunning example of baroque architecture. (Church usually open daily 9am-5pm.) The 12th-century **Igreja de Marvila** has a 16th-century Manueline portal and a 17th-century *azulejo* interior (closed for restoration in 1993). The early Gothic severity of nearby **Igreja**

da Graça contrasts with Marvila's exuberance. In the chapel to the right of the chancel is the tomb of Pedro Alvares Cabral, the explorer who discovered Brazil. Off R. São Martinho stands the medieval **Torre das Cabaças** (Tower of the Gourds), so-called because of the 8 earthen bowls installed in the 16th century to amplify the bell's ring. The main exhibit in the **Museu Arqueológico de São João do Alporão** is what little of Dom Duarte de Meneses his comrades could salvage from the battlefield: one tooth. (Open Tues.-Sun. 10am-12:30pm and 2-5:30pm. Free.)

Santarém has a **sweets fair** (from the last Wed. to Sun. in April) featuring calories from all over Portugal. Put some meat on those spindly bones at the **Festival e Seminário Nacional de Gastronomia** (the last 10 days of Oct.), in which each region of Portugal has a day to prepare a typical feast and entertainment.

The **Pensão do José,** (a.k.a. **Pensão da Dona Arminda**), Travessa do Frois, 14 and 18 (tel. (043) 230 88), under the sign that reads "rooms," has bright, clean singles for 2000$ and doubles for 3500$. **Residencial Abidis,** R. Guilherme de Azevedo, 4 (tel. (043) 220 17), down the street from the Central, is a 19th-century conception of luxury with modern conveniences, such as phones in most rooms. (Singles 2500$, with bath 4250$. Doubles 4200$, with bath 7000$.) **Restaurante Caravana,** Travessa do Frois, 24, serves toothsome food in a refreshingly clean, modest restaurant. (Entrees 650-800$. *Frango corado* (ruddy chicken) with fires 750$. Open Sun.-Fri. 8am-10:30pm.)

Buses leave every hour for Lisbon (1hr., 700$). To get to the tourist office from the **bus station,** walk through the park and cross busy Av. Marquês Sá da Bandeira. Turn right and then left, taking R. Pedro Canavarro uphill, and make a right on R. Capelo Ivêns. The **train station** is 2km outside town, with trains to Lisbon (every hr., 1hr., 500$) and Tomar (every 2hr., 1hr., 360$).

■■■ ÉVORA

One of the only major towns to relieve the empty and sparsely populated Alentejo, Évora rises like a megalith from the rolling plain of olive trees. Portugal's showpiece of medieval architecture, the town also contains a Roman Temple to Diana, Moorish arches, and a 16th-century university. Colorful tile façades and whitewashed walls glimmer in a tangle of verdant streets and wrought-iron balconies.

ORIENTATION AND PRACTICAL INFORMATION

Évora is easily accessible from Lisbon; several trains per day ply the routes from the capital and Faro. **Praça do Giraldo** is Évora's main square. In the old town on the hill, dozens of winding sidestreets lead in and out of the *praça,* home to most of the monuments and lodgings.

Tourist Office: Pr. Giraldo, 73 (tel. 226 71). Open Mon.-Fri. 9am-7pm, Sat.-Sun. 9am-12:30pm and 2-5:30pm; Oct.-May Mon.-Fri. 9am-6pm, Sat.-Sun. 9am-5:30pm.

Post Office: R. Olivença (tel. 233 11), 2 blocks north of Pr. Giraldo. Open for mail, **Posta Restante,** telephones, and **telegrams** Mon.-Fri. 8:30am-6:30pm. **Postal Code:** 7000.

Telephones: at the post office. **City Code:** 066.

Currency Exchange: Exchange machine outside tourist office. Open 24hrs.

Trains: (tel. 221 25), 1½km from town center. To: Lisbon (5/day, 3hr., 770$), Faro (1/day, 6hr., 1380$), Beja (4/day, 1½hr., 535$).

Buses: R. República (tel. 221 21), opposite Igreja de São Francisco. To: Lisbon (7/day, 2½hr., 1050$), Faro (3/day, 5hr., 1380$), and Porto (5/day, 7-8½hrs., 2100$). **Luggage Storage** in the station basement (80$/day).

Laundromat: Lavévora, Largo D'Alvaro Velho, 6 (tel. 238 83), off R. Miguel Bombardo. Open Mon.-Fri. 9am-1pm and 3-7pm. 350$/kg.

Bicycle Rental: Évora Rent-a-Bike (tel. 761 453). Bikes delivered to you. Half-day 1000$. Full day 1500$.

Hospital: R. Velasco (tel. 250 01, 221 32, or 221 33), close to the city wall and intersection with R. D. Augusto Eduardo Nunes.
Emergency: tel. 115. **Police:** R. Francisco Soares Lusitánia (tel. 74 11 20), near the Temple of Diana.

ACCOMMODATIONS AND CAMPING

Most *pensões* reside around the **Praça Giraldo.** *Quartos* cost 2000-3500$.

Pensão Giraldo, R. Mercadores (tel. 258 33), 2 blocks from Turismo. Small, tidy rooms just off the *praça*. Singles 2400$, with shower 3500$. Doubles 3500$, with shower 4800$.
Pensão Os Manueis, R. Raimundo, 35 (tel. 228 61), around the corner from Turismo and upstairs from a restaurant. The main building with rooms and baths is clean and sunny. The annex across the back street is less so, but rooms are still spacious. Singles 3000$, with bath 5000$. Doubles 3500$, with bath 5500$.
Pensão Residencial O Eborense, Largo da Misericórdia, 1 (tel. 220 31), first right as R. República hooks a left into the center of town. Ducal mansion turned renovated pension. Rooms seem taller than they are wide. Unique rugs in each room. All have bath and heating. Singles 7500$. Doubles 9000$. Breakfast included.
Camping Orbitur (tel. 251 90), a 2-star park on Estrada das Alcáçovas, which branches off the bottom of R. Raimundo. Only 1 bus to town daily; it's a 40-min. walk. Washers. Small market. Reception open 8am-10pm. 455$/person, 460$/tent, 390$/car. Showers 50$.

FOOD

A **public market** usually livens up the small square in front of Igreja de São Francisco and the public gardens.

Café-Restaurante A Gruta, Av. General Humberto Delgado, 2 (tel. 281 86), outside the city wall on the way to Pr. de Touros. Follow R. República toward the train station & turn right at the end of the park. It's in a cave! Inhale the thick aroma of roasting fowl as you pass by the monstrous grill. Half-chicken (500$). Open Sun.-Fri. 11am-3pm and 5-10pm.
Restaurante O Garfo, R. de Santa Catarina, 13-15 (tel. 292 56). Leave the square via R. Serpa Pinto & take the 1st right. Giant fork on the wall. *Gaspacho à Aleutejana com peixe frito* (900$). Entrees 900-1100$. Open daily 11am-midnight.

SIGHTS AND ENTERTAINMENT

Off the east side of the *praça*, Rua 5 de Outubro leads to the colossal 12th-century **sé.** The **Museu de Arte Sacra,** in a gallery above the nave, houses the cathedral's treasury and astonishing 13th-century ivory *Virgem do paraíso*. (Cloister and museum open Tues.-Sun. 9am-noon and 2-5pm. 200$.) Next door, the **Museu d'Évora** houses Roman artifacts unearthed nearby, and 16th- and 17th-century European paintings. (Open Tues.-Sun. 10am-12:30pm and 2-5pm. 200$.) Across from the museum, Évora's most famous monument, the remains of the 2nd-century **Templo de Diana,** stands outlined against the sky; it was used as a slaughterhouse for centuries. Facing the temple is the town's best-kept secret, **Igreja de São João Evangelista** (1485). The church is the private property of the Cadaval family, who live in their ancestors' ducal palace next door. (Open 9am-noon and 2-6pm. 200$.) The *pièce de resistance* of a visit to Évora is the **Igreja Real de São Francisco.** Its austere bulk encoffins the rapturously perverse **Capela de Ossos** (Chapel of Bones). Three tireless Franciscan monks ransacked assorted local cemeteries for the remains of 4000 people in order to construct it. Enormous femurs neatly panel every inch of wall space, while rows of skulls line the capitals and ceiling vaults. (Church and chapel open Mon.-Sat. 8:30am-1pm and 2:30-6pm, Sun. 10-11:30am and 2:30-6pm. To chapel 50$; 50$ to take pictures.)

Discoteca Slide, R. Serpa Pinto, 135, keeps the music blaring until 2am. Cover charges 1000$ and 500$ respectively; both charges include 2 beers. Évora's most popular café-bar hangout is **Portugal,** R. João de Deus, 55. Évora's festival, the **Feira de São João** (last week of June), celebrates the arrival of summer with a full-fledged, Portuguese-style country fair.

ALGARVE

This southern coast is in the process of selling its soul to commercial capitalism. After the Moors were driven from Portugal, the Algarve remained a quiet fishing backwater; now increasing tourism and overdevelopment are destroying its trademark villages. Portuguese often come in September, while in July and August foreigners predominate, lured by the region's beaches and sunny, dry weather. Ocean winds cool the mornings, while clear skies bless the evenings.

Hotels and *pensões* usually fill during the peak summer months; use the reasonably priced *quarto*. Ask at tourist offices or bars, keep your eyes peeled for signs, or take your chances with the room-pushers who accost incoming travelers at bus and train stations. Local delicacies include *caldeirada* (a chowder of fish and shellfish), *cataplana* (ham, clams, and sausage), and *lulas* (squid, often cooked in its own ink). Tourist offices sell *The Algarve News* (105$). It runs articles on trendy clubs, local festivals, special events, and topless beaches.

Faro, the Algarve's capital, is at once a transportation hub and a provincial Portuguese city. Low-tech Portuguese trains wheeze into town from Lisbon (6/day, 7hr., 1550$). Aside from the mobbed resorts (like **Albufeira**), plenty of villages welcome budget travelers (try Salema and Burgau). Other inexpensive spots are **Sagres** (ravishing isolated beaches and sheer cliffs) and the region between **Olhão** and the Spanish border (**Tavira,** for example). Reaching more remote beaches is a snap, as EVA has extensive bus services with convenient schedules and low fares. The train costs less than the bus but only connects major coastal cities, and in some towns the station is a hike from the center.

■■■ LAGOS

For many, many moons, swarms of Europeans have sojourned here to worship the almighty Sun. Most visitors don't care that Lagos was a major Moorish port, the official harbor for the fleet of Prince Henry the Navigator and a center of the African slave trade. The port and old town preserve a measure of local color; along the narrow pedestrian streets, cosmopolitan bars burble to imported pop or sway to jazz. To the west, rock tunnels through the sheer cliffs connect secluded sandy coves, while 4km of uninterrupted beach lounges to the east.

ORIENTATION AND PRACTICAL INFORMATION

Running the length of the river, **Avenida dos Descobrimentos** carries traffic in and out of the city. Rua das Portas de Portugal marks the gateway leading into **Praça Gil Eanes** and the town's glitzy tourist center. Most restaurants, accommodations, and services hover about the *praça* and **Rua 25 de Abril;** they are usually mobbed.

> **Tourist Office:** Largo Marquês de Pombal (tel. 76 30 31). Take the sidestreet R. Lina Lectão (off Pr. Gil Eanes) which leads to the Largo. Open Mon.-Fri. 9:30am-7pm, Sat.-Sun. 9:30am-12:30pm and 2-5:30pm.
>
> **Budget Travel: Club Algarve,** R. Marreiros Neto, 25 (tel. 76 23 37), uphill from the tourist office. Open Mon.-Fri. 9am-12:30pm, 2:30-6:30pm.
>
> **Post Office:** R. Portas de Portugal (tel. 76 31 11), between Pr. Gil Eanes and Av. Descobrimentos. Open Mon.-Fri. 9am-6pm; for **Posta Restante** 9am-noon. **Postal Code:** 8600.
>
> **Telephones:** In an air-conditioned building across from the post office. Open 8:30am-6pm. **City code:** 082.

Trains: tel. 76 29 87. On the eastern edge of town, across the river from the bus station. To Lisbon (6/day, 6½hr., 1550$) and Évora (3/day, 4½hr., 1380$).

Buses: Rodoviária (tel. 76 29 44), on the eastern edge of town. To Lisbon (4/day, 5hr., 1900$) and Faro (4/day, 2½hr., 850$).

Laundromat: Lavandaria Luso-Britânica, Pr. Gil Eanes, 11 (tel. 76 22 83). Wash and dry 1300$/4kg load. Dry cleaning: pants 1500$, shirt 320$. Open Mon.-Fri. 9am-1pm and 3-7pm, Sat. 9am-1pm.

Medical Services: Hospital, R. Castelo dos Governadores (tel. 76 30 34), next to Igreja Santa María. **Ambulance** (tel. 76 01 15). English spoken.

Police: General Alberto Silva (tel. 76 29 30), near Pr. da República. English spoken.

ACCOMMODATIONS, CAMPING, AND FOOD

Rooms in *casa particulars* go for 1500-3500$.

Pousada de Juventud de Lagos (HI), R. Lançarote de Freitas, 50 (tel. 76 19 70). From turismo, walk up R. Garrett, then hang a left onto R. Cândido dos Reis. The street is on your right. Central courtyard with tables. Excellent showers. All day reception, curfew 2am. HI card mandatory. Summer reservations recommended; make them through Movijoven, Av. Duque D'Avila, 137, Lisboa 1000. 1500$, low season 900$.

Residência Marazul, R. 25 de Abril, 13 (tel. 76 97 49), near Turismo. Access to hedonistic, wicker-chaired lounge. Elaborate wainscoted interior. Immaculate rooms, some with small terraces. Spotless baths. Singles 6000-8500$, doubles 7500-8500$; Oct.-May singles 2750-5200$, doubles 3000-5500$.

Camping: Sites are crowded and expensive, resembling high-tech shantytowns. Jam-packed **Parque de Campismo do Imulagos** (tel. 76 00 31) is annoyingly far away but linked to Lagos by a free shuttle bus. Reception open 8am-10pm. 738$/person, 410$/car. Nearer town on the beautiful Praia Dona Ana is **Camping da Trinidade** (tel. 76 38 92). 300$/person, 350$/tent, 270$/car. Free showers.

Restaurante Escondidinho, hidden in a dead-end alley in front of the GNR (from the *praça* walk down Av. dos Descobrimentos (upstream) and turn left up R. da Capelinha; it's on the left), is truly Portuguese, yet welcoming to foreigners. The toothsome grilled catch of the day is 800-1200$. **Mullens,** R. Cândido dos Reis, 86, is a Lagos hot spot. Servers dance to the tables with huge portions of spicy food, and the crowd quivers with a carnal pulse. (Chicken *piri-piri* smothered in hot sauce 995$. Open noon-2pm and 7-10:30pm.)

SIGHTS AND ENTERTAINMENT

Only the altar of **Igreja de Santo António** survived the 1755 earthquake; workers painstakingly rebuilt everything else exactly as before. Extraordinary gilded wood-work embellishes the interior. Adjoining the church, the **Museu Municipal** exhibits costumes, weapons, and mutant animal fetuses. (Open Tues.-Sun. 9:30am-12:30pm and 2-5pm. 200$, students and seniors free; Sun. free.) On either side of Pr. da República, near Igreja de Santa María da Misericórdia, molders the evil remains of the 16th-century **Antigo Mercado de Escravos,** modern Europe's first slave market. Ancient weathered cliffs surround the **beaches.** Follow Av. dos Descobrimentos (the main waterside avenue) west until the sign for **Praia de Pinhão.** Follow this to the shore and continue on the paths until you find a cove to your liking. The rocks afford tremendous views of the inlets.

The streets of Lagos pick up late into the evening; the area between Pr. Gil Eanes and Pr. Luís de Camões bursts with cafés. **Café Gil Eanes,** Pr. Gil Eanes, 20, snares especially large crowds.

NORTHERN PORTUGAL

Although their landscapes and shared Celtic past invite comparison with neighboring Galicia, the **Douro** and **Minho** regions are more populated and faster developing. South of the Rio Minho lies **Braga,** a busy commercial city whose concentration of religious architecture has earned it the title of the Portuguese Rome. Braga's people are considered by some the most pious, by others the most fanatic, and by all the most politically conservative in the country. Buses travel between Braga and Porto (1½hr., 570$).

Farther inland rises a mountainous region composed of three provinces: **Trás-os-Montes, Beira Alta,** and **Beira Baixa.** Recent agricultural boom and the success of the wine trade has transformed the region into a quirky center of upward mobility, but the transportation system remains downright archaic.

Cutting from the snowy mountains to the foggy coast south of Porto, the **Extremadura** region features an angry Atlantic, sharp cliffs, and whitewashed fishing villages. **Nazaré** is a quaint seaside town whose inhabitants paint their narrow wooden boats bright colors and preserve their unique form of dress. Nazaré is an easy bus trip from Lisbon (6/day, 2hr., 1000$).

■■■ COIMBRA

Portugal's former capital, Coimbra regained importance in the late 16th century as a center of the Inquisition. Centuries later, Salazar (Portugal's longtime Fascist dictator) attended the university. In spite of these unfortunate caveats, Coimbra has a self-assured elegance which belies its urban woes of grime, filth, and noise.

ORIENTATION AND PRACTICAL INFORMATION

Coimbra's center, a tangle of narrow streets, is split into 2 areas. The lower town lies between the triangle formed by the river, **Largo da Portagem,** and **Praça 8 de Maio.** The upper town spreads on the adjoining hill, accessible through the **Arco de Almedina.** Coimbra has 2 train stations: Coimbra-A, near the town center by the bridge, and Coimbra-B, 3km northwest of the center.

Tourist Office: Largo Portagem (tel. 238 86), 2 blocks east of Coimbra-A off Av. Emídio Navarro. Open Mon.-Fri. 9am-6pm, Sat.-Sun. 9am-12:30pm and 2-5:30pm.

Currency Exchange: Hotel Astória, across the *largo* from the tourist office. 800$ charge/transaction. Open 24hrs.

Post Office: R. Olímpio Nicolau Rui Fernandes (tel. 297 80), just past the Manga rotunda. Central office is in the pink powder puff on Av. Fernão de Magalhães. Both open Mon.-Fri. 8:30am-6:30pm, Sat. 9am-12:30pm. **Postal Code:** 3000.

Telephones: In post offices. **City Code:** 039.

Trains: Estação Coimbra-A, Largo das Âmeias (tel. 272 63). From the front entrance follow Av. Emidio Navarro along the river all the way to Turismo. **Estação Coimbra-B** (tel. 349 98). Trains from cities outside the region stop only here; regional trains stop at both stations. Frequent shuttles connect the two (5min., 100$). To: Porto (14/day, 3hr., 770$), Lisbon (14/day, 3hr., 1145$), Paris (1/day, 22hr., 18,640$).

Buses: Av. Fernão de Magalhães (tel. 270 83). To reach the tourist office, turn right from the station and follow the avenue to Coimbra-A and then Largo da Portagem (15min.). To: Lisbon (16/day, 3hr., 1150$), Porto (5/day, 6hr., 1000$), Évora (5/day, 6hr., 1400$), Faro (4/day, 12hr., 2400$).

Luggage Storage: At bus station: 120$/day. **Coimbra-A:** 200$/4hr., 1600$/day.

Public Transportation: Buses and street cars. Fares: 165$ (single ticket bought on board); 450$ (book of 10). Special tourist passes also available. Ticket books and passes sold in kiosks at Largo da Portagem and Pr. República, among other places.

Hospital: Hospital da Universidade de Coimbra (tel. 70 11 33 or 40 39 39). Near the Cruz de Celas stop on lines #3, 7, 7T, and 29.

Emergency: tel. 115. Police: R. Olímpio Nicolau Rui Fernandes (tel. 220 22).

ACCOMMODATIONS AND CAMPING

Notoriously cheap and seedy *ponsões* line **Rua da Sota** and the surrounding streets across from Coimbra-A. Anything decent starts at 3500$ for doubles.

Pousada de Juventude (HI), R. António Henriques Seco, 14 (tel. 229 55). From either Coimbra-A or Largo Portagem, take bus #7, 8, 29, or 46, then walk from Pr. República up R. Lourenço A. Azevedo, left of the Santa Cruz park, and take the 2nd right. Enormous sunlit rooms (84 beds), TV room with bar, and gray parrot (Jacó). Kitchen and hand laundry. Reception open 9am-noon and 6pm-midnight. Bag drop-off all day. Lockout noon-6pm. Curfew midnight. 1400$; Oct.-May 1000$. Breakfast included.

Pensão Rivoli, Pr. Comércio, 27 (tel. 255 59), in a mercifully quiet pedestrian plaza off busy R. Ferreira Borges, which originates in Largo da Portagem. Neat, well-furnished rooms with white walls. Lockout 1am, but you can borrow a key. Singles 2000$. Doubles 4000$.

Residência Lusa Atenas, Av. Fernão de Magalhães, 68 (tel. 293 57), on the main avenue between Coimbra-A and the bus station, 3 blocks north of the former and 10min. south of the latter. Comfy rooms with high ceilings and large windows. Uncanny cleanliness. Small private baths in each room. Winter heating. Singles 2500$, with bath 3500$. Doubles 4500$, with bath 5000$. Triples 6000$, with bath 6500$. Breakfast included.

Camping: Municipal Campground (tel. 70 14 97), in a recreation complex ringed by noisy avenues. The entrance is at the arch off Pr. 25 de Abril. Reception open 9am-10pm; Oct.-March 9am-6pm. 220$/person, 165$/tent, 200$/car. 5% IVA not included. Showers free.

FOOD

Scout out **Rua Direita,** west off Pr. 8 de Maio, the sidestreets to the west of Pr. Comércio, and Largo da Portagem and the university district around **Praça da República.** There are university *cantinas* (cafeterias) at several locations, including one in the old college courtyard. Students with ID or student-posers without (easy June-July when the university hosts foreign programs) will receive a better-than-average cafeteria meal for a mere 250$.

Churrasqueria do Mondego, R. Sargento Mór, 25, off R. Sota, 1 block west of the Largo da Portagem. Frequented by truck drivers, students, and tourists. The *frango no churrasco* (barbecued half-chicken) leaves Colonel Sanders in the dust (330$). Try the *piri-piri* sauce (it's *hot*). Open noon-3pm and 6-10:30pm.

Casino da Urca, R. da Baixo, in front of the old Santa Clara convent. Low beamed ceiling and antique farm implements. *Espetada a casa* (House Kebab, 800$) is mighty savory. Entrées, most 650-1100$. Open noon-3pm and 7pm-midnight.

Café Santa Cruz, Pr. 8 de Maio, in what used to be part of the cathedral. The most famous café in Coimbra. Espresso worshiping has replaced more conventional prayer. Filled with professors and students. Coffee 55$. Open 7am-2am.

SIGHTS AND ENTERTAINMENT

To reach the old center of town, pass through the **Arco de Almedina,** the remnant of a Muslim town wall. Up a narrow stone stairway looms the hulking 12th-century Romanesque **Sé Velha** (Old Cathedral). R. Borges Carneiro (behind the cathedral) leads to the **Museu Machado de Castro,** famous for its Gothic and Renaissance sculptures, illuminated by creepy lighting in the underground passageways of the old Roman forum. (Open Tues.-Sun. 10am-12:30pm and 2-5:30pm. 200$; students and seniors free; Sun. mornings free.)

Rua São Pedro, flanked by the grim façades of new university buildings, leads to the **Porta Férrea** (Iron Gate), a door to the old courtyard of the **universidade.** The staircase at the right leads up to the **Sala dos Capelos,** where portraits of Portugal's

PORTO (OPORTO)

kings (6 of whom were born in Coimbra) hang below a beautifully painted 17th-century ceiling. (Open dialy 9am-noon and 2-6pm.) Past the Baroque clock tower are the **capela da universidade** (university chapel) and the 18th-century **biblioteca da universidade** (university library). The library shelters 143,000 books in 3 lofty halls painted with Chinese motifs. (Open daily 9am-12:30pm and 2-5pm. 250$.)

The **Mosteiro de Santa Cruz** (Monastery of the Holy Cross) on Pr. 8 de Maio, at the far end of R. Ferreira Borges in the lower city, is a 12th-century monastery with all the usual fixin's: a splendid barrel-vaulted **Sacristía** (sacristy), an ornate **tumulos reais** (where the first 2 kings of Portugal lie buried), and a 16th-century **claustro.** (Open daily 9am-noon and 2-6pm. 150$.) In the 14th century, Queen Isabel ordered the construction of the great **Convento de Santa Clara-a-Velha**—smack on top of a swamp. The convent sinks a little deeper each year; today it's more than half underground. (Open 9am-12:30pm and 2-5:30pm.)

To hear the most unrestrained and heartfelt *fado* singers, go after dinner to **Diligência Bar,** R. Nova, 30 (tel. 276 67), off R. Sofia. (Open until midnight.) The happening discos are **Via Latina,** R. Almeida Garret, 1, near the Santa Cruz garden, and **Scotch,** across the river near Convento Santa-Clara-a-Nova. Both places peak between midnight and 2am. (Occasional cover. Beers about 300$.)

■■■ PORTO (OPORTO)

As the proverb says, "Coimbra sings, Braga prays, Lisbon shows off, and Porto works." Magnificently situated on a dramatic gorge cut by the Rio Douro, 6km from the sea, Portugal's second city is an attractive harbor town and the industrial and commercial hub of the north. For the 1415 invasion of Ceuta, residents slaughtered all their cattle, gave the meat to the Portuguese fleet, and kept only the entrails (tripe) for themselves. The ever-popular dish *tripas à moda do Porto* commemorates the culinary self-sacrifice. Porto's fame, however, springs from the taste of its *vinho.* Developed by English merchants in the early 18th century, the Port wine industry across the River Douro in Vila Nova de Gaia drives the city's economy.

ORIENTATION AND PRACTICAL INFORMATION

At the heart of Porto, **Avenida dos Aliados** forms a long rectangle bordered on the north by **Praça General Humberto Delgado** and on the south by **Praça da Liberdade.** The **Estação São Bento** lies smack in the middle of town, just off Pr. Liberdade. The **Ribeira,** or Esplanade, district is a few blocks to the south, directly across the bridge from **Vila Nova de Gaia,** the area of wine houses.

Tourist Office: R. Clube dos Fenianos, 25 (tel. 31 27 40), on the west side of city hall. Open Mon.-Fri. 9am-7pm, Sat. 9am-4pm, Sun. 10am-1pm; Oct.-June Mon.-Fri. 9am-12:30pm and 2-5:30pm, Sat. 9am-4pm.

American Express: Top Tours, R. Alferes Malheiro, 96 (tel. 208 27 85), up R. do Almada from the Turismo. Open Mon.-Fri. 9am-12:30pm and 2:30-6:30pm.

Currency Exchange: An office at the **airport** provides service Mon.-Fri. 9am-8pm, Sat. 9am-4pm. There's an **automatic exchange machine** (open 24hrs.) on Pr. Liberdade, right outside Banco Espírito Santo e Commercial de Lisboa.

Consulates: U.K., Av. Boavista, 3072 (tel. 68 47 89). Handles Canadian and Commonwealth affairs. Open Mon.-Fri. 9:30am-12:30pm and 3-5pm.

Post Office: Pr. General H. Delgado (tel. 208 02 51), across from the tourist office. Open for stamps Mon.-Fri. 8am-9pm, Sat.-Sun. 9am-6pm. **Postal Code:** 4000.

Telephones: at Pr. Liberdade, 62. Open 8am-11:30pm. Also at the post office. **City Code:** 02.

Flights: Aeroporto Francisco de Sá Carneiro (tel. 948 21 41), accessible by bus #44 and 56 from Pr. Lisboa. **TAP Air Portugal,** Pr. Mouzinho de Albuquerque, 105 (tel. 948 22 91). To Lisbon (13,400$) and Madrid (35,200$).

Trains: Estação de São Bento (tel. 200 27 22), centrally located 1 block off Pr. Liberdade. Receives some trains, mostly locals, and nearby regional routes.

Estação de Campanhã (tel. 56 41 41), Porto's main station west of the center. Frequent connections to Estação São Bento (5min., 90$). To: Coimbra (13/day, 2½hr., 770$), Lisbon (5/day, 4½hr., 1515$; ALFA 8/day, 3¼hr., 2950$), Madrid via Entroncamento (2/day, 12hr., 7500$), Paris (1/day, 27hr., 19,000$).

Buses: Garagem Atlântico, R. Alexandre Herculano, 366 (tel. 200 69 54). To: Coimbra (11/day, 1½hr., 950$), Lisbon (5/day, 5hr., 1600$).

Bookstore: Livraria Diário de Notícias, R. Sá de Bandeira, 5, across from Estação São Bento. Open Mon.-Fri. 9am-12:30pm and 2:30-7pm; winter Mon.-Fri. 9am-12:30pm, Sat. 9am-1pm.

Laundromat: Penguin, Av. Boavista (tel. 69 50 32), in shopping center Brasília. Follow the same route to the youth hostel, but walk uphill 1 block farther to the rotary. 1300$/5.5kg load. Open Mon.-Sat. 10am-11pm.

Medical Services: Hospital de Santo António, R. Prof. Vicente José de Carvalho (tel. 200 52 41).

Emergency: tel. 115. **Police:** R. Alexandre Herculano (tel. 200 68 21).

ACCOMMODATIONS AND CAMPING

Most *pensões* lie west of Av. Aliados. Rates for singles are absolutely criminal.

Pousada de Juventude do Porto (HI), R. Rodrigues Lobo, 98 (tel. 606 55 35), Take bus #3, 20, or 52 (10min., 140$) from the stop on the lower west end of Pr. Liberdade and hop off at R. Júlio Dinis (driver knows the hostel stop). Fine kitchen facilities, cramped rooms, game room, and library. If you arrive in town after 10am, don't bother. 3-day max. stay. Reception open 9-11am and 6pm-midnight. Curfew midnight. 1200$, Oct.-June 950$. Breakfast included.

Pensão Estoril, R. Cedofeita, 193 (tel. 200 51 52 or 200 27 51), on a street radiating from Pr. Carlos Alberto. Colossal, bright rooms in an elegant building with sea-green carpeting. All rooms have radios and winter heating. Lounge with satellite TV. Singles with shower 2500-3000$. Doubles with shower 3000-3500$. Triples with shower 4800$. Quads with shower 6000$.

Pensão dos Aliados, R. Elísio de Melo, 27 (tel. 200 48 53), on the left as you walk up Av. Aliados. Living room with TV. Sumptuous rooms with telephones and wall-to-wall carpeting; all have bath. Singles 5500$. Doubles 6500$. Breakfast included. In summer reserve several days in advance.

Camping: Prelada, Parque de Prelada (tel. 81 26 16), 5km from the beach. Take bus #6 from Pr. Liberdade. 390$/person, 310$/tent, 320$/car.

FOOD

The most colorful restaurants border the river in the Ribeira district, particularly on **Cais de Ribeira, Rua Reboleira,** and **Rua de Cima do Muro.** You'll find much seedier surroundings near Praça da Batalha on **Rua do Cimo de Vila** and **Rua do Cativo.** Replete with fresh flowers, fruit, and fish, the **Mercado de Bolhão** perfumes the corner of R. Formosa and R. Sá de Bandeira. (Open Mon.-Fri. 7am-5pm, Sat. 7am-1pm.)

Restaurante Abadia, Trav. Passos Manuel, 22. Waiters, white tablecloths, and the *menú* win. *Bacalhau à gomes de sá* (a codfish specialty, 1300$). Open daily noon-3pm and 7-10pm.

Churrasqueira Moura, R. Almada, 219-223. Dirt-cheap meals (most under 1000$) include *frango no churrasco* (barbecued chicken with fries, 660$). Open Mon.-Sat. 11:30am-10pm.

Taberna Típica, R. Reboleira, 12. Stone walls and nautical decor fit the riverside location. *Arroz de polvo* ("octopus rice" specialty, 790$). Satisfying *pratos do dia* 750-1300$. Open Thurs.-Tues. 11am-midnight.

SIGHTS

The heavy Romanesque husk of Porto's 13th-century **cathedral** glowers on a hill above the Ribeira. To the left of the high altar, the Capela do Santíssimo Sacramento shines with solid silver and plated gold. During the Napoleonic invasion, townspeople whitewashed the altar to protect it from vandalism. (Open daily 9am-noon and 2-5:30pm. To cloister 100$.) West of the cathedral, on Rua da Bolsa at Rua do Comércio do Porto, stands the **Palácio da Bolsa** (Stock Exchange), the epitome of 19th-century elegance. Magnificent parquet floors of inlaid Brazilian wood smell of cedar and jacaranda. Modeled after the Alhambra in Granada, the sparkling Sala Arabe took 18 years to decorate. (Open Mon.-Fri. 9am-6pm, Sat.-Sun. 10am-noon and 2-5pm; Oct.-May Mon.-Fri. 9am-5pm, Sat.-Sun. 10am-noon and 2-4pm. 400$, students 200$.) Originally Gothic but remodeled in the 17th and 18th centuries, the **Igreja de São Francisco** glitters with one of the most elaborate gilded wood interiors in Portugal. (Open Tues.-Sat. 9am-5pm. 110$.) South of the Bolsa, the **Ribeira** (Esplanade) is skirted by a marvelous quay filled with shops and restaurants. To see more of the Ribeira, take trolley #1 from the Igreja de São Francisco along the river to the **Foz do Douro,** Porto's beach community.

Just up R. Taipas from the museum and church rises the 82m **Torre dos Clérigos** (Tower of Clerics). Long the city's most prominent landmark, its granite tower glimmers like a splendid processional candle. Mount the 200 steps for a vista of the city and the Rio Douro valley. (Open Mon.-Sat. 7:30-9:30am, 10:30am-noon, and 3-6pm, Sun. 10:30am-1pm and 8-10pm. Free.)

Most of Porto's *caves* or *adegas* (wine lodges) lead free tours of the wineries, where both red and white port are aged and blended in huge oak barrels. Now as always, only human feet crush the grapes (à la Lucy and Ethel). Most of the 80-odd Port lodges ferment across the river, in **Vila Nova de Gaia.** Walk across the lower level of the Dom Luís I bridge and take a sharp right. Of the 15 lodges offering free tours and samples, the major ones, such as **Cintra, Vasconcellos,** and **Sandeman,** keep the most regular hours (ask at the tourist office).

Spain (España)

US$1	= 128ptas (pesetas, or ESP)		100ptas =	US$0.78
CDN$1	= 97ptas		100ptas =	CDN$1.03
UK£1	= 198ptas		100ptas =	UK£0.50
IR£1	= 186ptas		100ptas =	IR£0.54
AUS$1	= 83ptas		100ptas =	AUS$1.20
NZ$1	= 71ptas		100ptas =	NZ$1.42
SAR1	= 26ptas		100ptas =	SAR3.78
Country Code: 34			**International Dialing Prefix: 07**	

Spain is a subcontinent in its variety of scene, climate, landscape, artistic tradition, and ethnic groupings. A major theme in Spanish history is the perpetual opposing trends of unity and dissolution. The centrifugal tendencies (there are currently 17 "nations" in Spain) are attributable in part to the peninsula's historic condition as a crossroads of highly diverse cultures, and partly to the mountainous topography which makes it possible for communities to live largely in isolation.

Phoenicians, Carthaginians, Greeks, Romans, Visigoths, and Muslims were drawn to Spain's legendary mineral wealth and to its strategic position. The Romans brought their roads, irrigation canals, aqueducts, courtyards, rounded arches, brick masonry, legal code, and language. The Muslims, who invaded in 711, were transmitters and elaborators of classical Greek science and philosophy and of those Eastern artistic traditions crucial to the European Renaissance. Spain inspired the builder in its settlers, and the climate seems peculiarly well-suited for pickling old stone. In Andalucía, the mosque at Córdoba and the Alhambra in Granada are as much fountainheads of architecture as the Parthenon in Athens or Aya Sofya in İstanbul.

After three centuries of Muslim hegemony and another three centuries of Muslim, Jewish, and Christian vernacular syncretism (a prime example of which is Mudejar architecture, which applies Moorish use of tile, brick, and geometric patterns to European structures such as Gothic and Romanesque), Enrique de Trastámara won control of Castile in 1369 and began to build a Christian Spain modeled after high medieval, Latinate European traditions (including rigid religious orthodoxy and intolerance). In 1469, the marriage of Fernando de Aragón and Isabel de Castilla joined Iberia's two mightiest Christian kingdoms. By 1492, the unstoppable duo had captured Granada (the last Moorish stronghold) and had shipped off Columbus, among others, to explore the New World. The daughter of Fernando and Isabel, Juana La Loca (the Mad), married Felipe el Hermoso (the Fair), scion of the powerful Habsburg dynasty. Ms. Crazy and Mr. Handsome spawned Carlos V (Charles V, 1516-1556), who reigned supreme over an immense empire—what is today the Netherlands, and Belgium, as well as part of Germany, Austria, Spain and the colonies in the Americas. This era of imperial grandeur and exploitation lasted until Spain's American territories began to declare independence during the Napoleonic Wars. The 19th century saw rapid industrialization in some areas (although the majority of the country remained agricultural), and the growth of regional consciousness in nearly all. Sparked by international depression, these tensions erupted in the Spanish Civil War (1936-1939); aided crucially by Hitler and Mussolini, Francisco Franco emerged as the country's dictator and ruled until his death in 1975. Under King Juan Carlos, Franco's hand-picked successor, Spain has become a modern, stable, and democratic constitutional monarchy, and since 1982 has been led by Socialist Prime Minister Felipe González, under whose spending-intensive governance Spain became the fastest-growing European country from 1986-1990.

Every year, tourists more than double Spain's population of 40 million; much of the crunch comes in July and August. No infrastructure could possibly be expected to bear such a burden. This fact—and Andalucía's searing heat—counsel against summer travel in southern Spain; if you must travel then, choose central or northern itineraries.

> For more explicit, hot, and sweaty information about Spain, get your hands on a copy of *Let's Go: Spain & Portugal.*

GETTING THERE AND GETTING AROUND

Spanish **trains** are clean, somewhat punctual and reasonably priced, although they don't run to some small towns. **RENFE,** the Spanish national rail system, offers many types of service: *AVE* trains are the fastest but currently run only between Madrid and Sevilla. *Talgos* are elegant low-slung trains that zip passengers in air-conditioned compartments; *electro* are very comfortable and quick, but have more intermediate stops than talgo. *Talgo* 200s are talgo trains on *AVE* rails; currently they offer some services out of Madrid. *Expreso, estrella,* and *rápido* vary greatly in speed. *Cercanías* are commuter trains that radiate from larger cities to suburbs and nearby *pueblos,* making frequent stops and usually lacking air-conditioning. Don't bother with any *tranvía, semidirecto,* or *correo* train—these are ludicrously slow and are now uncommon. Unfortunately, no youth railpass exists (not even the old *Tarjeta Joven*). On blue days (almost every day except for holidays and Friday and Saturday afternoons), round-trip tickets are discounted 10%; sometimes those with student IDs enjoy further reductions. Buy tickets within 60 days of departure at RENFE travel offices, RENFE train stations and authorized travel agencies. RENFE will refund 85% (75% on "red days"—holidays) of the ticket price for cancellation up to 15 minutes before train departure. The only other train company in Spain is **FEVE,** actually a conglomeration of private companies which has short runs between northern towns not served by RENFE. Those with Eurailpasses need only pay a small reservations fee on trains in Spain.

Bus routes are far more exhaustive than the rail network, are the only public transportation to isolated areas, and almost always cost less. They're usually slightly slower than the equivalent trains, but highway improvements and expansions have cut travel time between major cities by as much as 50% in the past few years. Spain has a multitude of private companies rather than one national bus line, which makes trip planning an ordeal.

Rental cars cost considerably less than in other European countries. For rural drives, tourist offices often supply leaflets on local *"Rutas Turísticas."* **Hitching** is reportedly slow and can be dangerous. Spanish hospitality to hitchhikers has dwindled in the wake of increasing crime. The northern areas are regarded as relatively easy to hitch in, as is the Mediterranean coast. Inland hitching is said to be only fair; hitching out of Madrid—in any direction—is nearly impossible. In Andalucía, rides are infrequent and the sun can be intolerable.

SPAIN ESSENTIALS

Most towns have a centrally located **Oficina de Turismo** (tourist office, fondly called *Turismo*) that distributes information on sights and lodgings. They'll give you a free map that usually includes brief descriptions of sights and useful phone numbers. Although most don't book accommodations, many *Turismos* keep a list of approved establishments or can point you to a *casa particular* (private room). **Viajes TIVE,** the national chain of student travel agencies, peddle discount travel tickets, churn out ISICs and HI cards, and dispense transport information.

The northern regions are rightly called "wet" or "green" Spain, with a humid, temperate climate open to the sea, and a lush, often thickly wooded landscape (both features reappear in those mountain areas of the south and east whose ranges are high enough to catch moisture). The interior has a climate resembling that of Central Europe, with long winters and, in the lowlands, torrid summers. The eastern and southern coasts enjoy a Mediterranean climate, with mild winters. The northeast coast can be humid; the Guadalquivir river basin (including Seville and Córdoba) is the most sweltering part of the country.

Some Spanish men think that foreign women traveling without male or family companions do so *en busca de aventura* (in search of sexual adventure). Women should be extra cautious in big cities, and memorize the **Spanish emergency phone number (091).**

Banks, shops and offices shut down on **legal and religious holidays** in Spain: New Year's Day, Jan. 6, March 29, Maundy Thursday, Good Friday, Easter Sunday, May Day, Corpus Christi (the Thurs. following the 8th Sun. after Easter), July 25, Aug. 15, Oct. 12, Dec. 8, and Christmas. Some of these religious celebrations are no longer legal holidays, but business slows down anyway and sometimes stops altogether. The Semana Santa (Holy Week), the week before Easter, sees much celebration, especially in Andalusia. Throughout the week between Palm Sunday and Easter, cities and towns strive to outdo one another with ardent displays of adoration. The eve of San Juan (June 24) and Santiago (July 25), best observed in Santiago de Compostela, are cause for celebration across Spain. Bullfights feature prominently in most festivals between May and October.

Spanish workers ordinarily start at 9am, go home at 1:30 or 2pm for a long lunch, and go back around 4:30 or 5pm until 8pm. On Saturday, shops are usually open only in the morning, and Sunday is a day of rest for everyone except a few indispensables (not including tourist offices). The smallest denomination of paper **currency** is 1000ptas. Coins come in 1, 5, 10, 25, 100ptas, and the rare 50pta coins. In summer, **banking hours** are Monday through Friday 9am-2pm; in winter, banks are also open

Saturday 9am-1pm. The odd bank is open for an afternoon session too. Banks charge a minimum of 500-750ptas for currency exchange. **El Corte Inglés,** a Spanish department store chain, exchanges money from Monday to Saturday 10am-8pm at competitive rates: 1% commission (250ptas min. charge) on traveler's checks; 2% commission (500ptas min. charge) on currency.

Communication There are 4 official **languages** in Spain. Catalan is the language of choice in Catalonia, València and the Balearic Islands. The non-Indo-European Basque (Euskera) language is spoken in north central Spain, and Galician (related to Portuguese) is spoken in the once-Celtic northwest, though both are minority languages even in their own dominions. Spanish (Castilian, or Castellano) is spoken everywhere. In Spanish, "ll" is pronounced like English "y", "j" like "h", and in most of the country, soft "c" and "z" like "th".

Stamps are sold at post offices, hotels, and tobacconists. An airmail letter takes 10-14 business days to reach the U.S. and Canada; it's faster to the U.K. and Ireland, slower to Australia and New Zealand. Postage for a letter is 90ptas. The Spanish version of Poste Restante is **Lista de Correos.** Most post offices also have fax service. A telegram *(telegrama)* is the most reliable means of communication. Telegraph offices are inside post offices. A message costs 135ptas per word. **Phone** booths are marked by signs that say *Teléfono público* or *Locutorio.* Most bars also have pay phones. Local calls cost 15ptas. A three-minute call to anywhere in Spain is 100ptas. Phonecards in 1000 and 2000ptas denominations are more convenient than feeding coin after coin into a payphone; they're sold at tobacconists (although, mysteriously, they're often sold out). Direct-dialing from a phone booth is the cheapest way to make international calls. It can take up to 30 seconds after you dial to make the connection; dial 07, wait for the high-pitched dial tone, then its country code + city code + phone number. Collect calls *(cobro revertido)* are billed according to pricier person-to-person *(persona a persona)* rates, but may still be cheaper than calls from hotels. *Telefónica* is a central phone office. Other useful numbers include: Local Operator, 009; Local Police Emergency, 091; and *Guardia Civil,* 062. For MCI's **World Reach,** dial 900 99 0014.

Accommodations and Camping REAJ, the Spanish Hostelling International (HI) affiliate, runs about 100 youth hostels year-round and over 140 in summer. A bed costs about 700ptas per night. HI cards (1800ptas) are available at Viajes TIVE, other travel agencies and REAJ offices, but are rarely sold at youth hostels.

Accommodations have many an alias in Spain; each name indicates a specific type of establishment. Cheapest and barest are *hospedajes* (called *Cases de Huéspedes* in the south). The categories next higher in quality are *pensiones,* then *hostales,* then *hostal-residencias* (all three similar in amenities), the staples of many budget travelers. *Hostales* must have sinks in the bedrooms, while *hostal-residencias* verge on hotel poshness. These are rated by the government on a 2-star system; even one-star places in this category are usually very comfortable. The highest priced accommodations are *hoteles,* far beyond the reach of budget travelers. *Pensión completa* (full board: breakfast, lunch and dinner) usually costs about 2000ptas; *pensión media* (half-board: breakfast, dinner) is only occasionally offered.

Campgrounds are government-regulated on a 3-class system, rated and priced by the quality of amenities. Tourists offices stock the *Guía de Campings,* a fat guide to all official campgrounds in Spain.

In some areas, tourist authorities promote alternate types of accommodations. Look out for *casas particulares* (private residences), *casas rurales* (rural cottages), *casas rústicas* (farmhouses), *refugios* (rustic huts in the mountains), *colegios mayores* (state university student dorms), and monasteries or convents.

Food and Drink Spaniards start their day with a breakfast of coffee or thick, liquid chocolate and *bollos* (rolls) or *churros* (lightly fried fritters). As in the rest of

Europe, dinner ("lunch" to Americans) is served between 2 and 3pm, and traditionally consists of several courses. Supper at home is light and devoured around 8pm. Supper out begins after 9pm, usually at 10pm, and is a light, three-course meal.

Some restaurants are "open" from 8am until 1 or 2am, but most only serve meals from 1:30 or 2 to 4pm and from 8 until 11pm or midnight. Each city's tourist office rates its restaurants with a row of forks, 5 forks indicating luxury. *Cafeterías* are rated by a row of up to 3 cups. All cafeterias and one- and two-fork establishments are in the budget range. Prices for a full meal range from about 800ptas in the cheapest bar-restaurants to perhaps 1800ptas in a four-forker. Restaurants often offer a *plato combinados* (combination platter—includes a main course and side dishes on a single plate, plus bread, and sometimes beverage) or a *menú del día* (two dishes, bread, beverage, and dessert—roughly 800-1100ptas).

Nibbled on or snarfed down at bars, *tapas* are ever so conducive to convivial good spirits. Seek out these varied delights in *tascas* that specialize in given varieties. A *tasca,* often also called a *taberna,* is a bar or pub that serves *tapas* at a counter or a few tables in back. *Pinchos* are bite-size samples stabbed by a toothpick; *tapas* are regular appetizer-like servings. *Raciónes* may be equal to an entree in size. *Bocadillos* are *tapas* served as a sandwich on a hunk of thick bread—often a viable substitute for lunch. Your fork may find its way into: *champiñones al ajillo* (mushrooms in garlic sauce), *jamón serrano* (smoked ham), *atún* or *bonito* (tuna), *calamares fritos* (fried squid), *chorizo* (spicy sausage), *gambas* (shrimp), *ternera* (veal), *lomo* (pork), *judías verdes* (green beans), and *lenguado* (sole).

While the most well known Spanish dishes—*paella* (steamed saffron-flavored rice with chicken stock and an assortment of seafood), *gazpacho* (cold tomato-based soup), and *tortilla española* (potato omelette)—are from València, Andalusia, and Castile, respectively, the most sophisticated and varied cuisines on the peninsula were developed in Euskadi, Navarra, Catalunya, and Galiza. Rabbits are stewed with parsley and garlic, and appear on menus as *conejo al ajillo.*

Food is almost always washed down with alcohol, whether a glass of wine (*vino blanco* is white, *tinto* is red) or of beer *(cerveza).* Beer is served in bottles or on draught, in either a small glass *(caña),* or a tall one *(tubo).* Aguila, Estrella, and San Miguel are excellent national brands; Volldamm (Catalunya), and Alhambra (Andalusia) are fine regional brews. Rioja is a world-renowned grape-growing region, with especially good red wines; there are innumerable fine regional wines. Sangria is made of red wine, sugar, brandy, seltzer, and peaches. Another native beverage is sherry *(jerez),* from the city of the same name.

■■■ MADRID

The city's air (which 19th-century European princesses came to sniff when pregnant) has been likened to champagne, but it's Madrid's boundless energy that makes visitors swoon. Trapped smack in the hot, dry Castilian plain, residents of Spain's First City saunter amid broad, leafy boulevards, grandiose Renaissance and neoclassical monuments, sumptuous mansions, sidewalk *terrazas,* and endless theaters, museums, and cafés.

Although it witnessed the coronation of Fernando and Isabel, Madrid was of no great importance until paper-pushing Habsburg Felipe II plunked down the Spanish court here permanently in 1561; an unlikely choice of capital considering the city's distance from vital ports and rivers. Yet from that moment on, the city became the seat of wealth, culture, and imperial glory, watching over Spain's 16th- and 17th-century Golden Age of literature (Quevedo, Larra), art (Velázquez, Goya), and architecture. Today's Madrid owes much of its neoclassical flair, from the Palacio Real to the Museo del Prado, to the 18th-century urban renewal of Bourbon Felipe V. Passionately hostile to Franco's nationalists, the center was the last city to fall to the dictator save for València. Since then Madrid has kept up a furious pace. The capital of contemporary Spanish cultural life, surpassing Barcelona as the country's manufacturing and financial center, the city is anything but a museum piece.

ORIENTATION AND PRACTICAL INFORMATION

The *Plano de Madrid* and the *Plano de los Transportes* maps, free at the city tourist office, are both necessary and helpful, but not quite sufficient; pick up the Flak map (770ptas) at a newspaper kiosk. The epicenter of Madrid is the **Puerta del Sol,** an intersection where 8 streets meet above ground, and metro lines blue #1, red #2, and yellow #3 meet underneath. Four major streets conduct traffic in and out of Sol. Orient yourself with your back to the clock tower on the **police station** (a good landmark). The street leading traffic out of Sol (on your far left) is **Calle del Arenal.** Calle del Arenal runs into **Calle de Bailén** at its other end (in front of the Plaza de Oriente and Palacio Real). A right turn on Bailén leads to **Plaza de España,** with **Parque del Oeste** to the left. The street leading traffic into Sol is **Calle Mayor** (on your near left). Down this street is the **Plaza Mayor. Carrera San Jerónimo** emerges from the other side of Sol. **Plaza Canalejas** is just down the street; **Calle Príncipe** leads out of the right of the plaza to **Plaza Santa Ana** and an area of quality restaurants, bars, and *terrazas*. **C. Alcalá** (on your far right) leads from Sol to **Plaza de la Cibeles** and eventually to **Plaza de la Indepencia** and the **Parque del Retiro.**

South of Sol, amid a tangle of streets reached by **Calle de Carretas,** is **Calle de Atocha,** which runs downhill to **Estachión de Atocha** (train station). South of C. Atocha lies the *barrio* **Arganzuela.** North of Sol, bounded by the **Gran Vía,** is a major shopping area. **C. Montera,** the one street with car traffic amidst pedestrian *calles,* leads from Sol to Gran Vía and the eponymous Metro stop. To the left, Gran Vía runs by **Plaza de Callao** and heads downhill to **Pl. España.** Past Pl. España, the Gran Vía becomes C. Princesa, stretching uphill through the residential **Argüelles** and collegiate **Moncloa** *barrios.* Even farther north is the **Ciudad Universitaria** (1- to 1½-hr. walk). **C. Fuencarral** leads off the Gran Vía to the north and forms the eastern border of **Malasaña,** a lively middle-class *barrio.* Parallel to C. Fuencarral is C. Hortaleza, which heads into the working-class *barrio* **Chueca,** full of inexpensive restaurants, nightclubs and *hostales.* North of these zones, Madrid is increasingly modern, gentrified, and residential. **Paseo Prado, Recoletos,** and **Castellana** moves from historical and cultural sights north into financial and business centers.

Madrid is extremely safe compared to other major European cities, but the Puerta del Sol, Plaza 2 de Mayo in Malasaña, Plaza de Chueca, and Pl. España (to a lesser extent) are particularly intimidating late at night. As usual, we advise you to avoid the parks and quiet residential areas when it's dark.

Tourist Offices: Municipal, Pl. Mayor, 3 (tel. 366 54 77 or 366 48 74, fax 366 54 77). Metro: Sol. Open Mon.-Fri. 10am-8pm, Sat. 10am-2pm. **Regional/Provincial Office of the Comunidad de Madrid,** C. Princesa, 1, Torre de España (tel. 541 23 25), entrance faces Pl. España. Metro: Pl. España. A **2nd office** is at C. Duque Medinaceli, 2 (tel. 429 49 51), just off Pl. Cortes. Metro: Sol. Open Mon.-Fri. 9am-7pm, Sat. 9:30am-1:30pm. More offices at **Estación Chamartín** (tel. 315 99 76; open Mon.-Fri. 8am-8pm, Sat. 9am-1pm) and the **airport,** in the international arrivals area (tel. 305 86 56; open same hrs. as Chamartín).

Budget Travel: Viajes TIVE: C. Fernando el Católico, 88 (tel. 543 02 08 or 543 74 12). Metro: Moncloa. Branch at José Ortega y Gasset, 71 (tel. 347 77 00). Metro: Lista.

Embassies and Consulates: U.S. (both): C. Serrano, 75 (tel. 577 40 00). Metro: Ruben Dario. Open Mon.-Fri. 9am-1:30pm and 3-6pm. **Canadian (both):** C. Núñez de Balboa, 35 (tel. 431 43 00). Metro: Velazquez. Open for walk-in service Mon.-Fri. 9am-12:30pm, for phone service only also 2-5pm. **British Embassy:** C. Fernando el Santo, 16 (tel. 319 02 00). Metro: Colón. **Consulate,** C. Marqués de la Ensenada, 16 (tel. 308 52 01). Open Mon.-Fri. 8am-2:30pm. **Australian (both):** Po. Castellana, 143 (tel. 579 04 28, fax 570 02 04). Metro: Cuzco. Open Mon.-Thurs. 8:30am-5pm, Fri. 8:30am-2:15pm. **New Zealand (both):** Pl. Lealtad, 2,

Madrid

1 National Tourist Office
2 Regional Tourist Office
3 City Tourist Office
4 Budget Travel: Viajes TIVE
5 American Embassy
6 Australian Embassy
7 Canadian Embassy
8 New Zealand Embassy
9 U.K. Embassy
10 American Express Office
11 Main Post Office
12 Estación de Chamartín
13 Estación del Norte
14 Estación de Atocha
15 Estación de Nuevos Ministerios
16 Estación de Recoletos
17 Estación de la Plaza de Colón
18 Estación Sur de Autobuses
19 Main Police Station
20 Youth Hostel
21 San Pedro el Viejo
22 Palacio de Santa Cruz

23 Capilla del Obispo, Iglesia San Andrés, and San Isidro
24 Convento de las Descalzas Reales
25 Catedral de San Isidro
26 Palacio Real and Catedral de la Almudena
27 Calcografía Academia de San Fernando and Iglesia de San Francisco
28 Iglesia de San Francisco
29 Capilla de San Antonio
30 Museo del Prado
31 Centro Reina Sofía
32 Museo Municipal
33 Teatro de la Opera
34 Biblioteca Nacional
35 Palacio de las Cortes
36 Museo Lázaro Galdiano
37 Museo Arqueológico
38 Museo de Artes Decorativas
39 Museo de América
40 Museo Naval
41 Auditorio Nacional

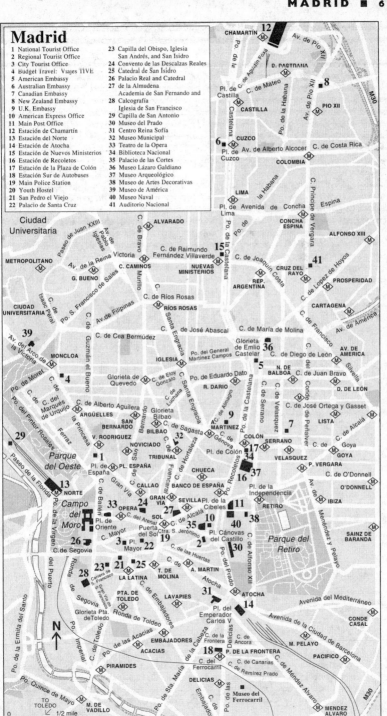

3rd floor (tel. 523 02 26). Metro: Banco de España. Open Mon.-Fri. 9am-1:30pm and 2:20-5:30pm. **South African Embassy:** Edificio Lista, C. de Claudio Coello 91-6, (tel. 527 31 53).

Currency Exchange: American Express has the best rates. Also at **El Corte Inglés,** C. Preciados, 3 (tel. 532 18 00; Metro: Sol); C. Goya, 76 (tel. 577 71 71; Metro: Goya); C. Princesa, 42 (tel. 542 48 00; Metro: Argüelles). Open Mon.-Sat. 10am-9pm, Sun. noon-8pm.

American Express: Pl. Cortes, 2, Madrid 28014 (tel. 322 55 00; 24-hr. lost Cheques toll-free tel. 900 99 44 26; fax 429 21 78). Open Mon.-Fri. 9am-5:30pm, Sat. 9am-noon.

Post Office: Palacio de Comunicaciones, Pl. Cibeles (tel. 536 01 10). Metro: Banco de España. Information open Mon.-Fri. 8am-10pm. Open for stamps and certified mail Mon.-Fri. 8am-10pm, Sun. 10am-1pm (through Door H); for Lista de Correos Mon.-Fri. 8am-9:30pm, Sat. 8:30am-2pm; for **telegrams** 24hrs. Telegram assistance available Mon.-Fri. 8am-10pm (at Window 27) and 8-10pm (through Door H), Sun. 8am-10pm (through Door H). English and French spoken at information desk. **Postal Code:** 28070.

Telephones: Telefónica, Gran Vía, 30, at C. Valverde. Metro: Gran Vía. Open Mon.-Sat. 9am-midnight, Sun. 10am-midnight. The **Palacio de Comunicaciones** (above) is infinitely quieter. Open Mon.-Fri. 8am-midnight, Sat.-Sun. and holidays 8am-10pm. **City Code:** 91.

Flights: Aeropuerto Internacional de Barajas, 15km northeast of Madrid. **Bus-Aeropuerto** to Plaza de Colón (300ptas). **Iberia:** C. Goya, 29 (tel. 587 81 56). For domestic and international reservations call 563 99 66, 24hrs.

Trains: Madrid has 3 *largo recorrido* (long distance) stations. **Estación Chamartín,** Agustín de Foxá (tel. 323 21 21). Metro: Chamartín, line #8 (1 stop from Pl. Castilla stop on blue line #1). Bus #5 runs to and from Sol (45min.); the stop is just beyond the lockers. Chamartín services towns throughout Spain, Portugal, and France. Ticket windows open daily 6:45am-11:35pm. **Estación Atocha,** Av. Ciudad de Barcelona (tel. 527 31 60). Metro: Atocha-Renfe (on blue line #1). Newly renovated, serves Castilla-La Mancha, Andalucía, València, Granada, Córdoba, Toledo, and Salamanca. Also has AVE (Alta Velocidad Española) service to Seville via Córdoba (tel. 534 05 05). Service to Portugal. Ticket windows open daily 6:30am-11:30pm. **Estación Príncipe Pío (or Norte),** Po. del Rey, 30 (tel. 247 00 00). Metro: Opera by way of extension "Norte" (follow signs in either direction). Trains to A Coruña, León, Salamanca. **RENFE Main Office,** C. Alcalá, 44 (tel. 563 02 02), where Gran Vía hits C. Alcalá. Metro: Banco de España. Arrive when it opens to avoid long waits. Open Mon.-Fri. 9:30am-8pm. Sample *regional-expres* and *largo recorrido* fares to: Ávila (8/day, 2hr., 710ptas); Segovia (8/day, 2hr., 650ptas); Toledo (9/day, 1hr., 535ptas); Salamanca (3/day, 3½hr.); Lisbon (11hr., 5600ptas); Paris (17-19hr., 12,715ptas).

Buses: Numerous private companies serve Madrid, each with its own station. Buses usually pass through the central **Estación Sur de Autobuses,** Canarias, 17 (tel. 468 45 11) en route. Metro: Palos de la Frontera, yellow line #3. Private companies include: **Estación Empresa Ruíz,** Rda. Atocha, 12 (tel. 468 08 50). Metro: Atocha. **Estación La Sepulvedana,** Po. de la Florida, 3 (tel. 547 52 61). Metro: Norte (take extension from Opera to the train station). **Estación Herranz,** C. Fernández de los Ríos (tel. 543 81 67), at C. Isaac Peral. Metro: Moncloa.

Luggage Storage: Estaciones de Chamartín and **Atocha** (see trains). Automatic lockers for backpacks 300ptas/day, for large packs and suitcases 500ptas/day. Open daily 7:30am-11:30pm. **Estación Sur de Autobuses** (see buses). Bags checked (80ptas/bag/day). Lockers also at the airport-bus terminal beneath Pl. Colón.

Public Transportation: Metro 125ptas; 10-ride ticket *(billete de diez)* 550ptas; tel. 435 22 66 and 552 49 00. Runs 6am-1:30am. The *Plano del Metro* is more concise than the unwieldy *Plano de los Transportes* which should be used to decipher the **bus** system (125ptas, 10-ride *bonobus* pass 550ptas). Buses run 6am-midnight. 11 nocturnal buses travel from Sol and Pl. Cibeles to the outskirts every ½hr. midnight-3am; every hr. 3-5am. Nocturnal buses (numbered N1-N11) are indicated on a special section on the *Plano*. There are N stops all along the marked routes, not just in Sol and Pl. Cibeles. **Information:** Empresa Municipal de Transportes (EMT; tel. 401 3100 or 555 72 96).

Hitchhiking: tel. 542 10 89 for route info. Neither popular nor safe. Hitchers take N-I (north) for Burgos; N-II (northeast) for Zaragoza and Barcelona; N-III (east) for València; N-IV (south) for Andalucía; N-VI (northwest) for Avila, Segovia, Salamanca, and Galicia; E-4 (west) for Portugal; 401 (southeast) for Toledo.

Taxi: Base fare is 150ptas, plus 70ptas/km, plus supplements. Tel. 445 90 08, 447 51 80. Service for the handicapped, tel. 547 82 00, 547 85 00, or 547 86 00.

Car Rental: Don't do it unless you're planning to zoom out of Madrid. **Atesa:** C. Orense, 83 (tel. 572 26 65). Metro: Tetuán. C. Francisco leads to C. Orense. Also at the airport (tel. 205 86 60). Open daily 7am-midnight.

English Bookstores: Librería Turner, C. Genova, 3 (tel. 319 28 67). Metro: Cólon. Classics and the very latest. Guidebooks. **Booksellers,** C. José Abascal, 48 (tel. 442 79 59).

Laundromat: Lavandería Donoso Cortés, C. Donoso Cortés, 17 (tel. 446 96 90). Metro: Quevedo. Self-service. Wash and dry 350ptas/5kg. Soap 60ptas. Open Mon.-Fri. 9am-7pm, Sat. 8:30am-1pm.

Late-Night Pharmacy: tel. 098, or check *Farmacias de Guardia* listings in local papers.

Crisis Hotlines: Rape, 574 01 10. **AIDS Information,** 445 23 28. **Women's Medical Issues,** 730 49 01. Open Mon.-Fri. 3:30-6:30pm. **English-Language Help,** 559 13 93. Open 7-11pm.

Medical Assistance: Anglo-American Medical Unit, Conde de Aranda, 1, 1st floor (tel. 435 18 23), to the left. Metro: Serrano. Not an emergency clinic.

Emergency: tel. 091 or 092. **Ambulance:** 061 or **Red Cross** (tel. 522 22 22). **Fire:** tel. 080. **Police:** C. Luna, 29 (tel. 521 12 36). Metro: Callao.

ACCOMMODATIONS

Demand for rooms rises dramatically in summer; make reservations. Expect to pay 1600 to 2500ptas/person for a typical *hostal* room. **Calle Fuencarral** is less expensive and closer to the nightlife of Malasaña and Chueca. The centrally located **Puerta del Sol** and **Palacio Real** zone is crawling with tourists.

Albergue Juvenil Santa Cruz de Marcenado (HI), C. Santa Cruz de Marcenado, 28 (tel. 547 45 32). Metro: Argüelles. Walk down C. Pricesa, turn left on C. Serrano Jover, and right on C. Santa Cruz de Marcenado. Modern, recently renovated facilities located near the student district. English spoken. New lockers. Reception open 9am-10:30pm. Strict curfew 1:30am. 650ptas, over 26 800ptas. Members only. Tiny breakfast included. Reservations in writing 15 days in advance; 3-day max. stay. *Pensión completa* 1450ptas, over 26 1700ptas.

Albergue Juvenil Richard Schirrman (HI), Casa de Campo (tel. 463 56 99). Metro: El Lago. Turn left (downhill) on leaving the station, left at the paved road which runs parallel to the Metro tracks, and look for signs for the hostel. On the outskirts of the city, in an enormous park, close to a lake and municipal swimming pool. Don't even contemplate walking alone through the unlit park at night. 130 bunk beds. Bar with TV, library, basketball court, laundry (500ptas/load). English spoken. Each austere 8-person room has a bath. New lockers. Members only. Reservations in writing 15 days in advance; 3-day max. stay. Same bed and meal prices as above.

Hostal-Residencia Cruz-Sol, Pl. Santa Cruz, 6, 4th floor (tel. 532 71 97), near the Pl. Mayor. Metro: Sol. Sizeable rooms, some with balconies overlooking the Iglesia de Santa Cruz. A forest for the creative mind: hardwood floors with greenish wallpaper. Ferns, too. Singles 2000ptas. Doubles 2500ptas, with bath 4000ptas. Hot showers 200ptas.

Hostal-Residencia Paz, C. Flora, 4, 1st floor (tel. 547 30 47). Metro: Sol or Opera. Spotless rooms hold new beds, mattresses, and well-maintained furniture. Some English spoken. Singles 2200ptas. Doubles 3200ptas, with shower 3600ptas. Triples 4500ptas. Call ahead for reservations.

Hostal-Residencia Jeyma, C. Arenal 24, 3rd floor (tel. 541 63 29). Metro: Opera. You won't find singles cheaper or quieter than these anywhere within a light year of Puerta del Sol. Singles 1300ptas, doubles 2600ptas.

Hostal-Residencia María del Mar, C. Marqués Viudo de Pontejo, 7, 2nd and 3rd floor (tel. 531 90 64). Metro: Sol. 40 recently renovated rooms with shining tile floors and blond, shapely furniture. Lounge with TV. Singles 1500ptas. Doubles 2800ptas, with bath (and bigger room) 5000 ptas.

Hostal-Residencia Miño, C. Arenal, 16, 2nd floor (tel. 531 50 79 or 531 97 89). Metro: Opera or Sol. A melting pot of rooms ranging from large with hardwood floors and balconies, to tight quarters with vinyl underfoot. Singles 2200ptas, with shower 2900ptas. Doubles with shower 3900ptas. Triples 6000ptas.

Hostal-Residencia Mondragón, Carrera San Jerónimo, 32, 4th floor (tel. 429 68 16). Metro: Sol. Glass-block and carved marble entry leads into a former palace full of *hostales*—over which Mondragón reigns supreme. Wide halls, clean rooms, and sun-splashed red-tiled terraces. Singles 1500ptas. Doubles 2300ptas, with shower 2500ptas. 3-person doubles 2800ptas, with shower 3000ptas. Showers 100ptas. No reservations. Open March-Dec.

Hostal Carreras, C. Príncipe, 18, 3rd floor (tel. 522 00 36), between Pl. Santa Ana and Pl. Canalejas. Metro: Antón Martín, Sol, or Sevilla. Recent renovation and expansion make for 2 worlds: the old (wood floors, big rooms) and the new (white tiled floors, new furniture). Advance payment required. Singles 2000ptas. Doubles 3000ptas, with shower 3700ptas. Triples with shower 4500ptas.

Hostal Alcázar Regis, Gran Vía, 61, 5th floor (tel. 547 93 17). Metro: Pl. España or Santo Domingo. Rooms are spacious though simpler than their stained-glass doors and opulent reception halls suggest. Singles 2500ptas. Doubles 4100ptas. Triples 5900ptas. Breakfast 350ptas. Fills up quickly; make reservations.

Hostal-Residencia Tanger, Gran Vía, 44, 9th floor (tel. 521 75 85). Metro: Callao. Dizzying views of the street. No cooties here—rooms are scrubbed down to the hardwood floors. Singles 1800ptas, with shower 2300ptas. Doubles with shower 3500ptas. Open Sept.-July.

Hostal-Residencia Josefina, Gran Vía, 44, 7th floor (tel. 521 81 31), two floors down from Tanger. Shadowy elegance and period furniture complemented by a certain poignant decay. *Blade Runner*-esque stairwell. Singles 1700ptas. Doubles 3000ptas, with shower 4200ptas. Triples 3500ptas, with shower 4200ptas.

Hostal Palacios-Ribadavia, C. Fuencarral, 25, 2nd floor (tel. 531 10 58 and 531 48 47). Metro: Gran Vía. Owner fervently swears, "My job is the bed—you *will* have fresh sheets daily." No slacking in other departments either. Major renovations planned. Singles 2100ptas, with shower 2300ptas. Doubles with shower 3600ptas. Triples with shower 5300ptas, with bath 6000ptas. No charge for children under 10. *Let's Go* bearers snag 10% discount.

Hostal-Residencia Abril, C. Fuencarral, 39, 4th floor (tel. 531 53 38). Metro: Tribunal. Cutesy prints of kitties and babies and garish mirrors amongst newborn furniture. Singles 1950ptas, with shower 2200ptas. Doubles 3000ptas, with shower 3400ptas. Triples with shower 4100ptas.

Camping

Tourist offices can provide information about the 13 or so campsites within 50km of Madrid. The same information is in their **Guía Oficial de Campings, España 93**. **Camping Osuna** (tel. 741 05 10, fax 320 63 65) is located on the Ajalvir-Vicálvaro road (15.5km). Take the metro to Canillejas, then cross the pedestrian overpass, walk through the parking lot, and turn right along the freeway. (475ptas/person, tent, or car). The campground can pass as an autonomous city; it has phones, hot showers, washers and dryers, safes, currency exchange, medical care, a playground, a bar, and a restaurant.

FOOD

Let's face it: eating out in Madrid is pricey. Restaurants open for lunch at either 1:30 or 2pm and for dinner at 8 or 9pm, although most diners prefer to arrive after 10pm. Madrid's delicacies include *caldereta de cordero* (lamb stewed with tomatoes and peppers), *cocido madrileño* (chickpea stew flavored with *chorizo* sausage), and *pisto manchego* (a vegetable stew). **Argüelles** and **Moncloa** are middle-class *barrios* near the Ciudad Universitaria. They're a bit out of the way, but have at least two restaurants per block. **Calles Echegaray** and **Manuel Fernández González** are the budget boulevards. In the following listings and Madrid in general, a *restaurante* or *casa* is open from 1 to 4:30pm and 8:30pm to midnight unless otherwise noted. Establishments such as *mesones*, *cafeterías*, *bares*, *cafés*, *terrazas*, and *tabernas* include a bar and serve drinks, *tapas*, *raciones*, and *bocadillos* all day until midnight.

A delightfully active alternative to a full sit-down meal is hopping from bar to bar gobbling *tapas* at the counter. Most *tapas* bars (a.k.a. *tascas* or *tabernas*) are open noon to 4pm and 8pm to midnight or later. Some, doubling as restaurants, flock about Plaza Mayor (tourist alert!) and Plaza Santa Ana. **Mercado de San Miguel,** just off the northwest corner of Pl. Mayor (open Mon.-Sat. 8am-2pm and 5:30-8pm) and **Mercado de la Cebada,** at the intersection of C. Toledo and Carrera de San Francisco, are two of the most convenient supermarkets.

Casa Ciriaco, C. Mayor, 84. Metro: Sol or Opera. Madrid fare without pretensions. Entrees average about 1500ptas; *menú* 1700ptas. Open Sept.-July Thurs.-Tues.

Madrid 1600, C. Cava de San Miguel. Metro: Sol. One of numerous "typical" restaurants on this street, an eensy stone-walled den. *Menú* 1200ptas. Open 1-4pm and 8pm-midnight.

Museo del Jamón, C. San Jerónimo, 6 (tel. 521 03 46), off Puerta del Sol. Metro: Sol. Five other locations in the city. The most overt expression of Spain's fascination with piggies. No hamless wall space. *Menú del día* 850 or 1000ptas. Open Mon.-Sat. 9am-12:30am, Sun. 10am-12:30am.

Mesón La Caserola, C. Echegaray, off C. San Jerónimo. Metro: Sol. Busy joint serving a solid *menú* (825ptas) to ravenous locals on lunch break. Cheap *raciones* and *tapas* during off-hours; many entrees around 600ptas.

Restaurante Integral Artemisa, C. Ventura de la Vega, 4, off C. San Jerónimo. Metro: Sol. A decent veggie place, despite slow service. Main dishes 800-1200ptas. Many salads around 900ptas. Non-vegetarian entrees available. A/C.

Casa Portal, C. Olivar, 3 (tel. 239 07 39). Metro: Lavapiés. Dandy Asturian specialties such as salmon and *tortilla de angulas* (eel tortilla, 1200ptas), but come for the homemade *sidra* (350ptas) decanted in true Asturian style (poured from a bottle held high above the shoulders into a glass on the floor so that it stays fizzy). Open Thurs.-Sat. and Mon.-Tues. noon-midnight, Sun. and Wed. for lunch only.

Taberna Carmencita, C. San Marcos, 36, on the corner with C. Libertad. Metro: Chueca. Popular with tourists and businesspeople, this classic restaurant, founded in 1830, evokes pre-War Madrid: brass fixtures, black and white photos of *toreros,* polychrome *azulejos,* lace curtains, and iron and marble tables. The *menú* is a steal at 1000ptas for its superb bread and wine, plus an appetizer.

Restaurante La Vaxcongada, Pl. Vázquez de Mella, 10, on the edge of Chueca toward Gran Vía. Typical dishes of Madrid and the País Vasco (Basque country). *Menú* 700ptas. Entrees 300-700ptas. High ceiling and A/C. The lone waiter manages to keep everyone happy and retain his sanity.

Restaurante Zara, C. Infantas, 7, off C. Hortaleza. Metro: Gran Vía. Tropical food with a stained-glass sunset backdrop. Half *pollo asado* (roast chicken) 700ptas.

La Gata Flora, C. 2 de Mayo, 1 (tel. 521 20 20), at C. San Vicente Ferrer. Metro: Noviciado or Tribunal. Tightly packed tables and a bohemian crowd in a marvelous Italian restaurant. Try the *cappelletti al pesto* (dumplings in a delicious basil sauce, 875ptas). Wash your meal down with fabulous sangria (875ptas). Open Sun.-Thurs. 2-4pm and 8pm-midnight, Fri.-Sat. 8:30pm-1am.

El Restaurante Vegetariano, C. Marqués de Santa Ana, 34, off Pl. Juan Pujol on the corner with C. Espíritu Santo. Metro: Tribunal. High-quality vegetarian concoctions. Chewy homemade bread. Main course 750-900ptas. Salad bar (small plate 535ptas, large 975ptas). A/C.

SIGHTS

From Plaza Mayor to Puerta de Toledo The arcaded **Plaza Mayor** (Metro: Sol) is topped with the Habsburgs' elegant black slate roofs and spindly, pagoda-like towers. It was completed in 1620 for Felipe III; his statue is also from the 17th century, although it took the city until 1847 to get it up. The public executions and bullfights that took place here are now but ghosts haunting the plaza's lively cafés. This most picturesque part of Old Madrid is not far from smaller and quieter **Plaza de la Villa.** Legend has it that François—Carlos V's archenemy—was held prisoner in the **Torre de los Lujanes,** a 15th-century building on the eastern side of the plaza. The characteristically Habsburg 17th-century **Ayuntamiento** (or Casa de la Villa) on the plaza was both the mayor's home and the city jail. South of Pl. Mayor on C. Toledo looms **Iglesia de San Isidro,** a 17th-century church where thin shafts of light squeeze their way through small stained-glass windows, and the walls drip with heavy gold leaf. The remains of San Isidro landed here after being tossed from church to church like a diseased hot potato. (Metro: Latina. Open for mass only.) The nearby **Basílica de San Francisco El Grande** has an enormous neoclassical dome, and paintings by Goya.

Between Central del Sol and Paseo del Prado Picasso's *Guernica* is part of (and the centerpiece in) the **Centro de Arte Reina Sofía,** a collection of 20th-century art at C. Santa Isabel, 52, opposite Estación Atocha near the south end of Po. Prado (Metro: Atocha). When Germans bombed the Basque town of Gernika for the Fascists in Spain's Civil War, Picasso painted this huge work of jumbled and distorted figures to denounce the bloodshed. When asked by Nationalist officials whether he was responsible for the picture, Picasso answered "No, you are." He gave the canvas to New York's Museum of Modern Art on condition that it return to Spain when democracy was restored. The move to the Reina Sofía sparked an international controversy—Picasso's *other* stipulation was that the painting hang only in the Prado, to prove his equality with Titian and Velázquez. Sorry, Pabs. As if Picasso's masterpiece wasn't enough, this pink neoclassical monolith of a museum contains a splendid art history library, bookstore, repertory cinema (art films in Spanish at noon and 4:30pm, 150ptas), and café. (Open Mon.-Sat. 10am-9pm, Sun. 10am-2:30pm. 400ptas, students free.)

In Madrid, only the Prado surpasses the collection of the **Museo de la Real Academia de Bellas Artes de San Fernando,** C. Alcalá, 13. (Metro: Sol or Sevilla. Bus #3, 5, 20, 51, or 52.) The museum contains works by Velázquez, Rubens, and Zurbarán; El Greco's *Saint Hieronymus,* Ribera's *Ecce Homo,* and Goya's *Escena de Inquisición.* (Open Mon.-Fri. 9am-7pm, Sat.-Mon. 10am-2pm. 200ptas, students free.) Next door the **Calcografia Real** (Royal Print and Drawing Collection) organizes excellent temporary exhibitions of works on paper.

The **Museo Thyssen Bornemizsa,** on the corner of Po. Prado and C. San Jerónimo (tel. 361 01 51; Metro: Banco de España) is an 18th-century palace transformed to house this fabulous and newly-purchased 775-piece collection of Old Masters and 20th-century art. Complementing the Prado perfectly, it fills out areas where the Prado is relatively weak, and is one of the treasures of Madrid. A must-see. (Open Tues.-Sun. 10am-7pm. No entry after 6:30pm. 600ptas, students and retired people 350ptas.)

The Retiro and Jerónimos **Parque del Retiro,** Madrid's top picnic and suntanning zone, was originally intended to be a *buen retiro* (nice retreat) for Felipe IV. The palace burned down, but the **Museo del Ejército** remains. Alfonso XII and his horse glare at the **Estanque Grande,** a rectangular lake in the middle of the park. You can row row row your boat here (boats available daily 10am-sunset; 400ptas for 2 people, 100ptas for each additional person).

Museo del Prado Spain's premier museum, and one of Europe's finest, is on Po. Prado at Pl. Cánovas del Castillo. (Metro: Banco de España or Atocha). The neoclassical building has sheltered the royal painting collection since the time of Fernando VII, who cared precious little for art and plenty about making an impression at home and abroad. Over 5000 paintings, many collected by Spanish monarchs between 1400 and 1700, include Spanish and foreign masterpieces, with particular strengths in the Flemish and Venetian Schools. The wonder of the Prado is that *every* work is a masterpiece. The second floor presents Spanish works from the 16th and 17th centuries, highlighted by the collection of Diego Velázquez. All his major works are here, including the fascinating *Las Hilanderas* (The Spinners), his exquisite portraits of the royal family, *The Forge of Vulcan,* and his ultimate masterpiece, *Las Meninas* (The Maids of Honor). Francisco de Goya is represented by *La Maja vestida* (Clothed Maja) and *La Maja desnuda* (Nude Maja), the hilariously unflattering *La Familia de Carlos IV* and *Los Fusilamientos del tercero de mayo,* which depicts the slaughter of Spaniards by Napoleon's army. Among the El Grecos are *La Trinidad* and *La Adoración de los Pastore.* Works of Spanish painters from the same era fill the first floor, including Murillo, Ribera, and Zurbarán. The Prado also has a formidable stash of Italian works by greats such as Titian, Fra Angelico, Raphael, Tintoretto, and Botticelli. Because the Spanish Habsburgs long ruled the Netherlands, the Flemish holdings are also top notch, with Hieronymus Bosch, Roger van der Weyden, Albrecht Dürer, Peter Brueghel, and Rubens. (Open Tues.-Sat. 9am-7pm, Sun. 9am-2pm. 400ptas, students with ISIC and citizens of EC countries under 21 with ID free.)

Your ticket to the Prado also admits you to the nearby **Casón del Buen Retiro,** C. Alfonso XII, 28, facing the Parque del Retiro (Metro: Retiro or Banco de España). Once part of Felipe IV's Palacio del Buen Retiro, then a porcelain factory, it was destroyed in the war against Napoleon. The rebuilt version has a superb collection of 19th-century Spanish paintings. (Same hrs. as the Prado.)

Along Paseo Recoletos For a sense of Spain's past—stretching back to prehistory—visit the **Museo Arqueológico Nacional,** C. Serrano, 13. (Metro: Colón or Serrano. Bus #1, 9, 19, 51, 53, or M-2.) Astounding tile mosaics, mummies, crowns of Visigoth kings, ivories from Muslim Andalucía, the suspicious *Dama de Elche,* and the hollow *Dama de Baza (*ashes of cremated bodies were deposited in this 4th-century statue, found in a tomb in the province of Granada). There's also Romanesque and Gothic sculpture, and Celtiberian silver and gold. (Open Tues.-Sat. 9:30am-8pm, Sun. 9:30am-6:30pm. 200ptas, students free.)

The Palacio Real and Environs With 20 square km of tapestry and the largest candelabra in Europe, the impossibly luxurious **Palacio Real** (Metro: Opera) was built for first Bourbon King Felipe V to replace the Alcázar, which burned down on Christmas Eve, 1734. The shell of it took 40 years and interior decoration of its 2000 rooms dragged on for a century. Spanish monarchs abandoned it in the war-torn 1930's. To see the Palacio's Versailles-esque collection of porcelain, tapestries, furniture, armor, and art, stroll around or take a guided tour (in Spanish or English, 40min.). (Metro: Opera. Buses #4, 15, 25, 33, or 39. Palace open, except during royal visits, Mon.-Sat. 9am-6pm, Sun. 9am-3pm. 500ptas, students 350ptas, Wed. free for EC citizens. Arrive early to avoid waiting.) The palace faces the **Plaza de Oriente,** a semicircle square enclosed on the northern side by the serene **Jardines de Sabatini,** the park of choice for romantics. Juan Carlos opened **Campo del Moro** (facing the canal) to the public only 12 years ago; the view of the palace rising majestically on a dark green slope is straight out of a fairy tale. In the heart of downtown, the **Convento de las Descalzas Reales** (Convent of the Royal Barefoot Ones), Pl. Descalzas, between Pl. Callao and Sol. Metro: Callao or Sol), founded in 1559, accepted only women of royal blood, thus acquiring an exceptional collection of religious artwork—tapestries, paintings, sculptures, and liturgical objects, not to mention discarded shoes. The Salón de Tapices contains 12 renowned tapestries woven from cartoons by Rubens. Other rooms hold paintings by Zurbarán, Titian, and Rubens. Mandatory tour in Spanish. (Open Tues.-Sat. 10am-12:30pm and 4-5:30pm, Fri. 10:30am-12:30pm, Sat. 11am-1:30pm. 350ptas, students 250ptas.)

Casa de Campo Catch the cable car *(teleférico* 250ptas, round-trip 360ptas; noon-9pm) down to the city's largest park, the **Casa de Campo.** Woods, a municipal pool, a zoo, and an amusement park all conspire to leave the city far behind. Don't attempt to explore the park on foot; it's so large it makes Madrid's center look like a clearing in the woods. Avoid straying beyond populated areas such as the zoo and amusement park after sunset. (Amusement park open Mon.-Fri. noon-11pm, Sat. noon-1am, Sun. noon-midnight. Metro: Lago or Batán. Bus #33 or 65.)

El Pardo An elegant Renaissance and Neoclassical country palace, painted butterscotch and white, **El Pardo** is a 15-minute bus ride from the city center. Set on the royal hunting grounds, it was a retreat of Castilian monarchs in the 16th century. The original hunting lodge was much enlarged and remodeled by the designer of the Palacio Real. Franco frequently chose to receive visitors here, and it still occasionally serves as the residence of visiting diplomats and heads of state. Inside there's a wealth of Flemish and Italian paintings and numerous tapestries designed by Goya. (Open Mon.-Sat. 9:30am-12:15pm and 3-6pm, Sun. 9:30am-1:40pm. You must wait for a group to form for the compulsory guided tour. 350ptas, 250ptas for students; Wed. free for EC citizens. Bus #601 from Paseo de Moret, near Moncloa Metro stop, 95ptas.) Next door, there's an interesting 18th-century **Iglesia** and a lavish **Casita del Príncipe** by Villanueva, creator of the Prado.

ENTERTAINMENT

Residents of Spain's first city like to say that no one goes to bed until they've killed the night. Lily-livered sleeping habits are scorned, so adjust your body clock accordingly. The weekly *Guía del Ocio* (75ptas at any kiosk) lists complete entertainment minutiae, as do the Friday supplement *(El Mundo's* "Metropoli," *El País's* "Guía," *Diario 16's* "Madrid") and the daily *cartelera* listings in any newspaper. Pl. 2 de Mayo in Malasaña, Pl. Chueca, Pl. España, and the Gran Vía can be intimidating and sleazy. For a city of its size, however, Madrid is fairly safe, and the only places to avoid late at night are the parks.

Classic Cafés Coffee at a classic café is expensive (200-250ptas)—but an hour or two spent at one of them is a most economical way to soak up a little Madrid (and a lot of second-hand smoke). **Café Comercial,** Glorieta de Bilbao, 7 (Metro: Bilbao), is a traditional establishment with high ceilings and huge mirrors frequented by artists and Republican aviators alike. Anti-Franco protests started here. (Beer 100ptas. Open daily 11am-midnight.) **Café Gijón,** Po. Recoletos, 21 (Metro: Colón), has both a breezy terrace and a smoky bar-restaurant. Long a favorite of the literati, this is the sort of place where people bring their books to study and their friends to talk. Coffee 250ptas at the tables. (Open daily noon-midnight.)

Nightlife: Cafés, Bars, Clubs, Discos As the sun sets and bathes the streets in gold, **terrazas** and **chiringuitos** (outdoor cafés/bars) spill across sidewalks all over Madrid. **Pl. Mayor** is handy for a glass of wine while digesting the tourist office's brochures. **C. Bailén,** by the Viaducto, has spectacular views of flaming sunsets (one thing urban pollution *is* good for). A number of kiosks and open-air *cafeterías* sprinkled about the **Casa del Campo. Pos. Castellana, Recoletos,** and **Prado** are fashionable and hip areas, hence a bit pricy. **Pl. 2 de Mayo** (Malasaña) and **Pl. Olavide** (Bilbao) host drink-sippers in the shade of umbrellas and trees. **El Viso,** west of the Auditorio Nacional to Po. Castellana and south to C. María de Molina is a pre-war garden city within the city in which villas, walled gardens, and winding streets exude a charming village-like aura. Hippies, intellectuals, bohemians, street musicians, and junkies check each other out in the **Plaza 2 de Mayo. C. San Vincente Ferrer,** with its tattoo parlors, second-hand clothing and leather stores, motorcycle repair shops, and countless pubs is a prime neighborhood

For **clubs and discos,** life begins at 1:30am. Many discos have "afternoon" sessions (usually 7-10pm, cover 250-1000ptas) for teens; but the "night" sessions (lasting until dawn) are for really letting your hair down. Don't be surprised if at 5:30am there's still a line of people waiting to get in. Really. Cover *(entrada)* can get as high as 1500ptas, and men may be charged 200ptas more than women. The cover charge often includes a drink. It's tough to make it to **Club Andy Warhol's,** C. Luchana, 20, in time to receive your 15 minutes of fame. (Open Mon.-Sat. 5am (yep, that's am)-10am, Sun. 5am-noon.) **Joy Eslava,** C. Arenal, 11 (Metro: Sol or Opera), is a three-tiered theater turned disco with 3 bars, laser lights, videoscreen and live entertainment. The young crowd parties to disco music. (Cover 1500ptas. Open Mon.-Thurs. 11:30pm on, Fri.-Sat. 7-10:15pm and 11:30pm-5:30am.)

A few establishments deserve specific mention. **Cervecería Alemana,** Pl. Santa Ana, 6, is an ex-Hemingway hangout with a slightly upscale crowd. It's one of a row of three *cervecerías* (brasseries) that all deserve exploration. (Open Sun.-Fri. noon-12:30am, Sat. noon-1:30am.) **Viva Madrid,** C. Manuel Fernández González, 7, next to Pl. Santa Ana (Metro: Antón Martín), is a U.S. expatriate hangout with wonderful tiles and animals carved in wood. (Beer and juice 400ptas, mixed drinks 700-800ptas. Open daily 8pm-3am.) In Malasaña, **La Tetera de la Abuela,** C. Espíritu Santo, 37, brings together writers, actors, and students. (Open Sun.-Thurs. 7:30pm-1am, Fri.-Sat. 7:30pm-2am.) The self-proclaimed House of Beer, **Cervecería Ratskeller's,** corner of C. Luchana and C. Palafox (by the cinema Palafox), is so crowded on weekends there's barely room to raise glass to mouth. (Open daily noon-3am.)

Film, Theater, and Sports The **Parque del Retiro** shows free movies nightly at 11pm. The state-subsidized *filmoteca* in the renovated Art Deco **Ciné Doré,** C. Santa Isabel, 3 (tel. 369 11 25; Metro: Antón Martín), is the best for repertory cinema. (Tickets 200-400ptas.) Subtitled films are shown in many private theaters, such as **Alphaville** and **Renoir 1** and **2**—check the V.O. (for *versión original)* listings in entertainment guides. The theater district is bounded by Pl. Santa Ana and Pl. Colón (south to north), and Po. Prado-Recoletos and Puerta del Sol (east to west). **Localidades Galicia,** Pl. Carmen, 1 (tel. 531 27 32; Metro: Sol), handles theater tickets, as well as those for soccer games and bullfights. (Open Mon.-Fri. 10am-1pm and 4:30-7pm.) The theater district is bounded by Pl. Santa Ana and Pl. Cólon (south-north) and Po. Prado-Recoletos and Puerta del Sol (east-west). **Teatro Español,** C. Príncipe, 25 (tel. 429 03 18, tickets and info tel. 429 62 97; Metro: Sevilla), hosts well-known Spanish plays. In summer, the city sponsors free movies and plays in the **Plaza Mayor, Plaza de Lavapiés,** and the **Plaza Villa de París.** Tickets around 1300-1700ptas, reduced prices on Wednesdays. The finest classical performances happen at the **Auditorio Nacional,** C. Príncipe de Vergara, 136 (tel. 337 01 00). In 1993 the grand, granite 19th-century **Teatro de la Opera,** on Pl. Opera, will reopen soon after years of reconditioning as the city's principal venue for classical ballet and the lyric genre. **Flamenco** in Madrid is tourist-oriented and expensive. If you must, try **Casa Patas,** C. Cañizares, 10 (tel. 369 04 96). The flamenco starts at midnight (Fri.-Sat.); the cover charge varies. (Open daily 8:30pm-2:30am.)

Spanish sport-fans go ballistic for **fútbol** (soccer)! Every Sunday, occasionally Saturday, between September and June, one of two big local teams plays at home. "Real Madrid" plays at Estadio Santiago Bernebeu, Po. Castellana, 104 (tel. 457 11 12; Metro: Lima; buses #27, 40, 43). "Atlético Madrid" plays at Estadio Vicente Calderón, C. Virgen del Puerto, 67 (tel. 366 47 07; Metro: Pirámides or Marqués de Vadillos). (Tickets for seats 2500ptas, for standing-room 1000ptas.) If tickets are sold out, shifty scalpers lurk by the stadium during the afternoon or evening a few days before the game. **Corridas** (bullfights) are held during the Festival of San Isidro and every Sunday in summer, less frequently the rest of the year. The season lasts from March to October. If you can stomach the killing of six beautiful *toros bravos* (and occasionally a reckless matador), keep your eyes open for posters in bars. **Plaza de las Ventas,** C. Alcalá, 237 (tel. 356 22 00), east of central Madrid, is the biggest ring in Spain. (Metro: Ventas. Bus #21, 53, 110.) Ticket outlets are at C. Victoria, 3, off C. San Jerónimo east of Puerta del Sol (Metro: Sol); Pl. Carmen, 1 (tel. 531 27 32); and Pl. Toros, C. Alcalá, 237 (Metro: Ventas). A seat is 2000-2500ptas.

■ Near Madrid

They called **El Escorial** the eighth wonder of the world, and they were right. It is a fascinating, severe complex that includes a monastery, two palaces, a church, two pantheons, a magnificent library, and innumerable artistic treasures. Located near the charming town of **San Lorenzo** and within easy striking distance of Madrid, El Escorial should be visited early in the day to see it all. Don't come on Monday, when the whole complex and most of the town shut down.

The **Monasterio de San Lorenzo de El Escorial** was a gift from Felipe II to God, himself, and the people, commemorating his victory over the French at the battle of San Quintín in 1557. The **Palacio Real** includes the *Salón del Trono* (Throne Room) and two **dwellings** in one—Felipe II's spartan 16th-century apartments and the more luxurious 18th-century rooms of Carlos III and Carlos IV. The astonishing **Panteón Real** (known affectionately as *el pudridero,* the rotting chamber) was another brainchild of Felipe II. Although he didn't live to see it finished, he's buried here with Carlos V and most of their royal descendants. Royal servants dumped bygone nobles in the small adjoining room so that they could dry before being stuffed into their permanent tombs. On the far side of the complex, the **Salas Capitulares** (chapter rooms), now contain an outstanding exhibition on the construction of El Escorial, with some wooden models of 16th-century machinery and the buildings themselves. Also in the Salas Capitulares is the **Pinacoteca,** which holds a collection of masterpieces by Bosch, Dürer, El Greco, Titian, Tintoretto, Velázquez, Zurbarán, Van Dyck, and others. (The entire complex of El Escorial is open Tues.-Sun. 10am-7pm; Nov.-March 10am-6pm. Last admission to palaces, pantheons and museums 1hr. or ½hr. before closing (depending on "zone"), 15min. for the *casitas.* To monastery 500ptas, students 300ptas, free Wed. for EC citizens. To the *casitas* 150ptas.)

Trains arrive at Ctra. Estación (tel. (91) 890 04 13), 2km from San Lorenzo where Ctra. Estación meets Pl. Virgen de Gracia. They run to Madrid's Atocha and Charmatín stations (28/day, 1hr., round-trip 580ptas); Avila (11/day, 1hr., 580ptas); and Segovia (same info as Avila). The **tourist office** is at C. Floridablanca, 10 (tel. (91) 890 15 54; open Mon.-Fri. 10am-2pm and 3-4:45pm, Sat. 10am-1:45pm). **Buses** stop at Pl. Virgen de Gracia. The **Autocares Herranz office** is at C. Reina Victoria, 3 (tel. (91) 890 41 22). Buy tickets at the Bar Casino, C. Rey, 3 (tel. (91) 890 41 00). Buses run to Madrid (15/day, 1hr., 325ptas, round-trip 600ptas).

In the shadows of the colossus, lively San Lorenzo willingly hosts those who need another day. The best accommodations can be found at **Hostal Vasco,** Pl. Santiago, 11 (tel. (91) 890 16 19), a charming 19th-century building with a terrace on the plaza and a lounge on each floor. (Singles 1400ptas. Doubles with shower 3500ptas. Triples 4900ptas. *Pensión completa* 5100ptas. Tempting aromas seep from the eponymous restaurant next door.) The **Mercado Publico,** C. del Rey 9, 2 blocks off C. Floridablanca, sells a large selection of fresh produce, deli meats, cheeses, and other staples. (Open Mon.-Sat. 9am-2pm and 6-9pm, except Thurs. closed mornings.) During the **Festivals of San Lorenzo** (Aug. 10-20), parades of giant figures line the streets and fireworks fill the sky.

CASTILE AND LEÓN

In the High Middle Ages, this Christian kingdom emerged from obscurity to lead the battle charge against Islam. The nobility grew immensely wealthy as it seized more and more land; and well before the famous union with Aragón in 1492, it was clear that Castilla had the whip in hand. The concept of a unified Spain—under Castilian command—took root here, and *castellano* (called simply "Spanish" by foreigners) became the dominant language throughout the nation. Green and rolling León (the provinces of León, Zamora, and Salamanca) retorts that it had 24 kings before Castilla even had laws. Between the imperial hauteur of Castilla and the provincial pride of León, the region overflows with ego.

Farmland, acres of primeval woods rich in game, and even more of it sheer wilderness, the landscape is studded with splendid cathedrals, sumptuous palaces, and well-defined urban personalities. The majestic Gothic cathedrals of Burgos and León; the slender Romanesque belfries along the Camino de Santiago in León; the warm, intricately chased sandstone of Salamanca; and the proud city walls of Avila emblazon themselves as images not only of Castilla and León but also of all Spain.

■■■ ARANJUEZ

Centuries of Habsburg and Bourbon royalty fled to Aranjuez to escape Madrid's scorching heat. This is a town with peace and quiet, strawberries and impossibly tall elms and plane trees. Like several other venerable royal retreats (such as La Granja), Aranjuez no longer hosts monarchs during the summer (it lost out to Mallorca a while back), but the decaying grandeur of its **Palacio Real** nonetheless warrants an excursion from Madrid. Room after opulent room displays finely worked Vatican mosaic paintings in natural marble, chandeliers and mirrors from the La Granja crystal factory, Buen Retiro porcelain, Flemish tapestries, Chinese points, and ornate French clocks. (Open Tues.-Sun. 10am-6:30pm; Oct.-May Tues.-Sun. 10am-6pm. Compulsory tour in Spanish. 400ptas, students 275ptas. Free Wed. to EC citizens.) More relaxing are the extensive gardens, especially the huge **Jardines del Príncipe,** created for the youthful amusement of the future Carlos IV. (Gardens open 10am-sunset.)

Hostal Infantas, C. Infantas, 4 (tel. 891 13 41), rents adequate rooms just minutes away from the traffic circle. All rooms have phones. (Singles with shower 1400ptas. Doubles 2400ptas, with shower 3900ptas.) The town's strawberries and asparagus have been famed for centuries. *Fresón con nata* (strawberries and cream, 300ptas) are staples at kiosks throughout town and in cafés on **Calle Infantas,** across from the tourist office. **Bar-Kiosco El Brillante,** at the beginning of C. Infantas, serves *tapas* and *platos combinados* (450-850ptas). The **mercado** hawks fresh produce, breads and deli foods in a 19th-century building between C. Gobernador and C. Abastos.

The **tourist office** (tel. 891 04 27), is temporarily housed in a kiosk opposite the construction in Pl. San Antonio and Pl. Rusiñol. To get to the **train station** (tel. 891 02 02), 1km out of town, take Ctra. Toledo away from the palace and follow the signs (10min). Frequent trains run to Toledo (½-1½hr., 240ptas) and Madrid (45min., round-trip 580ptas). **Buses** run to Madrid (8/day, 340ptas) from C. Infantas, 8 (tel. 891 01 83).

■■■ TOLEDO

Cervantes called it that "rocky gravity, glory of Spain and light of her cities." Baroque poet Góngora called it a perpetual avalanche. Toledo remains a treasury of Spanish culture, no matter how many armies of tourists and vendors of kitsch pass through, and peaceful coexistence and collaboration among Christians, Muslims, and Jews has left behind a dignified and mystical walled city. Successively a Roman settle-

TOLEDO

ment, capital of the Visigothic kingdom, stronghold of the Emirate of Córdoba and imperial city under Carlos V, Toledo bears a rich history and heritage surpassed by few others in Spain.

ORIENTATION AND PRACTICAL INFORMATION

Getting here is a snap from Madrid; many buses and trains make the 90-minute journey every day. From a stop to the right of the train station, or from the inside the bus station, city buses #5 and 6 go directly to **Plaza de Zocodóver,** the center of town (80ptas). No Castilian city is as labyrinthine as Toledo; to make things worse, many of the streets are unmarked. Many major sights are near or atop the central hill, which is almost exactly circular.

Tourist Office: (tel. 22 08 43; fax 25 26 48), just outside the Puerta Nueva de Bisagra and Po. de Merchán, on the north side of town. From Pl. Zocodóver, take the main street leading downhill, C. Armas, through various name changes to the gate; pass under and cross the intersection. Open Mon.-Fri. 9am-2pm and 4-6pm, Sat. 9am-3pm and 4-7pm, Sun. 9am-3pm. For a map and rudimentary info without the walk, queue up at the gray **information booth,** Pl. Zocodóver (tel. 22 12 02). Open Mon.-Sat. 10am-6pm, Sun. and holidays 10am-3pm.

Post Office: C. Plata, 1 (tel. 22 36 11). Open for all services, including **telegrams,** Mon.-Fri. 8am-9pm, Sat. 9am-2pm; also open Sat. 2-7pm for telegrams only. **Postal Code:** 45001.

Telephones: C. Plata, 20. Open Mon.-Fri. 9:30am-1:30pm and 5-9pm, Sat. 9:30am-2:30pm. **City Code:** 925.

Trains: Po. Rosa (tel. 22 30 99), in a neo-Mudejar building opposite the Puente de Azarquiel. To Madrid's Estación de Atocha (8/day, 1½hr., round-trip 820ptas). No direct line to Ávila (connection in Madrid) or Andalucía (connection in Algodor or Aranjuez, depending on destination).

Buses: (tel. 21 58 50) in the Zona Safón, northeast of the old city walls. **Continental/Galiano** (tel. 22 29 61). To Madrid (12/day, 1hr., 510ptas).

Laundromat: Juan Pascual, C. Bolivia, 2 (tel. 22 16 03). Wash and dry 1325ptas/5kg. Open Mon.-Fri. 9am-1:30pm and 4-8pm.

Medical Assistance: Hospital Virgen de la Salud (tel. 26 92 00), on Avenida de Barber, toward Ávila highway.

Emergencies: tel. 091. **Police: Municipal,** Ayuntamiento, 1 (tel. 23 34 07).

ACCOMMODATIONS AND CAMPING

Finding a bed during summer weekends can be difficult.

Residencia Juvenil "San Servando" (HI), Castillo San Servando (tel. 22 45 54), uphill on the left from the train station (15min.). Pool, TV room, and modern bathrooms. 96 rooms, each with 3 bunk beds, many with views. Anyone returning alone at night should take a cab. Reception open 7:50am-11:50pm. Curfew around 11:50pm. 650ptas. Breakfast included. Hot water 8:30-9:30am and 8-10pm. Reserve ahead; the hostel sometimes books large groups.

Hostal Residencia Labrador, C. Juan Labrador, 16 (tel. 22 26 20). From Pl. Zocodóver take C. Barrio Rey. Almost a hotel, the 3 floors are rarely filled. Rooms are neat and whitewashed; some are spacious. Singles 1600ptas. Doubles with shower 2700ptas. Triples with shower 3800ptas. Quads with bath 5500ptas. Prices don't include IVA.

Hostal Las Armas, C. Armas, 7 (tel. 22 16 68), just off the low end of Pl. Zocodóver. This 200-year-old house, with low ceilings, narrow twisty steps, impossible angles and flowering patio, is like an Escher print—or a mini Toledo. Curfew 1am. Singles 1800ptas. Doubles 2900ptas. Triples 4000ptas. Prices don't include IVA. Open April-Oct.

Pensión Descalzos, C. Descalzos, 30 (tel. 22 28 88), down the steps off Po. San Cristobal or down the Bajada Descalzos, in the southwest corner of town. Close to the Casa del Greco and Iglesia Santo Tomé (and bus lines #2 and #3). New and roomy, with soft toilet paper, liquid soap and truly hot showers. Rooms at the

back look out over San Marín's bridge. Half of the 14 rooms have a view of San
Marín's Bridge. Singles 1875ptas. Doubles 3000ptas, with bath 4900ptas. Triples
6600ptas. Jan.-March 17 1500ptas, 2500ptas, 4000ptas, 5400ptas.

Pensión Lumbreras, C. Juan Labrador, 9 (tel. 22 15 71), near Hostal-Residencia
Labrador. Tired beds in unexceptional rooms. Singles 1300ptas. Doubles
2100ptas. One ample triple 3500ptas. Quads 4400ptas. Breakfast 175ptas.

Camping: Camping El Greco (tel. 22 00 90), 1.5km from town on the road to
Madrid (C-401), easily reached by bus #7. Wooded and shady 1st-class site
between the Tajo and an olive grove. 450ptas/person, tent, or car.

Circo Romano, Av. Carlos III, 19 (tel. 22 04 42). 2nd class site. Closer but noisier
and often in disrepair. 450ptas/person, tent, or car.

FOOD

Two-fork restaurants and not-so-cheap *cafeterías* abound; sleuth around. *Menús*
may be pricy (1200-1600ptas and up) but have well-prepared regional specialties.

Restaurante La Cubana, Po. Rosa, 2, across the river in front of Puente Viejo de
Alcántara, down the road from the youth hostel. It's a coin-flipper—the wooded,
tavern-like restaurant or the outdoor *terraza* with overhanging grapevines? *Gazpacho* (390ptas) and *pollo al ajillo* (garlic chicken, 725ptas). Other dishes significantly more expensive. Open daily 1-4pm and 8-11pm.

Cafetería Fuensalida-Manila, Pl. de Conde, 2, in the southwest corner of town. A
brick-walled, cavernous establishment underneath the Fuensalida Palace. Many
salads around 400ptas. Open 8am-11pm.

SIGHTS AND ENTERTAINMENT

Vestiges of circus, aqueduct, and sewer remain of the **Roman settlement.** Fortified
walls, attributed to King Wamba (7th century), surround the city. South and uphill
from the plaza is the **Alcázar,** Toledo's most formidable landmark. Little remains of
the original 13th-century structure; the building was largely reduced to rubble during the Civil War, as besieged Fascist troops held out against acute Republican bombardment. The rooms above ground are now a gung-ho, nationalistic military
museum, dedicated to the arms, uniforms, and medals of the Spanish foot soldier.
(Open Tues.-Sun. 9:30am-1:30pm and 4-6:30pm. 125ptas.) To the west, the grandiose **cathedral,** with 5 naves, delicate stained glass, and endless ostentation, soars
from the city center. As the seat of the Primate of Spain, the cathedral contains an
embarrassment of riches. The *Sacristía* hoards El Grecos and 2 Van Dycks. (Cathedral open Mon.-Sat. 10:30am-1pm and 3:30-7pm, Sun. 10:30am-1pm and 4-7pm;
Sept.-June Mon.-Sat. 10:30am-1pm and 3:30-7:30pm, Sun. 10:30am-1pm and 4-6pm.
To the Sala Capitular, Capilla del Rey, and Sacristía 300ptas.)

Greek painter Domenico Theotocopuli, alias El Greco, was a *toledano* most of his
life, painting wild skies and spindly saints in a warped version of Titian's palette. The
Casa del Greco (House of El Greco), at C. Levi, 3, isn't really the house in which he
lived but contains an okay collection of his paintings. (Was closed for renovation in
1993.) The nearby **Iglesia de Santo Tomé** displays El Greco's *El Entierro del Conde
de Orgaz* (The Burial of Count Orgaz). (Open Tues.-Sat. 10am-1:45pm and 3:30-
6:45pm, Sun. 10am-1:45pm; off-season Tues.-Sat. 10am-2pm and 3:30-6pm, Sun.
10am-1:45pm. 100ptas.)

Two synagogues are all that remain of what was once Spain's largest Jewish community, both in the **Judería** on the west side. The **Sinagoga del Tránsito** (1366) is a
simple building with wonderful Mudejar plasterwork and an *artesonado* (coffered)
ceiling. Manuscripts, lids of sarcophagi, inscriptions, and amulets stuff themselves
into the **Museo Sefardí** inside the synagogue. (Open Tues.-Sat. 10am-2pm and 4-
6pm, Sun. 10am-2pm. 200ptas.) **Sinagoga de Santa María la Blanca** (1180), down
the street, was the city's principal synagogue but was later converted to a church.
(Open daily 10am-2pm and 3:30-7pm; off-season 10am-2pm and 3:30-6pm.
100ptas.) Less touristed are the remnants of the city's Islamic past, near the Puerta

del Sol off C. Real de Arrabal. Both a Muslim and a Christian house of worship at different points in its life, the **Mezquita del Cristo de la Luz** is Toledo's oldest building (it's been around since the 10th century). The columns support arches inspired by the mosque at Córdoba. The Emirate was also responsible for the **hammams** (baths) on C. Angel.

At night, congregations of young people scarf *tapas* and swill beer to the east and west of Pl. Zocodóver, along **Calle de Santa Fe** and **Calle de la Sillería. T Beo,** Callejón de la Sillería (just off C. Sillería), is the place to dance.

■■■ SEGOVIA

Rising majestically above the Castilian countryside, the old city of Segovia offers beautiful golden churches, twisting alleyways, and a people fiercely proud of their city and province. Today its tourist appeal is slightly sterilized by self-satisfaction and commercialization, as Segovians find new and ever more artful ways to separate the tourist from his or her money.

ORIENTATION AND PRACTICAL INFORMATION

Segovia lies 88km northwest of Madrid on the rail line to Medino del Campo and Valladolid. To get to the tourist office from the bus or train station, take bus #2B (every 15min., 75ptas) to **Plaza Mayor** (a.k.a. Plaza de Franco).

> **Tourist Office:** Pl. Mayor, 10 (tel. 43 03 28), in front of bus stop, on the south side of the plaza. Complete information on accommodations, bus, train, and sights posted in windows. Open Mon.-Sat. 9:30am-2pm and 5-7pm, Sun. 10am-2pm.
>
> **Post Office:** Pl. Dr. Laguna, 5 (tel. 43 16 11), up C. Lecea from Pl. Mayor. Open for stamps, Lista de Correos, and **telegrams** Mon.-Sat. 8am-9pm. **Postal Code:** 40006.
>
> **Telephones:** C. Juan Bravo, 6. Open Mon.-Fri. 10am-1pm and 5-8:45pm, Sat. 10am-1:45pm. **City Code:** 911.
>
> **Trains:** Po. Obispo Quesada (tel. 42 07 74). To Madrid (5-12/day, 2hr., 565ptas). One train Mon., Fri., and Sat. goes to Medina del Campo and León with connections to Salamanca. **Luggage Storage** (300ptas/checked bag). Open daily 5:45am-11:30pm.
>
> **Buses: Estacionamiento Municipal de Autobuses,** Po. Ezequile González, 10 (tel. 42 77 25), on Po. Conde de Sepúlveda at Av. Fernández Ladreda. To: Avila (4/day, 495ptas); Madrid (10-15/day, 690ptas); Barcelona (1/day, 5080ptas).
>
> **Medical Assistance: Hospital de la Misericordia,** Dr. Velasco, 3 (tel. 43 08 12). **Ambulance** (tel. 43 01 00).
>
> **Emergencies: Police Municipal** (day tel. 42 12 12; night tel. 43 12 12).

ACCOMMODATIONS, CAMPING, AND FOOD

During the summer, finding a *hostal* room may be a nightmare; reservations are vital. You may want to consider visiting Segovia as a daytrip. **Hostal Juan Bravo,** C. Juan Bravo, 12 (tel. 43 55 21), right on the main thoroughfare in the old town, has bright, carpeted rooms with snazzy pictures. (Doubles 3200ptas, with bath 4100ptas. Triples 4400ptas, with bath 5500ptas.) **Camping Acueducto,** Ctra. Nacional, 601 (tel. 42 50 00), 2km from Segovia toward La Granja, is a 2nd-class site in the shadow of the Sierra de Guadarrama. (360ptas/person or tent. Open April-Sept.)

Segovia is famed for sublimely tender roast suckling pig *(cochinillo)* and lamb, but steer clear of Pl. Mayor and Pl. Azoquejo. **Mesón del Campesino,** C. Infanta Isabel, 12, opposite Vogue 2, has tall tables, young crowds, and filling portions. *(Platos combinados* 300-700ptas. *Menú* 850-1500ptas. Open Fri.-Wed. 11am-4pm and 8:30pm-midnight.) **Bar-Mesón Cueva de San Estéban,** C. Valdelaguila, 15, off the top of Pl. San Estéban, reached by C. Escuderos, has stone and mortar walls, wooden pygmy footstools for seats, and reasonable *menú* (800ptas). Entrees are 400ptas and up, and cold beer flows from the font at the cave's rear (125ptas).

SIGHTS

Supported by 128 pillars that span 813m, the 2 tiers of 163 arches of the **Acueducto Romano** are constructed of great blocks of granite—with no mortar. View it at its maximum height (28.9m) from Plaza del Azoguejo, or catch its profile from the steps on the left side of the plaza. The **Alcázar,** an archetypal late-medieval castle, juts audaciously into space at the far northern end of the old quarter. Isabel was crowned Queen of Castile in the Alcázar in 1474 (hence the streets named in her honor). Inside, instruments of destruction and mounted knights in armor terrorize from every side. (Alcázar open daily 10am-7pm; Oct.-March 10am-6pm. 350ptas, seniors 250ptas.) Commissioned by Carlos V in 1525, the **cathedral** towers above Pl. Mayor in the center of town. The late Gothic naves are impressively high, with a striking ceiling pattern of rib vaulting, and the stained-glass windows are ethereal. Skip the snoozy taped tour (50ptas) and luxuriate in the tranquil cloisters. The **museum** contains a fine assortment of Flemish tapestries and paintings. (Cathedral open 11am-2pm and 4-6pm. Museum open Mon.-Sat. 9am-7pm; Oct.-March Mon.-Fri. 9:30am-1pm and 3-6pm, Sat.-Sun. 9:30am-6pm. 200ptas.)

Nighttime activity calls for the Pl. Mayor and its tributaries. Pubs crowd **Calles Infanta Isabel** and **Isabel la Católica** (nicknamed "the streets of the bars"). **Pub Oja Blanca,** Pl. Mayor, 6, attracts a more uptown crowd. Three km to the northwest, **Zamarramala** hosts the **Fiestas de Santa Agueda** (St. Agatha) on the 2nd weekend in February, when women symbolically take over the town's administration, dress up in beautiful, old-fashioned costumes, and parade through the streets.

■ Near Segovia

The royal palace and grounds of **La Granja,** 11km southeast from Segovia, were built by the first Bourbon King Felipe V; "The Versailles of Spain" was one of 4 royal summer retreats (with El Pardo, El Escorial, and Aranjuez). Marble everywhere, windows framed by original 250-year-old lace curtains, ceilings painted in false perspective, and lavish crystal chandeliers (made in San Ildefonso's renowned crystal factory) are just the tip of the iceberg. (Palace open daily 10am-6pm; Oct.-March Mon.-Sat. 10am-1:30pm and 3-5pm, Sun. 10am-2pm. 500ptas, students, professors, and seniors 200ptas. EC citizens free on Wed.) Frequent **buses** leave Segovia for La Granja (6-10/day, 20min., 95ptas).

■■■ AVILA

Avila's fame is forever ensured by St. Teresa of Avila (1515-1582)—mystic, writer, reformer of monastic life, the nun who founded the Order of the Discalced Carmelites and whose raptures were immortalized in marble by Bernini. Because the city sits on a rocky escarpment high above the Río Adaja valley, Avila keeps cool in the summer while the plain swelters below. Within the classic medieval walls, carved images of bulls and hogs are mute reminders of a Celtiberian culture much older than the ancient fortifications. Avila proudly wears the oldest, most complete fortified medieval belt of any Spanish city. Construction of the **murallas medievales** began in 1090, but most were realized in the next century; the concentrated burst of activity lent the walls their unusual uniformity. Eighty-two massive towers reinforce walls whose thickness averages 3m. The best view of the walls and of Avila itself is from the **Cuatro Postes,** a tiny 4-pillared structure past the Río Adaja on the highway to Salamanca, 1.5km to the northwest of the city. The walls can be climbed along the Parador Nacional in Pl. Concepción Arenal.

Some believe that the profile of the **cathedral** looming over the watchtowers inspired St. Teresa's metaphor of the soul as a diamond castle. Begun in the 2nd half of the 12th century, the oldest Spanish cathedral in the transitional Romanesque-to-Gothic style recalls the long, turbulent centuries of the Reconquista, when war and religion went hand in hand. The small **museum** has a fine collection of gold and silver work, sculptures, and paintings from the 12th to 18th centuries, including a small El Greco. (Cathedral open daily 8am-1pm and 3-7pm; Oct.-April daily only to 5pm. Free. Museum open daily 10am-1:30pm and 3-7pm; Oct.-April only to 6pm. 200ptas.) Most of St. Teresa's mystical experiences took place during the 30 years she spent in the **Convento de la Encarnación.** The tiny cell where she lived is through the farthest door in the farthest chapel. Upstairs from the cloister, a museum features a collection of furnishings, letters and other personal effects. (Open daily 9:30am-1:30pm and 3:30-6pm; winter 9:30am-1pm and 4-7pm. Obligatory tour in Spanish 75ptas.) Locals built the **Convento de Santa Teresa** in the 17th century on the site of her parents' home. The church's restrained façade offers no hint of the extravagance of the chapel built over Teresa's birth spot. Among other treasures, the convent supposedly holds one of Teresa's severed fingers; the other nine are somewhere else. (Open daily 9:30am-1:30pm and 3:30-7pm. Free.)

Accommodations, Food, and Practical Information Lodgings in Avila are expensive. Many visitors make this a (somewhat rushed) daytrip from Madrid. **Residencia Juvenil "Duperier" (HI),** Av. Juventud (tel. (918) 21 35 48), is cute but only has 10 beds. (Curfew 11pm. 650ptas/person. With 1 meal 1000ptas.) The **Hostal Santa Ana,** C. Alfonso Montalvo, 2 (tel. (918) 22 00 63), off Pl. Santa Ana, down Av. José Antonio from the train station, is an efficiently run *hostal;* sheets are snow-white, baths are spic and span. (Doubles 3000ptas. Triples 4000ptas. Oct.-July 14 2800ptas, 3700ptas. Showers 200ptas.)

The city won fame for its *ternera de Avila* (veal) and *mollejas* (sweetbread). The *yemas de Santa Teresa* or *yemas de Avila,* local confections made of egg yolks and honey, and *vino de Cebreros,* the smooth regional wine, are delectable. **Plaza de la Victoria** is a center of budget dining, though the atmosphere and prices are tourist-inspired. Every Friday (9am-2pm), a **mercado típico** in Pl. Victoria sells local food, flowers, and crafts. **Mesón El Rastro,** Pl. Rastro, 4, at C. Cepadas and C. Caballeros at the southern wall, is a large, noisy dining hall decked out like a hunting lodge. Expect to wait; it's popular. Choose from the 2 *menús del día* (1400ptas), both of which feature hearty portions. (Entrees 600-1500ptas. Open daily 1-4pm and 9:30-11pm.) Unpretentious **Restaurante El Ruedo,** C. Enrique Larreta, 7, serves regional specialties. (*Menú* 1190ptas. Open Wed.-Sun. 1:30-4:30pm and 8pm-midnight.)

Avila's **tourist office,** Pl. Catedral, 4 (tel. (918) 21 13 87), is directly opposite the cathedral. From Pl. Santa Teresa, walk through the main gate and turn right up winding C. Cruz Vieja. (Open Mon.-Fri. 9am-8pm, Sat. 9am-3pm, Sun. 11am-3pm; Oct.-May Mon.-Fri. 9am-2pm and 4-6pm, Sat. 9am-2pm.) The **bus station** is on Av. Madrid at Av. Portugal (tel. (918) 22 01 54), on the northeast side of town. Buses run to Segovia (1-5/day, 45min., 475ptas); Salamanca (5-9/day, 1½hr., 705ptas); and Madrid (3/day, 2hr., 650ptas). To reach the Pl. Santa Teresa, cross the street and walk down C. Duque de Alba. The **train station,** Av. Portugal, 17 (tel. (918) 22 01 88; info tel. 22 65 79), is at the end of Av. José António on the northeast side of town. Trains head to Medina del Campo (16/day, 1hr., 465ptas; change here for Segovia); Salamanca (13/day, 2hr., 565ptas); and Madrid (28/day, 2hr., 575-1000ptas). To reach Pl. Santa Teresa from the train station (northeast of the center), follow Avenida José António to Calle de Isaac Peral, bear right, and turn left on C. Duque de Alba. Municipal buses run from nearby the train station to the Pl. de la Victoria.

■■■ SALAMANCA

For centuries the "hand of Salamanca," the brass knocker traditionally found on the doors of this city, has welcomed students, scholars, rogues, royals, and saints. In the old city, golden sandstone has lent itself to every major architectural style from Romanesque to baroque; even the modern quarters are largely built from it. The university here is Spain's oldest (founded in 1218), and the perfect balance of the active and the contemplative life is the hallmark of the Salmantine way. In summer, a huge influx of foreign students adds a certain tang to the atmosphere, but the city in winter, with a thin layer of snow on the cathedrals, is hauntingly attractive.

ORIENTATION AND PRACTICAL INFORMATION

Most sights and a great deal of cheap food and accommodations lie south of the **Plaza Mayor.** The **Universidad** is south of the Plaza Mayor, near the **Pl. de Anaya.** Whether you arrive by bus or train, you'll be 20 minutes from the town center. From the train station, catch the bus that goes to **Plaza Mercado** (next to Pl. Mayor). From the bus station, either catch bus #4 to Pl. Mercado or walk down Calle de Filiberto Villalobos, cross the busy main road and plummet down Calle Ramón y Cajal; then turn left and immediately right up Calle Prior, which runs directly to Pl. Mayor.

Tourist Office: Municipal, Pl. Mayor (tel. 21 83 42). Open Mon.-Fri. 10am-1:30pm and 4-6pm, Sat. 10am-2pm. **Provincial,** Gran Vía, 39-41 (tel. 26 85 71). Open Mon.-Fri. 9:30am-2pm and 4:30-7pm, Sat. 10am-2pm, Sun. 11am-2pm.

Budget Travel: TIVE, Po. Carmelitas, 83 (tel. 26 77 31). Long lines; go early. Open Mon.-Fri. 9am-2pm. **Viajes Juventus,** Pl. Libertad, 14 (tel. 21 74 07).

Currency Exchange: American Express, Pl. del Campillo, 4 (tel. 43 70 02). Checks cashed; no mail pick-up. Open Mon.-Fri. 9:30am-1:30pm and 4:30-8pm, Sat. 10am-1:30pm; Nov.-May Mon.-Fri. 9:30am-1:30pm and 4-7:30pm, Sat. 10am-1:30pm. For lost checks call (900) 99 44 26. 24-hr. service.

Post Office: Gran Vía, 25 (tel. 24 30 11). Open for stamps and information Mon.-Fri. 9am-2pm and 4-6pm, Sat. 9am-2pm; for Lista de Correos Mon.-Fri. 9am-2pm; for **telegrams** Mon.-Sat. 9am-9pm. **Postal Code:** 37008.

Telephones: Pl. Peña Primera, 1, off Pl. Bandos. Open Mon.-Sat. 9am-3pm and 4-11pm. **City Code:** 923.

Trains: Po. Estación Ferrocarril (tel. 26 33 33). **RENFE office**, Pl. Libertad, 10 (tel. 21 24 54). Open Mon.-Fri. 9am-1pm and 5-7pm. To: Avila (5/day, 1hr., 620ptas); León (4-5/day, 3½hr., 1540ptas); Madrid (2-4/day, 3½hr., 123ptas); Barcelona (at 10:15pm, 14hr., 6000ptas); Porto, Portugal (2/day, 8½hr., 2855ptas).

Buses: Av. Filiberto Villalobos, 71 (tel. 23 67 17 or 23 22 66). To: Avila (1-4/day, 1-2hr., 740ptas); Segovia (Mon.-Sat. 3/day, 2hr., 1250ptas); Madrid (very frequent, 2½-3hr., 1525-1910ptas); León (4-6/day, 3hr., 1500ptas); Barcelona (2-3/day, 11½hr., 5700ptas).

Medical Assistance: Hospital Clínico, Po. San Vicente, 23 (tel. 29 11 00). **Ambulance** (tel. 24 09 16, 25 54 64, or 24 37 87).

Emergencies: tel. 092. **National Police** tel. 091. **Municipal Police** tel. 21 96 00, in Ayuntamiento.

ACCOMMODATIONS AND CAMPING

Many students, many rooms. Plenty of cheap *pensiones* off the side streets from Pl. Mayor, especially on **Calle Meléndez,** just south of the plaza.

Pensión Marina, C. Doctrinos, 4, 3rd floor. (tel. 21 65 69), between C. Compania and C. Prado. Mammoth bedrooms, bubbly owners, and 2 TV lounges. One single 1600ptas. Doubles 2200ptas.

Pensión Barez, C. Meléndez, 19 (tel. 21 74 95). Owners treat you like one of the family. Shiny clean. Balcony rooms with a view of San Benito. TV lounge with table. 1100ptas/person; Oct.-May 1000ptas. Showers 125ptas.

Hostal Carabela, Po. Canalejas, 10-12 (tel. 26 07 08), off Pl. España. Tends to be noisy; rooms are impeccable if uninspiring. Tight baths. Singles 2000ptas, with shower or bath 2600ptas. Doubles 2600ptas, with shower or bath 2900ptas. Nov.-Feb.: 1800ptas; 2300ptas; 2400ptas; 2600ptas. Showers 150ptas. Prices do not include IVA.

Hostal Oriental, C. Azafranal, 13 (tel. 21 21 15), halfway between Pl. Mayor and Pl. España. Wimpy singles and hefty doubles, some jazzed up by colorful floor tiles and teeny tables. Singles 1700ptas. Doubles 3200ptas. Showers free-250ptas.

Camping: Regio (tel. 13 88 88), 4km toward Madrid, has the nicest sites. Part of a complex that includes a 4-star hotel and pool. 450ptas/person, car, or tent. **Don**

Quijote (tel. 25 75 04), 4km toward Aldealengua. 300ptas/person, 325ptas/tent. Open March-Oct.

FOOD

Every clique has its favorite café in **Plaza Mayor;** all serve the same moderately good food at a standard, slightly inflated price. During the academic year (Oct.-May), drop in on the **Comedor Universitario,** the university dining hall open to the public. (Meals 600ptas or less.) Don't miss *jeta,* a local *tapas* specialty (fried pig lips). The daily **market** (8:30am-2pm) peddles on Pl. Mercado to the east of Pl. Mayor.

Restaurante El Bardo, C. Compania, 8. Three tiers serve excellent 3-course vegie and classic 2-course *menús* at lunch. Lively at midday; more sedate at night. A la carte meal 1500ptas. Open Nov.-Sept. Tues.-Sun. 11am-4pm and 7pm-midnight.

Imbis, R. Mayor, 31. Good selection of *tapas. Platos combinados* about 700ptas. *Menú* 1000-1100ptas. Open 8am-midnight.

Restaurante Vegetariano El Trigal, C. Libreros, 20 (tel. 21 56 99), near the cathedral and the Patio de las Escuelas. An intimate setting, with polished wood floors and birds. Lo and behold, it's a yoga center, too! Creative *menú* 775, 825, or 1300ptas. *Platos combinados* 675ptas. Open daily 1-4pm and 8:30-11pm.

SIGHTS

Here there are splendid examples of Roman, Romanesque, Gothic, Renaissance and baroque structures, all in sandstone. Nowhere is the golden glow more apparent than in the **Plaza Mayor,** a trapezoid begun in 1729 during the reign of Felipe V. Between the arches—almost 100 of them—hang medallions with bas-reliefs of famous Spaniards, from El Cid to Franco. One of the city's most celebrated land-marks, the 15th-century **Casa de las Conchas** (House of Shells), is adorned by rows of scallop shells chiseled in sandstone. Pilgrims who journeyed to Santiago de Compostela wore shells like these as a token of their visit to St. James the Apostle's tomb. (Closed while under renovations. Now a public library.)

The focal point of Salamanca, the **Universidad,** is entered from the **Patio de las Escuelas,** off C. Libreros. The university's **entryway** is one of the best examples of Spanish Plateresque, a style named for the filigree work of *plateros* (silversmiths). Some bystanders may be seeking out Salamanca's gray mascot: a smallish frog carved on a skull on the right side of the façade. It's said to represent the dankness of prison life, but those wacky students allege it brings them good luck on exams. Another bizarre tradition holds that if you spot it without help you'll be married within the year. Inside the **Escuelas Menores,** also on the Patio de las Escuelas, is the *Cielo de Salamanca* (Sky of Salamanca), a 15th-century fresco of the zodiac. (University open Mon.-Fri. 9:30am-1:30pm and 4:30-6:30pm, Sat. until 6pm, Sun. 10am-1pm. 200ptas, seniors 100ptas, students free.) To the right of the principal entrance to the university is the absorbing **Casa-Museo de Unamuno,** featuring the philosopher-poet's scatterbrained ruminations on his birth in the first window of manuscripts, and his dexterous origami in the study. (Open Tues.-Fri. 11am-1:30pm and 4:30-6:30pm, Sat.-Sun. 10am-2pm. Free.)

Begun in 1513 to accommodate the growing tide of Catholics, the spindly spires of the **catedral nueva** weren't finished until 1733. The Romanesque **catedral vieja** (1140) has an amazing central altarpiece by Nicolas Florentino that narrates the story of the Virgin Mary in 53 scenes. The **cathedral museum** features a paneled ceiling by Fernando Gallegos, Salamanca's most famous painter, and houses the Salinas organ, named for the blind musician to whom Fray Luís dedicated an ode. (Cathedrals open daily 10am-2pm and 4-8pm; Oct.-March 10am-1pm and 4-6pm. Old cathedral, cloister, and museum via new cathedral, 200ptas. New cathedral free.) In the center of the **Puente Romano,** a 2000-year-old Roman bridge spanning the Tormes, stands the **Toro Ibérico,** a huge headless granite bull. The bridge was part of an ancient Roman road called the Camino de la Plata (Silver Way) that went from Mérida, in Extremadura, to Astorga, near León.

Ambiente, an inexpensive pamphlet sold at kiosks, lists movies and special events. Posters at the **Colegio Mayor** (Palacio de Anaya) advertise university events, free films and student theater. The **Plaza Mayor** is the social as well as geographic center of town; people overflow from the plaza as far west as **San Vicente.** A lot of the student nightlife also concentrates on the **Gran Vía** and side streets. **Café Novelty,** on the northeast corner of Pl. Mayor, is the oldest café in town and a meeting place for students and professors. Miguel de Unamuno was a regular. Also try **Café El Corrillo,** Pl. Mayor by C. Juan del Rey. **Pub Rojo y Negro,** C. Espoz y Mina sells scrumptious coffee, liquor and ice cream concoctions (250-600ptas) in an old-fashioned red and black setting. There's a dance floor down below. (Open daily until 12:30am.) Dance at **Camelot,** C. Bordadores, near several other clubs/pubs.

■■■ LEÓN

In Spain the city is called *la ciudad azul* (the blue city), after the dominant hue of the cathedral's stained glass windows. Some think that, given the urban grime, it should be renamed *La Ciudad Dingy Grey*. Once a springboard for the Reconquista, León owes its continuing material comfort to the fertile agricultural hinterland, and to the deposits of iron and cobalt mined throughout the province.

Proud *Leóneses* claim that their **cathedral** is the most beautiful in the land. A splendid **museo** on the evolution of Romanesque sculpture hides beyond the vast cloister and twisting sculptures. (Museum open daily 9:30am-1:30pm and 4-7pm. Cloister and museum 300ptas, cloister only 100ptas.) The **Basílica de San Isidoro** was dedicated in the 11th century to San Isidoro of Sevilla, whose remains were brought to León while Muslims ruled the south. The corpses of León's royal family rest in the impressive **Panteón Real,** but more lively fun is overhead: remarkably vibrant tempera frescoes cover 2 crypt ceilings. (Open Mon.-Sat. 10am-1:30pm and 4-6:30pm, Sun. 10am-1:30pm. With tour 300ptas.) The city's **murallas romanas** are well preserved around the cathedral and San Isidoro.

Accommodations, Food, and Practical Information For lodging, look on **Avenida de Roma, Avenida de Ordoño II,** and their side streets, which lead into the new town from Pl. Guzmán el Bueno. The **Residencia Juvenil Infanta Doña Sancha (HI),** C. Corredera, 2 (tel. (987) 20 22 01, 20 38 11), 2 blocks past the Jardín San Francisco, is a clean university dorm during the school year. (Singles, doubles, and triples available. 700ptas/person. *Pensión media* 1200ptas. *Pensión completa* 1550ptas. Over 26: 900ptas; 800ptas; 1600ptas; 2100ptas. Often booked solid; call ahead. Open July-Aug.) **Consejo de Europa (HI),** Po. Parque, 2 (tel. (987) 20 02 06), off Pl. Toros, is recently renovated. (800ptas, over 26 950ptas. Often booked solid; call ahead. Open July-Aug.) The chatty proprietors of **Hostal Oviedo,** Av. Roma, 26 (tel. (987) 22 22 36) offer large rooms with many terraces. (Singles 1500ptas. Doubles 2500ptas. Triples 3300ptas. Showers 250ptas.)

Food in the buff is sold at **Mercado Municipal del Conde,** Pl. Conde, off C. General Mola. (Open Mon.-Sat. 9am-2pm.) Inexpensive places cluster by the cathedral on **C. Cid** and nearby streets. Also seek around **Plazas Mayor** and **San Martín. Bar-Restaurante Cortijo Susi,** C. López Castillón, 8, is a friendly, family-run place with a lively adjoining bar. A tasty *paella* starts off the 800pta *menu*. (Open Mon.-Sat. 1-4:30pm and 8:30-11:30pm.) The **Cafetería-Restaurante Catedral,** by the cathedral at C. Mariano Dominjuez Berrueta, 17, has impressive leather chairs for a needed respite after the filling 950pta *menu de la dia*. (Open Mon.-Sat. 1-4pm and 8pm-midnight.)

León's **tourist office** is at Pl. Regla, 3 (tel. (987) 23 70 82, fax 27 33 91), in front of the cathedral. (Open Mon.-Fri. 9am-2pm and 4-6pm, Sat. 10am-1pm.) The **telephone office** is at C. Burgo Nuevo, 15. (Open Mon.-Fri. 9am-2:30pm and 4-10:30pm, Sat. 9am-2pm and 4-9pm.) **Trains** leave from **RENFE,** Av. Astorga, 2 (tel. (987) 27 02 02), across the river from Pl. Guzmán el Bueno, at the bend in Av. Palencia. The 24-hr. ticket office is at C. Carmen, 4 (tel. (987) 22 05 25). Little engines that could run to: A Coruña (4/day, 7hr., 2600ptas), Madrid (5/day, 9½-11hr., 5900ptas), and other locales. **Buses** leave from Estación de Autobuses, Po. Ingeniero Saenz de Miera (tel. (987) 21 10 00); (Information open Mon.-Sat. 7:30am-9pm.) Buses chug to Madrid (7/day, 4½hr., 2225ptas) and Astorga (12/day, 1hr., 395ptas).

■■■ BURGOS

Everything in Burgos stands tall, from its starched citizens to the Gothic stone architecture for which it is famous. The *Cabeza de Castila* (Head of Castile), Burgos rose to prominence as capital of the province, then of the kingdom of Castile, claiming the purest form of Castilian. The town's other claim to fame is Rodrigo Díaz de Vivar, a.k.a. El Cid, Spain's real-life epic hero. Although not born here, his more memorable exploits took place in this suave, graceful city. Today, Burgos belies its conservative reputation with a lively youth culture and the international influence of backpacking pilgrims on their way to Santiago.

ORIENTATION AND PRACTICAL INFORMATION

Burgos lies about 240km north of Madrid on the main route between Madrid and France. The **cathedral** and most other monuments are found in the old city of plazas and curving streets. Across the river hulk the train and bus stations.

Tourist Office: Pl. Alonso Martínez, 7 (tel. 20 18 46). From Pl. José Antonio take Laín Calvo for 3 blocks. A variety of multilingual maps and brochures; even a computer to take you on a video tour of the region. Open Mon.-Fri. 9am-2pm and 4:30-6:30pm, Sat. 10am-1:30pm.

Budget Travel: Viajes TIVE (tel. 20 98 81), in the Casa de Cultura on Pl. San Juan. Unmarked door; hang a left after entering. Student IDs (500ptas) and HI card (1800ptas). Some English spoken. Open Mon.-Fri. 9am-2pm.

Post Office: Pl. Conde de Castro, 1 (tel. 26 27 50), across the river from Pl. Primo de Rivera. Open for stamps, *Lista de Correos*, and **telegrams** Mon.-Fri. 8am-9pm, Sat. 9am-2pm. **Postal Code:** 09000.

Telephones: Telefónica, C. San Lesmes, 18, off Pl. España. Sends but doesn't receive **faxes.** Open Mon.-Sat. 9am-1pm and 5-9pm. **City Code:** 947.

Trains: at the end of Av. Conde Guadalhorce, across the river from Pl. Castilla (tel. 20 35 60). A 10-min. walk southwest of the city center. Information open daily 7am-11pm. **RENFE,** C. Moneda, 21 (tel. 20 91 31). Open Mon.-Fri. 9am-1pm and 4-7pm, Sat. 9am-1pm. To: Donostia/San Sebastián (11/day, 3hr., 1900ptas); León (5/day, 2hr., 1500ptas); Madrid (8/day, 3½hr., 1900-2600ptas); Barcelona (3/day, 8hr., 5100ptas); Santiago (1/day, 7hr., 4400ptas).

Buses: C. Miranda, 4 (tel. 20 55 65), off Plaza de la Vega. To: Madrid (10/day, 3hr., 1680ptas); Barcelona (4/day, 7hr., 4455ptas); León (1/day, 2hr., 1515ptas).

Medical Assistance: Casa de Socorro, Conde de Vallellano, 4 (tel. 26 14 10), at C. Ramón y Cajal near the post office.

Emergencies: tel. 091 or 092. **Ambulance,** tel. 24 12 12. **Police,** tel. 28 88 34 or 39.

ACCOMMODATIONS, CAMPING, AND FOOD

Head either to the streets radiating from the far side of Pl. Mayor or the neighborhood around Pl. Vega. **Hostal-Restaurante Castellano,** C. Laín Calvo, 48 (tel. 20 50 40) is near the tourist office, 2 blocks up from Pl. José Antonio, but only doubles have windows. (Singles 2000ptas. Doubles 3000ptas, shower included. Closed Dec. 20-Feb. 2.) **Hostal Niza,** C. General Mola, 12 (tel. 26 19 17), has meticulously color-coordinated rooms, each with 2 endearing little puffy chairs. (Singles 2120ptas. Doubles 3180ptas. Triples 3400ptas. Showers 250ptas.) At **Hostal Hidalgo,** C. Almirante Bonifaz, 14 (tel. 20 34 81), all rooms have high ceilings and wood floors. (Singles 1700ptas. Doubles 2700ptas.) The "fuentes Blancas" bus (65ptas) voyages to

Camping Fuentes Blancas, 3.5km outside Burgos. (Open April-Sept., 425ptas/person, tent, or car.)

Landlocked Burgos means meat, meat and more meat. There are 2 markets: **Mercado Norte** near Pl. España and the smaller **Mercado de Abastos,** on C. Miranda near the bus station. (Open Mon.-Sat. 7am-3pm. Mercado Norte. Fri., 5:30-8pm.) **Mesón de los Herreros,** C. San Lorenzo, 20, between Pl. Mayor and Pl. Alonso Martínez, means *tapas*-o-rama. Only diehards eat the *morritos* (pig nose) or *sesos* (lamb brains). (*Raciones* 300-800ptas. Open Mon.-Sat. 9:30am-3:30pm and 6pm-12:30am, Sun. 11am-3:30pm and 6pm-midnight.) **Biodega Riojana,** Pl. Alonso Martínez, 9 , on the corner of C. San Juan has *cerveza*-induced exuberance and neighborly *tapas,* but weak decor. Open 9am-3pm and 7-10:30pm.)

SIGHTS AND ENTERTAINMENT

The slender, lacy spires of the **cathedral** soar above the city. A powerful group of 13th-century gentlemen sheep farmers (the Mesta) paid for this Gothic masterpiece with funds from their extraordinary merino wool. In the **Capilla Mayor,** at the east end, El Cid's bones and those of his wife Jimena commingle in marmoreal serenity. Before leaving the cathedral, look for the fly catcher high up near the main door in the central aisle. As it strikes the hours, this strange creature opens its mouth in imitation of the crowds gawking below. (Cathedral open 9:30am-1pm and 4-7pm. Free. Chapels or museum 350ptas, students 100ptas.) After the cathedral, the **Estatua de El Cid** in Pl. General Primo de Rivera is Burgos's most venerated landmark. Rodrigo Díaz de Vivar (Cid comes from the Arabic for Lord) won his fame through bold exploits at home and in battle against both Moors and Christians.

Past the **Casa del Cordón,** where Columbus met with Fernando and Isabel after his second trip to America, and Felipe el Hermoso (the Handsome) died after a trying game of *pelota* (jai-alai), is the **Museo de Pintura Marceliano Santa Maria.** Rich landscape scenes and portraits by Marceliano Santa María, a 20th-century local artist, hang within. (Open Tues.-Sat. 10am-2pm and 5-8pm, Sun. 10am-2pm. 25ptas, students free.)

Take the "Barrio del Pilar" bus from El Cid's statue in Pl. Primo de Rivera (55ptas), 1km west of Burgos to the **Museo-Monasterio de las Huelgas Reales**, a summer palace of Castilian kings and later a convent for Cistercian nuns. The convent only accepted the elite of the elite, led by an abbess who was rumored to be only slightly less regal than the queen herself. It now contains the **Museo de Telas** (textile museum) and Gothic cloister. (Open Tues.-Sat. 10:30am-2pm and 4-6:30pm, Sun. and holidays 10:30am-3pm. 400ptas, free Wed.). The **Cartuja de Miraflores** is a Carthusian monastery that houses the ornate tombs of King Juan II of Castile, Queen Isabel of Portugal, and their son Don Alfonso. Debate rages as to whether Alfonso's early death was caused by scheming noblemen or a bad cold. (Open Tues.-Sat. 10:15am-3pm and 4-6pm, Sun. and holidays 11:20am-12:30pm, 1-3pm, and 4-6pm. Mass Mon.-Sat. 9am, Sun. and holidays 7:30am and 10:15am. Free.) To get here, take the "Fuentes Blancas" bus (4/day from Pl. Primo de Rivera, 65ptas) or walk 3km east along the Paseo de La Quinta.

Nightlife in Burgos rivals that of Spain's larger cities. Students congregate in the zone next to the cathedral (known as **Las Llanas**) and **Pl. Huerto del Rey** (at the center of the zone). The elegant and relatively tranquil cafés along Paseo del Espolón draw a slightly more mature crowd. **La Trastienda,** just off the Paseo at the corner of C. Eduardo Martinez de Campo, 4, attracts young members of all sexual orientations. Draft beer 125ptas. Nightlife switches into high gear from June 23 to July 8, when Burgos honors its patron saints Peter and Paul with concerts, parades, fireworks, bullfights, and dances. The day after Corpus Christi, citizens parade through town with the *Pendón de las Navas,* a banner captured from the Moors in 1212.

NORTHERN SPAIN

For ages, religious pilgrims en route to Santiago de Compostela (Christianity's third most holy city after Jerusalem and Rome) have crossed the French border into northern Spain in search of spiritual knowledge. Whether you seek fulfillment in sun-worship, on a pair of skis, or in front of the fiery nostrils of a bewildered bull, the area remains a haven. The autonomous communities of Aragón, Navarra and Euskadi (the Basque Country) all share a border with France. Cantabria picks up where Euskadi leaves off along the North Atlantic coast, Asturias is west of Cantabria and tiny Galicia occupies the far northwest corner of the country. The Pyrenees loom along most of the border; use Jaca in Aragón as a base for mountain adventure. Out of the mountains in Navarra, Pamplona and its bulls are the most well-known attraction. When you tire of playing Hemingway's game, know that some of the most beautiful beaches in the world stretch along the Atlantic from San Sebastián (Donostia) to Santander (whence ferries leave for Plymouth, England). Both the inland scenery and the politics grow more complex in the restive Basque provinces.

A rest stop on the Celts' journey to Ireland around 900 BC, Galicia's past lives on in the form of rich supernatural folklore, *gaitas* (bagpipes), Celtic inscriptions, and *dólomes* (funerary chambers). Rivers wind through Galicia's rolling hills, stone-walled farms, and slate-roofed fishing villages, and gradually widen into the famous rías (inlets) that empty into the Cantabrian Sea and the Atlantic. Galicians maintain their own language, *gallego*, which is closer to Portuguese than to Castilian.

The Basques have called Iberia home for longer than any other ethnic group, tenaciously fighting off all incursions. The 3 Basque provinces of Guipúzcoa (Gipuzkoa), Vizcaya (Bizkaia) and Alava (Araba), and their respective major cities—San Sebastián (Donostia), Bilbao (Bilbo) and Vitoria-Gasteiz cozy up to France on the Atlantic coast. A distinct culture and unique language (which linguists have been unable to relate conclusively to any other) combine with a lingering resentment of the atrocities committed by the Nationalists during the Civil War to feed aspirations of greater autonomy. Most Basques wish to remain part of Spain, but the minority that does not, comprised of terrorist group ETA and their political counterparts, Herri Batasuna (HB), is extremely vociferous. Pro-ETA posters and graffiti abound, but waning support and police crackdowns have reduced the violence that once plagued the tempestuous landscapes and industrial conglomerations of the Basque country. The lightning-fast sport of *pelota* (jai alai) was born here, and Basque cooking is famous for its richness and variety. *Bacalao a la vizcaína* (salt cod in a tomato sauce) and *chipirones en su tinta* (cuttlefish in its own ink) have become popular throughout the Iberian peninsula.

■■■ SANTIAGO DE COMPOSTELA

Embraced by the Ríos Tambre and Ulla, Santiago was founded in 813, when, according to legend, Bishop Teodomiro informed Asturian King Alfonso II of the miraculous discovery of a tomb containing the remains of the Apostle St. James. In his Spanish incarnation, the gruesomely named St. James the Moorslayer (Santiago Matamoros) occasionally appeared on a white charger to lead the Christian forces into battle. Santiago thus became one of Christianity's three holy cities, and—like Rome and Jerusalem—the destination of pilgrimages. The clever Benedictine monks built monasteries to host the pilgrims on the way, giving rise to the first large-scale tourist industry in European history. Pilgrims from all over Spain and Europe still follow the superhighway (Ctra. 120) to Santiago. In 1993, an estimated 5 million tourists (believers and otherwise) added their forces to the 30,000 university students already here, overwhelming Santiago's population of 100,000.

ORIENTATION AND PRACTICAL INFORMATION

The **cathedral** marks the center of the old city, which is corralled in by **R. Fonte Santo Antonio (C. Calvo Sotelo)** and sits higher than the new city. Three streets lead directly to the cathedral from the south side of town (train station side): **Rúa do Franco** (Calle del Franco), **Rúa do Vilar** (Rúa del Villar) and **Rúa Nova** (Calle Nueva). From the train station, turn right at the top of the stairs and take C. Hórreo to **Praza de Galiza** (do *not* take Avenida de Lugo). From here, it's one more block to **Entrecalles**, from which the 3 cathedral-bound streets spring. From the bus station, take bus #10 to Pr. Galiza (every 10-15min., 70ptas).

Tourist Office: R. Villar, 43 (tel. 58 40 81), in the old town. Open Mon.-Fri. 9am-2pm and 4-7pm, Sat. 10am-1:30pm.

Budget Travel: TIVE, Plazuela del Matadero, s/n (tel. 57 24 26), up R. Fonte Santo Antonio (Calvo Sotelo) from Pr. Galiza. ISIC 500ptas. HI card 1800ptas. Open Mon.-Fri. 9am-2pm.

American Express: Ultratur Viajes, Av. Figueroa, 6 (tel. 58 70 00). Open Mon.-Fri. 9am-2pm and 4:30-7pm. Sat. 9am-2pm.

Post Office: Travesra Fonseca (tel. 58 12 52; fax 56 32 88), on the corner of R. Franco. Open for stamps and Lista de Correos Mon.-Fri. 8am-9pm, Sat. 9am-2pm; for **telegrams** Mon.-Fri. 8am-9pm, Sat. 9am-7pm; for **faxes** Mon.-Fri 8am-9pm, Sat. 9am-9pm. **Postal Code:** 15080.

Telephones: C. Bautizados, 13, in the old town off Pl. Toral. Open Mon.-Fri. 10am-11:30pm, Sat. 10am-8pm, Sun. 11am-3pm and 5-9:30pm. **Telephone Code:** 981.

Trains: R. General Franco (tel. 52 02 02). Information open Mon.-Sat. 7am-11pm, Sun. 7am-1pm. To: Madrid (2/day, 8hr., 4625-6810ptas); Pontevedra (11/day, 1¼hr., 375ptas); A Coruña (14/day, 1hr., 360-670ptas, *talgo* 845ptas); Barcelona (2/day, 7hr., 7210ptas).

Buses: Estación Central de Autobuses (tel. 58 77 00), C. San Cayetano. Nothing central about it, but #10 bus leaves every 15min. for center, 70ptas. Information open 8am-10pm. **ALSA** tel. 58 64 53. To: Madrid (2/day, 8-9hr., 5365ptas); Donostia/San Sebastián (1/day, 6hr., 3120ptas); Bilbo (2/day, 9½hr., 5895ptas). **Castromil** tel. 58 97 00. To: A Coruña (17/day, 1½hr., 675ptas); Pontevedra (15/day, 1½hr., 540ptas). **Empresa Freire** tel. 58 81 11. To Amsterdam, Paris, Hamburg, and Zürich.

Luggage Storage: At the **train station** (lockers 300ptas). Open 7:30am-11pm. At the **bus station** (75ptas/bag). Open 8am-10pm.

Laundromat: Lava-Express, C. República El Salvador, 21 (tel. 59 00 95), in the new town at the corner with C. Alfredo Brañas. Self-service wash and dry 550ptas/4kg. Open Mon.-Fri. 9:30am-2pm and 4-8:30pm, Sat. 10am-2pm.

Medical Assistance: Hospital Xeral, C. Galeras (tel. 54 00 00).

Emergency: Ambulance: tel. 59 36 56. **Policía municipal** tel. 092.

ACCOMMODATIONS, CAMPING, AND FOOD

Rúa do Vilar and **Calle Raiña** spill over with *fondas* and *pensiones,* and every other building in town has a hand-drawn *"habitaciones"* sign. **Hospedaje Ramos,** C. Raiña, 18, 2nd floor (tel. 58 18 59), is simple but comfortable and clean; rooms with private baths are sweeter and a far better deal (though the public bath is spotless). (Singles 1300ptas, with bath 1500ptas. Doubles 2200ptas, with bath 2500ptas.) **Hopedaje Sofia,** C. Cardenal Paya, 16 (tel. 58 51 50), has immense rooms and a caring owner who may let you use the kitchen if you're nice. And charming or not, everyone benefits from the hot, hot water in spotless bathrooms (Singles 1700ptas. Doubles 2900ptas. Prices lower in winter.) **Camping As Cancelas,** R. 25 de Xullo, 35 (tel. 58 02 66), sits 2km from the cathedral on the northern edge of town. Take bus #6 or 9. Souvenirs, laundry, supermarket and pool make this the Club Med of camping. (475ptas/person, 490ptas/car or tent.)

Pilgrims need to eat too; Santiago is a budget diner's dream. Most restaurants are in the old town east of the cathedral, notably on **Rúa del Villar, Rúa Franco,** and **Calle de la Raíña.** The open **market** stretches from Pl. San Felix to Convento de San

Augustín, north of the cathedral. (Open Mon.-Sat. 7:30am-2pm.) **Casa Manola,** R. Traviesa, 27, near the market and Pl. San Augustín, serves a 600pta *menú* of endless choices. Bread, wine, and a peach are included.) Snag a table beneath the archway outside at the **Café-Bar El Metro,** R. Nova, 12, and enjoy a 900pta pro-choice *menú* (Open daily 1-5pm and 8pm-midnight. Closed Christmas week and Semana Santa.)

SIGHTS AND ENTERTAINMENT

The entire old town has been designated a national monument; feast your art-historian's heart out on every door and square. The **cathedral's** kernel is an admirable Romanesque Latin cross with ambulatory and radiating chapels. The cathedral has 4 façades, each a masterpiece from a different period, and 4 separate entrances, each opening onto a different **plaza:** Pr. Platerías, Quintana, Obradoiro or Azabaxería. The **Pórtico de la Gloria,** facing the Praza da Obradoiro, is oft considered the crowning achievement of Spanish Romanesque sculpture. Inside the cathedral, Santiago's revered remains lie beneath the high altar in a silver coffer, while his more savory bejeweled bust sits above. The **museo** and **claustros** impress some people with gorgeous 16th-century tapestries, so detailed that they threaten to leave your eyes permanently crossed if you look too closely. (Museum open 10:30am-1:30pm and 4-6:30pm, holidays 10:30am-1:30pm. Museum and cloisters 200ptas.) Near Pr. Camino, both the **Museo do Pobo Galego** and the **Museo Municipal** exhibit interesting tidbits of Galician culture in the Gothic **Igrexa de Santo Domingo.** (Open Mon.-Sat. 10am-1pm and 4-7pm. Free.)

Crowds of all ages flood the city's cellars for mix-and-match nightlife. (All clubs open roughly 11pm-4am, with action starting well after midnight; women generally free, men 400-600ptas.) Santiago's **fiestas** occur July 18 to 31. The climax is the bacchanalian Féstival del Apóstol, on July 25.

■ Near Santiago: Rías Bajas (Rías Baixas)

Protected coves lure *galegos* to the *Rías* (estuaries) for weekend visits. Tourism is gradually eclipsing fishing as the main local industry, since foreigners as well as Spaniards realized there are reasons to travel to the Rías other than the surf. Quaint stone villages and Celtic ruins speckle the countryside. Public transportation between towns in this area is sparse; either rent a car or plan your itinerary carefully.

North of Santiago North of Santiago, the Rías Altas stretch their watery fingers into the land from the province of Lugo down to Cabo Finisterre. In the misty mountains of Galiza the weather is anything but predictable (even in summer), but views are spectacular year-round. Thanks to a healthy burst of summer tourism from landlocked Spaniards, the Rías Altas have the resources to augment a relatively unspoiled coastline. An excellent base for seeing the Rías Altas,

La Coruña (A Coruña) also has a stellar nightlife, a historic old town, plenty of waterfront restaurants, and a couple of decent beaches. Linked to train and bus to the rest of Galiza, it makes an ideal base for exploration. The **tourist office** is at Dársena de la Marina (tel. (981) 22 18 22), near the waterfront. (Open Mon.-Fri. 9am-2pm and 4-6pm, Sat. 10:30am-1pm.) **Trains** leave from C. Joaquín Planelles, s/n (tel. (981) 23 03 09) for Vigo (8/day, 3hr., 880ptas). **Buses** serve the Rías Altas and surrounding area from C. Caballeros (tel. (981) 23 96 44), across Av. Alcalde Molina from the train station. Bus #1 (85ptas) runs from the train and bus stations to Turismo and the post office. For accommodations, scour **Calle Riego de Agua** and the entire area from Pl. Maria Pita down to Pl. San Agustín and C. San Andrés. **Fonda María Pita,** C. Riego de Agua, 38, 3rd floor (tel. (981) 22 11 87), is pristine, with white lace curtains. The cheery rooms, some huge, some with balcony, are always clean. (Singles, usually full, 1400ptas. Doubles with sink 2500ptas. Showers 100ptas.) There are 3 other attractive *hostales* in this building.

Excursions to the Rías Altas are many. In La Coruña's northern coast, where buses and trains seldom run and hitching is useless, rain forests give way to soft, empty beaches around the **Rías de Cedeira, Ortigueira** and **Viveiro.** Buses and the occasional FEVE train run inland to Ortigueira from Ferrol, but the sporadic coastal bus from A Coruña is preferable—you can always hop off if you see a place you like.

South of Santiago   Chiefly a port city, sprawling **Vigo** is noisy, polluted, and largely unattractive, but its ferries, buses, and trains shuttle visitors efficiently to the nearby Ría de Vigo and Río Miño. The **tourist office** is at As Avenidas, s/n (tel. (986) 43 05 77; open Mon.-Fri. 9am-2pm and 4:30-6:30pm, Sat. 10am-12:30pm). **Trains** leave from RENFE, Pl. de la Estación, s/n (tel. (986) 43 11 14) to Pontevedra (14/day, 35min., 210ptas); Santiago de Compostela (9/day, 2hr., 650ptas); A Coruña (8/day, 3hr., 1005ptas) and Porto, Portugal (3/day, 1365ptas). **Buses** leave from **Estación de Autobuses,** Av. Madrid, s/n (tel. (986) 37 34 11), for Santiago de Compostela (17/day, 2hr., 600ptas); A Coruña (10/day, 2½hr., 1005ptas), and Bayona (every ½hr 190ptas).

Budgeters come from far and wide for Vigo's inexpensive rooms, especially those on **Calle Alfonso XIII** (to the right from the train station). **Hostal Ría de Vigo,** C. Cervantes, 14 (tel. 43 72 40), left off C. Alfonso XIII, is simple, spacious, and squeaky-clean. (Singles with bath 1800ptas. Doubles with bath 3200ptas.) **Hostal-Residencia Madrid,** C. Alfonso XIII, 63 (tel. (986) 22 55 23), has singles for 1500ptas and doubles for 1700-1800ptas. The **Gran Vía** and **C. Venezuela** are clotted with outdoor *terrazas* and shiny, bright *cafeterías* that aren't overly expensive. **Cafetería Lido,** Gran Vía, 3, has an elegant, long wood bar with tables in back. (Veggie sandwiches 275ptas. Open Tues.-Sun. 7:30am-2am.)

Cangas and Baiona make the best beach excursions from Vigo. A ferry ride across the Ría de Vigo, **Cangas** is hardly an unspoiled paradise, but it does retain a small-town feeling and a white **beach. Ferries** go from Vigo to Cangas (every ½-hr., 20min., round-trip 375ptas). Twenty-one km southwest of Vigo, snug in its own mini estuary, lies **Bayona** (Baiona), the first European town to receive word of the discovery of the Americas, when La Pinta returned to its port in March, 1493. Now Bayona is a beach town with one *parador nacional* and a handful of churches to its credit. **Buses** leave Vigo for Bayona (every ½-hr., ¾-1¼hr., 190ptas).

■■■ SAN SEBASTIÁN (DONOSTIA)

This provincial capital is a blue-blood resort in a come-here-to-die setting. By day, crowds flock to La Concha, the crescent-shaped strip of sand that hugs the Mar Cantábrico. On either side of this giant playground, 2 steep hills elbow their way into the sea. They call San Sebastián "the seashell with the pearl" because La Concha curves like an oyster round a pearl-like islet in the bay. The separatist tensions that once marred this pleasure-loving town have all but disappeared; residents seem eager to ignore the political graffiti lingering on walls, preferring to promote the enjoyment of sun and surf. Enjoy San Sebastián's commodities, but don't expect to cut corners; over a century and a half of exclusivity are still reflected in the prices.

ORIENTATION AND PRACTICAL INFORMATION

The Río Urumea splits San Sebastián in two. The city center and most of the monuments are on the west side of the river, in a peninsula that juts into the sea. In the north of the peninsula is the **parte vieja** (old city). To the south, the **Cathedral del Buen Pastor** sits on the edge of Calle de San Martín, in the commercial district. The main bridge, **Puente Santa Catalina,** turns into **Avenida de la Libertad** on the west side of the river and runs to the **Playa de la Concha,** which fronts a large bay. To the left, past the tunnel, is **Playa de Ondarreta;** to right is **Monte Urgull.** The east side of the river is home to the RENFE station. To get to the *parte vieja,* head straight to Puente María Christina, cross the bridge and then turn right along the river and walk 4 blocks north to Av. de la Libertad. Turn left and follow it to the **puerto** (port); the *parte vieja* fans out to the right. To get to the tourist office from the station, turn right after crossing Puente María Cristina (the southern bridge) and continue past Puente Santa Catalina; Calle Reina Regente will be on the left. The bus station is in the south of the city in Plaza de Pío XII. **Avenida de Sancho El Sabio** runs to the right (north), straight toward the ocean and the center of the city.

Tourist Office: Municipal: Centro de Atracción y Turismo (tel. 48 11 16), C. Reina Regente s/n, in the vast Teatro Victoria Eugenia. Open Mon.-Sat. 8am-8pm, Sun. 10am-1pm; Oct.-May Mon.-Fri. 9am-1:30pm and 3:30-6:30pm, Sat. 9am-1pm.

Budget Travel: TIVE, C. Tomás Gros, 3 (tel. 27 69 34), 1 block off Pl. Euskadi down C. Miracruz and then right; it's below street level. ISIC 500ptas. HI card 1800ptas. Open Mon.-Fri. 9am-2pm.

Currency Exchange: Banca Besné, C. Fuenterrabía, 4 (tel. 42 04 41), 4th left off Av. Libertad heading away from the river. Open Mon.-Sat. 9am-8pm, Sun. and holidays 9am-1pm; Oct.-June Mon.-Sat. 9am-1pm and 3:30-7pm.

Post Office: C. Urdaneta, s/n (tel. 46 49 14; fax 45 07 94), the street just south of the cathedral. Open for *Lista de Correos* Mon.-Fri. 8am-9pm, Sat. 9am-2pm; for stamps, **telegrams,** and **fax** same hrs., plus Sat. until 7pm. **Postal Code:** 20007.

Telephones: C. San Marcial, 29, 1 block from Av. Libertad, toward the cathedral. Open Mon.-Sat. 9:30am-11pm. **City Code:** 943.

Trains: Two stations. **RENFE, Estación del Norte,** Av. Francia, s/n (tel. 27 92 56), on the east side of Puente María Cristina. Information (tel. 28 35 99) open 7am-11pm. To: Pamplona (1-2/day, 1¾hr., 1200ptas); Burgos (4/day, 3½-4½hr., 2100ptas); Madrid (5/day, 7½hr., 4800ptas); Barcelona (1-2/day, 8-9hr., 4100ptas); Santiago de Compostela (2/day, 11hr., 5800ptas); Seville (Mon., Wed., and Fri., 15½hr., 6550ptas; change at Bilbao); València (1/day, 15hr., 6120ptas); Lisbon (1/day, 16hr., 7200ptas); Paris (5/day, 7400ptas; change at Hendaya). **ET/ FFVV, Estación de Amara** (tel. 45 01 31). Where Av. Libertad hits the Playa de la Concha, turn left on C. Easo and follow for 8 blocks. Information open 6am-10:45pm. Mostly for destinations within San Sebastián.

Buses: Several private companies run from different points in the city. Most leave from Pl. Pío XII (buy tickets at ticket booths along river).

Luggage Storage: From the RENFE station, cross Puente María Cristina, turn right, walk 1 block, then take C. San Martín to the left; after 5 blocks, head left on C. Easo (en route to Estación Amara, next to the firefighters). 100ptas/day, 250ptas overnight. Open summer 8:30am-9pm.

Laundromat: Lavomatique, C. San Juan, 13. Enter from C. Iñigo in the old quarter. Wash 450ptas/4kg. Dry 25ptas/4kg. Soap 25ptas. Ironing 50ptas. Open Mon.-Fri. 10am-1pm and 4-8pm, Sat.-Sun. and holidays 10am-1pm.

Medical Assistance: Casa de Socorro, C. Pedro Egaño, 8 (tel. 46 63 19, -41 20). **Red Cross:** C. Matías, 7. **Ambulance** (tel. 22 22 22, 21 46 00, or 21 51 64).

Emergencies: tel. 092. **Police: Municipal** (tel. 46 40 20).

ACCOMMODATIONS AND CAMPING

Desperate backpackers are always forced to scrounge and grovel for rooms in August. If you get away with 2500ptas a night, consider yourself lucky. Budget options congregate both in the *parte vieja* and around the **cathedral.**

Albergue Juvenil la Sirena (HI), Po. Igüeldo, 25 (group reservations tel. 31 20 56; fax 45 30 65), near Playa de Ondarreta, in the far west end of the city. Bus #16 (direction "Igüeldo") or 27 (direction "antiguo") runs there. Like an answered prayer; brand-new facilities. Rooms for 4, 6, or 8 all have bathrooms. Must be under 26. 1500ptas/person; winter 1000ptas. Breakfast included. Sheets 300ptas. Luggage storage and laundry service included. Wheelchair access.

Pensión Amaiur, C. 31 de Agosto, 44, 3rd floor (tel. 42 96 54). From Alameda del Boulevard go up C. San Jerónimo to the end and turn left. Recently renovated and scrupulously tended, with a gardened balcony. Dreamy mattresses. *Semana Santa* and June 22-Sept. 21: Doubles 4500ptas. Triples 6000ptas. After *Semana Santa* to June 21: 3000ptas; 4200ptas. Sept. 22 to before *Semana Santa*: 2500ptas; 3300ptas. Bring *Let's Go* and get 500ptas knocked off the price.

Pensión Loinaz, C. San Lorenzo, 17, 2nd floor (tel. 42 67 14). The people are delightful, the location ideal, the price fair, and the rooms choice. Semana Santa and July-Aug. Doubles 4000-4500ptas, triples 6000ptas. Semana Santa-June: 3000ptas; 4300ptas. Sept.-Semana Santa: 2500ptas; 3500ptas.

Pensión La Perla, C. Loyola, 10, 2nd floor (tel. 42 81 23), the street directly ahead of the cathedral. Handsome wood floors and doorframes; all rooms with balconies and showers. English-speaking owner. Winter heating. Singles 3000ptas. Doubles 4500ptas. Oct.-June: 2500ptas; 3000ptas.

Camping: Camping Igüeldo (tel. 21 45 02), 5km west of town. 268 *parcelas* fill in the blink of an eye. Bus #16 leaves from Alameda del Boulevard (roughly every hr. 6:50am-10:30pm, 80ptas.) *Parcela* 3000ptas, 2700ptas in spring and fall, 1300ptas in winter (includes car, tent, and up to 4 people).

FOOD

Tapas are a religion here. The bars in the old city spread an array of enticing tidbits-on-a-toothpick (10 *pinchos* and a drink, 1150ptas). Thirty-nine restaurants and bars breathe cheaply on **Calle Fermín Calbetón. Mercado de San Martín** inhabits C. San Marcial, between C. Loyola and Urbieta. (Open Mon.-Thurs. 7:30am-2pm and 4:30-7:30pm, Fri.-Sat. 6:30am-2pm and 4:30-7:30pm.)

Bar la Cepa, C. 31 de Agosto, 7, up C. Narrica from Alameda del Boulevard and to the left (the 7th street), in the *parte vieja.* There are hams and inverted wine bottles hanging from the ceiling, pictures of *matadores* on the walls, and a wagon-size wheel of Swiss cheese on the bar. *Tapas* city. *Bocadillos* 325-625ptas.

Bar Extaniz, C. Fermín Calbetón, 24, up C. San Jerónimo from Alameda del Boulevard; take the 3rd right. Refreshingly modern interior. 15 different tortillas. *Bocadillos* 325-650ptas. Open Thurs.-Tues. 10:30am-4pm and 6:30pm-midnight.

SIGHTS AND ENTERTAINMENT

The view of the bay—from anywhere—is especially spectacular on weekends after dark, when the base of Isla Santa Clara is lit by banks of floodlights so that it seems to float on a ring of light. The top of **Monte Igüeldo,** at the far side of the bay, provides the best view. For the **funicular** to the top, take the #16 "Igüeldo" bus from Alameda del Boulevard or walk along the beach and turn left just before the tennis courts. (Funicular every 15min. June 15-Sept. 15 10am-10pm; April-May 11am-8pm; 65ptas.) At the other end of the curved beach, gravel paths wind through the cool, shady woods of **Monte Urgull.** At one end of Paseo Nuevo (the wind-whipped road that rounds the peninsula), the **Museo de San Telmo,** housed in a former Dominican monastery, has an array of Basque artifacts dating to prehistory, a couple of dinosaur skeletons, some El Greco paintings, and exhibitions of contemporary art. (Open Mon.-Sat. 9:30am-1:30pm and 3:30-7pm, Sun. 10:30am-2pm. Free.)

The *parte vieja* pulls out all the stops after dark. The **Bar Uraitz** and **Bar Eibartarra,** C. Mayor, 26, are the two most packed bars on the street, itself virtually impassable after dark. In the mood to boogie? Check out the modern music and dance mixes of the giant **Iguana,** C. San Jerónimo, in the *parte vieja.* **La Piscina,** C. San Martín, 66, is where beautiful people go to vogue together.

San Sebastián's 4-day **Festival de Jazz** in the 3rd week of July is one of Europe's most ambitious. For information on the 1993 festival, contact the **Oficina del Festival de Jazz** at C. Reina Regente, s/n, 20003 San Sebastián (beneath the tourist office). The week of August 15, **Aste Nagustia** (Big Week), is ablaze with sports events, concerts, movies, and an international fireworks display.

■■■ PAMPLONA

La Fiesta de San Fermín—known to locals as **Los Sanfermines** (July 6-14)—is that orgy of bull worship celebrating Pamplona's patron saint San Fermín, who was martyred when bulls dragged him through the streets. The mayor kicks off 8 days of craziness by lighting the first *cohete* (rocket) from the Ayuntamiento's balcony. Then the fantastical **Raui Raui procession** winds through the streets. The **encierro** (running of the bulls) takes place at 8am every morning; hyper-adrenalized (and testosteroned) idiots in white shirts and red sashes flee from not-so-innocuous herbivores that charge 825m down the streets to the bull ring *(Plaza de Toros)*. It lasts about 2 minutes when the bulls stay packed; isolated bulls are far more dangerous, since they'll run into the crowds. Try not to cower in a doorway; 3 people were recently trapped and killed by bulls this way. Many are injured at the end of the course, where the river of adrenaline (and occasional chunk of flesh) cascades through a terribly narrow opening. If you decide to participate, watch an *encierro* first. At all costs avoid running with the dangerous, enormous weekend bunch: there's lots of pushing, shoving and pain. To witness the madness, be at the Santo Domingo stairs or inside Pl. Toros itself by 7am. The scene in the **bull ring** is exciting enough for those who would rather not be mauled, but seats (1500ptas or more a head) sell out fast. Two free sections are reserved in the stands for women and children. Another kind of running takes place here: large vats of sangria and canisters of flour are dumped on spectators, and heifers with sawed-off horns are periodically released on the crowd. At day's end, the hoopla moves into the streets with dancing in the alleys, spontaneous parades and a no-holds-barred party on Pl. Castillo. The truly inspired carousing takes place the first few days of the *fiesta*. Nearby towns sponsor *encierros* too—Tudela in the last week of July, Estella in the first week of August, Tafalla the week of August 15, and Sangüesa the week of September 12.

The clatter of cranky bovines somehow obscures Pamplona's varied architectural legacy. The pentagonal **Ciudadela**, with its duck pond, deer park and strollable gravel paths, sprawls next to the delicious **Jardines de la Taconera.** On weekends, the bars in the **Casco Antiguo** climax with youth activity.

Accommodations, Food, and Practical Information Only when your moon is in its 7th house and Jupiter aligns with Mars will you bed here during the *encierro* (reserve at least 2 months ahead for overpriced rooms). Check papers for **casas particulares** (from 2000ptas/person) or stay in a nearby town. The **tourist office** is here at C. Duque de Ahumada, 3 (tel. (948) 22 07 41), to help you. They have a functional map but provide little information on budget beds. Find the office from Pl. Castillo by turning left off Av. Carlos III onto C. Duque de Ahumada. Information on **currency exchange** and buses to campsites are on the office's bulletin board. (Open daily 10am-7pm; Oct.-June Mon.-Fri. 10am-2pm and 4-7pm, Sat. 10am-2pm.) Store packs at the bus station (July 5-14 open 24hrs., 200ptas/day). Be wary; theft multiplies during *Los Sanfermines,* and the areas by the walls in the *casco antiguo* are a nighttime no-no.

When the bulls stop running, snap up a bed on C. San Gregorio and its continuation, C. San Nicolás. **Hostal Bearán,** C. San Nicolás, 25 (tel. (948) 22 34 28), has comfy, pink-trimmed rooms. (Doubles with bath 4500ptas; Oct.-May 3500ptas.) Enact your favorite jailbird fantasy in **Hostal Otano,** C. San Nicolás, 5 (tel. 22 50 95), once a prison. It now has gorgeous rooms, tasteful, modern furniture, and oil paintings. (Singles 1500ptas, with bath 2500ptas. Doubles 3500ptas, with bath 4500ptas. You must pay up front.) A private bus runs from the bus station 4 times per day (9:10am-8:30pm) to **Camping Ezcaba** (tel. (948) 33 03 15; 400ptas/person, tent, car; open June-Sept.). Look on Calle Navarrería (near the cathedral), Calle Estafeta and Calle Mayor for frenzied feeding. On C. San Nicolás, **Restaurante Sarasate,** #19-21, serves a nutritious *menú* (850ptas) amid Indian tapestries and Dylan tunes. (Open Mon.-Thurs. 1:30-4pm, Fri.-Sat. 1:30-4pm and 9-11pm.)

Bus #9 (20min., 75ptas) runs from the train station to the head of Po. Sarasate, which leads to central Pl. Castillo. **RENFE** (tel. (948) 13 02 02, 22 72 82), off Av. San Jorge, has crappy connections to the outside world. Better to take swift **buses** from the station on C. Conde Oliveto (at the corner of C. Yanguas y Miranda) to Madrid, Barcelona, Zaragoza, San Sebastián, and the Navarrese Pyrenees.

JACA

■■■ JACA

Pilgrims to Santiago once recuperated from the trek through the Pyrenees at this first major stop on their route, the ancient capital of the Kingdom of Aragón. Today the pilgrimage has reversed directions; most people now head through Jaca *toward* the Aragonese Pyrenees for spectacular hiking and skiing. The **tourist office** at Av. Regimiento, 2 (tel. (974) 36 00 98), past C. Mayor, has lots of hiking information. (Open Mon.-Fri. 9am-2pm and 4:30-8pm, Sat. 10am-2pm and 5-8pm, Sun. 10am-2pm; Sept.-June Mon.-Fri. 9am-1pm and 4:30-7pm, Sat. 10am-1pm and 5-7pm. Closed afternoons on festival days.) City buses run between the **train station** and downtown (6/day, 6:30am-8:25pm, 50ptas). Trains run to Zaragoza (3/day, 3hr., 1025ptas) and Madrid (1/day, 6½hr., 3100ptas). **La Oscense** (tel. (974) 35 50 60) runs buses to: Sabiñánigo (2-3/day, 15min., 140ptas); Zaragoza (2-3/day, 2½hr., 1210ptas); and Pamplona (through Puente La Reina; 2/day, 2hr., 800ptas).

Jaca's *hostales* and *pensiones* are mainly grouped around C. Mayor and the cathedral. **Albergue Juvenil de Vacaciones (HI),** is at Av. Perimetral, 6 (tel. (974) 36 05 36), by the skating rink. This summer camp to the max has tightly-packed doubles, triples and quints that encourage camaraderie. (Reception in the smoke-filled bar open daily 1-4pm and 7pm-midnight. Members 550ptas, over 25 750ptas. Nonmembers 2000ptas. Winter heating.) **Habitaciones Martínez,** C. Mayor, 53 (tel. (974) 36 33 74), is run by a management that gushes over *Let's Go* travelers. Bar downstairs is occasionally noisy but always friendly. New rooms down the street have elegant bedspreads (1800ptas/person). Older rooms above bar are smaller (1500ptas/person). Camp at **Peña Oroel** (tel. (974) 36 02 15), 3½km down the road to Sabiñánigo, with its wooded grounds and first-rate facilities. (470ptas/person, tent, and car. Open *Semana Santa* and mid-June to mid-Sept.)

Parque Nacional de Ordesa y Monte Perdido The real things to see are the mountains and valleys that surround Jaca. A car is nearly indispensable, and Jaca is one of the few places those under 21 can rent one—**Aldecar** on Av. Jacetania, 60, left from the bus station and downhill. (Tel. (974) 36 07 81. 2500ptas/day, 25ptas/km.) More than worth the transport hassle is the **Parque Nacional de Ordesa y Monte Perdido,** northeast of Jaca near the French border. The stunning stacks of striated stone carved by the Río Arazas make scenery and hiking here incredible. It's an 8km hike (some hitch) from **Torla,** the closest town, which you can reach traveling bulk rate with the mail from Sabiñánigo. To spend the night, hike to the shelters within the park, or get the same feel at Torla's **Refugio L'Atalaya,** C. Francis, 45 (tel. (974) 48 60 22), for 900 ptas/night. If you want your own room, go farther up Torla's only crossroad, where **Fonda Ballarín,** C. Capuvita, 11 (tel. (974) 48 62 12) costs 1410ptas for singles, 2540ptas for doubles (mid-Sept. to June 1300ptas, 2330ptas). Get hiking maps and information about the park from the **ICONA office** in Torla on C. Francia (tel. (974) 48 62 12; open daily 8am-3pm) until the info center at the entrance to the park opens.

CATALONIA (CATALUNYA)

Hemmed in by the Pyrenees to the north and the Riu Ebro delta to the south, Catalunya is a privileged land. This prosperous region has always proudly held itself apart from the remainder of the country, retaining its own culture and tongue. Colonized by Greeks and Carthaginians, Catalunya (or Tarraconensis) was one of Rome's favored provinces. In the second half of the 18th century, Catalunya rapidly developed into one of Europe's premier textile manufacturing centers, and industrial expansion through the 19th century underpinned a flowering of the arts and sciences now known as a Catalan *Renaixença* (Renaissance). Having fought on the losing side in the Civil War, Catalunya lost its autonomy in 1939; Catalan instruction was widely suppressed, and publication in the language was limited. Since autonomy was recovered in 1977, Catalan media and arts have flourished. The language (it's not a dialect) is once again official in Spain and some are currently pushing for the right to speak Catalan in the Senate; the region itself is almost entirely bilingual.

Some worry that the use of Catalan in institutions such as universities will discourage talented Spaniards elsewhere from teaching, studying or doing research here, effectively sealing off the principality from the wider world. Vargas Llosa, for one, has spoken of the growing fascism of Catalunya. Others argue for more autonomy for the region, and some people advocate total political secession. Most visibly, during the 1992 Olympics Catalan president Jordi Pujol referred to the "country" of Catalunya in full-page ads in newspapers around the world. "Freedom for Catalunya" banners were not an uncommon sight, and Catalan was one of the 4 official languages of the Games. Whether by air, rail, bus, ferry or road, transportation in Catalunya is superb; only in the Pyrenees and on the Costa Brava do you need a car.

■■■ BARCELONA

Grand, sprawling, self-confident Barcelona embodies Catalunya's artistic genius and commercial resourcefulness. It boasts a long reputation for being the nation's most cosmopolitan, sophisticated, and progressive city.

By the Middle Ages, Barcelona was the capital of a fat commercial empire, but the discovery of the Americas turned the Atlantic into the hip trade route and left the poor Mediterranean neglected. Not until the 19th century did the Industrial Revolution's textile mills restore Barcelona's glory, feeding a budding bourgeoisie who shared the wealth with a pioneering generation of artists and musicians. The city tore down its medieval walls in 1859; the brilliant architects of *Modernismo*, led by native son Antoni Gaudí, responded with exuberant, fantastical creations. The 20th century brought political unrest and the rise of anarchism when, during the Spanish Civil War, the anti-Fascist coalition operated out of Barcelona. In recent decades the city has been receptive to the political activism of feminists, gays, and other groups.

Barcelona used the 1992 Olympics to reinvent itself. Substandard hotels fell to the wrecking ball, new parks and sculpture gardens were planted, pedestrian zones expanded, and over 50 monuments restored. Paris has been described as the capital of the 19th century; Barcelona may be remembered as the capital of the 1990s.

ORIENTATION AND PRACTICAL INFORMATION

On Spain's Mediterranean coast 200km from the French border and 5 to 8 hours due east of Madrid, Barcelona is Spain's second most important transport hub; most traffic to and from the rest of Europe passes through here. **Plaça de Catalunya** is the city's hub. From here, **Las Rambles** and **Via Laietana** run straight to the harbor. From the harbor end of Las Rambles as you face toward Pl. Catalunya, **Montjuïc,** site of the 1992 Olympic stadium, rises to the left, and the towering **Vila Olímpica** (Olympic Village) is along the shore to the right. The **Barri Gòtic,** centered on the cathedral and Plaça Sant Jaume, lies in between. On the left side of Las Rambles toward the port is **Barri Xinès,** the city's red-light district.

From Pl. Catalunya toward the mountains away from Las Rambles, the **Eixample** borders the Gran Via de les Corts Catalanes along its lower edge and is bisected by Passeig de Gràcia. The upper limit of the grid-planned neighborhood is Avinguda Diagonal, which separates the Eixample from the older neighborhood of **Gràcia,** in the foothills of the mountains encircling Barcelona.

Barcelona is a relatively safe city. Pickpocketing is the most common crime, mainly on and near Las Rambles and in the train stations. Plaça Reial and Carrer Escudellers should be avoided altogether after dark, and Barri Xinès is not safe for lone walkers at night.

BARCELONA

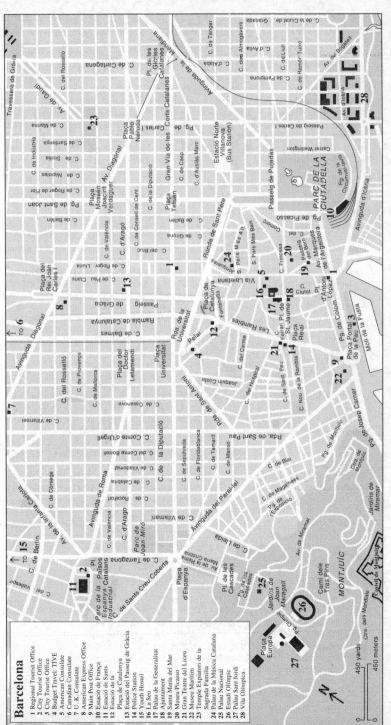

Barcelona

1 Regional Tourist Office
2 City Tourist Office
3 City Tourist Office
4 Budget Travel: TIVE
5 American Consulate
6 Canadian Consulate
7 U.K. Consulate
8 American Express Office
9 Main Post Office
10 Estació de França
11 Estació de Sants
12 Estació de la
   Plaça de Catalunya
13 Estació del Passeig de Gràcia
14 Police Station
15 Youth Hostel
16 La Seu
17 Palau de la Generalitat
18 Ajuntament
19 Santa Maria del Mar
20 Museu Picasso
21 Gran Teatre del Liceu
22 Museu Marítim
23 Temple Expiatori de la
   Sagrada Família
24 Palau de la Música Catalana
25 Palau Nacional
26 Estadi Olímpic
27 Palau Sant Jordi
28 Vila Olímpica

Tourist Offices: La Gran Via de les Corts Catalanes, 658 (tel. 301 74 43). Metro: Urquinaona (L1, L4) or Pl. Catalunya (L1, L3, L5). 2 blocks from the Pg. Gràcia intersection, in the Eixample. Open Mon.-Fri. 9am-7pm, Sat. 9am-2pm. **Estació Central de Barcelona-Sants,** Pl. Països Catalans, s/n (tel. 491 44 31). Metro: Sants-Estació (L1, L5). Info on Barcelona only. Open daily 8am-8pm. **Aeroport El Prat de Llobregat,** International Terminal (tel. 478 47 04); 25m to the left of the customs exit. Info on all of Spain. Open Mon.-Sat. 9:30am-8pm, Sun. 9:30am-3pm. **Estació França,** Av. Marqués de l'Argentera, s/n (tel. 319 57 58). Open 8am-2pm and 4-10pm, Sat.-Sun. 8am-8pm.

Budget Travel: TIVE (Oficina de Turismo Juvenil), C. Gravina, 1 (tel. 302 06 82). Metro: Universitat (L1). A block from Pl. Universitat off C. Pelai. Come here first and come early: in summer there's often a wait. Eurotrain tickets, cheap buses (Paris 7950ptas, Rome 11,350ptas, London 11,450ptas), flights, and ISICs (500ptas). Open 9am-2pm; Sept. 16-May 9am-1pm and 4-5pm. **Centre d'Informació: Assesorament per a Joves,** C. Avinyó, 7 (tel. 402 78 03). More student tourist office than travel agency. No tickets, but plenty of free advice. Excellent library of travel guides, including *Let's Go*. English spoken. Open Mon.-Fri. 10am-2pm and 4-8pm.

Consulates: U.S.: Pg. Reina Elisenda, 23 (tel. 280 22 27; fax 205 52 06). Metro: FFCC, Reina Elisenda. Open Mon.-Fri. 9am-1pm. **Canada:** Via Augusta, 125 (tel. 209 06 34). Metro: FFCC, Sant Gervase or Muntaner; any line from Pl. Catalunya except Tibidabo. Open Mon.-Fri. 9am-1pm. **U.K.:** Av. Diagonal, 477 (tel. 419 90 44; fax 405 24 11). Metro: Diagonal (L3, L5). Open Mon.-Fri. 10am-2pm. **Australia:** Gran Via Carles III, 98 (tel. 330 94 96; fax 411 09 04). Metro: María Cristina (L3). Open Mon.-Fri. 10am-2pm.

American Express: Pg. Gràcia, 101 (tel. 217 00 70; client fax and mail 415 37 00). Metro: Diagonal (L3, L5). 24-hr. multilingual service. 1% commission on bills, none on Travelers Cheques. ATM. Open Mon.-Fri. 9:30am-6pm, Sat. 10am-noon.

Currency Exchange: The best rates are at the **banks** in the Eixample; 1% commission on greenbacks (min. 300ptas). Banking hours are Mon.-Fri. 8:30am-2pm. **El Corte Inglés** (Pl. Catalunya; open Mon.-Sat. 9am-9pm) changes fiat and traveler's checks with no commission or minimum. On Sun. you can change money at **Estació de Sants** (tel. 490 77 70, ext. 93) for a 1% commission on checks and bills (500ptas min. on checks, 400ptas on bills). Open daily 8am-10pm, except Dec. 25, 26 and Jan. 1, 6. The exchanges on **Las Rambles** may be temptingly convenient on Sun., but they often charge the maximum commission (9.8%).

Post Office: Pl. Antoni López (tel. 318 38 31). Metro: Jaume I or Barceloneta (L4), at the end of Via Laietana near the port. Open for stamps Mon.-Sat. 9am-10pm; for *Lista de Correos* (window #17) Mon.-Sat. 9am-2pm; for **telegrams** Mon.-Sat. 8am-10pm. **Postal Code:** 08002.

Telephones: Central Telephone Exchange, C. Fontanella, 2. Metro: Catalunya (L1, L3), just off Pl. Catalunya. Open Mon.-Sat. 8:30am-9pm. Another is at Estació Sants. Metro: Sants-Estació (L3, L5). Open 7:45am-11pm. **City Code:** 93.

Flights: Airport at **El Prat de Llobregat** (tel. 370 10 11), 12km southwest of Barcelona. RENFE Trains (every ½hr., 20min., 220ptas) to **Estació Central-Sants** (Metro: L1, L5; on the southwestern edge of the city), then **Plaça de Catalunya** (Metro: L1, L3; in the center). Late-night **bus** service (bus EN) from the airport to the Plaça de Espanya (Metro: 21, 25) 11:15pm-2:40am, or from Pl. de Espanya to the airport 11:50pm-3:15am.

Trains: RENFE 24-hr. information (tel. 490 02 02; some English spoken). **Estació Sants** (Metro: Sants-Estació, L3, L4; open 6am-11pm) is the domestic and international hub. **Estació França** (Av. Marqués de L'Argentera, s/n; Metro: Barceloneta, L3; open 6am-11pm) is the terminal for: Madrid (6/day, 3800-5900ptas); València (10/day, 4½hr., 2400-3500ptas); Sevilla (3/day, 12-14hr., 6300-9000ptas); Milan (1/day, 18hr., 15,000ptas); Zürich (1/day, 13½hr., 12,500ptas).

Buses: Iberbus, Av. Paral-lel, 116 (tel. 441 54 94). Metro: Paral-lel (L3.) Open Mon.-Fri 8am-1:30pm, 3-7:30pm; Sat. 9am-1pm and 4-7pm. To: London (3/week, 24hr., 13,450ptas); Paris (1/day, 13hr., 9850ptas). **Enatcar,** Estació del Nord (tel. 245 25 28). Metro: Arc de Triomf (L1). Open Mon.-Sat. 6am-1am. To: Madrid (5/day, 8hr., 2600ptas); València (10/day, 4½hr., 2500ptas). **Julià Via,** C. Viriato (tel. 490 40

00). Metro: Estació-Sants (L3, L5). Open daily, 9am-8pm. To: Paris (15hr., 9850ptas), Frankfurt (16hr., 11,700ptas). **Sarfa,** Estació del Nord (tel. 265 11 58). Open daily 8am-5:30pm. The most convenient way to get many beach towns along the Costa Brava (2hr., 1000ptas).

Ferries: Transmediterrànea, Av. Drassanes, 6 (tel. 317 42 62). Metro: Drassanes (L3). Open Mon.-Fri. 9am-1pm and 4-6pm; Sat. 9am-noon. **Estació Marítima** (tel. 317 42 62 for tickets and departures). During the summer daily voyages between Barcelona and Mallorca (8hr.), Menorca (9hr.), and Eivissa (9½hr.).

Public Transportation: tel. 412 00 00. *Guía del Transport Públic,* available free at tourist offices and at the transport information booth in Pl. Catalunya, maps out all the city's metro lines and bus routes (day and night). Both metro and bus rides cost 115ptas (10-ride pass 560ptas). Hold onto your ticket or pass throughout the trip; riding the metro without a receipt earns you a 5000ptas fine. Metro open Mon.-Thurs. 5am-11pm; Fri., Sat., holidays 5am-1am; Sun. 6am-midnight. Routes vary, but day buses usually run 5am-10pm and night buses from 11pm-4am.

Taxis: tel. 358 11 11, 330 08 04, 357 77 55, or 300 38 11. The first 6min. or 1.9km cost 250ptas, then it's 100ptas/km.

Car Rental: Docar, C. Montnegre, 18 (tel. 322 90 08, 24-hr. reservations). Free delivery and pickup. 1900ptas/day, 19ptas each additional km. Mon.-Fri. 9am-7pm, Sat. 9am-1pm.

Hitchhiking: Those who choose to hitch to France take the metro to Fabra i Puig, then Av. Meridiana to reach A-7. Those en route to Tarragona and València take bus #7 from Rambla Catalunya at Gran Via or ride the green line to Zona Universitaria, at the southern end of Diagonal, and head for A-7 south. The *autopista* access lies near here. With the proper sign, this approach also puts hitchers on the A-2 to Zaragoza, the beginning of the trek to Madrid. Hitching on *autopistas* (toll roads, marked by an "A") is illegal, but it is permitted on national (N) highways. **Barnastop,** C. Sant Ramon, 24 (tel. 443 06 32), on the corner of Non de Rambla. Metro: Liceu (L3). Matches drivers with riders. 3ptas/km to driver on standard roads, 4ptas/km on highways, 1.2ptas/km commission. Open Mon.-Fri. 11am-2pm, or leave a message on the machine.

Luggage Storage: Estació Sants. Metro: Sants-Estacio (L1, L3); **Estació França.** Metro: Barceloneta (L1). Lockers 300 and 500ptas. Open 6:30am-11pm. **Estació del Nord,** Metro: Arc de Triomf (L1). Lockers 300ptas. Open Mon.-Fri. 7:30am-7pm, Sat. 8am-noon. Many of the hostels will store for about 150ptas/bag/day.

English Bookstores: Librería Francesa, Pg. Gràcia, 91 (tel. 215 14 17). Metro: Diagonal (L3, L5). Open Mon.-Fri. 9:30am-2:30pm and 4-8:30pm; Sat. 9:30am-2pm. Reading is fundamental, as is making the most of extra space in this book.

Laundromats: Lava Super, C. Carme, 63, off Las Rambles by the Palau Virreina. Wash and dry 1000ptas/5kg. Open Mon.-Fri. 8am-8pm, Sat. 8am-2pm.

24-hr. Pharmacy: Drugstore, Pg. Gràcia (tel. 215 70 74). Metro: Pg. Gràcia (L3, L4). Between C. Mallorca and C. València. Night buses N4, N6, and N7 pass by it.

Gay and Lesbian Associations: Front d'Allibrement Gai de Catalunya, C. Villaroel, 63 (tel. 254 63 98). Metro: Urgell (L1). At the corner of C. Consell de Cant and Villaroel. **Grup de Lesbianes Feministes de Barcelona,** Gran Via de les Corts Catalanes, 549, 4th floor (tel. 323 33 07). Metro: Pl. Catalunya (L1, L3). Less than 1 block from Pg. Gràcia heading away from Pl. Catalunya.

Medical Assistance: Hospitals: Hospital Clínic, Villarroel, 170 (tel. 323 14 14). Metro: Hospital Clínic (L5). Main entrance at intersection of C. Rosselló and Casanova. Hospitals also useful as an emergency drug store.

Crisis Services: Informatia Dona, C. València, 302 (tel. 487 80 92). Metro: Passeig de Gràcia (L3, L4). For female victims of violence. Mon.-Fri. 10am-2pm.

Emergencies: Ambulance: tel. 061. **Fire:** tel. 080. **Police:** New station at Las Rambles, 43 (tel. 301 90 60), across from the entrance to Pl. Real, next to C. Nou de la Rambla. Metro: Liceu (L3). English, French, German, and Italian spoken. **Municipal Police:** tel. 092. **National Police:** tel. 091.

ACCOMMODATIONS AND CAMPING

Hostal and *pensión* signs catch the eye every 3 doors. Quality varies, but the benefits of the 1992 Olympic frenzy are still evident—newly painted walls, upgraded bathrooms, and new beds, which become a rare commodity during peak season (July-Aug.). The summer and non-summer (generally Sept.-May) price distinction remains in Barcelona.

Hostels

Alberg Mare de Déu de Montserrat (HI), Pg. Mare de Deu del Coll, 41-51 (tel. 210 51 51), beyond Park Güell. Take bus #28 from Catalunya, or take the metro to Vallcarca (L3); walk up Av. República Argentina and across C. Viaducte de Vallcarca and follow the signs up the hill. A gorgeous neo-Moorish entrance, detailed Baroque salóns and institutionalized sleeping areas, its own private woods, and a hilltop view of Barcelona. 3-night max. stay. Reception open 7:30-9:30am, 5-7:30pm, and 8:30-10pm. Midnight curfew, but doors open at 1 and 2am sharp for the late-night crowd. 1000ptas, over 25 1500ptas, and 500ptas deposit for ID card. HI card required. Breakfast included. Sheets 350ptas. No reservations.

Alberg Juvenil Palau, C. Palau, 6 (tel. 412 50 80). Metro: Jaume I (L4). A block from Pl. Sant Jaume: take C. Ciutat to C. Templaris; take the 2nd left. Friendly, small hostel in the heart of the Barri Gòtic. Full kitchen and spacious dining salón with TV. 2-8 people/room. 1100ptas/bed, breakfast included. Reservations with 1 night's deposit.

Pensions

Hostal Marítima, Las Rambles, 4 (tel. 302 31 52). Metro: Drassanes (L3). At the port end of Las Rambles; follow the signs to *Museo de Cera* (wax museum) next door. Its prime location on the main drag can have noisy drawbacks. The speaker in each room can be turned off if the Doors and Dire Straits aren't your scene. Bathrooms leave too much to be desired. Singles 1700ptas. Doubles 2800ptas, with shower 3200ptas. Triples 4800ptas, with shower 5100ptas.

Casa de Huéspedes Mari-Luz, C. Palau, 4, 2nd floor (tel. 317 34 63). Metro: Jaume I (L4) or Liceu (L3). One block from Pl. Sant Jaume. Take C. Ciutat to C. Templaris, then the 2nd left. After dark do not approach by Escudellers. The kind owners offer basic rooms, sparkling new showers, use of their refrigerator, and a li'l extra TLC. 1200ptas/person (less in winter). Reservations for repeat visitors.

Pensión Fernando, C. Volta de Remei, 4 (tel. 301 79 93). Metro: Liceu (L3). On the left off C. Ferran walking from Las Rambles. Small, affordable rooms cramped with furniture and flowing with advice. Those in a for a longer haul get use of kitchen and other amenities. 1300ptas/person. Keys for 24-hr. access.

Hostal-Residencia Pintor, C. Gignás, 25 (tel. 315 47 08). Metro: Jaume I (L4). Gignás is the street that narrows from C. Angel Baixeras behind the post office. Each spacious room features new paint and furniture, a balcony, and thick red-and-black checked blankets. Singles and doubles 1500ptas/person.

Hostal-Residencia Romay, C. Avinyó, 58 (tel. 317 94 14). Metro: Drassanes (L3). Toward the end of Las Rambles, turn left onto C. Josep Clavé. C. Avinyó lies on the left after the church. Long, starch-white halls open to big rooms with furniture straight from the *Brady Bunch's* dining room. Keys provided for free entrance and exit. Singles 1500ptas. Doubles 2500ptas, with bath 3000ptas.

Hostal Levante, Baixada de San Miguel, 2 (tel. 317 95 65). Metro: Liceu (L3). Walk down C. Ferrau, and a right on C. Avinyo. Bda. Sant Miguel is the first left. Tiled floors that you could eat off of, new bathrooms, handsome wood interior and large windows. Singles 2000ptas. Doubles 3500ptas, with shower 4500ptas. Sept.-April 500ptas off. Reservations accepted.

Pensión Bienestar, C. Quintana, 3 (tel. 318 62 83). Metro: Liceu (L3).Two blocks from Las Rambles, off C. Ferrau. Quiet *pensión* has 28 beds with spotless white sheets and comfortable (if superfluous) thick red blankets. Singles 1700ptas. Doubles 2200ptas. Triples 3300ptas. Check-out 11:30am.

Pensión Segura, Junta de Comerç, 11 (tel. 302 51 74). Metro: Liceu (L3). From the metro walk down Las Rambles, turn right at C. de Hospital, then 1st left after Pl.

Sant Augustì. Huge central patio, firm beds, newly renovated, well-lit. Singles 1900ptas. Doubles 3000ptas, with bath 3500ptas. Breakfast 345ptas. Reservations for more than 1 person with deposit; postal code: 08001.

Hostal Capitol, Las Rambles, 138 (tel. 301 08 72; fax 412 31 42). Metro: Pl. Catalunya (L1, L3). Two steps from Pl. Catalunya. The English-speaking owner's parrot says one word, *guapo* (handsome), that sums up the whole operation. Color TV with cable and private phone in every room. Singles 2500ptas. Doubles 3800ptas, with shower 4300ptas. Quads 5600ptas, with shower 6300ptas. Prices don't include IVA. Credit cards and reservations gladly accepted.

Pensión Noya, Las Rambles, 133 (tel. 301 48 31). Above noisy restaurant Nuria, a 12-room retreat welcoming backpackers. Singles 1600ptas, doubles 2600ptas.

Residencia Australia, Ronda Universitat, 11 (tel. 317 41 77). A gregarious English-speaking owner shows that she cares with embroidered sheets and curtains, a spotless bathroom, ceiling fans, and winter heating. Singles 2300ptas. Doubles 3300ptas, with bath 3950ptas. Prices don't include IVA.

Pensión L'Isard, C. Tallers, 82 (tel. 302 51 83). Metro: Universitat (L1). Opposite the University. A dorm room's foil: quiet, relaxing rooms with new mattresses, tiling, sinks, and sliding glass doors onto the balcony. Singles 1800ptas. Doubles 3500ptas, with bath 4500ptas. Triples 4500ptas. Reservations with deposit.

Hostal Residencia Lausanne, Av. Porta de L'Angel, 24 (tel. 302 11 39). In the middle of the shopping promenade. Couches and chairs in many rooms. A terrace provides Swiss-like sanctuary from Barcelona's intensity. Singles 2000ptas. Doubles 3000ptas, with shower 3990ptas. Triples with shower 4500ptas.

Pensión Nevada, Ave. Porta de L'Angel, 16 (tel. 302 31 01). Just past Hostal Lausanne. Your cozy bedroom away from home on the range complete with firm beds, comfortable chairs, flowers on the balcony, and more. The good life at a good price. Singles 1800ptas. Doubles 3800ptas. Keys given for 24-hr. access.

Residencia Universitaria Victoria, C. Comtal, 9 (tel. 317 45 97). The first left on Av. Port de L'Angel walking from Pl. Catalunya. Popular with foreign students staying in Barcelona, this *pensión* is equipped with a full kitchen, TV, washer-dryer, and open-air dining room. Painting gallery in the reception with original works by the owner. Singles 2000ptas, per month 48,000ptas. Doubles 3000ptas.

Hostal-Residencia Oliva, Pg. Gràcia, 32, 4th floor (tel. 488 01 62), At Pg. Gràcia and C. Disputació. Metro: Pg. Gràcia (L4, L3). Sedate lounge with a long, polished wooden table encourages guests to write the great 20th-century novel. New bathrooms and frilly curtains and bedspreads. Some doubles are cramped. Singles 2650ptas. Doubles 4770ptas, with bath 5830ptas. Breakfast included.

Pensión L'Isard, C. Tallers, 82 (tel. 302 51 83). Metro: Universitat (L1). Beaming with youth at the end of the street off Pl. Universitat. New mattresses, tiling, sinks, the works. Neighborhood quiets down at night. English and German spoken. Singles 1700ptas. Doubles 3000ptas. Reservations with 1 night's deposit; postal code: 08001.

Hostal Lausanne, Av. Porta de l'Angel, 24, (tel. 302 11 39). Head toward the *Telefónica* but turn right; look for the blue square sign next to Cellini jewelry. Bright, airy rooms and a tranquil terrace out back for catching the evening breeze. Couches and chairs in many rooms, but some doubles are cramped. Singles 1800ptas. Doubles 3000ptas, with bath 3500ptas.

Pensión San Medín, C. Gran de Gràcia, 125 (tel. 217 30 68), down the street from the Fontana (L3) Metro stops. Hallways lined with faux-corkboard wallpaper and long Persian rugs. Each room has new furniture and a phone. Singles 2300ptas, with bath 3500ptas. Double 4300ptas, with bath 5300ptas. Shower 200ptas.

Hostal Dalí, C. Boquería, 12 (tel. 318 55 80). Metro: Luceu (L3). From the metro walk down Las Rambles to Pl. Boquería and turn left. No drooping watches, only sagging beds and slouching couches in the TV room downstairs. Singles 1700ptas, with bath 2100ptas. Doubles 2800ptas, with bath 3000ptas. Reservations only by phone and held until 6pm same day.

Hostal Líder, Rambla Catalunya, 84 (tel. 215 19 23). Metro: Pg. Gràcia (L3, L4). Intersection with C. Mallorca is one of Barcelona's swankiest shopping areas. Sacrifice aesthetic delight to be the first at the shops. Singles without showers 1700ptas. Doubles with showers 3200ptas.

Pensión Aris, C. Fontanella, 14 (tel. 318 10 17). On the right past the Telefónica. Ideal location, soundproofed by the 1½ blocks between here and Las Rambles. Spartan rooms ar being renovated, but the price is right. Singles 1400ptas. Doubles 2700ptas. Reservations with 1 night's deposit (postal code: 08010).

Camping

While there is no camping in Barcelona, inter-city buses (150ptas) run to these locations in 20 to 45 minutes. **El Toro Bravo** (tel. 637 34 62) is just south of El Prat in Vildecans, accessible by bus L93 from Pl. Universitat or L90 from Pl. Goya. (525ptas/person, 575ptas/tent.) **Filipinas** (tel. 658 28 95; 525ptas/person and 575ptas/tent) and **La Ballena Alegre** (tel. 658 05 04; 450ptas/person and 1100ptas/tent; both open May 15-Sept.) are also 1st-class sites another km down the road.

FOOD

Barcelona is a city of dining out; just about every block has 4 or 5 places to eat. In the Eixample, *patisseríes* and cafés offer expensively luscious treats under the shady trees. Closer to the port, bars and cafés are more harried. The Barri Gòtic is plastered with 850-950ptas *menús*. Catalan specialities include *mariluz a la romana* (white fish in tomato sauce), *butifarra con judias blancas* (sausage with white beans), and *crema catalona* (Catalan pudding).

"La Boquería," officially the **Mercat de Sant Josep,** off Rambla Sant Josep, 89, is Barcelona's best market, with fresh fish and produce in an all-steel *Modernista* structure. (Open Mon.-Sat. 8am-2:30pm, 5-8pm.) Bakeries are a cheap alternative, as they often sell cold *bocadillos*.

Restaurante Bidasoa, C. Serra, 21 (tel. 318 10 63). Metro: Drassanes (L3). Take 3rd left off C. Josep Anselm Clavé from Las Rambles. They'll stir up whatever your heart desires if you're not satisfied by the 43 permutations of eggs, salad, and fish. Meals under 1000ptas. Open Sept.-July Tues.-Sun. 1:30-4pm and 8-11pm.

Pakistani El Gallo Kirko, C. Avinyó, 19 (tel. 412 48 38). Metro: Liceu (L3). THe 4th left from C. Ferran. Specializes in *couscous* (with vegetables 450ptas) and curry (with beef and rice 450ptas). Slurp mango fruit shakes for 350ptas. Open daily noon-midnight. Credit cards accepted.

Els Quatre Gats, C. Montsió, 3-5 (tel. 302 41 40). Metro: Catalunya (L1,L3). The 2nd left off Av. Portal de L'Angel. A touristed spot with matching prices. The hangout of Picasso and other Lost Generation artists and intellectuals; their works adorn the walls. *Menú* 1500ptas (plus IVA) served Mon.-Fri. 1-4pm. Open Mon.-Sat. 8am-2am, Sun. 5pm-2am. Credit cards accepted.

Restaurante Self-Naturista, C. Santa Anna, 11-15 (tel. 318 23 88). Metro: Catalunya (L1, L3). A self-service vegetarian cafeteria where the variety of desserts and salads spills over the counter. Wholesome meatless *paella* (310ptas). Russian salad 320ptas. Open Mon.-Sat.11:30am-10pm; count on a line during *siesta*.

Restaurant Pitarra, C. Avinyò, 56 (tel. 301 16 47). Metro: Drassanes (L3). Turn left at the end of Las Rambles on C. Clavé, which becomes C. Ample; take the 3rd left after the church. The former home of the Catalan poet and dramatist Pitarra. The art lives on in dishes concocted by the former chef to Queen Sofia of Spain. Meal for 2 about 3000ptas. Open Sept.-July Mon.-Sat. 1-4pm and 8-11:30pm.

Restaurante Riera, C. Joaquím Costa, 30 (tel. 242 50 58). Metro: Universitat (L1). Off Ronda de Sant Antoni near Pl. Universitat. Top-notch rudimentary feast alongside flocks of gregarious regulars. 3-course meal with drink and homemade flan 575ptas. Open Sept.-July Mon.-Thurs. 1-4pm and 8:30-11pm, Fri. 1-4pm.

Bar Restaurante Los Toreros, C. Xuclá, 3-5 (tel. 318 23 25). Metro: Catalunya (L1, L3). On a narrow alley between C. Fortuny and C. Carme, both off Las Rambles. Red-cape colored floors and ads for bullfights. 70s music meant to anger the bull. *Platos combinados* from 500ptas. Open Mon.-Fri. 8am-1am, Sun. 8am-5pm.

Restaurante Nuria, Las Rambles, 133 (tel. 317 43 77). Metro: Catalunya (L1, L3). Two doors down from Burger King at the upper end of Las Rambles. Sandwiches downstairs and meals upstairs. Hell, there's even a condom machine in the bathroom. *Platos combinados* (750ptas). Open 8:30am-1:30am.

SIGHTS

During the summer (June 13-Sept. 27) the easiest way to take in the major sights of Barcelona is to hop on the **Transports Turistics Barcelona,** sponsored by the city's Patronat de Turisme. (Ajuntament tourist offices have a free pamphlet that maps out the bus route.) The tourist offices have a wealth of information and pamphlets. *Barcelona: One and Only* is a *barrio*-by-*barrio* description of the city; *El Barcelonés* is a quick and dirty glance. And don't leave the office without the Ajuntament's large map of the city, which lists all the museums and Gaudís in Barcelona.

Las Rambles and Barri Gòtic Dubbed "the most beautiful street in the world" by W. Somerset Maugham, tree-lined **Las Rambles** runs from Pl. Catalunya to the Monument de Colom at the port. Composed of 5 segments, this broad pedestrian lane is a bundle of urban nerves: street performers swallow knives, beggars hold out their hands and tourists fiddle with their fanny packs. At the port end, the **Monument de Colom,** erected in 1886, towers over the city. (Elevator to the top open 9am-9pm; Oct.-June 23 Tues.-Sat. 10am-2pm and 3:30-6:30pm, Sun. 10am-7pm. 200ptas. Ticket office open until ½hr. before closing.) Barcelona's drive to recover and refurbish its seafront has resulted in not only Vila Olímpica but also **Moll de la Fusta,** between Pg. Colom and the water, a wide new pedestrian zone that leads down to the docks, which are ideal for a slow evening *passeig.*

You can ride westward on the small ferry **Las Golondrinas** (tel. 412 59 14) through Barcelona's busy harbor, past a beautiful view of Montjuïc to the isolated peninsula at the breakwater. (July-Sept. 11am-9pm; Oct. and April-June Mon.-Fri. 11am-6pm, Sat.-Sun. 11am-7pm; Nov.-March Mon.-Fri. 11am-5pm, Sat.-Sun. 11am-6pm. Every ½hr., round-trip 300ptas.)

Strictly speaking, the **Barri Gòtic** (Gothic Quarter) is the area surrounding the cathedral, the Ajuntament, and the Generalitat, but the name also extends to the area between Las Rambles and Via Laietana. Since Roman times, the handsome **Plaça de Sant Jaume** has been the city's main square. The Gothic **Eglésia Catedral de la Santa Creu** is on C. Bisbe next to the Generalitat (look for its high-flying jagged spires) and the smallish **Plaça de la Seu.** (Tel. 315 35 55. Cathedral open 7:45am-1:30pm and 4-7:45pm. Cloister open 8:45am-1:30pm and 4-6:45pm. Museum open 11am-1pm. 50ptas. Ask a guard to let you see the *coro* for 25ptas.) On the opposite side of the cathedral, on C. Comtes, is the **Palau Reial** (Royal Palace). Inside, the **Museu Frederic Marés** holds the sculptor's idiosyncratic personal collection and the **Museu d'Historia de la Ciutat** has the ruins of a Roman colony. (Chambers of the royal palace open Tues.-Sat. 9am-8:30pm, Sun. 9am-1:30pm, Mon. 3:30-8pm. Museu d'Historia open Tues.-Sat. 10am-2pm and 4-8pm, Sun. 10am-2pm. 250ptas.)

Barri de la Ribera and Parc de la Ciutadella The venerated **Barri de la Ribera** section of the old city grew with Barcelona's development as a major sea power during the Middle Ages. The **Eglésia Santa María del Mar** on Pl. Santa María, is perhaps the zenith of 14th-century Catalan Gothic design. Entrance around back at Pg. del Born, 1. (Open 9am-12:30pm and 5-8pm, occasionally closed Sun. for concert preparations.) Off Pg. del Born, C. Montcada runs up to the world-famous **Museu Picasso** at #15-19, housed in what were once 2 adjacent medieval mansions. Thirty rooms trace the master's development during his turn-of-the-century stay in Barcelona. (Open Tues.-Sat. 10am-8pm, Sun. 10am-3pm. 500ptas.)

The peaceful **Parc de la Ciutadella** hosted the 1888 Universal Exposition; it now harbors several museums and a zoo. Little Snowflake (*Copito de Nieve*), the only captive albino gorilla in the world, is the main attraction at the **Parc Zoològic** (tel. 221 56 06), south of the Plaça d'Armes. (Open 9:30am-7:30pm. 850ptas.) On Pl.

Armes is Barcelona's **Museu d'Art Modern,** with a potpourri of paintings and sculptures mostly by 20th-century Catalan artists. (Open Wed.-Mon. 9am-7pm.)

The Eixample The 1859 demolition of Barcelona's medieval walls symbolically ushered in a *Renaixença* (Renaissance) of Catalan culture. Hausmann-wannabe Ildefon Cerdà's design for a new Barcelona, *Pla de Reforma i Eixample* (plan for renovation and broadening), reveals a grid of squares softened by the cropped corners of streets, which form octagonal intersections. The best way to approach this macro-museum of Catalan architecture is with 2 handy guides available free at the tourist office. *Discovering Modernist Art in Catalonia* offers a cogent look at the main buildings. *Gaudí* is a pamphlet describing 9 of the master's magnum opuses.

Many modernist buffs argue that the **Casa Milà** apartment building (popularly known as **La Pedrera**—Stone Quarry), Pg. Gràcia, 92, entrance on C. Provença (tel. 487 36 13), is Gaudí's masterpiece. Note the intricate ironwork around the balconies and the diversity of the front gate's egg-shaped window panes. The arches are not structural; they point to other Gaudí buildings. (Rooftop tours Mon.-Fri. 10am-1pm on the hour. Same-day reservations accepted in the early morning. Free.) Gaudí's life's work was the **Temple Expiatori de la Sagrada Família,** on C. Marina between C. Mallorca and C. Provença. (Metro: Sagrada Familia, L5). Seizing another architect's neo-Gothic plans, Gaudí made the church look like no other building on earth. Its 3 proposed façades symbolize Jesus' nativity, passion, and glory; only the first is finished. Take the elevator or walk up the stairs to wander among the towers, bridges, and crannies of the façade. The museum has a model of the complete structure. (Open daily 9am-9pm; Nov.-Feb. 9am-6pm; March-April and Oct. 9am-7pm; May and Sept. 9am-8pm. Church and museum 500ptas.

For a quick glimpse of buildings from the peak of *Modernismo,* check out the odd-numbered side of Pg. de Gràcia (called *la manzana de la discordia*—block of discord), between C. de Aragò and Consell de Cent. The upper 2 floors of the façade of **Casa Lleó i Morera** (1905) sprout flowers, and winged monsters snarl on the balconies. Gaudí's balconies undulate and the tiles sparkle on #43, **Casa Batlló,** whose interior resembles a German Expressionist film.

Montjuïc Throughout Barcelona's history, whoever controlled the strategically located **Montjuïc** (mountain of the Jews) ruled the city. Over the centuries, dozens of despotic rulers have modified the **fortress** built on top of the ancient Jewish cemetery at Montjuïc. **Poble Espanyol,** Barcelona's attempt to dissuade you from visiting the rest of Spain, features replicas of famous buildings and sites from every Spanish region: a Plaza Mayor (with a self-service cafeteria), a Calle de la Conquista, a Plazuela de la Iglesia, and so on. Prices here are high, but think of all the travel money it saves! Studded with happening bars and clubs, it's also a favorite weekend nightspot. (Open Mon. 9am-8pm, Tues.-Thurs. and Sun. 9am-2am, Fri.-Sat. 9am-4am. Craftspeople close shop 1hr early. 650ptas.)

The **Museu d'Art de Catalunya,** Palau Nacional, at Metro: Espanya (L1, L3), then bus #61, is in the stately **Palau Nacional.** The museum holds the world's finest Romanesque art collection, but is partially closed for renovations.

In 1929, Barcelona inaugurated the **Estadi Olímpic de Montjuïc** in its bid for the 1932 Olympic games. Over 50 years later, Catalan architects Federic Correa and Alfons Milá and Italian Vittorio Gregotti renovated the shell (open 10am-6pm) and lowered the playing field to maximize seating for the 1992 Games. The **Palau d'Esports Sant Jordi** is the most technologically sophisticated of the Olympic structures. About 100m down the road from the Olympic stadium is the **Fundació Joan Miró,** including works from all periods of Miró's career. (Open Tues.-Wed. and Fri.-Sat. 11am-7pm, Thurs. 11am-9:30pm, Sun. 10:30am-2:30pm. 500ptas, students 250ptas.) To get to Parc de Montjuïc, go first to Pl. Espanya (Metro: L1, L3), then take bus #61, which comes every 10 minutes and stops at various points on the mountain. The walk up, along Av. Reina María Cristina, is direct but lengthy.

Park Güell and Tibidabo Take bus #24 or take the metro to Lessups (L3) to see the **Park Güell,** conceived as a garden city for 60 houses with a splendid view of the city and sea. Gaudí designed its roads, walls, and service buildings. Inside, find an elegant white staircase lined with a multicolored salamander; in the back of the park, elevated paths swerve through hedges and prehistoric plants. The **Casa-Museu Gaudí** is here. (Open April-Oct. daily 10am-2pm and 4-7pm; Nov.-March 10am-2pm and 4-6:30pm. 150ptas. Park open daily 10am-9pm; April and Sept. 10am-8pm; March and Oct. 10am-7pm; Nov.-Feb. 10am-6pm. Free.)

To step back from all the architecture and art museums, head to the city's highest point at **Tibidabo,** perched atop the encircling mountains. To reach the top, either wait 15 minutes for the *tramvia blau* (blue streetcar; 125ptas) or walk up Av. Tibidabo in the same time. At the top of the street, you have to take a funicular. (Operates 7:15am to ½hr. after the Parc d'Atraccions closes. Round-trip 400ptas.)

ENTERTAINMENT

Every evening around 5pm, a man sets up a box in the middle of C. Porta de l'Angel before the Galerías Preciados and, as a crowd gathers, intersperses opera with commentary. Nightlife in Barcelona starts then and there, winding down about 14 hours later. Having caught word that the city is a perfect combination of exuberance and variety, international youths have poured in over the last few years. The best source of information on movies, concerts, cultural events, bars, and clubs is the weekly *Guía del Ocio* (75ptas), available at newsstands.

Discos, Pubs, and Bars The *passeig* is divided into 2 shifts: the post-siesta burst (around 5-7pm), then a 2nd wave after dinner (perhaps 9-11pm). The later *passeig* blends into the beginnings of a drink around 10 or 11pm, but only in a pub, café or bar. After the bars wind down around 2am, the crowds flood the discos for another 4 or 5 hours. Don't refer to a *disco* as a *club*; the latter means "brothel." The 700ptas cab ride to *Mirablau* is worth it to watch Barcelona light up in the evening.

The most fashionable, modern, and safe discos are located in the **Eixample.** Head out along **Carrer de Balmes, Avinguda Diagonal,** and any of their cross streets. (Metro: Diagonal, L3, L5.) **Otto Zutz,** C. Lincoln, 15 (tel. 238 07 22), is one of the largest and flashiest. (Metro: FFCC Muntaner. Uptown near Pl. Molina at C. Balmes and Via Augusta. Cover 2000ptas. Drink included. Open until 4:30am.) **La Fira,** C. Provença, 171 (tel. 323 72 71), Metro: Diagonal (L3, L5), contains bumper cars, swings, ferris wheel benches, and fun-house mirrors salvaged from amusement parks. No carnival dress: avoid shorts and sandals. (Open Mon.-Thurs. 7pm-3am, Fri.-Sat. 7pm-4am, Sun. 6pm-midnight.) **Studio 54,** Av. Paral-lel, 64 (tel. 329 54 54), is on the opposite side of Barri Xinés from Las Rambles, Metro: Paral-lel (L3). Unlike its departed New York counterpart, it has lost neither its popularity nor its cachet. Famous rock groups sometimes play here. (Open Fri.-Sun. midnight-dawn; cover 1000ptas. Early sessions Sat.-Sun. 6:30am-10pm; cover 750ptas. Drink included.)

Music, Theater, and Film The **Gran Teatre del Liceu,** Rambla de Caputxins, 61 (tel. 318 92 77; Metro: Liceu (L3)), founded in 1847, is one of the world's leading opera stages. (Sept.-July season. Box office open Mon.-Fri. 8am-8pm, Sat. 8am-1pm.) At the **Palau de la Música Catalana,** an extraordinary brick *Modernista* building, cleverly tucked away on C. Francesc de Paula, 2 (tel. 268 10 00), off Via Laietana near Pl. Urquinaona, concerts cover all varieties of symphonic and choral music, and tickets run 500-5000ptas. Ask about free Tuesday night winter concerts. (Box office open Mon.-Fri. 5-8pm; Sept.-May Mon.-Fri. 11am-1pm and 5-8pm.)

Films are popular in Barcelona. Besides Spanish and Catalan features, you should be able to find a Hollywood classic or the hottest new flick in English. It's customary to tip the usher (25ptas or so) who shows you to your seat. Check the schedule of the **Filmoteca,** Av. Sarrià, 33 (tel. 430 50 07), run by the Generalitat, for classic, cult,

GERONA (GIRONA)

exotic, and otherwise exceptional films. (Always subtitled if not a Castilian- or Catalan-language film. Metro: Hospital Clínic, L5. 300ptas.)

■ Near Barcelona

The **Costa Daurada** glitters southwest of Barcelona, where the unmistakable profile of the **Montserrat** mountain range, legendary site of the Holy Grail, juts out from the Riu Llobregat valley. Home of *La Verge de Montserrat*, a 10th-century bronze of the Virgin Mary, the mountain's **monastery** is the spiritual *patrona* of Catalunya. In the upper reaches of the mountain's silence, nature and deep meditation are yours for the breathing in a hiker's paradise. Take the FFCC trains from Barcelona's Pl. Espanya to Montserrat. The blinding beaches of **Sitges** are a prime daytrip, only 45 minutes from Barcelona's Sants train station (440ptas). A chic resort, Sitges earns its name with long ocean-side walks and whitewashed houses. This delightful town buzzes with activity year-round and is home to an international gay community.

Roman ruin fanatics will drool over **Tarragona,** a provincial capital that still proudly displays well-preserved Roman forums and chariot-racing arenas. From the train station (to Barcelona 475ptas), turn right to the winding stairs that lead you up to the outlook over the Mediterranean. The wide avenue stretching away from the sea is Rambla Nova, home of the **tourist office,** at #46 (tel. 23 21 43), on the way to the **youth hostel.** (Cross the traffic circle to Av. Pres. Lluis Companys and turn right after 2 blocks. 1000ptas; over 26 1500ptas. Make reservations in summer.)

COSTA BRAVA

The jagged cliffs of the Costa Brava cut into the Mediterranean Sea from Barcelona north to the French border. Craggy precipices and hairpin turns render certain parts of the coast unnavigable even by the most modern land transportation, and in winter the *tramontana*, a bitterly cold wind from the Pyrenees, can screech at 45 mph for 4 days straight. In July and August, the coast turns its other cheek of warm sun, cool breezes, and idyllic seaside vistas to attract vacationing European families.

■■■ GERONA (GIRONA)

Few travelers know what they're missing when, on their way from Barcelona to France, they bypass **Gerona.** The wonderfully schizophrenic Gerona is really two cities in one: a hushed medieval masterpiece of stone alleyways on one river bank and a thriving, modern city on the other. The city was home to the renowned *cabalistas de Girona,* who for centuries spread the teachings of mystical Judaism in the West. Today artists and students from the university fill the city's cafés and strut through streets lined by Gerona's orange, yellow and blue façades.

ORIENTATION AND PRACTICAL INFORMATION

The coffee-colored **Riu Onyar** divides the new city from the old. The **Pont de Pedra** connects the two banks and leads directly into the old quarter by way of C. Ciutadans, C. Carreras Peralta, and C. Força, off which are located the **Cathedral** and the historic Jewish neighborhood known as **el Call.**

Gerona is the Costa Brava's transport hub: all trains on the Barcelona-Portbou-Cerbère line stop here, scores of buses travel daily to the Costa Brava and nearby cities, and the major national and international car companies have offices here. The RENFE and bus terminals are off **Carrer de Barcelona** on the modern side of town.

Tourist Office: Rambla de la Libertat, 1 (tel. 419 54 19, fax 419 54 18), directly on the left as you cross Pont de Pedra from the new town. The staff has made Gerona

GERONA (GIRONA)

tourism its guiding passion. Transit schedules, restaurant and accommodations listings with locations marked on maps, and piles of brochures. English and all major European languages spoken. Least busy in early afternoon. (Open Mon.-Fri. 8am-8pm, Sat. 8am-2pm and 4-8pm; July-Aug, also open Sun. 9am-2pm.) **Train station branch:** tel. 21 62 96. Downstairs, on the left as you face away from the RENFE ticket counter. Open July-Aug. Mon.-Fri. 9am-2pm. The office posts indexed street map when closed, with directions to the main office.

Budget Travel: Direcciò General de Juventut, C. Juli Garreta, 14 (tel. 20 15 54), 1 block from the train station, off C. Bisbe Tomás de Lorenzana. In an unmarked building, 1 flight up on the *entresol* (mezzanine). Railpasses, buses to Europe, HI cards (1800ptas), ISICs (500ptas), *Guide to Budget Accommodations* (500ptas). They also run Gerona's youth hostel. Open Mon.-Fri. 8am-3pm; Oct.-May 9am-2pm.

Post Office: Av. Ramón Folch, 2 (tel. 20 32 36), at Gran Via de Jaume I. Turn right on the Gran Via from the old city. Open Mon.-Sat. 8am-9pm for stamps and *Lista de Correos*. **Telegrams** upstairs. Open Mon.-Sat. 9am-9pm. **Postal Code:** 17001.

Telephones: Gran Via de Jaume I, 58. Turn left on the Gran Via if coming from the old city and walk ½block. Open Mon.-Sat. 9am-9pm. **Telephone Code:** 972.

Trains: RENFE, Pl. Espanya (tel. 20 70 93). To: Figueres (25/day 6am-11pm, 26-52min., 240ptas); Portbou (22/day 6:10am-11:20pm, 50-70min., 360ptas); Barcelona (28/day 6:10am-10pm, including 2 *talgos;* 1-2hr.; 565ptas, *talgo* 1560ptas); València (1/day, 7:45am, 8hr., 3300ptas); Madrid (2/day, including 1 *talgo;* 12hr., *talgo* 9-10hr.; 5000ptas, *talgo* 6600ptas).

Buses: (tel. 21 23 19), around the corner from the train station. **Sarfa** (tel. 20 17 96). To: Tossa de Mar (1/day, July-mid-Sept. 3/day; 465ptas, Sat.-Sun. 530ptas). **Fills de Rafael Mas** (tel. 21 32 27). To: Lloret (3-5/day; 55min.; 395ptas, Sat.-Sun. 460ptas). **Barcelona Bus** (tel. 20 24 32). Express service to Barcelona and Figueres (4-13/day).

Medical Services: Hospital Municipal de Santa Caterina, Pl. Hospital 5 (tel. 20 14 50), across from library. **Hospital Doctor Josep Trueta** (tel. 20 27 00), on the highway to France. Interpreter in summer. **Red Cross:** (tel. 22 22 22). **Police: Policía Municipal,** C. Bacià, 4 (tel. 41 90 92). From Banco Central turn right on the Gran Via, then right on Bacià. In **emergency** dial 092.

ACCOMMODATIONS AND FOOD

Rooms are hardest to find in Gerona from October to June, when many small *pensiones* fill with local university students and workers. **Alberg-Residència de Girona (HI),** C. Ciutadans, 9 (tel. 21 80 03), lies in the heart of the old quarter, on the street which runs from Pont de Pedra. High-caliber staff, high-fashion sheets. (11pm curfew, but door opens again at midnight and 1am. 1000ptas, over 25 1500ptas. Reserve 2-3 days in advance, especially late May to early June.) **Pensio Viladomat,** C. Ciutadans, 5 (tel. 20 31 76), is on the same street and features yellow tilework, high ceilings and big bare rooms. This jumbo edifice usually fills with groups in July and early August. (Singles 1650ptas. Doubles 3000ptas.) Chow down at **Café la Torrada,** C. Ciutadans, 18, 1 block from the youth hostel, which draws an artsy university crowd. Catalan menu only. (Entrees 300-1000ptas. Open Mon.-Fri. 9am-4pm and 7pm-midnight, Sat.-Sun. 7pm-midnight.) **Larcada,** Rambla de la Libertat, 38 (tel. 20 10 15), has dozens of tables right on the Rambla. Linger over your meal in true Spanish style near amorous couples flaunting their bliss. Try their crispy, tangy variation on the pizza theme (650ptas).

SIGHTS AND ENTERTAINMENT

Most of Gerona's sights are in the old city. The **Call** begins at C. Sant Llorenç, a right turn off C. Força onto a narrow alleyway. The entrance to **Casa de Isaac el Cec** is off C. Sant Llorenç about halfway up the hill. The probable site of the last synagogue in Gerona, it now serves as a museum linking the baths and the butcher shop. (Open Tues.-Sat. 10am-2pm and 4-7pm, Sun. 10am-2pm. July-Aug. 10am-6pm. Free.) Gerona's cyclopean Gothic **catedral** rises up a record-breaking 90 Rococo steps from its *plaça*. The northern **Torre de Charlemany** is the only structure which remains from the 11th century; the cavernous interior has one rather than the customary 3 naves, making it the world's widest Gothic vault at 22m. In the trapezoidal cloister, the **Museu del Claustre** hoards some of Gerona's most precious possessions, including the intricate and animated **Tapis de la Creació**, which takes up the entire wall of Room IV. Woven in the 11th or 12th century, its illustrations depict the cycle of creation and biblical scenes. (Cathedral and museum open daily 10am-1:30pm and 4-8pm; Oct.16-Jan.7 and Feb.-April Tues.-Sun. 10am-2pm and 4-6pm. Museum only, 300ptas, students 200ptas.)

Bars such as **Class, Croquis, Fractal,** and **Azimut** draw the biggest crowds. Of Gerona's 4 discotheques, the mightiest is **La Sala de Cel,** C. Pedret, 118 (tel. 21 26 64), off Pl. Sant Pere in the northern quarter of the city. It's in a venerable building with a small pool and garden. (Open Sept.-July Thurs.-Sun. nights.)

■ Near Gerona

Tossa de Mar is a blissful resort on the lower part of the Costa Brava, about 40km north of Barcelona. Beaches aside, the chief lure is the *Vila Vella* (old town), a collection of 14th- and 15th-century buildings and fortifications on the rocky peninsula above the sea. Bus service is reasonably frequent (6-7/day) from Barcelona, but is so limited from Gerona that travelers may wish to head for Lloret de Mar (10km south) and catch the 15-minute bus ride from there to Tossa. The **tourist office** (tel. 34 01 08; fax 34 07 12), in the bus terminal at the corner of Av. Ferron Agullo and Av. Pelegrí, has a godsend map of the city, accommodations, campsites, and services. (Open Mon.-Sat. 9am-9pm, Sun. 10am-1pm; Sept.-June Mon.-Sat. 10am-1pm and 4-7pm.) **Fonda Lluna,** C. Roqueta, 20 (tel. 34 03 65) has small rooms, big beds, grand-parent-like attention, and a heartstopping rooftop view of the *Vila Vella* and the sea. (1600ptas with bath. Rates lower May-June. Open May-Aug.)

Tourists once ignored the rather unwelcoming and beachless **Figueres,** 40km north of Gerona. But since Salvador Dalí decided to build a museum for his works here, art buffs have swarmed to see the largest single collection of Spain's most notorious Surrealist. Transformed from an old municipal theater, the **Teatre-Museu Dalí,** in Pl. Gala i S. Dalí, parades the artist's capricious projects: erotically nightmarish drawings, extraterrestrial landscapes, and even a personal rock collection. (Open daily 9am-8:15pm; Oct.-June 10:30am-5:15pm. 600ptas, students and seniors 400ptas.) The **HI youth hostel,** C. Anicet de Pagés, 2 (tel. 50 12 13), is a bit of a hike from the train and bus stations. (Lock-in 11pm-8am. Lockout 1-5pm. 850ptas, over 25 1050ptas; members only. Reserve 1 month ahead in July and Aug. through the Barcelona office at (93) 402 11 66 or call the hostel 2-3 days before arrival if you can get there by 8pm.) The **tourist office** (tel. 50 31 55) on Plaça del Sol. offers the standard information about visiting Catalunya. (Open mid-June-Sept. Mon.-Sat. 8:30am-8pm; Oct.-June 20 Mon.-Fri. 8:30am-3pm, Sat. 9am-1pm.)

Teisa buses connect with Olot (3-5/day, 9:15am-5pm, 1¼hr., Mon.-Fri. 400ptas, Sat.-Sun. 510ptas), where there's service to Ripoll, an entrance to the Catalan Pyrenees. RENFE **trains** (tel. 50 46 61) make for Gerona (26/day including 2 *talgos*, 25min.-1hr., 220ptas) and Barcelona (15/day, 1½-2hr., 710ptas).

■■■ CATALAN PYRENEES

By and large, the old counties of Pallars, Urgell, and Cerdanya remain in idyllic isolation. Badly paved roads and limited bus service prevent easy access, but the splendor of Parc d'Aigüestortes, filled with clear glacial lakes and waterfalls, merits the journey. For each Catalan *comarca,* the Department of Commerce and Tourism distributes pamphlets with information on local winter sports or areas of scenic grandeur. Skiers will find the English-language guide *Snow in Catalonia* (free at tourist offices) especially useful. Cyclists should ask for *Valles Superiores del Segre/Ariège*. Editorial Alpina publishes a series of indispensable topographical maps.

Ripoll and Núria Ripoll is the point of entry for the area. From Gerona or the Costa Brava you can connect by bus; RENFE runs from Barcelona through Ripoll to **Puigcerdà,** where you are linked by bus to La Seu d'Urgell. The RENFE line connects to ski-resort **Núria,** and more complicated transport from Barcelona will get you to the lakes and hikes of the Parc d'Aigüestortes. Puigcerdà calls itself the "capital of snow," and you can indeed ski in the country of your choice (Spain, France or Andorra) at one of 19 ski areas within a 50km radius.

The **tourist office,** C. Querol, 1 (tel. (973) 88 05 42), a right turn off Pl. Ajuntament with your back to the view, has a good map packed with accommodations and entertainment listings. (Open Mon.-Thurs. 10am-1pm and 4-7pm, Fri.-Sat. 10am-1:30pm and 4-8:30pm, Sun. 10am-2pm; Oct.-June Tues.-Thurs. 10am-1pm and 4-7pm, Fri.-Sat. 10am-1:30pm and 4-8:30pm.) There's a **HI youth hostel** at the Mare de Déu de les Neus in La Molina-Alp on Ctra. Font Canaleta (tel. 89 20 12), 500m from the RENFE station at La Molina, 30 minutes by train from Puigcerdà. (Members only. 1000ptas, over 25 1500ptas. 170 beds. Slopes 1km away.) **RENFE** (tel. 88 01 65) runs to Ribes de Freser, then connects to Núria (7/day, 1¼hr., 230ptas), Ripoll (7/day, 1½hr., 290ptas) and Barcelona (6/day, 4½hr., 850ptas). **Alsina Graells** (tel. (973) 35 00 20) runs 3 buses per day to La Seu d'Urgell and back (1hr., 400ptas). The first departs Puigcerdà at 7:30am; the last returns from La Seu at 7pm. The train line to Puigcerdà also gets you to **Ripoll**, with its noted monastery, and connects you to the train to the alpine ski resort **Núria.**

BALEARIC ISLANDS (ILLES BALEARES)

The Balearic Islands are an autonomous province of Spain about 100km off the east coast between Barcelona and València; the most important islands are Mallorca, Menorca, Ibiza (Eivissa), and Formentera. Although numbers have dwindled somewhat, hundreds of thousands still descend upon the sun-drenched islands each summer, making for a prosperous economy. Those islanders not running a restaurant or *pensión* work in the olive, fig, and almond groves that blanket the countryside. **Mallorca** is home to the province's capital, Palma, and absorbs the bulk of invaders, particularly in July and August. Jagged limestone cliffs line the north coast, while lazy bays scoop into the rest of the coastline. **Palma** is a showy Balearic upstart; its streets hustle with conspicuously consuming shoppers, and the town boasts a swinging nightlife. **Ibiza,** once a haven of the counterculture, is a decadent entertainment capital with an active gay community. **Formentera** is the southernmost and most expensive of the Balearics, with a bevy of tranquil beaches. **Menorca** retains sloping green pastures cut by rugged stone fences, empty white beaches, hidden coves, and mysterious Bronze Age megaliths.

It's a cinch finding **rooms** on any of the islands until late July. The best weather shines in autumn and spring anyway, as summer days are hot and dry, save for the occasional northeasterly wind.

Transmediterránea has the monopoly on **ferry** movement between the mainland and all the islands except Ibiza and Formentera. Their ships depart from Barcelona (office at Estació Marítima, tel. (93) 317 42 62) and València (office at Av. Manuel Soto Ingeniero, 15, tel. (96) 367 65 12). **Flebasa** (tel. (96) 578 40 11, 78 42 00), in the city of Denia (on the FEVE rail line between València and Alacant), challenges Transmediterránea in Eivissa. Their boats dock in Port Sant Antoni. The high-speed ferry ticket comes with a bus connection from either of those cities or from Madrid, Albacete, and Benidorm (in summer). (One-way from Madrid 7610ptas, from Alacant or València 5570ptas.)

Flying is the best way to island-hop. **Iberia** flies from Palma to Eivissa (3-4/day, 20min., 4800ptas) and Maò (2-3/day, 20min., 4850ptas). Note that the stopover in Palma between Menorca and Eivissa can last up to 4 hours (2-3/day, 10,650ptas). Planes fill a couple of days in advance in summer, so make reservations. If flying round-trip, ask if the *tarifa-mini* fare is applicable.

Seafarers between the islands sail Transmediterránea, whose ships connect Palma with Eivissa City (2/week, 4½hr., 4870ptas) and Maò (1/week, 6½hr., 4750ptas). Mallorca, Menorca, and Eivissa all operate extensive intra-island **bus** systems. Travel costs on Mallorca, Menorca, or Eivissa add up, as bus fares between cities range from 100 to 700ptas each way. **Cars, mopeds, and bikes** provide self-operated transport to the islands' remote beaches. A full day in a car such as a SEAT Panda should cost around 5000ptas, including insurance; on a Vespa or moped, 2200ptas; on a bicycle, 800ptas.

VALÈNCIA

■■■ VALÈNCIA

Medieval song describes València as the land of water, light and love. Surrounded by the famed orange groves of the *huerta* (orchard), this lively, modern city is graced by numerous ancient buildings, museums and monuments. Greenthumbs are the majority in València; the lushly exuberant parks and gardens are a local obsession. The regional language is Valenciá, a dialect of Catalan, but residents also speak Castilian Spanish.

ORIENTATION AND PRACTICAL INFORMATION

Avinguda **M. de Sotelo** runs from the train station to **Plaça del Ajuntament,** where the city tourist office is located.

Regional Tourist Office, Estació del Nord, C. Xàtiva, 15 (tel. 352 85 73), on the right as you walk off the train. Plenty of pamphlets and maps on any little town in the Communidad València. Open Mon.-Fri. 9am-8pm, Sat.-Sun. 10am-7pm. **City Tourist Office:** Pl. Ajuntament, 1 (tel. 351 04 17). Open Mon.-Fri. 8:30am-2:15pm and 4:15-6:15pm, Sat. 9am-12:45pm.

Currency Exchange: El Corte Inglés, C. Pintor Sorolla, 26 (tel. 351 24 44). From Pl. Ajuntament, walk down C. Bareas as it turns into a pedestrian walk; El Corte Inglés sits on the left. **Currency exchange,** novels and guidebooks in English, haircutting, cafeteria, restaurant, **telephones,** and a humungoid grocery store on the 5th floor. Open Mon.-Sat. 10am-9pm.

Budget Travel: IVAJ, C. Hospital, 11 (tel. 386 97 00). ISIC 500ptas. HI card 1800ptas. Open Mon.-Fri. 9am-1:30pm and 4:30-6:30pm.

American Express: Duna Viajes, C. Cirilo Amorós, 88 (tel. 374 15 62). Next to Pl. America on the edge of Río Turia. Open Mon.-Fri. 9:30am-2pm and 5-8pm, Sat. 10am-2pm.

Post Office: Pl. Ajuntament, 24 (tel. 351 67 50). Open for stamps Mon.-Fri. 8am-9pm, Sat. 9am-2pm; for *Lista de Correos* Mon.-Fri. 9am-2pm; for **telegrams** (tel. 352 20 00 after hours) daily 8am-9pm. **Postal Code:** 14600.

Telephones: Pl. Ajuntament, 27. Open Mon.-Sat. 9am-11pm, Sun. 10am-2pm and 6-9pm. **Faxes** (fax 394 27 44) sent and received. **City Code:** 96.

Flights: The airport is 15km southwest of the city (tel. 350 95 00). CVT buses (tel. 340 47 15) link the airport with the bus station in València (almost every hr. 6am-8:20pm from airport, 200ptas). **Iberia,** C. Pau (Paz), 14 (tel. 352 05 00). Open Mon.-Fri. 9am-2pm and 4-7pm, Sat. 9am-1:30pm.

Trains: Estació del Nord, C. Xàtiva, 15 (tel. 351 36 12). Information office open daily 7am-10:30pm. To: Barcelona (9/day; 4-6hr.; 2400-3500ptas); Madrid (8/day, 5-7½hr., 2900-3800ptas); Seville (2/day; 8½-9½hr.).

Buses: Estació Terminal d'Autobuses, Av. Menéndez Pidal, 13 (tel. 349 72 22), across the river, a 25-min. walk northwest of the town center. From town center, take bus #8 (65ptas) at Pl. Ajuntament, 22. **Luggage storage** 100ptas. Open daily 7am-9pm.

Public Transportation: EMT Buses (tel. 352 83 99). Most leave from Pl. Ajuntament, 22. Buy tickets aboard or at any newsstand (75ptas, 10-ride ticket 490ptas).

Ferries: Transmediterránea, Av. Manuel Soto Ingeniero, 15 (tel. 367 07 04). To Palma de Mallorca (Mon.-Sat., 9hr., 5700ptas). Or buy tickets (on day of departure only) at the **port office,** Estación Marítima (tel. 367 39 72). Take bus #4 from Pl. Ajuntament. **Flebasa** (Denia office tel. 578 42 00) ferries to the Baleares leave from Denia (5700ptas includes 3hr. bus to Denia).

Laundromat: Lavandería El Mercat, Pl. Mercat, 12 (tel. 391 20 10), on the left past the market. Self-service wash or dry 425ptas. Open Mon.-Fri. 10am-2pm and 4-8pm, Sat. 10am-2pm.

24-hr. Pharmacy: Check listing in *Levante* (local paper, 100ptas) or the *farmacias de guardia* schedule posted outside any pharmacy.

Medical Assistance: Hospital Clínico Universitario, Av. Blasco Ibañez (tel. 386 26 00), at the corner of C. Dr. Ferrer. Take bus #30 or 40 from Av. M. de Sotelo in front of the train station. English-speaking doctor is often on duty.

Emergencies: tel. 091. **Ambulance** (tel. 352 67 50). **First Aid,** Pl. América, 6 (tel. 322 22 39). **Rape Crisis Hotline:** (tel. 900 58 08 88). **Police:** Jefatura Superior, Gran Via de Ramón y Cajal, 40 (tel. 351 08 62).

ACCOMMODATIONS

The business of València is business, so rooms are not hard to find during high tourist months. Avoid the areas by the *barrio chino* (red-light district) around Pl. Pilar. The best options cluster around **Pl. Ajuntament** and **Pl. Mercat.**

Alberg Colegio "La Paz" (HI), Av. Port, 69 (tel. 369 01 52). Take bus #19 from Pl. Ajuntament and ask the driver to signal the stop. Forbidding fortress disguises a peaceful ambience. 2-4 people/room. Lockout 10am-5pm; lock-in before 8:30am. Curfew midnight. Members only. 850ptas/person, over 26 1240ptas. Breakfast included. Sheets 300ptas. Open July-Sept. 15.

Hostal del Rincón, C. Carda, 11 (tel. 391 60 83). Ample hotel with starched white sheets and squeaky-clean bathrooms. Singles 1000ptas. Doubles 1800ptas.

Hostal-Residencia El Cid, C. Cerrajeros, 13 (tel. 392 23 23), off C. Vicente Mártir between Pl. Ajuntament and Pl. La Reina. *Faux* wooden floors, outgoing owner, and a little dog named Snoopy radiate a homey feel. Singles 950ptas. Doubles 1900ptas, with shower 2100ptas, with bath 3000ptas.

Hostal Moratin, C. Moratin, 15 (tel. 352 12 20), 1st street on the left off C. Barcas coming from Pl. Ajuntament. Brilliantly white rooms. Cozy dining room where owner often serves up a mean *paella*. Singles 1750ptas. Doubles 2900ptas. Triples 4350ptas. Prices higher in Aug. Breakfast 200ptas. Dinner 825ptas.

FOOD

València, of course, gave birth to *paella*. Custom dictates that this dish be eaten only at midday—just try to get some after sunset. Another regional favorite is *horchata*, a sweet, milky white drink pressed from locally-grown *chufas* (earth almonds). Buckets of fresh fish, meat, fruit and cereals sell at the **Mercat Central** on Pl. Mercat. (Open Mon.-Thurs. 7am-2pm, Fri. 7am-2pm and 5-8:30pm, Sat. 7am-3pm.)

Restaurante La Utielana, Pl. Picader de Dosaigües, 3 (tel. 352 94 14). Take C. Barcelonina off Pl. Ajuntament, turn left at its end, then a sharp right onto C. Procida. Devilish to find. Professional service, SoHo ambience, and not a plate on the menu over 650ptas. Choose from a super scoop of scrumptious seafood *paella* (a shocking 325ptas) or *gambas a la plancha* (425ptas). A meal you will not forget. A/C. Open Sept.-July Mon.-Fri. 1:15-4pm and 9-11pm, Sat. 1:15-4pm.

Café Valiente, C. Xàtiva, 8 (tel. 351 21 17). Stainless steel bar winds around the *restaurante,* accommodating patrons with one ambition—a large helping of *paella* scooped fresh from giant round pans (with chicken 450ptas, with seafood 515ptas). Expect a good 10-15min. wait. *Paella* served religiously 1-4pm. Open Mon.-Sat. 1-4pm and 7-10pm, Sun. 1-5pm.

La Lluna, C. Sant Ramón (tel. 392 21 46). Behind the hanging-bead curtain is a veg-gie restaurant to die for. A 4-course *menú* and whole-grain bread served only weekday afternoons (700ptas). Open Mon.-Sat. 1:15-3:45pm and 8:15-11:30pm.

SIGHTS AND ENTERTAINMENT

Most of the sights line the **Río Túria** or cluster near **Plaça de la Reina.** Taxonomists may lose it when they see the **Jardí Botànic,** a university-maintained open-air botan-ical garden that cultivates 43,000 plants (300 precisely-labeled species) from around the world. (Open daily 10am-9pm; Oct.-May daily 10am-6pm. 50ptas, students free.) The banks of the diverted **Túria** are now one of the world's largest urban parks, soon to be completed.

On C. Sant Pius V, the compelling **Museu Provincial de Belles Artes** displays superb 14th- to 16th-century Valencian "primitives" (influenced by Flemish paint-ers' marked attention to clothing) and works by later Spanish and foreign masters—a Hieronymous Bosch triptych, El Greco's *San Juan Bautista,* Velázquez's self-por-trait, Ribera's *Santa Teresa* and a slew of Goyas. (Open Oct.-July Tues.-Sat. 10am-2pm and 4-6pm, Sun. 10am-2pm; Aug. Tues.-Sun. 10am-2pm. Free.)

The Aragonese began the Gothic and Neoclassical **seu** (cathedral) in Pl. Zaragoza shortly after the *Reconquista.* Seized by a fit of Romantic hyperbole or simply ver-tigo, French novelist Victor Hugo counted 300 bell towers in the city from the **Mica-let** (the cathedral tower) in Pl. Reina—actually there are only about 100. (Tower open daily 10am-1pm and 4:30-7pm. 100 (not 300) ptas.)

Behind the cathedral on Pl. Mare de Déu, **Basílica de la Mare de Deú dels Desa-mparats** (Basilica of Our Lady of the Forsaken) is an elliptical edifice that houses a shining golden altar and thousands of burning candles. In Plaça del Mercat, the old **Llotja de la Seda** (Silk Exchange) testifies to València's medieval prominence in the silk trade. Handsome twisted pillars mask the upper chambers, with their master-fully sculpted ceiling. The ceiling is accessible by staircase from the Patio los Naran-jos. (Open Tues.-Sat. 10am-1:30pm and 5-9pm; Sun. 10am-2pm. Free.)

The newer sections of the city around Pl. Cánovas del Castillo and over the Túria near the university on Av. Blasco Ibañez are fertile ground for discos. One favorite is **Woody,** C. Menéndez y Pelayo, 137, with a blinking 70s-type dance floor. (Open Fri.-Sat. 11:30pm-7am. Cover 1000ptas.) **Distrito 10,** C. General Elío, 10, is another hot spot of mirrors, 3 floors of balconies and a gigantic video screen. (Open Sept.-July Thurs.-Sat. 6-9:30pm and midnight-7am, Sun. 6-9:30pm. Early session 400ptas, late session 1500ptas.) Gay men congregate at **Balkiss,** C. Dr. Monserrat, 23.

València's most illustrious traditional event is undoubtedly **Las Fallas,** March 12-19. The city's neighborhoods compete to build the most elaborate and satirical papier-mâché effigy; over 300 such *ninots* spring up in the streets. Parades, bull-fights, fireworks and street dancing enliven the annual excess, and on the final day—*la nit del foc* (fire night)—all the *ninots* simultaneously burn in one last, clam-orous release.

■■■ JÁTIVA (XÀTIVA) AND GANDÍA

Játiva The last foreigner of note to come through Játiva was Felipe V, and he burned it to the ground. With an imposing mountainous backdrop and land that lends itself equally to *huertas* (orchards) and to vineyards, it's no wonder that Felipe was just one in a long line of conquerors. Although it's quite accessible as a daytrip from València, few tourists visit the city, and its quiet charm remains intact.

The striking ramparts atop the hill in back of town lead to the city's **castell,** made up of two sections, the **castell machor** (larger), on the right as you come in, and the pre-Roman **castell chicolet** (smaller). The former, used from the 13th through 16th centuries, bears the scars of many a siege and earthquake. Its arched stone **prison** has held some famous wrong-doers, including King Fernando el Católico and the Comte d'Urgell, would-be usurper of the Aragonese throne. Referred to in Verdi's *Il Trovatore,* this man spent his final decades here before being buried in the castle's chapel. (Open Tues.-Sun. 10:30am-2pm and 4:30-7pm; in the off-season Tues.-Sun. 10:30am-2pm and 3:30-6pm. Free.)

The **tourist office** is at C. Noguera, 10. (Tel. (096) 227 33 46. Open Tues.-Sun. 9am-2:30pm; Sept. 16-June 14 Tues.-Fri. 9am-2pm and 4-6pm, Sat.-Sun. 10am-2pm.) **Trains** connect València to Játiva (35/day, 1hr., 290ptas, round-trip 405ptas).

Gandía Gandía is best known as the hang-out of the Borgias, especially of Francisco de Borgia, who renounced his title and wealth to become a Jesuit. Everything you need is a stone's throw from the train station on **Marqués de Campo.** Everything you want is at the **beach,** 4km away.

Simple flattery does not do justice to **Alberg Mar i Vent (HI),** C. Doctor Fleming, s/n (tel. 289 37 48), the hostel/beachfront resort in Platja de Piles, a town 10km south of Gandía. Take the **La Amistal bus** (tel. (96) 287 44 10), which departs from the right of the train station (check with the tourist office for times; 85ptas). Water laps at the door, there's an outdoor patio and basketball court and they rent bikes and windsurfers. Alcohol is strictly prohibited. (3-day max. stay. Curfew midnight. 770ptas. With 3 meals/day 1700ptas. Over 26 2225ptas. Open Feb.-Nov.)

The **tourist office** is at Marqués de Campo (tel. (96) 287 77 88), across from the train station in a small brick building. (Open Mon.-Fri. 10am-2pm and 4-8pm, Sat.-Sun. 10am-2pm.) Take a **train** to València (31/day, every ½hr.; 1hr.; 365ptas).

■■■ ALACANT (ALICANTE)

Beyond the polished pedestrian thoroughfares inlaid with meticulously cleaned red tiles lies the old city—paradoxically a modern, urban snarl of lively streets at the foot of the *castillo*. Grittier than their new-quarter counterparts, these streets are full of historic buildings and mouthwatering food. The beaches are nearby, the lodging is plentiful and cheap and the nightlife moves at a steady clip.

ORIENTATION AND PRACTICAL INFORMATION

Esplanada de Espanya stretches along the waterfront between 2 large jetties. Behind it, the old quarter is a web of streets and *plaças* off the main avenue, **Rambla Méndez Nuñez,** where nearly all services and points of interest cluster.

Tourist Office: Oficina de Información Turística, C. Portugal, 17 (tel. 514 92 95), next to the bus station. Open Mon.-Fri. 9am-2pm. **Tourist Office,** Esplanada d'Espanya, 2 (tel. 520 00 00). Information about the coast. Open Mon.-Sat. 10am-8pm; Sept. 16-June 14 Mon.-Sat. 10am-7pm.

Currency Exchange: El Corte Inglés, Maisonnave, 53. Zero commission. They've a map; they also offer novels and guidebooks in English, haircutting, a restaurant and **telephones.** Open Mon.-Sat. 10am-9pm.

Budget Travel: TIVE, Av. Aguilera, 1 (tel. 513 11 58), near the train station off Av. Oscar Esplá. No tickets sold. ISIC 500ptas. HI card 1800ptas. Open Mon.-Fri. 9am-1:30pm and 5-8pm.

Consulate: U.K., Pl. Calvo Sotelo, 1 (tel. 521 60 22), in the center of town at the end of C. Dr. Gadea. Open Mon.-Fri. 8:30am-2pm.

Post Office: Pl. Gabriel Miró (tel. 521 99 84), off C. Sant Ferran from the Rambla. Open Mon.-Fri. 8am-9pm, Sat. 9am-2pm. **Telegrams** (tel. 522 20 00). Open Mon.-Fri. 8am-9pm, Sat. 9am-7pm, Sun. 9am-2pm. **Postal Code:** 03000.

Telephones: Av. Constitució, 10 (tel. 004). Open daily 9am-10pm. Another office at the **bus station.** Open Mon.-Fri. 9:30am-2pm and 5-9:30pm, Sat.-Sun. 10am-2pm and 5-9pm. **City Code:** 96.

Flights: Aeroport Internacional El Altet (tel. 528 50 11), 17km from town. **Alcoyana** (tel. 513 01 04) sends 13 buses/day between the airport and Av. Constitución (departs town 7am-10pm, departs airport 6:30am-9:20pm; 125ptas). **Iberia,** C. F. Soto, 9 (tel. 521 85 10).

Trains: RENFE, Estació Término, Av. Salamanca (tel. 592 02 02), west of the city center. To reach Esplanada d'Espanya from here, walk down wide Av. la Estación to Plaza de los Luceros and hang a right onto Av. Federico Soto, which leads to the waterfront. Information open daily 7am-10pm. Most destinations require a transfer. Direct to: València (5/day, 3hr., 1500-2100ptas); Madrid (6/day, 9hr., 2900-4300ptas); Barcelona (5/day, 11hr., 3200-4900ptas). **Ferrocarrils de la Generalitat Valenciana, Estació de la Marina,** Av. Villajoyosa, 2 (tel. 526 27 31), far from town. Take bus C-1 from Pl. Espanya. Local service along the Costa Blanca. Also **night trains** to discos on the beaches near Alacant.

Buses: C. Portugal, 17 (tel. 513 07 00). To reach Esplanade d' Espanya, turn left onto Carrer d' Italia and right on Av. Dr. Gadea; follow Dr. Gadea until the park, then left on the waterfront toward Esplanada Espanya. For the Costa Blanca, go to **UBESA** (tel. 513 01 43). **Enatcar** (tel. 522 00 77) runs to Madrid (8/day, 5-6hr., 2695ptas); Granada (5/day, 7½hr., 2960ptas) and Barcelona (7/day, 8hr., 4115ptas). **Luggage storage** (200ptas/bag). Open daily 6:45am-10pm.

Ferries: Flebasa (tel. 578 20 00). Service from Denia (includes bus from Alacant to Denia, otherwise 350ptas) to Eivissa (1-2/day, 3hr., 5220ptas).

Medical Assistance: Hospital Clínico, C. Alicante Sant Joan (tel. 590 83 00). **Ambulance** (tel. 521 17 05, 523 06 01).

Emergency: tel. 091. **Police: Commisaría,** C. Médico Pascual Pérez, 33 (tel. 514 22 22).

ACCOMMODATIONS AND CAMPING

While there seems to be a *pensión* or *casa de huéspedes* on every corner, stay away from the places along C. Sant Ferran (where theft and prostitution are common) and around the Església de Santa María; opt instead for the newer section of town.

Residencia Juvenil (HI), Av. Orihuela, 97 (tel. 528 12 11). Take bus G from next to the bus station on the corner of C. Lorenzo and C. Portugal, and get off at the last stop (75ptas). HI card required. 3-day max. stay. 770ptas, with breakfast 850ptas, with 3 meals 1700ptas. Over 25: 910ptas, 1240ptas, 2225ptas.

Habitaciones México, C. Primo de Rivera, 10 (tel. 520 93 07), off the end of Av. Alfons X El Sabio. Pristine rooms with fresh towels and complimentary soap. Gregarious owner. Kitchen available for the culinary types and book swap for literary ones. Singles 1450ptas. Doubles 2800ptas, with bath 3400ptas. Triples 3600ptas.

Pensión Les Monges, C. Monjas, 2 (tel. 521 50 46). Follow C. San Isidro off Rambla Mendez Nuñez until it turns into C. Monjas. Each room individually decorated in the owner's whimsical taste—not to mention the Renaissance tapestry in the reception. Single 1500ptas, with sink 1700ptas, with shower 2000ptas, with bath 2500ptas. Doubles 3000ptas, with sink 3200ptas, with shower 3500ptas.

Camping: Camping Bahía (tel. 526 23 32), 4km away on the road to València. Take bus C-1. 400ptas/person, or tent. Open March 15-Oct. 15.

FOOD

Small family-run establishments in the **old city** (between the cathedral and the steps to the castle) and on side streets around town are the least traveled route. Locals devour tapas in the **C. Mayor.** The **market** near Av. Alfonso X El Sabio sells fresh fish, meats and produce, plus sandwich meats and bread.

La Venta del Lobo, C. Sant Ferran, 48. A 2-room neighborhood grill preparing specialties from all over Spain. Try *gazpacho Andaluz* for a taste of the south (370ptas) or Valencian *paella*. Revel in the house specialty dessert *lobo loco,* an incredible flan boat doused in fruit, chocolate ice cream, nuts, and whipped cream (385ptas). Open Tues.-Sat. 1-5pm and 8:30pm-12:30am, Sun. 1-5pm.

Mesón de Castilla, C. Sant Nicolau, 12. The shi-shi name does not do justice to the down-home cooking. The owner rotates 10 plates to accommodate the regulars. *Menú especial*—3 courses, fruit, bread, and drink—700ptas. *Paella* option Thurs. and Sun. Open Mon.-Fri. 1-4pm and 7-10pm, Sat.-Sun. 1-4pm.

Casa Miguel, C. Poeta Quintana, 4. Street parallel to Av. Alfons X el Sabio, near the central market. Specializes in vegetarian dishes, including succulent garlic mushrooms (300ptas) and wicked vegetarian *paella* (600ptas). Open Mon.-Fri. 1-4pm and 8:30-10pm, Sat. 1-4pm.

SIGHTS AND ENTERTAINMENT

Complete with drawbridges, clandestine tunnels, fishy passageways, and urine-splashed dungeons, the **Castell de Santa Bárbara** isn't just another castle. The Carthaginians were the first lucky owners of this 200m high fortress. After they left, the military used the castle as a prison. Now most of it has been reconstructed; there's a dry moat, a dungeon, and a spooky ammunition storeroom to review. Even if the citadel doesn't overwhelm, the view makes Alacant look like the Rió of Spain. (Open daily 9am-8pm; winter 9am-7pm. Free.) The **Concatedral de San Nicolás de Bari,** 1 block north of Méndez Núñez on C. San Isidro, reflects the sober Renaissance style of Agustín Bernadino, while the baroque communion chapel lavishly compensates for such restraint. Intricate wood carvings embellish the door to the cloister. (Open Mon.-Sat. 8am-2:30pm and 6-8:30pm, Sun. 9am-1:45pm.)

If Alacant's beach doesn't suit you, hop bus C-1 in Pl. Espanya (75ptas) or board the Alacant-Denia train (85ptas) for the 6km long **Platje de Sant Joan.** If crowds have soiled every square inch, try the **Platja del Saladar** in Urbanova. Buses from the Alacant bus station make the trip to Urbanova (3/day, 35min., 100ptas).

Alacant's hottest disco is **Buggatti,** C. Sant Ferran, 27 (tel. 521 06 46), featuring neon-lined bars and candle-lit tables. (Cover including 1 drink 1000ptas. Open nightly until 5:30am.) Gay men hang out at **Jardineto** on C. Baron de Finestrat. From June 21 to 29, the town bursts with bacchanalian celebration for the **Festival de Sant Joan,** comprised of romping *fogueres* (symbolic or satiric effigies).

ANDALUCÍA

Between the jagged Sierra Morena and the deep blue sea, Andalucía has always inspired fascination with its rich history. Home of several emperors and writers of the caliber of Seneca and Quintilian, it was one of the Roman Empire's richest, most sophisticated provinces. The Moors remained in control of eastern Andalucía longer than elsewhere (711-1492), but the region owes just as much to the Romans' irrigation, cool patios, and red and white stone architecture. The Moors maintained and perfected these techniques; more importantly they assimilated and elaborated the wisdom and science of Classical Greece and the East, which made the European Renaissance possible. Owing to the long summers, regional cooking is light, depending on such delicacies as *pescaíto frito* (lightly fried fish) and cold soups such as *gazpacho* served *con guarnición* (with garnish), often spooned by the waiter at your table.

■■■ SEVILLE (SEVILLA)

With its brilliant light, whitewashed grace, jasmined balconies, and orange trees laden with fat glowing globes, Seville may convince you that otherworldly cities do

SEVILLE (SEVILLA)

exist. Site of a small Roman acropolis founded by Julius Caesar, seat of Moorish culture, focal point of the Spanish Renaissance, and guardian angel of traditional Andalusian culture, Seville has never failed to spark the imagination of newcomers. The 16th-century maxim *"Qui non ha vista Sevilla non ha vista maravilla"*—who has not seen Seville has not seen a marvel—remains true 5 centuries later.

ORIENTATION

Seville is a major travel hub, connecting Portugal, Cádiz, Córdoba, and Madrid. **Río Guadalquivir** flows roughly north-south through Seville. Most of the city, including the alleyways of the old **Barrio de Santa Cruz**, is on the east bank; some of the most active nightlife and least expensive food are on the west bank in **Barrio de Triana** and **Barrio de los Remedios**. The **cathedral**, on **Avenida de la Constitución** marks Seville's center, where the main tourist office, post office, banks, and travel agencies cluster. Seville's shopping district lies north of the cathedral where Constitución fades into **Plaza Nueva**. The neighborhoods surrounding Plaza Nueva, as well as those northeast of the Barrio de Santa Cruz **(Barrio de la Puerta del Carne** and **Barrio de la Puerta de Carmona)** are hunting grounds for *pensión* and restaurant seekers. The **Estación Santa Justa** (train station), is a 40-minute walk from the city center. The main bus station at **Prado de San Sebastián** on C. Menéndez Pelazo is much closer (a 10-min. walk). Beware, Seville is the Spanish capital of pickpocketing and car theft.

PRACTICAL INFORMATION

Tourist Offices: Regional, Av. Constitución, 21B (tel. 422 14 04, fax 422 97 53), 1 block south of the cathedral. Open Mon.-Fri. 9:30am-7:30pm, Sat. 10am-2pm. **City,** Po. Delicias, 9 (tel. 423 44 65), across from Parque de María Luísa by Puente del Generalísimo. Open Mon.-Fri. 9am-1:15pm and 4:30-6:45pm.

Budget Travel: Viajes TIVE, C. Jesus de Veracruz, 26 (tel. 490 60 22). Downtown near El Corte Inglés. Open Mon.-Fri. 9am-1:30pm.

Consulates: U.S.: Po. Delicias, 7 (tel. 423 18 83 or 423 18 85). Open Mon.-Fri. 10am-1pm. In emergencies, call U.S. embassy in Madrid at tel. (91) 577 40 00. **Canada:** Av. Constitución, 30, 2nd floor, #4 (tel. 422 47 52; in emergency (91) 431 43 00). **U.K.:** Pl. Nueva, 8B (tel. 422 88 75). In emergencies, call Madrid for referral in Seville. Covers New Zealand affairs. Open Mon.-Fri. 9am-2pm.

American Express: Viajes Alhambra, Teniente Coronel Seguí, 6 (tel. 421 29 23), north of Pl. Nueva. Holds mail **(postal code:** 41001). Open Mon.-Fri. 9:30am-1:30pm and 4:30-8pm. Sat. 9:30am-1pm.

Currency Exchange: El Corte Inglés: Pl. Duque de la Victoria, 10, near C. Alfonso XII; C. Luis de Morales, 122, near the football stadium. 1% commission (250ptas min. charge). Open Mon.-Sat. 10am-9pm.

Post Office: Av. Constitución, 32 (tel. 421 95 85), across from the cathedral. Open for stamps and most mail services Mon.-Fri. 8am-9pm, Sat. 9am-7pm. Open for Lista de Correos Mon.-Fri. 8am-9pm, Sat. 8am-2pm. Open for **telegrams** (national tel. 422 00 00, international tel. 422 68 60) and **faxes** Mon.-Fri. 8am-9pm, Sat. 9am-8pm. **Postal Code:** 41070.

Telephones: Pl. Gavidia, 7, near Pl. Concordia. Open Mon.-Fri. 10am-2pm and 5:30-10pm, Sat. 10am-2pm. **Telephone Code:** 95.

Flights: Aeropuerto San Pablo, (tel. 451 61 11), 12km from town on Ctra. Madrid. A taxi to the airport from the center of town costs about 1000ptas. **Iberia,** C. Almirante Laco, 2 (tel. 422 89 01, reservations 901 33 111), is in front of Torre del Oro. To: Madrid (5/day, 12,500ptas); Barcelona (5/day, 19,500ptas).

Trains: Estación Santa Justa, Av. Kansas City, s/n (information tel. 441 41 11, reservations 442 15 62). Bus #70 links Estación Santa Justa and the Prado de San Sebastián bus station. Bus EA makes for the airport and for Puerta de Jerez, near the regional tourist office. Both buses stop on Av. Kansas City, to the left as you exit the station. There's now special high-speed AVE (*Alta Velocidad Española*) train service between Sevilla and Madrid that reduces travel time to 2¾hr. (6/day, 6000-8400ptas). **RENFE,** C. Zaragoza, 29 (tel. 421 79 98), near Pl. Nueva. Open

Mon.-Fri. 9am-1:15pm and 4-7pm. Sat. 9am-1pm. To: Córdoba (10/day; *AVE* 50min., 1700-2300ptas; *talgo* 1½hr., 1800ptas; *expreso* 1300ptas; *tranvía* 2hr., 670ptas); Cádiz (8/day; *talgo* 1¾hr., 1900ptas; *rápido* 1800ptas; *tranvía* 2hr., 826ptas); Algeciras (2/day, 1745ptas); Málaga (3/day, 3-4hr, 1235ptas); Granada (3/day, 4-5hr, 14900ptas), Madrid (12/day; *AVE* 3¼hr., 6000-7200ptas; *talgo* 6hr., 5900-6200ptas; *expreso* 6-8hr., 4200ptas); Barcelona (4/day, 10-13hr.; *talgo* 9000ptas; *rápido* 8800ptas; *expreso* 6800 ptas).

Buses: Prado de San Sebastián, C. José María Osborne, 11 (tel. 441 71 11). Bus #70 and C2 link Estación Santa Justa and Prado de San Sebastián. **Empresa Alsina Graells** (tel. 441 88 11). To: Córdoba (Mon.-Fri. 16/day, Sat. 8/day, Sun. 12/day, 1¾hr., 1000ptas); Granada (9/day, 3¼-4hr., 2920ptas); **Transportes Comes** (tel. 441 68 58). To: Jerez de la Frontera (8/day, 2hr., 1110ptas); Algeciras (5/day, 3½hr.,1975ptas).

Luggage Storage: At the main bus station, 160ptas/day, open 6:30am-10pm. At the train station, small locker 300ptas, medium locker 400ptas, large locker 500ptas/day; open 24 hr.

Women's Center: C. Alfonso XII, 52 (tel. 421 33 75). Information on feminist and lesbian organizations and gay matters, as well as legal and psychological services for rape victims.

Laundromat: Lavandería Robledo, C. F. Sánchez Bedoya, 18 (tel. 421 81 32), 1 block west of the cathedral, across Av. Constitución. Wash and dry 5kg 950ptas. Open Mon.-Fri. 10am-2pm and 5-8pm, Sat. 10am-2pm.

Hospital: Hospital Universitario, Av. Dr. Fedriani, s/n (tel. 437 84 00). English spoken.

Emergency: tel. 091. **Police:** (tel. 461 67 76), Av. Paseo de las Delicias.

ACCOMMODATIONS AND CAMPING

During Semana Santa and the Feria de Abril, rooms vanish and prices soar. Make reservations if you value your feet. Look in the **Barrio de Santa Cruz,** especially around C. Mateos Gago. Also try the **Plaza de Curtidores** and the **Plaza de Pilatos,** in the Barrios Puerta de la Carne and Puerta de Carmona.

2Seville Youth Hostel (HI), C. Isaac Peral, 2 (tel. 461 31 54), a few km out of town. Take the #34 bus. 3-day max stay. No curfew or lockout. English spoken. Members 954ptas, over 26 1166ptas; nonmembers 2968ptas.

Huéspedes Buen Dormir, C. Farnesio, 8 (tel. 421 74 92). From the cathedral follow Mateos Gago, bear left on the main thoroughfare, then turn right on Fabiola; look for the alley opposite #10. Room sizes vary radically. Over 50 birds fill the lobby, but they sleep at night, so you can *buen dormir.* Singles 1500ptas. Doubles 2500ptas, with bath 3000ptas.

Hostal-Residencia Córdoba, C. Farnesio, 12 (tel. 422 74 98). Family-run with modern bathrooms, stained-wood doors, and spacious rooms. Singles 2500ptas. Doubles 3500ptas, with bath 4700ptas.

Hostal Bienvenido, C. Archeros, 14 (tel. 441 36 55), near Pl. Curtidores, just off C. Mendez Pelaya. Welcoming managers. Rather small, dark rooms. Singles 1500ptas. Doubles 3000ptas.

Hostal La Gloria, C. San Eloy, 58 (tel. 422 26 73). Striking exterior with ornate brick-orange wood trim. Flawlessly tiled floors, firm beds. Slight bathroom stench mars otherwise pleasant atmosphere. Night attendant. Hot showers. A/C upstairs, where it's hottest. Singles 2000ptas, with bath 3000ptas. Doubles 3000ptas.

Hostal Romero, C. Gravina, 21 (tel. 421 13 53). Potted plants, antique furniture, and hanging brass pots embellish the typically Sevillian inner courtyard. Rooms are basic. Singles 2000ptas. Doubles 4000ptas. Triples 4500ptas.

Hotel Simón, C. García de Vinuesa, 19 (tel. 422 66 60), across Av. Constitución from the cathedral. An 18th-century mansion with beautiful inner courtyard and corked fountain that spouts ferns. Laundry service available. Singles 3600ptas, with bath 5800ptas. Doubles 5800ptas, with bath 9000ptas.

Camping Sevilla, Ctra. Madrid-Cádiz, km 534 (tel. 451 43 79), 12km out of town near the airport. From Estación Prado de San Sebastián, take the Empresa Casal bus toward Carmona (approximately every hr. 7am-9:30pm, 225ptas) or bus #70, which stops 800m away at Parque Alcosa. 490ptas/person, 460ptas/car, or tent. Children 390ptas.

Camping: Camping Villsom, Ctra. Sevilla-Cádiz, km 554, 8 (tel. 472 08 28), about 14km out of the city. Take the Los Amarillos bus that goes to Dos Hermanas via Barriada (every 20-25min. 6:30am-midnight, 115ptas). Adults 355ptas. 370ptas/car or tent.

FOOD

Seville is renowned for its jams, pastry, and candy, sold in **Plaza del Cabildo** near the cathedral. *Bar-restaurantes* gravitate around Estación de Córdoba on **Calle Arjona** and **Avenida Marqués de Paradas,** and on many streets of **El Arenal** and **Puerta de Carmona. Barrio Triana** is Seville's favored venue for the *tapeo* (tapas-bar hopping), a gloriously active alternative to sit-down dining. **Mercade del Arenal** is near the bullring on C. Pastor y Leandro, between C. Almansa and C. Arenal. Look there for *toro de lídia* (fresh bull meat) from next door. (Open Mon.-Sat. 9am-2pm.)

Cervecería Giralda, C. Mateos Gago, 1 (tel. 422 74 35), behind the cathedral. Andalusian tiled walls and Moorish arches. Hopping every night. Entrees 800-1200ptas, delicious *tapas* 175-200ptas. Divine *champiñones a la plancha* (grilled mushrooms in garlic and olive oil, 250ptas). Open 9am-midnight; kitchen open 1-4:30pm and 8pm-midnight.

Restaurante El Baratillo, C. Pavia, 12 (tel. 422 96 51), on a tiny street off C. Dos de Mayo. You'd never know it existed if it weren't for the local raves. Surprisingly generous *menú* 450ptas, including bread and beverage. *Platos combinados* 450-750ptas. Meals served Mon.-Fri. 8-10pm, Sat. noon-5pm.

Bar-Mesón El Serranito, C. Antonia Díaz, 11 (tel. 421 12 43), beside the bullring. Take C. García Vinuesa across from the cathedral and split left on C. Antonia Díaz. The stuffed bull's head was a gift from the *matador*—a friend of the owner. Behind the bar a framed Virgin Mary is suffered to sit with hanging hams and bull-fighting paraphernalia. *Platos combinados* 750ptas. Meat and fish dishes about 900ptas. Open Mon.-Sat. noon-4:30pm and 8pm-midnight.

Mesón La Barca, C. Santander, 6, across C. Temprado, up from Torre del Oro. Ample portions, small restaurant. *Platos combinados* 600ptas. Bambi gone classy: *estofado de venado* (venison, red wine, garlic, and vegetable stew; 750ptas). Open Sun.-Fri. 11am-midnight.

Jalea Real, Sor Angela de la Cruz, 37 (tel. 421 61 03), near Pl. Encarnación. From Pl. Encarnación, head 150m east on C. Laraña and turn left immediately before Iglesia de San Pedro. Excellent vegetarian fare—fruits and veggies coming out of the walls. Garlicky, creamy *gazpacho* 350ptas. Excellent, 2-course lunch *menú* with whole-wheat bread, wine and dessert 1150ptas. Gargantuan *platos combinados* 650ptas. Open Tues.-Sat. 1:30-5pm and 8:30-11:30pm, Sun. 1:30-4:30pm.

Freiduría Santana, C. Pureza, 61 (tel. 433 20 40), parallel to C. Betis, 1 block off the river. This wee green and red fried-fish stand is jammed with locals. 11 kinds of fried fish, all fresh and delicious. Open Sept.-July Tues.-Sun. 7pm-midnight.

Casa Manolo, C. San Jorge, 16 (tel. 433 47 92), north of Puente Isabel II. Local favorite; a madhouse during *fiestas.* Meat locker displays the merchandise for inspection. *Menú de la casa* 1600ptas, *pescado frito* (fried fish) 900ptas. Meals served Tues.-Sun. 9am-midnight.

SIGHTS AND ENTERTAINMENT

Sights Christians razed an Almohad mosque to clear space for Seville's cathedral in 1401, although the famed **La Giralda** minaret survived. The conquerors demonstrated their religious fervor by constructing a church so great that, in their own words, "those who come after us will take us for madmen." The largest Gothic edifice ever built, it took more than a century to complete. Black and gold coffin-bearers block the entrance, guarding one of Seville's most cherished possessions, the **Tumba de Cristóbal Colón** (Columbus's Tomb). The tower and its twins in Marrakech and Rabat are the oldest and largest surviving Almohad minarets. (Tower and cathedral open 9:30am-8pm. 500ptas includes guide to cathedral.)

The 9th-century crenellated walls of the **Alcázar** face the south side of the cathedral. The site was used as early as 712 by the Almohads to control the Guadalquivir, and this palace-fortress is the oldest still used by European royalty. (Open Tues.-Sat. 10:30am-1pm., Sun. 10am-2pm. 600ptas. Students free.) The 16th-century **Lonja** was built by Felipe II as a *casa de contratación* (commercial exchange) for the American trade. In 1784 it was turned into the *Archivo General de Indias* (Archive of the Indies), a collection of over 30,000 documents relating to the conquest of the "New World." Highlights include letters from Columbus to Fernando and Isabella. (Open Mon.-Fri. 10am-1pm. Free.) The **Museo de Arte Contemporáneo** next door (C. Santo Tomaso, 5) has some fab Mirós on the top floor. (Open July-Sept. Tues.-Fri. 10am-2pm; Oct.-June Tues.-Fri. 10am-7pm, Sat.-Sun. 10am-2pm. Free.) On C. Temprado, off C. Santander, two blocks west of the Lonja, is the **Hospital de la Caridad,** a compact 17th-century complex of arcaded courtyards. Its founder, Don Miguel de Mañara, is popularly believed to be the model for Don Juan. (Open Mon.-Sat. 10am-1pm and 3:30-6pm. Church 200ptas.)

King Fernando III forced Jews fleeing Toledo to live in the **Barrio de Santa Cruz,** now a neighborhood of winding alleys, flower pots, and excellent art galleries. North of Barrio Santa Cruz off Pl. Pilatos, the **Casa de Pilatos** is the most sumptuous Sevillian palace after the Alcázar. (Open 9am-7pm. 1000ptas.) The **Museo Provincial de Bellas Artes,** Pl. Museo, 9, in a 16th century Andalusian palace and a connected church, has a collection of Spanish masters second only to the Prado's. (Open Tues.-Fri. 10am-2pm and 4-7pm, Sat.-Sun. 10am-2pm. Free.)

Entertainment The tourist office distributes *El Giraldillo*, a free monthly magazine on entertainment in Seville. The venerable **Teatro Lope de Vega,** near Parque María Luísa, has long been the city's leading stage. (Ask about scheduled events at the tourist office or check the bulletin board in the university lobby on C. San Fernando.) There is a cluster of *chiringuitos,* outdoor bars that pipe in their own dance music, on the east bank of the river between Puente del Generalísimo and Puente de San Telmo. (Beer 125-200ptas. Open Mon.-Thurs. until about 5am, Fri.-Sat. until about 6:30am.) **La Carbonería,** C. Levies, 18, a few blocks west of C. Menéndez y Pelayo off C. Santa María la Blanca, was established 30 years ago to encourage artists and musicians censored during Franco's dictatorship and now functions as a popular nightspot (flamenco Sun.-Tues.). Lambada at **El Coto,** C. Luis de Morales, 118, across from El Corte Inglés near the football stadium (cover 800ptas, Sun. 1200ptas).

The best flamenco in town is on the western edge of Barrio Santa Cruz at **Los Gallos,** Pl. Santa Cruz, 11 (tel. 421 69 81). The cover (3000ptas) includes one drink (1st show 9:30pm, 2nd at midnight; if you pay for the 1st, the 2nd is free). Several booths on C. Sierpes, C. Velázquez and Pl. Toros sell **bullfight** tickets. For information on dates and prices, go to **Plaza de Toros de Sevilla** or call 422 31 52.

Seville's world-famous **Semana Santa** (Holy Week) festival lasts from Palm Sunday to Good Friday. Penitents in hoods guide 99 bejeweled floats, lit by hundred of candles, through the streets. The city explodes in the **Feria de Abril** (April Fair), a week-long festival that began as a popular revolt against foreign influence in the 19th century. The party rages in Seville with circuses, folklore displays, and bullfights.

■ Near Seville

Cádiz and Jerez de la Frontera The headquarters of the Spanish treasure fleet, Sir Francis Drake torched the Spanish Armada as it lay at anchor here in 1587. The city is energetically progressive: Cádiz's inhabitants fought fiercely against the Fascists during the Civil War, and today they consistently vote for leftist parties. Socially, the city has a roaring nightlife, open gay life, and the most extravagant carnival in all of Spain. Hunt around the harbor and Pl. San Juan de Dios for inexpensive lodgings. The **Hostal Colón,** C. Marques de Cádiz, 1 (tel. 28 53 51), offers hotel-ish comfort at hostel-ish prices. (Doubles 2800-3200ptas. Triples 3300ptas.) The **tourist office** is at C. Caldrón de la Barca, 1 (tel. 21 13 13). (Open Mon.-Fri. 9am-2pm and 5-7pm, Sat. 10am-1pm.)

You can see fermenting sherry in the *bodegas* (wine cellars) of **Jerez de la Frontera,** one of Andalucía's most commercial cities. **Harvey's of Bristol, González Byass,** and **Williams and Humbert, Ltd.** have multilingual tour guides who distill the complete sherry-making process as you sip free samples. (Late mornings, daily.) The **tourist office** is at C. Alameda Cristina, 7 (tel. 33 11 50, -62; open Mon.-Fri. 8am-3pm and 5:30-8pm, Sat. 10am-1:30pm; winter Mon.-Fri. 8am-3pm and 5-7pm, Sat. 10am-2pm). During the second week in September, the town erupts in the harvest celebration **Fiestas de la Vendimia**. Look for a place to stay along C. Medina, near the bus station, and C. Arcos, which intersects C. Medina at Pl. Romero Martínez. **Trains** run to Seville (10 *rápidos* and *expresos*/day, 1¼hr., 565ptas).

Arcos de la Frontera and Véjer da la Frontera Arcos de la Frontera is a historic monument of a city, a maze of alleyways, medieval ruins, and stone arches in the midst of fields of sunflowers and sherry-grape vines. The **Iglesia de Santa María** offers a dandy view of olive groves and low hills. Built in 1553, the church has a unique interior melange of Gothic, Renaissance, and baroque styles. A Spanish-speaking guide is available. (Open for mass daily 8:30pm, also Sun. noon; winter daily 8pm, also Sun. noon. Open Mon.-Fri. 11am-2pm and 4:30-7pm. 150ptas.) For sleeping, try **Fonda del Comercio,** C. Debajo del Corral, 15 (tel. 70 00 57), with its high-beamed ceilings, antique furniture, and thick white-washed walls. (Singles 1200ptas. Doubles 2400ptas.) The **tourist office** is at C. Cuesta de Belén, 1a (tel. 70 22 64), on the continuation of the Corredera. (Open Mon.-Sat. 9am-2pm; winter Mon.-Fri. 9am-3pm, Sat. 9am-2pm.)

Véjer de la Frontera is the archetypal charming and tourist-free Andalusian village. Whitewashed houses scatter at the base of a handsome Moorish castle, and an elegant church pokes above an imposing rock spike. The **Castillo Moro** offers the usual assortment of battlements and crenellated walls, along with a blinding view of the town's white houses. (Open July-Aug. 10am-2pm and 4-9pm, or ask at Ayuntamiento.) Sra. Luísa Doncel keeps clean and secure **rooms** in the nameless *pensión* on C. San Filmo, 12 (tel. 45 02 46; singles 1200ptas; doubles 2400ptas). Véjer's **tourist office** is in the Ayuntamiento on Pl. España (tel. 44 72 75; open Mon.-Fri. 8:30am-2:30pm). **Buses** run inland almost every hour from Cádiz (1¼hr., 485ptas) and (1¼hr., 595ptas).

■■■ CÓRDOBA

Córdoba has seen Christianity, Islam, and Judaism meet in harmony and strife for centuries. Arab occupation brought the town its greatest prosperity; for a time Córdoba, with its vast library, was one of the largest cities in medieval Europe. The city's whitewashed houses, serene patios and narrow streets typify Spanish Andalucía; Moorish influence lingers as both Muslims and Catholics still congregate in the Mezquita (mosque) every year on the anniversary of its construction.

ORIENTATION AND PRACTICAL INFORMATION

Córdoba sits atop the Andalusian triangle (north of Seville and Granada), about halfway between Madrid and Gibraltar. The city's more modern northern half extends from the train station on **Avenida de América** down to **Plaza de las Tendillas** in the center of the city; the older, mazelike southern half, known as the **Judería** (old Jewish quarter), extends from Pl. Tendillas down to the banks of the Guadalquivir, winding past the Mezquita and Alcázar.

Tourist Office: Provincial, C. Torrijos, 10 (tel. 47 12 35), on the western side of the Mezquita. English spoken. Open Mon.-Fri. 9:30am-2pm and 5-7pm, Sat. 10am-1pm; Nov.-March Mon.-Fri. 9:30am-2pm and 3:30-5:30pm, Sat. 10am-1pm.

Post Office: C. Cruz Conde, 15 (tel. 47 82 67), just north of Pl. Tendillas. Open for stamps and Lista de Correos Mon.-Fri. 8am-9pm, Sat. 9am-7pm. **Telegrams:** tel. 47 20 09, 47 03 45. Open Mon.-Fri. 8am-9pm, Sat. 9am-7pm. **Postal Code:** 14070.

Telephones: Pl. Tendillas, 7. Open Mon.-Fri. 9:30am-1:55pm and 5-10:55pm, Sat. 9:30am-1:55pm. **City Code:** 957.

Trains: Av. América, 130. (**Information:** tel. 49 02 02.) To: Seville (16/day, *AVE* 50min., 1700-2300ptas; *talgo* 1¾hr., 1800ptas; *rápido* 1½hr., 1100-1300ptas; *tranvía* 2hr., 670ptas); Algeciras (2/day, 5½hr., 1590ptas); Madrid (5/day; 4½-8hr.; *talgo* 4300-4900ptas, *rápido* 4400-6100ptas, *expreso* 3400ptas); València (3/day, *expreso* and *rápido* 5615ptas). **RENFE,** Ronda de los Tejares, 10 (tel. 47 58 54). Open Mon.-Fri. 9am-1:15pm and 5-7:30pm.

Buses: Transportes Ureña and **Empresa Bacoma,** Av. Cervantes, 22 (tel. 47 23 52). To: Madrid (3:30pm, 5½hr., 3030ptas); València (3/day, 4285ptas); Barcelona (2/day, 7140ptas). **Alsina-Graells Sur,** Av. Medina Azahara, 29 (tel. 23 64 74). To: Seville (16/day, 2-3hr., 1000ptas); Granada (7/day, 3-4hr., 1555ptas); Málaga (4/day, 3½hr., 1360ptas); Cádiz (1/day, 1955ptas).

Luggage Storage: Paquete-Exprés, next to the train station. 300ptas/locker.

Laundromat: Cordobesas, C. Barroso, 2, between Pl. Tendillas and the Mezquita. Not self-service; 1250ptas/5kg. Open Mon.-Fri. 9:30am-1:30pm and 5-8:30pm, Sat. 9:30am-1:30pm; winter Mon.-Fri. 9:30am-1:30pm and 4:30-8pm, Sat. 9:30am-1pm.

Medical Assistance: Urgencias Avenida de América, Av. América, s/n (tel. 47 23 82), ½km east of the train station.

Emergency: Ambulance: tel. 29 55 70. **Fire:** tel. 080. **National Police,** tel. 091. **Municipal Police,** tel. 092.

ACCOMMODATIONS AND CAMPING

Accommodations cluster near the train station, in and around the Judería, and off the Plaza de las Tendillas.

Residencia Juvenil Córdoba (HI), Pl. Judas Levi (tel. 29 01 66, fax 29 05 00), next to the municipal tourist office. Hostel heaven: impeccably clean, brand-new building with marble floors in the heart of the Judería. Each room has 2 firm beds and a sink. 3-day max stay. No curfew. Membership required, but available on the spot (500ptas, over 25 1000ptas). Call to reserve in the summer. 954ptas, over 25 1166ptas. With breakfast 1166ptas, over 25 1378ptas. *Media pensión* 1908ptas, over 25 2226ptas. *Pensión completa* 2438ptas, over 25 3074ptas.

Huéspedes Martínez Rücker, Martínez Rücker, 14 (tel. 47 25 62), just east of the Mezquita. Charming furnishings and rooms. Singles 1500ptas. Doubles 3000ptas.

Hostal-Residencia Séneca, C. Conde y Luque, 7 (tel. 47 32 34), 2 block north of the Mezquita. Impeccably maintained, but some rooms tiny. English and French spoken. Singles 1875ptas, 1675ptas in winter. Doubles 3500ptas, with bath 4500ptas. Triples 5000ptas. Doubles and triples 500ptas less in winter. Breakfast included.

Camping: Campamento Municipal, Av. Brillante (tel. 47 20 00; ask for *Camping Municipal*). About 2km north of the train station: turn left on Av. América, left again at Av. Brillante, then walk uphill. Buses #10 and 11, which leave from Av. Cervantes near the station, run to the campsite. Public pool next door. 401ptas/person, tent, or car, under 10 302ptas.

FOOD

The famous Mezquita attracts more high-priced eateries than Mohammed did followers. If you're counting pesetas, branch out into the Judería.

Sociedad de Plateros, C. San Francisco, 6 (tel. 47 00 42), between C. San Francisco and the top end of Pl. Potro. Casual atmosphere attracts families by day and British students by night. Wide selection of *tapas*. Fresh fish, including *japuta*, almost every day (450ptas). Bar open 8am-4:30pm and 6:30pm-1am; meals served 1-4pm and 8:30-10pm.

Taberna Salinas, C. Tundidores, 3 (tel. 48 01 35), just south of the Ayuntamiento. A shining example of traditional Cordovan cooking: *salmorejo, carne con tomate,* and an eye-popping (or Popeye-ing?) spinach mash. Service a bit rushed, but the patio setting is calm. *Raciones* 500-7600ptas. Open Mon.-Sat. noon-4pm and 8pm-midnight; winter Mon.-Sat. noon-4pm and 7:30-11:30pm.

Cafetín Halal, C. Rey Heredía, 28 (tel. 47 76 30). As much an Islamic center as a restaurant. Locals drink herbal teas (over 30 kinds) on Arabic sofa-tables. *Couscous* (800ptas). Food gets mixed reviews. Open noon-midnight.

SIGHTS AND ENTERTAINMENT

Begun in 784, the **Mezquita** was intended to surpass all other mosques in grandeur. Over the next 2 centuries the spectacular golden-brown building was gradually enlarged to cover an area equivalent to several city blocks. The courtyard features carefully spaced orange trees, palm trees, and fountains. Inside, 850 pink and blue marble, alabaster, and stone columns support hundreds of red- and white-striped 2-tiered arches. In 1523 drastic alterations stuck a full-blown Renaissance cathedral in the middle of the mosque. (Open April-Sept. 10am-7pm; Oct.-March 10am-1:30pm and 3:30-5:30pm. 500ptas, ages 8-11 250ptas, free Sun. 10am-1pm.)

Just west of the Mezquita and closer to the river lies the **Alcázar,** a palace for Catholic monarchs that headquartered the Inquisition between 1490 and 1821. Its walls surround a manicured hedge garden with flower beds, terraced goldfish ponds, fountains, and palm trees. (Open May-Sept. Tues.-Sat. 9:30am-1:30pm and 5-8pm, Sun. 9:30am-1:30pm; Oct.-April 9:30am-1:30pm and 4-7pm. Gardens illuminated May-Sept. 10pm-1am. 225ptas, free Tues.) Tucked away on C. Judíos, the **Sinagoga** is a solemn reminder of the 1492 expulsion of Spanish Jewry. (Open Tues.-Sat. 10am-2pm and 3:30-5:30pm, Sun. 10am-1:30pm. 50ptas.) The **Museo Taurino y de Arte Cordobés,** at Pl. Maimonides, a bullfighting museum, contains galleries full of the heads of bulls who killed matadors. (Open May-Sept. Tues.-Sat. 9:30am-1:30pm and 5-8pm, Sun. 9:30am-1:30pm; Oct.-April Tues.-Sat. 9:30am-1:30pm and 4-7pm, Sun. 9:30am-1:30pm. 200ptas, free Tues.)

To see some of the best **flamenco** in Spain with an audience o' tourists, head for the **Tablao Cardenal,** Cardenal Herrero, 14 (tel. 48 03 46), facing the Mezquita. (Shows Tues.-Sat. at 10:30pm. 2000ptas includes a drink.) The tourist office keeps a schedule of **bullfights** at Las Califas bullring; tickets range from 800 to 120,000ptas.

Constructed in the 10th century by Abderramán III, the **Medina Azahara** is a pleasure palace built into the Sierra Morena, 8km northwest of the city. It was divided into 3 terraces: the palace, the living quarters for the thousands of servants, and the gardens. Before its excavation in 1944, the existence of the site had been mere rumor. (Open May-Sept. Tues.-Sat. 10am-2pm and 6-8:30pm, Sun. 10am-2pm; Oct.-April Tues.-Sat. 10am-2pm and 4-6:30pm, Sun. 10am-2pm. 250ptas, EC citizens free.) Reaching Medina Azahara takes some effort; call ahead to make sure it's open (tel. 23 40 25). The O-1 bus (schedule information tel. 25 57 00) leaves from Av. Cervantes for Cruce Medina Azahara, stopping 3km from the site itself (about every hr. 6:30am-10:30pm, 90ptas).

■■■ GRANADA

As the Christian Reconquista advanced, the Moors enclosed the glorious city of Granada in layer upon layer of fortification. The citadel was bitterly contested until 1492, when Boabdil, its last Arab king, lost the city's keys to Catholic monarchs Fernando and Isabel. Though Granada's mosques were destroyed, the majestic clay-red Alhambra and snow-capped Sierra Nevada still lure travelers here. The 50,000 students of its University help make Granada a lively provincial capital.

ORIENTATION AND PRACTICAL INFORMATION

The center of Granada is **Plaza Nueva,** framed by handsome Renaissance buildings and outfitted with a wide variety of hotels and restaurants. Plaza Nueva sits just north of **Plaza de Isabel la Católica,** which is at the intersection of the two main arteries, **C. Reyes Católicos** and **Gran Vía de Colón.** From RENFE and all bus stations except Alsina Graells, follow Av. Constitución to Gran Vía de Colón, turn right and walk 15-20 minutes into town. Municipal buses cover nearly all areas of town; bus #11 (85ptas) connects a number of major streets, including Carretera de Madrid, the train and bus stations and the town center. If solo, avoid the small streets at the foot of the Albayzín northeast of Pl. Nueva after dark.

Tourist Office: Plaza Mariana Pineda, 10 (tel. 22 66 88). From Puerta Real follow Acera del Casino through Pl. Campollo into Pl. Mariana Pineda. Open Mon.-Fri. 9am-2pm and 4:30-7pm, Sat. 10am-1pm. **Branch Tourist Office:** Calle Mariana Pineda, s/n. Open Mon.-Fri. 10am-1pm and 5-7pm, Sat. 10am-1pm.

Budget Travel: Viajes TIVE, C. Martínez Campo, 21 (tel. 25 02 11). Open Mon.-Fri. 9am-1pm and 4:30-7:30pm.

Currency Exchange: Hipercor supermarket, C. Arabial at Sta. Clotilde, near the bus station. Good rates and long hours. Open Mon.-Sat. 9am-9:30pm.

American Express: Viajes Bonal, Av. Constitución, 19 (tel. 27 63 12), at the north end of Gran Vía de Colón. Open Mon.-Fri. 9:30am-1:30pm and 5-8pm. Currency exchange for cardholders only Mon.-Fri. 10am-1pm.

Post Office: Puerta Real, s/n (tel. 22 48 35; fax (58) 22 36 41). Open for stamps and Lista de Correos Mon.-Fri. 8am-9pm, Sat. 9am-2pm; for **telegrams** Mon.-Fri. 8am-9pm, Sat. 9am-7pm, Sun. 9am-2pm. **Fax** service. **Postal Code:** 18070.

Telephones: C. Reyes Católicos, 55, 1 bl. towards Pl. Nueva from Pl. Isabel la Católica. Open Mon.-Sat. 9am-2pm and 5-10pm. **Telephone Code:** 958.

Trains: C. Dr. Jaime García Royo, s/n (tel. 23 34 08), at the end of Av. Andaluces, which leads into fat Av. Constitución, due west of the city center. To: Málaga (3/day via Bobadilla, 4hr., 1030ptas); Córdoba (3/day, 4hr., 1285ptas); Seville (3/day, 4hr., 1500ptas); Algeciras (2/day, 5hr., 1540ptas); València (3/day, 8-12hr., 4450ptas); Madrid (2/day, 6-8hr., 3700ptas); Barcelona (2/day, 13hr., 6400ptas).

Buses: The usual mess of companies, including **Alsina Graells,** Camino de Ronda, 97 (tel. 25 13 58), near C. Emperatriz Eugenia in Andalucía, and **Bacoma,** Av. Andaluces, 12 (tel. 28 42 51), near the train station.

Laundromat: Lavandería Autoservicio Emperatriz Eugenia, C. Emperatriz Eugenia, 26 (tel. 27 88 20). Wash 300ptas. Dry 200ptas. Open Mon.-Sat. 9am-2pm and 4-8pm.

Luggage Storage: At the **train station** (200ptas). At the Alsina Graells **bus station** (300ptas).

Medical Services: Clínica de San Cecilio, Calle Doctor Oloriz, 16 (tel. 28 02 00).

Police: Municipal, C. Duquesa, 21 (tel. 092). **Guardia Civil** (tel. 25 11 00). **Policía Nacional,** Pl. Campos (tel. 091). English and French spoken (theoretically).

ACCOMMODATIONS, CAMPING, AND FOOD

The most convenient budget hotels are directly off **Pl. Nueva,** on the street that leads to the Alhambra. The **youth hostel** is closed for renovation. The **Pensión Doña Lupe,** Av. del Generalife, s/n (tel. 22 14 73), actually in the Alhambra, is a true oasis in the *Let's Go* pilgrimage. The clean, expansive rooms have baths, TV, and winter heating. There's also a pool and an English-speaking owner. (Students and/or *Let's Go* users: singles 1000ptas, doubles 1950ptas.) A sneaky rope mechanism unlocks the door to a hidden world of spacious, simply decorated rooms at the **Hostal Navarro-Ramos,** Cuesta de Gomérez, 21 (tel. 25 05 55; singles 1100ptas, with bath 1200ptas. Doubles 1900ptas, with bath 2900ptas.) **Huéspedes Romero,** C. Sillería, 1 (tel. 26 60 79), overlooks Pl. Trinidad at the end of C. Mesones. Each room is unique. Large double beds and tiled floors. (Singles 1200ptas. Doubles 2400ptas.) **Camping** is available at 4 locations near Granada, all of which charge 350-415ptas/person and /tent. **Sierra Nevada,** Av. Madrid, 107 (tel. 15 09 54), has

GRANADA

lots of shady trees, modern facilities, and free hot showers. (350-440ptas/person, tent, or car. Youngsters 315ptas.)

The area around Plaza Nueva oozes with restaurants. **Restaurante Alcaicería,** C. Oficios, 6, is one of the most highly regarded fooderies in town. Enter through the vine-covered archway and follow the sounds of the guitar. (*Menú* 1450ptas. Open daily 1-4pm and 8-11:30pm.) The unassuming façade of **Rincón de Pepe,** Escudo de Carmen, 17, off Pl. Carmen, hides good food and better prices. *Menú* 525-975ptas. (Open daily noon-4pm and 7:30-11pm.) The **market** overflows from Pl. Romanilla beside the cathedral, or at least until the architectural dig at the usual spot on C. San Augustín is done. (Open Mon.-Sat. 8am-3pm.)

SIGHTS

The **Alhambra** is the name of both the hill that dominates Granada and the sprawling palace-fortress atop it. Against the silvery backdrop of the Sierra Nevada, the Christians drove the first Nazarite King Alhamar from the Albayzín to this more strategic hill. Here he built a fortress called the **Alcazaba,** the oldest section of today's Alhambra. The **Alcázar** (Royal Palace) was built for the great Moorish rulers Yusuf I (1333-1354) and Muhammad V (1354-1391). Legend has it that an unexplained force murdered Yusuf I in an isolated basement chamber of the Alcázar; his son Muhammad V was left to complete the palace. After the Christian *Reconquista* drove the Moors from Spain, Fernando and Isabella respectfully restored the Alcázar. Little did they know that two generations later omnipotent Emperor Carlos V would demolish part of it to make way for his **Palacio de Carlos V,** a Renaissance masterpiece by Pedro Machuca, a disciple of Michelangelo. Although it is glaringly incongruous amidst all the Moorish splendor, experts agree that the Palacio is one of the most beautiful Renaissance buildings in Spain. Up the hill past the Alhambra's main entrance is the lush palace greenery of the **Generalife,** the spacious summer retreat of the Sultans that crowns the Alhambra's twin hill, *el cerro del sol* (the sun hill). Enter the Alhambra through Puerta de Granada, off Cuesta de Gomérez. (Alhambra open Mon.-Sat. 9am-7:45pm, Sun. 9am-5:45pm; Oct.-May 9am-5:45pm. 600ptas, Sun. after 3pm free. Generalife only, 150ptas. Box office shuts down about 45min. before closing time.)

Begun 30 years after the Christian reconquest of the city, the **cathedral** (entrance on Gran Vía), intended to outshine the Alhambra, does not even rise out of its shadow. The **Capilla Real** (Royal Chapel) contains the elaborate tomb of Fernando and Isabel, their nutty daughter Juana La Loca, and her husband Felipe el Hermoso (whose corpse Juana dragged around with her for a unpleasantly long time after his demise). (Both open daily 10:30am-1pm and 4-7pm; Oct.-Feb. daily 10:30am-1pm and 3:30-6pm. 200ptas, Sun. morning free.)

ENTERTAINMENT

Entertainment listings are near the back of the daily paper, the *Ideal* (90ptas), under the heading *Cine y Espectáculos.* The Friday supplement lists even more bars, concerts, and special events. At night, the university crowd tarries at pubs and bars in the area bounded by **Calle Pedro Antonio de Alarcón, Callejón de Nevot** and **Calle de Melchor Almagro.** The **Internacional Festival de Música y Danza** (mid-June to early July) sponsors open-air performances of classical music and ballet in the gardens of the Alhambra's Generalife. Prices for seats run 2000-7500ptas.

■ Near Granada

There are 7000 **caves** in the Guadix region and 2000 in **Guadix** itself. People began moving into caves because they couldn't afford houses; the fad spread like the plague. Forty percent of the population now lives in privately-owned caves, some of which date back more than 1000 years. Dug into soft clay hills 55km east of Granada, the caves have the whitewashed exteriors of typical Andalusian houses.

From the bus station, walk along Carretera de Almería (which becomes Avenida de Medina Olmos) to the **Plaza de las Palomas** (Square of the Doves, a.k.a. Plaza de la Constitución). Crowning the hill is the recently opened **Cueva Museu** in Pl. Ermita Nueva. Here visitors simulate cave life and examine costumes and tapestries from the region. The new multilingual **tourist office** (tel. 66 26 65) is on Ctra. Granada. (Open Mon.-Sat. 9:30am-2:30pm.) Come here by **bus** from Granada (11/day, 1½hr., 475ptas). The bus station in Guadix is at Urbanización Santa Rosa (tel. 66 11 02), near Ctra. Almería.

■■■ COSTA DEL SOL

The coast has sold its soul to the Devil, and now he's starting to collect. Artifice covers its once-natural charms as chic promenades and hotels seal off small towns from the shoreline. The former Phoenician, Greek, Roman, and Arab ports cater to an international clientele with wads of money and tons of attitude. Although the Costa del Sol officially extends from Tarifa in the southwest to Cabo de Gata east of Almería, the name most often refers to the resorts from Marbella, in the province of Málaga, to Motril, in the province of Granada. Post-industrial Málaga divides the Costa in two. To the northeast, the hills dip straight into the ocean, where the scenery is less spoiled but beaches are usually rocky. To the southeast, the Costa is more built up and water washes almost entirely against concrete.

Nothing can take away the coast's major attraction, however: 8 months of spring and 4 of summer per year. Sun-freaks swarm everywhere in July and August; make reservations or be ready for a search. Prices double in high season. Some sleep on the beaches (solo travelers and women should be cautious), a practice that is winked at on the outskirts of less elegant areas. Alternatively, ask around for *casas particulares*. June is the best time to visit, when summer weather has come to town but most vacationers haven't.

Trains go far as Málaga, Torremolinos, or Fuengirola; private bus lines supply connections along the coast itself. Railpasses are not valid, but prices are reasonable.

■ Málaga

More style than substance, the city is known gastronomically for wine (not cuisine) and economically for tourism (not industry). Poor Málaga, once celebrated by Hans Christian Andersen, Rubén Darío and native poet Vicente Aleixandre, has lost its looks. Its concrete arms extend down the coast, its beaches are unpleasant and its streets are crowded and dirty. As the 2nd-largest city in Andalucía and the area's transportation hub, Málaga is best used as a base for Costa-del-Sol-searching.

To see the city at its best, stroll the length of the palmy **Paseo del Parque;** it'll take you below the **Alcazaba,** the local Moorish palace. The palace contains a museum of Roman and Moorish art surrounded by flowering purple blossoms, palm trees, and cacti. (Open Tues.-Sat. 9:30am-1:30pm and 5-8pm, Sun. 10am-2pm; winter 4-7pm. 20ptas.) The **Museo de Bellas Artes,** C. San Augustín, 6, in the old palace of the Counts of Buenavista, hoards a wealth of mosaics, sculptures and paintings, including works by Murillo, Ribera, and native son Picasso. (Open daily 10am-1:30pm and 5-7pm. 250ptas, EC students under 21 free.) Po. Parque turns into **Almeda Principal** just east of the **Plaza de la Marina**. The city center, containing most sights and the **catedral** (called "the little lady with one arm" because no one ever bothered to finish the second tower) is north of Almeda Principal. (Open Mon.-Sat. 10am-12:45pm and 4-6pm. 100ptas.)

The most popular beach stretches to the east at **Pedregalejos.** (Take bus #11.) After dinner, in the restaurants along the beach, students swamp the bars a few blocks down. Others forage inland to **Calle Juan Sebastián Elcamo** in the **Echevarría** district, where crowds coagulate around 1am when the discos open.

Accommodations, Food, and Practical Information Many budget establishments cluster north of **Paseo del Parqued** and **Almeda Principal,** but Málaga's affordable rooms tend to look somewhat run-down. **Hostal Residencia Chinitas,** Pasaje Chinitas, 2 (tel. (95) 221 46 83), on an alley off Pl. Constitución, is a *hostal* with humor. There's a mellow reception area with a VCR and movie collection and the rooms are clean. (Singles 1500ptas. Doubles with bath 2800ptas.) For inexpensive food, try the *pasajes* of the older section of town around **Plaza de la Constitución** and **Calle Granada,** and also on the streets behind **Paseo Marítimo.** The main **market,** near the town center between the river and Almeda Principal, gets crowded after noon, but the selection is still pretty good. (Open Mon.-Sat. 8am-2pm.) Those in the know dine on the beachfront in **Pedregalejos,** near the eastern edge of town, where a row of crowded and inexpensive restaurants snatches up the day's catch. (Take bus #11 from Po. Parque.)

There's a multilingual **tourist office** at Pasaje de Chinitas, 4 (tel. (95) 221 34 45), off Pl. Constitución. (Open Mon.-Fri. 8:30am-2pm, Sat. 9am-1pm.) The **train station** is at C. Cuárteles (tel. 231 25 00), southwest of the city. To get to the town center, take bus #3 or 4 from the park opposite the station to Po. Parque; debark at Pl. Marina. Or else walk down C. Cuárteles, turn left on Po. Matadero (fronting the river), cross Puente Tetuán, and you'll be on Almeda Principal (15min.). **RENFE,** C. Strachan, 2 (tel. 221 31 22), is less crowded, more convenient for getting tickets and information. Open Mon.-Fri. 9am-1:30pm and 4:30-7:30pm. To: Granada via Bobadilla (2/day, 3½hr., 1030ptas); Seville (5/day, 2½-3½hr., 1235ptas); Córdoba (8/day, 2½hr., 1030ptas); Madrid (5/day, 7hr., 4600ptas); Barcelona (3/day, 11-14hr., 7000ptas). There's also an enormous central **bus station**, at Po. Tilos (tel. 235 00 61), behind RENFE.

■ Marbella

Glamorous Marbella, the jewel of the Costa del Sol, has but one function: the fleecing of the British, Germans, French, Swedes, and Americans who descend upon it each season in a vain attempt to rub elbows with the rich and famous. The city extorts *pesetas* quickly, efficiently, painlessly, and in 5 different languages, but it's also possible to steal away from this snooty city with a budgety good time. Marbella has a chic promenade over the beach, leaving its most valuable asset starved for space. If the press of flesh stifles, hop on the Fuengirola bus, stop at **Playa de las Chapas,** 10km east, and walk in either direction to find an open stretch.

If you don't have reservations, especially from mid-July through August, arrive early and pray. The area in the old part of town behind Av. Ramón y Cajal is loaded with little *hostales* and *fondas,* all of which fill up quickly. Several cheap guest houses line **Calle Ancha, Calle San Francisco, Calle Aduar** and **Calle de los Caballeros,** all of which are uphill on C. Huerta Chica, across C. Ramón y Cajal from the tourist office road. People at bars often know of *casas particulares.* **Hostal del Pilar,** C. Mesoncillo, 4 (tel. (95) 282 99 36), the 2nd left off C. Huerta Chica, has a relaxing bar/lounge with a sociable, youth-hostelish ambience. (Mattresses on the roof in warm months 800ptas/person. Singles 1500-1900ptas. Doubles 2400-2900ptas. Triples about 3600ptas.) **Casa-Huéspedes Aduar,** C. Aduar, 7 (tel. (95) 277 35 78), is positively overflowing with roses in summer. Unexceptional rooms open onto a brand new, tiled and plant-filled courtyard on the first floor; balconied rooms upstairs. (Singles 1500ptas. Doubles 2500ptas. Oct.-March: 1200ptas; 2200ptas.) **Bar El Gallo,** C. Lobatas, 46, sports a loud TV and louder locals, but lip-smackin' good food. (*San Jacobo*—pork stuffed with ham and swiss—and fries 400ptas. Open 9am-midnight, but meals not served at all times.)

Buses leave for Málaga (every 30min., 1½hr., 455ptas) from the station on Av. Ricardo Soriano (tel. (95) 277 21 92). To get to the town center, take a left on Avenida Ricardo Soriano until it becomes **Avenida Ramón y Cajal.** The old town is on the left; the waves crash to the right. The multilingual **tourist office** is at Av.

Miguel Cano, 1 (tel. (95) 277 14 42), behind the Almeda Park. (Open Mon.-Fri. 9:30am-9:30pm, Sat. 10am-8pm; winter Mon.-Fri. 9:30-8pm.)

■■■ RONDA

Ronda tops a rocky massif split by a spectacular 1000-ft. gorge, while far below the Río Guadalevín twinkles. Ronda's history runs as deep as that gorge. Pliny and Ptolemy mention it as *Arunda* (surrounded by mountains); during the Muslim occupation, the sneaky Al Mutadid ibn Abbad annexed the city for Seville by asphyxiating the previous lord in his bath. Only an hour from the resorts of the Costa del Sol, Ronda is both a welcome diversion from crowded beaches and a good base for exploring some of the *pueblos blancos* to the south.

The old and new parts of the city are connected by 3 bridges: the most impressive of these, the **Puente Nuevo** (1735), hangs nearly 100m high. Ronda's 2nd and 3rd bridges are the 17th-century **Puente Viejo** (rebuilt over an earlier Arab bridge) and the Roman **Puente San Miguel.** Nearby is the **Plaza de Toros,** the site where local hero Pedro Romero invented modern bullfighting *a pie* (on foot) and used the *muleta* (red cape) for the first time. Inside the 1784 structure, the **Museo Taurino** tells his glorious story and highlights Cayetano Ordóñez, apotheosized by Hemingway as the matador in *The Sun Also Rises.* (Open daily 10am-7pm; Oct.-May 10am-2pm. 200ptas; seniors and children free Fri. after 3pm.)

Accommodations, Food, and Practical Information There are plenty of rooms to go around, almost all of which are bunched in the new city along the streets perpendicular to **Carrera Espinel. Fonda La Española,** C. José Aparicio, 3 (tel. (952) 287 10 52), on a side street around the corner from Turismo, is sparkling clean, and has spacious rooms and a sundeck view of El Tajo. (Curfew 1am. 1200ptas.) **Hostal Ronda Sol,** C. Almendra, 11 (tel. (952) 287 44 97), near the corner with C. Sevilla, has a sunken courtyard and rooms with matching furniture. (Singles 1300ptas. Doubles 2300ptas.) The few budget eateries cluster near the center of town around **Plaza de España. Cervecería Marisquería "El Patio,"** Carrera Espinel, 100, has A/C inside, patio outside and some potent garlic chicken (450ptas). (Open Thurs.-Tues. noon-4pm and 8pm-1am.) **Mesón Santiago,** C. Marina, 3, off Pl. Socorro, has a vine-covered terrace in the summer and a cozy fireplace in winter. *Filete de ternera* (veal cutlet) 900ptas. (Open daily noon-5pm.)

Ronda's **tourist office,** Pl. España, 1 (tel. (952) 287 12 72), can help show you around. (Open Mon.-Fri. 9am-2pm.) Both the **train station,** Av. Andalucía (tel. (952) 287 16 73), and **bus station,** Av. Concepción García Redondo, 2, rumble on the western side of the new city to: Málaga (3/day, 2hr., 720ptas); Algeciras (6/day, 3hr., 545ptas); Granada (3/day, 4hr., 950ptas) and Seville (at noon, 4½hr., 1200ptas). Change at Bobadilla for destinations other than Algeciras. To reach the center of town, turn right on Av. Andalucía and follow it past the bus station (where the name changes to C. San José) until the street ends. Here, take a left on C. Jerez, follow it past the Almeda del Tajo (city park) and Pl. Toros (C. Jerez will change names to Virgen de la Paz) until it hits **Plaza de España.** Carrera Espinel intersects C. Virgen de la Paz directly across from the *corrida de toros,* immediately before Pl. España.

■■■ GIBRALTAR AND ALGECIRAS

The gateway to the Atlantic commands a breathtaking view of the **Straits of Gibraltar** all the way to the Moroccan coast. Nicknamed "Gib" by the locals, this British colony is a microcosm of modern Britain, complete with bobbies, fish 'n' chips, a changing of the guard, and Marks and Spencer. Gibraltar takes its Britishness very seriously, but unlike their counterparts in London, citizens can switch from the Queen's English to Andalusian Spanish with ease. British sovereignty and the Spanish presence haven't always coexisted peacefully: for 20 years, Franco cut off all contact between the Rock and Spain. In 1985, the Spanish government reopened the frontier gates; anyone with a passport may travel freely to and from the Rock.

The main **tourist office** is at 18-20 Bomb House Lane (tel. 742 89), in the Gibraltar Museum. Gibraltar has a separate country code (350); from Spain, dial 07 to access the international net. The USA Direct code is 88 00. Realistically, you have two rooming alternatives: 1) Stay in Algeciras, a bus ride away. 2) Ask around the restaurants near the La Línea bus station for info about *casas particulares*. The cheapest beds are at the **Toc H Hostel**, Line Wall Rd. (tel. 734 31). Show up by 9:30am with your lucky rabbit's foot. (£3/person. £15/week.) The other choice is **Miss Serruya Guest House,** 92/1a Irish Town. (Tel. 732 20. Singles £10. Doubles £14.) **Buses** run to **La Línea,** the nearest Spanish town on the border, from the Empresa Comes station in Algeciras behind Hotel Octavio (every ½hr., 40min., 195ptas).

Most people come to **Algeciras** to leave. Just 13km across the blue, on the Spanish side of the Bahía de Algeciras, the port offers cheap rooms and a passage to Morocco. All services necessary for transit to Morocco are clustered around the port. The **tourist office,** C. Juan de la Cierva, s/n (tel. 57 26 36), is the gigantic tube-shaped pink and red building. Open Mon.-Fri. 9am-2pm, Sat. 10am-1pm. **Trains** run to Málaga (2/day, 5hr., 1300ptas); Seville (3/day, 1900ptas), Granada (2/day, 2½hr., 1600ptas), and Madrid (2 direct night trains/day, 5300ptas). **Ferries** go to Ceuta (5-9/day, 1¼hr., 1500ptas, 7900-8500ptas/car) and Tangier (4-8/day, 2½hr., Class A 3440ptas/person, Class B 2700ptas/person, 8500ptas/car). Children 4-12 travel for ½-price; passengers with Eurailpasses get 20% discount.

Lots of convenient lodgings bunch around **Calle José Santacana,** parallel to Av. Marina and one block inland, and **Calle Duque de Almodóvar,** 2 blocks farther from the water. Check **Hostal Vizcaíno,** at C. José Santacana, 9. (Tel. (956) 65 57 56. Singles with bath 1000ptas. Doubles with bath 2000ptas.) **Hostal Residencia Gonzalez,** C. Jose Santacana, 7 (tel. 65 28 43), is another decent bargain close to the port with roomy, tasteful quarters and new wood furnishings. (Singles 1200ptas, with bath 1500ptas. Doubles 2400ptas, with bath 3000ptas.)

Turkey (Türkiye)

US$1 = 11,800TL (lira, or TRL)
CDN$1 = 9000TL
UK£1 = 18,400TL
IR£1 = 17,200TL
AUS$1 = 7700TL
NZ$1 = 6550TL
SAR1 = 2460TL
Country Code: 90

10,000TL =   US$8.45
10,000TL = CDN$1.11
10,000TL =   UK£0.54
10,000TL =   IR£0.58
10,000TL = AUS$1.30
10,000TL =   NZ$1.53
10,000TL =   SAR4.06
International Dialing Prefix: 99

> All prices are quoted in U.S. dollars because rampant inflation in Turkey tends to correspond roughly with the devaluation of the lira.

Turkey has served as both a battleground and a canvas for Eastern and Western cultures and traditions. The iron-forging Hittites controlled Asia Minor in the 2nd millennium BC, developed systems of government and law, and spoke one of the earliest known Indo-European languages. The Aegean coastal cities (Miletus, Ephesus, Pergamon, and Smyrna) enriched Greek culture as much as did Greece proper. Asia Minor became the cradle of the foundling religion of Christianity that ruled Europe for the next 1500 years. In the 11th century the region then shuddered with the advent of Seljuk Turk control. More recently, World War I witnessed a genocide of the Armenian people which has been likened to the Holocaust.

Perhaps the greatest empire the world has ever known, the Ottomans ruled Turkey (and, at times, a large part of the Eastern Mediterranean) from the early 15th century to the end of World War I. The reign of Süleyman the Magnificent, from 1520 to 1566, marked the apex of the empire, after which point it declined into a stagnant morass of corruption. That modern Turkey exists at all is a tribute to early 20th-century leader Mustafa Kemal (Atatürk) who led the forces that expelled the British, French, Greek and Russian armies. Equating modernization with Westernization, Atatürk abolished the Ottoman Caliphate, Romanized the alphabet, outlawed

Muslim tribunals and installed a facsimile of democratic government; for a time he went so far as to command *muezzin* (prayer callers) to sing in modern Turkish, even though, according to Muhammed, the Qur'an is perfect, immutable, and untranslatable in classical Arabic.

Atatürk's autocratic reforms, however, could go only so far. Beyond İstanbul and a few other large cities, traditional Islamic customs and attitudes prevail. In the late 1970s, the democracy began to falter as street warfare erupted in İstanbul, prompting military intervention. Elections in 1983 ushered in the right-wing party of Prime Minister Turgut Özal. Though the leader of the opposition remains in enforced exile, his party was recently reinstated and martial law withdrawn. Turkey was a crucial ally to the U.S. during the Cold War, but its current position has become more vague. In the summer of 1992, government conflict with armed Kurds reached a peak. Turkey's application to the EC is still pending consideration as of 1993. Snubbed by the West, Turkey has sought economic opportunity to the east, in the former Soviet republics of Kazakhstan, Tajikistan, and Uzbekistan.

For men, Turkey may be an ideal budget travel destination (some compare it to Greece 10 years ago, pre-tourist-influx), but restrictive customs which give women subordinate status (if unofficially) make it difficult, at best, for women traveling alone (see Women in Health, Safety and Climate below).

> For more detailed coverage of Turkey, consult *Let's Go: Greece & Turkey*.

GETTING THERE

Bus travel is one of the cheapest methods of arriving in Turkey. Amsterdam, Athens, London and Munich are all centers for private bus lines providing long-distance tours. **Magic Bus** offers cheap, direct service to Europe's major cities. Offices are located at 20 Filellinon St., Syntagma, Athens (tel. (01) 323 74 71); and 32 Tsimiski St., Thessaloniki (tel. (031) 28 32 80). **London Student Travel,** 52 Grosvenor Gardens, London SW1W OAG (tel. (071) 730 34 02) offers competitive rail, coach, and air fares all over the continent.

Trains to Turkey from Venice, Munich, and Vienna are relatively cheap. They are also relatively inconvenient: Eurail is invalid in Turkey, and the Turkish rail system is rivaled only by the Greek as Europe's most antiquated and least efficient. Be sure to ask for a top bunk and wrap the straps of your luggage around your limbs when you sleep to deter thieves.

Reservations are recommended for many **ferries;** be warned, however, that they run on very irregular schedules. You should check in at least 2 hours in advance. Make sure you bring along toilet paper and motion sickness medication. There is direct ferry service between Piraeus, Greece and İzmir, but it's cheaper to sail from one of the Greek islands. Three ferries per week also run between Pythagorion and Kuşadasi. You can also travel to Turkey by boat from points other than Greece, including Brindisi, Italy. Be prepared for the Turkish port tax—usually around US$9.

Turkish Airlines (THY) fares are exorbitant, but a 60% student reduction brings them in line with the budget carriers. THY also has regular service to Turkey from European countries and offers 50% discounts to ISIC holders and those under 22 on some international flights. If you have flown to Greece on certain European charter flights, you are required to stay in Greece for your vacation (in other words, you can't take advantage of cheap fares to Greece in order to visit Turkey). Both **Romanian Airlines (Tarom)** and **Pakistan Air** offer low fares to İstanbul from the U.S. and major European cities.

Many travelers cross Turkey on the way to other Asian countries. Most buses to the east depart directly from Ankara. Transit visas for Syria are easier to obtain than for Iran; Iraq seems a less likely bet. Reaching the former USSR from Turkey is a definite possibility; check locally or with the Russian embassy in Ankara.

TRAVELING IN TURKEY

Turkey is a budget traveler's dream. Frequent and cheap **buses** run between all size-able cities. Private bus lines sometimes offer students a 10% discount (flash the ol' ISIC). **Varan Tours** buses, though slightly more expensive, are faster and more comfortable for longer trips (they're air-conditioned). The trade-off for inexpensive **trains** (10% student discount) is the looong rides. Also, trains do not run along the western coast. **Shared taxis,** known as *dolmuş,* usually minibuses or vans, fill gaps left by the remarkably comprehensive bus system and also follow fixed routes. They are almost as cheap as buses and leave whenever they fill up *(dolma* means "stuffed"). You can get on and off *dolmuş* whenever you like. **Hitchhiking** in Turkey is reportedly quite common. Often the driver will ask for 50-100% of the bus fare. The hitching signal is a waving hand.

Those unwilling to suffer through Turkey's eternal bus and train rides should consider the low domestic fares on **Turkish Airlines;** the student (ages 12-24—bring ID) rate is US$42. There is no **ferry** system along the west coast except for a **Turkish Maritime Line** boat from İstanbul to İzmir (3/week; 1/week Oct.-June).

TURKEY ESSENTIALS

Turkish government tourist offices and tourist police exist in most major cities and resort areas. Some English, German or French is usually spoken. They help find accommodations and often provide the usual slew of services without charge. In places without an official office, travel agents often serve the same function.

The black market exchange rate in Turkey is only slightly better than the official rate. If you're coming from Greece, spend your *drachmae* before arriving; the few banks that change them do so at an egregious rate. Persistent haggling in shops, over accommodations, and over less regulated transportation fares can save you loads of money. Examine what you buy at bazaars carefully; exporting antiques is a jailable offense, even if you plead ignorance. *If you're caught doing drugs in Turkey, you're screwed.* The horror stories of lengthy prison sentences and dealer-informers are true; embassies are absolutely helpless in all cases. The minimum sentence for possession of even the smallest amount is 16 months. Turkish law also provides for "guilt by association"—those in the company of a person caught are subject to prosecution. As for the foolish notion of smuggling: anyone looking remotely like a backpacker gets searched with a fine-toothed comb arriving back in Europe from Turkey. If you still don't believe us, watch *Midnight Express* for some more detailed depictions of Turkish prisons.

Everything closes on the national **holidays:** January 1, April 23, May 19, August 30 and October 28-29. During Ramadan *(Ramazan* in Turkish; Feb. 11 to March 24 in 1994), pious Muslims will not eat, drink, smoke, or travel between dawn and sunset. Outside İstanbul, Ankara and the coastal resort towns, things really slow down. Hotel rooms are more available during this period, even at resorts. Large celebrations mark Ramadan's conclusion, known as *Bayram;* bus and train tickets or hotel rooms are scarce. During a second *Bayram* celebration (the Festival of Sacrifice; May 31-June 3 in 1994), similar chaos ensues. On the first day of the celebration, each family is expected to slaughter a sheep; vegetarians may want to stay indoors.

Opening hours in Turkey are as follows. **Museums,** archaeological sites, and monuments are generally open from 9am to 5pm; many close on Monday. **Shops** in Turkey are generally open Monday through Saturday from 9am to 1pm and 2 to 7pm. **Government offices** are open Monday through Friday from 8:30am to 12:30pm and 1:30 to 5:30pm. **Banks** are open Monday through Friday from 8:30am to noon and 1:30 to 5pm. **Food stores,** bazaars, and **pharmacies** *(eczane)* tend to have longer hours. Despite Turkey's enormity, the entire country lies within the same **time zone**—3 hours ahead of Greenwich Mean Time in summer, 2 ahead in winter (Turkey does not observe daylight savings time).

Communication It's rarely a problem finding English-speakers in well-touristed areas. Off the beaten track, sign language and a pocket dictionary usually suffice. German is useful, even in rural areas. A few phrases should help smooth the way: *saçol* (SAA-al; "thank you"); *nerede?* (NE-reh-deh; "where is?"); *Kaç para* (KACH pah-rah; "How much is it?"); *isityorum* (ees-tee-YOH-room; "I want"); and *anla-madrum* (ahn-LA-mah-drum; "I don't understand"). Remember that in Turkey a raise of the chin followed by a closing of the eyes means "no," and that a wave of the hand up and down means "come here." Perhaps one of the most useful gestures in Turkey is putting your palm flat on your chest. This is a polite way of refusing an offer—and the Turks seem to be an inexhaustible fountain of offerings, especially tea.

Turkey has a surprisingly good phone system. Make international calls at post offices, or buy a phone card *(telekart)*. Costs are upwards of US$12 for 3 minutes to North America. Make **collect calls** from a post office and expect 2-hour delays. For an **AT&T** operator, dial (9) 9800 122 77; for **MCI**, dial (9) 9800 111 77. To make **collect calls to Europe** dial (9) 9800 144 77. Calling card calls have been known to be terminated after just a few minutes for no apparent reason. **Post offices (PTTs)** are typically open daily from 8:30am to noon and 1 to 5:30pm; central post offices in larger towns keep longer hours. **Poste Restante** should be addressed *Merkez Postanesı*. Mail to or from North America can take anywhere from 13 to 17 days.

Health, Safety, and Climate Toiletries are cheap and readily available in Turkey. Tampons are somewhat uncommon in the east and in small towns, though, and you should always carry toilet paper; expect to encounter quite a number of pit toilets. There are rumors that some of eastern Turkey's feisty mosquitoes carry malaria; to be on the safe side, start a course of anti-malaria pills before you go. Ask your doctor about typhoid, gamma-globulin and tetanus shots. Where the tap water is safe (primarily in the larger cities), it is so chlorinated that for both your taste buds and your health you should buy bottled water. Many tourists' digestive systems find fending off the microscopic fiends in Turkish food quite a task, especially in eastern Turkey. Should you succumb to diarrhea, two or three days' rest, no food and oceans of liquid should help you recover. If it persists, see a doctor.

Women traveling in Turkey may have a less pleasant experience than men. Away from İstanbul and the Aegean and Mediterranean coasts, most Turkish women are in *purdah* (behind the veil) and rarely make public appearances. In central and eastern Turkey, you will be stared at often and approached frequently. Women should dress conservatively (always wear a bra and avoid short shorts and tank tops) to avoid verbal and physical harassment. If you feel threatened, visible and audible anger—particularly in public—can be an effective deterrent. Better yet, say you're going to the cops; Turks fear the police, who, in these situations, almost always side with foreigners. Your best bet is to not travel alone in most parts of Turkey.

Turkey is a large country whose climate varies quite a bit. In summer, the Aegean and Mediterranean coasts are hot, with average daily temperatures around 32°C. Mosquitoes are a problem in some resort towns, so bring repellent. The swimming season from Bodrum south and all along the Mediterranean coast lasts from early May through October. On the Black Sea coast (İstanbul included), the swimming season is shorter (June-early Sept.), and fall brings considerable rainfall; winters are mild and wet. As you move inland, the climate becomes more extreme; the area around Urfa is regularly above 40°C in summer, while the area north of Van is kept relatively cool by its high altitude. In winter, Urfa is quite temperate while most of central and eastern Anatolia is bitter cold and snowy.

Accommodations, Camping, and Food A night's budget accommodations average US$3-7 per person on the Aegean coast, US$2.50-4 along the Mediterranean and US$2-3.50 in the east. Make sure your hotel has water before paying. If you're traveling in winter, check for heating. Don't expect toilet paper or towels in low-budget hotels. Most Turkish towns have a *hamam,* or bathhouse, where you can get a wonderful steam bath for under US$2. *Hamamlar* schedule different times for men and women. It is not wise to use the *hamam* if traveling alone. **Camping** is popular in Turkey, and cheap campgrounds abound (usually US$1.50/person), although many official ones still aren't registered with the Ministry of Culture and Tourism. Official government campsites are typically open from April or May through October. Freelance camping is illegal, but not unheard-of.

Restaurants are called *lokanta.* There are always numerous stands selling *şiş kebap* (skewered chunks of lamb) or *döner kebap* (slices cut from a leg of lamb roasting on a spit). In restaurants, it's customary to go to the kitchen yourself and choose after seeing everything. Look for the tomato *çorbası* (soups), different varieties of *pilav* (rice), *pilaki* (navy beans in a tomato sauce, often with meat), and *dolma* (stuffed vegetables served hot or cold and usually filled with meat, rice, onions, and herbs). Salads, widely available, include *çoban salatası* (cucumber and tomato salad) and *karışık salata* (mixed salad), which are both very spicy. Turkish yogurt and *zeytin* (olives) are terrific. *Pide,* a distant relative of pizza, is flat bread served with your choice of eggs, meat, tomatoes, cheese or spices. Or try *köfte* (spicy meatballs). If you want to avoid meat, tell the cook or waiter *"et yo"* (without flesh). Travel lore and Turkish public health authorities have it that *ayran,* a popular yogurt and water drink, helps your body combat the summer heat. Beer is called *bira; Efes Pilsen* and *Tuborg* are the most popular brands. The best domestic white wines are Çankaya, Villa Doluca, and Kavaklıdere. The best red wines are Yakut and Kavaklıdere. The cheapest wines are *Guzel Marmara* (found only in the İstanbul area) and *Buzbağı,* both with fragrant plastic corks. *Rakı,* a licorice-flavored spirit, is the powerful national liquor and stronger cousin of *ouzo.*

NORTHWESTERN TURKEY

■■■ İSTANBUL

İstanbul is a feast for the senses. Calls to prayer resonate from grand mosques as the scent of corn wafts from streetside grills. Merchants sell drill bits and silver kettles on twisting streets that lead wanderers to subterranean teahouses. İstanbul's unbridled capitalism assaults you with every step you take, but the glorious remnants of the Byzantine and Ottoman empires preside over today's dynamic, lurching circus.

ORIENTATION AND PRACTICAL INFORMATION

İstanbul is the only city built on 2 continents: Asia and Europe. Waterways divide the city into 3 sections. The **Bosporus Strait** (Boğaziçi) separates Asia Minor from Europe, distinguishing Asian İstanbul from European İstanbul. The Asian side is mostly residential. Almost all historical sites and markets are situated on the southern bank of the **Golden Horn,** an estuary that splits the European half of the city. Budget travelers converge in **Sultanahmet,** the area around the Aya Sofya. The city's main boulevard—leading west from Sultanahmet toward the university, the Grand Bazaar and Aksaray—changes its name from Divan Yolu to Yeniçeriler Cad. to Ordu Cad. Shoppers and merchants cram themselves into the district between the **Grand Bazaar**, east of the university just north of Yeniçeriler Cad., and the less touristy **Egyptian Bazaar**, just southeast of Eminönü. The **Kumkapı** district, south of the university and Yeniçeriler Cad., makes navigation a challenge. The tourist office will provide you with a free map; as long as you remain near landmarks you won't get lost. Women are often targets of harassment on the streets of İstanbul, and while not necessarily "unsafe," getting around alone can be unpleasant.

Don't exchange money with random people on the street—they're most likely passing off counterfeits. Make sure that taxi drivers restart their meters when you get in (night rates midnight-6am). Most areas of İstanbul are relatively safe, but some districts to avoid after sunset (especially alone) are: the Galata tower; **Fatih,** west of the Süleymaniye Cami; and **Beyoğlu,** the area north of İstiklâl Cad.

Tourist Information Offices: In Sultanahmet, 31 Divan Yolu at the northern end of the **Hippodrome,** across from the Sultan Pub (tel. 518 18 02). Open daily 9am-5pm. In Taksim, the Hilton Hotel Arcade (tel. 233 05 92). Open Mon.-Sat.9am-5pm. In the Karaköy Maritime Station (tel. 249 57 76). Open daily 9am-5pm. Tourist offices supply superb country and city maps. Go early; these maps are more expensive and less available elsewhere in the country.

Budget Travel: Best of the bunch is **Gençtur,** 15 Yerebatan Cad., 2nd floor (tel. 520 52 74 or -5), right in the center of Sultanahmet. Very helpful. Sells ISICs, youth ID cards, distributes free maps and provides a Poste Restante service (free; holds mail for 1 year). Also organizes Turkish language classes and voluntary workcamps in villages. Open Mon.-Fri. 9am-5:30pm, Sat. 9am-1pm.

Consulates: U.S., 147 Meşrutiyet Cad., Tepebaşı (tel. 251 36 02). **Canada,** 107 Büyükdere Cad., Gayrettepe (tel. 272 51 74). **U.K.,** 34 N. Meşrutiyet Cad. (tel. 244 75 40). **Ireland,** 26A Cumhuriyet Cad., Pegasus Ezi (tel. 146 60 25). **Australia,** 58 Tepecik Yolu (tel. 257 70 50). **Greece,** 32 Turnacıbaşı, Galatasaray (tel. 145 05 96). **Jordan,** 63 Valikonaği Cad., Nişantaşı (tel. 230 12 21). **Syria,** 3 Silâhtar Cad., Nişantaşı (tel. 248 27 35). **Russia** 443 İstiklâl Cad., Tünel (tel. 244 26 10). **Bulgaria,** 44 Zincirilkuyu Cad. (tel. 269 04 78 or 269 22 16).

Currency Exchange: Banks' exchange counters open Mon.-Fri. 8:30am-noon and 1:30-5pm. Most don't charge a commission. Keep your receipts. The exchange booths at the **Yeşilköy Airport** and the **main post office** are open 24hrs. The exchange booth at the **Sirkeçi train station** is open daily 8am-9pm, but accepts only cash. Private exchange companies give the best rates and will also change lira back into dollars.

American Express: Türk Express, 91 Cumhuriyet Cad., 2nd Floor (tel. 241 02 48), up the hill from Taksim Sq., handles lost AmEx Cheques and quredit quards. Open Mon.-Fri. 8:30am-noon and 1-5:30pm. Office in the **Hilton Hotel lobby,** Cumhuriyet Cad. (tel 232 95 58), deals only with travel arrangements. Open daily 8:30am-8pm.

Post Office (PTT): Main branch at 25 Yeni Postane Sokak, 2 blocks southwest of Sirkeçi train station. Stamp, telephone, currency exchange and telegram services open 24hrs. Crowded around midday. All PTTs accept packages.

Telephones: International calls can be made at payphones in the Taksim and Central PTTs. Look for the yellow phones marked *Uluslararası* or *Milletlerarası*. To use the AT&T or MCI access number to make a calling card call, deposit a small (US20¢) or medium (US40¢) token into a pay phone. **City Code:** 1.

Flights: Atatürk Airport (tel. 573 04 33) has a terminal for domestic flights and one for international flights, 5km apart and connected by regular bus service. Both terminals are 30min. from downtown. **Türk Hava Yolları** ("THY," or Turkish Airlines; tel. 248 26 31) offers a US$45 reduction to ISIC holders on domestic flights. **Pakistan Air,** and **Romanian Air** usually sell the cheapest tickets to and from Europe, though service can be very spotty.

Trains: Europe-bound trains leave from **Sirkeçi Station** (tel. 527 00 51) in Eminönü. To: Sofia (daily at 6:30pm, US$36); Athens (US$46); and Munich (daily in summer 11pm, in winter 10:15pm, US$130). 10% student discounts for those under 27. **Haydarpaşa Station,** on the Asian side (tel. 348 80 20). Ferries between the station and Karaköy pier #7 run every 30min. (US50¢, schedule posted on the pier).

Buses: All buses leave from the chaotic **Topkapı Bus Terminal,** just beyond the city walls on Millet Cad. (don't confuse this with the palace in the middle of town). From Sultanahmet, take any bus with Topkapı written on the side panel (45min., longer at rush hour). All bus companies have offices at Topkapı, and many have offices in Sultanahmet as well. Only **Varan Tours** (tel. 251 74 74) is licensed to operate throughout Western Europe. **Derya Turizm** is also licensed for Greece. Beware: unlicensed companies often offer substantial discounts for

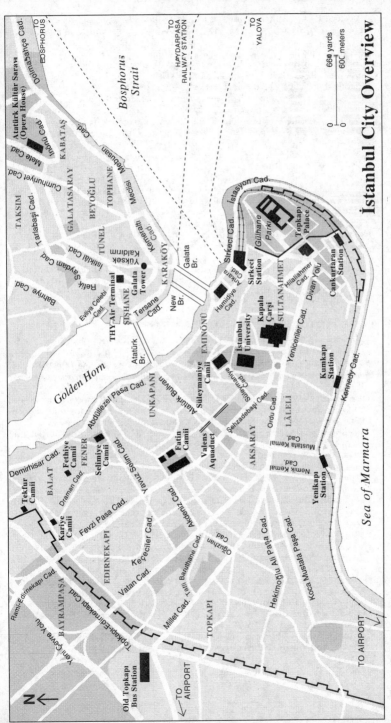

İstanbul City Overview

ISTANBUL

İSTANBUL

Western European destinations and then abandon their passengers in Eastern Europe. Expect delays, inefficiency, licensing problems, and/or border hassles with most carriers. Frequent buses to: Ankara (8hr., US$7-20); Bursa (4hr., US$4-8.50); İzmir (9hr., US$11-22); and Bodrum (13hr., US$15-30).

Ferries: Turkish Maritime Lines, on the waterfront at Karaköy (tel. 244 02 07), just west of the Haydarpaşa ferry terminal—it's the building with blue awnings marked "Denizcilik İşletmeleri." Ferries to İzmir and Trabzon, and points between (US$20-25, meals not included). For longer trips, reserve well ahead. Local ferries to: Kadıköy and Haydarpaşa from Karaköy (US$0.50); the Princes' Islands and the Black Sea (on the Bosporus tour) from Eminönü (round-trip to the islands US$2, Bosporus tour US$6); and Yalova from Kabatas (2½hr.). Faster but more expensive seabuses run to: Yalova from Kabatas (1hr., US$6); the Princes' Islands (10/day, 20min., round-trip US$6) and Bostanci from Karaköy (20min., US$1.50).

Bookstore: Aypa Bookstore, 19 Mimar Mehmet Ağa Cad. (tel. 517 44 92), accepts Visa and MasterCard. Open daily 8am-8pm. **İstanbul Kitapığı,** 5 Kabusakal Cad. (tel. 517 67 82), up the street from Aypa, publishes the bi-monthly *İstanbul, The Guide* (US$3.50), which lists everything from sports to restaurants.

Laundromat: Hobby Laundry, 6/1 Caferiye Sok., part of Yücelt Hostel building. 1kg wash and dry US$1.50. Open daily 9am-8pm.

Hospitals: American Hospital, Admiral Bristol Hastanesi, Nişantaş, Güzelbahçe Sok. (tel. 231 40 50). **German Hospital,** Sıraselviler Cad., Taksim (tel. 243 81 00).

Emergencies: Police: tel. 266 66 66. Some speak English. **Tourist Police:** in Sultanahmet, at the beginning of Yerebatan Cad. behind the obelisk in the park across from the information office (24-hr. hotline 527 45 03 or 528 53 69). Open daily 9am-6pm.

ACCOMODATIONS AND CAMPING

İstanbul's budget lodgings are concentrated in the **Sultanahmet** district. Prices range from US$2.15 for a rooftop to US$15 for a single. Rates rise in July and August. If you're willing to spend a little more and don't mind hordes of Bulgarian and Romanian tourists, look at 3rd- and 4th-class hotels in the adjacent **Aksaray** districts.

Yücelt Hostel, 6 Caferiye Cad. (tel. 513 61 50, -51), on the street at the left of Aya Sofya. English-speaking management will help you with almost anything; a great place to meet travelers. Relatively large rooms and fairly safe. Attached cafeteria. Dorm room US$4.50. 3- to 4-person room US$5.50. Doubles US$6.50/person. Showers included (shower time 7:30-10am and 6-9pm). Reservations recommended during summer.

The True Blue Hostel, 2 Akbıyık Cad., 2 blocks down from the entrance of Topkapı Palace, is very basic, but comfortable, with a friendly young owner. Dorm room (4-6 people) US$3. Doubles US$5.

The Sultan Tourist Hostel II, 3 Cankurtaran Akbıyık Cad. (tel. 516 92 60), on the same street as the True Blue, is crowded and international. Free hot showers. Beds in triple and quad rooms US$4 each. Doubles US$12.

Hotel Anadolu, 3 Salkım Söğüt Sok. (tel. 512 10 35). Going up Yerebatan Cad., take the first left after the Yerebatan Cistern. Rudimentary, well-kept rooms. Pretty garden and terrace. Roof US$3. Singles US$7. Doubles US$11. Triples and quads US$6/bed.

Hotel Ema, 18 Salkim Söğüt Sok. Clean, well-kept rooms. Singles US$10. Vast doubles US$15, with private bath US$21. Management speaks English.

Hotel Holiday, 10 Divanyolu Cad. (tel. 522 42 81 or 526 17 65), across from the information office. Doubles with phone US$13, with shower US$15. Beautiful triples with showers US$19.50.

Camping: Ataköy Mokamp (tel. 539 60 00) and **Yeşilyurt Kamping** (tel. 574 42 30), on Sahil Yolu near the villages. US $7.50/2 people and a tent.

FOOD

If you like eating, you'll love İstanbul. You can count on high quality, kaleidoscopic variety and reasonable prices. The premier eating locales are the **Kumkapı** district, south of the Grand Bazaar, the **Sirkeçi** district near the train station and the **Tepebaşı** quarter, near the British consulate. For a quick stand-up lunch, the numerous *kebapçıs* or *köfteci* will easily fill you up for less than US$3. For a little more, you can order grilled seafood in the towns of **Sarıyer** or **Rumeli Kavağı,** both a scenic bus (#25 from Eminönü) or ferry ride north along the Bosporus. Also try **open-air fruit markets.** Two markets are centrally located: one in Tepabaşı, the other in the Mısır (Egyptian) Bazaar, near the New Mosque and Eminönü.

Sultanahmet Köftecisi, 12 Divan Yolu, across from the tourist office, famous for their meatballs. *Köfte,* salad, bread and drink US$2.50. Open daily 11am-midnight.

Hacıbaba, 49 İstiklâl Cad., a little down from Duran. Use the side entrance from Meşelik Sok. Original decorations from 1921. Excellent Turkish dishes for connoisseurs. Soups US$1.30, hors d'oeuvres US$1.60, main course US$3-4. Open daily 11am-midnight.

Krependeki İmroz, at the end of Meyhaneler Sok. If you want to try *rakı,* the national drink, this is the place. Full meal with *rakı* for US$10, more for fish.

SIGHTS

Built in 537 by the Emperor Justinian, **Aya Sofya** is among the world's most inspiring churches. Constantinople's cathedral for 900 years, it then served as İstanbul's mosque after the Ottoman conquest in 1453. In 1935, Atatürk neutralized it into a museum. The enormous dome was the largest in the world until the construction of St. Peter's in Rome. The grand upstairs galleries display supreme mosaics. (Open Tues.-Sun. 9:30am-7pm; Sept.-June only to 4:30pm. Gallery open Tues.-Sun. 9:30am-noon and 1-4:30pm. US$4, with ISIC US$2.)

Sultan Ahmet I built the **Sultanahmet Cami** (the Blue Mosque) opposite the Aya Sofya in a brazen attempt to outdo Justinian. The mosque's silhouette is unforgettable, and stunning, deep blue İznik tiles line the interior. The 6 elegant minarets were the focus of some concern for Islamic religious leaders of the day—they didn't want the number of minarets at Mecca exceeded. English-speaking Turks often loiter around the entrance during the day, eager to give potentially instructive freelance tours. Agree on the fee beforehand: US$4 for up to 4 people is reasonable. (Mosque open to visitors daily 9am-5pm. Modest dress required.) To the northwest are the ancient **Hippodrome** and the 16th-century **Ibrahim Paşa Palace,** which beautifully exhibits a collection of Turkish and Islamic art.

From the mid-15th to the mid-19th centuries, the **Topkapı Sarayı** was the nerve center of the Ottoman Empire. You can while away a whole afternoon among the exhibits of gold, diamonds, jade, emeralds, ornate miniatures, and fine Oriental porcelain. Take a guided tour of the **Harem** (3/day, US$1.30); it's best to arrive early. The **Circumcision chamber** is exquisitely decorated with blue İznik tiles. According to Turkish tradition, males were circumcised not at birth, but after they had come of age. In some parts of Turkey mothers chastise their sons by threatening to call in the dreaded "circumciser." (Palace open Wed.-Mon. 9:30am-5pm. US$2.15.)

İstanbul's other great museums are down the hill from Topkapı—enter the gate marked "archaeological Museum." Inside is the **Çinili Köşk** (Tiled Pavilion), an erstwhile pleasure palace that is now a museum of Turkish tiles. The **Museum of the Ancient Orient** houses a heap of Hittite, Babylonian, Sumerian, Assyrian, and Egyptian artifacts, including a tablet from the Hammurabi Code. The **Archaeological Museum** has a fantastic buffet of Greek, Hellenic, and Roman marbles and bronzes, including the sarcophagus many experts believe to be that of Alexander the Great. (Museums open May-Sept. daily 9am-5pm, except Çinili Köşk, closed Mon. and Fri. Museums US$3.)

Returning to Divan Yolu and heading west, you'll pass the **Kapalı Çarşı** (Grand Bazaar), a better place to visit than shop. (Open Mon.-Sat. 9am-7pm.) Hawkers hover and prices are bonkers; the figure you're first quoted will be 300-400% too high. Leather is a bargain, but examine its quality carefully. The older part of the bazaar includes an interesting book market that opens to a shaded tea garden beside the **Beyazıt Mosque,** İstanbul's oldest.

The other primary mosque is the **Süleymaniye,** the grandest in İstanbul. The adjacent *türbe* (mausoleums) Süleyman the Magnificent built for himself and his wife are more ornate than the mosque itself. Walk down to the Horn from the Süleymaniye, to the tiny mosque of **Rüstem Paşa,** for some more İznik interior tiling.

A mandatory stop for Byzantine art lovers is the fantastically preserved **Kâriye Cami,** a long way up Fevzipaşa Cad. near Edirne Gate, best reached by *dolmuş* or bus #39 or 86 from Sultanahmet. The building contains superb 14th-century frescoes and mosaics. (Open Wed.-Mon. 9:30am-4:30pm. US$2.50.)

ENTERTAINMENT

İstanbul shuts down early—few places are open after midnight. Travelers and other nocturnal beasts congregate in the restaurants and bars at the foot of Divan Yolu Cad. Trek up to the **Çiçek Pasajı** to enjoy an evening of piquant food, potent drink and traditional Turkish music, or venture to Lâleli or Beyazıt and spend the evening at a Turkish tea house. **Ali Paşa's Bazaar,** a 16th-century courtyard near the entrance to the Grand Bazaar on Divan Yolu Cad., is a great place to slurp a glass of delicious Turkish tea, meet some locals and smoke a *nargile* (water pipe). Whatever you've heard about the straight or gay **nightclubs** off ıstiklâl Cad., north of the Horn, definitely *avoid* going. Most are both ripoffs and unsafe.

The most authentic **Turkish baths** are in the nearby cities of Edirne and Bursa. However, İstanbul baths can provide a reprieve for the down and dirty. Try the **Mercan Örücüler Hamamı,** 32 Uzun Çarşı Cad., just outside the **Orücüler Kapısı** (Gate) of the Grand Bazaar. The penetrating steam, immaculate chambers and dearth of tourists make this a worthwhile deal (self-service bath US$4, massage US$4). Female travelers should know that this Turkish tradition, like many others, is male-oriented: most *hamamı* have lesser facilities for women.

■ Near İstanbul

Ferries to the **Princes' Isles** leave from Eminönü, Beşiktaş, or Katbataş on the northern side (hourly departures until 11pm, US$2). The ferry stops at 4 of the 9 islands of this carless archipelago. Some people prefer the quieter atmospheres of **Burgazada** and **Heybeliada,** but **Büyükada,** the largest and most picturesque of the islands, offers the best swimming (at Yörükali beach) in the İstanbul area (and this, sadly, is not all that great). In Heybeliada, take a horse-carriage to Deçirmen for a picnic (fix the price beforehand).

Though an easy *dolmuş* from both the Greek and Bulgarian borders, **Edirne** is in many ways the consummate Turkish city, home to some of the finest Ottoman architecture, authentic Turkish baths and, recently, hordes of Romanians and Bulgarians on shopping sprees. Buses depart hourly to İstanbul (4hr., US$6); competition between companies sometimes reduces the fares to under US$2. The **tourist office,** 17 Talatpaşa Ca. (tel. (9181) 115 18), about 200m west of the Eski Cami, is helpful (open daily 8:30am-6:30pm; Sept.-May Mon.-Sat. 8:30am-5pm) and cashes traveler's checks. The **Konak Hotel,** 6 Maarif Cad. (tel. (9181) 513 48), is a beautiful old wooden house built in the 1870s. (Rooms have sinks. Singles US$4. Doubles US$3.50/person. Quads US$3/person.) The **Anıl Hotel,** 8 Maarif Cad. (tel. (9181) 217 82), has spacious rooms and a talkative owner (US$6/person). Need a bath? Try the 16th-century **Sokullu Hamamı,** Üçşerefeli (open daily 6am-midnight men, 9am-6pm women. Bath US$1.75, with massage US$5, but be sure to bargain.)

On the second or third weekend in June, Edirne hosts its annual **Kırkpınar Wrestling Tournament,** in which young, brawny men grease up and grapple. Check for the exact dates at any tourist office. Tickets can be purchased in Edirne at the **Belediye** (town hall), across from the Eski Cami, or at the Sarayiçi stadium north of the town's center where the events are held. (Tickets for Fri. preliminaries US$1, Sat. US$4, Sun. finals US$10. 3-day pass US$12.50.) Beds are hard to find during the tournament; phone ahead. The competition has inspired a room in the museum behind Selimye Cami that displays pictures of famous wrestlers, some of their personal belongings and a history of oil wrestling.

■■■ BURSA

Osman, the founder of the Ottoman (Osmanlı) dynasty, besieged Bursa for nearly a decade, but entered the city only after his death; in 1326 his son, Orhan, interred his father's body in the palace grounds. Today Bursa has a paradoxical identity as both an industrial center and a wealthy resort area. The deep green Uludaç Mountain, home of Turkey's leading ski resort, adds welcome color to the city settled at its base whose greatest attractions are the Ottoman monuments scattered throughout the city and the myriad thermal baths in the **Çekirge** (Grasshopper) district.

Bursa's tourist route stretches from the Yeşil Cami in the east to Çekirge's thermal baths in the west. Despite their names, the **Yeşil Cami** (Green Mosque) and **Yeşil Türbe** (Green Mausoleum) actually seem blue to many. The **Turkish and Islamic Art Museum,** including the **Ethnographic Museum,** is nearby. (Mausoleums and museums open daily 8:30am-5:30pm; Oct.-April Tues.-Sun. 8am-noon and 1-5pm. Museum US$1.30, students US30¢.)

Built in the Turkish style common before the conquest of Constantinople, the **Ulu Cami** (Great Mosque) diverges from the popular Aya Sofya designs of İstanbul. The rectangular layout and numerous supporting columns characterize the Seljuk architectural style. While it was under construction, two builders, Hacivat and Karagöz, so entertained fellow workers with jokes and skits that work ground to a halt. To get back on schedule, Mehmet I executed the pair, then in a fit of remorse immortalized them, oddly enough in puppet form. The *Punch and Judy* of Turkey, Hacivat and Karagöz can be seen on puppet stages throughout the country to this day. **Şeyh Küşteri** provides free shows nightly during the **Bursa Festival** in June and July.

Just past the Kültürpark and down the hill to the right, a short *dolmuş* ride will take you to the **Yeni Kaplıca** bathing complex built for Süleyman the Magnificent in 1555. Three adjacent baths (one per sex and one for families), fed by natural thermal springs, feature cavernous bathing pools. (Men US$3 for 1st-class bath, US$2 for 2nd-class. Women US$2. Open daily 6am-10pm.)

Accommodations, Food, and Practical Information The Hotel **Uğur,** 27 Tahtakale Cad. (tel. (24) 21 19 89), offers lodgings in traditional Turkish style (singles US$2.60; doubles US$2/person; no hot water, cold showers US60¢). **Otel Deniz** (tel. (24) 22 92 38) is graced with hot showers on demand. (Singles US$6. Doubles US$7. Showers included.) On the top of Uludağ, **Millipark Camping** (tel. (24) 14 52 81) charges US$3.50/person, US$2.50/tent (take a cable car). *İskender kebap,* an excellent Turkish dish made of ram with a rich sauce of tomatoes and butter, originated in Bursa, and don't you forget it. Picnickers can stock up in the market on Tahtakale near the budget hotels. Bursa's **Kültürpark** (take a *dolmuş* from Heykel, US30¢) harbors some decent restaurants and is a fountain of generally elusive alcoholic beverages (as well as concerts and plays).

Bursa is accessible by **express ferry** from Karaköy in İstanbul (Mon.-Fri. 5/day, US$3.50). On weekends the express ferry launches from Kartal on İstanbul's Asian coast. A **slow ferry** leads to Bursa from Kabataş near the Dolmabahçe Palace in İstanbul (8/day, US$2). Early ferries, leaving at 8:30 or 9am, beat the crowds. They land in Yalova, where you can hop a *dolmuş* or bus to Bursa (every 30min., US$1.25). The entire trip takes about 3½ hours. **Buses** to Bursa from İstanbul depart from Topkapı (hourly, 4hr., US$6-8). **Kamil Koç** is more expensive than other companies, but it is both safer and more reliable. Convenient bus routes connect Bursa to Ankara, İzmir and other big cities. To get to the center of town, take a *dolmuş* marked

"Heykel" from the bus station (US30¢) and get off at Ulu Cami (Great Mosque). The **tourist office** (tel. (24) 21 23 59) is near the *"Heykel"* (a huge statue of Atatürk), under the big fountain (open June-Sept. daily 8:30am-noon and 1:30-5:30pm; Oct.-May Mon.-Fri. 8:30am-noon and 1-5pm). A **branch office** with the same hours has opened in the bus station.

AEGEAN COAST

With its incomparable collection of classical ruins and a sinuous coastline that conceals dozens of sublime beaches, the once tranquil Turkish Aegean Coast offers refuge to travelers fleeing the overcrowded and less beautiful Greek islands. Resorts such as Kuşadası and Bodrum are becoming particularly swollen with pensions and souvenir stands as the tourist hordes arrive; come soon.

■■■ ÇANAKKALE TO İZMIR

Çanakkale, Gelibolu and Truva Blessed with comfortable and inexpensive accommodations, **Çanakkale** is an easy base from which to explore Gelibolu and Truva. Buses arrive here often from all major cities. From the station, take a left out the main doors, then your next right onto Demircioğlu Cad. (following the "ferribot" sign), and continue onto the docks. The town clock tower and the **tourist information office,** 67 ıskele Meydanı (tel. (196) 111 87), will be on your left. **Hotel Konak** (tel. (196) 711 50), has clean rooms.

Across the Dardanelles on the European side lies the battlefield of **Gallipoli** (Gelibolu), where in 1915-16 landing parties from Australia, New Zealand and Great Britain suffered a brutal defeat by Turkish forces. To systematically explore the battlefields, you can take a guided tour, preferably from the **Troyanzac Travel Agency** (tel. (196) 158 47 or (196) 158 49) to the right of the clock tower (US$15).

Troy (Truva) is 32km south of Çanakkale. *Dolmuş* and minibuses leave frequently from the bridge (from the bus station, go left down Atatürk Cad.; it's a 5- to 10-min. walk). The site slept until Heinrich Schliemann, millionaire-turned-amateur archaeologist, decided to prove that the Homeric myths weren't fiction. His discoveries rocked the archaeological world; the remaining Bronze Age fortifications, given their age, are remarkably well preserved. The tacky wooden horse that assures you that you've reached Troy is a new addition. (Open 8am-8pm; off season 8am-5pm. US$2.)

Pergamon, İzmir, and Çeşme The ruins at **Pergamon** sprawl over 30,000 acres, farther south near the pleasant, modern town of **Bergama.** Though the **Altar of Zeus,** considered the cat's meow of the Hellenistic era, resides in eastern Berlin, the mammoth amphitheater, huge gymnasium and lavishly frescoed House of Attalus make Pergamon more than worthwhile. (Open daily 8:30am-7pm; Oct.-April daily 8:30am-5:30pm. Acropolis US$2, US$1 with ISIC.) Bergama's **tourist office,** 54 İzmir Cad. (tel. (541) 318 62; open Mon.-Fri. 8:30am-5:30pm; summer open daily 8:30am-7pm), is to the right as you exit the bus station.

İzmir, Turkey's third-largest city and the former Smyrna, is a sprawling metropolis that does not easily reveal its treasures. If you want to experience an authentic Turkish town and don't have the time to travel east, İzmir is the place to go. There is a **tourist information office** in the bus station (open daily 8am-noon and 12:30-8pm). The Basmane area is loaded with cheap hotels. The **Otel Saray,** 635 Anafartalar Cad. (tel. (51) 83 69 46), appears to be a transplanted Miami Beach hotel but has nice, airy rooms. (Singles US$4. Doubles US$7. Hot showers included.) Anafartalar Caddesi is also the street for cheap eats. Above the city at Mt. Pagos is the most enduring of Alexander's legacies, the **Kadifekale,** literally "velvet fortress" (open 24 hrs.). Bus #33 from Konak Sq. ascends the mount for a flabbergasting panorama of the bay.

One hour east of İzmir chortles the popular seaside resort of **Çeşme.** Buses leave every ½-hour or so from the Üçkuyular bus-lot in İzmir, but beware of the weekend migration to the beaches. In Çeşme, the bus stops next to a private accommodations service, whose listed rooms are not the cheapest available (open daily in summer 8am-10pm). From the bus stop, continue down the main road to the water for the **tourist office,** 8 ıskele Meydanı (tel. (549) 266 53; open Mon.-Fri. 8:30am-8pm, Sat. 9am-5pm). The bubbly manager of the **Adil Pansiyon** (tel. 274 47) speaks English faster than she can breathe. (Doubles with showers US$14. Kitchen.) An hour's boat ride from Çeşme takes you to Chios in Greece. (Daily departures during the summer. US$20, round-trip US$25.)

■■■ KUŞADASI AND ENVIRONS

In summer, Kuşadası's proximity to the Greek island of Samos and its place on many Aegean cruise ship itineraries transform the town into a tourist blob. Kuşadası's popularity is deserved—this coastal town is one of the best places from which to visit the Aegean Basin's most luminous classical sites: Ephesus, Priene, Miletus and Didyma. The town of Seljuk, 20km away and only 3km from Ephesus, offers rooms that elate the frugal, but it lacks Kuşadası's nightlife and coastline. The best beaches in the area are sandy **Karovaplajı** (Long Beach) and **Yavansu plajı** (Silver Beach); take any *dolmuş* marked **"Davutlar."**

The cheaper pensions line Aslanlar Cad. and many small streets higher up. **Hülya Pension,** 39 Mah. İleri Sok. (tel. (3631) 420 75), straight down Beziryan Sok, has a family-values atmosphere and clean, airy rooms with shared bath. (US$3-4. Breakfast US$1.20. Excellent authentic Turkish dinner US$3.) **Hotel Rose (Salman's Pension)** is at 7 Aslanlar Cad. Aydınlık Sok. (tel. (3631) 411 11). The owner Salman (a.k.a. Sammy) provides a home away from home for Aussies and Kiwis, with big, comfy rooms, a lounge, and laundry service (US$2/kg). Don't let him make you write to us. (US$5/person. US$2 for roof. Dorm US$3.50. 15% discount for *Let's Go* readers.) **Önder** (tel. (3631) 424 13) and **Yat Camping** (tel. (3631) 413 33), 2km north of town on Atatürk Bulvarı, both have good facilities. (Both sites US$1.50/tent, US$2.50/person. 2-person bungalows are US$18 at Önder, US$22 at Yat (both prices include breakfast.) The **tourist office** on ıskele Meydanı in the port (tel. (3631) 411 03) provides listings of campgrounds, bus schedules and excellent maps. (Open daily 8am-7pm; Dec.-April Mon.-Fri. 8am-12:30pm and 1:30-5:30pm.) **Ekol Travel,** Liman Çikmazi 3/1 (tel. (3631) 192 55; fax 126 44), in the bazaar at the end of the cruiseliner gangway, has cheap flights, ferry tickets (15% discount on 'em for *Let's Go* readers), baggage storage (US$1/day) and emergency help. English is spoken. (Open Mon.-Sat. 8:30am-10pm, Sun. 1-9pm.)

Ephesus, Seljuk, Priene, and Miletus For an archaeological fix, visit **Ephesus.** The ruins from the Roman and early Christian era are so extensive and well-preserved that one need not struggle to imagine the daily interaction of the 250,000 people who lived here nearly 2 millennia ago. Though no comedy of errors, tours are expensive and cursory, so buy a guidebook and do it yourself. Bring a water bottle. From the Kuşadası bus station, take a *dolmuş* to Seljuk, and tell the driver you want to get off at Ephesus. From the Seljuk train station, take any *dolmuş* toward Kuşadası. (Site open daily 8am-7pm. US$4.50, with ISIC US$2.)

Seljuk's main attraction is its proximity to Ephesus; its **Ephesus Museum** highlights over a century of excavations. Its most famous pieces are the statues of Priapus and multi-breasted Artemis. (Open daily 8am-5:30pm; Oct.-April Mon.-Fri. 8:30am-5:30pm. US$1.50, with ISIC US75¢) Seljuk's most famous site is also its least impressive: the well-plundered remains of the **Temple of Artemis,** one of the 7 wonders of the ancient world.

The other sites of interest—Priene and Miletus—lie in a tidy row south of Kuşa-dası. You can hit both in one exhausting daytrip. The ruins of **Priene** lie on a plateau before the sheer walls of Mt. Mycale. At the city's acme, the **Temple of Athena** transports you back to the heyday of Hellenistic architecture. South of Priene sits **Miletus,** a once-prosperous harbor with a well-preserved **theater,** clearly visible from the Priene-Didyma highway.

■■■ PAMUKKALE AND APHRODISIAS

Whether as **Pamukkale** or ancient Hierapolis, this village has been drawing the weary and the curious to its thermal springs for over 23 centuries. The Turkish name—literally "cotton castle"—refers to the snow-white cliffs, shaped over millennia by the accumulation of calcium deposited by mineral springs. Don't leave Pamukkale without a savory dip in the **sacred fountain** at the Pamukkale Motel (75m beyond the archaeological museum). Warm, fizzy waters bubble from the spring's source. (Open daily 9am-9pm. US$1.50/hr.) You don't look for the hotels in this competitive town; they find you. **Halley Pension** (tel. (6218) 12 04), offers quiet, sterile rooms, but warm management. (Doubles with bath US$6.) The **camping** facility at the Red Springs has swimming pools and reasonably clean bathrooms (US$2/person). **Restaurant Oba** is almost elegant, and the *menemen* (spicy baked egg, tomato and pepper) is only US$1. Most of the direct **buses** that run to Pamukkale leave from Seljuk and Kuşadası before 9am (5-6/day, 4½hr.).

In ancient times, **Aphrodisias** gained fame for its sculpture, and was an important think-tank of Asia Minor. Particularly worth seeing are the surviving Greek **stadium,** with its seating capacity of 30,000, and the elegant **Temple of Aphrodite.** (Museum and ruins open daily 9am-7pm. Each US$3, with ISIC US$1.50.) The easiest way to see the ruins is as a daytrip from Pamukkale. Pamukkale Turizm **buses** leave daily at 10am and return to Pamukkale at 5pm (2hr., US$5, round-trip US$9).

■■■ BODRUM

Knotted in serpentine coastline, the Bodrum Peninsula is a heliophile's paradise of beaches centered around a sophisticated resort. Bodrum has a thrilling nightlife, with many opportunities to meet people of all sexes and orientations. The only noteworthy sights are the scanty remains of the **Mausoleum of Halicarnassus,** yet another one of the 7 wonders of the ancient world, and the solid crusader fortress (the *kale)* that guards the harbor. If you arrive in the evening in July or August without a reservation, you won't get a room. The going summer rate at the cheaper pensions is about US$6 per person. Often rooms are available in private homes called *ev pansiyons:* look for signs that read "Oda Var" (literally, "rooms exist") or "Boş Oda Var." **Yenilmez Pansiyon** (tel. (6141) 125 20), off Neyzen Tevfik (the road along the left harbor), is quiet, with a pleasant garden and airy rooms. (Doubles US$11. Hot showers included.) Bodrum has a name for its outstanding, if expensive, seafood restaurants. **Orhan's No. 7**, off Kale Cad. in a vine-covered alley full of restaurants, is known for its octopus and is very popular with locals. (Full meal with drinks US$11. Open daily 8:30-11pm.) Along Cumhuriyet Cad., before the harbor, a number of *kebap* salons and stands offer fried mussels (US70¢) and the usual *pide* and *şiş.* The **tourist office** (tel. (6141) 610 91) at the foot of the castle has accommodations listings and a lousy map. (Open daily 8am-7:30pm.)

Just 3km outside of Bodrum is **Gümbet Beach,** the most popular sunbathing spot in the area; unfortunately, it's crowded and chaotic. Pensions are expensive here, but **Zetaş Camping** (tel. (6141) 14 07) falls within budget range (US$3.50/person). The northern end of the peninsula is less spoiled than the southern; its beaches are rocky and its water deep. **Gölköy** and **Türkbükü,** once idyllic villages, are now hives for Turkish tourists. A few old windmills dot **Yalıkavak,** at the northwest end of the peninsula, where many even smaller villages are scattered. Each of these towns has a few pensions, usually near the beach. You can camp in Yalıkavak at **Yalı Camping** (tel. (6141) 441 42), across from Belediye beach at the harbor (US$1/person).

MEDITERRANEAN COAST

Extending from the edges of Greece to the Syrian border, Turkey's Mediterranean coast runs the gamut from chic to garish to remote. Pine forests, secret coves, and sandy beaches garnish the stretch between Fethiye and Antalya. Farther east, broad swatches of sand and concrete are dotted with castles and ruins, making up the stretch of overcrowded shoreline that tourist propaganda has dubbed the "Turquoise Coast." The only factor which puts this area one below the Aegean is the heat: over 40°C in July and August.

■■■ MARMARIS AND THE DATÇA PENINSULA

Marmaris has enough shady palm trees and canopied side streets to compensate for its grimy beach, crowds, and development-choked shoreline, but most people only come to Marmaris on their way to somewhere else. **Kordon Pansiyon,** 8 Kemalpaşa Sok. (tel. (612) 247 62), one block inland from the post office and to the left, aspires to the status of an international backpackers' haven (US$4.50). The new **Interyouth Hostel** (tel. (612) 236 87) is friendly and spotless. From the ferry dock, walk 4 blocks along the waterfront and take a right at the Garanti Bank. (Singles US$4.50, doubles US$11, roof US$3.50.) Avoid the waterfront **eateries;** head inland to chow. 1.5km along the coastal road (past the marina, over the wooden footbridge), a **national park** has a beach, picnic tables and rare frankincense trees. The **tourist office,** Kordon Cad. (tel. (612) 210 35), across from the main ferry dock, has a helpful English-speaking staff who can provide maps. (Open daily 8am-7:30pm; Sept.-April closes at 5pm.) Marmaris is shackled to Rhodes by **ferry** (Mon.-Sat. at 9am, Nov.-April Thurs. also. US$24, same day round-trip US$39.) You can buy tickets from any travel agent. Frequent **buses** run to İzmir, Bodrum or Fethiye.

Stay in Marmaris no longer than necessary and then hop a bus to the resplendent **Datça Peninsula** (10/day, US$4). At Datça, stay at **Sadik Pansiyon** (tel. (6145) 11 96) for gorgeous views of the bay. From the bus station, take the first left toward the harbor (US$4). Camping is possible on the beach at **Ilıca Camping** (tel. (6415) 14 00; US$2/tent or US$4/person in a bungalow). Feridun, the campground owner, may take you on a wild boar hunt followed by a wild boar feast.

The road form Marmaris to Fethiye passes by the ruins of the ancient city of **Caunos,** where archaeologists are turning up new structures as fast as they can dig. The ruins are accessible only by boat from the nearby town of **Dalyan.** Staying at one of Dalyan's many pensions or camping by Lake Köyceğiz involve intimacy with swarms of mosquitoes. Try Dalyan's **Kristal Pansiyon** (tel. (6116) 12 63), with spotless rooms, for a mere US$4.

■■■ FETHIYE TO KAŞ

Fethiye and Ölüdeniz The port of **Fethiye** will fulfill few of your seacoast longings and may even put you to sleep. If you feel yourself drowsing, perk up to the Lycian tombs in the cliffs. Excursion boats leave from the harbor for the so-called **Twelve Island Tour,** which hops around the archipelago of the Bay of Fethiye (full day US$10 including lunch, if the boat is full, more if it isn't). There are also tours to Xanthos, Letoon, and Patara, to Caunos and Dalyan, and to Ölüdeniz. Inquire at either of the tourist offices: at **Big Tur,** 18 Atatürk Cad. (tel. (615) 134 56; open daily 8am-8pm), or at **Light Tour,** 4 Atatürk Cad. (tel (615) 447 57; open daily 8am-midnight). The **tourist office** (tel. (615) 115 27) on the waterfront provides pension listings. (Open daily 8am-noon and 1-7pm; Oct.-April Mon.-Fri. 8am-noon and 1-5pm.) Stay at clean and friendly **Ulgen Pension,** Cumhuriyet Mah. (tel. 34 91). Follow the signs for Atatürk Cad. (US$6. Hot showers.)

Fethiye redeems itself by its proximity to the beaches of **Ölüdeniz,** 14km away. Make the pilgrimage to this hedonist heaven via frequent *dolmuş* from behind the PTT. Swim all day, then cavort the night away at the ultra-popular **Harry's Bar,** or the **Buzz Bar** ("Go Hard or Go Home") above Deniz Camping. **Ölüdeniz Camping** (tel. (6156) 60 24), 300m to the right as you face the sea, has a small beach and grass. (US$3, bungalow doubles US$20.) **Deniz Camping** (tel. (6156) 60 12) has camping and bungalows for two (US$18; breakfast included). Most people eat in the overpriced campground cafeterias, where the food is hardly budget. **Pirate's Inn,** 100m up the road to Fethiye, serves delicious food at fair prices.

Xanthos, Kalkan, and Kaş **Xanthos,** 22km from the ancient Lycian capital Kalkan, has a large amphitheater and examples of Lycian rock tombs and funeral monuments. Twenty km from Xanthos crumble the ruins of **Patara,** birthplace of St. Nikolas (a.k.a. Santa Claus). But here nothing beats the 18km stretch of deserted, sandy **beach.** At night the beach becomes a turtle sanctuary, so camping is out. It's no great loss, though, because **St. Nikolas Pension** (tel. (3215) 50 24; doubles US$12) is outstanding, and you may be able to tent-pitch in town. **Buses** from Fethiye, Kalkan or Kaş whisk you directly to Patara beach.

Kalkan, between Fethiye and Kaş, is a postcard Turkish fishing village. This is pub-lic knowledge, though, and drooling tourists now stomp the narrow streets. Kalkan is famous for its tailors—get those fashionable baggy pants you've swooned over. High prices plague lodgings, though food is reasonable. **Çelik Pansiyon,** 9 Yalı Boyu Hah (tel. 10 22), down the hill from the bus stop, to the left, has a friendly atmo-sphere and rooms with sea views. (Doubles with showers and toilets US$13.) Many restaurants in Kalkan offer all-you-can-eat-in-one-trip buffets. **Köşk Restaurant** lays a sumptuous table for about US$3.50 (veer left down the main street).

In the seductive village of **Kaş,** you can explore the mountainous, ruin-strewn countryside, take a boat trip around the coast, listen to 60s rock in a funky bar, or just sit on the waterfront and sip tea. The main attraction around Kaş is **Kekova,** a partially submerged Lycian city about 2 hours east (tours US$8). The trip ogles Byz-antine ruins and nearby fishing villages, one beneath a cliff honeycombed with Lycian tombs. You can visit Santa's last chimney dive at the **Christian Basilica** in **Demre;** in 1087, thieves plundered Santa's tomb, escaping to Bari, Italy with his bones and the cute little red hat. **Buses** running from Kaş to Antalya stop in Demre.

■■■ ANTALYA AND ALANYA

Perched above the sea a scenic 4½-hour bus ride from Kaş, **Antalya** is a great sponge for sucking up Roman ruins. East of Antalya lies the ancient Roman province of **Pamphylia** and its several important, partially excavated sites. The travel agencies that line Cumhuriyet will send you there. Antalya's **Archaeological Museum,** on Kenan Evren Bulvarı at the western end of town, showcases many of the artifacts found thus far. (Open Tues.-Sun. 9am-6pm. US$2.) A theater garnished with marble reliefs, a grand colonnaded avenue, and a supreme stadium conjure a vision of **Perge** in its 2nd-century heyday. To get here from Antalya, take a *dolmuş* to Aksu from the central *dolmuş* station, then walk 2km. No imaginative reconstruction is necessary at **Aspendos,** 49km from Antalya, thanks to the efforts of the Seljuk Turks who used it as a pilgrimage way station. The huge theater is one of the best-pre-served in the world; even the stage is almost completely intact.

Sack out cheaply in old Ottoman homes. The best pensions are in the old city (called "Kaleiçi"), southeast of the yacht harbor. A quiet courtyard makes **Adler Pansiyon** (tel. (31) 41 78 18), at Barbaros Mah. and Civelek Sok., one of the loveliest. (Singles US$6.) At the **Sabah Pansiyon,** 60 Hesapçi Şok (tel. 47 53 45 or 46), the rooms range from odd to luxurious, and the attached restaurant is great. (Terrace beds $3, singles $6, doubles $9-18.) To reach the main **tourist office** (tel. (31) 11 17 47) from the bus station, follow Kâzım Özalp Cad. toward town, turn right onto Cumhuriyet Cad. and go 100m past the statue of (you guessed it) Atatürk. (Open in summer daily 8am-6pm; off-season Mon.-Fri. 8am-5:30pm.) Connections to major Turkish cities are possible via **Turkish Airlines** (İstanbul US$70, İzmir US$60, Ankara US$60) and by **bus.**

Aside from its muscular fortress, **Alanya** offers little more than crowds, concrete and dirty beaches. If you're stuck here, try the simple but clean **Hotel Ankara Pala** on Müftüler Cad. (tel. (323) 188 64; US$3/person); the **tourist office** (tel. (323) 312 40; open daily 8am-7pm, off-season 8am-5:30pm) is in the shadow of the castle.

■■■ SILIFKE AND MERSIN

Buses travel daily from Alanya east to **Silifke** (7hr., US$7), whose mission in life is to provide bus links inland to Konya or Ankara. The nearby port of **Mersin,** sometimes called **İçel,** is Turkey's largest Mediterranean port, a good place to miss unless you need a ferry to Northern Cyprus. **Otel Murat 2** (tel. (74) 32 46 81), a block away from the bus station, has singles for US$6 and doubles for US$12. For the cheapest fresh fish on the Mediterranean, visit the **restaurants** near the fish market around the *Belediye,* the municipal government building (*mercan,* red coral fish, US$1). The friendly, multilingual crew at the main **tourist office** (tel. 36 63 58), at the harbor, just inland from the Turkish Maritime Line Agency (tel. 13 98 58), can provide maps and rooming suggestions. (Open daily 8am-5pm; off-season daily 9am-noon.)

■■■ ANTAKYA (HATAY)

Few tourists are to be found in idyllic Antakya (Hatay on Turkish publications), and a merciful breeze subdues the summer heat. Little remains from the Biblical days when this was Antioch—a city of half a million, one of the largest in the Mediterranean. Everything that's left—including spectacular mosaics—is in the **Archaeological Museum.** (Open Mon. 1:30-5pm, Tues.-Sun. 8am-noon and 1:30-5pm. US$1.50, students US80¢.) Two km from the town center towards Reyhanlı is **San Pierre Kilesi,** where St. Peter's original congregation coined the word "Christianity." (Open Tues.-Sun. 8am-noon and 1:30-5:30pm. Free.)

From the Atatürk statue in the city center, walk down Atatürk Cad. to the **tourist office** in the park on the opposite side of the circle. (Open daily 9am-noon and 1:30-6:30pm; off-season Mon.-Fri. 8:30am-noon and 1:30-5pm.) For accommodations, walk down İstiklâl Cad. from the bus station toward the town center. **Hotel Güney,** 8 İstiklâl Sok. (tel. (891) 117 78), has spic-and-span rooms. (Singles with bath US$6. Doubles US$9, with bath US$12.) If you have a Syrian visa (which you should get in İstanbul or Ankara), you can take a bus directly to Aleppo (*Halep* in Turkish), 100km away (US$7.50). You are supposed to exchange US$100 at the border. Daily buses also run to Jordan (*Ürdün* in Turkish, US$22.50).

CENTRAL TURKEY

The rolling miles of stoic Anatolian plateau contain the oldest and newest landmarks of Turkish civilization. Konya, once capital of the Seljuk Empire, bristles with exquisite mosques and tombs, while Ankara, Turkey's capital, testifies to the modernization imposed by the contemporary Turkish state. To the south, Cappadocia's ancient ruins attract the lion's share of tourists.

■■■ KONYA

Konya was the 12th-century capital of the Seljuk sultans and has been Turkey's religious center since the 13th century, when Afghani holy man Celâleddin Rumi, known to his followers as Mevlâna, settled here. Founder of the famous order of Whirling Dervishes, Mevlâna believed spiritual perfection and union with the divine was achieved through ecstatic dance. In 1925, Atatürk dissolved the order and now the Dervishes dance but once a year in December (if you can't make it, genuine Dervishes whirl year-round in İstanbul). You can spot the 13th-century **Mevlâna Tekke** by its radiant turquoise tower. Inside this one-time monastery are the *türbes* of Celâleddin and other Dervishes, as well as a fascinating museum with prayer rugs, musical instruments, and elaborately decorated garments. (Open Mon. 8:30am-3pm, Tues.-Sun. 8:30am-5:30pm. US$2.) Konya's other major attractions stud **Alaadin Tepesi** (Aladdin Hill), several hundred meters up Hükümet Cad. This mound supposedly contains layers of civilization stretching back to the Bronze Age. While in Konya, wander through the enchanting **market,** between the Aziziye Mosque and the **post office** (open 24hrs.) on Alaadin Cad.

The **tourist office** 21 Mevlâna Cad. (tel. 110 74), is across the street from the Mevlâna Tekke. **Çatal Pansiyon,** around the corner from the tourist office (tel. (33) 11 49 81), charges US$8.50 for a bed. Up Mevlâna Cad. 2 blocks and to the right is the cushy **Otel Çeşme,** 35 İstanbul Cad. (tel. 33 51/24 26; singles US$11-13.50; doubles US$16; triples with private bath UD$23). The local specialty is *firin kebap,* a chunk of oven-roasted lamb. Try it at **Lokanta Şima Restaurant,** near the tourist office.

Ten **buses** a day roam between Konya and Silifke (5hr., US$4), 15 times a day to and from Ankara (3hr., US$4) and İzmir (US$7.50). Night buses run to and from İstanbul. If you arrive at the bus station in the daytime, take a minibus marked "Mevlâna" to the center; at night try a 3-wheeled cart. After midnight, you'll have to take a taxi. To get back to the bus station take any *dolmuş* marked "Otogar."

■■■ ANKARA

Travelers have often scorned this sprawling, polluted, windy capital, but their criticisms are not entirely valid. Besides its roles as a transport center and museum city, Ankara has many European-style cafés in the **Kızılay** district. Catch the city on a sunny summer day, and you may find it more lively and engaging than its poor reputation would suggest.

ORIENTATION AND PRACTICAL INFORMATION

Get a map at the tourist office; you'll need it to survive in this huge and bewildering city. Most points of interest are in the **Ulus** and **Kızılay** districts. Continue straight on Cumhuriyet Bulvarı to the equestrian statue of Atatürk in the center of Ulus. Remember that the statue faces west; it is a key reference.

Tourist Office: Office at the airport. Main office at 121 Mustafa Kemal Bul. (tel. 488 70 07). From the bus or train stations, go under the train tracks to Tandoğan Sq., then left on Mustafa Kemal Bul. The office is on the ground floor of the Ministry of Tourism (Turizm Başkanlik) on your right. Open Mon.-Fri. 8:30am-7:30pm, Sat.-Sun. 9am-5pm.

Embassies: On Atatürk Bul., south of Hürriyet Sq.: **U.S.,** 110 Atatürk Bul. (tel. 426 54 70). **Canada,** 75 Nenehatun Cad. (tel. 436 12 90). **U.K.,** 46a Şehit Ersan Cad. (tel. 427 43 10). **Australia,** 83 Nenehatun Cad. (tel. 436 12 40). **Bulgaria,** 124 Atatürk Bul. (tel. 426 74 55). **Greece,** 911 Zia Ul-Rahman Cad. (tel. 436 88 60).

American Express: 7 Cinnah Cad. (tel. 167 73 34). Take any bus marked "Kavak-lidere" across from the Ulus post office. Mail held. Emergency cash for cardhold-ers. Wired money not accepted. Open Mon.-Fri. 9am-6pm, Sat. 9am-1pm.

Post Office: PTT, on Atatürk Bul. in Kızılay. Open 24hrs. Poste Restante open daily 9am-5pm. **Currency exchange** open 24hrs.

Telephones: At the post office (open 24hrs.), bus and train station. **City Code:** 4.

Airport: Direct flights to İstanbul (hourly 7am-10pm, 1hr.), Adana, Diyarbakır, Erzurum, İzmir, and Trabzon. Buses leave from the Turkish Airlines office (tel. 419 14 42) next to the train station 1½hr. before domestic and 2hr. before inter-national departures (US$1.50). All domestic flights US$62, students US$38.

Trains: The Otagar bus station is 500m south of the train station; it's quicker to travel between İstanbul and Ankara by bus, but overnight trains are more com-fortable. The *Mavi Tren* leaves both İstanbul and Ankara daily at 11pm (9hr., US$11). The *Anadolu Exspresi* leaves both cities at 9am and 9pm (11hr., US$7, couchette US$9). Ankara is also connected by rail to İzmir, Konya, Cappadocia, Erzurum, Trabzon, and other Turkish cities.

Buses: Frequent departures to Konya (hourly, 3hr., US$6), İstanbul (5hr., US$8-10), İzmir, Bodrum, Trabzon, Bursa, and Nevşehir, to name a few. Buses also run to Nevşehir and Ürgüp every hr. until 8pm. Daily to the Iranian border (US$15), Baghdad (US$30), and Aleppo, Syria. Lockers 25¢.

Hospital: Hacettepe University Hospital, Hasırcilar Cad. (tel. 310 35 45). From the statue in Ulus, head south for about 2km, turn left onto Talat Paşa Cad. and climb the hill to Hasircilar Cad. Emergency health care. Open 8:30am-5pm.

ACCOMMODATIONS AND FOOD

Most of the less expensive hotels are to the west of **Ulus**, toward the citadel, but this is a busy, noisy part of town, and hotels tend to be rather run-down. First try **San Otel,** Anafartlar Cad. Şan Sk. No. 8C, a spotless new hotel in a quieter area of town. (Singles US$7.50. Doubles US$13. Triples US$18.) The **Hisar Oteli** (tel. 311 98 89) is a little noisier, but clean, with a pleasant view. (Singles US$9, doubles $17). **Otel Yakut,** 19 Hilal Soq. (tel. 312 51 58), is on a mall street between the Hacı Bayram mosque and the Roman baths, and has sunny, carpeted rooms. (Singles US$8, with bath US$13. Doubles US$17). Ulus, like all of Turkey, is full of cheap *kebapçıs*. From Ulus, walk east on Hisarparkı Cad., turn right just before Anafartalar Cad. to find Ankara's big **food market,** with everything from sugared almonds to live chickens.

SIGHTS

The fantastic **Anadolu Medeniyetleri Müzesi** (Museum of Anatolian Civilizations) is near the southern end of the citadel that dominates the old town. Take a taxi (US$1.50) or walk east and up the hill from the Atatürk statue, then turn right onto Ipek Cad. The museum's nifty neolithic and Hittite collections justify a visit to Ankara. The setting is unique: a restored Ottoman *han* and *bedesten* (covered bazaar), its halls tweeting with scads of canaries, houses a collection of astoundingly old artifacts that traces Anatolian history from the dawn of civilization. (Open daily 9am-5:20pm. US$2.50, students US$1.25.) Take a taxi (US$1-3) or walk up the hill east from the statue of Atatürk, on Hisarparkı Cad., and right onto Ipek Cad. While in the area, stroll through the **bazaar,** the town-within-a-town inside the citadel walls, and the **Alâeddin Mosque.** Don't leave town without visiting **Anıt Kabir,** Atatürk's tomb. Its immense scale and the sheer number of Atatürk's personal effects manifest Turkey's reverence for its national hero. The site is in a vast park on the west side of town (a 25-min. walk from Kızılay). Southbound bus #63 on Atatürk Cad. will take you to the park. (Mausoleum open Tues.-Sun. 9am-noon and 1-5pm.)

■ Near Ankara

The sprawling ruins of **Hattuşaş,** the Hittite capital, are some 200km east of Ankara, 25km off the highway to Samsun. The first people to smelt iron, the Indo-European Hittites conquered Anatolia around 2200 BC. United under a central authority, the

Hittites vied with the Egyptians for control of the Fertile Crescent. Along the 9km wall encircling Hattuşaş, the **Yerkapı** (Earth Gate), a 70m-long tunnel/gate, begs a special visit. The Hittite high priest ruled from the inner sanctum of **Büyük Mabed** (Big Temple). To enter the chamber, subjects had to cross a drawbridge over 2 pools of water. Admission (US$2) also includes **Yazılıkaya,** an open-air temple where a cohort of the 1000 deities of the Hittite pantheon are represented in bas-relief, 4km south of Hattuşaş. To reach Hattuşaş, take a bus to Sungurlu (2½hr., US$4). There are unpredictable *dolmuşes* to Boğazkale, 1km from the ruins. Taxis are another option (US$3 is a good price; haggle with the driver). Otherwise, a private taxi costs US$15 for a one-way ride to Boğazkale, $20-30 for a full tour of the ruins. There is a tiny campsite next to the Aşıkoğlu motel. In Boğazkale, the **Baskent Pansiyon** has singles for US$10, doubles US$14, and triples US$20.

■■■ CAPPADOCIA

About 300km southeast of Ankara, Cappadocia is the most striking province in Turkey's central plateau. Peculiar, enchanting volcanic formations, clustered in valleys and along ridges, chisel the sharp-jawed landscape. When Christians arrived here in the 6th century they carved houses, churches and entire cities out of the soft volcanic rock. You'll want to spend a few days making daytrips from one of the 3 major towns in the region: Nevşehir is the best transportation hub, Ürgüp is a pretty, modern city and Göreme has the unique architecture and bizarre surroundings that lure travelers to Cappadocia. Each is within an hour's bus ride of the others.

Nevşehir Dusty, noisy Nevşehir is the region's transportation hub. Buses depart every morning for Ankara (4hr., US$6), Konya (3hr., US$5), Mersin and Adana (4hr., US$7), and overnight rides go to İzmir and İstanbul (12hr., US$11.50). The region's *dolmuş* routes are also centered here. Go to the **tourist office** (tel. 336 59), on Atatürk Bul., for maps, brochures, and information about certified guides. (Open daily 8am-noon and 1:30-6pm; off-season Mon.-Fri. 9:30am-5:30pm.) Coming down Atatürk, turn left on Lâle, and you'll find *dolmuş* for Göreme and Uçhisar (US30¢). A right on Lâle will bring you to the *dolmuş* for Ürgüp, Avanos, Niğde, Aksaray, and the underground cities of Kaymaklı and Derinkuyu (US$1-2). Municipal **buses,** cheaper than *dolmuş,* run 9 times a day between Nevşehir and Ürgüp (check schedule at the tourist office). Guided tours are cheapest in Göreme (US$15-27/person). Buses from the main bus station also rattle to Konya or the Mediterranean coast. If you must stay in Nevşehir, you can crash at **Ipek Palas Oteli,** at 99 Atatürk Bul. (tel. 314 78), 10 minutes west of the station (US$5.50/person; US$8/2 people). **Otel Nur,** 2 Belediye Cad. (tel. 314 44) has sparkling rooms, some with balconies (US$4/person). To get there from the bus station, turn left from Atatürk Bul.

Göreme and Ürgüp Göreme's proximity to rock-hewn churches and the valley of Zelve make it a convenient base. **Guided tours** of Cappadocia's major sites are available from several agencies in town for US$15-37. The most impressive of these are at the **Göreme Open-Air Museum,** 1km out of the village on the Ürgüp road. (Open 8am-6:30pm. US$5.50, students US$1.50.) The churches here are a legacy of Cappadocian Christianity in the Byzantine Empire. The monks of Cappadocia built the majority of the churches in Göreme between the 4th and 10th centuries, and inhabited the area until the formation of the modern Turkish Republic, when all Anatolian Greeks were relocated in exchange for the Turks living in Greece. Be certain to visit the Apple Church and the Chapel of the Sandal in the hill right before the main entrance; both feature superb frescoes. In the last few years, over 60 new pensions have carved a niche for themselves, charging a standard US$4 for a room without a bath. For cave-dwelling with the comfort of a hotel, try **Peri Pension** (tel. (4857) 11 36); its rooms are in a giant rock cone (US$4/person). The amiable **Rock Valley Pension** offers a true hospitality, lots of headroom and celestial showers

(US$4-6). Camp at **Göreme Dilek Camping,** where phallic rock formations penetrate the campsite, swimming pool and restaurant (US$4-6/tent).

The leafy town of **Ürgüp,** 20km east of Nevşehir, makes a pleasant base for exploring. A bus runs every half hour to Nevşehir (US30¢), where you must go before backtracking to Göreme. There are *dolmuş* and buses to Kayseri for connections to the east (on the hr., 7am-7pm, US$1). The Ürgüp **tourist office** (tel. (4868) 10 59) is on Kayseri Cad., inside the garden; they'll help you plan daytrips. (Open daily 8:30am-8:30pm; Oct.-March Mon.-Fri. 8am-5pm.) **Seymen Pansiyon** (tel. (4868) 23 80), conveniently facing Atatürk's back in the center of town, is friendly and comfortable (US$4/person). Try the *Saç Tava* (grilled meat and veggies) for US$3 at **Sofa Restaurant,** on Cumhuriyet Sq. (open daily 7:30am-11:30pm). Dance at **Legend Disco & Cave Bar,** literally a hole in the wall. Somewhat risky rental mopeds are an excellent way to see the sites in the area; try **Hepatu Rent-a-Motorcycle** (tel. 12 41; US$10/4hr.) if you have an international driver's license.

BLACK SEA COAST

Tourist propaganda encourages you to believe that Turkey has only two coasts: the Aegean and the Mediterranean. But the country's longest (and least visited) shore rises out of the Black Sea in steep, misted hills; the narrow lonely beaches are prodded by industrial cities and fishing villages. A highway traces the coast closely, so you can scan from your vehicle and choose what you want to explore. Hotels are available only in the larger cities, but campsites appear every 50km or so.

Breezy and amiable **Amasya** was the first capital of the Pontus kingdom which ended with the rise of Rome. Its residents live against the backdrop of monumental tombs carved into the cliffs above. For rooms on the river, first try **Konfor Palas Oteli** (tel. (3781) 12 60; US$5/person). Then seek the **Hotel Ap Aydın,** 86 Mustafa Kemal Cad. (tel. (3781) 24 63; single US$7.50). **Buses** run to Ankara (every 30min., 5hr., US$8), İstanbul (hourly, 11hr., US$14-18), and points south.

Sinop supports an American military base and a small tourist industry. The **Otel Gül Palas,** Cumhuriyet Cad. No. 3, (tel 1737) is 50m from the bus station. (Singles $5, doubles $7, triples $9.) Visit the medieval castle walls snaking through the city and the ruins of **Balatlar Church,** a 13th-century religious compound. A **tourist office** (tel. (3761) 19 96) is at the harbor. (Open daily 9am-8pm; closed off-season.)

EASTERN TURKEY

> Since 1984, the PKK (Kurdish Worker's Party), has been fighting for an independent Kurdish state. Violence is never directed against travelers, but bombs and fighting do pose a threat; for this reason *Let's Go* did not send researchers to Eastern Turkey in 1993. Think twice before traveling in this region.

Welcome to the final frontier of the European budget traveler. When journeying in Eastern Turkey, some caveats are in order. *Women will not feel comfortable alone;* even when traveling in pairs, wear long pants or skirts, long-sleeved blouses and scarves over your heads, and still prepare for unwanted attention. Bring some toiletries, especially toilet paper and tampons. Transportation can also pose difficulties. Buses often leave only when they're full, and schedules change according to demand and road conditions. If you get off a bus between stops it might be impossible to find another one later. Weather straddles every climatic extreme. Gaziantep, Urfa, Diyarbakır and Mardin are hot as *cehennem*—hell—in summer: temperatures there can top 110°F (43°C). In winter, deep snow periodically cuts off much of Turkey's northeastern end. Hakkâri is virtually inaccessible from November through March. Less-than-sanitary restaurants and hotels can pose a major problem; avoid the cheapest places, and don't eat dishes made with ground meat. Don't try the tap water, or any unboiled liquid foods; drink only the nationally distributed bottled water, fruit juice, or soda. If English leads nowhere, try German. Virtually every town large enough to stop in has a bank, but you should carry U.S. dollars (cash or small-denomination traveler's checks).

There is no such thing as a picturesque town in eastern Turkey—the cities are usually dusty, concrete and powerfully ugly. Nevertheless, the harsh plains and jagged peaks are incredibly captivating, and this leg can be one of the most rewarding of your Turkish adventure.

EASTERN EUROPE

Estonia (Eesti): Baltic States

Baltic States

Gulf of Finland

Baltic Sea

Hiiumaa

Saaremaa

Tallinn

Narva

RUSSIA

Lake Peipus

ESTONIA

Pärnu

Tartu

Gulf of Riga

Ventspils

Sigulda

Jurmala

Riga

LATVIA

Liepāja

Klaipeda

LITHUANIA

RUSSIA

Kaunas

Vilnius

RUSSIA

POLAND

0   40 mile

0   40 kilometer

US$1 = 13.00kr (kroons)	10kr = US$0.77
CDN$1 = 9.84kr	10kr = CDN$1.02
UK£1 = 20.10kr	10kr = UK£0.50
IR£1 = 18.80kr	10kr = IR£0.53
AUS$1 = 8.43kr	10kr = AUS$1.19
NZ$1 = 7.16kr	10kr = NZ$1.40
SAR1 = 2.69kr	10kr = SAR3.70
Country Code: 372	International Dialing Prefix: 810

Estonia took a historic step in the summer of 1992 when it became the first Baltic state to acquire its own post-Soviet constitution and currency. As the kroon gains some stability and a collection of Western ventures fills Tallinn with Volvos, cellular phones, and Jehovah's Witnesses, stoic Estonians deliberate over the best ways of reversing a 50-year social process that Russified their culture and Sovietized their supermarkets. After overcoming successive centuries of domination by the Danes, Swedes, and Russians, the Estonians' serene, patient pragmatism has matured into a dynamic and (some would say) Scandinavian attitude. Language is a stray link among ethnic Estonians (60% of the population) but divides them from the Russian immigrant community, who have to pass strict Estonian language tests in order to obtain citizenship in this new state. With a maximum span of less than 300km, Estonia is the smallest of the Baltic nations. Tallinn, its cosmopolitan, fast-paced capital, is home to half a million; Tartu, the Estonian Oxbridge, is a daytrip away; and Pärnu and the islands of Saaremaa and Hiiumaa shine as Baltic Coast resort areas.

GETTING THERE AND GETTING AROUND

In September 1993, most Estonian consulates could issue a 30-day, single-entry tourist visa (US$10) or a 1-year, multiple-entry visa (US$50) to citizens of Ireland and South Africa. Citizens of the U.S., U.K., Canada, Australia, and New Zealand do not need a visa to visit Estonia. The Estonian Consulate in the U.S. is located at 630 5th Ave. Suite 2415, New York, NY 10111 (tel. (212) 247-1450). Irish and South African citizens seeking visas should contact the Estonian Embassy,16 Hyde Park Gate, London SW7 5DG, U.K. A Latvian or Lithuanian visa is also valid for Estonia. It is possible to obtain a visa upon arriving in Estonia, but it is wiser to obtain one beforehand. Latvian visas are the cheapest of the 3.

Several **cruise lines** reach Tallinn from Helsinki. **Merelle,** Kluuvik 6, 00100 Helsinki (tel. 358 (0) 65 87 33 or 358 (0) 65 10 11) sells tickets for the *MIS Tallink* (daily, 3½hr.) and for the *MIS Georg Ots* (daily from Helsinki 10am, from Tallinn 6pm; 3½hr.; both ships one-way 120mk). The **Estonian New Line** has 3 hydrofoils, 2 of which make 2 daily round-trips in the summer, the 3rd only one (1½-2hr., 130mk, round-trip 230mk). Their cheapest fare, 100mk one-way, seats you on the ferry *Corbiere,* which leaves Helsinki at 8am and 8pm and arrives in Tallinn at 11:30am and 11:30pm daily. They also offer a one-day, visa-free tour of Tallinn (9:30am-5:30pm, 290mk). Tickets are available at travel bureaus or the Helsinki office at Kalevank 1 (tel. 358 (0) 680 24 99, summer only). From Stockholm, **Estline,** Estlineterminalen i Frihammnen, 11556 Stockholm (tel. 46 (8) 667 00 01), sails the *Nord Estonia* to Tallinn and back 3-4 times a week at 5:30pm. (14½hr., 385kr, students 295kr).

Finnair flies daily to Tallinn (round-trip 475mk, under 25 standby 420mk), and **Estonian Airlines** flies daily from Helsinki (round-trip 435mk). **SAS** flies from Stockholm to Tallinn daily (round-trip 1600 Swedish kr). **Buses** and **trains** radiate from Tallinn across Estonia, with connections to Russia, Latvia, and Lithuania. Train schedules are available at railway stations; purchase a useful schedule for other forms of transportation *(Tallinna transpordi teatmik)* at the Tourist Bureau in Tallinn. **Taxis** will take you anywhere for hard currency, although it is cheaper to pay in kroons.

ESTONIA ESSENTIALS

Try to get all the brochures and travel literature you can in Tallinn; most small towns offer only city maps. *The Baltic States: A Reference Book* offers data ranging from maps and hotels in every major town to a small "Who's Who" section for each country. Buy it for 200kr at Hotel Viru or in bookstores, where it'll be cheaper. All over the Baltics, St. John's (Jaanipäev), the eve of the summer solstice, inspires bonfires, festivals of song, and open-air revelry. In Estonia, Saaremaa throws the best bash. The main frolicking usually takes place on June 24th.

In Estonia, as in the rest of the Baltics, some restaurants and cafés take an hour break during the late afternoon or early evening. Most Estonian doorkeepers are friendly to Westerners, although you'll occasionally encounter a hard-headed Stalinist. Try smiling and speaking English, German, or French. If dining late, try to get in before 10pm. If possible, try making reservations around lunchtime.

Postcards to the U.S. require 2kr stamps. In 1993, public **phones** in Tallinn were free, as they had not been converted to accept Estonian senti pieces (100 senti=1 kroon). A new cardphone system will be introduced soon. Make calls to Europe from the central post office for 4-9kr per minute, and to the U.S. for 14kr per minute. Estonia's currency is the kroon; remember that rubles are no longer valid. Consider carrying a small backup supply of hard currency, as traveler's checks can be difficult to exchange.

Between the US$100-per-night Intourist abodes and the cheap, slightly drab hotels with no hot water, a few companies have set up youth hostels and started to arrange stays at private homes; contact the Tallinn tourist office. **FHS (Hua Ai Trade Ltd.),** Mere puiestee. 6, Tallinn (tel. and fax 372 (2) 44 11 87) and **CDS Reisid (Baltic Bed and Breakfast),** Raekoja plats 17, Tallinn (tel. 372 (2) 44 52 62; fax 372 (2) 31 36 66), offer rooms in homes throughout the Baltic countries. FHS costs US$9-15 per person; CDS is computerized and efficient, but costs US$25.

Estonians speak the best English in the Baltic states; most young people know at least a few phrases. If you use Russian, make it clear that it's not your only language. *Aitäh* (EYE-tah) means "thank you;" *palun* (PALL-oon), "please" or "here you are." "Yes" is *ja* and "no" is *ei* (rhymes with "hay"). "Do you speak English?" is *Kas Teie raagite inglis keelt?* (Kahs TEH-yeah REH-git-teh EEN-glis kehlt.)

■■■ TALLINN

An active port 80km from Helsinki, Tallinn and its old city are so beautiful that the Danes, the Germans, the Swedes, and the Soviets have all laid claim to them at some time. In the last 30 years, immigrants have almost doubled the city's population to half a million; ethnic Russians are the largest minority. Visitors to Tallinn may notice not-so-subtle signs of resentment towards the Russians living here: anger directed at the Soviet regime that annexed the country in 1939.

The heart of Tallinn is still very much a stony and medieval Nordic Florence, the cultural and political center of a nascent republic. The city is best enjoyed under the clear skies of the summer's white nights, when the sun sets for only 2 hours and leaves the sky a glowing pink from evening until morning.

ORIENTATION AND PRACTICAL INFORMATION

Tallinn's **Vanalinn** (Old Town) is an egg-shaped maze of streets from which four main roads branch forth. **Põhja puiestee,** which joins with Sadama, leads to the sea terminal, **Pärnu maantee** heads south, **Paldiski maantee** leads towards the Tallinn Zoo, and **Narva maantee** will take you to Pirita, Tartu, and Narva. The Old Town peaks in the fortress-rock of **Toompea,** whose 13th-century streets are level with the church steeples in the **All-linn** (low town). To get to the Old Town from the sea terminal, you can either take a taxi (don't pay more than US$3 or its kroon equivalent) or walk 5-7 min. west on Sadama, which turns into Põhja puiestee, then go left on Suur-Rannavärav and into Pikk. From the *Balti jaam* (train station), cross Toom puiestee and go straight through the park along Nunne; the stairway up Patkuli trepp on your right leads to Toompea.

Under Finnish influence, Tallinn's tourist literature is rapidly approaching Scandinavian standards. There are 3 city maps available, one in Russian, another in Estonian (which also covers the suburbs), and a third simplified one (with Estonian street names) for tourists. Buy them at newspaper stands at the Tourist Office at Raekoja Plats 8 in the center of the Old Town (tourist maps 18kr, *Tallinn This Week* 10kr). Also check out the extremely thorough *Tallinn, the Capital of Estonia: The Traveler's Guide*, sold in English and Russian.

Tourist Office: Tallinna Turismiamet, Raekoja Plats 8 (tel. 44 88 86 or 66 69 59; fax 44 12 21), across from the Town Hall in the Old Town. City maps, hotel lists, and other useful brochures. The friendly English- and German-speaking staff will quote schedules and prices and make reservations for transportation. They also have information about package tours and homestay organizations.

Consulates: U.S., Kentmanni 20 (tel. 31 20 21; fax 31 20 25). **U.K.,** Kentmanni 20 (tel. 45 53 28). **Canada,** Toomkooli 3 (tel. 44 90 56). **Russia,** Pikk 19 (tel. 44 30 14). **Latvia,** Tönismägi 10 (tel. 68 16 68). **Lithuania,** Vabaduse plats 10a (tel. 44 89 17). **Finland,** Liivalaia 12 (tel. 44 95 22). Travelers from **Australia** and **New Zealand** should contact the U.K. consulate.

Currency Exchange: Various *panki* (banks) in the city offer about the same rates and exchange traveler's checks from 9am-3pm. The bureaus at the train and bus stations offer slightly worse rates and are ostensibly open daily 9am-5pm, but sometimes close unpredictably. **Hansapank** (Viru 20), in the Old Town near Hotel Viru, is open daily 8am-8pm. Save the receipts to change money back.

Post Office: Main office at Narva maantee 1, across from the Hotel Viru. **Poste Restante.** Open Mon.Fri. 8am-8pm, Sat. 8am-5pm. **Postal Code:** EE0001.

Telephones: It's possible to call Helsinki directly from Tallinn. In Tallinn, use Finnish marks in the special phones at the airport and sea terminal. Other calls beyond the Baltics can be made from the main post office; order your call and wait for the connection. Open daily 7am-10pm. Local phones were free of charge in 1993, but a new cardphone system will be introduced soon. **City Code:** 22.

Trains: The **Balti jaam** (Balti station) on Toom puiestee can be reached by trams #1 and 2; in 1993 it was under renovation. If you don't speak Russian, Finnish, or Estonian, it's more convenient to get information and tickets at the tourist office than at the station. To: Moscow (3/day, 15-16hr., 96kr); St. Petersburg (2/day, 9hr., 49kr); Rīga (2/day, 9-10hr., 49kr); Warsaw (1/day, 8hr., 507kr). Rent lockers in the **luggage storage** area for 0.50kr.

Buses: The **Autobussijaam** (station) is on Masina, 1.5km southeast of the Old Town. Tram #4 and bus #22 connect to the city center. To: Rīga (4/day, 6hr., 32kr); St. Petersburg (1/day, 8½hr., 46kr); Tartu (4/day, 3hr., 21kr); and Pärnu (4/day, 2½hr., 16kr). Buses are faster and more expensive than trains.

Flights: The **Lennujaama** is in the eastern part of Tallinn. Bus #22 connects the airport with the train and bus stations, as well as with the city center in 20-24min. To: Helsinki (4/day, 35min., round-trip 435mk); Stockholm (3/day, 55min., round-trip 1600 Swedish kr); Kuressaare (2/day, 40min., 60kr).

Ferries: Tallinna Reisisadam (Tallinn Harbor) is a 15-min. walk from the city center. Serviced by trams #1 and 2. To: Helsinki (7/day; 2hr., 120mk); Stockholm (3-4/week; 14½ hr.; 385 Swedish kr). Purchase tickets from **WRIS** (tel. 44 13 64; fax 42 62 51).

Public Transportation: The public transportation system is changing rapidly; purchase a *Tallinna Transpordi Teatmik* (transportation schedule) from a bookstand or tourist office. Buses, trams, and trolleybuses cover the entire Tallinn suburban area and each category has separate stops marked with ideograms. They run from 6am-midnight and require tickets which can be purchased only at newsstands (0.40kr). Punch them on board. Monthly passes are 15kr.

Taxis: Around Hotel Viru, they'll rip you off. Find a *takso* stand, or call 43 03 30 (a private company) or 60 30 44 (state-run). Rides should run the kroon equivalent of US$2-8.

Emergencies: Ambulance: tel. 03. Police: tel. 02.

ACCOMMODATIONS

Alongside youth hostels, a new form of budget accommodation is emerging in Tallinn: a bed and breakfast option, which has the additional advantage of acquainting the traveler with local Estonians. **Family Hotel Service (Hua Ai Trade Ltd.),** Mere puiestee 6 (tel. and fax 372 (2) 44 11 87), provides a room with a family and access to the bathrooms and kitchen for US$10-15 per person. **CDS Reisid (Baltic Bed and Breakfast),** on the town hall square, Raekoja Plats 17 (tel. 372 (2) 44 52 62; fax 372 (2) 31 36 66), places travelers with English-speaking hosts (US$25 fee), and can arrange walking tours and wait-free visas to Russia. Make reservations in advance. The **Agnes youth hostel (HI)** at Narva maantee 7 (tel. 43 88 70), offers 34 rooms with communal showers and bathrooms, complemented by a friendly Russian-speaking staff who also know some English and German. Knock on the door to get in after midnight. From the train station, take tram #1 or 3 and get off just after the Hotel Viru. The hostel is in the courtyard. (94kr/person, 89kr with ISIC or student ID. Open April 1-Aug. 25.) The **Hotel Viitamin** (tel. 43 85 85), 2 doors down from Agnes on Narva, offers roughly the same healthy facilities as the hostel, but the bathrooms are shared by fewer people. Meet lots of Swedes and Finns here. (250kr.)

FOOD

Tallinn's Old Town and its surroundings are beginning to be filled with small restaurants (English is spoken at most places) whose low prices and large portions guarantee budget travelers' satisfaction. On Uus 7, a **24-hour store** with a pink panther insignia beckons the night owl. Tallinn is also filled with cozy, picturesque bars housed in old cellars. Try a few shots of *Vana Tallinn* (Old Tallinn) liqueur at **Bar Viarosse,** Lai 23, downstairs from the Noovsoo theater. (Imported beer 22kr; other drinks 6-8kr. Open Mon.-Fri. 10am-4pm and 6-11pm, Sat.-Sun. noon-11pm.) At the **Eeslitall Baar,** Voorimehe 3, sailors, tourists, and intellectuals convene to imbibe and dance the night away. (Open daily 4pm-4am, Estonian and Russian liquor 5-15kr; imported beer 25-30kr.)

Gnoom, Viru 2 (tel. 44 27 55). A restaurant, grill, bar, and café, whose medieval decor includes stiff-backed chairs and heavy silver candlesticks. Try the *seljanka* (thick fish soup, 10.50kr). Entrees 30-70kr. Restaurant, grill, and bar open daily noon-midnight; café open Mon.-Sat. 9am-9pm, Sun. 9am-6pm.

Rüütlibaar, Kohtu 2 (tel. 44 87 78), in a portico across from the *Toomkirik* (Cathedral). An oddly irreverent restaurant/bar with great prices: rainbow trout with home-fries 19kr, cheaper at lunch; *höögviin* (hot red wine) only 5kr. Entrees 10-20kr. Open daily noon-midnight.

Baar Vegan, Uus 22, serves (can you believe it?) several vegetable and grain dishes from which you compile your meal; each large teaspoonful costs 1kr. Fruit and vegetable juices are also available. Open weekdays 10am-6pm.

Eeslitall, Dunkri 2 (tel. 44 80 33). Meat and vegetarian dishes 20-50kr, tasty omelettes 9-20kr, in a crazy post-modern interior: wooden planks in the ceiling painted in floral patterns and futuristic landscape paintings. Open noon-2am.

Peetri Pizza, Pärnu maantee 22 and Lai 4 (tel. 66 67 11 and 60 16 53). Lots of toppings available (10-22kr). 1st location open 10am-3am; 2nd open 10am-11pm.

Maiasmokk Kohvik, Pikk 16 (tel. 60 13 96), the 1st marzipan and chocolate producer in Estonia (est. 1864), serves ice cream (8-15kr), tea, coffee, hot chocolate, salads, and pastries, as well as alcohol. Open 11am-10pm.

SIGHTS

You can get acquainted with the **Old City** by starting at Hotel Viru, walking down Narva maantee then continuing on along Viru past a 15th-century city gate to **Raekoja plats,** where handicrafts are sold on summer evenings and folk songs and dances are performed on a small outdoor stage. The **Raekoda** (Town Hall) was built during 1371-1404 and is guarded by **Vana Toomas** (Old Thomas), a cast-iron figurine of the legendary defender of Tallinn, which dates from 1530. Behind the Raekoda, at Raekoja 6, you'll find the **Rae Museum,** which served as the town jail in 1370. Nowadays it houses an interesting exhibit on early Estonian photography and some contemporary Estonian sculptures. (Open Thurs.-Tues. 10:30am-5:30pm. 1-2kr.) For a **view** of the northern towers and bastion of the medieval city, go up Vene, take a right on Olevimägi and up Uus. In front of the smaller tower, *Paks Margareeta* (Stout Margareeta), you'll find the **Meremuuseum's** (sea museum), Pikk 70, changing exhibits on Tallinn's history as a busy port. (Open Tues.-Sun. 10am-6pm. 2kr.) If you go down Pikk, you'll run into the **Oleviste kirik** (St. Olav's Church) on your right, the tallest church in town. (Open Sunday 10am-5pm, services on Mon. and Thurs. at 6:30pm.) Go to the end of Pikk and take a left onto Rataskaevu to see the mighty spire of **Niguliste kirik** (Nicholas Church), Oleviste's only rival among city churches. Inside is a fragment of Bernt Nothe's medieval masterpiece, *Danse Macabre.* (Open Wed. 2-9pm, Thurs.-Sun. 11am-6pm. 1-2kr.) If you walk down Rüütli, take a right and go up toward Toompea, you'll see on your left **Kiek in de Kök** (peek in the kitchen), an allusion to the fact that from this height, you could see into everyone's home in 16th-century Tallinn. The tower, still pockmarked with embedded cannonballs, was built in 1475 and has 6 levels of art and historical exhibits. (Open Tues.-Fri. 10:30am-5:30pm, Sat.-Sun. 11am-4:30pm. 0.50-1kr.) Straight ahead is the **Neitsitorni** (Virgin Tower), where you can drink *höögviin* and hobnob with bohemians. The doorman extracts a 3kr entrance fee, and another 3kr is charged for seating on the balcony. Up the street and on your left, you'll find the **Alexander Nevsky Cathedral,** begun under Tsar Alexander III and finished a few years before the Bolshevik Revolution. A marble marker from 1910 recalls Peter the Great's victory over the Swedes in 1710. (Open 8am-7pm.) The recently opened **Eesti Kunstmuuseum** (Estonian Art Museum) is across from the **Toomkirik** which is higher up on Toompea. It exhibits Estonian art from the 19th century to the 1940s. (Open Wed.-Mon. 11am-6pm.) The **Toompea Castle,** the present seat of the Estonian government, rises directly in front of you here, but the door is barred to prying eyes. At the **Tallinn City Museum** on 17 Vene, you'll find everything you've ever wanted to see from early 19th-century Tallinn. (Open 10:30am-6pm. 2kr.) On the eastern side of Tallinn, reachable by tram #1 or 3 is the **Kadriorg Palace,** Tallinn's museum of fine arts. The building, erected to honor Catherine the Great, houses a collection of Estonian paintings and sculptures and is located across the park from the "Kadriorg" tram stop. (Open Tues.-Sun. 11am-5pm. 3kr.) In July, **Rock Summer** draws students from all over the world to Tallinn (for more info call Makarov Music Management, 23 84 03).

In **Rocca-Al-Mare,** a peninsula 12km west of Tallinn, you'll find the quaint **Estonian Open-Air Museum,** Vabaõhumuuseumi 12 (tel. 55 91 76), a collection of wooden mills and farmsteads from the 18th-20th centuries. Take bus #21 from Balti jaam (30min.) or a taxi (50-70kr). (Open May-Oct. 10am-4pm.)

■■■ KURESSAARE

Sleepy but charming **Kuressaare** became the seat of the Saare-Laane bishopric in the 16th century. The town is small; you can walk from the west side's medieval episcopal castle (complete with moat), to the modern bus station on the eastern border in less than 15 minutes. To get downtown, walk along Tallinna for 3 blocks until you see a small square and an "Info" sign on your left. If flying in, take a taxi from the airport (6kr). On the way toward the castle, at **Raekoja plats** (the narrow town square), there is a monument to the 1918-1920 struggle for independence. On your left squats the **Kuressaare Town Hall,** a squarish building with an Estonian flag, built in 1670. (Open 7:30am-2:30pm.) Walk through the park on Lossihoovi towards the **Kuressaare Episcopal Castle,** the town's main attraction. The castle houses the **Saaremaa Regional Museum.** (15kr, students 5kr.) Pick up a map (1kr) at the castle entrance. (Open Wed.-Sun. 11am-7pm. Last entry 5:30pm.) The quiet and clean beaches of **Mändjala** and **Järve** are about 15km away from Kuressaare. Take a taxi to either from the city center (15kr). During the *Jaanipäev* (St. John's Day) celebrations, people flock to the country from the cities to sing, dance, and leap over bonfires throughout the night.

Accommodations, Food, and Practical Information The **Mardi Öömaja,** Vallimaa 5A (tel. 558 78, 574 36), is a youth hostel with spacious, newly-decorated rooms only a 10-minute walk from the square. Reception is on the second floor. A café downstairs serves breakfast. (100kr/person on the 2nd floor, 65kr/person on the 3rd, where there are fewer showers and smaller rooms. Breakfast included. No curfew.) The **Panga Pansionaad** (tel. 579 89, 577 02) at Tallina 27, has excellent singles for 270kr and 10 sparklingly clean doubles for 300kr. It's best to reserve a spot in advance. From the bus station, go around the back and cross Tallinna. The pension is behind the white building with the "Pank" sign; go through the small iron gate on the left.

Fan your appetite at **Kohvik (Café) Veski** (tel. 548 58), on the corner of Kaevu and Pärna, inside an old windmill. (Entrees 8-15kr. English menu. Open noon-5pm, 7pm-1am.) Three doors away from the town hall, the **Pirukad** bakery (Lossi 5) sells *pontsiki* (fried doughnuts).

The **tourist office** is in a small white building on the town's main square. The friendly, English-speaking staff can help you with accommodations, bike rentals, and sell you a map of the city (12kr). (Open 9am-5pm.) They also have info on the Saaremaa camping grounds. If you want to bike across town or around Saaremaa, rent one (30kr/day) from the **bicycle rental service** next to Mardi Öömaja, Vallimaa 5A (tel. 558 78 or 572 94). Catch a **bus** at the *Autobussijaam* at the intersection of Tallinna and Romandandi to: Tartu (2/day, 5hr., 32kr); Pärnu (4/day, 3-4hr., 26kr); and Tallinn (6/day, 4½hr., 26kr). **Plane** tickets are also available (9am-5pm); Estonian Airlines flies to Tallinn twice daily (60kr). The **airport,** in Roomassaare, can be reached by taxi (6kr).

■■■ PÄRNU

Pärnu is located 130km south of Tallinn on Estonia's western coast. The medieval center of the city has rapidly become commercialized, and staying on the main street, Rüütli, will give you an incomplete picture. Discover the charm of this coastal city by walking on the *Rand* (beach) or through the parks; the beach pavilions and beautiful houses on the *Esplanaadi* (boulevard) were built in the 19th century when Pärnu was famed for its waters and mud baths.

Facing Hotell Pärnu on Rüütli, you'll find the **Museum of the City of Pärnu,** a quintessential municipal museum full of old clothes and arrowheads. (Open Wed.-Sun. 11am-6pm, Sat.-Sun. 11am-5pm. 2kr, students 1kr.) This and the **Lydia Koidula Museum,** Jannseni 37, located at the childhood home of the 19th-century poet who led a revival in Estonian-language verse and drama, are the only museums in town. (Open Wed.-Sun. 10am-5pm, Sat.-Sun. 10am-4pm. 2kr, students 1kr.) If you turn left on Nikolai, you'll find the stern **Eliisabeti Kirik,** built in 1747. (Open daily 10am-2pm). Check out the Stalin-inspired **Endla Theater** (Keskväljak 1), used for festivals and special events. On Midsummer Night Pärnu hosts the **Fiesta jazz festival,** along with the **Baltic Scandal,** a modernist Baltic and Scandinavian theater extravaganza.

The broad, long, sandy beach, down Supeluse, is punctuated with signs such as the heartening "the water is too dirty for swimming," and, if you're lucky, a little sun. At its best, in August, the temperature won't get past 29°C.

Accommodations, Food, and Practical Information The most central rooms are at the **Hotell Pärnu,** Rüütli 44 (tel. 421 45 and 431 00), right by the bus station. They lack hot water but include breakfast. (Singles 180kr. Doubles

230kr.) You can change money here from 8am-midnight; the rates aren't great. They do take American Express and speak English, though. **Hotell Leharu,** Sääse 7 (tel. 458 95), in a former sanatorium, harbors English speakers and hot showers. Go to the fourth floor, and try to ignore the first-floor construction work. (Singles 200kr. Doubles 350kr.) **Hotell Kajakas,** Seedri 4 (tel. 430 98), has a sauna but no hot water. (Singles 110kr. Doubles 140kr.) **CDS** and **FHS** (see Tallinn) also arrange bed and breakfast with Pärnu families.

The colorful **Bar and Café Bristol** face each other at the corner of Hommiku and Rüütli; each offers a cozy, wood-paneled atmosphere. The *kohvipood* (café) serves clear vegetable soup (*puljong*), salads, and pastries. (1-3kr. Bar open 2pm-2am, café 8am-6pm.) **Komandandi Kelder Restaurant** is just off Rüütli, on the corner of Nikolai and Uus; ice cream, beverages, and entrees (16-20kr) are available in the basement from 10am-10pm.

Pärnu is best reached by **bus** since the station is in the very center, down Ringi from the bus parking lot on your right. There are 4 daily buses to Rīga (22kr), more than a dozen to Tallinn (15kr), 7 to Tartu (22kr), 1 to Kaliningrad, Russia (46kr), 1 to Vilnius (58kr), and 1 to Kaunas (62kr). The **train station** is east of the city center, by the corner of Riia maantee and Raja (Take buses #4 and 22 to and from the central post office.) There is a train twice daily to Rīga (4½ hr., 18kr) and to Tallinn (3½ hr., 6kr). Grab maps and information about Pärnu at **Reiser Travel Agency,** Rüütli 35 (tel. 372 (44) 445 00; fax 372 (44) 448 85). From the bus station, walk down Kirji and take a right on Rüütli; the **post office** on Akadeemia 7 is at the street's end. (Open Mon.-Fri. 8am-6pm, Sat. 9am-3pm.)

■■■ TARTU

Since the town has been burned to the ground 55 times, very little remains of medieval Tartu. When it's not smoldering, the town hosts **Tartu University,** which boasts 9 faculties and a student body of 7500. The summer traveler will see very little academia in action; when school is out, Tartu becomes a sleepy, provincial town to be enjoyed in an afternoon or two of strolls.

From the *Bussijaam* (bus station), walk down Turu, which turns into Vabaduse puiestee; the **town square** is your third left. Buy a much-needed map of Tartu (10kr) at the only **bookstore** on the square (on its north side). The remarkable architecture and long history of the **university** (founded in 1632, it's the oldest operating university in northern Europe) will amaze you; to reach it, go behind the **town hall** (the pink building on the south side of the square), take a right on Ülikooli , walk 2 blocks, then look for a building with white colonnades. The **Museum of Classical Art,** a small but charming gathering of Roman and Greek art, is inside. (Open Mon.-Fri. 11am-4:30pm. 3kr.) By befriending local students you may get a private tour of the university. The ruins of the 14th-century **Jaani Kirik** (St. John's Church) can be found on Ülikooli (which turns into Jaani). On top of the **Toomemägi** (Cathedral Hill) are the majestic remainders of the 13th-century **St. Peter and Paul Church.** The **Estonian National Museum** is at Veski 32 (open Wed.-Sun. 11am-6pm; 2kr), and features ethnographic exhibits from all over Estonia.

Accommodations, Food, and Practical Information For overnight stays, try the comfortable and central **Park Hotell,** Vallikraavi 23 (tel. 336 63; fax 343 82; walk along Lossi toward the hill, bear left, go under a bridge, continue on Liivi and take your first left after the Liivi fork), where singles go for 160-320kr. More expensive singles have a large bed that can be used by two. Doubles run from 220kr, with only a basin, to 600kr, for true luxury. Reservations are recommended. Another option is **Hotel Tartu,** Soola 3 (tel. 320 91), right behind the bus station. (Singles 160kr. Doubles 260kr. 15% discount with youth hostel card. Communal showers, sauna 50kr/hr.)

The jolliest restaurant in town is **Püssirohukelder** (Gunpowder Cellar), Lossi 28 (tel. 341 24), a two-level cellar *baar* with beautiful medieval walls. A full meal costs 40kr. Make reservations on Wednesday, Friday, and Saturday nights, because the variety show (9-11pm) usually draws a full house. (Open 2-7pm and 8pm midnight.) **Peetri Pizza** on Tiigi 11 (tel. 303 10), not far from the university's main library, offers pizzas for 10-22kr. (Open 11am-midnight.)

The **tourist office** is just off the main square (Raekoja plats) at Küütri 3 (tel. 321 41. Open Mon.-Fri. 10am-6pm). **Buses** depart 8 times daily from Tallinn (3hr., 23kr). If you come by **train** from Tallinn (4/day, 4hr., 14kr), you'll have to take a taxi from the railway station toward Raekoja plats (10-15kr).

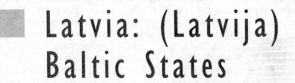

Latvia: (Latvija) Baltic States

> In the summer of 1993, Latvia had two monetary standards, the Latvian ruble (LVR) and the lat, which was equal to 200LVR, and will be adopted as the sole Latvian currency. *Let's Go* lists prices in Latvian rubles (LVR) except in cases where an establishment only accepts hard currency, in which case prices are listed in U.S. dollars (US$). Latvia was still using Russia's telephone system in 1993, as well.

US$1 = 126LVR	100LVR = US$0.80
CDN$1= 96LVR	100LVR = CDN$1.05
UK£1 = 196LVR	100LVR = UK£0.51
IR£1 = 182LVR	100LVR = IR£0.55
AUS$1 = 82LVR	100LVR = AUS$1.22
NZ$1 = 70LVR	100LVR = NZ$1.44
SAR1 = 26LVR	100LVR = SAR3.82
Country Code: 372	**International Dialing Prefix: 810**

Latvia, a nation of 2.7 million situated between Estonia and Lithuania on the Baltic coast, is no exception to the Baltics' history of foreign domination: Germany, Poland, Sweden, tsarist Russia, and the Soviet Union have all sought to maintain a grip on its gentle landscape and 5000 lakes. But Latvia has managed to retain its national identity, reflected in music, art, folk culture, and handicrafts; the Baltika festival (to be held in Rīga in July, 1994) is a good opportunity to see traditional-dress performances of folk songs and dances.

GETTING THERE AND GETTING AROUND

In September 1992, visas were required to enter Latvia. Latvian embassies or consulates are located at 4325 17th St. NW, Washington, DC 20011 (tel. (202) 726-8213), 79 Pegasus Trail, Scarborough, Ont. M1G 3N8 (tel. (416) 289-2617), 72 Queensborough Terrace, London W2 3SP and P.O. Box 23, Kew, Victoria 3101 NSW. The cost is US$5 for U.S. citizens and US$10 for others; the processing time is two weeks. Latvian visas are also valid for Estonia and Lithuania. Latvian visas are the cheapest of the 3.

Americans can arrive at the border with no visa. Flying or taking a ferry in, they can get a **visa** for up to 90 days; on a train, they can get a 2-day visa for US$20. They must then extend either visa at the Visa and Registration Department of the Ministry of Internal Affairs (Raiņa bulv. 5, tel. 21 97 21). Get there early and be prepared to wait. (Open 10am-1pm and 2-4pm.)

The least expensive way to reach Rīga if you're already in the Baltics is by train or bus from Tallinn or Vilnius. If you travel by train, be sure to secure a *coupé* or a first-class compartment. Flying into Rīga is also an option; **Finnair** goes from Helsinki (4/week; round-trip 1170 Finnish mk, student standby 970 Finnish mk). **Latvijas Avio-līnijas** flies from Helsinki (2/week, round-trip US$222), Copenhagen (1/day, round-trip US$418), and Stockholm (1/day, round-trip US$373). **SAS** flies in from Copenhagen (1/day, round-trip US$418) and Stockholm (1/day, round-trip US$375). **Baltic International** has begun flying from Frankfurt (5/week, round-trip US$370), Hamburg (2/week, round-trip US$425), and Berlin (2/week, round-trip US$444).

Sea travel is another possibility. **Baltic Lines** (tel. 46 (11) 15 15 11) makes a round-trip each week between Stockholm and Rīga. The ship leaves Stockholm on Tuesdays at 4pm, arrives in Rīga the next day at 9:30am, leaves Rīga at 6pm and is back in Stockholm on Thursday at 10am (US$120 in a quad).

LATVIA ESSENTIALS

Gather brochures and travel literature on Rīga and other destinations at **Latvia Tours,** which shares an office with **American Express** on Grēcinieku iela 22/24 (tel. 013 (2) 213 652; fax 013 (2) 213 666). A city map of Rīga is sold at newsstands (85LVR), and *Rīga This Week* and the excellent, encyclopedic *The Baltic States: A Reference Book* can be bought at main hotels and hard-currency shops. As in the rest of the Baltics, stores sometimes close for an hour or two between noon and 3pm, and restaurants may take a break between 5 and 7pm. Homemade Latvian bread and pastries are delicious and worth asking for; try *speka rauói,* a warm pastry, or *biezpienmaize,* bread with sweet curds. Latvian beer is strong and bitter, but very cheap; a bottle anywhere costs 60LVR or less.

Public city phones take *žetoni* (coins) with a single groove, while long-distance phones require žetoni with two grooves. Both are available at post offices and phone offices, where you can make calls outside the Baltic area. Note that timetables for buses and trains in the Baltics run horizontally instead of vertically. Latvians speak Russian, albeit reluctantly. Most young Latvians study English or German but probably aren't fluent. Start off in your own language, and break into Russian only after your native tongue has failed. Key words and phrases include *lõdzu* (LOOD-zoo; "please"), *paldies* (PAHL-dee-yes; "thank you") and *Vai jus runājiet angliski?* (VIE yoos roo-nah-yet ahn-GLEES-kee; "Do you speak English?").

Latvia is currently using two monetary standards; the Latvian ruble (LVR, at 126 rubles to the dollar) is gradually being taken over by the lat (1 lat = 200LVR) which will eventually stand as Latvia's single currency. All prices quoted here are in LVR; expect at least a 50-100% inflation rate over the next year. As in Estonia and Lithuania, Latvian establishments are struggling to adjust to walk-in customers instead of preprogrammed Intourist tours. No single tourist office has been established, but there are a few organizations that can help with accommodations and ticket reservations. **Tourservice** (Latvian Travel Company) at Elizabetes iela 27 (tel. 32 60 09; fax 16 11 83) has listings of budget accommodations and makes travel arrangements. (Open Mon.-Fri. 10am-6pm, Sat. 10am-2pm). **Patricia**, Elizabetes 22-4a (tel. 28 48 68; fax 286 650. Open Mon.-Fri. 9am-7pm), provides tourist info in English and arranges homestays (average US$10/night) as well as apartment rentals (US$30-40/night).

■ ■ ■ RĪGA

Latvia's capital has been subject to Western (specifically Germanic) influence for almost its entire existence. **Vecrīga** (the old town), full of 18th- and 19th-century architectural landmarks, occupies a small part of Rīga: the area between Kr. Valdemāra iela and Marijas ie. can be covered in a 15-minute walk, and the belt between Aspazijas bulv. and the right bank of the Daugava in about the same time. The center of Rīga is in turn-of-the-century *Jugendstil*, with sculpted parks that provide a sanctuary from the sprawling, noisy, dirty metropolis.

PRACTICAL INFORMATION

Tourist Office: There is no centralized office yet. **Latvia Tours,** Grēcinieku iela 22/24 (tel. 21 36 52; fax 21 36 66) is a good place to start as they can give you a lot of useful brochures, including *Rīga This Week*. Open Mon.-Fri. 9am-5pm. **Tourservice,** Elizabetes iela 27 (tel. 32 60 09; fax 16 11 83), and **Patricia,** Elizabetes iela 22-4a (tel. 28 48 68; fax 28 66 50), can provide plane and train info, and bookings for transportation and accommodations. A new, exhaustive Rīga City Map can be bought at many newsstands for 85LVR. Rīga also has a tourist information line (tel. 22 17 27), not always staffed by English speakers.

American Express: Latvia Tours (see above) provides AmEx services.

Embassies: U.S., 7 Raiņa bulv. (tel. 22 70 45, 21 00 06, or 22 26 11); **U.K.,** Elizabetes iela 2 (tel. 32 07 37 or 32 52 87); **Canada,** Elizabetes iela 45/47 (tel. 33 33 55); **Lithuania,** Elizabetes iela 2 (tel. 32 17 44, 32 15 19, or 32 09 48); **Sweden,** Lāčplēša 13 (tel. 28 62 76); **Finland,** Teātra 9 (tel. 21 60 52); **Denmark,** Pils laukums 11 (tel. 22 62 10). **Australians** and **New Zealanders** should call the U.K. Consulate.

Currency Exchange: There is an office in the train station. Open daily 10am-8pm. This and the change bureau in Hotel Latvija, Elizabetes iela 55 (open daily 10am-7pm), keep reliable hours, but their rates are worse than those of small makeshift offices all around town, identified by the "Valūtas Apmaiņa" signs.

Post Office: Stacijas laukums 1, near the railway station. Open Mon.-Fri. 8am-8pm, Sat. 8am-4pm, Sun. 10am-4pm. To send packages abroad, go to window #4. Letters and postcards going abroad need a 40LVR stamp. **Poste Restante:** 1050.

Telephones: Office at Brīvības 21 for calls abroad or purchasing žetoni. Open 24hrs. When calling internationally, dollars get you straight through; with rubles you may wait up to 2hr. To the U.S.: $3 or 160LVR/min. To Europe: $2 or 90LVR/min. **City code:** 2.

Flights: Lidosta Rīga (Rīga Airport), 8km southwest of the Old Town. Take bus #22, tram #7, or a taxi (don't pay more than 500-700LVR). Flight info available from the airport (tel. 20 70 09), or from **Latvijas Aviolīnijas** (tel. 22 31 75).

Ferries: Sea terminal (tel. 32 98 82) located 1km north of the Rīga castle along Eksporta iela; take a taxi (100-150LVR) from the city center.

Trains: Rigas centrālā stacija, Stacijas laukumā, just east of the Old Town along Marijas iela. To: Moscow (2/day, 17-18hr., 511LVR); St. Petersburg (2/day, 13-14hr., 320LVR); Kaliningrad, Russia (1/day, 12hr., 200LVR); Klaipeda (1/day, 6½hr., 230LVR); Vilnius (2/day, 8-9hr., 260LVR); Liepāja (4/day, 5-6hr., 270LVR). Get train information at the information window or by calling 007 (dial several times). If you can, buy train tickets to major cities in advance; black marketeers often buy them up to sell on the departure day for double or triple the price.

Buses: Autoosta, 200m south of the train station along Marijas. To: Liepāja (12/day, 4hr., 394LVR); Tallinn (6/day, 6hr., 510LVR); Vilnius (2/day, 6hr., 420LVR); Kaunas (3/day, 6hr., 370LVR). For inquiries, call 21 36 11.

Public Transportation: An efficient network of buses, trams, and trolleys covers the greater Rīga area, divided into 3 zones. Rides are 7LVR/zone; buy tickets in advance at a newsstand and punch them on board.

Taxis: A ride within Rīga should cost no more than 500LVR. Call 33 40 41.

Emergencies: Ambulance: tel. 03. **Fire:** tel. 01. **Police:** tel. 02.

ACCOMMODATIONS

Alternatives to the large, impersonal Intourist hotels are rapidly proliferating in Rīga in the form of cheery hostels and networks of private rooms. **Patricia,** Elizabetes iela 22-4a (tel. 28 48 68; fax 28 66 50), and the **Tourist Club of Latvia,** Skunu 22 (tel. 22 76 80 or 21 23 77), as well as **FHS** and **CDS** (see Tallinn, Estonia), place tourists into private homes for a small fee.

Rīga HI Youth Hostel. Rīga Youth and Family Hostel, Kalnciema iela 10/12 (tel. 22 64 63; fax 22 47 85). Take train #4 or 5, or bus #22, 37, or 41. On the 3rd floor of a student dorm not far from the Vanšu bridge in Āgenskalus, convenient to the Old Town. Spartan accommodations, hot water, and a friendly, English-speaking staff. No curfew or membership needs. US$10. Open June 1-August 31.

Laine, Skolas iela 11 (tel. 28 76 58 or 28 88 16). A hostel just off Elizabetes iela in the new center, occupying the 4th floor of the building, with communal bathrooms and showers. Bright, spacious rooms. Prices from US$10 singles to US$40 quads. Breakfast included. No curfew or membership requirements.

Victorija, A Čaka 55. (tel. 27 62 09 or 27 23 05), 1½km from the Old Town. The cheapest rooms share communal bathrooms and showers (occasional hot water). Doubles 800LVR. Rooms with shower, refrigerator, and TV cost 1700LVR for singles and 2500LVR for doubles.

Tūrists, Slokas iela 1 (tel. 61 54 55). Drab, but acceptable. Rooms with shower and bathroom, but temperamental hot water supply. Located in Āgenskalus. Singles US$30. Doubles US$50.

FOOD AND ENTERTAINMENT

Food in Rīga, for the most part, is a blur of the same *karbonadas, kotletas,* and *bifšteks* you'll find elsewhere in the Baltics. A few beer halls and cafés (*kafejnīca*) stand out for their atmosphere. The **central market** is in the hall behind the bus station on Prāgas iela; you can buy fresh fruits and vegetables, as well as meat and dairy products. (Open Sun.-Fri. 7am-6pm, Sat. 7am-3pm.)

Pie Kristapa, Jauniela 25/27 (tel. 22 75 30 or 22 48 36), has a restaurant upstairs and an incredible beer hall downstairs, which serves hearty portions of simple and delicious food, and home-brewed beer in big ceramic jugs. Make reservations around lunchtime by paying a 200LVR cover. Main dishes 100-300LVR. Open daily noon-6pm and 7pm-midnight.

Jana, Skunu 16 (tel. 22 62 58). Though small and overbooked (seats about 24), Jana is king among Rīga's restaurants. Try their pancakes with caviar. Entrees 450-600LVR. Reservations are a must. Open Mon.-Sun. 11am-11pm.

Hotel Latvija, Elizabetes 55. Two restaurants here: the main one (open 11am-10pm) and the "restaurant of national cuisine" (open 1pm-midnight); try their *karbonadas* and the hot mushroom dish as an appetizer. Entrees 150-350LVR.

Kafejnīca Pētergailis, Skārņu 25. A café with funky stained-glass windows facing the square between St. Peter's and St. John's churches. A good place for ice cream or dessert (25-60LVR). Open Mon.-Sat. 11am-10pm, Sun. noon-9pm.

Carlsberg Beer Garden. A great place to have a quiet beer and watch or be watched. Right across from the cathedral. Beer 90LVR/can, bratwurst 230LVR. Open daily 10am-11pm.

Forum, Kaļķu 24 (tel. 22 84 89). Small restaurant serving basic Western-tasting food. Main courses US$8-12. Hard currency only. Gamble the night away at the casino upstairs (US$3 cover charge includes 1 free drink). Open 11am-3am.

Like Cinderella, most of Rīga tries to head home around midnight; fill the gap with some culture. Birthplace of Mikhail Baryshnikov, Rīga is home to the **Latvian National Opera,** Nometņu 62 (tel. 61 57 73), the **Russian Drama Theater,** Kaļķu 16 (tel. 22 46 60), and the avant-garde **Experimental Theater Studio (ETS),** Brīv-ības 85 (tel. 53 29 06). For details on performances, look for posters around the city or consult *Rīga This Week.* Tickets to organ concerts in the Doma Cathedral can be purchased at Doma laukums 1 (tel. 21 34 98), opposite the main entrance at the *koncertzales kase.* (Open noon-3pm and 4-7pm.)

SIGHTS

To reach **Vecrīga** (the Old Town) from the bus station, go under the bridge at your left and across the street. From the train station, walk down Marijas iela toward the river for 3 or 4 minutes, then turn right on Vaļņu iela. Go down Vaļņu, take a left on

Audēju iela and you'll come to **Pēter baznīcas** (St. Peter's Church) on your right after a few blocks. For an amazing view of Rīga's rooftops, scale the **tower.** (Open 10am-8pm. 50LVR.) At a height of 72m (the top level), you can see the Baltic Sea. Just behind the church at Jāna 7 stands the **Jāna baznīca** (St. John's Church). (Open daily 10am-1pm.) To reach the **Doma Church,** go up Skārņu, north of St. Peter's. Skārņu turns into Škunu, and leads directly to the vast, irregular, and cobblestone expanse of **Doma laukums** (Cathedral Square). The Doma Church, the largest church in the Baltics, was first consecrated in 1226, and has since been modified by architects of various persuasions. Notice the German pipe organ that dates from 1844; boasting 6786 pipes, it's among the biggest (and best) in the world. (Church open to visitors Tues.-Fri. 1-5pm, Sat. 10am-2pm.) Upon leaving the church, go back to the square and walk north along Jēkaba. Take your first left, Mazā Pils iela. **Rīga Castle** awaits you at the end of the street; nowadays, it houses 3 museums. The **Museum of Latvian History** and the **Museum of Foreign Art** contain reproductions of classical sculptures, Latvian paintings, works of German and Dutch masters, and exhibits on the decorative arts. (Museums open Wed. and Fri. 1-7pm, Thurs., Sat., and Sun. 11am-5pm. 20LVR for main exhibit, 10LVR for each additional exhibit.) The **Rainis Museum of Literature** honors the memory of Latvia's greatest poet, Jānis Rainis, as well as other prominent Latvian literary figures. (Open Mon.-Tues. and Thurs.-Sat. 11am-5pm, Wed. 1-7pm. 20LVR.) North of the castle, a graceful **sculpture garden** teems with works by 20th-century Latvian sculptors. Torņa iela, which runs from this garden southeast towards Brīvības, is lined by several galleries and shops and will lead you to the **Pulvertornis** (Powder Tower), one of Rīga's oldest landmarks and the only city wall tower left. Nine cannonballs are still lodged in its 14th-century walls. Inside, visit the **Latvian Museum of War,** with exhibits on Latvian armed forces. (Open Thurs. noon-7pm, Tues.-Wed. and Fri.-Sun. 11am-6pm. 10LVR, students 6LVR.) Down Basteja bulv. and then left on Brīvības, you'll come across **Brīvības Piemineklis,** the beloved Latvian Freedom Memorial that was dedicated in 1935 when Latvia was an independent republic. A few blocks up Brīvības, in the Esplanāde, the **Orthodox Metropolitan Cathedral** rises over the greenery. Across the Esplanāde, near the corner of kr. Valdemāra and Elizabetes, you'll find the **State Museum of Latvian Art,** Rīga's foremost art museum boasting 19th- and 20th-century works by such artists as Kazaks, Tone, and the colorful Rēriks. (Open Wed.-Mon. 11am-5pm. 20LVR.)

■ Near Rīga

Only 20km west of Rīga, the sandy beaches of **Jūrmala** beckon on hot summer days. To get there, take a bus or one of the frequent trains (every 15-20 min., 4am-1am) from the rail station in Rīga. A handful of towns dot the Jūrmala coast; **Majori** (the 12th stop after Rīga's rail station, 40min., round-trip 36LVR), with its beaches and lively shopping area, is one of the most enjoyable. From the train stop, walk down the closest street you see, take your first right, and you'll be at Jomas, Majori's main street, which is lined with shops, cafés, restaurants, and bars. Every street to the left off Jomas leads to the beaches along Rīga bay. Majori's beach is clean, but the waters are not safe to swim in. Instead, rent a beach chair (50LVR for the day) and relax. **Café Omega,** behind the tourist bureau (Jomas 42), serves delicious warm sandwiches (45LVR). Vegetarians can ask for meatless ones. (Open Mon.-Fri. 3-10pm, Sat.-Sun. noon-10pm.)

Sigulda is a delightful daytrip. Located less than 60km northeast of Rīga and serviced by frequent trains (12/day, 1½hr., round-trip 88LVR), Sigulda stands at the entrance to the **Gauja National Park,** 920 sq. km of woods, caves, brooks, lakes, and ancient oaks. A map of the town (75LVR) can be purchased at a bookstore across the street from the train station at the corner of Ausekļa and Pils iela. To get to the region's main attractions, its **medieval castles,** walk down Raiņa iela (directly across from the train station; it changes its name to Gaujas iela) for about a kilometer. From the intersection of Cēesu and Gaujas, take the paved path that runs parallel to the left side of the road, and you'll see a building that houses an unnamed **café** serving pastries, ice cream, and sandwiches from 10am to 7pm. Ride on the cable car for a memorable crossing of the **Gauja gorge** (8min., 15LVR); the castles and cave await you on the other bank. Inside the park (10LVR), the walls of **Gūtmaņa cave** are covered with inscriptions, some dating to the 17th century. Go 500m up Turaidas road to reach the **Turaidas Castle Complex;** tickets are sold at the gate. (Open daily 9:30am-6pm. 10-20LVR.) The main tower holds a historical exhibit of various castle occupants' belongings, dating back to 1214; climb to the top for a magnificent view of the Gauja and the surrounding hills.

■ Lithuania (Lietuva): Baltic States

US$1	= 4.00LT (litas)		10LT =	US$0.25
CDN$1	= 3.04LT		10LT =	CDN$0.33
UK£1	= 6.20LT		10LT =	UK£0.16
IR£1	= 5.80LT		10LT =	IR£0.17
AUS$1	= 2.60LT		10LT =	AUS$0.38
NZ$1	= 2.21LT		10LT =	NZ$0.45
SAR1	= 0.83LT		10LT =	SAR1.20

Country Code: 372 **International Dialing Prefix: 810**

The only country in the Baltics with a history as an independent, expanding kingdom, Lithuania still likes to think of itself as the maverick, indomitable nation that once extended from the Baltic to the Black Sea. Subsumed into Poland by the 16th century, the late 18th century saw it come under the rule of tsarist Russia. Independent once again between the wars, Lithuania was annexed by the Soviet Union in 1939 and subjected to decades of attempted Russification. Yet the nation managed to maintain its own language and culture even during the Soviet period; today, 80% of the nation's 3½ million people are ethnically Lithuanian.

In March 1990, Lithuania shocked the world by declaring itself independent. The international community reacted uneasily, and Moscow immediately began reprisals, starting with a crippling shutoff of all oil supplies and culminating in an assault on Vilnius's radio and TV center in January 1991 that left 13 dead. Yet the Lithuanian declaration crucially focused world attention on the Baltics; the freedom that came in the wake of the failed *putsch* of August 1991 vindicated Lithuanian radicalism, and a goal that had seemed so improbable for 51 years suddenly became a reality.

On June 25, 1993, Lithuania established its own currency, the litas.

GETTING THERE AND GETTING AROUND

Citizens of the U.K. and the U.S. do not need visas to visit Lithuania; others will need need a valid passport to receive a visa. Ten-day visas may be obtained at the border for a fee of $40—it is always wise, however, to obtain a visa from your local embassy prior to your departure. A multiple-entry, 90-day visa costs US$25, and is valid for 6 months from the date of issue. The Lithuanian Embassy in the U.S. is at 2622 16th. St. NW, Washington, DC 20009 (tel. (202) 234-5860). The Baltics now constitute a "common visa zone:" Lithuanian visas are valid in Estonia and Latvia, and vice versa. Latvian visas are the cheapest of the three.

Klaipėda, Kaunas, and Vilnius are easily reached by **train** or **bus** from Latvia or Estonia; buses or first-class train compartments tend to be the best option. The pre-WWII rail route between Lithuania and Poland may be operational by the summer of 1994. Currently trains to Poland go through Belarus, requiring a transit visa of US$25. Several **airlines** service the decaying Vilnius airport: **SAS** flies from Copenhagen (7/week, round-trip US$332), **Lufthansa** from Frankfurt (3/week, round-trip US$441), **Hamburg Airlines** from Berlin (2/week, round-trip US$520), and the Polish carrier **LOT** from Warsaw (3/week, round-trip US$120). In Vilnius, you can buy tickets to Western destinations on the country's new airline, **Lietuvos Avialinijos,** to Berlin (3/week, one-way US$164), Frankfurt (3/week, one-way US$223), and Copenhagen (3/week, one-way US$232). You can also reach Klaipėda, on the Baltic Sea coast, by weekly **ferry** from Germany; book months in advance (call 01 (261) 578 49 in Klaipėda). **Greif Reisen,** Universitätsstr. 2, 5810 Witten-Heven, Germany (tel. 49 (02302) 240 44), can also give you ferry information and take reservations.

Within Lithuania, there is a reasonable train and bus network between cities.

LITHUANIA ESSENTIALS

There may be a tourist office in Vilnius by the summer of 1994; in the meantime, read the excellent *Vilnius in Your Pocket,* an exhaustive compendium about the capital. It's updated every 2 months and is available at newsstands in Vilnius (2.5LT). *The Baltic States: A Reference Book* and Inroads's *Guide to the Baltic States* will give you that extra informational edge. A sketchy map of Klaipėda can be found in **Klaipėda Today;** you can buy maps of Kaunas and Vilnius at newsstands or well-stocked local bookstores. Lithuania's own currency, the **Litas,** was reinstated on June 25, 1993. In the summer of 1993, some establishments still only accepted "hard" currency. All prices should be in litas by 1994.

Lithuanian is an Indo-European language which still preserves many archaic roots. Lithuanians speak Russian reluctantly, but won't mind as long as you clearly identify yourself as a Westerner. Some young people speak a little English or German. A few words will smooth your travels: *ačiū* (AH-choo) means "thank you" and *prašau* (prah-SHAU) means "please." "Yes" is *taip* (type), "no" is *ne,* "Do you speak English?" is *Ar kalbate angliškai?* (AHR KAHL-bah-teh an-GLEESH-kye) and "I don't understand" is *nesuprantu* (neh-soo-PRAHN-too). As in the rest of the Baltics, a bathroom door bedecked with a triangle whose point faces the infernal depths indicates "men;" with the point facing up, it indicates "women."

■■■ VILNIUS

Multilingual, sprawling and defiant, the capital city of Lithuania has stood at the crossroads of foreign influences for centuries without losing its preeminence as Lithuania's major cultural and social center. Known as the "Jerusalem of Europe," the city was the center of turn-of-the-century Eastern Europe's Yiddish literary and cultural life; half its population was Jewish. Even now, Vilnius is home to ethnic Russians, Poles, and Belarussians, though religiously it is firmly Catholic.

The River Neris winds through the city center; most of the Old Town is on the left bank. The railway and bus stations are only a few steps from the heart of the old city. A long street called Aušros Vartų, then Didžioji, then Pilies, runs 200m north from the station to the cathedral square and east of the Cathedral. The castle hill and its tower rise above the labyrinthine cobblestone streets of the Old Town.

PRACTICAL INFORMATION

Tourist Offices: Not yet; try the Lithuanian Youth Hostels' office, Kauno 1A-407 (tel. 79 66 50) or the service desks of the **Hotel Astorija,** Didžioji 35/2, or **Hotel Lietuva,** Ukmergės 20. You don't need a tourist office if you're toting *Vilnius In Your Pocket,* available in bookstores and newsstands (2.5LT). City information in Russian and Lithuanian (tel. 65 26 32).

VILNIUS

Embassies: U.S., Akmenų 6 (tel. 22 30 31; fax 22 27 79). **U.K.,** Antakalnio 2 (tel. 22 20 70; fax 35 75 79). **Canada,** c/o Hotel Draugystė in summer 1993 (tel. 66 17 31). **Estonia,** Turniškių 20 (tel. 77 85 32; fax 76 98 18). **Poland,** Aušros Vartų 7 (tel. 22 44 44; fax 22 34 54). **Sweden,** Jogailos 10 (tel. 22 64 67; fax 22 64 44). **Finland,** Klaipėdos 6 (tel. 22 16 21).

Currency Exchange: Look for Valiutos Keitykla signs and compare rates. A branch of **Vilniaus Bankas** has long hours at the **Central Post Office,** Gedimino 7 (tel. 61 67 59). Open 10am-6pm daily. Their main outlet at Gedimino 12 (tel. 62 60 43) cashes traveler's checks. Open Mon.-Fri. 9am-12:30pm and 2:30-5pm.

Post Office: Central Post Office at Gedimino 7 (tel. 61 66 14). Open Mon.-Fri. 8am-8pm, Sat.-Sun. 11am-7pm. Postcards abroad US15¢. **UPS** (tel. 22 61 11), **DHL** (tel. 62 21 18, 62 17 64), and **Federal Express** (tel. 76 55 06).

Telephones: Place calls abroad at the **Central Telegraph Office,** Vilniaus 33/2 (tel. 61 99 50). Open 24hrs. Local phones use flat *žetoni* or a 15K coin; long-distance phones use *žetoni* with grooves. You can call within Vilnius from these too, but first dial 8 22. When you call out of Vilnius, always dial 8 and then wait for the dial tone. **City Code:** 0122, from the West dial 370 (2).

Trains: Station at Geležinkelio 16, (tel. 63 00 88 or 63 00 86). The reservation bureau is at Šopeno 3, near the station (tel. 62 30 44). Ask for a "coupe" compartment or for *pirmas klassa* (1st-class). To: Moscow (7/day, 13hr., 10.20LT); St. Petersburg (7/day, 14hr., 12.70LT); Warsaw (4/day, 12hr., US$15); Rīga (6/day, 7hr., 10.20LT); Klaipėda (2/day, 10hr., 7.40LT); Tallinn (1/day, 14hr., 16.20LT); Berlin via Warsaw (2/day, 19hr., DM190); Prague (1/day, 36hr., US$65).

Buses: At **Autobusų Stotis,** Sodų 22, 50m from the railway station. To: Klaipėda (7/day, 5hr., 10.90LT); Rīga (5/day, 6hr., 13.40LT); Minsk (6/day; 5hr., express 3¼hr.; 6.60LT); 1 uncomfy overnight bus to Tallinn (12hr., 27.30LT); Warsaw (1/day, 9hr., US$14); Berlin (17hr., US$66); Kaunas (about 2/hr. 9am-9pm, 1¾hr., 3.70LT). Advance booking (tel. 26 29 77); international booking (tel. 63 52 77).

Public Transportation: Good system; doesn't run (but isn't necessary) in the Old Town. Rides US10¢, monthly passes 8.40LT. Buy tickets in advance at stands marked *spaudos*. Don't forget to punch them when you get on board.

Taxis: Call 22 88 88, or go to one of the numerous *takso* stops. A ride should not cost more than 5-10LT; don't pay in hard currency, or the price will double.

Emergency Numbers: Ambulance: tel. 03. **Fire:** tel. 01. **Police:** tel. 02.

ACCOMMODATIONS

There's a room crunch in Vilnius, and unfortunately, the new hotels-in-progress will cater to businesspeople. Outside of a youth hostel, travelers can expect the rock-bottom price for a room with most average conveniences to be around US$20-30.

Lithuanian Youth Hostels, Filaretų 17 (tel. 26 06 06, 75 66 50). Reached by bus #34 from the train station (6 stops); in a peaceful neighborhood in the outskirts of the Old Town. Hot breakfast served 9-10am in the sunny dining room. Clean communal showers, often lacking hot water. No curfew. US$5 with HI card.

Baltic Accommodation and Travel Service, Geležinio Vilko 27 (tel. 66 16 92 or 66 76 80). Poised on the edge of Vilnius's beltway; from the station take bus #16 to "Kaunas," backtrack onto Zemaitas, and take a left at the highway (Geležinin villio). Bleak rooms with communal showers and baths; kitchen and TV room. No curfew. Negotiable 3-day max. stay. US$10/night.

Hotel Vilnius, Gedimino 20/1 (tel. 62 41 57 or 62 36 65). Only 3 blocks away from the cathedral. The building in which the front desk is located has fair rooms without showers or bathrooms for US$17 (singles) and US$30 (doubles). The 2nd *corpus* (building) of the hotel is down the street and has slightly more run-down rooms with similar features for US$14 (singles) and US$24 (doubles).

FOOD AND ENTERTAINMENT

Vilnius has a handful of marvelous restaurants with excellent food and contrasting atmospheres. Order appetizers, ice cream, and an extra entree with your meal; it still won't cost more than US$3-4.

Literatų Svetainė (tel. 61 18 89), Gedimino 1 at the corner of T. Vrublevskio. You'll come back again and again to this cozy restaurant; the atmosphere is romantic and the service attentive. English menu. Beer and wine available for hard currency. Entrees 2.10-4.60LT. Open daily noon-11pm.

Viola, Kalvarijų 3, across from St. Raphael's Church. A lively Armenian restaurant, serving possibly the best food in Vilnius. Try the *shashliki,* the *kebab,* Armenian cheese, and Armenian meat salad. Menu in Russian. Live Russian jazz band at night. Entrees 2.0-5.3LT. Open daily 1pm-midnight.

Stihliai, Stihlių 18. A fashionable café with great ice cream. Also serves salads and small pizzas. Open Mon.-Fri. 9am-10pm, Sat. noon-10pm, Sun. 10am-10pm.

Blyninė, Pilies 8. Look for 2 bronze arms holding a plate of pancakes above the door. Great *blynai* (pancakes) with meat or cheese fillings smothered in cream or jelly. (0.9-1.5LT) Open Mon.-Fri. 11am-8pm, Sat. 9am-7pm, Sun 9am-6pm.

Dainava, Vienuolio 4 (tel. 61 74 81), plays songs that made the hit parade and has a sometimes risqué show at 10pm. (Open Tues.-Sun. noon-11pm, bar open 'til 2am.)

SIGHTS

One block north of the railway station, the **Aušros Vartai** (Gates of Dawn) welcome you into Vilnius's **Old Town,** the largest in the Baltics. Built in the 16th century, they feature griffins and the crest of Lithuania on their outer façade and house the chapel of **Our Lady of Vilnius.** Go through the gates, enter the first door on your right and go up one floor to see the Madonna's image, surrounded by miracle-seeking pilgrims. Going back down to the street and entering the doorway at the end of the building, you'll reach the **Church of St. Theresa,** a vivid example of early baroque art. On your way out, notice the worn crucifix by the door; the devout kiss its feet upon entering and leaving the church. The **Šv. Kazimiero** church, named after the country's patron saint, can be found further along Aušros Vartu. The oldest Baroque church in town, the Soviets turned it into a museum of atheism in 1966; it was restored as a church in 1989. After this landmark, Aušros becomes Didžioji and broadens to form **Museum Square.** On its center stands the **Town Hall,** home to the **Lietuvos Dailės Muziejus** (Lithuanian Art Museum), which holds a collection rich in late 19th- and 20th-century Lithuanian paintings. (Open Tues.-Sun. noon-6pm. US30¢.) Behind it stands the **Exhibition Palace of the Arts.** (Open 11am-7pm. Free.) The only **synagogue** left of the 96 that existed before 1940 can be found at Pylimo 39 (off Rūdininkų). The Nazis used it to store medical supplies and it's now undergoing its first exhaustive restoration.

At the corner of Pilies and Šv. Jono, you'll find the **University of Vilnius.** Go through the arches opposite from St. John's church and you'll see the remarkable **Astronomical Observatory,** a 17th-century building with zodiac signs on the frieze atop the façade. Go back to the main courtyard, pass the church on your right, and enter yet another courtyard to find **Littera,** the excellent university bookstore. Maps and guides to Vilnius are available here. (Open Mon.-Thurs. 10am-6pm, Fri. 10am-5pm.) If you turn right on Šv. Mykolo and walk for a block from Pilies, you'll face **St. Michael's,** a Renaissance church dating back to 1625, which now houses a bland Soviet-style **Museum of Architecture.** (Open Wed.-Mon. 11am-7pm. US20¢.) Across the street shines Vilnius's Gothic treasure, **St. Anne's Church and Bernardine Monastery,** the church Napoleon wanted to carry back to France. (Open Tues.-Sat. 10am-3pm and 6-8pm, Mon. 6-8pm.) At the end of Pilies, on Šventaragio, you'll find the white-walled, majestic **Katedros Aikštė** (Cathedral Square). The present cathedral dates back to the late 18th century; the contorted figures on the southern wall depict Lithuanian Grand Dukes in religious fervor. Inside, notice the early Baroque **Chapel of St. Casimir,** which houses a royal mausoleum. (Open Mon.-Fri. 7am-noon, 3-8pm, Sat.-Sun. 7am-2:30pm and 5:30-9pm.) Go up the Castle Hill and climb to the top of **Gediminas Tower** for an unparalleled view of Vilnius's spires and a modest historical museum. (Open Wed.-Mon. 10am-6pm. US30¢.)

Other museums in the area include the **A. Mickiewicz Memorial Apartment** on Bernardinų 11, housed in the poet's 1822 lodgings (open Fri. 2-6pm and Sat. 10am-2pm), and the **Lithuanian State Jewish Museum** at Pamėnkalnio 12 and Pylimo 4 (2 locations), which has exhibits on the Holocaust and the Old Vilnius Synagogue, respectively. (Open 9am-5pm. Free.) Across the Neris River, at Upės 8, 200m north of Hotel Lietuva, you'll find the **Nacionalinė Galerija,** with exhibits on the January 1991 crackdown in Vilnius and the deportations of the 1940s and 50s. (Open Wed.-Sun. 11am-6pm. US30¢.) One final must-see is the high baroque **St. Peter and St. Paul Church,** built around 1688. Located on Antakalnio, before the British embassy, it's a 10-min. walk from Cathedral Square. Look up at the ceiling, where over two thousand figures dance, sing, and levitate. (Open daily 8am-7pm).

■ Near Vilnius

Don't miss a visit to the peaceful lakeside village of **Trakai,** reachable through frequent bus and train service from Vilnius (30min., 1.1LT). The capital of the Grand Duchy of Lithuania in the 14th century, **Trakai Castle** is a *pièce de resistance.* The castle is on an island in Lake Galvė, accessible by bridge. From the bus station take a right, walk down Vytantos St. for 1½km and then take the bridge on your right. The watch tower is 30m high. (Open Tues.-Sun. 10am-6pm. US40¢) Rent a **rowboat** on the lake shores for 1LT per hour.

■■■ KAUNAS

Kaunas was a trade hub between Poland, Lithuania, and Russia in the 16th century, and served as Lithuania's capital during the interwar period when Vilnius was occupied by Poland. Now Kaunas, though still Lithuania's second-largest city, charms with a provincial spirit. Getting around central Kaunas is simple, since it lies on either side of one long thoroughfare: the pedestrian street **Laisvės alėja,** 1.3km long, lined with all the shops, restaurants, cafés, and bars of modern Kaunas. When the street bears left, it allows vehicle transit and becomes **Vilniaus gatve,** extending into the Old Town and the Town Hall Square.

Begin your tour of Kaunas by walking around the white, majestic **Russian Orthodox Church,** built in the 1880s. Sadly, the church is now in disrepair. (Open Mon.-Fri. 10am-4pm, Sat.-Sun. 9am-4pm.) Walk down Laisvės for 2 blocks, turn right on Daukanto and then take your first left. You'll be facing the **Freedom Statue,** deported by the Soviets in the 1940s and returned to its pedestal in 1989, and the **Kaunas Historical Museum.** (Open Wed.-Sun. 11am-6pm. US30¢.) The museum exhibits the aircraft in which two Lithuanian-Americans, Darius and Girėnas, tried to fly from New York to Kaunas non-stop in 1933 (they crashed in Germany). Go through the arcade with the cannons on your right as you leave the museum to find the **M. K. Čiurlionis Museum,** honoring the works of the prolific avant-garde artist who sought to combine painting and music into a single artistic medium. (Open Tues.-Sun. noon-6pm. Closed last Tues. of the month. US40¢.) Right across the street, at Putvinskio 64, you'll find the **A. Žmuidzinavičiaus Museum,** better known as the **Kaunas Devil's Museum,** which houses a collection of more than 200 devil figures, most of them folk Lithuanian carvings. Don't miss the sculpture that shows Devil Hitler and Devil Stalin chasing each other through a playground littered with human bones. (Open Tues.-Sun. noon-6pm. US40¢.) You'll soon come to a turn; continue on Vilniaus towards the Old Town. Four blocks later, you'll come to the **Kaunas Basilica,** the largest Gothic building in Lithuania. The interior is pristine, dynamic late Baroque. (Open Mon.-Sat. 10am-7pm, Sun. 2-7pm.) On your left, you'll find **Rotušės Aikštė** (Town Hall Square), crowned by the **White Swan,** the 18th-century Town Hall.

There's one last jewel in Kaunas: the **Pažaislis Monastery and Church,** a vibrant Baroque ensemble with rich frescoes, on the right bank of the Nemunas, 10km east of central Kaunas. The church was commissioned by the Chancellor of Lithuania, Kristunas Pacas, and was dedicated in 1674 after 60 years of labor and an expenditure of 2 million ducats. (Open Mon.-Sat. 10am-5pm, Sun. 10am-6pm.) Take trolley bus #5 from the Historical Museum or the railway station to the end of the line, then walk down the main road for 1km. The church is just past a small beach.

Accommodations, Food, and Practical Information At the grayish but comfortable **Hotel Baltija** at Vytanto 71 (tel. 22 36 39 or 22 87 85); spartan singles go for 11LT, doubles for 21LT. Dining in Kaunas offers no frills, but **Tulpe,** Laisvés 49, has immaculate tables, good service, and great ice cream. (Entrees 3-5.5LT. No alcohol. Open Tues.-Sun. noon-5pm and 6-11pm, Mon. noon-7pm.) At Laisvés 68, the well-known **Metropolis** beckons with red decor, meat-and-potatoes entrees (2-4.9LT), and live Lithuanian music from 9pm-midnight on weekends. Arrive early. (Cover 1LT. Open daily 11am-midnight.) In the Old Town, the dark **Medžiotoju Užeiga** (Hunters' Inn), at Rotušes aikštè 10, was a favorite haunt of Mickiewicz. (Full meal 3LT. Open daily 11am-10pm.) At Laisvés 102, you'll find the **Central Post Office.** (Open Mon.-Sat. 9am-6pm. **Poste Restante: 3000.**) To change money, look for *Valintos Keitykla* signs. Kaunas's **bus station** is at Vytanto 26; it's dirty, ruinous, and presently being renovated. Catch buses here for Warsaw (1/day, 11hr., US$16) and Vilnius (1/hour, 1¾hr., 3.7LT). One and a half blocks down Vytanto, at the corner with Čiurlionio stands the **train station,** with connections to Moscow (1/day, 17hr., 3.3LT) and Vilnius (15/day, 2hr., US89¢).

■■■ KLAIPĖDA

The third-largest city in Lithuania is rather cosmopolitan—it's one of the few places in Lithuania where you can dance 'til 3am. Unfortunately, it needs a cartographer; no updated map has been made since the 1940s. **Klaipėda Today,** available at hotels and gift shops, has a rough but useful map of the center.

Klaipėda faces a narrow peninsula that separates the Kuršių Marios, Lithuania's largest lake, from the Baltic Sea. The **Smiltyné beach** is on the peninsula and faces the Baltic; (ferries from the mainland every 15min., 0.3LT). The **ferry terminal** is near the city canal in the Old Town, not far from Tiltų. Years of environmental abuse have left the entire Baltic polluted, so it's better to stay on land and sunbathe.

Klaipėda's nightlife makes Lithuania's other cities pale by comparison, and is one of the city's prime attractions. **Pas Alberta,** at the corner of Sukilélių and Daržų in the Old Town, is the most popular place in town, despite the hefty cover charge. (6LT. Open 1pm-1am or so.) **Žilinskas,** at the corner of Karpių and Mèsininkų, is for cooler heads and well-lined pockets; champagne costs 7.5LT a bottle and there's a 5LT cover charge, but they'll bring you ice cream on a silver tray. There's dancing until midnight and live jazz in the afternoons. (Open 1pm-midnight.) The Old Town was razed during WWII, so Klaipėda's main attractions are the beach and the nightlife, but you can find one or two cultural things to do. Visit the **Museum of Lithuanian History** at Didžioji Vanders 6, just off Tiltų in the Old Town. Klaipėda's Lenin statue hides in the museum's backyard; before 1991 it stood on the square next to Hotel Klaipéda. (Open daily 11am-7pm. US10¢, students US5¢.) Down Turgaus, you'll find the city **theater,** a neoclassical building once visited by Wagner. (Tickets US40-80¢.)

Accommodations, Food, and Practical Information

Klaipėda has a few cozy hotels; the best deal is **Hotel Vètrungé,** Taikos 28 (tel. 548 08), 1½km away from the Old Town, serviced by buses #8 and 10. Rooms come with bathroom, shower, and phone (9-18LT). **Hotel Baltija,** Janonio 4 (tel. 149 67), is located closer to the bus and train stations but has communal showers. (Singles 16LT. Doubles 26LT.) The café **Juoda-Balta,** H. Manto 15, has a black and white interior with mirrors and red, green, and cool blue lighting, as well as delicious food.

(Entrees 3.5-6LT.) **Prūsija,** Šimhaus 6 (tel. 185 81), has a softer, less modern decor, with MTV blaring for jarring contrast. (Main courses 5-7.5LT. Open 10am-4pm, 5pm-midnight.) **Restaurant Klaipėda** in the Hotel Klaipėda is sunny and clean. Entrees run 4.5-6LT, and Lithuanian beer is also available. (Open Wed.-Mon. noon-4pm and 6:30pm-1am, Tues. noon-4pm and 6:30-10pm.)

Walk to the right from the railway station along Priestočio to reach **Manto gatvė,** the main thoroughfare running through Klaipėda. Manto continues north across the city channel and into the Old Town, where it becomes Tiltų; in the new part of town, the same street is called Taikos. You can exchange currency at the **central bank** on Turgaus 1 (open 10am-5pm), where the rate is not great, or at the innumerable kiosks around town, which give a better rate but no receipt. From the **bus station,** Butkų Juzės 9 (tel. 114 34, information 148 63), 2 blocks away from Manto along Vilties, buses head for Liepāja (5/day, 2½hr., 1.2LT), Kaunas (13/day, 5hr., 5.5LT), Vilnius (9/day, 6hr., 7.4LT), and Kaliningrad, Russia (3/day, 3½hr., 2.7LT). **Trains** chug from the station at Priestočio 7 (tel. 146 14), across the street from the bus station, to Kaunas (2/day, 7hr., 3.9LT) and Vilnius (2/day, 10hr., 5.9LT).

Bulgaria (България)

US$1	= 27.40Lv (leva, or BGL)	10Lv =	US$0.37
CDN$1	= 20.80Lv	10Lv =	CDN$0.48
UK£1	= 42.50Lv	10Lv =	UK£0.24
IR£1	= 39.70Lv	10Lv =	IR£0.25
AUS$1	= 17.80Lv	10Lv =	AUS$0.56
NZ$1	= 15.20Lv	10Lv =	NZ$0.66
SAR1	= 5.70Lv	10Lv =	SAR1.75
Country Code: 35		**International Dialing Prefix: 00 (EU)**	

Come to Bulgaria and you'll find a nation where Southern European charm and tranquility belie the sometimes inefficient nature of many institutions, where hospitality can win you lifelong friends, and where education is valued above all else. During WWII, Bulgaria was one of the only European countries that did not persecute its Jewish population; its religious tolerance may stem from the nation's joint Christian and Muslim heritage. The Stara Planina mountain range bisects Bulgaria horizontally from Sofia to Varna, sloping down toward the Danube in the north. The Rila and Pirin Mountains are south of Sofia, and the Rhodopi Mountains center around the resort of Pamporovo, south of Plovdiv. Between the Rhodopis and the Stara Planina hides the famous Valley of Roses.

In 681, Bulgar tribes imposed their state traditions over the more agricultural Slavic tribes settled in the Balkans, thus forming the first of the Slavic nations. Brothers Cyril and Methodius created the first Bulgarian alphabet, called *glagolitsa;* their disciple Kliment Ohridski was the author of the modern-day Cyrillic alphabet. With the recognition of Bulgarian church autonomy in 870, the country joined Christian Europe. After over 100 years of Byzantine rule, the powerful Second Bulgarian Kingdom emerged in 1187, stretching from the Black Sea to the Aegean and the Adriatic Seas. In the 14th century, the country was crushed by Ottoman invaders who valued the region's agricultural output and ruthlessly kept Bulgaria a nation of peasants for almost 5 centuries.

During the National Revival of the 19th century, the Bulgarians reestablished their own independent church and founded a school system. While Britain and France insisted on preserving the integrity of the Ottoman Empire, Russia began to be seen as Bulgaria's defender—a factor in Bulgaria's eventual alliance with the Soviet Union. The Soviets, however, dealt a crushing blow to the Bulgarian economy by making it dependent on Russian imports.

On November 10, 1989, the Bulgarian Communist Party retired Todor Zhivkov, the unpopular, conservative, and much-ridiculed leader, changed its name to the Socialist Party (BSP), and held elections. After the parliamentary elections of November 1991, Bulgaria established a non-Communist government. The country's first presidential elections in January 1992 re-elected philosopher Zhelyn Zheler and poet Blaga Dimitrova as president and vice-president. Personal freedoms in Bulgaria have bounded ahead, yet many Bulgarians are starting to feel the stranglehold of financial limitations and skyrocketing inflation. For tourists, some of the onerous regulations, such as visa requirements, have been relaxed, while others—like the statistical card issued at the border—remain.

GETTING THERE

As of September 1993, American citizens could visit Bulgaria **visa**-free for up to 30 days; but Canadian, British, Irish, Australian, and New Zealander citizens need either a 1-month tourist visa (US$34) or a 30-hour transit visa (US$24). Even in European capitals, visas usually take a week or more to process, so try to get one in your home country. The Bulgarian **U.S. embassy and consulate** are at 1621 22nd St. NW, Washington, DC 20008 (tel. (202) 387-7969, fax (202) 234-7973). Citizens of the United Kingdom, Canada, Australia, New Zealand, and South African can obtain 30-day single-entry tourist visas from their local consulate (US$34 for normal delivery, US$64 for express). U.S citizens are not required to obtain a visa for visits in Bulgaria of fewer than 30 days. For more information, contact the private agency **Balkan Holidays,** 41 East 42nd St., #508, New York, NY, 10017 (tel. (212) 573-5530, fax (212) 573-5538). Tourists may pay either in dollars or leva; hotels and private accommodations charge Westerners different prices than Bulgarians.

TRAVELING IN BULGARIA

Public transportation in Bulgaria costs about 15Lv/100km. The **train** system is quite comprehensive, but very slow and crowded; direct trains run between Sofia and all major towns. Trains come in 3 varieties: express (експрес), fast (бързи), and slow (пътнически). Couchettes are an option (usually 10Lv); purchase spots on the train. To buy an international ticket, you must go to the appropriate office, usually in the town center; look for **Rila Travel** (РИЛА). An ISIC will give you discounts only on tickets to Eastern European countries. You can only buy domestic tickets at the station, except for the Sofia Central Railway Station (Централна Гара-София), where they have an international ticket counter. Buying a ticket on the train doubles the cost. Stations are poorly marked, and signs are often only in Cyrillic. Try to find out the exact time you are due at your destination or take along a good map that shows your route. If you miss your stop on a main express line, get off at the next stop and try to get the express in the opposite direction (which should be coming in 15-30min.); otherwise you could blow the entire day trying to get back. Some useful words are влак *(vlak,* "train"), автобус *(avtobus,* "bus"), гара *(gara,* "station"), перон *(peron,* "platform"), коловоз *(kolovoz,* "track"), билет *(bilet,* "ticket"), заминавщи *(zaminavashti,* "departure"), пристигащи *(pristigashti,* "arrival"), пушачи *(pusha-chi,* "smoking"), and непушачи *(nepushachi,* "non-smoking").

The increase of train ticket prices has spurred serious **bus** competition. Prices often beat the trains and you can save up to 3 hours. Unfortunately, bus lines and hours are not well-advertised and buses often leave whenever they get full. Private buses don't always issue a ticket or receipt; hand in the money as you board. Tourist offices such as **Balkantourist** have comfortable express buses which are an excellent option for long distances. The once-cheap **Balkan Air** shuttle fares have swollen enormously over the past year. (Sofia to Varna one-way US$65.)

Hitchhiking, once popular and reliable in Bulgaria, is now a growing risk with worsening economic conditions, particularly for Westerners who are targets for theft. There have also been reports about attacks on drivers from hitchhikers recently. Transportation is so cheap that to have to wait and possibly get stuck under the scorching Balkan sun makes hitchhiking simply not worth it.

BULGARIA ESSENTIALS

Balkantourist, the former national tourist bureau, maintains offices throughout the country, although many have new names as a result of privatization. The staff changes money, and books hotel rooms and private accommodations. Hotels throughout the country often maintain tourist offices which can be of great help.

One leva (Lv), the standard monetary unit, is divided into 100 stotinki (st), but we list most prices in U.S. dollars (US$). The official rate of US$1 to approximately 27.5Lv closely coincides with the rates offered by private banks and numerous private exchange bureaus. The advantage of the latter is that they tend to have extended hours (24-hr. ones have a "Change Non-Stop" sign in English) but may not be able to buy all currencies (especially NZ$). Hotels have worse rates and people who approach you on the street to change money usually do not have the best intentions. Because of money reform in the early 1970s, any Bulgarian bill dated before 1974 is worthless—check carefully. You can cash **American Express** Traveler's Cheques in dollars or leva at major banks such as the **First Private Bank** which has branches throughout the country. (Commission: US$10 for every US$1000 regardless of the number of Cheques). There is an American Express Travel Service office at 1 Vitosha Blvd., off Ploshtad Sveta Nedelya (St. Nedelya's Square, площад Света Неделя), opposite the National Museum of History in Sofia.

Businesses open around 8-9am; while some banks may close as early as 2pm, tourist bureaus, post offices, and shops remain open later; in more touristy areas and bigger cities shops may close as late as 10pm, but they're often shut on weekends. Expect an hour lunch break around 1pm. Private shops, restaurants, cafés, and bars have more extended hours and are usually open on weekends. "Non-stop" signs in English indicate that the place is open 24 hours. National holidays are: January 1-2, March 3, a few days around Orthodox Easter, May 1, May 24 (Saints Cyril and Methodius's Day), and 3-4 days around Christmas.

While Bulgaria is becoming more accessible, budget travelers are apt to notice signs of the country's poor condition at the wrong time. Don't find out about the state of public bathrooms the hard way; pack a small bar of soap and some toilet paper. Safety concerns are of special importance in a country where hard currency is desired above all. If you take a taxi, choose your driver carefully and be sure of the price before you get in. (In summer 1993 the going rate was 4Lv/km.) On the same note, avoid walking alone after dark, even if you're sure of where you're going. There is a general lack of tolerance towards homosexuals in the country. The chances of being attacked are minimal; keep in mind, however, that life here will generally be made easier if you do not express your views or preferences outwardly. Basic medicines in Bulgaria have unfamiliar names; all cost under 15Lv and will usually be sold at a pharmacy (аптека, *apteka*). Request *analgin* for headaches, *analgin chinin* for a cold or the flu, *amidopxhen* for a high temperature and *saridon* for general pain relief. Band-aids are *sitoplast;* cotton wool is *pamuk.*

The climate in Bulgaria is mild: the average winter day is around 0°C while summer days max out at around 30°C with low humidity. Late fall is the rainiest, grayest season.

Communication See the Cyrillic transliteration table in the Russia section; Bulgarian is much the same, except that х is *h*, ш is *sht*, and ъ is sometimes transliterated as *â* (pronounced as in English b*u*g). Key phrases include добър ден (DO-bur den, "hello"), кога (ko-GA, "when"), къде (kuh-DEH, "where"), колко (KOL-ko, "how much"), благодаря (blahg-oh-dahr-YAH, "thank you"), моля (MOE-lya, "please"), довиждане (doh-VEEZH-dan-yeh, "good bye"), поща (PO-shta, "post office"), частна квартира (CHAHST-na kvar-TEE-ra, "private room"), and колко струва (KOHL-ko STROO-va; "how much does it cost?"). Russian is widely understood, but it is best to ask permission before using it. Many Bulgarians are learning English, but it is still not very widely spoken, especially in the countryside. Bulgarian-English phrasebooks are sold at bookstands and bookstores for about 30Lv. If you need an English speaker in one of the major towns during the school year (Sept. 15-June 30), ask for help at the language school (езикова гимназия; *yezikova gimnaziya*). Many older Bulgarians speak French, and German is popular in the resort towns along the Black Sea. Since Bulgarian head movements for "yes" and "no" are the reverse of the West's, try to confirm everything with *da* (yes) or *ne* (no). Also be aware that many street names will be changed as the country decommunizes, but many old signs have not yet been replaced. Use both the old and new street names, and, once there, try to find an accurate map (from 1993 or later).

Making international **telephone** calls from Bulgaria requires tremendous patience. The country does not have USA Direct service, but to call collect dial 0123 for an international operator or have the telephone office or hotel receptionist order the call for you. Calls to the U.S. average US$22 for 10 minutes. **Betkom** direct dial telephones with digital display screens are found at most major hotels and resort areas. They service only Europe and the Middle East and require a special calling card sold from a kiosk near the phone. In an emergency (such as visa complications or urgent phone calls) go to your embassy. **Postage** (including packages) is very cheap: 6-9Lv depending on the destination. Bulgaria is in the same time zone as Greece and Romania, and is 1 hour ahead of Western Europe.

Accommodations and Camping When you cross the border you will be given a yellow **statistical card** to document where you stay each night. If you lose it, you may have difficulty getting a hotel room. The establishment in which you stay will add its stamp to the card, which is collected when you leave the country. Years ago, tourists were fined if they didn't have a stamp for each night they had spent in Bulgaria; now, Bulgarian border officials tend to be much less strict, so any card with at least a couple of stamps on it should suffice.

Private rooms are arranged through Balkantourist or other tourist offices from US$8-13 a night, and can be an excellent opportunity to get to know a Bulgarian family. Be sure to ask for a central location and try to find out if any family members speak English. Bulgarian **hotels** are classed by stars; rooms in one-star hotels are almost identical to those in 2- and 3-star hotels but have no private bathrooms; they average about US$8 for singles and US$13 for doubles. Some discounts are available through Balkantourist. The majority of Bulgarian **Youth Hostels** are located in the countryside and are popular with student groups; try to make reservations through **ORBITA** or **Pirin Tours** in Sofia. Outside major towns, **campgrounds** give you a chance to meet Eastern European backpackers (US$1.80-3.10/person). Spartan wooden bungalows await at nearly every site but are often full. Freelance camping is popular, but you risk a fine. Camping in reserve areas is strictly prohibited; watch for the signs.

Food and Drink Food from kiosks is cheap (12-16Lv for a sandwich or burger and a Coke), and restaurants average 60Lv per meal. Kiosks sell *kebabcheta* (small hamburgers, 3Lv), salami sandwiches (5Lv), and *banitsa* (cheese-filled breads, 3Lv). Fruits and vegetables are usually sold in vegetable shops (зеленчуков магазин, *zelenchukov magazin)* or in markets (пазар, *pazar).* Some fruits are sold directly on the streets from stalls. *Shopska salata* is a widely available, an addictive salad of tomatoes, peppers, and cucumbers covered with feta cheese. Delicious! *Kiopolou* and *imam bayaldu* are eggplant dishes. A *gjuvetch* is a mixed vegetable stew with onion, eggplant, peppers, beans, potatoes, parsley, and peas. Also try *tarator*—a cold soup made with yogurt, cucumber, and garlic. Well-stirred *airan*, Bulgarian yogurt with a little water and a few ice cubes, can bring you back to life on a hot summer day. Another popular summer drink is *ais-nektar* (a thick fruit juice with a scoop of ice cream). Many restaurants are now serving Bulgarian specialties; try 'em all, but eat carefully. Don't drink the unpasteurized milk unless it's been very well heated. Eschew sour yogurt and resist rare hamburgers. Do not fear the water; it's probably purer than the stuff you're used to drinking back home. The fountains and taps scattered throughout the cities and countryside will save your life on more than one day under the hot Balkan sun. Bring a water bottle and a hearty spirit.

■■■ SOFIA (СОФИЯ)

Visitors to Sofia will probably be astonished to find a manageable, well-planned metropolis in the heart of the Balkans. The center of town, with its grid of enormously wide *bulevards* paved with yellow bricks, may make you feel like you've arrived in the Land of Oz. Most of the sights are within walking distance of the city center and easily found with the aid of a good map. Sofia is for the most part a new city—only a few medieval churches and 2 mosques survive— but its architecture reflects Bulgaria's role as a bridge between Turkey and Western Europe. Watch for small palaces and public buildings that look like a cross between the German baroque and Russian Imperial styles—the Sheraton Hotel building, for example. Most of these are surrounded by massive modern monuments; Sofia is a carnival of socialist architecture, topped only by the Stalinist monsters found in Moscow. Outside the center, the Emerald City ends and Sofia rapidly turns into an aesthetic nightmare of run-down neighborhoods and shoddy new high-rises.

ORIENTATION AND PRACTICAL INFORMATION

Sofia's 1.2 million inhabitants occupy the center of the Balkan peninsula, 500km southeast of Belgrade. International trains run to Belgrade, Thessaloniki, Athens, İstanbul, and Bucharest. **Ploshad Sveta Nedelya** (St. Nedelya Square, площад Света Неделя) is the center of Sofia. The central district is ringed by a road that changes names as it circles the city. Incoming roads intersect this ring; the most important starts life as bul. Vitosha (Витоша) and runs north through pl. Sveta Nedelya, where it changes its name to bul. Knyaginya Maria Luiza (Княгиня Мария Луиза) and bends around to reach the train station at the northern end of the city. Perpendicular to bul. Knyaginya Maria Luiza, bul. Stamboliiski (Стамболийски) and bul. Dondukov (Дондуков) are 2 other major thoroughfares. Maps are sold at tourist offices and at stalls on the street (30Lv). Practice your Cyrillic reading skills here; all the names are transliterated into the Roman alphabet.

Tourist Offices: Balkantourist, bul. Stamboliiski 27 (tel. 88 55 43). English-speaking staff books accommodations, exchanges money, makes ticket reservations. Open Mon.-Fri. 8-10pm. The office at bul. Vitosha 1 (tel. 433 31) includes an

American Express branch (open Mon.-Fri. 8am-8pm, Sat. 8:30am-1:30pm) and can give leva from most major credit cards for a 4% fee. Branch office at the airport (tel. 796 293) open Mon.-Fri. 8am-10:30pm. **Pirin Tours,** bul. Stamboliiski 30 (tel. 87 05 79 or 87 06 87), across from Balkantourist, helps arrange transportation and accommodations and provides youth hostel information. Open Mon.-Fri. 9-5:30.

Budget Travel: ORBITA Travel, Hristo Botev 48 (tel. 87 955 52). Branch office in the ORBITA Hotel: take tram #9 south past the Palace of Culture to the intersection with bul. Anton Ivanov and look behind Hotel Vitosha. Open Mon.-Fri. 9:30am-12:30pm and 1:30-4:30pm.

Embassies: U.S., ul. Suborna 1a (tel. 88 48 01 through 05), 3 blocks from pl. Sveta Nedelya behind the Sheraton Hotel. Library. Periodicals and video tapes. Open Mon.-Fri. 11:30am-4:30pm. Duty officer available 24hrs. Consular section at ul. Kapitan Andreev 1 (tel. 65 80 36), behind the Economic Tehnikum. Open Mon.-Fri. 9am-noon for visa applications, 1-5pm for other concerns. **U.K.,** bul. Vasil Levksi 65 (tel. 88 53 61), 3 blocks northwest of the Palace of Culture. Open Mon.-Thurs. 8:30am-12:30pm and 1:30-5pm, Fri. 8:30am-1pm. Both embassies hold mail. Citizens of **Canada, Australia,** and **New Zealand** should contact the British embassy. **Romania,** ul. Sitnjakovo 4 (tel. 70 70 67). **Greece,** bul. Evlogi Georgiev 68 (tel. 44 37 65 or 44 37 70). **Turkey,** bul. Vasil Levski 23 (tel. 87 23 06 or 87 29 84). Open Mon.-Fri. 9am-6pm.

Currency Exchange: At **Balkantourist** offices and all large hotels. Generally open daily 8am-10pm. There is an **American Express** office at Vitosha 1 which holds mail. **Lindor,** 31 Vitosha Blvd. (tel. 88 14 92) and **Inter,** 72 Vasil Levski Blvd. (tel. 81 57 40). Traveler's checks cashed at the **First Private Bank** at ul. Suborna 2a (tel. 46 51 28). Open Mon.-Fri. 9am-12:30pm.

Post Office: ul. General Gurko 2, at the park east of pl. Sveta Nedelya. **Poste Restante.** Generally open 7am-8:30pm. Many hotels also provide postal services. **DHL** (express postal service), bul. Tsar Osvoboditel 8 (tel. 71 46 60 or 71 33 60).

Telephones: Across from the post office. Open 24hrs. Expect long lines. To avoid them, call from the Hotel Sheraton's lobby phones, but be prepared to pay nearly twice the rate. For local calls, use 20st coins. **City Code:** 02.

Flights: Airport Sofia (tel. 712 01; 45 11 13 for international flights; 72 24 14 for domestic). Municipal buses #84 and 284 run regularly. **Bulgarian Balkan Airlines,** pl. Narodno Subranie 12 (tel. 88 44 33), is open Mon.-Fri. 7:30am-7:30pm and Sat. 8am-2pm. To Varna or Burgas (US$65), Moscow (US$246), and Warsaw (US$83). Also try the ticket office under the Palace of Culture (tel. 59 79 95). Always ask for **youth fares** if you're under 26; the savings can be more than 50%.

Trains: Sofia's central train station is north of the center on bul. Knyaginya Maria Luiza. Trams #1, 7, and 15 travel to pl. Sveta Nedelya. The windows at the station sell domestic tickets only; cop couchettes on board. For information, international tickets, and couchette reservations, visit the **Rila travel office** at ul. General Gurko 5 (tel. 87 07 77). Office open Mon.-Fri. 8-11:30am and noon-6pm (mid-afternoon hours are capricious), Sat. 8am-2pm. To: Athens (US$62), Belgrade (US$20), Bucharest (US$16), Budapest (US$38), and İstanbul (US$38). 20% discount on international rail travel with ISIC at Rila travel office. Also try the ticket office under the Palace of Culture (tel. 59 31 06).

Buses: Terminal at bul. Gen. H. Mihailov 23 (tel. 52 50 04) handles tickets for international routes. No ISIC discounts. Some private buses operate international routes. Check with Balkantourist about express buses.

Public Transportation: The system of trams, trolley buses, and buses is gleefully cheap (3Lv/ticket, 10Lv/all-day ticket). Buy tickets at kiosks or from the driver and punch 'em in the small machines between the bus windows. Operating hours: officially 4am-1am (although many routes stop before midnight).

Hitchhiking: Hitching in the Sofia area is getting increasingly dangerous. Those hitching to Rila Monastery take tram #5 to highway E79. Those headed to Koprivshtitsa take tram #3 from Sofia. They leave early to return the same day.

Laundromats: There aren't any per se in Bulgaria. The larger hotels are often unwilling to wash non-guests' clothing, even for hard currency. Don't despair;

SOFIA

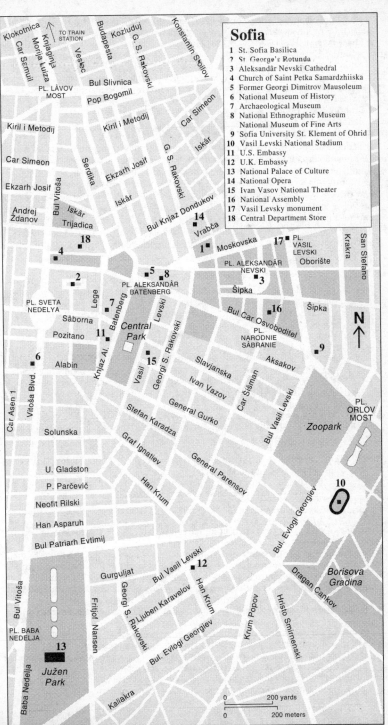

Sofia

1 St. Sofia Basilica
2 St. George's Rotunda
3 Aleksandâr Nevski Cathedral
4 Church of Saint Petka Samardzhiiska
5 Former Georgi Dimitrov Mausoleum
6 National Museum of History
7 Archaeological Museum
8 National Ethnographic Museum
  National Museum of Fine Arts
9 Sofia University St. Klement of Ohrid
10 Vasil Levski National Stadium
11 U.S. Embassy
12 U.K. Embassy
13 National Palace of Culture
14 National Opera
15 Ivan Vasov National Theater
16 National Assembly
17 Vasil Levsky monument
18 Central Department Store

the hot Balkan sun dries hand-washed clothes pretty quickly. If you're staying in a private room, arrange it with your hosts for a minimal charge.

Pharmacy: pl. Sveta Nedelya 5, (81 50 89). Open 24hrs. Night pharmacies throughout the city generally open 10pm-7am. Try **1st Private Pharmacy** at the intersection of Nafit Rilsker and Tsar Asen.

Medical Assistance: In a medical emergency, contact a hotel receptionist. Emergency aid for foreigners, offered by state-owned hospitals, is free of charge. **Hospital:** bul. Patriarh Evtimii 35 (tel. 87 95 32).

Emergencies: Police: tel. 166. **Ambulance:** tel. 150.

ACCOMMODATIONS AND CAMPING

Balkantourist and ORBITA (see above) arrange all types of private rooms for US$8-12/night. So do our friends at the train station. (Remember that these "cheap private room" pushers may not stamp your statistical card.) If you arrive in Sofia after Balkantourist closes, you're on your own. In the summer of 1993 the best option by far was private accommodations. For a minimal extra charge you may get tea, coffee, breakfast, and laundry facilities. The hotels are not always worth their prices and the cheapest ones can be unsafe. Apart from the Balkantourist office at bul. Stamboliiski 27, you may also find private lodgings at **Markela**, bul. Knyaginya Maria Luiza 17, across from the Central Department Store. (Singles 120Lv. Doubles 200Lv. Open Mon.-Fri. 9:30am-7pm, Sat. 9:30am-4pm.)

Hotel Tourist (Хотел Турист), ul. Rizki Prochod 1, (tel. 20 49 91). 20min. from the city center; take bus #77 from the train station to its last stop (жк. Красна Поляна) or tram #4. A hotel/youth hostel catering largely to students. Small café and TV room. Large, clean rooms with bath. Singles US$8 or US$6 with HI card. US$16. Doubles US$12.

Hotel Hemus (Хемус), bul. Cherni Vruh (Черни Връх) 31 (tel. 66 13 19 or 639 51). A 3-star hotel past the Palace of Culture at the southern extreme of downtown. Take tram #1, 7, or 15 to Palace of Culture, then head for the high-rise up bul. Cherni Vruh. Lots o' groups. Benign bathrooms with shower; rooms have radio, phone, and a capital view of the city. Friendly English-speaking receptionists. Singles US$40. Doubles US$60. (US$25 and US$40 through Balkantourist.) Major credit cards accepted.

Hotel Sevastopol (Севастопол), on ul. Rakovski (Раковски) near ul. General Gurko (tel. 87 59 41). Take the boulevard on the left of the Sheraton 5 blocks, then turn right onto ul. Rakovski. Centrally located on a noisy street. Mildly usable communal bathroom with shower but no hot water. Singles US$9. Doubles US$11.

Camping: Cherniya Kos, 11km southeast of city center (tel. 57 34 79). Take tram #5 from behind Museum of History, then a bus. Set on a wooded slope near the base of the Vitosha and Lyulin Mountains, this campground offers bungalows for US$13/person. 2-person bungalows US$16. Open May-Oct.

FOOD

From fast food to Bulgarian specialties, inexpensive meals are easy to find in Sofia.

Melnik Grill, inside the Sheraton Hotel; enter from the street (tel. 87 81 42). Named after a Bulgarian town in the Pirin Mountains. Often has live traditional music. Uncommonly wide variety of steaks, salads, soups, and desserts. Full meal about US$15-20. Menus in English. Open noon-4pm and 6-11:30pm. Last orders at 3pm and 10:45pm. Major credit cards accepted.

Pizza Palace (Пица), bul. Vitosha 34 (81 08 69). Delicious, medium-sized pizzas for US$2-4. Open daily 11am-2am. Menu in English.

Palace of Culture café, on the 8th floor. Coffee, sandwiches, and desserts with the best view in Sofia. Bring a camera. Open daily 9am-10pm.

Havana (Хавана), bul. Vitosha 27 (tel. 80 05 44). Take your pick: a restaurant, a café, and a cocktail bar inhabit this complex resembling an indoor Cuban city. The spicy fare from the restaurant downstairs might give even Castro heartburn. Café open 7am-2am. Restaurant open noon-midnight with music beginning 7pm.

Budapest (Будапеша), ul. Rakovski 145 (tel. 87 27 50). Hungarian cuisine. Full meals US$5. Bring your Bulgarian grandparents to help you read the menu. Open Mon.-Fri. 10am-11pm, Sat. 10am-midnight.

Amerikana (Американа) and **Chez Louis** (Шер Луи), at the Central Department Store, bul. Maria Luiza 2, on the 1st and 5th floors, respectively (tel. 87 96 21, ext. 248 for Amerikana, 246 for Chez Louis). Balkanized version of American fast food (full meal US$2-3). Chez Louis offers a wider selection, including pizza, pasta, burgers, and milk shakes. Both places open Mon.-Fri. 8am-8pm; Amerikana also open Sat. 8am-11pm, Sun. 10am-11pm.

SIGHTS AND ENTERTAINMENT

Sofia's two most venerable churches, the late Roman **St. George's Rotunda** and the early Byzantine **St. Sofia,** sprang up in the 4th and 6th centuries, respectively. St. George's hides in the courtyard of the Sheraton Hotel, while St. Sofia, the city's namesake, stands several blocks behind the Party house. Both are closed for restoration but worth seeing from the outside. Across the square from St. Sofia looms the massive, gold-domed **St. Alexander Nevsky Cathedral** (open Sun.-Fri. 8am-6pm, Sat. 8-10am and 4-8pm), erected in the early 20th century in memory of the 200,000 Russians who died in the 1877-78 Russo-Turkish War. The main attraction is in the **crypt,** a monstrous collection of painted icons and religious artifacts from the past 1000 years. (Crypt open Wed.-Mon. 10am-6pm.) In an underpass at pl. Sveta Nedelya is the tiny 14th-century **Church of Saint Petka Samardzhiiska,** which contains some eye-grabbing frescoes; despite its size, this is one of Sofia's finest churches. (Open daily 8am-6pm. Donations encouraged.)

The former **Georgi Dimitrov Mausoleum,** on pl. Aleksandr Batenberg (Александр Батенберг) is a memorial to Stalin's former right-hand man, long-hated and now officially vilified. While debate still rages over the fate of the building, Bulgarians have put it to practical use as a public bathroom. The labels in the **National Museum of History** off pl. Sveta Nedelya on Vitosha 2, are in Bulgarian only, but the magnificent Thracian treasures need no commentary. (Open Mon.-Fri. 9:30am-5:15pm. 3Lv with ISIC.) The **Archeological Museum,** at the southwestern end of pl. Aleksandr Batenberg, houses items from the Thracian, Greek, Roman, and Turkish settlements in Bulgaria. (Open Tues.-Sun. 10am-noon and 2-6pm.) For a look at traditional Bulgaria, be sure to check out the **National Ethnographic Museum** (open Wed.-Sun. 10am-noon and 1:30-6pm) and the **National Museum of Fine Arts** (open Tues.-Sun. 10am-6pm), also located on the square. (1Lv each with ISIC.) At the **Sofia Municipal Art Gallery,** ul. General Gurko 1, near ul. Sofiiska Komuna, you can taste Bulgarian impressionism and modern art. (Open Wed.-Sun. 10:30am-6:30pm. Free.)

Even a quiet city like Sofia can sweeten your social life. Try the **disco** underneath the Palace of Culture (cover 5Lv; open 7pm-4am) or the more congested **Yalta** club near the Hotel Sofia at pl. Narodno Subranie, across the street from the main gates of **Sofia University St. Klement of Ohrid** (Софийски Университет Св. Климент Охридски"). Yalta functions as a café during the day (open Sun.-Fri. 10am-8pm) and as a disco at night. (Open daily 10pm-4am.) Most of the newly opened entertainment spots are in the Student City (Студентски Град). **Bul. Vitosha,** down toward the Palace of Culture, is a popular hangout on summer nights; some of its cafés stay open until 2am. You can also purchase tickets to see one of Bulgaria's fine performing arts companies through Balkantourist or any of the fancy hotels in town.

■■■ RILA MONASTERY
(РИЛСКИ МАНАСТИР)

The **Rila Monastery,** 120km south of Sofia, is the largest and most famous monastery in Bulgaria. Founded by the hermit Ivan Rilski in the 10th century, it maintained the arts of icon painting and manuscript copying during the Turkish occupation. The 1200 frescoes on the central chapel and surrounding walls form an outdoor art gallery. Try to make one of the services at 6:30am or 5pm. The monastery also houses 3 museums (20Lv) with ornate religious objects and items from Bulgaria's past. In the hills surrounding the monastery there are excellent opportunities for both short and long **hikes.** Inquire at Pirin Tours in Sofia for more info.

To reach the monastery from Sofia, take the lone (6:30am) **train** to the Kocherinovo (Кочериново) station (12km from Kocherinovo town); buses run to the monastery every half-hour. Alternatively, hop a **bus** from the Ovcha Kupel (овча Купел) station in Sofia (take tram #5). **Hotel Rilets** (Рилетэ) Rila 2630, has singles for US$18, doubles US$23 with bath. You *may* be able to find a room in the monastery itself. **Camping Bor** is a 20-minute walk beyond Hotel Rilets. (US$2.50/person, US$2/tent; US$12 for 3-person bungalow. Open early June-late Sept.) Be sure to talk to George about the best hiking trails in the area. **Restaurant Rila,** just outside the western gate of the monastery, serves up a beautiful view of the mountains and monastery and delicious local trout (US$2-4).

■■■ BLAGOEVGRAD (БЛАГОЕВГРАД)

You can cover the major points of interest in Blagoevgrad in half an hour or so; it's more fun to spend time making friends with the students at the American University of Bulgaria (AUBG), most of whom speak flawless English. If you arrive by bus (10-12/day, 20Lv), from Sofia or from the Rila Monastery via the town of Rila (18Lv) walk back 50m or so when you get off. Turn right at the traffic lights and walk up bul. Kiril and Mathodius (Кирила и Методии), the city's main street. The railway station is the crimson building behind you at the end of the boulevard. Walk straight for 5-6 blocks until you reach a small square of white stone, and look to the left. This is the **American University of Bulgaria (AUBG),** the first U.S. college in Eastern Europe. The useful information office (tel. 25 4 21) is on the 1st floor. (Open Mon.-Fri. 8am-5pm.) The lobby holds the school's **bookstore** (open Mon.-Fri. 9am-1pm and 2pm-6pm) where you can buy condoms, phone cards, and books in English. In the **university café** across the corridor you can enjoy the coldest glass of Kool-aid in town and watch MTV or CNN via satellite. (Open Mon.-Fri. 7:30pm-5pm.) Don't miss the peacefulness of **Varosha** (the old town) and the **Regional Museum of History.** (Open Mon.-Fri. 9am-noon and 2-6pm. US$1.) The gun and sword collections are truly fascinating. In Varosha you can see the **Mitropolitska Church** (Митрополишка Църква); it boasts a very good choir. The water in the church yard is the purest you will ever taste. In the fall and winter, Blagoevgrad features excellent theater and a world-famous folk ensemble known as "Pirin" (Пирин).

Accommodations, Food, and Practical Information The **Hotel Volga** offers airy singles with refrigerator, balcony, and private bath for US$10 with student ID (tel. 20 9 91, 20 9 92, or 20 0 93 through the university switchboard). Another possibility is **Hotel Bor** (Хотел Бор), a long trudge away in southeastern Blagoevgrad (tel. 2 24 91). The hotel has 2 stars and features a restaurant, tavern, and disco. The path through the park to the hotel isn't lit at night. (Singles US$20. Doubles US$28.)

The food in Blagoevgrad is varied and inexpensive; the locals joke that there are more cafés than people. The 24-hour **Bar-Restaurant Evropa** (Бар-Ресторант Европа), located on the back of a block of apartments along the main commercial street, is tricky to find; ask for directions. It's worth the effort—a full lunch here will cost about US$1. Try the *pasta Bachinovo* (паста Бачиново), a local specialty.

You'll find most important places clustered around the bright white city square. The **Tourist Service** office (tel. 232 18), next door to the Alan Mak Hotel, is very knowledgeable concerning bus and train schedules to Sofia, Borsko, and Melnik. (Open Mon.-Fri. 8am-6pm.) Or simply call the bus station (tel. 237 50) or train station (tel. 236 95) for the latest schedules. The **Central Post Office** is located on pl. Hristo Botev. (**Telephones** open daily 7am-9:30pm; post office Mon.-Fri. 7:30am-

7:30pm and Sat. 8am-noon and 2-6pm.) **First Private Bank,** on the right side of pl. G. Izmirliev-Makedoncheto, will cash traveler's checks. (Open Mon.-Fri. 8:30am-12:30pm and 1:30-5:30pm, Sat. 8:30am-12:30pm.)

Bansko and Melnik   About 60km southeast of Blagoevgrad is **Bansko** (Банско), reachable 6 times daily by bus (1½hr.) from Blagoevgrad. Of great importance in the Bulgarian National Revival period, Bansko is also a popular youth skiing town in the winter. **Melnik** (Мелник), 80km to the south of Blagoevgrad, is more difficult to reach; some have found hitching to be the best method. The sandstone pyramids (пясъчните пирамиди) among which Melnik lies look incomprehensibly absurd from some angles. The town sports distinctive southeast Bulgarian architecture; take time to discover the Mediterranean elements in the façades. Also be sure to visit the ruins of the 13th-century **Boyar's House**—the only preserved medieval house in Bulgaria.

■■■ KOPRIVSHTITSA (КОПРИВЩИЦА)

With its picturesque wood-and-stone cottages and its proud history of revolt, Koprivshtitsa is one of Bulgaria's most enchanting villages, one of the few remaining where horses cart more than a histrionic duty. A hundred years ago, Todor Kableshkov drafted his momentous "letter of blood" here, announcing the April uprising against Ottoman rule—the most passionately glorified event in Bulgarian history. The Turks savagely crushed the insurgency, but their brutality sparked the Russo-Turkish War of 1877, leading to Bulgarian independence.

Koprivshtitsa flaunts brilliant examples of **National Revival architecture;** several houses now serve as museums of Bulgarian handicrafts. Buy an informative book about the town at the bookstore in the town center. (Open 8am-noon and 3-5:30pm.) Check out the two types of cottages: the first are sturdy, half-timbered, early 19th-century houses with open porches, high stone walls, and sparse ornamentation; the more common type features enclosed verandas and delicate woodwork.

Trains from Sofia to Varna stop at Koprivshtitsa station (6/day, 2hr., 10Lv), 8km away from the town. Koprivshtitsa is the station after Anton. A bus awaits to take you into town (10min.). Rooms for Westerners are scarce here, especially on weekends. Strongly consider seeing the village in a long daytrip from Sofia. **Balkantourist** is in the brown house facing the river behind the restaurant enclave in the center. The staff here speaks little English. (Open Mon.-Fri. 8am-5pm.) **Hotel Koprivshtitsa** (Хотел Копривщица; tel. 21 82) offers singles for US$10 and doubles for US$15. Cross the 2nd stone bridge from the center and ascend the steps. Some devious maps show a nonexistent campground. The picturesque **Restaurant Diado Liben** (ресторант "Дядо Либен"), in the blue house across the river from the center, serves grilled specialties including *sirene po trakiski* (сирене по тракийски; cheese with sausage). An excellent **cafeteria** is in the restaurant complex in the town center.

■■■ VALLEY OF ROSES (РОЗОВА ДОЛИНА)

Two and a half hours east from Sofia along the Sofia-Varna rail line is the small town of **Karlovo** (Карлово), huddled at the foot of the Stara Planina. If at all possible, visit this region during the first weekend of June; the annual week-long **Rose Festival** (Празник На Розата), features performances by traditional Bulgarian song-and-dance troupes, comedians, as well as soccer matches, bazaars, and the like. Ask travel agents for details. For a grand view of the festivities, book a room in the **Rozova Dolina Hotel.** (Singles US$20. Doubles US$30.) Karlovo's **Roza Tours** office occupies the hotel lobby.

Trains connect Karlovo with **Kazonlak** (Казанлък), the largest town in the valley, several times a day (1½hr., US50¢). During the summer months the air of Kazonlak is filled with the fragrance of roses. Check out the ethnographic **Rose Museum** (Музей на Розата) by jumping on bus #2 from the central square; ask the driver to stop at the museum. (Open daily 8:30am-5pm. 20Lv with ISIC.) The **Kazonlak Tomb,** in Tyulberto Park, dates back to the late 4th century BC. (Open daily 8am-noon and 1:30-6pm. 1Lv with ISIC.) A local tale has it that young men drinking water from the fountain off the city's central square are destined to marry a local maiden. Our researcher has nothing to report on its effects...yet.

Snag the best hotel deal in town at the **Hotel Roza,** ul. Rozova Dolina 2, facing the central square. (Singles US$20. Doubles US$40.) Make reservations for the festival. Or try the **Campground Kazonlushka Roza** (Къмпинг "Казанлъшка роза") 4km north of Kazonlak. (Open May-Sept.) Find an oasis of beauty among the overbearing, gray socialist blocks in the **women's monastery** (Женския Манастир), which only offers lodging to women travelers (sorry, boys). For dining in Kazonlak search out the restaurant **Strata Kushta** (Страта Къща) on ul. Dr. Baev 19. Heading into the central square take your second left onto ul. Gen. M. Skobelev and then the first right on ul. Gen Gurke. (Open daily 9am-1pm.)

The **tourist office** (tel. 251 52 or 210 87) is located on the 1st floor of Hotel Kazonlak, on the central square. (Open Mon.-Fri. 8:30-11:30am and 2-5pm.) Many private **bus** lines to nearby towns and cities (such as Karlovo, Gabrovo, and Stara Zagora) start from the bus and railway station just south of the center of town; buses to further points depart from the parking lot in front of the Hotel Kazonlak.

Ten km south of Kazonlak (US$4 by taxi) is **Lake Georgi Dimitrov,** a scenic, brownish lake on whose bottom lies the remains of the Thracian city Sevtopolis. At the northern extreme of the Valley of Roses looms the legendary **Shipka Pass** (Шипченски Проход), site of the bloody and pivotal battle where Russian and Bulgarian forces prevented the Turks from advancing beyond the Balkan Mountains. Take bus #6 from the city center.

■■■ PLOVDIV (ПЛОВДИВ)

A local guidebook notes that "Not seeing Plovdiv is not seeing Bulgaria." You may not believe this at first, as most of Bulgaria's second city seems to be the worst sprawl of gray apartment complexes and exhaust-ridden boulevards the country has to offer. Hold your disappointment until you stroll into the rambling stairway-streets of the **Old Town** via the **Trimontsium** (Трихълмието). In the Old Town, Bulgarian Revival houses hang their beamed, protruding upper stories over the cobblestones, windows stare down into alleyways at impossible angles, and churches and mosques hide in secluded corners. From the train station, take trolley #2 or 102, or bus #16, to the town center (5 stops). Start at the **Dzhumaya Mosque** (Джумая джамия) on ul. Knyaz Aleksandr I (Княз Александър I), and wander up ul. Suborna (Съборна). Turn to find the 2nd-century **Amphitheater of Philippopolis,** at the entrance to the tunnel that runs under the old town. If at all possible, try to see a performance in the amphitheater (such as June's Theater Festivities or the summer run of the National Opera, about 25Lv). Back on Suborna, continue a bit farther to the **National Ethnographic Museum** (Етнографски Музей), which contains a well-presented collection of artifacts from this period. (Open Tues.-Sun. 9am-noon and 2-5pm; closed Fri. mornings.) The most interesting and colorful baroque houses are down the hill from here, through the Roman gate. The **Georgiadi House** (къща Д. Георгиади) displays exhibits from the War of Liberation. Ask at the Puldin Tours office about tickets to the **Plovdiv Chamber Music Festival** (June-July).

Accommodations, Food, and Practical Information The gracious, English-speaking staff at the **Puldin Tours** office, bul. Bulgaria 106 (България; tel. (032) 55 38 48; open Mon.-Fri. 9am-8pm; in winter Mon.-Fri. 8am-6pm), proffers a city map and in-depth guides to Plovdiv's history (45Lv), arranges private accommodations, and changes traveler's checks (US$5 commission). To reach the office from the train station, take trolley #102 to bul. Bulgaria (the 9th stop) near Plovdiv's fairgrounds. Walk back one block—it's on your right. (Singles US$8, Doubles US$12.) **Hotel Leipzig** (Хотел Лайпциг; tel. (032) 23 22 50 or 23 20 01), bul. Ruski 70 (Руски), is just 3 blocks from the rail station and 10 minutes from the town center. Though located in a noisy area, the hotel has excellent prices and clean rooms. (Singles US$26. Doubles US$35.) **Hotel Bulgaria,** ul. Patriar Eftimi (Патриар Эфтими) 13 (tel. (032) 22 60 64), is another acceptable option and is just off pl. Tsentralen (Централен), the main square. (Singles US$22. Doubles with shower US$32. Receptionist speaks English.) **Trakia Camping** (tel. (032) 55 13 60) is open all year round. Bear in mind that during the biannual trade fairs (beginning on the 1st Mon. of May in spring, the last Mon. of Sept. in fall), accommodations prices swell by up to 500%.

Be sure to visit **Taverna Puldin** (Пълдин) in the heart of the Old Town, built right into the Roman walls at ul. Knjaz Tsereteli 1 (Княз Церетели). Take ul. Maksim Gorky (Максим Горкий) to its 4th right through the Turkish gate; it's your second right. (Full meal US$6-9. Open daily 11:30am-midnight.) Also in the Old Town, try the **Restaurant Alafrangite** (Алафрангите) at ul. Kiril Nektariev (Кирил Нектариев) 17, in an eye-catching National Revival house that once appeared in a *National Geographic* article. Their specialty is *vreteno,* a pork or veal steak with a cheese and mushroom filling. (Full meal US$2.50-4.50. Open daily 11am-12am.) From behind the Dzhumaya Mosque follow ul. Maxim Gorki; make the 3rd right. On a cool evening, head to the fountainside café in the Public Garden (formerly the Garden of King Boris), within walking distance from the Old Town. Multicolored strobes illuminate the fountain—the most popular hangout in town—and you can rent rowboats to splash your way around the small lake.

The **Rila** bureau has moved to ul. Liljiana Dimitrova (Лильяна Димитрова), just past the church. **Public transportation** in Plovdiv consists of buses and trolleys (20Lv). Domestic private **bus** lines operate from Hotel Trimontsium or the Central Railway Station (Централна ЖП гара); the most frequent international buses are to İstanbul, departing from Park-hotel Saint-Petersburg (Парк-хотел Санкт-Петербург) or bus station Rodopi (автогара "Родопи"). **Trains** from Sofia to İstanbul stop in Plovdiv, as do most Sofia-Burgas trains. Sofia-Plovdiv service runs about every 2 hours (2½hr., US$1). A system of faster, private **buses** has also opened up (1½hr., 20Lv).

Bachkovo Monastery About 28km south of Plovdiv is the Bachkovo Monastery (tel. (03327) 277 or 236), second largest in the country after Rila. Take a bus from the main station to Asenovgrad, where you can catch a bus to the monastery.

■■■ VELIKO TURNOVO
(ВЕЛИКО ТЪРНОВО)

Set dramatically on the steep banks of the River Jantra, Veliko Turnovo was once the capital of the powerful Second Bulgarian Kingdom. Amid the ruins of the palaces of Bulgarian tsars and patriarchs are fragments of mural paintings and mosaics that testify to the vibrancy of this center of medieval culture. From the Veliko Turnovo train station, take bus #13 or 15 to the town center (2Lv) or brace yourself for the uphill climb to the city (1km). From the bus station, take buses #7 or 10 five stops to the center. The ruins of the fortress **Tsarevets** (Церевец), which once housed the royal palace, litter the top of a large hill. (Open 8am-7pm daily. 25Lv.) As you wander to or from the fortress, stop at the **Archeological Museum,** off ul. Ivan Vazov (Иван Вазов), which contains wonderful Thracian pottery, a fine collection of medieval crafts from the Turnovo ruins, and copies of the most famous Bulgarian religious frescoes. (Open Tues.-Sun. 8am-noon and 1-6pm. 31Lv or 5Lv with ISIC.) You can see 20th-century depictions of Veliko Turnovo over the ages at the municipal **art**

museum, situated on the peninsula within the river's bend. (Open daily 10am-6pm.)

Accommodations, Food, and Practical Information Get private rooms from the currency exchange booth in the lobby of Hotel Etur on 1 Al. Stamboliiski (tel. (062) 241 95). Centrally located doubles with shower are available for US$6-8. (Open daily 9am-5pm.) Cheap lodging can be found at **Motel Sveta Gora** (tel. (062) 204 72), 2km west of town; take bus #14. (Doubles with shower and breakfast US$20. Bungalows (no shower) US$13. Camping for 2 people US$6.) There is now an excellent **youth hostel** in the Hotel Trapezitsa (Хотел Трапезица) at ul. Stefan Stambolov (Стефан Стамболов) 79 (tel. (062) 220 61) with private bathrooms. (Singles US$10, US$7 with ISIC. Doubles US$19, US$16 with ISIC.)

For a superb meal complete with quick, friendly service and a fantastic view, get a window seat at the **Panorama Complex** (Комплекс Панорама), next door to Hotel Trapezitsa. (Full meal under US$3. Open daily 6am-midnight.) In the small square across from the Hotel Trapezitsa, the **Mehana** (Механа) is a fine place to sample *shishlik* (lamb kebab) and live Bulgarian music. (Full meal US$2.50. Open daily 6am-11:30pm.) There's a *pazar* (market) at ul. Vasil Levski and ul. Dimitur Ivanov. The most sage café in the area is **Magi** (Маги), on ul. Nikola Pikolo.

Yantra Tourist (tel. (062) 202 36 or 281 65), is currently at the back of the Hotel Etur. They have useful brochures and 10Lv maps of the city. (Open Mon.-Fri. 8am-noon and 1-5:30pm.) Veliko Turnovo is half an hour by train or bus south of Gorna Oryahovitsa (Горна Оряховица), which is on the rail line connecting Sofia and Varna.

Etura About 50km southwest of Veliko Turnovo lies this **ethnographic museum park,** established in the 1960s to preserve the awareness of arts and crafts from the National Revival period; here you can watch the authentic production of flour, sheets, gold jewelry, and wool carpets. It's a bit out of the way, but well worth a half-day's visit; take the train west from Gorna Oryahovitsa and get off in Gabrovo. Etura is just on the outskirts of town.

■■■ RUSE (РУСЕ)

Bulgaria's largest Danubian city saw the construction of the first railway line in Bulgaria (1864), the opening of the first bookstore (1867), the first movies (1897), and the first newspaper printed in Bulgarian. The city's leading position was largely due to the strong Austro-Hungarian influence coming down the Danube (Дунаб). Ruse is known for its outstanding musical intelligentsia and traditions which have made it the setting of Bulgaria's biggest symphonic music festival—the **March Musical Days** (Мартенски Музикални Дни). To get to the city center, take bus #1 or 101, or trolley #23 or 25, from in front of the rail station for 3 stops. Walk 2 blocks up that street, ul. Borisovska (Борисовска), to reach the central square, most recently called Svoboda (Свобода). Here you'll find a beautiful Italian-style monument and a magnificent theater building reminiscent of Vienna. Ul. Alexandrovska (Александровска), lined with shops, cafés, and restaurants, extends from both sides of the square. It leads to Ruse's most popular park, **Mladezhki Park** (Младежки Парк), on the eastern side of the city.

Behind the statue on pl. Svoboda stands the former Communist Party headquarters, called *Koraba* ("the ship") because of its appearance. To the left is the Opera House and next to it the **Sveta Troitsa church** (Света Троица; main building open Sat.-Sun. 6am-8:30pm). The church, erected in 1632 during the Ottoman occupation, couldn't be built higher than any Turkish mosque in the city. Ruse is also the home of one of the few Catholic churches in Bulgaria—**St. Paul's Church** (Света Павел), currently under reconstruction. The city's youth hang out in the park east of the city center and near the Prista hostel.

Accommodations, Food, and Practical Information Private **accommodations** are generally your best option; cheaper but much less desirable rooms are offered at the old **Hotel Balkan** (Хотел Балкан; tel. (082) 27 91 89) along ul. Aleksandrovska (Александровска), the primary street (Singles US$4. Doubles US$8.)

For a solid, inexpensive meal, stop at any of the restaurants along the main street. **Restaurant Potsdam** (Ресторант Потсдам) is located to the east of the main square at ul. Aleksandrovska 79. (Full meal US$3. Open daily 11:30am-midnight.) About 8km west of the city center is the **campground** and **Restaurant Ribarska Koliba** (Рибарска Колиба), next to the tourist **hostel** Prista (Приста). To get there, hop on bus #6 or 16 from the city center. Bus #17 will take you to the highest TV tower in the Balkans, where Ruse's most renowned restaurant, **Leventa** (Левента), sports 11 distinctive halls, each decorated in a different style. Try the **café-bar** on top of the TV tower for a fab view and delicious *torta zapaw* (chocolate cake). (Café open daily 4-11:30pm. Restaurant open daily 11:30am-midnight.)

First Private Bank is located on the corner of ul. Aleksandrovska and Ferdinandova. (Open Mon.-Fri. 8:15-11:30am and 1-3:30pm, Sat. 8:30am-1:30pm.) The **central post office** is a little ways off pl. Svoboda. (Open Mon.-Fri. 7am-7pm, Sat. 7:30am-6pm, Sun. 8am-noon. **Telephones** open daily 7am-10pm.) The **Rila** bureau is on the right side of the central post office at ul. Knyazheska 33 (Княжеска; tel. 22 39 20; open Mon.-Fri. 8am-noon and 1-6pm, Sat. 8am-1pm).

Ruse can be reached by **train** from Bucharest and by train or **bus** from Sofia, Varna or Veliko Turnovo (3hr., 20Lv). The bus and train stations are adjacent to each other about 2km south of the city center. The tourist office **Dunav Tours** is located on ul. Lybomir Pipko to the right and behind the town hall. Check here for private accommodations. (Open Mon.-Fri. 8am-noon and 1-5:30pm.) Pick up a free map at the Riga Hotel 4 blocks north of Dunav Tours.

BLACK SEA COAST

Many Eastern and a growing contingent of Western Europeans come to the Black Sea Coast to bronze themselves in July and August; Varna and Burgas are the principal transportation centers. Strewn between the largest resorts are tiny villages where you can escape the crowds. Train travel from Sofia is excruciatingly crowded and slow, yet still a bargain at under US$3; buses are quicker, more comfortable, and sometimes cheaper. Balkantourist and ORBITA Hotel each have an express bus from Sofia to Burgas every day in the summer for about US$4 (6hr). Along the coast, frequent yet crowded buses run between most points of interest. Hydrofoils run between Varna, Nesebur, Burgas, Pomorie, and Sozopol. Service is infrequent and expensive (the price can be 3 times as much as bus fares); tickets go on sale 1 hour before departure. Inquire at the port.

■■■ VARNA (ВАРНА)

Varna, known as Bulgaria's sea capital, is understandably crowded in summer. On the bright side, it harbors an alluring old town, seaside gardens, and a beach complete with roller-skating young Bulgarians. By the time the Romans arrived in the 2nd century AD, Varna was already a trade and cultural center. In 1402, it was the last city to surrender to the Ottoman invaders, and remained the least influenced by them under their oppression. As you stroll along Varna's **seaside gardens**, have a look inside the **Marine Museum** (open 8am-6pm; 20Lv, 5Lv students) and check out the **Aquarium** (Аквариум; open Mon. 2-5pm, Tues.-Sat. 9am-5pm; 10Lv). The **Dolphinarium,** in the northern part of the park, has two 30-minute shows (Tues.-Sun. at 11am and 3pm). Take bus #8, 9, or 14. In the old part of the city, known as the

BURGAS

Greek neighborhood (Грыцка Махала), you can see the impressive **Roman baths** (Римски Терми; open Tues.-Sun. 9am-6pm; Oct.-April Mon.-Fri. 10am-5pm; 2Lv). The second-largest cathedral in the country, **Sv. Bogoroditsa,** is in the center of the city, where you can also have a look at the exquisite **art gallery** at ul. L. Karavelov (Л. Каравелов) 1. Chamber concerts are often held here; inquire at the tourist bureau for a schedule. (Open Tues.-Sun. 10am-7pm; the sign "free day Monday" means it's closed then. 3Lv.)

Varna's **beach** charges an appropriately nominal 6Lv entrance fee. For serious sunbathing, head out to Varna's renowned resort, **Golden Sands** (Златни Пясыци). While there, you can go parasailing (US$12) high above the Black Sea Coast and then plunge into a hearty seaside meal (often less than 130Lv). To get there, hop on bus #9, which leaves every half hour and stops near the center (by the cathedral) and by the Cherno More Hotel (4Lv each way). Golden Sands features many water-sports, nightclubs, and tourists. The **campgrounds** here charge 40Lv per person plus the same amount for a tent spot and wooden bungalows. A visit to the former royal and later high Communist officials' residence, **Evksinograd** (also reached by bus #9), will blow your mind with its meticulously kept park. Admission is 40Lv and tours start on the hour. The exceptionally infrequent bus #29 (8:35am, 11:30am, and 5pm daily; 2 additional buses at 7am and 3:30pm on weekends) takes you up to the exotic **monastery** (Скален Манастир) perched amid the rocks (3Lv).

Accommodations, Food, and Practical Information

Private rooms are easy to find here. (US$6-11 depending on the category and length of stay. 3-night min. stay). The unattractive but cheap **Hotel Musala,** ul. Musala (Мусала) 3 (tel. (052) 22 39 25), next door to the tourist bureau, offers singles for US$10 and doubles for US$14 (both with sink in room and hall showers). If you're alone the management might try to put someone in your extra bed. The **Cape Galata camp-ground,** 6km away, has bungalows. (Open mid-June to mid-Sept.) In summer, if everything is booked, travelers often crash in the park next to the train station; they check their luggage at the *Garderob* across from the station. (Open 6-11:30pm. 5Lv.)

Restaurants (meals average US$5) and **nightlife** center around pl. Nezavisimost and along ul. Knyaz Boris I. A very popular hangout for younger crowds is the festi-val complex (Фестивалния Комплекс). In the summer a good number of discos and bars open up by the beach.

To get to **Balkantourist** from the train station, go through the underpass and walk straight up the street onto which it opens, ul. Tsar Simeon I, until you come to the large Independence Sq. (пл. Независимост). The bureau is on the 2nd sidestreet to your right, at ul. Musala 3 (tel. 22 55 24; open daily 8am-6pm; Oct.-April closed Sun.). There is a helpful **Rila** international trains bureau at ul. Shipka 3 (Шипка; tel. (052) 22 62 88 or 22 62 73), a sidestreet off ul. Knyaz Boris I. (Open Mon.-Fri. 8am-4:30pm.) The **post office** and **telephones** can be found behind the Cathedral. (Tele-phones open daily 7am-2:40pm and 3-11pm. Post office open Mon.-Fri. 7am-7pm, Sat. 7:30am-7pm, Sun. 8am-noon.)

■■■ BURGAS (БУРГАС)

The Black Sea coast's other transportation hub, Burgas offers easy access to nearby villages and beaches. Burgas's citizens call their town "the city of talents" because of the many artists and international sports stars who were born here. Unfortunately, few remain after attaining success. The **"Primorets" Tourist Bureau** (tel. (056) 472 75) at ul. Aleksandrovska #2 (Александровска), has lots of private rooms available. (Singles 100Lv. Doubles with shower 160Lv.) The staff speaks English, has old maps in English and sells bus tickets to Sofia (60Lv) and İstanbul (1 leaves every night, US$18). The bureau is located at the corner of the pedestrian street which opens up to Station Square (*Garov pl.,* Гаров пл.), where the train, bus, and hydrofoil stations are located. (Open daily 8am-8pm; in winter daily 8am-6pm.) The **post office** is 2 blocks to the left of the train station along bul. Vazov, at ul. Tsar Petur I (Цар Петър I; open Mon.-Fri. 7am-noon and 1-8pm, Sat. 8am-6pm). **First Private Bank** is on 1 Tutrakam ul. (tel. (056) 470 51; open Mon.-Fri. 8:30am-2pm). The **Hotel Briz** (Бриз) (tel. (056) 431 80) overlooks the seaport from Station Square. (Singles US$7. Doubles US$12.) With your back to the hydrofoil port, take a right onto the main road to the seaside gardens. Walking along the beach, seek out the **Starata Gemiya** (Старата Гемия) restaurant (tel. 431 37), called "Fregatata" in town. It's behind the Hotel Primorets in the Maritime Park and seafood is their specialty. (Full meal US$3. Open daily 9am-midnight.) Avoid tap water in Burgas; its metal content burns tender Western stomachs.

Buses (6/day, 2½hr., 38Lv) connect Burgas with Varna's main bus station (in the northwest of town). In the summer of 1993 no **hydrofoil** service ran out of Burgas. This situation may change, so consult a local tourist bureau.

Sozopol and Nesebur The area south of Burgas is becoming increasingly popular; the stretch between Burgas and **Ahtopol** (Ахтопол) is lined with enchanting bays and beaches. There are about 15 campgrounds, and many small and inexpensive private hotels are now appearing. **Sozopol** (Созопол), 34km south of Burgas, is one of the most enticing coastal towns, resting on the site of an ancient Greek harbor. The Old Town sports a Mediterranean influence; old women still sell beautiful handmade lace on the street. Near where the bus lets you off from Burgas is **Sozopol Tourist Office** (tel. (05514) 17 84) but you may have trouble finding someone who speaks English. **Balkantourist** is located on Ropotamo ul. in a new and large white building (tel. 251; open daily 8am-10pm). **Hotel Radik** (Хотел "Радик"; tel. (05514) 17 06), at ul. Republikanska 4 (Републиканска), has a gorgeous panoramic view of the harbor. Rooms are small but comfortable. (US$4.50/bed.) There are **campgrounds** a few km away; try the **Zlatna Ribka** (Златна Рибка), **Gradina** (Градина), or **Chernomorets** (Черноморец). (All are open May-Sept. and charge US$1.50/person.) For a delicious meal and a romantic view of the sea, walk across the Old Town until you reach its northern end to **Restaurant Vyaturna Melnitsa** (Вятърна Мелница), on ul. Morski Skali (Морски Скали). (Menu in English; meals US$3; open daily 8am-1am). Sozopol is an easy daytrip from Burgas (buses every hr. from 5am-8pm, 16Lv each way).

The area north of Burgas caters to family and package-vacation crowds, making it grueling to find cheap lodgings. The big tourist ghetto here is the crowded **Sunny Beach** (Слынчев Бряг). Show up at any Balkantourist office and you will be ushered to one of the more expensive hotels. **Nesebur** (Несебър) is a charming museum town perched atop the peninsula at the southern end of Sunny Beach, a sweet alternative for a few nights' stay. Look for a private room in one of the authentic old houses; inquire at the **tourist bureau** near the harbor. (Open daily 8am-1pm and 1:30-5pm.) You can reach Sunny Beach and Nesebur by **bus** from Burgas's central station (every 30min., 10Lv).

Czech Republic (Česká Republika)

US$1 = 28.80kčs (koruny, or CSK)		10kčs = US$0.35	
CDN$1= 21.90kčs		10kčs = CDN$0.46	
UK£1 = 44.60kčs		10kčs = UK£0.22	
IR£1 = 41.70kčs		10kčs = IR£0.24	
AUS$1 = 18.70kčs		10kčs = AUS$0.53	
NZ$1 = 15.90kčs		10kčs = NZ$0.63	
SAR = 5.98kčs		10kčs = SAR0.67	
Country Code: 42		**International Dialing Prefix: 00**	

On New Year's Day, 1993, after more than three quarters of a century of relatively unabrasive coexistence, the Czech and Slovak Republics, formerly known as Czechoslovakia, split, bloodlessly. The notion of self-determination is a fairly new thing to the Czech people; from the Holy Roman Empire to the Nazis and the Soviets, foreign powers have driven their internal affairs: even Alexander Dubček's 1960s "Prague Spring" refroze in 1968 with the iron rumble of Soviet tanks. In 1989, Czechoslovakia finally blossomed with the exuberant Velvet Revolution, and Gustav Husák's puppet government quietly stepped down.

Today, former Czechoslovak playwright-*cum*-president Vaclav Havel is once again the political leader of the Czechs, but his people seem remarkably blasé about all this reform and transformation. Not surprisingly, few miss the Soviet dominance. The metamorphosis of their nation seems the natural consequence of freedom; many are champing at the bit to Westernize, trying to recover as soon as possible from the Communist debacle.

GETTING THERE AND GETTING AROUND

Visas Visa requirements for visitors to the Czech Republic have eroded steadily since the revolution. In September 1993, Americans did not need visas for stays up to 30 days; U.K. citizens could stay visa-free for 180 days. Canadians, Australians, and New Zealanders still needed either a 30-day tourist visa or a 48-hour transit visa (US$44 for Canadian tourist visa; US$21 for other countries). Embassies are located at 3900 Linnean Avenue, NW, Washington, DC 20008 (tel. (202) 363-6315); 50 Rideau Terrace, Ottawa, Ont. Canada K1M 2A1 (tel. (613) 749-4442 or 749-4450); 25 Kensington Palace Gardens, London W84 QX (tel. (071) 229 1255); and 169 Military Rd., Dover Heights, Sydney NSW 2030 (tel. (02) 371 88 77 or 78). Americans can prolong their stay to 180 days from within the Republic.

Transportation **EastRail** became valid in the Czech Republic in 1991, and Eurail may be by 1994, but since rail travel is still a bargain (about 48kčs/100km on a 2nd class *rychlík* train), they may not be such a great deal. The fastest trains are the *expresný;* the *rychlík* trains cost as much as the express, while the few *spešný* (semi-fast) trains cost less; avoid *osobný* (slow) trains. **ČSD,** the national train company, publishes the monster *Jízdní řád* (train schedule, 74kčs), helpful if only for its 2-page English explanation in front. *Odjezd* (departures) are on yellow posters, *prijezd* (arrivals) on white. Čedok gives ISIC holders up to 50% off international tickets bought at their offices. If you're heading out of the country, buy a ticket to the border and use a railpass or buy a ticket from there. Seat reservations (*místenka,* 6kčs) are required on almost all express and international trains, and for all first-class seating; snag them at the counter with a boxed "R" above it. A slip of paper with the destination, time, date, and an "R" expedites the transaction. Be sure to have transit visas to go through Slovakia, or else go through Vienna instead.

   Buses can be significantly faster and only slightly more expensive than trains, especially near Prague and for shorter distances, but be sure to check how many stops they make. **ČSAD,** the national bus company, also runs international routes. From Prague, buses run a few times per week to Munich, Milan, etc., and from Brno to Linz, Austria. Consult the timetables posted at stations or buy your own (25kčs) from bookstores and newsstands. **Hitchhiking** is popular in the Czech Republic, especially during the morning commuting hours (6-8am).

CZECH REPUBLIC ESSENTIALS

The importance of **Čedok,** the state tourist company and relic of centralized communist bureaucracy, has seriously diminished since the 1989 revolution. **CKM,** its junior affiliate, remains helpful for the student and budget traveler by acting as a clearinghouse for youth hostel beds and issuing ISICs and HI cards. The quality and trustworthiness of private tourist agencies varies. **Information offices** in major cities provide tons of print on sights, cultural events, hostels, and hotels. City maps (*plán města*) are available for almost all tourist destinations (19-45kčs).

   There is no longer any mandatory foreign **currency exchange** requirement, but keep a couple of exchange receipts in order to change money back upon leaving. Though still operating, the black market is graying around the temples, and since the official exchange rate has almost reached street levels, it's hardly worth the risk. Bring western currency in small denominations, as it is often preferred as payment in larger hotels and private accommodations in bigger cities. Banks are generally open from 7am to 3 or 5pm. Czech money is no longer valid in Slovakia.

   The country's **climate** ranges from relatively mild winters (about 30°F) to warm summers that average 70°F. Bring your own batteries and feminine hygiene supplies. **Crime** has climbed dramatically since the 1989 revolution; be especially aware of snatch-and-run and pickpocketing. In **emergencies,** make use of your embassy; local police may flounder in English. Lost wallets and purses sometimes appear at embassies with only the cash missing. The **emergency phone number** throughout the country is **158. National holidays** include New Year's Day, Easter

Sunday and Monday, May Day (May 1), the now-ironic Anniversary of Soviet-American Liberation (May 8), July 5-6 (State Holiday), October 28 (Independence Day), and Christmas (Dec. 25-26). Many establishments now close on other religious holidays such as Ascension Day (late May or early June). The National Theater closes in July and August across the Czech Republic.

Teaching English You can hook a position as an English teacher, especially if you're willing to teach outside of Prague. The message board at the **American Hospitality Center** (see Prague: Tourist Offices) posts requests, as do the classifieds of the English-language newspaper, *Prognosis*. Also czech out the **Academic Information Agency,** nám. Max. Gorkého 26 (tel. (02) 26 70 10), in Prague. Terms of employment vary, from monthly stipends plus housing, to lunch money and Czech lessons. Organizations which recruit volunteers include **Education for Democracy/ USA,** P.O. Box 40514, Mobile, AL 36640-0514 (tel. (205) 434-3889), and the **The Foundation for Civil Society,** 1270 Ave. of the Americas., Ste. 609, New York, NY 10020 (tel. (212) 332-2890).

Communication Russian *was* every student's mandatory second language, but English first will win you more friends. A few German phrases go even further, especially in Prague. Pronunciation of Czech words can be difficult. The č is "ch," as in Čedok (CHE-dok), the š is "sh," as in *guláš* (GOU-lash), ž sounds like "zh" as in "azure" or *nádraží* (NAH-dra-zhee), ň sounds like the Spanish ñ, though more subtle, ě is "yeh" as in "náměstí" (NAH-myes-tee). Before you leave home, pick up a *Say it in Czech* phrasebook. A few handy phrases in Czech will make you sound like less of an oaf: *Dobrý den!* (doh-BREE den, "hello"); *Na shledanou* (nah-SLEH-dah-noh-oo, "goodbye"); *Děkuji* (YEH-kwee, "thank you"); *Prosím* (PROH-seem, "please" and "you're welcome"); *Kolik?* (KOH-lik, "how much?"); and *Zaplatíme* (ZAH-plah-tyee-meh, "We're ready to pay"). Just this once, *no* (NOH) or *ano* (ah-NOH) means "yes," and *ne* (NEH) means "no." The **mail** works fine. International **phone** calls are possible, though finding a grey and blue pay phone that works can be challenging. Look for a phone with a globe above it; most in post offices work. Buy phone cards (100kčs) at most newsstands. In the orange boxes, the coin will fall automatically when you are connected. Local calls cost 1kčs regardless of length. For inter-city calling, insert additional coins when the warning tone sounds. For AT&T's **USA Direct,** dial 00 42 00 01 01. For **MCI,** dial 00 42 00 01 12.

Accommodations and Camping Converted **university dorms** run through CKM are the cheapest option in July and August. Comfy 2-to 4-bed rooms go for 150-250kčs per person. CKM also runs **Junior Hotels,** year-round hostels loosely affiliated with HI, which give discounts to both HI and ISIC holders and which are comfortable but often full. Wildcat hostel operations have usurped CKM's monopoly on youth lodgings, but not necessarily surpassed its reliability. Showers and bedding are almost always included, and breakfast is sometimes, especially outside of Prague.

Across the country, **private homes** have become a legal and feasible lodging opportunity. In Prague, hawkers offer expensive rooms (US$11-25, but don't agree to more than US$20), sometimes including breakfast; scan train stations for "hostel," "zimmer," or "accommodations" ads. Quality varies wildly. Make sure anything you accept is easily accessible by public transport. Outside of Prague, Čedok handles most private room booking, although private agencies are burgeoning around train and bus stations. Be prepared for a healthy commute to the center of town. If you're sticking to **hotels,** consider reserving ahead of time from June to September in Prague, Bratislava, and Brno, even if it requires pre-payment. Outside these cities, it's easier to find space. Hotels come in 5 flavors: A-star, A, B-star, B, and C. As cities scramble to attract tourists, many of the grungy C hotels have begun to disappear. In 1993, singles in a B hotel averaged 500kčs, doubles 750kčs (within Prague 800kčs and 1200kčs, respectively). Inexpensive **camping** is available everywhere (most sites open only mid-May to Sept.), ranging from 40-85kčs per person. The book *Uby-tování ČSR*, in decodable Czech, comprehensively lists the hotels, inns, hostels, huts, and campgrounds in Bohemia and Moravia. Bookstores also sell a fine hiking map of the country, *Soubor Turistických Map*, with an English key.

Food and Drink The health food craze has yet to hit the Czech Republic: the 4 basic food groups here are sausages (*párek, klobosa*), cheese (*sýr*), ice cream (*zmr-zlina*), and beer (*pivo*). The *Hotová Jídla* (ready dishes) section on menus consistently includes variations on *gulaš*, pork or beef doused in a creamy sauce. Some key words are: *vepřová* (pork), *hovězi* (beef), *kuře* (chicken), *ryby* (fish), *kapr* (carp), *pstruh* (trout), and *zelenia* (vegetables). *Smáženy* means fried. Signs which should command your salivary attention are *bufet, samoobsluha* (self-service), and *občerstveni*, all variations on the stand-up snack bar. A *hostinec* caters to a steady clientele of beer drinkers; *kavárny* and *cukrárny* serve coffee and exquisite pastry, but note that *káva* (coffee) is often a thick layer of grounds topped with boiling water. A *pivnice* is a beer hall and a *vinárna* a wine bar, usually specializing in fine Slovak wines; both are good places to eat. Czech beers are among the world's best. The most famous are *Plzeňský Prazdroj* (Pilsner Urquell) and *Budvar* (the original Budweiser), but the *Velképopovický* is a local favorite. From Saturday noon to Sunday morning, all grocery stores and some restaurants close. It's customary to round up the bill a few kčs, and often it will be done for you. At finer eateries, give a 10% tip as you pay; do not leave it on the table. Vegetarians can munch on *smaženy sýr* (fried cheese), a scrumptious Czech specialty sold at food stands, and produce from *ovoce zelenina* stores (greengrocers) or *potraviny* (general grocery stores). Vegetarian restaurants have begun to pop up in larger cities.

■ ■ ■ PRAGUE (PRAHA)

The Princess Libuše stood atop a hill overlooking the River Vltava and declared, "I see a city whose glory will touch the stars; it shall be called *Praha* (threshold)." Prague is the "city of a hundred spires," of soaring cathedrals and lavish baroque palaces. Its lively squares and avenues give the city a festival atmosphere which few can rival, and its museums, concert halls, and ballet and opera performances are world-class. Since the Velvet Revolution of 1989, the city has exploded from relative obscurity and isolation behind the Iron Curtain into a tourist destination rivalling the great capitals of Western Europe. And while many locals can't keep up with the rising prices, Prague is still a fabulous bargain by Western standards. Just don't flaunt your affluence; instead, immerse yourself in the humbling magnificence of this 1000-year-old capital in the heart of Bohemia.

ORIENTATION AND PRACTICAL INFORMATION

Prague straddles the **River Vltava** (Moldau in German), with direct rail and bus links to Vienna, Berlin, Munich, and Warsaw. All train and bus terminals are on or near the Metro; the **nám. Republiky** Metro station is closest to the principal tourist offices and accommodations agencies. *Tabak* stands and bookstores sell an indexed *plán města* (city map). Prague's English-language newspapers are *Prognosis* and *The Prague Post*.

At the top of the western bank of the Vltava lies **Hradčany**, Prague's castle district. Below it are the lovely palaces and gardens of **Malá Strana** (Lesser Town). From Malá Strana, the pedestrian-only **Karlův Most** (Charles Bridge) crosses the river and leads into **Staré Město** (Old Town), at the center of which is the huge, architecturally resplendent plaza, **Staroméstké náméstí**. North of Staroméstké náméstí lies **Josefov,** the old Jewish quarter. South of Staré Mésto are the rich 19th-century façades of the more commercial **Nové Mésto** (New Town).

The center of Prague is dominated by 3 streets which form a leaning *T*. The long base of the *T*, separating the Old and New Towns, is **Václavské náměstí** (Wenceslas Square; actually a grand boulevard); at the bottom of the *T* towers the brooding **National Museum**. The busy pedestrian street **Na příkopé** forms the right arm and leads to **náměstí Republiky**. On the left, 28 října becomes Národní after a block, leading to the **National Theater** on the river. A maze of small streets leads to Staroměstské nám. 2 blocks above the *T*.

Tourist Offices: Čedok, Na příkopé 18 (tel. 212 71 11). No longer essential, but a convenient place to buy train and bus tickets. Processing them can take over an hour in high season. Open Mon.-Fri. 8:30am-6pm, Sat. 8:30am-12:30pm. Next door at **Pražská Informační Služba** (Prague Information Service), Na příkopé 20 (tel. 54 44 44), grab a handful of brochures on upcoming concerts and city sights. Open Mon.-Fri. 9am-7pm, Sat. 9am-6pm. **CKM,** Žitna 12 (tel. 29 99 415), next to the Junior Hotel Praha. Metro: I.P. Pavlova. Information, accommodations, and transportation tickets. Open daily 9am-1pm, 2-6pm. Branch office at Jindřisská 28 (tel. 26 85 07). Metro: Můstek. Sells HI and ISICs. Open Mon.-Fri. 9am-1pm and 2-5pm, Sat. 9am-noon. Go to the **American Hospitality Center,** Na Mustkú 7 (26 15 74 or 26 20 45), for their message board, posted with requests for English tutors, cycling companions, notes to friends and the like. CNN, MTV, popcorn, and pizza, just north of the end of Vácklavske nám. Open daily 10am-10pm.

Embassies: U.S., Tržiště 15, Praha 12548 (tel. 53 66 41, ext. 2362 for consular services). Metro: Malostranská. Cross the Charles Bridge and enter Malostranské nám. (castle side), then left on Karmelitská and right on Tržiště. **Canada,** Mickiewiczova 6 (tel. 312 02 51). Open Mon.-Fri. 8:30am-noon and 2-4pm. **U.K.,** Thunovská 14 (tel. 53 33 47). Open daily 9am-12pm and 2:45-4pm. Travelers from **Australia** and **New Zealand** should contact the British embassy. All Western embassies will hold mail. **Hungary,** Badeního 1 (tel. 36 50 41). Same-day visa for citizens of Australia and New Zealand US$20 plus 2 photos. Open Mon.-Wed. and Fri. 9am-noon. **Poland,** Valdštejnská 8 (tel. 53 69 51); consular section Václavské nám. 49 (tel. 26 44 64). Same day visa service. Citizens of Australia and New Zealand pay US$28 plus 2 photos; students US$21 with ISIC. Open Mon.-Fri. 9am-1pm. **Russia,** Pod kaštany 1 (tel. 38 19 41). Consular section around corner at Korunovačni 34 (tel. 37 37 23). Visas US$25 with proper preparation; citizens of Australia pay US$50. Open Mon., Wed., and Fri. 9:30am-1pm. **Ukraine** (tel. 37 43 66). **Lithuania** (tel. 312 46 19).

Currency Exchange: Čedok offers the best rates on cash, in spite of a 2% commission. The state bank at Na příkopé 14 (a stone's throw from Čedok) will cash traveler's checks for US$ or DM. Open Mon.-Fri. 7:30am-noon and 1-3:30pm. Živnostenská bank, Na příkopé 20, does the same, and gives cash advances on Visa and MasterCard. Commission 1% on notes, 2% on traveler's checks. Open Mon.-Fri. 8am-9:30pm, Sat. 9:30am-12:30pm, 1:30-5:30pm. Beware the black market; you may end up with a wad of counterfeit bills that no one will take.

American Express: Václavské nám. 56 (tel. 26 17 47). Metro: Muzeum. Mail held at U.S. visitors counter at above address plus 113 26 Praha 1. Cardholders' personal checks cashed for kčs only. MasterCard advances, Express cash machine. Open Mon.-Fri. 9am-7pm, Sat. 9am-3pm.

Post Office: Jindřišská 14. **Poste Restante** at window 28, stamps at windows 20-23, letters and parcels under 2kg at windows 10-12. Open 24hrs. **Parcels** over 2kg can be mailed only at Pošta-Celnice, Plzeňská 139. Take tram #9 west, and ask for the stop. A bureaucratic pain. Airmail should arrive within 10 days. Open Mon.-Tues. and Thurs.-Fri. 7am-3pm, Wed. 7am-6pm, Sat. 8am-noon. Metro: Můstek.

Telephones: At the post office and most train and Metro stations. Phone cards (100 kčs) available at Post Office and many newsstands, giving about 2 min. calling time to the U.S. **City Code:** 02.

Flights: Ruzyné Airport (tel. 334 33 14), 20km northwest of city center. **ČSA** (tel. 36 78 14), the Czech airline, runs buses to the airport every 20-30min. from

ORIENTATION AND PRACTICAL INFORMATION

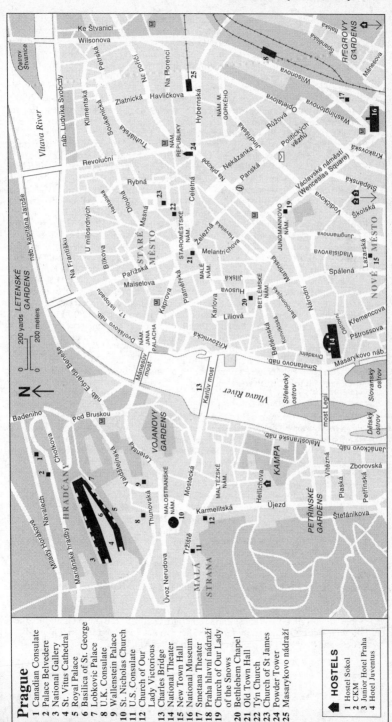

Prague

1 Canadian Consulate
2 Palace Belvedere
3 National Gallery
4 St. Vitus Cathedral
5 Royal Palace
6 Basilica of St. George
7 Lobkovic Palace
8 U.K. Consulate
9 Wallenstein Palace
10 St. Nicholas Church
11 U.S. Consulate
12 Church of Our
   Lady Victorious
13 Charles Bridge
14 National Theater
15 New Town Hall
16 National Museum
17 Smetana Theater
18 Praha hlavní nádraží
19 Church of Our Lady
   of the Snows
20 Bethlehem Chapel
21 Old Town Hall
22 Týn Church
23 Church of St James
24 Powder Tower
25 Masarykovo nádraží

▲ **HOSTELS**

1 Hostel Sokol
2 CKM
3 Junior Hotel Praha
4 Hotel Juventus

6am-6:30pm from Revoluční 25 (around back), 5 blocks north of Metro: nám. Republiky. Buy tickets (20kčs) on bus. Or take bus #119 from Metro: Dejvická.

Trains: There are 4 train stations in Prague. Always ask what your point of departure will be—the information may not be volunteered. **Praha-Holešovice:** the main international terminal—you'll probably arrive here or at hlavní nádraží; both on Metro line C. **Praha hlavní nádraží** (a.k.a. Woodrow Wilsonova station; Metro: hlavní nádraží) Some international and many domestic routes. To: Berlin (6/day, 6hr.), Budapest (6/day, 9hr.), Vienna (5/day, 5hr.), Warsaw (2/day, 10hr.). **Masarykovo nádraží,** on Hybernská, serves only domestic routes. **Praha-Smíchov** and **Masarykovo** (Metro: nám. Republiky) are across the river. Czech-speakers can call train information (tel. 24 44 41 or 26 49 30).

Buses: ČSAD has 3 terminals (*Autobusové nádraží*). The central one is **Praha-Florenc,** on Křižíkova (tel. 22 86 42 or 22 26 29), behind the Masarykovo nádraží railway station. Metro: Florenc. *Informace* desk staff speaks little English, but posted schedules are legible and extensive. Open Mon.-Fri. 6am-6:30pm, Sat. 6am-1pm, Sun. 8:30am-noon and 12:30-3:30pm. Buy tickets at least a day in advance, as they often sell out. To Milan and Munich (2/week), Venice (4/week), Vienna (daily). Extensive service throughout the Czech and Slovak Republics.

Public Transportation: tel. 22 95 52. The **Metro,** tram, and bus systems serve the city well. Tickets, good for all forms of transportation, cost 4kčs; stock up at newspaper stands and *tabak* shops as the orange *automat* machines in Metro stations require exact change. Čedok sells handy tourist passes, good on all 3 modes of transport (1 day, 30kčs; 2 days, 50kčs; 15kčs each additional day). Punch your ticket when boarding, and punch a new ticket when switching vehicles—except in the Metro, where your ticket is valid for 1hr. after punching on all lines as long as you don't go above ground. Fine for riding without a punched ticket: 200kčs. Metro runs daily 5am-midnight. Night trams 51-58 and buses 500-510 run midnight-5am (every 40min.); look for their dark blue signs at transport stops.

Taxis: tel. 35 03 20 or 35 04 91. Make sure the meter is running or set a price beforehand. Downtown to airport about 300kčs. To the hostel 150-200kčs.

Hitchhiking: Hitchhiking in and around Prague has become increasingly dangerous. Travelers going east take tram #1, 9, or 16 to the last stop. To points south, they take Metro C to Pražskeho povstáni, then go left 100m, crossing náměstí Hrdinů to 5 Květná, (a.k.a. highway D1). To Munich, they take tram #4 or 9 until the intersection of Plzeňská and Kukulova/Bucharova, then hitch south. Those going north take a tram or bus to Kobyliské nám., then bus #175 up Horňatecká.

Luggage Storage: Lockers (4kčs) in every train and bus station, except the main train station. Lockers (4kčs) there are usually full—try 24-hr. baggage storage in basement (9.50kčs/day for 1st 15kg). Beware of those who might relieve you of heavy baggage by watching while you set your 4-digit locker code.

Laundromat: If you stay in a private flat, ask if your laundry can be included with the family's. Often it will come back darned and ironed, even your underwear. If you're on your own, go to **Laundry Kings** at Dejvická 16, 1 block from Hradčanská metro stop. Self-service wash 40kčs/load, dry 15kčs/8min. Soap 10-20kčs. Full-service is an additional 30kčs and takes 24hr. in high season. Open Mon.-Fri. 6am-10pm, Sat.-Sun. 8am-10pm. Filled with similarly soiled and thirsty Americans.

Bookstore: The Globe Bookstore, Janouského 14. Metro: Vltavská. From the Metro, walk under the overpass on your right, then turn right onto Janouského. Large selection of used paperbacks (avg. 80kčs). Open daily 9am-5pm.

Pharmacy (*Lékárna*): Na příkopé 7 (tel. 22 00 81). Open 24hrs.

Emergencies: Ambulance (tel. 155). **Fire** (tel. 150). **Police** (tel. 158). **Medical Emergency Aid** in English and German: (tel. 29 93 81). English is shaky; try calling your embassy. **Police** headquarters at Olšanská 2 (tel. 21 21 11 11). Metro: Flora, then walk down Jičinská and right onto Olšanská; the station is about 200m on your right. Or take tram #9. Come here to get a **visa extension.** Open Mon., Tues., and Thurs. 8am-3pm, Wed. 8am-5pm, Fri. 8am-2pm.

ACCOMMODATIONS

The **Prague Information Service Guide Office,** Panská 5, off Na Příkopé, displays a list of all accommodations. (Open daily 9am-6pm.) Prices in Prague are rising rapidly, but beds are plentiful. Besides private flats, budget travelers have 3 main options: youth hostels, class B (2-star) or C (1-star) hotels, and campgrounds. In late June, universities empty for the summer, freeing up hundreds of cheap rooms.

Official Agencies

CKM, Žitná 12 (tel. 29 99 41 or 29 99 45; fax 235 48 59). Metro: nám. I.P. Pavlova, then backtrack down Žitná, or walk down Štěpánská from Václavské nám. Lists local dormitories and youth hostels that currently have beds available (220-450kčs) and provides metro and tram directions. Open daily 9am-1pm and 2-6pm.

Universitas Tour, Opleta lova 38 (tel. 22 35 431 or 22 35 50), 2 blocks north of the main train station. Metro: Hlavní nádraží. In July and Aug., books rooms in hostel/dorm on premises. 300 kčs/person in singles, doubles, triples, and quads. Hall baths. Rest of the year, scouts out a *penzión* (350kčs/person including breakfast and bath), private rooms (450-600kčs). Open Mon.-Sat. 8:30am-6pm; July-Aug. 8:30am-8:30pm.

Pragotur, U Obecního domu 2 (tel. 231 70 00 or 232 51 28), a side street off nám. Republiky, across from the Hotel Paříž. Metro: nám. Republiky. B- and C-class hotels (600-900kčs/person) and private homes. Doubling or tripling up with others may speed things up. No min. stay. Private rooms in center. Singles 665kčs. Doubles 875kčs. Open Mon.-Fri. 8am-7pm, Sat. 9am-6pm, Sun. 9am-3pm.

Private Agencies

When you first arrive in Prague, you may be besieged by individuals offering private rooms. The going rate hovers at about US$10-15 (250-450kčs), depending primarily on proximity to the town center. Try haggling. These are generally safe arrangements, but if you're wary of bargaining on the street, try private agencies which set up shop seemingly overnight in prominent areas of town. Make sure any rooms you accept are easily reachable by public transportation. Payment in US$ or DM is usually preferred, sometimes required, though kčs are generally accepted.

Top Tour, Rybná 3 (tel. 231 40 69 or 269 65 26), 1 block west of nám. Republiky. Dorm hostels (3 beds/room, 400kčs/person). Private singles 630-700kčs, doubles 1050-1150kčs. Open Mon.-Fri. 9am-8pm, Sat.-Sun. 10am-7pm.

Vesta, Wilsonova 80 (tel. 236 81 28), on the top floor of the Hlavní nádraží train station. Make sure you understand just what sort of accommodations you are paying for here; make them write it down. Private rooms 350-500kčs/person, hostels near the center 250kčs/person, and hotels 500-800kčs/person. Open Mon.-Sat. 8:30am-7:30pm, Sun. 8:30am-4:30pm.

Hello Ltd., Gorkého-Senovážné nám 3 (tel. 22 42 83). From nám. Republiky, walk down Hybernská and turn right on Dlážděná. Choose rooms from photos. Private rooms 400-600kčs. Private flats 800-900kčs/person. Open daily 9am-10pm.

Prague Suites, Melantrichoua 8 (tel. 26 77 70 or 26 93 84), 2 blocks north of intersection of Václavské nám and Na příkopé. Associated with American Hospitality Center. Private rooms US$15-20. Also handles long-term rooms. Open 24hrs.

AVE Ltd., Wilsonova 8 (tel. 24 22 32 26 or 24 22 35 21), top floor of the Hlavní nádraží train station. Convenient and speedy. Hostels from 200 kčs, private rooms from 400kčs, hotel singles from 800kčs, and doubles 1100kčs. Also in nádraží Holešovice. Open daily 6am-11:30pm; Sept.-June 6am-10pm.

Primo Agency, Žitná 17 (tel. 249 10 340), down the street from CKM. Hostels for 235kčs, private doubles from 700-1000kčs, flats from 900kčs/night total—a steal for groups. Open daily 9am-10pm; Sept.-June 11am-8pm.

Hostels (Studentska Kolej)

An enormous cluster is west of the river in the Strahov neighborhood, next to the Olympic stadium. Take bus #217 from Metro: Dejvická or #176 from Metro: Karlovo nám. to Stadion strahov (every ½hr.).

ESTEC Students House, "Kolej Strahov," Vaníčkova (was Spartakiádní), *blok* (building) 5 (tel. 52 73 44). Follow above directions, then walk around the stadium to the right. 500 beds from July to mid-Sept. Limited 1st-floor space available mid-Sept. to June. Lively bar—who needs to go downtown? Open 24hrs.; Sept.-June 5-10pm. Check-in 24hrs. Check-out 10am. No curfew. Doubles 240kčs/person. Breakfast 50kčs. Post office (open Mon.-Fri. 8am-3pm) and student grocery store (open Mon.-Fri. 7:30am-7pm, Sat.-Sun. 7:30am-noon) next door.

TJ Slavoj, V náklích (tel. 46 00 70). Take tram #3 or 17 to "Braník" (last stop). Lonely 10-min. walk from tram; look for it in the daytime. 48 beds in a boathouse by the river; 3-, 4-, and 5-bed rooms. No lockout. No curfew. 170kčs. Hearty meals 40kčs. Kind proprietors will leave your laundry folded on your bed for 30kčs.

Pensión V podzámčí, V podzámčí 27 (tel. 472 27 59), next to the TJ Sokol Krč gym. Metro: Budějovická, then bus #192 to 3rd stop. 6 rooms with 2 beds plus double twin-mattress loft. Clean and comfortable; some grateful travelers have left flowers for the gracious hosts. Kitchen. Reception open Mon.-Fri. 7:30am-10pm, Sat.-Sun. 7am-11pm. No lockout. 225kčs. Breakfast 30kčs. Make reservations.

Domov Mládeže, Dykova 20 (tel. 25 06 88 or 25 14 29). Take tram #16 from Ječná to 4th stop, or Metro: nám. Miru, then tram #16 up to 2nd stop, go right on Nitranská, left on Dykova. 60 beds in the peaceful Vinohrady district. Hall showers. Open 24hrs. No lockout. No curfew. 250kčs. Breakfast 30kčs.

Pension Novodvorská, Novodvorská 151 (tel. 47 18 414). Metro: Smíchovské nádraží, then bus #196 or 198 to "Sídl. Novodvorská." Many floors of student housing, often full. Reception open 24hrs. 420kčs, with breakfast.

TJ Sokol Karlin, Malého 1 (tel. 22 20 09), behind the Praha-Florenc bus station. Metro: Florenc. 5- to 12-bed dorms plus cots in a gymnasium. Usually has room. Reception open 6pm-midnight. Check-out 7am. Lockout 8am-6pm. 170kčs; cots 110kčs.

Hostel Sokol, Hellichova 1 (tel. 53 45 51, ext. 397). Metro: Malostranská. Take tram #12 or 22 to Hellichova and follow signs. Just 5min. from the Charles Bridge. Offers clean and comfortable 10- to 15-bed rooms, co-ed by floor. Reception open 6-10am and 3pm-12:30am. Curfew 12:30am, 18kčs charge to let you in after that. 180kčs. Breakfast 20kčs. Storage room for valuables. Open June-Sept.

Hostel Braník, Urbova 1233 (tel. 46 26 41 or 42). Metro: Smíchovské nádraží, then take bus #196 or 198 to Ve Studeném. 180 beds in singles, doubles, triples, and quads. Reception open 24hrs. No lockout. No curfew. 280 kčs/person, with breakfast.

Hotels

As privatization accelerates, dependable budget hotels are fading faster than you can say *demokracia*. The difference in price between B- and C- hotels and pensions is often dramatic, while quality levels are comparable. Beware that hotels sometimes try to bill you for a more expensive room than the one you stayed in. Come prepared with pen, paper, and receipts.

Hotel Juventus, Blanická 10 (tel. 25 51 51 or 25 51 52), 1 block from Metro: nám. Míru. Ideal location near the city center, between Francouzská and Korunní. Hall showers. Reception open 24hrs. Singles 695kčs. Doubles 1110kčs.

Junior Hotel Praha, Žitná 10 (tel. 29 29 84), right next to CKM. Rooms on the cutting edge of 70s revival decor. Private showers and baths. Singles 980kčs, doubles 1260kčs. Breakfast included. Reserve in advance.

Hotel Madape, Malešická 74 (tel. 89 31 04). Metro: Želiského, then bus #234 5 stops to "Vackow." Bus stop is around corner from Metro, beside cemetery where Kafka is buried. No English, some German spoken. B-category. Private baths. Doubles off hospital-like corridors, a cheap 290kčs/person.

Camping

The **Pražská Informační Služba** (Prague Information Service Guide Office), Panská 5, just around the corner from Čedok, has a list of all Prague's campgrounds. Call ahead to make sure there's room; German always spoken, English occasionally. There is a cluster of campgrounds north of the center in the Troja district of Prague. The largest is **Sokol Troja,** Trojská 171 (tel. 84 28 33). Take bus #112 from Metro: Nádraží Holešovice; get off at Kazanka (4th stop), and walk 100m. (90kčs/person, 70kčs/small tent, bungalows 170kčs/bed. Reservations recommended.) Or try **Sokol Dolní Počernice,** Dolní Počernice, Nad rybníkem (tel. 71 80 34). Take tram #9 to the end of the line, then bus #109 and ask for the campground.

FOOD

Restaurants in Prague eat careless travelers alive. After numerous hidden charges are added in, the bill can be nearly twice what you expected. Always ask to see a menu; most restaurants post them outside. Don't be fooled: *anything* they offer you to go with your meal will cost extra, and you'll be charged for everything they place on your table, including bread and even ketchup. Finally, take more care than usual to check the bill. Tipping involves rounding the bill up a few kčs. At posher places, 10% is adequate. Include the tip as you pay; don't leave it on the table. Traditional Czech dishes are generally cheapest; look for *Hotová Jídla.* For a quick bite, the numerous window stands selling tasty *párek v rohlíku* (sausage in a small roll with mustard) for 7-15kčs are a bargain. Many an outlying Metro stop becomes an impromptu marketplace during the summer; look for the daily **vegetable market** at the intersection of Havelská and Melantrichova in the Old Town.

Restaurace Črný Kůň (Black Horse), Vodičková 36 (tel. 22 41 53), downstairs in the Lucerna Bar complex. High ceiling and carved dark wood. Czech dishes 60kčs, veggie dishes 50kčs, European cuisine 90-130kčs. Open daily 11am-11pm.

U Palečka, Nitranská 22 (tel. 25 13 00). From Metro: Jiřího z Poděbrad, cross Vinohradská; Nitranská is the 1st street to the left. Gourmet Czech cuisine in an intimate setting. Pork steak smothered in cheese, ham, and asparagus (75kčs). Dress is casual but neat. Try to reserve ahead for dinner. Open daily 11am-midnight.

Poříčská Pekárna, 28 Na Poříčí. Metro: nám Republiky. Piles of freshly baked breads and pastries (4-8kčs), as well as carni- and herbivorous sandwiches, all for less than a Twix bar back home (19kčs). Open Mon.-Fri. 7am-7pm, Sat. 8am-1pm.

Café FX, Břlehradská 120, Metro: I.P. Pavlova. Stylish vegetarian café; a sanctum for ex-patriates and travelers alike. Greek salad 50kčs. Juices 20kčs. Poetry readings in English in the back (Sun. 6pm). Open daily 11am-5am.

Slovanska Hospada, Na Příkopé 22 (tel. and fax 25 12 10). Metro: nám Republiky. No-nonsense Czech fare. Owners headed the Czech National AIDS Awareness Week. Dishes around 40kčs. Open Mon.-Sat. 11am-10pm.

V Soudím dvoře, Karmelitská 19, Metro: Malostranská. Down from St. Nicholas cathedral in Malostranské nám. One-horse bistro home to many a quiet conversation. Entrees 45kčs, omelettes 18kčs, ½-liter beer 9kčs. Whisper daily 10am-11pm.

Supermarkets are generally small and packed with cheap fruits, vegetables, and other goodies. Try **Pomona,** Václavské nám 52, next to American Express (open Mon.-Fri. 7am-9pm, Sat. 9am-2pm, Sun. noon-9pm), and **Casa Pascual,** Národní 27, Metro: Národní třída. (Open Mon.-Fri. 8am-7pm, Sat. 8am-1pm.)

SIGHTS

Surrounded by a labyrinth of Old World alleyways, the luminous baroque elegance of **Staroměstské náměstí** is truly startling. This sweeping space is dominated by the **Old Town Hall,** which expanded from the original 14th-century tower to include several neighboring buildings. The town hall used to extend to within a few meters of the baroque **St. Nicholas Church,** but that section was demolished by the Nazi tanks on the very last day of WWII. Townspeople and tourists gather on the hour to see its fabulous **Astronomical Clock,** with 12 peering apostles and a bell-ringing skeleton representing death. The clockmaker's eyes were put out by his patron so he could not craft another. A statue of martyred Czech theologian and leader **Jan Hus** occupies the place of honor in the center of the square. Across from the Town Hall is **Týn Church.** The tower on the right represents Adam, who shields Eve, the tower on the left, from the midday sun. To the left of the church, the creamy 14th-century **House at Stone Bell** shows the gothic core which may lurk under many of Prague's baroque façades, and exhibits works from the Municipal Gallery of Prague. (Open Tues.-Sun. 10am-6pm.) Between Maiselova and Týn church is **Franz Kafka**'s former home, marked with a plaque. (Hard-core Kafka devotees can visit the writer's final resting place at the Jewish Graveyard right outside Metro: Želivského.) A short detour down Jilská will bring you to the **Bethlehem Chapel,** where Jan Hus preached to his loyal congregation from 1402 until he was burnt at the stake.

Josefov, the traditional Jewish quarter around Pařížská and Maiselova (Metro: Starométská), lost 80,000 of its 90,000 inhabitants to Nazi death camps during WWII. Tours to **Terezín** concentration camp depart every Sunday and Thursday at 10am from the Jewish Town Hall, Maiselova 18, and return at 3pm. Buses #17 and 20 also leave Florenc bus station and take about an hour. (Camp museum open daily 9am-4:30pm.)

Karlův most (Charles Bridge) may be Europe's most festive. Artisans, classical guitarists, and other street musicians fill the bridge day and night above a bevy of swans. Depicted at the base of hero Jan Nepomuk's statue in the center of the bridge is hapless Jan being tossed over the side for guarding his queen's confidences. Climb the Gothic **defense tower** on the Malá Strana side for a super view of Prague. (Open daily 10am-5:30pm. 20kčs, students 10kčs.) Head down the stairs on the left side of the bridge (as you face the castle district) to **Hroznová,** where a mural honors John Lennon and the peace movement of the 1960s. **Slovanskù ostrov** (island) and the larger **Střelecky ostrov** (accessible from most 1 Máje) offer soothing shade.

The **Malá Strana** (Lesser Town) is rich in palaces, ornate gardens, and grand baroque churches. The grandest is the 18th-century **St. Nicholas' Church,** the highest achievement of Czech baroque art. Mozart played the organ here. (Open daily 9am-5pm. 20kčs, students 10kčs.) Nearby on Karmelitská rises the more modest **Church of Our Lady Victorious,** repository of the wax statue of the Infant Jesus of Prague, reputed to have miraculous powers. A simple wooden gate at Letenská 10 (off Malostranské nám.) opens onto the **Valdštejnská zahrada** (Wallenstein Garden), one of Prague's best-kept secrets. This tranquil 17th-century baroque garden, adorned with statues and frescoes depicting scenes from the Trojan War, is enclosed by old buildings that glow golden on sunny afternoons.

You can spend days wandering about the edifices that comprise the **Pražský hrad** (Prague Castle), on Nerudova. All the styles of architecture that have made Prague so astonishingly beautiful are well-represented; the castle is crowned by the soaring **Katedrála sv. Vita** (St. Vitus's Cathedral), completed in 1930 after 600 years of construction. To the right of the high altar stands the **tomb of St. John Nepomuk,** 3 meters of solid, glistening silver, weighing in at 2 tons. Climb the 287 steps of the **Cathedral Tower** for a breathtaking view of the castle and the city. (Open daily 10am-4pm. 15kčs, students 8kčs.) In the nearby **Czech Chancellery,** 2 Habsburg officials were lobbed out the window by fed-up Bohemian noblemen in 1618. Though a dungheap broke their fall, the die was cast, and war ravaged Europe for the next 30 years. Built in 1485 to enhance the castle's fortifications, the **Powder Tower** houses a reconstructed alchemist's laboratory. (10kčs, students 5kčs.) Inside the **Lobkovický Palace,** a permanent exhibit details the history of the Slavs and contains a replica of the Czech coronation jewels. (30kčs, students 15kčs.) Higher up is a tiny street carved into the fortified wall, **Zlatá ulička** (Golden Lane), where the court alchemists supposedly toiled. (Buildings open Tues.-Sun. 9am-5pm; Oct.-March 9am-4pm.) Exiting the castle grounds across the Powder Bridge, you'll see the entrance to the peaceful **Royal Garden,** laid out in 1534 by Ferdinand I to include the glorious Renaissance palace **Belvedere** (under renovation in 1993). (Open Tues.-Sun. 10am-5:45pm. 5kčs, students 2kčs. For more information on the entire castle complex, go to the **Informační středisko** behind the cathedral.

A model of the Eiffel Tower tops the **Petřínské sady,** gardens on the hills to the south. (Open May daily 9am-10pm; July-Aug. 9am-11pm. 20kčs, students 5kčs.) A funicular to the top (4kčs—look for *lanové dráhy* signs) leaves from just above the intersection of Vítézná and žjezd. Not far from the station at the top is a wacky little castle offering juvenile bliss—a hall of mirrors. (Open daily April-Oct. 9am-6pm. 10kčs, students 5kčs.) Just east of the park lies **Strahov Stadium,** the world's largest, enclosing the area of 10 soccer fields.

For a magnificent view of the Old Town and castle from the east, stroll up forested **Pohled z Vítkova** (Vítkov Hill), topped by the world's largest equestrian monument; from this perch, one-eyed Hussite leader Jan Žižka keeps a watchful eye out for Crusaders, whom he stomped out on this spot in 1420. From Metro: Křižíkova, walk down Thámova, through the tunnel, and up the hill. (Open 24hrs. Free.)

A ½-hour walk south of Nové Mĕsto is the quiet fortress **Vyšehrad,** the Czech Republic's most revered landmark, and is delightfully tourist-free. On the mount above the river, the fortress encompasses a neo-Gothic church, a Romanesque rotunda, and the Vyšehrad Cemetery. (Complex open 24 hrs.) Take Metro C to "Vyšehrad." Even the subway stop has a movie-sweep vista of Prague.

As you exit the main gate of the castle, walk straight ahead; the lovely **Loretto** will be on your right, with an aggrandized replica of Jesus' birthplace and a diamond mine of a treasury. (Open Tues.-Sun. 9am-4:30pm. 30kčs, students 20kčs.)

Museums

National Museum, Václavské nám 68 (tel. 26 94 51 through 55). Metro: Museum. A vast collection including meteorites, enormous minerals, and fossils; don't miss the skeleton horse and rider. In January 1969, 20-year-old student Jan Palach set himself on fire here to protest the Prague Spring. Open Mon. and Wed.-Fri. 9am-5pm, Sat.-Sun. 10am-6pm. 20kčs, students 10kčs.

State Jewish Museum, (Státní Židovské Muzeum; tel. 231 06 81), Jáchymova 3, Metro: Staroméstké nám. Includes 5 synagogues, a cemetery, and a collection of artifacts from Bohemia and Moravia. Hitler ordered that these relics of Judaica be preserved for an intended museum of the extinct Jewish race. A unique collection of children's drawings and poems from the wartime Terezin ghetto also survives. The fascinating underground **Staronová Synagogue** is the oldest in Europe; parts date from 1270. Next to the synagogue is the pink rococo **Jewish Town Hall,** with its Hebrew clock which proceeds counter-clockwise. The **Pinkas Synagogue** houses the memorial to the Czech Jews who perished in the Holocaust. The nearby **Jewish cemetery** ripples with 12,000 tombstones. Town Hall and Staronová Synagogue open Sun.-Fri. 9:30am-5pm. 30kčs, students 15kčs. Cemetery and other synagogues open Sun.-Fri. 9:30am-5:30pm. 80kčs, students 30kčs.

National Gallery: collections housed in 9 different historical buildings. The **National Gallery of European Art** is in the **Šternberk Palace,** Hradčanské nám. 15, and includes works by Rubens, Breughel, Dürer, Picasso, and your favorite Impressionists. The **National Gallery of Bohemian Art,** Gothic to Baroque, is housed in St. George's Monastery inside Prague Castle. Includes works by Czech artists including Master Theodorik, court painter for Karel IV. To either gallery 40kčs, students 10kčs. Open Tues.-Sun. 10am-6pm.

Muzeúm Mozart, Mozartova 169 (tel. 54 38 93). Metro: Andřl, left on Pleňská, left on Mozartova, in Villa Bertramka, where Mozart lived in 1787 and reputedly wrote *Don Giovanni.* Open daily 9:30am-6pm. Garden concerts July-Aug. on Fri. at 7:30pm. Call ahead for tickets. 50kčs, students 30kčs.

The Prague Municipal Museum (Muzeum hlavního mésta Prahy), Na poříčí 52 (tel. 236 24 50). Metro: Florenc. The highlight is a meticulously precise 1:480

scale model of old Prague. Come see what your hostel looked like in 1834. 10kčs, students 5kčs. Open Tues.-Sun. 10am-6pm.

Museum of Decorative Arts, 17 listopadu 2 (tel. 232 00 51). Metro: Staroměstské, at Široká and 17 listopadu, right behind the Old Jewish Cemetery. Includes exquisite ceramics and richly carved and bejeweled furnishings from Renaissance and Baroque palaces. 2nd floor houses one of the world's largest glasswork collections (closed to the public in 1993, but should be open on weekends in 1994.) Open Tues.-Sun. 10am-6pm. 20kčs, students 10kčs.

ENTERTAINMENT

Both the *Prague Post* and *Prognosis* include an invaluable night-by-night listing of opera, ballet, and theater performances, as well as all classical, rock, and jazz concerts in town. The grandest of Prague's theaters are the **Národní Divadlo (National Theater),** Národní třida 2 (tel. 20 53 64; box office open Mon.-Fri. 10am-8pm, Sat.-Sun. 3-8pm), the **Státní Opera (State Opera),** Wilsonova třida, between Metro: Muzeum and Hlavní nádraži (tel. 26 53 53; box office open Mon.-Fri. 10am-6pm, Sat.-Sun. noon-6pm), and the newly renovated **Stavorské Divadlo (Estates Theater)** (tel. 22 86 58), Ovocnýtrh (between Celetná and Železná in the Old Town), which presented the premiere of Don Giovanni in 1787, with Mozart himself conducting. (Box office open Tues.-Sat. 10am-6pm, Sun.-Mon. noon-6pm.) All 3 theaters showcase world-class opera, drama, and ballet productions almost nightly at 7pm. (Tickets from about 40-400kčs; unsold tickets available ½hr. before showtime. Scalpers near the National Theater charge around 200kčs each.)

From mid-May to early June, the **Prague Spring Festival** draws musicians from around the world and outdoor concerts animate the city. Tickets (270-540kčs) can be bought at **Bohemia Ticket International,** Na příkopé 16 (tel. 22 87 38), next to Čedok. (Open Mon.-Fri. 9am-6pm, Sat. 9am-3pm, Sun. 9am-2pm.) The **Stavovske Divadlo** theater (tel. 22 72 82) at Ovocnùtrh in the Old Town (Metro: Mùstek) provides earphones for simultaneous English translation of its plays. (Box office in Kolowrat Palace around the corner open Mon.-Fri. 10am-6pm, Sat.-Sun. noon-6pm.) With an over 200-year-old tradition in Prague, marionette theater thrives at **říše Loutek** (National Marionette Theatre) at Žateckal in the Old Town (tel. 232 34 29; box office open Mon. and Tues. 2-8pm). A star tourist attraction is the **Laterna Magica,** Národní 4 (tel. 20 62 60), a cutesy but clever integration of film, drama, and dance. (Performances Mon.-Fri. at 8pm, Sat. also at 5pm. Box office open Mon.-Sat. 3-6pm. Tickets 300-450kčs. Often sold out in summer 2 weeks in advance.)

Václavské náměstí thumps with numerous dancespots, but the best way to enjoy Prague at night is to head to a *pivnice* or a *vinárna.*

U Fleků, Křemencova 11. Behind the National Theater; look for the huge clock. Prague's touristy answer to the German brew house, with homebrewed brown ale. 30kčs cover to sit outside for the oompa band. Open daily 9am-11pm.

Repre Club, downstairs from the beautiful art-nouveau Municipal House. Maybe the prettiest building you'll ever get wasted in. Live music nightly until midnight, DJ after that. Cover 50kčs. Open daily 9pm-5am. Around the corner at the **Thirsty Dog,** swap stories with other travelers over cheap drafts (15kčs).

Radost FX, Břlehradská 120 (tel. 25 12 10), below Café FX. An alternative dance club to make Comrade Stalin turn in his grave. Cover 50kčs. Open 9pm-6am daily.

Krušovická Pivnice, Široká 20, 2 blocks from Staroměstské nám off Pašížská. Traditional Czech *pivnice,* serving light, dark, and half-and-half. Beer 13kčs. Open Mon.-Sat. 11am-midnight.

Reduta, Národní 20 (tel. 20 38 25). A good jazz club with live music nightly and a clientele of artists drowning in tourists. Cover 80kčs. Open Mon.-Sat. 9pm-2am.

U sv. Tomáše, Letenská 12. Swinging monks founded it in 1358 as a monastery brewery. This *pivnice* serves possibly Prague's best beer—no small feat. 20kčs/ glass. 15kčs cover charge for the Czech folk band. Open 11am-midnight.

■ Near Prague

The Central Bohemian hills surrounding Prague contain 14 castles, some built as early as the 13th century. A 45-minute train ride from Prague (8kčs) brings you to **Karlštejn,** a walled and turreted fortress built by Charles IV to house his crown jewels and holy relics. The **Chapel of the Holy Cross** is decorated with over 2000 inlaid precious stones and 128 apocalyptic paintings (sadly faded) by medieval artist Master Theodorik. Take the Metro to the "Smíchovské nádraži" (Praha-Smíchov station) where trains cart gawkers hourly to Karlštejn castle. (Open Tues.-Sun. 9am-4pm. With foreign language guide 90kčs, students 40kčs; in Czech 10kčs, students 5kčs.) A **campground** (tel. 0311 942 63) is located on the left bank of the River Berounka. (Open 24hrs.)

Animal-rights activists might wish to avoid **Konopiště,** in Benešov (bus from Praha-Florenc station to the Katná Hora stop at Benešov, 1½ hrs.), a Renaissance palace with a luxurious interior preserved from the days when Archduke Franz Ferdinand bagged game here—over 300,000 animals. Fittingly, the **Weapons Hall** contains one of the finest collections of 16th- to 18th-century European arms.

An hour and a half southeast of Prague by bus is the former mining town of **Kutná Hora.** Soon after a silver vein was struck here in the 13th century, a royal mint—**Vlašskù dvůr**—was established to produce the Prague *groschen* (silver coin). The uninteresting coin museum has commentary written entirely in Czech, but up the stairs from the courtyard is a magnificent **Gothic Hall** with frescoes and lovely carved wooden triptychs. The most convincing evidence of the wealth that once flowed through the town is the fantastic, begargoyled **Cathedral of St. Barbara,** built to rival St. Vitus in Prague. Buses leave nearly hourly from Prague's Metro: Želivského, platform #2, and from Praha-Florenc station.

WESTERN BOHEMIA

Bohemia, the western half of the Czech Republic, is the traditional homeland of the Czech people. Common heritage did little to prevent squabbles, as the hundreds of prickly castles guarding former feudal principalities attest.

■■■ KARLOVY VARY

The springs of **Karlovy Vary** (Karlsbad in German), have a guest list that's a roster of 19th-century political and cultural icons: Goethe, Schiller, Tolstoy, Gogol, Beethoven, Metternich, and Marx sampled the waters here. People still throng to the town to attempt to cure their ailments and to enjoy the air of Victorian luxury and grandeur. Libation from the "13th spring" is a potent liqueur with a pastoral aftertaste called *Becherovka,* made from herbs and Karlovy Vary water. A fitting accompaniment to all Karlovy Vary ritual are the circular *oplatký* wafers which resemble 20cm beer coasters; they taste divine plain or chocolate-covered.

The Teplá River winds through the town, which lies in a narrow valley caught in the folds of steep hillsides. On the banks above the modern thermal sanatorium is a **public swimming pool.** (Open Mon.-Sat. 8am-9:30pm, Sun. 9am-9:30pm. 20kčs/hr.) The many-pillared **Mill Colonnade** on Mlýnské nábřeží contains a few thermal faucets. Bring your own cup, or buy one in a souvenir shop. The heart of Karlovy Vary is the **Vřídelní Colonnade** on Vřídelní, replete with gushing 12m fountain. Try the faucet's scalding water. The baroque **Church of Mary Magdalene** overlooks the colonnade. Hiking paths and the **Diana Funicular Railway** on Mariánská lead up to **Diana Tower** at the top. (Departures daily every 15min. 10am-6pm. 35kčs round-trip. Tower 5kčs.) The moderately-priced **Diana Restaurant** and **kavárna** sit atop the mountain. (Open daily 10:30am-6pm.) **Hiking trails** also appear on the Karlovy

Vary city map (19kčs), available in bookstores. Check out the white **Russian Orthodox Church,** which glitters with gold.

Accommodations, Food, and Practical Information The cheapest place to stay in Karlovy Vary is the attractive **Junior Hotel Alice (HI),** ul. Pétiletky 147 (tel. (017) 243 79), a lovely 3km hike out of town (undergoing renovations in 1993). From the city bus station (near the market), take bus #7 about 12 stops. Reserve in advance. (Members and ISIC holders 215kčs/person, nonmembers in singles 420kčs. Prices from 1991, when hostel was last open.) One stop past J. H. Alice is the A-star hotel **Sport Hotel Gejzír,** at bus stop Gejzír. (Singles 305kčs. Doubles 550kčs.) For B hotels, Čedok recommends reserving 3 to 4 months in advance, although these hotels often have rooms available. A 3-minute walk from the main bus station, up the hill, left on T. G. Masaryka, then right on Dr. Davida Bechera, at no. 18, is **Hotel Turist,** (tel. (017) 268 37; C category; doubles 750kčs; triples 1095kčs). The **Čedok** closest to the waters, at Karla IV 1 (tel. (017) 261 10), books pensions for 40DM per person. Take bus #13 from bus station to Lázně III. (Open Mon.-Fri. 9am-5pm, Sat. 9am-noon; Oct. to mid-May Mon.-Fri. 9am-4pm, Sat. 9am-noon.) **"W,"** nám. Republiky 3 (tel. (017) 277 68), near the bus station, also books private rooms. (US$10-15. Open Mon.-Fri. 9am-7pm, Sat. 10am-7pm.) Score cheap eats at the **občervstení grill** on Stará Louka, 2 bridges past the colonnade exit. (Pork cutlets 32kčs; grilled sausages 15-19kčs.) The **Fortuna Restaurant** at Zámecký vrch 14 cooks up Italian favorites. (Pizzas 59-90kčs. Open daily 11am-10pm.)

The **bus** is your ticket from Prague's Praha-Florenc to Karlovy Vary (every hr., 2½hr., 56kčs). Buy tickets 2 or 3 days in advance. Leave your bags at **dolní nádraží** train station, 300m down Varšovká (which becomes Západní) from the bus station.

■■■ MARIÁNSKÉ LÁZNÉ AND PLZEŇ

Mariánské Lázné   Forty km south of Karlovy Vary (1hr. 20min. by bus, 17kčs), Mariánské Lázné (Marienbad in German) is another spa popular among ailing European gentry and is cheaper and less touristy than its northern neighbor. The town is a stately park, designed and landscaped by Václav Skalník. At the **Lázeňska Colonnade,** the faucets go on and off magically when you wave your hand over them. There is a fountain concert every hour. (Open daily 6am-noon and 4-6pm.)

The **Čedok** office is next to the Hotel Evropa on Třebízského (tel. (0165) 25 00), in the center of town; take bus #5 from the station and get off at "Centrum." (Open Mon.-Fri. 8am-5pm.) The finest pad is easily CKM's beautiful **Junior Hotel Krakonoš (HI)** (tel. (0165) 26 24), 3km southeast of town in a gorgeous wooded location. From the train station, take bus #5 to "Centrum," then bus #12 to the top of the mountain. (HI members and ISIC holders 239kčs, nonmembers 350kčs. Reserve in advance.) Several **B-category hotels** line the main street (singles 450-600kčs, doubles 600-900kčs); the cheapest is the **Hotel Evropa** at Třebízského (tel. (0165) 20 63, -64; singles 350kčs, with bath 550kčs; doubles 550kčs, with bath 850kčs). Hotel restaurants are fairly similar in price and setting (full meals 150-250kčs). **Kavárna Charlie** (tel. (0165) 29 47) on Anglická 11 is outstanding and cheaper than most. (Full meal 150kčs. Open daily 11am-midnight.) Express **trains** come hither on the Prague-Nuremberg rail line (3/day, 3½hr., 105kčs).

Plzeň   Eighty km southwest of Prague, Plzeň is immortalized as the birthplace of beer and as the source of *Plzeňsky Prazdroj* (Pilsner Urquell). Improve the industrial view with several rounds of the town's finest at the **Pivnice Prazdroj,** U Prazdroja 1 (tel. (019) 356 08), right outside the brewery gates and within walking distance from the train station. (Open Mon.-Fri. 10am-10pm, Sat.-Sun. 11am-9pm.) If you find the art of beer-making compelling, visit the **Brewery Museum,** housed in a 15th-century brewery at Veleslavínova 6, in the town center. (Open daily 10am-

6pm. 30kčs, students 10kčs.) The heart of Plzeň is náměstí Republiky. The lone bronze tower of the Gothic **Cathedral of St. Bartholemew** is the highest in Bohemia (102m)—its mate was destroyed by lightning (surprise) in 1525. To spend the night, contact **Čedok,** at the corner of Sedláckova and Prešovská (tel. (019) 366 40; open Mon.-Fri. 9am-noon and 1-5pm, Sat. 9am-noon). The **Sport Hotel,** U Borského porku 21 (tel. 27 17 70) borders on lush Borský park, just south of the center. (Private bath, tennis courts, and TV. 380kčs.) From the train station, take tram #1 or 2 to the right (north), get off at the post office, then cross the major street and take tram #4 to the left (south) to the last stop. The **Bíla Hora autocamping** at 28 řijna (tel. (019) 356 11) has bungalows. (400kčs/person.) Take bus #20 5km north of town. (Open May-Sept.) Plzeň lies conveniently on the Prague-Munich **train** line; alternatively, it's 2 hours and 38kčs from Mariánské Lázné.

SOUTHERN BOHEMIA

České Budějovice Founded in 1265 as a royal town at the confluence of the rivers Vltava and Malše, České Budějovice grew fat in the 16th century and then thinned out during the Thirty Years War; it earned its fame as the original home of **Budvar** (Budweiser) beer. The Budějovice-to-Linz horse-drawn railway was the first in Europe. The center is **nám. Přemysla Otakara II,** one of the largest squares in Europe, flanked by pastel Renaissance and Baroque houses and lorded over by the 72m **Black Tower,** which rewards a hefty climb with a nifty view. (Open July-Aug. daily 10am-7pm; Sept.-May Tues.-Sun. 10am-6pm. 6kčs.) Once Gothic, **St. Nicholas's Cathedral** next door received a baroque facelift during 1641-1649.

Čedok, in the southwest corner of nám. Přem. Otakara II (tel. (038) 323 81), does little but change money. (Open Mon.-Fri. 9am-6pm, Sat. 9am-noon.) **CKM,** Karla IV 14, books hostels in July and August. (Open Mon.-Fri. 9am-6pm.) **CTS International Travel Service,** at the northwest corner of the square at Krajinská 1 (tel. (038) 250 61), books private rooms in town and all over southern Bohemia. (Singles 170-300kčs. Open daily 9am-7pm.) **AT Pension,** Dukelská 15 (tel. (038) 529 34), has fabulous 2- and 3-bed rooms, some with private bath, in 2 buildings near the center. (350kčs/person includes excellent breakfast. Reception open 24hrs.) From the train station walk down Žižkova, then left on U tří lvů, and left on Dukelská. The famous **Masné Krámy beer hall** crams tables into former Renaissance meat shops and is the most interesting spot in town for people-watching. (Entrees 35-100kčs. Budvar 15kčs/½liter. Open Sun.-Thurs. 10am-11pm, Fri.-Sat. 10am-midnight.) **U Paní emy,** Široká Ulice 25, is a local favorite. (Entrees 40-90kčs. Open daily 10am-3am.)

From Prague, **buses** run almost hourly to České Budějovice (3hr., 48kčs), which makes a superb springboard for visits to nearby towns such as becastled **Tábor, Jindřichuv Hradec,** and **Třeboň.** Many Czechs come to České Budějovice to visit the fairy-tale palace of **Hluboká nad Vltavou,** 12km to the north. Several buses per day make the trip. (Palace open Tues.-Sun. 8am-noon and 1-5pm.)

Český Krumlov Scenic Český Krumlov, 24km southwest of České Budějovice, seems frozen in time; it was declared by UNESCO second only to Venice in historical value. The 13th-century **castle** walls hide a lavish interior; don't miss the Eggenberg's golden carriage or the festively painted **Masquerade Hall.** (Castle grounds open 24hrs. Interior rooms only with guided tour: May-Sept. Tues.-Sun. 8am-4pm; April and Oct. Tues.-Sun. 9am-3pm. 1/day in English, at around 2pm.) The Vltava—more moat than river at this point—cradles the town, with the castle crowning the northern perimeter. To reach the town center, **nám. Svornosti,** from the bus station, simply head towards the castle watch tower, visible from the parking lot. Once there, you'll find a number of restaurants, including the one at the **Hotel Krumlov** at no. 14. (Entrees 60-150kčs. Open daily 11am-10pm.) For cheaper rooms, try the

Tourist Service office (tel. (0337) 46 05), just inside the castle grounds at Zámek 57 (open daily 9am-6pm), which arranges stays in private rooms (60-400kčs). In addition, **CTS Travel Service** has an office at Latrán 67 (tel. (0337) 28 21), but a better idea is to arrange a room at the CTS office in České Budějovice, if you're coming from there. The tiny hostel **U Vodníka,** Povodě 55, along the banks of the Vlatava, has room for 6 lucky guests. (180kčs/person. Write ahead to U Vodníka, Povodě 55, 381 01 Český Krumlov, to reserve.)

MORAVIA

■■■ BRNO

Midway on the rail line between Prague (3¼hr., 96kčs) and Bratislava (1½hr., 60kčs), Brno is the political and cultural capital of Moravia, the wine-making eastern half of the Czech Republic. To find the principal sights, simply look up: the **Cathedral of Sts. Peter and Paul** rears above the city in a kaleidoscope of stained-glass. Atop the hill behind the cathedral, the **Špilberk Castle** fell to both Napoleon and Hitler; the latter used it as SS headquarters and executed over 80,000 prisoners in the castle's dungeons. (Under renovations in summer 1993. Dungeon open Tues.-Sun. 9am-6pm. Box office closes at 5:15pm. 20kčs, students 10kčs.) The 41 mummified bodies of the **Capuchin Cloisters** repose in Kapucínské nám., downhill from the cathedral. (Open Tues.-Sat. 9-11:45am and 2-4:30pm, Sun. 11-11:45am and 2-4:30pm. 10kčs, students 7kčs. Not for the faint of heart.) Across the street is the **Reduta Theater,** where the 11-year-old Mozart conducted in 1767. (Closed for renovations in 1993.) **Nám. Zelný trh** hosts the daily **produce market** and the **Dietrichstein Palace,** which holds the **Moravian History Museum** at #8. (Open Tues.-Sun. 9am-6pm. To permanent exhibit 20kčs, to temporary exhibits 30kčs; students, 10kčs and 16kčs.)

The **Čedok** for foreigners is at Divadelní 3 (tel. (42) 21 30 66; open Mon.-Fri. 9am-6pm, Sat. 9am-noon). **CKM,** Česká 11 (tel. (42) 21 31 47), one block northwest of nám. Svobody, books hostel rooms for 200kčs, 180kčs for students. (Open Mon.-Fri. 10am-noon and 1-4pm.) The cheapest hotel is the **Hotel Avion,** Česká 20 (tel. (42) 21 50 36; fax (42) 21 40 55). Some rooms even come with their own TVs. (Singles 425kčs, with bath 615kčs. Doubles 750kčs, with bath 990kčs.) **Hotel U Jakuba,** Jakubské nám. 6 (tel. (42) 229 91), in the shadow of St. Jacob's Church, has singles for 886kčs and doubles for 1307kčs, all with private bath. Sample from the stand-up food factory known as the **Sputnik bufet,** Česká 1/3, right off nám. Svobody, where a full meal won't run more than 30-40kčs. (Open Mon.-Fri. 7am-7pm, Sat. 7am-2pm.) The **San Marco** Restaurant, near the skinny end of nám. Svobody on Panská 6, has a stunning wine list and a selection of Czech and Italian dishes. (Entrees 30-70kčs. Open daily 10am-midnight.)

■ Near Brno

Just 20km from Brno are the stalagmites and stalactites of the **Moravian Kras** (caves), home to 4 main networks of caverns open to visitors year-round. From Brno, take the bus to Blansko (7/day, 1hr., 15kčs), then hop on a bus to the caves. The 8am and 11am buses make a 4-hour tour that hits all of the major caverns (May-Sept.). Other runs go only so far as the **Punkevní jeskyně** (4kčs one-way), a main cavern offering a 75-minute tour of the gaping **Macocha Abyss,** created when the cave roof fell in,   d a boat ride on the subterranean Punkva River. (Open Mon.-Fri. 7am-4:30pm, Sat. and Sun. 7:30am-4pm; Oct.-March Mon.-Fri. 7:30am-3pm, Sat.-Sun. 7:30am-4pm. 20kčs, students 10kčs.) Bring a sweater or jacket; it gets mighty chilly, even in summer.

A major stop on the bus line from České Budějovice and Brno is the historically preserved Renaissance town of **Telč** (2hr. by bus from either city, 42kčs). Its pastel archways and stone watchtowers create a truly lovely square, **nám. Zachariáše z Hradce**, surprisingly free of gawking tourists. The main attraction is **Telč Castle,** erected in the late 14th and early 15th centuries. (Open Tues.-Sun. 8am-noon and 1-5pm; April and Sept.-Oct. 9am-noon and 1-4pm. 25kčs, students 10kčs.) The castle complex at the far, narrow end of the town square also houses a **museum** of Moravian and Telč history (same hrs. as above; 8kčs, students 4kčs), and a **gallery** of modern art by Jan Zrzavý, who once held the title of National Artist of Czechoslovakia. (Same hrs. as above, plus Nov.-March Tues.-Fri. and Sun. 9am-noon and 1-4pm, Sat. 9am-4pm. 10kčs, students 5kčs.) To reach the town square from the bus center, take a left out of the parking lot; at the end of the street, take a left down Masarykova and look for the green, red, and yellow trail markers at Na parkane. Follow the cobblestones to the left, then cross the stone bridge on the right. The **Hotel Černý orel** at #7 (tel. (066) 96 22 21; B-category) keeps comfortable rooms (singles 430kčs, with bath 490kčs; doubles 580kčs, with bath 750kčs), and a restaurant with patio seating on the square. (Entrees 25-150kčs; menu in English. Open Mon.-Sat. 7am-11pm, Sun. 7am-10pm.)

Hungary (Magyarország)

US$1	= 93Ft (forints, or HUF)	100Ft =	US$1.07
CDN$1	= 74Ft	100Ft =	CDN$1.41
UK£1	= 144Ft	100Ft =	UK£0.69
IR£1	= 135Ft	100Ft =	IR£0.74
AUS$1	= 61Ft	100Ft =	AUS$1.65
NZ$1	= 51Ft	100Ft =	NZ$1.94
SAR1	= 19Ft	100Ft =	SAR5.17
Country Code: 36		International Dialing Prefix: 00	

The people of Hungary combine an exacting attention to detail with a warm Mediterranean affability that has miraculously survived the apathy associated with the late communist system. Academic minds will marvel at the centuries-old tension between Magyar ethnicity and foreign domination. Mongols ravaged the country in the 13th century, and from the 16th to 19th century, Turks and Habsburgs plundered it. World War I redistributed two thirds of its territory, and after World War II, the Soviet Union transformed Hungary into a buffer state with a puppet government. In 1956, Hungarian patriots led by Imre Nagy rose up against this repression with a passion that was crushed only by Soviet tanks; the bullet holes that dot so many of Budapest's buildings recall this bloody uprising. In the fall of 1989 the Hungarian people fulfilled the aspirations of the previous generation and broke away from the Soviet orbit in a bloodless revolution.

Today, although still aglow with their political triumphs, Hungarians are beginning to experience a vicious economic hangover. Inflation is rapidly reducing one quarter of the population to poverty. High prices for necessities, widespread unemployment, and yawning inequities in wealth harshly remind Hungarians of the desperate side of liberty. The country is resigning itself to a painful decade of transition.

In the wake of the Communist abdication, Hungary struggles to dispel its reputation as an underdeveloped, "Eastern bloc" nation. Aside from transitional economic woes, the most visible vestiges of the old regime are benevolent: efficient public transportation, clean parks and streets, and a low incidence of violent crime. In addition, the architectural integrity of Hungary's beautiful city centers was mercifully preserved, although somber cement apartment blocks skirt major cities like so many massive gravestones.

Hungarian culture has flourished throughout the country's tumultuous history: musical contributions include 19th-century composer Ferenc (Franz) Liszt, as well as 20th-century geniuses Zoltán Kodály and Béla Bartók. Many current musical groups enjoy worldwide respect, and theater and film also thrive under the direction of such luminaries as István Szabó and Miklós Jancsó. Folk music collectors should look for tapes by Sebestyén Márta.

With a fifth of Hungary's population, Budapest dominates the country, and no provincial center is more than a 3-hour train ride—through fertile corn and sunflower fields—away from the capital city.

GETTING THERE AND GETTING AROUND

Budapest's **Ferihegy airport** handles all international traffic, including **MALÉV,** the national airline. Hungary's domestic transport network resembles a wheel with Budapest at the hub and rail lines as the spokes. Use buses to travel around the rim of the wheel, or return to Budapest for connections.

Hungarian **trains** *(vonat)* are reliable and inexpensive; Eurail is valid. *Személyvonat* are excruciatingly slow; *gyorsvonat* trains (listed in red) cost the same and move at least twice as fast. All of the larger provincial towns are accessible by the blue express rail lines *(sebesvonat or expressz)*. The express fare from Budapest to any of the provincial cities should cost between 300-700Ft each way, including a seat reservation (required on trains marked with an "R" on schedules). Hungarian train terms include *érkezés* (arrival), *indúlás* (departure), *vágány* (track), and *állomás* or *pályaudvar* (station, abbreviated *pu.*). All travelers under 26 get a 33% discount. The ISIC commands discounts of up to 50% on international tickets from IBUSZ, Express, and station ticket counters. Show your ISIC and repeat "student," or the Hungarian, *diák* (DEE-ahk). International tickets are no longer the bargain they once were (from Budapest to: Vienna one way second-class US$26; Prague US$46; Warsaw US$52). A trans-Siberian ticket, once US$48, now runs about US$300. Between countries in Eastern Europe, buying a ticket to the border and then another one on the train sometimes works out cheaper.

The extensive **bus** system is cheap but crowded; most routes between provincial cities pass through Budapest. The **Erzsébet tér** bus station in Budapest posts schedules and fares. Inter-city bus tickets are purchased on the bus (get there early if you want a seat), while tickets for local city buses must be bought in advance from a newsstand (18-27Ft) and punched on board. Those who **hitchhike** use main roads and wave their hands to signal approaching cars.

Either IBUSZ or Tourinform can provide a brochure about **cycling** in Hungary that includes maps, suggested tours, sights, accommodations, bike rental locations, repair shops, and recommended border-crossing points. Write to the tree-huggers at the **Hungarian Nature-Lovers' Federation (MTSZ),** 1065 Budapest, Bajcsy-Zsilinszky út 31, or the **Hungarian Cycling Federation,** 1146 Budapest, Szabó J. u. 3, for more information. Some rail stations rent bicycles to passengers.

HUNGARY ESSENTIALS

Perhaps the best word for foreigners in Hungary to know is **IBUSZ,** the Hungarian national travel bureau. Their offices throughout the country can make room arrangements, change money, sell train tickets, and charter tours. Snare the pamphlet *Tourist Information Hungary* and the monthly entertainment guides *Programme in Hungary* and *Budapest Panorama* (all free and written in English). **Express,** the former national student travel bureau, handles youth hostels and changes money. Regional travel agencies are more helpful than IBUSZ and Express in the outlying areas. **Tourinform** is a fantastically helpful non-profit information service with locations in 15 of Hungary's 19 counties. They have many free and helpful brochures and answer all your questions about Budapest and the rest of Hungary, often serving as interpreters.

Change money only as you need it. If you save exchange receipts and show your passport, you can convert 50% back into Western currency. Make sure to keep some Western cash to purchase visas, international train tickets, and (less often) private accommodations (as hard currency sometimes results in lower prices and better service). **American Express** offices in Budapest, and IBUSZ offices around the country, cash traveler's checks for a 6% commission. **Cash advances on credit cards** are available at a few locations in Budapest. All major credit cards are accepted at more expensive hotels and at many shops and restaurants; the smaller ones accept only American Express. The best rates during summer 1993 could be found at branches of the OTP, IBUSZ, and Agricultural banks. New Zealand dollars cannot be exchanged here, so pack another currency. At the few exchange offices with extended hours, the rates are generally poor. Black market exchanges are illegal yet common, but the rates offered are rarely favorable enough (an extra 10%) to risk the large chance of being swindled.

Many addresses are shedding their Russian names in the wake of the 1989 revolution. Tourist brochures, maps, subway-station signs, and even street signs may not reflect the latest purges, so get the most recent map available. Hungarian addresses usually involve one of the following: *utca,* abbreviated *u.* (street); *út* and the related *útja* (avenue); *tér* and the related *tere* (square; but may be a park, plaza, or boulevard); *híd* (bridge); and *körút,* abbreviated *krt.* (ring-boulevard). A single name such as Baross may be associated with several of these in completely separate parts of a city—i.e. Baross út, Baross u., Baross tér, etc. Numbers on the two sides of a street are not always in sync.

Business hours in Hungary are Monday to Friday from 9am to 6pm (7am-7pm for food stores). Banks close around 3pm on Friday, and many businesses close on Sundays, but hours keep expanding as Marx gives way to Mammon. Larger shopping centers and food stores may also sell food on Sundays. Tourist bureaus usually open Monday-Saturday 8-9am and close 5-6pm (some open until noon on Sun.) in summer; in winter these hours shrink to Monday through Friday 10am to 4pm. Museums are usually open Tuesday to Sunday 10am to 6pm, with occasional free days on Tuesday. With an ISIC you can often get in free or pay 50%. Nothing is open on national holidays, Christian holidays, May 1, and August 20, March 15, and Oct. 23.

Should you get sick, contact your embassy for lists of **English-speaking doctors** in Budapest. Some travelers have supported themselves in Budapest for years by teaching English at an English-language school or through private tutoring. Contracts run for a semester. For more information, contact the **English Teachers' Center** through the American Embassy, or look for listings in the libraries of the American and British embassies. You can also try calling the myriad private schools that advertise in *Budapest Week* or on posters.

Communication Hungarian belongs to the Finno-Ugric family of languages. Elementary German can be a great advantage when traveling here. English works in Budapest, but in the countryside, especially in Eastern Hungary, even German may fail. Western newspapers and magazines are available in many Budapest newsstands and in large hotels. Hungary's English-language paper *Daily News* is supposedly published weekly. The English language *Budapest Week* (62Ft at American Express) has excellent listings, survival tips, helpful hints, and insightful articles about life in Hungary. A few starters for pronunciation: *c* is pronounced "ts" as in *cats*; *cs* is "ch" as in *Ch*alupa; *gy* is "dy" as in the French *adieu*; *ly* is "y" as in *yam*, *s* is "*sh*" as in *sh*ovel; *sz* is "*s*" as in "Seattle"; *zs* is "*jh*" as in pleasure, and *a* is "*a*" as in *a*lways. The first syllable usually gets the emphasis. Some useful tidbits: *jó napot* (YOH naw-pot, "hello"); *köszönöm* (KUR-sur-nurm, "thank you"); *mikor?* (MI-kor? "when?"); *hol?* (where?); *kérem* (KAY-rem, "please"); *kérek* (KEH-rek, "I'd like..."); *viszontlátásra* (VI-sohn-tlah-tah-shraw, "goodbye"); *fizetni szeretnék* (VI-zet-ney

SEH-ret-nayk, "I'd like to pay"); *nem értem* (NEM AYR-tem, "I don't understand"); *beszél angolul/németül* (BES-el AWN-gohlul/NAY-met-yuhl, "Do you speak English/ German?"); *viz* ("water"); *sür* (SHUR, "beer"). In personal names, the family name precedes the given name.

Almost all telephone numbers in the countryside now have a "3" as their first digit. Hungary's pay **phones** require a 5Ft piece every 3 minutes for local calls. Wait for the tone and dial slowly. For long distance, dial 06 before the area code (2 digits long, except in Budapest). International calls require red phones or new, digital-display blue ones, found at large post offices, on the street, and in metro stations. The blue phones tend to cut you off after 3-9 minutes, but red phones are more difficult to find. At 200Ft per minute to the U.S., telephones suck money so fast you need a companion to feed them. Direct calls can also be made from the telephone office in Budapest, with a 3-minute minimum to the U.S. To call collect, dial 09 for the international operator. For AT&T's **USA Direct,** put in a 20Ft coin (which you'll get back), dial 00, wait for the second dial tone, then dial 36 01 11. June 1992 saw the installation of new telephones that used a phone-card, purchasable at post offices.

The **mail** works fine (airmail—*légiposta*—to the U.S. takes 5-10 days). Because Hungary's per capita telephone rate is the second-lowest in Europe (Albania wins), it is very common to send **telegrams,** even across town. Ask for a telegram form (*távirati ürlapot*) and fill it out before returning to the counter. Post offices are indicated by the sign POSTA. (Generally open Mon.-Fri. 8am-7pm, Sat. 8am-1pm.) When using hand signals for numbers, remember to start with the thumb for "1"—holding up your index finger means "wait."

Accommodations and Camping

Most travelers stay in **private homes** booked through a tourist agency. (Singles 700-1200Ft. Doubles 800-2000Ft.) If you stay fewer than 4 nights, you must pay a surcharge (30% of one night's stay). Singles are scarce; it's worth finding a roommate, because solo travelers often must pay for a double room. Agencies may initially try to foist off their most expensive quarters on you; be persistent. Outside of Budapest, the best and cheapest office is usually the regional one. After staying a few nights, you can often make arrangements with the owner directly, and avoid the tourist agencies' 20-30% commission. You can also ditch the agencies and find your own room where there is a sign for *szoba kiadó* or *Zimmer frei.* Make sure any private room you rent is near the center or easily accessible by public transport. Renting a private room is often less an introduction to Hungarian life than a business transaction. Many owners keep their quarters and lives walled off from the traveler; you receive a front-door key and sometimes kitchen access. Others, however, will offer a gracious welcome.

Some towns have cheap **hotels** (doubles 1200-1600Ft). As the hotel system develops and room prices rise, **hostels** will become more attractive. Many can be booked at **Express** or sometimes the regional tourist office after you arrive (250-700Ft). From late June through August, **university dorms** metamorphose into hostels. Locations change annually; register through an Express office in the off-season, at the dorm itself during the summer. The staff at Express generally speak German, sometimes English. They cannot book hostels in another city. In 1992 hostels required neither HI cards nor sleep sacks, though that may change as Hungary's tourist industry integrates with Western Europe's. Over 100 **campgrounds** are sprinkled throughout Hungary, charging about 500Ft per day for 2 people. You can often rent 2-person bungalows for 800-1200Ft and 4-person jobs for about 2000Ft, but you must pay for unfilled spaces. Most sites are open from May through September. Tourist offices offer the comprehensive booklet *Camping Hungary,* which is revised annually. For more information and maps, contact the **Hungarian Camping and Caravanning Club** in Budapest, or Tourinform.

Food and Drink

With its fantastic concoctions of meat, spices, and fresh vegetables, many find Magyar cuisine among the finest in Europe. Paprika, Hungary's chief agricultural export, colors most dishes red. In Hungarian restaurants, called *vendégl* or *étterem*, you may begin with *gulyásleves*, a delicious and hearty beef soup seasoned with paprika—often a meal in itself for only 100-120Ft. *Borjúpaprikás* is a veal dish with paprika, often accompanied by small potato-dumpling pastas called *gnocchi*. Vegetarians can find the tasty *rántott sajt* (fried cheese) and *gombapörkölt* (mushroom stew) on most menus. *Túrós táska* is a chewy pastry pocket filled with sweetened cottage cheese. *Somlói galuska,* Hungarian sponge cake, is a fantastically rich and delicious concoction of chocolate, nuts, and cream. Hungarians claim that the Austrians stole the recipe for *rétes* and called it *strudel.*

Few Hungarians can afford restaurants; finding a genuine, "local" eatery is a stretch. Gypsy music often spells tourist trap; it may be worth your while to plow through a few crowds and find a more remote Gypsy eatery. Menus are posted outside most every restaurant; check your bill, although discrepancies are rare. Bread is generally included in the meal, though a 10% gratuity has become standard, even if the bill includes a service charge (which goes to the management); give the money to the waiter when you pay. A gypsy musician expects about 150Ft from your table, depending on the number of listeners. A *csárda* is a traditional inn, a *bisztró* an inexpensive restaurant, and an *ön kiszolgáló étterem* a cheap cafeteria. Since precious few menus outside Budapest are written in English, a dictionary can spare you from a point-and-pray meal. For pastry and coffee, look for a *cukrászdá,* where a sweet-tooth can fulfill relentless desire for dangerously few forints. *Kávé* means espresso. **Salátabárs** vend deli concoctions.

Vegetarians may have trouble filling up in Hungarian restaurants, but fresh fruit and vegetables abound on stands and in produce markets. Supermarkets (look for the **"ABC"** sign) sell dry goods and dairy products; the fresh milk is delectable but turns sour within 48 hours. **Julius Meinl** is the largest national supermarket chain. Except "non-stops," most shops close from 1pm on Saturday to Sunday morning.

Hungarians are justly proud of their wines. Most famous are the red *Egri Bikavér* ("Bull's Blood of Eger") and the white *Tokaji* wines (150Ft/bottle at a store, 300Ft at a restaurant). Fruit schnapps *(pálinka)* are a national specialty; you can try them in most cafés and bars. Local beers are good; the most common is *Dreher.*

■■■ BUDAPEST

At once a cosmopolitan European capital and the stronghold of Magyar nationalism, Budapest has awakened from its 40-year Communist coma with the same vigor that helped rebuild the city from the rubble of WWII. Though endowed with an architectural majesty befitting the former number-2 city of the Habsburg empire and an intellectual and cultural scene often compared to that of Paris, the squares and cafés of Budapest retain a worn-at-the-elbows charm lacking in its more fastidious Western counterparts. Today, the city manages to maintain charm and spirit—refusing to buckle under the relentless siege of Western glitzification—while pursuing the total abnegation of all things Russian.

ORIENTATION AND PRACTICAL INFORMATION

Budapest straddles the **Danube River** in north-central Hungary, 250km downstream from Vienna. The city is enclosed by a traffic ring, more concrete to the east of the **Duna** (Danube)—where St. Istvan körút, Teréz körút, Erzsébet körút, József körút, and Ferenc körút firmly link arms—than in the nebulous west. **Óbuda** (Old Buda), in the northwest, was the center of the original Roman settlement. Hilly **Buda** on the west bank embraces the **Castle District;** on the east side buzzes **Pest,** the heart of the modern city. Three central bridges, **Széchenyi lánchíd** (Chain Bridge), slender, white **Erzsébet híd** (Elizabeth Bridge), and green **Szabadság híd,** bind the halves together. Streets arbitrarily change names from one block to the next.

Moszkva tér (Moscow Square), is where virtually all trams and buses start or end their routes. One Metro stop away, **Batthány tér** lies opposite the Parliament build-

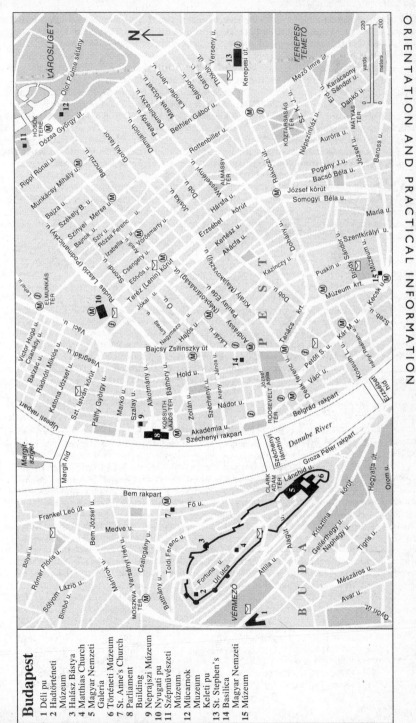

Budapest

1 Déli pu
2 Hadtörténeti
  Múzeum
3 Halász Bástya
4 Matthias Church
5 Magyar Nemzeti
  Galéria
6 Történeti Múzeum
7 St. Anne's Church
8 Parliament
  Building
9 Néprajszi Múzeum
10 Nyugati pu
11 Szépmüvészeti
  Múzeum
12 Mücarnok
  Muzeum
  Keleti pu
13 St. Stephen's
  Basilica
14 Magyar Nemzeti
  Múzeum
15 Múzeum

ing on the west bank; this is the starting node of the HÉV commuter railway. Budapest's 3 Metro lines converge at **Deák tér,** at the core of Pest's loosely concentric ring boulevards, beside the main international bus terminal at **Erzsébet tér.**

Addresses in Budapest begin with a Roman numeral representing one of the city's 22 districts. In mailing addresses, the middle 2 digits of the postal code correspond to the district number. Many street names occur more than once; always check the district as well. Streets are in the process of shedding their Communist names; an up-to-date map is essential. The American Express and Tourinform offices have excellent free tourist maps, or pick up the *Belaváros Idegenforgalmi Térképe* at any metro stop (80Ft).

Tourist Offices: Tourinform, V, Sütö u. 2 (tel. 117 98 00). Off Deák tér around the corner from Porsche Hungaria. M: "Deák tér." Remarkably helpful, multilingual tourist office providing info from sight-seeing tours to opera performances to the location of Aikido dojos. Open daily 8am-8pm. Sight-seeing, accommodation bookings and travel services available at **IBUSZ, Cooptourist,** and **Budapest Tourist** (offices in train stations and tourist centers). Ask for their free and very helpful quarterly *For Youth.*

Budget Travel: Express, V, Zoltán u. 10 (tel. 111 64 18), 2 blocks south of the Parliament building. M: "Kossuth Lajos." Some reduced international plane fares for the under-26 crowd, youth and ISIC fares on trains to Eastern Europe (same reductions available at station ticket offices). Open Mon.-Thurs. 8:30am-4:30pm, Fri. 8:30am-3pm. **Main office,** V, Szabadság tér 16 (tel. 131 77 77), sells ISICs (250Ft). Open daily 7am-7pm. **Accommodations office** in Keleti station (tel. 142 17 72) may be able to sell reduced tickets by 1994. Open daily 8am-7pm.

Embassies: Unless otherwise noted, embassy and consulate services are in the same building. **U.S.,** V, Szabadság tér 12 (tel. 112 64 50, after hours 153 05 66). M: "Kossuth Lajos," then walk 2 blocks down Akademia and take a left on Zoltán. Check out the plaque honoring Cardinal Jozef Mindszenty, an important figure in the 1956 revolt who spent his remaining years as a refugee in the embassy. Open Mon.-Fri. 8:30am-noon and 2-4pm. **Canada,** XII, Budakeszi út 32 (tel. 176 77 11). Take bus #22 5 stops from "Moszkva tér." Open Mon.-Fri. 8am-4pm. **U.K.,** V, Harmincad u. 6 (tel. 266 28 88), near *Café Gerbeaud.* M: "Vörösmarty tér." Open Mon.-Thurs. 9am-4:30pm, Fri. 9am-1:30pm. **New Zealanders** should contact the British embassy. **Australia,** VI, Délibáb u. 30 (tel. 153 42 33), parallel to Andrassy ut. M: "Hösök tér." Open Mon.-Fri. 8am-4pm. **Czech Republic,** VI, Szegfü u. 4 (tel. 142 17 54). Open Mon.-Fri. 8:30am-1pm. **Slovakia,** XIV, Stefánia út 22-24 (tel. 251 18 60). **Poland,** VI, Városligeti fasor 16 (tel. 122 84 37). **Russia,** VI, Bajza út. 35 (tel. 252 12 28). Open Mon., Wed., and Fri. 9am-3pm.

Currency Exchange: Save your receipts to change up to 50% of what you exchanged back into hard currency (at all IBUSZ offices and most other change bureaux). **OTP Bank** or **Penta Tours,** on Váci u. 19-21. Probably the best rates in town. Open Mon.-Fri. 9am-12:30pm and 1:30-5pm. **IBUSZ,** at V, Petőfi tér 3, just north of Elizabeth *(Erzsébet)* Bridge. Cash advances on Diners Club and Visa (forints only). Performs most AmEx banking services. Open 24hrs. **Magyar Külkeres Kedelmi Bank** (Foreign Trade Bank), V, Szent István tér 11. Open Mon.-Thurs. 8am-2pm and Fri. 8am-1pm. Another **branch** at V, Türr István u. 9, 1 block south of Vörösmarty tér. Open Mon.-Fri. 8am-8pm and Sat. 9am-2pm. Both offices give Visa and MasterCard cash advances (forints only) and cash traveler's checks in US$ for 2% commission.

American Express: V, Deák Ferenc u. 10 (tel. 266 86 80). M: "Vörösmarty tér." Sells Traveler's Cheques for cash, Moneygrams, or cardholders' personal checks. ATM for AmEx cards; cashes traveler's checks in US$ for a 6% commission. Cash advances only in forints. Free maps; on Thurs. and Fri. pick up the free *Budapest Week* here as well. Holds mail. Address mail as: "<u>SCHROEER</u>, Nikki, American Express, Hungary Kft., Deák Ferenc u. 10, H-1052 Budapest, Hungary." Open Mon.-Fri. 9am-6pm, Sat. 9am-2pm; Oct.-June Mon.-Fri. 9am-5pm, Sat. 9am-1pm.

Post Office: Poste Restante at V, Városház u. 18 (tel. 118 48 11). Open Mon.-Fri. 8am-8pm, Sat. 8am-3pm. 24-hr. **branches** at Nyugati station, VI, Teréz krt. 105-

107, and Keleti station, VIII, Baross tér 11c. After-hours staff does not speak English. You may be better off sending mail via American Express.

Telephones: V, Petőfi Sándor u. 17. English-speaking staff. **Fax.** Open Mon.-Fri. 8am-8pm, Sat.-Sun. 8am-3pm. At other times, try the post office. Budapest numbers begin with 1 or 2. **Local operator:** 01. Red phones for international calls. **City code:** 1.

Flights: Ferihegy Airport, tel. 157 21 22 for reservations, 157 71 55 for general information, 156 65 78 for departures, and 157 84 06 for arrivals. Easily reached by *Volánbusz,* every ½-hr. daily 5am-9pm to and from Erzsébet tér (M: "Deák tér," ½hr., 150Ft). Or take Metro line 3 to "Kőbánya-Kispest," then bus #93. Both the black and red buses go to terminal 1, but only the reds go to departures at terminal 2. **Youth** (under 26) as well as **standby** (under 25) **flight** tickets available at the **Malév** office V, Dorottya u. 2 (tel. 118 51 22), on Vörösmarty tér (open Mon.-Fri. 7:30am-4:30pm) or any other travel agency. There's a **hostel** (Asmara Youth Hostel, Bajcsy Zsilinszky u. 51) at the airport for early birds who fly at dawn.

Trains: (tel. 122 78 60 domestic, 142 91 50 international). Those under 26 get a 33% discount on international tickets. Show your ISIC. The 3 main *pályaudvar* (stations), (**Keleti pu., Nyugati pu.,** and **Déli pu.**) are also Metro stops. Trains to and from a given location do not necessarily stop at the same station. 2nd class to **Vienna** (10/day, 3½hrs., US$27), **Prague** (5/day, 8hr., US$47), Warsaw (2/day, US$53), Berlin (5/day, US$62), and Bucharest (6/day, US$88). Catch the **Orient Express** in Budapest—1 train daily from Berlin on its way to Bucharest.

Buses: Volánbusz (tel. 117 29 66 for domestic service, 117 25 62 for international service.) **Main station,** V, Erzsébet tér. M: "Deák tér." **Luggage storage** available. Several buses/week to İstanbul (US$50), Venice (US$55), and Bucharest. Buses to the Czech Republic, Slovakia, Poland, Romania, Turkey, and Ukraine depart from the **Népstadion** terminal on Hungária körút 48-52. M: "Népstadion." Domestic buses are usually cheaper than trains, but may take slightly longer. Buses to the Danube Bend leave from the **Árpád Híd** station.

Public Transportation: The **Metro** is rapid and punctual; built in 1896, it was the first in continental Europe. Three numbered lines—line 1 is yellow, line 2 is red, and line 3 is blue. An "M" indicates a stop, but you won't always find the sign on the street; it's better to look for stairs leading down. All *Trafik* shops and some sidewalk vendors sell tickets (*villamos jegy,* 25Ft) for buses, trams, and the Metro, valid through Óbuda. You're supposed to punch your ticket on board trams and buses, but few people do; the enforcement largely appears at the beginning of the month. Monthly passes (1100Ft) are valid from the 1st of one month through the 5th of the next. Some buses take over when the subway shuts down (Metro open 4:30am-11:10pm). The **HÉV commuter rail** runs between Batthyány tér in Buda and Szentendre, 40min. north on the Danube Bend. Trains leave about every 15min.

Hydrofoils: MAHART International Boat Station, V, Belgrád rakpart (tel. 118 12 23), near the *Erzsébet* bridge, has info and ticketing. Open Mon.-Fri. 8am-4pm. Or try the **IBUSZ** office at Károly Krt. 3 (tel. 122 24 73; M: "Astoria"). Open Mon.-Fri. 9am-5pm. Arrive at the docks 1hr. before departure for customs and passport control. Be sure to inquire about prices before setting off on an international voyage; the return ticket may be astronomically expensive. Eurailpasses may garner a discount on tickets bought through the Austrian company **DDSG.**

Taxis: Főtaxi, tel. 111 61 16. 32Ft/km. **Volántaxi,** tel. 166 66 66. 20Ft, plus 36Ft/km. Avoid the Mercedes-Benz taxis, which charge double the jalopy fee.

Hitchhiking: Hitching in the Budapest area has become especially dangerous of late. Those who are hitching south to Szeged and Belgrade (along M5 and E75) take tram #2 from "Soroksári út" to the end of the line; they then switch to bus #23, then bus #4. Hitchers heading west to Győr and Vienna or southwest to Lake Balaton and Zagreb take bus #12 from "Moszkva tér" out to "Budaörsi út," then switch to bus #72. **Kenguru,** VIII, Kofarago u. 15 (tel. 138 20 19; M: "Astoria") is a carpool service charging 4Ft/km. Open Mon.-Fri. 8am-6pm, Sat. 8am-2pm.

Bookstore: Kossuth Könyvesbolt, V, Vörösmarty tér 4, to the right of Café Gerbeaud. English-language tourist books and paperbacks. Open daily 10am-6pm.

Laundromat: Mosószalon, V, József Nádor tér 9. Wash: 210Ft/5kg. Dry: 90Ft/15min. Look for the gumball-hue tile column in the window. Open Mon., Wed., and Fri. 7am-3pm, Tues. and Thurs. 11am-7pm.

Gay and Lesbian Services: tel. 138 24 19; open daily 8am-4pm. Gay life in Budapest is almost underground; cafés and bars open and close in a few weeks. Public tolerance is lacking, and attacks from skinheads are not uncommon.

Pharmacies: The following are open 24hrs.: I, Széna tér 1 (tel. 202 18 16); VI, Teréz krt. 41 (tel. 111 44 39); IX, Boráros tér 3 (tel. 117 07 43); and IX, Üllöi út 121 (tel. 133 89 47). At night, ring the bell to rouse the owner; you will be charged a slight fee for the service.

Emergencies: Ambulance: tel. 04. **Fire:** tel. 05. **Police:** tel. 07. Emergency medical care is free for foreigners. List of English-speaking doctors available at the U.S. embassy. **24-hr. Emergency Medical Service** (English spoken) tel. 118 82 12.

ACCOMMODATIONS AND CAMPING

Travelers arriving in July and August will be swarmed at the train station by representatives of various hostels. If you'd rather rent a private room or flat, seek out a less voracious onlooker; just make sure the room is near public transportation and see your chamber before you pay (generally 600-1000Ft/person).

Private Accommodations Services

Nascent accommodation services and new branches of established organizations are springing up like wildfire. The rates (700-1200Ft/person) depend on the category and location. Arrive early (around 8am) and you may get a single for 600Ft or a double for 900Ft. It's hard to find a cheap, centrally located room for only 1 or 2 nights. Travelers who stay for more than 4 nights can haggle for a delicious rate.

IBUSZ 24-hr. accommodation office at V, Petőfi tér 3 (tel. 118 39 25 or 118 57 76). Offers the most rooms in Budapest. The streets outside IBUSZ offices swarm with Hungarians pushing "bargain" rooms; quality varies, but they're legal.

Budapest Tourist, V, Roosevelt tér 5 (tel. 117 35 55), near the *Forum Hotel,* 10min. from Deák tér, on the Pest end of the Chain Bridge. No min. stay. Singles 800-1000Ft. Doubles 1600-3000Ft. Open Mon.-Fri. 8am-6pm, Sat. 8am-2pm; Oct.-June Mon.-Fri. 8am-6pm. **Branch offices** around the city keep the same hours.

Cooptourist, VI, Bajcsy-Zsilinszky út. 17 (tel. 111 70 34 or 111 32 44). Doubles 1200-1600Ft. Triples 1500Ft. Claims all rooms are in districts VI and VII. 30% surcharge for stays of fewer than 3 nights. English spoken. Open Mon.-Fri. 9am-5pm.

Duna Tours (tel. 131 45 33 or 111 56 30), next to Cooptourist, allows travelers to see rooms before accepting them. Doubles 1500Ft. Quads 1600-1800Ft. English-speaking staff. Claims their rooms are only in district V and VI. Open Mon.-Thurs. 9:30am-noon and 12:30-5pm, Fri. 9:30am-noon and 12:30-4pm, Sat. 9am-1pm; Oct.-April Mon.-Fri. 8am-4:15pm.

To-Ma Tour, V, Oktober 6 út. 22 (tel. 153 08 19), promises to find you a central room, even if only for one night. Doubles 1200-2000Ft, with private bathroom 2400Ft. Triples 2200Ft. Reservations by phone or fax during the summer are recommended. Open Mon.-Fri. 9am-noon and 1-8pm, Sat.-Sun. 9am-5pm.

Hostels

Most hostel-type accommodations, including university dorm rooms, are under the aegis of **Express.** Try their office at V, Semmelweis u. 4 (tel. 117 66 34 or 117 86 00); leave Deák tér on Tanács krt., head right on Gerlóczy u., and the first left is Semmelweis u. Before accepting lodging at the rail station, make sure you're not being brought to a private hostel trying to wedge many people into an eensy 2-room flat.

Open year-round

Diaksportszálló, XIII, Dózsa György u. 152 (tel. 140 85 85 or 129 86 44). Entrance on Angyaföldi, 50m from the "Dózsa György" Metro stop. Dirt cheap and exceptionally social. Bar occupied 24hrs, as is reception. Quiet upstairs—don't worry.

This is hostel #4 of the "More Than Ways Company"—ask for it by name. 8-bed rooms 360Ft/person. Doubles 480Ft/person. Quads 460Ft/person.

Back Pack Guesthouse, XI, Takács Menyhért u. 33 (formerly Antal János u.; tel. 185 50 89). From *Keleti pu.* or the city center take bus #1, 7, or 7A (black numbers) heading toward Buda and disembark at "Tétenyi u ," after the rail bridge. From the bus stop, head back under the bridge, turn left, and follow the street parallel to the train tracks for 3 blocks. Look for the small green signs. One of the homiest hostels in the area. 26 beds; call ahead. The staff is young, friendly, and helpful. 5- and 8-bed rooms. Bulletin board lists trips, programs and information. Bike rental available. No curfew. 450-520Ft. Hot showers, breakfast, private locker, use of kitchen and TV included. Sheets 50Ft.

ASMARA youth hostel, XVIII, Bajcsy Zsilinszky u. 51, near the airport. Metro: "Köbánya-Kispest." From the Metro stop, take bus #93 and get off at "Majus 1. tér;" it's 2 blocks to the right. Common bathroom and kitchen. 560Ft.

Summer hostels

Almost all dorms of the **Technical University** *(Műegyetem)* become youth hostels in summer; they're conveniently located in district XI, around Móricz Zsigmond Körtér. Take the Metro to "Kalvin Ter," then ride tram #47 or 49 to "M. Zsigmond." For more information, call the **International Student Center** at 166 77 58 or 166 50 11, ext. 1469. During the summer the center also has an office in Schönherz.

Schönherz, XI, Irinyi u. 42 (tel. 166 54 60), one Metro stop after "Universitas." With 1300 beds, the largest dorm around. This high-rise has well-kept quads with bathrooms and refrigerators. Sauna 100Ft; open 7-9pm. 500Ft. Doubles 700Ft/person. Triples 600Ft/person. 50Ft surcharge without HI membership. Breakfast 100-250Ft. Information office open 8am-midnight.

Vasarhely, XI, Krusper u. 2-4 (tel. 185 37 94), on the southwestern corner of the Technical University. One of the fairest dorms of all—all rooms have a refrigerator and private shower. Doubles 700Ft/person. Quads 600Ft/person.

Bakfark hostel, Bakfark u. 1-3 (tel. 201 54 19). Metro: "Moszkva tér." Centrally located. From the Metro stop, stroll along Margit krt (formerly Mártírok útja); take the first sidestreet after Széna tér. 88 beds. Sheets, locker, and use of washing machine included. Reception open 24hrs. No curfew. Checkout 9am. Dorm beds 460Ft/person. Hostel van will pick you up at the *Keleti* rail station; call ahead.

Universitas, XI, Irinyi u. 9-11 (tel. 186 81 44). First stop after "Petőfi híd" on tram #4 or 6. Large dorm with comfortably clean doubles. 500 beds. Hall bathroom. Refrigerator in all rooms. Checkout 9am. 620Ft. Laundry machines 180Ft.

Bercsényi, XI, Bercsényi u. 28-30 (tel. 166 66 77), 1 more stop on tram #4 or 6 past Schönherz, on the sidestreet next to the large **Skala supermarket**. Newly refurbished rooms with sink and fridge. Hall bathrooms. Free parking. Reception open 24hrs. 65 doubles, 650Ft/person. Washing machine (120Ft) available.

Kek, XI, Szüret u. 2-18 (tel. 185 23 69). Take bus #27 2 stops from "Móricz Zsigmond Körtér." In a peaceful, green neighborhood on the side of the *Gellért Hill.* Kitchen. Doubles 780Ft/person, 1120Ft/person with shower.

Hotels

Budapest still has a few inexpensive hotels, often clogged with groups. Call ahead. Proprietors generally speak English. All should be registered with Tourinform.

Hotel Citadella, atop *Gellért Hill* (tel. 166 57 94). Take tram #47 or 49, 3 stops into Buda to "Móricz Zsigmond Körtér," then bus #27 to "Citadella." Perfect location. Dorm beds 420Ft. Quads with bathroom 2740Ft. Usually packed; call ahead.

Lido Hotel, III, Nánási u. 67 (tel. 188 68 65). M: "Arpád híd," then bus #106 to "Nánási." Near river and the *Aquincum* ruins. Singles 1550Ft. Doubles 2350Ft.

Hotel Kandó, III, Bécsi út 104-108 (tel. 168 20 36). Take bus #60, 7 stops from "Batthyány tér." Apartments with private showers and refrigerators. Open July-Aug. Doubles 1800Ft. Triples and quads 2000Ft.

Unikum Panzió, XI, Bod Péter u. 13 (tel. 186 12 80). M: "Deli pu.," then bus #139 south to "Zólyom Köz"; walk 2 blocks on Zólyom Köz and turn left. 15min. from the castle. Singles 2250Ft. Doubles 3000Ft. Both with shower. Breakfast included.

Camping

Camping Hungary, available at tourist offices, describes Budapest's campgrounds.

Zugligeti Niche Camping, Zugligeti út 101. Take bus #158 from "Moszkva tér" to the last stop. A chairlift at campground entrance ascends the Buda hills. Lovely wooded location. English spoken. 330Ft/person. Open March 15-Oct. 15.

Római Camping, III, Szentendrei út 189 (tel. 168 62 60). M: "Batthyány tér," then take the HÉV tram to "Római fürdö." Whopping 2000-person capacity. Disco, swimming pool, and huge green park on the site; Roman ruins nearby. Reception open 24hrs. Bungalows mid-April to mid-Oct. 960Ft for a bunk bed, 1490Ft for 2 beds side by side. Tents 425Ft/person, students 390Ft.

Hárs-hegy, II, Hárs-hegy út 5 (tel. 115 14 82). Take bus #22 from "Moszkva tér" to "Dénes utca." 2-person tent 780Ft. 2-person bungalows 1040Ft.

Diák Camping, III, Királyok útja 191. Take HÉV from "Batthyány tér" to "Római fürdö," then ride bus #34 for 10min. 160Ft/person, 80Ft/tent. Doubles, triples, quads, 10-bed dorm rooms 240Ft/person. Bike rental 30Ft/hr., 180Ft/day. Canoes 40Ft/hr., 240Ft/day.

FOOD

Even the most expensive restaurants in Budapest may be within your budget, though less costly family eateries may offer superior cuisine. Many restaurants have menus in German, some in English. An average meal runs 400-600Ft. Cafeterias lurk under **Önikiszolgáló Étterem** signs (entrees 50-160Ft). Seek out the *kifözde* or *kisvendégl* in your neighborhood for a taste of Hungarian life.

Pizzerias overrun the city, though their version is closer to the Italian pie than the popular American conception. The world's largest branch of Burger King glowers on the Oktogon, while co-conspirators Pizza Hut and McDonald's lurk nearby. Though hardly Hungarian, these juggernauts can prove life-savers with their late hours and quick service. Be as adventurous as you can; your intrigued palate will bless you for the extra effort later. Ask your hotel or hostel management to recommend a local favorite in order to avoid the many tourist traps. A 10% tip has come to be expected in many establishments.

Travelers may also rely on markets and raisin-sized 24-hour "Non-Stop" stores. Take a gander at the **produce market,** IX, Vámház krt. 1-3 at Fövám tér (open Mon. 6am-3pm), the **ABC Food Hall,** I, Batthyány tér 5-7 (open Sun. 7am-1pm) or the **Non-Stops** at V, Oktober 6, u. 5, and at V, Régi Posta u., off Váci u. past McDonald's.

Vegetárium, V, Cukor u. 3 (tel. 138 37 10). M: "Ferenciek tér." Walk up Ferenciek Tér (formerly Károlyi M. u.) to Irány u. on the right, and turn left. Vegetarian and macrobiotic dishes (tempura 300Ft). A great place to detox after a week of meat. Classical guitar in the evening. Smoke-free. English menu. Open daily noon-10pm.

Claudia, V, Bástya u., off of Kecskeméti u. (tel. 117 19 83). M: "Kálvin tér." Subterranean family restaurant with hearty, inexpensive food (entrees 220-510Ft). Generous helpings of exotic specials are a highlight. Open daily 11am-11pm.

Golden Gastronomie, V, Bécsi u. 8 (tel. 117 21 97), 2 doors down from American Express. The enticing deli fixings are provocatively displayed. Sample the salads (60-85Ft/100g) before making a choice. English spoken. Open 24hrs.

Paprika, V, Harmincad u. 4, just north of Vörösmarty tér, at the big red pepper. Hungarian fast food and a picture menu to help speed eye-hand-mouth coordination. Entrees 80-130Ft. Open Mon.-Fri. 11am-6pm, Sat.-Sun. 11am-4pm.

Shalom Restaurant, VII, Klauzál tér 2, a 10min. walk from Deák tér. (tel. 122 14 64). Elegant but inexpensive Kosher restaurant in the traditionally Jewish section of town. Entrees 300-400Ft. Open daily noon-11pm.

New York Bagels, IX, Ferenc krt. 20 (tel. 215 78 80). M: "Ferenc körút," the walk 200m toward the river. Eastern Europe's first and only bagel shop. Assorted bagels baked hourly (36Ft), with homemade spreads (140Ft). Yes, they even have lox (276Ft). Owned by a former *Let's Go* Researcher-Writer. Open 24hrs.

Sirály, VI, Bajcsy-Zsilinszky út. 9 (tel. 122 00 64 or 122 88 80). Metro: "Deák tér." Well-prepared Hungarian food (entrees 250-400Ft) and imported beer. Just the place to partake of some potent paprika. Fast and friendly service. Menus and service in English. Open daily noon-midnight.

Megálló ("Bus stop"), VII, Károly krt. 23, 2 doors to the left of the IBUSZ office. M: "Deák tér." Look beyond the ratty bearskin on the wall to the 130-item menu (available in English) which includes such temptations as "rumpsteak with gizzard in red wine." Dinner about 400Ft. Open daily 11am-11pm.

Söröző a Szent Jupáthoz, II, Dékán u. 3 (tel. 115 18 98). 50m from the "Moszkva tér" Metro stop, with an entrance on Retek. Venture down the modest stairway, then right back up into a lively garden. Portions are huge—be ready to roll yourself home. "Soup for Just Married Man" 139Ft. Entrees 200-500Ft. Open 24hrs.

Marxim, II, Kis Rókus u. 23 (tel. 115 50 36). M: "Moszkva tér." With your back to the castle, walk 200m along Margit krt. and turn left. KGB pizza and Lenin salad are among the revolutionary dishes served in barbed-wire-laden booths. Food prepared by the staff according to their abilities, consumed by the patrons according to their needs. Open Mon.-Fri. noon-1am, Sat. noon-2am, Sun. 6pm-1am.

Marcello's, XI, Bartók Béla út 40 (tel. 166 62 31). May be the only pizzeria in Budapest to use tomato sauce rather than ketchup. Pizzas 160-340Ft. Reservations suggested. Open Mon.-Sat. noon-10pm.

Cafés

The café in Budapest is more a living museum of a bygone era than just a place to be spoiled by scrumptious desserts and coffee; these amazing institutions were the training grounds for Budapest's literary, intellectual, and cultural elite. If you lounge in the hallowed eateries long enough, you'll be smothered by the atmosphere. Attendance in at least one café is *de rigeur* for any visitor; moreover, the absurdly ornate pastries are inexpensive, even in the most pretentious establishments.

Café New York, VII, Erzsébet krt. 9-11 (tel. 122 38 49). M: "Blaha Lujza tér." This remarkably embellished café was the favored locale of turn of the century "starving" *artistes*. Exquisite gilded ceilings. Cappuccino 100Ft. Ice cream and coffee delights 100-350Ft. Open daily 9am-midnight.

Ruszwurm, I, Szentháromság u. 7. Confecting since 1826 and strewn with period furniture. Stop by to relax after the majesty of *Mátyás Cathedral* down the street in the castle district. You won't be hurried on your way. Best ice cream in Budapest 20Ft/scoop. Cakes 50-70Ft. Open daily 10am-8pm.

Gerbeaud Cukrászda, V, Vörösmarty tér 7. M: "Vörösmarty tér." Formerly the meeting place of Budapest's literary elite, this café retains a stunning 19th-century elegance. Service is relaxed, what's your rush? About 90Ft. Open daily 7am-9pm.

Wiener Kaffeehaus (Bécsi Kávéház), inside the *Forum Hotel* on the Danube. Budapest's *crème de la cake.* You'd be amazed by what you can savor for 90Ft. Everything served by pink-clad Magyar maidens. Open daily 9am-9pm.

SIGHTS

Buda Strategically perched 100m above the Danube, Budapest's **Castle District** rests atop **Várhegy** (Castle Hill). Cross the **Széchenyi lánchíd** (chain bridge) and ride the *sikló* (cable car) to the top. (Open daily 7:30am-10pm. 80Ft.) Built in the 13th century, the **Budavári palota** (Royal Palace) was leveled by Mongols, Turks, Habsburgs, Nazis, and Soviets; bullet holes in the façade recall the 1956 uprising. In the post-post-war period, extensive excavations revealed artifacts from the earliest castle; they're now housed in the **Budapest History Museum.**

From the palace, stroll down Színház u. and Tárnok u. to breach **Trinity Square,** site of the Disneyesque **Fisherman's Bastion.** Behind the tower stands the neo-

Gothic **Mátyás templom** (Matthias Church), converted into a mosque literally over-night on September 2, 1541, when the Turks commenced their occupation of Buda; it remained a mosque for 145 years. (Open daily 7am-7pm.) Don't miss the stunning marble bust of Queen Elizabeth, in the **treasury.** The marble was hewn from the Italian Carrara mine—Michelangelo's master sculptures were all crafted from this material. (Treasury open daily 9am-5:30pm. 30Ft.) Outside the church is the grand **equestrian monument** of King Stephen, with his trademark double cross.

Next door sits the presumptuous **Budapest Hilton Hotel,** which incorporates the remains of Castle Hill's oldest church, an abbey built in the 13th century.

The **Liberation Monument,** a 100-foot bronze statue dedicated to the Soviet sol-diers who died "saving" Hungary from the Nazis, crowns neighboring **Gellért Hill.** Hike up to the **Citadella** from the Gellért Hotel, or take bus #27 from "Móricz Zs. körtér" 2 stops past the hotel. The view from the top is spectacular at night.

Overlooking the Elizabeth bridge near the base of Gellért Hill is the statue of **St. Gellért,** complete with colonnaded backdrop and glistening waterfall. Bishop Gellért was sent by the pope to the coronation of Hungary's first Christian King to assist the monarch in the conversion of the pagan Magyars. Disgruntled nonbeliev-ers hurled the bishop to his death from atop the hill that now bears his name.

The fabulous **Pál-völgyi caves** hide east of the *Vadaskert.* Enjoy such attractions as the Cave of the Stone Bat and the 25m-deep Radium Chamber, but be sure to wear your long johns, even in the summer—it's quite cool inside. Take the HÉV rail line from "Batthyány tér" to "Szépvölgyi," and walk away from the river to Kolosy tér; then take bus #65 or 65a across from the yellow church to "Pál-völgyi barlang." (Guided 45-min. tours May.-Sept. Tues.-Sun. on the hour 9am-4pm; Oct.-Dec. and Feb.-April Sat.-Sun. on the hour 9am-4pm. 50Ft, students 30Ft.)

Between the caves and the Castle, the **Margit híd** spans the *Duna* to the lovely **Margitsziget.** This vast island offers thermal baths, luxurious garden pathways, and shaded terraces. According to legend, King Béla IV vowed to rear his daughter Mar-garet as a nun if the nation survived the Mongol invasion of 1241. The Mongols left Hungary decimated but not destroyed, and Margaret was confined to the island con-vent. Take bus #26 from "Szt. István krt." to reach the island.

Pest Cross the Danube to reach Pest, the commercial and administrative center of the capital. Its heart is the **Inner City,** an old section rooted in the pedestrian zone of Váci u. and Vörösmarty tér. Pest's river bank sports the magnificent neo-Gothic **Parliament** building in Kossuth tér. (Tours through IBUSZ and Budapest Tourist; 1200-1500Ft.) **St. Stephen's Basilica,** 2 blocks north of Deák tér, is by far the city's largest church, with room for 8500 worshipers under its massive dome. The saint's **right hand,** one of the nation's most revered religious relics, is displayed here. (Open daily 8am-7pm. Free. Hand visible Mon.-Sat. 9am-5pm, Sun. 1-4pm; Oct.-March Mon.-Sat. 10am-4pm, Sun. 1-4pm.) The Budapest **Synagogue,** the largest active synagogue in Europe, is on the corner of Dohány and Wesselényi streets. Next door, the **Jewish Museum** devotes one haunting room to photos and docu-ments from the Holocaust. (Open April-Oct. Mon. and Thurs. 1-4pm; Tues., Wed., and Fri. 10am-1pm.)

Andrassy útja, probably the nation's grandest boulevard, extends from the edge of the Bélvaros in downtown Pest to **Hősök tere** (Heroes' Square), 2km away. *Hősök tere* is dominated by the **Millennium monument,** which showcases the nation's heroes from 896 to 1896, when the structure was erected for the great 1000th Anniversary celebration. Behind the monument, the **Városliget** (City Park) contains a permanent circus, an amusement park, a zoo, a castle, and the impressive **Széchenyi Baths.** The façade of **Vajdahunyad Castle,** intended to chronicle 1000 years of architecture, is a stone collage of Romanesque, Gothic, Renaissance, and Baroque. Rent a **rowboat** (June to mid-Sept. daily 9am-8pm, 150Ft/hr.) or **ice skates** (Nov.-March daily 9am-1pm 60Ft, daily 4-8pm 100Ft) on the lake next to the castle.

The ruins of the northern Budapest garrison town, **Aquincum,** the most impressive vestiges of the Roman occupation, continue to crumble in the outer regions of the 3rd district. The **museum** on the grounds contains a model of the ancient city, as well as musical instruments and household items. (Open April-Sept. 9am-6pm, Oct. 9am-5pm 20Ft.) The remains of the **Roman military baths** are displayed beside the overpass at Florian tér near the "Árpád híd" HÉV station. From the stop, just follow the main road away from the river.

Museums

Buda Castle (tel. 175 75 33). Contains several exhibits: the **Museum of Contemporary History** and the **Ludwig Museum,** a collection of international modern art. Open Tues.-Sun. 10am-6pm. 100Ft, students 50Ft. The **Hungarian National Gallery,** a vast hoard containing the best in Hungarian painting and sculpture over a millennium. Open Tues.-Sun. 10am-6pm. 60Ft, students 30Ft. One ticket valid for all 3 wings. **Budapest History Museum** chronicles the development of Óbuda, Buda, and Pest. Open Wed.-Sun. 10am-6pm. 60Ft, students 30Ft.

Hungarian National Museum, VIII, Múzeum Krt. 14-16 (tel. 138 21 22). Includes a chronicle of pre and post-Magyar settlements in Hungary, as well as the **Hungarian Crown Jewels,** supposedly the very crown and scepter used in the coronation of King Stephen on Christmas Day in the year 1000. Open Tues.-Sun. 10am-6pm. English guide book 75Ft. 50Ft, students 20Ft.

Néprajzi Múzeum (Museum of Ethnography), V, Kossuth Tér 12 (tel. 132 63 40). Outstanding exhibit of Hungarian folk culture, from the late 18th century to the First World War. It covers the whole cycle of peasant life and customs, from childhood to marriage (to taxes) to death. One of Budapest's best museums; in the erstwhile home of the Hungarian Supreme Court. Open Tues.-Sun. 10am-6pm. 50Ft, students free. Free on Tues.

Szépmüveszti Múzeum (Museum of Fine Arts), XIV, Hősök tere (tel. 142 97 59). Simply spectacular. One of Europe's finest collections, from Duccio to Picasso. Highlights include a room devoted to El Greco, and an exhaustive Renaissance display. Cameos from favorite impressionists. Open Tues.-Sun. 10am-6pm.

ENTERTAINMENT

Budapest offers a vast and varied cultural program. Pick up a copy of the English-language monthly *Program in Hungary* or *Budapest Panorama,* both available free at tourist offices; they contain daily listings of all concerts, operas, and theater performances in the city. The "Style" section of the weekly English-language *Budapest Sun* is another excellent source for schedules of entertainment happenings.

The **Central Theater Booking Office,** VI, Andrassy u. 18, next to the Opera House (tel. 112 00 00), and the branch at Moszkva tér (tel. 135 91 36) both sell tickets to most every performance in the city. (Open Mon.-Thurs. 10am-1pm and 2-6pm, Fri. 10am-3pm.) An extravaganza in the gilded, neo-Renaissance **State Opera House,** VI, Andrássy út 22 (tel. 153 01 70; M: "Opera"), can cost as little as 50Ft; the box-office sells unclaimed tickets for up to half off ½hr. before showtime. (Open Tues.-Sun. 10am-7pm.) The city's **Philharmonic Orchestra** is also world renowned; concerts thunder through town almost every evening from September through June. The ticket office, Vörösmarty tér 1 (tel. 117 62 22), is next to the Opera House. (Open Mon.-Fri. 10am-6pm, Sat. 10am-2pm. Tickets 600Ft.)

Summer theaters are sprinkled throughout the city. The **Margitsziget Theater,** XIII, on Margaret Island (tel. 111 24 96), features opera and Hungarian music concerts. Take tram #4 or 6 to "Margitsziget." **Mátyás Church** holds regular organ and choral recitals. (Tickets 100-320Ft.) The **Pest Concert Hall** (Vigadó), V, Vigadó tér 2, on the Danube bank near Vörösmarty tér, hosts operettas almost every other night. (Tickets 150-500Ft.) Folk-dancers stomp across the stage at the **Buda Park Theater,** XI, Kosztolányi Dezsö tér (tel. 117 62 22). Brochures and concert tickets flood from the ticket office at Vörösmarty tér 1. (Open Mon.-Fri. 11am-6pm. Tickets run 70-250Ft.) The **Budapest Spring Festival,** in late March, provides an excellent chance to see the best in Hungarian art and music.

To soak away weeks of city grime and crowded trains, sink into a **thermal bath,** a constitutive part of the Budapest experience. Post-bath massages vary from a 3-minute slap to a royal ½-hour indulgence. Many baths are meeting places for, but by no means exclusively for, Budapest's limited gay population. The **Gellért** baths are conveniently located inside *Hotel Gellért* at the base of *Gellért Hill.* Women and men frolic nude in separate baths. (Thermal bath and sauna 140Ft. 15-min. massage 160Ft. Open Mon.-Sat. 6am-7pm, Sun. 6am-4pm.) The gorgeous **Széchenyi** spread, XIV, Állatkerti u. 11 (tel. 121 03 10), beckons in the main city park *(Városliget),* near Heroes' Square. M: "Széchenyi Fürdó." Their thermal baths (130Ft) command a devoted following among the city's venerable gentry, while the large **outdoor swimming pool** (200Ft) delights their grandchildren.

Nightlife

Budapest's citizens are rapidly catching up on 35 years of foregone revelry. The clubs around the university generally attract the liveliest patrons.

Morrison's Music Pub, VI, Révay u. 25 (tel. 269 40 60), to the left of the State Opera House. M: "Opera." ½ pub, ½ hip dance club with cheap beer (80Ft). Young, international crowd. Cover 100-200Ft. Functional English red telephone booth inside. Open noon-4am.

Fregatt Pub, V, Moluár u. 26 (tel. 118 99 97), M: "Ferenciek tér," off Váci u. Filled with English-speaking 20-somethings. Beer 110Ft. Shuts down at midnight.

Véndiák (Former Student), V, Egyetem tér (tel. 117 46 03). M: "Kálvin tér," then walk up Kecskeméti u. This late-night bar also has a lively dance floor. Popular with local students. Really picks up around 2am. Cover 100Ft. Open 9pm-4am.

Tilos az Á ("A" is forbidden), VIII, Mikszáth Kálmán tér 2 (tel. 118 06 84). Walk down Baross u. from the "Kálvin tér" Metro station for 2 blocks, then turn left. This cryptic Magyar name should strike a chord with hard-core Winnie the Pooh fans. Live music and dancing until the wee hours. Open daily 8pm-4am.

Jazz Café, V, Balassi Bálint u. 25 (tel. 132 43 77). M: "Kossuth tér," across the square past the Parliament building. Live jazz nightly at 8pm. Closes at midnight.

Táncház, an itinerant folk-dancing club, where you can stomp with Transylvanians. Beginners' circle and an instructor. Locate them in *Pesti Mùsor* (Budapest's weekly entertainment guide, in Hungarian) or ask at Tourinform.

KEK, the "official" club of Eötvös Loránt University, V, Károlyi Mihály u. 9 (tel. 117 49 67). M: "Ferenciek tér." July-Aug. open Tues. 6-10pm, Thurs. 7pm-midnight.

Local, VII, at the intersection of Dob u. and Kertész u. just off Erzsébet krt. A gay club.

■■■ DANUBE BEND (DUNAKANYAR)

North of Budapest, the Danube sweeps south in a dramatic arc known as the Danube Bend *(Dunakanyar)* as it flows down from Vienna along the Slovakian border. Roman ruins from settlements of the first century dapple the countryside, and medieval palaces gaze upon the river in **Esztergom** and **Visegrád.** An artist colony thrives today amid the museums and churches of **Szentendre.** Lying within 45km of Budapest, the region offers winsome daytrips from the capital.

Hourly **buses** from Budapest's Árpád Híd metro station link these towns with the capital. If you're going directly to Esztergom, take the bus through Dorog; the 70-minute ride is almost an hour shorter than the route winding along the river through Visegrád (139Ft, stretches between the 3 cities cost 74Ft each). The suburban railway (HÉV) to Szentendre (every 15min.; 40min., 64Ft) starts from Batthyány tér in Budapest. **River boats** from Budapest are a pleasurable, if painstaking, way to visit the region; they cast off from Budapest's Vigadó tér dock 4 times per day and steam to Visegrád (3hr., 105Ft) and Esztergom (5hr., 120Ft), making short stops along the way. Not all boats stop at Szentendre (1hr., 75Ft). **Dunatours,** V, Bajcsy-Zsilinszky út. 17 (tel. 131 45 33), in Budapest, books private rooms in Szentendre. (Open Mon.-Thurs. 9:30am-noon and 12:30-5pm, Fri, 9:30am noon and 12:30-4pm.)

Szentendre Twenty km north of Budapest, Szentendre's diminutive pastel townhouses and surpassing galleries draw rampaging legions of tourists to its artsy streets. On **Templomdomb** (Church Hill) above Fő tér is Szentendre's first stone church, built in the 13th century. Across Alkotmány u. is the rival **Serbian Orthodox Church;** the church is open only for Sunday services, but the grounds house a museum of 18th-century Serbian religious art. (Open Wed.-Sun. 10am-6pm. 30Ft.) The most impressive of Szentendre's museums is the **Kovács Margit Múzeum,** at Vastagh György u. 1, which exhibits brilliant ceramic sculptures and tiles by the 20th-century Hungarian artist Margit Kovács (including the renowned *Pound Cake Madonna;* 60Ft, students free). Also worthwhile is the **Czóbel Museum** atop Church Hill, displaying the works of Hungary's foremost impressionist, Béla Czóbel.

From the HÉV and bus station, use the underpass and continue 10 minutes up Kossuth Lajos u. to the triangular center of the old town, Fő tér. Branching off at the top of the square to the right is Bogdányi u., where the **IBUSZ** office at #11 (tel. (26) 31 35 96 or 31 35 97) finds rooms (doubles 1300Ft) and rents bicycles. (800Ft/day. Open Mon.-Sat. 9am-4pm; Sept.-June Mon.-Fri. 9am-4pm.) **Dunatours,** Bogdányi u. 1 (tel. (26) 31 13 11), speaks rough-hewn English but can usually secure you a comparably priced room. (Open Tues.-Sun. 10am-12:30pm and 1:30-6pm.) Camping is available at **Pap-szigeti Camping** (tel. (26) 31 06 97), 800m north of Fő tér. (2 people with tent 520Ft. Open May-Sept.)

Visegrád Thirteen km upriver between the Pilis and Börsöny mountains, Visegrád was once the high-water mark of the Roman Empire. For nearly 2 centuries, Visegrád and Buda rotated as the capital of Hungary. After suffering one too many Mongol invasions, King Béla IV built a stone **citadel** on the hilltop in 1259—hike up to "Fellegvár" from the King Matthias statue near the wharf. (40min. Open daily 9am-5:30pm.) Hourly buses run from the town's first stop to the citadel in July and August (44Ft). Below the citadel, **Solomon's Tower** once formed part of a lower castle for regulating river traffic. The museum inside holds relics from the royal palace. (Open May-Oct. Tues.-Sun. 9am-4:30pm. 30Ft.) From the tower, cavort on Fő u. to the terraced ruins of the 14th-century **palace** of King Charles Robert. (Open Tues.-Sun. 9am-5pm; Nov.-March 8am-4pm. 30Ft.)

Few tourists sleep in Visegrád, which consists of only two major streets. The first of the bus's 3 stops is nearest the Tower and Palace, while the second is closer to the **hostel and campground** (tel. (26) 32 81 02; 450Ft/2 people and tent; open May-Sept.). Walk into town away from the river and take the first right after the green-tipped church for the Széchenyi u. **campground and hostel.** (330Ft/2 people and tent; hostel bed 300Ft.) Show your ISIC at both sites for 10% discounts. Fő u. runs parallel to the Danube and the main road to the cathedral at the other end of town. Near the green-tipped church at about Fő u. 100, several houses rent **private rooms** for about 1000Ft per person. The **snack bar** at the foot of the citadel is open during visiting hours and is better and cheaper than most of its breed.

Esztergom Esztergom witnessed the birth and coronation of Hungary's first king, Saint István (Stephen) in 1000 AD. Strategically located 20km beyond Visegrád at the western edge of the Danube Bend, the city has been invaded by Mongols, Turks, and the Austrian Habsburgs, and today is most famous as a stronghold of the Catholic church. **Esztergom Cathedral,** the largest church in Hungary, majestically crowns **Várhegy** (Castle Hill) to the north. Franz Liszt composed and conducted the consecration mass for this colossal grey marble structure, which was begun in 1010 AD. and completed in 1856. The **treasure room** contains the cross upon which all the kings of Hungary until 1916 took their oath. (Open daily 9am-4:30pm. 50Ft, students 10Ft.) From the cupola you can look across the river into Slovakia. (20Ft, students 10Ft.) The **Keresztény Múzeum (Christian Museum)**, on Berényi Zsigmond u. at the foot of Castle Hill, houses an exceptional collection of Hungarian and Italian religious artwork. Experience the country-town atmosphere of this one-time capital at the daily **vegetable market** on Simor János u. near the bus station (6am-5pm).

IBUSZ, Lőrinc u. 1 (tel. (33) 31 25 52), has city maps for 31Ft and doubles for 1300Ft. (Open Mon.-Fri. 8am-11:50am and 12:30-4pm, Sat. 8-11am.) From the bus station, walk up Simor János u. to the center, where those streets and Rákóczi meet in Széchenyi tér. Up the street at Lőrinc u. 6, **Komtourist** (tel. (33) 31 20 82) has rooms in pensions. (Doubles 1200-2000Ft. Open Mon.-Fri. 8am-4pm, Sat. 8-11am.) Walk along Lőrinc u. from Rákóczi tér until you reach a bridge, and turn left before crossing it to find **Márta Panzió,** Bocskoroskúti út 1 (tel. (33) 31 19 83), where double rooms with bathroom and breakfast are 1800Ft. Closer to the town center is **Pansion Platán,** Kis Duna sétany 11 (tel. (33) 31 13 55), where a double with communal bathroom goes for 1378Ft. **Vadvirág Camping** (tel. (33) 31 22 34), one of the three in town, is a 10-minute bus ride outside the city (the Visegrád bus leaves 5min. before the hour from the station). From IBUSZ, walk down Lőrinc u. to the Danube and turn right. (250Ft/person. 4-person bungalows with bathroom 2200Ft). A closer, if more crowded campground, is **Gran Camping**. From Rákóczi tér, walk down Lőrinc u. across the bridge and continue to the other side of the island, then go left. (280Ft/person, 250Ft/tent. 4-person bungalow with bath 3200Ft. ISIC discount 10%. Students-only dorm beds 320Ft. Open May to mid-Oct.)

For fish specialties, continue on Mártirok u. across the bridge and look left—under a straw roof, **Halászcsárda** serves the catch of the day for 140-250Ft. (Open daily noon-10pm.) **Alabárdos** on Bajcsy-Zsilinszky út 49 (tel. (33) 31 26 40) serves reasonably priced Hungarian specialties. (Entrees 350-500Ft. Open daily noon-11pm. Menu in English.)

■■■ EGER

A thousand years of invasions and bacchanalian revelry have made Eger one of the most beguiling towns in Hungary. Two hours northeast of Budapest by train, Eger serves as a launch pad for exploring the Baradla caves in Aggtelek and the Bükk and Mátra Mountains, the loftiest in the country. The potent **Egri Bikavér** (Bull's Blood) wine flows from Eger, the red-wine capital of Hungary. The **Szépasszonyvölgy** (Valley of Beautiful Women) in the southwestern part of the town shelters hundreds of wine cellars, of which **Ködmön** is the most famous, but not necessarily the best. Locals say that in the valley the wine is watered down; you'll have to judge for yourself. From Deák Ferenc U. and Eszterházy tér, go west from the center for 20 minutes on Telekessy István, which becomes Bacsó Béla u. and eventually Szépasszonyvölgy u., until you reach the bottom of the hill; it's the first restaurant on your left. Rowdy Hungarians drink and sing along with gypsy violinists in the candlelight, and the inexpensive food is as fine as the atmosphere. (Entrees 150-300Ft. Egri Bikavér only 100Ft/½L. Open daily noon-10pm; kitchen closes around 8pm.)

Eger's most venerable buildings date from the Baroque and Turkish periods. At medieval **Eger Castle,** István Dobó and his fighters repelled the unified Turkish army in 1552, halting the Ottoman advance for another 44 years. Hungarians still revere it as a symbol of national pride. The **István Dobó Museum** displays excavated doorways, weapons, and pottery. (Open Tues.-Sun. 9am-5pm. 60Ft, students free.) Reach the castle from Kossuth u. In Dobó tér, the comely Baroque **Minorite church** overlooks a statue of Captain Dobó and two co-defenders—one a woman poised to hurl a rock upon an unlucky Turk. The other end of Kossuth u. leads to the yellow **cathedral,** the second-largest church in Hungary, on Eszterházy. (Open daily 9am-6pm. Free.) Skillful artists have made it nigh impossible to distinguish real marble from the painted illusions. Opposite the cathedral, the Rococo, 18th-century **Lyceum** stages operettas and other performances (100Ft). Inside the Lyceum (now a teacher's college) is the magnificent **library** in room #48, whose frescoed ceiling depicts the Council of Trent. A **Museum of Astronomy** awaits on the 6th floor, a great view from a balcony on the 8th, and a **periscope** on the 9th, which projects live images onto a table in front of you (Lyceum open Tues.-Fri. 9:30am-1pm, Sat.-Sun. 9:30am-noon. 60Ft, students 15Ft. Have another Kodak moment of Eger from the **Turkish minaret,** the northernmost Turkish monument in Europe. (Ascend the huge stone pencil daily 10am-6pm. 20Ft.) The 18th-century **Serbian church** on Vitkovics u. (at the northern end of the center, parallel to Széchenyi u.) displays a magnificent altar and beautiful murals. (Open daily 10am-4pm. Free.)

Accommodations, Food, Practical Information

Express, Széchenyi István u. 28 (tel. (36) 31 07 57), relays information about summer youth hostels in university dorms. (Open Mon.-Fri. 8am-4pm.) **Egertourist,** Bajcsy-Zsilinszky u. 9 (tel. (36) 31 17 24), finds private rooms. (Singles from 750Ft. Doubles from 960Ft. Open Mon.-Fri. 8am-7pm, Sat. 8am-2pm.) Egertourist also runs **Egercamping** at Rákóczi u. 59-79 (tel. (36) 31 05 58), 1.2km out of town. (Take city buses #5, 10, 11, or 12.) Through the archway next to Egertourist is **IBUSZ,** Bajcsy-tömb belsö (tel. (36) 31 14 51), where doubles fetch 950Ft. (Open Mon.-Thurs. 8am-noon and 1-4pm, Fri. 8am-noon and 1-3pm.) Both Egertourist and IBUSZ sell 20Ft city maps. You can also go directly to the dormitories for rooms from 250Ft. Consider the **Berzeviczy Gizella Kollégium,** Leányka u. 2 (tel. (36) 31 23 99), and the nearby **Kun Béla Kollegium,** Leányka u. 6, both mere seconds from the castle. Ascend the steps to the right of the castle entrance; you can see the large, white Berzeviczy from there; Kun Béla is the gray block around the corner. Or head to the **Eszterházy Károly** dorm on Egészségház u. 4 (tel. (36) 31 23 77), off Kossuth Lajos u. (250Ft/person.) The **Hotel Unicornis** (tel. (36) 31 28 86) gets only 1 star for its 1 horn and has rooms at Dr. Hibak Károly u. 2. (Doubles 1220Ft, with shower 1450Ft.)

In town, in the shadow of the cathedral, **Kazamata** restaurant sits in a concrete cave. (Entrees 130-400Ft. Open daily 10am-11pm. Disco/bar 10pm-4am.) Country women hawk produce and flowers in the cavernous **indoor market,** near Centrum áruház department store in the center. (Open Mon.-Fri. 6am-6pm, Sat. 6am-1pm, Sun. 6-10am.) Upstairs, fabulous barbeque ribs sell for a paltry 100Ft. (Open Mon.-Fri. 8am-7:30pm, Sat.-Sun. 8:30am-7:30pm.) **HBH** (Bayerische Hofbräuhaus), Bajcsy Zs. u. 19, next to Dobó Jér, serves quick and inexpensive gourmet meals in enormous portions. Wash them down with local beer in the back of the restaurant. (Open daily 10am-10pm; Nov.-March Mon.-Sat. 10am-10pm. Entrees 170-350Ft. Menus in English.)

Trains from Budapest-Keleti station go directly to Eger or make a tight connection in Füzesabony (about every 3hrs., 2hr., 402Ft). Trains split in Hatran, so beware. From the train station, try to take the (infrequent) #3 bus 2 stops or walk to the right on Deák Ferenc út to the yellow cathedral on Eszterházy tér. Turn right on Kossuth Lajos u., then take a quick left along Eszterházy tér to reach Széchenyi István u., where **OTP Bank** posts information and hours for all **exchange bureaus** in town.

■ Near Eger

Eger's charm derives partly from its proximity to the **Bükk Mountains,** a small, densely forested range with a national park and numerous hiking trails. **Szilvásvárad,** a small town 27km north of Eger in the beautiful Szalajka Valley, is an excellent base for mountain merriment, and is also home to a stud farm of Lippizaner horses, of Vienna's Spanish Riding School fame. A bus makes the 1-hour trip from Eger nearly every hour. Szilvásvárad's camping surpasses Eger's as LG does OTL. Try **Hegyi Camping** at Egri út 36a (tel. (36) 35 52 07; open mid-April to mid-Oct.).

Beyond the Bükks, near the Slovak border, is the village of **Aggtelek.** Beneath the venerable houses stretch the **Baradla Caves,** whose 25m stalagmites and 2km lakes will blow your mind. They're accessible by bus from the bus station in Pyrker tér behind the Cathedral. (8:50am daily, return from the caves for Eger and Budapest at 3:05pm, 2¾hr., 344Ft. Cave admission 150Ft, students 75Ft. Tours leave on the hour daily 9am-4pm.) The bus drops you off at 2-star **Hotel Cseppkö** (tel. (36) 31 17 24), 200m from the caves and 3km from the Jósvafo-Aggtelek train station, accessible via Miskolc. (Doubles with private bath 2000Ft, including breakfast. Book ahead at Express in Eger.) **Camping** is available in the park outside the cave mouth. (115Ft/person, 161Ft/tent. Hostel beds 200Ft. 1st- and 3rd-class bungalows 1500Ft and 800Ft, respectively.)

■■■ GYŐR

Though usually associated with heavy industries such as the Rába truck factory, Győr (DYUR) is not without charm: it's still possible to see a horse-drawn firewood cart slowing down rush-hour traffic. All of Győr's major sights are within easy walking distance of each other and the bus station and can be seen in an afternoon. Three rivers that later become part of the Danube meet here, adding to the pleasant atmosphere. About 10 minutes up Aradi vértanúk from the station is **Köztársaság tér** (Republic Square), site of the very yellow **Carmelite Church** and the remains of a medieval castle. Follow Alkotmány u. away from the river to Széchenyi tér, the old town center, to drink *kávé* and people-watch. The marketplace on the river transmogrifies into a **bazaar** on Wednesday, Friday, and Saturday mornings. The town's **Cathedral** dates from the 11th century, and is an open-air museum of architectural styles; elements of the Romanesque, Gothic, and Baroque styles are all present. Inside, dozens of golden cherubim and the magnificently frescoed nave and side aisles make it one of the nation's loveliest. Don't miss the wide-eyed bust of Saint László in the Héderváry Chapel, a masterwork of Gothic goldsmithery. The **Margit Kovács Museum** on Rözsa Ferenc u. 1, 1 block north of Széchenyi tér, is one of Győr's hidden treasures, displaying the artist's distinctive ceramic sculptures and tiles. (Open Tues.-Sun. 10am-6pm; Nov.-March 10am-5pm. 20Ft, students 10Ft.) Győr frolics away its **summer festival** (late June-early July) with theater, ballet, and concerts.

Accommodations, Food, and Practical Information Győr is 2 hours from the Budapest-Keleti train station (6/day, 402Ft), and an easy daytrip from Sopron (6/day, 1hr., 254Ft). From the bus station, take the underpass to the train station (signs say Belváros) and emerge 40m to the right of the train station's main entrance. Straight ahead is Aradi Vértanúk u.; at its intersection with Szent István út. is **Ciklámen Tourist,** Aradi u. 22 (tel. (96) 31 15 57 or (96) 31 67 01), where an English-speaking staff rents singles for 750Ft, doubles for 1300Ft, and gives away a map. (Open Mon.-Thurs. 8am-4:30pm, Fri. 8am-3:30pm, Sat. 8am-1pm.) Otherwise, a right from Aradi onto Szent István for 2 blocks will bring you to Szent István út 29-31, where **IBUSZ** (tel. (96) 31 17 00 or 31 42 24) rents singles from 770Ft and doubles from 880Ft. (Open Mon.-Tues. and Thurs. 8-11:50am and 12:30-4pm; Wed. and Fri. 8-11:50am and 12:30-3:30pm.) Two blocks into the tourist area, take a right to Bajcsy-Zsilinszky út 41 (past the theater) where **Express** (tel. (96) 32 88 33) offers friendly service. (Open Mon.-Fri. 8am-noon and 12:30-3:45pm. Has doubles.)

Try **Hotel Aranypart** at Áldozat u. 12, 5 stops on bus #16 from Szabadság tér. (Doubles 1800Ft.) In July and August you can find beds in the unmarked but brightly colored **Kollegium** on Liszt Ferenc u. 42 (tel. (96) 31 36 55), which runs out of Széchenyi tér. (300Ft/person.) **Szárnyaskerék Hotel,** on Révai Miklós u. 5 (tel. (96) 31 46 29) at the railway station, has clean rooms but a non-English-speaking staff. (Doubles 1500Ft, with bath 1700Ft.) There's a **post office** down the street at Bajcsy-Zsilinszky út 46. (Open Mon.-Fri. 8am-8pm.) Bus #8 stops at **Kiskút-ligeti Camping** (formerly called Ciklámen Camping), Kiskút-liget (tel. (96) 31 89 86).

Camping and bungalows are open April 15 through October 15, and the motel is open year-round. (2-person bungalows 1500Ft. 300Ft/person in tent.)

Vaskakas (Iron Rooster) **Tavern,** in the dungeon of the castle on Köztársaság tér, has music and a great location. (Platters 150-520Ft. Open 11am-4am.) **Várkapu,** at Bécsikapu tér 7, serves excellent paprika garnished lightly with food. (Entrees 200-450Ft. Open daily 10am-11pm. English menu.) **Komédiás** at Czuczor G. u. 30 (tel. (96) 31 90 50), on the west side of the theater, is a cozy family-run restaurant with a limited selection, excellent service, and reasonable prices. (Entrees 150-380Ft.) A **Biergarten** huddles around the back (beer 90Ft).

■■■ SOPRON

Sopron is the Hungarian metropolis closest to Austria both geographically and culturally, lending the city's denizens an air of snobbery, and though it's one of the most expensive towns in Hungary, Sopron is still cheap enough for the Austrians who flock here every day. Most of Sopron's historic sights lies within the oval **Old Town,** bounded by Széchenyi tér in the south, Vár kerület to the east and north, and Öguabona tér to the west. Enter under the tall green **fire tower** (*tüztorony*), which presides over the shingled roofs. (Sights open Tues.-Sun. 10am-6pm. Museum 40Ft, 20Ft with ISIC.) On the right, **Storno-Ház,** a Renaissance palace, holds a marvelous collection of baroque items. Across the street on the right is the **Bencés Templom** (Goat Church), built by a happy herder whose goats found gold. The small Franciscan **monastery** next door dates from the late 13th century. Its textbook Gothic architecture is enriched by 10 small sculptures symbolizing human sins. (Open Sat.-Thurs. 10am-noon and 2-5pm. Free.) Walk down Új u. to 2 rare 14th-century **synagogues** at no. 11 (under renovation in 1994) and no. 22, which evoke life in the Jewish community, expelled in 1526. (Open Wed.-Mon. 9am-5pm.) Ten minutes outside the old town at the intersection of Május 1 and Csatkai Endre is the **Liszt Ferenc Múzeum** (Franz Liszt Museum). Don't be fooled; it's an ethnographic museum and has nothing to do with the composer. During the **Sopron Festival Weeks** (June-July), the town hosts a profusion of opera, ballet, and concerts, some set in the **Fertörákos Quarry** caverns, 10km away. (1 bus/hr. from main bus terminal. Admission 10Ft for students. Concerts 300-400Ft. Buy tickets for all events from the *Festival Bureau* on Széchenyi tér. across form the post office. Open Mon.-Fri. 10am-1pm and 2-5pm, Sat. 10am-1pm.)

Accommodations, Food, and Practical Information At **Lokomotiv,** Várkerület 90 (tel. (99) 31 11 11), you can get doubles for 1000-1200Ft. (Open Mon.-Fri. 8am-4pm, Sat. 8am-noon). The **IBUSZ** office at Várkerület 41 (tel. (99) 31 24 55), offers excellent exchange rates as well as singles and doubles for 1000Ft. (Open Mon.-Fri. 8am-4pm, Sat. 8am-noon.) At **Ciklámen Tourist,** Ógabona tér 8 (tel. (99) 31 20 40) doubles go for 1300Ft the first night, 1200Ft each night thereafter. (Open Mon.-Thurs. 7:30am-4pm, Fri.-Sat. 7:30am-8pm, Sun. 8:30am-noon; mid-Sept. to May Mon.-Fri. 7:30am-4pm, Sat. 7:30am-3:30pm.)

Talizmán Panzió is 1½km west of the center at Ady Eudre u. 85, but the comfortable rooms with TV and private shower are a steal at 800Ft per person. From the train station, walk up Mätyas Kiraály one block to Csengery, then catch bus #10 going left (west) on Csengery to the Panzió. In the comfortable *panzió* above the **Taverna** (see below), show 'em your *Let's Go* for a 200Ft discount on rooms. (Doubles 1200Ft, with bath 1500Ft.) Showers and TVs in every room and no curfew, make this a great spot to set up camp for a night or two. **Lövér Campground** (tel. (99) 31 17 15) on Köszegi u. at the south end of town, is often crammed. (Bungalow doubles 1100Ft. Bungalow triples 1400Ft.) Take bus #12 from Várkerület, and ask to be let off at the campground (every 30min. until 10:15pm).

At **Deák Étterem** at Erzsébet u. 20 on Deák tér (tel. (99) 31 16 86), you can meet the **English club,** which comes for a chat and beer every Tuesday evening from September to June. In the huge green garden, you can try to decipher your meal from the non-English menu. (Entrees 150-480Ft. Open Mon.-Sat. 10am-midnight, Sun. 10am-10pm.) To get there, walk toward the train station along Erzsébet u. from Széchenyi tér. **Taverna** is a mighty restaurant at Táncsics M. u. 15. Take bus #19 three stops from the train station. A huge wine cellar serves excellent food at very reasonable prices. (Entrees 140-450Ft.) Eat before the orchestra starts or you just might choke with laughter. (Open Mon.-Sat. 8am-10pm.) Less mighty wallets can stop at the **Non-Stop** grocery store on the corner of Móricz Zsigmond u. and Magyar u., or at the larger **Julius Meinl** grocery store on Várkerület.

Sopron rises from fertile farmland only a few **rail** hours from Budapest's Déli station (5/day, 3hr., 656Ft) and Vienna's Südbahnhof (7-9/day, 1½hr., US$17). From **Gysev pu.**, walk north on Mátyás Király út for 10 minutes to reach Várkerület, or take bus #1, 2, or 12 for 3 stops (22Ft at newsstands, 30Ft on the bus). The **bus station** is a short hop north of Ciklámen Tourist on Lackner Kristóf. A **post office** is on Széchenyi tér, at the southern end of the old town. (Open Mon.-Fri. 8am-8pm, Sat. 8am-noon.)

■ Near Sopron

Twenty-seven km east of Sopron in the small town of **Fertöd** stands the magnificent rococo **Eszterházy Palace,** nicknamed "The Hungarian Versailles," easily the finest palace in the country. Miklós Eszterházy, known as Miklós the Sumptuous, built the palace in 1766 to hold his multi-day orgiastic feasts. Franz Joseph Haydn wrote and conducted here, and stellar concerts still resound within. (Open Tues.-Sun. 8am-4pm.) **Buses** leave hourly for Fertöd from stage 5 in the station on Lackner Kristóf in Sopron (45min., 105Ft). Book dorm beds or doubles with Ciklámen Tourist in Sopron.

Roadside shrines and thriving farm villages lie along the bus route from Sopron to **Kőszeg.** (Take the Szombathely line; 3/day, 1½hr., 172Ft.) Kőszeg is also served by trains from Szombathely (about 15/day, 30min., 72Ft). The town prospered in the Middle Ages, when its castle helped battle Turkish invaders. Today, Kőszeg's central Jurisics tér retains its medieval cityscape; **St. James Church** is one of the country's most significant Gothic treasures. The bus from Sopron stops first at the train station and then closer to the center. Step off and turn right on Kossuth Lajos u.; 1 block up is **Várkör** (Castle Ring), the ovoid main street. From the train station, cross the little bridge and bear right up Rákóczi u. about 1km into the center. **Savaria Tourist** on Várkör 69 (tel. (94) 36 02 38), offers doubles in private homes for 1100Ft (German spoken). Next door, at the corner of Városház u. is an **Express** office (tel. (94) 36 02 47; open May-Oct.) with hotel rooms (doubles 1300Ft, with bathroom 1800Ft; 10% off with HI card), and 20m farther, **IBUSZ,** Városhaz 3 (tel. (94) 36 03 76) has doubles from 900Ft. (All tourist offices open Mon.-Fri. roughly 8am-4pm, Sat. 8am-noon.) There is also a **campground** in town near the beach on route #87. The **castle** (tel. (94) 36 02 27) at Rajnis u. 9 in Jurisics tér has tourist dorm rooms for 280Ft per person. **Irottkö Restaurant,** Fő tér 4, is good (entrees 180-430Ft; open daily 7am-10pm), and the more authentic **Kulacs Restaurant,** Várkör 12, 1½ blocks from Irottkö, is better yet. (Entrees 140-440Ft. Open daily 9am-10pm.)

■■■ LAKE BALATON

Shallow Balaton is the largest lake and one of the most coveted vacation spots in Central Europe. The first villas appeared during the Roman Empire; when a railroad linked Lake Balaton to the surrounding population in the 1860s, it mushroomed into a favorite summer playground. Today, mobs of Germans, Austrians, and Hungarians invade the region for its rich scenery and comparatively low prices.

Lake Balaton is easily accessible from Budapest through Balatonfüred on the northern shore or Siófok on the southern shore (5 **trains**/day, 350-400Ft), towns which sate vacationers with discos and bars but leave little for rainy days. **Buses** run from Balatonfüred to the quieter Tihany (1/hr., 6am-10pm, 44Ft), while ferries link the three towns. **MAHART ferries** are the most convenient and enjoyable way to travel to nearby towns on the lake; students get half off on all fares. (1/hr. mid-April to mid-Oct.; Siófok to Balatonfüred 1hr., to Tihany 80min.; 156Ft, students 78Ft). Bundles of tourist agencies book private rooms at the bus and train stations, and there are numerous *Zimmer Frei* signs for rooms for rent on the street.

Tihany Perched on a peninsular hilltop, Tihany (TEE-haw-nee) is the most luscious spot on the lake. The discos of the lowlands give way to the town's venerable baroque church and the inland lakes and hiking trails that lace the rolling hills. The price of peace is predictably high, and Tihany's isolation means fewer hedonistic diversions. Distinguish between the two ferry landings, Tihany and, to the southwest, Tihanyi-rév. The village is at the top of the hill, marked by the twin-towered church. The view from atop the village is the best anywhere on the lake. Take the bus (local ones leave frequently from both ferry wharves, or stay on the bus from Balatonfüred) up to town, or hike up the winding paths toward the church.

Lording over the peninsula and visible from Balatonfüred, the magnificent 1754 **Abbey Church** has baroque altars, pulpit, and organ. (Open daily 10am-5pm. 20Ft, students 10Ft.) Buried in the crypt is Andrew I, one of Hungary's first kings. His grant establishing the first church on the site in 1055 is one of the oldest extant Hungarian texts. Ask about the occasional organ concerts during the summer. Next door, an 18th-century monastery has been reincarnated as the **Tihany Museum,** with psychedelic dreamscapes, colorized etchings, and Roman inscriptions displayed in a cool, subterranean **lapidarium** (room with stone carvings). (Open March-Oct. Tues.-Sun. 10am-6pm. 30Ft.) Far from the madding crowd is the bizarre **garage-gallery** of "painter artist, writer, professor" Gergely Koós-Hutás, at Füdötelep 43, a 5-minute climb from the Tihany wharf. Works include massive canvases of a didactic Lenin as well as several of the artist himself in front of famous edifices around the world, such as Grauman's Chinese Restaurant in Hollywood. Signed photos are a steal at 20Ft. The promenade behind the church also leads to the **beach** (follow the "strand" signs), open daily 7am to 7pm (50Ft), though the side gate remains unlocked after hours.

Balatontourist, the **post office,** and the church all huddle next to the bus stop. Balatontourist, Kossuth u. 20 (tel. (86) 34 85 19) arranges private rooms in the village. (Doubles 1570Ft. Open in summer Mon.-Sat. 8am-6:30pm, Sun. 8am-1pm.) Set up your own accommodations at the numerous houses posting *Zimmer* signs. A room close to the lake isn't worth the expense, since the village is but a hop, skip, and a jump away. For an indoor panorama, choose **Echo Rest,** the round building at the end of the promenade. (250-550Ft. Open daily 10am-11pm.) Next to the abbey, **Rege Presso** (Panorama Teraze) has a more restricted view, but the best pastries on the peninsula. (50-60Ft. Open daily 9am-7pm.)

Keszthely Certainly the most civilized town on the whole lake and its largest port, the pride of Keszthely (KESS-tay) is the **Festetics Palace,** of whose 360 rooms you can only see the central wing. Built by one of the most powerful Austro-Hungarian families, it exemplifies the beauty and grandeur of the Baroque. Concerts are often held in the mirrored ballroom hall during summer. (Open Tues.-Sun. 9am-6pm. 250Ft, with ISIC 50Ft.) The surrounding park is a vast and well-kept strolling ground. The **Georgikon Major Múzeum** at Bercsényi u. 67 is an extremely amusing apotheosis of Gyorgy Festetics, who founded Europe's oldest agricultural university here in 1797. (Open April-Oct. Tues.-Sat. 10am-5pm, Sun. 10am-6pm. 30Ft, free with ISIC.)

Five **trains** per day head to and from the Budapest-Déli station in Budapest (546Ft) and skirt the southern shore of the lake. Be careful when arriving from Budapest; only the first 3 or 4 carriages of the train actually go to Keszthely. Once at the train station, ignore the signs saying MÁV tours and *Privatzimmer dienst;* these bureaus are largely unhelpful. The bus station is at the front of the train station; **buses** leave to nearby towns and even places as far away as Győr and Budapest. Walk straight ahead along Martirok útja until you reach the city's main street, Kossuth Lajos. Turn right and head for its pedestrian section. Arriving by bus from a different Balaton city, you may be let out on Szalasztó u. near Kossuth Lajos u. If so, turn right down Kossuth Lajos to the pedestrian zone and tourist office. Try **IBUSZ** at Széchenyi u. 1-3 for doubles from 1100Ft. Beware of rooms far from the shore, which cost the same. (Open Mon.-Fri. 8am-6pm, Sat. 8am-1pm and 4-8pm, Sun. 9am-1pm; mid-Sept. to May Mon.-Fri. 8am-4pm.) A **Tourinform** is at Kossuth Lajos u. 28. (Open Mon.-Sat. 9am-7pm, Sun. 9am-1pm.) There's also a **private-room bureau** at Római u. 2. (Open May-Sept. Mon.-Fri. 5-8pm, Sat. 8am-8pm, Sun 9am-1pm.) All tourist offices are located within a block of Fő tér. Mr. Attila Lukics's cosy **panzió** is at Jókai Mór u. 16 (tel. 31 12 32), a block down from Fő tér. Look for the signs. The 3 triples and 3 doubles each have baths; Mr. Lukics offers *Let's Go* readers a 20% discount. In July and August, head to the **Pethe Ferenc Kollégium** at Festetics György út 5 (tel. 31 12 90), the continuation of Kossuth Lajos in the southern part of Keszthely (triples with hall bath 300Ft/person), or try the **Helikon Tourist Hotel,** Honvéd u. 22 (tel. 31 14 24), for dorm beds with breakfast for 500Ft. **Sport Camping** (tel. 31 37 77) is a 5-minute walk south from the train station and across the tracks; it has tons of mosquitoes and doubles for 700Ft; a tent for two runs 550Ft per day. *Zimmer Frei* signs are most common in the neighborhood of the Tourist Hotel.

Restaurants here aim to make their yearly profits in the tourist season; don't be surprised by higher prices. **Béke Vendéglő,** Kossuth u. 50 (tel. 31 24 47), has a large shady garden and reasonable prices. (Entrees 140-460Ft.) Gypsy music plays in the evenings. (Open daily 8am-10pm.) **Park Vendéglő** is at Vörösmarty u. 1/a (tel. 31 16 54). From Fő tér, follow Vöröscsillag u. until it comes across Vörösmarty. *Let's Go* readers get yet another discount here: 10% off or a free glass of wine. (Entrees 280-550Ft. Open daily 11am-11pm. English menu.) **Reform,** Rákóczi tér 3, is one of a handful of Hungary's vegetarian restaurants. Pay 55Ft per 100g of whatever you choose. (Open daily 11am-9pm.)

Siófok　Siófok is the largest city on the southern shore of Lake Balaton and the tourist capital of the whole lake. Several high-rise, high-priced hotels line the crowded beachfront, making it the most modern, if least scenic, of Balaton's resorts. Public and private **beaches** (60Ft) alternate along Siófok's expensive coastline; both are equally packed in the summers. Numerous nightclubs line the lakefront, while amphibious lounge lizards revel on the **Disco Boat** from July 10-August 22, leaving the docks at 9:30pm (250Ft).

The bus and train stations are next to each other off the town's main drag, Fő u. From the stations, go right down Fő u. toward the large octagonal water tower. **Tourinform** is inside the tower's base. (Open Mon.-Fri. 8am-9pm, Sat. 8am-1pm and 4-8pm, Sun. 10am-noon.) **IBUSZ,** nearby, at Fő u. 174 (tel. (84) 31 10 66), has doubles near the center for 1500Ft. (Open Mon.-Fri. 8am-6pm, Sat. 8am-8pm, Sun. 8:30am-1pm.) Across the street at Szabadság tér 6, **Siotour** (tel. (84) 31 09 00) has doubles for 1000Ft. (Open Mon.-Sat. 8am-8pm, Sun. 9am-noon and 4-7pm.) Camping is available 5km east of the center at **Aranypart Camping** (tel. (84) 31 18 01), where 2 people can pitch a tent near the water for 630Ft. You can also pitch a tent in the backyard of the **Tuja Panzió,** Szent László u. 74 (tel. (84) 31 49 96), for 400Ft per person. The *panzió,* meanwhile, has doubles for 1200Ft per person. Szent László u. is just one block from the beach and is lined with *panziós* and *Zimmer Frei* signs; doubles here fetch 1500-2700Ft. The **Csárdás Restaurant,** Fő u. 105, offers traditional Hungarian dishes in a friendly atmosphere. (Entrees 275-500Ft. Open mid-May to mid-Oct. 11:30am-midnight.) The outdoor cafeteria-style counter near the ferry station serves a respectable spaghetti *bolognese* for 120Ft. **MAHART ferry** boats leave almost hourly to nearby ports from the docks next to the verdant **Jókai**

Park, just 10 minutes from the train station. **Trains** leave from Budapest-Deli station roughly every hour (2hr., 304Ft).

Balatonfüred On the swan-studded north shore of Lake Balaton, Balatonfüred is the lake's first spa and the nation's premier health center. While hordes of vaca-tioners come to bask in the glaring sun along the extensive beaches (in moderation, of course), thousands of heart patients every year make the pilgrimage to the world-renowned **cardiac hotel** to drink from the curative carbonic springs. The shady lakefront park and promenade east of the dock have been planted with trees as liv-ing monuments to famous people treated there. You can drink to your own health from the temple-like **Kossuth Lajos Well,** just above the park in **Gyógy tér** (Heath Square); a nearby sign documents the hotspring's mineral content. The **public beach** east of the dock is more central and costs 60Ft, while the **western beach** costs 50Ft. (Both are open 9am-6pm.)

If you arrive by **boat,** walk straight up the hill and turn right at the round, yellow church to find **Balatontourist,** at Blaha Lujza u. 5 (tel. (86) 34 28 23), where doubles go for 1500Ft. (Open Mon.-Sat. 8:30am-6:30pm, Sun. 9am-12:30pm; Sept.-May Mon.-Fri. 9am-4pm.) Across the street is the **Hotel Blaha Luzja** (tel. (86) 34 26 03), where doubles go for 2300Ft with breakfast. Further up, a left on Petőfi Sándor u. brings you to **IBUSZ** at no. 4a (tel. (86) 34 23 27), which offers doubles for 1800Ft, plus 30% the first night if you stay fewer than 4 nights. Walk up Vörösmarty u. 1 block and left on Kéthlykároly, where numerous *Zimmer Frei* signs await; rooms are 1000-1500Ft per person. The enormous **FICC Rally Camping,** Széchenyi u. 24 (tel. (86) 34 38 23), is a 20-minute walk west of the dock, where 2 people and a tent can stay by the lakefront for 750Ft. The 24-hour **Pizzeria Roma,** at the corner of Jokai Mór u. and Petőfi Sandor u., may be the cheapest place to eat in Füred. (Pizzas 200-220Ft.) Stand up and cheer at the huge **daily market** on Huray u., which has tons of vegetables, clothing, and crafts (9am-6pm).

■ ■ ■ PÉCS

Spiced with minarets from the Ottoman occupation and home to over a dozen museums and galleries, Pécs (PAYTCH) could well be the cultural capital of Hun-gary. In the Middle Ages the city's walls encircled an area larger than modern-day Vienna, and its architecture retains a pleasing mix of Central European and Mediter-ranean styles. The main square, Széchenyi tér, is dominated by the nation's largest **mosque,** dating from the 16th century and long converted to Christianity. Today it serves as the inner-city Parish Church—the stone window grilles alone belie its former faith. An impressive **synagogue** *(Kossuth tér)* recalls a once-thriving Jewish community. (Open May-Oct. Sun.-Fri. 9:30am-1pm and 1:30-5pm. 35Ft, students 25Ft, includes highly educational booklet.) West of Széchenyi lies the distinctive 4-towered **Cathedral,** whose earliest parts date back to the 4th century; it was restored in Romanesque style from 1881-92. (Open Mon.-Sat. 9am-1pm and 2-5pm, Sun. 1-5pm. 40Ft, students 20Ft.) The **Archaeological Museum,** Széchenyi tér 12, behind the Inner City Parish Church, traces the history of the city. Eight more muse-ums and galleries, some quite exceptional, are all clustered along Káptalan u. and can be seen on a leisurely but rewarding afternoon stroll. All are open Tuesday to Sunday 10am-6pm and are free with ISIC. The **Zsolnay Porcelain Museum** houses some exquisite creations, while the **Victor Vasarely Museum,** showcases arresting works by the famous Hungarian op-artist. Not to be missed is the **Csontváry Museum,** which houses the works of Tivadar Csontváry Koszka (1853-1919), Hun-gary's two-eared answer to Van Gogh. Snag a view of Pécs from the TV tower that looms above it. (Take bus #35. 50Ft.)

Accommodations, Food, and Practical Information   Rent a pri-vate room at the **MÁV travel office** (tel. (72) 32 45 23) in the railway station, 10 min-

SZEGED

utes from the city center by bus. (Open Mon.-Thurs. 9am-4:30pm, Fri. 9am-4pm; Sept.-May Mon.-Thurs. 8am-4:30pm, Fri. 8am-3:30pm. Doubles 1100Ft. English spoken.) Or take any bus that goes to Széchenyi tér (including #30 and 34) and head into one of the tourist offices on or just below the square. **IBUSZ,** Széchenyi tér 8 (tel. (72) 31 21 76), has doubles for 1100Ft. (Open Mon.-Thurs. 8am-noon and 12:30-4pm, Fri. 8am-noon and 12:30-3pm, Sat. 8am-noon.) The staff at **Mecsek Tourist,** Széchenyi tér 1 (tel. (72) 31 33 00), just across from IBUSZ, speaks more English, has doubles for 1050Ft and runs a campground (listed below). Disdain the 180Ft map from Meczek Tourist in favor of the 20Ft model from IBUSZ. For **student accommodations** call the AIESEC Center at the Economics University (tel. (72) 31 14 33, ext. 273; Mon.-Fri. 9am-4pm). The **student dorm** on Rákóczi út 52 (tel. (72) 31 59 57), across from the big Konzum department store is shabby but still liveable. (Doubles, triples, and quads 400Ft/person.) The best hostel is the farthest away, at Szántó Kovács u. 1 (tel. (72) 32 42 34); take bus #27 from Konzum Aruház. **Szent Mór Kollégium,** on 48-es tér 4 (tel. (72) 31 11 99), has cozy doubles (800Ft) and triples (1150Ft) in a gorgeous old building. In the **Kollégium** on Rókus u. 2 (tel. (72) 32 42 77, ext. 174), big sunny quads with bunkbeds go for 400Ft per person and doubles for 450Ft per person (550Ft with bath). Take bus #30 to the 4th stop after Széchenyi tér. Early in the day or outside of peak season, take bus #34 directly to the **campground** (tel. (72) 31 59 81), in the hills above the city, where tent sites (500Ft/2 people), 3-bed bungalows (1600Ft), and doubles in a 1-star hotel (2000Ft) are located at the entrance to hiking trails into the Mecsek Hills. (Camp open mid-April to mid-Oct.) Call the campsite for same-day reservations. For advance reservations, call Mescek Tourist (see above).

For cheap **food** near the center, try **Liceum Söröző,** in a cellar off Kossuth Lajos u. 35, across from the Liceum church. (Entrees 220-360Ft. Open Mon.-Fri. 11am-10pm. English menu.) Wander through the inner courtyard to **Iparos Kisvendéglő,** behind a house at Rákóczi út 24, for well-prepared and reasonably priced entrees (190-520Ft), though you may have trouble selecting the excellent steaks from a menu written only in Hungarian, German, or Croatian. (Open Sun.-Thurs. 11:30am-10pm, Fri.-Sat. 11:30am-midnight.) **DÓM Restaurant** inhabits a 2-level wooden model of a church. (Entrees 130-400Ft. Open daily 11am-11pm. Menu in German.) **Caflisch Cukrászda** at Kossuth Lajos u. 32 spoils visitors with delightful Hungarian sweets. (30-55Ft. Open Sun.-Thurs. 8am-10pm, Fri.-Sat. 8am-11pm.)

Several **trains** per day chug from Budapest-Déli station (3hr., 632Ft). The bus and train stations are about 800m apart at the bottom of the town's historic district. Bus #34 connects both with Széchenyi tér, the town's tourist center.

■ Near Pécs

From Pécs, consider a daytrip to the incredible sculpture park in **Nagyharsány,** hard by the Croatian border, 37km to the south. Located in and around a former quarry, the park contains pieces by artists from around the world. Facing the quarry, follow the path on the right for a climb to even better views of the town and the fruited plains below. First take a train to Villány (1hr., round-trip 220Ft); from the station, turn left and follow the main road (towards Siklós) about 4km. There is a map across from the ABC supermarket 1km along, or just ask for the *szoborpark.*

■■■ SZEGED

Szeged's easy-going charm belies the fact that it's Hungary's only planned city and a somewhat dynamic center of the southeastern plain. Glorious art-nouveau buildings are sprinkled among row after row of colorful neo-Renaissance façades, endowing Szeged's streets with remarkable beauty, and the savory scent of sweet paprika and spicy fish soup *(halászlé),* for which Szeged is famous, perfumes the air.

In 1879, the River Tisza burst its banks, destroying almost everything in town. Survivors of the flood constructed the neo-Romanesque **Votive Church** in Dóm tér, whose brick dome and 91m twin towers dominate the city's skyline. One of the largest churches in Hungary, its organ has over 10,000 pipes. (Open daily 9am-6pm, except during services Sun. 10-11am. Free.) Kissing the church is the 12th-century **Demetrius Tower,** Szeged's oldest monument. Note the sculptures of great Hungarian heroes in front of the cathedral. Behind the Votive Church is the less imposing **Serbian Church,** with precious Orthodox icons. In the center of town is **Széchenyi tér,** where the yellow **Town Hall** was restored after the deluge to its present eclectic form. Walk along the Vörösmarty u. side of the square to see the lavish, art nouveau **gyógyszertár** (pharmacy) building. Just southwest of Széchenyi tér, in Aradi Vértanúk tér, stands **Hősök Kapuja** (Heroes' Gate), guarded by stone likenesses of the fascist soldiers it was originally meant to honor. From July 20 to August 20 every year, the country's largest open-air festival, the **Szeged Weeks** in Dóm tér, tickles tens of thousands of visitors with opera, ballet, and folklore performances. (Tickets purchased through the tourist offices 100-500Ft).

In Roosevelt tér along the river is the **Móra Ferenc Museum,** a huge neo-classical building that houses cultural and artistic accomplishments from the region, as well as a fascinating display of the long-vanished Avar tribe who occupied the Carpathian Basin from the 6th to 9th centuries.

Accommodations, Food, and Practical Information

Head for the less expensive **Szeged Tourist** at Klauzál tér 7 (tel. (62) 32 18 00; singles 500-600Ft; doubles 900-1200Ft; open Mon.-Fri. 8:30am-5pm, Sat. 9am-1pm; Sept.-June 9am-5:30pm, Sat. 8am-noon). Across the street, **IBUSZ,** Klauzál tér 2 (tel. (62) 47 11 77), sells train tickets, finds rooms, and speaks better English; they also sell an accurate city map (150Ft). (Singles and doubles 1000F/person. Open Mon.-Fri. 8am-4pm, Sat. 8am-1pm, 45-min. lunch break around noon.) **Tourinform** is located on Victor Hugo u. 1, on the corner of Oskola u. (Open Mon.-Fri. 8am-6pm, Sat. 10am-2pm.) There are several decent **kollégiums** in Szeged. (Open July-Aug.) The most luxurious is **Ápáthy István Kollégium,** Ápáthy Istvan u. 1 (tel. (62) 32 31 55), with its perfect location right next to Dóm tér and its triples with private bath. (Singles and doubles 1400Ft. Triples 1800Ft.) Also in a prime location is the **Eötvös Loránd Kollégium,** Tisza Lajos krt. 103 (tel. (62) 31 06 41), just down the road from Hősök Kapuju, with singles for 477Ft and doubles for 901Ft. The **Talent Center,** Fürj u. 92b, in Újszeged (tel. (62) 31 27 11), has a very green campground and motel open all year. The motel has 4- and 6-bed rooms with bunk beds (320Ft/person). Eight-bed tents house people for 150Ft (May 1-Sept. 30; 2-person tent 275Ft). To get there take bus #71 (every 20min.) 6 stops from Széchenyi tér. Tram #1 takes you to another year-round motel, **Napfény,** Dorozsmai út 4 (tel. (62) 32 58 00; doubles 750Ft; quads 1900Ft). Debark at the last stop, ascend the steps of the overpass behind you, and walk to the right.

Two cafeteria-style establishments have low-priced entrees (100-150Ft): **Fesztival** (open daily 10am-9pm), on Oskola u. across the street from the Votive Church, is a little snazzier than **Boszorkány Konyhu** (The Witch's Kitchen), just off Széchenyi tér at Híd u. 8. (Open 9am-9pm.) For an upscale dining evening, try **Alabárdós,** Oskola u. 11, 2 blocks from Klauzal tér at the other end of Oroszlán. (280-700Ft. Open Mon.-Sat. 11:30am-2pm and 6pm-midnight.) Solid Hungarian food, vegetarian options, and pasta are served at **Restaurant Botond,** on the same side of the square at no. 12. (Menu in English. Entrees 140-420Ft. Open daily noon-midnight.) By far the busiest place in town is the **Kisvirág Cukrászda** in Klauzúl tér, which serves excellent pastries (50Ft) and an endless stream of ice cream. (15Ft/scoop. Open daily 8am-10pm.) The city's youth hang at the **Mojo Club,** Batthyány u. 12, and on the banks of the Tisza. (Open daily 6pm-2am.)

When training it to Budapest-Nyugati from Szeged, make sure to board the right car—the **train** splits midway (6 expresses/day, 2½hrs., 576Ft). Romania-bound

TOKAJ

trains pass through Békéscsaba, which has regular connections with Szeged. With your back to the train station, follow the tracks outside the front entrance (going right) for 15 minutes, or take tram #1 to Széchenyi tér (5 stops). One block back, on the other side of Híd u., is Klauzál tér, where **tourist agencies** live long and prosper.

■■■ TOKAJ

Tokaj lingers idyllically along the west bank of the gentle Tisza River, at the base of the vineyard-laden foothills of the Zempleni range, home to the world-renowned Tokaj wines, which Louis XVI proclaimed "the wine of Kings, the king of wines." Of these, the strikingly sweet Tokaj Aszú is the most famous.

In July and August, rest at the **Kollégium** at Bajcsy-Zsilinszky 15-17 (tel. (41) 35 23 55), where quads are 400Ft per person. The **Makk-Marci Panzió** at Ligetközl on the corner of Kossuthlajos across from the post office, has excellent rooms with private baths. (Singles 1166Ft. Doubles 1802Ft. Breakfast included.) Camping is available across the river along the banks of the Tisza at **Tisza Camping** (tel. (41) 35 20 12), across the less central of the town's two bridges. (2 people/bungalow 600Ft, in a tent 300Ft.) Renting a **canoe** from the campsite (100Ft/5hr.) and drifting down the Tisza may be the most enjoyable way to spend the afternoon in this sleepy village. Land-lubbers may prefer a **hike** between vineyards to the top of the Bald Peak high above town; take the road up from Kossuth tér. Try one of the several *halászcsárdá* (fish restaurants) along the main road, which serve the catch of the Tisza. Numerous **wine cellars** *(bor pince)* serve Tokaj's finest; the largest is the Rákóczi at Kossuth tér 15 (open daily 7am-7pm), though the tiny cellar 50m away on Ovar utea 40 may be more memorable. (Open daily 11am-11pm. Ring the buzzer if no one is there. Both places, bottles 300-700Ft.)

Tokaj is on the **rail** line between Miskolc and Nyiregyháza. Trains from Budapest-Keleti station leave for Miskolc almost hourly (2½hr., 440Ft); from Miskolc trains leave as frequently to Tokaj (1hr., 108Ft). From the railway station, go left until the overpass, then left again takes you to the town center.

Poland (Polska)

US$1 = 19,500zł (złoty, or PLZ)
CDN$1 = 14,800zł
UK£1 = 30200zł
IR£1 = 28300zł
AUS$1 = 12700zł
NZ$1 = 10800zł
SAR1 = 4060zł
Country Code: 48

1000zł = US$0.51
1000zł = CDN$0.67
1000zł = UK£0.33
1000zł = IR£0.35
1000zł = AUS$0.79
1000zł = NZ$0.93
1000zł = SAR0.25
International Dialing Prefix: 00

The first and most gracious of the 1989 Eastern European shakedowns unfolded in Poland with a diplomacy more typical of chess games than revolutions. After over 20 years of anti-government union strikes, economic distress, and political imprisonments, Wojciech Jaruzelski's Central Committee met with Lech Wałęsa and other Solidarity leaders during several weeks of "round-table" discussions. In return for Solidarity's pledge to end strikes, the government agreed to legalize the union, amend the constitution, and hold free elections. Solidarity members swept into all but one of the contested seats, and the editor of its newspaper was sworn in as Eastern Europe's first noncommunist Prime Minister in 40 years. Checkmate.

Now, the largest and most populous of the newly liberated Eastern European nations is gritting its teeth in a determined attempt to rejoin the modern world. In 1990, the Solidarity government opted to take the bitter dose of capitalism in one gulp. To woo western investment, the government eliminated subsidies, froze wages, and devalued currency, throwing the antiquated economy into recession and producing the first unemployment in 45 years. Consumer goods now fill the shelves, and budding capitalists truck in supplies to sell at sidewalk bazaars, though few people have any free cash to spend. Although prices have continued to increase, Poland is still a bargain for Westerners.

Whatever Poland is or becomes, it promises few dull moments. Struggle has been a way of life for Poles, who have enjoyed only 20 years of freedom in this century. Resilient and gracious, they have drawn strength from the Catholic Church and a rich intellectual tradition. Survivor of the devastating Second World War, mismanagement, and environmental carnage, the country offers many riches. The medieval amber shores of the Baltic coast to the north transform into poppy-strewn plains that dominate Poland's landscape. Along the southern border, the Sudety and Karpaty Mountains break the lull of the lowlands, culminating in the exhilarating, snowcapped peaks of the Tatry range where *górale* (mountaineer) folklore still thrives.

GETTING THERE

As of September 1993, citizens of the U.S. and U.K. need no visas for Poland for stays up to 90 days. Citizens of Canada, Ireland, Australia, South Africa, and New Zealand need visas. Single-entry visas (valid 3 months) cost US$32; transit visas (valid 48hrs.) cost US$16 (students US$12). In Canada and the U.S., their embassies are at 2603 Lakeshore Blvd., Toronto, Ont. M8V 1G5 (tel. (416) 252-5471), or 223 Madison Ave., New York, NY 10016 (tel. (212) 889-8360).

Getting to Poland means an easy if tiresome train trip from Berlin, Prague, or Budapest (often overnight); **Polferries'** ships (tel. 46 (965) 252 11)—from Ystad, Sweden (2/day; 260 Swedish kr, with ISIC 210 Swedish kr); or Copenhagen, Denmark (5/week; 280 Danish kr, with ISIC 230 Danish kr) to the port city of **Świnoujście** in northeast Poland; or from Öxelösund, Sweden or Helsinki, Finland to **Gdańsk** (1-3/week from each port)—are an excellent option. The Lithuanian road border to the northeast is open; bus and train travel to L'viv in Ukraine is quick if you can get a visa and a seat, and taking the train to St. Petersburg and Moscow is also possible from Warsaw. To Slovakia, cross by bus and foot through the Tatry Mountains from Zakopane or by train from Kraków to Prešov and Košice.

TRAVELING IN POLAND

Trains PKP trains run frequently with service to almost every town; although prices have dramatically increased, they remain an inexpensive mode of travel for Westerners. Train stations have large boards with alphabetical listings of towns, and posters with chronological listings of trains. *Odjazdy* (departures) are in yellow; *przyjazdy* (arrivals) appear in white. The few *ekspresowy* trains are listed in red with an "Ex" in front of the train number. *Pośpieszny* (direct trains, listed in red without the "Ex"), chug along almost as fast. *Osobowy* trains (listed in black) are the slowest and cheapest—about 35% less than direct fares. Once you figure out which train you want, note the *peron* (platform) number, write down the destination, type of train, date, and time; then hand the information to the clerk. All *expresowy* and some *pośpieszny* trains require seat reservations; if you see a boxed R on the schedule, ask the clerk for a *miejscówka* (22,000zł). A *bilet* (ticket) in *pierwsza klasa* (1st class) is 50% more and worth it for overnights—the seats fold back all the way. Buy your ticket aboard the train for a small surcharge, but you must find the conductor before he finds you or risk being slapped with an outrageous fine. Train tickets are only valid on the day of issue. **Polrail passes** are available from travel bureaus (ORBIS, for example), covering unlimited 1st-class train travel for 8, 15, or 21 days. International train tickets can now be purchased only with złoty. The ISIC entitles cardholders to 25% off on international fares (zip on domestic). **Eurotrain passes,** available at ALMATUR, offer 40% discounts on train tickets between European capitals for those under 26.

Buses, Flights, Hitching, and Urban Transportation

Bus travel has become cheaper than the train. **PKS buses** are a particularly good idea for short excursions, which can take hours on an *osobowy* train. Advance tickets may be purchased at the bus station. In the country, PKS markers (like yellow Mercedes-Benz symbols) indicate bus stops, but drivers will often halt elsewhere if you flag them down. Though the domestic **airline,** LOT, is not a real budget option, it does give students under 26 a 25% discount.

One may **hitch** on any road in the country; hand-waving, not a thumb, is the accepted sign. Though Polish hitchers are expected to pay, drivers usually refuse compensation from foreigners. The Polish government has encouraged hitching with the *Autostop Hitchhike Book,* available from PTTK for 36,000zł (valid May-Sept.); it includes an insurance policy, an ID card, a tourist information book, and vouchers that qualify one's drivers for prizes and compensation.

City public transportation *(komunikacja miejska)* is cheap and efficient. Buy tickets from any *Ruch* kiosk, and punch your ticket *(bilet)* on board. Students can usually ride for the lower *ulgowy* fare; this means buying the half-price ticket, or, if the ticket says *dwukrotnego,* punching only one end instead of both ends. In most cities, trams stop running as early as 10pm.

Taxis will probably rip you off. Search out official vehicles with the city coat-of-arms on the door, and insist that the driver use the meter. You will be asked to pay for the driver's return trip if you travel outside the city. Fares increase 50% at night.

POLAND ESSENTIALS

ORBIS is the Polish state travel bureau, with offices in most major hotels and elsewhere in major cities. They sell international *(międzinarodowe)* and domestic *(krajowe)* train tickets and international bus tickets. **ALMATUR,** the Polish student travel organization, sells the ISIC and Eurotrain passes; they can also help find inexpensive university housing during the summer. Both provide maps and brochures, as do **PTTK** and **IT** bureaus, on the main street of every town.

The Polish złoty is real money now but still not widely traded in the West. Change back before leaving. For cash, *kantor* offices (private exchange counters) offer marginally better rates than banks or hotels. Traveler's checks can be exchanged at most ORBIS offices in major cities, at each town's main office of the **Narodowy Bank Polski** and at the **Bank Pekao** in the Warsaw Marriott hotel. Normal banking hours are weekdays from 8am to 4pm, though some banks stay open until 6pm. Exchange windows in some ORBIS hotels stay open 24hrs. The black market is extinct. Currency reform remains a rumor; until then, take care not to confuse the 1000-zł bill with the 100,000-zł bill.

Large department stores are usually open from 9am to 8pm, grocery stores from 6am to 7pm and most small shops from 11am to 7pm. Most museums are open Tuesday through Sunday from 10am to 4pm. Legal holidays include New Year's Day, Easter, Workers' Day (May 1), Constitution Day (May 3), Corpus Christi (June 14), All Souls' Day (Nov. 1), National Day (Nov. 11), and Christmas (Dec. 25-26). New religious and national holidays may be officialized as state control atrophies. Museums ordinarily close the day after a holiday as well.

Public bathrooms, often identified with a triangle for men and a circle for women, are common (2000zł). Be prepared: carry your own roll of toilet paper.

A word on **fines:** don't do anything your mother wouldn't recommend. You can be seriously fined for (among other things) jaywalking, putting your shoes on a train seat, or riding a tram or bus without a validated ticket.

Dial 997 for the **police,** 998 for the **fire** department, and 999 for an **ambulance.**

Communication In cities, many Poles know some English. German is more common; try English before Russian. Students may know French as well. Polish spelling is fully phonetic and easy to figure out. Buy a phrasebook before you arrive. Some key words and phrases include: *Dzień dobry!* (jane DUH-brih, "hello"); *Ile kosztuje?* (EE-leh kosh-TOO-yeh, "how much is it?"); *Dziękuję* (jeng-KOO-yeh, "thank you"); *Do widzenia* (duh veed-ZANE-ya, "goodbye"). When you approach a stranger or a sales clerk, preface your question with *Proszę pana* (PRUH-sheh PAH-nah, "please, sir") or *Proszę pani* (PRUH-sheh PAH-nee, "please, ma'am"). Women traveling alone may have to deal with a drunken oaf or two; fire away a firm *Odczep się* (UHD-chep sheh, "get lost"). When all else fails, there's always *Nie mówię po polsku* (nyeh MOO-vyeh poh POHL-skoo, "I don't speak Polish").

   Mail to and from Poland is slow but becoming more reliable. Airmail *(lotnicza)* letters usually take 7-10 days to the U.S. For **Poste Restante,** put a "1" after the city name to make sure it goes to the main post office. Public pay **phones** now use tokens *(żetony),* which come in 2 denominations (A for inner-city calls, 600zł, and C for city-to-city calls, 6000zł). PPTT phone cards are available for all types of calls, even international ones, and come in several denominations (up to 60,000zł). Special phones have slots in which to slide the card, and instructions are in English. Both tokens and phone cards are available at the post office. AT&T's **USA Direct** is now available from phone card phones as well as post offices and private phones (dial 010 480 0111; outside Warsaw, dial 0 and wait for a tone first). To make a **collect call,** write the name of the city or country and the number plus "Rozmowa 'R' on a slip of paper, and hand it to a post office staff member; it'll take some time. Direct international calls to most Western European countries, as well as to the U.S., are available from private phones—just dial 0 plus the country code and the number you are calling.

Accommodations and Camping At the train station or outside the tourist office, you will likely make the acquaintance of grandmother types offering private rooms. These unofficial accommodations are usually safe, clean, and convenient, but do ask if the room is near the city center. Expect to pay about US$15 per person.

   HI youth hostels *(schroniska młodzieżowe)* are generally crowded, rather primitive and quite uncomfortable, but are absolutely everywhere and cost an average of 56,000zł per night (slightly less for "juniors" under 18 or 26, slightly more for non-members). Hot water is chancy. **PTSM** is the national hostel organization. **University dorms** are a smart option during the summer (July-Aug.), when they transform into sparse but cheap tourist housing. Ask at ALMATUR. **PTTK** runs a number of hotels called **Domy Turysty,** where you can stay in multi-bed rooms for 40,000-90,000zł. Many towns have a **Biuro Zakwaterowań,** which arranges stays in private homes. In summer, only Category I rooms are available.

   Tent sites average 25,000zł per person, 50,000zł with car. Bungalows are often available; a bed costs about 100,000zł. Look for the *Polska Mapa Campingów,* which lists all campgrounds. ALMATUR also runs a number of campgrounds in summer; ask for a list at one of their offices.

Food and Drink Food is quite cheap in Poland, and more expensive does not always mean better. A *restauracja* or *kawiarnia* has waiters; a *bar* is self-service. Do not tip. At sit-down restaurants, try *kotlet schabowy* (pork chop), *kaczka* (roast duck served with plums and apples), *flaczki* (tripe), and *węgorz* (eel). Soups are the highlight of Polish cuisine; try the famous beet broth, *barszcz,* or a cup of *żurek,* a creamy soup made with barley flour and loaded with crumbs, eggs, and sausage. Fruit and vegetable stands are on every corner, and fast-food trailers sell *zapiekanki* (mushrooms, melted cheese, and ketchup on french bread) for 8000zł and *hot dogi* and *hamburgery* for 10,000-15,000zł. *Naleśniki* (Polish crepes) are filled with fruit, cheese, jam, or whipped cream. Get a taste of real home cooking at super-cheap self-service cafeterias or at a *bar mleczny* (milk bar), which sells vegetarian dishes and often meat entrees as well. All wines are imported and can be expensive; most places list by the glass, not the bottle. Polish beer is dubious, but try to find *Żywiec* or *Okocim* (if you want it cold, say so). Polish vodka is a national specialty; *Wyborowa* is the best brand. Tea is consumed in glasses and never with milk.

■■■ WARSAW (WARSZAWA)

Contemnir procellas (to defy the storms) is Warsaw's motto. At least two-thirds of the city's population perished during WWII and by 1945, 85% of the capital's standing structures had fallen. Over 50 years after the German invasion, the faded but colorful façades of the *Stare Miasto* (old town), the cobblestone streets, and the tall, narrow buildings have all been painstakingly restored. Buildings that never existed rose above the rubble, built after plans found in old archives—a resurrection testifying to Warsaw's relentless, defiant spirit.

ORIENTATION AND PRACTICAL INFORMATION

Warsaw, the country's principal air and rail hub, lies in east-central Poland, about 150km from the Belorussian border. The *Śródmieście* (city center) and most major points of interest lie on the west bank of the **River Wisła,** which bisects the city. To the right of the main train station **Warszawa Centralna, ul. Marszałkowska** intersects **Aleje Jerozolimskie,** forming the center of the modern downtown. Beyond, Aleje Jerozolimskie extends toward the river to cross the next major street, **Nowy Świat.** A right on Nowy Świat leads down embassy row to Łazienki and Wilanów palaces; a left leads north to the old town. A good map with bus and tram lines is *essential;* purchase one at the *Ruch* (news and tobacco) stand on any street corner, in large hotels or bookstores, in the airport, or in bus and train stations.

Tourist Offices: ORBIS, ul. Bracka 16 (tel. 26 02 71). Entrance on Jerozolimskie near Nowy Świat. Train, plane, and bus tickets. Arrive early to avoid midday rush. Open Mon.-Fri. 8am-7pm, Sat. 8am-3pm. **Travel office branches** downtown sell international train tickets and plane tickets, and change money. Open Mon.-Fri. 8am-6pm. **Centrum Informacji Turystycznej** (Tourist Information Center), pl. Zamkowy 1-13 (tel. 635 18 81), in the old town. Doles out a guide to Warsaw listing all hotels, tourist offices, restaurants, and cafés (65,000zł), peddles city maps (15,000-25,000zł), and provides sight-seeing information. Open Mon.-Fri. 9am-6pm, Sat. 10am-6pm, Sun. 11am-6pm.

Budget Travel: ALMATUR, ul. Kopernika 23 (tel. 26 35 12 or 26 26 39), off Nowy Świat. Good place for travel information and English speakers. Sells Eurotrain passes and ISICs. Open Mon.-Fri. 9:30am-5pm, Sat. 10am-2pm. Main office at ul. Kopernika 15. **PTSM,** ul. Chocimska 28, #427 (tel. 49 81 28), near pl. Unii Lubelskiej, is the Polish youth hostel federation. Stockpiles lists of all Polish youth hostels as well as membership cards (50,000zł, students 35,000zł). Open Mon.-Fri. 9am-3pm. **PTTK,** Podwale Śródmieście 23 (tel. 31 80 65), in the old town. Info on its budget hotels *(Domy Turysty)* across Poland. Open Mon.-Fri. 11am-5pm. Camping, kayaking, and hiking information Tues. and Fri. 1-6pm.

Embassies: U.S., al. Ujazdowskie 29-31 (tel. 628 30 41); entrance around the corner at ul. Piękna 12. Open Mon.-Fri. 9am-noon. **Canada,** ul. Matejki 1-5 (tel. 29 80 51). Open Mon.-Fri. 8:30am-1pm and 2-5pm. **U.K.,** al. Róż 1 (tel. 628 10 01). Consular office at Wawelska 14 (tel. 25 80 31). Open Mon.-Fri. 9am-noon. **Australia,** ul. Estońska 3-5 (tel. 17 60 81). **New Zealand** citizens should contact the British embassy. **Czech Republic,** ul. Koszykowa 18 (tel. 628 72 21). Open Mon.-Fri. 9am-1pm. **Slovakia,** ul. Litewska 6. **Lithuania,** al. Ujazdowskie 13 (tel. 62 31 94 or 694 24 87). **Russia,** ul. Belwederska 25, bldg. C. Open Wed. and Fri. 8am-1pm. **Ukraine,** ul. Szuka 7 (tel. 29 32 01). **Belorus,** ul. Ateńska 67 (tel. 17 39 54).

Currency Exchange: For cash: all hotels, banks, and tourist offices as well as private *Kantor* counters (with slightly better rates) throughout the city. For traveler's checks: the **Narodowy Bank Polski** at Plac Powstańców Warszawy, on the 2nd fl. (open Mon.-Fri. 8am-6pm, Sat. 8am-1pm); the **Bank Pekao** at the Warsaw-

Marriott on al. Jerozolimskie, 3rd fl. (open Mon.-Fri. 8am-6pm); and most **ORBIS** offices. Credit card cash advances available at ORBIS on al. Jerozolimskie.

American Express: Marszałkowska 142 (tel. 27 80 31). Full service. Express cash machine, 24hrs. Postal code: 00-068. Open Mon.-Fri. 9am-5pm, Sat. 10am-2pm.

Post Office: At Swiętokrzyska and Jasna. Open 24hrs. **Poste Restante** at counter #12. **Fax** bureau (98,400zł/page to U.S.). **Postal code:** 00-001.

Telephones: At the post office. Long lines during the day. **City Code:** 022.

Flights: From the new and improved international **Port Lotniczy Warszawa-Okęcie** (Terminal 1), ul. Żwirki i Wigury; take bus #175 to the city center (after 11pm, bus #611). Procure bus tickets *(bilety)* at the *Ruch* stand in the departure hall or at the *kantor* office outside (4000zł). Domestic flights depart from **Warszawa-Okęcie** (Terminal 2), ul. 17 Stycznia.

Trains: Most trains use the well-organized **Warszawa Centralna** in the center of the city. Platforms are on the underground level, most services on the ground floor, main ticket windows 1 floor up, and international windows on the top floor. To: Berlin (3/day, 6-8hr., 620,000zł); Budapest (2/day, 14hr., 920,000zł); Paris (1/day, 22hr., 3,000,000zł); Prague (3/day, 10hr., 310,000zł); Moscow (2/day, 23hr., 960,000zł); and St. Petersburg (1/day, 26hr., 850,000zł).

Buses: The main bus station (tel. 23 64 94 or 23 64 95) is **PKS Warszawa Zachodnia,** next to the train station at al. Jerozolimiskie 144. From the train station, take bus M headed west (away from the city center). Ask at ORBIS about international bus tickets, and be persistent. Often direct bus routes exist where direct trains do not.

Luggage Storage: At Warszawa Centralna, use the **przechowalnia bagażu** on the level below the main hall (4000zł/piece/day, plus 0.6% of baggage value—an arbitrary calculation on your part). Up to 10 days.

Public Transportation: Bus and tram lines are marked on the standard city map. Fare 4000zł, students 2000zł; some express buses (which have letters rather than numbers) 8000zł. Night buses 12,000zł. Large baggage 4000zł/piece. You must buy tickets at a *Ruch* stand or street vendor; there are no conductors on buses or trams. Once in the bus or tram, punch both ends of the ticket in the machines on board. If caught without a punched ticket, you'll be nabbed for 200,000zł.

Taxis: Stands marked by blue and white signs. **Radiotaxi,** tel. 96 24. Avoid cabs at Warszawa Centralna or the Marszałkowska-al. Jerozolimskie rotary; you'll be over-charged.

Hitchhiking: A ride-finding service is available at the **Autostop Bureau,** ul. Narbutta 27a (tel. 49 62 08), located at the back of the building. Sells the *Hitchhike Book* for 25,000zł. Open Mon.-Fri. 9am-3pm.

Bookstores: Panorama, ul. Nowogrodzka 56 (tel. 21 19 18). A sizable collection of inexpensive books in English and French. Open Mon.-Fri. 10am-6pm. The **Klub Międzynarodowej Prasy i Książki,** Marszałkowska 104/122, carries stacks of Western magazines in English. Open Mon.-Fri. 9am-8pm, Sat. 9am-4pm.

Laundromat: At ul. Anielewicza and Karmelicka (tel. 31 73 17). Take bus #180 north from Marszałkowska. Open Mon.-Fri. 9am-7pm, Sat. 9am-1pm; get there early. Wash and dry 70,000zł/6kg. Dry additional 15min. 30,000zł. Bring your own detergent.

Emergencies: Ambulance: tel. 999. **Fire:** tel. 998. **Police:** tel. 997. **Headquarters:** tel. 26 24 24.

ACCOMMODATIONS AND CAMPING

The **Syrena** office, ul. Krucza 16 (tel. 628 75 40), pins down rooms in private homes; arrive early. From the train station, turn left (toward downtown) at al. Jerozolimskie, follow it to ul. Krucza and take a right. (Singles 160,000zł. Doubles 250,000zł. Open daily 8am-7pm.)

Schronisko Młodzieżowe (HI), ul. Smolna 30, top floor (tel. 27 89 52), across from the National Museum. Take bus #158 or 175, or tram #22 from al. Jerozolimskie. Clean but basic; usually full by the end of the evening. Excellent location. Lockout (including reception) 10am-5pm. Curfew 11pm. 56,000zł, under 18 50,000zł.

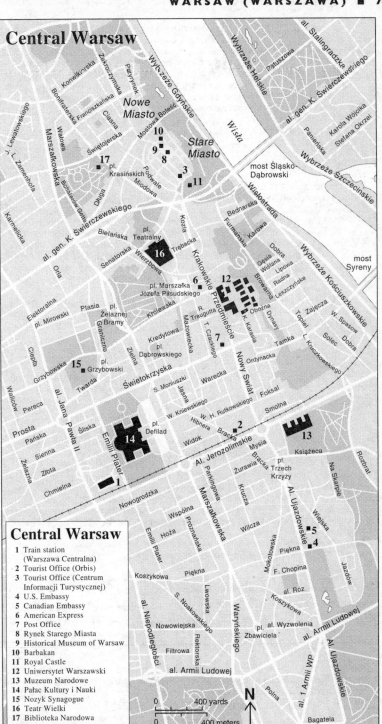

Central Warsaw

Nowe Miasto

Stare Miasto

Wisła

most Śląsko-Dąbrowski

most Syreny

Central Warsaw

1 Train station
   (Warszawa Centralna)
2 Tourist Office (Orbis)
3 Tourist Office (Centrum
   Informacji Turystycznej)
4 U.S. Embassy
5 Canadian Embassy
6 American Express
7 Post Office
8 Rynek Starego Miasta
9 Historical Museum of Warsaw
10 Barbakan
11 Royal Castle
12 Uniwersytet Warszawski
13 Muzeum Narodowe
14 Pałac Kultury i Nauki
15 Nozyk Synagogue
16 Teatr Wielki
17 Biblioteka Narodowa

0   400 yards

0   400 meters

N

Nonmembers 70,000zł. Sheets 10,000zł. Showers, kitchen, baggage room. English spoken. No wheelchair access.

Schronisko Młodzieżowe (HI), ul. Karolkowa 53a (tel. 32 88 29). Take tram #22 west from al. Jerozolimskie or the train station. Get off at "Okopowa." Left on al. Solidarności (Gen K. Swierczewskiego on maps). When you see ul. Karolkowa on the left, turn right. Pretty and out of the way. Lockout 10am-5pm. Curfew 11pm. 4- to 7-bed rooms 90,000zł. Kitchen. Baggage room 5000zł. No showers.

Dom Nauczyciela (Teacher's House), Wybrzeże Kościuszkowskie 31-33 (tel. 625 05 71). From Świętojerska, take bus #150 or 155 to Pomnik Syreny stop. Entrance on ul. Jaracza. Overlooks a park, the river, a highway, and an electric plant. Well-kept rooms. Reception opens at 2pm. Singles 210,000zł. Doubles 400,000zł.

Dom Chłopa, pl. Powstańców Warszawy 2 (tel. 27 92 51), between the Pałac Kultury and Nowy Świat. A real hotel, attracting an older clientele, but young Poles crowd the pool hall. Reception open 24hrs. Singles 360,000zł. Doubles 750,000zł. Breakfast included.

Hotel Harenda (PTTK), also known as **Dom Turysty,** ul. Krakowskie Przedmieście 4-6 (tel. 26 26 25). From train station, take bus #175 to "Uniwersytet." Walk *back* to the end of the block; take the first left on Obożna. Very near tourist zone, as the name would suggest. Clean, modern showers. Prices from 100,000zł/person for quads to 450,000zł for a single with bath. Reservations a must.

Hotel-Uniwersytet Warszawski, ul. Belwederska 26/30 (tel. 41 13 08). Take bus #131 or 180 from Marszałkowska to the "Spacerowa." An international tourist crowd beds down south of the Park Łazienkowski. Singles 380,000zł. Doubles 570,000zł. Breakfast included.

Hotel MDM, Plac Konstytucji 1 (tel. 628 25 26). A grand, graying edifice brooding over a noisy, commercial stretch of Marszałkowska south of the centrum. Singles 300,000zł. Doubles with bath 780,000-880,000zł. Breakfast included. Students with ID receive a 20% discount.

Camping: Camping Gromada, ul. Żwirki i Wigury 32 (tel. 25 43 91), at ul. Rokitnicka. Take bus #175 (direction "Port Lotniczy") one stop past "Pomnik Lotnika." 38,000zł/person, students 33,000zł, tent included. 2-person bungalows 116,000zł, 4-person 232,000zł. Open May 1-Sept. 30.

FOOD

Many of Warsaw's best restaurants bunch around the **Rynek Starego Miasta,** the market square of the old town. Few Poles can afford these places; Warsaw's proletarian cafeterias are infinitely more colorful and cheap. During the day, you can stop by a *sklep spożywczy* (grocery store) and test your food vocabulary.

Bazyliszek, Rynek Starego Miasta 5 (tel. 31 18 41). One of Warsaw's finest. Roast duck 190,000zł. Reserve ahead and dress sharp. Some vegetarian entrees. Open Mon.-Fri. noon-midnight, Sat.-Sun. noon-1am.

Zapiecek (tel. 31 56 93), at the corner of ul. Piwna and Zapiecek in the old town. Candle-lit intimacy with a German bent. Entrees 50,000-100,000zł. Open Mon.-Sat. 11am-11pm.

Blikle, Nowy Świat 35. The best pastries in the city by the same Swiss family since the 1870s. Delectables from 3000zł. Open mid-July to mid-June Mon.-Fri. 10am-6pm, Sat. 10am-3pm.

Bar Uniwersytecki, Krakowskie Przedmieście 16-18. Next to the university under the yellow awning. Big helpings of Polish food for low prices. Entrees 10,000zł. Open Mon.-Fri. 7am-8pm, Sat.-Sun. 9-11am.

Restaurant Maryla, ul. Nowogrodzka 24-26 (tel. 21 02 71), inside the Hotel Forum. Bland but generous helpings of traditional entrees (150,000-180,000zł). Open daily 11:30am-10pm. Across the hall, the **Rotisseria Soplica** serves up a lot more charm and a longer menu of international dishes. Open daily 7-11am and 1pm-midnight.

Kawiarnia Bazyliszek, Rynek Starego Miasta, on the old town market square. Its namesake restaurant's outdoor café. A relaxing place amid the restored splendor of Warsaw's old town. Cappuccino 19,000zł. Open daily 9am-9pm.

Lody W. Hoduń, ul. Nowomiejsk 11/13, in the old town. Divine ice cream in waffle cones for 2500zł a scoop. Open daily 10am-7pm.

Nowe Miasto, Rynek Nowego Miasta 13 (tel. 31 43 79). Says "Restauracja Ekologiczna" outside. Organically grown vegetarian entrees 48,000-67,000zł. Live music nightly. Open daily 10am-midnight. Credit cards accepted. Wheelchair accessible.

SIGHTS

Stare Miasto, Nowe Miasto, and Trakt Królewski

Warsaw's postwar reconstruction shows its finest face in the **Stare Miasto** (Old Town). Narrow, cobbled streets, colorful houses, and brick churches give the area a rustic atmosphere. The **Rynek Starego Miasta** (Old Town Market Square) has emerged from recent renovation in pristine condition. The house on the corner at no. 31 dates back to the 14th century. At no. 42, the **Historical Museum of Warsaw** chronicles the city's resilient past. (Open Tues. and Thurs. 11am-6pm; March 15-Nov. 14 Tues. and Thurs. noon-7pm; Wed., Fri., and Sat. 10am-3:30pm all year, Sun. 11am-4:30pm all year. 10,000zł, students 5000zł, Sun. free.) From the square, follow ul. Krzywe Koło to the **Barbakan,** a rare example of 16th-century Polish fortifications. To the north lies the **Nowe Miasto** (New Town)—actually the second-oldest district in the city— restored to its 18th- and 19th-century glory. The **Marie Skłodowska-Curie Museum** marks the Nobel prizewinner's birthplace at ul. Freta 16. (Open Tues.-Sat. 10am-4:30pm, Sun. 10am-2:30pm.) For a view of the old and new towns, take the Śląsko-Dąbrowski bridge to the other side of the Vistula.

Many of Warsaw's must-sees lie along the 4km **Trakt Królewski** (Royal Route). The city's most attractive thoroughfare, it begins in the *Stare Miasto* as Krakowskie Przedmieście. Here, the completely rebuilt **Royal Castle** at the entrance to the old city has long been a symbol of Polish independence. The castle ticket office is at ul. Świętojańska 2. (Open Tues.-Sat. 10am-5pm, Sun. 10am-4:30pm. 60,000zł, students 30,000zł; Sun. 50,000zł, students 20,000zł; Thurs. free.) Climb the **tower** on Krakowskie Przedmieście in the southeastern corner of plac Zamkowy for a bird's eye view. (Open April-Oct. Tues.-Fri. 10am-4pm, Sat.-Sun. noon-7pm. 10,000zł.) **Uniwersytet Warszawski** occupies a complex of rebuilt palaces; across the street, Fryderyk Chopin lived and composed at the Academy of Fine Arts in the **Pałac Czapskich.** His heart is stuck in an urn in the **św. Krzyża Church,** a block away. The **Chopin Museum** is at Okólnik 1 in the Ostrogski Castle (tel. 27 54 71).

The Royal Route continues down to aleje Jerozolimskie as **Nowy Świat,** lined with cafés, boutiques, and street vendors. At plac Trzech Krzyży, it changes names one last time to aleje Ujazdowskie, terminating at plac Na Rozdrożu in the **Park Łazienkowski.** With its swans and majestic peacocks, the park is an appropriate setting for the pulse-quickening neoclassical **Pałac Łazienkowski,** which harbors galleries of 17th- and 18th-century art. (Open Tues.-Sun. 10am-3pm barring rain. 20,000zł, students 12,000zł.)

Commercial District, Gardens, and the Ghetto

Warsaw's commercial district lies southwest of the old town along Marszałkowska. Here, at aleje Jerozolimskie 3, is the **Muzeum Narodowe** (National Museum), with stellar though sporadically gruesome collections of 8th- to 12th-century Coptic and medieval art. (Open Tues. and Sun. 10am-5pm, Wed. and Fri.-Sat. 10am-4pm, Thurs. noon-6pm. 10,000zł, students 5000zł.) The best panorama of Warsaw is from atop the 70-story "Stalin Gothic" **Pałac Kultury** (Palace of Culture), on Marszałkowska, as this is the only location from which the hulking beast itself is not visible. (Open Mon.-Sat. 9am-6pm, Sun. 10am-6pm. 30,000zł.)

Below, at the crossroads of Marszałkowska and Świętokrzyska, buzzes one of the capital's many post-communist bazaars. Shopping and commerce have flooded the streets since the inception of crash capitalism in January 1990; everything from kitchen sinks to kiwi fruit goes for what the market will bear. **Bazar Różyckiego** is across the river on ul. Targowa (open daily, tram #7 from al. Jerozolimskie); another bazaar unfolds every weekend across the river in the Praga district, around the **Stadion Dziesięciolecia.** Watch your wallet.

Meticulously manicured trees and an outstanding baroque palace garnish the **Wilanów Gardens,** reached by bus #180 and express bus B from ul. Marszałkowska. (Palace open Mon. and Wed.-Sun. 10am-2:30pm. Palace 22,000zł, students 12,000zł. Park 10,000zł, students 5000zł.) The **Muzeum Plakatu** is Europe's largest poster museum. (Open Tues.-Fri. 10am-4pm, Sat.-Sun. 11am-5pm. 10,000zł, students 5000zł.)

Still referred to as "the Ghetto," the modern Muranów neighborhood of Warsaw holds few vestiges of what was once a community numbering 400,000. The beautifully reconstructed **Nożyk Synagogue** on ul. Twarda 6 lies just north of the Pałac Kultury. Look for the **Ghetto Uprising Monument** on ul. Zamenhofa. The **Jewish Cemetery** on ul. Okopowa stretches for miles, a forest-covered treasure of gravestone art. (Open Mon.-Thurs. 9am-3pm, Fri. 9am-1pm.) At Umschlagplatz, a huge and moving monument marks the spot where 300,000 Jews were rounded up to be sent to death camps. Farther north, in the Żoliborz section, Father Jerzy Popiełuszko delivered outspoken anti-government sermons at the **św. Stanisława Kostki Church** until his brutal murder by the secret police in 1984. Today his grave is a shrine to both the Church and Solidarity. Take tram #6, 15, 31, or 36 to Plac Wilsona; the church is on ul. Kozietulskiego.

ENTERTAINMENT

Much of Warsaw's social life revolves around its *winiarnie* (wine cellars) and *kawiarnie* (cafés). The most popular outdoor cafés are those on the Rynek Starego Miasta and along Nowy Świat.

Gessler, Rynek Starego Miasta 27, in the *Stare Miasto.* A premier wine cellar for the past 300 years, now owned by the like-named folks on ul. Senatorska. Drinks 50,000-100,000zł. Open daily from 1pm until the last dram is drunk dry.

Pod Herbami, ul. Piwna 21-23 (tel. 31 64 47). A pleasant, decent tavern full of local folk. Open Sun.-Thurs. 11am-11pm, Fri.-Sat. 11am-1am.

Gwiazdeczka, ul. Piwna 40, in the old town. Lovers meet under the Renaissance arches of its open-air garden. Principally a café, but serves alcohol. Coffee 10,400zł. Wine 20,000-30,000zł/glass. Open daily 9am-10pm.

U Hopfera, ul. Krakowskie Przedmieście 53. Another fine Warsaw winery. Cure the munchies with a plateful of *pierogi* (36,600zł). Open daily 9am-3am.

Hybrydy, ul. Złota 9, near the commercial district. A major-rager for footloose students. Open Fri.-Sat. 6pm-3am, Sun. 6pm-11pm. Cover 40,000zł, students 20,000-30,000zł; Sun. 30,000zł, students 20,000zł. Informal dress.

Classical concerts fill the **Gallery of Sculptures** in the Pomarańczarnia near the Pałac Łazienkowski on Sundays in June and July. (Ticket inquiries at the palace or gallery.) The **Pomnik Chopina** (Chopin Monument) nearby in the Park Łazienkowski hosts free Sunday performances by some of Poland's most distinguished classical artists. (May-Oct. at noon and 4pm.) **Teatr Wielki,** Plac Teatralny 1 (tel. 26 30 01), Warsaw's main opera and ballet hall, offers performances almost daily, except during July. The **Filharmonia Narodowa** (National Philharmonic Orchestra; tel. 26 72 81) gives regular concerts in its hall on ul. Jasna, northeast of the train station. For information and tickets, visit the **ZASP** *kasy teatralne* (tel. 21 94 54 or 21 93 83) at al. Jerozolimskie 25. (Open Mon.-Fri. 11am-6pm, Sat. 11am-2pm.) **Akwarium,** ul. Emilii Plater 49 (tel. 20 50 72), behind the Pałac Kultury, is the top spot in the city for live jazz. (Open Mon.-Thurs. 11am-11pm, Fri.-Sun. 11am-3am.)

■■■ GDAŃSK

Gdańsk (Danzig, in German) revitalized Poland with the political tidal wave of Solidarity (Solidarność), but its history sets it apart from the rest of the country. For centuries a major partner in the Hanseatic League, the Treaty of Versailles declared Danzig a "free city" and removed it from German possession. Hitler's desire to "correct" this situation was a significant factor in his decision to invade Poland, and it was here that WWII's first shots were fired. Although traces of German influence remain—most notably in architecture and gravestone inscriptions—the most compelling edifice in Gdańsk today is distinctively Polish: the striking monument at the gates of the Gdańsk (formerly Lenin) Shipyard, honoring workers who died in the 1970 uprising against the economic policies of Party First Secretary Gomułka.

ORIENTATION AND PRACTICAL INFORMATION

Gdańsk dips its toes in the Baltic Sea, serving as Poland's principal port. With Sopot and Gdynia, Gdańsk forms the "tri-city" metropolitan area, popular with Poles for its seaside piers and beach resorts. From the Gdańsk-Główny train station, the old town center lies a few blocks south, across Wały Jagiellońskie, along the Motława River.

Tourist Office: Centrum Informacji Turystycznej (Tourist Information Center), ul. Heweliusza 25-33 (tel. 31 43 55; fax 31 66 37), up the street from the Hotel Hevelius. Loaded with maps, guides, and tickets to major sights. English spoken. Open Mon.-Fri. 8am-4pm. **ORBIS,** in the Hotel Hewelius at ul. Heweliusza #22, does international and domestic train tickets, international bus, and all ferry tickets. English spoken. Open Mon.-Fri. 10am-5pm, Sat. 10am-4pm.

Budget Travel: ALMATUR, Długi Targ 11, 2nd floor (tel. 31 29 31 or 31 24 03), in the center of town. ISICs and bus and train tickets. Open Mon.-Fri. 9am-5pm.

Currency Exchange: The post office, hotels, banks and *Kantor* desks throughout the city center. **Narodowy Bank Polski** is on ul. Bogusławskiego next to Targ Węglowy. Open Mon.-Fri. 8am-6pm, Sat. 8am-noon.

American Express: At the Hotel Hevelius. **ORBIS** office. Replaces lost Cheques and cashes Traveler's Cheques. Holds mail. Closest full-service office in Warsaw.

Post Office: ul. Pocztowa and ul. Długa, in the center of town. Open Mon.-Fri. 8am-8pm, Sat. 9am-1pm. Fax bureau. Currency exchange. **Postal Code:** 80-801.

Telephones: At the post office. Open Mon.-Fri. 7am-9pm, Sat.-Sun. 9am-5pm. **City Code:** 058.

Flights: The **airport** is 22km away at Rebiechowo. Buses #110 and B connect it with the train station. The orange **LOT** office is at ul. Wały Jagiellońskie 2-4 (tel. 31 11 61). Open Mon.-Fri. 8am-6pm. To London (Sat., 2,400,000zł) and Hamburg (Sun.-Fri., 1,400,000zł). All plane tickets also available at **ORBIS.**

Trains: For international expresses to Berlin (1/day; 502,500zł, including the overnight), take a local commuter train from Gdańsk-Główny north to Gdynia-Główna (every 6-12min.). From Gdańsk-Główny to Prague (1/day, 11hr., 348,000zł) and Warsaw (6/day, July-Aug. 11/day, 4hr., 72,000zł). Validate your local ticket by punching it at one of the yellow *kasownik* machines *before* getting on the train.

Buses: PKS station located behind train station. Enter through underground passageway. Tickets sold 5:30am-10:20pm. To: Toruń (3/day, 3 hr., 74,000zł), Malbork (4/day, 18,000zł), Vilnius (1day, 250,000zł).

Ferries: Reach the terminal at **Nowy Port** by commuter rail. From Gdańsk to Oxelösund, near Stockholm (Mon., Wed. and Sun.; Sept.-May Thurs.; US$67), Helsinki (Sun. and Thurs. US$58), Ystad in Sweden (mid-April to mid-Oct. Fri., US$76), and Kaliningrad in Russia (May-Sept. Tues., Thurs., and Sat., 4½hr., US$50). All ferry tickets available at ORBIS.

Hitchhiking: Those Warsaw-bound go to ul. Elblącka (near the stadium).

Medical Assistance: Ambulance service, ul. Nowe Ogrody 1/7 (tel. 41 10 00).

Emergencies: Ambulance: tel. 999. **Fire:** tel. 998. **Police:** tel. 997.

ACCOMMODATIONS AND CAMPING

Gdańsk and the resort town of Sopot up the coast claim Poland's most popular beaches and are commensurately swamped in summer. Reserve well in advance. For help in finding a room, try **Biuro Zakwaterowań,** at ul. Elżbietańska 10-11 (tel.

31 17 27, 31 38 49, or 31 93 71), across from the train station. Singles run 140,000zł; doubles 250,000zł. (Open daily 7:30am-7:30pm.)

Schronisko Młodzieżowe (HI), ul. Wałowa 21 (tel. 31 23 13). Cross street in front of the train station, head up ul. Heweliusza and turn left at ul. Łagiewniki. Most convenient of 4 area hostels. Smaller rooms available to escape the kiddie brigade. Kitchen. Showers in basement. Lockout 10am-5pm. Curfew 10pm. 44,000zł, students under 26 36,000zł. Sheets 11,000zł. Baggage room 5000zł.

Schronisko Młodzieżowe (HI), ul. Smoluchowskiego 11 (tel. 32 38 20). Take tram #2, 6, 12, 13, or 14 for 4 stops from the train station. Kitchen. Lockout 10am-5pm. Curfew 10pm. 44,000zł, under 21 36,000zł. Sheets 11,000zł. Breakfast 12,500zł. Baggage room 5000zł. Frequently booked.

Schronisko Młodzieżowe (HI), ul. Grunwalkzka 244 (tel. 41 16 60). Take tram #6 or 12 to al. Wojska Polskiego, walk down ul. Chopina and turn left. Immaculate, efficiently run, and a long walk even after the endless tram ride. Lockout 10am-5pm. Curfew 10pm. 44,000zł; ages 18-26 36,000zł. Sheets 10,000zł.

Hotel ZNP, ul. Jana Uphagena 28 (tel. 41 91 16), in the Wrzeszcz neighborhood northwest of the center. Take tram #6 or 12 for 7 stops. Lovely brick edifice dripping with ivy on a tree-lined sidestreet. Singles 140,000zł, with bath 250,000zł. Doubles 640,000zł, with bath 400,000zł. Triples 330,000zł, with bath 400,000zł.

Hotel Jantar, Długi Targ 19 (tel. 31 27 16), near the Green Gate. Ideally located, frequently booked. Singles 350,000zł. Doubles 530,000zł, with bath 660,000-750,000zł. Triples with bath 840,000zł.

Camping: Gdańsk-Jelitkowo, ul. Jelitkowska 23 (tel. 53 27 31). From Gdańsk-Główny, take tram #2, 4, or 6 to the last stop, then bus #143 one stop to the left. One block from the beach. 34,000zł/person. 20,000-48,000zł/tent. Bungalows 100,000zł/day. Open June to mid-Sept.

FOOD

From the river walkway, you can follow the aroma of fresh fish frying. For fresh food of all sorts, try the **Hala Targowa market** on ul. Podmłyńska. (Open Mon.-Fri. and 1st and last Sat. of the month 9am-6pm.) Appease a late-night craving at the **24-hr. store,** upstairs at Wały Jagiellońskie, across from the train station.

Bar Rybny Krewetka, ul. Elżbietańska 10, across from the train station. Cafeteria-style fish bonanza, for less than 20,000zł/meal. Halibut *sauté,* 12,500zł. Open Mon.-Fri. 10am-6pm, Sat. noon-6pm.

Bar Neptun, ul. Długa 33/34. A revamped milk bar now serving hearty, homestyle meat dishes alongside vegetarian entrees. But where on earth did they get those 7-Eleven uniforms? 20,000zł/feed. Open Mon.-Fri. 7am-7pm, Sat. 9am-5pm.

Palowa, ul. Długa 47, in the basement of the town hall. A popular pseudo-medieval café run by the Gdańsk students' union. Torte from 7000zł/slice. Coffee 4500-12,000zł. Mixed drinks 20,000-46,000zł. Open daily 10am-midnight.

Tawerna Restauracja, ul. Powrożnica 21/22 (tel. 31 41 14), at the end of Długi Targ near the Green Gate. Expensive but delicious, with generous servings. Try the *pstrąg* (trout) for 270,000zł, including side dishes. Open daily 11am-10pm.

Tan-Viet Restauracja, ul. Podmłyńska 1/5. Far East meets Eastern Europe at 50,000-129,000zł/entree. Several shrimp platters from 59,000zł. Open daily 11am-10pm.

SIGHTS AND ENTERTAINMENT

Gdańsk was one of the first Polish cities to undergo an exhaustive postwar facelift. The handsome market square, **Długi Targ,** forms the center of town, where the original 16th-century façade of the **Dwór Artusa** faces out onto the **Neptune Fountain**. The 14th-century **town hall,** next to the fountain, houses the **Gdańsk Historical Museum;** don't miss the fantastic conference chamber. A trip up the tower (open July-Aug.) includes a series of numbing photographs of Gdańsk just after the war, while the 4th floor exhibits Solidarity printing presses, photographs, and underground journals from 1980-81. (Open Tues.-Thurs. 10am-3:30pm, Sat. 10am-4pm, Sun. 11am-4pm. 10,000zł, students 5000zł.) One block north is Gdańsk's grandest house of worship, the **Kościół Mariacki.** Almost completely rebuilt after its destruction in WWII, the church reigns as Poland's largest brick cathedral. You can climb many steps up the steeple to rise above the din and clatter of the city. (Steeple open May to mid-Oct. daily 9am-5:30pm. 5000zł.) **Ul. Mariacka,** behind the cathedral, is perhaps Gdańsk's most beautiful. Follow it through the gate to the river and turn left to glimpse the enormous **Gothic crane** that unloaded medieval freighters.

Attend Sunday mass at Lech Wałęsa's parish—the simple brick **św. Brigydy** church just north of the old town at ul. Profesorka 17. The **Old Post Office,** on ul. Obrońców Poczty Polskiej, was the rallying point for Polish resistance during the German invasion and has become a patriotic symbol. Solidarity flags fly high once again at the **Gdańsk Shipyard** and at the **monument** to the 1970 uprising, north of the center of town, near ul. Jaracza and only 1 stop from the train station on tram #8. Take a ferry to the island of **Westerplatte,** where you can visit the site of the first shots of WWII. Boats leave from outside the Green Gate at the end of Długi Targ. (April-Nov. 4 /day; 9:30am-4pm. 30,000zł, students 25,000zł.)

The Gdańsk area enjoys more sunshine than any other in the country. To get to **Stogi Beach,** the city's best, take tram #8 or 13 (direction "Stogi") from the train station to the end, or bus #112 or 186 (also direction "Stogi") to the last stop, then follow ul. Nowotna and everyone else, although only the brave (or the foolish) actually venture in the water.

The young and the restless in Gdańsk frequent disco and jazz clubs like **Flisak,** on ul. Chlebnicka, a quiet hangout for local art students. (Open daily noon-2am.) The **Rudy Kot,** ul. Garncarska 18-20, features live music and a score of pool tables. (Open Mon.-Sat. 11am-11pm, Sun. 1pm-midnight.) Every year during the first 2 weeks of August, Gdańsk erupts in the street fair **Jarmark Dominikański.** The **Jantar Jazz Festival,** which visits the city during July and August, ushers in the September **Polish Film Festival,** held in the NOT building next to the Hotel Hevelius. All tickets are available at ORBIS.

■ Near Gdańsk

Malbork Castle, in the unassuming town of the same name, was the main residence of the Teutonic Knights in the 14th century. WWII reduced the fortress—then one of the largest castles in Europe—to just another pile of rubble; reconstruction continues to this day. To get to the castle, follow ul. Dworcowa from the train station towards the center and take the fork marked "Centrum." Go up the steps to cross the highway, then walk up ul. Kościuszki; you'll see the ruddy castle towers atop the hill. (Open Tues.-Sun. 8:30am-5pm; Oct.-April 9am-2:30pm. Admission only with guided tour (in Polish; other languages 45,000zł extra). Tour 45,000zł, students 30,000zł.)

The reconstructed **Hotel Zbyszko,** ul. Kościuski 43 (tel. (055) 33 94), is on the right as you head towards the castle. (Singles 120,000zł. Doubles 170,000zł. Triples 220,000zł.) The **Hotel Dedal** on ul. Marksa 5 (tel. (055) 31 37), originally built for military guests, now welcomes peaceful bed-seekers to its rooms. The **Hotel Sportowy** (tel. (055) 24 13) doubles as a campsite on the outskirts of town off ul. Portowa; follow signs from the center. (Singles 150,000zł. Doubles 170,000zł. Triples 270,000zł. Quads 320,000zł. Camping 30,000zł/person; tents 30,000zł. Bungalows 450,000zł.) There are plenty of **milk bars** on or near ul. Kościuszki, and the winding paths beneath the castle walls along the Nogat river make excellent picnicking grounds. The **Café Zamkowa,** next to the castle entrance, prepares a regal feast amidst the coats of arms and wrought-iron gates that hang on the walls. (Entrees 50,000-90,000zł. Open daily 10am-6pm.) From Gdańsk, Malbork is a half hour and 18,000zł away (5 trains/day, en route to Warsaw). The bus station is one street away from the train station.

Sopot, 15 minutes away by commuter train (9000zł, leaving every 6-12 min.), features miles of white beaches, and is also the music center outside Gdańsk. At **Molo Pier** admission is 3000zł (6000zł on weekends), but the water is cleaner than at the Grand Hotel. Rooms are cheap and convenient at **Hotel Teodora Dolacińska,** plac Konstytucji 3-go Maja 3 (tel. 51 15 25); or procure a private room from the **IT** office, nearby at no. 8/10 (tel. 51 26 17). Watch for the **Opera Lećna** festival in September and the Thursday **piano festivals** in the town hall. All tickets are available at the **ORBIS** office on ul. Monte Cassino 49 (open daily 10am-5pm); meals are 40,000-90,000zł at **Caffe Bazaar,** across the tracks at no. 5.

■■■ SZCZECIN

Settled in the 8th century and chartered in 1278, Szczecin (SHCHEH-cheen) has changed hands repeatedly due to the strategic value of its ports, a cosmopolitan history which found the city in German hands during the Allied bombings of 1944. A few original structures remain, but much of the city's beauty lies in its restorations.

A relic of the Prussian settlement, the baroque **Brama Portowa** (Port Gate) marks the downtown area. A block away on ul. Wyszyńskiego, the 13th-century **St. James Cathedral** looms over the town; restoration has yet to replace its windows. The giant, newly-restored **Palace of Pomeranian Princes** overlooks it all from Szczecin's oldest settlement site. (Open Tues.-Sun. 10am-6pm. 15,000zł, students 10,000zł.) Behind the palace bravely stands the abandoned **Maiden's Tower,** the only one of 37 original towers on the medieval town walls to survive WWII. The old **Ratusz** (Town Hall) holds one of the city's three branches of the **National Museum;** this one explains Szczecin's history from the Paleolithic to the present. Find the rest of the museum, chronicling Pomeranian art from the medieval to the modern, north of Castle Hill, 2 blocks west of the 15th-century Gothic Church of Sts. Peter and Paul. (Both branches open Sat.-Sun. 10am-4pm, Tues. and Thurs. 10am-5pm, Wed. and Fri. 9am-3:30pm. 15,000zł, students 10,000zł. Thurs. free. 1 ticket gets you into both galleries.)

Accommodations, Food, and Practical Information The **youth hostel** at ul. Unisławy 26 (tel. 23 25 66; take tram #3 to "Staszica," turn left on Kilińskiego) is cramped and lacks showers, but a bed and use of the kitchen costs only 37,500zł (non-members 50,000zł). The **Hotel Zwycięstwa** at pl. Zwycięstwa 1 (tel. 51 31 91) offers better-quality singles for 120,000zł, doubles for 180,000zł, triples for 210,000zł, and quints for 250,000zł. Further out in the suburbs, watch democracy in action at the **Foundation in Support of Local Democracy Hostel,** ul. Marii Skłodowskiej-Curie 4 (tel. 704 72). The service and facilities are worth the long trek. (Tram #9 to "Tragutta," continue 2 blocks, turn left, and walk to the end of the street. Singles 135,000zł. Doubles 270,000zł. Triples 285,000zł. Quads 360,000zł.)

Quick and convenient, the **Cafe Vega** at entrance H of the palace has an English menu and spicy entrees (20,000-40,000zł) to go with its endless liquor collection. (Open daily 10am-10pm.) **Bistro Aha** on ul. Farna is a friendly and modern café. (Open Mon.-Fri. 10am-10pm, Sat. 10am-8pm, and Sun. noon-8pm.)

For travel help, hit the **ORBIS** office at pl. Zwycięstwa 1 (tel. 431 06; open Mon.-Fri. 9am-5pm and Sat. 9am-1pm). **Informacja Turystyczna,** ul. Wyszyńskiego 26 (tel. 33 79 18), is a good first stop if you're looking for maps or brochures in English. (Open Mon.-Fri. 9am-5pm.) The **Post Office** and **telephones** are on al. Niepodległości, in a beautiful turn-of-the-century brick building. (Open Mon.-Sat. 8am-8pm. **Telephones** open 24hrs.) The train and bus stations are next to each other at the end of ul. 3-go Maja; take tram #3 to the center, or walk (10 min.). Trains run to Gdańsk (3/day, 5hr., 186,000zł), Poznań (5/day, 3hr., 86,000zł), and Berlin.

■■■ TORUŃ

An astounding number of tourist attractions are packed into Toruń's medieval ramparts. The old town, commanding the right bank of the Wisła River, was constructed by the Teutonic Knights in the 13th century and is the birthplace of renowned astronomer Nicolas Copernicus (the guy on the 1000-zł bill). Visit his birthplace, **Dom Kopernika,** at ul. Kopernika 17. (Open Tues.-Sun. 10am-4pm. 5000zł, students 3000zł, Sun. free.) The **Ratusz** (Town Hall) is the center of the tourist district and sells tickets to most of the sights in town. Inside its lovely woodworked doors is an art gallery with changing exhibits by Polish painters. (Open Tues.-Sun. 10am-4pm. 10,000zł, students 5000zł. Sun. free.) Relics of the Teuton founders include Toruń's crooked **Tower,** a part of the town wall near the bridge now too unstable to climb, and the **castle ruins** on ul. Przedzamcze, a maze of crumbling brick foundations. (Open daily 9:30am-4pm. 3000zł.) Stop by the **Kościół Marii** (Church of the Virgin Mary) just off the market on Panny Marii, and appreciate its eerily high aisle and stained glass of geometric designs and pictures. To view the length of the town, stroll along the **Bulwar Filadelfijski,** named for Toruń's sister City of Brotherly Love, among fishermen and lingering couples who line the stone steps to the river.

Accommodations, Food, and Practical Information PTTK runs a **Dom Turysty (Wycieczkowy)** on ul. Legionów 24 (tel. (056) 238 55). Take bus #10 from pl. Rapackiego outside the old town gate to the 3rd stop. (Doubles 180,000zł. Triples 270,000zł. Quads 320,000zł.) The **Hotel Trzy Korony** (tel. (056) 260 31) faces the *Ratusz* at Rynek Staromiejski 21. (Singles 150,000zł. Doubles 220,000zł. Triples 330,000zł.) The **Hotel Polonia** (tel. 230 28), pl. Teatralny 5, opposite the municipal theater, has large single beds, and double rooms with sinks. (Singles with bath 250,000zł. Doubles 400,000zł. Triples 720,000zł.) The **Hotel Pod Orłem,** ul. Mostowa 15 (tel. (056) 250 24) has huge, comfortable rooms. (Singles 150,000zł. Doubles 250,000zł, with bath 350,000zł. Triples 350,000zł, with bath 450,000zł.) The campground **Tramp** (tel. (056) 241 87) is across ul. Kujawska from the train station at #33. (20,000zł/person. 4-person bungalows 160,000zł.)

A large collection of **fruit and vegetable stands** line up a block east of the *Rynek;* most restaurants are in the old town. **Bar Mleczny,** ul. Różana 1, serves strawberry omelettes for 5700zł and big ol' bowls of soup for 3100zł. (Open Mon.-Fri. 9am-6pm, Sat. 9am-4pm.) **Zajazd Staropolski,** ul. Żeglarska 14, offers traditional dishes in a modernized (by 1970s standards) medieval chamber. (Entrees 20,000-60,000zł. Open daily 7am-10pm.) Reacquaint your taste buds with oregano and tomato sauce at the **Staromiejska Italian Restaurant,** ul. Szczytna 4 (tel. (056) 242 71), where you can order Italian *pierogi* (otherwise known as tortellini) for 33,000zł. **Kawiarnia Pod Atlantem,** ul. św. Ducha 3, swims in imported alcohol. (Open daily 10am-10pm.)

Toruń's train station is across the river from the town center. Buses #13, 22, and 33 from the station cross the bridge into town and stop at the gate to the old town. **ORBIS,** ul. Żeglarska 31 (tel. (056) 243 46), in the old town, sells train and bus tickets and distributes free information on Toruń and Copernicus. (Open Mon.-Fri. 9am-5pm.) **PTTK,** ul. Pl. Rapackiego 2 (tel. (056) 249 26), sells maps and brochures. (Open Mon.-Fri. 8am-5pm, Sat. 9am-1pm, Sun. 9am-1pm.) Toruń lies 3 hours by **train** northwest of Warsaw. (3/day, 3hr. 20min., 64,000zł.) Find the **post office** and **telephones** at Rynek Staromiejski 15 (**postal code:** 87-100; telephones open 24hrs.).

■■■ POZNAŃ

Poznań (known as Posen to its Prussian (1793-1918) and German (1939-45) rulers) first hosted the biannual International Trade Fair in 1921; in fall and spring, business folk from around the world descend upon the city, filling up hotel rooms and bolstering the local economy. Downtown, in the **Stary Rynek,** opulent 15th-century merchant homes surround the Renaissance **Ratusz,** which houses a museum detailing the town's history. (Open Mon.-Tues. 10am-4pm, Wed. 10am-6pm, Thurs. and Sun. 10am-3pm. 10,000zł, students 6000zł.) Resplendent with frescoes and pink marble, the **Kościół Farny** (Parish Church) blesses the end of ul. Świętosławska; in the square, the **Museum of Historic Musical Instruments,** Stary Rynek 45, stars Chopin's own piano. (Open Tues. 11am-5pm, Wed. and Fri. 10am-4pm, Sat. 10am-5pm, and Sun. 10am-3pm. 10,000zł, students 6000zł.) In 1956, workers protesting high food prices clashed with government troops, and 74 people died. The bloody incident is commemorated in the park on ul. Niepodległości at ul. św. Marcin by two stark crosses knotted together with steel cable and emblazoned with successive dates recalling workers' uprisings across Poland.

Accommodations, Food, and Practical Information There are 2 youth hostels in Poznań open year-round. **The HI youth hostel** is at Berwińskiego 2/3 (tel. (061) 66 36 80). Located in a school with many kids in the vicinity, it's a 10-minute walk west of the train station. (Sr. 45,000zł. Jr. 24,000zł.) The **Wojewódzki Ośrodek Mełodyrzny,** a clean hostel/hotel, is at ul. Niepodległości 34 (tel. (061) 53 22 51; 78,000zł). Take bus #51 from the train station to the Hotel Polonez and walk back 1 block. The **ALMATUR** office, on ul. Fredry 7 at the corner of ul. Kościuski (tel. (061) 52 03 44), will give you the scoop on summer hostels; for private rooms, try **Przemysłal,** ul Głogowska 16 (tel. (061) 66 39 83), or Pl. Gen Dabrowskiego 1. Fall out of bed and onto the old market square at the **Dom Turysty** at Stary Rynek 91 (tel. (061) 52 88 93; singles 300,000zł, with bath 350,000zł; doubles 500,000zł, with bath 600,000zł; multi-bed rooms 80,000zł/person). The centrally located **Hotel Rzymski** (formerly Poznański), ul. Marcinkowskiego 22 (tel. (061) 52 81 21), has small, shiny rooms and a multilingual staff. (Singles 250,000zł, with bath 400,000zł. Doubles 420,000zł, with bath 570,000zł.) **Hotel Wielkopolska,** ul. św. Marcin 69 (tel. (061) 52 76 31), is near the university in the commercial district. (Singles 240,000zł, with bath 340,000zł. Doubles 460,000zł, with bath 520,000zł.)

Inside the golden walls of the **U Dylla bistro** at Rynek Starego Miasta 37, entrees are 40,000-70,000zł. (Open daily 9am-midnight.) For cheap eats, the **Aranti** restaurant and café, at the train station, serves up tasty spaghetti for a mere 7000-10,000zł. (Open daily 9am-11pm.) At night, the chic café **Amigo** serves desserts for 15,000zł at the corner of Libelta and ul. Niepodległości. (Open daily 10am-2am.)

The **ORBIS** office, which books rail tickets, is next to the Hotel Rzymski, at ul. Marcinkowskiego 21. (Open Mon.-Sat. 10am-5pm.) Travelers' Cheques are cashed at the **American Express** office at Pl. Gen. Dąbrowskiego 1. The **U.S. Consulate,** ul. Chopina 4 (tel. (061) 52 95 86) is open Mon.-Fri. 8:30am-5pm; the phone line is always open for emergencies. The main **train** station is in the southwestern corner of the city. To get to the center, take bus #51, 68, or 76 to the end of ul. Dworcowa and transfer to any tram headed to the right. Consider breaking up the Berlin-to-Warsaw train journey in Poznań.

■■■ WROCŁAW

Wrocław (better known to many by its German name, Breslau) is the active capital of Lower Silesia (Śląsk Dolny), straddling the Odra River. Under Prussian rule between 1741 and 1945, the city's elaborate postwar reconstruction is another example of the fiery Polish spirit. Stately cathedrals give the **Ostrów Tumski** (Cathedral Island) section its dignified character; this oldest neighborhood lies across the river from the center of town, next to the **Botanical Gardens.** On the more populated bank, within the **Panorama Racławicka,** a 120m mural lining circles the inside of a round building on ul. Purkiniego, which recounts the peasant insurrection led by Kościuszko after Poland lost its independence in the late 18th century. (Open Tues.-Sun. 8am-7pm.) In the heart of town, the somber Renaissance and Gothic

Ratusz (town hall) on the old town's *Rynek Główny* (main market square) houses the **city museum.** (Open Wed.-Fri. 10am-4pm, Sat. 11am-5pm, Sun. 10am-6pm. 10,000zł. Wed. free.) In the southern area of the city, the **Operetka,** the **Teatr Polski,** and the **Filharmonia** are all on the same stretch of ul. Piłsudskiego. (Ask at ORBIS for tickets.)

Accommodations, Food, and Practical Information   The **Biuro Usług Turystycznych** (Tourist Services Center), ul. Piłsudskiego 98 (tel. (071) 44 41 01), will find you a room. (Singles 160,000zł. Doubles 280,000zł. Open Mon.-Fri. 8:30am-4pm, Sat. 9am-2pm.) Nearby, the **Hotel Odra,** marked "Piast II" (tel. (071) 44 54 47) on ul. Stawowa off the main avenue, has refurbished quarters. (Singles 115,000zł. Doubles 220,000zł, with bath 280,000zł. Breakfast 40,000zł.) The **Hotel Piast,** ul. Piłsudskiego 98 (tel. (071) 300 33), offers comparable rooms at steeper prices. (Singles 180,000zł. Doubles 300,000zł.)

To satisfy stomach rumblings, forage around the *rynek.* The **Vega Bar** dishes out vegetarian entrees (full meal under 30,000zł) at Rynek/Ratusz 27a. (Open Mon.-Fri. 8am-7pm, Sat.-Sun. 9am-5pm.) Try a cafeteria style meal for under 20,000zł at **Bar "Mis,"** ul. Kuźnicza 48. (Open Mon.-Fri. 6:30am-6pm, Sat. 8am-5pm.) At night, the day-time denizens of the *rynek* are replaced by a younger, hipper crowd; try the clubs here or on nearby ul. Łazienna. Stop by in June for the international **Jazz nad Odra** festival (tickets available at ORBIS).

Direct **trains** link Wrocław daily to Berlin, Frankfurt, Leipzig, Dresden, Munich, Prague, Budapest, and points in Poland. There are **ORBIS** offices at ul. Piłsudskiego 62 (open Mon.-Fri. 9am-5pm, Sat. 10am-2pm) and on the *rynek* at the corner of ul. Oławska. (Open Mon.-Fri. 10am-5pm, Sat. 10am-2pm.) **ALMATUR** (tel. (071) 44 39 51) is at ul. Kościuszki 34. (Open Mon. and Fri. 9am-4pm, Tues.-Thurs. 9am-5pm, Sat. 10am-2pm.)

■■■ JELENIA GÓRA AND THE SUDETY

Jelenia Góra   In the southwestern corner of Poland, the landscape buckles and rolls along the Czech border to form the Sudety mountain range. The crisp air and mineral springs in the **Jelenia Góra Valley** provide a welcome respite for city dwellers tired of the stagnant, industrial Silesian lowlands. At the foot of the Karkonosze Range, Jelenia Góra makes a starting point for loftier hiking, skiing, and resort areas (ask at the **IT bureau** on ul. 1-go Maja 4½); the town also wins points for its serene setting. The **Plac Ratuszowy** surprises, with singularly white baroque merchant houses and low-arched walkways. The 18th-century **Ratusz** in the center stretches to the peerless blue skies, and just west of the Plac, the **Castle Tower Gate** on ul. Jasna is all that remains of the town's medieval fortifications.

The cramped **youth hostel Bartek** (tel. (075) 257 46) is 2 streets south of the train station on ul. Bartka Zwycięzcy 10, off ul. J. Kochanowskiego (40,000zł). The **Hotel Europa,** ul. 1-go Maja 16 (tel. (075) 232 31), is carpeted and spacious. (Singles 230,000zł, with bath 340,000zł. Doubles 330,000zł, with bath 490,000zł. Multi-bed rooms 80,000zł/person.) The **Park campground** and **hotel** (tel. (075) 269 42) on ul. Świerciewskiego 42 is 15 minutes east of the old town on foot. (Hotel doubles 180,000zł. Triples 210,000zł. Camping 30,000zł/person. 30,000-35,000zł/tent.) The Plac Ratuszowy is the best dining hub for famished foreigners. The **Retro,** at no. 13/14, serves huge portions of meaty Polish entrees; *gołąbki* (cabbage rolls stuffed with meat and rice) are 55,000zł (Open 10am-9pm.) The **Staropolska Karczma** on ul. 1-go Maja 33 serves tavern chow from 21,000-40,000zł. (Open daily 9am-8pm.) For coffee and ice cream, relax beneath the gleaming white arches of the **Hortus Kawiarnia** at Plac Ratuszowy 39. (Open 10am-6pm.)

The local **ORBIS** office on ul. 1-go Maja 1 sells transportation tickets (tel. (075) 262 11; open Mon.-Fri. 9am-5pm, Sat. 10am-2pm), but will not cash traveler's checks; instead, go to the **Narodowy Bank Polski,** ul. 15-go Grudnia 18. (Open Mon.-Fri. 8am-5pm, Sat. 8am-noon.)

Karpacz and Sobieszów About 18km southeast of Jelenia Góra lies **Karpacz,** a popular hiking and skiing destination. **Ul. Konstytucji 3-go Maja** is the main drag. The train and bus stations are at the bottom of the hill; the road wanders up **Mt. Śnieżka** past the **campground Pod Lipami** at no. 8 (tel. 193 16). At the intersection with ul. Obrońców Pokoju, wooden information posts list the town's slew of *pensjonats,* but it's hard to find a room without the help of the **Biuro Turystyczne "Karpacs,"** (tel. 195 47), at no. 52. (Open Mon.-Fri. 10am-6pm, Sat. 10am-4pm. 40,000zł/person, with bath 70,000-80,000zł. The bus stops next door.) At the same address is **Restauracja Pohulanka,** one of the many Polish standards along the main roads. (Entrees 40,000-60,000zł. Open Tues.-Sun. 10am-9pm.) **Bar Maja** at Ul. Mickiewicza is cheaper (meals under 30,000zł) and open every day (9am-5pm).

Several trails leave from the Biały Jar bus stop, one more stop uphill. The **Kopa chairlift** is 1000m away (trails take 20min.-2½hrs.) Three stops beyond Biały Jar, the **Wang Temple** attracts church-hounds to its tiny but ornate, 12th-century timber chapel, transported from Norway in 1844 by the king of Prussia. (Open Mon.-Fri. 9am-1pm and 2-6pm, Sun. 11:30am-1pm. 5000zł, students 3000zł.)

In the village of **Sobieszów,** south of Jelenia Góra, a day hike through a corner of the **Karkonosze National Park** leads to **Zamek Chojnik** (Chojnik Castle), perched atop a summit. (8000zł, students 4000zł.) From Jelenia Góra, take bus #9 or 15 to the village (20min.), get off at ul. Cieplicka and ul. Chałubińskiego. Look for signs— "*Do Zamku*" or "*Chojnik*"—that lead to the dirt path up the mountain. PTTK runs a **mountain hostel** (tel. 535 35) next to the castle (50,000zł).

From Jelenia Góra to Karpacz, take the **train** (4/day, 45min., 6000zł) or the more frequent **buses** from the stop outside the train station (15/day, 1hr., 6000zł). From Jelenia Góra, 11 trains per day (55min., 6000zł) depart for Szklarska Poręba Górna. Trains also depart for Wrocław (4/day, 2¼hr., 17,000zł), Warsaw (3/day, 8hr., 90,000zł), and Kraków via overnight train (10:38pm, 9hr., 65,000zł).

■■■ KRAKÓW

Kraków is a jewel among European cities. Unlike most of Poland, the city miraculously escaped the obliteration of WWII; instead, the Nazis desecrated Wawel Castle, using Kraków's most precious landmark as their headquarters. Many of its beguiling buildings now bear instead the scars of severe air pollution from the smokestacks of industrial Nowa Huta, Kraków's "model" socialist suburb to the east. Nevertheless, a stroll through Kraków's cobblestone alleys punctuated with baroque cupolas and church spires transports you to a more innocent century.

ORIENTATION AND PRACTICAL INFORMATION

The city fans outward in roughly concentric circles from the large Renaissance **Rynek Główny** (main market square), at the heart of the **Stare Miasto** (old town). The refreshingly green belt of the **Planty** gardens rings the Stare Miasto, and the **Wisła River** skims the southwest corner and **Wawel Hill.** For maps, try **ORBIS** or **COIT,** near the train station.

Tourist Offices: ORBIS, in the Hotel Cracovia, al. Piłsudskiego 1 (tel. 21 98 80). Open Mon.-Fri. 8am-8pm, Sat.-Sun. 8am-4pm; Oct.-April Mon.-Fri. 8am-4pm, or at Plac Szczepański 2 on the Rynek Główny (same hours; tel. 22 61 47).

Budget Travel: ALMATUR, Rynek Główny 7-8 (tel. 22 63 52; fax 22 67 08), in the courtyard in back. Open Mon.-Fri. 8:30am-5:30pm, Sat. 10am-2pm. Eurotrain cards and ISICs.

Consulate: U.S., ul. Stolarska 9 (tel. 22 97 64). Library open Mon.-Fri. noon-4:45pm.

Currency Exchange: At **Kantor** booths all over the city, ORBIS offices, and hotels. Traveler's checks cashed at the **Narodowy Bank Polski,** ul. Basztowa 20. Open Mon. and Fri. 7:45am-1pm, Tues.-Thurs. 7:45am-5pm.

American Express: At the **ORBIS** office on al. Piłsudskiego (see Tourist Offices). Lost checks replaced, but no wired money accepted nor Traveler's Cheques sold. Holds mail for US$1/piece. Nearest full-service office is in Warsaw.

Post Office: Main branch at Westerplatte and Starowiślna has **Poste Restante.** Open Mon.-Fri. 7:30am-8:30pm, Sat. 8am-2pm, Sun. 9-11am. **Postal Code:** 30001.

Telephones: At post office main branch. Open 24hrs. **City Code:** 012.

Flights: The **airport** is 16km away in Balice. From the train station, take bus #208 (40min.). Downtown **LOT** office at ul. Basztowa 15 (tel. 22 50 76 or 22 70 78). Open Mon.-Fri. 8am-7pm, Sat. 8am-3pm.

Trains: Alight at **Kraków Główny** (tel. 22 41 82 or 22 22 48) on pl. Kolejowy, an easy 10-min. walk northeast from the center of town. To Warsaw (9/day, 2¾hr.). Some trains to southeastern Polish cities leave from **Kraków Płaszów,** south of the city center. Tickets sold at stations or at ORBIS.

Buses: PKS station (tel. 936) opposite the train station. To Oświęcim (10/day, 1hr. 40min., 21,000zł); Nowy Sącz (hourly, 3hr.); Częstochowa (1/day, 2½hr.), and Warsaw (3/day, 4½-6hr.).

Emergencies: Ambulance: tel. 999. **Fire:** tel. 998. **Police:** tel. 997.

ACCOMMODATIONS AND CAMPING

Friendly neighborhood room-retrievers **Wawel Tourist** (tel. 22 19 21) reside next to the tourist office at ul. Pawia 8. (Open Mon.-Fri. 8am-9pm, Sat. 9am-3pm. Singles 90,000-120,000zł. Doubles 160,000-200,000zł.) Reservations are vital in summer. **ALMATUR, IT,** or **PTTK** can call ahead for you.

Schronisko Młodzieżowe (HI), ul. Oleandry 4 (tel. 33 82 22). Take tram #15 (west from the train station) or 18; or walk (15min. from the *Stare Miasto*). Flexible lockout 10am-5pm. Curfew 11pm. Nonmembers welcome. Clean and pleasant if you can get a double (juniors 70,000zł; seniors 80,000zł) or a 3- to 5-bed room (juniors 60,000zł; seniors 70,000zł).

Schronisko Młodzieżowe (HI), ul. Kościuszki 88 (tel. 22 19 51), inside the convent gate. Take tram #2 from Westerplatte. Run by nuns in a heavenly setting—a Renaissance courtyard tucked away behind the high convent walls. Reception open Mon.-Fri. 8am-3pm and 5-11pm, Sat. 8am-2pm and 5-11pm, Sun. 8-10am and 5-11pm. Curfew 11pm. Juniors 38,000zł. Seniors 54,000zł. Nonmembers 60,000zł. Sheets 11,000zł.

Student Hotel Żaczek, ul. 3-go Maja 5 (tel. 33 54 77). Next to the youth hostel. Vast, friendly, and stark. Take tram #15 or bus #119 from the train station. Singles 160,000zł. Doubles 240,000zł. Triples 360,000zł.

Hotel Polonia, ul. Basztowa 25 (tel. 22 12 81), next to the Hotel Warszawski. First-rate and cosmopolitan. Singles 250,000zł. Doubles 370,000zł. Triples 420,000zł.

PTTK Dom Turysty, Westerplatte 15-16 (tel. 22 95 66), near the central post office. Big, brown, and efficient. Dandy location on park and near Rynek Główny. 8-bed dorms 95,000zł/person. Reception open noon-10pm.

Camping: Motel and Camping Krak, ul. Radzikowskiego 99 (tel. 37 21 22 or 37 58 40). Take tram #4, 8, 12, or 44 to Fizyków and walk north. Open May 15-Sept. 15.

FOOD

Obwarzanki (soft pretzels with poppy seeds) are Kraków's street-stand specialty. All the places listed below are within a few blocks of the Rynek Główny.

Balaton, ul. Grodzka 37. Divine Hungarian cuisine always attracts crowds. Entrees 12,000-46,000zł. Try the *placki ziemniaczane po węgiersku* (potato pancakes, 46,000zł). Open daily 9am-10pm.

Staropolska, ul. Sienna 4. Traditional Polish fare served with simple elegance. Entrees 25,000-80,000zł. Open daily 9am-11pm.

Kawiarnia u Zalipanek, ul. Szewska 24. An entertaining outdoor café on the *Planty* garnished with local folk art. Tortes 9,300-11,900zł/slice. *Miód grzany* (honey "warmed over") 19,000zł. Open daily 9am-10pm.

Bar Mleczny Uniwersytecki, on the corner of ul. Piłsudskiego and Podwale, across from the Jagiellonian University. A last bastion of proletarian dining—a full meal comes to under 15,000zł. Open Mon.-Fri. 6am-8pm, Sat. 7am-4pm, Sun. 7am-3pm.

Raffa, s/w Jana 3. Elegant French pastries under 8,000zł. Open Mon.-Sat. 7am-7pm.

Różowy Skoń Salad Bar, next to the Bar Uniwersytecki. Pop art decor and delicious salads (8,000zł/dkg). Open Mon.-Sat. 9am-9pm, Sun 11am-9pm.

SIGHTS

At the center of the old town is the **Rynek Główny,** one of the largest and most distinctive market squares in Europe. In its northeastern corner rise the red towers of the **Kościół Mariacki,** a richly decorated cathedral. The invading Nazis dismantled the 500-year-old carved-wood altarpiece and stashed it away; Allied forces discovered the buried pieces in Germany at war's end. Reassembled, it is ceremoniously unveiled at noon each day. Diagonally across the square stands the lonely **Ratusz** (Town Hall) **Tower,** spared when the rest of the building was torn down in 1820. (Open Wed. and Fri.-Sun. 9am-4pm, Thurs. 11am-6pm. 7000zł.) Dividing the square in half, the Italianate **Sukiennice** (Cloth Hall) is as mercantile now as it was in guild times; the ground floor is an enormous souvenir shop. Upstairs, the **Muzeum Narodowe** (National Museum) houses 18th- and 19th-century Polish classics. (Open Wed. and Fri.-Sun. 10am-3:30pm, Thurs. noon-5:30pm. 20,000zł, students 10,000zł, Thurs. free.) During the academic year, Polish students cruise the area around the statue of Adam Mickiewicz, Poland's most celebrated Romantic poet.

The **Zamek Wawelski** (Wawel Castle) is one of the finest surviving pieces of Renaissance architecture in Poland. Begun in the 10th century, the castle has 71 chambers, a magnificent sequence of 16th-century tapestries commissioned by the royal family, and a series of 8 tapestries from Arras depicting the story of Noah's Ark. An English guidebook is available; a tour in English runs daily 10:25am. (Open Tues., Thurs., and Sat.-Sun. 10am-2:45pm, Wed. and Fri. 10am-3:45pm. Buy tickets early. 15,000zł, students 5000zł.) Next door is Kraków's **Cathedral,** where Poland's kings were crowned and buried. Its former archbishop is now Pope John Paul II. (Open Mon.-Sat. 9am-5:30pm, Sun. 12:15-5:15pm. Ticket window for graves and the *dzwona* (bell) *Zygmunta* open Mon.-Fri. 9am-5:15pm, Sat. 9am-4:45pm, Sun. 12:15-5:15pm. 10,000zł, students 5000zł.) Outside, look for the statue of Tadeusz Kościuszko, the Polish patriot who joined the American Revolution and died resisting Russian invaders in the late 18th century. Beneath Wawel hill is the **Smocza Jama** (Dragon's Den), the dungeon which in legend is home to Kraków's fire-breathing mascot.

The old town has a few small but excellent museums. Religious art from the 15th to 18th centuries resides in the **Kamienica Szołayskich,** plac Szczepański 9. (Open Mon. and Fri.-Sun. 10am-3:30pm, Tues. noon-5:30pm. 10,000zł, students 5000zł.) The **Zbiory Czartoryskich,** ul. św. Jana 19, shelters paintings from the Renaissance to the 18th century. (Open Mon.-Tues. and Sat.-Sun. 10am-3:30pm, Fri. noon-5:30pm. 10,000zł, students 5000zł.)

Kraków's **Jagiellonian University,** over 600 years ancient, is the second-oldest in Eastern Europe after Prague's. Astronomer Nicholas Copernicus and drama scholar Agnieszka Marszałek are among its distinguished alumni. The university's oldest building is the 15th-century **Collegium Maius,** on ul. Jagiellońska 15 in the old town, with a bewitching Gothic courtyard and vaulted walkway. (Open Mon.-Fri. 11am-2:30pm, Sat. 11:30am-1:30pm to groups only—join or form one. 10,000zł, students 5000zł.) South of the old town center lies **Kazimierz,** the 400-year-old Jewish quarter (take tram #6, 8, 10, 18, or 19). You can still see remnants of what was once a large and vital community; Poland's oldest synagogue, the **Stara Synagoga** at Szeroka 24, is now a museum. (Open Wed.-Thurs. and Sat.-Sun. 9am-3pm, Fri. 11am-6pm.)

ENTERTAINMENT

Student clubs romp from about 8pm to midnight or 1am, and charge a minimal cover. **Pod Jaszczurami,** Rynek Główny 8, features quality jazz (Mon. 6-10pm and Tues. 8pm-1:30am) and a popular disco (Wed.-Thurs. and Sun. 8pm-1am, Fri.-Sat 9pm-3:30am). The **Rotunda,** ul. Oleandry 1, across from the hostel, has a popular dance floor and jazz on Thursdays from 8pm. *The* place to be seen is **Maxime,** ul. Floriańska 32. (Open daily 5pm-4am). Kraków's best-known café, **Jama Michalika,** Floriańska 45, home of the Green Balloon cabaret, is festooned with political caricatures and eclectic, plush decor. (Open daily 9am-10pm).

Cricot 2, an avant-garde group once led by the late Tadeusz Kantor, has a museum of its works at ul. Konoicza 5. (Open Mon.-Fri. 10am-2pm.) The **Filharmonia Krakowska** plays regularly in its hall at ul. Zwierzyniecka 2.

■ Near Kraków

Oświęcim and Wieliczka The Nazi concentration camps at **Auschwitz** (Oświęcim) and **Birkenau** (Brzezinka) are places of unspeakable horror, debris of an apocalypse that many have begun to forget. Millions were murdered here; thousands more suffered hideously at the hands of the Nazis. The camps are in the town of **Oświęcim; buses** leave from the central Dworzec PKS across from Kraków Główny (10/day, 1½hr., 16,000zł). **Trains** leave from Kraków Główny to reach the site (4/day, 1¾hr., 21,000zł).

Prisoners were originally kept at the smaller **Konzentrazionlager Auschwitz I,** within the city limits. By foot, turn right as you exit the train station, go 1 block and turn left; the camp driveway is 1.6km down on your right. Or catch bus #2, 3, 4, or 5; all will drop you near the kiosks outside the driveway. The camp itself is now a museum; barracks and crematoria hold displays detailing Nazi atrocities. An excellent English guidebook is available at the entrance. Begin your visit with the utterly terrifying film shot here by the Soviet Army on January 27, 1945. (Camp open 24hrs. Museum areas open daily 8am-7pm; May and Sept. 8am-6pm; April and Oct. 8am-5pm; March and Nov.-Dec. 15 8am-4pm; Dec. 15-Feb. 8am-3pm. Free.) You must not leave Oświęcim without visiting the starker and vaster **Konzentrationlager Auschwitz II-Birkenau.** In the countryside, 3km from the original camp and a good half-hour's walk west of the train station, Birkenau was constructed later in the war. There are no pamphlets, brochures, or display cases, only endless rows of barracks and watchtowers and the untouched, collapsing remains of gas chambers and crematoria. In the far right corner of the camp is a pond still gray from the tons of ashes deposited there nearly half a century ago.

Thirteen km southeast of Kraków, visit the 1000-year-old salt mine at **Wieliczka,** where pious Poles have carved an immense 20-chapel complex in salt 100m underground. (Open daily 8am-6pm; Nov.-March 8am-4pm. Obligatory guided tours; last leaves 1½hr. before closing. 70,000zł, students 40,000zł.) **Trains** travel from Kraków (hourly, 25min., 6000zł). Follow the tracks' former path and then the *do kopalni* (to the mine) signs. Guidebook in English available at kiosks (20,000zł).

Tarnów and Częstochowa The Romany culture still thrives in **Tarnów,** 1½ hours west of Kraków by train (hourly, 21,000zł). The main street, ul. Krakowska, leads from the train station to the *Rynek;* at the corner of ul. Urszulańska the **Ethnographic Museum** exhibits a permanent display on Gypsy arts and culture, with an outdoor Gypsy camp in summer. In the *Rynek,* the **Town Hall Museum** shows off frescoes, furniture, and porcelain; the **Diocesan Museum,** behind the golden 16th-century **cathedral,** holds an enormous collection of sacred art and folk art. (Open Tues.-Sat. 10am-3pm, Sun. 9am-2pm.) **Restauracja Ke Moro,** ul. Żydowskiego 13, serves hearty, spicy Gypsy cuisine from 1pm until the guests go home; there's live Gypsy music nightly. (Entrees 40,000-70,000zł.) Local artists hang out at **Café Galeria** on Rynek 4. (Open Mon.-Sat. 10am-midnight; Sun. 3pm-midnight.) The cheery pastel **Dom Wycieczkowy,** ul. Żydowska 16 (tel. (40) 21 62 29), offers a place in a 6- to 8-bed room for only 45,000zł. (Singles 120,000zł. Doubles 170,000zł.)

As Mecca is to Muslims, so is **Częstochowa** to Catholic Poles. Every year hundreds of thousands of natives and foreigners make the pilgrimage to the most sacred of Polish icons, the **Black Madonna** in the towering monastery of **Jasna Góra.** (Chapel housing the icon open 6am-noon.) Countless crutches, medallions, and rosaries strung upon the chapel walls attest to its miraculous powers. During the 17th-century Swedish invasion of Poland, the Madonna shed tears, giving the Poles the strength to defend their country. Częstochowa is most accessible from Kraków by train (2hr.). The **Hotel Mały,** ul. Katedralna 18 (tel. 433 71), is just behind the train station, off ul. Pilsudskiego. (Doubles 150,000zł, with bath 220,000zł. Triples 180,000-210,000zł. Quads 240,000-260,000zł.) The restaurant **Roma,** al. Wolności 18, serves generous portions in a clever split-level setup. **ORBIS** (tel. 417 69, 420 56, or 412 83) has its ticket office at the corner of al. NMP and ul. Klińskiego. In summer, contact **ALMATUR,** al. NMP 37 (tel. 443 68), about student accommodations and summer youth hostels. (Open Mon.-Fri. 9am-5pm, Sat. 10am-2pm.)

■■■ ZAKOPANE

Directly south of Kraków, the placid Polish landscape shoots up 2500m to form the Tatry Mountains. **Zakopane** is the crowded center of the region. Set in a valley surrounded by jagged peaks and soul-stirring alpine meadows, the town is Poland's premier ski and hiking resort. Short **mountain hikes** are a specialty of the region. A map is essential. The entrance to the **National Park** at the end of ul. Strążyska is a starting point for hikes of 2½-6 hours. (5000zł, students 3000zł.) **Giewont** (1090m) is 4½ hours away. The mountain lake of **Morskie Oko** dazzles herds of tourists; take a bus (3hr., 20,000zł round-trip) from Zakopane, then hike 10km (6hr.). For a more dramatic vista, catch a bus to **Kuźnice,** 20 minutes south of central Zakopane, and hop on the **Kasprowy Wierch** chairlift. (Daily 7:30am-8:10pm; Dec.-Feb. 8am-4pm; March-May and Oct. 7:30am-5:40pm; June 7:30am-6:10pm. 40,000zł round-trip.)

Accommodations, Food, and Practical Information The big, friendly **youth hostel (HI)** is at Nowotarska 45 (tel. (0165) 662 03); walk down ul. Kościuszki toward town, then take the second right onto ul. Sienkiewicza and walk 2 blocks. (Lockout 10am-4pm. Curfew 11pm. 62,000zł.) Turn left at the youth hostel and walk 1 block; on your left is the powerful **Juventur Hotel Słoneczny,** ul. Słoneczna 2a. (tel. (0165) 662 53. Singles 150,000zł, with bath 210,000zł. Doubles 300,000zł, with bath 420,000zł. Triples with bath 630,000zł.). The **PTTK Dom Wycieczkowy,** ul. Zaruskiego 5 (tel. (0165) 32 81 or 32 82), is in a large traditional chalet. (Multi-bed rooms 40,000-50,000zł/person.) **Camping Pod Krokwią,** ul. Zeromskiego (tel. (0165) 22 56), across the street from the base of the ski jump, usually has space. (18,000zł/person, 12,000-20,000zł/tent. Open May-Aug.)

To soothe your palate or rest your knees after a day on trail, hit the **Kawiarnia** at the Hotel Orbis Giewont (at ul. Krupówka and ul. Kościuszki) for tasty tortes (9000-18,000zł) or *naleśniki* (crepes, 30,000zł). (Open daily 8am-8pm.) The **Karczma Redykołka** at the corner of ul. Krupówka and ul. Kościeliska (entrees 20,000-56,000zł; open 10am-8pm), is an irresistible tourist haunt fashioned after the traditional *chaty góralskie* (mountain huts). Off the beaten path, the **Karczma Obrochtówka** on ul. Kraszewskiego 10a is worth the search for its fabulous kitchen and charming folk atmosphere. (Open Tues.-Sun. noon-10pm.)

Bus and (slower) **rail** lines link Zakopane to Katowice, Kraków, and Warsaw; a direct train connects to Budapest (Mon., Thurs., and Sat.). See the chapter on the Slovak Republic for cross-border **bus** information. Scoop up maps and hiking tips from the **IT Bureau** on ul. Jagiellońska 1 (tel. 122 12; open Mon.-Fri. 8am-8pm).

■■■ LUBLIN

In the heart of Małopolska, where horse-drawn ploughs still outnumber tractors, Lublin has long occupied an eminent place in Poland's history. In 1569, the Treaty of Lublin officially united the Kingdom of Poland and the Grand Duchy of Lithuania to form one of Europe's largest and most prosperous empires for nearly two centuries. Thereafter, successive invasions by Swedes, Russians, Austrians, and Germans left many stains upon the city. Today Lublin is a pleasant compromise between a convenient modern city and a living museum.

ORIENTATION AND PRACTICAL INFORMATION

Lublin lies 175km southeast of Warsaw on the historic trade route to L'viv and Ukraine. All principal sights roost on or near **Krakowskie Przedmieście,** which stretches west from the *Stare Miasto* (old town), turning into al. Racławickie before reaching the Ogród Saski (Saxon Gardens) and the Catholic University.

Tourist Office: IT, ul. Krakowskie Przedmieście 78 (tel. 244 12). Ladles out maps (26,000zł). Friendly, but spotty English speakers. Open Mon.-Fri. 9am-5pm, Sat. 10am-2pm. **ORBIS,** at ul. Narutowicza and ul. Okopowy (tel. 222 56). International and domestic train and bus tickets. Open Mon.-Fri. 9am-6pm, Sat. 11am-4pm.

Budget Travel: ALMATUR, ul. Langiewicza 10 (tel. 332 38), in the university district. Currency exchange, train tickets. Sells ISICs. Open Mon.-Fri. 9am-4pm, Sat. 10am-2pm.

Currency Exchange: Kantor counters across the city have the best rates. Traveler's checks exchanged at the **Narodowy Bank Polski,** Krakowskie Przedmieście 37. Open Mon.-Fri. 8am-1pm, Sat. 8am-noon.

Post Office: ul. Krakowskie Przedmieście 52, opposite Plac Litewski. Open Mon.-Fri. 7am-9pm, Sat. 8am-2pm. Fax bureau. **Postal Code:** 20001.

Telephones: At the post office (side entrance). Open 24hrs. **City Code:** 081.

Trains: tel. 202 19. **Lublin Główny,** pl. Dworcowy 1, south of the old town. Take trolleybus #150 to the center. To Warsaw (9/day, 3hr.) and Kraków (2/day, 4hr.).

Buses: PKS station, ul. Tysiąclecia 4, below the Lublin castle, near the old town. To: Warsaw (11/day, 3hr., 38,000zł); Kraków (1/day, 6hr. 20min., 74,000zł) and Zamość (14/day, 2hr., 25,000zł).

Pharmacy: ul. Krakowskie Przedmieście 49. Open daily 8am-8pm.

Medical Assistance: ul. Jaczewskiego 1/3 (tel. 77 55 71).

Emergencies: Ambulance: tel. 999. **Fire:** tel. 998. **Police:** tel. 997.

ACCOMMODATIONS AND CAMPING

Lublin lacks a private room-finding agency, but reasonable alternatives are within walking distance of the historic center.

Schronisko Młodzieżowe (HI), ul. Długosza 6a (tel. 306 28), west of the center near the Catholic University. Take bus #150 from the train station to the end of the Saxon Gardens (1 stop after the turnoff onto al. Racławickie). Quaint bathrooms and lots of insects, but friendly owners. Kitchen and camping facilities. Lockout 10am-5pm. Curfew 10pm. Both flexible. Luggage storage. Jr. 20,000-35,000zł. Sr. 22,000-40,000zł. Nonmembers 24,000-45,000zł. Sheets 9600zł.

ZNP Dom Noclegowy, ul. Akademicka 4 (tel. 382 85). Take bus #150 from the train station just past Ogród Saski. Walk back to u. Hłopacińskiego, turn right. Hostel-esque. Singles 100,000zł. Doubles 130,000zł. 6-person rooms 500,000zł. 1 shower each level.

Hotel Lublinianka, ul. Krakowskie Przedmieście 56 (tel. 242 61). Ideal location. Lofty ceilings. Decent bathrooms. Singles 200,000zł. Doubles 300,000zł. 7-person 50,000zł/person.

Motel PZM, ul. B. Prusa 8 (tel. 342 32). Follow ul. 3-go Maja from Krakowskie Przedmieście. Courteous service, pleasant atmosphere. Singles 160,000zł, with bath 180,000zł. Doubles 260,000zł, with bath 300,000-320,000zł.

ZAKOPANE

Camping, ul. Sławinkowska 46 (tel. 322 31). Take bus #18 from the center, or else take your tent to ul. Długosza and crash on the youth hostel grounds—it's closer. Camping 15,000zł/person, 11,000-15,000zł/tent. Open May-Sept.

FOOD

Restauracja Powszechna, ul. Krakowskie Przedmieście 56, across ul. Kołłątaja from the post office. Café-restaurant caters to a yuppie crowd. Crisp, thin pizza is the house specialty. House music and pizza to order (50,000-100,000zł). Imported alcohol. Open Mon.-Sat. noon-midnight, Sun. noon-11pm.

Restaurant Europa, ul. Krakowskie Przedmieście 29 (tel. 220 12). A central lunch spot. Elegant, slightly stuffy atmosphere. Entrees 30,000-60,000zł. Open Mon. noon-10pm, Tues.-Fri. noon-midnight, Sat. noon-2am.

Restaurant Karczma Słupska, Aleje Racławickie 24, past the Catholic University. Concocts Polish specialties (19,000-29,000zł) in a tavern atmosphere, complete with carved wooden benches. Orchestra belts out the Lawrence Welk hit parade from 4:30pm Fri.-Tues. Open Thurs.-Tues. 10am-10pm, Wed. 10am-8pm.

Bar Mleczny, Krakowskie Przedmieście 29, next to the Hotel Europa. Breakfast foods 6000zł. Open Mon.-Sat. 8am-5pm.

Lunch Bar, ul. Królewska 11, outside the old town. Despite the English name (an ever-growing trend), it's Polish food on plastic dishes. Soups and salads 7000-15,000zł, entrees 20,000-30,000zł. Open Mon.-Sat. 10am-8pm, Sun. noon-8pm.

Kawiarnia Trzosik, ul. Grodzka 5, in the old town. Charming courtyard beyond the archway. Delicious desserts 13,000zł. Open daily 10am-8pm.

SIGHTS AND ENTERTAINMENT

The 19th-century ochre façades of **Krakowskie Przedmieście,** Lublin's main artery, introduce the more ancient buildings of the medieval *Stare Miasto* (old town). If you walk east from **Plac Litewski** and the central post office, you soon pass the 18th-century **Kościół i Klasztor Kapucynów** (Capuchin Church and Cloister) on your right. Continue to reach the fortified **Kraków gate,** which ushers you into the old town. Take a right on narrow ul. Trybunalska; halfway down an archway, the street leads to the grand **cathedral** and its opulent frescoes and gilded altar. Cross back through the arch and head straight to the early Renaissance painted façades of the **Rynek** (market square). A right on cobblestone ul. Grodzka takes you down the hill, past weather-worn houses to a small square with a lookout through the willows. If you go to Lublin for no other reason you should go to see this view of Lublin's modern suburbs against the massive **Lublin Castle,** originally built in the 14th century but redone in the 19th with an Arabian Nights theme. Once court of a feudal kingdom, the castle served as Gestapo headquarters during WWII. The fortified walls now house a **museum of the history of Lublin,** along with archaeological and ethnographic displays. (Open Wed.-Sat. 9am-4pm, Sun. 9am-5pm. 12,000zł, students 8000zł; free Sun.) If you can make it across the bazaar across al. Tysiąclecia, climb the hill for a view of the city from the **Kościół Sw. Mikokaja Biskupa,** a church built in 1700 and restored in 1873.

The hottest dance spots change frequently; ask students in the university town or watch for posters. The old town has a number of bars; **Piwnice Mieszczki** on ul. Grodzka 7 serves beer for 13,000zł in tiny catacombs. Go to the student cafeteria during the academic year, located in the Marie Curie University district opposite the **ALMATUR** office. Behind the modern entrance to Lublin's **Catholic University** on ul. Racławicka is an airy courtyard with perpetually young crowds. For **Filharmonia** tickets, head for the booking office at ul. Kapucyńska 7 (Sept.-June season).

■ Near Lublin

Majdanek and Kazimierz Dolny The largest concentration camp after Auschwitz, **Majdanek** is the site of 360,000 murders. The former cell-blocks now house moving exhibits chronicling the operations of this death factory, spread over the 5km Black Road near Lublin's southeastern suburbs. City buses #28, 153, 156,

158, and 159 from the center stop just before the huge granite monument marking the entrance to the grounds. (Open Tues.-Sun. 8am-6pm; Oct.-April Tues.-Sun. 8am-3pm. English brochure 1500zł.)

For a less grim excursion, take a day out of town to visit the bewitching village of **Kazimierz Dolny,** on the sandy banks of the Wisła River some 45km west of Lublin. The **ruins** of a 14th-century castle overshadow the town, which, as usual, centers around the whitewashed façades of the **Rynek** (market square). Hike up to the castle tower·and pause along the way at the towering 16th-century baroque **Fara** church to survey one of Poland's oldest and best preserved organs, dating from 1620. Concerts are held Saturdays at 7pm. (Ruins and tower open daily 9am-5pm. Buy ticket at ruins and save for the tower. 4000zł, students 3000zł.) Off the *rynek*, the **Muzeum Nadwiślańskie**, ul. Senatorska 11/13, houses a collection of paintings inspired by the town's enchanting layout. (Open Tues.-Sun. 10am-4pm; Oct.-April Tues.-Sun. 10am-5pm. 5000zł, students 3000zł.)

PTTK at Rynek 27 (tel. 100 46) sells guides to the town and arranges stays in private rooms. (Singles 80,000-95,000zł. Doubles 108,000-140,000zł. Triples 123,000-162,000zł. Open Mon.-Fri. 8am-6pm, Sat. 1-5pm, Sun. 9am-1pm.) PTTK also operates the gorgeous, whitewashed **pensjonat Murka**, ul. Krakowska 59 (tel. 100 36), 20 minutes away by foot through the village. (Singles 170,000zł. Doubles 300,000zł. Triples 390,000zł. Breakfast included.) There's a **campground** next door. (25,000zł/person. Tents 25,000-30,000zł.) At the tiny **Domek Campingowy,** ul. Krakowska 35 (tel. 108 14), Anna Stachyra provides a bathroom, sink, and double room for 45,000zł, garden view included. **Restauracja Esterka,** Ryn 1, is dark and lovely with entrees 20,000-50,000zł. (Open Mon.-Sat. noon-8pm.) **Buses** to Kazimierz Dolny leave every hour from platform 3 of the Lublin bus station (direction "Puławy," 1½hr., 18,000zł), making frequent stops in the countryside.

Sandomierz and Zamość Another retreat into southeastern Poland's captivating countryside leads to **Sandomierz,** 2½ hours southwest of Lublin. Beneath the spacious, sloping *rynek* winds a mysterious **underground tourist route,** stone and brick 14th-century chambers inhabited by Tartar ghosts. (Tours on the ½-hr. daily 10am-5pm. 10,000zł, students 6000zł.) The **Hotel Pod Cizemką,** Rynek 27 (tel. 236 68), is the only act in town, but the location can't be beat. (Doubles 240,000zł. Triples 300,000zł. Quads 400,000zł. All with bath.) Across the *rynek* is **Kawiarnia Kasztelanka.** (Entrees 10,000-25,000zł. Open daily 9am-midnight.) PKS buses run from Lublin to Sandomierz (5/day, 35,000zł). **ORBIS** (tel. 230 40) is at Rynek 24. (Open Mon.-Sat. 9am-4pm.) **PTTK** sits next door. (Open Mon.-Fri. 8am-3pm.)

"The Renaissance Pearl" of Poland, the "Padua of the North," the town of **Zamość** is not just another set of pretty façades. Stop by the **PTTK** office under the Ratusz or the **ORBIS** office at ul. Grodzka 18 to pick up brochures in English on the town's architecture. (ORBIS open Mon.-Fri. 10am-4:30pm, Sat. 11am-3:30pm.) Don't leave without visiting the **Rotunda** at the end of ul. Męczemników Rotundy. This 19th-century brick fort was converted during WWI to a crematorium and camp; the number of executions may be as high as 50,000. (Open 9am-6pm; Oct.-April 14 10am-5pm. Free.) The PTTK **Dom Wycieczkowy** (tel. (084) 26 39) at ul. Zamenhoffa 11 is hostel-like. (Doubles and triples 75,000zł/person. 4- to 8-bed rooms 65,000zł/person.) The modern **Hotel Renesans** (tel. (084) 20 01) is on ul. Grecka 6. (Singles 190,000zł. Doubles 290,000zł. Triples 360,000zł.) Food pickings are slim; try the **bar mleczny** on ul. Staszicka 10 with meals under 20,000zł (open daily 8am-5pm), or the **Restauracja Centralka** on ul. Żeromskiego. (Open daily 10am-10pm.) The **Piwnica Pod Arkadami** attracts enchanting and fashionable youth at ul. Staszica 25 on the *rynek*. (Open daily noon-midnight.) To reach Zamość from Lublin, take the **train** (3/day) or **bus** (29/day, 2hr., 37,000zł).

■■■ PRZEMYŚL AND ŁAŃCUT

Przemyśl Less than a *kupon*'s toss from the Ukrainian border, Przemyśl exhibits an Eastern flair that no other Polish city can match. Stroll among churches and up twisting cobblestone streets to the **cathedral** on ul. Grodzka and Katedralna; above on ul. Zamkowa is the white Renaissance **zamek** (castle), with its view of the town and the San River below. (To tower 4000zł, students 2000zł. Open 9am-6pm.) The **Carmelite Monastery** on ul. Kapitulna boasts Italian-cast bells that ring on the hour.

If you spend the night, **ORBIS** on Plac Legionów (tel. (010) 33 66) will help you find rather pricey accommodations. (Open Mon.-Fri. 7am-6pm, Sat. 7am-2pm.) Otherwise, sleep at the **Dom Wycieczkowy** (tel. (010) 40 32), ul. Sowińskiego just to the right of ORBIS, but plan to wash elsewhere and use the WC before you arrive. The **Karpacka Restaurant** on ul. Kościuski 5, near the bridge, serves a mean *żurek* soup (12,000zł) but is a haven for heavy drinkers after dark. (Open daily 11am-midnight.) Seven **trains** arrive daily from Kraków (3½-4 hrs., 94,500zł), while 3 per day head for L'viv (3½hr.). **Buses** also cross the border to L'viv (4/day, 3hr., 100,000zł).

Łańcut The **palace** at Łańcut may be the most splendid building in Poland. Built in 1620 as a fortification, it was transformed in the 18th century by Elżbieta Lubomirska, a princess with French tastes and an eye for fine art. The grounds are to this day maintained perfectly. (Grounds open, 5am-11pm; palace open Apr.-Oct. Mon.-Sat. 9am-2:30pm, Sun. 9am-4pm; Feb.-April and Oct.-Nov. Tues.-Sun. 10am-2:30pm. 30,000zł, students 20,000zł.) The palace is the site of a May **chamber music festival** and regular concerts. Outside the museum, save your tickets for the **Orangeria** and **coach museum**. The palace is a 25-minute walk from the train station; head up ul. Żeromskiego and right on ul. Gródzka (or grab a local bus or taxi). A bed at **Dom Wycieczkowy**, ul. Dominikańska (tel. 45 12), runs from 36,000-60,000zł. Entrees at **Restauracja Karczma**, ul. 3-go Maja 1, are inexpensive and hearty. (Open daily 9:30am-9pm.) Łańcut is 2¾ hours east of Kraków by **train** (42,000zł).

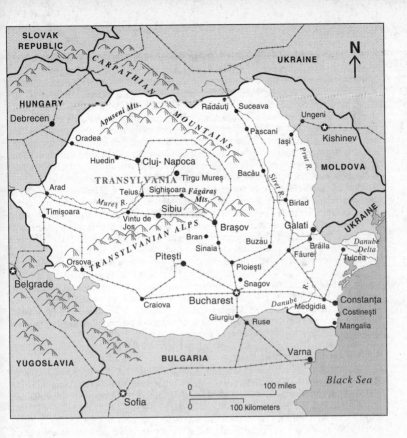

Romania

US$1	= 850lei (ROL)	1000lei =	US$0.18
CDN$1	= 646lei	1000lei =	CDN$1.55
UK£1	= 1320lei	1000lei =	UK£1.55
IR£1	= 1230lei	1000lei =	IR£0.81
AUS$1	= 553lei	1000lei =	AUS$1.81
NZ$1	= 470lei	1000lei =	NZ$2.13
SAR1	= 177lei	1000lei =	SAR5.66
Country Code: 40		**International Dialing Prefixes: EU: 00; USA: 011**	

Deep in the mysterious Carpathian Mountains, Romanian peasants preserve folk traditions lost to the rest of Europe for centuries. The fortified towns of Transylvania
still look like medieval woodcuts, and the green hills of Moldavia remain as serene as
the frescoes on their monastery walls. The country's stains—soot-blackened, ruined
towns and decades of forced resettlement in urban industrial nightmares like Bucharest—date from the days when Romania was the poorest and most totalitarian country in the Soviet bloc; to retire the country's US$11 million foreign debt, the
Romanian dictator Nicolae Ceauşescu ruthlessly bled his people. In a process called

"systemization," he destroyed rural villages and herded their inhabitants into factory towns. The Romanian people were deadened by fear and gnawing hunger.

In December 1989, Romania erupted in a revolution as bloody, crude, and excessive as the man it extinguished. The overthrow was quick and violent, lasting only eight days. The military fought alongside a ragtag citizens' army against Ceauşescu's dreaded Securitate force. Hostilities centered on control of Bucharest's TV and radio stations in a grotesque demonstration of the power of media. Ceauşescu and his wife were captured, "tried," and summarily executed. But the bloody revolution ultimately proved fleeting, as Ion Iliescu's neo-communist National Salvation Front replaced Ceauşescu, garnering an astonishing 82% of the vote. By June 1991, the protesters were back and more boisterous than ever, and today pro-monarchist feelings are growing stronger, economic headaches are further destabilizing the fledgling government's legitimacy, and huge social and economic contrasts have developed among the population. The government has begun to cut exports, channel goods and electricity back to the people, and focus on Romania's potentially rich agricultural sector. Yet the country has a long and painful climb ahead. Ragged beggars can be seen in front of flashy shop windows in the bigger cities.

The hospitality of the Romanian people will surely be a high point of your visit; though many do not speak English, most will make an effort to understand you. Be aware, though, that due to the extreme difficulty of life here, some Romanians might befriend you in the hopes of receiving an invitation to your country (which facilitates their visa process). Westerners are walking gold mines to Romanians: US$55 equals a month's wages here. Be careful, but not paranoid; register with your embassy, and watch your wallet at all times.

GETTING THERE

In September 1993, citizens of the U.S., Canada, Ireland, the U.K., Australia, New Zealand, and South Africa all needed visas for Romania; single-entry visas (US$31) and multiple-entry visas (US$68) both allow a 6-month stay. Romanian embassies are at 1607 23rd St. NW, Washington, DC 20008 (tel. (202) 232 4747 or 232 4749), and 655 Rideau St., Ottawa, Ont. K1N 6A3 (tel. (613) 789 3709 or 789 5345, fax (613) 789 4365). You can also obtain a visa at the border. By train, the best access points are Sofia, Belgrade, and Budapest; other trains run from Poland, Slovakia, Russia, and Ukraine, while buses connect from Bucharest and Constanta to Varna, İstanbul, and Athens.

TRAVELING IN ROMANIA

Trains **Agentie de Voiaj CFR** (CHE-FE-RE; in Bucharest, appears as SNCFR) sells domestic and international train tickets. There is always an information desk (not necessarily English-speaking) where you inquire about which counter sells tickets to your destination. Knowing the number of the train you want is crucial; get a copy of the train timetable *(Mersul Trenurilor;* 200 lei, US27¢; instructions in Romanian, French, Russian, and German). Tickets can be purchased at CFR offices up to 24hrs. before the train leaves; after that the train station will only sell tickets from 2 hours before the scheduled departure. Remember that Eurail is not yet valid in Romania.

There are 3 types of trains: *rapid* (indicated in green on timetables and at train stations), *accelerat* (red), and *persoane* (black). Try to travel in 1st class *(clasa-întîi,* wagons marked by a yellow stripe on the side) and by *rapid* or *accelerat* trains. The difference in price between 1st and 2nd class is minimal by Western standards (around 200 lei), and the comfort and security are much higher. Even in 1st class, however, there will be no curtains and most likely no lights. If you want to take an overnight train, again opt for 1st class in a sleeping carriage *(vagon de dormit).* During holiday periods, it's a good idea to purchase tickets for *rapid* trains at least 5 days in advance. Lock your compartment, stay with your belongings at all times, and don't fall asleep unless you're sure the people around you are trustworthy.

To buy **international tickets,** go to the CFR office in larger towns and be prepared to wait a while. Budapest-bound trains may exit Romania through either Arad or Oradea; you'll need to specify one when buying a ticket. In southern Romania, it is customary to give your smaller change to the desk officer after purchasing your ticket. It is now possible to pay for international train tickets with lei, but the conditions may test your physical fitness: at the counter you may be given a special receipt saying how much you have to pay; if this happens you must change money at a nearby bank or bureau and then return with the validated receipt. An ISIC entitles you to discounts on tickets throughout Eastern Europe.

Buses, Flights, and Hitching Use the extensive local **bus** system only when trains are not available; though cheaper than trains, they are usually packed and poorly ventilated. Look for the signs for the bus station *(autogară)* in each town. Before heading out, ask for a copy of the bus schedule *(mersul autobuzelor).* **Flying,** once a worthwhile alternative, now requires Western currency and is relatively expensive (Bucharest-Constanta US$65). In addition, old, rickety aircraft make domestic flights on TAROM a harrowing experience. **Hitchhiking,** though risky, remains popular throughout the country. Drivers may expect a payment equivalent to 50-100% of the bus fare for giving you a lift. A wave of the hand, rather than a thumb, is the recognized sign. As always, women traveling alone will want to find another means of transportation.

ROMANIA ESSENTIALS

ONT (sometimes called "OJT"), the national tourist bureau, doesn't always give reliable info about the price and availability of cheap rooms. Branches in expensive hotels are often more useful than the main offices. **CTT,** the youth travel agency, is designed for organized groups and will be utterly befuddled by your presence.

In 1991, Romania released banknotes of 500, 1000, and 5000 lei. Bills worth 100 lei are still in circulation, but are nearly worthless and looked at with suspicion. You can pay for almost anything except plane tickets in lei; due to currency fluctuations, however, *Let's Go* lists many prices in US$. It's a good idea to keep all receipts for money exchanged and folk art purchased in Romania. Lots of private exchange bureaus can be found throughout the country now; there's little variation among their rates and commissions. Avoid changing money on the street. Although unofficial trading is still illegal, getting jailed is now less of a risk than getting cheated; train stations demand special wariness. Try befriending English-speaking Romanian students; they'll help you find better lodgings and can assist in restaurants where you might otherwise be overcharged. It is customary to give inexact change, especially if it is under 10-15 lei. **Prices listed below are at US$1=745 lei.**

Be wary of weekend **business hours.** Under Ceauşescu, weekends meant shorter work days for Romanians, not days off. The new government immediately gave everyone weekends off but has since had second thoughts. Many banks and more important businesses may be closed on Friday afternoons. Tourist and CFR bureaus are usually open Monday through Friday 8am to 8pm. They may be open on Saturday mornings as well, but almost everything is closed on Sundays. Many shops (even privatized ones) tend to close by 6pm. Twenty-four-hour cafés and food stores can be found in some cities. **National holidays** are New Year's Day (stores closed Jan. 1-3), 3-4 days for Orthodox Easter (a week later than Roman Catholic Easter), May Day (May 1), and Christmas (some businesses may be closed Dec. 25-31). Romania is in the same time zone as Bulgaria, one hour ahead of Western Europe.

Gypsies are widely mistrusted in Romania, and not without reason: they will likely be the greatest threat to your belongings. You'll also see numerous gypsies lying on the street or sitting at corners, begging.

Many Romanians hold conservative attitudes towards sexuality. Unfortunately, these attitudes may translate into harrassment of gay, lesbian, and bisexual travelers.

ROMANIA ESSENTIALS

Public hygiene in Romania will challenge Westerners. Most public restrooms lack soap, towels, and toilet paper. Even "privatized" public bathrooms that charge 10-20 lei may give you only a tiny amount of toilet paper. Feminine hygiene products can sometimes be found in stores now, but will be expensive. (Camera film has also gone the way of capitalism; a roll of 35mm film may cost US$8.) Stash basic medicines in your backpack as well; drug stores *(farmacie)* may not have what you need. If you do buy medicines in Romania, know what you're purchasing: *antinevralgic* for headaches, *piramidon* for colds and the flu, and *saprosan* for diarrhea.

Communication Romanian is a Romance language; travelers familiar with French, Italian, Spanish, or Portuguese can usually decipher public signs. However, spoken Romanian is a trial for the average visitor. Some transliterations of Romanian letters are: *ş* as in ca*sh*; *î* or *â* as in str*i*ng, *ă* as in b*u*s and *c* as in *ch*eese when followed by *i* or *e* (otherwise, as in *co*ol). A few key phrases in Romanian will smooth your travels considerably. Try the following: *vă rog* (VUH-rog; "please"), *multumesc frumos* (mul-tsu-MESK fru-MOZ; "thank you very much"), *bună dimineata/ ziua/seara* (BU-na di-mi-NYAH-tsah/ZI-huah/SAH-rah; "good morning/day/ evening"), *unde* (UN-de; "where?"), *ce* (CHE, "what?"), *cînd* (KUHND, "when?"), *cît costă* (KUT KOH-stah; "How much does it cost?"). In Transylvania, German and Hungarian are widely spoken. Throughout the country, French is the second language for the older generation, English for the younger.

Making **international phone calls** is no easy task in Romania. At the phone office, write down where you want to call, how long you want to talk and the telephone number. Operators shout your telephone destination in the most incoherent way possible, so stay nearby. You will pay up front (always ask for the rate per minute). Since rates rise the longer you stay on, it is cheaper to call collect *(telefon cu taxă inversă)*. The country still does not have USA Direct; even at the central post office in major cities (where it's best to call from), there may not be any phones that make international calls. Only telephones beginning with 12 in Bucharest can dial direct internationally. **City calls** cost 1 lei but you'll sometimes get a wrong number even though you may have dialed correctly. Calls within the same area are usually 10 lei per minute and 20 lei per minute to outside areas. To dial another city use the prefix 9, followed by the city code. You can easily find intercity telephones *(telefon interurban)* on the street. Some of them dial Bucharest without requiring any prefix.

Accommodations and Camping Private accommodations are generally the way to go, but hosts rarely speak English, and travelers should be aware that renting a room "together" means sharing the same bed. Through ONT, they run about US$12 per person (breakfast included). Always fix a price before you accept anything. Freelance housing offers should cost under US$6. Make sure that the person has written references from other travelers that may make their offer more credible. Your hosts may also expect you to change money with them at a favorable rate. Many towns reserve **university dorms** for foreign students at insanely low prices. Ask at the local university rectorate; the ONT *may* be able to help you. Prices at category II hotels start at US$12 for singles and US$24 for doubles (showers cost US$4-5 more). **Campgrounds** are crowded, and their bathrooms redefine the word "foul." Bungalows are relatively cheap but often full in summer (about US$5-10). The tourist map called *Popasuri Turistice* (in French), lists most sites.

Food and Drink Finding food in Romania is no longer such a problem; marketplaces are excellent sources of inexpensive food. It's a good idea to carry a water bottle. There are taps—often actual wells—in train stations and spaced regularly along major roads, although it's always a safer bet to buy bottled water. Wines of the Murfatlar region, near the Black Sea, are world-famous and wonderfully inexpensive (US$3-5/bottle). A good, cheap local drink is *tuică* (ts-WI-ca, plum brandy). Three or four shots will be enough to dull your hunger pangs.

With the current exchange rate, even some of the most expensive restaurants are cheap (full meals US$10-12). But double-check your bill and politely ask for an explanation if the amount appears incorrect. Many restaurants list prices per serving of 100 grams, so be sure both you and your waiter understand how much you plan to spend. Except in the more expensive establishments, you are expected to seat yourself wherever there is space available, including at a partially occupied table. Restaurants are generally open from 7am to 10pm but stop serving an hour before closing. Tip by rounding up the bill to the nearest 50 or 100 lei.

∎∎∎ BUCHAREST (BUCUREŞTI)

In the 1920s and 30s, Bucharest was a city of beautiful boulevards, parks, and fine neoclassical architecture. It takes a vivid imagination to recreate this vision today: Ceauşescu's government demolished historic neighborhoods, replacing them with concrete-box housing projects. If you misguidedly plan to spend time here, flee to the lakes, parks, and suburbs, where a glimmer of Bucharest's old personality remains.

ORIENTATION AND PRACTICAL INFORMATION

Bucharest is in southeastern Romania, 70km north of the Bulgarian border. Direct trains connect the city with most Eastern European capitals. Armed with a city map (secured at the train station with any luck), head east on **Calea Grivitei** and take a right onto **Calea Victoriei,** which leads to most sights and tourist spots. Walk down another 4 blocks on Strada Biserica Amzei, the continuation of Grivitei, to **Bulevardul Magheru** (which becomes Bd. Bălcescu and then Bd. Brătianu), the main artery in Bucharest. Bus #133, trolley #79, or the metro to Piata Romană will take you to Bd. Magheru. A taxi to Piata Romană should cost under 2000 lei (US$2.50).

Tourist Offices: The **ONT** office at the Gara de Nord is apparently just for show. Open Mon.-Fri. 7:30am-8pm, Sat. 7:30am-3pm, Sun. 7:30am-2pm. For reliable help, go to the main office, Bd. Magheru 7 (tel. 14 51 60), next to the *Magazinul Eva* (EVA store), for maps (500 lei, US70¢) and information on sights, accommodations, and camping throughout the country. Private rooms US$15/bed (showers and breakfast included); ask a for central location. Open Mon.-Fri. 8am-8pm, Sat. 8am-3pm, and for money exchange only Sun. 8am-1pm. Most major hotels have ONT desks or newly privatized tourist offices.

Budget Travel: CTT, Str. Dem Dobrescu 4-6 (tel. 14 05 66), at the 2nd traffic light to the right of ONT. Intended for groups, but ask about the events sponsored by CTT for students (e.g., International Folklore Festival). Open Mon.-Fri. 8am-5pm.

Embassies: U.S., Str. Tudor Arghezi 7-9, 1 block behind Hotel Intercontinental. For services, go to the adjacent consulate on Str. Snagov 25 (tel. 10 40 40). Open Mon.-Fri. 8am-5pm. **Canada,** Str. Nicolae Iorga 36 (tel. 50 61 40), near Piata Romană. Open Mon.-Fri. 9am-5pm. **U.K.,** Str. Jules Michelet 24 (tel. 12 03 03). Open Mon.-Thurs. 8:30am-5pm, Fri. 8am-1pm. Citizens of **Australia** and **New Zealand** should contact the British embassy. **Bulgaria,** Str. Rabat 5 (tel. 33 21 50). Open Mon.-Fri. 8:30am-12:30pm and 2-5pm. **Hungary,** Str. Jean-Louis Calderon 63 (tel. 14 66 21, 14 66 22, and 14 66 23). Open Mon.-Thurs. 8am-4:30pm, Fri. 8am-3:30pm. **Russia,** Şoseaua Kiseleff 46 (tel. 17 13 09). Open Mon., Wed., and Fri. 9am-1pm. Try also the Russian consulate (tel. 17 01 20 through -29).

Currency Exchange: Avoid changing money on the street. **ONT** offices change most currencies and traveler's checks (2.5% commission); or look in the newspaper for the bank offering the best rate. Major credit cards are accepted at expensive hotels and restaurants, but usually at an unfavorable rate.

American Express: Bd. Magheru (tel. 312 25 96), on the 2nd floor in the entryway next to the ONT office. Replaces lost cards and Cheques, but won't accept wired money. Issues Traveler's Cheques to card holders. Holds mail. Open Mon.-Fri. 8:30am-5pm.

Post Office: Str. Matei Millo 10, off Calea Victoriei. Open Mon.-Fri. 7:30am-8pm, Sat. 7:30am-2pm. **Poste Restante** down the street next to the Hotel Carpati. **Postal Code:** 70154.

Telephones: Make international calls from Calea Victoriei 37, near the theaters. Open 24 hrs. At night, go around the side. Expect to wait; ask to make collect calls. Calls to the US average US$1.50/min. For directory assistance, call 11 51 50. Wait for the English-speaking operator. Other useful numbers include: 051 (general inquiries), 052 (CFR/railway info), 055 (police), 065 (pharmacies), 071 (international phone calls), and 091 (intercity phone calls). **City Code:** 90.

Flights: Otopeni Airport (tel. 33 66 02, information tel. 33 31 37), 16km away, handles international traffic. Buses to Otopeni leave from the TAROM office every 1-2hr.; buy tickets on board. Coming from Otopeni, buses let you off near the Hotel Intercontinental on Bd. Magheru. **Báneasa Airport,** connected with Piata Romană by tram #131, handles domestic flights. Buy international tickets at Str. Brezoianu 10 (tel. 46 33 46; see directions under Trains below); domestic tickets at the **TAROM** office, Piata Victoriei (tel. 59 41 85 or 59 41 25). Both offices are open Mon.-Fri. 7:30am-7pm.

Trains: Gara de Nord (tel. 052) is the principal station; it's unlikely that you'll have to visit **Basarab, Báneasa,** or **Obor.** Gara de Nord has one baggage check for foreigners and one for locals. **Domestic** tickets can be purchased in advance (though not in English) at the **Agence de Voyage, CFR,** which has 2 offices: one at Calea Grivitei 132 (tel. 50 42 47), 2 blocks down from the train station; the other at Str. Brezoianu 10, 1st floor (tel. 13 26 44), 2 blocks south of Bd. Mihail Kogălniceanu between Calea Victoriei and Cişmigiu Park (use the TAROM entrance). Learn the phrase *Un bilet pentru...* ("One ticket to..."). To: Constanta (class I, 2000 lei, US$2.70); Braşov (class I, 1200 lei, US$1.60); Cluj-Napoca (class I, 3400 lei, US$4.50). **International** tickets must be bought at the CFR office in Piata Unirii. All offices open Mon.-Fri. 7:30am-7pm, Sat. 7:30am-noon.

Buses: Three stations serve Bucharest. **Filaret,** Piata Gării Filaret 1 (tel. 41 06 92), and **Rahova,** Şos. Alexandriei 164 (tel. 76 47 95), are both in the southern suburbs; **Báneasa,** Str. I. Ionescu de la Brad 5 (tel. 79 56 45), is to the north. All are madhouses. Scores of buses to İstanbul via Bulgaria leave from the main train station (17hr., US$15; outside and to the right, one company charges US$10). Each representative will *claim* that their bus is air-conditioned. Suspicious dealings with customs officials are common. For buses to Athens, inquire at Hotel Majestic or at the office in room 129 in Hotel Union, Str. I Cîmpineanu (tel. 13 26 40).

Public Transportation: Buses, trolleys, and trams all cost 20 lei. Tickets available at kiosks near most stops or on the buses. Buses are packed to the gills on busy routes—people literally hang out the doors. Hold on to your valuables. The metro offers reliable service to all major points in Bucharest for 50 lei; open 5am-11pm.

Taxis: tel. 053. Expect 240 lei/km. Try to hail "state taxis" with the number 053 on the rear passenger door. Arrange the price (*pretil*) before you accept a ride (*bine* means "good").

Hitchhiking: Those hitching north take tram #149 (or the TAROM shuttle) to the airport. Those heading to the Black Sea and Constanta take tram #13 east; to Giurgiu and Bulgaria, tram #12; to Piteşti and western Romania, tram #13 west.

Pharmacies: At Bd. Magheru 18 (tel. 59 61 15) just across from the ONT office and in the train station. Open 24hrs. Ring the bell at night.

Medical Assistance: Clinica Batiótei, Str. Tudor Arghezi 28, behind the Hotel Intercontinental. The only hospital authorized to treat foreigners.

Emergencies: Police (tel. 055). Also, call your consulate.

ACCOMMODATIONS

The ONT office can arrange private rooms (US$15) or accommodations in hotels starting at US$20. You're better off avoiding offers for private accommodation by individuals at the train station. During the school year (early Sept.-late June), Romanian students will often share their rather drab rooms. Try the dormitories of the **Polytechnic Institute** near the Semănătoarea Metro stop. Hotel Cişmigiu on Bd.

Kogălniceanu, 2 blocks east of Grădina Cişmigiu, has been recently turned into a student dorm for the Film and Visual Arts Institute.

Category II hotels are the best value for the budget traveler and are most likely to have space available. Most of the rooms in these hotels are similar; the difference lurks in price and location. Check the signboard posted outside the ONT office in the train station for more information. All of these establishments recommend that you make reservations.

Hotel Dunărea, Calea Griviței 140 (tel. 617 32 20), across from the Gare du Nord train station. One of the least expensive hotels in Bucharest. Rooms are bearable for short layovers, and it's a short ride to the city center. Singles with sink 9000 lei (US$12), with shower 10,000 lei (US$13), with bath 11,000 lei (US$15). Doubles with shower 15,000 lei (US$20), with bath 18,000 lei (US$24).

Hotel Negoiu, Str. Ion Câmpineanu 16 (tel. 615 52 50). Turn right onto the side-street across from the Hotel Intercontinental off Bd. Nicolae Balcescu. Old and stately, with private baths. Singles US$22, doubles US$34.

Hotel Union, Str. Decembrie 11 (tel. 613 26 40), across the street from Negoiu at #13. Singles with sink US$15, with shower US$28, with bath US$42. Doubles US$24, US$44, US$66. Triples with sink US$39, with bath US$69.

Hotel Muntenia, Str. Academiei 21 (tel. 614 60 10). To the right of Hotel Union. Many boisterous groups. Singles and doubles US$27, with shower US$34.

Hotel Carpati, no. 16 Str. Matei Millo (tel. 617 76 90). On a quiet side street near the central post office. Singles with sink US$21. Doubles US$41.

FOOD

There is an open-air market on Str. Piata Amzei between Calea Victoriei and Bd. Magheru. Kiosks sell inexpensive snacks, soft drinks, and fruit on the streets.

Restaurant Elegant-Efes, Bd. Magheru 24A (tel. 659 54 30), across from the main ONT office. Opened in the early summer of 1993 and quickly found a following for its *pui* (roasted ½-chicken, US$4) and *crenwurst* (pork sausages, US$1). Wash the meal down with a pint of *habla* (cold draft beer) imported from Turkey. Open daily 10am-3pm.

Restaurant Dunana, Bd. Nicolae Balescu 315 (tel. 615 40 13), across from the Hotel Intercontinental. Tends to be a bit overpriced but offers an excellent vantage point from its outdoor terrace over Piata Universitatii. Soft drinks an astounding US$1.50/can, but the pizza is a delicious bargain at US$1. Open daily 10am-11pm. Nightly disco music club 9pm-4am. 1000 lei.

Hanul Lui Manuc, Str. 30 Decembrie 62 (tel. 613 14 15), near the southern end of Calea Victoriei. Traditional cuisine in a beautifully restored 17th-century manor that's also a pricey hotel. Restaurant inside, day bar in courtyard, café in cellar. Meals about US$6-8 (make sure waiters don't overcharge you). Restaurant open daily 7am-midnight. *Crama* (cellar) open Mon.-Fri. 11am-11pm, Sat.-Sun. 10am-midnight. *Bar de Zi* (day bar) open Mon.-Fri. 10am-10pm, Sat.-Sun. 10am-11pm.

Snack Bar Negoiu, at the side of the hotel of the same name. Popular with a younger Romanian crowd. Loud music and lots of cigarette smoke. Try the Italo-Romanian spaghetti with *chiftele*. Meals about US$3. Open Mon.-Sat. 8am-11pm.

SIGHTS

You can see the remnants of old Bucharest on the circuit formed by **Calea Victoriei, Strada Lipscani,** and **Bulevardul Magheru.** Most of the elegant buildings making up the palace on **Piata Victoriei** are now government offices. If it's open, visit the extensive collection of Western and Romanian art at the **Muzeul de Arta al Romaniei** on Str. ştirbei Vodă. Several private art collections have been combined in the **Museul Colectiilor de Arta,** farther down Calea Victoriei at #111. Farther south, past the open-air market at Piata Unirii, are the excavations of a **Roman settlement.**

In 1989, anti-government rebels broadcast as Securitate forces stormed the **TV station.** Entrance is forbidden, but the bullet-scarred buildings in the vicinity attest to the importance of the media in modern society. (Take bus #131 from Piata Romana to "Piata Aviatorilor".) Heading south on Blvd. 1848 past Piata Unirii, go right onto **Bulevardul Unirii;** Ceaușescu demolished 20% of Bucharest to build this street of luxury apartments, including a palace, the **House of the People,** for himself and his retainers. The monument to megalomania was strictly off-limits to ordinary citizens before the revolution.

Although there is no substitute for traveling through the countryside of Moldavia or Maramureș to discover Romanian folklore, the open-air **Village Museum** in Parcul Herăstrău re-creates peasant dwellings from all regions of Romania. From Magheru Bd., take bus #131 or 331 north to the Arcul de Triumf. (Open Tues.-Sun. 9am-8pm, Mon. 9am-5pm.) The **Museum of the History of the City of Bucharest,** on Piata Universității, has an authentic parchment dated September 20, 1459—the earliest use of the name "București" in any written document. The parchment bears the signature of Vlad Dracul, father of more famous son Vlad Tepeș, "the Impaler" (alias Count Dracula). (Open Tues.-Sun. 10am-6pm. 15 lei.)

Bucharest is replete with parks, to compensate for its urban wastescape. Wander through well-groomed central **Cişmigiu Park,** a few blocks west of Calea Victoriei, or the picturesque **Herăstrău Park** to the north, focal points for much of the city's social life. Elderly pensioners, young couples, soccer players, and chess whizzes are everywhere. The bars in Herăstrău Park provide ample opportunity to rub elbows with the locals. You can also join the crowds at **Parcul Studentilor** (Student Park) on Lacul Tei; swim or play volleyball, basketball, tennis, or ping pong here. Take bus #35 or trolley #86 to the end and follow the signs.

ENTERTAINMENT

Whatever you do in the evening, pack a map and cab fare; the streets are very poorly lit and buses are unreliable. At the **Casa de Culture Studentilor,** Calea Plevnei 61 (near the Eroilor metro stop), behind the Opera, there's a disco where you can gyrate with Romanian students, many of whom speak English. The staff may be more interested in your Western money than in serving you well, however. (Open Thurs.-Sun. 7:30pm-midnight.) The **Vox Maris** disco on Bd. M. Kogalniceanu under the Cercul Militar National is one of the most trendy nightspots in Bucharest. (Open nightly 10pm-4am. US$4.)

The **Club Ski-Nautic Báneasa,** Str. Madrigalului 24, Section 1, behind the Herăstrău restaurant in the park of the same name, lets you forget you're in Bucharest. In summer, nightly performances animate the theaters on Calea Victoriei north of Bd. Gheorghiu. Buy tickets at the *casa de billete,* Calea Victoriei 48. (Open 9am-1pm and 2-8pm for Theater Tandarica; 10am-1pm and 4:30-7:30pm for Theater Giulesti.)

The seasons for the **Romanian Opera, Philharmonic,** and the **Operetta Theater** (tickets 100 lei) run from mid-October to late March. The **National Theater,** Bd. Bălcescu 2, and the **C. Nottara,** Bd. Magheru 20 (tel. 15 93 02), are also renowned. Tickets are sold for the following week's performance on Saturday at each theater's box office. Bucharest also has the only **Jewish State Theater** *(Teatre Evreesk)* in Europe, at Str. Iuliu Baraș 15, which performs throughout the summer. The shows are in Yiddish, though the simultaneous headphone translations into Romanian should make everything clear. Right.

■ Near Bucharest

If Bucharest drives you mad, take a daytrip to **Snagov,** a tiny village half an hour north of Bucharest by car or train. (Sat.-Sun. 8:30am and 4pm, returning 10am and 6pm; one-way US$1.) Many people hitch. In summer, hordes descend upon **Snagov Park,** 5km west of Snagov village, where you can swim in the brownish lake or rent a rowboat (11 lei/1½hr.) and row to **Snagov Monastery** (½-hr. trip). Here lies the grave of the infamous Vlad Tepeș. The so-called Count Dracula earned his reputation by defying the Ottomans and impaling the heads of the Turkish police on spikes, setting them around the walls of his capital. Women may wish to do the same to the monastery keepers—only men may enter.

Another option is to escape to **Sinaia**. This high mountain resort town lies 1¾ hours from Bucharest toward Braşov by train. Here looms the 19th-century summer castle of King Carol I, the first King of Romania. Be sure also to visit the **Sinaia Monastery,** built in the 17th century and used as a refuge during the Russo-Turkish War.

BLACK SEA COAST

Romania's Black Sea coast is jam-packed in summer, if only because it is the only holiday most Romanians can afford. Trains run from Bucharest to Constanta (4/day, 3hr., I class 2000 lei (US$2.70)), where you can catch a bus to the Black Sea resorts.

Constanta The city, a Greek harbor some 2500 years ago, received its name from the daughter of Emperor Constantine; some residents playfully regard Constantinople as "the fatherland." Escape the innumerable gray apartment blocks that stifle the city by exploring the old town. Take a walk along the waterfront **promenade** past the imposingly elegant *Cazino*. The **mosque** on Str. Muzeelor is one of the few reminders of Turkish domination and offers a bird's eye view of the town. In Piata Ovidiu, behold the **Statue of Ovid,** commemorating the Roman writer who wrote his most famous poems in exile here, then head to the **Archeological Museum.** (Open daily 9am-8pm. 100 lei, students 50 lei.) The park around Lacul Tăbăcăriei houses a **dolphinarium** and a **planetarium.**

The **ONT office** (tel. 61 48 00) on Bd. Tomis 66 speaks English and can help you arrange private accommodations or provide useful info on the prices and availability of resort hotels in the surrounding area. Take trolley #40 or 43 from the train station and get off where Bd. Tomis intersects Bd. Republicii (about 5 stops). (Open Mon.-Fri. 8am-7pm, Sat. 8am-1pm.) Down Bd. Tomis from the ONT office at #20-26, **Hotel Tineretului** (tel. (91) 61 35 90) has bright and airy rooms with TVs, phones, and private baths. (Singles US$18.50. Doubles US$37.) Bd. Tomis is the main street, cutting across the whole city, but most shops and restaurants are located on ştefan Cel Mare. At Piata Unirii, next to Bd. Republicii, you can find a large **food store** and a **fruit and vegetable market**. The old town, though very small, is a more pleasant place for a meal or coffee. The **central post office** is at Bd. Tomis 79. In the **CFR bureau** at Str. Vasile Canarache (tel. (91) 61 49 60), towards the seaport from Piata Ovidiu, you can buy domestic tickets and tickets to İstanbul (I class US$66), Sofia (I class US$22), and Athens. (Open Mon.-Fri. 7am-7pm, Sat. 7am-1pm.) Call (91) 66 66 13 to find out about **buses** to Dobrich and Varna, Bulgaria.

Near Constanta The last stop on bus #40 or tram #100 from the main train station brings you to the seaside resort of **Mamaia** just north of Constanta. Only serious tan-freaks willing to pay extra for accommodation should venture here. Contact the **Hotel Lotus** (tel. (91) 83 17 46) or the **Hotel Delfin** (tel. (91) 38 16 40) for information and current student discounts.

There are buses from the train station nearly every half-hour marked for **Mangalia** and the rest of Romania's southernmost seaside resorts (150 lei). Bypass humdrum **Eforie Nord** and **Eforie Sud,** the first resorts to the south, and go straight to **Costineşti,** a dynamic seaside hotspot catering to an exclusively young crowd. You can hike the 3km from the bus stop; hitchers say it's easy enough to get a ride. The complex is open May-Sept. and is most crowded after July 15, when Romanian universities begin their summer break. Try to call ahead (tel. (91) 74 29 77 or 74 28 50; ext. 162). The **Vile Belvedere** (tel. 74 15 07 or 74 38 50) offers clean and comfortable rooms without bath (US$11/person). Bungalows and other less desirable rooms abound. Continuing farther south, you'll pass through the intergalactic resorts **Neptun, Jupiter, Venus,** and **Saturn** before reaching Mangalia. The picturesque landscape and lakes of Neptun, one of the newer resorts, are well worth a visit. If planning to stay overnight, try to get a room in **Hotel Adriana** or **Hotel Raluca** in Venus. (Singles US$10-12. Doubles US$15-17.)

Probably the village least spoiled by the heavy tourist industry, **2 Mai** is located on the southern end of the Romanian coast. There are no hotels, so bring a tent or arrange private accommodations (set the price before you move into the room). This village seems to be popular among intellectuals, artists, and bohemian students. From here you can make a short trip on foot to Bulgaria.

Danube Delta The scenic Danube Delta occupies the northern half of the coast. **Tulcea** is its main gateway, 5 hours from Bucharest by fast train via Medgidia, and 4 hours from Constanta by slow train. The terrain between the three arms of the Danube from Tulcea to the Black Sea is a world of natural and artificial canals cutting their way through kilometers of roads—a paradise for anglers, birdwatchers, and adventurers armed with small boats. This huge ecosystem undergoes perceptible changes within a single lifetime; 40m of land are created every year. Ask Tulcea's ONT office in the **Hotel Delta** about excursions through the delta; the tourist map of the area has cute pictures of the local birdies and beasties. Close to the bus station and in Tulcea is the ultra-cheap **Three Star Hotel** on Str. Carpat 1-300. This place is a dive, but for US$1.75 (650 lei/bed) you can have a room all to yourself. Cross over Str. Issaccea in front of the central department store on the waterfront and the hotel is a short walk up the hill. **Navlomar,** Delta Sport Tours, sells boat tickets to the Ukrainian city of Ismail (Wed. and Sat. 8am, US$7) and can arrange excursions around the Delta. Their office is farther down the pier past the bus station.

TRANSYLVANIA

For centuries, Hungarians, Romanians, Russians, and Turks have fought over the rich Transylvanian plateaus in northwestern Romania. The evidence remains—villages built around fortified churches and citadel ruins stand on nearly every hill. Romania's Hungarians, the country's largest minority group, are concentrated here, especially in the northwest. Many people still speak German or Hungarian better than Romanian. Two different train routes from Budapest merge at Braşov before continuing to Bucharest: trains through Arad stop either in Sibiu or Sighişoara, while those through Oradea stop at Cluj-Napoca and Sighişoara.

■■■ BRAŞOV

Braşov, rising from the foot of Mt. Timpa, is one of the most beautifully restored cities in Romania and a good base for excursions to the Carpathian mountains. **Piata Sfatului,** in the center of the old town, and the nearby Str. Republicii, provide splendid strolling ground and give a sad glimpse of the beauty Romania lost when the housing projects took over. The fairy-tale-esque **Orthodox Cathedral** in the square was built in 1858 of marble and delicate gold. The **History Museum,** in the middle of the square, was formerly a courthouse; legend holds that the condemned had to jump from the tower to their deaths. (Open Tues.-Sun. 10am-6pm. Closed for restorations in summer 1993.) Uphill from the square along Str. Gh. Baritiu looms the **Black Church,** the most celebrated Gothic building in the country; it received its name after being charred in a fire in 1689. (Open Mon.-Sat. 10am-6:30pm. 50 lei, students 25 lei.) Walk right from the Hotel Aro Palace along Bd. Eroilor for an **ethnographic museum** which houses exhibits of traditional Transylvanian folk costumes and ceramics. (Open Tues.-Sun. 10am-6pm. Students 50 lei.) A few doors down at no. 21 is the **Muzeul de Arta** (National Art Museum), featuring the work of Romania's newest talents. (Open Tues.-Sun. 10am-6pm. Students 25 lei.)

Accommodations, Food, and Practical Information EXO (tel. (92) 14 45 91 or (92) 14 39 75), a very helpful private accommodations bureau, is located at Str. Postăvarului 6. (Open Mon.-Fri. 11am-8pm, Sun. 11am-2pm.) As you face Hotel Aro Palace, walk 350m left and then make a quick right onto Str. Republicii. Turn left at the first crossing, walk for a block, and turn right onto Str. Postă varului. (**Private accommodations** US$6.) Larger groups may be able to secure a bungalow in the nearby ski resort Poiana Braşov for 600 lei per bed. Students in the **dormitory** complex off Str. Memorandului may offer to share their quarters (school year early Sept.-late June). You may be approached at the train station by the jovial and energetic **Mr. Babes Aurel**, who offers rooms in his house for US$5. He and his wife (who speaks French) go out of their way to make you feel at home (Str. Cerbului 32; tel. (29) 14 05 17). The **Hotel Aro Sport,** Str. Sf. Ioan 6 (tel. 14 38 40), at the back of the Hotel Aro Palace, is the cheapest in Braşov. Spartan but clean rooms with communal bathrooms cost US$22 for singles, US$36 for doubles.

Restaurants cluster near the main square. **Gustări** offers traditional Romanian fare. (Full meals US$2. Open daily 9am-9pm.) For dessert, head across the square and take a right onto Str. Muresenilor to the **Mamamia,** where banana splits, milkshakes, and sundaes are expensive (about US$3), but well worth the treat. Riding up the **Mount Tîmpa** cable car (Tues.-Sun., round-trip 400 lei) wins you both a transfixing view and a reasonably priced restaurant, the **Panoramic** (tel. 11 98 51), at the top.

From the train station, ride bus #4 for 10 minutes. On Bd. Eroilor, you'll see the Hotel Aro Palace on your left facing a park; the ONT **tourist office** (tel. (92) 14 16 48) in its lobby has maps and information on hotel accommodations. (Open daily 8am-8pm.) To walk from the station (2km), head straight on Bd. Victoriei, follow the road to the right around the civic center, then turn right on Bd. 15 Noiembrie, which becomes Bd. Eroilor after Piata Teatrului. The **CFR** office is on Str. Republicii 53. (Open Mon.-Fri. 7am-7:30pm. Braşov to Bucharest 1200 lei (US$160), to Sighişoara US$128.) The city is Transylvania's major **train** hub, 2½-3 hours from Bucharest by train; all Budapest-Bucharest trains stop here.

■ Near Braşov

Poiana Braşov, one of Romania's most popular resorts, is only 10km away (buses leave from in front of the main building of the university on Bd. Eroilar; 200 lei). Ask for "maşina de Poiana." The resort has about 15 category I hotels and many restaurants in a beautifully green, open area among the mountains, perfect for hiking or skiing.

Bran, 23km southwest of Braşov, is a picturesque town housing the famed **Castle of Vlad Tepeş.** Ostensibly home to the count who inspired Bram Stoker's novel *Dracula,* the castle still poses majestically, though not very mysteriously, on its hill. (Open Tues.-Sun. 9am-4pm.) Actually, Count Dracula had nothing at all to do with this castle; the rumor started because the place needed money for reconstruction. Still, it merits a look. The locals try to keep it interesting with the **Muzeul Vama Bran,** which contains old photos and relics from the place, and with an **ethnographic museum** of Transylvania. (Open Tues.-Sun. 10am-4pm. To castle and museum 75 lei, with ISIC 25 lei.) To get to Bran from Braşov, take the **bus** marked "Bran" from the station on Bd. Eroilor (every hr., 200 lei).

■■■ SIGHIŞOARA (SEGESVÁR, SCHÄSSBURG)

Of all the medieval towns in Transylvania, **Sighişoara** is perhaps the least spoiled and most enchanting. Surrounded by mountains and crowning a green hill on the railroad line between Cluj and Braşov, its guild towers, old clock tower, steeples, and irregular tile roofs are almost entirely unobstructed by modern buildings. The old walled town is preserved as a museum, and visitors can wander into the surrounding hilly, green farmland. In recent years, Sighişoara's citizens have struggled to make their town more cosmopolitan: they call the small modern housing estate near the Orthodox Cathedral "the Vatican," the poor Gypsy neighborhood at the end of the town is known as "Congo," and you can have a pint of beer at a local pub called "Dallas." The **History Museum** in the clock tower offers a glimpse into the city's more provincial past as well as an outstanding panorama of the surrounding area. (Open Tues.-Sun. 9am-6:30pm. 60 lei, students 30 lei.) Nearby is the **Museum of Medieval Armory,** whose 3 rooms display cannonballs, Middle-Eastern-style swords *(iatagan),* and other weapons of Dark-Age domination. (Open Tues.-Sun. 10am-3:30pm. 20 lei, with ISIC 10 lei.) Check out the old Saxon **church** (closed for renovations in the summer of 1993) and graveyard, at the top of a 175-step covered wooden staircase.

Accommodations, Food, and Practical Information From the train station, take a right, then a quick left, walk across the river, and bear right onto Str. 1 Decembrie to reach the town's main hotel and tourist office, **Birolilade Turism** (tel. (950) 710 72; open Mon.-Fri. 8am-5pm, Sat. 9am-noon). The staff speaks English and are very helpful in providing everything from maps to private accommodations. They even offer private tours of the city for less than US$2. The **CFR** office is on the corner of Str. 1 Decembrie and Str. Gen. Grigorescu. (Open Mon.-Fri. 7am-8pm.) Farther down Str. 1 Decembrie is the **telephone office** (open daily 7am-10pm) and the **post office.** (Open Mon.-Fri. 7:30am-noon and 5-7pm.)

Right next door **Hotel Steaua** ("star," tel. (950) 719 30) is not nearly as luminous as the name suggests, but the price of the room includes breakfast. (Singles US$14, with bath US$17. Doubles US$25, with bath US$31. Triples with bath US$35.) Just 4km outside town on the road to Sibiu is the **campground** and restaurant **Hula Danes** (tel. (950) 710 52). Bungalows for two cost US$8.50 per bed. Five buses per day head in the direction of the campground from the bus station (50 lei).

In the old town, you can have an excellent meal of local delicacies; try the corner house on the 2nd sidestreet after entering through the clock tower (full meal US$3). Vlad Dracul's son was born here in 1331; bite into **Restaurant Vlad Dracul** (tel. (950) 71 596; open daily noon-10pm), which really picks up at night, especially in the dungeon-like *berarie* downstairs. If you take the first sidestreet after the clock tower and walk toward the Lutheran church atop the hill, you'll come to a small square where **Cofetarie Boema** is located. This cozy café offers magnificent cakes with aromatic coffee. (Open daily 9am-9pm.)

The **Făgăraş Mountains** lie just to the south of the rail line between Subiu and Braşov. You can day-hike past snowfields and shepherds' huts and stay cheap in a *cabana* (a primitive mountain lodge with an outhouse and occasionally electricity). The view of the Wallachian plains to the south and the Transylvanian plateau to the north will make up for any fatigue. Bring a map and food—the only available grub may be the Romanian equivalent of Spam—and disinfect water from the streams.

■■■ CLUJ-NAPOCA

Proud of its Roman past, Cluj even has a statue of Lupina Capitolana with Romulus and Remus sent by "Mother Rome." Cluj is officially a bilingual city, and though many ethnic Hungarians are moving back to Hungary, the town's operas and two theaters still perform in both Romanian and Hungarian. The university also adds a foreign flavor to the atmosphere, with many Arab and Greek students. Watch your belongings carefully, but otherwise the city is enjoyable.

To get to the city center from the train station, take either bus #3 or 4 (50 lei) or head straight down the main street and across the river to the old town (2km). A walk around the central square, over which the Gothic steeple of the **Catholic Cathedral** rises majestically, should help you to orient yourself. Cluj has a few interesting museums and churches. A walk up Str. Făcliei will bring you to the 15th-century **Biserica Reformată** (Reform Church), which often holds organ concerts. On neighboring Piata Victoriei, the **Catedrala Arhiepiscopală** (Orthodox Cathedral) holds services. (Mon.-Sat. 7:30-9:30am and 6-7pm, Sun. 8:30am-12:30pm and 6-7pm.) Also worth seeing are the **Museum of Transylvanian History,** Str. Constantin Daicoviciu 2 (open Tues. and Thurs.-Sun. 10am-5pm), the **Village Museum** in Park Hoia, and the **Ethnographic Museum of Transylvania,** Str. Memorandumului 21. ISICs earn discounts on admission. On Str. Universității, beginning from the southern end of Piata Unirii, you'll discover the student section of town. The hottest nightspot in town is the **Bianco e Niro** disco and bar, Str. Universității 7-9, with a high tech sound and light system to keep you moving (300 lei, with ISIC). The **Nicula Monastery,** 60km towards Heudin, is accessible by bus, while the nearby **Apuseni Mountains** are a wonderful hiking area.

Accommodations and Food   Check the accommodations board at the train station for directions to the hotels in Cluj-Napoca. The **Hotel Vladeasă,** at Str. Gh. Doja 20 (tel. (95) 11 84 91), is the best value for both location and price. (Doubles US$23, with bath US$28. Triples US$34, with bath US$37.) Farther from the town center towards the train station is the old yellow **Hotel Astoria** (tel. (95) 13 01 66) on Str. Horea 3, whose rooms are spacious but bland. (Singles US$17, with bath US$21. Doubles US$28, with bath US$32. Triples US$40, with bath US$43.) As a last resort, walk across the street from the train station to the **Hotel Pax** (tel. (95) 13 61 01). Noisy singles with bath are US$17; doubles US$28, with bath US$34; triples US$41. **Camping Făget** (tel. (95) 11 62 34) is 8km from the city towards Bucharest. (US$4 for 1 person, US$5 for 2 people, US$6 for 3 people. Open May-Oct. 15.)

Back on the central square, you can sip a cup of coffee and eat piece of cake at **Cofetarie Carpati** for under 200 lei. (Open Mon.-Fri. 7am-10pm, Sat.-Sun. 8am-4pm.) Enjoy the regional specialties and the excellent view overlooking the town square at **Restaurant Someş,** Str. Iuliu Maniu 2, near the Catholic Cathedral; it's among the most expensive restaurants in town, but a full meal costs only US$4. (Open daily 10am-10pm.) **Pizza Pizza,** Str. Gh. Doja 27, across from the Hotel Vladeasă, gives a Romanian twist to this popular favorite for just 500 lei per slice. (Open daily 9am-9pm.) At **Cofeteria Tineratului,** university types sip coffee between classes. (Open Mon.-Fri. 8am-8pm, Sat. 9am-5pm.) There's a big **market** on Riata Nihai Viteazu. (Covered section open Tues.-Sat. 8am-4pm.)

Practical Information   The tourist office **KmO** is located at Piata Unirii 10 (tel. (95) 11 65 57; open Mon.-Fri. 9am-5pm, Sat. 10am-1pm). Buy a map of the city (200 lei), change money, or arrange for a private room somewhere close to the city's center (US$4, breakfast included). The office may even be able to give you information on renting a room in the university dorms. Next to KmO is the **CFR** office where you can buy tickets around Romania or to neighboring Hungary. The exchange office **Shaker** on Str. Memorandumulsi 9, around the corner from KmO, offered the best rates for changing money in summer 1993. (Open Mon.-Fri. 9am-5pm, Sat. 9am-1pm). The **Central Post Office** with the international telephones located around back is on Str. Gh. Doja 33. (Open daily 7am-10pm.) On the central square screams an insanely crowded **telephone office.** (Open daily 8am-9pm.) On Riata Nihai Viteazu at no. 11, you'll find the **TAROM** office (tel. (95) 13 02 34; open Mon.-Fri. 7am-2pm and 3-7pm, Sat. 7am-1pm), where you can buy tickets for hard currency only. (To Bucharest, US$38; to Constanta, US$48.) Cluj-Napoca can be reached by **train** (from Budapest, 6½hr.; from Bucharest, 8hr.; from Braşov, 3hr.).

Russia (Россия)

Due to the instability of the ruble, allow for an inflation rate of up to 100% over the next year. Furthermore, the hard-currency equivalent may fluctuate.

Kakim byt Sovetskomu Soyuzu?—What will become of the Soviet Union?— was the question asked in Minsk, Belarus in October 1991, when Yeltsin and others gathered to decide the fate of the crumbling Soviet empire in the wake of a failed conservative coup. The answer: *nikakim*—nothing—and so the Commonwealth of Independent States (CIS), a loose confederation of 12 of the former Soviet republics, was born. Russia is now redefining itself as a country of nationality as opposed to ideology, and has metamorphosed from the world's largest bastion of socialist power into an enormous, sprawling yard sale. Red banners are visible only in souvenir shops, *babushki* (elderly women) peddle the contents of their *dachas* (summer cottages), and enterprising young capitalists buy and sell Western goods on street corners. Privately owned stores *(kommercheskie magazini)* flourish, though their selection of goods is often arbitrary; a pair of old boots, a Sony Walkman, and a dried herring may all find themselves at the same kiosk. Russians manage to endure with unique resourcefulness and a heavy dose of black humor, saving, bartering, growing vegetables on their windowsills, and taking refuge around the kitchen table with homemade pickles and a bottle of vodka.

Since the Mongol invasion of the 13th century, Russia has been a nation in a virtually perpetual state of emergency. At the beginning of the 18th century, Peter the Great's crash Westernization cost thousands of lives and precipitated a permanent crisis of cultural identity. Serfdom persisted in Russia up to 1861; in the late 1800s, famine, peasant unrest, and a wave of strikes culminated in the failed 1905 revolution. In 1917, the enormous destruction of World War I cost the tsars their crown.

The rise of Soviet power could not staunch the flow of catastrophe. After the Bolshevik Revolution, civil war and a wave of political executions claimed an untold number of lives. Under Stalin, purges that left tens of millions dead laid the groundwork for totalitarianism, and at least 25 million more died in the campaigns of World War II. The country finally began to recover under Nikita Khrushchev, whose economic reforms and political liberalization led to the "thaw" of the early 1960s before he was ousted in the "Brezhnev coup" of 1964. After Brezhnev, Andropov, and Chernenko expired within a 3-year span, Gorbachev came to power in 1985, but what began with 6 years of *glasnost* (openness) and *perestroika* (rebuilding) gradually turned into a bewildering hodgepodge of semi-anarchy, deepened economic crisis, cynicism, and reinforced apathy. Ironically, the failed coup claimed Gorbachev, winner of the 1990 Nobel Peace Prize for his efforts to lead Russia out of the communist era, as one of its victims; growing discontent among Russians led him to resign in December 1991, leaving Boris Yeltsin, president of the Russian Federation, to occupy Gorbachev's diminished office in the Kremlin.

Russia itself is not a monolith, but rather a vast patchwork of autonomous regions and minority nationalities, subject to the same pressures that broke apart the larger union. The Yakuts (who sit on huge mineral resources) have declared themselves independent, the Tatars—a Muslim enclave in the Orthodox Russian heartland—also want autonomy, and ethnic Russians and their neighbors are fighting over territory (and self-determination) all along the southwestern borders of Russia. Growing discontent with living conditions and general frustration with the slow pace of reform threaten, once again, the powers that be. The hardship of travel here is rewarded by a glimpse of history in the making, in a place of bewildering logic, surprising variety, and so much potential wealth.

GETTING THERE

Flights, Trains, Buses, and Ferries

Flying on Aeroflot or Delta to St. Petersburg or Moscow is the easiest way to reach the former Soviet Union, but there are few discount fares. It may be cheaper to fly somewhere else in Europe and then take the train. **Rail travel** from Helsinki is a fine option; you can reserve in advance by telephone (358 (0) 62 52 16) and pick up your ticket at a special office in the Helsinki station. The Finnish Moscow-bound train crosses the border before midnight; make sure your visa is valid from the date you leave Helsinki. Daily trains also run to Moscow and St. Petersburg from Eastern European capitals. Rail travel from the Baltic capitals is an especially cheap and reliable option. **Buses** run by **Finnord** leave for Petersburg 4 times daily from Lahti, Finland (7hr., 190-220mk); reserve well in advance at tel. (358 (0) 96 00 40 90). The **ferries** that cross from Stockholm and Helsinki to St. Petersburg carry organized tours only.

It is generally OK to enter Russia through a city not specifically listed on your visa. Make sure to buy a round-trip ticket; return tickets to the West can be extraordinarily difficult to obtain, especially if you don't speak Russian.

Visas

Russia remains among the most difficult countries to enter on your own. Getting a visa for individual travel essentially requires that you have someone to guarantee your well-being in Russia, whether this is an official organization, an individual with special approval, or a travel agency. The **Russia Youth Hostel Federation (RYHF)** can arrange visas for the duration of your stay at their St. Petersburg or Moscow hostels (US$10 fee). RYHF can also provide support for business visas (up to 3 months) whether or not the individual is staying at one of the hostels. Contact them at 409 N. Pacific Coast Highway, Building 106, #390, Redondo Beach, CA 90277 (tel. (310) 379-4316; fax (310) 379-8420). If you are arriving through the Baltics the Tallinn based **CDS Reiser** offers visas for a US$25 fee. Contact them at Raekoja plats 17, Tallinn (tel. 372 (2) 445 262; fax 372 (2) 313 666). It is also possible to buy invitations through certain **travel agencies** in the U.S. (around US$60-100). This is technically illegal (since you have no connection with the organization which "invited" you), but many people try it successfully. Be sure to research carefully the agency you choose.

Individual travelers to Russia can also try to work through a **registered Russian organization** with official permission to invite foreigners. The process can take 3 to a dozen weeks; since mail to the former Soviet Union is not reliable, stick to phones, telexes, and fax machines. The organization will need to know your dates of visitation, your full name, address, citizenship, occupation, date and place of birth, passport number, plus its place and dates of issue and expiration. When you receive your invitation, send a photocopy of it, a photocopy of the front pages of your passport, a completed application (contact the embassy or a travel agent for blanks), 3 photographs, a self-addressed, stamped envelope, a cover letter, and the visa fee (most recently US$30) to the Russian Embassy; processing normally takes up to 2 weeks, but can be expedited for a surcharge. You may prefer to have this final step handled through a visa service with experience in Russian visas. **Private Russian citizens** can invite foreigners, but it's arduous; the process from your end is the same as through a registered organization—but start 6 months in advance.

If you have been invited by an official organization, you can extend your visa by presenting a letter from your sponsor at the OVIR office. Officially, you can freely travel anywhere that isn't off-limits to foreigners (such as military bases and power plants), but local administration may give you a hard time.

Visa-Free Cruises

If you're already in Europe and want only a quick taste of Russia, these short trips (from a few hours to a couple of days) are the way to go. They're operated by Scandinavian ferry companies; though nominally "visa-free," you must still supply the ferry operator with passport details from up to 2 weeks in advance. From Finland, **Kristina Cruises** is the largest operator, running overnight cruises from Kotka, Finland (west of Helsinki) to Vyborg, Russia (near St. Petersburg) year-round (from 195mk); in summer, they have 3- to 4-day Helsinki-St. Petersburg trips (from 440mk). Contact them at Korkeavuorenkatu 2, 48100 Kotka, Finland (tel. 358 (52) 18 10 11), or in Helsinki (tel. 358 (0) 62 99 68). In the U.S., **Eurocruises** (tel. (800) 688-3876) can book most of these trips.

Group Tours

A group tour is the most convenient way to visit Russia without sapping your wallet. You need not sacrifice your individuality—it is possible and advisable to miss group excursions and meals (despite the protests of your guide), and to set off on your own with a map. Official excursions do bypass lengthy admission lines and bring you to sights that are otherwise inaccessible. Tours rarely include transport to and from Russia.

The tours of Russia and Ukraine offered by **Scandinavian Student Travel Service (SSTS)** have been discontinued. Their former overseas agent, STA Travel, was working on filling this gap in group travel when this book went to press. Contact STA for updated information (see the Essentials, at the beginning of this book for addresses). If you're already in Europe, **Finnsov Tours** is perhaps the biggest Finnish tour company; contact them at Eerikinkatu 3, 00100 Helsinki, Finland (tel. 358 (0) 694 20 11).

Many organizations in the U.S. run special educational tours to Russia. Try contacting **CIEE** (tel. (212) 661-1414; see Essentials, at the beginning of this book) or the **American Council of Teachers of Russian** (ACTR), 1776 Massachusetts Ave. NW, Suite 300, Washington, DC 20036 (tel. (202) 833-7522). **Volunteers For Peace,** 43 Tiffany Rd., Belmont, VT 05730 (tel. (802) 259-2759) has innovative workcamps and language programs across the former Soviet Union which run about US$300-700; group airfare to Russia for the programs runs US$950 round-trip.

Customs Formalities

Customs enforcement is arbitrary and unpredictable. There's not much you can do except be polite; one day they'll tear your pack apart, the next they'll just nod and dismiss you. If you fly in—especially with a group—your baggage will probably not be inspected. You may encounter more difficulty if you arrive by train or car. Weapons and narcotics are definitely off-limits; if you have doubts about anything, check with the Russian embassy before you go. Politely answer the questions the border officials ask, but *do not* offer any information that they don't specifically ask about.

You cannot bring rubles into or out of the country, not that you would ever want to. At the border, you will be given a **Customs Declaration Form** on which to declare all your valuables and foreign currency. *Don't* lose it. Everything listed on the customs form must be on your person when you leave the country. Keep all exchange slips and receipts from *beryozka* (hard-currency) stores so that you can prove that no Western cash disappeared through illegal channels. In order to export works of art, icons, old *samovars* (not the electric kind), and antique books—technically, anything published before 1945, you'll need either an official receipt from a *beryozka* store, or a difficult-to-obtain permit (plus a 100% duty charge) if the item was a gift or was purchased for rubles. Military items such as army belts and flags are nominally contraband, but authorities rarely bother with them anymore.

TRAVELING IN RUSSIA

Restrictions, Flights, and Trains Foreigners are allowed free movement as long as they notify OVIR before heading out of their "home base" city and stay away from closed areas (primarily nuclear zones and cities connected to the military). You are officially required to buy internal plane and train tickets at inflated Intourist prices, but with Russian friends and a car, you can surely get away with a trip into the countryside. Short commuter rail journeys are also unlikely to be a problem, especially to standard tourist destinations. Although it's illegal, at press time, those who speak fluent Russian could procure long-distance train tickets at the ticket office (not always in the train station) for just a handful of rubles. Russian trains are crowded; you may be stranded if all return seats are booked. Also, you *are* breaking the law; if you wander into a closed area and are noticed by the police, you risk prompt deportation and the possible denial of subsequent visas.

Russia boasts an extensive **rail** network and a vast, not-so-reliable **air** system monopolized by **Aeroflot** (Аэрофлот). **Train** cars are divided into 3 classes: luxury 2-bed "SV" compartments, 4-bed cozy "coupés," and *platskarti* (open-car couchettes). *Elektrichka* (commuter rail, marked on train station signs as пригородные поезда; *prigorodnye poezda*) have their own platforms at each train station; buy tickets from machines with exact change, or from the *kassa* (касса; ticket counter).

Public Transportation and Taxis Within Russian cities, overcrowded **buses, trams,** and (in major metropoli) unbelievably efficient **Metro** systems ferry citizens for 10-15R per ride. In the Metro, you drop the coins into machines that let you onto escalators. Buy bus tickets at newsstands or from the *babushki* at Metro stations. For longer stays, ask at a ticket window for a *yediny bilet,* a pass valid on all forms of public transport for one calendar month. On the bus you must validate your ticket in one of the little hole-punchers. Since it's often bone-crushingly crowded, riders often ask their neighbors to pass tickets up to be punched. The same goes for purchasing tickets, which can sometimes be done from the driver. It is also customary for passengers to tap each other on the shoulder and ask if they are getting off at the next stop (Вы выходите?—it sounds like "Vee vee-HOAD-it-yeh") so that everyone can push their way to an exit. Metro stations are all in Cyrillic; if you don't read Russian, you can usually recognize stations by memorizing the first and last letters. When two lines intersect, there's a different station name for each line. You'll want to know the words *vkhod* (вход; entrance), *vykhod* (выход; exit), *vykhod v gorod* (выход в город; exit to the city), and *perekhod* (переход; passage to another line). Metro stations are marked above ground by a fluorescent red *M*. Try to acquire the newest city map possible, for Metro stations and street names have been changing wildly in recent years, as tastes in politics have spun.

Hailing a **taxi** can be an adventure, particularly late at night (when it is unwise to take a cab alone). Many of those who stop for you will be private citizens, taking passengers to make a little extra cash. Step off the curb and hold out your hand; when a car stops, tell the driver your destination before getting in. He will either refuse the destination and speed off, or nod his head, at which point you can haggle about the price. Meters are non-operational. If you do not speak Russian, you will get ripped off; if you get away for less than 300R, you should feel lucky. Cab drivers often double as roving minimarts, carrying *shampanskoye* (champagne), *vino* (wine), or *vodka* (vodka—convenient, eh?) in the trunk at twice the standard price.

RUSSIA ESSENTIALS

Be flexible. Expect airport delays, tour cancellations, hotel changes, cold showers, and bathrooms *sans* toilet paper. Careful packing can make all the difference. Bring any feminine hygiene supplies and contraceptives that you might need with you; although the former are available in hard-currency stores, you can never be sure. Plastic bags and toilet paper will come in handy. Roach traps can be a godsend if you are staying in a dormitory. Women traveling alone should try not to make prolonged eye contact with unknown men; this invites attention, and in rare cases, danger. Resolutely say *otstan ot menya* ("leave me alone")

Currency and Shopping

The Russian **ruble** is nonconvertible and close to worthless. The bankrupt governments, especially the offices that deal with tourists, are understandably committed to prying every possible dollar from foreign visitors. Any excursion or theater ticket purchased from Intourist will be billed in Western currency. The state operates overpriced hard-currency *(valyoota)* stores called *beryozka*, where foreign tourists can buy lacquerware, furs, and liquor. In these and in privately owned stores, prices are generally listed in US$, so if you're there to buy, bring dollars along. Note that comparably of the gorgeous products on sale in hard-currency stores are also sold (for rubles or other hard currency) in the many open markets such as the Arbat and Izmailovski Park. A matryoshka listed at US$60 in a beryozka might go for US$35 from an individual artisan—capitalism at work for the individual!

You can exchange your money for rubles at state banks, exchange offices in stores, and in many Intourist hotels. You are officially required to produce your customs form; you will be given a State Bank Certificate listing the amount exchanged. When leaving the country, you must show your Customs Form and all State Bank Certificates in order to exchange unused rubles back into foreign currency; you cannot re-convert more rubles than you legally exchanged. At times it is impossible to re-convert unspent rubles, so change only small sums of hard currency at a time.

If you happen by a tourist-dense area, you may well be approached by Russians with a fascination for all things Western. Many of these will be *fartsovchiki* (black marketeers) who want to change money—this is quite risky, since some try to rip off unsuspecting tourists. Beware of dealers who won't change money in public, and *always* count your rubles before handing over your hard currency.

Russia can be a user-unfriendly society: state shops are crowded, with few products and long lines. If the first response to your request is *"nyot!"* don't despair: this rarely means that something is impossible. You just have to learn the system. A 3-line process is the rule in stores. In the first line, ogle the products and find out their prices. Then stand in line to tell the cashier their departments and prices; pay and take the receipt. In the 3rd line, present the receipt to the salesperson and pick up your purchase—unless the store has already run out. This process will only work in Russian; if you're linguistically challenged, have a local friend show you the ropes.

To thank your friends, a tour guide, or a helpful hotel attendant, bring along some small gifts. Postcards of Western cities, keychains with logos of American companies, pens, and toiletries are highly valued. For grander gift-giving, bestow cassette tapes of Western rock music, T-shirts, books, coffee, tea, or cigarettes. A bottle of imported wine makes a very special present.

Communication

Mail, Telegrams, Faxes, and E-Mail There is neither rhyme nor reason to the former Soviet Union's **mail service.** Delivery can take anywhere from 2 weeks to eternity. Write addresses with the country and zip code first. Overseas letters from Russia cost 130R, post cards 100R; stamps and postcards can be purchased at post offices (почта) and major Intourist hotels. Mail fleeing Russia usually has a better chance of surviving than mail trying to get in. You can send mail "express" to the States for 750R; it might take a mere 3 weeks. Parcels must be brought unwrapped to specially designated post offices. Leave price tags on and bring receipts with you. **Telegrams** (sent from телеграф offices, usually connected to post offices) are relatively cheap (350R/word to the U.S.). Look for a stack of blanks (the international forms say Международная Телеграмма), fill one out in Roman characters and bring it to the window. Central post offices are also now equipped to send and receive **faxes.** The international **electronic mail** network offers an instant and free connection to selected universities and institutes inside the country; ask student friends about setting up a trans-oceanic connection home.

Telephones Local telephones in Moscow take 15-kopek or 1-R pieces, sold at selected kiosks for 15-25R; in St. Petersburg they take metro tokens. Phones are notoriously unreliable. You can make intercity calls from private homes, telegraph offices, your hotel room, or special phone booths (marked междугородные) in each city. Dial 8, wait for the tone, then dial the city code. Direct international calls buzz from telegraph offices and hotel rooms: Dial 8, wait for the tone, then dial 10 and the country code. Outside Moscow and St. Petersburg, out-of-area calls must be ordered a day in advance at hotels or telegraph offices. You'll probably have to speak Russian to pull this off. Calls to North America cost 800-1800R per minute with a 3-minute minimum; calls to Europe are 600-1200R per minute. You cannot call collect. Several hotels in Moscow now have direct-dial booths operated by a special card or credit card. The cost is astronomical (at least US$12/min. to the U.S.). To be reached quickly in an emergency, leave the number of your tour group with someone at home; your embassy should be able to find you. If traveling independently, leave a copy of your itinerary with the embassy, along with your name, address, date and place of birth and passport number. Calling into the country can be equally frustrating. The U.S. and Canada as well as most European countries have direct dial to Moscow and St. Petersburg. For other cities, go through the operator. It may take 30 tries, giving you ample opportunity to chomp into *War and Peace*.

After a week or so in the former Soviet Union, you may begin to feel hopelessly out of touch with the outside world. Most Intourist hotels stock recent issues of *Time, Newsweek,* and the *International Herald Tribune* (US$2). If you plan on being in Russia or Ukraine for an extended period of time, a short-wave radio is invaluable. In Moscow, the BBC World Service comes in at around 1508MHz. If it is news of Russia you seek, try the *Moscow Times*. You can also dropProspect by the reading room of the U.S. Commercial Office in Moscow, Novinski bul. 15 (formerly ul. Tchaikovskovo; open Mon.-Fri. 9am-5pm), or the U.S. Consulate in St. Petersburg.

Language Though more and more people speak English in the former Soviet Union, take some time to familiarize yourself with the Cyrillic alphabet. It's not as difficult as it looks and will make getting around and getting by immeasurably easier.

Cyrillic	English	Pronunciation	Cyrillic	English	Pronunciation
А, а	a	*A*lways	Р, р	r	B*r*ad
Б, б	b	*B*altimore	С, с	s	*S*arala
В, в	v	The *V*illage People	Т, т	t	*Th*omas
Г, г	g	*G*alina	У, у	u	kit 'n' cab*oo*dle
Д, д	d	*D*avid	Ф, ф	f	*F*riend
Е, е	ye	*ye*llowtail	Х, х	xh	*ch*utzpah
Ё, ё	yo	*yo* momma	Ц, ц	ts	*ts*ar
Ж, ж	zh	Bre*zh*nev	Ч, ч	ch	*ch*icken tender
З, з	z	*Z*ack	Ш, ш	sh	*sh*it
И, и	i	W*ee*vil	Щ, щ	shch	Khru*shch*ev
Й, й	y or j	(no sound)	Ъ, ъ	(hard sign)	(no sound)
К, к	*k*	*C*orrigan	Ы, ы	y	glottal "i"
Л, л	l	*L*oopy	Ь, ь	(soft sign)	(no sound)
М, м	m	*M*ary Grace	Э, э	eh	Al*e*xander
Н, н	n	*N*ancy	Ю, ю	yoo	*you*
О, о	o	swing l*o*w	Я, я	yah	*Ya*hoo!
П, п	p	*p*uffin			

On the list of handy phrases-to-know: добрый день (DOH-bree DYEHN; "Good day"), спасибо (spa-SEE-bah; "thank you"), хорошо (hah-rah-SHOH; "OK"), извините (eez-vee-NEET-syeh; "excuse me"), где (gdyeh; "where"), касса (KAH-sah; "cash register" or "ticket office"), and метро (meh-TROH; "metro"). In the Slavic world, plurals of words are usually formed by adding the letter "ы" or "и" to the end, so the plural of *matryoshka* is *matryoshki*. Note that улица (*ulitsa;* abbreviated ул.) means "street"; проспект (*prospect;* пр.) means "avenue"; площадь (*ploshad;* пл.) means "square"; and бульвар (*bulvar;* бул.) is "boulevard." Once you get the hang of recognizing the letters, you can pronounce just about any Russian word—have a go!

ACCOMMODATIONS

Western-style **youth hostels** have begun to arrive in Russia. The **Moscow Travelers' Guest House** and the **St. Petersburg International Hostel** provide comfortable facilities in the two Russian capitals. Both arrange visas for your stay. Especially during summer, reserve well in advance. On an **arranged tour,** Intourist or Sputnik, the state travel organizations which operate hotel chains, will set up accommodations. **Intourist** hotels offer comfortable rooms with a shower, phone, and television. **Sputnik** accommodations tend to be more spartan and less clean, sometimes with communal bathrooms. All meals are included and served in the hotel restaurant. All Intourist hotels have a small hard-currency store, dollar bar, restaurant, and post office. In Moscow and St. Petersburg, hot water often gets turned off during part of the summer for pipe repairs, so you may have to make do with cold showers.

New services have sprung up lately that rent **apartments** to foreigners for longer stays. These can be much more economical but are more challenging to arrange. Make sure that the service will provide an invitation and arrange for your visa. In Russia, find addresses in the *Moscow Times, Petersburg Chronicle,* and in metros.

Another cheap option is to stay in a **university** or institute dorm; many will take in foreign students for a few dollars a night. Rooms are liveable, but don't expect sparkling bathrooms or reliable hot water. Make arrangements with an institute from the

West. Staying with friends or relatives in Russia requires a personal invitation (see Getting to Russia, above). As soon as you arrive, go down to the central ОВИР (OVIR) office (in Moscow, at ul. Chernyshevskaya 42 and called УВИР) to register.

FOOD

Searching for palatable commercial food in Russia will strain your ability, patience, and stomach. But rest assured, you will not starve, and if you remember to look upon food for its principal value—nourishment—you will get by. The standard hotel menu includes салат (salad), often cucumbers and tomatoes garnished with sour cream; суп (soup), usually hearty and cabbage-based; мясо (meat), unidentifiable and most often chopped or else sliced with alternating veins of gristle; potatoes; chopped beets or cabbage; and, for dessert, чай (tea) or кофе (coffee) with extra-creamy мороженое (ice cream, usually vanilla).

If you are not on a hotel meal plan, the quest for food will require advance planning and dogged determination. To be completely sure of eating at a particular place, make an evening reservation in the morning. Reservations are absolutely necessary in Moscow and St. Petersburg; after 10pm, you may squeeze in.

At privately run **"cooperative" restaurants,** the service is generally more attentive and the menu more extensive than in state-run establishments. When you reserve, ask for a *chisti stol* (clean table) to be sure the table is free of *zakuski* (appetizers): many places will garnish your table with salads, caviar, and cold cuts prior to your arrival, which, if you eat them, will cost you dearly. You can ask them to remove uninvited *zakuski* to save money. Georgian cooperatives almost always serve at least one non-meat entree. The food at столовая (*stolovaya;* cafeterias) is dirt-cheap but repulsive and unsanitary. Кафе (cafés) are a step up and usually offer a decent chicken dish (around 500R).

Delicious Russian white and black bread and sweet rolls cost next to nothing at ubiquitous булочная (*bulochnaya;* **bakeries**). For fruits and vegetables, head for a рынок (*rynok;* **market**), where farmers sell their privately grown goods for a profit. Wash everything before eating it; pesticides here can knock off large mammals as easily as bugs. Bring your own shopping bag and haggle. Мороженое (ice cream) sells well even in the middle of winter (100-700R). Buy quickly; stands exist as transiently, popping up and disappearing as fast as the little purple guys in Whack-a-mole.

Several **all-night liquor stores** have opened in the larger cities. *Zolotoye koltso, Russkaya,* and *Zubrovka* are the best vodkas around, *Stolichnaya* and *Moskovskaya* are very well known, and the generic brand gets the job done. Vodkas and wines are available in hard-currency stores too, for a price. A beer hall is a great place to meet locals, though Russian brew is nothing to celebrate. Most major restaurants and hotels have foreign-currency bars. Don't buy alcohol from street kiosks; dangerous home-brews and tap water are sometimes sold under well-known labels.

The **water** in Moscow is mostly potable, but best taken in limited doses; to be safe, boil it for a few minutes. The water in St. Petersburg, however, is a stomach-pounder—it's infected with a bacteria called **giardia,** a friend you *don't* want to make. It is easily curable with U.S. medicine (buy it in advance). Without such treatment, a bout with giardia will make you feel like your intestines have declared independence and eliminated all visa requirements. Water purification (iodine) tablets, sold at camping stores, and boiling (at least 10min.) will kill giardia. Talk to a physician before going, as contact with the contaminated water is unavoidable. Preferably, drink bottled water sold at hard currency stores. A gamma globulin shot will lower your risk of hepatitis. One final word of advice: Take Pepto-Bismol and snack foods such as peanut butter, instant soup, and granola to tide you over on those days when you can't face another sour cream salad. Bon appetit!

ORIENTATION AND PRACTICAL INFORMATION

■ ■ ■ MOSCOW (МОСКВА)

Moscow is exhausting and apocalyptic (in a comicbook-like way): morbid and infinitely interesting. The city where Ivan the Great's Kremlin stands shoulder-to-shoulder with Stalin's monstrous Gothic skyscrapers (15 in all; one for each former republic) is really an enormous, sprawling peasant village—haphazard and semi-anarchic—onto which an illusion of order was imposed through vast housing and cultural projects. Its 9 million denizens include members of every Soviet nationality, and its borders encompass dozens of forests, monasteries, industrial parks, and even farms. While a large part of the city dates from the last 50 years, the result of relentless church-destruction and boulevard-widening, the older neighborhoods still speak of the days when "Moscow of the Thousand Churches" was the capital of the tsars and seat of the Russian Orthodox Patriarchy. The city still harbors many beautiful spots—monasteries untouched by the wrecker's ball, huge parks and palaces—but these must be discovered amid the present rows of pre-fab housing blocks and monolithic avenues, beneath an anti-utopian and nightmarish skyline.

Founded by Prince Yuri Dolgoruki in 1147, Moscow became the center of the Russian government in the 14th century. When Peter the Great moved the capital to St. Petersburg in 1712, the saying arose that while St. Petersburg might be Russia's head, Moscow was its heart. Today, many non-Muscovites, resentful of the capital's power and wealth, beg to differ. This is Russia's rudest, noisiest, pushiest, but most energetic and happening metropolis—a city where all the political, social, and cultural ferment that rocked the Soviet Union in the past few years has found an outlet. The new generation of shopkeepers and peddlers, prostitutes, and hired gunmen-mafiosos in flashy Italian suits are eating away at Stalin's orderly foundations and replacing them with corruption and lawlessness, an army of termites eating away at the carcass of the communist whale. As the struggle between the center and the periphery continues, Moscow remains fixed at center stage.

ORIENTATION AND PRACTICAL INFORMATION

Moscow is laid out in a series of concentric rings, emanating from the Kremlin. The outermost "ring road" forms the city boundary (and, in 1993, technically the limits of your visa), but most sights of interest to visitors lie within the inner "garden ring" (corresponding to the Ring Line of the Metro). **Red Square** (*Krasnaya Ploshad*, Красная Площадь) and the **Kremlin** (Кремль) mark the center of the city; nearby start Moscow's popular shopping streets, **Novi Arbat** (Новый Арбат, formerly prospekt Kalinina), running west parallel to the Metro's blue lines, and **ulitsa Tverskaya** (Тверская), which goes north along the green line. Ul. Tverskaya was formerly called ulitsa Gorkovo; the upper half, which leads to the **Garden Ring** (Садовое Кольцо), the original limit of 19th-century Moscow, is now known as ulitsa Pervaya Tverskaya-Yamskaya. Below it runs the Metro's circle line. Learn Cyrillic, orient yourself by the **Metro**, and you can never get really lost. All buses and trams eventually stop at one of the stations, marked by a blue neon **M**. An extensive map of Moscow, including all public transportation routes and a street index, sells at many kiosks for 1000R.

Tourist Offices: Central Excursion Bureau, ul. Belinskovo 4A (tel. 203 8016), around the corner from the Intourist Hotel and 2 blocks from Red Square. A good resource center if you feel like spending lots of Western currency, but they'll be reluctant to tell you about anything payable in rubles. If you don't speak Russian, you may have to buy your out-of-town excursions here. Open daily 9am-9pm. The **Moscow Excursion Bureau,** ul. Rozhdestvenka 5 (tel. 923 89 53), behind Detski Mir. If you speak some Russian, your best bet for out-of-town excursions, walking tours, etc. Historic tours of Moscow plus daytrips to Vladimir and Suzdal, all for rubles. Open daily 10am-2pm and 3-6pm.

Embassies: U.S., Novinski bul. (formerly ulitsa Tchaikovskovo) 19/23 (tel. 252 24 51 through 252 24 59). M: Баррикадная (Barikadnaya). Open Mon.-Fri. 9am-6pm.

Canada, Starokonyusheni per. 23 (tel. 241 58 82 or 241 11 11). Open Mon.-Fri. 8:30am-1pm and 2-5pm. **U.K.,** nab. Sofiskaya (formerly nab. Morisa Toreza) 14 (tel. 230 63 33, fax 233 35 63). Open Mon.-Fri. 9am-12:30pm and 2:30-6pm. **Australia,** Kropotkinski per. 13 (tel. 246 50 12 through 246 50 16). Open Mon.-Fri. 9am-12:30pm and 1:30-5pm. **New Zealand,** ul. Povarskaya (formerly ul. Vorovskovo) 44 (tel. 290 12 77 or 290 34 85). Open Mon.-Fri. 8:30am-12:30pm and 1:30-5pm; Sept.-May 9am-12:30pm and 1:30-5:30pm.

Currency Exchange: The best official deal in town is probably at Moscow's **Central Telegraph.** With an American Express card, you can change travelers' checks for dollars in the **Dialog Bank** at the Hotel Slavyanskaya, in back of the Kievskaya (Киевская) metro station. Open Mon.-Fri. 10am-1pm and 2-5pm.

American Express: ul. Sadovaya-Kudrinskaya 21a (tel. 956 90 00 or 956 90 01). M: Mayakovskaya (Маяковская). Take a left out of the metro station to ul. Sadovaya-Bolshaya, which becomes ul. Sadovaya-Kudrinskaya. All banking services for cardholders. **Express Cash** machine. Open Mon.-Fri. 9am-5pm. AmEx window at Dialog Bank as well.

Post Office: Moscow Central Telegraph, ul. Tverskaya 7, a few blocks from the Kremlin. Look for the globe and the digital clock out front. **Poste Restante:** 103009. **International mail.** Open Mon.-Fri. 8am-2pm and 3-9pm, Sat. 8am-2pm and 3-7pm, Sun. 9am-2pm and 3-7pm. A less crowded branch at **Novi Arbat 22** near Dom Knigi. Express Mail Service 9am-noon, 1-4:30pm. Open Mon.-Fri. 8am-8pm, Sat. 8am-6pm, Sun. 10am-6pm. Poste Restante also at the **Intourist Hotel Post Office,** ul. Tverskaya 3/5. Address mail to До Востребования *(Do Vostrebovania),* K-600, Intourist Hotel, ul. Tverskaya 3/5, Moscow, Post Office at ul. Myasnitskaya 26. To mail **packages,** especially books, bring them unwrapped to the Intourist Hotel Post Office or to Moscow Central Telegraph; they will be wrapped and mailed while you wait (4600R for 3kg airmail). Open Mon.-Fri. 9am-1pm and 2-5pm, Sat. 9am-1pm and 2-4pm.

Telephones: At **Moscow Central Telegraph.** You can either order a call or use an overseas direct-dial telephone; be prepared to wait 1-3 hours either way. Depending on the time of day, calls to the States cost 690-1725R/min. Cheaper on weekends. **Telegrams** at windows 7-9 (450R/word). **Faxes** 1300R/page. Open daily 8am-8pm. Branch office at 22 is less crowded. International telephone cabinets (международный телефон; *mezhduharodni telefon)* at M: Boykovskaya (Бойковская) with much less of a wait. Major hotels have direct-dial international phone booths at exorbitant prices (1min. to the U.S.: US$12-25!). International calls can also be placed from private homes (direct dial: 8+10+country code+phone number) at 920R/min, 9pm-9am. **Local calls** require either a 15 kopek coin or a 1 ruble coin: these are sold at some (not all) kiosks for 10-25 rubles. **City Code:** 095.

Fax and Photocopy Services: Alphagraphics, ul. Pervaya Tverskaya-Yamskaya 50 (tel. 251 12 15). Canadian-Soviet joint venture provides photocopying, laser printing, and faxing services for hard currency, but with a smile. Also **DHL express mail** (½lb. US$46 to the U.S.). Open Mon.-Fri. 9am-6pm.

Train and Plane Tickets: Intourist Main Office, ul. Petrovka 15/13, (tel. 927 11 81, fax 921 19 96), to the right of the Bolshoi Theater. In the courtyard of building #15; enter under the archway on ul. Petrovka. Open Mon.-Fri. 9am-6pm. Purchase cheap same-day or next-day tickets at the Intourist window of the appropriate train station for the local Russian price and US$4 commission. Foreigners are required to buy tickets only through Intourist, but if you're traveling with a Russian friend, it's easier and cheaper to buy the ticket from the station (if you speak good Russian) or have your friend do it for you. Don't travel alone with a non-Intourist ticket; if the conductor suspects you're a foreigner, he may try to scare you into paying a bribe or otherwise harass you.

Flights: Moscow has 3 main airports, all outside the city limits. International flights arrive at **Sheremetyevo-2** (Шереметьево-2) to the north. M: Aeroport (Аэропорт), then an airport bus (orange) that stops at the terminals. Buses stop around 9pm; cabs will rip you off like you've never seen, up to 5000R, but you have no choice. Most domestic flights originate at **Vnukovo** (Внуково), **Domodedovo** (Домодедово), or **Sheremetyevo-1.** Buses link all 3 airports; com-

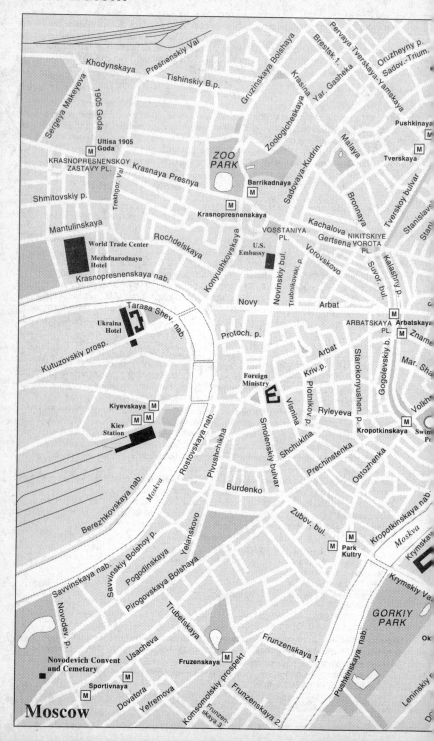

Moscow

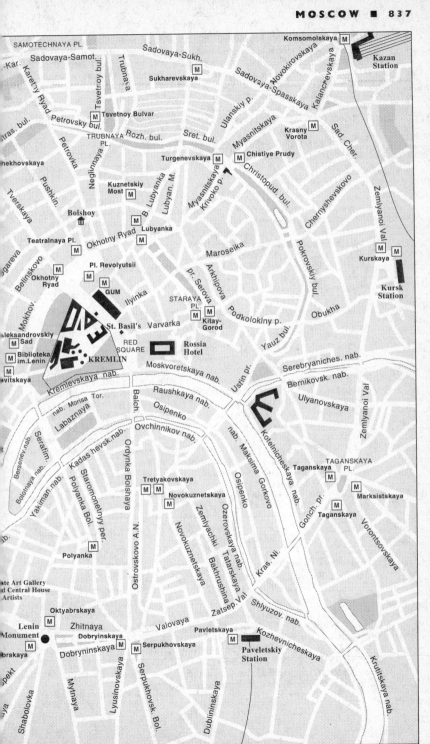

ACCOMMODATIONS

muter rail goes to Vnukovo and Domodedovo. **Foreign airline representatives: Finnair,** proyezd Khudozhestvennovo Teatra 6 (tel. 292 87 88). Open Mon.-Fri. 9am-5pm. **Lufthansa,** pr. Olympinski 18/1 (tel. 975 2501). Open Mon.-Fri. 9am-5:30pm, Sat. 9am-1pm. **Delta,** Hotel Mezhdunarodnaya II, Krasnopresenskaya nab. 12 (tel. 253 26 60 or 253 26 59). Open Mon.-Fri. 5:30pm. **SAS,** Kuznetski most 3 (tel. 925 47 47). Open Mon.-Fri. 9am-6pm.

Trains: Moscow has 8 main stations, most clustered around the Metro's Ring Line. Trains to St. Petersburg and some to Estonia depart from **Leningradski vokzal** (Ленинградский Вокзал; Leningrad station). M: Komsomolskaya (Комсомолская). Across the street are **Kazanski vokzal** (Казанский Вокзал; Kazan station) and **Yaroslavski vokzal** (Ярославский Вокзал; Yaroslav station), where the Trans-Siberian leaves (3/week, US$150-240.) Other stations are served by similarly named Metro stops. **Paveletski voksal** (Павелетский Вокзал) and **Kurski vokzal** (Курский Вокзал) serve the south. **Rizhski vokzal** (Рижский Вокзал) serves Rīga, Latvia (3/day, 16hr., 1900R) and Estonia. Trains from Warsaw (2/day, 22hr., US$52) and Vilnius, Lithuania (3/day, 18hr. 2300R) arrive at **Byelorusski vokzal** (Белорусский Вокзал). Trains to Ukraine, the Czech Republic, Slovakia, Bulgaria, and Romania use **Kievski vokzal** (Киевский Вокзал). Train info: tel. 266 9000 through 266 9009.

Taxis: tel. 927 21 08, 927 00 00, or 457 90 05. If you don't speak Russian, it's nearly impossible to get anyone to take you for rubles. Ask around for the going rate before you get in a cab, and be sure to agree on a price before you set off (should not be more than 6000R within Moscow). Taxi stands are indicated by a round sign with a green "T." Meters are purely ornamental.

Public Transportation: The **Metro** will impress upon you the importance and ease of learning the Cyrillic alphabet. Remember: Вход means entrance, Выход exit, Выход в город exit to the street, and Переход passage to a different line and often to a new station: a station which serves more than one line will generally have different names. Trains run 6am-1am (fare 10R). Buses and trolleys cost 10R/ride; tickets available in metro station *kassi* (кассы) and sometimes from the driver. *Yedinye bileti* (единые билеты; month-passes) are 1200R from ticket windows. Get Metro maps at street kiosks (about 100R). **Lost and found:** tel. 222 20 85 (for the Metro) and 923 87 53 (for trolleys, trams, and buses).

Laundromat: Look for a sign saying прачечичныаьа. **Ceylon Tea Laundromat,** ul. Krasikova 10. Open Tues.-Fri. 7:30am-9pm, Sat. and Mon. 9-am-6pm. If you venture into a laundromat, plan to spend most of the day. Use only cold water in the machine, and put your wet clothes in the spinner before tossing them in the dryer. Your bathtub might be more convenient.

Medical Assistance: European Medical Center, Gruzinski per. 3, korpus 2 (tel. 253 07 03). French joint venture offering walk-in medical care for hard currency (US$76/visit, students US$61). Open Mon.-Fri. 9am-6pm.

Emergencies: Ambulance: tel. 03. **Fire:** tel. 01. **Police:** tel. 02. Good luck. No coins needed from pay phones. Also try the U.S. Embassy's emergency number (tel. 252 24 51).

ACCOMMODATIONS

The **Travellers Guest House,** ul Bolshaya Pereyaslavskaya 50 (tel. 971 40 59, fax 280 76 86; M: Prospect Mira; walk north along pr. Mira and take a right onto p. Bani to ul. Bolshaya Pereyaslavskaya) is the first real hostel in Moscow. In addition to comfortable dorm rooms and kitchen facilities, it offers visa services, train tickets, tourist info for guests and non-guests, and an enthusiastic English-speaking staff. (No curfew. US$10/bed in 3- to 4-person room. Singles US$20. Doubles US$26.) The **RA Tour Agency,** ul. Bolshaya Gruzinskaya 52 (tel. 254 07 45, 254 70 20, or 254 57 11; fax 254 32 97), requires advance reservations for dormitory accommodations for large groups (US$5/person) or rooms at the Hotel Izmailova for individuals. (Singles US$25. Doubles US$36.) To rent an apartment, look through ads in the *Moscow Times, Moscow Tribune,* and *Moscow Guardian.*

FOOD

Moscow's restaurants are the best in Russia, especially since the opening of new, privately run cooperatives, but *everybody* knows it. Adopt an early eating schedule; even mediocre places have long lines after 5pm. Eating out is a rare and expensive occasion for Russians—they usually linger for several hours—and most establishments only serve once per mealtime, so places fill up fast and reservations are recommended. The best strategy is to make a round of calls around noon to reserve for dinner; otherwise, you may be out of luck. Make sure that the meal will be payable in rubles and that you're getting a *chisti stol* (clean table—without a large assortment of appetizers that you will pay for dearly). Before you pay for a meal with a credit card, find out the exchange rate the restaurant uses. Menus usually come in Cyrillic. Joint-venture restaurants often offer higher quality food and considerably larger bills. Cafés are substantially cheaper than restaurants, and often quite good.

Cooperative stands selling quick, tasty kebab plates and meat sandwiches, as well as all of your favorite American fast food joints, have blossomed all over Moscow. In addition to the original **McDonald's** at Pushkin Square, there are now 2 others: one on the Arbat and one on ul. Belinskovo across from the Central Telegraph. All are marvels of efficiency and cleanliness. (Big Mac 1350R. Open 10am-10pm.) **Pizza Hut** has slices for 1000R. **Baskin-Robbins** is in the Hotel Rossiya and on the Arbat (open daily noon-1pm and 2-10pm), while **Pinguin,** a Swiss-Soviet joint venture, scoops out exotic-flavored ices on ul. Tverskaya, in the Moskva Hotel, and on the Arbat. (150R a cone. Open daily 10am-10pm.)

Private restaurants are steadily out-pacing state restaurants, but as the latter go under, their staffs shrink, making reservations all the more necessary.

Aragvi (Арагви), ul. Tverskaya 6 (tel. 229 37 62). M: Okhotni Ryad (Охотный Ряд), Entrance on pl. Sovetskaya. Georgian cuisine; specialities include *satsivi* (cold chicken in walnut sauce), *kharcho* (spicy soup), and caviar. Have a bottle of *Mukuzani* or *Tsinandali* with your meal. Full dinner with alcohol about 20,000R. Open daily noon-midnight. Last entry 11:30pm.

Uzbekistan (Узбекистан), ul. Neglinnaya 29 (tel. 924 60 53). M: Pushkinskaya (Пушкинская). A hangout for homesick Uzbeks, Kazakhs, and Tadzhiks; also popular with tourists. Try *tkhumdulma* (boiled egg with a fried meat patty), followed by *shashlyk* (shish kebab) Uzbek-style. Try the Uzbek bread, baked on the premises. Open daily noon-11pm. Last entry 11:30pm. Reservations necessary at dinner time; insist on the main ruble hall where main courses are priced 720-2100R (full dinner with alcohol in a private cabinet US$30/person). Women may not feel comfortable alone in this area at night.

Slavyanski Bazar (Славянский Базар), ul. Nikolskaya (formerly ul. 25 Oktyabrya) 17. (tel. 221 18 72). M: Okhotni Ryad. A haunt for private Soviet millionaires and mafiosi. Start off with a shot of vodka and *ikra* (caviar). Entrees 670-2560R. Open daily 11am-5pm and 6-11pm. Last entry 10:30pm.

Hotel Moskva (Москва), Manezhnaya pl., next to Red Square. Restaurant entrance around the back. *Shvedski stol* (buffet smorgasbord) especially popular with the bureaucrats across the street at Gosplan. Open daily for breakfast (2000R, 8-10:30am) and lunch (4000R, noon-4pm).

Cooperatives

Guria, pr. Komsomolski 7 (tel. 246 0378). M: Park Kultury. Go around the left of the building to enter this homey restaurant that serves delicious Georgian fare for low prices (main dishes 500-3000R). A vegetarian meal of *lobio* (beans), *khachapuri,* salad, and Georgian yogurt comes to 2500R. Bring your own drinks. Open daily noon-11pm.

Café Margarita (Маргарита), ul. Malaya Bronnaya 28 (tel. 299 65 34). Trendy café opposite the Patriarch's Ponds, where Bulgakov's *The Master and Margarita* begins. Enjoy the speciality of the house, tomatoes stuffed with garlic and cheese, or just sip a cup of tea and watch the artsy crowd smoke away the af-

FOOD

ternoon. Live piano music nightly (cover 1000R.) Main courses 2000-3300R. Open daily 2-4pm and 6pm-2am.

Mziuri, Arbat 42 (tel. 241 36 51). Downstairs at the Georgian cultural center; tasty meals in an elegant setting. Entrees 3000-5000R. Open noon-4pm and 7-11pm.

U Pirosmani (У Пиросмани), pr. Novodevichi 4 (tel. 247 19 26), across from the Novodevichi Convent. M: Sportivnaya (Спортивная). Specializing in delicately spiced Georgian cuisine, a cooperative above the rest for its flavorful dishes, served with panache. Menu on a chalkboard at the entrance; ask the waiter to decipher. Meals US$1.50-5. Open daily noon-10pm. Dinner reservations a must.

Delhi (Дели), ul. Krasnaya Presnya 23-b (tel. 252 17 66). M: ul. 1905 goda (ул. 1905 года). Turn left as you exit the station, heading toward the Stalinist tower at the end of the avenue. Next to the Olimp (Олимп) sports store, in the blond-brick block of stores. Gracious service, tasty meats, and iced drinks make this a luxurious oasis. A number of vegetarian options. Menu in Russian, Urdu, and English. Show up at noon for lunch or reserve for dinner; specify that you want to eat in the ruble room. Entrees 1500-1800R. Open noon-5pm, 7-11pm.

Aist (Аист), ul. Malaya Bronnaya 1/8 (tel. 291 66 92). M: Pushkinskaya. Hearty soups and appetizers make this a cozy spot to sample solid Russian food. Wraparound red velvet decor simulates a '70s opium den. Main courses 1600-3900R. Open daily noon-5pm and 6-10pm.

Zaidi i Poprobuy (Зайди и Попробуй), pr. Mira 124 (tel. 286 8165). M: Novo-Alekseyevskaya (Ново-Алексеевская), then take the trolley bus a couple of stops north. Entrance on ul. Malaya Moskovskaya (Малая Московская). The name of this establishment means "Drop in & Try," which is what the mafia did 3 years ago when they firebombed the place for refusing to hand over protection money. Undaunted, the owners rebuilt and added an armed Van Damme to guard the entrance. Entrees 4300-4700R. Open daily noon-11pm.

Cafés

Kombi's at 2 locations: pr. Mira 48 and off Tverskaya at M: Mayakovskaya. A western-style sandwich shop with subs (1200-2000), freshly-squeezed orange juice (1300R), and milkshakes (900R). Open daily 11am-10pm.

Baku-Liban, ul. Tverskaya 24. Middle Eastern kebabs and falafel (700R) at this stand-up co-op. Open daily 10am-10pm.

Blinchiki (Блинчики). Strastnoi bulvar. Not a café, but a stand, off Tverskaya, diagonally opposite McDonald's. Scrumptious apricot-filled *blini* (Russian crêpes) 150R. Open daily 10am-8pm.

Kafe Stoleshniki (Столешники), Stoleshnikov per. 6 (tel. 229-2050). Heading up Tverskaya from the Kremlin, take a right on Sovyetskaya Ploshad and walk down a block. Entrance on side alley to the right. Noteworthy for its intimate atmosphere—bare brick walls and candlelight. 3000R cover includes a selection of appetizers. Main dishes 800-2200R. Open daily noon-11pm.

Café Oladi (Оладьи), ul. Pushkinskaya 9 or ul. Gertsena 15, just past the Tchaikovsky Conservatory. Both branches share the same namesake dish: small, sweet pancakes. 75R. Pushkinskaya branch open daily 9am-7pm. Gertsena branch open Mon.-Sat. 10am-8pm.

Markets

To replenish your diet after too many potato and sour cream salads, go to a farmer's market—*rynok* (рынок; pronounced "REE-nuk")—where Russians, as well as Georgians, Armenians, Uzbeks, and peasants from all over truck in their fresh fruit and flowers to sell for whatever the market will bear. The best, though priciest, market is the Tsentralni Rynok (M: Tsvetnoi Bulvar). Other good ones are at M: Baumanskaya (Бауманская) and M: Aeroport (Аэропорт).

A number of Western-style **supermarkets** have popped up recently; they accept hard currency only but stock all the yogurt, frozen pizza, and kiwi fruit you can eat, and most of them staff English-speakers. **The Irish House,** 11 Novi Arbat, M: Arbatskaya, is a supermarket-clothing-electronics store. A well-stocked Russian supermarket, **Novoarbatski Gastronom,** flanks the Irish House at the left. (Open Mon.-

Sat. 8am-9pm and Sun. 10am-7pm.) **Stockmann,** M: Paveletskaya (Павелетская), is a Finnish grocery emporium for credit cards only. Prices are in dollars. Get out on the side of the street opposite the train station, and walk up left 2 blocks; past the *blini* (блины) stand on your left and behind the white curtains is the glassed-in store. (Open daily 10am-8pm.) **Colognia,** Bolshaya-Sadovaya 5/1, is part of the Peking Hotel. (Open daily 10am-8pm.)

SIGHTS

Red Square Lenin's historical legacy has finally come into question, and his name and face are coming down all over Moscow. The Party, so to speak, is finally over. The *pièce de résistance* of Leninmania is the **Lenin Mausoleum,** that red marble bunker in Red Square, where his pale and refrigerated remains went on display after he died in 1924. This particular monument may be priced to move—no one wants to hang on to the Marx-misinterpreter too closely, and there have been rumors of a potential museum or collector purchase. Two games for inside: guess if He's real, and count the soldiers guarding him—why so many still? (Open Tues.-Thurs. and Sat. 10am-1pm, Sun. 10am-2pm. Free.) Check your camera and bag in the building to the left of the line; they don't want any McCarthyist tourists bringing in a tool to profane their icon. Time your visit to see the changing of the guard (11am)—whether goosestepping or standing at attention, they make the Buckingham Palace Guards look like fidgety children. Behind, the **Kremlin Wall,** burial site of Soviet greats such as Josef Stalin, Leonid Brezhnev, Maxim Gorki, Yuri Gagarin, and American John Reed (!), is accessible only as part of the mausoleum tour.

If you have a real appetite for Lenin memorabilia, there's no better place to satiate it than the **Central Lenin Museum.** Containing everything from his Rolls-Royce to his underpants, the Graceland of Russia is located at pl. Revolyutsii 2, just off Red Square. (Open Tues.-Thurs. 10:30am-7pm, Fri.-Sun. 9:30am-6pm. Free.) For a heavy dose of irony, head up to the 3rd floor, where a Western-style store peddles fax machines and other tools of the capitalist bourgeoisie.

Across Red Square stands Russia's most famous architectural achievement: **St. Basil's Cathedral** (собор Василия Блаженово; *Sobor Vasiliya Blazhenovo).* The stone interior, straight from the Middle Ages, is filled with beautiful icons and historical artifacts; it's definitely worth the trip inside. Note the flat brick ceilings, which according to some engineers defy the laws of physics. (Open Wed.-Mon. 9:30am-5:30pm. Ticket office open 9:30am-4:30pm. 100R.)

Directly across Red Square from the Kremlin stands **GUM** (ГУМ; "goom"), the arch-department store of the former Soviet Union. The store's architecture alone makes it worth a visit, but recent renovations and scores of Western businesses make GUM a Russian shopper's paradise as well. (Open Mon.-Sat. 8am-8pm.) Turn right out of GUM's front doors and follow ul. Nikolskaya to **Lubyanskaya ploshad,** named for the infamous political prison that witnessed untold numbers of tortures and murders during the Stalinist purges half a century ago.

The Kremlin The ultimate icon of Soviet power and centralization, the 69-acre **Kremlin** is truly Moscow's centerpiece. The 20m-high, 10m-thick walls date from the 14th-century reign of Ivan III (the Great, not the Terrible). The **Annunciation Cathedral,** with an iconostasis by the great painters Andrei Rublev and Theophan the Greek, stands near the **Archangel Cathedral,** where Ivan the Terrible and other tsars repose. Not far away looms the huge **Assumption Cathedral;** Ivan the Terrible's custom-made coronation throne still resides proudly by the south portal. Napoleon, always respectful of tradition, set up his stables here. The very plain **Church of the Twelve Apostles** was Patriarch Nikon's 17th-century answer to the 16th-century extravagance of St. Basil's. Purchase tickets for the cathedrals at booths in **Aleksandrovsky Gardens** just outside the Kremlin Wall along pr. Marksa. (Open Fri.-Wed. 10am-5pm. 1000R plus 200R/cathedral. Ticket booth open 10am-5:30pm. Group tours of the Kremlin grounds and cathedrals arranged through Intourist.)

Shorts and large bags are officially no-nos inside the Kremlin complex; take your chances or check your bags near the gate. To experience the glory and wealth of tsarist Russia, visit the **Armory Museum.** Located next to Borovitsky Gate, the Armory contains the armor, gowns, jewels, thrones, and carriages of the tsars. Get your tickets through Intourist or buy them more cheaply at the ticket office in Aleksandrovsky Gardens. (Open Tues.-Sun. 1000R for 10am, noon, 2:30pm, and 4:30pm excursions.) The **Diamond Fund,** an annex of the Armory, houses Catherine the Great's crown of 5000 diamonds and the dazzling, famous Fabergé eggs. (Group tours only; arrange through Intourist. Admission up to US$10 with ISIC, but worth it.)

Any dark-suited men stepping out of black limousines are likely heading for the yellow **Grand Kremlin Palace,** where the Supreme Soviet, Russia's newly democratic parliament, meets. The modern white-marble **Palace of Congresses** stages ballet and opera performances throughout the summer. (Tickets through Intourist or hotel ticket offices US$25.) After the thwarted coup of August 1991, it was here that the Congress of People's Deputies met to dissolve itself and appoint an interim State Council to run the country. Leaving the Kremlin from Trinity Gate, next to the palace, you enter the **Aleksandrovsky Gardens.** At the northern end, the eternal flame of the **Tomb of the Unknown Soldier** flickers in memory of the Soviet Union's 25 million World War II dead. Urns containing soil from the 12 "hero cities" of World War II bear silent testimony to the country's losses.

For the best views of the Kremlin, walk behind St. Basil's, across the bridge and along the far bank of the Moskva River, or take a ride on one of the **sight-seeing boats.** The boats stop at every bridge downstream to Kolomenskoye or upstream to Gorky Park (every 20min., 250R). Guided tour boats leave from the Rossiya Hotel (behind St. Basil's; Mon., Wed., and Fri. at 3:30pm, 2hr., 2000R.)

Pushkin Square, Patriarch's Ponds, and the Arbat Halfway up ul. Tverskaya from Red Square, **Pushkin Square** (M: Pushkinskaya) is Moscow's favorite rendezvous spot. Amateur politicians gather on the square to argue and hand out petitions. Follow ul. Bolshaya Bronnaya, next to McDonald's, down to the bottom of the hill, turn right and follow ul. Malaya Bronnaya to the **Patriarch's Ponds,** where the action of Mikhail Bulgakov's novel *The Master and Margarita* begins. Several blocks away, at M: Arbatskaya, the **Arbat,** a pedestrian shopping arcade, was once a showpiece of *glasnost,* a haven for political radicals, Hare Krishnas, street poets, and *metallisti* (heavy metal rockers). Midway up, on a sidestreet, is a graffiti wall dedicated to the memory of rocker Victor Tsoi of the Soviet group Kino, who served as an idol to many young Russians before his death in a car crash 2 years ago.

Art Galleries Across the street from the Gorky Park entrance looms the huge modern **Tsentralni Dom Khudozhnika** (Центральный Дом Художника; Main Exhibition Hall), which sometimes shows independent avant-garde artists along with the usual retrospectives. (Open Tues.-Sun. 11am-8pm. 20R.) The entrance to the **New Tretyakov Art Gallery,** which hosts changing exhibits (in 1993 there was a large retrospective of Russian avant-garde art from the 1910s and 20s), lies on the long side of this building. (Open Tues.-Sun. 10am-8pm. 80R. Recorded info about current exhibits tel. 230 77 88.) One of Russia's premier art galleries, the **Tretyakov Art Gallery** (M: Tretyakovskaya/Третяковская; straight out of the Metro on Ordynski tupik and to the right) houses a superb collection of Russian and Soviet art beneath its traditional peaked roofs. The museum is undergoing major reconstruction, but a state-of-the-art wing has just been reopened and now showcases a collection of Russia's most famous works, including the 12th-century Vladimir icon of the Mother of God and Malevich's "Black Square" from the modernist movement of the 20th century. (Open Tues.-Sun. 10am-8pm. 80R.) The **Pushkin Museum of Fine Arts** at ul. Volkhonka 12 (M: Kropotkinskaya/Кропоткинская) boasts a respectable collection of

European Renaissance and Classical art, as well some Salvador Dalí drawings. (Open Wed.-Sun. 10am-8pm, Tues. 10am-9pm, holidays 10am-6pm. 70R.)

The **Metro** is a museum of a different kind. Each station sports original artwork and phantasmagoric chandeliers. Ring line stations are the most spectacular, notably Komsomolskaya (Комсомольская). The polished chrome and mosaics of Mayakovskaya (Маяковская) station also deserve a look, as do the statues fashioned in the Socialist Realist style at Ploshad Revolyutsii (Площадь Революции).

Authors' Houses and Monasteries

Russians take immense pride in their formidable literary history, preserving authors' houses in their original state, down to the half-empty teacups on the mantelpiece. Each is guarded by a team of *babushki* fiercely loyal to their master's memory. At ul. Lva Tolstovo 21 is the **Leo Tolstoy House Museum,** where Tolstoy lived and worked from 1882-1901. (M: Frunzenskaya/Фрунзенская. Cross the street outside the metro and take a trolleybus up 2 stops. Open Tues.-Sun. 10am-5:30pm; off-season 10am-3pm. Closed the last Fri. of every month. 60R.) At ul. Sadovaya-Kudrinskaya 6 is **Chekhov's House Museum,** where Chekhov lived from 1886-1890. (M: Barikadnaya/Баррикадная. Open Tues., Thurs., and Sat.-Sun. 11am-6pm, Wed. and Fri. 2-8pm. 50R.) **Gorky's Flat Museum,** ul. Kachalova 6-2, off ul. Sadovaya-Kudrinskaya just north of ul. Gertsena (M: Barikadnaya), is particularly interesting for its interior. The main staircase is designed to project the feeling and movement of waves on the sea. (Open Wed. and Fri. noon-8pm, Thurs. and Sat. 10am-5:45pm, Sun. 10am-5:30pm. Closed the last Thurs. of the month. Free.) **Dostoevsky's Flat Museum** is at ul. Dostoyevskovo 2 behind the star-shaped Red Army Theater. (M: Novoslobodskaya/Новослободская. Open Sat.-Mon. and Thurs. 11am-6pm, Wed. 10am-4pm, Fri. 1-9pm. 60R.) The **Mayakovsky Museum,** a fascinating achievement in Futurist museum design, is located at ul. Serova off Lubyanskaya ploshad. Look for the bust of Mayakovsky surrounded by huge red metal shards; the museum is in the building behind it. (Open Thurs.-Tues. 11am-5pm. Free.)

When you can't take the grime and bedlam any more, escape to one of Moscow's hidden parks or monasteries. Among these is the **Novodevichi Monastir** (convent) (Новодевичи Монастырь), near M: Sportivnaya (Спортивная). Take the exit out of the metro that *doesn't* go to the stadium, then take a right on that street. The convent is several blocks down on the left. Tsars and nobles kept the coffers filled by exiling their well-dowried wives and daughters here when they grew tired of them. The great Russian philosopher Solovyov is buried within the monastery's walls. **Smolenski Cathedral** in the center of the convent is exquisite. To the right and down the street, the convent's **cemetery** cradles the graves of Gogol, Chekhov, Stanislavsky, Khrushchev, Shostakovich, Mayakovsky, and other luminaries. The gravestones are often highly creative representations—visual or symbolic—of the deceased. Avoid visiting the convent on Sundays, when tour buses hog the place. Open Tues.-Sun. 11am-4pm. 100R; cemetary ticket office is in a light-blue kiosk across the street from the entrance.)

Parks

Another relatively untourised respite from Moscow's chaos is the tsars' **Kolomenskoye Summer Residence,** on a wooded rise above the Moskva River and a 10-minute walk south from M: Kolomenskaya (Коломенская). Peter the Great's 1702 log cabin and Bratsk Prison, where the persecuted Archpriest Avvakum wrote his celebrated autobiography, have been moved here from Arkhangelsk and Siberia respectively. (Grounds open daily 7am-10pm. Free. Museums open Wed.-Thurs. 1-8pm; Oct.-April Wed.-Sun. 11am-6pm. 100R.)

Izmailovski Park (Измайловский Парк; M: Izmailovskaya/Измайловская) spreads to the northeast of the city center, flooded in winter by hordes of gung-ho cross-country skiers. On Saturdays and Sundays, get off at M: Izmailovski Park and walk toward the stadium for Moscow's largest bazaar; haggle over Ukrainian painted eggs, old coins, *samovars* (enormous tea pots), pins, lacquer boxes, and *matryoshki*. These last items are the charming nested dolls that come in all sizes and themes, from the traditional Russian peasant family to a collection of Soviet premiers. You can bargain for some amazing works of art here, for prices much lower than at hard-currency stores.

Near Moscow State University, in the Lenin Hills (a leafy enclave overlooking the city center) is a viewing area from which you can see the **Luzhniki Sports Complex,** the **Lenin Stadium,** site of the 1980 Olympics, and all of Moscow behind it. On the way back, stop off at M: Kropotkinskaya. Nearby is the **Moscow Swimming Pool,** a heated outdoor tub where a beautiful cathedral twice as tall as the Statue of Liberty once soared. Stalin tore it down, intending to erect a palace of Soviets, but the ground proved too soft (many say it's a curse). Take care if you decide to swim; the water may not be the best, and fellow bathers may take an interest in your valuables. (Open Mon.-Sat. 6:55am-9:15pm, Sun. 7am-7:45pm. 50R/45-min. session.)

From M: Park Kultury (Парк Культуры), cross the **Krimski Most** bridge to **Gorky Park.** This is Moscow's amusement park, where droves of out-of-towners and young Muscovites promenade and relax. Huge outdoor speakers blare energetic tunes day in and day out, and in winter the paths are flooded to create a park-wide ice rink. (70R. Open 9am-10pm.)

Worship: Religion, Education, and Shopping To get a real feeling for Russian culture, attend an Orthodox service. One 17th-century jewel of a place is the **Church of St. Nicholas** at Komsomolski pr. and ul. Frunze (M: Frunzenskaya). Daily services are at 8:00am and 5pm; women must cover their heads. Keep respectfully silent or a Rasputin-like figure may ask you to leave. The **Yelokhovski Cathedral,** ul. Spartakovskaya 15 (M: Baumanskaya/Бауманская), is Moscow's largest and perhaps most beautiful operational church. (Services Mon. and Sat. 8am and 6pm, Sun. and holidays 7am and 10am.) Another ecclesiastic gem is the 18th-century **Church of Ionna Voina,** on ul. Dimitrova (M: Oktyabrskaya/Октябрская), named after the patron saint of the tsar's musketeers. (Services daily 8am and 6pm.)

The **Moscow State University** (known as МГУ; EM-GEH-OO) a hefty walk from M: Universitet (Университет), lies within a single Stalinist edifice; to fully appreciate its size, you must see it at close range. You need a pass to enter the university premises, but talking to a guard (try to do it in Russian, however broken) may get you in.

Shop with Russians along **Novi Arbat,** Moscow's most glamorous retail boulevard. At the **Melodiya** record store, Novi Arbat 40, you can find hard-to-get Russian classics and records by popular Russian and Western artists. Records run 90R (chamber music) to 5000R (Run DMC); CDs cost 5000-14,000R. (Open Mon.-Sat. 9am-8pm.) **Dom Knigi** (Дом Книги), Novi Arbat 26, stocks a wide variety of books. (Open Mon.-Sat. 10am-7pm.) The **Book Beryozka,** ul. Prechistenka (formerly Kropotkinskaya) 31 (M: Kropotkinskaya), sells Russian classics in the original (a good gift for Russian friends) and art books in English. Pick up your photo guide to the Moscow metro here. (Open. Mon.-Sat. 10am-6pm.) Moscow's outdoor **pet market** (птичый рынок) happens every Sunday on a suburban back street; *babushki* line the sidewalk trading kittens, salamanders, and goldfish. From M: Taganskaya (Таганская), take tram #35 up 2 stops.

ENTERTAINMENT

To find out what's going on in the capital, choose among English language newspapers and journals, including **The Moscow Times, The Moscow Tribune,** and **The Moscow Guardian.** The Friday edition of the **Moscow Times** has arts and entertainment listings for the upcoming week. All are available free of charge at hotels and hard-currency stores. **The Moscow Times: Quarterly** can be purchased for US$5, and contains up-to-date tips on restaurants and night-clubs.

There's a lively club scene in Moscow for expatriates and tourists. For an early start, hit the **Arbat Blues Club,** per. Aksakova 11 (tel. 291 15 46; open Fri.-Sat. 7:30pm-midnight; cover US$5 or ruble equivalent). **Club 011** gets going around midnight, behind AmEx at ul. Sadovaya-Kudrinskaya 19. (Open Thurs.-Sat. 10pm until everyone leaves. Cover US$5.) Drop in at **Rosie O'Grady's,** ul. Znamenka 9 (tel. 203 9087), for a beer. (Open Sun.-Thurs. noon-midnight, Fri.-Sat. noon-1:30am.)

Your best bet for traditional entertainment in Moscow is the official stuff: the ballet, the symphony, and—yes—the circus and puppet theater. The **Bolshoi Ballet** (tel. 292 00 90) is usually away on tour over the summer, and Intourist-arranged substitutes can be disappointing. Try the program at the mammoth **Tchaikovsky Concert Hall,** ul. Bolshaya Sadovaya 20 (tel. 299 03 78), next to M: Mayakovskaya. Catch a quartet or a symphony for mere pennies at the world-famous **Tchaikovsky Conservatory** (tel. 229 81 83), down the block at ul. Gertsena. Moscow's theaters have been trying avant-garde productions of late; if your Russian is less than fluent, this makes them all the more difficult to understand. Still, it's worth looking into some of the better companies: the **Moscow Art Theater** (better known by the acronym MXAT, pronounced "EM-khat"; tel. 229 87 60 or 203 73 99), with a new home at Tverskoi bul. 22 and a tradition going back 90 years; the **Sovremennik Theater,** at Chistoprudni bul. 19a (tel. 921 64 73; M: Kirovskaya/Кировская); and the **Taganka Theater of Drama and Comedy,** at ul. Chkalova 76 (tel. 272 63 00; M: Taganskaya). The **Stanislavsky Theater,** ul. Pervaya Tverskaya-Yamskaya 21 (M: Pushkinskaya), is a favorite among Moscow's intellectuals. (Tickets easily available at the *kassa* during the day for evening performances.) Moscow's famed **Obraztsov Puppet Theater,** ul. Sadovo-Samotekhnaya 3 (tel. 299 33 10), isn't just for kids, and the technically impressive slapstick productions hurdle all language barriers. Don't turn up your nose at Moscow's top-notch **Old** and **New Circuses** (цирк; tel. 200 17 59); besides showing first-rate acrobatics, tiger taming, and clowns, they're an excellent window into Russian working-class culture.

Tickets to these events can be purchased for rubles at street kiosks; one of the better ones is on ul. Pervaya Tverskaya-Yamskaya. (Prices range from 100 to 3000R.) Also try the **Central Excursion Bureau** (see Tourist Offices above) early in the morning of the day you wish to see a performance; they often sell out sooner than kiosks and you'll have to pay hard currency, but their information is centralized and in English. (US$15-50.) Major hotels often have helpful service bureaus. If you are told an event is sold out, be dogged and look elsewhere. Small gifts may make an uncooperative cashier more resourceful, and you can sometimes get a ticket in front of the theater just before curtain time.

■ Near Moscow

There are scores of fascinating sights beyond the 25km limit of your visa. If something out there interests you, the legal solution is the Central Excursion Bureau (see Tourist Offices above). They'll prepare the visa in about a day and charge a flat rate in hard currency for the excursion, including transportation. However, enforcement has loosened nearly to the point of non-existence; if they are discreet and can decipher Cyrillic, travelers can easily hop on the *elektrichka* (commuter rail) and join all the other Muscovites for an afternoon much more rewarding than the Intourist bus routine. Bringing a Russian friend will smooth the passage.

Zagorsk (Загорск), about 60km from Moscow, hosts one of Russia's 4 active monasteries and some of the most beautiful cathedrals you will find in all of Russia, some with original icon screens by Rublev and his followers. The one-day Intourist tour leaves 9am Friday from the Intourist Hotel. (US$38. Monastery museum open Tues.-Sun. 10am-6pm. 100R.) To get there by yourself, take the "Alesandrovsk" (Александровск) *elektrichka* from Moscow's Yaroslavski station (1½hr., round-trip 52R). The monastery is visible from the Zagorsk train station.

A daytrip to **Vladimir** (Владимир) and **Suzdal** (Суздаль), both 230km from Moscow, is a treat. Vladimir, the capital of medieval Muscovy, has a beautiful church that inspired the Assumption Cathedral in the Kremlin. Suzdal was famous for its churches-to-inhabitants ratio of 1:4; the town is well-preserved as a showcase "museum city" and still hosts 5 monasteries in a pastoral setting of distinctly Russian beauty. Intourist tours leave Sunday at 8am from the Central Excursion Bureau (15hr., US$78); there's so much to see and the towns are so distant from Moscow that it may really be worth the step-by-step narrative and enforced guided tours. If you understand Russian, the Moscow Excursion Bureau offers much cheaper excursions to Vladimir and Suzdal (about 16,800R each); check the schedule inside their office at Rozhdestvenka 5.

■■■ ST. PETERSBURG
(САНКТ-ПЕТЕРБУРГ)

Upon returning from a tour of Western Europe in 1703, Peter the Great decided that his backward empire needed a new capital, a cosmopolis on the level of Paris and Berlin, to replace hopelessly provincial Moscow—and so St. Petersburg was built on the swampy Neva delta at the edge of the Gulf of Finland. During the 18th and 19th centuries, the Russian aristocracy imported French and Italian architects to bedeck the city with Baroque and Neoclassical mansions, landscaped parks, and carefully planned canals and streets. Marxism took root here in the 1870s, setting in motion the vanguard that brought the Bolshevik Revolution in 1917 and Russified the city's name to Petrograd. In 1924, after Lenin's death, it was officially renamed **Leningrad** (Ленинград). During WWII, a 900-day siege by the German army took the lives of more than 650,000 citizens; even today, almost every family in the city can claim at least 1 victim.

Three quarters of a century of communist rule have left an indelible mark on St. Petersburg. As in other cities of the former Soviet Union, long lines snake around generic "Bread" and "Meat" stores punched into the crumbling façades of former mansions. Yet here and there a bit of the old glitter remains: St. Petersburg boasts some of the world's finest art museums, gorgeous Imperial palaces in the suburbs, and the literary landscape of Dostoevsky and Gogol.

St. Petersburg is today more provincial than Moscow, but its rich cultural past makes it irresistible, a city of madness and fantasy—the mythical creation of Peter the Great on the one hand and Pushkin on the other. In a June 1991 referendum, Leningrad residents voted to change the city's name back to St. Petersburg; now the traditional November 7 holiday commemorating the Bolshevik revolution has become "Vivat Sankt-Peterburg" day—"Long live St. Petersburg."

ORIENTATION AND PRACTICAL INFORMATION

St. Petersburg is in northwestern Russia, just 6 hours' train ride east of Helsinki, Finland and 9 hours northwest of Moscow. Built on a series of islands in the swampy delta of the **Neva River,** the city is laced with canals. The historical heart of the city is the **Peter and Paul Fortress** (Петропавловская Крепость), where Peter the Great made his first settlement in 1703. St. Petersburg's major thoroughfare, **Nevsky Prospekt** (Невский Проспект), starts at Palace Square (Дворцовая пл.), a few blocks south and across the river from the fortress, and heads east toward the Alexander Nevsky Monastery complex.

Tourist Office: You're on your own. Try the **Intourist Service Bureau,** in the Astoria Hotel, Isaakievskaya pl. 2 (tel. 210 50 46 for tours and theater info). Excursions leave several times a week to Pushkin, Pavlovsk, Petrodvorets, Peter and Paul Fortress, the Hermitage, and St. Isaac's Cathedral (US$9-13).

Consulates: U.S., ul. Furshtadtskaya (Фурштадтская, formerly Petra Lavrova) 15 (tel. 274 85 68). M: Chernyshevskaya (Чернышевская). Open Mon.-Fri. 9am-5:30pm. **Finland,** ul. Chaikovshovo (Чайковского) 71 (tel. 153 35 49). Open Mon.-Fri. 9am-5pm.

Currency Exchange: Look for the Obmen Valyuta (Обмен Валюта) signs. A decent rate for your dollars and traveler's checks can always be had at the **Central Exchange Office,** ul. Mikhailovskaya (Михайловская, formerly ul. Brodskovo) 4,

ORIENTATION AND PRACTICAL INFORMATION

St. Petersburg

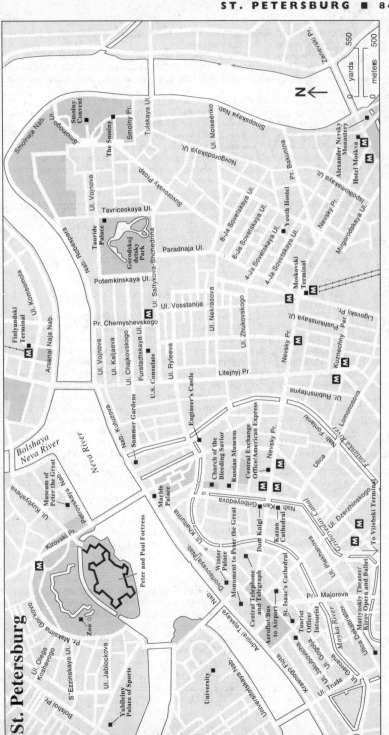

off Nevsky pr. and across from the Grand Hotel Europe. M: Gostiny dvor (Гостиный Двор). Open daily 9:30am-6pm.

American Express: ul. Mikhailovskaya 1/7 (tel. 315 74 87 or 315 65 17), in the Grand Hotel Europe. Provides travel service, replaces lost and stolen cards, refunds and sells Traveler's Cheques. Mail held for cardholders. Open Mon.-Fri. 9am-5pm.

Post Office: ul. Pochtamtshaya (Почтамптская) 9. Stamps to U.S. 130R, telegrams 350R/min. Open Mon.-Sat. 9am-8pm, Sun. 10am-6pm. Address **Poste Restante** to Do Vostrebovama (До Востребовама). **Postal Code:** 190 000. Addressing the envelope in Cyrillic will expedite delivery, but isn't essential.

Telephones: Central Telephone and Telegraph, ul. Gertsena (Герцена) 3-5, off Nevsky Prospect near Palace Square. A call to the U.S. runs about 1600R/min. for direct-dial service in the front room. Local calls can be made from any phone booth on the street; use one of the *mezhdugorodni* (междугородный, intercity) phone booths at the Central Telephone office; they take special grooved *zhetoni* (жетоны, coins) that are sold across from the booths. **Telegrams** 350R/word, to the U.S. 7500R/page. Open 24hrs., except 12:30-1pm. **City Code:** 812.

Flights: The main **airport** is **Pulkovo** (Пулково). Buses link it with the downtown **Aeroflot** office at ul. Gogolya (Гоголя) roughly every hr. (500R). You can also take bus #39 from M: Moskovshaya (Московская; every 20-40 min., 15min. ride). **Foreign airline offices** include: **Delta,** ul. Gertsena (tel. 311 58 20). Open Mon.-Fri. 9am-5pm. **Finnair,** ul. Gogolya 19 (tel. 104 34 39). Open Mon. 9am-5pm, Tues.-Thurs. 9am-8pm, Fri.-Sun. noon-8pm. **Austrian Airlines** and **SwissAir,** Nevsky pr. 57 (tel. 314 50 86). **Bulgarian Airlines,** ul. Gertsena 36 (tel. 315 50 30). Open daily 9am-1pm and 2-5pm.

Trains: St. Petersburg has 4 main railway stations, all accessible by Metro. Trains to Estonia, Lithuania, Latvia, and Poland leave from the **Varshavski** (Варшавский) station, M: Baltiskaya (Балтийская). To Ukraine and Byelorussia from the **Vitebski** (Витебский) station, M: Pushkinskaya (Пушкинская). To Moscow (15 daily; 9hr.; US$4, 1600R) and all other points in Russia from the **Moskovski** (Московский) station, M: pl. Vostaniya (Восстания). To Helsinki (2/day, 6hr., US$65) from the **Finlyandski** (Финляндский) station, M: pl. Lenina (Ленина). The **central ticket office** for rail travel (Централные Железнодорожные Кассы) is at Canal Griboyedova 24 (канал Грибоедова). Open Mon.-Sat. 8am-8pm, Sun. 8am-4pm. Foreign tourists must purchase tickets with a US$4 surcharge at the special **Intourist** department inside the ticket office (windows 100-104 on 2nd floor); they also handle international tickets (windows 90-99). Open daily 8am-noon and 1-7pm.

Public Transportation: Buses, trolleys, and an unbelievably efficient Metro system keep St. Petersburg humming (6am-1am). The crush on buses is guaranteed to thin you down. Metro fare 15R; buy bus and trolley tickets at newsstands and kiosks (15R). Maps with all routes can be purchased at most kiosks (250R). A 1500R *yedini bilet* (единый билет) pays for all public transportation (metro, bus, trolley, and tram) for a calendar month.

Laundromat: Your bathtub. Be sure to bring detergent from home; the Russian variety is hard to find and devours clothes (and even skin) voraciously.

Emergencies: Ambulance: tel. 03. Also try the **main hospital** at 558 60 06 for medical assistance. **Fire:** tel. 01. **Police:** tel. 02.

ACCOMMODATION

To date, only 1 hostel exists in St. Petersburg. Run by California-based **Russian Youth Hostels,** it opened its doors in early June 1992. The restored 5-story building is near M: pl. Vostaniya (пл. Восстания) on 3rd ul. Sovyetskaya 28 (третая Советская). The neighborhood is quiet and pleasant; the hostel itself is clean and modern, even by Western standards. Rooms have 2, 3, or 4 beds each (50 beds total). Each floor has its own kitchen (stove and sink; small refrigerator downstairs) and bathroom. Women, men, and showers on different floors. (Reception open 24hrs. Check in by 9:30pm. Check-out 11am. No lockout. US$15.) The hostel will arrange your visa for the duration of your stay; reservation confirmation and visa runs US$10 plus consular charges. In Russia, call (812) 277 05 69, or fax (812) 277 51 02; otherwise call the

California office at (310) 379-4316, or fax (310) 379-8420. Make reservations outside Russia at least 3-4 weeks in advance; reservations from within Russia are accepted within 2 weeks of arrival. **CDS Reisid (Baltic Bed and Breakfast),** Raekoja Plats 17, Tallinn, Estonia (tel. 372 (2) 445 262; fax 372 (2) 313 666), places travelers with English-speaking hosts in the Baltic States and CIS (US$25 fee), and can also arrange wait-free visas to Russia.

FOOD

St. Petersburg may lack Moscow's broader choice of new cooperative restaurants, but travelers still have a number of options. Besides establishments serving local specialties, a number of Western-style eateries have recently opened their doors. Restaurants usually close at 11pm, and reservations are highly advisable. Call or drop by in person around noon to secure a dinner spot for the same evening; otherwise you may be left with few options come nightfall. *Tap water is not safe to drink in St. Petersburg, and the bottled variety is putrid.* Get foreign mineral water at hard-currency stores, boil or filter your own, or snag a bottle of Western soda. It's best to avoid unpackaged snacks sold on the street. **Markets** stock fresh produce, meat, cheese, and honey but are comparatively much more expensive than state-owned stores; 1kg of tomatoes is likely to go for about 1500R at the market, and a single pineapple will cost around 5000R. The **covered market** at Kuznechni pereulok 3, just around the corner from M: Vladimirskaya (Владимирская), and the **Patent Cooperative Trade Center,** ul. Nekrasova 53 (Некрасова), at the top of Ligovski pr. (open Tues.-Sun. 8am-7pm, Mon. 8am-4pm), are both excellent. In the listings below, restaurants have table service; at cafés you order from a counter.

Restaurants

Tbilisi, ul. Sytninskaya (Сытнинская) 10 (tel. 232 93 91). M: Gorkovskaya (Горьковская); follow the iron-wrought fence that wraps around the park until you see the Sytny (Сытный) market. Tbilisi is just around the corner. A wide selection of tasty Georgian appetizers (300-1350R) and hot dishes (750-2400R). A good option for vegetarians. Menu in Russian, English, and Finnish. You can buy wine at the Sytny market to accompany your meal. Open daily 11am-11pm.

Demyanova Ukha (Демьянова Уха), pr. Kronverski 53 (tel. 232 80 90), at M: Gorkovskaya (Горьковская). Fresh-fish dishes in an atmospheric restaurant. Main courses 905-2530R. Open 11am-10pm. Reservations needed even for lunch.

Koryeiski Domik (Корейский Домик, Korea House), nab. Reki Fontanki (наб. Реки Фонтанки) 20 (tel. 275 72 03), through an archway from the canal. Korean-style meat cooked before you. Mmmm.... Also serves soup, rice, noodles, and dumplings. Full meal about 4000-5000R. Open 1-9pm.

Chaika (Чайка), Kanal Griboyedeva 14 (tel. 312 46 31), off Nevsky pr. German fare, hard liquor, caviar, and cheesecake for hard currency. Extensive menu. Main dishes run DM5.50-18. Open daily 11am-5am.

Café Tet-a-Tet (Кафе Тет-а-Тет), pr. Bolshoi (Большой) 65 (tel. 232 10 35) at M: Petrogradshaya (Петроградская). An elegant, intimate restaurant; live music on grand piano and tables for 2. Standard Russian fare, entrees 1500-4000R. Open 1-6pm and 8pm-1am. Make reservations in person noon-1pm.

Balkany (Балканы), Nevsky pr. 27 (tel. 315 47 48), between the Kazan Cathedral and Gostiny Dvor. Standard Russian fare; just pick a table, sit down, and ask for a menu. Main courses 2100-2600R. Open daily 11am-10pm.

Shanghai, ul. Sadovaya (Садовая) 12 (tel. 311 27 51). M: Gostiny Dvor, off Nevsky pr. 1st floor serves Russian food during the day and Chinese food in the evening; 2nd floor offers Chinese fare all day. 2nd-floor menus in Chinese, Russian, and English. The English menu is more extensive but prices can be as much as 3 times higher as those on the Russian one. Several vegetarian main dishes. Entrees (Russian menu) from 1500R. Open daily noon-11pm.

Literaturnoye Café (Литературное Кафе), Nevsky pr. 18 (tel. 312 85 36). A famous 19th-century chat spot for writers and artists, gracefully restored to its original elegance. Pushkin had his last meal here before departing for his fatal duel.

Pricey, but unbeatable for champagne and sweets in the afternoon. *Prix fixe* meal for 15000R includes champagne, wine, and soda. Cover 1000R. Come early to snag a ticket. Open daily noon-5pm and 7-10pm.

Moskva (Москва), in the Moskva Hotel (tel. 164 59 44). M: pl. Aleksandra Nevskovo. Pleasant surroundings, decent Russian-style food. Entrees at the 1st floor á la carte 500-2600R. Open daily noon-10pm. All-you-can-eat on the 2nd floor.

Cafés

Metekhi (Метехи), ul. Belinskovo 3 (tel. 272 3361), just off the Fontanka canal. This Georgian cooperative café ladles out a terrific bowl of *kharcho* soup and *lobio* (vegetarian chili) for about 400R each. Open 11am-8pm.

Vody Lagidze (Воды Лагидзе), next door to Metekhi. Cheesy *khachipuri* (a Georgian national treasure, 300R). Open 11am-3pm and 4-10pm.

Dessert Hall (Десерт Хол). Also next door to Metekhi, but farther down Belinskovo. Great place for a cheap snack. Salad, open-faced sandwiches, and pastries all under 150R. Vodka and champagne 200-350R. Open 11am-3pm and 4-10pm.

Baghdad (Багдад), ul. Furshtadtskaya 35. This small cafe located downstairs from the street serves a hearty bowl of *lagman* (soup with meat) and rice *plov*. Down a full meal for 1500R. Open 11am-11pm.

Grill Diez (Гриль Диш), pr. Kamenostrovski 16 (tel. 232 42 55). Whole chicken roasted on skewers (2000R), pita bread (500R). Open 10am-8pm. Chicken available on the ½hour. (Cuckoo.)

Gino Ginelli, on canal Griboyedova, just off Nevsky pr. near Dom Knigi. Next to Chaika. DM5.50-7.50 buys American-style pizza or cheeseburgers for homesick Westerners. Ice cream DM2/scoop. Open 10am-1am.

Le Café, pr. Nevsky 142, convenient to the hostel. Oasis for Westerners with its caviar-topped salads (US$4-6.50) and omelettes (US$3.50). Open 11am-11pm.

Kafe Morozhenoye (Кафе Мороженое), Nevsky pr. 24, opposite the Kavkazki. St. Petersburg's premier ice cream parlor. Faded elegance and pastel green walls. Ice cream 230R/200g, with chocolate shavings 100R extra. Open daily 10am-2pm and 3-10pm.

Baskin Robbins 31 Flavors, on Nevsky pr. M: Ploshad Vostaniya. Across from the metro. Just like in the U.S. Small cone 700R. Open daily 10am-10pm.

SIGHTS

Winter Palace, Russian Museum, and St. Isaac's Cathedral St. Petersburg's cultural highlight is the magnificent green-and-gold **Winter Palace** in spacious Palace Square, the site of a mass town meeting during the 1991 coup attempt. The building, inhabited by tsars up until the Revolution, is a true symbol of the enormous power of Russia's pre-revolutionary autocracy. The palace now houses the **Hermitage** (Эрмитаж) museum, one of the world's finest. The Hermitage collection started with Catherine the Great's 24 paintings; it now includes 2½ million items, kept in about 1000 rooms. In Spanish works, it is surpassed only by the Prado in Madrid, while in Dutch paintings (especially Rembrandts) it has no equal. The museum also displays Flemish masters such as Rubens and works by da Vinci, Michelangelo, and Titian. The Impressionist and 20th-century collections are superlative. The building itself is a paragon of extravagance. Among the main halls where the tsars reigned and entertained is the awesome **Malachite Hall,** where Kerensky's Provisional Government met for the last time on November 7, 1917, when Lenin's Bolshevik forces stormed the palace. From that point, the Communists controlled the government. (Hermitage open Tues.-Sun. 9am-6pm. 7000R.) Try to go with a tour group, or else arrive early.

At the **Russian Museum** (Русский Музей) on the north side of pl. Iskustv (Искусств), down ul. Mikhailovskaya just off Nevsky pr., Russian art runs chronologically from an exquisite collection of 12th- to 16th-century icons through 18th- and 19th-century portraiture. Unfortunately, the permanent exhibit stops at the end of the 19th century with Vrubel, just as the nation begins to come into its own. (Open Wed.-Mon. 10am-6pm. *Kassa* located downstairs to the right. 5000R, students

2500R, Russians 100R. Solitary visitors get in free on 1st Wed. of the month Sept. 15-May 15.)

For a splendid view of the city, climb to the dome of **St. Isaac's Cathedral** (Исаак-иевский Собор), on Isakievskaya pl., a massive example of 19th-century civic-religious architecture. The dome of the cathedral is coated with 100kg of pure gold. The murals and mosaics inside are the works of some of Russia's greatest artists; the chips in the marble columns appear courtesy of German artillery fire during the siege of Leningrad. (Museum open daily 10am-6pm. Colonnades open 10am-5pm. To museum 50R, students 15R. To colonnades 25R, students 5R.)

Peter and Paul Fortress

There are several museums inside the Peter and Paul Fortress, across the river from the Hermitage. The **cathedral**'s golden steeple rises far above the Neva River. In its baroque interior are displayed the graves of several tsars, including Peter the Great; note the icons that illustrate their "divine right." (Open Thurs.-Tues. 11am-6pm. 200R. Purchase tickets at the *kassa* outside the main gate.) Just outside the church is Mikhail Shemyakin's controversial rendering of Peter the Great in stone, which at once fascinates and offends Russians from all walks of life. Another museum worth visiting is the **State Museum of the History of St. Petersburg**, just to the left of Shemyakin's statue. (Open Thurs.-Tues. 11am-6pm. *Kassa* closes at 5pm. 300R, students 100R.) Beyond the archway that leads out to the Neva are plaques commemorating the terrible floods that have repeatedly devastated the city. The last few tsars used the fortress as a political prison where they hanged many young radicals, including Lenin's older brother. (Open Thurs.-Mon. 10am-7pm, Tues. 10am-4pm; Sept.-May Thurs.-Mon. 11am-6pm, Tues. 11am-4pm; closed last Tues. of each month. 500R, Russians 200R.) Stroll around the palace to the City Beach, where people tan standing up by catching the warmth radiating from the walls.

Nevsky Prospect

(Невский Проспект) It may seem like all 5 million of St. Petersburg's residents are jammed onto the sidewalk of Nevsky Prospect, and that 50% of them want to change money or sell you a rabbit hat. Few other streets have played so prominent a role in Russian literature—Nikolai Gogol devoted a whole novel to it. The street begins at the **Admiraltestvo** (Адмиралтество), whose golden spire, painted black during WWII to disguise it from German artillery bombers, towers over the Admiralty gardens and Palace Square. Check out the memorial statues of Russian literary and musical greats surrounding the fountain. A few blocks down Nevsky at #28 is **Dom Knigi** (Дом Книги), once St. Petersburg's definitive bookstore but now more of a landmark, though some titles are still available here. Its rooftop globe dates from the building's pre-revolutionary days as Russian headquarters of the Singer sewing machine company. Check out the collection of posters on the 2nd floor. (Open Mon.-Sat. 10am-8pm.)

The colossal edifice across the street, modeled after St. Peter's in the Vatican, is the **Kazan Cathedral** (Казанский Собор; Kazanski Sobor), which has served as the **Museum of the History of Religion and Atheism** since the Revolution. At the moment it functions neither as a full-fledged museum nor as an Orthodox church. Its collection of Russian religious artifacts and copies of famous icons is still quite good, however. (Open Tues.-Thurs. 11am-6pm. 60R.) The plaza between the cathedral's wings is the center of St. Petersburg's political and religious activity. New political parties deliver speeches from the east wing; discussion circles gather starting about 8pm. Stop to admire the monarchists, anarchists, fascists, hypnotists, Christian fundamentalist missionaries, and Hare Krishnas—and meet Russians ravenous for contact with the West. Women should not wander around this area alone in the evening; the wings of the cathedral are reportedly a favorite meeting spot for prostitutes and their customers.

Farther down Nevsky pr. at no. 35 stands the pale yellow **Gostiny Dvor** (Гостиный Двор), St. Petersburg's largest department store. Lots of lacquer boxes, Ukrainian

SIGHTS

painted eggs, and *matryoshka* dolls are on sale here. (Open Mon.-Sat. 10am-8pm). Check out the prices at Gostiny Dvor before venturing across the street to the center of St. Petersburg's chintzy tourist **art market** in front of the Grand Hotel Europe. Be sure to *hold on* to your moneybelt here with both hands; art markets, which offer a fascinating collection of some of Russia's greatest talents, are also a haven of black-market activity and professional pickpockets, since it's mostly foreigners who can afford the steep prices.

The halfway point of Nevsky Prospect is marked by the Moscow train station, which faces **Uprising Square** (Площадь Восстания; *Ploshad Vostania*). From the square, it's only 1 Metro stop (M: pl. Aleksandra Nevskovo) to the top of St. Petersburg's main street, where the Neva River again swings into view. Here, within the **Alexander Nevsky Lavra** monastery (Лавра Александра Невского) are 2 **cemeteries**; such luminaries as Tchaikovsky, Lomonosov, and Dostoevsky repose here. Tickets to the tomb museum are sold in the *kassa* outside of the monastery walls. (Open Fri.-Wed. 11am-7pm. 400R, students 250R, Russians 60R.) The **Large Choral Synagogue of St. Petersburg,** St. Petersburg's only functioning synagogue, located at Lermontovski pr. 2, has morning and evening services daily (8am and 6pm). **Nikolski Cathedral,** the magnificent blue-and-gold structure a few blocks east of the synagogue on ul. Rimskovo-Korsakovo (Римского-Корсаково), near the Kirov theater and conservatory, has services daily at 10am and 6pm.

Riverbanks and Canals You can escape the bedlam of Nevsky Prospect along the banks of the Neva, the smaller Moika and Fontanka Rivers, and the Griboyedov canal (канал Грибоедова). A promenade along the **Palace Embankment** (Дворцовая Набережная) of the Neva toward the lovely **Summer Garden** (Летний Сад) will take you past many former embassies and resplendent examples of 19th-century neoclassical architecture. Within the Summer Garden stands the small but elegant **Summer Palace** of Peter the Great. (Open May-Sept. 15 Wed.-Mon. 11am-6:30pm; Sept. 16-Nov. 9 Wed.-Mon. 10am-5:30pm. 500R, Russians 60R.) Among the bevy of literary museums in St. Petersburg is the **Pushkin Apartment,** Moika nab. 12. (Open Mon.-Wed.10:30am-6pm. 250R, Russians 40R. Come early; tickets go fast.) The **Dostoevsky Museum** (Достоевский Музей) is in the writer's apartment at Kuznechny per. 5/2, around the corner from M: Vladimirskaya (Владимирская); *The Brothers Karamazov* (quite possibly the universe's greatest novel) was penned here. On display are the writer's notes for various novels; Dostoevsky's study is preserved as it was when he died, and the clock on the table points to the exact hour of his death. (Open Tues.-Sun. 10:30am-6:30pm; closed last Wed. of month. 400R, students 200R, Russians 50R.) The **Anna Akhmatova Museum,** a showcase for one of the greatest poets of the Soviet era, is housed in a yellow edifice at Fontanka 34; the entrance to the museum is located at Liteyni pr. 51. (Open Tues.-Sun. 10:30am-6:30pm. 50R.)

The magnificent cathedral on the Griboyedov canal, the **Church of the Bleeding Savior** (Спас На Крови; *Spas Na Krovi*), sits on the site of Tsar Alexander II's 1881 assassination. Though the cathedral has been under repair for the past 20 years and remains closed to the public, the minutely detailed mosaics on its exterior merit a close look. Among St. Petersburg's many memorials to the victims of WWII is the **Piskarevskoye Memorial Cemetery** (Пискаревское Мемориалское Кладбище). A visit to the cemetery is guaranteed to help you understand the degree of suffering endured by the Russians during the war. Many of the victims of the siege of Leningrad are buried here in mass graves whose plaques indicate only the year in which the grave was dug. The inscription "No one is forgotten, nothing is forgotten" is etched on a stone wall behind the awe-inspiring statue of the Motherland at the cemetery's far end, and an eternal flame burns at the cemetery's entrance, one of many such flames in Russia's major cities dedicated to the memory of WWII victims. To reach the cemetery, take bus #75 about 10 stops from M: pl. Muzhestva (Мужества, a word meaning "courage" and "spirit"); the cemetery is on the left-hand side of the road across from a large flower shop. The **site of Pushkin's fatal duel** can be reached by taking the Metro to "Pionerskaya" (Пионерская) and then walking along Kolomyazhki pr. (Коломяжкий).

St. Petersburg has a number of good **hard-currency stores.** The best-stocked are the **Neva Star** at the Hotel Moskva (Гостиница Москва) and the **Baltic Star** at the Hotel Pribaltiskaya (Гостиница Прибалтиская). The hard-currency store at the Hotel Astoria stocks electronics as well as drinks, some clothing, and snack food.

ENTERTAINMENT

St. Petersburg's famed White Nights lend the night sky a pale, bewitching glow from mid-June to early July. Unfortunately, most activities in St. Petersburg draw to a close by 11pm, so there's diddly to do but wander about and watch the drawbridges go up at about 1:30am. This can be quite romantic, but remember to do it from the *same* side of the bridge your hotel is on: the bridges don't go back down again until 3am. During the 3rd week in June, when the sun barely touches the horizon, the city holds a series of outdoor evening concerts as a part of the **White Nights Festival.** Check kiosks and posters for more information. The theater season comes to an end around the time of this festival and opens up again in early September, but check for summer performances at ticket offices. (Tickets 50-2500R at Nevsky pr. 42, across from Gostiny Dvor, or from kiosks and tables near St. Isaac's Cathedral and along Nevsky pr.) Possibly the world's finest ballet company, the **Kirov Opera and Ballet,** housed at Teatralnaya pl. (Театральная) in the former **Marinski Theater,** witnessed the classic performances of Pavlova and Shalyapin and the premieres of famous Russian operas. Another choice is choreographer Boris Eifmann's **Sovremenniye (Contemporary) Ballets;** call Hotel Astoria's Service Bureau for information. (Open Mon.-Sat. 9am-8pm, Sun. 10am-7pm.) The **St. Petersburg Philharmonic** at ul. Mikhailovskaya 2, opposite the Grand Hotel Europe, offers world-class classical music performances for just a few rubles. Dmitri Shostakovich's Seventh Symphony rang out in defiance here on August 9, 1942, while the city endured the Nazi siege. (Tickets at Nevsky Prospect 30.) For more placid entertainment, take a **boat ride** up and down the Neva River. Tours leave across from the Hermitage (90-min. ride 4000R, Russians 200R). Tours of the city's canals leave daily 11:30am to 8:30pm from the Fontanka river, just off Nevsky pr. (1¼hr. ride 3000R).

St. Petersburg's rock scene, besides being the liveliest in Russia, is of tremendous social importance; in recent years it has spurred the emergence of a separate youth culture, something unheard-of under the Soviet regime. Tickets to weird, tacky stadium shows can be purchased at kiosks along Nevsky pr. To find out about more worthwhile bands, drop by the **St. Petersburg Rock Club** (Рок Клуб; tel. 312 34 83) at ul. Rubinshteina 13, in the courtyard and through the right door on the far wall. Soviet rock superstars like Kino and Igry got their starts in this dingy old building. The newly-opened **Rock Café Nord** (Рок Кафе Норд) at pr. Ligovski 153 caters to a younger generation (500R cover). Your jazz cravings can be slaked at the St. Petersburg **Jazz Club** (Джаз Клуб), Russia's oldest and finest, at Zagorodny pr. 27 (Загородный; tel. 164 85 65), offering Dixie or cool jazz most nights from 8pm (300R cover). If you have an itch to go dancing, try the disco **Joy** (Джой) at Kanal Griboedova (Канал Грибоедова) 30. (Open 10pm-5am. Cover US$10.)

■ Near St. Petersburg

A string of sumptuous 18th-century summer palaces and estates repose around St. Petersburg. Erected by the families of the tsars in the heyday of pre-revolutionary Russia, the palaces stand as a testament to the splendor of the Romanovs in much the same way that Versailles today symbolizes the excesses of the French Bourbons.

The 3 major palaces stand on what was German territory during the siege of Leningrad in 1942-44. Tragically, all were burned to the ground during the Nazis' retreat, but in one of the great paradoxes of the Soviet regime, Stalin provided the staggering sums of money necessary to completely rebuild these symbols of the tsars during the postwar reconstruction of the Soviet Union. All of the palaces are accessible by bus, electric train, or, in the case of Peter the Great's summer place, by hydrofoil from the Hermitage art museum in St. Petersburg.

Petrodvorets (Петродворец; literally "Peter's Palace"), will remind you of Versailles from the moment you enter the grounds: a lovely palace surrounded by a cascade of golden fountains and waterfalls. The complex, begun by Peter the Great, is unfortunately deteriorating, because the sluggish economy has severely cut back the maintenance of this and other state parks. The main fountain is under restoration, and the once beautifully kept lower gardens are now dotted with dandelions and crabgrass. The upper gardens and palace interior still impress, however, and the gardens are a good place to get away from the breakneck pace of downtown St. Petersburg. Once inside the lower gardens, follow the sound of children's shrieks and giggles to the **"joke fountains,"** which, activated by one misstep, suddenly splash their unwitting victims. (Palace open Tues.-Sun. 11am-6pm; closed last Tues. of the month. 2200R, Russians 100R.) **Hydrofoils** leave between 9am and 7pm from a dock in front of the Winter Palace (2/hr.; 20min.; 1500R; return ticket must be purchased at the palace entrance to the grounds 1000R, Russians 200R). **Trains** leave frequently from Baltiski Station (2/hr., 45min., 16R).

Twenty-five km south of the city, **Pushkin** (Пушкин), formerly known as Tsarskoye Selo ("Tsar's Village"), harbors Catherine the Great's magnificent summer residence, a gorgeous azure, white, and gold baroque palace snugly enclosed in tailored French gardens. Don't miss a tour; the palace interior is truly extraordinary. Pictures of the ravaged palace, taken after the Nazi siege, adorn the halls as a testament to the work that has been put into restoring it. The main ballroom, decorated with floor-to-ceiling mirrors, delicate wall carvings, and gilded trim is perhaps the single most impressive room in all of St. Petersburg. (Open Wed.-Mon. noon-5pm, only with guided tours. 3000R, Russians 200R.) Don't miss the **Pushkin museum** located in the poet's boarding school, next to the Catherine Palace. (Open Wed.-Mon. noon-5pm. 1500R, Russians 100R.) After a tour of the palace and the Gymnasium, stroll through the surrounding park, rent a **boat,** and row out onto the pond surrounded by dreamy pavilions. (Palace open Fri.-Wed. noon-6pm, closed last Fri. of the month. Park open daily 6am-10pm.) **Trains** leave from Vitebski station every 20 min. (25R). **Pavlovsk's palace** and parks are located further along the same train line.

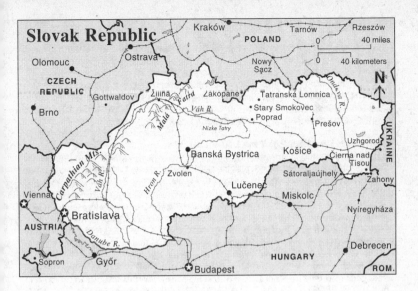

Slovak Republic (Slovensko)

US$1 = 32.10SK (Koruny)	10SK = US$0.31
CDN$1 = 24.40SK	10SK = CDN$0.41
UK£1 = 49.70SK	10SK = UK£0.20
IR£ = 46.50SK	10SK = IR£0.22
AUS$1 = 20.90SK	10SK = AUS$0.48
NZ$1 = 17.70SK	10SK = NZ$0.57
SAR1 = 6.67SK	10SK = SAR1.50
Country Code: 42	

Survivor of centuries of Tartar invasions, Hungarian domination, and Soviet industrialization, Slovakia has emerged triumphant as a mature country. Natural wonders cover the map: the north is mountainous and forested, sloping into the gorgeous landscapes of central Slovakia. Hiking and skiing are national pastimes. The countryside is dotted with castle ruins, relics of the defense against the Tartars. In the smaller towns, even the suburban factories have not destroyed the old-time atmosphere. Slovakia is still coping with national debt and an industry-heavy economy, but domestic production is on the rise and the financial future looks hopeful. Take a deep draught of Slovak wine, put on the hiking boots, and enjoy the freedom.

TRAVELING IN SLOVAKIA

The main Slovakian **railway** starts in Košice and ends in Bratislava; links to Prague, Budapest, Vienna, and Kraków are frequent and 35% cheaper for students. EastRail is valid in the Slovak Republic; Eurail is not. **ŽSR** is the national train company; every information desk has a copy of **Cestovný poriadok** (58SK), the master schedule. *Odchody* (departures) and *prichody* (arrivals) are on the left and right sides, respectively, of schedules and posters, but be sure to check revolving timetables, as the train platform *(naštupište)* often changes from the printed one. A reservation *(mies-tenka,* 6-7SK) is required for international voyages (including the Czech Republic), *expresný* trains, and for 1st-class seats but not domestic *rychlík* (fast), *spešný* (semi-fast), or *osobný* (local) trains. Buy a reservation at the boxed-R counter before you buy a ticket. The Czechoslovak **bus** company, **ČSAD,** still operates and also pub-lishes a master schedule; however, it's generally easier to let the information desk decipher it. **Bicycling** is popular; **hitchhiking** is legal.

SLOVAKIA ESSENTIALS

Čedok, the Czechoslovak travel bureau, still exists in the Slovak Republic but is being phased out. **CKM,** the Čedok of Czechoslovak youth, is in the same boat, but offices tend to be less rushed; go there for info on domestic travel, hostels, and ISICs. **Slovakoturist** is gaining steam but still has trouble dealing with foreigners.

Czechoslovak **coins** are valid in both countries. Both stamped and unstamped **bills** are valid in Slovakia. Telephones and ticket machines tend to accept the 10SK coin as well as the old kčs, but not the brand-new 1SK or 2SK coins. You cannot buy Czech crowns in Slovakia without a Slovak passport; find a Slovak friend or change back to western currency first if you're crossing the border.

The **mail** service is quite modern; Poste Restante mail with a "1" after the city name goes to the main post office. Local **telephone** calls cost 2SK; drop the coin in after you've been connected. The AT&T **USA Direct** number is 00 42 00 01 01. International calls are easiest at the post office or from phones with a globe on top.

Slovaks understand both Czech and Polish; many know German, and English and French are common in Bratislava. The diligent tourist can turn heads with a phrase or two in Slovak: *Dobrý den!* (DOH-bree den, "hello"); *Do videnia* (DOH vee-dane-yah, "goodbye"); *D'akujem* (DYAK-oo-yem, "Thank-you"); *Prosím* (PROH-seem, "please" and "you're welcome"); *Kol'ko?* (KOYL-koh, "how much?"); *Zaplatím* (ZAH-plah-tyeem, "I'm ready to pay"). *Áno* (AH-noh) or *Hej* (HEY) means "yes" and *Nie* (NYEH) means "no." A city map is a *mapa mésta* (MAH-pah MEH-stah).

Summers average 71°F; winters 34°F. The **emergency phone number** is 158. Everything closes on New Year's Day, Easter Sunday and Monday, Cyril and Method-ius Day (July 4), October 28, and Christmas (Dec. 25-26). If a holiday falls on a Sun-day, the next day becomes a holiday. The week between Christmas and New Year's is almost void of commerce and public transport.

Accommodations and Camping In Bratislava, **summertime hostels** open when university students leave; get info at CKM. **Juniorhotels (HI),** though uncom-mon, are a step above the usual brand of hostel. In the mountains, **chaty** (chalets) range from plush quarters for 400SK a night to a friendly bunk and outhouse for 70 SK. **Hotels** in the boonies provide comparable service to those in cities but are far cheaper. **Campgrounds** abound near the country's 5 national parks but are often open only in summer. A campground map is intermittently available at CKM offices.

Food and Drink Sausages and roasted game delight the Slovak palate, but fine wines and cheeses also form an indispensable part of the national diet. Look for *bryndza,* a soft ewe's milk cheese, served with bread or potatoes. *Syr* (cheese) is usually an option even if not on the menu. At a *bufet, samoobsluha,* or *občerstveni,* you can chow with the boys; a *kaviareň* or *viniareň* serves coffee, tea, and wine. All grocery stores close between Saturday noon and Monday morning. *Potraviny* (groceries) and *ovocie zelenina* (greengrocers) pop up on every other corner. Almost every major city has a vegetarian restaurant.

■■■ BRATISLAVA

The proud, new Bratislava-as-capital is reveling in its recaptured role as cultural cen-ter. The narrow streets of the old town are fluid and turbulent with reconstruction and renewal; outside the walls they open out into commercial avenues that hold the metropolis together. The city's highways and concrete towers defy the sleepy agricultural surroundings, but on peaceful Castle Hill, the traffic is distant and the urban roar quieter; the staid palace peers down sternly on the hubbub below.

ORIENTATION AND PRACTICAL INFORMATION

Bratislava lies on the banks of the Danube, a proverbial stone's throw from the Austrian and Hungarian borders. Trains and buses connect the city with Budapest and Vienna; hydrofoils also serve Vienna. Traveling by rail to Prague sometimes requires a change at Brno. Avoid debarking at the Nové Mesto train station, which is much farther from the center than Bratislava's *Hlavná stanica* (main station).

The Danube runs west-to-east across Bratislava. The old town, with its cluster of tourist offices and restaurants, sits just north of the river bank, bordered by the **Staromestská** highway to the west, **námestie SNP** to the north, **Stúrova** to the east, and **Hviezdoslavovo námestie** to the south. To reach the old town from the train station, take tram #13. Buy tickets (5SK) for the tram from the orange automat machines (near major tram stops). The green-and-orange *mapa mésta* (34SK) shows Bratislava's tram routes and tourist destinations in 5 languages.

Tourist Offices: BIS (Bratislava Information Service), Pańska 18 (tel. 33 37 15 or 33 43 25). Books rooms at Bernolak hostel and provides info in English on current cultural events. Open Mon.-Fri. 8am-6pm, Sat. 8am-1pm; Oct.-May Mon.-Fri. 8am-4:30pm, Sat. 8am-1pm. **Slovakoturist,** Pańska 13 (tel. 33 57 22). Good source of info about the rest of Slovakia, but little on Bratislava. Open Mon.-Fri. 9am-6pm, Sat. 8am-noon.

Consulates: US, Hviezdoslavovo nám. 4 (tel. 33 33 38). **Czech Republic,** Panenská 33. **Austria,** Holubyho 11 (tel. 31 11 03). **Hungary,** Palisády 54 (tel. 33 56 01). **Poland,** Hummelova 4 (tel. 31 52 22).

Currency Exchange: Čedok and **VÚB** (Vseobecna úverová Bank) take traveler's checks; for cash, private exchange offices have better rates.

Post Office: At nám. SNP 35. **Poste Restante** counter #5. Open Mon.-Fri. 7am-9pm, Sat. 7am-5pm, Sun. 9am-1pm. **Postal Code:** Bratislava 1, 810 00.

Telephones: Kolárska 12. Open 24hrs. **City Code:** 07.

Trains: Tel. 469 45. **ČSD Hlavná stanica** is at the northern end of town off Šancová. To: Prague (6/day, 6hr.), Budapest (3/day, 3hr.), and Vienna (5/day, 1hr.). International tickets at counter #8 or 9.

Buses: ČSAD Autobusová stanica, at Mlynské nivy (tel. 632 13 or 21 22 22). Take bus #215 or 220 to the town center, and bus #210 to the train station. To: Prague (9/day, 4hr., 124SK), Budapest (2/day, 4¾hr., 140SK), and Vienna (6/day, 1¾hr., 224SK). Check Vienna ticket for bus number *(č. aut.),* since a whole fleet leaves simultaneously at departure time.

Hydrofoils: BDT, Fajnorovo nábrezie 2, on the river bank next to the Slovak National Museum. To Vienna (2/day, 1¼hr., 330SK). Open Mon.-Fri. 6am-6pm, Sat.-Sun. 6-8am and 4-6pm.

Hitchhiking: Those hitching to Vienna cross the SNP bridge and walk down Viedenská cesta. The same road takes them to Hungary via Győr, though fewer cars head in that direction. Those headed to Prague take bus #104 from the center up Pražská to the Patronka stop.

Pharmacy: Look for *Lekáršen,* Špitálska 3 (tel. 51 01 14). Open 24hrs.

Emergencies: Ambulance: tel. 155. **Fire:** tel. 150. **Police:** tel. 158. Station at Mestskásprava VB, Špitálska 14 (tel. 593 41 or 531 71).

ACCOMMODATIONS AND CAMPING

Bratislava is hopping with student accommodations, largely due to the Vienna-bound crowds in the summer. **CKM,** Hviezdoslavovo nám. 16 (tel. 33 16 07; open Mon.-Fri. 9am-noon and 1-4:30pm), can lead you to inexpensive summer dorms, with directions to boot. Čedok can arrange private rooms 20 minutes by bus or tram from the center (150-450SK/person).

Youth Hostel Bernolak (studenský domov Jura Hronca), Bernolákova 1 (tel. 4977 21). Take trolleybus #210 to Račianske mýto and take the street just right of the monument. High-rise student dorm 15 min. from the old town. Singles 525SK. Doubles 195SK, with ISIC 170SK. Triples 175SK, with ISIC 155SK. Open July-Aug.

Mladá Garda, Račianska 103 (tel. 25 31 36). Small friendly rooms in the suburbs. Take tram #3 to the Mladá Garda stop. 90SK/person. Open July 10-Aug. 30.

YMCA na Slovensku, Karpatska 2 (tel. 49 80 05). 2 blocks down Šancová from the train station in an old, terraced dwelling; cinema on 1st floor. Reception open 8am-11pm. Doubles, triples, and quints 200SK/person. Open mid-July to mid-Aug.

Ustav vzdelávania ve stavebnictve, Bárdosova 33 (tel. 37 20 60). Ride tram #44 for 2 stops from train station to Bárdošova; hike up to the 3-story white and glass building with the name on top. This academic residence moonlights as a hotel, providing cheap, comfortable beds in the suburbs. Uphill climb and it may be full; call first. Doubles with bath 340SK. Triples 510SK.

Juniorhotel Sputnik CKM (HI), ul. Drienová 14 (tel. 29 41 67 or 23 43 40). Take bus #22 to 7th stop or tram #8 from train station to the 8th or 9th stop and look for a small lake on your left: across it lies the hotel. Deluxe student lodging. Disco, café, and restaurant. Members and ISIC holders 400SK/person. Nonmembers: singles 950SK; doubles 1450SK. Reservations recommended. English spoken.

Motel Zlaté Piesky, ul. Vajnorská (tel. 633 06), in suburban Trnávka. Take tram #2 or 4 to last stop or bus #110 from Trnavské mýto to last stop. Campground and bungalows down by the lakeside, way out of town. Camping 127SK/person. 4-person bungalow 507SK.

FOOD

Bratislavans grow up on grilled meats and superb Slovak wine. *Denný* bars, offering an array of salads, sandwiches, and other ready-to-eat foods, are everywhere. For groceries, go to the huge **Prior** department store downtown at Kamenné nám.

Stará Sladovňa, Cintorínska 32. 15 min. northeast of the old town. Men carouse nightly in this boisterous beer hall. Budvar 13SK/½L. Open daily 10am-11pm.

Arkadia, Beblavého 3 (tel. 33 56 50), next to the castle gate. Top-drawer elegance on the top of Castle Hill. Succulent dishes 100-450SK. Open daily noon-11pm.

Astor Reštauracie (tel. 21 43 12), across from the YMCA, at the corner of Žilinská and Šankova. Pleasant, inexpensive eatery near the train station attracts the local dinner crowd. Entrees 21-100SK. Mongo Astor special for 2, 1415SK. Open Mon.-Fri. 11am-11pm, Sat.-Sun. noon-11pm.

Vegetariánska Jedáleň, Laurinska 6. Cafeteria-style vegetarian chow. Open Mon.-Fri. 11am-8pm.

SIGHTS AND ENTERTAINMENT

The imperial residences of the **Bratislavský hrad** (Bratislava Castle) burned during the Napoleonic Wars and were resurrected only after WWII. The castle now houses the Slovak National Assembly and the principal branch of the **Mestské Múzeum** (City Museum). For a crash course in 20th-century Slovak history, art, and culture, visit the 3rd floor. (Open Tues.-Fri. 9am-5pm, Sat.-Sun. 10am-6pm. 40SK, with ISIC 12SK.) From Castle Hill, **ul. Zámocká** leads across the highway to the **Staré Mésto** (Old Town) and **St. Martin's Cathedral,** the early Gothic coronation site of Hungarian monarchs. The **Mirbach Palace,** Františkánske nám. 11, houses the Municipal Art Gallery, with temporary exhibits of modern Slovak paintings and a beautiful series of 17th-century English tapestries. Take time to listen to the recorded description of the tapestries' mysterious appearance in Bratislava. (Open Tues.-Sun. 9am-5pm. 5SK, students 2SK.) The best-preserved section of the town wall is the **Michalská veža,** a baroque tower metalled with weapons. The **Franciscan Church,** at Františkánske nám. 1, is an impossibly harmonious hybrid of Gothic, Renaissance, and baroque styles.

For concert and theater schedules, pick up a copy of *Kám* (6SK) at BIS. Although not in English, the information is easy enough to decipher. The **Slovak Philharmonic** plays regularly on ul. Palackého; buy tickets at the Reduta office behind the concert hall up to 1 hour before performances. **National Theatre** tickets are also sold here; the theatre is on Komenskeho nam. Also look for performances by the internationally-known **Bohdan Warchal Quartet,** based in Bratislava in summer.

■■■ BANSKÁ BYSTRICA

Every Slovak town has a nam. SNP—it refers to the Slovak National Uprising, a massive 1944 rebellion against the Nazis. Banska Bystricá is where it all happened. Looming over the edge of the old town like a spaceship, the bowl-shaped **Monument of the Slovak National Uprising** houses a **museum** commemorating the events. (Open Tues.-Sun. 8am-6pm. 8SK, students 4SK.) Here in the heart of picturesque Central Slovakia, even the war did little to detract from the Renaissance ambiance of the old town square, **nám. SNP,** one block from the monument up Kapitulska. The steeples of the **Church of the Virgin Mary** and the **barbican watch tower** dominate the northeast corner of the square. At nám. SNP 4, the **Museum of Central Slovakia,** housed in a former burgher's palace, provides a historical overview of the region. (Open Mon.-Fri. 8:30am-noon and 1-5pm, Sun. 9am-noon and 1-5pm. 8SK, students 5SK.)

To get to the town center from either the bus or train station, head toward the towering Hotel Lux. From there, you'll see the SNP monument and the old town spires beyond. **Čedok** has offices at nám. Slobody 4 (tel. (088) 425 75 or 425 76; open Mon.-Fri. 9am-6pm, Sat. 9am-2pm). The **CKM Juniorhotel (HI),** Národna 12 (tel. (088) 233 67 or 255 93), has bargain rooms of civilized quality, and a CKM office in the lobby. (Office tel. (088) 258 46. Open Mon.-Fri. 9am-4:30pm. Singles 180SK, doubles 290SK. With ISIC or HI membership, all beds 120SK/person.) Around the corner, the **Hotel Urpín,** J. Cikkera 7 (tel. (088) 245 56), soothes the rankled tourist. (Singles with bath 420SK. Doubles with bath 600SK.)

The **Slovenská Reštauracia** on nám. SNP has a friendly staff to go with the friendly prices. (Open Sun.-Fri. 11am-10pm. Entrees 18-64SK.) Down the street at Horná ul. 39, the **Vegetarianská Reštauracia ALFA BIO** is warm and elegant. (Entrees 18.50-39.60SK; fish dishes more expensive. Open Mon.-Sat. 11am-11pm.) Next to the monument, **Bašta** restaurant is open daily 11am to midnight.

Buses provide more frequent and direct connections than trains. Several make the trip per day to Bratislava (3¼hr, 122SK), Košice (4½hr., 90SK), Žilina (2hr., 52SK), Zvolen (19/day, 12SK), and Bojnice (6/day, 17SK). One 8-hour overnight bus departs each evening at 10:15pm for Prague (254SK). If you're headed for the High Tatras, 4 early-morning buses depart for Tatranská Lomnica (50SK) before 10am; afternoon travelers should take the bus to Poprad (3hr., 44SK). Daytrips to **Zvolen Castle,** only a few km south of Banská Bystrica, as well as **Bojnice Chateau** to the east, take less than half an hour by bus.

■■■ SLOVENSKÝ RAJ

On the other side of the Low Tatras, less than 1½ hours by bus from Poprad, the **Slovenský Raj National Park** begins. A paradise of stately pines and untamed wilds, the park also contains several breathtaking caves. The **Dobšinská Jadova Jaskyňa** (Dobšiná Ice Caves) are the most accessible. From the Dobšinská bus stop, head uphill along the blue and yellow path for 20 minutes. (At top, obligatory 20min. tours leave on the hour 9am-4pm, May 9-Oct. 15. The caves are inaccessible during winter. Min. 20 people/tour. 36SK, students 12SK. Prices double for tour in English.) The more extensive caves at **Ochtina** are easier to reach from Rožnava, the end of the bus line from Poprad.

A large map of local chalets is posted at the entrance to the park. **Chata Ruffíni** (tel. (0942) 981 77) provides first-rate rooms. (Singles with bath 220SK. Doubles with bath 400SK.) Take the dirt road to the right of the post office. The **restaurant** at Hotel Ľudova is reasonably-priced. (Entrees 24-57SK. Open daily 7:30am-8:30pm.)

From Poprad, **buses** head for Dobšina (6/day, 20SK). One bus daily from Banská Bystrica also reaches the site (3hr., 64SK), and a line from Košice is imminent. Service to Rožnava (10/day, 30min.) makes the other parts of the park accessible.

■■■ THE HIGH TATRAS (VYSOKÉ TATRY)

Mountains throw their powerful shadows over much of Slovakia's frontier. Rearing over the **Nízké Tatry** (Low Tatras) to the south, the **Malá Fatra** (Little Fatra) to the west, and the Tatras Mountains across the Hungarian border is the **Vysoké Tatry** (High Tatras) range. A scant 26km long, it is the most compact high mountain range in the world. The dizzying ridges conceal 150 glacial lakes *(pleso);* the forests harbor deer, bear, and edelweiss. Two indispensable maps are *Vysoké Tatry 21* (17SK) for hiking trails, and *Tatranské Strediská* (Centers of the High Tatras, 13SK) for roads.

Poprad-Tatry is the springboard for the main rail system to the High Tatras. The city is a frequent stop for **trains** running from Košice to Prague (3/day, 8hr., 112SK) or Bratislava (10/day, 5hr., 112SK). The same trains also stop in Žilina, 2 hours west of Poprad. Poprad itself is an unattractive city, but 10 paces from the train station door, **Hotel Europa** charges only 150SK for singles and 220SK for doubles.

From the train station's upper-level platform, the narrow-gauge Tatras Electric Railway (TEŽ) train runs to **Starý Smokovec,** the administrative and transportation center of the Tatras (2/hr. 6am-5:30pm, 1/hr. 2-6am and 5:30-10:30pm; ½hr.; 7SK). The bright red trains also connect Starý Smokovec with woodsier **Tatranská Lomnica** (10min., 4SK) and the swankier ski resort of **Štrbské Pleso** (50min., 7SK) every half hour (5am-10:30pm). Regular trains *(motorové)* also run directly to Tatranská Lomnica via Studeny Potok (15min., 6SK) and depart from platforms on the ground level every hour. If traveling directly from Poprad-Tatry, buy a through ticket even if you change at Starý Smokovec. Save coins to use the automat machines when ticket windows close.

■ Starý Smokovec

A thriving Tatras settlement for 200 years, Starý Smokovec is a tourist hub for every season. A prodigious funicular (2/hr., 6am-7:45pm, 10SK) leads up to the ski resort **Hrebienok** (1285m). An easy 20-minute hike from Hrebienok leads to the foaming *Studenovodské vodopada* (waterfall). Continue downhill along the blue trail through towering pines to Tatranská Lomnica (1½hr.), or face the challenge of the 6km **Veľka Studená dolina,** (aptly named "Big Cold Valley"), leading to the **Zbojnicka Chatka** (3hr.) in the opposite direction. (Beds 120SK/person). The green trail passes through **Malá Studená dolina** (Little Cold Valley) and rises in steep terraces to Téryho Chalet (3hr.).

Back in town just above the train station, **Čedok** (tel. (0969) 24 97 or 29 50) provides hiking information, books beds in **Popradské Pleso** and **Sliezsky Dom** (345SK). English spoken. (Open Mon.-Fri. 8am-4pm, Sat. 8am-noon.) The other 4 mountain huts are handled by **Slovakoturist** (tel. (0969) 20 31 or 28 27), 1 stop beyond Starý Smokovec on the train to Tatranská Lomnica. The cheapest accommodations reside at the **CKM Juniorhotel Vysoké Tatry (HI)** in Horný Smokovec (tel. (0969) 26 61), 2 stops on the way to Tatranská Lomnica (ISIC and HI cardholders 130SK, non-members 200SK). **Hotel Bystrina** (tel. (0969) 26 18) is on the road behind Grand Hotel, about 200m towards Nový Smokovec. (Doubles 950SK, breakfast included.) The nearest **campground** is Tatracamp, 3km away down the road or rail line to Poprad, but it is open only mid-July to mid-August. (95SK).

Next to Čedok, a grocery store, department store (open Mon.-Fri. 7:30am-6pm, Sat. 7:30am-noon), and a **stand-up bistro** (open Mon.-Fri. 7:30am-6pm, Sat. 7:30am-1pm) all form part of the same complex, making it possible to buy groceries, hiking equipment, and pancakes within a few minutes.

■ Tatranská Lomnica

High above Tatranská Lomnica, a monster ski-lift runs like a prickly spine up **Lomnický Štít** (2632m). From the train station, follow the signs for 15 minutes to "Kabinova lanovka." (Wed.-Mon. 7am-8pm. 30SK.) Arrive early to make sure you get a place. At Skalnaté Pleso, perambulate around pondlike **Glacia Lake,** or continue on the chairlift to Lomnický Sedla for a jaw-dropping view of the Tatra range. (Open Tues.-Sun. 8am-5:30pm. 20SK round-trip). A gutsier option is to take the impossibly vertical cabin lift to the top of the rocky peak. (Open Tues.-Sun. 7:30am-5:30pm. 50SK round-trip). Hikers can follow the red (Magistrála) or blue trail across the mountains. In town, the **Tatras National Park Museum** has exhibits on the natural history and human settlements of the area. (Open Mon.-Fri. 8:30am-noon and 1-5pm, Sat.-Sun. 8am-noon. 6SK.) **Mountain bike rental** is available at Milič Blahout, across from the Hotel Slovakia on the main road. (Full day 180SK.)

Hotel Lomnica (tel. (0969) 96 72 51), across the tracks from the train station to the right, offers spacious rooms for reasonable prices. (Doubles 900SK, with bath 1200SK. Triples 1200SK, with bath 1400SK.) Campers flock to the humongous **Eurocamp FICC** (tel. (0969) 96 77 41). They charge 70SK per person and per tent for their extensive facilities; 4-person bungalows are 1350SK. Take any *motorové* train to the Eurocamp stop (6SK); during July and August, you can catch a bus at the parking lot next to Hotel Lomnica (every ½-hr.). The cheaper but less fancy **Tatranec** (tel. (0969) 96 77 04) is one bus stop earlier. (40SK/person, 45SK/tent. 6-person bungalow 677SK. Open June-Sept.)

Across from the train station, **Slovenská Restauracia** serves Slovak specialties. (Entrees 20-61SK. Open daily noon-8pm.) Next door, **Piccolo Pizza** has developed a small American cult following for its personal-size pizzas. (30-56SK. Open daily 10am-8pm.) The **grocery store** behind the station stocks victuals for the trail. (Open Mon.-Fri. 7:45am-5:30pm, Sat. 8am-noon.)

To cross into Poland from the High Tatras, either wait until Wednesday for the 1:10pm bus to Zakopane (1½hr.) and Kraków (3½hr.), or else take a bus from either Starý Smokovec or Tatranská Lomnica north to Łysa Polana (15/day, 16SK). The bus will drop you off in a parking lot right before the **border crossing.** Walk across the bridge to have your passport stamped, then wait at the bus stop on the main road for either a private "mini-bus" (30min.), which will try to charge you blind, or a PKS bus (every other hour, more frequent June-Sept.; 13,000zł, baggage 2000zł) to Zakopane, Poland. You won't mind the shuffle when you see the gorgeous mountain scenery along the way.

■ Malá Fatra

Smaller peaks and smaller crowds await to the west of the High Tatras in the Malá Fatra, where queer rock formations and jagged slopes are softened by pine forests and bubbling springs, and the Vrátna Valley is marked by stark stone. Drab but convenient **Žilina** is the starting point for a day on the trails; the town is 112SK away by train from Košice or Bratislava. Buses to the Vrátna Valley leave from platform #10 in the bus station. Blue trails (easy) leave from most bus stops along the park road; red (medium) and black (difficult) trails from the dark Chata Vrátna chalet (the last bus stop). Wander up to the Chleb peak (1647m) and Ošiepková Mulda skiing area. **Chairlifts** head for Grúň Peak (989m; 8:30am-7pm, 16SK round-trip) from an earlier park bus stop, and for Chleb Peak (8:30am-6pm, 50SK round-trip, min. 20 people) from Chata Vrátna. Rangers at the **Mountain Rescue Service** near the Grúň Peak lift struggle valiantly to explain hiking options in English (tel. (089) 952 32; open daily

7am-7:30pm). Pick up the *Malá Fatra Vrátna 12* trail map and *Vrátna-Martinské hole* ski map here, at Chata Vrátna, or in metropolitan bookstores.

Back in Žilina, **CKM** (tel. (089) 235 18) is in the right hand corner of Mariánske námestie, the newly-renovated town square. (Open Mon.-Fri. 9am-noon, 12:30pm-4pm.) To get there from the train station, stroll along ul. Národná for 15 minutes. For accommodations, the **Hotel Metropol** (tel. (089) 239 00) is efficient and sufficient (singles, doubles, and triples 200SK/person; showers 15SK), and back-to-back with the bus station. The **Hotel Boboly** in the park charges more. (Singles 360SK. Doubles 520SK.) **Campsites** abound; there's one near every bus stop. Prices range from 25SK to 65SK per person. The **Chata Vrátna** chalet may be full; if it's not, expect to dole out 400SK per bed. The **Hotel Polom restaurant** is open late for midnight ramblers. (Entrees 27-138SK. Open daily 7am-2am.) Next door to CKM, the **Vegetariánska Reštaurácia** caters to the hip and healthy. (Open Mon.-Fri. 9am-11pm, Sat.-Sun. 10am-11pm.) Have some tofu with those potatoes (26.90SK).

■■■ KOŠICE

Capital of the country's easternmost province (East Slovakia), Košice boasts an old town studded with 460 historic buildings. It became a free royal city in 1347 and peaked in the 15th century as the third-largest town in what was then Hungary; a gypsy flavor lingers today.

Hlavná is the main thoroughfare; the train and bus stations are a block east through the park. At the base of Hlavná, the **Cathedral of St. Elizabeth** faces off against the **National Theater.** (Crypt open Tues.-Sat. 9am-5pm, Sun. 9am-1pm.) These grandiose edifices dwarf the ancient **tower** between them, which now contains the **metallurgical museum** (10SK, students 5SK), but if you can find your way through the jumble of cast-iron bells, pewter doorknockers, and gold candlesticks, the top floor reveals a stunning view of the old town and the distant, sinister suburbs. At the north end of Hlavná, the **East Slovak Museum** devotes itself to archeology, prehistory, and precious gold coins. (Museums open Tues.-Sat. 9am-5pm, Sun. 9am-1pm. 20SK, students 10SK.)

On the south end of Hlavná, snuggling up to the 4-star Slovan Hotel, **Čedok** (tel. (095) 231 21) speaks English and changes money fluently. (Open Mon.-Fri. 8:30am-4:30pm, Sat. 9am-noon.) **Hotel Coral**, Kasárenské nam. 5 (tel. (095) 260 95 or 268 49), behind the Prior department store, is clean and modern. (Singles 330SK. Doubles with bath 450SK.) **Hotel Europa** (tel. (095) 238 97), on your left as you exit the park, charges a bit more but the facility is worth it. (Singles 420SK, doubles 720SK.) The formerly rickety **Clubhotel**, Nerudova 2 (tel. (095) 276 78), near the *Zimný Štadion* stop, is currently undergoing renovations, and will probably be considerably less rickety by next year. For **Auto Camping Salaš Barca** (tel. (095) 583 09), take a tram south from the Slovan Hotel to the overpass and walk west 500m. (Open April-Sept. 65SK/person.)

Try the delicious soy entrees and "vitamin bomb" salads (40SK) at **Ajvega**, ul. Orlia 10, left off Mylynská from the rain station. (Open daily 10am-11pm.) The **Hotel Sloven Restaurant** is more sedate, with a multilingual menu and attractive entrees. (21-153SK. Open daily noon-10pm.) At night, **Restaurácia Solo** caters to Košice youth at Hlavná 76. (Open noon-11pm daily.) The **open-air market** unfolds 1 block west of the cathedral (Mon.-Fri. 9am-5pm).

Košice is Eastern Europe's sleeper **train** hub, along most routes from Poland to Bulgaria and Romania and near the halfway point of the 13-hour Kraków-Budapest slog. Other connections to Budapest require a change at Miskolc. Two trains per day from Prague cross the Ukrainian border to L'viv (8hr.) and Kyyiv (17hr.) in Ukraine, and ultimately Moscow. Service rolls to Prague (6/day, 9hr., 215SK), Bratislava (7/day, 6hr., 186SK), Poprad-Tatry (1½hr., 64SK), and Žilina (2½hr., 112SK).

Ukraine (Україна)

US$1	= 16,000KRB (Kupony, or coupons)	10,000KRB =	US$0.62
CDN$1	= 12,200KRB	10,000KRB =	CDN$0.82
UK£1	= 24,800KRB	10,000KRB =	UK£0.40
IR£1	= 23,200KRB	10,000KRB =	IR£0.43
AUS$1	= 10,400KRB	10,000KRB =	AUS$0.96
NZ$1	= 8850KRB	10,000KRB =	NZ$1.13
SAR1	= 3330KRB	10,000KRB =	SAR3.00

Country Code: 7   **International Dialing Prefix: 810**

In September 1993, the Ukrainian currency situation was extremely confusing. *Kupony* (money coupons) were the main form of currency and were exchanged at the rate of 9000 coupons per US$. Last year *kupony* were exchanged at the rate of 230 per US$. Ukraine was researched in July 1993; expect inflation to severely alter prices by 1994.

Despite Russian influence, Ukraine has held fast to a distinct political and literary tradition for hundreds of years. The fruit of the republic's farms, factories, and mines was shipped to Moscow during the Soviet era, and was a primary reason why Ukraine was considered the "breadbasket" of the Soviet republics, but on December 1, 1991, an overwhelming 90% of Ukraine's citizens voted for complete independence. Ukrainian currency and visas have since appeared, and, ironically, a postwar power play by Stalin (trying to get more votes for the USSR) means that Ukraine already has a seat at the United Nations.

Ukrainian nationalism resurfaced in the 19th century under the banner of the poet Taras Shevchenko, who led a campaign to revitalize the Ukrainian language and safeguard it from Polish and Russian cultural imperialism. In this century, the movement drew strength from Soviet acts of mistreatment such as Stalin's forced famine of 1931 (which claimed 7 million lives), the long-standing ban on the teaching of Ukrainian in Soviet schools, and the Chernobyl disaster of 1986. Russian is spoken reluctantly, yet skillfully, by eastern Ukrainians (those living in "left-bank Ukraine," the area east of the Dnieper (Дніпро) River); Western Ukraine, never Russified to the extent of its eastern neighbor, claims Polish as its second language and has now taken up the struggle to preserve and reassert Ukrainian nationality.

With patience and a positive attitude, the traveler to Ukraine will be rewarded with an experience that offers a glimpse not only at beautiful landscapes and the rich cultural heritage of this land, but also of the extraordinary process that is now redefining life in Ukraine. With democratization and the free market finally starting to appear, the changes taking place reflect nothing less than history in the making.

GETTING THERE

As of September 1993, visas are needed to visit or pass through Ukraine. Regular visa processing from an embassy abroad takes up to two weeks and costs US$30. (Priority processing—less than 7 days—is US$60, while express—same day service—costs US$100.) The Ukrainian Embassy in the U.S. is located at 3350 M. Street, NW Washington, DC 2007 (tel. (202) 333-0606). Getting a visa for Ukraine requires a letter of invitation from a Ukrainian citizen or organization, or a tourist voucher from a travel agency. If you find yourself in Europe with no invitation and do have the sudden urge to visit Ukraine, see what the nearest Ukrainian embassy will do about your visa situation. If you are determined and have the time to spare then head to the border, where they may simply let you in or issue you a 24-hr. travel pass to go directly to Kyyiv and petition for a visa. Remember that once you leave the country for any reason your Ukrainian visa becomes invalid. Even if you do have the proper visa, it's a wise idea to bring along photocopies of your invitation or travel vouchers as mementos for doubtful border guards.

Home & Hostel (tel. 1-800-SOVIET-U in the U.S.) can be very helpful in providing information on how to obtain a visa officially and finding out more about travel to Ukraine; it may be much more expensive than doing it yourself, but can save time and provide peace of mind for someone planning a trip. Another option is **Kobasniuk Travel, Inc.,** 157 Second Ave., New York, NY 10003 (tel. (212) 254-8779; fax (212) 454-4005), which handles all aspects of travel to Ukraine.

A round-trip flight is by far the best option to reach Ukraine. **Air Ukraine** offers a round-trip ticket from New York to Kyyiv (Kiev) for US$700. **Trains** and **buses** from countries bordering Ukraine are cheaper and a much more flexible option but are usually very crowded. (Trains from Bucharest, Romania to Kyyiv or Odessa via Kishinev, Moldova every Fri. and Sat. at 10:30pm, 17hr., US$40. Buses from Warsaw, Poland to L'viv, 10hr., US$6; from Varna to Odessa, 24hr., US$28.) Expect at least 3 hours at the border for customs. **Boat service** from coastal cities in Turkey, Bulgaria, and Romania exists in principle but was in such a state of flux during the summer of 1993 that it is impossible to provide accurate information concerning schedules and prices. Ask at travel offices or the office of the harbor master in the city from which you plan to depart. A regular ferry, however, does operate from the Romanian city of Tulcea to the Ukrainian port of Izmail (Tues. and Sat. 8am, US$6, 2hr.).

TRAVELING IN UKRAINE

Domestic **train** routes reach into every corner of Ukraine and remain inexpensive. Tickets are divided into 4 categories depending on the type of compartment: Спальный, Купейный, Плацкарт, or Общий. Спальный Вагон is a compartment with separate beds and seating for 2. This is the top of the line for train accommodations but women traveling alone may wish to avoid the uncomfortable position of sharing a room with a stranger. More crowded but just as bearable is the Купейный Вагон with 4 couchettes. Clean sheets and hot tea are usually available on overnight trains for less than US$1. Unless you have a penchant for the noise, smells, and stares of the locals avoid the other types of compartment. **Buses** follow many of the same routes as trains and for shorter trips they can be quicker. Buying tickets in advance should assure you of a seat, but it's also possible to buy a standing-room spot directly from the driver. Some buses may also have a minimal charge for baggage. Air Ukraine has **flights** to most major cities in Ukraine, but you must pay in hard currency, usually US$. Don't rely too heavily on their schedules; fuel shortages or enough unsold seats will frequently cancel a flight.

Public transportation in the larger cities consists of **trams, trolleybuses, buses,** and, in Kyyiv only, a fairly efficient **metro system.** Expect a maddening crunch at rush hours and don't be afraid to push your way on board. You can purchase tickets from the kiosks near each stop or, in some cases, directly from the driver. Monthly passes allow unlimited access to all forms of public transportation (under US$1). The meter rate for **state taxis** in the summer of 1993 was 1000 coupons per km, but many drivers prefer to negotiate the fare. **Private transport** and taxis alike can be hailed by holding your hand at a downward salute. Try to stick to state taxis at night, which you can spot by their checkered sign or from the model of the car, Volga sedans.

UKRAINE ESSENTIALS

The breakup of the Soviet Union also brought about the demise of the official state travel agency, **Intourist,** which was responsible for foreigners traveling to Ukraine. **Private tourist offices** are just now starting to make an appearance, and can be useful places to get maps or hard-to-find train tickets. These offices are more used to dealing with groups than with individual travelers, so be sure to smile a lot, speak slowly, and be persistent. Phrases like, "It is too difficult to do" or "There are no more available" are generally signals for you to offer something a little extra (never call it a bribe) to speed things along. Making friends in any travel office can work wonders for your travels throughout Ukraine.

The colorful *karbovinets* is the official Ukrainian **currency;** they are colloquially known as *kupony* (coupons). The U.S. dollar functions almost as a second form of currency, and is often preferred to the unstable coupon which was losing its value rapidly due to hyperinflation in the summer of 1993. Make sure that any foreign currency you bring with you is not torn or too worn out; changers will refuse bills if they are in bad condition. The easiest places to exchange money and sometimes travelers checks (for a 2.5% commission) is in the lobbies of the more expensive hotels that cater to a Western clientele. Go early in the morning (they sometimes run out of money) and bring your passport. Although the **black market** is technically illegal, a brisk trade of dollars for coupons exists. The exchange rate jumped so significantly over a period of days during the summer of 1993 that it was worth changing only small amounts on a daily basis to take advantage of such currency fluctuations.

The loosening of state control and the worsening economic situation in Ukraine has led to an increase in crime. Foreigners can be an appealing target; be discreet with your valuables and never expose large sums of cash, particularly just after changing money. Try not to walk alone after dark, and steer clear of unlit parks and side streets. If you need a ride at night take a state taxi and choose your driver carefully. Women travelers should simply ignore unwanted advances from amorous

Ukrainian men and seek out the assistance of the militia (Милиция) if the annoyance persists. If need be, turn to an older woman for help in an uncomfortable situation; her stern rebukes will usually be enough to embarrass the most persistent jerks.

It's a wise idea to register with your embassy once you arrive in Ukraine. Besides making the process of recovering lost passports much quicker, the embassy staff may be able to offer important information on travel or the situation in Ukraine.

Communication Due to a recent joint-venture established between the Ukrainian government and a Western telecommunications firm, the price of international **phone** calls from Ukraine has skyrocketed. A call to the U.S. averages US$2.50 per minute, and at least 3 minutes are required to order a call. Collect calls and calling cards were both impossible in the summer of 1993. **Mail** is much cheaper and will usually reach a destination outside Ukraine (with luck) after at least 2 weeks.

Your trip to Ukraine will go much more smoothly if you already know a few words in Russian or take the time to learn a few key phrases in Ukrainian. English-speakers are rare and most likely to be found among Ukrainian students who generally speak a second language. Pick up a Ukranian phrase book before setting out and try to memorize the following phrases: Добрый день (Doh-bree-DYEHN; "Good day"), До Побачення (Doh-poh-BAH-chen-ya; "Good-bye"), Прошу (PRO-shoo; "Please"), Добре (DOH-breh, "Good"), Перепрошую (Peh-reh-PRO-shoo-yoo; "Excuse me"), Коли (Koh-LEH; "When?"), Де (Deh; "Where?"), Скильки (SKIL-kee; "How much?"), Дякую (DYA-kou-yoo; "Thank you").

Accommodations, Camping, and Food The open road to capitalism and the influx of foreign businessmen have brought about a sharp rise in the cost of **hotels** in Ukraine, but you can still find decent lodgings for about US$12-18 for a double. More inexpensive and restful arrangements can be had in **campgrounds,** usually located just outside the city limits. Bring a tent or rough it in a bungalow for under US$10 a night. Vacant **dorm rooms** in the universities are another option, but finding out who is in charge or what permission is needed requires patience and solid language abilities. While it's likely that you may be offered a place to stay at a Ukrainian's home after meeting a local on a train or bus, there's no office or bureau in Ukraine as of yet which can arrange **private accommodations.** In the U.S., however, **Home & Hostel** (tel. 1-800-SOVIET-U), can set up homestays and reserve train tickets well in advance of your arrival. A homestay with a Ukrainian family in Kyyiv with breakfast included costs US$65.

You can eat well in Ukraine for a pittance. Sidewalk cafés and restaurants line the main thoroughfares, offering everything from desserts and cool drinks to traditional Ukrainian, Russian, or Georgian food. Ask for the tasty mushroom hors d'oeuvres, typically baked in sour cream, a serving of borsch, or the delicious potato or cheese-filled dumplings known as *vareniki. Shashlik,* a beef or lamb shish kabob, will make your mouth water. Be aware that the meat or fish appetizers (*zakuski*) are usually the most expensive and least filling items on the menu. Expect to pay US$2-5 per person for a full meal including alcohol.

■■■ KYYIV (КИЇВ)

Sometimes called the "Mother of all Rus," Kyyiv was a sizeable metropolis when Moscow was just a grove of pines and St. Petersburg a cluster of swampy islets. The capital of Kyyivan Rus, a kingdom that stretched from Lake Lagoda to just below Kyyiv, the city really took off after Prince Vladimir the Great proclaimed his kingdom's conversion to Christianity in 988 AD.

Today Kyyiv is rapidly becoming an international center of business, politics, and culture. The construction projects, new businesses, and closer connections with the rest of the world reflect Kyyiv as it moves into the next century; in the hills above downtown you can catch a glimpse of the city's much older character. Here, along shady, chestnut-lined avenues, the golden cupolas of ancient churches and monasteries reveal traditions of faith and culture that stretch back for centuries and still exert an influence on the life of the country and the broader Slavic world.

ORIENTATION AND PRACTICAL INFORMATION

Situated on the lush, steep banks of the Dnieper (Дніпро) River, Kyyiv is a busy port serving ships headed south to the Black Sea and north to Russia. The city itself is divided into 2 parts: upper Kyyiv clings to the hills, while lower Kyyiv skirts the riverbanks. **Khreshchatik** (Хрещатик), the city's main boulevard, is lined with theaters, shops, and cafés. Running parallel, **vulitsya Volodimirska** (вулиця Володимирська) hosts a variety of historical sights.

Tourist Office: No central tourist office in Kyyiv yet. On vul. Hospitalna 12, just behind the Respublikanski Stadion, the office of **Intourist Kyyiv** does little more than arrange domestic and international flights as well as train tickets (tel. flights: domestic 224 10 45, international 224 29 50; train tickets 224-2559). Expect to pay a commission on all tickets. Down the hill at no. 9 is the **Hotel Rus** (tel. 220 42 55 or 220 52 33), where you can pick up a detailed map of the city for US$1 or join one of their tours of the city for US$10. The **Balkantour Travel Company** (tel. 229 04 67) on vul. Lenina 10 or the **Tourist** (tel. 225 30 71) farther up at 26 offer similar services. Keep your eyes open for a free copy of the **Kyyiv Times,** an English-language newspaper which provides excellent coverage of both local and national events.

Embassies: U.S.: Ironically located in the old Communist Party headquarters at vul. Yuriya Kotsyubinskoho 10 (tel. 224 73 44 or 224 73 49). **Canada:** vul. Yaroslaviv val 31 (tel. 212 02 12). **U.K.:** vul. Desyatinna 9 (tel. 288 05 04). **Australians** should contact the British Embassy.

Currency Exchange: The more expensive hotels typically have the worst rates but can change most major currencies. The only place in Kyyiv that handles traveler's checks is **Hotel Intourist** on vul. Hospitalna 12, which cashes them into either US$ or Ukrainian coupons for a 2.5% commission. (Open Mon.-Fri. 8am-12pm and 1-7:30pm, Sat.-Sun. 8am-5pm.) A better rate can be found by checking out the numerous orange **kiosks** marked Обмін Валют which appear on almost every other street corner. In front of the **department store,** Универмаг, on Plosha Peremohi, people wait to buy or sell dollars. Теочнишаллы, what they are doing is illegal, but not much appears to be done by the government to stop it. If you have second thoughts, the lobby of the department store has an orange exchange kiosk.

Post Office and Telephones: Khreshchatik 24. Open daily 8am-10pm. Telephones and fax. Look for the large Поштамт sign partially covered by ivy. Telephones open daily 8am-10pm; post office open Mon.-Fri. 8am-9pm, Sat. 9am-7pm. **City Code:** 044.

Trains: Kyyiv-Passazhirski (Київ-Пассажирський), Vokzalna pl., at the end of vul. Komiterny from bul. Taras Shevchenka. M: Vokzalna (Вокзальна). **Train tickets** can be purchased at the **Central Ticket Office** (tel. 223 11 10) on vul. Tarasa Shevchenka. M: Universitet (Университет), then head left out of the station and walk down a few blocks. The 3-story building will be across the street on your right. Train schedules available; for planes, buses, and boats they're notoriously unreliable. Window #39 on the 2nd floor sells tickets to foreigners. Bring your passport and be prepared to wait. (Open Mon.-Fri. 8am-1pm and 2-6pm, Sat.-Sun. 9am-1pm and 2-3pm.) Night trains to L'viv (US$4) and to Odessa (US$5). Tourist agencies are more convenient but charge more than double the price. Find bargains among the **scalpers** who hang out around the entrance to the ticket office.

Public Transportation: Kyyiv's metro system (tickets 15 coupons) is clean and efficient; the central point is station Maidán Nezalezhnosti (Майдан Незалежності). *Perekhid* (перехід) indicates a walkway to another station, while *vikhid u micto* (вихід у місто) indicates an exit onto the street. Buy tickets for the extensive trolley and bus network from kiosks near each stop, or buy a pass for unlimited rides on all public transportation (under US$1), sold at the beginning of each month.

Taxis: To hail a cab, stand by the road and hold out your hand. Rides within the city should cost about 50 coupons/km; fares jump when the sun goes down. Private cars are usually cheaper than taxis.

Flights: Boryspil Airport (tel. 225 22 52) can be reached by the bus marked Полёт from Plosha Peremohi every 30min. **Air Ukraine** offices are at the Intourist Kyyiv and at Plosha Peremohi behind the circus. Both open Mon.-Sat. 8am-1pm and 2-8pm, Sun. 8am-1pm and 2-6pm. To: New York (US$1702), Moscow (US$116), L'viv (US$72), and Odessa (US$70). **Hungarian Airlines,** vul. Vladimirskaya 20 (tel. 229 36 61). Open Mon.-Fri. 10am-5pm. **LOT Polish Airlines,** Khreshchatik 14 (tel. 269 59 95). Open Mon.-Fri. 9am-5pm, Sat. 10am-2pm.

Pharmacy: In the lobby of the Hotel Intourist. Well-stocked with Western products. Hard currency only. Open Mon.-Fri. 9am-1pm and 2-6pm.

Emergencies: Medical: tel. 03 or your embassy. **Fire:** tel. 01. **Police:** tel. 02.

ACCOMMODATIONS

It's hard as hell to find affordable accommodations in Kyyiv; even the most undesirable hotels have sharply increased their prices to greet the growing numbers of foreign visitors. Still, there are a few options. About 10km outside the city in a quiet pine forest lies the **Motel Prolisok** (Мотел Проліcок; tel. 444 12 93) on prospect Peremohi 179, a motel and campground only a 30-minute commute by public transportation from the city center. (Doubles US$65 with telephone, television, and bath. Tents US$4. 6-bed bungalows with shower US$8/person.) Within the complex itself are a restaurant, exchange bureau, and even a sauna. Take the metro from Maydan Nezaezhnosti to the last stop, "Святошино." From there transfer to trolleybus #7 and get off at "Автостанция Дачна." Continue down the road for about 2km; the motel will be on your right. Within the city, try the **Hotel Libid** (Готель Лыбидь; tel. 274 00 63). The rooms are definitely not worth the US$53 but the hotel is centrally located at Plosha Peremohi, close to the train station and airport bus. (Take tram #2 from the train station to the first stop.)

FOOD

Kyyiv's streets, particularly in summer, reflect the bounty of Ukraine's harvest. Attraction number one is the fresh fruit-flavored **sherbet,** usually apricot or strawberry. Ask for *sto hram* (100g) if you want a medium-sized cone.

Café Winter Garden (Зимовий Сад) is a short trip from downtown (take tram #5 or trolleybus #80 to "Соломяновка пл."), but the delicious Beef Stroganoff and the pleasant location makes the commute well worth it. In the park across from the stop. Full meal US$4. Open daily noon-9pm.

Restaurant Spasheena (Спашина), vul. Spask (Спаськ) 8, is quiet and traditionally Ukrainian. Open Mon.-Fri. noon-5pm and 6-11pm, Sat.-Sun. 5-11pm.

Café Virmenia (Вирмения), Andriyivsky uzviz 11 (tel. 416 42 79), down from St. Andrew's Cathedral. Sit on the terrace to a mouth-watering grilled lamb *shashlik* loaded with vegetables and french fries. Full meal US$5/person.

Kureni (Курені), Parkova Aleya 19 (tel. 293 40 62), behind the Hotel Dnipro, just past the Dynamo stadium. In little clay and grass huts: unbeatable atmosphere but improvable food. Meals US$3. Open noon-5pm and 6-11pm.

Bistro Maxim (Бистро Максіть), vul Lenina 21 (tel. 224 70 21), just across from the opera house. Cordially crowded. US$2 gets you soup, salad, and dish of meat and potatoes. Open Mon.-Sat. 11am-4pm.

The hard currency supermarket **NIKA** on bul. Taras Shevchenko can satisfy almost any craving for Western food products. (Open Mon.-Sat. 10am-8pm, Sun. 10am-6pm.) Across the street, the **Bessarabian Rynok** (Бессарабський Ринок) has fresh fruits and veggies. (Open Tues.-Sun. 7am-7pm, Mon. 7am-5pm.) A slightly less expensive market is at the **Livoberezhna** (Ливобережна) metro stop; coming from the city center take a right off the platform and look for the entrance to the market behind the cafe. Note: Chernobyl-related radiation via ingested flora is not dangerous.

SIGHTS

You can sense Kyyiv's character by strolling down **Khreshchatik.** The street begins at Bessarabska pl., which also marks the start of bul. Taras Shevchenko. Continuing along Khreshchatik, you'll pass a number of fountains and stores, including Kyyiv's **Central Department Store** (ЦУМ), vul. Lenina 2. (Open Mon.-Sat. 9am-9pm.) Farther down, the façade of the Hotel Moskva commands **Maydan Nezalezhnosti** (Independence Square). By the square's circular central fountain, vendors hawk alternative newspapers, while circles form to discuss politics past and present. The end of Khreshchatik opens onto **Komsomolska pl.,** where the **Central Park of Culture and Rest** provides sweeping views of the Dnieper River from the area near the **Arch of Brotherhood** (a huge silver croquet wicket commemorating the union of Russia and Ukraine), jokingly referred to by locals as the "the yoke." Follow the uphill path to an outdoor theater, where Kyyiv's grandfathers while away the daytime hours playing chess. The park also boasts the **Monument to the Brave Soccer Players.** As the story goes, Nazi troops forced the team to play a "death match" against a German SS team. Stirred by local pride, Kyyiv's Dynamo played their hardest, won the match 3-0, and were promptly executed.

From Khreshchatik, **Vul. Engels** will take you uphill and away from the tourists and traffic into a quiet, older neighborhood. A walk up **bul. Taras Shevchenko** brings you to **Kyyiv State University,** where nearly 22,000 students attend class. (M: Universitet.) Further up bul. Taras Shevchenko at #20 stands the many-domed ochre **Vladimirska Cathedral,** built to commemorate the 900th anniversary of Christianity in Kyyiv. The spectacular interior blends Byzantine styles with art nouveau. At no. 12 stands the **Taras Shevchenko Museum,** one of the largest and most beautiful literary museums in the former Soviet Union. The museum is well-kept for good reason: Shevchenko, Ukraine's most beloved poet, was the 19th-century father of Ukraine's nationalist movement. Exhibits are labeled in Ukrainian and Russian, but an English-speaking guide is under US$1. (Open Tues.-Sun. 10am-5pm. Closed on last Fri. of the month. 100 coupons, students 20 coupons.)

A walk up **vulitsya Volodimirska** ushers you into Kyyiv's past. Up the hill from the opera house are the **Golden Gates** (Золоті Ворота), constructed in 1037. Recently restored, they now house a museum. (Open Fri.-Wed. 10am-6pm. 50 coupons, students 25 coupons.) The entrance to the **St. Sophia Monastery Complex** is at vul. Volodimirska 24, the cultural center of Kyyivan Rus and the site of the first library in Rus. Exquisite Byzantine icons from the 11th century make the building's interior worth a visit. (Museum open Fri.-Wed. 10am-5:30pm. 100 coupons, students 30 coupons; additional charge to photograph.) At the end of vul. Volodimirska stands another gorgeous church, **St. Andrew's Cathedral,** currently under repair. The surrounding grounds host a number of museums and monuments, including the **State Museum of the History of Kyyiv.** Take a stroll downhill on Andriyivsky uzviz away from St. Andrew's and into lower Kyyiv and the historic Podol district. Halfway down, at no. 13, is **Bulgakov's House.** (Open Tues.-Sun.) Kyyiv's alternative artistic and theatrical scene revolves around this street. Check out the small, independent galleries. To get back to upper Kyyiv, hop the scenic **funicular railway** (фунікулер). Constructed in 1905, it's the oldest of its kind in the former Soviet Union. Take the metro to "Poshtova pl." (Поштова пл.). (Open daily 6:30-11pm. 10 coupons; Sun. free.)

Two major points of interest lie outside the city's main district. The **Monument to Mother Ukraine** towers over the city skyline and houses a World War II museum in its base. Plans are underway to tear down this iron lady and replace her with a memorial to the victims of Chernobyl, so be sure to snap a photo while it still stands. Down the road on vul. Sichnevovo Povstanya is the fascinating **Pecherska Lavra monastery** (Печерска Лавра Софіївський собор), founded in 1051 and considered one of the holiest places in Ukraine and Russia. The museums established on the monastery grounds during the Soviet period are gradually being returned to the Orthodox Church. Although the expansive view from the bell tower is a highlight of the visit

(150 coupons), the most memorable part of the grounds are the **catacombs,** a series of caves where monks lived and were buried in the Middle Ages. Women must cover their heads when visiting the caves (no shorts or short skirts). To get to the grounds, take a cab or trolleybus #20 from the Днипро Hotel downtown to the last stop. (Open Wed.-Mon. 10am-5pm. To grounds 200 coupons, students 100 coupons; US$1 for cameras, US$5 for guide.)

Farther along the outskirts of Kyyiv is the moving World War II monument at **Babi Yar** (Бабий Яр). A large group of carved figures commemorates the place where victims of the Nazis were buried starting in September of 1941. Although the plaques state that 100,000 Kyyivans died during this time, newer estimates double that figure. Many of the victims, most of them Jews, were buried alive. Take trolleybus #27 eight stops from the Petrivka (Петрівка) metro stop or the #16 trolleybus from Maydan Nezalezhnosti. The monument stands in the park, near the TV tower.

To see where Kyyivans hang out during the hot summer days, take the metro to **Gidropark** (Гідропарк), where you'll find an amusement park and beach on an island in the Dnieper. Tucked in a corner near the bridge is the Venice Beach of Ukraine, where young Kyyivan men lift spare automobile parts to keep in shape.

ENTERTAINMENT

In the summer, locals café-hop up and down Kreshchatik, and gather to talk at the fountains of Maydan Nezalezhnosti, which are lit up at night. If you desire more spirited company, **Slavuta,** vul. Horkoho 12 (tel. 227 03 91), is open until midnight and has beer on tap (US$3/½L). Late-nighters in Kyyiv gravitate to the **24hr mini-bar** on vul. Chervonoarmeiska just across the street from Respublikanski Stadion. The new hard-currency sports bar **Playoffs Intl.,** on the 3rd floor of the Hotel Libid at Plosha Peremohi, is an oasis of Western-style night life in the middle of Kyyiv. Order a draft beer or pizza and burgers while you play pool, catch a glimpse of their satellite TV, or dance with a hip crowd to the music of a live DJ. (Open Sun.-Thurs. 7pm-3:30am, Fri.-Sat. 7pm-5am. Cover charge US$10; before 9pm free; students US$2 on Wed.)

The local arts scene thrives at a number of **theaters;** some of the more interesting ones are the small independent companies that line Andriyevski uviz including the **Koleso** theater-café, the **Theater Studio "Na Podoli"** (tel. 416 01 94), and the tiny, recently established **Life-Art Cabaret** in the Academia at no. 34, which often hosts folk singers. Most of them close down in the summer. For tickets to the **opera, philharmonic,** or other performances check with the ticket office (Театральна каса), vul. Lenina 26. (Open Tues.-Sun. 9am-5pm.) If you're in Kyyiv during **soccer** season (late spring to mid-autumn), see a **Dynamo Kyyiv** game. Kyyivans go bonkers with good reason: their team is one of the best anywhere. Buy tickets at the stadium on vul. Chervonoarmeiska. (M: "Respublikanski Stadion" (Республиканский Стадион).)

Pick up Ukrainian ceramics, baskets, and embroidered goods for coupons at the **Ukrainian Souvenir** (Український Сувенір) store, vul. Chervonoarmeiska. (Open Mon.-Fri. 10am-2pm and 3-7pm, Sat. 10am-6pm.) The daily and weekend **bazaars** in the summertime in Respublikanski Stadion are an experience in themselves even if you don't buy anything from the myriad goods hauled here from all over Eastern Europe and the former Soviet Union. Try to come to Kyyiv on **Ukraine Sovereignty Day** (July 16), when the city becomes a moveable feast.

■■■ L'VIV (ЛЬВІВ)

L'viv, alternately called L'vov (by the Russians), Lwów (by the Poles), and Lemberg (by the Germans), dates back to 1256, when the city's first fortress arose in a valley at the confluence of Eastern European trade routes. From the start an integral part of East Central Europe rather than the Russian empire, its narrow cobblestone alleys and magnificent Gothic and baroque cathedrals are startlingly reminiscent of such former Austro-Hungarian jewels as Prague and Kraków. In 1939 Western Ukraine was cut out of Poland and annexed to the rest of the Ukrainian Soviet Socialist Republic, L'viv's predominantly Polish population was deported, scarlet banners were hung, and decades of Sovietization ensued.

In the post-Soviet age, L'viv has become the center of Ukrainian national revival. L'viv's many Greek Orthodox churches are being handed back to their congregations after decades of closure. The yellow and blue Ukrainian flag flies over the headquarters of the democratically elected city council, and *Rukh*, the Ukrainian popular front, maintains its headquarters here. Nonetheless, life goes on quietly in the city's medieval squares and coffeehouses as locals contemplate a way out of the drab, crumbling Soviet legacy.

ORIENTATION AND PRACTICAL INFORMATION

L'viv fans outward from **plosha Rynok** (пл. Ринок), the heart of the old city. The principal shopping street is the shady **prospect Svobodi** (пр. Свободи, formerly pr. Lenina), which runs from the **Opera House** to pl. Mickiewicza. Many street names have been changed recently, either back to their prewar appellations or to new, noncommunist versions. Ask locals for help in deciphering maps.

Tourist Office: The **Travel Bureau** (tel. 72 67 51) is in the lobby of the Hotel Intourist on pl. Mickiewicza. Maps of the city (500 coupons), tours, bus and train tickets, and info about camping on the outskirts of the city. Open Mon.-Fri. 9am-6pm. The **Travel Agency** (tel. 798 57 21) in the Hotel Dnestr, bordering the park Ivan Franko across from L'viv University, has maps (250 coupons) and a German- and English-speaking staff. Open Mon.-Fri. 9am-1pm and 2-6pm.

Currency Exchange: Exchange bureaus in the **Hotel Dnestr** (open daily 8am-1pm and 2-6pm) and the **Hotel Intourist.** (Open Mon.-Sat. 9am-5pm, Sun. 9am-3pm.) Only the latter changes traveler's checks (2.5% commission).

Post Office: vul. Slovatskovo 1 (Словацьково), one block from park Ivan Franko, to the right as you face the university. Open Mon.-Fri. 8am-8pm, Sat. 8am-6pm, Sun. and holidays 8am-2pm. Poste Restante.

Telephones: Doroshenka 39, around the corner from the post office. Order your call and wait at least an hour for it to be put through. Open 24hrs. **Fax:** (0322) 76 15 85. US$7.50 to send; 1000 coupons to receive. Open Mon.-Fri. 8am-10pm. Pay phones take special coins which can be bought at the telephone office for 30 coupons each. **City Code:** 0322.

Trains: From the station, tram #6 goes into center city. Trains daily to and from Budapest, Prague, Vienna, Bucharest, and most major former Soviet cities. Tickets are a pain in the butt to get, so try one of the tourist offices listed above for help.

Public Transportation: No metro, but an extensive system of (crowded) trams.

ACCOMMODATIONS

Hotel Independence (Готель Незалежність), vul. Marchenka 6A (tel. 75 72 14), was once the exclusive rest stop for Communist party officials. Service is excellent; the restaurant will prepare whatever your palate desires. Doubles US$7; ½-price if you arrive alone. Apartments with sitting room and refrigerator US$10.

Hotel Intourist, pl. Mickiewicza 1 (tel. 79 90 11), in the heart of the city. Built in 1901, this hotel was undergoing extensive renovations to its exterior in the summer of 1993. Spacious rooms with high ceilings and decor that hints at a more elegant past. Ask for a room above the 2nd floor to escape the street noise below. Singles US$14. Doubles US$17; with bath, TV, and piano US$58.

Hotel Ukraine (Готель Україна), pl. Mickiewicza 4. Rundown but bearable. You'll be glad you paid extra for your own bathroom. Rooms US$3-8.

Hotel Sputnik (Готель Спутник), vul. Knahini Olgi 116 (tel. 64 58 22). One of the newer hotels in L'viv. 15-min. ride from the city center (tram #3 to the last stop). Modern rooms with bath, TV, and telephone. Singles US$26. Doubles US$38.

FOOD

A number of L'viv's better restaurants are in the vicinity of pl. Rynok in the old section of town.

Stari Royal (Старий Рояль; Grand Piano), at vul. Stavropitivska Dnestr, next to the pharmacy museum. The city's first cooperative welcomes guests to the soft strains of its namesake piano. Full meal with borsch, vareniki, and pork cutlet just under US$2. Open daily noon-11pm.

Pid Levom (Пид Левом; Under the Lion), pl. Rinok 20, behind the gate with the brass lion's head. Large hall at street level supplemented by atmospheric brick cellar. Salad 400 coupons, borsch 900 coupons, main course 2400 coupons.

Grono (Гроно), vul. Ryleeva 12, up the hill to the left of the Dniester Hotel. Food is Georgian and tasty, the service friendly, and the atmosphere comfortable. Menu may soon be changing to Ukrainian fare; fighting in the Caucasus has disrupted supplies of Georgian foods and wine. Open Mon.-Sat. noon-9pm, Sun. 1-10pm.

Restaurant Lyuks (Люкс), Kopernika 6/7, across from the Mickiewicz column. Step upstairs past the hall of mirrors to the turn-of-the-century dining room; the food and service have not kept up with the stylish decor, but you can have the standard cucumbers, meat, and potatoes. Open daily noon-5pm and 6-11pm.

Cafe Bilya Fontana (Cafe White Fountain), prospect Svobody, across from Lyuks. Inexpensive place where the menu hangs unceremoniously on the wall. Soup 900 coupons, vareniki 400. Open daily 9am-8pm.

Restaurant Festival (Фестивальний), vul. Sichovich Strilsti 12 (tel. 72 20 59), behind the main university building. Traditional Ukrainian fare under US$3. Music and cabaret show 7:30-8:30pm, 1000 coupons. Open daily noon-11pm.

Pizza Pronto on vul. Gorodska 61, just down the street from the circus. A busy little restaurant serving up hot pizza by the slice (900 coupons) or whole pizza (US$2). Open daily 10am-9pm.

Reflecting its Polish and Austro-Hungarian heritage, L'viv is a city of coffee and cafés. Although few elegant coffeehouses remain, there are a couple of spots to sit down and have a cup with friends. If you're greeted with the Ukrainian *"kavy nemaye"* (no coffee), walk on down to the next place. On pl. Rynok, wander into the **Kofein-aya** (Кофейная), vul. Virmenska 19, a popular hangout with local artists. If there's no room inside, take your Turkish coffee (200 coupons) and a pastry outside onto the street to mingle with those in a similar predicament. (Open daily 9am-3pm and 4-8pm.) A crowded spot for ice cream is **Corona** (Корона) on prospect Svobody. (Small cone 4000 coupons. Open daily 10am-3pm and 4-8pm.) The **Halytski Rynok** (Галицький Ринок), behind the flower stands across from the Church of St. Andrew, has fresh berries, honey, and vegetables. (Open summer 7am-6pm.) For nifty-gifty knick-knacks, check out **Ukrainian Souvenirs** (Український Сувенір), Gorodska 33. (Open Mon.-Sat. 10am-6pm.)

SIGHTS AND ENTERTAINMENT

L'viv's historical center is fairly compact and best seen on foot. Start your walk on **prospect Svobodi,** next to the ornate neoclassical **Opera and Ballet Theater** (Театр Опери та Балету). The opera opens onto a pedestrian mall that runs down the middle of the boulevard, splitting it in two. As you face the center, with your back to the opera, walk on the right side of pr. Svobodi to get a look at the city's principal shops and hotels, lodged in the ochre façades of old Polish apartments. A third of the way up pr. Svobodi, at the intersection with vul. Hnatyuka, is the **Ethnographic Museum** (Музей Етнографії), with a statue of Liberty on a parapet outside. The museum harbors a detailed exhibit of Ukrainian dress, archeological artifacts, painted eggs, and embroidery. (Open Wed.-Sun. 10am-6pm. 200 coupons, students 100 coupons.) If you turn off onto vul. Hnatyuka you will come to a fork in the road; head left to the **park of Ivan Franko,** fronting on **L'viv University.** Back on pr. Svobodi, you eventually reach the **Mickiewicz column,** honoring the Polish poet. Turn left at the Ukraine movie theater and head toward the stone-gray façade of the former 17th-century Bernardine Monastery, now the Greek Catholic **Church of St. Andrew.** The church boasts a cavernous interior covered in frescoes, and a massive gilt altar of rich gold and black granite. To reach the very heart of the old city, make a sharp left here and take one of the narrow streets leading up to **pl. Rynok,** the historic market square, presenting a collage of 4-story, richly decorated merchant homes dating from the 16th to the 18th centuries. A couple of interesting museums cluster around the square. Among the interesting museums clustered around the square are the **Historical Museum,** at pl. Rinok 4 (open Thurs.-Tues. 10am-6pm; 100 coupons) and the adjoining **Italian Courtyard** at pl. Rinok 6. The **Pharmacy Museum** (Аптека Музей), housed in L'viv's oldest drugstore, sells small bottles of iron-fortified "wine" designed to cure all your ills. (Ask for the 300-coupon *vino.* Open Mon.-Sat. 9am-7pm, Sun. 10am-5pm.) On pl. Katedralna rises the Polish **Roman Catholic Cathedral.** (Open Mon.-Sat. 6am-noon and 6-8pm, Sun. and holidays 6am-3pm and 5:30-8pm.) Next door stands a small Renaissance chapel, whose portal displays a frieze of delicately sculpted stone. At the east end of the square are the massive **Assumption Church** (next to the 60m Korniak belltower) and the baroque cupola of the **Museum of Religion,** formerly a Dominican monastery and church, whose masterfully carved wooden figures are worth a look. (Open Fri.-Sun. 11am-6pm. 100 coupons, students 50 coupons.) Up above the old city, where the television tower now stands, rises **High Castle Hill** (*Vysoki Zamok;* Высокий Замок), from whose top a stunning panorama of L'viv unfolds. Continuing farther east, take tram #2 or walk along vul. Lichakivska to vul. Krupyarska (Крупярська). Walk up the street on the left to the outdoor **Museum of Architecture,** also known as the **Shevchenskivski Hai** (Шевченьскивський Гай). Lying on a vast park, the museum harbors a collection of authentic wooden houses brought here from around western Ukraine. (Open Tues.-Fri. and Sun. 10am-6pm, Sat. 11am-7pm.) Back on Lichakivska, head down vul. Mechnikova to the whitewashed chapel and the **Lichakivski Cemetery** (Личакiвський Цвинтар). On the terrain of L'viv's most famous necropolis are the graves of Polish and American nobles beside the simple graves of local residents from throughout the centuries. Tram #2 takes you from the cemetery back to town. (From downtown, take #4.) **Striski Park** (Стрийський парк) is a splendidly manicured park complete with swans and a greenhouse.

When the night comes, L'viv offers comparatively little. Near the arsenal on vul. Vinnichenka is **Pid Veshayu** (Пiд Вежею; Under the Tower), a popular, rowdy beer hall. Coffee is served upstairs, draft beer in the smoky grotto basement. Part of L'viv's original city wall (c. 1256) is visible downstairs near the bar. (Open daily 9am-3pm and 4-8pm, but beer sleeps late: on tap after 10am. Women traveling alone may feel more comfortable elsewhere.) Catch a performance at the **Opera** or the **Symphony,** vul. Chaikovskoho 7. The ticket desks (*teatralni kasi;* театральни каси), pr. Svobodi 37, sell, well, you guess. (Open Mon.-Sat. 11am-2pm and 4-7pm.)

■ Near L'viv

A couple of hours west and south by car or train rise the pine-covered Carpathian Mountains; steep valleys carpeted with wildflowers and chalets overlook crystal streams. The Carpathians are worth a daytrip if you have the time. The tourist offices can advise you as to the best way to get around outside L'viv.

■■■ ODESSA (ОДЕССА)

Odessa looks out from the shadows of Ukraine and Russia to the sea and a larger world. The city began as an Ottoman coastal fort, then fell to the Russian Empire in 1789 and grew into a major seaport and industrial center. By the turn of the 19th century, waves of Russian, Ukrainian, Jewish, and other European settlers had turned Odessa into a thriving metropolis of decidedly cosmopolitan character. In more recent years, summer visitors have flocked to Odessa to enjoy the cool waters and sandy beaches of the Black Sea.

ORIENTATION AND PRACTICAL INFORMATION

The main street in Odessa is **ul. Deribasovskaya** (ул. Дерибасовскай), closed in part to traffic to allow pedestrians to enjoy its many shops and cafes. The northern end of Deribasovskaya intersects **ul. Sovietskoi Army,** (ул. Советской Армий); in the opposite direction, heading towards the sea, it comes across **ul. Pushkinskaya** (ул. Пушкинская). A right onto Pushkinskaya from Deribasovskaya will eventually lead to the train station, while turning left ushers you onto **Primorski Boulevard** (Приморский Бул.), a tree-lined promenade favored for its panoramic views of the sea.

Tourist Offices: Not much help in finding rooms or reliable maps, but may be of some help for train and bus tickets. **Intourist Office,** ul. Pushkinskaya 17, in the lobby of the Hotel Krasnaya (Готель Краснай). Open Mon.-Fri. 9am-6pm. **Service bureau** in the Hotel Chornoye Morye (Готель Чёрное Море), ul. Lenina 59, close to the train station. Open Mon.-Fri. 9am-5pm.

Currency Exchange: The Porto Franko Bank (Порто-Франко Банк), ul. Pushkinskaya 10, will change dollars into coupons. Open Mon.-Fri. 9am-6pm. Across the street at no. 17 the exchange bureau in the **Hotel Krasnaya** is 1 of the few places in Odessa that handles traveler's checks (2.5% commission) but arrive early; they frequently run out of money. Open Mon.-Fri. 9am-5pm and Sat. 10am-1pm.

Central Post Office and Telephones: bul. Sadovaya 4, (бул. Садовая). International telephone office open 24hrs.; pay phones for calls within Odessa are free of charge; good luck finding one that works. The post office is open daily 8am-8pm. The newsstand in the main hall sells helpful city maps (30 coupons).

Trains: **Train station** on Privokzalnaya pl. (Привокзальная пл.), at the southern end of ul. Pushkinskaya. Trolleybus #1 takes you to the city center near Deribasovskaya. Buy tickets at least 2 days early at the **Central Ticket Bureau** on ul. Srednefontanskaya (Среднефонтанская). Take bus #146 or #136 and look for the large sign "Центральные Железнодорожные кассы." Scalpers at the station help if all else fails.

Buses: The main bus station is on ul. Dzerzhinskovo 58 (Дзержинского). Tram #5 goes to the train station; #15 leads downtown. **Tinra** (Тинра), ul. Zhukovskovo, (ул. Жуковского), 26. Service to Varna, Bulgaria (Tues. 7am, 24hr., US$28).

Flights: Aeroflot, ul. Karl Marx 17 (tel. 22-2300), handles all flights from Odessa. Take bus #101. To: Moscow (US$125) and Kyyiv (US$74). Open daily 8am-6pm.

Boats: Routes exist, but schedules are unpredictable. Ask for info at the booking office of the **Black Sea Steamship Line** on Potemkin pl. at the top of the stairs by the same name. Open Mon.-Fri. 8:30am-5pm, Sat.-Sun. 10am-2pm. The **Morskoi Vokzal** (Морской Вокзал), down the bottom of the Potemkin stairs at ul Suvorova (ул. Суворова), 6 also has a ticket booth in the main terminal. To the left of the main dock are the ferries that run to the beaches surrounding Odessa.

ACCOMMODATIONS

The most inexpensive hotels are located downtown along ul. Deribasovskaya or ul. Sovietskoi Army. The **Hotel Central** (Готель Центральная) is on ul. Sovietskoi Army 40 just across the street from a park. The receptionists here are friendly and will speak the little English they know if you coax them long enough. (Doubles US$11; with sitting room and private bath US$19.) Right next door at no. 34 is the **Hotel Passage** (Пассаж), with tidy rooms preferred by Turkish businessmen. (Singles with bath US$14. Doubles with bath US$18.) Take a right out of the hotel and another quick right onto ul. Deribasovskaya for 2 other options. Just past a small city park is the **Grand Moscow Hotel** (Большая Москва) at no. 29. Rooms here are clean and spacious with high ceilings and private bathrooms and include TV, phone, and fridge. (Singles US$16. Doubles US$22.) Finally, just down the road at no. 25 is the **Hotel Spartak** (Спартак), like the highly attractive Mexico assistant-editor of a similar name, is well kept and makes for a comfortable night's sleep. (All rooms US$14; some have bath.) If you're willing to spend US$30 and up to be close to the beach then head south to **Arcadia Beach** (Аркадия) and look into one of the many pricey hotels that cater to summer crowds.

FOOD

The area around Deribasovskaya holds enough restaurants and cafés to keep even the most active appetites in check. The new and trendy **Galaxy Restaurant** downstairs at ul. Sovietskoi Army 23 has a bar room and 2 different halls, one of which offers live music beginning at 8pm. (Full meal US$4; menu in English. Open daily noon-midnight.) On one edge of the small city park on ul. Deribasovskaya, the **Pecheskato café** (Печескато Кафе) features a delicious menu of grilled hamburgers, chicken, and *shashlik* for US$2. If you can't find a table in this extremely popular eatery then order directly with the chef and take your meal into the nearby park where the atmosphere is just as pleasant. (Open daily 11am-8pm.) One street over from Deribasovskaya, the **Restaurant Fav** (Фав), ul. Trecheskaya 50, serves traditional Ukrainian and Russian specialties in an old theater; the restaurant still makes good use of the stage with nightly cabaret performances. (Dinner and show about US$6. Open daily 6pm-4am.) At the end of Primorski bul. (bordering on Vorontsov's Palace), the quaint **Café Old Odessa** (Старая Одесса) offers strictly outdoor eating. You can munch sandwiches, order *shashlik*, and wash it down with a cup of Turkish coffee or a cocktail while gazing at the magnificent view of the harbor, all for only US$3. On weekends an endless stream of newlyweds parades by the café to have their pictures taken at the nearby bridge.

SIGHTS AND ENTERTAINMENT

Start a walking tour of Odessa from the point where ul. Deribasovskaya and ul. Sovietskoi Army intersect. The park here is known on maps as pl. Sovietskoi Army but the locals refer to it as Sobornaya pl. to recall the large cathedral which once stood in the center. The church was destroyed by the Soviets and a **statue of Mikhail Vorontsov,** an early governor of Odessa, was erected in its place. Turn yourself around and proceed down ul. Deribasovskaya towards the sea. On the left you'll notice the **city park** where artists and craftsmen sell their work on weekends. Take your 3rd left onto ul. Lenina and continue to the majestic **Opera and Ballet Theater** (Театр Оперы и Балета), built from 1884-1887; it was being renovated in the summer of 1993. Check out the ticket office on the side of the theater for a schedule of performances. (Tickets 25-200 coupons. Open daily 10am-5pm.)

Three interesting museums lie to the left of the theater just down ul. Lastochkina. The first is the **Museum of the Black Sea Fleet** (Музей Морского Флота), whose exhibits recount the history of Odessa as a vital naval port. (Open Fri.-Wed. 10am-5pm. 100 coupons.) Cross over the next street heading in the same direction and you'll see the yellow building of the **Archeological Museum of Odessa** (Археологичний Музей), which houses artifacts found in the Black Sea region, dating back to ancient Greece and Rome. Especially worth a look is the collection of gold coins stored in a basement vault. (Open Tues.-Sun. 10am-5pm. 300 coupons, students 100 coupons.) The **Literature Museum** (Литературний Музей), housed in a 18th century palace, offers a fascinating account of the city's history through its many books, prints and photographs. Consider hiring an English-speaking guide (500 coupons) for the full story, since the museum's exhibits are labeled only in Russian. (Open Tues.-Sun. 10am-5pm. 50 coupons, 25 for students.) Retrace your steps and take a right at the Archeological Museum onto the shady, tree-lined **Primorski Boulevard,** the most popular spot in Odessa to stroll and people watch. The statue of the great Russian writer **Alexander Pushkin** (c. 1881) has his back unceremoniously turned to city hall, since the local government refused to help fund its construction. On either side of city hall are the figures of **Fortuna,** goddess of fate and **Mercury,** god of trade, the two symbols of the city of Odessa. Strolling down Primorski bul. you'll come upon another statue, this one of the **Duc de Richelieu,** whose concrete stare looks down toward the **Potemkin stairs** and the more distant **Morskoi Vokzal.** Director Serge Eisenstein used these stairs in his epic 1925 film, "Battleship Potemkin," and since then the name has stuck. A left at this point will bring you to a monument commemorating the actual mutiny of that famous ship. Continue farther

O D E S S A

along to the end of Primorski to the **Palace of Vorontsov** (c.1826), now a club for schoolchildren, and you'll understand why this early governor of Odessa had his home built at this spot. The view is spectacular and gets better as the sun sinks down, casting its final rays over the city and the ships berthed in the harbor below. To your left is the long, white **Mother-in-Law Bridge,** built, they say, so an elderly lady could more easily visit her son-in-law, a high ranking official in the local Communist party. It sways and creaks with each sea breeze (the bridge, not the Party).

For those who wish to take full advantage of their time at the seashore, head to Odessa's southern beaches for a day of swimming and sun bathing. **Arcadia Beach** (Аркадия) is one of the better ones around and can be reached by tram (#5) or by one of the more irregular ferries that depart from the Morskoi Vokzal.

LET'S USE CTS

THE YOUTH & STUDENT TRAVEL SPECIALISTS

FROM LONDON

in US$ ✈ one way	
Amsterdam 66	Munich 108
Athens.............118	New York 175
Berlin 108	Paris 61
Bangkok 289	Pisa(Florence) 129
Dublin 52	Prague 119
Edinburgh 61	Rome 90
Los Angeles....252	Sydney 525
Madrid 90	Tel Aviv 133
Miami 169	Venice.............100

ACCOMMODATION WORLDWIDE

in US$ 🛏 one night	
London........... **23**	Paris................. 33
Amsterdam 27	Prague 16
Edinburgh........ 33	Rome 21
Florence............15	Venice 22
Dublin.............. 18	

Tours around Europe

7/14/21-day all around Europe from/to London at 40 USD per day. And also sightseeings, excursions, tours, rent-a-car, transfers and other services for the budget minded traveller.

Europe by train

EUROTRAIN EXPLORER • $ 127 Dutch Explorer • London- Amsterdam-Brussels-Brugges-London • $293 Rome Explorer • London-Paris-Pisa-Florence-Lucerne-Strasbourg-Luxemburg-Brussels-London
EUROPE BY COACH • **9 days all inclusive from $550**

 CENTRO TURISTICO STUDENTESCO E GIOVANILE   Major Credit Cards accepted   SATA ISTC

YOUTH & STUDENT TRAVEL CENTRE

LONDON
44 Goodge Street W1P 2AD
tel. (071) 5804554-6375601
Underground station:
Goodge Street

LONDON
220 Kensington High Street,
W8 7RA
tel. (071) 9373265
Underground station:
High Street Kensington

ROME
via Genova, 16 (corner via
Nazionale) tel. (06) 46791
Underground station: Repubblica

ROME
Corso Vitt. Emanuele II, 297
tel. (06) 6872672-3-4

FLORENCE
via de'Ginori, 25-R
tel. (055) 289721-289570

MILAN
via S. Antonio, 2
tel. (02) 58304121

NAPLES
via Mezzocannone, 25
tel. (081) 5527975-5527960

VENICE
Dorso Duro Ca' Foscari, 3252,
tel. (041) 5205660-5205655

PARIS
20, rue des Carmes
tel. (1) 43250076
75005 Latin quarter
Underground station:
Maubert Mutualité

INDEX

Villa Borghese

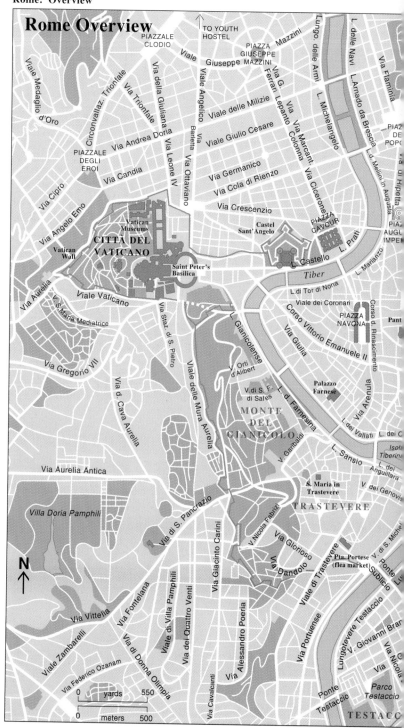

Rome: Transportation

Rome Transport

TO YOUTH HOSTEL

A-LINE
B-LINE

Stations:
OTTAVIANO
LEPANTO
FLAMINIO
SPAGNA
BARBERINI
REPUBBLICA
TERMINI
CASA PRETORIO
VITTORIO
CAVOUR
S. PIETRO

Urban Train Service (F.S.)

Landmarks:
VILLA BORGHESE
PIAZZA DEL POPOLO
PIAZZA CAVOUR
PIAZZA GIUSEPPE MAZZINI
PIAZZA COLONNA
PIAZZA NAVONA
PIAZZA VENEZIA
Pantheon
Trevi Fountain
Palazzo del Quirinale
Palazzo Farnese
Castel Sant'Angelo
St. Peter's Basilica
Vatican
Stazione Termini
C. d. Rinascimento

Streets:
Viale Regina Margherita
Via Nomentana
Via Nizza
Via Po
Corso d'Italia
Via Salaria
Via Piave
Via XX Settembre
Via V. Veneto
Via Sistina
Via del due Macelli
Via del Babuino
Via del Corso
Via di Ripetta
Via Flaminia
Viale del Muro Torta
Via G. Ferrari
Via Marcant. Colonna
Via Cicerone
Via Lepanto
Viale Giulio Cesare
Viale delle Milizie
Via Cola di Rienzo
Via Crescenzio
Viale Angelico
Via Ottaviano
Via Leone IV
Viale dei Coronari
Corso Vittorio Emanuele II
Via Giulia
Viale Trastevere
Via Cavour
Via Nazionale
Via Merulana
Via Giov. Lanza
Via dei Fori Imp.
V. d. Quattro Fontane
Via Barberini
Via Cestio Pretorio
Via Marsala
Via Giuseppe Mazzini
Tiber

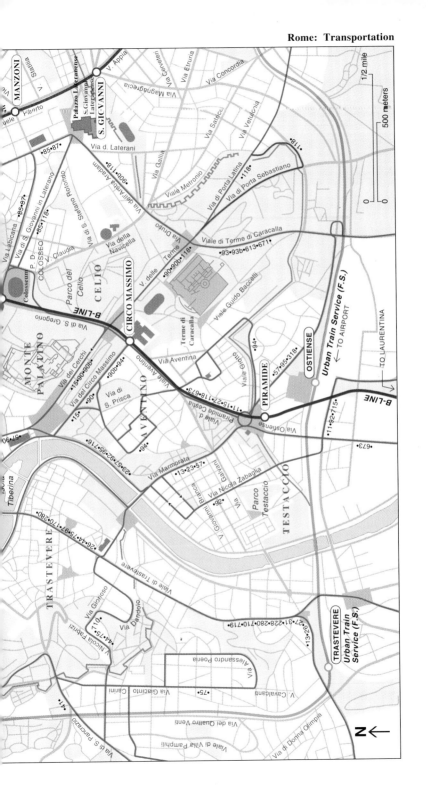

Rome: Transportation

VILLA BORGHESE

VILLA MEDICI

V. del Muro Torto

Spagna

PIAZZA TRINITÀ D. MONTE

Via d. Due Macelli

PIAZZA DI SPAGNA

Via Propaganda

Via Mario de Fiori

Via Belvedere

Via Trinità dei Monti

Via del Babuino

Via della Croce

Via della Carozze

Via d. Condotti

Via Borgogna

Via Frattina

Via delle Vite

Via della Mercede

PIAZZA S. SILVESTRO

Via del Corso

Via Vittorio

Via del Tritone

Via del Monti

PIAZZA DEL POPOLO

Via di Ripetta

Via Canova

LARGO D. SCHIAVONI

Via Brunati

Via del Vantaggio

PIAZZA AUGUSTO IMPERATORE

Via Borghese

Via Tomacelli

PIAZZA DEL PARLIAMENTO

Via Campo di Marzo

Via Prefetti

Via F. di Savoia

Lung. in Augusta

PIAZZA D. PORTO DI RIPETTA

Via della Scrofa

Via Clementino

Lungotevere Marzio

Tiber River

Lung. dei Mellini

Ponte Cavour

Lung. Prati

Ponte Umberto I

Nona

PIAZZA D. LIBERTA

Ponte Margherita

Via Feder. Cesi

Via G. Belli

Via P. Cossa

Via V. Colonna

Via Ulpiano

PIAZZA DEI TRIBUNALI

Via Orsini

Via Cola di Rienzo

Via E. Q. Visconti

Via Lucr. Caro

PIAZZA CAVOUR

Via Cicerone

Via Tacito

Via Triboniano

Lungotevere Castello

Via Cassiodoro

Via Ovidio

Via Boezio

Via Crescenzio

PIAZZA ADRIANA

Castel Sant' Angelo

Ponte S. Angelo

Lung. Vaticano

Via Alberico II

Via Vitelleschi

PIAZZA PIA

Via della Conciliazione

Walks

1 Piazza del Popolo
2 Ara Pacis
3 Mausoleum of Augustus
4 Palazzo Borghese
5 Spanish Steps
6 Trevi Fountain
7 Vittorio Emanuele Monument
8 Campidoglio
9 Teatro Marcello
10 Isola Tiberina
11 Palazzo Doria Pamphili
12 Church of Santi Apostoli
13 Church of San Marcello
14 Piazza di S. Ignazio
15 Piazza di Pietra
16 Piazza Colonna/ Column of Marcus Aurelius
17 Palazzo Chigi
18 Pantheon
19 Giolitti
20 Piazza Minerva
21 Church of Santa Maria Sopra Minerva
22 Church of San Luigi dei Francesi
23 Piazza Navona
24 Church of Sant'Antonio dei Portoghesi
25 Museo Napoleonico
26 Il Gesù
27 Largo Argentina
28 Church of Sant'Andrea delle Valle
29 Palazzo del Cancelleria
30 Chiesa Nuova
31 Piazza Sforza Cesarini
32 Campo dei Fiori
33 Piazza Farnese
34 Piazza della Quercia
35 Monte di Pietà
36 Church of Santissima Trinità dei Pellegrini

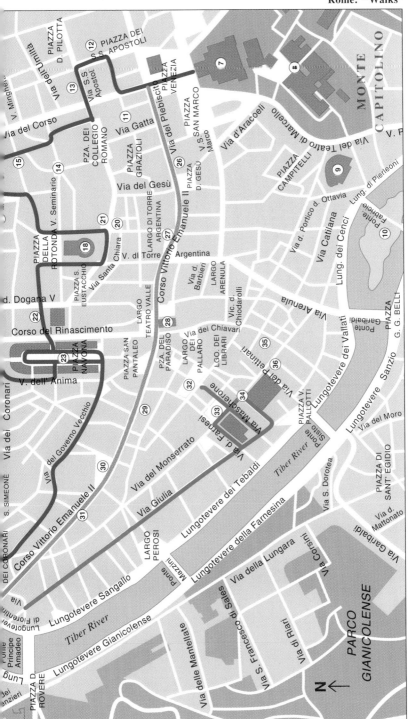

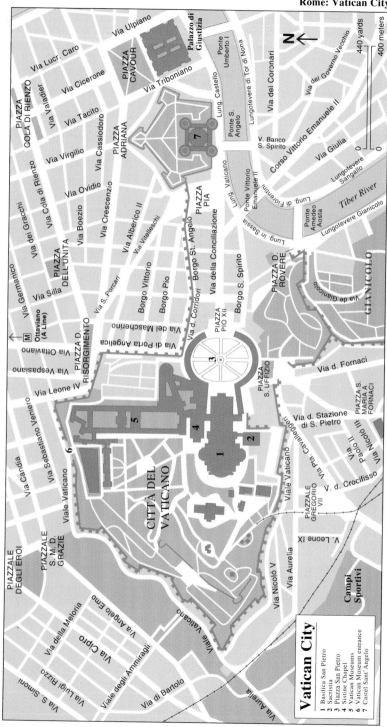

Rome: Vatican City

N

440 yards
400 meters

Vatican City

1 Basilica San Pietro
2 Sacristia
3 Piazza San Pietro
4 Sistine Chapel
5 Vatican Museums
6 Vatican Museum entrance
7 Castel Sant'Angelo

CITTÀ DEL VATICANO

Palazzo di Giustizia

PIAZZA CAVOUR

PIAZZA COLA DI RIENZO

PIAZZA ADRIANA

PIAZZA DELL'UNITA

PIAZZA PIA

PIAZZA PIO XII

PIAZZA S. UFFIZIO

PIAZZA D. ROVERE

GIANICOLO

PIAZZA D. RISORGIMENTO

PIAZZALE DEGLI EROI

PIAZZALE S. M. D. GRAZIE

PIAZZA S. MARIA A. FORNACI

PIAZZALE GREGORIO VII

Campi Sportivi

Tiber River

Via Ulpiano
Via Lucr. Caro
Via Cicerone
Via Valadier
Via Tacito
Via Cassiodoro
Via Virgilio
Via Ovidio
Via Cola di Rienzo
Via Boezio
Via Crescenzio
Via dei Gracchi
Via Germanico
Via Silla
Via Vespasiano
Via Ottaviano
Via Leone IV
Via Sebastiano Veniero
Via Candia
Viale Vaticano
Via Angelo Emo
Viale Vaticano
Via della Meloria
Via Cipro
Via Luigi Rizzo
Via S. Simoni
Viale degli Ammiragli
Via di Bartolo
Via Aurelia
Via Nicolò V
Via Leone IX
V. d. Crocifisso
Via d. Stazione di S. Pietro
Via d. Fornaci
Via Nicolò III
Via Paolo II
Via Paolo III
Via d. Cavalleggeri
Viale Vaticano
Via di Porta Angelica
Via del Mascherino
Via d. Corridori
Via S. Porcari
Borgo Vittorio
Borgo Pio
Borgo S. Angelo
Borgo della Conciliazione
Borgo S. Spirito
Via Alberico II
Via Vitelleschi
Lung. Vaticano
Lung. in Sassia
Ponte Vittorio Emanuele II
Lung. di Fiorentini
Ponte Amedeo Aosta
Lungotevere Gianicolo
Via de Gianicolo
Ponte S. Angelo
Lung. Castello
Ponte Umberto I
Lungotevere di Tor di Nona
Via dei Coronari
Via del Governo Vecchio
Corso Vittorio Emanuele II
V. Banco S. Spirito
Via Giulia
Lungotevere Sangallo
Via Triboniano
Ottaviano (A Line)

M Ottaviano (A Line)

1
2
3
4
5
6
7

Paris Metro

*The stations Liège and Rennes are closed after 8pm and on Sundays and holidays.

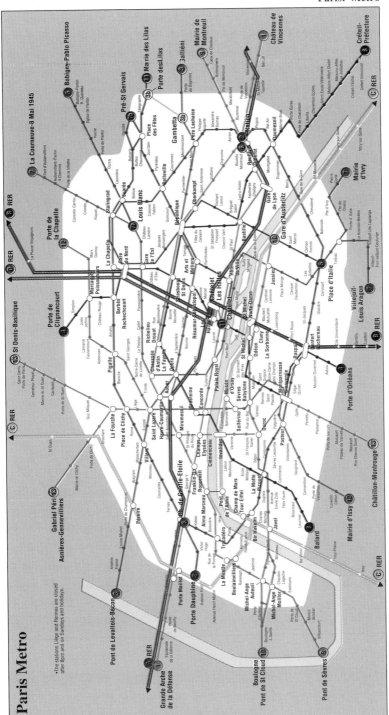

Paris: 1er and 2e

9e

Rue Chaussée d'Antin

Rue St-Lazare

R. d'Amsterdam

Richelieu

St Lazare

Chaussée d'Antin

Havre-Caumartin

Boulevard Haussmann

Bd. Haussmann

Rue Auber

Rue

Opéra

Boulevard des Italiens

Rue Pasquier

Rue Tronchet

Auber

Scribe

Bd. des Capucines

Opéra

Rue du Quatre

Sep

Quatre Septembre

Bd. de la Madeleine

Rue des Capucines

Rue de la Paix

Rue des Petit Champs

Biblio
Na

Madeleine

Rue Boissy d'Anglas

Madeleine

La Colonne

PLACE VENDÔME

Pyramides

Avenue de l'Opéra

Rue de Richelieu

Rue Royale

8e

Rue St-Honoré

Rue de Castiglione

Rue des Pyramides

1er

Musée Bouilhet
Christofle

Rue St-Honoré

PLACE
ANDRE-MALRAUX

Concorde

Rue de Rivoli

Tuileries

Palais F

Jeu de Paume

PLACE
CARROL

PLACE DE
LA CONCORDE

JARDIN DES
TUILERIES

L'Orangerie

Quai des Tuileries

Pt. de la
Concorde

Seine

Pont
Solférino

Pont
Royal

Pont du
Carrousel

Quai Anatole France

Quai Voltaire

Assemblée
Nationale

Chambre des
Deputés

Musée
D'Orsay

Musée
d'Orsay

Rue de Lille

7e

Rue de l'Université

Ecole Natio
Superieure
Beaux-

| 0 | 1/8 mile |
| 0 | 125 meters |

Bd St-Germain

Solférino

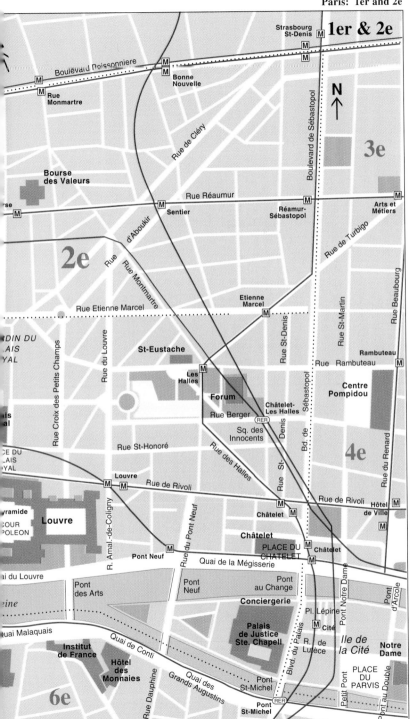

1er & 2e

Strasbourg
St-Denis M

Boulevard Poissonnière

Bonne
Nouvelle

N
↑

Rue
Monmartre

3e

Rue de Cléry

Bourse
des Valeurs

Rue Réaumur

Boulevard de Sébastopol

Réaumur-
Sébastopol

Arts et
Métiers

se M

Sentier

2e

Rue d'Aboukir

Rue

Rue Montmartre

Rue de Turbigo

Etienne
Marcel

Rue Etienne Marcel

Etienne
Marcel
M

DIN DU
AIS
YAL

Rue Croix des Petits Champs

Rue du Louvre

St-Eustache

Rue St-Denis

Rue St-Martin

Rue Beaubourg

ais
al

Les
Halles

Forum

Rue Rambuteau

Rambuteau M

Centre
Pompidou

E DU
AIS
YAL

Rue Berger

Châtelet-
Les Halles
RER

Boulevard de Sébastopol

Rue St-Honoré

Sq. des
Innocents

Bd. de

4e

Rue du Renard

Rue des Halles

Rue St-Denis

yramide
COUR
POLEON

Louvre

Louvre
M M

Rue de Rivoli

M

Rue de Rivoli

Hôtel
de Ville M

M

R. Amal.-de-Coligny

Rue du Pont Neuf

Châtelet

M

Châtelet

Pont Neuf

Châtelet

M Châtelet

PLACE DU
CHÂTELET

ai du Louvre

Quai de la Mégisserie

Pont
des Arts

Pont
Neuf

Pont
au Change

eine

Conciergerie

Pl. Lépine

Pont Notre Dame

Pont
d'Arcole

uai Malaquais

Institut
de France

Quai de Conti

Palais
de Justice
Ste. Chapell

M Cité

Ile de
la Cité

Notre
Dame

Hôtel
des
Monnaies

Quai des
Grands Augustins

Rue Dauphine

R. de
Lutèce

Blvd. du Palais

Pont
St-Michel

Petit Pont

PLACE
DU
PARVIS

Pont au Double

6e

Pont
St-Michel
RER

Pont Neuf

Châtelet M

Palais du Louvre

Pont Neuf M

Quai du Louvre

1er

Pont au Change

Pont du Carrousel

Pont des Arts

Pont Neuf

Cité

Conciergerie

Ste-Chapelle

Hôte Dieu

Quai Malaquais

Quai de Conti

Bd. du Palais

Cité M

Ile de la Cité

Ecole Nationale Superieure des Beaux Arts

R. Bonaparte

Institut de France

Hôtel des Monnaies

Rue Mazarine

Quai des Grands Augustins

Pont St-Michel

Rue de la Cité

Rue des Sts-Pères

Rue Jacob

Rue de Seine

Rue Dauphine

Pont St-Michel RER

St-Michel M

Pl. St-Michel

Rue St-Jaques

R. de l'Abbaye

PLACE ST-GERMAIN-DES-PRÉS M

St-Germain Des Prés

Rue St-André des Arts

Rue Danton

Bd. St-Germain

7e

Bd. St-Germain

St-Germain des Prés M

M

Mabillon

Odéon M

Boulevard

Musée du Cluny

R. du Four

Rue de Tournon

Rue de l'Odéon

Rue Racine

St-Michel

Sorbonne

R. de Sèvres

R. du Vieux Colombier

R. du Saint Sulpice

PLACE ST-SULPICE

St-Sulpice

PLACE DE L'ODÉON

PLACE DE LA SORBONNE

R. du Cherche Midi

M **St-Sulpice**

R. de Rennes

R. d'Assas

R. de Vaugirard

Palais du Luxembourg

Rue Soufflot

Luxembourg M

Bd. Raspail

Rennes M

6e

Rue Gay-Lussac

St Placide M

JARDIN DU LUXEMBOURG

Rue de Montparnasse

Notre-Dame des Champs

Rue Vavin

Rue Notre-Dame des Champs

Rue d'Assas

Boulevard St-Michel

Rue St-Jaques

Montparnasse Bienvenüe M

Vavin M

Boulevard du Montparnasse

Avenue de la Observatoire

Port Royal

R. du Depart

Boulevard Raspail

14e

Edgar Quinet M

Boulevard Edgar Quinet

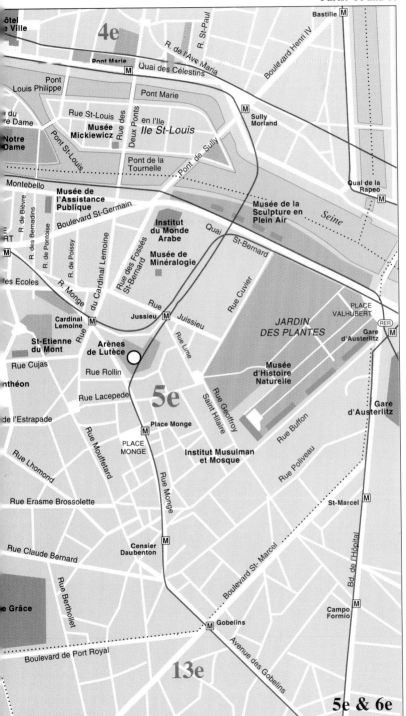

Bastille [M]

ôtel
e Ville

4e

R. St-Paul

R. de l'Ave Maria

R. St-Paul

Boulevard Henri IV

Pont Marie [M]

Quai des Célestins

Pont
Louis Philippe

Pont Marie

Rue St-Louis

e du
re Dame

Musée
Mickiewicz

Rue des Deux Ponts

en l'Île
Ile St-Louis

[M]

Sully
Morland

Notre
Dame

Pont St-Louis

Pont de la
Tournelle

Pont de Sully

Quai de la
Rapeo

[M]

Montebello

Musée de
l'Assistance
Publique

Boulevard St-Germain

Musée de la
Sculpture en
Plein Air

Seine

R. de Bièvre

R. des Bernardins

R. de Pontoise

R. de Poissy

R. du Cardinal Lemoine

Rue des Fosses
St-Bernard

Institut
du Monde
Arabe

Musée de
Minéralogie

Quai

St-Bernard

RT

[M]

es Ecoles

R. Monge

Rue Cuvier

PLACE
VALHUBERT

[RER]

Cardinal
Lemoine [M]

Rue

Jussieu [M]

Juissieu

Rue Linne

JARDIN
DES PLANTES

Gare
d'Austerlitz

[RER] [M]

St-Etienne
du Mont

Arènes
de Lutèce

Rue Cujas

Rue Rollin

5e

Musée
d'Histoire
Naturelle

Gare
d'Austerlitz

nthéon

Rue Lacepede

Rue Geoffroy
Saint Hilaire

Rue Buffon

de l'Estrapade

[M] Place Monge

Rue Mouffetard

PLACE
MONGE

Institut Musulman
et Mosque

Rue Lhomond

Rue Monge

Rue Poliveau

Rue Erasme Brossolette

St-Marcel [M]

Rue Claude Bernard

Censier
Daubenton [M]

Bd. de l'Hôpital

Campo
Formio [M]

Rue Berthollet

e Grâce

[M] Gobelins

Boulevard St-Marcel

Boulevard de Port Royal

Avenue des Gobelins

13e

Paris: RER

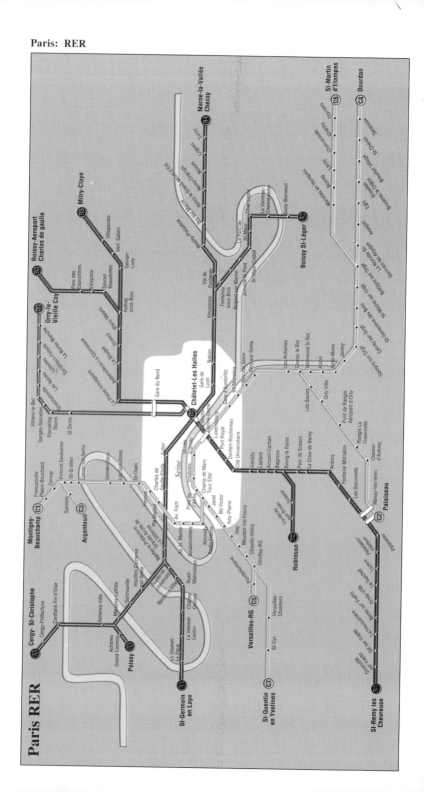

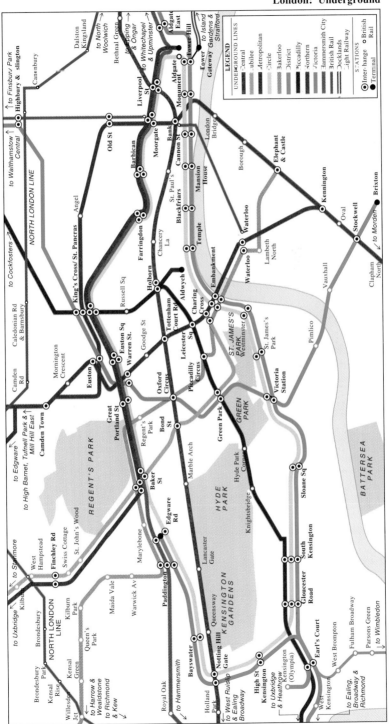

London: Underground

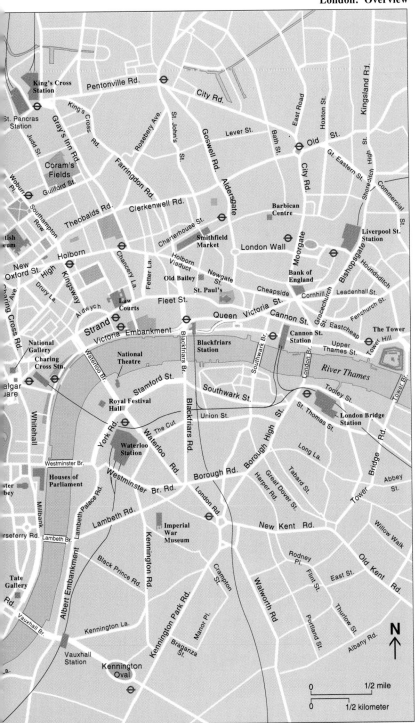

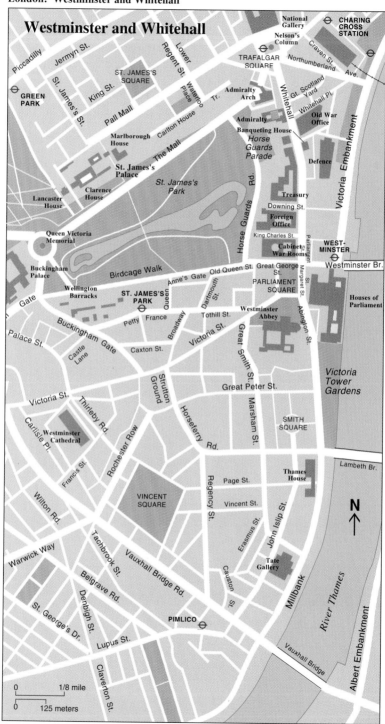

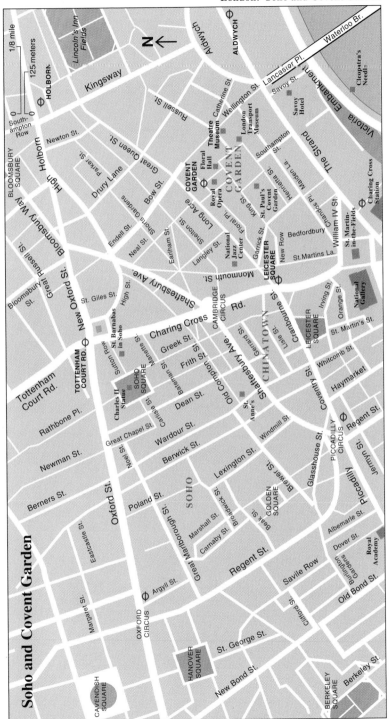

Soho and Covent Garden

London: Soho and Covent Garden

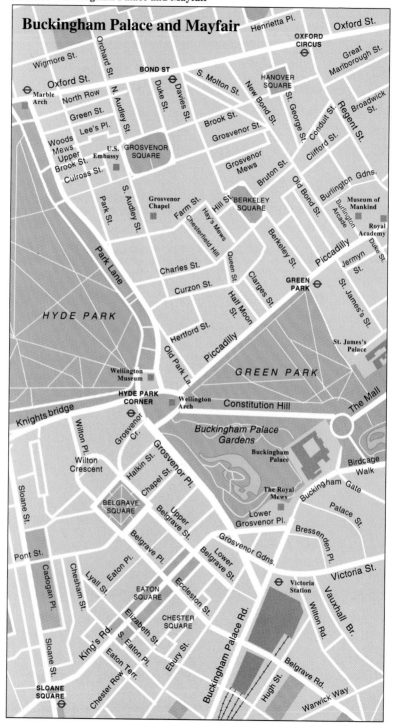

Buckingham Palace and Mayfair

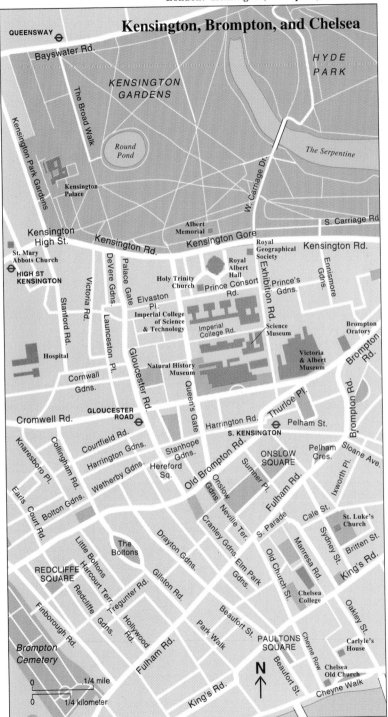

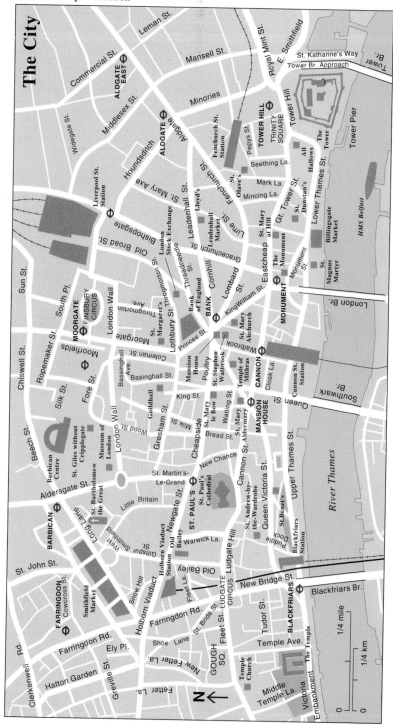

London: City of London

The City